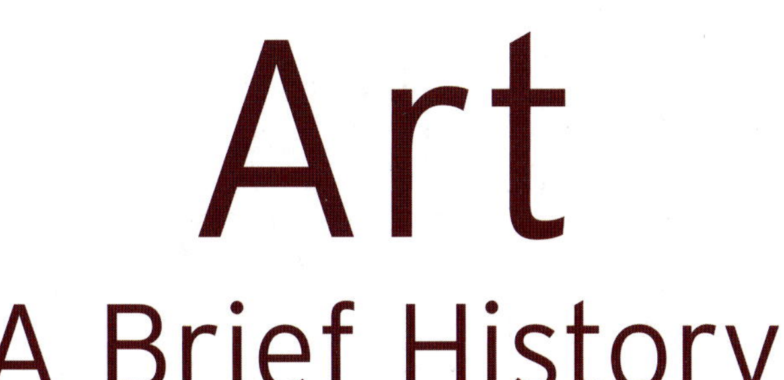

Art
A Brief History

FOURTH EDITION

Marilyn Stokstad

PROFESSOR EMERITA
THE UNIVERSITY OF KANSAS

Michael W. Cothren

PROFESSOR
SWARTHMORE COLLEGE

Prentice Hall
Upper Saddle River London Singapore
Toronto Tokyo Sydney Hong Kong Mexico City

Editorial Director: Leah Jewell
Editor-in-Chief: Sarah Touborg
Senior Sponsoring Editor: Helen Ronan
Editorial Project Manager: David Nitti
Editorial Assistant: Carla Worner
Media Director: Brian Hyland
Media Editor: Alison Lorber
Director of Marketing: Brandy Dawson
Senior Marketing Manager: Laura Lee Manley
Marketing Assistant: Ashley Fallon
Senior Managing Editor: Ann Marie McCarthy
Assistant Managing Editor: Melissa Feimer
Senior Operations Specialist: Brian Mackey
Production Liaisons: Barbara Cappuccio and Marlene Gassler
AV Project Manager: Gail Cocker
Cartography: Peter Bull Art Studio
Senior Art Director: Pat Smythe
Site Supervisor, Pearson Imaging Center: Joe Conti
Pearson Imaging Center: Corin Skidds, Robert Uibelhoer, and Ron Walko
Cover Printer: Lehigh-Phoenix Color
Printer/Binder: Courier/Kendallville

This book was designed by
Laurence King Publishing Ltd, London
www.laurenceking.com

Production Controller: Simon Walsh
Page Design: Andrew Shoolbred/Gregory Taylor
Photo Researcher: Evi Peroulaki
Copy Editor: Jennifer Speake
Proofreader: Lisa Cutmore

Cover photo and page iii: **Antoní Gaudi**. *Casa Batllò*, 43 Passeig de Gracia. 1904–1907.
Photo: Ricard Pla. Back inside cover photo: Vincent Abbey Photography.

Credits and acknowledgments borrowed from other sources and reproduced, with permission, in this textbook appear on the appropriate page within text or on the credit pages in the back of this book.

Library of Congress Cataloging-in-Publication Data

Stokstad, Marilyn -
[Art history]
Art : a brief history / Marilyn Stokstad. -- 4th ed.
p. cm.
Abridgment of the author's Art history.
Includes bibliographical references and index.
ISBN 978-0-13-605909-7 (pbk. : alk. paper)
1. Art--History. I. Title.
N5300.S923 2010
709--dc22
2009018338

10 9 8 7 6 5 4

Prentice Hall
is an imprint of

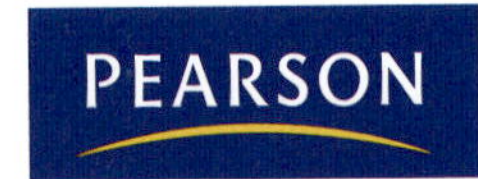

www.pearsonhighered.com

ISBN 10: 0-13-605909-0
ISBN 13: 978-0-13-605909-7
Exam Copy ISBN 10: 0-205-69517-5
ISBN 13: 978-0-205-69517-1

BRIEF CONTENTS

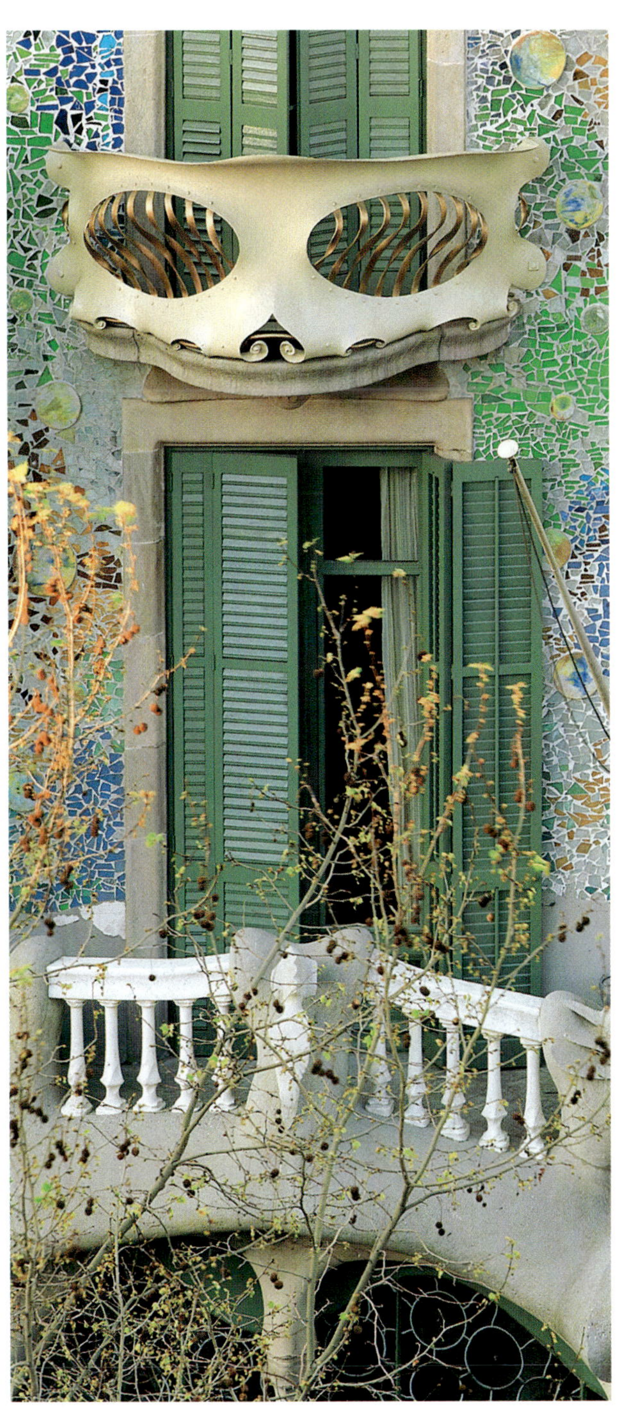

CONTENTS

This new edition of *Art: A Brief History* is the result of a happy and productive collaboration between two scholar-teachers who share a common vision. In certain ways, we also share a common history. Neither of us expected to become professors of art history. Marilyn Stokstad took her first art history course as a requirement of her studio arts program. Michael Cothren discovered the discipline almost by chance during a semester abroad in Provence when a painting instructor sent him on a field trip to learn from the formal intricacies of Romanesque sculpture. Perhaps as a result of the unexpected delight we found in these revelatory formative experiences, we share a conviction that first courses in the history of art should be filled with as much enjoyment as erudition; that they should foster an enthusiastic, as well as an educated, public for the visual arts. With this end firmly in mind we will continue to create books intended to help students enjoy learning the essentials of a vast and complex field of study. For millennia human beings have embodied their most cherished ideas and values in visual and tangible form. We have learned that by engaging with these works from the past, we can all enrich our lives in the present, especially because we are living in a present when images have become an increasingly important aspect of how we communicate with each other.

Like its predecessors, this new edition seeks to balance formal and iconographic analysis with contextual art history in order to craft interpretations that will engage with a diverse student population. Throughout the text, the visual arts are treated as part of a larger world, in which geography, politics, religion, economics, philosophy, social life, and the other fine arts were related components of a vibrant cultural landscape. This is a daunting agenda for a "Brief" book. But we believe it is essential. Art and architecture have played a central role in human history, and they continue to do so today. Our book will fulfill its purpose if it introduces a broad spectrum of students to some of the richest human achievements created through the centuries and across the globe, and if it inspires those students both to respect and to cherish their historical legacy in the visual arts. Perhaps it will convince some to dedicate themselves to assuring that our own age leaves a comparable artistic legacy, thereby continuing the ever-evolving history of art.

So ... What's New in This Edition?

We believe that even an established introductory art history text should continually respond to the changing needs of its audience—both students and educators. In this way it is more likely to make a greater difference in the role that art can and will assume in its readers' lives, both at the time of use and long into the future—indeed, long after the need for the next revision arises.

Our goal was to make this revised text an improvement over its earlier incarnations in sensitivity, readability, and accessibility without losing anything in comprehensiveness, in scholarly precision, or in its ability to engage the reader. Incorporating feedback from our many users and reviewers, I believe we have succeeded.

Some highlights of the new edition include the following.

- Every chapter now ends with a full-page timeline to help students coordinate the history of art with other aspects of human history.
- A new series of maps has been created to enhance the clarity and accuracy of the relationship between the art discussed and its geographical location and political affiliation.
- Throughout, images have been updated whenever new and improved images were available. New works have been added to the discussion in many chapters to enhance and enrich what is said in the text.
- The language used to characterize works of art—especially those that attempt to capture the lifelike appearance of the natural world—has been refined and clarified to bring greater precision and nuance.
- Depth has been added to the coverage of work by women and minorities, especially in the last few chapters.
- In response to readers' requests, discussion of many major monuments has been expanded.
- Several chapters have been reorganized for greater clarity. The art of the Ancient Near East and Ancient Egypt now have dedicated chapters of their own, while the art of the Hellenistic Mediterranean, the Etruscans, the Neo-Babylonians and the

Persians, has been moved into the chapters on the Ancient Near East, Ancient Greece, and Ancient Rome. Reorganization has also strengthened the chapter on Early Medieval and Romanesque Art, as well as the chapter on Neoclassicism, Realism, and Romanticism.

- In keeping with this book's tradition of inclusivity, an even broader spectrum of media is addressed here, with expanded attention, for example, to Gothic stained glass and Navajo textiles.

New Scholarship

Over the many years we have taught undergraduate beginners, we have always enjoyed sharing—both with our students and our fellow educators—the new discoveries and fresh interpretive perspectives that are constantly enriching the history of art. We relished the opportunity here to incorporate some of the latest thinking and most recent discoveries—whether this involved revising the dating and interpretation of well-known Prehistoric monuments like Stonehenge (fig. 1–16), presenting fascinating new recreations of familiar masterworks such as the "colorized" Aegina archer from Ancient Greece (fig. 5–18), or including a new theory on the meaning of Jan van Eyck's masterful *Double Portrait* (fig. 12–1). Indeed, changes have been made on many levels—from the introduction to the bibliography, and from captions to chapter introductions and conclusions. Every change aims to make the text more useful to the instructors and students in today's art history classrooms.

In Gratitude

As its predecessors did, this Fourth Edition of *Art: A Brief History* benefited from the reflections and assessments of a distinguished team of scholars and educators. We are grateful to the following academic reviewers for their numerous insights and suggestions for improvement:

Scott Brennan-Smith, Cuesta College
Marla Burg, Ventura College
Harold Cole, Baldwin Wallace College
Frances Connelly, University of Missouri – Kansas City
Eva D'Ambra, Vassar College
Sheri Dickson, Tri-County Tech College
Robert Dohrmann, University of Oklahoma
Regina Gee, Montana State University
Marian J Hollinger, Fairmont State University
Susanne Howard, Columbus State University
Anne Leader, City College of New York
Necia Turner Miller, Rose State College
Bonnie J. Noble, University of North Carolina, Charlotte
Susan Slocum, Columbia College
James Swensen, Brigham Young University
Rochelle Weinstein, City College of New York

Chapter by Chapter Revisions

Some of the more prominent highlights of this new edition include the following:

CHAPTER 1

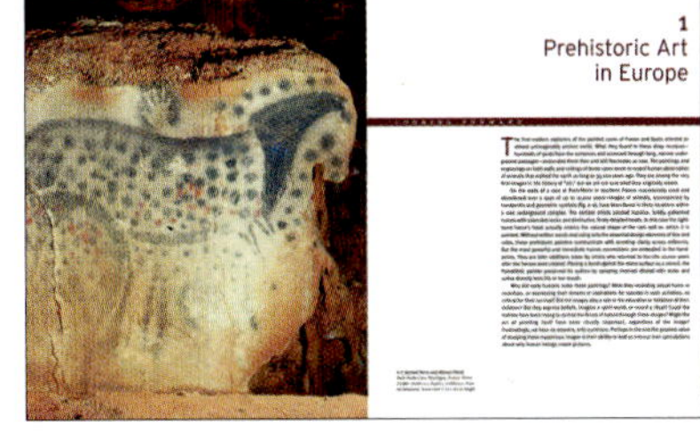

Now focuses only on European prehistoric art and opens with the newly introduced cave paintings of Pech-Merle, with their extraordinary records of actual human hands. The Tuc d'Audoubert bisons add weight to the discussion of prehistoric sculpture, and a "Closer Look" highlights the clay figures from Cernavoda. The interpretation of Stonehenge has been expanded to incorporate the results of important excavations over the past five years.

CHAPTER 2

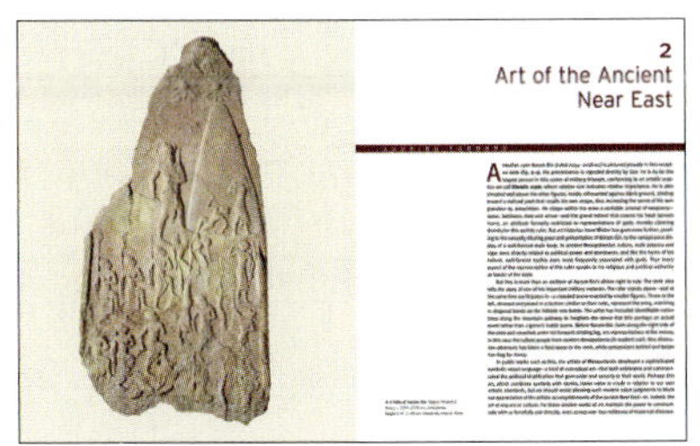

The Ancient Near East is afforded its own chapter, now surveying a broader time-span extending from Mesopotamian Sumer to the expansive Persian Empire. Additional headings clarify the relationship between dynastic succession and artistic developments. A new opener focusing on the Stele of Naram-Sin, incorporates compelling ideas from recent scholarship. A new box on "Art as Spoils of War" cites the impact of the recent Iraq war on local antiquities.

CHAPTER 3

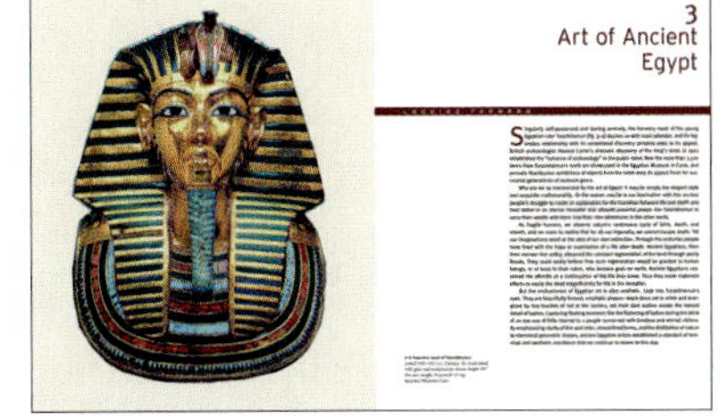

A new box on Periods of Ancient Egyptian Art extracts material formerly in the text to make it more accessible to students. Discussion of Old Kingdom architecture is consolidated and expanded, and a new sculpted portrait of Hatshepsut allows discussion of the constitution of her royal image as well as the design of her funerary temple. A newly-developed box on the Tomb of Ramose highlights a spectacular example of New Kingdom art and clarifies the dramatic change in a new direction that will soon occur under the reign of Akhenaten. A Fayum mummy added at the end projects the history of Egyptian art forward into the Roman period.

CHAPTER 4

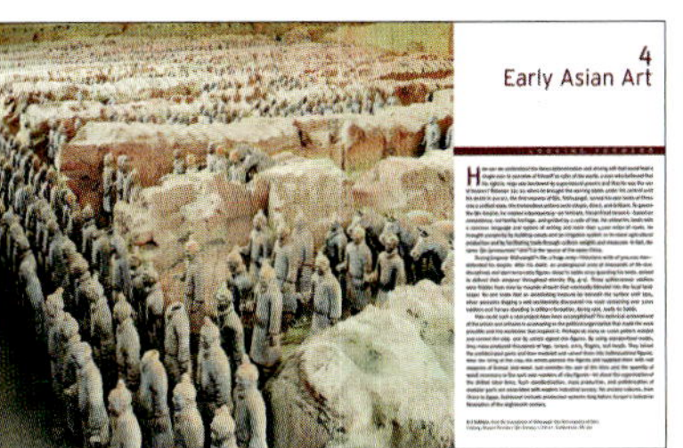

A male torso from Harappa has been added to represent the art of the Indus Valley in a way that is more consistent with the interpretive narrative of this chapter. A newly developed map shows the geographic relationship among the great river cultures of Asia and those of Africa and the Near East discussed in the previous two chapters.

CHAPTER 5

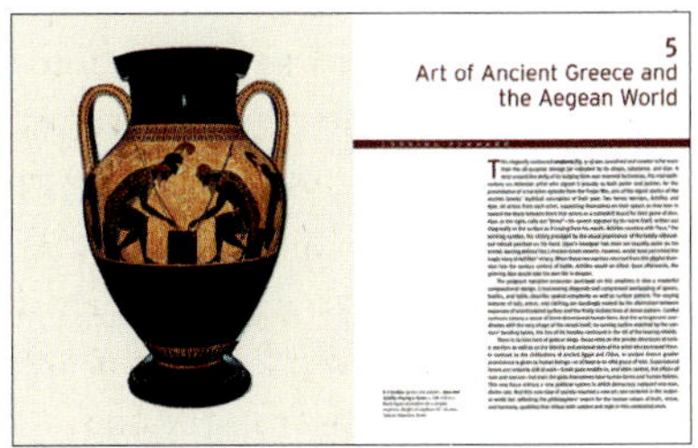

Through a reorganization of chapter divisions, the history of ancient Greek art has been extended here into the Hellenistic period. A new opener highlights the narrative power of Greek painting by showcasing a masterpiece by Exekias. An expanded box on temple design integrates a discussion of planning with the decorative system of Greek Orders. A new box on color in Greek sculpture reports on revealing new research. Discussion of the Celts gives cultural identity to the dying warrior from Pergamon.

CHAPTER 6

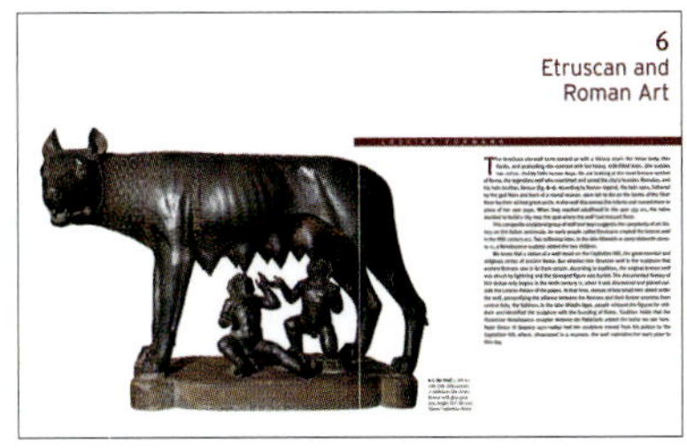

Discussion of the Etruscans has been moved to the beginning of this chapter. Many figures have been improved with better images, notably the Ara Pacis, which is shown in its new architectural setting. An added box addresses the place of portraiture in the Roman funeral ritual. Discussion of portraits is expanded throughout to enrich student understanding of varying idealized modalities—classicizing and tetrarchic, as well as veristic. The Basilica Ulpia is now illustrated with a reconstructed view of the interior, and discussion of the Arch of Constantine is consolidated at the end of the chapter.

CHAPTER 7

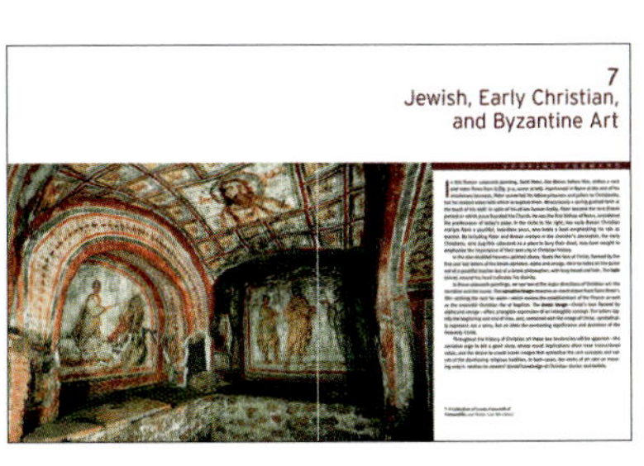

A new "Closer Look" on Dura-Europos recounts the story of the preservation and rediscovery of important monuments of early Jewish and Christian architectural art. A reworked and expanded box on longitudinal and central planning characterizes these important architectural types in Early Christian architecture, and a much transformed box on the naming of Christian churches brings clarity to a topic that often confuses students. Iconoclasm is the subject of another new box, addressing not only the suppression of images in Byzantium, but more modern instances of iconoclastic fervor.

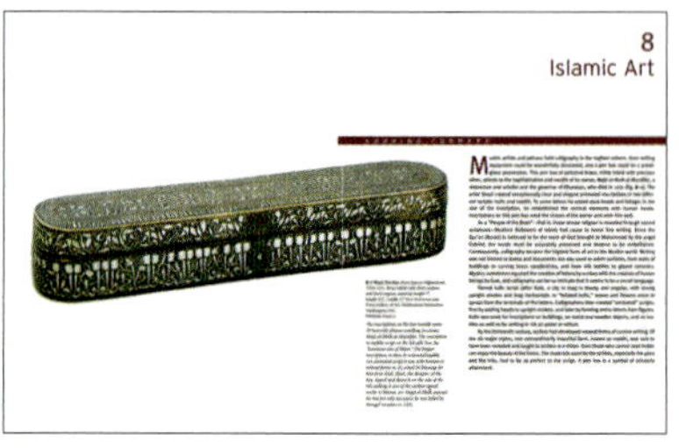

CHAPTER 8

The early part of the chapter is reorganized to consolidate the architectural discussion first, and introduce calligraphy afterwards. Plans of mosques have been juxtaposed with pictures of each building rather than grouped within a box. A picture by legendary painter Bihzad is added to the discussion of Persian manuscripts. Hasan Fathy's modern Egyptian mosque closes the chapter to underline that Islamic art is not a phenomenon restricted to the past.

CHAPTER 9

The text has been revised for greater accuracy and clarity, and three images are new to this edition.

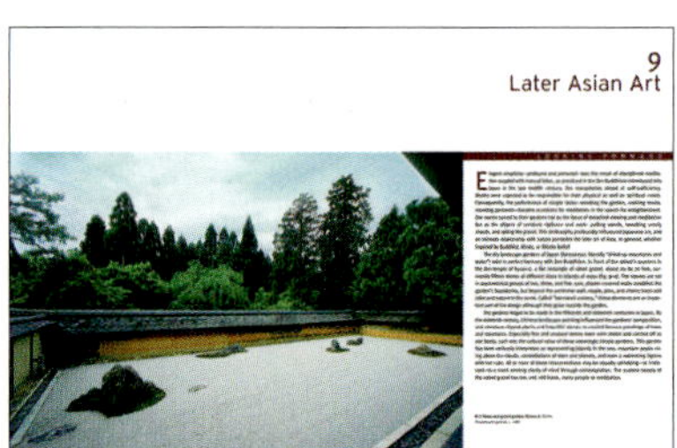

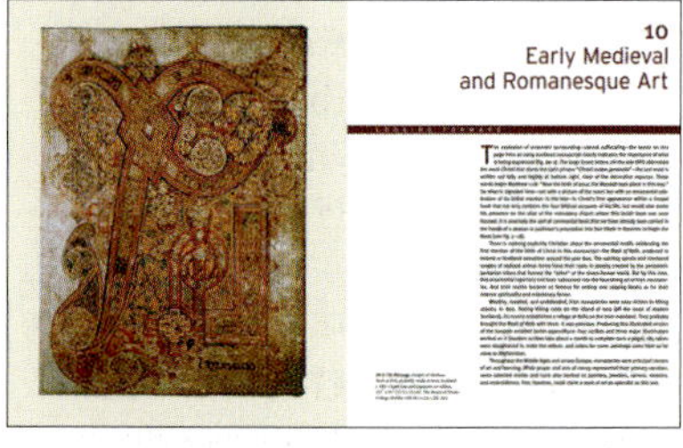

CHAPTER 10

This chapter has been significantly reorganized, important new works added or substituted, and treatment of major monuments expanded. The chapter begins with the spectacularly complex *Chi Rho* page of the Book of Kells. With the inclusion of additional pages from Carolingian gospel books and a two-page painting from an astonishingly expressionistic Spanish Beatus manuscript, as the chapter builds, students will gain a better sense of the rich stylistic diversity in Early Medieval book arts. The introduction of the *Gero Crucifix* allows an expansion of attention to Ottonian sculpture. New boxes focus on the Bayeux Embroidery and the paintings of Hildegard of Bingen.

CHAPTER 11

Selective pruning and a refocus on major monuments bring clarity to the discussion of architecture, sculpture, and illuminated books. The addition of the *Flight into Egypt* from a window at Saint-Denis, along with a more developed technique box, enriches the discussion of the stained glass that is so central to the history of Gothic art and architecture. The entire breadth of Ambrogio Lorenzetti's *Effects of Good Government* fresco is now illustrated. The illustration of the Raising of Lazarus from Duccio's *Maestà* allows a fuller discussion of the narrative styles of early fourteenth-century Italian painting. A new box on fresco technique balances the box on panel painting repeated from the previous edition.

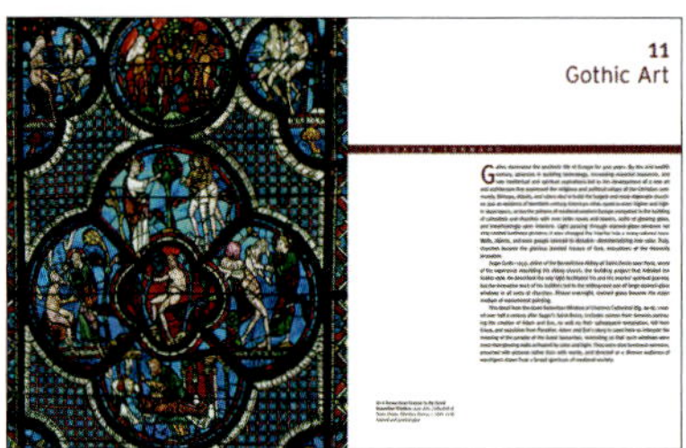

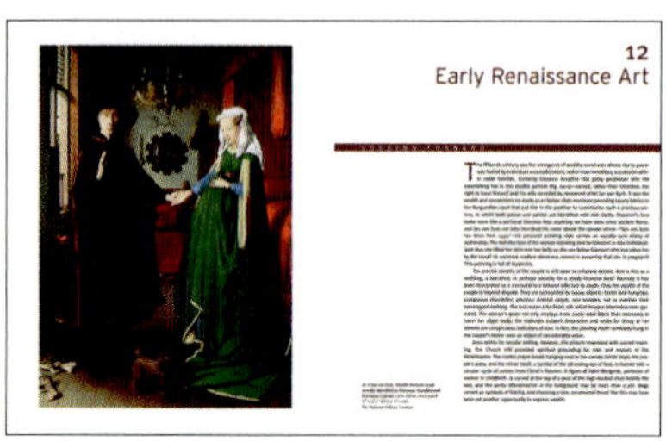

CHAPTER 12

A new opener on Jan van Eyck's *Double Portrait* expands discussion of new interpretive theories on the meaning of this seminal work and provides a smoother transition into the northern painting with which this chapter begins. A new box addresses the technique of oil painting that was so central to the work of van Eyck and his Flemish contemporaries. A new "Closer Look" explores the competition between Ghiberti and Brunelleschi to secure the commission for the Duomo Baptistery bronze doors at the dawn of the Florentine Renaissance. Expanded treatment of Ghiberti's subsequent *Doors of Paradise* adds the illustration of a single panel as well as the whole ensemble.

CHAPTER 13

A new picture of Michelangelo's Sistine Ceiling is supplemented by a juxtaposed diagram identifying the subjects portrayed. Treatment of the French Renaissance is expanded to include Clouet's portrait of Francis I—important in relation to Holbein's portrait of Henry VIII. A sculptural panel by Properizia de' Rossi expands further on the increasingly prominent role women artists acquired during the Renaissance. There is also reworked and expanded treatment of Titan's *Venus of Urbino* and Grünewald's *Isenheim Altarpiece*, and Cranach's *Nymph of the Spring* replaces Altdorfer's *Danube Landscape*.

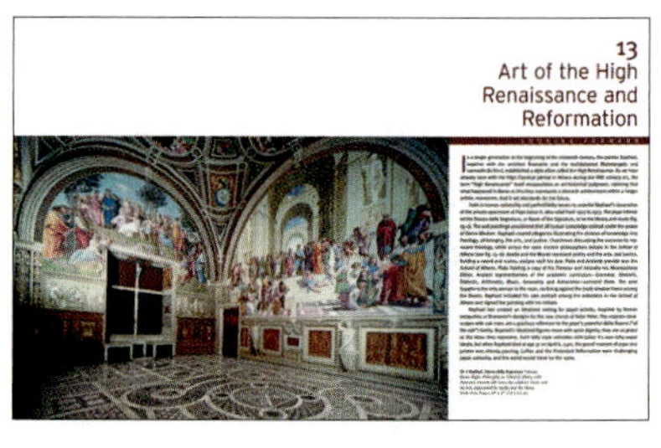

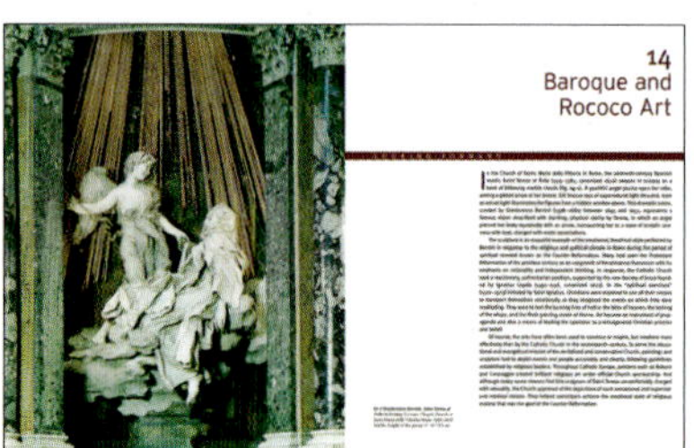

CHAPTER 14

An overall view of the Contarelli Chapel allows Caravaggio's *Calling of Saint Matthew* to be seen in context, and *Bacchus* has been added to represent Caravaggio's secular paintings. Responding to readers' requests, treatment of major monuments such as Velázquez's *Las Meninas* has been expanded.

Substitution of a more intimate portrait by Hals gives greater range to the treatment of Dutch painting, and Rembrandt's *Anatomy Lesson of Dr. Tulp* has been added to coordinate with the discussion of science and art, moved up from the end of the chapter and into the treatment of painting in Holland. The chapter now ends with the Rococo.

CHAPTER 15

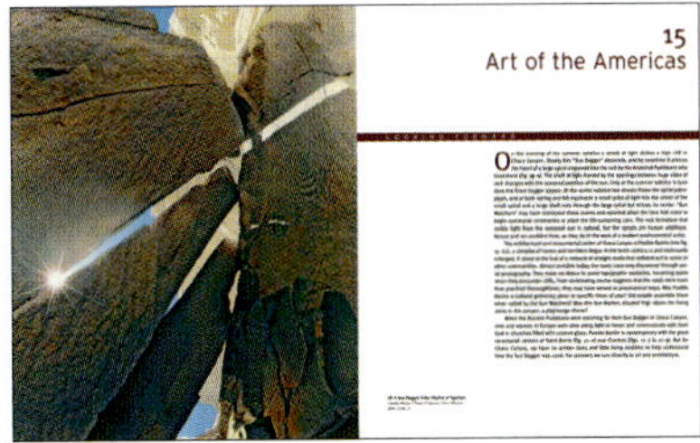

A new opener on Chaco Canyon evokes the use of ancient Native American art in social life and ritual. A contemporary textile by Julia Jumbo brings a Navajo work into the consideration of art in the North American southwest.

CHAPTER 16

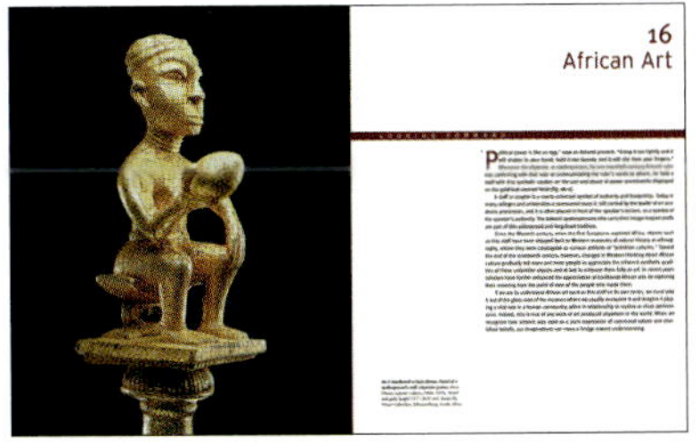

A new text for the opener, additional discursive captions, and some reorganization bring further clarity to the presentation of African art. The box on lost-wax casting technique was moved into this chapter within the context of the Benin bronzes.

CHAPTER 17

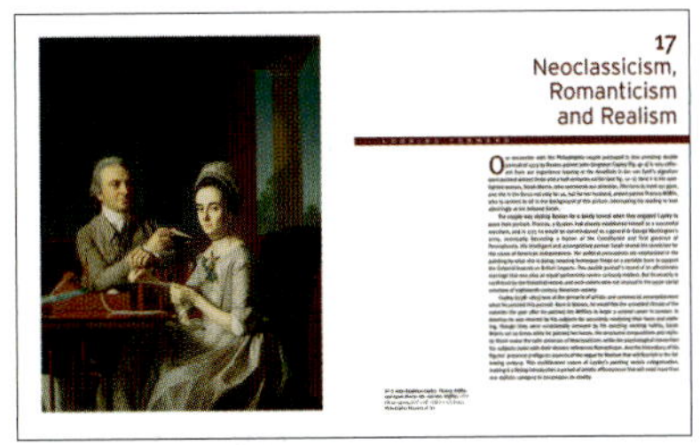

A new opener focuses on the way Copley's portraits of couples establish the strong role of women in American colonial history. The chapter has been completely reorganized to clarify the way the art historical categories of Neoclassicism, Romanticism, and Realism have been used to organize the discussion of European and American art from the late eighteenth to the middle of the nineteenth century. New paintings by Delacroix, Millet, and Turner strengthen the discussion of these major artists.

CHAPTER 18

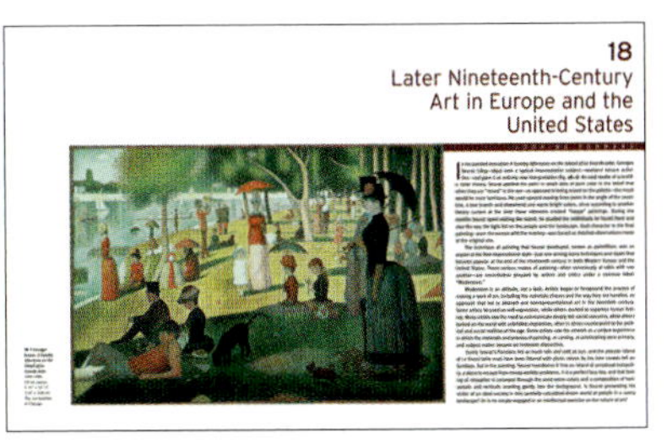

Reorganization of the chapter has brought clarity to the presentation of this complex but critical period in the history of art. Gaudí now is represented by the more characteristic Casa Batllò. Greater attention is given to Whistler through the discussion of one of his *Nocturnes*—in relation to the influential trial that pitted him against the critic John Ruskin. Manet is incorporated into the discussion of Realism rather than Impressionism, conforming to standard art historical practice and consistent with the character of his paintings. Greater attention has been given to Eakins, especially his *Gross Clinic*. A new box on Japonisme also provides extended treatment of van Gogh.

CHAPTER 19

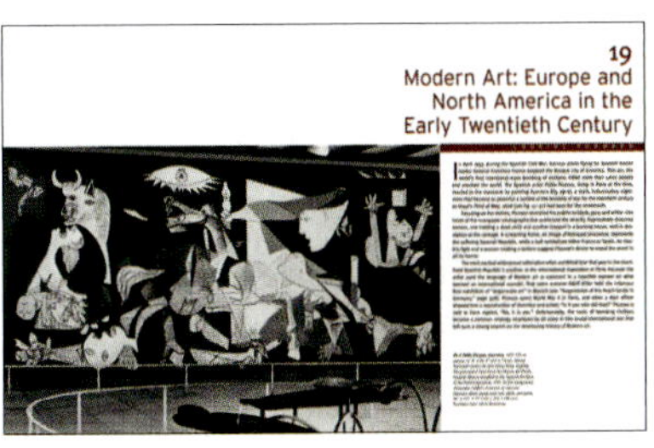

Picasso's *Guernica* is the new, more compelling opener. Artists introduced to the chapter include Léger, Popova, and Mary Colter. Kandinsky, Stieglitz, Miro, and Le Corbusier are represented by new works. A new "Closer Look" on Marsden Hartley reveals the personal meanings that often stand behind abstract art. New exterior views of the Schröder House and the Woolworth Building strengthen treatment of architecture. Treatment of European art between the wars is reorganized to integrate the discussion of architecture with related developments in other arts. The image of Frank Lloyd Wright's Fallingwater in the winter has been replaced with an autumnal view when the water is actually "falling."

CHAPTER 20

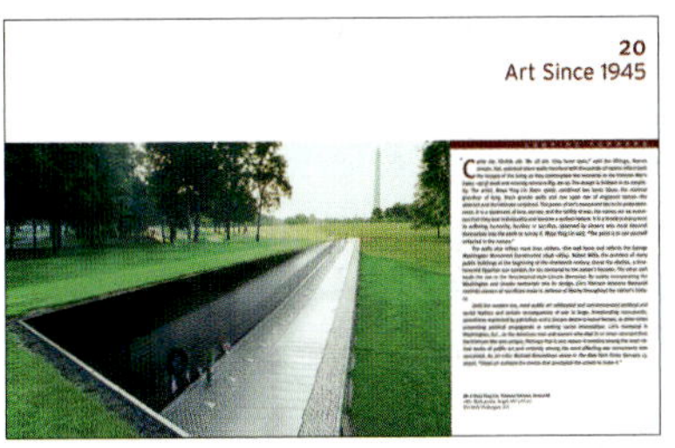

An added picture of Jackson Pollock painting gives visual form to action painting. New works by Jaune Quick-to-See Smith, Judith Baca, and Kerry James Marshall expand the representation of artists of diverse ethnic backgrounds and works that call for social change. Illustration of a pioneering domestic work of Robert Venturi develops the discussion of Postmodern architecture. The addition of a 2008 work by Hiroyuki Hamada and the reorganization of the conclusion to focus on Santiago Calatrava's Transportation Hub at the site of the World Trade Center in New York extend the works of art in this chapter well into the first decade of the twenty-first century.

Faculty and Student Resources for Teaching & Learning with *Art: A Brief History*

Pearson/Prentice Hall. We are pleased to present an outstanding array of high quality resources for teaching and learning with Stokstad's *Art: A Brief History*. Please contact your local Prentice Hall representative (use our rep locator at www.pearsonhighered.com) for more details on how to obtain these items, or send us an email at art.service@pearson.com.

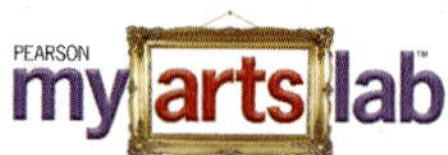

www.myartslab.com Save time, improve results. MyArtsLab is a robust online learning environment providing you and your students with the following resources:

- Complete and dynamic e-book
- Illustrated and printable flashcards
- Unique "Closer Look" tours of over 125 key works of art
- Pre-and post-tests for every chapter of the book
- Customized study plan that helps students focus in on key areas
- Primary Sources with critical thinking questions
- Writing Tutorials for the most common writing assignments

Available at no additional charge when packaged with the text. Learn more about the power of MyArtsLab and register today at www.myartslab.com

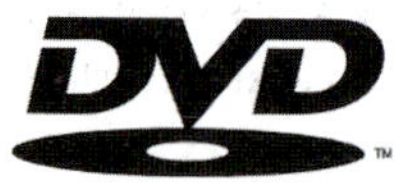

The Prentice Hall Digital Art Library. Instructors who adopt Stokstad's *Art: A Brief History* are eligible to receive this unparalleled resource containing every image in *Art: A Brief History* in the highest resolution (over 300 dpi) and pixellation possible for optimal projection and easy download. Developed and endorsed by a panel of visual curators and instructors across the country, this resource features over 1,600 illustrations in jpeg and in PowerPoint, an instant download function for easy import into any presentation software, along with a zoom feature, and a compare/contrast function, both of which are unique and were developed exclusively for Prentice Hall.

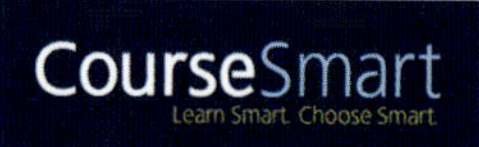

CourseSmart eTextbooks Online is an exciting new choice for students looking to save money. As an alternative to purchasing the print textbook, students can subscribe to the same content online and save up to 50% off the suggested list price of the print text. With a CourseSmart eTextbook, students can search the text, make notes online, print out reading assignments that incorporate lecture notes, and bookmark important passages for later review. For more information, or to subscribe to the CourseSmart eTextbook, visit www.coursesmart.com.

Classroom Response System (CRS) In Class Questions (ISBN: 0-205-76545-9). Get instant, class-wide responses to beautifully illustrated chapter-specific questions during a lecture to gauge student comprehension—and keep them engaged. Contact your local Prentice Hall sales representative for details.

MyTest (ISBN: 0-205-76544-0) is a commercial-quality computerized test management program available for both Microsoft Windows and Macintosh environments.

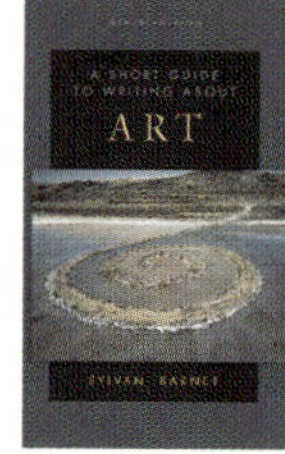

A Short Guide to Writing About Art, 10/e (ISBN: 0-205-70825-0) by Sylvan Barnet. This best-selling text has guided tens of thousands of art students throught the writing process. Students are shown how to analyze pictures (drawings, paintings, photographs), sculptures, and architecture, and are prepared with the tools they need to present their ideas through effective writing. Available at a discount when purchased with the text.

Instructor's Resource Manual with Test Bank (ISBN: 0-205-76543-2, download only) is an invaluable professional resource and reference for new and experienced faculty, containing sample syllabi, hundreds of sample test questions, and guidance on incorporating media technology into your course.

Art: A Brief History is a concise version of *Art History,* which was first published in 1995 by Harry N. Abrams, Inc. and Prentice Hall, Inc. Because this new edition builds on the revisions of previous editions of both *Art History* and *Art: A Brief History,* the work of many colleagues and friends who contributed to the original texts and their subsequent revisions is reflected here. We extend to them our long-term gratitude.

We worked closely with two gifted and dedicated editors at Pearson/Prentice Hall, Sarah Touborg and Helen Ronan, to craft a book that would incorporate effective pedagogical features into a shortened art historical narrative. At Pearson, Helen Ronan, Barbara Cappuccio, Marlene Gassler, Cory Skidds, Brian Mackey, David Nitti, and Carla Worner supported us in our work. At Laurence King Publishing, Donald Dinwiddie, Kara Hattersley-Smith, Julia Ruxton, Evi Peroulaki, and Simon Walsh oversaw the production of this new edition. Much appreciation also goes to Brandy Dawson, Director of Marketing, and Laura Lee Manley, Marketing Manager, as well as the entire Social Sciences and Arts team at Prentice Hall.

From Marilyn Stokstad:

I extend my thanks to Robert D. Mowry and Claudia Brown for their contributions and assistance with Asian art, Patrick Frank for Modern and Latin American art, D. Fairchild Ruggles for Islamic art, Sara E. Orel for art of the Pacific Islands, and Patricia J. Darish and David A. Binkley for African art.

Of course, my very special thanks go to my sister, Karen Leider, and my niece, Anna Leider.

From Michael W. Cothren:

Words are barely adequate to express my gratitude to Marilyn Stokstad for welcoming me with such trust, enthusiasm, and warmth into the collaborative adventure of revising this book. Working alongside her—and our extraordinary editors Sarah Touborg and Helen Ronan—has been delightful and rewarding, enriching and challenging. I look forward to continuing the partnership.

I have been supported by a host of colleagues at Swarthmore College. Generations of students challenged me to hone my pedagogical skills and steady my focus on what is at stake in telling the history of art. I am particularly indebted to Susan Eberhard (class of 2009), who introduced me to the astonishing Copley portrait that now opens Chapter 17. The staff of McCabe Library—especially my friend Mary Marissen—located, or even acquired, the books I needed at the moment they were necessary. Special thanks to List Gallery Director Andrea Packard, who brought the work of Hiroyuki Hamada to campus and set in motion my connection with him that led ultimately to his inclusion in this edition. My fellow teachers in the Art Department—especially Randall Exon, Nikki Greene, Constance Cain Hungerford, Janine Mileaf, Kathryn O'Rourke, Patricia Reilly, and Tomoko Sakomura—have answered all sorts of questions, shared innumerable insights on works in their areas of expertise, and offered unending encouragement and support. I am so lucky to work with them.

Many art historians have generously provided assistance, and I am especially grateful to Betina Bergman, Cheri Falkenstien-Doyle, Ann Kuttner, Elizabeth Marlowe, Thomas Morton, Mary Shepard, David Simon, Donna Sadler, and Jeffrey Chipps Smith.

I was fortunate to have the support of friends David Eldridge, Stephen Lehmann, and Bianca O'Keefe, who patiently listened and truly relished my enjoyment of this work. My extraordinary daughters Emma and Nora are a constant inspiration. I am so grateful for their delight in my passion for art's history, and for their dedication to keeping me from taking myself too seriously. My deepest gratitude is reserved for Susan Lowry, my wife and soulmate, who brings joy to every facet of my life. She was not only patient and supportive during the long distraction of my work on this book, she also provided help in so very many ways. The greatest accomplishment of my life in art history occurred on the day I met her at Columbia in 1973.

If the arts are ultimately an expression of human faith and integrity as well as human thought and creativity, then writing and producing books that introduce new viewers to the wonders of art's history, and to the courage and visions of the artists and art historians that stand behind it—remains a noble undertaking. We feel honored to be a part of such a worthy project.

Marilyn Stokstad
Lawrence, Kansas

Michael W. Cothren
Swarthmore, PA

Spring 2009

Use Notes

The various features of this book reinforce each other, helping the reader to become comfortable with terminology and concepts that are specific to art history.

Starter Kit and Introduction The Starter Kit is a highly concise primer of basic concepts and tools. The outer margins of the Starter Kit pages are tinted to make them easy to find. The Introduction is an invitation to the many pleasures of art history.

Captions There are two kinds of captions in this book: short and long. Short captions identify information specific to the work of art or architecture illustrated:

artist (when known)
title or descriptive name of work
date
original location (if moved to a museum or other site)
material or materials a work is made of
size (height before width) in feet and inches, with meters and centimeters in parentheses
present location

The order of these elements varies, depending on the type of work illustrated. Dimensions are not given for architecture, for most wall paintings, or for most architectural sculpture. Some captions have one or more lines of small print below the identification section of the caption that gives museum or collection information. This is rarely required reading.

Long captions contain information that complements the narrative of the main text.

Definitions of Terms You will encounter the basic terms of art history in three places:

IN THE TEXT, where words appearing in **boldface** type are defined, or glossed, at their first use. Some terms are boldfaced and explained more than once, especially those that experience shows are hard to remember.

IN BOXED FEATURES on technique and other subjects, where labeled drawings and diagrams visually reinforce the use of terms.

IN THE GLOSSARY at the end of the volume, which contains all the words in **boldface** type in the text and boxes. The Glossary begins on page 605, and the outer margins are tinted to make it easy to find.

Maps and Timelines At the beginning of each chapter you will find a map with all the places mentioned in the chapter. At the end if each chapter, a timeline runs from the earliest through the latest years covered in that chapter.

Boxes Special material that complements, enhances, explains, or extends the text is set off in three types of tinted boxes. Elements of Architecture boxes clarify specifically architectural features, such as "Post-and-Lintel and Corbel Construction" in Chapter 1 (page 33). Technique boxes (see "Stained-Glass Windows," page 275) amplify the methodology by which a type of artwork is created. Other boxes treat special-interest material related to the text.

Bibliography The bibliography at the end of this book beginning on page 613 contains books in English, organized by general works and by chapter, that are basic to the study of art history today, as well as works cited in the text.

Dates, Abbreviations, and Other Conventions This book uses the designations BCE and CE, abbreviations for "before the Common Era" and "Common Era," instead of BC ("before Christ") and AD ("Anno Domini," "the year of our Lord"). The first century BCE is the period from 99 BCE to 1 BCE; the first century CE is from the year 1 CE to 99 CE. Similarly, the second century BCE is the period from 199 BCE to 100 BCE; the second century CE extends from 100 CE to 199 CE.

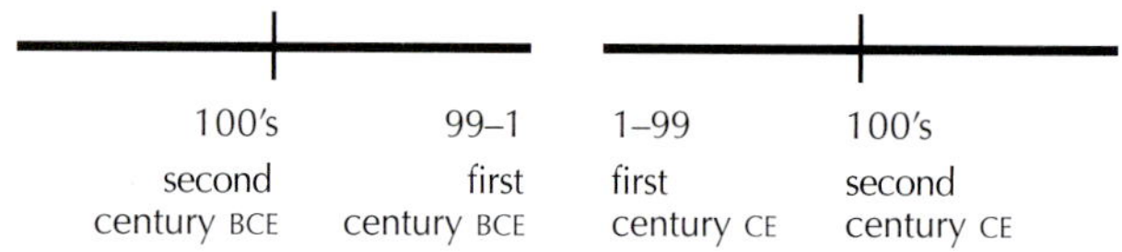

Circa ("about" or "approximately") is used with dates, spelled out in the text and abbreviated to "c." in the captions, when an exact date is not yet verified.

An illustration is called a "figure," or "fig." Thus, figure 6–7 is the seventh numbered illustration in Chapter 6. Figures Intro–1 through Intro–30 are in the Introduction. There are two types of figures: photographs of artworks or of models, and line drawings. Drawings are used when a work cannot be photographed or when a diagram or simple drawing is the clearest way to illustrate an object or a place.

When introducing artists, we use the words active and documented with dates, in addition to "b." (for "born") and "d." (for "died"). "Active" means that an artist worked during the years given. "Documented" means that documents link the person to that date.

Accents are used for words in French, German, Italian, and Spanish only.

With few exceptions, names of museums and other cultural bodies in Western European countries are given in the form used in that country.

Titles of Works of Art Most paintings and works of sculpture created in Europe and North America in the past 500 years have been given formal titles, either by the artist or by critics and art historians. Such formal titles are printed in italics. In other traditions and cultures, a single title is not important or even recognized. In this book we use formal descriptive titles of artworks where titles are not established. If a work is best known by its non-English title, such as Manet's *Le Déjeuner sur l'herbe* (*The Luncheon on the Grass*), the original language precedes the translation.

Starter Kit

Art history focuses on the visual arts—painting, drawing, sculpture, prints, photography, ceramics, metalwork, architecture, and more. This Starter Kit contains basic information and addresses concepts that underlie and support the study of art history. It provides a quick reference guide to the vocabulary used to classify and describe art objects. Understanding these terms is indispensable since you will encounter them again and again in reading, talking, and writing about art.

Let us begin with the basic properties of art. A work of art is a material object having both form and content. It is often described and categorized according to its STYLE and MEDIUM.

FORM

Referring to purely visual aspects of art and architecture, the term *form* encompasses qualities of LINE, SHAPE, COLOR, LIGHT, TEXTURE, SPACE, MASS, VOLUME, and COMPOSITION. These qualities are known as FORMAL ELEMENTS. When art historians use the term *formal,* they mean "relating to form."

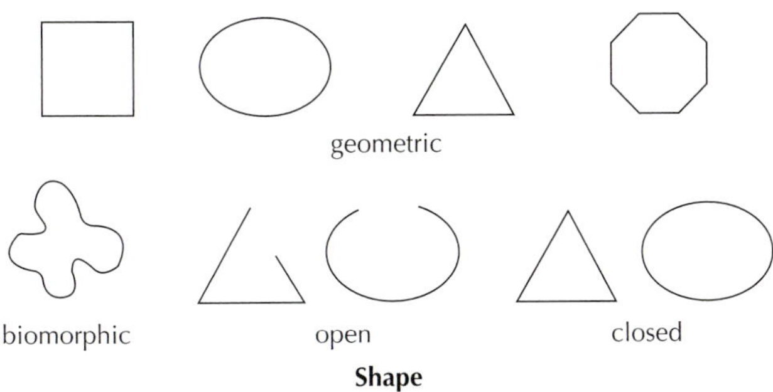

Shape

Line and **shape** are attributes of form. Line is a form—usually drawn or painted—the length of which is so much greater than the width that we perceive it as having only length. Line can be actual, as when the line is visible, or it can be implied, as when the movement of the viewer's eyes over the surface of a work follows a path determined by the artist. Shape, on the other hand, is the two-dimensional, or flat, area defined by the borders of an enclosing *outline* or *contour.* Shape can be *geometric, biomorphic* (suggesting living things; sometimes called *organic*), *closed,* or *open.* The *outline* or *contour* of a three-dimensional object can also be perceived as line.

Color has several attributes. These include HUE, VALUE, and SATURATION.

HUE is what we think of when we hear the word *color,* and the terms are interchangeable. We perceive hues as the result of differing wavelengths of electromagnetic energy. The visible spectrum, which can be seen in a rainbow, runs from red through violet. When the ends of the spectrum are connected through the hue red-violet, the result may be diagrammed as a color wheel. The primary hues (numbered 1) are red, yellow, and

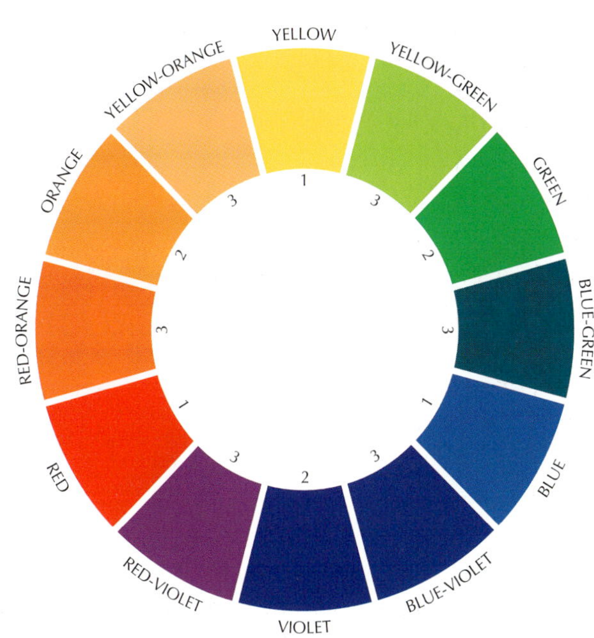

blue. They are known as primaries because all other colors are made by combining these hues. Orange, green, and violet result from the mixture of two primaries and are known as secondary hues (numbered 2). Intermediate hues, or tertiaries (numbered 3), result from the mixture of a primary and a secondary. Complementary colors are the two colors directly opposite one another on the color wheel, such as red and green. Red, orange, and yellow are regarded as warm colors and appear to advance toward us. Blue, green, and violet, which seem to recede, are called cool colors. Black and white are not considered colors but neutrals; in terms of light, black is understood as the absence of color and white as the mixture of all colors.

VALUE is the relative degree of lightness or darkness of a given color and is created by the amount of light reflected from an object's surface. A dark green has a deeper value than a light green, for example. In black-and-white reproductions of colored objects, you see only value, and some artworks—for example, a drawing made with black ink—possesses only value, not hue or saturation.

Value scale from white to black.

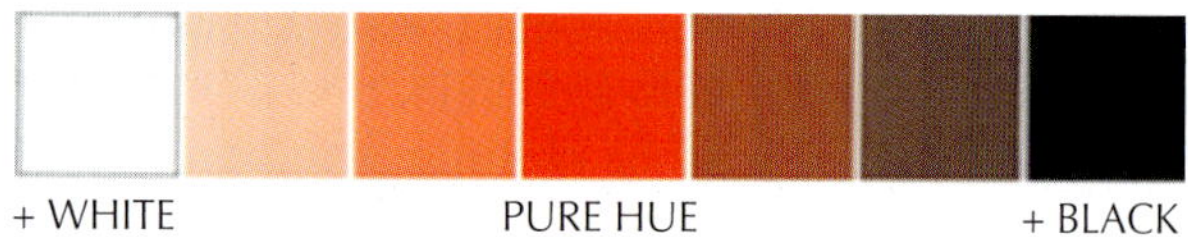

Value variation in red.

SATURATION, also sometimes referred to as INTENSITY, is a color's quality of brightness or dullness. A color described as highly saturated looks vivid and pure; a hue of low saturation may look a little muddy or dark.

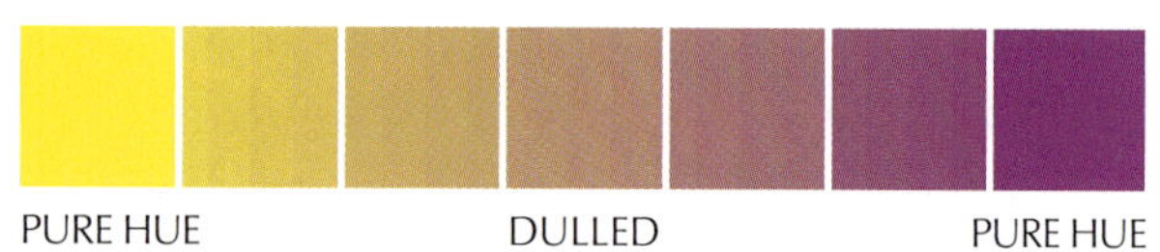

Intensity scale from bright to dull.

Texture, another attribute of form, is the tactile (or touch-perceived) quality of a surface. It is described by words such as *smooth, polished, rough, prickly, grainy,* or *oily.* Texture takes two forms: the texture of the actual surface of the work of art and the implied (illusionistically described) surface of the object represented in the work.

Space is what contains objects. It may be actual and three-dimensional, as it is with sculpture and architecture, or it may be fictional, represented illusionistically in two dimensions, as when artists represent recession into the distance on a flat surface—such as a wall or a canvas—by using various systems of perspective.

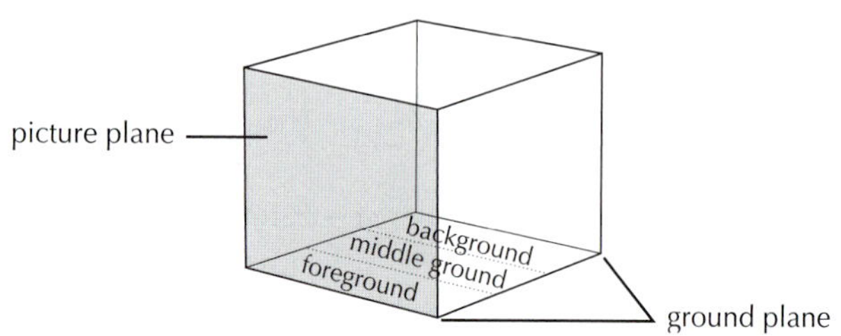

Mass and **volume** are properties of three-dimensional things. Mass is matter—whether sculpture or architecture—that takes up space. Volume is space that is enclosed or defined, and may be either solid or hollow. Like space, mass and volume may be represented illusionistically on a two-dimensional surface, such as a painting or a photograph.

Composition is the organization, or arrangement, of forms in a work of art. Shapes and colors may be repeated or varied, balanced symmetrically or asymmetrically; they may be stable or dynamic. The possibilities are nearly endless and depend both on the time and place where the work was created as well as the objectives of individual artists. PICTORIAL DEPTH (spatial recession) is a specialized aspect of composition in which the three-dimensional world is represented on a flat surface, or PICTURE PLANE. The area "behind" the picture plane is called the PICTURE SPACE and conventionally contains three "zones": FOREGROUND, MIDDLE GROUND, and BACKGROUND.

Various techniques for conveying a sense of pictorial depth have been devised by artists in different cultures and at different times. A number of them are diagrammed here. In some Western art, the use of various systems of PERSPECTIVE has sought to create highly convincing illusions of recession into space. At other times and in other cultures, perspective is not the most favored way to treat objects in space.

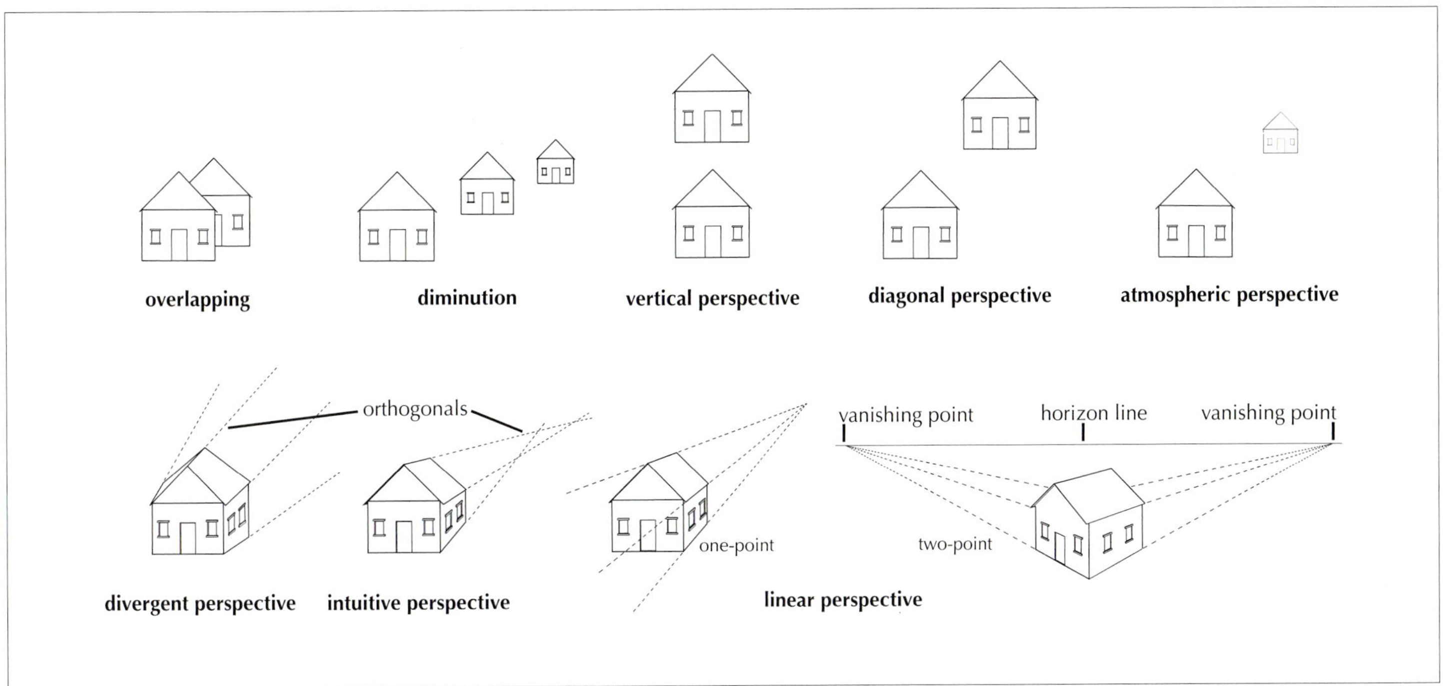

Pictorial devices for depicting recession in space

The top row shows several comparatively simple devices, including OVERLAPPING, in which partially covered elements are meant to be seen as located behind those covering them, and DIMINUTION OF SCALE, in which smaller elements are to be perceived as being farther away than larger ones. In VERTICAL PERSPECTIVE (space in registers), elements are stacked vertically, with the higher elements intended to be perceived as deeper in space. Another way of suggesting depth is through ATMOSPHERIC PERSPECTIVE, which depicts objects in the far distance, often in bluish-gray hues, with less clarity than nearer objects and treats sky as paler near the horizon than higher up.

In the lower row, DIVERGENT or REVERSE PERSPECTIVE, in which forms widen slightly and lines diverge as they recede in space. INTUITIVE PERSPECTIVE takes the opposite approach: Forms become narrower and converge the farther they are from the viewer, approximating the optical experience of spatial recession. LINEAR PERSPECTIVE, also called SCIENTIFIC, MATHEMATICAL, ONE-POINT, and RENAISSANCE PERSPECTIVE, is an elaboration and standardization of intuitive perspective and was developed in fifteenth-century Italy. It uses mathematical formulas to construct illusionistic images in which all elements are shaped by, or arranged along, imaginary lines called ORTHOGONALS that converge in one or more VANISHING POINTS on a HORIZON LINE. Linear perspective is the system that most people living in Western cultures think of as perspective. Because it is the traditional visual code they are accustomed to reading, they accept as "truth" the distortions it imposes. One of these distortions is the assumption of a single viewpoint.

CONTENT

Content includes SUBJECT MATTER, which is what a work of art represents. Not all works of art have subject matter; many buildings, paintings, sculptures, and other art objects include no recognizable references to things in nature, focusing instead on lines, colors, masses, volumes, and other formal elements. However, all works of art—even those without recognizable subject matter—have content, or meaning, insofar as they seek to communicate ideas, convey feelings, or affirm the beliefs and values of their makers, their patrons, and usually the people who originally viewed or used them.

Content may derive from the social, political, religious, and economic CONTEXTS in which a work was created, the INTENTION of the artist, and the RECEPTION of the work by beholders (the audience). Art historians, applying different methods of INTERPRETATION, often arrive at different conclusions regarding the content of a work of art, and single works of art can contain more than one meaning because they are occasionally directed at more than one audience.

The study of subject matter is called ICONOGRAPHY (literally, "the writing of images") and includes the identification of SYMBOLS—images that take on meaning through association, resemblance, or convention.

STYLE

Expressed very broadly, *style* is the combination of form and composition that makes a work distinctive. STYLISTIC ANALYSIS is one of art history's most developed practices, because it is how art historians recognize the work of an individual artist or the characteristic manner of several artists working in a particular time or place. Some of the most commonly used terms to discuss ARTISTIC STYLES include PERIOD STYLE, REGIONAL STYLE, REPRESENTATIONAL STYLE, ABSTRACT STYLE, LINEAR STYLE, and PAINTERLY STYLE.

Period style refers to the common traits detectable in works of art and architecture from a particular historical era. It is good practice not to use the words "style" and "period" interchangeably. Style is the sum of many influences and characteristics, including the time period during which it was created. An example of proper usage would be "an American house from the Colonial period built in the Georgian style."

Regional style refers to stylistic traits that persist in a geographic region. An art historian whose specialty is medieval art can recognize Spanish style through many successive medieval periods and can distinguish individual objects created in medieval Spain from other medieval objects that were created in, for example, Italy.

Representational styles are those that describe the appearance of recognizable subject matter in ways that make it seem lifelike.

REALISM and NATURALISM are terms that some people used interchangeably to characterize artists' attempts to represent the observable world in a manner that appears to describe its visual appearance accurately. When capitalized, Realism refers to a specific period style discussed in Chapter 17.

IDEALIZATION strives to create images of physical perfection according to the prevailing values of a culture. The artist may work in a representational style and idealize it to capture an underlying or expressive reality. Both *The Medici Venus* and Utamaro's *Woman at the Height of Her Beauty* (see figs. Intro–6 and Intro–8) can be considered IDEALIZED.

ILLUSIONISM refers to a highly detailed style that seeks to create a convincing illusion of physical reality. *Flower Piece with Curtain* is a good example of this *trompe l'oeil* (trick-the-eye) form of realism (see fig. Intro–2).

Abstract styles depart from mimicking lifelike appearance to capture the essence of a form. An abstract artist may work from nature or from a memory image of nature's forms and colors, which are simplified, stylized, perfected, distorted, elaborated, or otherwise transformed to achieve a desired expressive effect. Georgia O'Keeffe's *Red Canna* and the Indian bronze statue of *Punitavati* are both abstracted representations of nature (see figs. Intro–4 and Intro–9). NONREPRESENTATIONAL ART and EXPRESSIONISM are particular kinds of abstract styles.

NONREPRESENTATIONAL (OR NONOBJECTIVE) ART is a form that does not produce recognizable natural imagery. *Cubi XVII, XVIII*, and *XIX* are nonrepresentational (see fig. Intro–5).

EXPRESSIONISM refers to styles in which the artist exaggerates aspects of form to draw out the beholder's subjective response or to project the artist's own subjective feelings. Munch's *The Scream* is expressionistic (see fig. 18–30).

Linear describes both style and techniques. In linear styles artists use line as the primary means of definition. Utamaro's *Woman at the Height of Her Beauty* is created in a linear style (see fig. Intro–8). But linear paintings can also incorporate MODELING—creating an illusion of three-dimensional substance through shading, usually executed so that brushstrokes nearly disappear. Raphael's *The Small Cowper Madonna* combines linear outlines and modeled sculptural forms (see fig. 13–5).

Painterly describes a style of representation in which vigorous, evident brushstrokes dominate and outlines, shadows, and highlights are brushed in freely. Rembrandt's *Self-Portrait* of 1658 is a good example (see fig. 14–24). Sculpture in which complex surfaces emphasize moving light and shade is also called "painterly." Claudel's *The Waltz* is painterly sculpture (see fig. 18–34).

MEDIUM AND TECHNIQUE

What is meant by *medium* or *media* (the plural) refers to the material or materials from which a work of art is made. Today, literally anything can be used to make a work of art, including not only traditional materials like paint, ink, and stone, but also rubbish, food, and the earth itself.

Technique is the process that transforms the media into a work of art. Various techniques are explained throughout this book in Technique boxes. Two-dimensional media and techniques include painting, drawing, prints, and photography. Three-dimensional media and techniques are sculpture (for example, using stone, wood, clay or cast metal), architecture, and many small-scale arts (such as jewelry, containers, or vessels) in media such as ceramics, metal, or wood.

Painting includes wall painting and fresco, illumination (the decoration of books with paintings), panel painting (painting on wood panels) and painting on canvas, and handscroll and hanging scroll painting. The paint in these examples is pigment mixed with a liquid vehicle, or binder. Some art historians also consider pictorial media such as mosaic and stained glass—where the pigment is arranged in solid form—a type of painting.

Graphic arts are those that involve the application of lines and strokes to a two-dimensional surface or support, most often paper. Drawing is a graphic art, as are the various forms of printmaking. Drawings may be sketches (quick visual notes made in preparation for larger drawings or paintings); studies (more carefully drawn analyses of details or entire compositions); cartoons (full-scale drawings made in preparation for work in another medium, such as fresco, stained glass, or tapestry); or complete artworks in themselves. Drawings are made with such materials as ink, charcoal, crayon, and pencil. Prints, unlike drawings, are made in multiple copies. The various forms of printmaking include woodcut, the intaglio processes (engraving, etching, drypoint), and lithography.

Photography (literally, "light writing") is a medium that involves the rendering of optical images on light-sensitive surfaces. Photographic images are typically recorded by a camera.

Sculpture is three-dimensional art that is CARVED, MODELED, CAST, or ASSEMBLED. Carved sculpture is subtractive in the sense that the image is created by taking away material. Wood, stone, and ivory are common materials used to create carved sculptures. Modeled sculpture is considered additive, meaning that the object is built up from a material, such as clay, that is soft enough to be molded and shaped. Metal sculpture is usually cast (see "Lost-Wax Casting," page 446) or is assembled by welding or a similar means of permanent joining.

Sculpture is either free-standing (that is, surrounded by space) or in relief. Relief sculpture projects from the background surface of the same piece of material. High-relief sculpture projects far from its background; low-relief sculpture is only slightly raised; and sunken relief, found mainly in Egyptian art, is carved into the surface, with the highest part of the relief being the flat surface.

Ephemeral arts include processions, ceremonies, or ritual dances (often with décor, costumes, or masks); performance art; earthworks; cinema and video art; and some forms of digital or computer art. All have a central temporal aspect in that the artwork is either viewable for only a finite period of time and then disappears forever, is in a constant state of change, or must be replayed to be experienced again.

Architecture creates enclosures for human activity or habitation. It is three-dimensional, highly spatial, functional, and closely bound with developments in technology and materials. Since it is difficult to capture in a photograph, several types of schematic drawings are commonly used to enable the visualization of a building:

PLANS depict a structure's masses and voids, presenting a view from above of the building's footprint or as if it had been sliced horizontally at about waist height.

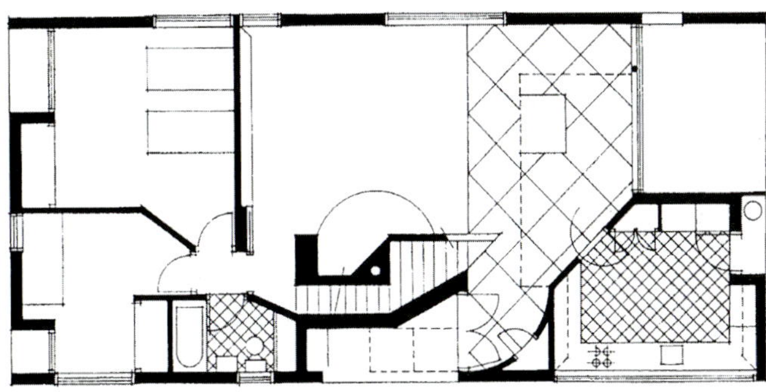

Plan: Philadelphia, Vanna Venturi House

SECTIONS reveal the interior of a building as if it had been cut vertically from top to bottom.

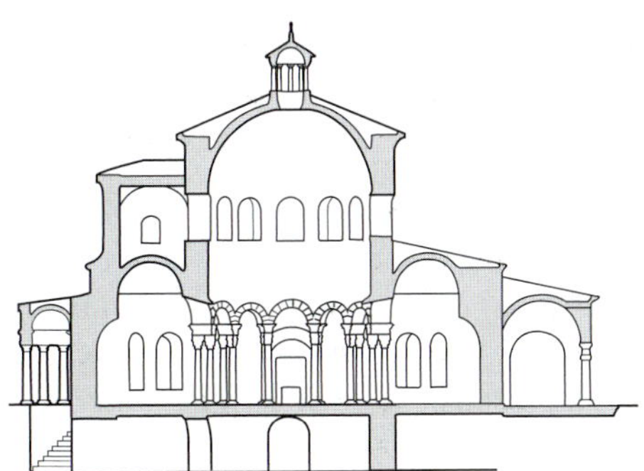

Section: Rome, Santa Costanza

ISOMETRIC DRAWINGS show buildings from oblique angles either seen from above ("bird's-eye view") to reveal their basic three-dimensional forms (often also cut away so we can peak inside) or from below ("worm's-eye view") to represent the arrangement of interior spaces and the upward projection of structural elements.

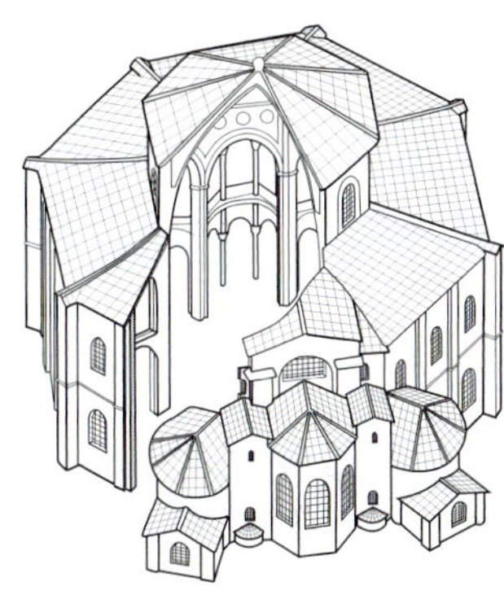

Isometric cutaway from above: Ravenna, San Vitale

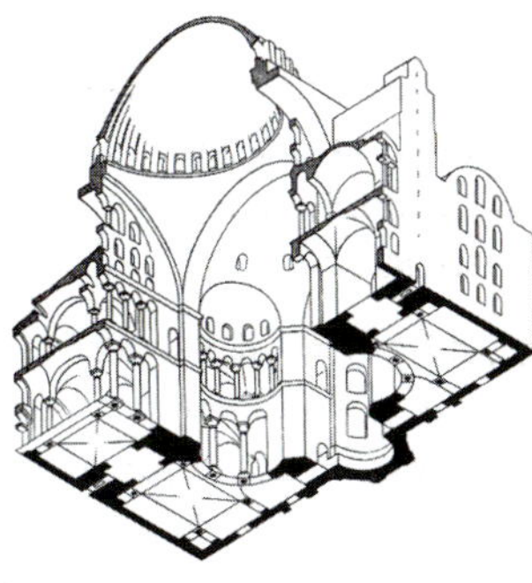

Isometric projection from below: Istanbul, Hagia Sophia

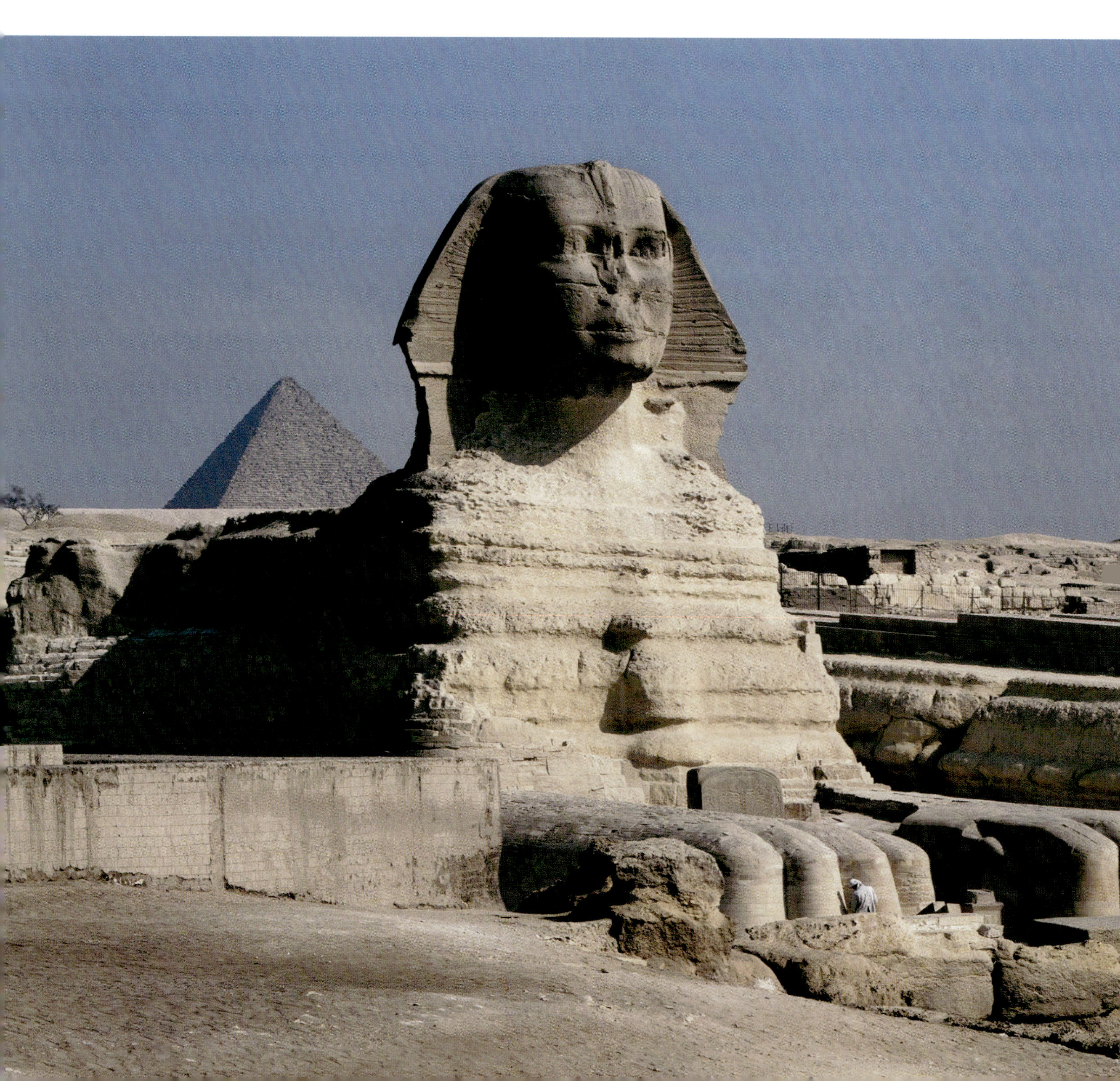

Introduction

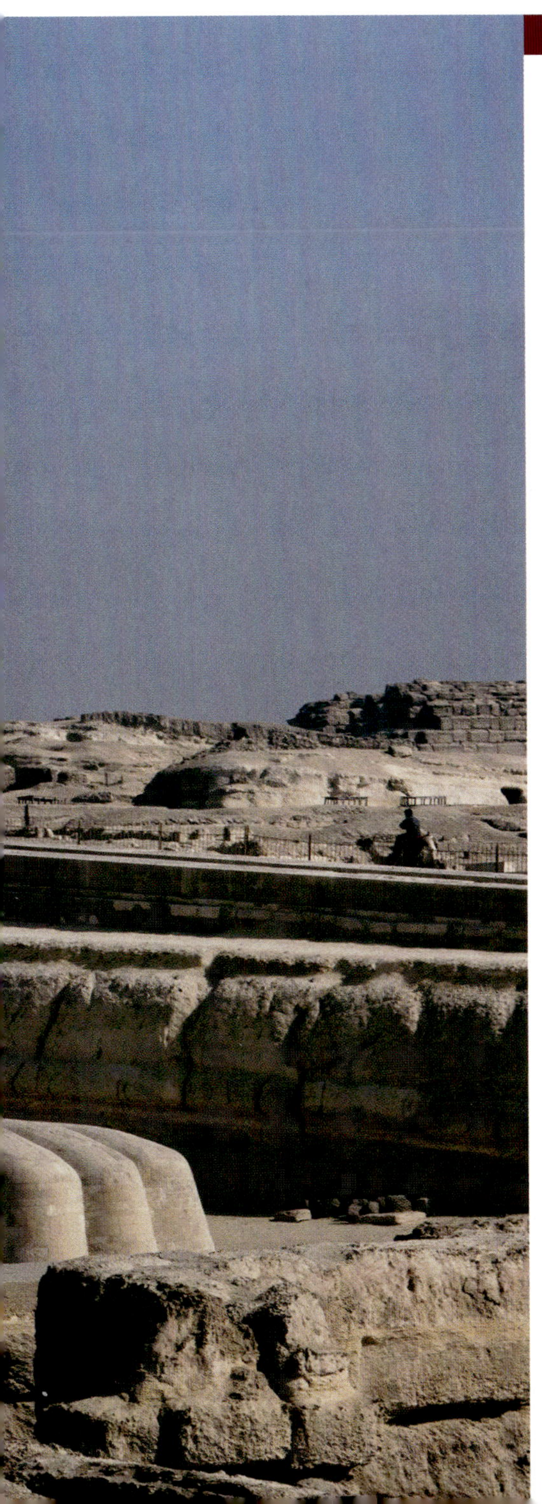

Crouching in front of the pyramids and carved from the living rock of the Giza plateau in Egypt, the Great Sphinx is one of the world's best-known monuments (fig. **Intro–1**). By placing the head of the ancient Egyptian king Khafre on the body of a huge lion, the sculptors joined human intelligence and animal strength in a single image to evoke the superhuman power of a ruler. For some 4,600 years, the Sphinx has defied encroaching desert sands and other assaults of nature; today it also must withstand the human-made sprawl of greater Cairo and the impact of air pollution. The Sphinx, in its majesty, symbolizes mysterious wisdom and dreams of permanence, of immortality. But is such a monument a work of art? Does it matter that the people who carved the Sphinx—unlike today's seemingly independent, individualistic, innovating artists—followed time-honored, formulaic conventions and the precise instructions of their patrons? No matter how viewers of the time may have labeled it, today most people would answer, "Certainly, this is art. Human imagination conceived this amazing hybrid man-lion, and human skill gave material form to the concept behind it." Does the human combination of imagination and skill constitute a work of art? What is art?

What Is Art?

Answering this question was once easier than it is today. Still, for us the severe geometric forms of the Great Sphinx and of the pyramids behind it on the Giza plateau unquestionably fit into the category of "art." They demonstrate a combination of imagination, skill, training, and observation on the part of their human creators. They embody some of the most cherished beliefs of the culture that created them. They appeal to our own taste for order and harmony; perhaps we consider them beautiful. Once one might have said, "They please the eye," but now more than ever we realize that beauty lies in the eye of the beholder, and that our aesthetic responses may be inconsistent with the responses of those in the past who created and originally saw the works we feel confident labeling as art.

Intro–1 The Great Sphinx, Giza, Egypt. Dynasty 4, c. 2613–2494 BCE. Sandstone, height approx. 65' (19.8 m)

Today, the definition of art can also incorporate notions of the artists' intentions, as well as the patrons' aspirations in commissioning the work. It relies, too, on the responses of viewers—both those today and those who saw the work when it was new. The role of art history is to answer complex questions that probe these notions. Who are these artists and patrons? What is this thing they have created? When and how was the work fashioned? What were the ideas and expectations that original viewers brought to its use or understanding? Only after exploring questions like these can we achieve a historical understanding and appreciation of those special artifacts we recognize as works of art.

Modes of Representation

The ancient Greeks admired the work of artists who were especially skillful at capturing the visual appearance of the natural world, as illustrated in a famous story about a competition between rival Greek painters named Zeuxis and Parrhasios held in the late fifth century BCE. Zeuxis painted a picture of grapes so detailed that birds flew down to peck at them. Then Parrhasios took his turn, and when Zeuxis asked his rival to remove the curtain hanging over the picture, Parrhasios gleefully pointed out that the curtain was his painting. Zeuxis agreed that Parrhasios had won the competition since he, Zeuxis, had fooled only birds, but Parrhasios had tricked an intelligent fellow artist.

In the seventeenth century, painter Adriaen van der Spelt (1630–1673) and his artist friend Frans van Mieris (1635–1681) paid homage to the story of Parrhasios' curtain with their painting of blue satin drapery drawn aside to show a garland of flowers (fig. **Intro–2**). More than a *tour-de-force* of ***trompe l'oeil*** painting (pictures that attempt to fool viewers into thinking what they are seeing is real, not a painted representation of the real), this work is an intellectual delight. The artists not only re-created Parrhasios' curtain

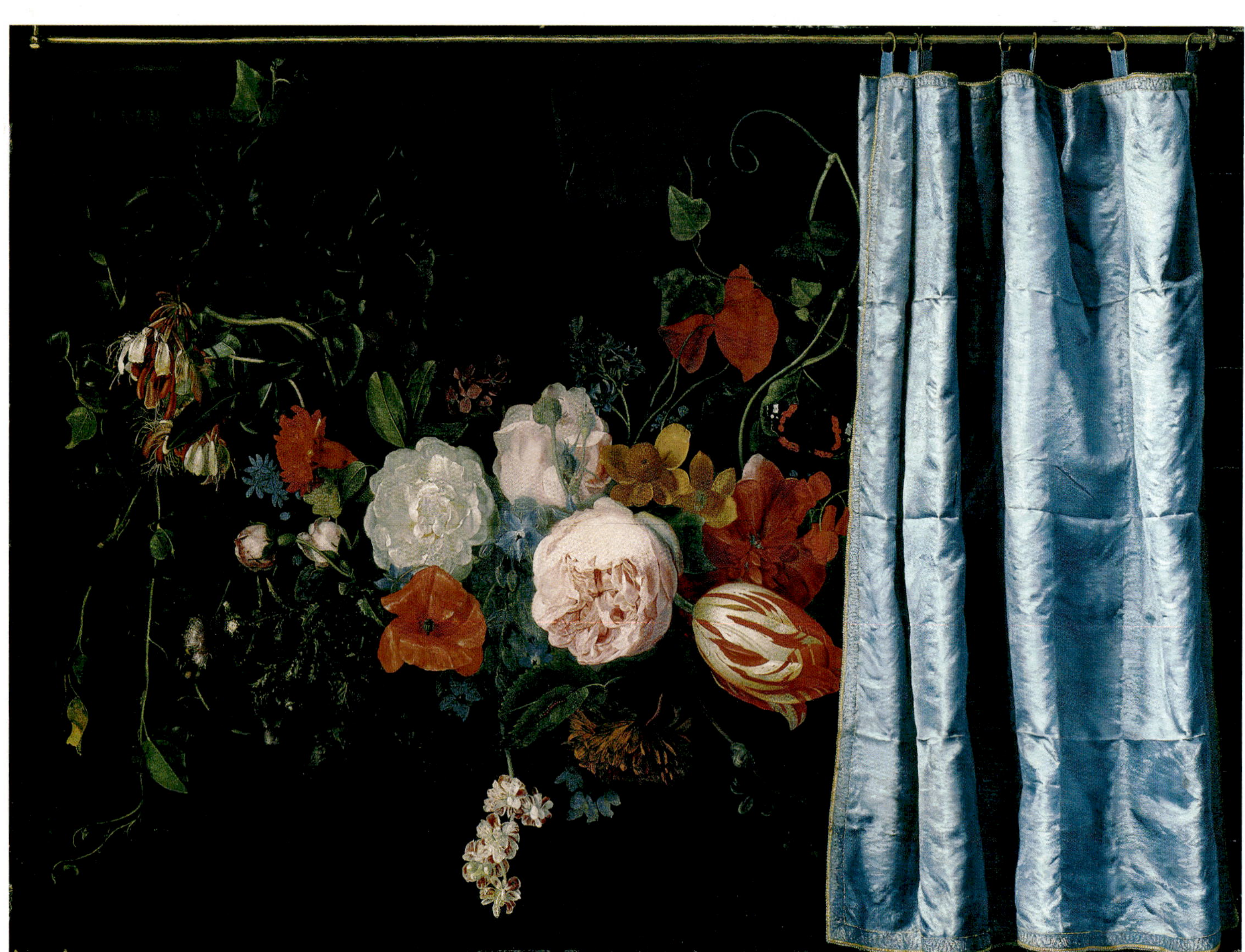

Intro–2 Adriaen van der Spelt and Frans van Mieris. *Flower Piece with Curtain*. 1658. Oil on panel, 18¼" × 25¼" (46.5 × 64 cm). The Art Institute of Chicago
WIRT D. WALKER FUND (1949.585)

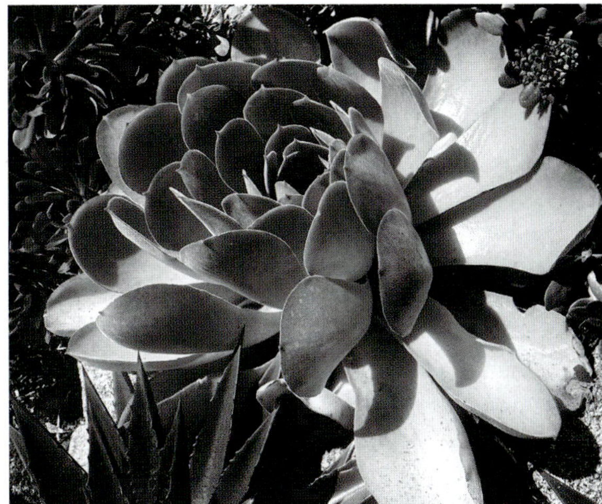

Intro–3 Edward Weston. *Succulent.* 1930. Gelatin-silver print, 7½" × 9½" (19.1 × 24 cm). Collection Center for Creative Photography, University of Arizona, Tucson

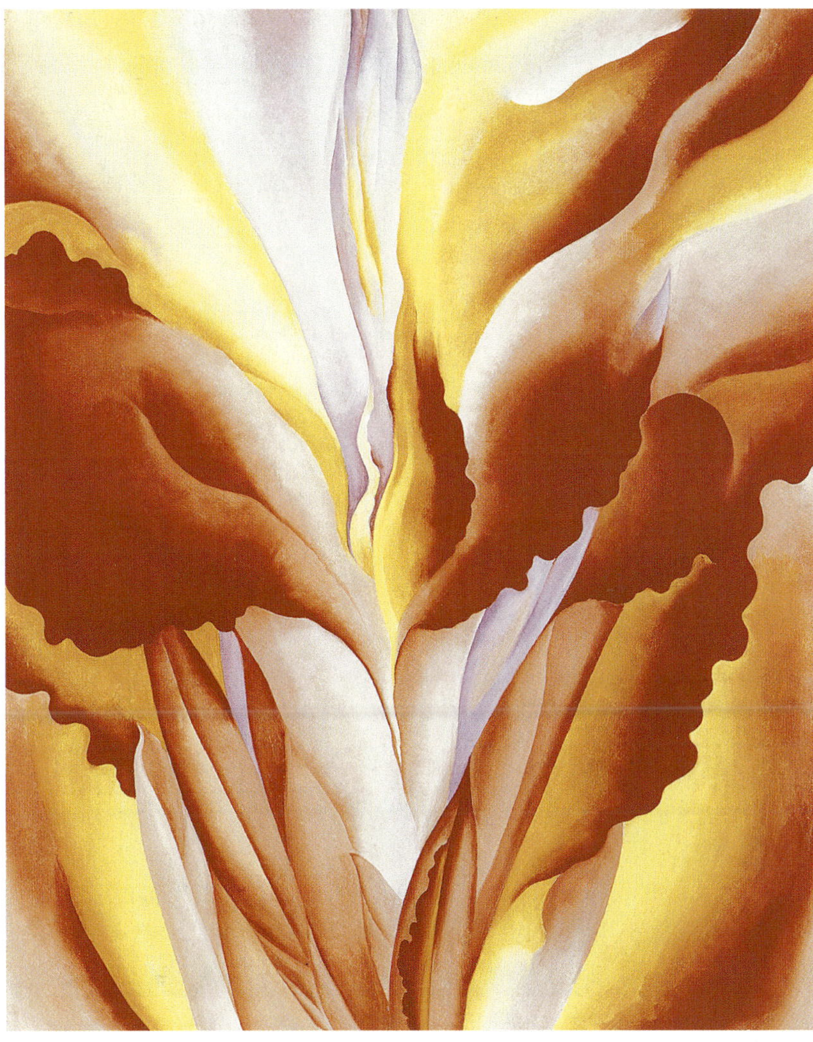

Intro–4 (RIGHT) **Georgia O'Keeffe. *Red Canna.*** 1924. Oil on canvas mounted on Masonite, 36" × 29⅞" (91.44 × 75.88 cm). Collection of the University of Arizona Museum of Art, Tucson
GIFT OF OLIVER JAMES (1950.1.4)

illusion but also included a reference to another Greek story that was popular in the fourth century BCE, the tale of Pausias, who depicted in a painting the exquisite floral garlands made by a young woman, Glykera. This second story raises the troubling and possibly unanswerable question of who was the true artist—the painter who copied nature in his art or the garland-maker who made works of art out of nature. The seventeenth-century people who bought such popular **still lifes** (paintings that portray inanimate objects) knew those stories and appreciated the artists' Classical references as well as their skills in drawing and manipulating colors.

Even today some people think that the mode of representation that seeks lifelike descriptions of the visual appearance of the natural world (sometimes referred to as **naturalistic** or **realistic**), represents the highest accomplishment in art. Not everyone agrees. The first artist to argue persuasively that precise observation alone produced "mere likeness," not art, was the Italian master Leonardo da Vinci (1452–1519), who said that the painter who copied the external forms of nature was acting only as a mirror. He believed that the true artist should engage in intellectual activity of a higher order and attempt to capture the inner life—the energy and power—rather than just the outward appearance of a subject.

Like van der Spelt and van Mieris, Edward Weston (1886–1958) and Georgia O'Keeffe (1887–1986) studied living plants. In his photograph *Succulent*, Weston used straightforward camera work, without manipulating framing or exposure in the darkroom in order to portray his subject accurately (fig. **Intro–3**). But he argued that even if the camera sees more than the human eye, the quality of the photographic image depends not on the camera, but on the choices made by the artist who uses it. When Georgia O'Keeffe painted *Red Canna*, she, too, sought to capture the plant's essence, not merely its appearance (fig. **Intro–4**). By painting the canna lily's organic energy rather than the way it actually looked, she created a new abstract beauty, conveying in paint the pure vigor of the flower's life force. This move away from recording precise visual appearance and toward **abstraction**—in which artists transform recognizable natural subjects into stylized patterns—is another mode of representation common throughout the history of art.

Furthest of all from the naturalistic mode are the pure geometric creations of polished stainless steel made by David Smith

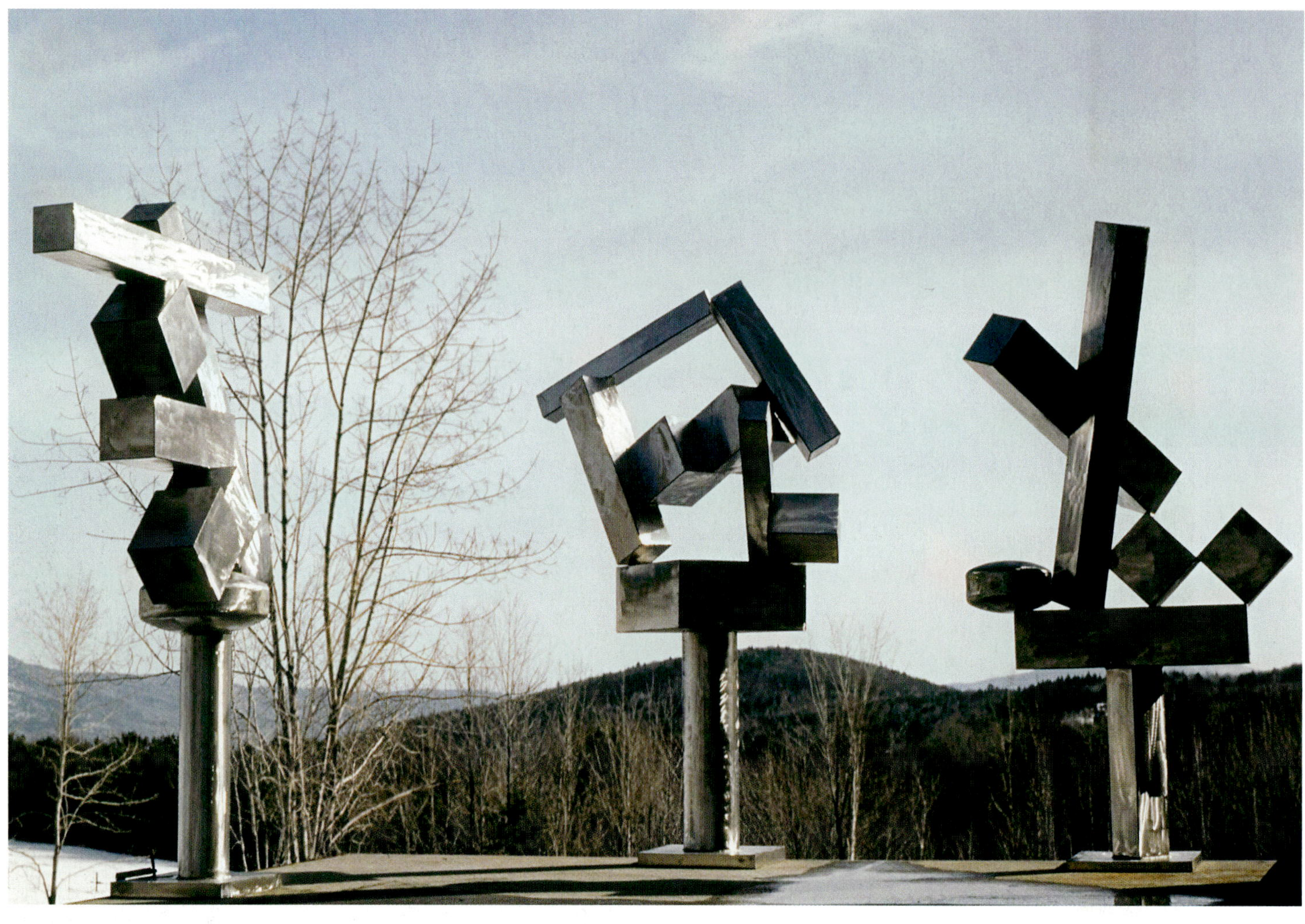

Intro–5 David Smith. ***Cubi XVIII*** (LEFT). 1964. Stainless steel, 9' 8" (2.94 m). Museum of Fine Arts, Boston. ***Cubi XVII*** (CENTER). 1963. Stainless steel, 9' 2" (2.79 m). Dallas Museum of Fine Arts, Dallas. ***Cubi XIX*** (RIGHT). 1964. Stainless steel, 9' 5⅜" (2.88 m). Tate Gallery, London. Shown installed at Bolton Landing, New York in 1965
PHOTO BY DAVID SMITH

(1906–1965). His *Cubi* works, such as the sculptures in figure **Intro–5**, are usually called **nonrepresentational** art (art that does not depict a recognizable natural subject). With works such as *Cubi XVII*, *XVIII*, and *XIX*, it is important to distinguish between subject matter and content. Abstract art like O'Keeffe's has both subject matter and content, or meaning. Nonrepresentational art does not have subject matter, but it does have meaning, generated when the artist's intention and the viewer's interpretation interact. Some viewers may see the *Cubi* works as robotic plants sprung from the core of an unyielding earth, a reflection of today's mechanistic society that challenges the natural forms of trees and hills.

Because meaning can change over time, a central goal of art history is to identify the cultural factors that originally contributed to the production and reception of works of art, to speculate on what they meant for the artists who made them and the original audiences who understood them. Art historians acknowledge that no historical explanation is definitive, that the interpretation of works of art changes and develops through time as new evidence emerges and new approaches are established.

The Human Body as the "Real" and the "Ideal"

Ever since people first made what we call art, they have been fascinated with their own image and have used the human body to express ideas and ideals. Popular culture in the twenty-first century continues to be obsessed with beautiful people—with Miss Universe pageants and lists of the Ten Best-Dressed Women and the Fifty Sexiest Men, just to name a few examples. Today *The Medici Venus* (fig. **Intro–6**), with her plump arms and legs and sturdy body, would surely be expected to slim down, yet for generations such a figure represented the peak of female beauty.

This image of the goddess of love inspired artists and those who commissioned their work from the fifteenth through the nineteenth century. Clearly artists had the skill to represent women as they actually appeared but instead chose to generalize the female form and adhere to the Classical **canon** (rule) of proportions in order to create a universal image, an ideal rather than a specific woman.

The Medici Venus represents a goddess, but artists also represented living people as idealized figures, creating symbolic portraits rather than accurate likenesses. The sculptor Leone Leoni

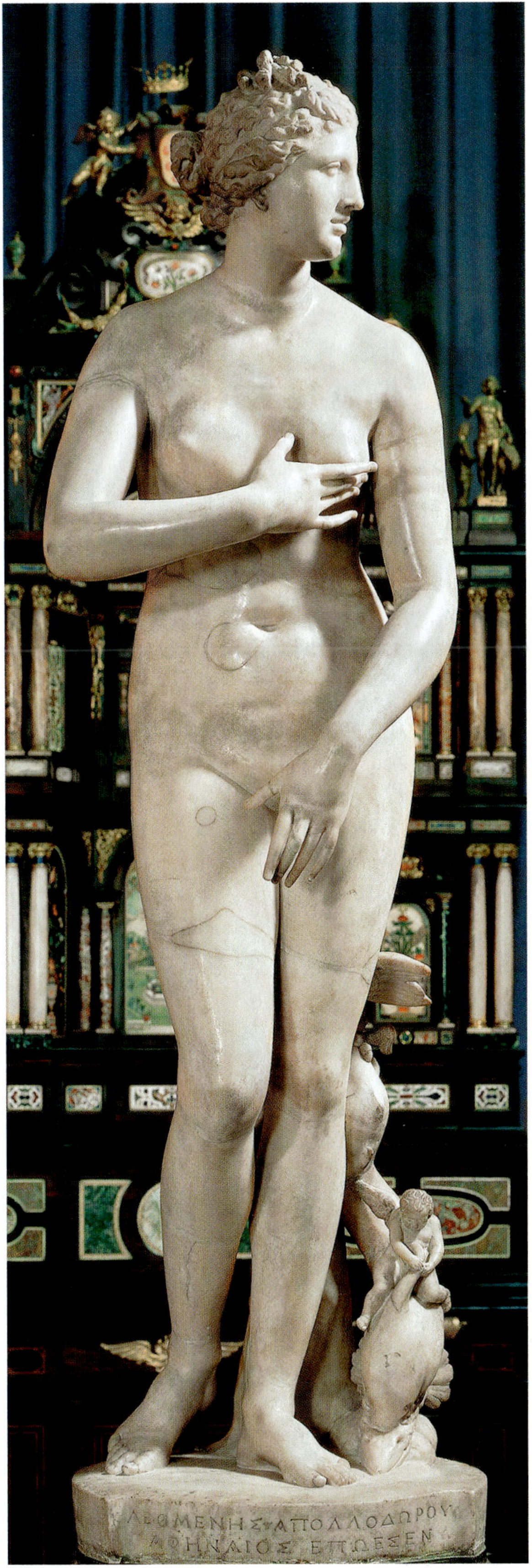

Intro–6 ***The Medici Venus.*** Roman copy of a 1st-century BCE Greek statue. Marble, height without base 5' (1.53 m). Villa Medici, Florence, Italy

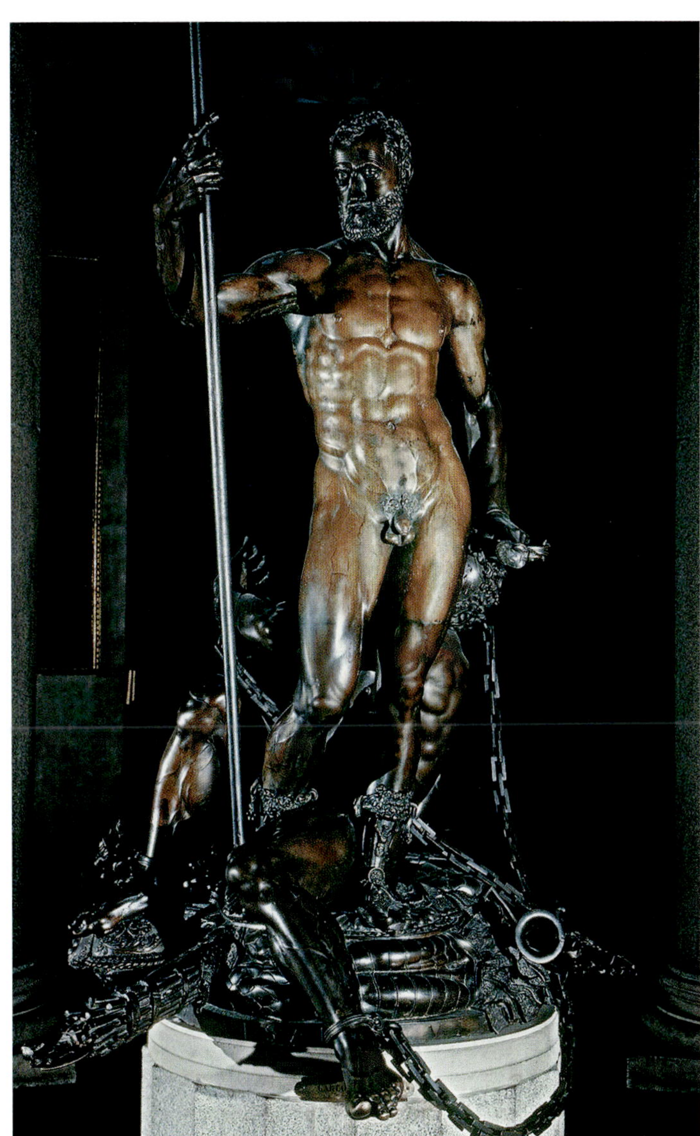

Intro–7 Leone Leoni. ***Charles V Triumphing over Fury, without Armor.*** c. 1549–1555. Bronze, height to top of head 5' 8" (1.74 m). Museo Nacional del Prado, Madrid, Spain

(1509–1590), commissioned to create a monumental bronze statue of Charles V (ruled 1519–1556), expressed the power of this ruler of the Holy Roman Empire just as vividly as did the sculptors of the Egyptian king Khafre, the subject of the Great Sphinx (see fig. Intro–1). Whereas in the Sphinx, Khafre took on the body of a vigilant crouching lion, in *Charles V Triumphing over Fury* the emperor has been endowed with the muscular torso and proportions of the Classical ideal male athlete (fig. **Intro–7**). Charles does not inhabit a fragile human body; rather, in his muscular nakedness, he embodies the idea of triumphant authoritarian rule. Not everyone approved of this representational mode. In fact, a full suit of armor was made for the statue, and today museum officials usually exhibit the sculpture clad in armor rather than nude.

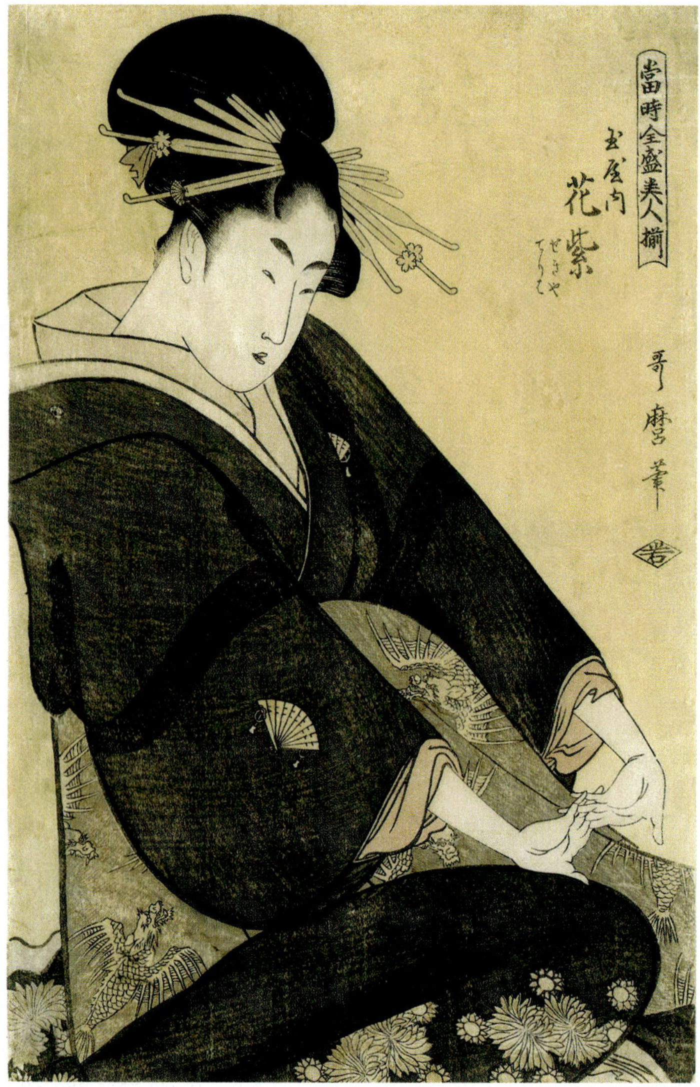

Intro–8 Kitagawa Utamaro. ***Woman at the Height of Her Beauty.*** Mid-1790s. Color woodblock print, 15⅛" × 10" (38.5 × 25.5 cm). Spencer Museum of Art, University of Kansas, Lawrence
WILLIAM BRIDGES THAYER MEMORIAL (1928.7879)

Another example of ideal beauty is the stylized vision of a woman depicted in a woodblock print (fig. **Intro–8**) by Japanese artist Kitagawa Utamaro (1753–1806). His portrayal reflects a complex society strictly regulated by convention and ritual. Simplified shapes depict the woman's garments and at the same time suggest the underlying form of her body. But the treatment of the rich textiles emphasizes surface pattern rather than bodily form, and the elaborate pattern of hair pins distract us from the shape of her coiffure. Utamaro has rendered the decorative silks and carved pins meticulously, but only suggested the woman's face and hands with a few carefully chosen, sweeping lines. The delight in surface detail and the effort to capture the essence of form with supreme economy are characteristic of the art of Utamaro's time and place. Images of men were equally simplified and elegant.

A fifteenth-century bronze sculpture from India conforms to an ideal of female beauty that is disquietingly distinct from those encountered thus far. Punitavati, a beautiful and generous woman who was deeply devoted to the Hindu god Shiva, was abandoned by her husband because she gave one of his mangoes to a beggar. So Punitavati offered her beauty to Shiva, and the god accepted the offering, and by taking her loveliness away turned her into an emaciated, fanged hag (fig. **Intro–9**). According to legend, Punitavati and her clanging cymbals, provide the music for Shiva as he keeps the universe in motion by dancing the cosmic dance of destruction and creation. The bronze sculpture, by depicting Punitavati's hideous appearance, seeks to evoke the spiritual beauty of her generosity and sacrifice.

Today, when images—including those of great physical and/or spiritual beauty—can be captured with a camera, why should an artist or sculptor draw, paint, or chip away at a knob of stone? Does art continue to play a significant role in our world? Attempting to answer these and other questions that consider the role of art is a branch of philosophy called **aesthetics**, which considers the nature

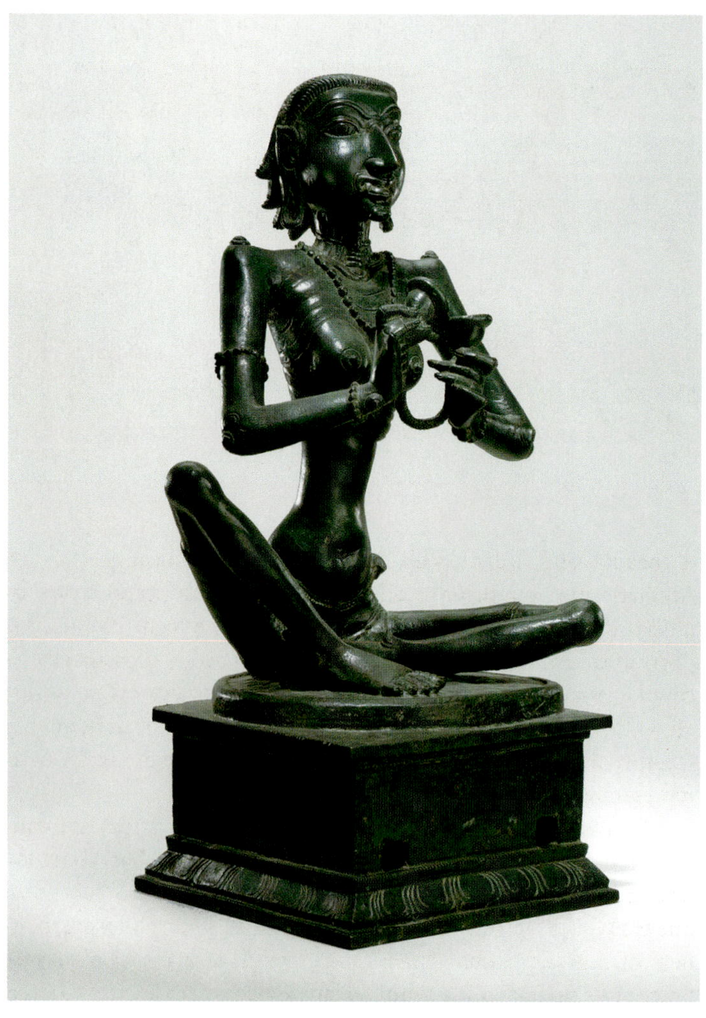

Intro–9 ***Punitavati (Karaikkalammaiyar)***, Shiva saint, from Karaikka, India. c. 1050. Bronze, height 19⅝" (49.8 cm). The Nelson-Atkins Museum of Art, Kansas City, Missouri
PURCHASE: WILLIAM ROCKHILL NELSON TRUST (33–533)

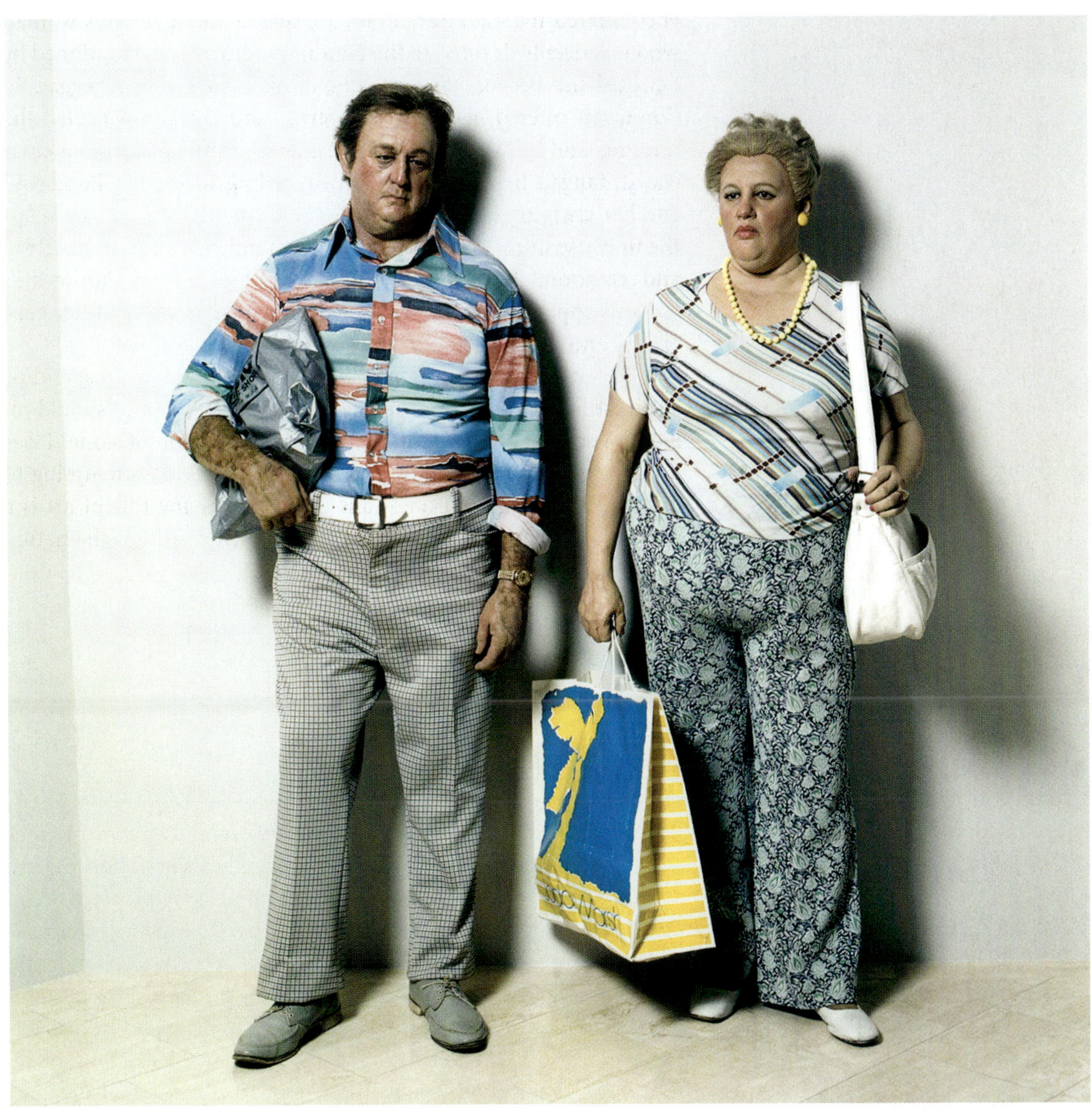

Intro–10 Duane Hanson. The Shoppers. 1976. Cast vinyl, polychromed in oil with accessories, life-size. Collection of the Nerman Family

of beauty and art, as well as the creation of beauty and art. Aestheticians would compare Duane Hanson's sculptural representations of two shoppers (fig. **Intro–10**) with the Medici Venus, the portrait of Charles V, and the sculpture of Punitavati. Is Hanson's couple more beautiful or less beautiful than these other works? How do we define beauty? What is the significance of determining whether these works seem beautiful to us, either individually or as representatives of our culture?

Whether or not we find these figural works beautiful, the similarities and differences among them have much to teach us about the time in which they were made. Historically, styles often vary from one era to another and from one culture to another. Differing manners of representation—"naturalistic" or "abstract"—also may be practiced simultaneously within a single culture. In ancient Greece, for example, the philosophers Aristotle (384–322 BCE) and Plato (428–348/7 BCE) both considered the nature of art and beauty in purely intellectual terms, but the two thinkers arrived at divergent conclusions. Aristotle believed that works of art should be evaluated on the basis of mimesis ("imitation"), that is on how faithfully artists recorded the appearance of the natural world. According to this approach, Hanson's work of the two shoppers might be considered the finest of the three. But of course, we need to be aware that while artists may work in a realistic or naturalistic style, they can employ it to portray imaginary creatures such as unicorns, dragons, or even sphinxes, and make them appear startlingly lifelike.

In contrast to Aristotle, Plato looked beyond nature for a definition of art. In his view even the most lifelike painting or sculpture was only a shadow or approximation of the material world. Rather than focus on an exact copy of the particular details seen in nature, Plato encouraged a focus on ideals, that is, on representations exhibiting perfect symmetry and proportion. Following such principles, sculptors could use human reason to triumph over nature, eliminating all irregularities to ensure a balanced and harmonious work of art. To accomplish Plato's ideals and represent things "as they ought to be" rather than as they are, Classical sculpture and painting established ideals that have inspired Western art ever since.

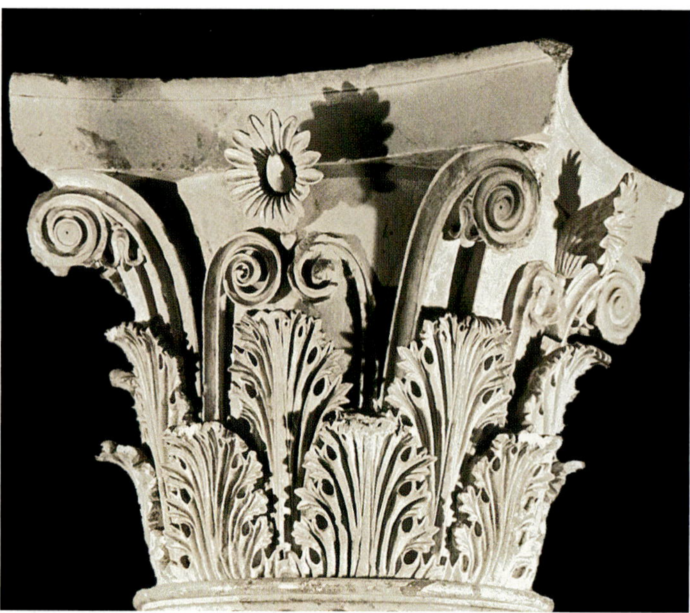

Intro–11 Corinthian capital from the *tholos* at Epidaurus. c. 350 BCE. Archaeological Museum, Epidaurus, Greece

A simple example from architecture may illustrate this Platonic tendency in Classicism more clearly than representations of the human figure. The carved top, or **capital**, of a Corinthian column—popular in ancient Greece during the fourth century BCE—has an inverted bell shape surrounded by acanthus leaves (fig. **Intro–11**). Although this foliage was inspired by the appearance of natural vegetation, the sculptors who carved the leaves eliminated blemishes to create perfect leaves rather than any particular leaf, first looking at nature and then carving the essence of the form, the Platonic ideal of acanthus foliage.

The terms "classic" and "classical," which derive from the style of art in the period in ancient Greek history when this type of idealism emerged, have come to characterize the art of ancient Greece and Rome in general and are used even more broadly today as synonyms for the peak of perfection in any period or product. Today, for example, we commonly use the adjective "classic" when speaking of exemplary films, automobiles, clothing, even colas.

Questions (and Answers) About Art

Underlying all our assumptions about works of art—whether in the past or the present—is the belief that art carries a message, that it can inform, challenge, and/or persuade viewers. But what gives an image meaning and expressive power? Why do some images fascinate and inspire us, while others frighten or astonish us? Why have people treasured some things and not others? These are difficult questions; even specialists disagree about answers. Sometimes even the most informed people conclude, "I just don't know."

Studying art history, therefore, may not provide us with definitive answers to all our questions, but it can help us better understand the value of asking the questions as well as exploring possible answers. Art history is grounded in the study of material objects that are the tangible embodiment of the ideas—and ideals—of a culture. For example, when we become captivated by the mysteriousness of a striking creation such as the Great Sphinx, art history can help us understand its particular imagery and meaning. Art history can also help us understand the larger cultural context of the work—that is, the social, economic, and political situation of the historical period that produced it, and the ways in which it originally expressed or engaged with its situation, and preserves it for us through the passage of time.

On their own, exceptional works of art speak to us with enduring eloquence over great expanses of time, but sometimes viewers need to understand a work's **iconography** (conventional subjects and symbols) before its meanings become clear. For example, in *Flower Piece with Curtain* (fig. Intro–2), the brilliant red and white tulip just to the left of the blue curtain was the most desirable and expensive flower in the seventeenth century; thus, it symbolizes wealth and power, and not simply natural beauty. Yet insects creep out of it, and a butterfly—fragile and transitory—hovers above it. Consequently, these flowers also symbolize the passage of time and the fleeting quality of human wealth. Understood within its cultural context, this painting becomes more than simply an exquisite still life.

Why Do We Need Art?

Before we begin to journey through time, examining and thinking about works of art and architecture historically, let us consider a few general questions that we should keep in mind as we proceed: "Why do we need art?," "Who are artists?," "What role do patrons and audiences play?," "What is art history?," and "What is a viewer's role and responsibility, both in the past and in the present?" By grappling with such questions, our experience of art can be greatly enhanced.

Some biologists account for the human desire for art by explaining that human beings have very large brains that demand stimulation. Curious, active, and inventive, we humans constantly explore, and in so doing invent things that appeal to our senses: fine art, fine food, fine scents, fine fabrics, and fine music. Ever since our prehistoric ancestors developed their ability to draw and speak, we have visually and verbally been communicating with each other. We use works of art to speculate on the nature of things and the meaning of life. In fulfilling our need to understand and our need to communicate, the arts serve a vital function. Through making art and viewing art we become fully alive.

Art and the Search for Meaning, Public and Private

Throughout history art has played an important part in our search for the meaning of the human experience. In an effort to understand the world and our place in it, we turn both to introspective personal art and to communal public art. Following a personal vision, James Hampton (1909–1964) created profoundly stirring religious art. Hampton worked as a janitor to support himself while, in a rented garage, he built *Throne of the Third Heaven of the Nations' Millennium General Assembly* (fig. **Intro–12**), his monument to his faith. In rising tiers, thrones and altars have been prepared for Jesus and Moses. Placing New Testament imagery on the

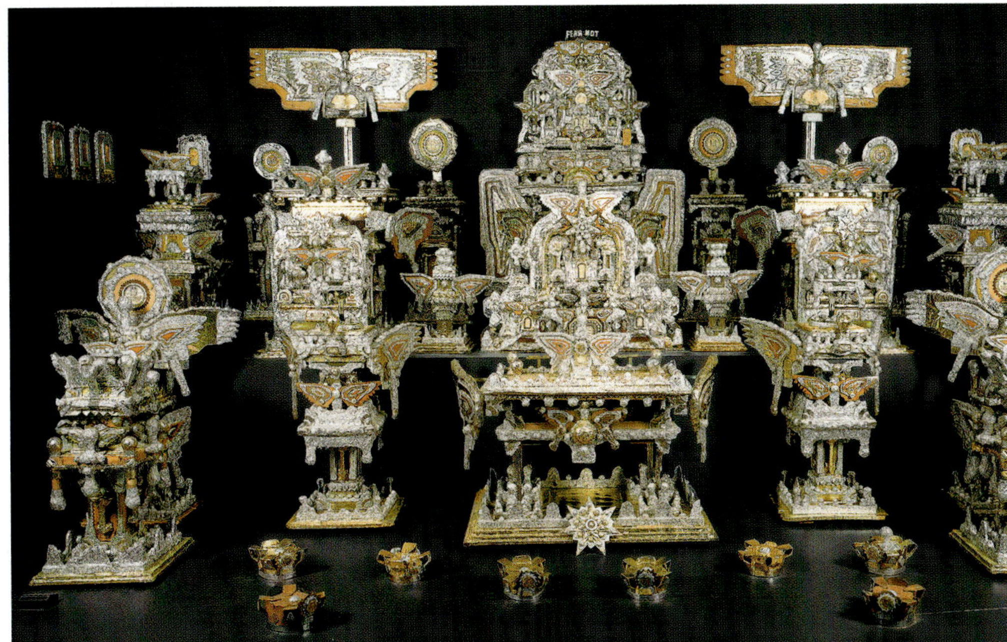

Intro–12 James Hampton. *Throne of the Third Heaven of the Nations' Millennium General Assembly*. c. 1950–1964. Gold and silver aluminum foil, colored Kraft paper, and plastic sheets over wood, paperboard, and glass, 10' 6" × 27' × 14' 6" (3.2 × 8.23 × 4.42 m). Smithsonian American Art Museum, Smithsonian Institution, Washington, D.C. GIFT OF ANONYMOUS DONORS (1970.353.1)

right and imagery from the Hebrew Bible on the left, Hampton labeled and described everything. He even invented his own language to express his visions. On one of many placards he wrote his credo: "Where there is no vision, the people perish" (Proverbs 29:18). Hampton made this fabulous assemblage out of discarded furniture, flashbulbs, and all sorts of refuse tacked together and wrapped in gold and silver aluminum foil and purple tissue paper. How can such worthless materials be turned into such an exalted work of art? Today we recognize that works of art can transcend the physical materials from which they are made.

In contrast to James Hampton, whose life work was created in private and only came to public attention after his death, most artists and viewers participate in more public expressions of art and belief. Some works are created for use in rituals that seek to establish ties to unseen powers and sometimes to connect the present with the past and the future. These special objects used in ritual, such as statues, masks, and vessels, may be valued as works of art by outsiders unaware of the circumstance and ceremonies that originally brought them to life. Two offering bowls—a European chalice and an African cup—are cases in point.

The cup known as the Chalice of Abbot Suger was used for what remains for many the central ritual of the Christian faith (fig. **Intro–13**). For Christians, communication between God and humans happens in the ceremonial commemoration of Jesus' Last Supper with his friends and disciples, known as Holy Communion or the **Eucharist**. For Roman Catholics, during this ritual reenactment at a consecrated altar, ordinary wine becomes the blood of Christ, while for Protestants, the wine remains symbolic of that blood. But for both groups the chalice (a vessel for the sacramental wine) plays a central role. Abbot Suger, twelfth-century leader of the French monastery dedicated to Saint Denis near Paris, found an antique agate vase in the storage chests of the abbey. He ordered his goldsmiths to add a foot, a rim, and handles, embellished with

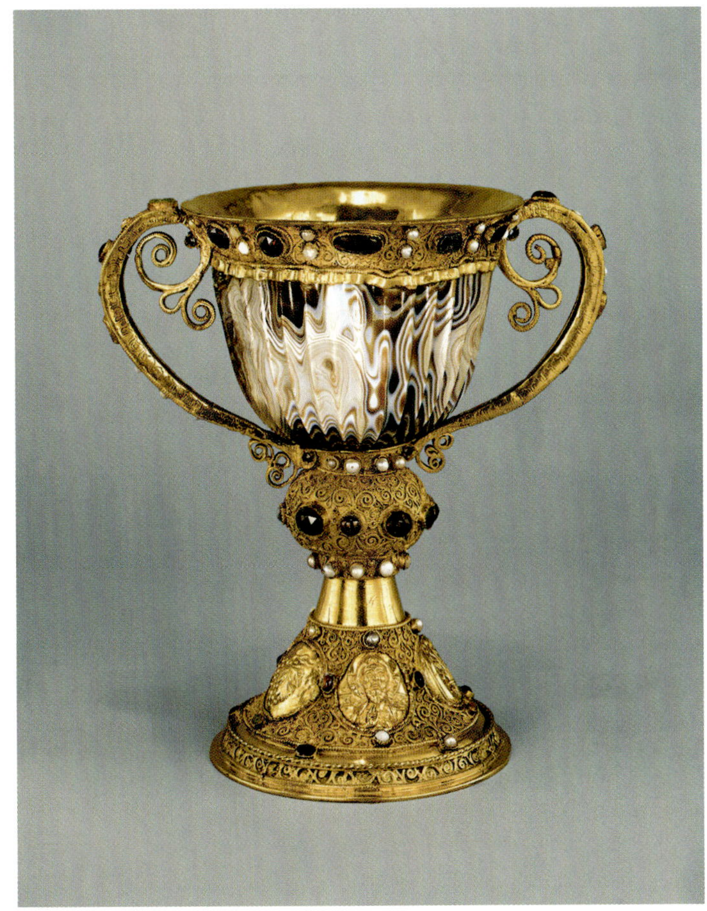

Intro–13 Chalice of Abbot Suger, from Abbey Church of Saint-Denis, France. Cup: Ptolemaic Egypt (2nd–1st century BCE) or Byzantine 11th century, sardonyx; mounts: France, 1137–1140, silver gilt, adorned with filigree, semiprecious stones, pearls, glass insets, and opaque white glass with modern replacements, 7½" × 4¼" (19 × 10.8 cm). National Gallery of Art, Washington, D.C.

semiprecious stones and medallions to this vase, transforming a secular object of prestige and delight into a sacred chalice to be used at the altar of his church in the celebration of the Eucharist.

The offering bowl created by the Yoruba people of West Africa, like Suger's chalice, served in rituals designed to communicate with gods (fig. **Intro–14**). It once held the palm nuts offered at the beginning of ceremonies in which people call on the god Olodumare (or Olorun) to reveal their destiny. Carved by the master Olówè of Isè in about 1925, this sculpture appears to portray a woman with a child on her back holding an ornate, covered cup. Men and women underneath it help the woman support the bowl, and more women link arms in a ritual dance on the lid. The child suggests the life-giving power of women and perhaps ultimately of Olodumare. The richly decorative and symbolic wood carving, even when isolated in a museum case, reminds us of all who sought to learn from Olodumare, the god of destiny, certainty, and order. But both Suger's chalice and Olówè's cup stand empty today. Encased in museum displays, these ritual vessels take on a new secular life, enshrined as precious works of art. By linking today's viewers with people in the distant past and in faraway places, they serve a purpose very different from the original intention of their patrons and makers.

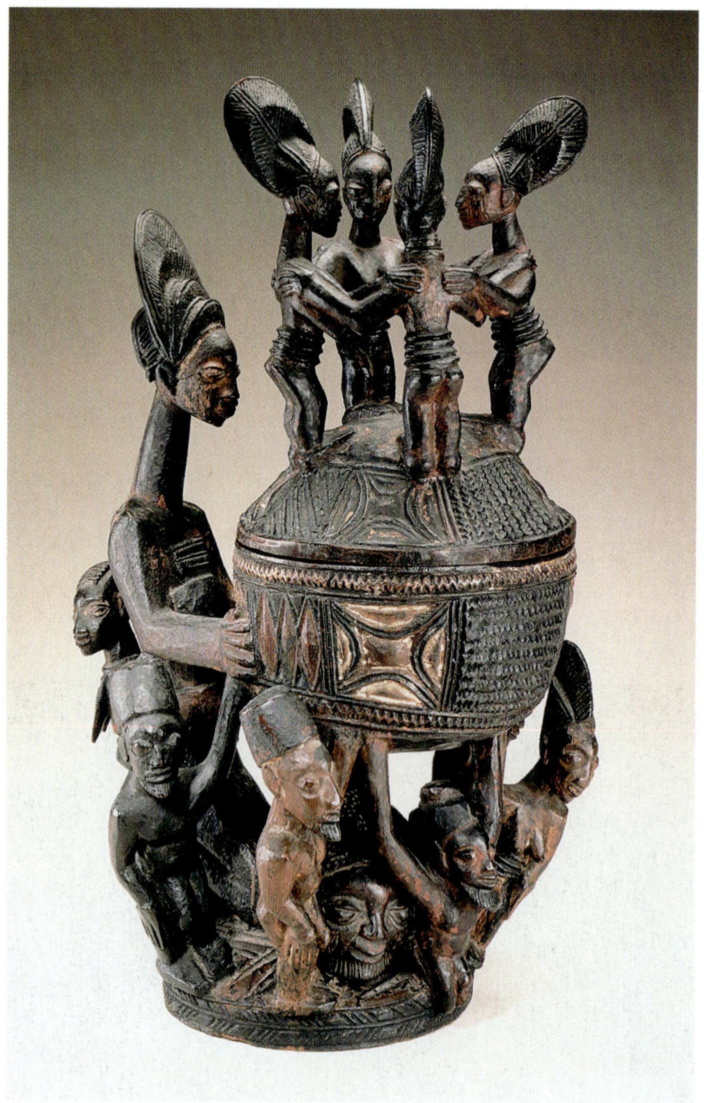

Intro–14 Olówè of Isè. Offering bowl, Nigeria. c. 1925. Wood and pigment, height 25$\frac{1}{16}$" (63.7 cm). National Museum of African Art, Smithsonian Institution, Washington, D.C.
BEQUEST OF WILLIAM A. MCCARTY-COOPER (95-10-1)

Art and Social Context

The visual arts are among the most sophisticated forms of human communication, at once shaping and being shaped by their social context. Artists may unconsciously interpret their times, but they also may be enlisted to serve social ends consciously in ways that range from heavy-handed propaganda (the portrait of Charles V in fig. Intro–7, for example) to subtle suggestion. From ancient Egyptian priests to elected officials today, religious and political leaders have understood the educational and motivational value of the visual arts.

Governments and civic leaders can use the power of art to strengthen the unity that nourishes society. In sixteenth-century Venice, for example, city officials ordered Veronese (Paolo Caliari, 1528–1588) and his assistants to fill the ceiling of the Great Council Hall in the ruler's palace with a huge and colorful painting, *The Triumph of Venice* (fig. **Intro–15**). Their contract with the artist survives to document their intentions. What they wanted was a painting that showed their beloved Venice surrounded by peace, abundance, fame, happiness, honor, security, and freedom—all to be realized in vivid colors and idealized forms. Veronese complied by painting the city personified as a mature, beautiful, and splendidly robed woman enthroned between the towers of the Arsenal, a building where ships were built for worldwide trade, the source of the city's wealth and power. Enthusiastic crowds of citizens cheer, while personifications of Fame blow trumpets and Victory crowns Venice with a wreath. Supporting this happy throng, bound prisoners and piles of armor attest to Venetian military power. The Lion of Venice—the symbol of the city and of its patron, Saint Mark—oversees the triumph. Although Veronese created this splendid display of propaganda to serve the purposes of his patrons, was his artistic vision as individualistic as that of James Hampton, whose art was pure self-expression?

Uncovering Sociopolitical Intentions

Although powerful patrons have used artworks throughout history to promote their political interests, modern artists are often independent-minded, astute critics of the powers that be. For example, among Honoré Daumier's most powerful critiques of the French government is his print *Rue Transonain, Le 15 Avril 1834* (fig. **Intro–16**). During a period of urban unrest, the French National Guard fired on unarmed citizens, killing 14 people. For his depiction of the massacre, Daumier used **lithography**—a cheap new medium that would enable him to spread his message as widely as possible. Indeed, his political commentary created such horror and revulsion that the government reacted by buying and destroying all the newspapers in which the print appeared. As this example shows, art historians sometimes need to consider not just the historical

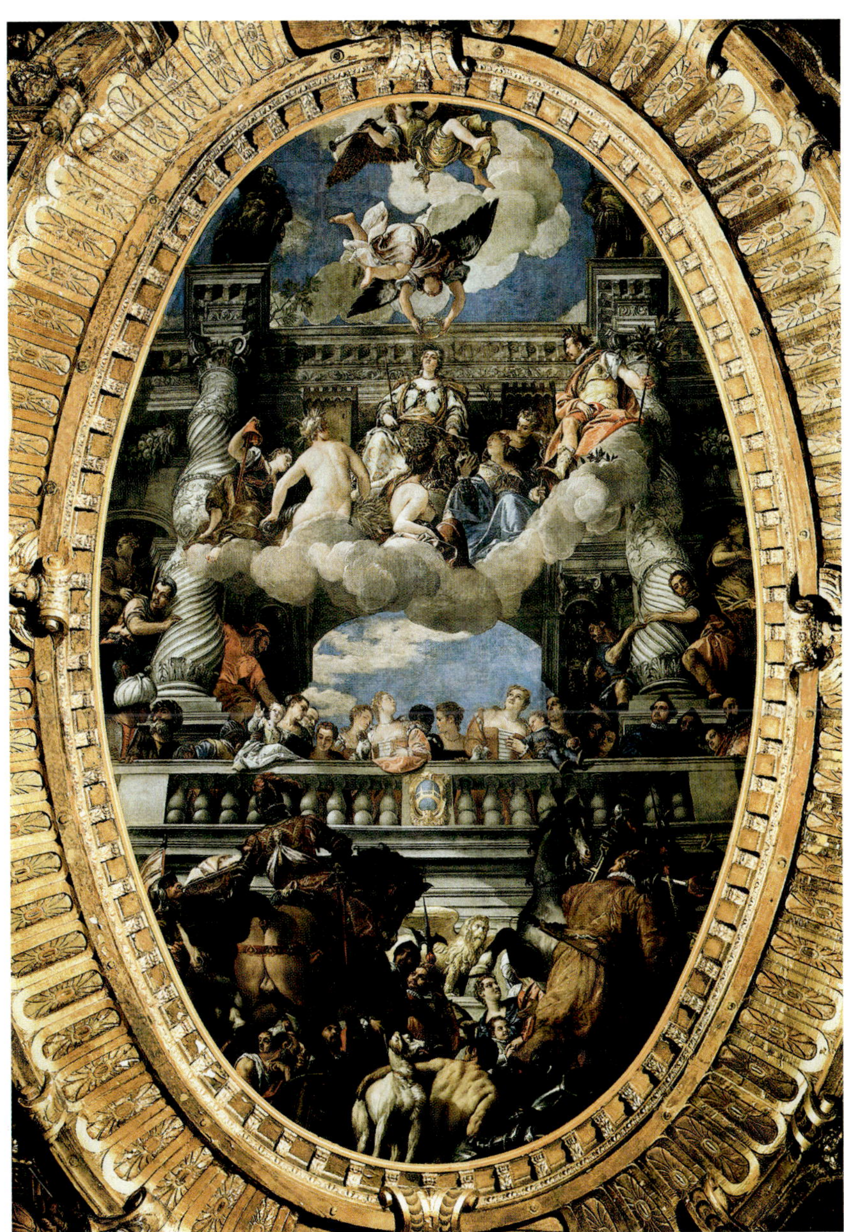

Intro–15 **Veronese.** ***The Triumph of Venice***, ceiling painting in the Council Chamber, Palazzo Ducale, Venice, Italy. c. 1585. Oil on canvas, 29' 8" × 19' (9.04 × 5.79 m)

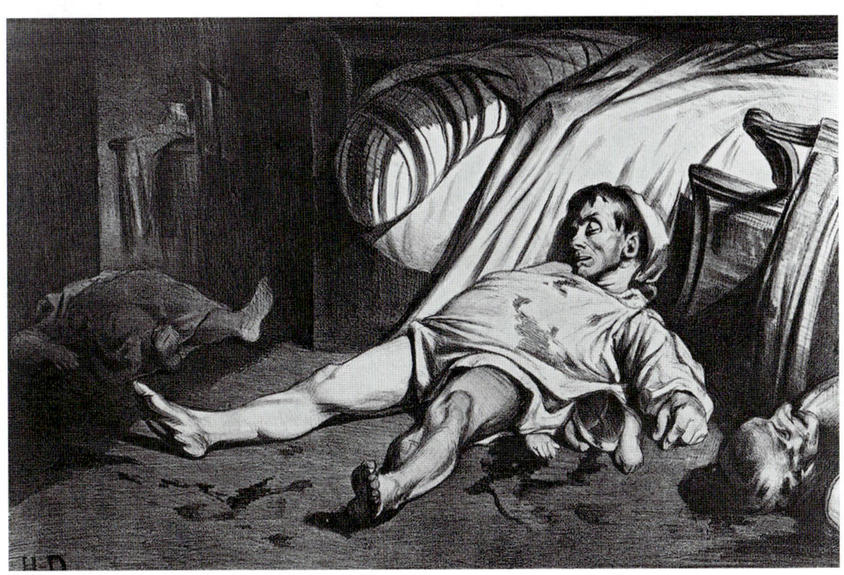

Intro–16 **Honoré Daumier.** ***Rue Transonain, Le 15 Avril 1834.*** Lithograph, 11" × 17⅜" (28 × 44 cm). Kupferstichkabinett, Staatliche Kunstsammlungen, Dresden, Germany

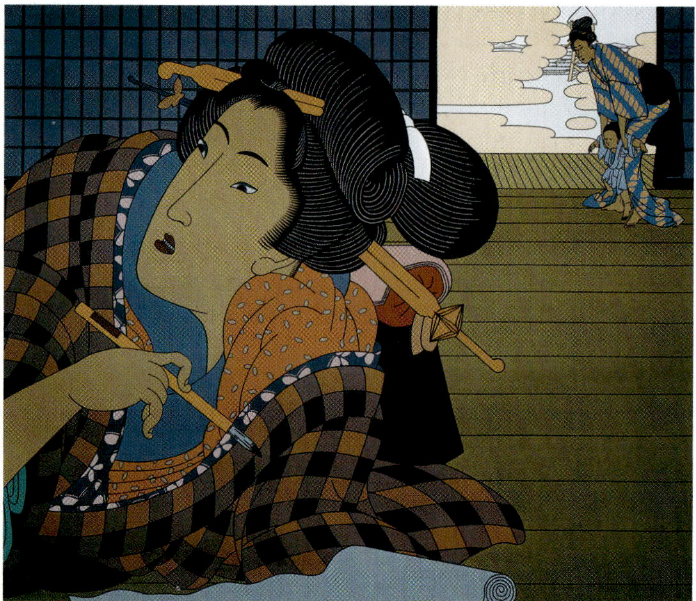

Intro–17 Roger Shimomura. ***Diary (Minidoka Series #3).*** 1978. Acrylic on canvas, 4' 11⅞" × 6' 1/16" (1.52 × 1.83 m). Spencer Museum of Art, University of Kansas, Lawrence
MUSEUM PURCHASE, STATE FUNDS (1979.51)

context of a work of art but also its political content and medium to gain a fuller understanding of it.

A more recent work with a challenging critical message recalls how American citizens of Japanese ancestry were removed from their homes and confined in internment camps during World War II. In 1978, Roger Shimomura (born 1939) painted *Diary*, illustrating his grandmother's account of the family's experience in one such camp in Idaho (fig. **Intro–17**). Shimomura has painted his grandmother in the close foreground, writing in her diary, while he (the toddler) and his mother stand further back by an open door—not signifying freedom but opening on to a field bounded by barbed wire. In this commentary on discrimination and injustice, Shimomura combines two formal traditions—the Japanese art of color woodblock prints (see fig. Intro–8) and American Pop art of the 1960s—to create a personal style that expresses his own dual cultural heritage.

Who Are Artists?

We have focused so far mostly on works of art. But what of the artists who make them? How artists have viewed themselves and have been viewed by those around them has changed dramatically over time. In Western art, painters and sculptors were at first considered artisans or craftspeople, in other words, laborers. The ancient Greeks and Romans ranked painters and sculptors among the skilled workers; what they admired were the creations, but not the creators. The Greek word for art, *tekne*, is the source for the English word "technique," and the English words "art" and "artist" come from the Latin word *ars*, which means "skill." People in the Middle Ages went to the opposite extreme, sometimes attributing especially fine works of art to angels or to Saint Luke. Artists continued to be seen as craftspeople—admired, often prosperous, but not particularly special—until the Renaissance, when artists such as Leonardo da Vinci proclaimed themselves to be geniuses with unique God-given abilities.

Soon after the Renaissance, Italian painter Guercino (Giovanni Francesco Barbieri, 1591–1666) synthesized the idea that saints and angels have miraculously made art with the concept that human

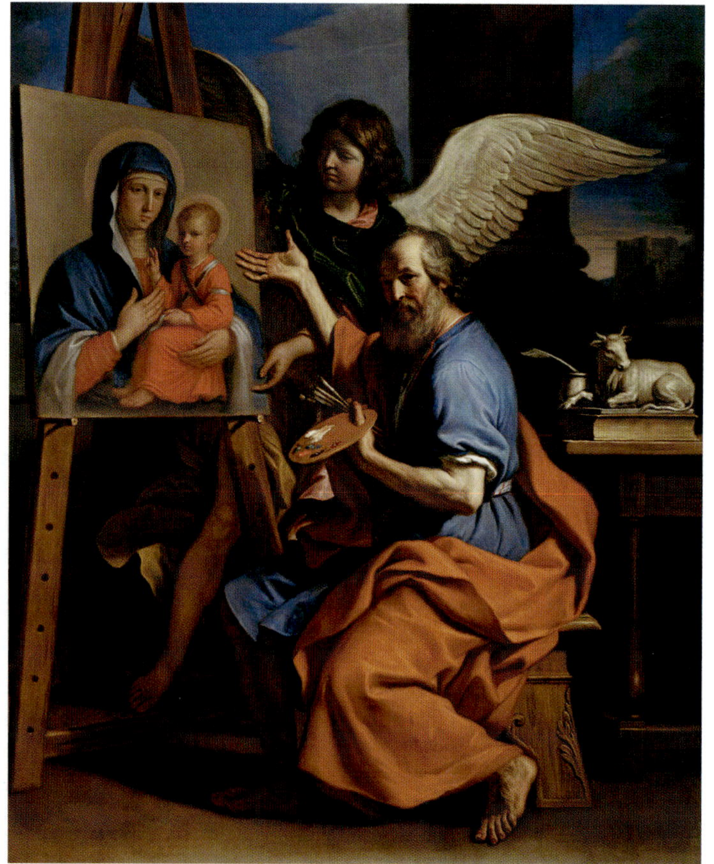

Intro–18 Il Guercino. ***Saint Luke Displaying a Painting of the Virgin.*** 1652–1653. Oil on canvas, 7' 3" × 5' 11" (2.21 × 1.81 m). The Nelson-Atkins Museum of Art, Kansas City, Missouri
PURCHASE (F83-55)

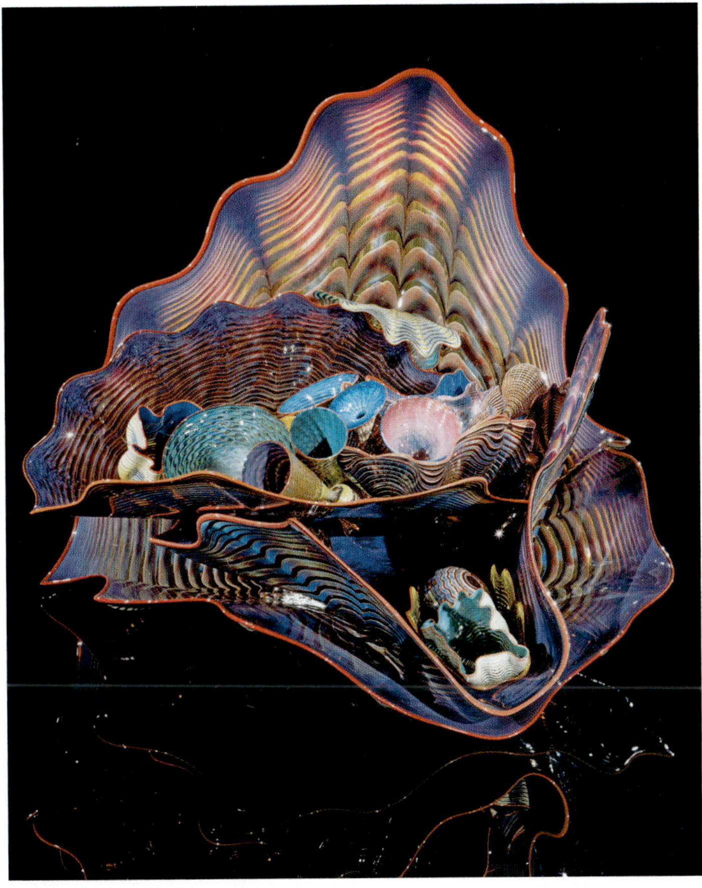

Intro–19 Dale Chihuly. ***Violet Persian Set with Red Lip Wraps.*** 1990. Glass, 26" × 30" × 25" (66 × 76.2 × 63.5 cm). Spencer Museum of Art, University of Kansas, Lawrence
MUSEUM PURCHASE: PETER T. BOHAN ART ACQUISITION FUND (1992.0002)

painters have special, even divinely inspired, gifts. In his painting *Saint Luke Displaying a Painting of the Virgin* (fig. **Intro–18**), Guercino portrays the evangelist who was regarded as the patron saint of artists because of a belief that Luke had painted a portrait of the Virgin Mary holding the Christ Child. In Guercino's work, Luke, seated before just such a painting and assisted by an angel, holds his palette and brushes. A book, a quill pen, and an inkpot decorated with a statue of an ox (Saint Luke's symbol) rest on a table, reminders of his status as author of a gospel. Guercino seems to say that if Saint Luke is a divinely endowed artist, then surely all other artists share in this special power and status. This image of the artist as an inspired genius has persisted.

Even after the idea of "specially endowed" creators emerged, numerous artists continued to conduct their work as craftspeople leading workshops of assistants. Artwork often continued to be a team effort. In the eighteenth century, for example, Utamaro's color woodblock prints (see fig. Intro–8) were the product of a number of people working together. Utamaro painted pictures, and others transferred the images to blocks of wood to be printed on paper. Nevertheless, Utamaro—as the one who conceived the work—is considered the "creator" or "artist" whose name is associated with the final product.

Such collaborative approaches continue today in the complex glassworks of American artist Dale Chihuly (born 1941). His team of artist-craftspeople is skilled in the ancient art of glassmaking, but Chihuly remains the controlling mind and imagination behind the works. Once created, his multipart pieces may be transformed when they are assembled for display; they take on a new life in accordance with the will of every owner, who may arrange the pieces to reflect personal preference, thus becoming part of Chihuly's creative team. Originally fabricated in 1990, *Violet Persian Set with Red Lip Wraps* (fig. **Intro–19**) has 20 separate pieces, but the person who assembles them determines their composition.

Whether artists work individually or communally, even the most brilliant ones typically spend years in study and apprenticeship. In his painting *The Drawing Lesson*, Dutch artist Jan Steen (1626–1679) takes us into an artist's studio where two people—a boy apprentice and a young woman—are learning the rudiments of their art (fig. **Intro–20**). The pupil has been drawing from sculpture and plaster casts because women were not permitted to work from nude models. *The Drawing Lesson* records contemporary educational practice and is a valuable record of an artist's workplace in the seventeenth century.

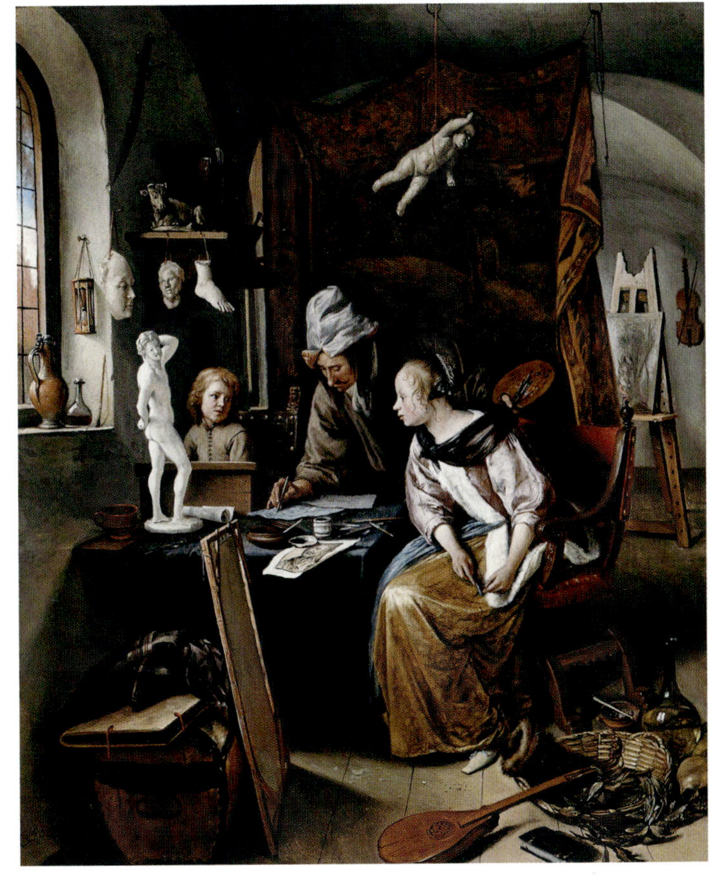

Intro–20 Jan Steen. ***The Drawing Lesson.*** 1665. Oil on wood, 19⅜" × 16¼" (49.3 × 41 cm). The J. Paul Getty Museum, Los Angeles, California

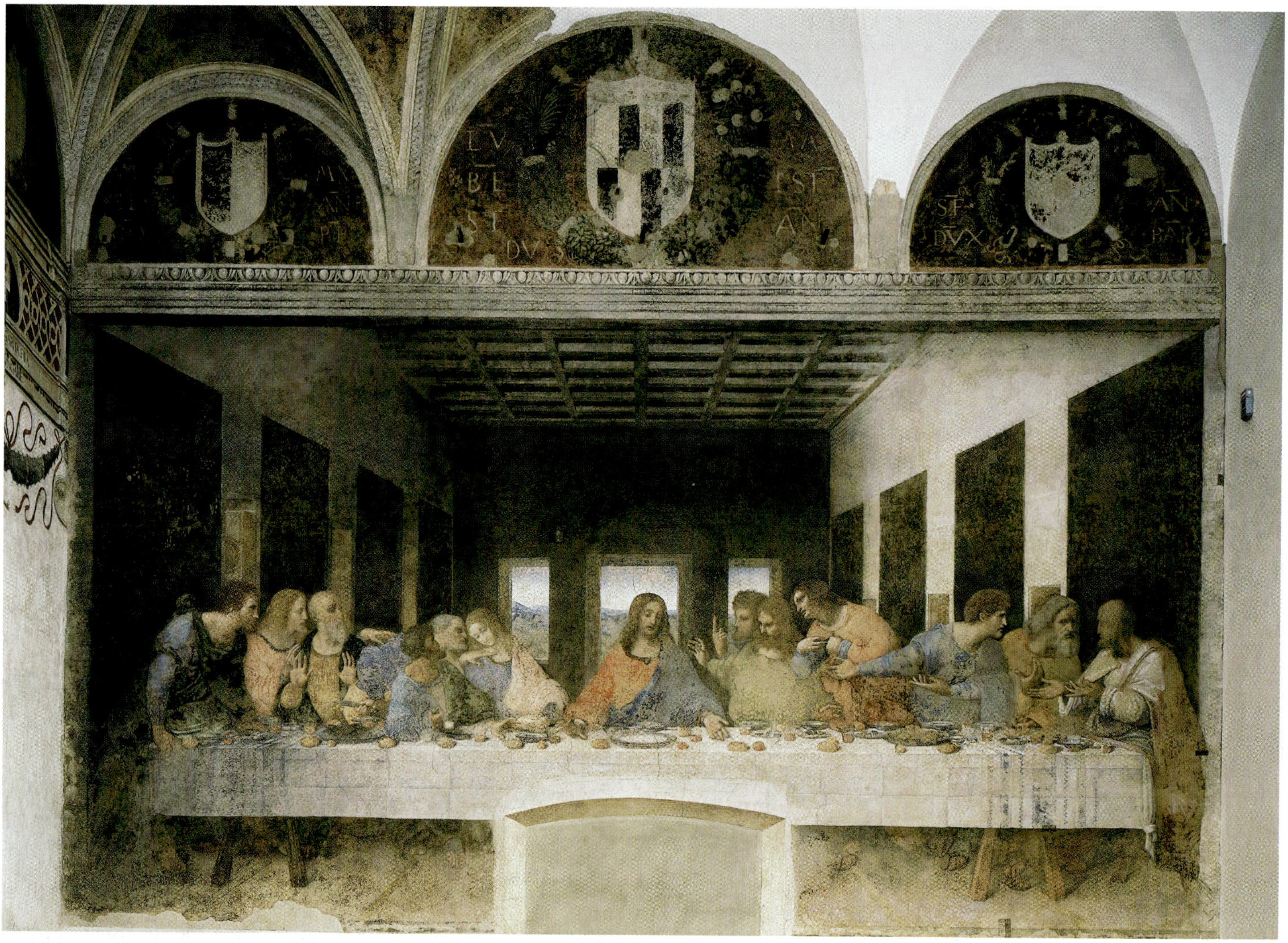

Intro–21 (ABOVE) **Leonardo da Vinci. *The Last Supper*,** wall painting in the refectory, Monastery of Santa Maria delle Grazie, Milan, Italy. 1495–1498. Tempera and oil on plaster, 15' 2" × 28' 10" (4.6 × 8.8 m)

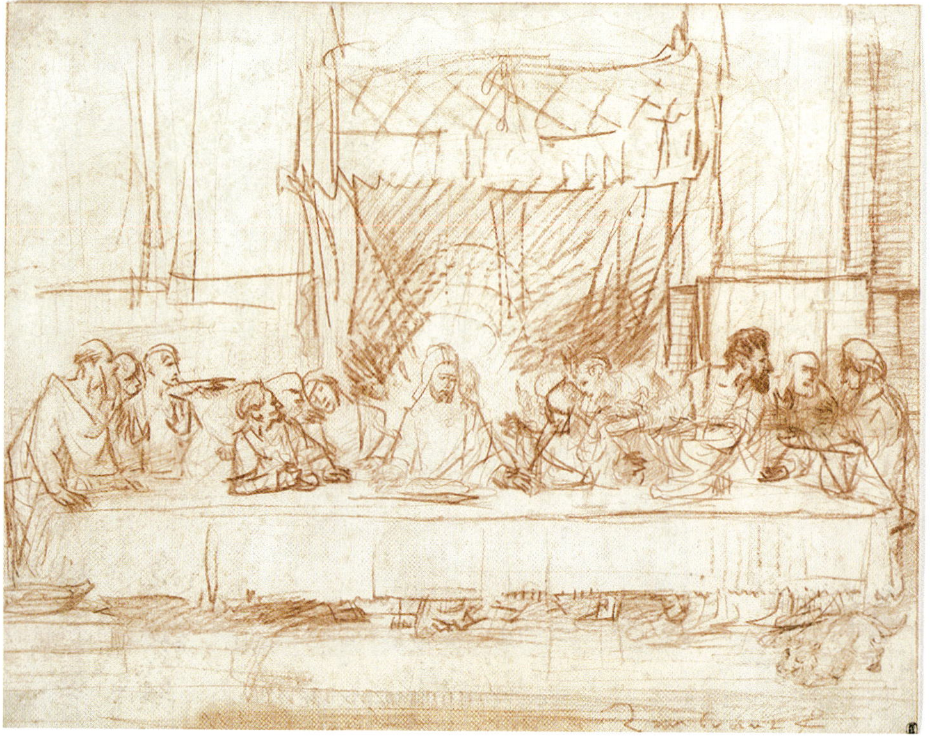

Intro–22 (LEFT) **Rembrandt van Rijn. *The Last Supper*,** after Leonardo da Vinci. Mid-1630s. Drawing in red chalk, 14⅜" × 18¾" (36.5 × 47.5 cm). The Metropolitan Museum of Art, New York
ROBERT LEHMAN COLLECTION, 1975 (1975.1.794)

Even the most mature artists learned from each other. In the seventeenth century, Rembrandt van Rijn carefully studied Leonardo's painting of *The Last Supper* (fig. **Intro–21**). Leonardo had turned this traditional theme into a powerful human drama by portraying the moment when Christ announced that one of the assembled apostles would betray him. The men react with surprise and horror to this shocking news, yet Leonardo depicts the scene as a symmetrical composition with the apostles in balanced groups of three on each side of Christ. The regularly spaced tapestries and ceiling panels lead the viewers' eyes directly to Christ, who is silhouetted in front of an open window.

Rembrandt, working 130 years later in the Netherlands, could only have known the Italian master's painting from a print, since he never went to Italy. Rembrandt "copied" *The Last Supper* in hard red chalk (fig. **Intro–22**). Then he reworked the drawing in a softer chalk, assimilating Leonardo's lessons but revising the composition and changing the mood of the original. With heavy overdrawing he re-created the scene, shifting Jesus' position to the left, giving Judas more emphasis, and adding a dog at the right. Gone are the wall hangings and ceiling, replaced by a huge canopy. The space is undetermined and expansive rather than focused. Rembrandt's drawing is more than an academic exercise; it is a sincere tribute from one great master to another. The artist must have been pleased with his version of Leonardo's masterpiece because he signed his drawing boldly in the lower right-hand corner.

What Role Do Patrons Play?

As we have seen, the person or group who commissions or finances a work of art—the **patron**—can have a significant impact on it. The Great Sphinx (see fig. Intro–1) was "designed" following the conventions of priests in ancient Egypt; the statue of Charles V was cast to glorify totalitarian rule (see fig. Intro–7); the content of Veronese's *Triumph of Venice* (see fig. Intro–15) was determined by that city's government officials; and Chihuly's glassworks (see fig. Intro–19) may be reassembled according to the collector's wishes or whims.

Although some artists work speculatively, hoping to sell their work on the open market, throughout history both individuals and institutions have acted as patrons of the arts or of certain artists. During periods of artistic efflorescence or at moments which saw major artistic development or change, enlightened patronage has been critical. Today, not only individuals but also museums and other institutions, such as government agencies (for example, the National Endowment for the Arts in the United States) provide financial support for the arts.

Individual Patrons

People who collect art constitute a very special audience for artists. Many patrons collect out of a love of art, but some collect art to enhance their own prestige, seeking an aura of power and importance by association. Individual patronage can also spring from, or develop into, cordial relationships between patrons and artists, as is evident in an early fifteenth-century manuscript illustration in which the author, Christine de Pizan, presents her work to Isabeau, the Queen of France (fig. **Intro–23**). Christine, a widow who supported her family by writing, hired painters and scribes to copy, illustrate, and decorate her books. She especially admired the painting created by a woman named Anastaise, whose work she considered unsurpassed in the city of Paris. Queen Isabeau was Christine's patron; Christine was Anastaise's patron; and all the women seen in the painting were patrons of the brilliant textile workers who supplied the brocades for their gowns, the tapestries for the wall, and

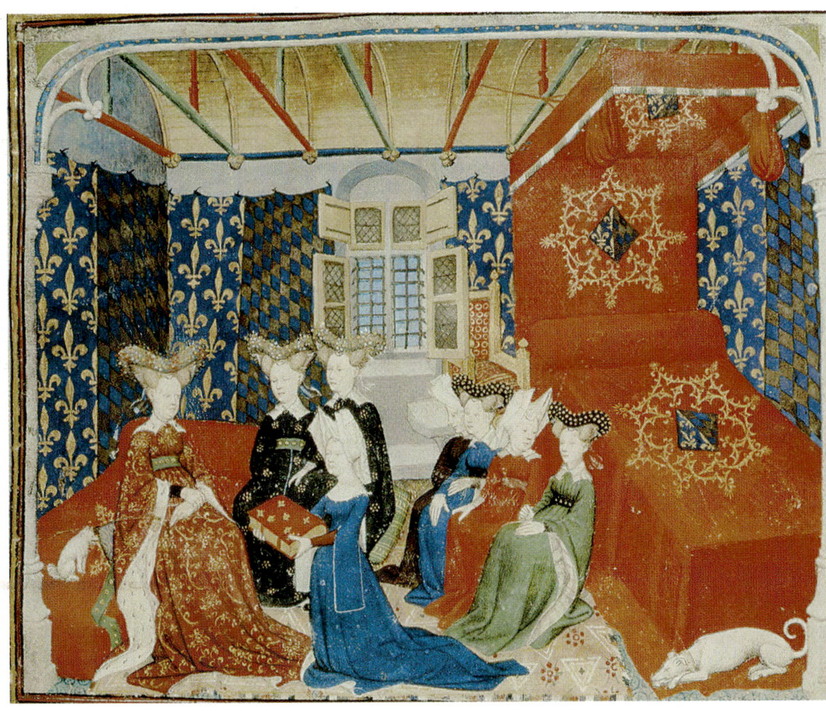

Intro–23 ***Christine de Pizan Presenting Her Book to the Queen of France.*** 1410–1415. Tempera and gold on vellum, image approx. 5½" × 6¾" (14 × 17 cm). The British Library, London (MS. Harley 4431, fol. 3)

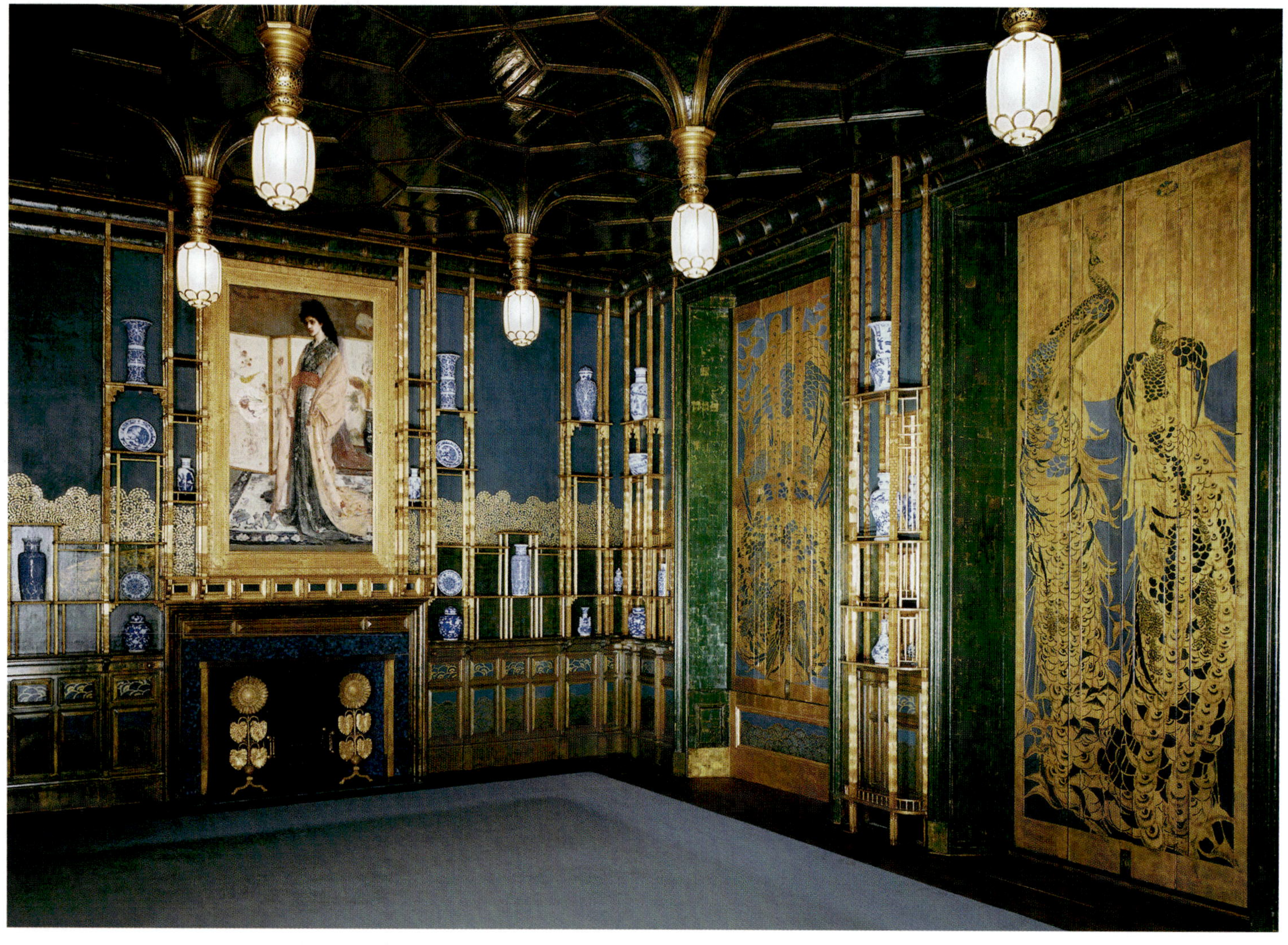

Intro–24 James McNeill Whistler. ***Harmony in Blue and Gold***, the Peacock Room, northeast corner, from a house owned by Frederick Leyland, London. 1876–1877. Oil paint and metal leaf on canvas, leather, and wood, 13' 11⅞" × 33' 2" × 19' 11½" (4.26 × 10.11 × 6.83 m). Over the fireplace, Whistler's *The Princess from the Land of Porcelain.* Freer Gallery of Art, Smithsonian Institution, Washington, D.C.
GIFT OF CHARLES LANG FREER (F1904.61)

the embroideries for the bed. Such networks of patronage and creation shape a culture.

But relations between artists and patrons do not always prove to be as congenial as these. Patrons may change their minds and sometimes fail to pay their bills. Artists may ignore their patron's wishes, to the dismay of everyone. In the late nineteenth century, the Liverpool shipping magnate Frederick Leyland asked James McNeill Whistler (1834–1903), an American painter living in London, what color to paint the shutters in the dining room where he planned to hang Whistler's painting *The Princess from the Land of Porcelain.* The room had been decorated with expensive embossed and gilded leather and finely crafted shelves to show off Leyland's collection of Chinese blue-and-white porcelain. Whistler, inspired by the Japanese theme of his own painting as well as by the porcelain, painted the window shutters with splendid turquoise, blue, and gold peacocks. But he did not stop there: While Leyland was away, Whistler painted the entire room, covering the gilded leather on the walls with turquoise peacock feathers (fig. **Intro–24**). Leyland, shocked and angry at what seemed to him to be wanton destruction of the room, paid Whistler less than half the agreed price. Luckily, he did not destroy Whistler's "Peacock Room" (which Whistler called simply *Harmony in Blue and Gold*). It was sold at Leyland's death to Charles Lang Freer (1854–1919), who installed it in his home in Detroit. When Freer died, the Peacock Room was moved to the Freer Gallery of Art in Washington, D.C.

Institutional Patronage: Museums and Civic Bodies

From the earliest times, people have gathered and preserved precious objects that convey the idea of power and prestige. Today, both private and public museums are major patrons, collectors, and preservers of art. Curators of such collections acquire works of art for their museums and often assist patrons in obtaining especially fine pieces, although the idea of what is best and what is worth collecting and preserving often changes from one generation to another.

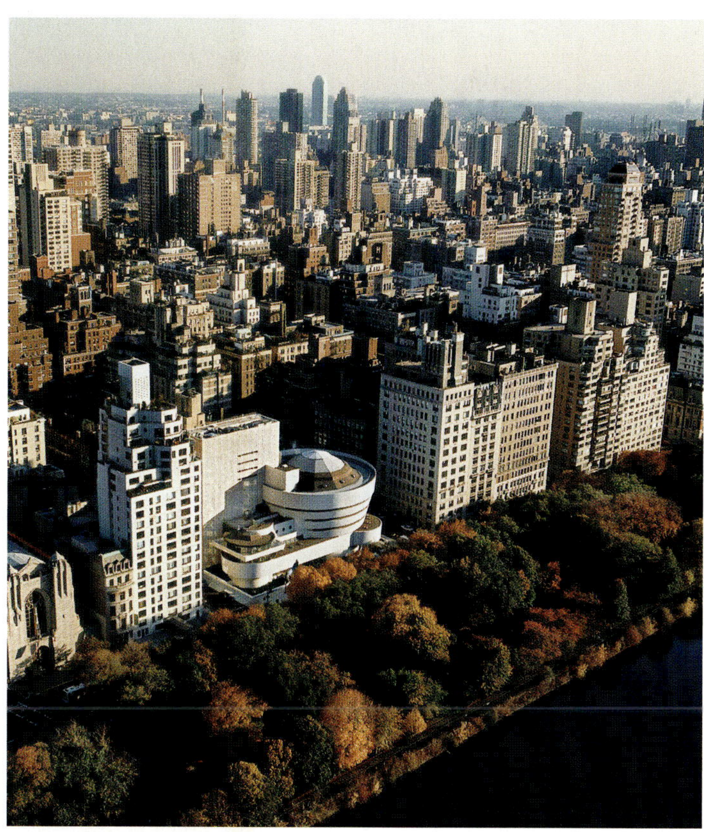

Intro–25 Frank Lloyd Wright. Solomon R. Guggenheim Museum, New York City. 1956–1959. Aerial view

PHOTOGRAPH BY DAVID HEALD © THE SOLOMON R. GUGGENHEIM FOUNDATION, NY

For example, the collection of abstract and nonrepresentational art formed by members of the Guggenheim family was once considered so radical that few people—and certainly no civic or governmental group—would have considered the art worth collecting at all. Today, the collection fills more than one major museum.

Frank Lloyd Wright's Solomon R. Guggenheim Museum (fig. **Intro–25**), with its snail-like, continuous spiral ramp, is a suitably **avant-garde** (strikingly new or radical for its time, "on the cutting edge") home for the collection in New York City. Sited on Fifth Avenue, beside the public green space of Central Park and surrounded on the other three sides by quadrangles of city buildings, the Guggenheim Museum challenges and relieves the verticality and right angles of the modern city. The Guggenheim Foundation recently opened another home for art, in Bilbao, Spain (see fig. 20–46), designed by Frank Gehry, a leader of the twenty-first-century avant-garde in architecture. As both Guggenheim museums show, such structures can do more than house collections; they can be works of art themselves.

Civic sponsorship of art is epitomized by fifth-century BCE Athens, a Greek city-state whose citizens practiced an early form of democracy. Led by the statesman and general Perikles, the Athenians defeated the Persians, and then rebuilt Athens's civic and religious center, the Acropolis, as a tribute to the goddess Athena and a testament to the glory of Athens. In figure **Intro–26**, a nineteenth-century British artist, Sir Lawrence Alma-Tadema, celebrates the accomplishment of the Athenian architects, sculptors, and painters, who were led by supervising artist Phidias. Alma-Tadema imagines the moment when Phidias showed the carved and painted frieze at the top of the wall of Athena's temple, the Parthenon, to Perikles and a privileged group of Athenian citizens, his civic sponsors.

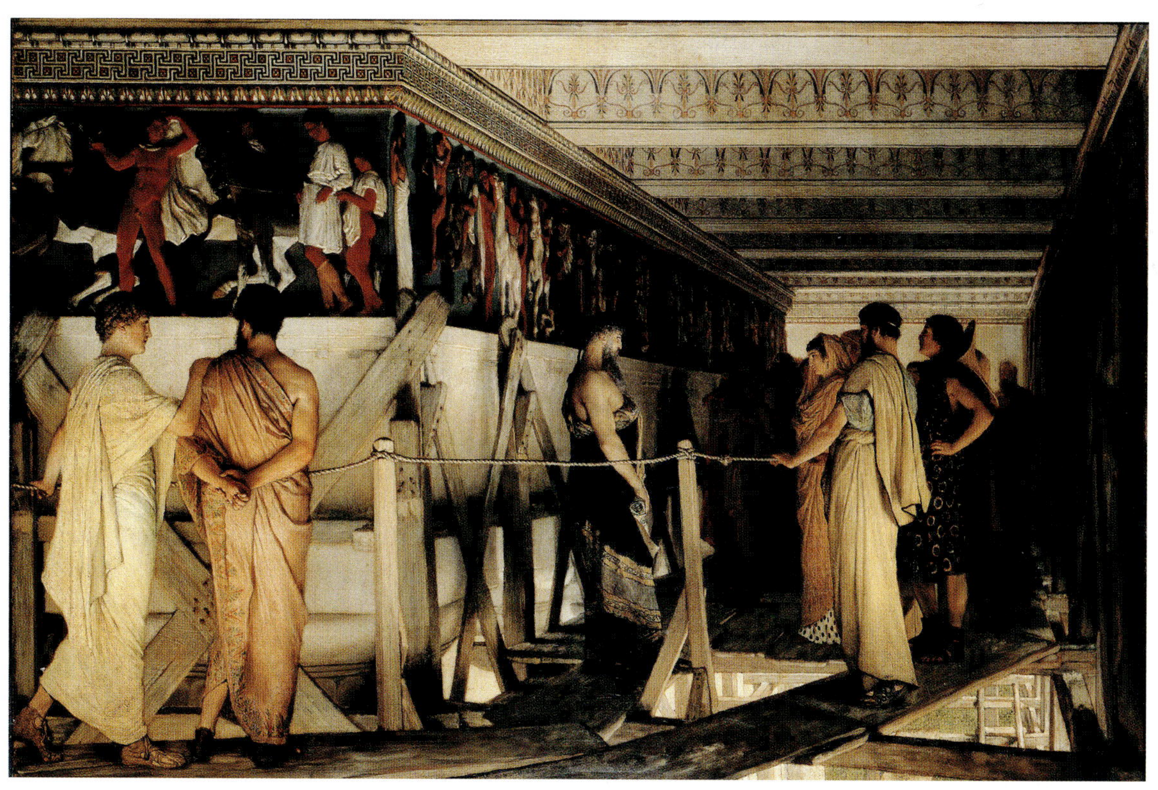

Intro–26 Lawrence Alma-Tadema. ***Phidias and the Frieze of the Parthenon, Athens.*** 1868. Oil on canvas, 29⅝" × 42½" (75.3 × 108 cm). Birmingham Museums and Art Gallery, England

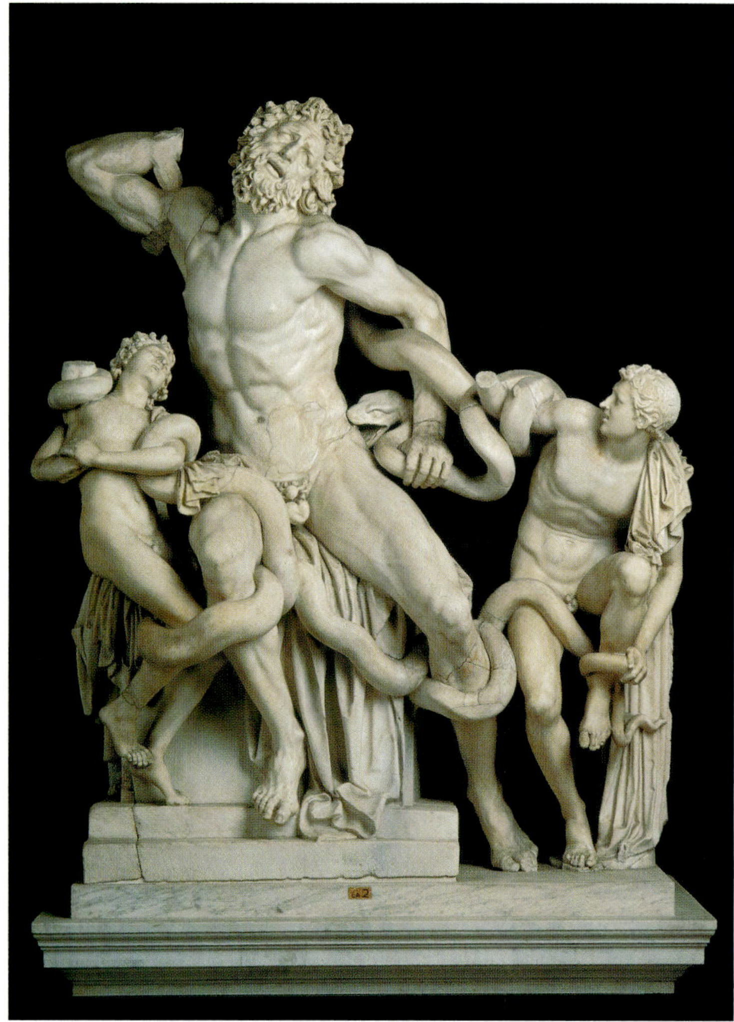

Intro–27 Hagesandros, Polydoros, and Athanodoros of Rhodes. ***Laocoön and his Sons***, as restored today. Probably the original of the 1st century CE or a Roman copy of the 1st century CE. Marble, height 8' (2.44 m). Musei Vaticani, Museo Pio Clementino, Cortile Ottagono, Rome, Italy

What Is Art History?

Art history became an academic field of study in colleges and universities only relatively recently, but many art historians trace the discipline itself to the 1550 publication of *Lives of the Most Excellent Italian Architects, Painters, and Sculptors* by the Italian artist and writer Giorgio Vasari (1511–1574). Some would push the origins earlier, to the work of ancient Roman commentator Pliny the Elder (33–79), who recorded the story of the competition between Greek painters Zeuxis and Parrhasios that we have already explored. Others would prioritize the work of Johann Joachim Winckelmann (1717–1768), who redirected attention away from artists' lives and toward the primacy of artistic values, especially Classicism. But the pioneering example of sixth-century Chinese painter Xie He's "Six Laws of Painting," demonstrates that the development of art history extends beyond the Western world. There are many forebears.

As the term "art history" implies, this interpretive enterprise combines two distinct but ultimately interrelated aspects: the study of individual works of art outside time and place (formal analysis and certain types of critical theory) and the historical study of art as a product of its broad cultural context (contextualism), the primary approach taken in this book. The scope of art history is immense, commensurate with the many and varied ways human beings have represented their world and expressed their ideas and ideals in visual form.

Studying Art Formally and Contextually

One method of scrutinizing individual art objects is known as **connoisseurship**. Through years of close contact with, and study of, the formal qualities that make up a work of art's style (such as design, composition, the manipulation of materials), connoisseurs categorize an unidentified work by comparing it with related pieces, being in this way able to attribute it to a period, to a place, and sometimes even to a specific artist. Today, such experts also make use of scientific testing—such as x-ray radiography, electron microscopy, infrared spectroscopy, and x-ray diffraction—but ultimately, connoisseurs depend on their visual memory and their skills in close formal analysis.

As a humanistic discipline, however, art history adds theoretical and contextual studies to the formal analysis of works of art. Art historians draw on biography to learn about artists' lives; on social history to evaluate the economic and political forces shaping artists, their patrons, and their public; and on the history of ideas to gain an

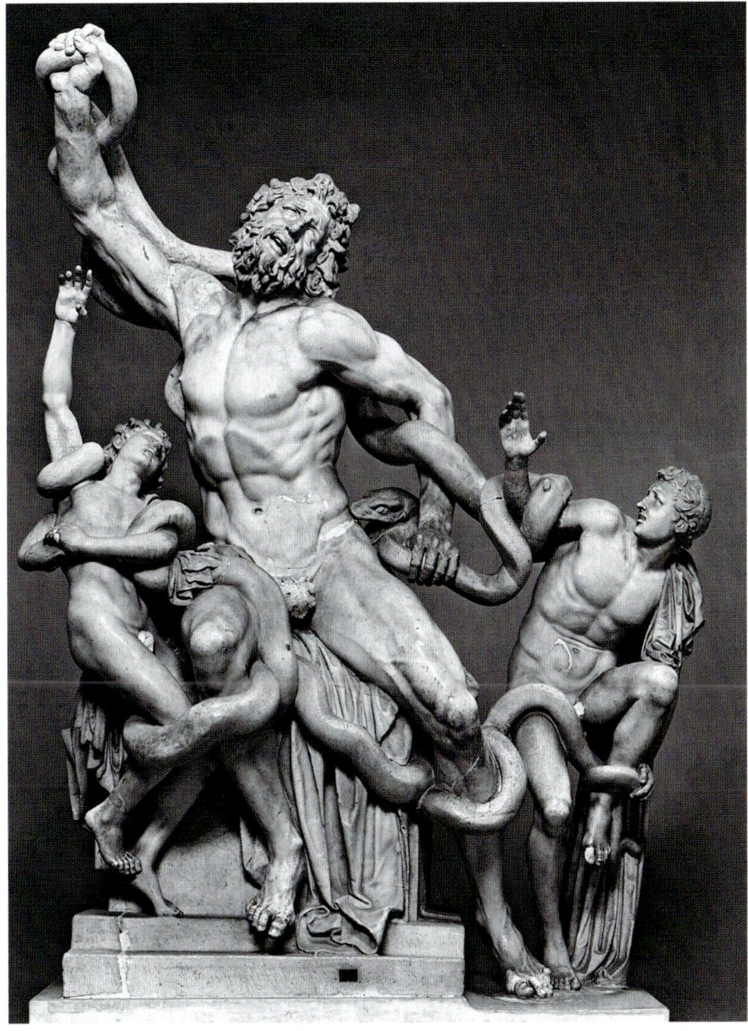

Intro–28 Hagesandros, Polydoros, and Athanodoros of Rhodes. ***Laocoön and his Sons,*** in an earlier restoration

understanding of the intellectual currents influencing artists' work and its reception. They also study the history of other arts, including music, drama, and literature, to gain a richer sense of the broader cultural context of the visual arts. Intense art historical study is also enhanced by the work of anthropologists and archaeologists, who reconstruct the social context of newly discovered works of material culture, but do not single out individual works of perceived excellence—labeled as "art"—for special attention.

Today, however, art historians themselves study a wider range of works than ever before. Many reject altogether the idea of a fixed canon of superior masterpieces. The distinction between elite fine arts and popular utilitarian arts has become increasingly blurred, and the notion that some media, techniques, or subjects are better than others has almost disappeared. This is one of the most telling characteristics of current art history, along with the breadth of studies it now encompasses and its changing attitude to challenges such as preservation and restoration.

Defending Endangered Objects

Today's art historians are also concerned with past and present natural and human threats to the very survival of works of art. Even as methodological sophistication and technological advances soar, art historians face special challenges when interpreting works that have been damaged or restored. As we try to understand such works of art, we must remain quizzical and flexible, recognizing, for example, that the legs of a marble figure may have been replaced, a section of wall in a mural painting may have been repainted, and many important historical buildings have been consolidated or transformed through continual use.

The challenges posed by restorations are clearly illustrated by two reworkings, hundreds of years apart, of the renowned ancient Greek sculpture *Laocoön and his Sons.* Laocoön was a priest who warned the Trojans of an invasion by the Greeks in Homer's account of the Trojan War. Although Laocoön told the truth, the goddess Athena, who took the Greeks' side in the war, dispatched serpents to strangle him and his sons. A tragic hero, Laocoön represents a virtuous man destroyed by unjust forces. In this powerful sculpture, his features twist in agony, and the muscles of his and his sons' superhuman torsos and arms extend and knot as they struggle (figs. **Intro–27** and **Intro–28**). When the sculpture was discovered in Rome in 1506, Michelangelo rushed to watch it being excavated, an astonishing validation of his own ideal, heroic style coming straight

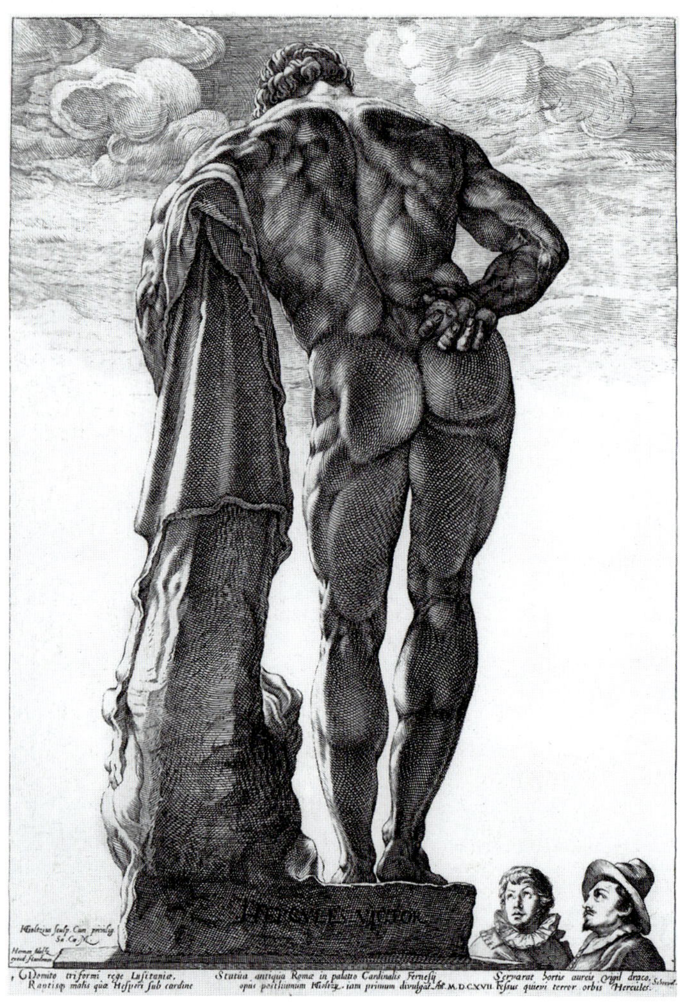

Intro–29 Hendrick Goltzius. *Dutch Visitors to Rome Looking at the Farnese Hercules.* c. 1592. Engraving, 16" × 11½" (40.5 × 29.4 cm)

After Goltzius returned from a trip to Rome in 1591–1592, he made engravings based on his drawings. These men have been identified as two of his Dutch friends.

out of the earth. The pope acquired it for the papal collection, and it can still be seen in the Vatican Museums.

In piecing together the past of this one work, we know that mistakes were made during the initial restoration. The broken pieces of the *Laocoön* group were first reassembled with the figures flinging their arms out in the melodramatic fashion seen in figure Intro–28. This would have been the sculpture seen by Renaissance and Baroque artists. Modern conservation methods, however, have produced a different image with a changed mood (see fig. Intro–27). Lost pieces are not replaced and Laocoön's right arm turns back upon his body, making a compact composition that internalizes the men's agony, perhaps speaking more directly to a self-centered twenty-first-century audience than the heroic struggle emphasized in the earlier reconstruction. We can only wonder what will be highlighted in the next transformation.

Such restorations of works like the *Laocoön* are undertaken to conserve art that is considered precious. But throughout the world, human beings intentionally or mindlessly threaten the very survival of works of art and architecture—and this is not only a recent problem. Greedy thieves plundered and vandalized Egyptian tombs centuries ago, and such theft continues to this day. Objects of cultural and artistic value in Iraq and Central America, for example, are being taken from official and unofficial excavation sites, then sold illegally. In industrialized regions of the world, emissions from cars, trucks, buses, and factories turn into corrosive rain that damages and sometimes literally destroys the works of art and architecture on which it falls.

For art, however, war may be the most destructive of all human enterprises. History is filled with examples of plundered works of art that, as spoils of war, were taken elsewhere and paraded and protected. But countless numbers of churches, synagogues, mosques, temples, and shrines have been burned, bombed, and stripped of decoration in the name of winning a war or confirming an ideology. In modern times, with weapons of mass destruction, so much that is lost is absolutely irrecoverable.

Nature, too, has played its part. Floods, hurricanes, tornadoes, avalanches, mudslides, and earthquakes all damage and destroy priceless treasures. For example, an earthquake on the morning of September 27, 1997, convulsed the small Italian town of Assisi, where Saint Francis was born and where he founded the Franciscan order. It shook the thirteenth-century Basilica of Saint Francis of Assisi—one of the richest repositories of Italian Gothic and Early Renaissance wall painting—causing great damage to architecture and paintings. Frescoes crumbled from the vaults and fell to the floor, but with the help of documentary photographs, the generous support of donors, and the painstaking work of restorers, these

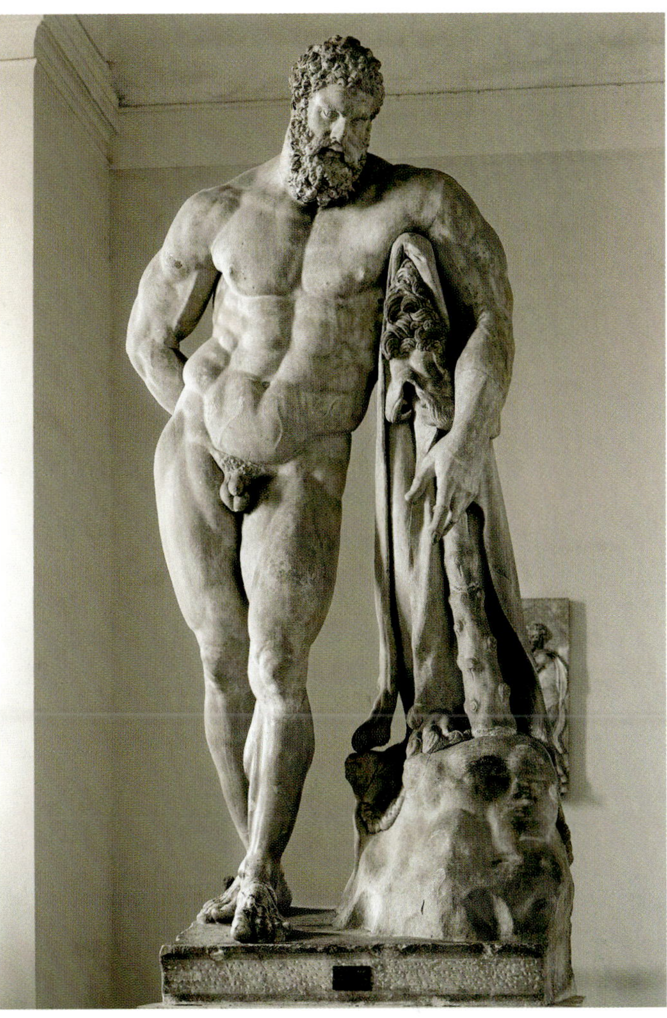

Intro–30 ***The Farnese Hercules***, copy of *The Weary Hercules* by Lysippos. 3rd century BCE. Found in the Baths of Caracalla in 1546; exhibited in the Farnese Palace until 1787. Marble, 10' 6" (3.17 m). Signed "Glykon" on the rock under the club. Left arm restored. Museo Archaelogico Nazionale, Naples, Italy

fragments have been reassembled with such skill that visitors today would hardly guess that an earthquake had brought down the ceiling only slightly more than a decade ago.

What Is a Viewer's Role and Responsibility?

As viewers we enter into an agreement with artists, who in turn make special demands on us. We re-create the works of art for ourselves as we bring to them our own experiences, our intelligence, and even our prejudices. Without our participation, artworks are only chunks of stone or smears of paint. But remember, all is change. From extreme lifelike description at one end of the spectrum to nonrepresentational abstraction at the other, artists have worked with varying degrees of naturalism, idealism, and abstraction. The challenge for the student of art history is to discover not only how but also why those styles evolved, and ultimately what significance these changes hold for us, for our culture, for our future.

Our involvement with art may be casual or intense, naïve or sophisticated, self-contained or interactive. At first we may simply react instinctively to a painting or a building or a sculpture, but this level of "feeling" about art—"I know what I like"—can never be fully satisfying, because ultimately it is self-centered. The work of art becomes a mirror that reflects back to us only the reactions we bring to it. Or, like these late sixteenth-century awestruck visitors—friends of Dutch artist Hendrick Goltzius, whose engraving (fig. **Intro–29**) derives from a drawing he made while they all shared a visit to a gallery in Rome—we can admire and ponder the ancient statue of Hercules (fig. **Intro–30**), taking in its forms and ideas and returning our own questions and reflections in a virtual conversation of give and take that crosses over barriers of time and space. In this way, as viewers we participate in the continual re-creation of works of art, allowing their meanings to change and evolve from individual to individual, from era to era. And in art history, our conversation opens to include friends and colleagues who, by sharing our interest in engaging with these cherished works from human history, enrich not only our communal understanding of the past, but also can refine our aspirations for the future.

For once we welcome works of art into our lives on their own terms, we have a ready source of sustenance and challenge that grows, changes, mellows, and deepens our daily experience. This book introduces us to works of art in their historical context, but no matter how much we study or read about art and artists, eventually we may return to the contemplation of an original work itself, the enduring tangible evidence of the ever-questing human spirit.

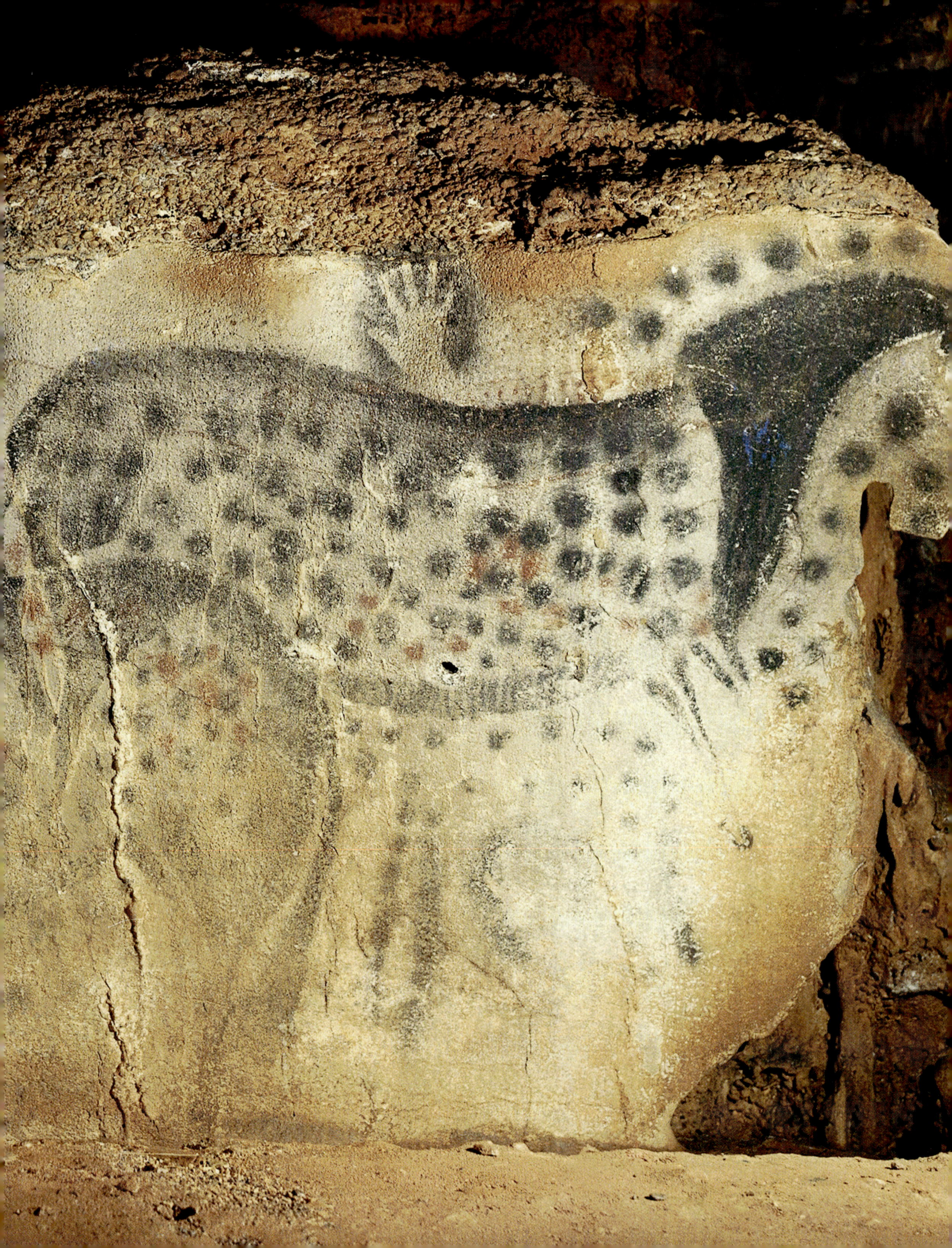

1
Prehistoric Art in Europe

LOOKING FORWARD

The first modern explorers of the painted caves of France and Spain entered an almost unimaginably ancient world. What they found in these deep recesses—hundreds of yards from the entrances and accessed through long, narrow underground passages—astounded them then and still fascinates us now. The paintings and engravings on both walls and ceilings of these caves seem to record human observation of animals that walked the earth as long as 35,000 years ago. They are among the very first images in the history of "art," but we are not sure what they originally meant.

On the walls of a cave at Pech-Merle in southern France—successively used and abandoned over a span of up to 10,000 years—images of animals, accompanied by handprints and geometric symbols (fig. **1–1**), have been found in 30 locations within a vast underground complex. The earliest artists painted massive, boldly patterned horses with extended necks and diminutive, finely detailed heads. In this case the right-hand horse's head actually mimics the natural shape of the rock wall on which it is painted. Without written words and using only the essential design elements of line and color, these prehistoric painters communicate with arresting clarity across millennia. But the most powerful and immediate human connections are embodied in the handprints. They are later additions made by artists who returned to the site 10,000 years after the horses were created. Placing a hand against the stone surface as a stencil, the Paleolithic painter preserved its outline by spraying charcoal diluted with water and saliva directly from his or her mouth.

Why did early humans make these paintings? Were they recording actual hunts or roundups, or expressing their dreams or aspirations for success in such activities, so critical for their survival? Did the images play a role in the education or initiation of their children? Did they express beliefs, imagine a spirit world, or record a ritual? Could the makers have been trying to control the forces of nature through these images? Might the act of painting itself have been ritually important, regardless of the image? Frustratingly, we have no answers, only questions. Perhaps in the end the greatest value of studying these mysterious images is their ability to lead us into our own speculations about why human beings create pictures.

1–1 ***Spotted Horse and Human Hand,*** Pech-Merle Cave, Dordogne, France. Horse 25,000–24,000 BCE; hand c. 15,000 BCE. Paint on limestone, horse over 5' (1.5 m) in length

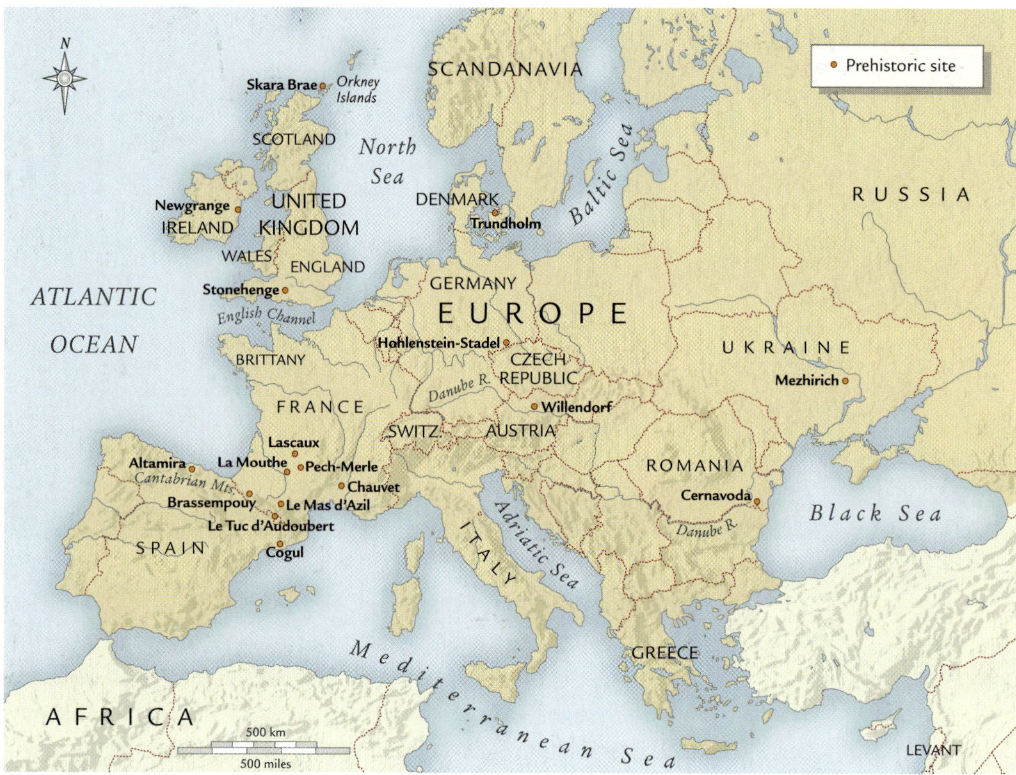

Map 1–1 Prehistoric Europe

Human beings made tools long before they made what today we call "art." *Homo habilis* ("handy human"), who first flaked and chipped (knapped) flint pebbles into blades and scrapers with cutting edges, lived in Africa 2 million years ago. By 200,000 years ago, *Homo sapiens* ("wise human") had moved into North Africa and Europe, and Asia as far as China. Evolutionary changes continued to take place; by 100,000 years ago, a well-developed type of *Homo sapiens* called Neanderthal inhabited Europe (see map **1–1**). Neanderthals used many different stone tools and carefully buried their dead with funerary offerings. By 35,000 years ago, they had disappeared, and Cro-Magnon humans inhabited the continent. The Cro-Magnons made tools of reindeer antler and bone as well as very fine chipped-stone implements. Clearly social beings, Cro-Magnons must have had social organization, rituals, and beliefs that led them to create art. They engraved, carved, drew, and painted with colored ochers, earthy mineral oxides of iron that could be ground into pigments. These people are our ancestors, and with their sculpture and painting the history of art begins.

Scholars began to study prehistory systematically—that is, to examine the thousands of years of human civilization before written historical records—less than 200 years ago. Struck by the wealth of stone tools, weapons, and figures found at ancient living sites, nineteenth-century archaeologists named the whole period of early human development the "Stone Age." Today's researchers further divide the time span into the Paleolithic, or Old Stone Age (from the Greek *paleo*, "old," and *lithos*, "stone")—which has Lower (earliest), Middle, and Upper phases—and the Neolithic, or New Stone Age (from the Greek *neo*, "new"). In this chapter we will consider the art of the Paleolithic and Neolithic periods and also the earliest age of metals—the Bronze and Iron Ages in Europe. Later chapters will consider the prehistoric art of other continents and cultures.

Upper Paleolithic Art

Our hunter-gatherer ancestors lived in small nomadic groups and created works of art and architecture as early as the Upper (later) Paleolithic period (c. 42,000–8000 BCE). During this time, the glaciers of the last Ice Age still covered northern stretches of Europe, North America, and Asia. Some of the most ancient Paleolithic artifacts are small figures, or figurines, of people and animals, made of bone, ivory, stone, or clay. Today, we interpret such self-contained, three-dimensional works as examples of **sculpture in the round**. Prehistoric carvers also produced **relief sculpture** in stone, bone, or ivory. In relief sculpture, the surrounding material is carved away, forming a recessed background from which the figures emerge toward us. Whatever their original significance, Paleolithic works of sculpture show a distinctive sense of design and the ability both to pose and to solve problems.

An early and puzzling example of a sculpture in the round is a human figure—probably male—with a feline head (fig. **1–2**), made about 30,000 BCE. Archaeologists excavating at Hohlenstein-Stadel, Germany, found broken pieces of ivory (from the tusk of a now-extinct woolly mammoth) that they realized were parts of an entire figure. Nearly a foot tall, the remarkable statue that they reconstructed from these fragments surpasses in size and complexity

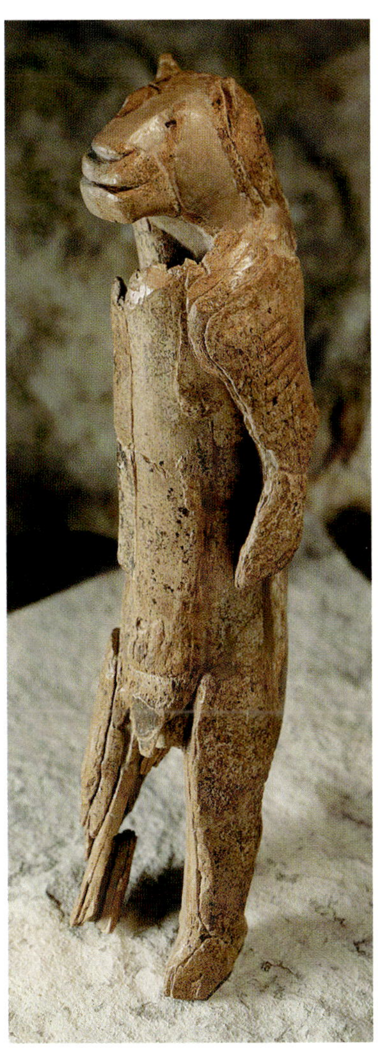

1–2 *Lion-Human*, from Hohlenstein-Stadel, Germany. c. 30,000 BCE. Mammoth ivory, height 11⅝" (29.6 cm). Ulmer Museum, Ulm, Germany

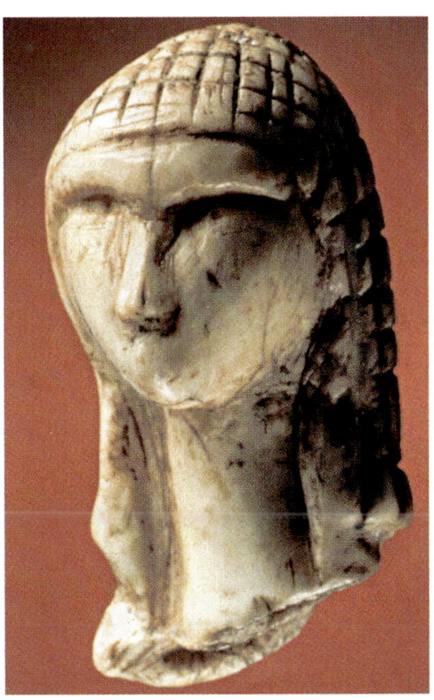

1–3 *Woman from Brassempouy*, Grotte du Pape, Brassempouy, Landes, France. c. 30,000 BCE. Ivory, height 1¼" (3.6 cm). Musée des Antiquités Nationales, St.-Germain-en-Laye, France

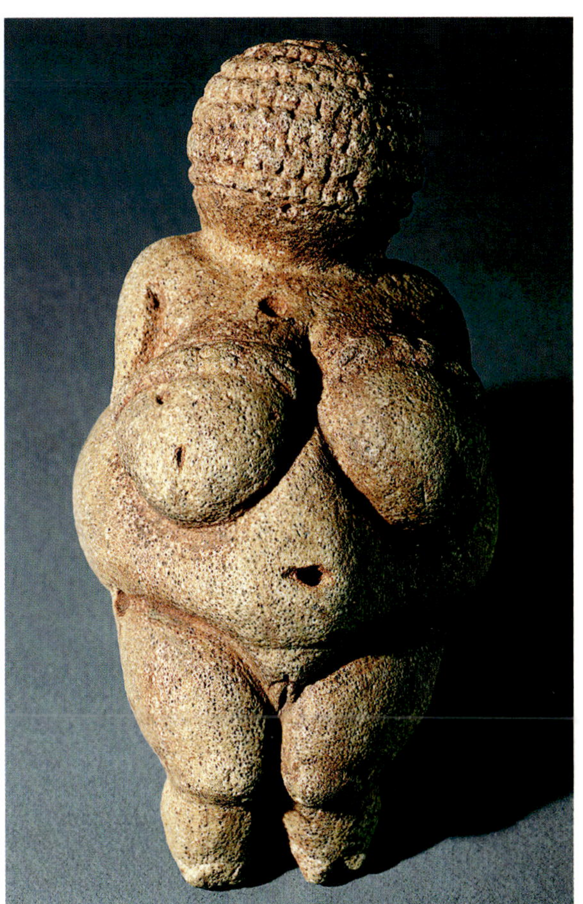

1–4 *Woman from Willendorf*, Austria. c. 24,000 BCE. Limestone, height 4⅜" (11 cm). Naturhistorisches Museum, Vienna, Austria

most early figurines. Instead of copying what he or she saw in nature, the carver created an imaginary creature, part man and part beast. Was the figure intended to represent a person wearing a ritual lion mask? Or has the man taken on the appearance and power of an animal? One of the few indisputable things that can be said about the *Lion-Human* is that it shows complex thinking and creative imagination: the ability to conceive and represent a hybrid creature never seen in nature.

Paleolithic sculptors depicted women more frequently than other subjects, and examples have been found in dozens of sites from France to Ukraine. The carver of the *Woman from Brassempouy* (fig. **1–3**) captured the essence of a head or what psychologists call the "memory image"—those generalized elements that reside in our standard memory of a human head. An egg shape rests atop a long neck; a wide nose and a strongly defined browline suggest deep-set eyes; and an engraved squared patterning may be hair or a headdress. This is an example of **abstraction** or **stylization**, which is the reduction of shapes and appearances to basic yet recognizable forms that are not intended to be exact replications of nature. The result in this case looks uncannily modern to the contemporary viewer. Today, when such a piece is isolated in a museum case or as a book illustration, we enjoy the ivory head as an aesthetic object, divorced from its cultural context. Actually, we know nothing of the motivation for creating this work, from which only the head survives. Perhaps the maker associated the woman with spiritual or magical powers. Perhaps the figure ensured her community's continuity as a fertility figure assuring the abundance of nature. These can only be speculations. No written records survive to document the thoughts and deeds of those who made and those who used such works.

The most famous Paleolithic female figurine, the *Woman from Willendorf* (fig. **1–4**), dates from about 24,000 BCE (see "The Power of Naming," page 26). Carved from limestone and originally colored with red ocher, the statuette's swelling, rounded forms make it seem much larger than its actual 4⅜-inch height. The sculptor exaggerated the figure's female **attributes** by giving it pendulous breasts, a bulging belly with a deep navel (a natural indentation in the stone), wide hips, dimpled knees and buttocks, and solid thighs. By carving a woman with a well-nourished body, the artist may be stressing her health and fertility, which could ensure the ability to produce strong children, thus guaranteeing the survival of the community.

Whatever their original significance, Paleolithic sculptures combine a sense of the formal complexity that results when human beings attempt to pose and solve problems of visual design. Similar

THE POWER OF NAMING

Our ideas about works of art are powerfully affected by the names we use to identify them, even in the captions of a textbook. Before the twentieth century, artists did not usually title their works. Titles were supplied by owners or scholars, and they often carried the cultural prejudices of the times when they lived.

An excellent example of such distortion is provided by the names early scholars gave to the hundreds of small prehistoric statues of women. For example, the sculpture in figure 1–4 was originally labeled *Venus of Willendorf*, joining the name of the Roman goddess of love and beauty with the geographical location where the statuette had been found. The use of this name sent a message that the figure was associated with religious belief, that it represented an ideal of womanhood, and that it initiated a long line of images of idealized feminine beauty.

Soon, similar works of Paleolithic sculpture came to be known as Venuses. But there is no proof that any of these figures had religious associations. They have been interpreted as representations of actual women, fertility symbols, expressions of ideal beauty, erotic totems, ancestor figures, or even dolls meant to help young girls learn women's roles. They could have been any or all of these.

Our ability to understand and interpret works of art is compromised by distorting and limiting labels. Even knowing that the figure was once named *Venus of Willendorf* influences the way we look at it. Calling a prehistoric figure "woman" instead of "Venus" frees us to think about it in new and creative ways.

talents are revealed in the structures of the period even if some object to the use of the word "architecture" in conjunction with prehistoric buildings. But even a simple structure requires a degree of imagination and planning, and Paleolithic builders in some regions used great ingenuity in constructing shelters that were far from simply utilitarian.

The people of the treeless grasslands of Russia and Ukraine created settlements of up to ten houses using the bones and hide of the woolly mammoth, whose long, curving tusks made excellent roof supports and arched door openings (fig. **1–5**). One such village, dating from 16,000–10,000 BCE, was discovered near the Ukrainian village of Mezhirich. Its turf-and-hide-covered houses were cleverly constructed with dozens of skulls, shoulder blades, pelvis bones, jawbones, and tusks. The largest house is an impressive 24 by 33 feet, and inside, archaeologists found 15 small hearths containing ashes and charred bones left by its last occupants. Clearly, life revolved around the hearth, the source of light and heat in the dark winter months.

Cave and rock-shelter paintings from the Upper Paleolithic period may provide the most powerful connections with our early ancestors. Rock art survives in many places around the world, but the oldest known examples come from Western Europe. People began to paint, engrave, draw, and model images in caves as early as 35,000 years ago, producing many cave paintings in southern France and northern Spain between about 30,000 and 10,000 BCE. The images represent animals—such as wild horses, bison, mammoths, aurochs (ancestors of cattle)—and a few people; many handprints; and hundreds of geometric markings, such as grids, circles, and dots. In some caves, painters decorated not only large caverns but also tiny chambers and recesses whose natural surfaces inspired images resembling low-relief sculpture. They must have worked in the light of small stone lamps fueled by animal fat, using charcoal and red and brown pigments of ground ochers, applied with fingers, "paint brushes" made of hair and moss, or blown directly from the mouth of the artist in a fine spray (see fig. 1–1).

Among the oldest securely dated European cave paintings are those at Chauvet Cave in southeastern France, a site which was discovered only in 1994 (fig. **1–6**). These accomplished paintings of animals, whose forms seem to bulge from the wall as they shift and move, were made around 30,000–28,000 BCE by artists who were in full command of their art. They have transformed their memories of active, three-dimensional creatures into two-dimensional representations by capturing the essence of well-observed animals—meat-bearing flanks, powerful legs, dangerous horns or tusks. The real significance of such cave paintings is unknown, but many theories have been suggested (see "The Meaning(s) of Prehistoric Paintings," page 27).

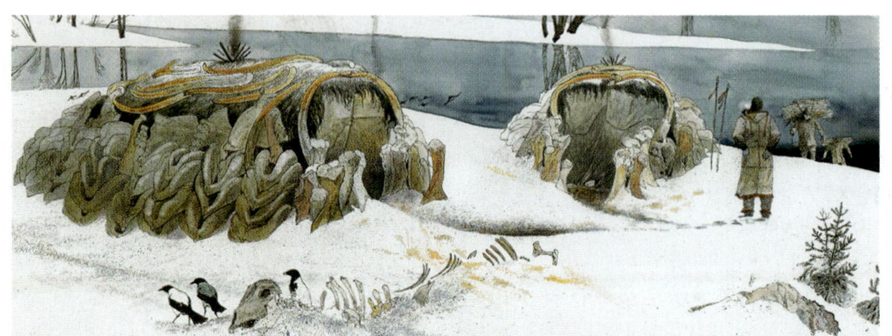

1–5 Reconstruction drawing of mammoth-bone house from Ukraine. c. 16,000–10,000 BCE

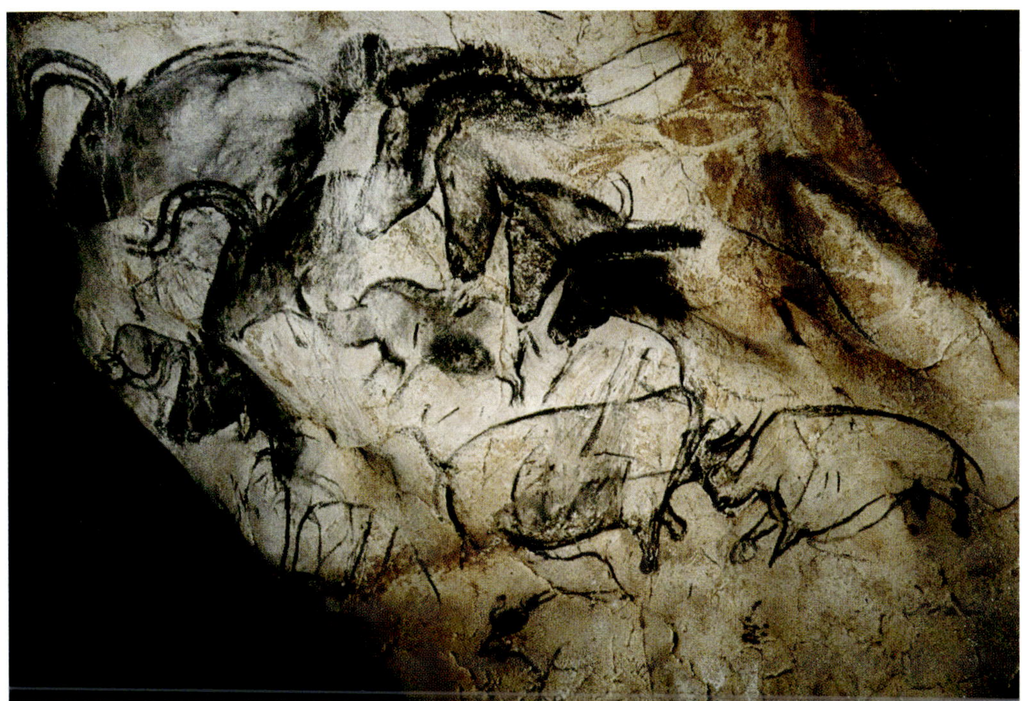

1–6 Wall painting with horses, aurochs (ancient oxen), and rhinoceroses, Chauvet Cave, Vallon-Pont-d'Arc, Ardèche Gorge, France. c. 30,000–28,000 BCE. Paint on limestone

In addition to animals, also included in the wall paintings of Chauvet Cave (named for one of the people who found it) are occasional humans (both male and female), many handprints, and hundreds of geometric designs. Footprints left in soft clay by a child go to a chamber containing bear skulls. According to radiocarbon dating, the charcoal used to depict the rhinos is 32,410 years old (give or take 720 years)!

THE MEANING(S) OF PREHISTORIC PAINTINGS

Anthropologists and art historians have put forward numerous theories to explain cave painting, often revealing as much about themselves and their times as about prehistoric art.

In the nineteenth century, the idea that human beings inherently desire to decorate themselves and their surroundings—an innate "aesthetic sense"—found ready acceptance. Some artists at the time promoted the idea of "art-for-art's sake," creating works of art for the sheer love of beauty. However, the effort and organization required to accomplish the great paintings of Lascaux and elsewhere suggest that their creators were motivated by more than pure aesthetics.

Early in the twentieth century, scholars rejected the idea of "art-for-art's sake" as a dated, romantic explanation. Led by Salomon Reinach, who believed that art fulfills a social function, they proposed that prehistoric cave paintings might be associated with ceremonies performed to enhance the fertility of the animals on which people depended for food. Reinach suggested that cave paintings were also expressions of "sympathetic magic," that prehistoric painters may have produced pictures of bison lying down to ensure that hunters found their prey asleep, or, by symbolically killing pictures of bison, guarantee the hunters' triumph over the beast itself. Abbé Henri Breuil extended these ideas to claim that caves were used as places of worship and settings for initiation rites.

In the second half of the twentieth century, scholars tended to base interpretations on scientific methods and current social theory. French scholars such as André Leroi-Gourhan and Annette Laming-Emperaire dismissed the "hunting magic" theory because debris from human settlements revealed that the animals used most frequently for food were not the ones traditionally portrayed in caves. These scholars discovered that cave images were often systematically organized, with different animals predominating in different areas of a cave. More recently, Leslie G. Freeman, has concluded that the reclining bison in the Altamira cave are neither dead, asleep, nor disabled—as others had assumed—but dust-wallowing, common behavior during the mating season.

Although hypotheses that seek to explain cave art have changed, and will continue to change over time, scholars are now in agreement that decorated caves must have had special meaning. People returned to them time after time over many generations, in some cases over thousands of years. Perhaps this art was the product of rituals intended to gain the favor of supernatural powers. Perhaps its significance had less to do with the finished painting than with the very act of creation. Artifacts and footprints suggest that the subterranean galleries, which were far from living quarters, had religious or magical functions. Perhaps the very experience of exploring the cave had significance for the image-makers. The discovery of musical instruments, such as bone flutes, may imply that even acoustical properties may have played a role, that caves were the site of performance as well as painting.

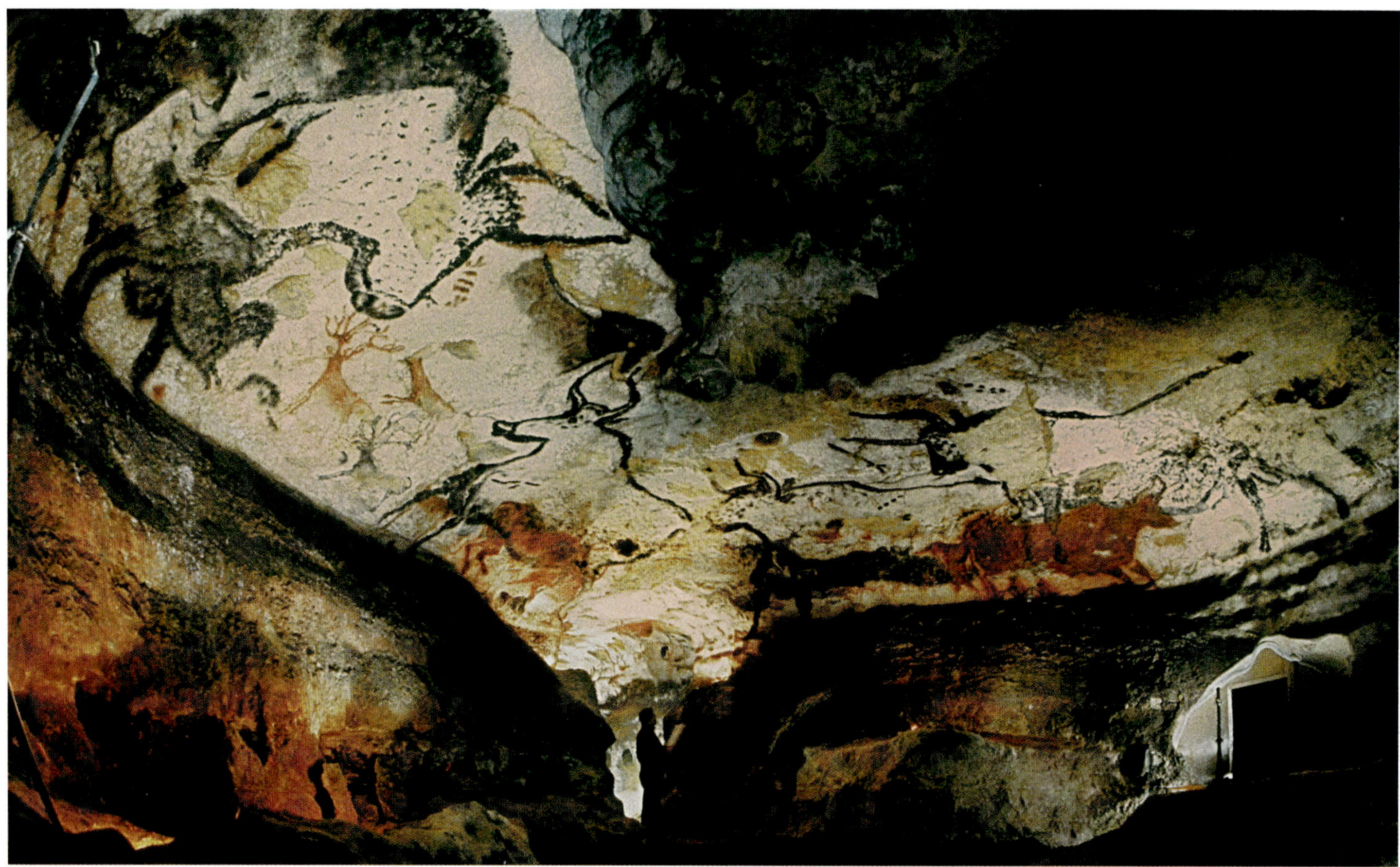

1–7 Hall of Bulls, Lascaux Caves. c. 15,000 BCE. Paint on limestone

Discovered in 1940 and opened to the public after World War II, the prehistoric "museum" at Lascaux soon became one of the most popular tourist sites in France—too popular, for the many visitors sowed the seeds of the paintings' destruction in the form of heat, humidity, exhaled carbon dioxide, and other contaminants. The cave was closed to the public in 1963 so that conservators might battle with an aggressive fungus that had attacked the paintings, and the authorities then created a facsimile of it. Visitors at what is called Lascaux II may now view copies of the painted images without harming the precious originals.

The best-known cave paintings today are those at Lascaux, in southern France (figs. **1–7** and **1–8**), where paintings of cows, bulls, horses, and deer date from about 15,000 BCE. The animals appear singly, in rows, face-to-face, tail-to-tail, and even painted on top of one another. Perhaps to ensure a complete image, the horns, eyes, and hooves are shown as seen from the front, while heads and bodies are rendered in profile. One scene at Lascaux is unusual not only because it includes a human figure but also because it is a rare example of a painting that seems to tell a story (see fig. 1–8). But what is this scene telling us? Why did the artist portray the man as only a stick-like figure with a bird's head when the bison was rendered with such accurate detail? It may be that the painting illustrates a myth regarding the death of a hero. Perhaps it illustrates an actual event. A compelling theory is that it depicts the vision of a shaman. As we know shamanism from practitioners today, shamans were thought to have special powers, an ability to foretell events and assist their people through contact with spirits in the form of animals or birds. Shamans typically make use of trance states, in which they believe they fly and receive communications from their spirit guides. The images they use to record their visions tend to be highly imaginative, incorporating geometric figures and combinations of human and animal forms such as the bird-headed or masked man in this scene from Lascaux or the lion-headed figure discussed earlier (see fig. 1–2).

The cave paintings at Altamira, in northern Spain (fig. **1–9**), were the first to be discovered, but scholars are still uncovering new information about them. As recently as 2008, specialists used an innovative scientific technique called uranium series dating to discover that prehistoric artists worked here over a very broad time span. The earliest paintings are now placed between 35,000 and 25,000 BCE, and the most recent date from 11,000 BCE. In this cave artists capitalized on natural sculptural effects by painting the bodies of their animals over and around geological protuberances in the cave's walls and ceilings. To produce the herd of bison on the ceiling of the main cavern, they used rich red and brown ochers to paint the large areas of the animals' shoulders, backs, and flanks, then sharpened the contours and added the details of the legs, tails, heads, and horns in black and brown, mixing yellow and brown from ochers with iron to make the red tones and deriving black from manganese or charcoal.

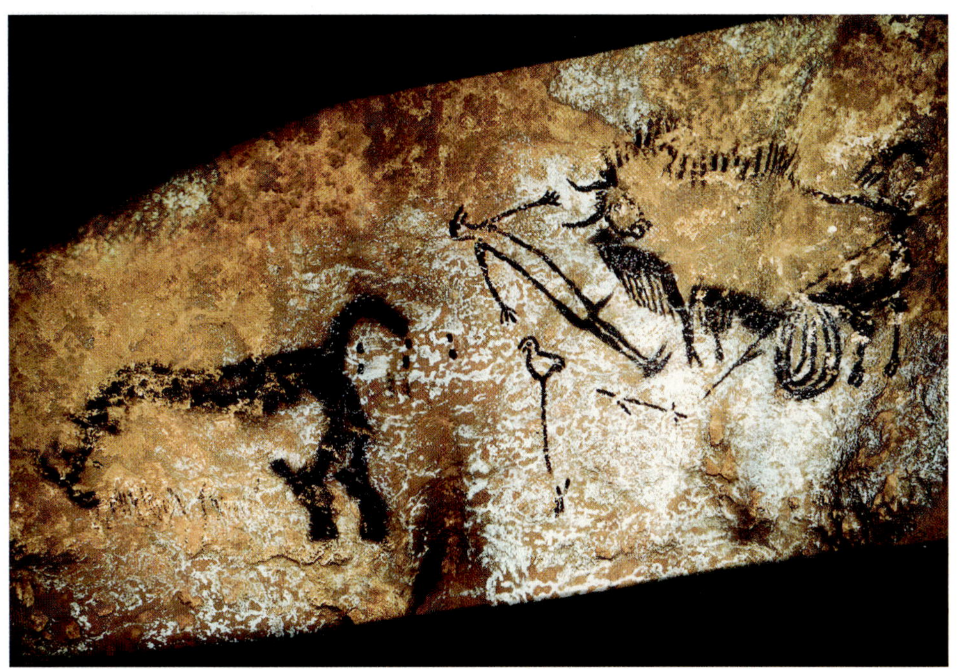

1–8 *Bird-Headed Man with Bison*, Lascaux Caves. c. 15,000 BCE. Paint on limestone, length approx. 9' (2.75 m)

A figure who could be a hunter, highly stylized but recognizably male and wearing a bird's-head mask, appears to be lying on the ground. A great bison looms above him. Below him lie a staff, or baton, and a spear thrower—a device that allowed hunters to throw farther and with greater force—the outer end of which has been carved in the shape of a bird. The long diagonal line slanting across the bison's hindquarters is a spear. The bison has been disemboweled.

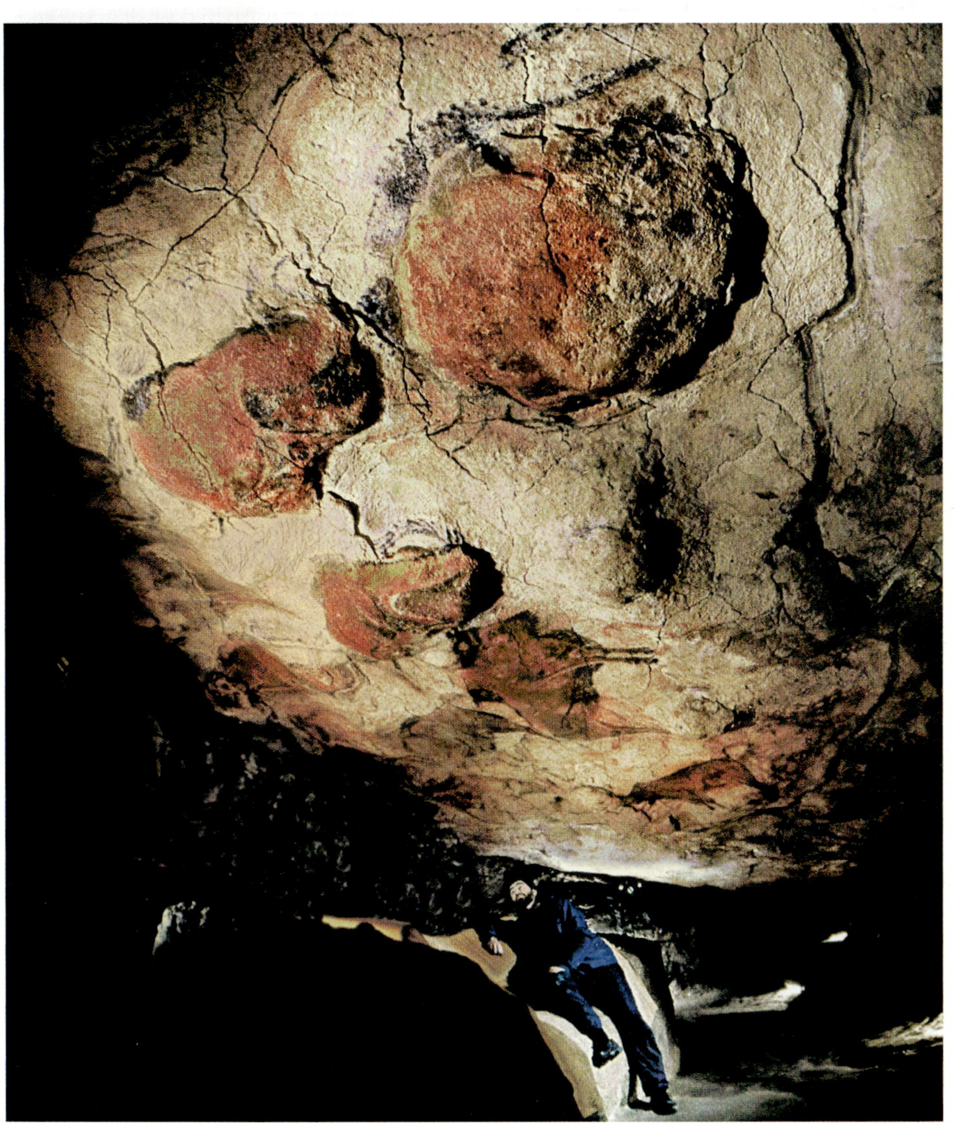

1–9 *Bison*, on the ceiling of a cave at Altamira, Spain. Sometime between 35,000 and 11,000 BCE. Paint on limestone, length approx. 8' 3" (2.5 m)

No one knew of the existence of prehistoric cave painting until one day in 1879, when a young girl exploring with her father on the family estate in Altamira crawled through a small opening in the ground and found herself in a cave chamber whose ceiling was covered with painted animals. Her father searched the rest of the cave, and then told authorities about the remarkable find. Few people believed that these amazing works could have been done by "primitive" people, and the scientific community declared the paintings a hoax. They were accepted as authentic only in 1902, after many other cave paintings, drawings, and engravings had been discovered at other spots in northern Spain and in France.

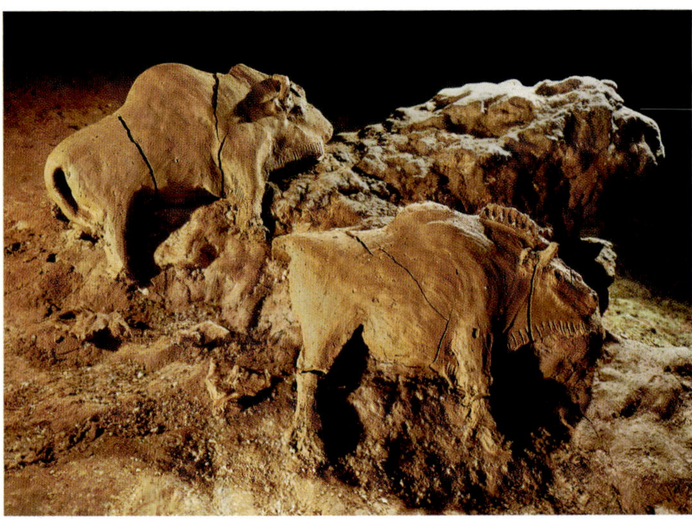

1–10 ***Bison***, Le Tuc d'Audoubert, France. c. 13,000 BCE. Unbaked clay, length 25" (63.5 cm) and 24" (60.9 cm)

In addition to paintings, caves sometimes had relief sculpture created by **modeling**, or shaping, the damp clay of the cave's floor. An excellent example from about 13,000 BCE is preserved at Le Tuc d'Audoubert, south of the Dordogne region of France. Here the sculptor created two bison leaning against a ridge of rock (fig. **1–10**). Although these beasts are modeled in very high relief (they extend well forward from the background), they display the same conventions employed in paintings, with emphasis on the broad masses of the meat-bearing flanks and shoulders. To make the animals even more lifelike, their creator engraved short parallel lines below their necks to represent their shaggy coats. Numerous small footprints found in the clay floor of this cave suggest that important group rites took place here.

Art in the Neolithic Period

Fundamental social and cultural changes mark the beginning of the Neolithic period. These include the development of organized agriculture, the maintenance of herds of domesticated animals (animal husbandry), and the foundation of year-round settlements. The Neolithic period ended with the introduction of metalworking—the Bronze Age—around 3400 BCE in the Near East and about 2300 BCE in Europe.

Much of what we know of Neolithic daily life comes from material remains of art and architecture. At Cogul, in the province of Lleida in Catalunya, the broad surfaces of a rock shelter were decorated between 4000 and 2000 BCE with elaborate narrative scenes involving dozens of small figures—men, women, children, animals, even insects—seemingly going about daily activities (fig. **1–11**). In the detail shown here, a number of women gracefully stroll or stand about; some in pairs hold hands. The women's small waists are emphasized by skirts with scalloped hemlines revealing large calves and sturdy ankles, and all the women appear to have shoulder-length hair. The women stand near several large animals, some of which are shown leaping forward with legs fully extended. This

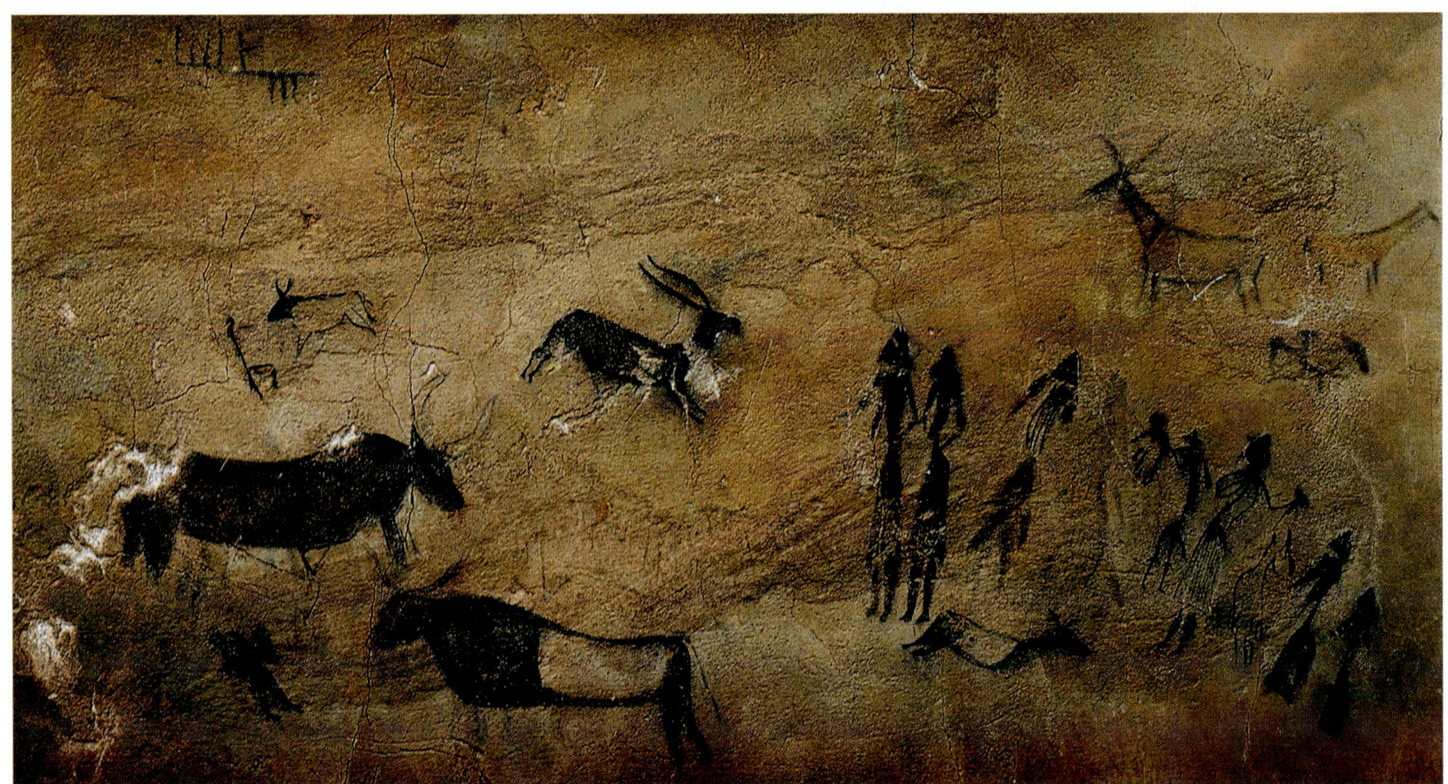

1–11 ***People and Animals***, detail of a rock-shelter painting in Cogul, Lleida, Spain. c. 4000–2000 BCE. Museu Arqueològic, Barcelona, Spain

CLOSER LOOK

For all we know, the artist who created these figures almost 5,500 years ago had nothing particular in mind—people had been modeling clay figures in southeastern Europe for a long time. Could a woman who was making cooking and storage pots out of clay have amused herself by fashioning images of people she saw around her? But because these figures were found in a grave in Cernavoda, Romania, they suggest to us an otherworldly message.

The woman, spread-hipped and big-bellied, appears to sit directly on the ground. She exudes stability, and her ample hips and thighs seem to stress her fecundity. But in a lively, even coquettish, gesture, she joins her hands on one raised knee, curls up her toes, and tilts her head upward. Though earthbound, is she communing with a celestial spirit world? Or does her upwardly tilted head suggest that she is watching the smoke rising from the hearth, or worrying about holes in the roof, or admiring hanging containers of laboriously gathered drying berries, or even gazing adoringly at her partner. The man is rather slim, but his legs and shoulders are powerful. He rests his head on his hands in a brooding, pensive posture, evoking thoughtfulness in a pose that would be made famous millennia later by French sculptor Auguste Rodin.

We can interpret the Cernavoda woman and man in many ways, but we cannot know what they meant to their makers or owners. Depending on how they are displayed, we spin out different stories about them. When set facing each other, side by side as they are in these photographs, we tend to see them as a couple—a woman and man in a relationship. In fact, we do not know whether the artist conceived of them in this way, or even made them at the same time. For all their visual eloquence, their secrets remain hidden from us.

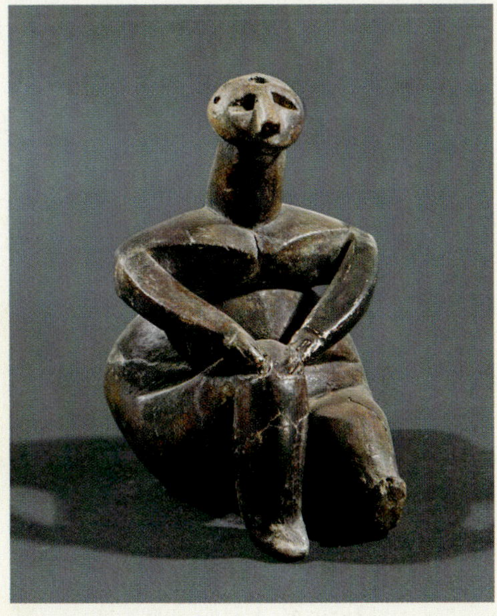

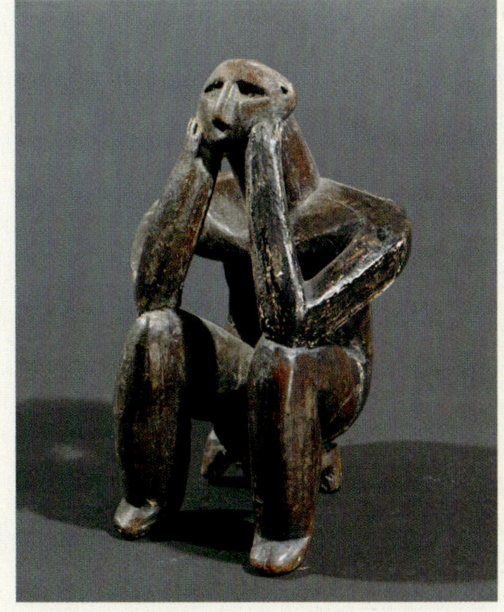

1–12 *Woman and Man*, from Cernavoda, Romania. c. 3500 BCE. Ceramic, height 4½" (11.5 cm). National Historical Museum, Bucharest

pose, called a **flying gallop**, has been used to indicate speed in a running animal from prehistory to the present. These rock shelters contain so much information that it is tempting to imagine them as records of daily life, but they probably served a greater social function. Perhaps they had an educational or religious use, for in some places the images were repainted many times.

In addition to painting on stone, Neolithic artists commonly used clay. Their **ceramics**, or wares made of baked clay—whether vessels or figures of people and animals—display a high degree of technical skill and aesthetic imagination. To produce ceramic works, artists had to add certain substances to the clay—bone ash was a common additive—and then subject the objects formed of that mixture to high heat for a period of time, thus hardening them and creating an entirely new material. Among the ceramic figures discovered at a pottery-production center in the Danube River valley at Cernavoda, Romania, are a seated man and woman (fig. **1–12**). The artist who made them shaped their bodies out of simple cylinders of clay but managed to pose them in ways that make them seem true to life.

1–13 Plan, village of Skara Brae, Orkney Islands, Scotland. c. 3100 BCE. (Numbers refer to individual houses.)

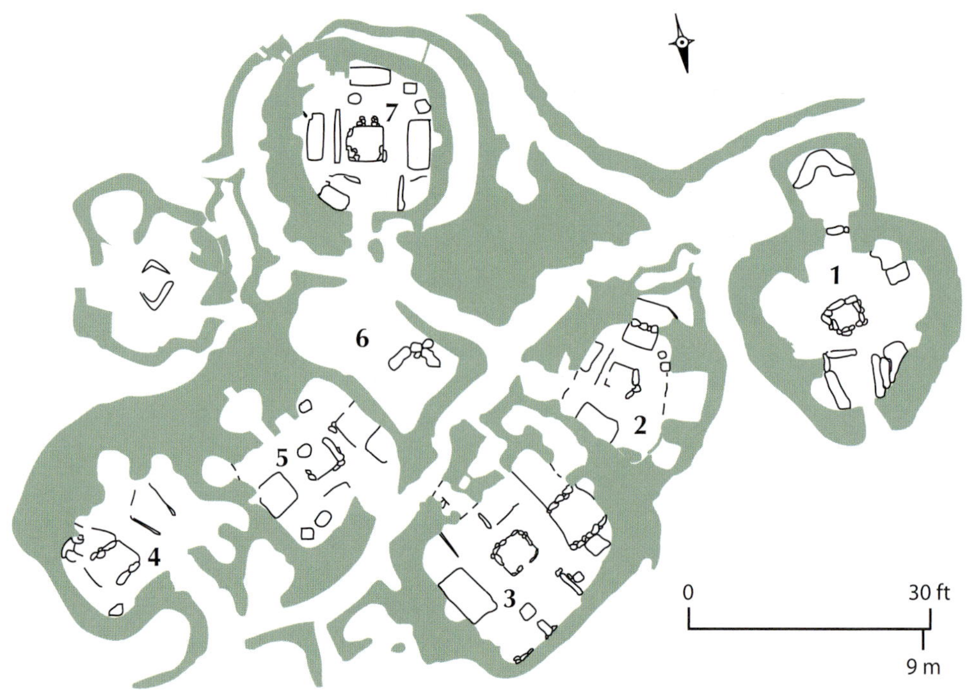

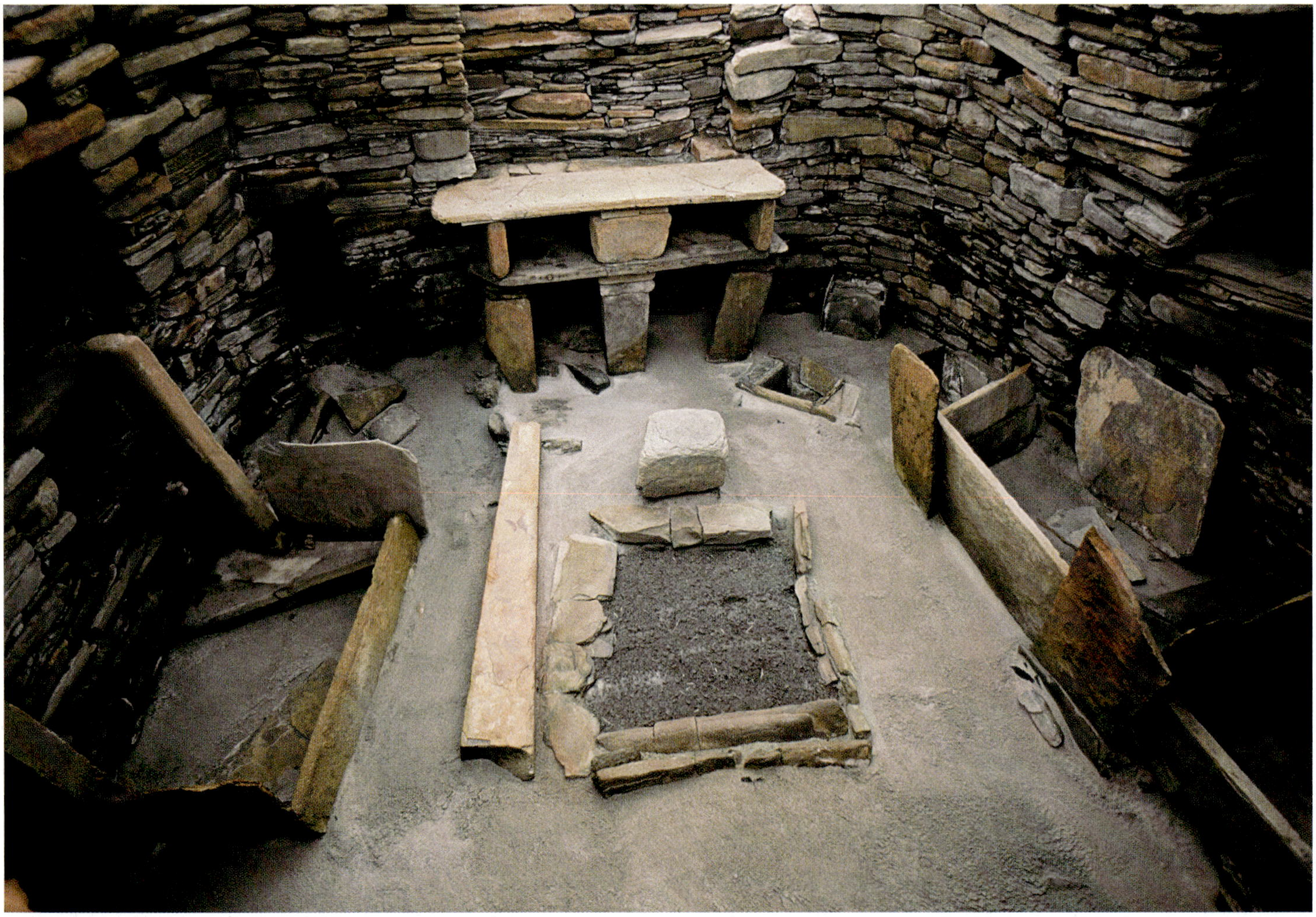

1–14 House interior, Skara Brae (house 7 in fig. 1–13)

ELEMENTS OF Architecture

Post-and-Lintel and Corbel Construction

Of all the methods for spanning space, post-and-lintel construction is the simplest. At its most basic, two uprights (posts) support a horizontal element (lintel). There are countless variations, from the wood structures, dolmens, and other underground burial chambers of prehistory, to Egyptian and Greek stone construction, to medieval timber-frame buildings, and even to present-day cast-iron and steel construction. Its limitation as a space spanner is the degree of tensile strength of the lintel material: the more tensile, the greater the possible span. Another early method for creating openings in walls and covering space is corbeling, in which rows or layers of stone are laid with the end of each row projecting beyond the row beneath, progressing until opposing layers almost meet and can then be capped with a stone (capstone) that rests across the tops of both layers.

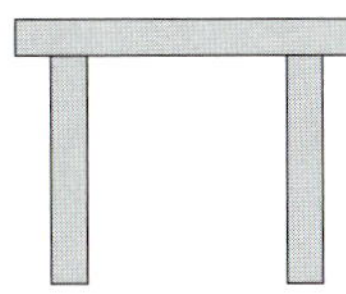

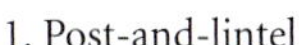

1. Post-and-lintel

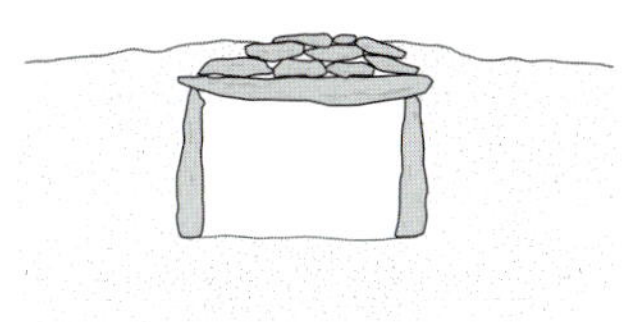

2. Cross-section of post-and-lintel underground burial chamber

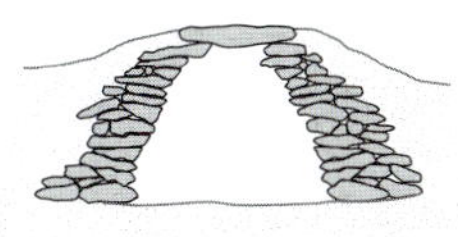

3. Cross-section of corbeled underground burial chamber

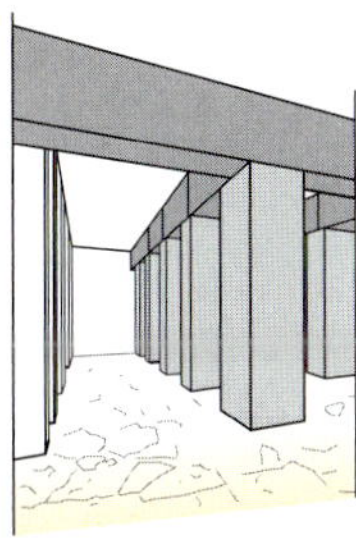

4. Granite post-and-lintel construction, Valley Temple of Khafre, Giza, Egypt, c. 2500 BCE

Architecture

As humans adopted a settled, agricultural way of life, they began to build large structures to serve as dwellings, storage spaces, and animal shelters. In Europe, timber became abundant after the retreat of the glaciers, and Neolithic people, like their Paleolithic predecessors, used wood and other plant materials that have left but scant traces, such as post holes, in the earth. They clustered their dwellings in villages, and they built large tombs and ritual centers outside their settlements. Luckily for us, sometimes they used stone.

A Neolithic settlement (occupied 3100–2600 BCE) is preserved in the sea sands at Skara Brae, on the Orkney Islands off the northern coast of Scotland (fig. **1–13**). The excavated village consists of a compact cluster of stone dwellings linked together by covered passageways. The largest house measures 20 by 21 feet, the smallest 13 by 14 feet. Layers of flat stones without mortar form walls, with each layer, or **course**, projecting slightly inward over the one below in a type of construction called **corbeling**. At Skara Brae the walls stopped short of meeting, and the remaining open space was covered with a roof of hides or turf. The interiors, such as the one shown (fig. **1–14**), were equipped with space-saving built-in furniture. Rectangular stone beds, some of them engraved with simple markings, flank the walls on either side of the large rectangular hearth. These box-like beds would probably have been filled with heather "mattresses" and covered with warm furs. On the back wall is a sizable storage niche and a two-shelf cabinet erected using post-and-lintel construction.

Megalithic Architecture

Massive tombs and monuments built from huge stones first appeared in the Neolithic period, when human societies became more stratified and complex. These structures are known as megalithic architecture, from the Greek roots for "large" (*megas*) and "stone" (*lithos*). Their construction required not only laborers to transport the giant boulders, but also skilled workers—predecessors of architects and engineers—to create designs and devise methods to shape and align the stones. In addition to a coordinated workforce to construct them, megalithic structures also required powerful political and religious leaders to dictate society's need for them.

Many megalithic tombs are preserved in Europe, where they were used for both single and multiple burials. In the simplest type, the **dolmen**, a tomb chamber was formed of huge upright stones supporting one or more table-like rocks, or **capstones**, in a post-and-lintel system. The structure was then mounded over with smaller rocks and dirt to form a **cairn** or artificial hill.

Many more elaborate burial sites called **passage graves**, with one or more corridors leading into a large burial chamber, also

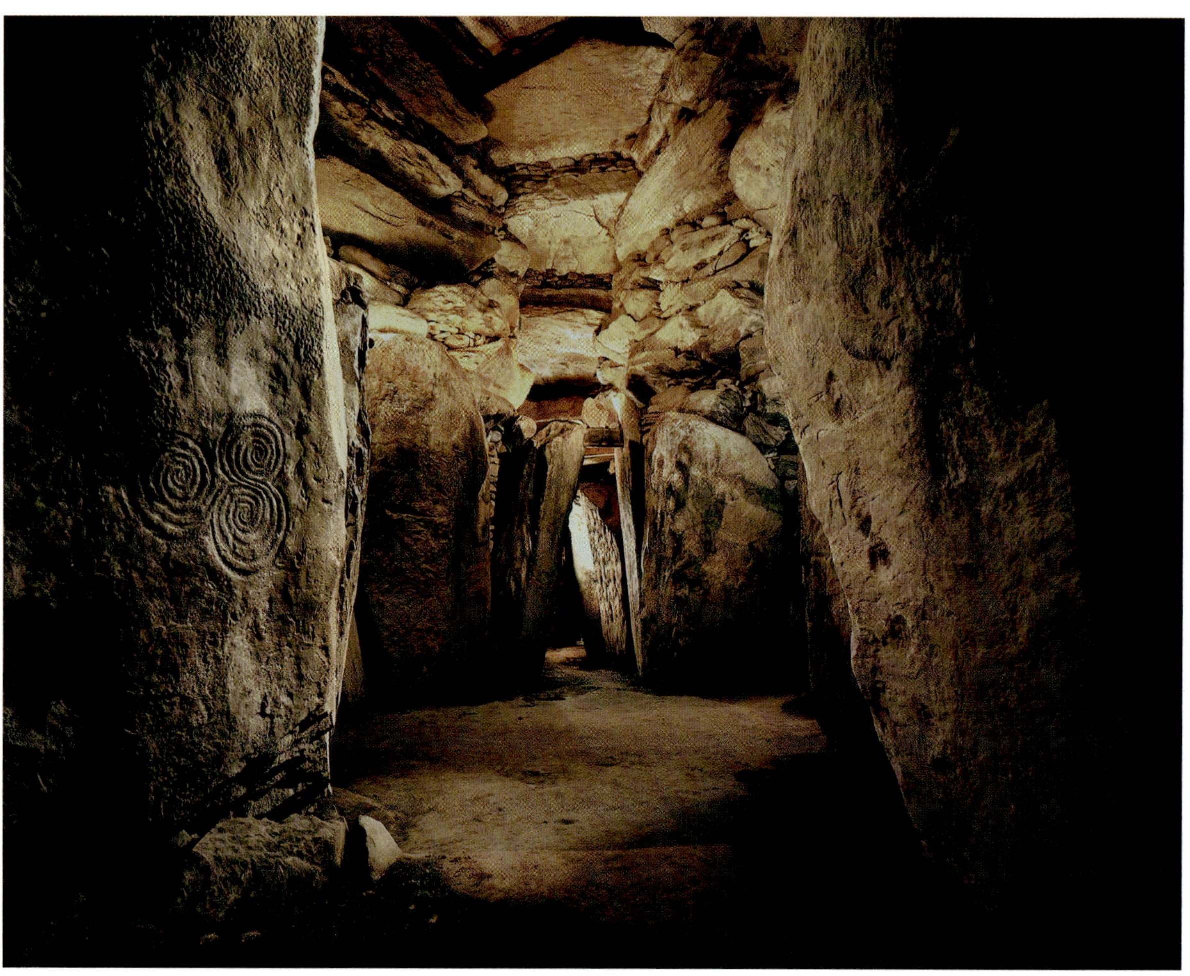

1–15 Tomb interior with engraved stones, Newgrange, Ireland. c. 3000–2500 BCE

survive. At Newgrange in Ireland a huge passage grave was constructed about 3000–2500 BCE (fig. **1–15**). Rings, spirals, diamond shapes, and other linear designs were engraved on the stones at its entrance, around the base of the cairn, and along its entrance passageway. These patterns may have been marked out using strings or compasses, and then carved by pecking at the rock surface with tools made of antlers and hard stones. A cairn that measured about 280 feet in diameter and 44 feet tall concealed a chamber with alcoves and a corbel vault rising to a height of 19 feet. The ritual purpose of Newgrange is still a mystery; however, some powerful solar symbolism must have played a part. The builders oriented the passage to the rising sun in midsummer, at which time light enters through a semiconcealed opening down the length of the passage to the tomb chamber and falls on a shallow, scooped-out, platter-like stone.

Besides tombs, Neolithic and post-Neolithic cultures built megalithic monuments and sculptures for ritual purposes that are still not fully understood by today's scholars. The best-known of these megalithic constructions, and another solar structure, is Stonehenge in southern England (figs. **1–16** and **1–17**). A **henge** is a circle of stones or posts, often surrounded by a ditch with built-up embankments. While Stonehenge is not the largest such circle from the Neolithic period, it is the most complex, reworked over at least four major building phases.

The main elements of Stonehenge are illustrated in the accompanying aerial photograph and diagram. The earliest circle, created about 3000 BCE, was a ditch with a 6-foot earthwork embankment, about 330 feet in diameter, and a surrounding circle of white chalk marks in the earth. Later generations transformed this circle into a more complex structure over the course of a millennium. They built a ring of gray sarsen (sandstone) uprights about 13 feet 6 inches tall and topped by a continuous lintel. Inside the sarsen circle they placed a ring of smaller bluestones, made of a bluish dolerite that they transported from a Welsh quarry 250 miles away that was also a prehistoric healing site. These circles surround a horseshoe-shaped arrangement of five trilithons, or pairs of stones topped by lintels (three stones in total), and a second horseshoe of bluestones. The largest of the trilithons stood 24 feet high. At the very center of this complex lies the so-called "altar stone." The actual role of this stone is unknown; designating it as an altar, which has religious connotations, is a modern presumption (see "The Power of Naming," page 26). The opening of the horseshoe focuses on what is known today as the Heel Stone, a single, 35-ton, 16-feet high sarsen megalith, brought from quarries 23 miles away. It stands outside the henge to the northeast and connects to the opening by a causeway.

One aspect of this megalithic monument more than any other has captured the public's imagination. Anyone standing at the exact

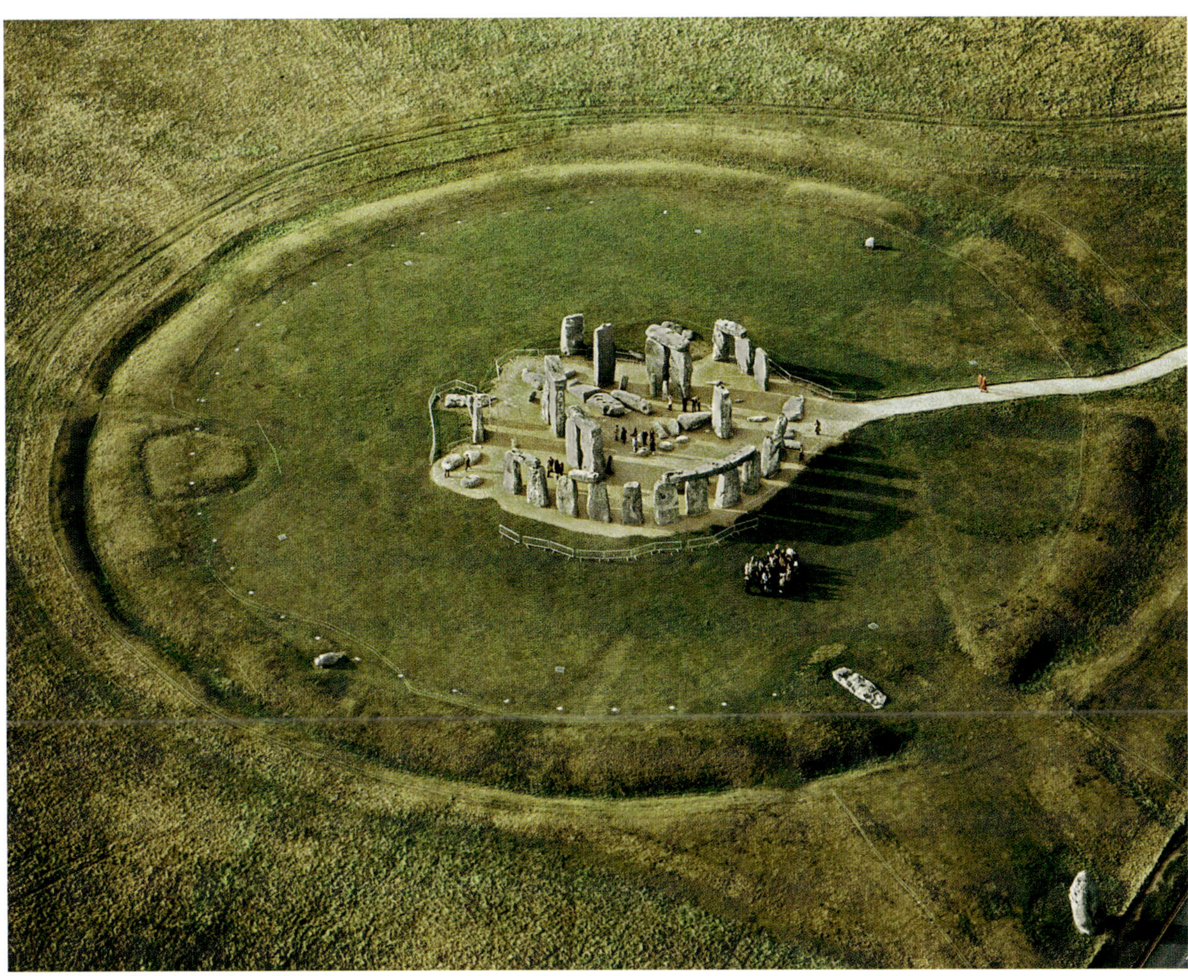

1–16 Stonehenge, Salisbury Plain, Wiltshire, England. c. 3000–1500 BCE

center of Stonehenge on the morning of the summer solstice 4,000 years ago would have seen the sun rise directly over the Heel Stone; at the winter solstice the monument seems to have been aligned with sunset rather than dawn. The midsummer sunrise still inspires hundreds of people to gather annually at Stonehenge. Given the relationship between the monument's orientation and the sun, some scholars think Stonehenge may have been a kind of observatory that helped astronomers to track cosmic events.

Excavations since 2002, however, have pointed to another possible significance for this and another nearby Neolithic site. While Stonehenge and its environs have emerged as the most extensive known Neolithic cemetery in England, with as many as 240 discovered graves, concurrent excavations at the nearby, and much larger, Woodhenge at Durrington Walls revealed remains of a thriving community of about 300 wooden houses, the largest-known Neolithic settlement in Britain. Archaeologists have suggested that these two contemporary sites could have been linked, one where people lived and the other where the most important among them were buried, both connected to the nearby Avon river by broad processional avenues.

But even more recently, in 2008, excavations within the circle at Stonehenge itself demonstrated that the first ring of bluestones was added to the site between 2400 and 2200 BCE, much later than archaeologists had previously believed. The theory emerging from this discovery holds that Stonehenge was at this time a healing center—a sort of prehistoric Lourdes. People from as far away as the Alps in mainland Europe made pilgrimages here, seeking relief from the effects of disease and injury by using water that had taken on therapeutic powers from the same bluestones that had been imported as construction material from a healing spring in Wales.

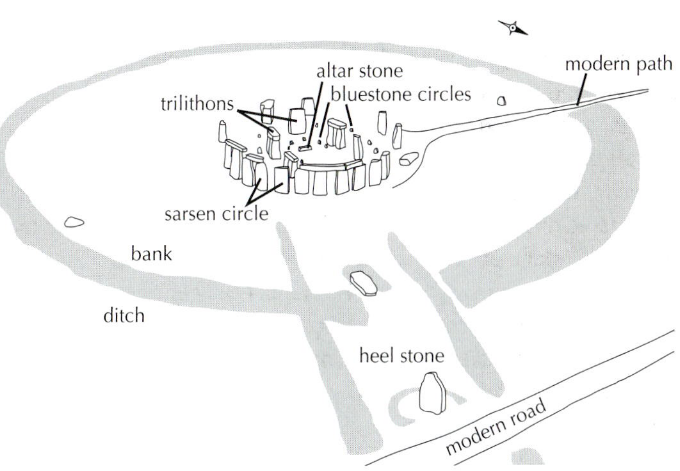

1–17 Diagram of Stonehenge showing elements discussed in text

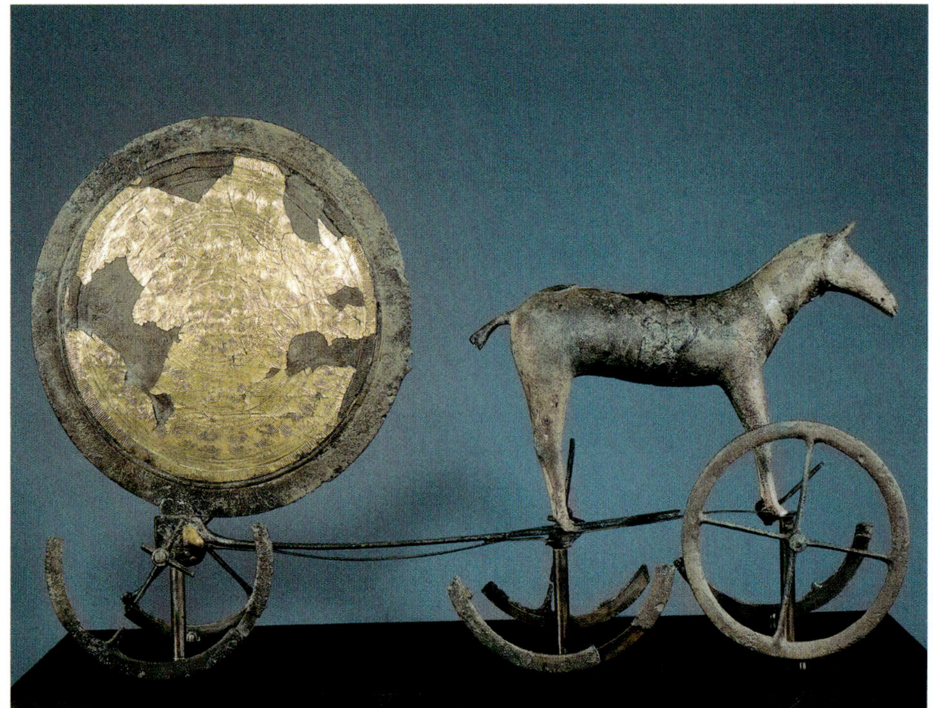

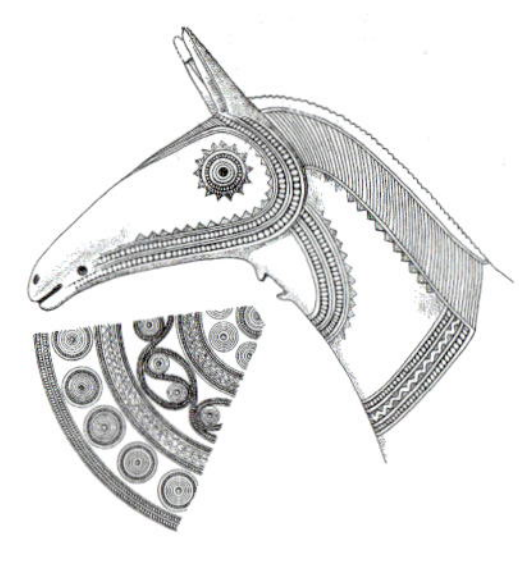

1–18 ***Horse and Sun-Chariot*** from Trundholm, Zealand, Denmark. c. 1800–1600 BCE. Bronze and gold, length 23¼" (59.2 cm). National Museum, Copenhagen. (Insert is a drawing of incised designs.)

Bronze and Iron Ages in Europe

Neolithic culture persisted in northern Europe until about 2300–2000 BCE. Metals had made their appearance about 2300 BCE, although gold and copper had been used in southern Europe and the Near East much earlier. The period that follows the introduction of metalworking is commonly called the Bronze Age.

A remarkable metal sculpture of between 1800 and 1600 BCE found in Denmark depicts a horse pulling a wheeled cart laden with a large, upright disk, thought to represent the sun (fig. **1–18**). As we saw at Stonehenge, a widespread sun cult seems to have existed as early as circa 3000 BCE in the north. Could this horse, with its gleaming load, have been rolled from place to place in a ritual reenactment of the sun's passage across the sky? The valuable materials from which the sculpture was made attest to its importance. The horse, cart, and disk were cast in bronze and delicately engraved with an abstract design of concentric rings, zigzags, circles, spirals, and loops. A thin sheet of beaten gold was then applied to the bronze disk and pressed into the **incised** patterns. The continuous and curvilinear patterns suggest the movement of the sun itself.

By 1000 BCE, iron technology had spread across Europe, although bronze remained the preferred material for luxury goods. Cheaper and more readily available than other metals, iron was most commonly used for practical items. The blacksmiths who forged the warriors' swords and the farmers' plowshares held a privileged position among artisans, for they practiced a craft that seemed akin to magic as they transformed iron by heat and hammer work into tools. A hierarchy of metals emerged based on each material's resistance to corrosion: Gold, the most permanent and precious metal, ranked first, followed by silver, bronze, and finally practical but rust-prone iron.

Looking Back

Long before men and women communicated with written words, they made images and objects. Sculpture began as a skillful flaking and chipping of flint tools and later developed into the decoration of bone and horn implements with simple patterns of engraved lines. As early as 30,000 BCE, small figures of people and animals made of bone, ivory, stone, and clay appeared in Europe, and at about the same time images of animals, geometric figures, and human hands were applied to the walls of caves. Drawn, painted, and engraved—at times incorporating the natural formations and irregularities of the cave walls themselves—these images are remarkable for their realism and for their rich colors. But it is unlikely that these oldest-known artists were simply embellishing cave walls in the sense that we use the words "decorating" and "ornament." Perhaps they believed that what they were doing was essential to their very existence and that of their fellow humans.

Our prehistoric ancestors also found ingenious and imaginative ways of providing themselves with shelters. As they adopted a settled, agricultural way of life, they began to build large structures clustered in villages and extensive tombs and ritual centers outside their settlements. As we stand awestruck in front of Stonehenge, we wonder how human beings could have imagined, planned, and then achieved, such a marvelous and complicated creation, moving special stones from far-away sacred places to create and expand this exceptional site over at least a thousand years. Was it a solar observatory, a funerary district, or a healing shrine? Perhaps it was all three, but it certainly holds additional secrets for later archaeologists to discover and later scholars to interpret. Writing the history of art is a continuing adventure that is never complete.

IN PERSPECTIVE

42000 BCE

◀ **Upper Paleolithic,** 42,000–8000 BCE

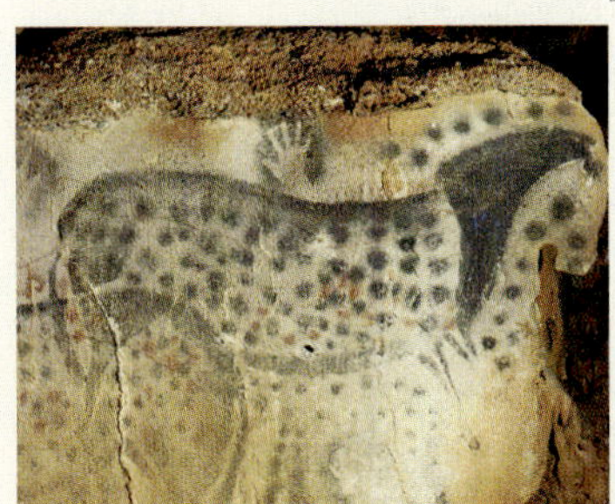

SPOTTED HORSE AND HUMAN HAND, c. 25,000–24,000 BCE

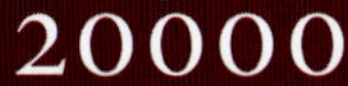
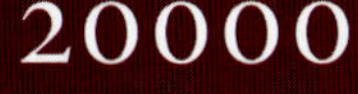
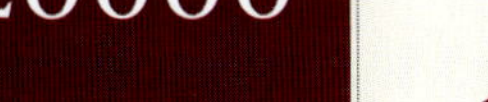

20000

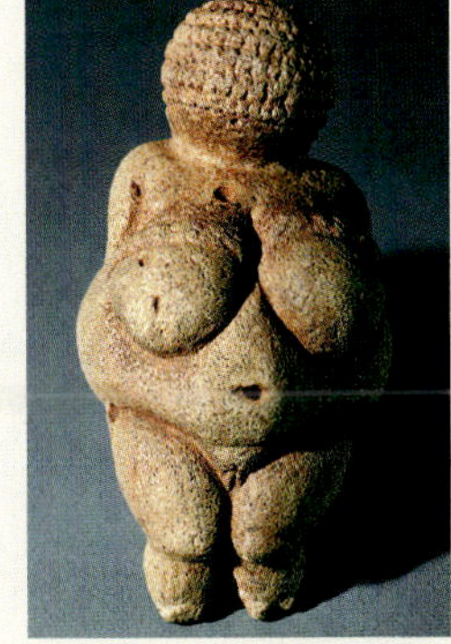

WOMAN FROM WILLENDORF, c. 24,000 BCE

◀ **Last Ice Age,** 18,000–15,000 BCE

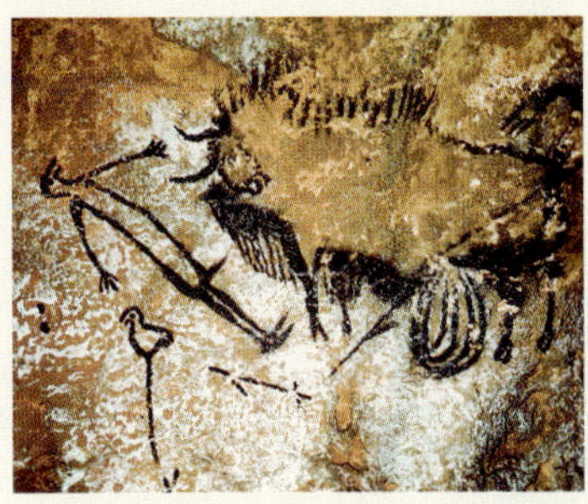

BIRD-HEADED MAN WITH BISON, c. 15,000 BCE

◀ **Paleolithic-Neolithic Overlap,** 9000–4000 BCE

◀ **Neolithic,** 6500–1200 BCE

5000

◀ **Farming in Europe,** c. 5000 BCE

◀ **Metallurgy,** c. 5000 BCE

◀ **Domestication of Horses,** c. 4000 BCE

◀ **Plow in Use,** c. 4000 BCE

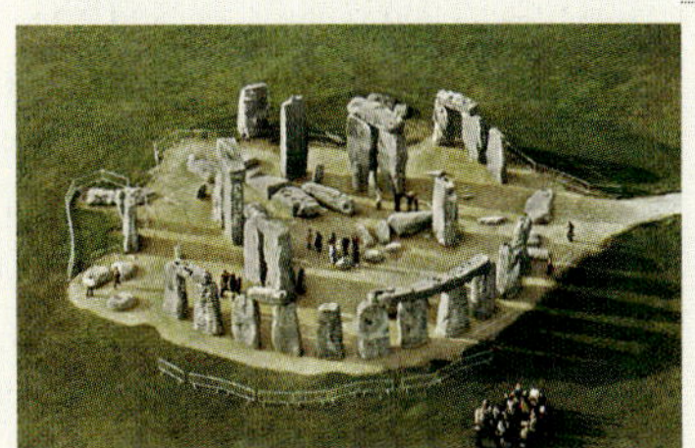

STONEHENGE, c. 3000–1500 BCE

◀ **Potter's Wheel in Use,** c. 3250 BCE

◀ **Invention of Writing,** c. 3100 BCE

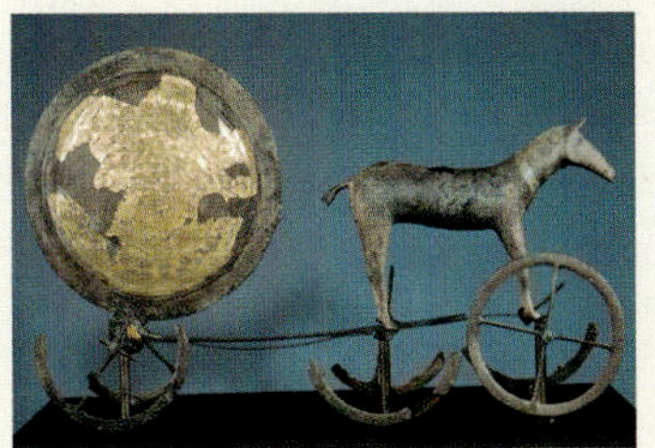

HORSE AND SUN-CHARIOT, c. 1800–1600 BCE

◀ **Bronze Age in Europe,** c. 2300–1000 BCE

1000 BCE

◀ **Iron Age in Europe,** c. 1000–400 BCE

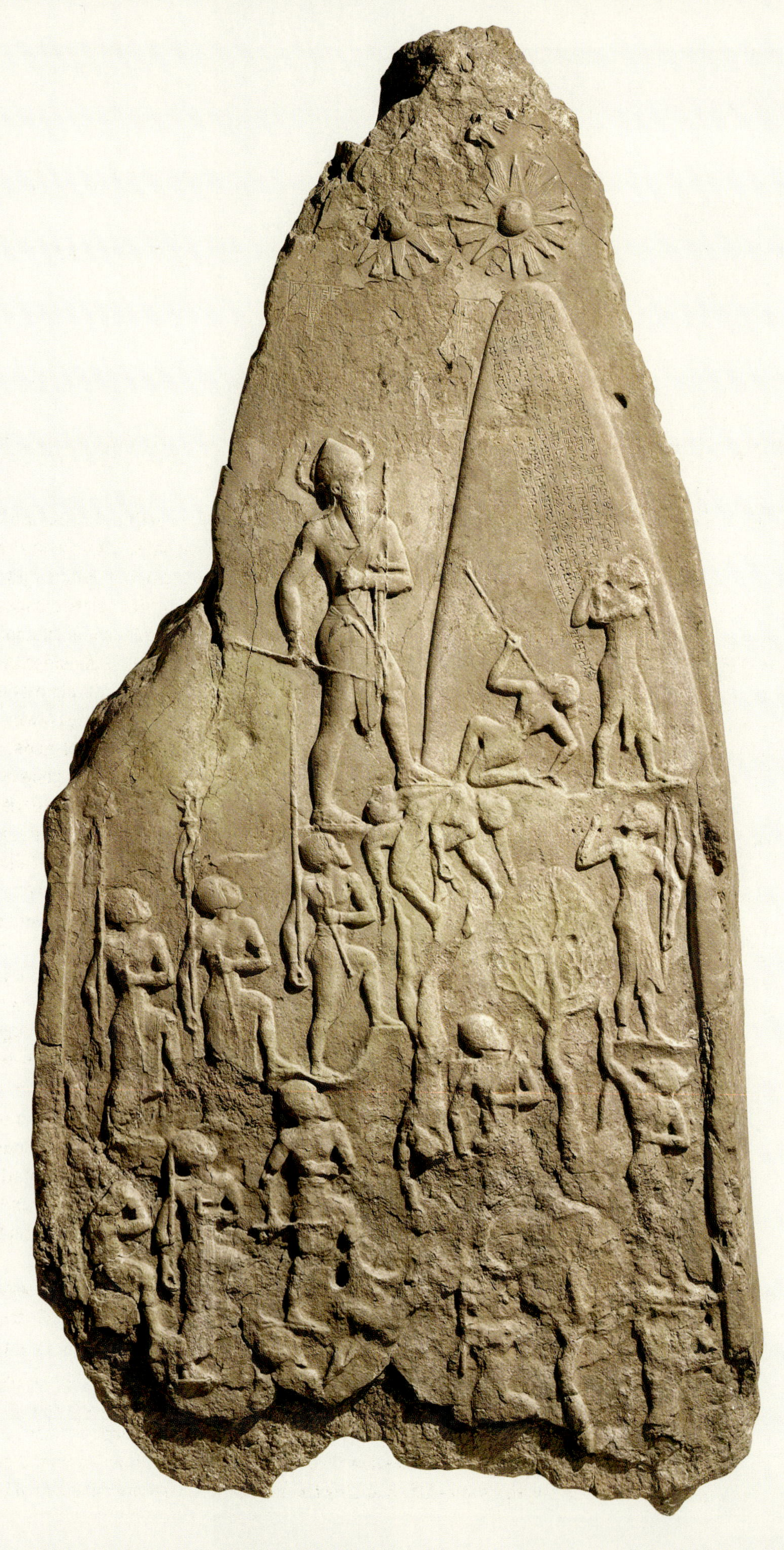

2
Art of the Ancient Near East

LOOKING FORWARD

Akkadian ruler Naram-Sin (ruled 2254–2218 BCE) is pictured proudly in this sculpted stele (fig. 2–1). His preeminence is signaled directly by size: he is by far the largest person in this scene of military triumph, conforming to an artistic practice we call **hieratic scale**, where relative size indicates relative importance. He is also elevated well above the other figures, boldly silhouetted against blank ground, striding toward a stylized peak that recalls his own shape, thus increasing the sense of his own grandeur by association. He clasps within his arms a veritable arsenal of weaponry—spear, battleaxe, bow and arrow—and the grand helmet that crowns his head sprouts horns, an attribute formerly restricted to representations of gods, thereby claiming divinity for this earthly ruler. But art historian Irene Winter has gone even further, pointing to the sexually alluring pose and presentation of Naram-Sin, to the conspicuous display of a well-formed male body. In ancient Mesopotamian culture, male potency and vigor were directly related to political power and dominance, and like the horns of his helmet, well-formed bodies were most frequently associated with gods. Thus every aspect of the representation of this ruler speaks to his religious and political authority as leader of the state.

But this is more than an emblem of Naram-Sin's divine right to rule. The stele also tells the story of one of his important military victories. The ruler stands above—and at the same time participates in—a crowded scene enacted by smaller figures. Those to the left, dressed and posed in a fashion similar to their ruler, represent the army, marching in diagonal bands up the hillside into battle. The artist has included identifiable native trees along the mountain pathway to heighten the sense that this portrays an actual event rather than a generic battle scene. Before Naram-Sin, both along the right side of the stele and smashed under his forward-striding leg, are representations of the enemy, in this case the Lullubi people from eastern Mesopotamia (in modern Iran). One diminutive adversary has taken a fatal spear to the neck, while companions behind and below him beg for mercy.

In public works such as this, the artists of Mesopotamia developed a sophisticated symbolic visual language—a kind of conceptual art—that both celebrated and communicated the political stratification that gave order and security to their world. Perhaps this art, which combines symbols with stories, looks naïve or crude in relation to our own artistic standards, but we should avoid allowing such modern value judgments to block our appreciation of the artistic accomplishments of the ancient Near East—or, indeed, the art of any era or culture. For these ancient works of art maintain the power to communicate with us forcefully and directly, even across over four millennia of historical distance.

2–1 Stele of Naram-Sin, Sippar (found at Susa). c. 2254–2218 BCE. Limestone, height 6' 6" (1.98 m). Musée du Louvre, Paris, France

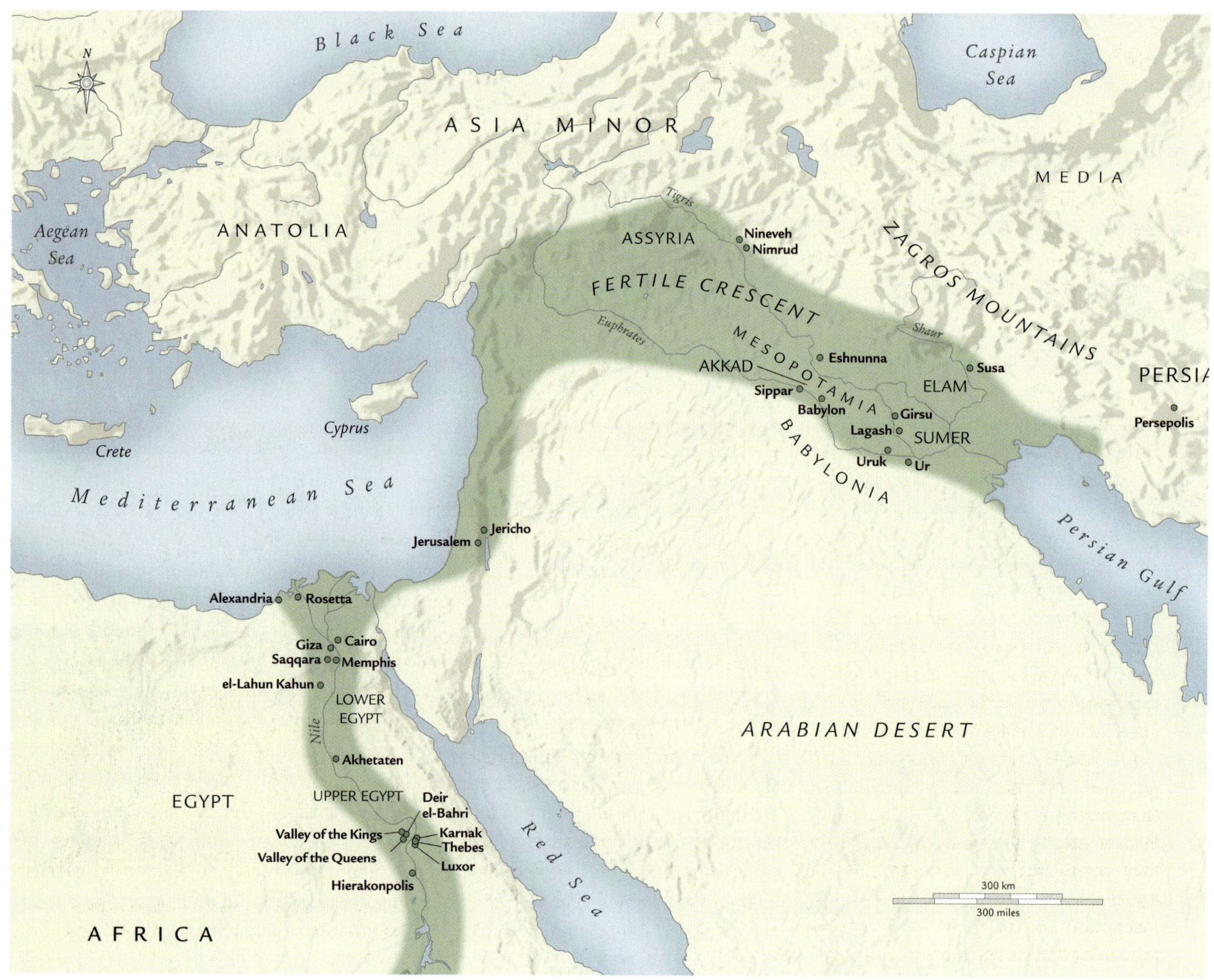

Map 2–1 The Ancient Near East. Green represents fertile agricultural areas

Well before farming communities appeared in Europe, people in Asia Minor and the ancient Near East domesticated grains in an area known today as the Fertile Crescent (see map **2–1**). A little later, in the sixth or fifth millennium BCE, agriculture developed in the alluvial plains between the Tigris and Euphrates rivers, which the Greeks called *Mesopotamia*, meaning the "land between the rivers," now in present-day Iraq. In a land prone to both drought and flood, there was a need for large-scale systems to control the water supply. Meeting this need may have contributed to the development of the first cities.

Between 4000 and 3000 BCE, a major cultural shift seems to have taken place. Agricultural villages evolved into cities simultaneously and independently in both northern and southern Mesopotamia. These prosperous cities joined with their surrounding territories to create what are known as city-states, each with its own gods and government. Social hierarchies—rulers and workers—emerged with the development of specialized skills beyond those needed for agricultural work. To grain mills and ovens were added brick and pottery kilns and textile and metal workshops. With extra goods and even modest affluence came increased trade and contact with other cultures.

Mesopotamia's wealth and agricultural resources, as well as its few natural defenses, made it vulnerable to political upheaval. Over the centuries, the balance of power shifted between north and south and between local powers and outside invaders. First the Sumerians controlled the south, but were eclipsed by the Akkadians, their neighbors to the north. When invaders from farther north conquered the Akkadians, the Sumerians regained power locally. The Babylonians next dominated the south. Later, the center of power shifted to the Assyrians in the north, then back again to the Babylonians (Neo-Babylonian period). Throughout this time, important cultural centers arose outside Mesopotamia, such as Elam on the plain between the Tigris River and the Zagros Mountains to the east, the Hittite kingdom in Anatolia (in present-day Turkey), and,

ART AS SPOILS OF WAR—PROTECTION OR THEFT?

Art has always been a casualty in times of social unrest. One of the most recent examples is the looting of the head of a woman from Warka (perhaps originally attached to a wooden statue of a goddess, c. 3000 BCE), when an angry mob in Baghdad broke into the unguarded Iraq National Museum in April 2003. The delicate marble sculpture was later returned, but not without significant damage. Also stolen was the Uruk vessel (see fig. 2–3), eventually returned to the museum shattered into 14 pieces.

Some of the most bitter resentment spawned by war—whether in Mesopotamia in the twelfth century BCE or in our own time—has involved the taking by the victors of art objects of great value to the conquered population. Museums around the world hold works either snatched by invading armies or acquired as a result of conquest. Two historically priceless objects unearthed in Elamite Susa, for example—the Akkadian Stele of Naram-Sin (see fig. 2–1) and the Babylonian Stele of Hammurabi (see fig. 2–10)—were not Elamite at all, but Mesopotamian. Both had been brought there as military trophies by an Elamite king, who added an inscription to the Stele of Naram-Sin explaining that he had merely "protected" it. The stele came originally from Sippar, an Akkadian city on the Euphrates River, in what is now Iraq. Raiders from Elam took it to Susa as booty in the twelfth century BCE.

The same rationale has been used in modern times. The Rosetta Stone, the key to deciphering Egyptian hieroglyphics, was discovered in Egypt by French troops in 1799, fell into British hands when they forced the French from Egypt, and ultimately ended up in the British Museum in London. In the early nineteenth century, the British Lord Elgin purchased and removed classical Greek reliefs from the Parthenon in Athens with the permission of the Ottoman authorities who governed Greece at the time (see page 122). His actions may indeed have protected the reliefs from neglect and damage in later wars, and they have remained installed, like the Rosetta Stone, in the British Museum, despite continuing protests from Greece.

The Ishtar Gate from Babylon (see fig. 2–16) is now reconstructed in Berlin, Germany. Many German collections include works that were similarly "protected" at the end of World War II and are surfacing now. In the United States, Native Americans are increasingly vocal in their demands that artifacts and human remains collected by anthropologists and archaeologists be returned to them.

"To the victor," it is said, "belong the spoils." It continues to be a matter of passionate debate whether this notion is appropriate in the case of revered cultural artifacts.

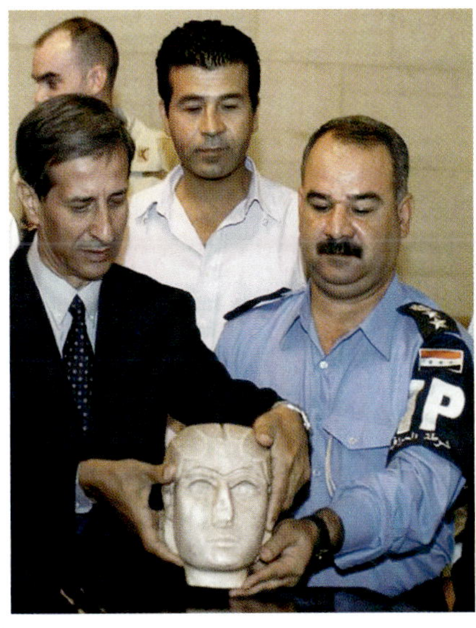

Photo of the face of a woman known as the *Warka Head*, displayed by Iraqi authorities on its recovery.

beginning in the sixth century BCE, the land of the Achaemenid Persians in present-day Iran. The Persians eventually established an empire that included the entire ancient Near East.

Sumer

The cities and city-states that developed along the rivers of southern Mesopotamia between about 3500 and 2340 BCE are known collectively as Sumer. The Sumerians have been credited with many "firsts." They may have invented the wagon wheel, the plow, and copper and bronze casting. But their greatest contribution to later civilizations may have been the invention in about 3100 BCE of a form of writing on clay tablets, apparently as an accounting system for goods traded at the city of Uruk. Simple pictures, or **pictographs**, were drawn in wet clay with a pointed tool, each representing a thing or a concept. Between 2900 and 2400 BCE, the pictographs evolved into phonograms—representations of syllable sounds—thus becoming a true writing system. **Scribes** (professionals who wrote and maintained records) developed a writing instrument called a **stylus**, with a triangular wedge at one end and point at the other. Mesopotamian writing is termed **cuneiform** (Latin for "wedge-shaped") after the shape of the marks made by this stylus.

In architecture, the Sumerians' most imposing buildings were **ziggurats**, stepped pyramidal structures with a temple or shrine on top. Towering over the flat plains, ziggurats proclaimed the wealth, prestige, and stability of a city's rulers and glorified its gods. They functioned as lofty meeting places between the earth and the heavens, where humans encountered their deities. The peoples of the ancient Near East were polytheistic; they worshiped many gods and goddesses, attributing to them power over human activities and the forces of nature. Each city had one special protective deity, and people believed that the fate of the city depended on the power of that deity. Religious specialists, eventually developing into a priest class,

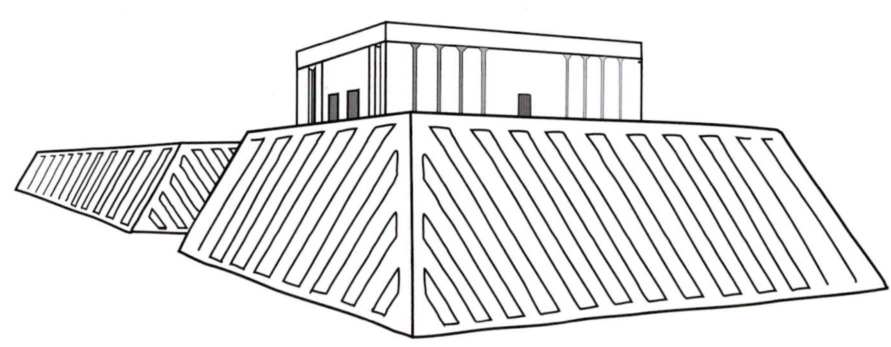

2–2 Reconstruction drawing of the Anu Ziggurat and White Temple, Uruk (modern Warka, Iraq). c. 3100 BCE

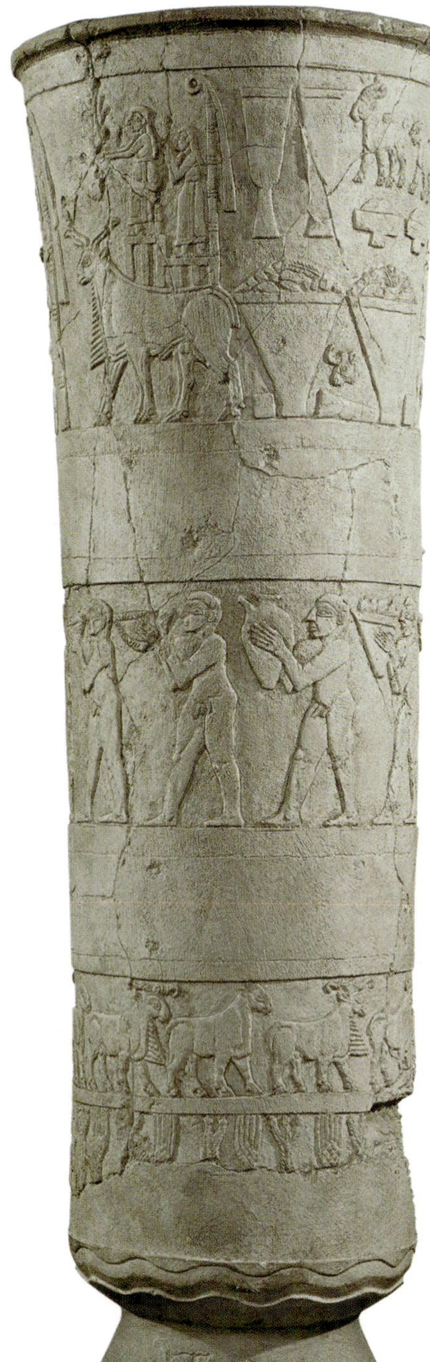

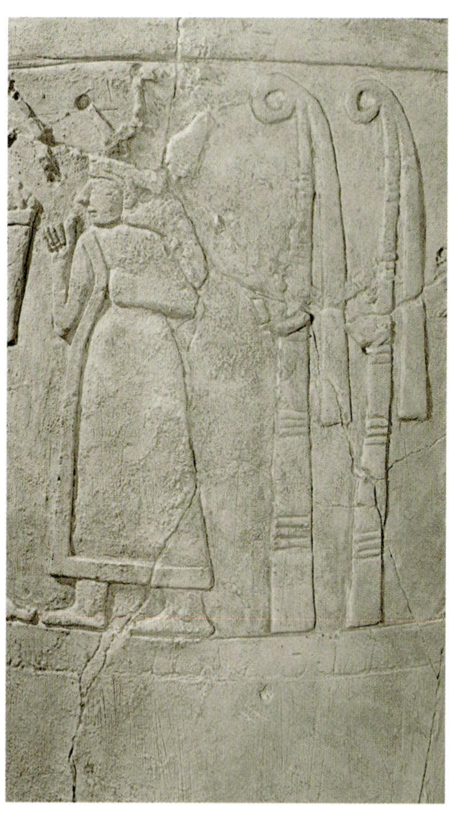

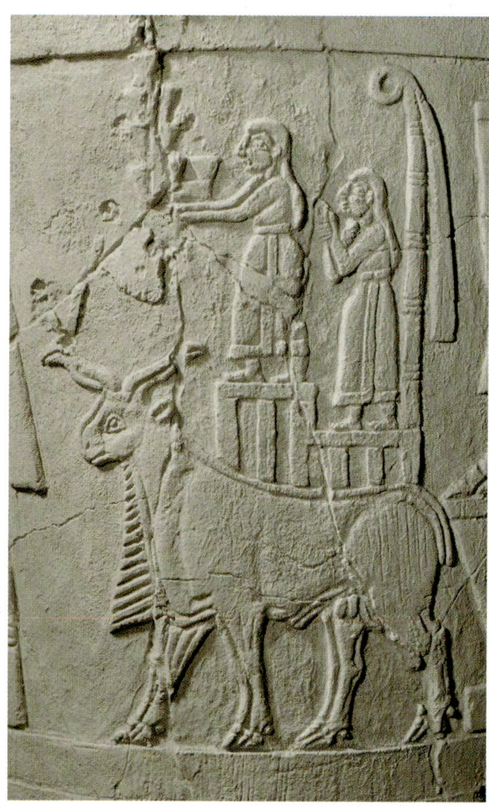

2–3 Carved vessel (with two details), from Uruk (modern Warka, Iraq). c. 3300–3000 BCE. Alabaster, height 36" (91 cm). Iraq Museum, Baghdad

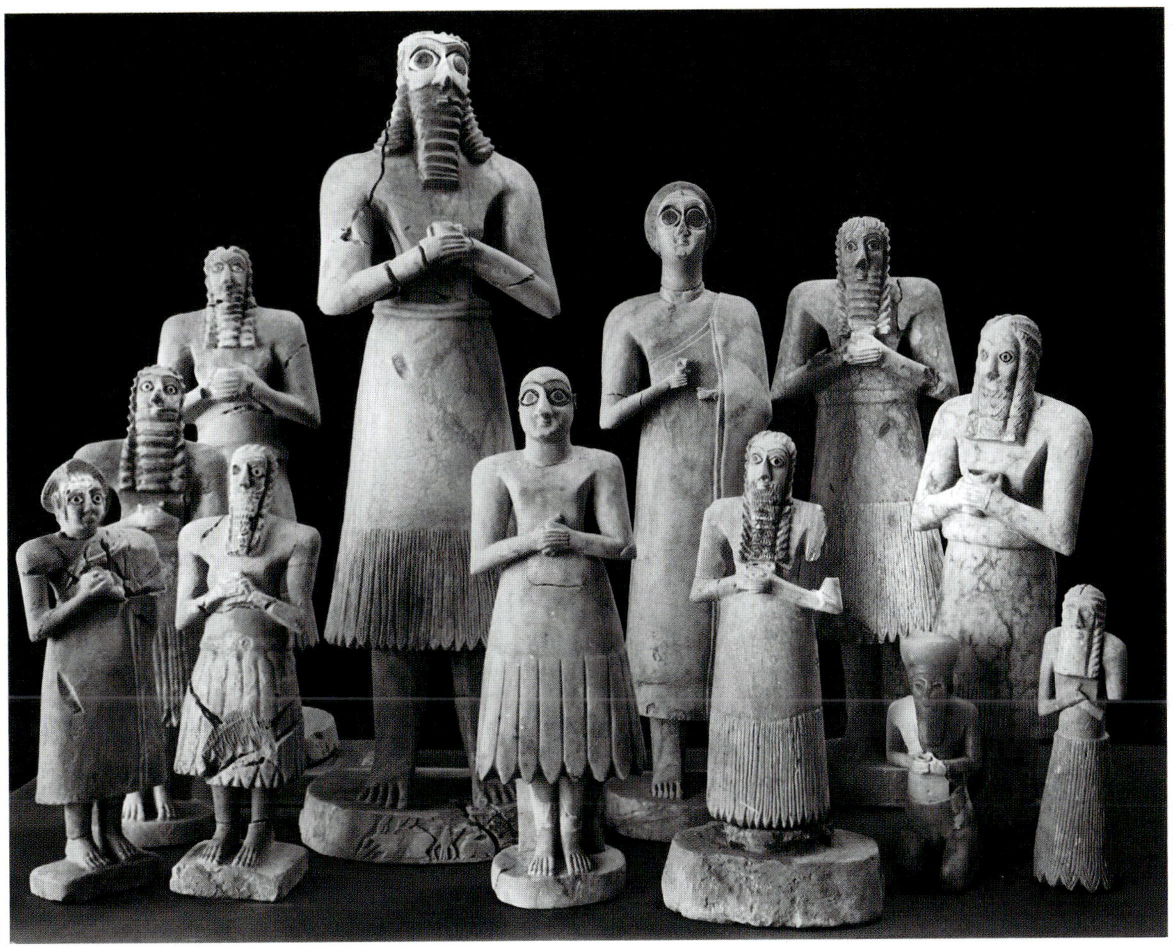

2–4 Votive statues from the Square Temple, Eshnunna (modern Tell Asmar, Iraq). c. 2900–2600 BCE. Limestone, alabaster, and gypsum, height of largest figure approx. 30" (76.3 cm). The Oriental Institute of the University of Chicago

controlled rituals and sacred sites, ensuring that the gods were honored properly. Temple complexes—clusters of religious, administrative, and service buildings—stood in each city's center.

Two large temple complexes at Uruk (modern Warka, Iraq) mark the first independent Sumerian city-state. A ziggurat dedicated to the sky god Anu, built up in stages over the centuries, ultimately rose to a height of about 40 feet. Around 3100 BCE, a whitewashed brick temple that modern archaeologists call the White Temple was erected on top (fig. **2–2**). The other complex was dedicated to Inanna, the goddess of fertility.

A tall vessel of carved **alabaster** (a fine, white stone), found near Inanna's temple, shows how Mesopotamian sculptors told stories in stone—here and for the next 2,500 years—with great clarity and economy (fig. **2–3**). They organized the visual narrative into three **registers**, or horizontal bands, and condensed the story into its essential elements. The lower register shows the natural world, beginning with water and plants variously identified by scholars as date palm and barley, wheat and flax. Above the plants, alternating rams and ewes march single file along a solid ground line. In the middle register, naked men carry baskets of foodstuffs, and in the top register, the goddess Inanna accepts an offering from two standing figures. Inanna stands in front of her shrine and storehouse, identified by two reed door-poles hung with banners. Facing her are two men, thought to be first a naked priest or acolyte presenting the offering-filled basket, followed by a ceremonially dressed figure of the priest-king, only partially preserved. The scene has been interpreted as the ritual marriage between the goddess and the priest-king to ensure the fertility of crops, animals, and people, and thus the continued survival of Uruk.

Stone statues dated to about 2900–2600 BCE from the Square Temple in Eshnunna (fig. **2–4**) reveal another aspect of Sumerian religious art. These **votive figures** (images dedicated to the gods) are directly related to an ancient Near Eastern devotional practice in which individual worshipers who could afford it would set up images of themselves before a larger, more elaborate image of a god in a shrine. A simple inscription might identify the figure as "one who offers prayers." Larger inscriptions might recount all the things accomplished in the god's honor.

The carvers of these votive figures followed the **conventions** of Sumerian art—that is, the traditional ways of representing forms. The faces, bodies, and dress are stylized and streamlined to emphasize the cylindrical forms of the figures. Stocky, muscular, bare-chested, the men in this group wear sheepskin kilts. The female figures are as massive as the men. Just right of center, one wears a dress wrapped diagonally to expose one breast. Some of the figures hold small vessels, probably similar to those that visitors to the temple

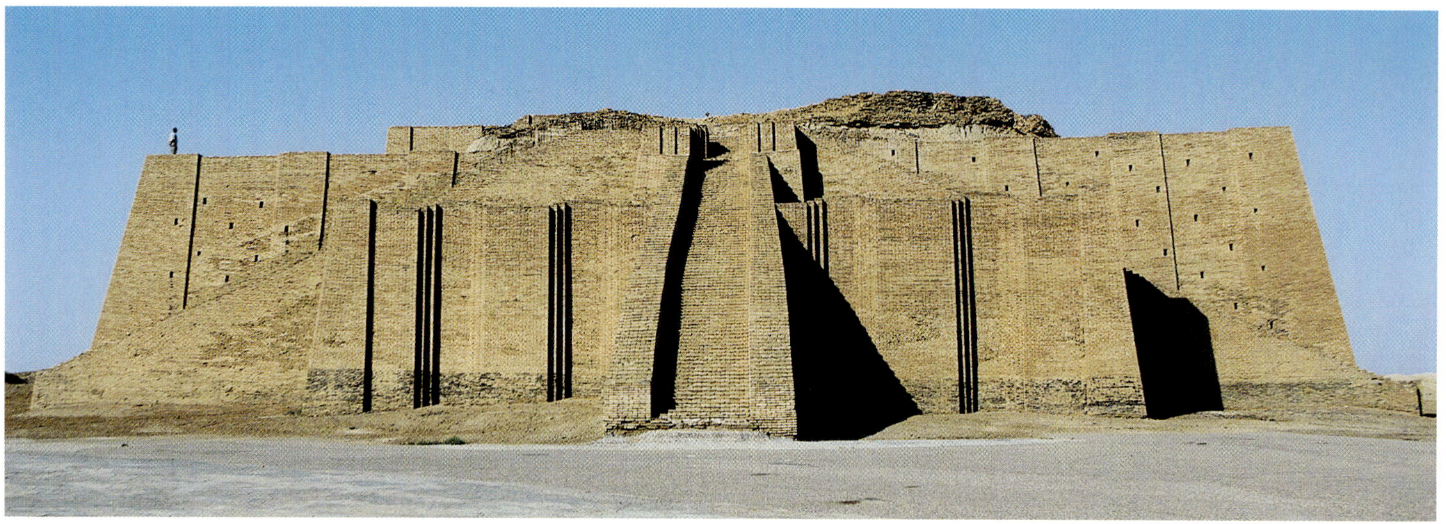

2–5 Nanna Ziggurat, Ur (modern Muqaiyir, Iraq). c. 2100–2050 BCE

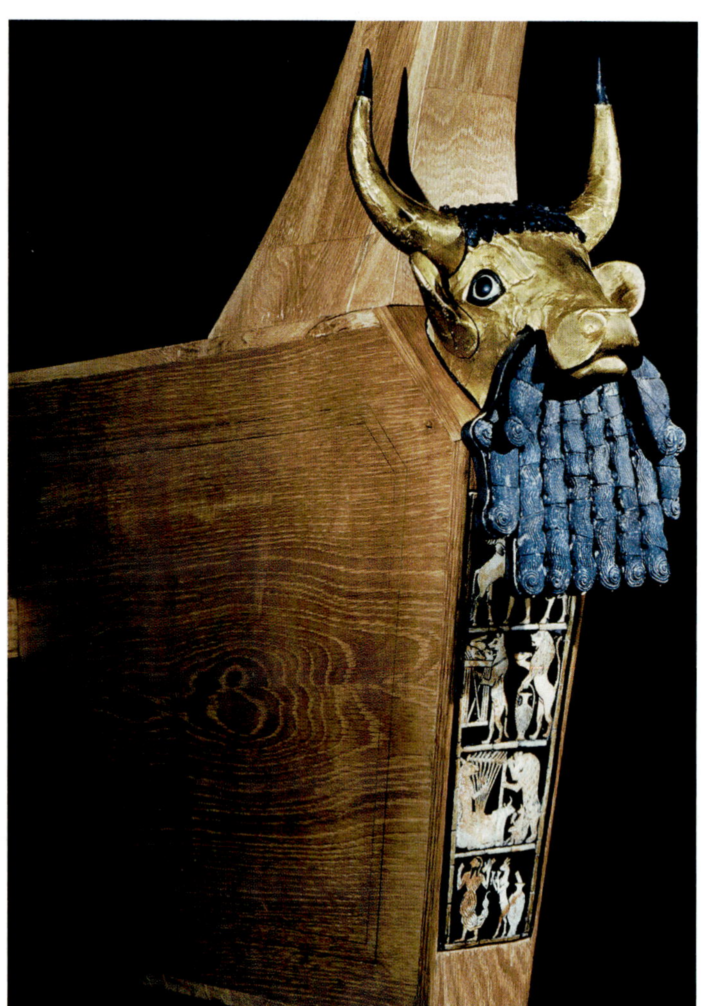

2–6 Bull lyre, from a royal tomb, Ur (modern Muqaiyir, Iraq). c. 2550–2400 BCE. Wood with gold, silver, lapis lazuli, bitumen, and shell, reassembled in modern wood support; height of plaque 13" (33 cm); maximum length of lyre 55½" (140 cm); height of upright back arm 46½" (117 cm). Penn Museum, Philadelphia
PENN MUSEUM OBJECT B17694, IMAGE 160104

used during ritual activities. They stand at respectful attention for all eternity, and their wide, staring inlaid eyes indicate communication between them and the god.

About a thousand years after the completion of the White Temple in Uruk, the people of Ur, a city on the Euphrates south of Uruk, built a mud-brick ziggurat dedicated to the moon god Nanna (fig. **2–5**). Here three staircases converge at an imposing entrance gate atop the first platform. Each platform is angled outward from top to base, probably to prevent rainwater from forming puddles and eroding the pavement. The first two levels of the Nanna Ziggurat and their retaining walls were reconstructed in recent times, and little remains of the upper level and the temple. Such temples were known as "the offering table of heaven" and "the waiting room of the gods," but we know nothing of the rituals performed in them.

The artists of Ur became accomplished in many arts: music, oral storytelling (which later became literature), work in precious materials, as well as stone sculpture and architecture. A superb example of their skill is a lyre—a kind of harp—from a royal tomb of Ur (c. 2550–2400 BCE), which combines wood, gold, lapis lazuli, and shell (fig. **2–6**). Archaeologists have restored the lost wooden parts of the lyre and reassembled the surviving pieces. On one end of the sound box, surmounting a panel with inlaid shell images of animals (fig. **2–7**), sits the gold, sculpted head of a magnificent bearded bull, intensely lifelike despite the decoratively patterned blue beard, created out of the semiprecious stone lapis lazuli. Since this material had to be imported from Afghanistan, it is enduring evidence of widespread trade in the region at this time.

In addition to inventing cuneiform writing, Sumerian temple staff and merchants developed flat stamps and more elaborate cylinder seals to secure and identify documents and signify property ownership. **Cylinder seals**, usually less than 2 inches high, were made of hard and sometimes semiprecious stones with designs incised into the surface. Rolled across a damp clay surface, the seal leaves a mirror image of its design that cannot easily be altered once

CLOSER LOOK

As in the animal fables of the legendary Greek author Aesop, the animals in the panels that decorate the bull lyre from a Sumerian royal tomb (fig. 2–7) personify humans. In one of the four registers, a seated donkey plucks the strings of a bull lyre—similar to the instrument on which this set of images originally appeared (fig. 2–6)—stabilized by a standing bear, while a fox accompanies him with a rattle. The next register shows upright animals who seem to be bringing food and drink for a feast. On the left, a hyena—assuming the role of a butcher with a knife in his belt—carries a table piled high with meat. A lion follows him with a large jar and pouring vessel. The top and bottom registers are particularly intriguing because they seem to illustrate scenes that could have been inspired by the *Epic of Gilgamesh*, a 3,000-line epic poem that is Sumer's great contribution to world literature. Rich in descriptions of heroic feats and fabulous creatures, Gilgamesh's story probes the question of immortality and expresses the heroic aim to understand hostile surroundings and to find meaning in human existence. What is especially interesting is that the poem was first written down nearly 700 years after the harp was decorated, suggesting that a very long oral tradition is visualized here. In the *Epic*, Gilgamesh encounters scorpion-men, like the one pictured in the lowest register. It is easy to see the hero himself in the commanding but unprotected bearded figure centered in the top register, naked except for a wide belt, masterfully controlling in his grasp the two powerfully rearing human-headed bulls that flank him. With the invention of writing, we are no longer dealing only with speculations as we did with prehistoric art. We can begin to identify and study subject matter and meaning with some confidence.

On another level, because the lyre and others like it were found in royal tomb chambers and were used in funeral rites, the imagery we see here may depict a funeral banquet in the realm of the dead. The animals shown are the traditional guardians of the gateway through which the newly dead person had to pass. Cuneiform tablets preserve songs of mourning, which may have been chanted by priests to lyre music at funerals. One begins: "Oh, lady, the harp of mourning is placed on the ground."

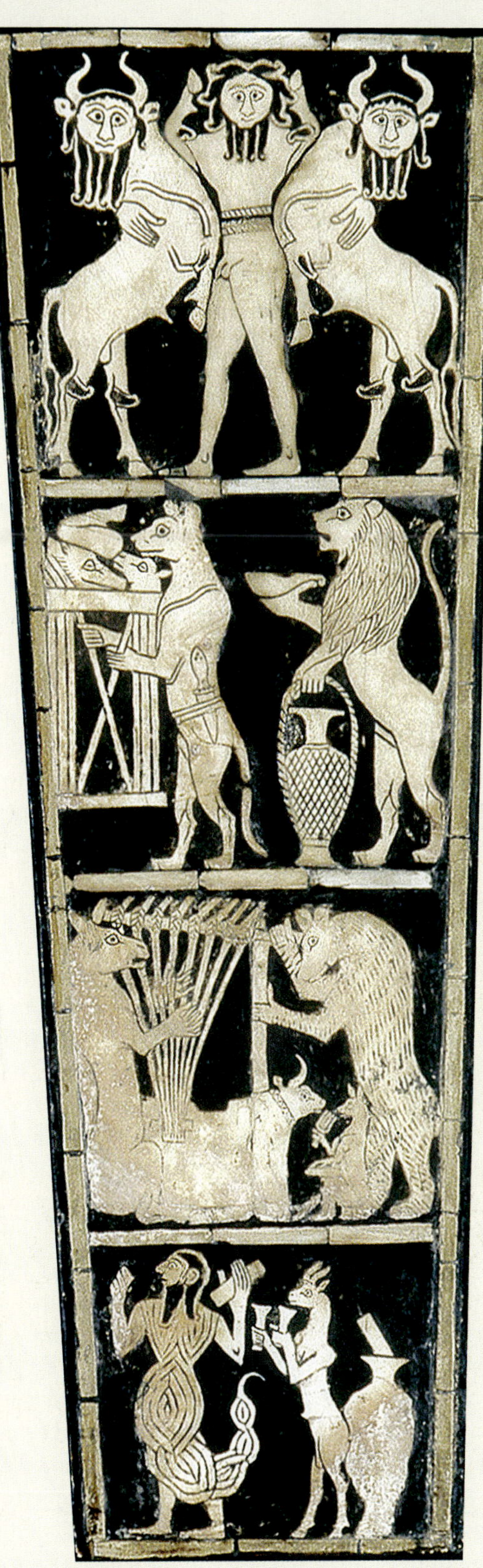

2–7 Mythological figures, detail of the sound box of the bull lyre in fig. 2–6. Wood with shell inlay, 12¼" × 4¼" (31.1 × 11 cm). Penn Museum, Philadelphia

PENN MUSEUM OBJECT B17694, IMAGE 150848

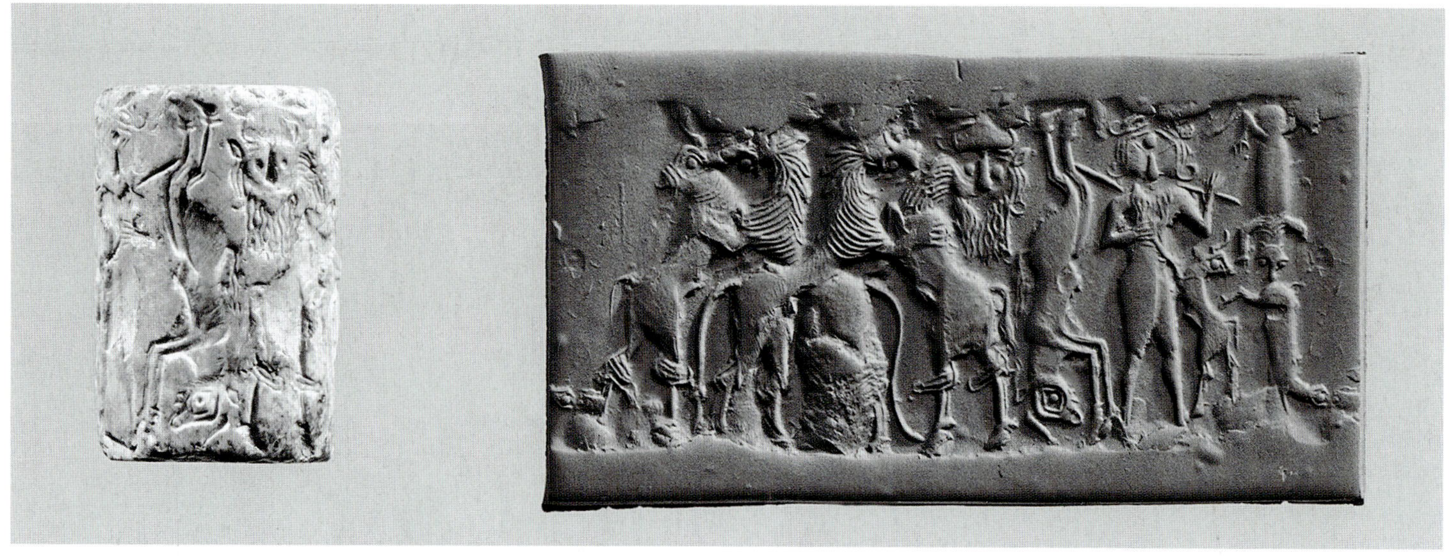

2–8 Cylinder seal from Sumer and its impression. c. 2500 BCE. Marble, height approx. 1¾" (4.5 cm).
The Metropolitan Museum of Art, New York
GIFT OF WALTER HAUSER, 1955 (55.65.4)

dry. The distinctive design on the stone cylinder seal shown in figure **2–8** belonged only to its owner. When rolled across the soft clay or a written document as a signature, or over the material used to seal something closed—the lid of a jar, the knot securing a bundle, or the door to a store room—the cylinder left a raised image or a band of repeated raised images of the incised design. Sealing discouraged unauthorized people from secretly gaining access to goods or information and guaranteed the authenticity of a document.

Akkad and Lagash

During the Sumerian period, a people known as the Akkadians had settled north of Uruk. They adopted Sumerian culture, but unlike the Sumerians, the Akkadians spoke a Semitic language (the same family of languages that includes Arabic and Hebrew). Under the powerful military and political figure Sargon I (ruled c. 2332–2279 BCE), they conquered most of Mesopotamia. For more than half a century, Sargon, "King of the Four Quarters of the World," ruled this empire from his capital at Akkad, the actual site of which is yet to be discovered.

The Stele of Naram-Sin, from about 2254–2218 BCE (fig. 2–1), commemorates a military victory of Sargon's grandson and successor Naram-Sin. Watched over by a cluster of solar deities, symbolized by the radiating suns at the top of the stele, the king, wearing the horned crown of a deity, stands above his soldiers and fallen foes near the top of the scene. The shape of the **stele** (upright stone slab) is used as a dynamic part of the composition. Its pointed outline accommodates and emphasizes the carved mountain depicted within it, and Naram-Sin is also posed to reflect its shape. In addition, he is larger to indicate his greater relative importance, a convention that art historians call hieratic scale, which is also prominent in the art of other cultures.

The Akkadian Empire fell around 2180 BCE to the Guti, a mountain people from the northeast. For a brief time the Guti controlled most of the Mesopotamian plain, except for the city-state of Lagash, which remained independent under Gudea, who ruled from the capital city of Girsu on the Tigris River. Gudea built and restored many temples, and within them, following a venerable Mesopotamian tradition, he placed votive statues in diorite (a very hard imported stone) of himself as the embodiment of just rule. Twenty have survived, making Gudea's face a familiar one in the study of ancient Near Eastern art. In the cuneiform inscription on the statue shown here (fig. **2–9**) Gudea dedicates himself, the sculpture, and the temple in which the sculpture resided to the goddess Geshtinanna, the divine poet and interpreter of dreams. Gudea's prominent face, framed below a patterned wide-brimmed hat, is youthful and serene; his oversized, wide-open eyes perpetually confront the gaze of the deity. He holds in front of him a vessel from which life-giving water flows in two streams filled with leaping fish.

Babylon

The land between the rivers remained a much-contested prize. Periods of political turmoil and stable government alternated until the Amorites, a Semitic-speaking people from the Arabian Desert to the west, moved into the area and reunited Sumer under Hammurabi (ruled 1792–1750 BCE). Their capital city was Babylon, and its residents were called Babylonians.

Among Hammurabi's achievements was a written legal code that recorded the laws of his realm and the penalties for breaking them. The code, incised in cuneiform script on a stele, appears under a portrait of the ruler standing before the enthroned supreme judge and sun god, Shamash, patron of law and justice (fig. **2–10**). In the introductory section of the stele's long inscription,

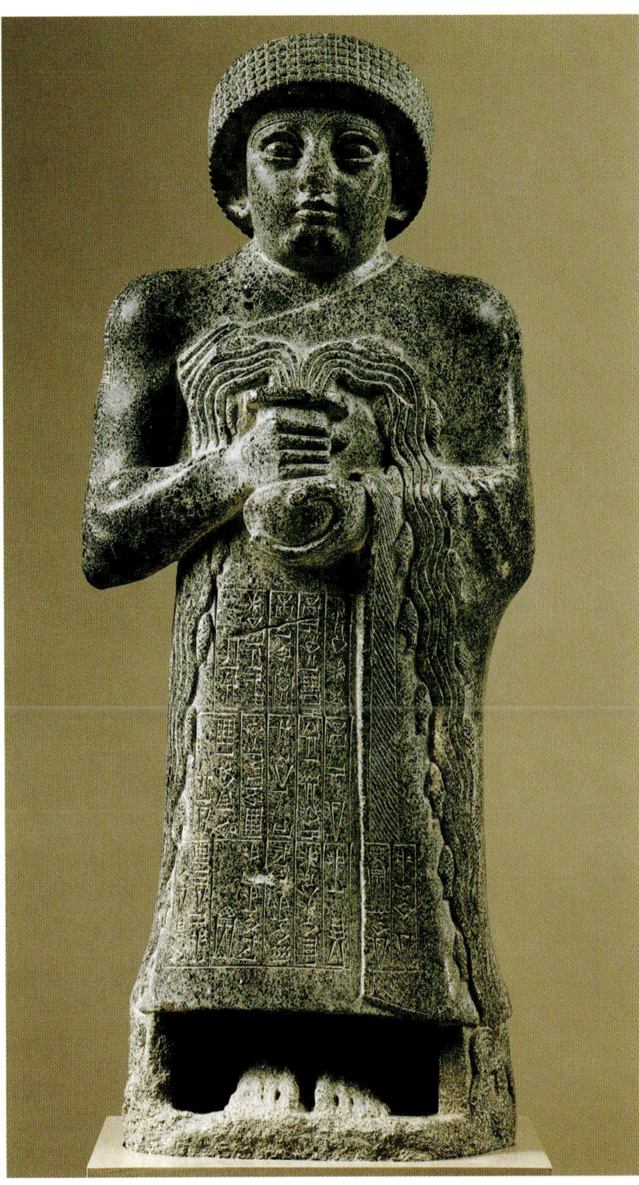

2–9 Votive statue of Gudea, from Girsu (modern Telloh, Iraq). c. 2090 BCE. Diorite, height 29" (73.7 cm). Musée du Louvre, Paris

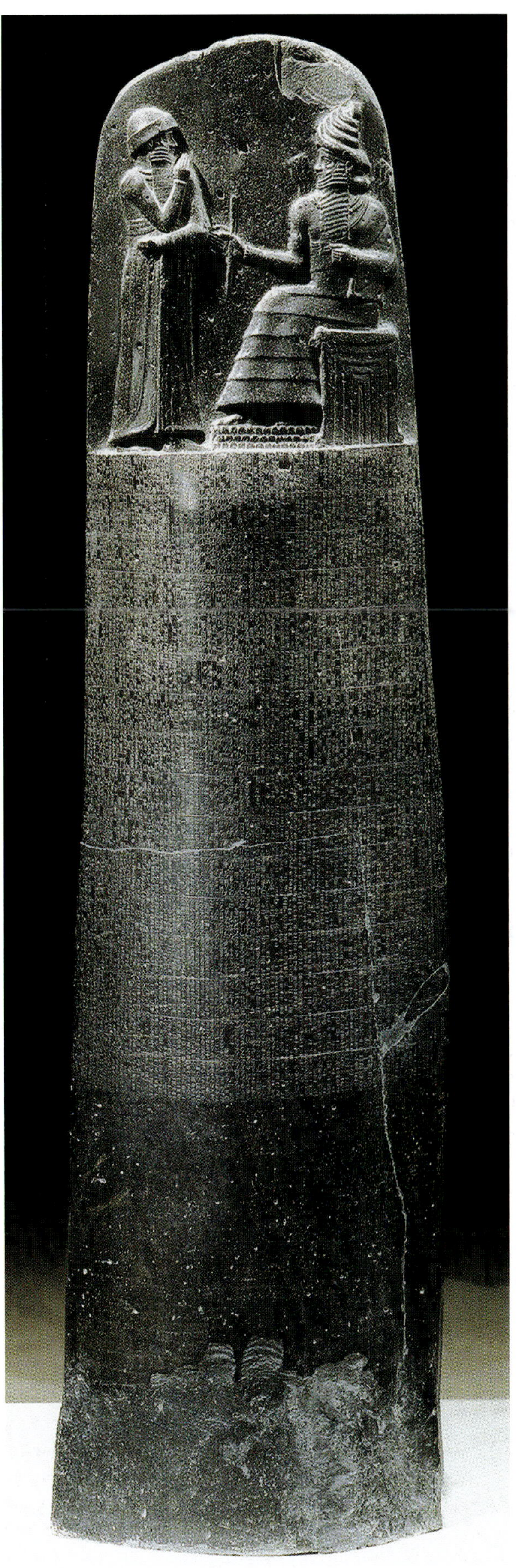

2–10 Stele of Hammurabi, from Susa (modern Shush, Iran). c. 1792–1750 BCE. Diorite, height of stele approx. 7' (2.13 m), height of relief 28" (71.1 cm). Musée du Louvre, Paris

A prologue on the front of the stele and an epilogue on the back glorify Hammurabi and his accomplishments, but most of the inscription outlines laws guaranteeing uniform treatment of people throughout the Babylonian kingdom. Most famous are the instances when punishments are specifically tailored to fit specific crimes—an eye for an eye, a tooth for a tooth, a broken bone for a broken bone. The death penalty is imposed for crimes such as stealing from a temple or palace, helping a slave to escape, or insubordination in the army. Trial by water and fire could also be imposed, as when an adulterous woman and her lover were sentenced to be thrown into the water; if they did not drown, they were judged innocent. Some of the punishments seem excessive today, but Hammurabi was breaking new ground by regulating laws and punishments rather than leaving them to the whims of rulers and officials.

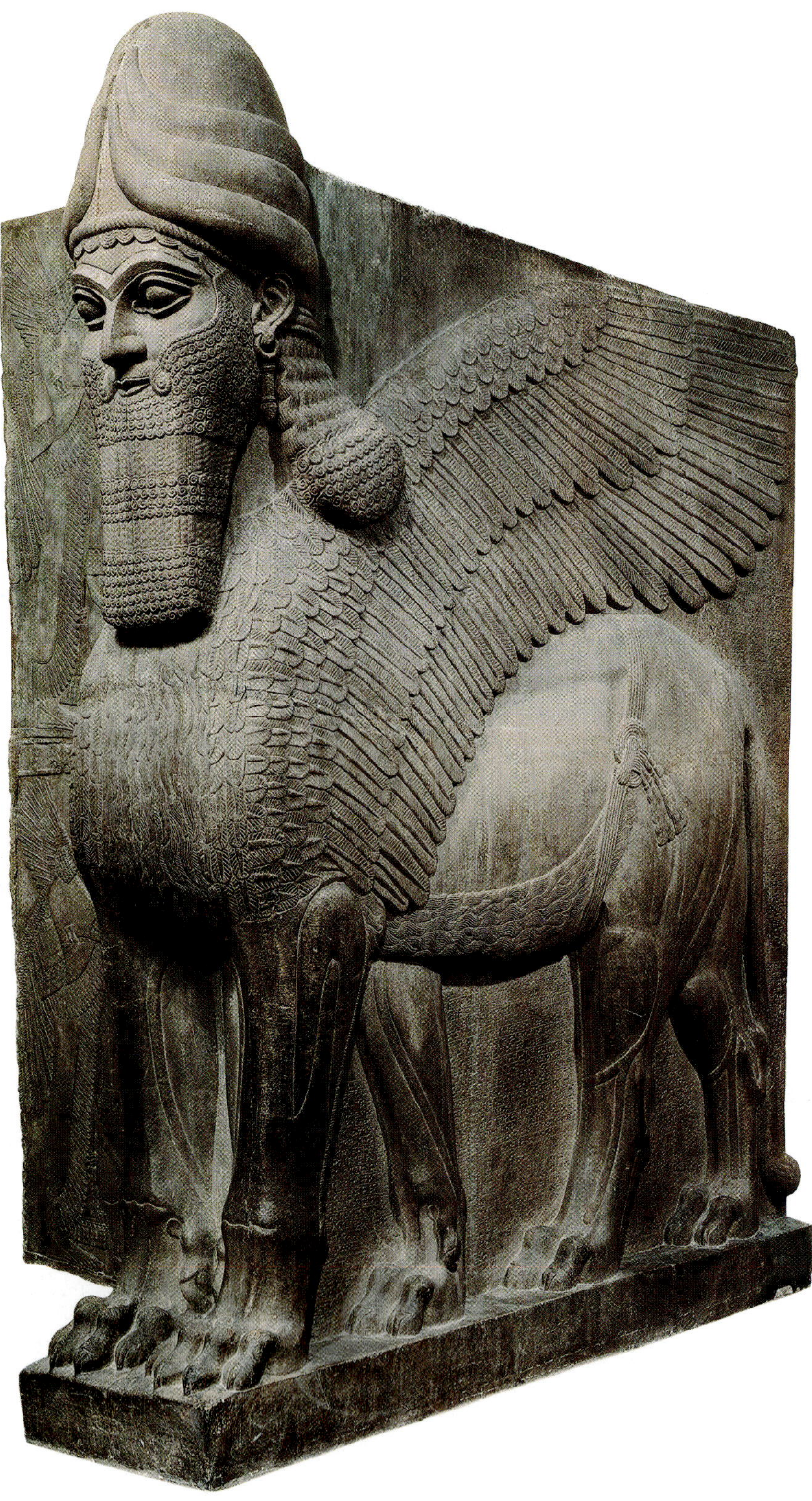

2–11 Human-Headed Winged Lion (Lamassus), from the palace of Assurnasirpal II, Nimrud (Iraq). 883–859 BCE. Alabaster, height 10' 2" (3.11 m). The Metropolitan Museum of Art, New York
GIFT OF JOHN D. ROCKEFELLER, JR., 1932 (32.143.2)

Hammurabi declared that with this code of law he intended "to cause justice to prevail in the land to destroy the wicked and the evil, that the strong might not oppress the weak nor the weak the strong." Most of the 300 or so entries that follow deal with commercial and property matters. Only 68 relate to domestic life, and a mere 20 deal with physical assault. Punishments were based on the wealth, social standing, and gender of the offender. The rights of the wealthy are favored over the poor, citizens over slaves, men over women.

Assyria

Around 1400 BCE the Assyrians rose to dominance in northern Mesopotamia. They controlled most of Mesopotamia by the end of the ninth century BCE, and by the early seventh century, they had extended their influence as far west as Egypt. Strongly influenced by Sumerian culture, the Assyrians adopted the ziggurat form and preserved Sumerian texts. The most complete surviving version of the *Epic of Gilgamesh* was found in the library of the powerful Assyrian king Assurbanipal (ruled 669–c. 627 BCE).

Assyrian rulers built fortified capital cities within which they constructed huge palaces decorated with wall paintings and stone reliefs of battle and hunting scenes, royal life or ceremonies, and religious imagery. During his reign (883–859 BCE), Assurnasirpal II established his capital at Kalhu (modern Nimrud, Iraq), on the east bank of the Tigris and undertook an ambitious building program, fortifying the new city with mud-brick walls 5 miles long and 42 feet high. Most of the buildings were made of mud brick; more impressive and durable limestone and alabaster were used to veneer walls for architectural decoration. Colossal guardian figures, called lamassus, flanked the major portals (fig. **2–11**), and panels carved with scenes in low relief covered the walls. In a vivid lion-hunting scene (fig. **2–12**), Assurnasirpal II stands in a chariot pulled by galloping horses and draws his bow against an attacking lion, advancing from the rear and with arrows already protruding from his body. Another expiring beast collapses on the ground under the horses. The immediacy of this image marks a shift in Mesopotamian art, away from a sense of timeless solemnity and toward an engaging sense of visual narrative that draws the viewer into the drama and emotionalism of the event portrayed.

Assurbanipal, king of the Assyrians two centuries later, maintained his capital at Nineveh (modern Kuyunjik, Iraq). He also had his palace

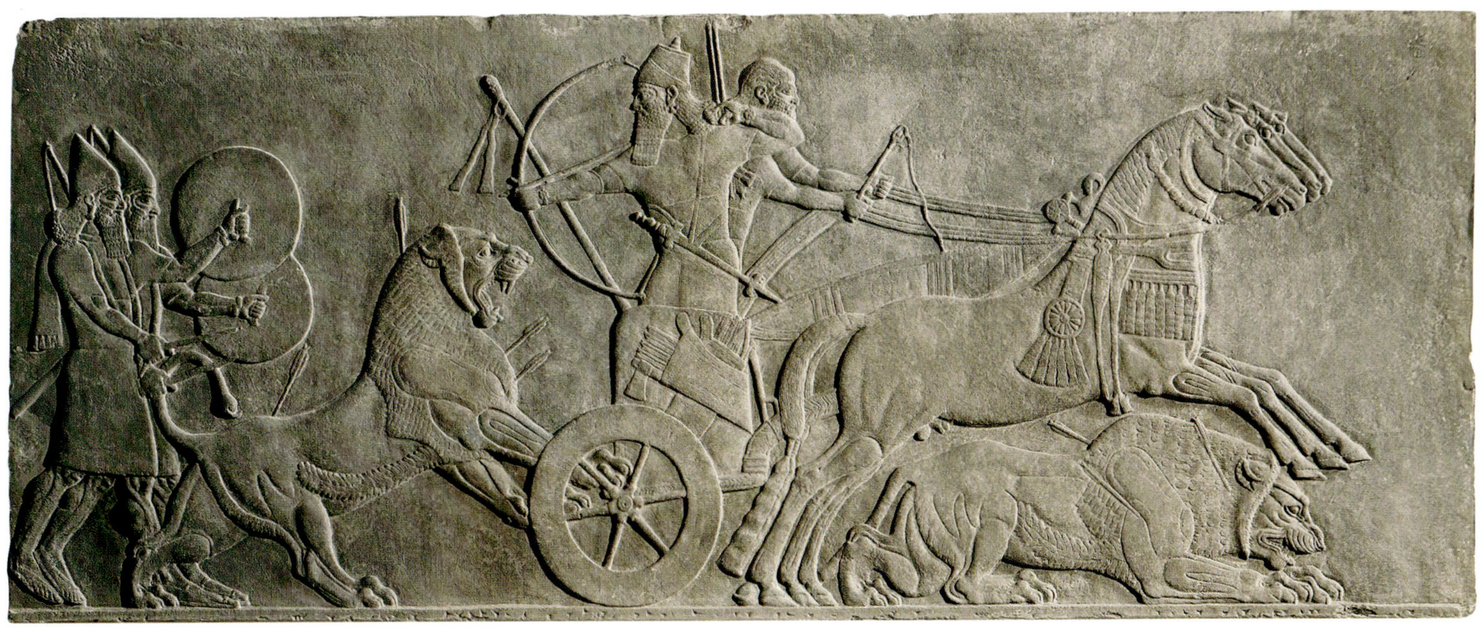

2–12 ***Assurnasirpal II Killing Lions***, from the palace complex of Assurnasirpal II, Nimrud (Iraq). c. 850 BCE. Alabaster, height approx. 39" (99.1 cm). The British Museum, London

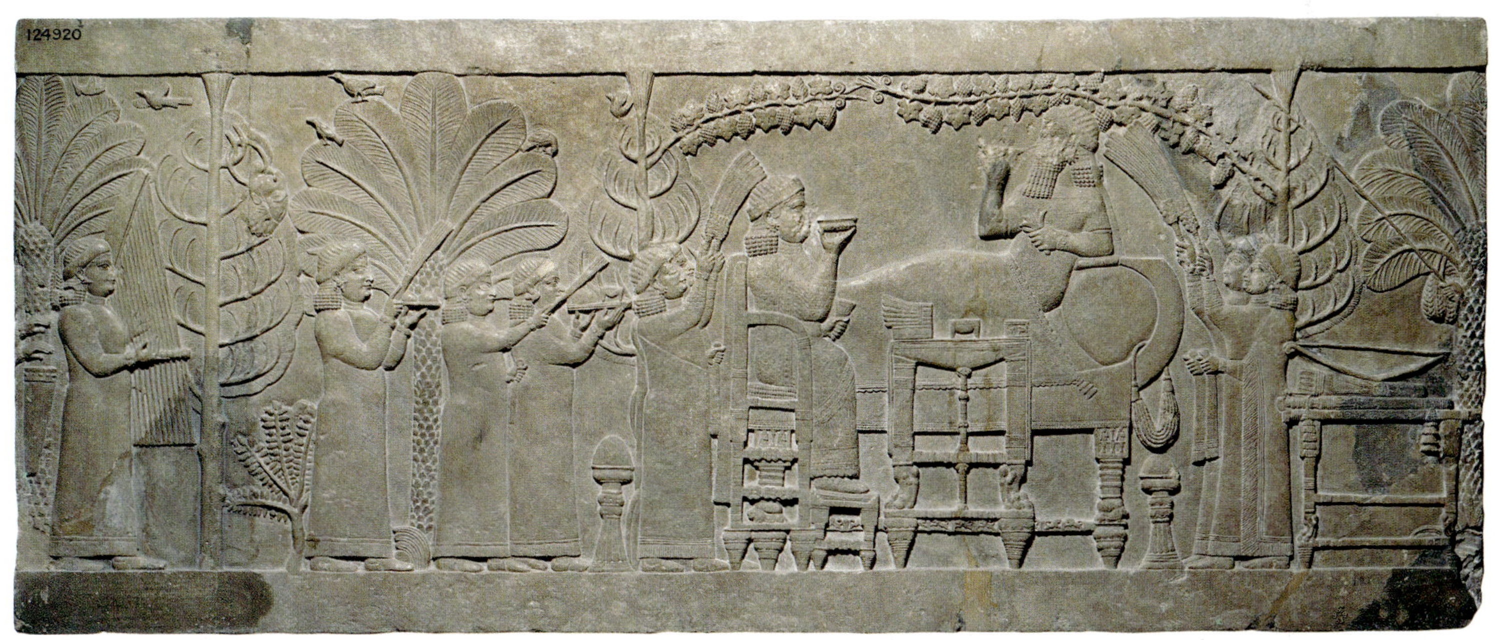

2–13 ***Assurbanipal and his Queen in the Garden***, from the palace at Nineveh (modern Kuyunjik, Iraq). c. 647 BCE. Alabaster, height approx. 21" (53.3 cm). The British Museum, London

decorated with panels of alabaster, carved with pictorial narratives in low relief. Most depict the king in battle or hunting, but one panel shows the king and queen relaxing in a pleasure garden (fig. **2–13**). The ruler, reclining on a couch, and his seated queen are surrounded by servants bringing trays of food and whisking away insects. The king has taken off his rich necklace and hung it on his couch, and he has laid aside his weapons, seen on the table behind him, but this tranquil domestic scene is actually a victory celebration. A grisly trophy, the upside-down severed head of his vanquished enemy, hangs from a tree at the far left.

THE FIBER ARTS

Fragments of fired clay impressed with cloth have been dated to 25,000 BCE, showing that fiber arts, including various weaving and knotting techniques, vie with ceramics as the earliest evidence of human creative and technical skill. Since prehistoric times, weaving appears to have been women's work—probably because women, with primary responsibility for childcare, could spin and weave no matter how frequently they were interrupted by family needs. Men, as shepherds and farmers, produced the raw materials for spinning and, as merchants, they distributed the fabrics not needed by the family. Early Assyrian cuneiform tablets preserve the correspondence between merchants traveling by caravan and their wives, who were running the production end of the business back home. The women often complain about late payments and changed orders. It is no coincidence that the woman shown spinning in the fragment from Susa (fig. 2–14) is an imposing figure, adorned with many ornaments. She sits barefoot and cross-legged on a lion-footed stool covered with sheepskin, spinning thread with a large spindle. A fish lies on an offering stand in front of her, together with six round objects (perhaps fruit). A young servant stands behind the woman as she works, fanning her.

The production of textiles is complex. First, thread must be produced. Fibers gathered from plants (such as flax for linen cloth or hemp for rope) or from animals (wool from sheep, goats, and camels or hair from humans and horses) are cleaned, combed, and sorted. Only then can they be twisted and drawn out under tension—that is, spun—into the long, strong, flexible fibers needed for textiles or cords. Spinning tools include a long, stick-like spindle to gather the spun fibers, a whorl (weight) to help rotate the spindle and stretch the thread, and a distaff (a word still used to describe women and their work) to hold the raw materials. Because textiles are fragile and rapidly decompose, the indestructible stone- or clay-fired spindle whorls are usually the only surviving evidence of threadmaking.

Weaving begins on a loom. **Warp** threads are laid out at right angles to **weft** threads, which are passed over and under the warp. In the earliest, vertical looms, warp threads were hung from a beam, their tension created either by wrapping them around a lower beam (a tapestry loom) or by tying them to heavy stones (a warp-weighted loom, which the woman from Susa would have used). Although weaving was usually a home industry, palaces and temples had large shops staffed by slave women, who specialized as spinners, warpers, weavers, and finishers.

Early fiber artists depended on the natural color of their materials and on natural dyes from the earth (ochers), from plants (madder for red, woad or indigo for blue, and safflower or crocus for yellow), and from animals (royal purple—known as Tyrian purple after its city of origin—from marine mollusks). Ancient Egyptians seem to have preferred white linen for their garments, which were elaborately folded and pleated. The Minoans of Crete created multicolored patterned fabrics with fancy borders, and Greeks excelled in the art of pictorial tapestries. The people of the ancient Near East used woven and dyed patterns and developed knotted pile (the so-called Persian carpet) and felt (a cloth of fibers bound by heat and pressure without spinning, weaving, or knitting).

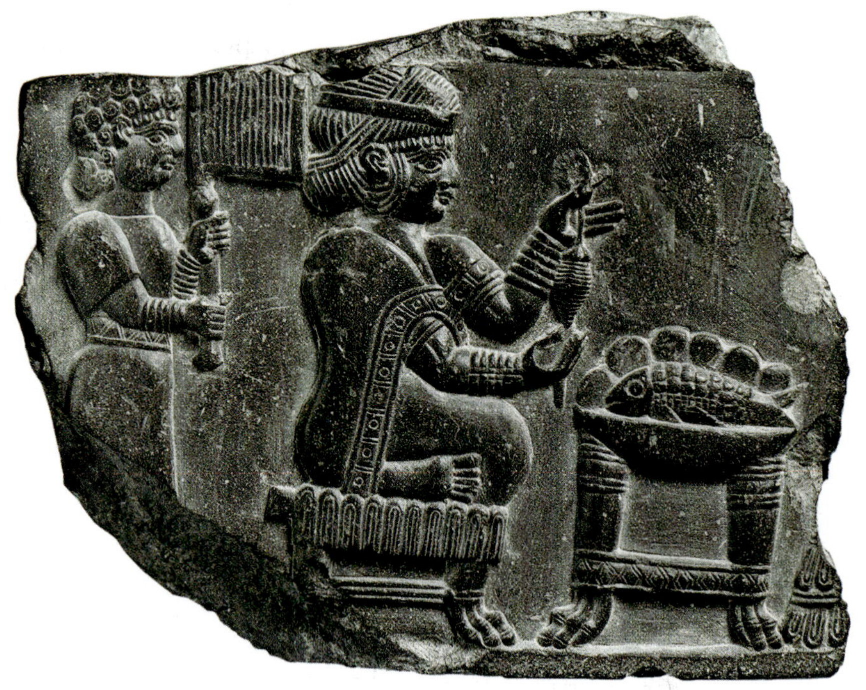

2–14 ***Woman Spinning***, from Susa (modern Shush, Iran). c. 8th–7th century BCE. Bitumen compound, 3⅝" × 5⅛" (9.12 × 13 cm). Musée du Louvre, Paris

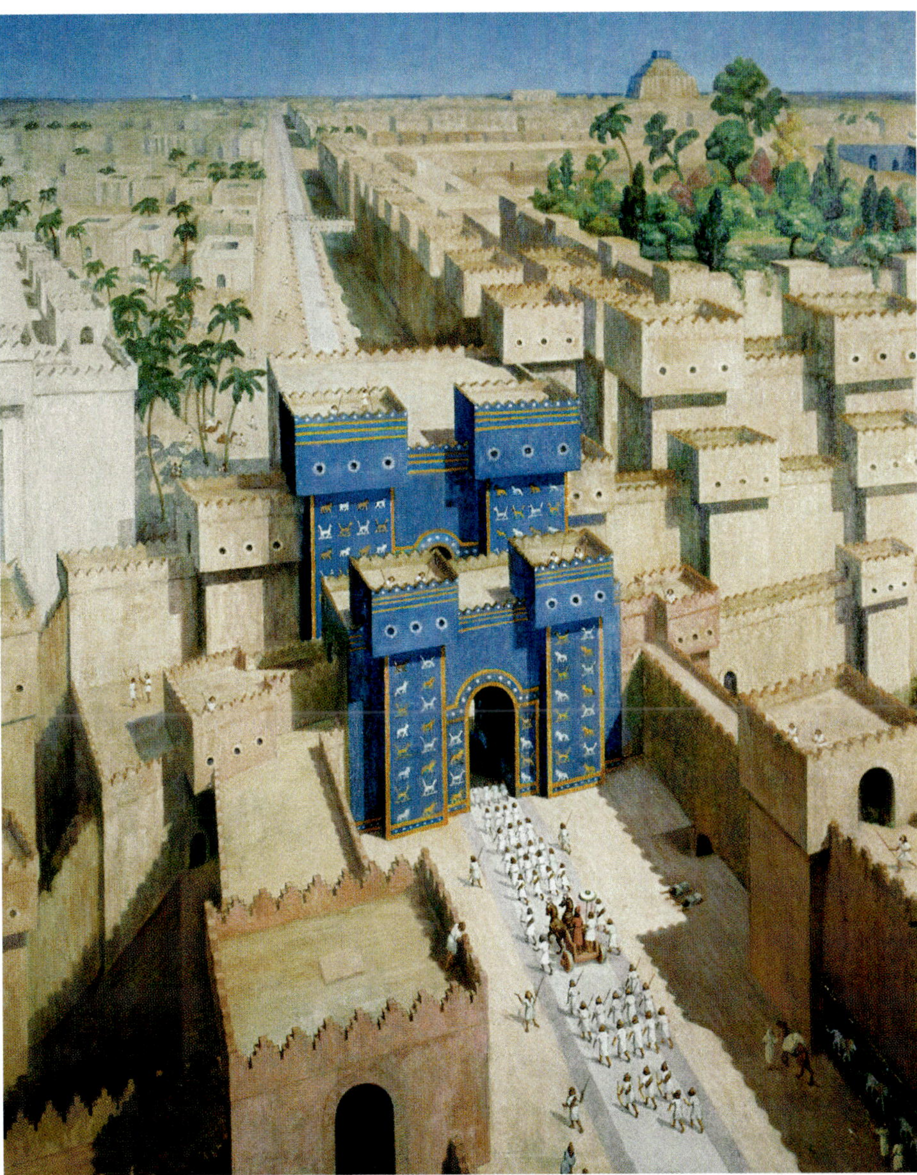

2–15 Reconstruction drawing of Babylon in the 6th century BCE
COURTESY OF THE ORIENTAL INSTITUTE OF THE UNIVERSITY OF CHICAGO

In this view, the palace of Nebuchadnezzar II, with its famous Hanging Gardens, can be seen just behind and to the right of the Ishtar Gate, to the west of the Processional Way. The Marduk Ziggurat looms up in the far distance on the east bank of the Euphrates. This structure was at times believed to be the biblical Tower of Babel—Bab-il was an early form of the city's name.

Neo-Babylonia

At the end of the seventh century BCE, the Medes, a people from western Iran, allied with the Babylonians and the Scythians, a nomadic people from northern Asia (present-day Russia and the Ukraine) invaded Assyria. In 612 BCE, this army captured Nineveh. When the dust settled, Assyria was no more and the Neo-Babylonians—so named because they recaptured the splendor that had marked Babylon 12 centuries earlier under Hammurabi—controlled a region that stretched from modern Turkey to northern Arabia and from Mesopotamia to the Mediterranean Sea.

The most famous Neo-Babylonian ruler was Nebuchadnezzar II (ruled 604–562 BCE), notorious today for his suppression of the Jews, as recorded in the book of Daniel in the Hebrew Bible. A great patron of architecture, he built temples throughout his realm and transformed Babylon—the cultural, political, and economic hub of his empire—into one of the most splendid cities of its day. A broad avenue, called the Processional Way because it was the route taken by religious processions honoring the city's patron god, Marduk, crossed the eastern sector of the city (fig. **2–15**). Up to 66 feet wide at points, the avenue was paved with large stone slabs. Colorful glazed bricks faced the walls along the route on both sides. The Processional Way ended at the Ishtar Gate, a main entrance to the city. Named after the goddess known as Inanna in Sumer and Ishtar in the Semitic-speaking regions of Mesopotamia, the gate with its four **crenellated** (notched) towers symbolized Babylonian power.

Persia

The Persians settled in southwestern Iran at the beginning of the first millennium BCE. Originally subservient to the Medes, the Persians obtained their independence in 549 BCE under Cyrus II "the

C L O S E R L O O K

Greek tales of the magnificent palaces, temples, and hanging gardens of ancient Babylon can still fire the imagination, and biblical accounts of the tyranny and decadence of Babylon's rulers conjure up images of licentious splendor. The Jews had reason to record Babylonian faults, since twice—in 597 BCE and 587 BCE—Babylonian armies destroyed Jerusalem and its temple and carried off the Jews into exile and captivity. In Babylon, one of these exiles, Daniel, survived an ordeal in the den of the king's lions, living to tell his story. The "Babylonian Captivity" became a turning point in Jewish history and prompted the poetic lamentations of the prophets Isaiah and Ezekiel.

Babylon was a huge city covering more than 3½ square miles on both sides of the Euphrates River in what is now Iraq. A wide Processional Way (see fig. 2–15) running parallel to the river joined temples and palaces and led to the northern palace complex. A moat, double walls, and gates with double towers defended the city. The northern gate (fig. **2–16**) in the royal sector was dedicated to Ishtar, goddess of love and war. The deep-blue surfaces of this so-called Ishtar Gate are decorated with alternating rows of bulls with blue forelocks—associated with Adad, the sky and weather god—and dragons, sacred to the city god, Marduk. Between 1905 and 1914, German archaeologists excavated the northern palace area. They recovered the brilliant glazed-tile decoration of part of the Processional Way, the Ishtar Gate, and Nebuchadnezzar's throne room, much of which they shipped to Germany, where it was reassembled in Berlin.

Using glazed bricks to decorate these enormous surfaces required careful planning and great technical skill. Just one of the dragons, for example, required as many as 75 to 80 bricks. Since firing caused the bricks to shrink, each brick had to be slightly larger than its allotted space in the final design. To enhance the splendid effect, brilliantly colored glass-based **glazes** were applied to the reliefs. (When fired, glaze produces a shiny, waterproof surface.)

Now reconstructed inside a Berlin museum (fig. 2–16 shows its installation), the Ishtar Gate sits next to a panel from the throne room in Nebuchadnezzar's nearby palace. In the portion seen here, an intricate design of striding lions, tall date palm trees with blue fronds, and patterns of white and yellow rosettes and palmettes are set against a deep blue background. The palm was associated with Ishtar in her role as protectress of the date storehouses. Lions were associated in the ancient Near East with royal power. Both motifs reminded Ishtar's devotees that she controlled both food and safety—the physical well-being and survival of her people.

In such a setting, described in the biblical book of Daniel, Nebuchadnezzar could have set up his golden idol, and Belshazzar could have used gold and silver vessels stolen from the Jewish Temple to serve wine at his infamous feast, causing Daniel to proclaim, "You have been weighed in the balance and found wanting!" (Daniel 5:27). Indeed Belshazzar's feast was his last, for the Persians entered the gates in 539 BCE—among them the Ishtar Gate—and destroyed Babylon that very night.

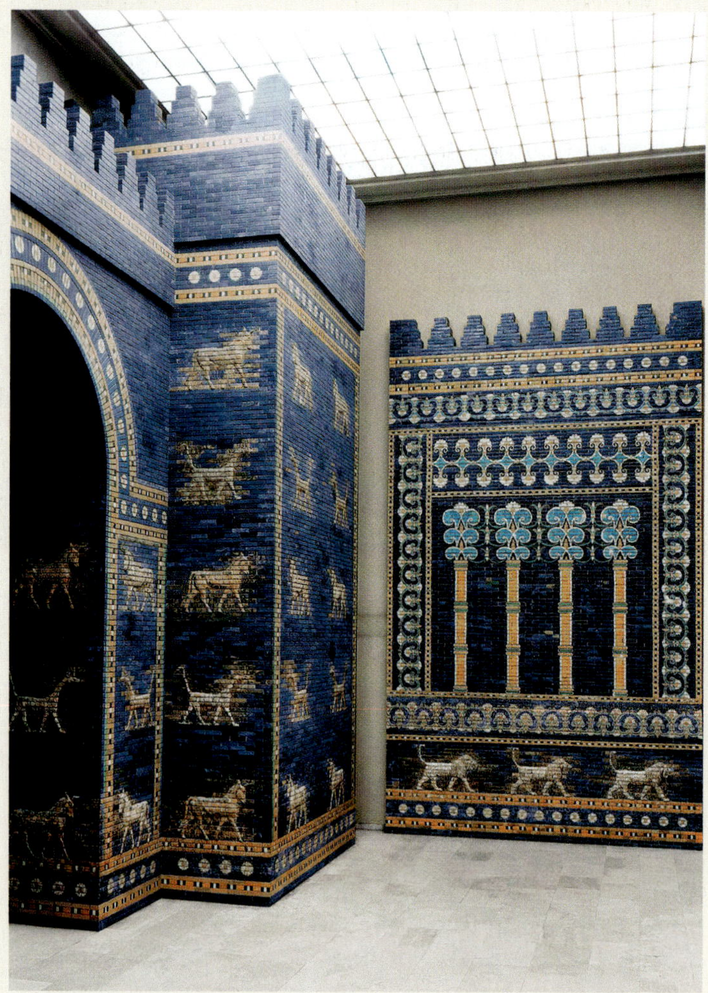

2–16 Reconstructed Ishtar Gate and throne room wall, from Babylon (Iraq). c. 575 BCE. Glazed brick, height of gate originally 40' (12.2 m) with towers rising 100' (30.5 m). Vorderasiatisches Museum, Staatliche Museen zu Berlin, Preussischer Kulturbesitz

Great," who ruled 559–530 BCE. He led the Persians in an astonishing series of conquests, and by the time of his death, the Persian Empire included Babylonia (vanquished by Persia in 539 BCE) and stretched from Iran into Anatolia. Cyrus' son Cambyses II (ruled 529–522 BCE) added Egypt and Cyprus to the empire. By the time Darius I (ruled 521–486 BCE) took the throne, he could boast: "I am Darius, great King, King of Kings, King of countries, King of this earth." Darius and his successors were known as the Achaemenid monarchs after a semilegendary ancestor, Achaemenes. They ruled for nearly two centuries, expanding the Achaemenid Empire both eastward and westward.

An able administrator, Darius organized the Persian lands into 20 tribute-paying areas under Persian governors, and he often left lesser local rulers in place. This practice, along with a tolerance for diverse native customs and religions, won the Persians the loyalty of many of their subjects. Darius also developed a system of fair taxation, issued a standardized currency, and improved communication throughout the empire.

Like many powerful rulers, Darius created monuments to serve as visible symbols of his authority. About 515 BCE, he began building a new capital in the Persian homeland, today known by its Greek name: Persepolis. He employed materials, workers, and artists from all over his empire. The result was a new multicultural style of art that combined many different traditions—Persian, Mede, Mesopotamian, Egyptian, and Greek.

In Assyrian fashion, the imperial complex at Persepolis was set on a raised platform, 40 feet high, and like Egyptian and Greek cities, it was laid out on a rectangular grid. The platform was accessible only from a single ramp made of wide, shallow steps to allow horsemen to ride up rather than having to dismount and climb on foot. Construction extended over nearly 60 years, and Darius lived to see the erection of only a treasury, the Apadana (Audience Hall), and a small palace for himself.

Darius' Apadana (fig. **2–17**), set above the rest of the complex on a second terrace, had a square hall large enough to hold several thousand people. The sides of the staircases and the walls of the platform were covered with sculpture in low relief. On the walls, ranks of warriors seem ready to defend the palace, while on the staircase, lions attack bulls at each side of the Persian generals. These animal combats (a popular theme throughout the Near East) emphasize the ferocity of the leaders and their men. Persian reliefs, like Greek friezes, were once brightly painted, and metal objects,

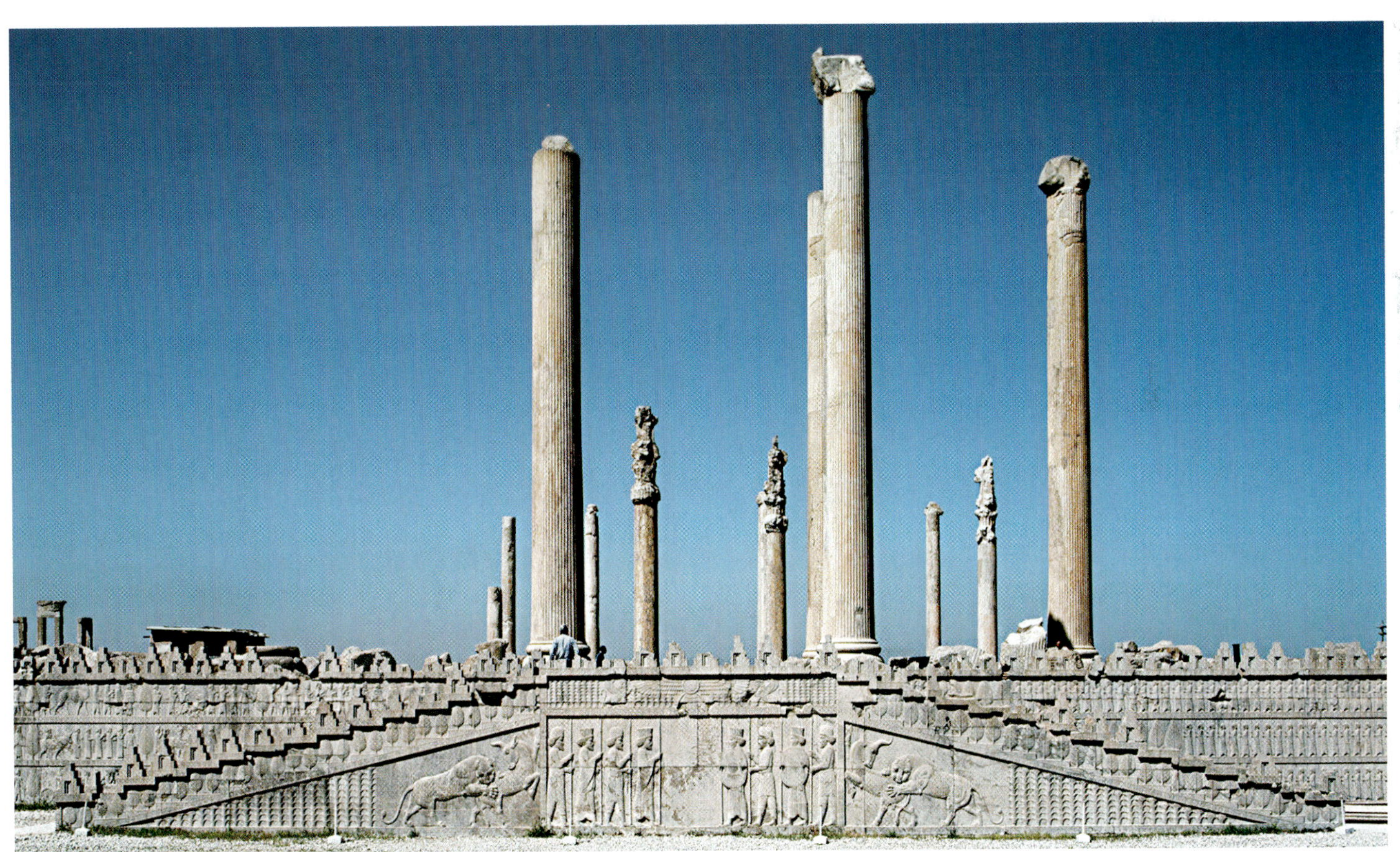

2–17 Apadana (Audience Hall) of Darius I and Xerxes I, ceremonial complex, Persepolis, Iran. 518–c. 460 BCE

The historian Cleitarchus of Alexandria relates that Alexander the Great and his troops accidentally torched the royal compound at Persepolis during a wild banquet in celebration of their victory over the Persians. It is more probable that Alexander had it destroyed deliberately. The site was never rebuilt, and its ruins were never buried. Scholars have been measuring, mapping, and studying what remains of the complex for generations. Various pieces of architectural ornament have been stripped from Persepolis for display in museums around the world.

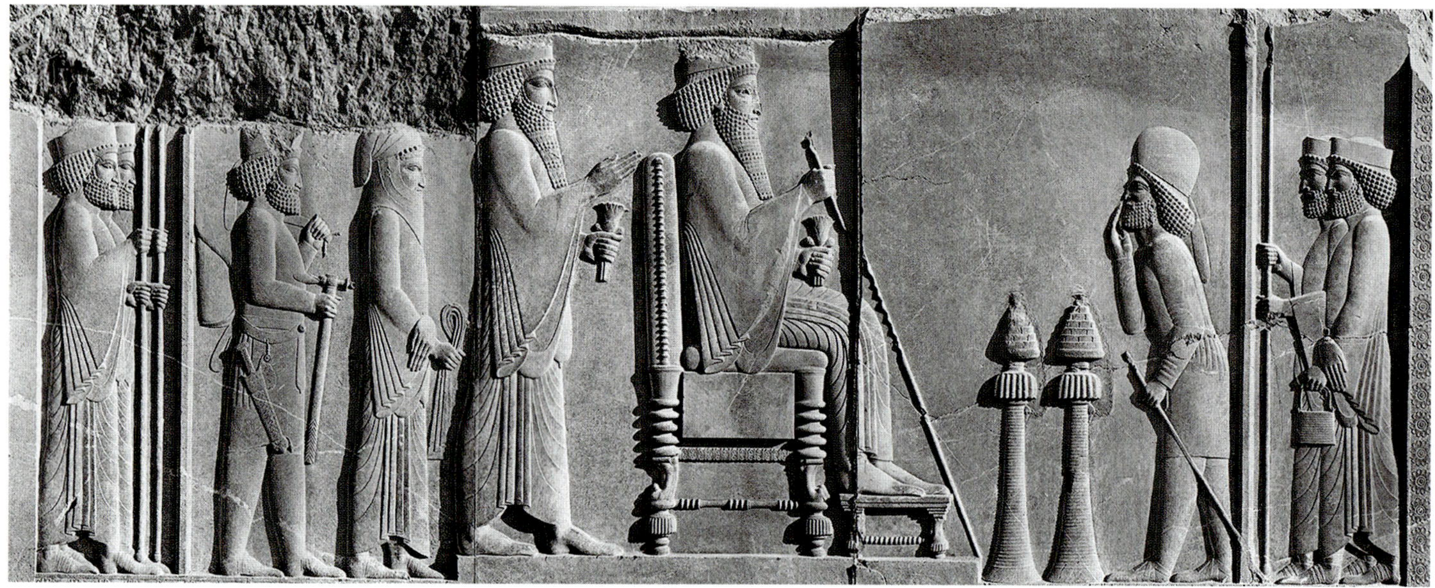

2–18 ***Darius and Xerxes Receiving Tribute***, detail of a relief from the stairway leading to the Apadana, ceremonial complex, Persepolis, Iran. 491–486 BCE. Limestone, height 8' 4" (2.54 m). Courtesy of the Oriental Institute of the University of Chicago

such as Darius' crown, were covered in **gold leaf** (thin sheets of hammered gold). Other reliefs throughout Persepolis depict displays of allegiance or economic prosperity. In one example, Darius holds an audience while his son and heir, Xerxes, listens from behind the throne (fig. **2–18**). During his own reign, Xerxes I (ruled 484–465 BCE) added a sprawling palace complex, enlarged the treasury building, and began a vast new public reception space, the Hall of 100 Columns.

At its height, the Persian Empire ruled by Darius and his successors extended from Africa to India. Only mainland Greeks successfully resisted the armies of the Achaemenids, and it was a Greek who ultimately put an end to their rule. Alexander the Great of Macedonia crossed into Anatolia and swept through Mesopotamia in 334 BCE, subsequently defeating Darius III and sacking Persepolis in 330. The lands of Persia then became part of the Hellenistic world.

Looking Back

Thousands of clay tablets covered with cuneiform writing document the evolution of writing in Mesopotamia, as well as an organized system of justice and the world's first epic literature. In Sumer, Akkad, Lagash, and Babylonia, agricultural advances and control of the rivers, increased food production. This made urban life possible. And population density gave rise to the development of specialized skills and social hierarchies. Priests communicated with the gods; rulers led and governed; warriors defended the greater community; and artisans and farmers supplied material needs.

Art became a means of communication. A distinctive architecture arose as people built colorful stepped ziggurats. Sculptors created compact cylindrical figures animated by wide staring eyes. By the ninth century, the Assyrians in northern Mesopotamia had built enormous city palaces and fortresses, placed guardian figures at the gates, and covered the walls with relief-sculptured narratives telling in vivid detail the Assyrians' daring exploits in nearly constant warfare. Later, Babylon in the south became a luxurious city, whose temples and ziggurats, palaces and ceremonial avenues were lined with brilliantly colored images made of glazed bricks. Finally, the Achaemenid Persians formed a spectacularly rich empire that drew from a series of cultural traditions to express its wealth and power in a huge palace complex at Persepolis.

But the evolving artistic achievements in the Near East are not without parallel in the ancient world. We will next explore another ancient river culture that established itself about the same time along the banks of the Nile in Egypt. Here too the early development of writing provides us with rich historical information, allowing us to understand much about the art and architecture it left behind. We will see other parallels—such as the establishment of a conceptual representational system for humans and their activity, as well as developing architectural technologies that allow the building of imposing statements of political power—but in Egypt there will be a marked emphasis on continuity rather than change.

IN PERSPECTIVE

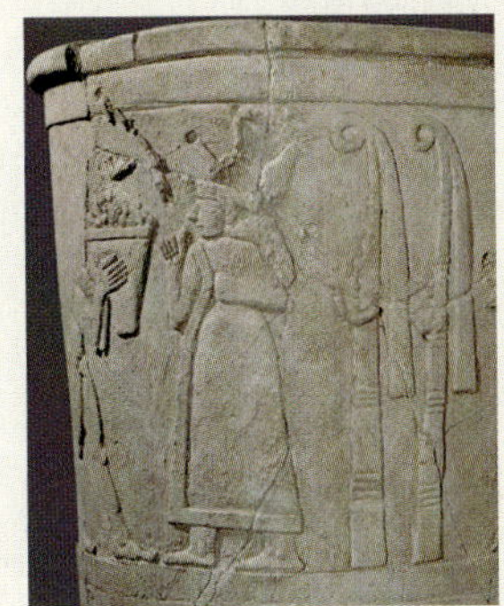

URUK VESSEL,
c. 3300–3000 BCE

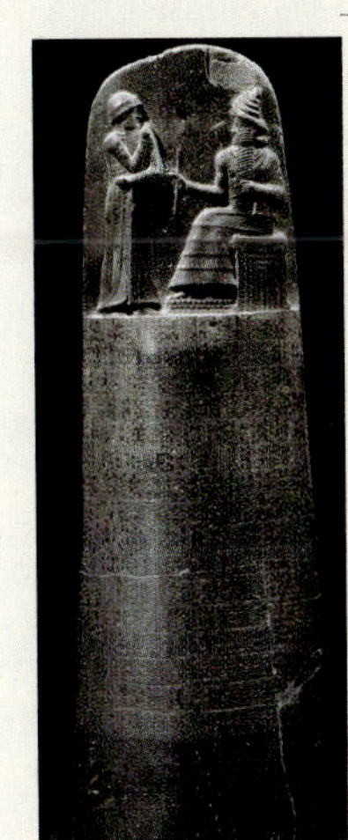

STELE OF NARAM-SIN,
c. 2254–2218 BCE

STELE OF HAMMURABI,
c. 1792–1750 BCE

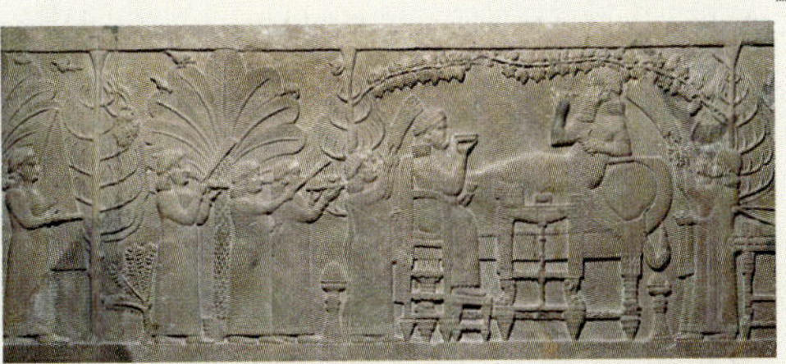

ASSURBANIPAL AND HIS QUEEN IN THE GARDEN,
c. 647 BCE

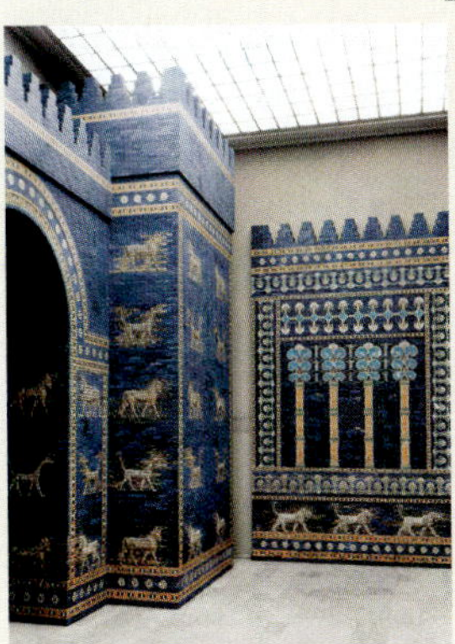

RECONSTRUCTED ISHTAR GATE
AND THRONE ROOM WALL,
c. 575 BCE

4000
BCE

◀ **Sumer,** c. 3500–2340 BCE

◀ **Potter's Wheel in Use,** c. 3250 BCE

◀ **Invention of Writing,** c. 3100 BCE

3000

◀ **Akkad,** c. 2340–2180 BCE

◀ **Naram-Sin,** ruled c. 2254–2218 BCE

◀ **Lagash,** c. 2150–2046 BCE

◀ **Hammurabi,** ruled c. 1792–1750 BCE

◀ **Hittite (Anatolia),** c. 1600–1200 BCE

1000

◀ **Assyrian Empire,** c. 1000–612 BCE

◀ **Assurnasirpal II,** ruled 883–859 BCE

◀ **Assurbanipal,** ruled 669–c. 627 BCE

◀ **Neo-Babylonia,** c. 612–539 BCE

◀ **Nebuchadnezzar II,** ruled 604–562 BCE

◀ **Persia,** c. 549–330 BCE

◀ **Darius I,** ruled 521–486 BCE

500
BCE

◀ **Alexander the Great sweeps through Mesopotamia,** 334 BCE

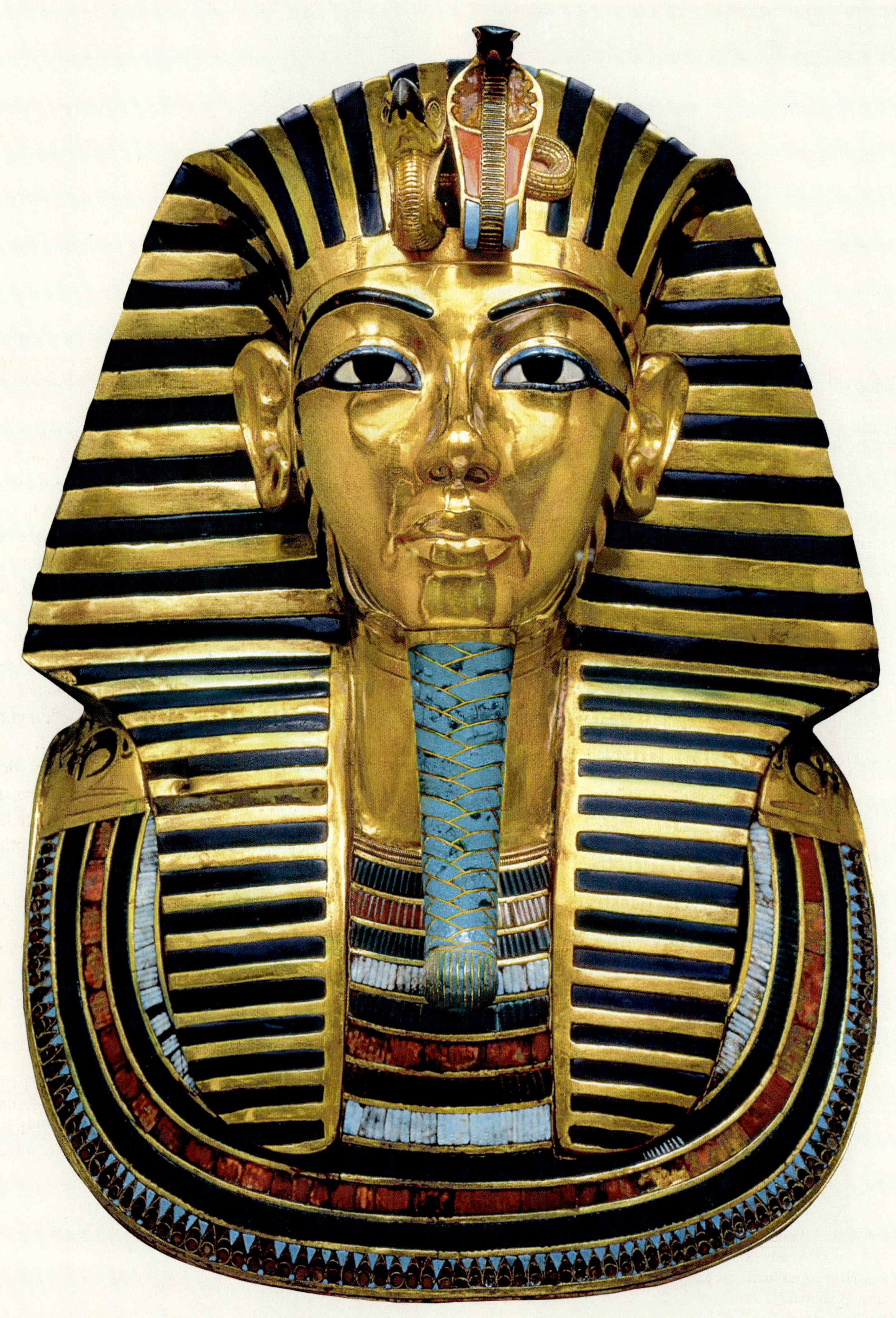

3
Art of Ancient Egypt

LOOKING FORWARD

Singularly self-possessed and staring serenely, the funerary mask of the young Egyptian ruler Tutankhamun (fig. **3–1**) dazzles us with royal splendor, and its legendary relationship with its sensational discovery certainly adds to its appeal. British archaeologist Howard Carter's dramatic discovery of the king's tomb in 1922 established the "romance of archaeology" in the public mind. Now the more than 3,500 items from Tutankhamun's tomb are showcased in the Egyptian Museum in Cairo, and periodic blockbuster exhibitions of objects from the tomb keep its appeal fresh for successive generations of museum-goers.

Why are we so mesmerized by the art of Egypt? It may be simply the elegant style and exquisite craftsmanship. Or the reason may lie in our fascination with this ancient people's struggle to create an explanation for the transition between life and death and their belief in an eternal hereafter that allowed powerful people like Tutankhamun to carry their wealth with them into their new adventures in the other world.

As fragile humans, we observe nature's continuous cycle of birth, death, and rebirth, and we come to realize that for all our ingenuity, we cannot escape death. Yet our imaginations recoil at the idea of our own extinction. Through the centuries people have lived with the hope or expectation of a life after death. Ancient Egyptians, from their narrow river valley, observed the constant regeneration of the land through yearly floods. They could easily believe that such regeneration would be granted to human beings, or at least to their rulers, who became gods on earth. Ancient Egyptians conceived the afterlife as a continuation of the life they knew. Thus they made elaborate efforts to equip the dead magnificently for life in the hereafter.

But the enchantment of Egyptian art is also aesthetic. Look into Tutankhamun's eyes. They are beautifully formed, emphatic shapes—black discs set in white and energized by tiny touches of red at the corners, yet their dark outline avoids the natural detail of lashes. Capturing fleeting moments like the fluttering of lashes during the blink of an eye was of little interest to a people concerned with timeless and eternal visions. By emphasizing clarity of line and color, streamlined forms, and the distillation of nature to elemental geometric shapes, ancient Egyptian artists established a standard of technical and aesthetic excellence that we continue to revere to this day.

3–1 Funerary mask of Tutankhamun
(ruled 1332–1322 BCE, Dynasty 18). Gold inlaid with glass and semiprecious stones, height 21¼" (54 cm), weight 24 pounds (11 kg).
Egyptian Museum, Cairo

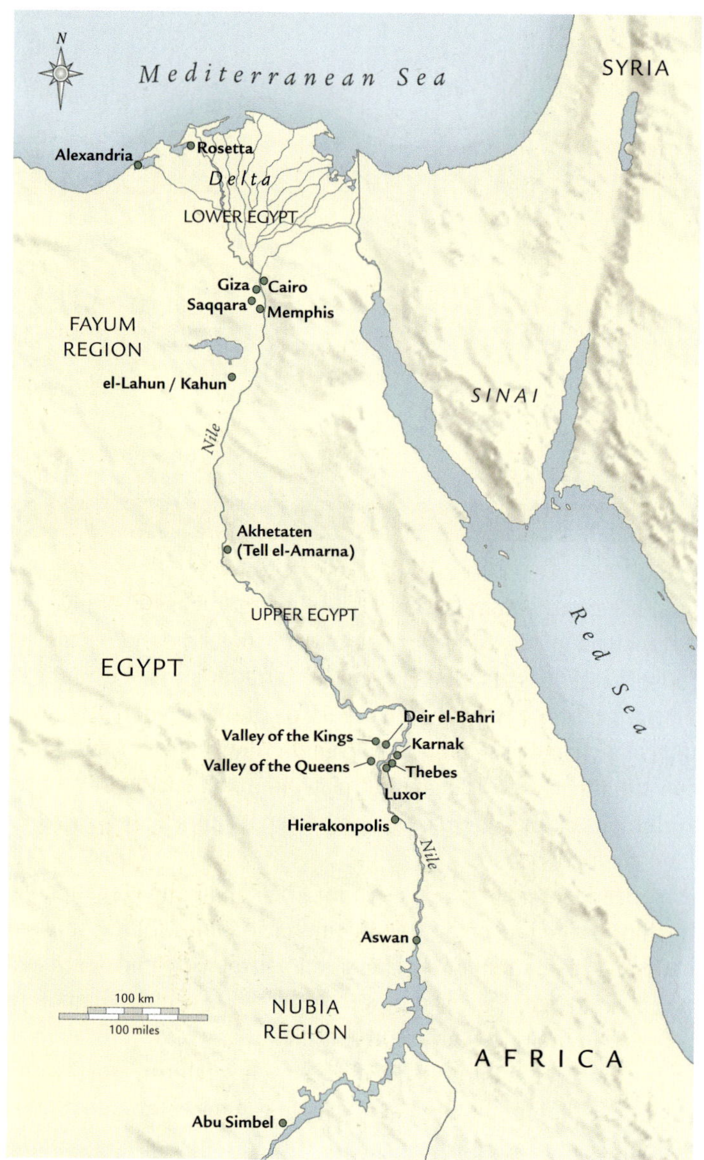

Map 3–1 Ancient Egypt

Periods of Ancient Egyptian Art	
c. 5000–2950 BCE	Predynastic Period
c. 2950–2575 BCE	Early Dynastic Period (Dynasties 1–2)
c. 2575–2150 BCE	Old Kingdom (Dynasties 3–6)
c. 2125–1975 BCE	First Intermediate Period
c. 1975–c. 1640 BCE	Middle Kingdom (Dynasties 11–14)
c. 1630–1520 BCE	Second Intermediate Period
c. 1539–1075 BCE	New Kingdom (Dynasties 18–20)
c. 715–332 BCE	Late Period
332–305 BCE	Macedonian Period
c. 323–30 BCE	Ptolemaic Period (which ends with the death of Cleopatra and the conquest by the Romans)

At the same time that city-states such as Sumer began to develop in Mesopotamia, a rich civilization arose in Egypt in the fertile valley and delta of the Nile (see map **3–1**). Around 5000 BCE, the valley's inhabitants adopted the agricultural village life associated with Neolithic culture. Farming communities along the Nile co-operated to control the river's flow, and, as in Mesopotamia, soon formed alliances. Over time, these rudimentary federations expanded by conquering and absorbing weaker communities, and by about 3500 BCE, there were several larger chiefdoms in the lower Nile Valley. Soon, Egypt was politically unified under a succession of kings from powerful families or dynasties.

In the third century BCE, an Egyptian priest and historian named Manetho collected and recorded the names of Egyptian kings, basing his work on temple records and inscriptions. Manetho grouped the kings into 30 dynasties that ruled the country between its unification around 3000 BCE and its conquest by Alexander the Great of Macedonia in 332 BCE. Egyptologists have since organized these dynasties into larger time spans or kingdoms reflecting broad historical developments.

Early Dynastic and Old Kingdom Egypt

With the start of the Early Dynastic period, Egypt became a consolidated state along the banks of the River Nile. According to Egyptian tradition, the country had previously evolved into two kingdoms: Upper Egypt in the south and Lower Egypt in the north. ("Upper" and "Lower" refer to the flow of the Nile.) An Upper Egyptian ruler,

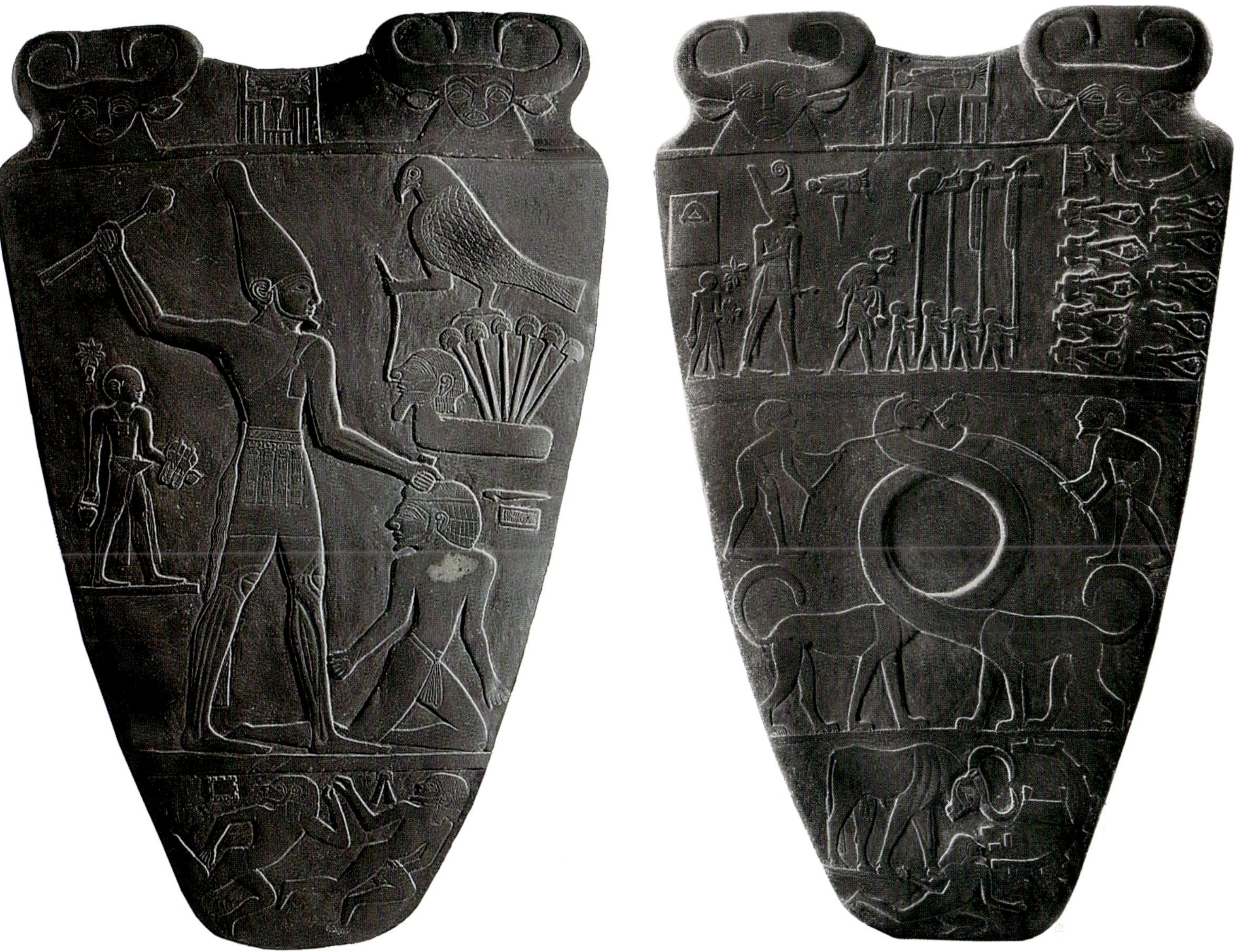

3–2 Palette of Narmer, from Hierakonpolis. Early Dynastic Period, c. 2950–2775 BCE. Green schist, height 25" (63.5 cm). Egyptian Museum, Cairo

referred to in an ancient document as "Menes king-Menes god," conquered Lower Egypt and first merged the lands into a single kingdom.

It is possible that Menes can be identified with a king named Narmer (ruled c. 3100 BCE), known from a stone palette (fig. **3–2**) found in the temple of Horus at Hierakonpolis. **Palettes**, flat stones with a circular depression carved on one side, were used to grind paint that was applied around the eyes to reduce the glare of the sun. The Palette of Narmer has the same form as these common objects but is much larger and must have had a ceremonial function.

King Narmer dominates the scene on both sides of the palette. His name appears at the top in pictographs: a horizontal fish (*nar*) above a vertical chisel (*mer*) set within a stylized palace façade. Following the convention of hieratic scale, he is shown larger than the other humans to signal his importance. On one side (fig. 3–2, left), Narmer, wearing the White Crown of Upper Egypt (see "Egyptian Symbols," page 66) and standing barefoot (an attendant behind him holds his sandals), holds the hair of a captive, perhaps the conquered ruler of Lower Egypt. The god Horus—a falcon with a human hand—holds a rope tied around the neck of a man whose head is attached to a block sprouting stylized papyrus symbolizing Lower Egypt. This combination of symbols makes it clear that Lower Egypt has been conquered and Narmer now rules both lands. On the other side of the palette (fig. 3–2, right), Narmer appears at top left wearing the Red Crown of Lower Egypt. The decapitated bodies of Lower Egyptian warriors have been placed in two neat rows to the right, their heads tucked between their feet.

Many figures on the palette are shown in poses that would be impossible to assume in real life. The artists chose a conceptual—rather than a perceptual—approach to the representation of the human figure. Heads are shown in profile, to capture most clearly their identifying features, while eyes, most recognizable and expressive when seen from the front, are rendered frontally. Shoulders are also frontal, but hips, legs, and feet are drawn in profile. These enduring conventions of Egyptian painting and relief sculpture would be followed for millennia, especially in depictions of royalty and other dignitaries. Persons of lesser social rank tended to be represented in ways that seem to us more lifelike.

Central to ancient Egyptian belief was the idea that every human being had a life force—the *ka*, or spirit—which lived on after the death of the body, forever engaged in the activities it had enjoyed during its earthly existence. Even after death, however, the *ka* needed a body to inhabit—either a carved likeness of the deceased or his or her actual corpse, preserved by mummification (see "Mummies," page 73).

The need to fulfill the requirements of the *ka* led not only to the creation of statues as substitute bodies, but also to the development of elaborate funerary rites and tombs filled with supplies and furnishings that the *ka* might require throughout eternity. In the Early Dynastic period, the most common type of tomb structure in Egypt was the **mastaba**, a flat-topped, one-story structure with slanted walls erected above an underground burial chamber. These tended to be grouped together in a **necropolis**—literally, "city of the dead"—at the edge of the desert on the west bank of the Nile where the sun set. Two of the most extensive of these early necropolises are those at Saqqara and Giza, near modern Cairo.

For his tomb complex at Saqqara, the Third Dynasty King Djoser (ruled c. 2650–2631 BCE) commissioned the earliest known monumental architecture in Egypt. The designer of the complex—Imhotep, prime minister and royal advisor—laid out Djoser's tomb as a stepped pyramid consisting of six mastaba-like elements stacked on top of each other and originally covered with a limestone facing, or veneer (fig. **3–3**). Although the final structure superficially resembles the ziggurats of Mesopotamia, it differs in both concept and purpose. It is built of finely cut stone, not mud brick; it rises in stages without ramps; and it protects a tomb. From its top, a 92-foot shaft descended to a granite-lined burial vault. Adjacent to the stepped pyramid, a funerary temple was used for continuing worship of the dead king, and sham buildings (fig. **3–4**)—simple masonry shells filled with debris—formed a miniature replica of the king's earthly realm, intended for the use of his *ka* in the hereafter.

The architectural form most closely identified with Egypt is the true pyramid with a square base and four sloping triangular sides (see "Mastaba to Pyramid," below). Most famous are the three Great Pyramids at Giza (fig. **3–5**), part of tomb complexes built by three successive Fourth Dynasty kings Khufu, Khafre, and Menkaure, whose reigns spanned circa 2551–2472 BCE. The oldest and largest of

ELEMENTS OF Architecture

Mastaba to Pyramid

The Egyptian burial structure—the gateway to the afterlife for kings and members of the royal court—began as a low rectangular mastaba with an internal room and chapel. Later, mastaba forms of decreasing size were stacked over underground burial chambers to form stepped pyramids. The culmination of the Egyptian burial structure is the pyramid, which housed an aboveground tomb and included false chambers, false doors, and confusing passageways to foil potential tomb robbers.

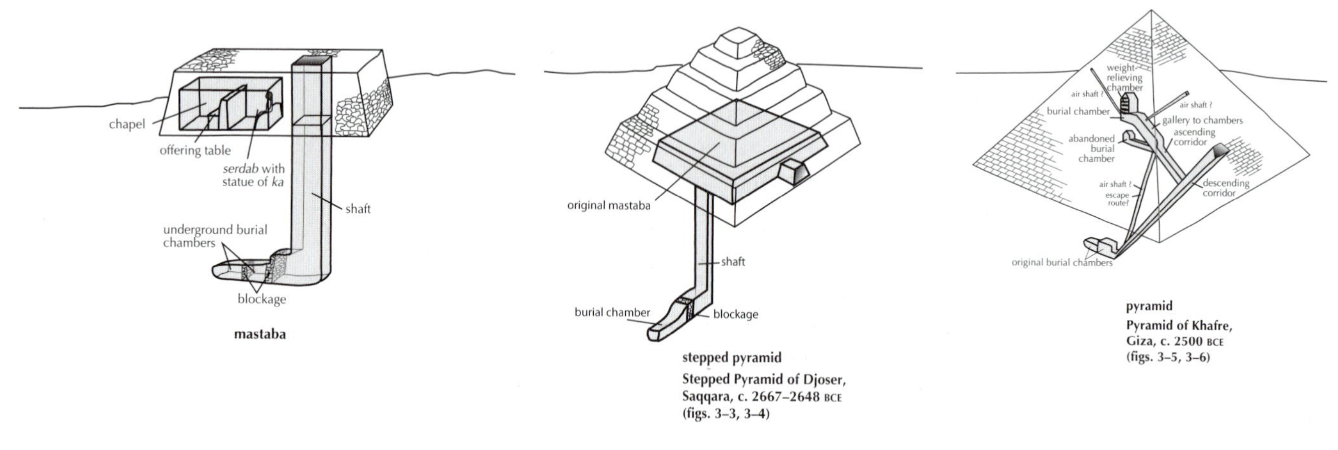

mastaba

stepped pyramid
Stepped Pyramid of Djoser, Saqqara, c. 2667–2648 BCE (figs. 3–3, 3–4)

pyramid
Pyramid of Khafre, Giza, c. 2500 BCE (figs. 3–5, 3–6)

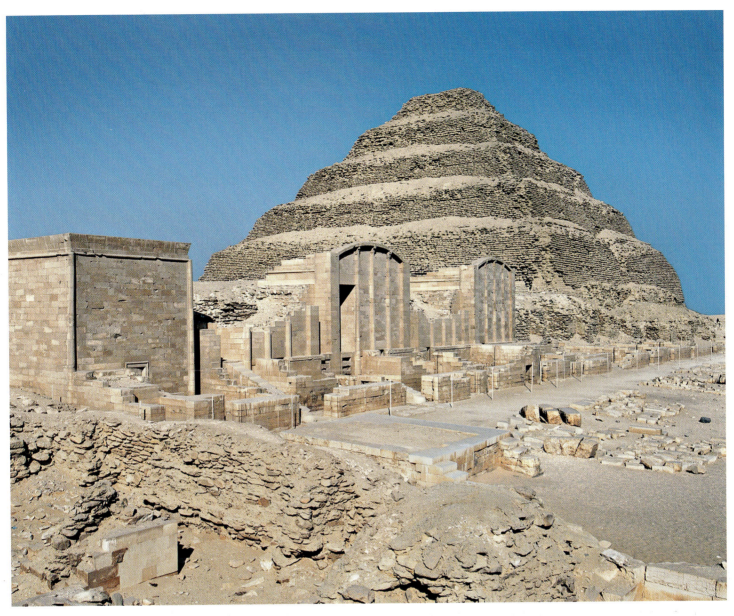

3–3 Stepped pyramid and sham buildings of the funerary complex of Djoser, Saqqara (c. 2630–2575 BCE, Dynasty 3). Limestone, height of pyramid 204' (62 m)

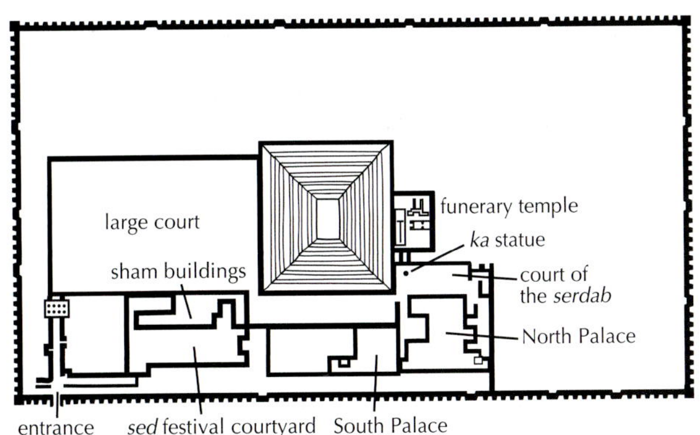

3–4 Plan of Djoser's funerary complex, Saqqara

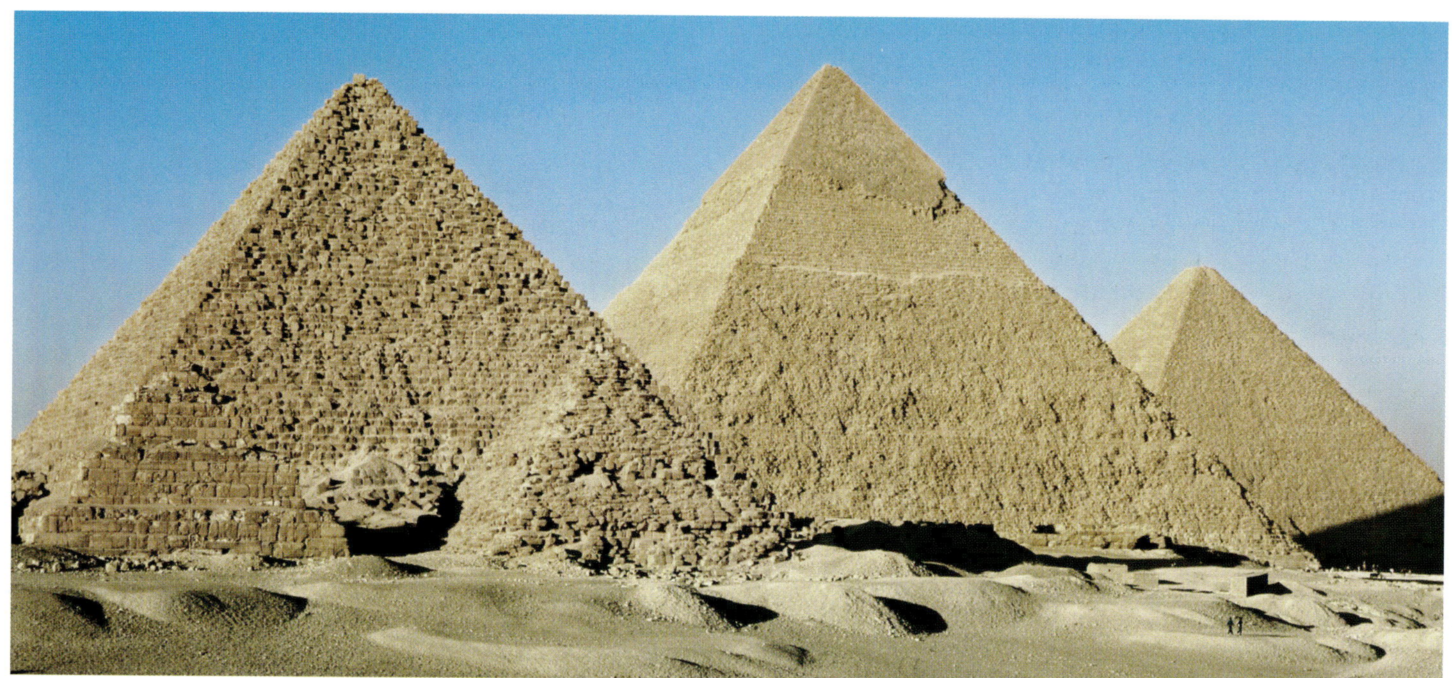

3–5 (ABOVE) **Great Pyramids**, Giza. Dynasty 4. c. 2575–2450 BCE. Erected by (from left) Menkaure, Khafre, and Khufu. Granite and limestone, height of pyramid of Khufu 450' (137 m)

The designers of the pyramids tried to ensure that the king and his tomb "home" would never be disturbed. Khufu's builders placed his tomb chamber in the very heart of the mountain of masonry, at the end of a long, narrow, steeply rising passageway, sealed off after the king's burial by a 50-ton stone block. Three false passageways, either deliberately meant to mislead or the result of changes in plan as construction progressed, obscured the location of the tomb. Despite such precautions, early looters managed to penetrate to the tomb chamber and make off with Khufu's funeral treasure.

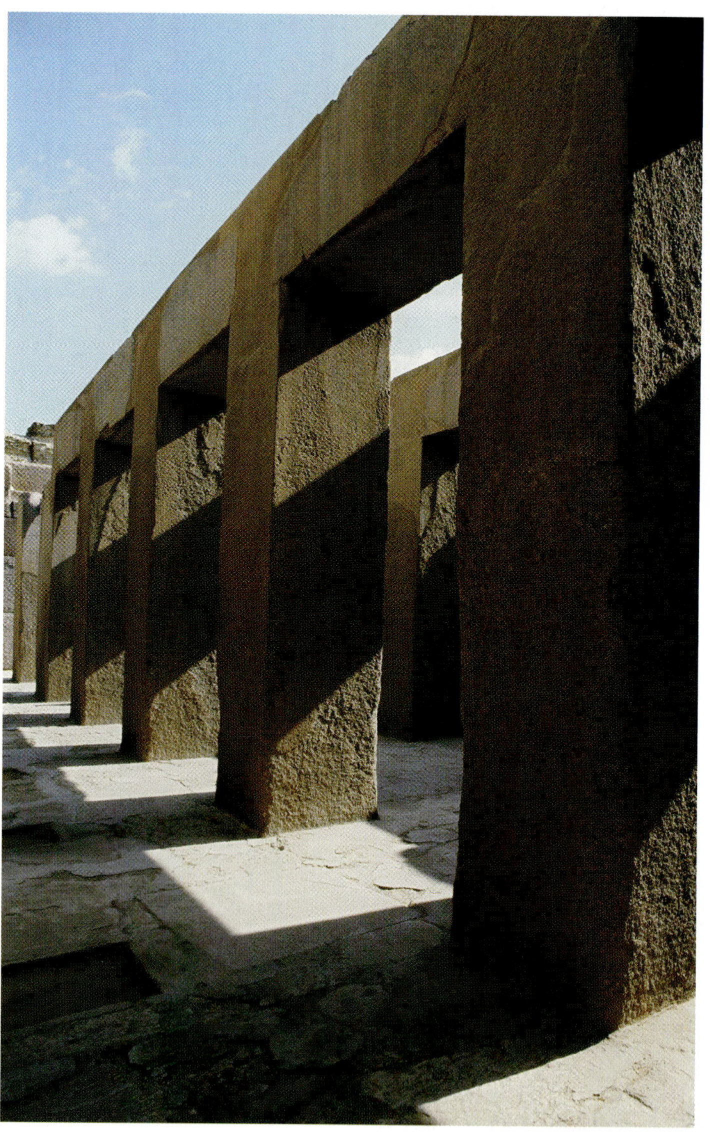

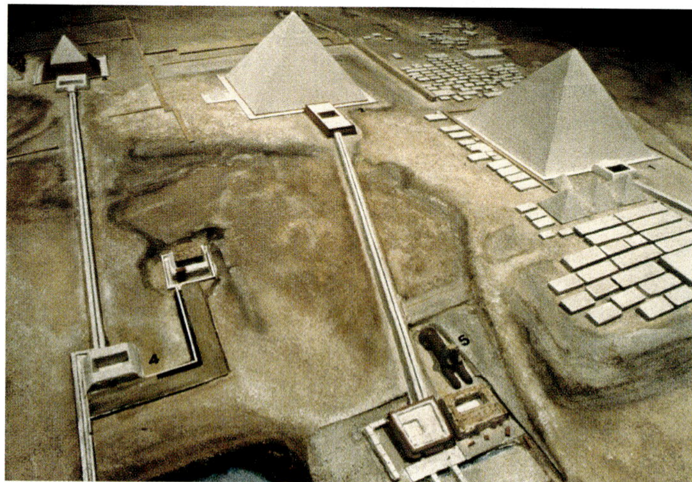

3–6 (ABOVE) **Model of the Giza plateau.** From left to right: temples and pyramids of Menkaure, Khafre, and Khufu. Prepared for the exhibition "The Sphinx and the Pyramids: One Hundred Years of American Archaeology at Giza," held in 1998 at the Harvard University Semitic Museum. Harvard University Semitic Museum, Cambridge, Massachusetts

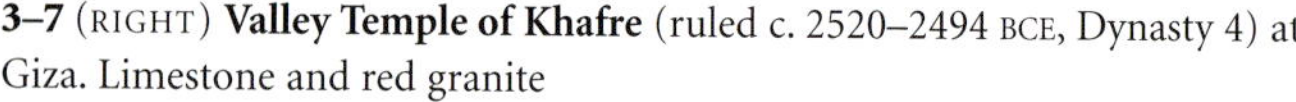

3–7 (RIGHT) **Valley Temple of Khafre** (ruled c. 2520–2494 BCE, Dynasty 4) at Giza. Limestone and red granite

the Giza pyramids is that of Khufu, which covers 13 acres at its base and originally rose to a height of about 480 feet—some 30 feet above the current summit which was originally faced with a sheath of polished limestone.

Next to each of the three pyramids was a funerary temple connected by a causeway, or elevated road, to a valley temple on the bank of the Nile (fig. **3–6**). When a king died, his body was ferried across the Nile from the royal palace to his valley temple, where it was received with elaborate ceremony. It was then carried up the causeway to the funerary temple and placed in its chapel, where further rites took place. Finally, the body was entombed in a well-hidden vault inside the pyramid.

The complex of Khafre (ruled c. 2520–2494 BCE) is the best preserved. It may be most famous for the colossal portrait of the king as a sphinx that combines his head with the body of a crouching lion (see fig. Intro–1; no. 5 on fig. 3–6). In the valley temple (fig. **3–7**) next to the sphinx, massive blocks of red granite form walls and piers supporting a flat roof, using the post-and-lintel system of stone construction (see "Post-and-Lintel and Corbel Construction," page 33). Sunlight, admitted by **clerestory** windows in the upper walls, reflected off the polished alabaster floors and illuminated the powerful statues of the king once lined up along the interior.

In three-dimensional sculpture, Egyptian artists were capable of carving arrestingly lifelike figures, particularly when representing people other than their rulers. Nevertheless a rigidly frontal, cubic conception continued to control sculpted forms, especially for members of the royal family. The compact, rectilinear solidity of Egyptian forms—a striking contrast with the cylindrical shapes of early Mesopotamian sculpture—may derive from the desire to give these statues a sense of strength and permanence, enhanced by the practical difficulties of carving hard stone such as diorite.

An over-life-size statue of Khafre (fig. **3–8**) from the valley temple of his pyramid complex represents the ruler enthroned and protected by the falcon-god Horus, who perches behind the king's head, enfolding it in his wings. Khafre wears the traditional royal costume: a short kilt, a false beard symbolic of kingship, and a folded linen headdress. He conveys a strong sense of dignity, calm, and, above all, permanence. The statue's compactness—arms pressed

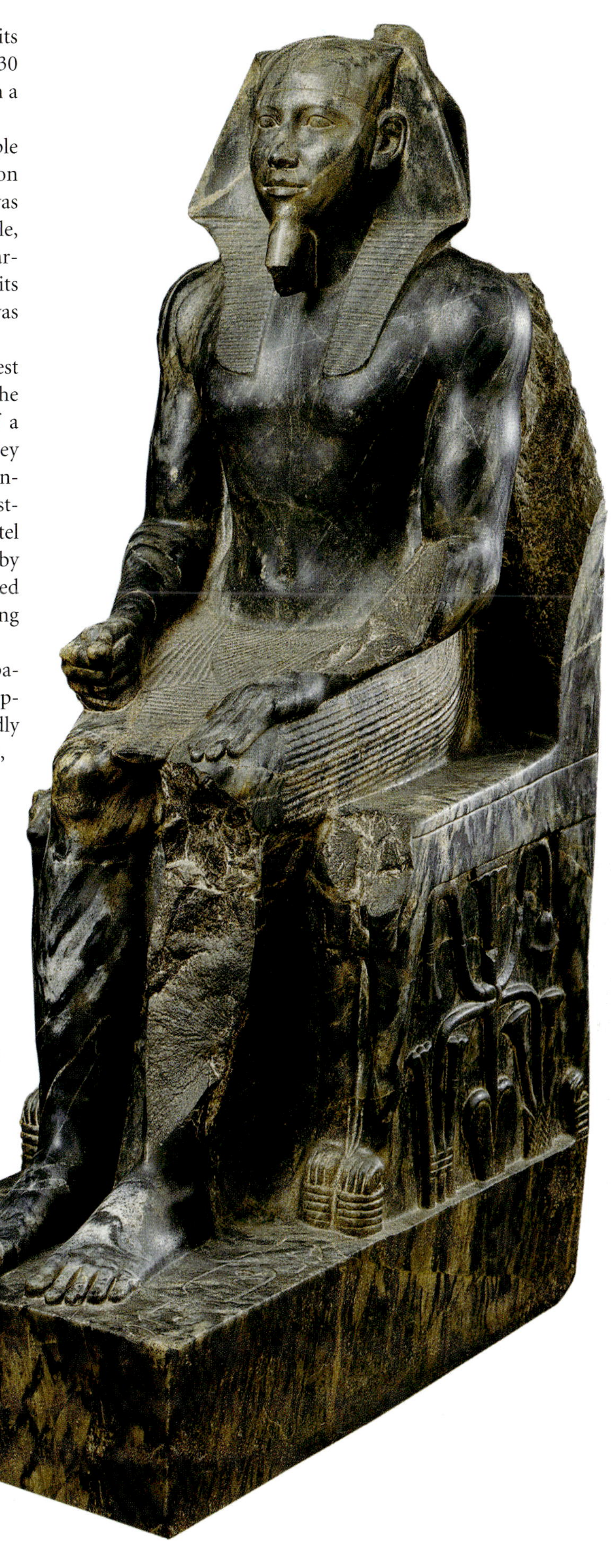

3–8 ***Khafre*** (ruled c. 2520–2494 BCE, Dynasty 4), from Giza. Anorthosite gneiss, height 5' 6⅛" (1.68 m). Egyptian Museum, Cairo

The statue was carved in an unusual material imported from Nubia. This stone produces a rare optical effect in sunlight; it glows a deep blue, the celestial color of Horus. In its original location in the valley temple, the sun would have shown through clerestory windows illuminating the alabaster floor and the figure, and creating a blue radiance around the figure.

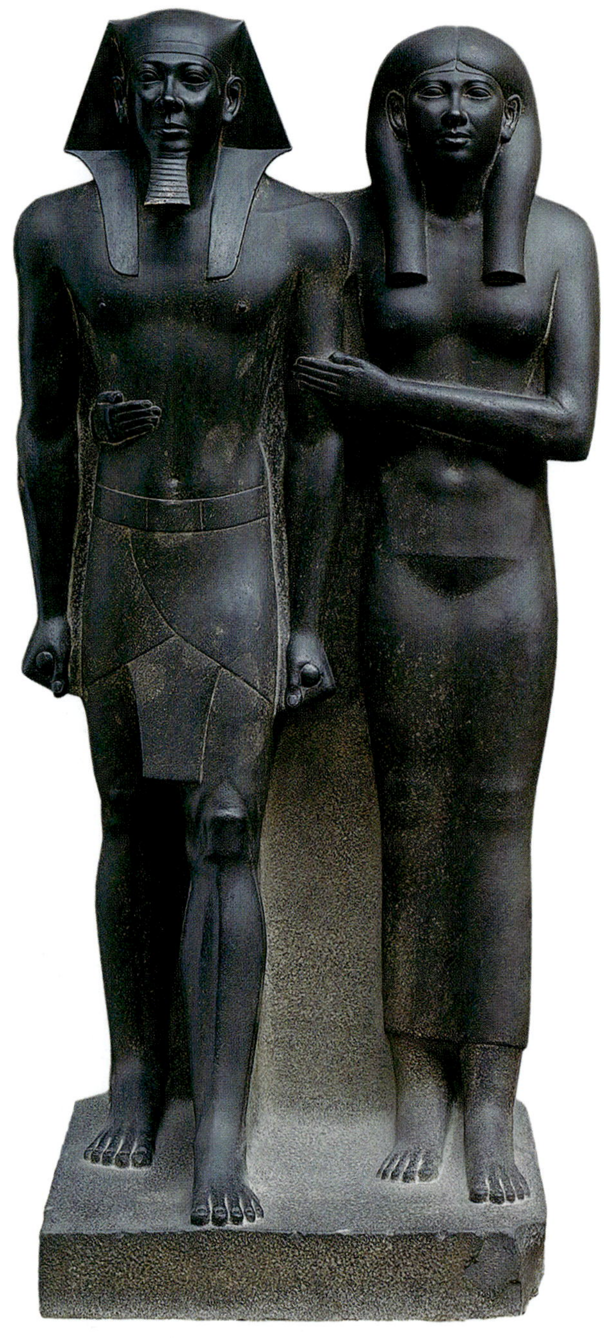

3–9 *Menkaure and a Queen, probably his principal wife Khamerernebty II* (ruled 2490–2472 BCE, Dynasty 4), from Giza. Graywacke with traces of red and black paint, height 54½" (142.3 cm). Museum of Fine Arts, Boston
PHOTOGRAPH © MUSEUM OF FINE ARTS, BOSTON, BOSTON MUSEUM OF FINE ARTS EXPEDITION (11.1738)

tightly to the body, body firmly anchored in the block—projects a sense of unwavering power in an athletic body caught at the peak of perfection.

These same formal and expressive features characterize a double portrait of Khafre's son, Menkaure (ruled c. 2490–2472 BCE), and a queen, probably his principal wife Khamerernebty II (fig. **3–9**), discovered in his valley temple. The figures, carved from a single block of stone, are visually joined by the queen's symbolic gesture of embrace. The king, depicted in accordance with cultural and political ideals as an athletic, youthful figure nude to the waist, stands in a conventional balanced pose with one foot extended, his arms straight at his sides, and his fists clenched over cylindrical objects. His equally youthful queen echoes his striding pose with a smaller step forward, and her sheer, tight-fitting garment reveals the soft curves of her body, a foil for the tight muscularity of the king.

Although not found within the three Great Pyramids, elaborate paintings and reliefs often decorated the interiors of the tombs of royalty and wealthy individuals. These images frequently show the dead person going about the duties and pleasures of earthly life, but they may also have had symbolic or religious meanings. A scene in the mastaba of a government official named Ti shows him supervising a hippopotamus hunt from a shallow boat (fig. **3–10**). The conventionally stylized, commanding figure of Ti, looms over this vibrant Nile environment. The river is depicted as a series of wavy lines, as if seen from above, but the creatures within are shown in profile to highlight their teeming activity, matched by the animals stalking birds within the papyrus at the top of the scene. In a separate boat ahead of Ti, the actual hunters, being of lesser rank and engaged in more strenuous activities, are rendered in a more lifelike and lively fashion than their master. They are captured at the

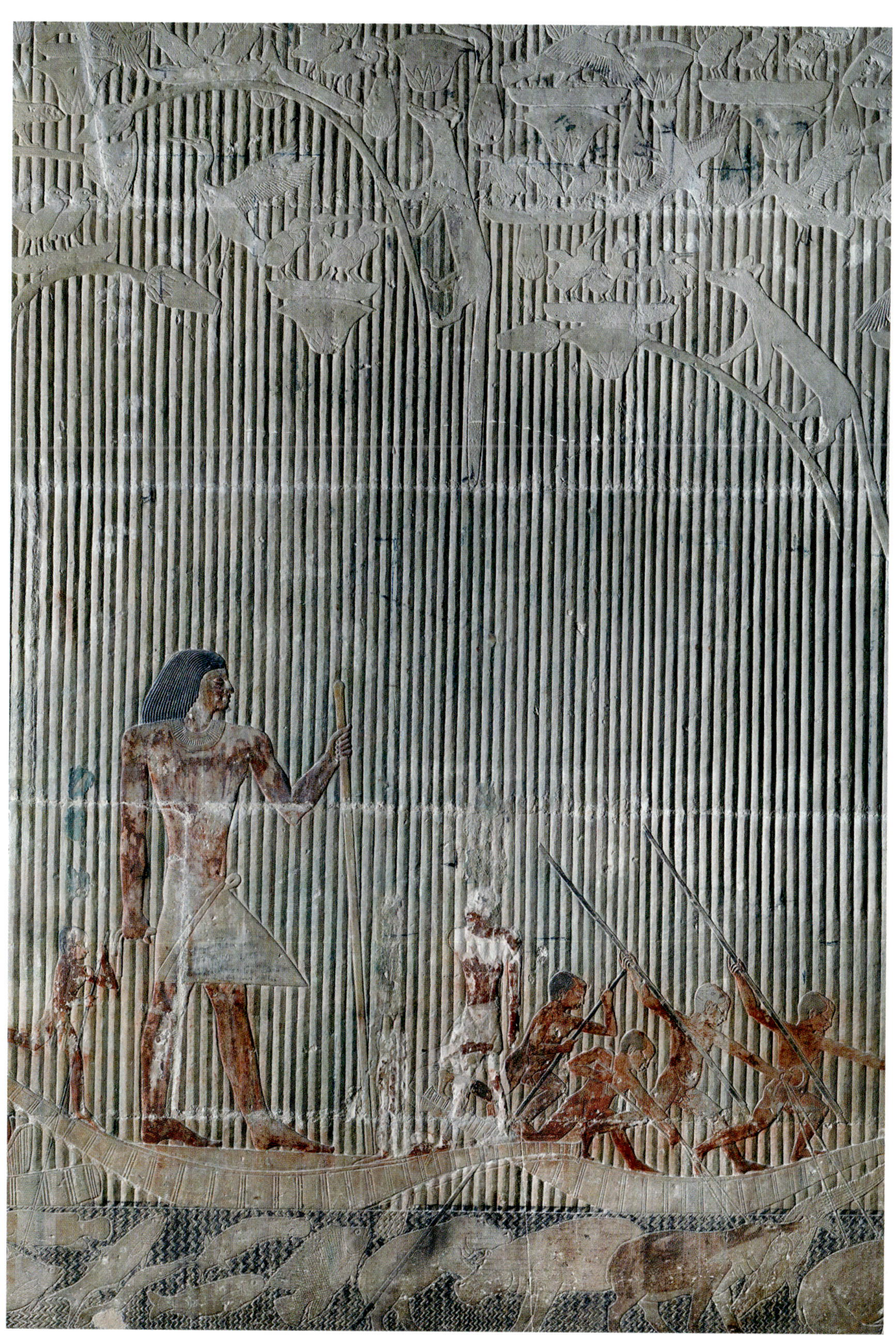

3–10 *Ti Watching a Hippopotamus Hunt*, Tomb of Ti, Saqqara. c. 2450–2325 BCE, Dynasty 5. Painted limestone relief, height approx. 45" (114.3 cm)

Surveying hippopotamus hunts was a duty of court officials like Ti. It was believed that Seth, the god of darkness, disguised himself as a hippo. Hippos were thought to be destructive since they wandered into fields, damaging crops. Thus tomb depictions of hippo hunts document the valor of the deceased and symbolize the triumph of good over evil.

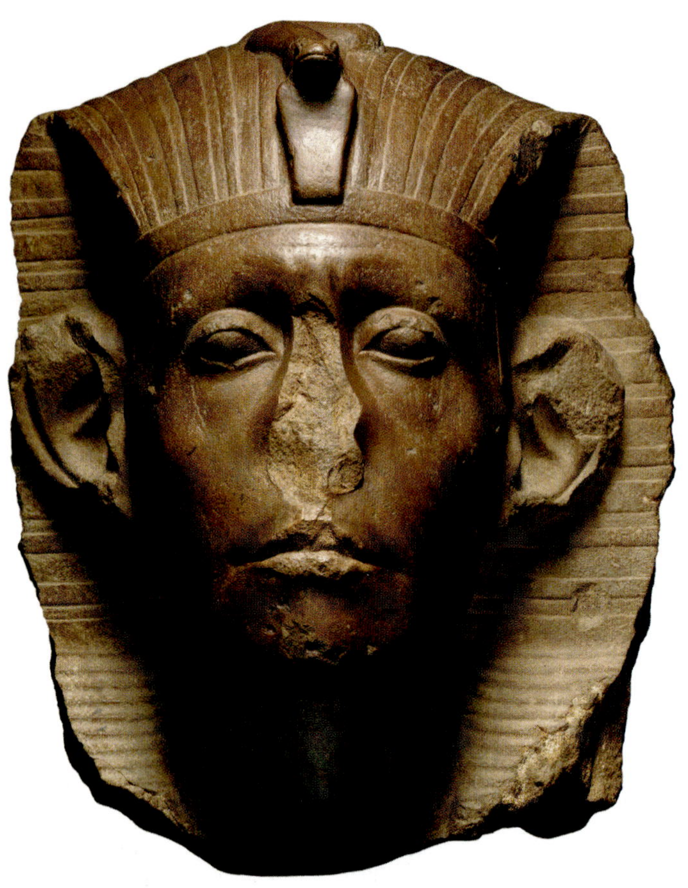

3–11 (LEFT) **Head of Senusret III** (ruled c. 1836–1818 BCE, Dynasty 12). Yellow quartzite, 17¾" × 13½" × 17" (45.1 × 34.3 × 43.2 cm). The Nelson-Atkins Museum of Art, Kansas City, Missouri

PURCHASE: WILLIAM ROCKHILL NELSON TRUST (62-11). PHOTOGRAPH: JAMISON MILLER

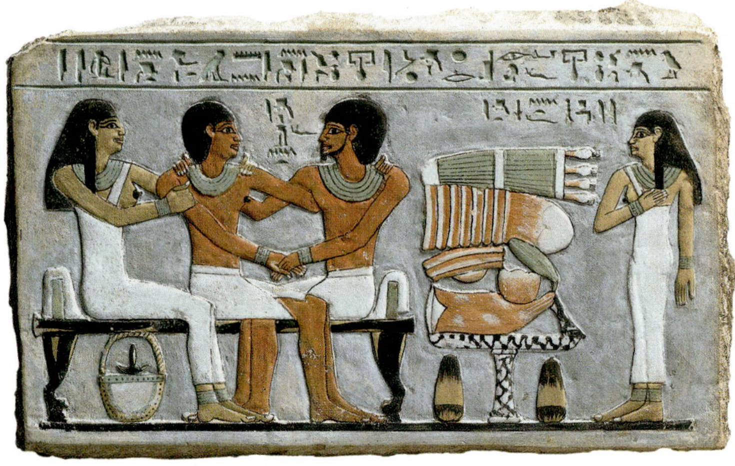

3–12 Funerary stele of Amenemhat, from Assasif (ruled c. 1938–1908 BCE, Dynasty 12). Painted limestone, 11" × 15" (30 × 50 cm). Egyptian Museum, Cairo. The Metropolitan Museum of Art, New York

EXCAVATION 1915–16

EGYPTIAN SYMBOLS

Crowned figures, symbolizing kingship, are everywhere in Egyptian art. The false beard of a god or a god-king is long and braided, and it ends in a knob. A living king is portrayed with a shorter, squared-off beard (see fig. 3–8). The cobra—"she who rears up"—was a symbol equated with the sun, the king, and other deities.

The god Horus, king of the earth and a force for good, is represented most characteristically as a falcon. The eye of Horus (*wedjat*) was regarded as symbolic of both the sun and moon. The *wedjat* here is the solar eye. The *ankh* is symbolic of everlasting life, and the scarab (beetle) was associated with the rising sun and the creator-god, Atum.

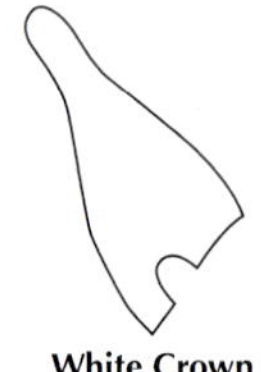

White Crown of Upper Egypt

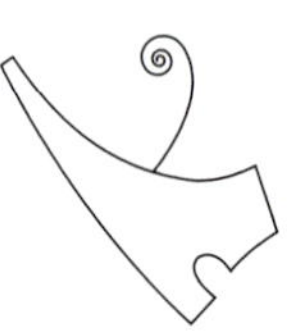

Red Crown of Lower Egypt

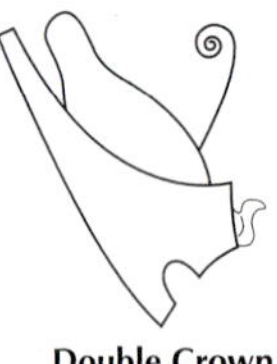

Double Crown of unified Egypt

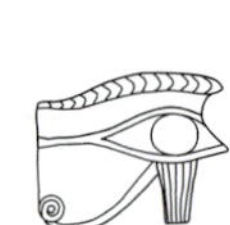

wedjat (eye of Horus)

falcon (the god Horus)

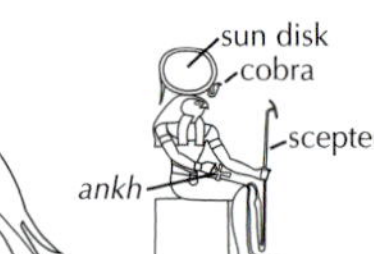

Horus

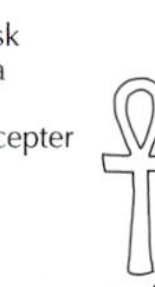

ankh

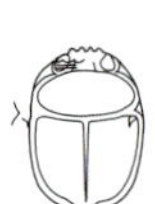

scarab

charged moment of closing in on their prey, spears positioned at the ready, legs extended for the critical lunge forward.

Middle Kingdom

About 2010 BCE, three successive kings named Mentuhotep (ruled c. 2010–c. 1938 BCE) reestablished royal power and reunited Egypt after several centuries of political disorganization. Under a stable, unified government, art and literature flourished in the Middle Kingdom, and it reflected a burgeoning awareness of the political upheaval of recent history.

Royal portraits of the Middle Kingdom do not always exhibit the self-confident formality of Old Kingdom examples. Some subjects appear to betray a special awareness of the hardship and fragility of human existence. A statue of Senusret III (ruled c. 1836–1818 BCE), dating from the Twelfth Dynasty, exudes this new sensibility (fig. **3–11**). Senusret was a dynamic king and successful general who led four military expeditions into Nubia (Egypt's neighbor to the south), overhauled the central administration at home, and did much toward regaining control over the country's increasingly independent nobles. Rather than proclaiming these achievements, however, his portrait statue seems to reveal something of his personality, even his inner thoughts. Senusret may appear wise in the ways of the world, but his sunken cheeks, drooping eyelids, and sternly set jaw suggest loneliness and melancholy. It is easy to see in this head a man burdened by the weight of his responsibilities.

In contrast, the family of Amenemhat presents a united and confident front. On his funeral stele (fig. **3–12**) a table heaped with food is watched over by a young woman named Hapi. The family sits, united by crisscrossing embraces, on a lion-legged bench. Everyone wears green jewelry and white linen garments, produced by the women in the household. Amenemhat (at the right) and his son Antel link arms and clasp hands while Iji holds her son's arm and shoulder with a firm but tender gesture, introducing a hint of narrative into this stylized tableau. Hieroglyphs identify the participants and preserve their prayers to the god Osiris.

There is little indication of how ancient Egyptians viewed the artists who created portraits of kings and nobles and recorded so many details of contemporary life, but artists must have been admired and respected. Some certainly had a high opinion of themselves. The tombstone of a Middle Kingdom sculptor claims, "I am an artist who excels in my art, a man above the common herd in knowledge. I know the proper attitude for a statue [of a man]; I know how a woman holds herself, [and how] a spearman lifts his arm. . . . There is no man famous for this knowledge other than I myself and my eldest son" (cited in Montet, page 159).

New Kingdom

During the New Kingdom (1539–1075 BCE), Egypt prospered both politically and economically. Its kings amassed great wealth and used their powerful army to surround the homeland with an empire. One of the most dynamic kings, Tutmose III of the Eighteenth Dynasty (ruled 1479–1425 BCE), even extended Egypt's influence along the eastern Mediterranean coast as far as modern Syria. Tutmose III was the first ruler to refer to himself as "pharaoh." The term means "great house" and was used the same way that people in the United States refer to the current president as "the White House." The successors of Tutmose III continued to call themselves pharaohs, and the title found its way into the Hebrew Bible and ultimately into modern usage.

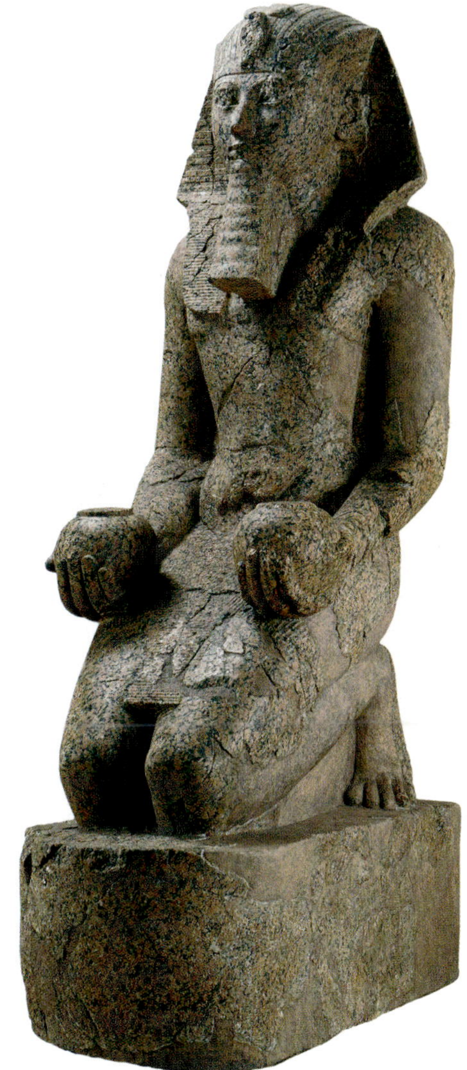

3–13 Kneeling figure of Hatshepsut, from Deir el-Bahri (ruled c. 1473–1458 BCE, Dynasty 18). Red granite, height 8' 6" (2.59 m). The Metropolitan Museum of Art, New York

One of the most intriguing political figures of the New Kingdom is Hatshepsut, wife of Tutmose III's father, Tutmose II. At her husband's death in circa 1473, Hatshepsut was declared ruler by the priests of Amun, delaying the succession of Tutmose III by 20 years. There was no artistic formula for a woman ruler in Egyptian art, yet Hatshepsut had to be portrayed in her new role. What happened reveals something fundamental about the art of ancient Egypt. She was represented as a male king (fig. **3–13**), wearing a kilt and linen headdress, occasionally even a king's false beard. The formula was not adapted to suit one individual; she was adapted to conform to convention. There could hardly be a more powerful manifestation of the premium on tradition in Egyptian royal art.

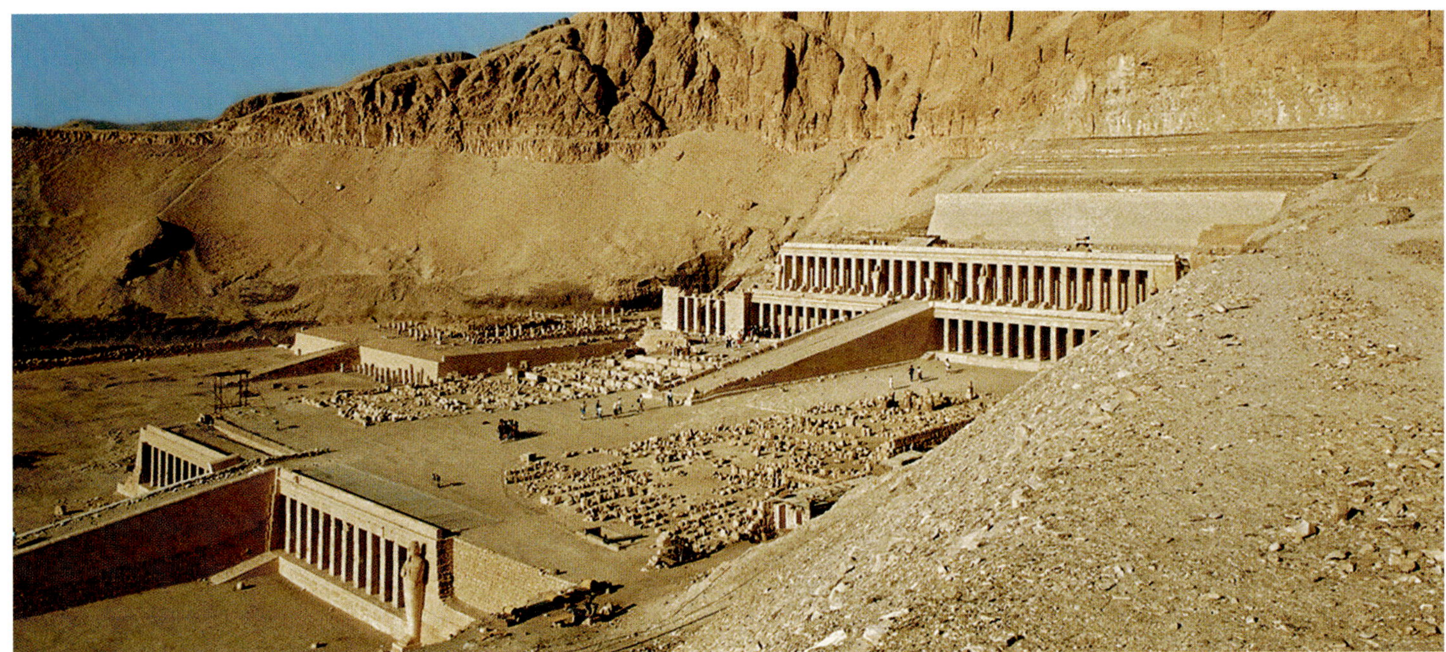

3–14 Funerary temple of Hatshepsut, Deir el-Bahri (ruled c. 1473–1458 BCE, Dynasty 18)

At the height of the New Kingdom, rulers again undertook extensive building programs, and Hatshepsut is responsible for one of the most spectacular: her funerary temple located at Deir el-Bahri (fig. **3–14**) across the Nile from the New Kingdom capital city of Thebes. This imposing complex was designed for funeral rites and commemorative ceremonies. Hatshepsut's actual tomb was hidden in the hills about a mile away. Reversing the scale relationship familiar from the Old Kingdom pyramids of Giza, here the temple is actually much larger and more prominent than the tomb itself.

Magnificently positioned against high cliffs and sensitively reflecting the natural three-part layering in the rise of the landscape—from flat desert, through a sloping hillside, to the crescendo of sheer stone cliffs—Hatshepsut's temple was constructed on three levels connected by ramps and fronted by **colonnades** (rows of columns). The colonnade on the top level led to a **hypostyle hall**, a vast column-filled space, with chapels dedicated to Hatshepsut, her father Tutmose I, and the gods Amun and Ra-Horakhty. Rare myrrh trees brought from Nubia and pools of water decorated the temple's terraces, and an elevated causeway lined with sphinxes connected the complex to a valley temple on the Nile.

Early in the New Kingdom, the priests of the god Amun in Thebes had gained such dominance that temples to the Theban triad of deities—Amun, his wife Mut, and their son Khons—became a major focus of royal patronage, rivaling the tombs and temples erected to glorify the kings themselves. Two principal temple districts arose near Thebes—one at Karnak to the north and the other at Luxor to the south.

The heart of the Great Temple of Amun at Karnak (fig. **3–15**) is a sanctuary containing the god's statue, accessed through a huge courtyard, a hypostyle hall, and a number of smaller halls and courts. Massive gateways called **pylons** set off each of these separate elements. Only kings and priests were allowed to enter the sanctuary of Amun, where priests washed and dressed the god's statue every morning. Twice a day, they offered it tempting meals.

The dominant feature of the temple complex is an enormous hypostyle hall erected in the reigns of the Nineteenth Dynasty rulers Sety I (ruled c. 1294–1279 BCE) and his son Rameses II (ruled c. 1279–1213 BCE) (fig. **3–16**). The hall, which may have been used for coronation ceremonies, is 340 feet wide and 170 feet long. Its 134 closely spaced columns supported a stepped roof of flat stones, the center section of which, resting on massive columns with lotus-flower **capitals** (sculpted block at the top of a column), rose some 30 feet above the flanking spaces (fig. **3–17**). Smaller columns with lotus-bud capitals support the roofs on each side. Piercing the side walls of the higher central section was a long row of **clerestory** (top story) window openings, which may not have provided much light, but did permit a cooling flow of air through the hall. Despite the dimness of much of the interior, artists covered nearly every inch of the columns, walls, and crossbeams with carved and painted images and inscriptions.

The traditional figural arts of New Kingdom Egypt—using a representational system that had dominated Egyptian figural art since the time of Narmer (see fig. 3–2)—reached a zenith of refinement and sophistication during the Eighteenth Dynasty reign of Amenhotep III (ruled c. 1391–1353 BCE), especially in the reliefs carved for the unfinished tomb of his vizier Ramose near Thebes (fig. **3–18**). But in this refined world of stable convention, something very jarring took place during the reign of Amenhotep III's successor. Amenhotep IV (ruled c. 1353–1336 BCE) founded a new religion honoring a single god, the life-giving sun disk Aten, and changed his own name to Akhenaten ("One Who Is Effective on Behalf of Aten"). Abandoning Thebes, the capital of Egypt since the beginning of the Eighteenth Dynasty and a stronghold of the priests of Amun, Akhenaten built a new capital city down the Nile between

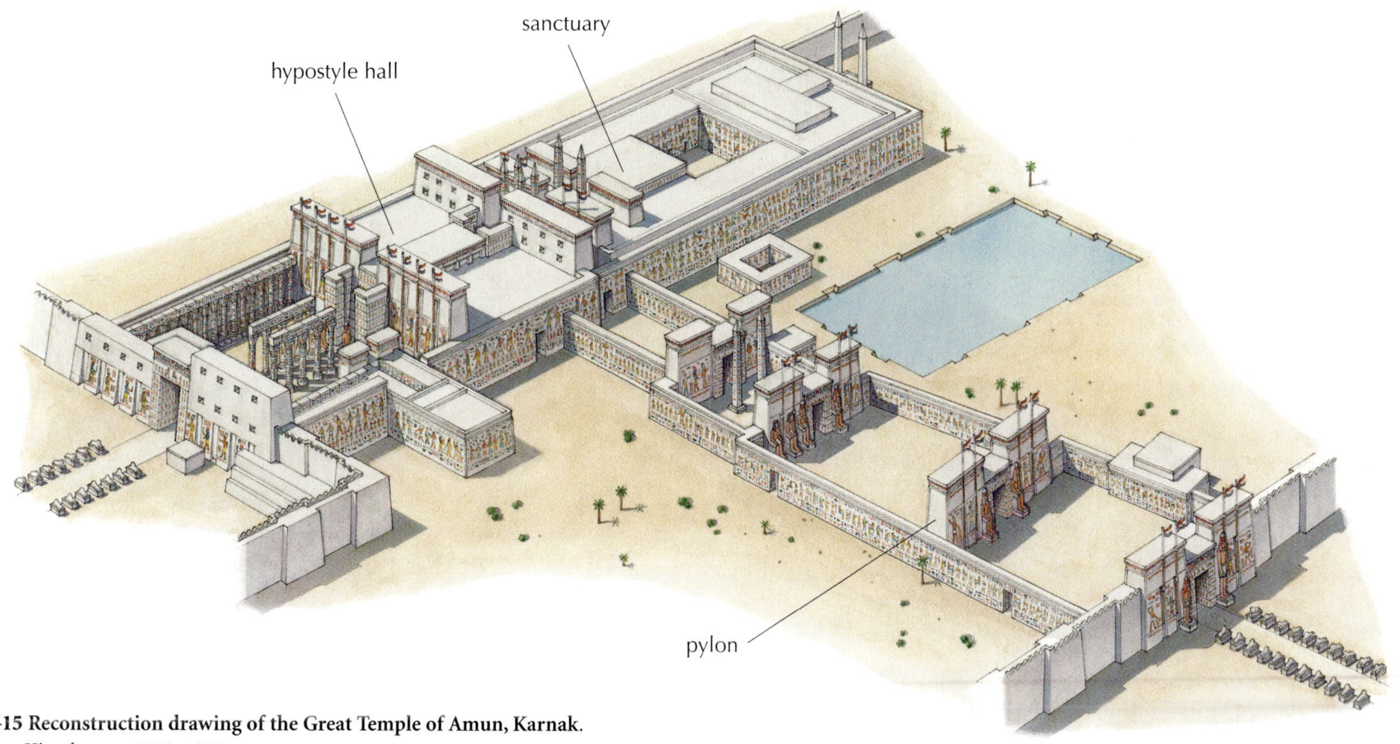

3–15 Reconstruction drawing of the Great Temple of Amun, Karnak. New Kingdom, c. 1579–1075 BCE

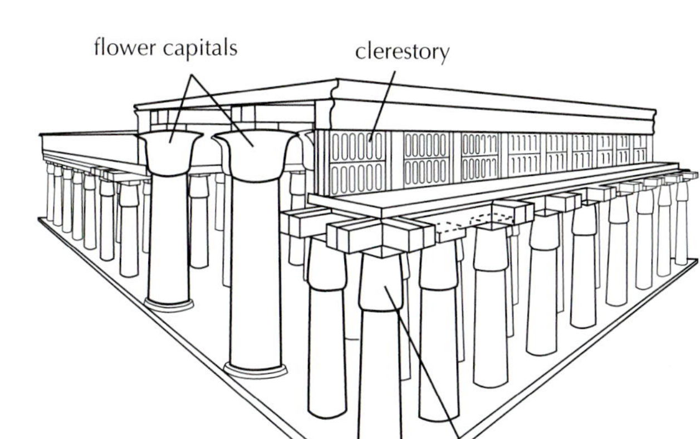

3–16 Reconstruction drawing of the hypostyle hall, Great Temple of Amun, Karnak. c. 1292–1190 BCE, Dynasty 19

Giza and Thebes, naming it Akhetaten ("Horizon of the Aten"). Using the modern name for this site, Tell el-Amarna, historians refer to Akhenaten's reign as the Amarna period.

Akhenaten saw himself as Aten's son, and he presided over the worship of Aten as a divine priest. His principal queen, Nefertiti, served as a divine priestess. Temples to Aten were open courtyards, where altars could be bathed in the direct rays of the sun. In art, Aten is depicted as a round sun disk sending down long, thin rays ending in human hands, some of which hold the *ankh* (see "Egyptian Symbols," page 66).

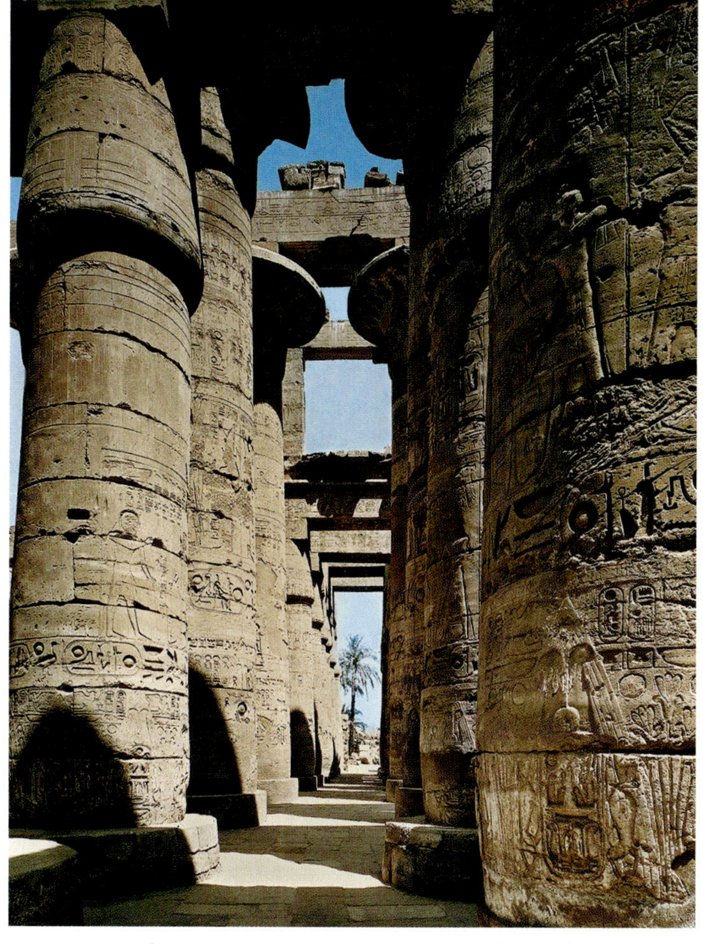

3–17 Flower and bud columns, hypostyle hall, Great Temple of Amun, Karnak

CLOSER LOOK

As mayor of Thebes and vizier (principal royal advisor or minister) to both Amenhotep III (ruled c. 1391–1353 BCE) and Amenhotep IV (ruled 1353–c. 1336 BCE), Ramose was second only to the pharaoh himself in power and prestige. Soon after his ascent to political prominence, he began construction of an elaborate tomb comprised of four rooms, including an imposing transverse hypostyle hall 80 feet wide. Walls were covered with paintings or with shallow relief carvings, celebrating the accomplishments, affiliations, and lineage of Ramose and his wife Merytptah, or visualizing the funeral rites that would take place after their death. But the tomb was not used by Ramose. Decoration ceased in the fourth year of Amenhotep IV's reign, when he renamed himself Akhenaten and relocated the court from Thebes to the new city of Akhetaten. Presumably Ramose moved with the court to the new capital, but neither his name nor a new tomb has been discovered there.

The tomb was abandoned in various stages of incompletion. The reliefs were never painted, and some walls preserve only preliminary sketches that would have guided the sculptors. But the works that were executed are among the most sophisticated relief carvings in the history of art. On one wall, Ramose and his wife appear, hosting a banquet for their family. All are portrayed at the same moment of youthful perfection, even though they represent two successive generations. We stand in awe of the technical skill demonstrated in the depiction of these untroubled and majestic couples: the dazzling textural differentiation of skin, hair, and cloth; the easy elegance of linear continuity realized in a medium where fluidity is not simple to obtain; the convincing sense of three-dimensionality managed within an extraordinarily shallow depth of relief. In this detail of Ramose's brother and sister-in-law (fig. **3–18**), the traditional ancient Egyptian marital embrace (see figs. 3–9, 3–12) takes on a new tenderness, recalling—especially within the eternal stillness of a tomb—the words of a New Kingdom love poem:

> While unhurried days come and go,
> Let us turn to each other in quiet affection,
> Walk in peace to the edge of old age.
> (Foster, page 18)

The conceptual conventions of Egyptian figural representation are rendered in the tomb of Ramose reliefs with such warmth, refinement, and technical virtuosity that they become almost believable. Our rational awareness of their artificiality is momentarily eclipsed by their sheer beauty.

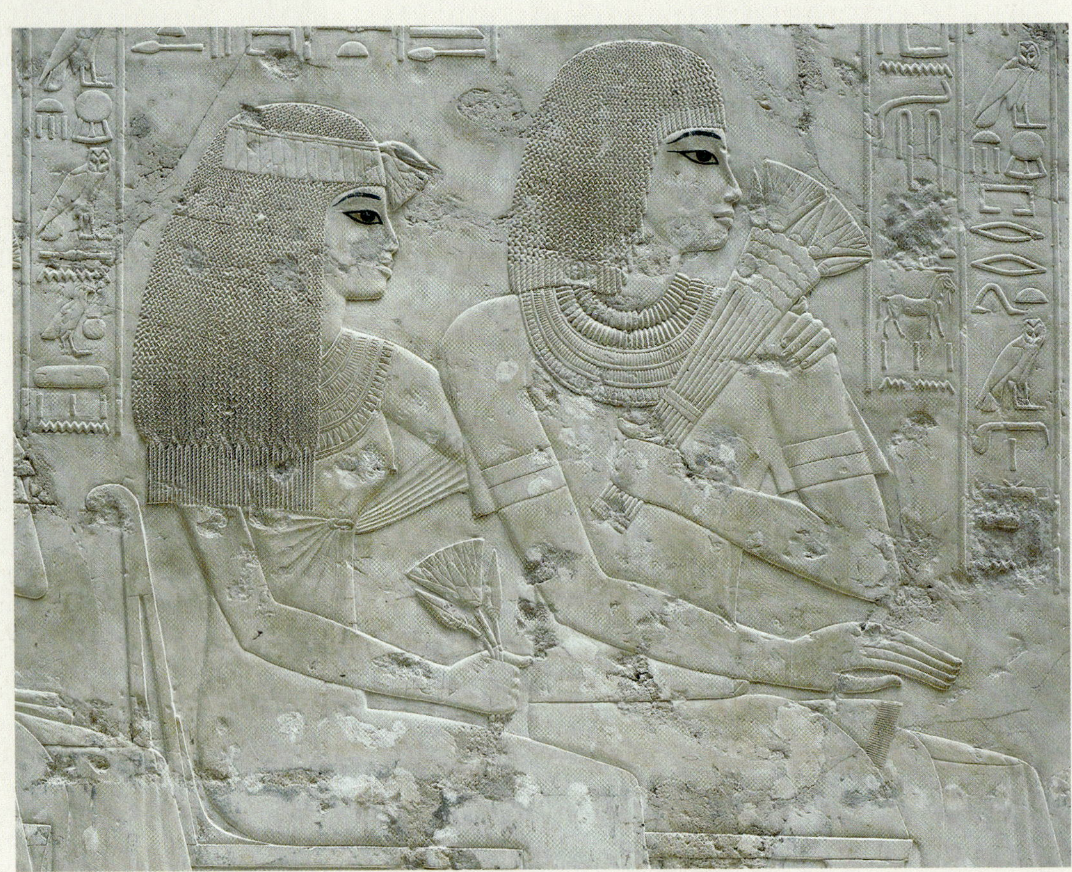

3–18 ***Ramose's brother Mai and his wife Urel***, from the tomb of Ramose, Thebes. c. 1375–1365 BCE, Dynasty 18

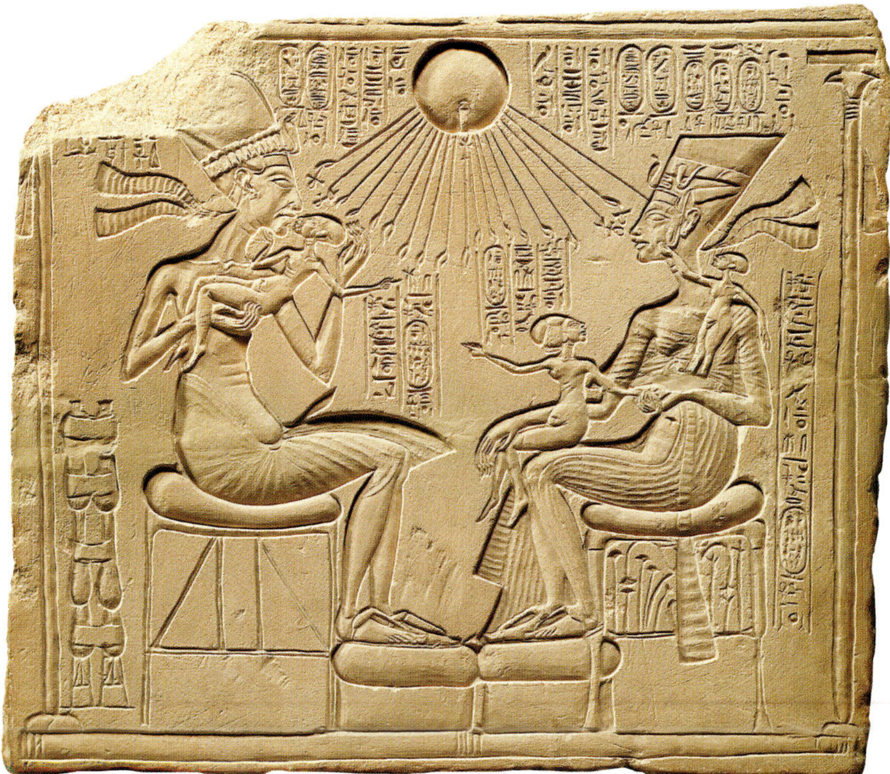

3–19 ***Akhenaten and his Family***, from Akhetaten (modern Tell el-Amarna). c. 1353–1336 BCE, Dynasty 18. Painted limestone relief, 12¼" × 15¼" (31.1 × 38.7 cm). Staatliche Museen zu Berlin, Preussischer Kulturbesitz, Ägyptisches Museum

Egyptian relief sculptors often employed the technique seen here, called ***sunken relief****. In ordinary reliefs, the background is carved back so that the figures project out from the finished surface. In sunken relief, the original flat surface of the stone is reserved as background, and the outlines of the figures are deeply incised, permitting the development of three-dimensional forms within the stone block.*

Akhenaten's reign not only saw the creation of a new capital and the rise of a new religion; it also led to radical changes in artistic conventions. In portraits of the king, artists subjected his representation to startling stylizations, even physical distortions: spindly arms and legs; a protruding stomach; swelling thighs; full breasts; and an attenuated, thin neck supporting an elongated, misshapen skull. A relief of Akhenaten, Queen Nefertiti, and three of their daughters exemplifies the new style (fig. **3–19**). What a striking contrast with the relief from Ramose's tomb! The king and queen sit on cushioned thrones playing with their nude children, whose elongated shaved heads conform to the newly minted figural type. The artist has conveyed the fidgety, engaging behavior of the children and the loving involvement of their parents in a manner not even hinted at in earlier royal portraiture. The couple receives the blessings of Aten, whose rays ending in hands penetrate the open pavilion to offer *ankh*s before the royal nostrils, giving them the "breath of life."

In a famed portrait of Nefertiti by the Akhetaten sculptor Tutmose, her refined, regular features, long neck, and heavy-lidded eyes seem almost too perfect to be human (fig. **3–20**), but eerily

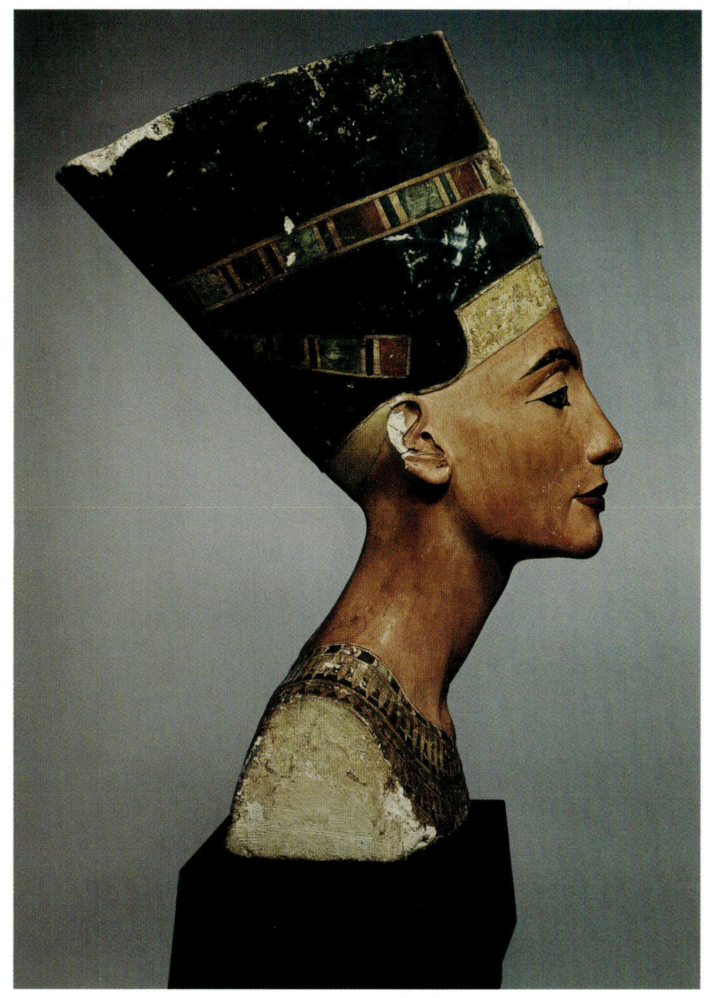

3–20 Tutmose. ***Nefertiti***, from Akhetaten (modern Tell el-Amarna). c. 1353–1336 BCE, Dynasty 18. Painted limestone, height 20" (51 cm). Staatliche Museen zu Berlin, Preussischer Kulturbesitz, Ägyptisches Museum

This famous head was discovered, along with drawings and other items relating to commissions for the royal family, in the studio of the sculptor Tutmose at Akhetaten, the capital city during the Amarna period. Bust portraits, consisting solely of the head and shoulders, were rare in New Kingdom art. Scholars believe that Tutmose may have made this one as a finished model to follow in carving or painting other images of his royal patron.

consistent with standards of beauty in our own culture. Part of the appeal of this head may be the artist's dramatic use of color. The hues of the blue headdress and its striped band are repeated in the rich red, blue, green, and gold of the jeweled necklace. The dark density of their patterns set off the sleek, elegant contours of her revealed neck and head.

Akhenaten's goals were actively supported not only by Nefertiti but also by his mother, Queen Tiy, who played a significant role in affairs of state during the reign of Akhenaten's father, Amenhotep III. Queen Tiy's personality emerges from a miniature portrait-head that reveals the exquisite bone structure of her dark-skinned face, with its arched brows, uptilted eyes, and slightly pouting lips (fig. **3–21**).

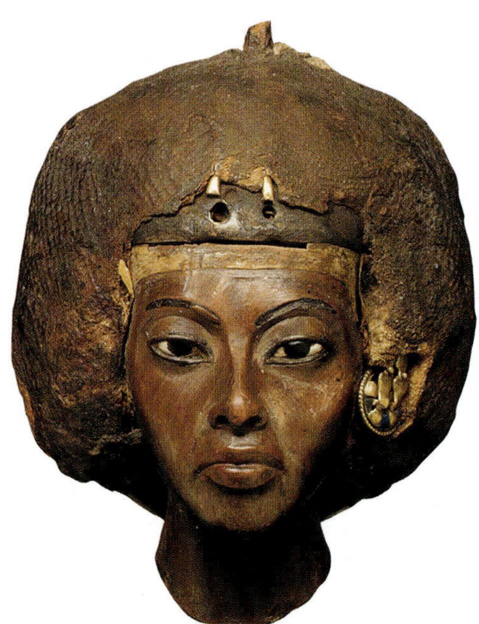

3–21 ***Queen Tiy***, from Kom Medinet el-Ghurab (near el-Lahun). c. 1352 BCE, Dynasty 18. Boxwood, ebony, glass, gold, lapis lazuli, cloth, clay, and wax, height 3¾" (9.4 cm). Staatliche Museen zu Berlin, Preussischer Kulturbesitz, Ägyptisches Museum

Akhenaten's new religion and revolutionary reconception of pharaonic art outlived him by only a few years, at which time the priesthood of Amun quickly regained its former power. The young king Tutankhaten (ruled c. 1332–1322 BCE) returned the capital to Thebes and reasserted traditional religious beliefs, changing his name, which meant "Living Image of the Aten," to Tutankhamun, "Living Image of Amun." He died young and was buried in the Valley of the Kings, across the Nile from Thebes. The undisturbed inner chambers of Tutankhamun's tomb, discovered in 1922, contained great treasures, including jewelry, textiles, furniture, a carved and inlaid throne, and four gold chariots. The king's mummified body, crowned with a spectacular mask preserving his royal likeness (fig. 3–1), lay inside three nested coffins. Like the funerary mask, the innermost coffin (fig. **3–22**) was made of solid gold, decorated with colored enamelwork, semiprecious stones, and very finely incised linear designs. The king holds a crook (a shepherd's staff) and a flail (a harvesting tool used to separate grains from their husks) that symbolize his power as provider and protector to his people, and that associate him with Osiris, a fertility and vegetation god who presided over the dead and the underworld.

Egyptian funerary practices revolved around Osiris, his resurrection, and a belief in the continuity of life after death for the righteous. The dead were thought to undergo a "last judgment" consisting of two tests presided over by Osiris and supervised by the god Anubis, jackel-headed overseer of funerals and cemeteries. The deceased were first questioned by a delegation of deities about their behavior in life. Then their hearts, which the Egyptians believed to be the seat of the soul, were weighed on a scale against an ostrich

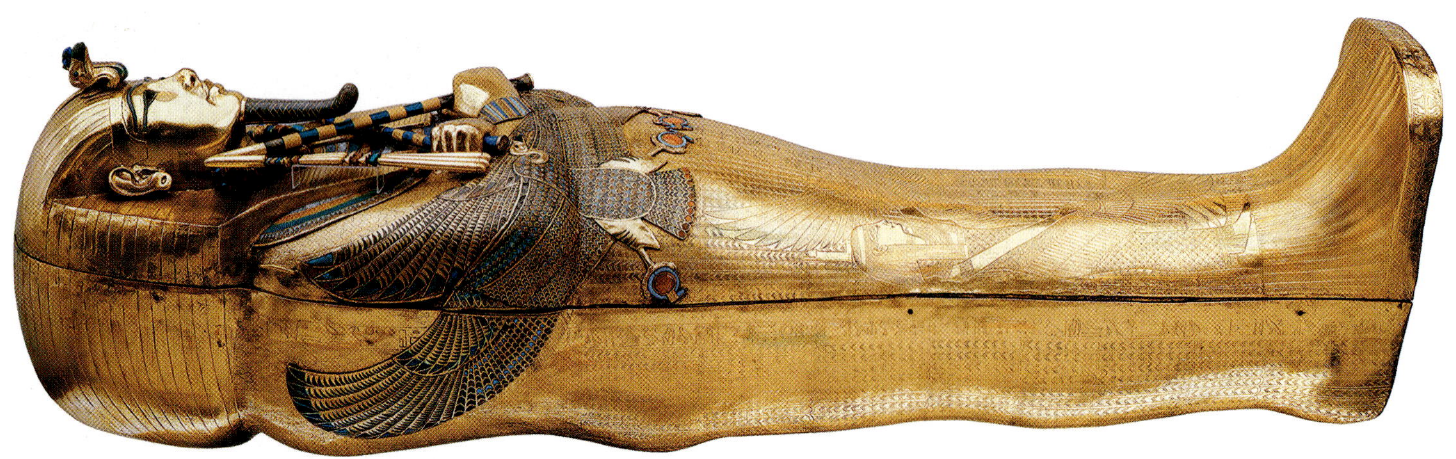

3–22 Inner coffin of Tutankhamun, from the tomb of Tutankhamun, Valley of the Kings (ruled 1332–1322 BCE, Dynasty 18). Gold inlaid with glass and semiprecious stones, height 6' ⅞" (1.85 m), weight nearly 243 lbs (110.4 kg). Egyptian Museum, Cairo

MUMMIES

No actual ancient Egyptian recipes for preserving the dead have been found, but the basic process can be gleaned from several sources, including images found in tombs, the descriptions of later Greek writers, scientific analysis of mummies, and modern experiments. The process was roughly as follows.

The dead body was taken to a mortuary, a special structure used exclusively for embalming. Under the supervision of a priest, embalmers removed the brain, generally through the nose, and emptied the body cavity through an incision in the left side. They then placed the body, together with its major internal organs, in a vat of natron, a naturally occurring salt. The body was left to steep in this solution for a period of a month or more, which caused the skin to blacken. Once workers had retrieved the body from the vat and carefully dried it, they often dyed it to restore something of its color; they used red ocher for a man and yellow ocher for a woman. Embalmers then packed the body cavity with clean linen—provided by the family of the deceased—that had been soaked in various herbs and ointments. They wrapped the major organs in separate packets, either putting them in special containers called "canopic jars" to be placed in the tomb chamber or stuffing them back in the body.

The tedious ritual of wrapping the body could now begin. Embalmers first wound the trunk and each of the limbs separately with cloth strips and then wrapped the whole body in a shroud before winding it in additional strips of cloth, layer after layer, to produce the familiar mummy shape. Good luck charms and other small objects were often inserted among the wrappings. If the family provided one, a Book of the Dead (see fig. 3–23)—a selection of magic spells meant to help the deceased survive a "last judgment" and win everlasting life—was tucked in between the mummy's legs.

feather, the symbol of Maat, goddess of truth. A monster named Ammit, the "Eater of the Dead," waited beside the scale to devour those who tipped the balance.

These beliefs gave rise to additional funerary practices especially popular among the nonroyal classes. Family members commissioned papyrus scrolls—"Books of the Dead"—containing magical texts or spells to help the dead survive and pass the tests (see "Mummies," above). A scene from a Nineteenth Dynasty example, created for a man named Hunefer, shows him at successive stages in his induction into the afterlife (fig. **3–23**). At the left, Anubis leads Hunefer to the spot where he will weigh the man's heart in a tiny jar. After passing the test recorded by the ibis-headed god, Thoth, Hunefer is presented by the god Horus to the enthroned Osiris, holding his usual crook and flail.

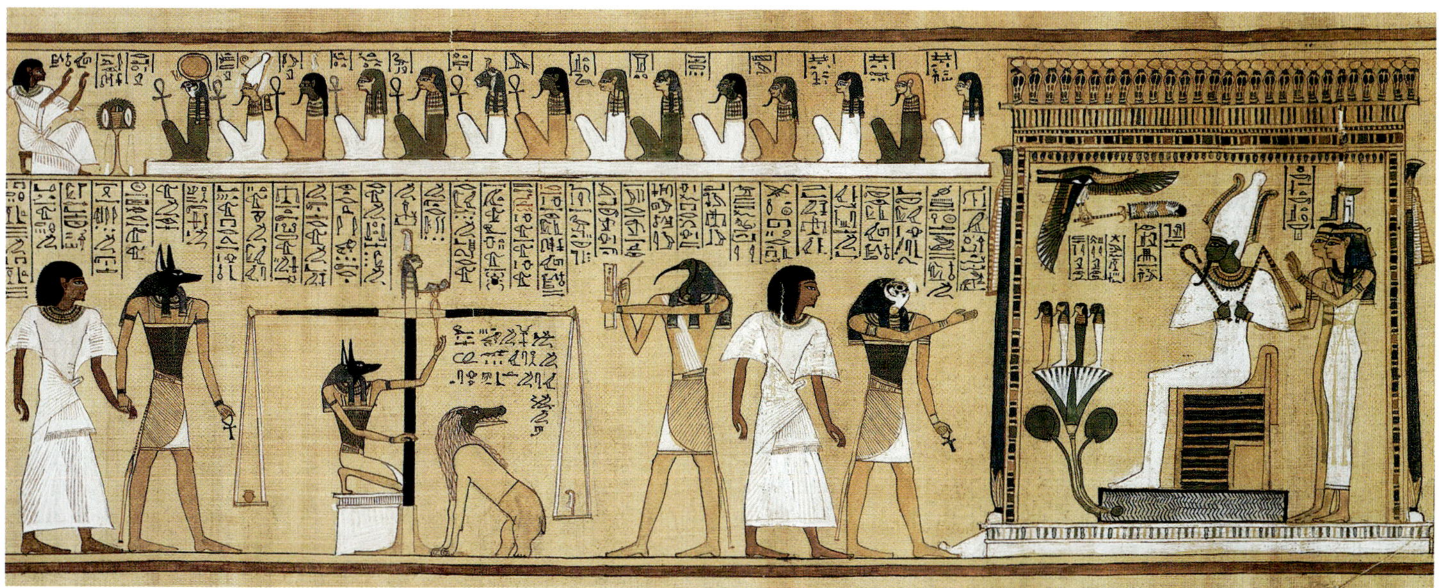

3–23 ***Judgment of Hunefer before Osiris***, illustration from a Book of the Dead. c. 1285 BCE, Dynasty 19. Painted papyrus, height 15⅝" (39.8 cm). The British Museum, London

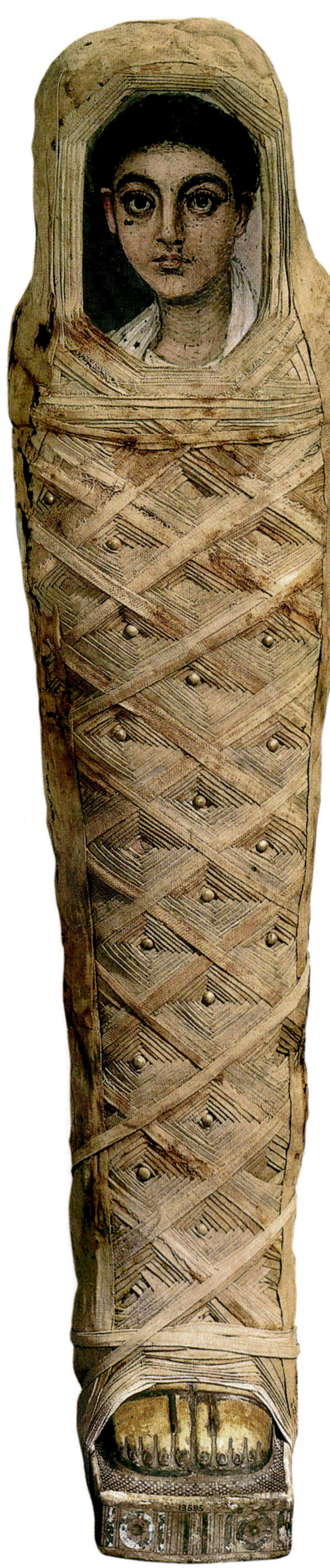

Late Egyptian Art

In 332 BCE, the Macedonian Greeks, led by Alexander the Great, conquered Egypt. After Alexander's death in 323 BCE, his generals divided up his empire. Ptolemy took Egypt, declaring himself king in 305. The Ptolemaic Dynasty ended with the death of Cleopatra VII (ruled 51–30 BCE), when Egypt became part of the Roman Empire.

Not surprisingly, works from this late period combined the conventions of Greco-Roman and Egyptian art. For example, the tradition of mummifying the dead continued well into Egypt's Roman period, and hundreds of mummies from that time have been found in the Fayum region of Lower Egypt. The mummy becomes a "soft sculpture," and instead of a stylized mask (see fig. 3–1), a Roman-style portrait (fig. **3–24**) painted on a wood panel in **encaustic** (hot colored wax) is inserted over the face. Although great staring eyes invariably dominate such images—as they had in the funerary mask of Tutankhamun—their artists carefully recorded individual features of the deceased, providing a link between Egyptian art and emphasis on portraiture that we will discover in the art of ancient Rome.

Looking Back

All cultures have rules for representing people, things, and ideas, but Egyptian conventions are among the most distinctive and long-lived in the history of art. Everything is represented from its most characteristic viewpoint: profile heads sit on frontal shoulders and stare out at viewers with frontal eyes. And Egyptian art is geometrically conceived and sleekly stylized, often abstract and conceptual in design. Symbols are established early on and endure for almost two millennia. Stability was clearly valued over change.

Egyptian art and history has been divided into three principal periods known as the Old, Middle, and New Kingdoms. The Old Kingdom was a heroic age of funerary art and architecture whose most famous works—the pyramids and sphinx at Giza—define the essence of Egyptian art for most people. The Middle Kingdom saw an increase in sensitive and more personal art. In the New Kingdom, proud rulers focused extraordinary resources on building temples and expanding the Egyptian Empire. During the Eighteenth Dynasty, Akhenaten even attempted to redirect the course of history, religion, and art, but the powerful conventions he tried to replace returned in the rule of his successor Tutankhamun. The discovery of this late pharaoh's tomb in 1922 ignited an international enthusiasm for Egyptian art that lasts to this day.

3–24 Mummy wrapping of a young boy, Hawara. c. 100–120 CE, Roman period. Linen with gilded stucco buttons and inserted portrait in encaustic on wood, height of mummy 53⅜" (133 cm); portrait 9½" × 6½" (24 × 16.5 cm). The British Museum, London

IN PERSPECTIVE

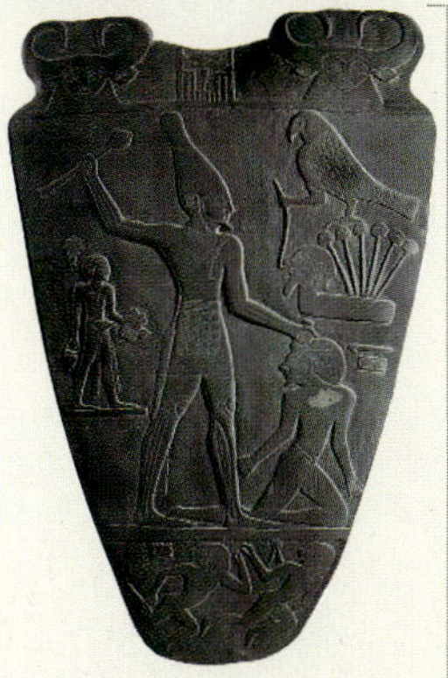

PALETTE OF NARMER, c. 2950–2775 BCE

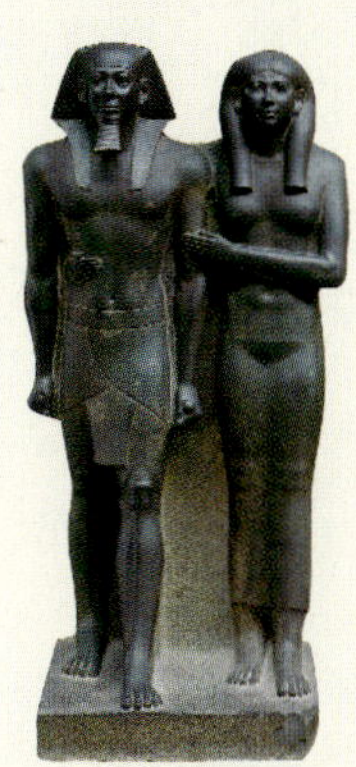

MENKAURE AND QUEEN, ruled 2490–2472 BCE

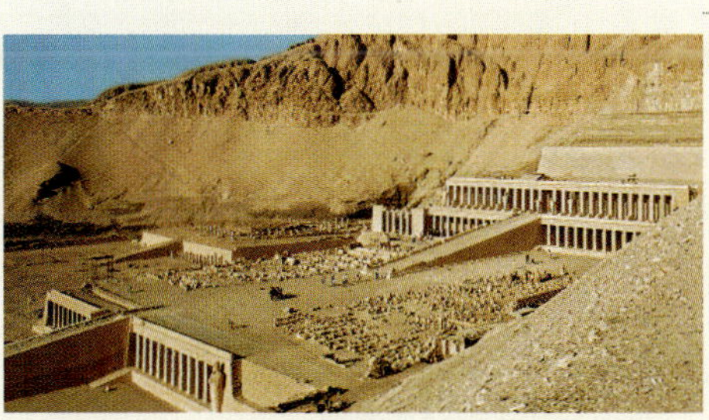

FUNERARY TEMPLE OF HATSHEPSUT, ruled c. 1473–1458 BCE

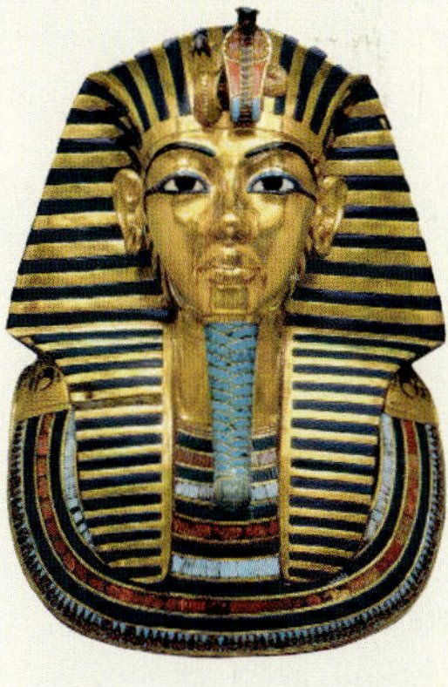

FUNERARY MASK OF TUTANKHAMUN, ruled 1332–1322 BCE

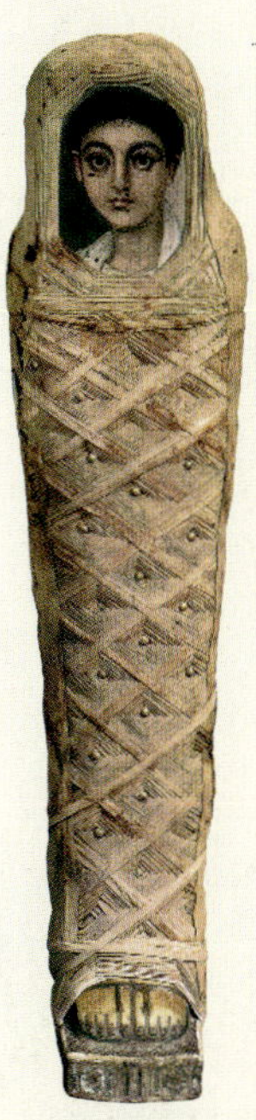

MUMMY WRAPPING OF A YOUNG BOY, c. 100–120 CE

3500 BCE

- **Early Dynastic,** c. 2950–2575 BCE
- **Djoser,** ruled c. 2650–2631 BCE

2500

- **Old Kingdom,** c. 2575–2150 BCE
- **Khafre,** ruled c. 2520–2494 BCE
- **First Intermediate Period,** c. 2125–1975 BCE

2000

- **Middle Kingdom,** c. 1975–c. 1640 BCE
- **Senusret III,** ruled c. 1836–1818 BCE
- **Second Intermediate Period,** c. 1630–1520 BCE

1500

- **New Kingdom,** c. 1579–1075 BCE
- **Hatshepsut,** ruled c. 1473–1458 BCE
- **Amarna,** c. 1353–1336 BCE
- **Akhenaten,** ruled c. 1353–1336 BCE
- **Tutankhamun,** ruled c. 1332–1322 BCE

1000

- **Third Intermediate Period,** c. 1075–715 BCE
- **Late Period,** c. 715–332 BCE

500

- **Conquest of Alexander the Great,** in 332 BCE
- **Ptolemaic Period,** c. 323–30 BCE
- **Roman Period,** c. 30 BCE–395 CE

1 CE

500

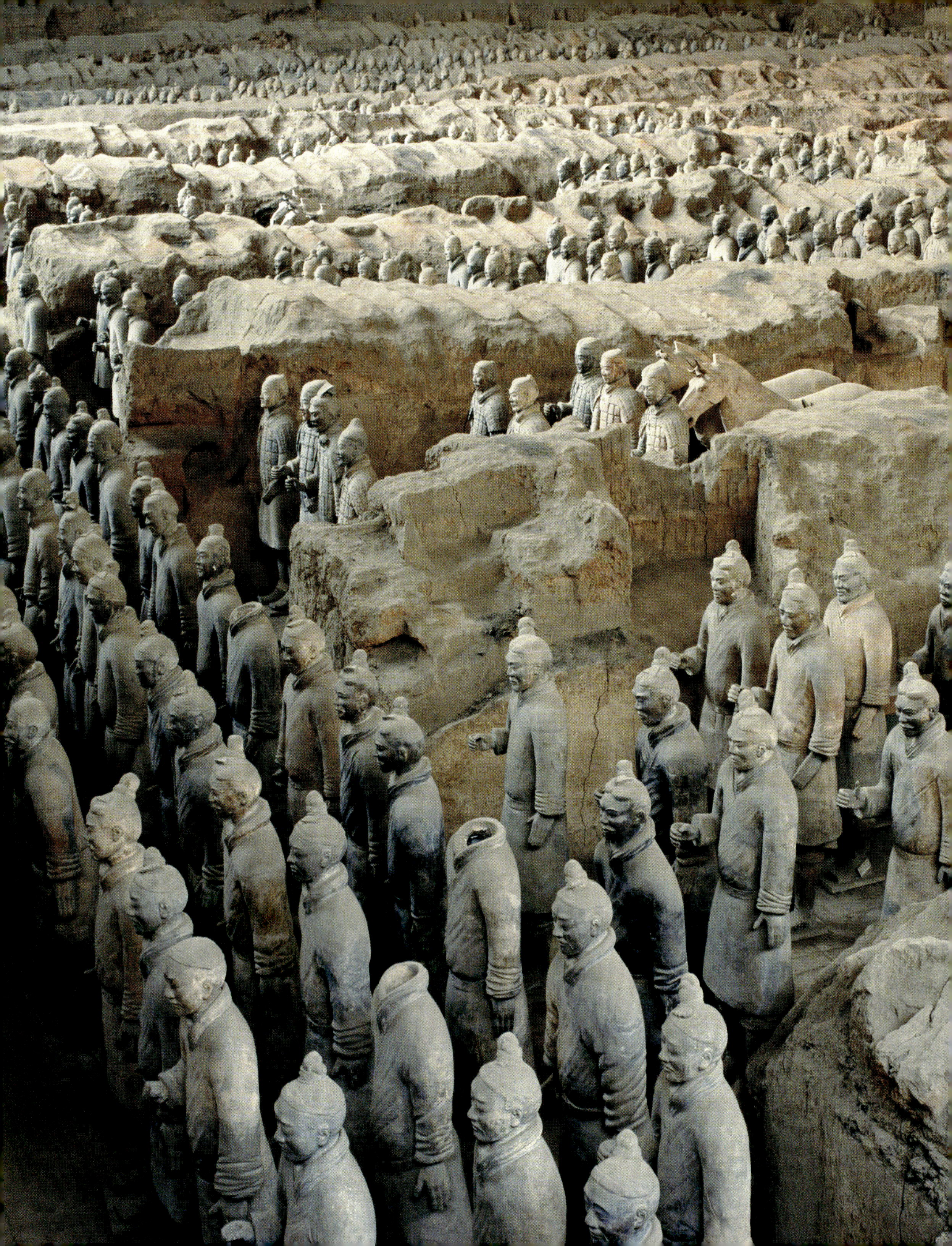

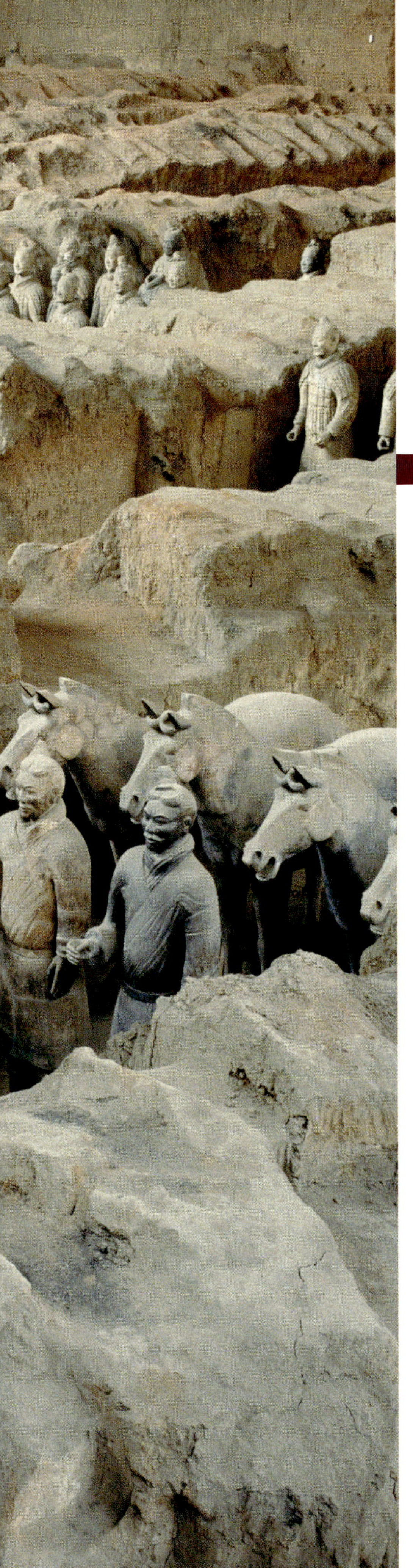

4 Early Asian Art

LOOKING FORWARD

How can we understand the fierce determination and driving will that could lead a single man to conceive of himself as ruler of the world, a man who believed that his right to reign was bestowed by supernatural powers and that he was the son of heaven? Between 221 BCE when he brought the warring states under his control until his death in 210 BCE, the first emperor of Qin, Shihuangdi, turned his vast lands of China into a unified state. His tremendous actions were simple, direct, and brilliant. To govern the Qin Empire, he created a bureaucracy—an intricate, hierarchical network—based on competence, not family heritage, and guided by a code of law. He united his lands with a common language and system of writing and more than 4,000 miles of roads. He brought prosperity by building canals and an irrigation system to increase agricultural production and by facilitating trade through uniform weights and measures. In fact, the name Qin (pronounced "chin") is the source of the name China.

During Emperor Shihuangdi's life, a huge army—historians write of 300,000 men—defended his empire. After his death, an underground army of thousands of life-size, disciplined and alert terracotta figures stood in battle array guarding his tomb, poised to defend their emperor throughout eternity (fig. **4–1**). These subterranean soldiers were hidden from view by mounds of earth that eventually blended into the local landscape. No one knew that an astonishing treasure lay beneath the surface until 1974, when peasants digging a well accidentally discovered the vault containing over 7,000 soldiers and horses standing in military formation, facing east, ready for battle.

How could such a vast project have been accomplished? The technical achievement of the artists and artisans is as amazing as the political organization that made the work possible and the worldview that inspired it. Perhaps as many as 1,000 potters molded and carved the clay, and 85 artists signed the figures. By using standardized molds, they mass-produced thousands of legs, torsos, arms, fingers, and heads. They joined the prefabricated parts and then modeled and carved them into individualized figures. After the firing of the clay, the artists painted the figures and supplied them with real weapons of bronze and wood. Just consider the size of the kilns and the quantity of wood necessary to fire such vast numbers of clay figures—let alone the organization of the skilled labor force. Such standardization, mass production, and prefabrication of modular parts are associated with modern industrial society. Yet ancient cultures, from China to Egypt, fashioned intricate production systems long before Europe's Industrial Revolution of the eighteenth century.

4–1 Soldiers, from the mausoleum of Shihuangdi (the first emperor of Qin), Lintong, Shaanxi Province. Qin Dynasty, c. 210 BCE. Earthenware, life-size

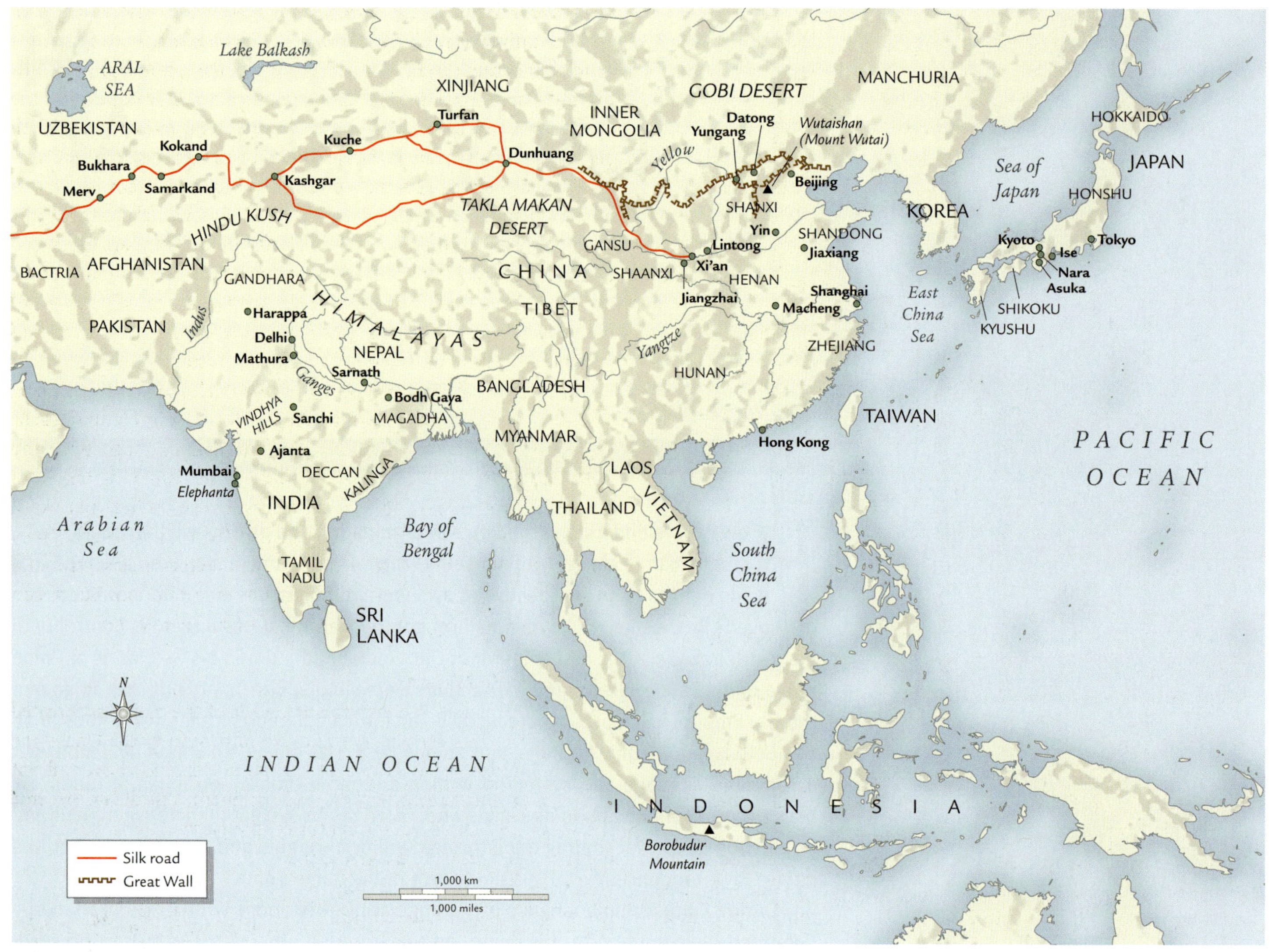

Map 4–1 Early Asia

The civilizations of South and East Asia are among the world's oldest and rank among the most culturally rich. Together, the South Asian subcontinent and the East Asian lands of China and Japan witnessed the birth of six great, still-active religions and/or philosophies: Buddhism, Hinduism, and Jainism in India; Confucianism and Daoism in China; and Shinto in Japan. The eastward spread of Buddhism—from the Indian subcontinent through Central Asia to the lands of present-day China, Korea, and Japan—united these regions philosophically and artistically. At the same time, the work of Indian, Chinese, and Japanese artists proudly reflects the profound differences between their aesthetic traditions (see map **4–1**).

The Indian Subcontinent

The Indian or South Asian subcontinent includes present-day India, southeastern Afghanistan, Pakistan, Nepal, Bangladesh, and Sri Lanka. Throughout the history of the area, these places have been culturally linked. Differences in language, climate, and terrain within India have fostered distinct regional and cultural characteristics and artistic traditions. However, despite such regional diversity, several overarching traits tend to unite Indian art. Most evident is a distinctive sense of beauty, with voluptuous forms and a profusion of ornament, texture, and color. Visual abundance reflects a belief in the generosity and favor of the gods. Another characteristic is the pervasive symbolism that enriches all Indian arts with intellectual and emotional layers. Third, and perhaps most important, is an emphasis on capturing the vibrant quality of a world seen as infused with the dynamics of the divine. Gods and humans, ideas and abstractions, are given tactile, sensuous forms, radiant with inner spirit.

The Indus Valley Civilization

The earliest civilization of South Asia arose in the lower reaches of the Indus River (in present-day Pakistan and in northwestern India). This Indus Valley, or Harappan, civilization (after Harappa, the first discovered site) flourished from approximately 2600–1900

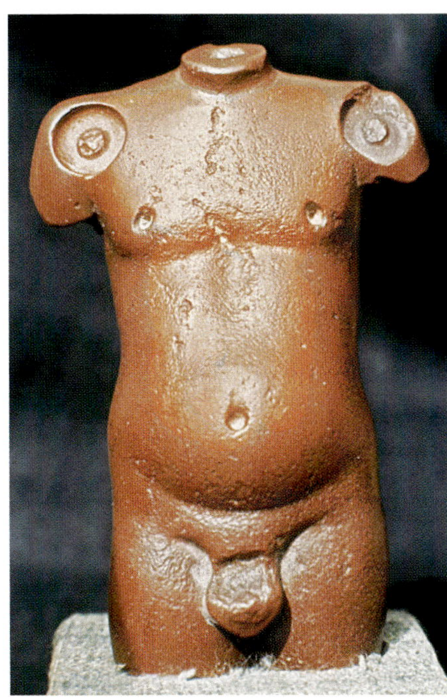

4–2 Torso, from Harappa, Indus Valley civilization. c. 2000 BCE. Red sandstone, height 3¾" (9.5 cm). National Museum, New Delhi

BCE, during roughly the same time as Egypt's Old Kingdom and the dynasty of Ur in Mesopotamia. Indeed, with Egypt and Mesopotamia, it is considered one of the world's earliest urban river valley civilizations.

A nude male torso found in Harappa is an example of the naturalistic style that flourished in the Indus Valley (fig. **4–2**). Less than four inches tall, it is one of the most extraordinary portrayals of the human form to survive from any early civilization. In contrast to the tightly controlled athletic male ideal developed in ancient Egypt, this sculpture emphasizes the soft texture of the organic human body and the subtle nuances of a moving muscular form. The abdomen is relaxed in the manner of a yogi able to control his breath. With these characteristics the Harappa torso forecasts the essential aesthetic attributes of later Indian sculpture.

For unknown reasons, the Indus Valley civilization declined between 2000 and 1750 BCE, and a seminomadic warrior people known as the Aryans entered India from the northwest, bringing with them an Indo-European language called Sanskrit and a hierarchical social order. The Vedic period that followed was named for the Vedas, a body of sacred writings. It lasted from about 1500 BCE until the rise of the first unified empire in the South Asian subcontinent in the late fourth century BCE.

The Vedic Period

The Vedic period is marked by the development of religiously sanctioned social classes or castes, which became hereditary, and by the beginnings of Buddhism, Hinduism, and Jainism—three of the four great religions of India. (The fourth is Islam.) The metaphysical texts known as the *Upanishads* were also written during this period. Examining the meaning of earlier, more cryptic Vedic hymns, the *Upanishads* focus on the relationship between the individual soul and the universal soul, or *Brahman*. The *Upanishads* advance concepts that became central to subsequent Indian philosophy, including the assertions that the material world is illusory and only the *Brahman* is real and eternal; that existence is cyclical; and that all beings are caught in *samsara*, which is a relentless cycle of birth, life, death, and rebirth. The goal of religious life is to attain *nirvana*—liberation from this cycle—by uniting our individual soul with the eternal, universal *Brahman*. These philosophical ideas are expressed in a more accessible and popular way in India's great literary epics, the *Mahabharata* and the *Ramayana*. Appearing toward the end of the Vedic period, these texts relate stories of gods and humans that later became immensely important in Hinduism.

In this stimulating religious, philosophical, and literary climate, numerous religious communities arose. The most influential teachers were Shakyamuni Buddha (see "Buddhism," page 80), and Mahavira (599–527 BCE), the founder of the Jain religion. Both espoused such basic Upanishadic tenets as the cyclical nature of existence and the desirability of escape from it. However, they rejected the authority of the Vedas and the hereditary class structure of Vedic society, with its powerful, exclusive priesthood. Buddhism and Jainism were open to all, regardless of social position.

The Rise of Buddhism

Buddhism provided the impetus for much of the major art created between the third century BCE and the fifth century CE. Under the Maurya Empire (c. 322–185 BCE), whose rule extended over all but the southernmost regions of the subcontinent, Buddhism became the state religion. For many centuries, the painting and sculpture of India were associated with imperial sponsorship of the religion. The Mauryan lion capital (fig. **4–3**), dated to about 250 BCE, is a prime example of one emperor's promotion of Buddhism. This capital once topped a 50-foot-high pillar of highly polished sandstone located on the grounds of the monastery at Sarnath, site of the Buddha's first teaching. One of many so-called Ashokan pillars, it was erected by Emperor Ashoka, who first sponsored Buddhism as the state religion. The capital rises with a cushion of downturned lotus petals, on which rests a

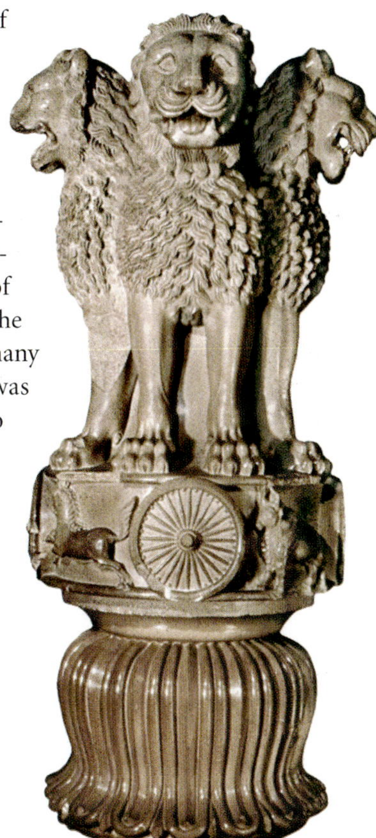

4–3 Lion capital, from an Ashokan pillar at Sarnath, Uttar Pradesh, India. Maurya Empire, c. 250 BCE. Polished sandstone, height 7' (2.13 m). Archaeological Museum, Sarnath

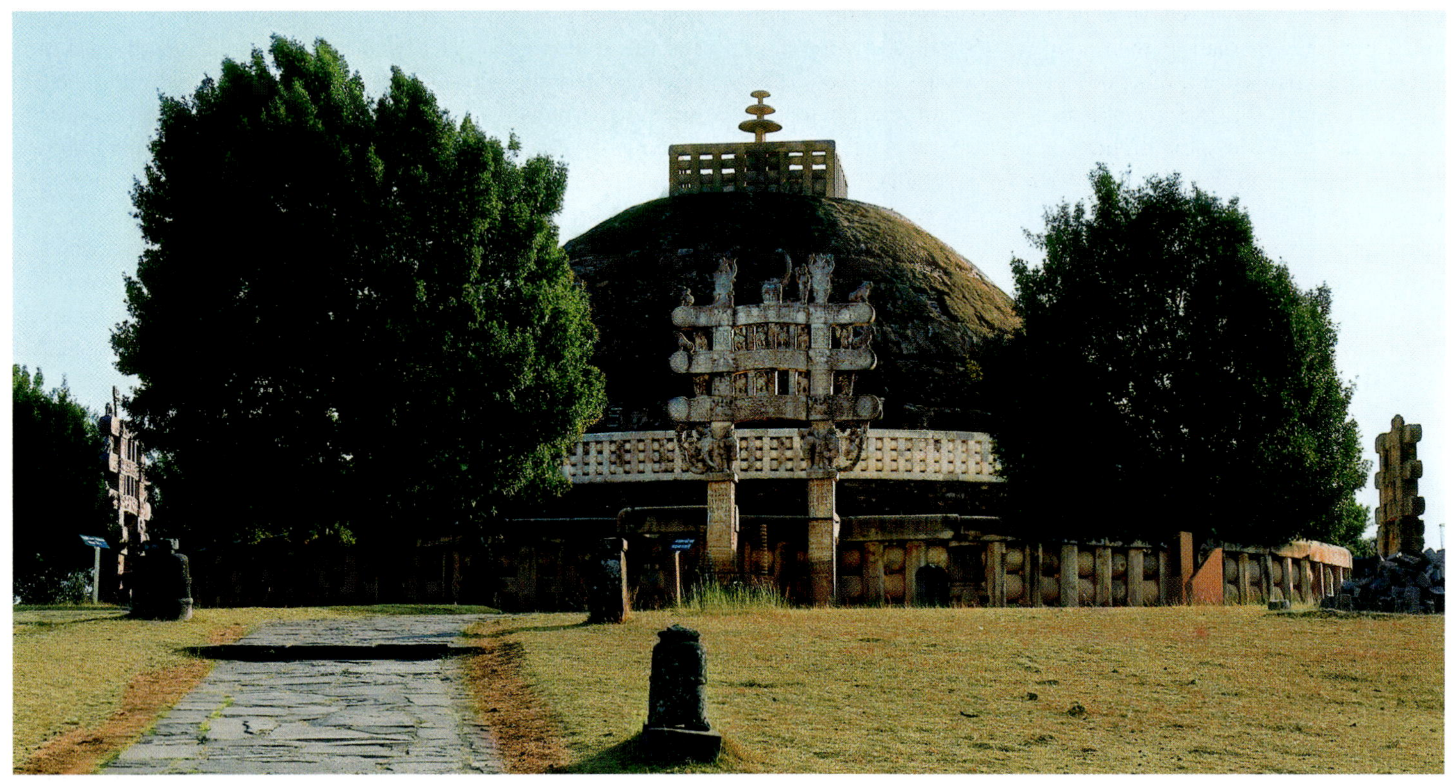

4–4 Great Stupa, Sanchi, Madhya Pradesh, India. Erected 3rd century BCE; enlarged c. 150–50 BCE

BUDDHISM

The Buddhist religion developed from the teachings of Shakyamuni Buddha (traditionally dated c. 563–483 BCE, though some scholars now put his death at c. 400 BCE), who lived and taught in the present-day regions of Nepal and northeast India. Born Prince Siddhartha Gautama in a small kingdom of the Shakya clan, he left his family and home at age 29 to live as an ascetic in the wilderness. He was deeply troubled by the inevitable sufferings of the human condition—old age, sickness, and death—and the repetitions of these sufferings through the continual cycle of rebirth. But after six long years of meditation, while sitting under a pipal (bodhi) tree at Bodh Gaya, Siddhartha Gautama attained complete enlightenment, or understanding of true reality, becoming the Buddha (meaning "enlightened one").

In his teachings, Shakyamuni Buddha expounded the Four Noble Truths, which are the foundation of Buddhism: (1) life is suffering; (2) this suffering has a cause, which is desire; (3) desire can be overcome and extinguished; and (4) the way to overcome desire is by following the eightfold path of right view, right resolve, right speech, right action, right livelihood, right effort, right mindfulness, and right concentration.

The early form of Buddhism, known as Theravada, stresses self-cultivation for the purpose of attaining *nirvana*. In Mahayana Buddhism, which developed later and became popular in northern India, China, Korea, and Japan, the goal was expanded from attaining *nirvana* for oneself to the attainment of buddhahood for all beings. A buddha is not a god but rather one who sees the ultimate nature of the world and is therefore no longer subject to the cycle of birth, death, and rebirth. Compassion for all became a primary motivating force of the religion.

Mahayana Buddhism recognizes not only Shakyamuni Buddha but also numerous other buddhas, such as Maitreya, the Buddha of the Future, and Amitabha (called Amida in Japan), the Buddha of Infinite Light and Infinite Life (that is, incorporating all space and time). Mahayana Buddhism developed the concept of **bodhisattvas**, saintly beings on the brink of buddhahood who have vowed to help others become buddhas before crossing over themselves. The appearance of bodhisattvas in art is based on the princely image of Siddhartha Gautama before he became the Buddha. Their rich clothing, jewelry, and long hair make them easily distinguished from buddhas, who wear a monk's robe, no jewelry, and short hair.

deep, round collar carved with four animals—lion, horse, bull, and elephant—alternating with four wheels called *chakra*s (see "Buddhist Symbols," page 83). Four lions stand back-to-back facing the four cardinal directions, emblematic of the universal nature of Buddhism. Their heraldic stance and the strong stylization of elements such as leg tendons and veins, claws, manes, and toothy muzzles, endow the lions with almost supernatural presence. When India gained its independence in 1947, this capital became the national emblem.

Between the second century BCE and the early first century CE, Buddhism continued as the main inspiration for art in the region, and some of the most important and magnificent early Buddhist structures were created. In early Buddhist art, the Buddha himself is not shown in human form. Instead, he is represented by symbols such as his footprints, an empty "enlightenment" seat, or a **stupa** (see "Stupas," below). Perhaps no early Indian monument is more famous than the Great Stupa at Sanchi in central India (fig. **4–4**). Stupas derive from burial mounds and their solid, dome-shaped earthen core contains **relics**, or material remains associated with a holy person. The first Buddhist stupas, holding the remains of the Buddha after his cremation, were venerated as his body and, by extension, his enlightenment and attainment of *nirvana*. Rituals of veneration at the stupa included circumambulation, or walking around the stupa in a clockwise direction, following the sun's path across the sky.

Originally built during the Mauryan period and enlarged about 150–50 BCE, the Great Stupa at Sanchi was part of a large monastery complex crowning a hilltop. The stupa's brick dome, once covered with shining white plaster, is topped by a square stone railing symbolizing the domain of the gods atop the cosmic mountain. The railing encloses the top of a mast bearing three stone disks, or "parasols," of decreasing size, which signal high rank and status. The mast itself is an ***axis mundi*** (axis of the world) assumed to connect the cosmic waters below the earth with the celestial realm above it and to anchor everything in its proper place.

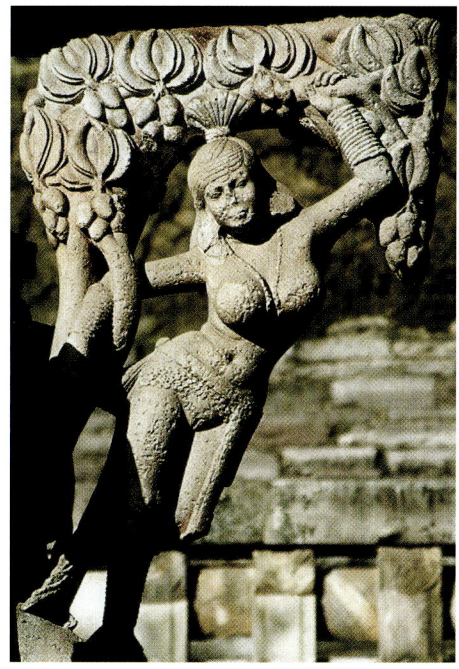

4–5 *Yakshi* bracket figure, detail of the east *torana*, Great Stupa, Sanchi. Stone, height approx. 60" (152.4 cm)

A 10-foot-high stone railing—punctuated by four stone gateways, or **toranas**—rings the entire stupa. As in much religious architecture, the railing provides a physical and symbolic boundary between the inner, sacred area and the outer, profane world. Each gateway is decorated with a profusion of carved incidents from the Buddha's life and past lives, as well as figural sculpture depicting subjects such as *Yakshi*s, female spirits associated with the beauty and fertility of nature (fig. **4–5**). The swelling, arching curves of the *Yakshi*'s body evoke her procreative and bountiful essence. Since her thin, diaphanous garment is noticeable only by its hems, she appears almost nude. As the personification of the waters, she is also the source of life. Here she symbolizes the sap of the tree, which flowers at her touch.

ELEMENTS OF Architecture

Stupas

Stupas began in India as simple, solid dome-shaped structures containing Buddhist relics. Later, a multistoried form of the stupa developed in India's Gandhara region during the Kushan Dynasty (c. 50–250 CE). As Buddhism spread northeastward along the Silk Route, the form of the multilevel stupa was merged with that of the watchtower of Han Dynasty China, leading to the creation of multistoried masonry structures with projecting tiled roofs known as pagodas.

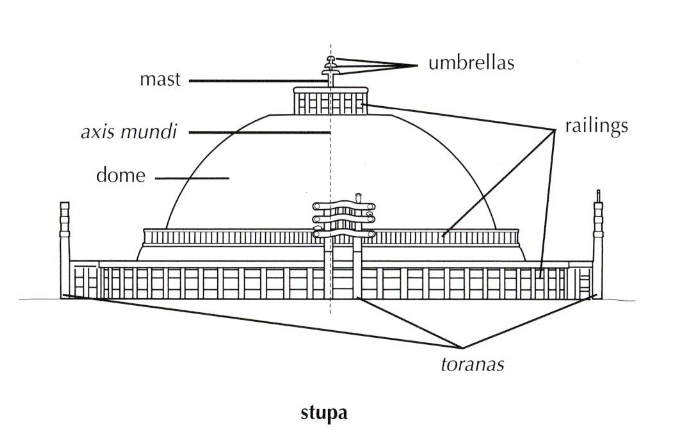

stupa

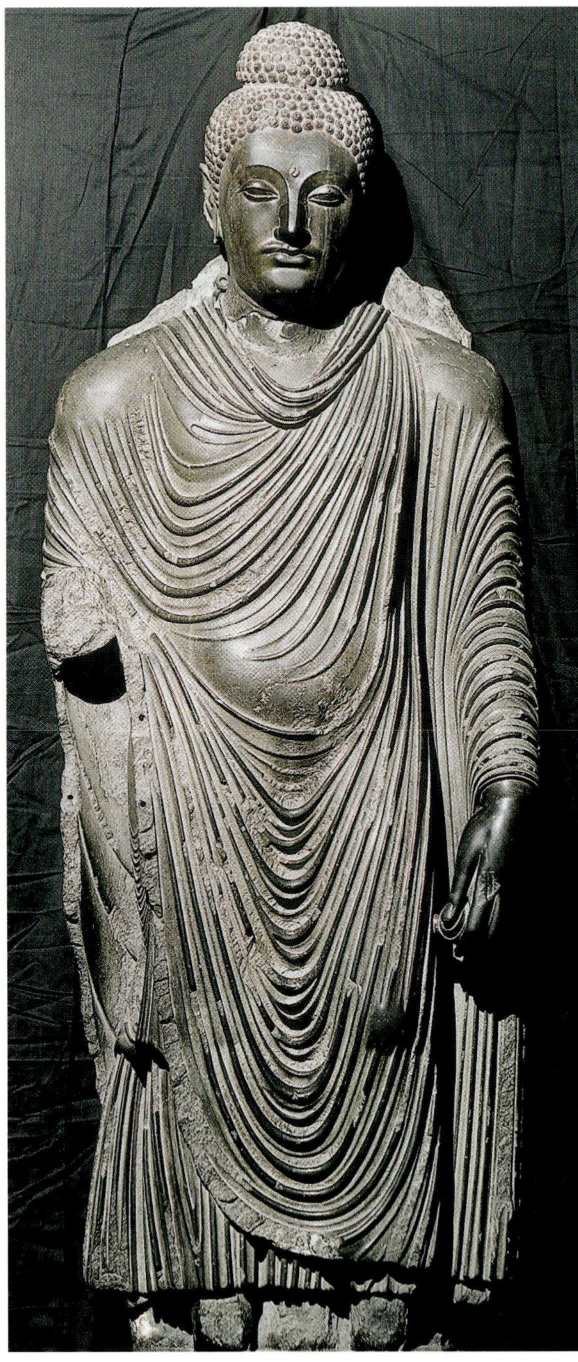

4–6 ***Standing Buddha***, from Gandhara (Pakistan). Kushan period, c. 2nd–3rd century CE. Schist, height 7' 6" (2.28 m). Lahore Museum, Lahore

Gandhara and Mathura Styles

During the first century CE, the regions of present-day Afghanistan, Pakistan, and North India came under the control of the Kushans, a nomadic people from Central Asia. During this period Buddhism underwent profound change, resulting in the development of a form of Buddhism known as Mahayana (see "Buddhism," page 80). Closely related to this new movement was the appearance of the first images of the Buddha himself. The two earliest styles of Buddha images arose in Kushan-ruled areas: Gandhara in the northwest (present-day Pakistan and Afghanistan) and Mathura in central India. Slightly later, a third stylistic tradition, known as the Amaravati school after its most famous site, developed to the south in the region ruled by the Andhra Dynasty.

In images from all three schools and throughout Asian art, the Buddha is readily recognized by certain visual characteristics. He wears a simple monk's robe, and because he had been a prince in his youth and had worn the customary heavy earrings, his earlobes are distended. The top of his head has a protuberance (*ushnisha*), which in images often resembles a bun or topknot, a symbol of his enlightenment. Between his eyes is the *urna*, a tuft of white hair.

A typical image from the Gandhara school portrays the Buddha as a powerful, over-life-size figure (fig. **4–6**). His robe is carved in tight, rib-like folds alternating with delicate creases, setting up a clear, rhythmic pattern of deep and shallow lines. This complex pattern of folds resembles the treatment of togas in some sculptural works from ancient Rome (see figs. 6–8 and 6–14), a stylistic influence resulting from the region's long history of contact with the Western world. The Gandhara style, transmitted across Central Asia, also exerted a strong influence on portrayals of the Buddha in East Asia.

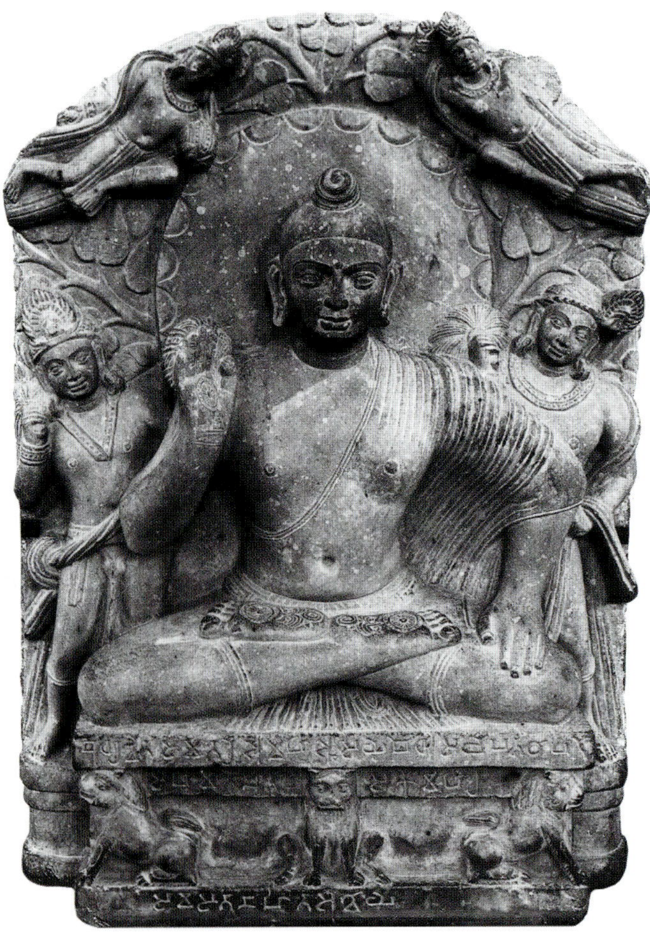

4–7 ***Buddha and Attendants***, from Katra Keshavdev, Mathura, Madhya Pradesh, India. Kushan period, c. late 1st–early 2nd century CE. Red sandstone, height 27¼" (69.2 cm). Government Museum, Mathura

At Mathura, the image of Buddha developed not through contact with the Greco-Roman tradition but within the indigenous sculptural tradition as represented by statues of *yakshas*, the native male nature deities. In one of the finest of the early Mathura images of Buddha (fig. **4–7**), the thin robe is pulled tightly over the body, allowing the fleshy form to be seen as almost nude. The Buddha is seated in a yogic posture, and his right hand is raised in a ***mudra***, or symbolic gesture, meaning "have no fear." His distinctive features and the impressions of *chakras*, or wheels, on his feet and right hand are all clearly visible (see "Buddhist Symbols," below). In the background are the branches of the pipal, or bodhi, tree, under which the Buddha was sitting when he achieved enlightenment.

BUDDHIST SYMBOLS

Buddhist symbols have myriad variations. A few of the most important are described here in their most generalized forms.

Lotus flower: Usually shown as a white water lily, the lotus (Sanskrit, *padma*) symbolizes spiritual purity, the wholeness of creation, and cosmic harmony. The flower's stem is an *axis mundi*.

Lotus throne: Buddhas are frequently shown seated on an open lotus, either single or double, which is a representation of *nirvana*.

Chakra: An ancient sun symbol, this wheel symbolizes both the various states of existence (the Wheel of Life) and the Buddhist doctrine (the Wheel of the Law). A *chakra*'s exact meaning depends on its number of spokes.

Attributes of a buddha: A buddha is distinguished by 32 physical attributes (*lakshanas*). Among them are a bulge on top of the head (*ushnisha*), a tuft of hair between the eyebrows (*urna*), elongated earlobes, and thousand-spoked circles (*chakras*) on the soles of the feet.

Mudras: These ancient symbolic hand gestures signify different states of being. In this diagram, the joined hands in the Buddha's lap form the Ohyana Mudra, a gesture of meditation and balance, symbolizing the path toward enlightenment. In fig. 4–7, Buddha's open palmed gesture is the Abhaya Mudra ("have no fear"), conveying reassurance, blessing, and protection. The Vitarka Mudra of the Bodhisattva in fig. 4–8 stands for intellectual debate.

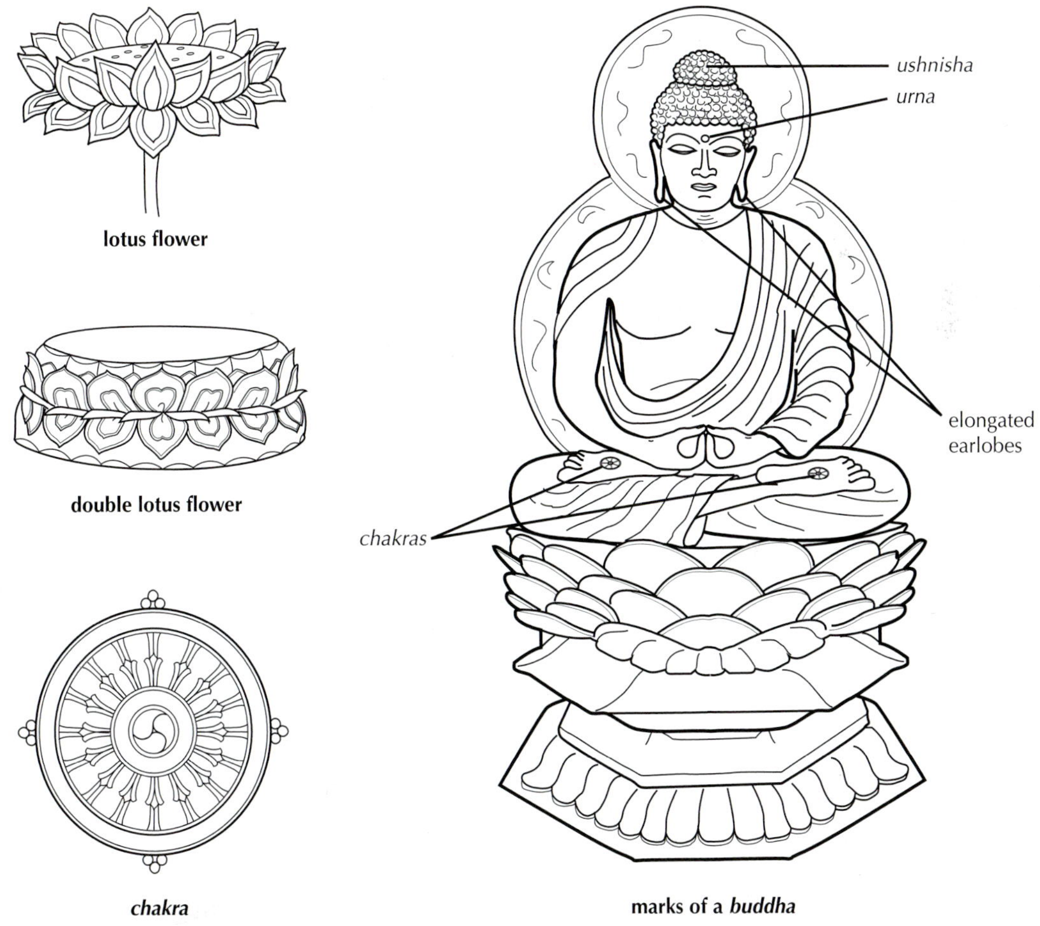

lotus flower

double lotus flower

chakra

marks of a *buddha*

Gupta Period

Buddhism reached its greatest influence in India during the Gupta period (c. 320–500 CE), named for the founders of a dynasty that ruled much of India at that time. Some of the finest surviving artworks of the Gupta period are **murals** (wall paintings) from the Buddhist rock-cut temples and halls of Ajanta, in western India (fig. **4–8**). Since ancient times, caves, frequently the abode of holy ones and ascetics, have been considered hallowed places in India. During the second century BCE, Buddhist monks began to excavate two types of rock-cut halls from the plateaus of the Deccan region. The type known as the *vihara* was used for the living quarters of the monks, and that known as *chaitya*, meaning "sacred," usually enshrined a stupa. Cave I at Ajanta, carved around 475 CE, is a *vihara* with monks' chambers around the sides and a shrine chamber in the back. Flanking the entrance of the shrine are murals of two bodhisattvas dressed in lavishly adorned, princely garments and crowns festooned with pearls (fig. 4–8). The graceful bending posture conveys his sympathetic attitude, while his spiritual power is suggested by his large size in comparison with the surrounding figures. In no other known example of Indian painting do bodhisattvas appear so magnanimous and graciously divine yet at the same time so human.

Even as Buddhism flourished, Hinduism, sponsored by Gupta monarchs, began the ascendancy that led to its eventual domination of Indian religious life (see "Hinduism," page 85). Hindu temples—and sculpture of the Hindu gods—rose with increasing frequency during the Gupta period and the post-Gupta era of the sixth to mid-seventh century.

In the mid-sixth century, a rock-cut cave-temple devoted to the major Hindu god Shiva was carved on the island of Elephanta, off the coast of Mumbai (formerly Bombay) in western India (fig. **4–9**). Impressive in its size and grandeur, the cave-temple's interior is

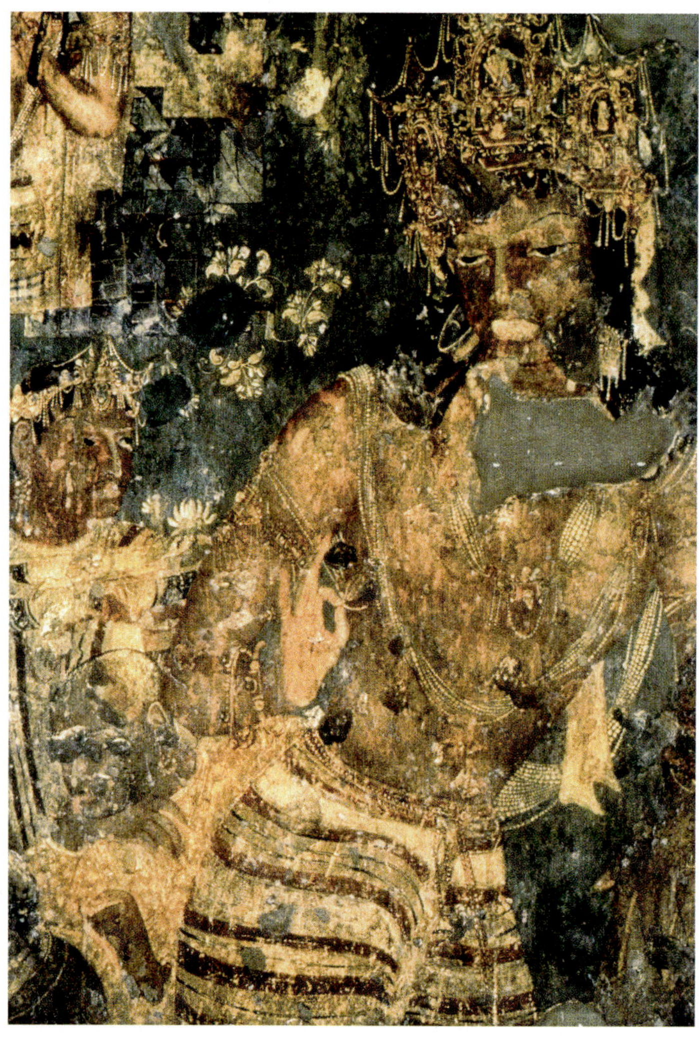

4–8 ***Bodhisattva***, detail of a wall painting in Cave I, Ajanta, Maharashtra, India. Gupta period, c. 475 CE

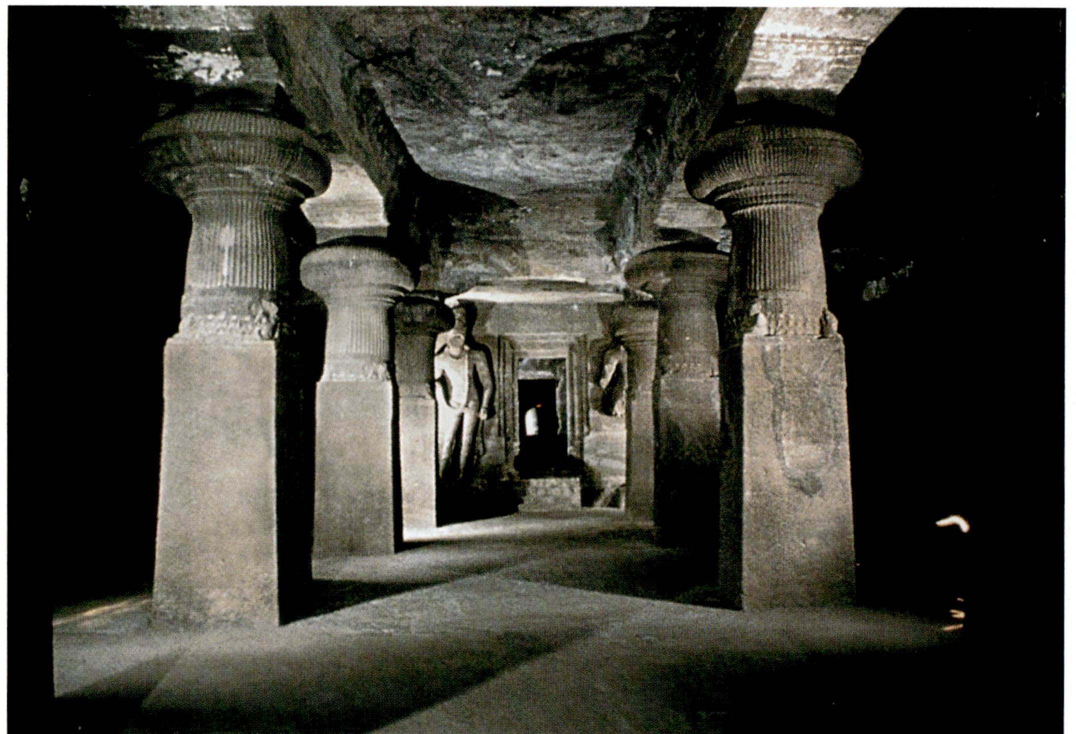

4–9 Cave-Temple of Shiva at Elephanta, Maharashtra, India. Mid-6th century CE. View along the east–west axis to the Shiva shrine

Large pillars cut from the living rock appear to support the beams of the low ceiling, although, as with all architectural elements in a cave-temple, they are not structural. Each pillar has a billowing "cushion" capital. Columns and capitals are delicately fluted, adding a surprising refinement to these otherwise heavy forms. The focus is on the lingam, the phallic symbol of Shiva, shown here at the center of the illustration.

HINDUISM

Hinduism is not one religion but many related beliefs and innumerable sects. It results from the mingling of Vedic beliefs with indigenous, local beliefs and practices. All three major Hindu sects draw upon the texts of the Vedas, which are believed to be sacred revelations set down about 1200–800 BCE. The gods lie outside the finite world, but they can appear in visible form to believers. Each Hindu sect takes its particular deity as supreme. By worshiping gods with rituals, meditation, and intense love, individuals may be reborn into increasingly higher positions until they escape the cycle of life, death, and rebirth. The most popular deities are Vishnu, Shiva, and the Great Goddess, Devi. Deities are revealed and depicted in multiple aspects.

Vishnu: A benevolent god who works for the order and well-being of the world. He is often represented lying in a trance or asleep on the Cosmic Waters where he dreams the world into existence. His symbols are the wheel and a conch shell. A huge figure, he usually has four arms and wears a crown and lavish jewelry. He rides a man-bird, Garuda. Vishnu appears in ten different incarnations, including Rama and Krishna, who have their own cults. Rama embodies virtue, and—assisted by the monkey king—he fights the demon Ravana. As Krishna, Vishnu is a supremely beautiful, blue-skinned youth who lives with the cowherds, loves the maiden Radha, and battles the demon Kansa.

Shiva: Lord of Existence, is both creative and destructive, light and dark, male and female. His symbol is the lingam, an upright phallus, which is represented as a low pillar. As an expression of his power and creative energy, he is often represented as the Cosmic Dancer, who dances the destruction and re-creation of the world (see fig. 9–4). He dances within a ring of fire, his four hands holding fire, a drum, and gesturing to the worshipers. Shiva's animal is the bull. His consort is Parvati, and their sons are the elephant-headed Ganesha, god of prosperity, and the six-faced Karttikeya, god of war.

Devi: The Great Goddess, controls material riches and fertility. She has forms indicative of beauty, wealth, and auspiciousness, but also forms of wrath, pestilence, and power. As the embodiment of cosmic energy, she provides the vital force to all the male gods. Her symbol is an abstract depiction of female genitals, often associated with the lingam of Shiva. When armed and riding a lion (as the goddess Durga), Devi personifies righteous fury. As the goddess Lakshmi, she is the goddess of wealth and beauty. She is often represented by the basic geometric forms of squares, circles, and triangles.

There are countless other deities, including Brahma, the creator, who once had his own cult. Brahma embodies spiritual wisdom. His four heads symbolize the four cosmic cycles, four earthly directions, and four classes of society: priests (brahmins), warriors, merchants, and laborers.

Central to Hindu practice are *puja* (forms of worship) and *darshan* (beholding a deity), generally performed to obtain a deity's favor and in the hope that this favor will lead to liberation from *samsara*. Because desire for the fruits of our actions traps us, the ideal is to consider all earthly endeavors as sacrificial offerings to the gods. Pleased with our devotion, a god may then grant us an eternal state of pure being, pure consciousness, and pure bliss.

designed along two main axes, one running north–south, and the other east–west. The three entrances provide the only source of light, and the resulting cross- and back-lighting effects add to the sense of the cave as a place of mysterious and confusing complexity. A worshiper is thrown off-balance—in preparation for a meeting with Shiva.

Shiva (meaning "the auspicious one") embodies the entire universe and exhibits a wide range of aspects or forms, both gentle and wild (see "Hinduism," above). He is the Great Yogi who dwells for vast periods of time in meditation in the Himalaya, the husband par excellence who makes love to the goddess Parvati for eons at a time, the Slayer of Demons, and the Cosmic Dancer.

Many forms of Shiva appear in monumental relief panels adorning the cave-temple at Elephanta. A huge bust of the deity represents his Sadashiva, or Eternal Shiva, aspect (fig. **4–10**). Carved out of the cave wall, three heads are shown in the photo resting

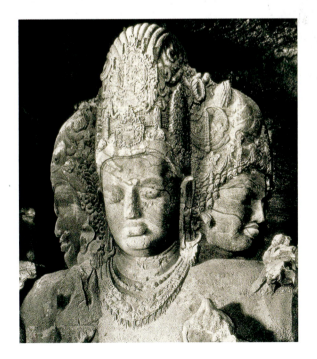

4–10 ***Eternal Shiva***, rock-cut relief in the cave-temple of Shiva at Elephanta. Mid-6th century CE. Height approx. 11' (3.4 m)

upon the broad shoulders of the upper body. A fourth head may have faced the stone wall since a four-faced Shiva (*chaturmuk*) is plausible in this setting and also a more common Hindu image. Typically the heads summarize Shiva's fivefold nature as creator (back), protector (left shoulder), destroyer (right shoulder), obscurer (front), and releaser (top). On his left shoulder, his protector nature is depicted as female, with curled hair and a pearl-festooned crown. On his right, the wrathful destroyer nature wears a fierce expression, and in front, the god is shown in deep introspection, with the piled-up hair of a yogi. The releaser contemplates the heavens. Indian artists often convey the many aspects or essential nature of a deity through multiple heads or arms. Their intent is to portray these additions with such convincing naturalism that we readily accept them. Here, for example, the artist has united three heads onto a single body so skillfully that we still relate to the statue as an essentially human presence.

Southeast Asia

Buddhism spread rapidly across Asia. At the end of the eighth century in Java, a family of rulers known as the Lords of the Mountains (the Sailendra Dynasty) began building a magnificent temple in the form of a sacred mountain at Borobudur (fig. **4–11**). The builders turned a natural hill into a three-step platform, measuring more than 400 feet across and oriented to the four cardinal directions. On this platform, slightly later builders erected five more platforms and covered the walls with relief sculpture. Then they built three round terraces that support 22 small stupas and a large central stupa. The entire complex rises more than 100 feet above the ground. The stupas hold images of the Buddha, and the vertical walls of the three terraces are carved with the Wheel of Life—birth, life, death, and rebirth—the life of the Buddha, and the stages of enlightenment and paradise. The people who came to Borobudur followed the path established by these corridors of sculpture, and circling clockwise they climbed the sacred mountain. They hoped to achieve enlightenment when they reached the stupa on the final platform.

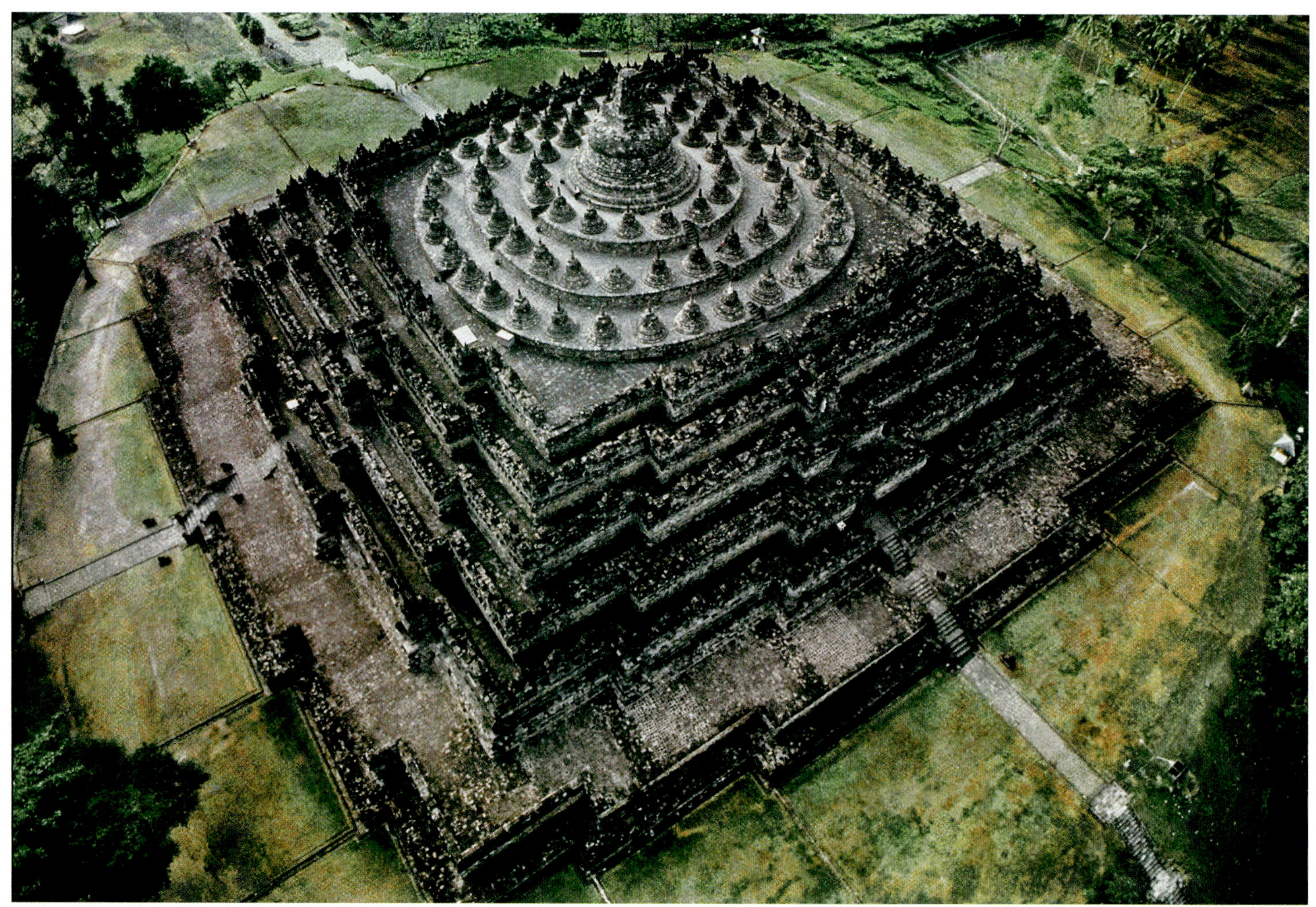

4–11 Buddhist Temple of Borobudur, Java, Indonesia. Sailendra Dynasty, 835–60 CE. Lava stone, perimeter of lowest gallery 1, 180' (360 m), diameter of crowning stupa 52' (16 m)

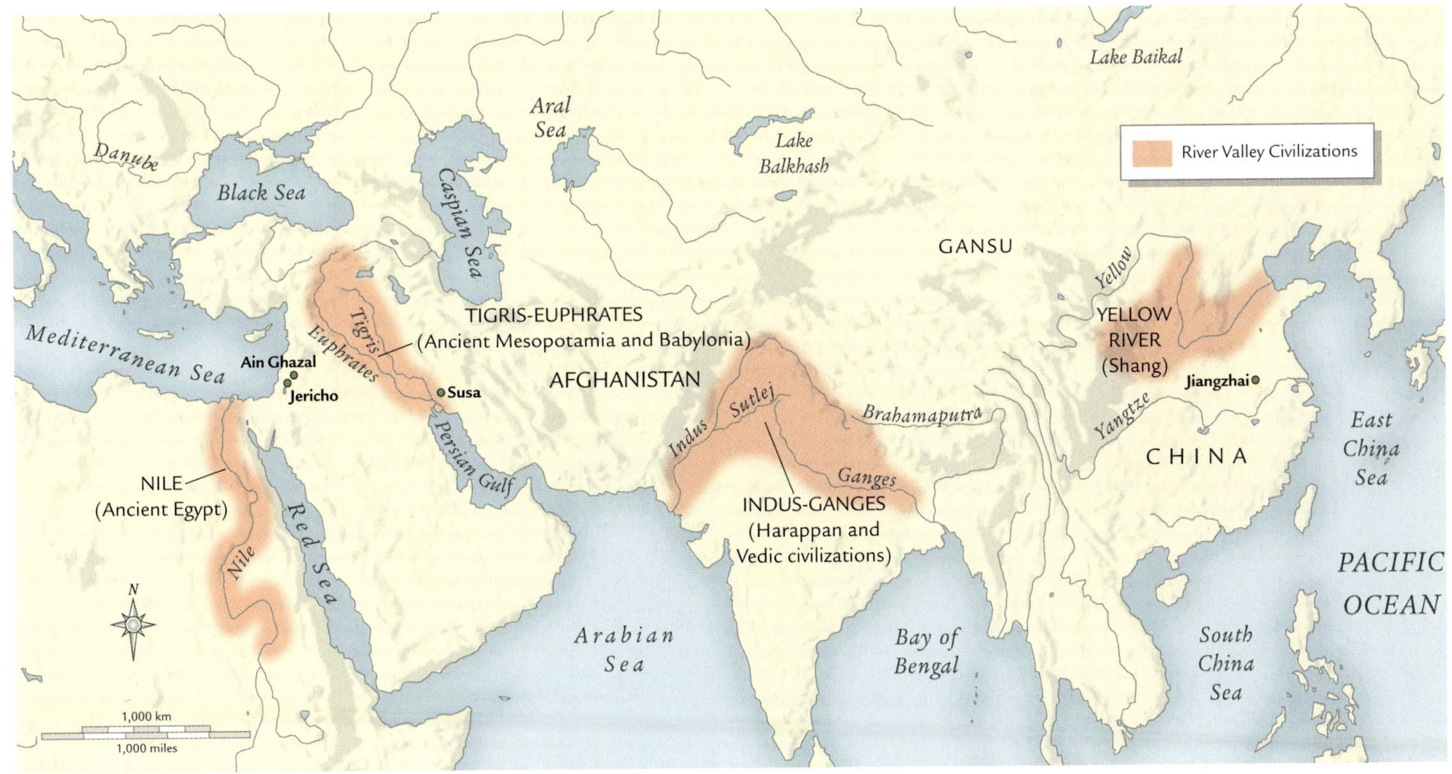

Map 4–2 Four Great River Valley Civilizations of the Ancient World

China

Among the cultures of the world, China is distinguished by its long, uninterrupted development, which has been traced back some 8,000 years. Even more remarkably, while rulers have come and gone, the country has been, with only a few breaks, unified since 221 BCE. Geographically, China is notable for its size, occupying a landmass slightly larger than the continental United States.

The country's historical and cultural heart—sometimes called Inner China—is the land watered by its three great rivers, the so-called "Yellow River" (Huang He), the Yangzi, and the Xi (see map **4–2**). Chinese towns and cities first emerged in the Neolithic period in fertile river valleys, especially around the deep southern bend of the Yellow River, nicknamed "China's Sorrow" because of its disastrous floods.

Agriculture based on rice and millet arose independently in East Asia before 5000 BCE. One of the clearest signs of Neolithic culture in China is the vigorous emergence of towns and cities. At Jiangzhai, near modern Xi'an, the foundations of more than 100 dwellings have been discovered surrounding the remains of a community center, a cemetery, and a kiln. Dated to about 4000 BCE, the ruins point to the existence of a highly developed early society.

The Bronze Age

The first Chinese kingdoms date to the Bronze Age, which began in China before 1600 BCE. Traditional histories tell of three Bronze Age dynasties: the Xia, the Shang, and the Zhou. Modern scholars once dismissed the Xia and Shang as legends, not actual civilizations, but twentieth-century archaeological discoveries fully established the historical existence of the Shang (c. 1700–1100 BCE) and point strongly to the historical existence of the Xia as well.

Shang kings ruled from a succession of capitals in the Yellow River valley, where archaeologists have found walled cities, palaces, and vast royal tombs. Society seems to have been highly stratified, with a ruling group that possessed the bronze technology needed to make weapons. They maintained their authority in part by claiming power as intermediaries between humans and the supernatural realm. Nature and fertility spirits were also honored, and regular sacrifices were made to the spirits of dead ancestors so that they might help the living.

Bronze vessels are the most admired and studied of Shang artifacts. They were connected with ritual practices, serving as containers for offerings of food and wine. The bronze *fang ding* illustrated here is a square vessel with four legs (fig. **4–12**). This is one of the largest of hundreds of vessels recovered from royal tombs near the last of the Shang capitals, Yin (present-day Anyang). In typical Shang style, its surface is decorated with a complex array of images based on animal forms. A large stylized, mask-like face (*taotie*) adorns the center of each side; more appear on the legs; and the rest of the surface is filled with images resembling birds, dragons, and other fantastic creatures. The deeper significance of such motifs remains mysterious.

Around 1100 BCE, the Shang were conquered by the Zhou from western China. During the Zhou Dynasty (1100–221 BCE), a feudal society developed, with a king, his relatives, and retainers ruling over

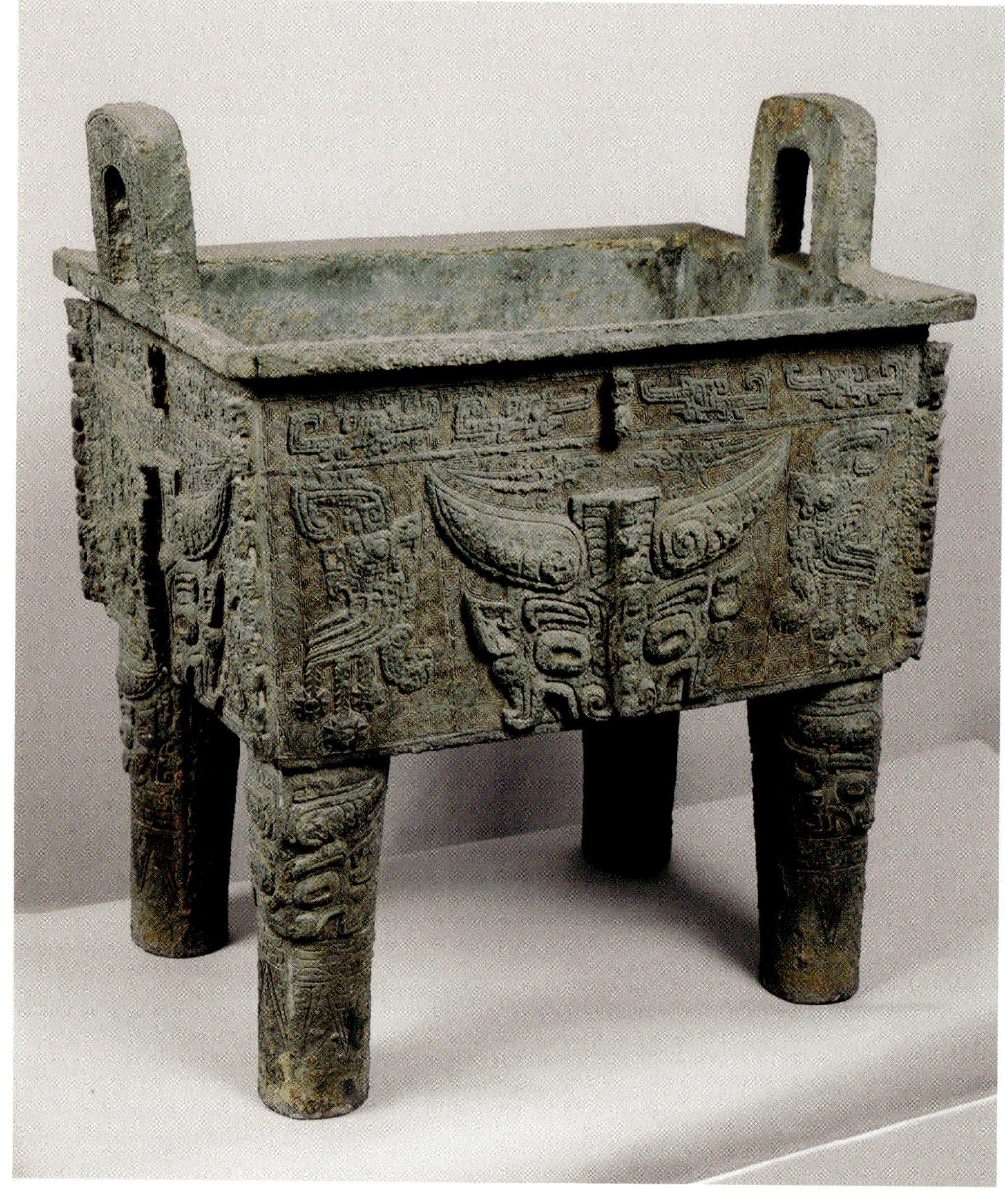

4–12 ***Fang ding***, from the tomb of Lady Hao, Anyang, Henan Province, People's Republic of China. Shang Dynasty, c. 1200 BCE. Bronze, height 1' 4¾" (42.5 cm). Commissioned by Lady Hao or her family. Cultural Relics Bureau, Beijing

numerous small states. The supreme deity became known as Tian, or Heaven, and the king ruled as the Son of Heaven—that is, as the representative of Tian on earth. All subsequent Chinese ruling dynasties also continued to follow the belief that imperial rule was mandated from heaven.

Many of China's great philosophers lived during the Zhou Dynasty, thinkers such as Confucius, Laozi, and Mozi. During the lifetime of Confucius (551–479 BCE)—a scholar born into an aristocratic family—warfare for supremacy among the various states of China had begun, and the traditional social fabric seemed to be breaking down. Looking back to the early Zhou Dynasty as a golden age, Confucius thought about how a just and harmonious society could once again emerge (see "Confucianism," page 89). He never found a ruler who would put his ideas into effect, but his philosophy, Confucianism, eventually became central to Chinese thought and culture.

Chinese Empires: Qin, Han, and Tang

Toward the middle of the third century BCE, the state of Qin launched military campaigns that led to its triumph over the other Chinese states by 221 BCE. For the first time, China was united under a single ruler, the powerful Shihuangdi (see "Looking Forward," page 77). Anxious to ensure personal immortality, this first emperor of Qin built his own underground **mausoleum** (a building used as a tomb) at Lintong in Shaanxi Province. Archaeologists who began to excavate a pit near the tomb in 1974 were stunned to discover a vast subterranean army of terracotta soldiers and horses (see fig. 4–1).

Although harsh and repressive as rulers, the Qin emperors nevertheless are also responsible for establishing a centralized bureaucracy and administrative framework, aspects of which are still used in China today. The country was divided into provinces and prefectures, the writing system and coinage were standardized, and forts on the northern frontier were connected to build an early form of the Great Wall.

During the peaceful and prosperous Han Dynasty that followed (206 BCE–220 CE), the country's borders were extended and secured. Chinese control over strategic stretches of Central Asia led to the opening of the famous Silk Route that linked China by trade to Europe. The philosophies of Daoism and Confucianism flourished as well. Daoism emphasizes the close relationship between humans and nature. It is concerned with bringing the quiet and humble individual life into harmony with the *Dao*, or Way, of the universe. On a popular level, Daoism developed into an organized religion, absorbing many traditional folk practices such as shamanism and the search for immortality.

A popular Daoist legend, which tells of the Isles of the Immortals in the Eastern Sea, is depicted on a bronze incense burner from the tomb of Prince Liu Sheng, who died in 113 BCE (fig. **4–13**). Around the bowl, gold **inlay** outlines the stylized waves of the sea. Above them rises the mountainous island, crowded with birds, animals, and people who have discovered the secret of immortality. This visionary world would have been shrouded in the shifting mist of incense when the burner was in use.

In contrast to the metaphysical focus of Daoism, Confucianism is concerned with the human world, and its goal is the attainment of equity. To this end, it proposes an ethical system based on reverence for ancestors and correct relationships among people (see "Confucianism," below). Attracted by this emphasis on social order and respect for authority, the Han emperor Wudi (ruled 141–87 BCE) made Confucianism the official philosophy. It remained the state ideology of China until the end of imperial rule in the twentieth century and eventually assumed the form and force of a religion.

Confucian subjects appear frequently in Han art. Among the most famous examples are the reliefs from the Wu family shrines built in 151 CE in Jiaxiang. Carved and engraved in low relief on stone slabs, the scenes were meant to teach such basic Confucian tenets as respect for the emperor, filial piety, and wifely devotion.

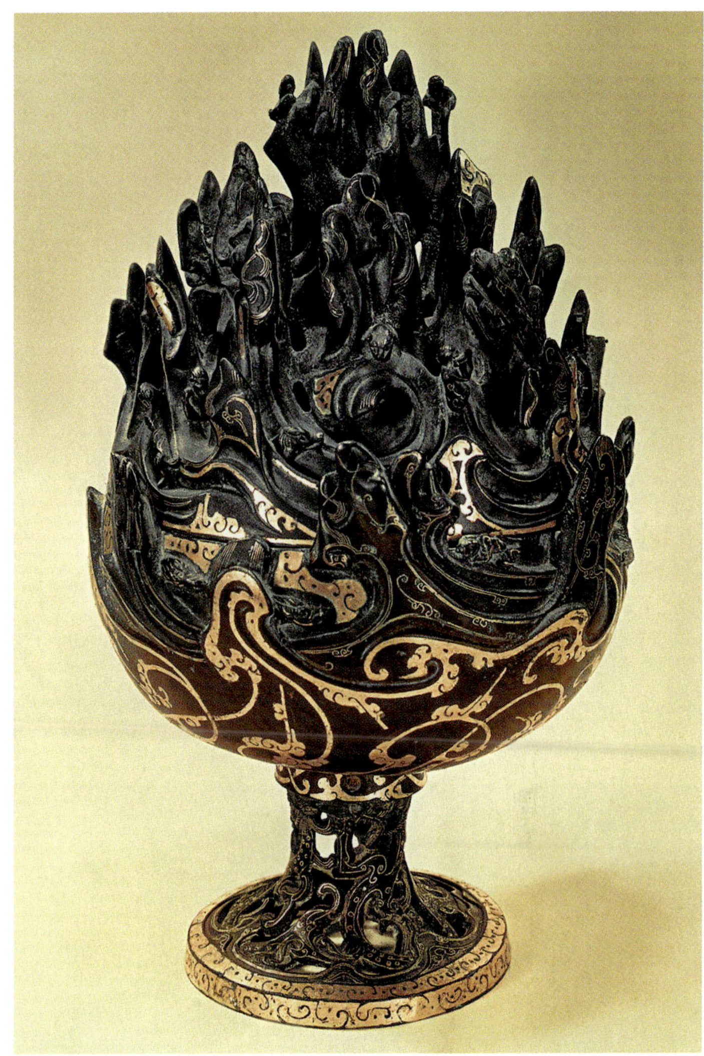

4–13 Incense burner, from the tomb of Prince Liu Sheng, Macheng, Hebei. Han Dynasty, 113 BCE. Bronze with gold inlay, height 10½" (26 cm). Hebei Provincial Museum, Shijiazhuang

CONFUCIANISM

Confucianism is based on the teachings of the Chinese scholar Confucius (551–479 BCE). His words have come down to us through a book known in English as the *Analects*, which records sayings of the philosopher collected by his disciples and their followers. At the heart of Confucian thought is the concept of *ren*, or human-heartedness. *Ren*, which emphasizes morality and empathy as the basic standards for all human interactions, is most fully realized in the Confucian ideal of the *junzi*, or gentleman. Originally indicating noble birth, the term *junzi* was redirected to mean one who through education and self-cultivation becomes a superior person, right-thinking and right-acting in all situations.

Confucius also emphasized the importance of *li*, etiquette. The formalities of social interaction—scrupulous manners as well as ritual, ceremony, and protocol—choreographed life so that an entire society moved in harmony.

Both *ren* and *li* operated in the realm of the Five Constant Relationships defining Confucian society: ruler and subject, parent and child, husband and wife, elder sibling and younger sibling, and elder friend and younger friend. Deference based on age and sex is built into this view, as is the deference to authority that made Confucianism popular with emperors. Yet responsibilities also flow the other way: The duty of a ruler is to earn the loyalty of subjects, of a husband to earn the respect of his wife, and of age to guide youth wisely.

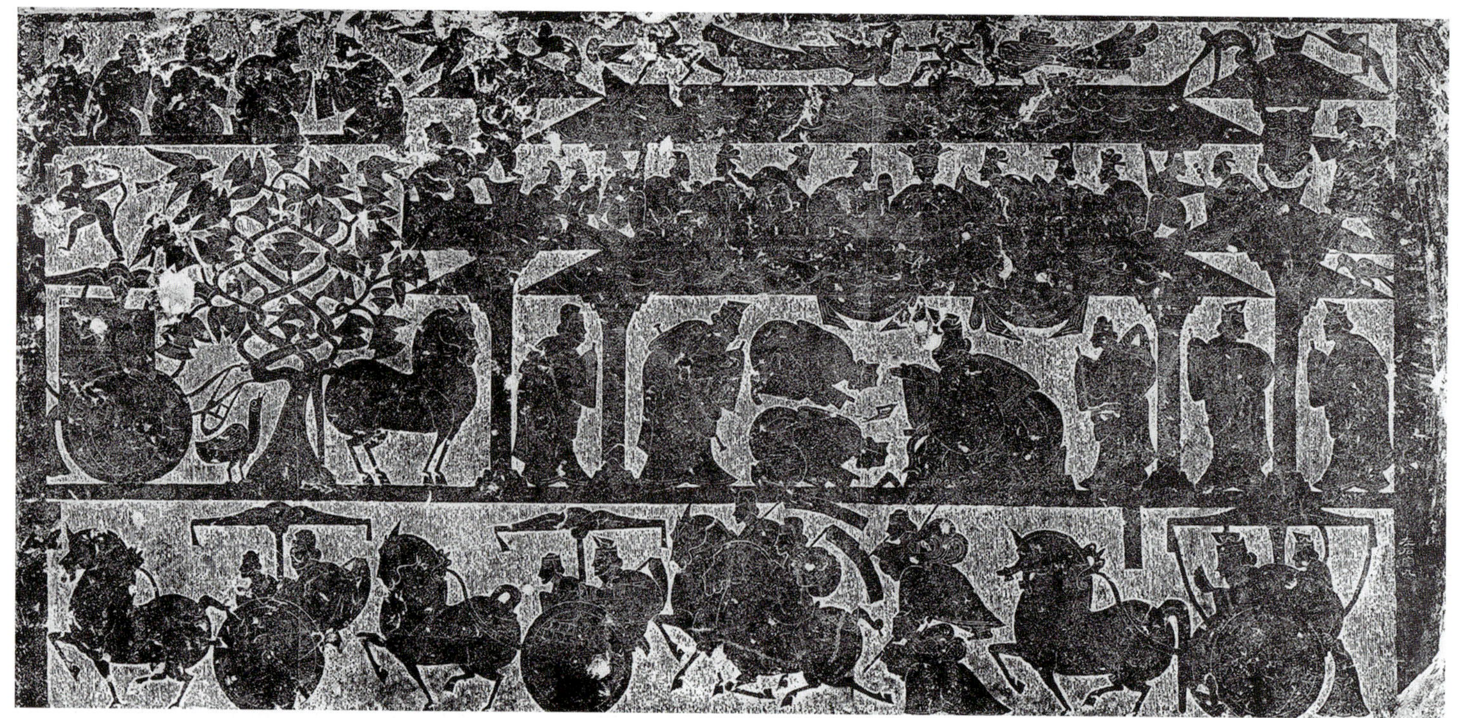

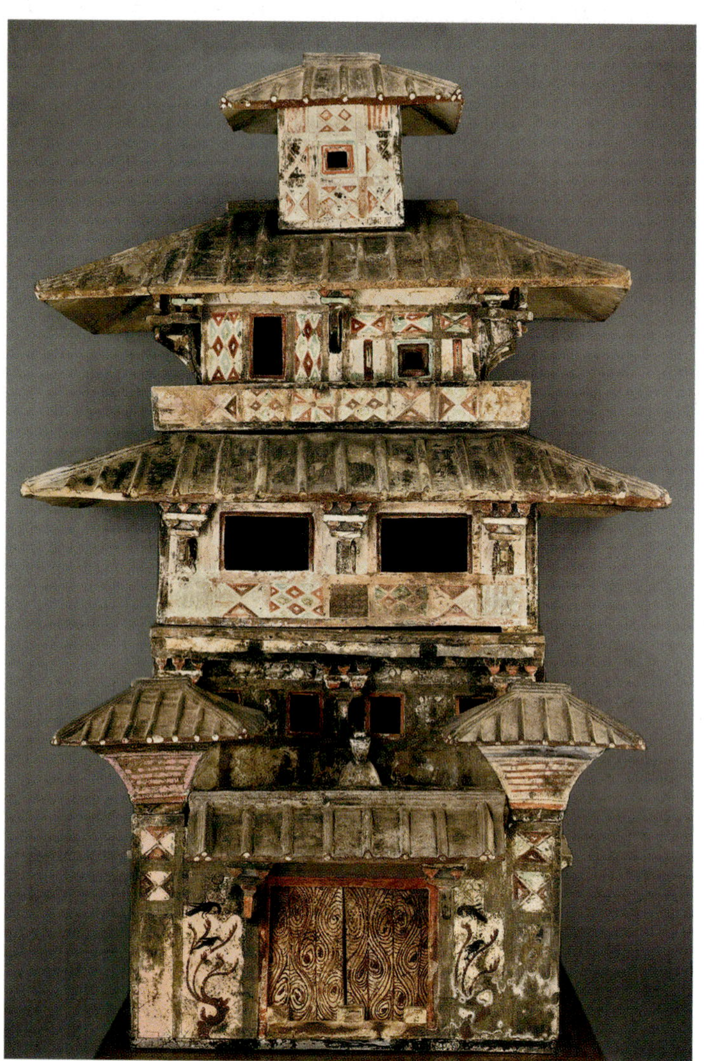

4–14 Detail from a rubbing of a relief in the Wu family shrine (Wuliangci), Jiaxiang, Shandong. Han Dynasty, 151 CE. Stone, 27½" × 66½" (70 × 169 cm)

4–15 Tomb model of house. Eastern Han Dynasty, 1st–mid 2nd century CE. Painted earthenware, 52" × 33½" × 27" (132.1 × 85.1 × 68.6 cm). The Nelson-Atkins Museum of Art, Kansas City, Missouri

PURCHASE: WILLIAM ROCKHILL NELSON TRUST (33-521). PHOTOGRAPH: JOHN LAMBERTON

One relief (fig. **4–14**) seems to depict homage to the first emperor of the Han Dynasty, who is sheltered in a two-story building and distinguished by his larger size. Birds and small figures on the roof may represent mythical creatures and immortals, while to the left the legendary archer Yi shoots at one of the sun-crows. In Yi's story, he shot all but one of the ten crows of the ten suns so that the earth would not dry out. Across the lower register, a procession brings more dignitaries to the reception.

Contemporary literary sources are eloquent on the wonders of the Han capital but, unfortunately, only ceramic models of Han architecture survive. One model of a house found in a tomb represents a typical Han dwelling (fig. **4–15**). Its four stories are crowned with a watchtower and face a small walled courtyard. Aside from the multilevel construction, the most interesting feature of the house is the bracketing system supporting the broad eaves of its tiled roofs. The painting on the exterior walls illustrates structural features such as posts and lintels. Trees with crows in their branches flank the entrance. Literary sources describe the walls of Han palaces as decorated with paint and lacquer and also inlaid with precious metals and stones.

With the fall of the Han Dynasty in 220 CE, China splintered into independent, warring kingdoms. This launched a period of almost constant turmoil, broadly known as the period of the Northern and Southern Dynasties, and lasted until 579 CE. Many intellectuals turned to Daoism, which contained a strong escapist element. Yet ultimately it was a new system of belief, Buddhism, that brought the greatest comfort to people of the time. Buddhism spread gradually north from India into Central Asia. With the increased transportation of people, goods, and ideas along the Silk Route during the Han Dynasty, Buddhism eventually reached China (see "The Silk Route and the Making of Silk," page 92). To the Chinese of the post-Han period, beset by constant warfare and social devastation, Buddhism offered consolation in life and the promise of life after death.

The most impressive surviving works of Buddhist art from the period of the Northern and Southern Dynasties are hundreds of caves carved from the solid rock of cliffs. The rock-cut caves at Yungang in Shanxi Province, for instance, contain many impressive examples of early Chinese Buddhist sculpture. The monumental seated Buddha illustrated here was carved in the latter half of the fifth century (fig. **4–16**). Because the front part of the cave has crumbled away, the 45-foot statue is now exposed to the open air. The overall effect of this colossus is remote and even austere, less human than the more sensuous expression of earlier sculptures in India. The image of the Buddha became increasingly formal and unearthly as it traveled east from its origins, reflecting a fundamental difference in the way the Chinese and the Indians visualize their deities.

In 581 CE, a northern general reunified China and established a short-lived dynasty of his own, the Sui. The Sui paved the way for one of the greatest dynasties in Chinese history, the Tang (618–907 CE). Even today many Chinese living abroad call themselves "Tang people," emphasizing that part of the Chinese character that is strong and vigorous, noble and idealistic, but also realistic and pragmatic. Cosmopolitan and tolerant, too, the Tang were both self-confident and curious about the world. Many foreigners came to the splendid new capital, Chang'an (present-day Xi'an), and the Chinese depicted them in witty detail. A ceramic statue of a camel

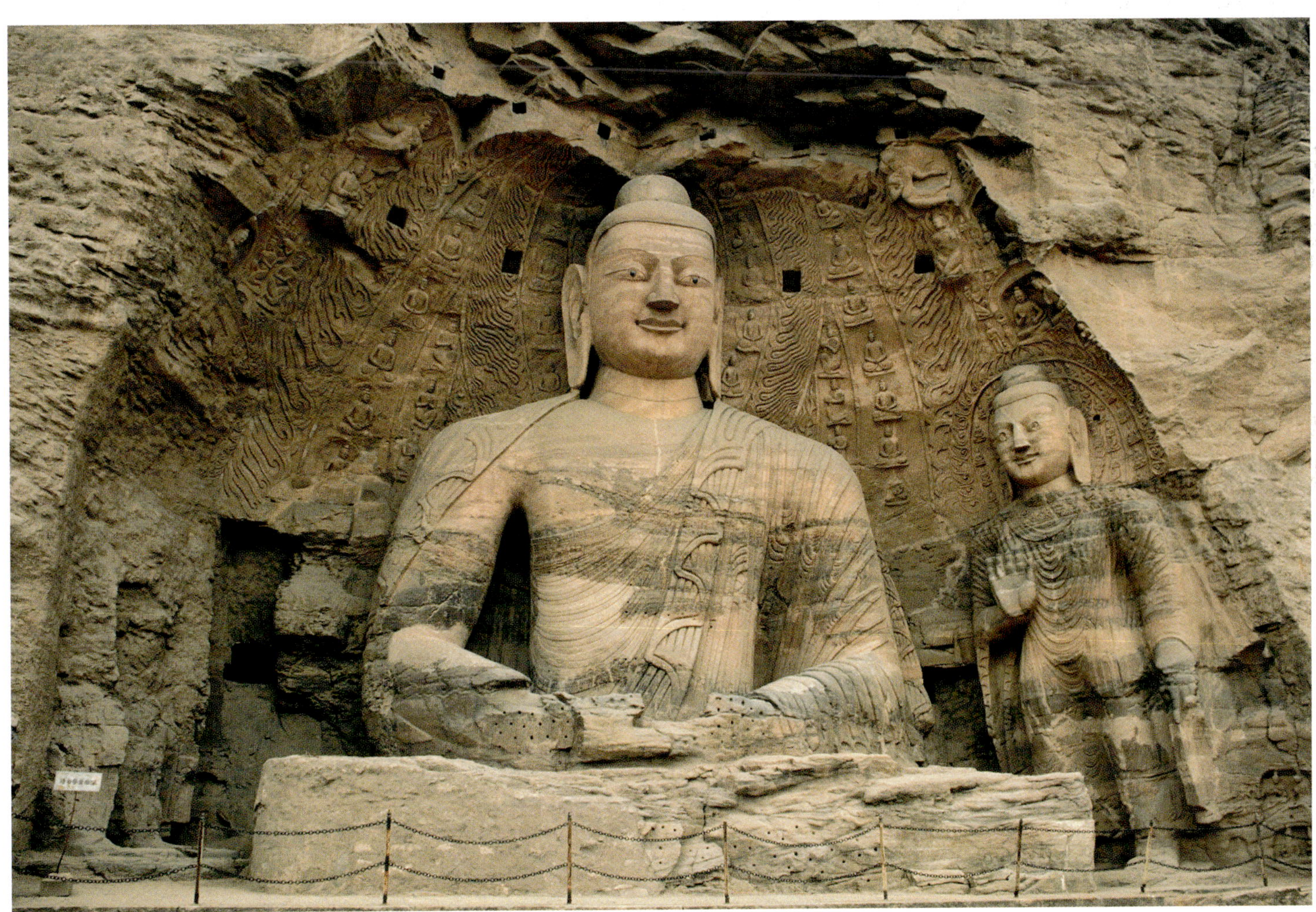

4–16 ***Seated Buddha***, Cave 20, Yungang Datong, Shanxi Province. Northern Wei Dynasty, c. 460 CE. Stone, height 45' (13.7 m)

*The elongated ears, protuberance on the head (*ushnisha*), and monk's robe are traditional attributes of the Buddha. The mask-like face, massive shoulders, and shallow, stylized drapery indicate a strong Central Asian influence.*

THE SILK ROUTE AND THE MAKING OF SILK

The fabled trade routes between East Asia and the West, called the Silk Route, were a 5,000-mile-long network of caravan and sea routes stretching from Chang'an to the westernmost point of the Great Wall of China—then all the way to Rome. Caravans carried Chinese luxury goods to the West, and bought back gold in payment. They passed through some of the most hostile regions in Asia and the Middle East, although no one caravan had to make the entire trip; goods would be passed from trader to trader on both the overland and sea routes. The Silk Route's importance fluctuated with the politics of the various regions through which it passed, as did the level of safety for its travelers. Rarely in its long history was it entirely open and comparatively safe.

Among the many precious goods carried along the Silk Route were spices and other foodstuffs, horses for trade, metals, gems, and, of course, silk. The cultivation and weaving of silk had been a closely guarded secret in China since about 2640 BCE, and it was not until about 550 CE, when two Christian missionaries smuggled a few silkworm larvae to Constantinople, that the Chinese lost their virtual monopoly. However, from as early as the third century BCE, silk cloth had been exported to Europe. It was treasured in ancient Greece and Rome, and it became a protected palace industry in the Byzantine Empire. Eventually, sericulture (the cultivation of silkworms) and luxury textile weaving took hold in southern Europe. For this and many other reasons, the use of the Silk Route declined. By the sixteenth century, it was no longer in use.

carrying a troupe of musicians reflects the Tang fascination with the "exotic" Turkic cultures of Central Asia (fig. **4–17**).

Such ceramic figurines, produced by the thousand for tombs, were decorated using a three-color-glaze technique that was a specialty of Tang ceramists. The glazes—usually chosen from a restricted palette of amber, yellow, green, and white—were splashed freely and allowed to run over the surface during firing to convey a feeling of spontaneity that complements the lively gestures and expressive faces of both camel and riders.

The early Tang emperors proclaimed a policy of religious tolerance, and virtually the entire country adopted the flourishing Buddhist faith. However, thousands of Buddhist temples, shrines, and monasteries were destroyed and innumerable bronze statues melted down when Confucianism was reasserted during the ninth century and Buddhism was briefly persecuted as a "foreign" religion.

Nanchan Temple, located on Mount Wutai in the eastern part of Shanxi Province, is not only one of the rare wooden Buddhist structures surviving from the Tang Dynasty but also the first important surviving example of Chinese woodframe architecture (fig. **4–18**). Constructed in 782 CE, its curved and tiled roof has broad overhanging eaves supported by **brackets** (architectural supports projecting from the walls). Bracketing became a standard element of East Asian architecture, especially in palaces and temples. Also typical is the **bay** system of construction, in which a cubic unit of space, a bay, is formed by four posts and their lintels. The bay functioned in Chinese architecture as a sort of **module**, a basic unit of construction. To create larger structures, an architect multiplied the number of bays. Thus the three-bayed Nanchan Temple, modest in scope, gives an idea of the vast, multistoried, lost palaces of the Tang.

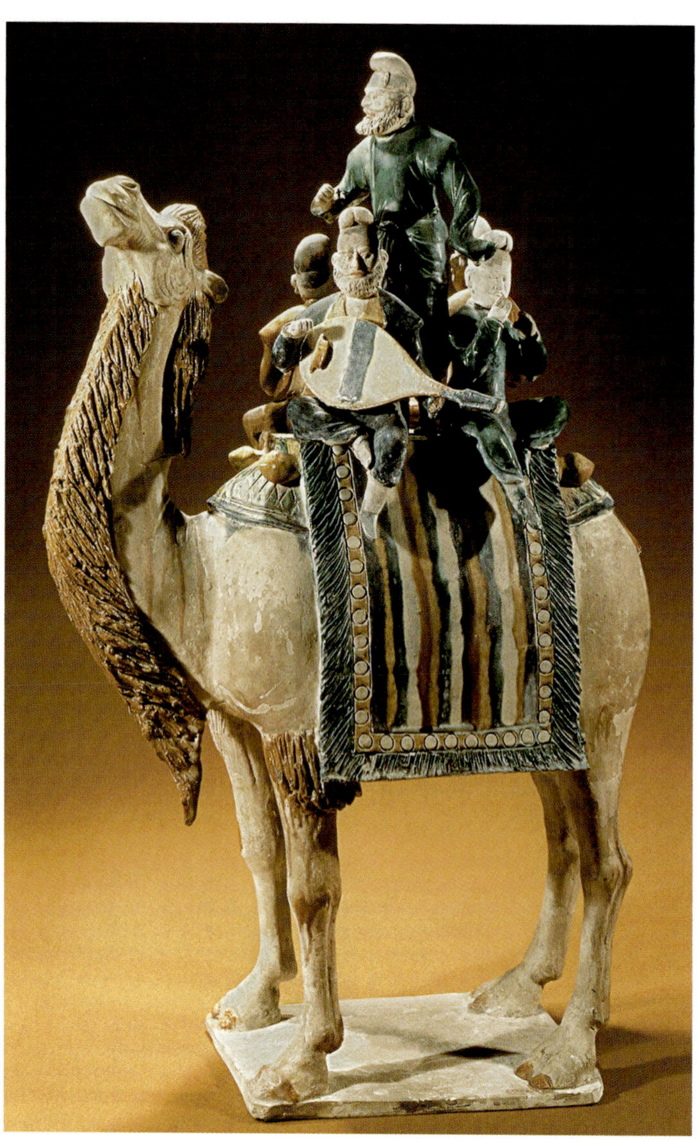

4–17 ***Camel Carrying a Group of Musicians*** from a tomb near Xi'an, Shaanxi Province. Tang Dynasty, c. mid-8th century CE. Earthenware with three-color glaze, height 26⅛" (66.5 cm). National Museum, Beijing

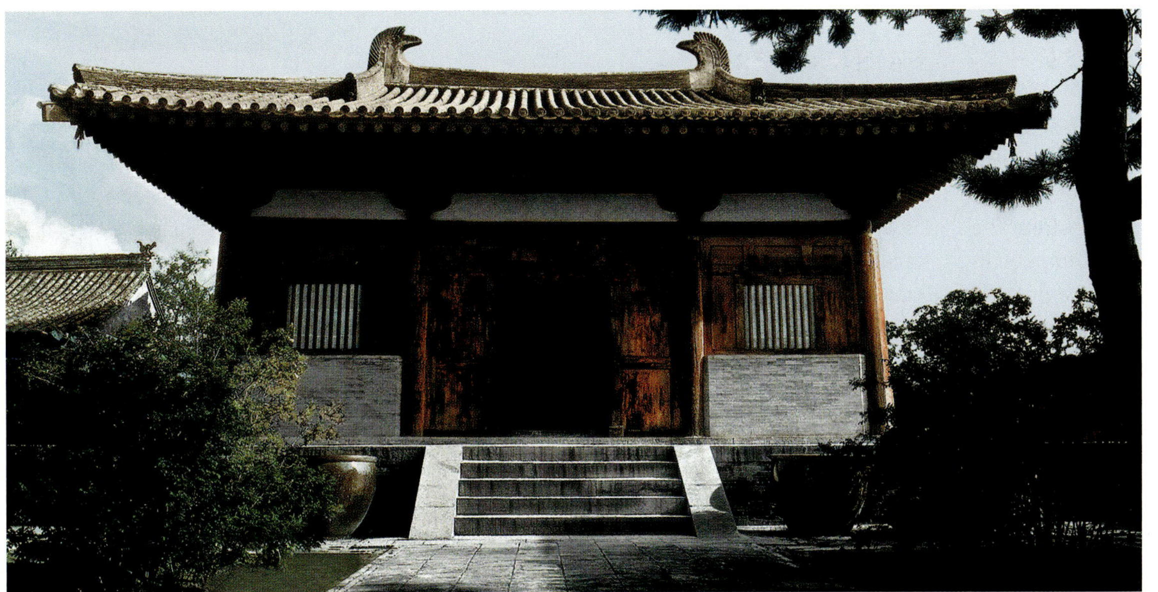

4–18 Nanchan Temple, Wutaishan, Shanxi Province. Tang Dynasty, 782 CE

The tiled roof, first seen in the Han tomb model (see fig. 4–15), has taken on a curved silhouette that becomes increasingly pronounced in later centuries. The very broad overhanging eaves are supported by a correspondingly elaborate bracketing system.

CLOSER LOOK

In Xi'an, the ancient capital of China, the Great Wild Goose Pagoda of the Ci'en Temple (fig. **4–19**) rises majestically above small buildings and low foliage. Massive walls, punctuated by roof after horizontal roof, dominate the surroundings with grace and power. The temple was constructed in 645 CE for the famous monk Xuan Zang on his return from a 16-year pilgrimage to India. At the Ci'en Temple, Xuan Zang taught and translated the Sanskrit Buddhist scriptures that he had brought back with him. His dedication to scholarship gave the temple special meaning for his students. Over the years, when students passed their official examinations, they went to the temple and inscribed their names, creating a veritable history of Chinese calligraphy.

Pagodas—towers associated with East Asian Buddhist temples—serve as reminders of the extent and influence of Buddhism. Like the stupas of South Asia, early East Asian pagodas were nearly solid, with small spaces for relics, and they retained *axis mundi* masts. In China the multistoried wooden pagodas with upward-curving roofs supported by elaborate bracketing are much like their prototypes, the earlier Han watchtowers. Later pagodas often provided access to the ground floor and sometimes to the upper levels as well. Although modified and repaired in later years (its seven stories were originally five, and a new finial has been added), the Great Wild Goose Pagoda still preserves the essence of Tang architecture in its simplicity, symmetry, proportions, and grace.

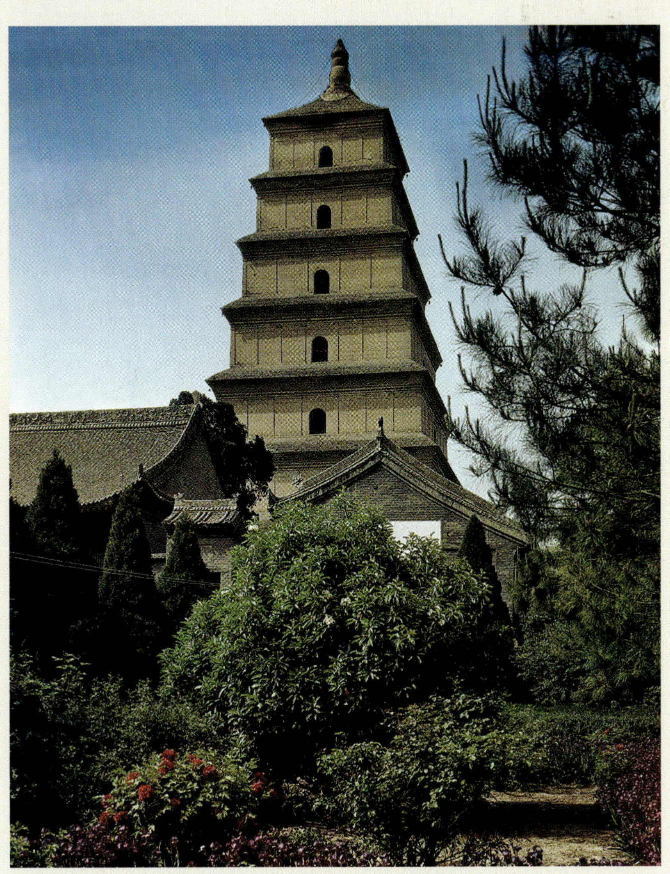

4–19 Great Wild Goose Pagoda of the Ci'en Temple, Chang'an, Shaanxi Province. Tang Dynasty, first erected 645 CE; rebuilt mid-8th century CE

CALLIGRAPHY

The emphasis on expressiveness and structural importance of brushstrokes finds its purest embodiment in calligraphy (the word comes from the Greek meaning "beautiful writing"). In China, calligraphy is regarded as one of the highest forms of artistic expression. For more than 2,000 years, China's literati, all of them Confucian scholars, have enjoyed being connoisseurs and practitioners of this art form. During the fourth century, calligraphy came to full maturity. The most important practitioner of the day was Wang Xizhi (c. 303–361 CE), whose works have served as models of excellence for all subsequent generations (fig. **4–20**).

Calligraphy is created by combining stylized strokes, executed with a brush and ink, to form the characters of Chinese writing. Chinese characters, unlike Western letterforms, evolved from pictographs, a picture or sign representing a thing or concept. Chinese calligraphic styles, from which Japanese and Korean calligraphy developed, are based on seven standard strokes, also known as the "Seven Mysteries": a horizontal line, a vertical line, a dot, sharp curves curling either to the left or right, and diagonal strokes executed at various angles, sweeping downward either toward the left or right.

Several styles of calligraphy developed in Asia over the centuries, each with its own unique traits and purpose. The characters in calligraphy used for meditation or poetry, for example, may appear far different from the characters seen in bureaucratic documents or official seals. Depending on the intent of the calligrapher, the width and length of strokes may vary between styles as may the sharpness of edges and corners and the concentration of ink on the page. (Compare, for example, the uniformly placed, compact characters with sharp strokes in figure 9–14 from China to the fluidity and wild curls that compose the elongated characters in figure 9–20 from Japan.)

The stamped characters that appear on Chinese artworks are seals, or personal emblems. The use of seals dates from the Zhou Dynasty, and to this day seals traditionally employ the archaic characters, known appropriately as "seal script," of the Zhou or Qin. Cut in stone, a seal may state a formal, given name, or it may state any of the numerous personal names that China's painters and writers may have adopted throughout their lives. A treasured work of art often bears not only the seal of its maker but also those of collectors and admirers through the centuries. In the Chinese view, these do not disfigure the work but add another layer of interest and history. This sample of Wang Xizhi's calligraphy, for example, bears the seals of two Song Dynasty emperors, a Song official, a famous collector of the sixteenth century, and two emperors of the Qing Dynasty of the eighteenth and nineteenth centuries.

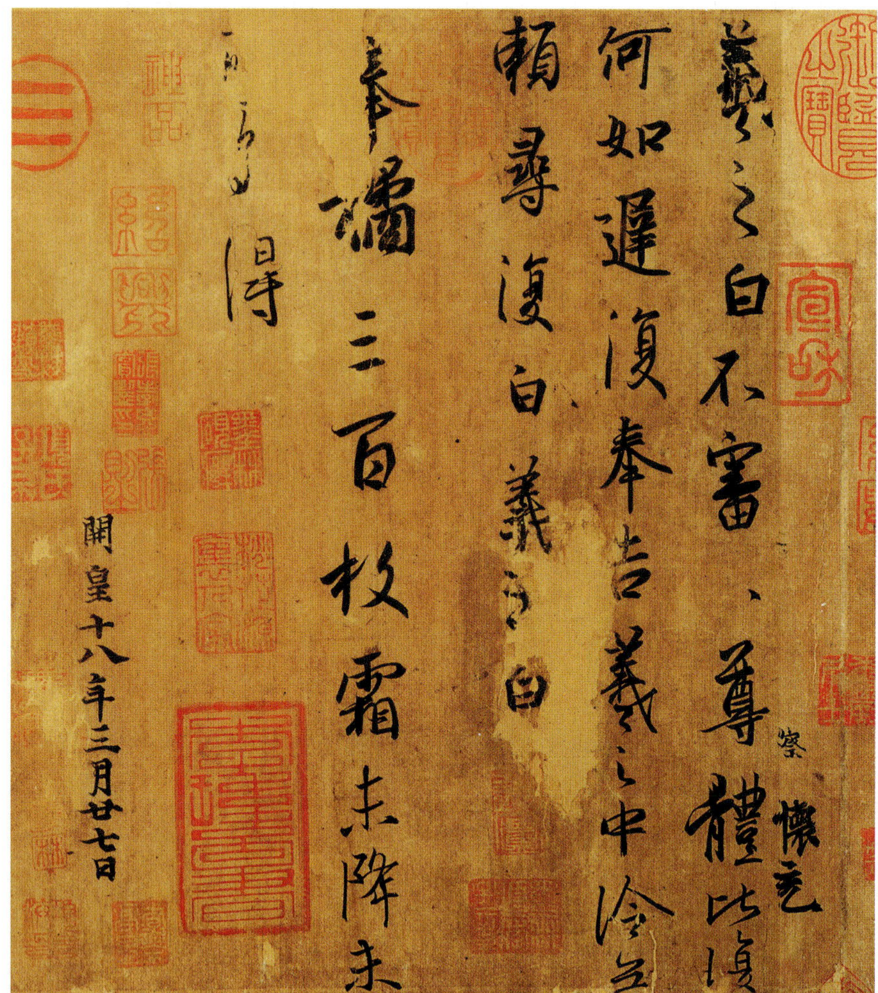

4–20 Wang Xizhi. Portion of a letter from the *Feng Ju* album.
Northern and Southern Dynasties, mid-4th century CE. Ink on paper, 9½" × 18½" (24.7 × 46.9 cm). National Palace Museum, Taipei, Taiwan, Republic of China

The Great Wild Goose Pagoda of the Ci'en Temple in Chang'an, the Tang capital, is another important monument of Tang architecture (see "Closer Look," page 93). Originally built of mud bricks between 645 and 652 CE, and rebuilt in the mid-eighth century of brick with wooden floors and steps, the Great Wild Goose Pagoda imitates the forms of wooden architecture of the time. The walls are decorated in low relief to resemble bays, and bracket systems are reproduced under the projecting roofs of each story. The pagoda helps us to visualize the splendor of Tang civilization and the architecture of the great cities of China.

Korea

In the late second century BCE, Emperor Wudi of China brought the northern part of the Korean peninsula into the Chinese Empire. By this time, the Korean people already had a long tradition as skilled ceramists and metalworkers. During the fourth century, Chinese settlers introduced Buddhism into the Korean peninsula and with it a demand for the figurative arts. The Koreans, in turn, transmitted their own blend of Chinese and Korean culture and religion to the Japanese islands at this time, introducing Buddhism there in 552 CE.

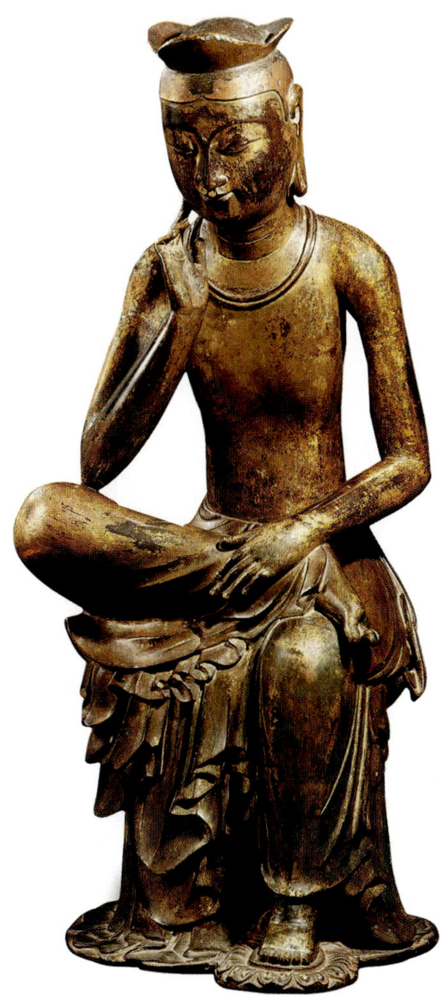

4–21 ***Bodhisattva Seated in Meditation***, Korea. Three Kingdoms period, early 7th century. Gilt bronze, height 35¾" (91 cm). National Museum of Korea, Seoul, Republic of Korea

The elegant gilded bronze figure of a seated bodhisattva (fig. **4–21**) illustrates the refined and courtly style achieved by Korean artists in the sixth and seventh centuries. The slender figure leans on one knee, striking a graceful pose associated with meditation. The garments cling to his body, the low relief of their folds forming linear patterns—repeated arcs over the legs and sharply pleated folds at the sides. This sophisticated style of Korean art spread to the Japanese islands, where it became the aesthetic basis for an international style of Buddhist art shared by artists in Korea, China, and Japan.

Japan

Human habitation on the Japanese islands dates back at least 30,000 years, to a time when the islands were still linked to the East Asian landmass and the Sea of Japan was only a lake. Some 15,000 years ago, melting Ice Age glaciers caused the sea level to rise, creating the islands we know today. A distinctive Japanese culture began to emerge during the Jomon period (c. 12,000–300 BCE), which was remarkable for its creation of the world's earliest surviving fired pottery vessels.

From ancient times, indigenous Japanese taste has been distinguished by a respect for and a delight in natural materials. Wooden architecture—farmhouses or Shinto shrines—was often left unpainted, and ceramics frequently were, and are, only partly glazed in order to display the clay bodies underneath. Japanese artists delighted in asymmetry. Paintings and prints that may seem off-balance to Westerners are actually adroitly composed. In addition, a sense of humor and playfulness sometimes surfaces in unexpected contexts, even in religious art of great power and depth. Finally, the Japanese have preserved their cultural heritage while welcoming and creatively transforming foreign influences—first from China and Korea and more recently from Europe and North America.

Immigrants from Korea during the Yayoi (c. 300 BCE–300 CE) and Kofun (c. 300–552 CE) periods helped to transform Japan into an agricultural nation, where rice cultivation became widespread. The emergence of a class structure can be dated to the Yayoi period, as can the development of metal technology—first bronze and then iron.

The Kofun Period

During the ensuing Kofun, or "old tombs," period—named for its large royal tombs—a pattern of venerating leaders grew into the beginnings of an imperial system. This system, still in existence today in Japan, eventually equated the emperor (or, very rarely, empress) with the all-powerful sun goddess.

When a Kofun emperor died, chamber tombs furnished with pottery and other grave goods were constructed. Some tomb sites extend over more than 400 acres, with artificial hills built over the tombs themselves. The hills were topped with hollow ceramic works of sculpture called ***haniwa*** to further distinguish the sites.

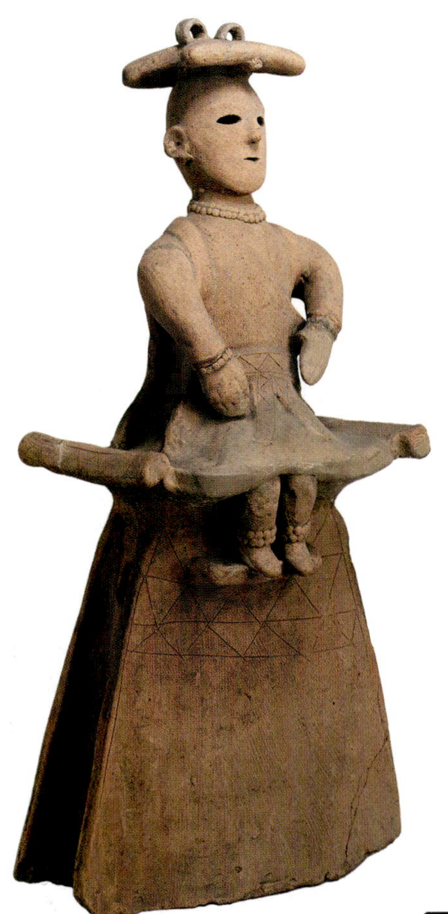

The first *haniwa* were simple cylinders that may have held jars with ceremonial offerings. Gradually these cylinders came to be made in the shapes of ceremonial objects—houses, boats, and, later, birds and animals. Finally, *haniwa* in human shapes were crafted, both female and male, representing all professions and classes. The *haniwa* illustrated here (fig. **4–22**) has been identified as a seated female shaman. Like shamans themselves, *haniwa* figures seem to have served as some kind of link between the world of the dead and the world of the living.

Haniwa figures may also reflect some of the beliefs of Shinto. This indigenous religion of Japan can be characterized as a loose confederation of beliefs in nature deities (*kami*). *Kami* were thought to inhabit many different aspects of nature, including particularly hoary and magnificent trees and rocks, as well as waterfalls, and living creatures such as deer. Shinto also emphasizes ritual purification of the ordinary world. In response to the arrival of Buddhism in Japan in the sixth century CE, Shinto became somewhat more systematized, with shrines, a hierarchy of deities, and more strictly regulated ceremonies.

One of the great Shinto sites is at Ise, on the coast southwest of Tokyo (fig. **4–23**), dedicated to the sun goddess, legendary ancestor of Japan's imperial family. For nearly 2,000 years, the shrine has been ritually rebuilt at 20-year intervals (most recently in 1993), by carpenters who train for the task from childhood. Stylistically and

4–22 *Haniwa* from Kyoto. Kofun period, 6th century CE. Earthenware, height 27" (68.5 cm). Tokyo National Museum

Haniwa *illustrate several characteristics of Japanese taste. They were left unglazed to reveal their clay bodies, and their makers explored the expressive potentials of simple and bold form.* Haniwa *shapes are never perfectly symmetrical; the slightly off-center placement of the eye slits, the irregular cylindrical bodies, and the unequal arms give them greater liveliness and individuality.*

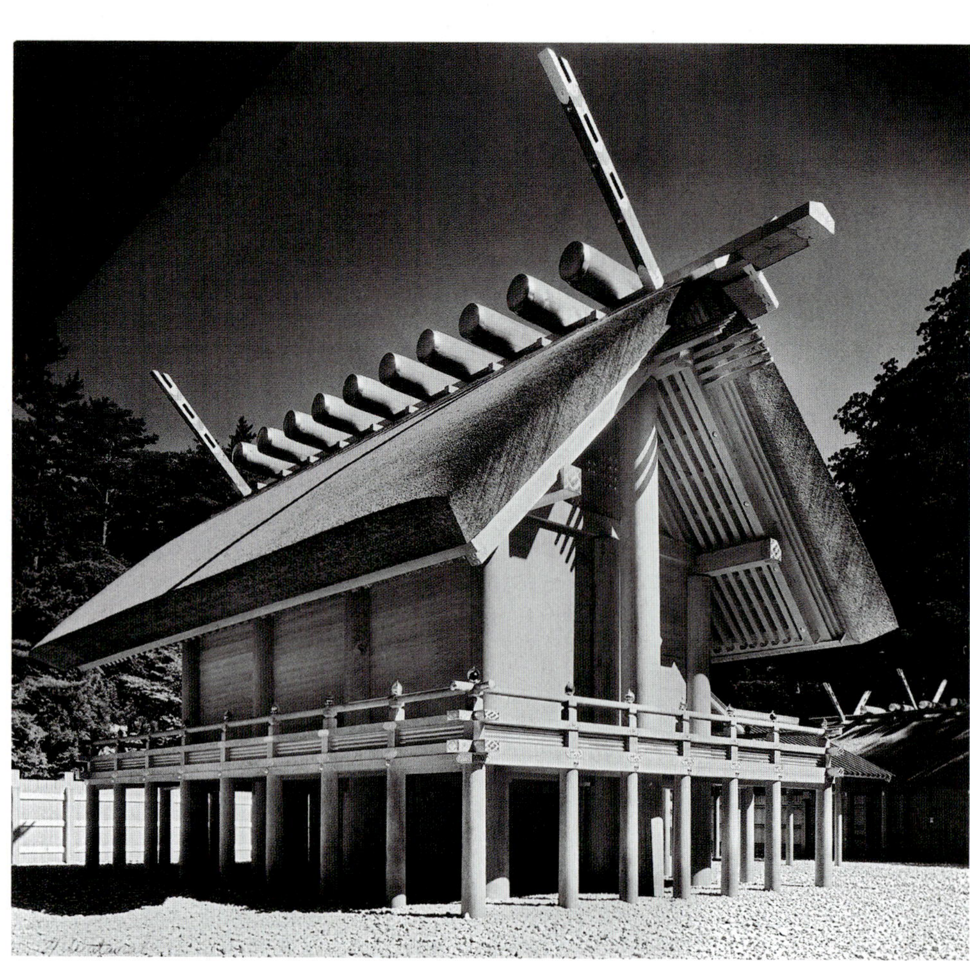

4–23 Inner Shrine, Ise, Mie Prefecture. Early 1st century CE; rebuilt 1993

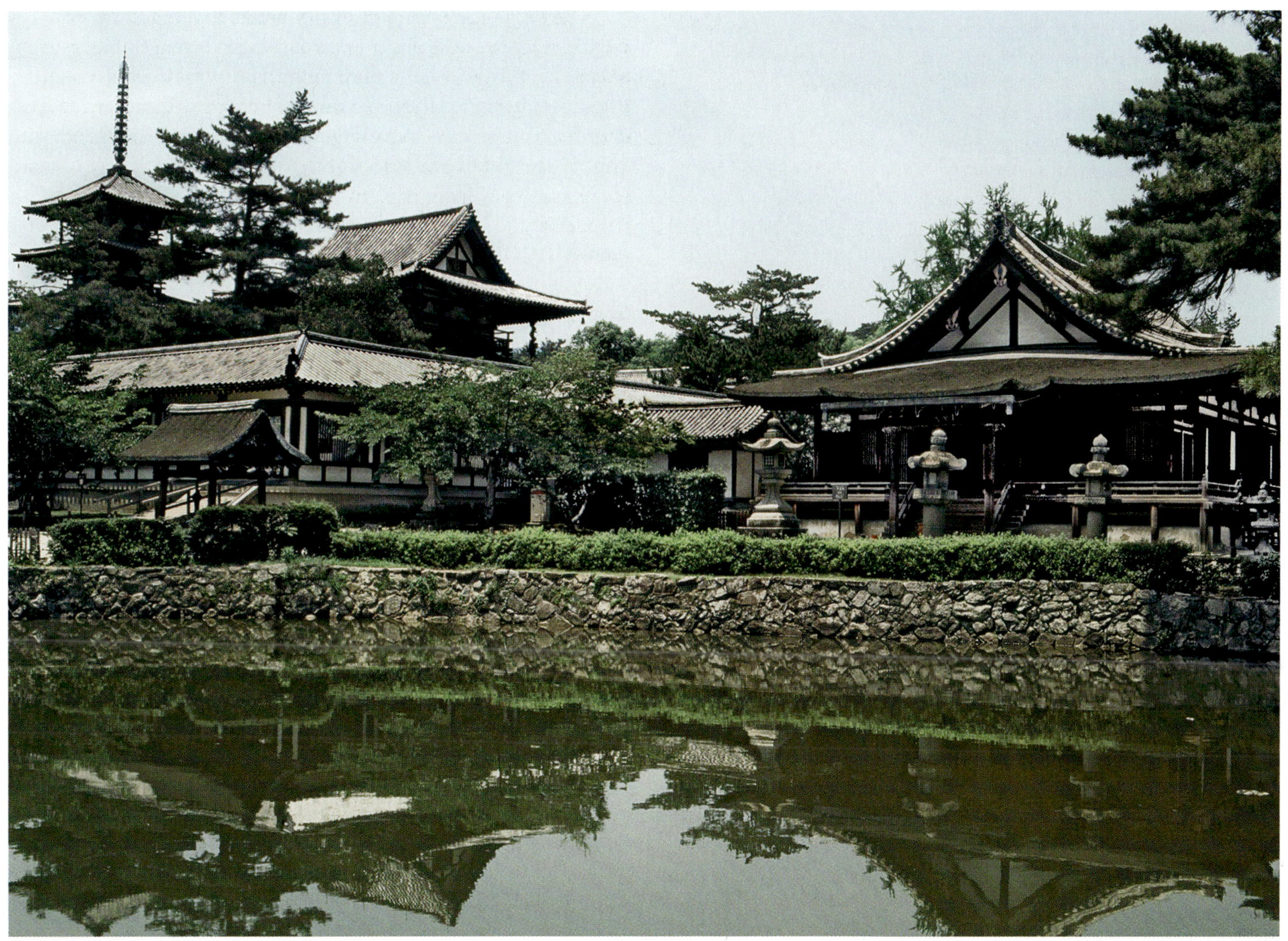

4–24 Main compound, Horyu-ji, Nara Prefecture. Asuka period, 7th century CE

technically, the shrine is typical of Shinto architecture: The builder used wooden piles to raise the building off the ground and unpainted cypress wood as a construction material; horizontal logs hold a thatched roof in place. These traditional features, which convey a sense of natural simplicity, ultimately derive from the architecture of ancient (first century CE) raised granaries used to store food. The Inner Shrine at Ise houses spiritual rather than corporal nourishment—a sword, a mirror, and a jewel—the three sacred symbols of Shinto.

The Asuka Period

During the Asuka period (552–646 CE), a time of intense cultural transformation, the Japanese adopted from China a system of writing and a centralized governmental structure. At the same time Buddhism was introduced from China and Korea, coexisting with Shinto. Reaching Japan in Mahayana form, with its many buddhas and bodhisattvas (see "Buddhism," page 80), Buddhism soon became a state religion. The imported religion introduced not only different gods but also an entirely new concept of religion itself. Where Shinto had found deities in nature, Buddhism offered a rich cosmology with profound teachings of meditation and enlightenment, as well as a human founder.

The most significant surviving early Japanese Buddhist temple is Horyu-ji (fig. **4–24**), located not far from Nara. Founded in 607 CE and rebuilt after a fire in 670, Horyu-ji includes the oldest surviving wooden structure in the world. The main compound consists of a rectangular courtyard surrounded by covered corridors. Within are two buildings, a large *kondo*, or golden hall, and a slender, five-story pagoda. Both are Chinese-style woodframe buildings with tiled roofs. The *kondo* is filled with Buddhist images and is used for worship and ceremonies. The pagoda serves as a **reliquary** (a repository for sacred relics) and is not entered. Other monastery buildings, such as a repository for sacred texts and dormitories for monks, lie outside the main compound.

Among the many treasures preserved in Horyu-ji is a miniature shrine decorated with paintings in **lacquer** (a type of hard, glossy

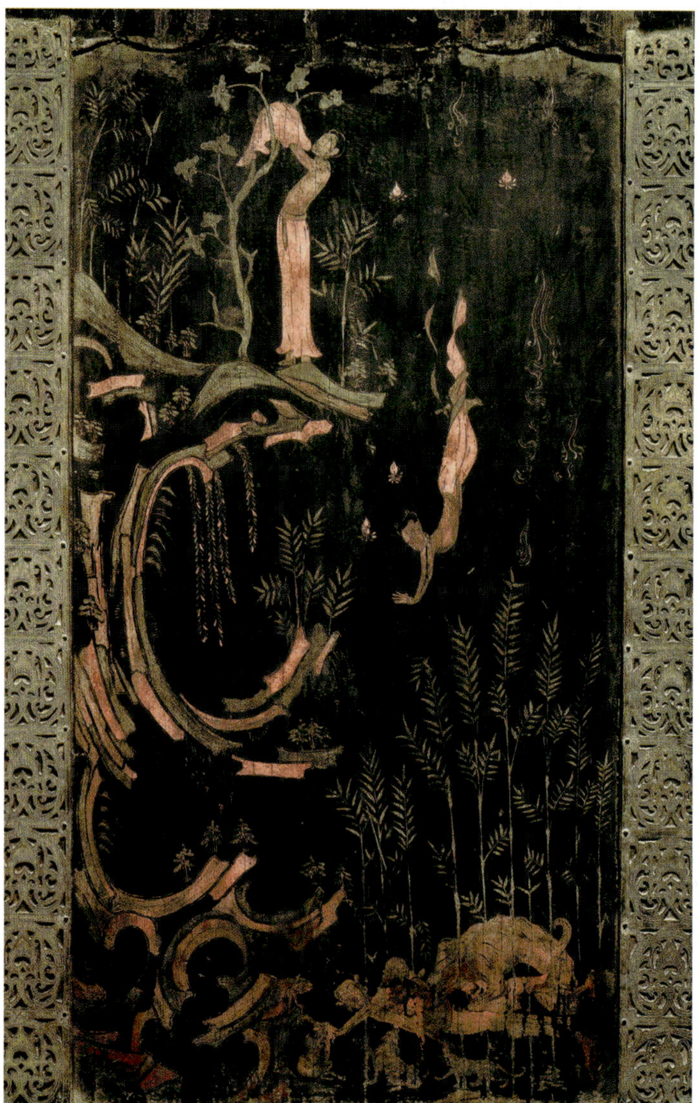

4–25 ***Hungry Tigress Jataka*****,** panel of the Tamamushi Shrine, Horyu-ji. Asuka period, c. 650 CE. Lacquer on wood, height of shrine 7' 7¾" (2.33 m). Horyu-ji Treasure House

varnish) (fig. **4–25**). It is known as the Tamamushi Shrine after the tamamushi beetle, whose iridescent wings were originally affixed to the shrine to make it glitter. The shrine may have been crafted in Korea or Japan, or perhaps by Korean artisans working in Japan, testifying to the international range of Buddhist art at this period.

The paintings ornamenting the Tamamushi Shrine are among the few two-dimensional works of art to survive from the Asuka period. The painting illustrated here tells a story from a former life of the Buddha, who is shown nobly sacrificing his life in order to feed his body to a starving tigress and her cubs. The tigers are at first too weak to eat him, so he jumps off a cliff to break open his flesh. The elegantly slender rendition of the Buddha's figure—shown three times in the three sequential stages of the story contained within this single frame—and the stylized treatment of the cliff, trees, and bamboo, represent a Buddhist style shared during this time by Chinese, Korean, and Japanese artists.

During the seventh and eighth centuries, Buddhism so thoroughly permeated the upper levels of society that an empress sought to cede her throne to a Buddhist monk. Her advisors intervened, but Buddhism remained the single most significant element in Japanese culture, comfortably coexisting with Shinto, just as it had with Hinduism in India and with Confucianism and Daoism in China.

Looking Back

The civilizations of South and East Asia—including those that flourished in what are today India, China, Korea, Japan, and Indonesia—are among the world's oldest and also rank among the most culturally rich. Early Asian cultures evolved from simple societies into complex, highly organized political and economic systems. They were bolstered by belief systems and rituals that evolved into religions that are still widely practiced today. Indigenous beliefs such as Hinduism in India, Confucianism in China, and Shinto in Japan contributed to distinctive styles and subjects of art in the locations where these religions proliferated. Buddhism, which originated in India, spread throughout the continent, making the Buddha a common subject throughout Asian art.

The rich philosophical and spiritual life of early Asian cultures was paralleled by increasing technical refinement and artistic skill in many media. Writing evolved into a complex and stylized pictographic script—**calligraphy**—in which the image of every character is a miniature work of art. Together with poetry, the mastery of such expressive linguistic images came to be considered the highest form of art, a situation we will encounter again in the more recent art of Islam.

IN PERSPECTIVE

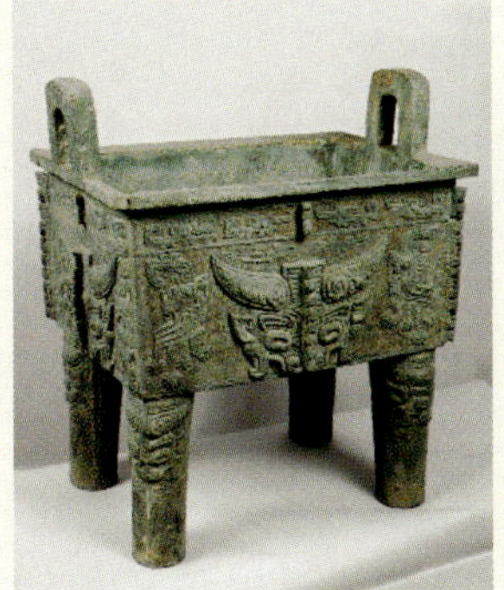

FANG DING, c. 1200 BCE

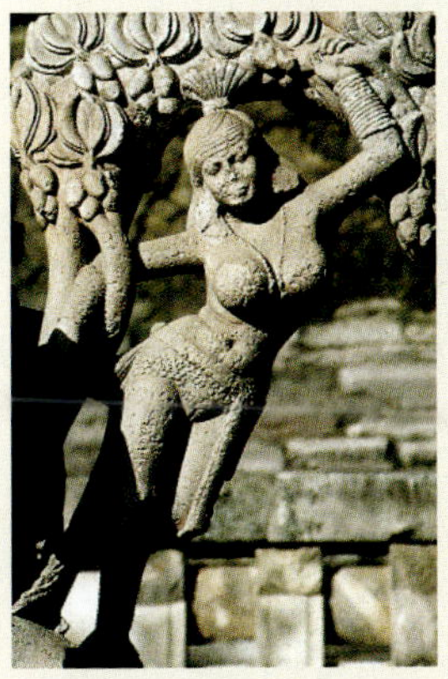

YAKSHI BRACKET FIGURE, c. 150–50 BCE

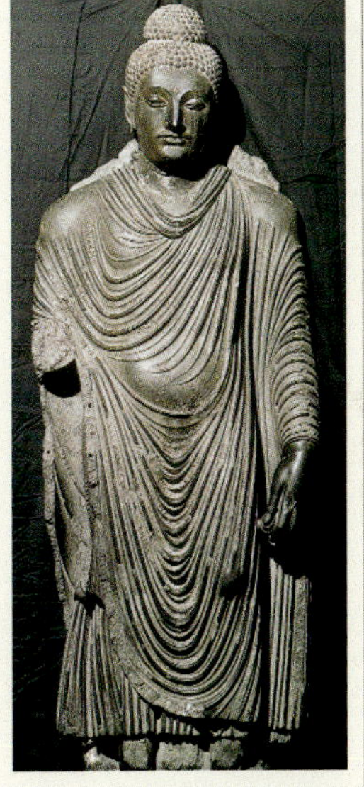

GANDHARAN BUDDHA, c. 2nd–3rd century CE

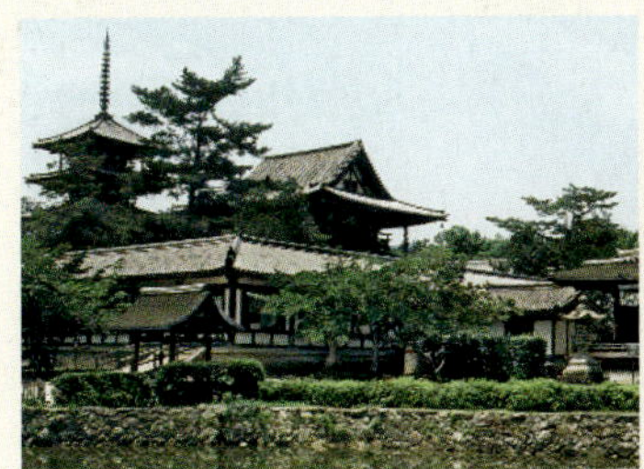

HORYU-JI, 7th century CE

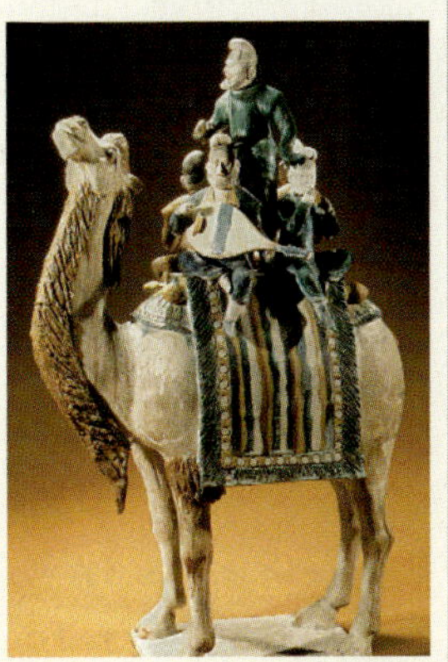

CERAMIC CAMEL, c. mid-8th century CE

3000 BCE

- **Indus Valley Civilization,** c. 2600–1900 BCE

2000

- **Vedic Period in India,** c. 1750–322 BCE
- **Shang Dynasty in China,** c. 1700–1100 BCE

1000

- **Confucius,** 551–479 BCE
- **Shakyamuni Buddha,** c. 563–483 BCE
- **Qin Dynasty in China,** 221–206 BCE
- **Han Dynasty in China,** 206 BCE–220 CE

0

- **Kofun Period in Japan,** c. 300–552 CE
- **Gupta Period in India,** c. 320–500 CE

500 CE

- **Asuka Period in Japan,** 552–646 CE
- **Tang Dynasty in China,** 618–907 CE

1000

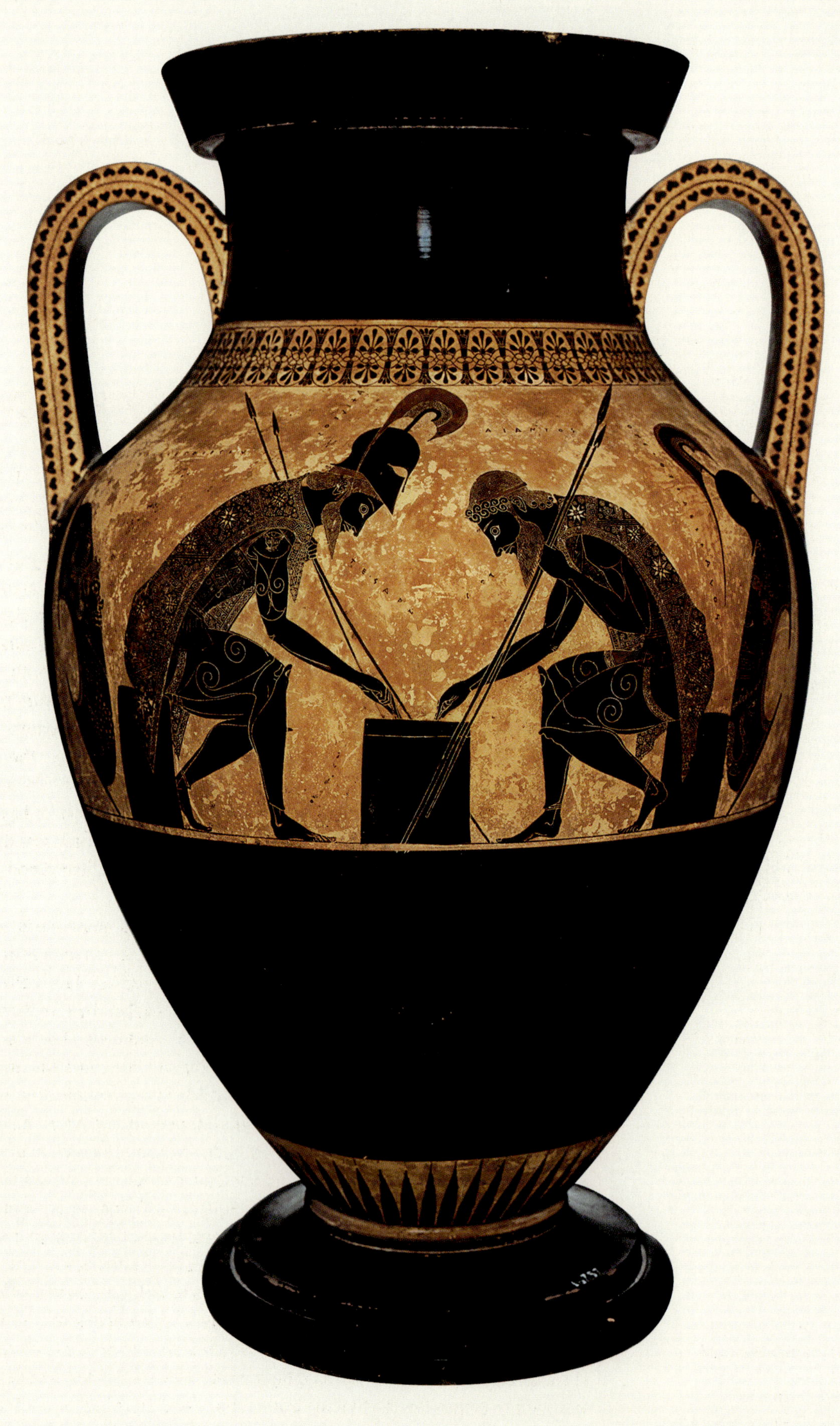

5
Art of Ancient Greece and the Aegean World

LOOKING FORWARD

This elegantly contoured **amphora** (fig. **5–1**) was conceived and created to be more than the all-purpose storage jar indicated by its shape, substance, and size. A strip around the belly of its bulging form was reserved by Exekias, the mid-sixth-century BCE Athenian artist who signed it proudly as both potter and painter, for the presentation of a narrative episode from the Trojan War, one of the signal stories of the ancient Greeks' mythical conception of their past. Two heroic warriors, Achilles and Ajax, sit across from each other, supporting themselves on their spears as they lean in toward the block between them that serves as a makeshift board for their game of dice. Ajax, to the right, calls out "three"—his speech signaled by the word itself, written out diagonally on the surface as if issuing from his mouth. Achilles counters with "four," the winning number, his victory presaged by the visual prominence of the boldly silhouetted helmet perched on his head. (Ajax's headgear has been set casually aside on his shield, leaning behind him.) Ancient Greek viewers, however, would have perceived the tragic irony of Achilles' victory. When these two warriors returned from this playful diversion into the serious contest of battle, Achilles would be killed. Soon afterwards, the grieving Ajax would take his own life in despair.

The poignant narrative encounter portrayed on this amphora is also a masterful compositional design. Crisscrossing diagonals and compressed overlapping of spears, bodies, and table, describe spatial complexity as well as surface pattern. The varying textures of hair, armor, and clothing are dazzlingly evoked by the alternation between expanses of unarticulated surface and the finely incised lines of dense pattern. Careful contours convey a sense of three-dimensional human form. And the arrangement coordinates with the very shape of the vessel itself, its curving outline matched by the warriors' bending backs, the line of its handles continued in the tilt of the leaning shields.

There is no hint here of gods or kings. Focus rests on the private diversions of heroic warriors as well as on the identity and personal style of the artist who portrayed them. In contrast to the civilizations of ancient Egypt and China, in ancient Greece greater prominence is given to human beings—or at least to an elite group of men. Supernatural forces are certainly still at work—Greek gods meddle in, and often control, the affairs of men and women—but even the gods themselves have human forms and human foibles. This new focus mirrors a new political system in which democracy replaced one-man, divine rule. And this new view of society required a new art: one centered in the material world but reflecting the philosophers' search for the human values of truth, virtue, and harmony, qualities that imbue both subject and style in this celebrated work.

5–1 Exekias (potter and painter). ***Ajax and Achilles Playing a Game.*** c. 540–530 BCE. Black-figure decoration on a ceramic amphora. Height of amphora 24" (61 cm). Vatican Museums, Rome

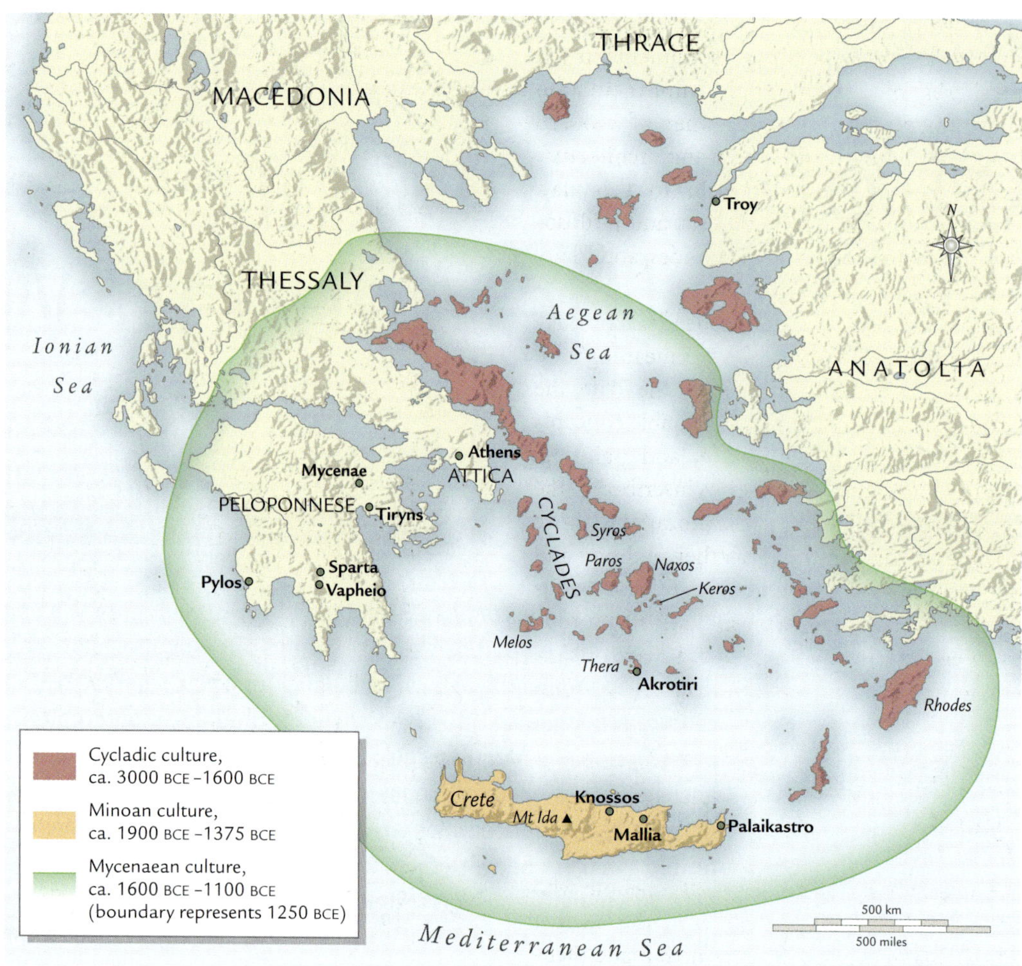

Map 5–1 The Aegean World and Ancient Greece

The Aegean region of Europe is an area composed of the Greek peninsula and a cluster of nearby islands in the Aegean Sea between the mainland and the large island of Crete. Being natives of a rocky peninsula and many islands, Aegean peoples became seafaring and adventurous by necessity. Unlike most of the early civilizations we have already considered, which arose in fertile river valleys, the people of Greece, the Cyclades, and Crete looked to the surrounding seas for both security and resources (see map **5–1**). And, from the third millennium BCE, through the Classical art of fifth-century BCE Athens, and extending into the broader development of the Hellenistic period beginning at the end of the next century, they created visual arts of arresting quality and originality.

Human settlements were established as early as 6000 BCE in the Cyclades, but since they left no written records, the prosperous Bronze Age society that developed there about 3000 BCE remains a mystery. The art they left behind has become a principal source of information about them.

At the start of the Aegean Bronze Age, about 3100 BCE, a culture marked by the use of bronze weapons and tools began to take shape on the island of Crete, south of the Cyclades. By around 1900 BCE it developed into the culture modern archaeologists have called Minoan. Strategically located, Minoan Crete became a great sea power, reaching its height between 1750 and 1470 BCE, the so-called New Palace period. Excavations in and around immense architectural complexes, dating from as early as 1900 BCE, have revealed the richness of Minoan art and ceremony and have uncovered ceramics, sculpture, wall paintings, and spectacular work in ivory and gold.

Minoan Crete declined after 1500 BCE, and dominance in the Aegean region shifted to a mainland Greek culture known as Mycenaean, after one of its major cities, Mycenae. The Mycenaeans, who spoke an early form of the Greek language, built fortified strongholds ruled by local princes or kings, warlords whose exploits were memorialized in later Greek epics such as the *Iliad* and the *Odyssey*.

The Aegean Bronze Age ended about 1100 BCE, when Mycenaean civilization collapsed for unknown reasons. A period of disorganization followed, and not until around 900 BCE did the inhabitants of the Aegean region begin to flourish again. These were the people who came to be called the Greeks. Linked by language—most spoke some form of Greek by then—they lived in self-sufficient, close-knit communities scattered throughout the region, which eventually developed into independently governed city-states.

Over the ensuing 700 years, the Greeks were spectacularly creative. We still credit them with groundbreaking experiments in science, mathematics, and herbal medicine; with the implementation of a representative government that is a forerunner of modern democracy; and with an astounding legacy of art and architecture that continues to influence the Western world to this day. Admiration for the works of Greek poets, dramatists, and philosophers, including Homer, Aeschylus, Sophocles, Euripides, and Plato, has also endured for more than two millennia.

Ancient Greek philosophers sought to define the ideal community, the actions of responsible citizenship, and the meaning of a good life by speculating on the nature of the Good, the True, the Beautiful. Artists responded by embodying such intangible concepts in the material forms of sculpture, architecture, and painting. "Know thyself" and "Nothing in excess" are maxims inscribed in the sanctuary of the sun god, Apollo, at Delphi in the mountains above the Gulf of Corinth. These words and the ideas they embody and inspire seem to have been imprinted on the heart and hands of every Greek artist: focus on human beings; study the variety found within the natural world in which we live; and strive to simplify and clarify these impressions in order to capture an ideal essence of life.

The Cycladic Islands

During the late Neolithic and early Bronze Ages, the people who lived on the Cyclades—like their contemporaries in the ancient Near East and Egypt (see Chapters 2 and 3)—farmed, made utensils, and engaged in trade. They used local stone to build fortified towns and hillside burial chambers, and they produced ceramic pottery and clay figurines of humans and animals.

Human figurines made of a fine white marble, abundant especially on the islands of Naxos and Paros, have been unearthed in and around Cycladic graves. Most depict women, although a few male statuettes have been found, including depictions of musicians and acrobats. Now starkly white, the statuettes originally had painted faces and hair. Since they were unearthed at grave sites, they may have been used in religious or burial rituals.

The *Seated Harp Player* is a fully developed sculpture in the round (fig. **5–2**). The figure has been reduced to geometric essentials, yet with careful attention to those elements that best characterize an actual musician. The harpist sits on a high-backed chair with a splayed base, head tilted back as if singing, knees and feet apart for stability, and arms raised, ready to pluck the strings. So expressive is the pose that we can almost hear the music.

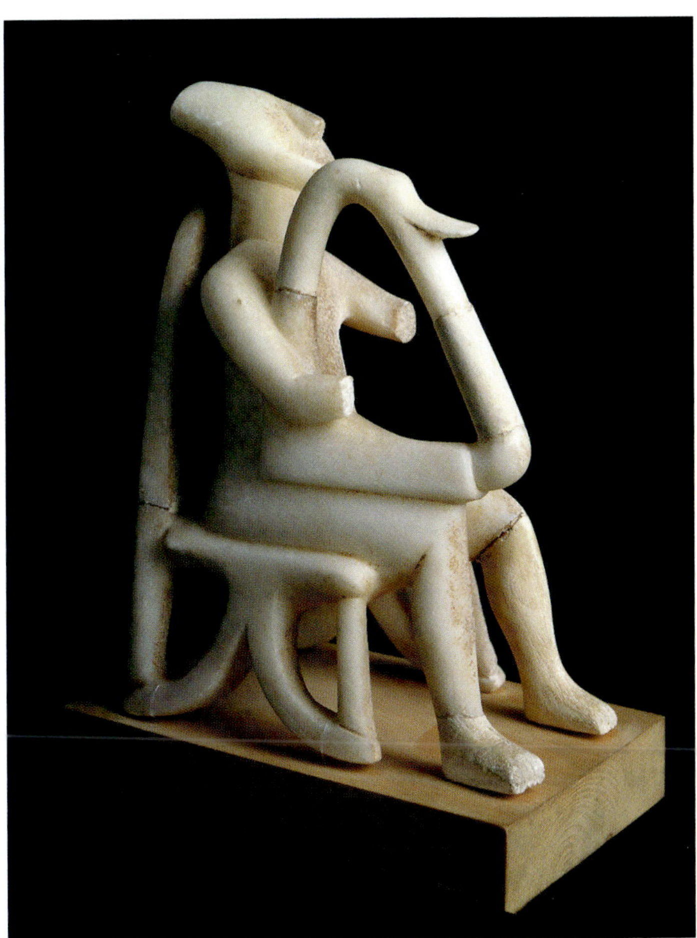

5–2 ***Seated Harp Player***, from Keros, Cyclades. c. 2700–2500 BCE. Marble, approx. 11½" (29.2 cm) high. Museum of Cycladic Art, Athens

Minoan Crete

The Minoan culture of the island of Crete flourished between c. 1900 and 1375 BCE. The word "Minoan" comes from a Greek legend about King Minos of Crete, who was said to have kept a human-eating monster called a Minotaur (half human and half bull) at the center of a labyrinth, or maze.

Crete, the largest of the Aegean islands, is 155 miles long and 36 miles wide. The earliest Minoans were self-sufficient agriculturally; they produced grains and fruit and raised cattle and sheep, which they traded for various luxury goods and for the copper and tin ores they needed to make bronze. Ancient Minoan traders must have been highly skilled sailors, traveling to ports in places as distant as Egypt, the Near East, and Anatolia (western Turkey).

Relatively little is known about daily life during the Minoan period, although a number of written records have been found at archaeological sites. The two earliest forms of Minoan writing, a form of hieroglyphs and a script called Linear A, still defy translation, but surviving documents in a later script, Linear B, give insights into Minoan material culture.

Minoan civilization remained very much a mystery until a British archaeologist, Sir Arthur Evans (1851–1941), excavated the buried ruins of an extraordinary building complex at Knossos, near Crete's north coast, in the early twentieth century. Great complexes such as Knossos were called "palaces" by modern archaeologists even though we do not know enough about the socio-political structure of Minoan Crete to be sure that there were kings. Safeguarded by watchtowers and stone walls, they were used simultaneously as administrative, commercial, and religious centers. The

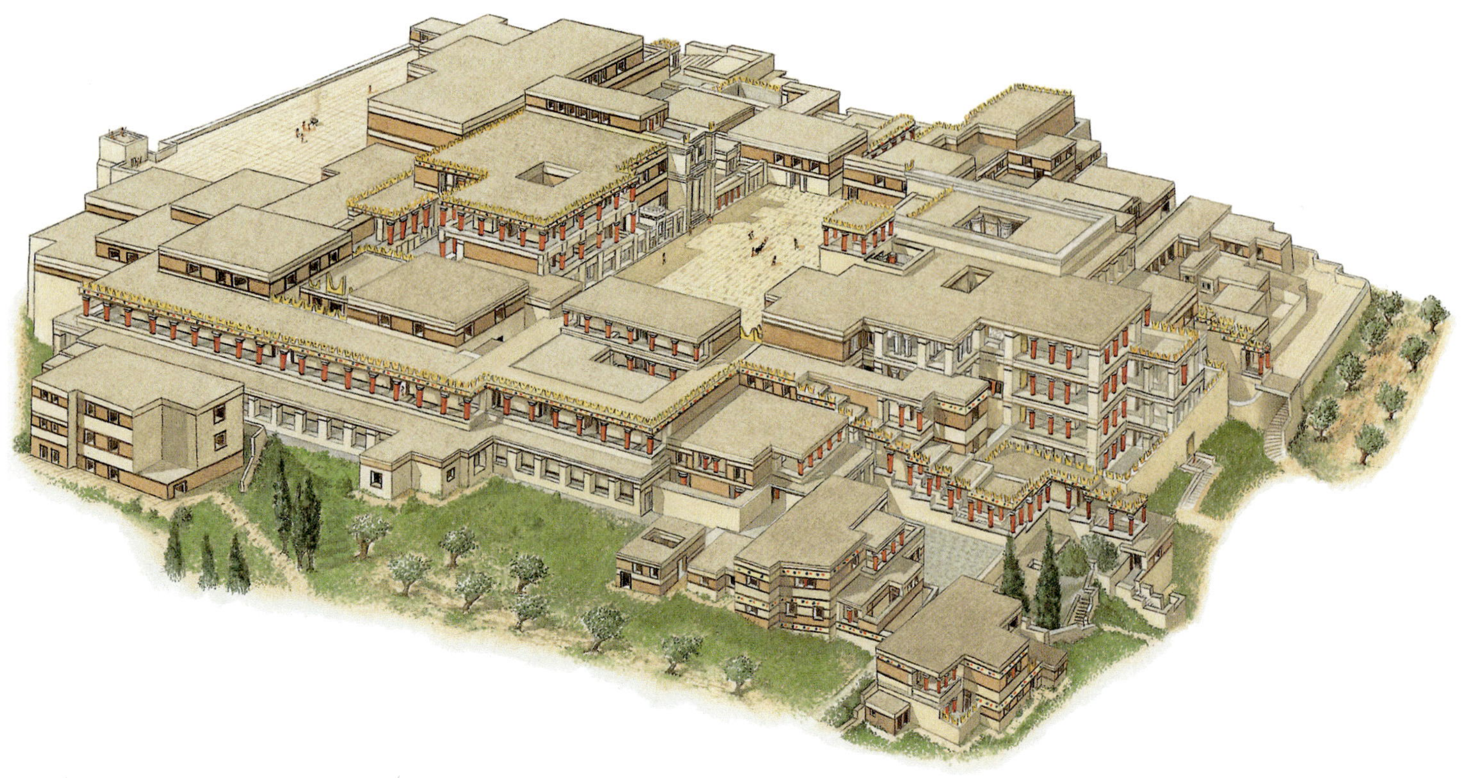

5–3 Reconstruction of the palace complex, Knossos, Crete. Site occupied 2000–1375 BCE

The architectural complex depicted in this drawing is the one built after destructive earthquakes and fires in c. 1700 BCE. It would be destroyed again about 1375 BCE. From the central courtyard, corridors and stairs led to several levels of suites of rooms, additional smaller courtyards, and light-wells.

builders devised an almost earthquake-proof flexible wall system of timber supports and braces with light, mud-brick infill. Only façades and lower walls were faced with **dressed stone** (cut and highly finished).

But even so, damage to several palaces including Knossos from a major earthquake about 1700 BCE required repair, and in the process many were enlarged. The resulting "new palaces"—multistoried, flat-roofed, and with many columns—were designed with staggered levels, open stairwells, and strategically placed air shafts and light-wells to maximize air and light. Residential, manufacturing, and warehouse areas surrounded a large, central courtyard.

During its heyday, the palace complex at Knossos covered 6 acres (fig. **5–3**). Its residential quarters had many luxuries: sunlit courtyards, richly colored murals, and an extraordinarily sophisticated plumbing system. Clusters of workshops in and around Knossos and other complexes formed commercial centers. Huge storerooms point to the centralized management of trade in foodstuffs. In a single storeroom at Knossos, excavators found enough large ceramic jars to hold 20,000 gallons of olive oil.

Minoan painters worked on a large scale, covering the walls of palace rooms with geometric borders, views of nature, and scenes of human activity. Elegantly drawn linear contours are filled with bright colors. There is a preference for profile or full-faced views, and a love of stylization that turns natural forms into decorative patterns but at the same time captures the appearance of the human body in motion. These conventions can be seen in the vivid murals surviving at Akrotiri, an outpouring of Minoan culture on the island of Thera (also called Santorini), north of Crete. One of the houses at Akrotiri has rooms dedicated to young women's initiation ceremonies. In the detail shown here, a young woman picks the purple flowers of the fall crocus, whose stigmas (also called saffron) were valued for their use as a yellow dye, as a flavoring for food, and as a medicinal plant to alleviate menstrual cramps (fig. **5–4**). The girl wears the typically colorful Minoan flounced skirt with a short-sleeved, open-breasted bodice, large earrings, and bracelets. Notice that she still has the shaved head, fringed hair, and long ponytail of a child, but the light blue color of her scalp indicates that hair is beginning to grow out.

One of the most famous paintings that has survived from the palace at Knossos shows two women and a man engaging in the dangerous ritual of bull leaping (fig. **5–5**). (Minoan painters followed the convention of depicting women with pale skin and men with dark skin already seen in ancient Egypt, fig. 3–12.) The woman at right is preparing to catch the man who is in the midst of his leap, and the woman at left is grasping the bull by its horns, perhaps ready to begin her own leap. The painting may show an initiation or fertility ritual, or it may honor a god by displaying human courage.

Painting on a smaller scale decorated ceramics produced in palace workshops. A striking vessel from the east Cretan site of Palaikastro, a bottle known as the Octopus Flask, dates from about

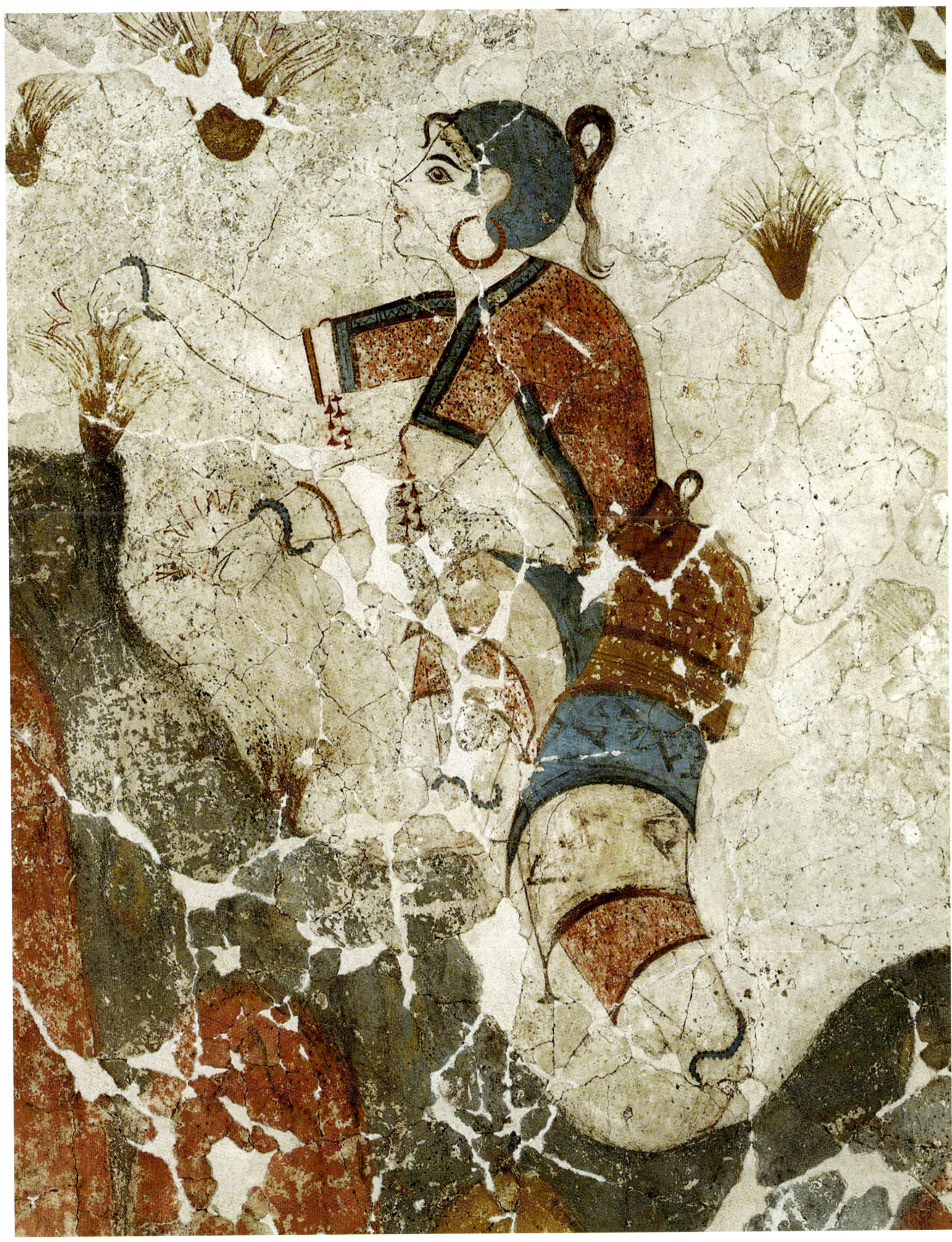

5–4 ***Young Girl Gathering Saffron Crocus Flowers***, detail of wall painting, Room 3 of House Xeste, Akrotiri, Thera. Before 1630 BCE. Thera Foundation, Petros M. Nomikos, Greece

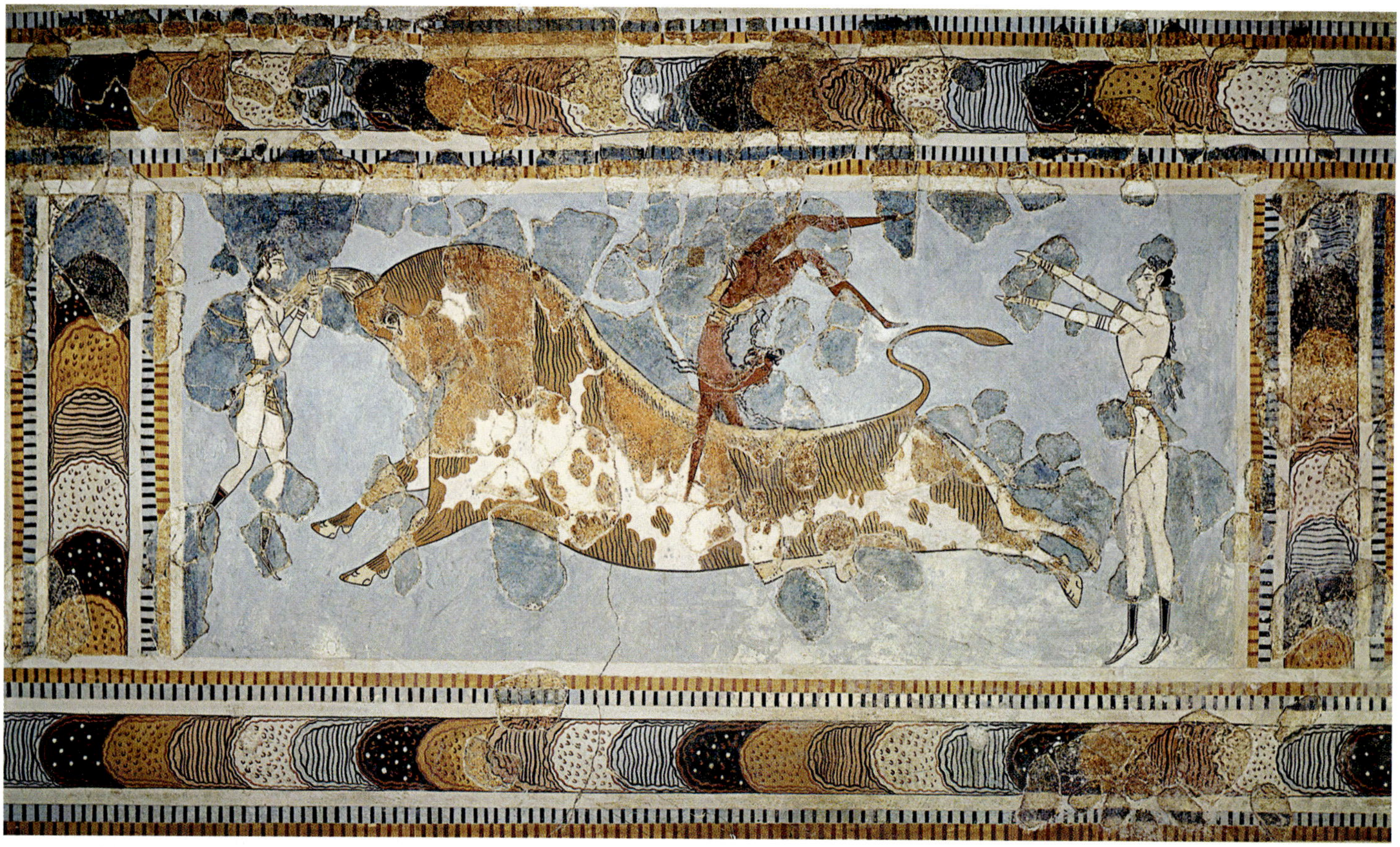

5–5 *Bull Jumping*, reconstructed wall painting, from the palace complex, Knossos, Crete. Late Minoan period, c. 1550–1450 BCE. Height approx. 24½" (62.3 cm). Archaeological Museum, Iraklion, Crete

Careful sifting during excavation preserved many fragments of the paintings that once covered the walls at Knossos. The pieces were painstakingly sorted and cleaned by restorers and reassembled into puzzle pictures that still had more pieces missing than found. Colors similar to the original ones have been used to fill the gaps, making it obvious which are the restored portions, but allowing viewers to have a sense of the image.

1500–1450 BCE (fig. **5–6**) and is decorated with a dynamic arrangement of marine life, seemingly in celebration of Cretan maritime power. Like microscopic life teeming in a drop of seawater, sea creatures float among an octopus's curling, sucker-lined tentacles. The painter captures the grace and energy of natural forms while presenting them as a stylized design in conspicuous harmony with the vessel's bulging shape.

The skills of Minoan metalsmiths made their work highly sought after in mainland Greece. Jewelers became adept at decorating goldwork with minute granules, or balls, of the precious metal fused to the surface, a technique known as **granulation**. This type of ornamentation enlivens a pendant perhaps made for a necklace in

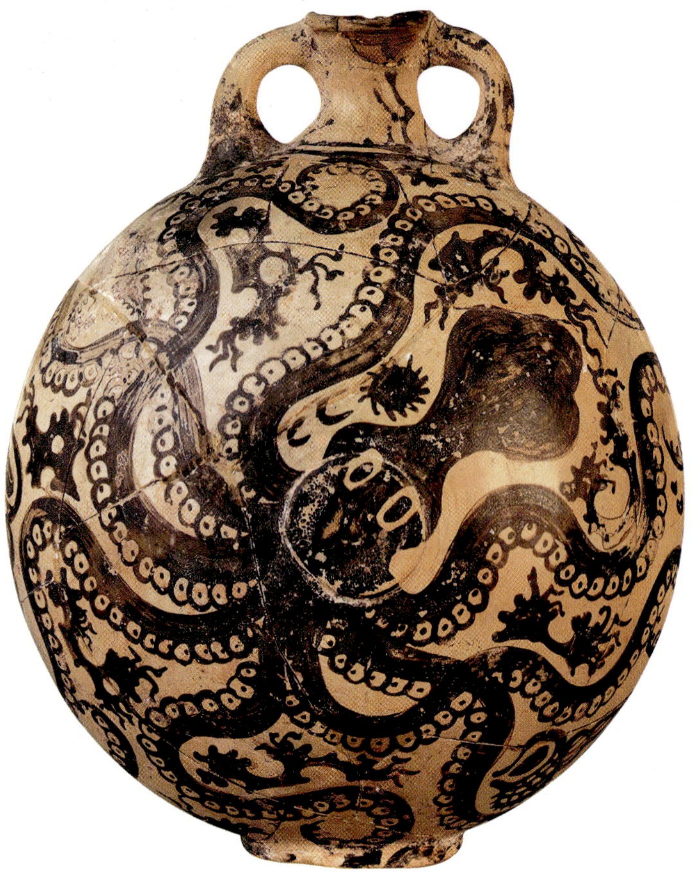

5–6 Octopus Flask, from Palaikastro, Crete. c. 1500–1450 BCE. Ceramic, height 11" (28 cm). Archaeological Museum, Iraklion, Crete

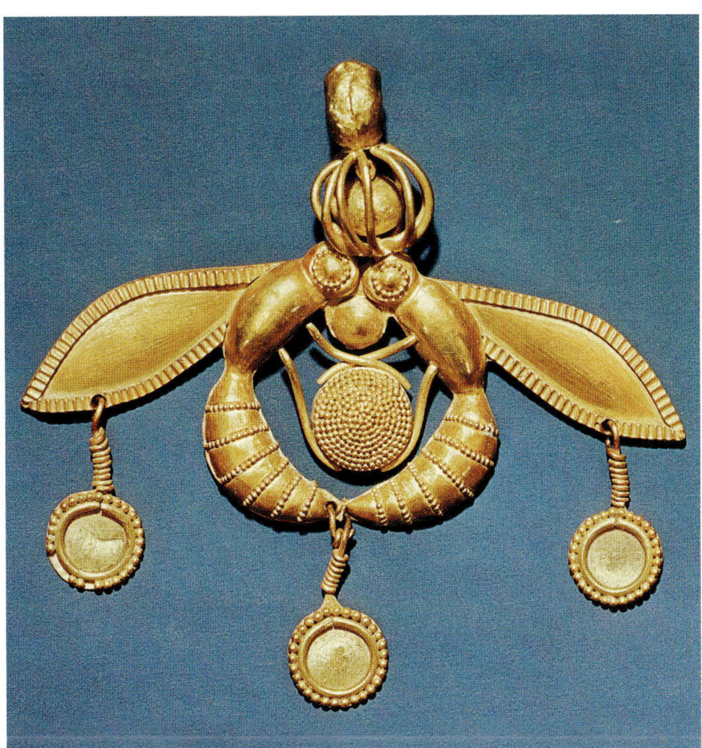

5–7 Pendant in the form of two bees or wasps from Chryssolakkos near Mallia, Crete. c. 1700–1550 BCE. Gold, height approx. 1 13/16" (4.6 cm). Archaeological Museum, Iraklion, Crete

about 1700–1550 BCE (fig. **5–7**). The artist arched a pair of bees or wasps around a circular drop of honey covered with granulation. Their sleek bodies, decorated with parallel rows of granules, are framed by a single pair of outspread wings.

Mycenean (Late Bronze Age) Civilization

At some time about 3000 BCE, Greek-speaking peoples invaded the Greek peninsula. They brought advanced metalworking, ceramic, and architectural techniques and displaced the indigenous Neolithic culture. Archaeologists use the term "Helladic" (from *Hellas*, the Greek name for Greece) to designate this Bronze Age period of mainland Greece. The Helladic period extends from about 3000 to 1000 BCE, overlapping the Cycladic and Minoan cultures. When Minoan culture declined after about 1500 BCE, a late Helladic mainland culture known as Mycenaean rose to dominance in the Aegean.

Life in the fortified city of Mycenae and other mainland strongholds probably contrasted sharply with life in the open palace complexes on the island of Crete. Mycenaean communities centered around strongholds controlled by local princes or kings. Evidence from shaft graves (deep vertical pits used for burial) dating from between 1600 and 1500 BCE suggests a society that became increasingly wealthy and stratified. Excavated by the German archaeologist Heinrich Schliemann (1822–1890) in 1876, the magnificent swords, daggers, scepters, jewelry, and drinking cups found within Mycenaean graves mark the burials of an elite class of warriors.

Three bronze dagger blades found in one of these shaft graves are decorated with inlaid scenes. The artist cut shapes out of different-colored metals—copper, silver, and gold—and inlaid them in the bronze blades, adding fine details in **niello** (a black sulfur alloy often inlaid into details incised into silver or gold). In the *Iliad*,

MYTHOLOGY

Human beings are storytellers, and virtually every society has created its own traditional stories that give form to its religious beliefs and attempt to explain the unexplained, including the origin of the universe, the meaning of birth and death, and the nature of good and evil. Throughout the world, mythological characters and their stories are the most frequently represented subjects in the history of art. The main characters of Classical mythology—that of Greek and Roman civilizations—are gods, demigods, heroes, and monsters. The behavior, relationships, and attitudes of such mythical characters mirror the beliefs and values of the society that created them.

Some myths seem to have originated in actual events. The Greek war against Troy in Asia Minor, for example, is now believed to have happened more than 300 years before it was mythologized in the *Iliad* and the *Odyssey*, by the poet known as Homer, in the eighth century BCE.

Homer tells of a Greek siege of the city of Troy, generally believed to have stood on the site of Hissarlik, in what is now Turkey. Paris, son of the Trojan king, abducted Helen, the most beautiful woman in the world and wife of King Menelaus of Sparta. Menelaus and his brother, King Agamemnon of Mycenae, the sons of Atreus, led the Greek troops in retaliation against Troy. Human warriors, gods, and goddesses took sides in the ten-year war. It is not clear whether Helen, Menelaus, or Agamemnon existed, or if even the Trojan War actually took place, but the story probably had roots in a real battle or raid. Ancient Greek historians, accepting the Trojan War as history, dated it anywhere from 1334 BCE to 1150 BCE, certainly long before Homer turned it into a legendary combat.

5–8 **Dagger blade** from Shaft Grave IV, Grave Circle A, Mycenae, Greece. c. 1550–1500 BCE. Bronze inlaid with gold, silver, and niello, length 9⅜" (23.8 cm). National Archaeological Museum, Athens

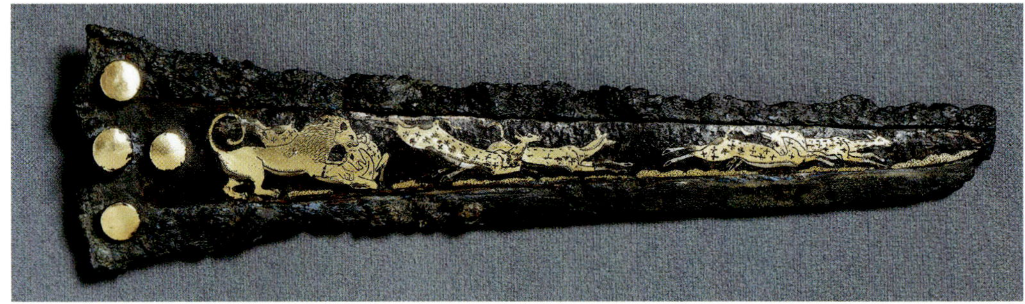

Homer's epic poem about the Trojan War, the poet describes similar decoration on Agamemnon's armor and Achilles' shield. The decoration on the blade shown here (fig. **5–8**) depicts a lion attacking a deer with four more terrified animals in full flight. Like the bull in figure 5–5, the animals spring forward in the "flying gallop" pose to indicate their speed and energy.

Other legends tell of a race of giants, the Cyclops, who moved the huge stones and gave the name "cyclopean" to the large-stone masonry seen in Mycenaean citadels and tombs. More than 100 above-ground burial places—referred to as **tholos tombs**—have been found on mainland Greece, nine of them in the vicinity of Mycenae. They were constructed for members of Helladic ruling families after shaft graves were no longer used. Perhaps the most impressive is the so-called "Treasury of Atreus," built around 1300–1200 BCE (fig. **5–9**).

An uncovered, walled passageway about 114 feet long and 20 feet wide led to the door of a conical structure, the **beehive tomb**. The spacious circular main chamber—47½ feet in diameter and 43 feet high—is formed by a **corbeled vault**: a stone ceiling built up in regular **courses** (layers) of dressed stone in overlapping and ever-decreasing rings carefully calculated to meet in a single **capstone** at the peak (fig. **5–10**). Like the Neolithic passage graves constructed in Western Europe (see fig. 1–15), the stone structure was covered by earth to form an artificial mound.

Megalithic walls, broken by a monumental entrance and one or two secret emergency exits, encircled the fortress of Mycenae (fig. **5–11**). The ruler's residence had a large audience hall called a **megaron**, or "great room." The main courtyard led to a porch, a vestibule, and then to the megaron where four large columns around a central hearth supported the ceiling. The roof section above the hearth was either raised or open to admit light and air and to permit smoke to escape. The imposing Lion Gate (c. 1250 BCE) led into the citadel (fig. **5–12**). The gate consists of a post-and-lintel frame that once held massive wood and metal doors, topped by a **relieving arch**, in this case, a corbel arch spanning the open space with layers of stones, each layer projecting over the preceding layer. In the opening over the door, a pair of lions nearly 9 feet tall flank a Minoan-style column that may symbolize the king's palace, and thus his royal power. The animals have lost their heads, but holes in the stones suggest that the heads were removable and probably fashioned of some precious material. If the lion heads were indeed made of bronze or gold, they must have created an imposing presence. From this gate, a long, stone passageway leads into the citadel, at the center of which stood the king's palace.

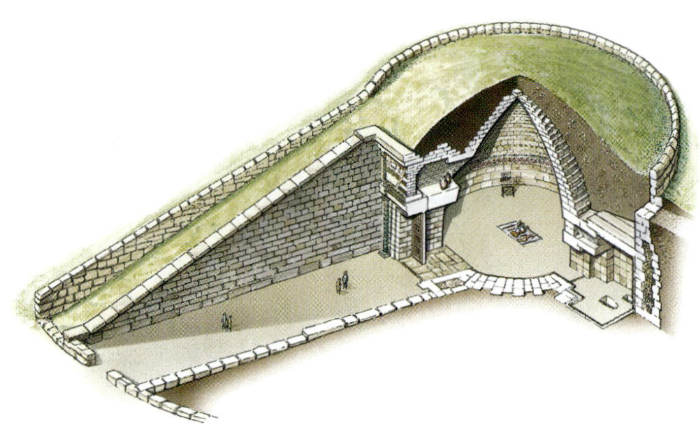

5–9 **Cutaway drawing of tholos tomb** (the so-called Treasury of Atreus), Mycenae, Greece. c. 1300–1200 BCE

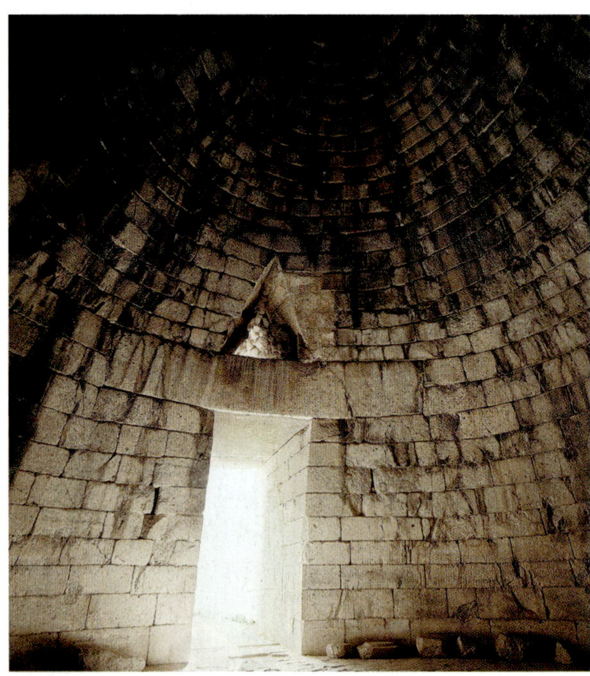

5–10 **Corbeled vault**, interior of tholos tomb (the so-called Treasury of Atreus), Mycenae, Greece. Limestone, height of vault approx. 43' (13 m), diameter 47' 6" (14.48 m)

For over a thousand years after it was constructed, this vast vaulted chamber remained the largest unobstructed interior space built in Europe. It was exceeded in size only by the Roman Pantheon (see fig. 6–27), built c. 118–128 BCE.

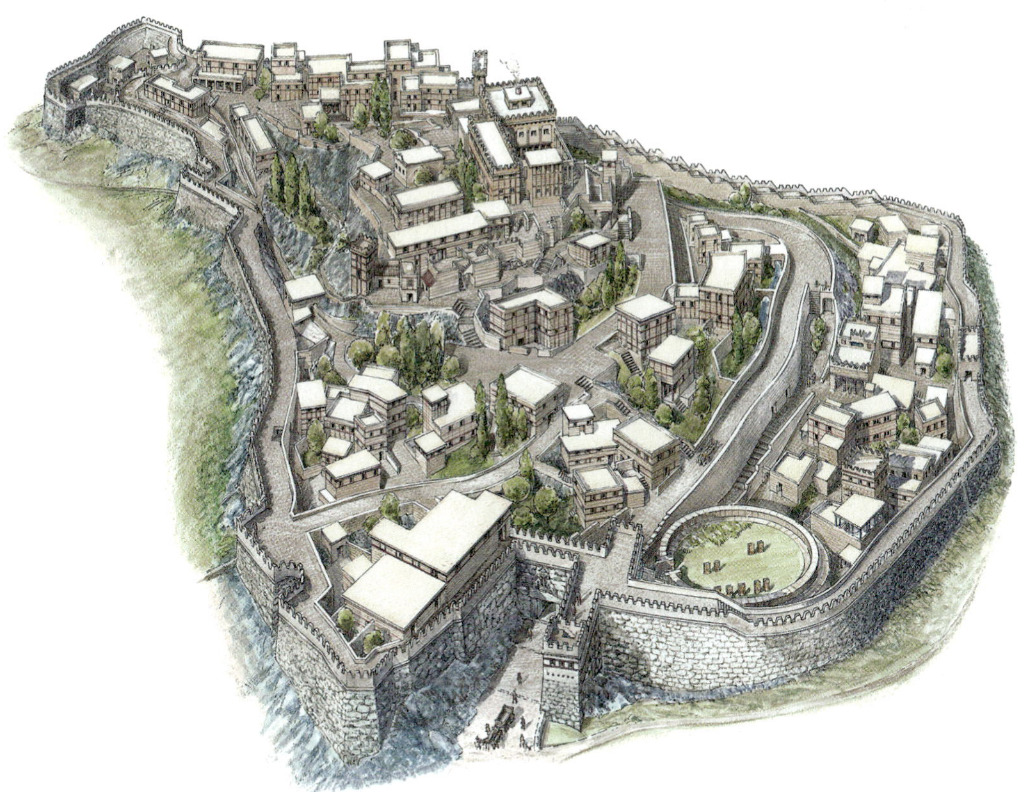

5–11 Reconstruction of the Citadel at Mycenae, Greece. Occupied c. 1600–1200 BCE (walls built c. 1340–1200 BCE)

Note the citadel's hilltop position and fortified ring wall. The Lion Gate (see fig. 5–12) is at the lower left, approached by a path flanked by wall sections. A grave circle is at the lower center.

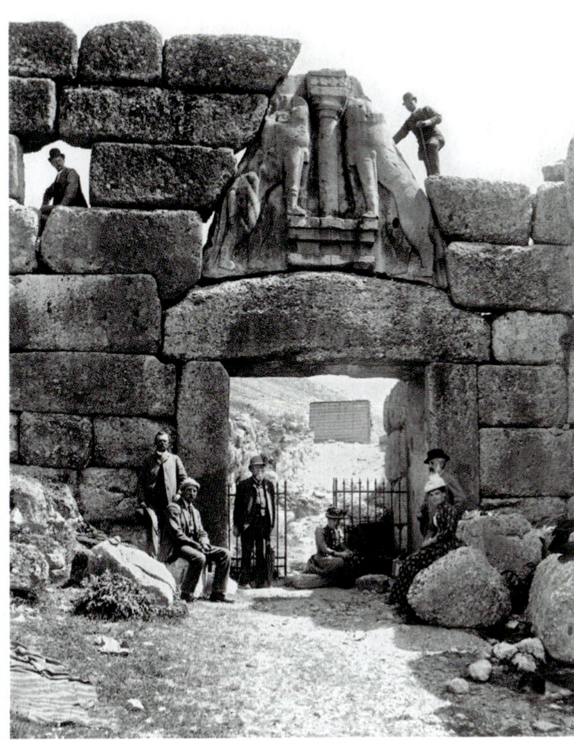

5–12 Lion Gate, Mycenae. c. 1250 BCE. Limestone relief, height of sculpture approx. 9' 6" (2.9 m)

In this historic photograph, Heinrich Schliemann, director of the excavation, stands to the left of the gate and his wife and partner in archaeology, Sophia, sits to the right.

Mycenaean civilization does not have a long history. By 1200 BCE, invaders are believed to have crossed into mainland Greece and taken control of the major cities and citadels. The period between about 1100 and 900 BCE was a "dark age" in the Aegean, marked by political and economic instability and upheaval. But a new culture was forming—one that looked back to the exploits of the Helladic warrior princes and the glories of a heroic age, while setting the stage for a truly new Greek civilization.

The Emergence of Greek Civilization

Ancient Greece was a mountainous land of spectacular natural beauty, where olive trees and grapevines grew on steep hillsides, producing oil and wine. But with little good farmland, the Greeks turned to commerce and colonization to alleviate food shortages as the population grew. In towns, skilled artisans provided metal and ceramic wares to exchange abroad for grain and raw materials. Greek merchant ships carried pots, olive oil, and bronzes around the Mediterranean Sea. Greek colonies in Italy, Sicily, and Asia Minor rapidly became powerful independent commercial and cultural centers, but they remained tied to the homeland by common language, traditions, religion, and history (see map **5–2**).

During the ninth and eighth centuries BCE, the Greeks began to form independently governed city-states—autonomous regions with a city such as Athens, Sparta, or Corinth, as its political, economic, religious, and cultural center—each with its own form of government and economy. By the sixth century, Athens began to

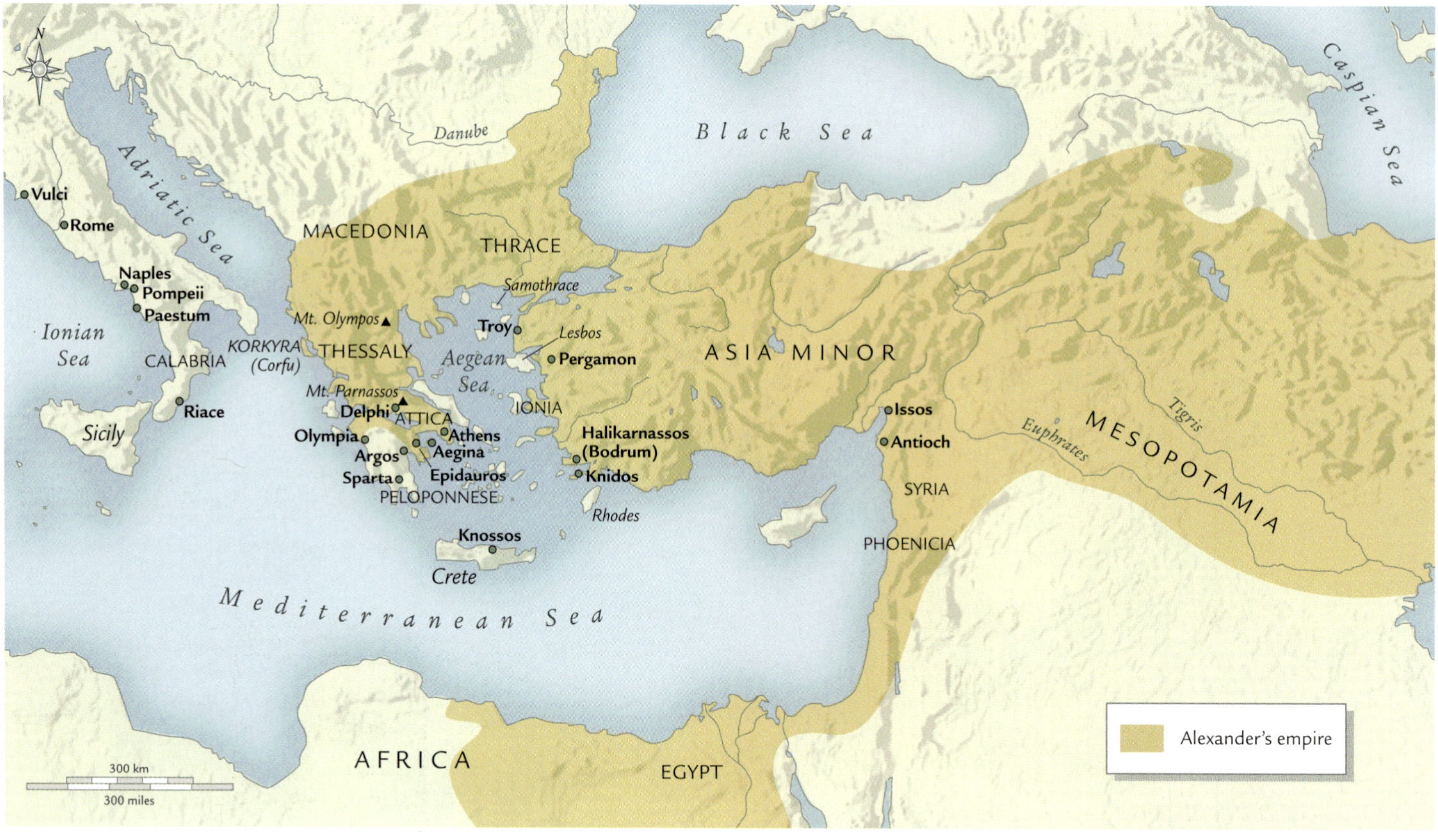

Map 5–2 Ancient Greece

assume cultural and commercial preeminence. Soon it had also established the notion that all citizens should share in the rights and responsibilities of government. This notion blossomed under Kleisthenes (d. 508 BCE, often called the father of democracy) into a system that was democratic in principle, but was in fact open only to Athenian men. Since they were not considered citizens, women took no official part in government, nor did slaves or men born outside Athens.

Within a remarkably brief time, Greek artists developed focused and distinctive ideals of human beauty and architectural design that continue to exert a profound influence today. From about 900 BCE until about 100 BCE, they concentrated on a new, rather narrow range of subjects and produced an impressive body of work with clear stylistic aspirations in a variety of media. Greek artists were restless. They continually sought to change and improve existing artistic trends and fashions, effecting striking stylistic change over the course of a few centuries. This is in stark contrast to the situation we discovered in ancient Egypt, where a desire for permanence and continuity maintained stable artistic conventions for nearly 3,000 years. Art historians have named the first three stages in the progressive development of ancient Greek art Geometric, Archaic, and Classical.

The Geometric Style

What we call the Geometric style flourished between about 900 and 700 BCE. One of a series of large Athenian ceramic vessels exemplifies the complex, linear, sylized decoration that gives this period its

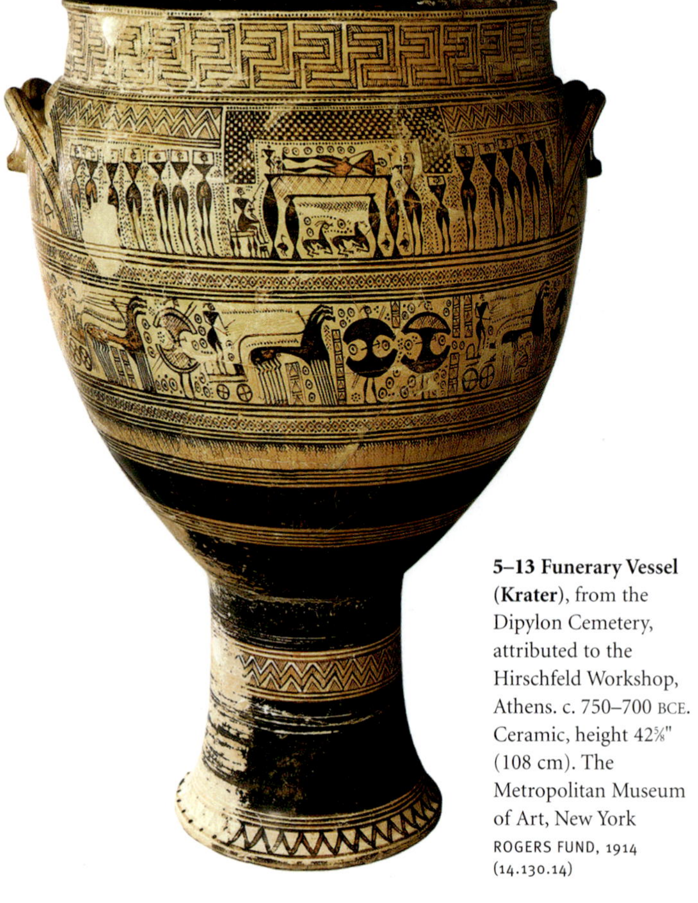

5–13 Funerary Vessel (Krater), from the Dipylon Cemetery, attributed to the Hirschfeld Workshop, Athens. c. 750–700 BCE. Ceramic, height 42⅝" (108 cm). The Metropolitan Museum of Art, New York
ROGERS FUND, 1914 (14.130.14)

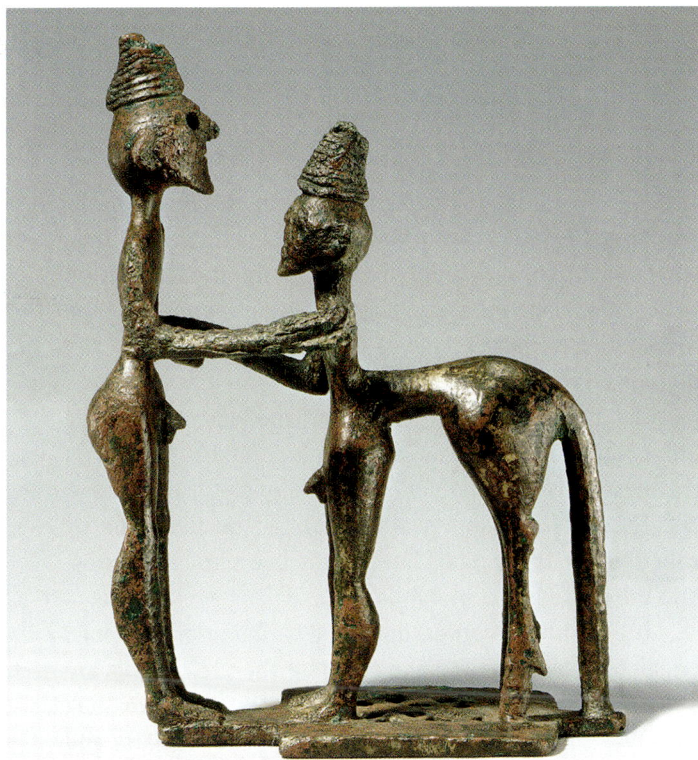

5–14 ***Man and Centaur***, perhaps from Olympia. c. 750 BCE. Bronze, height 4⅜" (11.1 cm). The Metropolitan Museum of Art, New York
GIFT OF J. PIERPONT MORGAN, 1917 (17.190.2072)

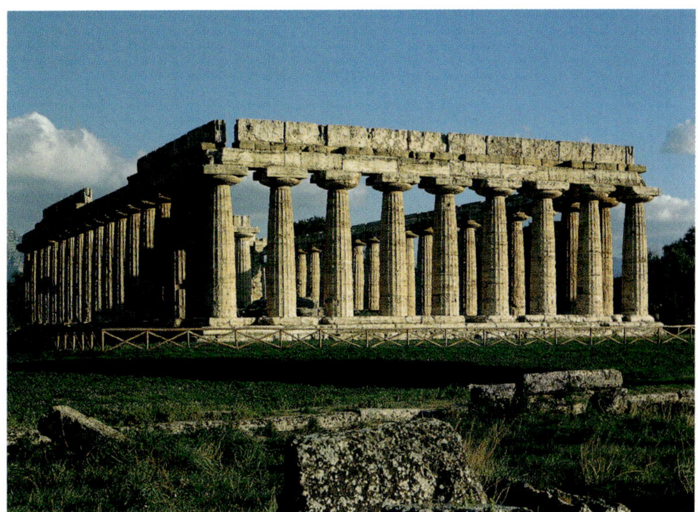

5–15a Temple of Hera I, Paestum, Italy. c. 550 BCE

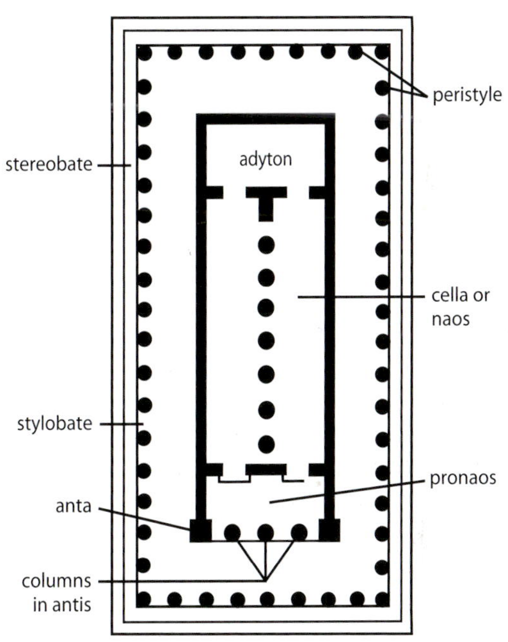

5–15b Plan of the temple of Hera I

name (fig. **5–13**). Dated about 750 BCE, this huge pot was a grave marker made to hold offerings. Funerary rituals are recorded in two bands, or registers, of decoration. In the top register, the body of the deceased lies on its side on a platform. Accompanying figures with their hands on their heads may be tearing their hair with grief. Triangles represent torsos; round dots stand for eyes in profile heads; lines depicting arms and legs swell into bulging thighs and calves. Below, a procession of horse-drawn chariots and foot soldiers, who look like walking shields, recall the athletic competitions or funeral games held to honor dead men. Figures are shown in either full-frontal or full-profile views. Any sense of three-dimensionality or receding space has been avoided to emphasize flat patterns and crisp outlines.

Artists of the Geometric period also produced small figurines cast in bronze. A tiny *Man and Centaur* dates from about 750 BCE (fig. **5–14**). Like the painter of the contemporary funerary vessel (see fig. 5–13), the sculptor has reduced body parts to simple geometric shapes. The identity of the two figures—charged with the energy of their encounter—is unknown, but they might be the legendary hero Achilles and the centaur Chiron, his teacher. Since such figurines have been found in sanctuary sites sacred to one or more of the Greek gods, they may have served as votive offerings.

The Archaic Period

The Archaic period (c. 600–480 BCE) does not deserve its name. "Archaic" means "antiquated" or "old-fashioned," even "primitive," but this was a time of great new achievement. It was when Sappho wrote her inspired poetry on the island of Lesbos, when the legendary storyteller Aesop crafted his animal fables. Artists and architects shared in the growing prosperity as city councils and wealthy individuals sponsored the creation of sculpture, fine ceramics, and civic buildings such as council chambers, public fountains (see fig. 5–20), and temples.

The earliest standing Greek temples date from the Archaic period. A temple was conceived both as earthly home and treasury for its honored god or goddess. Essentially, it is an idealized shelter, built in conformity to a standard plan and strict proportional relationships and decorated in conformity to a regulated decorative system we call the Greek **orders** (see "The Greek Temple," page 112).

ELEMENTS OF **Architecture**

The Greek Temple

Plans

Most Archaic and Classical Greek temples (see figs. 5–15b and 5–26b) have a main room, called the **cella** or **naos**, preceded by a vestibule, called the **pronaos**. Sometimes these are supplemented by additional, smaller interior spaces. Surrounding these enclosures is a single or double row of free-standing columns known as the **peristyle**. The platform or base of the entire building is called the **stylobate**, which rests on top of a series of steep steps, the **stereobate**.

Orders

The three Greek architectural orders are **Doric**, **Ionic**, and **Corinthian**. Each order is composed of a system of interdependent parts whose proportions are based on mathematical ratios. No element of an order could be changed without producing a corresponding change in the other elements.

The basic components of each Greek order are the **column** and **entablature**, which function as the post and lintel of the structural system. All types of columns have a vertical **shaft** topped by a **capital**; some also have a **base**. The column shafts are formed of round sections, or **drums**, which are joined inside by metal pegs. The **entablature** consists of an **architrave**, **frieze**, and **cornice**.

The Doric and Ionic orders were well developed by about 600 BCE. The Doric order is the oldest and plainest of the three. Shafts—**fluted**, or channeled, with sharp edges—rise directly from the stylobate without a base. Perhaps the most distinctive features are the **capitals**, where a cushion-like **echinus** signals the transition between **abacus** and shaft, and the frieze composed of the rhythmic alternation between projecting **triglyphs** and **metopes**, the latter sometimes filled with figural sculpture.

The more elongated, delicate, and decorative Ionic order is named after Ionia, a region occupied by Greeks on the west coast of Anatolia and the islands off that coast. The flutes of the shafts are separated by flat surfaces called **fillets**, the capitals have distinctive scrolled **volutes**, and the frieze is a continuous strip.

The Corinthian order, initially a variation of the Ionic, began to appear around 450 BCE. Its elaborate capitals are sheathed with stylized **acanthus** leaves below the volutes.

Over the centuries, beginning with the Romans and continuing to the present day, Western architects have invoked the Greek orders to express rationality and restraint, or to create playful variations on a traditional decorative system.

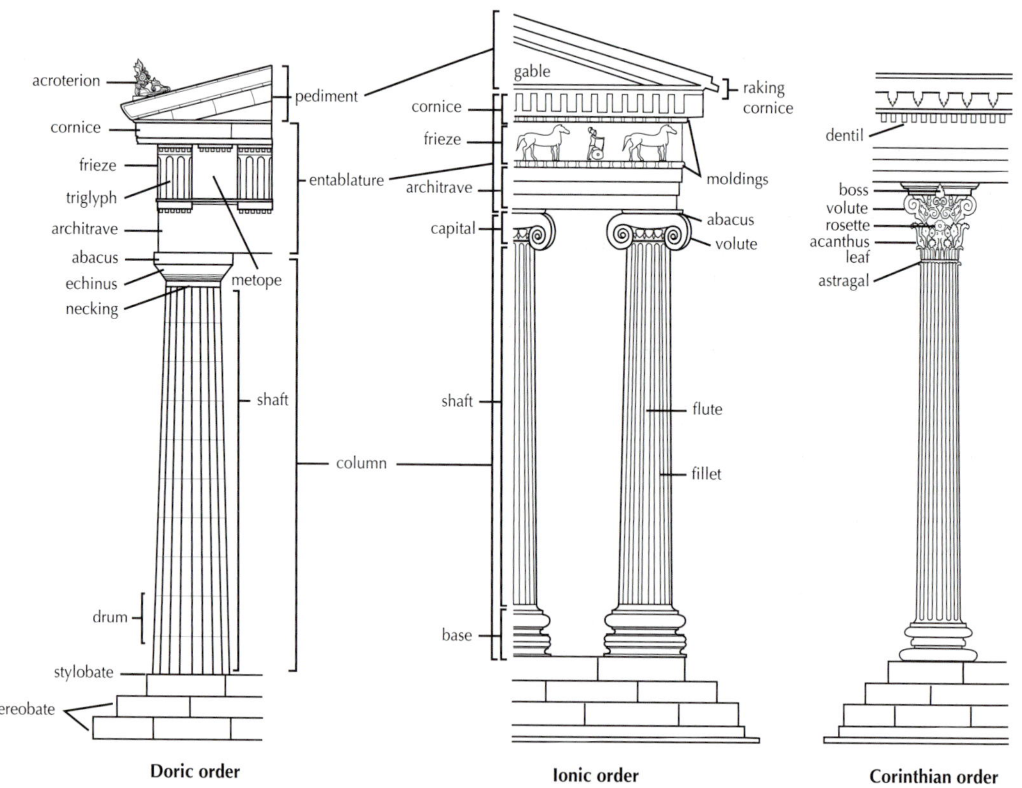

A particularly well-preserved Archaic period temple, built about 550 BCE, still stands at Paestum (Poseidonia), a Greek colony founded about 50 miles south of the modern city of Naples, Italy. Dedicated to Hera, queen of the gods, the temple (figs. **5–15a** and **b**) is known today as Hera I to distinguish it from a second temple to Hera built adjacent to it about a century later. The builders used the **Doric order**. Fluted **columns** without **bases**, resting directly on the **stylobate**, rise to unadorned, cushion-like capitals. The especially robust columns—each topped with a capital composed on a widely flaring **echinus** and a broad, blocky **abacus**—create a strong impression of permanence and stability. But because the columns swell in the middle and contract toward the top (a refinement known as **entasis**), the building retains a sense of energy and upward lift. Above the columns, a horizontal entablature (composed of **architrave**, **frieze**, and **cornice**) and the triangular **pediments** (forming the triangular gable ends) would have supported the temple's roof. In the Doric order, pediments and usually **metopes** were filled with sculpture, and fragments of painted terracotta decoration has been found in the rubble around Hera I.

In addition to carving sculpture for temple exteriors, Archaic sculptors also created free-standing statues. Usually life-size or larger, most were made of white marble and originally were painted in bright colors to enhance their lifelike qualities (see "Color in Greek Sculpture," page 115). Some bore inscriptions indicating that they had been commissioned by individual men or women for a commemorative purpose. While some marked graves, most stood in sanctuaries, where they lined the sacred way from the entrance to the main temple in perpetual attendance on the god or goddess.

Traditionally, a female statue of this type is called a **kore** (plural, *korai*), Greek for "young woman," and a male statue is called a **kouros** (plural, *kouroi*), meaning "young man." The Archaic *korai*, wearing long garments and jewelry, represented deities, priestesses, or nymphs. The *kouroi*, nearly always nude, have been variously identified as gods, warriors, and victorious athletes. Because the Greeks associated young athletic males with fertility and family continuity, the *kouroi* may have symbolized ancestors.

A statue known as the *Anavysos Kouros* dating from about 530 BCE (fig. **5–16**) exemplifies the Archaic Greek ideal. Reminiscent of standing males in Egyptian sculpture (see fig. 3–9), this young Greek is shown frontally, arms at his sides, fists clenched, and one leg striding in front of the other. Unlike ancient Egyptian stone statuary, however, is the figure's rounded athletic body and the way the sculptor has freed the arms and legs from the block of stone to make the figure more free and energetic. The carefully rendered anatomy and bulging muscularity enhance this sense of lifelike power and presence. The eyes are unnaturally large and wide open, and the mouth forms a characteristic closed expression, known as the Archaic smile, apparently used to enliven the expressiveness of the face. Unlike his partially clothed Egyptian counterpart, this young

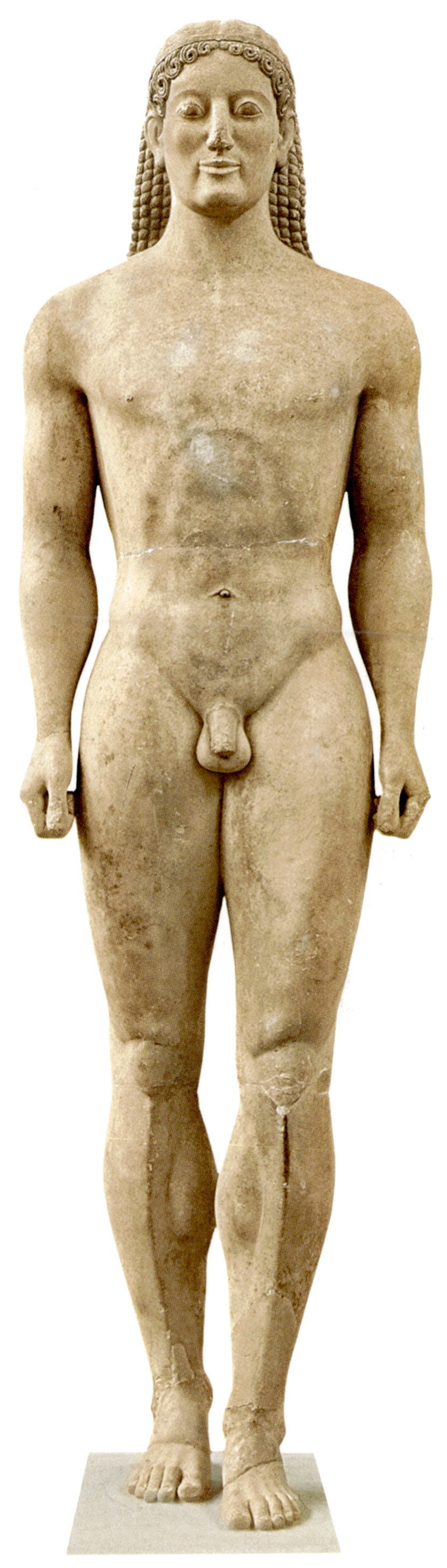

5–16 ***Anavysos Kouros***, from cemetery at Anavysos, near Athens. c. 530 BCE. Marble with remnants of paint, height 6' 4" (1.93 m). National Archaeological Museum, Athens

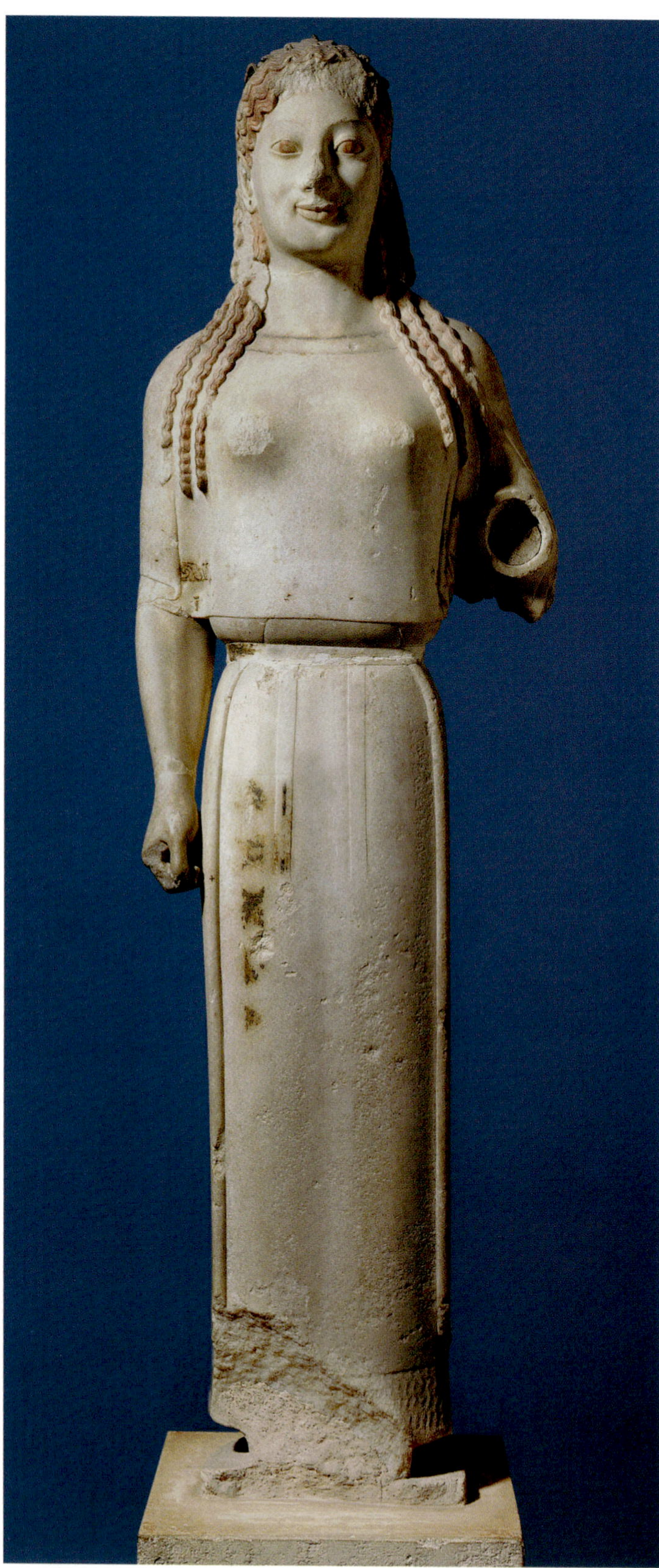

5–17 *"Peplos" Kore*, from the Acropolis, Athens. c. 530 BCE. Marble, height 48" (121 cm). Acropolis Museum, Athens

Greek's total nudity serves to remove the figure from a specific place, time, or social class. He is a symbol or type rather than a specific individual.

The *"Peplos" Kore* (fig. **5–17**), dated about the same time as the *Anavysos Kouros*, exhibits comparably rounded body forms, even though she is clothed. Her arms and head convey a sense of soft flesh covering an anatomically correct bone structure, and the smooth, feminine curves of her body are apparent under her garment. The original painted colors on both body and clothing must have made her seem even more lifelike, and she also once wore a metal crown and jewelry. The name we use for this figure is based on an assessment of her clothing, but it has recently been shown that she is not wearing the simple *peplos* of a young girl but a sheath-like garment—originally painted with a frieze of animals—identifying her instead as a goddess, perhaps Athena or Artemis. Her missing left forearm—which was made of a separate piece of marble fitted into the still-visible socket—would have extended forward horizontally and may have held an attribute that provided the key to her identity.

In the painting of Archaic ceramic vessels, artists presented not independent figures, but scenes evoking a story. Abandoning the narrow bands of decoration characteristic of the Geometric period (see fig. 5–13), Athenian painters gradually increased the size of figures until one or two narrative scenes occupied the body of a vessel. An amphora—a large, all-purpose storage jar—contemporary with the *kouros* and *kore* just discussed illustrates well this development (see fig. 5–1). One side shows the Trojan War heroes Ajax and Achilles in a rare moment of relaxation playing dice. This is an episode not included in any literary source, but for Greeks familiar with the story, this anecdotal portrayal of friendly play would have been a poignant reminder that before the end of the war, the heroes would both be dead, Achilles in battle and Ajax by suicide. Knowing the story was critical to engaging with such paintings, and artists often included identifying labels beside the characters to guide viewers to the narrative source.

In painting this amphora, Exekias used a technique known as **black-figure**, the principal mode of ceramic painting in the sixth century BCE. The painter used **slip** (a mixture of clay and water) to silhouette the shapes of figures against the unpainted clay of the background. Details were incised into the slip with a sharp tool inside the silhouetted shapes. The characteristic color contrast occurred only in the firing process when the slip emerged from the kiln as black and the body clay of the vessel turned red. On some pieces, touches of white and reddish-purple gloss, made of metallic pigments mixed with slip, enhanced the decorative effect.

Although painters were still creating handsome black-figure wares in the last third of the sixth century BCE, some turned away from this meticulous process to a new, more fluid **red-figure** technique—so called because red figures stand out against a black background. Painters first covered the pot with slip but left or "reserved" the shapes of the figures unpainted to reveal the underlying clay body. Instead of engraving details within a silhouetted area covered by slip, painters drew on the reserved areas with a fine brush dipped in liquid slip. As with the black-figure technique, after firing, the slip turned black and the clay body red. But here the result was a lustrous dark vessel with red-colored figures articulated with black

COLOR IN GREEK SCULPTURE

For many modern viewers, it comes as a real surprise, even a shock, that the stone sculptures of ancient Greece did not always have stark white, pure marble surfaces, comparable in appearance to—and consistent in taste with—the more recent, but still classicizing sculptures of Michelangelo or Canova (see figs. 13–8 and 17–2). But they were originally painted with brilliant colors. A close examination of Greek sculpture and architecture has long revealed evidence of polychromy, even to the unaided eye, but our understanding of the original appearance of these works has been greatly enhanced recently. Since the 1980s, German scholar Vinzenz Brinkmann has used extensive visual and scientific analysis to evaluate the traces of painting that remain on ancient Greek sculpture, employing tools such as ultraviolet and x-ray fluorescence, microscopy, and pigment analysis. Based on this research, he and his colleague Ulrike Koch-Brinkmann have fashioned reconstructions that allow us to imagine the exuberant effect these works would have had when they were new.

Illustrated here (fig. **5–18**) is their painted reconstruction of a kneeling archer from about 500 BCE that once formed part of the west pediment of the Temple of Aphaia at Aegina. To begin with they have replaced features of the sculpture—ringlet hair extensions, a bow, a quiver, and arrows—probably made of bronze or lead and attached to the stone after it was carved, using the holes still evident in the current state of the figure's hip and head (fig. **5–19**). Most stunning, however, is the diamond-shaped patterns that were painted on his leggings and sleeves, using pigments derived from malachite, azurite, arsenic, cinnabar, and charcoal. And the surfaces of such figures were not simply colored in. Artists created a sophisticated integration of three-dimensional form, color, and design. The patterning applied to this archer's leggings actually changes in size and shape in relation to the body beneath it, stretching out on expansive thighs and constricting on tapering ankles. Ancient authors indicate that sculpture was painted to make figures more lifelike, and these recent reconstructions certainly back them up.

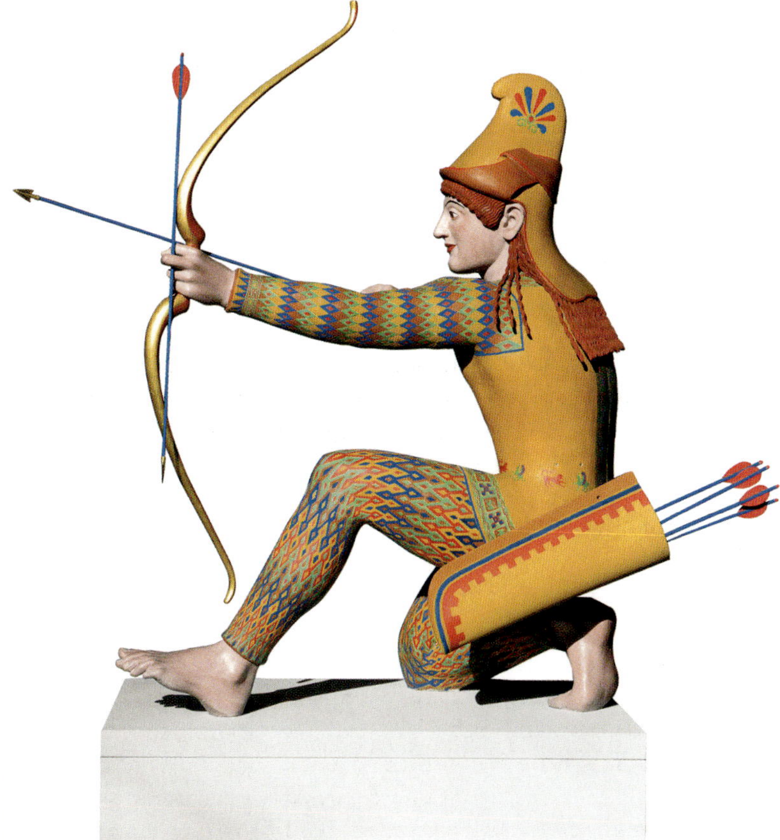

5–18 Vinzenz Brinkmann and Ulrike Koch-Brinkmann. Reconstruction of *Archer* from the west pediment of the Temple of Aphaia, Aegina. 2004 CE. Staatliche Antikensammlungen und Glyptothek, Munich

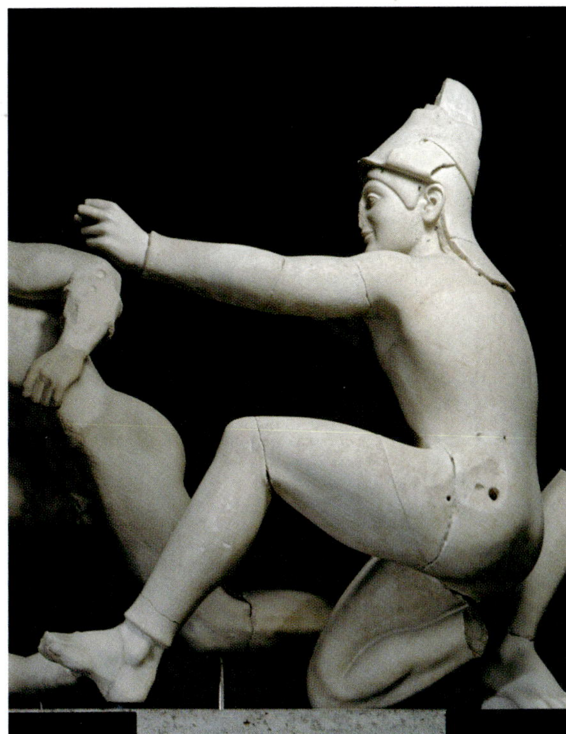

5–19 ***Archer*** **("Paris")**, from the west pediment of the Temple of Aphaia, Aegina. c. 500 BCE. Marble. Staatliche Antikensammlungen und Glyptothek, Munich

CLOSER LOOK

Here, the Priam Painter provides an interesting insight into everyday Greek city life as well as a view of an important public building in use (fig. **5–20**). Most women in ancient Greece were confined to their homes, so their daily trip to the communal well, or fountain house, was an important event. At a fountain house, in the shade of a Doric-columned porch, three women patiently fill hydriae (water vessels) like the one on which they are painted. A fourth balances her empty jug on her head as she waits, while a fifth woman, without a jug, appears to be waving a greeting to someone. The women's skin is painted white, a convention similar to the pale female figures found in Egyptian and Minoan art. Incising and touches of reddish-purple paint create fine details in the architecture and in the figures' clothing and hair.

The composition of this vase painting finely balances vertical, horizontal, rectangular, and rounded elements. The Doric columns, the decorative vertical borders, and even the streams of water flowing from the animal-head spigots echo the upright figures of the women. The wide black band forming the ground line, the architrave above the colonnade, and the left-to-right movement of the horse-drawn chariots across the flattened shoulder emphasize the horizontal, frieze-like arrangement of the women across the body of the pot. This geometric framework is softened by the rounded contours of the female bodies, the globular water vessels, the spigots, the circular **palmettes** (fan-shaped petal designs) framing the main scene, and the arching bodies of the galloping horses on the shoulder.

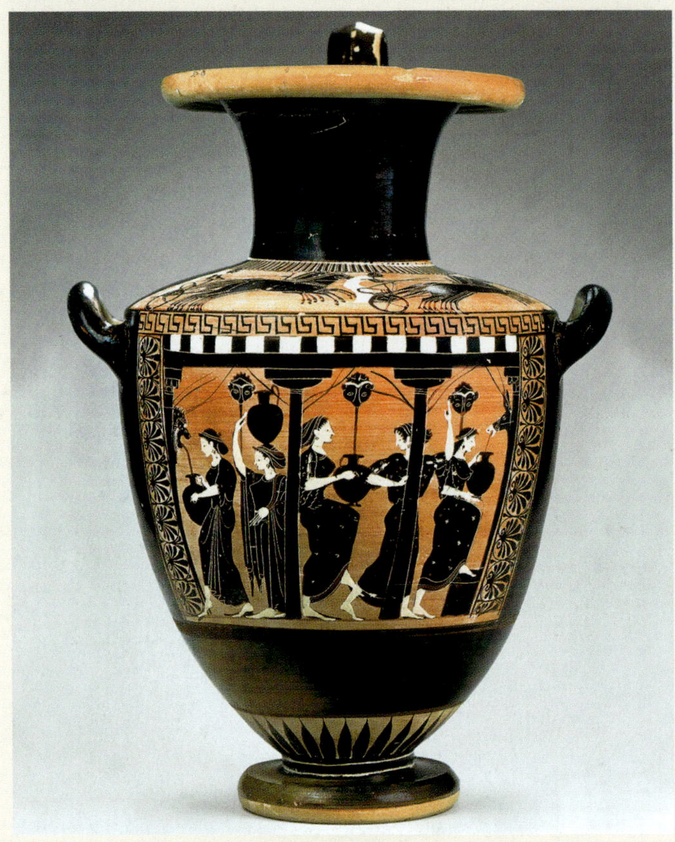

5–20 Priam Painter. ***Women at a Fountain House***, black-figure decoration on a hydria. 520–510 BCE. Ceramic, height of hydria 20⅞" (53 cm). Museum of Fine Arts, Boston

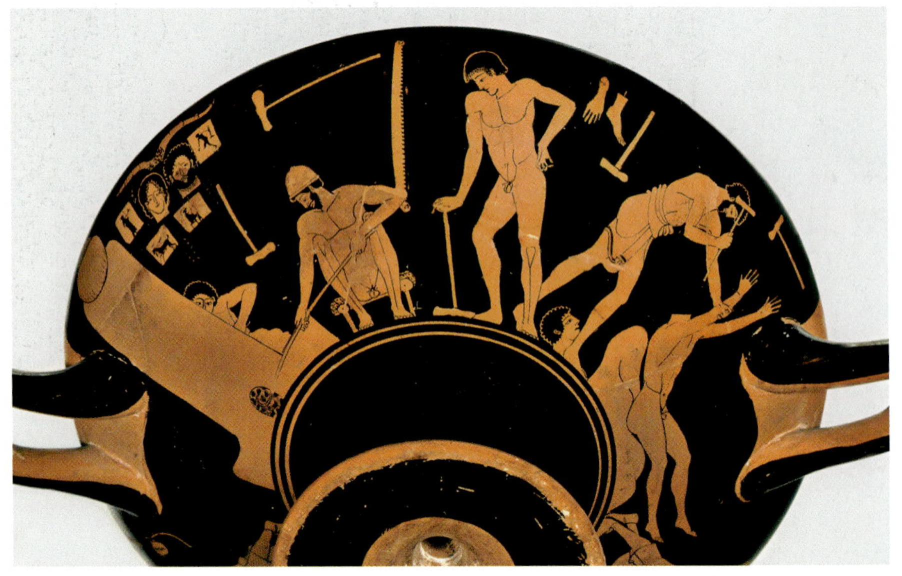

5–21 Foundry Painter. ***A Bronze Foundry***, red-figure decoration on a kylix found in Vulci, Italy. 490–480 BCE. Ceramic, diameter of kylix 12" (31 cm). Staatliche Museen zu Berlin, Preussischer Kulturbesitz, Antikensammlung

The painter uses the red-figure technique to convey the mass and energy of the figures and also draws in details of muscles and facial features. The men work in a real space defined by their furnace and other equipment as well as by their foreshortened bodies and limbs, especially the legs of the man tending the furnace.

painted details (see fig. 5–21). The greater ease, speed, and flexibility of this technique allowed artists to create more lively figures with a more developed sense of bodily form. Painters quickly adopted it as the preferred method of painting on ceramics.

An early fifth-century red-figure **kylix** (a shallow, two-handled drinking cup) displays one painter's virtuosity at adapting a scene to the shape of the vessel (fig. **5–21**) and in drawing individual figures caught in both action and repose. The artist, known as the Foundry Painter, used the circular underside of the cup to illustrate the workings of a foundry for casting bronze figures. On the walls of the pictured workshop hang tools and other paraphernalia: hammers, molds of a human foot and hand, and several sketches. A helmeted worker seated on a low stool attends to a furnace at left, while an adjacent man—perhaps the supervisor—leans casually on a staff. A third worker assembles the already-cast parts of a leaping bronze figure, whose head lies at the worker's feet. The Foundry Painter has created a lively and lifelike scene in an awkward compositional space, giving us insight into the working methods of bronze sculptors during the late Archaic period.

Greek Gods and Goddesses	
Zeus	king of the gods
Hera	Zeus' wife and sister, queen of the gods
Athena	goddess of wisdom and civilization
Ares	god of war
Apollo	god of the sun, creativity, and the fine arts
Aphrodite	goddess of love and beauty
Artemis	goddess of the moon and hunting (twin sister of Apollo)
Hermes	god of commerce; also messenger of the gods
Hades	god of the underworld
Dionysos	god of wine
Hephaestus	god of fire and metalworking
Hestia	goddess of hearth and family
Demeter	goddess of crops and the harvest
Poseidon	god of the sea and earthquakes (brother of Zeus)
Eros	god of love (son of Aphrodite)

Although sometimes worshiped as a god, the hero Herakles, a son of Zeus, is a demigod known for his physical strength.

The Early Classical Period

Historically, the early fifth century BCE was marked by a series of invasions from Persia. Greek city-states banded together against their common foe, and by 479 BCE an alliance led by Athens and Sparta had driven out the invaders. Perhaps this success against the Persians gave the Greeks a self-confidence that inspired and accelerated artistic development, for during the next two decades their art took a new stylistic direction, away from elegant stylization and toward a sense of greater faithfulness to the natural appearance of human beings and their world. This period of marked change and evolution that scholars have called the Early Classical period lasted from the end of the Persian Wars to about 450 BCE.

In free-standing sculpture, the Greeks shifted in only a few generations from the rigid frontality of Archaic *kouroi* to more relaxed, lifelike figures such as the so-called *Kritios Boy* (fig. **5–22**).

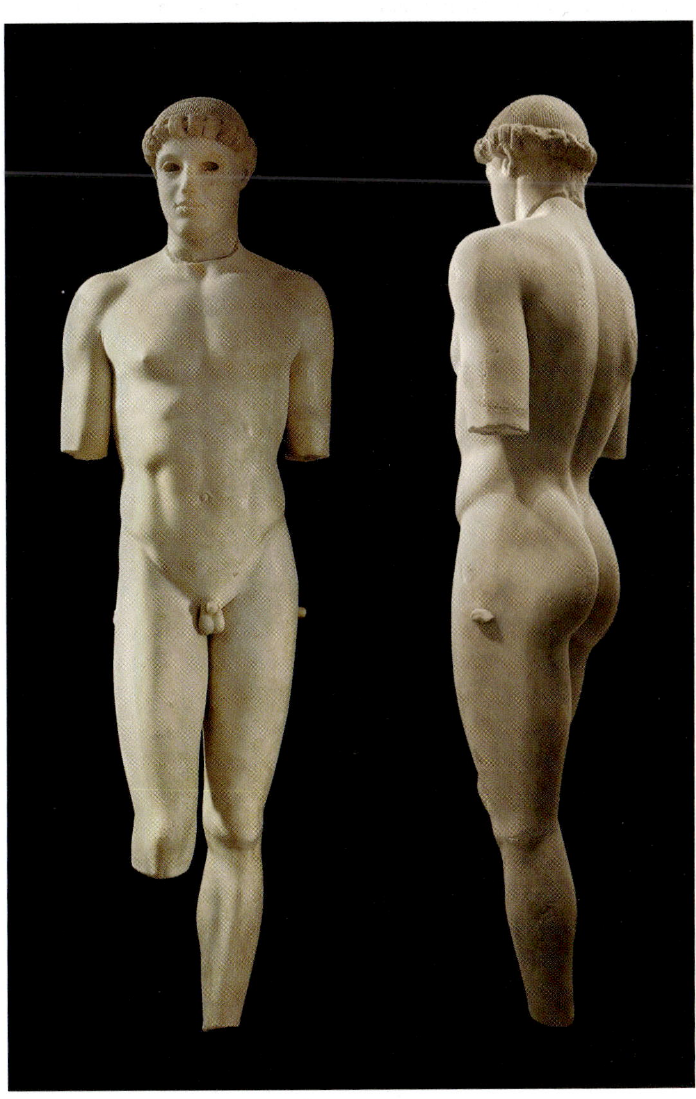

5–22 *Kritios Boy*. c. 480 BCE. Marble, height 3' 10" (1.17 m). Acropolis Museum, Athens

When the Kritios Boy *was excavated from debris at the Acropolis of Athens, the statue was thought by its finders to be a work of the Greek sculptor Kritios.*

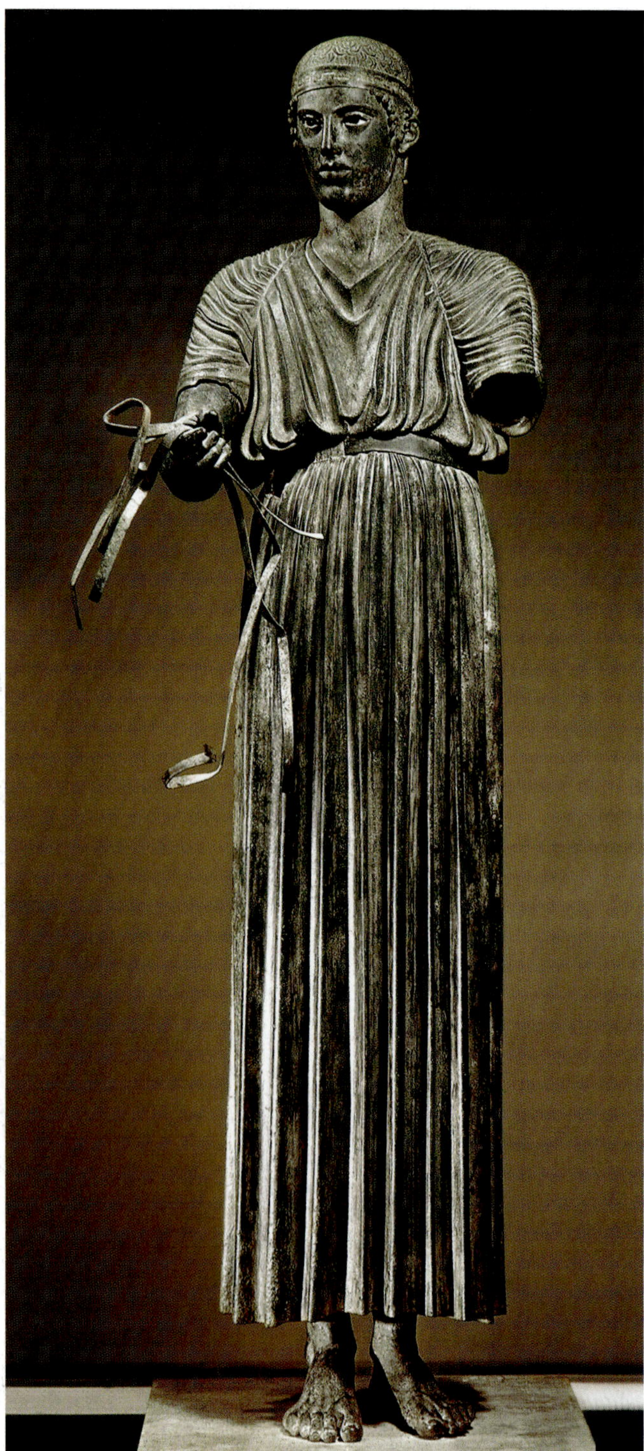

5–23 *Charioteer*, from the Sanctuary of Apollo, Delphi. c. 470 BCE. Bronze, height 5' 11" (1.8 m). Archaeological Museum, Delphi

The setting of a work of art affects our reaction to it. Today, this stunning figure is exhibited on a low base in the peaceful surroundings of a museum, isolated from other works and spotlighted for close examination. Its effect would have been very different in its original outdoor location, standing in a horse-drawn chariot atop a tall monument. Viewers in ancient times, exhausted from the steep climb to the sanctuary, possibly jostled by crowds of fellow pilgrims, could have absorbed only its overall effect, not the fine details of the face, robe, and hand visible to today's viewers.

In contrast to the over-life-size *Anavysos Kouros* (see fig. 5–16), the *Kritios Boy* originally stood only about 4 feet tall. The softly rounded body forms, broad facial features, and calm expression—lacking even a trace of the tight Archaic smile—give the figure an air of quiet solemnity. The easy pose contrasts markedly with the more rigid bearing of Archaic *kouroi.* The boy's weight rests on his left leg (the "engaged" leg), and his relaxed right leg bends slightly at the knee. The curve in his spine counters the slight shifting of his hips and the subtle drop of one shoulder. Through the asymmetry of this pose (known as **contrapposto**) the sculptor captures the figure's sense of life and potential for movement, which had been eclipsed by formal stylization in the Archaic *kouroi.*

The technique of modeling and hollow-casting bronze which was developed at the end of the Archaic period (see fig. 5–21) made possible more complex action poses with outstretched arms and legs far apart, which would be difficult to carve in stone. A life-size bronze *Charioteer* (fig. **5–23**) illustrates the skill of Early Classical metalworkers. It was found in the Sanctuary of Apollo at Delphi together with fragments of a bronze chariot and horses. An earthquake in 373 BCE toppled the monument with its sculptures and buried them in debris, saving the *Charioteer* from the fate of many ancient bronzes: being melted down to recycle the metal for another purpose. According to its inscription, the sculptural group commemorated a victory by the driver sponsored by King Polyzalos of Gela (Sicily) in the Pythian Games (an event like the Olympics but held at Delphi and honoring Apollo) of 478 or 474 BCE. The face of this handsome youth is idealized, but aspects of the figure are highly individualized. The single remaining hand and the feet look so real that they seem to have been cast from molds made from an actual person. The robe falls neatly into folds, yet the garment seems capable of swaying or rippling from a slight movement or sudden breeze. The lifelike quality of the *Charioteer* calls to mind the report by the Roman historian and naturalist Pliny the Elder (in the first century BCE) that three-time winners in Greek competitions had their features memorialized in statues.

A pair of over-life-size bronze figures known as the *Riace Warriors* (fig. **5–24**) illustrates the developing skill of ancient Greek sculptors in depicting the male nude figure. Found by a diver on the seabed near Riace, a town on the eastern Italian coast of Calabria, the statues, dating from about 460–450 BCE, may have been thrown from a sinking ship by sailors trying to lighten the load or may have been lost in a shipwreck. They reveal a striking balance between the idealized smoothness of "perfected" anatomy conforming to Early Classical standards and the reproduction of details observed from nature, such as the swelling veins in the backs of the hands. Contrapposto is even more evident here than in the *Kritios Boy,* and—especially in the illustrated warrior—the toned musculature suggests a youthfulness inconsistent with the maturity of the heavy beard and almost haggard face. The lifelike quality of this bronze is further heightened by inserted eyeballs of bone and colored glass, silver plating on the teeth, copper inlays on lips and nipples, and attached eyelashes and eyebrows of separately cast strands of bronze. This accommodation of the intense study of the human figure with idealism that belies the irregularity of nature would be continued by artists in the "High" Classical period.

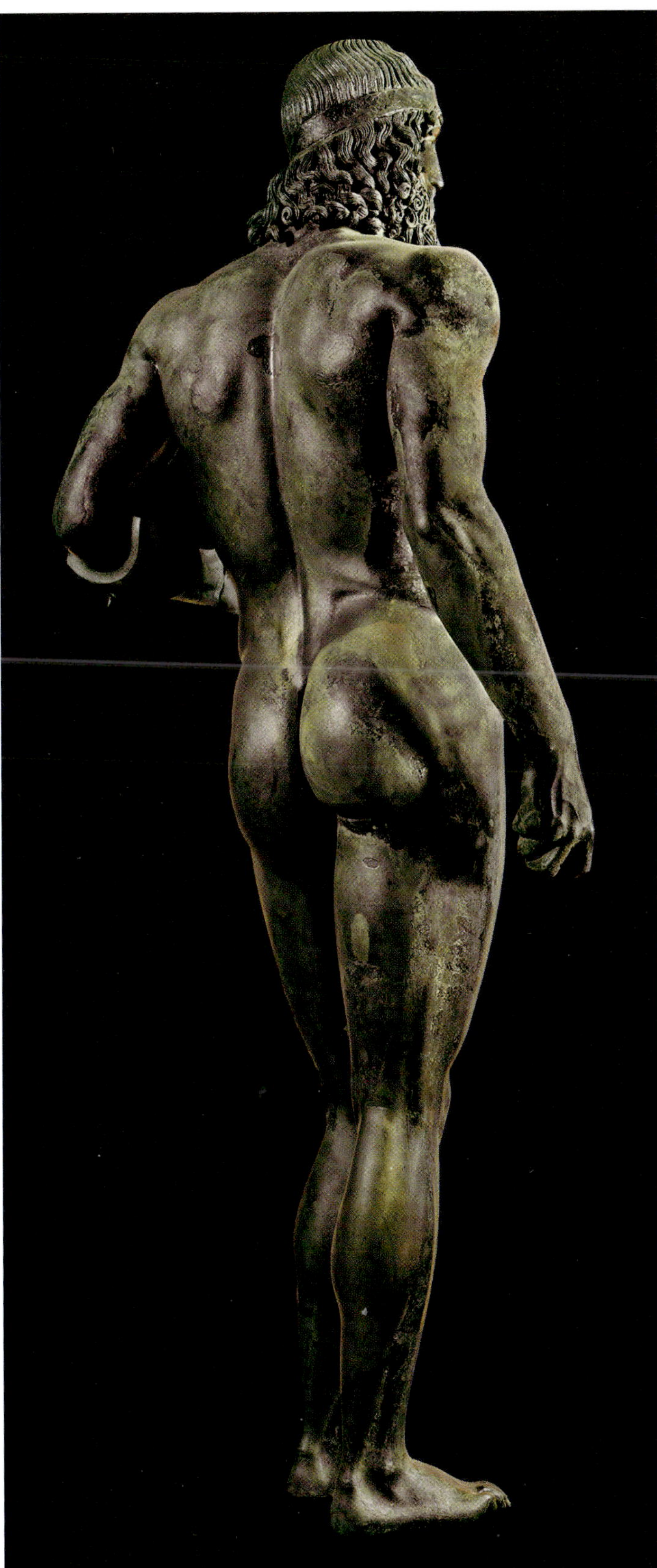

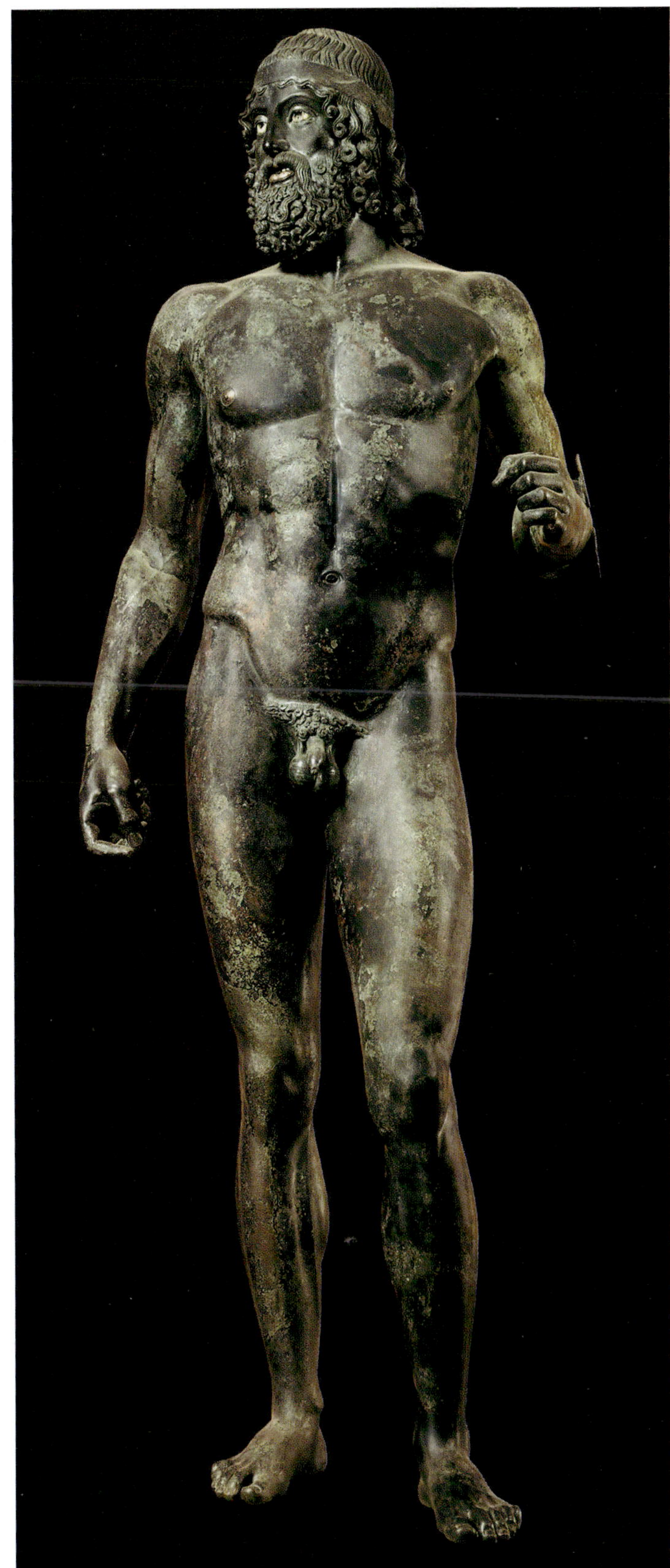

5–24 ***Warrior*** found in the sea off Riace, Italy. c. 460–450 BCE. Bronze with bone and glass eyes, silver teeth, and copper lips and nipples, height 6' 9" (2.05 m). Museo Archaeològico Nazionale, Reggio Calabria, Italy

The man held a shield (parts are still visible) on his left arm and a spear in his right hand. He may have been part of a monument commemorating a military victory, perhaps against the Persians.

CLASSIC AND CLASSICAL

Our words "classic" and "classical" come from the Latin word *classis*, referring to the division of the people in a society into classes based on wealth. Consequently, "classic" has come to mean "first class," "the highest rank," and "the standard of excellence." Greek artists in the fifth century BCE sought to create ideal images based on perfect mathematical proportions. Since Roman artists were also inspired by these ideals, the term "Classical" in this context refers to the cultures of ancient Greece and Rome. By extension, the word may also mean "in the style of ancient Greece and Rome," whenever or wherever that style is used. In the most general usage, a classic is something—whether a literary work, automobile, or film—of lasting quality and universal esteem.

The "High" Classical Period

The "High" Classical period of Greek art lasted only from about 450 to 400 BCE. The use of the word "high" to qualify the art of this time reflects the value judgments of art historians who have considered this period a pinnacle of artistic refinement, producing works that set a standard of unsurpassed excellence. Some have even referred to this half-century as Greece's "Golden Age," although these decades were also marked by the turmoil and destruction of the Peloponnesian War. Without a common enemy, Sparta and Athens turned on each other. Sparta dominated the Peloponnese peninsula and much of the rest of mainland Greece, while Athens controlled the Aegean and became the wealthy and influential center of a maritime empire. Today we remember Athens more for its cultural and intellectual brilliance and its experiments with democratic government, which reached its zenith in the fifth century BCE under the charismatic leader Perikles (c. 495–429 BCE), than for the imperialistic tendencies of its considerable commercial power.

The Parthenon

The Athenian Acropolis, the hill that formed the city's ceremonial center, visually expressed the city's values and its civic pride. The Persians had destroyed the site's earlier buildings and statues in 480 BCE, and Perikles promoted and organized the rebuilding of its monuments, beginning with the Parthenon in 447 BCE. According to Greek mythology, Athena, goddess of wisdom and civilization, claimed Athens as her city, and this new temple, dedicated to the Virgin Athena (*Athena Parthenos* in Greek), would proclaim this association, rising triumphantly over the city. The Parthenon, designed and built by the architects Kallikrates and Iktinos, was meant to dominate the other structures on the hilltop site (fig. **5–25**). The builders used the finest white marble, even replacing the customary terracotta roof with marble slabs. The renowned sculptor Phidias designed its sculptural decorations and also supervised the entire project of rebuilding the monuments of the Acropolis. The building itself was completed in 438 BCE, and its sculpture, executed by Phidias and other sculptors in his workshop, was finished in 432 BCE.

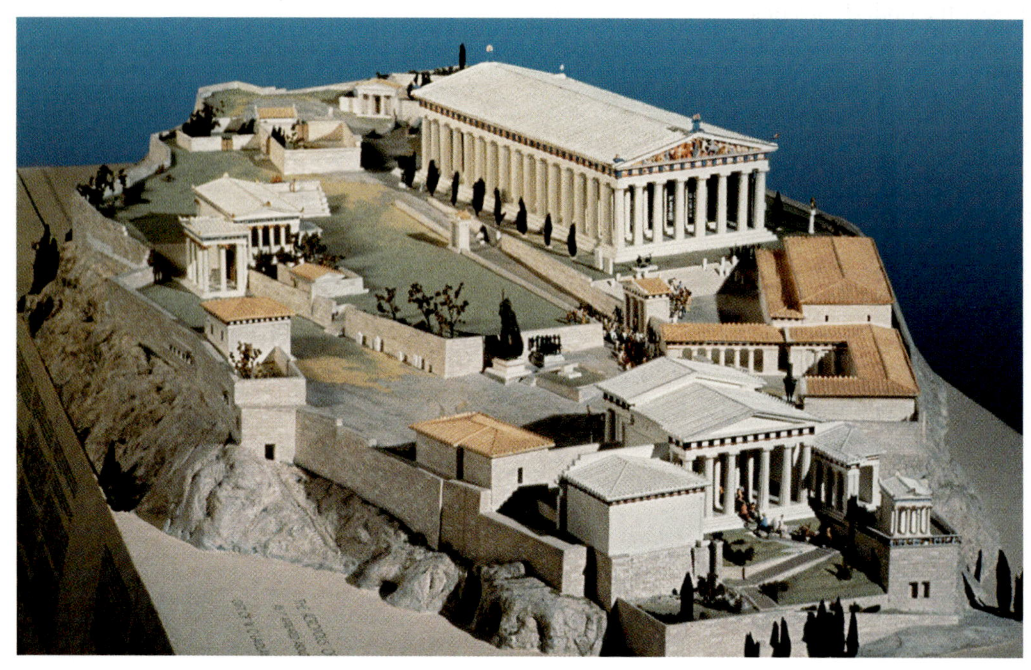

5–25 Model of the Athenian Acropolis in c. 400 BCE. Royal Ontario Museum, Toronto

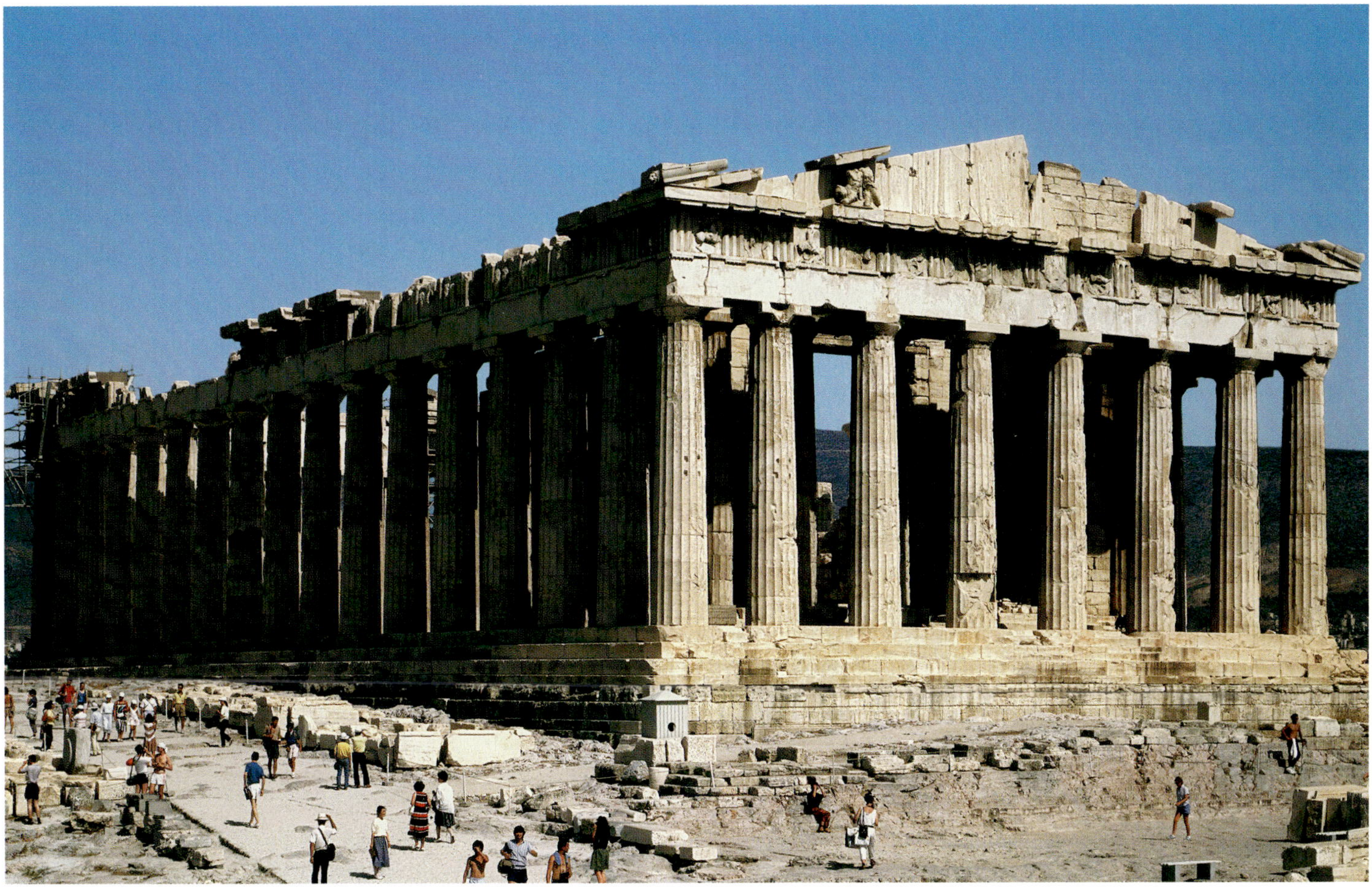

5–26a **Kallikrates and Iktinos. Parthenon,** Acropolis, Athens. c. 447–432 BCE. View from northwest

In its structure and design, the Parthenon illustrates the refinement of ancient Greek architecture (fig. **5–26a** and **b**). It follows the traditional cella and peristyle plan and uses the Doric order (see "The Greek Temple," page 112). To counteract the optical illusions that would distort its appearance when seen from a distance, the architects made many subtle adjustments to strict regularity. Since long horizontal lines appear to sag in the center, the architects designed both the base of the temple and the entablature to curve slightly upward toward the center. The columns have a subtle swelling, or **entasis**, and tilt inward slightly toward the center of the building. In addition, the corners are strengthened visually by reducing the space between columns at the ends of the colonnades. These subtle refinements in the arrangement of elements give the Parthenon a buoyant organic appearance and prevent it from looking like a heavy, lifeless stone box.

As in most temples, sculpture carved in the round filled both pediments of the Parthenon. The figures stood on the projecting shelves of the horizontal cornice (the top of the entablature) secured to the pediment wall with metal pins. The sculptor, whether Phidias or someone working in the Phidian style, expertly rendered the human form beneath the clinging draperies that create curvilinear patterns rippling over torsos, breasts, and knees. Most of the works of sculpture from the Parthenon have been damaged or lost over the

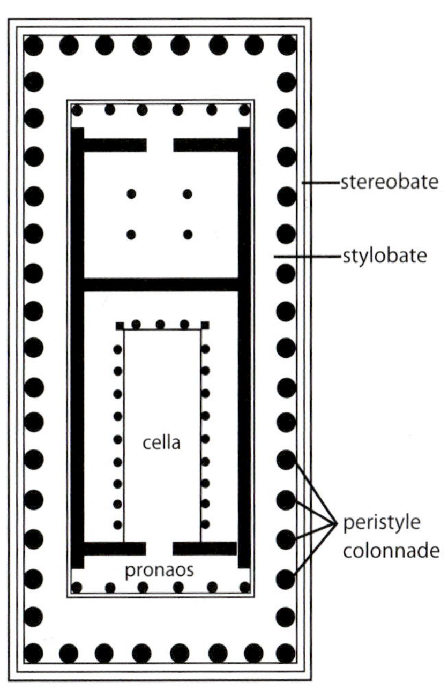

5–26b Plan of Parthenon, Athens. c. 447–432 BCE

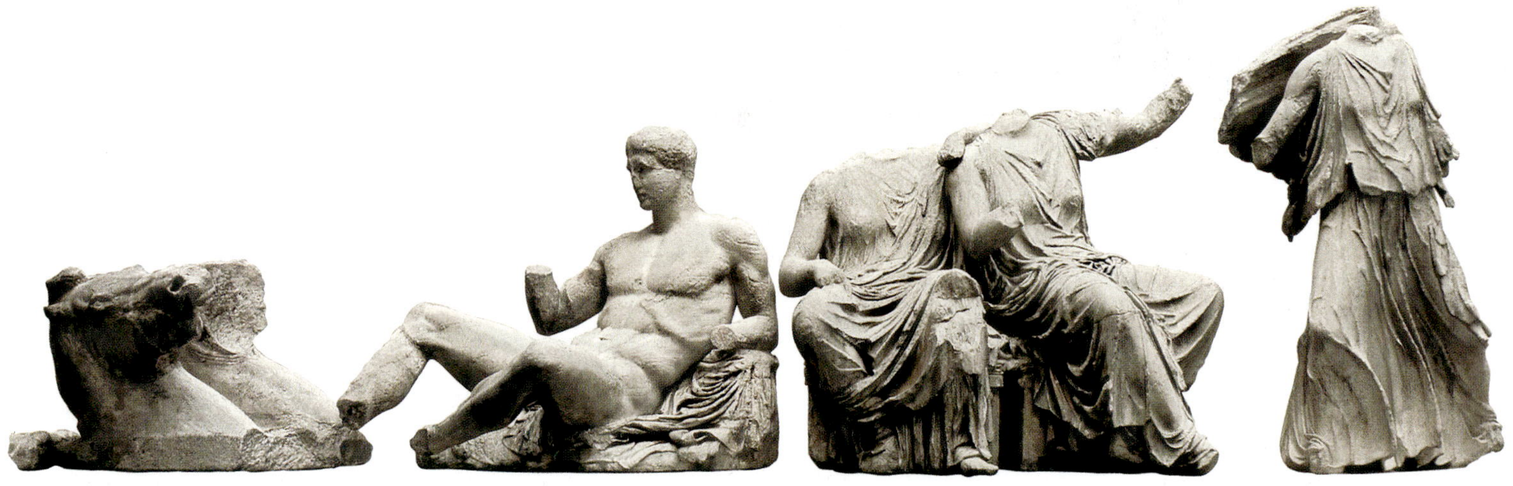

5–27 Photographic mock-up of the east pediment of the Parthenon (using photographs of the extant marble sculpture). c. 447–432 BCE. The British Museum, London

At the beginning of the nineteenth century, Thomas Bruce, the Earl of Elgin and British ambassador to Constantinople, acquired much of the surviving sculpture from the Parthenon, which was being used by the Turks for military purposes at the time. He shipped the pieces back to London in 1801 to decorate his lavish mansion, but after a financial dispute and other difficulties, he sold them to the British government in 1816. Referred to as the Elgin Marbles, most of the sculpture is now in London's British Museum, including all elements seen here. In recent times, the Greek government has tried unsuccessfully to have the Elgin Marbles returned.

centuries, but using the locations of existing pinholes, scholars have determined the placement of the surviving statues and can speculate on the poses of the missing ones.

The east pediment above the entrance to the cella is the better preserved of the two (fig. **5–27**). Originally over 90 feet long, the pediment lacks its central part, amounting to about 40 feet, probably destroyed in the fifth century when Christians turned the Parthenon into a church and built an apse at the east end. The ensemble illustrated the birth of Athena. The missing statues in the center probably showed Zeus seated on a throne, and standing next to him, Athena, who according to mythology had emerged fully grown from his head. The male nude, who fits so easily into the sloping pediment toward the left, has been identified as the hero Herakles with his lion skin or the god Dionysos lying on a panther skin. The two seated women next to him may be the earth and grain goddesses, Demeter and Persephone. The running woman is the messenger of the gods, Iris, who is spreading the news of Athena's birth. The three female figures on the right side are probably Hestia (a sister of Zeus and goddess of the hearth), Dione (one of Zeus's many consorts), and her daughter Aphrodite (goddess of love), who reclines like her male counterpart on the other side of the pediment to conform to its tapering triangular shape. The horses' heads represent (at far left) the ascending chariot of the sun god, Helios (Apollo), and (at far right) the descending moon goddess, Selene.

Originally, the Parthenon's white marble columns and inner walls supported bands of brightly painted low-relief sculpture. (Sir Lawrence Alma-Tadema fantasized the effect in his painting of 1868, entitled *Phidias and the Frieze of the Parthenon, Athens* [see fig. Intro–26]). The exterior Doric frieze included 92 carved metopes with scenes of victory. On the south side, they depicted the fight between half-human centaurs and a legendary Greek tribe known as the Lapiths. The Lapith victory over the centaurs may have symbolized the triumph of reason over animal passions. In one relief (fig. **5–28**), what should be a death struggle seems more like a

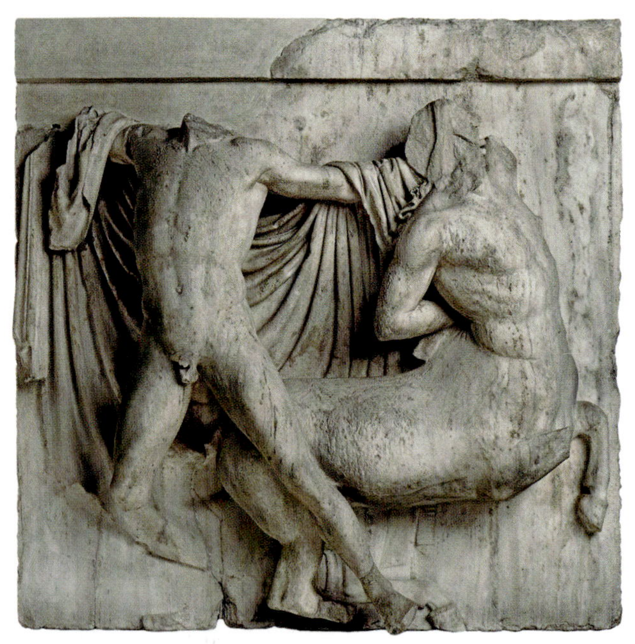

5–28 ***Lapith Fighting a Centaur***, metope relief from the Doric frieze on the south side of the Parthenon. c. 447–432 BCE. Marble, height 56" (1.42 m). The British Museum, London

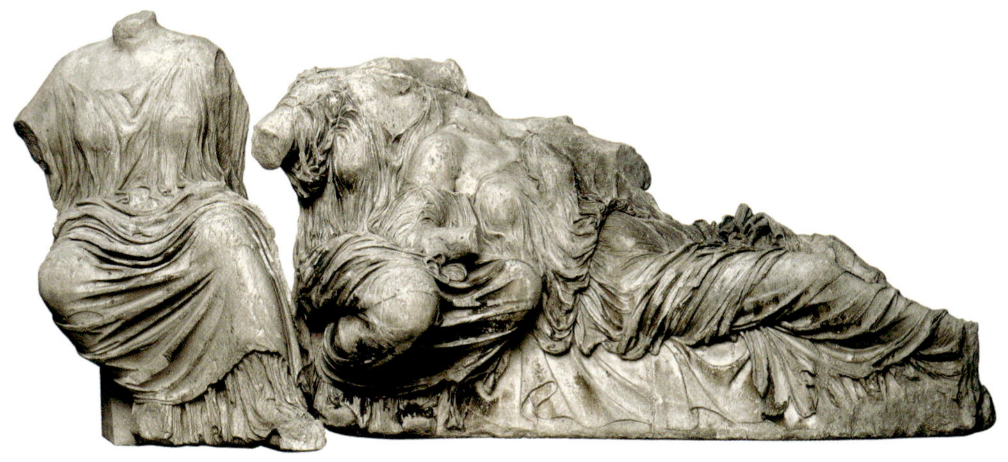

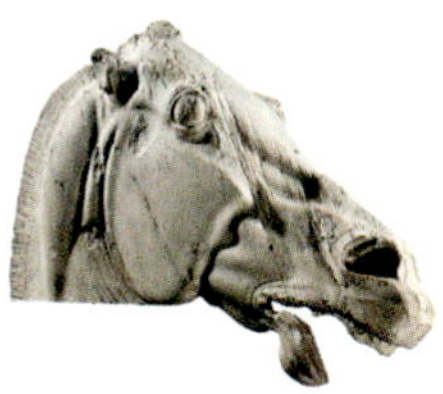

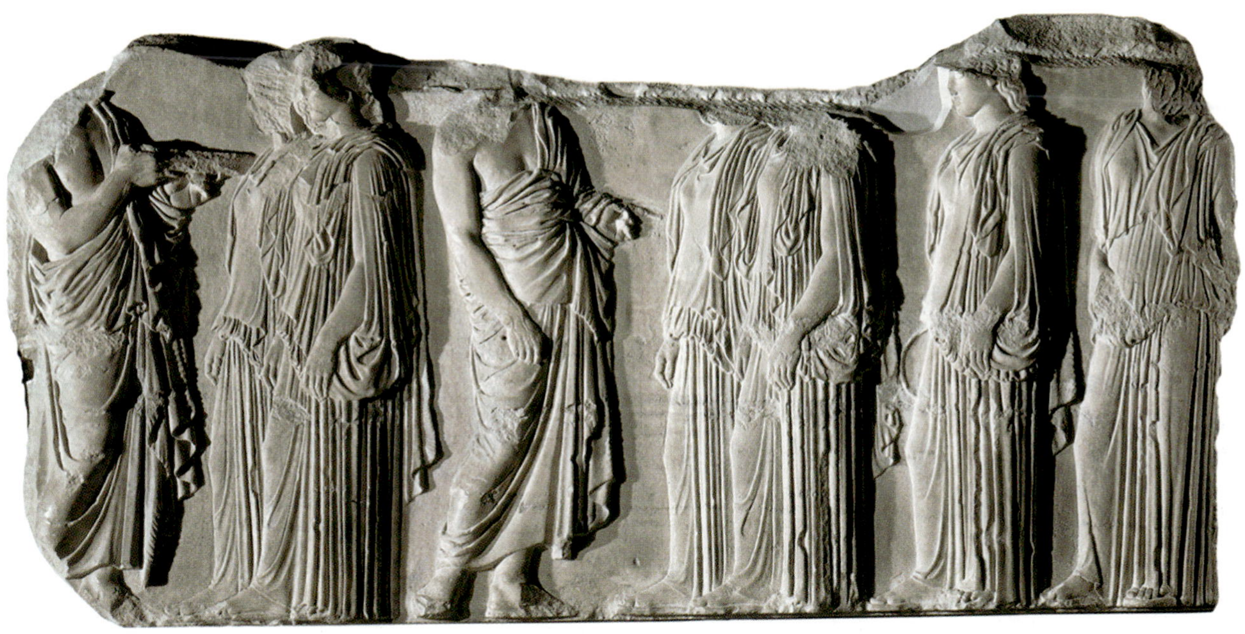

5–29 *Marshals and Young Women*, detail of the *Procession*, from the Ionic frieze on the east side of the Parthenon. c. 447–432 BCE. Marble, height 3' 6" (1.08 m). Musée du Louvre, Paris

The east façade presents a totally integrated program of images: the birth of the goddess in the pediment, her honoring by the citizens who present her with a newly woven peplos *on the Ionic frieze, and, seen through the doors, the glorious ivory and gold figure of Athena herself, the cult image.*

choreographed, athletic ballet, displaying the Lapith's muscles and graceful movements against the implausible backdrop of his carefully draped cloak.

Inside the Parthenon's Doric peristyle, an Ionic frieze (see "The Greek Temple," page 112) decorated the upper temple wall (fig. **5–29**). Unlike the staccato alternation of metope and triglyph in the Doric frieze, the Ionic frieze consisted of a continuous band of sculpture. Here, along the 525-foot-long strip, a procession unfolds, traditionally interpreted as an evocation of the great Panathenaic festival when the women of Athens carried a new wool *peplos* to the Acropolis sanctuary to clothe an ancient wooden cult statue of Athena housed in the Erechtheion there. Throughout the frieze, carefully planned rhythmic variations enliven the composition. Horses plunge ahead at full gallop; women proceed with a slow, stately step; parade marshals pause to look back at the progress of those behind; and gods and goddesses seated on benches await the arrival of the marchers.

The maidens in this detail, who walk with such grace and dignity, represent the Greek ideal of young womanhood, just as the muscular but poised marshals idealize manhood. The procession they participate in is an ideal one, outside time and place. The marble sculpture of the frieze was originally painted in dark blue, red, and ocher, and details such as the bridles and reins of the horses were added in bronze. To compensate for the dim lighting inside the peristyle, the top of the frieze band is carved in slightly higher relief than the lower part, tilting the figures outward to catch reflected light from the pavement. The procession of maidens attended by parade marshals, although only a fragment of the architectural decoration, epitomizes of the extraordinary quality characterizing every detail of the temple.

Other Buildings of the Athenian Acropolis

Upon completion of the Parthenon, Perikles commissioned an architect named Mnesikles to design a monumental gatehouse for the Acropolis, the Propylaia. Work began on it in 437 and stopped in 432, with the structure still incomplete. The Propylaia had no sculptural decoration, but its north wing eventually became the earliest known museum (meaning "home of the Muses"), a gallery built specifically to house a collection of paintings for public view.

We do not know the name of the designer of the Erechtheion, the second important temple erected on the Acropolis under Perikles' building program (fig. **5–30**), begun in the 430s and completed in 405 BCE, just before the fall of Athens to Sparta. The asymmetrical plan on several levels reflects the building's multiple functions in housing many different shrines, and it also conforms to the sharply sloping terrain on which it is located. The Erechtheion stands on the site of the mythical contest between the sea god, Poseidon, and Athena for patronage over Athens. During this contest, Poseidon struck a rock with his trident (three-pronged harpoon), bringing forth a spout of water, but Athena gave an olive tree and won the contest. The Athenians enclosed what they believed to be this sacred rock, bearing the marks of the trident, in the Erechtheion's north porch. Another area housed a sacred spring dedicated to Erechtheus, a legendary king of Athens, during whose reign the goddess Demeter was said to have instructed the Athenians in the arts of growing crops and other vegetation. It also housed the venerable wooden cult statue of Athena that was the focus of the Panathenaic festival.

The north and east porches of the Erechtheion have come to epitomize the Ionic order, serving as an important model for European architects since the eighteenth century. Taller and more slender in proportion than the Doric, the Ionic order also has richer and more elaborately carved decoration (see "The Greek Temple," page 112). The columns rise from molded bases and end in **volute** (spiral scroll) capitals, and the frieze is continuous. At the west end of the south side, six **caryatids** (female figures acting as columns) support the entablature of yet another porch (fig. **5–31**).

A second Ionic temple, dedicated to Athena Nike (Victory), stands near the entrance to the Acropolis precinct. Between 410 and 405 BCE, this temple was surrounded by a low wall faced with relief panels of Athena presiding over her winged attendants (known as Nikes or Victories) as they prepared for a victory celebration. One of the most admired panels depicts a Nike adjusting her sandal (fig. **5–32**). What a contrast with the restrained, stocky caryatids of the Erechtheion! The figure bends forward gracefully, allowing her ample robe to slip off one shoulder. Though now mostly lost, her large wings, one open and one closed, effectively balance this unstable pose. Unlike the swirls of heavy fabric covering the Parthenon goddesses or the weighty pleats of the robes of the Erechtheion caryatids, the textile covering this Nike appears delicate and light, clinging to her body like wet silk. The objectives of both artist and

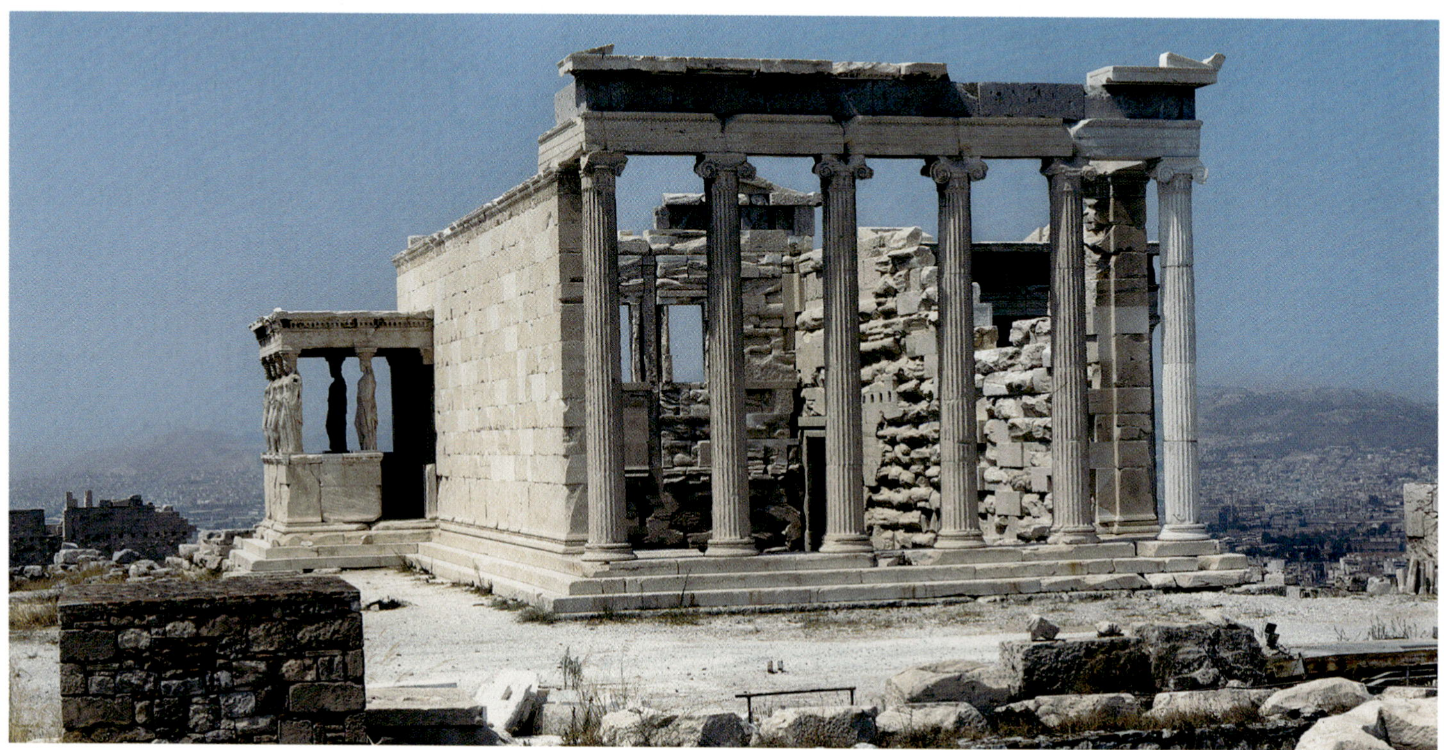

5–30 Erechtheion, Acropolis, Athens. c. 430–405 BCE. View from the east

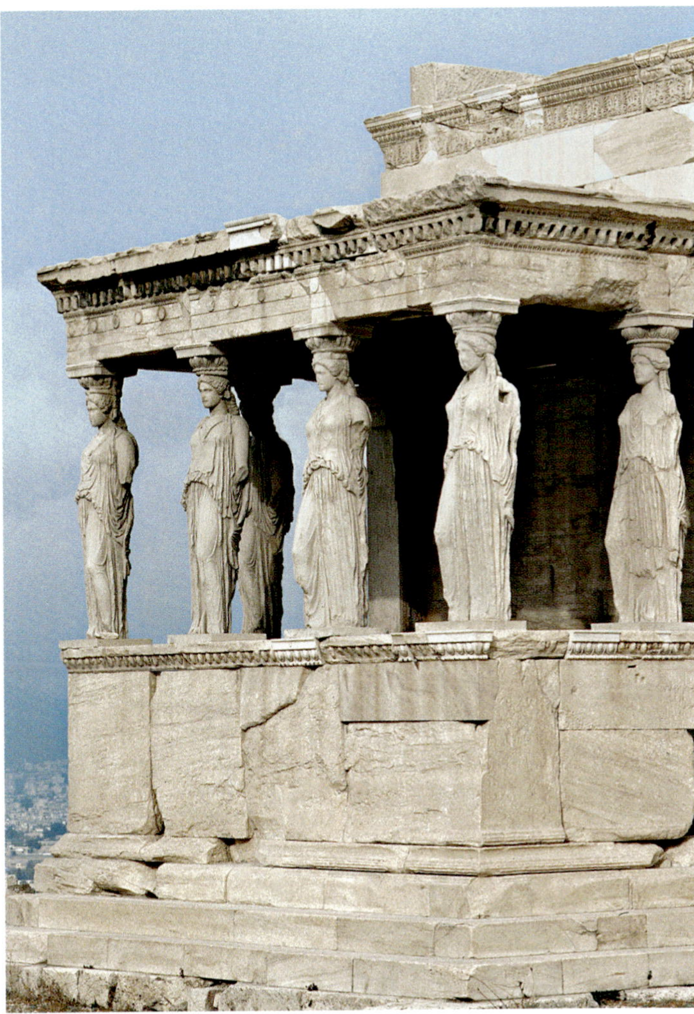

5–31 Porch of the Maidens (South Porch), Erechtheion, Acropolis, Athens. 421–405 BCE

Standing in Classical contrapposto, each caryatid stands on one engaged leg, while the other relaxes to bend at the knee. The vertical fall of the drapery on the supporting leg resembles the fluting of a column shaft, while the gracefully bent leg enlivens the columnar form like the entasis of the Doric shaft.

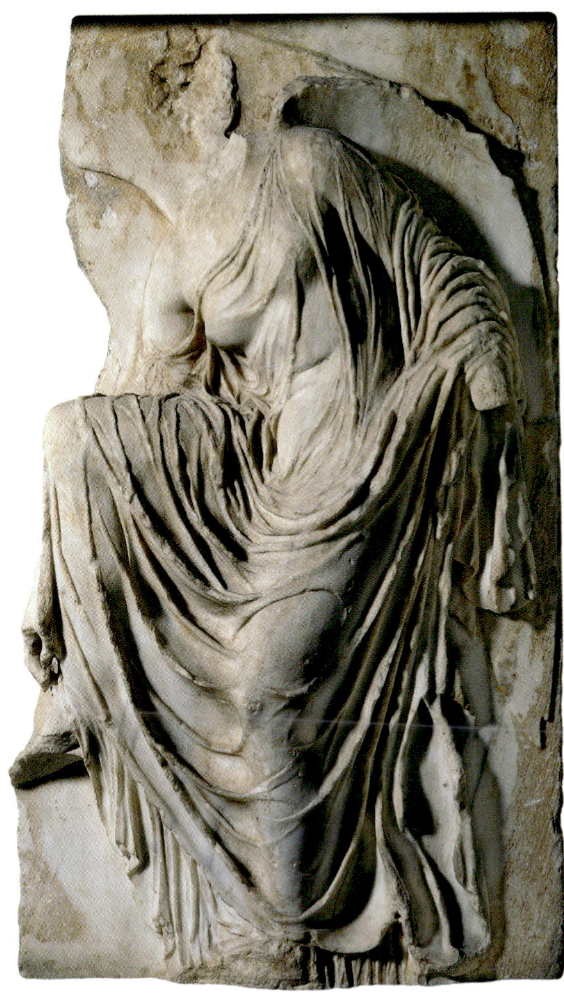

5–32 *Nike (Victory) Adjusting Her Sandal*, fragment of relief decoration from the parapet (now destroyed), Temple of Athena Nike, Acropolis, Athens. c. 410–405 BCE. Marble, height 3' 6" (1.06 m). Acropolis Museum, Athens

patron, as well as the cultural expectations of their audience, had changed dramatically since the creation of the "*Peplos*" *Kore* (see fig. 5–17).

High Classical Greek sculptors sought to create timeless images of men and women by embodying within them an ideal notion of human appearance and deportment. They accomplished this by first observing, and then paring down, the irregularities they saw in nature, and by using their knowledge of geometry to find what they believed were perfect proportions (see "The Canon of Polykleitos," page 126). And, to achieve the rhythmic harmony presented in narrative works such as the *Procession* frieze (see fig. 5–29)—in which each form is distinct and individual yet all are united into a balanced and interconnected whole—the artists must have carefully observed and distilled the incidents of many similar events. This quest to explore the relationship between the actual and the ideal was matched in the work of the Greek philosopher Socrates (c. 470–399 BCE) and his disciple Plato (c. 429–347 BCE), both of whom argued that all objects in the physical world were mere reflections of ideal forms that could be discovered through reason.

Late Classical Art of the Fourth Century BCE

In 404 BCE, the Peloponnesian War concluded with the defeat of Athens by Sparta. Ancient Athens never regained its dominant political and military status, yet Sparta failed to establish a lasting preeminence over the other Greek lands. The quarreling city-states finally fell under the dominance of Philip II of Macedonia in 338 BCE and, after Philip's assassination two years later, his 20-year-old son, Alexander the Great, incorporated the Greek city-states into an empire that extended from India to Egypt.

Remarkably, Greek art continued to evolve during this turbulent period. In their restless search for an ideal human form, sculptors, most notably Praxiteles and Lysippos in the fourth century BCE, developed a new canon of proportions for figures. Polykleitos'

THE CANON OF POLYKLEITOS

Just as Greek architects defined and followed a set of strict standards for ideal temple design, Greek sculptors sought an ideal for representations of the human body. Studying human appearances closely, the sculptors of the Classical period selected those attributes they considered most desirable and beautiful, such as regular facial features, smooth skin, and particular body proportions, and combined them into a single ideal.

The best-known art theorist of the Classical period was the sculptor Polykleitos of Argos. About 450 BCE he developed a set of rules for constructing the ideal human figure, which he set down in a treatise called "The Canon" (*kanon* is Greek for "measure," "rule," or "law"). To illustrate his theory, Polykleitos created a larger-than-life bronze statue of a man carrying a spear—perhaps the hero Achilles (fig. **5–33**). Neither the treatise nor the original statue has survived, but both were widely discussed in the writings of his contemporaries, and later Roman artists made marble copies of the *Spear Bearer* (*Doryphoros*). By studying these copies, scholars have tried to determine the set of measurements that defined the ideal proportions in Polykleitos' canon.

The canon included a system of ratios between a basic unit and the length of various body parts. Some studies suggest that his basic unit may have been the length of the figure's index finger or the width of its hand across the knuckles; others suggest that it was the height of the head from chin to hairline. The canon also included guidelines for *symmetria* ("commensurability"), by which Polykleitos meant the relationship of body parts to one another. In the statue he made to illustrate his treatise, he explored not only proportions but also the relationships among weight-bearing and relaxed legs and arms in a perfectly balanced figure. The cross-balancing of supporting and free elements in a figure is sometimes referred to as contrapposto.

In true Classical fashion, Polykleitos balanced careful observation with idealization to create what he considered the perfect human figure. The Roman marble replica of the Greek bronze illustrated here shows a male athlete, perfectly balanced with the whole weight of the upper body supported by the straight (engaged) right leg. The left leg is bent at the knee, with the left foot poised on the ball of the foot, suggesting movement. The pattern of tension and relaxation is reversed in the arrangement of the arms, with the right relaxed on the engaged side and the left bent to support the weight of the (missing) spear. This dynamically balanced body pose—characteristic of Classical standing figure sculpture—evolves out of the pose of the *Kritios Boy* (see fig. 5–22) of a generation earlier. The tilt of the hipline in the *Doryphoros* is a little more pronounced to accommodate the raising of the left foot onto its ball, and the head is turned toward the same side as the engaged leg.

To Polykleitos and others of the time, the beautiful was synonymous with the good, and sculptors sought a mathematical definition of the beautiful as it applied to the human figure, aspiring to make it possible to evoke notions of human perfection in the tangible form of sculpture.

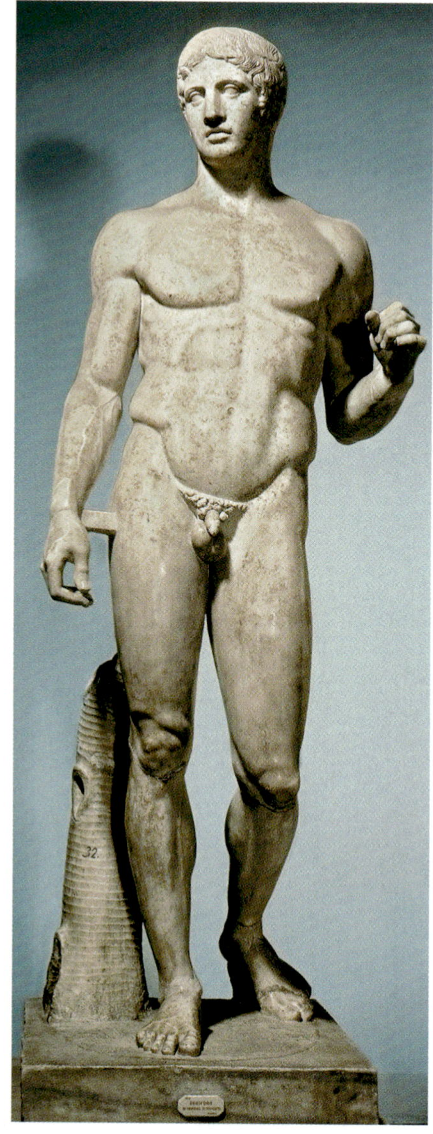

5–33 Polykleitos. ***Spear Bearer*** **(*Doryphoros*)**, perhaps Achilles. Roman copy after the original bronze of c. 450–440 BCE (tree trunk and bracing strut are Roman additions). Marble, height 6' 11" (2.12 m). Museo Archaeològico Nazionale, Naples

fifth-century BCE canon called for figures 6½ or 7 times the height of the head. Praxiteles, who worked in Athens from about 370 to 335 BCE or later, created figures about 8 or more "heads" tall. A marble sculpture of *Hermes and the Infant Dionysos* (fig. **5–34**)—probably a Hellenistic or Roman copy but so fine that generations of scholars believed it to be an original statue by Praxiteles—has a smaller head and a more sensual and sinuous body than Polykleitos' *Spear Bearer* (see fig. 5–33). Its off-balance, S-curve pose contrasts sharply with that of the tenser earlier work. And the subject is less detached. Indeed, there is a hint of human narrative: Hermes teases the infant god of wine with a bunch of grapes. But the soft modulations in the musculature, the deep folds in the draperies, and the rough locks of hair create a sensuous play of light and shadow over the figure's surface, emphasizing textural distinctions found in nature.

Around 350 BCE, Praxiteles created a daring statue of Aphrodite, the goddess of love (fig. **5–35**). For the first time, a well-known

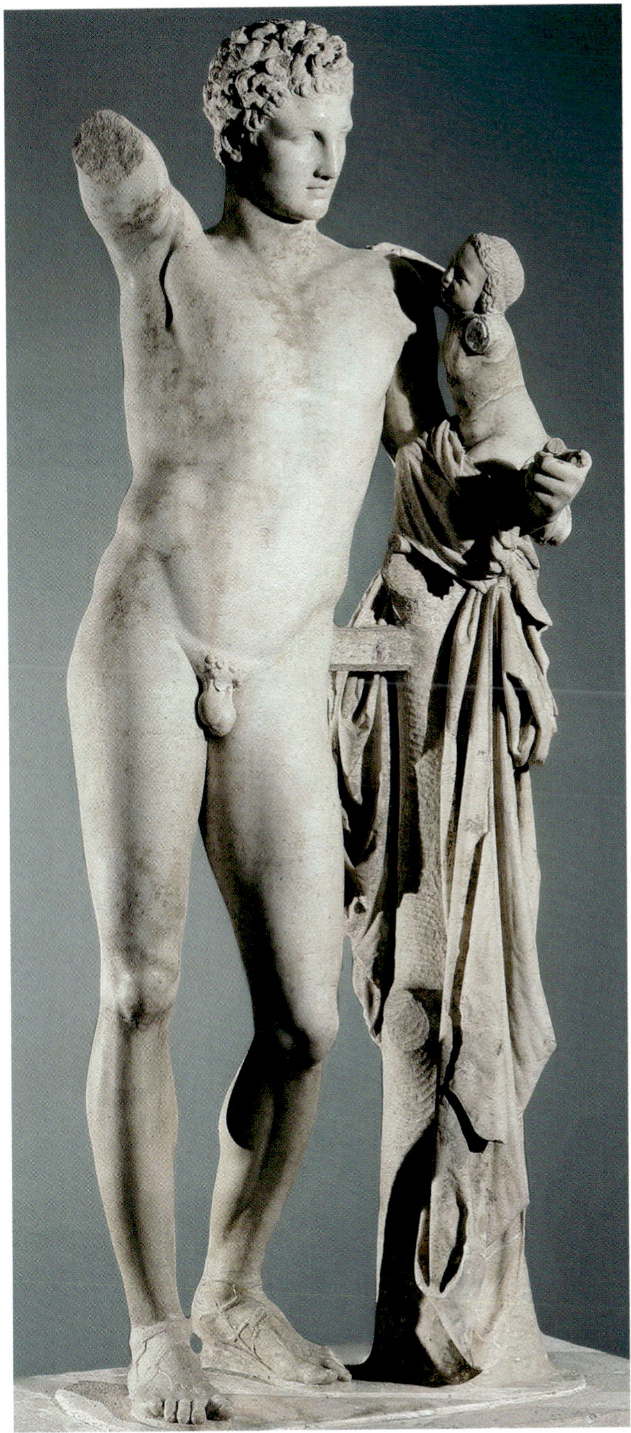

5–34 Praxiteles or his followers. ***Hermes and the Infant Dionysos***, probably a Hellenistic or Roman copy after a 4th-century BCE original. Marble, with remnants of red paint on the lips and hair, height 7' 1" (2.15 m). National Archaeological Museum, Olympia

Discovered in the rubble of the ruined Temple of Hera at Olympia in 1875, this statue is now widely accepted as an outstanding Roman or Hellenistic copy. Support for this conclusion comes from certain elements typical of Roman sculpture: Hermes' sandals, which recent studies suggest are not accurate for a fourth-century BCE date; the supporting element of crumpled fabric covering a tree stump; and the use of a reinforcing strut, or brace, between Hermes' hip and the tree stump.

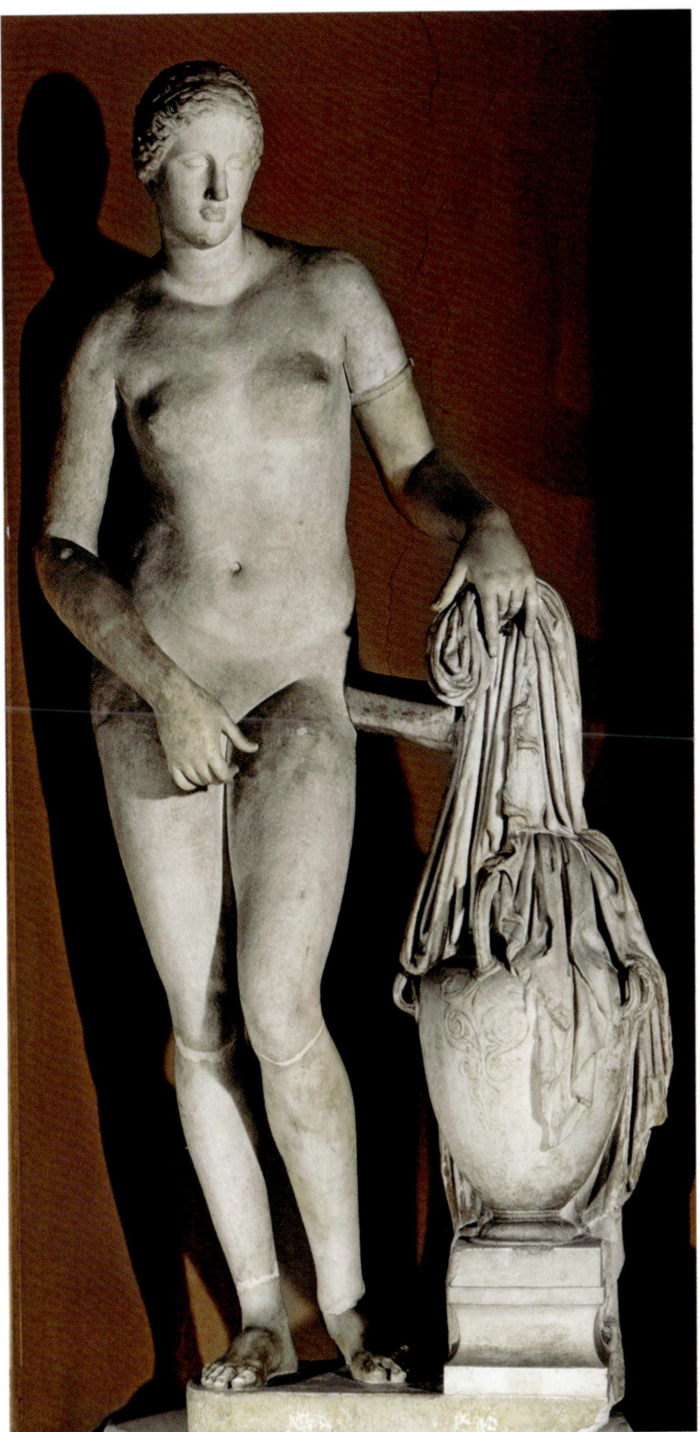

5–35 Praxiteles. ***Aphrodite of Knidos.*** Composite of two similar Roman copies after the original marble of c. 350 BCE. Marble, height 6' 8" (2 m). Vatican Museums, Museo Pio Clementino, Gabinetto delle Maschere, Rome

The head of this figure is from one Roman copy, the body from another. Seventeenth- and eighteenth-century CE restorers added the nose, the neck, the right forearm and hand, most of the left arm, and the feet and parts of the legs. This kind of restoration would rarely be undertaken today, but it was frequently done and considered quite acceptable in the past, when archaeologists were trying to put together a body of work documenting the appearances of lost Greek statues.

WOMEN ARTISTS IN GREECE

Although comparatively few artists in ancient Greece were women, there is evidence that women artists worked in many media. Ancient writers noted women painters; Pliny the Elder, for example, listed Aristarete, Eirene, Iaia, Kalypso, Olympias, and Timarete. Helen, a painter from Egypt who had been taught by her father, is known to have worked in the fourth century BCE and may have been responsible for the original wall painting of *Alexander the Great Confronts Darius III at the Battle of Issos* (see fig. 5–37). Greek women excelled in creating narrative or pictorial tapestries, and they also worked in pottery-making workshops. The hydria shown here (fig. **5–36**), dating from about 450 BCE, shows a woman and three men painting in such a workshop. In the center Athena, patron of crafts and the arts, holds a wreath, and Nikes crown the men, symbolizing victory in an artistic competition.

The woman sits on a raised dais at far right, painting the largest vase in the workshop but isolated from the other artists as well as the awards ceremony. Perhaps most women were excluded from public artistic competitions, as they were from men's athletic competitions. But could this woman be the head of this workshop? Athenian women could control property that they gained through inheritance. Secure in her own status, this woman may have encouraged her assistants to enter contests to further their careers and to bring glory to her workshop.

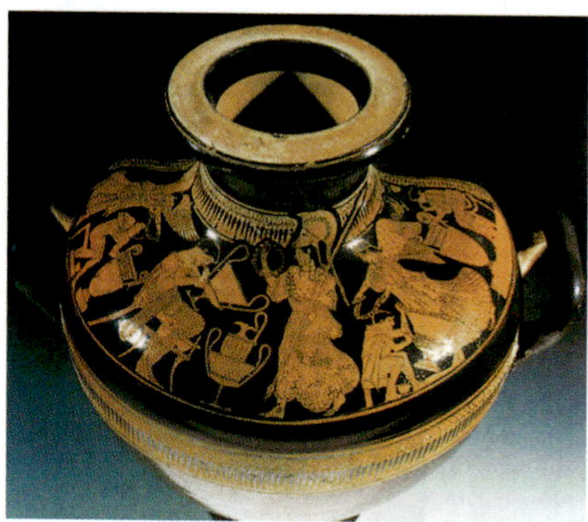

5–36 The Leningrad Painter. ***A Ceramic Painter and Assistants Crowned by Athena and Victories.*** Red-figure decoration on a hydria from Athens. c. 450 BCE. Private Collection, Milan

Greek sculptor depicted a goddess as a completely nude woman. The citizens of Knidos in Asia Minor purchased the sculpture and displayed it proudly in a shrine open on all four sides. The original sculpture is lost, but many Roman copies survive. As with the statue of Hermes, Praxiteles has incorporated a sense of narrative. The goddess is preparing to take a bath. Her right hand is caught in a gesture of modesty that actually calls attention to her nudity. She leans forward slightly with one knee bent in a seductive pose that emphasizes the swelling forms of her thighs, abdomen, and breasts. According to an old legend, Aphrodite herself journeyed to Knidos to see Praxiteles' statue and cried out in shock, "Where did Praxiteles see me naked?"

The other major sculptor of the fourth century BCE whose name and fame come down to us is Lysippos. Not one of his original statues survives, but we know that when summoned to create a portrait of Alexander the Great, he portrayed the ruler standing and holding a scepter in the same way he represented Zeus, king of the gods. According to the Roman historian Plutarch, Lysippos depicted

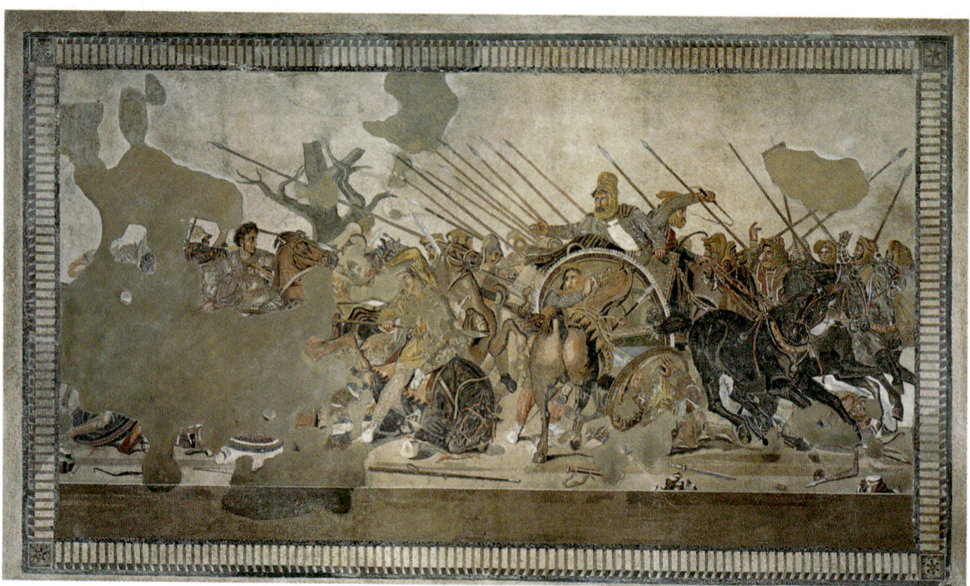

5–37 ***Alexander the Great Confronts Darius III at the Battle of Issos.*** 1st century CE floor mosaic from Pompeii, Italy, copied after a Greek painting of c. 310 BCE, perhaps by Philoxenos or Helen of Egypt. Museo Archeològico Nazionale, Naples

Alexander with his head slightly turned and his face raised upward toward the sky, as though the ruler, contemplating grave decisions, is waiting to receive divine advice.

Hellenistic Art

After establishing an empire that stretched from Greece south to Egypt, and as far east as India, Alexander died of a fever in Babylon at the age of 33 in 323 BCE. Alexander's premature death, and the subsequent breakup of his vast empire, marks the end of the Classical period in Greek art.

His untimely end left his empire with no administrative structure and no appointed successor. Almost immediately, his generals turned against one another, and local leaders tried to regain their lost autonomy. By the early third century BCE, three major powers had emerged from the chaos, ruled by three of Alexander's generals and their heirs: Antigonus, Ptolemy, and Seleucus. The Antigonids controlled Macedonia and mainland Greece; the Ptolemies ruled Egypt; and the Seleucids controlled Anatolia, Syria, Mesopotamia, and Persia. Each of these regions followed a different political course, but they were unified artistically and culturally by Greek ideas and Greek art. This Hellenistic world would last until the rise of Rome in the second and first centuries BCE.

Artists of the Hellenistic period developed visions discernibly distinct from those of their Classical Greek predecessors. Whereas earlier artists often sought to capture a canonical and generalized ideal in art, Hellenistic artists shifted focus to the individual and the specific. They turned increasingly from the heroic to the everyday, from aloof serenity to individual emotion, and from decorous drama to emotional melodrama. Their works appeal to the senses through luscious or lustrous surface treatments and to our hearts as well as our intellects through expressive subjects and poses. Although such tendencies are already evident during the fourth century BCE, they became much more pronounced in Hellenistic art.

Hellenistic painting reflects the new taste for dramatic narrative subject matter. Little remains of original Greek wall paintings, but as with Greek sculpture, later Roman patrons greatly admired Greek murals and commissioned copies in the form of wall paintings or mosaics. The first-century CE floor **mosaic** (a picture created from **tesserae**, small cubes of colored stone or marble) from Pompeii illustrated in figure **5–37**, showing a battle between Alexander the Great and Darius III of Persia, is a Roman copy of a Greek wall painting of about 310 BCE. The historian Pliny the Elder mentions a painting of this subject by the Greek painter Philoxenos of Eretria, but a recent theory claims this as a work of Helen of Egypt, one of a number of women painters recorded in ancient Greece.

The dramatic scene is one of violent action, diagonal disruption, and radical **foreshortening** (a technique that shows things as if they were receding or projecting forward within space). It elicits a strong response in the viewer. Astride a rearing horse at the left, his hair blowing free and his neck bare, Alexander challenges the helmeted and armored Persian leader, who stretches out his arm in a gesture of defeat and apprehension as his charioteer whisks him back toward safety within the Persian ranks. Presumably in close imitation of the original painting, the mosaicist created the illusion of solid figures through **modeling**, mimicking the play of light on three-dimensional surfaces by highlighting protruding areas and shading receding ones.

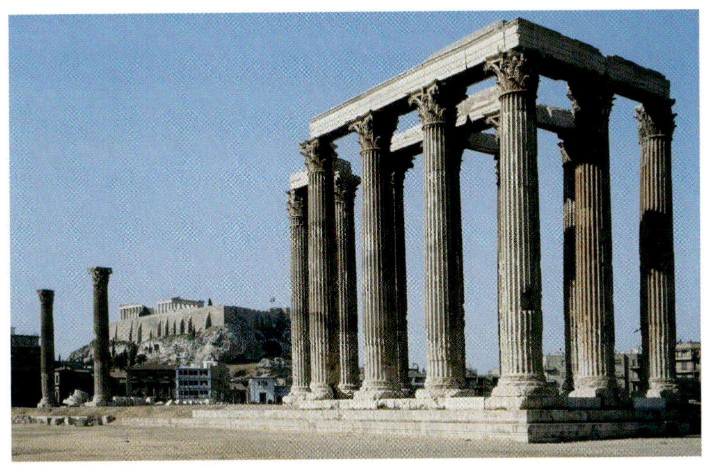

5–38 Temple of the Olympian Zeus, Athens. Height of columns 55' 5" (16.83 m). Building and rebuilding phases: foundation c. 520–510 BCE using the Doric order; temple designed by Cossutius, begun 175 BCE, left unfinished 164 BCE, completed 132 CE using Cossutius' design and Corinthian order. (Acropolis and Parthenon can be seen in the background.)

During the Hellenistic period, there was also increasing innovation in public architecture. For example, a variant of the Ionic order featuring a tall, slender column with an elaborate foliate capital began to challenge the dominance of the Doric and Ionic orders. Invented in the late fifth century BCE, and called Corinthian by later Romans, this highly ornate capital had previously been reserved for interiors (see fig. Intro–11). But in the new Temple of the Olympian Zeus (fig. **5–38**), located in the lower city of Athens near the foot of the Acropolis, a large-scale Corinthian peristyle fronts the exterior. In the second century BCE, building atop the huge foundation (measuring 135 by 354 feet) of a mid-sixth-century BCE Doric temple, the Roman architect Cossutius designed this new temple, but it was not completed until three centuries later under the Roman emperor Hadrian. The columns and entablature soar an imposing 57 feet above the base. Indeed, viewed through the remaining upright columns, the Parthenon seems almost modest in scale. But for all its height and luxurious decoration, the Temple of the Olympian Zeus followed long-established design norms. It was an enclosed rectangular building surrounded by a screen of columns and standing on a three-stepped base. Its proportions and details followed traditional standards. Quite simply, it is a Greek temple grown very large (see "The Greek Temple," page 112).

Hellenistic sculptors produced an enormous variety of work in a wide range of materials, techniques, and styles. The period was marked by two broad and conflicting trends. One (sometimes called anti-Classical) abandoned Classical strictures and experimented freely with new forms and subjects. This radical style was practiced in Pergamon and other eastern centers of Greek culture. The other trend emulated earlier Classical models, selecting aspects of certain favored works by fourth-century BCE sculptors—especially Praxiteles and Lysippos—to incorporate into their own works.

ELEMENTS OF Architecture

Greek Theaters

In ancient Greece, the theater offered more than entertainment; it was a vehicle for the communal expression of religious beliefs through music, poetry, and dance. During the fifth century BCE, the plays were primarily tragedies in verse based on popular myths and were performed at festivals dedicated to Dionysos. The three great Greek tragedians of the time were Aeschylus, Sophocles, and Euripides. They created works that defined tragedy for centuries.

Because ancient theaters were used continuously and were modified frequently over many centuries, no early theaters have survived in their original form. The largely intact theater at Epidauros, however, which dates from the fourth century BCE, presents a good example of the characteristics of early theaters (figs. **5–39** and **5–40**). A semicircle of tiered seats built into a hillside overlooks a circular performance area, called the *orkhestra* (from a Greek word meaning "to dance"), at the center of which was an altar to Dionysos. Rising behind the orchestra was a two-tiered stage structure made up of the vertical *skene* (scene)—an architectural backdrop for performances that also screened the backstage area from view—and the *proskenion* (*proscenium*), a raised platform in front of the *skene* that was increasingly used over time as an extension of the orchestra. Ramps connecting the *proskenion* with lateral passageways provided access to the stage for performers. Steps gave the audience access to the 55 rows of seats and divided the seating area into uniform wedge-shaped sections. (At Epidauros, the tiers of seats above the wide corridor, or gangway, were added at a much later date.) This standard design provided uninterrupted sight lines, excellent acoustics, and efficient crowd control for 12,000 spectators—a basic plan not greatly improved upon since.

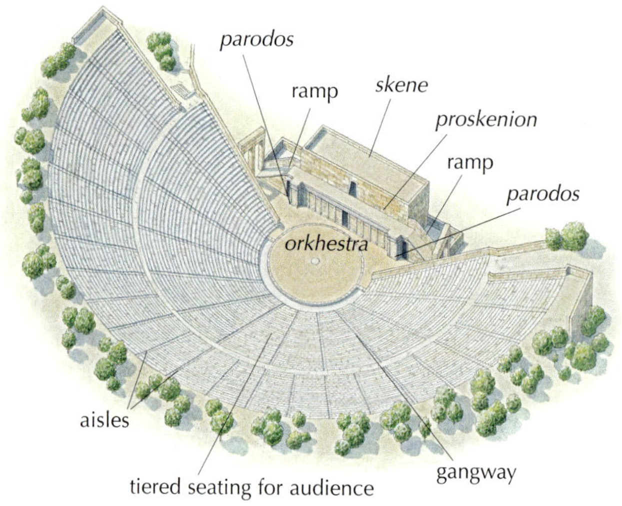

5–39 Reconstruction drawing of the theater of Epidauros

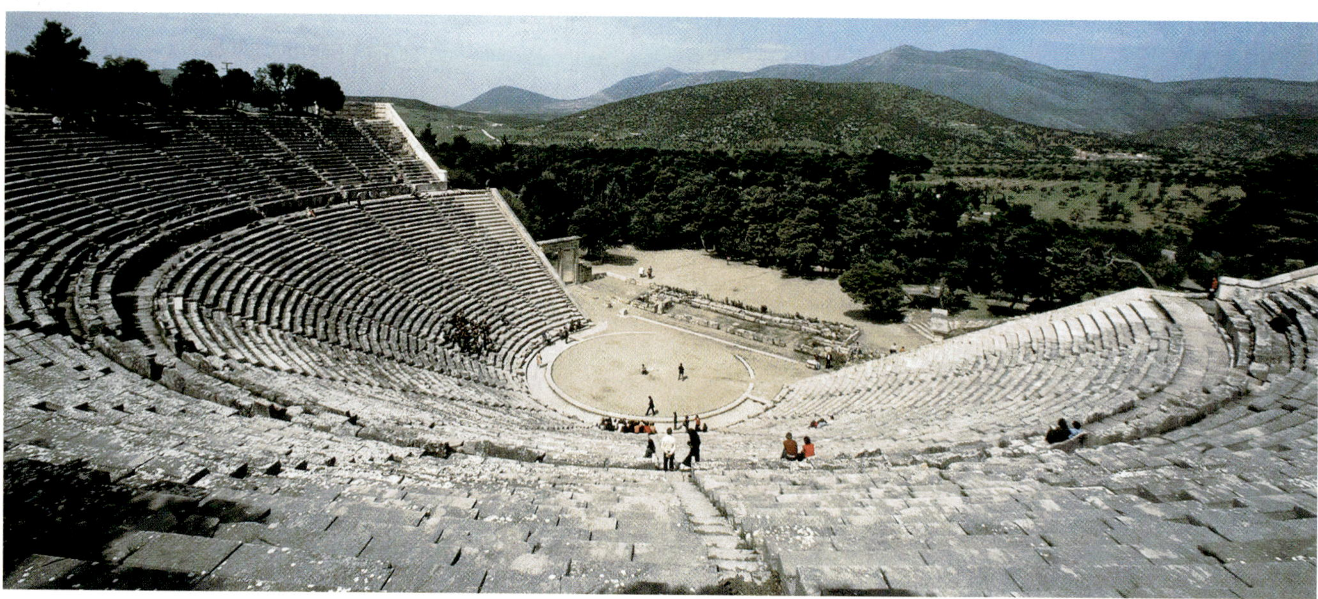

5–40 Theater, Epidauros. 4th century BCE and later

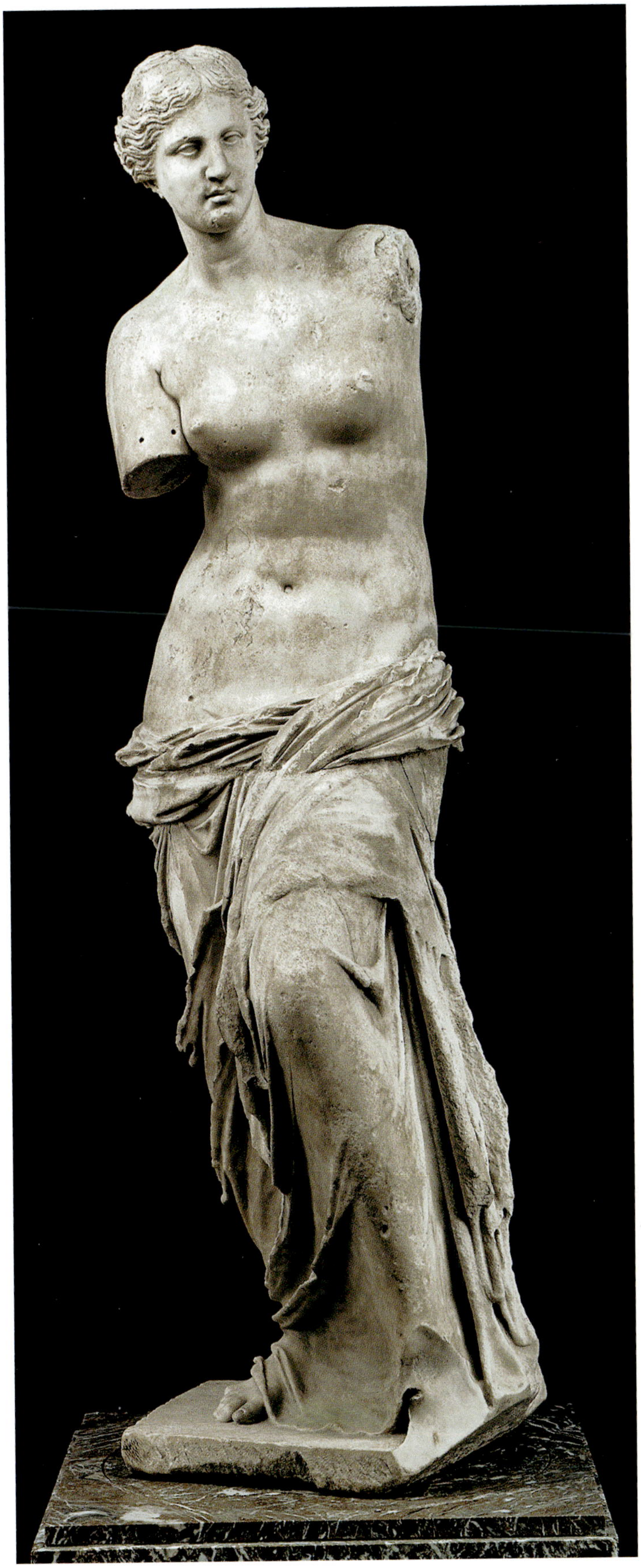

This nostalgic interest in Late Classical style is exemplified by the *Aphrodite of Melos* (fig. **5–41**), found on the Aegean island of Melos by French excavators in the early nineteenth century. This sculpture was intended by its maker to recall the *Aphrodite of Knidos* by Praxiteles (see fig. 5–35), and indeed the head, with its dreamy gaze, suggests the lost Praxitelean work. But the twisting stance and strong projection of the knee, as well as the rich, three-dimensional quality of the drapery, are typical of Hellenistic art. Moreover, the sensuous juxtaposition of soft flesh with the crisper texture of drapery, especially since it seems to be slipping off the figure, adds an insistent note of erotic tension that is thoroughly Hellenistic in concept and intent.

The Late Classical normative beauty of the *Aphrodite of Melos* contrasts sharply with the seemingly unvarnished portrayal of an elderly woman carrying a basket of vegetables and a chicken, also carved in the second century BCE (fig. **5–42**). At first glance she

5–41 ***Aphrodite of Melos*** (also called *Venus de Milo*). c. 150–100 BCE. Marble, height 6' 8" (2 m). Musée du Louvre, Paris

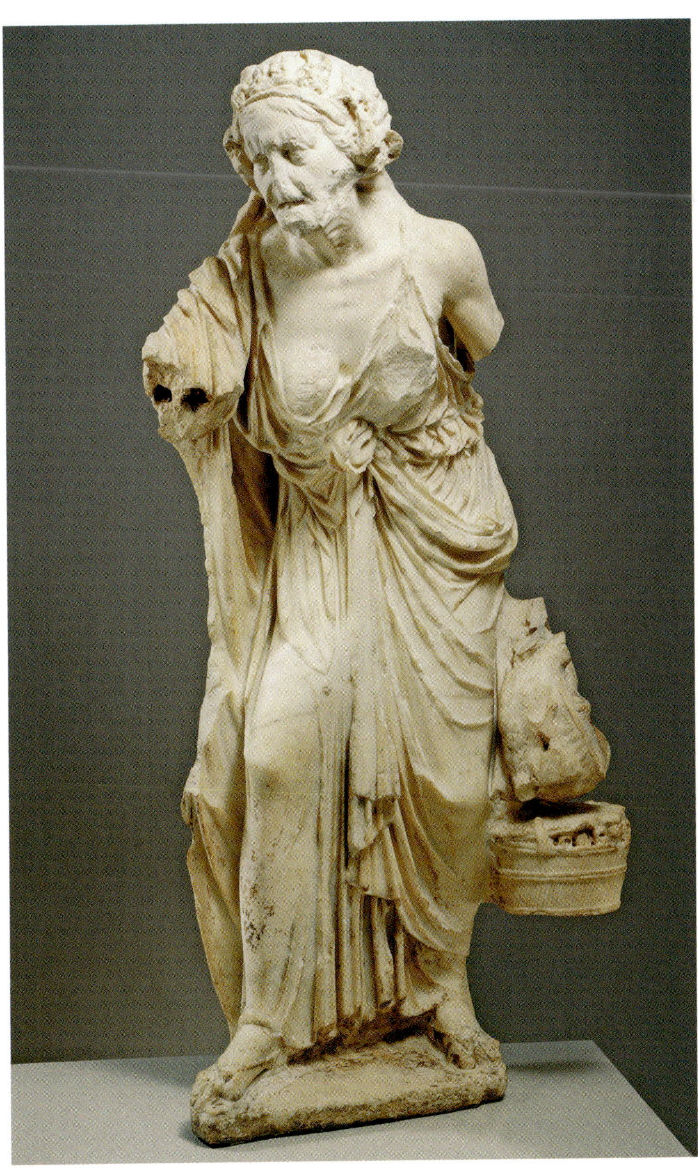

5–42 ***Market Woman***. Roman copy of 1st century CE. Marble, height 49½" (1.25 m). The Metropolitan Museum of Art, New York
ROGERS FUND, 1909 (09.19)

seems to be simply an old peasant woman doing her marketing. However, the disarray of her dress and her unfocused stare suggest that she represents an aging, dissolute follower of the wine god Dionysos, struggling on her way to make an offering. Such representations of people from all levels of society, as well as a taste for unusual physical types, became popular during the Hellenistic period.

Even more dramatic in its depiction of action is the *Nike (Victory) of Samothrace* (fig. **5–43**). The forward momentum of this 8-foot-high victory goddess is balanced by the powerful backward thrust of her enormous wings. She has just landed on the prow of the stone ship that formed the original base of the statue. The ensemble originally stood in a hillside niche high above the sanctuary of the Samothracian gods, perhaps drenched with spray from a fountain.

Some of the best-known examples of Hellenistic art were made in the third and second centuries BCE in the kingdom of Pergamon, a Greek state on the west coast of Asia Minor. After gaining independence in the early third century BCE, Pergamon quickly became a leading center of the arts and the hub of a new sculptural style that had far-reaching influence. That style is exemplified by sculpture from a monument commemorating the victory in 230 BCE of Attalos I (ruled 241–197 BCE) over the Gauls, a Celtic people who invaded from the north (fig. **5–44**). These bronze figures, known today from

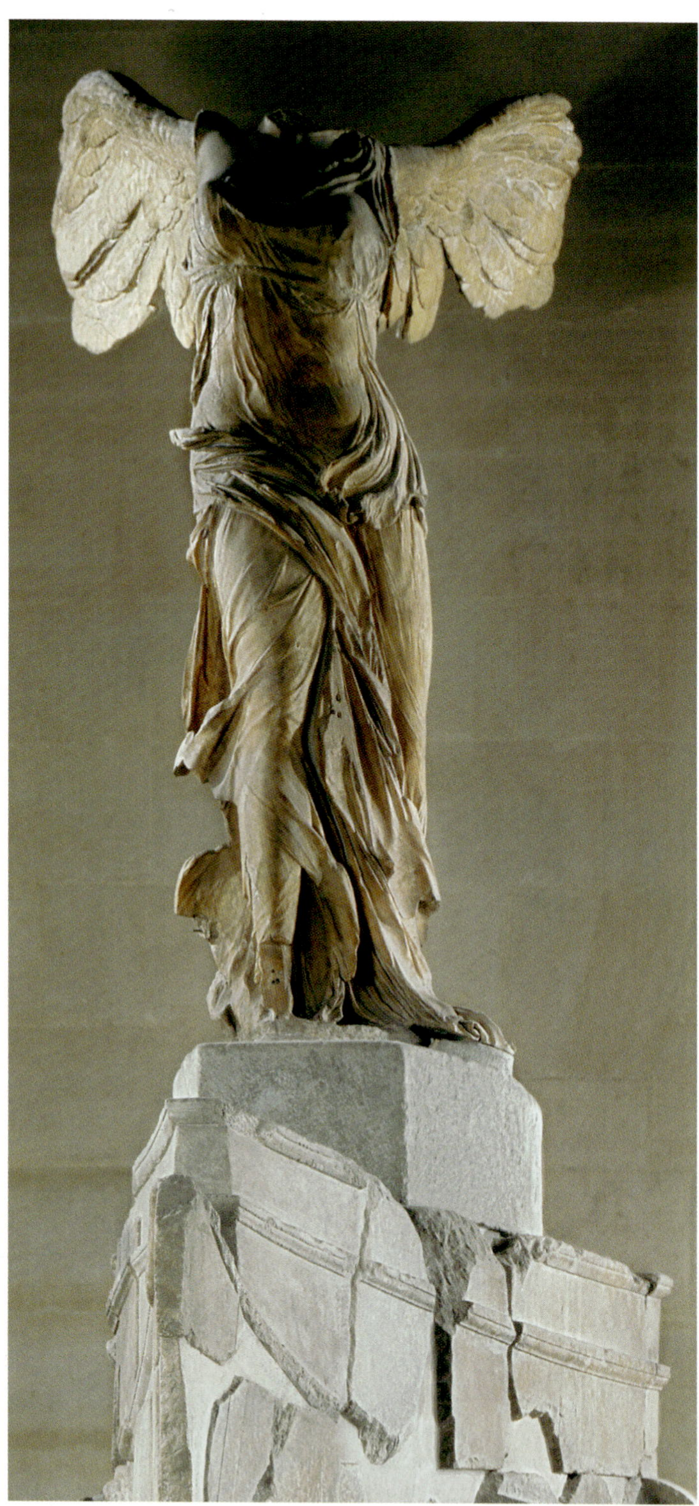

5–43 ***Nike (Victory) of Samothrace***, from the Sanctuary of the Great Gods, Samothrace. c. 180 BCE (?). Marble, height 8' 1" (2.45 m). Musée du Louvre, Paris

The wind-whipped garment and raised wings of this Victory indicate that she has just alighted on the prow of the stone ship that formed the original base of the statue. The work probably commemorated an important naval victory, perhaps the Rhodian triumph over the Seleucid king Antiochus III in 190 BCE. The Nike (lacking its head and arms) and a fragment of its stone ship base were discovered in the ruins of the Sanctuary of the Great Gods by a French explorer in 1863 (additional fragments were discovered later). Soon after, the sculpture entered the collection of the Louvre.

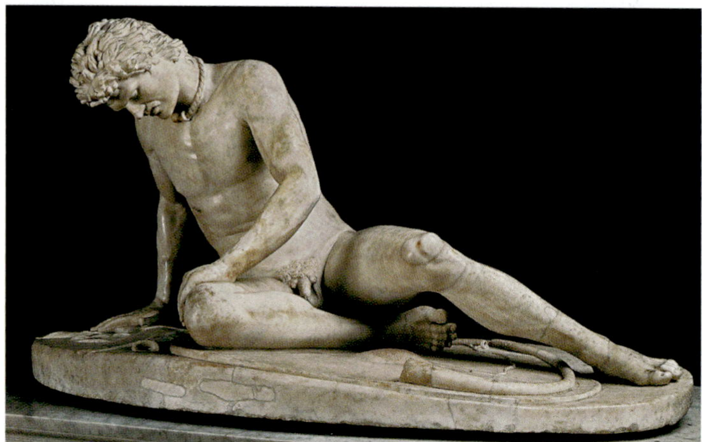

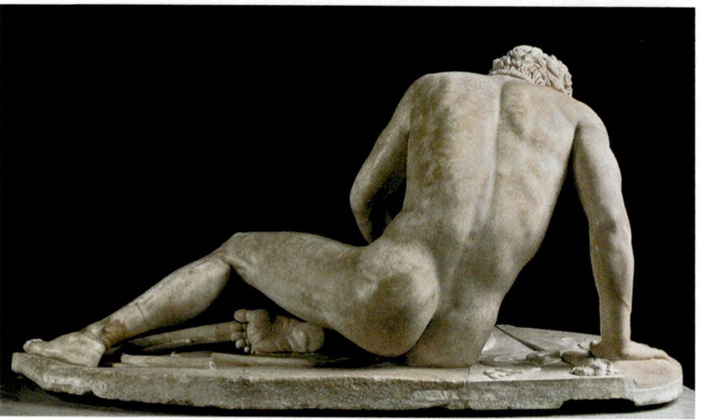

5–44 Epigonos (?). ***Dying Gallic Trumpeter***, Roman copy after the original bronze of c. 220 BCE. Marble, life-size, height 36½" (93 cm). Museo Capitolino, Rome

THE CELTS

During the first millennium BCE, Celtic peoples inhabited most of central and western Europe. The Celtic Gauls portrayed in the Hellenistic Pergamene victory monument (fig. 5–44) moved into Asia Minor from Thrace during the third century BCE. The ancient Greeks referred to these neighbors as barbarians, as they did to all outsiders. Pushed out by migrating people, attacked and defeated by challenged kingdoms like that at Pergamon, and then finally by the Roman armies of Julius Caesar, the Celts ultimately were driven into the northwesternmost parts of the continent: Ireland, Cornwall, and Brittany. Their wooden sculpture and dwellings and their colorful woven textiles have disintegrated, but spectacular funerary goods such as jewelry, weapons, and tableware have survived.

This golden torc (fig. **5–45**), dating sometime between the third and first centuries BCE, was excavated in 1866 from a Celtic tomb in northern France, but it is strikingly similar to the neck ring worn by the noble dying trumpeter illustrated in fig. 5–44. Torcs were worn by noblemen and were sometimes awarded to warriors for heroic performance in combat. Like all Celtic jewelry, the decorative design of this work consists not of natural forms but of completely abstract ornament, in this case created by the careful twisting and wrapping of strands of pure gold, resolved securely by the definitive bulges of two knobs. In Celtic hands, pattern becomes an integral part of the object itself, not an applied decoration. In stark contrast to the culture of the ancient Greeks, where the human figure was at the heart of all artistic development, here it is abstract, nonrepresentational form and its continual refinement that is the central artistic preoccupation.

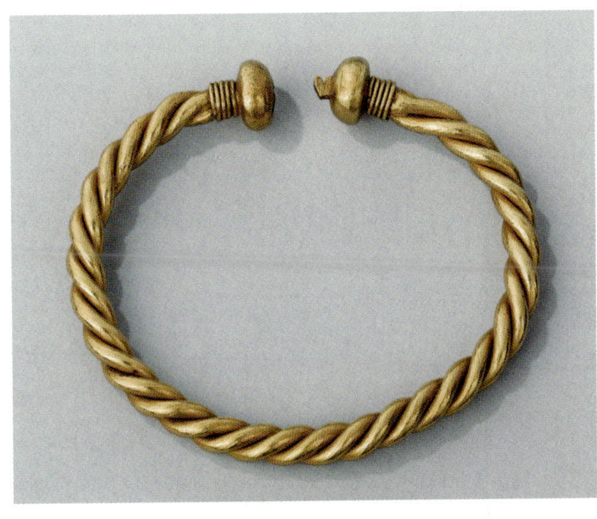

5–45 Torc, found at Soucy, France. Celtic Gaul, 3rd–1st century BCE. Gold. Musée Nationale du Moyen-Age, Paris

Roman marble copies, were mounted on a large pedestal. One of them, with the name Epigonos inscribed on the base, shows the agonizing death of a wounded Celtic soldier-trumpeter. His wiry, lime-spiked hair, his mustache, and his neck ring, or **torc** (reputedly the only item of dress the Gauls wore in battle), identify him as a "barbarian." But the sculpture also depicts his dignity and heroism in defeat, inspiring in viewers both admiration and pity for this fallen warrior. There is a sense of arrested motion as the trumpeter supports himself on his right arm, struggling to remain upright. This kind of deliberate attempt to elicit a specific emotional response in the viewer, a form of "expressionism," became another characteristic of Hellenistic art.

The style and approach seen in the monument to the defeated Gauls culminated in the celebrated frieze of the Pergamon Altar enclosure. Wrapped around the base of a huge Ionic colonnade that enclosed an altar to Zeus on a mountainside at Pergamon (fig. **5–46**), this frieze was probably executed during the reign of Eumenes II (ruled 197–159 BCE). It depicts the battle between the gods and the giants, a mythical struggle used by the Greeks as a metaphor for contemporary conflicts between themselves and people they considered barbaric enemies. In this case the subject invokes Pergamon's victory over the Celtic barbarian Gauls.

The panels are each about 7½ feet tall, and show Greek gods fighting human-looking giants and grotesque hybrids emerging from the bowels of the earth. In one section of the frieze, the goddess Athena has forced a winged monster to his knees (fig. **5–47**). Inscriptions along the base of the sculpture identify the monster as Alkyoneos, a son of the earth goddess, Ge, who rises in maternal wrath from the ground on the right. At the far right, a winged Victory foretells the outcome of this struggle, as she reaches to crown the victorious Athena.

The Pergamon frieze is carved in high relief with deep undercutting that creates dramatic contrasts of light and shade that play over the complex forms. Compositionally, the Pergamene sculptors sought to balance opposing forces in three-dimensional space along diagonal lines, whereas Classical Greek artists of the fifth century BCE sought equilibrium and control on a grid of horizontals and verticals (compare figs. 5–28 and 5–29). Some figures in the Pergamon frieze even extend beyond the architectural setting onto the steps, where visitors had to pass them on their way up to the shrine (see fig. 5–46, sculptural figures at far left). Many consider this theatrical interaction of deep space and complex form to be another hallmark of the Hellenistic style, just as they consider the controlled restraint of the Parthenon sculpture characteristic of the

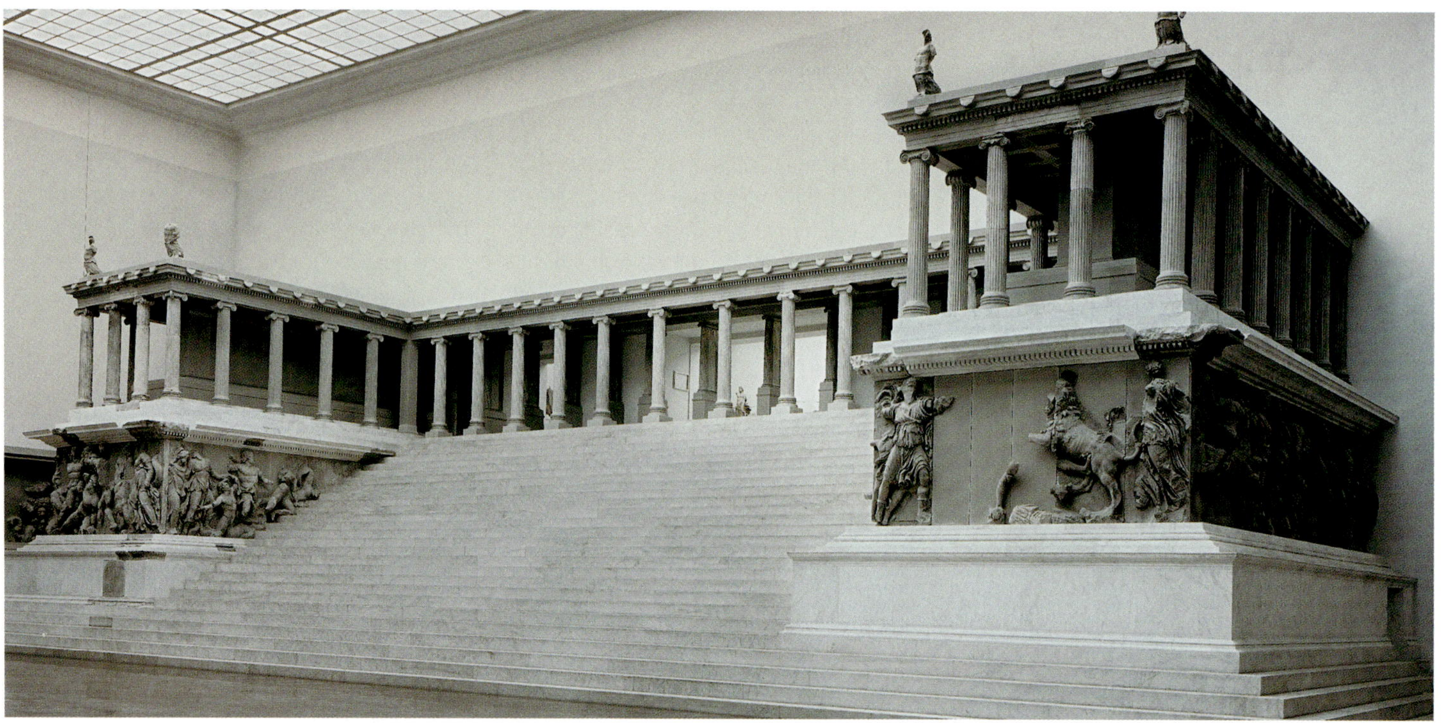

5–46 Reconstructed west front of the altar from Pergamon, Turkey. c. 175–150 BCE. Marble. Staatliche Museen zu Berlin, Preussischer Kulturbesitz, Antikensammlung

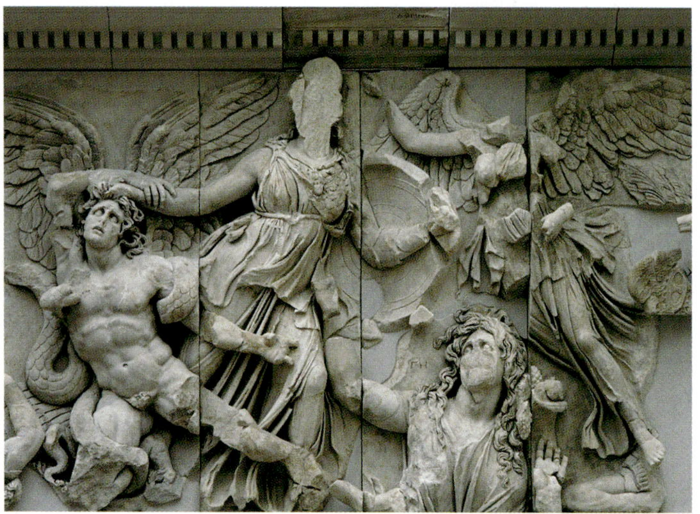

5–47 *Athena Attacking the Giants*, detail of the frieze from the east front of the altar from Pergamon. Marble, frieze height 7' 6" (2.3 m). Staatliche Museen zu Berlin, Preussischer Kulturbesitz, Antikensammlung

"High" Classical style. Similarly, the detached composure admired in Classical art gives way in the Hellenistic period to expressions of powerful emotions, such as pain, stress, anger, fear, or despair. (See also the Hellenistic sculpture of *Laocoön and his Sons* in fig. Intro–27.) Whereas the Classical artist asked only for an intellectual commitment, the Hellenistic artist demanded that the viewer also empathize.

Looking Back

At one time High Classical Greek art and architecture of the fifth century BCE were considered the pinnacle of artistic achievement. Today we also admire and study the vibrant richness of earlier Aegean art, as well as the dramatic intensity of the later art of the Hellenistic world. From the work of Minoan painters as early as the seventeenth century BCE through the dramatic virtuosity of Hellenistic sculptors who worked on the public monuments of Pergamon almost a millennium and a half later, Greek artists studied their surroundings with intense interest, focusing on every detail from the acanthus leaf, to the sleek tension of developed musculature, to the folds of their own clothing. But they did more than represent what they saw. They tempered their depictions of the natural world to conform to a series of changing ideals of artistic perfection.

In this way, idealized artistic representations could express the profoundest ideas and values of Greek society at large, themes paralleled in the works and aspirations of contemporary philosophers, playwrights, and politicians. For instance, the outburst of intellectual and aesthetic energy in "High" Classical Greece is concurrent with the evolution of a new democratic form of government, especially in Athens. Certainly, this new ideal of individual freedom—even if it seems limited by modern standards—created an environment in which new ideas could blossom and flourish.

And we are not the first to esteem the splendid works of art that emerged from this long period of creativity and experimentation. We will find in the next chapter that the ancient Romans admired the artistic production of their Greek predecessors to such an extent that they emulated and copied it, making Greek art and architecture one of several foundations for the glories that were Rome.

IN PERSPECTIVE

3000 BCE

◀ **Aegean Bronze Age,** c. 3100–1100 BCE

◀ **Cycladic Culture,** c. 3000–1600 BCE

2000

◀ **Minoan Culture on Crete,** c. 1900–1375 BCE

◀ **Mycenaean Culture,** c. 1600–1100 BCE

1000

◀ **Geometric Period,** c. 900–700 BCE

◀ **Earliest surviving list of Olympic game winners,** c. 776 BCE

◀ **Archaic Period,** c. 600–480 BCE

500

◀ **Perikles,** c. 495–429 BCE

◀ **Early Classical Period,** c. 480–450 BCE

◀ **Athenian and Spartan alliance defeats the Persians,** 479 BCE

◀ **Socrates,** c. 470–399 BCE

◀ **High Classical Period,** c. 450–400 BCE

◀ **Plato,** c. 429–347 BCE

◀ **Conclusion of Peloponnesian War,** 404 BCE

◀ **Late Classical Period,** c. 400–323 BCE

◀ **Death of Alexander the Great,** 323 BCE

◀ **Hellenistic Period,** c. 323–31 BCE

0

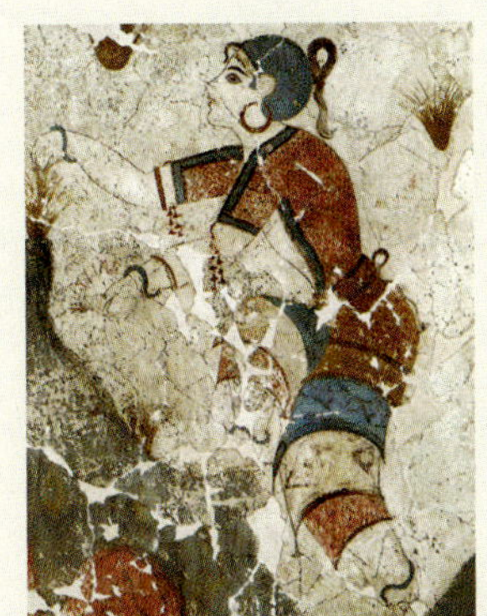

YOUNG GIRL GATHERING CROCUS, before 1630 BCE

KRITIOS BOY, c. 480 BCE

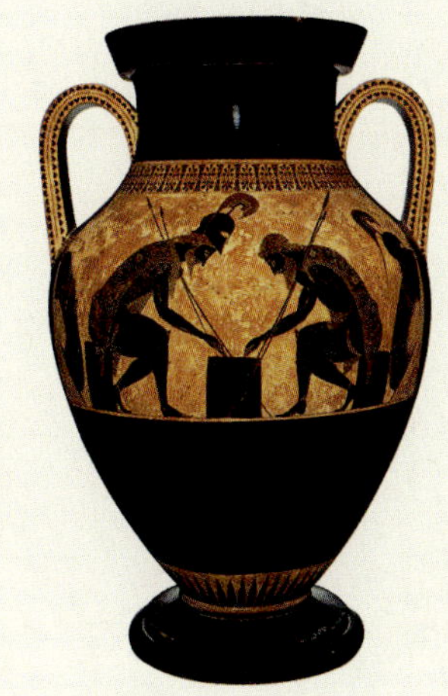

EXEKIAS, **AJAX AND ACHILLES,** c. 540–530 BCE

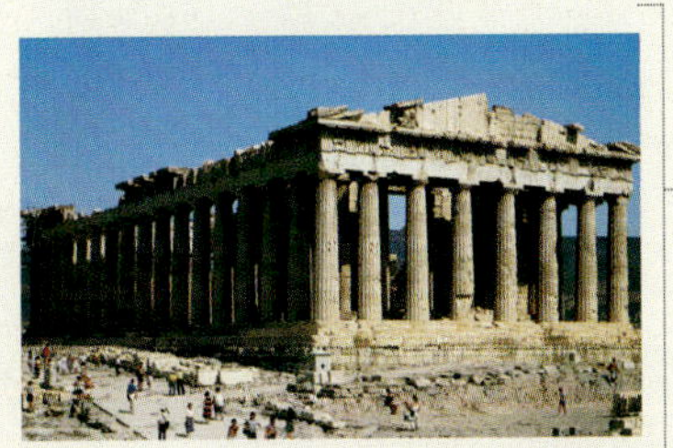

KALLIKRATES AND IKTINOS, **PARTHENON,** c. 447–432 BCE

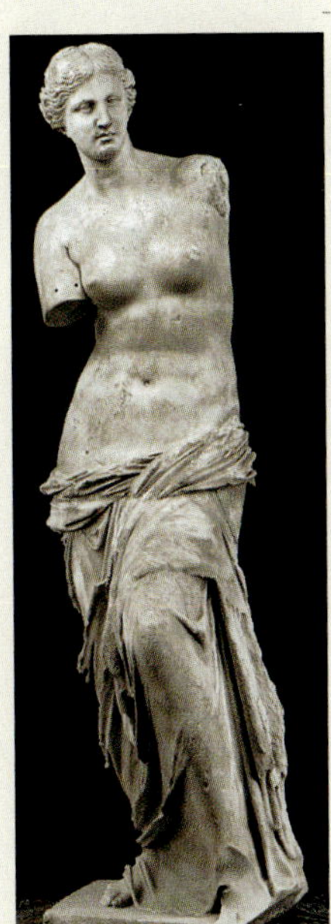

APHRODITE OF MELOS, c. 150–100 BCE

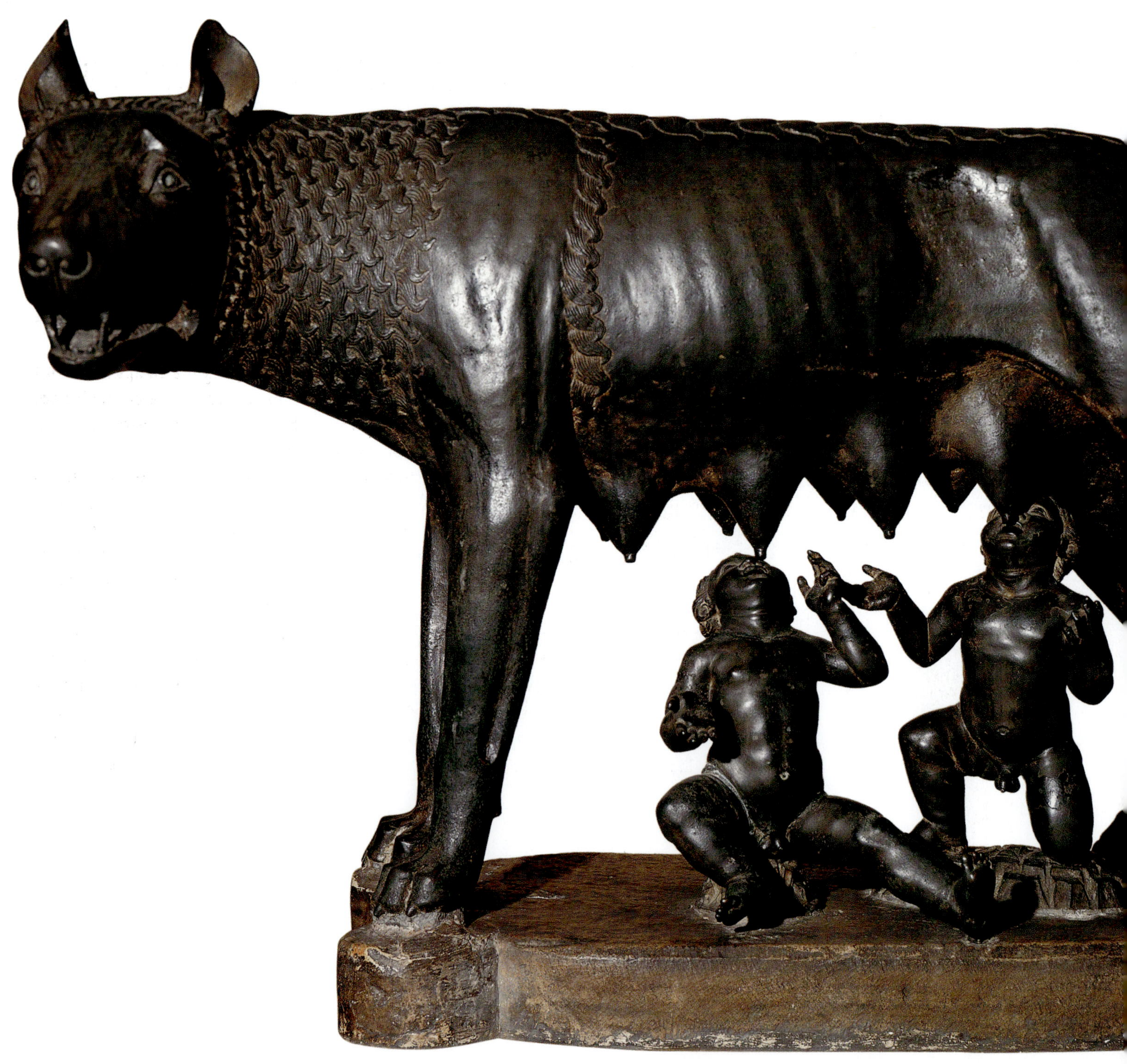

6 Etruscan and Roman Art

LOOKING FORWARD

The ferocious she-wolf turns toward us with a vicious snarl. Her tense body, thin flanks, and protruding ribs contrast with her heavy, milk-filled teats. She suckles two active, chubby little human boys. We are looking at the most famous symbol of Rome, the legendary wolf who nourished and saved the city's founder, Romulus, and his twin brother, Remus (fig. **6–1**). According to Roman legend, the twin sons, fathered by the god Mars and born of a mortal woman, were left to die on the banks of the Tiber River by their wicked great-uncle. A she-wolf discovered the infants and nursed them in place of her own pups. When they reached adulthood in the year 753 BCE, the twins decided to build a city near the spot where the wolf had rescued them.

This composite sculptural group of wolf and boys suggests the complexity of art history on the Italian peninsula. An early people called Etruscans created the bronze wolf in the fifth century BCE. Two millennia later, in the late fifteenth or early sixteenth century CE, a Renaissance sculptor added the two children.

We know that a statue of a wolf stood on the Capitoline Hill, the governmental and religious center of ancient Rome. But whether this Etruscan wolf is the sculpture that ancient Romans saw is far from certain. According to tradition, the original bronze wolf was struck by lightning and the damaged figure was buried. The documented history of this statue only begins in the tenth century CE, when it was discovered and placed outside the Lateran Palace of the popes. At that time, statues of two small men stood under the wolf, personifying the alliance between the Romans and their former enemies from central Italy, the Sabines. In the later Middle Ages, people mistook the figures for children and identified the sculpture with the founding of Rome. Tradition holds that the Florentine Renaissance sculptor Antonio del Pollaiuolo added the twins we see here. Pope Sixtus IV (papacy 1471–1484) had the sculpture moved from his palace to the Capitoline Hill, where, showcased in a museum, the wolf maintains her wary pose to this day.

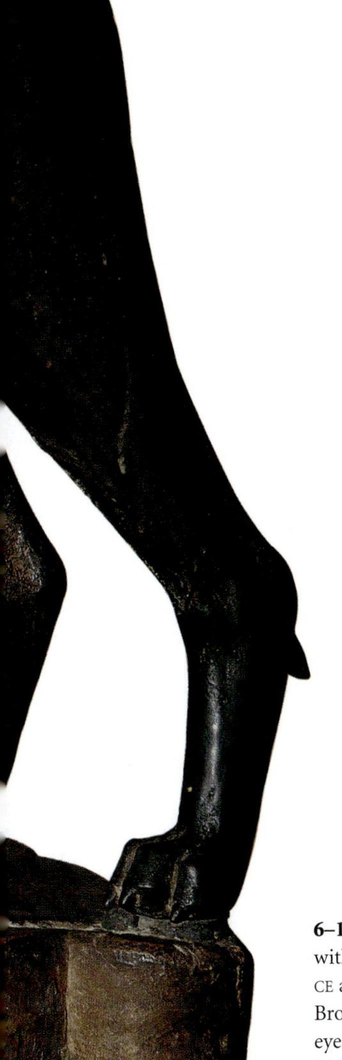

6–1 ***She-Wolf.*** c. 500 BCE with 15th–16th-century CE additions (the twins). Bronze with glass paste eyes, height 33½" (85 cm). Museo Capitolino, Rome

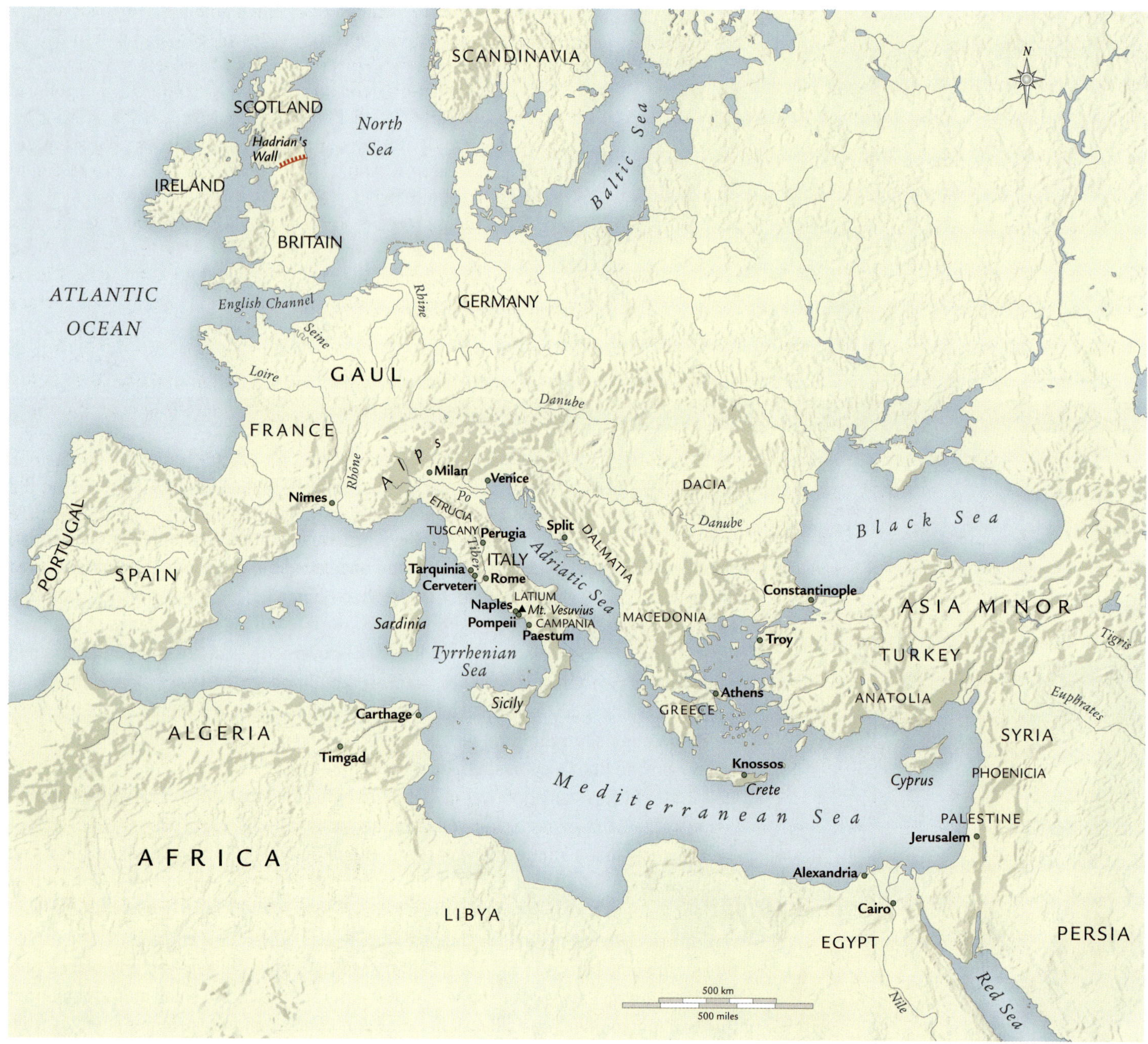

Map 6–1 The Ancient Roman World

The Etruscans

The ancient inhabitants of the boot-shaped Italian peninsula (see map **6–1**) were exposed through maritime trading and exploration to the rich cultural interplay among Near Eastern, Egyptian, and Greek civilizations. Etruscan society emerged in the seventh century BCE in Etruria (modern Tuscany), perhaps descending from a people called the Villanovans, who had occupied the northern and western regions of Italy since the Bronze Age. The Etruscans reached the height of their power in the sixth century BCE, when they formed a loose federation of a dozen cities. The fertile soil of Etruria and its rich lodes of metal ore formed the basis of their wealth.

Etruscan artists excelled at making monumental sculpture not out of stone, but with terracotta, a task requiring great technical and physical skill. Artists had to construct the pieces so that they would not collapse under their own weight while the raw clay was still heavy with moisture. In addition, they had to regulate the kiln temperature during the long firing process. The life-size figure of the god Apollo (fig. **6–2**) was made about 500 BCE. Its well-developed body and "Archaic smile" demonstrate that Etruscan sculptors knew the work of their Archaic Greek counterparts (see figs. 5–16 and 5–17). But while the Greeks represented men nude, the Etruscans did not. Here Apollo is partly concealed by a rippling robe, and his dynamic striding pose has a vigor that contrasts with the rigid

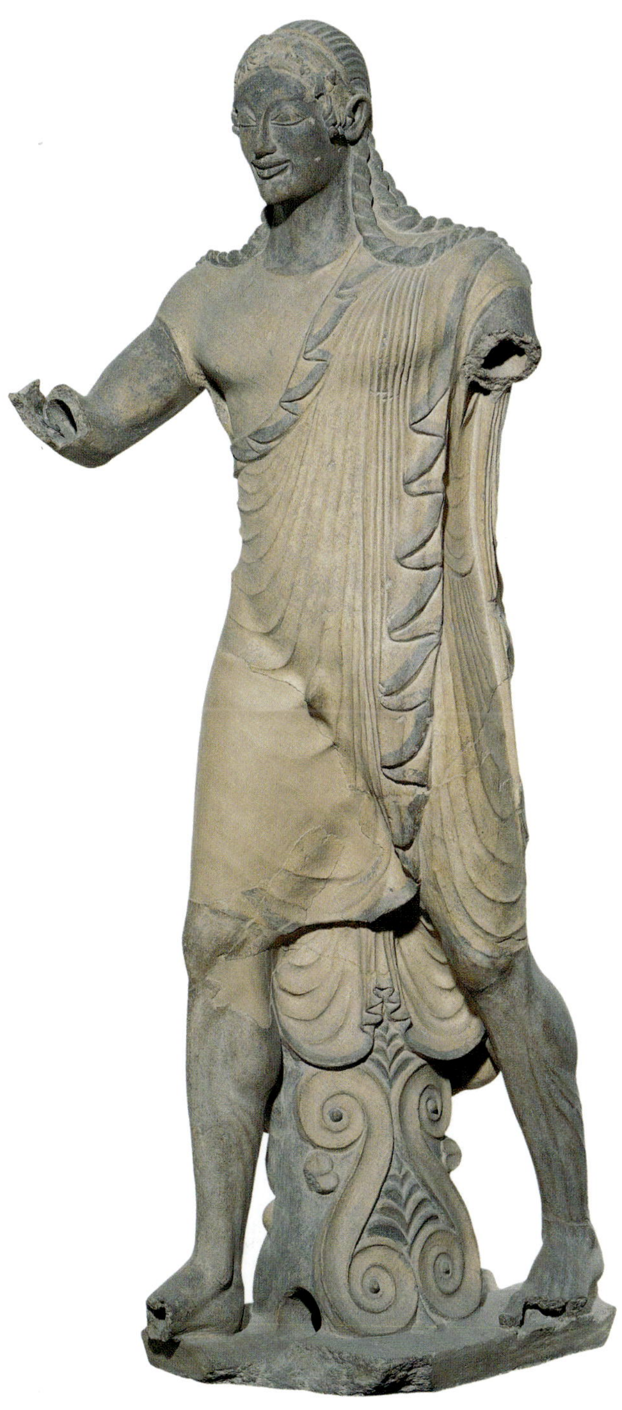

6–2 ***Apollo***, from the Temple of Minerva, Portenaccio, Veii. Master sculptor Vulca (?), c. 510–500 BCE. Painted terra cotta, height 5' 10" (1.8 m). Museo Nazionale di Villa Giulia, Rome

stance of Archaic Greek *kouroi*. This figure was originally placed along the roof ridge of an Etruscan temple at Veii as part of a four-figure narrative scene depicting a labor of Herakles that involved his fight with Apollo for possession of a deer sacred to Artemis, goddess of the moon and hunting. The dynamic Apollo looks as if he is stepping over the decorative scroll that helped support the sculpture when it was atop a temple. This sense of purposeful movement characterizes both Etruscan sculpture and painting.

According to the first-century BCE Roman architect and theorist Vitruvius, in certain ways Etruscan temples resembled Greek temples. For example, Etruscan builders also used post-and-lintel structure and gable roofs. The bases, column shafts, and capitals recall those of either the Greek Doric or Ionic order, and the entablature might have a frieze. Vitruvius used the term "Tuscan Order" to describe the characteristic variation of an unfluted shaft with a simplified base, capital, and entablature (see "Roman Architectural Orders," page 155). But although the Etruscans also built their temples on a high base, they had but a single flight of stairs leading to a columned porch on one short side of the rectangular temple, not the uniformly stepped stereobate and continuous peristyle colonnade that surrounded Greek temples (see "The Greek Temple," page 112). The deep porch led in turn to a cella, which was divided into three parallel rooms (fig. **6–3**).

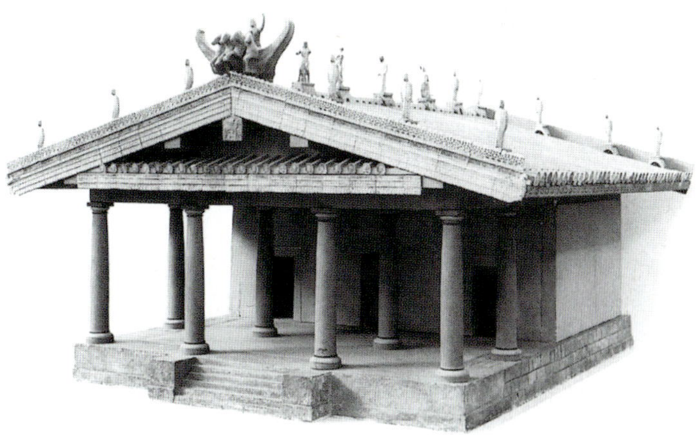

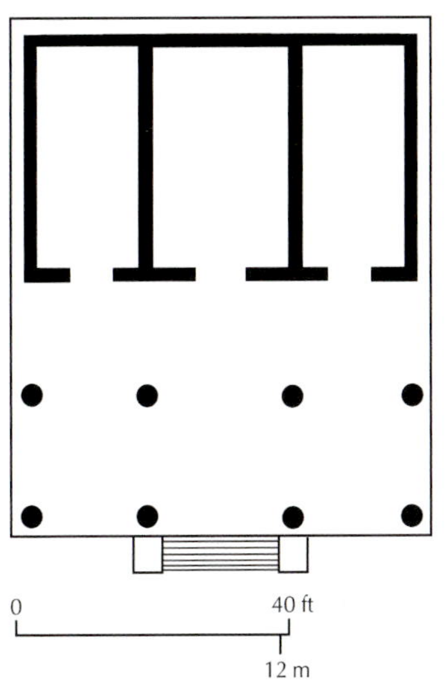

6–3 Reconstruction and plan of an Etruscan temple based on descriptions by Vitruvius. (Reconstruction: University of Rome, Istituto di Etruscologia e Antichità Italiche)

Although Etruscan temples were simple in form, they were embellished with dazzling displays of painting and terracotta sculpture. The temple roof, rather than the pediment, served as a base for large statue groups.

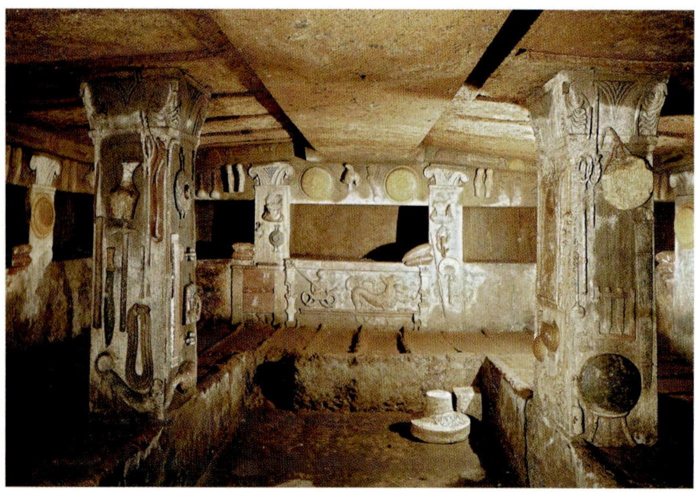

6–4 Burial chamber, Tomb of the Reliefs, Cerveteri. 3rd century BCE

The typical Etruscan home was a rectangular mud-brick structure built either around a central courtyard or around an **atrium**, a room with a shallow indoor pool for drinking, cooking, and bathing, fed by rainwater through a large opening in the roof. The burial chamber of the Tomb of the Reliefs at Cerveteri (near Rome) was carved to imitate such a house in the third century BCE (fig. **6–4**). The tomb's walls were plastered and painted, and the tomb was provided with a full selection of furnishings, some carved, others simulated in **stucco**, a slow-drying type of plaster that can easily be modeled or molded. Simulated pots, jugs, robes, axes, and other household items look like real objects hanging on hooks, and rendered in low relief at the bottom of the pillar left of center is the family dog.

Some tombs were painted, not carved. In the Tomb of the Triclinium at Tarquinia, dating from about 480–470 BCE, friezes of figural scenes surround a room whose ceiling is enlivened with colorful geometric decoration (fig. **6–5**). Energetic dancers—alternating between lighter-skinned women and their swarthy male partners, conforming to a coloristic convention for gender differentiation already familiar from the ancient art of Egypt and Greece—line the side walls, and at the end of the room couples recline on couches enjoying a banquet while cats prowl under the table looking for scraps. The immediacy of this wall painting is striking. Both dancers and diners are engaging in the joyful customs and diversions of human life as we know it, not enacting the formal rituals of a remote, long-dead civilization.

Etruscan **sarcophagi** (large carved tomb chests) also reflected domestic life. Rather than a cold, somber memorial to the dead, sculpted terracotta figures of a husband and wife recline comfortably on the lid of a sarcophagus made to look like a couch (fig. **6–6**). Two happy individuals, with almond-shaped eyes and benign smiles, seem to greet the viewer with lively gestures—the man once raised a drinking vessel. They might almost be attending a banquet or enjoying a performance of music or dance, the same convivial festivities recorded in paintings on Etruscan tomb walls.

Etruscan art and architectural forms left an indelible stamp on the art and architecture of early Rome, second only to the influence of Greece. By 88 BCE, when the Etruscans had been granted Roman citizenship, their art had already been absorbed into the developing Roman culture that would soon dominate the entire Mediterranean region and even beyond.

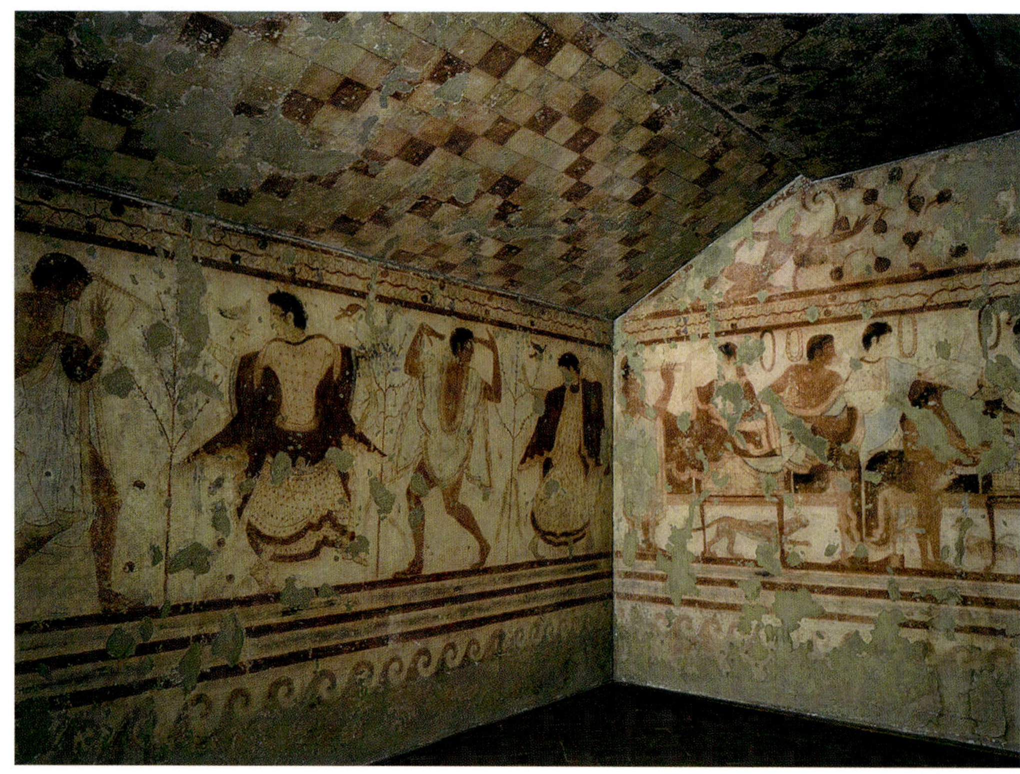

6–5 ***Dancers and Diners*** from a burial chamber, Tomb of the Triclinium, Tarquinia. c. 480–470 BCE

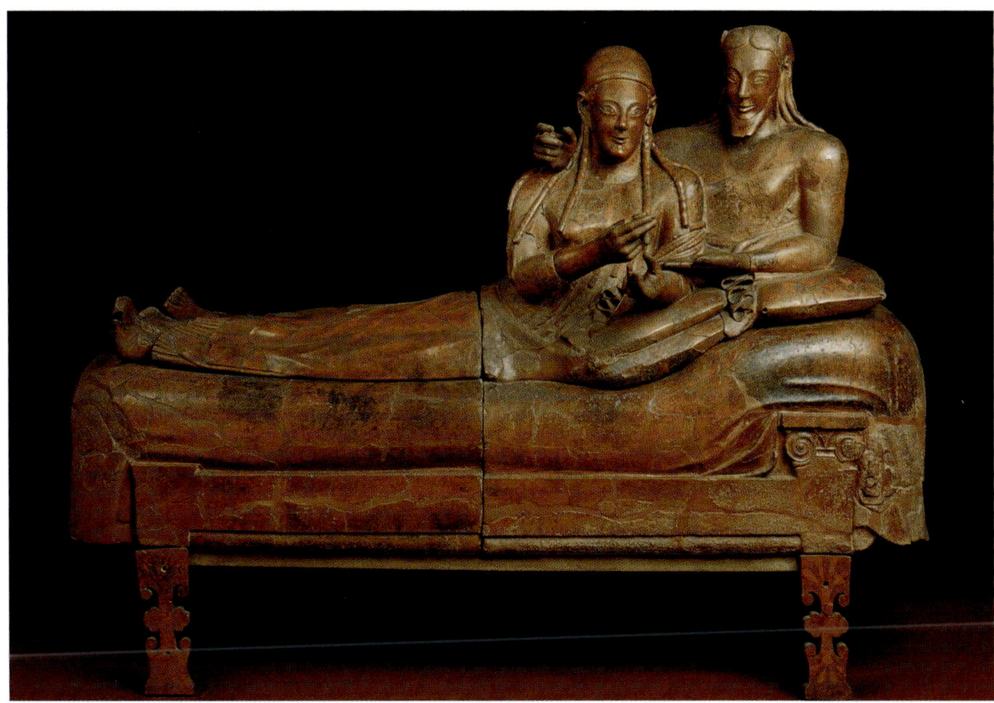

6–6 Sarcophagus, from Cerveteri. c. 520 BCE. Terracotta, length 6' 7" (2.06 m). Museo Nazionale di Villa Giulia, Rome

The Romans

At the same time that Etruscan civilization was flourishing in Etruria and Greek culture dominated the southern part of the peninsula in the colony around Paestum (see fig. 5–15), the Latin-speaking inhabitants of Rome began to develop into a formidable power. By the end of the third century BCE, the Etruscans themselves were absorbed into the Roman Republic, which was at that time expanding in many directions. At the height of their power—in the early second century CE—Romans would rule all the lands around the Mediterranean Sea, which they proudly referred to as *mare nostrum*, "our sea." Their empire stretched east to the Euphrates, south to Egypt, and northwest as far as Scotland.

To spur growth and to simplify administration of this vast empire, the Roman government undertook building programs of unprecedented scale and complexity, constructing central administrative and commercial centers (**forums** with basilicas), racetracks, theaters, public baths and water systems, apartment buildings, and even entire new cities. To speed communication and to facilitate commerce and the movement of troops, the Romans built a vast network of roads between their capital and the empire's farthest reaches. In fact, many modern European highways still follow the routes laid down by ancient Roman engineers, and Roman-era foundations underlie the streets of many European cities.

Culturally, the Romans borrowed heavily from Greece and the larger Hellenistic world. They incorporated Greek orders into their architecture, imported Greek art, and employed Greek artists. Like the Etruscans, they also adopted the Greek gods and heroes as their own, giving them Latin names (see "Roman Counterparts of Greek Gods," right). In Western Europe, the sophisticated legal, administrative, and cultural systems that the Romans imposed on the people they conquered endured for some 500 years. And in the eastern

Roman Counterparts of Greek Gods

ROMAN NAME	GREEK NAME
Jupiter	Zeus
Juno	Hera
Minerva	Athena
Mars	Ares
Apollo	Apollo
Venus	Aphrodite
Diana	Artemis
Mercury	Hermes
Pluto	Hades
Bacchus	Dionysos
Vulcan	Hephaistos
Vesta	Hestia
Ceres	Demeter
Neptune	Poseidon
Cupid (*or* Amor)	Eros
Hercules	Herakles (a demigod)

Distinctively Roman Gods

Fortuna—goddess of fate (Fortune)

Priapus—god of fertility

Janus—god of beginnings and endings (his two faces look forward and back)

Terminus—god of boundaries

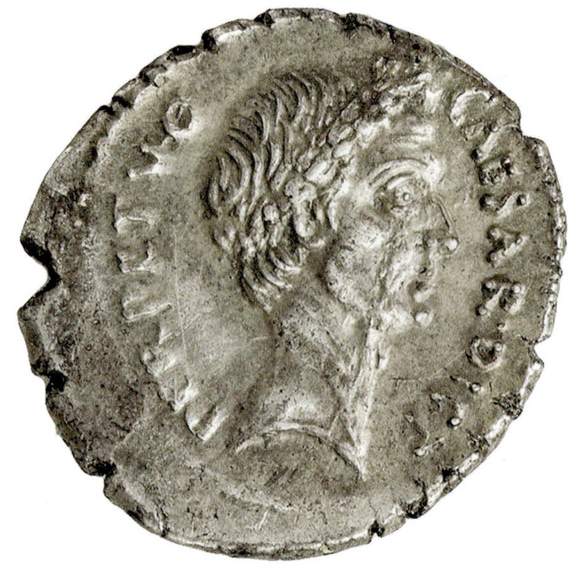

6–7 *Denarius* with portrait of Julius Caesar. 44 BCE. Silver, diameter approximately ¾" (1.9 cm). American Numismatic Society, New York

Mediterranean, the Classical traditions and styles of ancient Rome survived into the fifteenth century as Byzantine art.

The Republican Period

Early Rome was governed by a series of kings and an advisory body called the Senate, made up of upper-class citizens. The last kings of Rome were overthrown in 509 BCE, marking the beginning of what is known as the period of the Republic (509–27 BCE). Rome's conquest of lands outside the Italian peninsula strained its political system, weakening the authority of the Senate and leading to a series of civil wars among powerful generals. In 49 BCE Julius Caesar invaded Italy from his post in France, and in 46 BCE the general, who had ruled Rome with Pompey and Crassus in the First Triumvirate, emerged victorious over his rivals. He held power as dictator until his assassination in 44 BCE.

Artists of the Republican period sought to create lifelike images that convey the strong sense that they were based on careful observation. Viewing a portrait of Julius Caesar on a coin of 44 BCE (fig. **6–7**), we believe we know what he actually looked like. The tiny relief sculpture presents an elder ruler's careworn features and alert expression. This new idea of placing a living ruler's portrait on one side of a coin, and on the other a symbol of the country or an image that recalls some important action or event, was adopted by Caesar's successors, allowing us to follow the progression of Roman history through imperial portraits, values, and accomplishments.

The convention of emphasizing the effects of aging in portraits that appear to be accurate and faithful descriptions of actual individuals may have derived from the practice of making death masks of deceased relatives. During the Republican period, patrons clearly admired such seemingly realistic portraits and often turned to skilled Etruscan artists to execute them. The life-size bronze portrait of *Aulus Metellus* (fig. **6–8**)—the Roman official's name is inscribed on the hem of his garment in Etruscan letters—depicts the man addressing a gathering, his arm outstretched and slightly raised, a pose expressive of rhetorical persuasiveness. The orator wears the folded and draped garment called a toga, which would become the characteristic costume of Roman officials. According to Pliny the Elder, large statues like this were often placed atop columns as memorials to the individuals portrayed.

Art and architecture during the Republic initially reflected both Etruscan and Greek influences. In religious architecture, the Romans favored urban temples set, in the Etruscan manner, in the midst of congested commercial centers, rather than isolated temples in sacred precincts as preferred by the ancient Greeks. An early example is a small, rectangular temple built in the late second century BCE beside the Tiber River in Rome, perhaps dedicated to

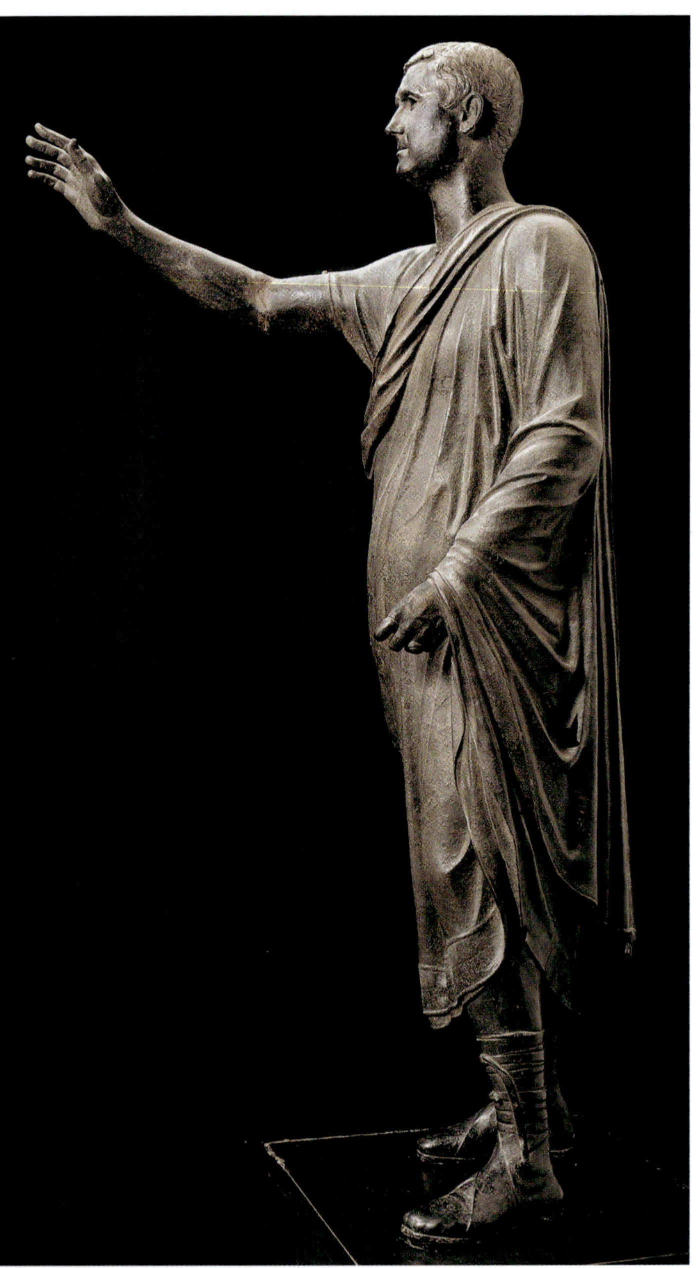

6–8 *Aulus Metellus*, found near Perugia. Late 2nd or early 1st century BCE. Bronze, height 5' 11" (1.8 m). Museo Archeològico Nazionale, Florence

CLOSER LOOK

The strong emphasis on portraiture in Roman art may stem from the early practice of creating likenesses—in some cases actual wax death masks—of revered figures and distinguished ancestors for display on public occasions, most notably funerals. Contemporary historians have left colorful evocations of this distinctively Roman custom. Polybius, a Greek exiled to Rome in the middle of the second century BCE, wrote home with the following description:

> ...after the interment [of the illustrious man] and the performance of the usual ceremonies, they place the image of the departed in the most conspicuous position in the house, enclosed in a wooden shrine. This image is a mask reproducing with remarkable fidelity both the features and the complexion of the deceased. On the occasion of public sacrifices, they display these images, and decorate them with much care, and when any distinguished member of the family dies they take them to the funeral, putting them on men who seem to bear the closest resemblance to the original in stature and carriage....There could not easily be a more ennobling spectacle for a young man who aspires to fame and virtue. For who would not be inspired by the sight of the images of men renowned for their excellence, all together and as if alive and breathing?....By this means, by the constant renewal of the good report of brave men, the celebrity of those who performed noble deeds is rendered immortal, while at the same time the fame of those who did good services to their country becomes known to the people and a heritage for future generations.
> (*Histories*, VI, pages 53–54)

Growing out of this heritage, Roman Republican portraiture is frequently associated with the notion of **verism**—an interest in the faithful reproduction of the immediate visual and tactile appearance of subjects. Since we find in these portrait busts the same sorts of individualizing physiognomic features that allow us to differentiate among the people we know in our own world, it is easy to assume that they are exact reproductions of their subjects as they appeared during their lifetime. Of course, this is impossible to verify, but our strong desire to believe it must realize the intentions of the artists who made these portraits and the patrons for whom they were made.

A life-size marble statue of a Roman patrician (fig. **6–9**), dating from the period of the emperor Augustus, embodies the practices documented much earlier by Polybius and links the man portrayed with a revered tradition and its laudatory associations. The large marble format emulates a Greek notion of sculpture, and its use here signals not only this man's wealth but also his sophisticated artistic tastes, characteristics he shared with the emperor himself. His toga, however, is not Greek but indigenous and signifies his respectability as a Roman citizen of some standing. The busts of ancestors that he holds in his hands document his distinguished lineage in the privileged upper class—there were laws regulating which members of society could own such collections—and the statue as a whole proclaims his adherence to the family tradition by having his own portrait created.

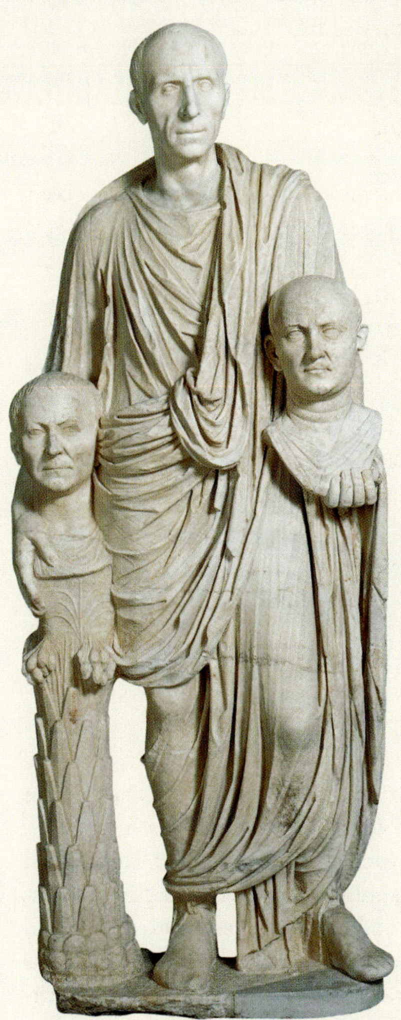

6–9 ***Patrician Carrying Two Portrait Busts of his Ancestors.*** End of 1st century BCE or beginning of 1st century CE. Marble, height 5' 5" (1.65 m). Palazzo de Conservatori, Rome

The head of this standing figure, though ancient Roman in origin, is a later replacement and not original to this statue. The separation of head and body in this work is understandable since in many instances the bodies of full-length portraits were produced in advance, waiting in the the sculptor's workshop for a patron to commission a head with his or her own likeness that could be attached to it. Presumably the busts carried by this patrician were likewise only blocked out until they could be carved with the faces of the commissioner's ancestors. These faces share a striking family resemblance, and the stylistic difference between the two bust formats reveals that these men lived in successive generations. They could be the father and grandfather of the man who carries them.

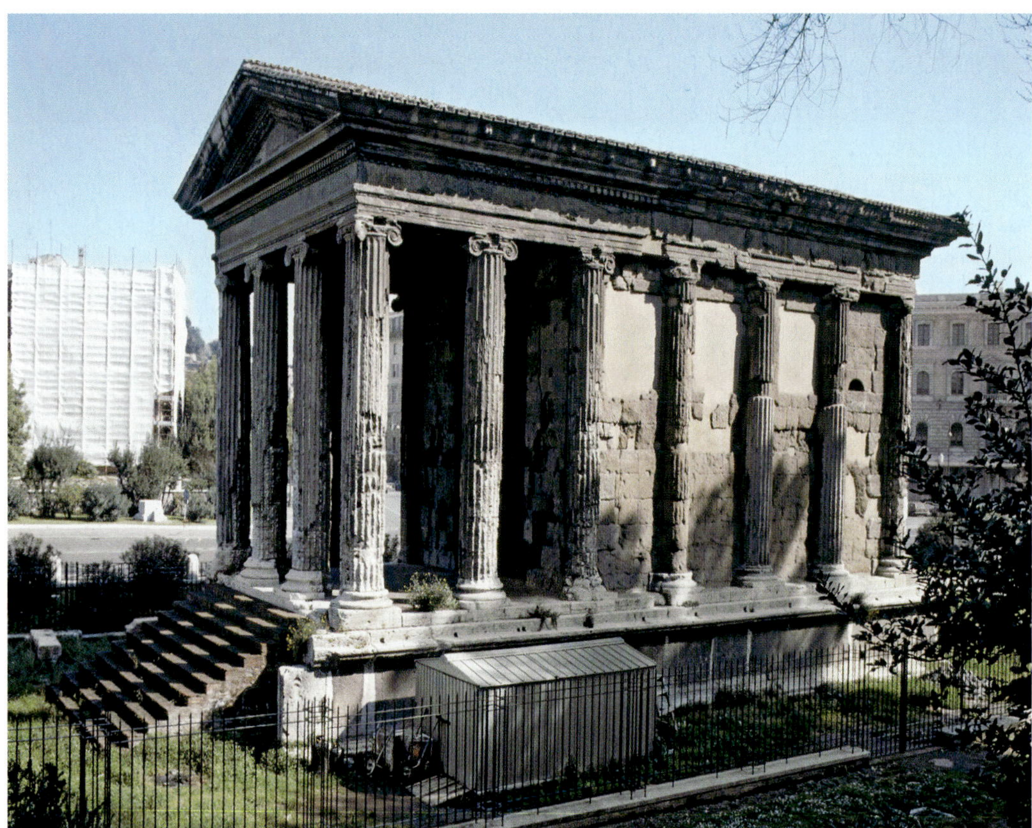

6–10 (LEFT AND BELOW) **Temple (perhaps dedicated to Portunus) and plan**, Forum Boarium (cattle market), Rome. Late 2nd century BCE

6–11 (OPPOSITE) **Pont du Gard, Nîmes,** France. Late 1st century BCE

The three arcades of the aqueduct rise 160 feet (49 m) above the river. They exemplify the simplest use of the arch as a structural element. The thick base arcade supports a roadbed approximately 20 feet wide. The arches of the second arcade are narrower than the first and are set at one side of the roadbed. The narrow third arcade supports the water channel, 900 feet long on 35 arches, each of which is 23 feet high.

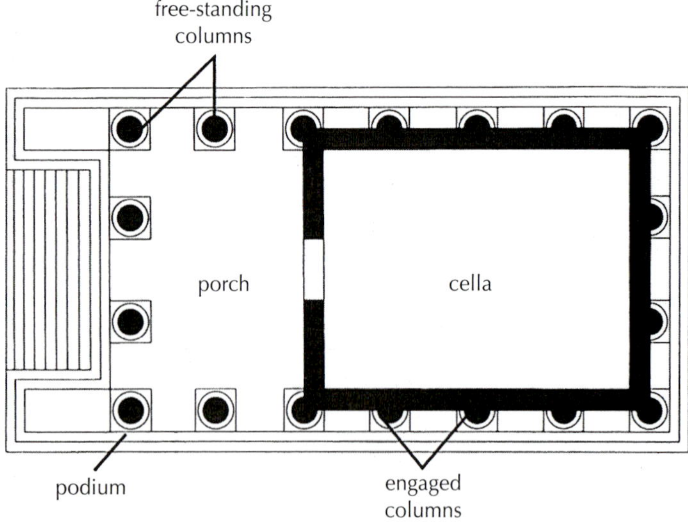

Portunus, the god of harbors and ports (fig. **6–10**). This typical Roman temple rests on a raised platform, or **podium**. It has a rectangular cella (interior room) and a colonnaded porch at one end that is approached by a broad, inviting staircase. The Romans adopted the Greek Ionic order here, but in contrast to Greek temples, only the columns on the porch are free-standing. Those around the cella are no longer structural but are employed here as **engaged** half-columns applied to articulate the wall. In another departure from the Greek temple tradition—which had encouraged viewers to walk around the buildings exploring their uniformly articulated sculptural mass—Roman temples are defined in relation to interior spaces, which viewers are invited to enter through one opening along the longitudinal axis of a symmetrical plan.

As city dwellers, Romans also devoted their ingenuity and resources to secular architecture. In fact, it was public building projects related to the transport and storage of food and water that made Roman cities viable. In many areas of Europe, especially around the Mediterranean, impressive examples of Roman engineering still stand. The Pont du Gard near Nîmes in southern France (fig. **6–11**) was designed to carry water over the Gard River. This **aqueduct**, as such structures with water conduits are called, was part of a system that used gravity to bring water to Nîmes from springs 30 miles to the north. At the time it was built, probably about 20 BCE, the aqueduct could provide 100 gallons of water a day for every person in Nîmes.

The Pont du Gard was constructed of precisely cut stones from a nearby quarry. It consists of a stack of three **arcades** (series of regularly spaced arched openings) formed by fitting together wedge-shaped pieces, called **voussoirs**, which are locked together at the top center by a final piece, called a **keystone** (see "Arch and Vault," page 145). A utilitarian structure, the aqueduct was left undecorated, and the projecting blocks that supported scaffolding during construction were left to provide easy access for repairs. Nevertheless, the Pont du Gard and other Roman aqueducts convey a sense of proportion and rhythm and seem to harmonize with their settings.

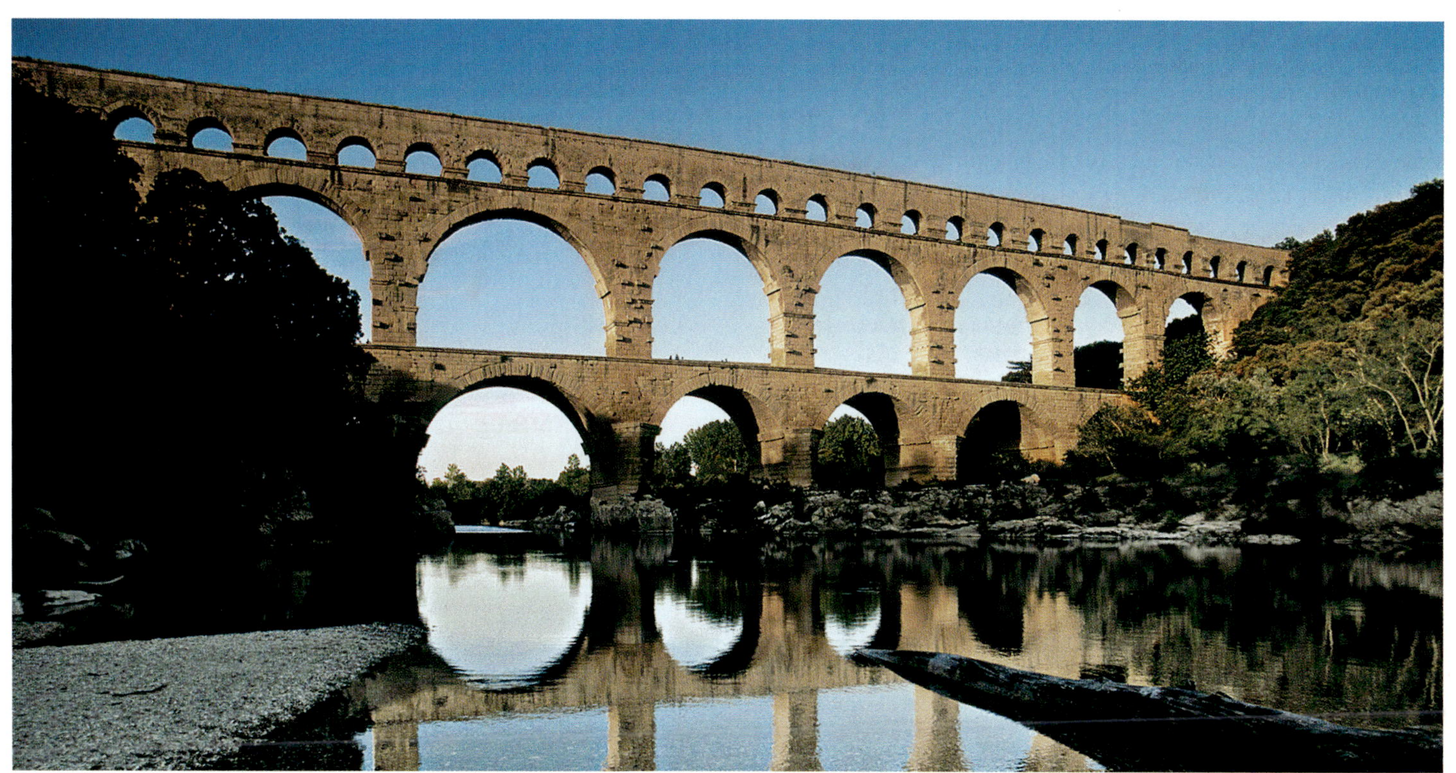

ELEMENTS OF Architecture

Arch and Vault

The round arch is a basic unit of Roman architecture. It is designed to displace most of the weight above it to its curving sides, and from there to the ground through supporting upright elements (**piers**, columns, or door or window jambs). Within a succession of arches, the unit made up of one arch and its supports is called a **bay**. Wall areas adjacent to curves of an arch are called **spandrels**. In the illustration at right, arrows indicate the outward thrust and downward gravity pull (weight) of the arch or vault.

A simple round arch can be lengthened to form a cylindrical **barrel vault**. In a barrel vault, however, the outward pressure exerted by its long curving sides usually requires added external support, called **buttressing**. When two barrel-vaulted spaces intersect each other at right angles, the result is a **groin vault**. The round arch and barrel vault were known and put to limited use by the ancient Mesopotamians, Egyptians, and Greeks. And they were employed more extensively by the Etruscans. But it was the Romans who realized the potential strength and versatility of these architectural elements and who exploited them to the fullest degree.

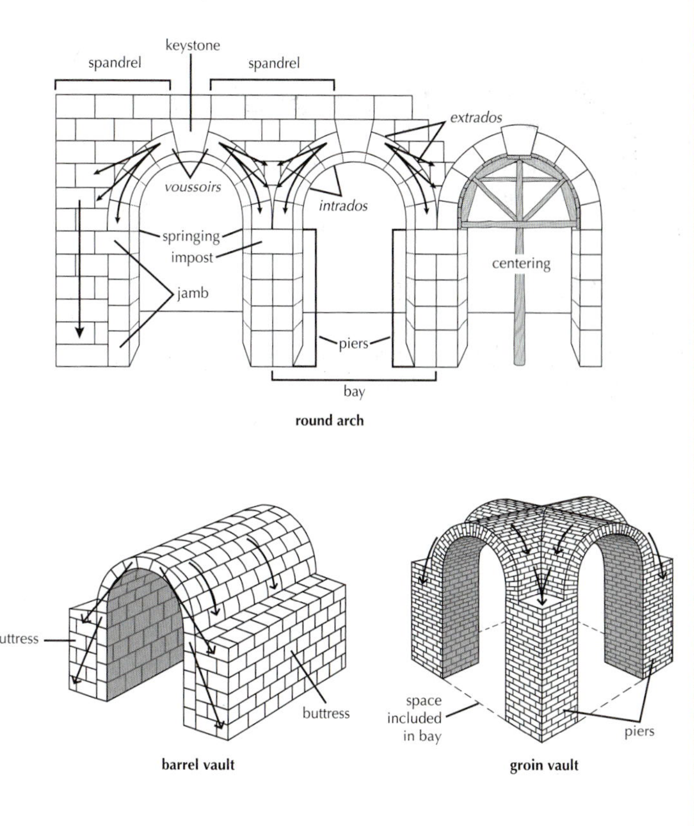

The Age of Augustus

After Julius Caesar's death and a period of renewed fighting, his great-nephew and adopted son, Octavian, assumed power. Although Octavian kept the forms of Republican government, he concentrated real authority in himself, and his ascension marks the end of the Republic. Under Augustus Caesar, as Octavian was titled by the Senate in 27 BCE, the Romans began to use imperial portraiture as political propaganda. An over-life-size statue of the emperor discovered in the villa of his wife Livia, the *Augustus of Primaporta* (fig. **6–12**), exemplifies the form. We see Augustus as he wanted to be seen and remembered. His image is inspired by heroic Greek figures such as the *Spear Bearer* (see fig. 5–33) and portrays him in the physical prime of his youth rather than the more advanced age memorialized in the coin portrait of Julius Caesar. At the same time the emperor's head is rendered with sufficient naturalistic detail to make him easily recognizable. Augustus wears a cuirass (body armor) that portrays defeated barbarians and scenes of his military victory, and he holds a commander's baton. His bare feet have led some scholars to propose that the work was made after his death to commemorate his **apotheosis**, or elevation to divine status.

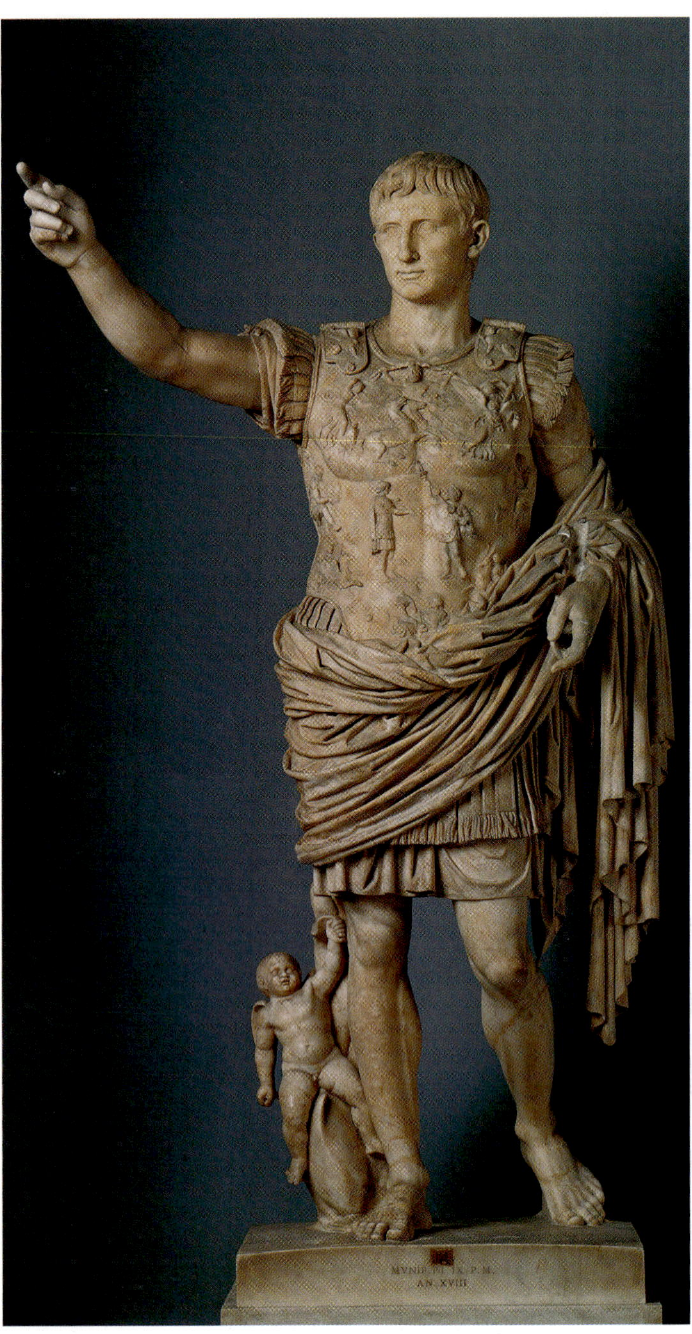

6–12 ***Augustus of Primaporta.*** Early 1st century CE (perhaps a copy of a bronze statue of c. 20 BCE). Marble, originally painted, height 6' 8" (2.03 m). Musei Vaticani, Braccio Nuovo, Rome

Roman sculptors were commissioned to create imperial propaganda by celebrating contemporary events on commemorative arches, columns, and tombs. Augustus' *Ara Pacis*, or Altar of Augustan Peace (fig. **6–13**), was as famous in its day as the *Vietnam Veterans Memorial* is in ours (see fig. 20–1). Begun in 13 BCE and dedicated in 9 BCE, the altar commemorates Augustus' triumphal return to Rome after establishing Roman rule in Gaul. The walled rectangular enclosure—the altar itself is inside and was approached by a flight of steep steps—was originally outdoors like Greek altars, not contained within a building as in more traditional Roman practice. The decoration is a thoughtful union of portraiture and allegory, religion and politics, public and private. Relief panels along the exterior of the north and south sides of the enclosure depict senators and members of the imperial family who would have attended the victory celebrations (fig. **6–14**).

Unlike the Greek sculptors who created an ideal Panathenaic procession for the Parthenon frieze (see fig. 5–29), the Roman sculptors of the *Ara Pacis* depicted actual individuals participating in a specific event at a known time. To suggest a double line of marchers in space, they varied the depth of the carving, with the closest elements in higher relief and those farther back in increasingly lower relief. The design draws us, as spectators, into the event by making the feet of the nearest figures project into our space.

The marriage of Augustus and Livia was childless, so the emperor's successor was Tiberius, one of Livia's two sons by her first marriage to Tiberius Claudius Nero. A large onyx **cameo** (a semiprecious stone or gemstone carved in low relief) known as *Gemma Augustea* evokes the apotheosis of Augustus after his death (fig. **6–15**). The emperor, crowned with a victor's wreath, sits at the center right of the upper register. He has assumed the identity of Jupiter, king of the gods; an eagle, sacred to Jupiter, stands at his feet. Sitting next to him is a personification of Rome that has Livia's features. The sea goat in the roundel between them may represent Capricorn, the emperor's zodiac sign. At the left, Tiberius holds a lance and steps out of a chariot. Returning victorious from the German front, he will assume the imperial throne as the adopted son and designated heir of Augustus. Below this realm of godly rulers is the earth, where Roman soldiers are raising a trophy (a post or standard on which armor captured from a defeated enemy is displayed). The cowering, chained barbarians at the bottom right wait to be tied to it. The *Gemma Augustea* brilliantly combines idealized, heroic figures of a kind characteristic of Classical Greek art with recognizable portraits, the dramatic action of Hellenistic art, and a purely Roman penchant for the portrayal of historical events.

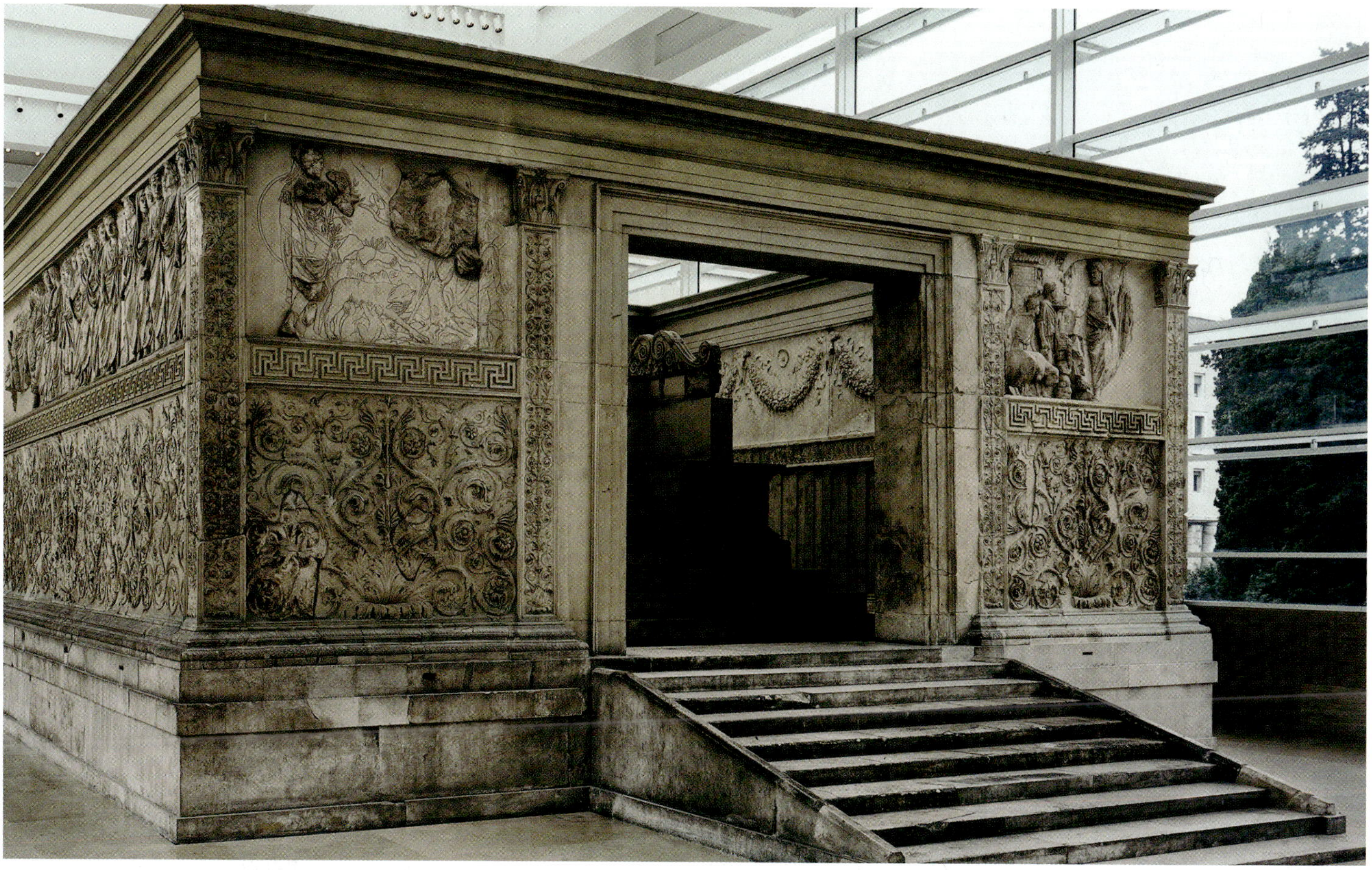

6–13 ***Ara Pacis***, Rome. 13–9 BCE. Marble, approx. 34' 5" × 38' (10.5 × 11.6 m). (The actual altar stands at the top of the stairs, visible through the door in the enclosure wall.)

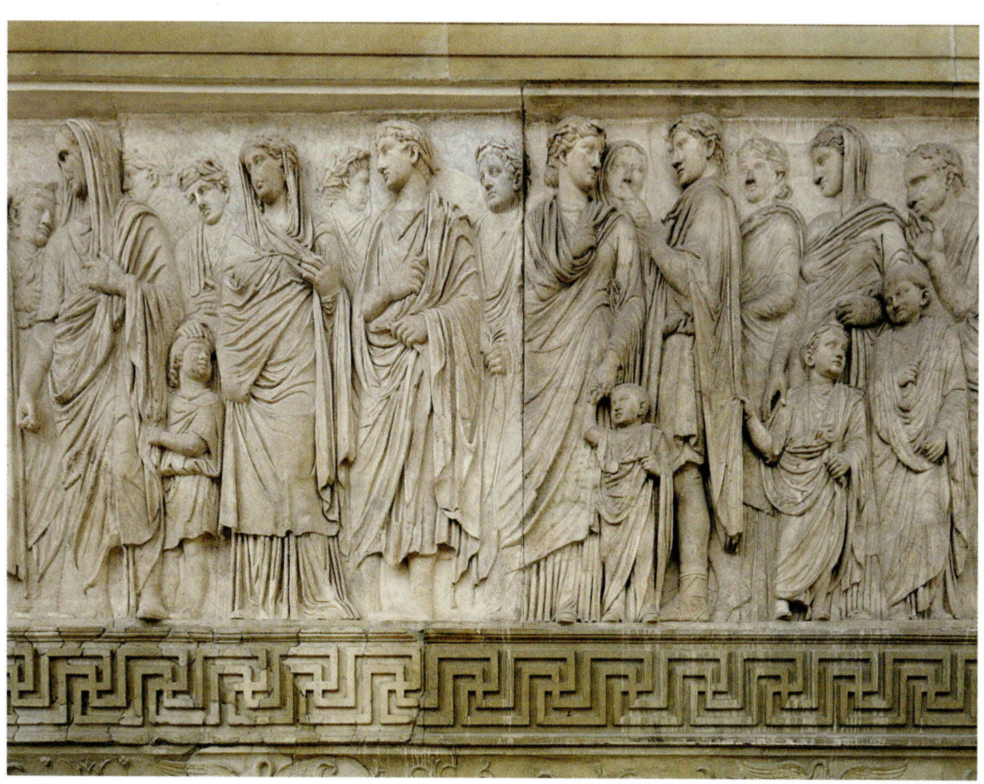

6–14 Imperial Procession, detail of a relief on the *Ara Pacis*. Height 5' 2" (1.6 m)

The middle-aged man with the shrouded head at the far left is Marcus Agrippa, who would have been Augustus' successor had he not died in 12 BCE. The bored but well-behaved youngster pulling at Agrippa's robe—and being restrained gently by the hand of the man behind him—is probably Agrippa's son, Gaius Caesar. The heavily swathed woman next to Agrippa on the right is probably Augustus' wife, Livia, followed by the elder of her two sons, Tiberius, who would become the next emperor. Behind Tiberius is Antonia, the niece of Augustus, looking back at her husband, Drusus, Livia's younger son. She grasps the hand of Germanicus, one of her younger children. Behind their uncle Drusus are Gnaeus and Domitia, children of Antonia's older sister, who can be seen standing quietly beside them. The depiction of children in an official relief was new to the Augustan period and reflects Augustus' desire to promote private family life and proclaim dynastic succession.

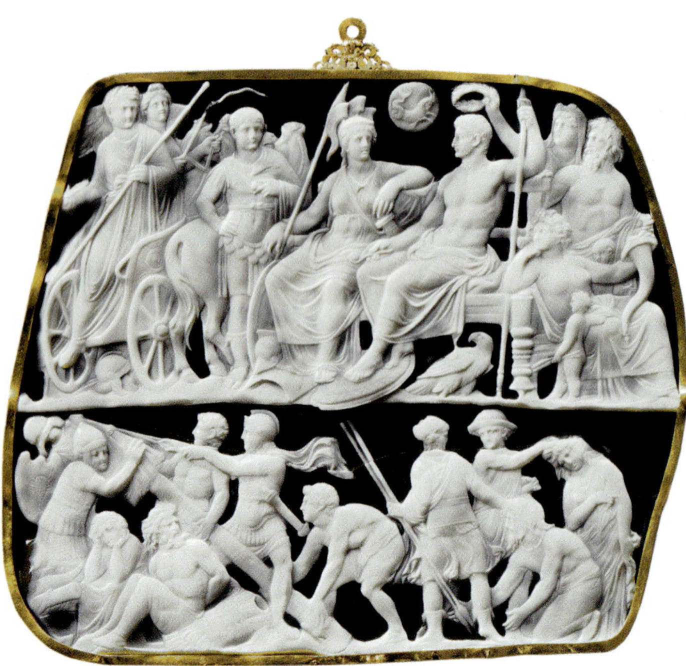

6–15 ***Gemma Augustea.*** Early 1st century CE. Onyx, 7½" × 9" (19 × 23 cm). Kunsthistorisches Museum, Vienna

The Roman House and its Decoration

In large cities, most Romans lived in two- or three-story apartment buildings with shared walls, and in towns, they often lived in houses behind or above rows of shops. The nature-loving Romans softened the regularity of their homes with beautifully planted gardens. Even in towns and cities wealthy people built gracious private residences with one or more gardens (fig. **6–16**). These large, elegant houses had rooms opening onto a central atrium, a partially roofed space with a pool for catching rainwater. In dry climates, the rainwater coming through the roof opening might instead be drained into a deep cistern.

Many fine examples of private residences can be seen at Pompeii, near modern Naples. Located near Mount Vesuvius, Pompeii was buried in volcanic ash after the eruption of 79 CE and remained remarkably well preserved until its rediscovery in the eighteenth century. The so-called House of the Silver Wedding is typical (fig. **6–17**). Behind the atrium and its surrounding rooms lay a second open area known as a peristyle court, an interior garden courtyard surrounded by a colonnaded walkway or portico. The mild climate of Pompeii permitted gardens to flourish year-round, and an aqueduct provided a reliable water supply. The more private family quarters, such as the bedrooms, dining room, and servants' quarters, were usually entered through the peristyle court. This courtyard functioned as an outdoor living room with painted walls, sculpture, and fountains.

Mosaics became popular as decoration for Roman floors and fountains, where durability and waterproofing were desired. Mosaic designs were created with pebbles or with small tesserae—cubes of marble, other stones, and sometimes pottery. Some mosaicists were so accomplished that they created works that resemble paintings. In fact, at the request of patrons, they often copied well-known paintings, employing very small tesserae to create subtle shadings and color changes. The "Alexander mosaic" (see fig. 5–37), once the floor of a house in Pompeii, is a superb example. And in *The Unswept Floor* mosaic (fig. **6–18**), Heraklitos adapted the ***trompe l'oeil*** ("fool the eye") representation of a floor littered with debris from a table by an earlier Hellenistic painter named Sosos. Heraklitos' mosaic version, made three centuries later, even shows a mouse among the table scraps. Bones of fish and fowl, fruit, and nuts are all re-created in meticulous detail, even casting shadows on the floor.

Realistic effects are also pronounced in the paintings with which Romans decorated the walls of the important rooms of their homes. The interior walls of Roman houses were smooth plaster surfaces with few architectural features. On these invitingly plain surfaces, artists painted decorations using pigment in a solution of lime and soap, sometimes with a little wax. In the earliest paintings, beginning about 200 BCE, artists created the illusion of thin slabs of colored marble covering the walls. They also modeled shallow architectural moldings and columns in plaster. By about 80 BCE, painters began to extend the space of a room visually with scenes of figures on a shallow platform or with a landscape or cityscape. Architectural details such as columns were painted rather than modeled from plaster. As time passed, such illusionistic architecture

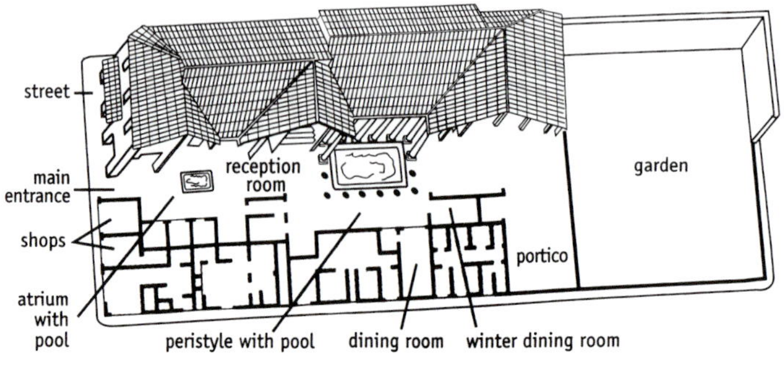

6–16 Reconstruction drawing and plan of the House of Pansa, Pompeii. 2nd century BCE

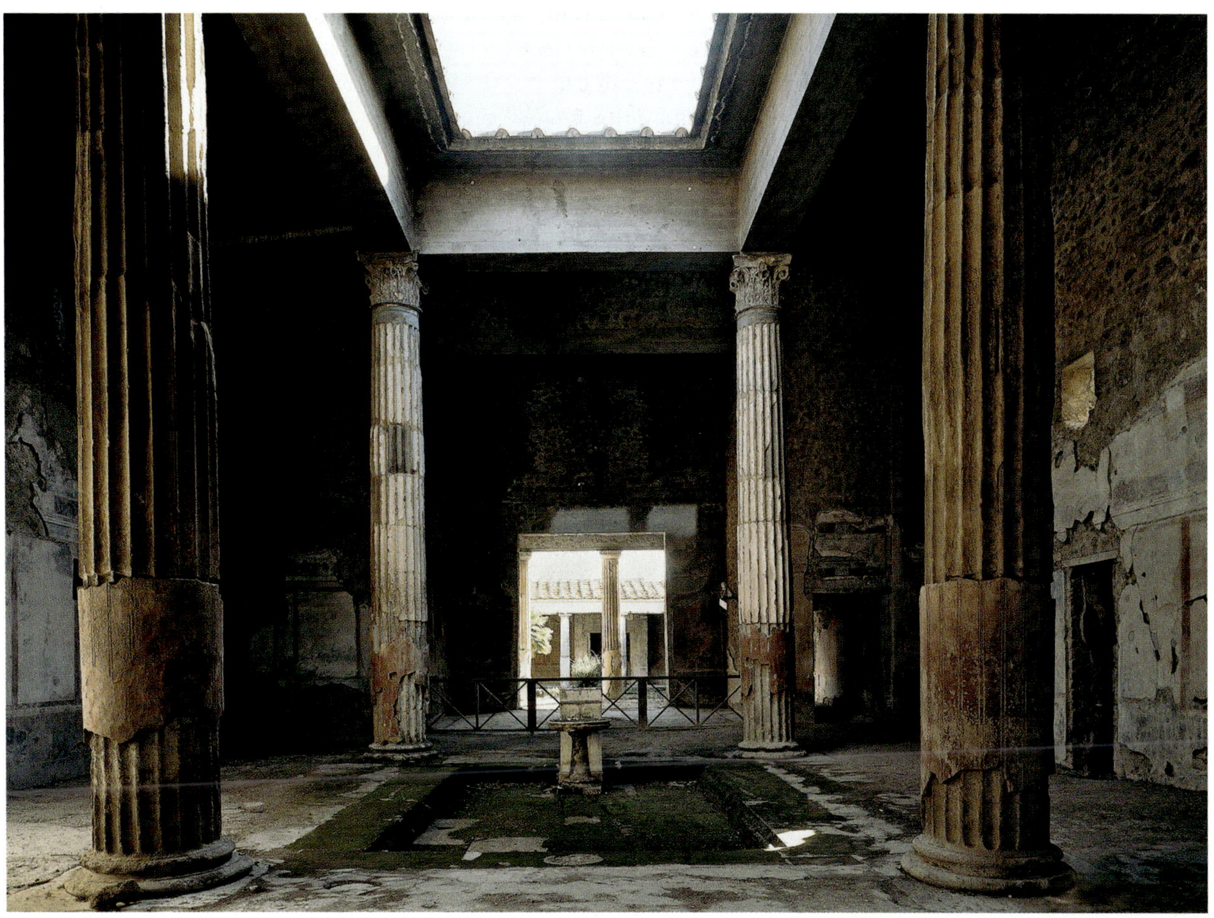

6–17 Atrium, House of the Silver Wedding, Pompeii. Early 1st century CE

This house received its unusual name as a commemorative gesture unrelated to his ancient history. It was excavated in 1893, the year of the silver wedding anniversary of Italy's King Humbert and his wife, Margaret of Savoy, who had supported archaeological fieldwork at Pompeii.

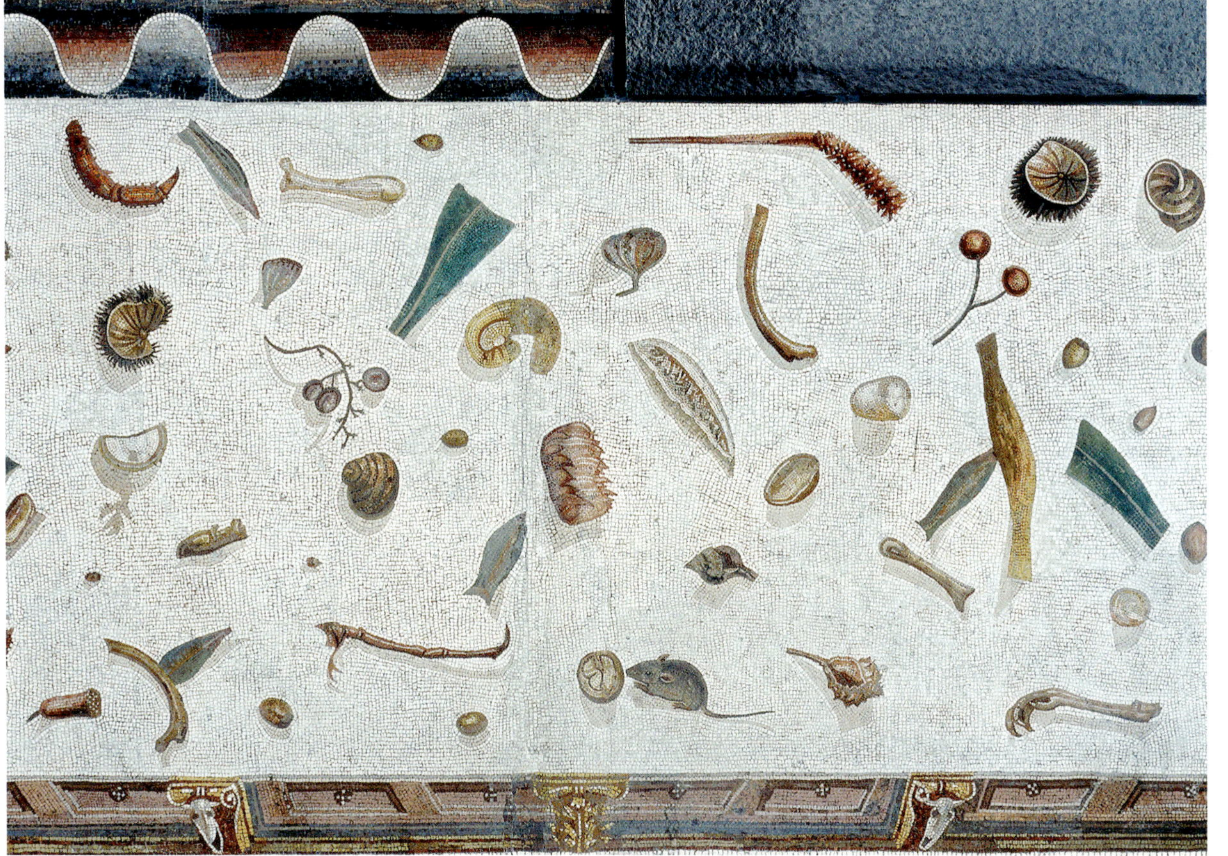

6–18 Heraklitos. *The Unswept Floor*, mosaic version of a 2nd-century BCE painting by Sosos of Pergamon. 2nd century CE. 13' 3½" (4.05 m). Musei Vaticani, Museo Gregoriano Profano, ex Lateranese, Rome

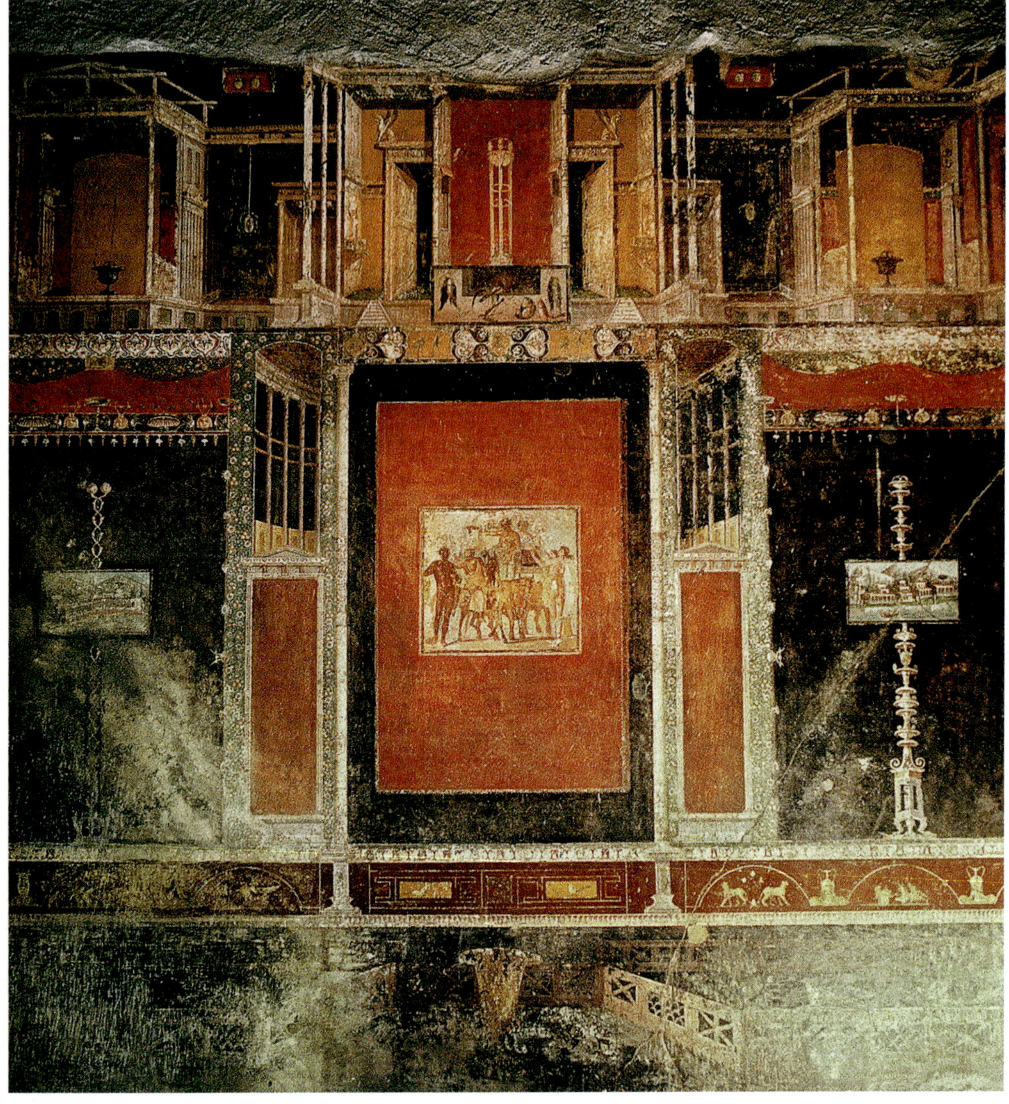

6–19 Detail of a wall painting in the House of M. Lucretius Fronto, Pompeii. Mid-1st century CE

became increasingly fanciful. Solid colored walls were decorated with slender, whimsical architectural and floral details and small, delicate vignettes. The wall surfaces seem to recede or even disappear behind a maze of floating architectural forms.

Artists used two different conventions to create the illusion of space: intuitive perspective and atmospheric perspective. In **intuitive perspective**, the architectural details follow diagonal lines that the eye interprets as parallel lines receding into the distance. Objects meant to be perceived as far away from the surface plane of the wall are shown slightly smaller than those intended to appear nearby. The artist created the illusion of looking out over a low, paneled wall, thus "painting away" the wall surface above. In **atmospheric perspective**, the colors become slightly grayer in the far background, reproducing the tendency of distant objects to appear hazy.

In the House of M. Lucretius Fronto in Pompeii, from the mid-first century CE (fig. **6–19**), the artist painted a room with panels of black and red, bordered with architectural moldings. These architectural elements are fantasies that play with perspective, free from any demand to be logical or consistent. The scene with figures, at the center, seems to be mounted on the large red panel. It is flanked by two small simulated window openings protected by grilles and two small pictures of villas in landscapes that appear to be held up by intricate bronze easels.

One of the most famous painted rooms in Roman art is in the so-called Villa of the Mysteries at Pompeii (fig. **6–20**). The rites of mystery religions were often performed in private homes as well as in special buildings or temples, and this room, at the corner of a suburban villa, may have been a shrine or a meeting place for such a cult. A reminder of the wide variety of religious practices tolerated by the Romans, the murals depict initiation rites—probably into the cult of Bacchus, who was the god of vegetation and fertility as well as wine, and was one of the most popular deities in Pompeii. The entirely painted architectural setting consists of a "marble" **dado** (the lower part of a wall) and, around the top of the wall, an elegant frieze supported by **pilasters** (engaged strips). The action unfolds on a shallow stage running around the entire room, and against a background of a brilliant, deep red that was very popular with Roman painters; this has come to be called "Pompeian red."

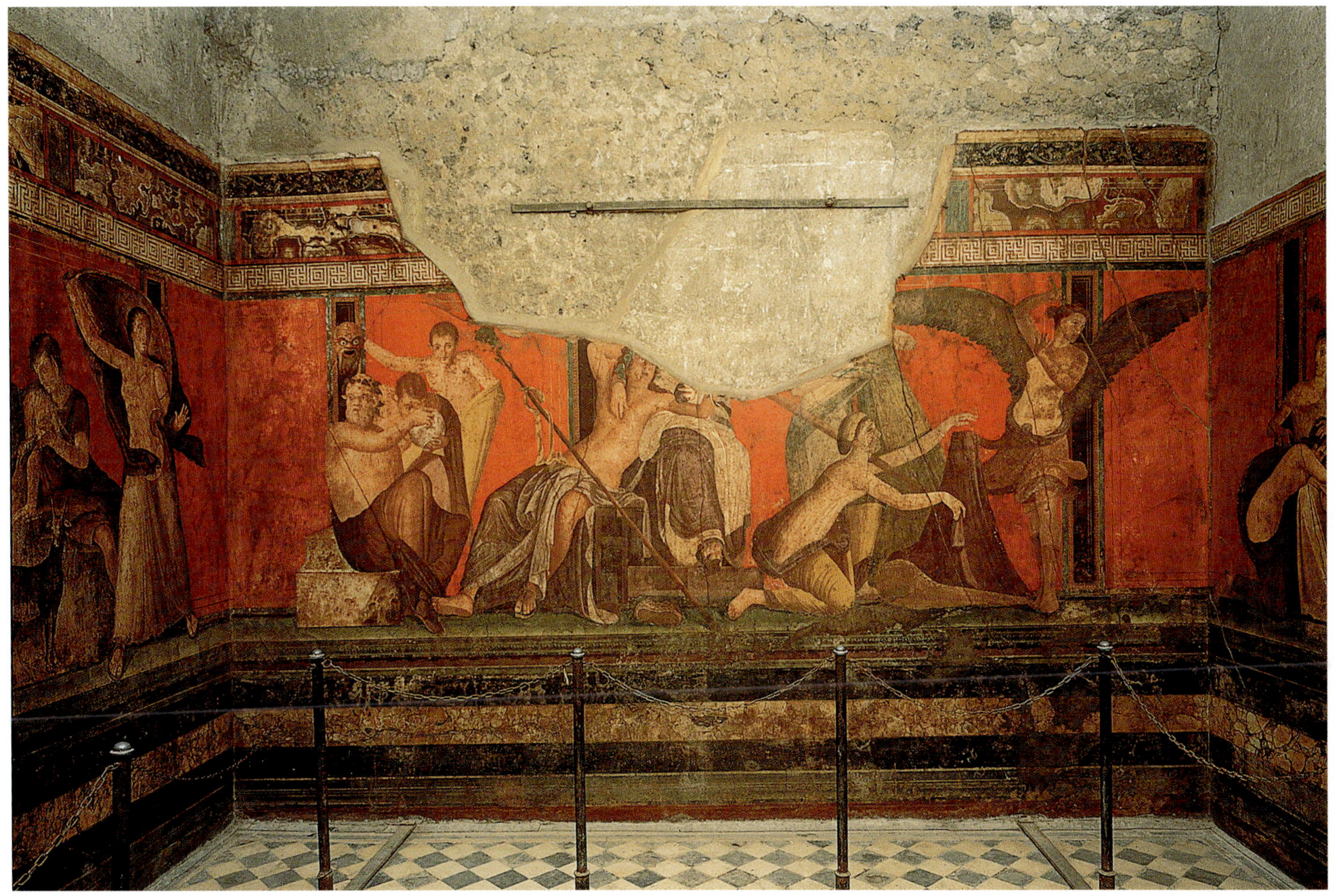

6–20 Wall painting, Villa of the Mysteries, Pompeii. c. 60–50 BCE

The Empire

The sequence of related Roman rulers that follows Augustus, beginning with Tiberius and ending with the reign of the despotic and capricious Nero, is known as the Julio-Claudian dynasty (14–68 CE). A powerful general named Vespasian seized control of the government after Nero's death to found the Flavian dynasty (69–96 CE). The Flavian emperors, Vespasian (ruled 69–79 CE), Titus (ruled 79–81 CE), and Domitian (ruled 81–96 CE), restored imperial finances and stabilized the empire's frontiers. Five outstanding rulers succeeded the Flavians: Nerva (ruled 96–98 CE), Trajan (ruled 98–117 CE), Hadrian (ruled 117–138 CE), Antoninus Pius (ruled 138–161 CE), and Marcus Aurelius (ruled 161–180 CE). Known as the "Five Good Emperors," they oversaw a long period of stability and prosperity. Under Trajan, the Roman Empire reached its greatest extent, annexing Dacia (roughly, modern Romania) in 106 CE and expanding the empire's boundaries in the Near East.

Imperial Art and Architecture

Romans were huge fans of sports events, and the Flavian emperors catered to their taste by building enormous arenas, including the Colosseum, one of Rome's most influential monuments (fig. **6–21**). Construction began in 72 CE during the reign of Vespasian, and the Colosseum—originally called the Flavian Amphitheater—was dedicated by Titus in 80 CE. (The name "Colosseum," by which it came to be known, derived from the Colossus, an over-life-size statue of Nero standing next to it.) The Flavians erected the arena to bolster their popularity in Rome, and in this enormous entertainment center, audiences watched blood sports and spectacles including animal hunts, fights to the death between gladiators or between gladiators and wild animals, and performances of trained animals and acrobats. The opening performance in 80 CE lasted 100 days, during which time, it was claimed, 9,000 wild animals and 2,000 gladiators died. For its ease of crowd movement and unobstructed views, the design of the Colosseum, which held about 50,000 spectators, has never been improved upon. Architects still copy features of it today.

The Colosseum was built entirely of masonry: travertine and tufa blocks and concrete faced with stone. Eighty barrel vaults built to cover corridors and stairs radiate from the arena's center. These form groin vaults where they intersect the barrel ring vaults that cover the passageways around the perimeter (see "Arch and Vault," page 145). These complex curved shapes could be formed of concrete faster and more cheaply than from stone blocks, which have to be cut by trained masons. The concrete consisted of stone rubble

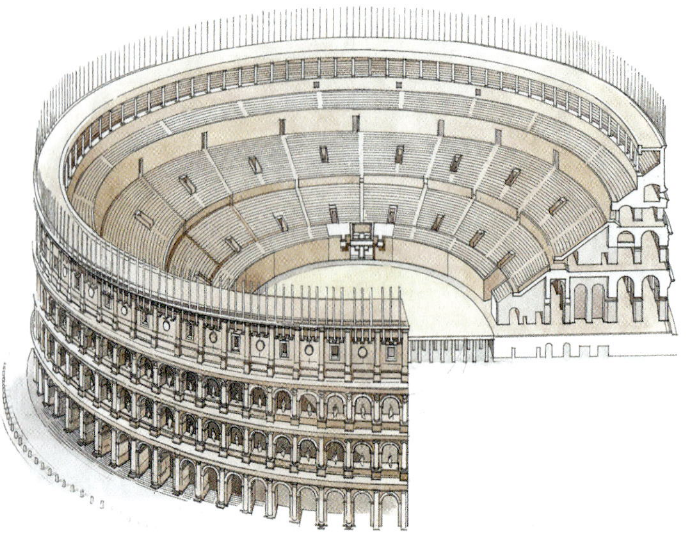

6–21 Reconstruction drawing of the Colosseum, Rome. 72–80 CE

(*caementa*) in a binder made from volcanic sand and water. This rough but strong core was faced with finer, worked stone.

The curving outer wall of the Colosseum consists of three levels of arcades surmounted by a wall-like top, or **attic story** (fig. **6–22**). Every arch is framed by engaged columns, which support friezes that mark the division between levels. Each level uses a different architectural order, and the levels become increasingly decorative as they rise. The ground floor is ornamented with columns in the Tuscan order (generally similar to the Greek Doric order except that the unfluted columns have bases). The Ionic order is used on the second level, the Corinthian on the third, and flat Corinthian pilasters adorn the fourth story. All these elements are purely decorative and serve no structural function. The systematic use of the orders in a logical succession from sturdy Tuscan to delicate Corinthian follows a tradition inherited from Hellenistic architecture and is still popular today as a way of articulating and organizing the façades of large buildings.

When Domitian became emperor in 81 CE, he immediately commissioned a triumphal arch to honor his brother and deified predecessor, Titus (fig. **6–23**). The Arch of Titus, which commemorates Titus' capture of Jerusalem in 70 CE, is essentially a large

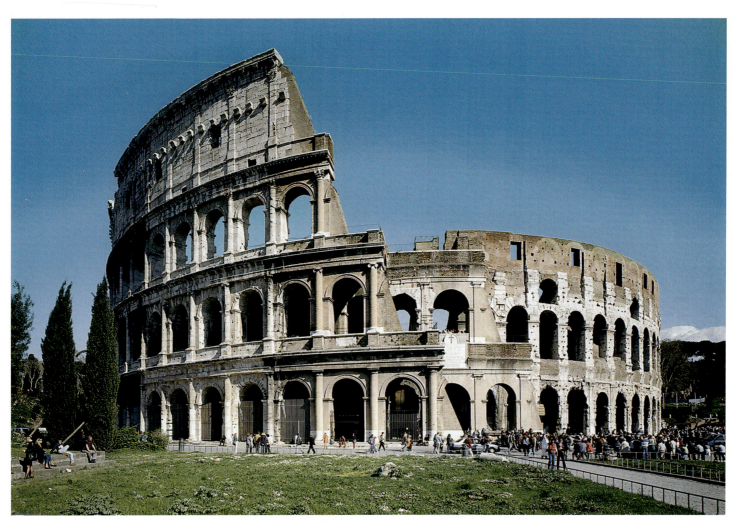

6–22 Colosseum, Rome. 72–80 CE

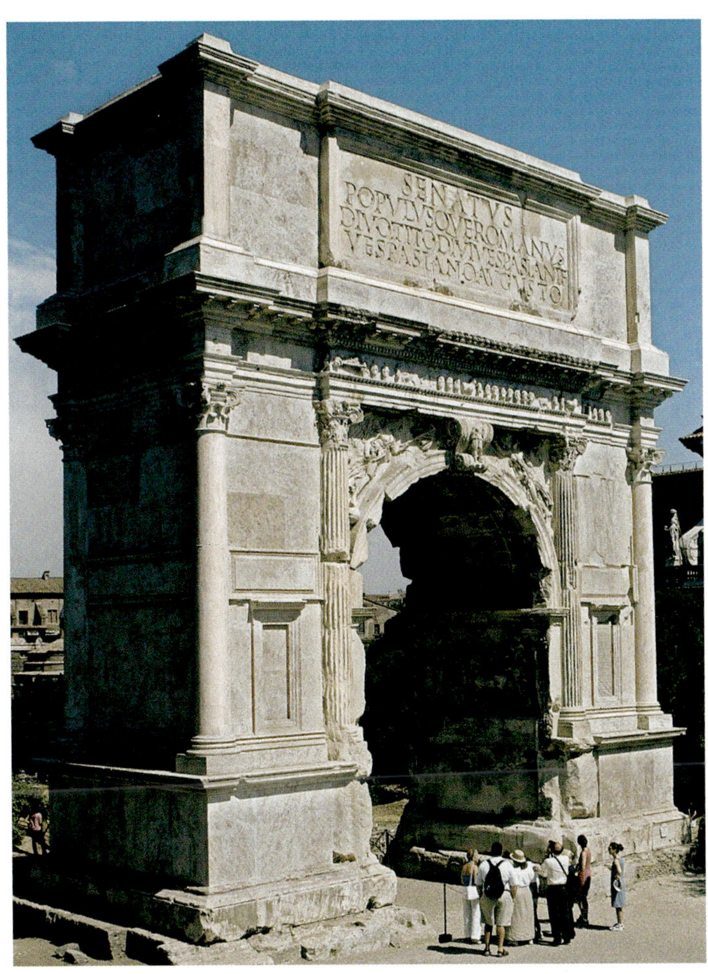

6–23 Arch of Titus, Rome. c. 81 CE. Concrete and white marble, height 50' (15 m)

The dedication inscribed across the tall attic story above the arch opening reads: "The Senate and the Roman People to the Deified Titus Flavius Vespasianus Augustus, son of the Deified Vespasian." The Romans typically recorded historic occasions and identified monuments with solemn prose and beautiful inscriptions in stone. The sculptors' use of elegant Roman capital letters—perfectly sized and spaced to be read from a distance and cut with sharp terminals (serifs) to catch the light—established a standard that calligraphers and alphabet designers still follow.

free-standing arch, the interior of which is a short barrel-vaulted passageway. The exterior of the arch is ornamented with engaged Composite columns (see "Roman Architectural Orders," page 155). Originally the 50-foot-high arch served as a giant base for a monumental bronze statue of a four-horse chariot and driver, a typical Roman triumphal symbol.

Titus' capture of Jerusalem ended a fierce campaign to crush a revolt of the Jews in Palestine. His troops looted and destroyed the Second Temple of Jerusalem and carted off its sacred treasures. These spoils were displayed in Rome during Titus' triumphal procession. According to the Jewish eyewitness and historian Flavius Josephus, the prizes included "the law of the Jews," a gold table, and a seven-branched lamp stand, or menorah.

The reliefs on the inside walls of the arch depict Titus' soldiers carrying this booty through the streets of Rome (fig. **6–24**). Viewing this crowd as through a window, the observer can easily imagine the boisterous scene. The varying depth of the relief elements creates

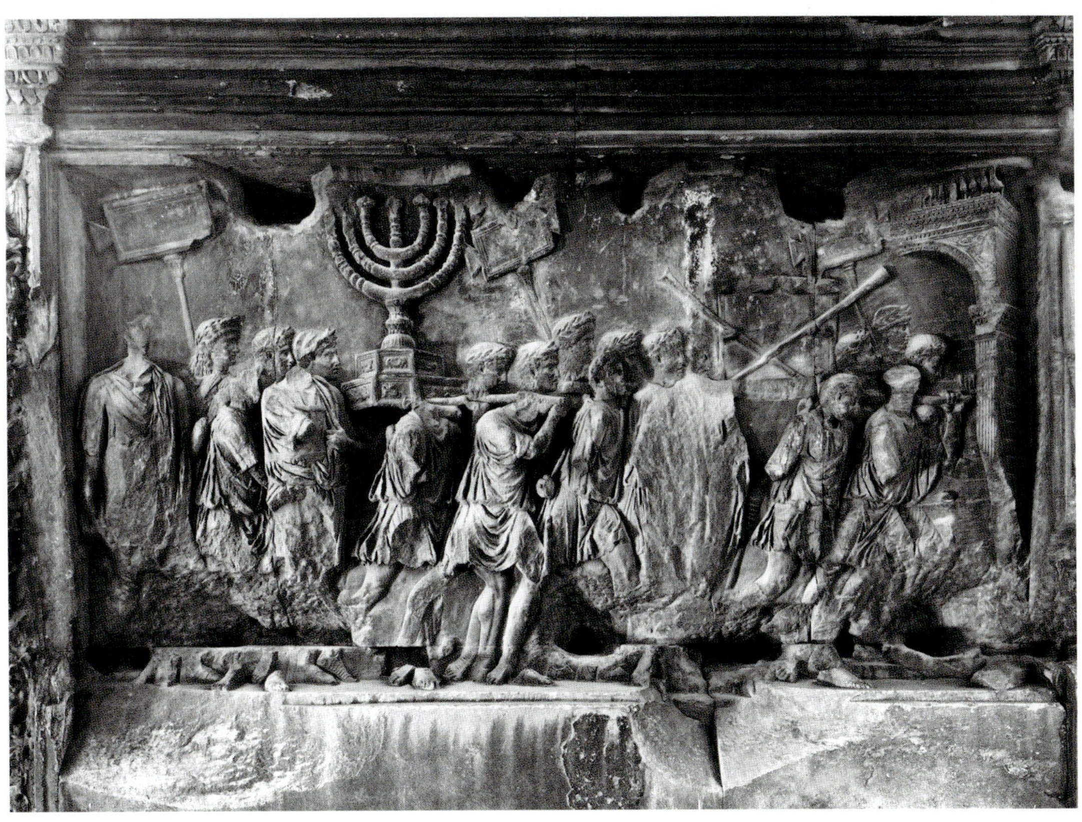

6–24 *Spoils from the Temple of Solomon in Jerusalem*, relief in the passageway of the Arch of Titus, Rome. Marble, height 6' 8" (2.03 m)

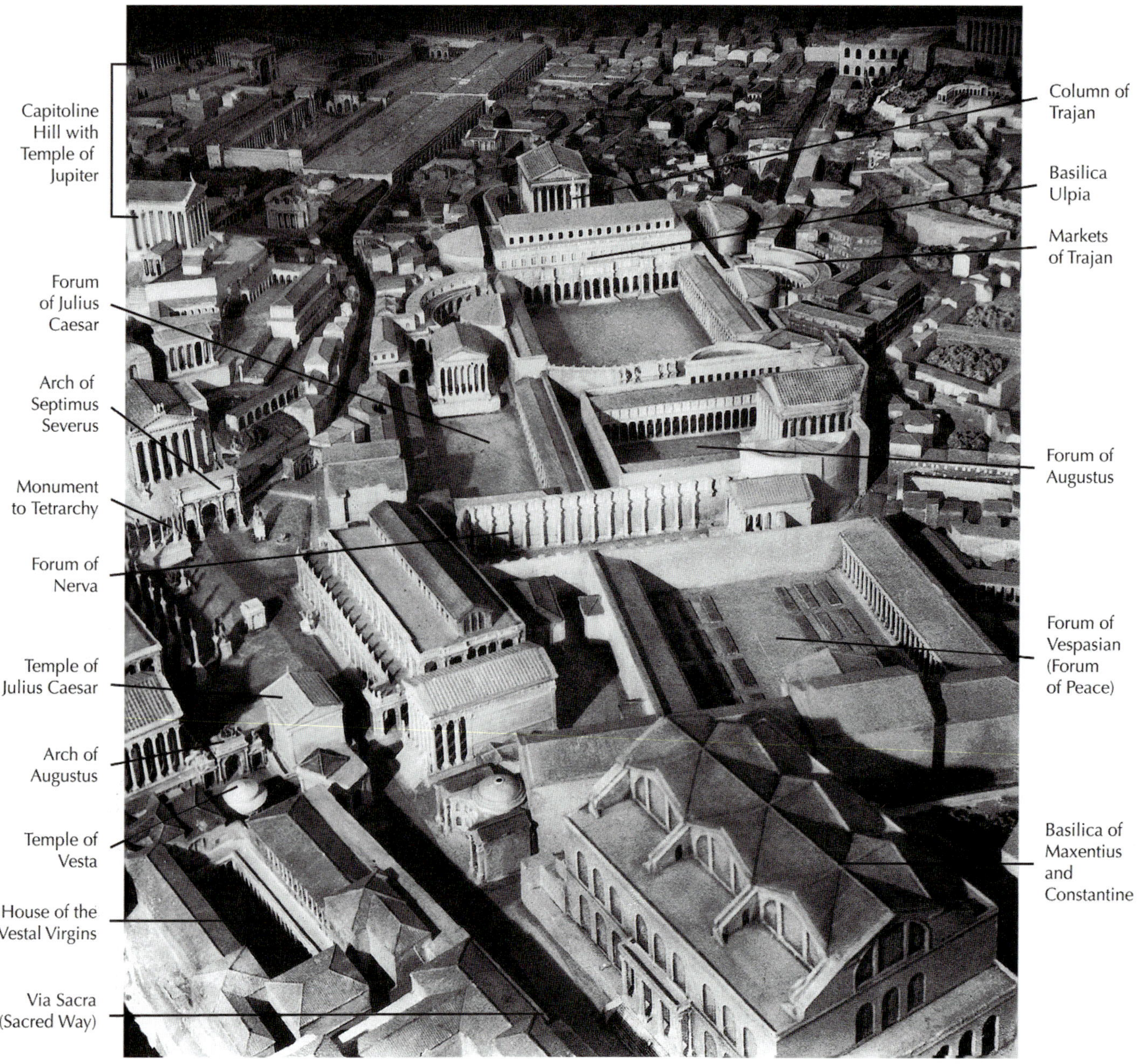

6–25 Model of the Forum Romanum and Imperial Forum, Rome. c. 46. BCE–325 CE

the impression that the marchers are moving toward the viewer and then turning to move away at the right through a distant arch. Spatial relationships, achieved by rendering close elements in higher relief than more distant ones, also produce a clear illusion of deeper and more complex space than that in the earlier reliefs of the *Ara Pacis*.

As mentioned, Romans built throughout the empire. Projects such as the imperial forums of the capital were repeated elsewhere on a smaller scale. A **forum**, the civic center, consisted of a large open square or oblong space generally surrounded by colonnades leading to a temple and sometimes a **basilica**. A general-purpose administrative structure, a basilica could be adapted to many uses. It could serve as an imperial audience chamber, an army drill hall, court of law, or school. The spacious and adaptable interior made the basilica form attractive to Christians, who would later appropriate it for churches.

Two basilicas can be seen in figure **6–25**: the Basilica Ulpia in Trajan's Forum, and the vaulted Basilica of Maxentius and Constantine. The Basilica Ulpia (fig. **6–26**), named for Trajan's family, was dedicated as a court of law in 113 CE. It was a grand, rectangular building partitioned into a large central area called a **nave**, flanked by two lower colonnaded **aisles** and entered through

ELEMENTS OF **Architecture**

Roman Architectural Orders

The Etruscans and Romans adapted Greek architectural orders to their own tastes, often using them as applied decoration on a wall. For example, the Etruscans modified the Greek Doric order by adding a base to the column. The Romans created the Composite order by combining the volute of the Greek Ionic capital with the acanthus leaves of the Corinthian order. The sturdy, unfluted Tuscan order combined the Greek Doric order and Etruscan models. In this diagram, the Roman orders are shown on pedestals, which consist of a plinth, a dado, and a cornice.

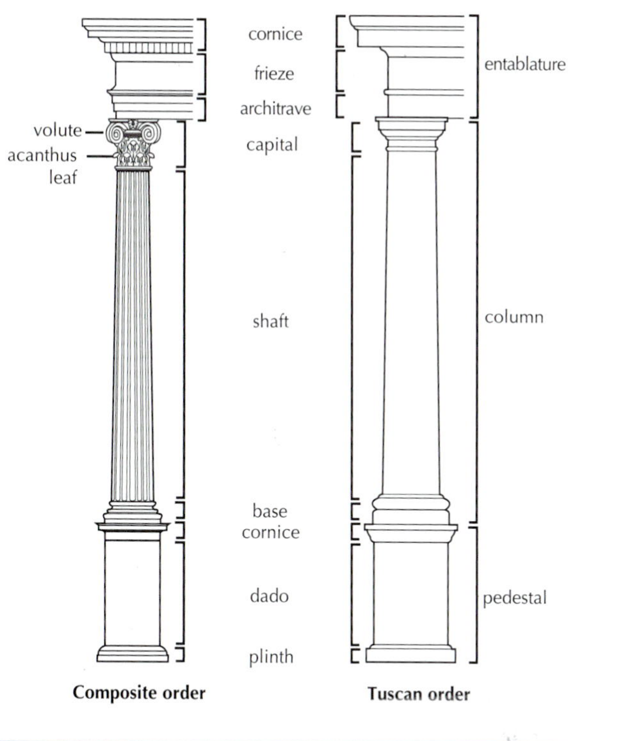

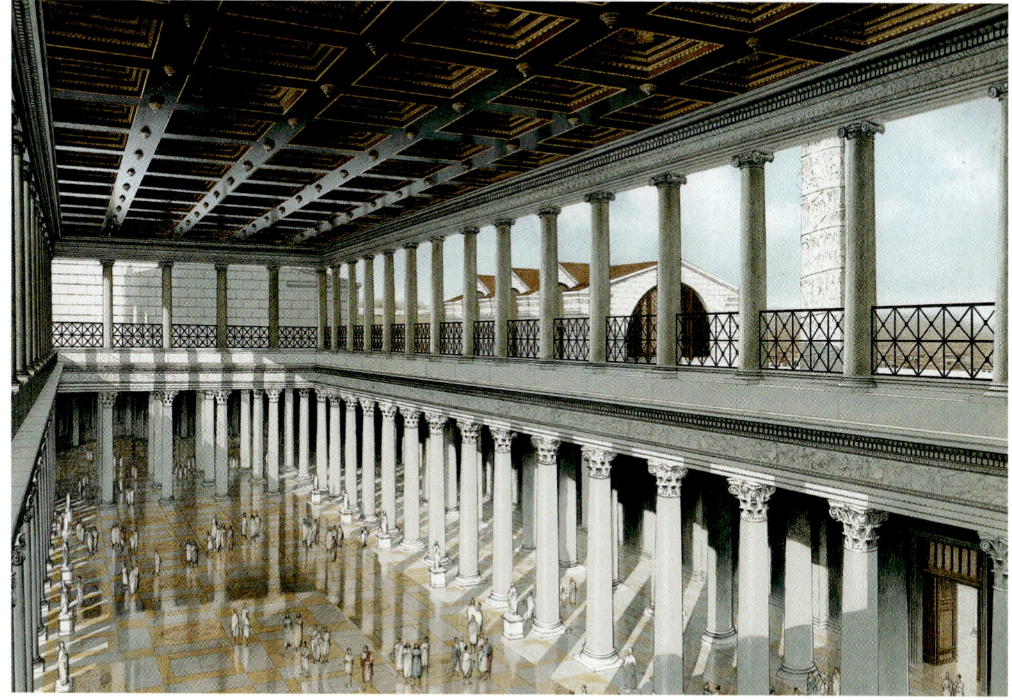

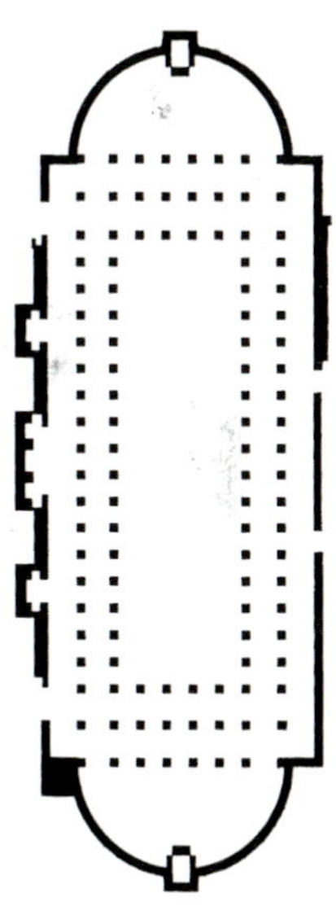

6–26 Restored view and plan of the interior of the Basilica Ulpia, from the Forum of Trajan, Rome. c. 113 CE (drawn by Gilbert Gorski)

several doors on the long side of the building that faced the open square of the Forum of Trajan.

Beyond the Basilica Ulpia was Trajan's tomb, surmounted by a column carved with spiraling reliefs depicting his victory over the Dacians. Later the forum complex was completed with a temple to the deified emperor. A large market was built into an adjacent hillside. The collective structures and spaces that make up the Forum of Trajan exemplify the finest in imperial city planning, satisfying both the needs of the citizens and the imperial desire for impressive public works and memorializing propaganda.

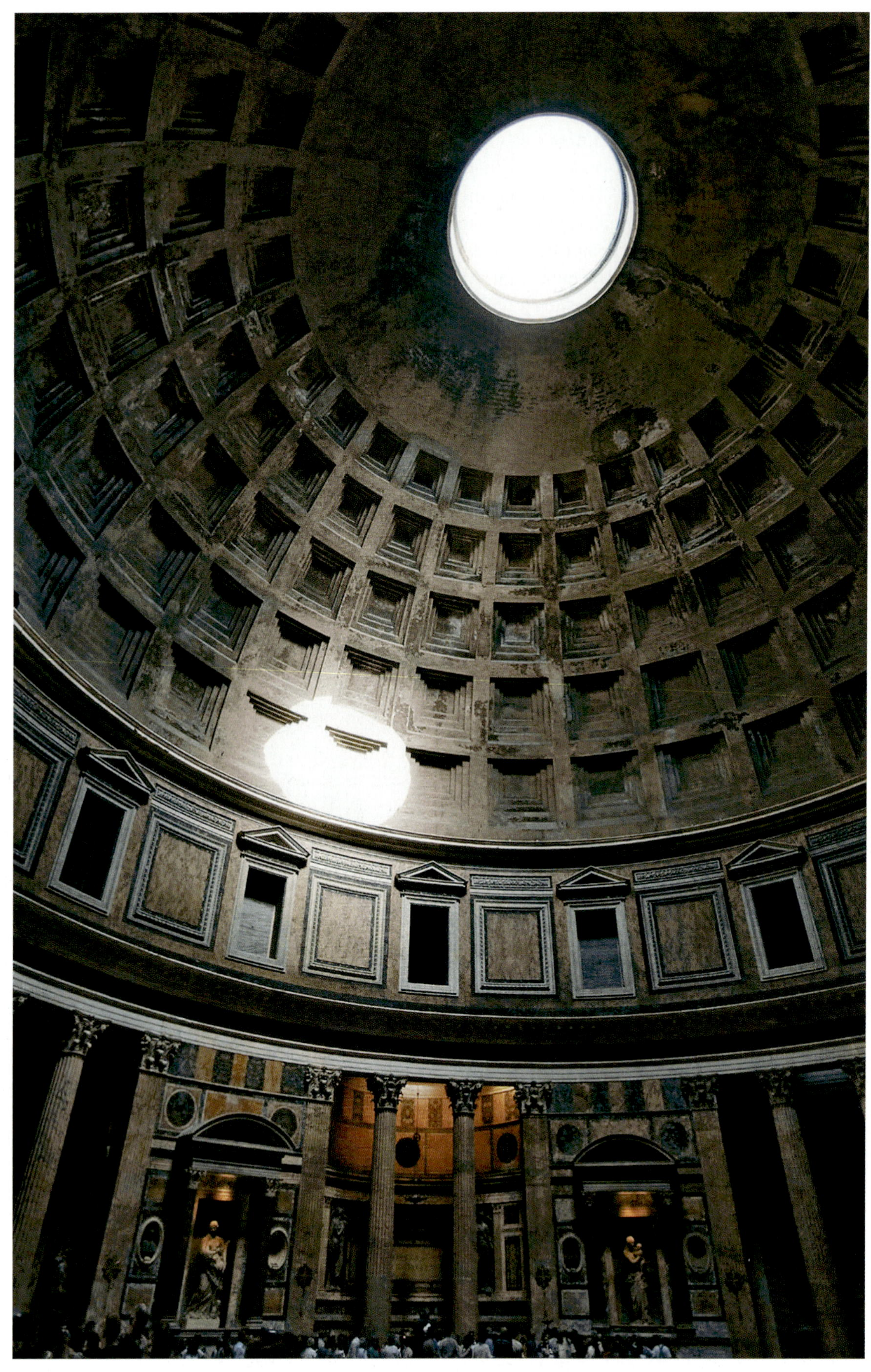

6–27 Dome of the Pantheon with light from the oculus on its coffered ceiling

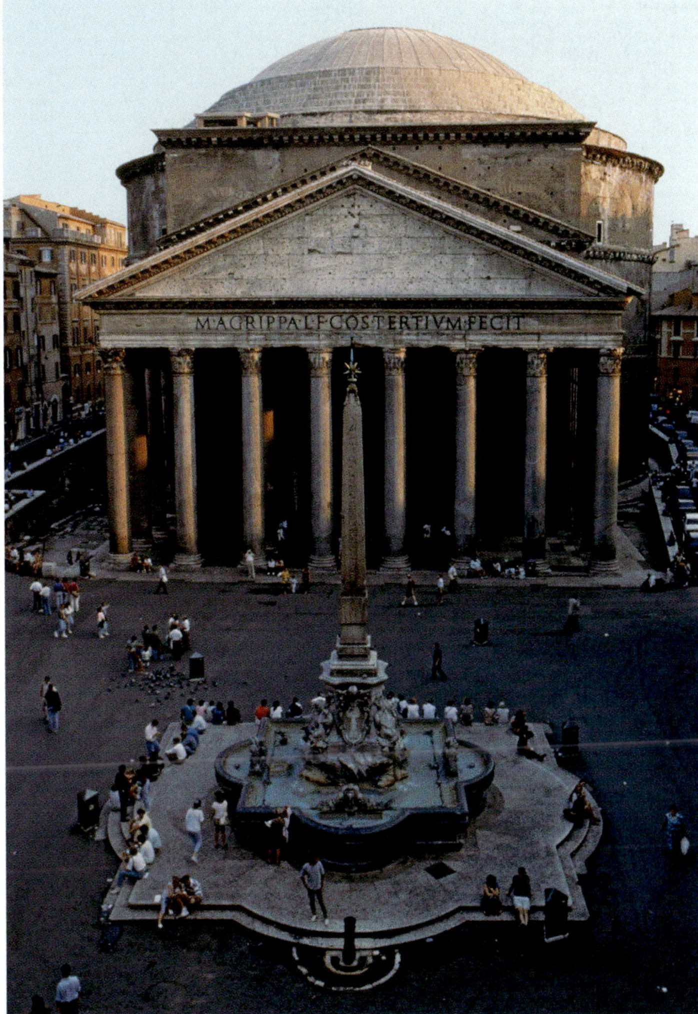

6–28 Pantheon, Rome. 118–128 CE

In the foreground of the photograph is a monumental fountain by G. della Porta, 1578. In 1711 Pope Clement XI added the ancient Egyptian obelisk.

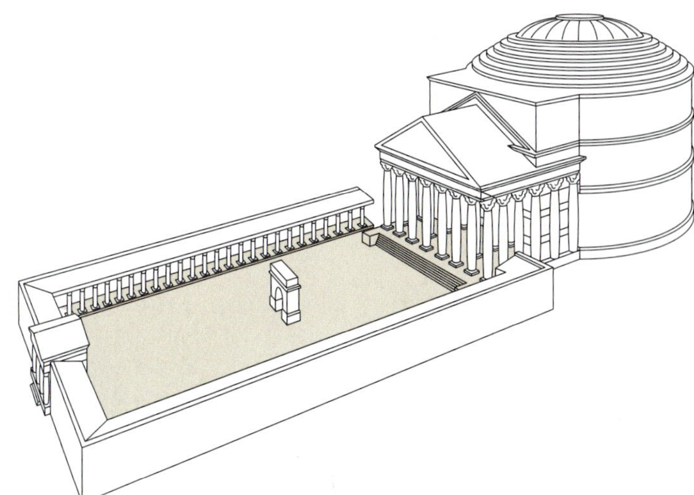

6–29 Schematic drawing of the Pantheon situated at the end of its original rectangular forecourt

Trajan's successor, Hadrian, was well educated and widely traveled. His admiration for Greek culture spurred new building programs throughout the empire. To the splendid architecture of Rome itself, he added the remarkable temple to the Olympian gods known as the Pantheon ("all the gods"), built between 118 and 128 CE (figs. **6–27** and **6–28**). The entrance porch, made to resemble the façade of a typical rectangular Roman temple, was all that original viewers could see as they approached the Pantheon through an enclosed courtyard (fig. **6–29**). The actual shape of the building was concealed. This theatrical presentation allowed the soaring and enclosing space of the giant **rotunda** (circular room) surmounted with a huge, bowl-shaped dome, 143 feet in diameter and 143 feet from the floor to its summit, to be a surprise encountered by viewers only after they passed through the rectilinear and restricted aisles of the portico toward the huge main door. Even without the courtyard approach, encountering this glorious space today is still an overwhelming experience for many of us, one that is repeated even on successive visits to the rotunda.

Often seen as the climax of the spatial experimentation and structural audacity characterizing Roman imperial architecture, the Pantheon has inspired hundreds of copies, variants, and eclectic borrowings. The true complexity of its construction, however, has only recently been fully understood. The circular wall, or **drum**, of the rotunda, which supports and buttresses the dome, is formed of brick arches and concrete that are concealed beneath the delicate architectonic patterns of marble veneer. Structurally, a dome works as an arch pivoted 360 degrees around the top of a drum. In the Pantheon, the usual keystone is replaced by a central circular opening, or **oculus**—a daring concept. The repetition of square against circle, established on a large scale by juxtaposing the rectilinear portico against the circular rotunda, is found throughout the building's ornamentation. Seven interior niches, rectangular alternating with semicircular, originally held statues of the gods. Inside the dome, square, box-like **coffers** (recessed ceiling panels) help lighten the weight of the masonry and may once have contained gilded bronze rosettes or stars suggesting the heavens.

Inside, our eyes are drawn upward over the pattern made by the coffers to the light entering through the 29-foot-wide oculus (see fig. 6–27), which creates a brilliant circle against the surface of the dome, a disk that moves around this microcosm throughout the day like a sun. Clouds can be seen traveling across the opening on some days; on others, rain falls through and then drains off through conduits planned by the original engineer. Occasionally, a bird flies in. This open, luminous space imparts the sense that one could rise buoyantly upward to escape the spherical hollow of the building and commune with the cosmos.

Portraits in Sculpture and Painting

The development of art in Rome depended on private as well as public patronage. For their homes, wealthy individuals might commission wall paintings, mosaics, or portraits in marble or bronze. Roman patrons usually demanded recognizable likenesses in their

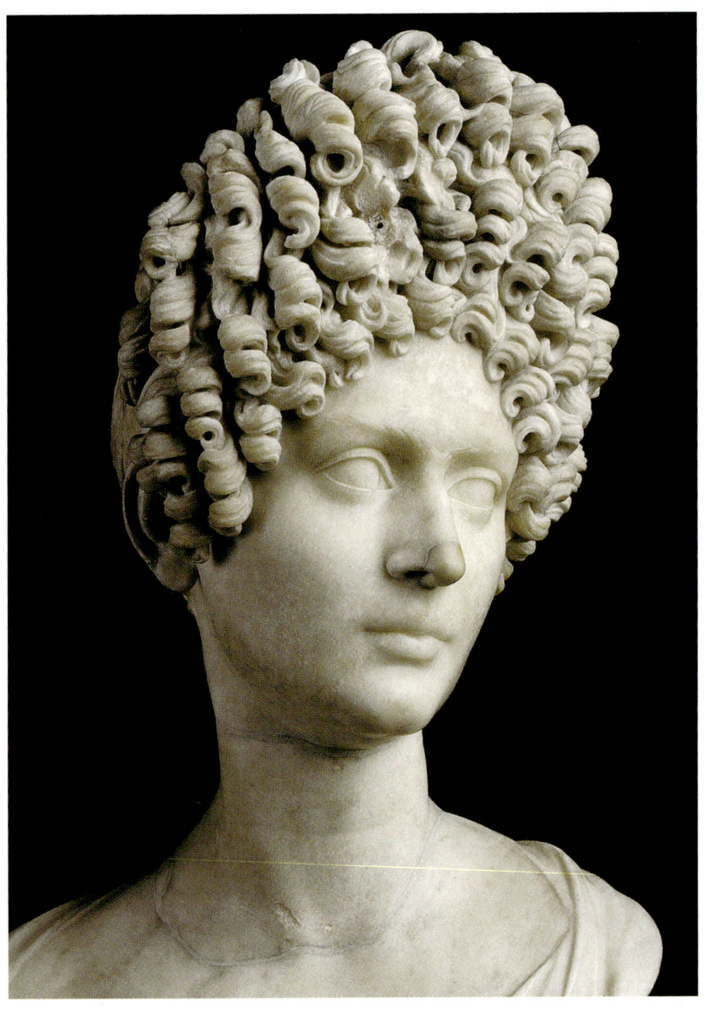

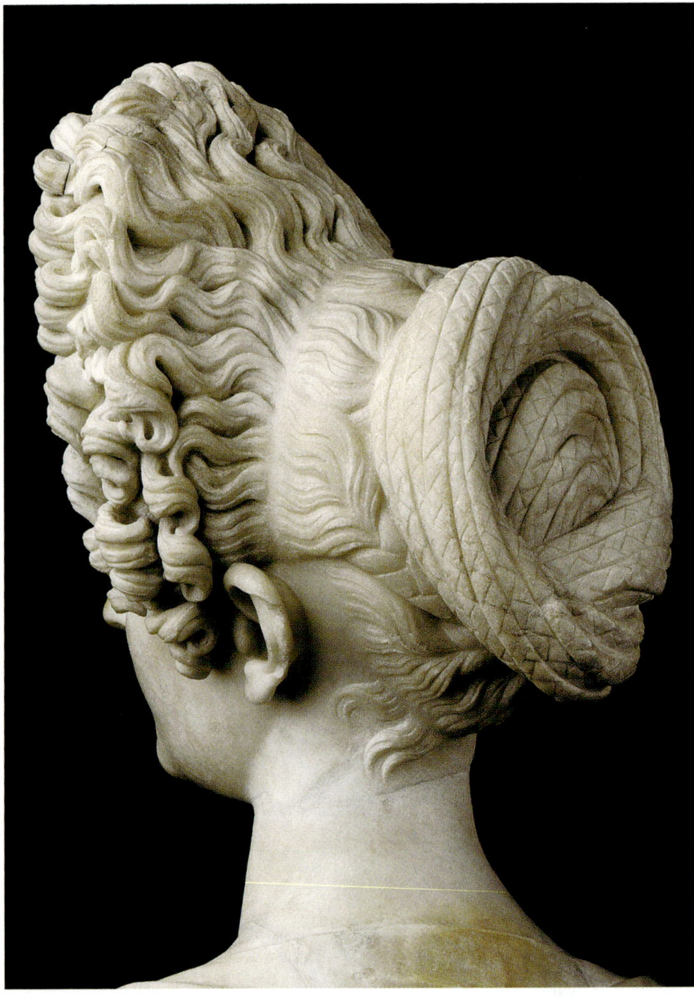

6–30 ***Young Flavian Woman.*** c. 90 CE. Marble, height 25" (65.5 cm). Museo Capitolino, Rome

The typical Flavian hairstyle seen on this woman required a patient hairdresser handy with a curling iron and with a special knack for turning the back of the head into an intricate basketweave of braids. Male writers loved to scoff at the results. Martial described the style precisely as "a globe of hair." Statius spoke of "the glory of woman's lofty front, her storied hair." And Juvenal waxed comically poetic: "See her from the front; she is Andromache [an epic heroine]. From behind she looks half the size—a different woman you would think" (cited in Balsdon, page 256).

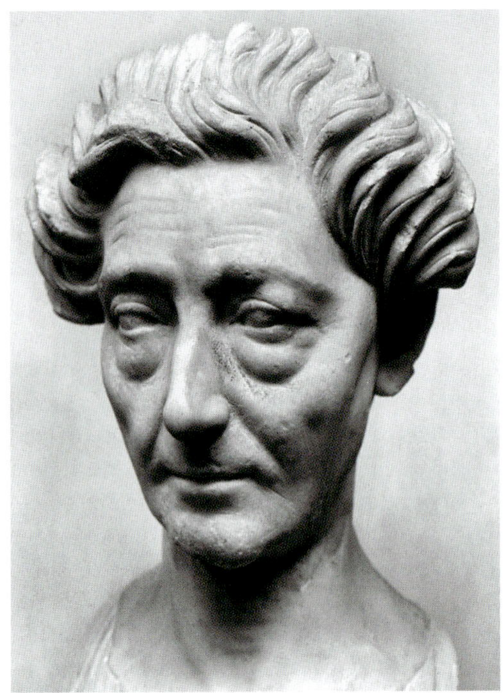

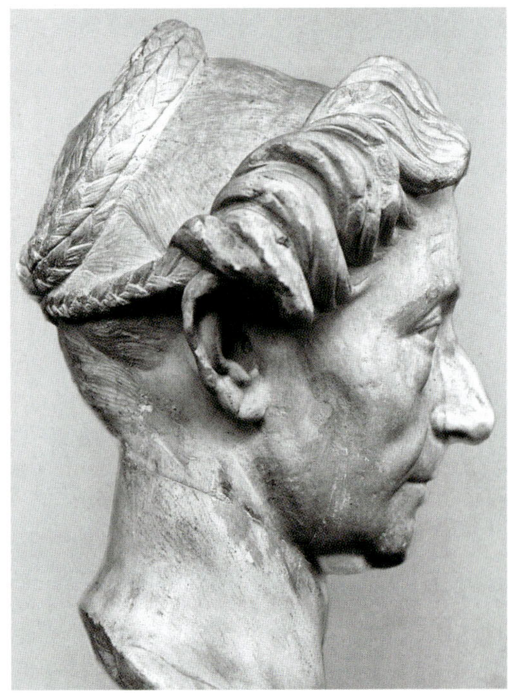

6–31 ***Middle-Aged Flavian Woman.*** Late 1st century CE. Marble, height 9½" (24.1 cm). Musei Vaticani, Museo Gregoriano Profano, ex-Lateranese, Rome

portrait heads, but this did not preclude some idealization. The portrait of an unidentified *Young Flavian Woman* (fig. **6–30**) is idealized in a manner similar to the *Augustus of Primaporta* (see fig. 6–12). The well-observed, recognizable features—strong nose and jaw, heavy brows, deep-set eyes, and long neck—contrast with the smoothly rendered flesh and soft, sensual lips. The hair is piled high in an extraordinary mass of ringlets following the latest court fashion. Executing the head required skillful chiseling and **drillwork**, a technique for rapidly cutting deep grooves with straight sides, as was done here to render the holes in the center of the curls. The overall effect, especially from a distance, is quite lifelike. The play of natural light over the more subtly sculpted marble surfaces simulates the textures of real skin and hair.

A contemporary bust of an older woman (fig. **6–31**) presents a strikingly different image of its subject. Although she also wears her hair in the latest fashion, this woman was apparently not as preoccupied with her appearance as her more youthful counterpart. The work she commissioned emphasized not the fresh sheen of an unblemished face, but a visage clearly marked by the passage of time during a life well lived. We may experience this portrait as less idealized and more naturalistic, but for a Roman viewer, it may also have conformed to an ideal of age and accomplishment by showcasing facial features cherished since the Republican period as reflections of virtue and venerability.

Portraits were also popular in wall paintings. A late first-century CE **tondo** (circular panel) from a house in Pompeii contains a portrait known as *Young Woman Writing* (fig. **6–32**). In a convention popular for women patrons, she is shown with the tip of a writing stylus raised to her lips. She holds a set of wood tablets coated with wax that were used in much the same way that we might use a pad of paper; letters engraved in soft wax with a stylus could be smoothed over and rewritten. When a text or letter was considered ready, it was copied onto expensive papyrus or parchment. As in a modern studio photograph, with its careful lighting and retouching and its reliance on a standardized set of poses, the young woman in this painting is portrayed in a conventional and idealized fashion.

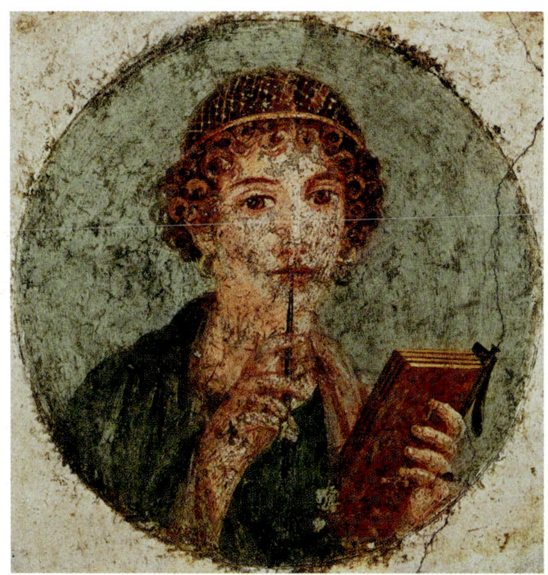

6–32 ***Young Woman Writing***, detail of a wall painting from Pompeii. Late 1st century CE. Diameter 14⅝" (37 cm). Museo Archeològico Nazionale, Naples

The fashionable young woman seems to be pondering what she will write about with her stylus on the beribboned writing tablet that she holds in her other hand. Romans used pointed styluses to engrave letters on thin, wax-coated ivory or wood tablets in much the way we might use a pad of paper. Tablets like these were also used by schoolchildren for their homework.

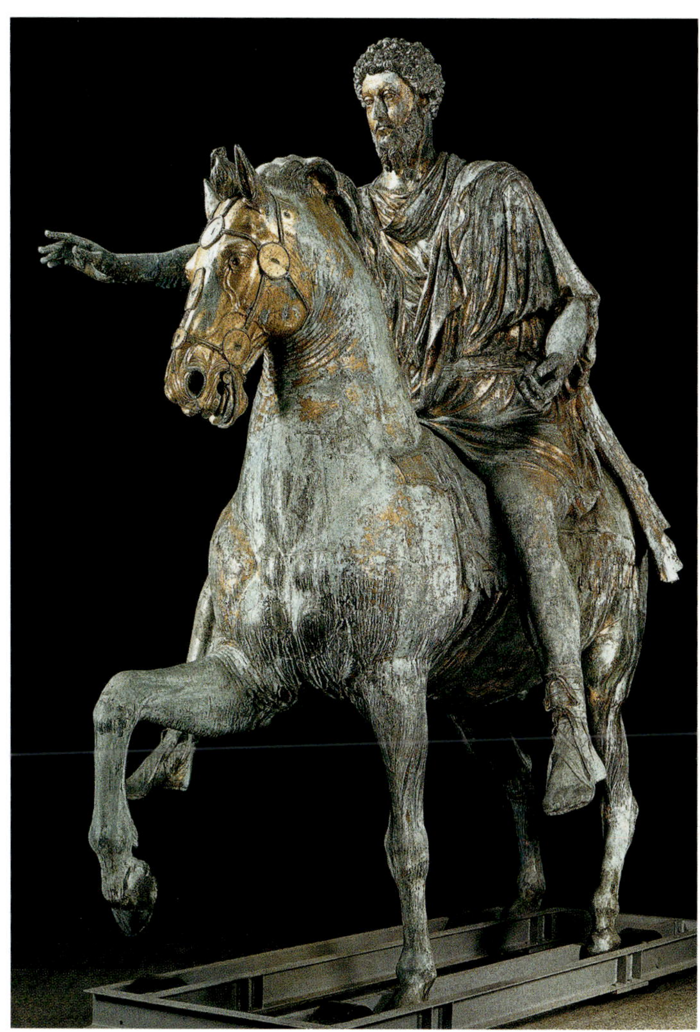

6–33 ***Marcus Aurelius***. c. 176 CE. Bronze, originally gilded, height of statue 11' 6" (3.5 m). Museo Capitolino, Rome

Hadrian's successor, Marcus Aurelius, was renowned both for his intellectual and his military achievements. In a gilded bronze equestrian statue, the emperor appears as a commander dressed in a tunic and short, heavy cloak (fig. **6–33**). The raised foreleg of his horse is poised to trample a defeated foe (now lost). The emperor wears no armor and carries no weapons; like the Egyptian kings, he conquers effortlessly by the will of the gods. And like his illustrious predecessor Augustus (see fig. 6–12), he raises his arm in a conventional gesture of address to his troops. In a lucky error or twist of fate, this statue came mistakenly to be revered during the Middle Ages as a portrait of Constantine, the first Christian emperor. Consequently, it escaped being melted down, a fate that befell many other bronze statues from antiquity.

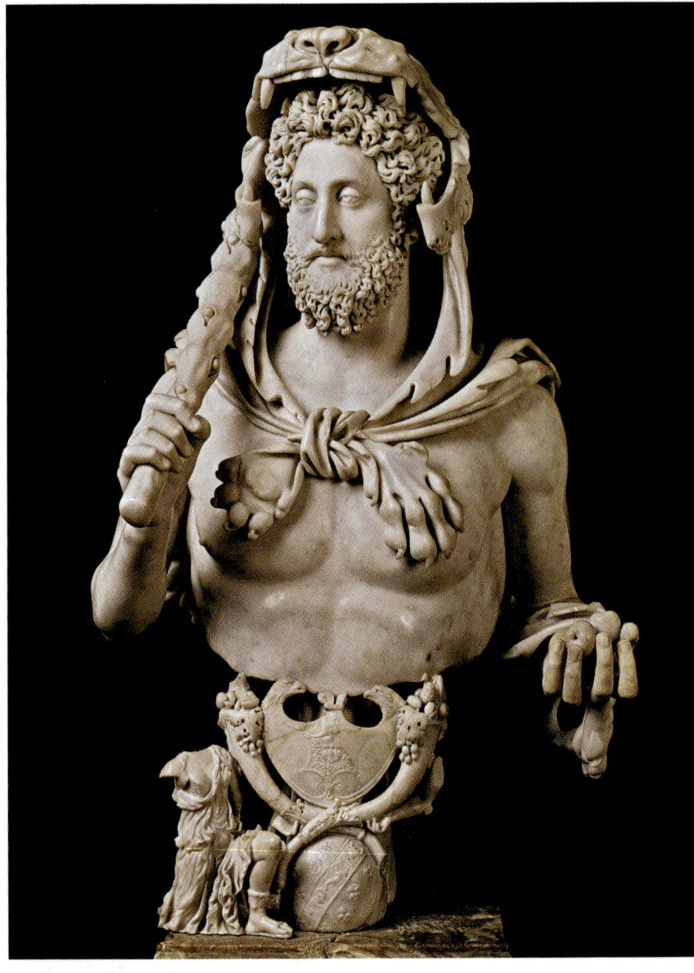

6–34 Commodus as Hercules, from the Esquiline Hill, Rome. c. 191–192 CE. Marble, height 46½" (118 cm). Palazzo dei Conservatori, Rome

Marcus Aurelius was succeeded by his son Commodus, a man without political skill, administrative competence, or intellectual distinction. During his unfortunate reign (180–192 CE), Commodus devoted himself to luxury and frivolous pursuits. He did, however, attract some of the finest artists of the day for his commissions. A marble bust of Commodus (fig. **6–34**) conveys the illusion of life and movement and emphasizes his family resemblance to his more illustrious and powerful father (see fig. 6–33), but it also captures its subject's vanity through the grand pretensions of his costume and the classical associations of his body type. The emperor is shown here in the guise of Hercules, adorned with references to the hero's legendary labors: his club, the skin and head of the Nemean Lion, and the golden apples from the gardens of the Hesperides (see fig. Intro–30).

The Late Empire

The reign of Commodus marked the beginning of a period of political and economic decline. During the rule of the succeeding Severan emperors (193–235 CE), migrating peoples from the north and east began to cross Rome's frontiers, disrupting provincial government. Imperial rule became increasingly autocratic, and soon the army controlled the government.

The anarchy of the mid-third century ended with the rise to power of the emperor Diocletian (ruled 284–305 CE). This brilliant politician and general reversed the empire's declining fortunes, but he also initiated an increasingly dictatorial government, eventually dividing the empire among four rulers known as the Tetrarchy. This political restructuring is paralleled by the introduction of a radically new, hard style of geometricized abstraction, especially notable in portraits of the tetrarchs themselves. A powerful porphyry bust of a tetrarch, startlingly alert with searing eyes (fig. **6–35**), embodies this stylistic shift toward the antithesis of the suave classicism seen in the portrait of Commodus as Hercules (see fig. 6–34). There is no clear sense of likeness. Who this individual is seems to be less significant than the powerful position he holds. Some art historians have interpreted this change in style as a conscious embodiment of Diocletian's new concept of government, while others have pointed to parallels with the provincial art of Diocletian's Dalmatian homeland or with the Neoplatonic aesthetics of Plotinus, a third-century CE philosopher who was widely read in the late Roman world. In any event, these riveting works represent not a degeneration of the classical tradition but its conscious replacement by a different aesthetic viewpoint.

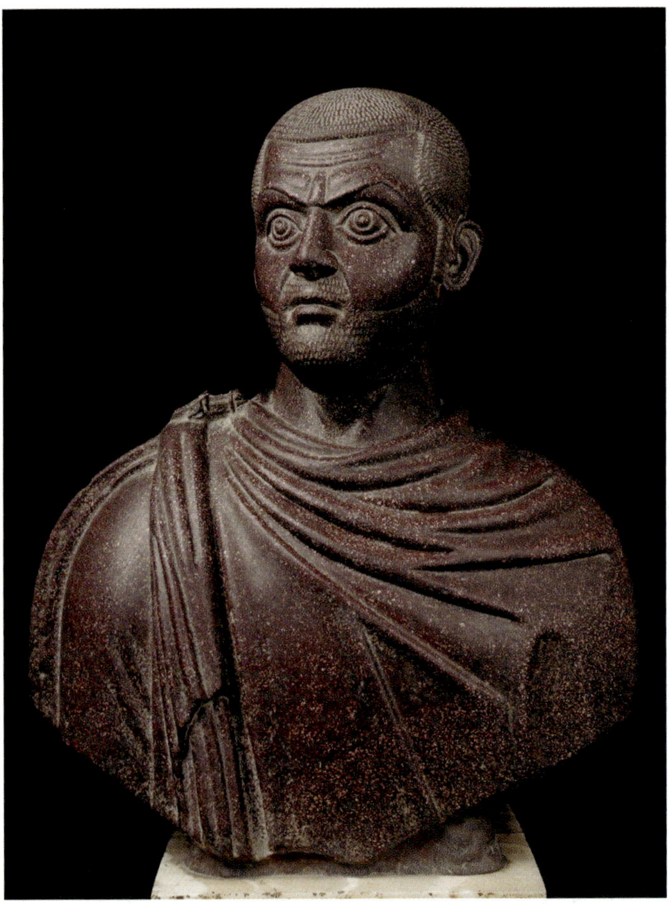

6–35 *Tetrarch* (Galerius?). Early 4th century CE. Porphyry, 2' 5½" (75 cm). Egyptian Museum, Cairo

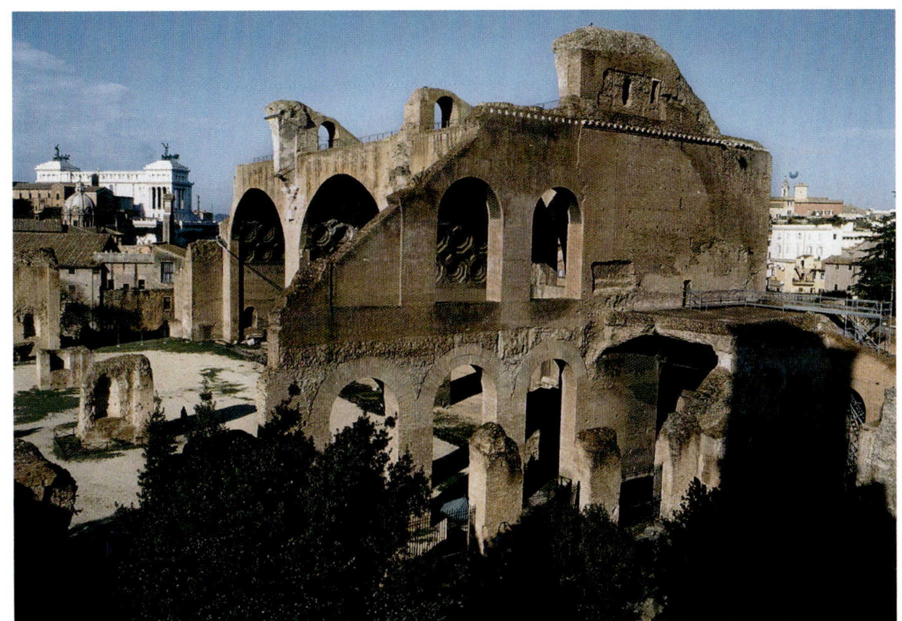

6–36 Basilica of Maxentius and Constantine, Rome. 306–313 CE

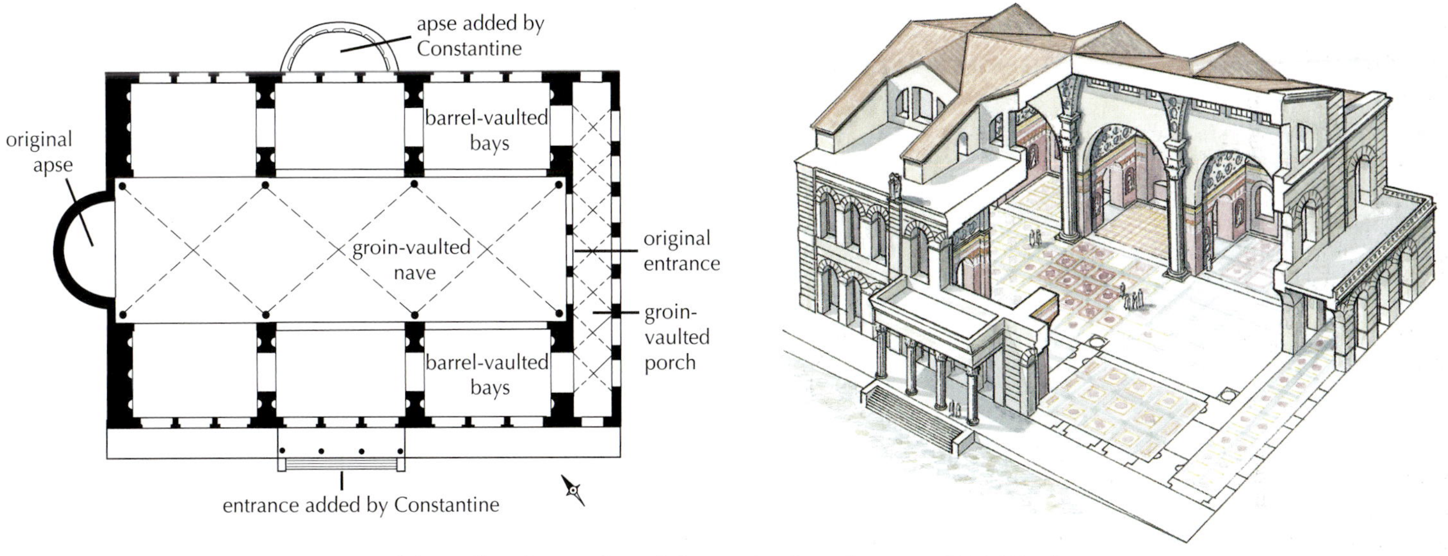

6–37 Plan and isometric reconstruction of the Basilica of Maxentius and Constantine, Rome (constructed 306–313 CE)

The orderly succession that Diocletian had hoped for failed to occur. After his own abdication and retirement in 305 CE, a struggle for position and advantage ensued almost immediately. Thereafter, two main contenders—both sons of tetrarchs—emerged in the western part of the empire: Maxentius, who controlled the Italian peninsula, and Constantine.

Although the city of Rome had declined in importance by this time, building did not end altogether. Maxentius (ruled 306–312 CE) ordered the repair of many buildings in Rome and had others built there during his short reign. His most impressive undertaking was a huge new basilica called the Basilica Nova, or New Basilica (figs. **6–36** and **6–37**). Now known as the Basilica of Maxentius and Constantine (whose architects modified and completed it), this was the last important imperial government building erected in Rome itself. It functioned as an administrative center and provided a magnificent setting for the emperor when he appeared as supreme judge. Three gigantic brick-and-concrete barrel vaults from a side aisle still loom over the streets of modern Rome (fig. 6–36). The central hall was covered with huge groin vaults (see "Arch and Vault," page 145) buttressed by the barrel vaults of the side aisles. Such strong support for the central groin vaults allowed the opening of generous windows in the clerestory. A groin-vaulted porch extended across one short side sheltering a triple entrance to the central hall. At the opposite end an apse acted as a focal point for the interior. The directional focus along a longitudinal axis from the entrance to the apse emphasized the presence of the emperor, or at least his statue. A monumental portrait of Constantine, found in the basilica, served as a stand-in for the emperor and a powerful

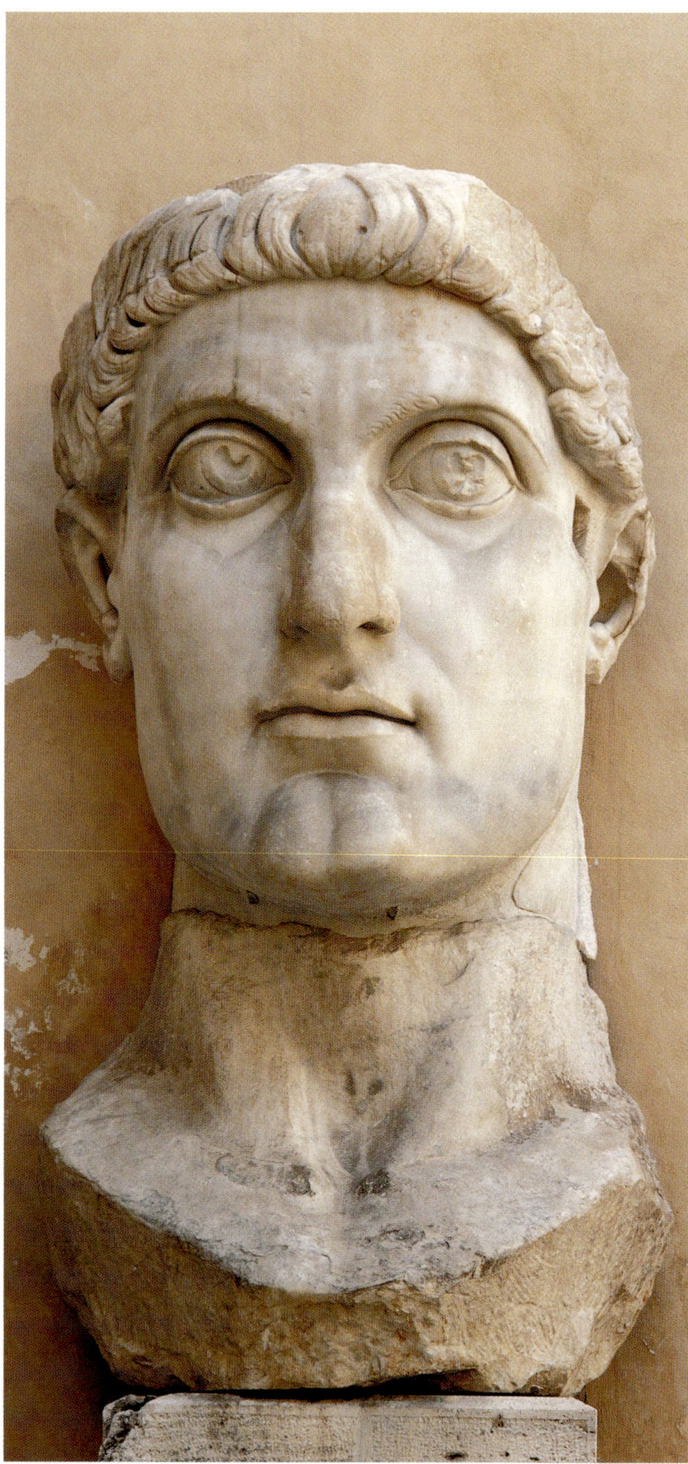

6–38 Constantine the Great, from the Basilica of Maxentius and Constantine, Rome. 325–326 CE. Marble, height of head 8' 6" (2.6 m). Palazzo dei Conservatori, Rome

This fragment came from a statue of the seated emperor. The original sculpture combined marble and probably bronze supported on a core of wood and bricks. Only a few marble fragments survive—the head, a hand, a knee, an elbow, and a foot. The body might have been made either of colored stone or of a scaffold of wood and bricks sheathed in bronze. The complete statue must have been awe-inspiring. Constantine was a master of the use of portrait statues to spread imperial propaganda.

reminder of his imperial power when he himself was unable to be present (fig. **6–38**).

After defeating Maxentius at the Battle of the Milvian Bridge in 312 CE, Constantine became sole ruler in the west (306–337). According to tradition, Constantine had a vision the night before the battle in which he saw a flaming cross in the sky bearing these words: "In this sign you shall conquer" (*in hoc signo vinces*). The next morning he ordered that his army's shields and standards be inscribed with the monogram XP (the Greek letters *chi* and *rho* for *Christos* or Christ, but also an abbreviation of the Greek word *chrestos*, meaning auspicious), and they won the battle. In 313 CE, Constantine issued the Edict of Milan granting freedom to all religious groups, including Christians.

A complex triumphal arch was constructed in Rome to commemorate Constantine's defeat of Maxentius. This memorial, placed next to the Colosseum, took the form of a huge triple arch (fig. **6–39**) that dwarfs the nearby Arch of Titus (see fig. 6–23). Three barrel-vaulted passageways are flanked by columns on high pedestals and surmounted by a large attic story bearing a laudatory inscription indicating that the arch was dedicated to Constantine by the Senate and the Roman people. Some of the sculpture decorating the arch came from other monuments made for Constantine's illustrious predecessors, the "good emperors" Trajan, Hadrian, and Marcus Aurelius. The reused items in effect transferred to Constantine the virtues of strength, courage, and piety associated with these earlier emperors. New reliefs made for the arch recount the story of Constantine's victory and remind viewers of his power and generosity. A rectangular panel above one arch (below the two roundels; fig. **6–40**) depicts Constantine's first public speech after defeating Maxentius. Toward the center of the panel, the emperor (his head is missing) stands on a temporary speaker's platform. He is flanked by standing officials and seated statues of Marcus Aurelius and Hadrian. In the background, the Basilica Julia and the Arch of Tiberius are to the left and the Arch of Septimius Severus is to the right, identifying the site of the speech as the Republican Forum.

Although the new reliefs reflect the long-standing Roman fondness for depicting important events with recognizable detail, in style and subject matter they contrast with the reused elements in the arch in their faithfulness to the avant-garde tetrarchic style. The forceful, blocky, mostly frontal figures, are compressed into the foreground plane. The participants below the standing Constantine almost congeal into a uniformly patterned mass that isolates "the new Augustus" and connects him visually with the seated statues of his illustrious predecessors on pedestals to each side. This two-dimensional, hierarchical approach, with its emphasis on authority and power rather than on individualized outward form, was among the styles adopted by the emerging Christian Church.

After 324 CE, Constantine—who had earned the epithet "the Great"—ruled as sole Roman emperor of the reunited empire until his death in 337. He made the port city of Byzantium the new capital and renamed it Constantinople (modern Istanbul, Turkey). After Constantinople was dedicated in 330, Rome, which had already ceased to be the seat of government in the west, further declined in importance.

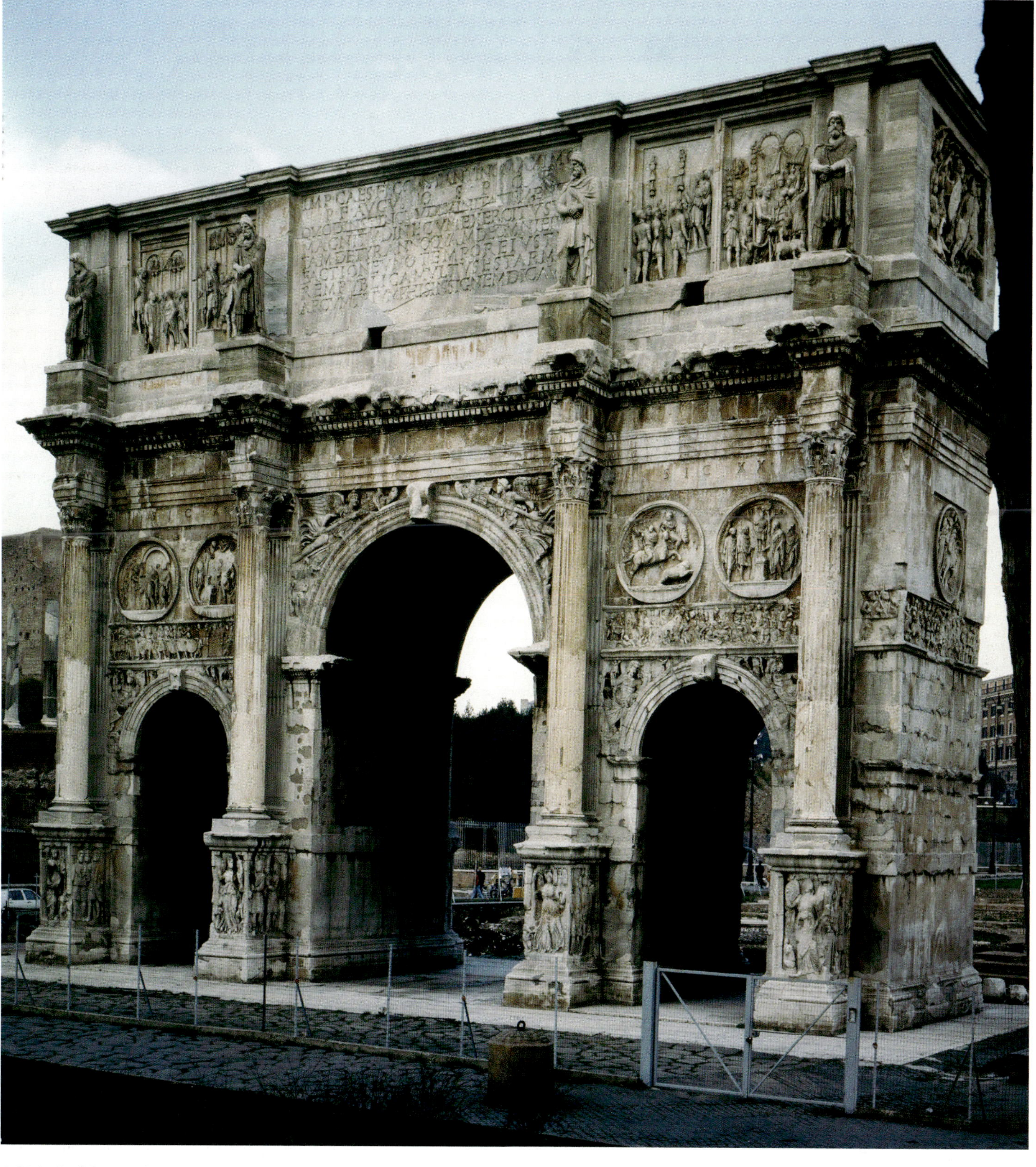

6–39 Arch of Constantine, Rome. 312–315 CE (dedicated July 25, 315 CE)

This massive, triple-arched monument to Emperor Constantine's victory over Maxentius in 312 CE *is a wonder of recycled sculpture. On the attic story, flanking the inscription over the central arch, are relief panels taken from a monument celebrating the victory of Marcus Aurelius over the Germans in 174* CE*. On the attached piers framing these panels are large statues of prisoners made to celebrate Trajan's victory over the Dacians in the early second century* CE*. On the inner walls of the central arch are reliefs also commemorating Trajan's conquest of Dacia. Over each of the side arches are pairs of giant roundels taken from a monument to Hadrian. The rest of the decoration is contemporary with the arch.*

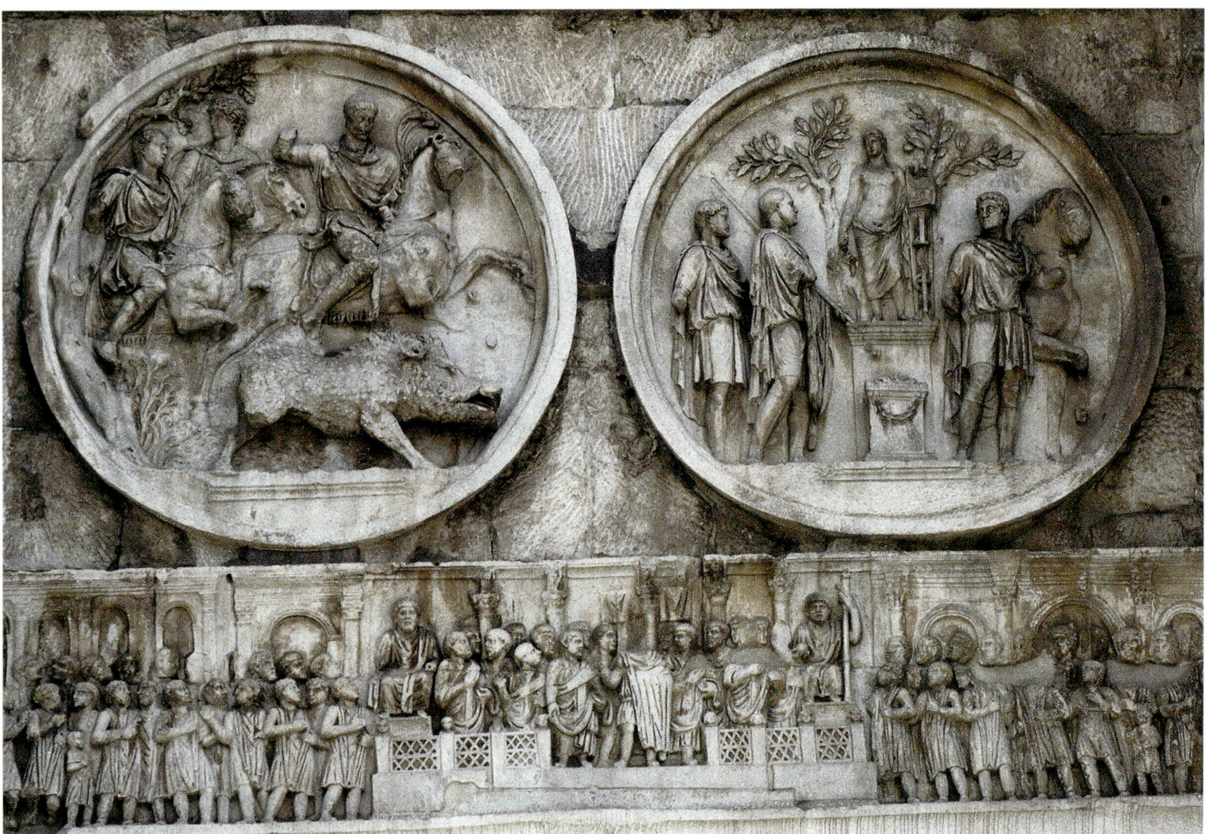

6–40 ***Hadrian Hunting Boar and Sacrificing to Apollo.*** Two roundels made c. 130–138 CE for a monument to Hadrian and reused on the Arch of Constantine. Marble, diameter 40" (102 cm); ***Constantine Addressing the Roman People in the Roman Forum.*** Arch of Constantine, Rome. 312–315 CE. Marble

The two circular reliefs were originally part of a lost monument erected by the emperor Hadrian (ruled 117–138 CE). The boar hunt demonstrates his courage and physical prowess, and his sacrificial offering to Apollo shows his piety and gratitude to the gods for their support. The classicizing heads, form-enhancing drapery, and graceful poses of the figures betray a debt to the style of late classical Greek art. In the fourth century CE, Constantine had these roundels removed from the Hadrianic monument, had Hadrian's head recarved with his own or his father's features, and incorporated them into his own triumphal arch (fig. 6–39) so that the power and piety of this predecessor could reflect on him and his reign. In a strip of relief underneath the roundels, sculptors from his own time portrayed a ceremony performed by Constantine during his celebration of the victory over this rival, Maxentius, at the Battle of the Milvian Bridge (312 CE). Rather than the Hellenizing mode popular during Hadrian's reign, the Constantinian sculptors employ the blocky and abstract stylizations that were fashionable during the Tetrarchy.

Looking Back

The ancient Romans conquered and ruled a vast territory around the Mediterranean Sea. As the empire absorbed the peoples it conquered, it imposed on them a legal, administrative, and cultural structure that endured for centuries and left a lasting mark on the civilizations that later emerged in Europe and surrounding regions.

As sophisticated visual propaganda, Roman art served the state and imperial authority. Creating both official images and representations of private individuals, Roman sculptors developed portraiture as a major art form. They also recorded contemporary historical events on commemorative arches, columns, and mausoleums erected in public places. But one of the greatest achievements of Roman culture was architectural: the development and exploitation of concrete as a building material. In contrast to stone, the components of concrete are cheap, light, and easily transported, and its use requires a large, but only semiskilled, workforce directed by a few trained and experienced supervisors following the plans of gifted designers. The use of concrete allowed ancient builders to move beyond the limitations of post-and-lintel architecture and enclose soaring architectural spaces with vast arching vaults.

Drawing artistic inspiration from their Etruscan and Greek predecessors and combining this with their own ambitiousness and creativity, Roman artists and architects created works that established enduring models of excellence in the West. And as Roman authority gave way to local rule, the newly powerful "barbarian" tribes continued to appreciate and even treasure the Classical learning and artistic innovations that the Romans left behind. It is the basis for the art of the Middle Ages; it will be "revived" during the Italian Renaissance; and we still draw on it heavily today.

IN PERSPECTIVE

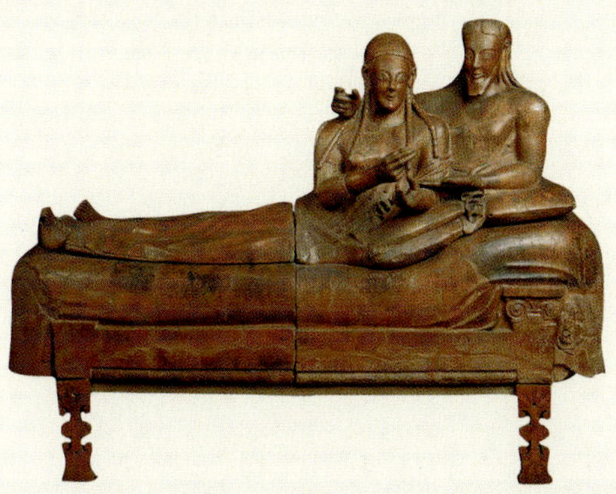

SARCOPHAGUS FROM CERVETERI,
C. 520 BCE

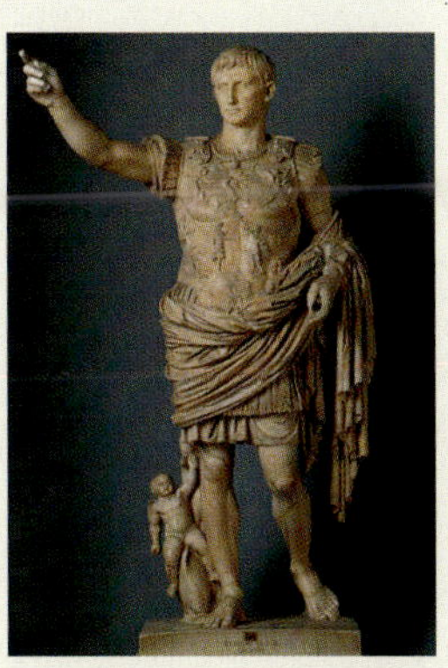

AUGUSTUS OF PRIMAPORTA,
EARLY 1ST CENTURY CE

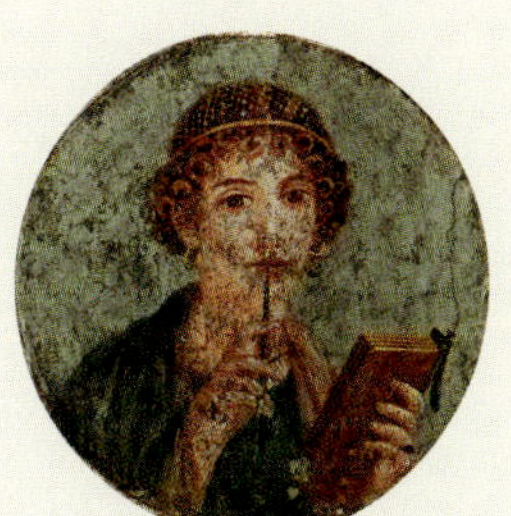

YOUNG WOMAN WRITING,
LATE 1ST CENTURY CE

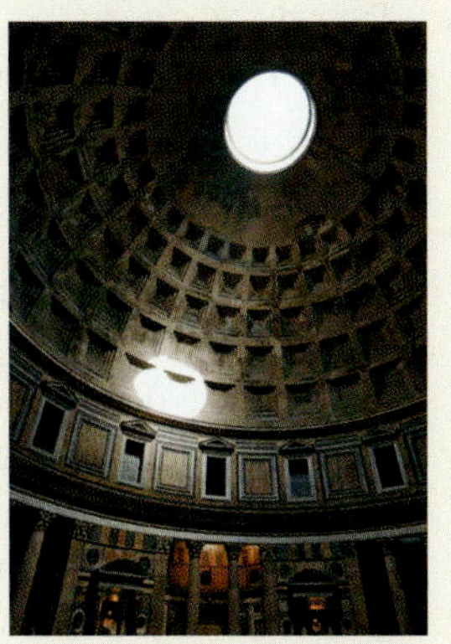

DOME OF THE PANTHEON,
118–128 CE

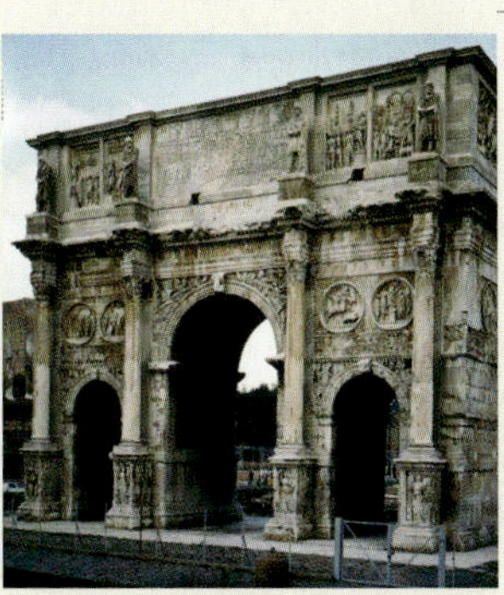

ARCH OF CONSTANTINE,
312–315 CE

700 BCE

- **Etruscan Supremacy,** c. 700–509 BCE

500

- **Persian Empire,** 549–330 BCE
- **Roman Republic,** 509–27 BCE
- **Classical Greek Culture,** 479–323 BCE
- **Conclusion of Peloponnesian War,** 404 BCE

300

100

- **Julius Caesar Assassinated,** 44 BCE
- **Roman Empire,** 27 BCE–395 CE
- **Emperor Augustus,** ruled 27 BCE–14 CE
- **Emperor Nero,** ruled 54–68 CE
- **Flavian Dynasty,** 69–96 CE
- **Titus' conquest of Jerusalem,** 70 CE
- **Eruption of Mount Vesuvius that buried Pompeii,** 79 CE

100 CE

- **Emperor Trajan,** ruled 98–117 CE
- **Emperor Hadrian,** ruled 117–138 CE
- **Emperor Marcus Aurelius,** ruled 161–180 CE
- **Diocletian establishes the Tetrarchy,** 284 CE

300

- **Emperor Constantine,** ruled 306–337 CE
- **Battle of Milvian Bridge,** 312 CE
- **Dedication of Constantinople as eastern Capital,** 330 CE

400

- **Division of Empire,** 395 CE

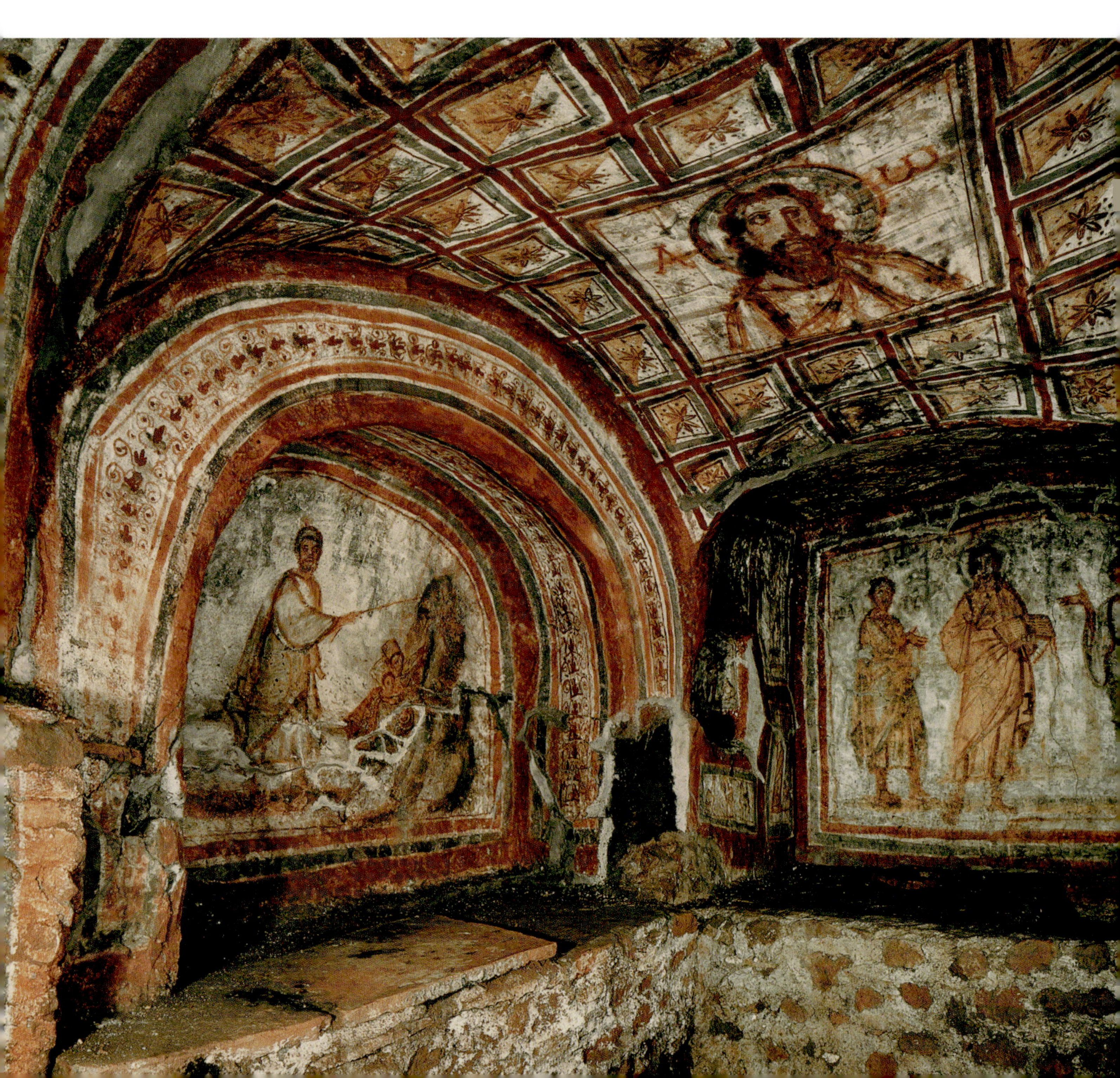

7 Jewish, Early Christian, and Byzantine Art

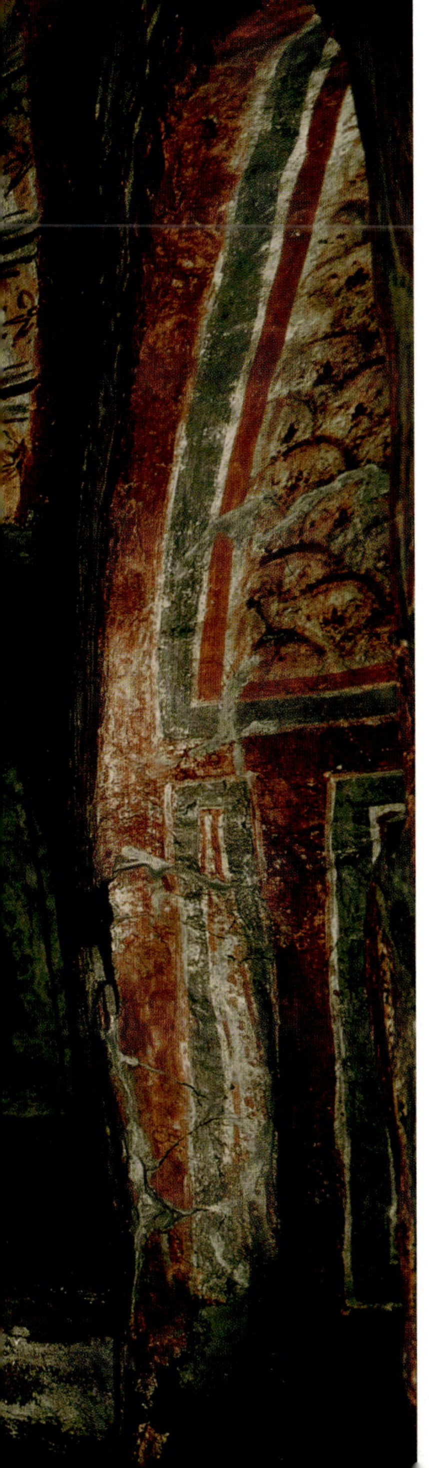

LOOKING FORWARD

In this Roman catacomb painting, Saint Peter, like Moses before him, strikes a rock and water flows from it (fig. **7–1**, scene at left). Imprisoned in Rome at the end of his missionary journeys, Peter converted his fellow prisoners and jailers to Christianity, but he needed water with which to baptize them. Miraculously a spring gushed forth at the touch of his staff. In spite of his all too human frailty, Peter became the rock (Greek *petros*) on which Jesus founded the Church. He was the first bishop of Rome, considered the predecessor of today's pope. In the niche to the right, two early Roman Christian martyrs flank a youthful, beardless Jesus, who holds a book emphasizing his role as teacher. By including Peter and Roman martyrs in the chamber's decoration, the early Christians, who dug this catacomb as a place to bury their dead, may have sought to emphasize the importance of their own city in Christian history.

In the star-studded heavens painted above, floats the face of Christ, flanked by the first and last letters of the Greek alphabet, alpha and omega. Here he takes on the guise not of a youthful teacher but of a Greek philosopher, with long beard and hair. The **halo** (circle) around his head indicates his divinity.

In these catacomb paintings, we see two of the major directions of Christian art: the narrative and the iconic. The **narrative image** recounts an event drawn from Saint Peter's life—striking the rock for water—which evokes the establishment of the Church as well as the essential Christian rite of baptism. The **iconic image**—Christ's face flanked by alpha and omega—offers a tangible expression of an intangible concept. The letters signify the beginning and end of time, and, combined with the image of Christ, symbolically represent not a story, but an idea: the everlasting significance and dominion of the heavenly Christ.

Throughout the history of Christian art these two tendencies will be apparent—the narrative urge to tell a good story, whose moral implications often have instructional value, and the desire to create iconic images that symbolize the core concepts and values of the developing religious tradition. In both cases, the works of art take on meaning only in relation to viewers' stored knowledge of Christian stories and beliefs.

7–1 Cubiculum of Leonis, Catacomb of Commodilla, near Rome. Late 4th century

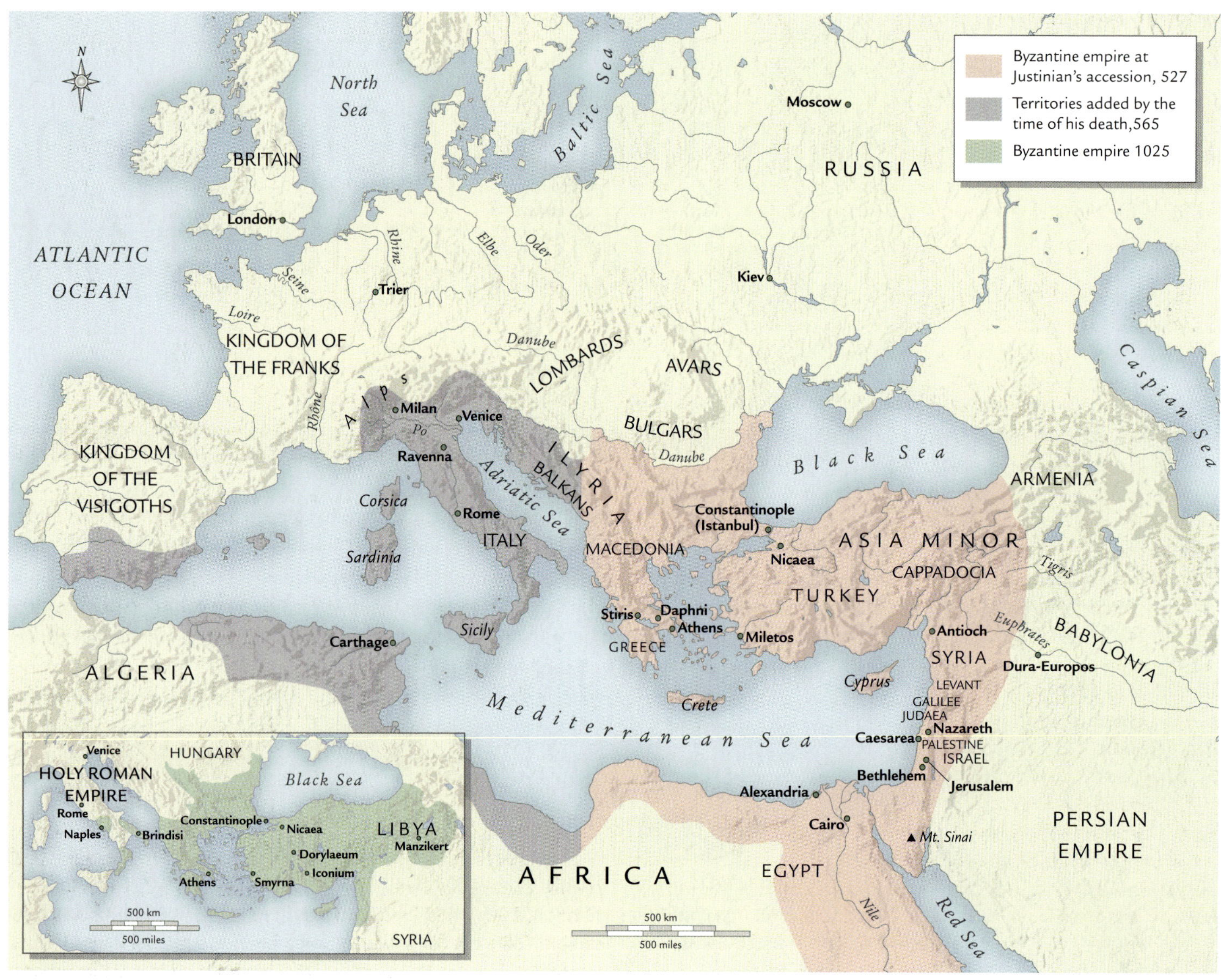

Map 7–1 The Late Roman and Byzantine World

Three religions that arose in the Near East and flourished across the Mediterranean Roman world (see map **7–1**) continue to inspire spiritual life of those in the Western world today: Judaism and Christianity, discussed in this chapter, and Islam, treated in Chapter 8. All three religions are monotheistic, meaning that their followers believe that only one god created and rules the universe. They are known as "religions of the book" because they have written records of God's will and words: the Hebrew Bible; the Christian Bible, which includes both the Hebrew Bible as its "Old Testament" and the Christian New Testament; and the Muslim Qur'an (or Koran), the word of God (Allah) revealed through the angel Gabriel to the Prophet Muhammad. Each religion builds on the beliefs and traditions of the earlier one. Traditional Jews believe that God made a covenant, or pact, with their ancestors and that they are God's chosen people. They await the coming of a savior, the Messiah, "the anointed one." Traditional Christians maintain that Jesus of Nazareth was that Messiah (the title "Christ" is derived from a Greek word meaning "Messiah"). They believe that in Jesus God took human form, preached among men and women, was put to death on a cross, and then rose from the dead and ascended into heaven, having established the Christian Church under the leadership of the apostles (his closest disciples). The followers of Islam, called Muslims, while accepting the Hebrew prophets and Jesus as divinely inspired, believe Muhammad to be Allah's last and greatest prophet, through whom Islam was revealed some six centuries after Jesus's earthly lifetime.

Jewish, Christian, and Muslim art combine in varying degrees Greek, Roman, and Near Eastern themes and forms. Jews and Christians embody in the visual arts their foundational stories and create visual symbols to signify their core beliefs, using both narrative and iconic imagery for the ornamental enrichment of sacred buildings and books. Muslims also decorate buildings and books with ornamental forms and abstract styles but prefer to convey religious meaning through the artistic enhancement of words rather than through figural images.

Jewish Art

The Jewish people trace their ancestry to a Semitic people called the Hebrews, who lived in the land of Canaan. Canaan, known from the second century CE by the Roman name of Palestine, was located between the Mediterranean Sea and the Jordan River. According to the Torah (the first five books of the Hebrew Scriptures), God promised the patriarch Abraham that Canaan would be a homeland for the Jewish people (Genesis 17:8), a belief that remains important among Jews to this day.

Jewish settlement of Canaan probably began sometime in the second millennium BCE. According to Exodus, the second book of the Torah, the prophet Moses led the Hebrews out of slavery in Egypt to the promised land of Canaan. At one crucial point during the journey, Moses climbed alone to the top of Mount Sinai, where God gave him the Ten Commandments, the cornerstone of Jewish law. These commandments, inscribed on tablets, were kept in a gold-covered wooden box, the Ark of the Covenant.

In the tenth century BCE, King Solomon built a temple in Jerusalem to house the Ark of the Covenant. The Temple consisted of courtyards, a porch, a hall, and the holy of holies housing the Ark with its guardian **cherubim** (high-ranking angels closely associated with God). Solomon sent to nearby Phoenicia for cedar, cypress, and sandalwood, and for a master craftsman to supervise the Temple's construction (II Chronicles 2:3–16). The Temple was the spiritual center of Jewish life.

In 586 BCE, the Neo-Babylonians, under King Nebuchadnezzar II, conquered Jerusalem (see Chapter 2). They destroyed the Temple, exiled the Jews, and carried off the Ark of the Covenant. When Cyrus the Great of Persia conquered Babylonia in 538 BCE, the Jews were permitted to return to Jerusalem and build the Second Temple, but from that time forward, Canaan existed primarily under foreign rule and eventually became part of the Roman Empire. In 70 CE Roman forces led by the future emperor, Titus, destroyed the Second Temple and Jerusalem (see fig. 6–24).

Jews continued to live in dispersed communities throughout the Roman Empire. Most of the earliest surviving examples of Jewish art date from the Hellenistic and Roman periods. Six Jewish **catacombs**, or underground burial chambers, were discovered just outside the city of Rome and had been in use from the first to the fourth century CE. They display wall paintings with Jewish themes. In one example, from the third century CE, two **menorahs**, or seven-branched lamps, flank the long-lost Ark of the Covenant (fig. **7–2**). The conspicuous representation on the Arch of Titus of the menorah looted from the Second Temple in Jerusalem kept the memory of these treasures alive in Rome. The menorah form probably derives from the ancient Near Eastern Tree of Life, symbolizing both the end of exile and the paradise to come.

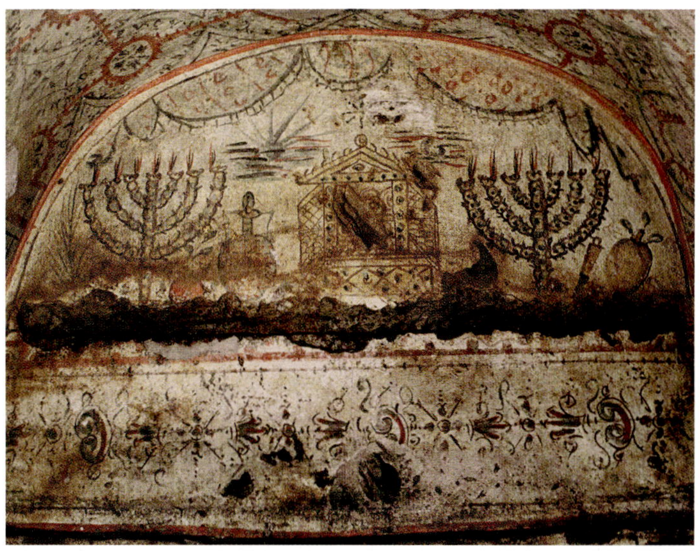

7–2 *Menorahs and Ark of the Covenant*, wall painting in a Jewish catacomb, Villa Torlonia, Rome. 3rd century. 3' 11" × 5' 9" (1.19 × 1.8 m)

Judaism has long emphasized religious learning. Jews gather in synagogues for study and worship; a synagogue can be any large room where the Torah scrolls are kept and read publicly. The destroyed Temple in Jerusalem had been a special, central holy place for all Jews, but synagogues could be constructed in any Jewish community. Some Jewish places of worship were located in private homes or in buildings originally constructed as homes. Far less Jewish art than Christian or Islamic art has survived, but a number of synagogues have been discovered or excavated. Their architecture and ornament reflect late Roman artistic traditions but incorporate specifically Jewish symbols.

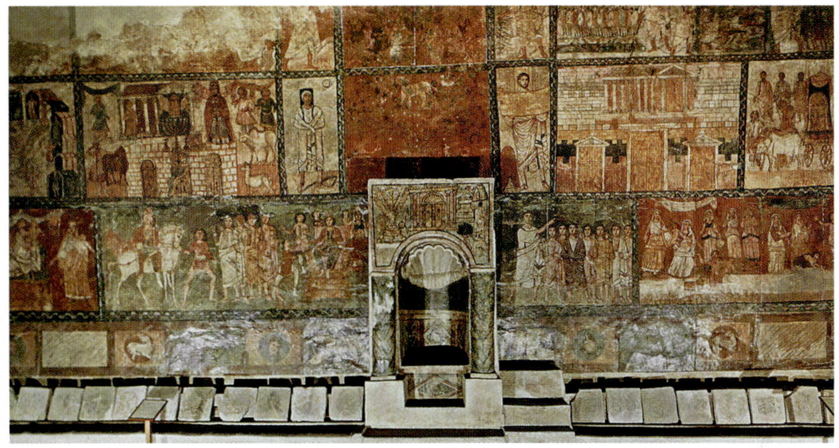

7–3 Wall with Torah niche, from a house-synagogue, Dura-Europos, Syria. 244–245. Tempera on plaster. Reconstructed in the National Museum, Damascus, Syria

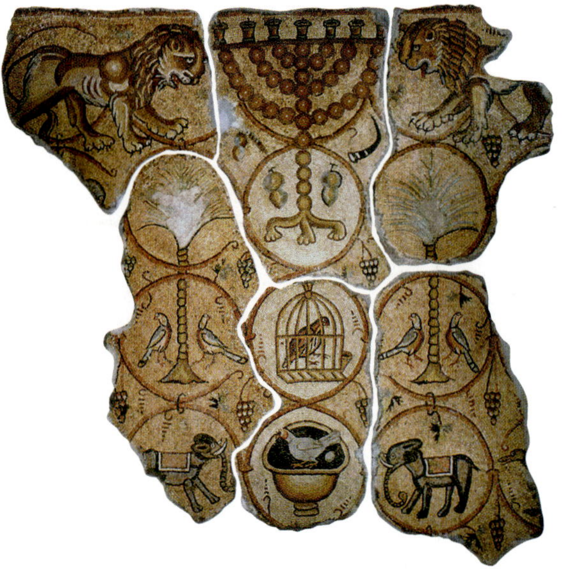

7–4 Synagogue floor, Maon (Menois). c. 530. Mosaic. The Israel Museum, Jerusalem

In the Roman city of Dura-Europos, in modern Syria, excavators discovered a Jewish house-synagogue, or synagogue built within a private home (see also "Closer Look," page 172). The first Dura-Europos synagogue consisted of an assembly hall, a separate alcove for women, and a courtyard. After a remodeling of the building, completed in 244–245 CE, men and women shared the hall, and residential rooms were added. Two architectural features distinguished the assembly hall: a bench along its walls and a niche for the Torah scrolls (fig. **7–3**). Scenes from Jewish history cover the walls. The story of Moses unfolds in a continuous narrative around the room, employing the Roman tradition of epic historical representation. The frontal poses, strong outlines, and flat colors are pictorial devices associated with Near Eastern art.

Jews also built synagogues designed on the model of the ancient Roman basilica. A typical basilica synagogue had a central nave with aisles; a semicircular apse in the wall facing in the direction of Jerusalem; and perhaps an atrium (courtyard) and a porch, or narthex. A Torah was kept in a shrine in the apse.

Synagogues contained almost no representational sculpture in conformance with Jewish law forbidding the creation or veneration of graven images. Paintings and mosaics, on the other hand, often decorated walls and floors. A fragment of a mosaic floor (fig. **7–4**) from a sixth-century synagogue at Maon (in Gaza) features traditional Jewish symbols along with a variety of stylized plants, birds, and animals. Two lions of Judah flank a menorah. Beside it is a *shofar*, or ram's horn, blown on ceremonial occasions, and three gourd-shaped *etrogs*, or citrons, used to celebrate the harvest festival of Sukkot. The *etrog* symbolizes the bounty of the earth and the unity of all Jews. Two palm trees refer to another Sukkot emblem, the *lulav*, a sheaf of palm, myrtle, and willow branches. The variety of placid birds and elephants may symbolize the universal peace as prophesied by Isaiah (11:6–9 and 65:25). The pairing of images to either side of a central element, such as the birds flanking the palm trees or the lions facing the menorah, is a characteristic motif of Near Eastern art. But the stylized grapevine that forms circular medallions to frame the images derives from the Greco-Roman tradition.

In 395, the Roman Empire split permanently in two, becoming the Western (Roman) Empire, which collapsed in 476, and the Eastern, or Byzantine, Empire, which lasted until 1453, when it fell to the Ottoman Turks. By this time most Jews lived outside Palestine, in communities spread across the Near East, North Africa, and Europe. Because their religious practice set them apart, and their numbers made them a minority, they faced special taxes, restrictions on the occupations they could enter, and sometimes violent persecution. The history of Jewish art is fragmented because many artworks were destroyed when Jewish homes and synagogues were attacked and burned. The artworks that survive reflect the interplay of many styles, centuries, and regions.

Early Christianity

Christianity began with the life and teachings of Jesus of Nazareth, a Jew born sometime between 8 and 4 BCE and crucified at age 33. Early Christians believed that Jesus was the Son of God, born in a human body to a virgin woman, Mary, and resurrected after death. Christian doctrine proclaimed one God manifest in three Persons, a Trinity of Father (God), Son (Jesus Christ), and Holy Spirit. In later years Christians also began to acknowledge saints—devout individuals connected with verifiable miracles and canonized, or officially honored, by the Church for upholding and practicing Christian beliefs, often at the cost of martyrdom (execution). Worshipers may ask saints to intercede for them with God, but saints are not worshiped as gods in their own right.

The Christian New Testament describes the life of Jesus in its first four books, known as the Gospels (the Good News). The Gospels relate that Jesus was a descendant of the Jewish royal house of King David and that he was born in Bethlehem in Judaea, where his mother, Mary, and her husband, Joseph, had gone to be registered in the Roman census. He grew up in Nazareth in Galilee, where Joseph was a carpenter. At age 30, Jesus began his public ministry, gathering about him a group of disciples, male and female followers. He performed miracles of healing and preached love for God and neighbor, the sanctity of social justice, the forgiveness of sins, and the promise of life after death. From his followers, he chose 12 apostles to carry on his work after his crucifixion and resurrection.

Jesus limited his ministry primarily to Jews; it was his apostles—including Paul, a later addition to the group—who took Jesus' teachings to non-Jews. Despite persecution, Christianity persisted and spread throughout the Roman Empire. The Roman emperor Constantine (see Chapter 6) permitted the Christians freedom of worship with the Edict of Milan in 313 CE. By the end of the fourth century, Christianity had become the official religion of the empire and non-Christians became the targets of persecution.

Throughout the Roman Empire, even before their religion was recognized, Christians met in private houses for worship. In Rome itself, they also excavated underground cemeteries, or catacombs, consisting of narrow passages and small burial chambers lined with rectangular burial niches (see fig. 7–1). These niches were filled with stone sarcophagi or sealed with tiles or stone slabs. The painted walls and ceilings of such catacombs provide some of the earliest

THE LIFE OF JESUS

Episodes from the life of Jesus as recounted in the Gospels form the principal subject matter of Christian visual art. What follows is a list of main events in his life with parenthetical references to figures within this book reproducing works of art that visualize them.

INCARNATION AND CHILDHOOD OF JESUS

Annunciation: The archangel Gabriel informs the Virgin Mary that God has chosen her to bear his son. A dove often represents the *Incarnation*, her miraculous conception of Jesus through the Holy Spirit. (10–15, 11–13, 11–16, 11–23, 12–4, 12–5, 12–27)

Visitation: The pregnant Mary visits her older cousin Elizabeth, pregnant with the future Saint John the Baptist. (11–13)

Nativity: Jesus is born in Bethlehem. The Holy Family—Jesus, Mary, and her husband, Joseph—is usually portrayed in a stable, or, in Byzantine art, a cave. (7–26, 10–15, 12–8)

Annunciation to and Adoration of the Shepherds: Angels announce Jesus' birth to shepherds, who hurry to Bethlehem to honor him. (12–8)

Adoration of the Magi: Wise men from the East follow a bright star to Bethlehem to honor Jesus as King of the Jews, presenting him with precious gifts. Eventually these Magi became identified as three kings, often differentiated through facial type as young, middle-aged, and old. (10–15, 11–23)

Presentation in the Temple: Mary and Joseph bring the infant Jesus to the Temple in Jerusalem, where he is presented to the high priest. (10–15)

Flight into Egypt: An angel warns Joseph that King Herod, to eliminate the threat of a newborn rival king, plans to murder all male babies in Bethlehem. The Holy Family flees to Egypt. (10–27, 11–4)

JESUS' MINISTRY

Baptism: At age 30, Jesus is baptized by John the Baptist in the Jordan River. He sees the Holy Spirit and hears a heavenly voice proclaiming him God's son.

Marriage at Cana: At his mother's request Jesus turns water into wine at a wedding feast, his first public miracle. (11–33)

Miracles of Healing: Jesus performs miracles of healing the blind, possessed (mentally ill), paralytic, and lepers; he also resurrects the dead.

Miraculous Draft of Fishes: At Jesus' command, Peter lowers the nets and catches so many fish that James and John have to help bring them into the boat. (13–7)

Calling of Levi/Matthew: Jesus calls to Levi, a tax collector, "Follow me." Levi complies, becoming the disciple Matthew. (14–10)

Raising of Lazarus: Jesus brings his friend Lazarus back to life four days after death. (11–29, 11–33)

Transfiguration: Jesus reveals his divinity in a dazzling vision on Mount Tabor as his closest disciples—Peter, James, and John—look on.

Tribute Money: Challenged to pay the temple tax, Jesus sends Peter to catch a fish, which has the required coin in its mouth. (12–26)

JESUS' PASSION, DEATH, AND RESURRECTION

Entry into Jerusalem: Jesus, riding an ass and accompanied by his disciples, enters Jerusalem, while crowds honor him, spreading clothes and palm fronds in their path. (13–33)

Last Supper: During the Jewish Passover seder, Jesus reveals his impending death to his disciples. Instructing them to drink wine (his blood) and eat bread (his body) in remembrance of him, he lays the foundation for the Christian Eucharist (Mass). (Intro–21, 13–23, 13–33)

Washing the Disciples' Feet: At the Last Supper, Jesus washes the disciples' feet, setting an example of humility. (10–18)

Agony in the Garden: In the Garden of Gethsemane on the Mount of Olives, Jesus struggles between his human fear of pain and death and his divine strength to overcome them. The apostles sleep nearby, oblivious. (13–33)

Betrayal (Arrest): Judas Iscariot (a disciple) has accepted a bribe to betray Jesus to an armed band of his enemies by kissing him. (11–16)

Jesus Before Pilate: Jesus is taken to Pontius Pilate, Roman governor of Judaea, and charged with treason for calling himself King of the Jews. Pilate proposes freeing Jesus but is shouted down by the mob, which demands Jesus be crucified. Pilate washes his hands to signify that the blood of Jesus is not on his hands, but on the hands of the crowd. (10–15)

Crucifixion: Jesus is executed on a cross, often shown between two crucified criminals and accompanied by the Virgin Mary, John the Evangelist, Mary Magdalen, and other followers at the foot of the cross; Roman soldiers sometimes torment Jesus—one extending a sponge on a pole with vinegar instead of water for him to drink, another stabbing him in the side with a spear. A skull can identify the execution ground as Golgotha, "the place of the skull." (10–12, 10–15, 13–34, 14–23)

Descent from the Cross (Deposition): Jesus' followers take his body down from the cross. (12–6, 13–27)

Lamentation/Pietà: Jesus' sorrowful followers gather around his body to mourn. An image of the grieving Virgin alone with Jesus across her lap is known as a **pietà** (from Latin *pietas*, "pity"). (11–33, 13–34)

Resurrection: Three days after his entombment, Christ rises from the dead.

Descent into Limbo (Harrowing of Hell *or* Anastasis): The resurrected Jesus descends into limbo, or hell, to free deserving predecessors, among them Adam, Eve, David, and Moses. (7–28)

Holy Women at the Tomb: Christ's female followers—usually including Mary Magdalen and Mary the mother of the apostle James—discover his empty tomb. An angel announces Christ's resurrection. (10–15)

Noli Me Tangere ("Do Not Touch Me"): Christ appears to Mary Magdalen as she weeps at his tomb. When she reaches out to him, he warns her not to touch him. (10–15, 11–33, 13–30)

Ascension: Christ ascends to heaven from the Mount of Olives, disappearing in a cloud, while his apostles watch.

CLOSER LOOK

Our understanding of buildings used for worship by third-century Jews and Christians was greatly enhanced, even revolutionized, by the spectacular discoveries made in the 1930s while excavating the Roman military garrison and border town of Dura-Europos (in modern Syria). In 256, threatened by the Parthians attacking from the east, residents of Dura built a huge earthwork mound around their town in an attempt to protect themselves from the invading armies. In the process—since they were located on the city's margins right against its defensive stone wall—the houses used by Jews and Christians as places of worship were buried under the earthwork perimeter. In spite of this enhanced fortification, the Parthians conquered Dura-Europos. But since the victors never unearthed the submerged margins of the city, an intact Jewish house-synagogue and Christian house-church remained underground awaiting the explorations of modern archaeologists.

We have already seen the extensive strip narratives flanking the Torah shrine in the house-synagogue. The discovery of this expansive pictorial decoration contradicted a long-held scholarly belief that Jews of this period avoided figural decoration of any sort in conformity with Mosaic law (Exodus 20:4). And a few blocks down the street that ran along the city wall, a typical Roman house built around a central courtyard held another surprise. Only a discreet red cross above the door distinguished it from the other houses on its block, but the arrangement of the interior clearly documents its use as a Christian place of worship. A large assembly hall that could seat 60–70 people lies on one side of the courtyard, and across from it is a smaller but extensively decorated room with a water tank set aside for baptism, the central rite of Christian initiation (fig. **7–5**). Along the walls were scenes from Christ's miracles and a monumental portrayal of the women visiting his tomb about to discover his resurrection (below). Above the baptismal basin is a lunette (semicircular wall section) featuring the Good Shepherd with his flock, but also including at lower left diminutive figures of Adam and Eve covering themselves in shame after their sinful disobedience (fig. **7–6**). Even this early in Christian art, sacred spaces were decorated with pictures proclaiming the theological meaning of the rituals they housed. In this painting Adam and Eve's fall from grace is juxtaposed with a larger image of the Good Shepherd (representing Jesus) who came to earth to care for and guide his sheep (Christian believers) toward redemption and eternal life—a message especially appropriate juxtaposed with the rite of Christian baptism, which signaled the converts' passage from sin to salvation.

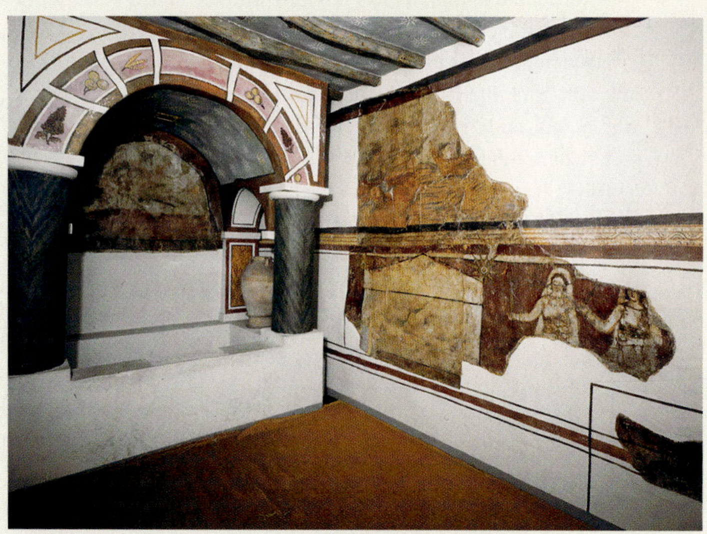

7–5 Model of walls and font, from the baptistry of a Christian house-church, Dura-Europos, Syria. Before 256. Fresco. Yale University Art Gallery, New Haven, Connecticut

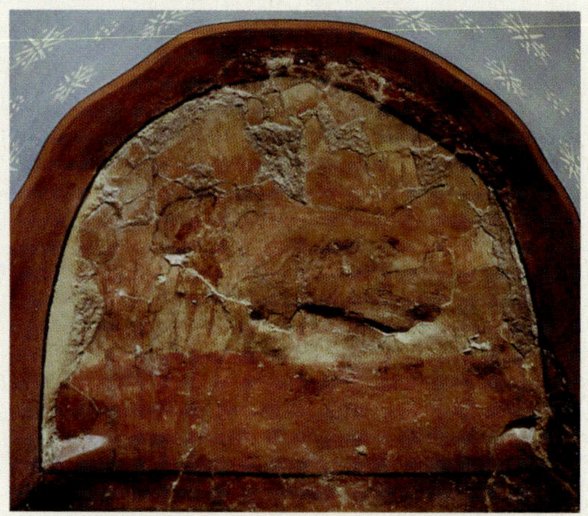

7–6 The Good Shepherd with Adam and Eve after the Fall, detail of wall painting in fig. 7–5

surviving examples of Christian art. By the fourth century, pictorial programs included narrative scenes, pictures of individuals, and iconic symbols. But even earlier paintings, from the middle of the third century, were discovered on the fringes of the empire in a house-church excavated at Dura-Europos (see "Closer Look," above), uncovered at the same time as the house-synagogue already discussed as an example of early Jewish narrative painting (see fig. 7–3).

Early Christian sculpture before the fourth century is even rarer than painting. What survives is mainly sarcophagi and small statues or reliefs, many of them featuring the Good Shepherd, a classical pagan motif associated with notions of the afterlife as a pastoral idyll that becomes an allegorical representation of Jesus for Christians familiar with their oral traditions or scriptural heritage (e.g., Luke 15:3–7; John 10:11–18). A remarkable set of small marble statues discovered in Asia Minor during the 1960s includes a sensitive carving of the Good Shepherd (fig. **7–7**) which must have been created for a Christian patron since it was found with sculptures portraying the life of Jonah, another very popular theme in Early Christian art.

The era of religious toleration, which began with the Edict of Milan and Constantine's active support of Christianity, spurred the building of Christian churches and shrines on a much larger scale. Constantine ordered a monumental basilica constructed at the place where Christians believed Saint Peter, the leader of the apostles, was buried. Peter (d. c. 64 CE) had led the first Christian community in Rome. As the city's first bishop (spiritual and administrative church leader), he was later recognized as the precursor of the popes (heads of the Christian Church in the West). The Constantinian Basilica of Saint Peter (called "Old" Saint Peter's because it was wantonly destroyed and replaced by a new building during the Renaissance) became the pope's church and came to signify his authority over all Christendom.

Old Saint Peter's (see "Longitudinal-Plan and Central-Plan Churches," page 174) included architectural elements arranged in a way that has characterized Christian basilica churches ever since it was built. **Transepts**—wings that intersected with the nave and aisles at a right angle—met the need for more space near the tomb of the saint, where a large number of clergy and pilgrims gathered for elaborate rituals. Christians believed that Saint Peter's bones lay beneath the high altar; indeed early Christian and pagan tombs did lie under the church, and the interior of the church itself initially served as a funerary space, with sarcophagi lined up along the aisles. Thus Old Saint Peter's served a variety of functions: as a burial place, as a pilgrimage shrine containing the relics of Saint Peter, and as a congregational church that could hold at least 14,000 worshipers. It remained the largest church in Christendom until the eleventh century.

Old Saint Peter's is gone, but some idea of a typical Early Christian basilica can be gained from the Roman Church of Santa Sabina. The interior, constructed by Peter of Illyria between 422 and 432, appears much as it did when first built (fig. **7–10**). The basic elements of the basilica church are clearly visible: a nave lit by clerestory (upper wall) windows, and side aisles that end in a rounded apse. Santa Sabina's interior displays a wealth of marble veneer and 24 fluted marble columns with Corinthian capitals reused from a second-century pagan building. The columns support arches creating a **nave arcade** (in contrast to Old Saint Peter's **nave colonnade**, with straight architrave rather than arcade). The **spandrels**, above the columns and between the arches are inlaid with marble images of the chalice (wine cup) and paten (bread plate)—the essential items for the **Eucharistic** (Mass or Holy Communion) rite that took place at the altar.

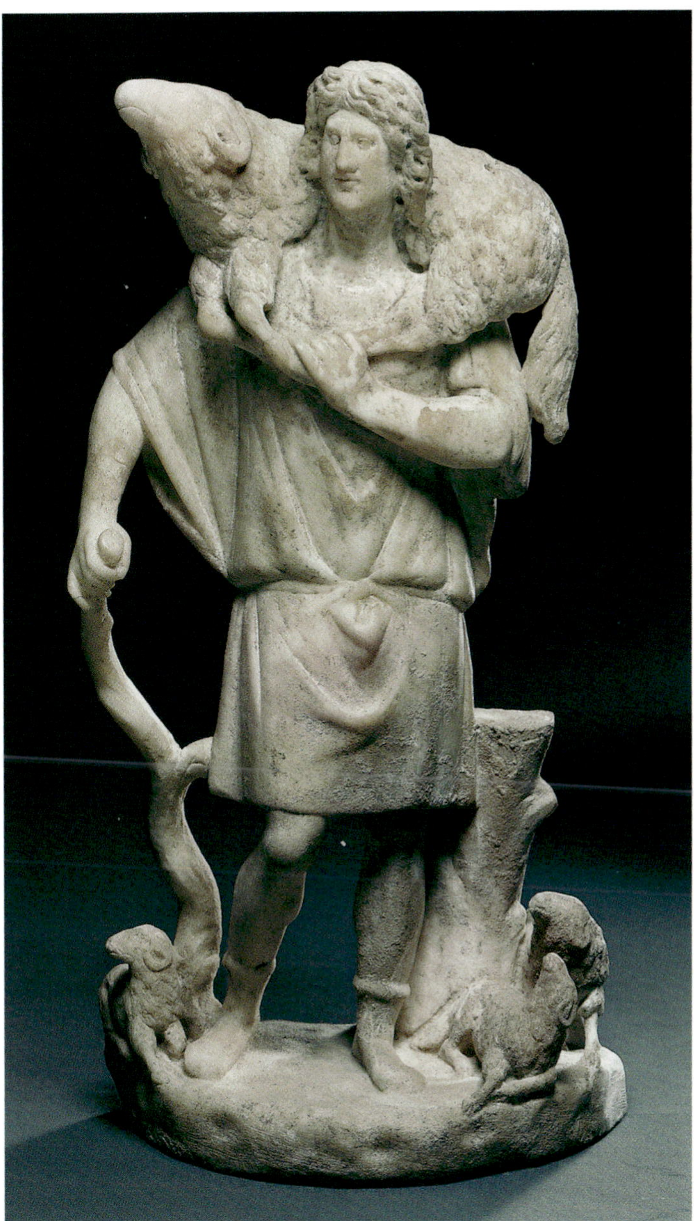

7–7 ***The Good Shepherd***, from Asia Minor (modern Turkey). c. 280–290. Marble, height 19¾" (50.2 cm), width 16" (15.9 cm). The Cleveland Museum of Art
JOHN L. SEVERANCE FUND (1965.241)

The beauty and richness of Early Christian church interiors can still be experienced in several fifth- and sixth-century buildings in Ravenna. By the fifth, Rome had lost its political, although not its spiritual, importance. The capital of the Western Roman Empire was moved to Milan in the late fourth century and then to Ravenna at the beginning of the fifth century. Ravenna offered direct access by sea to Constantinople, the capital of the Eastern (Byzantine) Roman Empire.

One of the earliest surviving Christian structures in Ravenna is a small, cross-shaped **oratory** (small chapel) once attached to the church of the imperial palace. It is named after the remarkable Galla Placidia, daughter of the Western Roman emperor, wife of a Gothic king, sister of Emperor Honorius, and mother of Emperor Valentinian. As regent for her son after 425, she ruled the Western

ELEMENTS OF **Architecture**

Longitudinal-Plan and Central-Plan Churches

The forms of early Christian buildings were based on two Roman prototypes: rectangular basilicas (see figs. 6–26, 6–37) and circular or squared structures, including rotundas like the Pantheon (see figs. 6–27, 6–28, 6–29). As in the basilica of Old Saint Peter's in Rome (fig. **7–8**), **longitudinal-plan** churches are characterized by a forecourt, the **atrium**, leading to an entrance porch, the **narthex**, which spans one of the building's short ends. Doorways—known collectively as the church's portals—lead from the narthex into a long, congregational area called a **nave**. Rows of columns separate the high-ceilinged nave from one or two lower **aisles** on either side. The nave can be lit by windows along its upper level just under the ceiling, called a **clerestory**, that rises above the side aisles' roofs. At the opposite end of the nave from the narthex is a semicircular projection, the **apse**. The apse functions as the building's focal point where the altar, raised on a platform, is located. Sometimes there is also a **transept**, a wing that crosses the nave in front of the apse, making the building T-shaped. When additional space (a liturgical choir) comes between the transept and the apse, the plan is known as a Latin cross.

Central-plan buildings were first used by Christians, like their pagan Roman forebears, as tombs. Central planning was also employed for baptistries (where Christians "died"—giving up their old life—and were reborn as believers) and for churches dedicated to martyrs (e.g., San Vitale, see fig. 7–16), often built directly over their tombs. Like basilicas, central-plan churches can have an atrium, a narthex, and an apse. But instead of the longitudinal axis of basilican churches, which draws worshipers forward along a line from the entrance toward the apse, central-plan buildings, such as the mausoleum of Constantina—rededicated in 1256 as the church of Santa Costanza (fig. **7–9**)—have a more vertical axis, from the center up through the dome, which may have functioned as a symbolic "vault of heaven."

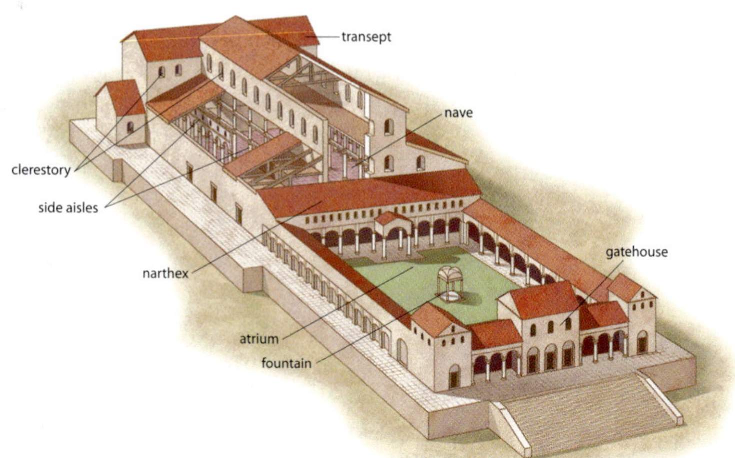

7–8 Reconstruction drawing and plan of Old Saint Peter's, Rome. c. 320–327; atrium added in later 4th century. Approx. 394' (120 m) long and 210' (64 m) wide

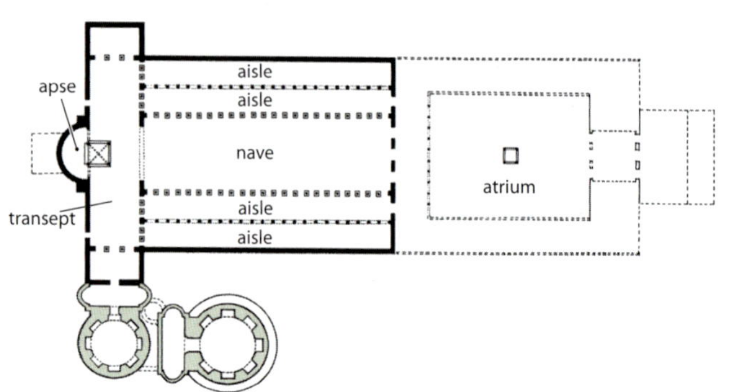

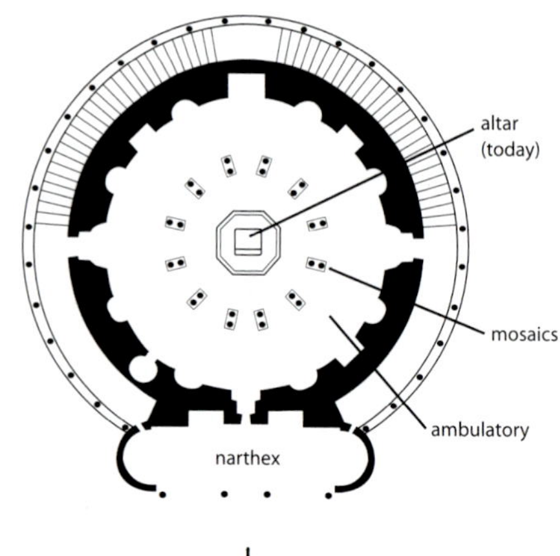

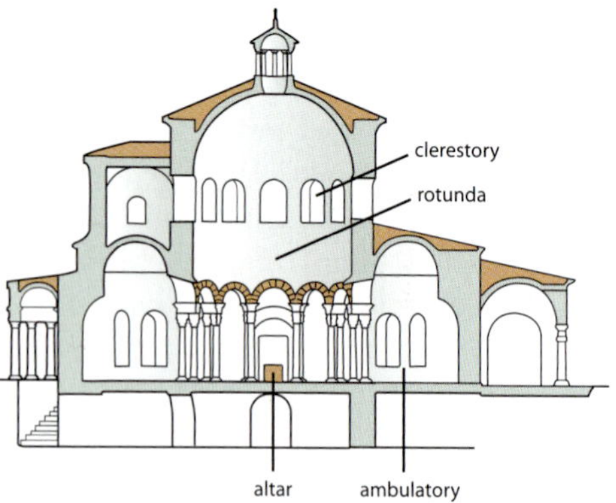

7–9 Plan and section drawing of Santa Costanza (originally mausoleum of Constantina, daughter of Constantine), Rome. c. 350

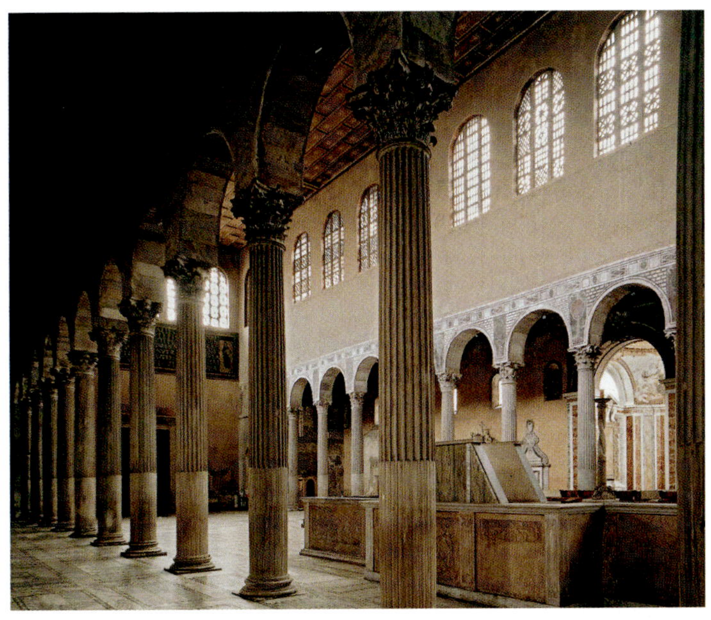

7–10 Interior, Church of Santa Sabina, Rome. 422–432

Empire. The upper walls and vaults of the tiny chapel are richly decorated with mosaics; panels of veined marble cover the walls below (fig. **7–11**). Floral and geometric patterns decorate the four central arches and vaults, and the walls above them are filled with figures of standing apostles gesturing like orators. Saint Lawrence is represented in the central **lunette** (semicircular wall section under the vault) at the end of one arm of the cross-shaped building. The triumphant martyr carries a cross over his shoulder like a trophy and stands next to the fire-engulfed metal grill on which he was literally roasted to death. Left of the grill stands a tall cabinet containing the books of the Gospels, signifying the faith for which Lawrence gave his life. Opposite Saint Lawrence, in a lunette over the entrance portal, is a mosaic of Jesus as the *Good Shepherd* (fig. **7–12**, and "Closer Look," page 176).

Early Byzantine Art

During the fifth and sixth centuries, the Italian peninsula was invaded by the Visigoths, Vandals, and Ostrogoths—Germanic peoples

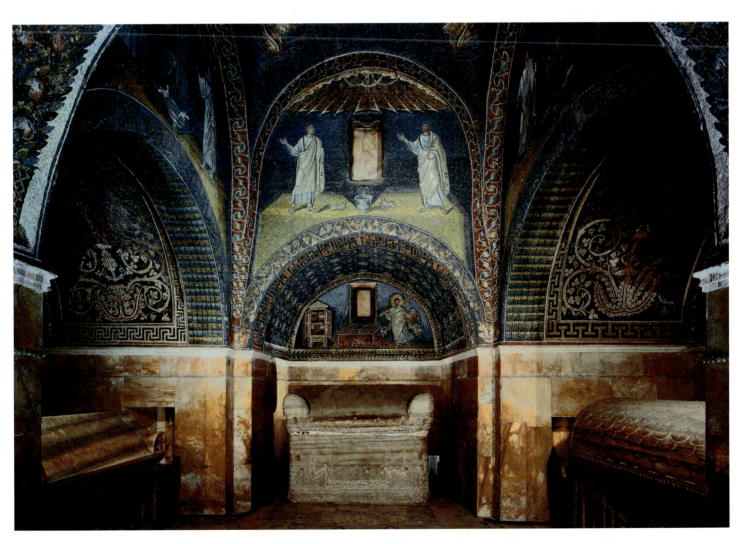

7–11 View from the entrance of the Oratory of Galla Placidia, Ravenna, Italy. c. 425–426. The three visible arms of the cross-shaped building hold sarcophagi. The lunette mosaic portrays the martyrdom of Saint Lawrence; upper walls, apostles

CLOSER LOOK

Few images are as appealing as the Good Shepherd, with its associations of loving, caring, protectiveness, and strength (fig. **7–12**). Originating in agrarian societies, the theme of the shepherd watching over a flock of sheep or carrying home a weak or lost lamb became a powerful and positive image, even in urban cultures. Today the Good Shepherd may be thought of as a Christian symbol, but it was not conceived as such. Ancient Greeks and Romans sometimes represented Hermes as a shepherd carrying a lamb or calf, and Orpheus was believed to have charmed flocks with his music. Jewish patriarchs measured their wealth in herds of sheep and camels, and one of the best known of the songs of King David envisions God as an all-providing shepherd (Psalm 23). Not surprisingly, Christians adopted this imagery for Jesus as early at the third century (see figs. 7–6 and 7–7). He had used it himself in his parables as an effective way to make God's love understandable to his listeners (Luke 15:3–7 and Matthew 18:12–14). According to John (10:11–16), Jesus called himself the good shepherd who lays down his life for his sheep. And so the imagery communicated a common theme for Jews and Christians alike in both the West and the East.

By the fifth century, with Christianity relatively secure as an established religion, an artist might add, or a patron might request to include, specifically Christian symbols in a work. In this mosaic from Ravenna, Jesus sits with his sheep in a luxuriant landscape, like a young Orpheus. But his shepherd's crook has become a golden cross standard. Indeed, Jesus is no longer the boy in a simple tunic used in Early Christian works, but a young emperor who wears purple and gold imperial robes and whose imperial majesty is signaled by the golden halo surrounding his head. When this mosaic was made, Christianity had for some time been the official state religion, and over a century had passed since the last official persecution of Christians. The patrons of the mosaic chose to assert the glory of Jesus Christ in mosaic, the richest known medium of architectural decoration, an imperial image still imbued with pagan spirit but now signaling the triumph of the new faith.

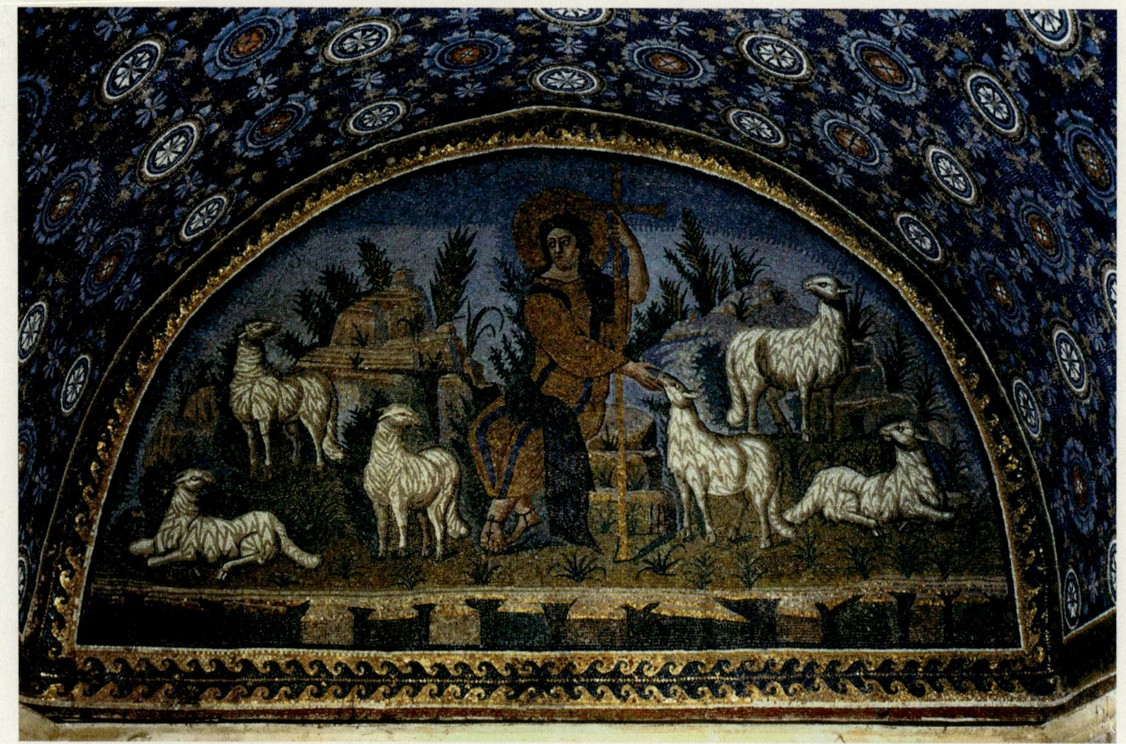

7–12 ***Good Shepherd***, mosaic in the lunette over the west entrance, Oratory of Galla Placidia, Ravenna, Italy. c. 425–426

The rocky band at the bottom of the scene, resembling a cliff face riddled with clefts, separates the divine image from worshipers, as if it were taking place on a stage that extends above and beyond the oratory in which they stand.

from the north. Rome was sacked twice, in 410 and 455. The Western Roman Empire collapsed in 476, and Italy fell to the Ostrogoths.

During the same period, the Eastern Roman (or Byzantine) Empire and its capital city of Constantinople flourished. Byzantine political power, wealth, and culture peaked in the sixth century, under Emperor Justinian I (ruled 527–565), ably seconded by Empress Theodora (c. 500–548). At its most expansive under Justinian, the Byzantine Empire included the lands that are now Greece, the Balkans, and Turkey; the Levant from Syria south to Arabia; Egypt; part of Spain; and a long strip along the Mediterranean coast of Africa. Justinian also reconquered Italy and Sicily, establishing Ravenna as the administrative capital on the Italian peninsula.

In Constantinople, Justinian began a campaign of building and renovation in the wake of the devastating urban Nika Riots in 532, but little remains of his architectural projects or of the old imperial city. The Church of Hagia Sophia (Holy Wisdom) is a spectacular exception (figs. **7–13** and **7–14**). Designed by two scholar-theoreticians, Anthemius of Tralles and Isidorus of Miletus, it embodies both imperial power and Christian glory. Anthemius was a specialist in geometry and optics, and Isidorus was a specialist in physics who had studied vaulted construction. Their crowning achievement was the original dome of Hagia Sophia, which provided a golden, light-filled canopy high above a processional space (fig. **7–15**). Procopius of Caesarea, who chronicled Justinian's reign, claimed poetically that the dome seemed to hang suspended on a "golden chain from heaven." It was rumored that Hagia Sophia was constructed by angels, but mortal builders achieved the feat in only five years (532–537).

Hagia Sophia is an innovative and audacious hybrid of longitudinal and central architectural planning. The building is clearly dominated by the hovering form of its gigantic dome (see fig. 7–15). But flanking **conches** (semidomes) form a longitudinal nave that expands outward from the central dome to connect with the narthex on one end and the sanctuary apse on the other. This processional core is flanked by side aisles, and galleries above them overlook the nave space (see figs. 7–14 and 7–15). The Byzantine church required galleries to accommodate female worshipers, who were not allowed to stand directly on the church floor.

Since this idiosyncratic mixture of basilica and rotunda precludes a drum—the ring of masonry underneath a dome that provides support around its circumference (as in the Pantheon, see fig. 6–27)—the main dome of Hagia Sophia rests instead on four **pendentives** (triangular curving wall sections) that connect the base of the dome with the huge supporting **piers** (large masonry supports) at the four corners of the square area beneath it (see "Pendentives and Squinches," page 179). And since these piers are essentially submerged back into the aisles, rather than expressed within the nave space itself (see fig. 7–14), the dome seems to float mysteriously over a void. The miraculous, weightless effect was reinforced by the light-reflecting gold mosaic that covered the surfaces of dome and pendentives alike, as well as the band of 40 windows that perforate the base of the dome where it meets its support. This daring move challenged architectural logic by seeming to weaken the integrity of the masonry at the very place where it needs to be

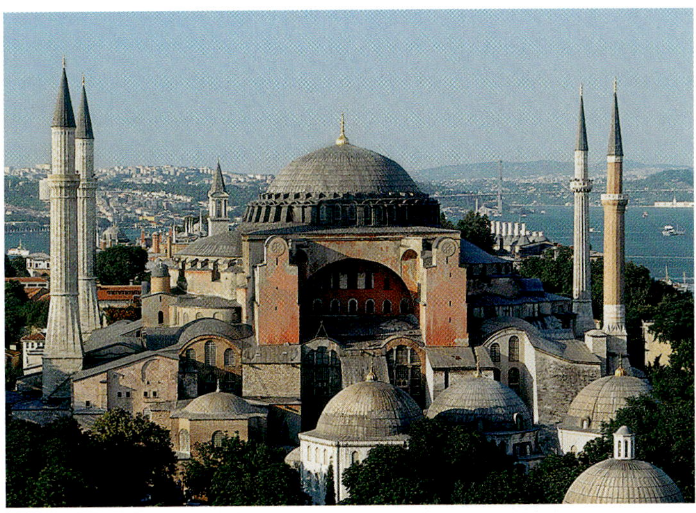

7–13 Anthemius of Tralles and Isidorus of Miletus. Church of Hagia Sophia, Istanbul, Turkey. 532–537. View from the southwest

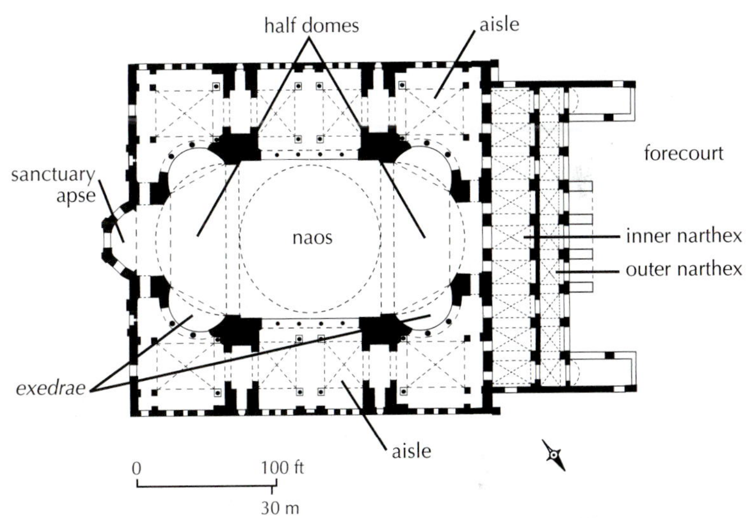

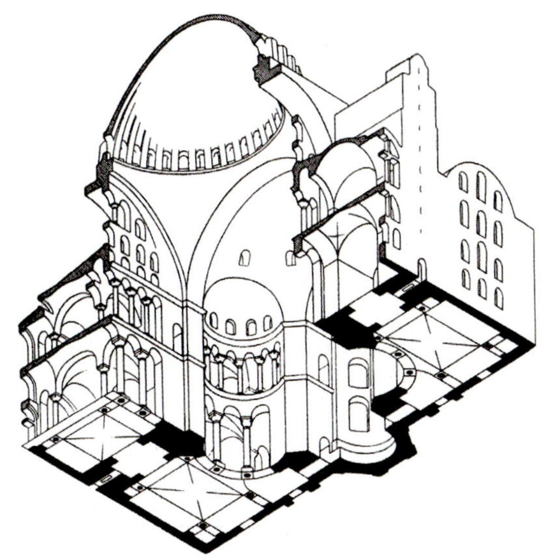

7–14 Plan and isometric drawing of the Church of Hagia Sophia

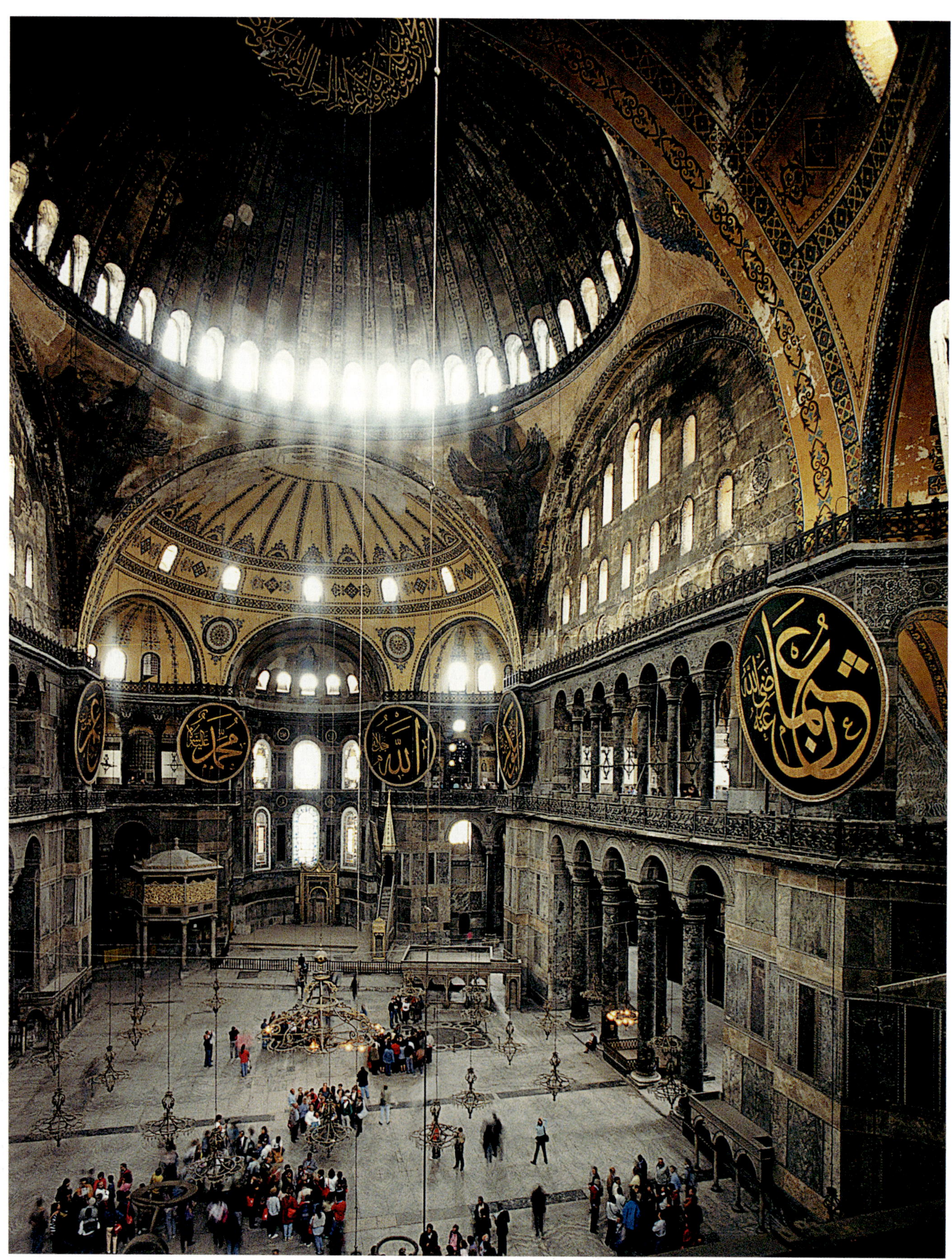

7–15 Church of Hagia Sophia

ELEMENTS OF Architecture

Pendentives and Squinches

Pendentives and **squinches** are two methods of supporting a round dome or its drum over a square space. Pendentives are spherical triangles between arches that rise upward and inward to form a circular opening on which the dome sits. Squinches are diagonal lintels supported on bracket-like constructions placed across the walls' upper corners. Because squinches create an octagon, which is close in shape to a circle, they provide a solid base around the perimeter of the dome, usually elevated on a drum, whereas pendentives project the dome inward, over the space it covers, making it seem to float over a void. Byzantine builders preferred pendentives (as at Hagia Sophia, see fig. 7–15) and elaborate squinch-supported domes became a hallmark of Islamic architecture (see fig. 8–12).

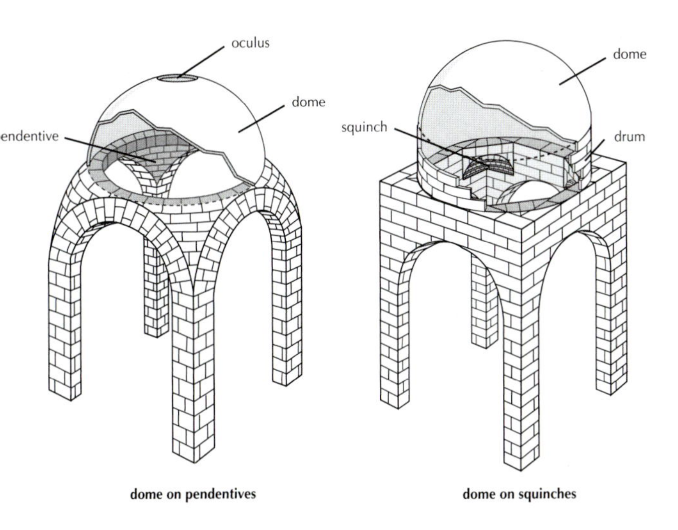

strong, but the windows created the circle of light that helps the dome appear to hover, and a reinforcement of buttressing on the exterior made the solution sound as well as shimmering. The origin of the dome on pendentives, which became the preferred method for supporting domes in Byzantine architecture, is obscure, but its large-scale use at Hagia Sophia was totally unprecedented and represents one of the boldest architectural experiments in the history of architecture.

Among the most important sixth-century Byzantine churches built outside Constantinople is the Church of San Vitale in Ravenna. It was commissioned by a local bishop, Ecclesius, when Italy was under Ostrogothic rule, but it was completed only after Justinian's conquest of Ravenna. The church was dedicated in 547 to the Early Christian martyr, Saint Vitalis. Its design is basically a dome-covered octagon surrounded by eight **exedrae**, or semicircular niches (fig. **7–16**), one of which is extended through the aisle to form the sanctuary. The rectangular sanctuary is flanked by circular rooms. A narthex once led to the palace.

The floor plan of San Vitale only begins to convey the effect of the complex, interpenetrating interior spaces of the church. The

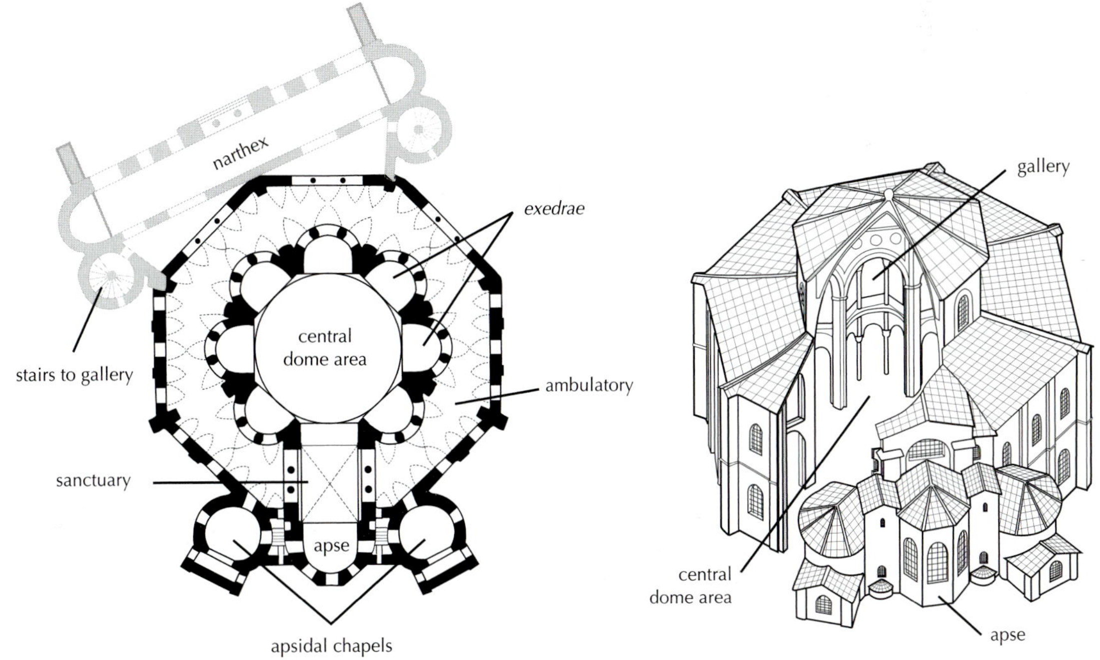

7–16 Plan and cutaway drawing of the Church of San Vitale, Ravenna, Italy. Under construction from c. 520; consecrated 547; mosaics c. 526–548

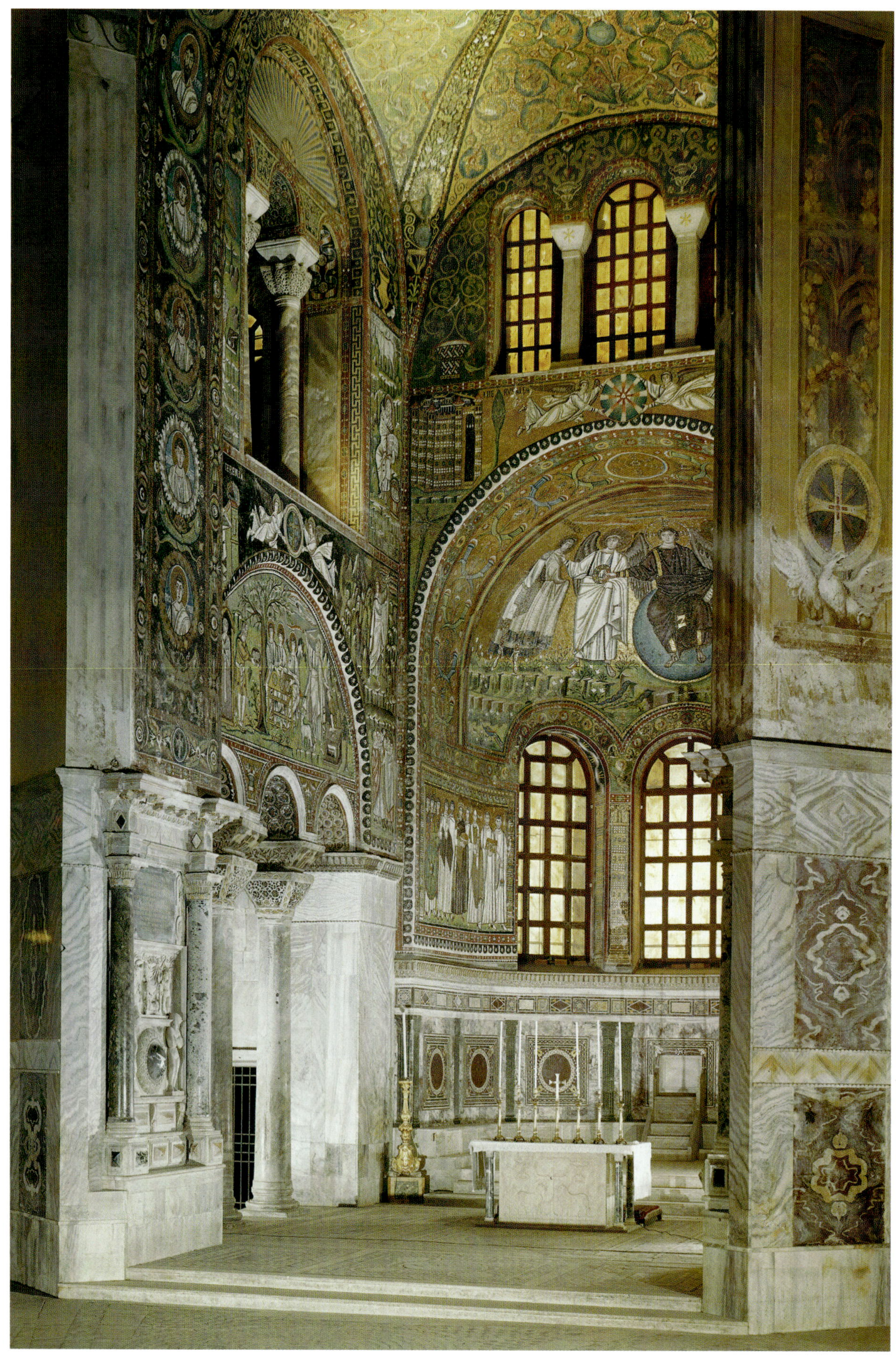

7–17 Church of San Vitale. View into the sanctuary toward the northeast

NAMING CHRISTIAN CHURCHES: DESIGNATION ✕ DEDICATION ✕ LOCATION

Christian churches are identified by a three-part descriptive title combining (1) designation (or type), with (2) dedication (usually to a saint), and finally (3) geographical location, and are cited in that order.

Designation: There are various types of churches, fulfilling a variety of liturgical and administrative objectives, and the identification of a specific church often begins with an indication of its function within the system. For example, an *abbey church* is the place of worship within a monastery or convent; a *pilgrimage church* is a site that attracts visitors wishing to venerate **relics** (material remains or objects associated with a saint) as well as attend services. A *cathedral* is a bishop's primary church (the word derives from the Latin *cathedra*, meaning throne, since the throne of a bishop is contained within his cathedral). A bishop's domain is called a *diocese*, and there can be only one church in the diocese designated as its bishop's cathedral, but the diocese is full of *parish churches* where local residents attend regular services.

Dedication: Christian churches are always dedicated to a saint or a sacred concept, for example Saint Peter's Basilica or the Church of Hagia Sophia ("divine wisdom"). In short-hand identification, when we omit the church designation at the beginning, we always add an apostrophe *s* to the saint's name, as when using "Saint Peter's" to refer to the Vatican Basilica of Saint Peter in Rome.

Location: The final piece of information that clearly pinpoints the specific church referred to in a title is its geographic location, as in Church of San Vitale in Ravenna or the Cathedral of Notre-Dame (French for "Our Lady," referring to the Virgin Mary) in Paris, even though its dedication—"Notre-Dame"—alone usually refers to this Parisian cathedral, in spite of the fact that many contemporary cathedrals (e.g., at Chartres and Reims) were also dedicated to "Notre-Dame." Similarly, "Saint Peter's" usually means the Vatican church of the pope in Rome.

dome rests on eight large piers that frame the exedrae and the sanctuary. The undulating, two-story exedrae open through superimposed arcades into outer aisles on the ground floor and into galleries on the second floor. They billow out from the cylindrical central space and create a swelling spatial sensation. The diaphonous quality of the walls is reinforced by the liberal use of reflective veined marble veneer and colored glass and gold mosaics in the surface decoration. In the conch of the sanctuary apse (fig. **7–17**), an image of Christ is imperially enthroned in paradise on a cosmic orb and flanked by archangels. Saint Vitalis (on his far right) is receiving from Christ a crown of martyrdom and Bishop Ecclesius (on Christ's far left) presents to Christ a model of the church itself.

Justinian and Theodora may never have set foot in Ravenna, but two large mosaic panels that face each other across the sanctuary of San Vitale, below the scene of Christ holding court in paradise, not only make their presences known, but capture it for perpetuity. In one panel, Justinian (fig. **7–18**), accompanied by Bishop Maximianus and leaders of church and state, presents the paten that will be used to hold the Eucharistic host. In the other, Theodora (fig. **7–19**), followed by her sisters and ladies of the court, carries a huge golden chalice studded with jewels. The rulers present these as precious offerings to Christ—emulating most immediately bishop Ecclesius who offers a model of the church to Christ in the apse, as well as the Magi, wise men from the East, whom Christians believe brought valuable gifts to Jesus at his birth. Note that the three Magi are depicted in the embroidered panel at the bottom of Theodora's purple cloak. The chalice and paten offered by the royal couple will be used by this church to offer Eucharistic bread and wine to the local Christian community during the liturgy. At the core of this central ceremony of Christian worship is the identification of the sacrificial body and blood of Christ with the substances of bread and wine, which Jesus had instructed his followers to eat and drink in remembrance of him, and which became emblematic of his offering of himself on the cross for their redemption. In this way the entire program of mosaic decoration revolves around the themes of offerings and Eucharist.

Theodora's group stands beside a fountain, presumably at the entrance to the women's gallery. The open doorway and curtain are classical space-creating devices, but here the mosaicists have deliberately avoided allowing their illusionistic power to overwhelm their ability also to create flat surface patterns. Notice, too, that the figures cast no shadows, and though modeled, their outlines as silhouetted shapes are more prominent than their sense of three-dimensionality. Still, especially in Justinian's panel, a complex and carefully controlled system of overlapping allows us to see these figures clearly and logically situated within a shallow space, moving in a stately procession from left to right toward the entrance to the church and the beginning of the liturgy. So the scenes portrayed in these mosaic paintings are both flattened and three-dimensional, abstract and representational, patterned and individualized. Like Justinian and Theodora, they are both there and not there at the same time.

Christians also commissioned books for religious services and clerical instruction, for personal study and meditation, or as expressions of prestige by wealthy leaders of church and state. We have seen Gospel books in the cabinet on the Saint Lawrence lunette (see fig. 7–11), and a book with a jeweled cover is carried by a deacon in Justinian's procession at San Vitale (see fig. 7–18). Until the invention of printing, all books were **manuscripts**—that is, they were written by hand on **parchment**, specially prepared animal skin. If they were decorated or illustrated, today we call them **illuminated**.

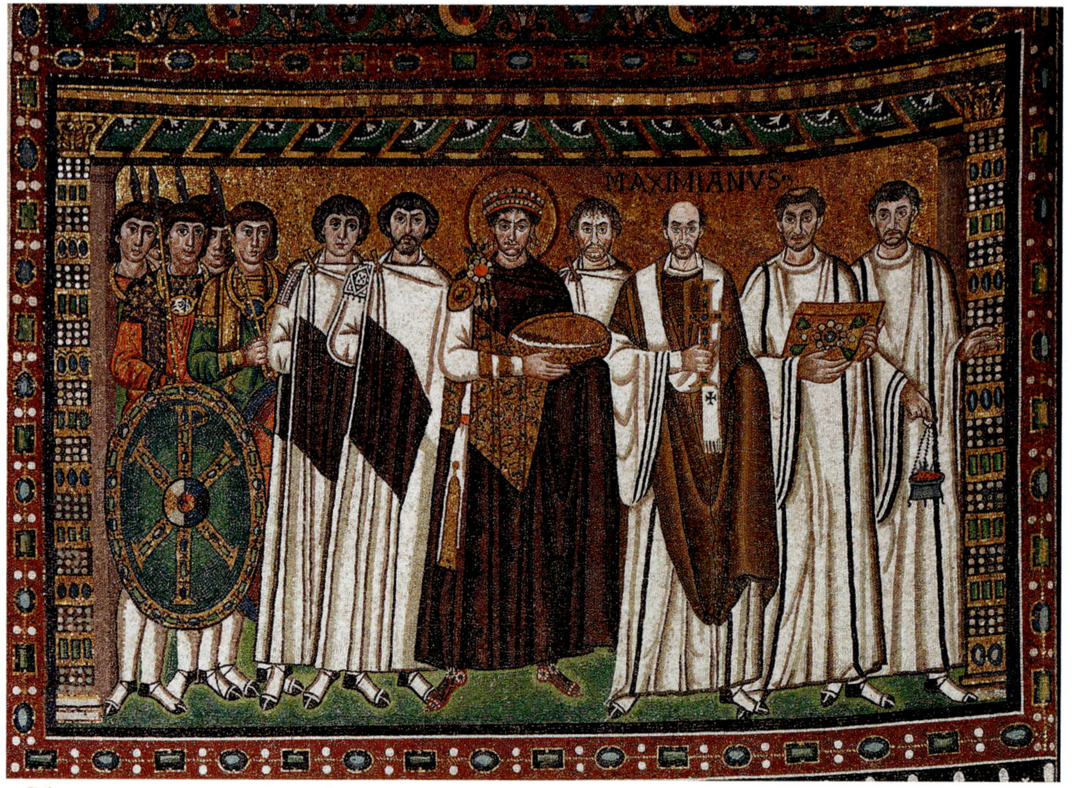

7–18 ***Emperor Justinian and his Attendants***, from north sanctuary wall of the Church of San Vitale, Ravenna, Italy. c. 547. Mosaic, 8' 8" × 12' (2.64 × 3.65 m)

As head of state, Justinian—nimbed (head surrounded by a nimbus or halo) and wearing a huge jeweled crown and a purple cloak—carries a large golden paten that he is donating to San Vitale for the celebration of the Mass. Bishop Maximianus at his left holds a jeweled cross and another churchman holds a jewel-covered book. Government officials stand at Justinian's right, followed by barbarian mercenary soldiers, one of whom wears a neck torc, another a classical cameo cloak clasp.

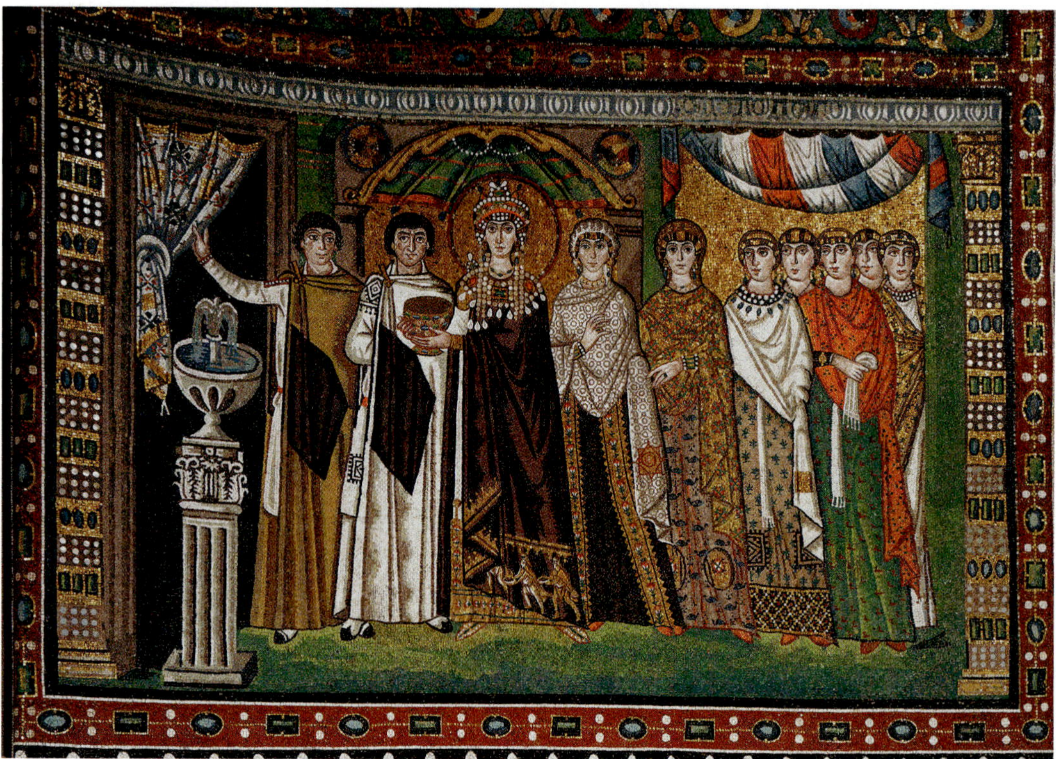

7–19 ***Empress Theodora and her Attendants***, from south sanctuary wall of the Church of San Vitale. c. 547. Mosaic, 8' 8" × 12' (2.64 × 3.65 m)

Theodora and her ladies wear the rich textiles and jewelry of the Byzantine court. Both men and women dressed in linen or silk tunics and cloaks. The men's cloaks are fastened on the right shoulder with a fibula *(brooch) and are decorated with a rectangular embroidered panel (*tablion*). Women wore a second full, long-sleeved garment over their tunics and a large rectangular shawl. Like Justinian, Theodora has a halo and wears imperial purple. Her elaborate jewelry includes a wide collar of embroidered and jeweled cloth. A crown, hung with long strands of pearls (thought to protect the wearer from disease), frames her face.*

During the Byzantine period and the European Middle Ages, many illuminated manuscripts were made not only in professional workshops, but also in monasteries and convents, religious communities where devout men and women (monks and nuns) withdrew from the secular world to devote their lives to study and prayer.

The manuscript page (called a **folio**) illustrated in figure **7–20** comes from a **codex** (bound, rectangular book in the modern sense, rather than a scroll), written in Greek on purple **vellum** (fine animal skin prepared for writing). The purple color indicates that it may have been done for an imperial patron; the costly purple dye, made

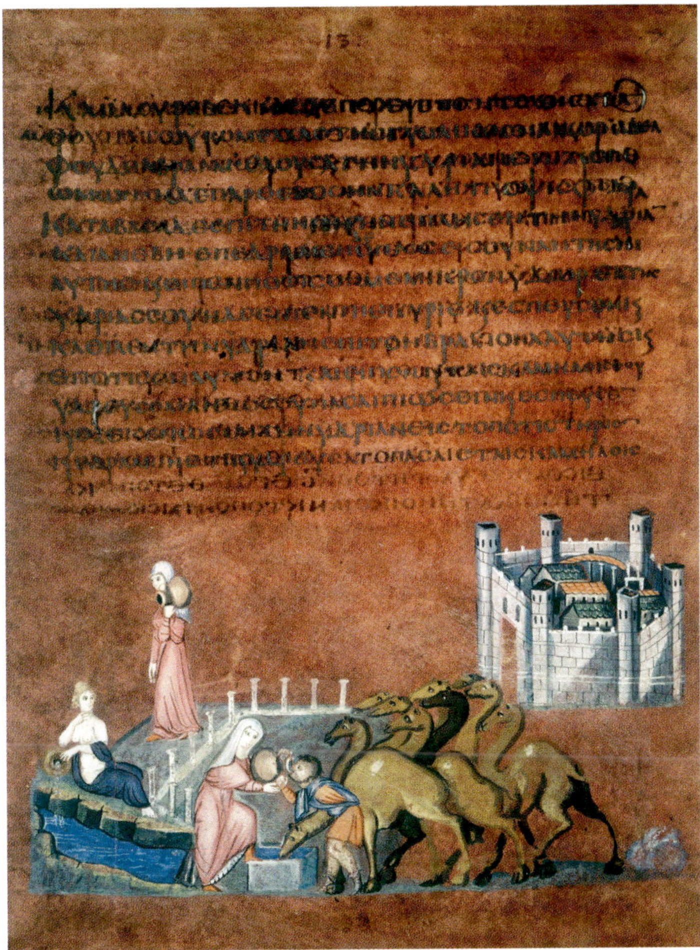

7–20 Manuscript page with *Rebecca at the Well*, from the book of Genesis, probably made in Syria or Palestine. Early 6th century. Tempera, gold, and silver paint on purple-dyed vellum, 13½" × 9⅞" (33.7 × 25 cm). Österreichische Nationalbibliothek, Vienna

from the shells of murex mollusks, was usually restricted to imperial use. Illustrations appear below the text at the bottom of the page. The story of Rebecca at the well (Genesis 24) on this leaf appears to be a single scene, but the painter—clinging to the continuous narrative tradition that had characterized the illustration of scrolls—combines events that take place at different times in the story within a single narrative space. Rebecca appears at the left walking away from the walled city of Nahor with a large jug on her shoulder, going to fetch water. A colonnaded road leads to a spring, personified by a reclining pagan water nymph holding a flowing jar. In the foreground, Rebecca appears again. Her jug now full, she encounters a thirsty camel driver and offers him a drink. Since he is Abraham's servant Eliezer, who is searching for a bride for Abraham's son, Isaac, Rebecca's generosity leads to her marriage. The lifelike poses and rounded, full-bodied figures of this narrative scene conform to the conventions of traditional Roman painting. The sumptuous purple of the background and the glittering metallic letters of the text situate the book within the world of the privileged and powerful in Christian society.

Icons and Iconoclasm

Many Christians in the Byzantine world prayed to Christ, Mary, and the saints while looking at images of them in manuscripts, on the walls of churches, or on independent painted panels known as **icons** (not to be confused with the word **iconic** which refers in general to images that represent symbols or ideas). Church doctrine toward the veneration of icons distinguished between idolatry—the worship of images—and the veneration of an idea or holy person depicted in a work of art. Icons were thus accepted as aids to meditation and prayer; the images were thought to act as intermediaries between worshipers and the holy personages they depicted, and honor showed to the image was believed to transfer directly to its spiritual prototype.

Early icons are rare. Among the most representative is the *Virgin and Child with Saints and Angels* (fig. **7–21**). The Virgin Mary, as the earthly mother of Jesus (called in Greek *Theotokos*, bearer of God), was viewed as a powerful intercessor, or go-between, who could appeal to her divine Son for mercy on behalf of repentant Christians. She was also considered the Seat of Wisdom, and like many images, this icon shows her holding Jesus on her lap in a way that suggests that she has become his imperial throne. Mother and

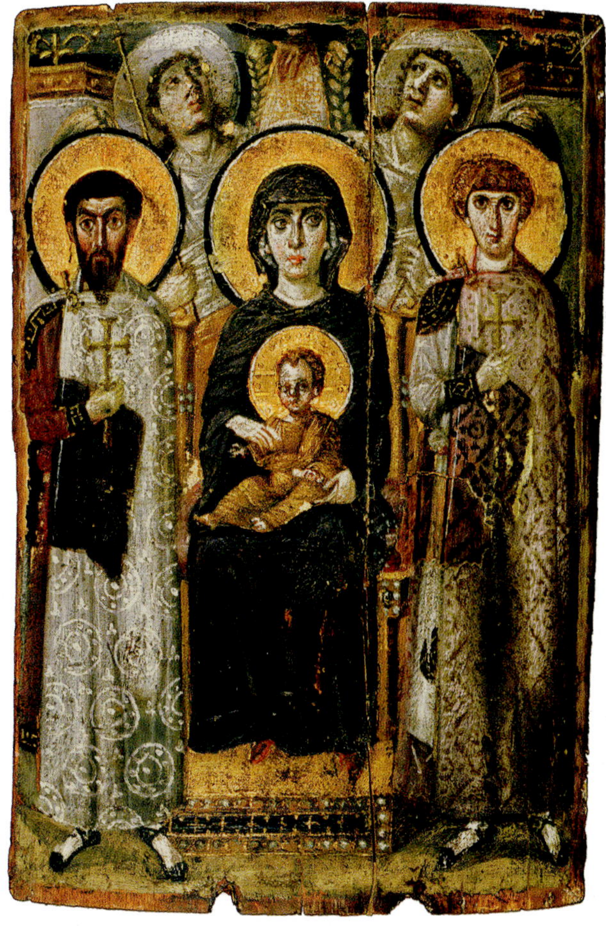

7–21 *Virgin and Child with Saints and Angels*, icon in the Monastery of Saint Catherine, Mount Sinai, Egypt. Second half of 6th century. Encaustic on wood, 27" × 18⅞" (69 × 48 cm)

ICONOCLASM

Iconoclasm (literally "image breaking," derived from the Greek words *eikon* for "image" and *klao* meaning "break" or "destroy") is the prohibition and destruction of works of visual art, usually because they are considered inappropriate in religious contexts.

During the eighth century, mounting discomfort with the place of icons in Christian devotion grew into a major controversy in the Byzantine world and in 726 Emperor Leo III (ruled 717–741) imposed iconoclasm, initiating the systematic destruction of images of saints and sacred stories on icons and in churches, as well as the persecution of those who made them and defended their use, policies and practices that were enforced with even greater fervor by his successor Constantine V (ruled 741–775). Iconoclasm endured as imperial policy until 843, when the widowed Empress Theodora reversed her late husband Theophilus' policy and reinstated the central place of images in Byzantine devotional practice.

A number of explanations have been proposed for this interlude of Byzantine iconoclasm. Some church leaders feared that the use of images in worship could lead to idolatry or at least distract worshipers from their spiritual exercises. Specifically there were questions surrounding the relationship between images and the Eucharist, the latter considered by iconoclasts as sufficient representation of the presence of Christ in the church. But there was also anxiety in Byzantium about the weakening state of the empire, especially in relation to the advances of Arab armies into Byzantine territory. It was easy to pin these hard times on God's displeasure with the idolatrous use of images. Coincidentally, Leo III's success fighting the Arabs could be interpreted as divine sanction of his iconoclastic position, and its very adoption might appease the iconoclastic Islamic enemy itself. Finally, since the production and promotion of icons was centered in monasteries—at that time rivaling the state in strength and wealth—attacking the use of images might check their growing power. Perhaps all these factors played a part, but at the triumph of the iconophiles (literally "lovers of images") in 843, the place of images in worship was again secure: icons proclaimed Christ as God incarnate and facilitated Christian worship by acting as intermediaries between humans and saints. Those who had suppressed icons were branded heretics (fig. **7–22**).

But iconoclasm is not restricted to Byzantine history. It reappears from time to time through the history of art. Some Protestant reformers of sixteenth-century Europe adopted what they saw as the iconoclastic position of the Hebrew Bible (Exodus 20:4), and many works of Catholic art were destroyed by zealous reformers and their followers. Even more recently, in 2001, the Taliban rulers of Afghanistan dynamited two gigantic sixth-century CE statues of the Buddha carved into the rock cliffs of the Bamiyan Valley, specifically because they believed such "idols" violated Islamic law.

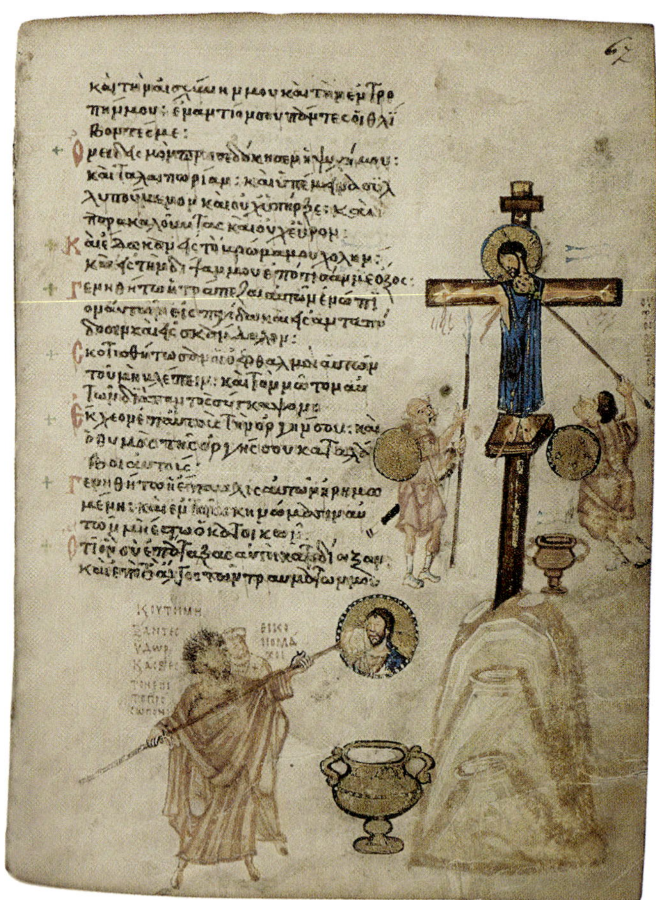

7–22 *Crucifixion and Iconoclasts* from the Chludov Psalter. Mid-9th century. Tempera on vellum, 7¾" × 6" (19.5 × 15 cm). State Historical Museum, Moscow (MS D.29, fol. 67r)

This page and its illustration of Psalm 21, made soon after the end of the iconoclastic controversy in 843, records the iconophiles' harsh judgment of the iconoclasts. Painted in the margin at the right, a scene of the Crucifixion shows a soldier tormenting Christ with a vinegar-soaked sponge. In a striking visual parallel, two named iconoclasts—identified by inscription—in the adjacent picture along the bottom margin employ a whitewash-soaked sponge to obliterate an icon portrait of Christ, thus linking their actions with those who had crucified him.

child are flanked here by the Christian warrior-saints Theodore (left) and George (right), two legendary figures said to have slain dragons. Symbolically the warrior-saints represent the triumph of the Church over the "evil serpent" of paganism. The artist has painted the Christ Child, the Virgin, and the angels in an illusionistic, Roman manner that renders them lifelike in appearance. But the warrior-saints are more stylized; the artist barely hints at bodily form beneath the richly patterned textiles of their cloaks and their tense faces are frozen in frontal stares of gripping intensity.

In the eighth century, in a reaction against the veneration of images known as **iconoclasm**, reactionary emperors ordered the systematic destruction of icons and forbade the use of images in Christian worship. A few survived in isolated places such as Mount Sinai in Egypt, which was no longer part of the Byzantine empire at this time. But iconoclasm did not last. In 843, Empress Theodora, then regent for her son Michael, reinstated the veneration of images, and icons would play an increasingly important role as the history of Byzantine art developed.

Middle Byzantine Art

After the defeat of the iconoclasts Byzantine art flourished again, beginning in 867 under the leadership of an imperial dynasty from Macedonia and continuing until Christian crusaders from the West occupied Constantinople in 1204. The Westerners were eventually expelled, however, and Byzantine culture was revived in the fourteenth and early fifteenth centuries until Muslim Ottoman Turks conquered Constantinople in 1453 and renamed it Istanbul.

During the tenth, eleventh, and twelfth centuries, artists produced sumptuous works for the Byzantine church and court, using precious materials such as silver and gold, jewels and enamels, and working them with extraordinary skill and refinement. One of the prizes the crusaders carried home to Venice in 1204 was a silver gilt and enamel icon of the archangel Michael (fig. **7–23**). The angel's head and hands are executed in relief in the **repoussé** technique (pounded out from the back of the metal sheet). Halo, wings, garments, and the roundels in the borders are detailed in delicate **cloisonné** enamel. (Cloisonné is produced by soldering fine wires in the desired pattern to a metal plate and then filling the cells—**cloisons**—with powdered colored glass. When the object is heated, the glass powder melts and fuses onto the surface of the metal to create small, jewel-like sections.) The angel is portrayed as a timeless youth, but the halo and the stylized and dazzling patterns of the wings and bodice remove the figure from our physical world. The sheer artistry of this icon seems to lift the image to a plane where light and color supplant form, and material substance dissolves into pure spirit.

While little Byzantine art survives from Constantinople, the northeastern Italian city of Venice holds many rich treasures of middle and late Byzantine art. At the end of the tenth century, Constantinople granted Venice a special trade status that allowed its merchants to control much of the commercial exchange between Western Europe and the Eastern Empire. With untold wealth flowing into the city's coffers, Venice's ruler, the doge, in 1063 commissioned a splendid church to replace an older chapel holding the relics of the martyred patron saint of Venice, Saint Mark the Apostle. Venetian architects looked to Byzantine domed churches for inspiration, especially the Church of the Holy Apostles in Constantinople. This important church—commemorating Constantine as well as the Apostles—had a Greek cross plan of five square units, each surmounted by a dome on pendentives; this was

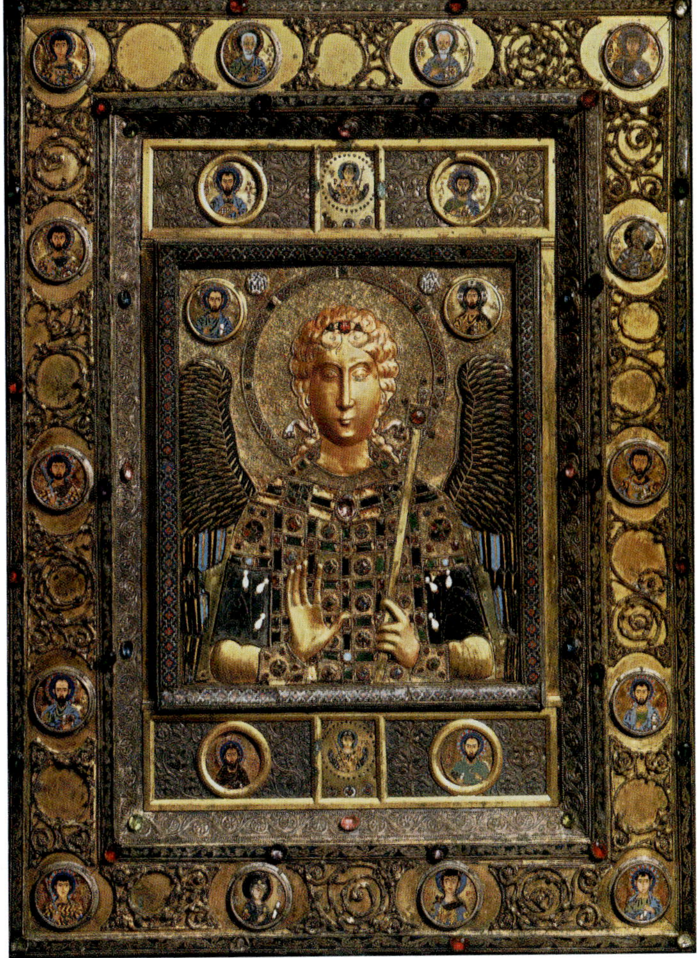

7–23 ***Archangel Michael***, icon. Late 10th or early 11th century. Silver gilt and enamel, 19" × 14" (48 × 36 cm). Treasury of the Cathedral of Saint Mark, Venice

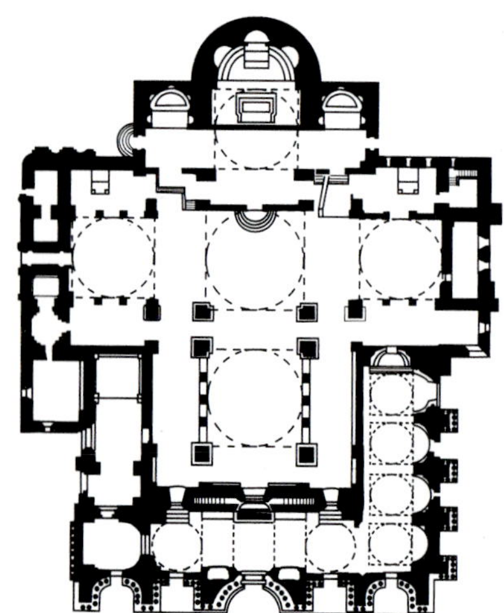

7–24 Plan of the Cathedral of Saint Mark, Venice. Begun 1063

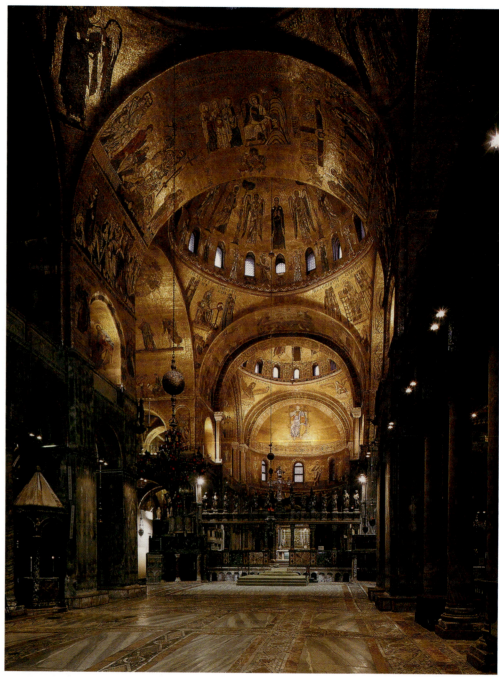

7–25 Cathedral of Saint Mark, Venice. Begun 1063

This church is the third one built on the site. It was both the palace chapel of the doge and the resting place for the bones of the patron of Venice, Saint Mark.

adopted by the builders of Saint Mark's (fig. **7–24**). Inside the church, these domed compartments, separated by barrel vaults and lit by circles of windows, produce a complex space in which each individual dome vies for attention (fig. **7–25**). As a result, Saint Mark's, and the Holy Apostles before it, lacks the powerful focus of Hagia Sophia, with its sweeping upward and forward movement focused by the unity of the single dome. But such intricate compartmentalization appealed to later Byzantine builders, and the Greek-cross five-dome plan was readily adopted as far away as the Ukraine.

Greece lay within the Byzantine Empire in the tenth and eleventh centuries, and the two churches of the Monastery of Hosios Loukas (near Stiris) are excellent examples of later Byzantine architecture (fig. **7–26**). The Katholikon (the major church) is a compact, central-plan structure, whose builders seems to have reveled in architectural complexity. The high central space carries the eye of the worshiper upward into the main dome soaring above a ring of tall arched openings. Single, double, and triple windows create intricate and unusual patterns of light. Curving surfaces are covered with a rich program of mosaics, and flat walls are sheathed in intricate marble veneers. Visible here are images of the Virgin and Child in the apse, Pentecost (the Lamb of God hovering over the Twelve Apostles) in the sanctuary dome, and the Nativity and standing saints in the vaults. (A mosaic of the Pantokrator once in the central dome fell and was replaced by a painting.) An icon screen (**iconostasis**) separates the sanctuary from the congregation.

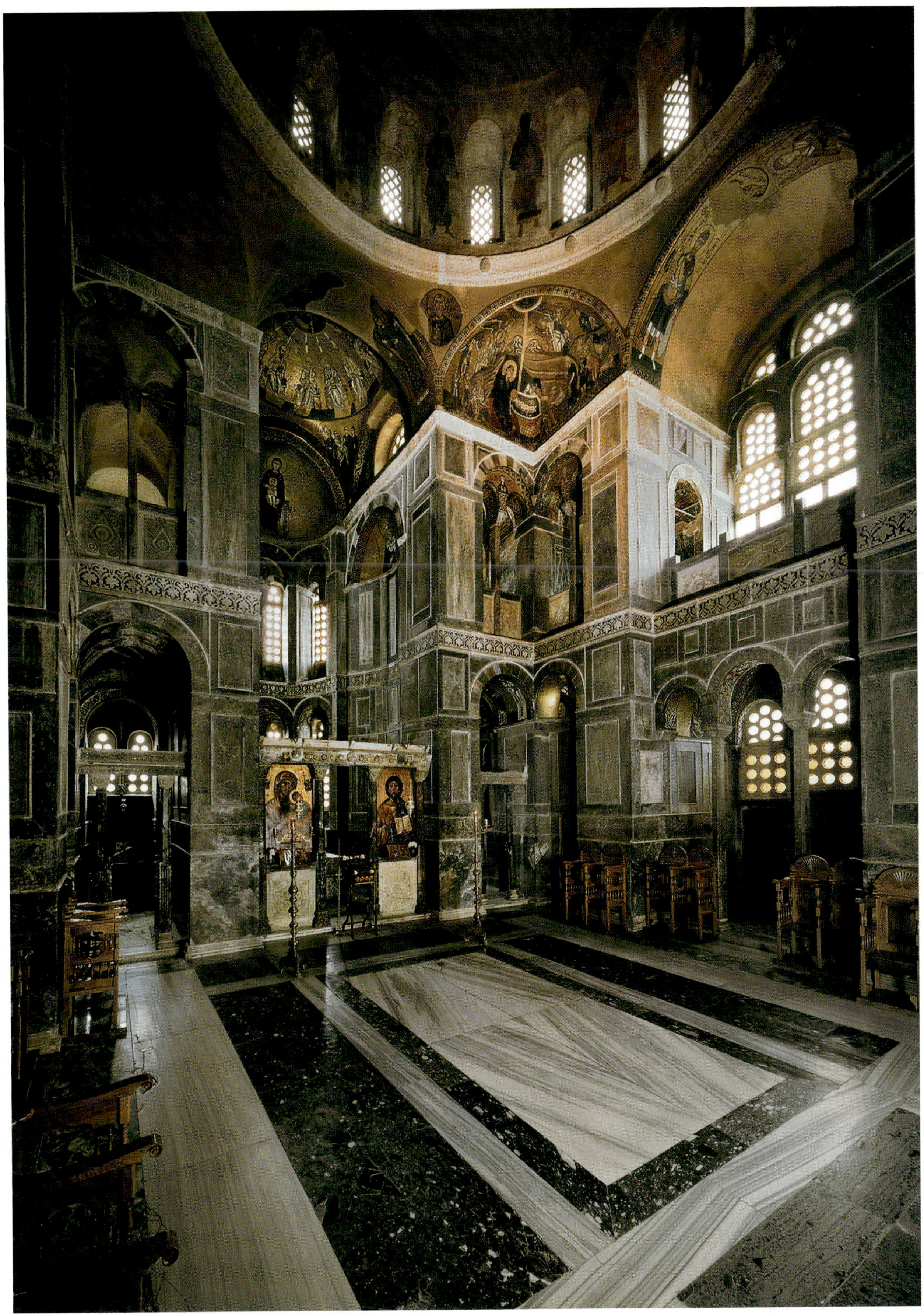

7–26 Central dome and apse, Katholikon, Monastery of Hosios Loukas, near Stiris, Greece. Early 11th century and later

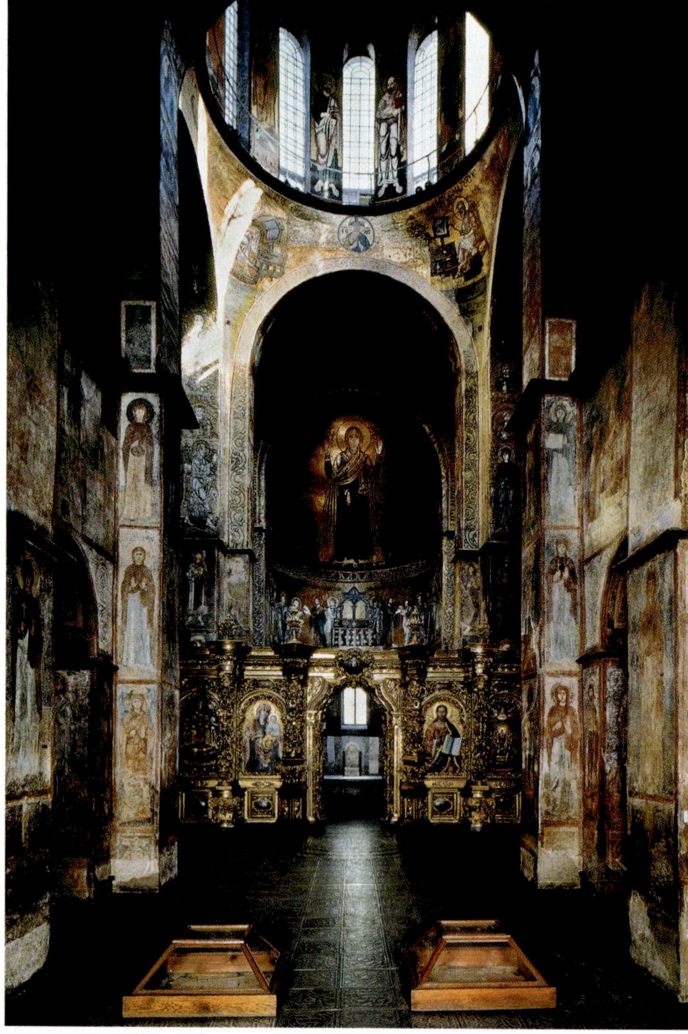

7–27 Interior, Cathedral of Santa Sophia, Kiev, Ukraine. 1037–1046

Ukraine and Russia

The rulers of the Rus (modern Ukraine, Belarus, and Russia) also fell under the spell of Constantinople and adopted Orthodox Christianity. These lands had been settled by Eastern Slavs in the fifth and sixth centuries, but later were ruled by eastern Scandinavian Vikings (the Rus) who established headquarters in the upper Volga regions and in the city of Kiev. The first Christian member of the Kievan ruling family was Princess Olga (c. 890–969), who was baptized in Constantinople by the patriarch himself, with the Byzantine emperor as her godfather.

In the eleventh century, Princess Olga's great-grandson, Grand Prince Yaroslav (ruled 1036–1054), founded the Cathedral of Santa Sophia in Kiev (fig. **7–27**). The increasing complexity seen in Greek Byzantine structures culminates in the Ukrainian and Russian churches. In Kiev, the finished building had double side aisles, five apses, a large central dome, and 12 smaller domes. The small domes were said to represent the Twelve Apostles gathered around Christ Pantokrator (the Ruler of the Universe), symbolized by the central dome. The many individual bays, each of which is an almost independent vertical unit, create a compartmentalized interior. The walls glow with lavish decoration: Mosaics glitter from the central dome, the apse, and the arches of the crossing, and the remaining surfaces are painted with fresco scenes from the lives of Christ, the Virgin, the apostles Peter and Paul, and the archangels.

The Kiev design established an iconographical system that came to be followed in Russian Orthodox churches. The Pantokrator fills the curving crest of the highest dome (not visible above the window-pierced drum in figure 7–27). Just beneath, the apostles stand between the windows of the drum, with the Four Evangelists occupying the pendentives. The Virgin Mary, arms raised in a traditional posture for prayer (the orant pose), seems to float in a golden heaven, filling the half-dome of the apse. In the mosaic on the wall below the Virgin is the Communion of the Apostles. Christ appears not once but twice in this scene, offering Eucharistic bread and wine to the apostles, six on each side of the altar. With such extravagant use of costly mosaic, Prince Yaroslav made a powerful political declaration of his own importance and wealth, and that of the Kievan church as well.

Late Byzantine Art

A last great age of Byzantine art began after crusaders, who occupied Constantinople in 1204, were expelled from the city in 1261. The patronage of emperors and wealthy courtiers stimulated renewed church building and renovation. For example, in the early fourteenth century, Theodore Metochites—poet, scientist, and imperial treasurer—commissioned an elaborately painted funerary chapel off the Constantinopolitan Church of the Monastery of Christ in Chora (later a mosque, Kariye Camii, and now a museum, Kariye Müzesi). A painting of the Resurrection of Christ, known in Greek as the *Anastasis*, is situated in the chapel's apse (fig. **7–28**). Artists in Western Europe usually depicted the Resurrection as the triumphant Christ emerging in glory from his tomb, but in the Eastern Church Christ is shown descending into hell to rescue Adam and Eve and others among his devout Jewish ancestors from Satan's grip. Here, Christ is dressed in shimmering white silk, his dynamic lunge forward reinforced by a tilted, star-studded **mandorla** (almond-shaped body halo). He has trampled down the doors of hell, tied Satan into a helpless bundle, and shattered hell's locks and chains, which lie scattered over the ground. He drags the elderly Adam and Eve from their open sarcophagi with such force that their bodies almost seem airborne.

The practice of venerating icons, and consequently the production of icons, continued in the Late Byzantine period. A remarkable work from this time is *Three Angels Visiting Abraham (Old Testament Trinity)*, a large icon created between 1410 and 1425 by the famed Russian artist-monk Andrey Rublyov (fig. **7–29**). It was commissioned in honor of Abbot Sergius of the Trinity-Sergius Monastery, near Moscow. The theme of the Trinity is always a great challenge for artists. One late medieval solution was to show three identical divine individuals—here, three angels—to suggest the idea. Rublyov's composition was inspired by a story in the Hebrew

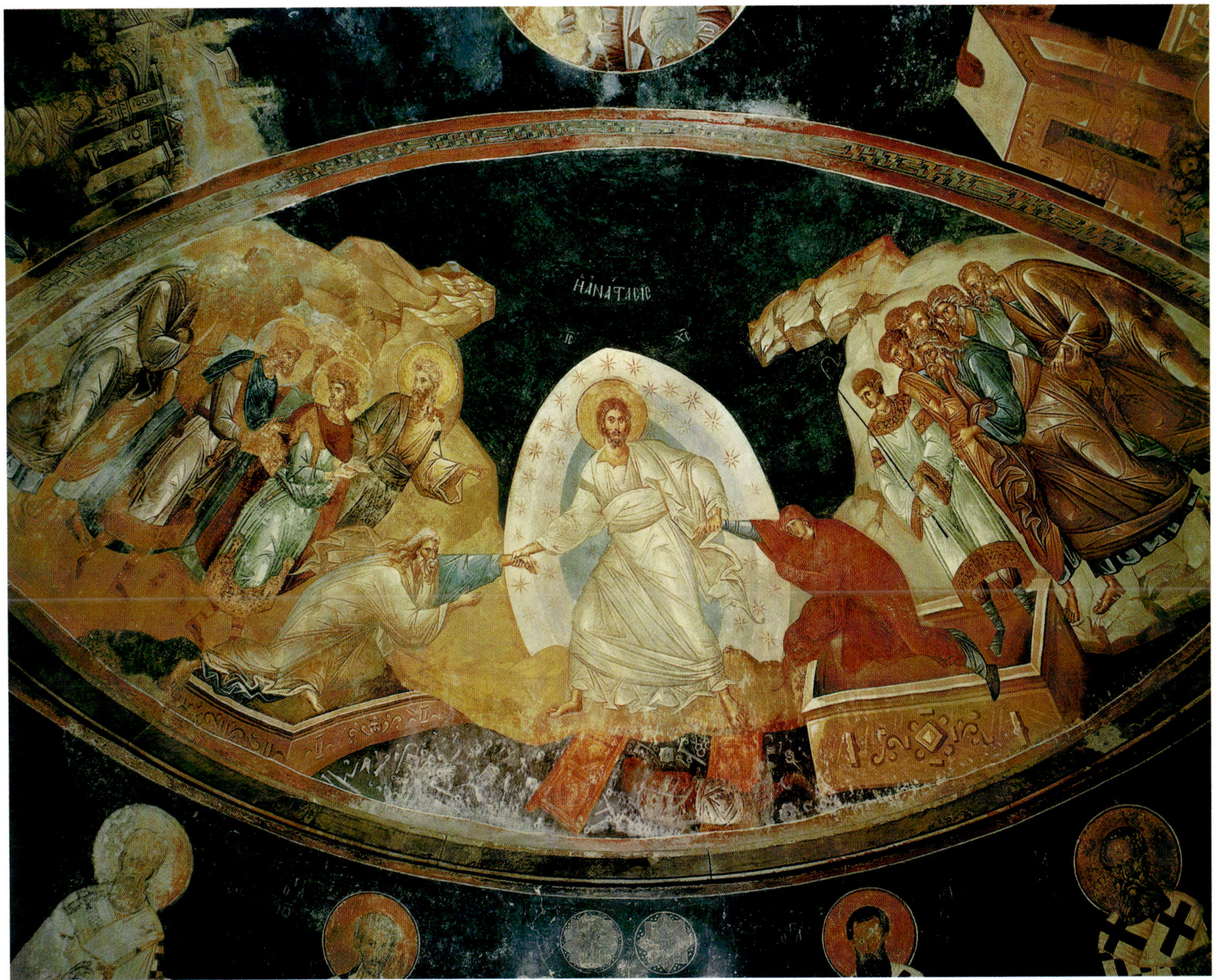

7–28 ***Anastasis.*** Painting in the apse of funerary chapel, Church of the Monastery of Christ in Chora (now Kariye Müzesi), Istanbul, Turkey. c. 1315–1321
WIM SWAAN PHOTOGRAPH COLLECTION (96.P.21)

Bible of the patriarch Abraham and his wife, Sarah, who entertained three strangers who were in fact God represented by three divine beings in human form (Genesis 18). Tiny images of Abraham and Sarah's home and the oak of Mamre can be seen above the angels; on the table, the food the couple offered to the strangers becomes a chalice on an altar-like table.

Rublyov's icon clearly illustrates how Late Byzantine artists relied on mathematical conventions to create ideal figures, as did the ancient Greeks, thus giving their work remarkable consistency. Unlike the Greeks, who based their formulas on close observation of nature, however, Byzantine artists invented an ideal geometry to evoke a heavenly realm and conformed their representations of the human to it. Here, as elsewhere, the circle—most apparent in the haloes—is the basic underlying structure for the composition. Despite the formulaic, somewhat uniform approach, Rublyov—and other talented artists like him—managed to create a personal expressive style. He relied on Byzantine conventions such as salient contours, elongation of the body, and a focus on a limited number of figures to capture the sense of the spiritual in his work, yet he distinguished his art by imbuing it with a sweet, poetic ambience. In his hands, the Byzantine style took on a graceful and eloquent new life.

The Byzantine tradition continues in the art of the Eastern Orthodox Church until today. But in Constantinople, Byzantine art—and the empire itself—came to a decisive end in 1453 when the forces of the Ottoman sultan Muhammad II overran the capital. The Eastern Empire then became part of the Islamic world, which absorbed aspects of the Byzantine art tradition into a very rich aesthetic heritage of its own. Leadership of the Orthodox Church shifted to Russia, where rulers declared Moscow to be the third Rome and themselves the heirs of Caesars (czars).

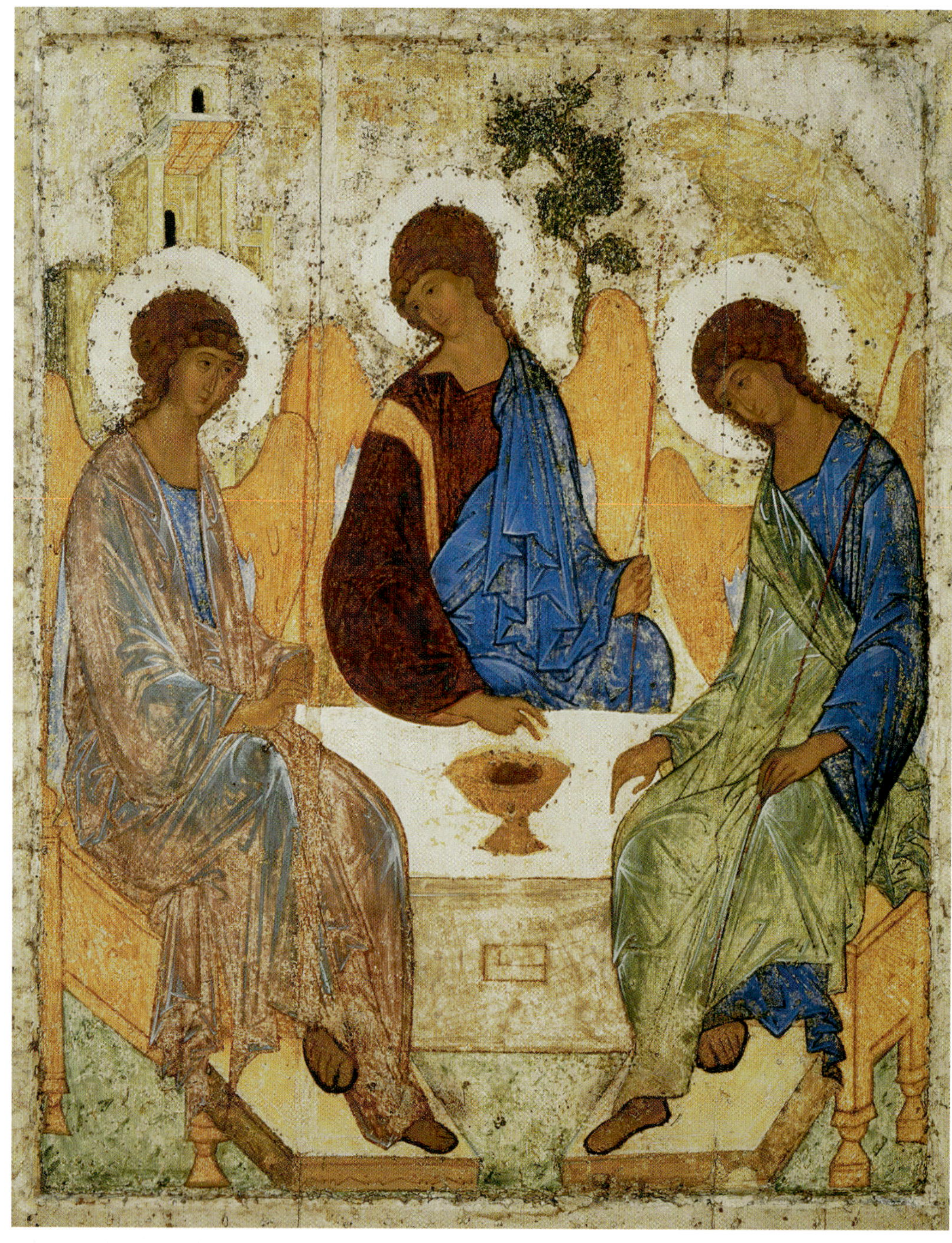

7–29 Andrey Rublyov. ***Three Angels Visiting Abraham (Old Testament Trinity)***, icon. c. 1410–1425. Tempera on panel, 55½" × 44½" (141 × 113 cm). Tretyakov Gallery, Moscow

Looking Back

Both Jews and Christians believe in a single god and seek to conform their lives and their societies to the will of that god as revealed and recorded in sacred Scripture. But they expressed their aspirations and core beliefs in pictures as well as words. Even though strictures within Jewish law forbidding the creation and worship of idols made the representational arts suspect, artists working for Jewish patrons depicted both symbolic and narrative Jewish subjects.

Believing that God came to earth in human form—Jesus Christ—Christians also created a powerful figurative art using human beings as expressive symbols, creating a tradition that would extend beyond the collapse of the Western Roman Empire to flourish in the Byzantine East for a thousand years, until Constantinople fell to the Islamic Ottoman Turks in 1453.

But during the formative third and fourth centuries, both Jews and Christians had looked to Near Eastern and Roman art for inspiration. These same two sources will coalesce around different social and religious principles in the formation of Islamic art, the subject of the next chapter.

IN PERSPECTIVE

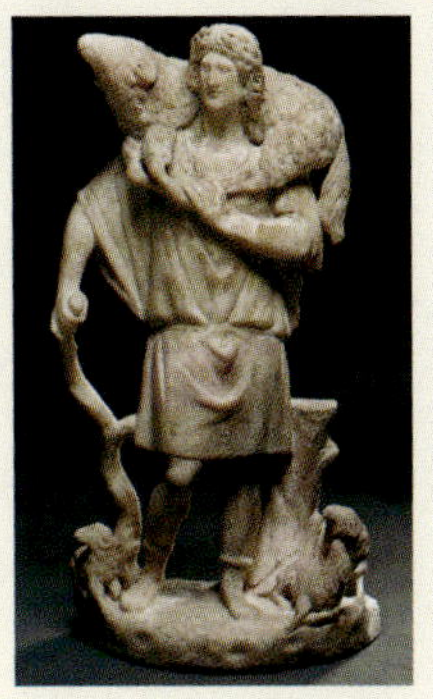

GOOD SHEPHERD, C. 280–290

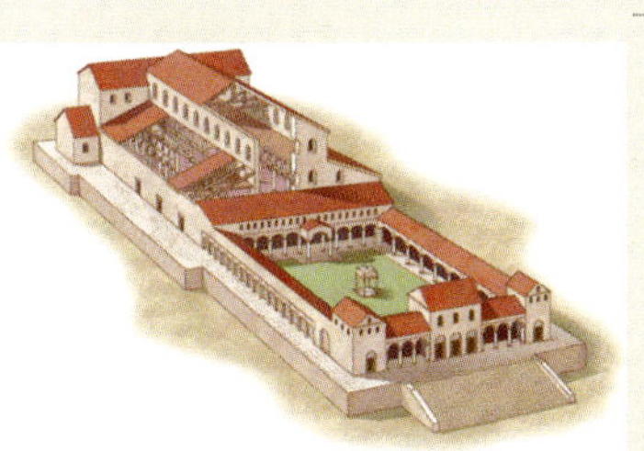

OLD SAINT PETER'S, C. 320–327

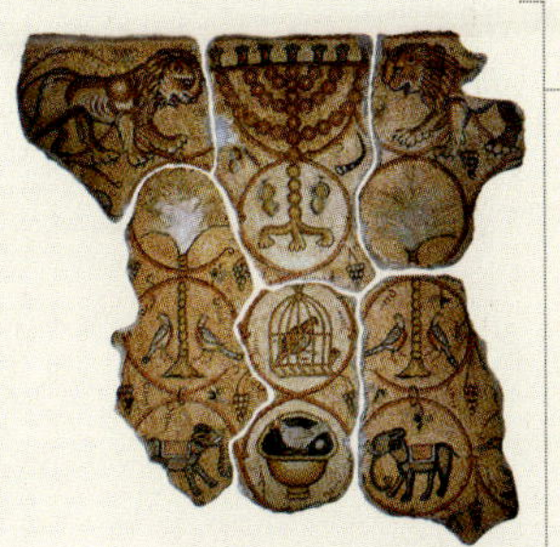

SYNAGOGUE FLOOR, C. 530

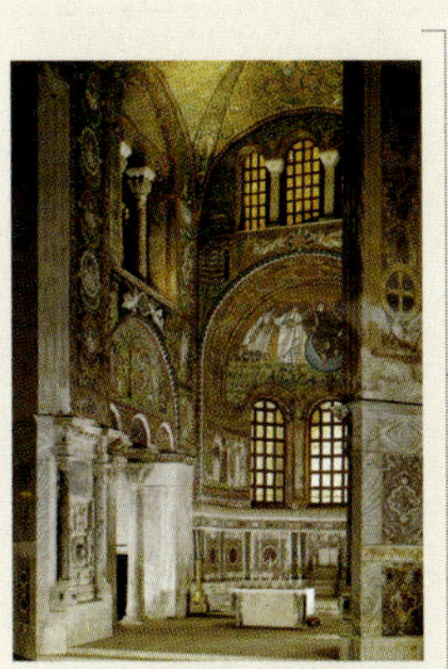

CHURCH OF SAN VITALE, CONSECRATED 547

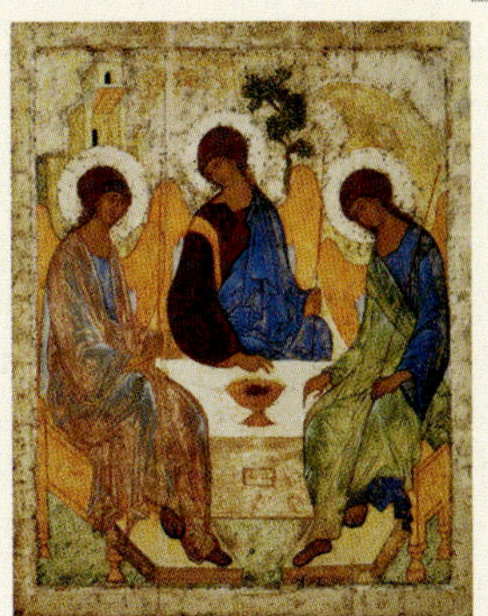

RUBLYOV
OLD TESTAMENT TRINITY, C. 1410–1425

100 CE

◀ **Roman destruction of the Temple in Jerusalem,** 70

◀ **Parthians conquer Dura-Europos,** 256

300

◀ **Edict of Milan legalizes Christianity in the Roman Empire,** 313

◀ **Council of Nicaea,** 325

◀ **End of the Western Roman Empire,** 476

500

◀ **Justinian,** ruled 527–565

700

◀ **Iconoclasm,** 726–843

900

◀ **Russia becomes Christian,** 988

◀ **Division of Church into Roman Catholic and Eastern Orthodox,** 1054

◀ **First Crusade,** 1095–1099

1100

◀ **Western Rule of Constantinople,** 1204–1261

◀ **Fall of Constantinople to the Ottoman Turks, signaling the end of the Roman Empire,** 1453

1500

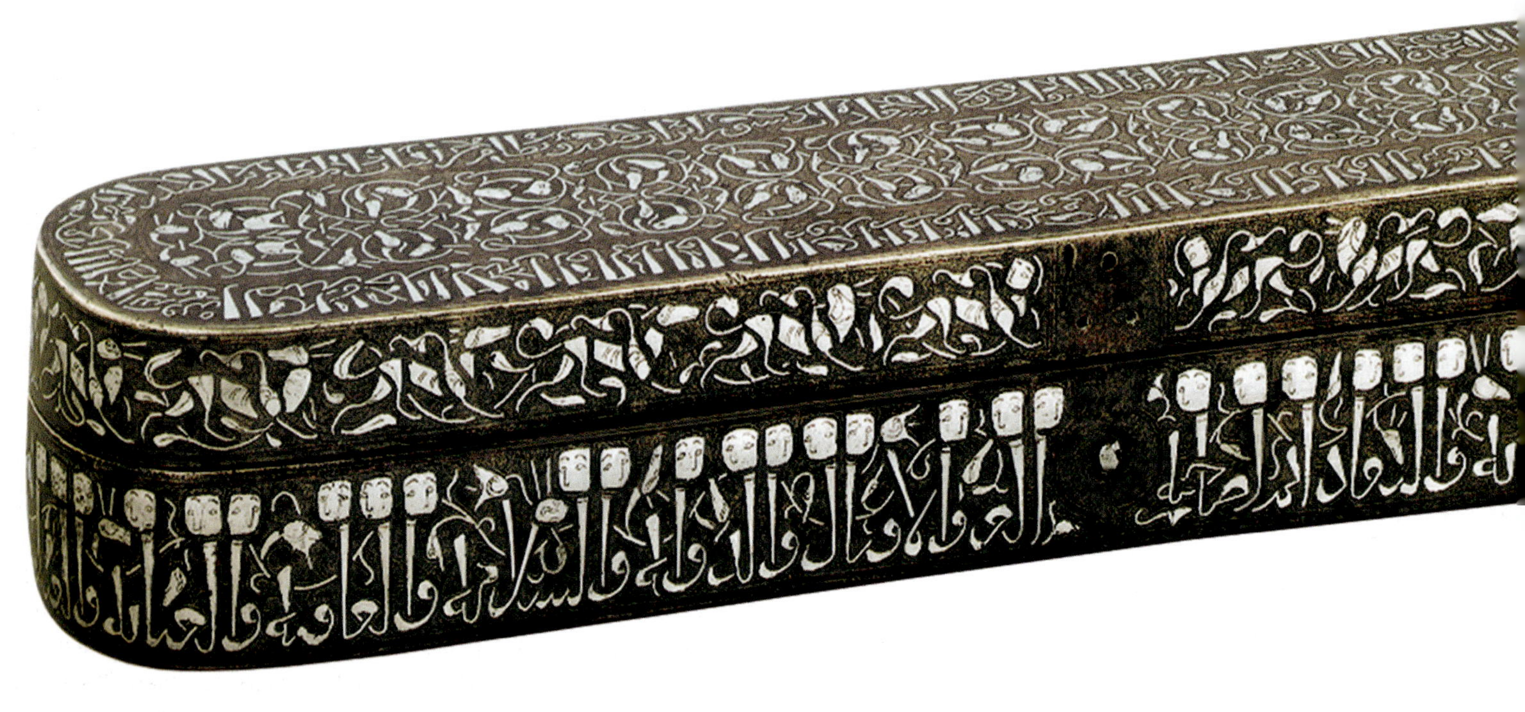

8
Islamic Art

LOOKING FORWARD

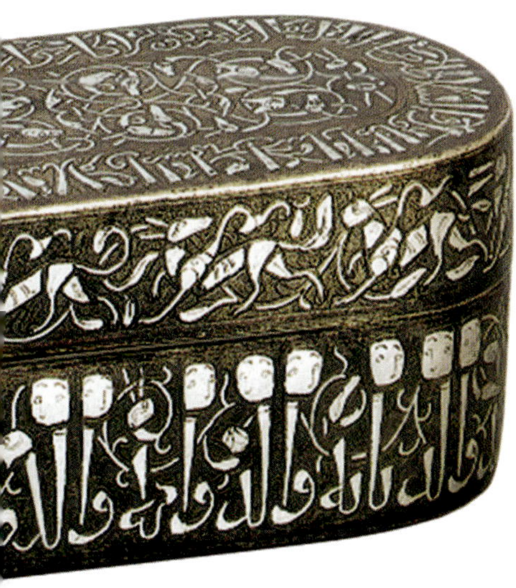

8–1 Shazi. Pen box, from Iran or Afghanistan. 1210–1211. Brass inlaid with silver, copper, and black organic material, height 2", length 12⅜", width 2½" (5 × 31.4 × 6.4 cm). Freer Gallery of Art, Smithsonian Institution Washington, D.C.
PURCHASE (F1936.7)

The inscriptions on the box include some 20 honorific phrases extolling its owner, Majd al-Mulk al-Muzaffar. The inscription in naskhi *script on the lid calls him the "luminous star of Islam." The largest inscription, written in animated* naskhi *(an animated script is one with human or animal forms in it), asked 24 blessings for him from God. Shazi, the designer of the box, signed and dated it on the side of the lid, making it one of the earliest signed works in Islamic art. Majd al-Mulk enjoyed his box for only ten years; he was killed by Mongol invaders in 1221.*

Muslim artists and patrons held calligraphy in the highest esteem. Even writing equipment could be wonderfully decorated, and a pen box could be a prestigious possession. This pen box of polished brass, richly inlaid with precious silver, attests to the sophistication and wealth of its owner, Majd al-Mulk al-Muzaffar, a statesman and scholar and the governor of Khurasan, who died in 1221 (fig. **8–1**). The artist Shazi created exceptionally clear and elegant animated inscriptions in two different scripts: kufic and *naskhi*. To some letters he added duck heads and foliage; in the rest of the inscription, he embellished the vertical elements with human heads. Inscriptions on this pen box extol the virtues of the owner and wish him well.

As a "People of the Book"—that is, those whose religion is revealed through sacred scriptures—Muslims (followers of Islam) had cause to honor fine writing. Since the Qur'an (Koran) is believed to be the word of God brought to Muhammad by the angel Gabriel, the words must be accurately preserved and deserve to be embellished. Consequently, calligraphy became the highest form of art in the Muslim world. Writing was not limited to books and documents but was used to adorn surfaces, from walls of buildings to curving brass candlesticks, and from silk textiles to glazed ceramics. Mystics sometimes equated the creation of letters by scribes with the creation of human beings by God, and calligraphy can be so intricate that it seems to be a secret language.

Formal kufic script (after Kufa, a city in Iraq) is blocky and angular, with strong upright strokes and long horizontals. In "foliated kufic," leaves and flowers seem to sprout from the terminals of the letters. Calligraphers later created "animated" scripts, first by adding heads to upright strokes, and later by forming entire letters from figures. Kufic was used for inscriptions on buildings, on metal and wooden objects, and on textiles as well as for writing in ink on paper or vellum.

By the thirteenth century, scribes had developed several forms of cursive writing. Of the six major styles, one extraordinarily beautiful form, known as *naskhi*, was said to have been revealed and taught to scribes in a vision. Even those who cannot read Arabic can enjoy the beauty of the forms. The materials used by the scribes, especially the pens and the inks, had to be as perfect as the script. A pen box is a symbol of scholarly attainment.

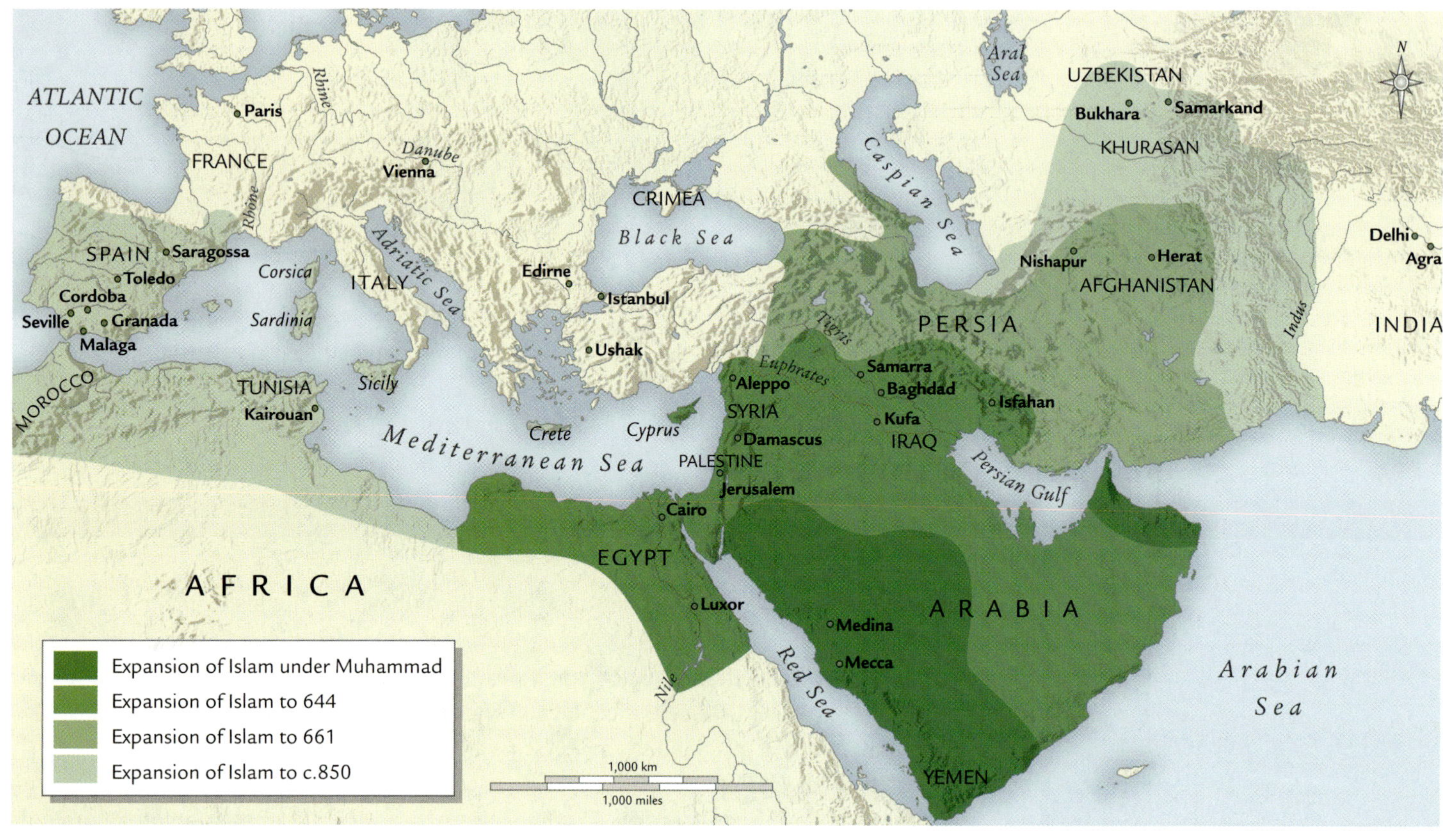

Map 8–1 The Islamic World

The religion called Islam (meaning "submission to [God's will]") originated in Arabia in the early seventh century. Under the leadership of its founder, the Prophet Muhammad (c. 570–632), and his successors, Islam spread rapidly, encompassing large areas of Africa, Europe, and Asia. Under four of Muhammad's closest associates, who assumed in turn the title of caliph (successor), Muslim armies conquered Persia (Iran), Egypt, and the Byzantine provinces of Syria and Palestine. The last of these caliphs, Ali (ruled 656–661), was succeeded by a rival, Muawiya (ruled 661–680), who founded the Umayyad dynasty. By the early eighth century, the aggressively expansionist Umayyads had reached India, conquered all of North Africa and Spain, and penetrated France to within 100 miles of Paris before being turned back. Today Islam is the world's fastest growing religion (see map **8–1**).

At first, Islamic art absorbed local traditions—as diverse as Roman, Byzantine, and Persian—in art and architecture. Because conservative Muslims discouraged the representation of humans, especially in religious contexts, artists living in Islamic lands developed a particularly rich vocabulary of ornament, including complex geometric designs and the scrolling vines known outside the Islamic world as **arabesques**. Artists excelled in surface decoration, manipulating an infinite variety of highly controlled patterns, and often highlighting the interplay between nonrepresentational designs and organic shapes and forms. For some people, such designs help free the mind from a focus on material form, opening it to contemplation of the enormity of divine presence.

Art During the Early Caliphates

Architecture

Under caliphs of the Umayyad dynasty (661–750), the political center of the Muslim world moved from the Arabian peninsula to the city of Damascus, in modern Syria. Inspired by the Roman and Byzantine architecture of the eastern Mediterranean, the Umayyads became enthusiastic builders of shrines, mosques, and palaces. After Mecca and Medina—sites directly associated with the life of Muhammad—Jerusalem was the holiest site in Islam. In the center of the city rises the Haram al-Sharif ("Noble Sanctuary"), a rocky outcrop that Muslims identify as the place from which Muhammad ascended to the presence of God on the "Night Journey" described in the Qur'an. The same rock is also associated with the creation of Adam; the place where the patriarch Abraham prepared to sacrifice his son, Isaac, at the command of God; and the site of the temple of Solomon, making it important to Jews and Christians, as well as Muslims.

In 692, the Umayyads constructed a shrine over the rock (fig. **8–2**) using Syrian artisans trained in the Byzantine tradition. The Dome of the Rock is the first great monument of Islamic art, decorated on the interior with a mosaic frieze containing the earliest written text of the Qur'an. Its centralized octagonal plan is derived from both Byzantine and local Christian architecture. Muslim patrons and builders, however, delighted in complex mathematical forms; for example, the plan of the octagonal structure is based on

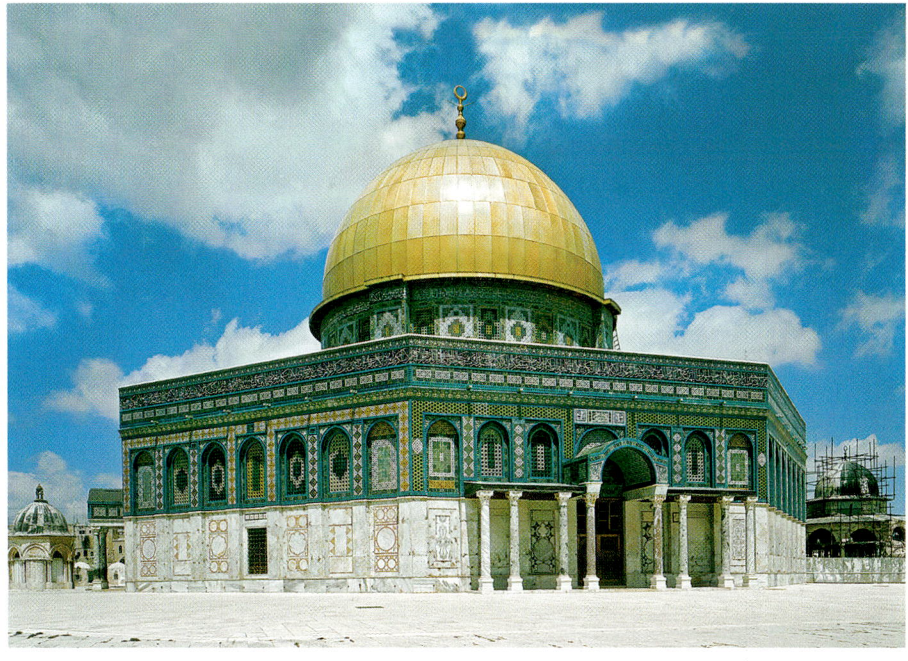

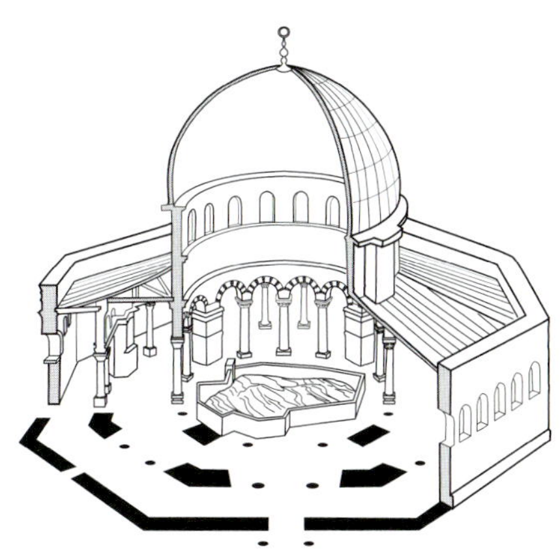

8–2 Exterior view and cutaway drawing of the Dome of the Rock, Jerusalem, Israel. Begun 692

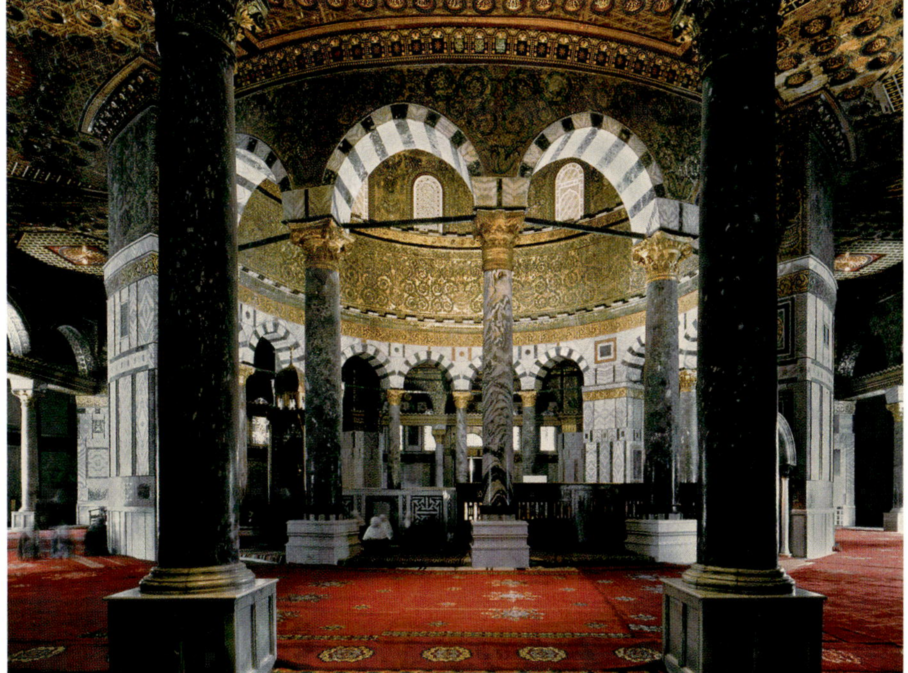

8–3 Interior, Dome of the Rock, Jerusalem, Israel

*Concentric aisles (**ambulatories**) permit the devout visitor to circumambulate the rock. Inscriptions from the Qur'an interspersed with passages from other texts and commentaries, including information about the building, form a frieze around the inner wall in gold mosaic on a turquoise-green ground. The pilgrim must walk around the central space first clockwise and then counterclockwise to read the inscriptions. The carpets and ceiling are modern but probably reflect the original intention.*

the eight-pointed star, formed by two intersecting squares. The central space is covered by a dome on a tall drum supported by an arcade. Two concentric aisles enclose the rock.

Marble veneer at ground level and glass mosaics above decorate the building's interior. Originally, glass mosaics also covered the upper half of the octagon's outer walls, but they deteriorated over time. The lower part of the octagon walls retains its original white marble facings, inset with patterns in colored stone. In the sixteenth century, the Ottoman Sultan Suleyman ordered the mosaics replaced with magnificent, colorful ceramic tiles, specialties of Turkish builders of that time.

A broad mosaic frieze on the inner wall depicts thick, symmetrical vine scrolls and trees in turquoise, blue, and green, embellished with imitation jewels, over a gold ground. The mosaics are variously thought to represent the gardens of Paradise and trophies of Muslim victories offered to God. The focal point of the building, remarkably enough, is not the decorative program—nor even something that can initially be seen. From the entrance one sees only pure light streaming down to the unseen rock, surrounded by color and pattern (fig. **8–3**). After penetrating the space, the viewer/worshiper realizes that the light falls on the precious rock, envisioning the very passage of Muhammad to the heavens.

ISLAM AND THE PROPHET MUHAMMAD

Islam originated in the Arabian peninsula in the seventh century. According to Islamic belief, God (Allah) transmitted his message through the archangel Gabriel to an Arab merchant, Muhammad. These revelations form the basis of the Islamic religion. Believers (Muslims) are those who submit to God and acknowledge Muhammad as their Prophet. Muslims also recognize earlier prophets—Moses, Abraham, Jesus—and share with Jews and Christians the belief in one God. Originally God's revelations were committed to memory and passed down orally, but after Muhammad's death an official transcription was made in the Qur'an.

The Prophet Muhammad was born about 570 in Mecca, a city in west-central Arabia. Mecca was the site of the Kaaba, an ancient, cube-shaped stone building believed to be the house Abraham built for God. Muhammad received his first revelations in 610 and soon thereafter was accepted as the Prophet of God by his friends and family. After failing to convert the local population, Muhammad and his companions were forced to flee in 622 to the oasis of Yathrib, which was renamed Medina, "the [Prophet's] City." It is to this event, called the *Hegira* (emigration), that Muslims date the beginning of their history.

Muhammad regained control of Mecca in 630, and the inhabitants eventually accepted the new religion. The Kaaba became Islam's sacred center, toward which Muslims around the world still face when praying. Muhammad died in Medina in 632. Only after his death was the Qur'an written down and assembled in 114 chapters, or *surahs*, each divided into verses, which make up the sacred scripture of Islam.

Muslims believe in a single, all-powerful God and in Muhammad as the last in the succession of true prophets. Islam also requires Muslims to follow the Five Pillars of Islam, sometimes symbolized by an open hand with five extended fingers. The most important pillar is the statement of faith: "There is no god but God and Muhammad is his messenger." The second pillar is ritual worship five times a day. (Muslims establish a direct, personal relationship with God through worship. The faithful prostrate themselves facing the Kaaba in Mecca.) The remaining pillars are charity to the poor, fasting during the month of Ramadan, and, if possible, a pilgrimage to Mecca. Muslims participate in congregational worship and listen to a sermon at a mosque (prayer hall) on Fridays.

After Muhammad's death, his father-in-law Abu Bakr became the first caliph, or successor to the Prophet. Ali—the husband of Muhammad's daughter Fatima—became the fourth caliph. The power struggle that ended in Ali's death led to the division of Islamic communities into Sunni (traditional) and Shi'ite (followers of Ali) Muslims.

The Dome of the Rock is a special shrine. **Mosques**, in contrast, provide a place for regular public worship. In detail, the plans of mosques (in Arabic, *masjid*, a "place of prostration") may vary, but they are all usually entered through a courtyard, and each must have a large covered space to accommodate the worshiping community at Friday prayers. All mosques are oriented in the direction of Mecca (***qibla***), and worshipers arrange themselves in rows to pray facing Mecca. A niche called a ***mihrab*** identifies the *qibla* wall, a practice deriving from a long tradition of using niches to signify holy places: the Torah shrine in a synagogue, the recessed frame for sculpture of gods and ancestors in Roman architecture, the apse in a Christian church. The ***maqsura***, an enclosure in front of the *mihrab* for the ruler and other dignitaries, became a feature of the principal congregational mosque after an assassination attempt on an Umayyad ruler. The ***minbar***, or pulpit, stands by the *mihrab* as a raised platform for the prayer leader and a symbol of his authority. The faithful gather for Friday prayers and listen to a sermon in the principal mosque of the city, called the Great Mosque or Masjid-i Jami ("Friday" or "Congregational Mosque).

The earliest mosques were very simple, modeled on Muhammad's house with its courtyard and porticoes, where early followers gathered for worship and to hear the Prophet speak from his raised seat. The Great Mosque of Kairouan, Tunisia (fig. **8–4**), although built in the ninth century, reflects this early form of the

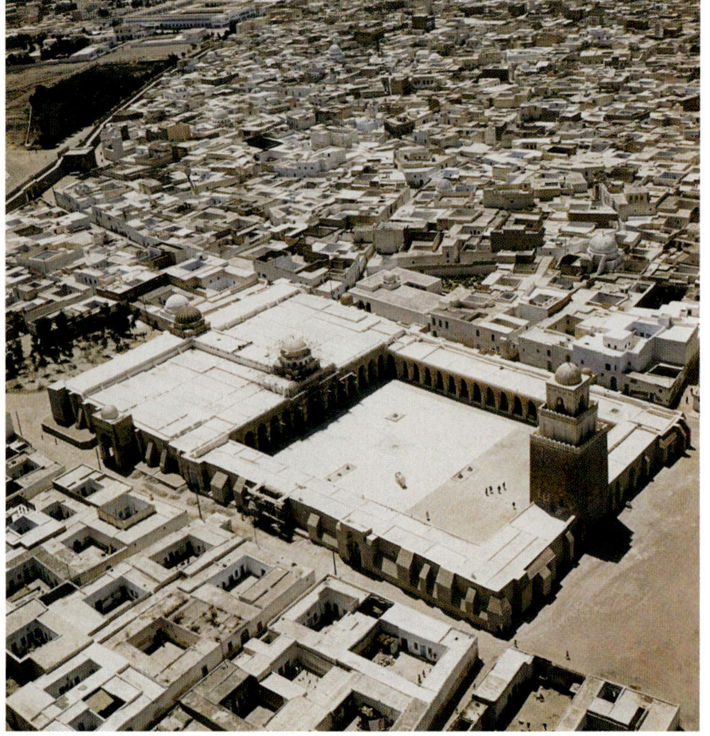

8–4 The Great Mosque, Kairouan, Tunisia. 836–875

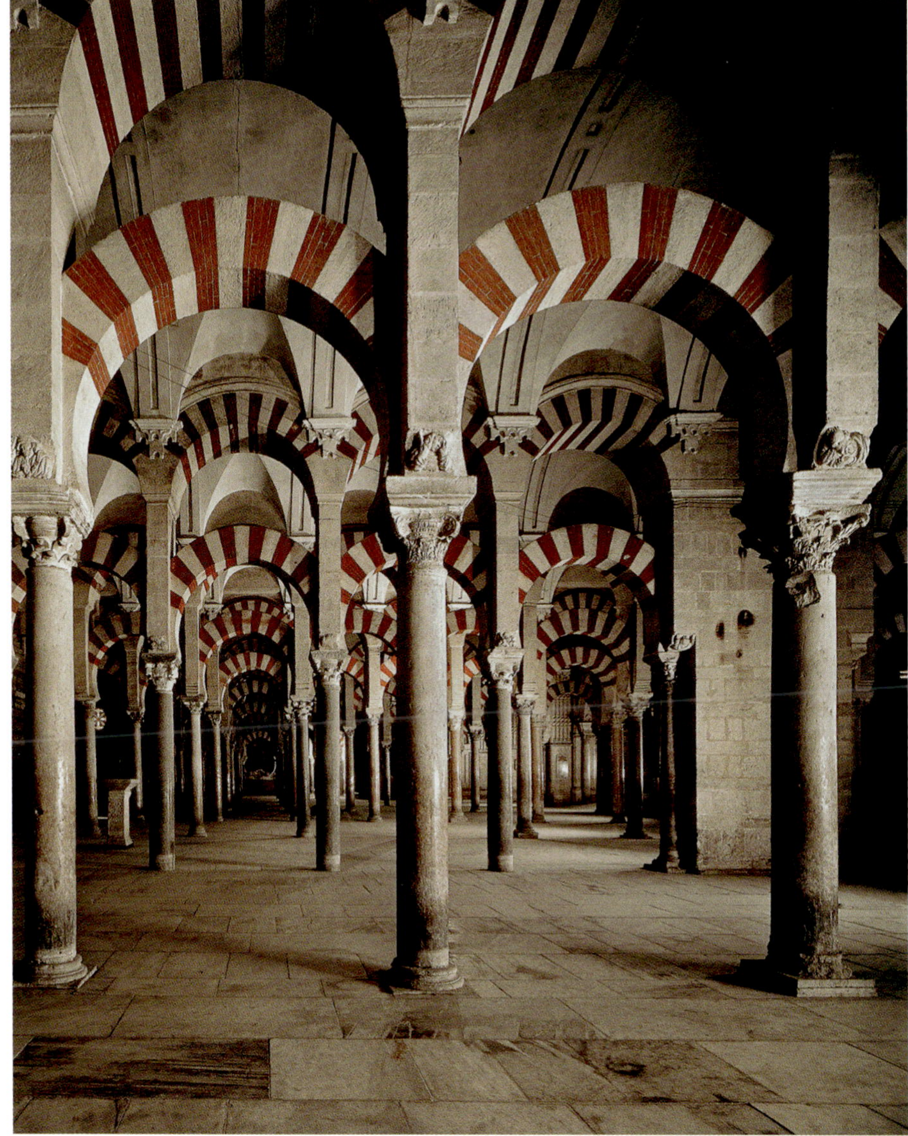

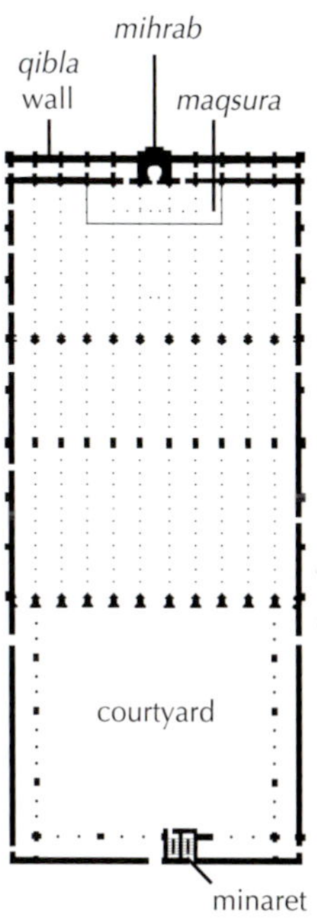

8–5 Prayer hall and plan of mosque, Great Mosque, Cordoba, Spain. Begun 785–786

The plan represents the state of the mosque after the renovations of al-Hakam II (ruled 961–976).

mosque. Its large rectangular plan is divided between a courtyard and a hypostyle prayer hall with a flat roof. The system of repeated bays and aisles can easily be extended as the congregation grows in size. A huge tower (the **minaret**, from which criers call the faithful to prayer) rises opposite the *mihrab*. A standard and increasingly visible feature of mosques, minarets will come to signify Islam's presence in a city.

When the Abbasids overthrew the Umayyads in 750, and Abbasid caliphs ruled the central and eastern lands of Islam from their capitals at Baghdad and Samarra (in modern Iraq) until 1258, the Umayyads maintained control in the far western lands of Islam. As the Abbasid caliphs took power, a survivor of the Umayyad dynasty, Abd al-Rahman I, fled across North Africa into southern Spain (al-Andalus in Arabic), establishing himself there as provincial ruler, or emir (ruled 756–788). From a new capital at Cordoba, the Umayyads governed al-Andalus until 1031, first as emirs and then, beginning with Abd al-Rahman III (ruled 912–961), as caliphs, setting themselves up as equals to the Abbasids. Their court at Cordoba became a renowned international center for scholars, scientists, poets, and musicians.

The finest surviving example of Spanish Umayyad architecture is the Great Mosque of Cordoba. This sprawling structure was begun in 785 by appropriating the site of a Christian church and was repeatedly enlarged to meet the needs of an expanding urban population. The marble columns and capitals in the first hypostyle prayer hall (fig. **8–5**) were recycled from the local ruins of classical buildings in this formerly wealthy Roman province. Two tiers of arches, one above the other, surmount the columns. The double-tiered design increases the height of the interior space and strengthens the structure. The distinctively shaped horseshoe arches—a form known from ancient Roman times—came to be closely associated with Islamic architecture in the west. At the Great Mosque in Cordoba, these arches are distinguished by the alternation of pale stone voussoirs (wedge-shaped stone blocks) and red bricks. While the alternating colors and textures are decorative, the use of contrasting materials is also functional. The stone gives strength, and

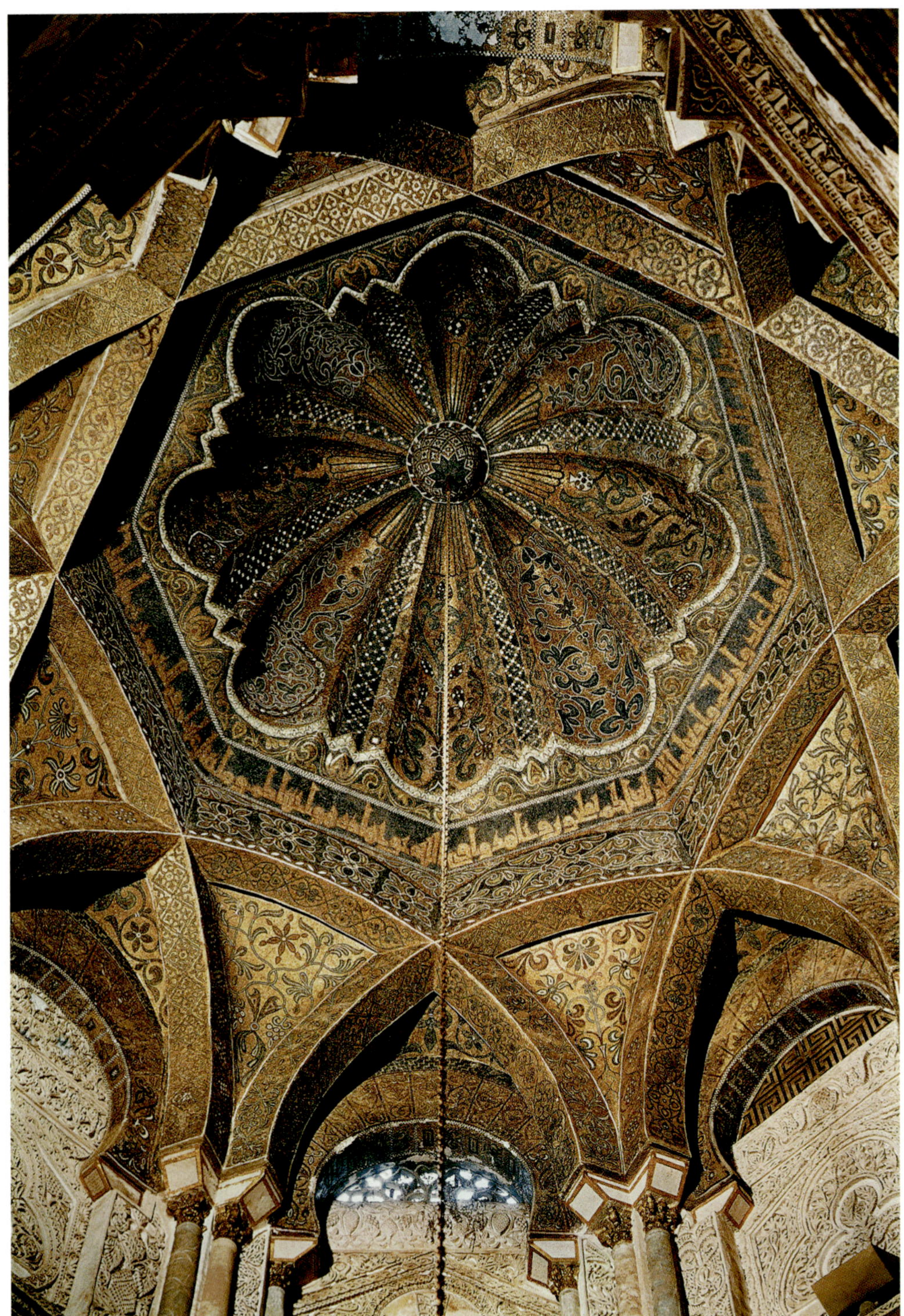

8–6 Dome in front of the *mihrab*, Great Mosque, Cordoba. 965

The costly and luxurious decoration of the additions that al-Hakam II (ruled 961–976) made to the Great Mosque disturbed many of his subjects. The caliph attempted to answer their objections with an inscription giving thanks to God, who "helped him in the building of this eternal place, with the goal of making this mosque more spacious for his subjects, something which both he and they greatly wanted" (Dodds, page 23).

the brick lends flexibility and ease in achieving the circular form of the arch. Roman and Byzantine builders also used the technique, but usually in utilitarian structures like defensive walls. The Muslims saw the decorative possibilities of the technique and realized its ornamental potential.

In the final century of Umayyad rule, Cordoba emerged as a major commercial and intellectual hub and a flourishing center for the arts, surpassing Christian European cities economically and in science, literature, and philosophy. As a sign of this new prestige and power, Abd al-Rahman III boldly reclaimed the title of caliph in 929. He and his son al-Hakam II (ruled 961–976) made the Great Mosque a focus of patronage, commissioning costly and luxurious renovations such as a new *mihrab* with three bays in front of it. Just in front of the *mihrab*, a melon-shaped, ribbed dome seems to float over a support of intersecting arches (fig. **8–6**). Lushly patterned mosaics with inscriptions, geometric motifs, and stylized vegetation clothe both this dome and the *mihrab* below in brilliant color and gold. These were installed by a Byzantine master who was sent by the emperor in Constantinople, bearing boxes of the small glazed ceramic and glass cubes (tesserae) used to create mosaics. Such artistic exchange is emblematic of the interconnectedness of the medieval Mediterranean—through trade, diplomacy, and competition.

Calligraphy

From the beginning, Arabic language and script have been revered in Islamic society. As the language of the Qur'an, Arabic is a powerful unifying force. From the eighth through the eleventh centuries, it was the universal scholarly language in Muslim lands. Reverence for the Qur'an as the word of God extends by association to the act of writing itself, and calligraphy—the art of fine hand lettering—becomes one of the glories of Islamic art.

Kufic, the earliest formal script, is blocky and angular and may have evolved from inscriptions on stone monuments. A page from a ninth-century Qur'an exemplifies a style of kufic writing common from the eighth to tenth century (fig. **8–7**). Red diacritical marks (pronunciation guides) accent the black ink. Horizontal strokes are elongated, and fat-bodied letters are emphasized. The *surah* ("chapter") title is embedded in the golden ornamental strip at the bottom of the page. This Qur'an is written on vellum, an especially fine parchment (prepared animal skin). Paper, a Chinese invention, was made in the Islamic world by the mid-eighth century but did not fully replace parchment until after the year 1000 (see "Indian Painting on Paper," page 218).

Beautifully designed script was not limited to books and documents, however. It was also displayed on walls of buildings and on metalwork, textiles, glass, and ceramics. Kufic-style inscriptions were popular decorations on ceramics made in the ninth and tenth centuries, even in distant centers like Nishapur (or Khurasan, in modern northeastern Iran) and Samarkand (in modern

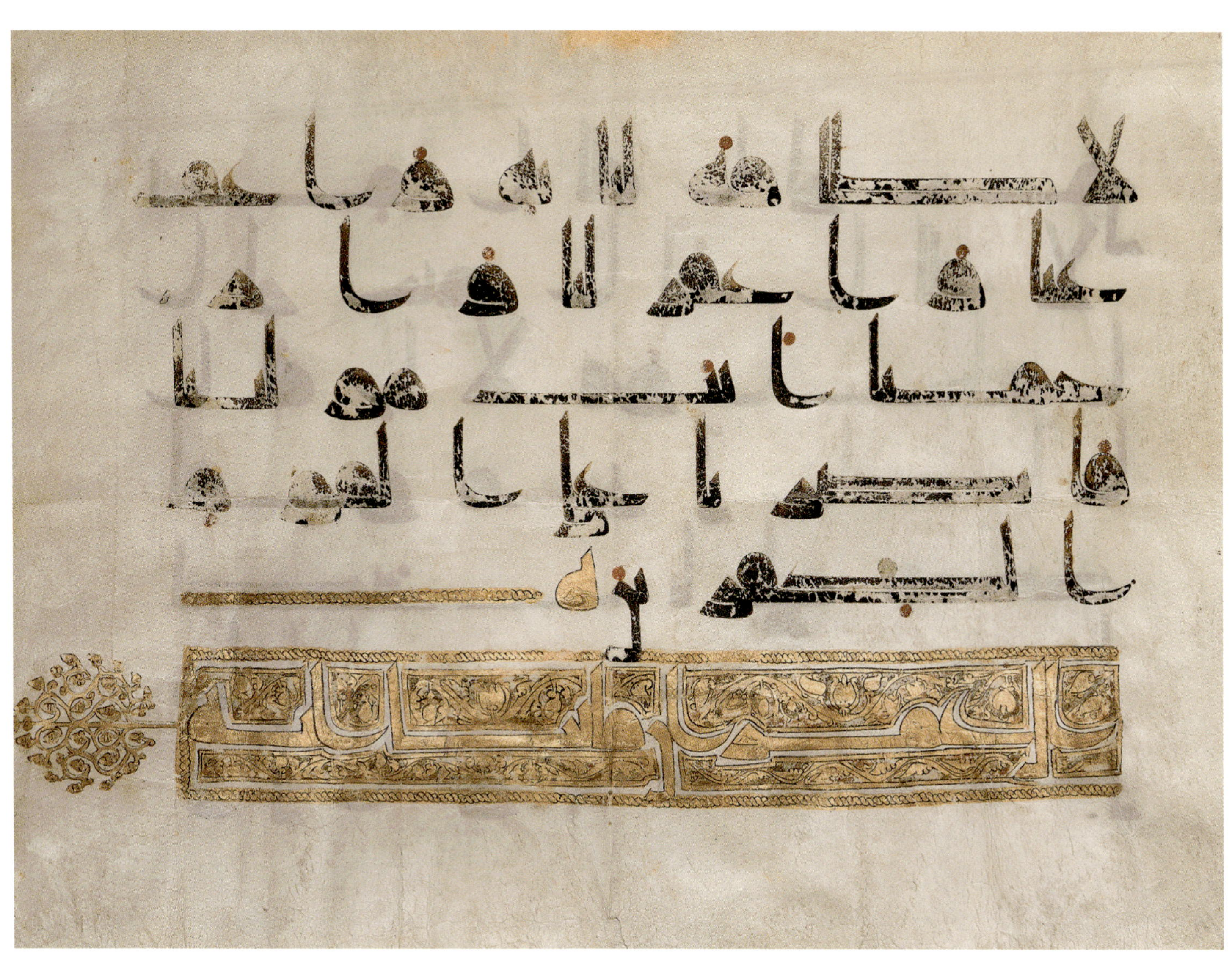

8–7 Page from the Qur'an (*surah* II: 286 and title *surah* III) in kufic script, from Syria or Iraq. 9th century. Ink, pigments, and gold on vellum, 8⁵⁄₁₆" × 11½" (21.1 × 29.2 cm). The Metropolitan Museum of Art, New York
ROGERS FUND, 1937 (37.99.2). PHOTOGRAPH © 1994 THE METROPOLITAN MUSEUM OF ART, NEW YORK

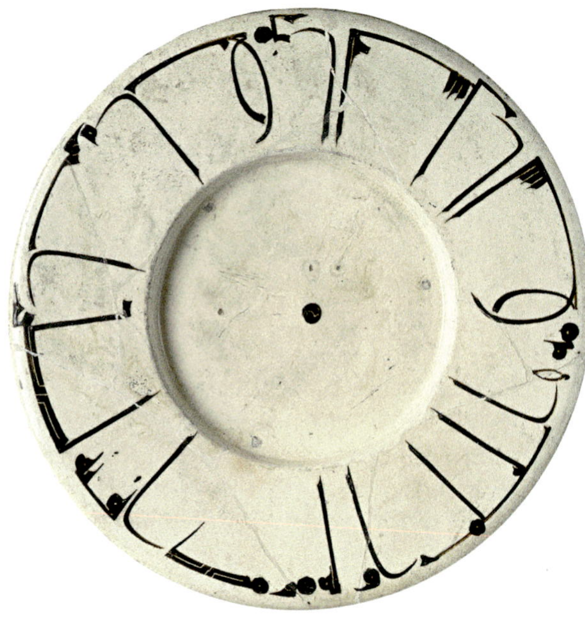

8–8 Plate with kufic border, Samarkand, Uzbekistan. 9th–10th century. Earthenware with slip, pigment, and lead glaze, diameter 14½" (37 cm). Musée du Louvre, Paris

The white ground of this plate imitated prized Chinese porcelains made of fine white kaolin clay. Since Samarkand was connected to the Silk Route (see page 92), the great caravan route to China, it was a center of intercultural exchange.

Uzbekistan). These elegant earthenware bowls and plates are characterized by a clear lead glaze applied over a black inscription on a white, slip-painted ceramic ground (fig. **8–8**). Here the script has been elongated to fill the plate's rim, stressing the letters' verticality in such a way that they seem to radiate from the bold spot at the center of the circle. But this is not abstract decoration. The inscription translates: "Knowledge, the beginning of it is bitter to taste, but the end is sweeter than honey." Inscriptions on Samarkand ware provide a storehouse of such popular sayings and folk wisdom.

Later Islamic Art

The Saljuqs in Persia

In the eleventh century, power in the Islamic world fell into the hands of more or less independent regional rulers. As the Abbasid caliphate disintegrated, the Saljuqs rose to power. A Turkic people from Central Asia who converted to Islam in the tenth century, the Saljuqs first conquered Persia in 1037–1040, establishing there the Great Saljuq Dynasty (c. 1037–1157). In 1055 they took over the Abbasid capital city of Baghdad, although the Abbasids survived as token rulers until 1258. Riven by dynastic in-fighting, the empire of the Great Saljuqs was divided up between many different Saljuq branches. In 1071, one of these branches, who became known as the Saljuq Dynasty of Rum, defeated the Byzantine army and went on to conquer most of the eastern Mediterranean including Anatolia

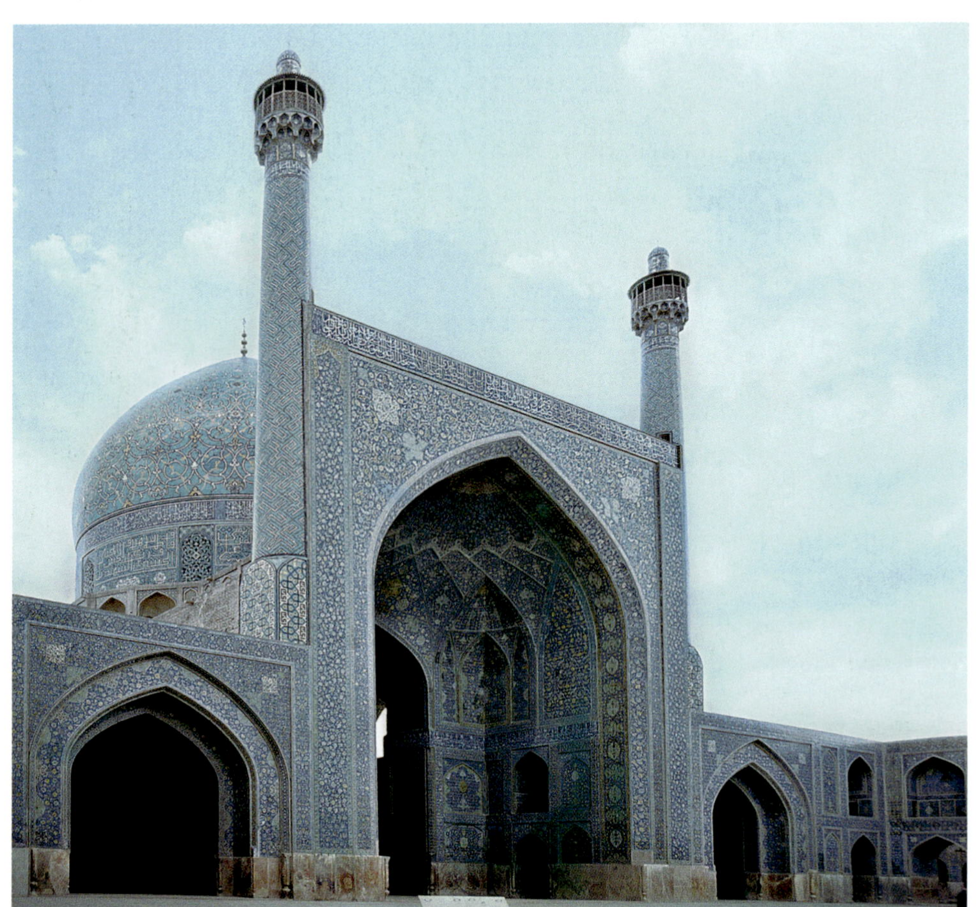

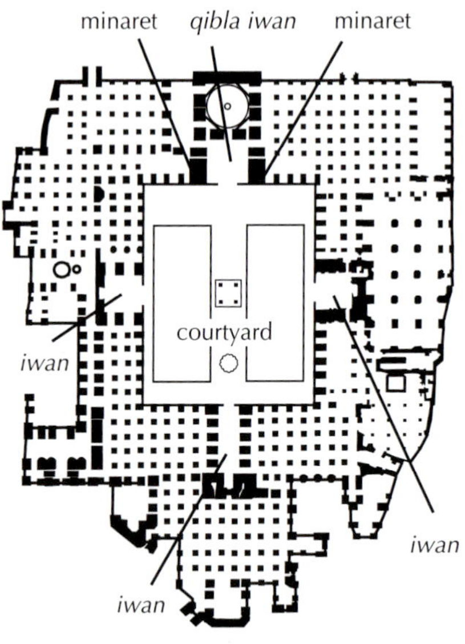

8–9 Courtyard view toward *qibla iwan* and plan of mosque, Masjid-i Jami (Congregational Mosque), Isfahan, Persia (Iran). 11th–18th century

(modern Turkey), which they held until the fourteenth century. In the meantime, Mongols, led by Ghenghiz Khan (ruled 1206–1227) and his successors thundered in to the region to capture a vast empire between northern China and Egypt. In the west, Umayyad Spain broke up into small kingdoms centered around major cities such as Saragossa, Málaga, Granada, and Seville. They engaged in constant warfare with Christian armies, who were determined to expel them from the Iberian peninsula. This military action (or Reconquest as the Christians call it) continued over a 400-year period, ending only in 1492 with the overthrow of the Nasrid Dynasty in the Kingdom of Granada.

The rulers of the Great Saljuq Dynasty proved themselves enlightened patrons of the arts. They built on a grand scale—mosques, ***madrasas*** (schools for advanced study), palaces, urban hostels, and remote caravanserais (inns) for traveling merchants to encourage long-distance trade. They adopted the Persian ***iwan***, a vaulted open room, and they perfected a mosque/madrasas plan in which four *iwans* are arranged around an internal courtyard. The Masjid-i Jami ("Congregational" or "Friday" Mosque) in the Saljuq capital of Isfahan (in modern Iran) has a four-iwan plan (fig. **8–9**). The *qibla iwan* on the south was vaulted with ***muqarnas*** (niche-like cells) in the fourteenth century. The tall, slender minarets and brilliant blue tiles were added in the seventeenth century.

Such tile work—another highlight of Islamic art—can be seen in a fourteenth-century tile mosaic *mihrab* originally from a *madrasa* in Isfahan (fig. **8–10**). More than 11 feet tall, the dazzling surface pattern was made by painstakingly cutting each piece of tile, including the pieces making up the calligraphy on the curving surface of the niche, and assembling them like a complicated puzzle set in mortar. The dense decoration includes regular organic and geometric forms that contrast with the sinuous irregularity of the inscriptions. The colors—white against turquoise and cobalt blue with accents of dark yellow and green—are characteristic of Persian tilework.

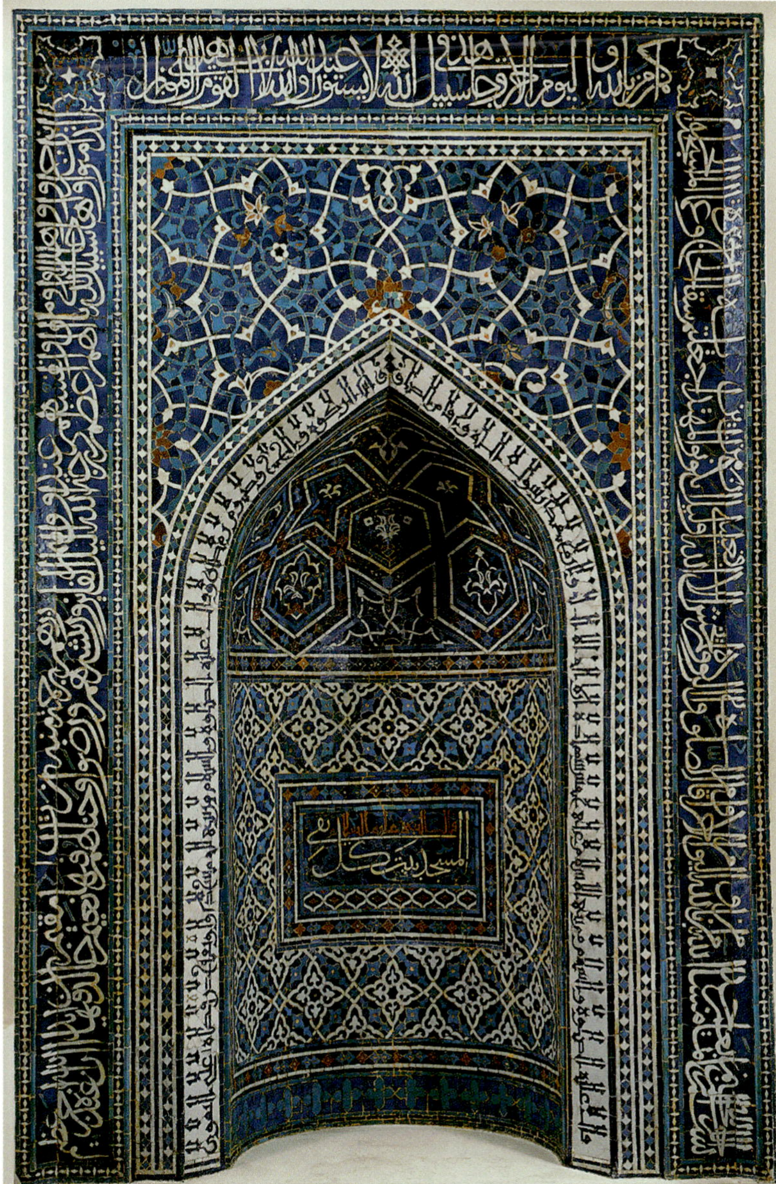

8–10 Tile mosaic *mihrab*, from the Madrasa Imami, Isfahan, Persia (Iran). c. 1354 (restored). Glazed and cut ceramic, 11' 3" × 7' 6" (3.43 × 2.29 m). The Metropolitan Museum of Art, New York

HARRIS BRISBANE DICK FUND (39.20). PHOTOGRAPH © 1982 THE METROPOLITAN MUSEUM OF ART, NEW YORK

One of the three Qur'anic inscriptions on this mihrab *dates it to approximately 1354. Note the combination of decorated kufic (inner inscription) and cursive* muhaqqaq *(outer inscription) scripts. The outer inscription tells of the duties of believers and the heavenly rewards for the builders of mosques. The inner arch gives the Five Pillars of Islam in kufic. The framed center panel says: "The mosque is the house of every pious person."*

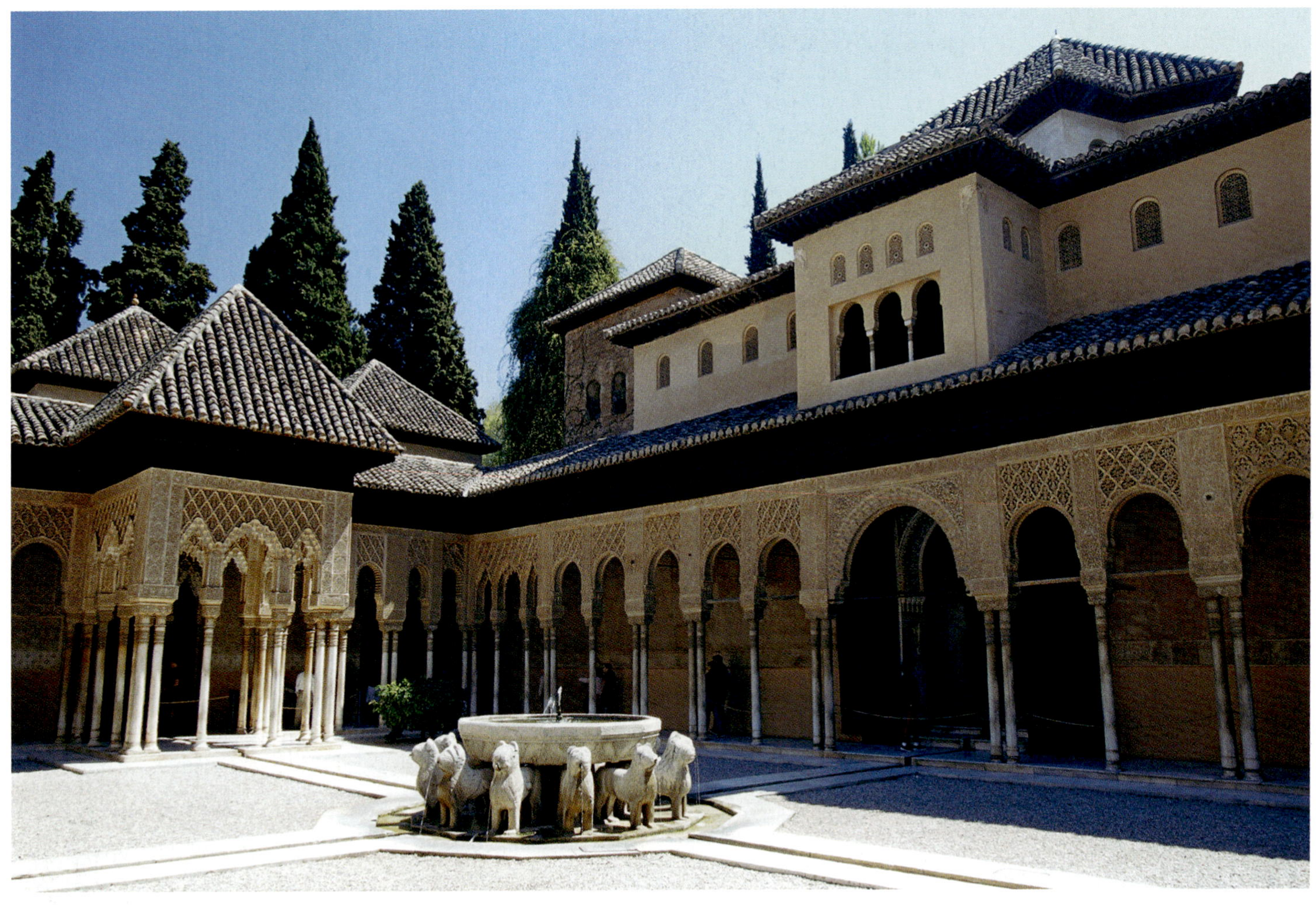

8–11 Court of the Lions, Alhambra, Granada, Spain. 1354–1391

Granada, with its ample water supply, had long been known as a city of gardens. The 12 stone lions of the fountain in the center of this court were salvaged from the ruins of an earlier palatial complex on the Alhambra hill. The earlier structure was begun in the late eleventh century by a high Granadan official of Jewish origin named Samuel ibn Naghralla and completed by his son Yusuf in the early twelfth century. Commentators of the time praised this complex, with its pools, fountains, and gardens. No doubt it was a source of inspiration for the builders of the later palaces.

The Nasrids in Spain

Muslim architects also created luxurious palaces set in beautiful gardens, such as the Alhambra in the southeastern Spanish capital of Granada. A fortified hilltop palace complex, it was the home of the Nasrids, the last Spanish Muslim dynasty (1232–1492), which controlled the area around Granada. The Alhambra gained its present form in the fourteenth century. The builders combined a fortress and royal residences with a small town, including mosques, baths, servants' quarters, barracks, stables, workshops, and a mint, that extends for about half a mile along the crest of a high hill overlooking the city of Granada.

An especially luxurious section of the palace is the Palace of the Lions, a private retreat built by Muhammad V (ruled 1354–1359, 1362–1391). At its heart is the rectangular Court of the Lions (fig. **8–11**), named for a fountain whose basin is supported on the backs of 12 stylized stone lions. The courtyard is enclosed by an arcade of carved stucco arches supported by slender columns, often clustered in groups of two or three. Although the central courtyard is filled with gravel today, it was originally a sunken garden with raised fountains and waterways. Aromatic shrubs, flowers, and small citrus trees were planted between the water channels that radiate from the fountain—evocative of the rivers of paradise—and divide the courtyard into quarters. The architectural focus of the Alhambra was largely directed inward, toward these lushly planted courtyards, which embody the Muslim vision of paradise as a well-watered, walled garden. Indeed, the English word *paradise* comes from *pairidiz*, the old Persian term for an enclosed park.

Pavilions used for dining and the performance of music and poetry open onto the Court of the Lions. One of these, the so-called Hall of the Abencerrajes, on the south side (probably a music room) is covered by a spectacularly intricate ceiling (fig. **8–12**). The eight-pointed-star-shaped dome rests on the clustered profusion of small

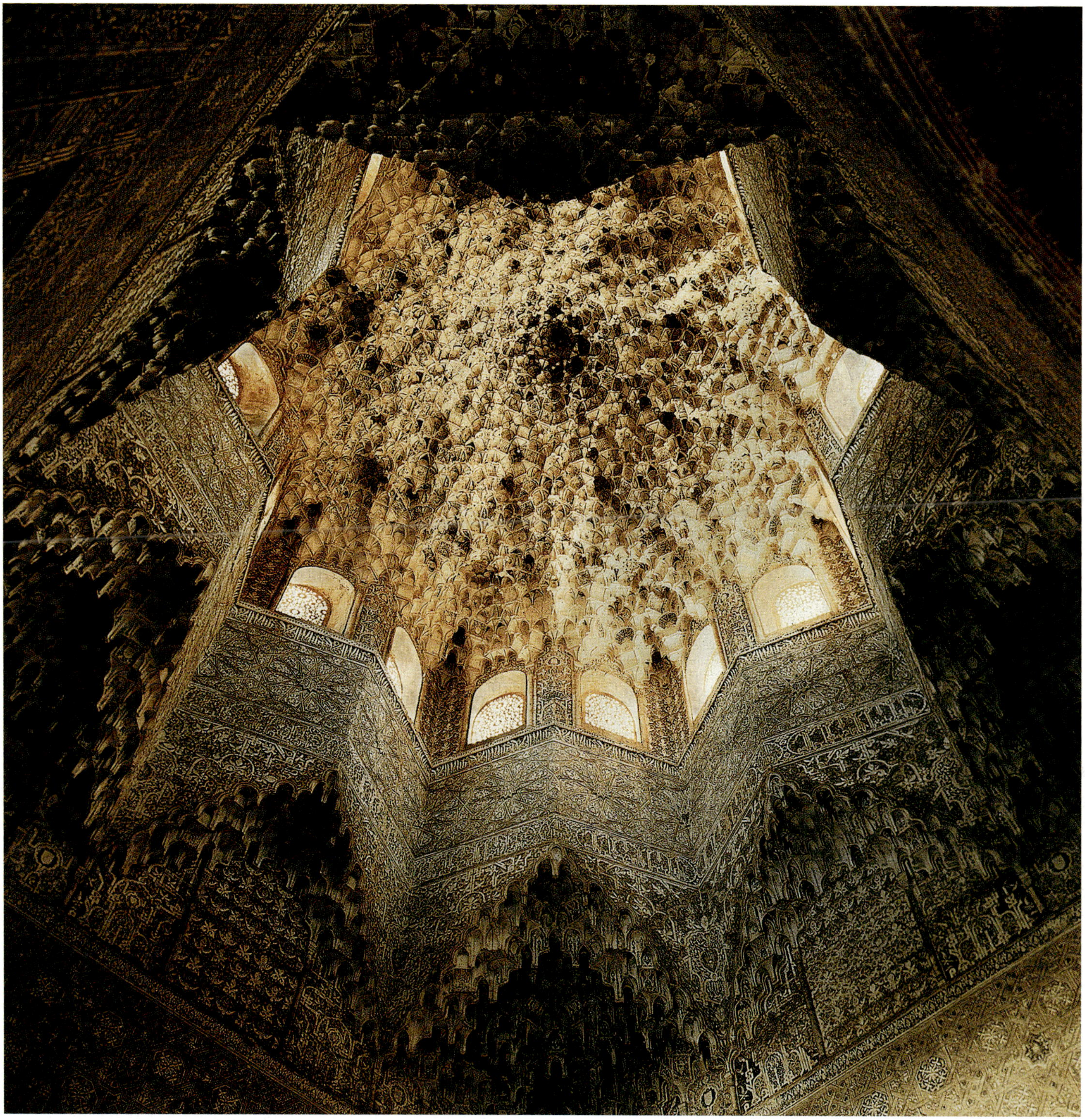

8–12 *Muqarnas* dome, Hall of the Abencerrajes, Palace of the Lions, Alhambra. 1354–1391

Structurally, muqarnas *are small niche-like components unique to Islamic architecture that are clustered in multiples as interlocking load-bearing, vaulting units. Over time they became increasingly ornamental and appeared as intricately faceted surfaces that created seemingly dissolving honeycombed spaces.*

squinches, or niche-like cells (*muqarnas*), and a honeycomb of *muqarnas* also covers the dome. The effect is a dematerialization of architectural form into an ephemeral illusion of dazzling—almost kinetic—heavenly space. The experience is heightened by a ring of windows just under the springing of the dome itself, bathing it in a splash of light that varies in balance and intensity throughout the day.

Luxury Arts

In cosmopolitan Islamic societies, exquisite craftsmanship was lavished not only on palaces but also on portable objects, highly valued for their beauty and usefulness and for the status they bestowed on their owners. Glass, made with the most ordinary ingredients—sand and ash—becomes the most ethereal of materials. According to the twelfth-century poet al-Hariri, glass is "congealed of air, condensed of sunbeam motes, molded of the light of the open plain, or peeled from a white pearl" (Jenkins, page 3). Glassmakers generally adapted earlier practices to new forms because the tools and techniques of making glass have changed very little since ancient times. A tall, elegant enameled bottle from the mid-fourteenth century exemplifies their skill in the application of enameled decoration in gold and various colors (fig. **8–13**). Probably made in a Syrian workshop, it bears a large inscription in cursive script naming and

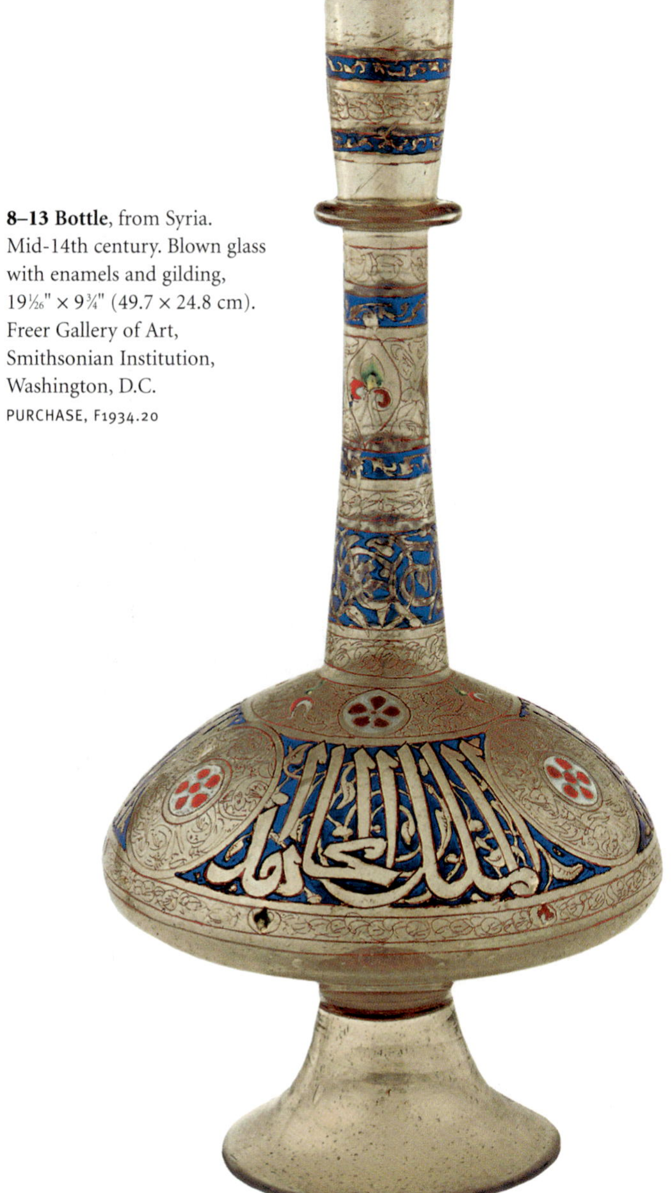

8–13 Bottle, from Syria. Mid-14th century. Blown glass with enamels and gilding, $19\frac{9}{16}$" × $9\frac{3}{4}$" (49.7 × 24.8 cm). Freer Gallery of Art, Smithsonian Institution, Washington, D.C.
PURCHASE, F1934.20

Technique

Carpet Making

Because textiles, especially floor coverings, are destroyed through use, very few carpets from before the sixteenth century have survived. There are two basic types of carpets: flat-weaves and pile, or knotted. Both can be made on either vertical or horizontal looms. The best-known flat-weaves today are Turkish kilims, which are typically woven in wool with bold, geometric patterns and sometimes with brocaded details. Kilim weaving is done in a tapestry technique called slit tapestry (see diagram a).

Knotted carpets are an ancient invention. The oldest known example, excavated in Siberia and dating to the fourth or fifth century BCE, has designs evocative of Achaemenid Persian art, suggesting that the technique may have originated in Central Asia. In knotted carpets (e.g. fig. **8–14**), the pile—the plush, thickly tufted surface—is made by tying colored strands of yarn, usually wool but occasionally silk for deluxe carpets, onto the vertical elements (warp) of a yarn grid (b or c). These knotted loops are later trimmed and sheared to form the plush surface of the carpet. The weft strands (crosswise threads) are shot horizontally, usually twice, after each row of knots is tied, to hold the knots in place and to form the horizontal element common to all woven structures. The weft is usually

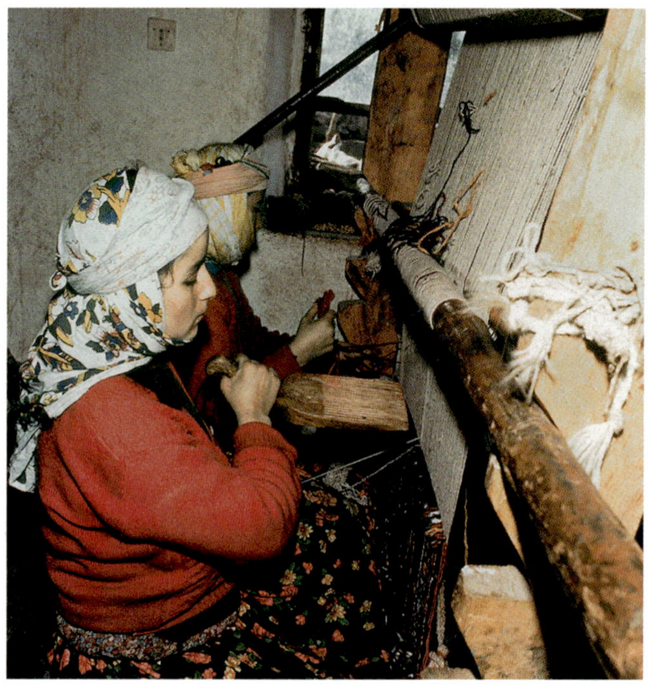

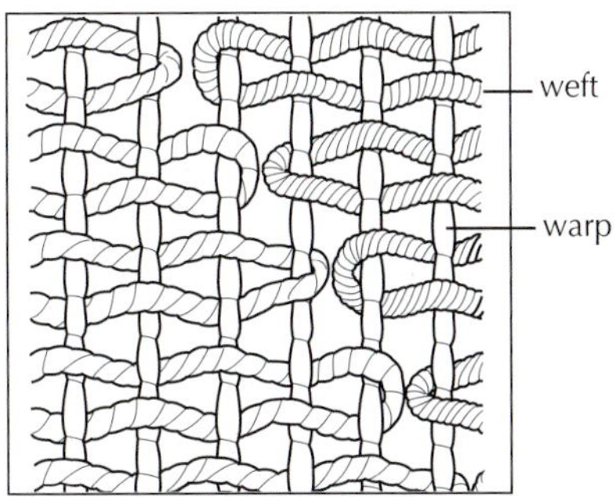

a. Kilim weaving pattern used in flat-weaving

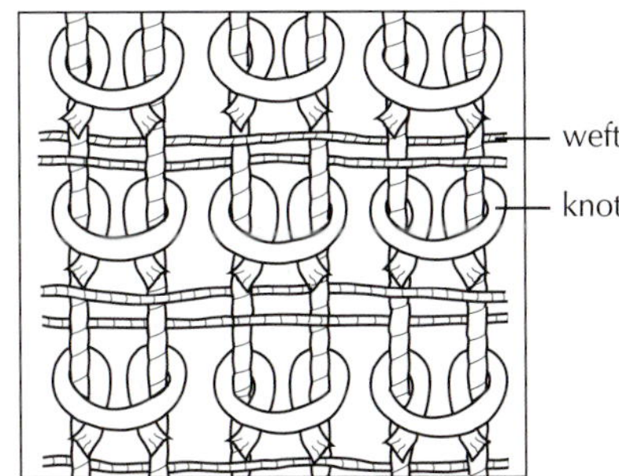

b. Symmetrical knot, used extensively in Iran

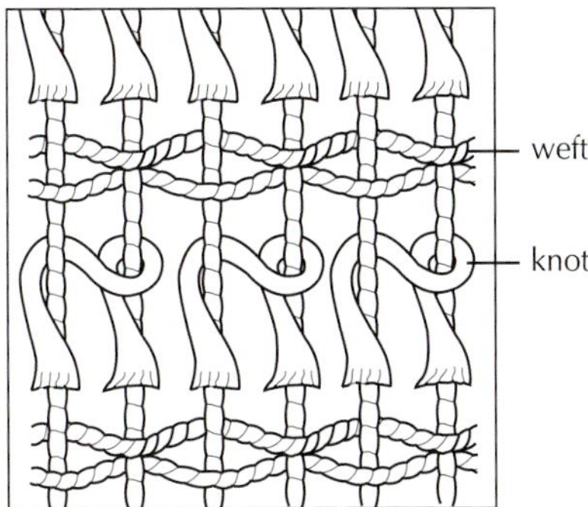

c. Asymmetrical knot, used extensively in Turkey

an undyed yarn and is hidden by the colored knots of the warp. Two common tying techniques are the symmetrical knot (b), extensively used in Iran, Egypt, and Central Asia (formerly termed the Sehna knot) and the asymmetrical knot (c), used extensively in Turkey (formerly called the Gördes knot). The greater the number of knots, the shorter the pile. The finest carpets have up to 2,400 knots per square inch, each one tied separately by hand.

Although royal workshops produced the most luxurious carpets, most knotted rugs have traditionally been made in tents and homes. Carpets were woven by either women or men, depending on local custom. The photograph in this box shows two women, sisters in Çanakkale province in Turkey, weaving a large carpet in a typical Turkish pattern. The woman in the foreground pushes a row of knots tightly against the row below it with a wood comb called a beater. The other woman pulls a dark red weft yarn against the warp threads before tying a knot. Working between September and May, these women may weave five carpets, tying up to 5,000 knots a day. A Çanakkale rug will usually have only 40–50 knots per square inch. Generally, an older woman works with a young girl, who learns the art of carpet weaving at the loom and eventually passes it on to the next generation.

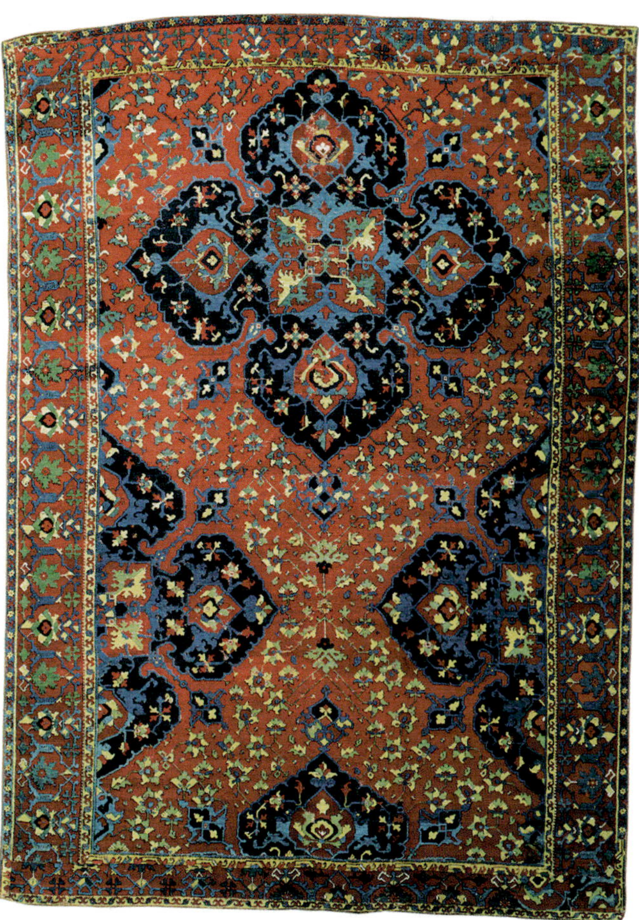

8–14 Medallion Rug, Variant Star Ushak style. Anatolia (modern Turkey). 16th century. Wool, 10' 3" × 7' 6¼" (3.13 × 2.29 m). St. Louis Art Museum
JAMES F. BALLARD COLLECTION/Z. PERKINS

honoring its owner, a sultan from Yemen. The five-petaled red rosette is an insignia of the Yemeni dynasty.

Leaders administering lands for caliphs and emirs commissioned works in metal, ivory, and precious stones, as well as glass. Like glassmakers, metalworkers inherited the techniques of their Roman, Byzantine, and Sassanian predecessors, applying their artistic heritage to new forms. Personalized containers for pens, ink, and blotting sand became emblems of the educated class. An artist named Shazi created an exquisitely engraved, embossed, and inlaid pen box for Majd al-Mulk al-Muzaffar, the governor of Khurasan (see fig. 8–1). Scrolls, interlacing designs, and human and bird heads enliven its calligraphic inscriptions, as if the words themselves were engaged in a lively exchange. A severe silver shortage in the mid-twelfth century may have prompted the development of inlaid brass pieces like this one that used the more precious metal sparingly. Humbler brassware was also available for those of more modest means.

Rugs and mats have long been used for Muslim prayer, which involves repeatedly prostrating oneself (kneeling and touching the forehead to the floor) before God. Many mosques were literally "carpeted" with wool-pile rugs received as pious donations; wealthy patrons gave large prayer rugs. Since the late Middle Ages, carpets have been the Islamic art form best known in Europe. Rugs from Persia, Turkey, and elsewhere were highly prized among wealthy Westerners, who often displayed them on tables rather than floors.

A carpet from Ushak in western Anatolia (modern Turkey), created in the first half of the sixteenth century, retains its wonderful colors (fig. **8–14**). Large, deeply serrated quatrefoil medallions establish the underlying star pattern, but arabesques flow in every direction. This "infinite arabesque," as it is called by experts (the pattern repeats infinitely in all directions), is characteristic of Ushak carpets. Carpets were usually at least three times as long as they were wide; the asymmetry of this carpet may indicate that it has been shortened.

Books

The art of book production also flourished throughout the Muslim world. An emphasis on the study of the Qur'an created a high level of literacy among both women and men in Islamic societies, and calligraphers were the first artists to emerge from anonymity and achieve individual distinction and recognition. Books on a wide range of secular as well as religious subjects were available, although even books copied on paper were costly. Libraries, often associated with *madrasas*, were endowed by members of the educated elite. Books made for royal patrons had luxurious bindings and highly embellished pages, the result of workshop collaboration between noted calligraphers and painters. New scripts were developed for new literary forms.

In addition to religious works, scribes copied and recopied famous secular texts: scientific treatises, manuals of all kinds, fiction, and especially poetry. Painters supplied illustrations for these books, and they later created independent small-scale paintings, or miniatures, that were collected by the wealthy and placed in albums. One of the great royal centers of miniature painting was at Herat (in modern Afghanistan). A school of painting and calligraphy was

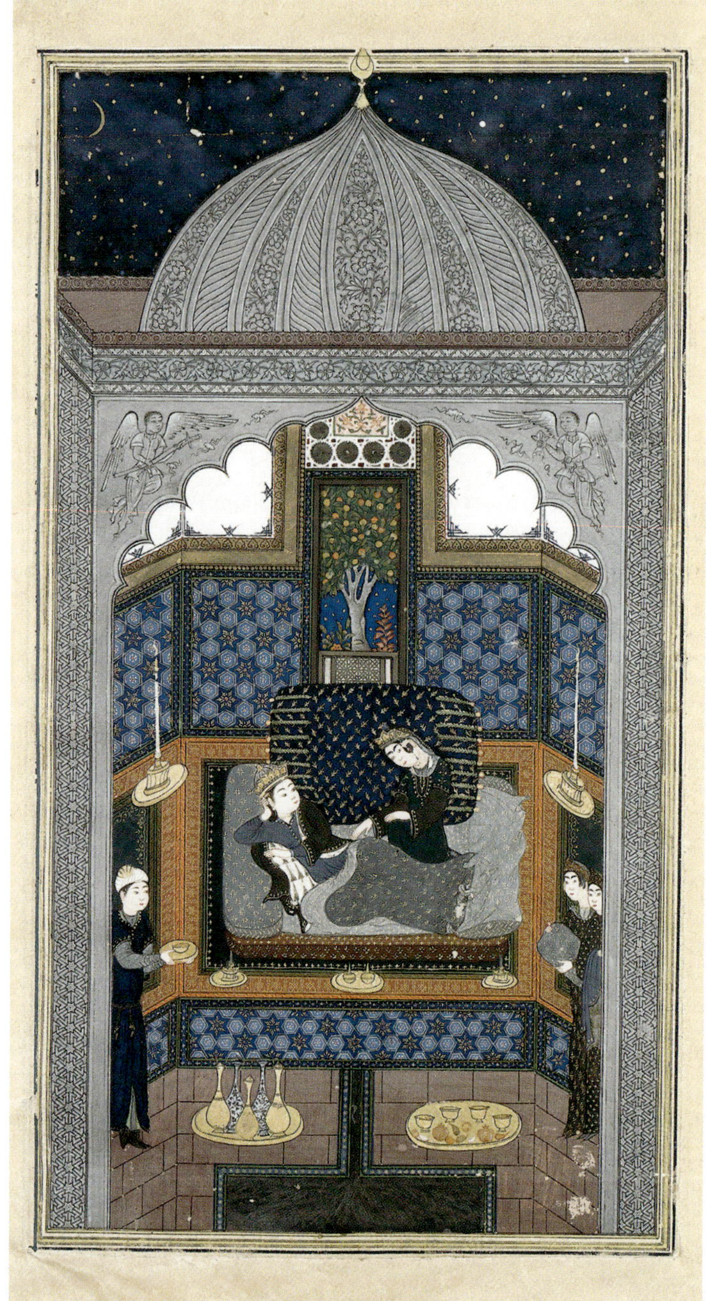

8–15 ***Bahram Gur with the Indian Princess in her Black Pavilion***, folio 23 from a *Haft Paykar* (*Seven Portraits*), by Nizami, Herat, Afghanistan. c. 1426. Color and gilt on paper, 8¼" × 4⅝" (20.9 × 11.7 cm). The Metropolitan Museum of Art, New York

GIFT OF ALEXANDER SMITH COCHRAN, 1913 (13.227.13)

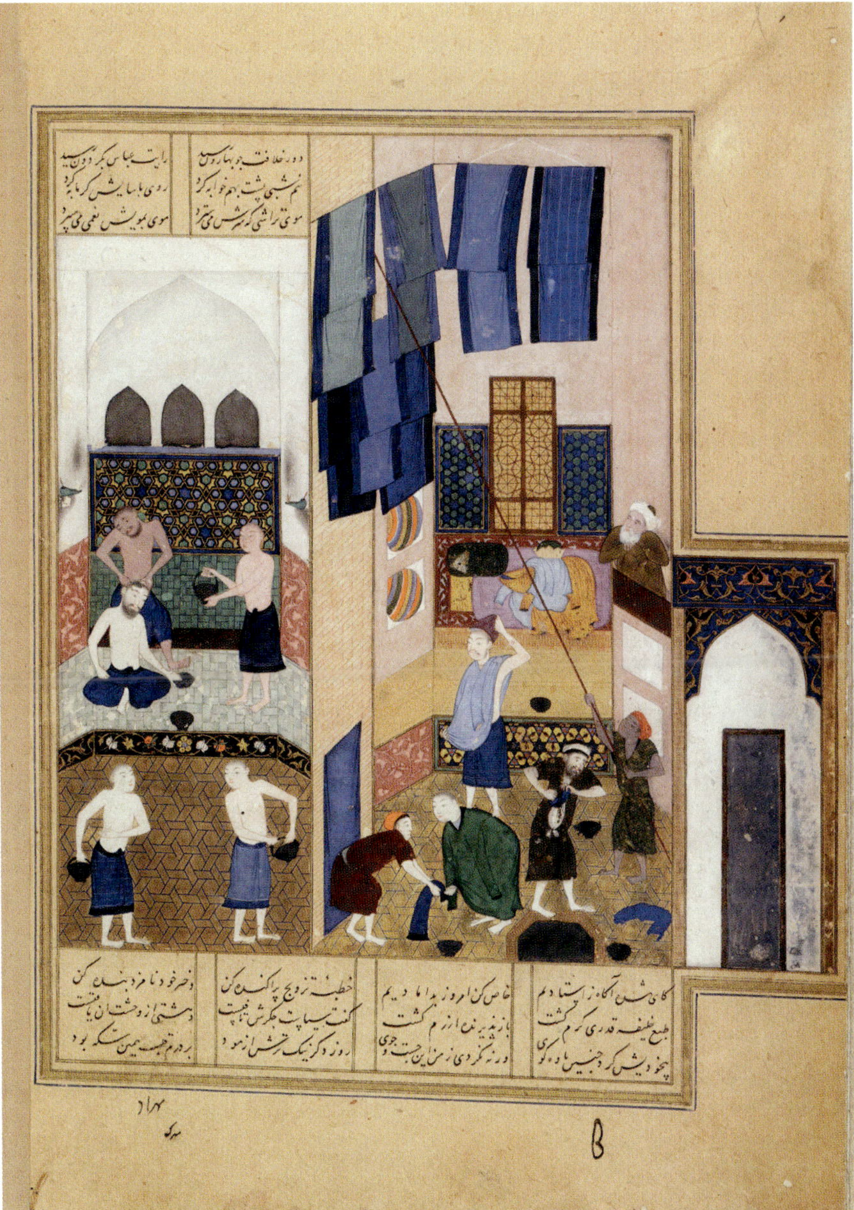

8–16 Kamal al-Din Bihzad. *The Caliph Harun al-Rashid Visits the Turkish Bath*, from a copy of the *Khamsa* (*Five Poems*) of Nizami. Herat, Afghanistan. c. 1494. Ink and pigments on paper, approx. 7" × 6" (17.8 × 15.3 cm). The British Library, London. Oriental and India Office Collections (Ms. Or. 6810, fol. 27v)

*Despite early warnings against it as a place for the dangerous indulgence of the pleasures of the flesh, the bathhouse (*hammam*), adapted from Roman and Hellenistic predecessors, became an important social center in much of the Islamic world. The remains of an eighth-century* hammam *still stand in Jordan, and a twelfth-century* hammam *is still in use in Damascus.* Hammams *had a small entrance to keep in the heat, which was supplied by steam ducts running under the floors. The main room had pipes in the wall with steam vents. Unlike the Romans, who bathed and swam in pools of water, Muslims preferred to splash themselves from basins, and the floors were slanted for drainage. A* hammam *was frequently located near a mosque, part of the commercial complex that generated income for the mosque's upkeep.*

founded there in the early fifteenth century under the cultured patronage of the Timurid dynasty (c. 1370–1507).

Prince Baysonghur held court in Herat during the early fifteenth century. A great patron of painting and calligraphy, he commissioned superb illuminated manuscripts, including an illustrated version of the story of the Sassanian prince Bahram Gur—who married seven princesses, one for each night of the week—written by the twelfth-century Persian mystic poet Nizami. The painting of *Bahram Gur with the Indian Princess in her Black Pavilion* illustrates the lyrical idealism that characterized the early Timurid style (fig. **8–15**). Although the scene takes place at night, the colors are clear and bright without a trace of shadow. Only the star-studded sky and the two tall candles in the pavilion signal to the viewer that night has fallen. The interior of the black pavilion is decorated with brilliant blue tiles, and through a central opening a lavish garden is visible. In the foreground a stream of silver water runs into a silver pool (the silver has now tarnished to black). Note how skillfully the artist shifts viewpoints—the tree, pavilion, tiled walls and step, the huge pillow, and the items on trays are seen straight on, while the floor, pool, platform, and bed are seen from a bird's-eye view. Obviously, this painter delighted in the representation of intricate decorative details, especially the tiles, fabrics, and the garden foliage. The amorous couple, their servants, and especially the setting, become part of the idealized, lyrical world of this Persian miniature.

In the second half of the fifteenth century, the leader of the Herat school was Kamal al-Din Bihzad (c. 1450–1514), who was considered by many contemporaries as the greatest of Persian painters. Around 1494, he illustrated a *Khamsa* (*Five Poems*, also written by Nizami). *The Caliph Harun al-Rashid Visits the Turkish Bath* (fig. **8–16**) demonstrates his renowned ability to render human activity convincingly and set his scenes within complex, stage-like architectural spaces that also conform to Timurid conventions, creating a visual balance between bustling activity and complex architecture. The bathhouse, its tiled entrance to the right leading to a high-ceilinged dressing room with brick walls, provides the structuring element. Attendants wash long, blue towels and hang them to dry on overhead clothes lines. A worker reaches for one of the towels with a long pole, and a client prepares to wrap himself discreetly in a towel before removing his outer garments. The blue door on the left leads to a room where a barber grooms the caliph while attendants bring water for his bath. The asymmetrical composition depends on a balanced placement of colors and architectural ornaments within each section.

The Mughal Empire

Islam first touched the Indian subcontinent in the eighth century, when Arab armies captured a small territory near the Indus River. In the eleventh century, the Turks began a war of conquest, and, by the beginning of the thirteenth century, Turkic dynasties ruled portions of the subcontinent from the northern city of Delhi. Although these early dynasties left their mark, it was in the sixteenth and seventeenth centuries that the Mughals made a lasting impression on Indian art.

The Mughals, like the Turks, originally came from Central Asia. The first Mughal emperor, Babur (ruled 1526–1530), conquered an empire stretching from Afghanistan to Delhi. Later Akbar (ruled 1556–1605) extended Mughal control over most of North India, and under his two successors, Jahangir and Shah Jahan, northern India was generally a unified Mughal Empire by 1658.

Probably no one had more impact on the creation of Mughal art than the emperor Akbar. A dynamic, humane, and just leader, Akbar especially loved painting. He created an imperial **atelier** (workshop) of painters, which he placed under the direction of two artists from the Persian court. Learning from these masters, Mughal painters soon tempered Persian idealized lyricism with robust Indian naturalism.

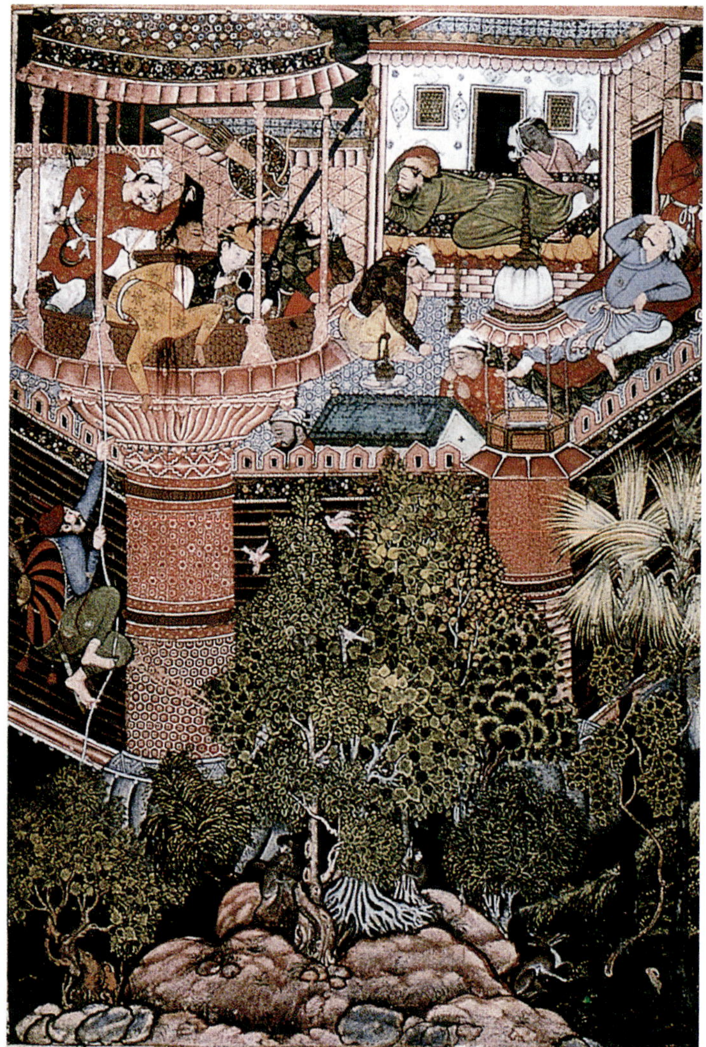

8–17 ***Hamza's Spies Scale the Fortress***, from the *Hamza-nama*. North India. Mughal period, reign of Akbar, c. 1567–1582. Gouache on cotton, 30" × 24" (76 × 61 cm). Museum of Applied Arts, Vienna

One of the most famous and extraordinary examples is an illustrated manuscript of the *Hamza-nama*, a Persian classic about the adventures of Hamza, uncle of the Prophet Muhammad. Painted on cotton cloth, each illustration is 30 inches high. The entire project gathered 1,400 illustrations into 12 volumes and took 15 years to complete.

One illustration shows Hamza's spies scaling a fortress wall and surprising some men as they sleep (fig. **8–17**). One man climbs a rope; another has already beheaded a figure in yellow and lifts his head aloft. The architecture, viewed from a slightly elevated vantage point, describes a three-dimensional setting, yet the sense of depth is boldly undercut by the flat geometric patterns of the tile work. The energy exuded by the large human figures, as well as the visual descriptions of their lifelike details, are characteristic of painting under Akbar—even the sleepers seem active in their varying postures. This vigorous figure style contrasts with the decorative linear qualities derived from Persian painting.

Nearly as prominent as the architectural setting with its vivid human action is the sensuous landscape in the foreground, where monkeys, foxes, and birds inhabit a grove of trees that shimmer and glow against the darkened background. The treatment of the gold-edged leaves at first calls to mind the patterned geometry of the tilework, but a closer look reveals a sense of naturalism rooted in careful observation. Each tree species is distinguishable by the shape of its trunk and leaves and its overall form. Pink and blue rocks with lumpy, softly outlined forms add still further interest to this painting, whose every inch is dense with intriguing details.

Mughal architects were the heirs to a 300-year-old tradition of Islamic building using arches and domes and benefited from indigenous virtuosity in stone carving. Mughal building culminated in the most famous of all Indian Islamic structures, the Taj Mahal (fig. **8–18**), sited on the bank of the Yamuna River at Agra in northern India. Built between 1631 and 1648, it was commissioned as a mausoleum for his wife by the emperor Shah Jahan (ruled 1628–1658), who is believed to have taken a major part in overseeing its design and construction.

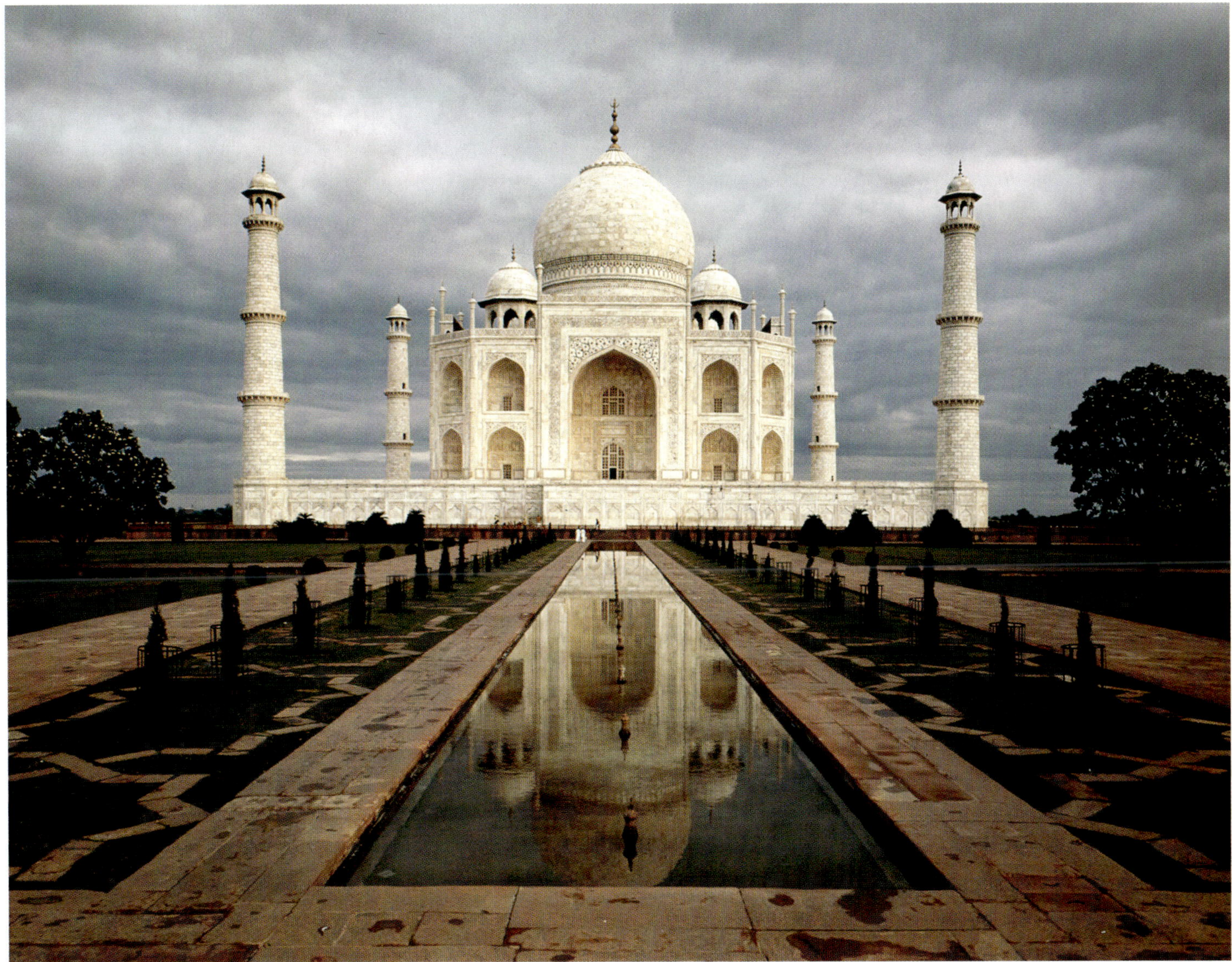

8–18 Taj Mahal, Agra, India. Mughal period, reign of Shah Jahan, 1631–1648

As visitors enter through a monumental, hall-like gate, the tomb looms before them across a spacious garden—measuring some 1,000 by 1,900 feet—set with long reflecting pools. In Shah Jahan's time, fruit trees and cypresses—symbolic of life and death—lined the walkways, and fountains played in the shallow pools. Truly, the senses were beguiled in this earthly evocation of paradise as described in the Qur'an.

A lucid geometric symmetry pervades the entire design. Each façade of the tomb is identical, with a central *iwan* flanked by two stories of smaller *iwan*s. By creating voids in the façades, these *iwan*s contribute to the building's sense of weightlessness. The dome rises gracefully on its drum, allowing the swelling curves and lyrical lines of its beautifully proportioned, surprisingly large form to emerge with perfect clarity. Four minarets surround the central structure, each crowned with a pavilion. Traditional embellishments of Indian palaces, these pavilions quickly passed into the vocabulary of Islamic architecture in India. Four more pavilions, this time on the roof, create a visual transition from the minarets to the lofty dome.

The pristine surfaces of the Taj Mahal are embellished with utmost subtlety. The sides of the platform are carved in relief with a blind arcade motif, and carved relief panels of flowers adorn the base of the building. The portals are framed with verses from the Qur'an inlaid in black marble, while the spandrels are decorated with floral arabesques inlaid in colored semiprecious stones. Not strong enough to detract from the overall purity of the white marble, the embellishments enliven the surfaces of this impressive yet delicate masterpiece.

The Ottoman Empire

In the early fourteenth century, the Ottoman Turks replaced the Saljuqs as rulers of northwestern Anatolia, eventually conquering most of the eastern Mediterranean, Egypt, and the Sudan, as well as the Balkans in eastern Europe. In 1453, they captured Constantinople (renaming it Istanbul) and brought the Byzantine

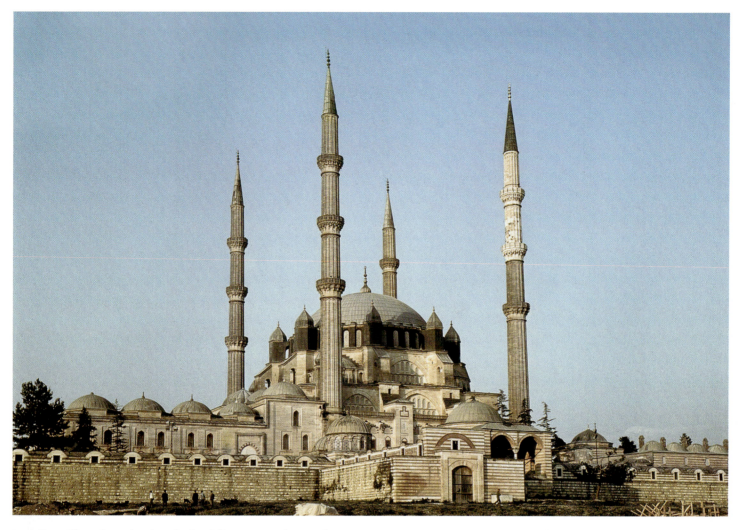

8–19 Sinan. Plan and exterior view of Sultan Selim Mosque, Edirne, Turkey. 1568–75

The minarets that pierce the sky around the prayer hall of this mosque, their sleek, fluted walls and needle-nosed spires soaring to more than 295 feet, are only 12½ feet in diameter at the base, an impressive feat of engineering.

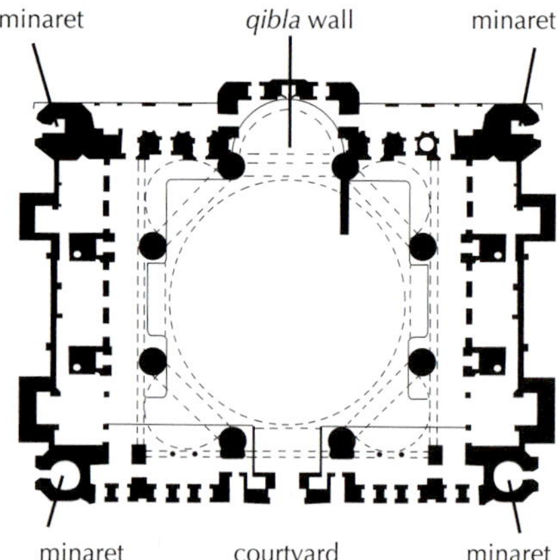

(and thus Roman) Empire to an end. The Church of Hagia Sophia (see fig. 7–15) became a mosque framed by the addition of four graceful Ottoman minarets. The church's mosaics were destroyed or plastered over and huge disks with the names of God, Muhammad, and the early caliphs were added over the pendentives in the mid-nineteenth century (see fig. 7–15). At present, Hagia Sophia is neither a church nor a mosque, but a state museum.

Inspired by this great Byzantine structure, Ottoman architects developed the domed, central-plan mosque. The finest examples of this new form were designed by the architect Sinan (c. 1489–1588). In 1528, he became chief architect for Suleyman I, known as "the Magnificent," the tenth Ottoman sultan (ruled 1520–1566). Suleyman's reign marked the height of Ottoman power, and the sultan sponsored a building program on a scale not seen since the days of the Roman Empire. Serving Suleyman and his successor, Sinan is credited with more than 300 imperial commissions, including palaces, *madrasas* and Qur'an schools, tombs, public kitchens and hospitals, caravanserais, baths, bridges, viaducts, and 124 mosques.

Sinan's crowning accomplishment, completed about 1575, when he was over 80 years old, was a mosque he designed in the provincial capital of Edirne for Suleyman's son Selim II (ruled 1566–1574) (fig. **8–19**). The gigantic hemispheric dome that tops this structure is more than 102 feet in diameter, larger than the dome of Hagia Sophia, as Sinan proudly pointed out. The dome crowns a building of extraordinary architectural coherence. In addition to the mosque, the complex housed a *madrasa* and other educational buildings, a cemetery, a hospital, and charity kitchens, as well as the income-producing covered market and baths. Framed by

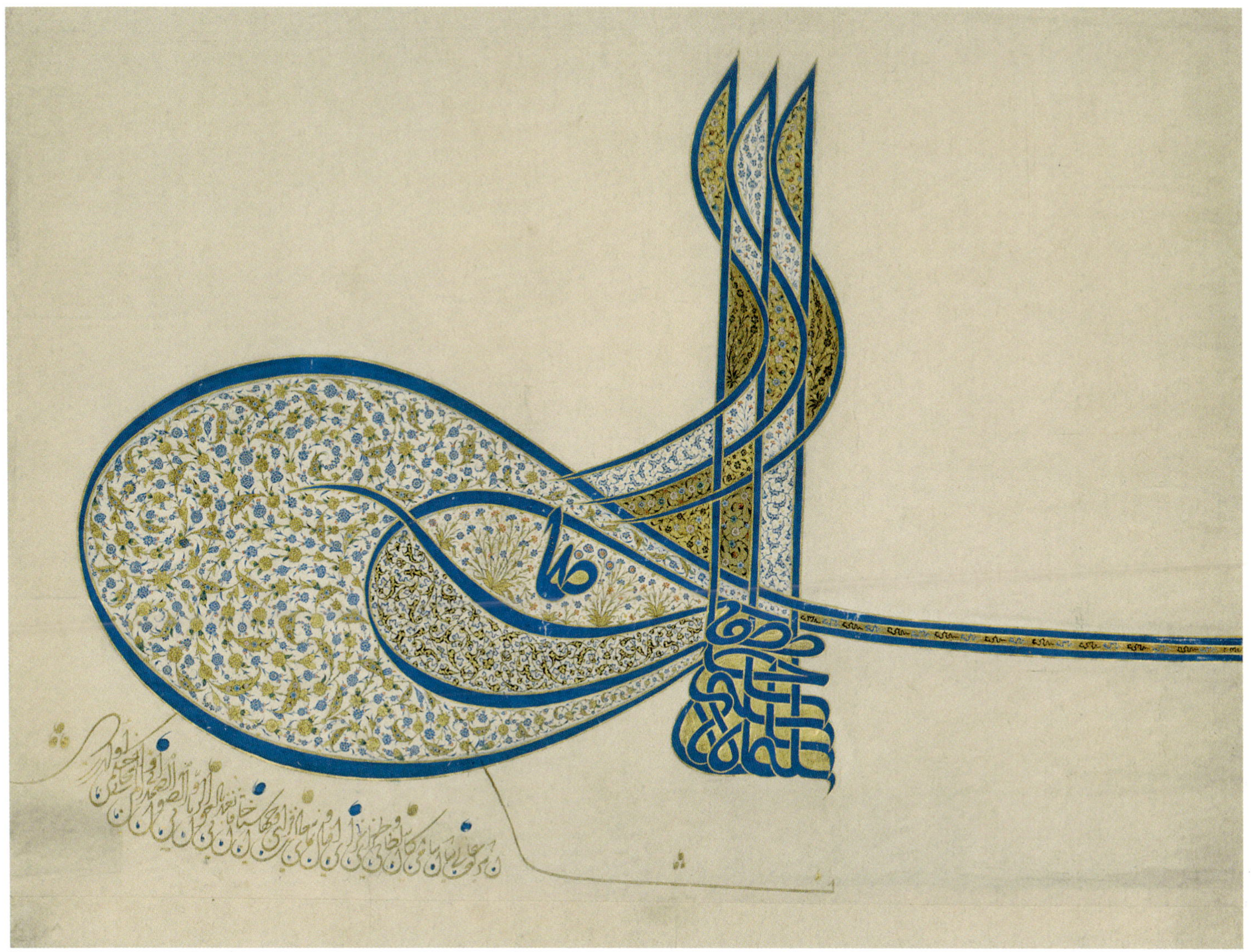

8–20 Illuminated *tugra* of Sultan Suleyman I, Istanbul, Turkey. c. 1555–1560. Ink, paint, and gold on paper, removed from a *firman* (official document) and trimmed to 20½" × 25⅜" (52.1 × 64.5 cm). The Metropolitan Museum of Art, New York
ROGERS FUND, 1938 (38.149.1)

the vertical lines of four minarets and raised on a platform at the city's edge, the Mosque of Selim proudly dominates the skyline.

Following a practice begun by the Saljuqs, the Ottomans put calligraphy to political use, developing the design of imperial ciphers—***tugras***—into a specialized art form. Ottoman *tugras* combined the ruler's name and title with the motto "Eternally Victorious" into a monogram. Symbolizing the authority of the sultan, *tugras* appeared on seals, coins, and buildings, as well as on official documents. Suleyman issued hundreds of edicts, and a high court official supervised specialist calligraphers and illuminators who produced documents that required particularly elaborate *tugras*. The *tugra* shown here (fig. **8–20**) is from a document endowing a charitable institution in Jerusalem that had been established by Suleyman's wife, Sultana Hurrem.

Tugras were drawn in black or blue ink with three long, vertical strokes (*tug* means "horsetail") to the right of two concentric horizontal teardrops. Decorative foliage patterns fill the spaces. *Tugras* required great skill to execute. The sweeping, fluid lines had to be drawn with perfect control according to set proportions, and a mistake meant starting over. The color scheme of the delicate floral interlace enclosed in the body of the *tugra* may have been inspired by Chinese blue-and-white ceramics, and similar designs appear on Ottoman ceramics and textiles. The Ottoman *tugra* is a sophisticated merging of stylization with naturalism, boldness with delicacy, political power with refined patronage, and function—both utilitarian and symbolic—with adornment.

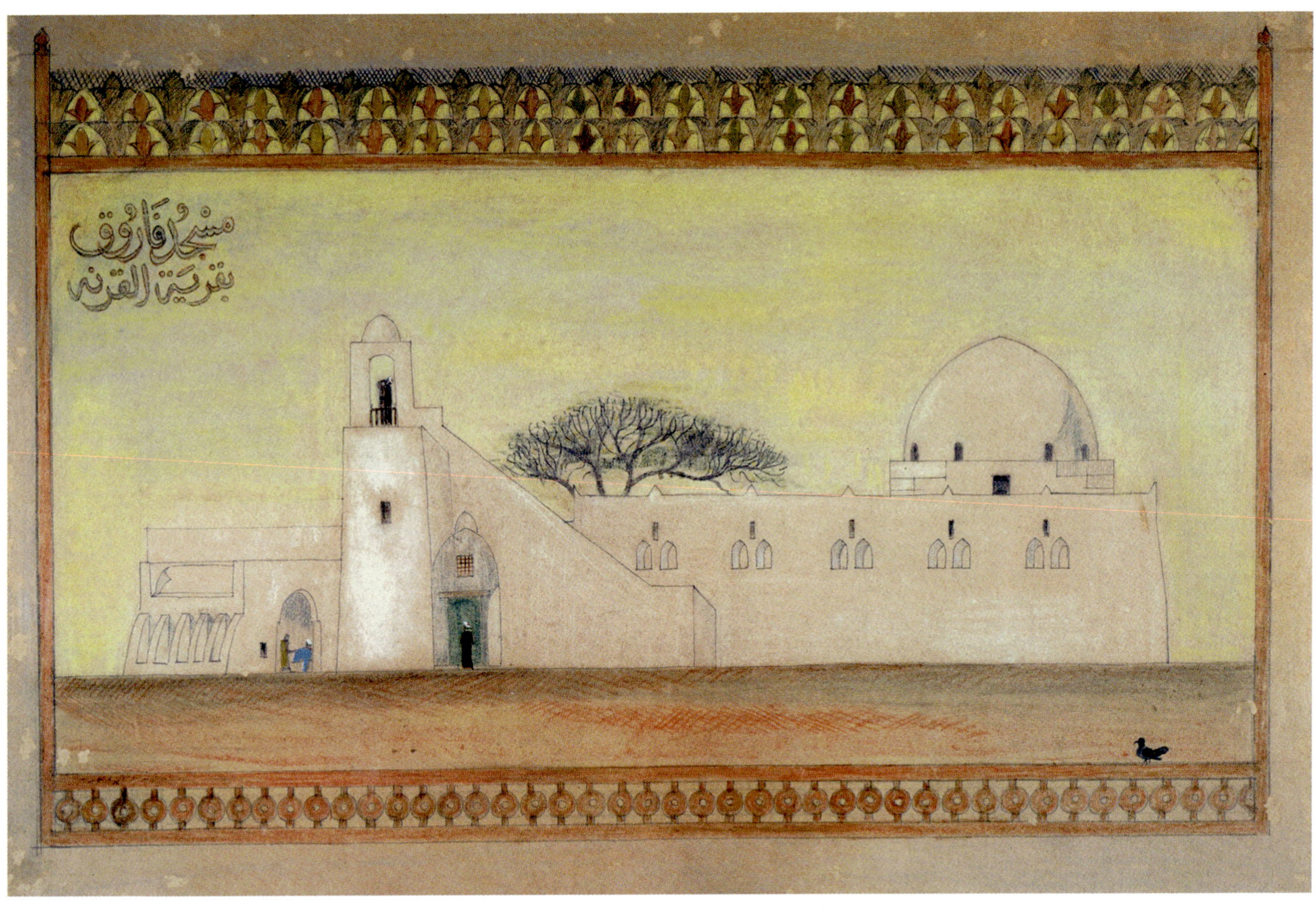

8–21 Hasan Fathy. ***Mosque at New Gourna***, Luxor, Egypt. 1945–1947. Gouache on paper, 22½" × 17⅞" (52.8 × 45.2 cm). Collection: Aga Khan Award for Architecture, Geneva, Switzerland

Modern Islam

Islamic art is not restricted to the distant past. But with the dissolution of the great Islamic empires and the formation of smaller nation-states during the twentieth century, questions of identity and its expression in art changed significantly. Muslim artists and architects began to participate in international movements that swept away many of the visible signs that formerly expressed their cultural character and difference. When architects in Islamic countries were debating whether modernity promised opportunities for new expression or simply another form of Western domination, the Egyptian Hasan Fathy (1900–1989) asked whether abstraction could serve the cause of social justice. He revived traditional, inexpensive, and locally obtainable materials such as mud brick and forms such as wind scoops (an inexpensive means of catching breezes to cool a building's interior) to build affordable housing for the poor. Fathy's New Gourna Village (designed 1945–1947) in Luxor, Egypt, became a model of environmental sustainability realized in pure geometric forms that resonated with references to Egypt's architectural past (fig. **8–21**). In their simplicity, his watercolor paintings are as beautiful as his buildings.

Looking Back

For Islam, God's word in the Qur'an, rather than any likeness in heaven or on earth, held a position of primary cultural importance. As a result, calligraphy emerged as the most highly valued form of art, and the written word was raised to a level of sophistication and expressiveness only matched in the neighboring cultures of East Asia. Islamic artists employed calligraphy everywhere, from monumental architectural inscriptions to the hand-written texts of luxury manuscripts (where those who penned the words were paid much more than those who painted the pictures), from clay plates to metalwork boxes, from luxurious silk fabrics to fragile glass bottles. Appearing in works of every medium, produced in every geographical location, the dominance of calligraphy, more than anything else, binds Islamic art into a cohesive cultural system across time and space, and even into the modern world.

IN PERSPECTIVE

600

- Founding of Islam, 622
- Early Caliphs, 633–61
- Umayyad Dynasty, c. 661–750
- Abbasid Dynasty, c. 750–1258
- Spanish Umayyad Dynasty, c. 756–1031

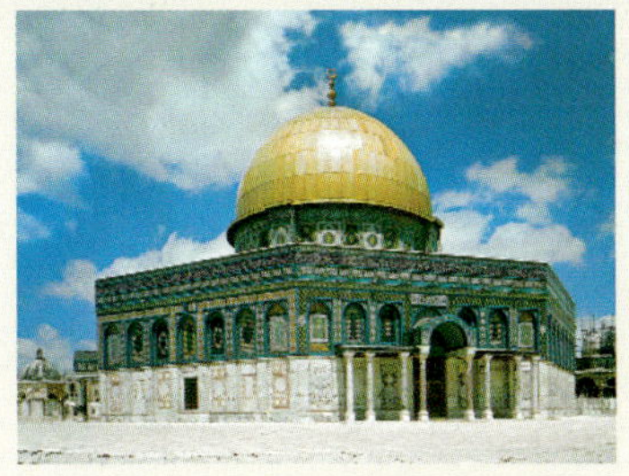

DOME OF THE ROCK, BEGUN 692

800

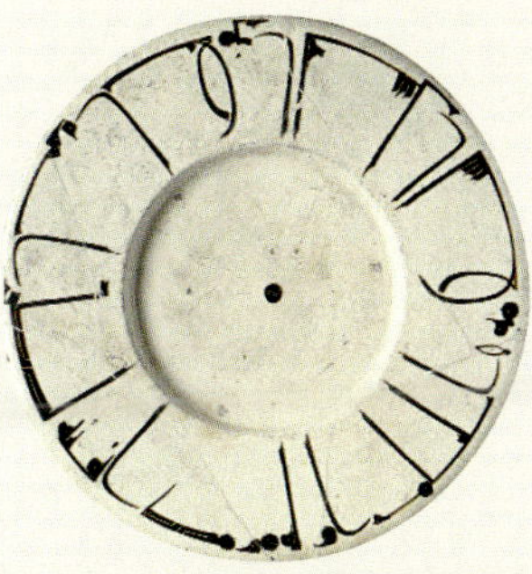

PLATE WITH KUFIC BORDER, 9TH–10TH CENTURY

- Fatimid Dynasty, c. 909–1171

1000

- Great Saljuq Dynasty, c. 1037–1157
- Saljuq Dynasty of Rum, late 11th–early 14th century

1200

- Spanish Nasrid Dynasty, c. 1232–1492
- Egyptian Mamluk Dynasty, c. 1250–1517
- Ottoman Empire, c. 1281–1918
- Timurid Dynasty, c. 1370–1507

1400

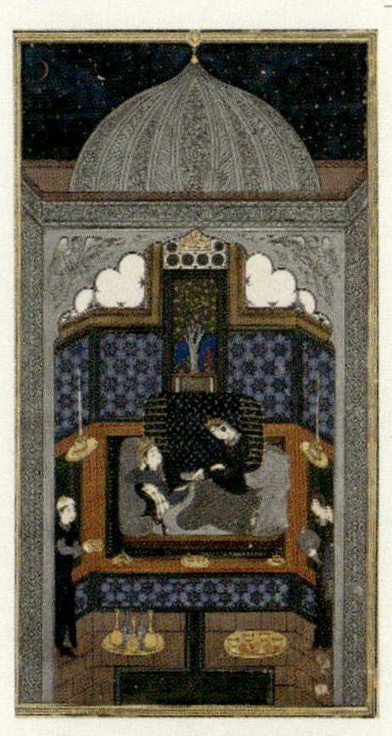

BAHRAM GUR WITH THE INDIAN PRINCESS IN HER BLACK PAVILION, c. 1426

- Fall of Constantinople to Ottoman Turks, 1453

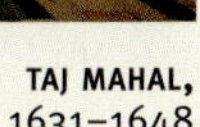

TAJ MAHAL, 1631–1648

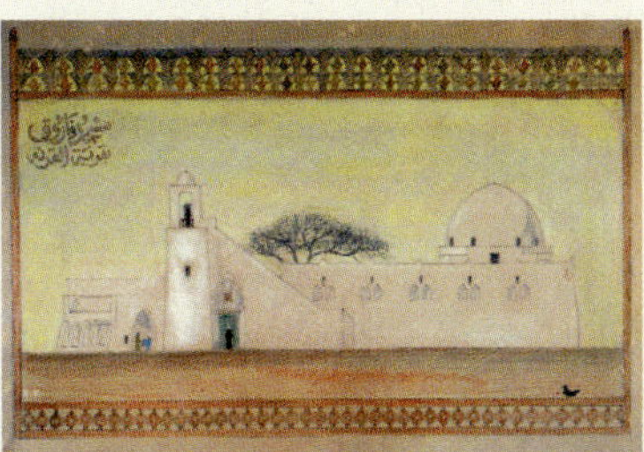

HASAN FATHY, **MOSQUE AT NEW GOURNA,** 1945–1947

- Modern Turkey Founded, 1918

2000

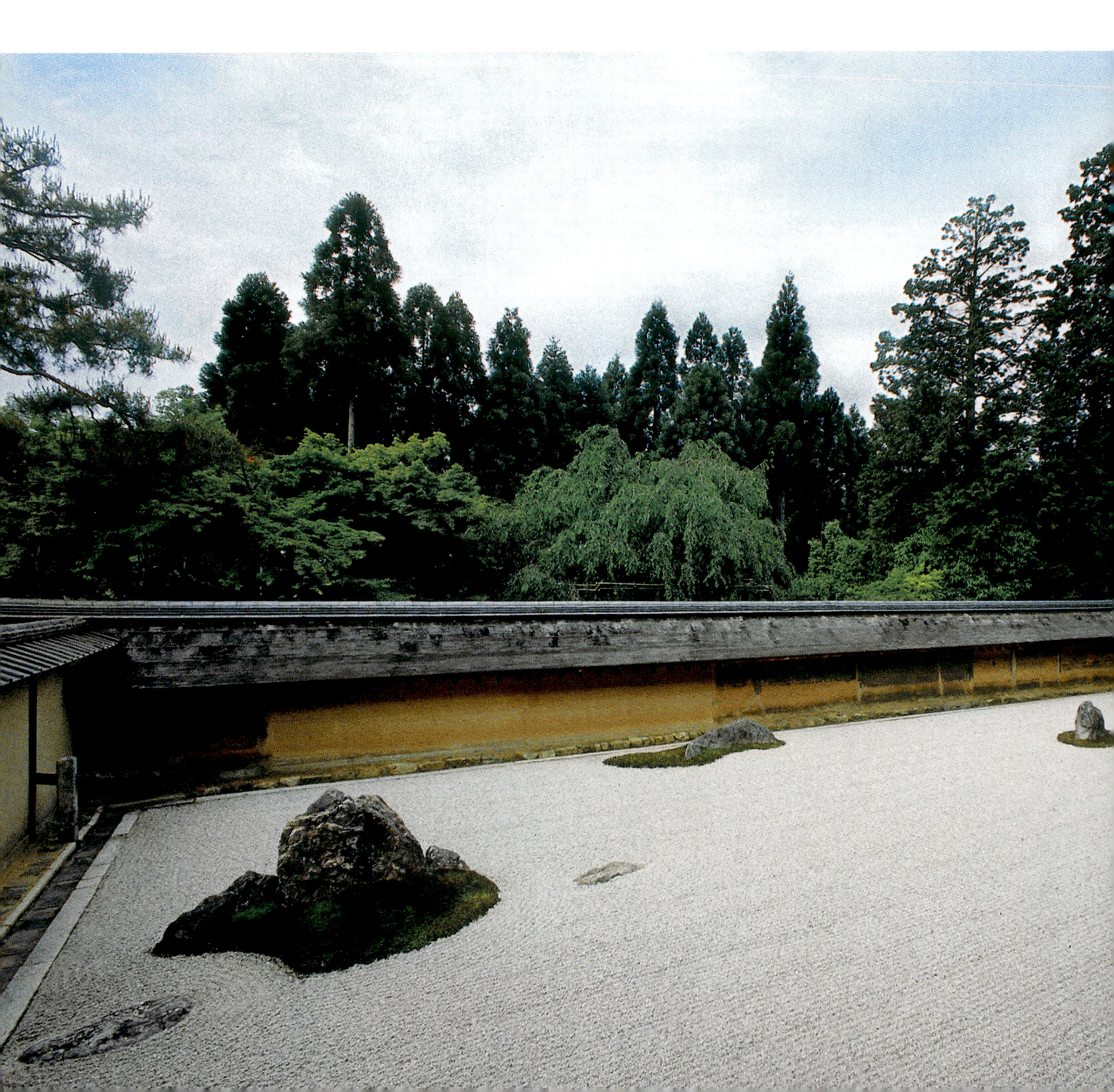

9
Later Asian Art

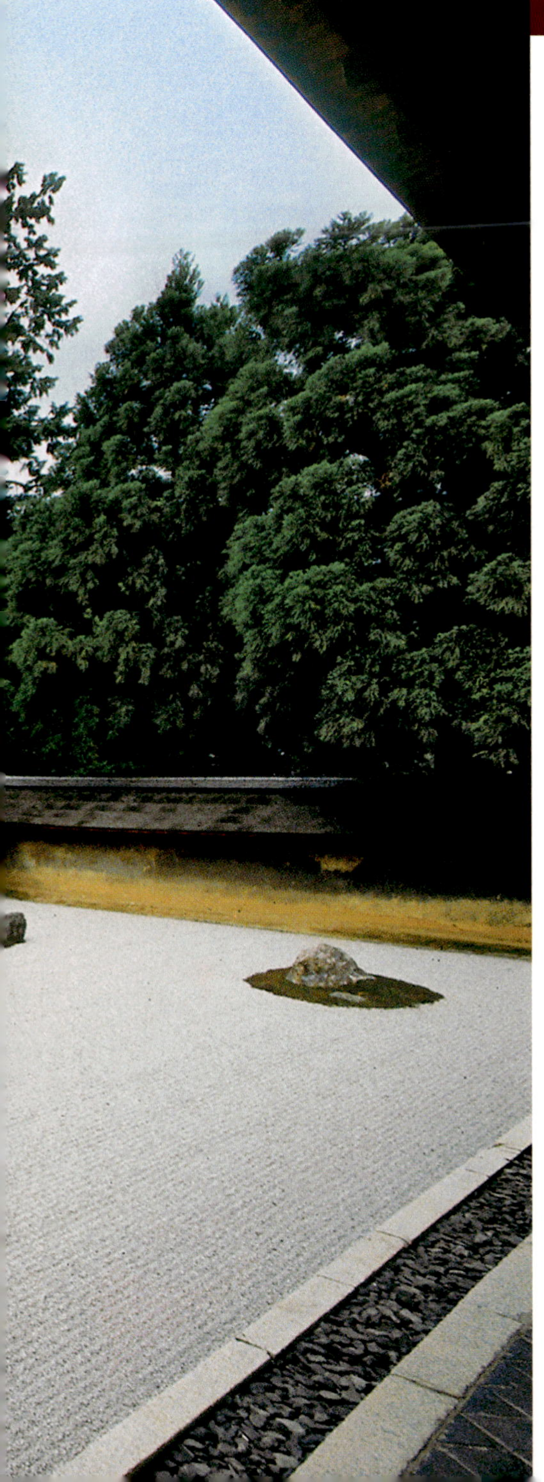

LOOKING FORWARD

Elegant simplicity—profound and personal—was the result of disciplined meditation coupled with manual labor, as practiced in the Zen Buddhism introduced into Japan in the late twelfth century. Zen monasteries aimed at self-sufficiency. Monks were expected to be responsible for their physical as well as spiritual needs. Consequently, the performance of simple tasks—weeding the garden, cooking meals, mending garments—became occasions for meditation in the search for enlightenment. Zen monks turned to their gardens not as the focus of detached viewing and meditation but as the objects of constant vigilance and work: pulling weeds, tweaking unruly shoots, and raking the gravel. This philosophy profoundly influenced Japanese art, and an intimate relationship with nature pervades the later art of Asia, in general, whether inspired by Buddhist, Hindu, or Shinto belief.

The dry landscape gardens of Japan (*karesansui*, literally "dried-up mountains and water") exist in perfect harmony with Zen Buddhism. In front of the abbot's quarters in the Zen temple of Ryoan-ji, a flat rectangle of raked gravel, about 29 by 70 feet, surrounds 15 stones of different sizes in islands of moss (fig. **9–1**). The stones are set in asymmetrical groups of two, three, and five. Low, plaster-covered walls establish the garden's boundaries, but beyond the perimeter wall, maple, pine, and cherry trees add color and texture to the scene. Called "borrowed scenery," these elements are an important part of the design although they grow outside the garden.

Dry gardens began to be made in the fifteenth and sixteenth centuries in Japan. By the sixteenth century, Chinese landscape painting influenced the gardens' composition, and miniature clipped plants and beautiful stones re-created famous paintings of trees and mountains. Especially fine and unusual stones were even stolen and carried off as war booty, such was the cultural value of these seemingly simple gardens. This garden has been variously interpreted as representing islands in the sea, mountain peaks rising above the clouds, constellations of stars and planets, and even a swimming tigress with her cubs. All or none of these interpretations may be equally satisfying—or irrelevant—to a monk seeking clarity of mind through contemplation. The austere beauty of the naked gravel has led, and still leads, many people to meditation.

9–1 Stone and gravel garden, Ryoan-ji, Kyoto.
Muromachi period, c. 1480

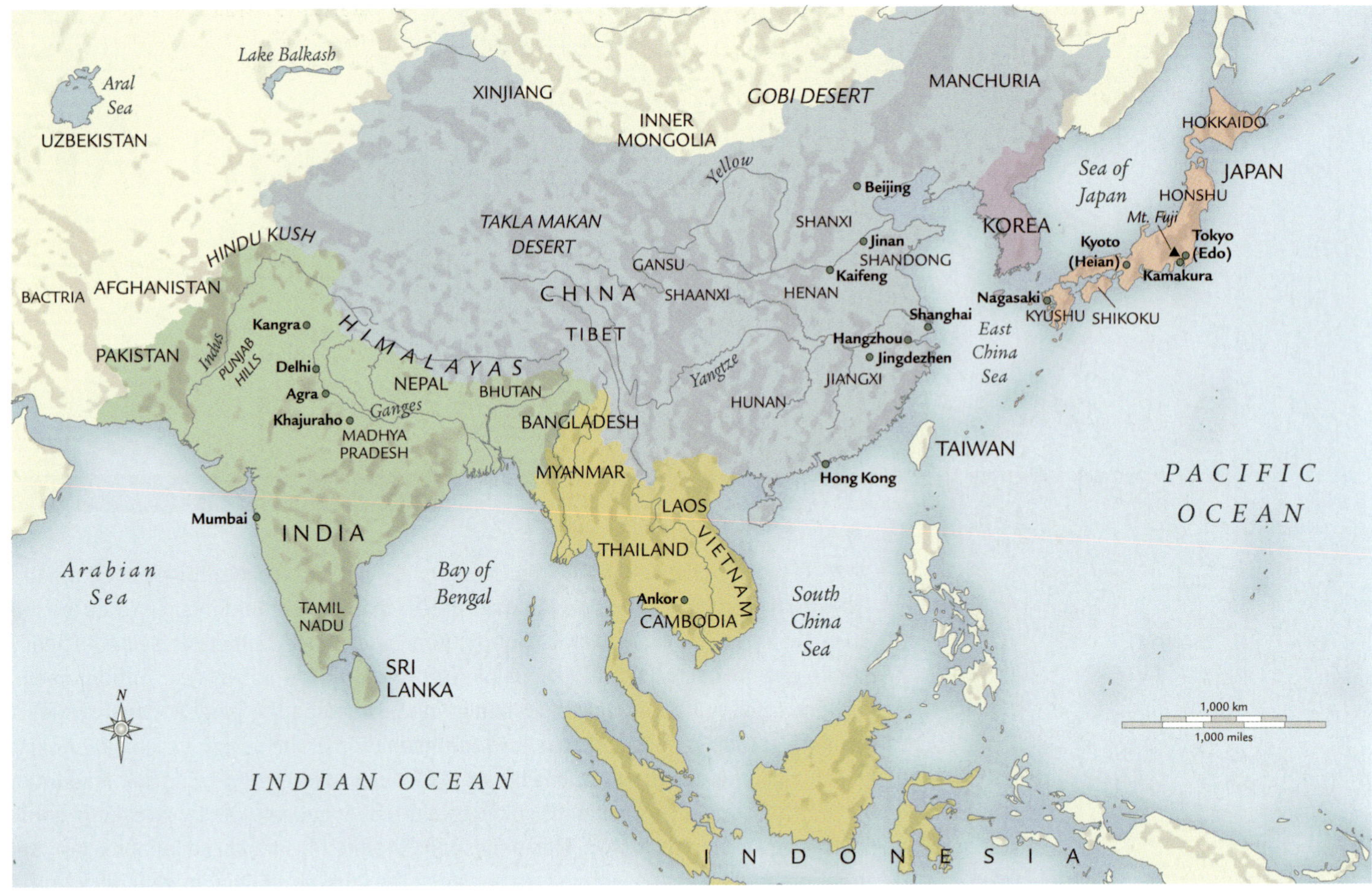

Map 9–1 Asia

The long period between c. 650 and 1526 was a time of transition in India (see map **9–1**). Buddhism declined as a cultural force, while artistic achievements under Hinduism soared. The monumental architecture of Hindu temples was rich in symbolism and ritual function, with each region of India developing its own variation. Later, Turkic people carried Islam to the South Asian subcontinent, and Muslim art expanded the already rich mix of styles, especially in the north, reaching its height under the Mughals (1526–1857).

During roughly the same period that Hinduism was displacing Buddhist primacy in India, Buddhism reached its height in China under the Tang Dynasty (618–907) (see Chapter 4). But soon there was a reaction to this flowering of a foreign religion on Chinese soil. Then, under the Song Dynasty (960–1279), openness to foreign influence gave way to greater cultivation of China's own traditions, including the revival of Confucianism. Landscape emerged as a very important subject and was used to express both philosophical and personal concerns.

Introduced from India by way of China and Korea, Buddhism was an important force in Japanese culture by the beginning of the Heian period (794–1185). New forms of Buddhism evolved: first Esoteric Buddhism and Pure Land Buddhism, and later, Zen. By the end of the fourteenth century, Zen Buddhism began to influence many aspects of Japanese life and culture, and soon Zen beliefs were expressed in sophisticated painting, calligraphy, ceramics, and gardens.

The South Asian Subcontinent

As Hinduism with its many gods and varied sects, flourished in the Indian subcontinent, temple architecture developed rapidly. Local rulers rivaled each other in the building of temples to their favored deities—Shiva, Vishnu, and the Great Goddess Devi—until the middle of the thirteenth century when Hindu temples reached unparalleled heights of grandeur and complexity.

A typical Hindu temple is the so-called northern type (figs. **9–2** and **9–3**), exemplified by the Kandariya Mahadeva temple (c. 1000 CE) dedicated to the god Shiva, one of more than 80 temples at Khajuraho in central India. It is dominated by a superstructure called a ***shikhara***, which rises as a solid mass above the flat, stone ceiling of a windowless sanctuary housing an image of the temple's "resident" deity. Crowning the *shikhara* is a circular, cushion-like element, known as an *amalaka*. A **finial** (knob-like decoration at the top of an architectural form) leads the eye to the point where earthly and cosmic worlds are thought to join. An imaginary *axis mundi* (line connecting the center of the earth to the heavens) runs from

9–2 Kandariya Mahadeva temple, Khajuraho, Madhya Pradesh, India. Chandella Dynasty, c. 1000 CE

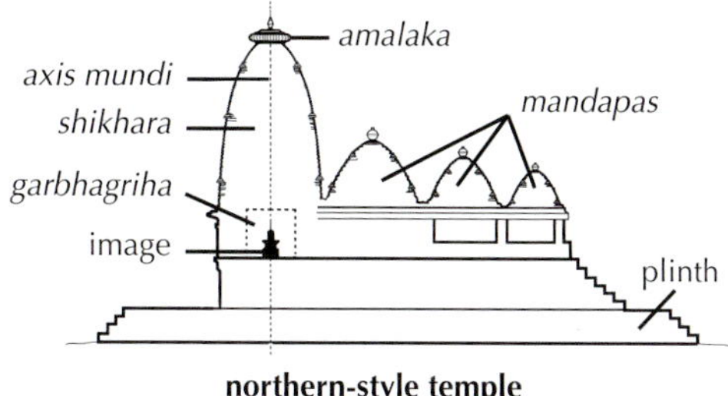

9–3 Schematic drawing of one of the main Indian temple forms: the northern style

the finial down the *shikhara* through the image of the deity into the ground below. In this way the temple becomes a conduit between celestial realms and the earth, a concept familiar from Buddhist stupas. At the Kandariya Mahadeva temple, the *shikhara* is bolstered by the clustering of many smaller *shikhara* motifs bundled around it. Below, porches surround the body of the temple, and at the front (to the right in figure 9–3), a steep flight of stairs leads into a series of three halls, known as *mandapa*s, preceding the sanctuary and capped on the exterior with a sequence of projecting forms that step down to form a smooth diagonal in front of the tall *shikhara* as they progress toward the temple front. The halls serve as a place for rituals, such as dances performed for the deity, and for the presentation of offerings. Symbolically, the halls represent the second or Subtle Body stage of Shiva's threefold emanation—from Formless One (state of being), to Subtle Body (the world), to Gross Body (assistance for living beings). The surface of the temple is encrusted with decorative architectural motifs (miniature *shikhara*s) and sculpted gods and goddesses that both soften and enrich the delineation of architectural forms.

At the time when this temple was built, two major religious movements affected Hindu practice and its art: the tantric, or esoteric, movement primarily in the north and the *bhakti*, or devotional, movement primarily in the south. The *bhakti* movement, based on ideas expressed in ancient texts, especially the *Bhagavad-Gita*, is concerned with the ideal relationship between humans and deities. *Bhakti* involves an intimate, personal, and loving relationship with a god, involving singular devotion and the abandonment of the self. This movement profoundly influenced the Chola Dynasty, rulers in the far south of India from the mid-ninth into the late thirteenth century. Inspired by *bhakti*, southern artists produced some of India's greatest and most humanistic works of sculpture, cast in bronze.

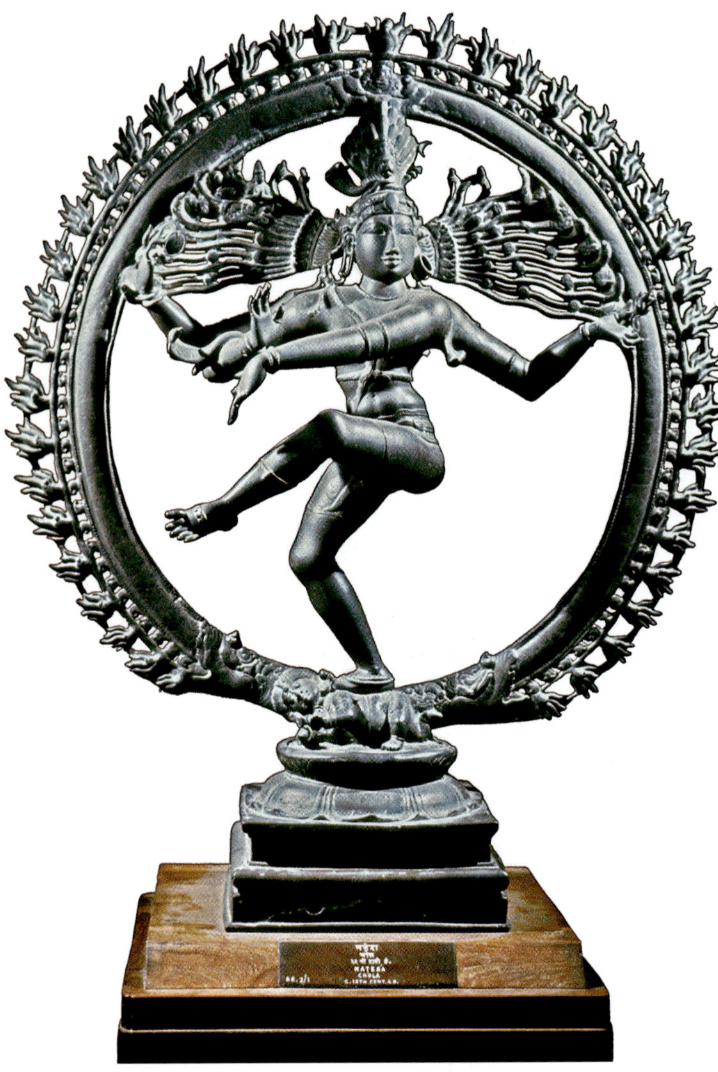

9–4 ***Shiva Nataraja (Lord of Dance)***, Tamil Nadu, South India. Chola Dynasty, 12th century CE. Bronze, height 32" (81.25 cm). National Museum of India, New Delhi, India

The bronze *Shiva Nataraja (Lord of Dance)* (fig. **9–4**), embodies the *bhakti* movement at its most fervent. No longer does the deity appear self-absorbed and introspective (see fig. 4–10). Instead, he generously displays himself to the devotee in full awareness of his benevolent powers. Dancing within a ring of fire, Shiva's extended left hand holds a spray of flames, emblematic of the destruction of the universe as well as of our ego-centeredness. Shiva's back right hand holds a drum, whose ceaseless beat represents the unstoppable rhythms of creation and destruction, birth and death. With his right front hand, he makes the "have no fear" gesture. His left front arm, gracefully stretched across his body with the hand pointing to his raised foot and leg, symbolizes the promise of liberation. The earlier Hindu emphasis on ritual and the depiction of the gods' heroic feats are here subsumed into a pervasive and humanizing quality of grace. The Hindu successors of the Chola continued this ever more sophisticated tradition of bronze sculpture in South India. (See also fig. Intro-9.)

The *bhakti* movement spread subsequently to North India and flourished in the courts of local Hindu princes such as the Rajputs. This period also witnessed the spread of Islam in India. The Muslim conquerors brought Islamic architectural design to the subcontinent, but it was the Mughal Dynasty that made the most lasting Islamic contribution to the art and architecture of India, both in painting (see fig. 8–17) and in buildings such as the Taj Mahal (see fig. 8–18).

Rajput Painting

Apart from the Mughal strongholds at Delhi and Agra, much of northern India was governed by local Hindu princes, descendants of the Rajput warrior clans, who were allowed to keep their lands in return for allegiance to the Mughals. Like the Mughals, Rajput rulers frequently established painting workshops at their courts. In Kangra, a large Rajput kingdom in the Punjab Hills (foothills of the Himalayas north of Delhi), a strong school of painting developed in the middle of the eighteenth century.

INDIAN PAINTING ON PAPER

Before the fourteenth century, most painting in India was on walls or palm leaves. With the introduction of paper and the painting techniques adapted from Persia, Indian artists produced jewel-toned paintings of arresting beauty. They used brushes made from the curved hairs of a squirrel's tail, arranged to taper from a thick base to a few hairs at the tip. The paint was mineral and vegetable pigments, ground to a paste with water, then bound with a solution of gum from the acacia plant.

Artists frequently worked from a collection of sketches in a master painter's studio. Sometimes sketches were pricked with small holes, and wet color was dabbed over the holes to transfer the drawing to a blank sheet beneath. The dots were connected into outlines, and the painting began. First, the painter applied a wash, or thin coat, of chalk-based white, which sealed the surface of the paper while allowing the underlying sketch to show through. Next, the artist filled the outlines with opaque color. When the colors dried, the painting was placed face down on a smooth marble surface and burnished (rubbed) with a rounded agate stone. The indirect pressure against the marble polished the pigments to a high luster. Then outlines, details, and modeling were added with a fine brush. Raised details such as the pearls of a necklace were made with thick, chalk-based paint, each pearl a single droplet hardened into a tiny raised mound.

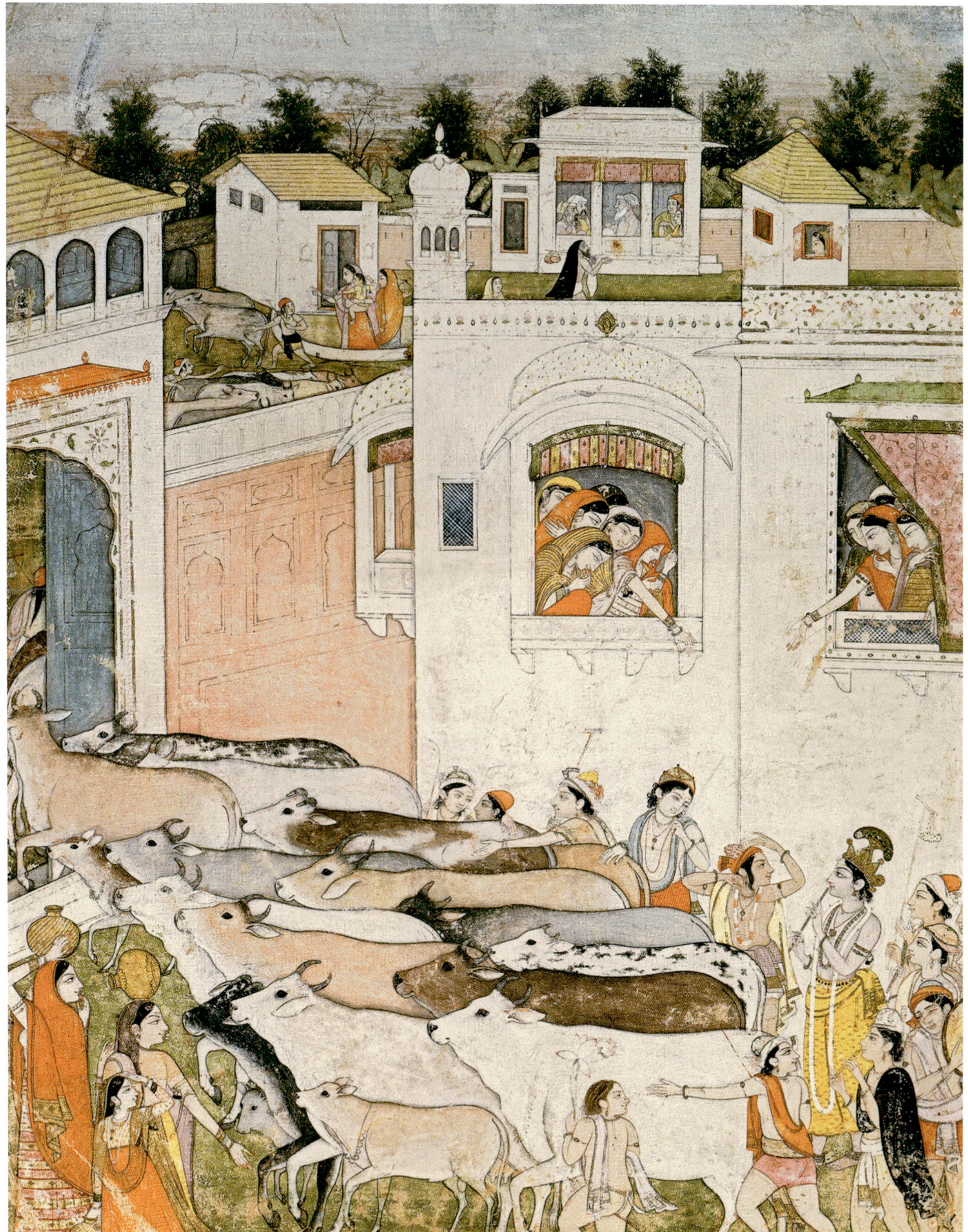

9–5 *The Hour of Cowdust*, Pahari. c. 1810–1815. Kangra school, Punjab Hills, Northern India. Attributed to the Family of Nainsukh. Opaque watercolor and gold on paper, 14$^{15}/_{16}$" × 12$^{9}/_{16}$" (38 × 31.9 cm). Museum of Fine Arts, Boston

Inspired by a revival of the emotional *bhakti* movement, poets wrote of the love of the god Vishnu for human beings, metaphorically expressed as the love of Krishna for the cow maiden Radha. *The Hour of Cowdust* (fig. **9–5**) depicts Krishna, who is living with the cowherds to escape the demons. Wearing his peacock crown, garland of flowers, jewelry, and yellow garment, the blue-skinned god plays his flute as he returns to the village with his fellow cowherds and their cattle. All eyes are upon him, for his music enchants all who hear it. Women with water jugs on their heads turn to look; others lean from windows to watch and call out to him. We

CLOSER LOOK

The decorative arts of India represent the height of opulent luxury. Ornament embellishes even the invisible backs of pendants and the bottoms of containers. Technically superb and crafted from precious materials, tableware, jewelry, furniture, and containers enhance the prestige of their owners and give visual pleasure as well. Metalwork and work in rock crystal, agate, and jade, carving in ivory, and intricate jewelry are all characteristic Indian arts. Because of the intrinsic value of their materials, however, pieces have been disassembled, melted down, and reworked, making the study of Indian luxury arts very difficult. Many pieces, like the carved ivory panel illustrated here (fig. **9–6**), have no date or records of manufacture or ownership.

Frozen in timeless delight, carved in ivory against a golden ground where openwork, stylized vines with spiky leaves weave an elegant arabesque, loving couples dally under the arcades of a palace courtyard, the thin columns and cusped arches of which resemble the arcades of the palace of Tirumala Nayak (ruled 1622–1662) in Madurai (Tamil Nadu) where this ivory plaque was made. The Nayak rulers commissioned sculpture and painting, but wood and ivory carving ranks among their artists' highest achievements, hardly a minor art. This plaque must have decorated a container for precious objects—note the keyhole at top center and the small holes in the borders where nails would have attached it to the side of a wooden box.

The huge eyes set under the figures' heavy brows suggest the intensity of their gaze, and the artist's choice of profile view emphasizes long noses and sensuously thick lips. Their hair is tightly controlled; the men wear their uncut hair in huge knots, and the women have long braids hanging down their backs. Are they divine lovers? After all, Krishna lived and loved on earth among the cow maidens. Or are we observing scenes of courtly romance?

The rich jewelry and well-fed bodies of the couples indicate a high station in life. Men as well as women have voluptuous figures with rounded buttocks and thighs. Some have ample tummies hanging over jeweled belts. The sharply indented slim waists of the women emphasize seductive breasts. All this smooth flesh contrasts with diaphanous fabrics that swath plump legs. Their long arms and elegant gestures seem designed to show off rich jewelry—bracelets, armbands, necklaces, and huge earrings. Such amorous couples symbolize harmony as well as fertility.

The erotic imagery suggests that the panel illustrated here might have adorned a container for personal belongings such as jewelry, perfume, or cosmetics. In any event, the ivory relief is a brilliant example of South Indian secular arts.

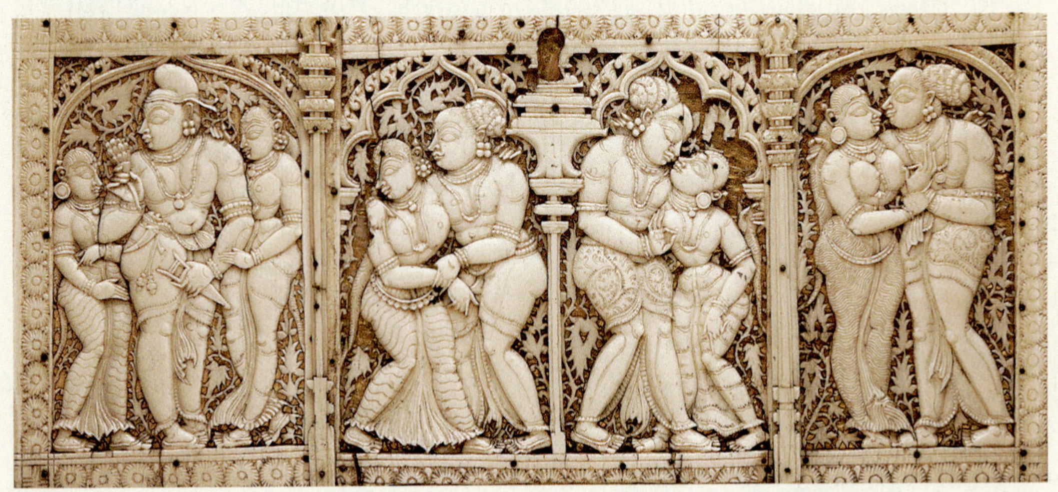

9–6 Panel from a box, Tamil Nadu, India. Late 17th–18th century. Ivory backed with gilded paper, 6" × 12⅜" × ⅛" (15.2 × 31.4 × 0.3 cm). Virginia Museum of Fine Arts

THE ARTHUR AND MARGARET GLASGOW FUND. 80.171. KATHERINE WETZEL © VIRGINIA MUSEUM OF FINE ARTS, RICHMOND

follow the path of the cattle as they move along a diagonal, surging through the gate and into the courtyard beyond. Pastel walls define receding space, where we glimpse other villagers going about their work or sitting within their houses. A rim of dark trees softens the horizon, and a rose-tinted sky completes the aura of enchantment. The scene reflects the sublime purity and grace of the divine, which, as in so much Indian art, is evoked within our human world to coexist with us as one.

In the southern Indian state of Tamil Nadu, the high quality of luxury arts—work in rock crystal, ivory (fig. **9–6**), mother-of-pearl, metalwork, and jewelry—made them renowned even outside India, and beginning in the sixteenth century, objects were made for export as well as for local sale. Sikhs took over the kingdom in 1826, and the British followed in 1846, effectively putting an end to the distinctive local styles.

Cambodia

Cambodia lies between India and China geographically and culturally. Buddhism and Hinduism supplanted local religions, and the indigenous Khmer people eventually developed a distinctive synthesis of beliefs that evolved into a state religion under a divine king who ruled at Angkor ("capital city") from the ninth to the thirteenth century. The concept of the World Mountain—Mount Meru—whether natural or human-made, underlaid the design of the monuments they built.

Suryavarman II (ruled c. 1112–1153) began the royal complex known to us as Angkor Wat (fig. **9–7**). Dedicated to Vishnu, the vast array of structures is both a temple and a symbolic cosmic mountain, home to the deity and axis of the world. Originally, the visitor approached the building over a bridge across a wide moat and, after passing through a monumental gateway, continued up a long avenue between two water-filled tanks to the building itself. The building has a simple plan of squares within squares defined by galleries surrounding a tall central tower with four lesser towers. Additional towers at the outer corners define the extent of the huge complex.

Sculpture covers every possible surface, depicting the many incarnations of the god Vishnu in dizzying detail. After the Siamese conquered the Khmer kingdom in 1437, the buildings of Angkor fell into neglect. By the time they were rediscovered in the nineteenth century, the jungle had covered them. Although Angkor Wat is now under the protection of UNESCO, twentieth-century wars and twenty-first-century thieves continue to imperil the existence of the site.

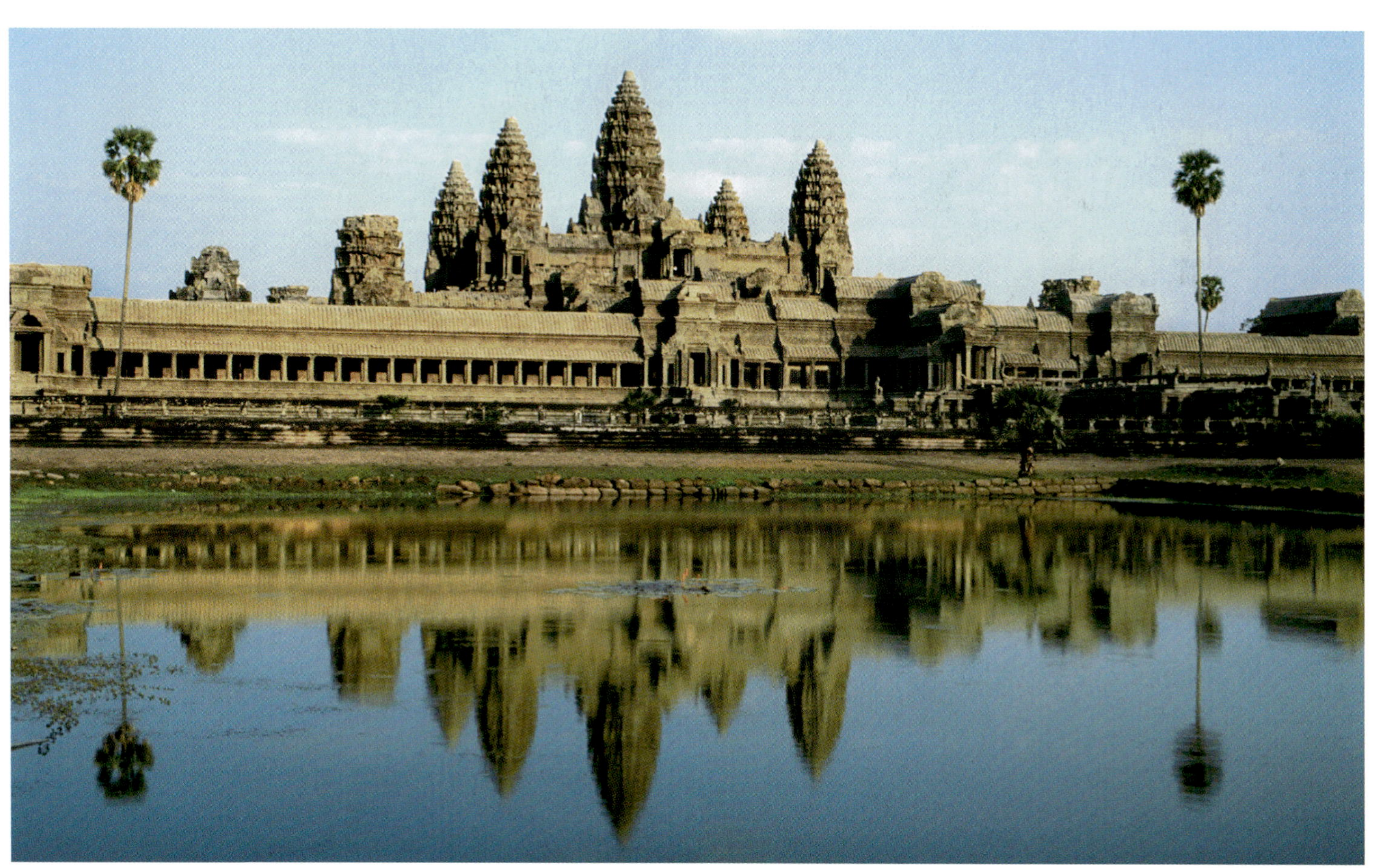

9–7 Angkor Wat, Kampuchea (Cambodia), west entrance. c. 1120–1150. The temple wall is 3,363' × 2,625' (1025.042 × 800.1 m) and the moats are 623' (189.89 m) wide

China

A brief period of disintegration followed the fall of the Tang Dynasty in 907, but the Liao Dynasty (907–1125) exerted some semblance of power. China was only united again under the Song Dynasty (960–1279). In 1126, invaders from Manchuria defeated the Song, sacking the capital Bianjing (present-day Kaifeng) and occupying much of the northern part of the country. Song forces withdrew south and established a new capital at Hangzhou. The dynasty from this point on is known as Southern Song (1127–1279), whereas the earlier years are called Northern Song (960–1126).

In spite of the changing political fortunes, artists continued to create splendid works. No hint of chaos or despair intrudes on the sublime grace and beauty of the *Seated Guanyin Bodhisattva* (fig. **9–8**). Bodhisattvas, beings who voluntarily remain on earth to help others achieve enlightenment, are represented as young princes wearing royal garments and jewelry, their finery indicative of their worldly but virtuous lives. Guanyin is the Bodhisattva of Infinite Compassion, who appears in many guises. Here, as the Water and Moon Guanyin, he sits on rocks by the sea, in the posture known as "royal ease." His right arm rests on his raised and bent right knee and his left arm and foot hang down, the foot touching a lotus blossom. The wooden figure was carved between the tenth and twelfth centuries, but the painting and gilding date from the sixteenth century.

During the Song period, the martial vigor of the Tang and Liao gave way to a culture of increasing refinement and scholarship. The study of history, literature, and philosophy flourished while Song philosophers revived Confucianism. Drawing on both Buddhism and Daoism they provided Confucianism with a metaphysical basis, a systematic and comprehensive explanation of the universe called Neo-Confucianism. It teaches that the universe consists of two

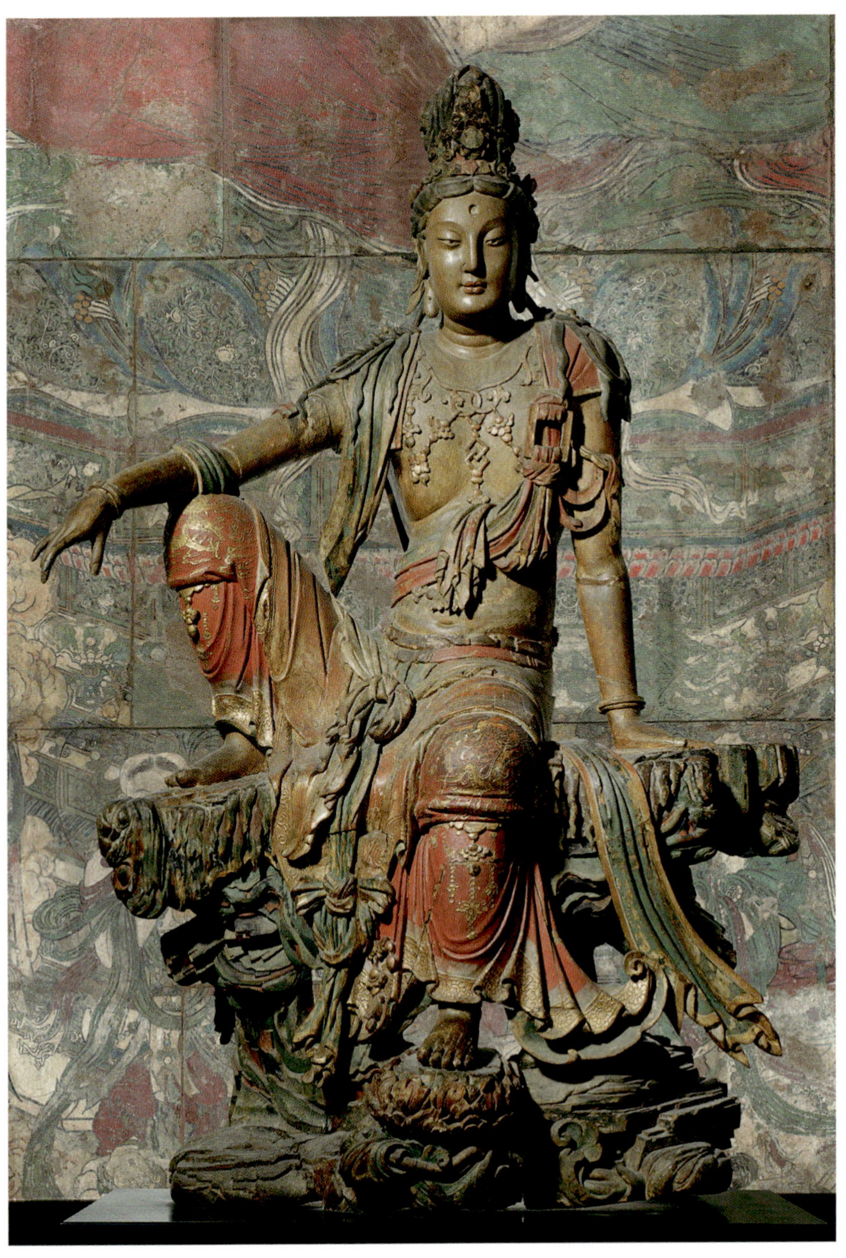

9–8 ***Seated Guanyin Bodhisattva.*** Liao Dynasty, 10th–12th century CE. Wood with paint, height 95" (241.3 cm). The Nelson-Atkins Museum of Art, Kansas City, Missouri
PURCHASE: WILLIAM ROCKHILL NELSON TRUST (34-10). PHOTOGRAPH BY JAMISON MILLER

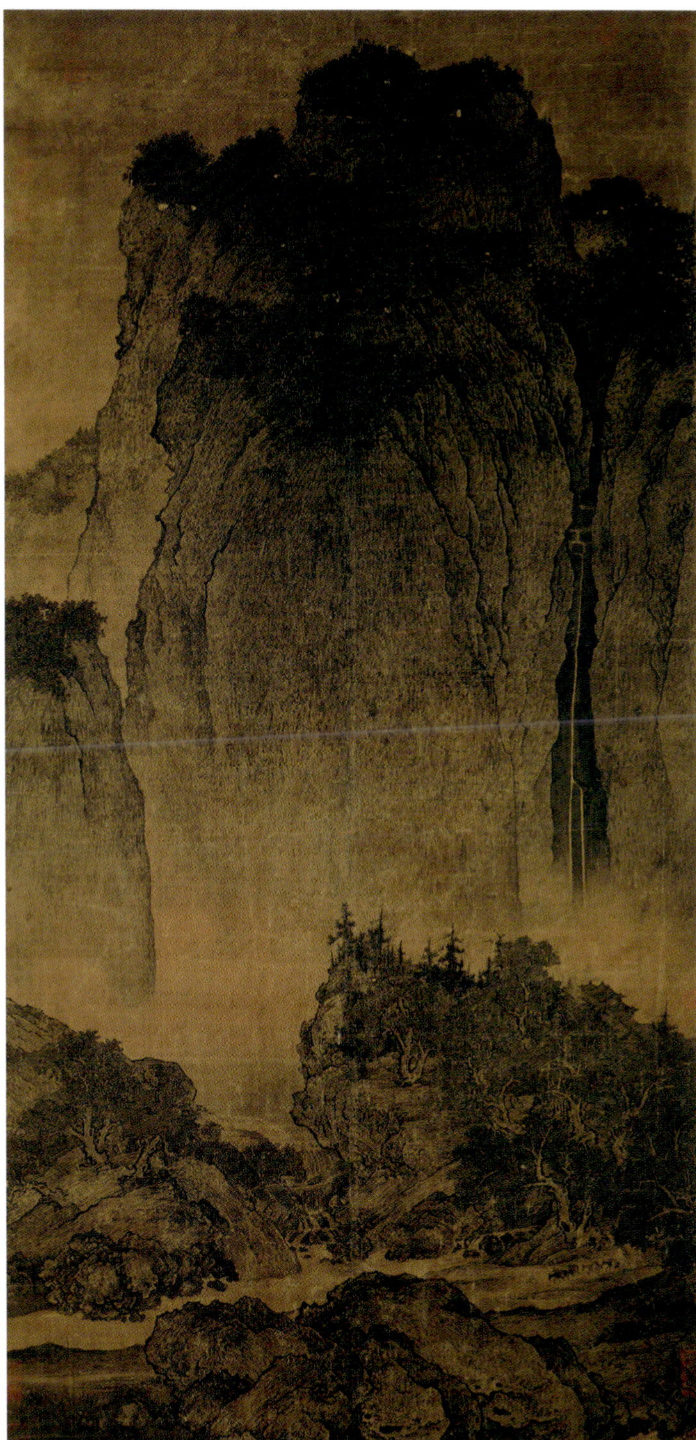

9–9 Fan Kuan. ***Travelers Among Mountains and Streams.*** Northern Song Dynasty, early 11th century. Hanging scroll, ink and colors on silk, height 6' 9¼" (2.06 m). National Palace Museum, Taipei, Taiwan, Republic of China

interacting forces known as *li* (principle or idea) and *qi* (matter). All pine trees, for instance, consist of an underlying *li* that we might call the "Pine Tree Idea," brought into the world through *qi*, the living tree. All the *li* of the universe, including humans, are but aspects of an eternal first principle known as the Great Ultimate. The task of humans is to purify their *qi* through education and self-cultivation so that their *li* may achieve union with the Great Ultimate.

Neo-Confucian ideas were visualized in landscape painting, which became the most highly esteemed subject for painters. Northern Song artists studied nature closely to master its varied appearances: the way each species of tree grew, the distinctive character of rock formations, the signs of changing seasons, and the myriad birds, blossoms, and insects around them. This study was integral to the artist's self-cultivation; mastering outward forms showed an understanding of the principles behind them. Yet despite their faithful visual description of individual forms, Song paintings do not seek to record specific views. The artist's goal was to paint the eternal aspect of "mountain," for example, not to reproduce the particular appearance of one mountain. Thus landscape painting expresses the desire for spiritual communion with nature as a key to enlightenment. Over the centuries, painting landscape also became a vehicle for conveying human emotions, potentially for expressing profound personal feelings.

One of the first great masters of Song landscape was Fan Kuan (active c. 990–1030), whose monumental *Travelers Among Mountains and Streams* is generally regarded as among the greatest monuments in the history of Chinese art (fig. **9–9**). The composition unfolds in three stages, comparable to the three acts of a sequentially visualized drama, moving step by step as we explore the world of the painting from front to back, bottom to top. A low-lying group of rocks at the bottom establishes the extreme foreground, anticipating, on a small scale, the shape and substance of the mountains to come. In the middle ground, travelers and their mules enter from the right. We are somewhat startled to suddenly realize our relative scale—the humans are quite small set against the vastness of the natural world. This middle ground, like the second act of a play, shows variation and development. Instead of a solid mass, the rocks are separated here into two groups by a waterfall. At right, the rooftops of a temple stand out above the trees.

Mist veils the transition to the background, so the mountain seems to loom up suddenly. This background area, almost twice as large as the foreground and middle ground combined, is the climactic third act of the drama. As our eyes begin their ascent, the mountain solidifies, its ponderous weight increasing as it billows upward, ultimately bursting into sprays of energetic brushstrokes that describe the scrubby growth on top. To the right, a slender waterfall—white against black—plummets, not to balance the powerful upward thrust of the sheer face of the mountain, but to enhance its monumentality through linear contrast. The painting as a whole summons up the feeling of climbing a high mountain, leaving the human world behind to come face-to-face in a spiritual communion with the Great Ultimate.

The ability of Chinese landscape painters to take us out of ourselves and let us wander freely through their visions of the natural world is closely linked to the avoidance of the **linear perspective**

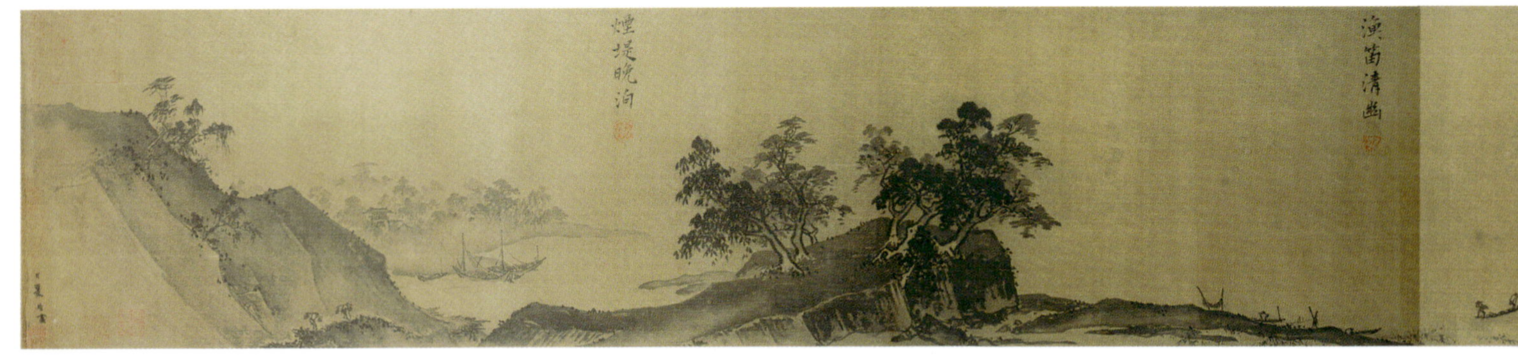

9–10 Xia Gui. Section of *Twelve Views from a Thatched Hut*. Southern Song Dynasty, early 13th century. Handscroll, ink on silk. Height 11" (28 cm), length of extant portion 7' 7¼" (2.31 m). The Nelson-Atkins Museum of Art, Kansas City, Missouri
PURCHASE: WILLIAM ROCKHILL NELSON TRUST (32-159/2). PHOTOGRAPH BY JOHN LAMBERTON

used in European painting, after fifteenth-century Florentine painters had developed a "scientific" system for recording or imagining views of a world seen from a single, fixed vantage point (see "Renaissance Perspective Systems," page 324). The goal of Chinese painting is precisely to avoid such controlling limitations and instead show a panoramic totality that transcends any one single viewpoint by capturing a combination of viewpoints.

Chinese landscape painting took a very different course after the fall of the Northern Song in 1126 and the removal of the court to Hangzhou. The work of Xia Gui (c. 1180–1230), a member of a reestablished imperial painting academy, is representative of this change. In sharp contrast to the majestic, austere landscapes of the Northern Song painters, his *Twelve Views from a Thatched Hut* (fig. **9–10**) presents an intimate and lyrical view of nature. In the surviving four of twelve views that originally made up this long **handscroll** (narrow, horizontal painting), subtly modulated ink washes describe a landscape veiled in mists. A few deft brushstrokes suffice to suggest details showing through the mist—the grasses growing by the bank, the fishermen at their work, the trees laden with moisture, the two bent-backed figures carrying their heavy load along the path that skirts the hill. Simplified forms, stark contrasts of light and dark, asymmetrical compositions, and great expanses of blank space suggest a fleeting, intangible world that can be grasped only in glimpses.

This development in Song painting from the rational and intellectual to the emotional and intuitive had a parallel in philosophy. During the late twelfth century, a new school of Neo-Confucianism called the School of the Mind insisted that self-cultivation could be achieved through contemplation, which might lead to sudden enlightenment. The idea of sudden enlightenment may have come from Chan Buddhism, better known in the West by its Japanese name, Zen. Chan Buddhists used meditation and techniques designed to "short-circuit" the rational mind. Xia Gui's painting seems also to follow this intuitive approach.

The highly cultivated audience that appreciated subtle and sophisticated Song painting was equally discerning in other arts, such as ceramics. Of the many types of Song ceramics, one of the most prized was Guan ware, made mainly for imperial use (fig. **9–11**). The shape of this graceful vase flows without interruption from base to lip, but the potter intentionally allowed a pattern of irregular, spontaneous cracks to develop in the lustrous off-white glaze. This creates an interplay of ordered and unplanned elements, setting the controlled regularity of the vessel's form against the uncontrollable spontaneity of the linear network in the glaze. Such ceramics have an understated quality as eloquent as the blank spaces and fugitive forms in Xia Gui's painting.

Closely related to Chinese Guan ware is the Korean celadon made during the Goryeo Dynasty (918–1392). At first the Korean potters copied Chinese ceramics, but soon they developed distinctive forms and new forms of decoration. Their most notable innovation was inlaid decoration, in which black and white slips were inlaid into lines incised or stamped in the clay body, creating underglaze designs in contrasting colors. The bottle in fig. **9–12** displays such an inlaid pictorial scene. A clump of bamboo intertwines with the branches of a blossoming plum tree at the edge of a lake. Geese swim by and dragonflies flutter above. Such broad-shouldered bottles were used as storage jars for wine, vinegar, and other liquids, and a small, bell-shaped cover originally capped the vessel, protecting its contents at the same time as it complemented its curves.

In 1279, the Southern Song Dynasty fell to the armies of the Mongol leader Kublai Khan, and China became part of the vast Mongol Empire. Kublai Khan founded the Yuan Dynasty (1279–1368), setting up his capital in the northeast, in what is now Beijing. The center of Chinese culture remained in the south, however, and southern Chinese scholars found themselves alienated from the Mongol court. Denied normal access to the government positions for which they were educated, these scholars, the literati, retreated into alternative outlets for their talents, including the arts.

The southerner Zhao Mengfu (1254–1322), a descendant of the imperial line of Song, is typical in this regard; a painter, calligrapher, and poet, he produced works for an elite audience of cultivated southern literati. Unlike many of his southern contemporaries, though, he eventually served the Yuan government in Beijing and was made a high official. Zhao painted *Autumn Colors on the Qiao*

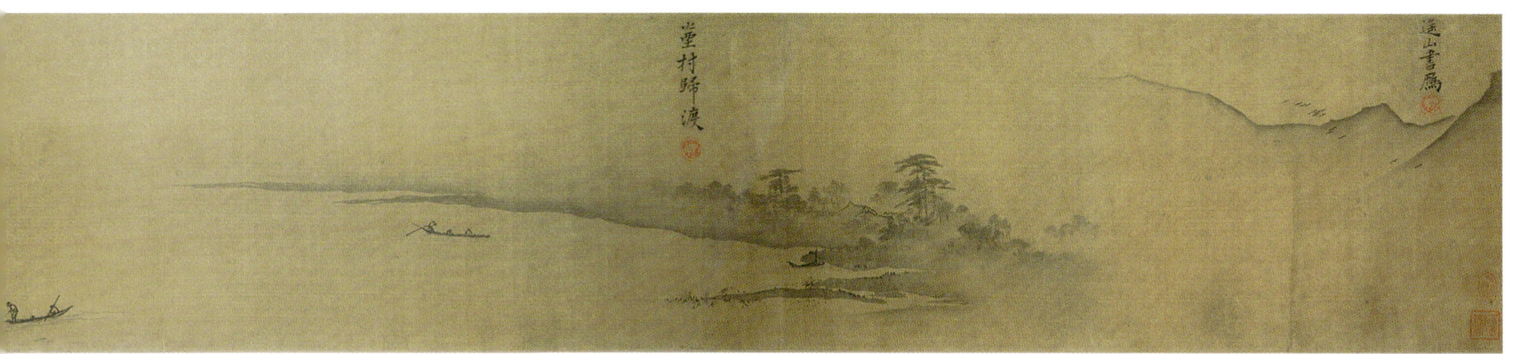

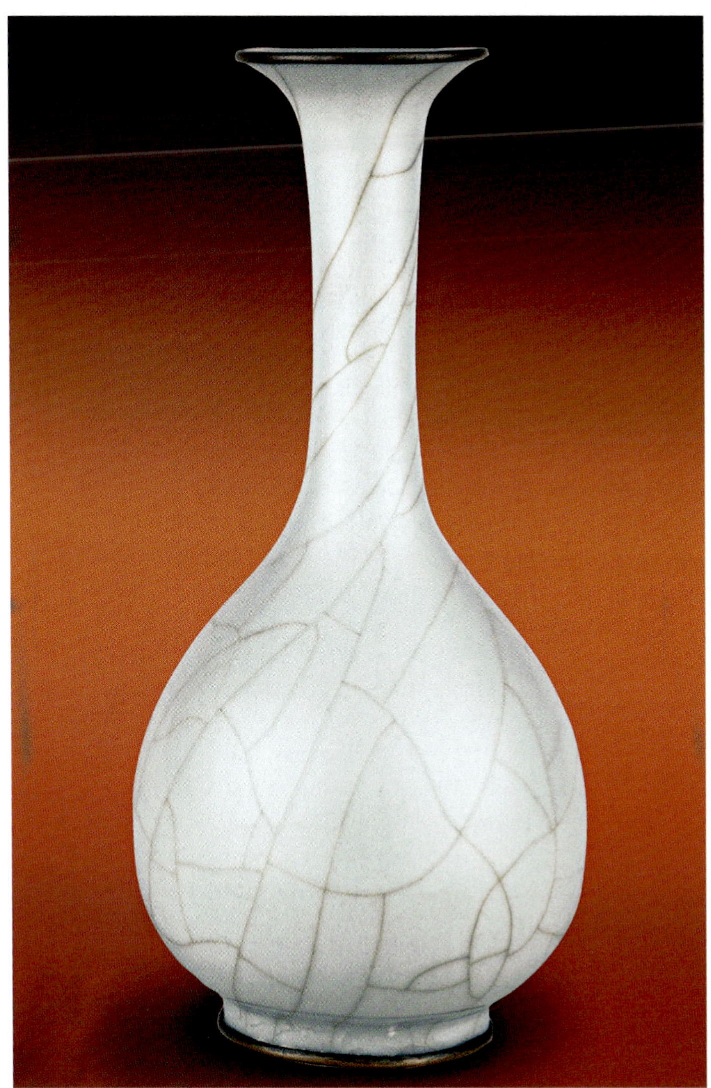

9–11 Guan ware vase. Southern Song Dynasty, 12th–13th century. Stoneware with crackled glaze, height 6⅞" (18 cm)
PERCIVAL DAVID FOUNDATION OF CHINESE ART, LONDON

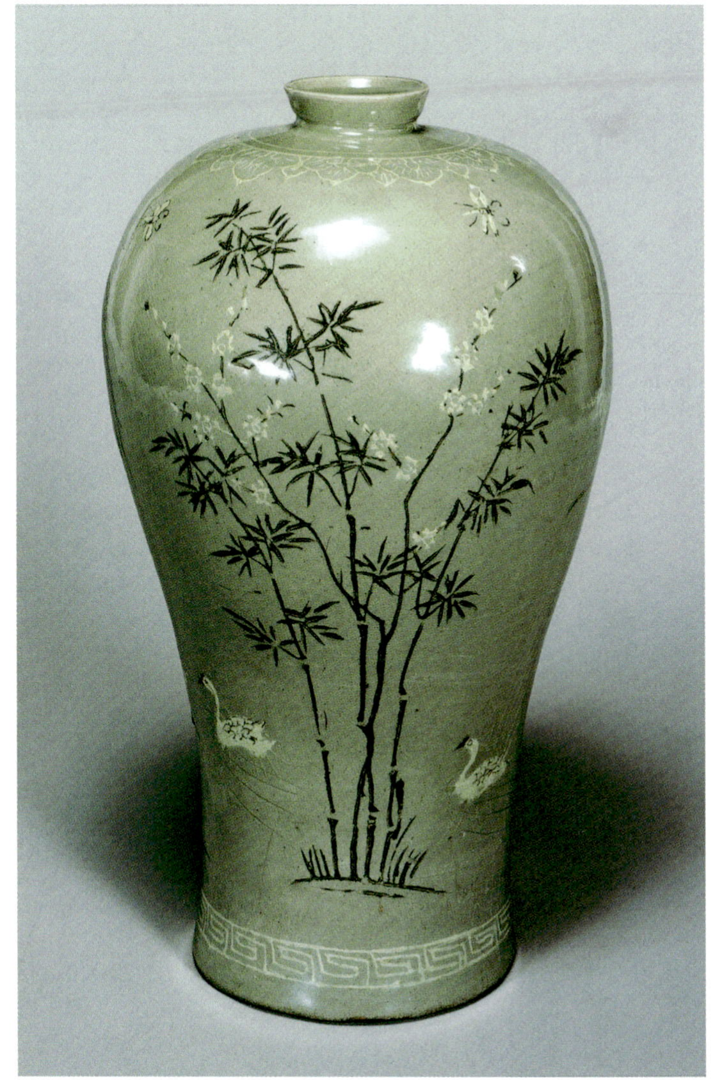

9–12 Maebyeong bottle with decoration of bamboo and blossoming plum tree. Korean. Goryeo Dynasty, late 12th–early 13th century. Celadon ware inlaid with black and white slip under the glaze, height 13¼" (33.7 cm). Tokyo National Museum, Japan

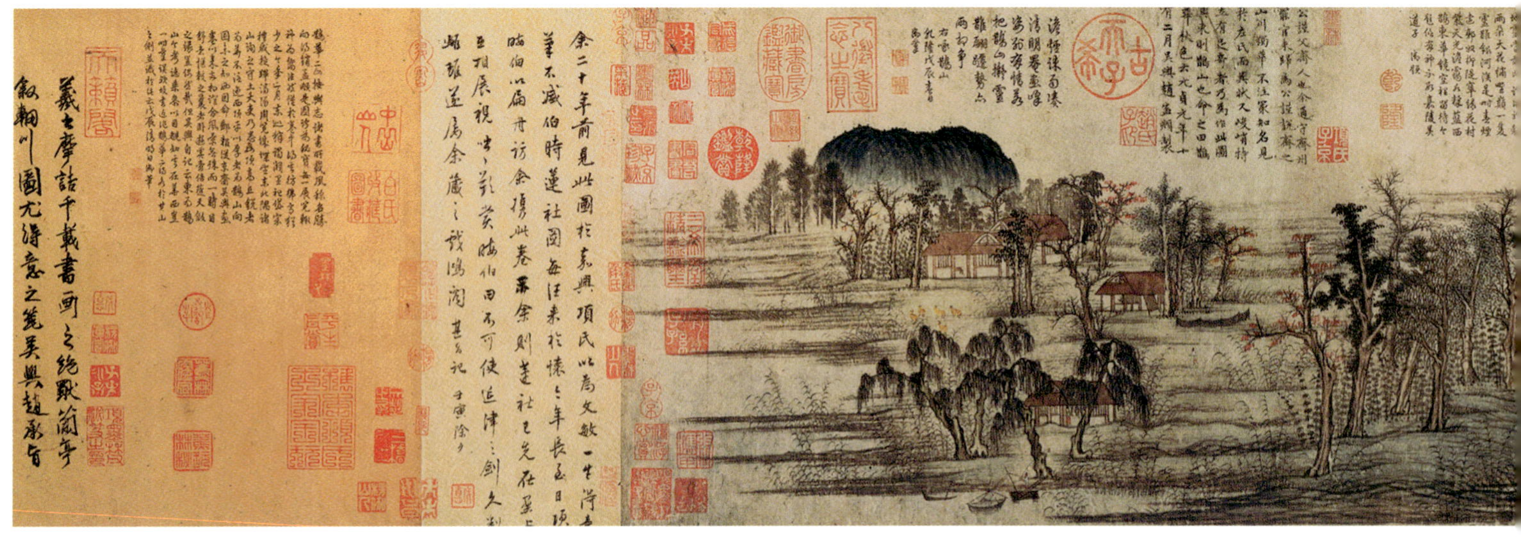

Technique

Formats of Chinese Painting

Aside from wall paintings that decorated palaces, temples, and tombs, most Chinese paintings were done in ink and water-based colors on silk or paper. Finished works were usually mounted as hand-scrolls, hanging scrolls, in albums, or on fans.

An album comprises a set of paintings of similar size, and usually of related subject matter, mounted in an accordion-fold book. Album-size paintings could also be mounted as a hand-scroll, a horizontal format generally about 12 inches high and anywhere from a few feet to dozens of feet long. More typically, however, a hand-scroll would be a single continuous painting, generally preceded by a panel giving the work's title and often followed by a long panel bearing colophons—inscriptions, such as poems, in praise of the work or comments by its owners over the centuries. Seals of the maker and also those of collectors and admirers through the centuries added another layer of interest.

Hand-scrolls were not meant to be displayed all at once, the way they are commonly presented today in museums. Rather, they were kept rolled up and only occasionally taken out for viewing. The viewer would unroll the scroll gradually, moving slowly through its entire length from right to left, lingering over favorite details.

Like hand-scrolls, hanging scrolls were not displayed permanently but taken out for a limited time—a day, a week, or a season. Unlike hand-scrolls, however, the hanging scroll was viewed as a whole, unrolled and hung on a wall, with the wooden roller at the lower end acting as a weight to help the scroll hang flat.

colophon panel

frontispiece

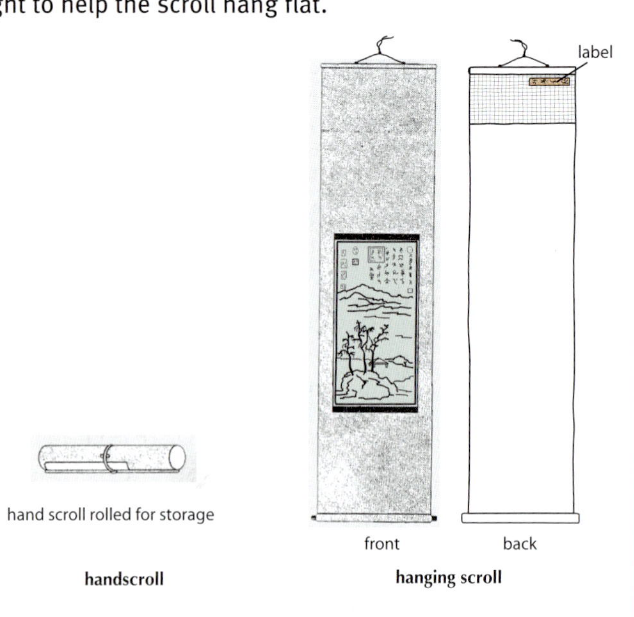

handscroll

hanging scroll

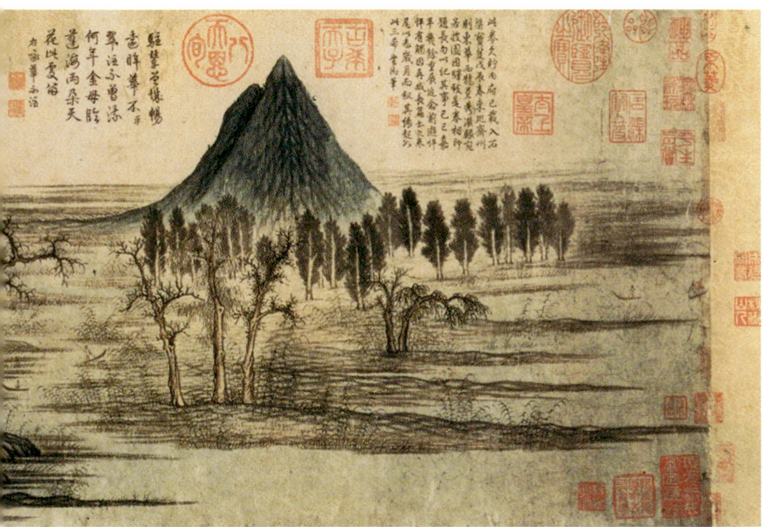

9–13 Zhao Mengfu. Section of *Autumn Colors on the Qiao and Hua Mountains*. Yuan Dynasty, 1296. Hand-scroll, ink and color on paper, 11¼" × 36¾" (28.6 × 93.3 cm). National Palace Museum, Taipei, Taiwan, Republic of China

and Hua Mountains (fig. **9–13**) for a friend living in the south and supposedly depicts the friend's ancestral home, Jinan, in the north. The mountains are not painted in the evocative, descriptive mode perfected by Song painters but rather in an elegant, archaic manner that recalls the much earlier art of the Tang Dynasty. In this way Zhao imbues his painting with a feeling of nostalgia, not only for his friend's distant homeland, but also for China's past.

This educated elite taste for antique styles became an enduring aspect of literati painting. Also typical of the tradition are the unassuming brushwork, the subtle colors sparingly used, and even the choice of a close friend as the intended audience. The literati painted not for public display but for each other. They favored hand-scrolls, hanging scrolls, or album leaves, which could easily be transported to show to friends or small gatherings (see "Formats of Chinese Painting," page 226).

The contrast between the opulent display and the austere aesthetic ideals of the literati is a defining feature of painting during the subsequent Ming Dynasty (1368–1644). Whereas court painters revived academic traditions of the Song, many literati painters built on the styles created by their Yuan predecessors. One of the major literati artists of the Ming period is Shen Zhou (1427–1509), who spent most of his life in the southern city of Suzhou, far from the court in Beijing. Shen Zhou studied Yuan painters avidly and tried to recapture their spirit in such works as *Poet on a Mountaintop* (fig. **9–14**). Here the poet has climbed a mountain and dominates the landscape. Before his gaze, a poem hangs in the air, like a projection of his thoughts. Not only the landscape painting, but also the poem is a vehicle for Shen Zhou's self-expression, having more to do with the artist's response to nature than with the physical world itself. With its perfect synthesis of poetry, calligraphy, and painting, and its harmony of mind and landscape, *Poet on a Mountaintop* represents the very essence of literati painting.

The cities of the south, such as Suzhou, were full of newly wealthy merchants who collected paintings, antiques, and art objects. The court, too, was prosperous and patronized the arts on a lavish scale. In such a setting, the decorative arts thrived.

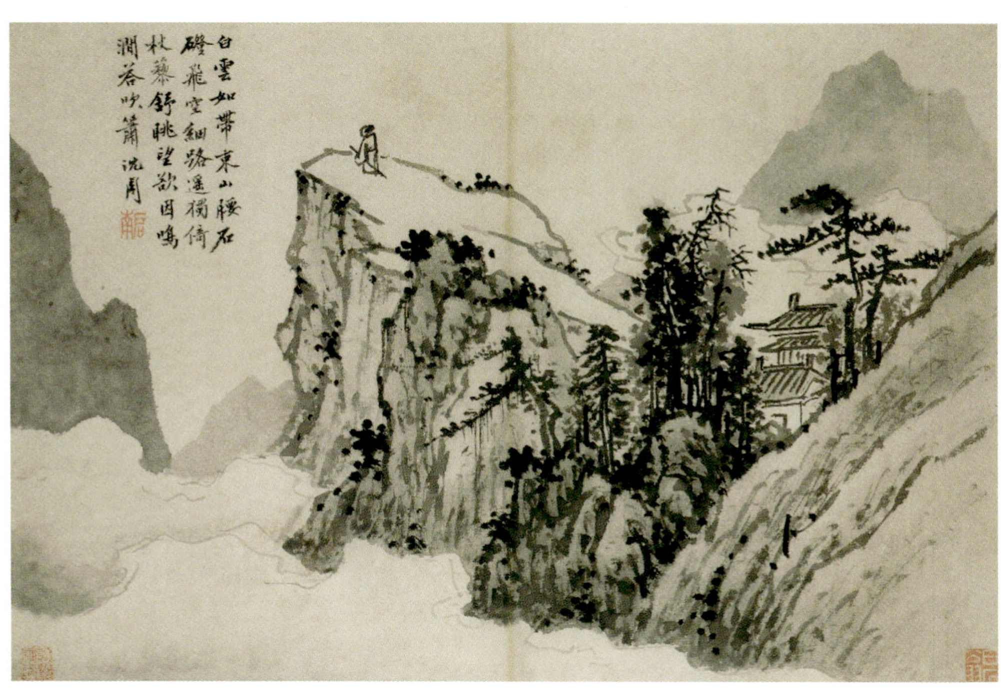

9–14 Shen Zhou. *Poet on a Mountaintop*, leaf from an album of landscape paintings, now mounted as part of a hand-scroll. Ming Dynasty, c. 1500. Ink and color on paper, 15¼" × 23¾" (38.1 × 60.2 cm). The Nelson-Atkins Museum of Art, Kansas City, Missouri PURCHASE: WILLIAM ROCKHILL NELSON TRUST (46–5½).

The poem at the upper left reads:

White clouds like a belt encircle the mountain's waist
A stone ledge flying in space and the far thin road.
I lean alone on my bramble staff and gazing contented into space
Wish the sounding torrent would answer to your flute.
(Translated by Richard Edwards, *Eight Dynasties of Chinese Paintings*, page 185)

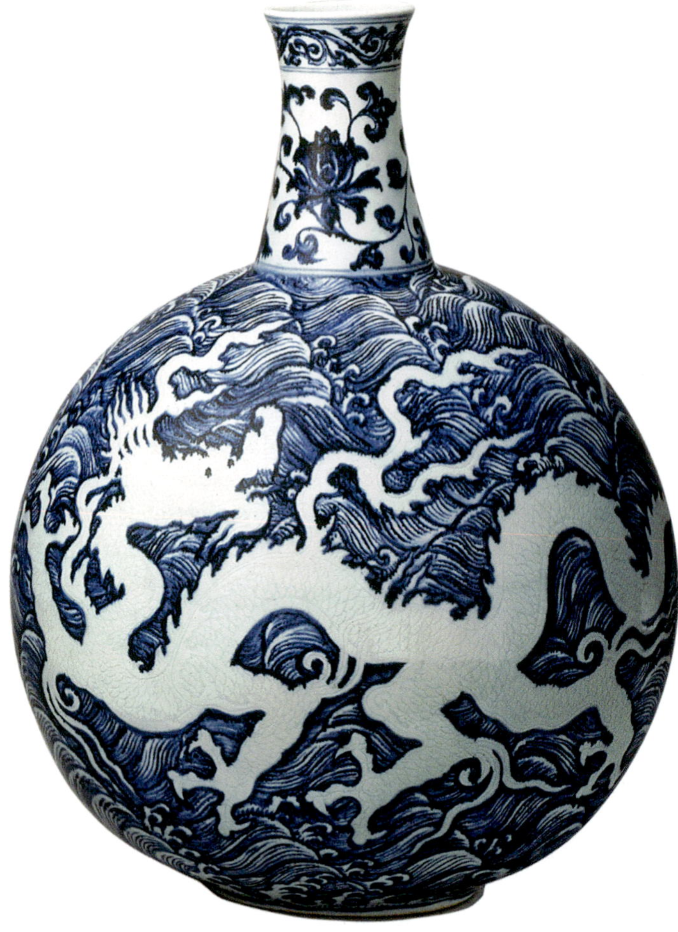

9–15 Porcelain flask with decoration in blue underglaze. Ming Dynasty, c. 1425–1435. Palace Museum, Beijing

Dragons have featured prominently in Chinese folklore from earliest times—Neolithic examples have been found painted on pottery and carved in jade. In Bronze Age China, dragons came to be associated with powerful and sudden manifestations of nature, such as wind, thunder, and lightning. At the same time, dragons became associated with superior beings such as virtuous rulers and sages. With the emergence of China's first firmly established empire during the Han Dynasty, the dragon was appropriated as an imperial symbol, and it remained so throughout Chinese history. Dragon sightings were duly recorded and considered auspicious. Yet even the Son of Heaven could not monopolize the dragon. During the Tang and Song dynasties the practice arose of painting pictures of dragons to pray for rain, and for Chan (Zen) Buddhists, the dragon was a symbol of enlightenment.

The Ming became famous the world over for its exquisite ceramics, especially **porcelain**. Porcelain is made from kaolin, an extremely refined white clay, and petuntze, a variety of the mineral feldspar. When properly combined and fired at a high temperature, the two materials fuse into a glass-like, translucent ceramic that is far stronger than it looks.

The porcelain flask in figure **9–15** came from the imperial kilns in Jingdezhen, in Jiangxi province, the most renowned center for porcelain in Ming China. The blue decoration—made from cobalt oxide, finely ground and mixed with water—was painted directly onto the unfired porcelain vessel in a technique known as **underglazing**. Next, the painter applied a clear glaze over the entire surface. After firing the flask emerged from the kiln with its blue decoration set sharply against white. In this case a dragon is reserved in white against a background painted with blue patterning. The subtle shape, the refined yet vigorous decoration of dragons writhing in the sea, and the flawless glazing typify the high achievement of Ming artisans.

Ming ceramists were not alone in their creativity and technical skill. Ming architects created the most important surviving example of traditional Chinese architecture: the Forbidden City, the imperial palace compound in Beijing (fig. **9–16**). The basic plan of Beijing was the work of the Mongols, who laid out their capital city according to Chinese principles, creating a walled rectangle with gates oriented to the four cardinal directions and streets running north–south and east–west arranged as a grid. The palace enclosure occupied the center of the northern part of the city. Under the Ming Dynasty Emperor Yongle (who ruled 1402–1424), the Forbidden City was rebuilt as we see it today.

Visitors to the Forbidden City entered on the south and passed through the South Gate, the monumental U-shaped complex near the middle of figure 9–16. Inside the gate, a bow-shaped canal spanned by five arched marble bridges crosses a broad courtyard. On the north side of the courtyard is the Gate of Supreme Harmony, opening into the larger Outer Court. This area houses three ceremonial halls raised on a broad platform, classic examples of Chinese palace architecture, with brilliant terracotta tile roofs and red lacquered columns. In the first and largest, the Hall of Supreme Harmony, the emperor sat on his throne during important state occasions. He faced south, looking out toward his city and, by extension, his realm. His back was to the north, the source of evil spirits, not to mention military threats from non-Chinese peoples beyond

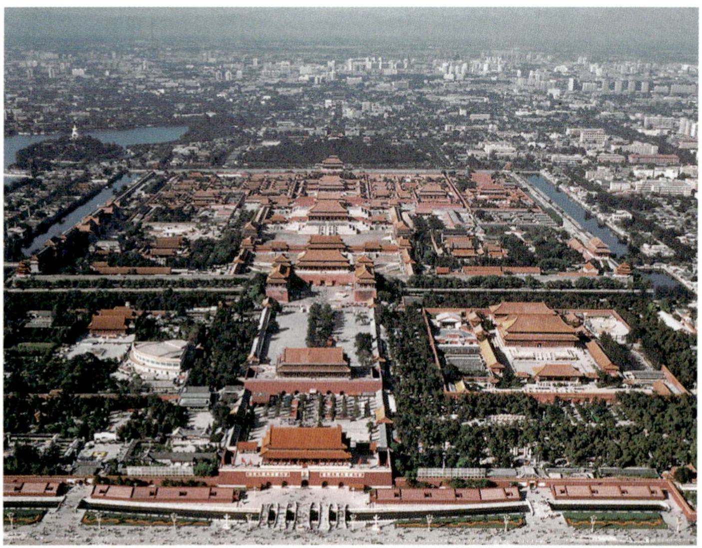

9–16 The Forbidden City, now the Palace Museum, Beijing. Mostly Ming Dynasty. View from the southwest

the Great Wall. Continuing on to the north in the Forbidden City, the visitor encounters the secluded and smaller Inner Court, which also has a progression of three buildings. This is where the emperor lived and conducted more private business affairs.

In its directional orientation and symmetrical arrangement, the plan of the Forbidden City reflects ancient Chinese beliefs about the harmony of the universe and emphasizes the emperor's role as the Son of Heaven, whose duty was to maintain the cosmic order from his throne in the middle of the world.

Japan

In Japan, by the Heian period (794–1185), Buddhism was practiced throughout the land, although it did not completely supplant the country's indigenous religion, Shinto. Buddhism offers paradisiacal realms and enlightenment, whereas Shinto offers the intercession of the gods in the affairs of this world. Since these two ideals did not fundamentally clash, modes of mutual accommodation were found. To this day, most Japanese see nothing inconsistent about having Shinto weddings and Buddhist funerals.

The general peacefulness of the Heian period contributed to a new cultural self-reliance on the part of the Japanese. Ties to China were severed in the mid-ninth century, and the Heian imperial government was sustained by support from aristocratic families. During these four centuries of splendor and refinement, two new schools of Buddhism became prominent: first, Esoteric Buddhism and later, Pure Land Buddhism.

In Esoteric Buddhism, the historical Shakyamuni Buddha became less important. Teaching centered instead on a universal or cosmic Buddha (in Japanese, *Dainichi*, "Great Sun") who was believed to preside over the universe. He was accompanied by a huge pantheon of buddhas, bodhisattvas, and fierce guardian deities. Esoteric Buddhism is hierarchical, and the complex relationship among its deities was often portrayed visually in **mandalas**, cosmic diagrams that position the deities in schematic order. The Womb World mandala from To-ji (fig. **9–17**) is entirely filled with gods. Dainichi at the center, is surrounded by attendant buddhas, bodhisattvas, and deities, in diagrammatic order and differentiated by symbolic attributes of their power. The leisured aristocracy favored Esoteric Buddhism, whose network of deities, hierarchy, and ritual found a parallel in the elaborate social divisions of the Heian court.

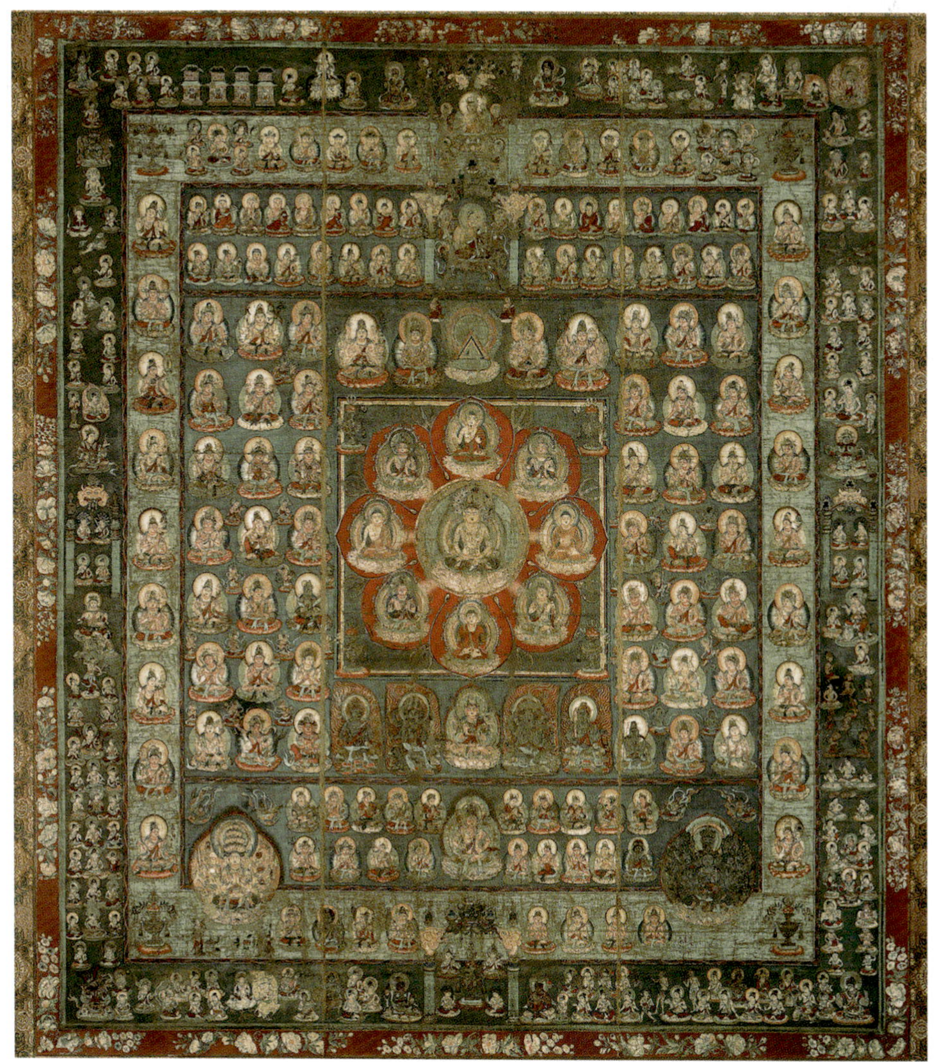

9–17 *Womb World Mandala*, To-ji, Kyoto. Heian period, late 9th century. Hanging scroll, colors on silk, 6' × 5' 1½" (1.83 × 1.54 m)

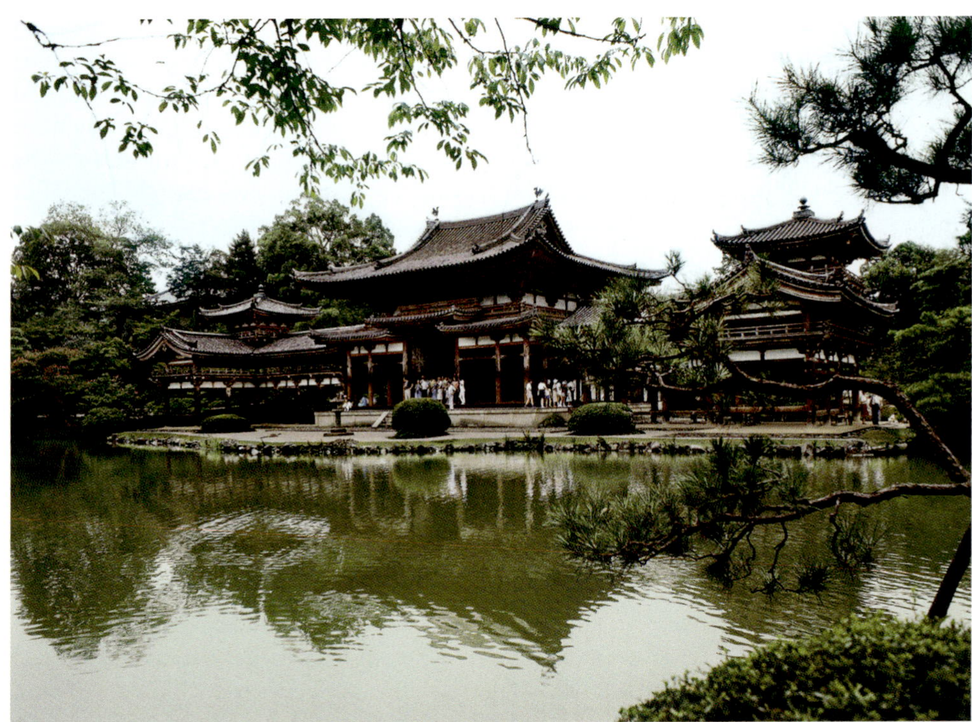

9–18 Byodo-in, Uji, Kyoto Prefecture. Heian period, c. 1053

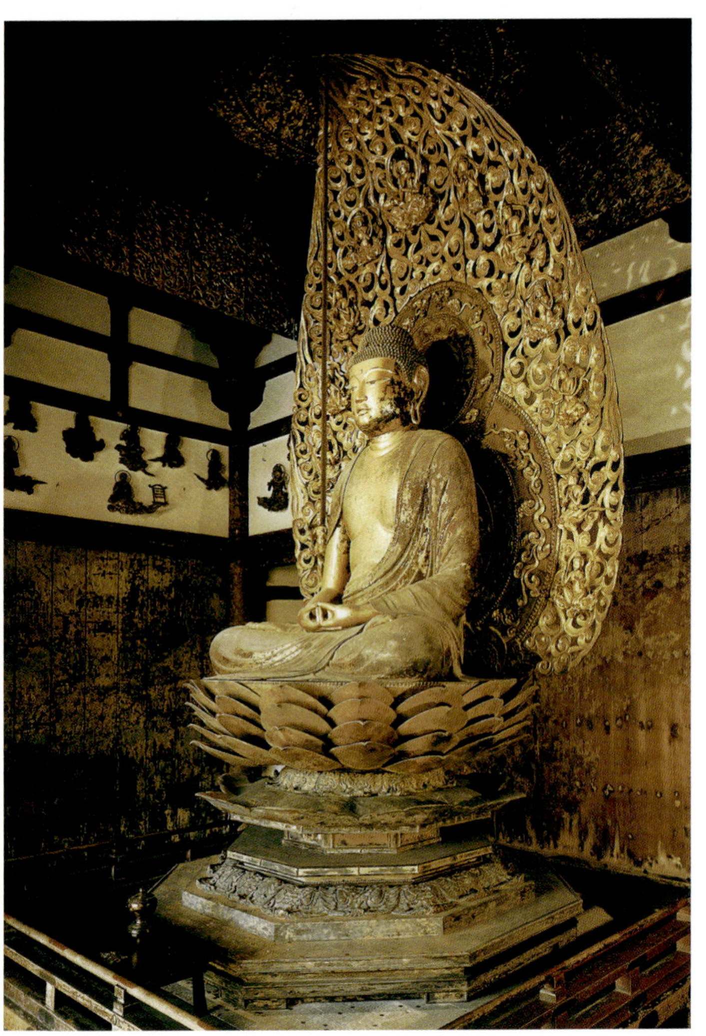

9–19 Jocho. *Amida Buddha*, Byodo-in. Heian period, c. 1053. Gold leaf and lacquer on wood, height 9' 8" (2.95 m)

Pure Land Buddhism came to prominence in the latter half of the Heian period, when a rising military class threatened the peace and tranquility of court life. In these uncertain years, many Japanese were ready for a form of Buddhism that would offer a means of salvation more direct than through the elaborate rituals of the Esoteric sects. Pure Land Buddhism taught that the Western Paradise (the Pure Land) of Amida Buddha could be reached through faith alone. In its ultimate form, Pure Land Buddhism held that the mere chanting of a mantra—the phrase *Namu Amida Butsu* ("Hail to Amida Buddha")—would lead to rebirth in Amida's paradise. This doctrine, spread by traveling monks who took the chant to all parts of the country, has made Pure Land Buddhism the most popular form of Buddhism in Japan to this day.

One of the most beautiful temples of Pure Land Buddhism is the Phoenix Hall at the Byodo-in (built c. 1053), located by the Uji River southeast of Kyoto (fig. **9–18**). Originally the summer retreat of a powerful aristocrat, it was later converted into a temple. The hall and its garden combine to evoke the palace of Amida in the Western Paradise. The lightness of its thin columns gives the Phoenix Hall a sense of airiness, as though the entire structure could easily rise up through the sky to the Western Paradise. In front of the hall is an artificial pond created in the shape of the Sanskrit letter *A*, the sacred symbol for Amida.

The Byodo-in's serene and compassionate central image of Amida (fig. **9–19**) was carved by the master sculptor Jocho (d. 1057). This figure was not created from a single block of wood like earlier sculpture but constructed of several individually carved

WRITING, LANGUAGE, AND CULTURE

Written Chinese was the international language of scholarship in East Asia, much as Latin was in medieval Europe. Educated Koreans, for example, wrote almost exclusively in Chinese until the fifteenth century. In Japan, Chinese continued to be used for certain kinds of writing, such as philosophical and legal texts, into the nineteenth century.

When the Japanese first began to write, they borrowed Chinese characters, which they refer to as *kanji*. However, differences between the Chinese and Japanese languages made this system extremely unwieldy, so during the ninth century the Japanese developed two syllabaries (*kana*), *katakana* and *hiragana*, to transcribe the sounds of their own language. (A syllabary is a system in which each symbol stands for a syllable.) *Katakana*, now generally used for writing foreign words, consists of mostly angular symbols, while *hiragana*, which is used for Japanese words, has graceful, cursive symbols.

A charming poem originated in Heian times to teach the new writing system. In two stanzas of four lines each, it uses almost all of the syllable sounds of spoken Japanese and thus almost every *kana* symbol. It was memorized as we would write our ABCs. The first stanza translates

Although flowers glow with color
They are quickly fallen,
And who in this world of ours
Is free from change?
(Translation by Earl Miner)

Below is the stanza written three ways. At the right, it appears in *katakana* glossed with the original phonetic value of each symbol. (Modern pronunciation has shifted slightly.) In the center, the stanza appears in flowing *hiragana*. At left is the mixture of Chinese characters and *kana* that eventually became standard. This alternating rhythm of simple *kana* symbols and more complex Chinese characters gives a special flavor to Japanese calligraphy. In all three versions of the stanza, the text is written, like Chinese, in columns from top to bottom and across the page from right to left. Following this logic, Chinese and Japanese narrative paintings also read from right to left.

イ I- ロ ro ハ ha- ニ ni- ホ ho- ヘ he- ト to
チ Chi- リ ri- ヌ nu- ル ru ヲ wo
ワ Wa- カ ka ヨ yo タ ta- レ re ソ so
ツ Tsu- ネ ne ナ na- ラ ra- ム mu

katakana

いろはにほへと
ちりぬるを
わかよたれそ
つねならむ

hiragana

色は匂へど
散りぬるを
我世誰ぞ
常ならむ

kanji and *kana*

blocks in Jocho's innovative **joined-wood method**, which allowed sculptors to create larger but lighter statues. Reflected in the water of the pond in front of it, the Amida image, heightened with gold leaf and lacquer (a hard, glossy surface varnish), seems to shimmer in its private retreat. The Buddha sits on an open lotus, a Buddhist symbol of purity. The flower's stem is an *axis mundi*, connecting the earthly and celestial realms.

While Buddhism dominated the Heian era, the refined secular culture that arose at court has never been equaled in Japan. A new system of writing developed, known as *kana* script (see "Writing, Language, and Culture," above). With its simple, flowing symbols interspersed with more complex Chinese characters, *kana* allowed Japanese writers to create a distinctive calligraphy quite unlike that of China.

Kana was used during the Heian period to write down a large body of literature, including many *tanka*, or five-line love poems. The poems of one famous Heian anthology, the *Thirty-Six Immortal Poets*, are still familiar to educated Japanese today. This anthology was produced in sets of albums, the *Ishiyama-gire*, which display elegantly written *tanka* on high-quality papers decorated with painting, block printing, scattered gold and silver, and sometimes paper **collage** (pasted colored papers).

The page shown here reproduces two *tanka* by the courtier Ki no Tsurayuki (fig. **9–20**). Both poems express sadness for the loss of a lover, the first lamenting:

Until yesterday
I could meet her,
But today she is gone—
Like clouds over the mountain
She has been wafted away.
(Translated by Stephen Addiss)

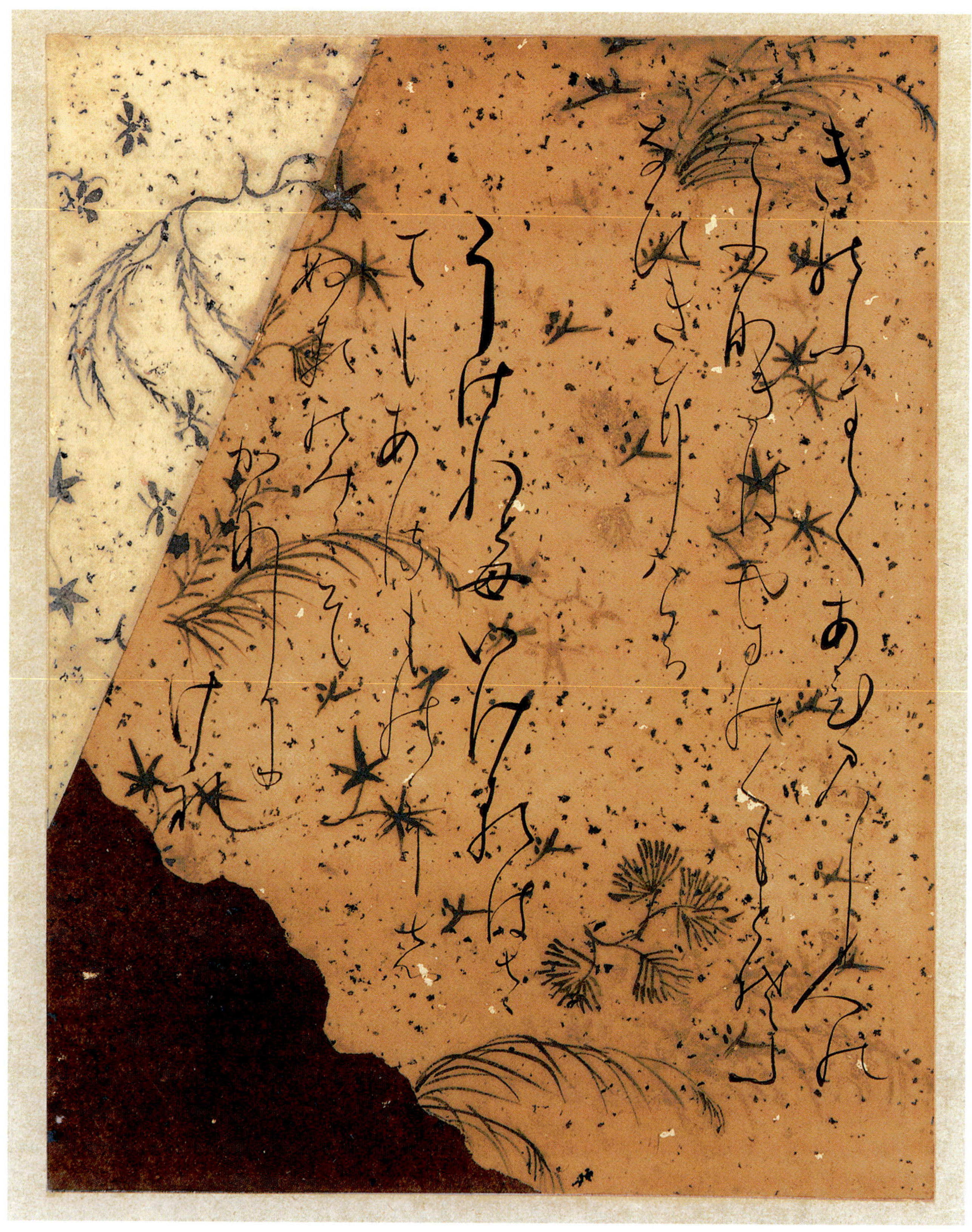

9–20 Album leaf from the *Ishiyama-gire*. Heian period, early 12th century. Ink with gold and silver on decorated and collaged paper, 8" × 6⅜" (20.3 × 16.1 cm). Freer Gallery of Art, Smithsonian Institution, Washington, D.C.

Although the style of Japanese calligraphy such as that in the Ishiyama-gire *was considered "women's hand," it is not known how much of the calligraphy of the time was actually written by women. It is certain, however, that women were a vital force in Heian society. Although the place of women in Japanese society was to decline in later periods, they contributed greatly to art at the Heian court.*

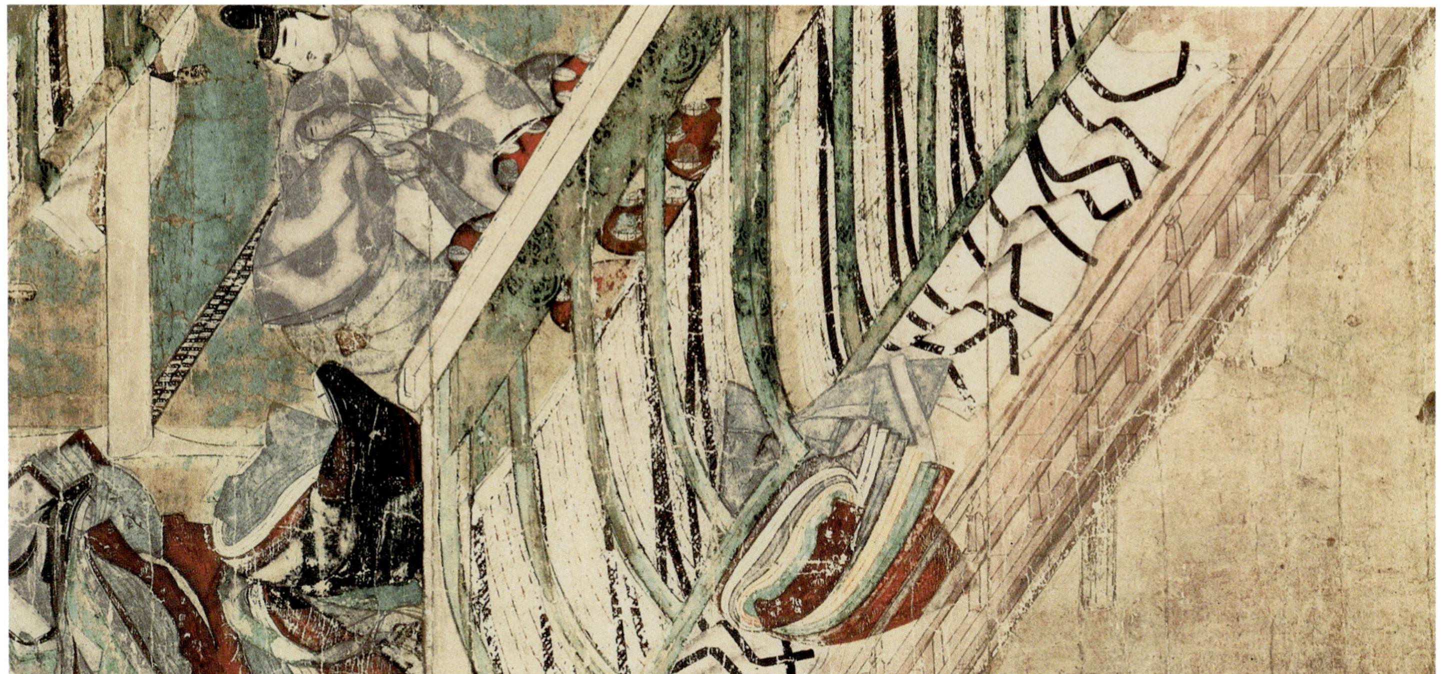

9–21 Scene from *The Tale of Genji*. Heian period, 12th century. Hand-scroll, ink and colors on paper, 8⅝" × 18⅞" (21.9 × 47.9 cm). Tokugawa Art Museum, Nagoya

Each scroll seems to have been produced by a team of artists. One was the calligrapher, most likely a member of the nobility. Another was the master painter, who outlined two or three illustrations per chapter in fine brushstrokes and indicated the color scheme. Next, colorists went to work, applying layer after layer of color to build up patterns and textures. After they had finished, the master painter returned to reinforce outlines and apply the finishing touches, among them the details of faces.

The wiry, flowing calligraphy, the patterning of the papers, the rich use of gold, and the suggestion of natural imagery epitomize courtly Japanese taste.

The world's first known novel, *The Tale of Genji*, written in Japanese at the beginning of the eleventh century by Lady Murasaki, immortalizes the lifestyle of the Heian court. Underlying the story of the love affairs of Prince Genji and his companions is the Japanese conception of fleeting pleasures and ultimate sadness in life, an echo of the Buddhist view of the vanity of earthly pleasures.

Among the earliest extant secular paintings from Japan are illustrations of *The Tale of Genji*, done in the twelfth century by unknown artists in a style sometimes described as "women's hand." This style was characterized by emphasis on bold shapes and delicate lines, strong if sometimes muted colors, and asymmetrical compositions in which interiors of buildings are viewed from above through invisible, "blown-away" roofs. The painters convey feelings by colors and poses rather than through movement or facial expressions. One scene portrays a seemingly happy Prince Genji holding a baby boy borne by his wife, Nyosan, in profile below him (fig. **9–21**). In fact, the baby was fathered by another court noble. Since Genji himself has not been faithful to Nyosan, he does not complain; meanwhile the true father of the child has died, unable to acknowledge his only son. The irony is even greater because Genji himself is the illegitimate son of an emperor. Thus what should be a joyous scene has undercurrents of sorrow. This is evoked visually by the muted colors of Genji's clothing, which contrast with the bright colors around him.

The courtiers of the Heian era became so engrossed in their own search for refinement that they neglected their responsibilities for governing the country. Clans of warriors, known as samurai, grew increasingly strong and soon became the real powers in Japan. The Kamakura era (1185–1392) began when the samurai Minamoto Yoritomo (1147–1199) assumed power in Japan as shogun (general-in-chief). He established a military capital at the seaside town of Kamakura, far from Kyoto. While paying respects to the emperor, Yoritomo kept both military and political power for himself. He thus began a tradition of rule by shogun that lasted in various forms until 1868.

Toward the latter part of the Kamakura period, Zen Buddhism reached Japan from China. In some ways, Zen resembles the original teachings of the historical Buddha in stressing that individuals must achieve their own enlightenment through meditation, without the help of deities or magical chants promoted by other schools of Buddhism.

An abbot named Kao at an early Zen temple was a pioneer in a kind of rough and simple painting in black ink that so directly expresses the Zen spirit. In a remarkable portrait of a monk sewing his robe (fig. **9–22**), we are drawn into the activity portrayed in the painting rather than merely focusing on it as a work of art. The almost humorous compression of the monk's face, coupled with the

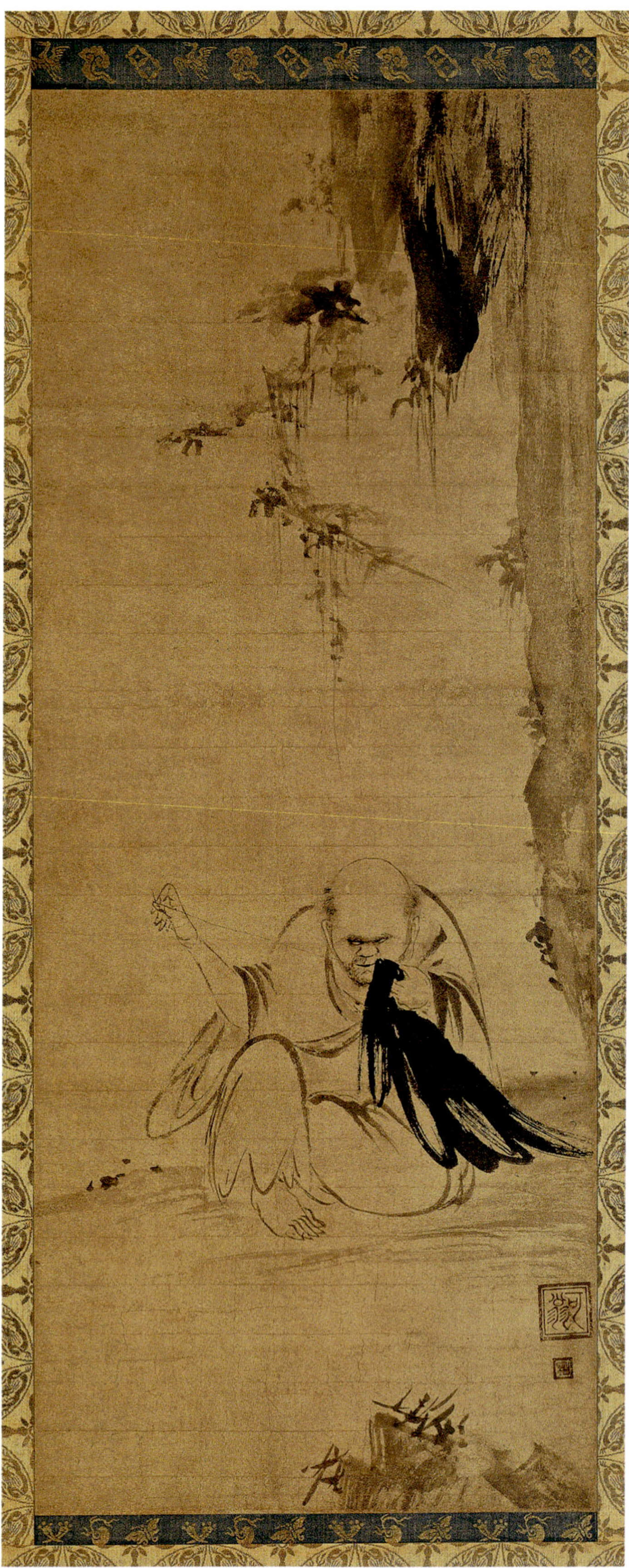

9–22 Attributed to Kao Ninga. ***Monk Sewing.*** Kamakura period, early 14th century. Ink on paper, 32⅞" × 13¾" (83.5 × 35.4 cm). The Cleveland Museum of Art
JOHN L. SEVERANCE FUND, 62.163

position of the darker robe, focuses our attention on his eyes, which then lead us out to his hand pulling the needle.

By the beginning of the Muromachi period (1392–1568), Zen dominated many aspects of Japanese culture. One of the most renowned Zen creations in Japan, built during the Muromachi era, is the "dry landscape garden" at the temple of Ryoan-ji in Kyoto (see fig. 9–1). There is a record of a famous cherry tree at this spot, so the completely severe nature of the garden may have come about some time after its original founding in the late fifteenth century. Nevertheless, the garden—which is only a part of the larger grounds of Ryoan-ji—is today celebrated for its serene sense of space and emptiness.

During the Momoyama period (1568–1603), civil wars swept through Japan, fought among samurai loyal to their own feudal lords rather than to the central government. Portuguese explorers and traders arrived, and with them European muskets and cannon, which soon changed the nature of Japanese warfare. In response to the new weapons, monumental fortified castles were built in the early seventeenth century. Many were sumptuously decorated, offering artists unprecedented opportunities to work on a grand scale. Large murals on *fusuma* (paper-covered sliding doors) were particular features of Momoyama design, as were folding screens with gold-leaf backgrounds. Temples, too, commissioned large-scale decorative paintings for rebuilding projects after the devastation of the civil wars.

Daitoku-ji, a celebrated Zen monastery in Kyoto, has a number of subtemples that are treasure troves of Japanese art. One, the Juko-in, features *fusuma* by Kano Eitoku (1543–1590), one of the most brilliant painters from the Kano family school, a professional school of artists patronized by government leaders for several centuries. The illustration here shows two of three walls of *fusuma* panels painted when the artist was in his mid-twenties (fig. **9–23**). The subject to the left is a popular Kano-school theme of cranes and pines, both symbols of long life; to the right is a great gnarled plum tree, a symbol of spring and renewal. An island situated where two walls meet in a corner provides a focus for the outreaching trees. Ingeniously, it belongs to both compositions at the same time, thus uniting them into a single organic whole.

During the Momoyama period, there continued to be interest in the quiet, the restrained, and the natural. This introspective mood found expression in the tea ceremony. "Tea ceremony" is an unsatisfactory term for *cha no yu*, the Japanese ritual of preparing and drinking tea, for which there is no counterpart in Western culture. The most famous tea master in Japanese history, Sen no Rikyu (1522–1591), conceived of the tea ceremony as an intimate gathering in which a few people would enter a small, rustic room, drink tea carefully prepared in front of them by their host, and quietly discuss the tea utensils or a work of art displayed for their enjoyment.

The age-old Japanese admiration for the natural and the asymmetrical is reflected in certain types of tea ceramics. A teabowl would be judged by such factors as how well it fit into the hands, how subtly its shape and texture appealed to the eye, and who had previously used and admired it. If a bowl had been given a name by a leading tea master, it was especially treasured by later generations. One of the finest teabowls extant (fig. **9–24**) was crafted by Hon'ami

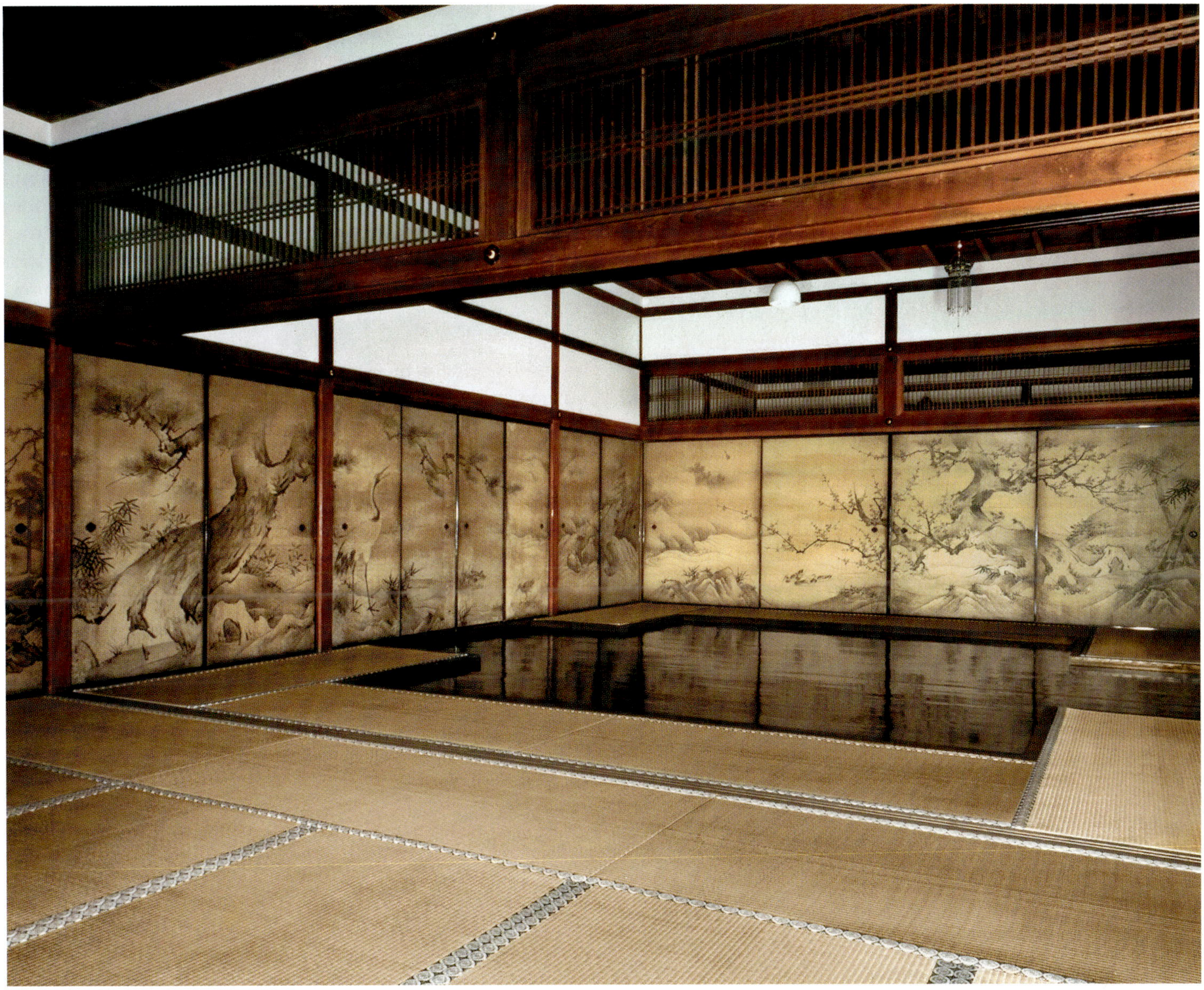

9–23 Kano Eitoku. ***Fusuma*** depicting pine and cranes (left) and plum tree (right), from the central room of the Juko-in, Daitoku-ji, Kyoto. Momoyama period, c. 1563–1573. Ink and gold on paper, height 5' 9⅛" (1.76 m)

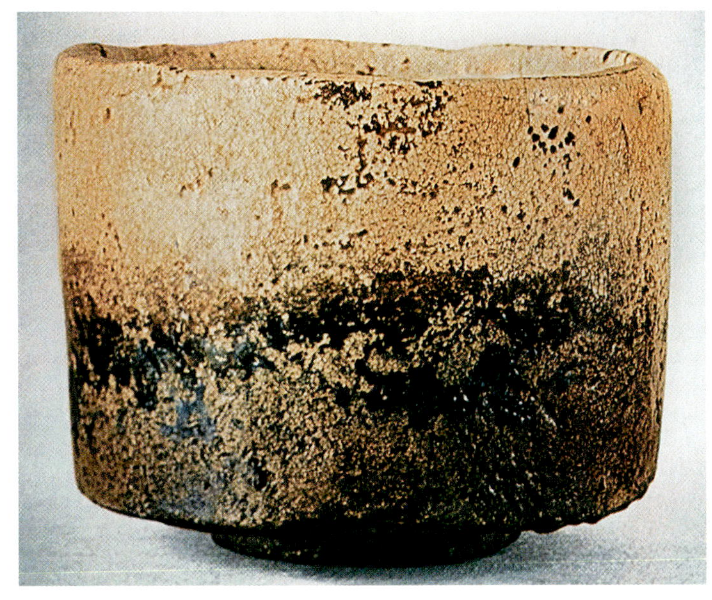

9–24 Hon'ami Koetsu. Teabowl, called *Mount Fuji*. Edo period, early 17th century. *Raku* ware, height 3⅜" (8.5 cm). Sakai Collection, Tokyo. Sunritz Hattori Museum of Arts, Japan

A specialized vocabulary developed to allow connoisseurs to discuss the subtle aesthetics of tea. A favorite term was sabi, *which summoned up the particular beauty to be found in stillness or even deprivation.* Sabi *was borrowed from the critical vocabulary of poetry, where it was first established as a positive ideal by the early thirteenth-century poet Fujiwara Shunzei. Other virtues were* wabi, *conveying a sense of great loneliness or humble and admirable shabbiness, and* shibui, *meaning plain and astringent.*

Koetsu (1558–1637). Named *Mount Fuji* after Japan's most sacred peak, it is an example of *raku*, a hand-built, low-fired ceramic developed especially for use in the tea ceremony. With its small foot, straight sides, slightly irregular shape, and crackled texture, this bowl exemplifies the entire ceremony. Merely looking at it suggests the feeling one would get from holding it, warm with tea, in one's hands.

Korean Painting

In Korea, the Joseon Dynasty (1392–1910) bridged the centuries and the cultural change from domination by China to entry into the modern world. The seventeenth and eighteenth centuries were a time of intellectual revival, bringing a new creativity to the arts, especially literature and painting. Buddhism gave way to Confucian religious belief and practice. In Korea, as in Japan, an admiration for natural effects and practical solutions emerged. Korean painters turned to their own landscape for inspiration, and both writers and painters used Korean themes. Genre paintings were also popular at the time. With an energy and pride that recall the seventeenth-century Dutch Republic or nineteenth-century America, Korean artists found inspiration in their own lives and country.

Typical of this turn to Korean themes is the landscape painting of Jeong Seon (1676–1759). Inspired by the Chinese scholar-painters of the Ming Dynasty, he used traditional techniques and media as he recorded actual appearances. In this scroll (fig. **9–25**), for example, he represents the Diamond Mountains, a celebrated range along Korea's east coast, aptly capturing its craggy, needle-like peaks emerging from the mist. The subject is Korean, and so is the energetic spirit and the intensely personal style, with its crystalline mountains, distant clouds of delicate ink wash, and individualistic brushwork. The free and spontaneous quality of Jeong Seon's elaborate brushwork became a Korean characteristic.

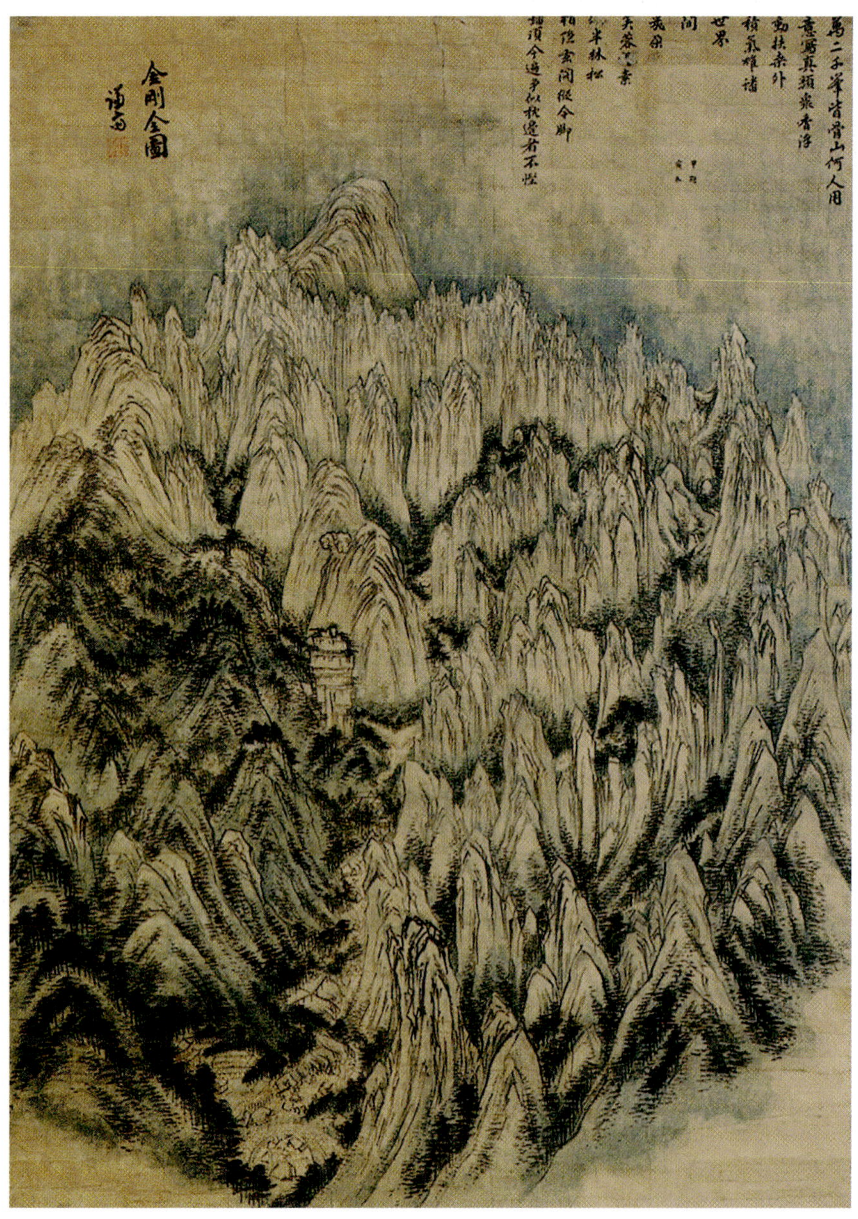

9–25 Jeong Seon. *Panoramic View of the Diamond Mountains (Geumgang-san).* Joseon Dynasty, 1734. Hanging scroll, ink and colors on paper, 40⅞" × 37" (130.1 × 94 cm). Lee'um, Samsung Museum, Seoul, Republic of Korea

Pictures of the Floating World

During the Edo period (1603–1868), when the *Mount Fuji* bowl was made, peace and prosperity came to Japan at the price of an increasingly rigid and often repressive form of government. Zen Buddhism was replaced as the prevailing intellectual force by a form of Neo-Confucianism, the philosophy formulated in Song Dynasty China that emphasized loyalty to the state. The government discouraged foreign ideas and foreign contacts, forbidding Japanese from traveling abroad and barring outsiders from Japan, with the exception of small Chinese and Dutch trading communities on an island off the southern port of Nagasaki.

Across Japan, and especially in the bustling new capital of Edo (modern Tokyo), people savored the delights of their peaceful society. Wealthy merchants patronized painters in the middle and later Edo periods, and even artisans and tradespeople could purchase less costly works of art—above all, woodblock prints.

Ukiyo-e ("pictures of the floating world"), as these woodblock prints are called in Japanese, represent the combined expertise of three people: the artist, the carver, and the printer. The artist supplied the master drawing for the print, executing its outlines in ink on tissue-thin paper. The carver pasted the drawing face-down on a hardwood block and cut around the lines—always working in the same direction as the original brushstrokes—with a sharp knife. The rest of the block was chiseled away, leaving the outlines standing in relief. This block, which reproduced the master drawing, was called the **key block**. If the print was to have several colors, the carver made a separate block for each color. A printer brushed water-based ink or color over the blocks, beginning with the key block; placed a piece of paper on top; and then rubbed with a smooth, padded device called a *baren* to make an impression. A publisher coordinated and funded the endeavor and distributed the prints to stores or itinerant peddlers.

The first artist to design polychrome prints was Suzuki Harunobu (1724–1770). One print that displays the charm and wit of his art is *Geisha as Daruma Crossing the Sea* (fig. **9–26**), in which a gracefully robed young woman is shown floating across the water on a reed. This is a playful reference to one of the legends about Bodhidharma, a semilegendary Indian monk, known in Japan as Daruma, and recognized as the founder of the Zen tradition in China. Many paintings were made of this monk standing on a reed to cross the Yangtze River. To see a young woman rather than a grizzled Zen master peering ahead to the other shore must have greatly amused the Japanese audience, but there was another layer of meaning in this image since geishas (meaning "artists," traditional Japanese entertainers) were sometimes compared with Buddhist teachers or deities in their ability to bring earthly pleasure, akin to enlightenment, to humans.

Popular *ukiyo-e* subjects included courtesans and actors (see fig. Intro–8), and beginning in the nineteenth century, landscapes, such as *Thirty-Six Views of Mount Fuji* by Katsushika Hokusai (1760–1849), came into fashion. Hokusai's blocks were printed again and again until they were worn out. Then they were recarved and more copies printed. Thousands of prints from this series still survive.

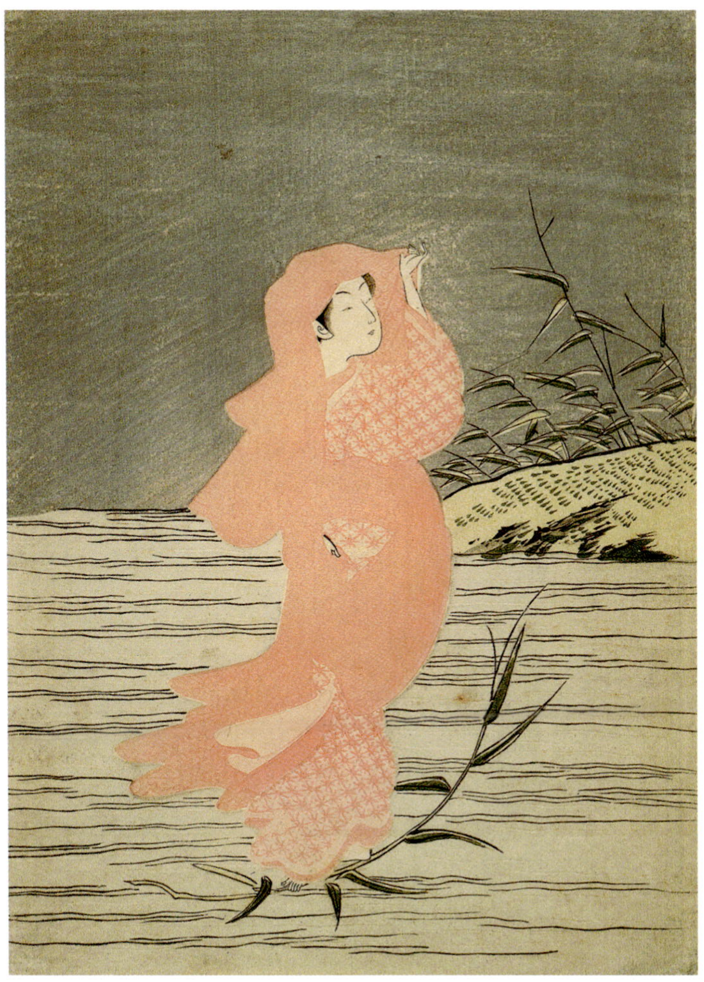

9–26 Suzuki Harunobu. ***Geisha as Daruma Crossing the Sea.*** Edo period, mid-18th century. Polychrome woodblock print on paper, 10⅞" × 8¼" (27.6 × 21 cm). Philadelphia Museum of Art

GIFT OF MRS. EMILE GEYELIN, IN MEMORY OF ANNE HAMPTON BARNES

The Great Wave (fig. **9–27**) may be the most famous scene from *Thirty-Six Views of Mount Fuji.* Hokusai was already in his 70s, with a 50-year career behind him, when he designed this image. Such was his modesty that he felt that his Fuji series represented only the beginning of his creativity, and he wrote that if he could live to be 100, he would finally learn how to become an artist.

When first seen in Europe and America, these and other Japanese prints were immediately acclaimed, and they strongly influenced late nineteenth- and early twentieth-century Western art (see "Japonisme," page 517). Not only was the first book on Hokusai published in France, but the value of these prints as collectable works of art was recognized in the West before it was in Japan. Only within the past 50 years or so have Japanese museums and **connoisseurs** fully recognized the value of this originally "plebeian" form of art. In the twentieth century, artists such as Roger Shimomura (see Intro–17) have rediscovered the power of such prints and incorporated references in their own work.

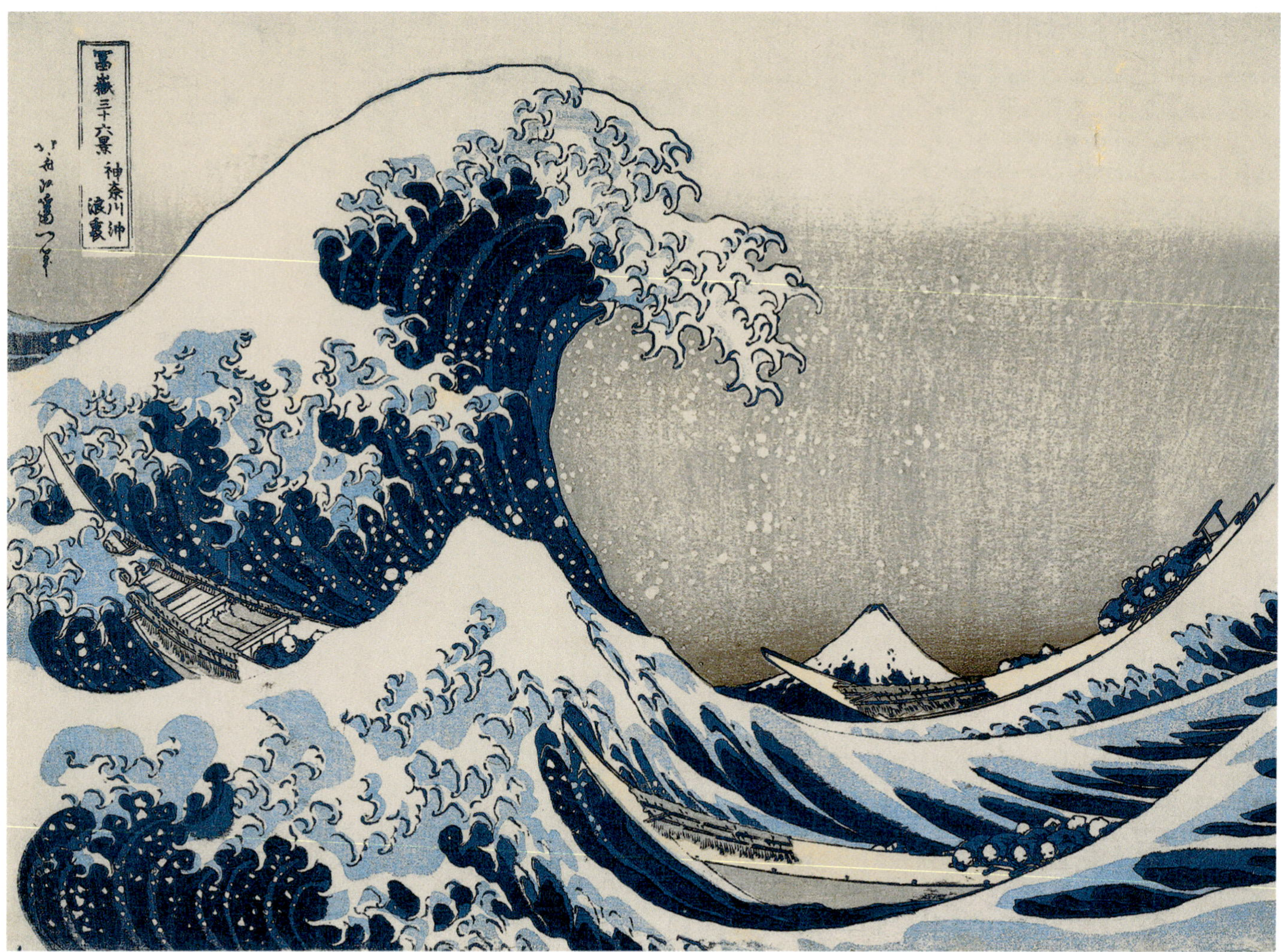

9–27 Katsushika Hokusai. *The Great Wave*. Edo period, c. 1831. Polychrome woodblock print on paper, 9⅞" × 14⅝" (25 × 37.1 cm). Honolulu Academy of Arts, Hawaii
THE JAMES A. MICHENER COLLECTION (HAA 13,695)

The great wave rears up like a dragon with claws of foam, ready to crash down on the figures huddled in the boats below. Far in the distance rises Japan's most sacred peak, Mount Fuji, whose slopes, we suddenly realize, swing up like waves and whose snowy crown is like foam—comparisons the artist makes clear in the wave nearest us, caught just at the moment of greatest resemblance.

Looking Back

Asian art combines material splendor and philosophical depth with an affinity for giving visual form to the spirituality of natural world. Wealthy rulers devoted staggering resources to creating spectacular architectural complexes: temples in India and Angkor Wat, and the Forbidden City in Beijing. Calligraphy continued to be refined into an ever more subtle and sophisticated art. But we usually associate the finest later Asian art with more intimate and intricate creations: small bronzes in India; ink painting and ceramics in China, Korea, and Japan; or that most ephemeral of the arts, gardening.

IN PERSPECTIVE

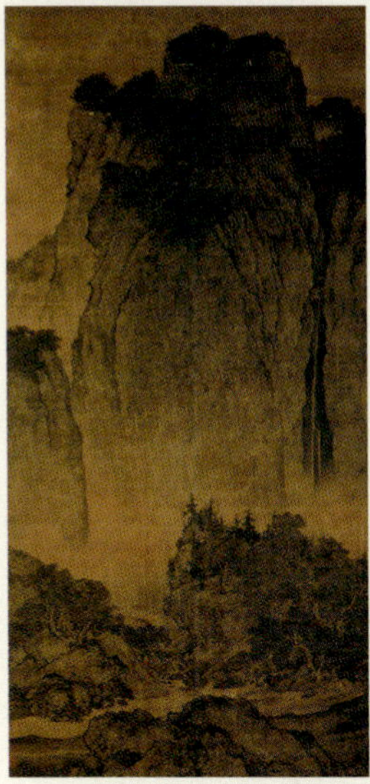

FAN KUAN,
TRAVELERS AMONG MOUNTAINS AND STREAMS,
EARLY 11TH CENTURY

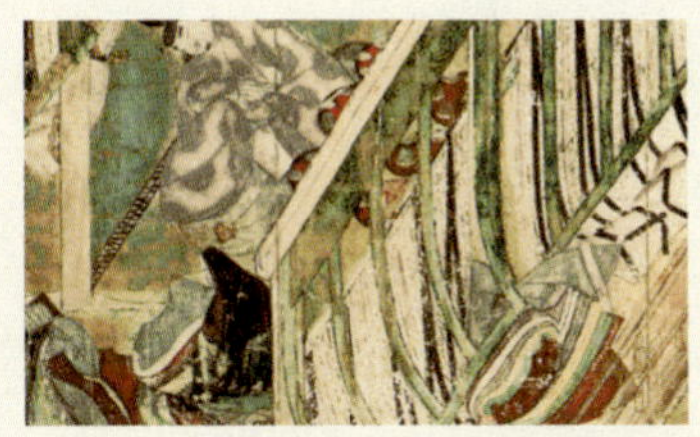

SCENE FROM THE TALE OF GENJI,
12TH CENTURY

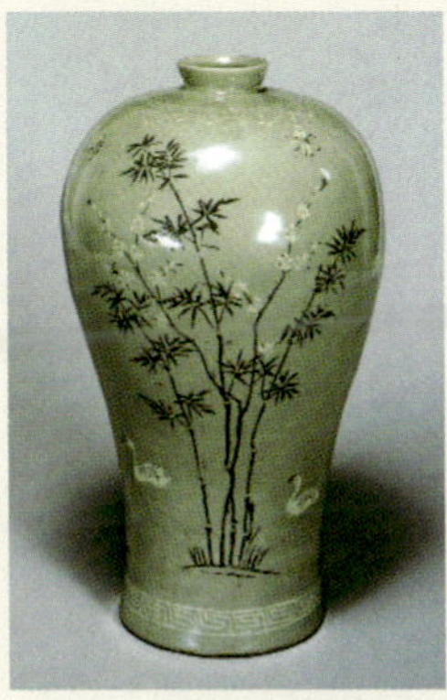

MAEBYEONG BOTTLE,
LATE 12TH–EARLY 13TH CENTURY

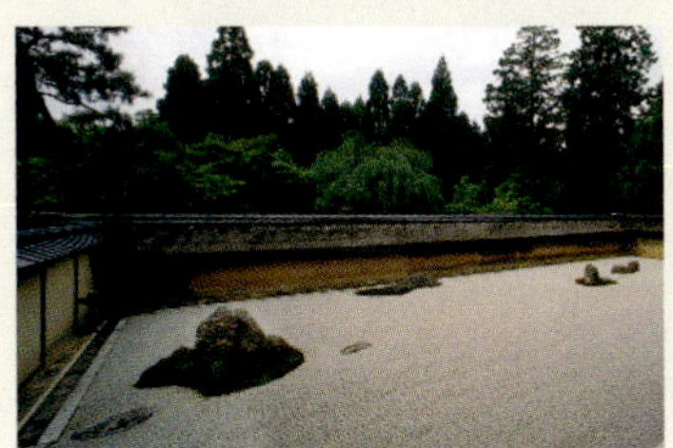

RYOAN-JI GARDEN,
C. 1480

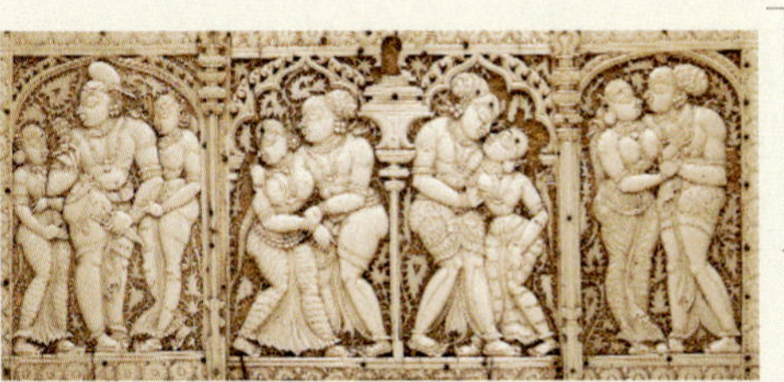

TAMIL IVORY BOX PANEL,
LATE 17TH–18TH CENTURY

1000

◀ **Heian Period in Japan,** 794–1185

◀ **Song Dynasty in China,** 960–1279

1200

◀ **Kamakura Era in Japan,** 1185–1392

◀ **Yuan Dynasty in China,** 1279–1368

◀ **Ming Dynasty in China,** 1368–1644

◀ **Muromachi Period in Japan,** 1392–1568

1400

◀ **Joseon Dynasty in Korea,** 1392–1910

◀ **Mughal Dynasty in India,** 1526–1857

◀ **Momoyama Period,** 1568–1603

1600

◀ **British East India Company Begins Activity in India,** c. 1600

◀ **Edo Period in Japan,** 1603–1868

1800

◀ **Peak of British Imperial Power in India,** 1848–1947

◀ **Republic of China (Mainland),** 1911–1949

◀ **Modern Turkey Founded,** 1918

◀ **South Korea,** 1945 to present

◀ **North Korea,** 1945 to present

◀ **Indian Independence,** 1947

◀ **People's Republic of China,** 1949 to present

2000

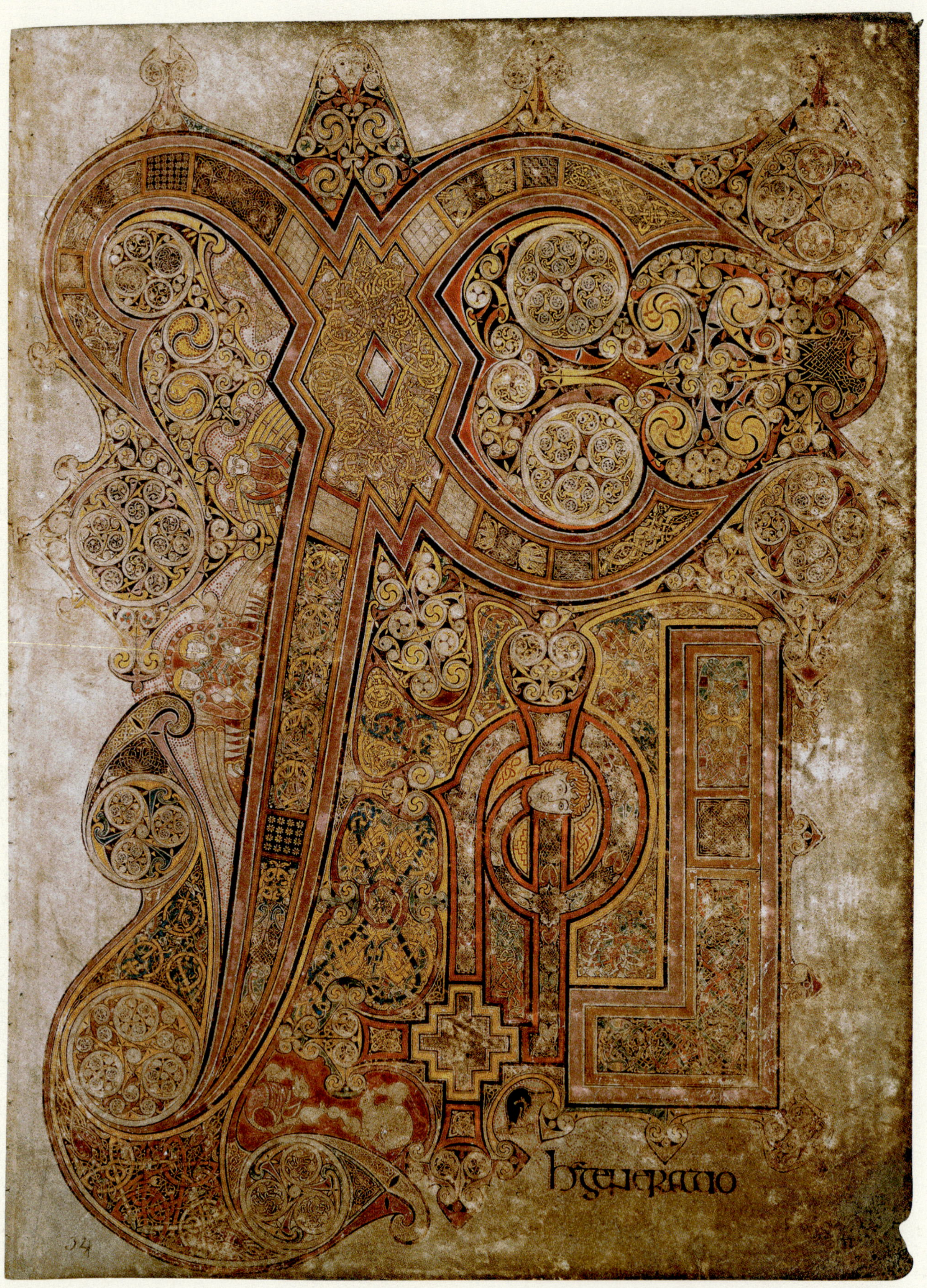
h generatio

10
Early Medieval and Romanesque Art

LOOKING FORWARD

The explosion of ornament surrounding—almost suffocating—the words on this page from an early medieval manuscript clearly indicates the importance of what is being expressed (fig. **10–1**). The large Greek letters *chi rho iota* (*XPI*) abbreviate the word *Christi* that starts the Latin phrase "*Christi autem generatio*"—the last word is written out fully and legibly at bottom right, clear of the decorative expanse. These words begin Matthew 1:18: "Now the birth of Jesus the Messiah took place in this way." So what is signaled here—not with a picture of the event but with an ornamental celebration of its initial mention in the text—is Christ's first appearance within a Gospel book that not only contains the four biblical accounts of his life, but would also evoke his presence on the altar of the monastery church where this lavish book was once housed. It is precisely the sort of ceremonial book that we have already seen carried in the hands of a deacon in Justinian's procession into San Vitale in Ravenna to begin the Mass (see fig. 7–18).

There is nothing explicitly Christian about the ornamental motifs celebrating the first mention of the birth of Christ in this manuscript—the *Book of Kells*, produced in Ireland or Scotland sometime around the year 800. The swirling spirals and interlaced tangles of stylized animal forms have their roots in jewelry created by the peripatetic barbarian tribes that formed the "other" of the Greco-Roman world. But by this time, this ornamental repertory had been subsumed into the flourishing art of Irish monasteries. And Irish monks became as famous for writing and copying books as for their intense spirituality and missionary fervor.

Wealthy, isolated, and undefended, Irish monasteries were easy victims to Viking attacks. In 806, fleeing Viking raids on the island of Iona (off the coast of modern Scotland), its monks established a refuge at Kells on the Irish mainland. They probably brought the *Book of Kells* with them. It was precious. Producing this illustrated version of the Gospels entailed lavish expenditure: Four scribes and three major illuminators worked on it (modern scribes take about a month to complete such a page); 185 calves were slaughtered to make the vellum; and colors for some paintings came from as far away as Afghanistan.

Throughout the Middle Ages and across Europe, monasteries were principal centers of art and learning. While prayer and acts of mercy represented their primary vocation, some talented monks and nuns also worked as painters, jewelers, carvers, weavers, and embroiderers. Few, however, could claim a work of art as splendid as this one.

10–1 ***Chi Rho* page**, Gospel of Matthew, *Book of Kells*, probably made at Iona, Scotland. c. 800. Oxgall inks and pigments on vellum, 12¾" × 9½" (32.5 × 24 cm). The Board of Trinity College, Dublin (MS 58 (A.1.6.), fol. 34v)

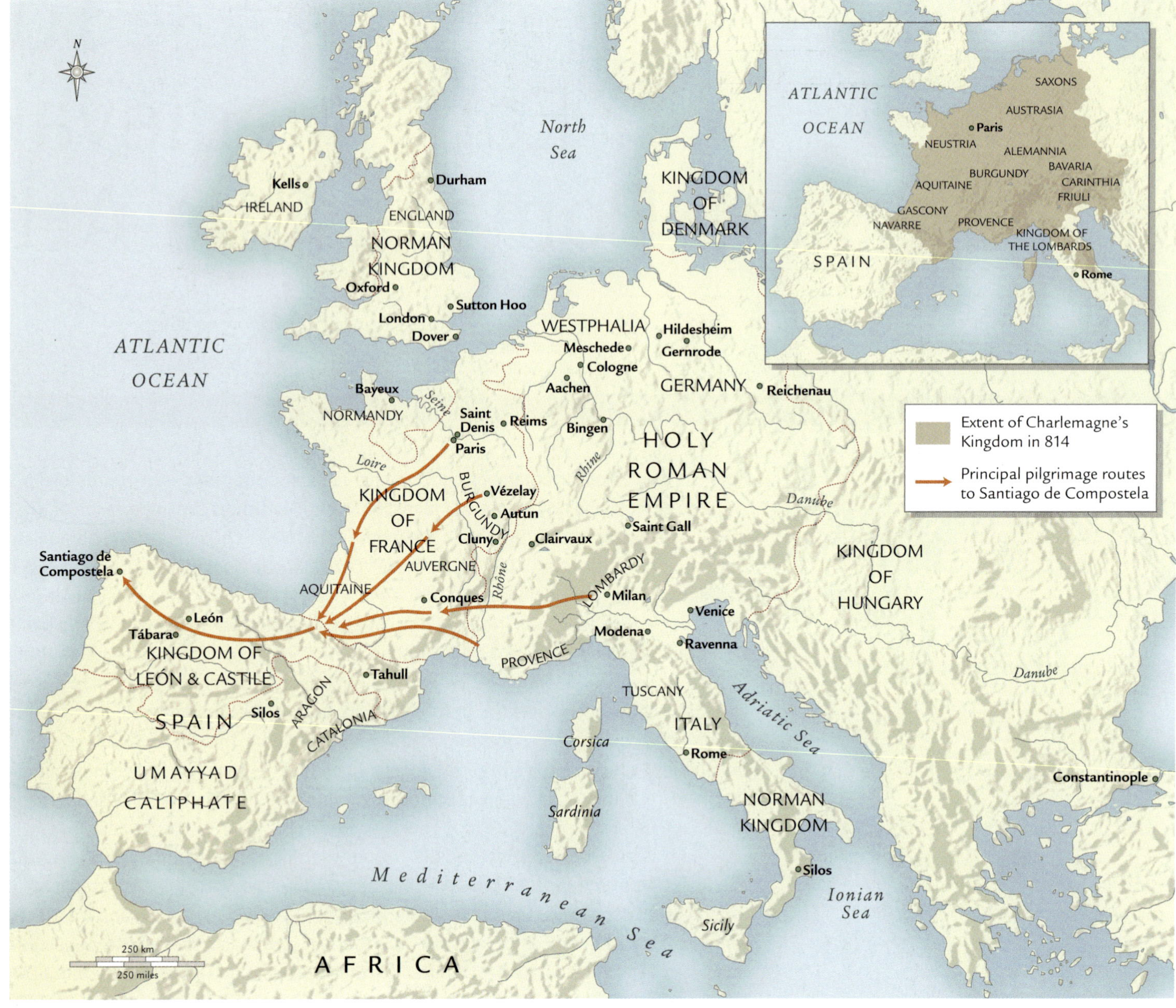

Map 10–1 Medieval Europe Around 1100

As Roman authority crumbled at the dissolution of the Western Empire, Christianity gained steadily in strength, and political power in Western Europe passed to bishops as well as to secular lords. The Church helped unify Europe's heterogeneous population—now an amalgam of Romans and barbarians—and Christianity spread into lands far from its Mediterranean origins, such as Ireland and eventually Scandinavia, which had never been ruled by Rome. The result was a vibrant, if sometimes tense, multiculturalism in which a variety of traditions intermingled to form a new medieval culture.

The Christian Church, as the repository of Roman tradition and learning, provided intellectual and artistic as well as spiritual leadership. As patrons of the arts, the clergy sponsored the building of churches and creation of equipment for use in rituals, including crosses, reliquaries (shrines containing holy relics), and copies of sacred books. Secular leaders—in the wake of the fifth century, mainly Germanic peoples, including Ostrogoths, Visigoths, Angles, Saxons, and Franks—built castles and commissioned the making of secular works of art such as jewelry, textiles, and armor, little of which survives. Stylistically, early medieval art reflects the fusion of the Germanic and late Roman traditions of the former Western Empire, as well as the influence of both pre-Christian art from Northern Europe and the Islamic art of Spain (see map **10–1**).

Western Europeans in this early medieval period looked with dismay on the rapid advance of Islam. The Muslims were also "People of the Book." Monotheistic, they accepted Judaism and Christianity as forerunners of their own prophet, Muhammad, and Muslim rulers were often tolerant of Christians and Jews in their

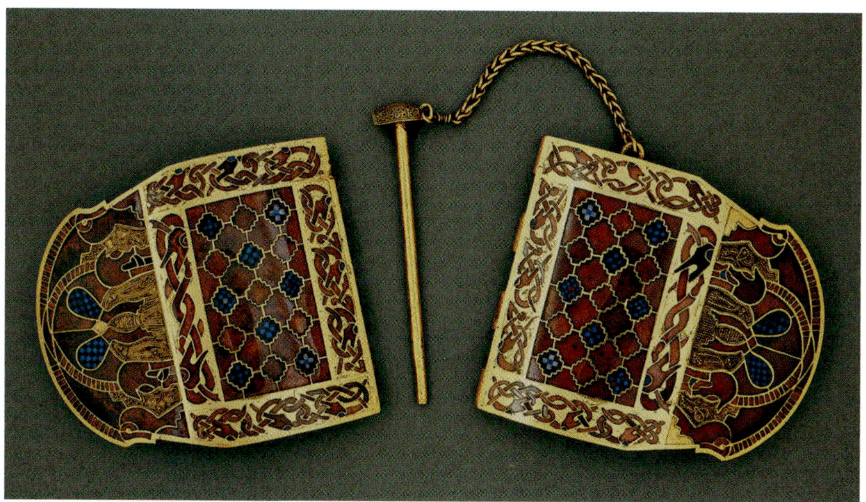

10–2 Hinged clasp, from the Sutton Hoo burial, Suffolk, England. First half of 7th century. Gold plaques with granulation and inlays of garnet and millefiore glass, length 5" (12.7 cm). The British Museum, London

territories. But less broad-minded western and northern European leaders viewed Muslims not only as unwanted foreigners but also as dangerous infidels. The presence of Muslims in Spain from the eighth century on raised fears among Christians of further Islamic inroads into Europe. The Franks, however, checked the advancing Muslim armies in the eighth century, safeguarding the development of the rest of Europe as a Christian land. By the end of the eleventh century, it was Christians who went on the crusading offensive, mounting holy wars against the Muslims to "free" what they considered their Holy Land.

Early Medieval Art in the British Isles

Another clash of cultures had occurred much earlier in the British Isles. The Romans subjugated the native Celtic inhabitants of Britain in 43 CE but did not invade Ireland. During the period of Roman rule, which lasted until the beginning of the fifth century, Christianity took root in Britain and spread to Ireland. After the fall of the Roman Empire in the fifth century, British chieftains took control, vying for dominance with the help of soldiers from continental Europe, thus giving rise to the legends of King Arthur and the Round Table. The Angles, Saxons, and Jutes from the Continent soon established kingdoms of their own, and the people under their rule adopted Anglo-Saxon speech and customs. Over the next 200 years, a new Anglo-Saxon and Hiberno-Saxon culture (*Hibernia* was the Roman name for Ireland) formed out of a fusion of Celtic, Germanic, and surviving Roman traditions.

Metalworking is one of the glories of Anglo-Saxon art. References to splendid jewelry and military equipment decorated with gold and silver fill Anglo-Saxon literature, such as the epic poem *Beowulf.* An early seventh-century burial mound, excavated in the English region of East Anglia at a site called Sutton Hoo (*hoo* means "hill"), concealed a hoard of such treasures, representing the broad cultural heritage that characterized the British Isles at this time: Celtic, Scandinavian, and classical Roman, as well as Anglo-Saxon. There was even a Byzantine silver bowl. The grave's still unidentified occupant was buried in an 86-foot-long ship. The vessel held weapons, armor, and other equipment for the afterlife, and such luxury items as an exquisite clasp of pure gold that once secured over his shoulder the leather body armor of its wealthy and powerful owner (fig. **10–2**).

The two sides of the clasp—essentially identical in design—connected when a long gold pin, attached to one half by a delicate but strong gold chain, was inserted through a series of aligned channels on the back side of the inner edge of each. The exquisite decoration of this work is created by thin pieces of garnet and blue-checkered glass (known as **millefiori**, from the Italian for "a thousand flowers") cut into precisely stepped geometric shapes or to follow the sinuous contours of stylized animal forms. The cut shapes were then inserted into channels—not unlike the cloissons that held enamels in Byzantine metalwork (see fig. 7–23)—and supplemented by granulation (the use of minute granules of gold fused to the surface, see also fig. 5–7). Under the stepped geometric pieces that form a rectangular patterned field on each side, jewelers placed gold foil stamped with incised motifs that reflect light back up through the transparent garnet to spectacular effect. Around these carpet-like rectangles are borders of interlacing snakes, and in the curving compartments to the outside stand pairs of semitransparent, overlapping boars stylized in ways that reflect the traditions of Scandinavian jewelry. Their curly pig's tails overlap their strong rumps at the outer edges on each side of the clasp, and following the visible vertebrae along the arched forms of their backs, we arrive at their heads, with floppy ears and extended tusks. Boars represented strength and bravery, important virtues in warring Anglo-Saxon society.

Among the richest surviving works of Hiberno-Saxon Christian art were lavishly decorated Gospel books, essential not only for the spiritual life within established monasteries, but also critical for the missionary activities of the Irish Church since a Gospel book was required in each new foundation. Often bound in gold and jeweled covers, they were placed on the altars of churches, carried in procession, and even thought to protect the faithful from enemies, disease, and various misfortunes. Such sumptuous books were produced by monks in local monastic workshops called **scriptoria**.

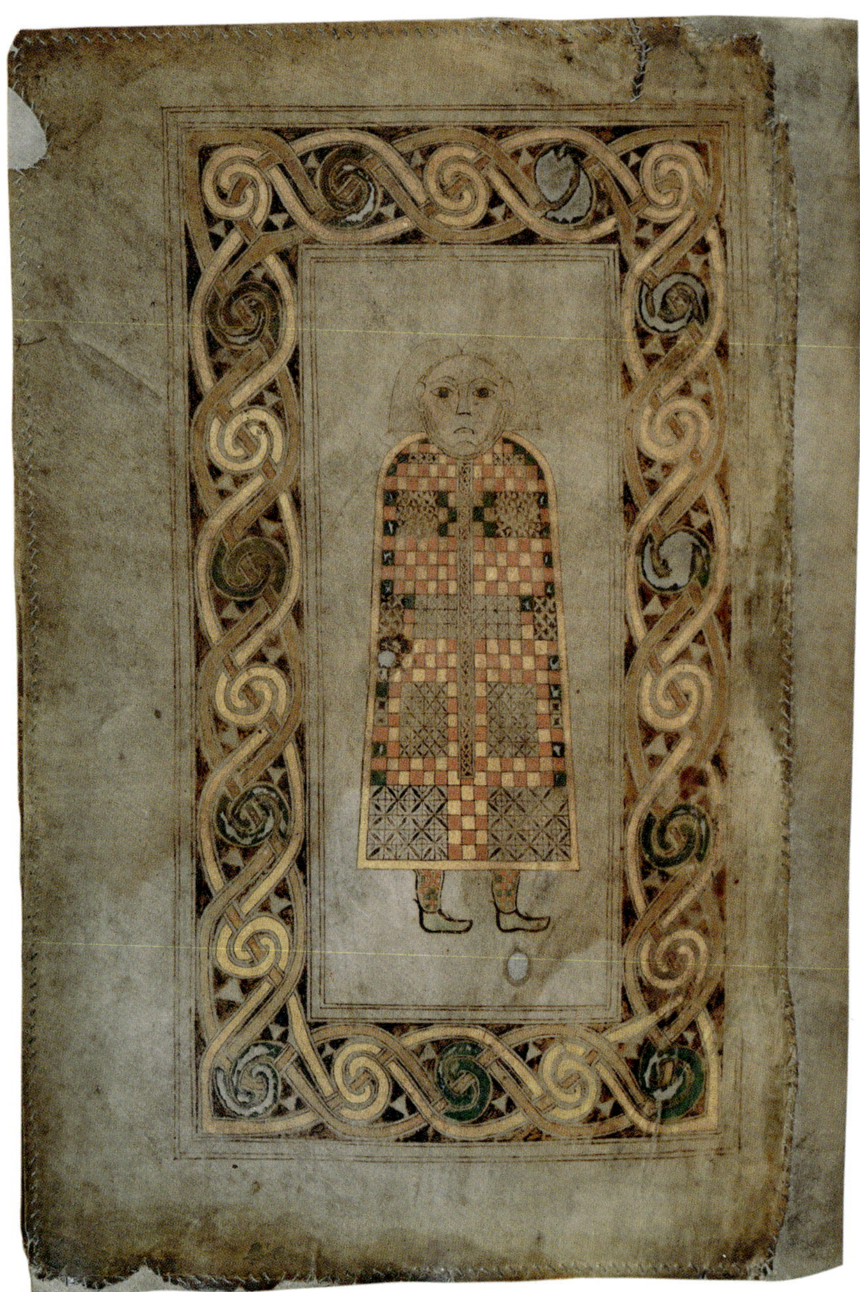

10–3 Man (Symbol of Saint Matthew), Gospel of Matthew, *Book of Durrow*. Hiberno-Saxon, second half of 7th century. Ink and tempera on parchment, 9⅝" × 6⅛" (24.4 × 15.5 cm). The Board of Trinity College Dublin (MS 57, fol. 21v)

One of the earliest Hiberno-Saxon Gospel books is the *Book of Durrow*, dating to the second half of the seventh century. The book's format reflects Roman Christian models. Each Gospel is introduced by a three-part decorative sequence: a page with the symbol of its evangelist author is followed by a page of pure ornament, and then elaborate decoration highlights the initial words of the text. The page in fig. **10–3** portrays the symbol for Matthew: the figure of a man. But what a difference from the way humans were represented in the ancient Roman tradition. Matthew's body is formed here by a flat field of checkered ornament, recalling the rectangular panels on the Sutton Hoo clasp (see fig. 10–2). A schematically symmetrical, frontal face stares at the viewer over the body's rounded shoulders, and the tiny feet that emerge at its other end are seen from contrasting profile view, as if to deny any hint of lifelike form or earthly spatial placement. Equally prominent as the figure is the bold band of complicated but coherent interlacing ornament that forms the border of the figure's field.

Comparable priority of ornament over figure also characterizes the *Book of Kells*, one of the most spectacular and inventive of the surviving Hiberno-Saxon Gospels, probably made around 800 in an Irish monastery on Iona, an island off the west coast of Scotland. Its most celebrated page may be the one that begins the account of Jesus' birth in Matthew's Gospel (see fig. 10–1). The Greek letters *chi*, *rho*, and *iota* create an irregular shape that resembles a cluster of gold and enamel brooches. At first glance, the page seems filled only with letters and abstract ornament, but hidden in the dense thicket of spirals and interlaces are human and animal forms. The spiral of the *rho* at the lower-right center of the page ends in the head of a red-headed youth, possibly Christ. At left center, three angels hold the edge of the plunging *chi.* At bottom center, just at right of the end of this longest stroke, two cats each capture a mouse, and to their right an otter catches a salmon. The cat-and-mouse scene may signal the triumph of good (embodied in the cats) over evil (embodied in the mice who try to eat the host—the Communion wafer, the mystical body of Christ).

Even as monks finished the *Book of Kells*, Hiberno-Saxon culture came under threat from abroad. At the end of the eighth century, seafaring bands of western Scandinavians known as Vikings began to appear on the coasts of the British Isles, lured by the wealth of church treasuries and fertile land. Intermittently looting and destroying coastal and inland river communities, they were a terrifying presence throughout Europe for nearly 300 years, eventually settling in what is now Iceland, Greenland, Ireland, England, France, Scotland, and Russia. About the year 1000, they even established a short-lived outpost in eastern North America.

Scandinavian Art

The Scandinavian homeland of the Vikings was a vital artistic center long before their raiding explorations and continued to flourish long after they had resettled in their foreign homes. Artists had exhibited a fondness for abstract patterning from prehistoric times (see fig. 1–18). Since Scandinavia was never part of the Roman Empire, by the fifth century CE pure animal style, untouched by the classical Mediterranean world, still dominated the arts. The Gummersmark brooch (fig. **10–4**), a large silver-gilt pin made in Denmark during the sixth century, was probably one of a pair used to fasten a cloak around the owner's shoulders. The brooch displays

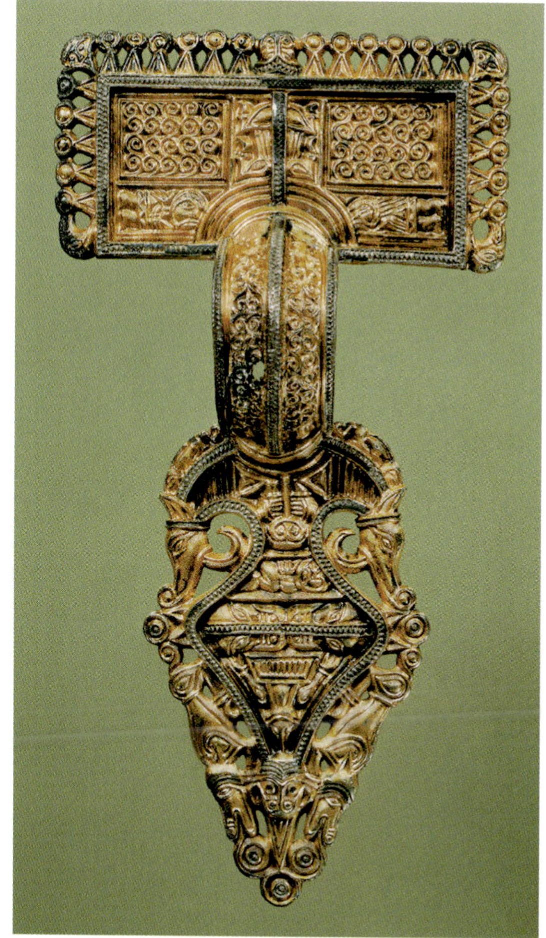

10–4 Gummersmark brooch, Denmark. 6th century. Silver gilt, height 5¾" (14.6 cm). Nationalmuseet, Copenhagen

THE MEDIEVAL SCRIPTORIUM

Today, presses can produce hundreds of thousands of identical copies of any book. In medieval Europe, however, before the invention of printing from movable type in the mid-1400s, books were made by hand, one at a time, with pen, ink, brush, and paint. Each one was a time-consuming and expensive undertaking.

At first, medieval books were usually made by monks and nuns in a workshop called a **scriptorium** (plural, scriptoria), which was usually in a monastery or convent. As the demand for books increased, rulers set up palace workshops employing both religious and lay scribes, and supervised by scholars.

Before paper came into common use in the early 1400s, books were written on **parchment**—prepared animal skins which were cleaned and scraped to create a smooth surface for writing and painting. The finest material—called **vellum**—was made from calfskin. Ink and paint also required time and experience to prepare, and many pigments, particularly blues and greens, were made from costly semi-precious stones. In very important manuscripts, artists also used gold in the form of gold leaf or gold paint.

Work on a book was often divided between scribes, who copied the text, and one or more artists, who painted illustrations, large initials, or other decorations. Although most books were produced anonymously, scribes and illustrators sometimes signed their work or provided background information in a **colophon** (notes on the book's production at the end of the manuscript).

The earliest books, scrolls, were made of sheets pasted or stitched together and were kept rolled up for protection and storage. About 400 CE, the **codex**, in which a number of folded sheets are stitched or glued together, began to assume greater favor than other book forms in Europe and remains the most common kind of book today. The scroll remained popular in Asia.

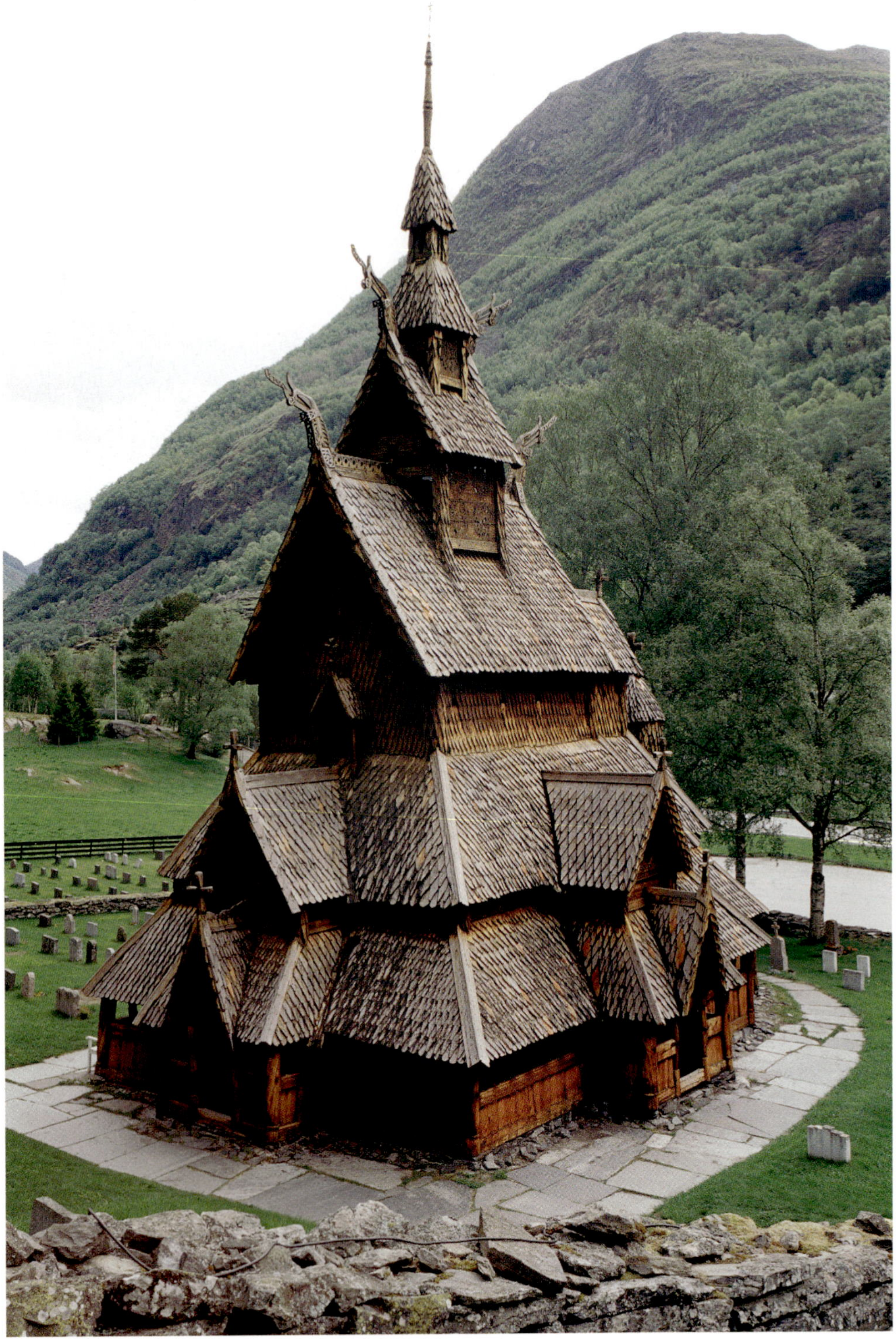

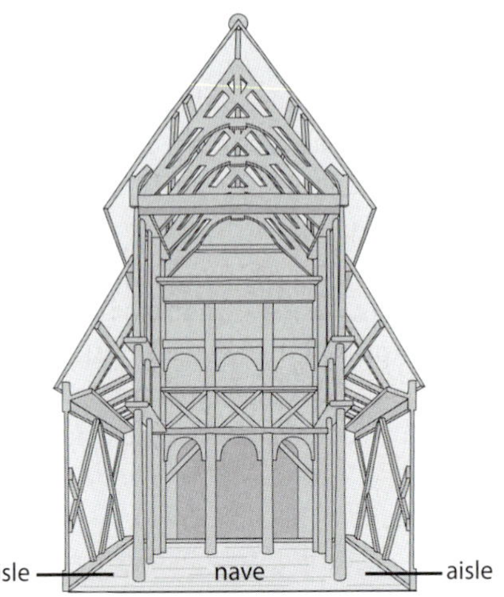

10–5 Exterior and section drawing of Borgund stave church, Sogn, Norway. c. 1125–1150

an impressive array of generally symmetrical designs, seething with fantastic animal forms. Ribs and spinal columns are exposed as if they had been x-rayed; hip and shoulder joints are pear-shaped; tongues and jaws extend and curl, and legs end in long claws. The stylistic origins of the boars on the Sutton Hoo clasp are easily seen here.

The vast forests of Scandinavia provided the materials for timber buildings of many kinds, but, since they were subject to decay and fire, the earliest of these structures have disappeared, leaving few traces. In rural Norway, however, twelfth-century **stave churches**—named for the four huge timbers (staves) that form their structural core—have survived, and they seem to record the structure and appearance of timber architectural traditions that once predominated in the northern European landscape of the Middle Ages. Borgund church, built about 1125–1150, is one of the finest (fig. **10–5**). Four corner staves support the central roof, with additional interior posts that create the effect of a nave and side aisles. A rounded apse covered with a timber tower is attached to the choir. The steeply pitched roofs protect the walls from the rain and snow. On all the gables, either crosses or dragon heads protect the church and its congregation from trolls and demons. The same basic wooden structure was used for almost all building types: on a large scale for palaces, assembly halls, and churches; on a small scale for domestic shelters which people shared with their animals.

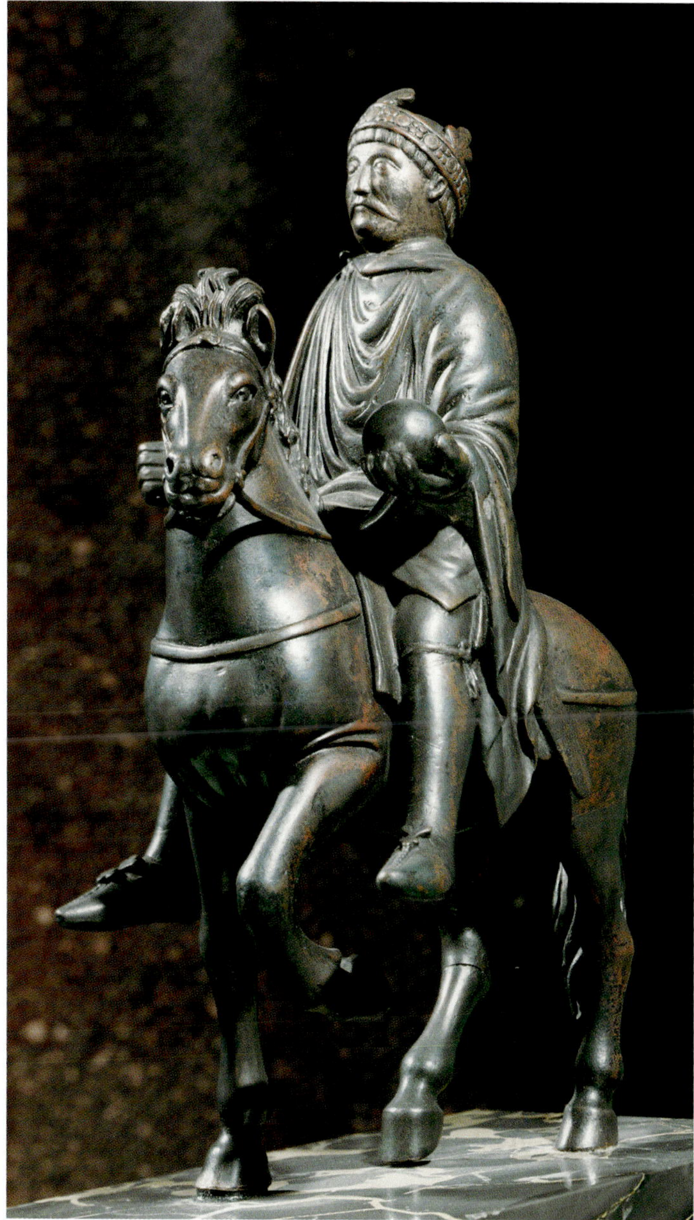

10–6 Equestrian Portrait of Charles the Bald (?). 9th century. Bronze, height 9½" (24.4 cm). Musée du Louvre, Paris

Carolingian Art

By the end of the fifth century, Frankish barbarians had settled in northern Gaul (modern France), and it was Frankish warriors who in 732 turned back the Muslim invasion of Gaul. The leaders of the Franks established a dynasty of rulers known as the Carolingians, after their greatest member Charles the Great, called Charlemagne (ruled 768–814). Charlemagne's empire in continental Europe encompassed at its greatest extent modern France, western Germany, Belgium, Holland, Luxembourg, and the Lombard kingdom in Italy. Charlemagne imposed Christianity throughout this territory, and in 800 Pope Leo III (ruled 795–816) granted Charlemagne the title of emperor, declaring him the rightful successor to the first Christian Roman emperor, Constantine. This event served to reinforce Charlemagne's authority over his realm and strengthened the bonds between the papacy and secular government in the West.

The Carolingian rulers' ascent to the Roman imperium, and the political pretensions it implied, are clearly signaled in a small bronze equestrian statue of a Carolingian emperor—once thought to be a portrait of Charlemagne himself but now usually identified as his grandson Charles the Bald (fig. **10–6**). The idea of representing an emperor as a proud equestrian figure recalls the much larger image of Marcus Aurelius (see fig. 6–33) that was believed during the Middle Ages to portray Constantine, the first Christian emperor and an ideal prototype for the ruler of the Franks, newly legitimized by the pope. But unlike the bearded Roman, this Carolingian king sports a mustache, a Frankish sign of nobility that had also been common among the Celts (see fig. 5–44). Works of art such as this are not the result of a slavish mimicking of Roman prototypes, but the creative appropriation of Roman imperial typology to glorify manifestly Carolingian rulers.

To proclaim the glory of the new empire in monumental form, Charlemagne's architects turned to the two former Western imperial capitals, Rome and Ravenna, for inspiration. Charlemagne's biographer, Einhard, reported that the ruler, "beyond all sacred and venerable places…loved the church of the holy apostle Peter at Rome." Not surprisingly, Constantine's basilica of Saint Peter, with its long nave and side aisles ending in a transept and projecting apse (see fig. 7–8), served as a model for many important churches in Charlemagne's empire.

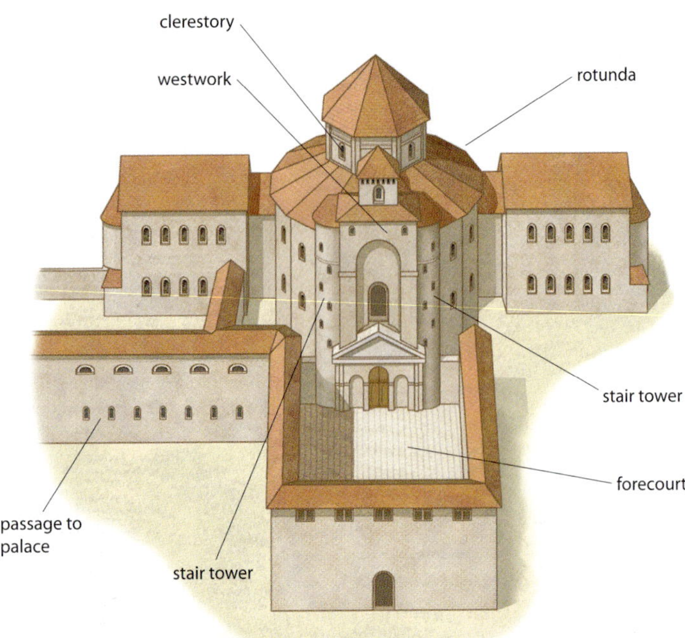

10–7 Reconstruction drawing of the Palace Chapel of Charlemagne, Aachen, Germany. Constructed 792–805

The chapel of his own palace at Aachen (in Germany) also has clear Italian roots. This building (fig. **10–7**) served several functions. It was the emperor's private chapel, the church of his imperial court, housed the precious relics of saints, and, after Charlemagne's death, was his mausoleum. The central octagonal plan recalls the Church of San Vitale in Ravenna (see fig. 7–16). The soaring core of the building (fig. **10–8**) is surrounded at the ground level by an ambulatory (curving aisle passageway) and, on the second floor, ringed by a gallery (a passageway overlooking the nave). Columns and railings at the gallery level form a screen that reemphasizes the flat, pierced walls of the octagon and enhances the clarity and planar geometry of its design. The effect is quite different from the dynamic spatial play and undulating exedrae of San Vitale, but the rich materials—some imported from Italy—and mosaics covering the walls at Aachen were clearly inspired by Byzantine architecture.

A new architectural feature created by Carolingian architects is the **westwork**, or monumental entrance block. At Aachen on the second floor of this projecting porch a throne room and chapel face the apse, giving the emperor an unobstructed view of the liturgy at the high altar, and at the same time ensuring his privacy and safety. Twin stair towers flank this entrance complex and create a distinctive western façade. The vertical emphasis of the western towers and the equally upward rising thrust of the interior seem to be northern contributions to Christian architecture. Early Christian basilicas were generally more horizontal in appearance.

Charlemagne turned to the Church to help stabilize his empire through religion and education. He looked most especially to Benedictine monks whom he called his "cultural army." Carolingian monks followed the *Rule for Monasteries*, written by Saint Benedict of Nursia (c. 480–c. 547), a set of practical guidelines for secluded communal life that outlined monastic vocation as a combination of work and prayer (liturgical services as well as private devotion). While contemplating how best to house such a community, Abbot Haito of Reichenau developed, at the request of Abbot Gozbert of Saint Gall, an ideal plan for the layout of monasteries. This extraordinary ninth-century drawing survives in the library of the Abbey of Saint Gall in modern Switzerland (fig. **10–9**). This is not a "blueprint" in the modern sense, prepared to guide the construction of an actual monastery, but an intellectual record of Carolingian meditations on the nature of monastic life. At its center is the cloister, an enclosed courtyard from which open all the buildings that are most central to the life of the monk. Most prominent is a large basilican church with towers, multiple altars with relics, and at the east (assuming the church was oriented in standard medieval fashion) a sanctuary where monks would gather for communal prayer

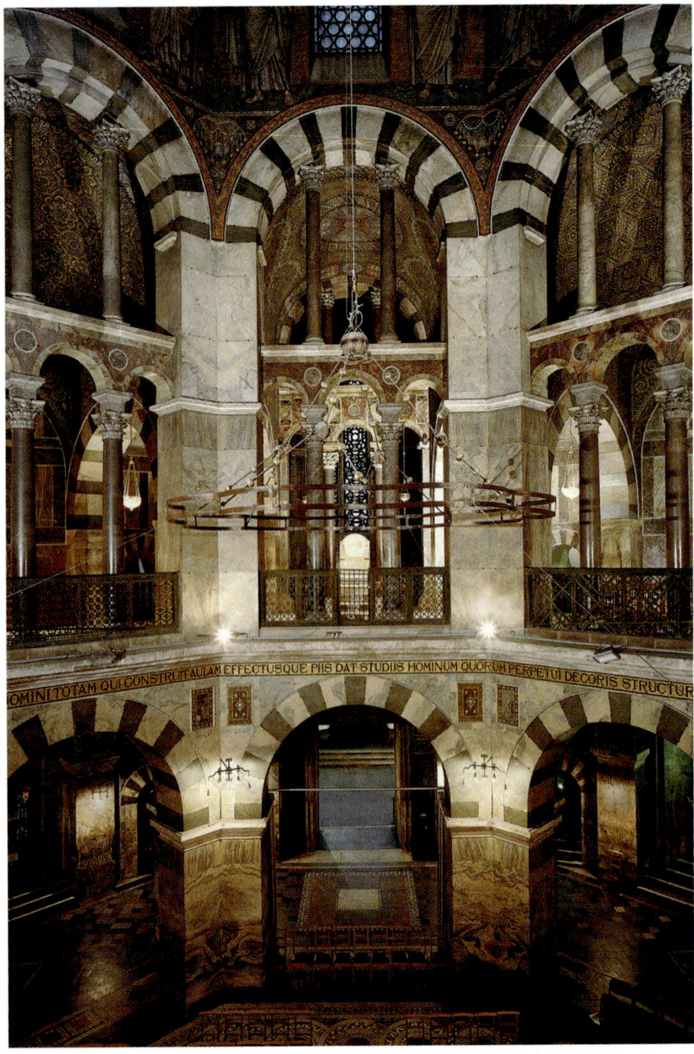

10–8 Palace Chapel of Charlemagne, interior view, Aachen (Aix-la-Chapelle), Germany. 792–805

Extensive renovations took place in the nineteenth century, when the chapel was reconsecrated as the cathedral of Aachen, and in the twentieth century, after it was damaged in World War II.

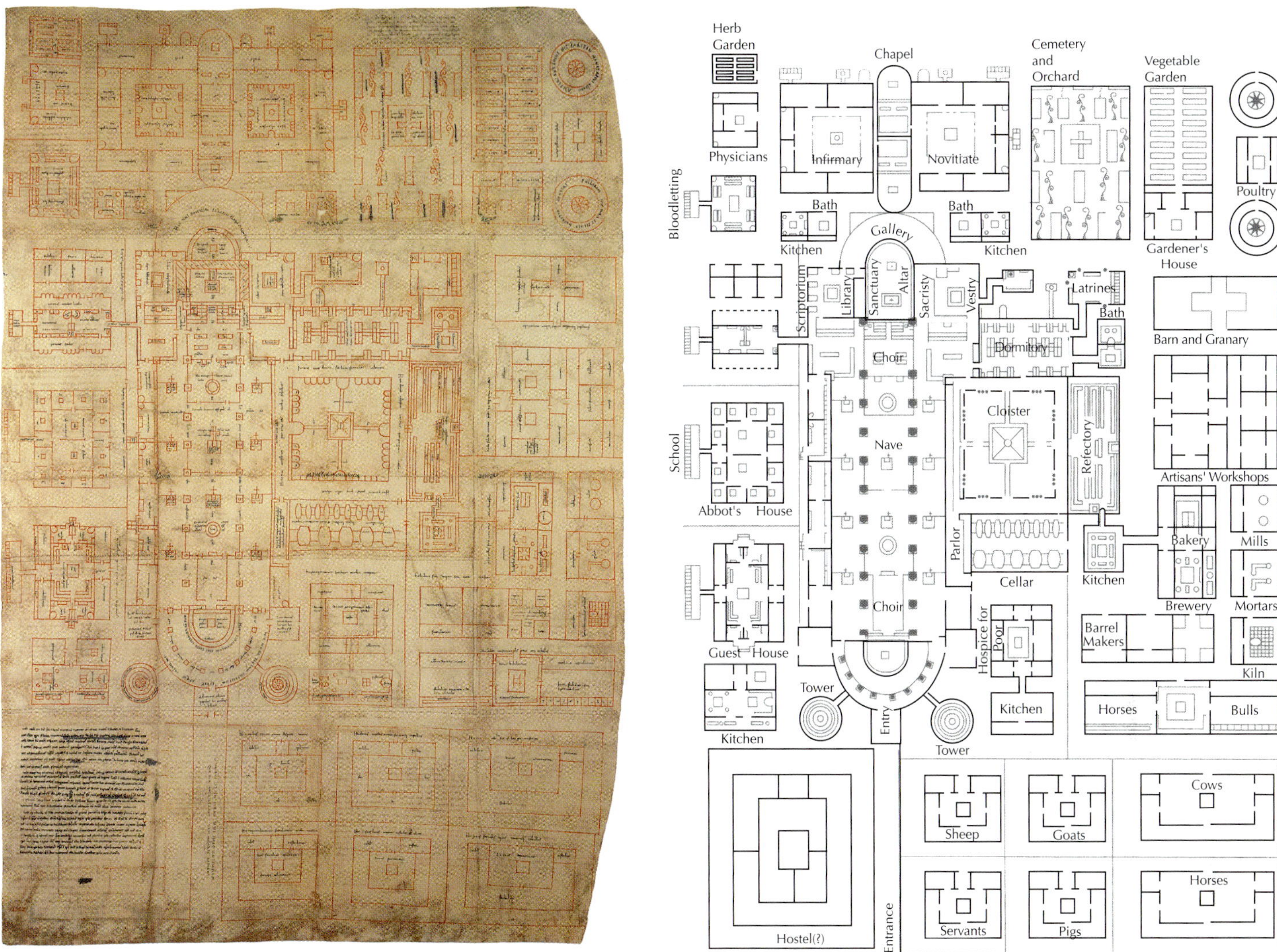

10–9 Plan of the Abbey of Saint Gall (original and redrawn with captions). c. 820. Original red ink on parchment, 28" × 44½" (71.1 × 112.1 cm). Stiftsbibliothek, St. Gallen, Switzerland (Cod. Sang. 1092)

throughout the day and night. The monks' quarters lie off the southern and eastern sides of the cloister, with dormitory, refectory (dining room), and workrooms. Further east are the cemetery, hospital, and school for novices (monks in training). To the north stand the abbot's residence, guest quarters, and a hospice for the poor. Buildings for lay farm workers and shelter for animals surrounded this central core. So efficient and functional was this plan that Benedictine monasteries often still follow the layout today.

As part of their monastic work life, some monks and nuns produced books. Books were central to the Carolingian renewal of learning. Charlemagne himself sponsored the scrupulous editing and copying of key ancient and religious texts, written in a new, clear script called Carolingian minuscule, based on ancient Roman forms but with a uniform lower-case alphabet that increased legibility and streamlined production. Like the builders and sculptors who transformed revived Roman types, such as basilicas, central-plan chapels, or equestrian imperial portraits, into creative new works, scribes and illuminators revived and revitalized the Christian manuscript tradition. Notably they returned the representation of human figures to a central position.

For example, the evangelist portraits—as opposed to evangelist symbols used to represent authors in the *Book of Durrow* (see fig. 10–3)—of the early ninth-century *Coronation Gospels* conform to the principles of idealized, lifelike representation consistent with the Greco-Roman classical tradition. The full-bodied, white-robed figure of Matthew (fig. **10–10**) is modeled in brilliant white and subtle shading and seated on the cushion of a folding chair set within a freely painted landscape. The way his foot lifts up to rest on the solid base of his writing desk emphasizes his three-dimensional placement within a described outdoor setting. Conventions for creating the illusion of solid figures in space may have been learned from Byzantine manuscripts in a monastic library, or artists from Byzantium—refugees from the iconoclastic controversy (726–843) that had sent painters fleeing the Byzantine world (see "Iconoclasm," page 184)—may have actually been working at the Carolingian court.

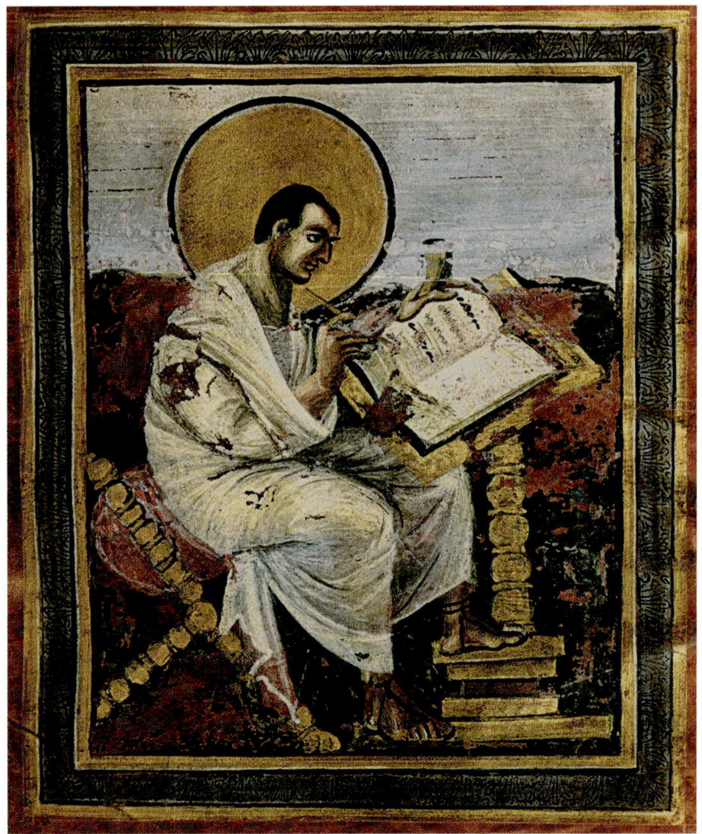

10–10 Page with *Matthew the Evangelist*, *Coronation Gospels*. Early 9th century. Ink and colors on vellum, 12¾" × 9⅞" (36.3 × 25 cm). Kunsthistorische Museum, Vienna

Tradition holds that this Gospel Book was buried with Charlemagne in 814, and that in the year 1000 Emperor Otto III removed it from his tomb. Its title derives from its use in the coronation ceremonies of later German emperors.

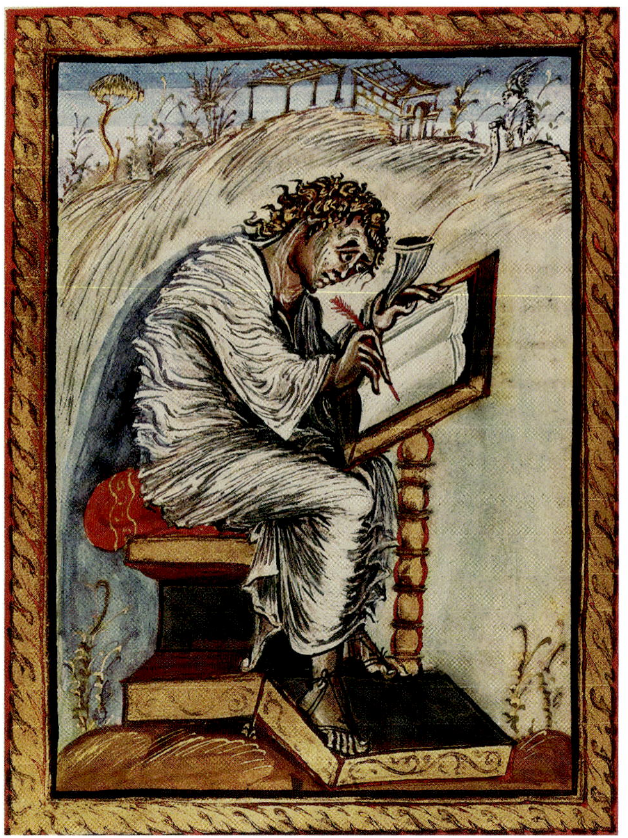

10–11 Page with *Matthew the Evangelist*, *Ebbo Gospels*. Second quarter of the 9th century. Ink and colors on vellum, 10¼" × 8¾" (26 × 22.2 cm). Bibliothèque Municipale, Epernay, France (MS 1, fol. 18v)

But as was the case with architecture, the incorporation of the Roman tradition in manuscript painting became the basis for a series of creative Carolingian variations. One of the most splendid is a Gospel book made for Archbishop Ebbo of Reims (816–835, 840–841) at the nearby Abbey of Hautevillers (fig. **10–11**). The calm, carefully painted grandeur characterizing Matthew's portrait in the Coronation Gospels (see fig. 10–10) has given way here to spontaneous, calligraphic painting suffused with unbridled passion. This may be most immediately apparent in the intensity of Matthew's gaze, but the whole composition is charged with energy, from the evangelist's wiry hairdo and rippling drapery, to the rapidly sketched landscape, and even extending into the acanthus leaves of the frame. This expressionism evokes the evangelist's spiritual excitement as he hastens to transcribe the Word of God delivered by the angel (also serving as Matthew's symbol), who is almost lost in the upper-right corner. As if to echo the saint's turbulent emotions, the footstool tilts precariously, and the top of the desk seems about to detach itself from the pedestal.

Sumptuous books such as these represent an enormous investment of time, talent, and materials. They were protected with heavy wooden covers that were sometimes sheathed in sheets of pure gold embellished with jeweled decoration. One of the richest of these (fig. **10–12**)—covering the *Lindau Gospels* and probably made between 870 and 880 in a workshop sponsored by Emperor Charles the Bald (ruled 840–877)—combines jewels and pearls with sculpture in gold. The Crucifixion is represented by figures formed from the gold background using the repoussé technique, as in the Byzantine icon of the archangel Michael (see fig. 7–23). Grieving angels hover above the arms of the cross, and earthbound mourners twist in agony below. Over Jesus' head figures representing the sun and moon hide their faces. In contrast to these gracefully agitated figures, the artist modeled a more monumental Jesus in a rounded, lifelike style that suggests a classical source. He seems to stand in front of the cross—straight and wide-eyed with outstretched arms, as if to prefigure his ultimate triumph over death. The jewels, rounded to form cabochons (polished, not faceted, stones), are raised on tiny feet or architectural configurations so as to allow light to penetrate under them, thus enhancing their luster and reminding medieval believers of biblical descriptions of the heavenly Jerusalem.

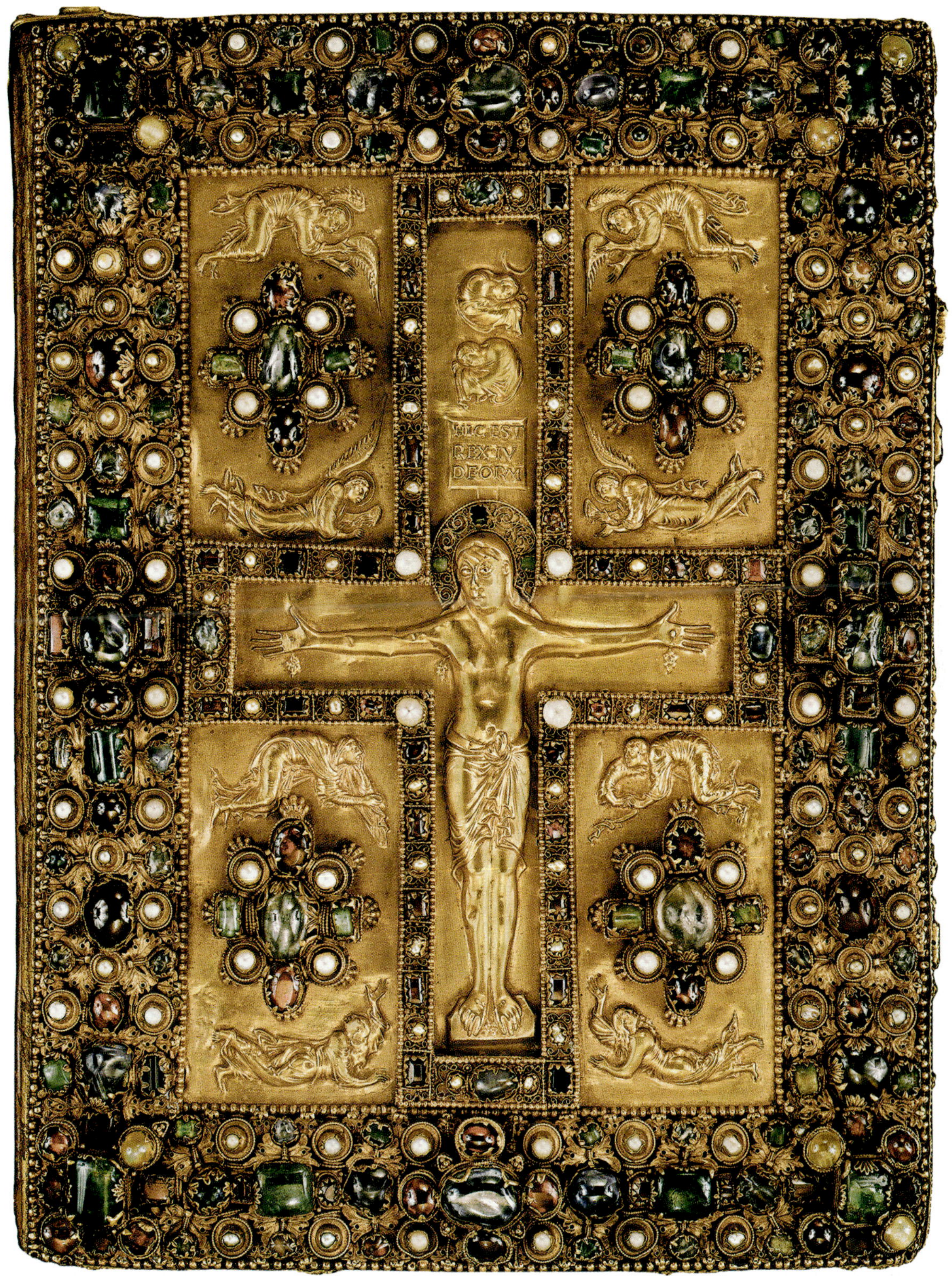

10–12 ***Crucifixion with Angels and Mourning Figures***, outer cover of the *Lindau Gospels*. c. 870–880. Gold, pearls, sapphires, garnets, and emeralds, 13¾" × 10⅜" (34.9 × 26.7 cm). The Pierpont Morgan Library, New York (MS M1)

Spanish Art

Christian and Islamic worlds met in medieval Spain. When Muslim armies arrived in the early eighth century, Spain was governed by the Visigoths, a Germanic people who had ruled over the indigenous Spanish population since the fall of the Western Roman Empire. The Islamic conquest of Spain in 711 ended Visigothic rule. With some exceptions, the Muslims allowed Christians and Jews to follow their own religious practices. Christian artists adapted many features of Islamic style to fit their traditional themes and developed a hybrid style known today as **Mozarabic**.

Antagonisms among Muslims, orthodox Christians, and the followers of various heretical Christian beliefs provided fertile material for Spanish theologians, and writing biblical commentaries to refute heretical beliefs became a major task of the monasteries of northern Spain. Beatus (d. 798), the abbot of the monastery of Liébana near the north coast, compiled around 776 the most influential commentary on the Apocalypse, describing the final and fiery destruction of the world before the Last Judgment and triumph of Christ. Illustrated manuscripts of this text are among the glories of early medieval art in Spain.

A particularly splendid copy was produced around 940–945, probably at the Monastery of San Salvator at Tábara, by an artist named Maius (d. 968), who both wrote the text and painted the illustrations. His gripping portrayal of the *Woman Clothed with the Sun* (fig. **10–13**), based on the biblical text of Apocalypse

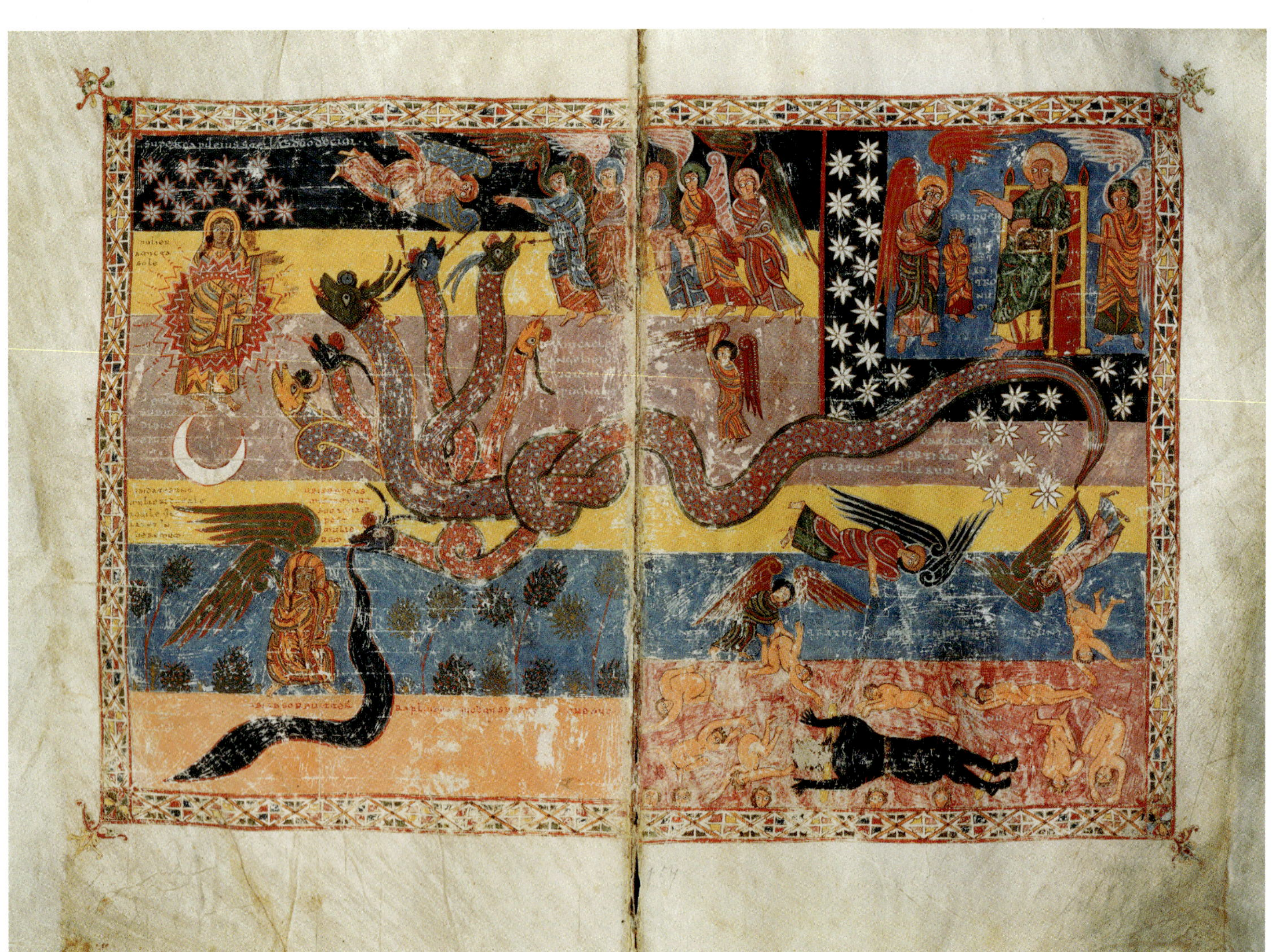

10–13 Maius. *Seven-Headed Dragon and Woman Clothed with the Sun*, from the *Morgan Beatus*, probably made at San Salvator at Tábara, Spain. 940–945. Tempera on vellum, 15⅛" × 22 1/16" (38.5 × 56 cm). The Pierpont Morgan Library, New York (MS M644, fols. 152v–153r)

When French painter Fernand Léger (1881–1955; see fig. 19–12) was visiting the great art historian Meyer Schapiro (1904–1996) in New York during World War II, the artist asked the scholar to suggest the single work of art that was most important for him to see while there. Schapiro took him to the Morgan Library to leaf through this manuscript, and the strong impact it had on Léger can be clearly seen in his later paintings.

(Revelation 12:1–18), extends over two pages to cover an entire opening of the book. Maius has stayed close to the text in composing his tableau, which is dominated by the long, seven-headed, red dragon that slithers across practically the entire width of the picture to threaten at top left the "woman clothed with the sun, with the moon under her feet, and on her head a crown of twelve stars" (12:1). With his tail, at upper right, he sweeps a third of heaven's stars toward the earth while the woman's male child appears before the throne of God. Maius presents this complex allegory of the triumph of the Church over its enemies with a forceful, abstract, ornamental style that accentuates the dramatic, nightmarish qualities of the events outlined in the text. The background has been distilled into horizontal strips of color; the figures become striped bundles of drapery capped with faces dominated by staring eyes and silhouetted, framing halos. Momentous apocalyptic events have been transformed by Maius into exotic abstractions that still maintain their power to captivate our attention.

Ottonian Art

By the third generation of the Carolingian dynasty, the empire had been divided into three parts, setting the stage for the modern partitioning of Europe. The western portion eventually became France. In the tenth century, control of the eastern portion—corresponding roughly to modern Germany, Switzerland, and Austria—passed to a dynasty of Saxon rulers known as the Ottonians, after its three principal figures: Otto I (ruled 936–973), Otto II (ruled 973–983), and Otto III (ruled 983–1002). Otto I gained control of Italy in 951, and the pope crowned him emperor in 962.

In the tenth and eleventh centuries, Ottonian artists in northern Europe, drawing on Roman, Byzantine, and Carolingian models, began a new tradition of large sculpture in wood and bronze that would have a significant influence on later medieval art. The *Gero Crucifix* (fig. **10–14**) is one of the few large works of carved wood to survive. Archbishop Gero of Cologne (ruled 969–976) commissioned the sculpture for his cathedral about 970. The figure of Christ is over-life-size, and the focus here, following Byzantine models, is on Jesus' suffering. He is shown as a tortured martyr, not as the triumphant hero of the *Lindau Gospels* cover (see fig. 10–12). Jesus' broken dead body sags on the cross, head falling forward, eyes closed. The crisp, linear folds of his golden drapery heightens the impact of his drawn face, emaciated arms and legs, sagging torso, and limp, bloodied hands. This is an image of distilled anguish, meant to inspire pity and awe in the empathetic responses of its viewers.

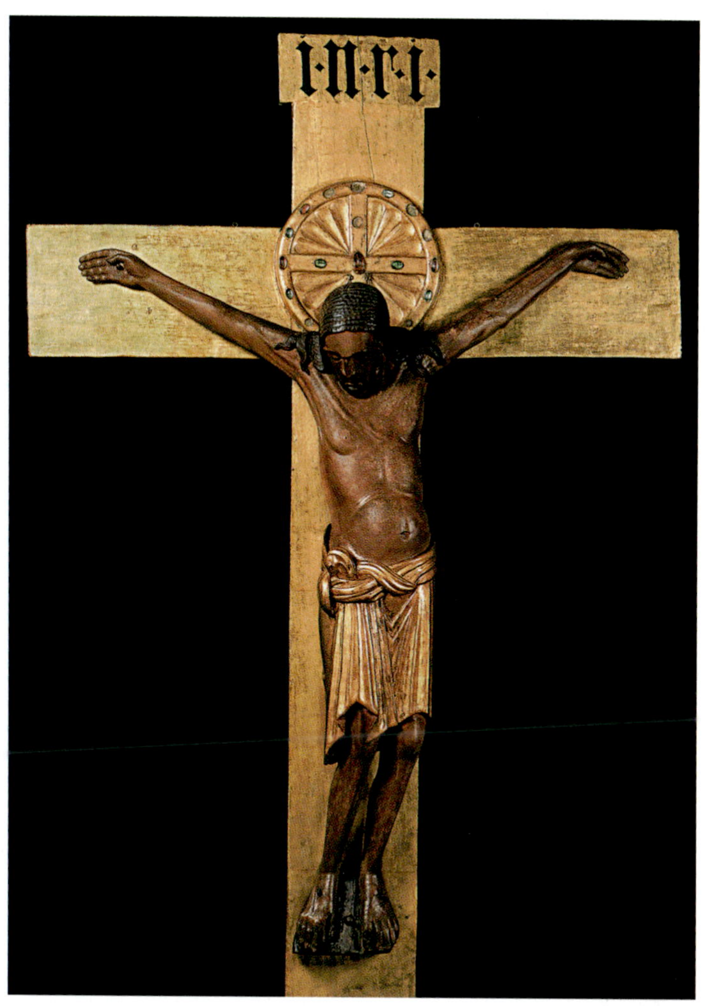

10–14 ***Gero Crucifix***, Cologne Cathedral, Germany. c. 970. Painted and gilded oak, height of figure 6' 2" (1.88 m)

This life-size sculpture is both a crucifix to be suspended over an altar and a special kind of reliquary. A cavity in the back of the head was made to hold a piece of the Host, or communion bread, already consecrated by the priest. Consequently, the figure not only represents the body of the dying Jesus but also contains within it the body of Christ obtained through the Eucharist.

An important patron was Bishop Bernward of Hildesheim in Germany, who was himself a skilled goldsmith. A pair of bronze doors made under his direction for his Abbey Church of Saint Michael represents the most ambitious and complex bronze-casting project—each door was cast as a single piece!—since antiquity (fig. **10–15**). The inscription in the band running across the center of the doors states that Bishop Bernward installed them in 1015.

The doors, standing more than 16 feet tall, are decorated with scenes from the Hebrew Bible on the left (read down from the Creation of Eve at the top to Cain's murder of Abel at the bottom) and New Testament scenes on the right (read upward from the Annunciation at the bottom to the *Noli me tangere* at the top; see "The Life of Jesus," page 171). In each pair of scenes, the event from the Hebrew Bible can be interpreted as a prefiguration or illumination of the adjacent New Testament event. For instance, the third panel down on the left shows Adam and Eve picking the forbidden fruit of Knowledge in the Garden of Eden, believed by Christians to be the source of human sin, suffering, and death. This scene is paired on the right with the Crucifixion of Jesus, whose sacrifice was believed to have atoned for Adam and Eve's Original Sin, bringing the promise of eternal life. At the center of the doors, six panels down—between the door pulls—Eve (left) and Mary (right) sit side

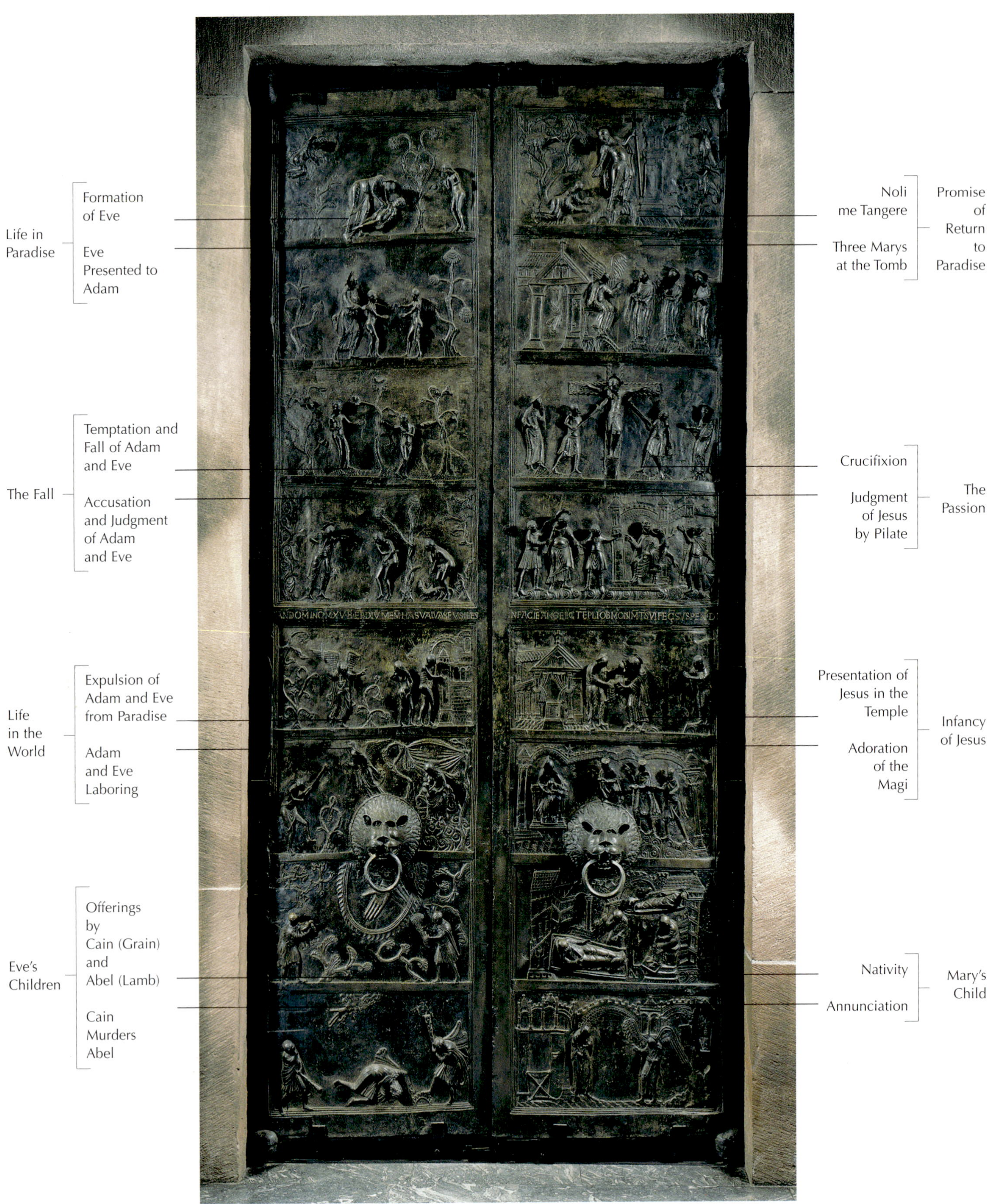

10–15 Bronze doors of Bishop Bernward, made for the Abbey Church of Saint Michael, Hildesheim, Germany. 1015. Bronze, height 16' 6" (5 m)

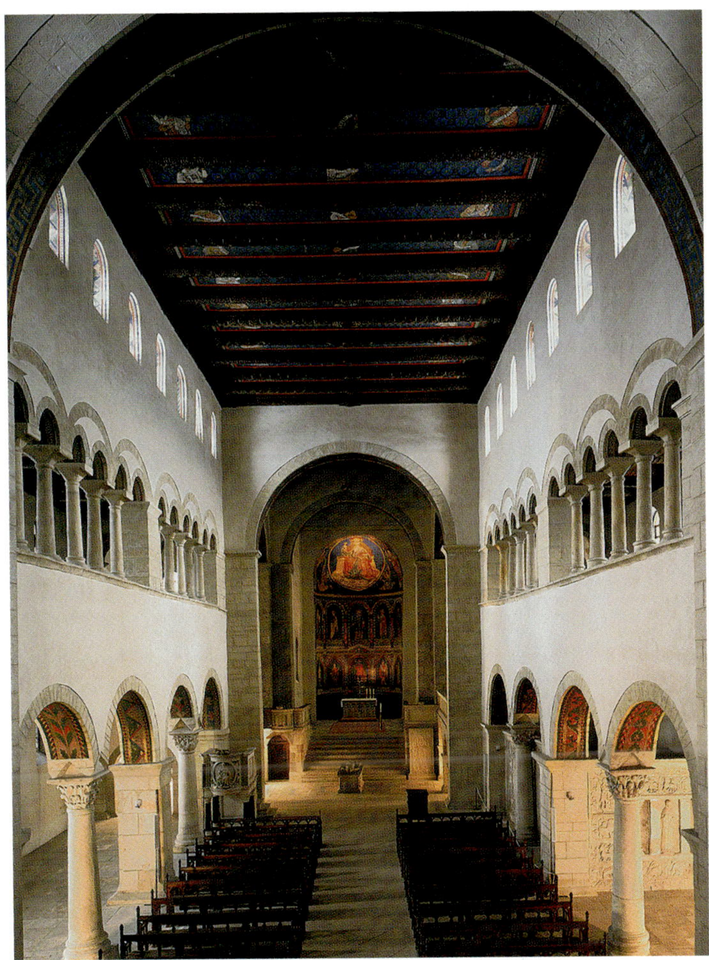

10–16 Nave, Church of Saint Cyriakus, Gernrode, Germany. Begun 961, consecrated 973

by side, holding their sons: Cain (who murdered his brother) and Jesus (who was unjustly executed) signify the opposition of evil and good, damnation and salvation. Other telling pairs are the murder of Abel (the first sin) with the Annunciation (the advent of salvation) at the bottom, and fourth from the top, the passing of blame from Adam and Eve to the serpent paired with Pilate washing his hands of any responsibility for the execution of Jesus.

Aristocratic Ottonian women often held positions of authority, especially as leaders of religious communities. When Margrave Gero (the provincial military governor) founded the convent of Saint Cyriakus in Gernrode, he made his widowed daughter-in-law its first abbess and began building the convent church (fig. **10–16**) in 961. Like an Early Christian or Carolingian basilica, the church has a nave flanked by side aisles. But the design of the three-level wall elevation—nave arcade, gallery, and clerestory—creates a rhythmic effect distinct from the uniformity that had characterized earlier basilicas. Rectangular piers alternate with round columns in the two levels of arcades, and at gallery level, pairs of openings are framed by larger arches and then grouped in threes. The central rectangular piers, aligned on the two levels, bisect the walls vertically into two units, each composed of two broad arches of the nave arcade surmounted by three pairs of arches at the gallery level. This seemingly simple design, with its rhythmic alternation of heavy and light supports, its balance of rectangular and rounded forms, and its combination of horizontal and vertical movements, seems to prefigure the aesthetic exploration of wall design that will characterize the Romanesque architecture of the succeeding two centuries.

Like their Carolingian predecessors, Ottonian monks and nuns created richly illuminated manuscripts, often patronized by secular rulers. Styles varied from place to place, depending on the traditions of the particular scriptorium and the models available in its library. The presentation page of a Gospel book made in the early eleventh century for Abbess Hitda (d. 1041) of Meschede, near Cologne (fig. **10–17**) represents one of the most distinctive local styles. The abbess offers her book to Saint Walpurga, her convent's patron saint. The artist has angled the buildings of the sprawling convent in the background to frame the figures and draw attention to their interaction. The size of the architectural complex underscores the abbess's position of authority. The foreground setting—a rocky, undulating strip of landscape—is meant to be understood as holy ground, separated from the rest of the world by golden trees and the huge arch-shaped aura that silhouettes Saint Walpurga. The energetic spontaneity of

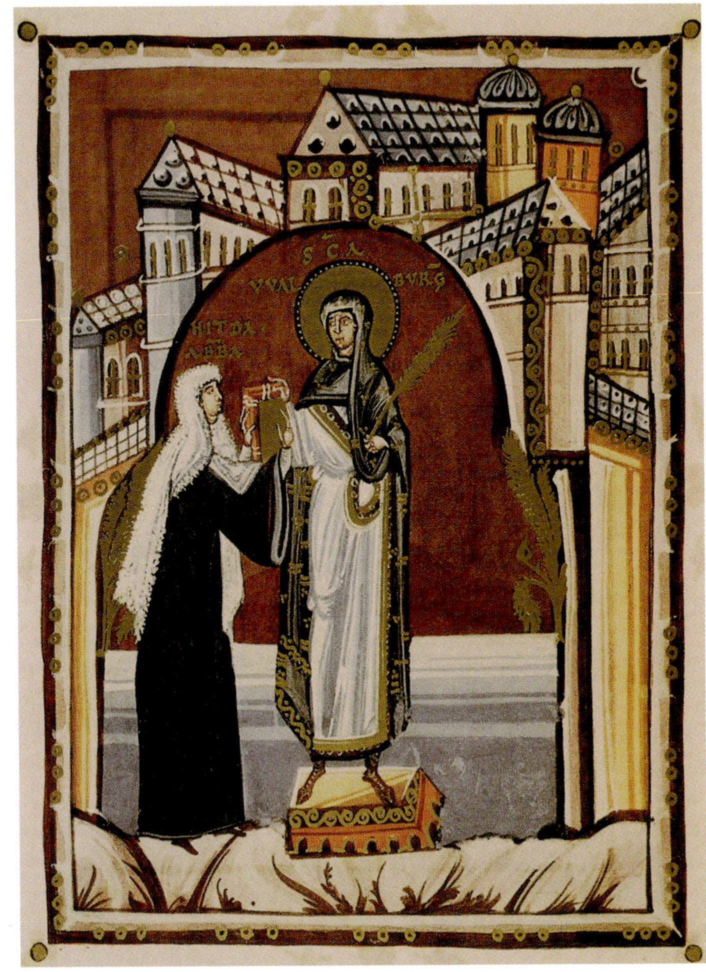

10–17 Presentation page with *Abbess Hitda* and *Saint Walpurga*, *Hitda Gospels*. Early 11th century. Ink and colors on vellum, $11\frac{3}{8}$" × $5\frac{5}{8}$" (29 × 14.2 cm). Hessische Landesund Hochschulbibliothek, Darmstadt, Germany

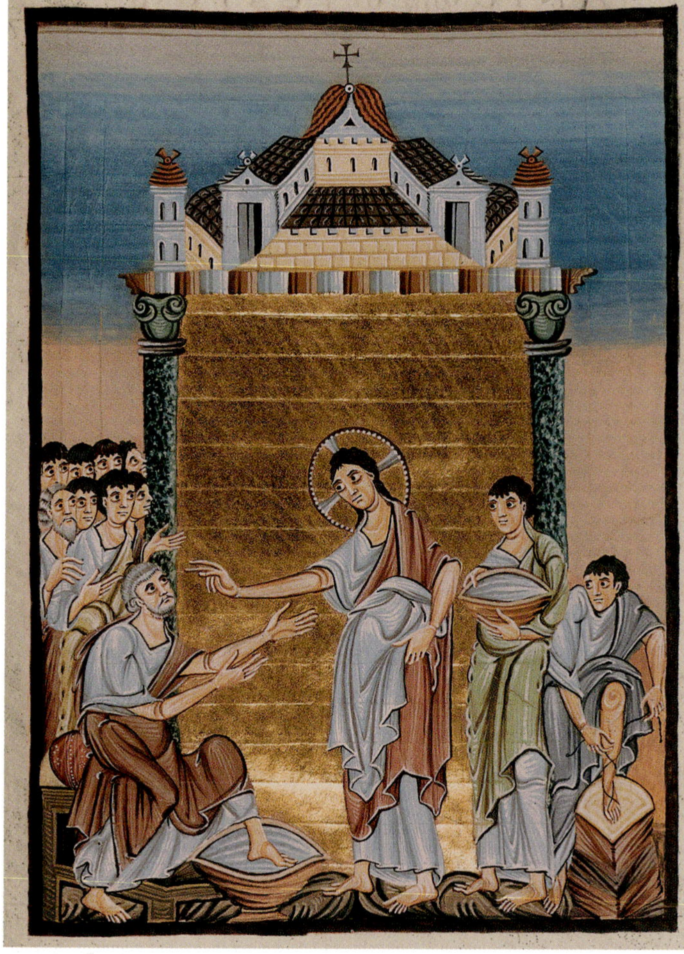

10–18 Page with *Christ Washing the Feet of His Disciples*, *Gospels of Otto III*. c. 1000. Ink, gold, and colors on vellum, 13⅛" × 9½" (33.4 × 24.2 cm). Staatsbibliothek, Munich (Clm 4453, fol. 237r)

the painting style suffuses the scene with a sense of religious fervor appropriate to the visionary saintly encounter.

The *Gospels of Otto III* (fig. **10–18**), made in a German monastery near Reichenau about 1000, shows another Ottonian painting style, in this case inspired by Byzantine art in the use of sharply outlined drawing and lavish fields of gold. Backed by a more controlled and balanced architectural canopy than that sheltering Hitda and Saint Walpurga (see fig. 10–17), these tall, slender men gesture dramatically with long, thin fingers. The scene depicts the moment when Jesus washes the feet of his disciples during their final meal together (John 13:1–17). Peter, who had tried to stop his Savior from performing this ancient ritual of hospitality, appears at left, one leg reluctantly poised over the basin while a centrally silhouetted and slightly overscaled Jesus gestures emphatically to underscore the necessity and significance of the act. Another disciple at far right enthusiastically lifts his leg to untie his sandals so he can be next in line. Selective stylization has allowed the artist of this picture to transform the received classical tradition into a style of stunning expressiveness and narrative power, features that will also characterize the figural styles associated with the Romanesque.

Romanesque Art

During the eleventh century, European life changed from a largely agricultural economy controlled by a landholding aristocracy to one where craft industries and trade allowed greater personal freedom and well-being. At the same time, more efficient farming facilitated population growth, and people began to move from agricultural villages into burgeoning urban areas. By the twelfth century, popular mass movements such as the crusades and pilgrimages began to end European isolation. Although the crusades were brutal military failures, the Western crusaders' encounters with the sophisticated Byzantine and Islamic cultures introduced new technology and ideas into Europe. People from all levels of society traveled together on pilgrimages to the three holiest places of Christendom: the tombs of Christ (the Holy Sepulcher) in Jerusalem, Saint Peter in Rome, and Saint James in Santiago de Compostela. Travel and trade led to the rise of an increasingly knowledgeable and urbane society, and foreign contacts helped to nourish a period of rich intellectual and artistic development.

Art historians have called the art produced from the mid-eleventh through the twelfth centuries *Romanesque* ("Roman-like"). Early nineteenth-century scholars first used the word with a pejorative edge to describe architecture that had the solid masonry walls, rounded arches, and masonry vaults characteristic of ancient Roman building but were not quite up to classical standards. Today we admire the remarkable vitality and variety of art and architecture that developed during the "Romanesque" period, drawing on many artistic traditions, not only Roman, but also Carolingian, Ottonian, Mozarabic, and Byzantine, blending with various local practices to form the Romanesque style, considered by many to be the first truly trans-European movement in the history of art.

Architecture

By the eleventh and twelfth centuries, increased prosperity provided the resources for burgeoning building activity in Europe. The need to provide for personal security in a period of constant local warfare and political upheaval, as well as the desire to glorify the house of the Lord and his saints, meant that building activity was focused on castles and churches. Those buildings that still stand—despite the ravages of weather, vandalism, neglect, and war—testify to the creativity and technical skills of the builders and the power and religious faith of the patrons.

In the twelfth century, Dover Castle (fig. **10–19**), safeguarding the coast of England from invasion, illustrates the way in which a key defensive position developed over the centuries. The Romans had built a lighthouse on the point, to which the Anglo-Saxons added a church (both can be seen surrounded by earthworks in the upper center of the illustration). Earthworks topped by wooden walls provided a measure of security, but the advantage of building stronger, fire-resistant walls was obvious. In the twelfth and thirteenth centuries, military engineers replaced the walls with stone and added the massive stone towers we see today. The Great Tower, as it was called in the Middle Ages (later known as a keep or donjon), had a courtyard (bailey) surrounded by additional walls. Ditches added to the height of the walls; in some castles, ditches

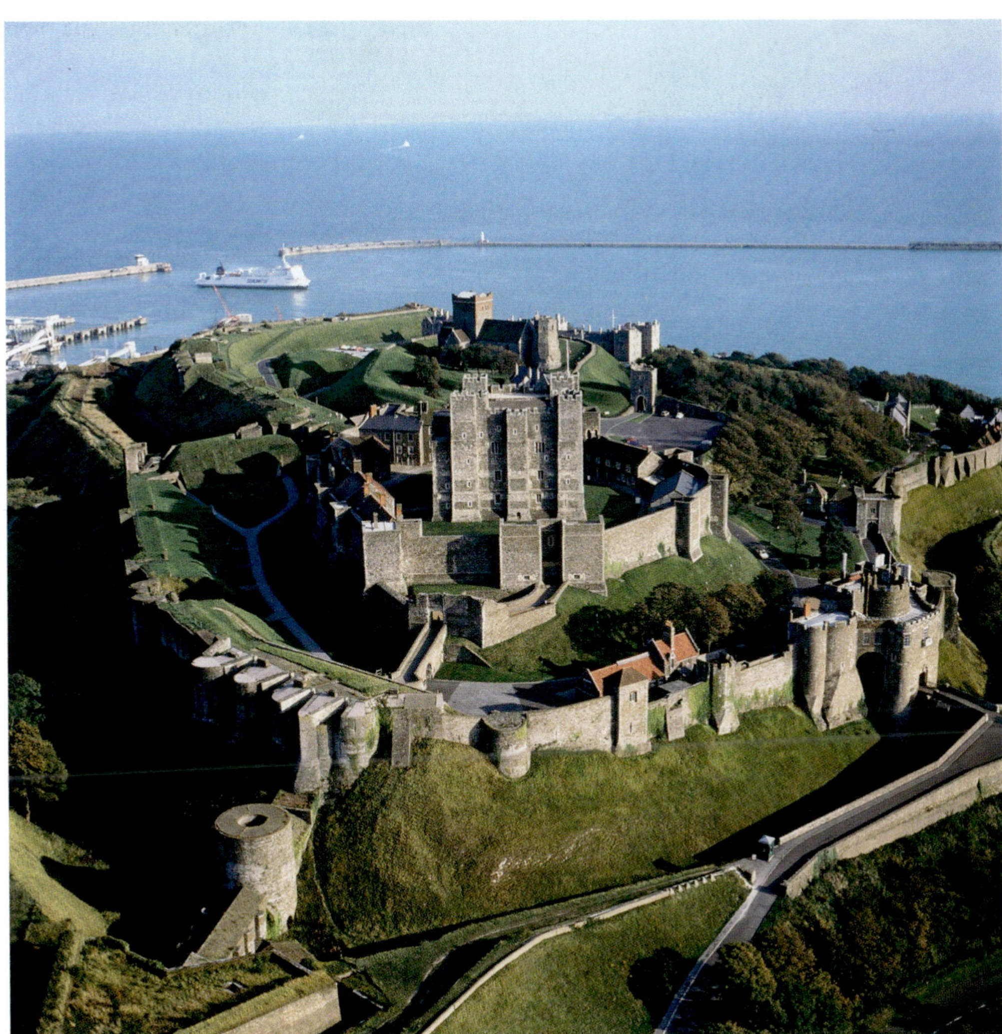

10–19 Dover Castle, air view overlooking the harbor and the English Channel. Center distance: Roman lighthouse tower, rebuilt Anglo-Saxon church, earthworks. Center: Norman Great Tower, surrounding earthworks and walls, 12th century. Outer walls, 13th century. Modern buildings have red-tiled roofs. The castle was used in World War II and is now a museum

were filled with water to form moats. The castle yard was filled with buildings, often including a great hall used for feasts and ceremonial occasions. Timber buildings housed troops, servants, and animals. Barns and workshops, ovens and wells were also needed since the castle had to be self-sufficient. A gatehouse, perhaps with a drawbridge, controlled the entrance. If enemies broke through the outer walls, the castle's defenders retreated to the Great Tower. In the thirteenth century, the walls at Dover were doubled and strengthened with towers, although the castle's position on cliffs overlooking the sea made scaling the walls nearly impossible. A castle's garrison could be forced to surrender only by starving its occupants. Dover is well preserved, but in most places broken walls and ruined towers stand as grim reminders of long sieges and the precariousness of medieval life.

If the castle of the secular lord was to be an imposing masonry structure, the house of God needed to be equally powerful and impressive. As one medieval monk put it, the Christian faithful were so relieved to have passed through the apocalyptic anxiety that had gripped their world at the millennial change around the year 1000, that in gratitude Europe was "clothed everywhere in a white garment of churches" (Radulphus Glaber, cited in Holt, page 18). Romanesque churches, like their early medieval predecessors, are often based on the basilican plan, but since designs varied from region to region, place to place, there is no such thing as a typical Romanesque church. Although timber remained a common building material, especially in northern Europe, Romanesque builders used masonry when conditions permitted. It was stronger and more fire-resistant, and masonry vaults enhanced the acoustical effect of the Gregorian chants sung inside. Stone barrel vaults or four-part groin vaults (see "Arch and Vault," page 145) reinforced by powerful supporting arches called ribs—a medieval innovation—covered aisles and even naves. **Buttresses** (thick masses of masonry) reinforced walls at critical points and made taller buildings possible. Towers emphasized both the **crossing** (where the nave and transept intersect) and the west façade, which usually contained the principal entrance to the church, often an elaborate portal encrusted with ornamental and figural sculpture.

When a large congregation or many clergy required that the sanctuary be expanded to include more than a single main altar, two plans evolved for the east end of a church. At Modena, Italy, the

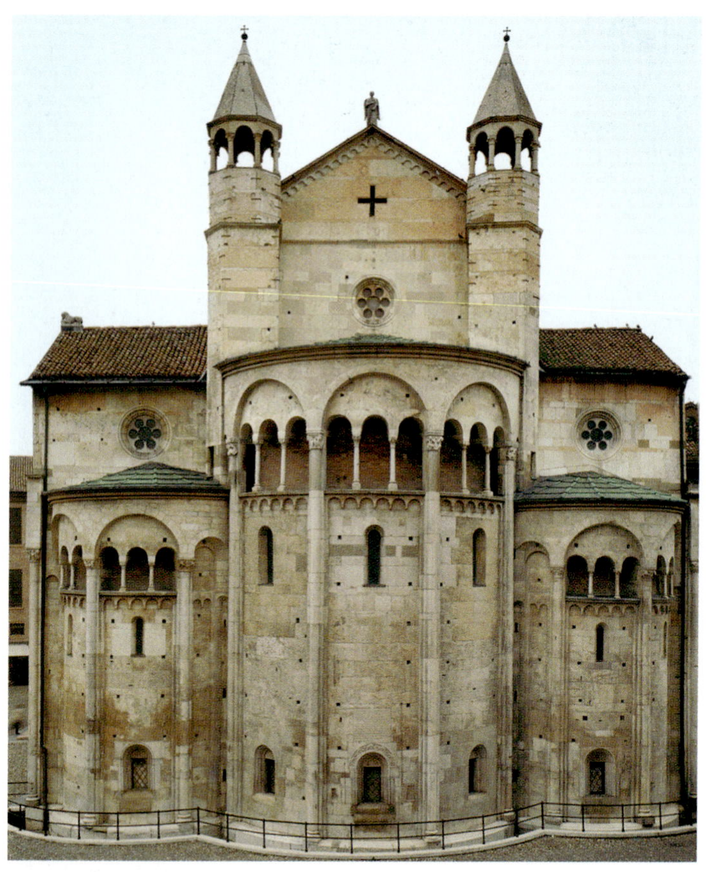

10–20 Modena Cathedral, view from east. Modena, Emilia, Italy. Building begun 1099, mainly 12th century

cathedral (fig. **10–20**) employed three apses at its east, or sanctuary, end. A large apse, housing the high altar at the end of the tall nave space, is flanked by smaller apses to each side. In this church horizontal arcades, or external galleries, composed of large arches enclosing three smaller arches, circle the exterior walls of all three apses, giving a geometric unity to the design at the same time as it distinguishes between major and subsidiary sanctuaries.

The second Romanesque plan responded not only to the need for additional altars for the clergy but also to the increasing demands on interior space for pilgrims venerating relics. Pilgrimage churches had to accommodate huge crowds and permit pilgrims to move from shrine to shrine. Additional altars and chapels were needed as collections of relics grew. Romanesque builders solved both objectives by adding chapels on the east side of a wide transept and by adding an ambulatory, or walkway, around the apse, encircled by chapels housing additional altars and relics (figs. **10–21** and **10–22**). This permitted pilgrims to circulate freely from chapel to chapel without disrupting regular church services in the main apse.

On entering a church like Santiago de Compostela, the viewer's attention is focused forward on the principal altar but is also drawn upward. Barrel vaults, whose strongly expressed transverse arches continue the vertical line of the piers, cover the high spaces of both nave and transepts (fig. **10–23**). Groin vaults cover the aisles, and in the upper-level galleries, half-barrel vaults (also called quadrant vaults) strengthen the building by countering the outward thrust of the high vaults and transferring it to the outer walls and buttresses.

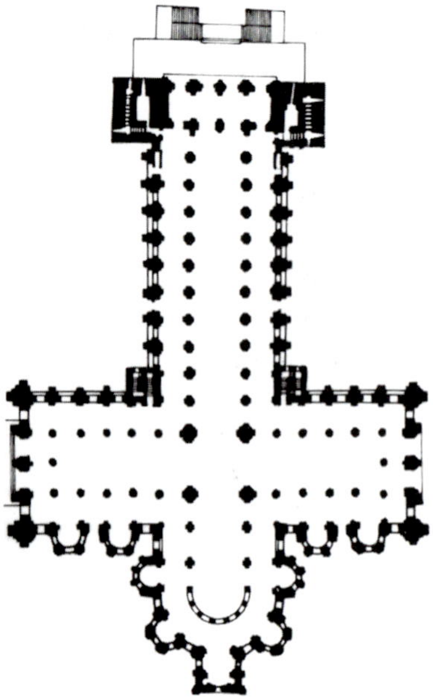

10–21 Plan of Cathedral of Saint James, Santiago de Compostela, Galicia, Spain. c. 1078–1122, with later additions

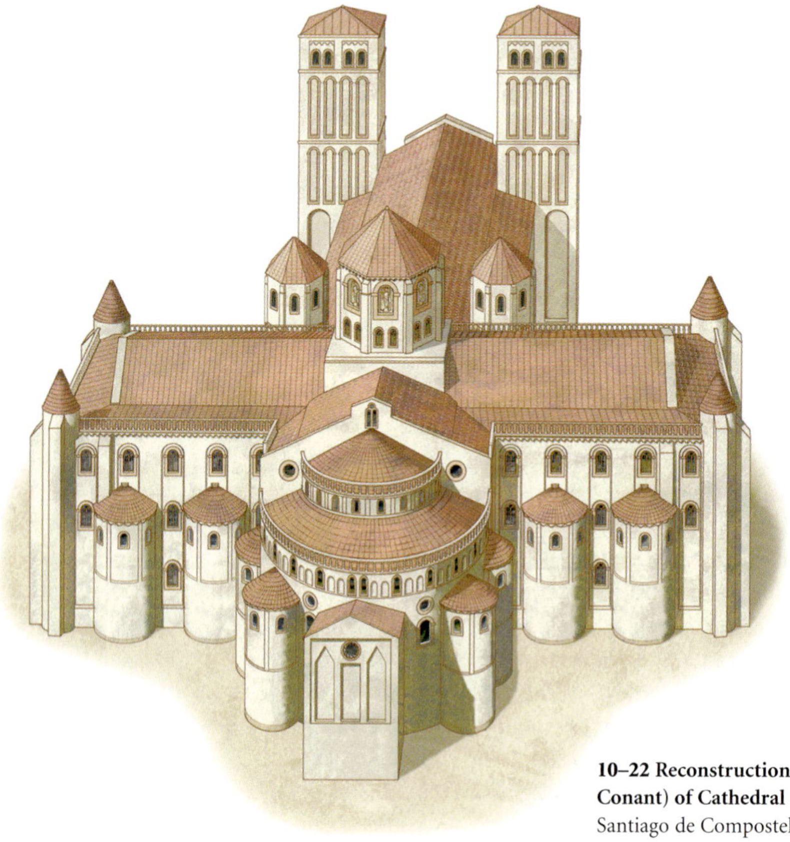

10–22 Reconstruction drawing (after Conant) of Cathedral of Saint James, Santiago de Compostela

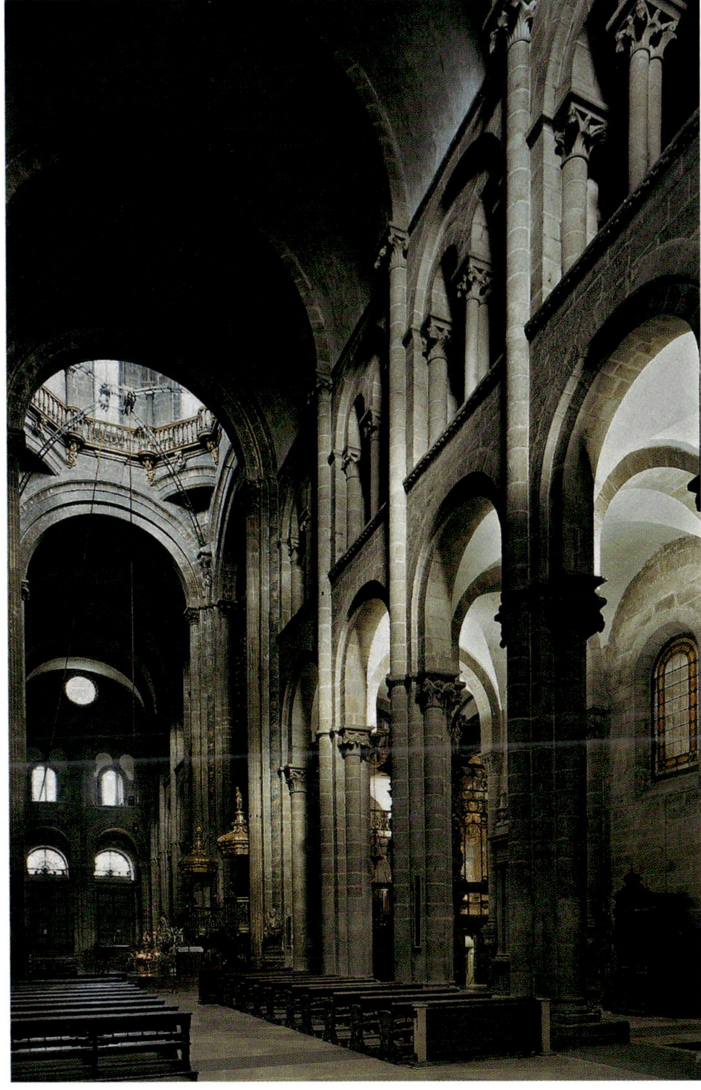

10–23 Transept, Cathedral of Saint James, Santiago de Compostela. Looking from the south transept portal toward the crossing. c. 1078–1122

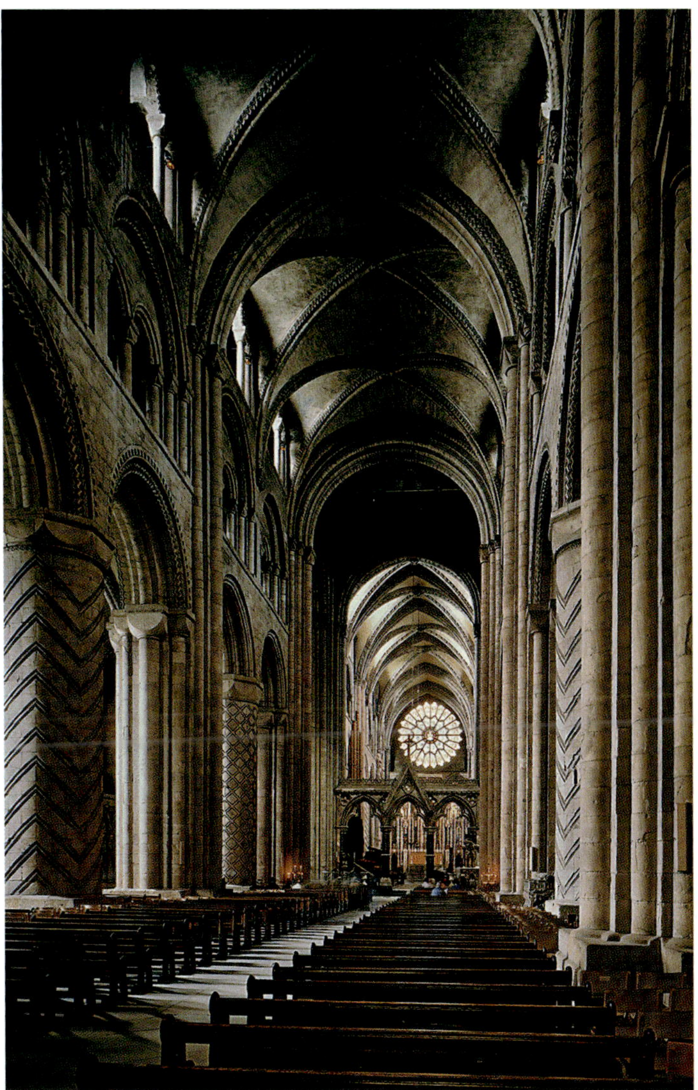

10–24 View from the west of nave and plan of Durham Cathedral. 1087–1133. Plan shows original choir, which was replaced in 1242–c. 1280. Vault height 73' (22.2 m)

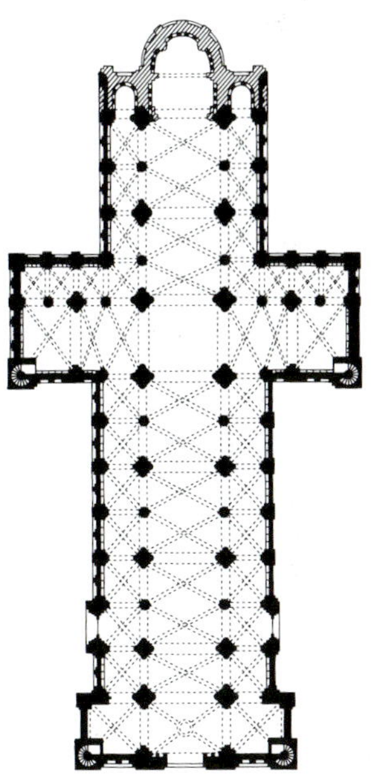

Above the church's square crossing, a windowed, octagonal lantern tower admits daylight as a beacon, directing the worshipers' attention toward the altar. Throughout the church, half-columns are attached to all four sides of the piers (for this reason they are known as **compound piers**). Working in concert with the transverse arches that punctuate the vaults, the compound piers divide the building into modular spatial units or bays. And the sculptural form they give to church interiors lent a sense of stability and monumentality to Romanesque architecture.

Builders working far to the north in Durham (fig. **10–24**) made what proved to be very significant advances in the Romanesque structural system. Strategically located on England's northern frontier with Scotland, after Duke William of Normandy's conquest of England in 1066, Durham grew into a fortified complex with a castle, cathedral, monastery, and village, over which the count-bishop held both secular and religious power. His cathedral is one of the most impressive of all medieval buildings as well as one of the most original.

Between 1093 and 1133, the Durham builders developed a new system of vaulting that was carried back to the Norman homeland in France. Massive compound piers alternate with chunky columnar piers to support the nave arcade, gallery, clerestory openings, and vaults. The round piers are carved with **chevrons** (zigzagging *V*s), spiral fluting, and diamond patterns, and topped by scalloped capitals. The ornamental effect was originally enhanced by painting. Above these decorative, but still sculptural, nave walls, the masons modified the Romanesque groin-vaulting system by applying two pairs of crisscrossing ribs within each long bay. The diagonal ribs create a complex but unifying pattern along the length of the nave, while the boldly projecting transverse arches that separate bay from bay continue the punctuation initiated below by the projecting half-columns of the compound piers. This rib vault and rectangular bay system was passed on as part of the Romanesque heritage of Gothic architecture.

Architectural Sculpture and Painting

Romanesque architectural sculpture was used primarily on the façade and entrance of a church and on the capitals of interior and exterior columns. Originally this sculpture was painted, and the interior walls of the churches were also frequently covered with paintings. Both sculpture and painting carried moralizing and inspirational messages. People arriving at the church, whether pilgrims from afar or members of the local parish or monastic community, must have stopped to contemplate the sculpture. At the beginning of the eleventh century, Bishop Bernward had used the bronze doors of his church at Hildesheim (see fig. 10–15) to embody theological truths. During the Romanesque period, the sculpture and painting on the walls of churches expanded the ability of buildings to proclaim religious messages.

The sculpture at Modena Cathedral is pervaded by the spirit of ancient Rome (fig. **10–25**). Horizontal bands of relief on the west façade are among the earliest narrative portal sculpture in Italy (c. 1099). An inscription reads: "Among sculptors, your work shines forth, Wiligelmus." Seemingly inspired by the style of antique sarcophagi, Wiligelmus took his subjects from the book of Genesis, focusing on events from the Creation to the Flood. This panel shows the *Creation and Fall of Adam and Eve.* On the far left is a half-length God with a cruciform halo, indicating two persons—Father and Son—framed by a mandorla (almond-shaped nimbus) supported by two angels. Following this iconic image, the narrative develops in three scenes from left to right: God creating Adam, then bringing Eve from Adam's side, and finally Adam and Eve covering themselves in shame as they greedily eat fruit from the forbidden tree, around which the wily serpent twists. Deft modeling and undercutting give these low-relief figures a strong three-dimensionality. The framing arcade establishes a stage-like spatial setting, with rock and tree serving as stage props. Wiligelmus's figures exude life and personality. They convey the emotional depth of the narrative they enact, and bright paint, now almost totally lost, must have increased their impact.

The **tympanum** (arched, half-circle) above the west portal of the Cathedral of Saint-Lazare at Autun in France greets visitors with a gripping portrayal of the Last Judgment (fig. **10–26**). A monumental Christ, enclosed in a mandorla held by two svelte angels, presides in judgment over the cowering, naked figures of the resurrected humans at his feet. To worshipers entering the church, the

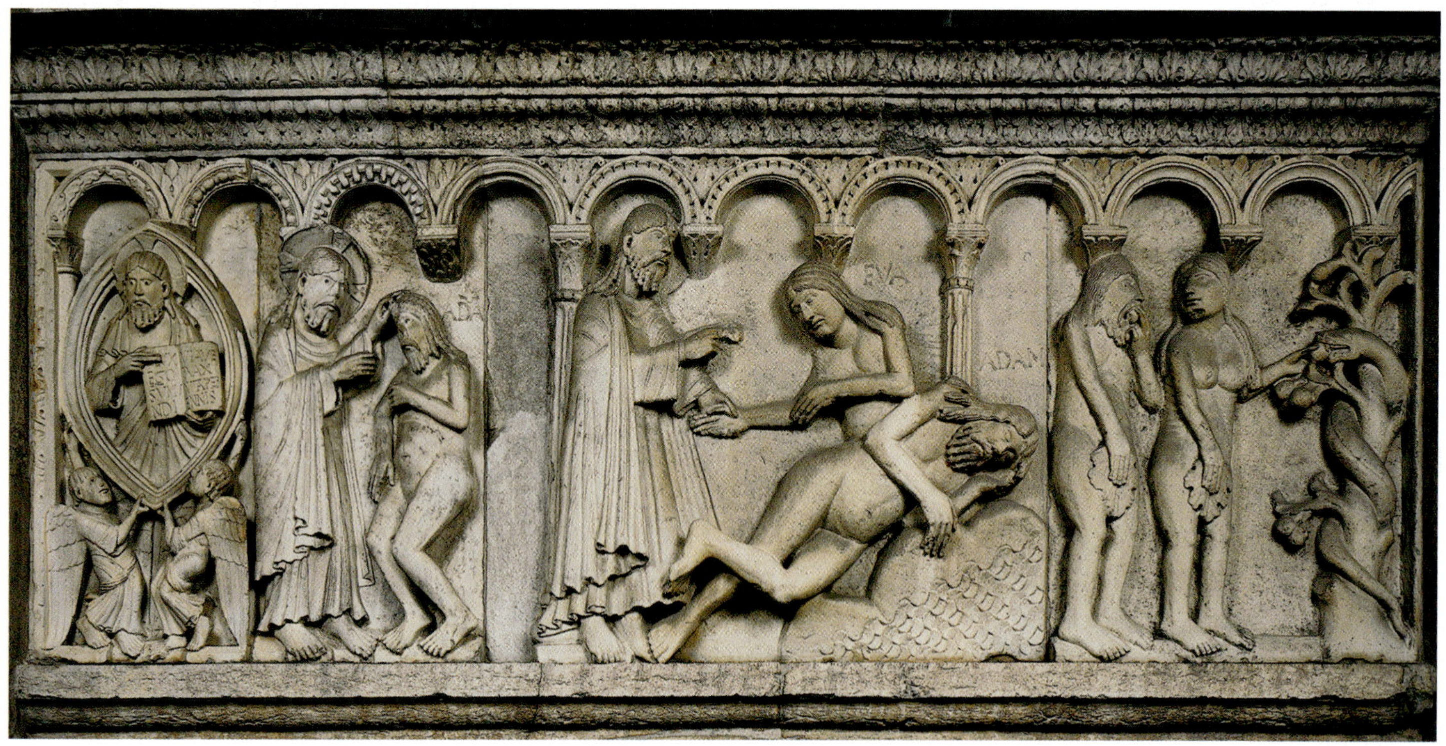

10–25 Wiligelmus. ***Creation and Fall of Adam and Eve.*** Modena Cathedral, west façade. c. 1099. Height approx. 3' (92 cm)

ELEMENTS OF **Architecture**

The Romanesque Church Portal

Portal sculpture (located around and above the main entrances) was one of the most notable features of Romanesque architecture. The most important carving was located on the lintel, the **tympanum** (the semicircular area above the door lintel), the **archivolts** (the moldings or blocks that follow the contour of the arch), and the **trumeau** (the central supporting post) and **jambs** (side posts) of the door.

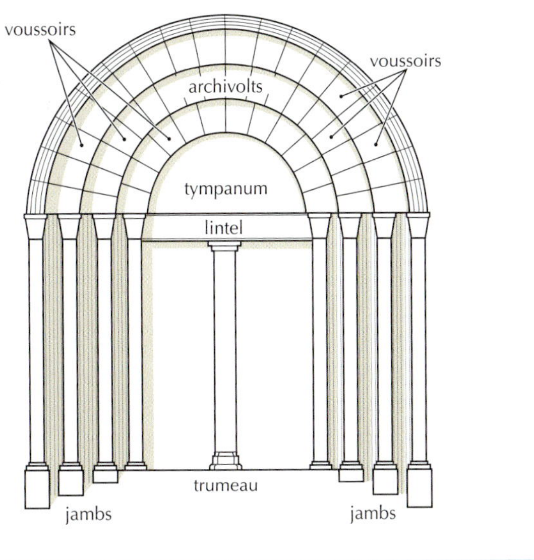

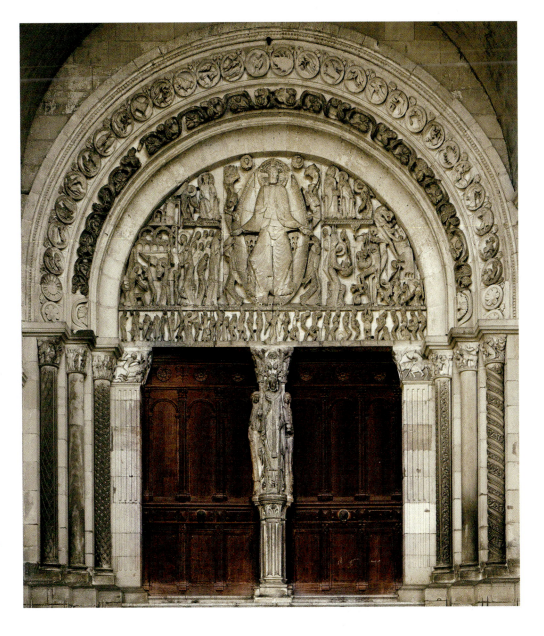

10–26 Gislebertus (?). *The Last Judgment*, west portal, Cathedral (originally Abbey Church) of Saint-Lazare, Autun, Burgundy, France. c. 1120–1130 or 1130–1145

An inscription just under the feet of the large figure of Christ at the center of this portal proclaims "Gislebertus hoc fecit" ("Gislebertus made this"). Traditionally, art historians have seen this as a rare instance of a twelfth-century artist's signature, assigning this façade and related sculpture to an individual named Gislebertus, who was at the head of a large workshop of sculptors. Recently, however, art historian Linda Seidel has challenged this reading of the inscription, arguing that Gislebertus was actually a late Carolingian count who had made significant donations to local churches. Like the names inscribed on many academic buildings of American universities, this legendary donor's name would have been evoked here as a reminder of the rich and long history of secular financial support in Autun, and perhaps also as a challenge to those currently in power to respect and continue that venerable tradition of patronage themselves.

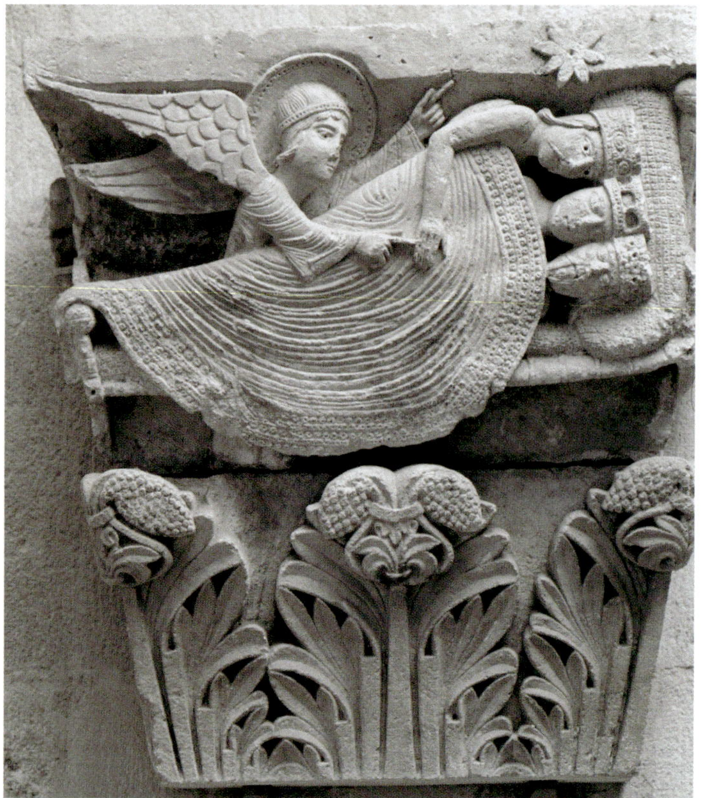

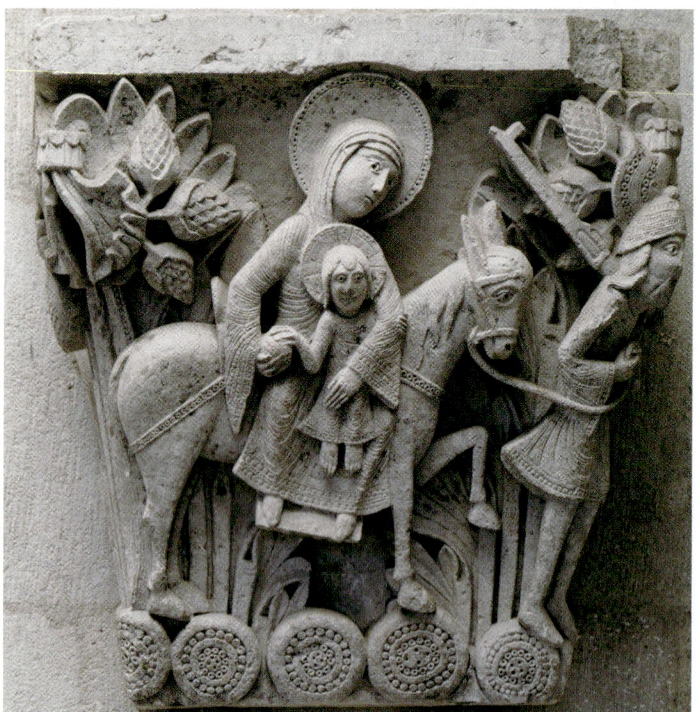

10–27 *The Magi Asleep* and *The Flight into Egypt*, two capitals from the choir, Cathedral of Saint-Lazare, Autun. c. 1125

The decorative wheel forms that appear under the feet of the donkey in the Flight into Egypt *are probably a reference to the rolling wooden statues used as props in liturgical dramas that would have been performed in Romanesque churches.*

message is clear. The damned writhe in torment on Christ's left (the "sinister" side, on the viewer's right) while the saved reach toward an architectural vision of heaven on Christ's right. Since the scene is filled with human interest, viewers can easily project themselves into what is going on. On the lintel, angels physically assist those rising from their sarcophagi, while a pair of giant, pincer-like hands descends aggressively at the right to snatch one of the damned directly into hell. Above these hands, the archangel Michael competes with devils for the souls of those weighed on the scales of good and evil. One of the risen has climbed to the top of the scale, hand raised to his face to project his pleas to Christ for help; another hides in the hems of the archangel's long robes, hoping to avoid judgment. By far the most riveting players in this drama are the wild, grotesque, screaming demons who grab and torment the damned and even try, in vain, to cheat by yanking the scales to favor damnation.

The creation of lively narrative scenes within the geometric confines of capitals (called **historiated capitals**) was an important Romanesque innovation in architectural sculpture. The same sculptors who worked on the Autun tympanum carved historiated capitals for pier pilasters inside the church. These two (fig. **10–27**) depict scenes from the childhood of Jesus drawn from Matthew 2:1–18. In one capital, the Magi—who have previously adored and offered gifts to the child Jesus—are interrupted in their sleep by an angel who warns them not to stop by on their way home to inform King Herod of the location of the newborn King of the Jews. In an ingenious compositional device, the sculptor has shown the reclining Magi and the head of their bed as if viewed from above, whereas the angel and the foot of the bed are viewed from the side. This allows us to see clearly the angel—who is appearing to them in a dream—as it touches the hand of the upper magus, whose eyes have suddenly popped open. As on the façade, the sculptor has conceived this scene in ways that emphasize the human qualities of its story, not its deep theological significance. With its charming, doll-like figures, the other capital shows an event that occurred just after the dream of the Magi: Joseph, Mary, and Jesus are journeying toward Egypt to escape the paranoid King Herod's order to murder all young boys to eliminate the young royal rival the Magi had journeyed to venerate.

Much as we admire the fine masonry of walls laid bare by centuries of the neglect or ill-advised cleaning of Romanesque churches, we must remember that people in the Middle Ages expected their churches to be filled with colorful and meaningful paintings, mosaics, or textiles. In an apse painting from the Church of San Climent in Taull (fig. **10–28**), in the Catalunyan Pyrenees of northern Spain, the Romanesque artist has almost re-created a Byzantine Pantokrator—Christ as ruler and judge of the world. Byzantine features include the modeling of forms through the use of repeated colored lines of varying width and shades, and such iconographical features as the alpha and omega (the first and last letters of the Greek alphabet) and the depiction of Christ holding a book inscribed in Latin, *ego sum lux mundi* ("I am the light of the world"; John 8:12). But the painter adapts the Byzantine style to the local taste for geometry and ornamental form, turning facial features and draperies into elegant patterns. And the background of wide stripes of color recalls earlier Spanish Beatus manuscripts (see fig. 10–13).

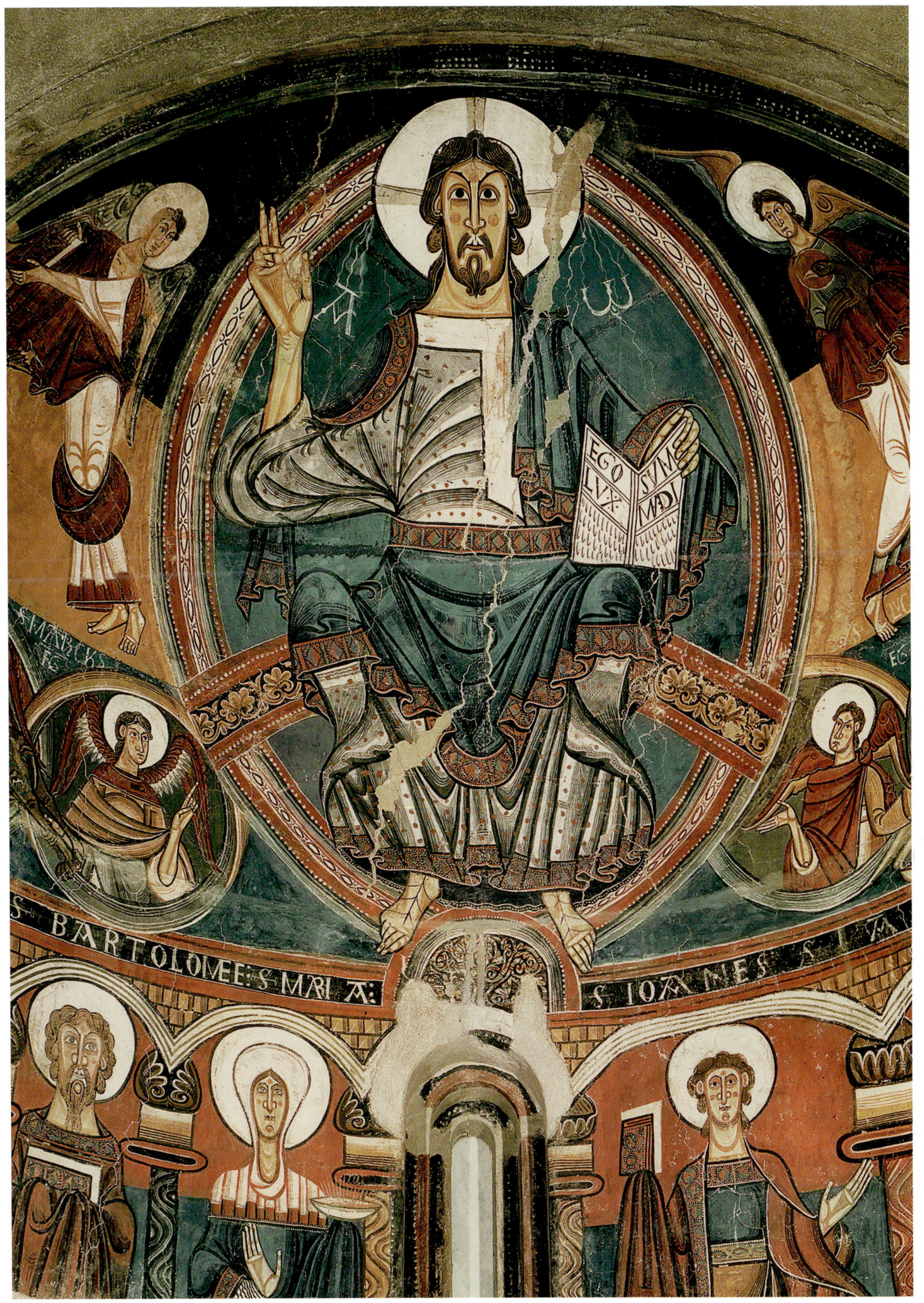

10–28 ***Christ in Majesty***, detail of apse painting from the Church of San Climent, Taull, Catalunya, Spain. c. 1123. Museu Nacional d'Art de Catalunya, Barcelona

CLOSER LOOK

Rarely has art spoken more vividly than in this strip of embroidered linen that recounts the history of the Norman conquest of England in 1066 with a staggering number of images (e.g., fig. **10–29**). In the 50 surviving scenes are more than 600 human figures, 700 horses, dogs, and other creatures, and 2,000 inch-high letters.

Although traditionally referred to as the Bayeux Tapestry, it should be called the Bayeux Embroidery. In **tapestry**, the colored threads that form the patterns, or pictures, are woven in during the process of making the fabric itself; **embroidery** consists of stitches applied on top of an already-woven fabric ground. The embroiderers, probably Anglo-Saxon women, worked in tightly twisted wool that was dyed in eight colors. They used only two stitches: the quick, overlapping stem stitch that produced a slightly jagged line or outline (e.g., the letters in fig. **10–30**), and the time-consuming laid-and-couched work used to form blocks of color. For the latter, the embroiderer first "laid" a series of long, parallel covering threads; then anchored them with a second layer of regularly spaced crosswise stitches; and finally tacked all the strands down with tiny "couching" stitches. Some of the laid-and-couched work was done in contrasting colors to achieve particular effects. The creative coloring is often fanciful; for example, some horses have legs in four different colors. Skin and other light-toned areas were represented by the bare linen cloth that formed the ground of the work.

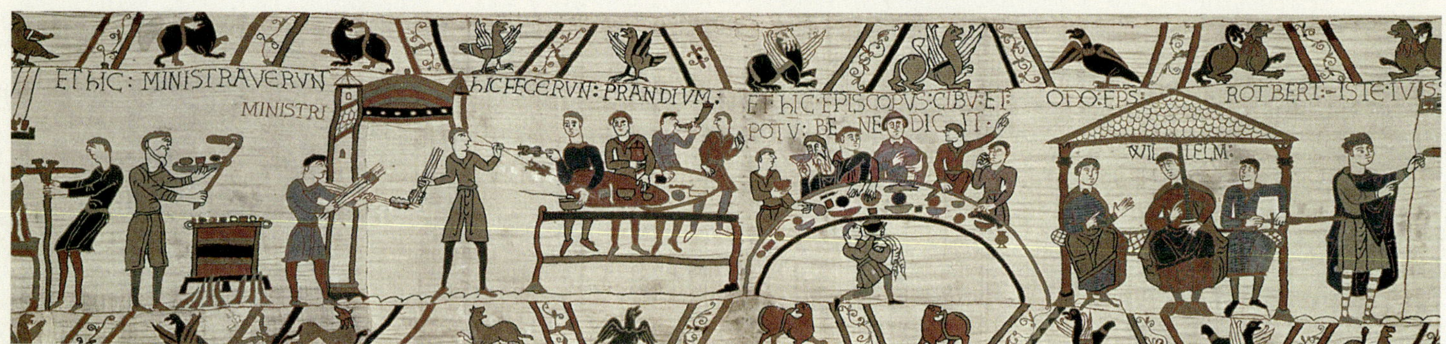

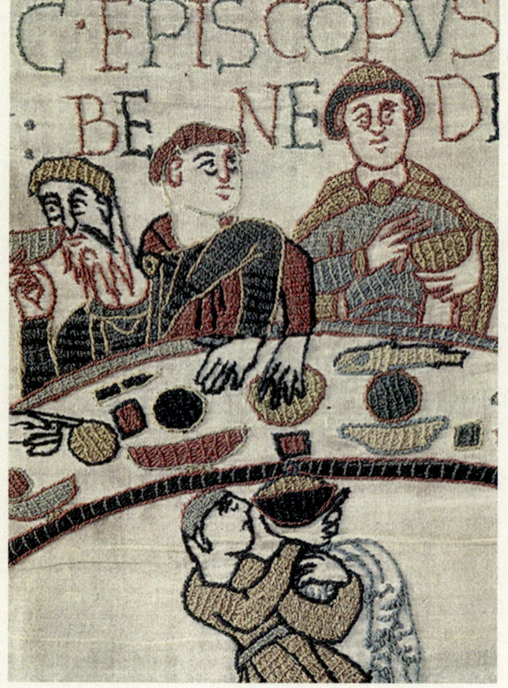

10–29 (ABOVE) ***Bishop Odo Blessing the Feast***, from the Bayeux Embroidery, Norman–Anglo-Saxon embroidery from England or France. c. 1066–1082. Linen with wool, height 20" (50.8 cm). Centre Guillaume le Conquérant, Bayeux, France

Odo and William are feasting before the battle. Attendants bring in roasted birds on skewers, placing them on a makeshift table made of the knights' shields set on trestles. The diners, summoned by the blowing of a horn, gather at a curved table laden with food and drink. Bishop Odo—seated at the center, head and shoulders above William to his right—blesses the meal while others eat. The kneeling servant in the middle proffers a basin and towel so that the diners may wash their hands. The man on Odo's left points impatiently to the next event, a council of war between William (now the central and tallest figure), Odo, and a third man labeled "Rotbert," probably Robert of Mortain, another of William's half-brothers.

*Translation of text: "...and here the servants (*ministra*) perform their duty./Here they prepare the meal (*prandium*)/and here the bishop blesses the food and drink (*cibu et potu*). Bishop Odo. William. Robert."*

10–30 (LEFT) **Detail of *Odo Blessing*** in fig. 10–29

Manuscripts, Textiles, and Woodcarving

Among the most admired arts during the Middle Ages are those that later critics patronizingly called the "decorative arts." Although small in scale, these works are often produced with very precious materials, and they were vital to the Christian mission and devotion of the institutions that housed them.

Artists in the eleventh and twelfth centuries were still often monks and nuns. They labored within monasteries as calligraphers and painters in the scriptorium to produce books and as metalworkers to craft the enamel-, and jewel-encrusted works used in liturgical services. And they embroidered the vestments, altar coverings, and wall hangings that clothed both celebrants and settings in the Mass. Increasingly, however, secular urban workshops supplied the aristocratic and royal courts with textiles, tableware, books, and weapons, as well as occasional donations to religious institutions.

Elaborate textiles, including embroideries and tapestries, enhanced a noble's status and were thus necessary features in castles and palaces. The Bayeux Embroidery is one of the earliest examples to have survived. This long narrative strip chronicles the events leading to Duke William of Normandy's conquest of England in 1066. Figure **10–29** shows William and his brothers Odo (Bishop of Bayeux 1049–1097) and Robert, feasting with the Norman troops before the battle. The images depicted on this long embroidered band may have been drawn by a Norman participant, since there is a clear Norman bias in the telling of the story, but style suggests that it may have been Anglo-Saxons who did the actual embroidery. This work represents the kind of secular art that must once have been part of most royal courts. It could be rolled up and transported from residence to residence as the noble Norman owner traveled throughout his domain, and some have speculated that it may have been the backdrop at banquets for stories sung by professional performers who could have received their cues from the identifying descriptions that accompany most scenes. Eventually the Embroidery was given to Bayeux Cathedral, perhaps by Bishop Odo, William's brother; we know it was displayed around the walls of the cathedral on the feast of the relics.

Another Romanesque chronicle is the earliest known illustrated history book: the *Worcester Chronicle* (fig. **10–31**), written in the twelfth century by a monk named John. The pages shown here concern Henry I (ruled 1100–1135), the second of William the

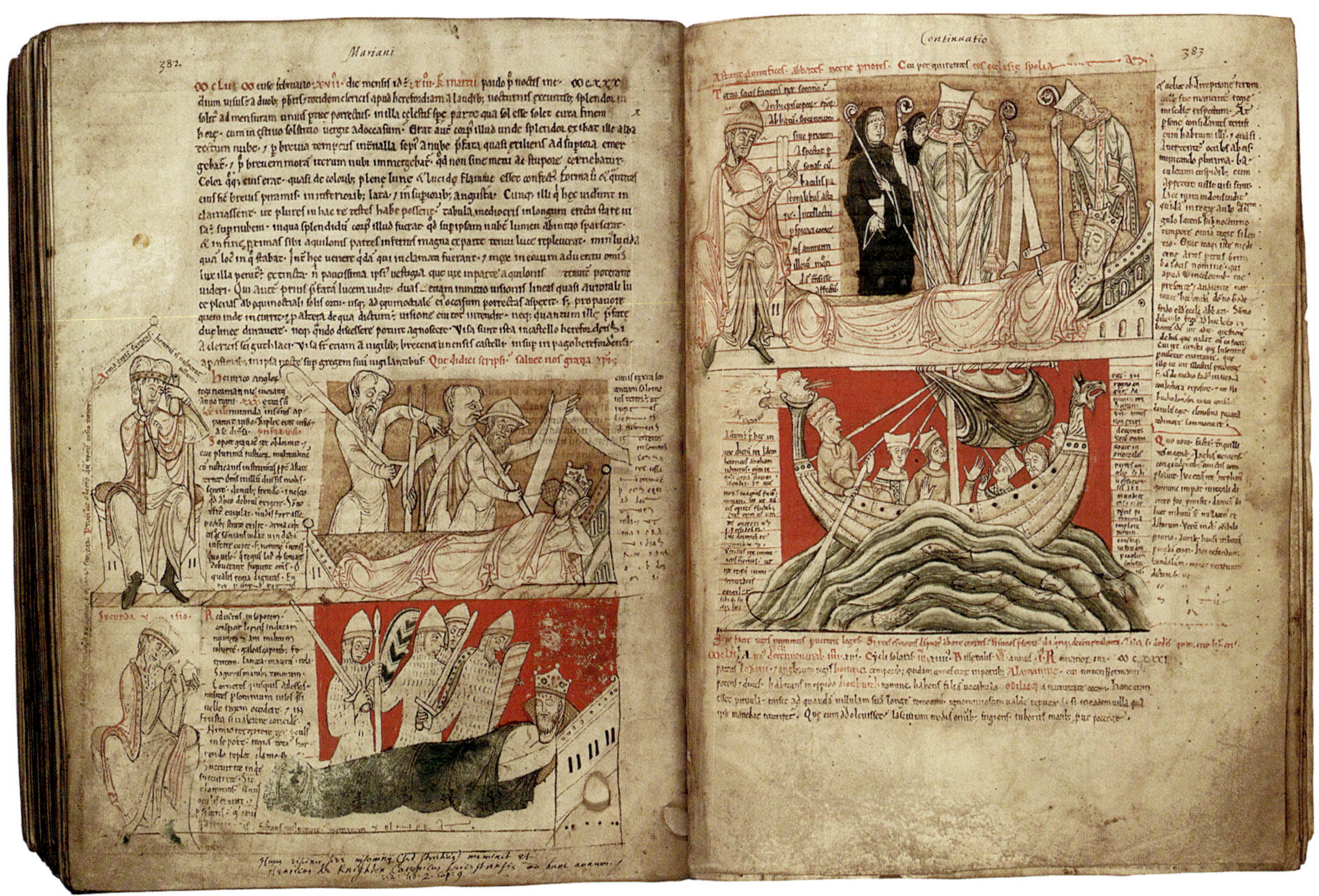

10–31 John of Worcester. Pages with *Dream of Henry I, Worcester Chronicle*, Worcester, England. c. 1140.
Ink and tempera on vellum, 12¾" × 9⅜" (32.5 × 23.7 cm). Each page Corpus Christi College, Oxford

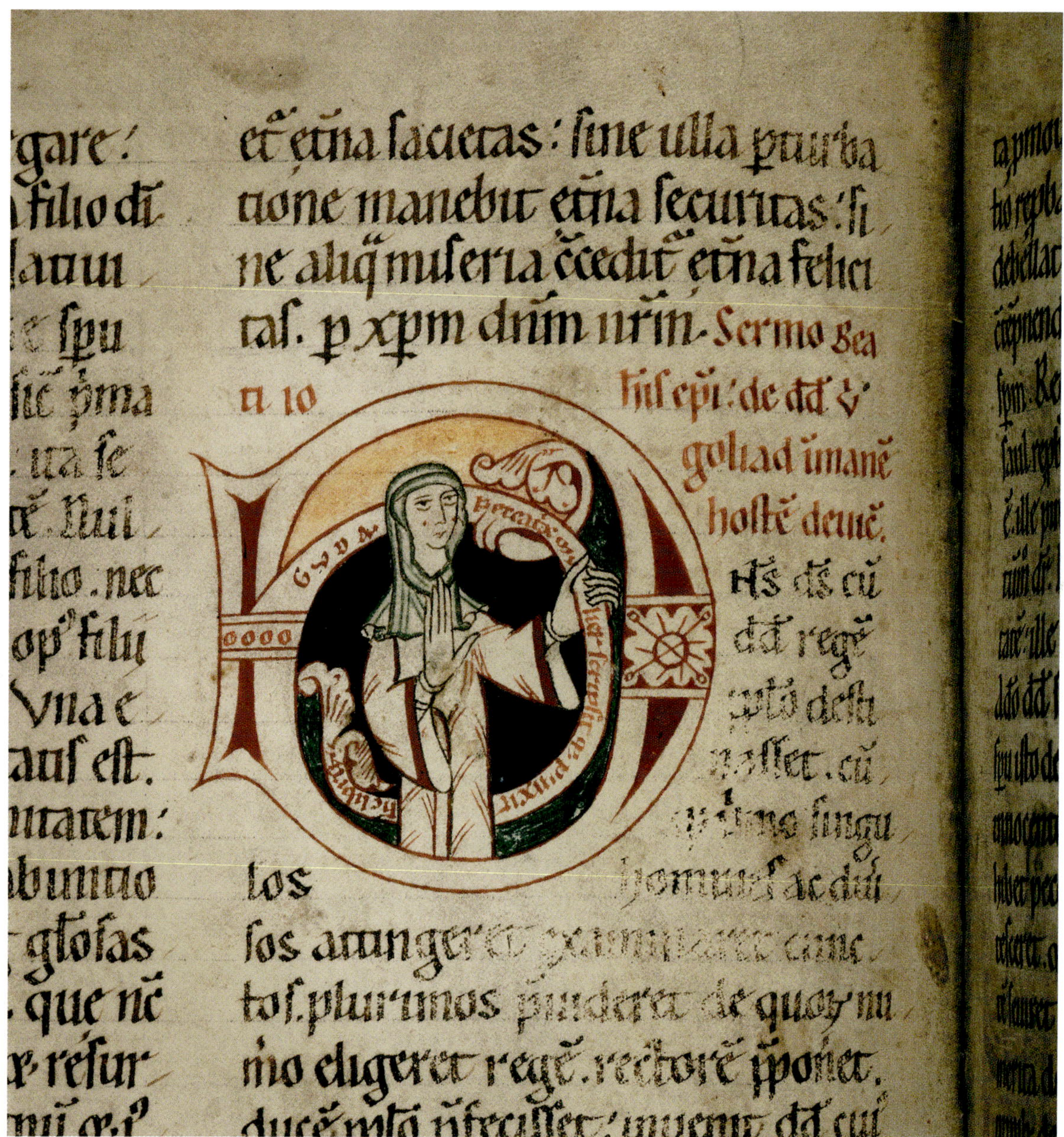

10–32 Self-portrait of Guda, from a *Book of Homilies*. Early 12th century. Ink on parchment. Stadtund Universitätsbibliothek Frankfurt, Germany (MS Barth. 42, fol. 110v)

Conqueror's sons to sit on the English throne. The text relates a series of dreams the king had in 1130, in which his subjects demanded tax relief, and the artist has portrayed these dreams with energetic directness. On the first night, angry farmers confront the sleeping king; on the second, armed knights surround his bed; and on the third, monks, abbots, and bishops present their case. In the fourth illustration, the king travels in a storm-tossed ship and saves himself by promising God that he will rescind the tax increase for seven years. The author of the *Worcester Chronicle* assured his readers that this story came from a reliable source, the royal physician Grimbald, who appears in the margins next to three of the scenes. The angry farmers capture our attention today because we seldom see working men with their equipment and simple clothing depicted in painting from this time. Although chancery (government) scriptoria existed, it was in monastic scriptoria that most books were produced. While we often study the most spectacularly beautiful manuscripts, the majority of books were functional items with few or no illustrations.

In the Romanesque period, as earlier in the Middle Ages, women were involved in the production of books as authors, scribes, painters, and patrons. A Spanish nun named Ende signed a tenth-century manuscript of Beatus' commentaries on the Apocalypse with the words "painter and servant of God." As we have seen, the eleventh-century Abbess Hitda (see fig. 10–17) had been a patron. Working in the early twelfth century, the nun Guda, from Westphalia, was both a scribe and painter. In a book of homilies (sermons), Guda inserted her self-portrait into the letter D and signed the image "Guda, a sinful woman, wrote and illuminated this book" (fig. **10–32**). Guda and her monastic sisters played an important role in the production of books in the twelfth century, and this image is the earliest signed self-portrait by a woman in Western Europe.

HILDEGARD OF BINGEN

We might expect women to have a subordinate position in the hierarchical and militaristic society of the twelfth century. On the contrary, aristocratic women took responsibility for managing estates during their male relatives' frequent absences during wars or while serving at court. And women also achieved positions of authority and influence as the heads of religious communities. Notable among them was Hildegard of Bingen (1098–1179). Born into an aristocratic German family, Hildegard transcended the barriers that limited most medieval women. She began serving as leader of her convent in 1136, and about 1147 she founded a new convent near Bingen. Hildegard also wrote important treatises on medicine and natural science, invented an alternate alphabet, and was one of the most gifted and innovative composers of her age, writing not only motets and liturgical settings, but also a musical drama that is considered by many to be the first opera. Clearly a major, multitalented figure in the intellectual and artistic life of her time—comparison with the later Leonardo da Vinci is almost unavoidable—she also corresponded with emperors, popes, and the powerful abbots Bernard of Clairvaux and Suger of Saint-Denis.

Following a command she received from God in 1141, and with the assistance of her nuns and the monk Volmar, Hildegard began to record the mystical visions she had been experiencing since she was five years old. The resulting book, called the *Scivias* (from the Latin *scite vias lucis*, "know the ways of the light"), is filled not only with words but with striking images of the strange and wonderful visions themselves. The opening page (fig. **10–33**) shows Hildegard receiving a flash of divine insight, represented by the tongues of flame encircling her head—she wrote, "a fiery light, flashing intensely, came from the open vault of heaven and poured through my whole brain"—while her scribe Volmar writes to her dictation. But was she also responsible for the arresting pictures that accompany the text in this book? Art historian Madeline Caviness thinks so. Perhaps Hildegard is using the large stylus to sketch on the wax tablets in her lap the pictures of her visions that were meant to accompany the verbal descriptions she dictates to Volmar, who sits at the right with a book in his hand, ready to write them down.

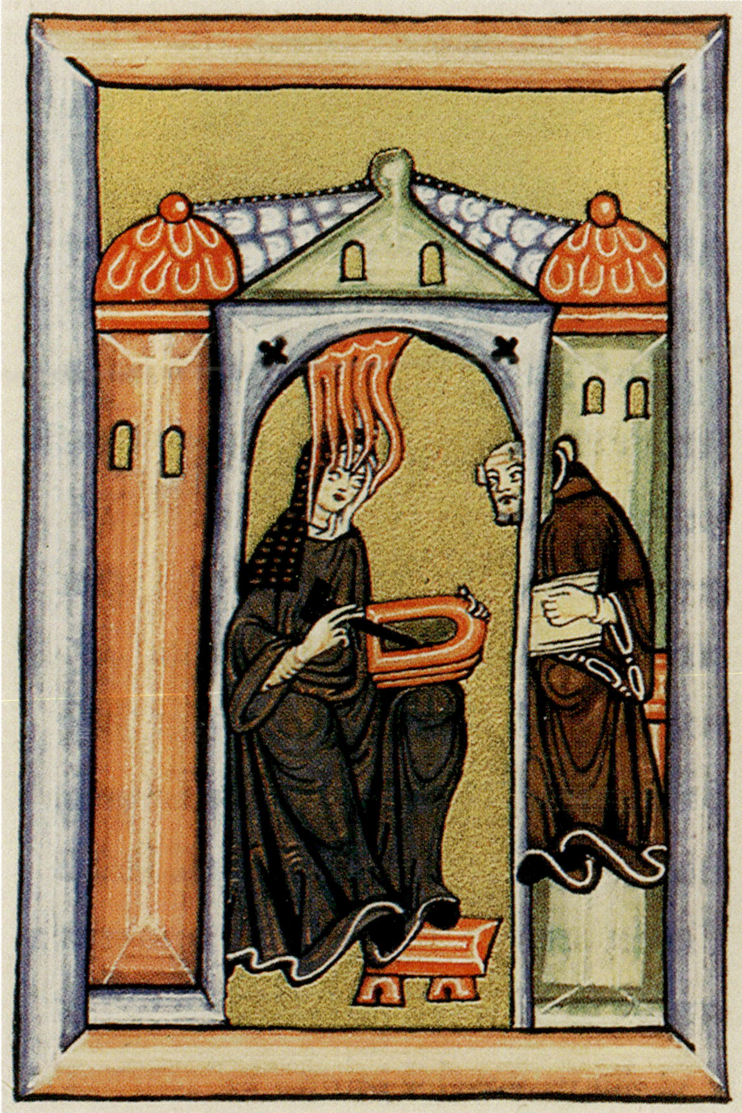

10–33 *Hildegard and Volmar*, from a facsimile of the frontispiece of the *Liber Scivias* of Hildegard of Bingen. Original, c. 1150–1175

This author portrait was once part of a manuscript of Hildegard's Scivias *that many believe was made during her own lifetime, but it was lost during World War II. Today we can study its images only from black-and-white photographs or from a full-color facsimile copy that was lovingly hand-painted by nuns in 1923–1933, the source of the figure reproduced here.*

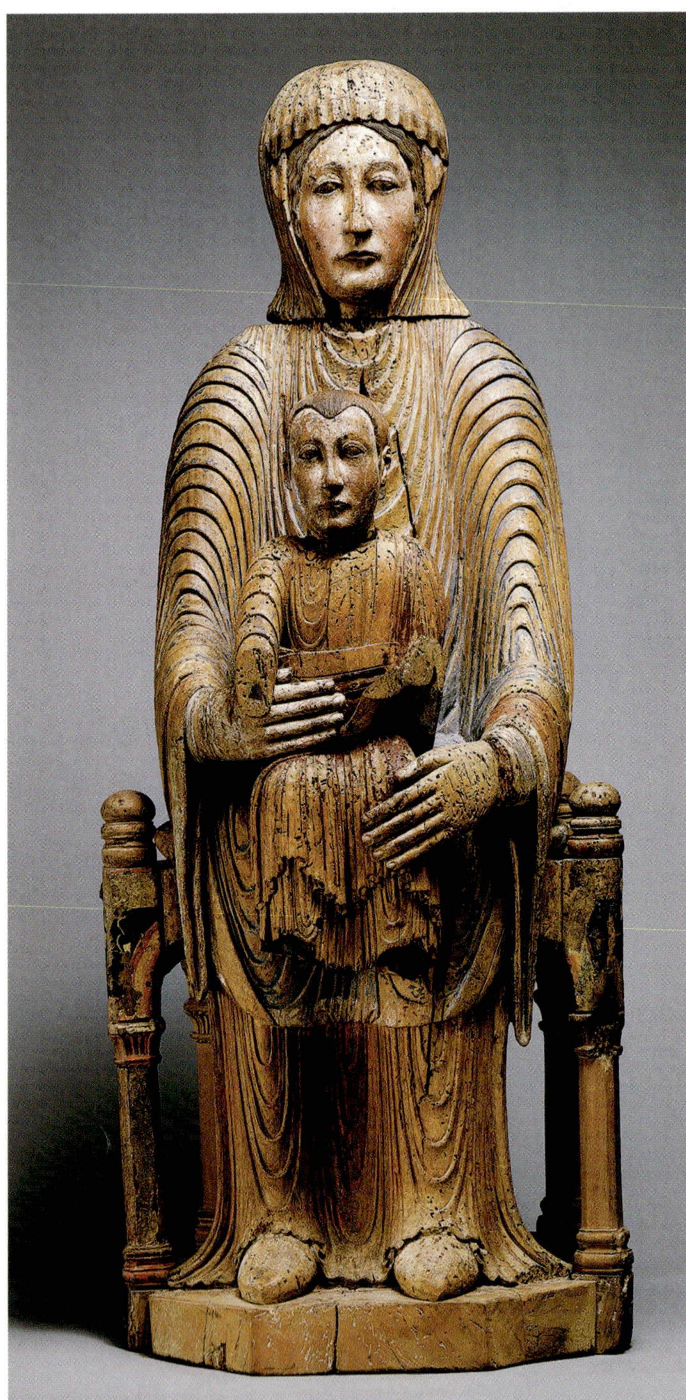

10–34 ***Virgin and Child***, from Auvergne region, France. Late 12th century. Oak with polychromy, height 31" (78.7 cm). The Metropolitan Museum of Art, New York
GIFT OF J. PIERPONT MORGAN, 1916 (16.32.194)

Since only the wealthiest churches could afford works in precious metals and jewels, wooden sculpture often satisfied the need for devotional images. Statues of the Virgin Mary holding the Christ Child on her lap, a type known as the Throne of Wisdom, became increasingly popular (fig. **10–34**). Here, Mary is seated on a throne-like bench symbolizing the throne of Solomon, the biblical king who most symbolized wisdom. She supports Jesus securely with both hands, and together the regal pair is posed frontally and rigidly. Jesus once held a book—scriptural wisdom—in his left hand and raised his right hand in blessing. For the medieval believer, the wisdom of God became human in Christ; in the medieval scholar's language, he is the Word incarnate. Mary represented the Church, as well as the earthly mother who gave Jesus his human nature and the throne on which he sits in majesty. As a fourteenth-century member of the clergy would write, "the throne of the true Solomon is the Most Blessed Virgin Mary, in which sat Jesus Christ, the true Wisdom" (trans. Forsyth, page 27).

Looking Back

As the political order of the Western Roman Empire disintegrated, the Christian Church assumed an ever-greater social and intellectual, as well as spiritual role in Western Europe. Christian bishops replaced Roman provincial governors as sources of political power; monasteries grew mightily in importance; and the pope emerged as the supreme leader of the Western Church. Although the empire itself was no longer a vital entity, the idea of imperial Rome—both as a secular empire and as the headquarters of the Christian Church—remained strong in people's minds. For example, as Charlemagne gained power and founded a Frankish dynasty, he allied himself with the pope, and used the emulation of Roman forms of art and architecture to proclaim his newly acquired status as emperor. In Carolingian art, ancient Classical forms blended with the Celtic and Germanic styles of the former barbarians, leading to the development of a new narrative and figurative art that was also richly decorative and expressive.

Christians had long used art to glorify God and convey religious ideas and ideals, and during the Romanesque period the practice blossomed into monumental sculpture and painting integrated into buildings of conspicuous scale and daring structural experimentation. Eleventh- and twelfth-century artists—men and women whose names were mostly unnoted by the historical record—worked in a variety of media and continually developed new forms of artistic expression. Although they made most of their works for religious contexts, their focus was on human beings, their stories and struggles, their fears and beliefs. In doing so they were not only satisfying the desires of patrons and viewers of their own time; they were also laying the groundwork for the Gothic art that was to follow.

IN PERSPECTIVE

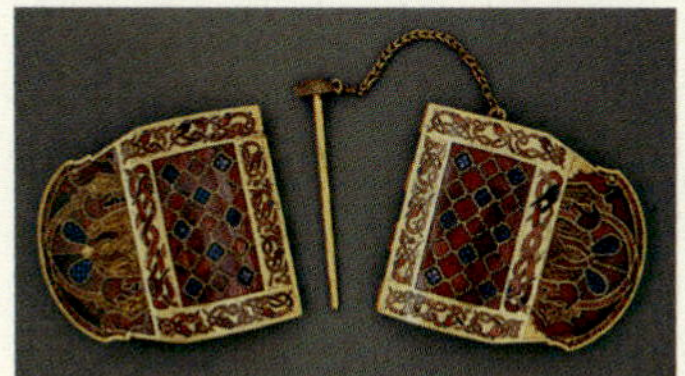
SUTTON HOO CLASP, FIRST HALF OF THE 7TH CENTURY

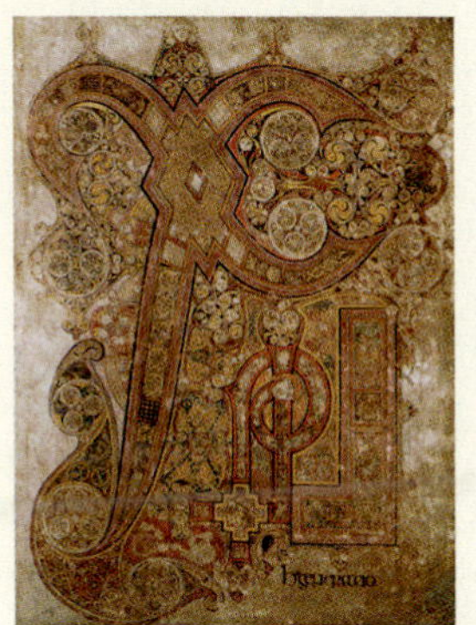
BOOK OF KELLS, c. 800

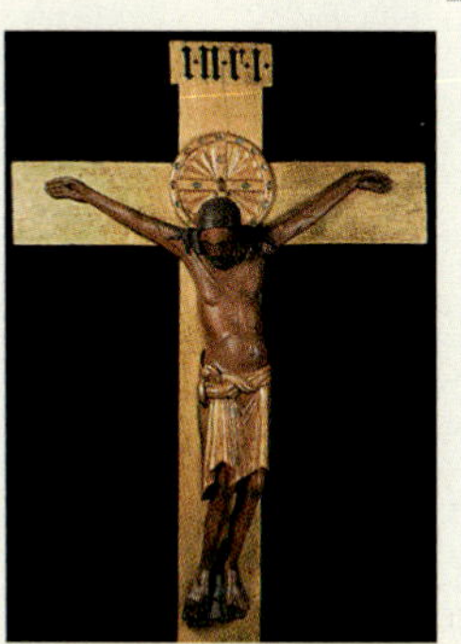
GERO CRUCIFIX, c. 970

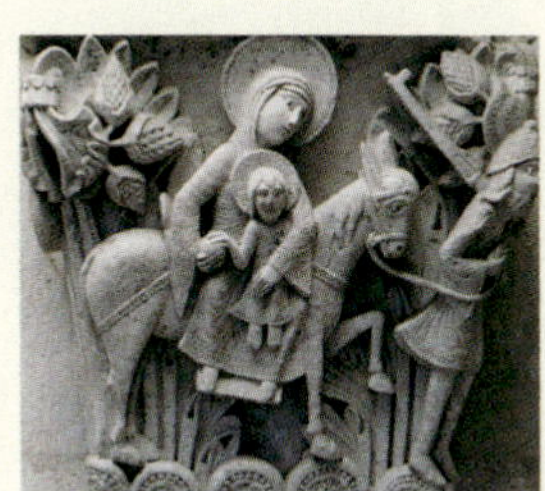
FLIGHT INTO EGYPT, c. 1125

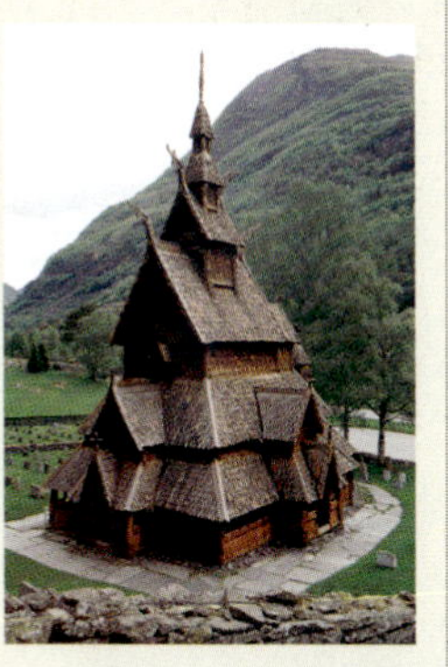
BORGUND STAVE CHURCH, c. 1125–1150

500

- **Saint Patrick in Ireland,** c. 433–461
- **Rule of Saint Benedict,** c. 530
- **Visigoths in Spain adopt Christianity,** c. 589

700

- **Islamic Conquest of Spain,** 711
- **Viking Raids Begin,** 793
- **Charlemagne Crowned Emperor by the Pope in Rome,** 800 (empire lasts until 887)

900

- **Ottonian Empire,** c. 919–1024
- **Viking Settlement in North America,** 1000
- **William of Normandy Invades England,** 1066
- **First Crusade,** 1095–1099

1100

- **Cistercian Order Founded,** 1098
- **Hildegard of Bingen Writes and Illustrates *Scivias*,** c. 1141–1151
- **Second Crusade,** 1147–1149

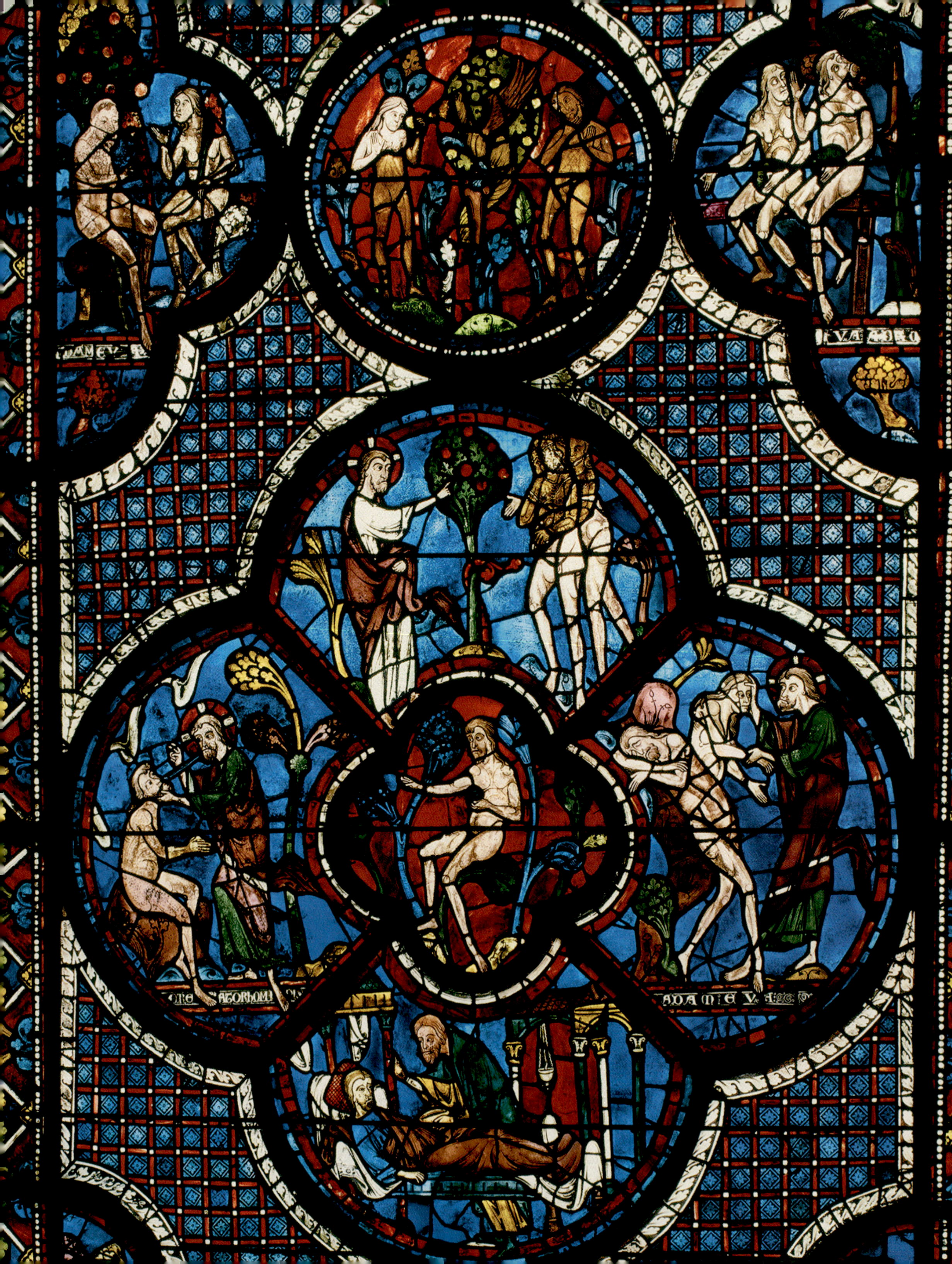

11
Gothic Art

LOOKING FORWARD

Gothic dominated the aesthetic life of Europe for 400 years. By the mid-twelfth century, advances in building technology, increasing material resources, and new intellectual and spiritual aspirations led to the development of a new art and architecture that expressed the religious and political values of the Christian community. Bishops, abbots, and rulers vied to build the largest and most elaborate churches. Just as residents of twentieth-century American cities raced to erect higher and higher skyscrapers, so too the patrons of medieval Western Europe competed in the building of cathedrals and churches with ever taller naves and towers, walls of glowing glass, and breathtakingly open interiors. Light passing through stained-glass windows not only created luminous pictures; it also changed the interior into a many-colored haze. Walls, objects, and even people seemed to dissolve—dematerializing into color. Truly, churches became the glorious jeweled houses of God, evocations of the Heavenly Jerusalem.

Suger (1081–1151), abbot of the Benedictine Abbey of Saint-Denis near Paris, wrote of his experience rebuilding his abbey church, the building project that initiated the Gothic style. He described the way light facilitated his and his monks' spiritual journey, but the innovative work of his builders led to the widespread use of large stained-glass windows in all sorts of churches. Almost overnight, stained glass became the major medium of monumental painting.

This detail from the Good Samaritan Window at Chartres Cathedral (fig. **11–1**), created over half a century after Suger's Saint-Denis, includes scenes from Genesis portraying the creation of Adam and Eve, as well as their subsequent temptation, fall from Grace, and expulsion from Paradise. Adam and Eve's story is used here to interpret the meaning of the parable of the Good Samaritan, reminding us that such windows were more than glowing walls activated by color and light. They were also luminous sermons, preached with pictures rather than with words, and directed at a diverse audience of worshipers drawn from a broad spectrum of medieval society.

11–1 Scenes from Genesis in the Good Samaritan Window, nave aisle, Cathedral of Notre-Dame, Chartres, France. c. 1200–1210. Stained and painted glass

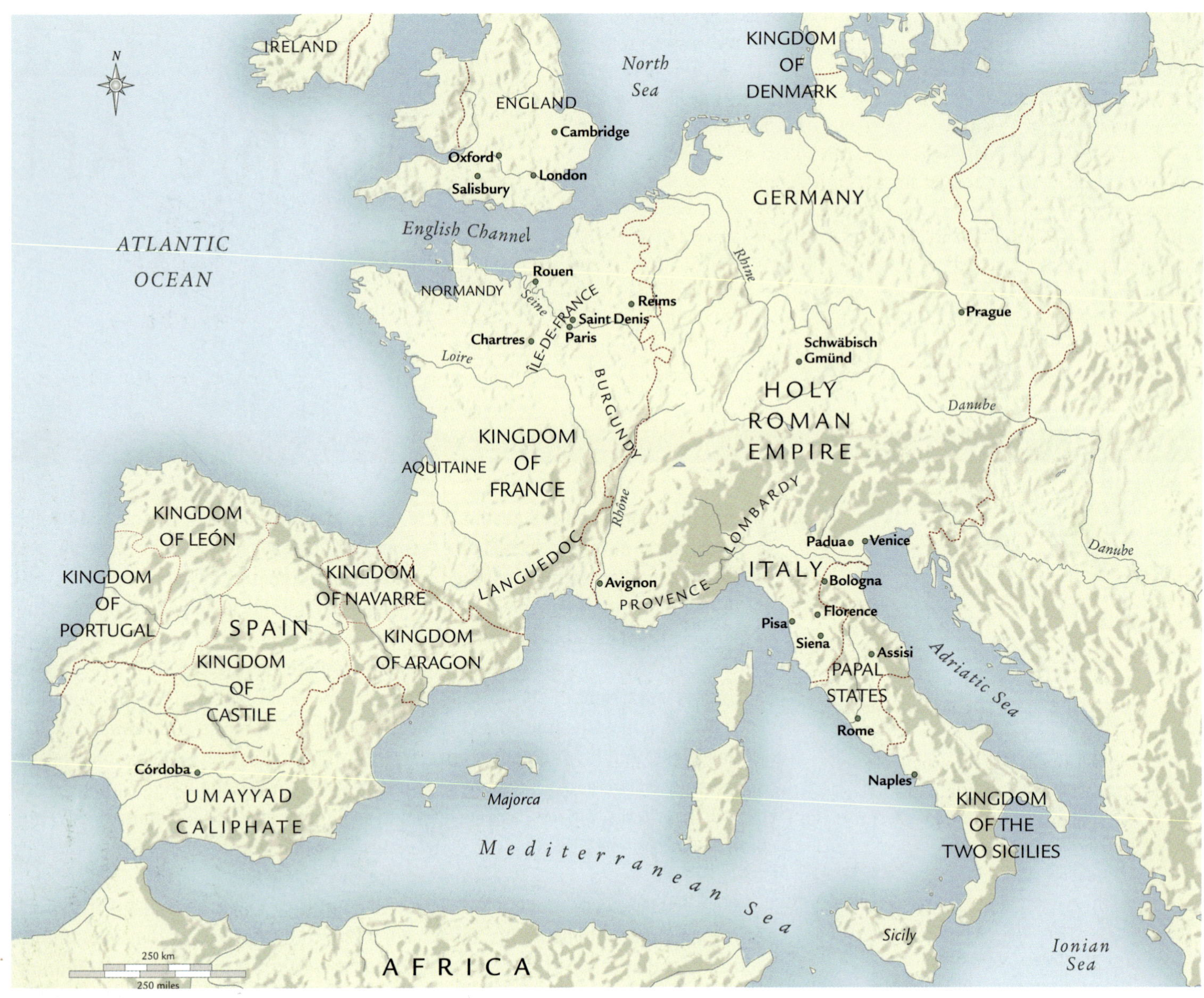

Map 11–1 Gothic Europe Around 1200

In the middle of the twelfth century, a distinctive new architecture known today as Gothic emerged in the Île-de-France, the French king's domain around Paris, coincident with the growing power of the French monarchy itself. Within 100 years an estimated 2,700 Gothic churches, shimmering with stained glass, were built in the Île-de-France region alone. Advances in building technology allowed progressively larger windows and ever loftier vaults supported by complex skeletal buttressing. From the capital of Paris the Gothic style spread throughout Europe and prevailed until about 1400, lingering even longer in some regions (see map **11–1**).

The term "Gothic" was introduced in the sixteenth century by the Italian artist and historian Giorgio Vasari, who disparagingly attributed the by-then-old-fashioned style to the Goths, the Germanic invaders who had "destroyed" the Classical civilization of the Roman Empire that he preferred. In its own day the Gothic style was simply called "modern art" or the "French style." As it spread from the Île-de-France, it took on regional characteristics and was adapted to all types of structures, including town halls, residences, and Jewish synagogues, as well as Christian churches.

During the flowering of the Gothic style in the twelfth and thirteenth centuries, Europe enjoyed a period of vigorous growth and prosperity. Towns gained increasing prominence, becoming important centers of artistic and intellectual life, while urban universities—first in Bologna, and later in Paris and Oxford—supplanted rural monastic schools as centers of learning. Two new religious orders arose to serve the expanding urban populations, the Franciscans and the Dominicans. The friars, as these monks were called, went out into the world to preach and minister to those in need, rather than confining themselves to a life of seclusion in the monastic complex.

Crusades and pilgrimages continued, and increasing contact with the Byzantine and Islamic worlds brought greater access to learned works from Classical antiquity. These writings, particularly those of Aristotle, promoted rational inquiry rather than an unquestioning faith as the path to truth, but the thirteenth-century scholar Thomas Aquinas was able to integrate faith and reason in Scholastic philosophy. Artists and master builders of the time, like the Scholastic thinkers, saw divine harmony in rational geometric relationships and expressed these in their art. Unlike their more freewheeling Romanesque predecessors, who used stylization and distortion to achieve emotional impact, thirteenth-century sculptors created more lifelike forms even though they were increasingly suffused with courtly affectation. Gothic religious imagery, like Romanesque imagery, aimed to embody Christian belief, but its effects are more subtle and cerebral, and it incorporates an even wider range of subjects drawn from the natural world. But above all, in Gothic cathedrals medieval worshipers experienced the earthly church as the embodiment of the Heavenly Jerusalem, radiant with divine light.

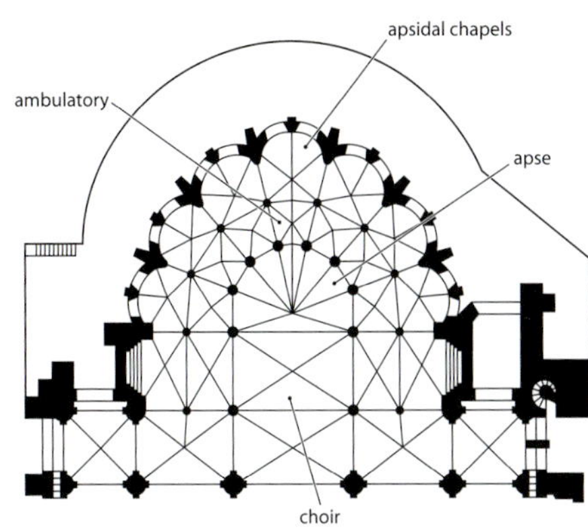

11–2 Plan of the choir of the Abbey Church of Saint-Denis, France. 1140–1144

Gothic Art in France

The first Gothic building was the Abbey Church of Saint-Denis, just north of Paris. This monastery had been founded in the fifth century over the tomb of Saint Denis, the early Christian martyr who had been sent from Rome to convert the local pagan population. As early as the seventh century, the monastery had also developed royal significance. Saint-Denis housed the tombs of French kings, the regalia used in royal coronations, and the relics of this patron saint of France.

Construction began on a new church in the 1130s under the supervision of Abbot Suger (abbot 1122–1151), who argued that the older building was inadequate to accommodate the crowds of pilgrims who arrived on feast days to venerate the body of Saint Denis and too modest to express the importance of the saint himself. In working with builders to conceive a radically new church design, he turned for inspiration to texts that were attributed erroneously to a follower of Saint Paul named Dionysius (the Greek form of Denis), who considered radiant light a physical manifestation of God. Through the centuries, this Pseudo-Dionysius also became identified with the martyred Denis whose body was venerated at the abbey, so Suger was adapting what he believed was the patron saint's concept of divine luminosity to a redesign of the abbey church that would showcase walls composed essentially of stained-glass windows. In inscriptions he composed for the bronze doors (now lost), he is specific about the motivations for the church's new architectural style: "Bright is the noble work; but being nobly bright, the work should lighten the minds, so that they may travel through the true lights, to the True Light where Christ is the true door" (Panofsky's translation, page 49).

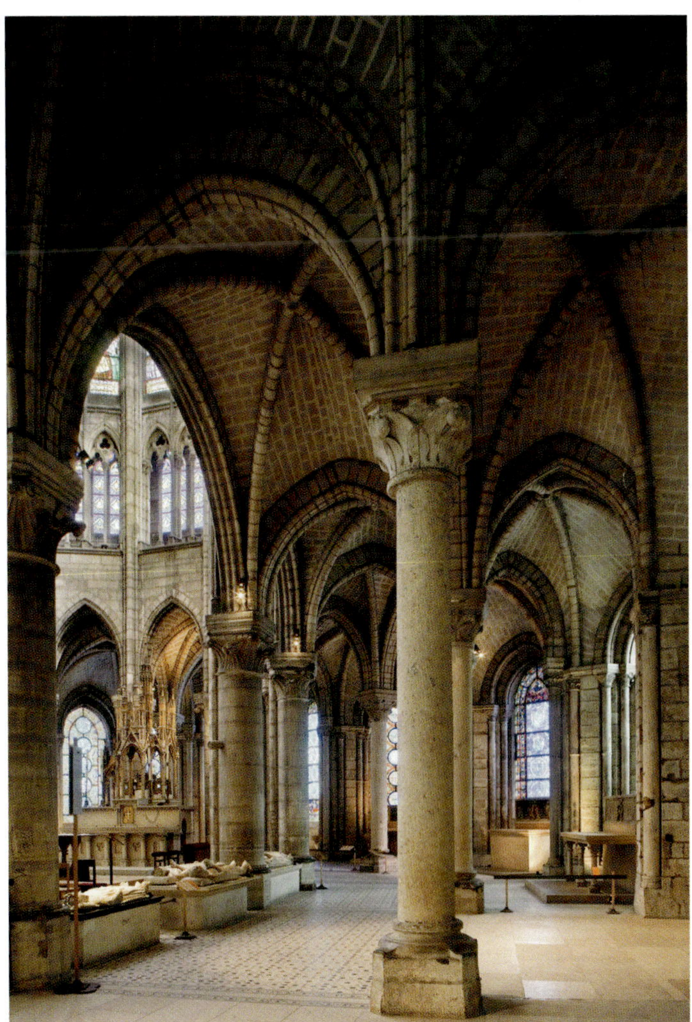

11–3 Ambulatory and chapels, Abbey Church of Saint-Denis

The plan of the choir (fig. **11–2**), built 1140–1144, retains key features of the Romanesque pilgrimage church (see fig. 10–21): a semicircular apse surrounded by an ambulatory from which radiate seven chapels of uniform size. The structural elements of the choir, too, had already appeared in Romanesque buildings, including pointed arches, ribbed groin vaults, and external buttressing that relieves stress on tall walls. The dramatic achievement of Suger's builders was the coordinated use of these features to create an architectural whole that emphasized open, flowing space, enclosed by non-load-bearing walls of colorful, glowing stained glass (fig. **11–3**). As Suger himself put it, the church becomes "a circular string of chapels by virtue of which the whole would shine with the wonderful and uninterrupted light of most luminous windows,

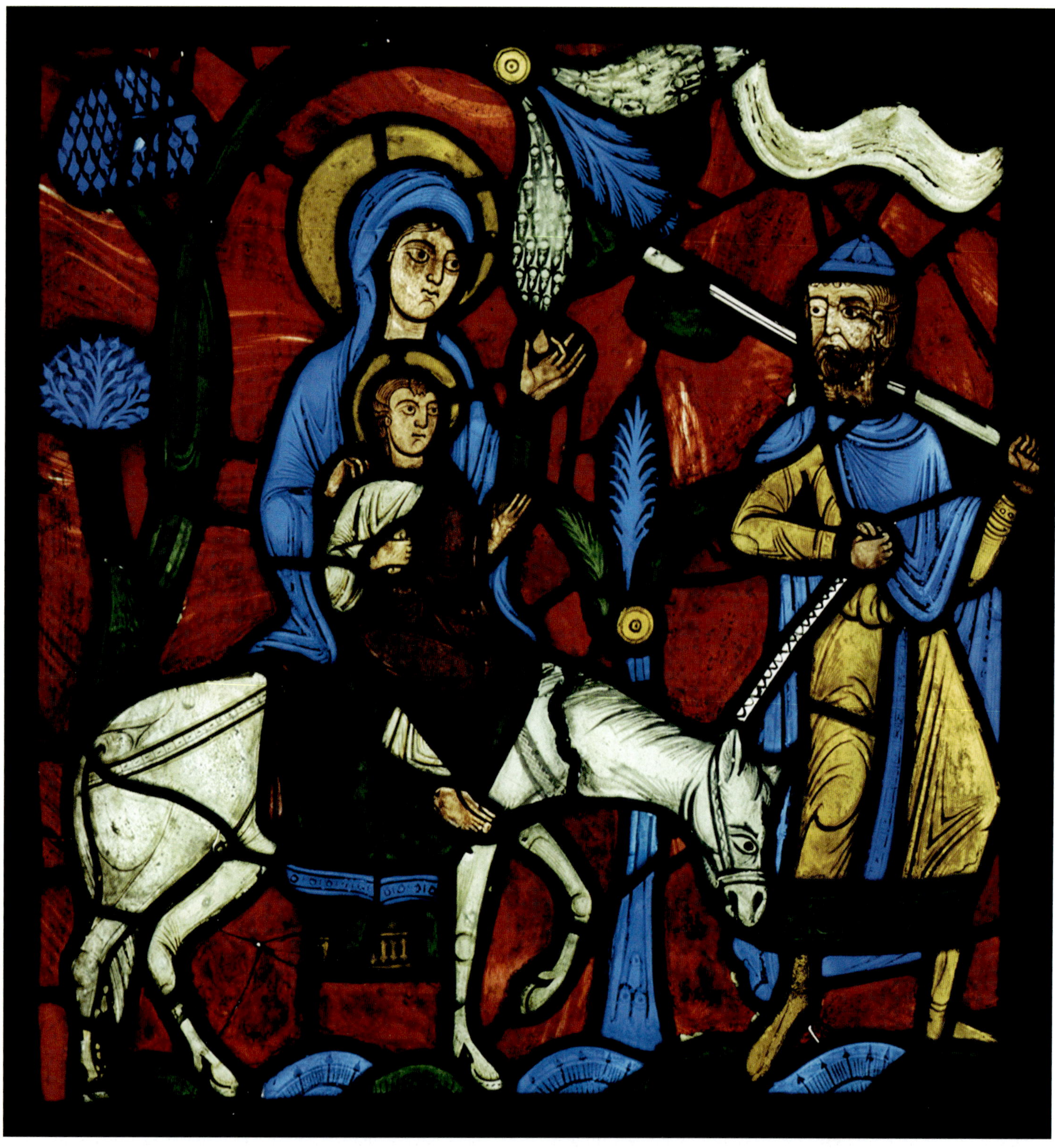

11–4 ***Flight into Egypt,*** **from the Infancy of Christ Window**, axial choir chapel, Abbey Church of Saint-Denis. c. 1140–1144. The Glencairn Museum, Bryn Athyn, Pennsylvania

Technique

Stained-Glass Windows

The "wonderful and uninterrupted light" that Suger sought in the reconstruction of the choir of Saint-Denis in the 1140s was provided by stained-glass artists that, as he tells us, he called in from many nations to create glowing walls for the radiating chapels, perhaps the clerestory as well. As a result of their exquisite work, this influential building program not only constituted a new architectural style; it catapulted what had been a minor curiosity among pictorial techniques into the major medium of monumental European painting. For several centuries, stained glass would be integral to architectural design, not decoration added subsequently to a completed building. Windows were produced at the same time as masons were building walls and carving capitals and moldings.

Our knowledge about the medieval art of stained glass is based on a twelfth-century text, *De diversis artibus* (*On the Various Arts*), written by a German monk who called himself Theophilus Presbyter. In fact, the basic procedure for making a stained-glass window has changed little since the Middle Ages. It is not a lost art, but it is a complex and costly process. The glass itself was made by bringing sand and ash to the molten state under intense heat, and "staining" it with color through the addition of metallic oxides. This molten material was then blown and flattened into sheets. Using a **cartoon** (full-scale drawing) painted on a white-washed board as a guide, the glass painter would cut from these sheets the individual shapes of color that would make up a figural scene or ornamental passage. This was done with a hot iron that would crack the glass into a rough approximation that could be refined by chipping away at the edges carefully with an iron tool—a process called grozing—to achieve the precise shape needed in the composition.

The artists used a vitreous paint (made, Theophilus tells us, of iron filings and ground glass suspended in wine or urine) full strength to block light and delineate features such as facial expressions or drapery folds. It could also be diluted to create modeling washes. Once painted, the pieces of glass would be fired in a kiln to fuse the painting with the glass surface. Only then did the artists assemble these shapes of color—like pieces of a complex compositional puzzle—with strips of lead (called **cames**), and subsequently affix a series of these individual panels to an iron framework within the architectural opening to form an ensemble we call a stained-glass window. Lead was used in the assembly process because it was strong enough to hold the glass pieces together but flexible enough to bend around their complex shapes and—perhaps more critically—to absorb the impact from gusts of wind and prevent the glass itself from cracking under pressure.

pervading the interior beauty" (Panofsky's translation, page 101). And since Suger saw the contemplation of light as a means of illuminating the soul and uniting it with God, he was providing his monks with an environment especially conducive to their primary vocation of prayer and meditation.

The revolutionary stained-glass windows of Suger's Saint-Denis were almost lost in the wake of the French Revolution, when this royal abbey represented everything the new leaders were intent on suppressing. Thanks to an enterprising antiquarian named Alexandre Lenoir, however, the twelfth-century windows, though removed from their architectural setting, were saved from destruction. During the nineteenth century, parts of them were returned to the abbey, but many panels are now in museums. One of the best-preserved panels, from a window that narrated Jesus' childhood, portrays the *Flight into Egypt* (fig. **11–4**). The crisp elegance of the delineation of faces, foliage, and drapery—painted with vitreous enamel on the vibrantly colored pieces of glass that make up the panel (see "Stained-Glass Windows," above)—is as clear today as it was when the windows were new. One unusual detail—the Virgin reaching out to pick a date from a palm tree that has bent down at the infant Jesus' command to accommodate her hungry grasp—is based on an apocryphal Gospel that was not included in the canonical Christian Scriptures but was a very popular source for twelfth-century artists.

The Abbey Church of Saint-Denis became the prototype for a new architecture of space and light based on a highly adaptable skeletal framework that supported rib vaulting with pinpoint piers and external buttressing systems. It initiated a period of competitive experimentation in the Île-de-France and surrounding regions that resulted in ever-taller churches enclosing increasingly lofty and broad interior spaces walled with ever-greater expanses of stained glass.

At the Cathedral of Notre-Dame in Chartres, southwest of Paris, masons built on the concepts pioneered at Saint-Denis. Constructed in several stages beginning in the mid-twelfth century and extending into the mid-thirteenth, Chartres is an amalgam of

ELEMENTS OF **Architecture**

Rib Vaulting

One of the chief technical contributions of Romanesque builders to Gothic architecture was rib vaulting. Rib vaults are a form of groin vault (see "Arch and Vault," page 145), in which the ridges (groins) formed by the intersecting vaults may rest on and be covered by curved, projecting moldings, called ribs. These ribs may have been structural as well as decorative, perhaps strengthening the joins and helping channel the vaults' thrust outward and downward. The ribs were constructed first, being supported themselves by scaffolding, and then they in turn supported the scaffolding necessary to build the webbing of the vault. Ribs developed over time into an intricate masonry "skeleton" filled with an increasingly lightweight masonry "skin."

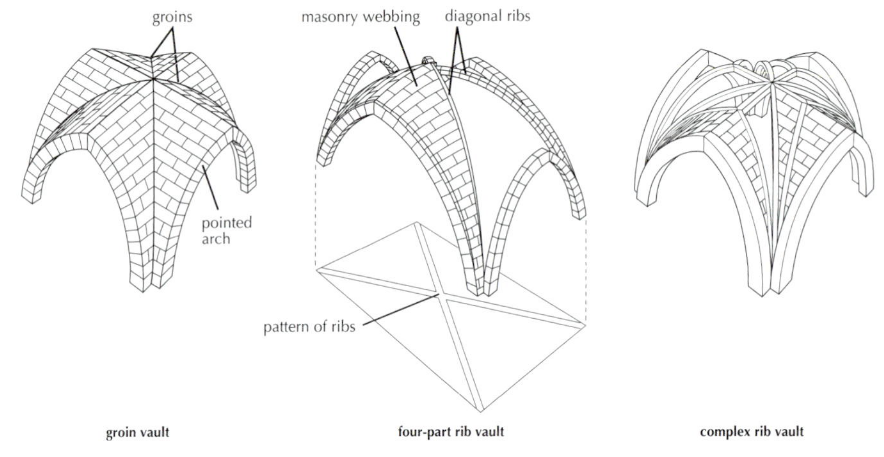

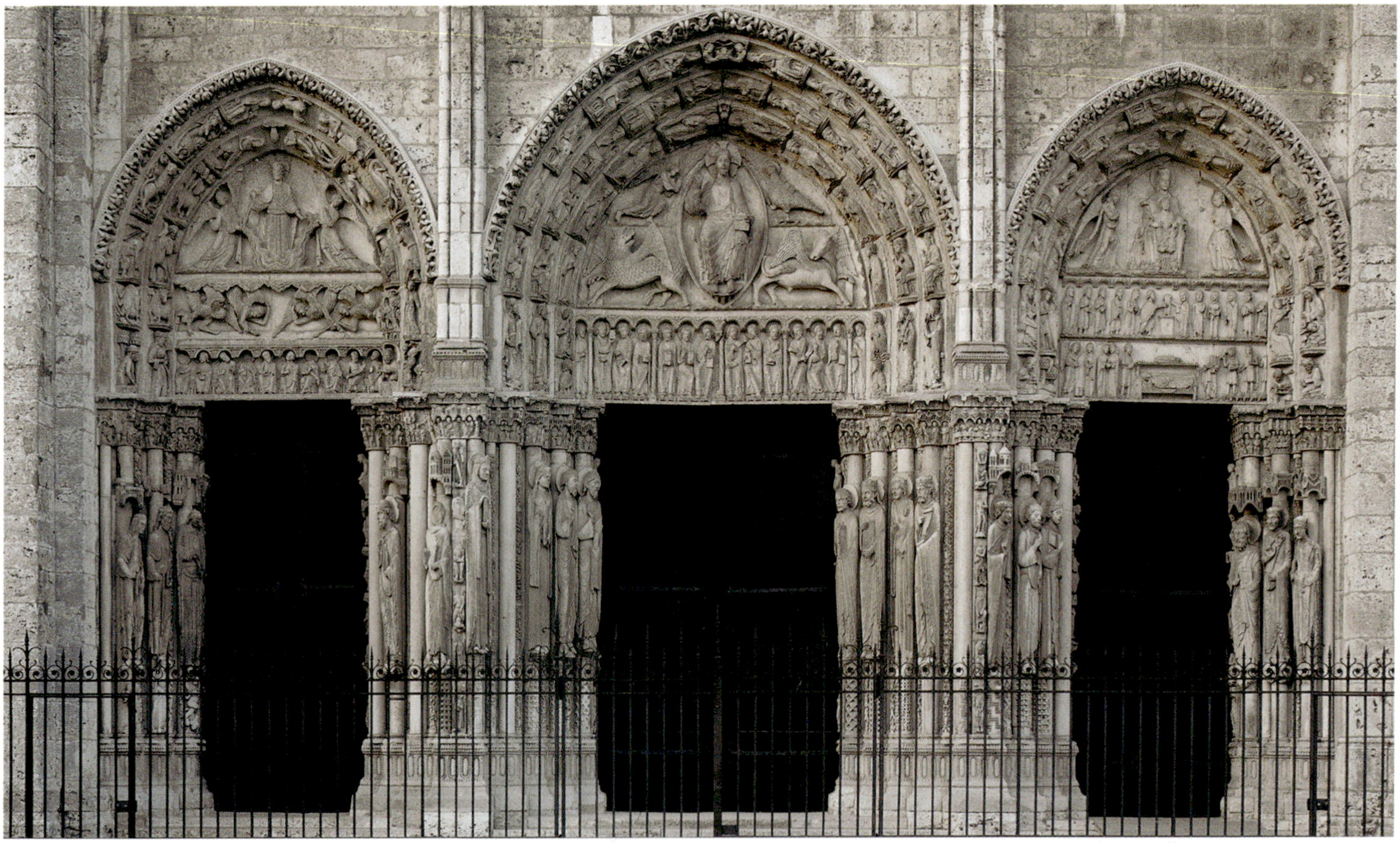

11–5 Royal Portal, west façade, Chartres Cathedral. c. 1145–1155

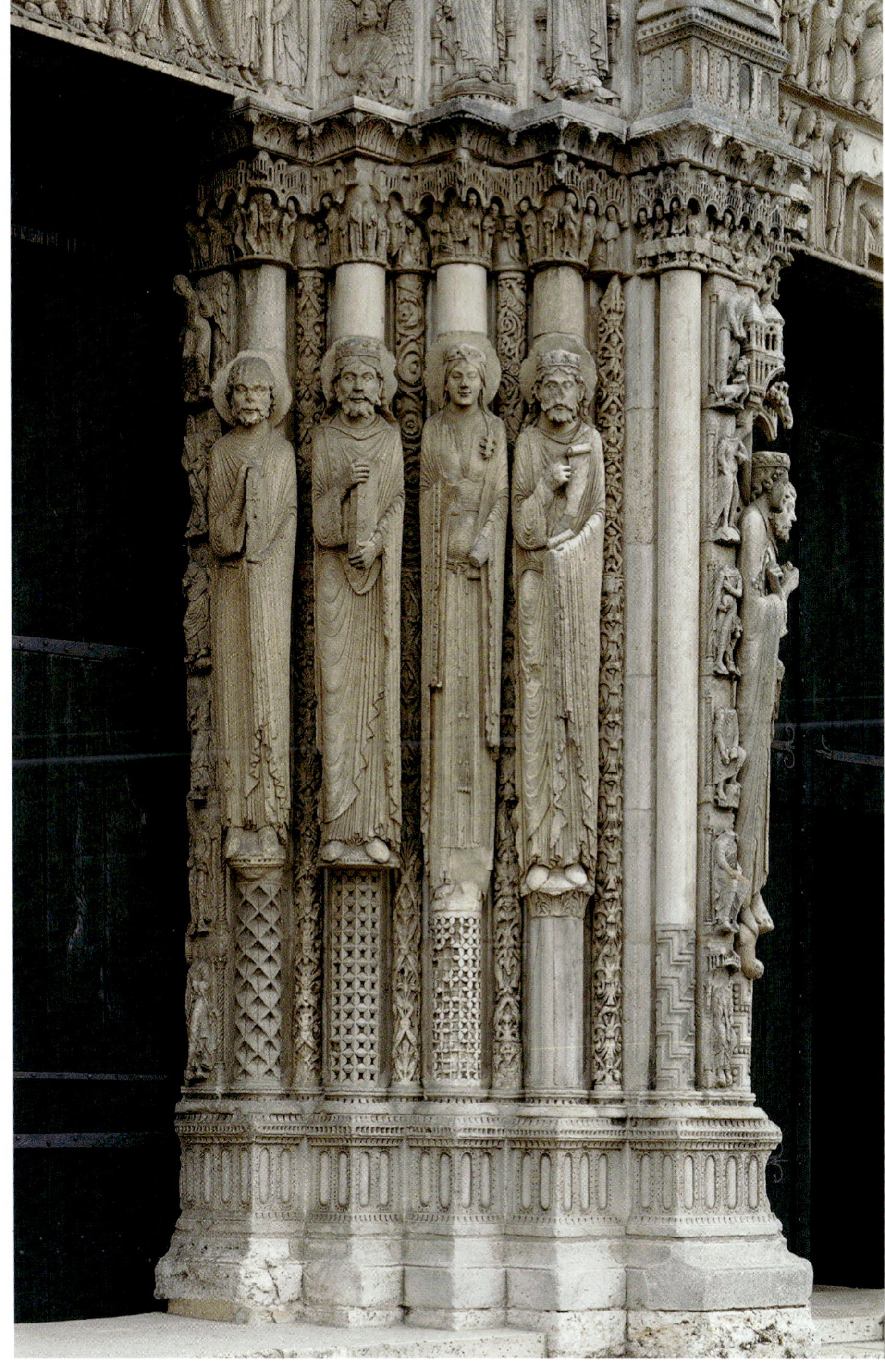

11–6 Jamb statues from the Royal Portal, right side of central west portal, Chartres Cathedral, c. 1145–1155

early and mature Gothic style. The west façade contains a sculptural program contemporary with the reconstruction of Saint-Denis. Surrounding these three doors—the so-called Royal Portal (fig. **11–5**)—high-relief figures calmly and comfortably fill their architectural settings. On the central tympanum Christ is enthroned in majesty, returning at the end of time. On the right tympanum are scenes from his infancy (representing the Incarnation, his first earthly appearance), and on the left is the Ascension (Jesus' return from earth to heaven). Flanking the three doorway openings are erect, frontal **statue columns** (fig. **11–6**), whose elegantly elongated proportions and linear but lifelike drapery, echo the cylindrical shafts behind them. Their meticulously carved, idealized heads radiate a sense of spiritual serenity. The prominence of kings and queens among these jamb statues—presumably representing Christ's royal ancestry in the Hebrew Bible—has given the Royal Portal its name.

The bulk of Chartres Cathedral was constructed after a fire in 1194 destroyed an earlier Romanesque church. Its builders codified what were to become the typical Gothic structural devices: pointed arches and ribbed groin vaults rising from compound piers over rectangular bays, supported by exterior **flying buttresses** (figs.

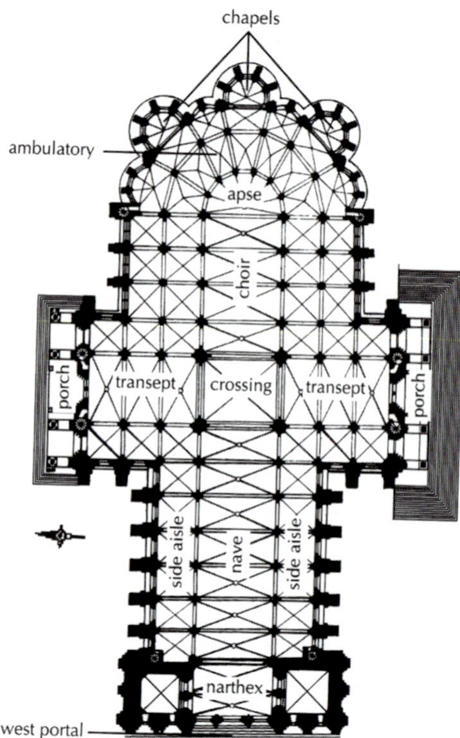

11–7 Plan of Chartres Cathedral. c. 1194–1250

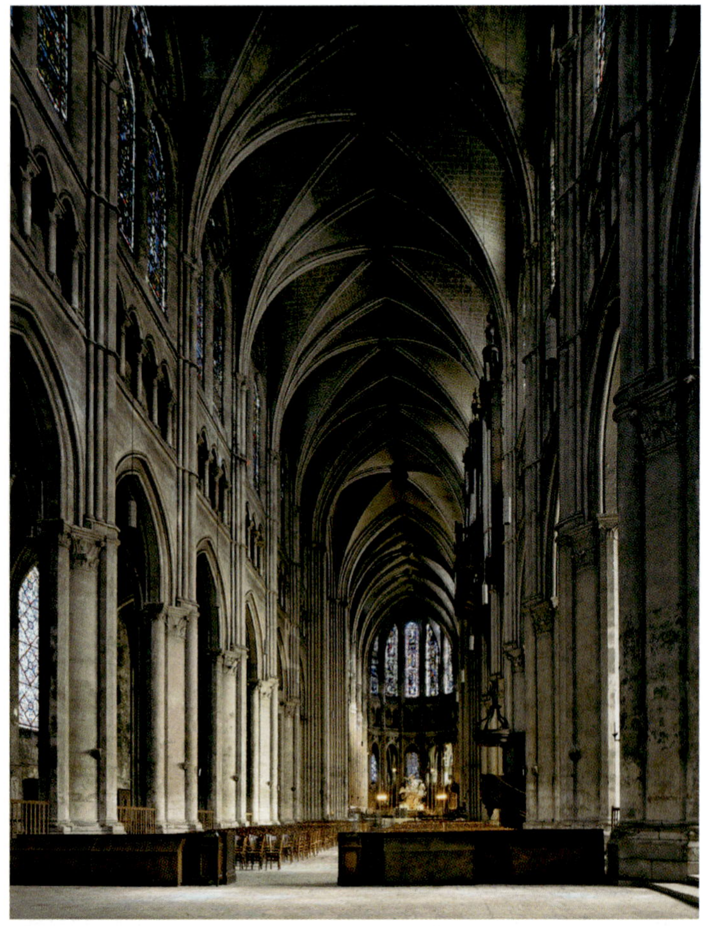

11–8 View of interior from the west, Chartres Cathedral. c. 1200–1250

ELEMENTS OF Architecture

The Gothic Church

Most large Gothic churches in Western Europe were built on the Latin-cross plan, with a projecting transept marking the transition from nave to choir, an arrangement that derives ultimately from the fourth-century Constantinian basilica of Old Saint Peter's (see fig. 7–8). The main entrance portal was generally on the west, with the choir and its apse on the east. A western narthex could precede entrance to the nave and side aisles. An ambulatory with radiating chapels circled the apse and facilitated the movement of worshipers through the church. Many churches have a three-story elevation, with a triforium sandwiched between nave arcade and a glazed clerestory. Rib vaulting usually covered all spaces in the Gothic period. **Flying buttresses** helped support the soaring nave vaults by transferring their outward thrust over the aisles to massive, free-standing, external buttresses. Church walls were decorated inside and out with arcades of round or pointed arches, engaged columns and colonnettes, an applied filigree of tracery, and horizontal moldings called **stringcourses**. The pitched roofs above the vaults—necessary to evacuate rainwater from the building—were supported by a wooden framework. A spire or crossing tower above the junction of the transept and nave was usually planned, though often never finished. Portal façades were also customarily marked by high, flanking towers or gabled porches ornamented with **pinnacles** and finials. Architectural sculpture proliferated on each portal's tympanum, **archivolts**, and **jambs**, and in France a magnificent rose window typically formed the centerpiece of the flat portal façades.

11–9 Schematic drawing of Chartres Cathedral

11–7, **11–8**, and **11–9**). This system permitted masons to reserve huge openings for stained-glass windows in the clerestory wall and reduce the **triforium** to a mid-level passageway with an arcaded screen, rather than a flat wall (see fig. 7–10) or a full gallery (see fig. 10–23). This elegant glass-and-masonry shell encloses an enormous open space, with vaults rising 118–120 feet above the floor. In Romanesque churches, worshipers are mainly drawn forward

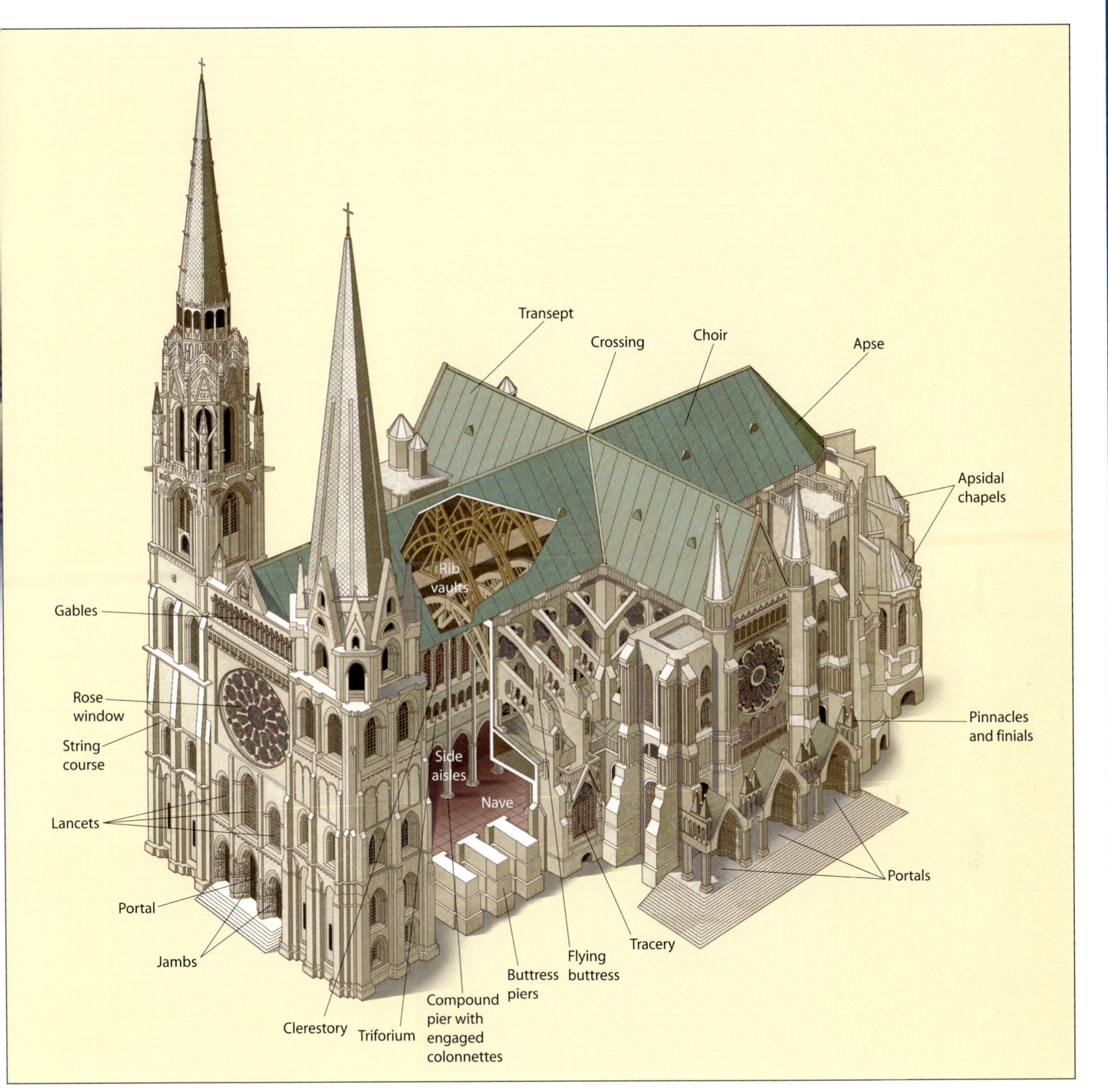

toward the apse; at Chartres they are drawn upward as well, to the clerestory windows illuminating the soaring vaults overhead (fig. 11–9).

Unlike the majority of French Gothic buildings, most of Chartres' windows have survived, comprising about 22,000 square feet of stained glass installed between 1200 and 1250. The Good Samaritan Window in the nave aisle—visible and legible to viewers, both medieval and modern—illustrates the complexity of Gothic narrative art with a learned allegory on sin and salvation (see fig. 11–1). The principal subject is a parable Jesus told his followers to teach a moral truth (Luke 10:25–37). The protagonist is a traveling Samaritan who cares for a stranger, beaten, robbed, and left for dead by thieves on the side of a road. Jesus' parable is an allegory for his imminent redemption of humanity's sins, and within this window a

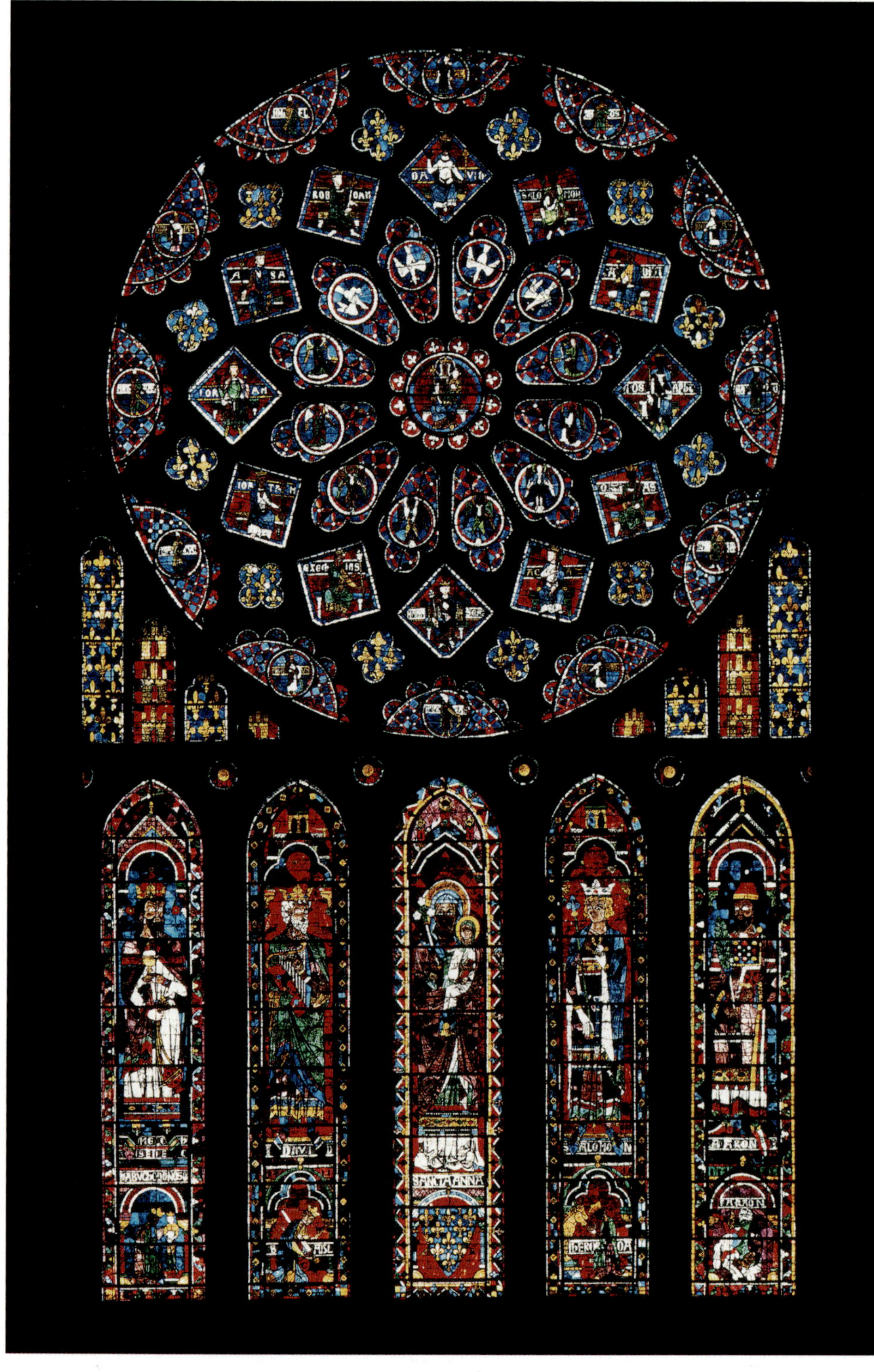

11–10 Rose and lancets, north transept, Chartres Cathedral. c. 1230–1235

story from Genesis is juxtaposed with the parable to underscore that association. Adam and Eve's fall introduced sin into the world, but Christ (the Good Samaritan) rescues humanity (the traveler) from sin (the thieves) and ministers to them within the Church, just as the Good Samaritan takes the wounded traveler to an inn (bottom scene, fig. 11–1). Stylistically, these willowy, expressive figures avoid the classicizing stockiness in Wiligelmus's folksy Romanesque rendering of the Genesis narrative at Modena (see fig. 10–25). Instead they adopt the dance-like postures that will come to characterize Gothic figures as the style spreads across Europe in ensuing centuries.

Other windows tell similarly moralizing tales of saints and holy heroes, providing the faithful with role models for a life well lived. But not all windows at Chartres are narrative. Monumental iconic ensembles were easier "read" in lofty openings more removed from viewers, such as the huge north transept rose with five slender lancets beneath it (fig. **11–10**), which proclaims the Virgin Mary's royal and priestly heritage. In the central lancet, Saint Anne holds

CLOSER LOOK

The soaring Cathedral Church of Notre-Dame (Our Lady) of Paris that we see today (fig. **11–11**) began as an early Gothic building bridging the period between Abbot Suger's Abbey Church of Saint-Denis and the thirteenth-century Cathedral of Chartres. Begun in 1163, construction on the choir of Notre-Dame was far enough along for the altar to be consecrated 20 years later. The nave, rising to 115 feet, dates to 1180–1200. The west façade, erected between 1200 and 1250, incorporated an earlier portal dedicated to Mary (Our Lady). By this time, the massive walls, buttresses, and six-part vaults, adopted from Norman Romanesque architecture, must have seemed very old-fashioned.

After 1225, a new master modernized and lightened the building by reworking the clerestory with the large double-lancet and rose windows we see today. Notre-Dame may have had the first true flying buttresses (experts are still arguing) although those seen at the right of the photograph, rising dramatically to support the high vault of the choir, result from later remodeling. (The 290-foot spire over the crossing is the work of the nineteenth-century architect Eugène Emmanuel Viollet-le-Duc.)

For all its spiritual and technological glory, Notre-Dame barely survived the French Revolution. The revolutionaries decapitated the statues associated with deposed nobility and their "superstitious" religion, and transformed the cathedral into a secular "Temple of Reason" (1793–1795). But it would not be long until Notre-Dame was returned to religious use. Napoleon crowned himself emperor at its altar in 1804, and Parisians gathered there to celebrate the liberation of Paris from the Nazis in August, 1944. Today, boats filled with tourists glide under bridges that link the island where the cathedral stands with the Left Bank, the traditional students' and artists' quarter. Notre-Dame so resonates with life and history that it has become more than a house of worship and work of art; it is a symbol of Paris and part of the shared culture of humankind.

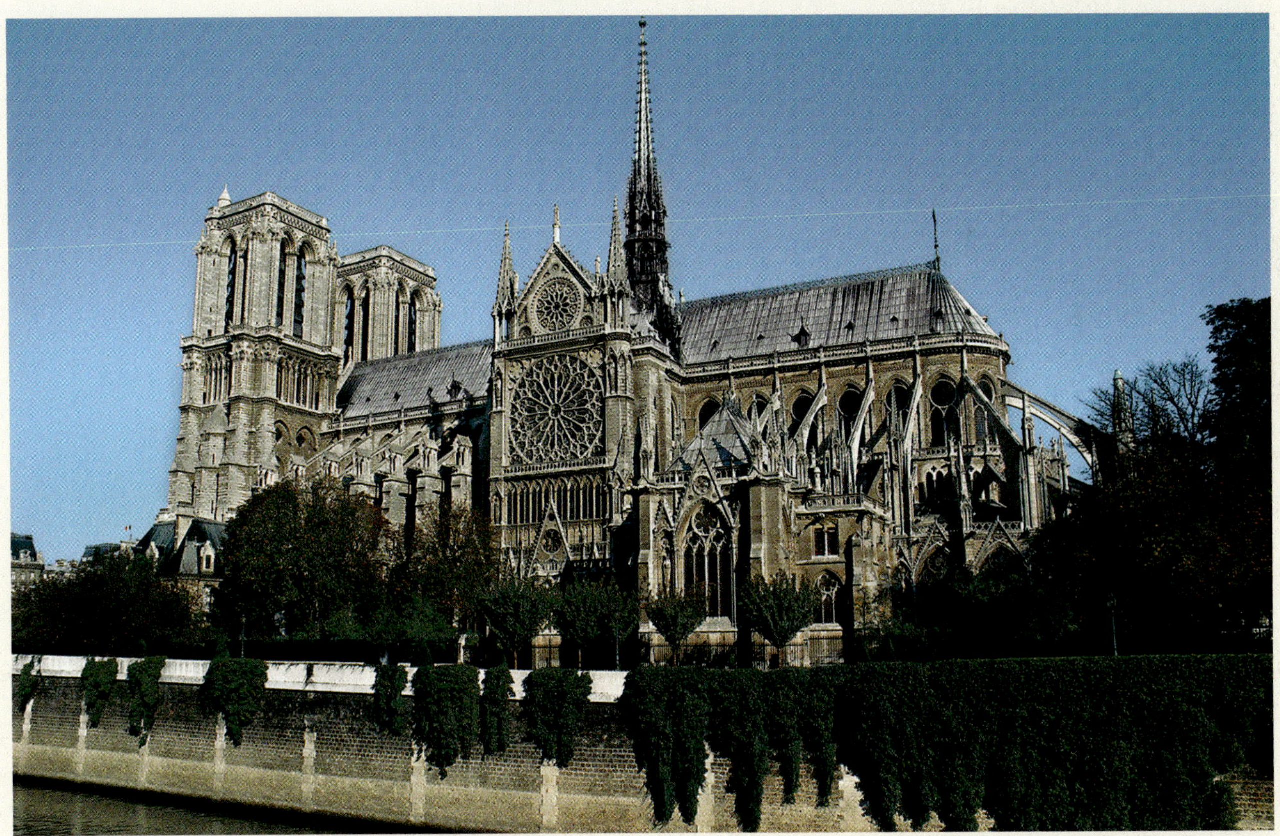

11–11 Cathedral of Notre-Dame, view from the southeast. Paris, France. Begun 1163

her daughter, the baby Mary, flanked left to right by statuesque figures of Melchizedek, David, Solomon, and Aaron. Above, in the very center of the rose itself, Mary and Jesus are enthroned, surrounded by a radiating array of doves, angels, and kings and prophets from the Hebrew Bible. This window was a gift from the young King Louis IX (ruled 1226–1270), probably arranged by his powerful mother Queen Blanche of Castile (1188–1252), who ruled as regent 1226–1234 during Louis's minority. Royal heraldic emblems secure the window's association with the king. The arms of France—golden fleurs-de-lys on a blue ground—fill a shield under Saint Anne, centered below. Fleurs-de-lys also appear in the graduated lancets bracketing the base of the rose and in a series of quatrefoils within the rose itself. But also prominent is the Castilian device of golden castles on a red ground, a reference to the royal lineage of Louis's powerful mother. Light radiating from the deep blues and reds create a hazy purple atmosphere in the soft light of the north side of the building. On a sunny day the masonry may seem to dissolve in color, but the theological message of the rose remains clear.

Important buildings were also under construction in Paris (see "Closer Look," page 281) and Reims (fig. **11–12**), where the cathedral was the coronation church of the French kings. A technique known as **bar tracery**, perfected at Reims, made possible especially expansive walls of glass. In bar tracery, thin stone bars, called **mullions**, form a lacy frame for the glass, replacing the older practice called **plate tracery** in which glass was inserted directly into openings reserved when constructing the wall itself. Reims is especially famous for the quantity and quality of its sculpture, which not only encrusts the entire perimeter of the exterior, but even appears on the interior surface of the western wall, where stories enacted by prophets and ancestors of Christ from the Hebrew Bible served as moral guides for monarchs who faced them when leaving the church after coronation.

The magnificent west façade at Reims has massive gabled portals with soaring peaks sheltering tympana filled with stained-glass windows rather than sculpture. The sheer magnitude of sculpture envisioned for this elaborate cathedral front required the skills of many sculptors, working in an impressive variety of styles over several decades. Four figures from the right jamb of the central portal illustrate this rich stylistic diversity (fig. **11–13**). The pair on the right portrays the *Visitation*, in which Mary (left), pregnant with

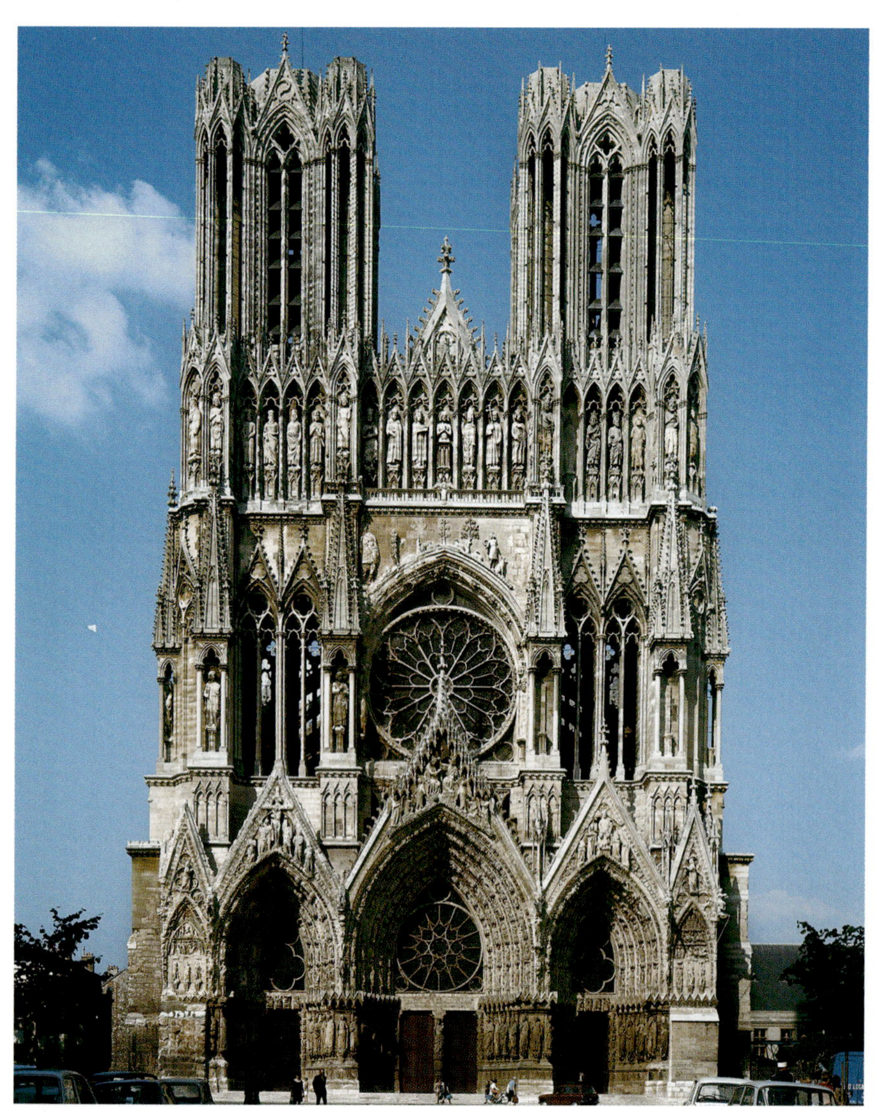

11–12 West façade, Reims Cathedral.
1230s–1260; towers mid-15th century

The towers were later additions to this massive cathedral front, as was the row of statues (the so-called Kings' Gallery) stretching across the façade at the base of the towers. The spires were never completed.

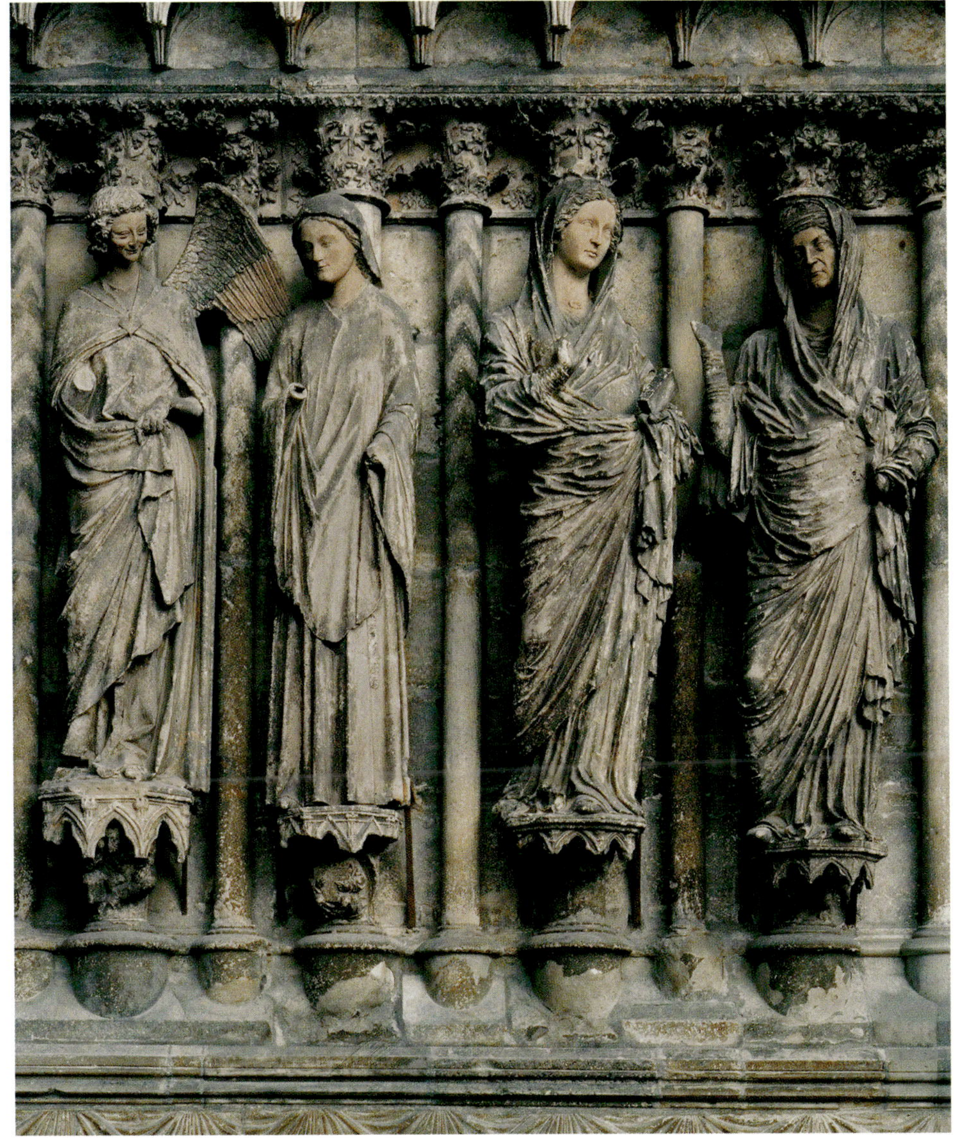

11–13 ***Annunciation*** (left pair: archangel Gabriel c. 1255, Mary c. 1245) and ***Visitation*** (right pair: c. 1230), right side, central portal, west façade, Reims Cathedral

Jesus, visits her older cousin, Elizabeth (right), pregnant with Saint John the Baptist. The sculptor of these figures, active in Reims about 1230–1235, drew heavily on ancient sources. The bulky bodies show the same solidity seen in Roman sculpture (see fig. 6–14), and the women's full faces, wavy hair, and heavy mantles recall imperial portrait statuary, even in their use of the two Roman facial ideals of unblemished youth (Mary) and aged accomplishment (Elizabeth) (compare figs. 6–31 and 6–32). The figures shift their weight to one leg in *contrapposto* as they turn toward each other in conversation.

The pair to the left of the *Visitation* illustrates the *Annunciation*, in which the archangel Gabriel announces to Mary that she will bear Jesus. Mary's slight body, restrained gesture, inward focus, and delicate features, contrast markedly with the bold tangibility of Mary in the *Visitation* next to her. She is clearly the work of a second sculptor. The angel Gabriel (at the far left) represents a third artist, active at the middle of the century. This sculptor created tall, gracefully swaying figures with small, fine-featured heads, whose affected expressions, carefully crafted hairdos, and poses of aristocratic refinement grew increasingly to characterize the figural arts in later Gothic sculpture and painting, becoming the basis for what is called the International Gothic Style, fashionable across Europe well into the fifteenth century.

By the middle of the thirteenth century builders had thoroughly mastered the design principles and building technology of Gothic architecture and began to focus attention on elaborating and refining the visual elements of the style. They enlarged windows, disguised walls behind carved bundles of moldings and shafts, and experimented with the linear quality that ribs gave to vaulting. The builders of a new royal palace chapel in Paris, called the Sainte-Chapelle, pushed the use of stained glass to its limit, almost completely obliterating any sense of a stone wall.

Constructed in 1243–1248 to house King Louis IX's prized collection of relics, the Sainte-Chapelle resembles a giant reliquary made of painted stone and glass instead of gold and gems, but turned inside out so that we experience it from within, rather than exclusively from the exterior. A ground-level chapel was accessible from the palace courtyard, but a larger private upper chapel could be entered only from the royal apartments. Entering the king's

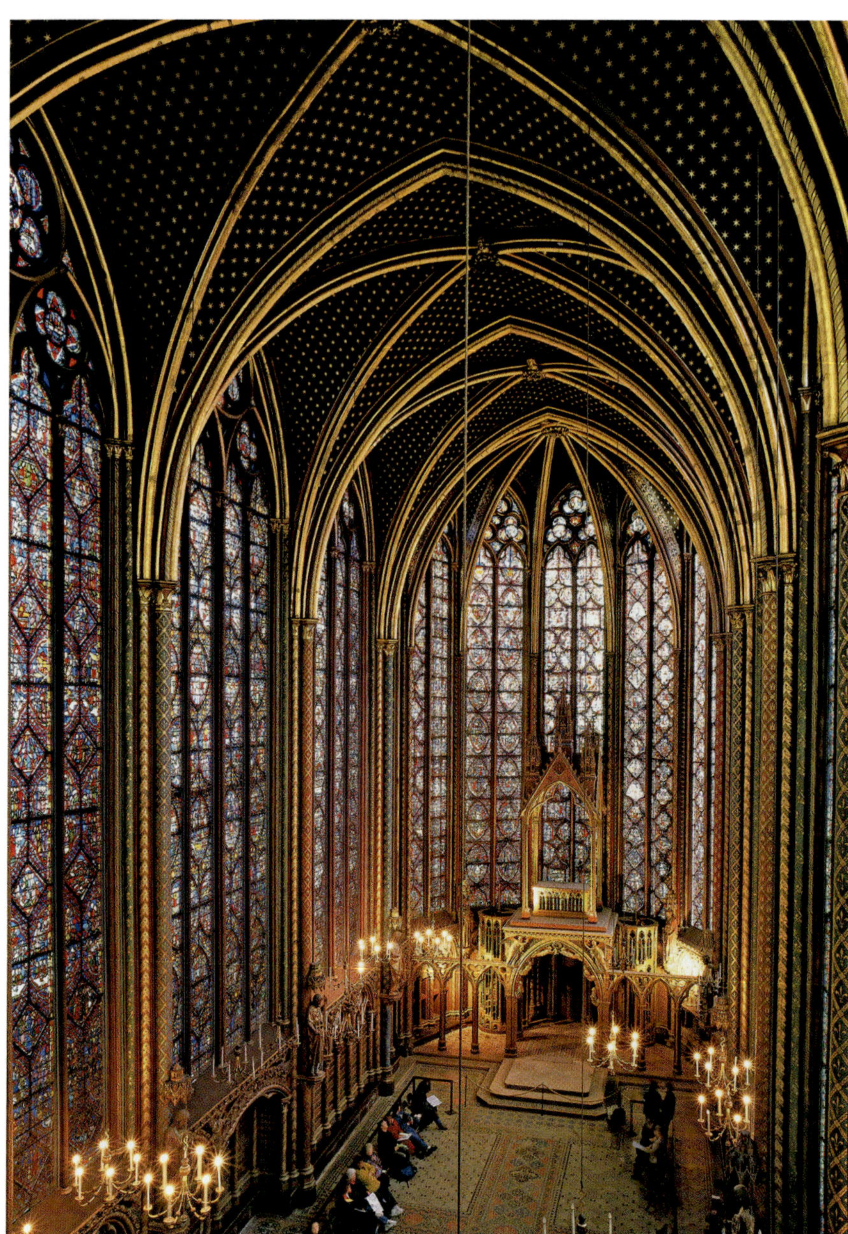

11–14 Interior, upper chapel, the Sainte-Chapelle, Paris. 1243–1248

The direct inspiration for Louis IX's construction of this new royal chapel was the acquisition in 1239 of the regal relic of Christ's crown of thorns, purchased from Baldwin II, Latin ruler of Constantinople. In the charter of 1244 that established services in the Sainte-Chapelle, Pope Innocent IV claimed that Christ had crowned Louis with his own crown, strong confirmation for Louis's own sense of the sacred underpinnings of his kingship.

upper chapel is like emerging into a glowing jewel box (fig. **11–14**), but this arresting visual impression is only part of the story. The stained-glass windows present extensive narrative cycles related to the special function of this chapel. Since they are painted in a bold, energetic style, the stories are easily legible, in spite of their breadth and complexity. Around the sanctuary's **hemicycle** (semicircular space surrounding the altar) are standard themes, such as the Infancy and Passion of Christ, relating to the celebration of the Mass. But along the straight side walls are broader, four-lancet windows whose narrative expanse is dominated by the exploits of the kings and queens of Judah as outlined in the Hebrew Bible, heroes Louis claimed as his own royal ancestors. Above the recessed niche where Louis himself sat at Mass was a window filled with biblical kings, whereas above the corresponding niche on the other side of the chapel where his mother, Queen Blanche of Castile, and his wife, Queen Marguerite of Provence, sat, were windows devoted to the lives of Judith and Esther, seen as appropriate role models for medieval queens. Everywhere we look we see kings being crowned, leading soldiers into holy warfare, or performing various royal duties, all framed with heraldic references to Louis and the French royal house. There is even a window that includes scenes from the life of Louis IX himself.

The style of the stained glass and sculpture of the Sainte-Chapelle is sometimes called the Court Style since its association with the Parisian court of Louis IX was one reason it spread to the courts of other European rulers. And Paris gained renown not only for Gothic architecture, stained glass, and sculpture, but also for illustrated books such as small Bibles used by students at the Parisian University, and extravagant devotional and theological works filled with exquisite miniatures for the use of wealthy patrons.

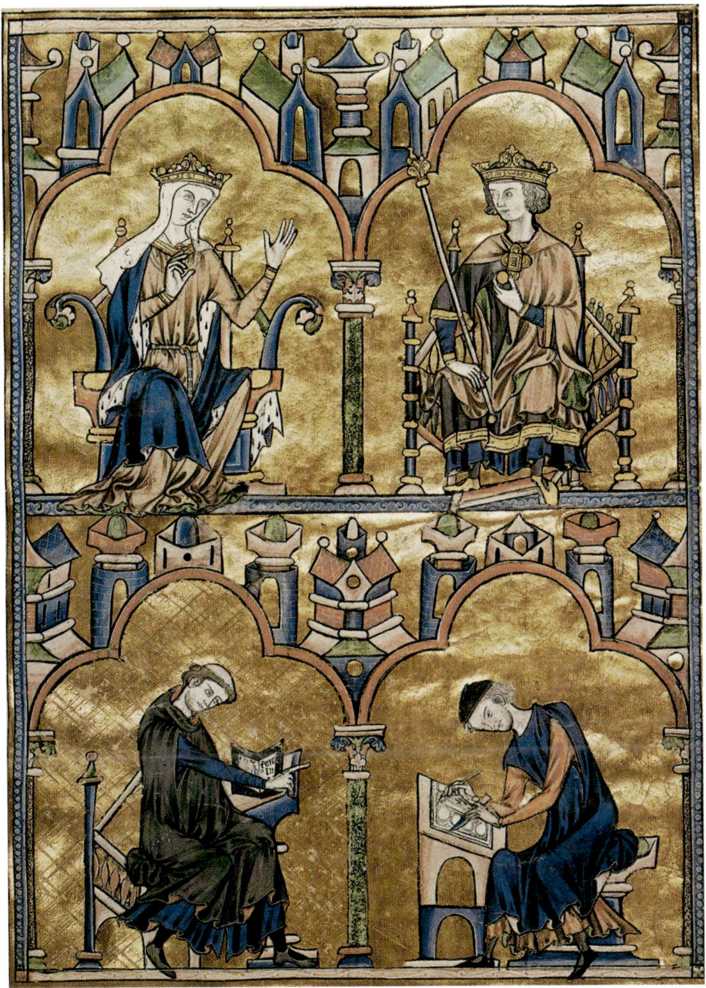

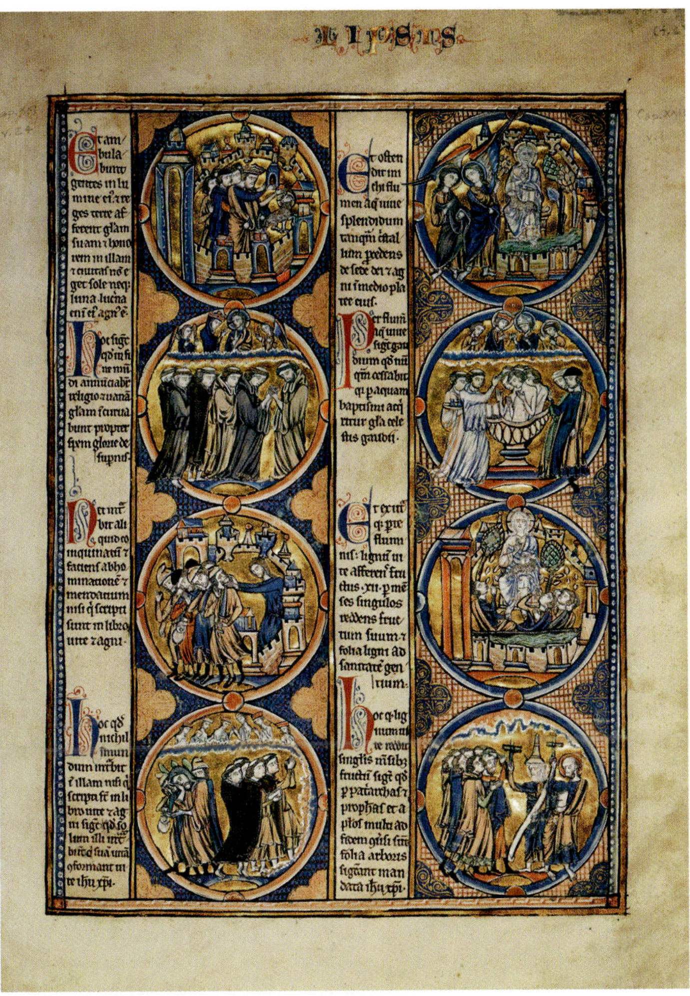

11–15 Two Pages from a Moralized Bible: (a) *Louis IX and Queen Blanche of Castile* and (b) scenes from and moralizations on the Apocalypse, made in Paris. 1226–1234. Ink, tempera, and gold leaf on vellum, each page 15" × 10½" (38 × 26.6 cm). The Pierpont Morgan Library, New York, MS M240, fol. 6 and 8

This three-volume book of biblical commentary in pictures and words seems to have been commissioned by Louis and Blanche as a gift for the Cathedral of Toledo in Spain, where most of it still resides. These two illustrations are from eight leaves of the manuscript that somehow made their way out of Toledo and into the collection of J. Pierpont Morgan.

One sumptuous example is a three-volume Moralized Bible from c. 1230, in which selected scriptural passages are paired with allegorical, or moralized, interpretations, using pictures as well as words to convey the message. The dedication page (fig. **11–15a**) shows the teenage King Louis IX and his mother, Queen Blanche of Castile, who served as regent of France until he came of age. The royal pair—emphasized by their elaborate thrones and slightly oversized heads—sits against a solid gold-leaf background under a multicolored architectural framework. Below them at left, a clerical scholar dictates to a scribe, who seems to be working on a page from this very manuscript, with a column of roundels already outlined for paintings.

This design of stacked medallions, forming the layout for each page of this monumental manuscript (fig. **11–15b**), clearly derives from stained-glass lancets with their columns of superimposed images (see fig. 11–14). But here the schema combines pictures with words. Each page has two vertical strips of painted scenes set against a mosaic-like repeated pattern and filled out by half-quatrefoils in the interstices—the standard format of mid-thirteenth-century windows. Adjacent to each medallion is an excerpt of text, either a summary of a scriptural passage or event or its terse contemporary interpretation or allegory. Both pictures and texts alternate between scriptural summaries and their moralizing explications, outlined in words and visualized with pictures. This adds up to a very learned and complicated compilation, perhaps devised by clerical scholars at the University of Paris, but certainly painted by some of the most important professional artists in the cosmopolitan French capital.

Beginning in the late thirteenth century a new kind of private prayer book became popular among wealthy patrons. Called **Books of Hours** because they contain special prayers to be recited at the eight canonical "hours," literally around the clock, these books focused on devotion to the Virgin, but they were often personalized for individual patrons with prayers to patron saints, a calendar showing saints' festivals, and sometimes prayers said for the dead.

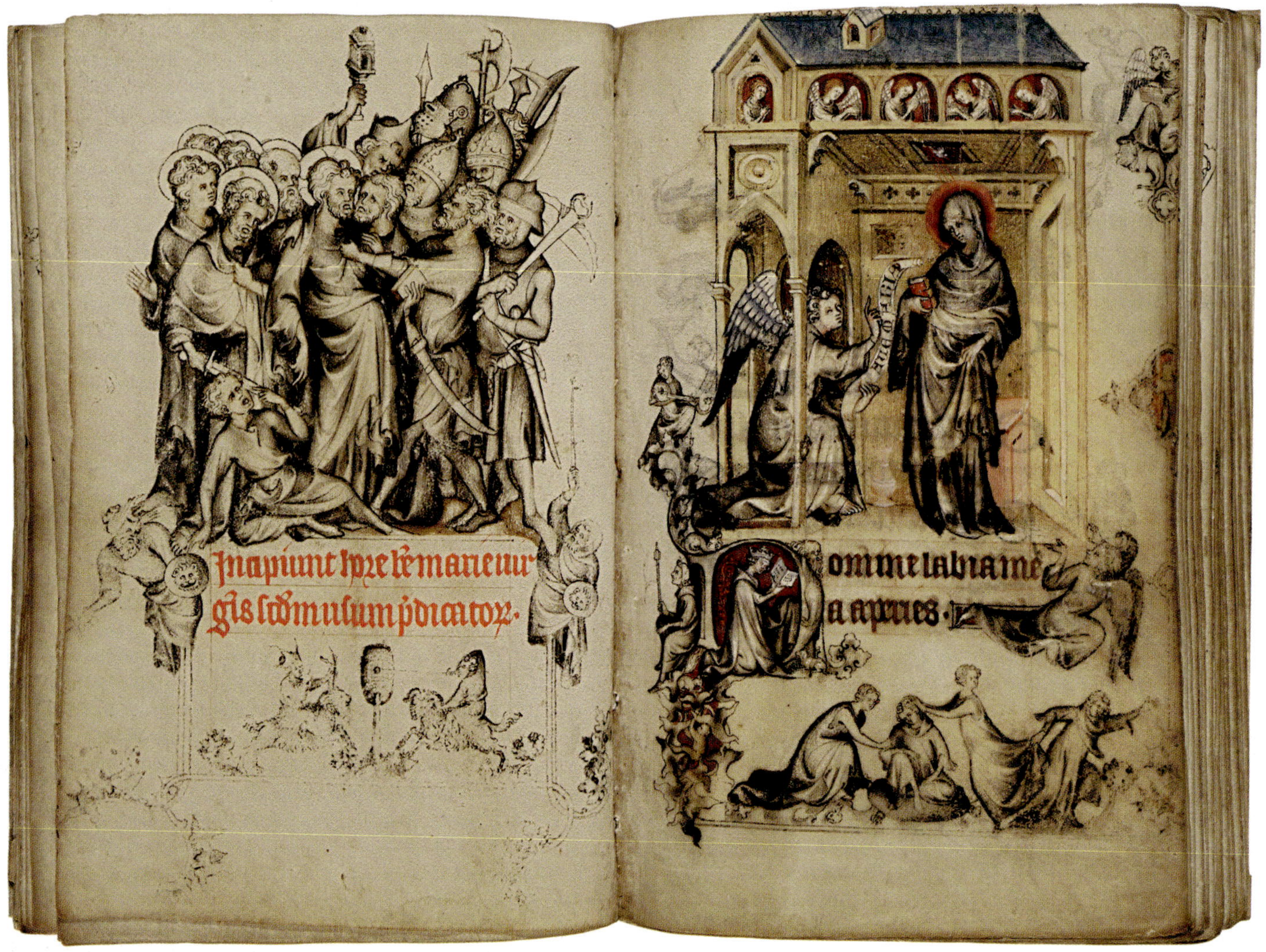

11–16 Jean Pucelle. Two-page opening showing *Betrayal and Arrest of Christ*, fol. 15v (left) and ***Annunciation*,** fol. 16r (right). *Hours of Jeanne d'Evreux*, from Paris. c. 1325–1328. Grisaille and color on vellum, each page 3½" × 2¼" (8.2 × 5.6 cm). The Metropolitan Museum of Art, New York
THE CLOISTERS COLLECTION, 1954 (54.1.2)

A tiny, exquisite Book of Hours given by King Charles IV of France (ruled 1322–1328) to his wife, Queen Jeanne d'Evreux, around the time of their marriage in 1325, is the work of a painter named Jean Pucelle (fig. **11–16**). Abandoning the intense colors used by earlier illuminators, Pucelle worked in **grisaille** (paintings executed only in shades of gray) adding only delicate touches of color. In the *Annunciation*, to the right on this two-page opening, an elegantly swaying Mary receives the archangel Gabriel in her Gothic-style home that seems to project outward from the page toward the viewer. Queen Jeanne herself appears in the initial "D" below the Annunciation, kneeling before a lectern and reading from her Book of Hours, perhaps beginning her private devotions with the very words written on this page: "*Domine labia mea aperies*" (Psalm 51:15—"O Lord open thou my lips"). This inclusion of the praying patron's portrait, a practice that continued in monumental painting and sculpture through the fifteenth century (see figs. 12–4 and 12–8), conveyed the idea that the pictures were not scenes illustrating a continuing story, but personal "visions" inspired by meditation. In the *Betrayal* on the left page, the traitorous disciple Judas Iscariot embraces Jesus, identifying him to soldiers who have come to seize him and setting in motion the events that lead to the crucifixion. The spoof of military training sketched below, showing "knights" riding goats and jousting at a barrel stuck on a pole, may be a commentary on the lack of valor shown by the soldiers assaulting Jesus.

Both pages show Pucelle's debt to the sculptural and painting style associated with the French court. Softly modeled, voluminous draperies are gathered loosely, falling in projecting diagonal folds around tall, elegantly posed figures with carefully arranged curly hair and broad foreheads. Jesus on the left and Mary on the right stand in the swaying S-curve pose typical of French art since the middle of the thirteenth century (see fig. 11–13, leftmost figure).

Besides carving the stone sculpture integrated into churches, Gothic sculptors also found a lucrative outlet for their work in a growing demand for small religious statues intended for homes and personal chapels, or as donations by wealthy patrons to favorite

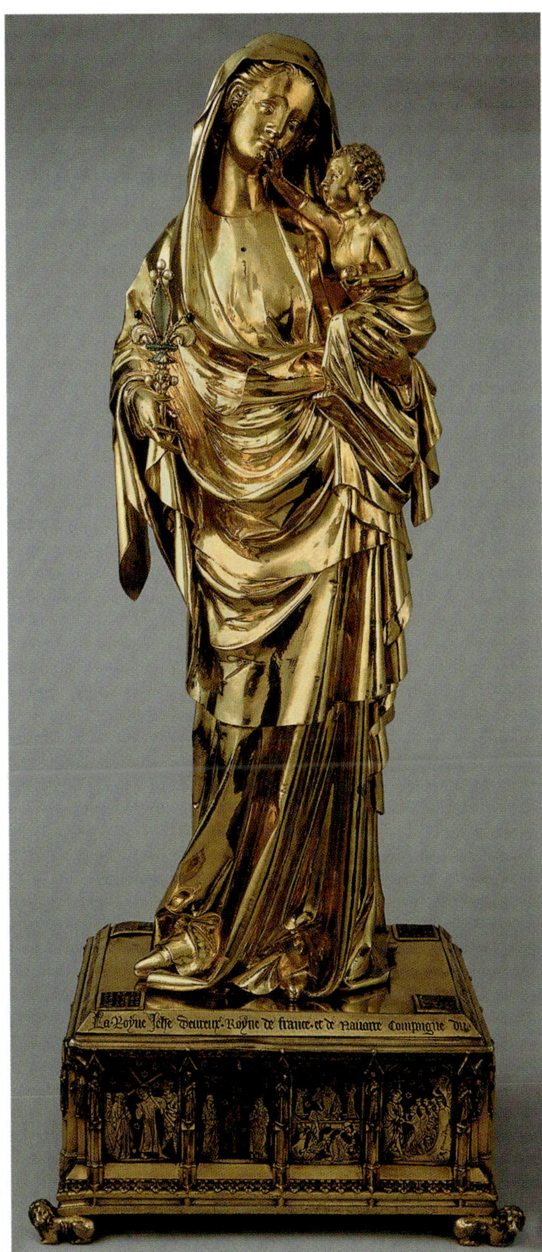

11–17 ***Virgin and Child***, from the Abbey Church of Saint-Denis. c. 1339. Silver gilt and enamel, height 27⅛" (69 cm). Musée du Louvre, Paris

churches. Among the treasures at the Abbey Church of Saint-Denis was the silver-gilt reliquary statue, slightly more than 2 feet tall, of a standing *Virgin and Child* (fig. **11–17**) containing hairs said to come from her head. An inscription on the base bears the date 1339 and the name of Queen Jeanne d'Evreux, whom we already know from her prayer book. The Virgin cradles her son in her left arm, and supports her weight on her left leg, creating the graceful S-curve pose that was a stylistic signature of the period.

Secular Art

Although the Gothic style developed in religious architecture, it spread to secular structures such as castles, town halls, and manor houses. Castles evolved during the Romanesque and Gothic period from enclosed strongholds to elaborate fortified residential complexes (see fig. 10–19). The ruined towers and walls of early medieval castles seem rather romantic and picturesque today, but they originally had both a military and a political function, projecting an aura of family power and wealth. By the end of the Middle Ages, however, castles became luxurious residences, their military aspect often more symbolic than real. Private rooms for ladies, for example, were added to great halls. One early fifteenth-century manuscript illumination shows the queen of France in a room with tapestry-hung walls, painted woodwork, and glass windows as well as magnificent furniture (see fig. Intro–23). Woven and embroidered textiles provided both insulation and enrichment. The use of heraldry (a symbolic language defining lineage) highlighted an owner's power and political rights.

The lid of an ivory box depicts a tournament taking place in front of castle walls (fig. **11–18**). Such mock battles were originally military training exercises, but they became popular aristocratic sporting events. In fact, during the twelfth and thirteenth centuries, the military ideal gave way to a new ideal of romantic love in literature and music as well as in the visual arts. In the scene on the left, ardent knights assault the Castle of Love, firing roses from crossbows and the deadly trebuchet (the most powerful medieval siege weapon), while women pelt the men with roses. The god of love

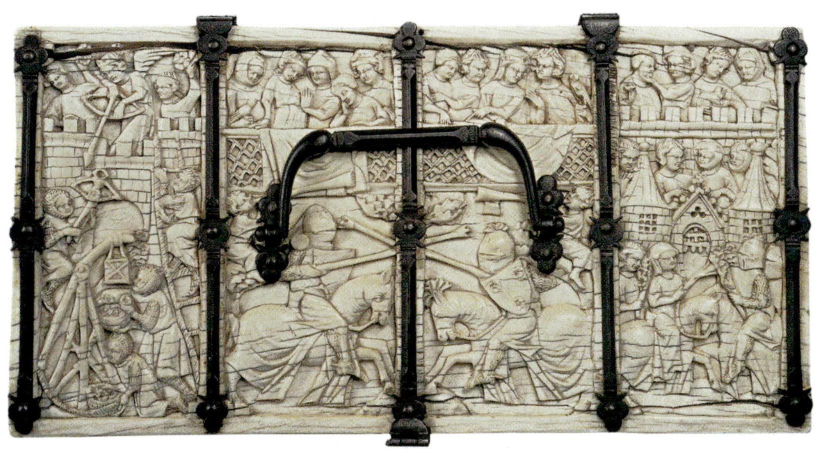

11–18 ***Attack on the Castle of Love***. Ivory panel. Paris. c. 1330–1350. 4½" × 9 11/16" (11.5 × 24.6 cm). Walters Art Gallery, Baltimore

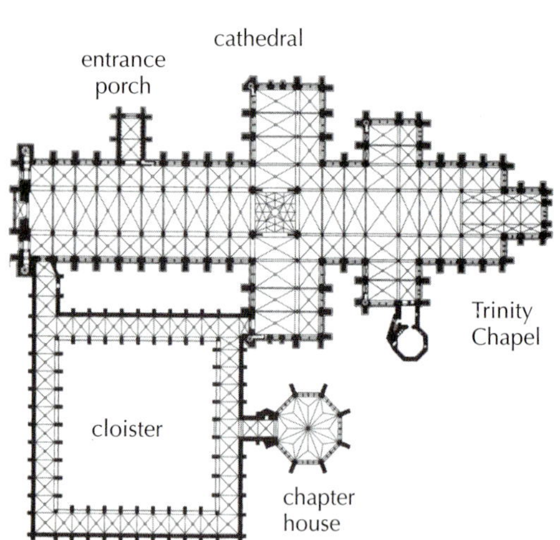

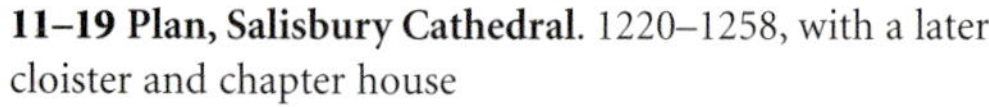
11–19 Plan, Salisbury Cathedral. 1220–1258, with a later cloister and chapter house

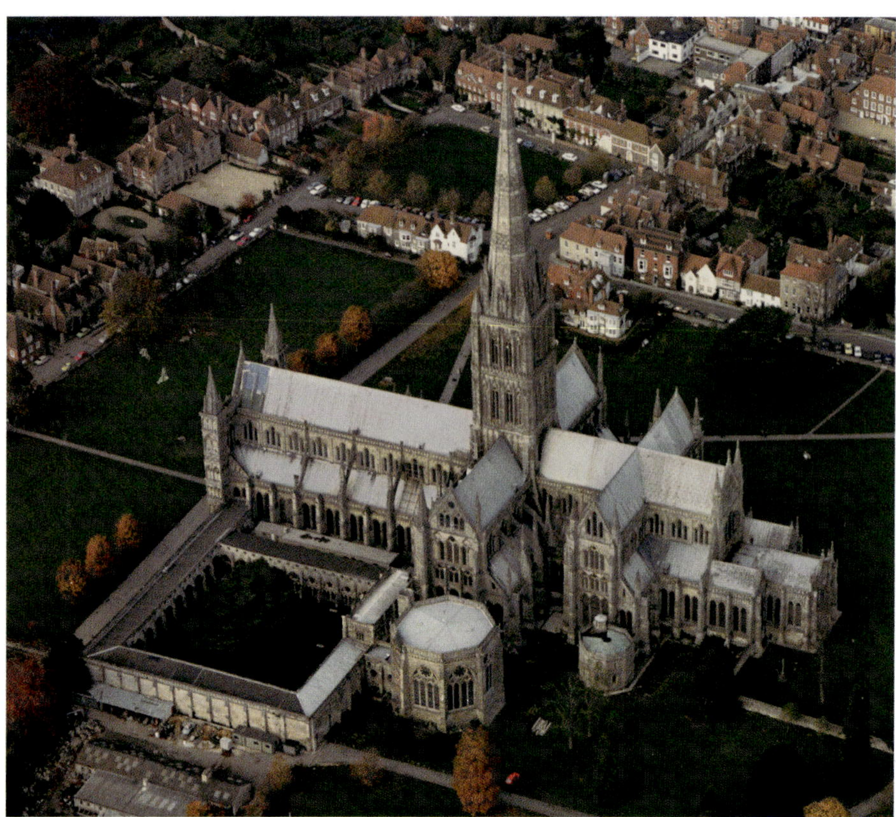
11–20 Salisbury Cathedral, Wiltshire, England. 1220–1258; west façade 1265; spire c. 1320–1330

joins the fray and aims his arrows at the attackers. The tournament spread over the middle two panels represents an allegorical battle of love. Elegant ladies and gentlemen watch two jousting knights, charging with visors down and lances set. The action concludes in the scene on the right, where the tournament's victor and his lady love meet in a playful joust of their own, while other couples engage in flirtations on the castle walls. This miniature castle has the crenellated walls and towers that remain symbols of an aristocratic medieval residence.

Gothic Art in England

As the Gothic style spread outside France, it not only became an international style in Europe but—in the thirteenth and fourteenth centuries—also took on innovative regional forms. In England, for instance, cathedral builders were less concerned with height than were their French counterparts, and they constructed long, broad naves and galleries. English builders focused their decorative efforts on walls, which, even if they retained a Romanesque sense of solidity and horizontal continuity, were enlivened by an elaborate profusion of arch moldings and by clusters of applied colonnettes.

Salisbury Cathedral, as its principal structure was built in a relatively short period of time (1220–1258), has a consistency of style that makes it an ideal representative of English Gothic architecture (figs. **11–19** and **11–20**). Typically English is the park-like setting

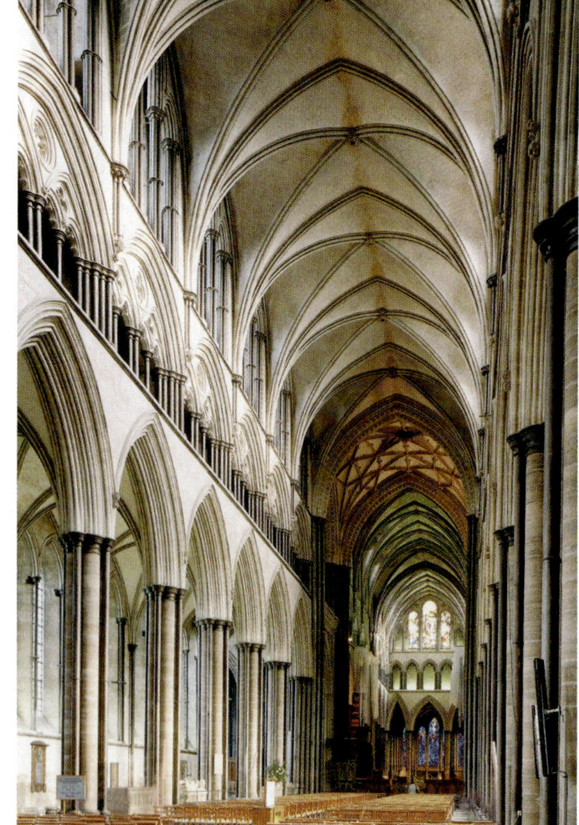
11–21 Nave, Salisbury Cathedral. 1220–1258. Looking east toward the high altar

(the cathedral close, or precinct) and attached cloister and chapter house for the cathedral clergy. Many English churches were completed with splendid towers and spires in the fourteenth century, and at Salisbury Cathedral, about 1320–1330, Master Richard of Farleigh built a crossing tower with a spire rising to the extraordinary height of 400 feet. Taller than anything visualized by the original builders, the spire required extra buttressing, so the builders added flying buttresses.

Typical of English cathedrals, Salisbury has wide projecting transepts (double transepts, in this case), a square apse, and a spacious sanctuary (fig. **11–21**). The interior reflects enduring Norman traditions (see fig. 10–24), with its heavy walls and tall nave arcade surmounted by a gallery and a clerestory with simple lancet windows, but the effect is quite different. A strong emphasis on the horizontal movement of the arcades, unbroken by any continuous vertical projections from the compound piers, directs worshipers' attention forward to the altar, rather than upward into the vaults. The shafts supporting the four-part rib vaults are made of a darker stone called Purbeck marble that polishes to a soft, brownish-black, fossil-laden glow, and is in stark contrast to the lighter stone of the rest of the interior.

Like the French, the English also made richly decorated books. The dazzling artistry and delight in ambiguities that had marked earlier medieval manuscripts in the British Isles (see fig. 10–1) still appear in the *Windmill Psalter* (c. 1270–1280). The letter *B*—the first letter of Psalm 1, which begins with the words *Beatus vir qui non abit in consilio impiorum* ("Happy are those who do not follow the advice of the wicked")—fills the entire left page of this opening and outlines a densely interlaced thicket of tendrils and figures (fig. **11–22**). This is a Tree of Jesse, a genealogical diagram of Jesus' royal and spiritual ancestors in the Hebrew Bible based on a prophecy in Isaiah 11:1–3. An oversized, reclining figure of Jesse, father of King David, appears sheathed in a red mantle, with the blue trunk of a vine-like tree emerging from his side. Above him is his majestically enthroned royal son, who, as an ancestor of Mary just above him, is also an ancestor of Jesus, who appears at the top of the sequence. In the circling foliage flanking this sacred royal family tree are a series of prophets, representing Jesus' spiritual heritage.

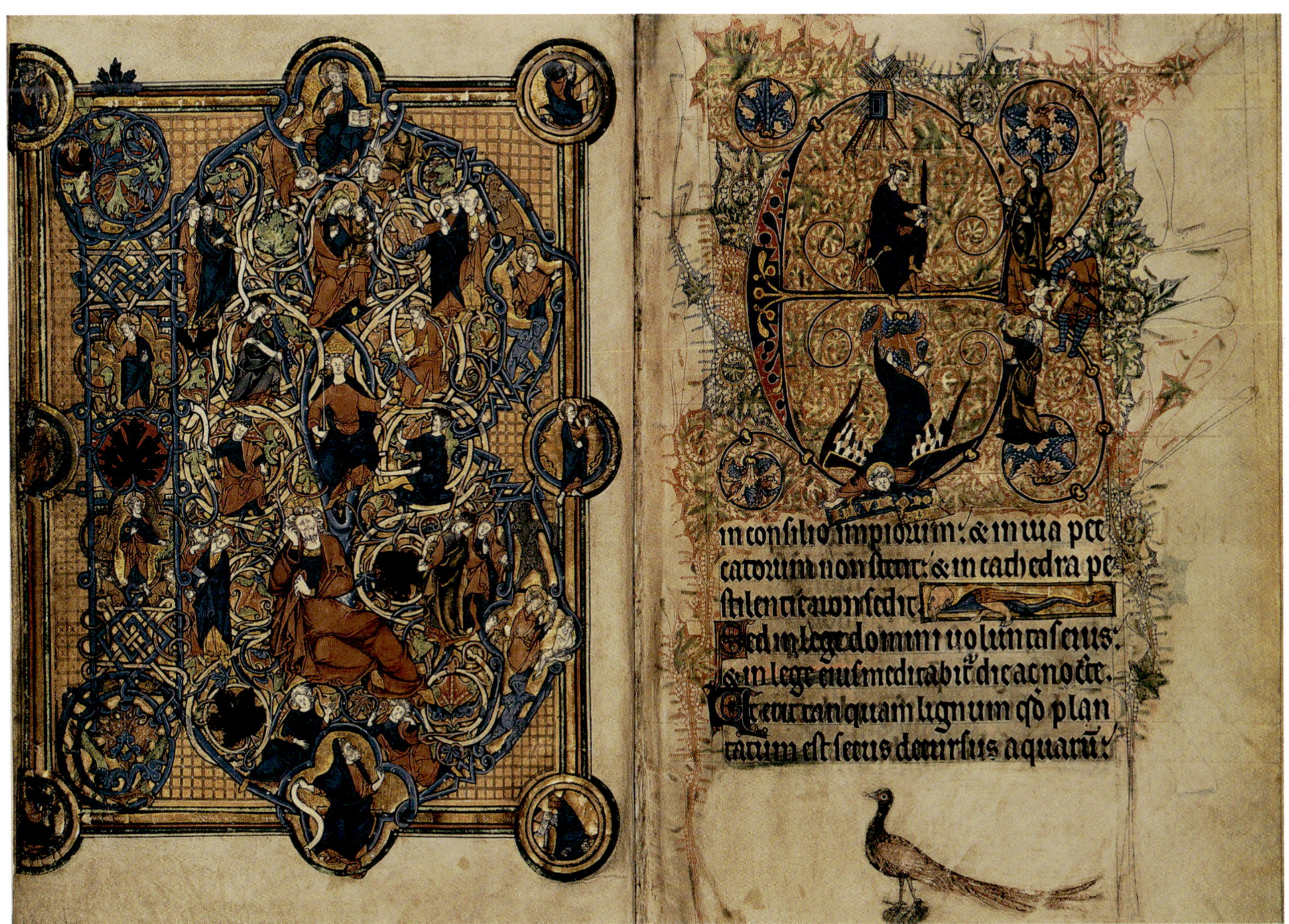

11–22 Two-page opening with *Psalm 1*, *Windmill Psalter*, from London. c. 1270–1280. Ink, pigments, and gold on vellum, each page 12¾" × 8¾" (32.3 × 22.2 cm). The Pierpont Morgan Library, New York M. 102, F. IV-2

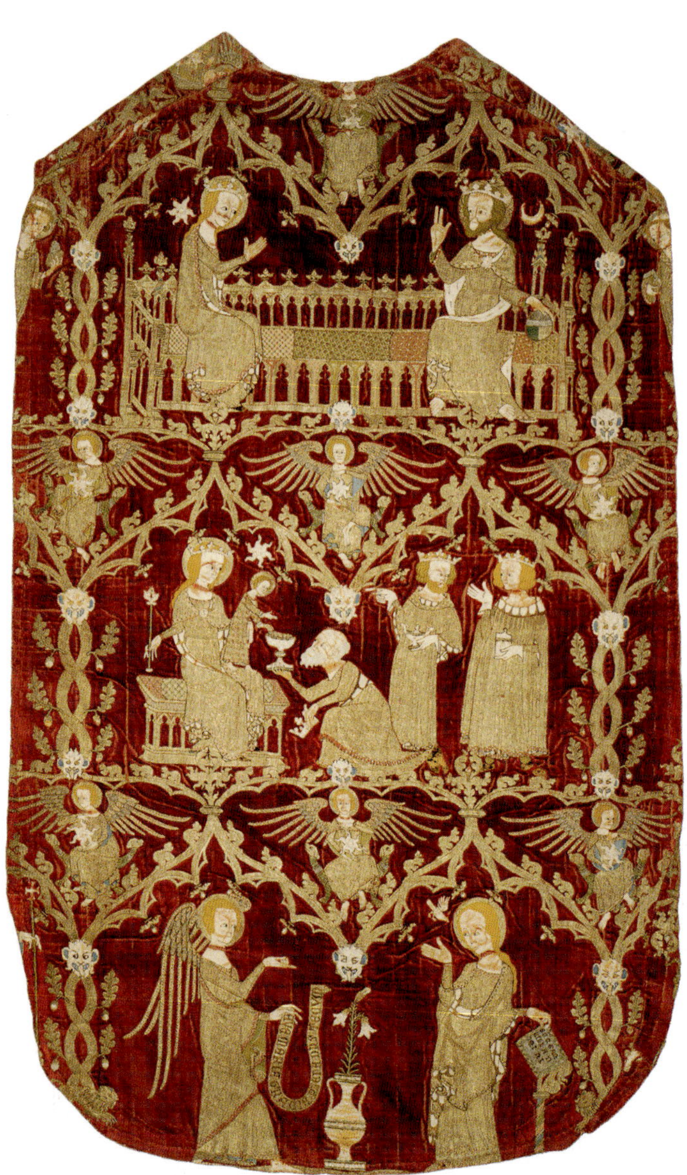

11–23 ***Scenes from the Life of the Virgin*****, back of the Chichester-Constable chasuble**, from a set of vestments embroidered in *opus anglicanum* in southern England. 1330–1350. Red velvet with silk, metallic thread, and seed pearls; length 4' 3" (1.29 m), width 30" (76 cm). The Metropolitan Museum of Art, New York
FLETCHER FUND, 1927 (2.7 162.1).

E, the second letter of the psalm's first word, only appears at the top of the right page and is formed from large tendrils emerging from delicate background vegetation to support the figures of characters in the story of the Judgment of Solomon portrayed within it (I Kings 3:16–27). Two women (one above the other at the right) claiming the same baby appear before King Solomon (enthroned on the crossbar) to settle their dispute. The king's judgment is to order a guard to slice the baby in half with his sword and give each woman her share. This trick exposed the real mother, who hastened to give up her claim in order to save the baby's life. The rest of the psalm's opening words appear on a banner carried by an angel who swoops down at the bottom of the *E*.

Surprising images proliferate among the pages' foliage; many are visual puns on the text. For example, the large windmill at the top of the initial *E* that gives the Psalter its name evokes the statement in the psalm that the wicked would not survive Judgment but would become "like chaff driven by the wind" (Psalm 1:4). Such imagery would have stimulated the user's contemplation of the inner meanings of the text's familiar messages.

The English also became renowned for pictorial needlework, using colored silk and gold thread to create images as detailed as the painters produced in manuscripts. Popular throughout Europe, the art came to be called *opus anglicanum* (English work). The names of several prominent embroiderers are known, but in her own day no one surpassed Mabel of Bury St. Edmunds, who worked for King Henry III. She created both religious and secular pieces, and the grateful king paid her in money and rich gifts. None of Mabel's work has been identified, but it must have resembled the embroidery on the Chichester-Constable chasuble (fig. **11–23**)—a type of garment worn by priests celebrating the Mass. Here, the images are formed by subtle gradations of colored silk. Three Marian scenes—(from bottom up) the Annunciation, the Adoration of the Magi, and the Coronation of the Virgin—are arranged in three registers framed by cusped, crocketed arches, supported on animal-heads and twisting branches sprouting oak leaves with seed-pearl acorns. As the priest moved, the vestment would have glinted in the candlelight. So heavy did such gold and bejeweled garments become that their wearers often needed help to move.

Gothic Art in the Germanic Lands

East of England and France, in the Germanic lands, a new type of Gothic architecture developed in the thirteenth century in response to the increasing importance of sermons within church services. These so-called **hall churches** featured a nave and side aisles with vaults of equal height, creating a spacious and open interior that could accommodate the large crowds drawn by charismatic preachers.

In the fourteenth century, Germanic architects—and especially the Parler family—perfected the hall church. Heinrich Parler designed and began the Church of the Holy Cross in Schwäbisch Gmünd, Swabia, in 1317 (fig. **11–24**). In 1351, his son Peter (c. 1330–1399), the most brilliant architect of this talented family, joined the workshop. He designed the choir in the manner of a hall church whose triple-aisled form was enlarged by a ring of deep chapels between the buttresses. The unity of the entire space was enhanced by the complex web vault that de-emphasized the division of the interior space into bays. Charles IV of Bohemia (ruled 1346–1375) recognized Peter's talent and in 1353 called on him to build the Cathedral of Prague, Charles's capital city. Henceforth Peter Parler and his heirs were the most influential architects in the Holy Roman Empire.

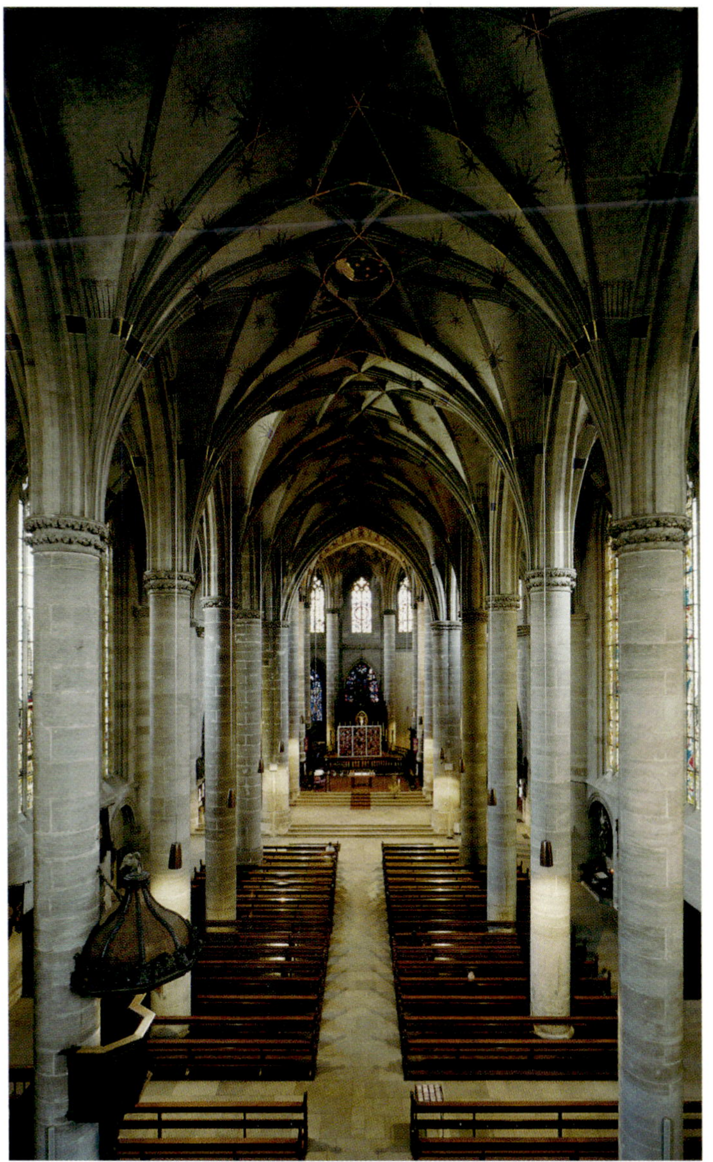

11–24 Heinrich and Peter Parler. Church of the Holy Cross, Schwäbisch Gmünd, Germany. Begun 1317; choir 1351; vaulting completed 16th century

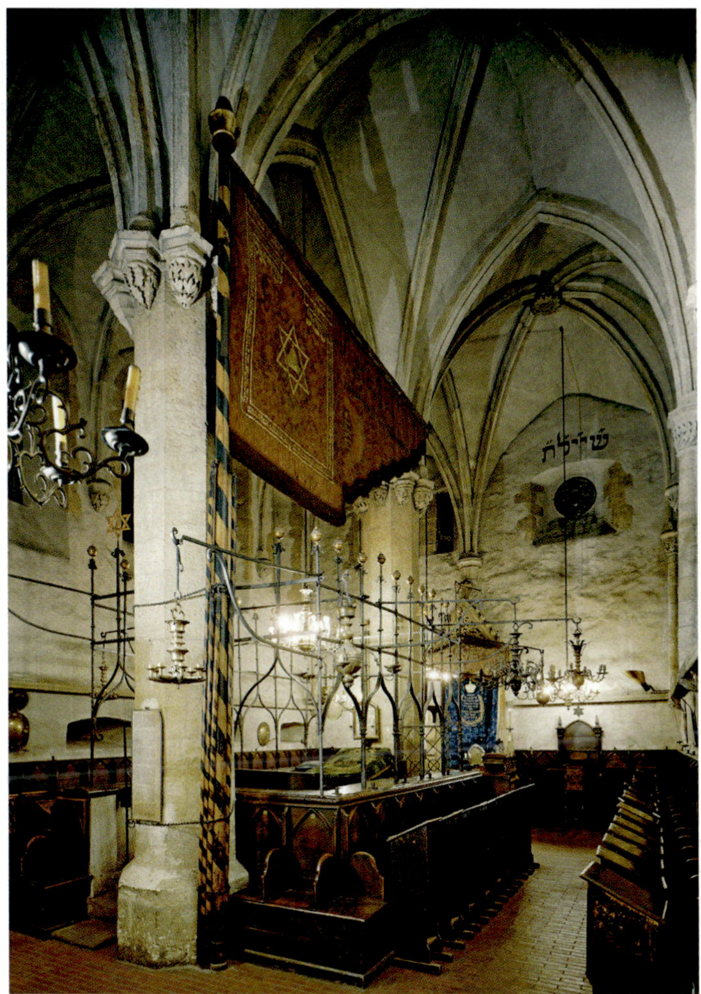

11–25 Interior, Altneuschul, Prague, Bohemia (Czech Republic). c. late 13th century; *bimah* after 1483

The flexible design of these great hall churches was soon widely adopted for civic and residential buildings. Also built in this style is the oldest functioning synagogue in Europe, Prague's Altneuschul (Old-New Synagogue), probably built in the late thirteenth or early fourteenth century (fig. **11–25**). As in a hall church, the vaults of the synagogue are all the same height. But unlike a church, with its division into nave and side aisles, the Altneuschul has two aisles, each with three bays of rib vaulting, to which a nonfunctional fifth rib has been added, perhaps to undo the cross symbolism inherent in the four-part vault.

The synagogue has two focal points, the *aron*, or shrine for the Torah scrolls, located on the east wall, toward Jerusalem, and a central raised reading platform called the *bimah*. The *bimah* can be seen here straddling the two central bays. The interior of the synagogue was originally richly adorned with murals. Men worshiped and studied in the principal space; women were sequestered in annexes.

Gothic Art in Italy

The thirteenth century was a period of political division and economic expansion for the Italian peninsula. The papacy had emerged from a conflict with the Holy Roman Empire as a significant international force, but its temporal success weakened its spiritual authority and brought it into conflict with the growing power of the kings of France and England. In 1309, after the election of a French pope, the papal court moved from Rome to Avignon, in southern France. During the Great Schism of 1378 to 1417, there were two rival lines of popes, one in Rome and one in Avignon, each claiming legitimacy.

Northern Italy was dominated by several independent and wealthy city-states controlled by a few powerful families. A growing sense of individualism promoted patronage of the arts. Artists began to emerge as independent agents, and although their methods and working conditions remained largely unchanged, they now formed powerful urban guilds and contracted freely with wealthy townspeople and nobles as well as with civic and religious institutions. Their ambitiousness and their sense of stylistic individualism reflected their economic and social freedom.

In 1338, the Siena city council commissioned Ambrogio Lorenzetti to paint murals in a room called the Sala della Pace (Chamber of Peace) in the city hall. The theme was to be the contrast between the effects of good and bad government on people's lives (fig. **11–26**). For the *Effects of Good Government in the City* (the left half of the mural), Ambrogio paid tribute to his patrons by painting a recognizable portrait of Siena—cathedral dome and distinctive striped campanile (its free-standing bell tower) visible in the upper left-hand corner—with streets filled by joyful and productive citizens. Ambrogio's achievement here was twofold. First, he maintained an overall visual coherence despite the shifts in vantage point and scale, helping to keep all parts of the flowing composition intelligible. Second, he created a feeling of lifelike scale in the relationship between figures and environment, an effect that continues into the *Effects of Good Government in the Country* at the right, where noble equestrian travelers leave the gate of the city, encountering farmers with pigs and produce on their way in. Throughout the two-part mural, from young people dancing to a tambourine outside a shoemaker's shop, to the travelers and merchants, to the masons on a scaffold, to the prosperous peasants tending fertile fields and lush vineyards, the work conveys a powerful vision of an orderly society marked by peace and plenty. Sadly, famine, poverty, and the horrible Black Death overtook Siena just a few years after this work was completed.

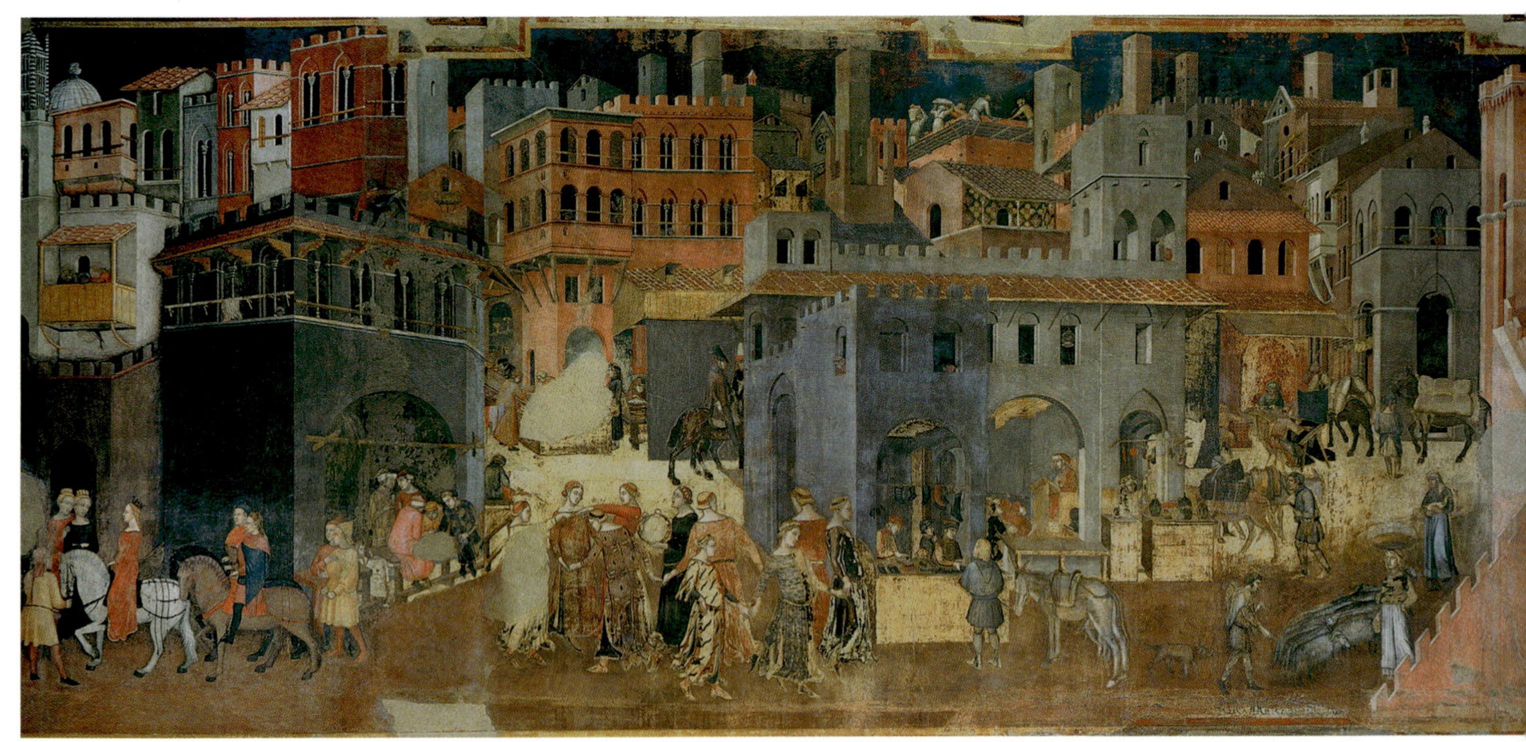

11–26 Ambrogio Lorenzetti. *Effects of Good Government in the City and in the Country*, fresco in the Sala della Pace, Palazzo Pubblico, Siena, Italy. 1338–1340

Sculpture

In the first half of the thirteenth century, Holy Roman Emperor Frederick II had fostered a Classical revival at his southern Italian court, a revival that inspired artists to turn to Roman sculpture for inspiration. Nicola Pisano (active c. 1258–1278), who moved from the south to Tuscany at mid-century, became the leading exponent of this classicizing style. An inscription on a free-standing marble pulpit (fig. **11–27**) in the Pisa Cathedral baptistery identifies Nicola as a supremely self-confident sculptor: "In the year 1260 Nicola Pisano carved this noble work. May so gifted a hand be praised as it deserves." The six-sided structure, open on one side for a stairway, is supported by columns topped with leafy Corinthian capitals. Standing figures and an angel flank Gothic trefoil arches. Three columns rest on the backs of shaggy-maned lions guarding their prey, and the center column stands on crouching human figures. The rectangular panels forming the pulpit's enclosure illustrate New Testament subjects, each framed as an independent composition. The sculptural treatment of the deeply cut, full-bodied forms is almost Roman, as are the heavy, placid faces; the congested layout and the use of hierarchical scale are less so. The format, style, and technique of Roman sarcophagus reliefs—readily visible in the burial ground next to the cathedral—may have provided Nicola's inspiration.

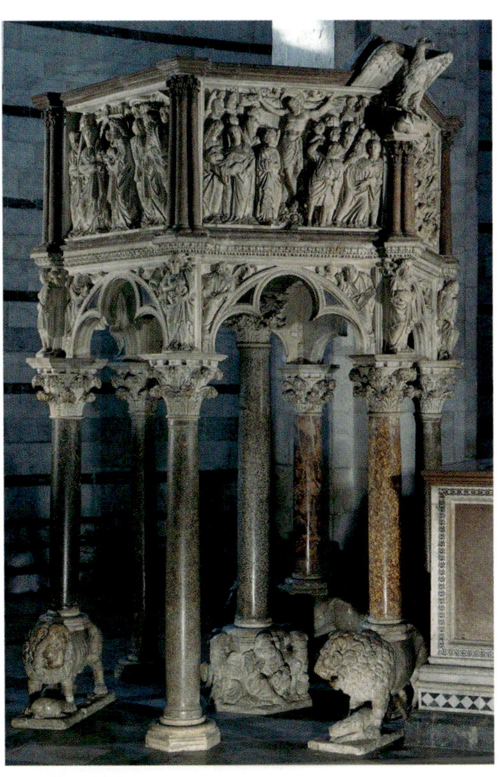

11–27 Nicola Pisano. Pulpit, Baptistery, Cathedral of Pisa. 1260. Marble, height approx. 15' (4.6 m)

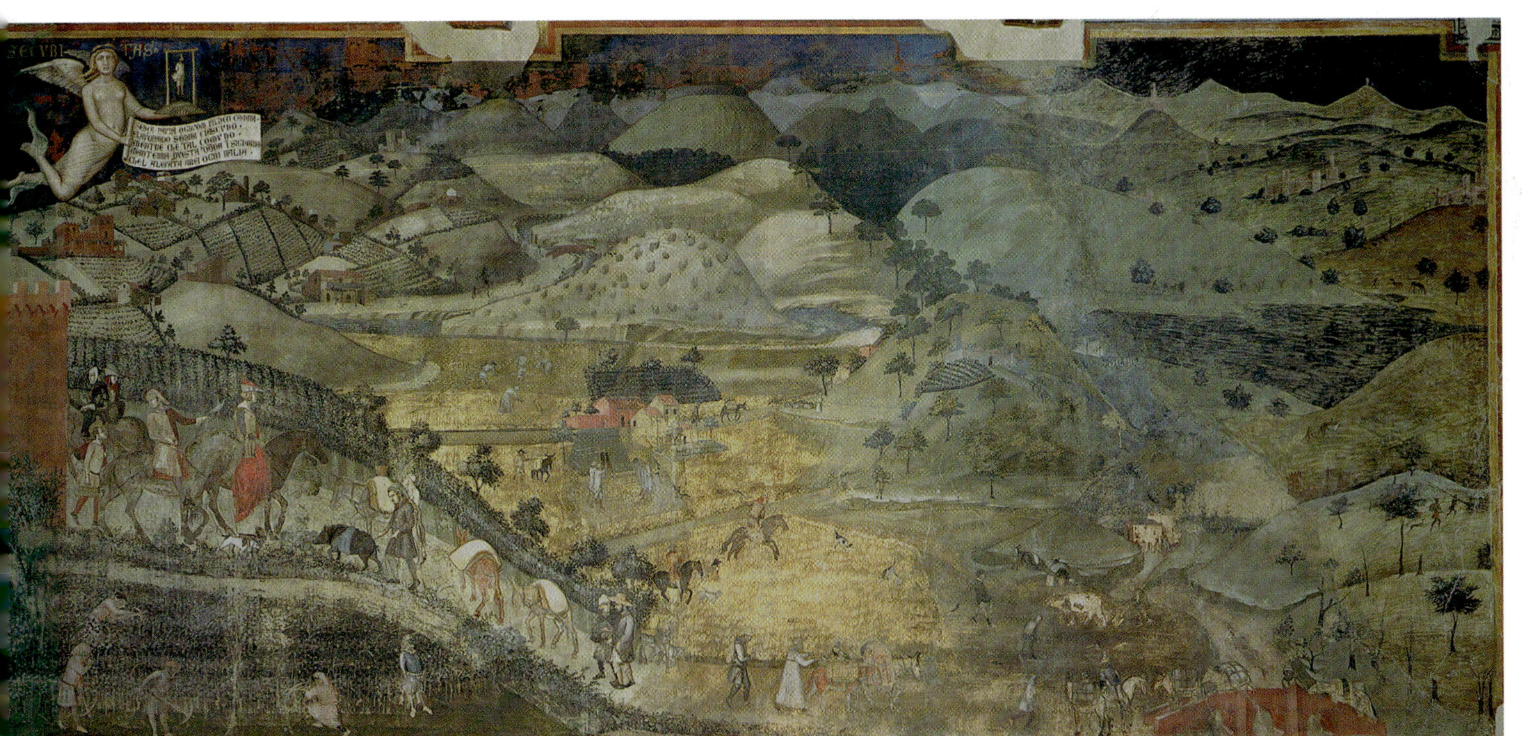

Hovering above the outside gate is a woman clad in a wisp of transparent drapery, a scroll in one hand and a miniature gallows complete with hanged man in the other. She represents security, and her scroll bids those entering the city to come in peace. The gallows is a sharp reminder of the consequences of not doing so.

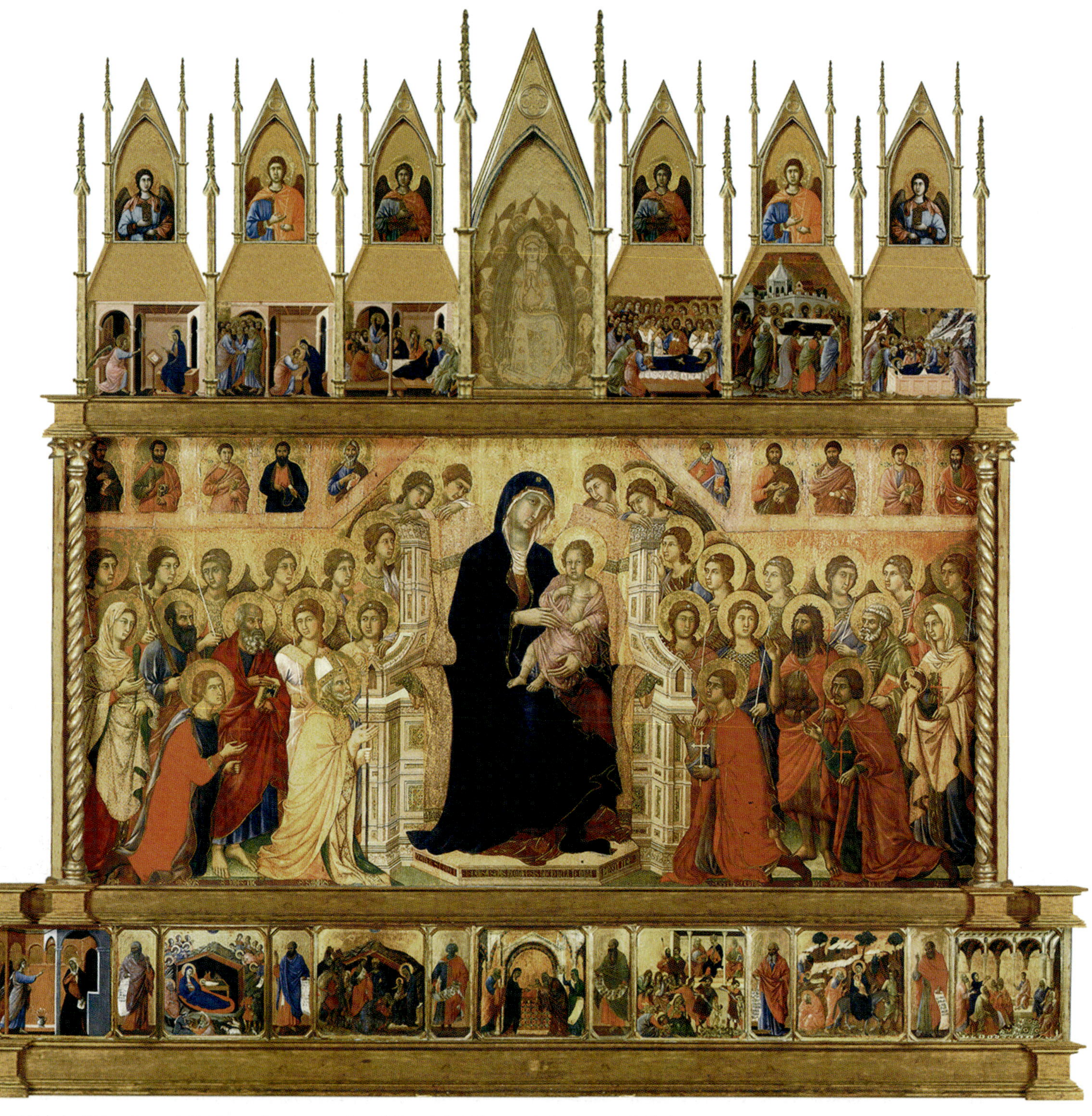

11–28 Duccio di Buoninsegna. Conjectural reconstruction of *Maestà* altarpiece, made for Siena Cathedral. 1308–1311. Tempera and gold on wood, main panel 7' × 13' (2.13 × 4.12 m)

The inscription running around the base of the majestic throne of the Virgin includes the artist's signature: "Holy Mother of God, be thou the cause of peace for Siena and life to Duccio because he painted thee thus." Duccio had in 1288 designed a splendid stained-glass window portraying the Death, Assumption, and Coronation of the Virgin for the huge circular opening in the east wall of the sanctuary. It would have hovered over the installed Maestà *when it was placed on the altar in 1311.*

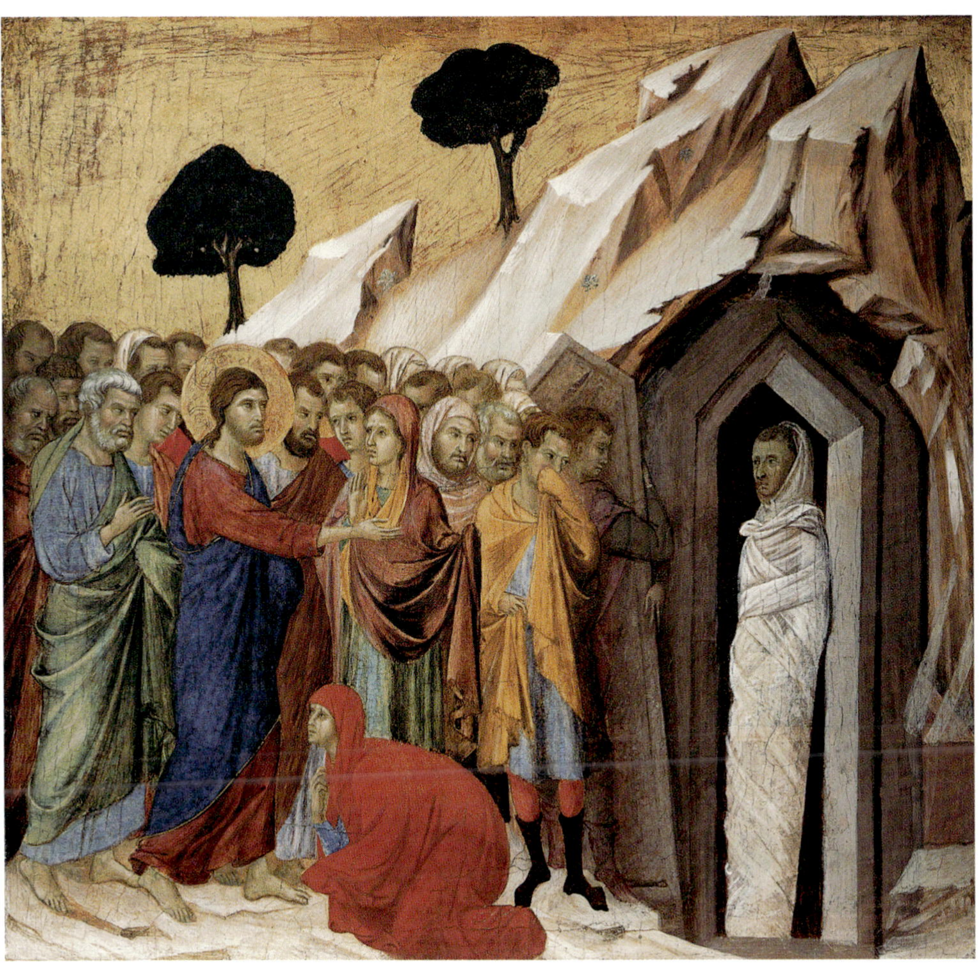

11–29 Duccio di Buoninsegna. *Raising of Lazarus*. From the back of the *Maestà* altarpiece, Siena Cathedral. 1308–1311. Tempera and gold on wood, 17⅛" × 18¼" (43.5 × 46.4 cm). Kimbell Art Museum, Fort Worth, Texas
APX (1975.01)

Panel and Mural Painting

Two very important schools of Italian Gothic painting emerged in Siena and Florence, rivals in this as in everything else. Siena's foremost painter was Duccio di Buoninsegna (active 1278–1318), whose creative synthesis of Byzantine and French Gothic sources transformed the tradition in which he worked. Between 1308 and 1311, Duccio and his workshop painted a huge altarpiece commissioned by Siena Cathedral and known as the *Maestà* (*Majesty*) (fig. **11–28**). Creating this altarpiece—assembled from many wood panels bonded together before painting—was an arduous undertaking. The work was large (the central panel alone was 7 by 13 feet) and it had to be painted on both sides since it could be seen from all directions when standing on the main altar at the center of the sanctuary. Duccio combines a softened figure style adapted from later Byzantine art with the linear grace and easy relationship between figures and their settings that is characteristic of French Gothic art.

Because the *Maestà* was dismantled in 1771, its power and beauty can only be imagined from scattered parts, some still in Siena but others elsewhere. Figure 11–28 is a reconstruction of how the original altarpiece must have looked. The main scene of the front face depicts the *Virgin and Child in Majesty* (hence its title *Maestà*), flanked by 20 angels and ten saints. Above and below were smaller-scale narrative scenes from the Life of the Virgin and the Infancy of Christ.

On the back were episodes from the Life of Christ, focusing on his Passion. Characteristic of Duccio's narrative style is the scene of the *Raising of Lazarus* (fig. **11–29**). Lyrical figures enact the event with graceful decorum, but their highly charged glances and expressive gestures convey a strong sense of dramatic urgency. The shading of drapery and the modeling of faces faithfully describe the figures' three-dimensionality, but the crisp outlines of the jewel-colored shapes created by their drapery, as well as the sinuous continuity of folds and gestures, generate rhythmic patterns across the surface. Experimentation with the portrayal of space extends from the receding rocks of the mountainous landscape to carefully studied interiors, here the tomb of Lazarus whose heavy door was removed by the straining hug of a bystander to reveal the shrouded figure of Jesus' resurrected friend, leaning against the door jamb.

The enthusiasm with which the citizens of a city greeted a great painting or altarpiece like the *Maestà* demonstrates the power of the images it represented as well as the association of the magnificent work with the glory of the city itself. We are fortunate to have a contemporary account of the day Duccio's completed altarpiece for Siena Cathedral was carried from his workshop on December 20, 1311, in a joyous procession:

> On the day that it was carried to the [cathedral] the shops were shut, and the bishop conducted a great and devout

company of priests and friars in solemn procession, accompanied by … all the officers of the commune, and all the people, and one after another the worthiest with lighted candles in their hands took places near the picture, and behind came the women and children with great devotion. And they accompanied the said picture up to the [cathedral], making the procession around the campo [square], as is the custom, all the bells ringing joyously, out of reverence for so noble a picture as is this.
(Holt, page 135)

In Florence the transformation of the Italo-Byzantine style began somewhat earlier than in Siena. Duccio's Florentine counterpart was an older painter named Cenni di Pepi (active c. 1272–1302), better known by his nickname, Cimabue. Cimabue is believed to have painted the *Virgin and Child Enthroned* (fig. **11–30**) in about 1280 for the main altar of the Church of the Santa Trinità (Holy Trinity) in Florence. Almost 13 feet high, this enormous panel painting seems to have set a precedent for monumental altarpieces. Surrounded by saints, angels, and prophets, as in Duccio's altarpiece, a huge Mary holds the infant Jesus in her lap and gestures toward him as the path to salvation, adopting a formula popular in Byzantine art at least since the seventh century (see fig. 7–21).

Cimabue also followed Byzantine practice in determining the proportions of the figures, the placement of their features, even the tilts of their haloed heads. To render the draperies of holy figures, he used the Byzantine technique of highlighting the base color with thin lines of gold. Mary's huge throne, painted to represent gold with inset enamels and gems, provides an architectural framework for the positioning of figures. The mixture of vantage points suspends the viewer in space in front of the image, simultaneously looking down on the projecting elements of the throne and Mary's lap, but straight at the prophets at the base of the throne and the splendid winged seraphim who appear one above another on either side. These spatial ambiguities, as well as subtle asymmetries throughout the composition, the Virgin's engaging gaze, and the

Technique

Cennini on Panel Painting

Cennino Cennini's *Il Libro dell'Arte* (*The Handbook of the Crafts*), a compendium of early fifteenth-century Florentine artistic techniques, includes step-by-step instructions for making panel paintings.

The wood for the panels, he specified, should be fine-grained, free of blemishes, and thoroughly seasoned by slow drying.The first step in preparing such a panel for painting was to cover its surface with clean white linen strips soaked in a gesso made from gypsum, a task best done on a dry, windy day. Gesso provides a ground, or surface, on which to paint, and Cennini specified that at least nine layers should be applied, with a minimum of two-and-a-half days' drying time between layers. The gessoed surface should then be burnished until it resembled ivory. The artist could now sketch the composition of the work with charcoal made from burned willow twigs. At this point, advised the author, "When you have finished drawing your figure, especially if it is in a very valuable [altarpiece], so that you are counting on profit and reputation from it, leave it alone for a few days, going back to it now and then to look it over and improve it wherever it still needs something … (and bear in mind that you may copy and examine things done by other good masters; that it is no shame to you)" (Thompson, page 75).

The final version of the design, he directed, should be inked in with a fine squirrel-hair brush, and the charcoal brushed off with a feather. Gold leaf was to be affixed next on a humid day over a reddish clay ground called bole, and the tissue-thin gold sheets carefully glued down with a mixture of fine powdered clay and egg white and burnished with a gemstone or the tooth of a carnivorous animal. Punched and incised patterning would be added later.

Italian painters at this time worked in a type of paint known as tempera: powdered pigments mixed most often with egg yolk, a little water, and an occasional touch of glue. Apprentices were kept busy grinding pigments and mixing paints according to their masters' recipes, setting them out for more senior painters in wooden bowls or shell dishes. Cennini claimed that panel painting was a gentleman's job, but given its laborious complexity, that was wishful thinking. His claim does, however, reflect the rising social status of painters.

Cennini outlined a highly formulaic painting process. Faces, for example, were always to be done last, with flesh tones applied over two coats of a light greenish pigment and highlighted with touches of red and white. The finished painting was given a layer of varnish to protect it and intensify its colors. Reflecting the increasing specialization that developed in the thirteenth century, Cennini assumed that an elaborate frame would have been produced by someone else according to the painter's specifications and brought fully assembled to the studio.

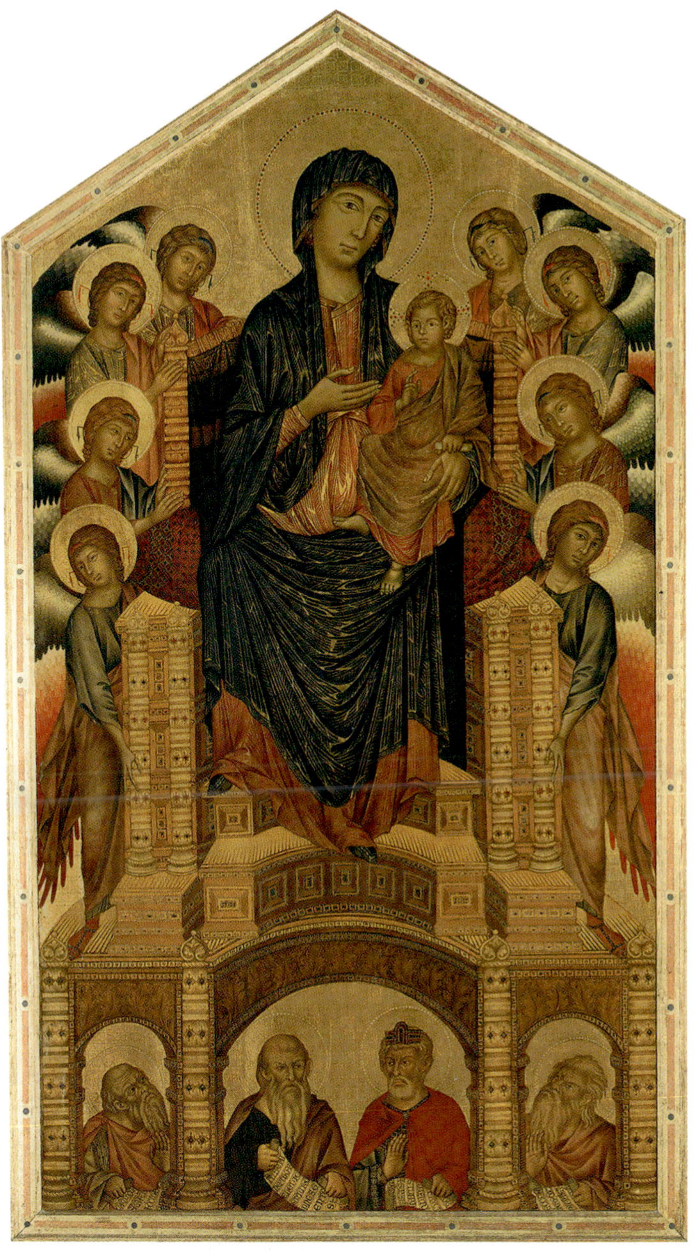

11–30 Cimabue. ***Virgin and Child Enthroned***, from the Church of Santa Trinità, Florence. c. 1280. Tempera and gold on wood, 12' 17" × 7' 4" (3.53 × 2.2 m). Galleria degli Uffizi, Florence

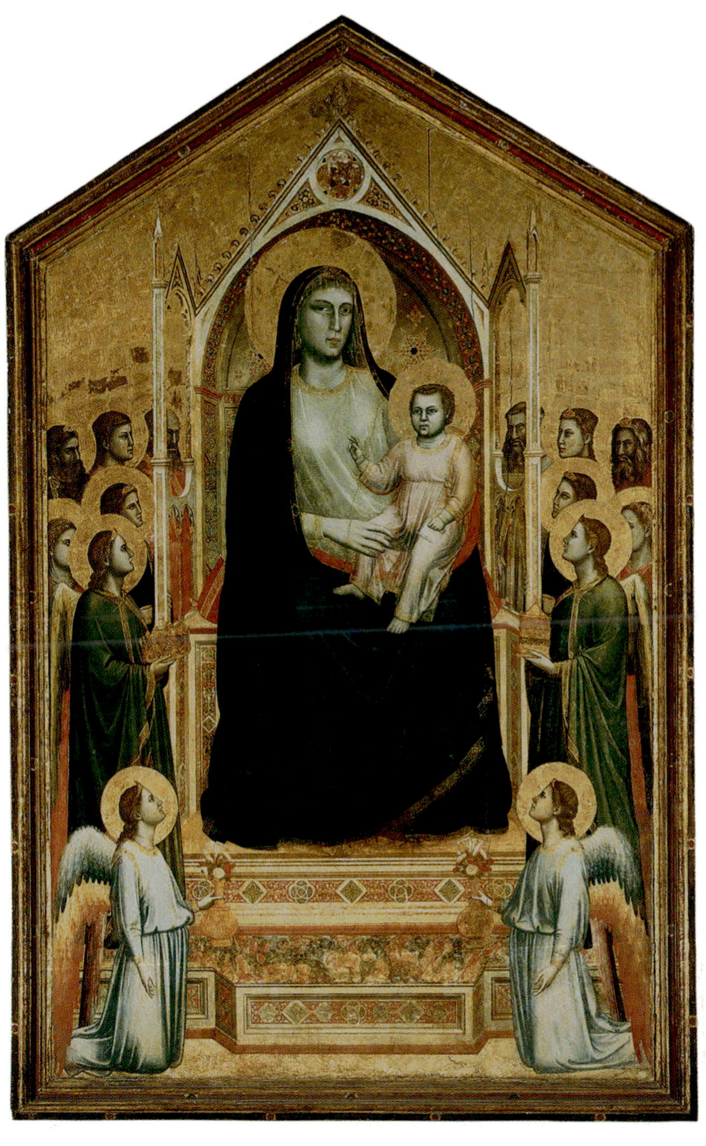

11–31 Giotto di Bondone. ***Virgin and Child Enthroned***, from the Church of the Ognissanti, Florence. 1305–1310. Tempera and gold on wood, 10' 8" × 6' 8¼" (3.53 × 2.05 m). Galleria degli Uffizi, Florence

well-observed faces of the old men, are all departures from tradition that serve to enliven the picture.

According to the sixteenth-century art chronicler Giorgio Vasari, Cimabue discovered a talented shepherd boy, Giotto di Bondone, and taught him how to paint. Then, "Giotto obscured the fame of Cimabue, as a great light outshines a lesser." Vasari also credited Giotto (active c. 1300–1337) with "setting art upon the path that may be called the true one [for he] learned to draw accurately from life and thus put an end to the crude Greek [i.e., Italo-Byzantine] manners" (trans. J. C. and P. Bondanella). The painter and commentator Cennino Cennini (c. 1370–1440) (see "Cennini on Panel Painting," page 296), writing in the late fourteenth century, was struck by the accessibility and modernity of Giotto's art, which, though it retained traces of the "Greek manner," was moving toward the depiction of a humanized world anchored in three-dimensional form.

Giotto's 1310 painting of the *Virgin and Child Enthroned* (fig. **11–31**) for the Church of the Ognissanti (All Saints) in Florence reflects Cimabue's influence in the positioning of figures within a largely symmetrical composition. Gone, however, are the Virgin's modestly inclined head and delicate gold-lined drapery; instead, light and shadow play gently across her substantial form. This

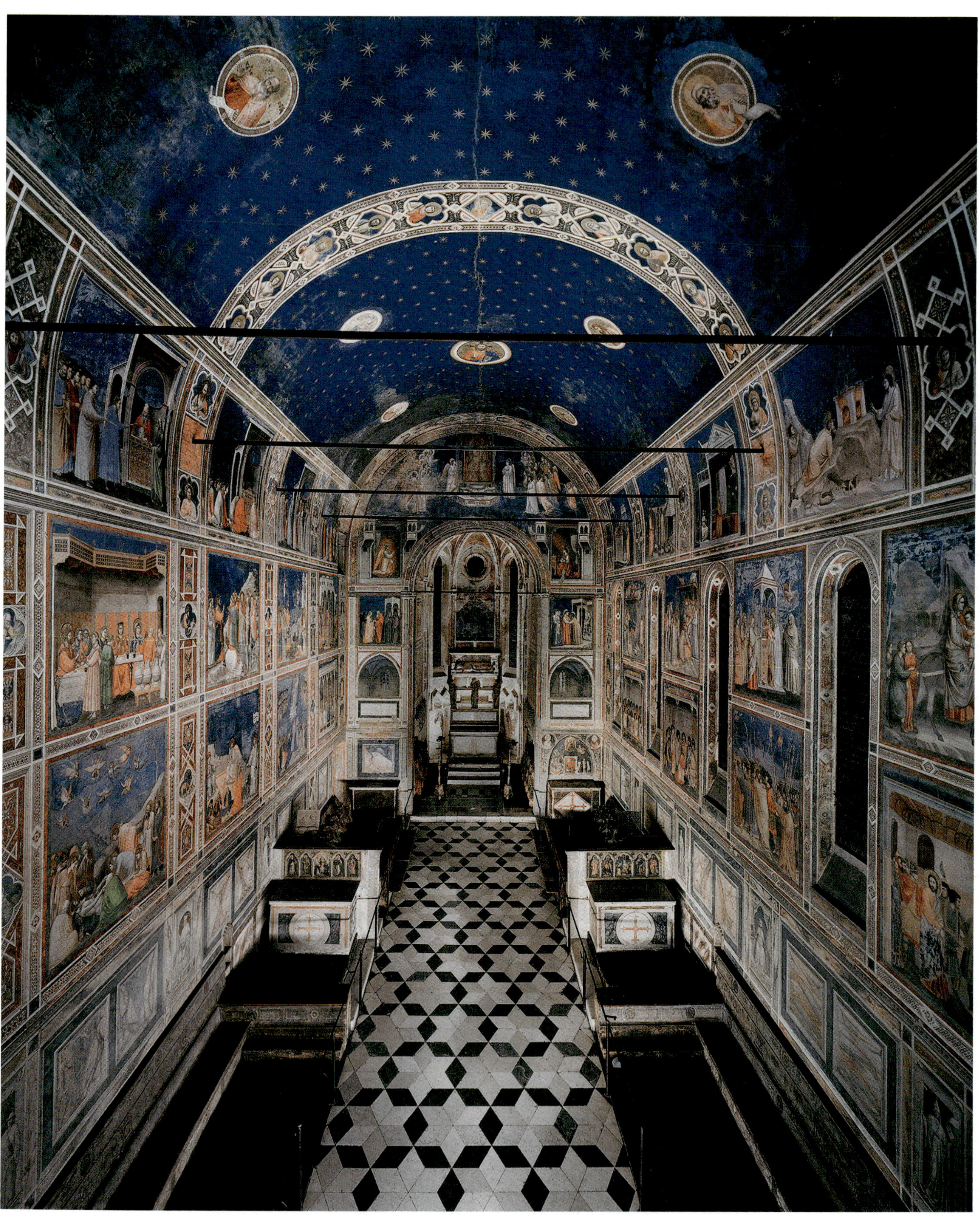

11–32 Giotto di Bondone. Frescoes of the Arena (Scrovegni) Chapel, Padua. View toward the east wall. 1305–1306

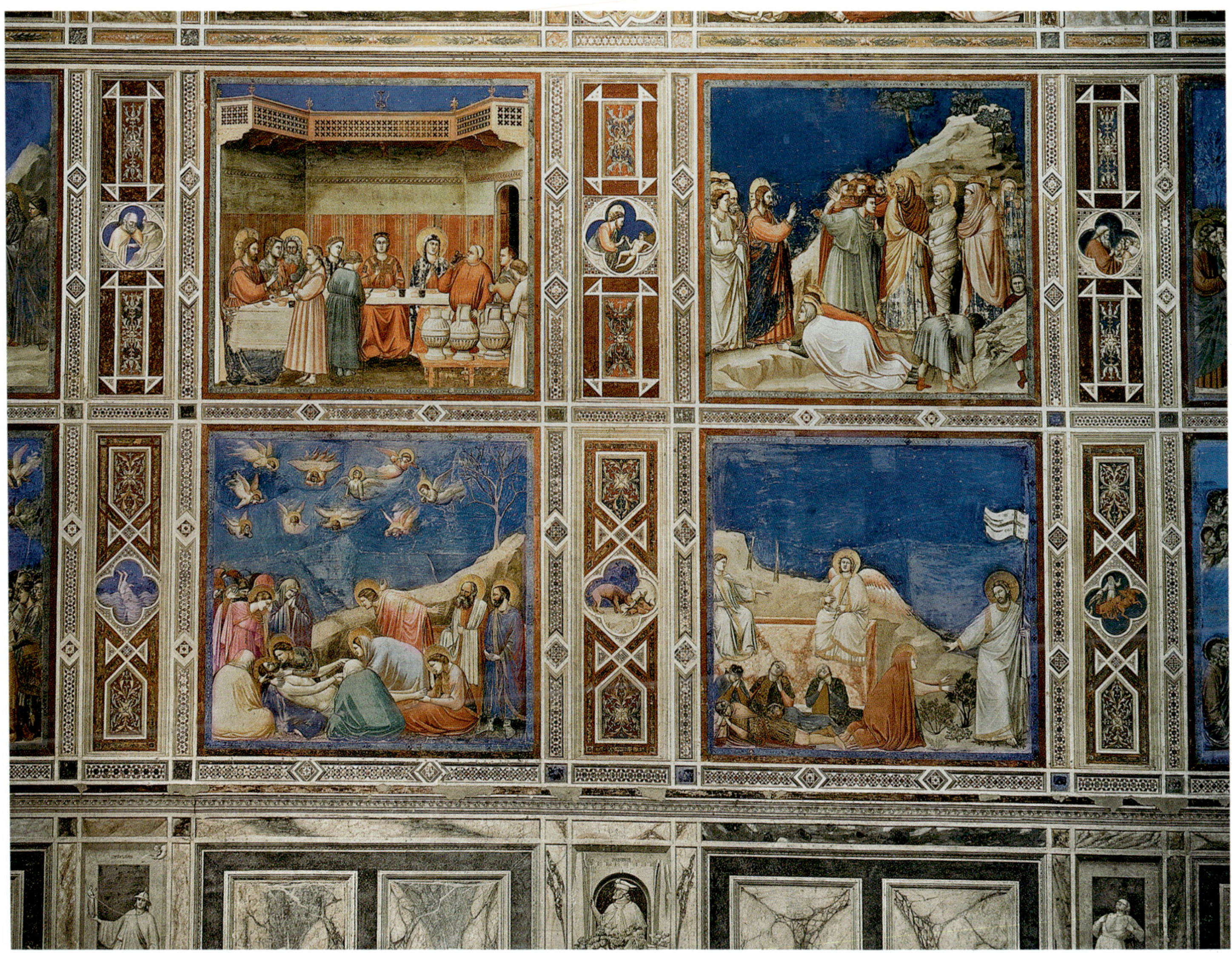

11–33 Giotto di Bondone. *Marriage at Cana, Raising of Lazarus, Lamentation,* and *Resurrection* (from top left), frescoes from north wall of Arena (Scrovegni) Chapel, Padua (see fig. 11–32, left-hand wall). 1305–1306

colossal Mary seems to overwhelm her slender Gothic throne. Despite Giotto's retention of hieratic scale and the formal, enthroned image type, he has created the sense that his figures are fully three-dimensional beings, whose plainly draped, bulky bodies inhabit real space. Gone are the courtly surface patterns emphasized in Duccio's work by sharp outlines and correspondences among curvilinear drapery folds.

Giotto's masterpiece is the frescoed interior of the Scrovegni family chapel in Padua, painted about 1305 (fig. **11–32**). Architecturally, the chapel (also known as the Arena Chapel because of its location near an ancient Roman arena) is a simple, barrel-vaulted room. Giotto covered the entrance wall with the Last Judgment and the sanctuary wall with highlighted scenes from the Life of Christ, notably the Annunciation spread over the two painted architectural frameworks on either side of the high arched opening into the sanctuary itself. He subdivided the side walls (fig. **11–33**) with a dado of allegorical grisaille paintings of Virtues and Vices, from which rise vertical bands containing quatrefoil portrait medallions set within a framework painted to resemble marble inlay and carved relief. The central band of medallions spans the vault (fig. 11–32), crossing a star-spangled sky in which large portrait disks float like glowing moons. Set into this framework are rectangular scenes aligned in three horizontal bands of narrative, portraying the life of the Virgin and her parents at the top and the life of Jesus along the middle and lower registers. Both the individual scenes and the overall program display Giotto's genius for distilling complex stories into a series of compelling moments. He concentrates on the human dimensions of the unfolding drama—from touches of anecdotal humor to expressions of profound anguish—rather than on its symbolic or theological weight.

Giotto's prodigious narrative skills are apparent in the pictures on the north side wall illustrated in fig. 11–33. At top left Jesus performs his first miracle, changing water into wine at the wedding feast at Cana. The wine steward—looking very much like the jars of

Technique

Buon Fresco

The two techniques used in mural painting are ***buon*** ("true") ***fresco*** ("fresh"), in which color is applied with water-based paints on wet plaster, and ***fresco secco*** ("dry"), in which paint is applied to a dry plastered wall.

The advantage of *buon fresco* is its durability. As the painted plaster dries, a chemical reaction bonds the pigments into the wall surface. In *fresco secco*, by contrast, the color does not become part of the plaster wall and, therefore, over time will tend to flake off. The chief disadvantage of *buon fresco* is that it must be done quickly, without mistakes. The painter plasters and paints only as much as can be completed in a day, which explains the Italian term for each of the sections: ***giornata***, or day's work. The size of a *giornata* varies according to the complexity of the painting within it. A face, for instance, can occupy an entire day, whereas large areas of sky can be painted quite rapidly. In Giotto's Scrovegni Chapel scholars have identified 852 separate *giornate*, some worked on concurrently within a single day by assistants in Giotto's workshop.

In medieval and Renaissance Italy, a wall to be frescoed was first prepared with a rough, thick undercoat of plaster. When this was dry, assistants copied the master painter's composition onto it with charcoal, at times corrected by the master. These drawings, known as *sinopia*, have an immediacy and freshness lost in the finished painting. Work proceeded in irregularly shaped *giornate* conforming to the contours of major figures and objects. Assistants covered one section at a time with a fresh, thin coat of very fine plaster over the *sinopia*, and when this was "set" but not dry, artists painted it with pigments mixed with water, working from the top down so that drips fell on unfinished portions. Some areas requiring pigments such as ultramarine blue (which was unstable in *buon fresco*), as well as areas requiring gilding, would be added after the wall was dry using the *fresco secco* technique.

new wine himself—tastes the results. To the right is the *Raising of Lazarus.* The basic elements of the scene are familiar from Duccio's rendering (fig. 11–29), but the comparison highlights with real clarity the distinctiveness of Giotto's narrative and pictorial style. He has sacrificed the elegantly cut and jewel-toned pattern of silhouettes within a solid figural mass in order to emphasize the bold modeling of individualized, solid figures who twist in space, using postures and gestures to react to the human drama by pleading for Jesus' help or by expressing astonishment at the miracle or revulsion at the smell of death. And Jesus is separated from the crowd, his transforming gesture highlighted against the dark blue of the background, his profile face locked in communication with the similarly isolated Lazarus, whose eyes, still fixed in death, let us know that the miracle is just about to happen. On the lower register, Jesus' grief-stricken followers lament over his dead body. This somber, quiet prelude gives way on the right to the Resurrection, indicated by the weighty angels flanking the empty tomb and by Jesus' own sense of movement, so forcefully conveyed by his raised leg that he seems almost ready to leave the earthly stage by walking out of the picture.

But the theological importance of these moments in Jesus' life is not completely eclipsed by Giotto's stirring attention to the human condition. Educated worshipers would also see in Jesus' miracle at Cana a prefiguration of the miraculous transubstantiation of bread and wine into Jesus' body and blood in the Mass. And the resurrection of the ghoulish Lazarus prefigures Jesus' own Resurrection, placed just below to encourage the comparison. These are traditional medieval associations. What is new here is the way Giotto draws his viewers into the experience of the events. This direct emotional appeal not only allows viewers to imagine scenes in relation to their own life experiences. It also embodies a new Franciscan value on personal devotion rooted in empathetic responses to sacred stories.

Looking Back

The art and architecture of Gothic France experienced a rich and rapid evolution, and achieved a growing international impact, as it emerged from Abbot Suger's vision of light-saturated monastic spirituality in the 1140s, through the great cathedral projects of the first half of the thirteenth century, and into King Louis IX's Parisian jewel-box Sainte-Chapelle of the 1240s. To enhance the desired effects of light and color, architects made buildings taller, walls lighter, and windows larger.

The fourteenth century saw regional architectural variations in centers throughout Europe, and the strong impact of Gothic painting in Italy, notable in the elegant, graceful figures that enact sacred stories in Duccio's Sienese *Maestà* of the early 1300s. But even if Sienese painting was a key contributor to the development of mainstream European Gothic art, it was Florentine painting, in the style championed by Giotto and kept alive by his pupils and their followers, that would be more fundamental to the development of Italian Renaissance art over the next two centuries.

IN PERSPECTIVE

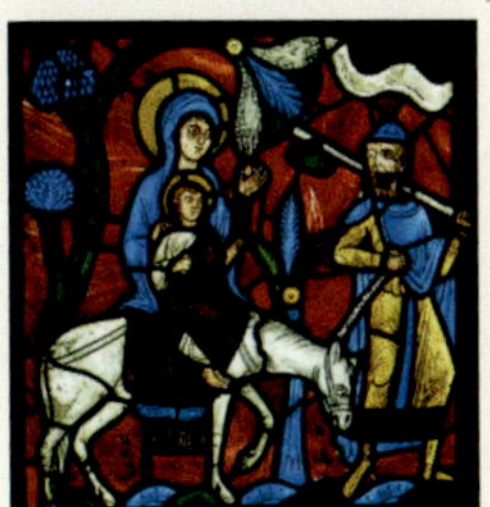

SAINT-DENIS STAINED GLASS,
C. 1140–1144

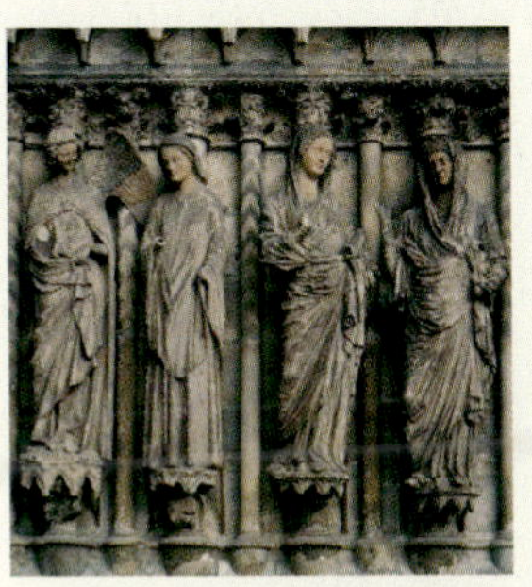

REIMS VISITATION AND ANNUNCIATION,
C. 1230–1255

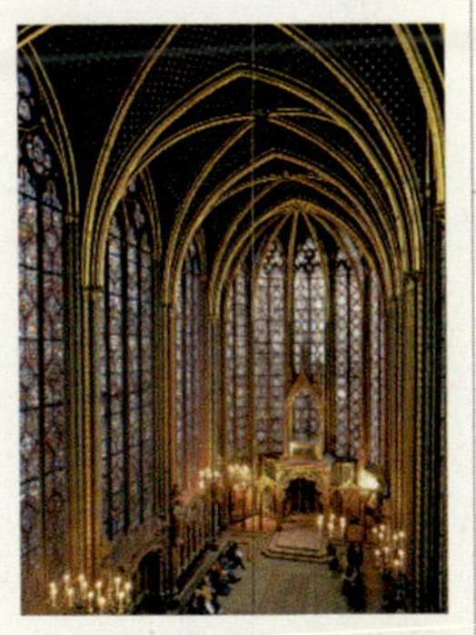

SAINTE-CHAPELLE,
1243–1248

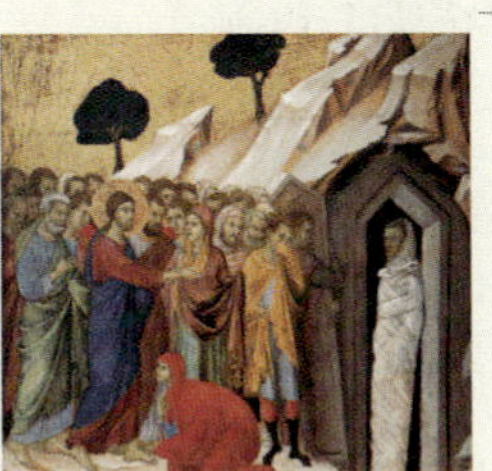

DUCCIO,
RAISING OF LAZARUS,
1308–1311

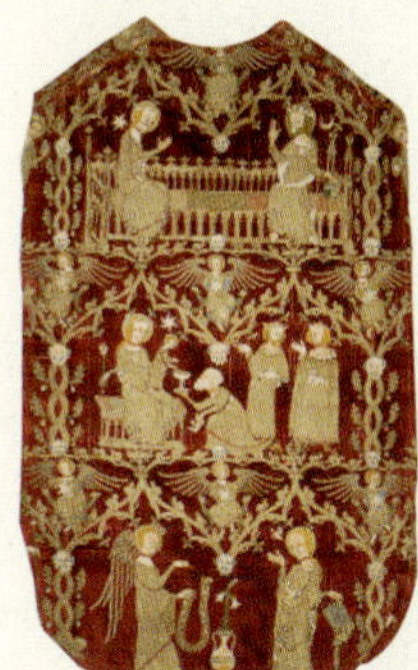

CHICHESTER-CONSTABLE CHASUBLE,
1330–1350

1100

◀ **Suger, abbot of Saint-Denis,** 1122–1151

1150

◀ **Second Crusade,** 1147–1149

◀ **Plantagenet Dynasty Ruled England,** 1154–1485

◀ **Third Crusade,** 1188–1192

◀ **Queen Blanche of Castile,** 1188–1252

1200

◀ **Fourth Crusade Takes Constantinople,** 1204

◀ **Franciscan Order Founded,** 1209

◀ **Louis IX (Saint Louis), King of France,** ruled 1226–1270

1250

◀ **Western Control of Constantinople Ends,** 1261

◀ **Thomas Aquinas Begins Writing *Summa Theologica*,** 1266

1300

◀ **Papacy Resides in Avignon,** 1309–1377

◀ **Queen Jeanne d'Evreux,** 1310–1371

◀ **Hundred Years' War,** 1337–1453

◀ **Black Death Begins,** 1348

1350

◀ **Boccaccio Begins Writing *The Decameron*,** 1348

◀ **Great Schism,** 1378–1417

◀ **Chaucer Starts Work on *The Canterbury Tales*,** 1387

1400

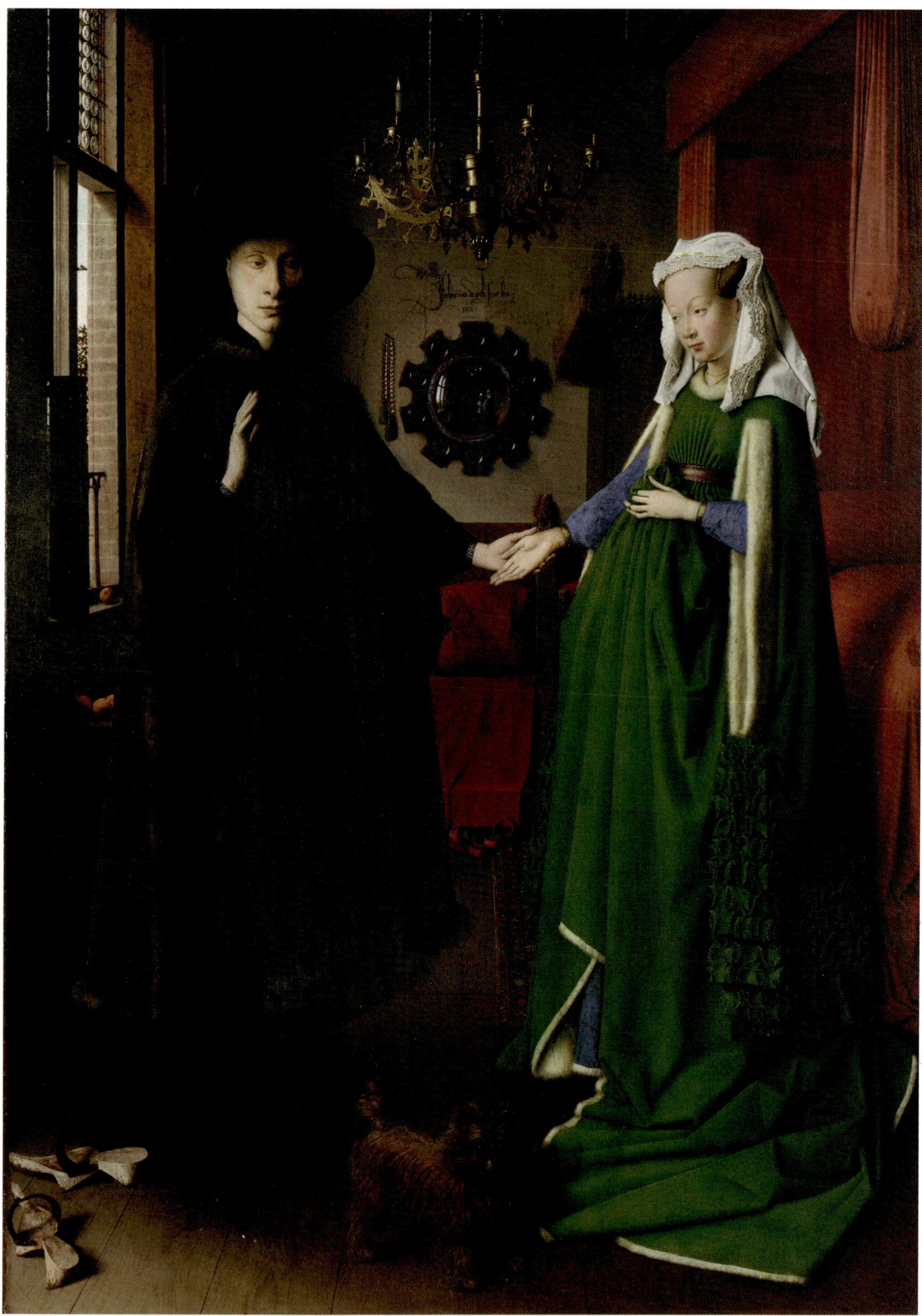

12
Early Renaissance Art

LOOKING FORWARD

The fifteenth century saw the emergence of wealthy merchants whose rise to power was fueled by individual accomplishment, rather than hereditary succession within noble families. Certainly Giovanni Arnolfini—the pasty gentleman with the astonishing hat in this double portrait (fig. **12–1**)—earned, rather than inherited, the right to have himself and his wife recorded by renowned artist Jan van Eyck. It was the wealth and connections he made as an Italian cloth merchant providing luxury fabrics to the Burgundian court that put him in the position to commission such a precious picture, in which both patron and painter are identified with real clarity. Giovanni's face looks more like a personal likeness than anything we have seen since ancient Rome, and Jan van Eyck not only inscribed his name above the convex mirror—"Jan van Eyck has been here 1434"—his personal painting style carries an equally sure stamp of authorship. The doll-like face of the woman standing next to Giovanni is less individualized. Has she lifted her skirt over her belly so she can follow Giovanni who has taken her by the hand? Or are most modern observers correct in assuming that she is pregnant? This painting is full of mysteries.

The precise identity of the couple is still open to scholarly debate. And is this a wedding, a betrothal, or perhaps security for a shady financial deal? Recently it has been interpreted as a memorial to a beloved wife lost to death. Only the wealth of the couple is beyond dispute. They are surrounded by luxury objects: lavish bed hangings, sumptuous chandelier, precious oriental carpet, rare oranges, not to mention their extravagant clothing. The man wears a fur-lined, silk velvet *heuque* (sleeveless over-garment). The woman's gown not only employs more costly wool fabric than necessary to cover her slight body; the elaborate cutwork decoration and white fur lining of her sleeves are conspicuous indicators of cost. In fact, the painting itself—probably hung in the couple's home—was an object of considerable value.

Even within its secular setting, however, the picture resonated with sacred meaning. The Church still provided spiritual grounding for men and women of the Renaissance. The crystal prayer beads hanging next to the convex mirror imply the couple's piety, and the mirror itself, a symbol of the all-seeing eye of God, is framed with a circular cycle of scenes from Christ's Passion. A figure of Saint Margaret, protector of women in childbirth, is carved at the top of a post of the high-backed chair beside the bed, and the perky affenpinscher in the foreground may be more than a pet. Dogs served as symbols of fidelity, and choosing a rare, ornamental breed like this may have been yet another opportunity to express wealth.

12–1 Jan van Eyck. ***Double Portrait: traditionally identified as Giovanni Arnolfini and Giovanna Cenami.*** 1434. Oil on wood panel, 33" × 22½" (83.8 × 57.2 cm). The National Gallery, London

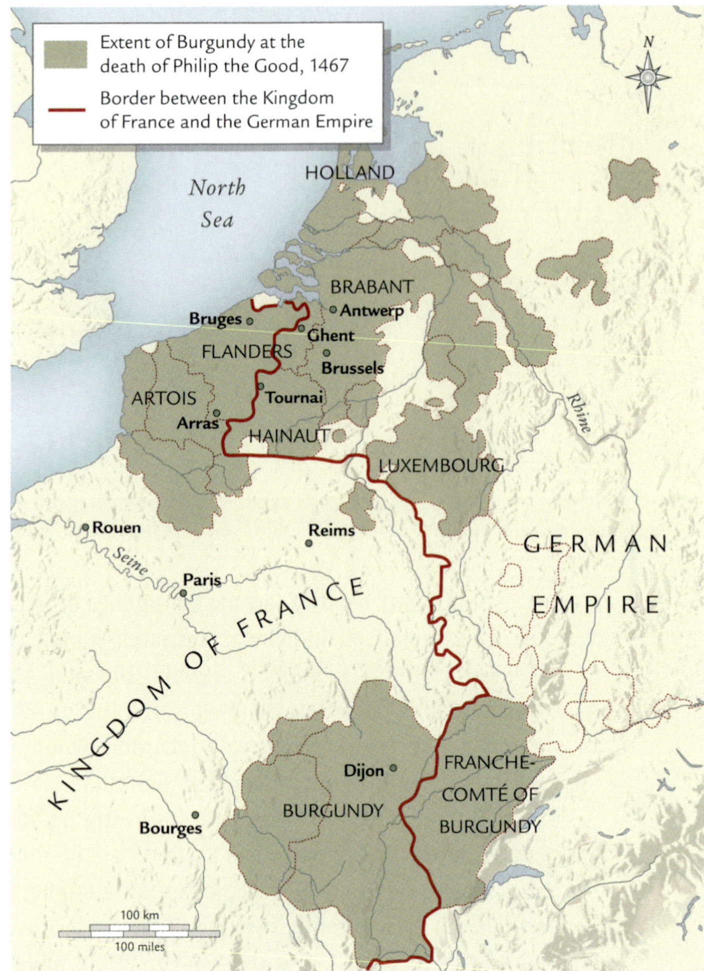

Map 12–1 Centers of Northern European Art during the Fifteenth Century

Fascinated by what they saw around them, fifteenth-century artists sought to observe and represent the variety of textures, shapes, and spaces they experienced in their world. They carefully described with paint the colors and textures of surfaces, and they developed intellectual systems, such as linear perspective, for pictorial simulations of three-dimensional forms arranged in space. They and their patrons were guided by a new emphasis on Humanist thinking, which placed great value on science, reason, and the individual, while never abandoning a steadfast religious faith.

Though the actual term "Renaissance" (French for "rebirth") was applied to this period by later historians, its origins lie in the thought of Petrarch and other fourteenth-century scholars, who believed in the power and potential of human beings for great individual accomplishment. These Italian humanists also looked back at the 1,000 years extending from the disintegration of the Western Roman Empire to their own day and determined that the human achievements of the Classical world was followed by a period of decline—a "middle" or "dark" age. They saw their own era as a third age characterized by a revival, rebirth, or renaissance, when humanity began to emerge from what they saw as intellectual and cultural stagnation and to appreciate once more the achievement of the ancients and the value of rational, scientific investigation. Clearly new things are happening in art as well as in intellectual life during the fifteenth century, and not only in Italy but also in Northern Europe. We will find, however, that northern and Italian artists will take somewhat divergent paths as they explore new ways of representing the natural world and the social and spiritual systems that sustained it.

Northern Renaissance Art

In Northern Europe (see map **12–1**), where the Gothic style had emerged from native traditions, artists came to the Renaissance by way of an intense curiosity about the natural world. Gothic artists in France, the Germanic lands, and the Low Countries (present-day Belgium, the Netherlands, and Luxembourg) had already captured the visual appearance of birds, plants, and animals with breathtaking virtuosity in manuscript painting, textiles, and sculpture. They enlarged on these interests in the fourteenth century by highlighting such effects as reflections on water, steamy breath on a cold winter's day, and the sheen of metal basins. In the fifteenth century,

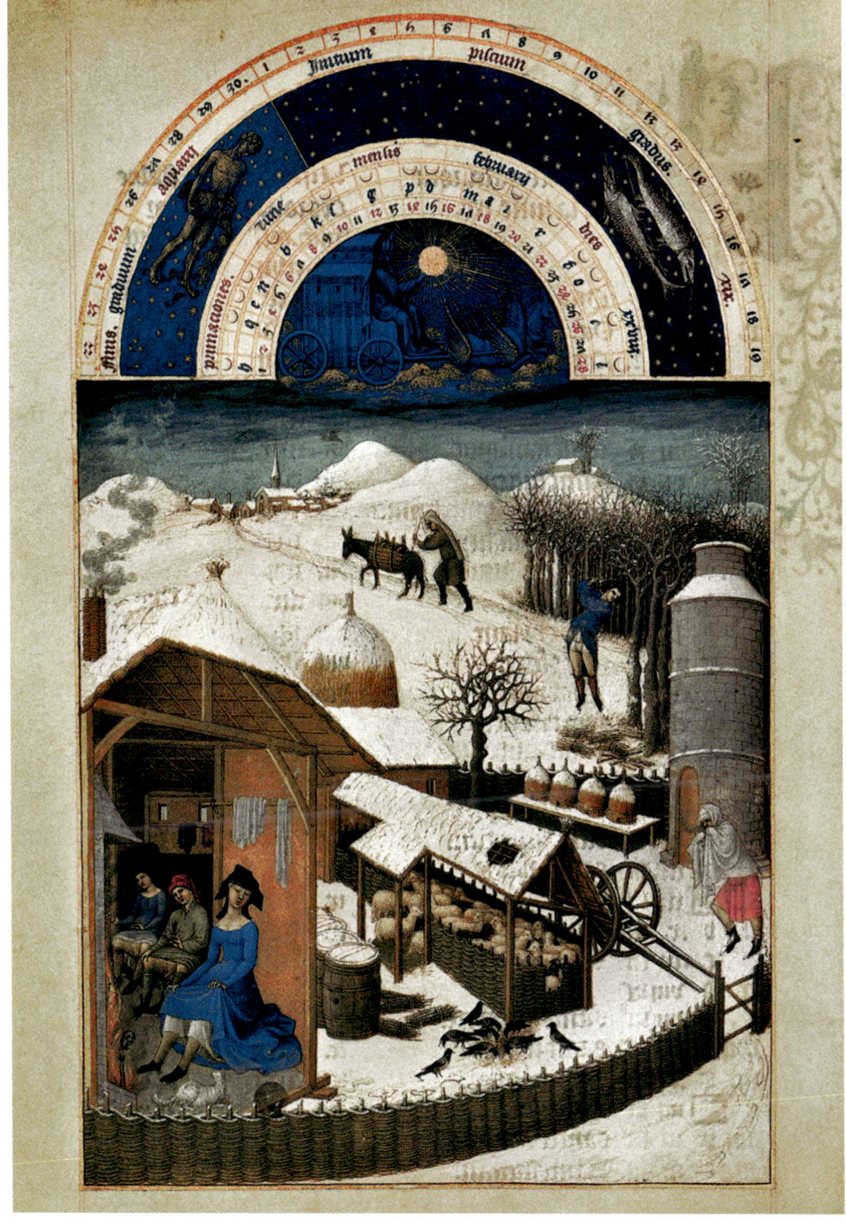

12–2 Paul, Herman, and Jean Limbourg. Page with *February, Très Riches Heures*. 1411–1416. Colors and ink on parchment, 8⅞" × 5⅜" (22.5 × 13.7 cm). Musée Condé, Chantilly, France

they worked to incorporate these details within scenes that seem to replicate their actual material world. Similarly, fifteenth-century portraits appear astonishingly lifelike, and even in religious paintings, saints and angels have distinct personalities, as if based on pecific human models.

At the beginning of the fifteenth century, the most famous illuminators of Northern Europe were three brothers, Paul, Herman, and Jean, commonly known as the Limbourg brothers because they came from the region of Limbourg in the Low Countries. At the time, people generally did not have family names in the modern sense, but were known instead by their first names, often followed by a reference to their place of origin, parentage, or occupation. For instance, the name Jan van Eyck means "Jan from [the town of] Eyck."

The Limbourg brothers are first recorded as apprentice goldsmiths in Paris in about 1390. About 1404, they entered the service of Duke John of Berry, for whom they produced their most famous work, the so-called *Très Riches Heures* (*Very Sumptuous Hours*), between 1411 and 1416. This Book of Hours included a calendar section with full-page paintings introducing each month. The subjects alternated between peasants' labors and aristocratic pleasures. On the February page (fig. **12–2**), farm folks relax before a blazing fire. Although many country people at this time lived in hovels, this farm looks comfortable and well maintained, with timber-frame buildings, a row of beehives, a sheepfold, and neatly woven fences. Most remarkably, the details of the painting convey the feeling of the cold winter weather: the leaden sky, the bare trees, the soft snow, the steamy breath of the bundled-up worker blowing on his hands, and the comforting smoke curling up from the farmhouse chimney.

The painting clearly maintains several Gothic conventions (see fig. 11–16), common in Northern Renaissance art well into the first

WOMEN ARTISTS IN THE LATE MIDDLE AGES AND THE RENAISSANCE

Since most formal apprenticeships were closed to them, medieval and Renaissance women artists learned their trade either from family members or in convents. Despite such obstacles, however, a few highly skilled women received major commissions. In the fourteenth century, Bourgot, the daughter of the miniaturist Jean le Noir, illuminated books for Charles V of France and John, Duke of Berry. Christine de Pizan supported herself and her children by writing for these same patrons. She oversaw the production of her books and wrote of one artist named Anastaise, "who is so learned and skillful in painting manuscript borders and miniature backgrounds that one cannot find an artisan who can surpass her...nor whose work is more highly esteemed" (*Le Libre de la Cité des Dames*, I.41.4, translated by Earl J. Richards). Also in the fourteenth century, Jeanne de Montbaston and her husband, Richart, worked together as book illuminators under the auspices of the University of Paris. After Richart's death, Jeanne continued the workshop and was sworn in as a *libraire* (publisher) by the university in 1343.

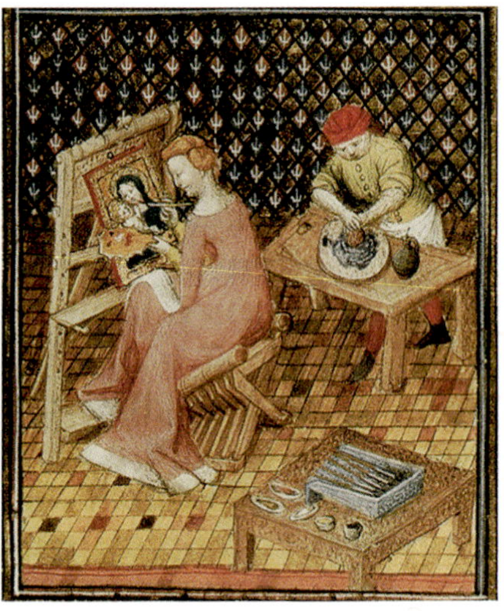

12–3 Miniature with *Thamyris* from Giovanni Boccaccio's *De Claris Mulieribus (Concerning Famous Women)*. 1402. Ink and tempera on vellum. Bibliothèque Nationale, Paris

In the fifteenth century, women were admitted to the artists' guilds (professional organizations) in some cities, including the Flemish towns of Ghent, Bruges, and Antwerp. The painter Agnes van den Bassche of Ghent, for example, operated a painting workshop with her artist husband and became a free master of the painters' guild after his death. A study of the painters' guild of Bruges has shown that by the 1480s one-quarter of its members were female.

The position of women artists in Italy was not as strong as in Flanders. The Humanists' emphasis on academic study rather than apprenticeship for artists, the tie between mathematics and the new linear perspective, and the emphasis on anatomical study—forbidden to women—and figure drawing from models prevented women from following careers in painting. Some women nevertheless learned from their fathers or husbands and helped in the family business.

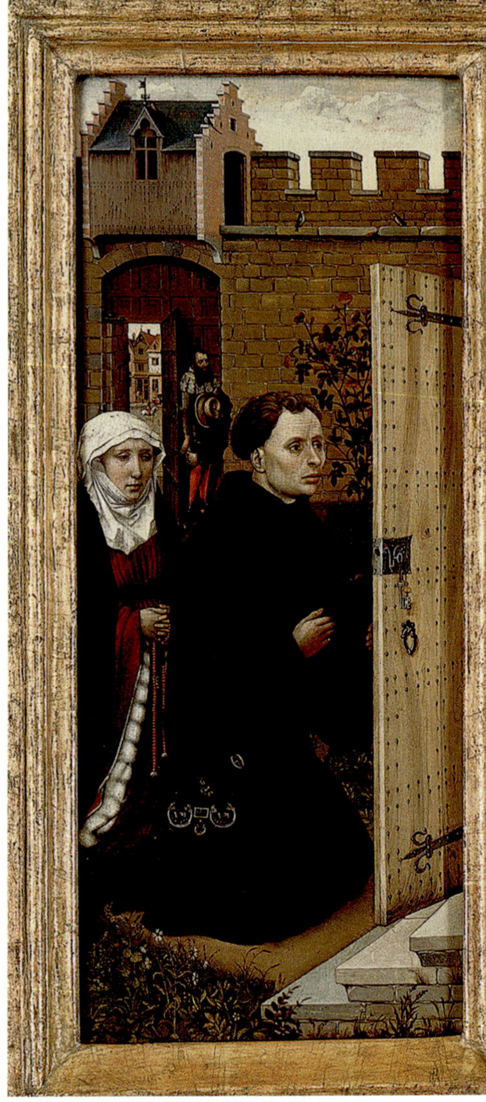

half of the fifteenth century. These include removing the front wall of the house in order to show inside activities, paying special attention to anecdotal detail, and placing the horizon line high within the framed space. But even if integration of figures and animals into the landscape has been accomplished within the prevailing Gothic style, scale relationships seem more consistent with our experience in the natural world, since the landscape recedes and the size of figures and buildings diminishes progressively in stages from foreground to middle ground to background.

Throughout most of the fifteenth century, Flemish artists (Flanders is roughly equivalent to the present-day lands of western Belgium, the southwestern Netherlands, and a small area of northern France) were considered among the very best in Europe. Flanders, which included part of the domain of the duke of Burgundy and the major seaport and cosmopolitan mercantile city of Bruges, was also the commercial center of Northern Europe, rivaling the Italian city-states of Florence and Venice, and attracting an international cadre of ambitious merchants like Giovanni Arnolfini from Lucca, whose portrait we have already explored (fig. 12–1).

The most outstanding exponents of Flemish painting during the first half of the fifteenth century were Robert Campin, Jan van

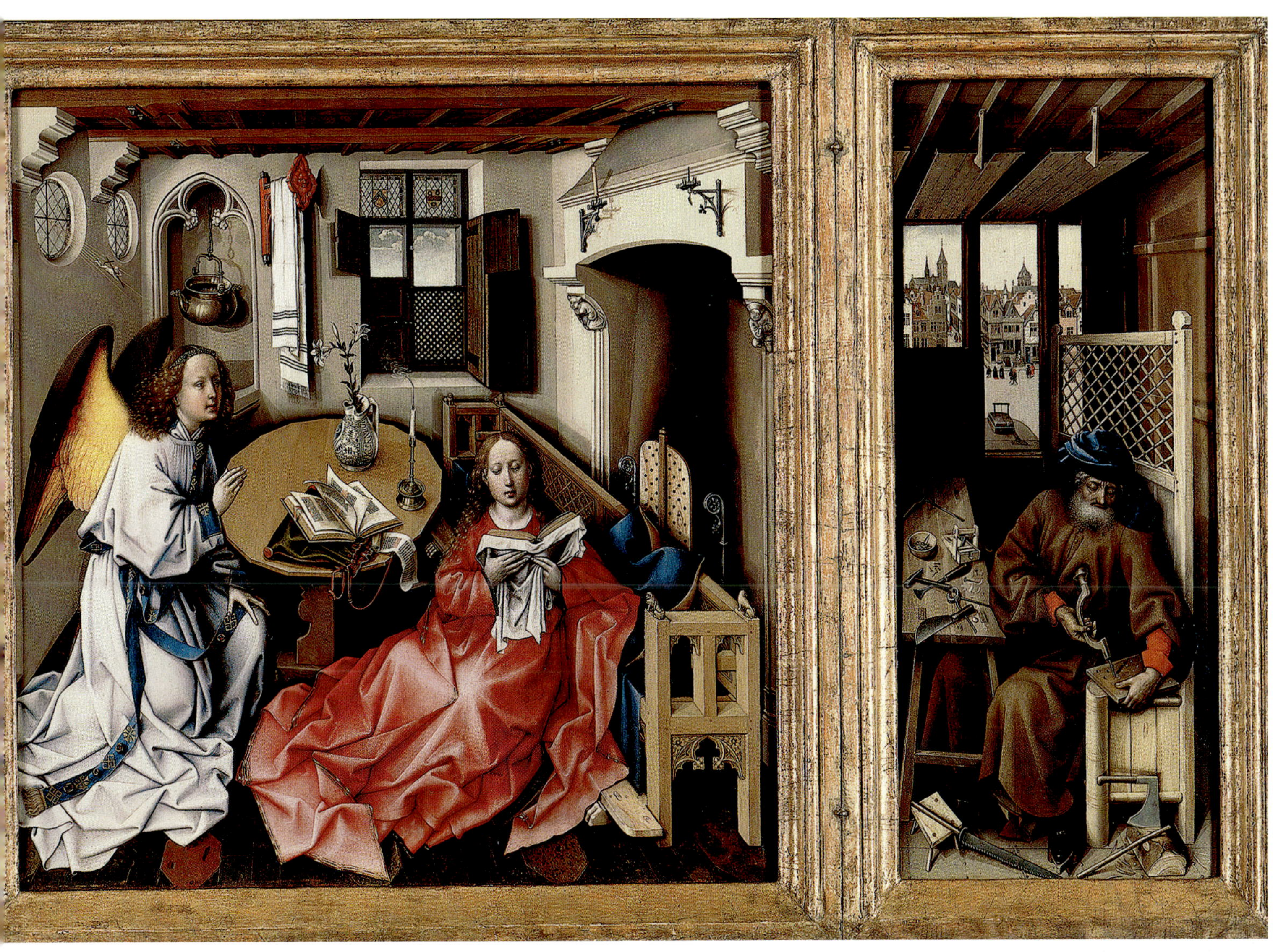

12–4 Robert Campin. *Mérode Altarpiece (Triptych of the Annunciation)* (open).
c. 1425–1428. Oil on wood panel, center 25¼" × 24⅞" (64.1 × 63.2 cm), each wing approx. 25⅜" × 10⅞" (64.5 × 27.6 cm).
The Metropolitan Museum of Art, New York
THE CLOISTERS COLLECTION, 1956 (56.70)

Eyck, and Rogier van der Weyden. About 1425–1428, Campin (documented from 1406; died 1444) painted an altarpiece now known as the *Mérode Altarpiece* (fig. **12–4**) after the name of its former owners. Its relatively small size (slightly more than 2 feet tall and about 4 feet wide with the wings open) suggests that it was made for a private chapel. Campin portrayed the Annunciation as if the Virgin lived in a Flemish home. Into this contemporary setting he incorporated everyday household objects that could also be seen as religious symbols. The lilies on the table, for example, were a traditional element of Annunciation imagery, symbolizing Mary's virginity. The hanging water pot in the background niche refers to Mary's purity and her sacred role as the vessel for the Incarnation of Christ. What seems at first to be a towel hung over the prominent, hinged rack next to the niche may be a tallis (Jewish prayer shawl). To us these objects may appear to be "hidden" or "disguised" symbols because they are treated as a normal part of the scene, but their religious meanings would have been quite clear to the intended audience of this altarpiece.

In the left-hand panel of the *Mérode Altarpiece*, the two people who commissioned it kneel in a garden before the open door of the house where the Annunciation takes place, suggesting that the scene we see is their vision induced by prayers and meditation. Such a presentation, popular with Flemish artists, allowed those who commissioned a religious work to appear in the same space and time, and often on the same scale, as the religious figures represented. In the right-hand panel, the view out of Saint Joseph's window depicts

Technique

Oil Painting

Whereas Italian artists favored tempera, using it almost exclusively for panel painting until the end of the fifteenth century (see "Cennini on Panel Painting," page 296), Flemish artists preferred oil paints, in which powdered pigments are suspended in linseed—and occasionally walnut—oil. They exploited the potential of this medium during the fifteenth century with a virtuosity that has never been surpassed.

Tempera had to be applied in a very precise manner because it dried almost as quickly as it was laid down. Shading was restricted to careful overlying strokes in graded tones ranging from white and gray to dark brown and black. Because tempera is opaque, light striking its surface does not penetrate to lower layers of color and reflect back, so the resulting surface is **matte**, or dull, taking on a sheen only with an overlay of varnish.

On the other hand, oil paint is a viscous medium which takes much longer to dry, and while it is still wet, changes can easily be made. Once applied, the paint has time to smooth out during the drying process, erasing traces of individual brushstrokes on the surface of the finished panel. Perhaps even more importantly, oil paint is translucent when applied in very thin layers, called **glazes**. Light striking a surface built up of glazes penetrates to the lower layers and is reflected back, creating the appearance of an interior glow. These luminous effects enabled artists to capture jewel-like colors and the varying effects of light on changing textures, enhancing the illusion that viewers are looking at real objects rather than their painted imitation.

So brilliant was Jan van Eyck's use of oil paint that he was credited by Giorgio Vasari with inventing the medium. Actually, it had been in use at least since the twelfth century when it is described in Theophilus Presbyter's *De diversis artibus* (see "Stained-Glass Windows," page 275).

a snapshot of a bustling Flemish street scene. The mousetraps on the workbench and extended windowsill of Joseph's carpentry shop are references to a passage written by the theologian Saint Augustine, referring to Christ as the bait in a trap set by God to catch Satan.

The complex and consistent treatment of light in the central panel of the *Mérode Altarpiece* represents a major preoccupation of Flemish painters. The strongest illumination comes from an unseen source at the upper left in front of the **picture plane** (corresponding with the picture's surface), as if sunlight were entering through the opened front of the room that allows the viewer to observe the scene. More light comes from the rear windows, and a few actually depicted linear rays from the round window at left are a symbolic vehicle for the Christ Child's descent. Jesus seems to slide down the rays of light linking God with Mary, carrying the cross of human salvation over his shoulder. The light falling on the Virgin's lap emphasizes this connection, and the transmission of the symbolic light through a transparent panel of glass (which remains intact) recalls the virginal nature of Jesus' conception.

Jan van Eyck (c. 1370/90–1441), Campin's contemporary, was court painter to Philip the Good, Duke of Burgundy, who was the uncle of the king of France and one of the wealthiest and most sophisticated men in Europe. He made Jan one of his confidential employees and even sent him on an embassy to Portugal. In a letter of 1434–1435, Duke Philip confessed that he could find no other painter equal to his taste or so excellent in art and science. But the duke was not Jan's only patron. In the Low Countries—where cities were largely independent of the landed nobility—civic leaders, town councils, and rich merchants were also important art patrons.

Jan's *Annunciation* (fig. **12–5**), a small panel that may have been part of an altarpiece, is an excellent example of the Flemish desire to paint in dizzying detail more than the eye can take in quickly with a single glance, capturing a luminosity possible only in the oil painting technique preferred by Flemish painters (see "Oil Painting," above). We can enjoy the painting for its visual characteristics—the virtuosity of the drawing, and the arrangement of shapes and colors—but we need information about its cultural context to grasp the way the original viewers understood it. The Annunciation (based on Luke 1:26–38) takes place in a richly appointed church, not Mary's house, as we saw in Robert Campin's painting. Gabriel, a youth with splendid multicolored wings and extravagant cloak, has interrupted Mary's reading. The two figures gesture gracefully upward toward a dove flying down through golden beams of light. As the angel Gabriel tells the Virgin Mary that she will bear Christ, the Son of God, golden letters spell out the angel's greeting, "Hail, full of grace," and Mary's response, "Behold the handmaiden of the Lord." Mary's words are written upside down since they are addressed to God. Most aspects of the painting are saturated with symbolic meaning. The dove signifies the Holy Spirit that will incarnate Jesus within Mary; the white lilies are symbols of Mary's purity. Visible in the floor tiling are medallions with signs of the zodiac signaling the traditional date of the Annunciation (March 25) and scenes from the exploits of heroes David and Samson, prefiguring in the Hebrew Bible the future triumphs of Mary's son.

Jan's best-known painting today is the distinctive double portrait of the couple traditionally identified as Giovanni Arnolfini and his wife, Giovanna Cenami (fig. 12–1). Early interpreters saw this riveting work as representing a wedding or betrothal. Above the mirror on the back wall, the artist inscribed the words: *Johannes de eyck fuit hic 1434* ("Jan van Eyck has been here 1434"). More normal on a signature would have been, "Jan van Eyck made this" (compare fig. 12–7), but the phrase "has been here" has suggested to some that Jan served as a witness to a matrimonial episode portrayed in the painting. And he is not the only witness recorded here. The convex mirror between the figures reflects not only the back of the couple but a front view of two visitors standing in the doorway, entering the room. Perhaps one of them is the artist himself.

New research has complicated this developing interpretation by revealing that Giovanni Arnolfini married Giovanna Cenami only in 1447, long after the date on the wall and Jan van Eyck's death. One scholar has proposed that the picture is actually a prospective portrait of Giovanni and Giovanna's marriage in the future, painted in 1434 to secure the early transfer of the dowry from her father to her future husband. Others have more recently suggested the man portrayed here is a different Giovanni Arnolfini, accompanied either by his putative second wife or a memorial portrait of his first wife, Costanza Trenta, who died the year before this picture was painted. The true meaning of this fascinating masterpiece may remain a mystery, but it is doubtful that scholars will stop trying to solve it.

Rogier van der Weyden (c. 1399–1464), an artist slightly younger than Jan, maintained a large workshop in Brussels—where he was official city painter—attracting apprentices and assistants from as far away as Italy. Nevertheless, not a single existing work of art bears his signature. To establish the stylistic character of Rogier's art, scholars have turned to a large panel painting (more than 7 by 8 feet) that depicts the Deposition, or removal of Christ's body from

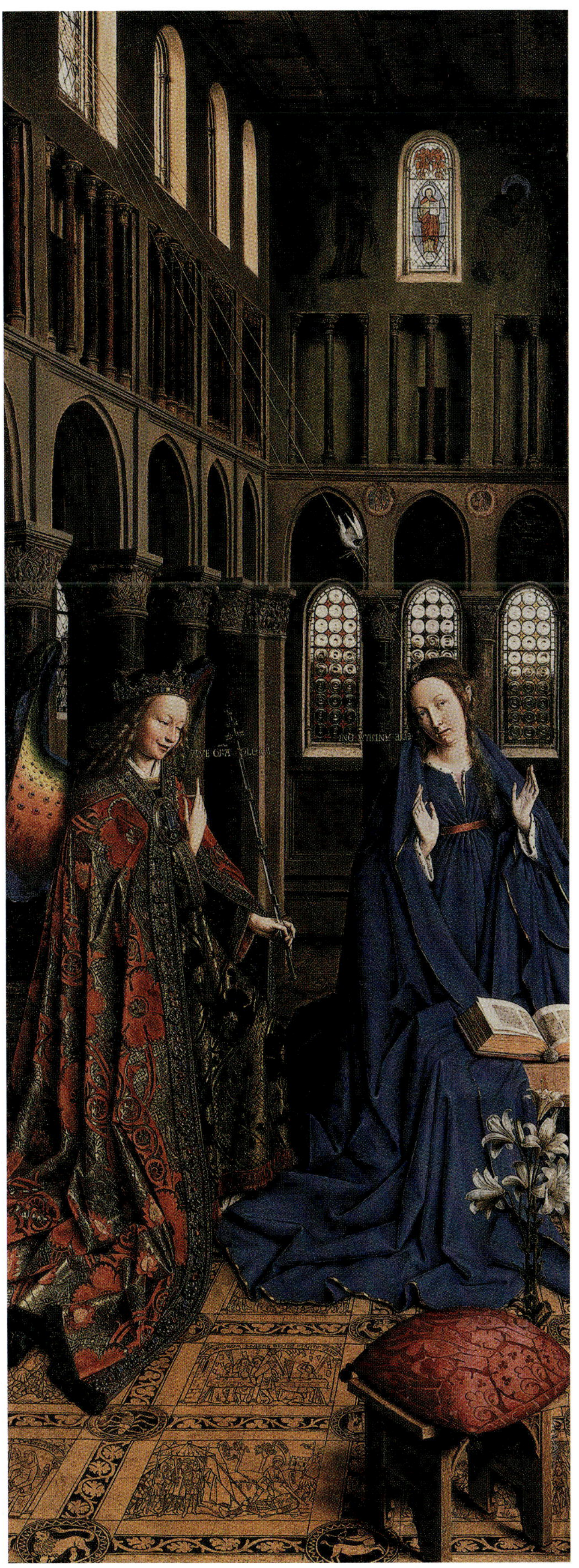

12–5 Jan van Eyck. ***The Annunciation***. c. 1434–1436. Oil on canvas, transferred from wood panel, painted surface, 35⅜" × 13⅞" (90.2 × 34.1 cm). National Gallery of Art, Washington, D.C.
ANDREW W. MELLON COLLECTION (1937.1.39)

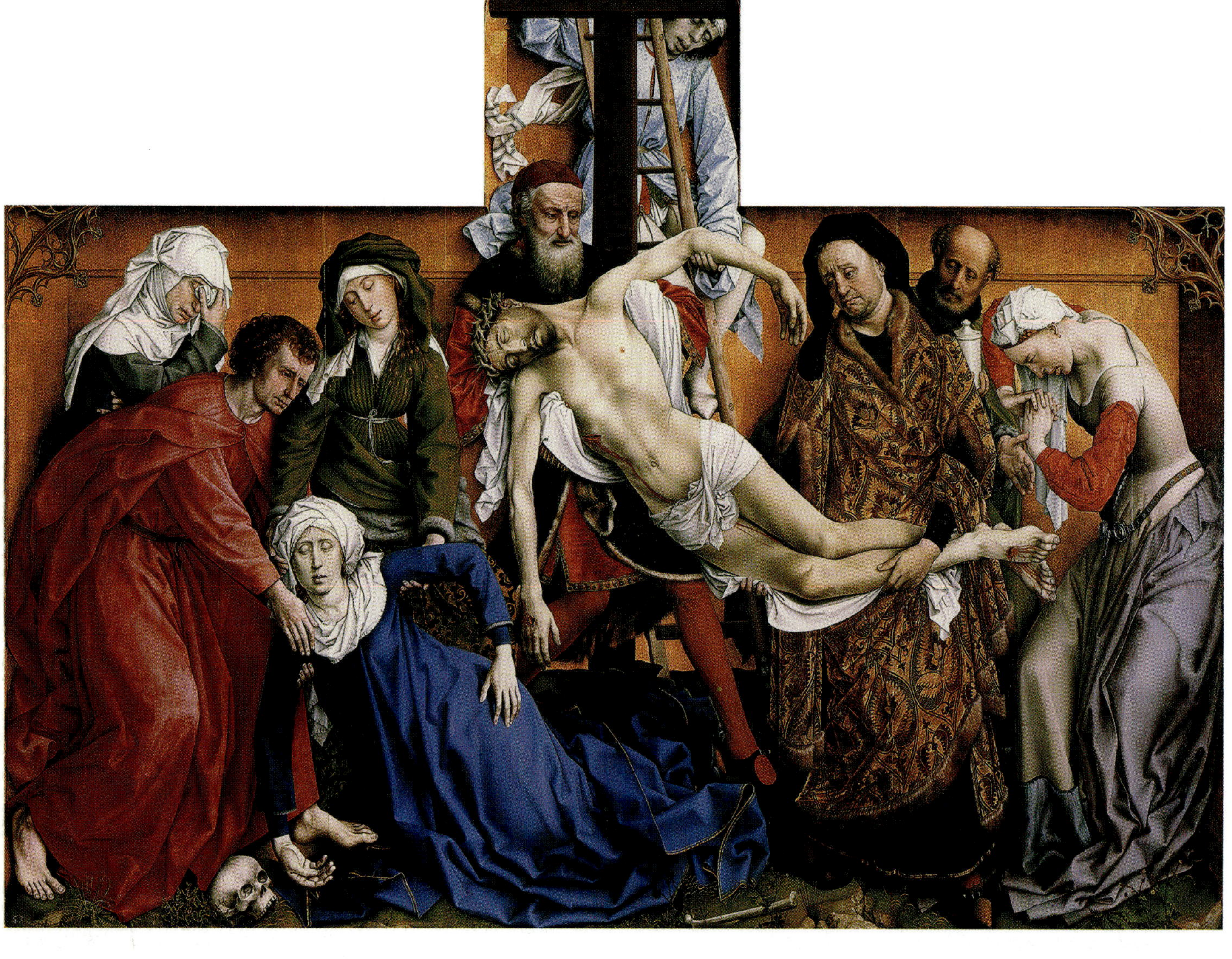

12–6 Rogier van der Weyden. ***Deposition***, from an altarpiece commissioned before 1443 by the Crossbowmen's Guild, Louvain, Brabant, Belgium. Oil on wood panel, 7' 2⅝" × 8' 7⅛" (2.2 × 2.62 m). Museo Nacional del Prado, Madrid

the cross (fig. **12–6**). This was likely the central panel of an altarpiece, commissioned by the Louvain Crossbowmen's Guild sometime around 1442, that once included now-lost panels representing the Four Evangelists and Christ's Resurrection.

The Deposition was a popular theme in the fifteenth century because of its potential for dramatic, personally engaging portrayal. In Rogier's painting, Jesus' suffering and death are made palpably real by the display of the life-sized corpse dominating the center of the composition. Rogier has arranged the figure in a languid curve, framed by jarringly thin, angular arms. His pose is echoed by the rhyming form of the fainting Virgin. It is as if mother and son share in the redemptive passion of his death on the cross, encouraging viewers to identify with both of them or join their gathered companions in mourning their fate. The white accents of the winding cloth and the tunic of the youth on the ladder set off Jesus' pale body, just as the white veil wrapped like a turban and shawl emphasizes the ashen face of Mary. The vibrant, solidly modeled figures, compressed and intertwined in a shallow, box-like space, press forward, allowing viewers no escape from their engaging expression of heartrending grief. Although united by their sorrow, the mourning figures react in personal ways, from the intensity of Mary Magdalen at far right, wringing her hands in anguish, to John the Evangelist's blank stare at left, lost in grief as he reaches to support the collapsing Virgin. The anguish of the woman behind him, mopping her tear-soaked eyes with the edge of her veil, is almost unbearably poignant.

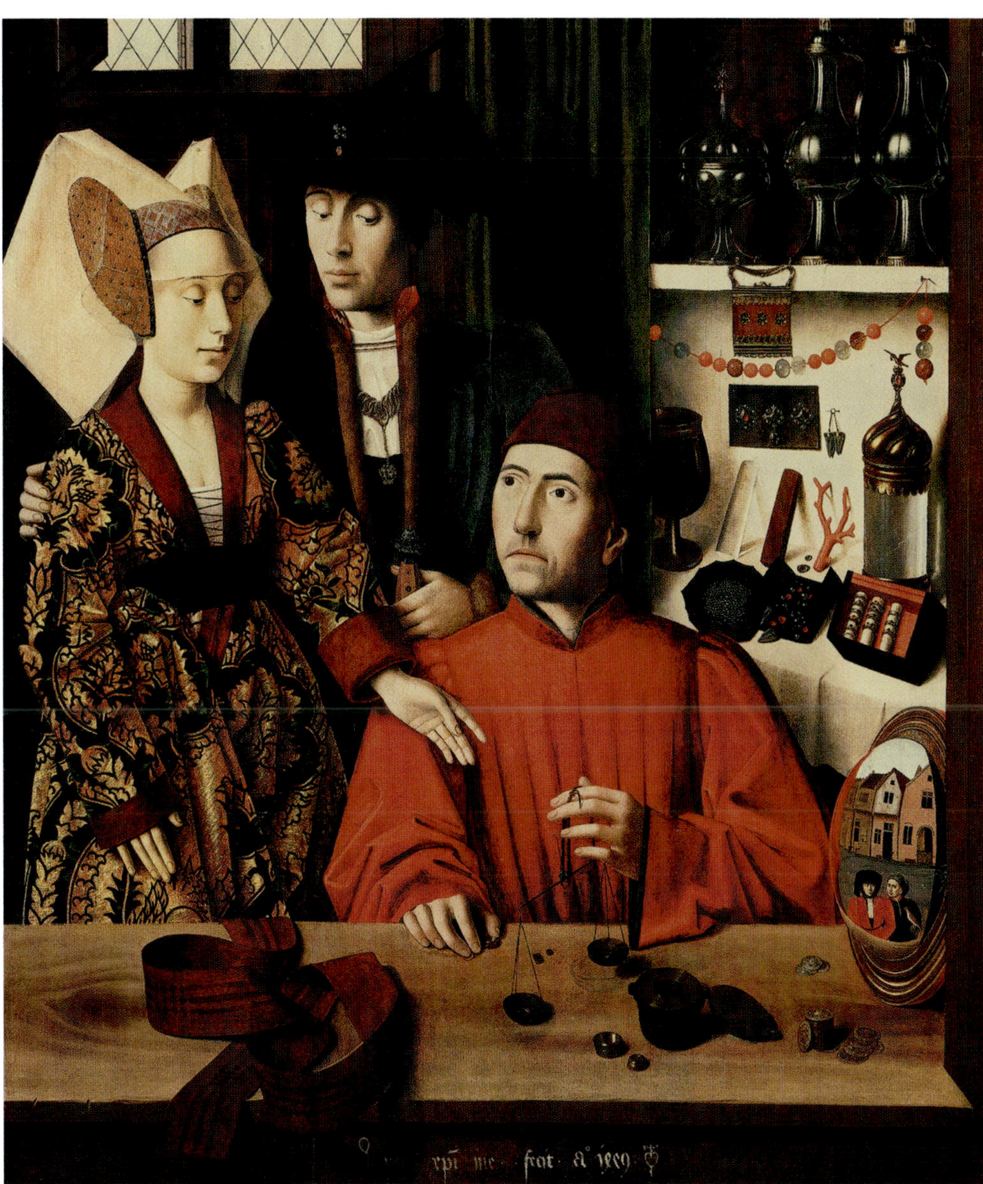

12–7 Petrus Christus. ***A Goldsmith in his Shop, Possibly Saint Eligius.*** 1449. Oil on oak panel, 38⅝" × 33½" (98 × 85 cm). The Metropolitan Museum of Art, New York
ROBERT LEHMAN COLLECTION, 1975 (1975.1.110)

The artist signed and dated his work in a bold inscription that appears just under the tabletop at the bottom of the painting: "Master Petrus Christus made me in the year 1449."

Second-Generation Painters

The extraordinary achievements of Robert Campin, Jan van Eyck, and Rogier van der Weyden attracted many followers. Petrus Christus (documented from 1444; died c. 1475), who worked in Bruges, probably came from the northern duchy of Brabant (now part of the southern Netherlands and north-central Belgium). In 1449, Christus painted one of his most admired works, *A Goldsmith in his Shop* (fig. **12–7**), perhaps conceived as a representation of Saint Eligius, patron saint of metalworkers. According to Christian legend, Eligius, a seventh-century ecclesiastic, goldsmith, and mint-master for the French court, used his wealth to ransom Christian captives. Here he weighs a ring to determine its value, as a handsome couple looks on. The young people are dressed in the height of Burgundian court fashion. The woman wears a rich Italian brocade gown and jeweled headdress; the man wears fur-lined black wool. A box of rings, a crystal reliquary with a gold dome, rosary beads, silver cups and flagons, and other treasures rest on a shelf in the background, affording us a tantalizing glimpse into a fifteenth-century goldsmith's shop.

As in Jan van Eyck's double portrait (see fig. 12–1), a convex mirror extends the viewer's field of vision, in this case showing two men on the street outside the window through which we ourselves view the interior of this shop. Whether or not the reflected image has symbolic or narrative meaning, within a shop it would have had a practical value, allowing the goldsmith to observe the approach of potential customers.

The painter Hugo van der Goes (c. 1440–1482) united the intellectual prowess of Jan van Eyck with the emotional intensity of Rogier van der Weyden to create an entirely new personal style. Hugo's major work was an exceptionally large altarpiece, more than 8 feet tall, commissioned by Tommaso Portinari for the family chapel in Florence and probably painted between 1474 and 1476

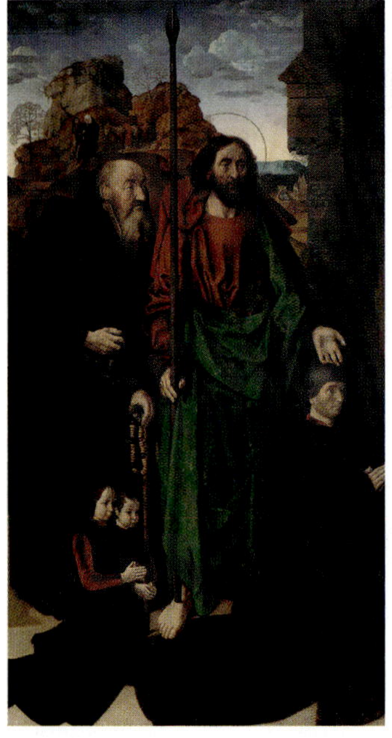
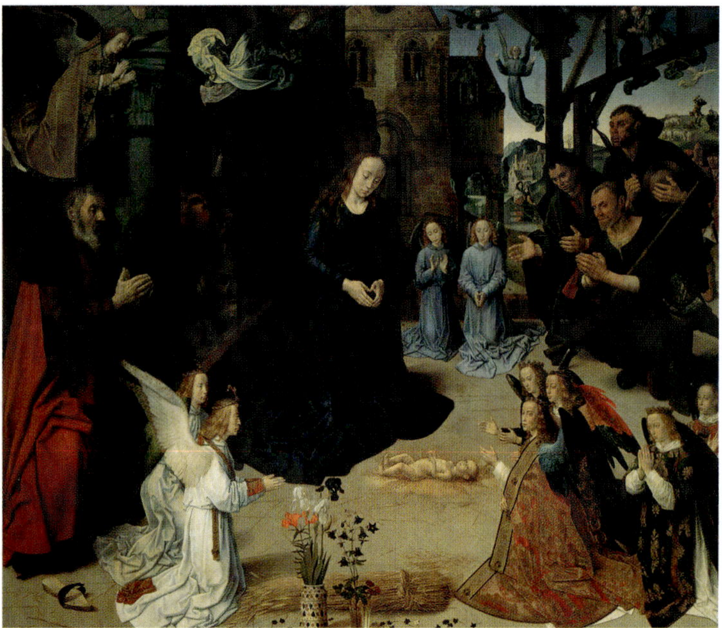
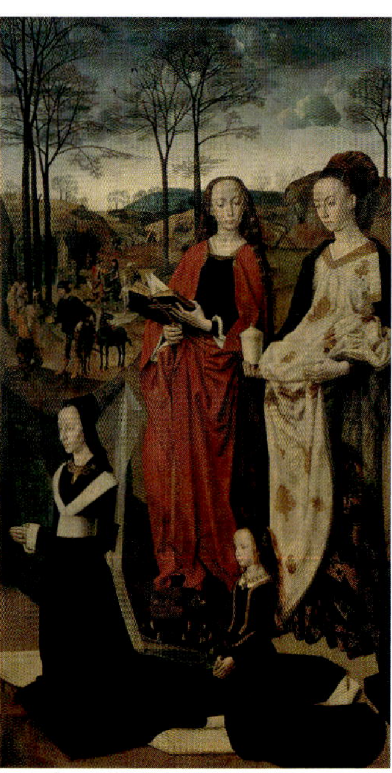

12–8 Hugo van der Goes. ***Portinari Altarpiece*** (open). c. 1474–1476. Tempera and oil on panel, center 8' 3½" × 10' (2.53 × 3.01 m); wings each 8' 3½" × 4' 7½" (2.53 × 1.41 m). Galleria degli Uffizi, Florence

(fig. **12–8**). Portinari, a Florentine living in Bruges, was the local manager of the bank owned by the powerful Medici family. He and his wife, Maria Baroncelli, are seen kneeling with their three eldest children, accompanied by patron saints, on the interiors of the hinged side panels. The central panel represents the Adoration of the newborn Jesus by Mary and Joseph, a host of angels, and a few shepherds who have rushed in from the fields. The monumental figures of Joseph, Mary, and the shepherds are the same size as the patron saints on the wings; the Portinari family and the angels are small in comparison.

In the center, the Christ Child rests naked and vulnerable on the ground with rays of light emanating from his body. This image was based on the visionary writing of the medieval Swedish mystic Bridget (declared a saint in 1391). Saint Bridget described Mary kneeling to adore the Child immediately after giving birth. The glass vessel in the foreground still life alludes to Christ's entry into Mary's womb without destroying her virginity, the way light passes through glass without breaking it. The seven blue columbines it holds symbolize the Virgin's future sorrows; and the violets scattered on the ground symbolize her humility. The **majolica** (glazed earthenware) *albarelo*, or drug jar, a luxury ceramic imported from Spain, holds three irises—white for purity and purple for Christ's royal ancestry—and a red lily, representing the blood of Christ.

Hugo's artistic vision goes far beyond formal religious symbolism. Although the brilliant palette and meticulous rendering of detail recall Jan van Eyck, and the intense but controlled feelings recall the emotional content of Rogier van der Weyden's works, the composition and figural types are entirely Hugo's. The shepherds, for example, who stand in unaffected awe before the miraculous event, are among the most sympathetically rendered images of common people to be found in the art of this, or any, period, and the portraits of the Portinari children are unusually sensitive renderings of the delicate features of youthful faces.

The work of Hugo and other Northern Renaissance painters presents a stark contrast to what we will discover in contemporary Florentine art. During the sixteenth century, Michelangelo sharply criticized the detailed realism of Flemish art in an often-quoted assessment:

> In Flanders they paint with a view to external exactness or such things as may cheer you and of which you cannot speak ill, as for example saints and prophets. They paint stuffs and masonry and the green grass of the fields and the shadows of trees, and rivers and bridges, which they call landscapes, with many figures on this side and many figures on that, and all this, though it pleases some persons, is done without reason or art, without symmetry or proportion, without skillful choice of boldness and, finally, without substance or vigor.
> (Snyder, page 88)

This was a minority viewpoint from someone who championed alternative values. In fact, Flemish art was so admired in the fifteenth century that many artists visited Flanders to study the work. Only at the end of the century did European patrons begin to favor the new styles of art and architecture developing in Italy.

Tapestries

The importance of textiles in the fifteenth century cannot be overemphasized. Major weaving centers arose in Brussels, Tournai, Arras, and in the Loire Valley, where Flemish and French artists produced outstanding tapestries that served both as sumptuous wall coverings and as a form of portable wealth. Indeed, the wealth of

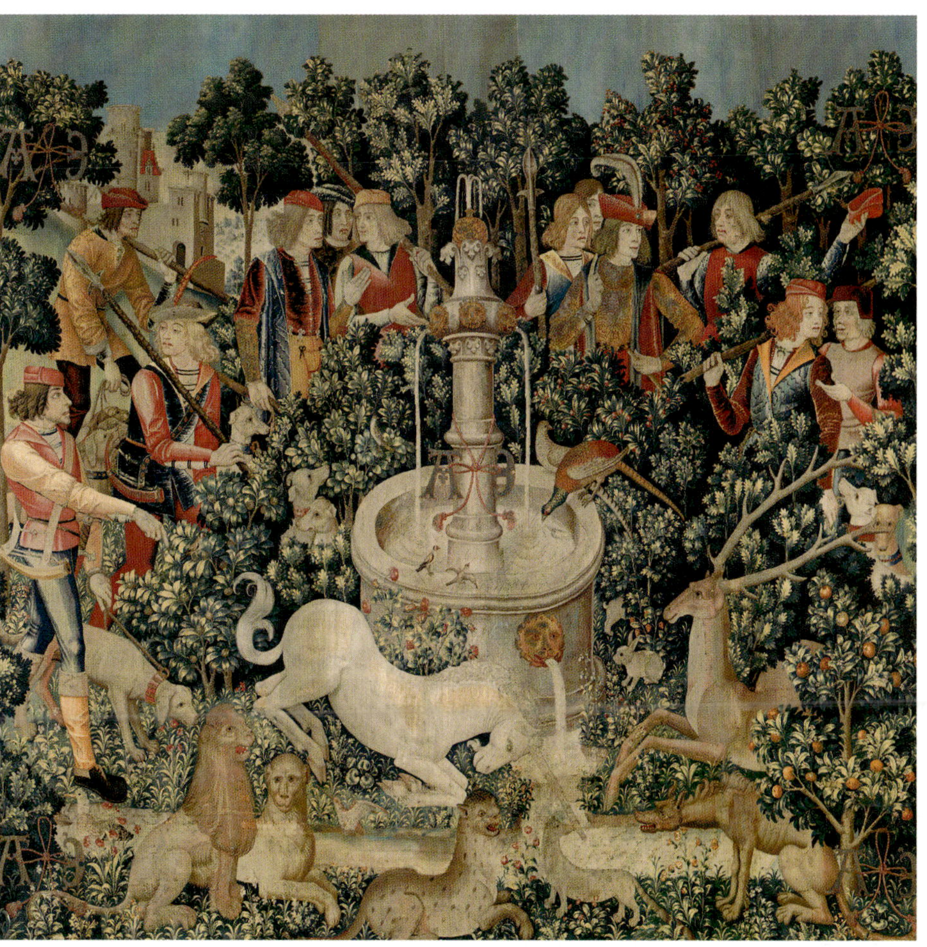

individuals can often be judged from the number of tapestries listed in their household inventories. The painting of Christine de Pizan presenting her manuscript to the queen of France (fig. Intro–23) gives a good idea of the effect achieved by luxurious wall hangings.

One of the finest examples of Renaissance tapestry is a series of wall hangings called the *Hunt of the Unicorn*, which includes *The Unicorn Is Found* (fig. **12–9**). The tapestries might have been made for Anne of Brittany whose initials, AE, hang on a cord from the fountain and at the four corners of the composition. The unicorn, a mythical horse-like beast with a single horn, could be captured only by a young virgin, to whom it came willingly. The animal symbolized the Incarnation, with Christ as the unicorn captured by the Virgin Mary; in the secular world, the unicorn hunt became a metaphor for romantic love and a suitable subject for wedding tapestries. The unicorn's horn was believed to be an antidote for poison; thus, the unicorn here is shown dipping its horn into the stream and so purifying the water from the fountain.

12–9 *The Unicorn is Found*, from the *Hunt of the Unicorn* tapestry series. c. 1498–1500. Wool, silk, and metal threads (13–21 warp threads per inch), 12' 1" × 12' 5" (3.68 × 3.78 m). The Metropolitan Museum of Art, New York
GIFT OF JOHN D. ROCKEFELLER JR. THE CLOISTERS COLLECTION, 1937 (37.8.2)

The price of a tapestry depended on the materials used. Rarely was a fine, commissioned series woven only with wool; instead tapestry producers enhanced it to varying degrees with colored silk and silver and gold threads. The richest kind of tapestry was one made entirely of silk and gold. Because the silver and gold threads used silk wrapped with real metal, people later burned many tapestries in order to retrieve the precious materials. As a result of this practice, few French royal tapestries have survived. Many existing works show obvious signs that the metallic threads were painstakingly pulled out in order to get the gold but preserve the tapestries.

The figures in this tapestry appear in a dense forest filled with flowers, with a distant view of a castle. The many birds and animals have symbolic meanings: the lion represents valor and faith; the stag, the Resurrection and protection against evil; rabbits, fertility; and dogs, fidelity. Among the birds, the pair of pheasants perched on the fountain (at right) are emblems of human love and marriage, and the goldfinches (also on the fountain rim) are another fertility symbol. The plants, depicted with botanical precision, reinforce the theme of protective and curative powers: the strawberry stands for sexual love, the pansy for remembrance, the oak for fidelity, the holly for protection, and the orange for fertility. The tapestry captures the vision of the biblical Song of Songs (4:12): "You are an enclosed garden, my sister, my bride, an enclosed garden, a fountain sealed."

The Graphic Arts

Printmaking emerged in Europe with the wider availability of paper and the development of printing presses at the end of the fourteenth century. The techniques used by printmakers during the Renaissance were woodcut and engraving (see "Woodcuts and Engravings," page 315).

People had long used woodblocks cut in relief to print designs on cloth, but only in the fifteenth century did the printing of images and texts on paper and the production of books in multiple copies begin to replace the copying of books individually by hand. Both illustrations in printed books and single-sheet printed images were sometimes hand-colored with watercolor paints.

At first, woodcuts were made by woodworkers with little art training. Soon printers began to hire artists to draw images for the artisans to cut from the block. Simply executed devotional images sold as souvenirs to pilgrims at holy sites became very popular. An example is *The Buxheim Saint Christopher* (found in the Carthusian Monastery of Buxheim, in southern Germany), dated 1423 (fig. **12–10**). This patron saint of travelers and protector from the plague, carries the Christ Child across a river; his charitable action is witnessed by a monk but ignored by two workers at a water mill.

Engravings, on the other hand, seem to have developed from the highly skilled metalworking techniques used by goldsmiths and armorers who recorded their work by rubbing lampblack into the engraved lines and pressing paper over the plate. German artist Martin Schongauer (c. 1435–1491), who learned engraving from his goldsmith father, was an immensely skillful printmaker who excelled both in drawing and in the difficult technique of shading from deep black to faintest grays. In his *Temptation of Saint Anthony*, engraved about 1480–1490 (fig. **12–11**), Schongauer illustrated the original biblical meaning of temptation as a physical assault rather than a subtle inducement. Wildly acrobatic slithery, spiky demons lift Anthony off the ground to torment and terrify him in midair. The engraver intensified the horror of the moment by condensing the action into a swirling vortex of figures beating, scratching, poking, tugging, and no doubt shrieking at the stoical saint, who remains impervious to all their torments because of his strong faith.

In Italy, the new Renaissance interest in Classical sculpture and anatomical research inspired an engraving by the Florentine goldsmith and sculptor Antonio del Pollaiuolo (c. 1432–1498): *Battle of the Nudes* (fig. **12–12**). Pollaiuolo may have intended this, his only known—but highly influential—print, as a study of the human

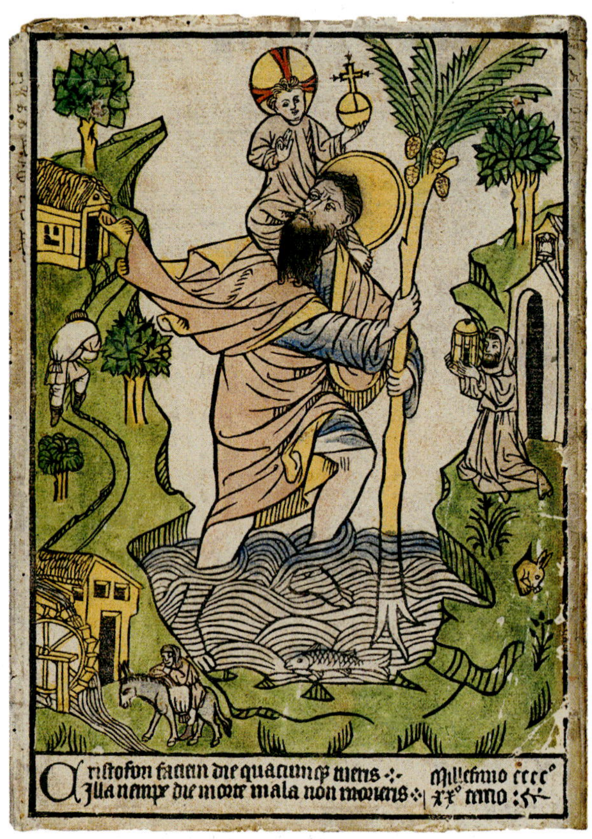

12–10 *The Buxheim Saint Christopher*. 1423. Hand-colored woodcut. The John Rylands University Library

COURTESY OF THE DIRECTOR AND LIBRARIAN, THE JOHN RYLANDS UNIVERSITY LIBRARY OF MANCHESTER, ENGLAND

The Latin text reads, "Whenever you look at the face of Christopher, in truth, you will not die a terrible death that day. 1423"

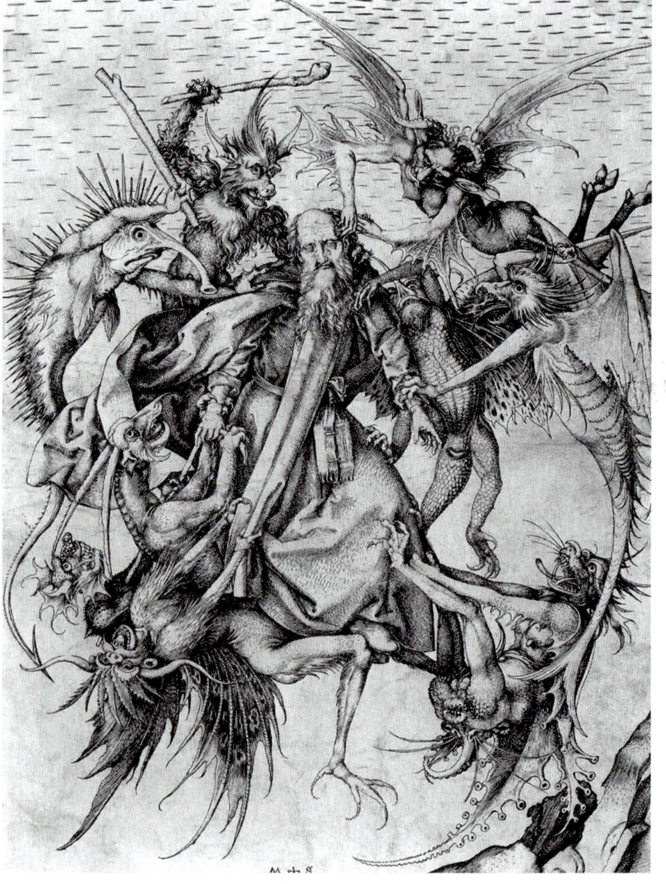

12–11 Martin Schongauer. *Temptation of Saint Anthony*. c. 1480–1490. Engraving, 12¼" × 9" (31.1 × 22.9 cm). The Metropolitan Museum of Art, New York

ROGERS FUND, 1920 (20.5.2)

Technique

Woodcuts and Engravings

An artist making a **woodcut** draws a design on a smooth block of fine-grained wood, then cuts away all the areas around the lines with a sharp tool called a gouge, leaving them in high relief. When the block's surface is inked and a piece of paper pressed down hard on it, the ink on the relief areas is transferred to the paper to create a reverse image.

Engraving on metal, in contrast, requires a technique called **intaglio**, in which lines are **incised** (cut into) the plate with tools called gravers or **burins**. Ink is applied over the whole plate and forced down into the lines, after which the surface of the plate is carefully wiped clean. The ink in the recessed lines transfers to a sheet of paper pressed hard against the plate with the aid of a press.

Whichever technique is used, the great advantage of printmaking is that woodblocks and metal plates can be used repeatedly to make nearly identical images.

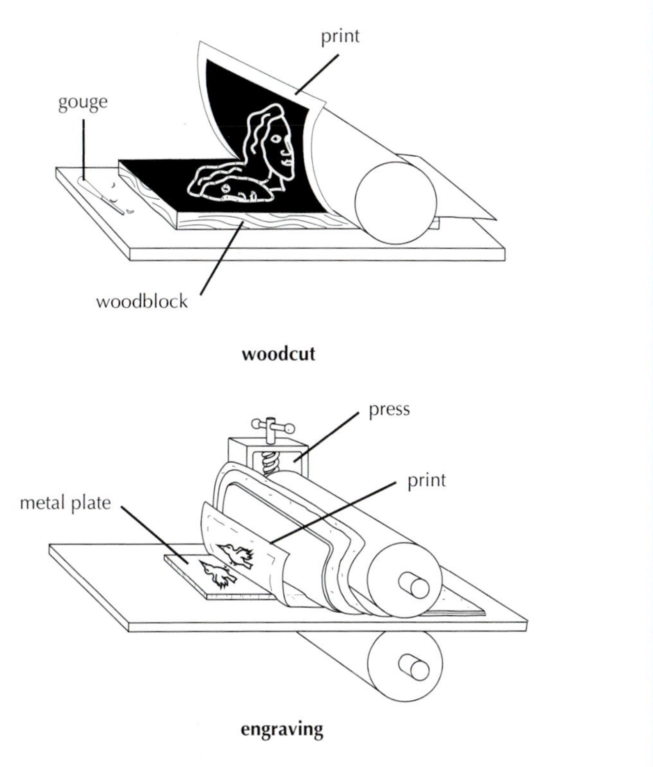

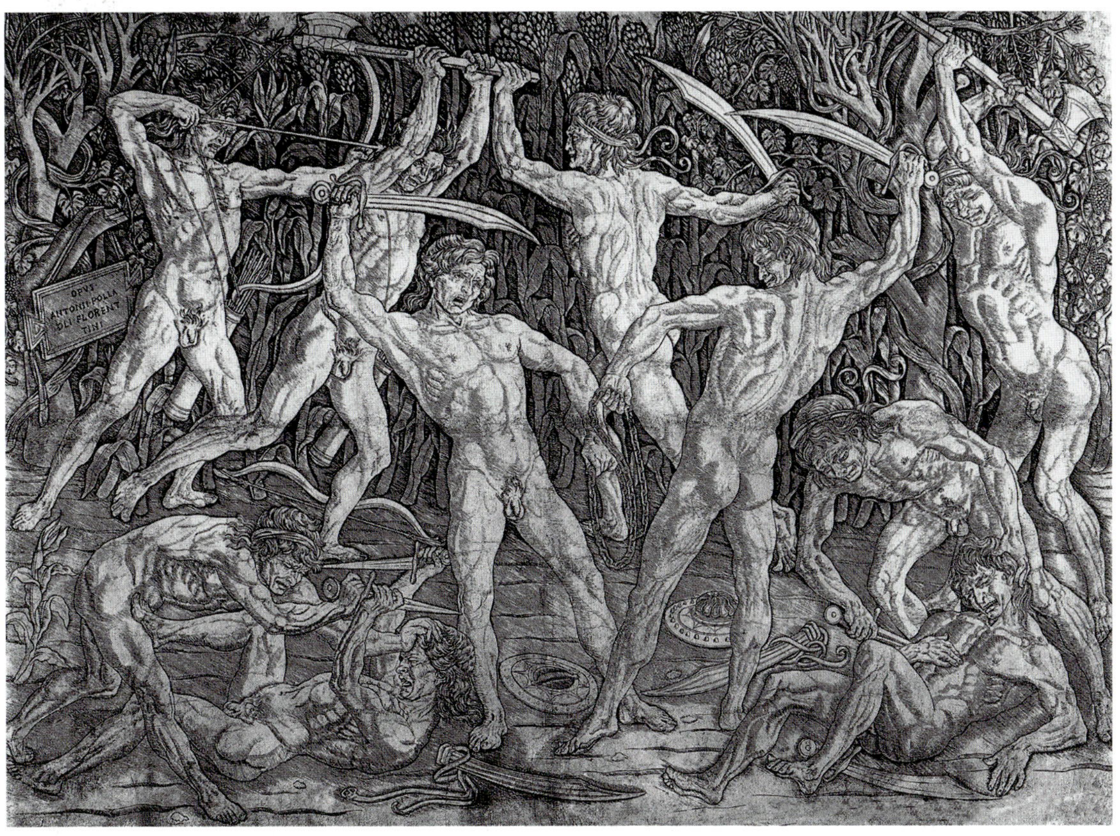

12–12 Antonio del Pollaiuolo. ***Battle of the Nudes.*** c. 1465–1470. Engraving, 15⅛" × 23¼" (38.3 × 59 cm).
Cincinnati Art Museum, Ohio
BEQUEST OF HERBERT GREER FRENCH. 1943.118

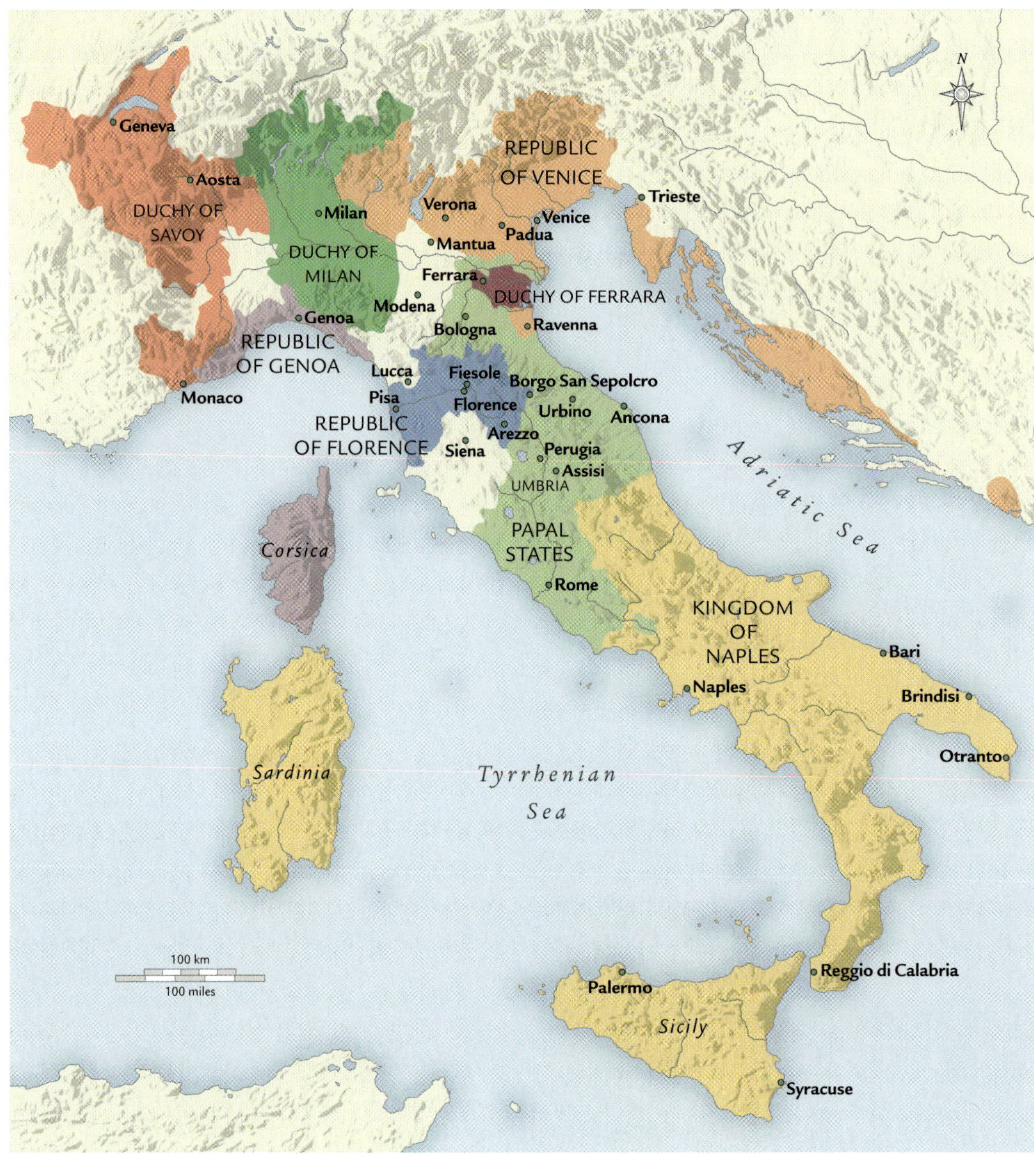

Map 12–2 Fifteenth-Century Italy

figure in action. The naked men ferociously fighting against a tapestry-like background of foliage seem to have been drawn from a single model. They strike poses which seem to have been inspired by Classical sculpture. Much of our fascination with the engraving lies in how Pollaiuolo depicts muscles of the male body reacting under tension. Like their Flemish counterparts, Italian artists moved gradually toward a greater precision in rendering the illusion of physical reality. But as we shall see, Italians studied the figure more analytically than Flemish artists, with the goal of achieving perfected but generic figures set within a rationally ordered, rather than a visually described space.

Renaissance Art in Italy

By the end of the Middle Ages, the most important Italian cultural centers were north of Rome at Florence, Milan, Venice, and the smaller duchies of Mantua, Ferrara, and Urbino (see map **12–2**). Much of the power was in the hands of wealthy families: the Medici in Florence, the Visconti and Sforza in Milan, the Gonzaga in Mantua, the Este in Ferrara, and the Montefeltro in Urbino. Cities grew in wealth and independence. As in Northern Europe, commerce became increasingly important. Money conferred status, and a shrewd business or political leader could become very powerful. Patronage of the arts was an important public activity with political overtones. One Florentine merchant, Giovanni Rucellai, succinctly noted that he supported the arts "because they serve the glory of God, the honour of the city, and the commemoration of myself" (Baxandall, page 2).

Beginning around 1400, Italian painters and sculptors, like their Flemish counterparts, increasingly focused their attention on

CLOSER LOOK

In 1401, the building supervisors of the baptistery of Florence Cathedral decided to commission a new pair of bronze doors, funded by the powerful wool merchants' guild. Instead of choosing a well-established sculptor with a strong reputation, they announced a competition for the commission. This prestigious project would be awarded to the artist who demonstrated the greatest talent and skill in executing a trial piece: a bronze relief representing Abraham's sacrifice of Isaac (Genesis 22:1–13) composed within the same Gothic quatrefoil framework used in Andrea Pisano's first set of bronze doors for the baptistery, made in the 1330s. The narrative subject was full of dramatic potential: Abraham, commanded by God to slay his beloved son Isaac as a burnt offering, has traveled to the mountains for the sacrifice, but just as he is about to slaughter Isaac, an angel appears, commanding him to release his son and substitute a ram tangled in the bushes behind him.

Two competition panels have survived, those submitted by the presumed finalists: Filippo Brunelleschi and Lorenzo Ghiberti, both young artists in their early 20s. Brunelleschi's composition (fig. **12–13**) is rugged and explosive, marked by raw dramatic intensity. Abraham rushes in from the left, grabbing his son by the neck, while the angel swoops energetically to stay his hand just as the knife is about to strike. Isaac's awkward pose embodies his fear and struggle. Ghiberti's version (fig. **12–14**) is quite different—suave and graceful rather than powerful and dramatic. Poses are controlled and choreographed; the harmonious pairing of son and father contrasts sharply with the wrenching struggle in Brunelleschi's rendering. And Ghiberti's Isaac is not a stretched, scrawny youth, but a fully idealized Classical figure, exuding calm composure.

The cloth merchants chose Ghiberti to make the doors. Perhaps they preferred the suave elegance of his figural composition. Perhaps they liked the prominence of elegantly disposed swags of cloth, reminders of the source of their patronage and prosperity. But they also could have been swayed by the technical superiority of Ghiberti's relief. Unlike Brunelleschi, Ghiberti cast background and figures mostly as a single piece, making his bronze stronger, lighter, and less expensive to produce. The finished doors, installed in the baptistery in 1424, were so successful that Ghiberti was commissioned to create a third set (see fig. 12–23), his most famous work, hailed by Michelangelo as the "Gates of Paradise." Brunelleschi would refocus his career on buildings rather than bronzes, becoming one of the most important architects of the Italian Renaissance.

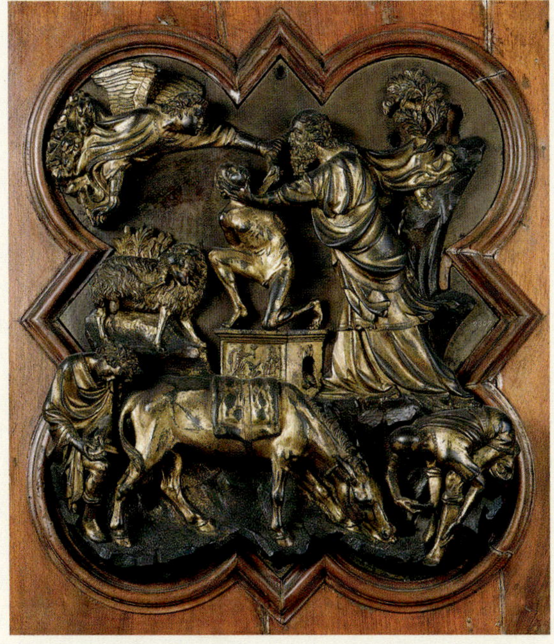

12–13 Filippo Brunelleschi. ***Sacrifice of Isaac.*** 1401–1402. Bronze with gilding, 21" × 17½" (53 × 44 cm) inside molding. Museo Nazionale del Bargello, Florence

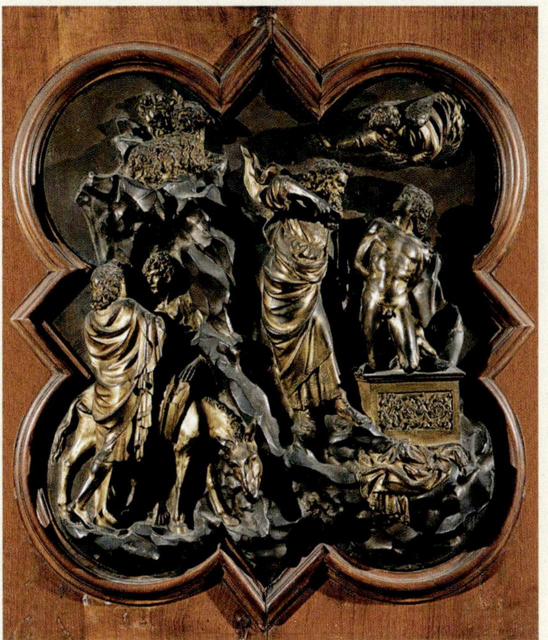

12–14 Lorenzo Ghiberti. ***Sacrifice of Isaac.*** 1401–1402. Bronze with gilding, 21" × 17½" (53 × 44 cm) inside molding. Museo Nazionale del Bargello, Florence

rendering the illusion of physical reality, building on the achievements of their great Florentine forebear Giotto. However, rather than seeking to replicate the detailed visual appearance of nature, as the Flemings did, Italian artists aimed at achieving lifelike but idealized figures—perfected, generic types—set within a rationally configured space organized through the strict use of linear perspective. At the same time, Italian architects began to use mathematically derived design principles and the Classical architectural orders to create buildings conforming to ideals of symmetry and restraint.

Towering figures of early Renaissance art—the architect Brunelleschi, the sculptor Donatello, and the painter Masaccio—came from Florence, the birthplace of the ideas that blossomed into the Italian Renaissance. They studied the physical remains of ancient Rome, and they integrated detailed knowledge of the past into their own highly original works.

Architecture

Filippo Brunelleschi (1377–1446), a young sculptor-turned-architect, was one of the major pioneers of Florentine Renaissance architecture. His design for the vast dome of Florence Cathedral (fig. **12–15**) was a great technical accomplishment. The dome is essentially a Gothic construction based on the pointed arch, using internal ribs to support the vault. It has an octagonal outer shell and a lower inner shell connected through a system of arches and horizontal sandstone rings. Brunelleschi invented an ingenious structural system—more efficient, less costly, and safer than earlier systems—by which each portion of the dome reinforced the next one as it was built up layer by layer. When completed, this self-buttressed unit required no external support. To this day, the dome remains the source of immense local pride.

Brunelleschi also produced remarkably innovative plans for smaller projects in Florence. Between 1419 and 1423, he built the elegant Capponi Chapel in the Church of Santa Felicità (see fig. 13–26). At the same time he was commissioned to redesign the Church of San Lorenzo, the parish church of the Medici family (fig. **12–16**). In both, Brunelleschi used classically inspired moldings and pilasters of pietra serena (a gray stone) against white walls to emphasize the mathematical basis of his design. Like many Romanesque and Gothic builders before him, he worked out his church plans using a module, or basic unit of measure, that could be multiplied or divided to generate every element of the design. The result was a series of clear, rational interior spaces in harmony with one another. Unlike the Romanesque and Gothic system, however, the result was human-scaled architecture full of Classical details.

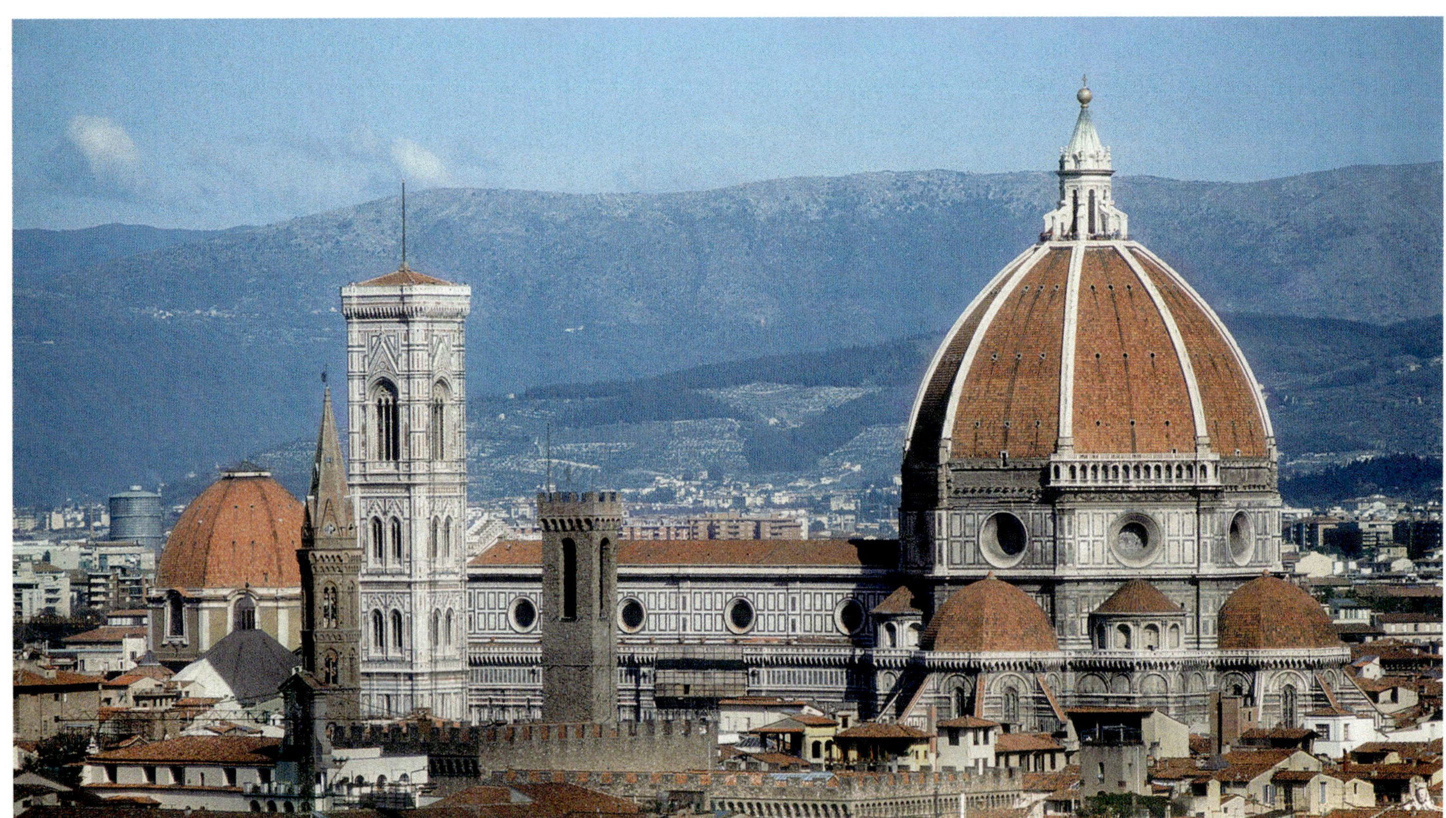

12–15 Filippo Brunelleschi. Dome of Florence Cathedral. 1417–1436; lantern completed 1471

The cathedral of Florence has a long and complex history. Arnolfo di Cambio's original plan was approved in 1294, but political unrest in the 1330s brought construction to a halt until 1357. Most of the building we see today was constructed between 1357 and 1378, but Brunelleschi's great dome—now the dominant architectural feature—was only begun in 1420. This dome was a source of immense local pride from the moment of its completion. Renaissance architect and theorist Leon Battista Alberti described it as rising "above the skies, large enough to cover all the peoples of Tuscany with its shadow" (Goldwater and Traves, page 33).

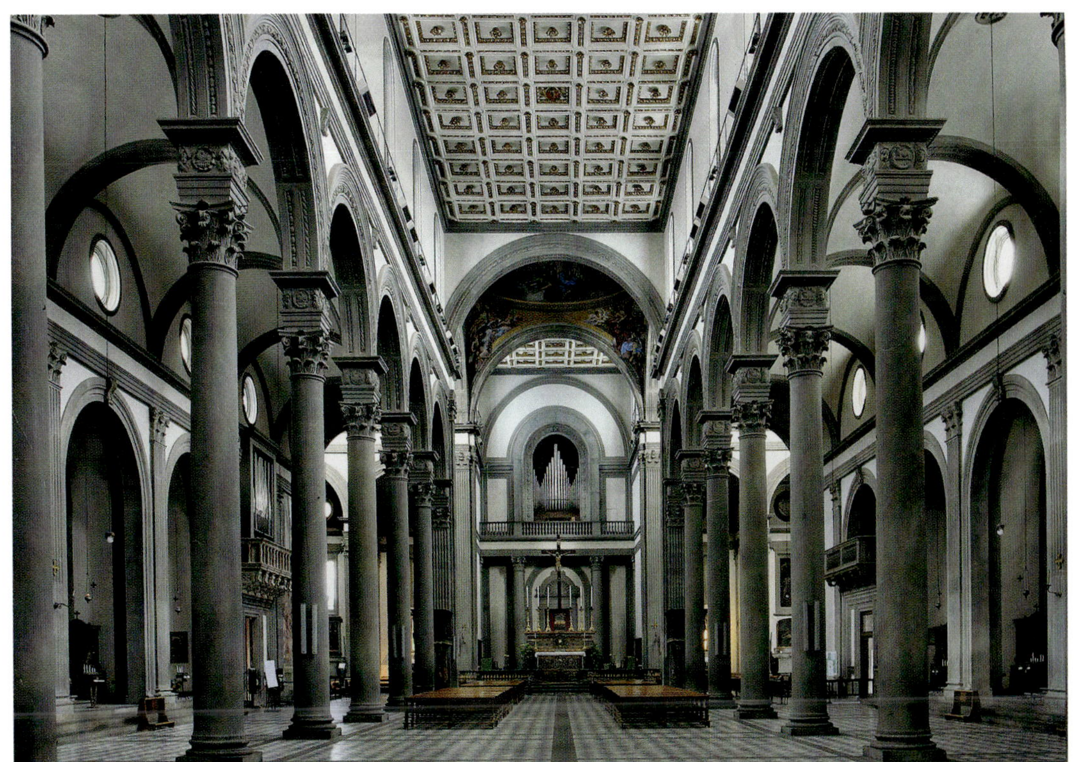

12–16 Filippo Brunelleschi. Nave, Church of San Lorenzo, Florence. Begun c. 1421

The Church of San Lorenzo is an austere basilica with a long nave flanked by single side aisles opening into shallow chapels and covered with a flat ceiling inset with coffers, like a Roman basilica. A hemispherical dome on pendentives covers the crossing. Each nave arch springs from an **impost block**, or section of entablature, resting on slender Corinthian columns. With this arrangement, Brunelleschi managed to bend, without exactly breaking, the rules of Classical architecture, in which piers, rather than columns, supported arches, and columns only supported entablatures. In the side aisles, the arched openings to the chapels are surmounted by arched lunettes that mirror the shape of the nave arcade. The Church of San Lorenzo was an experimental building combining old and new elements, but Brunelleschi's rational approach, unique sense of order, and innovative incorporation of Classical motifs inspired later Renaissance architects, many of whom learned from his work first-hand by completing his unfinished projects.

Brunelleschi's role in the Medici Palace in Florence (now known as the Palazzo Medici-Riccardi), begun in 1446, is unclear (fig. **12–17**). According to Giorgio Vasari, the sixteenth-century

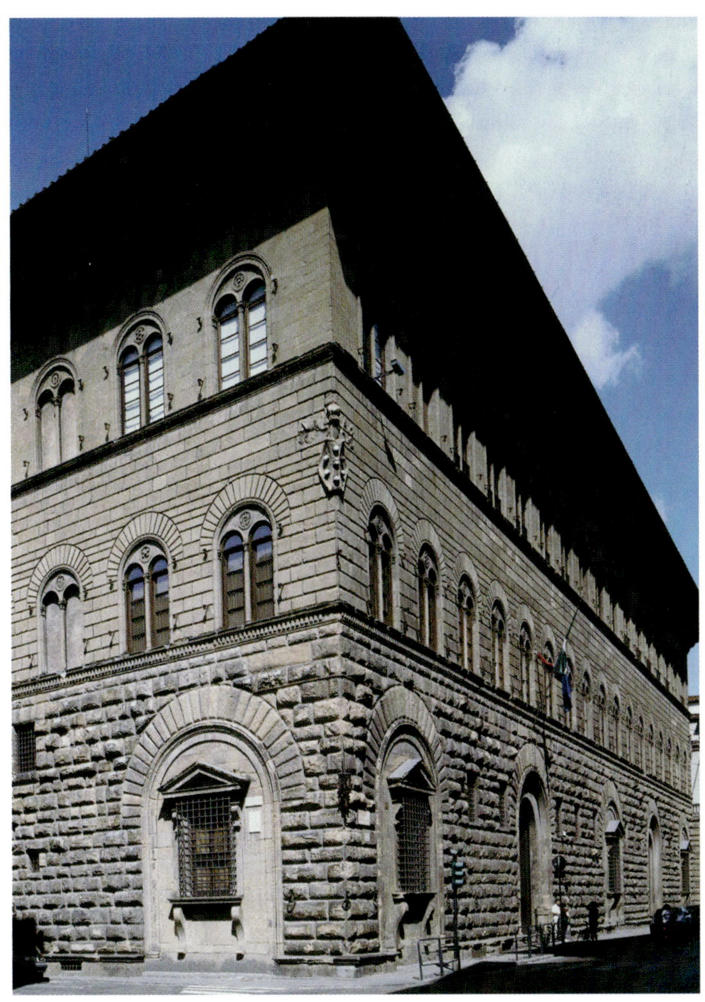

12–17 Attributed to Michelozzo di Bartolomeo. Palazzo Medici-Riccardi, Florence. Begun 1446

Cosimo de' Medici the Elder did not decide to build a new palace just to provide more living space for his family. He also incorporated into the plans offices and storage rooms for conducting his business affairs. For the palace site, he chose the Via de' Gori at the corner of the Via Larga, the widest city street at that time. Despite his practical reasons for constructing a large residence and the fact that he chose simplicity and austerity over grandeur in the exterior design, his detractors commented and gossiped. As one exaggerated: "[Cosimo] has begun a palace which throws even the Colosseum at Rome into the shade."

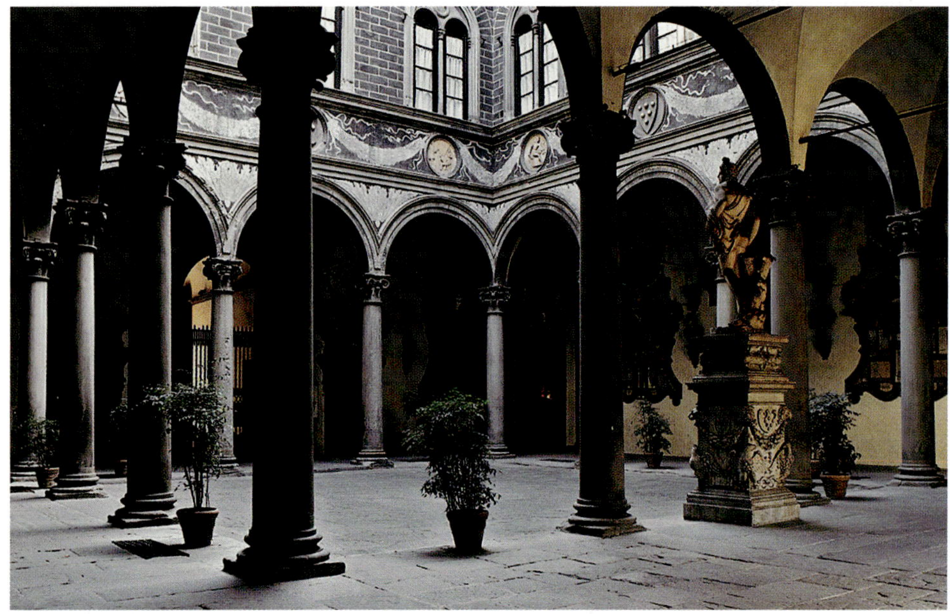

12–18 Courtyard with *sgraffito* decoration, Palazzo Medici-Riccardi, Florence. Begun 1446

artist and theorist who wrote what some consider the first history of art, Brunelleschi's model for the ***palazzo*** (any large house was called a *palazzo*, or palace) was rejected as too grand by Cosimo de' Medici the Elder. Today many scholars believe that Cosimo then hired Michelozzo to redesign the building. The relatively plain exterior was in keeping with political and religious thinking in Florence, where Christian ideals of poverty and charity were in vogue. Private homes were supposedly limited to a dozen rooms, but Cosimo actually acquired and demolished 20 small houses to provide the site for his imposing new residence, each story over 20 feet in height. In Florence the house was not only a dwelling place; it symbolized the family and established its proper place in the Florentine social hierarchy.

Though huge in size, this *palazzo* is marked by fine proportions and careful attention to detail. On one side, the ground floor originally opened through large, round arches onto the street, providing space for the family business. These arches were walled up in the sixteenth century and windows were designed by Michelangelo. The large **rusticated** stone blocks—that is, blocks with their outer faces left rough—facing the lower story clearly set it off from the two upper levels. In fact, all three stories are distinguished by stone surfaces that vary from sculptural at the ground level to almost smooth on the third floor.

Inside, the *palazzo* conforms to the time-honored tradition of placing rooms around a central courtyard. Unlike irregular

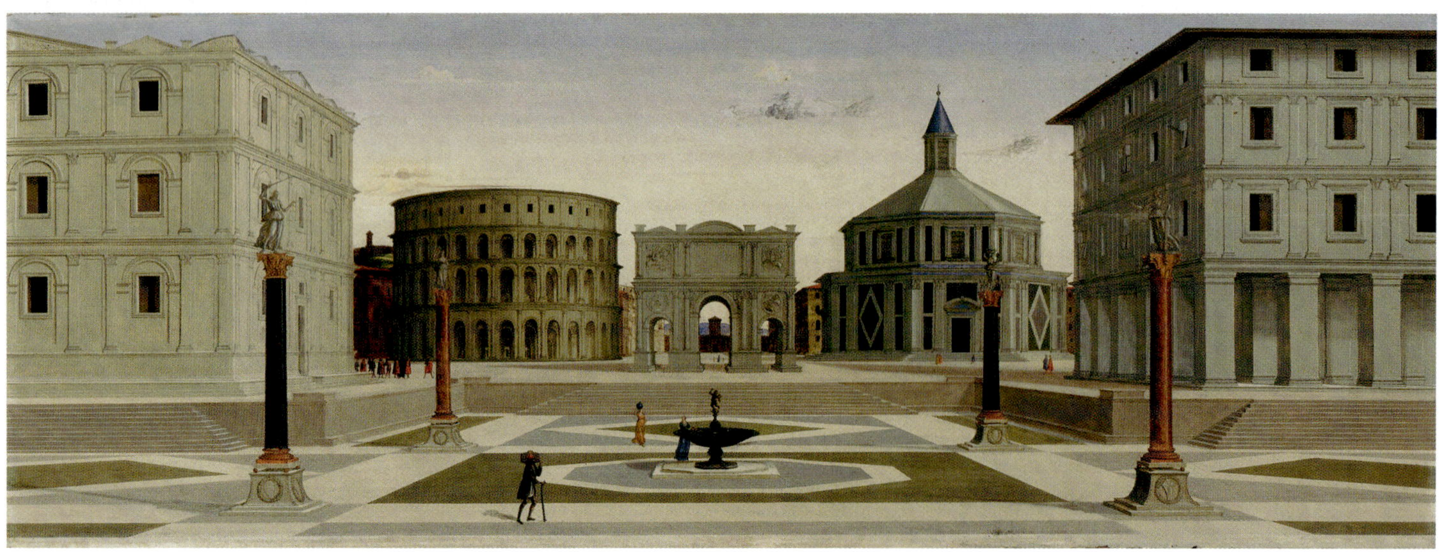

12–19 Anonymous. *View of an Ideal City*. c. 1500. Oil on panel, 30½" × 7' 1⅜" (77.4 cm × 2.17 m). Walters Art Museum, Baltimore

medieval plans, the Medici Palace courtyard is square with rooms arranged symmetrically (fig. **12–18**). Round arches on slender columns form a continuous arcade under an enclosed second story. The tall windows in the second story match the exterior windows on this same level. Disks bearing the Medici arms surmount each arch in a frieze decorated with swags in **sgraffito** (decoration produced by scratching through a layer of darker plaster or glaze). Such classicizing elements, inspired by the study of Roman ruins, gave the great house an aura of dignity and stability that enhanced the status of its owners. The Medici Palace inaugurated a new fashion for monumentality and regularity in residential Florentine architecture, followed by other wealthy Florentine families in their houses.

A developing intellectual interest in architectural design and urban planning inspired Italian Renaissance artists to imagine and paint vistas of ideal cities. The central Italian artist who invented the ideal city-center in fig. **12–19** included a triumphal arch and a mini-Colosseum amid contemporary townhouses. The octagonal church or baptistery in the right background suggests the influence of Leon Battista Alberti (1404–1472), a humanist-turned-architect. In his 1452 treatise *De re aedificatoria* (*On Architecture*), Alberti expressed his preference, based on his understanding of Classical buildings such as the Pantheon, for churches that were either circular or polygonal, because "most things which are generated, made or directed by Nature are round." The roofs of the houses are the same height, as Alberti recommended in his description of an ideal city. Only a few tiny figures walk the strikingly wide and clean streets in this visionary urban space—clearly distinguishing it from the crowded and twisted alleyways that crisscrossed virtually all fifteenth-century cities. The Four Cardinal Virtues—Justice, Prudence, Patience, and Fortitude—stand on columns in the four corners of the square, a reminder that in the dreams of Renaissance theorists, ideal cities would bring out the best qualities in their citizens.

Sculpture

Donatello, born Donato di Niccolò Bardi (c. 1386–1466), was one of the most influential and innovative figures of the early Italian Renaissance. He approached each commission as a new experiment. All his sculptures broke new ground. For example, Donatello's rendition of the biblical hero David, who slew the giant Goliath with a stone from his slingshot, is the earliest known life-size free-standing bronze nude in European art since antiquity (fig. **12–20**). Exactly when Donatello made the statue is unknown, but it was first recorded in 1469 in the courtyard of the Medici Palace in Florence, mounted on a base engraved with an inscription extolling Florentine heroism and virtue. Although the work clearly draws on the Classical tradition of heroic nudity, this sensuous adolescent boy in a jaunty hat and boots, standing on his enemy's severed head, has long piqued art-historical interest. Some have interpreted David's angular pose, dreamy expression, and underdeveloped torso, as Donatello's attempt to heighten the spectacular heroism of this child who takes on the adult responsibility of challenging and defeating a giant enemy warrior.

Donatello's work was not confined to Florence. He was probably called to Padua in 1443 to execute an equestrian statue

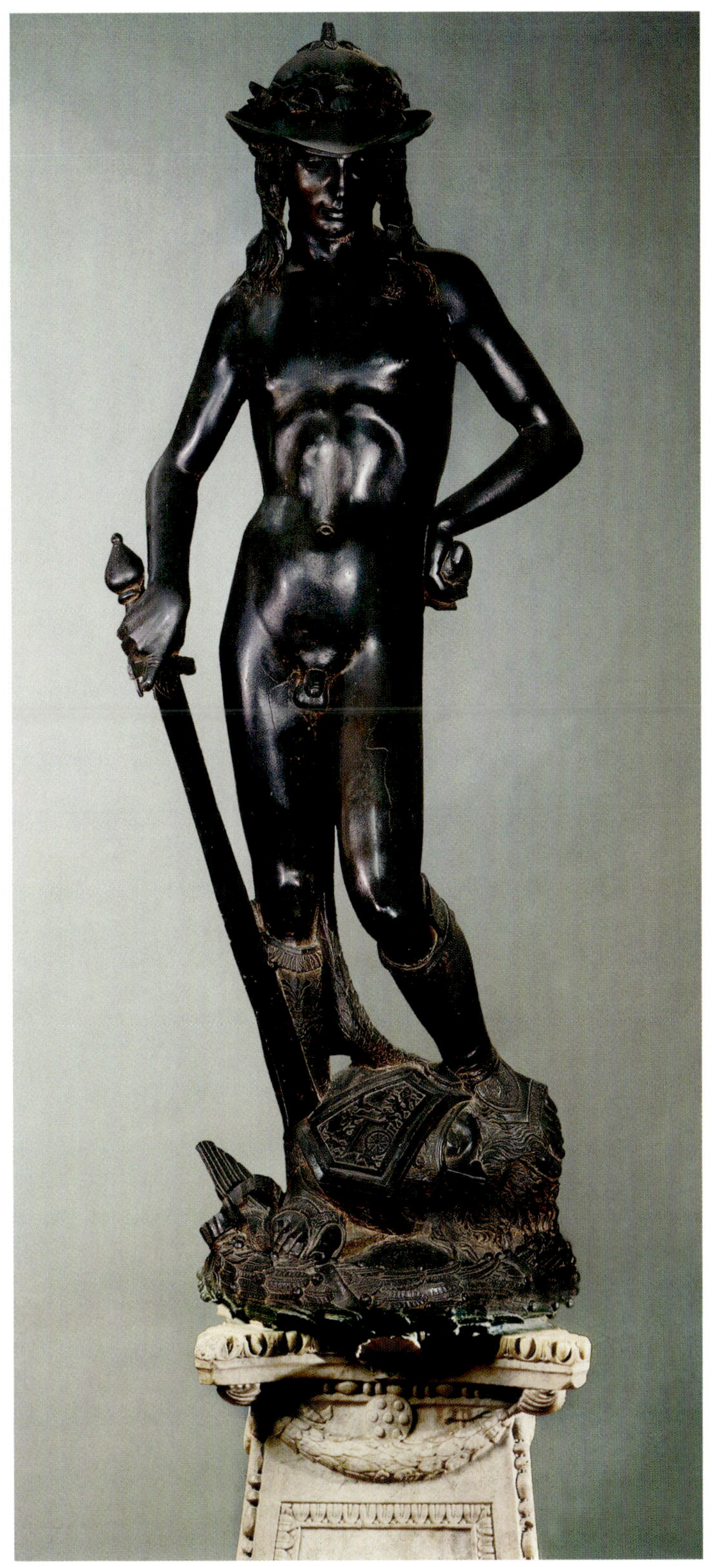

12–20 Donatello. *David*. 1450s or 1460s. Bronze, height 5' 2¼" (1.58 m). Museo Nazionale del Bargello, Florence

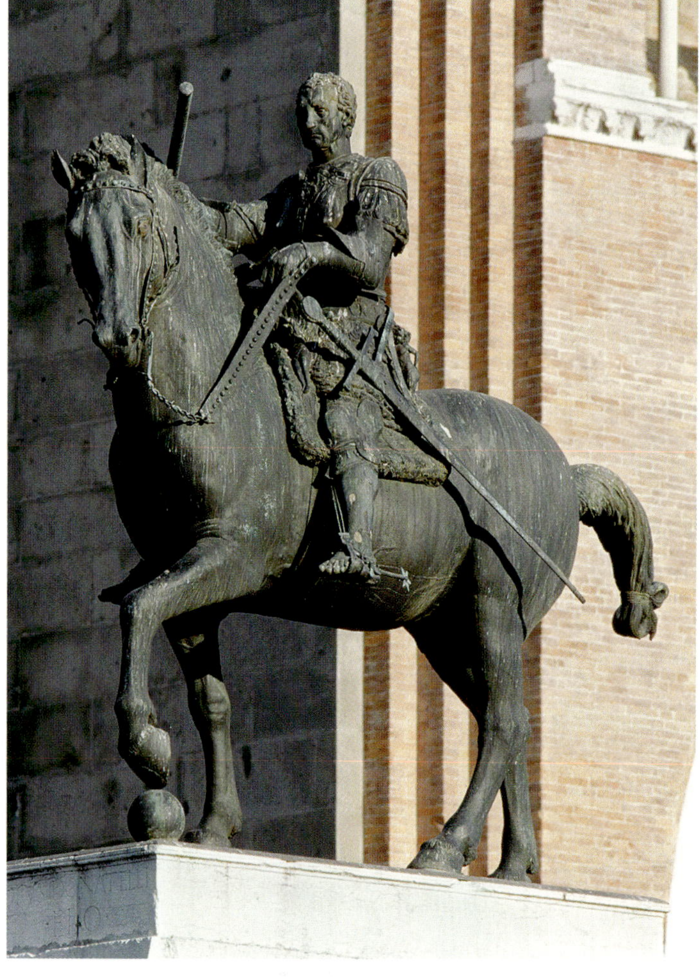

12–21 Donatello. Equestrian monument of Erasmo da Narni *(Gattamelata)*, Piazza del Santo, Padua. 1443–1453. Bronze, height approx. 12' 2" (3.71 m)

commemorating the Venetian general Erasmo da Narni, nicknamed *Gattamelata* (Honeyed Cat) (fig. **12–21**). His sources for this statue were two surviving Roman bronze equestrian portraits—one (now lost) in the north Italian city of Pavia, and the other of the emperor Marcus Aurelius (see fig. 6–33), which the sculptor certainly saw and probably sketched during a visit to Rome. The completed *Gattamelata*, installed on a high base in front of the church of Saint Anthony, was the first life-size bronze equestrian statue since antiquity. Viewed from a distance, this juggernaut of man and animal seems capable of thrusting forward at the first threat. Seen from up close, however, the man's sunken cheeks, sagging jaw, ropey neck, and stern but sad expression suggest a warrior grown old and tired at the end of a distinguished military career.

While Donatello was working in Padua, his rival Lorenzo Ghiberti (1378–1455) gained the prestigious commission in Florence for a third set of gilded bronze doors (see "Closer Look," page 317, for Ghiberti's choice for the second set) to be installed in the baptistery facing the cathedral's west façade. Ghiberti's doors (figs. **12–22** and **12–23**), installed in 1452, were reportedly said by Michelangelo to be worthy of being the Gates of Paradise, a name by which they are still known. Overall gilding unifies the ten large, square reliefs. Ghiberti organized the space depicted within each panel either by a system of linear perspective, approximating the one described by Alberti in his 1435 treatise on painting (see "Renaissance Perspective Systems," page 324), or by a series of arches, rocks, or trees leading the eye into the distance. Foreground figures are grouped in the lower third of each panel, while the other figures decrease gradually in size, suggesting deep space. In some panels, the tall buildings suggest ancient Roman architecture and illustrate the emerging antiquarian tone in Renaissance art.

The story of Jacob and Esau (Genesis 25 and 27) fills the relief in the center panel of the left door. Ghiberti creates a coherent and measurable space peopled by graceful, idealized figures (see fig. 12–22). He pays careful attention to one-point perspective in laying out the architectural setting. Squares in the pavement establish the receding lines of the orthogonals that converge to a central vanishing point under the loggia, while towering arches overlap and gradually diminish in size from foreground to background to define the receding space above the figures. The story unfolds in a series of individual episodes, beginning in the background. On the rooftop (upper right) Rebecca stands, listening as God warns of her unborn sons' future conflict; under the left-hand arch she gives birth to the twins. The adult Esau sells his rights as oldest son to his brother Jacob, and when he goes hunting (center right), Rebecca and Jacob plot against him. Finally, in the right foreground, Jacob receives Isaac's blessing, while in the center, Esau faces his father. Ghiberti's portrayal of this scene relates more closely to developments in painting than to contemporary sculpture.

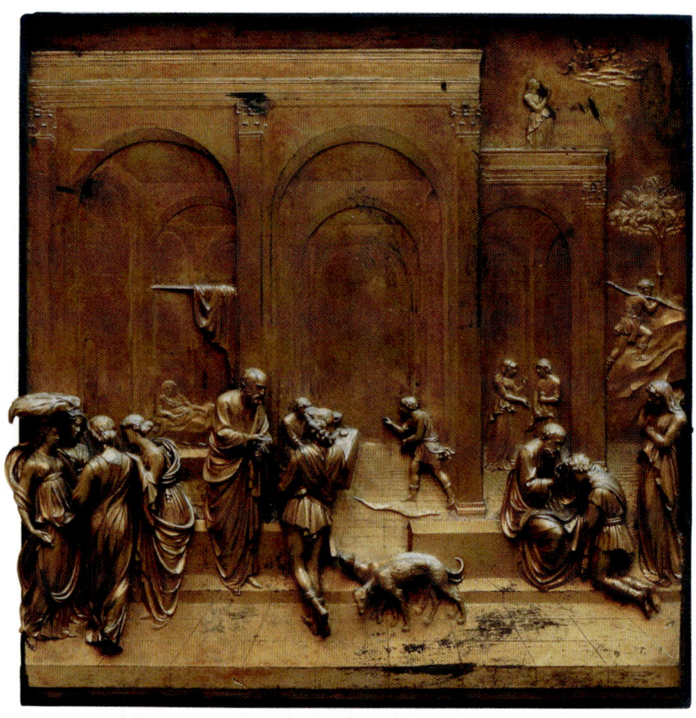

12–22 Lorenzo Ghiberti. *Jacob and Esau.* Panel from the Gates of Paradise (East Doors), from the Baptistery of San Giovanni, Florence. c. 1435. Gilded bronze, 31¼" (79 cm) square. Museo dell'Opera del Duomo, Florence

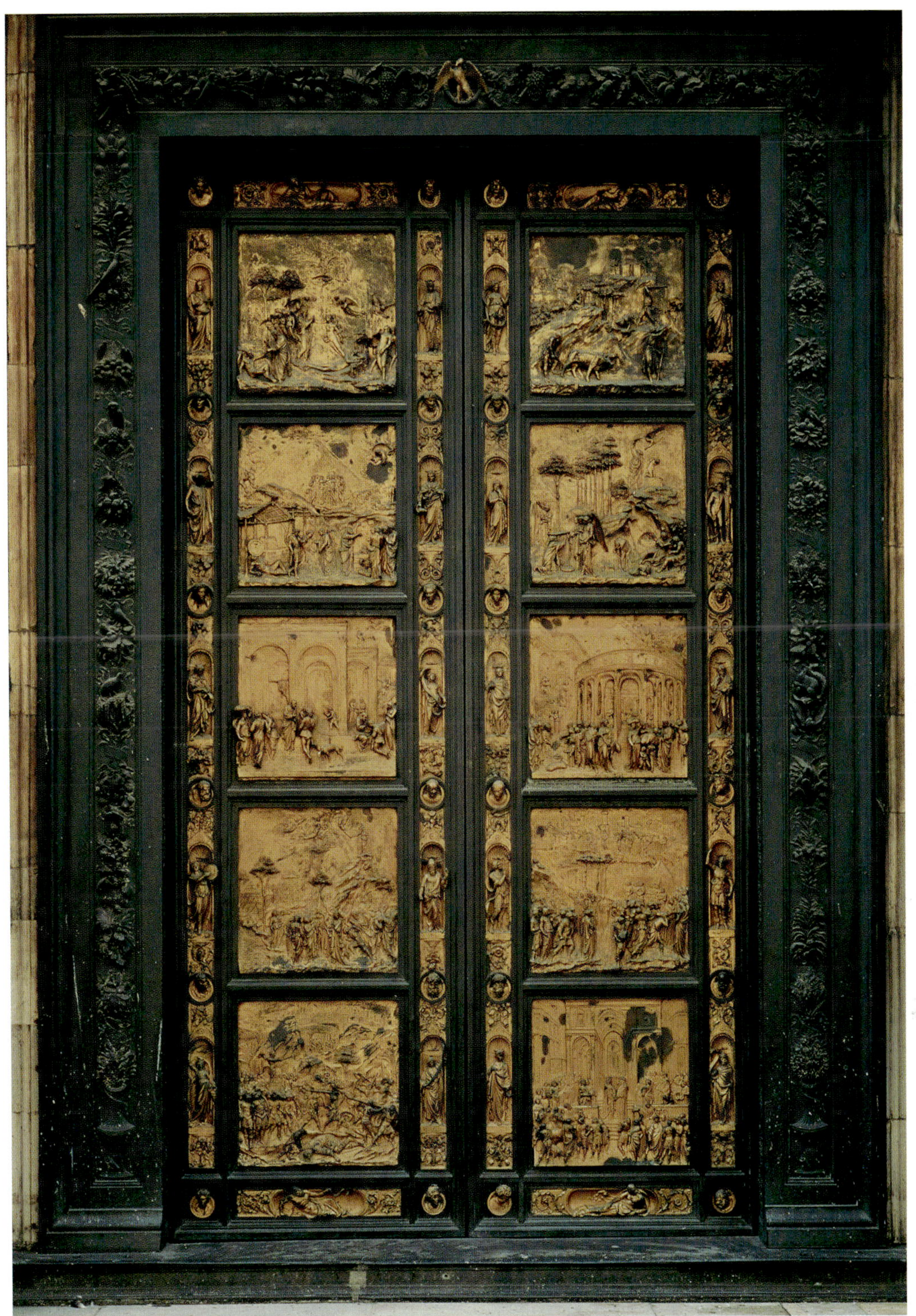

12–23 Lorenzo Ghiberti. Gates of Paradise (East Doors), from the Baptistery of San Giovanni, Florence. 1425–1452. Gilded bronze, height 15' (4.57 m). Museo dell'Opera del Duomo, Florence

The door panels, commissioned by the wool manufacturers' guild, depict ten scenes from the Hebrew Bible beginning with the Creation in the upper left panel. The murder of Abel by his brother, Cain, follows in the upper right panel, succeeded in the same left-right paired order by the Flood and the drunkenness of Noah, Abraham sacrificing Isaac, the story of Jacob and Esau, Joseph sold into slavery by his brothers, Moses receiving the Tablets of the Law, Joshua and the fall of Jericho, David and Goliath, and finally Solomon and the Queen of Sheba. Ghiberti placed his own portrait in the frame beside the Jacob and Esau panel. He wrote in his Commentaries *(c. 1450–1455): "I strove to imitate nature as clearly as I could, and with all the perspective I could produce, to have excellent compositions with many figures."*

Technique

Renaissance Perspective Systems

Fifteenth-century Italian artists developed a system known as **linear**, or **mathematical perspective** that enabled them to represent three dimensions on a two-dimensional surface, simulating the recession of space in the visible world pictorially in a way they found convincing. The sculptor and architect Filippo Brunelleschi first demonstrated the system about 1420, and the theorist and architect Leon Battista Alberti codified it in 1436 in his treatise *Della Pittura* (*On Painting*).

For Alberti, a picture's surface was conceived as a flat plane that intersected the viewer's field of vision at right angles. This highly artificial concept presumed that a viewer would stand dead center at a prescribed distance from a work of art. From this single fixed vantage point, everything would appear to recede into the distance at the same rate, following imaginary lines called **orthogonals** that met at a single **vanishing point** on the horizon. By using orthogonals in concert with controlled diminution of the scale as forms move back toward the vanishing point, artists could replicate the optical illusion that things appear to grow smaller, rise higher, and come closer together as they get farther away from us. Linear perspective makes pictorial spaces seem almost like extensions of the viewer's real space, creating a compelling, even exaggerated sense of depth (fig. **12–24**).

Linear perspective is not the only way to simulate spatial recession in two-dimensional painting. In **atmospheric perspective**, variations in color and clarity convey the feeling of distance when objects and landscape are portrayed less clear, and colors become more grayed, in the background, imitating the natural effects of a loss of clarity and color when viewing things in the distance through an atmospheric haze. Perugino uses both linear and atmospheric perspective in his *Delivery of the Keys to Saint Peter*.

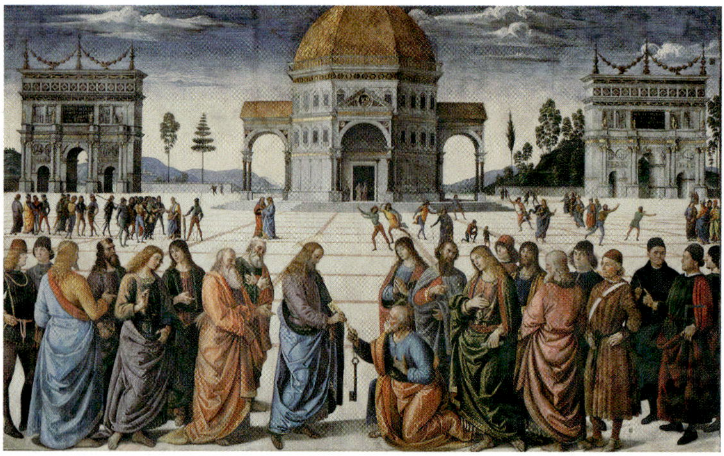

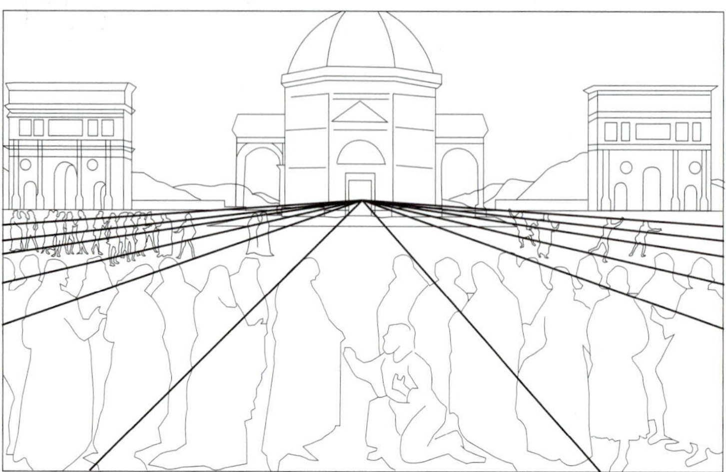

12–24 Pietro Perugino. ***Delivery of the Keys to Saint Peter***, Sistine Chapel, Vatican, Rome. 1481. Fresco, 11' 5½" × 18' 8½" (3.48 × 5.7 m)

Delivery of the Keys to Saint Peter *is a remarkable study in linear perspective. The clear demarcation of the paving stones of the piazza provides a geometric grid of orthogonal and horizontal lines against which the figures stand like chess pieces on the squares. People and buildings are scaled to size according to their distance from the picture plane and modeled by a consistent light source from the upper left. Horizontally, the composition is divided between the foreground frieze of figures and the widely spaced background buildings, vertically by the open space at the center between Christ and Peter and by the symmetrical architectural forms on either side of this central axis. Perugino's painting is, among other things, a representation of Alberti's ideal city (see fig. 12–19), described in* De re aedificatoria *as having a "temple" (that is, a church) at the very center of a great open space raised on a dais and separate from any other buildings so that it would always be visible.*

Painting

One of the major achievements of Italian Renaissance artists was the consistently scaled integration of human figures into rational architectural settings using linear perspective. This was accomplished early on in the works of the Florentine artist Tommaso di Ser Giovanni di Mone Cassai (1401–1428), nicknamed Masaccio ("big, ugly Tom"). In his short but brilliant career of less than a decade, Masaccio established a new direction in Florentine painting, much as Giotto had done a century earlier. The exact chronology of his works is uncertain, but his fresco of the *Trinity* in the Church of Santa Maria Novella in Florence falls sometime between 1425 and 1428 (fig. **12–25**).

The fresco was meant to give the illusion of a stone funerary monument and altar table set in a deep **aedicula** (framed niche) in the wall. Masaccio created the appearance of the niche through precisely rendered linear perspective in which the vanishing point lies on a horizon line just above the base of the cross at the eye level of an adult viewer standing in the church. The niche itself resembles the architecture of San Lorenzo (see fig. 12–16), demonstrating Masaccio's intimate knowledge of both Brunelleschi's perspective experiments and his architectural style. A consistent illumination, whose "source" seems to lie behind the viewer, models the figures and casts reflections on the painted coffers (recessed panels) of the vault.

In Masaccio's *Trinity*, a looming figure of God the Father holds the cross on which Jesus hangs, while the dove of the Holy Spirit seems poised in downward flight between Jesus' tilted halo and the Father's head. Mary and Saint John the Evangelist stand at the foot of the cross. Outside and in front of the niche the donors kneel in prayer. Mary gazes calmly out at us, her raised hand gesturing toward the Trinity. Below, in an open sarcophagus, a skeleton provides a grim reminder that death awaits us all and that our only hope is redemption and life in the hereafter through Christian belief. The inscription above the skeleton reads: "I was once that which you are, and what I am you also will be."

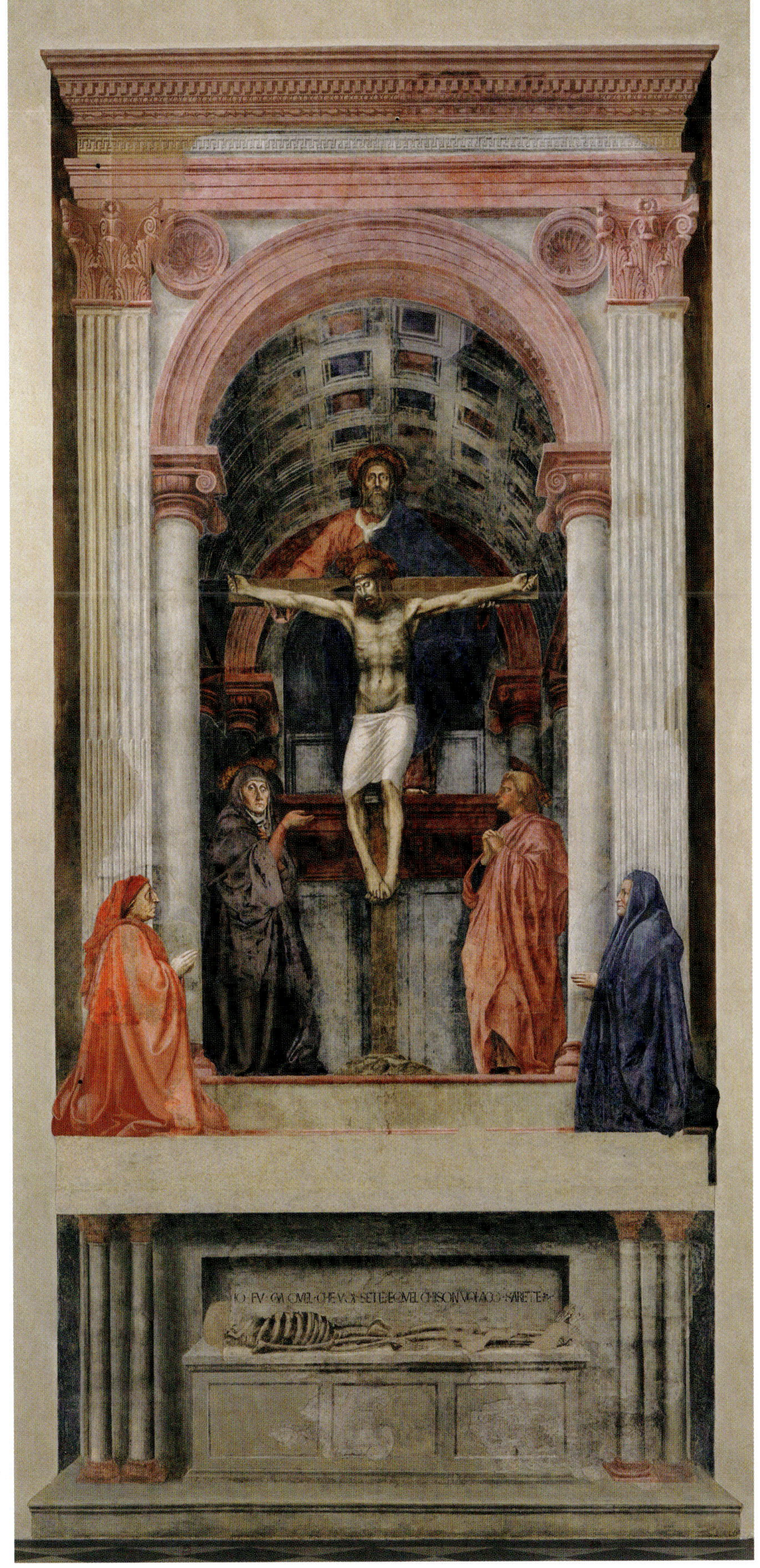

12–25 Masaccio. ***Trinity with the Virgin, Saint John the Evangelist, and Donors***, Church of Santa Maria Novella, Florence. c. 1425–1428. Fresco, 21' × 10' 5" (6.4 × 3.17 m)

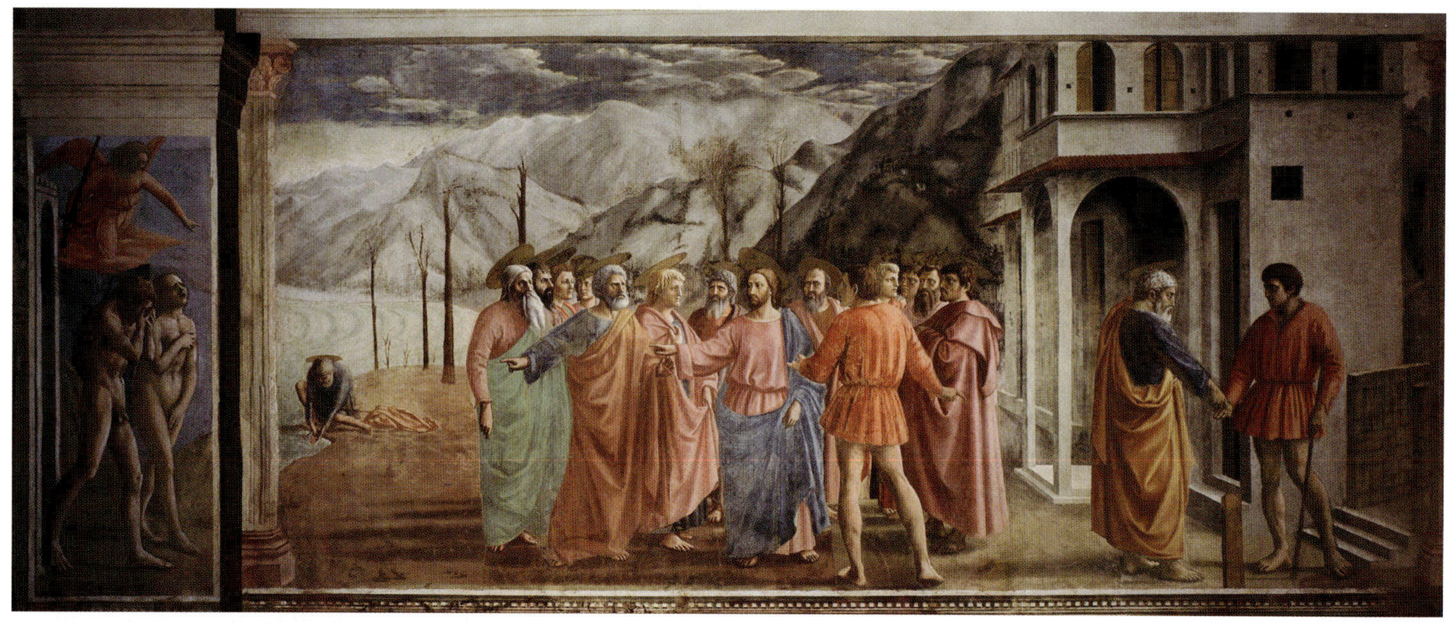

12–26 Masaccio. ***The Expulsion from Paradise*** **and** ***The Tribute Money*****,** Brancacci Chapel, Church of Santa Maria del Carmine, Florence. c. 1427. Fresco, 8' 1" × 19' 7" (2.46 × 6 m)

Much valuable new information about the Brancacci Chapel frescoes was discovered during the course of a cleaning and restoration carried out between 1981 and 1991. Art historians now have a more accurate picture of how the frescoes were done and in what sequence. One interesting discovery was that all of the figures in The Tribute Money, *except those of the temple tax collector, originally had gold-leaf haloes, several of which had flaked off. Rather than silhouette the heads against flat gold circles in the medieval manner, Masaccio conceived of the halo as a foreshortened gold disk hovering in space above each head.*

Masaccio's brief career culminated in the frescoes he painted on the walls of the Brancacci Chapel in the Church of Santa Maria del Carmine in Florence (fig. **12–26**). Reproduced here are the two best-known scenes: *The Expulsion from Paradise* (at left) and *The Tribute Money* (right). Adam and Eve are represented as monumental nude figures, presumably based on Masaccio's study of both the human figure and ancient Roman sculpture. The mass of their bodies reveals the underlying structure of bone and muscle, and a single light source emphasizes their modeled forms which cast clear shadows on the ground. Departing from earlier traditions that emphasized wrongdoing and original sin in representing this event, Masaccio concerns himself with the psychological impact of shame on humans who have been cast out of Paradise mourning and protesting, thrown naked and unprepared into the world.

In *The Tribute Money* (fig. 12–26, right), Masaccio portrays an incident from the Life of Jesus that highlights Saint Peter (Matthew 17:24–27), to whom this chapel was originally dedicated. In the central scene, a tax collector (dressed in a short red tunic and seen from behind) asks Peter (in the left foreground with the short gray beard) if Jesus pays the Jewish temple tax. Jesus instructs Peter to "go to the sea, drop in a hook, and take the first fish that comes up," which Peter does at the far left. In the fish's mouth, Peter finds a coin which he gives to the tax collector at the far right.

The Tribute Money is particularly remarkable for its early use of both linear and atmospheric perspective to integrate figures, architecture, and landscape into a consistent whole. The group of disciples around Jesus forms a clear central focus, behind which the landscape seems to recede logically into the far distance. To foster this illusion, Masaccio used linear perspective in the depiction of the house, and then reinforced it by diminishing the sizes of the barren trees and reducing the size of the crouching Peter at far left. The orthogonals implied by the architectural rendering lead viewers' eyes to the head of Jesus, which the painter has placed at the central vanishing point. A second vanishing point determines the position of the steps and stone rail at the right. The cleaning of the fresco during the 1980s revealed that it was painted in 32 ***giornate*** (a *giornata* is a section of fresh plaster that could be prepared and painted in one day). The cleaning also uncovered Mascaccio's subtle use of color to create atmospheric perspective in the distant landscape. The mountains fade from grayish green to grayish white and the houses and trees on their slopes are more sketchy, to simulate the lack of clear definition when viewing things in the distance through haze.

As with *The Expulsion from Paradise*, Masaccio models figures here with bold highlights and shadows, giving a strong sense of volumetric solidity. Figures cast their long shadows on the ground toward the left, implying a light source at the far right, as if the scene were lit by the actual window in the rear wall of the chapel. Not only does the lighting give the forms sculptural definition, but the colors vary in tone according to the strength of the illumination. Masaccio used a wide range of hues—pale pink, mauve, gold, seafoam green,

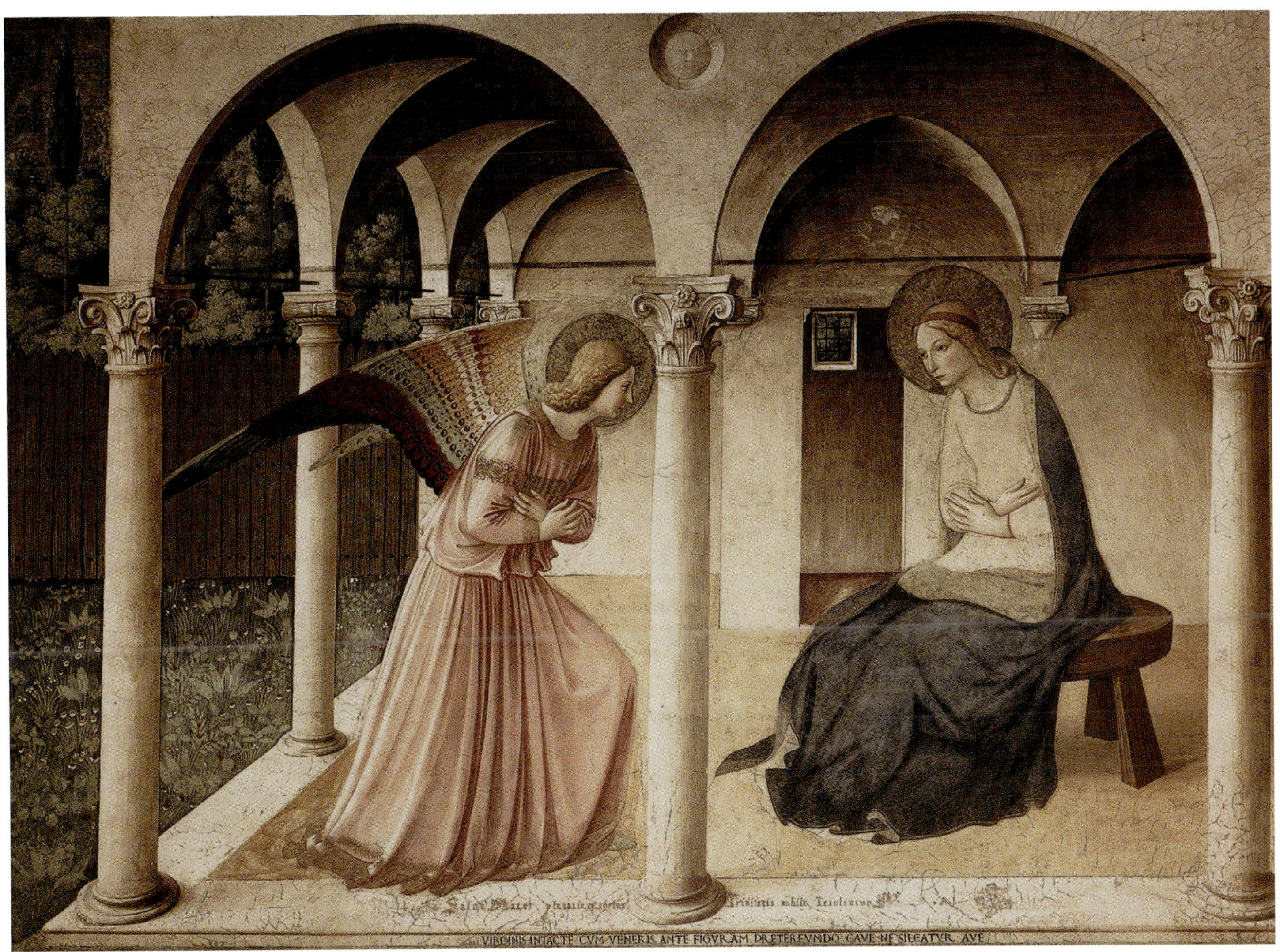

12–27 Fra Angelico. ***Annunciation***, Monastery of San Marco, Florence, north corridor. c. 1438–1445. Fresco, 7' 1" × 10' 6" (2.2 × 3.2 m)

apple green, and peach—and a sophisticated shading technique using contrasting colors (for example, Saint Andrew's green mantle is shaded with red instead of darker green). When restorers cleaned the painting, they also discovered a wealth of linear detail, especially in the settings, that had been obscured by dirt and overpainting. The landscape and buildings are much closer in appearance to the paintings by Masaccio's Northern European contemporaries than previously thought. In contrast to the Flemish artists, however, Masaccio's figures exhibit the artist's debt to Roman sculpture and the painting of Giotto and his followers, which he could have seen in fifteenth-century Florence.

Some stylistic innovations take time to be fully accepted, and Masaccio's innovative depictions of volumetric solidity, consistent lighting, and spatial integration were best appreciated by a later generation of painters. Many important sixteenth-century Italian artists, including Michelangelo (see Chapter 13), studied and sketched Masaccio's Brancacci Chapel frescoes, as they did in Giotto's Arena Chapel (see Chapter 11).

The tradition of covering walls with paintings in fresco, however, continued uninterrupted through the fifteenth century. Between 1435 and 1445 the decoration of the Dominican Monastery of San Marco in Florence, where Fra Angelico served as the prior, was one of the most important projects. Born Guido di Pietro da Mugello (c. 1395/1400–1455) and known to his peers as Fra Giovanni da Fiesole, Fra Angelico (Angelic Brother) earned his nickname through his piety as well as his painting. He is documented painting in Florence in 1417–1418, and he remained an active painter after taking vows as a Dominican monk in nearby Fiesole between 1418 and 1421.

In the Monastery of San Marco, Fra Angelico and his assistants created a painting to inspire meditation in each monk's cell, 44 in all. They also added paintings to the chapter house and the corridors. At the top of the stairs in the north corridor where the monks would pass on their way to their individual cells, Fra Angelico painted a serene scene of the Annunciation (fig. **12–27**). The illusion of space created by precise linear perspective seems to extend the

CLOSER LOOK

This ferocious but bloodless battle could take place only in our dreams. Under an elegantly fluttering banner, the Florentine general Niccolò da Tolentino leads his men against the Sienese at the Battle of San Romano, which took place June 1, 1432. Niccolò holds aloft his baton of command, a sign of his absolute authority. His gesture, together with his white horse and fashionable crimson and gold damask hat, ensure that he dominates the scene. The general's knights charge into the fray, and when they fall, like the soldier at the lower left, they join the many broken lances on the ground—all arranged in conformity with the new mathematical depiction of space called linear perspective.

The battle rages across a shallow stage, defined by the debris of warfare arranged in a neat pattern on the pink ground and backed by a tapestry-like hedge of blooming orange trees and rosebushes. In the cultivated hills beyond, crossbowmen prepare their lethal bolts. An eccentric Florentine nicknamed Paolo Uccello ("Paul Bird") created this panel painting, now housed in London's National Gallery (fig. **12–28**). It was part of a three-panel group, now separated. The other two paintings hang in major museums in Florence and Paris.

The strange history of these paintings has only recently come to light. Lionardo Bartolini Salimbeni (1409–1479), who headed Florence's governing Council of Ten during the war against Lucca and Siena, probably commissioned the paintings. Uccello's remarkable accuracy when depicting armor, heraldic banners, and even fashionable fabrics and crests from the 1430s would appeal to Florentine civic pride. The hedges of oranges, roses, and pomegranates—all ancient fertility symbols—suggest that Lionardo might have commissioned the paintings at the time of his wedding in 1438. He and his wife, Maddalena, had six sons, two of whom inherited the paintings. According to a complaint brought by one of the heirs, Damiano, Lorenzo de' Medici, de-facto ruler of Florence, "forcibly removed" the paintings from Damiano's house. They were never returned, and Uccello's masterpieces are recorded in a 1492 inventory as hanging in Lorenzo's private chamber in the Medici Palace. There, with their carved and gilded frames, the three paintings would have formed a brilliant and heroic frieze. Perhaps Lorenzo, who was called "the Magnificent," saw Uccello's heroic pageant as a trophy more worthy of a Medici merchant prince.

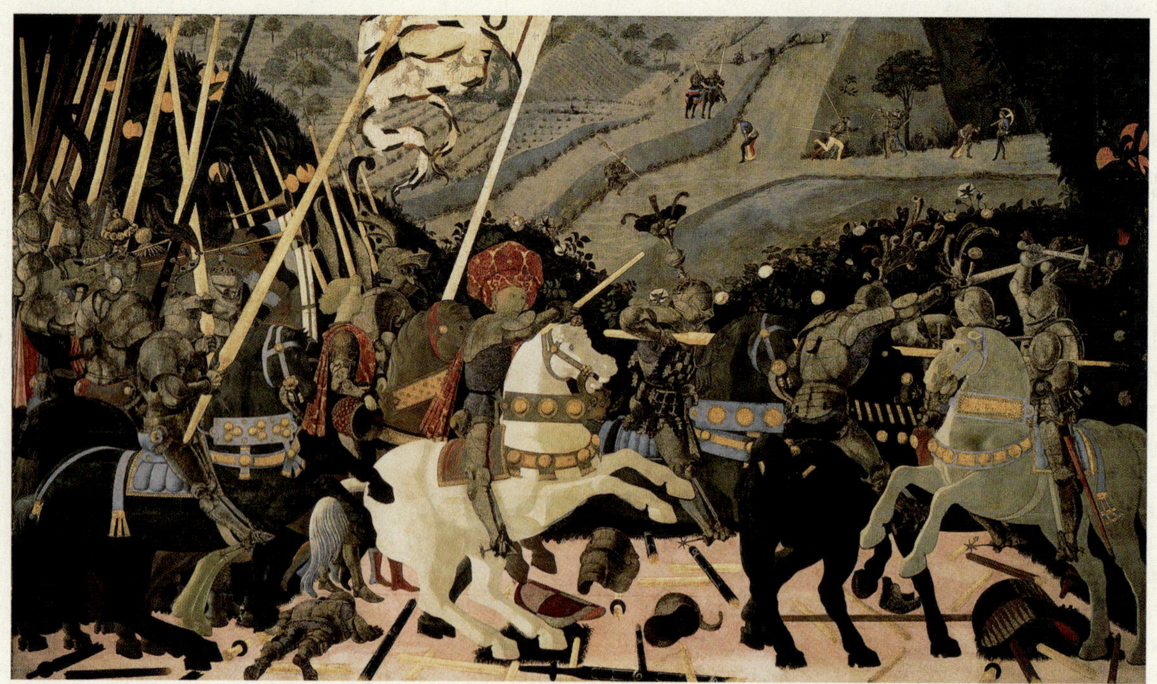

12–28 Paolo Uccello. ***The Battle of San Romano.*** 1438–1440. Tempera on wood panel, 6' × 10' 5" (1.83 × 3.23 m). The National Gallery, London

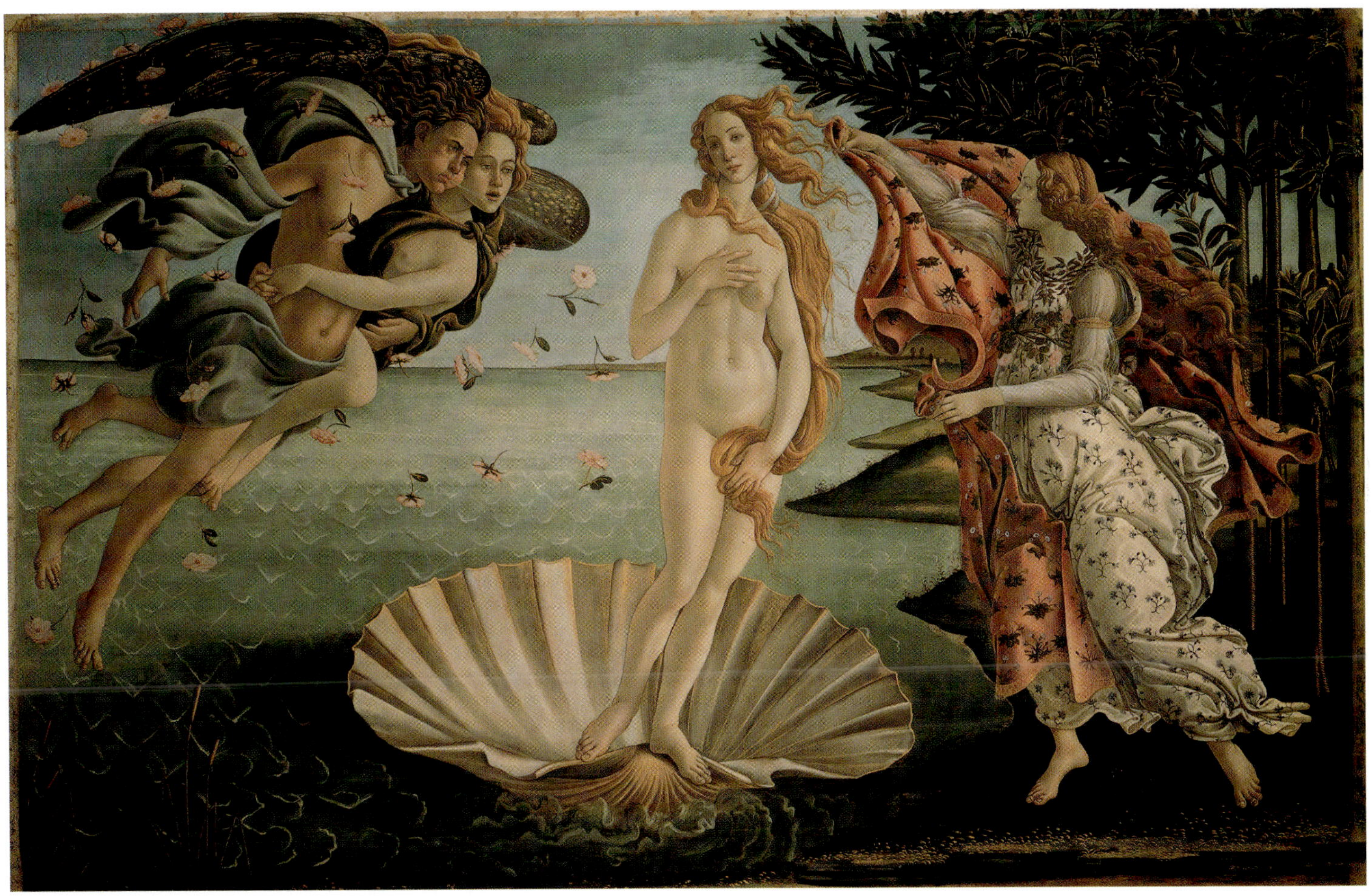

12–29 Sandro Botticelli. *Birth of Venus*. c. 1484–1486. Tempera on canvas, 5' 8⅞" × 9' 1⅞" (1.8 × 2.8 m). Galleria degli Uffizi, Florence

stairway and corridor outward into an arcaded portico and enclosed garden beside the Virgin's home, where the demure archangel Gabriel greets the modest, youthful Mary. The slender, graceful figures wearing quietly flowing draperies assume modest poses. Natural light falling from the left models their forms gently, casting an almost supernatural radiance over their faces and hands. The scene is a vision that welcomes the monks to the most private areas of the monastery and prepares them for their private meditations.

Pope Eugene IV summoned Fra Angelico to Rome in 1445, and the painter's assistants completed the frescoes in Florence. The pope may have hoped to appoint the painter archbishop of Florence, but finally chose the vicar of San Marco, Antonino Pierozzi, for the post in January 1446. When Pierozzi was proposed for canonization in the early sixteenth century, several people testified that Pope Eugene's first choice for archbishop had been Fra Angelico, who declined the honor and recommended his Dominican brother Antonino. The world of art was left richer by the choice, however, for Fra Angelico dedicated the rest of his life to his painting, including the pope's private chapel in the Vatican Palace.

At mid-century, when Fra Angelico was still painting his radiant visions of Mary and Jesus in the Monastery of San Marco, a new generation of artists emerged. Thoroughly conversant with the theories of Brunelleschi and Alberti, they had mastered the techniques (and tricks) of depicting figures in a constructed architectural space. Some artists became specialists. The eccentric painter Paolo di Dono (c. 1397–1475), called Paolo Uccello ("Paul Bird"), devoted his life to the study of linear perspective (see fig. 12–28). Vasari devoted a chapter in his history of art to Uccello, whom he described as a man so obsessed with the science of perspective that he neglected his painting, his family, and even his pet birds. Finally Uccello became, in Vasari's words, "solitary, eccentric, melancholy, and impoverished" (Vasari, page 79). According to Vasari, Uccello's wife complained that he sat up drawing all night and when she called to him to come to bed he would say, "Oh, what a sweet mistress is this perspective!"

Contrasting sharply with Uccello's scientific obsession is the fascination of the Florentine painter Sandro Botticelli (1445–1510) with fluid, linear, graceful figures resembling dancers. Among Botticelli's best-known works are paintings of mythological subjects, among them the *Birth of Venus* (fig. **12–29**). The date of this painting is controversial, but it was probably made around 1484–1486 for the private collection of Lorenzo de' Medici, who had become ruler of Florence in 1469. The central image, a type known as the modest Venus, is based on the antique statue of Venus in the Medici collection (see fig. Intro–6). The Classical goddess of love and beauty, born of sea foam, floats ashore on a scallop shell

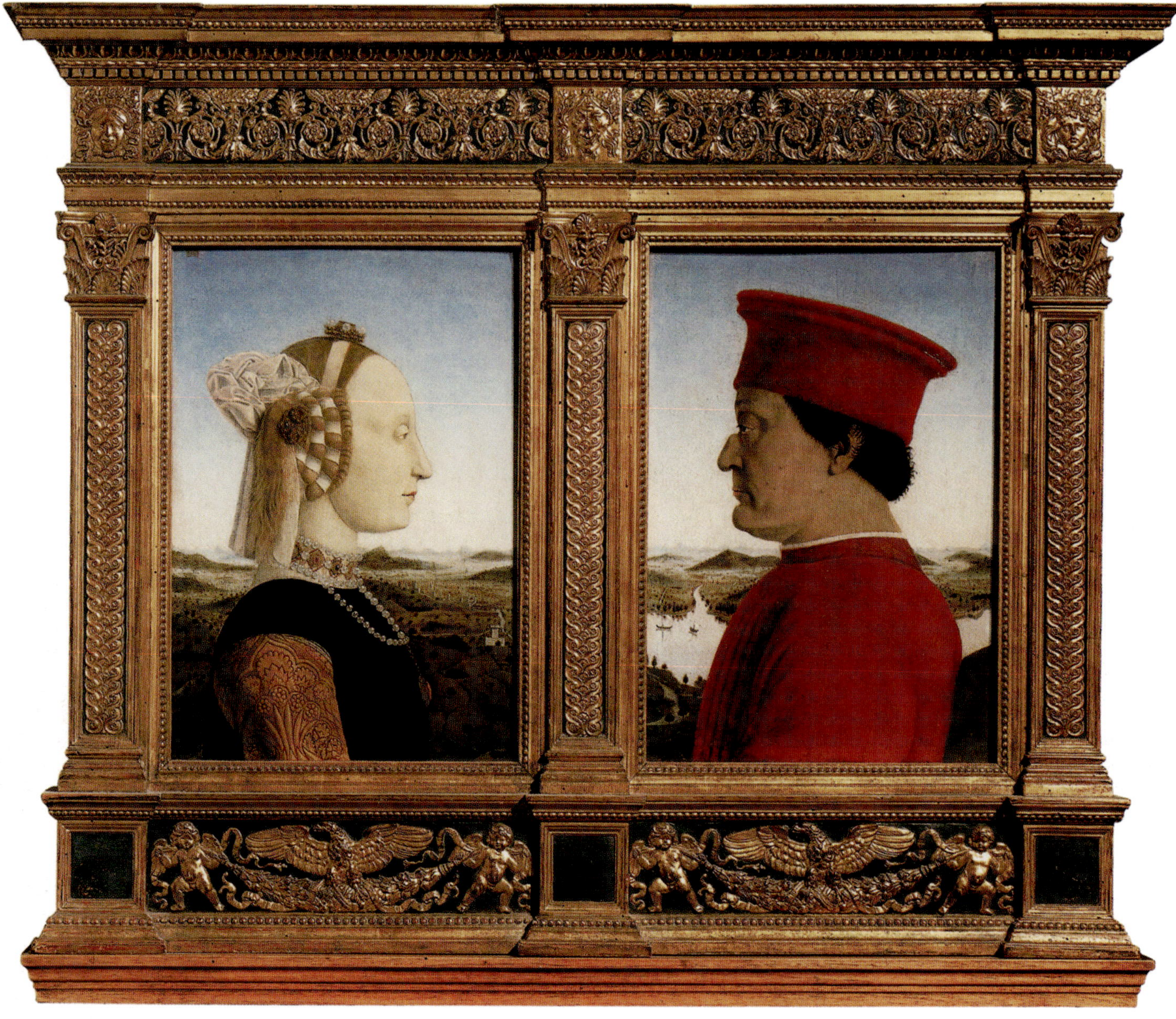

12–30 Piero della Francesca. ***Battista Sforza*** (left) and ***Federico da Montefeltro*** (right). c. 1474. Oil on wood panel, each 18½" × 13" (47 × 33 cm). Galleria degli Uffizi, Florence

gracefully arranging her hands and hair to hide—or enhance—her sexuality. Blown by the wind god Zephyr (and his love, the nymph Chloris), and welcomed on the right by a devotee holding a garment embroidered with flowers, Venus arrives at her earthly home. Botticelli seems to have interpreted the birth of Venus as the advent of the idea of beauty.

An artist profoundly influenced by Masaccio was Piero della Francesca (c. 1406/12–1492). Born in the small Tuscan town of Borgo San Sepulcro, Piero worked in Florence in the 1430s. He knew current thinking in art and art theory, including Brunelleschi's system of spatial illusion and linear perspective, Masaccio's powerful modeling of forms and use of atmospheric perspective, and Alberti's theoretical treatises. He was also an accomplished mathematician, generally credited with the modern rediscovery of Euclid. Piero was one of the few practicing artists who also wrote his own theories of art. Not surprisingly, in his treatises on mathematics and perspective he emphasized the geometry and the volumetric construction of forms and spaces that were so prominent in his own paintings. In fact, the organizing geometry of Piero's pictures was related to a mathematical skill called gauging, used by the very merchants who commissioned many of his paintings to estimate the volume and value of the commodities in which they traded. This link between the intellectual and commercial practices of painters and their patrons indicates the strong integration of Italian Renaissance art with the culture within which it developed.

Piero traveled widely to fulfill commissions, including a sojourn at the court of Federico da Montefeltro in Urbino. There, around 1474, he painted a pair of companion portraits of Federico

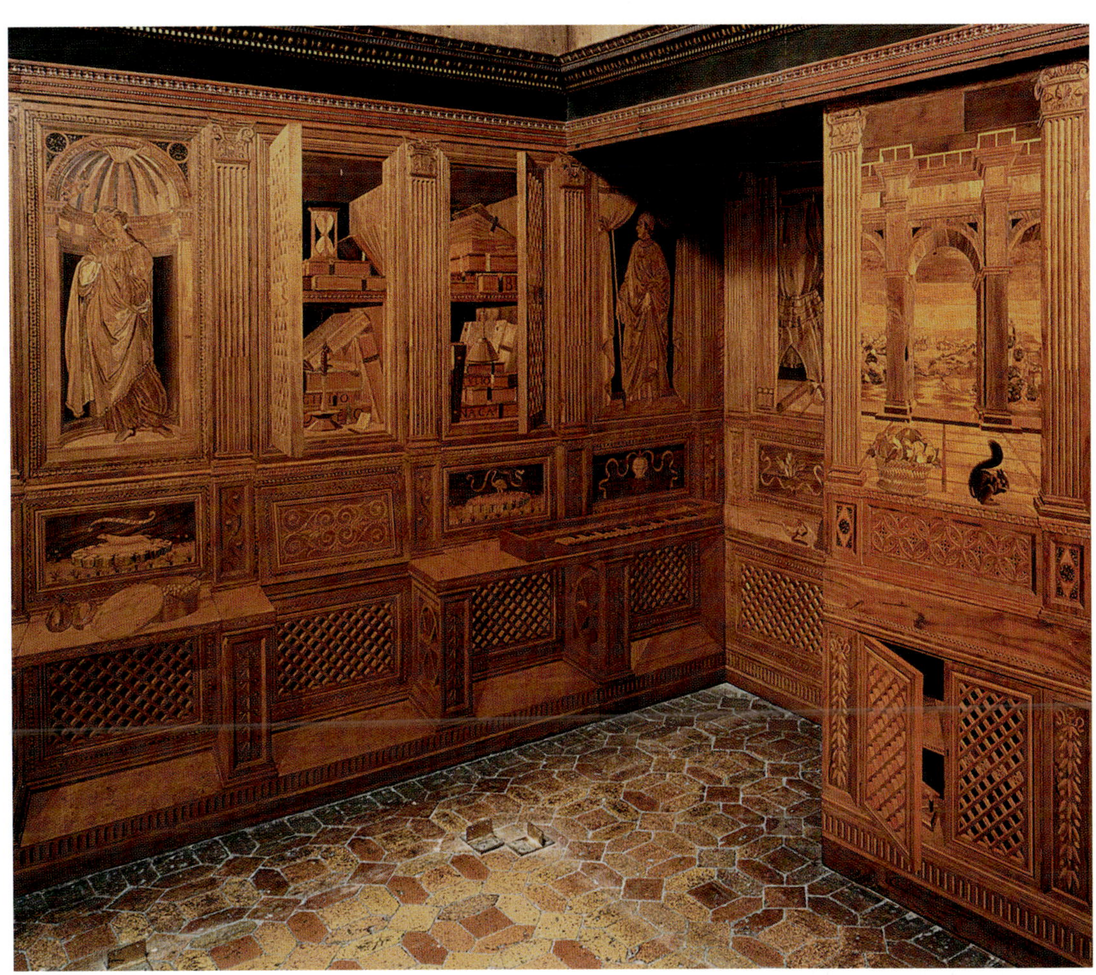

12–31 Giuliano da Maiano (?). Studiolo of Federico da Montefeltro, Ducal Palace, Urbino. 1476. Intarsia, height 7' 3" (2.21 m)

and his recently deceased wife, Battista Sforza (fig. **12–30**). Like portraits on Roman coins and cameos, the figures appear in strict profile, unengaged with the viewer. Piero emphasized the underlying geometry of the forms, rendering the figures with an absolute stillness. At the same time, he used the Northern technique of atmospheric perspective, with landscape features becoming lighter and paler as they recede systematically into the background. Piero used another Northern European device in the harbor view near the center of Federico's panel, where the water narrows into a river that leads us into the distant landscape. The portraits may have been joined as a **diptych** (a pair of panels) as they are now framed, since the landscape appears continuous across the two panels. On the back of the panels, in an allegory of personal virtue and triumph, the couple rides on horse-drawn wagons through another continuous landscape.

In the second half of the fifteenth century, a younger generation of artists turned the walls of chapels and palaces into brilliant displays of the good life as it was lived by the rich and powerful citizens of the Italian city-states Florence, Mantua, Urbino, and elsewhere. The subject of the murals might be religious or historical, but patrons wanted to see themselves at work, at prayer, and at play, showing off their jewelry, clothing, and household goods, and surrounded by images of their neighbors, families, servants, fine horses, and dogs. The interest in material possessions, an interest that religious reformers claimed reached the point of obsession, is apparent in the dazzling display of wealth even in purportedly religious scenes. In his palace in Urbino, Federico da Montefeltro had a small private room (fig. **12–31**), called a *studiolo* (a study). There he kept his fine books and art objects and there he could hold private conversations away from the huge halls filled with courtiers. In the *studiolo* architect and woodworker Giuliano da Maiano (1432–1490) used **intarsia** (wood inlay) to achieve remarkable ***trompe l'oeil*** ("fool the eye") effects, giving the illusion of pilasters, cupboards with latticed doors, niches with statues, benches, and tables—even the duke's armor, hanging like a suit in a closet. He accomplished these surprising effects by scrupulously applying the rules of linear perspective and foreshortening (a contraction of forms that supports the overall perspectival system) and carefully rendering every detail.

North of Urbino and the Montefeltro court, the Renaissance appeared in Venice and in Padua, where both Giotto (in the fourteenth century) and Donatello (in the mid-fifteenth) had lived and worked. Donatello was in Padua during the formative years of the young artist Andrea Mantegna (1431–1506), who pushed the system of linear perspective to its limits with his radical views and strongly foreshortened figures.

Mantegna's mature style is exemplified by the frescoes of the Camera Picta (Painted Room) in the ducal palace of Mantua. The

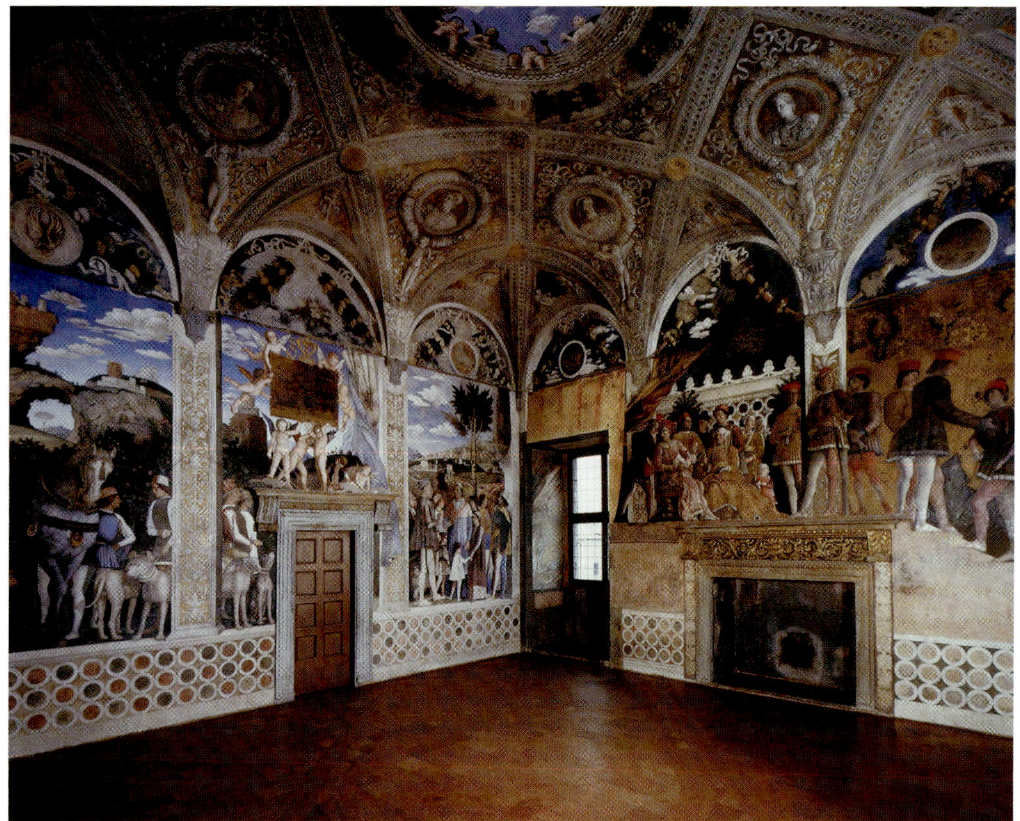

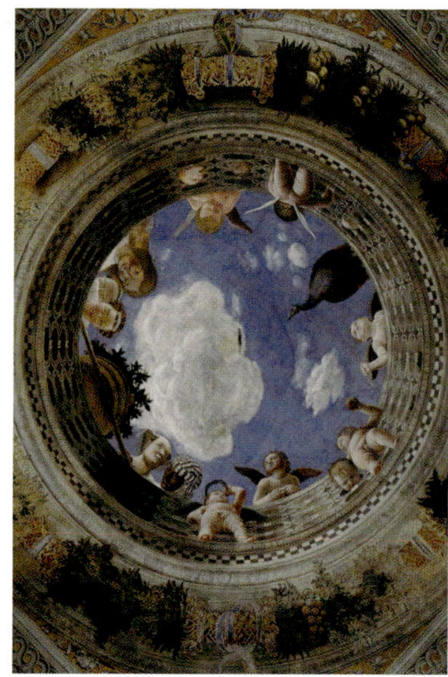

12–32 Andrea Mantegna.
Two views of the Camera Picta.
Ducal Palace, Mantua. 1465–1474. Fresco

artist decorated this tower chamber between 1465 and 1474 for Ludovico Gonzaga, the ruler of Mantua. On the vaulted ceiling, Mantegna painted a *tour-de-force* of perspective in creating a viewpoint called *di sotto in sù* (seen directly from below), which began a long tradition of illusionistic ceiling painting (fig. **12–32**). The room appears to be open to a cloud-filled sky through a large oculus in a simulated marble and mosaic-covered vault. On each side of a precariously balanced planter, three young women and an exotically turbaned African man peer at us over a marble parapet. A fourth young woman in a veil looks dreamily upward. Joined by a large peacock, several **putti** (a *putto* is a little boy, often shown naked and winged) frolic around the opening. Mantegna completed the decoration of the room with murals featuring portraits of members of the Gonzaga family.

Late in the fifteenth century, the city of Rome also became a magnet for Renaissance artists. Pope Sixtus IV summoned the finest painters to decorate the walls of his newly built Sistine Chapel, among them Pietro Vannucci, called Perugino (c. 1445–1523), who, though active in Florence, came from near the town of Perugia in Umbria. In 1482, he painted the *Delivery of the Keys to Saint Peter* (see fig. 12–24), an event not actually described in the Bible but suggested in Matthew 16:19. The event came to signify the supremacy of papal authority: Christ is shown giving the keys to the kingdom of heaven to the apostle Peter, who, as the first bishop of Rome, was also considered the first pope. As Perugino and other Florentine artists were called to the Vatican to fulfill papal commissions, the focus of Italian art began to shift from Florence to Rome.

Looking Back

Western European art of the fifteenth century reflects the values and worldview of a new social order. A spirit of inquiry was fueled by the study of Classical texts begun in the fourteenth century. The kind of logical discourse formerly reserved for theological debate now was applied to the material world. Theories based on the close observation of natural phenomena were put forward to be challenged and defended. Individuals gained importance, not only as inquiring minds but as the subject of inquiry. Artists, too, emerged from anonymity and were recognized as distinct personalities with individual talents and distinguishable styles.

Patrons wanted to see themselves and their possessions depicted as they actually looked. Fifteenth-century portraits have an arrestingly lifelike quality, combining careful—sometimes unflattering—description with an uncanny sense of vitality. The patrons' desire for faithfully observed representations extended to their surroundings; they wanted identifiable views of the buildings and countryside where they worked and played, fought and died. Artists explored and adopted new ways of representing space and organizing pictures using linear and atmospheric perspective. By the end of the fifteenth century, for patrons and painters, the visual mastery of the material world must have seemed complete. Careful observation, technical advancements, and scientific compositional systems had transformed both secular and religious art.

IN PERSPECTIVE

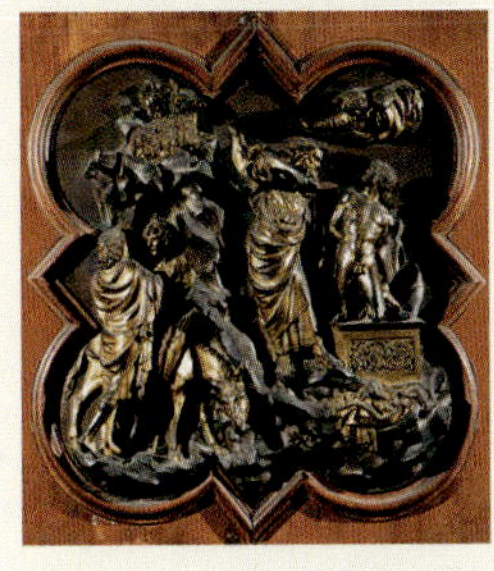
GHIBERTI,
SACRIFICE OF ISAAC,
1401–1402

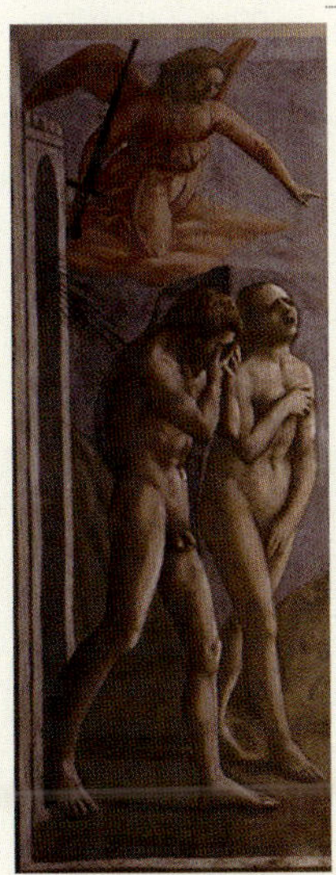
MASACCIO,
EXPULSION FROM PARADISE,
C. 1427

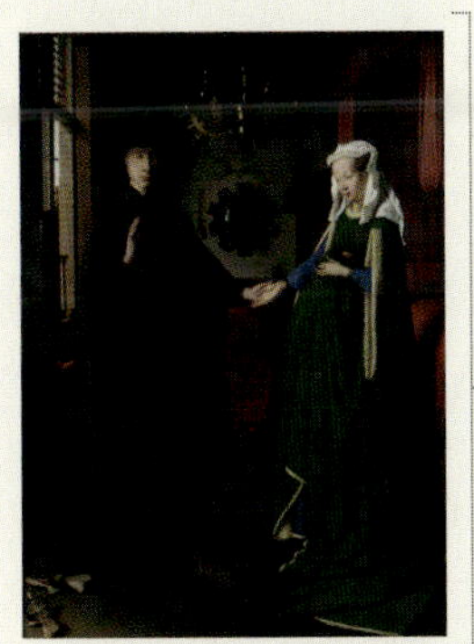
JAN VAN EYCK,
ARNOLFINI DOUBLE PORTRAIT,
1434

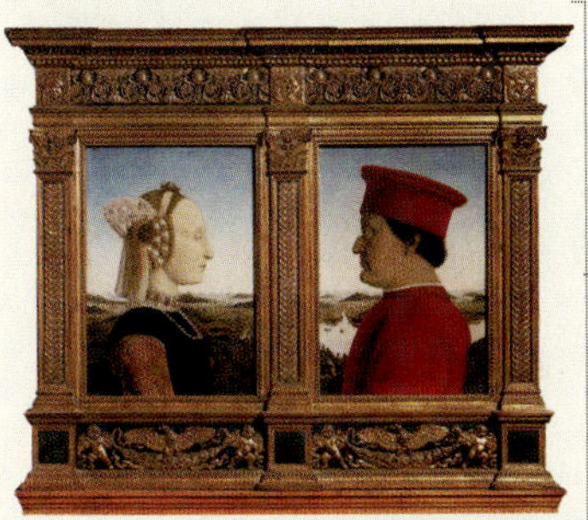
PIERO DELLA FRANCESCA,
BATTISTA SFORZA AND FEDERICO DA MONTEFELTRO,
C. 1474

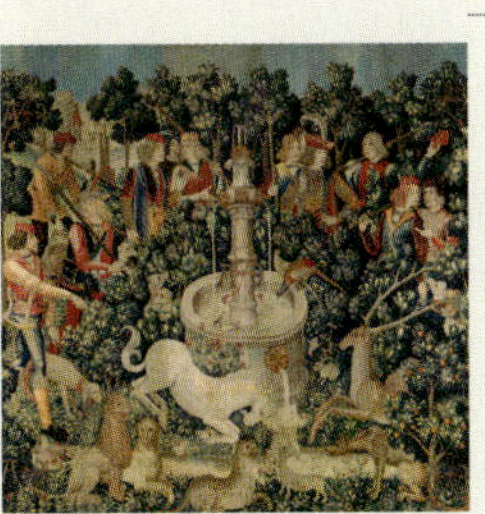
UNICORN IS FOUND,
C. 1498–1500

1400

◀ **Great Schism Ends,** 1417

1425

◀ **Alberti Writes *Della Pittura* (*On Painting*),** 1436

1450

◀ **Ghiberti Writes *Commentaries*,** C. 1450–1455

◀ **Habsburgs Begin Rule of Holy Roman Empire,** 1452

◀ **Hundred Years' War Ends,** 1453

◀ **Guttenberg Prints *Bible*,** 1455

◀ **Lorenzo de' Medici Rules Florence,** 1469–1492

1475

◀ **William Caxton Establishes First English Printing House,** 1476

◀ **Columbus Reaches the West Indies,** 1492

◀ **Savonarola Executed,** 1498

1500

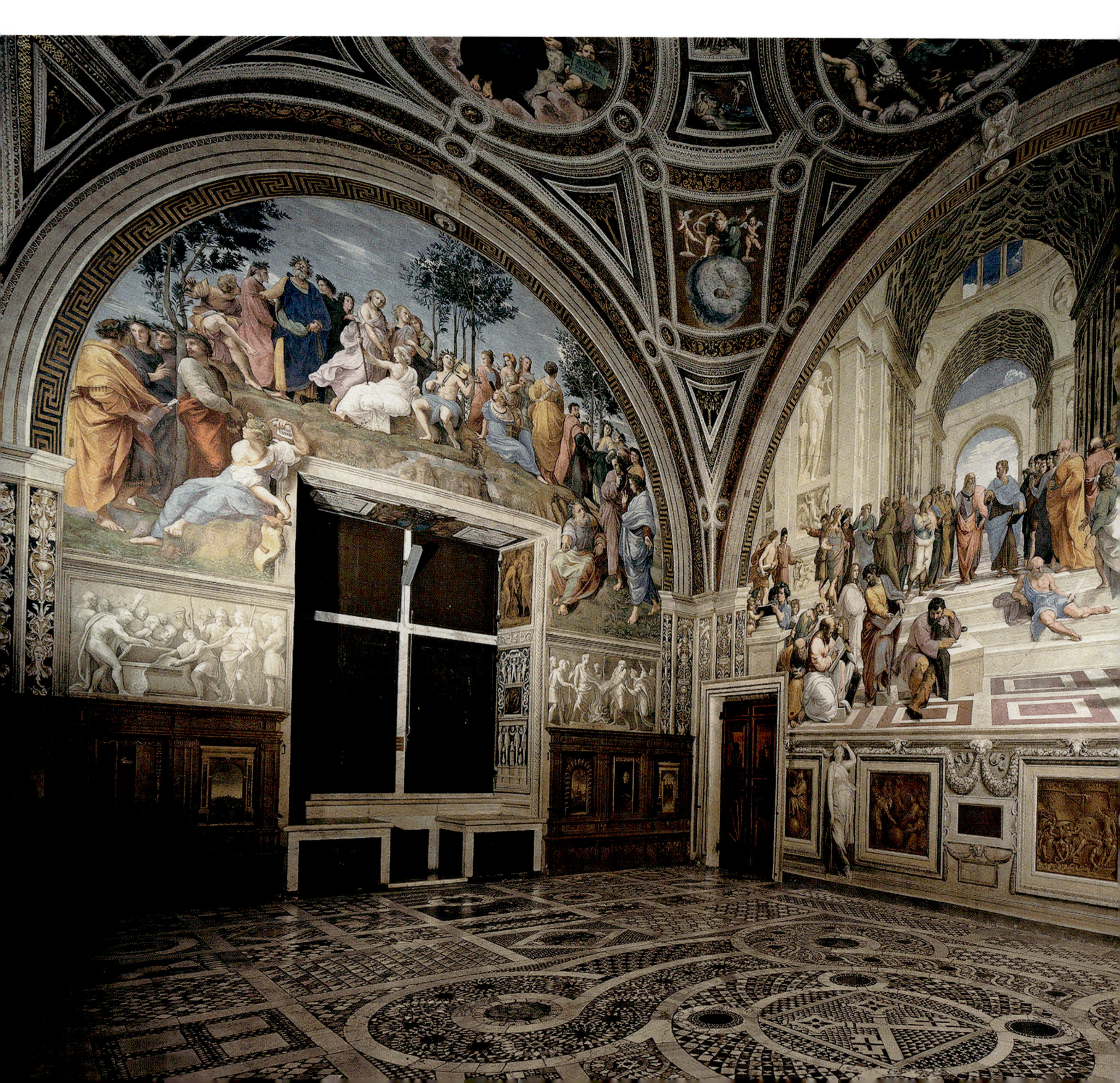

13 Art of the High Renaissance and Reformation

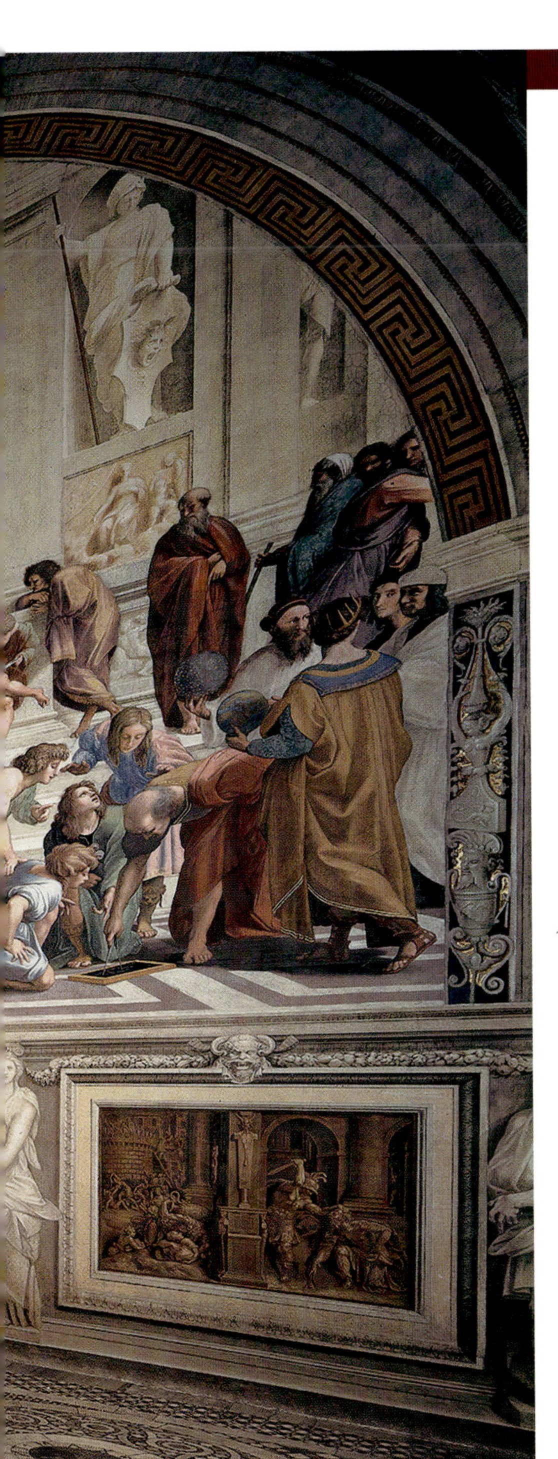

LOOKING FORWARD

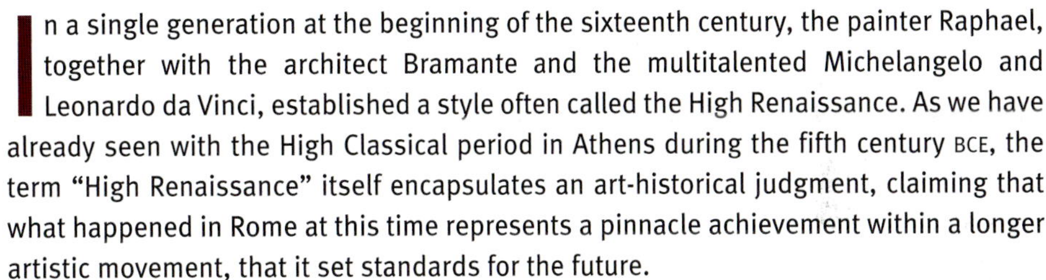

In a single generation at the beginning of the sixteenth century, the painter Raphael, together with the architect Bramante and the multitalented Michelangelo and Leonardo da Vinci, established a style often called the High Renaissance. As we have already seen with the High Classical period in Athens during the fifth century BCE, the term "High Renaissance" itself encapsulates an art-historical judgment, claiming that what happened in Rome at this time represents a pinnacle achievement within a longer artistic movement, that it set standards for the future.

Faith in human rationality and perfectibility seems to underlie Raphael's decoration of the private apartment of Pope Julius II, who ruled from 1503 to 1513. The pope intended the Stanza della Segnatura, or Room of the Signature, to be his library and study (fig. **13–1**). The wall paintings proclaimed that all human knowledge existed under the power of Divine Wisdom. Raphael created allegories illustrating the division of knowledge into theology, philosophy, the arts, and justice. Churchmen discussing the sacraments represent theology, while across the room ancient philosophers debate in the *School of Athens* (see fig. 13–6). Apollo and the Muses represent poetry and the arts; and Justice, holding a sword and scales, assigns each his due. Plato and Aristotle preside over the *School of Athens*, Plato holding a copy of his *Timaeus* and Aristotle his *Nicomachean Ethics*. Ancient representatives of the academic curriculum—Grammar, Rhetoric, Dialectic, Arithmetic, Music, Geometry, and Astronomy—surround them. The poet Sappho is the only woman in the room, reclining against the (real) window frame among the Muses. Raphael included his own portrait among the onlookers in the *School of Athens* and signed the painting with his initials.

Raphael has created an idealized setting for papal activity, inspired by Roman antiquities or Bramante's designs for the new church of Saint Peter. The majestic landscapes with oak trees are a gracious reference to the pope's powerful della Rovere ("of the oak") family. Raphael's idealized figures move with quiet dignity; they are as grand as the ideas they represent. Such lofty style coincides with Julian II's own lofty papal ideals, but when Raphael died at age 37 on April 6, 1520, the grand moment of pope and painter was already passing; Luther and the Protestant Reformation were challenging papal authority, and the world would never be the same.

13–1 Raphael. Stanza della Segnatura, Vatican, Rome. Right: *Philosophy*, or *School of Athens, with Plato and Aristotle*; left: (over the window) *Poetry and the Arts*, represented by Apollo and the Muses. 1510–1511. Fresco, 19' × 27' (5.8 × 8.2 m)

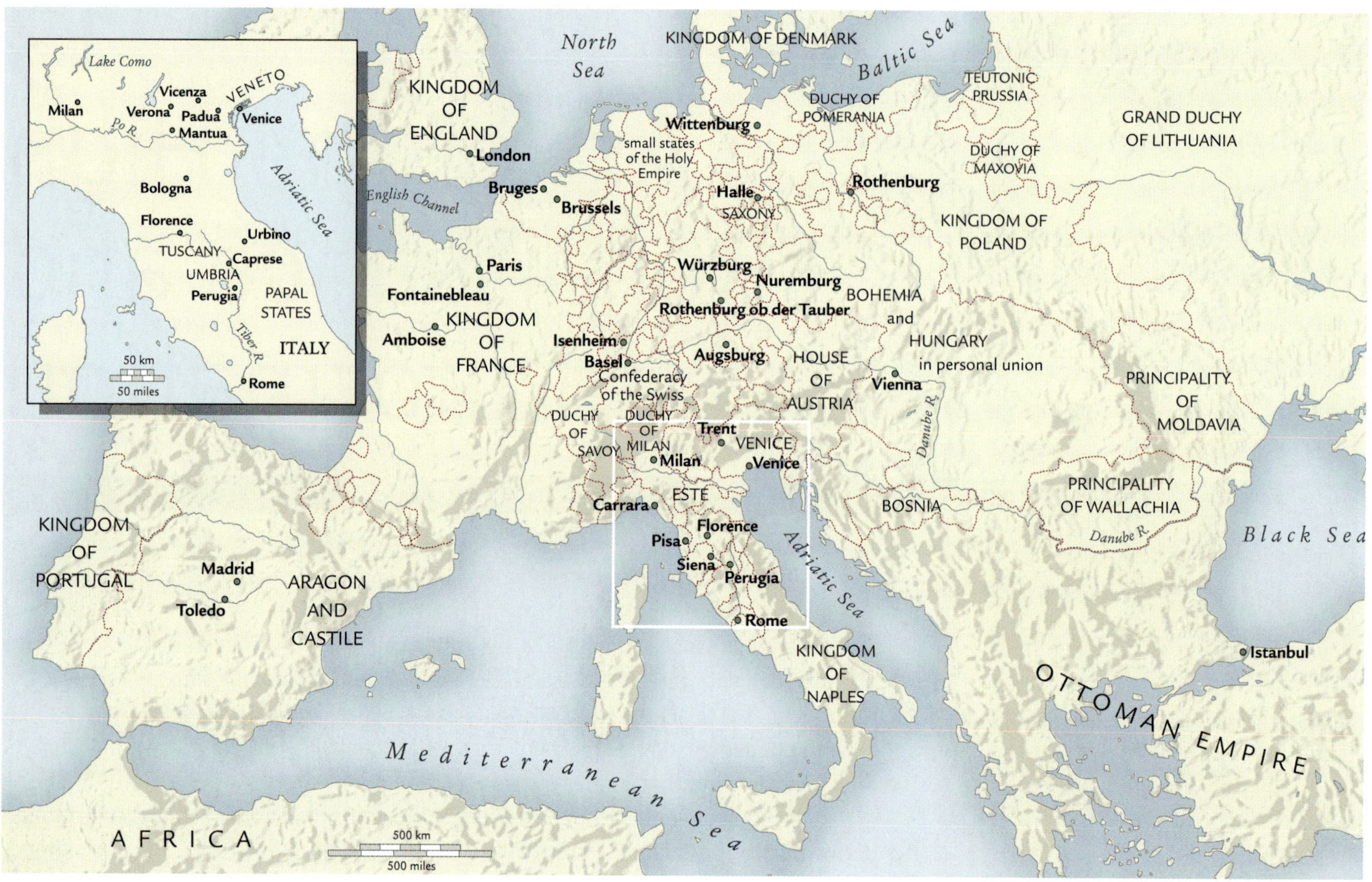

Map 13–1 Renaissance Europe

During the sixteenth century, early Renaissance Humanism underwent a radical shift. Its medieval roots and often uncritical acceptance of the authority of Classical texts, slowly gave way to an intensified spirit of inquiry. Scholars investigated the natural world around them, conducted scientific and mechanical experiments, and explored lands in Africa, Asia, and the Americas previously unknown to Europeans. They even questioned the authority of the pope in the movement known as the Reformation. The influential writings and leadership of important reformers, such as Martin Luther (1483–1546) in Germany, led to the establishment of Protestant churches in Northern Europe. And, at the Council of Trent (1545–1563), the Roman Catholic hierarchy responded with a program to counter the Reformation.

During the sixteenth century, travel in Europe became easier and safer, and artists often journeyed from city to city, even country to country; consequently, styles and techniques became less regional and more international (see map **13–1**). The materials artists worked with changed, too. Although fresco painting was still common, more and more artists painted with oil on canvas. They could produce oil paintings in their studios and easily transport and install them anywhere. Artists of stature became sought-after international celebrities, and their social status rose as painting, sculpture, and works of architecture came to be seen as liberal rather than manual arts, requiring intellectual activity rather than merely technical skill.

Italian Art

The painting, sculpture, and architecture produced during the early sixteenth century reflect a self-confident Humanism, an abiding admiration for Classical forms, and a dominating sense of stability and order. These characteristics are found above all in the work of four towering figures of the Italian Renaissance: Leonardo, Raphael, Michelangelo, and Titian. The achievements of these artists are so remarkable that nineteenth-century scholars called the period in Italy from about 1495 until the death of Raphael in 1520 the "High" Renaissance.

Leonardo da Vinci (1452–1519) received his training in Florence in the workshop of the painter and sculptor Verrocchio. Leonardo's fame as an artist is based on only a few known works of art, for his fertile mind jumped from one subject to another, and he seldom finished his projects. He had a passion for the study of mathematics, science, and engineering, and he compiled volumes of detailed drawings and notes on anatomy, botany, geology, meteorology, architectural design, and mechanics (see "The Vitruvian Man," page 338). At the court of Duke Ludovico Sforza of Milan, where Leonardo worked from as early as 1481 until 1498, he spent much of his time on military and civil-engineering projects, including an urban renewal plan for the city. But at Duke Ludovico's request, Leonardo also created one of the defining monuments of Renaissance art: an image of the Last Supper painted on the wall of the refectory (dining room) in the Monastery of Santa Maria delle Grazie in Milan (fig. **13–2** and fig. Intro–21).

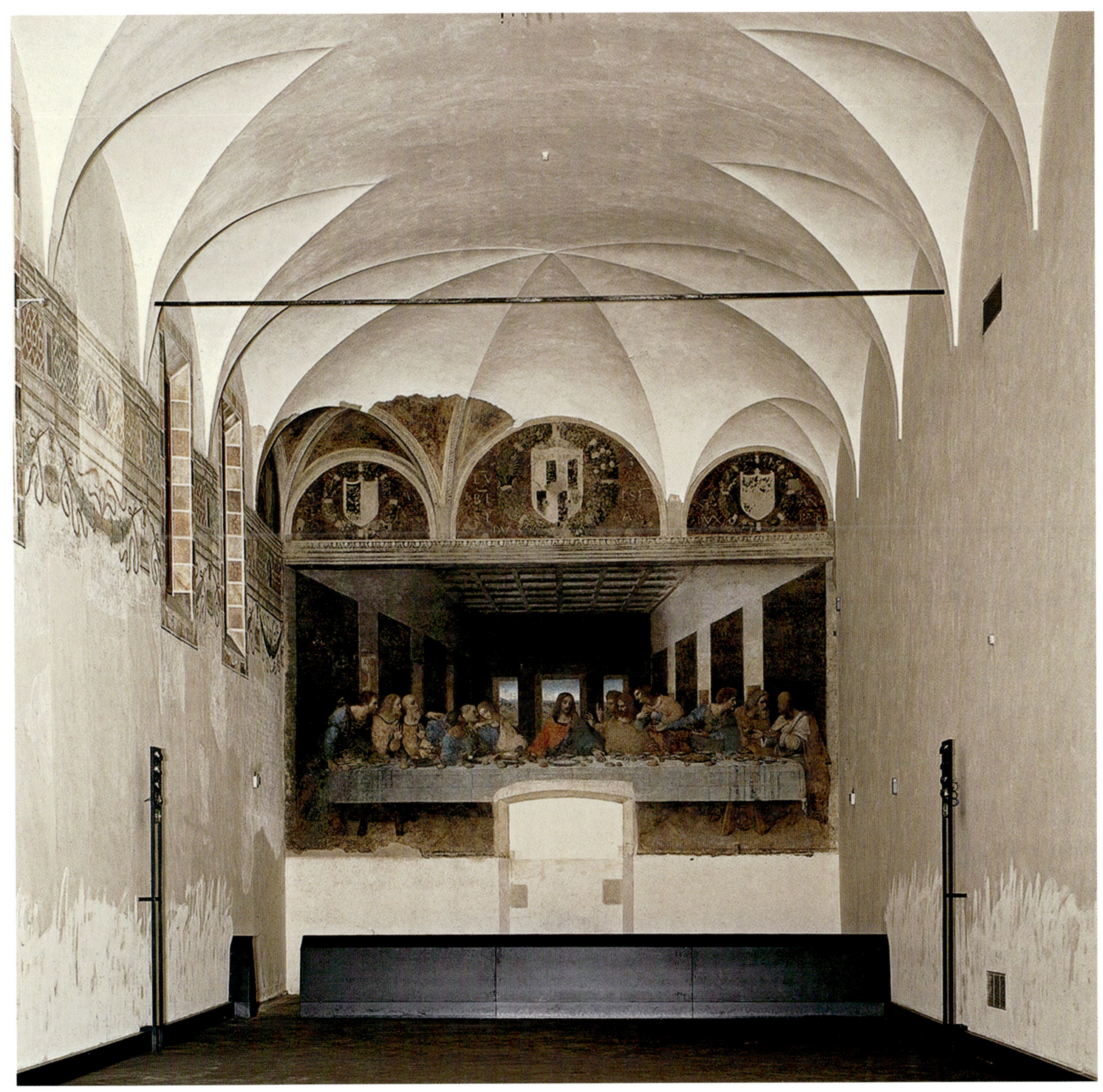

13–2 Leonardo da Vinci. ***Last Supper***, wall painting in the refectory, Monastery of Santa Maria delle Grazie, Milan. 1495–1498. Tempera and oil on plaster, 15' 2" × 28' 10" (4.6 × 8.8 m). (See fig. Intro–21.)

Instead of painting in fresco, Leonardo devised an experimental technique for this mural. Hoping to achieve the freedom and flexibility of painting on panel, he worked directly on dry intonaco *(a thin layer of smooth plaster) with an oil tempera paint whose formula is unknown. The result was disastrous. Within a short time, the painting began to deteriorate, and by the middle of the sixteenth century its figures could be seen only with difficulty. In the seventeenth century, the monks saw no harm in cutting a doorway through the lower center of the composition. Since then the work has barely survived, despite many attempts to halt its deterioration and restore its original appearance. The painting narrowly escaped complete destruction in World War II, when the refectory was bombed to rubble around its heavily sandbagged wall. The most recent restoration was completed in May 1999. The coats of arms at the top are those of patron Ludovico Sforza (ruled 1494–1499) and his wife Beatrice.*

THE VITRUVIAN MAN

Artists throughout history have turned to geometric shapes and mathematical proportions to seek the ideal representation of the human form. Leonardo, and before him the first-century BCE Roman architect and engineer (Marcus) Vitruvius (Pollio), equated the ideal man with both circle and square.

In his ten-volume *De architectura* (*On Architecture*), Vitruvius wrote:

> For if a man be placed flat on his back, with his hands and feet extended, and a pair of compasses centered at his navel, the fingers and toes of his two hands and feet will touch the circumference of a circle described therefrom. And just as the human body yields a circular outline, so too a square figure may be found from it. For if we measure the distance from the soles of the feet to the top of the head, and then apply that measure to the outstretched arms, the breadth will be found to be the same as the height.
> (book III, chapter 1, section 2)

Vitruvius determined that the ideal body should be eight heads high. Leonardo added his own observations—in the reversed writing he always used for his notebooks—when he created his well-known diagram for the ideal male figure, called the *Vitruvian Man*.

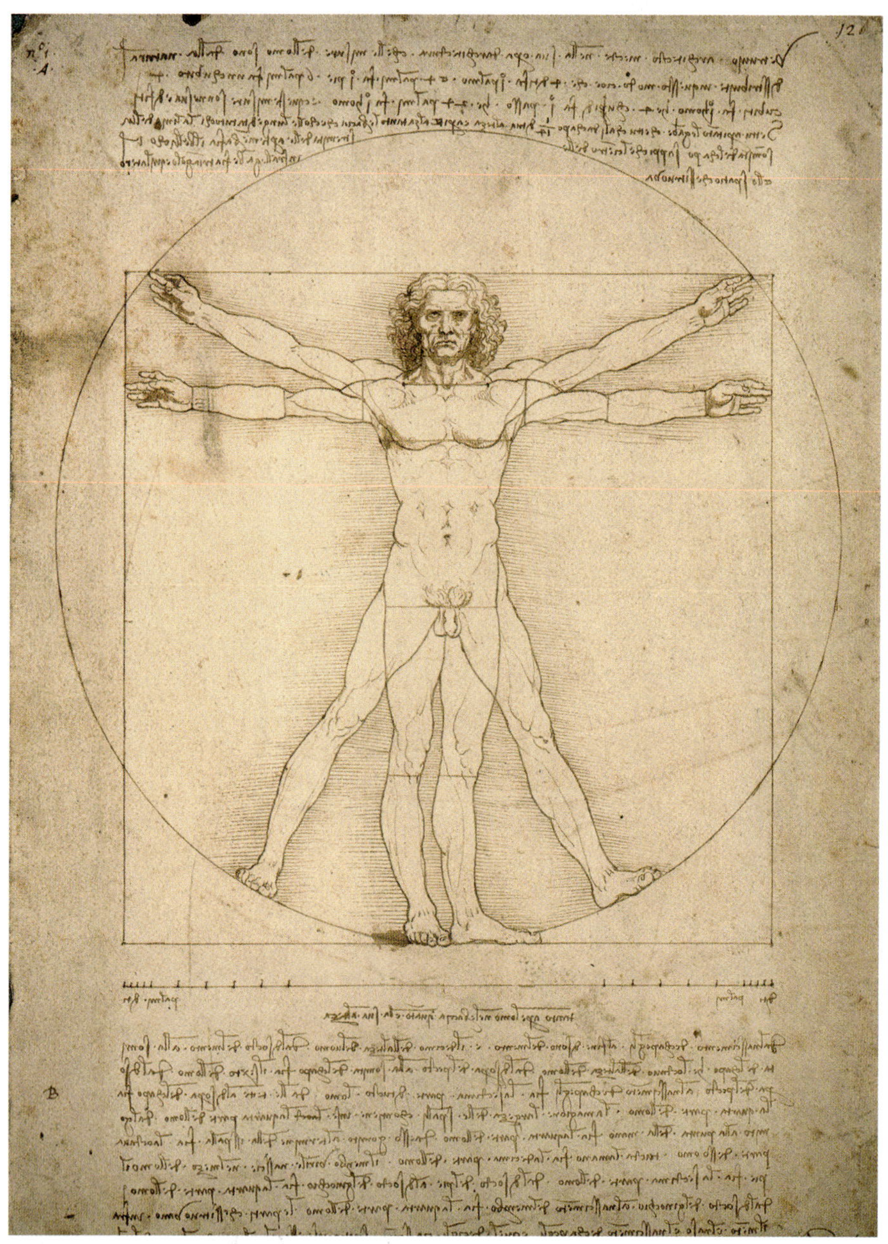

13–3 Leonardo da Vinci. ***Vitruvian Man.*** c. 1490. Ink, approx. 13½" × 9⅝" (34.3 × 24.5 cm). Galleria dell'Accademia, Venice

On one level, Leonardo painted a scene from a life story, capturing the moment when Jesus tells his companions during their last *seder* meal that one of them will betray him. They react individually, with shock, disbelief, or horror, presenting a study of human emotions. On another level, the *Last Supper* is a symbolic evocation of Jesus' coming sacrifice for the salvation of humankind, the foundation of institution of the Mass, even a prefiguration of the gathering of this local monastic community in this room for its communal meals. Leonardo has arranged the disciples in four groups of three flanking the stable, pyramidal form of Jesus, who

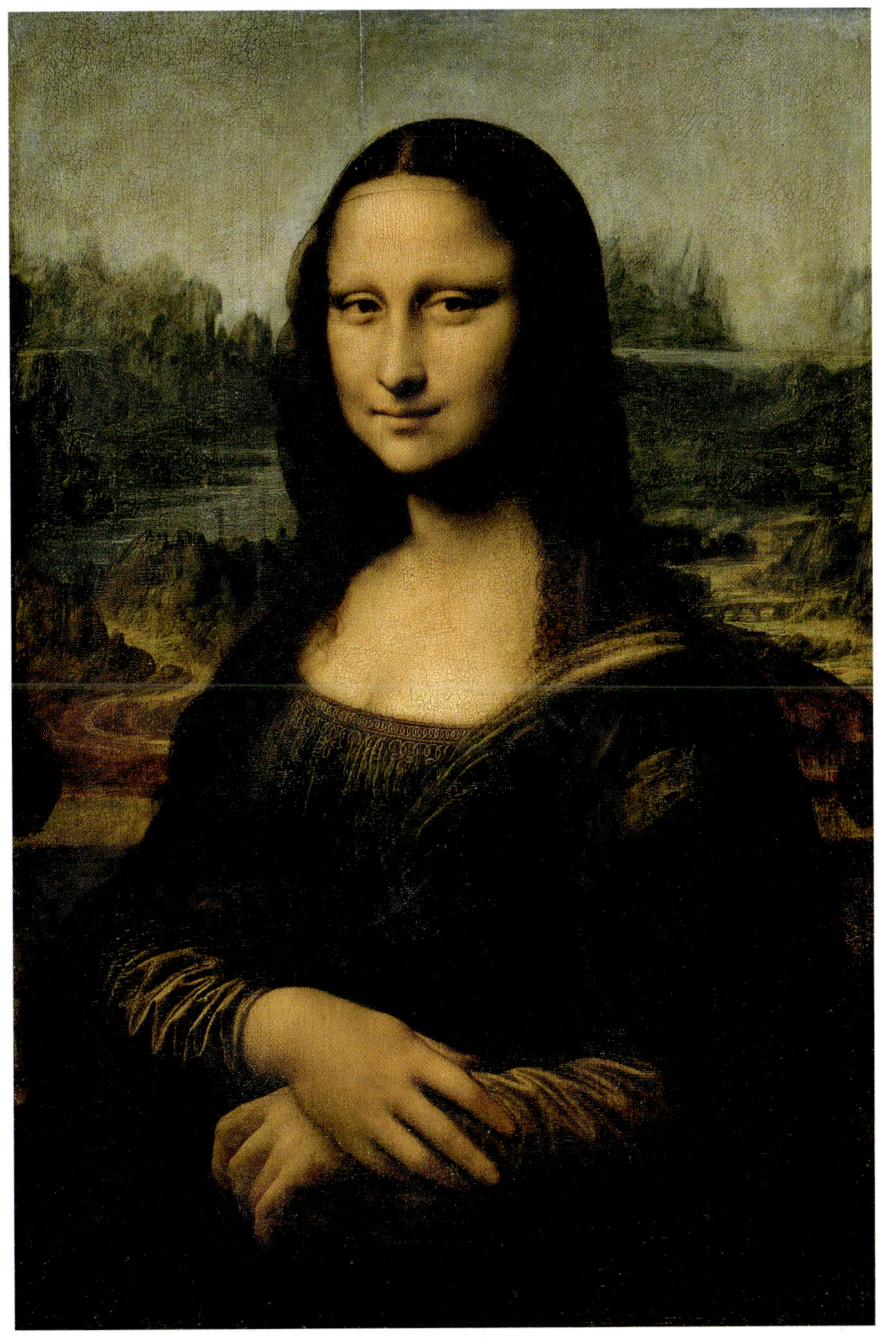

13–4 Leonardo da Vinci. ***Mona Lisa.*** c. 1503–1506. Oil on panel, 30¼" × 21" (76.8 × 53.3 cm). Musée du Louvre, Paris

sits calmly in the middle of the general commotion. Leonardo placed Judas in the first triad to the left of Jesus, along with the young John the Evangelist and the elderly Peter. Judas, Peter, and John were each to play essential roles in Jesus' mission: Judas, to set in motion the events leading to the Crucifixion; Peter, to lead the Church after Jesus' death; and John, the visionary, to foretell the Second Coming of Christ and the Last Judgment in the Apocalypse.

The composition enhances the meaning of the painting. The scene is set in a stage-like recession that extends the space of the room itself with a careful geometry. The one-point linear perspective is emphasized by the tapestries on the side walls. Orthogonals converge on the head of Jesus at mathematical center, behind which three windows form a natural—rather than symbolic—halo of light. Leonardo modeled the figures in a rich **chiaroscuro** (an Italian word combining "*chiaro*" [light] and "*scuro*" [dark], used to describe the artistic practice of using the gradual transition from highlight to shadow to create the illusion of three-dimensional form), which over time had been obscured by the deterioration of his experimental medium of oil paint on plaster, but is now more visible after a recent restoration.

In 1498, Leonardo left Milan and resettled in Florence. There he painted his renowned portrait *Mona Lisa* (fig. **13–4**), between about 1503 and 1506. The subject may have been 24-year-old Lisa Gherardini del Giocondo, the wife of a prominent Florentine merchant. (Mona was a respectful title, madonna). The solid, pyramidal form of her half-length figure was once framed by columns (lost when thieves cut the painting from its frame). It is silhouetted against distant mountains, whose desolate grandeur reinforces the mysterious atmosphere of the painting. To achieve this atmosphere and to help unify his compositions, Leonardo partly covered his paintings with a thin, lightly tinted varnish, which helped create the effect of an overall smoky haze, or ***sfumato.*** Because early evening light is likely to produce a similar effect naturally, he considered dusk the finest time of day, and recommended that painters set up their studios in a courtyard with black walls and a linen sheet stretched overhead to reproduce the effects of twilight.

Mona Lisa's facial expression has been called "enigmatic" because her gentle smile is not accompanied by the warmth one would expect to see in her eyes, which have boldly shifted to the side to look straight out at the viewer. It is this expressive complexity, and the sense of psychological presence it gives to the painted face, especially in the context of the mask-like detachment that was more characteristic of earlier Renaissance portraits (compare fig. 12–30), that makes the innovative *Mona Lisa* so arresting, even today. The implied challenge of her direct stare, contrasting with her apparent serenity, has made the *Mona Lisa* one of the most studied and written about, and best-known, paintings in the history of art.

Leonardo returned to Milan in 1508 and lived there until 1513. He also lived for a time in the Vatican at the invitation of Pope Leo X, but there is no evidence that he produced any works of art during his stay. In 1516, he accepted the French king Francis I's invitation to relocate to France as an advisor on architecture, taking the *Mona Lisa* with him. He lived there until his death in 1519 (see page 363).

About 1505—while Leonardo was working on the *Mona Lisa*—Raphael (Raffaello Santi or Sanzio, 1483–1520) arrived in Florence. He had come from his native Urbino after studying in Perugia with the leading artist of that city, Perugino (see fig. 12–24). Raphael quickly became successful in Florence. His paintings of the Virgin and Child, such as *The Small Cowper Madonna* (named for a modern owner) of about 1505 (fig. **13–5**), brought him fame and attracted patrons. The monumental, pyramidal form of the Virgin and Child, the carefully modeled draperies, and rich colors show that Raphael must have studied the work of Leonardo. However, the clear, even light that softly but solidly models the figures contrasts with the hazy *sfumato* favored by Leonardo. *The Small Cowper Madonna* recalls instead the atmospheric clarity and brilliant colors, as well as the courtly and playful poses of Perugino's paintings. In the distance on a hilltop, Raphael has painted a scene he knew well from his childhood, the domed Church of San Bernardino, two miles outside Urbino, which contains the tombs of the dukes of Urbino, Federico and Guidobaldo da Montefeltro, and their wives (see fig. 12–30).

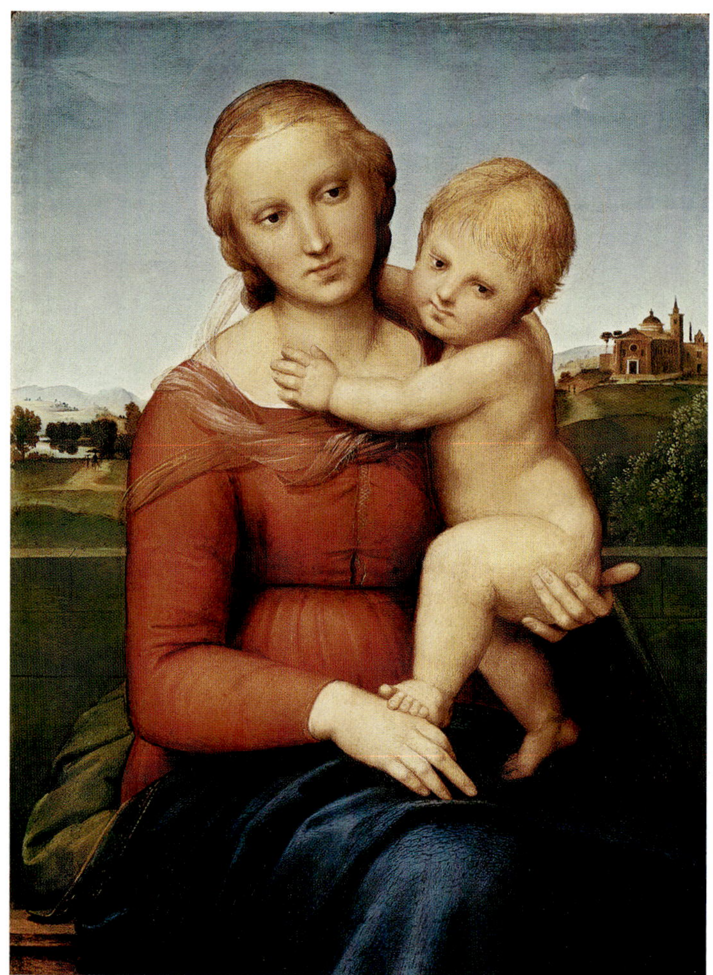

13–5 Raphael. *The Small Cowper Madonna.* c. 1505. Oil on panel, 23⅜" × 17⅜" (59.4 × 44.1 cm). National Gallery of Art, Washington, D.C.
WIDENER COLLECTION (42.9.57)

Raphael's greatest achievements came during a dozen years in Rome, where he arrived around 1508. As the fortunes of the ruling families of Florence and Milan fluctuated sharply because of political struggles, Rome rose to become the most active Italian artistic and intellectual center. Pope Julius II began a campaign to rebuild Rome and the Vatican, and he put Raphael to work almost immediately decorating the papal apartments. In the pope's library, Raphael painted the four branches of knowledge as conceived in the sixteenth century: theology (the *Disputa,* depicting the discussions concerning the true presence of Christ in the Eucharistic Host), philosophy (the *School of Athens*), poetry and the arts (*Parnassus,* home of the Muses), and law, or jurisprudence (the *Cardinal Virtues under Justice*).

Raphael's most influential achievement in these rooms was the *School of Athens* (fig. **13–6**), painted during 1510–1511. The painting seems to summarize the ideals of the Renaissance papacy in its grand conception of harmoniously arranged forms and rational space, as well as the calm dignity of its figures.

The shape of the walls and vault of the room itself inspired the composition of the painting. The viewer gazes at the scene through an illusionistic arch. The classical Greek philosophers Plato and Aristotle command center stage, emphasized by the light entering the central architectural opening very much like that behind the figure of Jesus in Leonardo's *Last Supper.* At the left, Plato gestures toward the heavens as the ultimate source of his philosophy, while

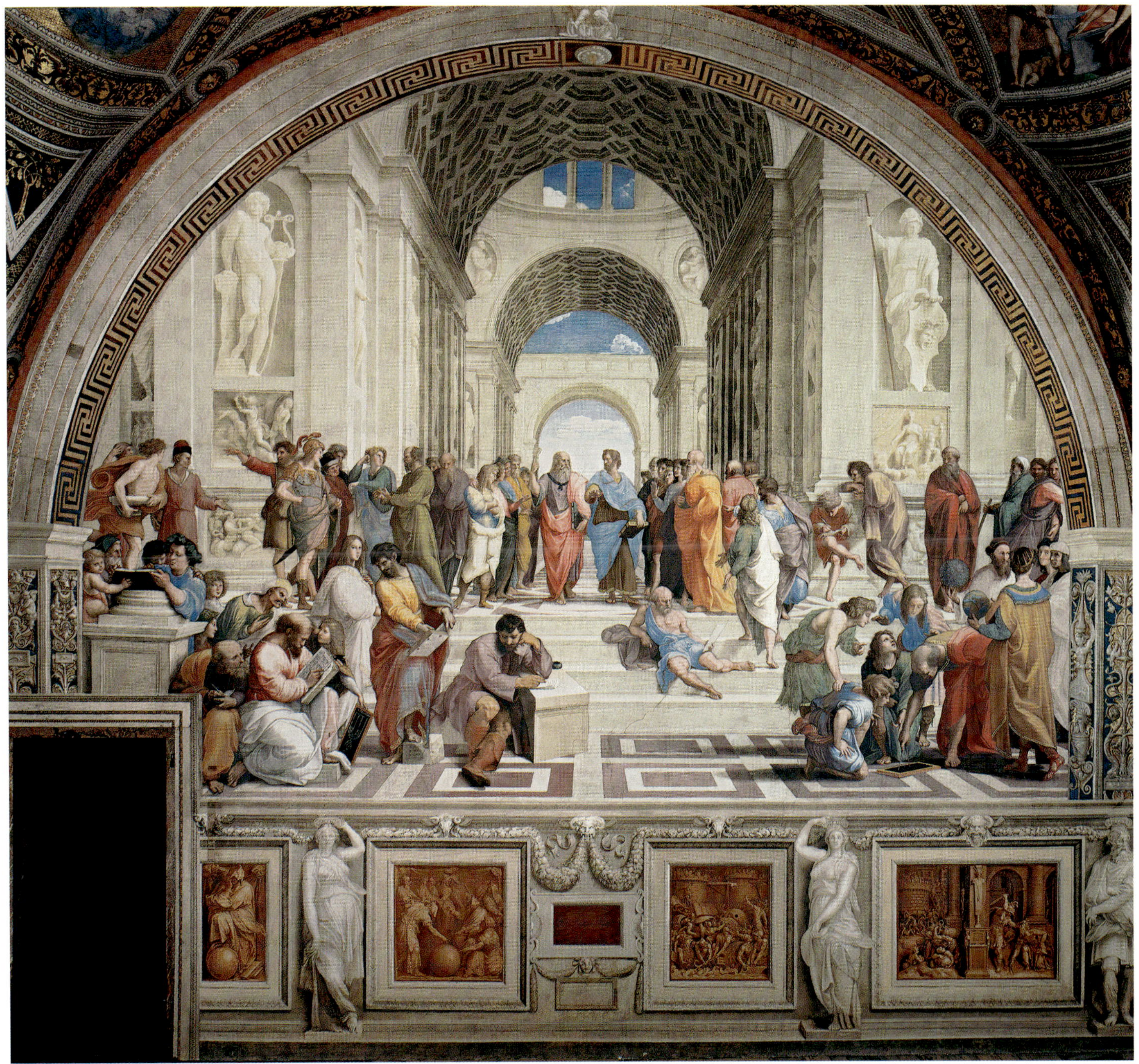

13–6 Raphael. ***School of Athens***, Stanza della Segnatura, Vatican, Rome. 1510–1511. Fresco, 19' × 27' (5.79 × 8.24 m)

Raphael gave many of the figures in his imaginary gathering of philosophers the features of his friends and colleagues. Plato, standing immediately to the left of the central axis and pointing to the sky, was said to have been modeled after Leonardo da Vinci; Euclid, shown inscribing a slate with a compass at the lower right, was a portrait of Raphael's friend, the architect Donato Bramante. Michelangelo, who was at work on the Sistine Chapel ceiling only steps away from the room where Raphael was painting this fresco, is shown as the solitary figure at the lower left center, leaning on a block of marble and sketching, in a pose reminiscent of the figures of sibyls and prophets on his great ceiling. Raphael's own features appear on the overlapped second figure in the front group at the far right, as the face of a young man listening to a discourse by the astronomer Ptolemy.

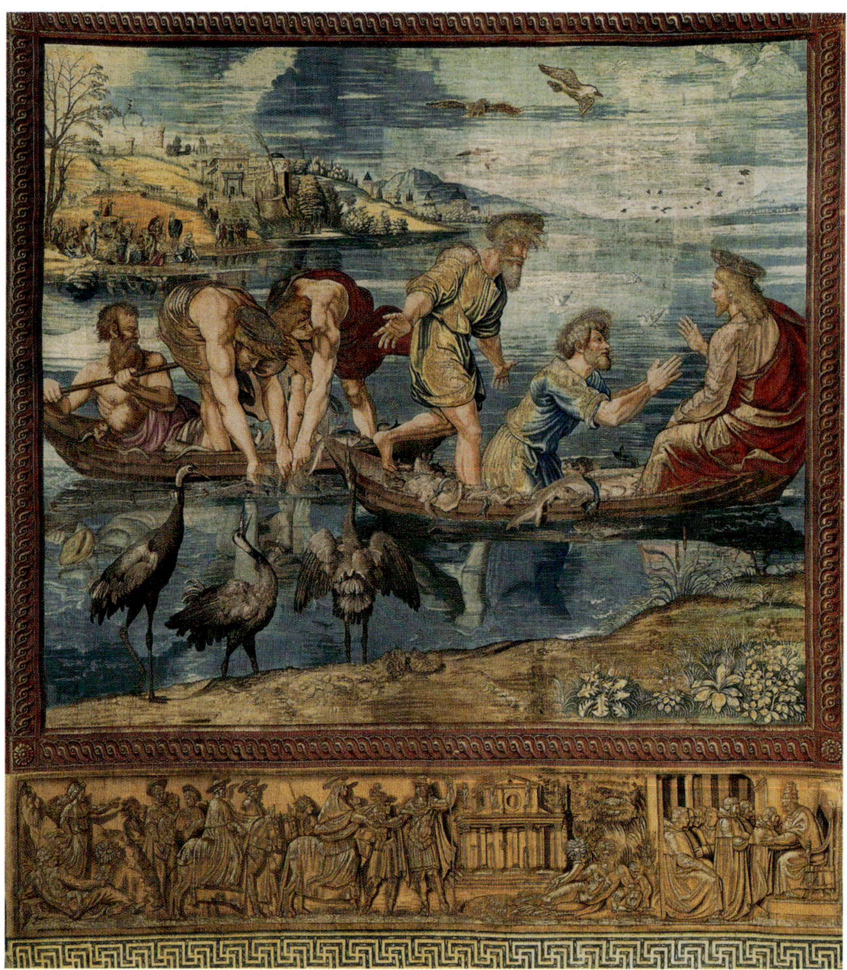

13–7 Shop of Pieter van Aelst, Brussels, after cartoons by Raphael and assistants. ***Miraculous Draft of Fishes on the Sea of Galilee***, from the nine-piece *Acts of the Apostles* series; lower border, two incidents from the life of Giovanni de' Medici, later Pope Leo X. 1515–1516; woven 1517, installed 1519 in the Sistine Chapel. Wool and silk with silver-gilt wrapped threads, 16' 1" × 21' (5.9 × 6.4 m). Musei Vaticani, Pinacoteca, Rome

Aristotle, his outstretched hand palm down, seems to emphasize the importance of gathering scientific knowledge empirically by observing the natural world. Looking down from niches in the walls are Minerva (on the right), the Roman goddess of wisdom, and Apollo (holding a lyre), the Greek and Roman god of the sun, rationality, poetry, and music. Around Plato and Aristotle are mathematicians, naturalists, astronomers, geographers, and other philosophers. For all their serene idealism, the figures within the painting break Classical conventions in their dynamically foreshortened contrapposto poses. The scene, flooded with light from a single source, takes place in an immense barrel-vaulted interior seemingly inspired by the new design for Saint Peter's, which was being rebuilt on a plan by the architect Bramante. The grandeur of the building is matched by the monumental dignity of the philosophers themselves, each of whom has a distinct physical and intellectual presence. The sweeping arcs of the composition are activated by the variety and energy of their poses, creating a dynamic unity that is characteristic of High Renaissance style.

Like Leonardo, Raphael had mastered several arts. In 1515–1516, he provided **cartoons** (paintings to serve as models for the proposed finished works) on themes from the Acts of the Apostles to be made into tapestries to cover the wall below the fifteenth-century wall paintings of the Sistine Chapel (see fig. 13–10). For the production of tapestries—woven in workshops in France and Flanders and extremely expensive—the artist made charcoal drawings, then painted over them with glue-based colors for the weavers to match. The first tapestry in Raphael's series was the *Miraculous Draft of Fishes on the Sea of Galilee* (John 21:1–11) (fig. **13–7**). The apostle Peter, who kneels here before the seated Christ, became the cornerstone on which the pope claimed absolute authority. The huge, straining figures in this composition remind us that Raphael felt himself in clear competition with Michelangelo, whose Sistine ceiling had been completed only three years earlier.

The two boats establish a frieze-like composition, not unlike the *School of Athens*. The panoramic landscape behind the fishermen includes a crowd on the shore and the city of Rome with its walls and churches. In the foreground the three cranes are not a simple pictorial device; in the sixteenth century, they symbolized the ever-alert and watchful pope, a timely addition because when the tapestries were first displayed in the Sistine Chapel on December 26, 1519, papal authority was already being challenged by reformers including Martin Luther.

Raphael died after a brief illness in 1520. After a state funeral, he was buried in the ancient Roman Pantheon, originally a Classical temple to the gods of Rome, but at that time a Christian church dedicated to the Virgin Mary (see fig. 6–28). In the view of many art historians, Raphael's death marks the end of the classical phase of the High Renaissance.

Michelangelo Buonarroti (1475–1564), was born in the Tuscan town of Caprese, but he grew up in Florence, and spent his long career working there as well as in Rome. At age 13, he was apprenticed to the painter Domenico Ghirlandaio. He soon joined the household of Lorenzo de' Medici, the Magnificent (1449–1492), where he studied sculpture with Bertoldo di Giovanni, a pupil of Donatello. Bertoldo worked primarily in bronze, and Michelangelo later claimed that he had taught himself to carve marble by studying the Medici collection of Classical statues.

While living in the Medici household, Michelangelo also came in contact with Neoplatonic philosophers who were part of Lorenzo the Magnificent's circle. Neoplatonism was a philosophy long favored by the Medici. Cosimo de' Medici the Elder (1389–1464) had founded an academy in Florence devoted to the study of Classical texts, especially the works of Plato and his followers. Neoplatonism takes various forms at different times and places, but basically it is characterized by a sharp opposition of the spiritual (the ideal or idea) and the physical (carnal matter that can be overcome by severe discipline and aversion to the world of the senses). Within discussions in the Medici academy, the perfectibility of the sculptural form was seen as a metaphor for the human ability to strive for perfection in a virtuous life. The sculptor's ability to release artistic form from a stone block was seen as equivalent to discovering and expressing the moral truth of the soul within the physical form of a human being. Such powerful ideas had a formative impact on the young Michelangelo, who was just coming into his own as a sculptor.

Michelangelo's major early work, at the turn of the century and well after his departure from the Medici household after Lorenzo's death in 1492, was a marble sculpture of the *Pietà*, commissioned by a French cardinal and installed as a tomb monument in Old Saint Peter's in the Vatican (fig. **13–8**). Michelangelo traveled to the

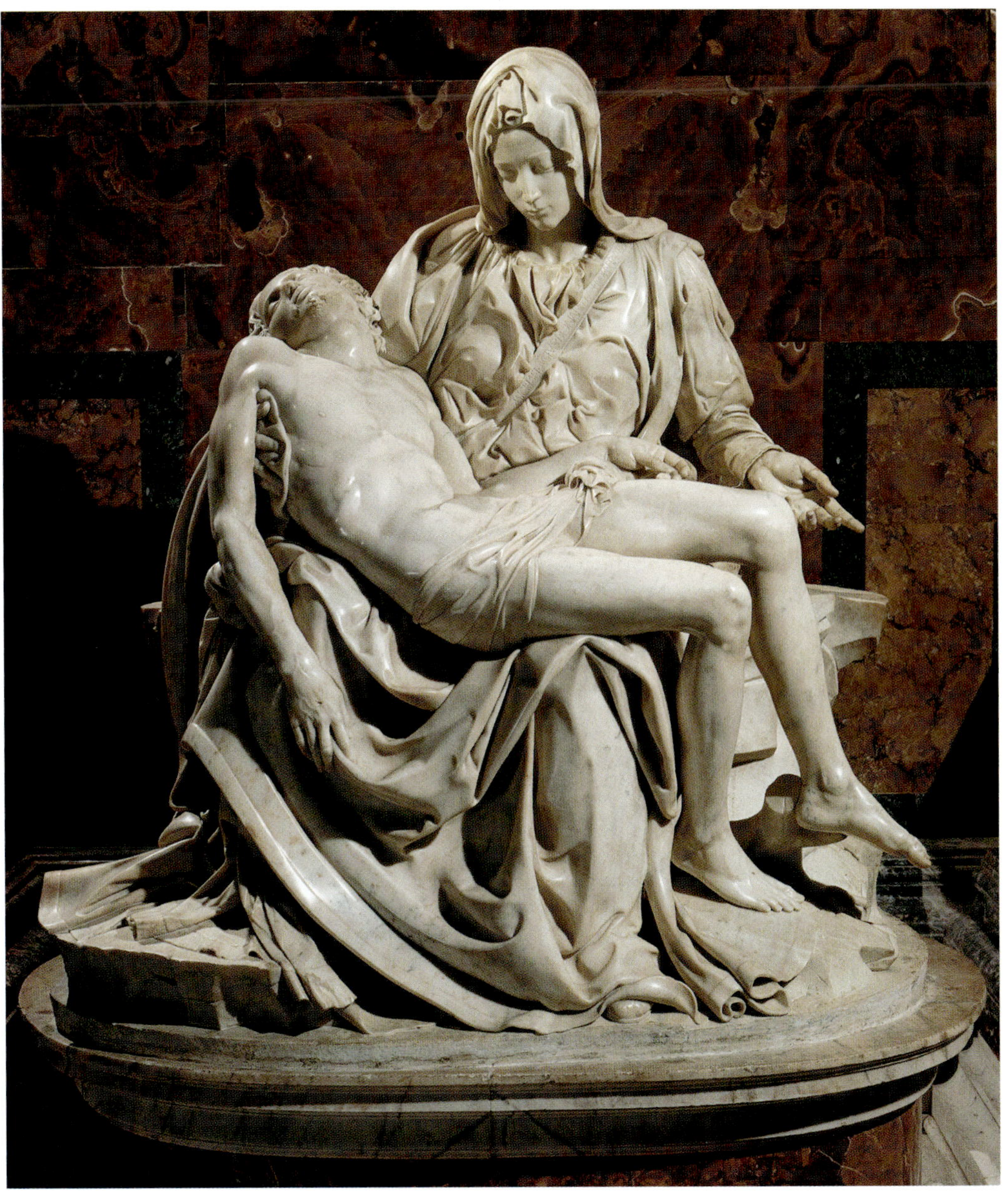

13–8 Michelangelo. ***Pietà***, from Old Saint Peter's. c. 1500. Marble, height 5' 8½" (1.74 m). Saint Peter's, Vatican, Rome

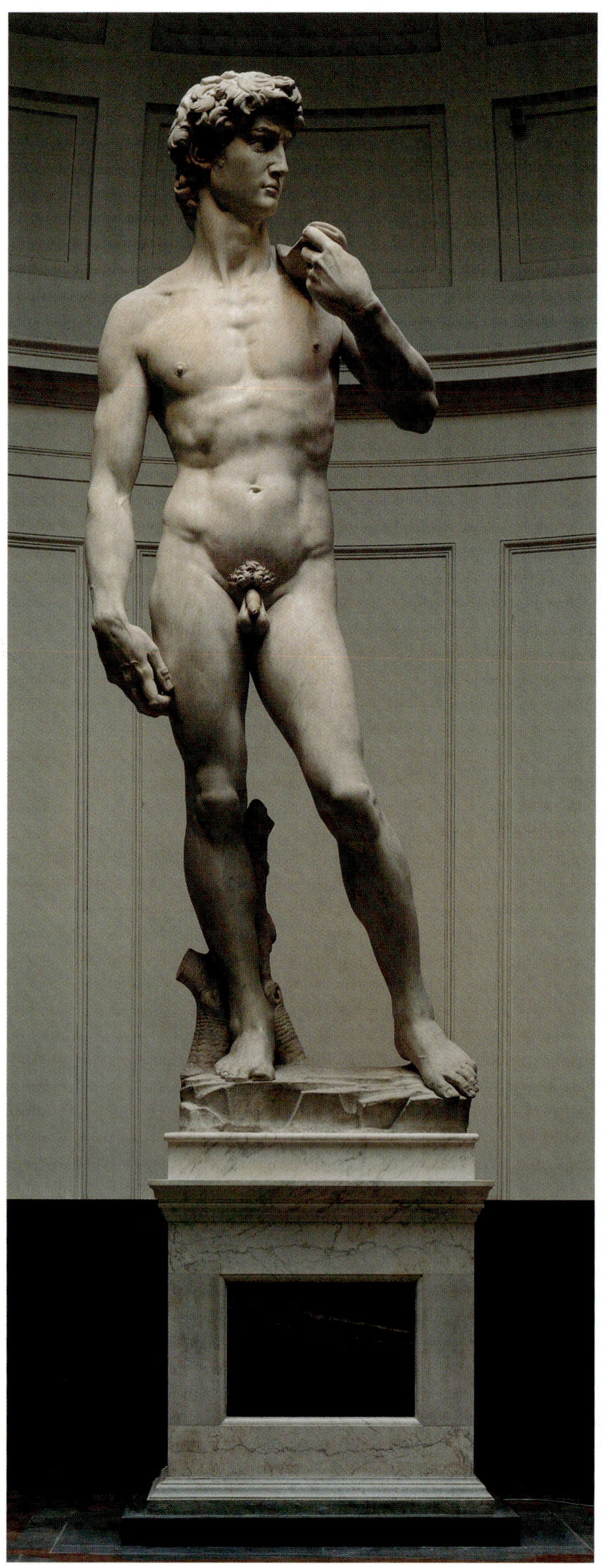

marble quarries at Carrara in central Italy to select the block from which to make this large work, a practice that he was to follow for nearly all his sculpture. The choice of the stone was important to him because, as in the metaphor of the Neoplatonists, he envisioned his sculpture as already existing within the marble, needing only his tools to "set it free."

The **pietà**—a representation of the Virgin supporting and mourning the dead Jesus—had long been a popular subject in Northern Europe, but was rare in Italian art at the time. Italians generally preferred the Lamentation, a narrative tableau including many of Christ's followers (see fig. 11–32, lower left). Michelangelo's Virgin is startlingly youthful—perhaps an outward manifestation of her inner virtue. She is heroic in stature, holding the unnaturally smaller, smoothly modeled body of her grown son. Inconsistencies in scale and age are forgotten, however, when contemplating the sweetness of expression, technical virtuosity of the carving, and the smooth modeling of the luscious forms. Michelangelo's compelling vision of beauty was meant to be seen up close at the statue's own level, so that the viewer can look into Jesus' face. The 25-year-old artist is said to have slipped into the church after it was finished, to sign the statue on a strap across the Virgin's breast thus answering directly questions that had come up about the identity of its creator.

In 1501, Michelangelo accepted a Florentine commission for a statue of the biblical hero David (fig. **13–9**) to be placed high atop a buttress of the cathedral. But when it was finished in 1504, the *David* was so admired that the city council placed it in the principal city square, next to the Palazzo della Signoria, the building housing the city's government. Although the statue embodies the antique ideal of the athletic, nude male, the emotional power of the facial expression and concentrated gaze is new. Unlike Donatello's bronze *David* (see fig. 12–20), this is not a triumphant hero with the head of the giant Goliath already under his feet. Slingshot over his shoulder and a rock in his right hand, Michelangelo's *David* knits his brow and stares into space, seemingly preparing himself psychologically for the danger ahead. No match for his opponent in experience, weaponry, or physical strength, Michelangelo's powerful David stands for the supremacy of right over might. He was a perfect symbol for the Florentines, who had recently fought the forces of Milan, Siena, and Pisa, and still faced political and military pressure.

Michelangelo had a contract to make other statues for the cathedral, but in 1505 Pope Julius II arranged for him to come to Rome to work on the spectacular tomb the pope envisioned for himself at the center of the new Saint Peter's. Julius set this commission aside in 1506, however, and ordered Michelangelo to redecorate the ceiling of his private chapel in the Vatican, the Sistine Chapel (fig. **13–10**). Julius's initial directions for the ceiling specified a simple *trompe l'oeil* architectural decoration; later he wanted the Twelve Apostles. According to Michelangelo, when the artist objected to the limitations of Julius' plan, the pope told him to paint whatever he liked. This Michelangelo presumably did, although he surely had a theological advisor.

13–9 Michelangelo. ***David***. 1501–1504. Marble, height 17' (5.18 m). Galleria dell'Accademia, Florence

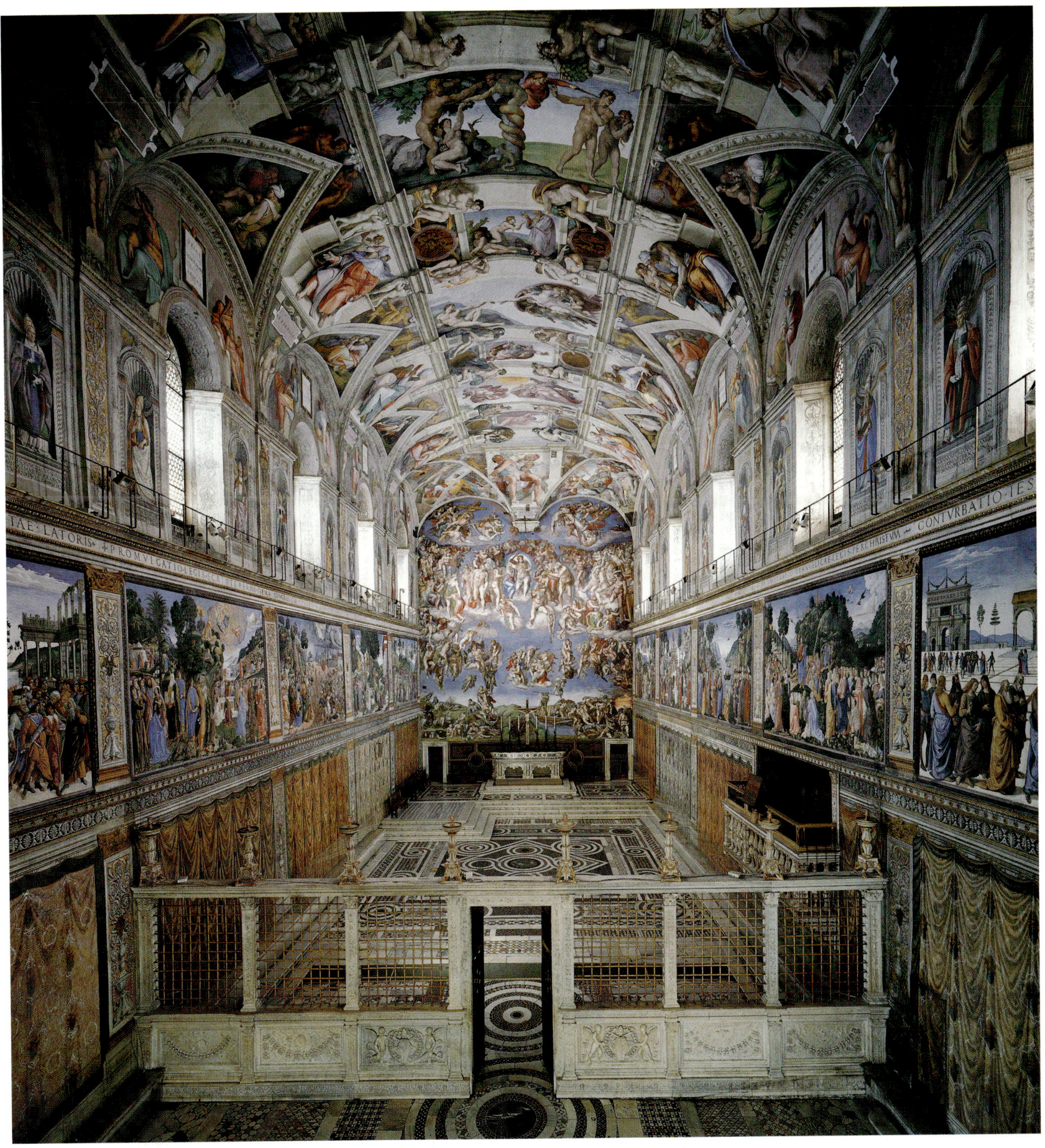

13–10 Interior, Sistine Chapel, Vatican, Rome. Built 1475–1481. Wall frescoes 1481–1483; ceiling painted 1508–1512; wall behind altar painted 1536–1541

Named after its builder, Pope Sixtus IV, the chapel is slightly more than 130 feet long and about 43½ feet wide, approximately the same measurements recorded in the Hebrew Bible for the Temple of Solomon. The floor mosaic was recut from stones used in the floor of an earlier papal chapel. The side walls were painted in fresco between 1481 and 1483 with scenes from the life of Moses and the life of Christ by Perugino, Botticelli, Ghirlandaio, and others. (The left side of Perugino's painting (see fig. 12–24), can be seen at the right edge of the photograph.) Below these are trompe l'oeil *painted draperies, where Raphael's tapestries illustrating the Acts of the Apostles once hung. Michelangelo's famous ceiling frescoes begin with the lunette scenes above the window arches (see fig. 13–11). On the end above the altar is his* Last Judgment, *finished in 1541 (see fig. 13–13).*

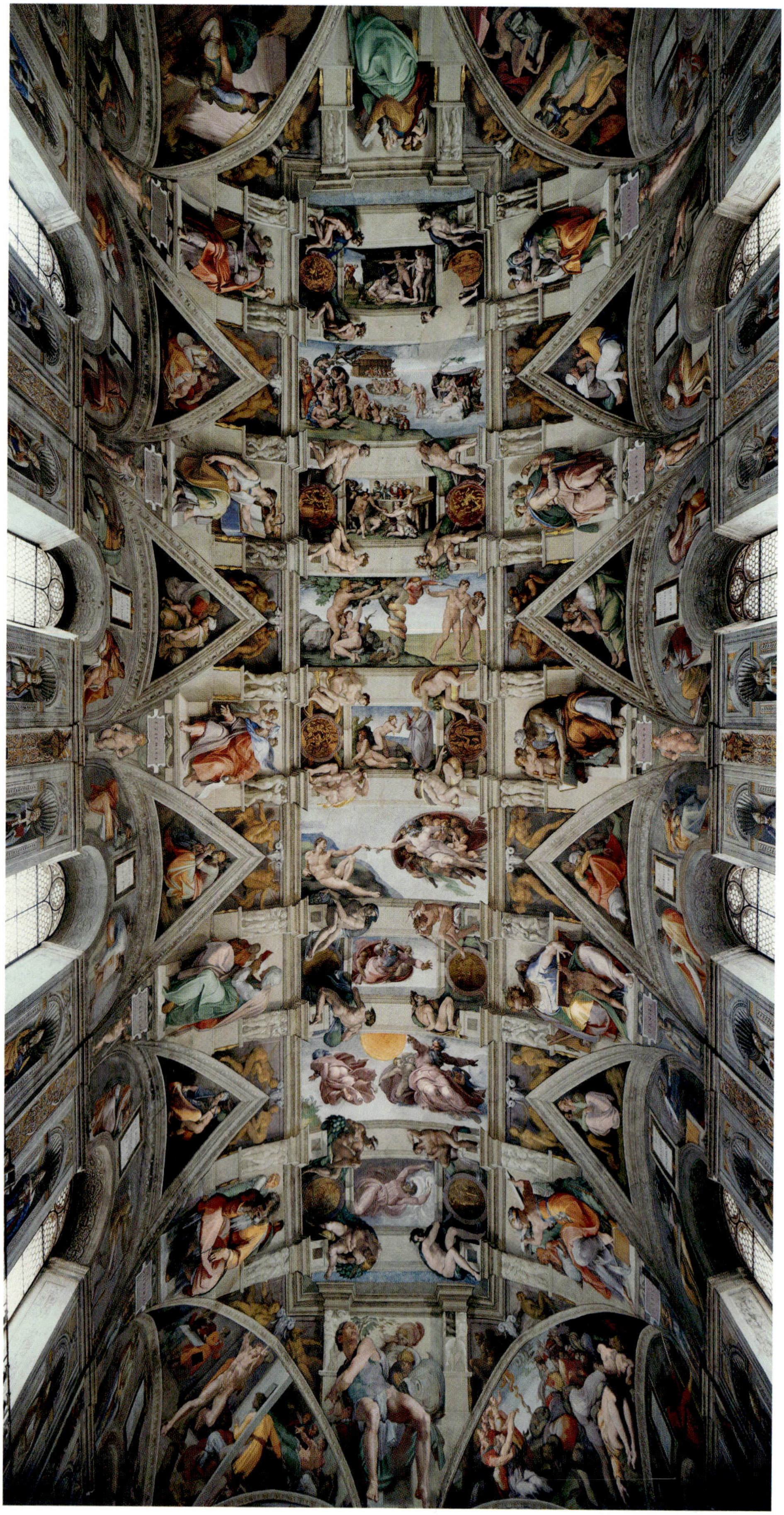

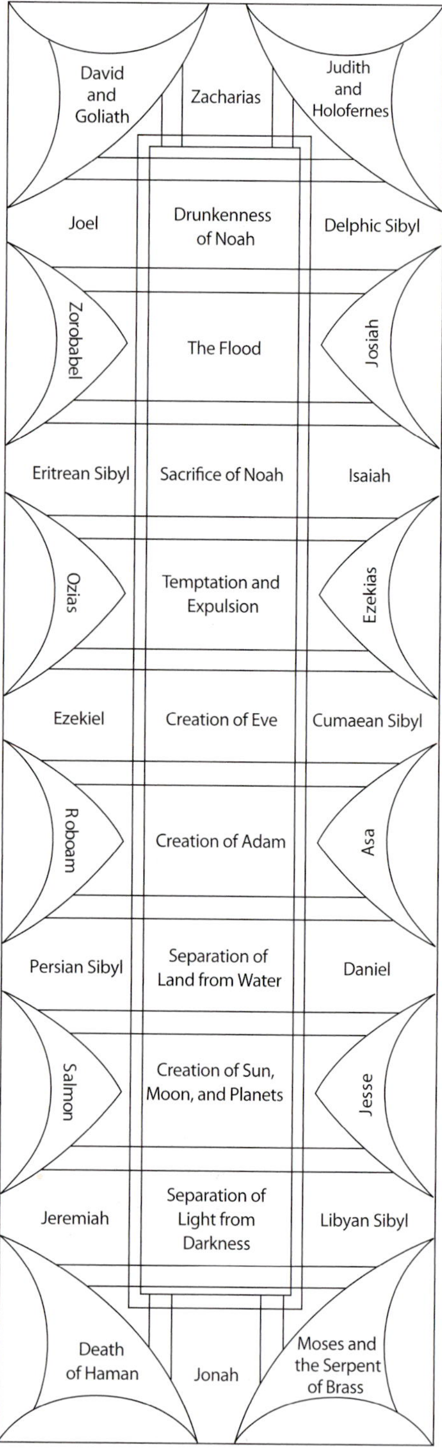

13–11 Michelangelo. Ceiling, Sistine Chapel. 1508–1512. Fresco

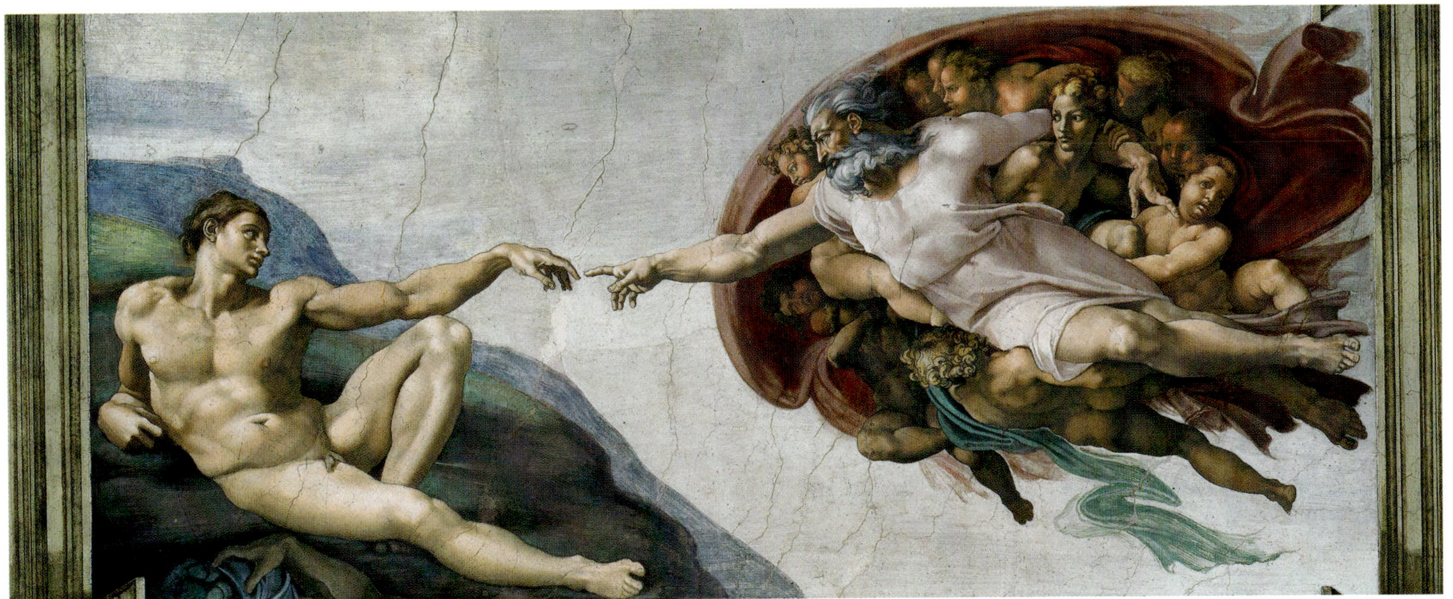

13–12 Michelangelo. ***Creation of Adam*****,** Sistine Chapel ceiling. 1511–1512

Michelangelo's design for the Sistine ceiling consists of an illusionistic marble architectural structure, filled with individual figures and narrative scenes. Running completely around the ceiling is a painted cornice with projections supported by pilasters decorated with sculptured *putti* (fig. **13–11**). Between the pilasters are prophets from the Hebrew Bible and Classical sibyls (female prophets) who were believed to have foretold Jesus' birth. Figures of nude young men (*ignudi*) sit in a variety of poses on pedestals above the fictive cornice. Rising behind the youths, the equally fictive ribs of the vault divide the ceiling into nine compartments, containing depictions of scenes from Genesis, including the Creation of Adam and Eve, their disobedience and expulsion from Paradise, and the story of Noah and the Flood. Eight triangular compartments over the windows contain paintings of the ancestors of Jesus.

Near the ceiling's center is the *Creation of Adam* (fig. **13–12**), in which Michelangelo captures the moment when God charges the languorous Adam with the spark of life. As if to echo the biblical text, Adam's heroic body, outstretched arm, and profile almost mirror those of God, in whose image he has been created. Emerging under God's other arm, and looking across him in the direction of her future companion, is the robust and energetic figure of Eve before her creation.

A quarter of a century after finishing the ceiling, Michelangelo again went to work in the Sistine Chapel, this time on the *Last Judgment*, painted some time between 1536 and 1541 on the large end wall behind the altar (fig. **13–13**). Michelangelo, now entering his 60s, had complained for years of feeling old, yet he accepted this important and demanding task, which took him two years to finish. He painted a writhing swarm of resurrected humanity, with the saved dragged from their graves and pushed up into a vortex of figures around Christ. Despite the efforts of several saints to save them at the last minute, the damned plunge toward hell on the right. To the right of Christ's feet is Saint Bartholomew, who in legend was martyred by being skinned alive, holding his flayed skin, the distorted face of which is painted with Michelangelo's own features. On the lowest level of the mural, directly above the altar, is the gaping, fiery mouth of Hell, toward which the demonic boatman Charon propels his craft on the River Styx, which encircles the underworld. The painting is a grim and constant reminder to the celebrants of the Mass—the pope and his cardinals—that they too will face stern judgment at the end of time.

In addition to his success as a sculptor and painter, Michelangelo was also an influential architect. After the completion of the *Last Judgment*, he took on his most important building commission: the rebuilding of Saint Peter's in Rome. The project had begun in 1506, when Pope Julius II made the astonishing decision to demolish the venerable but crumbling Constantinian basilica over Saint Peter's tomb (see fig. 7–8). To design and build the magnificent new church, the pope appointed the architect Donato Bramante (1443/4–1514), like Raphael a native of Urbino. Bramante envisioned the new Saint Peter's as a central-plan building, a Greek cross with four arms of equal length, crowned with an enormous dome over the central square crossing (see "Saint Peter's Basilica," page 350). Although there may have been a reference to the early Christian tradition of ***martyria*** (central-plan churches over martyrs' tombs, see "Longitudinal-Plan and Central-Plan Churches," page 174), in Renaissance thinking, the central plan and dome also symbolized the perfection of God.

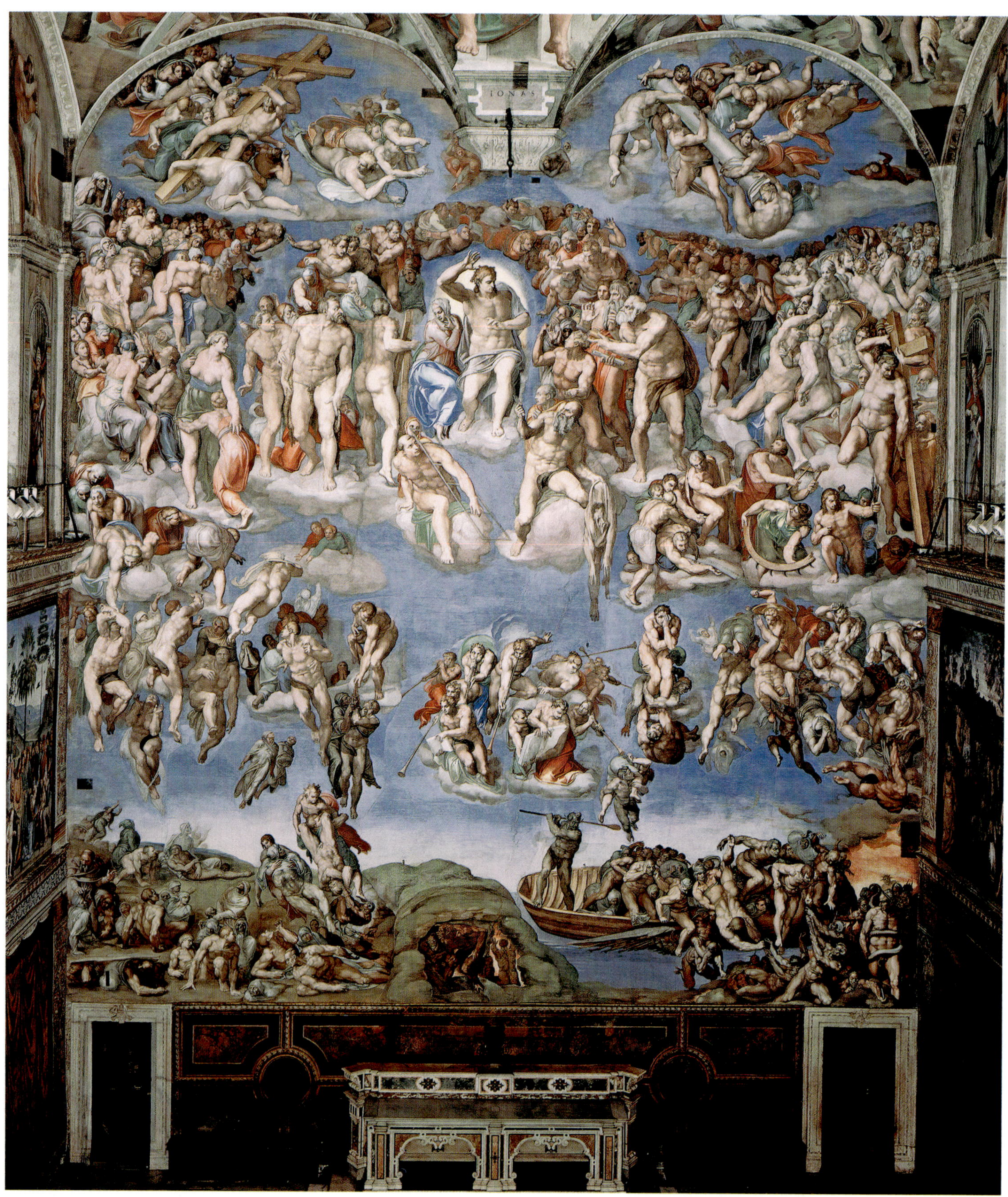

13–13 Michelangelo. ***Last Judgment***, Sistine Chapel. 1536–1541. Fresco, 48' × 44' (encompassing approx. 190 square meters or 2,100 square feet of surface)

Conservative clergy criticized this painting because of its frank nudity, and after Michelangelo's death they ordered bits of drapery to be painted by artist Daniele da Volterra to censor the offending passages, earning Daniele the unfortunate nickname Il Braghettone ("breeches painter").

13–14 Michelangelo. Saint Peter's Basilica, Vatican, Rome. c. 1546–1564 (dome completed 1590 by Giacomo della Porta). View from the southwest

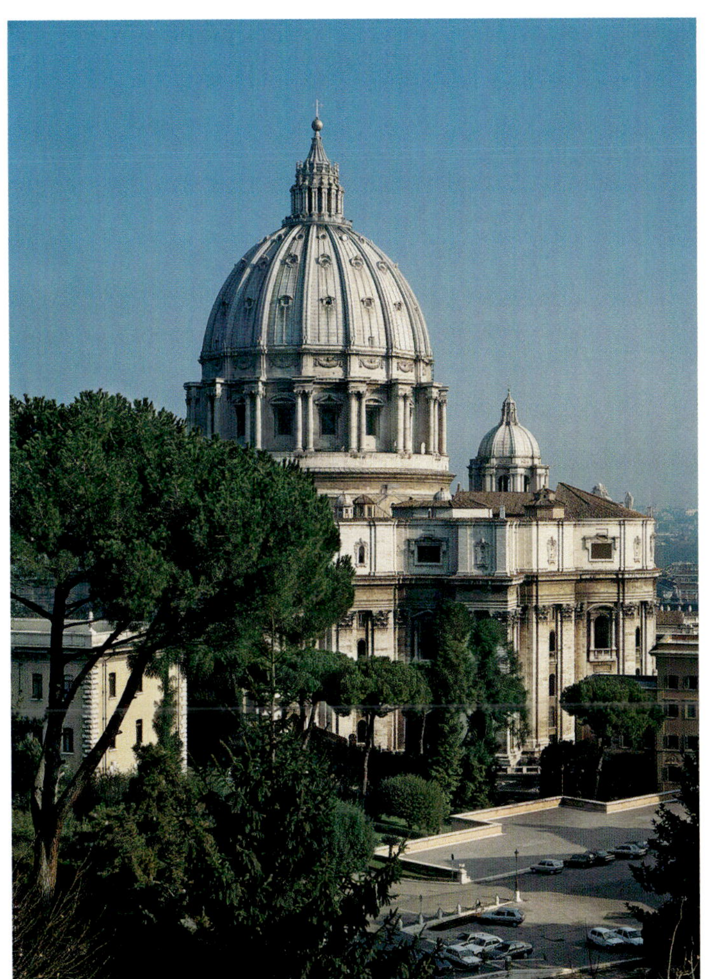

Ultimately, Michelangelo transformed the building into a central-plan church of magnificent proportions and superhuman scale (fig. **13–14**). Seventeenth-century additions and renovations dramatically changed the original plan of the church and the appearance of its interior (see figs. 14–2 and 14–3). However, Michelangelo's Saint Peter's can still be seen in the contrasting forms of the flat and angled exterior walls and the three surviving **hemicycles** (semicircular projections). Colossal pilasters (flat, engaged column-like elements extending through two or more stories), **blind windows** (frames without openings), and niches surround the sanctuary of the church. How Michelangelo would have built the great dome is not known; most scholars believe that it would have been hemispherical. The current dome retains Michelangelo's basic design: segmented with regularly spaced ribs, seated on a high drum with pedimented windows between paired columns, and surmounted by a tall lantern shaped like a circular temple.

Over the course of his lengthy career, Michelangelo continually explored the expressive potential of his art. Late in life, he discovered new stylistic directions that would inspire succeeding generations of artists. Michelangelo was an intense man who believed that his art was divinely inspired and who alternated between periods of depression and frenzied activity. He was difficult and often arrogant, yet he was devoted to his friends and helpful to young artists. In old age, he became deeply absorbed in religion and dedicated himself chiefly to religious works—many unfinished—that subverted Renaissance ideals of human perfectibility and denied his own youthful idealism. In the process he uncovered new forms that seem to mirror tensions evident in Europe during the second half of the sixteenth century.

In this age of artistic giants, very few women had the opportunity or inclination to become sculptors. Properzia de' Rossi (c. 1490–1529/30), who lived in Bologna, was an exception. She mastered many arts, including engraving, and was famous for her miniature sculptures, including an entire Last Supper carved on a peach pit! She created several pieces in marble for the Cathedral of San Petronio in Bologna—two sibyls, two angels, and this relief of *Joseph and Potiphar's Wife* (fig. **13–15**), where the biblical hero escapes, running, as the partially clad seductress snatches at his cloak. Properzia is the only woman whom sixteenth-century historian Vasari included in the 1550 edition of his *Lives of the Artists*, where he reports that a rival male sculptor prevented her from being paid fairly and from securing additional commissions.

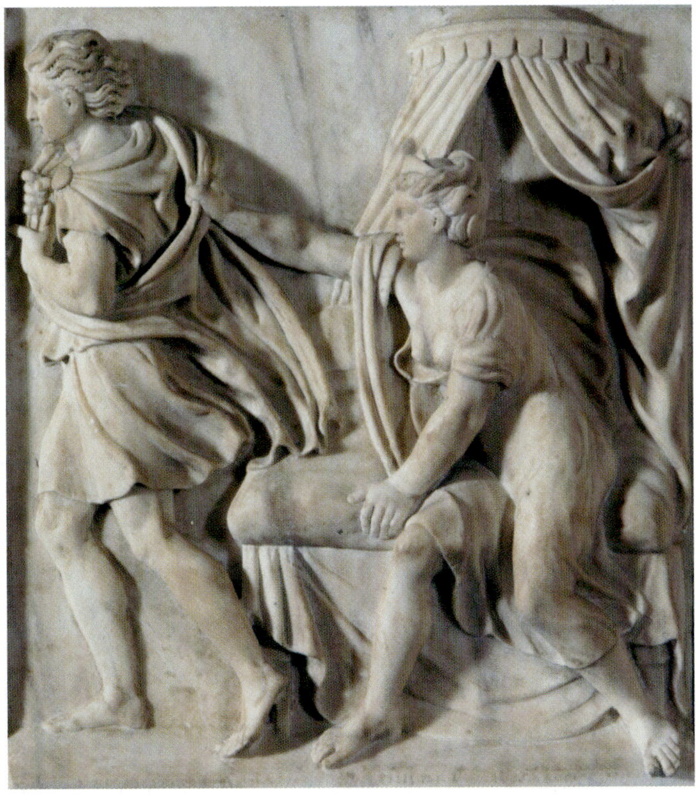

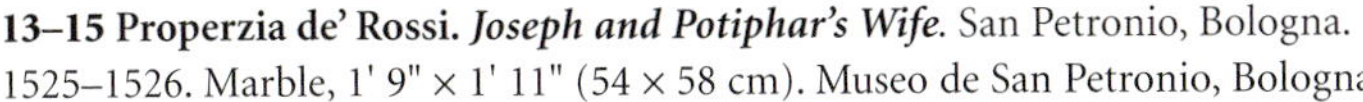

13–15 Properzia de' Rossi. *Joseph and Potiphar's Wife.* San Petronio, Bologna. 1525–1526. Marble, 1' 9" × 1' 11" (54 × 58 cm). Museo de San Petronio, Bologna

ELEMENTS OF Architecture

Saint Peter's Basilica

The original church of Saint Peter's was built in the fourth century CE by Constantine, the first Christian Roman emperor, to mark the grave of the apostle Peter, the first bishop of Rome and therefore the first pope. Constantine's architect erected an Imperial Roman basilica with a nave, flanking side aisles set off by colonnades, and an apse. To allow large numbers of clergy and pilgrims to approach the shrine, they also added a transept. The rest of the church was, in effect, a covered cemetery, carpeted with the tombs of believers who wanted to be buried near the grave of the apostle. When it was built, Constantine's basilica was one of the largest buildings in the world with an interior length of 368 feet (112.17 m) and width of 190 feet (57.91 m), and for more than a thousand years it was the most important pilgrimage site in Europe.

That anyone, even a pope, would pull down such a venerated building is an indication of the extraordinary self-assurance of the Renaissance—and especially of Pope Julius II himself. The deaths of both the pope and the architect Bramante in 1513–1514 put a temporary halt to the project. Successive plans by Raphael and others changed the Greek-cross plan to a Latin-cross plan in order to provide the church with a full-length nave. However, when Michelangelo was appointed architect in 1546, he returned to the Greek-cross plan and simplified Bramante's design to create a single, unified space. The dome was finally completed (1588–1590) some years after Michelangelo's death by Giacomo della Porta, who retained Michelangelo's basic design but gave the dome a taller and slimmer profile and changed the shape of its openings.

By the early seventeenth century, demands on the church had changed. During the Counter-Reformation, the Church emphasized congregational worship, so more space was needed for people and processions. Moreover, it was felt that the new church should more closely resemble Old Saint Peter's and should extend over roughly the same area, including the ground covered by the original atrium. In 1606, Pope Paul V commissioned the architect Carlo Maderno to change Michelangelo's Greek-cross plan back once again to a Latin-cross plan. Maderno extended the nave to its final length of slightly more than 636 feet and added a Baroque façade (see fig. 14–3), thus completing Saint Peter's as it is today. Later in the seventeenth century, the sculptor and architect Gianlorenzo Bernini monumentalized the square in front of the basilica by surrounding it with a great colonnade, like a huge set of arms extended to embrace the faithful as they approached the principal church of European Christendom.

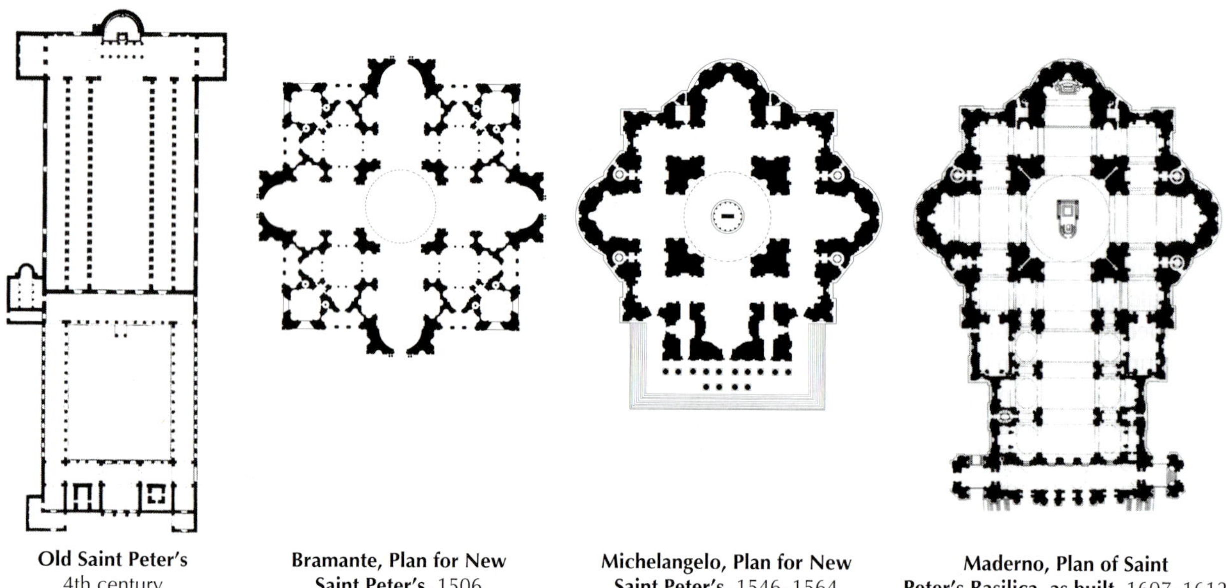

Old Saint Peter's 4th century

Bramante, Plan for New Saint Peter's. 1506

Michelangelo, Plan for New Saint Peter's. 1546–1564

Maderno, Plan of Saint Peter's Basilica, as built. 1607–1612

Venice and the Veneto

In the last quarter of the fifteenth century, Venice emerged as a major artistic center. Venetian painters embraced the oil medium from the late 1470s, earlier than most other Italian artists. It was the use of oil glazes that permitted the brilliant color and lighting effect desired by Venice's most famous Renaissance painters: Bellini, Titian, Tintoretto, and Veronese. By the sixteenth century, Venetians did not see themselves as rivals of Florence and Rome, but rather as superiors.

Giovanni Bellini (c. 1430–1516) amazed and attracted patrons with his artistic virtuosity for almost 60 years, beginning in the second half of the fifteenth century but extending well into the sixteenth, when he produced many of his greatest paintings in a mature, simplified, idealized style. In the San Zaccaria Altarpiece of 1505, the Virgin and Child, four saints, and an angelic musician appear in an ambiguous spatial setting: part church with a glittering gold mosaic semidome; part loggia open to the natural world of trees and cloudy sky (fig. **13–16**). The architecture of the altarpiece frame continues in the arches and pilasters of the painting. Light streams in from the left, the north side in a church, counter to the laws of nature. The figures bow their heads, reading and meditating; a single line of music breaks the stillness. Art historians have given a special name, *sacra conversazione* ("holy conversation"), to this type of composition showing saints, angels, and sometimes even the painting's donors in the same pictorial space with the enthroned

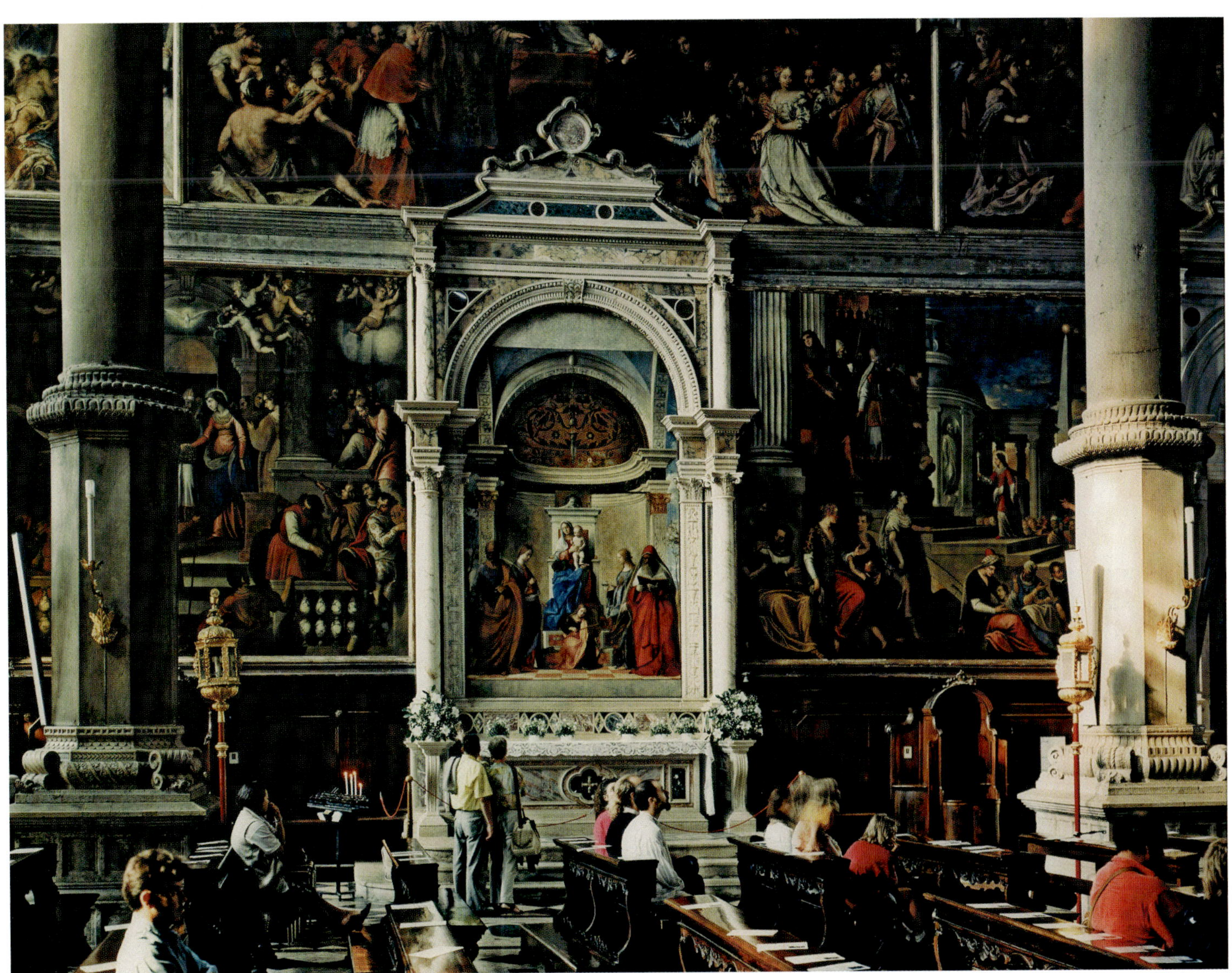

13–16 Giovanni Bellini. *The Virgin and Child Enthroned with Saints.* 1505. Altarpiece in the Church of San Zaccaria, as photographed, in context, by Thomas Struth in his monumental photograph, *San Zaccaria, Venice, 1995.* The painting: oil on panel, transferred to canvas. Photograph: 5' 10" × 7' 6" (1.7 × 2.2 m)

The church has become a museum filled with people who have come to study and admire the painting rather than worship at the altar.

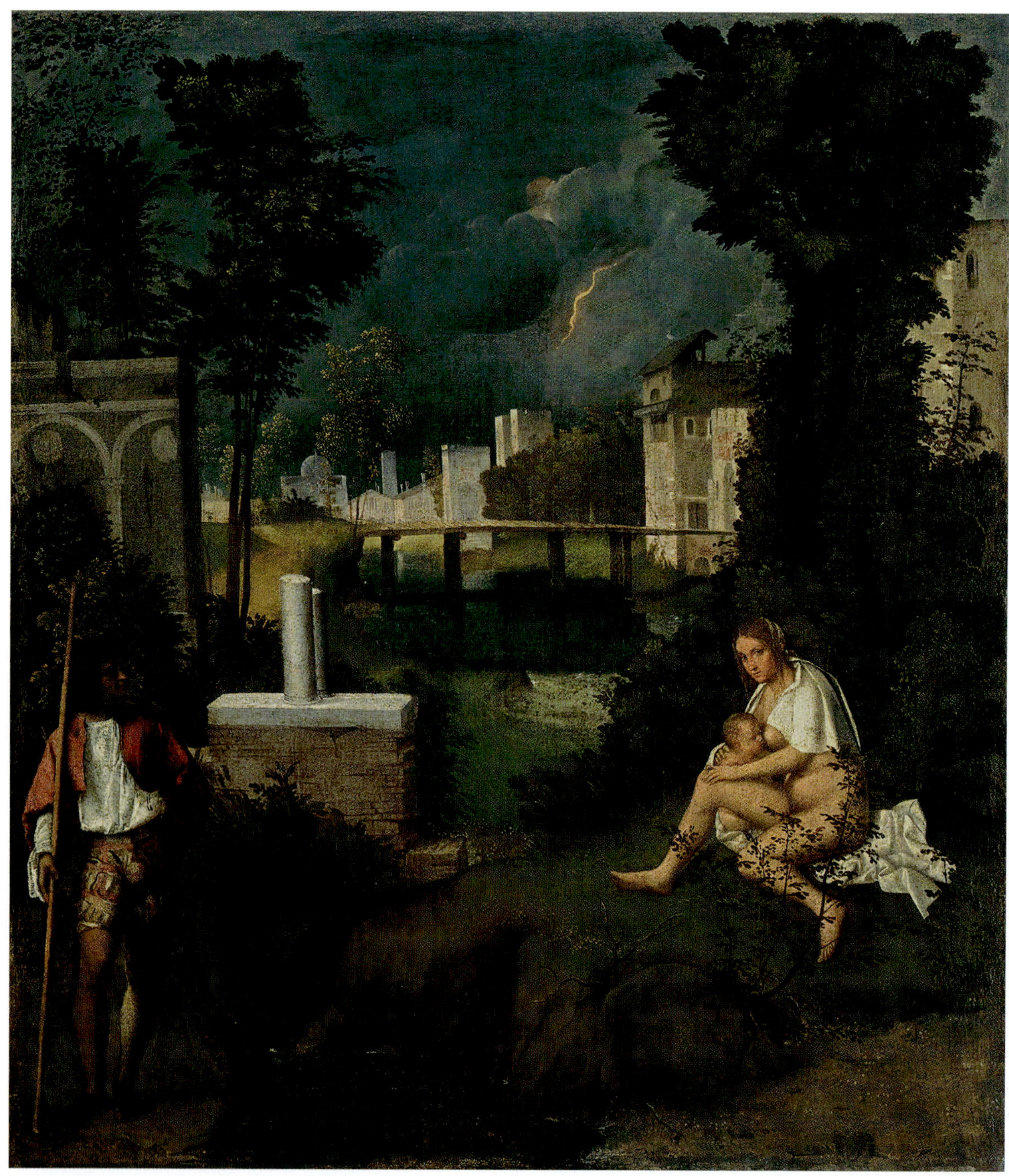

13–17 Giorgione. ***The Tempest.*** 1505–1510. Oil on canvas, 31" × 28¾" (79.4 × 73 cm). Galleria dell'Accademia, Venice

Virgin and Child. Despite the name, no conversation or other interaction among the figures takes place in a literal sense. Instead, the individuals portrayed are joined in a mystical and eternal communion occurring outside time, in which the viewer is invited to share.

The career of Giorgione (Giorgio da Castelfranco, c. 1475–1510), another Venetian artist, was much briefer—he died from the plague—and most scholars accept only four or five paintings as entirely by his hand. But his importance to Venetian painting is critical. He introduced new, enigmatic pastoral themes, known as *poesie* (or painted poems), that were inspired by the contemporary literary revival of ancient pastoral poetry. He is significant for his sensuous nude figures, and, above all, for his appreciation of nature in landscape painting, which played an increasingly important role in sixteenth-century art. Giorgione's early life and training are undocumented, but his work suggests that he studied with Giovanni Bellini. Perhaps Leonardo's subtle lighting system and mysterious, intensely observed landscapes also inspired him.

Giorgione's most famous work, called today *The Tempest* (fig. **13–17**), was painted shortly before his death, potentially in response to personal, private impulses—as with many modern artists—rather than to fulfill an external commission. Simply trying to understand what is happening in the picture piques our interest. At

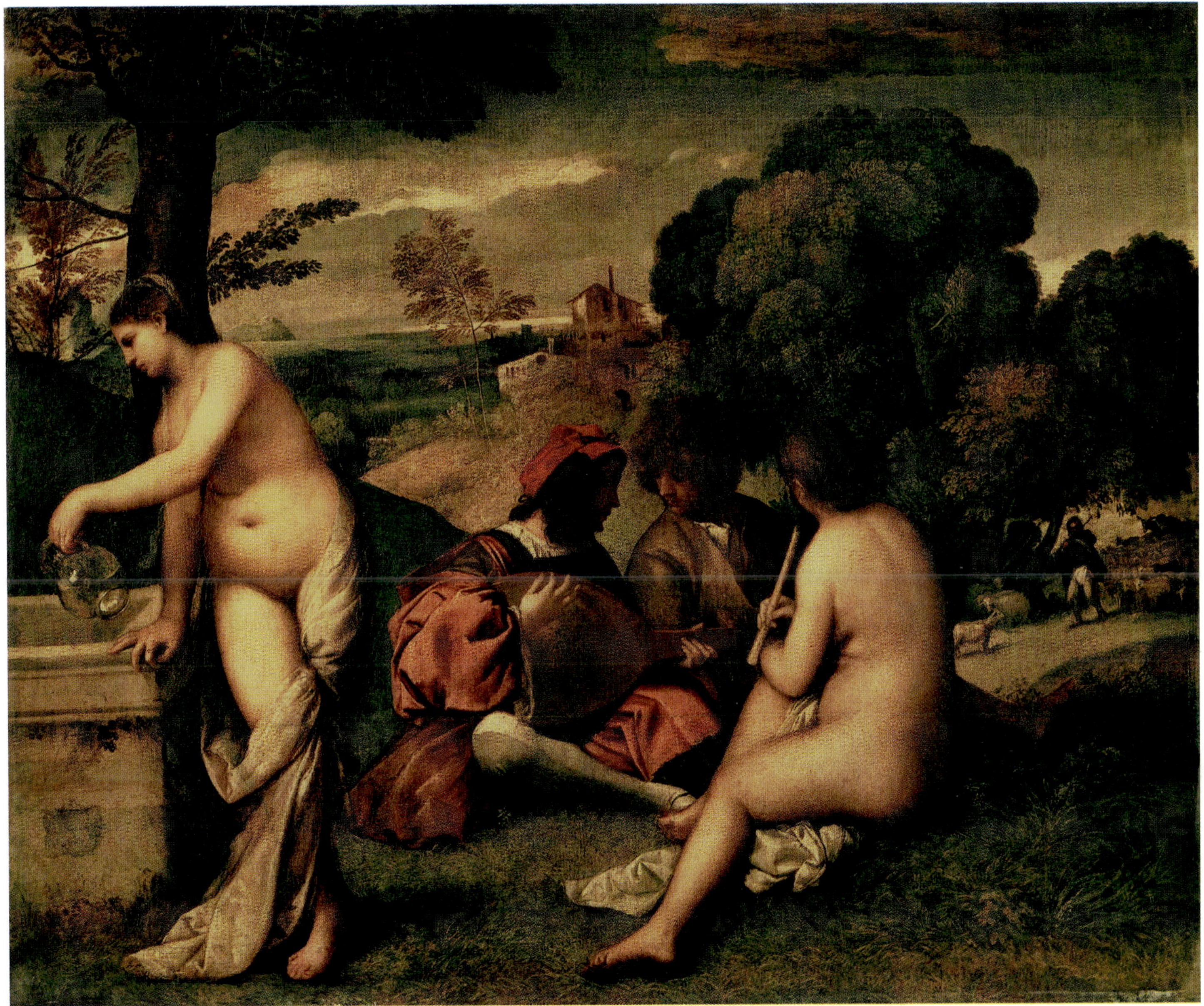

13–18 Titian (formerly attributed to Giorgione). ***Pastoral Concert.*** c. 1509–1510. Oil on canvas, 43¼" × 54⅜" (109 × 132 cm).
Musée du Louvre, Paris

the right, a woman is seated on the ground, nude except for the end of a long white cloth thrown over her shoulders. Her nudity seems maternal rather than erotic as she nurses the baby at her side. Across the dark, rock-edged spring stands a man wearing the uniform of a German mercenary soldier. His head is turned toward the woman, but he appears to have paused for a moment before continuing to turn toward the viewer. X-rays of the painting show that Giorgione altered his composition while he was still at work on it—the soldier replaces a second nude woman on the left. Inexplicably, a spring gushes forth between the figures, feeding a lake surrounded by substantial houses, and in the far distance a bolt of lightning splits the darkening sky. The artist's attention seems more focused on the unruly elements of nature rather than on the figures, giving landscape an importance that is new in Western painting.

In 1507, Giorgione took on a new assistant, Tiziano Vecellio, better known today as Titian (c. 1488–1576). The painting called *Pastoral Concert* (fig. **13–18**) is dated to a few years after this time. Perhaps Giorgione began the painting and Titian completed it after Giorgione's death, or Titian, inspired by Giorgione, may have painted it alone. In this puzzling picture, two young men, one richly dressed, the other a barefoot peasant, relax in a verdant landscape that, as in *The Tempest*, is one of the principal subjects of the painting. The men seem almost oblivious to the two nude women beside them and the shepherd tending his flock in the background. While the meaning of the juxtaposition of the nude and clothed figures is obscure, in a general sense this scene of an outdoor concert evokes the romantic ideal of a lost golden age, some misty time in remote antiquity when people led a carefree pastoral life, a theme much

WOMEN PATRONS OF THE ARTS

In the sixteenth century, many wealthy women—both from the aristocracy and from the merchant class—were enthusiastic patrons of the arts. Two English queens, the Tudor half-sisters Mary I and Elizabeth I, glorified their reigns with the aid of court artists, as did most sovereigns of the period. And the Habsburg princesses Margaret of Austria and Mary of Hungary presided over brilliant Humanist courts when they were regents. But perhaps the Renaissance's greatest woman patron of the arts was Isabella d'Este, Marchesa of Mantua (1474–1539) (fig. **13–19**), who gathered painters, musicians, composers, writers, and literary scholars around her. Married to Francesco II Gonzaga at age 15, she had great beauty, great wealth, and a brilliant mind that made her a successful diplomat and administrator. She was a true Renaissance woman, her motto the epitome of rational thinking: "Neither Hope nor Fear." An avid reader and collector of manuscripts and books, she sponsored an edition of Virgil while still in her 20s. She also collected ancient art and objects, as well as works by contemporary Italian artists such as Botticelli, Mantegna, Perugino, Correggio, and Titian. Her *grotto*, or cave, as she called her study in the Mantuan palace, was a veritable museum for her collections. The walls above the storage and display cabinets were painted in fresco by Mantegna, and the carved-wood ceiling was covered with mottoes and visual references to Isabella's impressive literary interests.

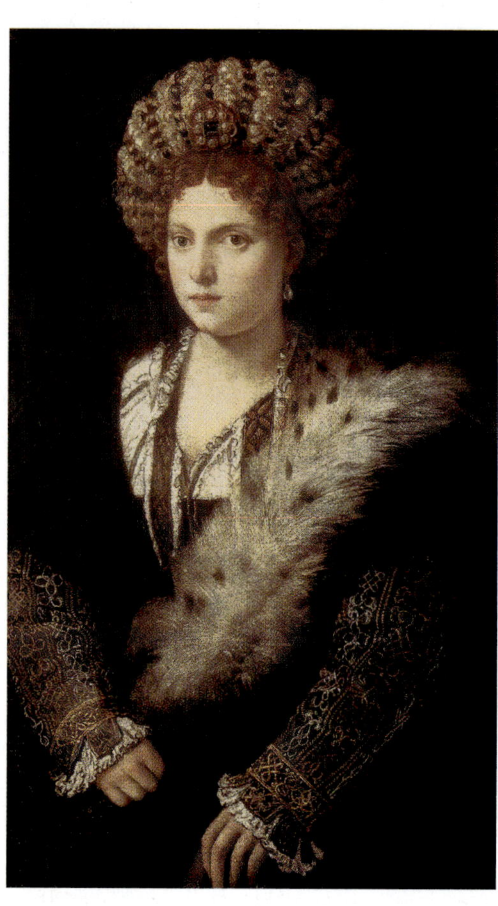

13–19 Titian. *Isabella d'Este*. 1534–1536. Oil on canvas, 40⅛" × 25¼" (102 × 64.1 cm). Kunsthistorisches Museum, Vienna

This great Humanist and patron of the arts was 60 years old when Titian painted her portrait, but he had studied an earlier portrait of her in order to capture her youthful beauty.

loved by Classical and early Renaissance poets. In fact, the painting is now interpreted as an allegory on the invention of poetry. Titian showcases here his renowned talent for painting sensuous female nudes whose swelling flesh seems to glow with an incandescent light. Titian seems to have been as inspired by flesh-and-blood beauty as by any source from poetry or art.

The early life of Titian is obscure. He supposedly began an apprenticeship as a mosaicist and then studied painting under Giovanni Bellini before working with Giorgione. In 1516, he became official painter to the Republic of Venice. Three years later, the powerful Pesaro family commissioned him to paint an altarpiece in Venice for the Franciscan Church of Santa Maria Gloriosa dei Frari—a Madonna and Child surrounded by members of the Pesaro family (fig. **13–20**). In the left foreground of the so-called *Pesaro Madonna*, Jacopo Pesaro, Bishop of Paphos, kneels directly in front of the Virgin. No doubt he merited this honored spot because he had led the papal army to victory over the Turks in 1502. A turbaned Turkish captive stands behind him, and a knight holds a banner displaying the arms of Pope Alexander VI. Saint Peter, a monumental seated figure with the key of heaven at his feet, looks approvingly at Jacopo, while Saint Francis, at right, gazes upward at the Christ Child. The grandeur of the scene, with its massive columns and marble staircase, enhances the power and glory of the Pesaros. No photograph can convey the vibrancy of the paint surfaces, which Titian built up in layers of pure colors, chiefly red, white, yellow, and black. The powerful intersecting diagonals of the composition reach from Jacopo Pesaro to the Virgin (innovatively placed off-center), and from the family at the lower right to the tilting banner at the

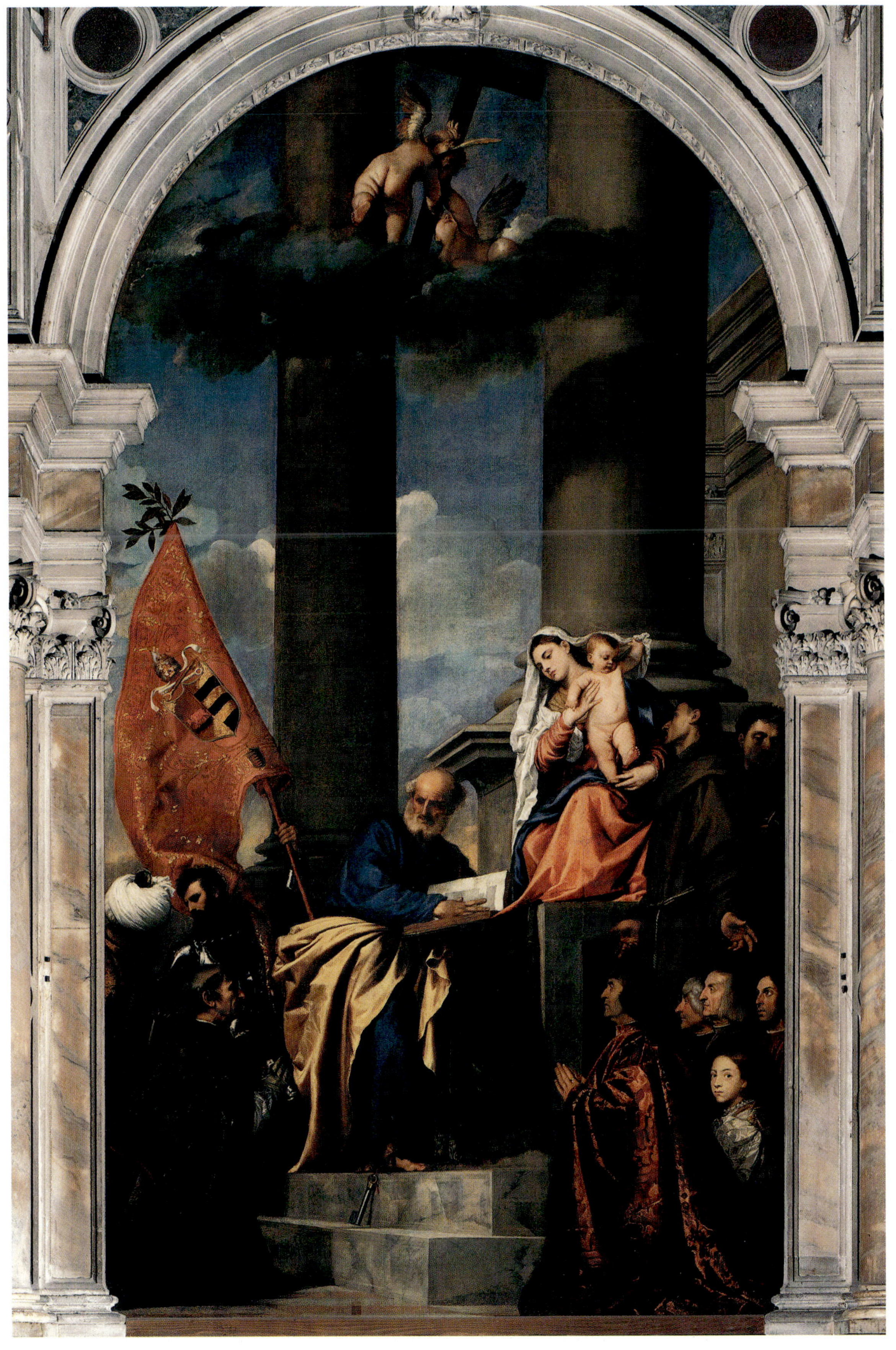

13–20 Titian. ***Pesaro Madonna.*** Pesaro Chapel, Santa Maria Gloriosa dei Frari, Venice. 1519–1526. Oil on canvas, 15' 11" × 8' 10" (4.85 × 2.69 m)

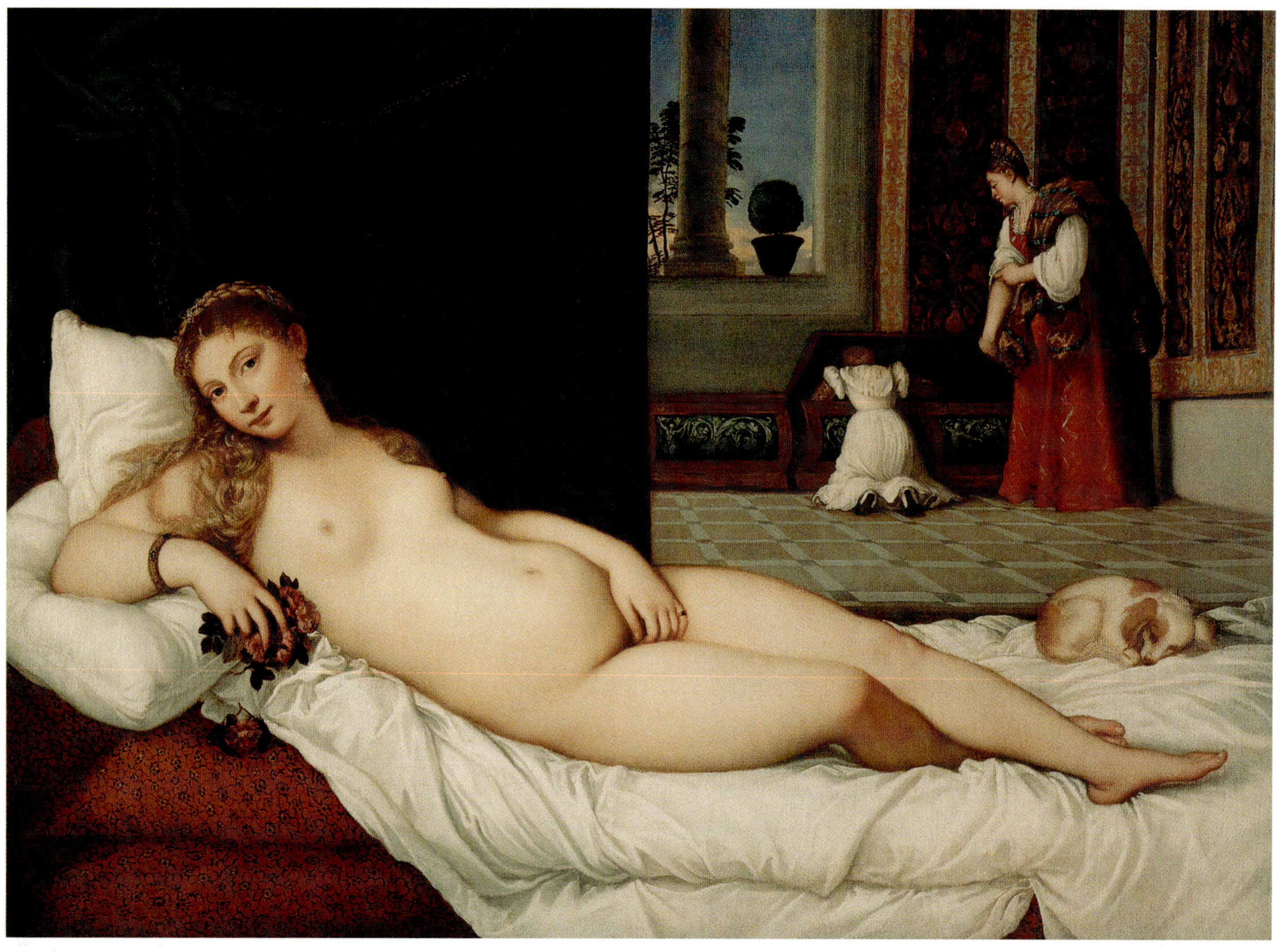

13–21 Titian. ***Venus of Urbino.*** c. 1538. Oil on canvas, 3' 11" × 5' 5" (1.19 × 1.65 m). Galleria degli Uffizi, Florence

upper left. The arresting visage of the youth who turns to meet our gaze at lower right guarantees our engagement.

Paintings of nude reclining women became especially popular in sophisticated court circles, where male patrons could enjoy and appreciate "Venuses" under the cloak of respectable classical mythology. Seemingly typical of such paintings is the "Venus" that Titian delivered to Guidobaldo della Rovere (Duke of Urbino, 1539–1574) in spring 1538 (fig. **13–21**). Here, we seem to see a beautiful Venetian courtesan with deliberately provocative gestures, stretching languidly on her couch in a spacious palace, her glowing flesh and golden hair set off by white sheets and pillows. But for its original audience, art historian Rona Goffen has argued, the painting was more about marriage than mythology or seductiveness. The multiple matrimonial references in this work include the *cassone* (marriage or trousseau storage chest) in the background where servants are removing or returning the woman's clothing, the bridal associations of the myrtle and roses she holds in her hand, and even the spaniel snoozing at her feet, a traditional symbol of fidelity and domesticity, especially when sleeping so peacefully. Titian's picture might be associated with Guidobaldo's marriage in 1534 to the 10-year-old Giulia Verano. Four years later, when this painting arrived, she would have been considered an adult rather than a child bride. Could this painting represent not a Roman goddess nor a Venetian courtesan, but a faithful wife welcoming her husband into their lavish home?

Paolo Caliari (1528–1588), called Veronese after his hometown of Verona, is nearly synonymous today with the popular image of Venetian splendor and pageantry. Like Titian, Veronese employed elaborate architectural settings and costumes for religious images, but he also added still lifes, anecdotal vignettes, and other details unconnected with the main subject that proved immensely appealing to Venetian patrons. One of Veronese's most famous works is the painting now called *Feast in the House of Levi* (fig. **13–22**), painted for the Dominican Monastery of Santi Giovanni e Paolo, Venice. At

CLOSER LOOK

According to the New Testament, Jesus revealed his impending death to his disciples during a *seder*, a meal celebrating the Jewish festival of Passover. This occasion, known to Christians as the Last Supper, and situated in the Gospels on the evening before the Crucifixion, was a popular subject in sixteenth-century European art. But in 1573, when the painter Veronese delivered an enormous canvas of this subject to fulfill a commission (fig. **13–22**), the patrons were shocked. Some were offended by the grandiose pageantry of the scene. Others protested the impiety of surrounding Jesus with a man picking his teeth, scruffy dogs, and foreign soldiers. As a result of the furor, Veronese was called before the Inquisition. There he justified himself first by asserting that the picture actually depicted not the Last Supper, but rather the Feast in the House of Simon, a small dinner held shortly before Jesus' final entry into Jerusalem. He also noted that artists customarily invent details in their pictures and that he had received a commission to paint the piece "as I saw fit." His argument fell on unsympathetic ears, and he was ordered to change the painting. Later he sidestepped the issue by changing its title to that of another banquet, one given by the tax collector Levi, whom Jesus had called to follow him (Luke 5:27–32). Perhaps with this change of subject, Veronese had modest revenge on the Inquisitors: when Jesus himself was criticized for associating with such unsavory people at this meal, he replied, "I have not come to call the righteous to repentance but sinners" (Luke 5:32).

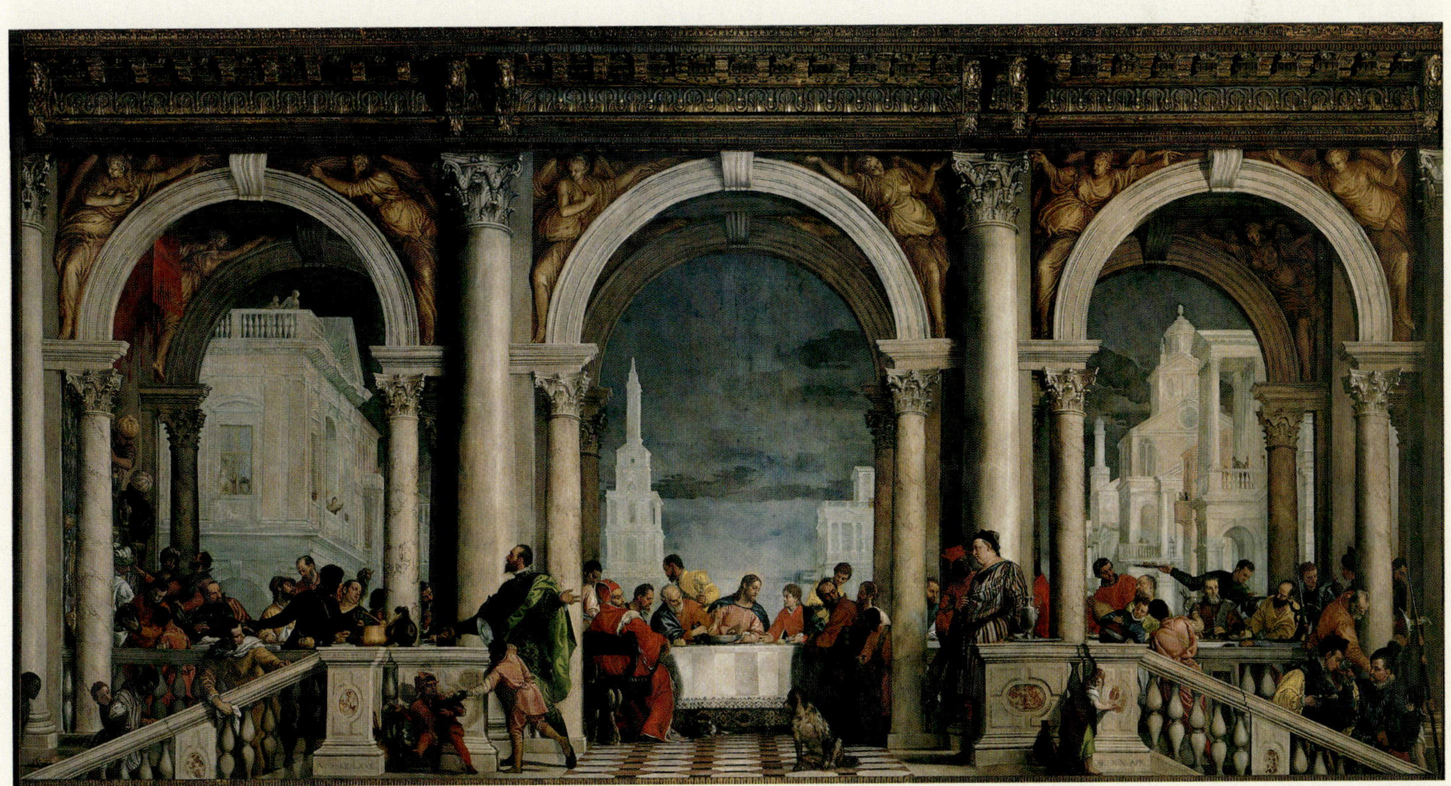

13–22 Veronese. ***Feast in the House of Levi***, from the Monastery of Santi Giovanni e Paolo, Venice. 1573. Oil on canvas, 18' 3" × 42' (5.56 × 12.8 m). Galleria dell'Accademia, Venice

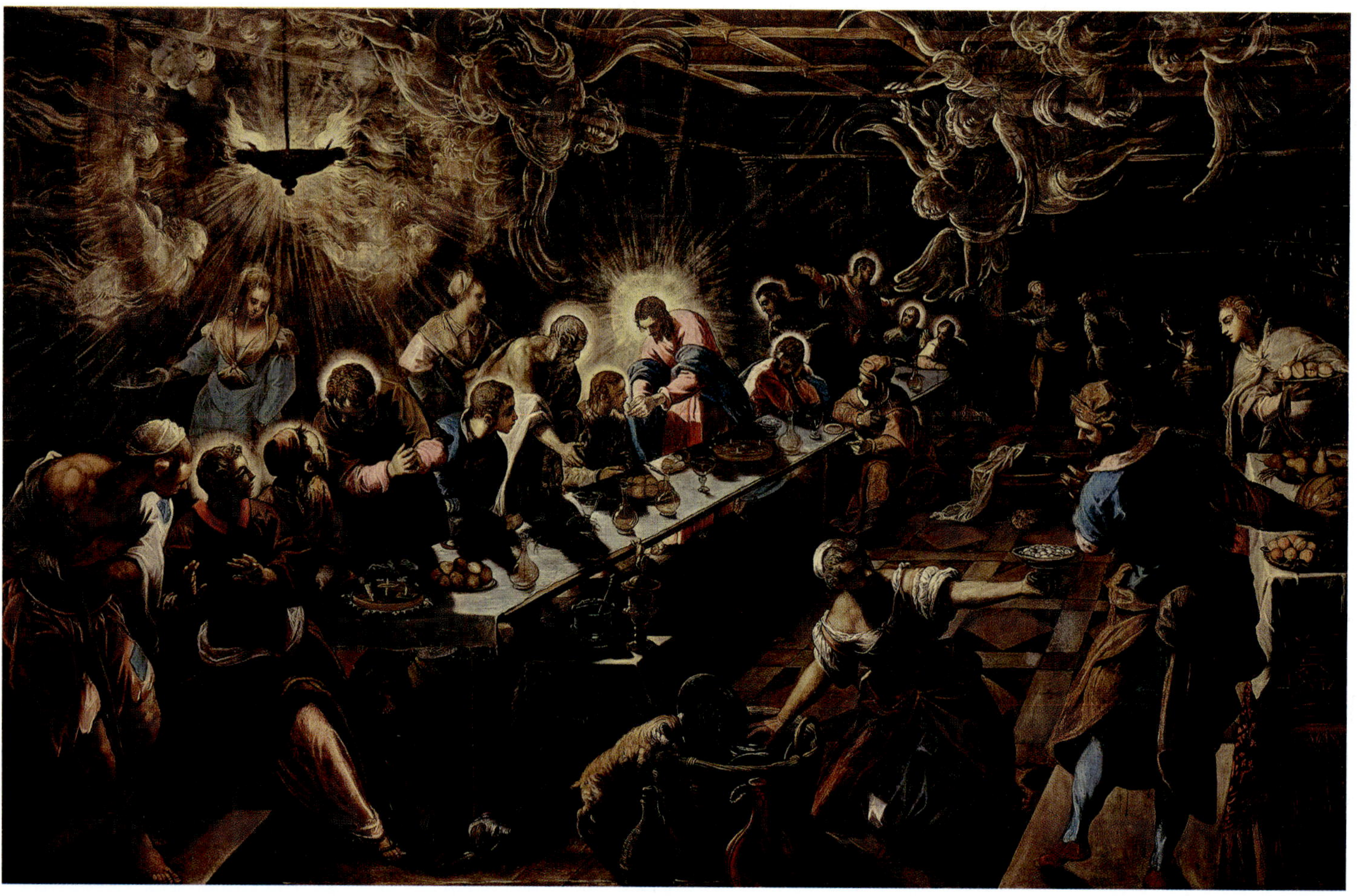

13–23 Tintoretto. ***Last Supper.*** Church of San Giorgio Maggiore, Venice. 1592–1594. Oil on canvas, 12' × 18' 8" (3.7 × 5.7 m)

first glance the true subject of this painting seems to be architecture; the inhabitants of the space only secondary. Beyond the enormous loggia, entered through colossal triumphal arches, an imaginary city of white marble gleams in the distance. The size of the canvas allowed Veronese to make his figures realistically proportional to the architectural setting without losing their substance. His painting *The Triumph of Venice* in the Doge's Palace in Venice (fig. Intro–15) is equally glorious.

Jacopo Robusti (1518–1594), called Tintoretto ("little dyer") after his father's trade, carried Venetian Renaissance painting in another direction. He is said to have been an apprentice in Titian's shop, where he proclaimed as his goal the combination of his master's color with the drawing of Michelangelo. The speed with which Tintoretto drew and painted was the subject of comment in his own time and of legends thereafter. Perhaps he seemed to paint so rapidly because he employed a large workshop, which included other members of his family. Of his eight children, four became artists. His oldest child, Marietta Robusti, worked with him as a portrait painter, and two or perhaps three of his sons also joined the shop. Another daughter, famous for her needlework, became a nun. Marietta, in spite of her fame and many commissions, stayed in her father's shop until she died, at age 30. So skillfully did she capture her father's style and technique that today art historians cannot be certain which paintings are hers.

Tintoretto often developed a composition by creating a small-scale model like a miniature stage set, which he populated with wax figures. He then adjusted the positions of the figures and the lighting until he was satisfied with the entire scene. Using a grid of horizontal and vertical threads placed in front of this model, he could easily sketch the composition onto squared paper for his assistants to recopy onto a large canvas. Assistants also primed the canvas and blocked in the areas of dark and light. The artist himself finished the painting, concentrating his attention on the more difficult passages.

With his dynamic technique, strong colors, and bright highlights, Tintoretto created a pictorial mood of intense spirituality. The *Last Supper* (fig. **13–23**), one of his last paintings, is filled with the kind of everyday details that Veronese also included, such as a servant kneeling by a basket of provisions, which is inspected by a curious cat. But these realistic elements are transformed by the plunging, off-center perspective and by the brilliant, otherworldly light emanating from Jesus and the disciples, which takes the place of traditional haloes. Bands of angels swoop in from above as the supernatural and secular worlds become one. Compared with the timeless, rigorous geometry of Leonardo da Vinci's *Last Supper* (see fig. Intro–21), Tintoretto's composition—seen from the corner rather than head on—is sweeping motion and twisting, gesturing figures. The spectator is drawn irresistibly inward, caught up in the sacred drama. And the narrative emphasis has shifted from Leonardo's study of personal betrayal to Tintoretto's reference to the institution of the Eucharist. Jesus offers bread and wine to a disciple in the manner of a priest administering the sacrament.

Andrea Palladio (Andrea di Pietro, 1508–1580) was the most important architect of this period in Venice. He began his career as a stonecutter in Padua, but after moving to Vicenza (in a region ruled by Venice), he became the protegé of a Humanist scholar and amateur architect, Giangiorgio Trissino, with whom he made three trips to Rome, studying and drawing ancient Roman remains. From this background, he developed into a scholar and an architectural theorist as well as a designer of buildings. His famous and influential *I quattro libri dell'architettura* (*Four Books of Architecture*), published in 1570, provided ideal plans for country estates, using proportions derived from ancient Roman structures, and despite their theoretical bent, were often more practical than earlier treatises. Perhaps his early experience as a stonemason provided him with the knowledge and self-confidence to approach technical problems and discuss them as clearly as he did theories of ideal proportion and uses of the Classical orders. The early eighteenth century witnessed an important Palladian revival, and Palladio's *Four Books of Architecture* was a standard part of the library of educated people of the time.

Palladio's versatility is already apparent in numerous **villas** (country houses, usually on large estates) built early in his career. His famous Villa Rotonda, just outside Vicenza (fig. **13–24**), was completed in 1569. Although the term "villa" implies a working farm, Palladio designed this one as a retreat for relaxation, literally a party house. To maximize vistas of the countryside, he placed a porch and a wide staircase on each face of the building. Called the Villa Rotonda because it had been inspired by another round building, the Roman Pantheon (see fig. 6–28), it was renamed Villa Capra after its purchase in 1591 by the Capra family. The plan (fig. **13–25**) shows the geometrical clarity of Palladio's conception: a circle inscribed in a small square inside a larger square, with symmetrical rectangular rooms and identical rectangular porticoes and staircases projecting from each of its faces.

The use of a central dome on a domestic building was a daring innovation that effectively secularized the dome. The Villa Rotonda initiated what was to become a long tradition of domed country houses, particularly in England and the United States, including Monticello, Thomas Jefferson's country house in Virginia (see fig. 17–12). Jefferson was one of the first people in Colonial America to have a copy of Palladio's writings. Interestingly, Palladio himself had described the setting for the Villa Rotonda as "sopra un monticello" (on a small hill).

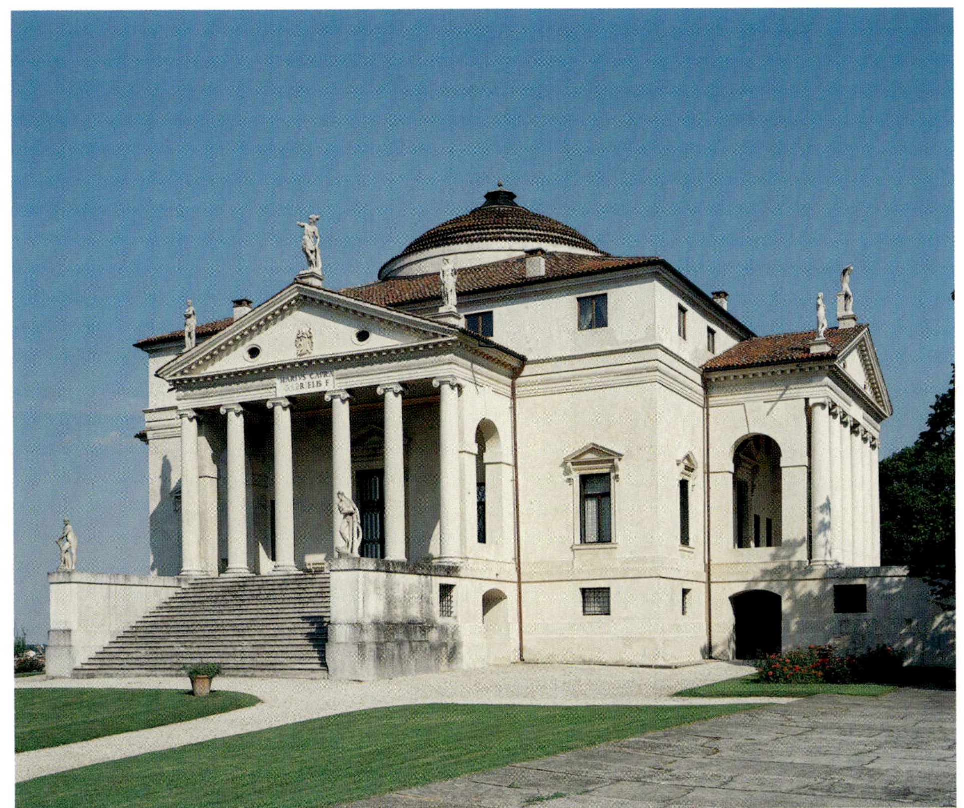

13–24 Andrea Palladio. Villa Rotonda (Villa Capra), Vicenza, Italy. Begun 1550

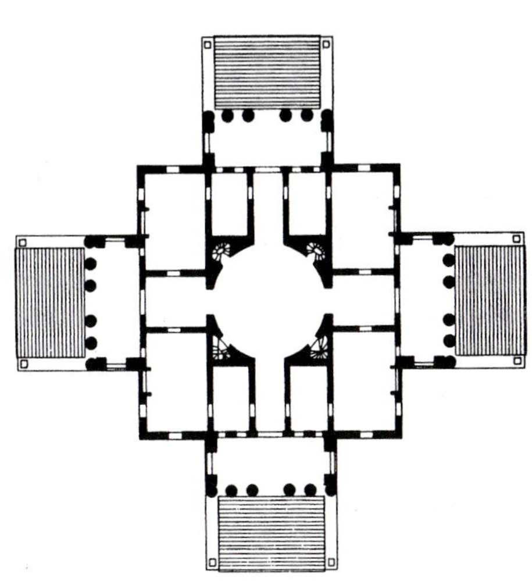

13–25 Andrea Palladio. Plan of the Villa Rotonda

Mannerism

Italy

A new style developed in Florence and Rome in the 1520s that art historians have associated with the death of Raphael and labeled "Mannerism," a word deriving from the Italian *maniera* (meaning "style"). Mannerism was an anticlassical movement in which artificiality, grace, and elegance took priority over the ordered balance and lifelike references that were hallmarks of High Renaissance art. Patrons favored esoteric subjects, displays of extraordinary technical virtuosity, and the self-conscious pursuit of beauty for its own sake. Artists fearlessly manipulated and distorted accepted formal conventions, creating contrived compositions, irrational spatial environments, and figures with elongated proportions, complicated artificial poses, enigmatic gestures, and dreamy expressions. Painters quoted from ancient and modern works of art in much the same manner as contemporary poets and authors were quoting from ancient and modern literary classics. Mannerist sculpture—often small in size and made from precious metals—also stylizes body forms and foregrounds displays of technical skill. The designs of Mannerist architecture defy uniformity and balance as well as the conventional use of Classical orders.

Mannerist painters worked in Florence in the 1520s. The frescoes and altarpiece created by Jacopo da Pontormo (1494–1557) between 1525 and 1528 for the 100-year-old Capponi Chapel in the Church of Santa Felicità in Florence bear the hallmarks of the style (fig. **13–26**). Open on two sides, Brunelleschi's chapel creates the effect of a loggia in which frescoes on the right-hand wall (in the photograph) depict the Annunciation and **tondos** (circular pictures) under the cupola represent the Four Evangelists. The altarpiece on the adjoining wall depicts the Deposition. In the *Annunciation* the Virgin accepts the angel's message but also seems moved by a vision of her future sorrow as, in the adjoining painting, she sees her son's dead body lowered from the Cross (fig. **13–27**). Here Pontormo's ambiguous composition enhances the visionary

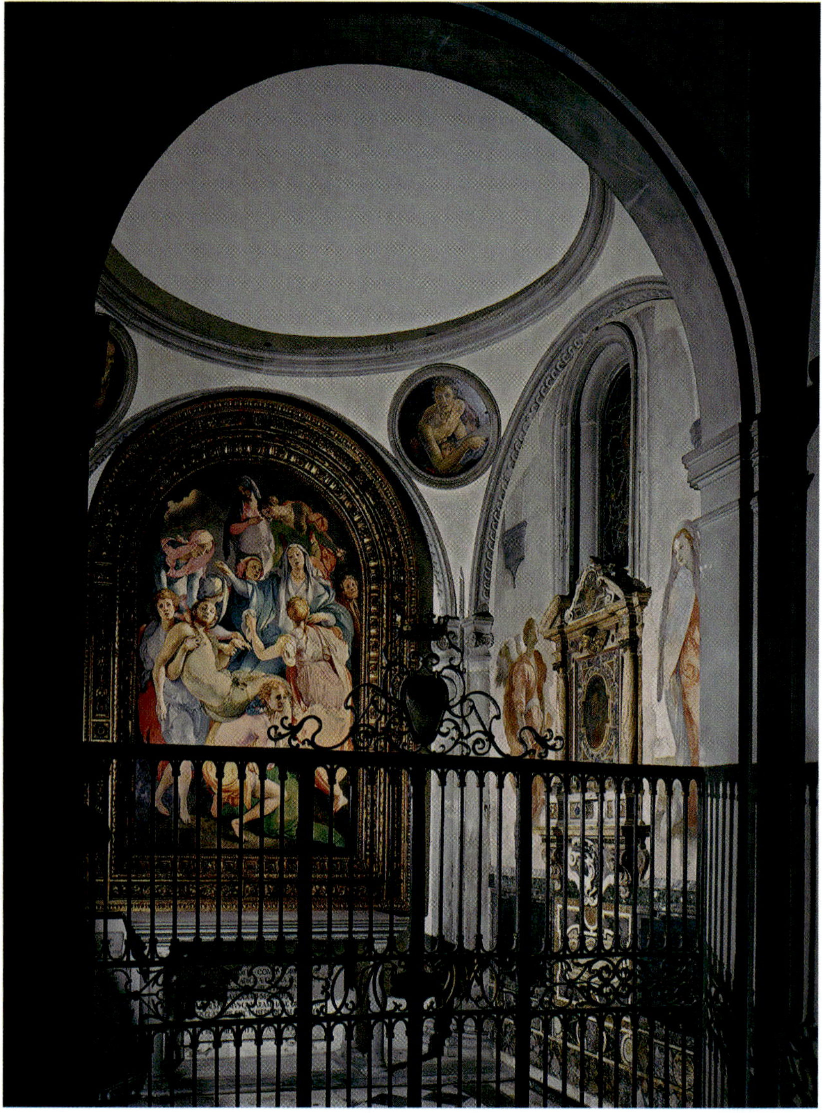

13–26 Capponi Chapel, Church of Santa Felicità, Florence. Early Renaissance chapel by Filippo Brunelleschi, 1419–1423; Pontormo, tondos with the four evangelists and mural painting of the Annunciation, on the window wall, fresco, 1525–1528; Pontormo, altarpiece, *Deposition*, oil on panel, 1525–1527

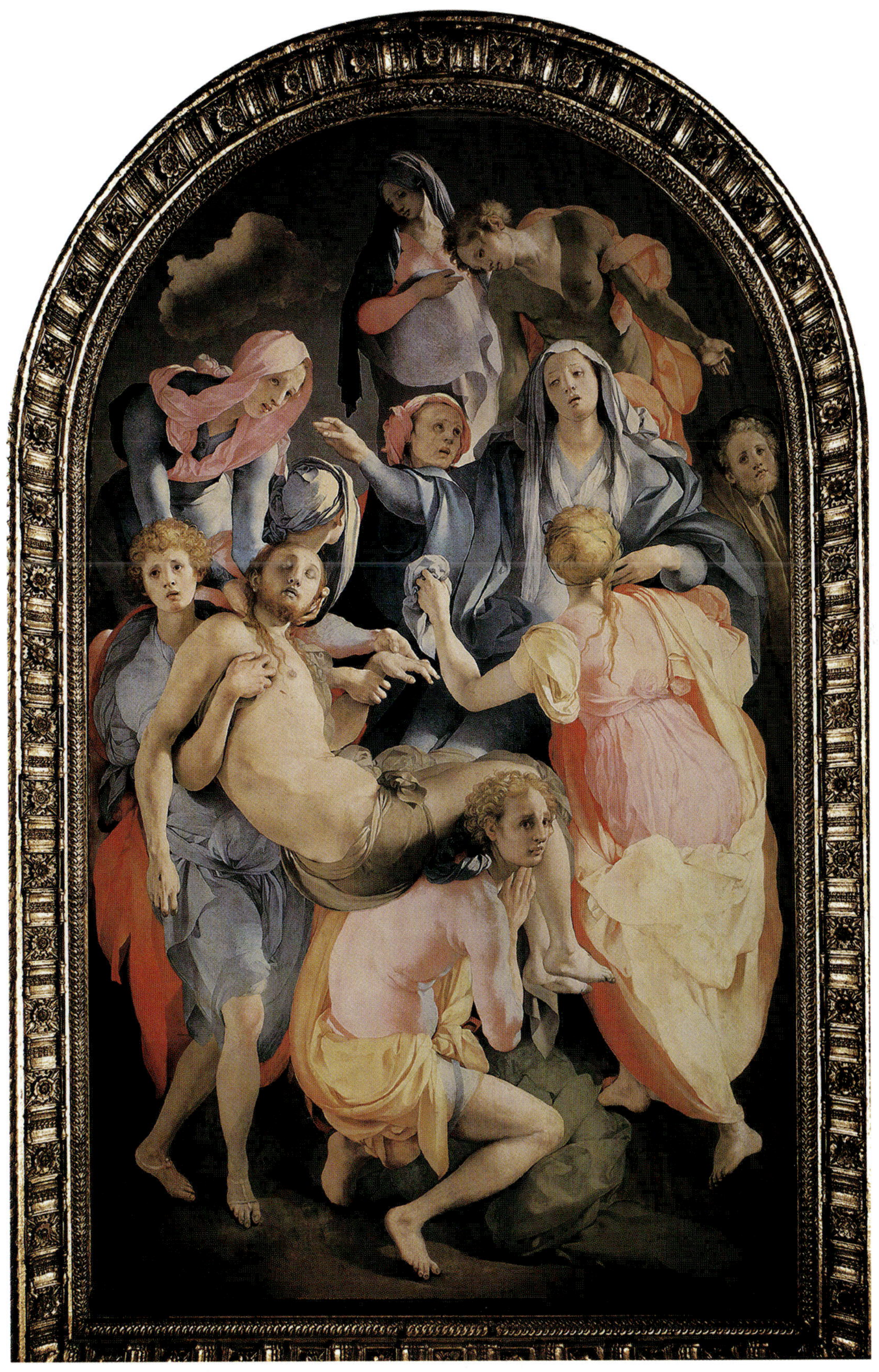

13–27 Jacopo da Pontormo. *Deposition*. Capponi Chapel, Church of Santa Felicità, Florence. 1525–1527. Oil on panel, 10' 3" × 6' 4" (3.12 × 1.93 m)

The pose of Christ's corpse in this scene would have reminded sophisticated viewers of Michelangelo's famous Vatican Pietà *(see fig. 13–8).*

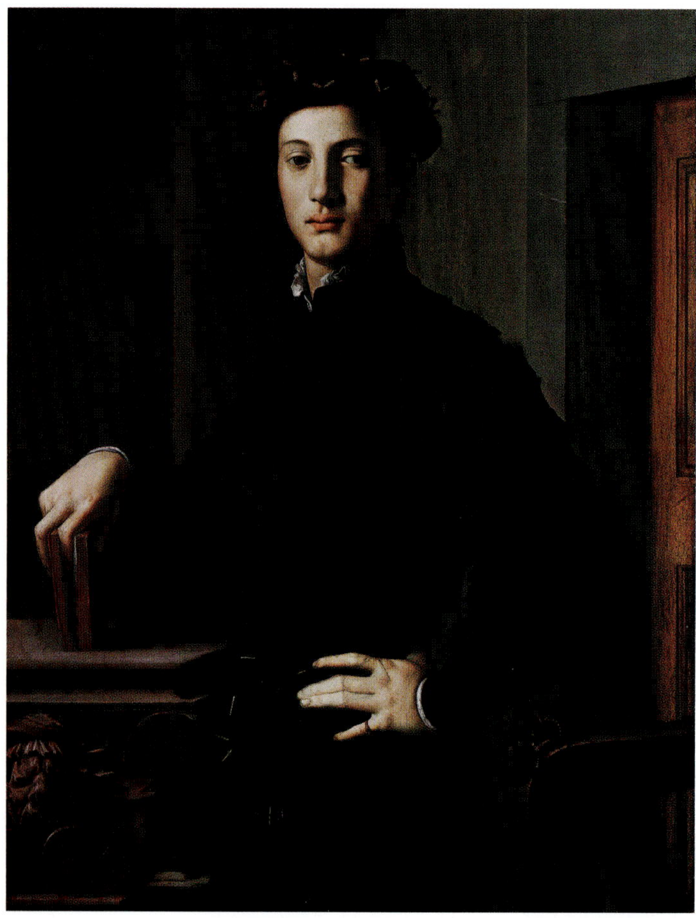

13–28 Agnolo Bronzino. *Portrait of a Young Man*. c. 1540–1545. Oil on wood panel, 37⅝" × 29½" (95.5 × 74.9 cm). The Metropolitan Museum of Art, New York
THE H. O. HAVEMAYER COLLECTION, BEQUEST OF MRS. H. O. HAVEMEYER, 1929 (29.100.16)

quality of this painting. Shadowy ground and cloudy sky give little sense of a specific location. Some figures press forward into the viewer's space, while others seem to levitate or stand precariously on tiptoe. Pontormo chose a moment just after the removal of Jesus' body from the cross, when the youths who have lowered him pause to regain their hold. Odd poses and drastic shifts in scale charge the scene emotionally, but perhaps most striking is the use of astonishing colors—baby blue and pink with accents of olive green, yellow, and scarlet—arranged in odd juxtapositions. The overall tone of the picture is set by the unstable youth crouching in the foreground, whose skintight bright pink shirt is shaded in iridescent, pale gray-green, and whose anxious expression is directed out of the painting at the viewer.

Pontormo's assistant at this time was Agnolo di Cosimo (1503–1572), whose nickname "Bronzino" means "Copper-Colored" (just as we might call someone "Red"). In 1540, Bronzino became the Medici court painter. Although he was a versatile artist who produced altarpieces, frescoes, and tapestry designs over his long career, he is best known today for his elegant Mannerist portraits. Bronzino's virtuosity in rendering costumes and settings creates a rather cold and formal effect, but the self-contained demeanor of his subjects admirably conveys their haughty personalities. A *Portrait of a Young Man* (fig. **13–28**) demonstrates Bronzino's characteristic portrayal of his subjects as intelligent, aloof, elegant, and self-assured. The youth toys with a book, suggesting his scholarly interests, but his wall-eyed stare creates a slightly unsettling, artificial effect, associating his face with the carved masks on the furniture. His costume seems more present than his personality.

Many sixteenth-century Italian artists continued to draw inspiration from the great leaders of the earlier generation, especially Raphael and Michelangelo. In 1557, the father of Sofonisba Anguissola (1528–1625), a gifted portrait painter from Cremona, consulted Michelangelo about his daughter's artistic talents. He asked Michelangelo for a drawing that she might copy and hoped the master would critique her work. Michelangelo obliged. Sofonisba was also a skilled miniaturist, an important kind of painting in the sixteenth century, when people had few means of recording the features of a lover, friend, or family member. She painted her

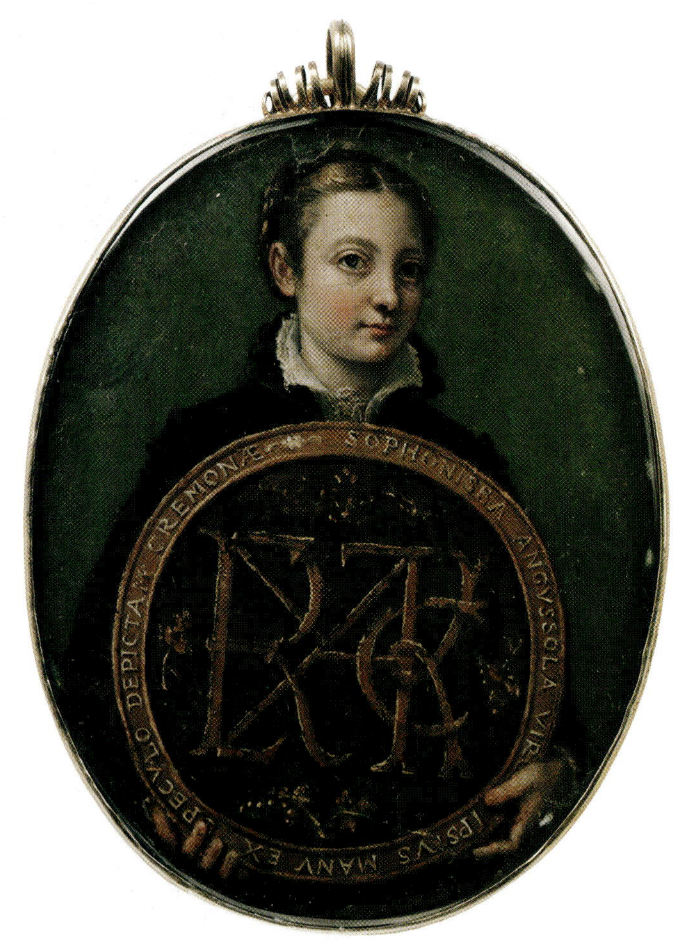

13–29 Sofonisba Anguissola. *Self-Portrait*. c. 1552. Oil on parchment on cardboard, 2½" × 3¼" (6.4 × 8.3 cm). Museum of Fine Arts, Boston
PHOTOGRAPH © 2010 MUSEUM OF FINE ARTS, BOSTON. EMMA F. MUNROE FUND (60.155)

Sofonisba was not the only talented Anguissola daughter. Her sisters Elena, Lucia, Minerva, Europa, and Anna were all painters, too. Only their brother, Asdrubale, evidently lacked the family talent, but as a member of the city council of Cremona he focused on his political career.

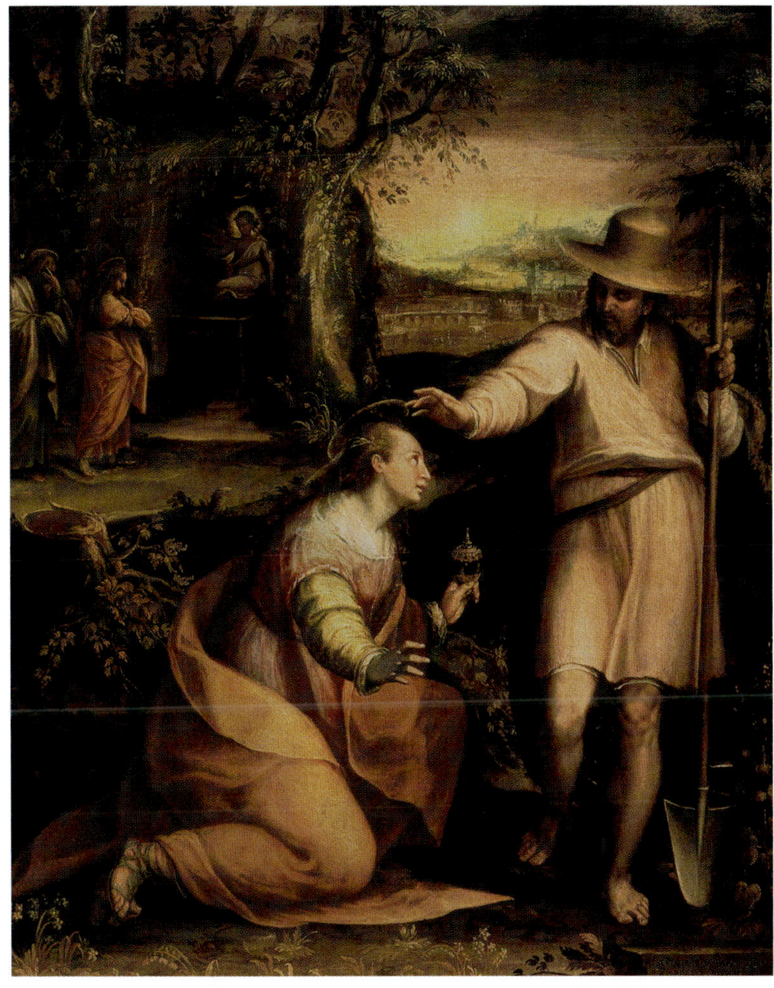

13–30 Lavinia Fontana. *Noli Me Tangere.* 1581. Oil on canvas, 47⅜" × 36⅝" (120.3 × 93 cm). Galleria degli Uffizi, Florence

own miniature portrait holding a medallion, the border of which spells out her name and hometown (fig. **13–29**). The interlaced letters at the center of the medallion are a riddle; they seem to form a monogram with the first letters of her sisters' names: Minerva, Europa, Elena—names that reflect the enthusiasm for the Classical world in Renaissance Italy.

In 1560, Sofonisba accepted the invitation of the queen of Spain to become a lady in waiting and court painter, a post she held for 20 years. Unfortunately, most of her Spanish works were lost in a seventeenth-century palace fire. After her years at court, she retired to Sicily (a Spanish territory), where she died at age 92. Anthony van Dyck met Sofonisba in Palermo in 1624, where he sketched her and claimed that she was then 96 years old. He wrote that she advised him on positioning the lights for her portrait, asking that the light not be placed too high because the strong shadows would bring out her wrinkles.

Bologna was especially hospitable to accomplished women at this time. It boasted some two dozen women painters as well as a number of women scholars who lectured at the university. Lavinia Fontana (1552–1614) learned to paint from her father, a Bolognese follower of Raphael. By the 1570s, her success was so well rewarded, that her husband, the painter Gian Paolo Zappi, gave up his own career to care for their large family and help his wife by building frames for her paintings. In 1603, she moved to Rome as an official painter to the papal court. She also soon came to the attention of the Habsburgs, who became major patrons of her work.

In 1581, while still in her 20s, Lavinia Fontana painted a *Noli Me Tangere* (fig. **13–30**), where Christ reveals himself for the first time to Mary Magdalen following his Resurrection (John 20:17). The Latin title of the painting means "Do not touch me," Christ's words when Mary moved to embrace him, explaining to her that he now existed in a new form somewhere between physical and spiritual. The biblical account claims that Mary Magdalen at first mistook Christ for a gardener, so Fontana represented him with a broad-brimmed hat and spade. In the middle ground of the painting she portrays a second version of the Resurrection, where women followers of Christ discover an angel in his empty tomb. This secondary scene's unsettling diagonal plunge into depth and temporal disconnect is a typical feature of late Mannerist painting in Italy.

France

Painters from Italy carried the Mannerist style to France, where King Francis I (ruled 1515–1547) was an important patron of the arts and an enthusiastic devotee of Italian Renaissance style. Francis even persuaded Leonardo to join him in 1516 at the French royal **château** at Amboise, where the artist spent the last two years of his life, offering advice on architectural projects and, as the king said, providing the pleasure of his conversation.

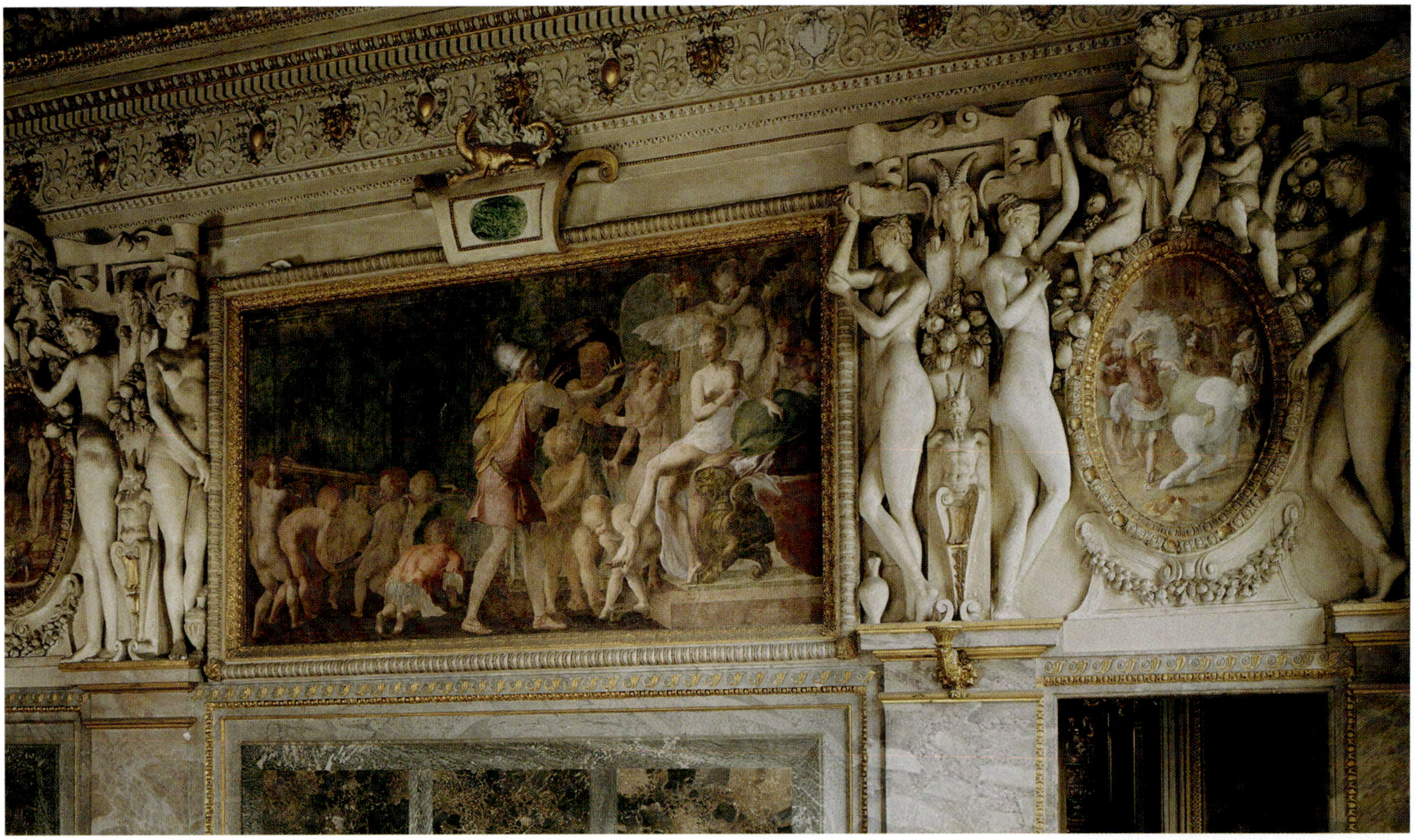

13–31 Primaticcio. Stucco and wall painting. Chamber of the Duchess of Étampes, Château of Fontainebleau. 1540s

This was originally the bedroom of Francis I's mistress, the Duchess of Étampes, but in 1749 Louis XV had the space transformed as part of a new grand staircase providing access to his apartments.

Eventually choosing a medieval hunting lodge at Fontainebleau as his primary residence, Francis began transforming it in 1526 into a grand country palace, or château. In 1530, he imported a Florentine artist, the Mannerist painter Rosso Fiorentino (1495–1540), to direct the project. After Rosso died, he was succeeded by his Italian colleague Francesco Primaticcio (1504–1570), who spent the rest of his career at Fontainebleau working on the decoration of the château from 1532 until his death. During that time, he also commissioned and imported a large number of copies and casts made from original Roman sculpture, including the *Apollo Belvedere* in the Vatican gardens, the newly discovered *Laocoön* (see fig. Intro–27), and even the relief decoration on the Column of Trajan. These works provided an invaluable visual resource for the northern artists employed on the project.

Among Primaticcio's first projects at Fontainebleau was the redecoration, in the 1540s, of the chambers of the king's official mistress, Anne, Duchess of Étampes (fig. **13–31**). The artist combined the arts of woodworking, stucco relief, and fresco painting in his

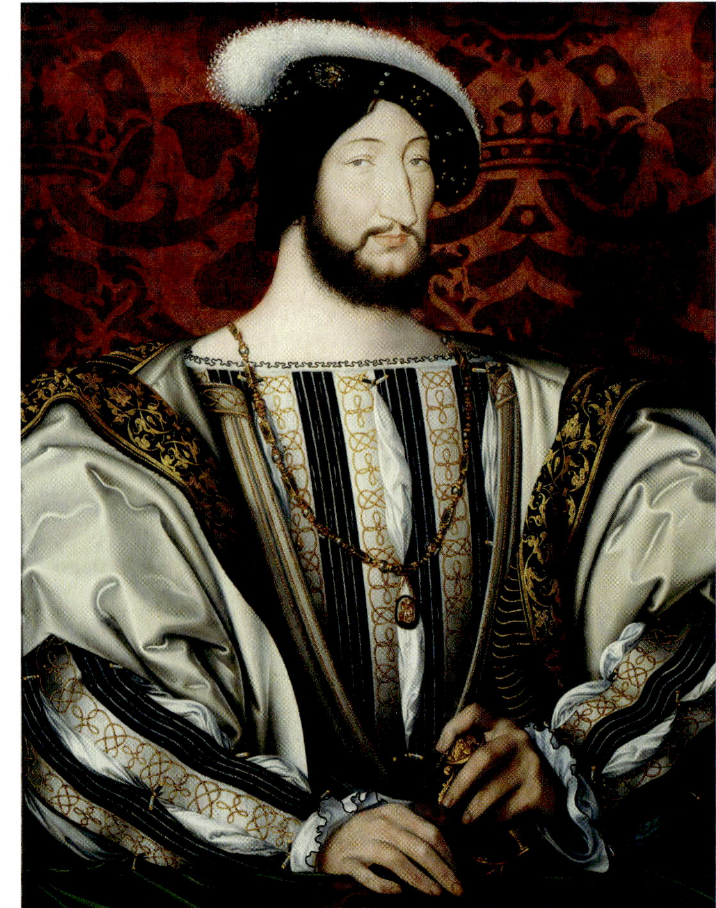

13–32 Jean Clouet. Francis I. 1525–1530. Oil and tempera on wood panel, 37¾" × 29⅛" (95.9 × 74 cm). Musée du Louvre, Paris

complex but lighthearted and graceful interior design. The lithe figures of his stucco nymphs recall Pontormo's painting style (see fig. 13–27), with their elongated bodies and small heads. Their spiraling postures and teasing bits of clinging drapery charge the work with a playfully eroticism. Garlands, mythological figures, and Roman architectural ornament almost overwhelm the walls with lavish visual enrichment. This first School of Fontainebleau established an Italianate tradition of Mannerism in painting and interior design that spread to other centers in France and the Netherlands.

But not all the artists working at the court of Francis I were Italian. The Flemish artist Jean Clouet (c. 1485–c. 1540), working in France as early as 1509, found great favor as the royal portrait painter during the 1520s. In his official portrait of the king (fig. **13–32**), Clouet created a flattering but lifelike image by modulating Francis's distinctive features with subtle shading and highlighting the nervous activity of his fingers. At the same time he created an image of pure power. Elaborate, puffy sleeves broadened the king's shoulders to fill the entire width of the panel, much as Renaissance parade armor turned scrawny men into giants. The detailed rendering of the delicately worked costume of silk, satin, velvet, jewels, and gold embroidery could be painted separately from the portrait itself. Royal clothing was often loaned to the artist or modeled by a servant to spare the "sitter" the boredom of posing. In creating such official portraits, the artist sketched the subject, then painted a prototype that, upon approval, was the model for numerous replicas made for diplomatic and family purposes.

German Art

German sculptors of the sixteenth century worked in every medium, and they produced some of their finest and most original work in the wood of the fine-grained linden (limewood) tree, which grew abundantly in central and southern Germany. Tilman Riemenschneider (1460–1531) directed the largest sculpture workshop in Würzburg; he was also politically active in the city's government. Riemenschneider's work attracted patrons from other cities, and in 1501 he signed a contract for one of his major creations, the *Altarpiece of the Holy Blood*, for the Church of Saint James in Rothenburg, which housed an important relic: a drop of what was believed to be Jesus' blood. The altarpiece was to be nearly 30 feet high. Erhart Harschner, a specialist in carving shrines, began work on the frame in 1499, and Riemenschneider created the figures. The relative value that the patrons placed on the contributions can be judged from the fact that Harschner received 50 florins and Riemenschneider only a little more—60 florins.

The main panel of the altarpiece represents the Last Supper (fig. **13–33**). Like his Italian contemporary Leonardo (see fig. 13–2), Riemenschneider depicted the moment of Jesus' revelation that one of his disciples would betray him. Unlike Leonardo, however, Riemenschneider composed his group with Jesus off-center at the left and the disciples crowded around him. Judas, at center stage, holds a money bag as a symbol of the 30 pieces of silver he received for his treachery. Jesus extends a morsel of food to Judas, signifying that he is the one destined to set in motion the events that will lead

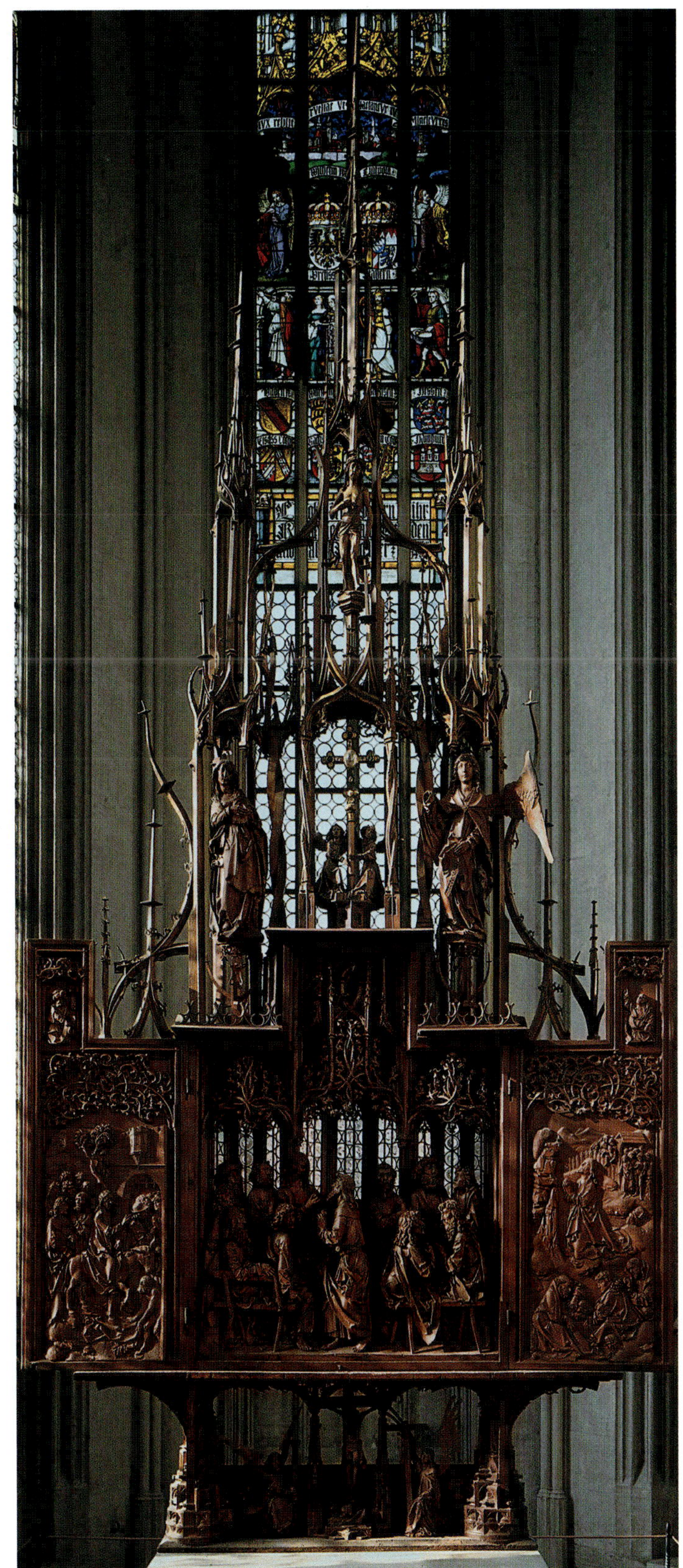

13–33 Tilman Riemenschneider. *Altarpiece of the Holy Blood*: *Last Supper* (center); *Entry into Jerusalem* (left wing); *Agony in the Garden* (right wing); *Annunciation* (upper figures); *The Resurrected Christ* (top-most figure). 1499–1505. Limewood and glass, height of tallest figure 39" (99.1 cm), height of altar 29' 6" (9 m).Sankt Jakobskirche, Rothenburg ob der Tauber, Germany

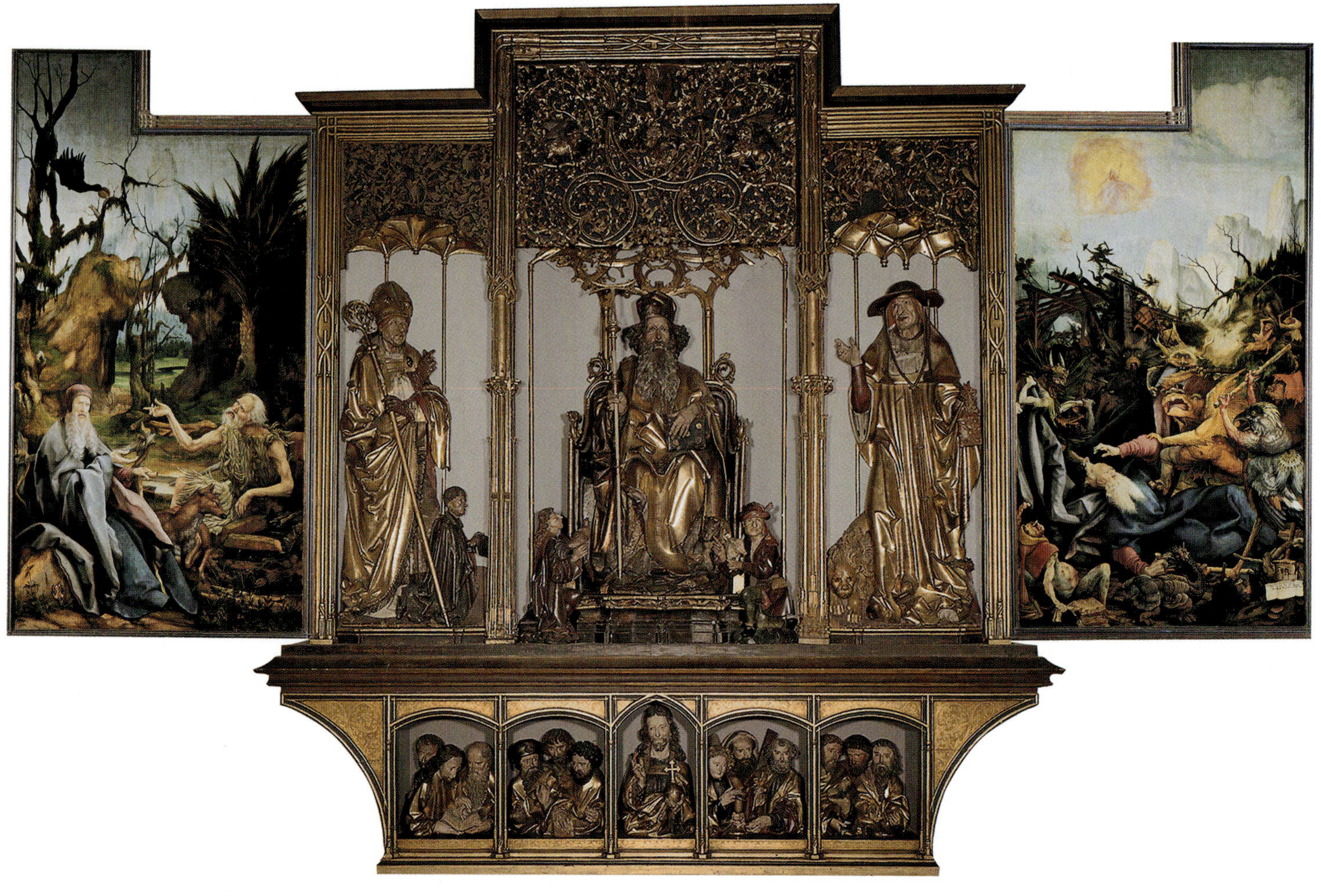

13–34 Nikolaus Hagenauer and Matthias Grünewald. ***Isenheim Altarpiece***, open (above) and closed (right), from the Community of Saint Anthony, Isenheim, France. Sculpture c. 1500, painting c. 1510–1515. Painted and gilt limewood, oil on panel; center painted panels 9' 9" × 10' 9" (2.97 × 3.28 m); each wing 8' 2" × 3' ½" (2.49 × 0.93 m); predella 2' 5½" × 11' 2" (0.75 × 3.4 m). Musée d'Unterlinden, Colmar, France

to Jesus' death (John 13:21–30). One apostle (John) leans to point down toward the altar where the relic of the Holy Blood would have been displayed.

Rather than creating individual portraits, Riemenschneider repeated a limited number of types. His figures have large heads, prominent features, and elaborate hair treatments that feature thick wavy locks and deeply drilled curls. The muscles, tendons, and raised veins of hands and feet are especially lifelike, as are the pronounced cheekbones, sagging jowls, and baggy eyes. Voluminous draperies cover the slim figures; the deep folds and active patterning create strong highlights and dark shadows that unify the figural composition with the intricate carving of the framework. Although earlier sculpture had been painted and gilded, Riemenschneider introduced the use of a natural wood finish with clear varnish. The scene is set in a stage-like space with real windows in the back wall glazed with bull's-eye glass. Natural lighting bathes the sculpture with constantly changing effects, according to the time of day and the weather.

In 1525, Riemenschneider supported the peasants, who, because of economic and religious oppression, rose up against their feudal overlords in the Peasants' War, an early manifestation of the Protestant movement. His involvement led to his being fined and imprisoned. Riemenschneider survived, but created no more sculpture and died just six years later.

Painting and Prints

In painting, two very different German artists, Matthias Gothardt, known as Matthias Grünewald (c. 1470/75–1528), and Albrecht Dürer (1471–1528), dominated the early sixteenth century. Grünewald continued a long indigenous tradition of mysticism and emotionalism, while Dürer's intense observation of the natural world represented new interests in empirical study and linear perspective and a new ideal for the human figure.

Grünewald is best known today for the wings he painted between 1510 and 1515 to protect an altarpiece of carved images of saints created around 1500 by Nikolaus Hagenauer for the

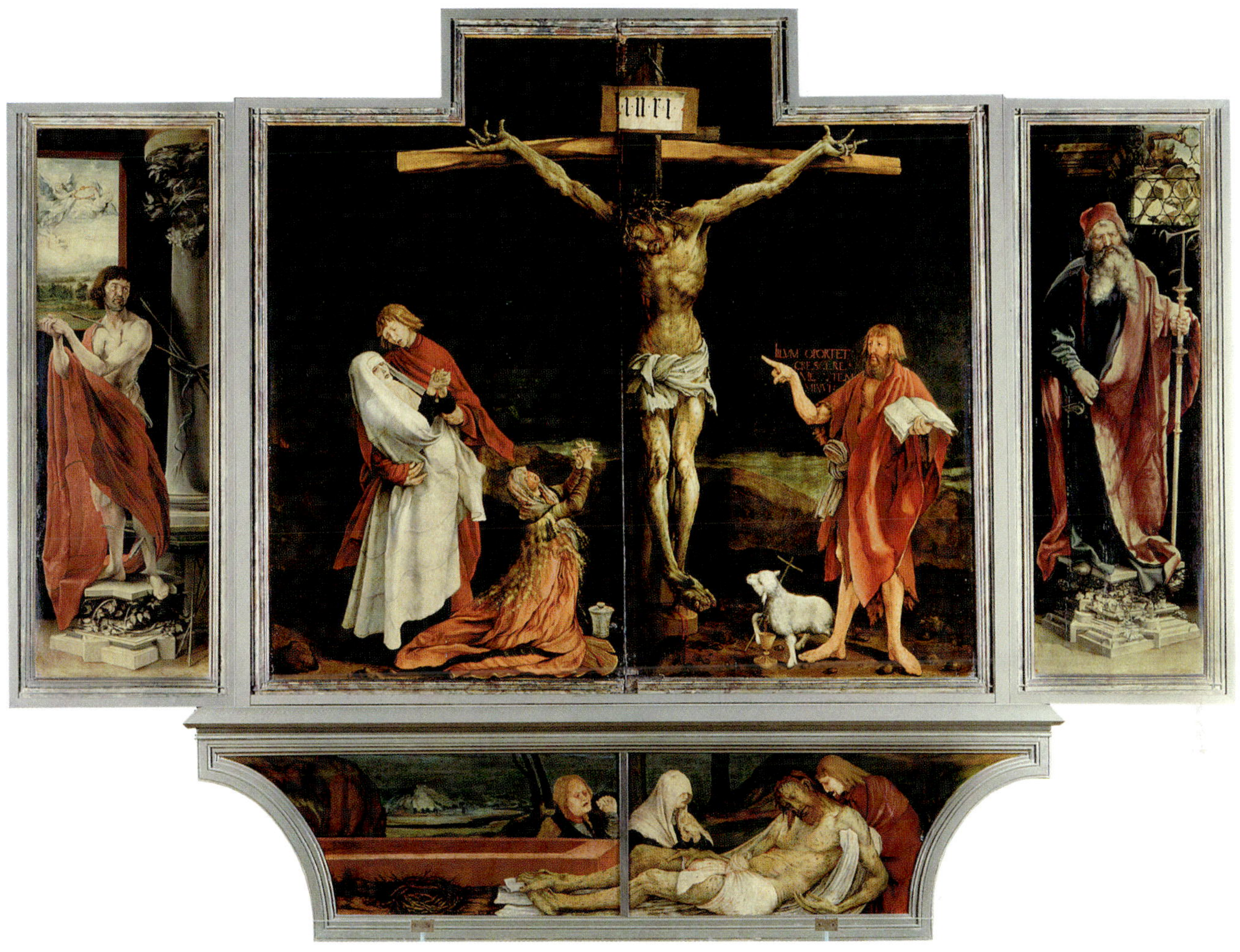

Community of Saint Anthony in Isenheim, whose hospital specialized in diseases of the skin, including plague and leprosy. The completed *Isenheim Altarpiece* (fig. **13–34**) was thought to have healing properties itself, and viewing it was part of the treatment given to patients who entered the hospital. Made with both fixed and movable wings, the altarpiece was displayed in different configurations depending upon the Church calendar. On normal weekdays, when it was closed (fig. 13–34, lower image), viewers saw a shocking portrayal of the Crucifixion in a darkened landscape, flanked by life-size figures of Saints Sebastian and Anthony Abbot standing like statues on pedestals. Grünewald represented the tortured body of Jesus in horrific detail, covered with gashes and pierced by the thorns used to crown his head. Not only do the figure's ashen color, open mouth, and blue lips indicate that he is dead, but he seems already to be decaying, an effect enhanced by the palette of putrescent greens, yellows, and purplish red. A ghost-like Virgin Mary has collapsed in the arms of an emaciated John the Evangelist, and Mary Magdalen has fallen in anguish to her knees. Her clasped hands with exaggerated fingers echo Jesus' claw-like fingers, cramped in rigor mortis, as well as the emphatically pointing finger of John the Baptist to the right. In the predella, or supporting platform, below, Jesus' bereaved mother and friends prepare his body for burial, a scene that must have been familiar in the hospital.

The altarpiece was completely opened to reveal Hagenauer's sculpture (fig. 13–34, left image) only for the special festivals of Saint Anthony. Grünewald's paintings on the wings as seen in this configuration, show at right Saint Anthony attacked by horrible demons, perhaps inspired by the horrors of the diseased patients. On the left wing is the meeting of Saint Anthony with the hermit Saint Paul in a wilderness landscape full of the medicinal plants used in the hospital's therapy. Grünewald painted the face of Paul with his own self-portrait, while Anthony is a portrait of the donor and administrator of the hospital, the Italian Guido Guersi, whose coat of arms Grünewald painted on the rock next to him.

Like Riemenschneider, Grünewald's involvement with the Peasants' War damaged his artistic career. The artist spent his

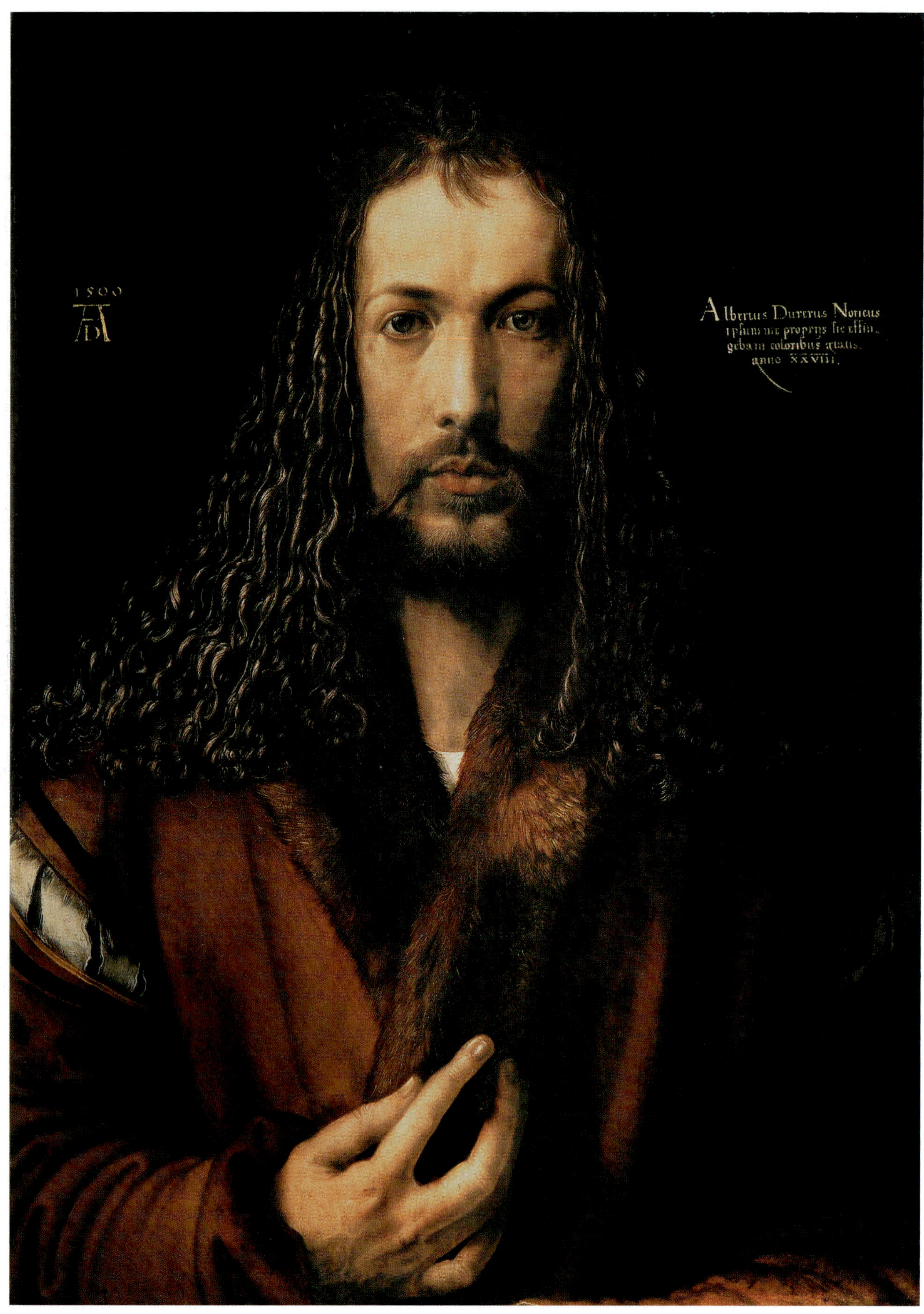
1500
Albertus Durerus Noricus
ipsum me propriis sic effin-
gebam coloribus aetatis
anno XXVIII.

13–35 Albrecht Dürer. ***Self-Portrait.*** 1500. Oil on wood panel, 26¼" × 19¼" (66.3 × 49 cm). Alte Pinakothek, Munich

last years in Halle, whose ruler was the chief protector of Martin Luther and a longtime patron of Grünewald's contemporary, Albrecht Dürer.

Studious, analytical, meticulous, and as self-confident as Michelangelo, Albrecht Dürer was the foremost artist of the German Renaissance. He was the son of a Nuremberg goldsmith and served apprenticeships in painting, stained-glass design, and printmaking. He became familiar with the latest developments in Italian Renaissance art during two trips to the Italian peninsula, in 1494–1495 and 1505–1506. He seems to have resolved to reform German art by publishing theoretical writings and manuals that discussed Renaissance problems of perspective, ideal human proportions, and the techniques of painting.

During Dürer's first trip to Italy he absorbed both the idealism associated with Italian art and the concept of the artist as an independent creative genius. In his self-portrait of 1500 (fig. **13–35**), he represents himself as an idealized, even Christ-like, figure in a severely frontal pose, meeting the viewer's eyes like an icon. His rich, fur-lined robes and flowing locks of curly hair create a monumental equilateral triangle, a timeless symbol of unity.

Dürer's early interest in Italian art and his theoretical investigations continued in his 1504 engraving of *Adam and Eve* (fig. **13–36**). These figures represent his first documented use of an ideal of human proportions based on Roman copies of Greek statues, probably known to him through prints or small sculpture in the antique manner. But behind his idealized figures, he recorded the flora and fauna of their setting with typically northern descriptive detail. Embedded in the landscape are symbols of the four humors, referencing the belief that after Adam and Eve disobeyed God, they and their descendants became vulnerable to imbalances in body fluids that altered human temperament. An excess of black bile from the liver produced melancholy, despair, and greed; yellow bile caused anger, pride, and impatience; phlegm in the lungs resulted in lethargy, disinterest, and a lack of emotion; and an excess of blood made a person unusually optimistic but also compulsively interested in the pleasures of the flesh. These four human temperaments are symbolized here by the melancholy elk, the choleric cat, the phlegmatic ox, and the sensual rabbit. The scurrying mouse is an emblem of Satan, and the parrot may symbolize false wisdom, since it can only repeat mindlessly what it hears. Dürer's pride in his engraving can be seen in the prominence of his signature—a placard bearing his full name and date hanging on a branch next to Adam.

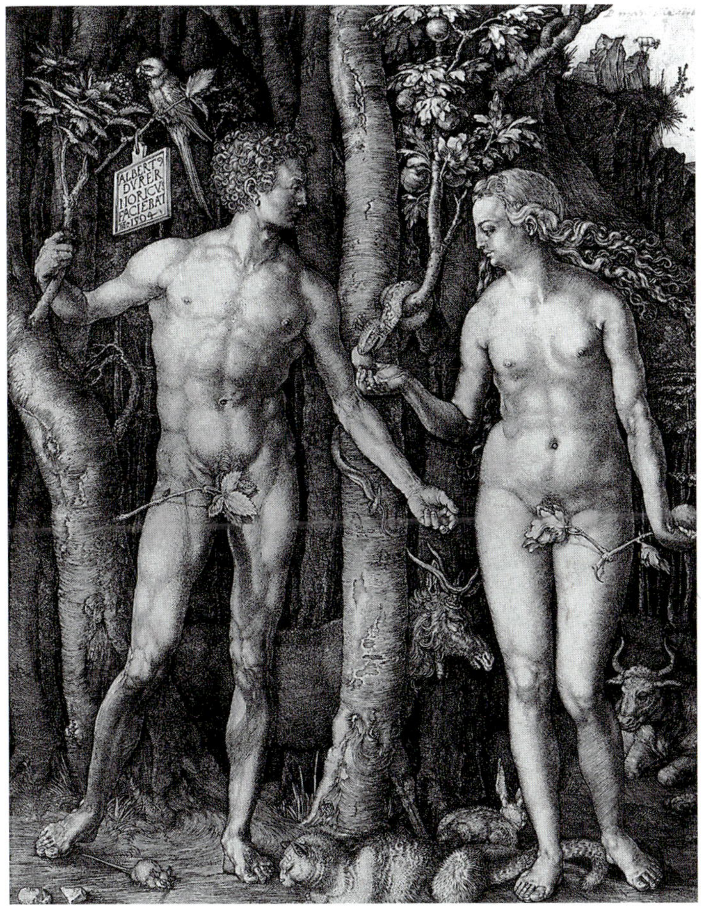

13–36 Albrecht Dürer. ***Adam and Eve.*** 1504. Engraving, 9⅞" × 7⅝" (25.1 × 19.4 cm). Philadelphia Museum of Art
PURCHASED: LISA NORA ELKINS FUND (1951-96-4)

The Reformation and the Arts

Against a backdrop of broad dissatisfaction with financial abuses and lavish lifestyles among the clergy, religious reformers began to challenge specific practices and beliefs of the Catholic Church, especially the sale of indulgences (guarantees of relief from the punishment required after death for forgiven sins). From their protests, the reformers came to be called Protestants, and their insistence on church reform gave rise to a movement called the Reformation. Two of the most important reformers in the early sixteenth century were themselves Catholic priests and trained theologians: Desiderius Erasmus of Rotterdam (1466?–1536), a Dutchman; and Martin Luther (1483–1546), a German. The two men questioned official Church teachings and the pope's supremacy, and they emphasized individual faith and saw ultimate religious authority in the Bible. Failing in their attempt to reform the practices of the Catholic Church, Protestants broke away from Rome. This, in turn, prompted Rome to launch a Counter-Reformation. At the Council of Trent (1545–1563), the Roman Catholic hierarchy formulated a program that included the Inquisition, with its special tribunals to root out heresy.

The effects of the Reformation on art were also significant and at times destructive. Some Protestants considered religious imagery to be idolatrous and in some areas actually destroyed religious art and whitewashed church interiors in fits of iconoclasm. As a result, many artists turned to portraiture and other secular subjects to make their livings. In Catholic regions, people still venerated traditional images of Christ and the saints, but officials from the Church scrutinized works of art for heretical or profane subject matter.

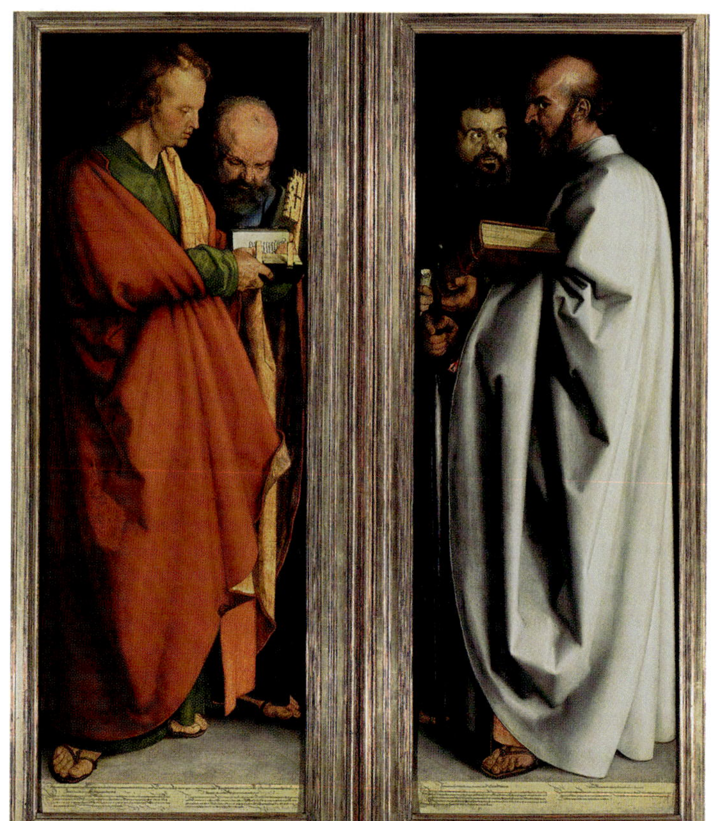

13–37 Albrecht Dürer. ***Four Apostles***. 1526. Oil on wood panel, each panel 7' 1/2" × 2' 6" (2.15 × 0.76 m). Alte Pinakothek, Munich

A long inscription on the frame warns the viewer not to be led astray by "false prophets" but to heed the words of the New Testament as recorded by these "four excellent men." Below each figure are excerpts from their letters and from the Gospel of Mark warning against those who do not understand the true word of God. In the inscriptions, Dürer used Luther's German translation of the New Testament. The paintings were surely meant to demonstrate that a Protestant art was possible.

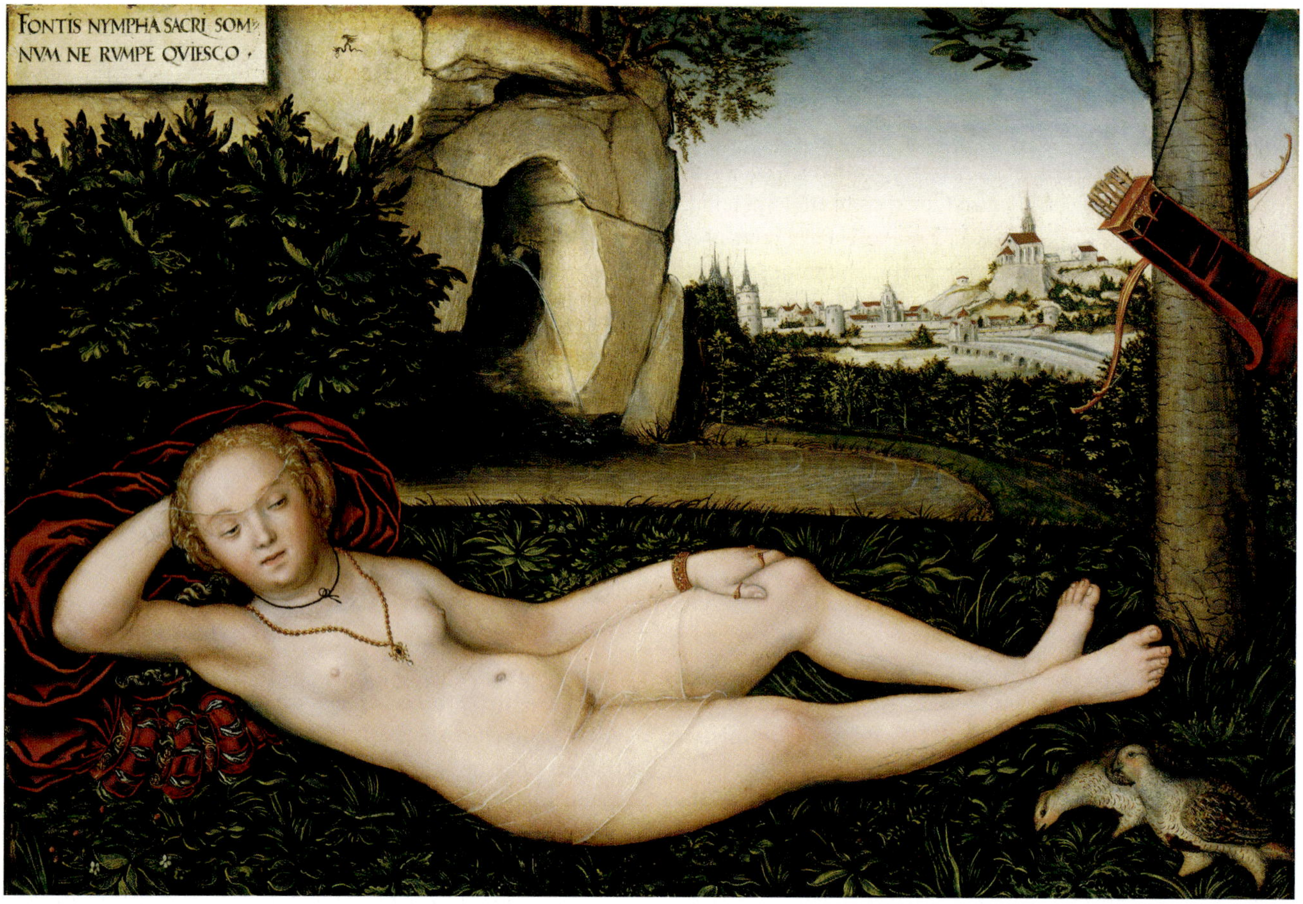

13–38 Lucas Cranach the Elder. ***Nymph of the Spring***. c. 1537. Oil on panel, 19" × 28 1/2" (48.5 × 72.9 cm). National Gallery of Art, Washington, D.C.

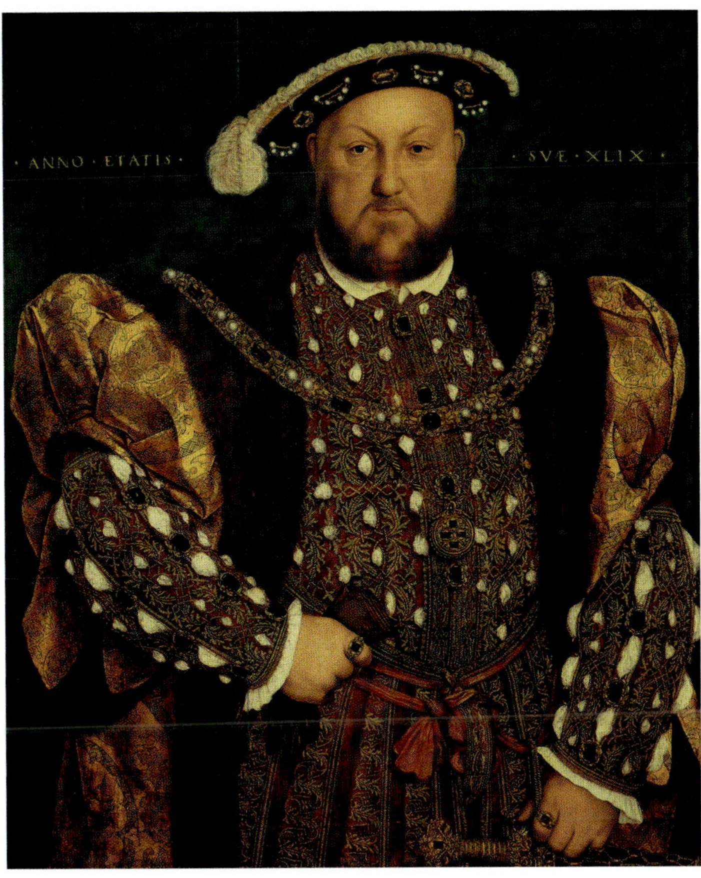

13–39 Hans Holbein the Younger. ***Henry VIII***. 1540. Oil on wood panel, 32½" × 29½" (82.6 × 75 cm). Galleria Nazionale d'Arte Antica, Rome

Martin Luther, himself, never supported the destruction of religious art, and Dürer, who admired Luther's writings, may have painted a pair of large panels commonly referred to as the *Four Apostles* (fig. **13–37**) in order to demonstrate that Protestant imagery was possible. The paintings depict John, Peter, Paul, and Mark. On the left panel, the elderly Saint Peter, the first pope, seems to shrink behind the young Saint John, Luther's favorite evangelist. On the right panel, the Evangelist Mark is nearly hidden behind Saint Paul, whose teachings and epistles were greatly admired by the Protestants. Dürer presented the panels, painted in 1526, to the city of Nuremberg, which had already adopted Lutheranism (then almost synonymous with Protestantism) as its official religion. Dürer wrote, "For a Christian would no more be led to superstition by a picture or effigy than an honest man to commit murder because he carries a weapon by his side. He must indeed be an unthinking man who would worship picture, wood, or stone. A picture therefore brings more good than harm, when it is honourably, artistically, and well made" (cited in Snyder, 2nd ed., page 333).

One of Dürer's friends, and Martin Luther's favorite painter, Lucas Cranach the Elder (1472–1553) was appointed court painter to Frederick the Wise of Saxony. There he met Italian artists who evidently inspired him to take on the subject of the female nude. Just how far the German artist's style and conception of figure and her environment differ from Italian Renaissance norms is easily seen in his *Nymph of the Spring* (fig. **13–38**), especially when compared with Titian's *Venus of Urbino* (see fig. 13–21). Cranach was inspired by a fifteenth-century inscription on a fountain beside the Danube, cited in the upper left corner of the painting: "I am the nymph of the sacred font. Do not interrupt my sleep for I am at peace." Cranach records the Danube landscape with Northern attention to detail and turns his nymph into a highly provocative young woman, who glances slyly out at the viewer through half-closed eyes. She has cast aside a fashionable red velvet gown, but still wears her jewelry, which together with her transparent veil enhances rather than conceals her nudity. Unlike other artists working for Protestant patrons, many of whom looked on earthly beauty as a sinful vanity, Cranach seems delighted by earthly things: the lush foliage that provides the nymph's couch, the pair of partridges (symbols of Venus and married love), and Cupid's bow and quiver of arrows hanging on the tree. Could this nymph be a living beauty in the Wittenburg court? She is surely not an idealized embodiment of a classical Venus.

In the context of the volatile German religious and political climate, some Roman Catholic artists left their homes to seek patronage abroad. Hans Holbein the Younger (1497–1543), born in Augsburg, spent much of his early career in Basel, Switzerland, but worked in Antwerp and London from 1526 to 1528 to escape religious turmoil. Although he had officially become a Protestant by 1532, harassment from reformers sent him once again to England, where he served as court painter to the Tudor monarch Henry VIII (ruled 1509–1547).

One of Holbein's official portraits of Henry (fig. **13–39**), painted about 1540, recalls Clouet's portrait of Francis I (see fig. 13–32)

for good reason. Henry was so fascinated by the elegant French king that he attempted to emulate and even surpass him in appearance. After Francis started a new trend by growing a beard, Henry grew a similar one, as seen in this portrait. Holbein used the English king's great size—he was well over 6 feet tall and had a 54-inch waist in his maturity—to advantage for this official image, enhancing Henry's majestic figure with the latest style of dress. He is outfitted here for his wedding to his fourth wife, Anne of Cleves, on April 5, 1540, in a short puffed-sleeved cloak of heavy brocade trimmed in dark fur, a narrow, stiff white collar fastened at the front, and a doublet slit to expose his silk shirt and encrusted with gemstones and gold braid. It is one of the most imposing images of power in the history of art.

Netherlandish and Spanish Art

Politically, the Netherlands (a region that at the time included Holland and Belgium) and Spain were united under the Habsburg Empire during the sixteenth century. The art made by Netherlandish and Spanish artists, however, was far from unified. Some artists continued the styles of the late fifteenth century; others looked back to even earlier Flemish painters for models. Some became Mannerists in the Italian mode. A few, such as the Netherlandish artist Hieronymus Bosch, were so individualistic that they seem unique.

Hieronymus Bosch (c. 1450–1516) created a world of fantastic imagery in paintings such as the *Garden of Earthly Delights* (fig.

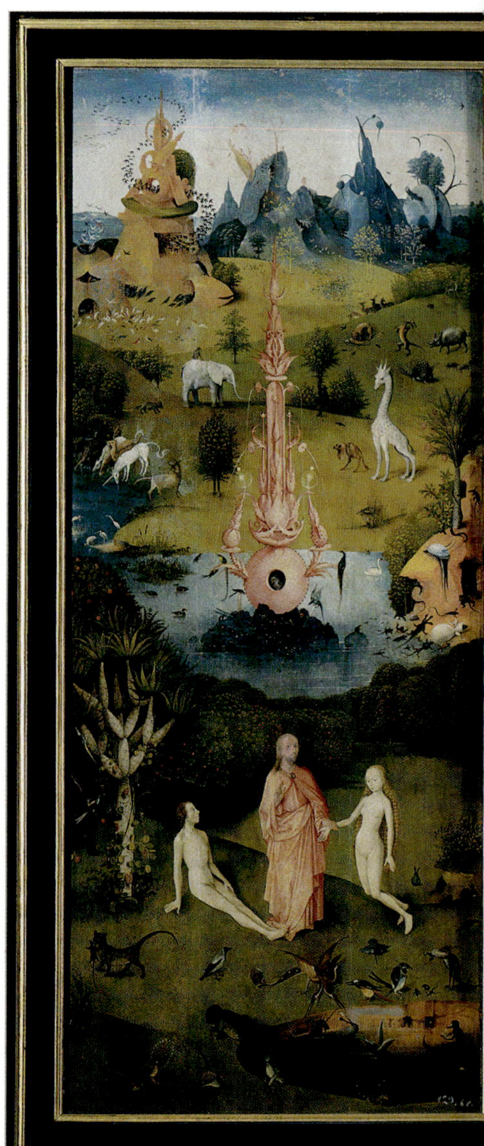

13–40 Hieronymus Bosch. ***Garden of Earthly Delights*** (center); *Creation* (left wing); *The Damned* (right wing). c. 1505–1515. Oil on wood panel, center panel 7' 2½" × 6' 4¾" (2.2 × 1.95 m), each wing 7' 2½" × 3'2" (2.2 × 0.97 m). Museo Nacional del Prado, Madrid

This work was commissioned by an aristocrat for his Brussels townhouse, and the artist's choice of a triptych format, which suggests an altarpiece, may have been an understated irony. As a secular work, the Garden of Earthly Delights *may well have inspired lively discussion and even ribald comment, much as it does today in its museum setting. Despite—or perhaps because of—its bizarre subject matter, the triptych was copied in 1566 in tapestry versions, one (now in El Escorial, Madrid) for a cardinal and another for Francis I. At least one painted copy was made as well. Bosch's original triptych was sold at the onset of the Netherlands' revolt and sent in 1568 to Spain, where it entered the collection of Philip II.*

13–40). There are many interpretations of the triptych. The subject seems to be based on the Christian belief in humanity's natural state of sinfulness. The imagery begins with the Creation of the World (on the wing exteriors, not shown), continues with the Creation of Adam and Eve on the left wing, and ends with the Last Judgment on the right. The fact that only the damned and not the saved are shown in the Judgment scene seems to warn that damnation is the natural outcome of a life lived in ignorance and folly, that humans ensure their own damnation through the self-centered pursuit of the pleasures of the flesh. The central panel illustrates just such activity, where seemingly harmless diversions such as games, romance, and music turn into sins such as lust, gluttony, and sloth. Luscious fruits—strawberries, cherries, grapes, and pomegranates—appear everywhere in the *Garden*, serving as food, as shelter, and in one instance even as a boat. Herbalists believed these fruits enhanced sexual desire and fertility. In the painting the fruits also suggest that life is as fleeting and insubstantial as the taste of a strawberry.

The works of Bosch were so popular that, nearly a half century after his death, the painter Pieter Bruegel the Elder (c. 1525–1569) began his career by imitating them. Fortunately, Bruegel's talents went far beyond those of a copyist, and he soon developed his own style and themes. Working first in Antwerp and then in Brussels, he produced artfully composed works that reflected contemporary social, political, and religious conditions. Between 1551 and 1554, Bruegel traveled through the Alps to Rome, Naples, and all the way

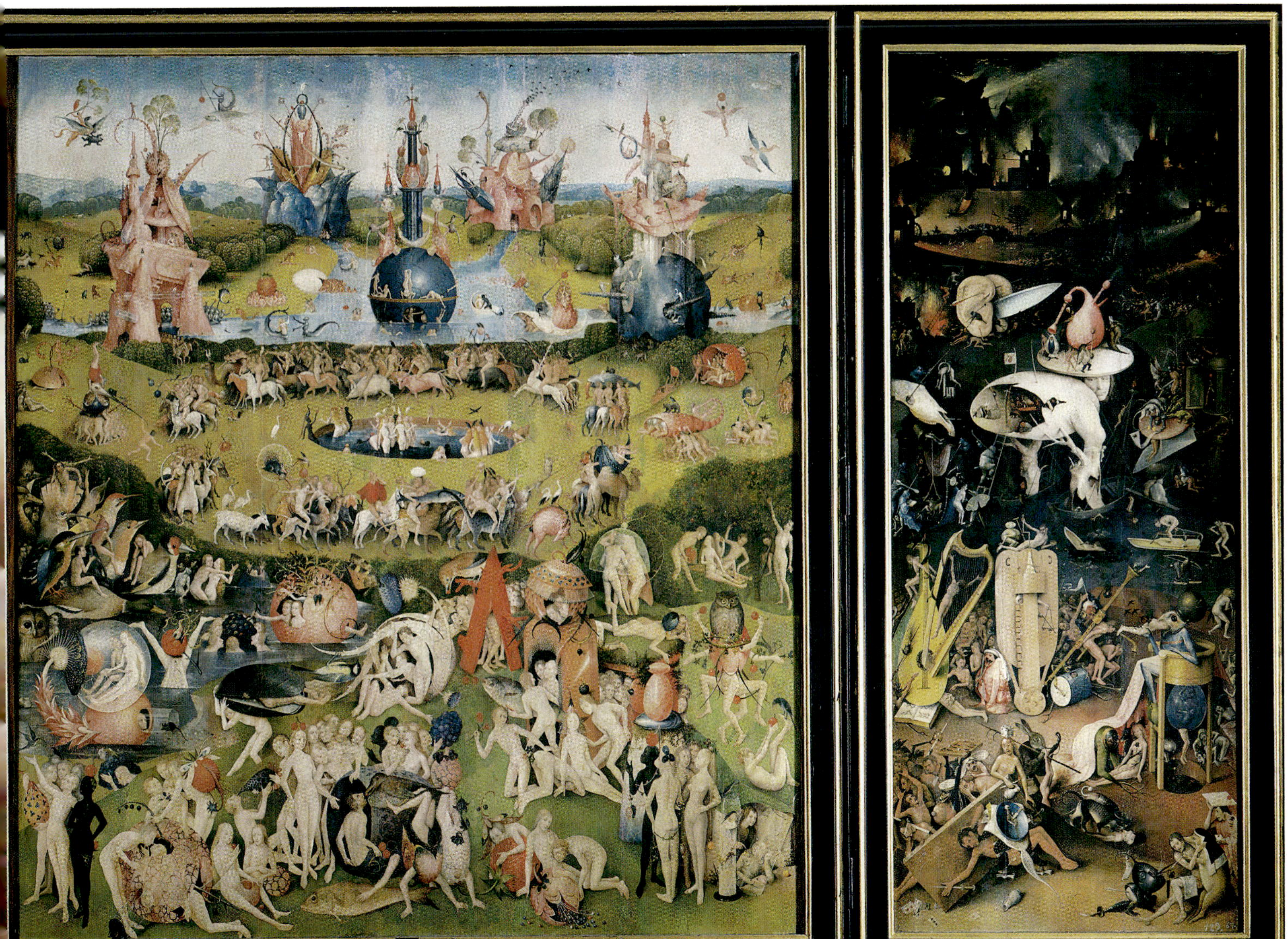

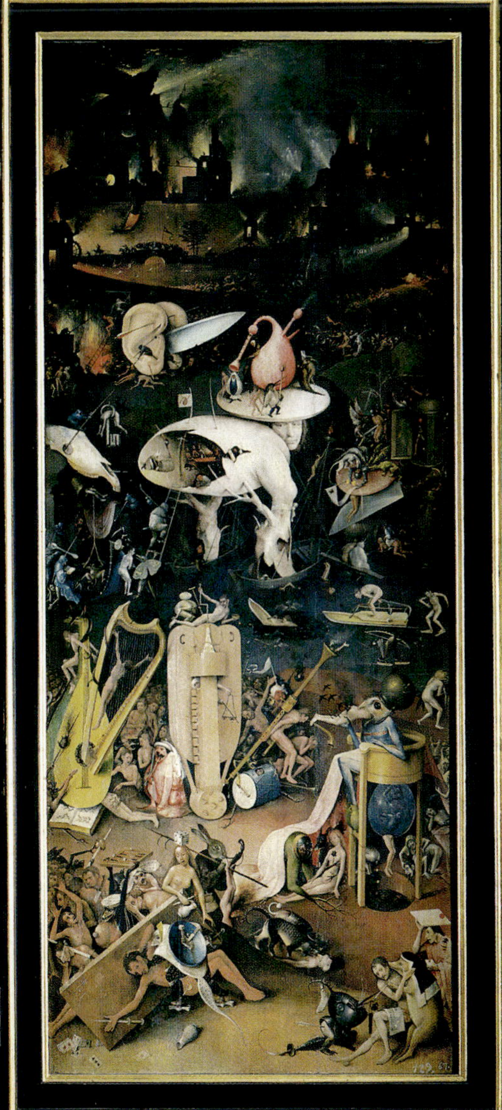

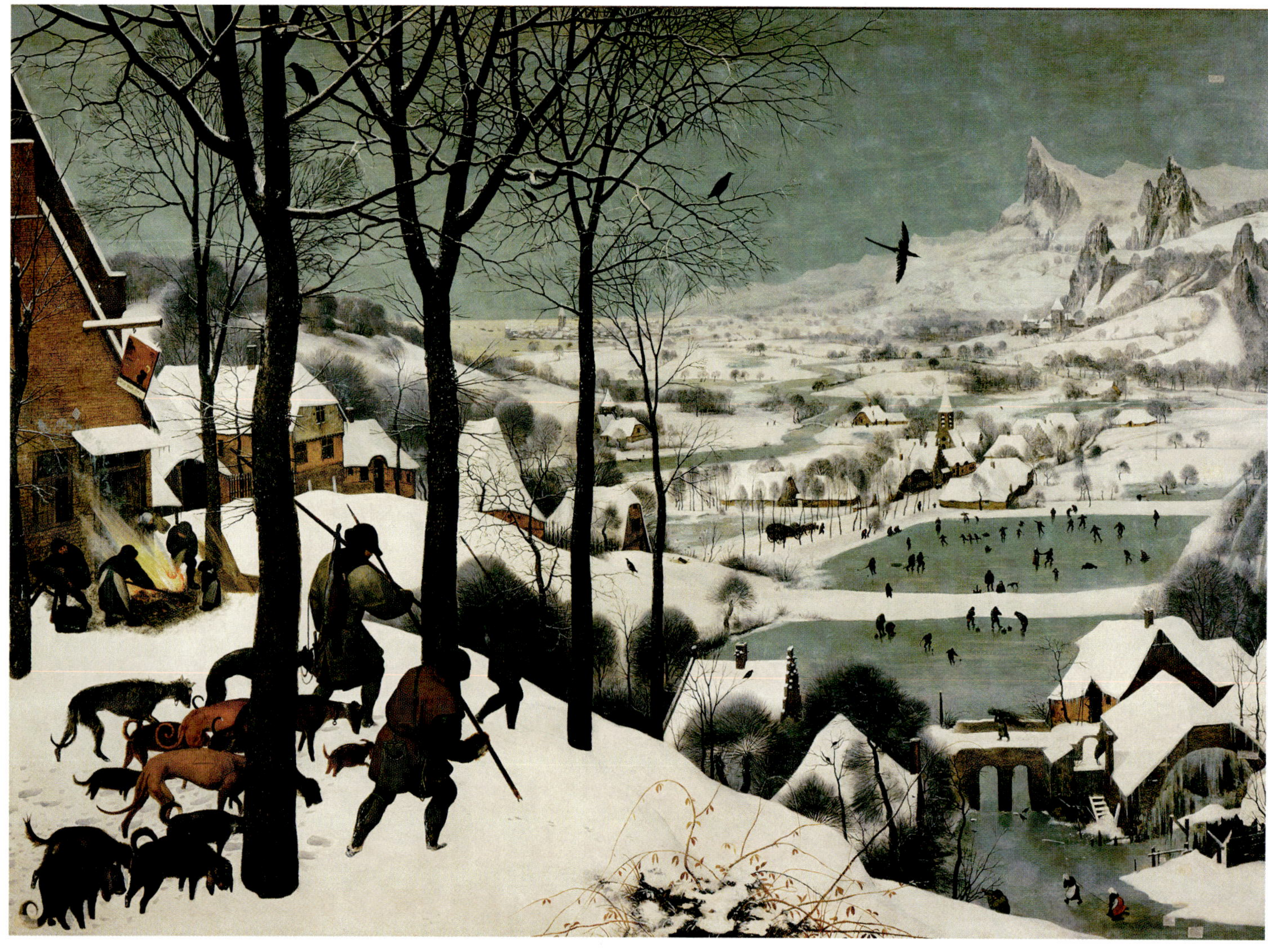

13–41 Pieter Bruegel the Elder. ***Return of the Hunters.*** 1565. Oil on wood panel, 3' 10½" × 5' 3¾" (1.18 × 1.61 m). Kunsthistorisches Museum, Vienna

to Sicily. Unlike many Renaissance artists, he did not record the ruins of ancient Rome or the wonders of Italian cities. Instead he was fascinated by the landscape, particularly the formidable jagged rocks and sweeping panoramic views of Alpine valleys, which he recorded in detailed drawings. Back home in his studio, he painted the flat and rolling lands of Flanders as broad panoramas, but added imaginary mountains on the horizon.

Cycles, or series, of paintings on a single allegorical subject such as the Times of Day, the Seasons, or the Five Senses became popular decorations in Flemish upper-class homes. Bruegel's *Return of the Hunters* (fig. **13–41**) of 1565, from a cycle of six panels, in which each represents a pair of months, describes November and December. The artist captures the damp, cold winter with its early nightfall much as his compatriots the Limbourgs did 150 years earlier (see fig. 12–2). In contrast to much Renaissance and Mannerist art, the subject matter in this painting appears neutral and descriptive, rather than narrative or allegorical. The hunters slog stoically by, trailed by their dogs, while workers at an inn singe a pig in a fire before they finish the butchering. The viewer's eye, plunging across the wide valley toward the distant peaks, is deliberately slowed by the careful balance of the vertical tree trunks and the horizontal rectangles of frozen water.

As religious art declined in the face of Protestant disapproval, portraits became a major source of work for artists. Caterina van Hemessen (1528–1587) of Antwerp, who learned to paint from her father, developed an illustrious international reputation as a portraitist. Typically she portrayed her subjects in three-quarter view, carefully including background elements that could be shown perspectivally, such as the easel in her *Self-Portrait* (fig. **13–42**). In delineating her own features, Caterina presented a serious young person without personal vanity yet seemingly already self-assured about her artistic abilities. The inscription on the painting reads: "I Caterina van Hemessen painted myself in 1548. Her age 20."

Early in van Hemessen's career, she became a favored court artist of Mary of Hungary, sister of Emperor Charles V and regent of the Netherlands. Caterina married Chretien de Morien, the organist of Antwerp Cathedral in 1554, and when Mary ceased to be regent in 1556, the couple accompanied her to Spain. At the death of their patron in 1558, the couple received a lifetime pension. Now financially secure, Caterina seems to have given up her painting career.

Philip II of Spain (ruled 1556–1598) was a great patron of Titian and collected the work of Bosch, but he did not like the works of the man who in the twentieth century became one of Spain's most famous painters: Kyriakos (Domenikos) Theotokopoulos (1541–1614), who arrived in Spain in 1577 after working for ten years in Italy. El Greco ("the Greek"), as he was called, began his career as a Byzantine icon painter in his native Crete. He entered Titian's shop in Venice around 1566, but about 1570 he moved to Rome. His mature style combined the intense emotionalism of late Byzantine art (see fig. 7–28) with rich color and loose brushwork reminiscent of Tintoretto. This distinctive pictorial vision expressed in paint the intense spirituality of a fervent religious revival in late sixteenth-century Spain.

In 1586, the artist was commissioned by the Orgaz family to honor an illustrious ancestor who had been a great benefactor of the Church. At his funeral in 1323, Saints Augustine and Stephen were said to have appeared to lower this Count Orgaz's body into his tomb, while his soul was seen ascending to heaven. In El Greco's *Burial of Count Orgaz* (fig. **13–43**), an angel in the center lifts Orgaz's tiny ghostly soul as the miraculous burial takes place below. Portraits of local aristocrats and religious notables fill the background of the picture. Following Italian Mannerist practice, there is no reference to a specific setting (see fig. 13–27). El Greco placed his own 8-year-old son at the lower left next to Saint Stephen and signed the painting on the boy's white kerchief. He may have put his own features on the man above Saint Stephen's head, who, like the child, looks straight out at the viewer.

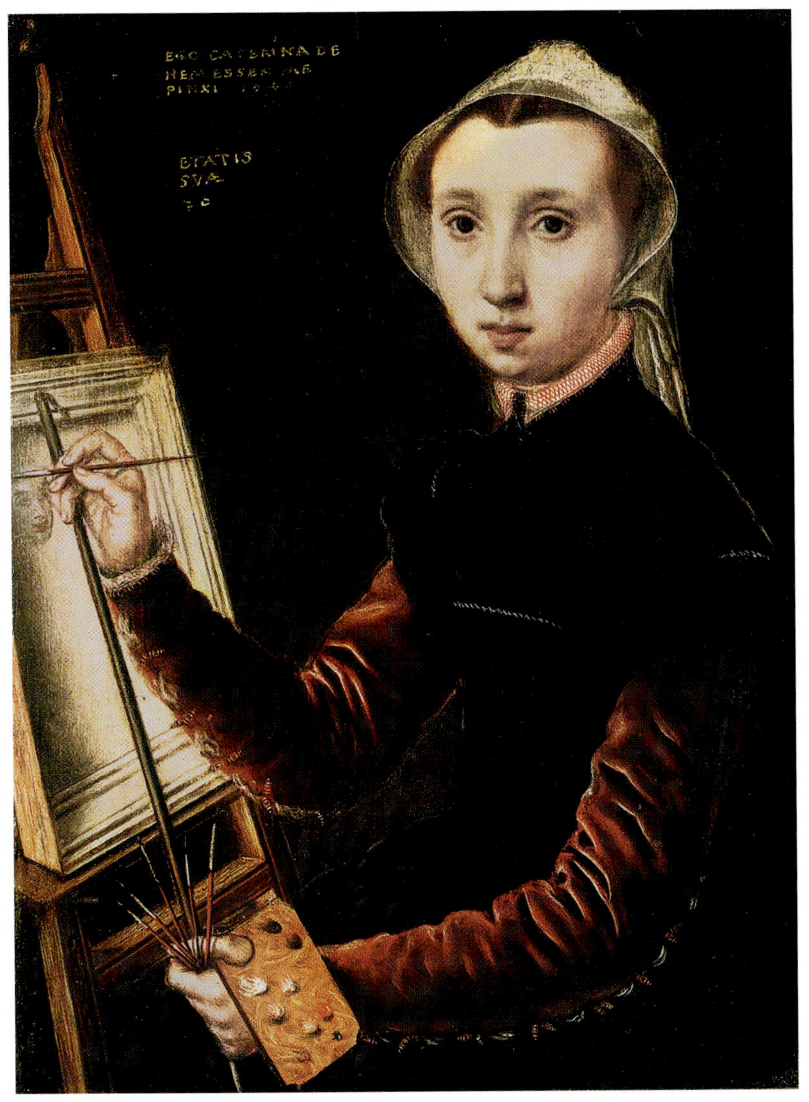

13–42 Caterina van Hemessen. ***Self-Portrait.*** 1548.
Oil on panel, 12¼" × 9¼" (31.1 × 23.5 cm).
Öffentliche Kunstsammlung, Basel, Switzerland
PERMANENT LOAN FROM THE PROF. J.J. BACHOFEN-BURCKHARDT FOUNDATION, 1921 (1361)

This self-portrait of the artist at work provides a glimpse into an artist's studio and working methods. The panel on the easel already has its frame, against which the painter leans her mahlstick—an essential painter's tool used to steady the hand while doing fine, detailed work.

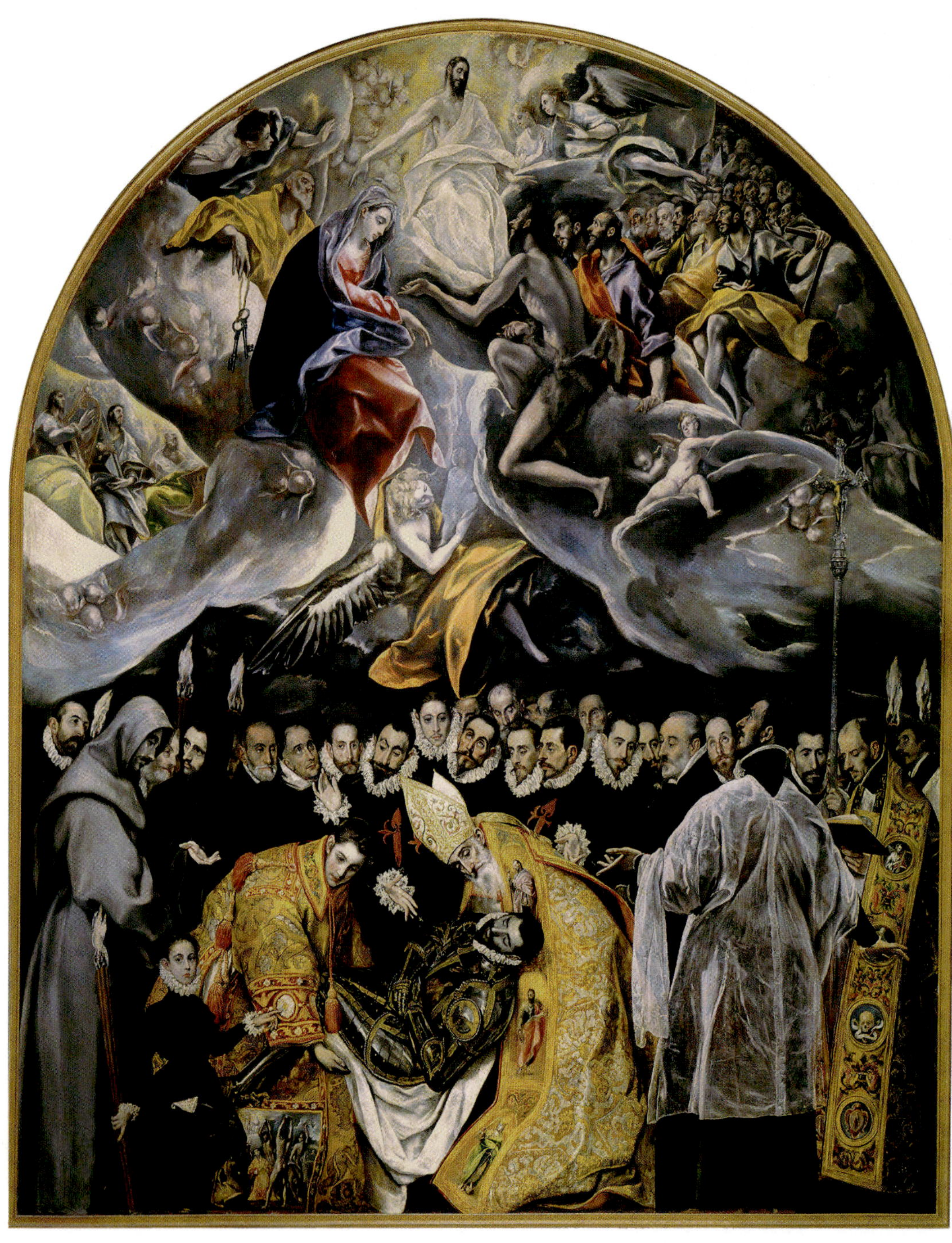

13–43 El Greco. ***Burial of Count Orgaz***, Church of Santo Tomé, Toledo, Spain. 1586. Oil on canvas, 16' × 11' 10" (4.88 × 3.61 m)

Looking Back

In the fifteenth and sixteenth centuries in Europe, artists and scholars began to explore the natural world with the kind of intensity that their medieval predecessors had devoted to heaven and hell. Of course they continued theological debates, but they also studied human and animal anatomy, botany and geology, astronomy and mathematics. Italian artists followed a conceptual, almost mathematical, bent, while Flemish and French artists followed a more perceptual approach in describing the appearance of their world. The conception of a painting, sculpture, or work of architecture began to be seen as a liberal—rather than a manual—art, one that required liberal education as well as technical training.

The Protestants carried on the tradition of using the visual arts to promote a cause, to profess beliefs, and to glorify—just as the Catholic Church had over the centuries used great church buildings and religious art for their theological as well as aesthetic value. The effects of the Reformation and the Counter-Reformation would continue to reverberate in the arts of the following century throughout Europe and, across the Atlantic, in America.

IN PERSPECTIVE

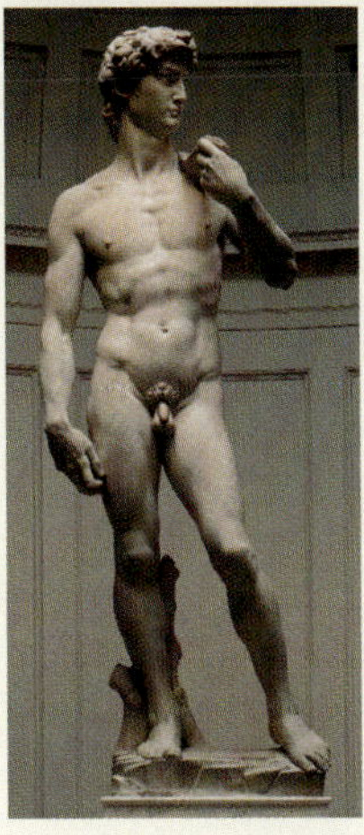

MICHELANGELO,
DAVID,
1501–1504

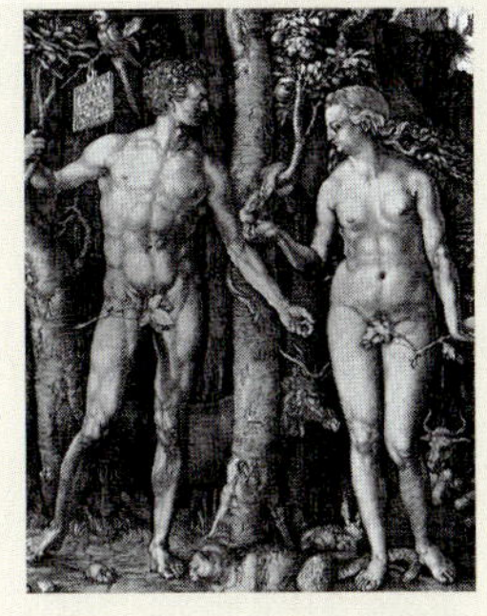

DÜRER,
ADAM AND EVE,
1504

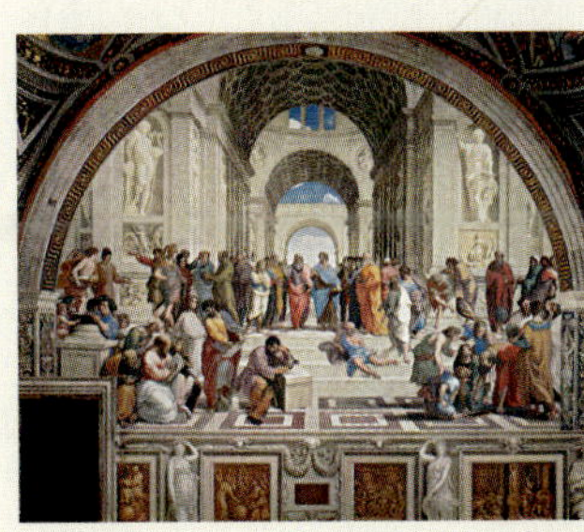

RAPHAEL,
SCHOOL OF ATHENS,
1510–1511

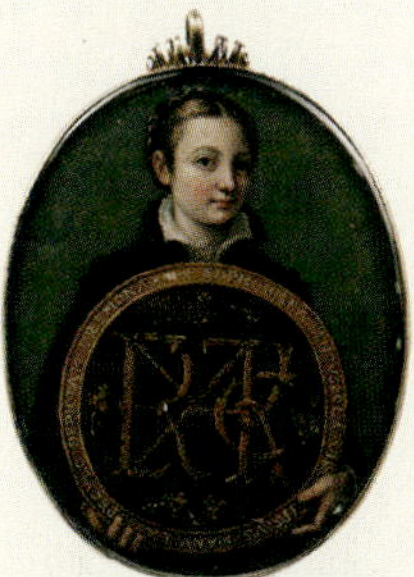

ANGUISSOLA,
SELF-PORTRAIT,
C. 1552

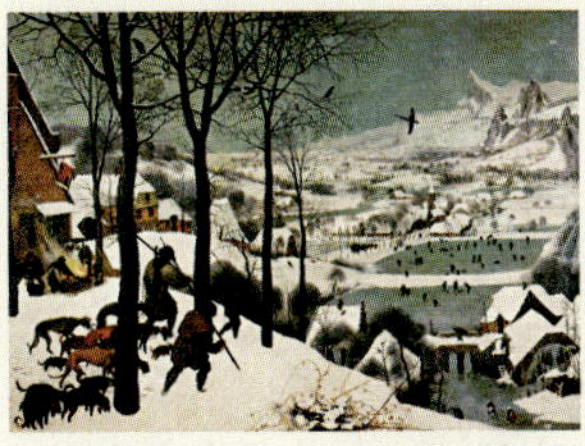

BRUEGEL,
RETURN OF THE HUNTERS,
1565

1500

◀ **Pope Julius II,** ruled 1503–1513

◀ **Henry VIII, King of England,** ruled 1509–1547

◀ **Francis I, King of France,** ruled 1515–1547

◀ **Luther Officially Protests Church's Sale of Indulgences,** 1517

◀ **Death of Leonardo at the court of French king Francis I,** 1519

◀ **Charles V Holy Roman Emperor,** ruled 1519–1556

1520

◀ **Death of Raphael,** 1520

◀ **First Circumnavigation of Earth,** 1522

◀ **Peasants' War,** 1524–1526

◀ **Charles V Orders Sack of Rome,** 1527

1540

◀ **Jesuit Order Confirmed,** 1540

◀ **Pope Paul III Institutes Inquisition,** 1542

◀ **Council of Trent,** 1545–1563

◀ **Vasari's *Lives* Published,** 1550

◀ **Philip II, King of Spain,** ruled 1556–1598

◀ **Elizabeth I Queen of England,** ruled 1558–1603

1560

◀ **Death of Michelangelo,** 1564

◀ **Veronese Appears Before the Inquisition,** 1573

1580

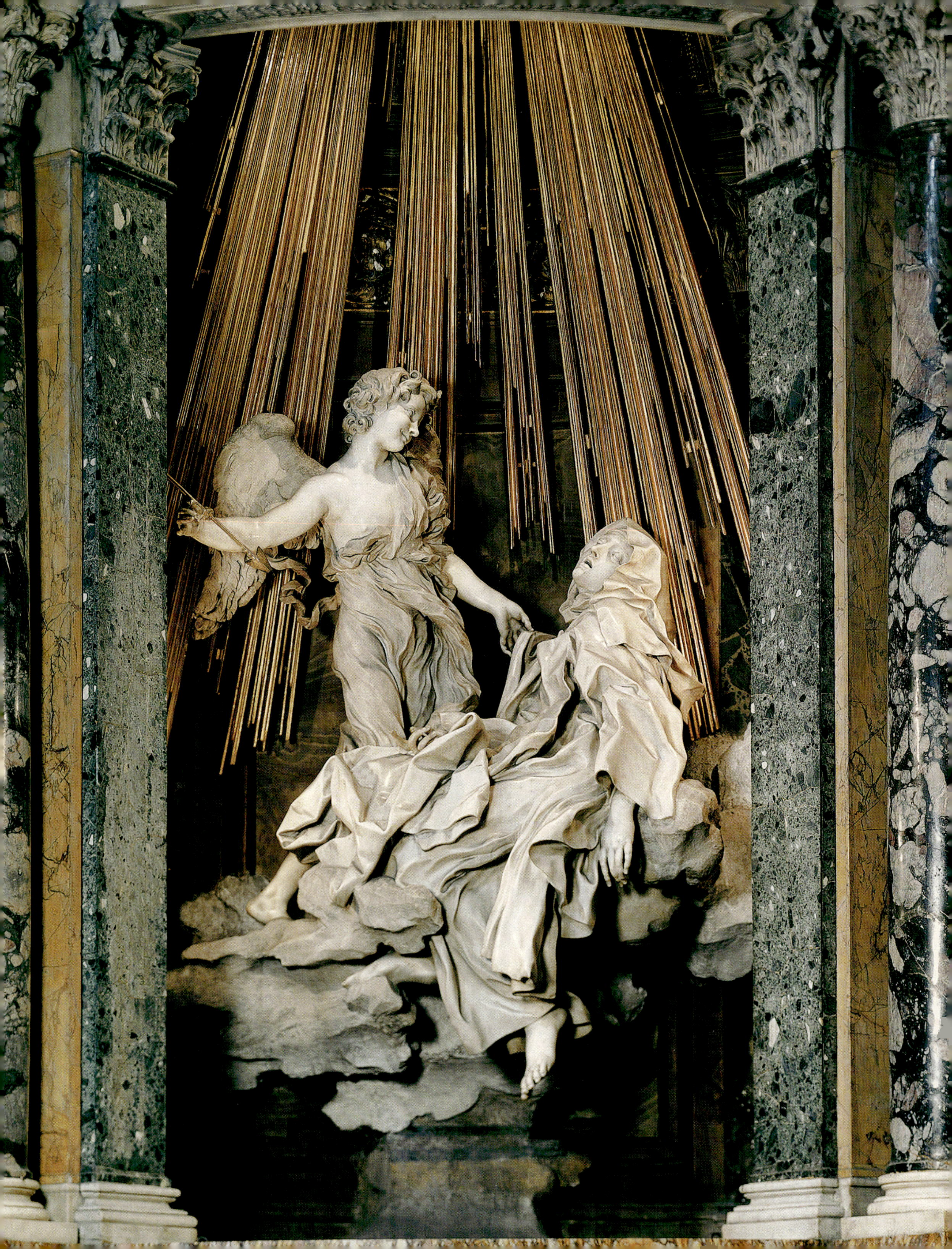

14 Baroque and Rococo Art

LOOKING FORWARD

In the Church of Santa Maria della Vittoria in Rome, the sixteenth-century Spanish mystic Saint Teresa of Ávila (1515–1582, canonized 1622) swoons in ecstasy on a bank of billowing marble clouds (fig. **14–1**). A youthful angel plucks open her robe, aiming a gilded arrow at her breast. Gilt bronze rays of supernatural light descend, even as actual light illuminates the figures from a hidden window above. This dramatic scene, created by Gianlorenzo Bernini (1598–1680) between 1645 and 1652, represents a famous vision described with startling, physical clarity by Teresa, in which an angel pierced her body repeatedly with an arrow, transporting her to a state of ecstatic oneness with God, charged with erotic associations.

The sculpture is an exquisite example of the emotional, theatrical style perfected by Bernini in response to the religious and political climate in Rome during the period of spiritual renewal known as the Counter-Reformation. Many had seen the Protestant Reformation of the previous century as an outgrowth of Renaissance Humanism with its emphasis on rationality and independent thinking. In response, the Catholic Church took a reactionary, authoritarian position, supported by the new Society of Jesus founded by Ignatius Loyola (1491–1556, canonized 1622). In the "spiritual exercises" (1522–1523) initiated by Saint Ignatius, Christians were enjoined to use all their senses to transport themselves emotionally as they imagined the events on which they were meditating. They were to feel the burning fires of hell or the bliss of heaven, the lashing of the whips, and the flesh-piercing crown of thorns. Art became an instrument of propaganda and also a means of leading the spectator to a reinvigorated Christian practice and belief.

Of course, the arts have often been used to convince or inspire, but nowhere more effectively than by the Catholic Church in the seventeenth century. To serve the educational and evangelical mission of the revitalized and conservative Church, paintings and sculpture had to depict events and people accurately and clearly, following guidelines established by religious leaders. Throughout Catholic Europe, painters such as Rubens and Caravaggio created brilliant religious art under official Church sponsorship. And although today some viewers find this sculpture of Saint Teresa uncomfortably charged with sexuality, the Church approved of the depictions of such sensational and supernatural mystical visions. They helped worshipers achieve the emotional state of religious ecstasy that was the goal of the Counter-Reformation.

14–1 Gianlorenzo Bernini. ***Saint Teresa of Ávila in Ecstasy.*** Cornaro Chapel, Church of Santa Maria della Vittoria, Rome. 1645–1652. Marble, height of the group 11' 16" (3.5 m)

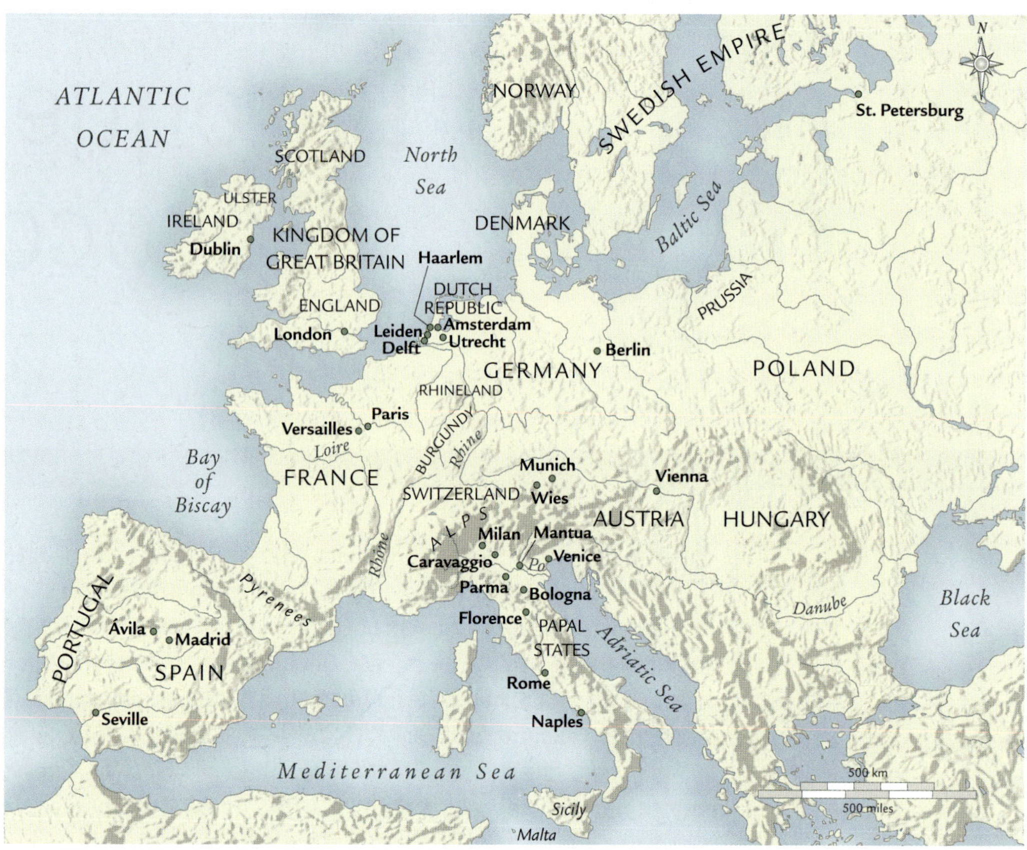

Map 14–1 Seventeenth-Century Europe

The intellectual and political struggles set in motion by the Renaissance and Reformation of the fifteenth and sixteenth centuries intensified in the seventeenth century. Religious wars continued, although gradually the Protestant forces gained control in the north, where Spain recognized the independence of the Dutch Republic in 1648. In Rome an energized papacy, aided by the new Jesuit Order, maintained the primacy of Catholicism in southern Europe, the Holy Roman Empire, and France (see map **14–1**). As rulers' economic strength began to slip away, artists found patrons in the Church and the secular state, as well as in the newly confident and prosperous urban middle class. What evolved was a style known as the Baroque. The label may be related to the Italian word *barocco*, a jeweler's term for an irregularly shaped pearl—something beautiful, fascinating, and strange.

Much Baroque art deliberately evokes intense emotional responses from viewers. Dramatically lit, theatrical compositions often combine several media within a single work, and also foreground displays of technical virtuosity. But the Baroque period also saw its own version of Classicism, a more emotional and dramatic variant of Renaissance ideals and principles featuring idealization based on observation of the material world; balanced (though often asymmetrical) compositions; diagonal movement in space; rich, harmonious colors; and the inclusion of visual references to ancient Greece and Rome. Many Baroque artists sought lifelike depiction of their world in portraiture, **genre paintings** (scenes from everyday life), **still life** (paintings of inanimate objects such as food, fruit, or flowers), and religious scenes enacted by ordinary people in ordinary settings. Intense emotional involvement, lifelike renderings, and Classical references may exist in the same work.

During the eighteenth century, a refined Baroque manner known as the Rococo emerged. Developing first in Italy, this style soon spread into France, central Europe, and even Russia. The Rococo style, characterized by fanciful architectural decoration, a pastel palette, and often a mood of playful melancholy, remained popular along with earlier Baroque styles until the rise of Neoclassicism in the third quarter of the eighteenth century.

Italian Art for the Counter-Reformation Church

The patronage of the Church and those aristocratic Roman families—such as the Borghese, the Barberini, and the Farnese—allied with the papacy dominated Italian art from the late sixteenth to the late seventeenth century. Following the directives of the Counter-Reformation, splendid religious architecture was embellished with painting and sculpture to help convince the faithful of the power of traditional religion. In Rome, the Borghese Pope Paul V (pope 1605–1621) ordered the expansion and modernization of the new Saint Peter's Basilica. In 1606, he commissioned the architect Carlo

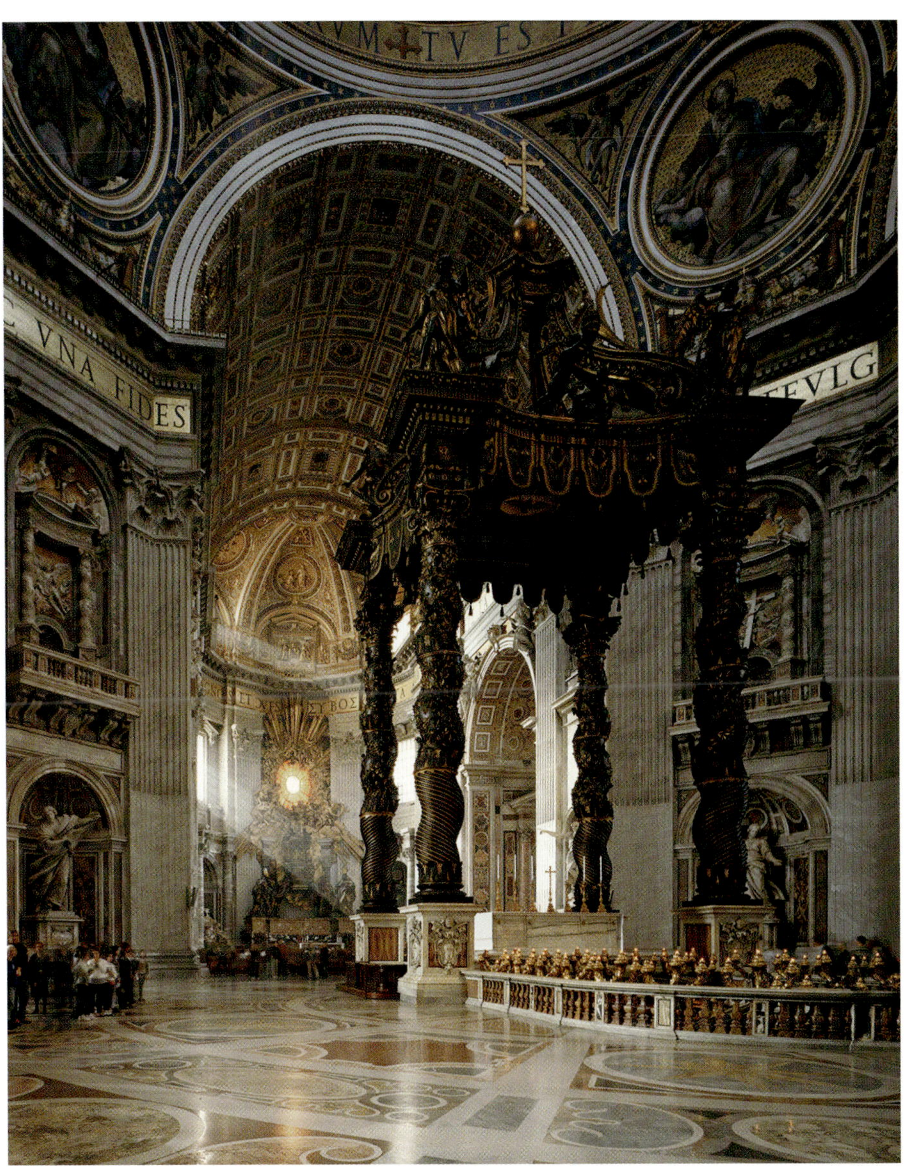

14–2 Gianlorenzo Bernini. ***Baldacchino.*** Located in the crossing of Saint Peter's Basilica, Vatican, Rome. 1624–1633. Gilt bronze, height 100' (30.48 m). Chair of Saint Peter (visible at the back) 1657–1666, gilt bronze, marble, stucco, and glass. Pier decorations 1627–1641, gilt bronze and marble

Maderno (1556–1629) to add a longer nave and a new façade to Michelangelo's Greek-cross building, only a half century old (see "Saint Peter's Basilica," page 350).

When Maffeo Barberini was elected pope as Urban VIII (pope 1623–1644), he unhesitatingly gave the young Bernini the task of designing an enormous bronze **baldachin**, or canopy, over the main altar of Saint Peter's. The resulting *Baldacchino* (fig. **14–2**), which stands about 100 feet high, exemplifies the Baroque tendency toward grandiose displays. Winding bronze grapevines decorate twisted columns inspired by columns, believed to have come from Solomon's Temple in Jerusalem, that were a part of the altar shrine in Old Saint Peter's. Since grapevines are an ancient symbol of the wine of the Eucharist, Bernini's columns combine symbolism from Judaism and Christianity, conforming to the view of Christian scholars that Solomon's Temple supports the Christian Church just as the Hebrew Bible is the foundation of the New Testament. Crowning the structure is an orb and a cross representing universal dominion of Christ. The angels and *putti*, as well as the tasseled panels imitating textiles on the entablature, are all cast of bronze. The work marks the tomb of Saint Peter but also serves as a tribute to Urban VIII and his family, the Barberini, whose emblems—honeybees, suns, and laurel leaves—are prominently displayed.

Visible through the *Baldacchino*'s columns is a huge bronze reliquary containing an ancient wooden throne known as the Chair of Saint Peter. It symbolizes the direct descent of Christian authority from the apostle Peter to the reigning pope, a belief rejected by many Protestants and therefore deliberately emphasized in Counter-Reformation Catholicism. The chair is lifted upward by four theologians amid a surge of gilded clouds toward an explosion of angels, *putti*, and gilded rays of glory, surrounding a stained-glass window depicting the dove of the Holy Spirit. The actual sunlight and the flickering candles, reflected and multiplied by the gilded bronze, are a calculated part of the sculpture.

When Maderno died in 1629, Saint Peter's Basilica was complete as we know it today. However, Bernini, Maderno's collaborator of five years, later designed and supervised the building of a

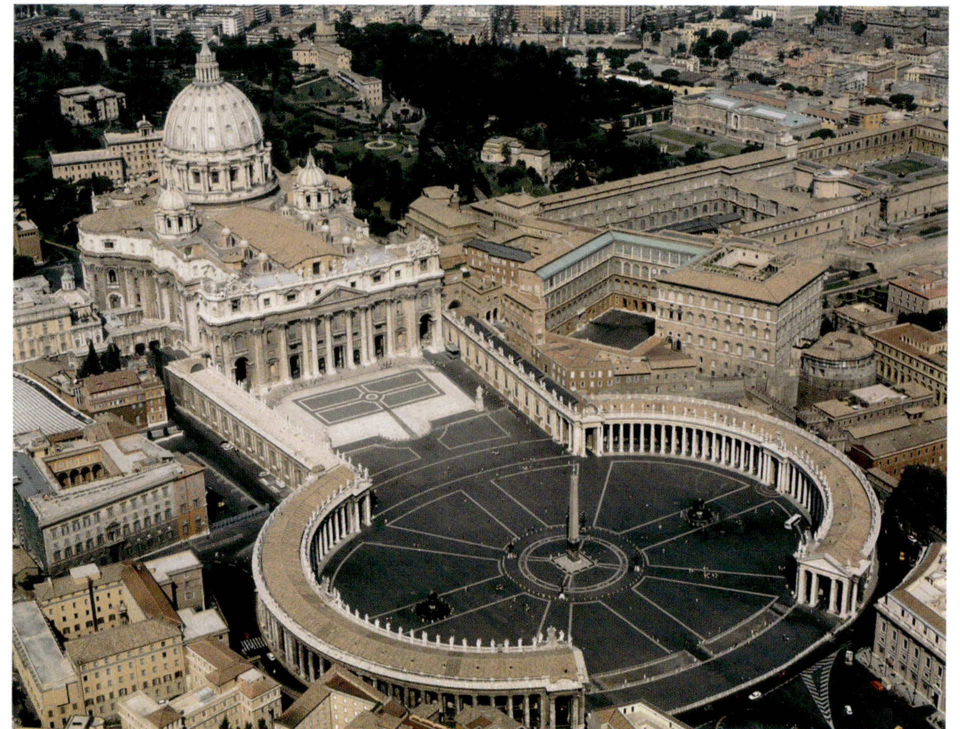

14–3 Gianlorenzo Bernini. Saint Peter's Basilica and Square, Vatican, Rome. Carlo Maderno, façade 1607–1615; Bernini, square designed c. 1656–1657

Perhaps only a Baroque artist of Bernini's talents could have unified the many styles that come together in Saint Peter's Basilica. The visitor today does not see a piecing together of parts made by different builders at different times, starting with Bramante's original design for the building in the sixteenth century, but rather encounters a triumphal unity of all the parts in one coherent whole.

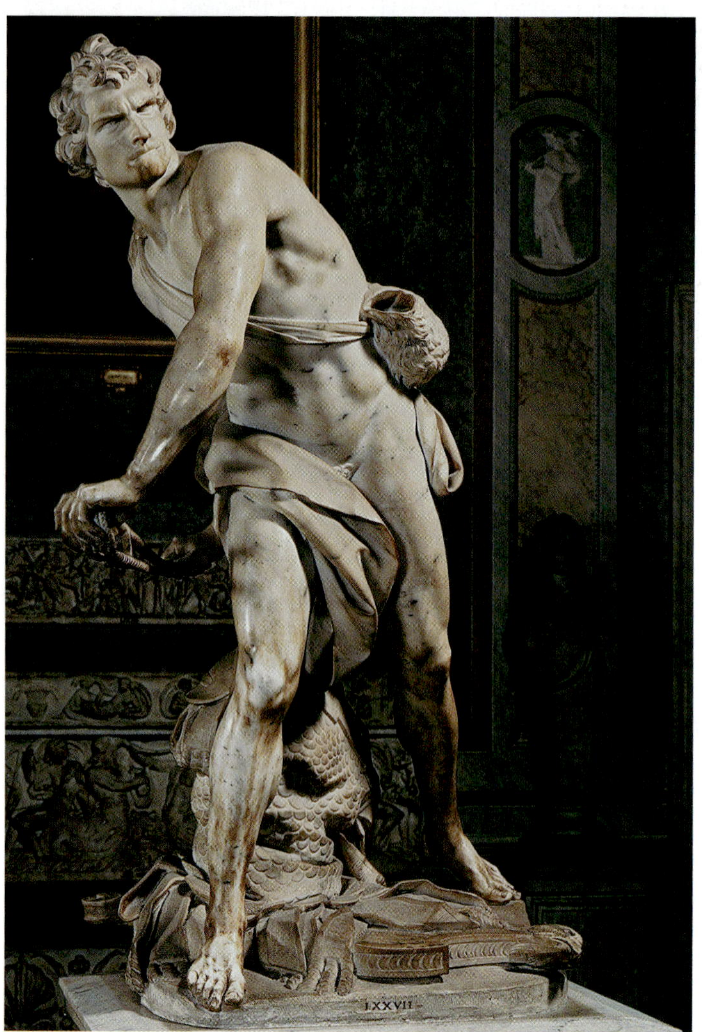

14–4 Gianlorenzo Bernini. ***David.*** 1623. Marble, height 5' 7" (1.7 m). Galleria Borghese, Rome

colonnade to enclose the square in front of the church (fig. **14–3**). The space at Bernini's disposal was irregular and already contained an Egyptian obelisk (moved there in 1586) and a fountain (to the right, made by Maderno in 1613), which had to be incorporated into the overall plan. In a remarkable design, Bernini framed the square with two enormous, curved covered walkways using giant Doric columns. These connect with two straight but diverging porticoes that lead up a slight incline to the two ends of Maderno's church façade. Later, in 1675, Bernini added a second matching fountain at the left of the obelisk, enhancing the sense of balance in the vast space.

Bernini characterized his design as the "motherly arms of the church" reaching out to the world. He intended to build a third section of the colonnade closing the open side so that only after pilgrims had crossed the Tiber River bridge and made their way through narrow streets, would they encounter the enormous open space in front of the imposing church. This element of surprise would have made the basilica and its setting an even more awe-inspiring sight. The approach today—along the grand avenue of the Via della Conciliazione running from the Tiber to the basilica—was conceived by Mussolini in 1936 as part of his masterplan to transform Rome into a grand fascist capital.

Bernini began his career as a sculptor, not as an architect, and he continued to work in that medium throughout his career for both the papacy and private clients. His *David* (fig. **14–4**), made for the nephew of Pope Paul V in 1623, introduced a new type of three-dimensional composition that intrudes forcefully into the viewer's

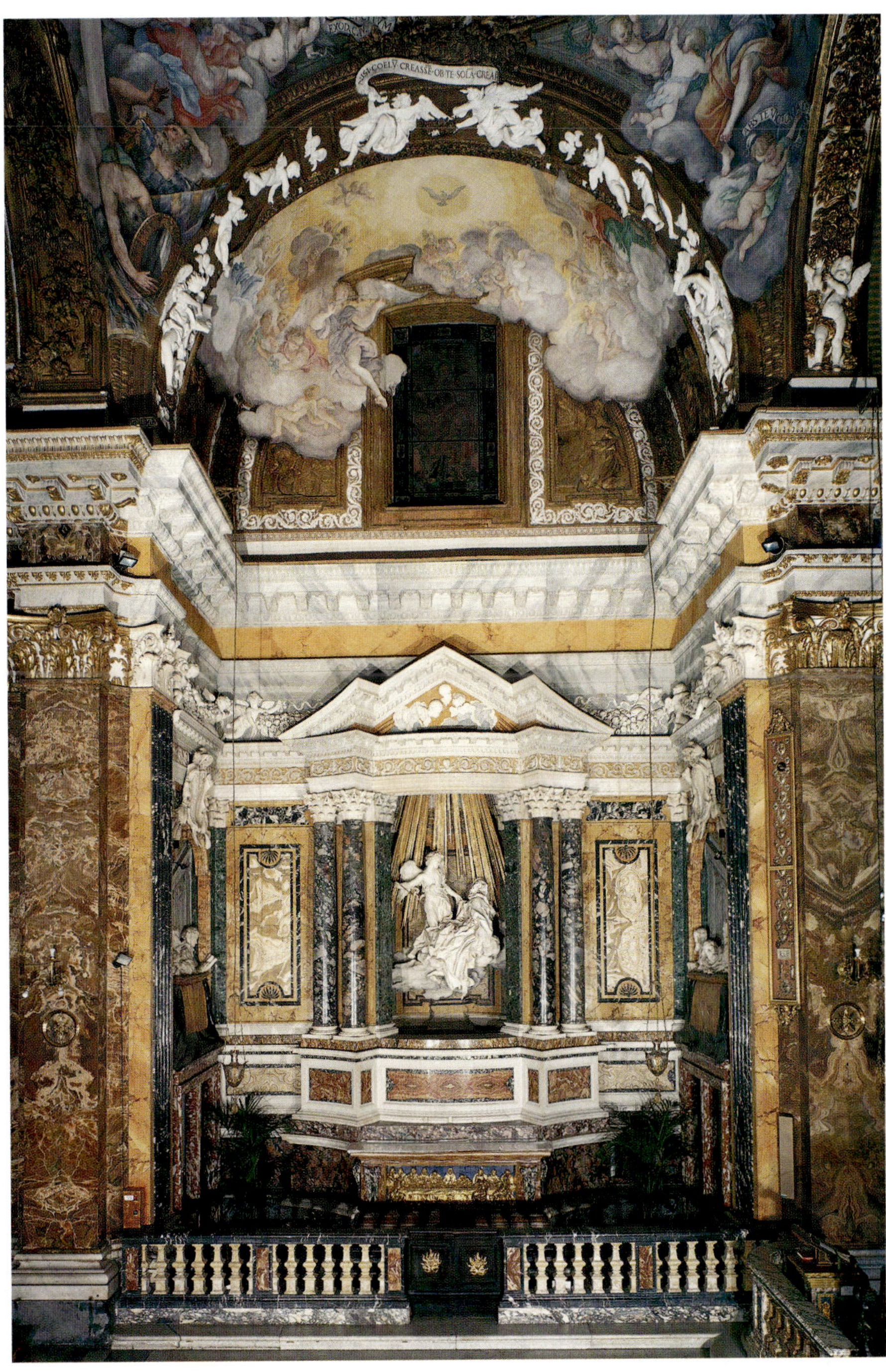

14–5 Gianlorenzo Bernini. Cornaro Chapel, Church of Santa Maria della Vittoria, Rome. 1642–1652

space. The hero bends at the waist and twists far to one side, ready to launch the fatal rock at Goliath. Unlike Donatello's already victorious, introspective adolescent (see fig. 12–20), or Michelangelo's pensive young man, contemplating the task ahead (see fig. 13–9), Bernini's more mature David, with his lean, sinewy body, clenched mouth, and straining muscles, is all tension, action, and determination. By creating a twisting figure caught in movement, Bernini incorporates the surrounding space within his composition, implying the presence of the unseen adversary somewhere behind the viewer, who becomes a part of the action, rather than its displaced and dispassionate observer.

Even after Bernini's appointment as Vatican architect in 1629, his large workshop enabled him to accept outside commissions, such as the decoration of the funerary chapel of Cardinal Federigo Cornaro in the Church of Santa Maria della Vittoria (fig. **14–5**). For this project, carried out from 1642 to 1652, Bernini covered the walls of the tall, shallow chapel with colored marble panels and created the sculptural group of *Saint Teresa of Ávila in Ecstasy* (see fig. 14–1) above the altar. On the chapel's high back wall, the curved ceiling surrounding the window appears to dissolve into a painted vision of clouds and angels, and on the side walls, kneeling against what appear to be balconies, are portrait statues of members of the

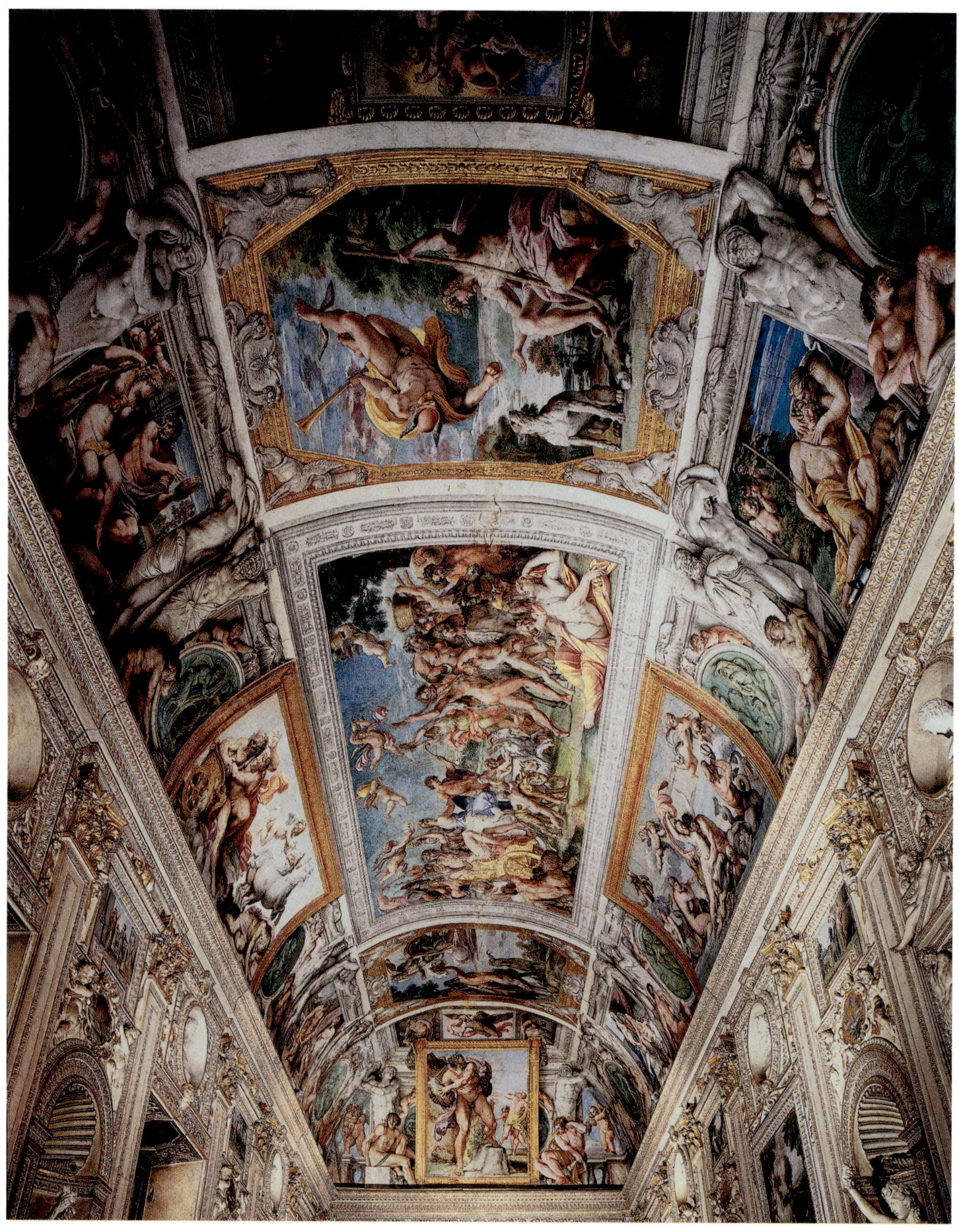

14–6 Annibale Carracci. Ceiling of Gallery, Palazzo Farnese, Rome. 1597–1601. Fresco, approx. 68' × 21' (20.7 × 6.4 m)

Cornaro family. Two are reading from their prayer books; others converse; and one leans out from his seat, apparently to look at someone entering the chapel. Bernini's complex, theatrical interplay of the levels of illusion in the chapel was imitated by sculptors throughout Europe.

Baroque illusionism reached its peak in ceiling decorations for churches, civic buildings, palaces, and villas. Many were covered entirely by *trompe l'oeil* painting, but some were complex constructions combining architecture, painting, and stucco sculpture. A ceiling painted by Annibale Carracci (1560–1609) in the Roman palace of the powerful Farnese family is considered the major monument of early Baroque Classicism. Commissioned to celebrate the wedding of Duke Ranuccio Farnese of Parma, it presents an exuberant mythological tribute to earthly love (fig. **14–6**). Annibale, cofounder with his family of an art academy in Bologna, was assisted by his brother Agostino (1557–1602) on this

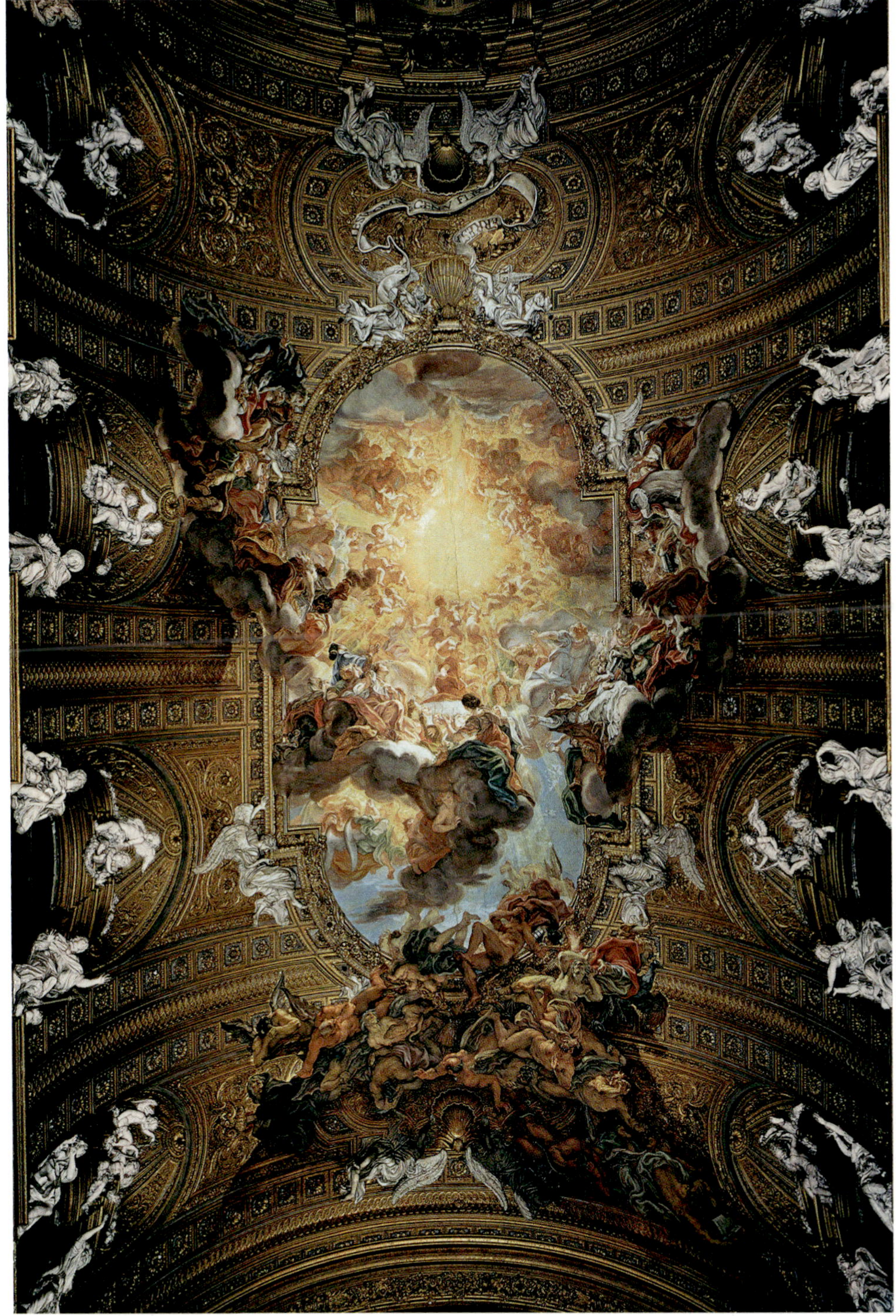

14–7 Giovanni Battista Gaulli. *The Triumph of the Name of Jesus and the Fall of the Damned*, vault of the Church of Il Gesù, Rome. 1672–1685. Fresco with stucco figures

spectacular project, painted at the turn of the century (1597–1601). The ceiling painting creates the illusion of framed paintings, stone sculpture, bronze medallions, and nude youths in an architectural framework, and was clearly inspired by Michelangelo's Sistine Chapel ceiling (see figs. 13–10 and 13–11). But instead of Michelangelo's cool illumination and intellectual detachment, the Farnese ceiling glows with a warm light that recalls the work of the Venetian painters Titian and Veronese. The ceiling became famous almost immediately, and since the Farnese family, proud of the gallery, generously allowed young artists to sketch there, Annibale's great work influenced Italian art well into the seventeenth century.

Closer in spirit and style to Bernini's art, is *The Triumph of the Name of Jesus* (fig. **14–7**), which fills the nave vault of the Church of Il Gesù, mother church of the Society of Jesus (the Jesuits), in Rome. The vault was originally unpainted, but Giovanni Battista Gaulli (1639–1709), also called Baciccio, created the ceiling we see today

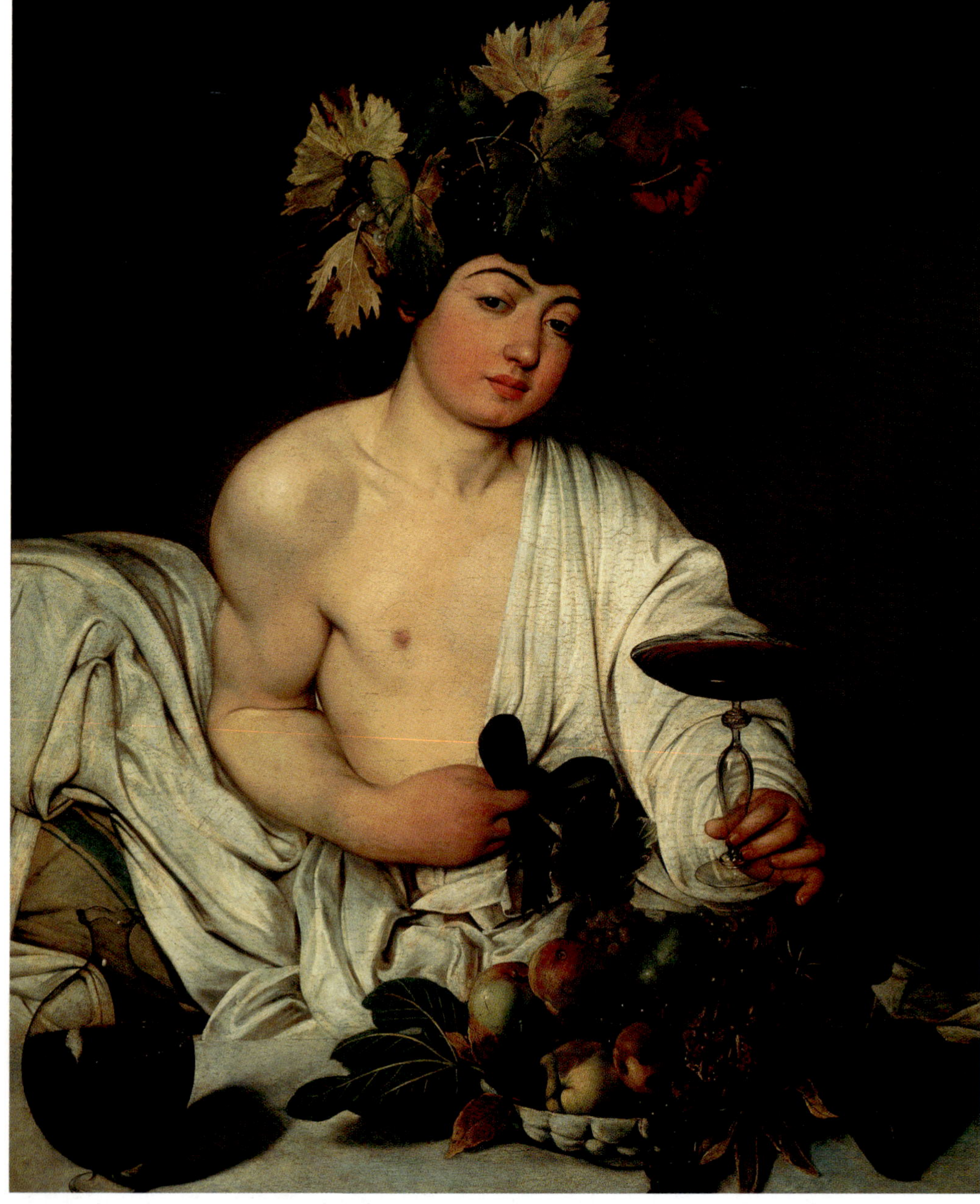

14–8 Michelangelo Merisi, known as Caravaggio. *Bacchus*. 1595–1596. Oil on canvas, 37" × 33½" (94 × 85 cm). Galleria degli Uffizi, Florence

between 1676 and 1679. He had worked during his youth for Bernini, from whom he absorbed a Baroque taste for drama and spectacle. But this astonishing creation went beyond anything that had preceded it. Architecture, sculpture, and painting combine to produce the illusion that clouds and angels have floated down through an opening at the top of the church. The focus, off-center, is the brilliant golden aura surrounding the letters IHS (barely visible in figure 14–7), the monogram of Jesus and the insignia of the Jesuits. The larger subject is the Last Judgment, with the elect rising toward the name of God and the damned plummeting through the ceiling toward the nave floor. The sweeping extension of the work into the nave space, the powerful appeal to the viewers' emotions, and the near-total unity of the multimedia visual effect—all hallmarks of Italian Baroque—were never surpassed.

But not all Roman Baroque art was meant to overwhelm the viewer by sheer spectacle. Michelangelo Merisi (1571–1610), known as Caravaggio after his birthplace in northern Italy, introduced a powerful new realism and a dramatic use of light and gesture to Italian Baroque art. After his arrival in Rome in 1592, Caravaggio at first painted for a small sophisticated circle associated with the household of art patron Cardinal del Monte, where the artist was invited to reside. His subjects from the 1590s include still lifes and scenes featuring fortunetellers, cardsharps, and glamorous young men dressed as musicians or mythological figures. The *Bacchus* of 1595–1596 (fig. **14–8**) is among the most polished of these early works. Caravaggio seems to have painted exactly what he saw, reproducing the tanned character of those parts of this undressed youth—hands and face—that have been exposed to the sun as well as the dirt under his fingernails. The figure himself is strikingly androgynous. Made up with painted lips and smoothly arching eyebrows, he seems to offer the viewer the gorgeous glass goblet of wine held delicately in his hands, while fingering the black bow that holds his clothing together at the waist. Is this a provocative invitation to an erotic encounter or a young actor outfitted for the role of Bacchus, god of wine? Does the juxtaposition of the youth's invitation with a still life of rotting fruit transform this into an image about the transitory nature of sensual pleasure, either admonishing the viewer to avoid sins of the flesh or encouraging him to enjoy life's pleasures while he can? The ambiguity seems to make the painting even more provocative.

Most of Caravaggio's commissions after 1600 were for religious art, and reactions to these paintings were mixed. On occasion, patrons rejected his powerful, sometimes brutal, naturalism as unsuitable to the elevated subject matter. However, this very realism recalls Counter-Reformation ideas of spirituality, as put forward in the meditations, or *Spiritual Exercises*, of Saint Ignatius Loyola, the founder of the Jesuit Order. It was also connected to the populist theology of the preacher Filippo de' Neri (1515–1595, canonized in 1622), who consciously strove to make Christian history and doctrine understandable and meaningful to common people.

One of Caravaggio's earliest religious commissions was the 1599–1600 decorative program of the private chapel of the Cointrel family (Contarelli in Italian) in the French community's church in Rome (fig. **14–9**). Unlike in earlier chapels and churches, where frescoes were applied directly to the walls of a chapel, Caravaggio produced three huge oil paintings on canvas in

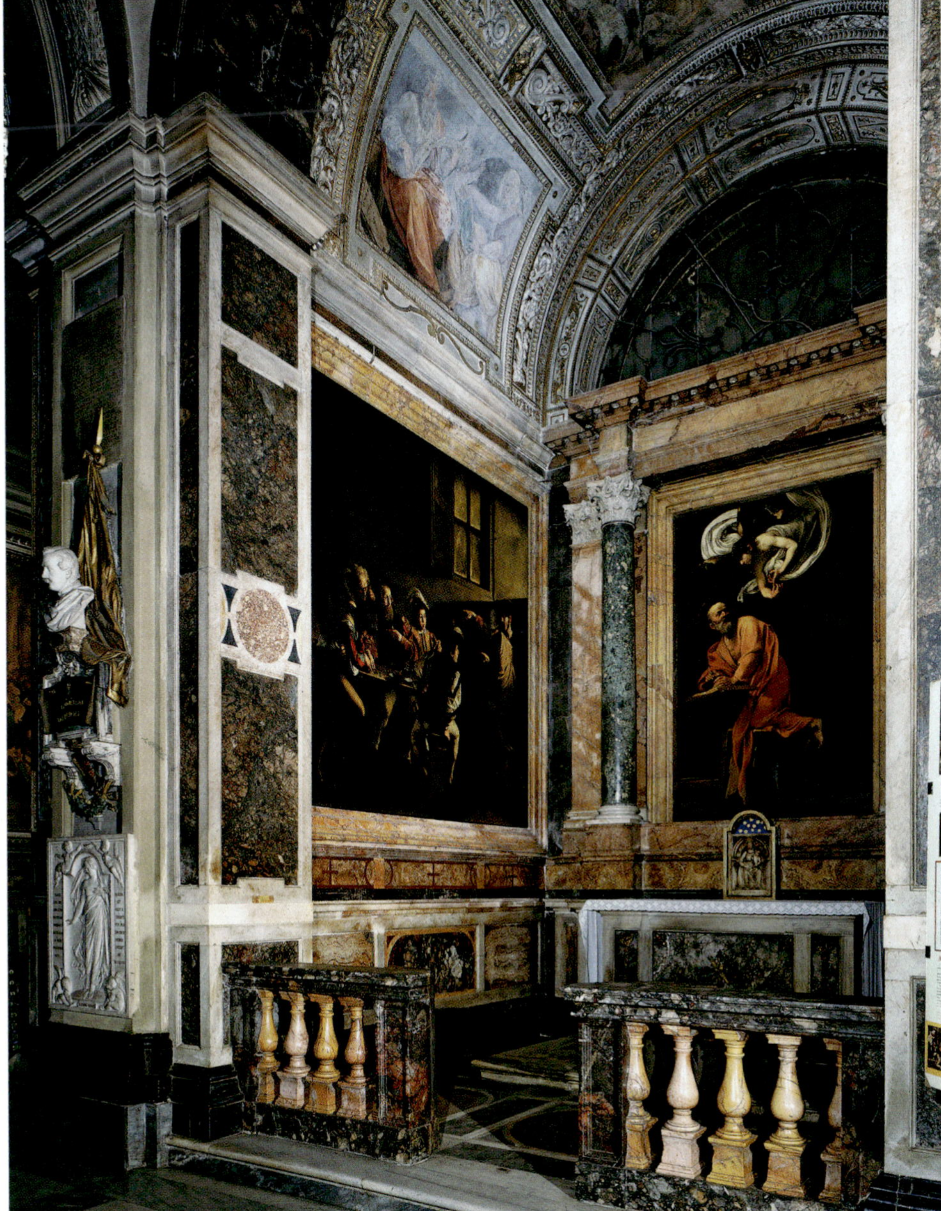

14–9 Contarelli Chapel, Church of San Luigi dei Francesi, Rome

*Whereas Caravaggio was commissioned in 1599 for the paintings on the side walls of this chapel—*The Calling of Saint Matthew *(visible at left) and across from it* The Martyrdom of Saint Matthew *(not visible here)—it was only in 1602 that he was contracted to paint the portrait of Matthew writing his Gospel to hang over the altar. He delivered the painting in that same year, but it was rejected because the saint looked too crude and common to satisfy clerical taste, and the fleshiness of the angel, who sidles up to Matthew with striking coziness, was considered inappropriately risqué. Caravaggio painted a second, more decorous version, seen here, with a nobler Matthew and more distant angel, and the rejected version was snapped up by the Roman collector, Vincenzo Giustiniani, who actually paid for the replacement in order to acquire the more sensational original. Unfortunately, this first painting was destroyed in the bombing of Berlin during World War II.*

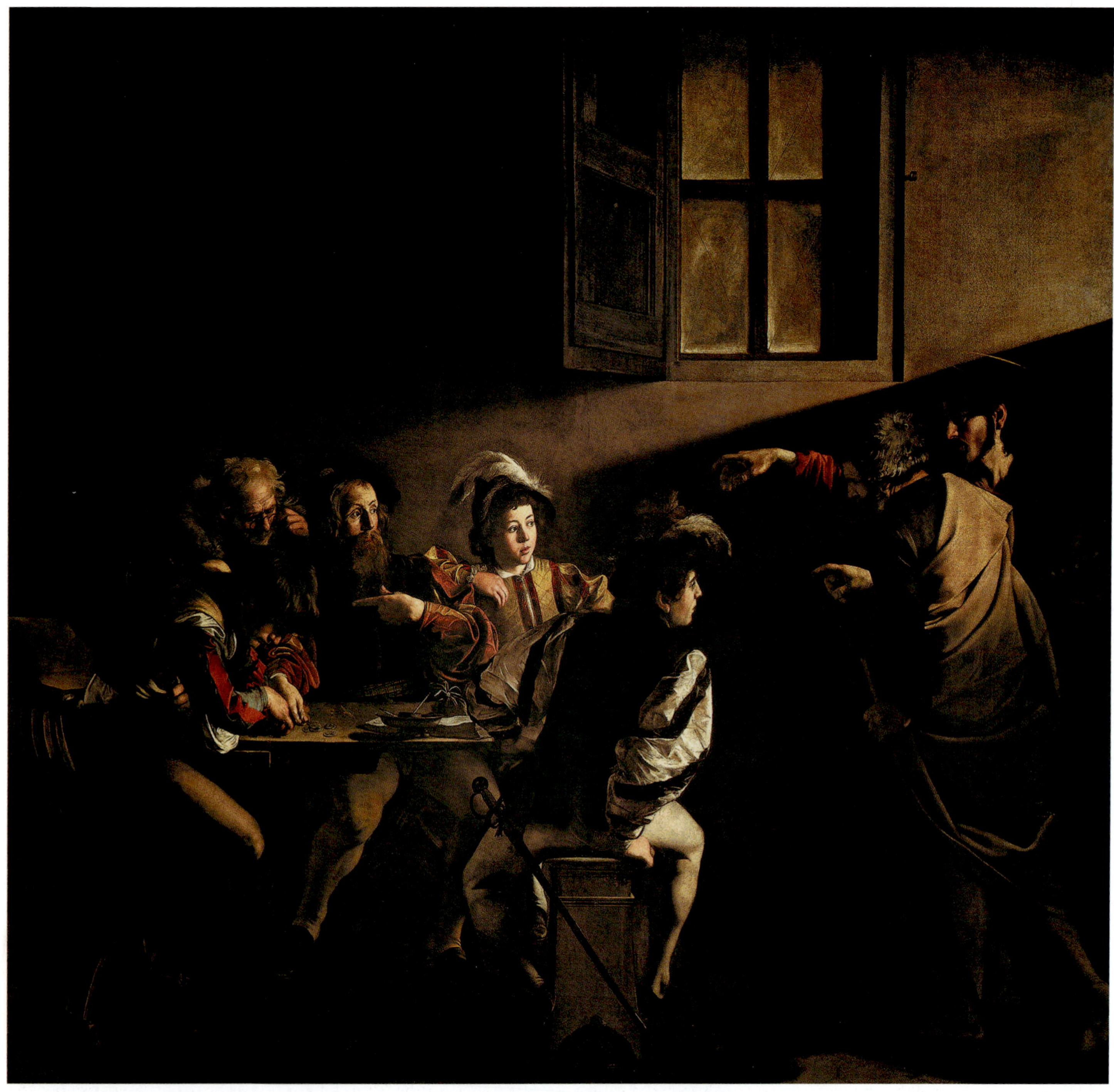

14–10 Caravaggio. *The Calling of Saint Matthew*. Contarelli Chapel, Church of San Luigi dei Francesi, Rome. 1599–1600. Oil on canvas, 10' 7½" × 11' 2" (3.24 × 3.4 m)

his studio, only later installing them within the chapel as a coordinated ensemble: two scenes from the life of Saint Matthew on the side walls, and the saint's portrait as Gospel writer over the altar.

The Calling of Saint Matthew (fig. **14–10**) depicts the moment when Jesus chooses the tax collector Levi to become one of his apostles (Mark 2:14, Matthew 9:9). Levi—who will become Saint Matthew—sits at a table counting or collecting money, surrounded by elegant young men in plumed hats, velvet doublets, and satin shirts. Nearly hidden behind the back of the beckoning Saint Peter, the gaunt-faced Jesus points dramatically at Levi with a gesture that is repeated in the tax collector's own surprised response, pointing to himself as if to say, "Who? Me?" An intense raking light enters the painting from upper right, as if it were coming from the chapel's actual window above the altar to spotlight the important features of this darkened scene. Viewers, encountering the painting obliquely across the empty space in front of Saint Matthew, seem to be

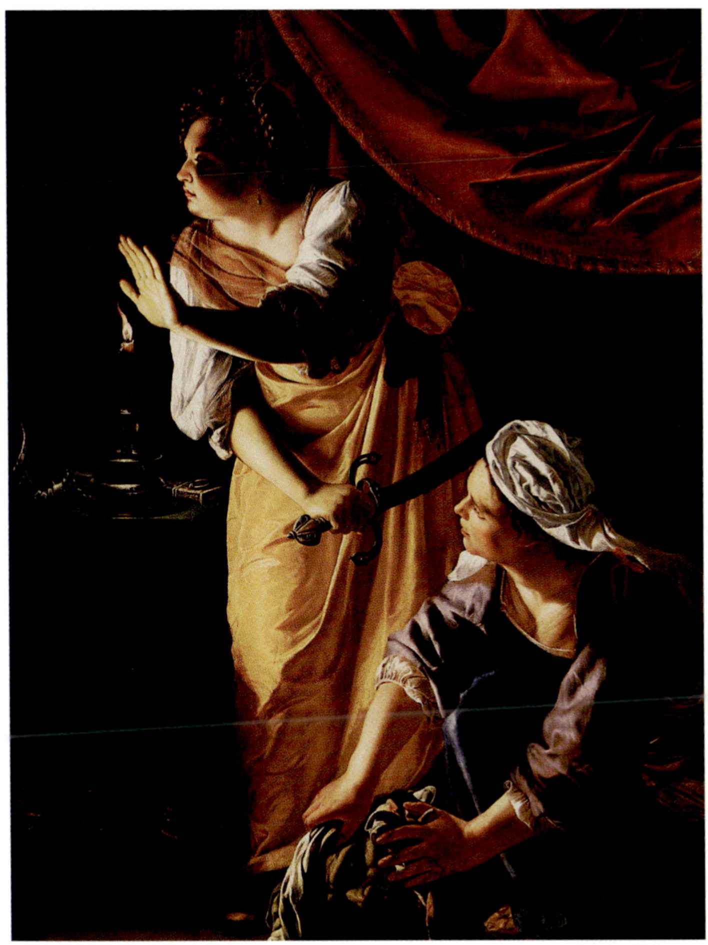

14–11 Artemisia Gentileschi. *Judith and her Maidservant with the Head of Holofernes*. c. 1625. Oil on canvas, 72½" × 55¾" (184.2 × 141.6 cm). The Detroit Institute of Arts, Detroit, Michigan

GIFT OF LESLIE H. GREEN

The beautiful Jewish widow Judith saved her people from the Assyrian army by entering the enemy camp and enticing the general Holofernes to eat and drink until he fell into a stupor. Then she cut off his head and escaped, carrying the trophy as evidence of her heroic act.

witnessing the scene as it is occurring, elevated on a recessed stage before them.

Despite the esteem in which Caravaggio was held as an artist, his violent temper repeatedly got him into trouble. During the last decade of his life, he was frequently arrested, initially for minor offenses—throwing a plate of artichokes at a waiter, carrying arms illegally, or street brawling—but in May 1606 he killed a man in a duel fought over a disputed tennis match and had to flee from Rome as a fugitive under a death sentence. He supported himself on the run by painting in Naples, Malta, and Sicily, before dying on July 18, 1610, just short of his 39th birthday, of a fever contracted during a journey back to Rome where he expected to be pardoned for his capital offense.

Caravaggio inspired an entire generation of painters with his unvarnished realism and his **tenebrism** (an exaggerated and theatrical type of chiaroscuro where selected forms emerge strongly highlighted from a pervasively dark background). One of his most gifted Italian followers was Artemisia Gentileschi (1593–c. 1652/3), whose international reputation helped spread the Caravaggesque style beyond Rome. Artemisia first studied and worked under her father, a Roman follower of Caravaggio. In 1616, she moved to Florence, where she was elected to the Florentine Academy of Design. In one of several versions of the Jewish heroine Judith's triumph over the Assyrian general Holofernes (fig. **14–11**), Artemisia uses Baroque naturalism and tenebrist effects, dramatically spotlighting Judith still holding the bloody sword and shielding the candle's light, as her maid stuffs the general's head into a sack. Throughout her life, Artemisia painted images of heroic and abused women, including Judith, Susanna, Bathsheba, and Esther.

Art in the Habsburg Empire

The leaders of the Church lived like princes, but they were not the only patrons of the arts in seventeenth-century Europe. With the growth of nation-states and absolute monarchies, kings and nobles realized that impressive buildings and splendid portraits could secure and enhance their status by surrounding them with an aura of power. Spain's Habsburg kings Philip II, Philip III, Philip IV, and Charles II saw the political and economic decline of the Spanish part of their empire. What had seemed an endless flow of gold and silver from the Americas diminished, and Protestant England and the Dutch Republic were an increasingly serious threat to Spanish trade and colonial possessions. Agriculture, industry, and trade all suffered, and there were repeated local rebellions, culminating in 1640, when Portugal reestablished its independence.

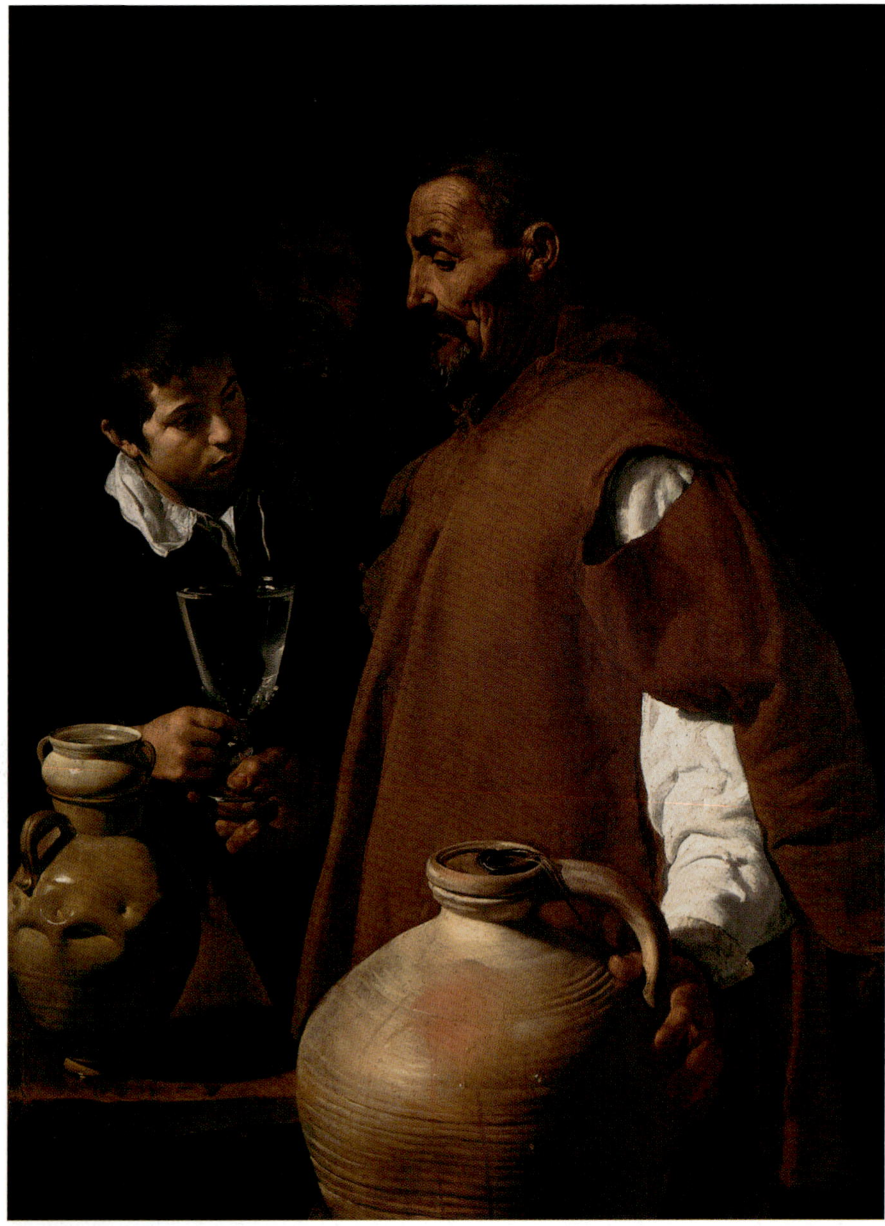

14–12 Diego Velázquez. *Water Carrier of Seville*. c. 1619. Oil on canvas, 41½" × 31½" (105.3 × 80 cm). Wellington Museum, London

In the oppressively hot climate of Seville, Spain, where this painting was made, water vendors walked the streets selling their cool liquid from large clay jars like the one in the foreground. In this scene, the clarity and purity of the water are proudly demonstrated by its seller, who offers the customer a sample poured into a glass goblet. The jug contents were usually sweetened by the addition of a piece of fresh fruit or a sprinkle of aromatic herbs.

Spain

In spite of economic decline, Spanish artists and writers created a "Golden Age" during the seventeenth century, which included one of the most brilliant painters of any age: Diego Rodriguez de Silva y Velázquez (1599–1660). Velázquez entered the painters' guild of Seville in 1617. Like many artists in Spain and Spanish-ruled Naples in the early seventeenth century, at the beginning of his career he was profoundly influenced by Caravaggio. As a young artist, Velázquez, who worked from life, painted tavern, market, and kitchen scenes, showing ordinary people amid still lifes of various foods and kitchen utensils. The model for the *Water Carrier of Seville* (fig. **14–12**), a painting of about 1619, was a well-known character in that city. The objects and figures in the painting, arranged with mathematical rigor, allowed the artist to exhibit his virtuosity in rendering sculptural volumes and contrasting textures such as pottery, glass, and fabrics. Selected elements in the picture are illuminated by dramatic dramatic splashes of natural light—Velázquez's version of Caravaggio's tenebrism.

In 1623, Velázquez moved to Madrid, where the young artist became a courtier and the official painter for the young Philip IV (ruled 1621–1665), a powerful position that he held until his death in 1660. Visits to Italy in 1629–1631 and again in 1649–1651, where Velázquez studied narrative paintings with complex figural compositions, influenced the evolution of the artist's style.

Perhaps Velázquez's most striking and enigmatic work is the enormous multiple portrait known as *Las Meninas*, or *The Maids of Honor*, painted in 1656, near the end of his life (fig. **14–13**). Here, Velázquez draws the spectator directly into the scene. In one interpretation, the viewer stands in the very space occupied by King Philip and his queen, whose reflections can be seen in the large mirror on the back wall, perhaps a clever reference to Jan van Eyck's Arnolfini double portrait (see fig. 12–1), which was part of the

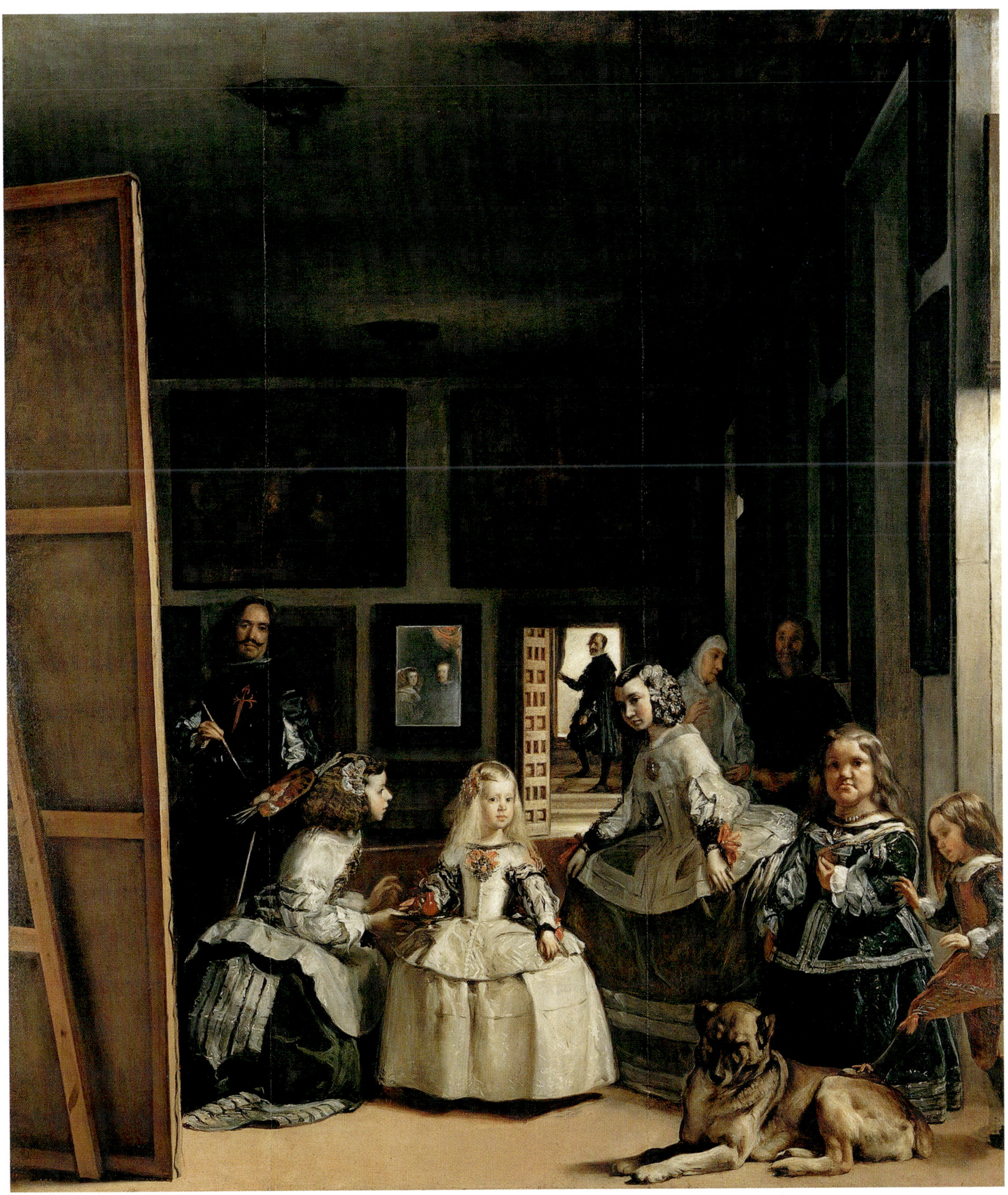

14–13 Diego Velázquez. ***Las Meninas (The Maids of Honor).*** 1656. Oil on canvas, 10' 5" × 9' ½" (3.18 × 2.76 m). Museo Nacional del Prado, Madrid

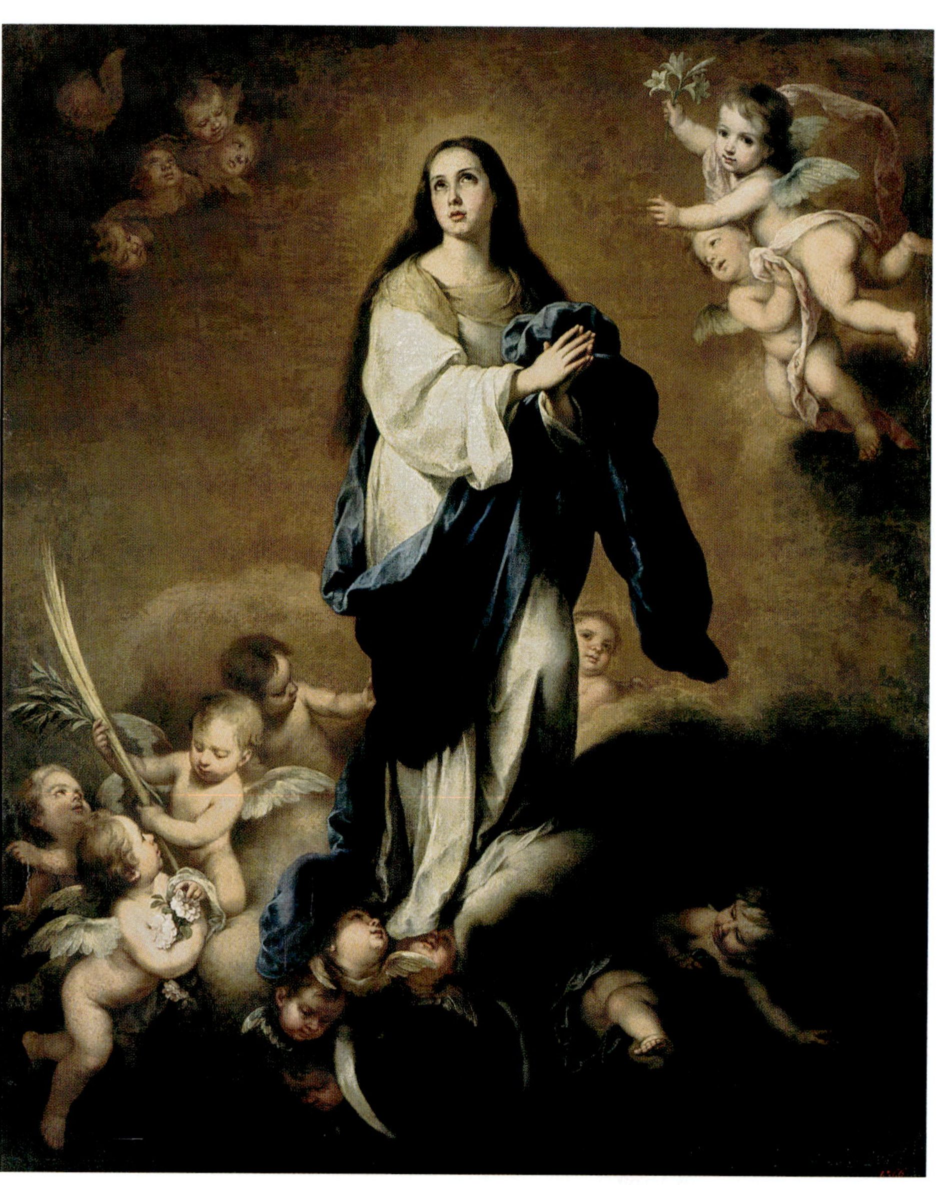

14–14 Bartolomé Esteban Murillo. *The Esquilache Immaculate Conception.*
c. 1645–1650. Oil on canvas,
7' 8" × 6' 5" (2.35 × 1.96 m).
State Hermitage Museum, St. Petersburg, Russia

Spanish royal collection at this time. Echoing pictorially the claim made in Jan's signature, Velázquez himself is also present, brushes and palette in hand, beside a huge canvas. However, the central focus of the painting is neither the artist nor the royal couple but their brilliantly illuminated 5-year-old daughter, the Infanta (Princess) Margarita. She is surrounded by attendants, most of whom are identifiable portraits. In his characteristic bravura style of painting, Velázquez built up his forms with layers of loosely applied paint and finished off the surfaces with dashing highlights in white, lemon yellow, and pale orange. His technique captures the appearance of light reflecting from surfaces, while on close inspection his forms dissolve into a complex maze of individual strokes of paint.

No consensus exists today on the precise meaning of this monumental painting. It is a royal portrait, as well as a self-portrait of the artist himself, standing at his easel. But fundamentally, *Las Meninas* is a personal artistic statement. Throughout his life, Velázquez had sought respect and acclaim for himself and for the art of painting. Here, dressed as a courtier, the Order of Santiago covering his chest (added later) and the keys of the palace tucked into his sash, Velázquez proclaims the dignity and importance of painting as one of the liberal arts.

Velázquez's younger colleague from Seville, Bartolomé Esteban Murillo, was one of the most popular painters of his day. Known for his rich colors and skillful technique, Murillo specialized in religious art and especially in paintings of the Immaculate Conception (fig. **14–14**), the controversial idea that the Virgin Mary was born free from Original Sin. Devotion to Mary grew during the seventeenth and eighteenth centuries, and Counter-Reformation authorities had provided specific instructions for artists who painted the Virgin of the Immaculate Conception. She was to be dressed in blue and white, hands folded in prayer, surrounded by an unearthly light ("clothed in the sun"), and standing on a crescent moon as she is carried upward by angels who often carry palms and symbols of the Virgin, such as a mirror, fountain, roses, and lilies.

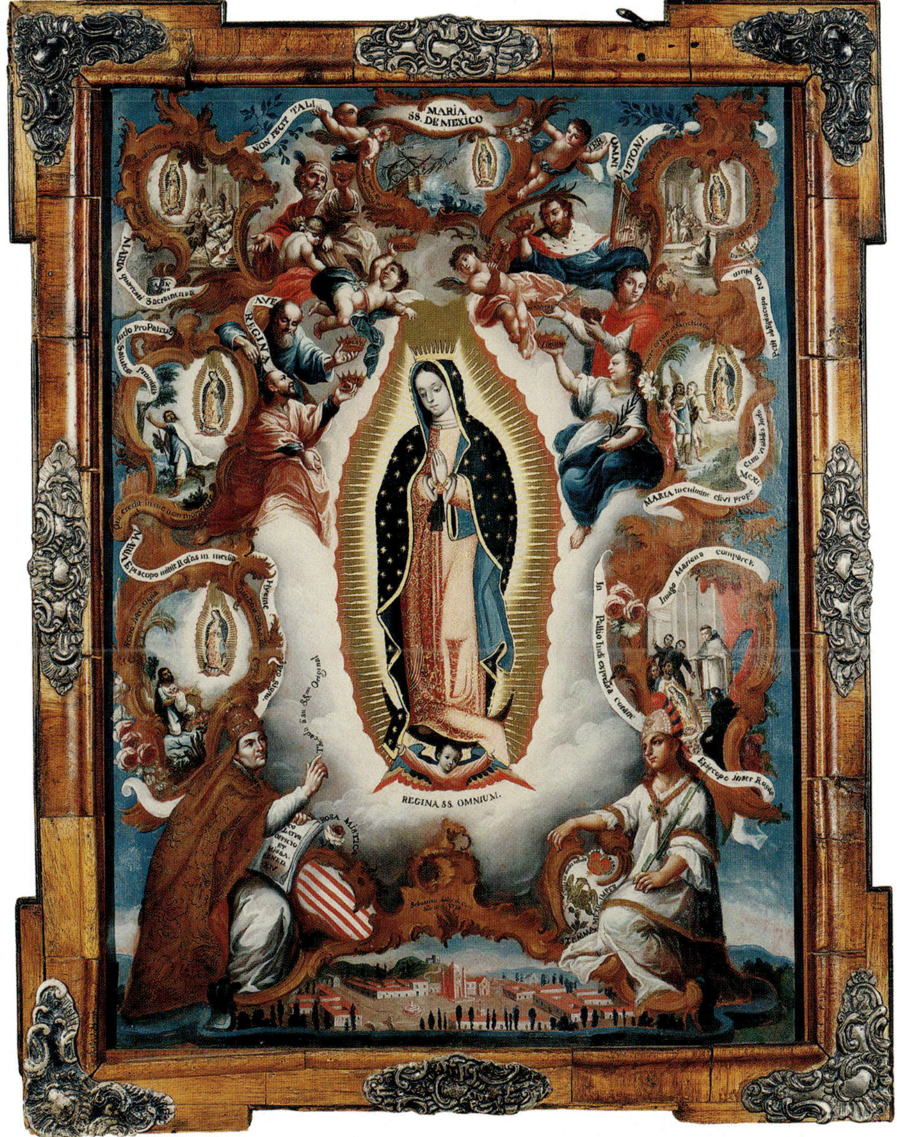

14–15 Sebastian Salcedo. *Our Lady of Guadalupe*. 1779. Oil on panel and copper, 25" × 19" (63.5 × 48.3 cm). Denver Art Museum

COLLECTION, FUNDS CONTRIBUTED BY MR. AND MRS. GEORGE G. ANDERMAN AND AN ANONYMOUS DONOR (1976–56)

At the bottom right is the female personification of New Spain (Mexico) and at the left is Pope Benedict XIV, who in 1754 declared the Virgin of Guadalupe to be the patron of the Americas. Between the figures, the sanctuary of Guadalupe in Mexico looms in the distance. The four small scenes circling the Virgin represent the story of Juan Diego, and at the top, three scenes depict Mary's miracles. The six figures above the Virgin represent prophets and patriarchs of the Hebrew Bible and apostles and saints of the New Testament.

The Spanish colonization of the Americas dates to 1519, when Hernan Cortés arrived off the coast of Mexico. Within two years, after forging alliances with enemies of the dominant Aztec people, Cortés succeeded in taking the Aztec capital, Tenochtitlan (on the site of present-day Mexico City). Over the next several years, Spanish forces established Mexico as a colony of Spain. In the wake of the conquest, the European conquerors suppressed local beliefs and practices and imposed Roman Catholicism throughout Spanish America. Murillo's home, Seville, was a center for trade with the Spanish colonies, and the Church exported many paintings by the artist to the New World. When the native population began to visualize the Christian story, Murillo's paintings were often the models.

Catholics in Mexico gained their own patron saint after the Virgin Mary appeared in 1531 to an indigenous convert named Juan Diego, asking that a church dedicated to her be built on a hill where the goddess Coatlicue had once been worshiped. As evidence of this vision, Juan Diego brought the archbishop flowers that the Virgin had caused to bloom. He carried the flowers wrapped in his cloak, and when he opened his bundle, the cloak bore the image of a dark-skinned Mary in the guise of the Virgin of the Immaculate Conception. An eighteenth-century work by the painter Sebastian Salcedo depicts such an image of Mary, surrounded by scenes from the story of Juan Diego (fig. **14–15**). The site of the vision was renamed Guadalupe, after Our Lady of Guadalupe in Spain, and became a venerated pilgrimage center. In 1754, the pope declared the Virgin of Guadalupe to be the patron saint of the Americas.

Flanders

Flanders was part of the Spanish Habsburg domain during most of the Baroque period. After a period of relative autonomy under Habsburg regents from 1598 to 1633, the region came under direct and often oppressive Spanish rule. In spite of the shifting political climate, however, artists of great talent flourished in the cultural

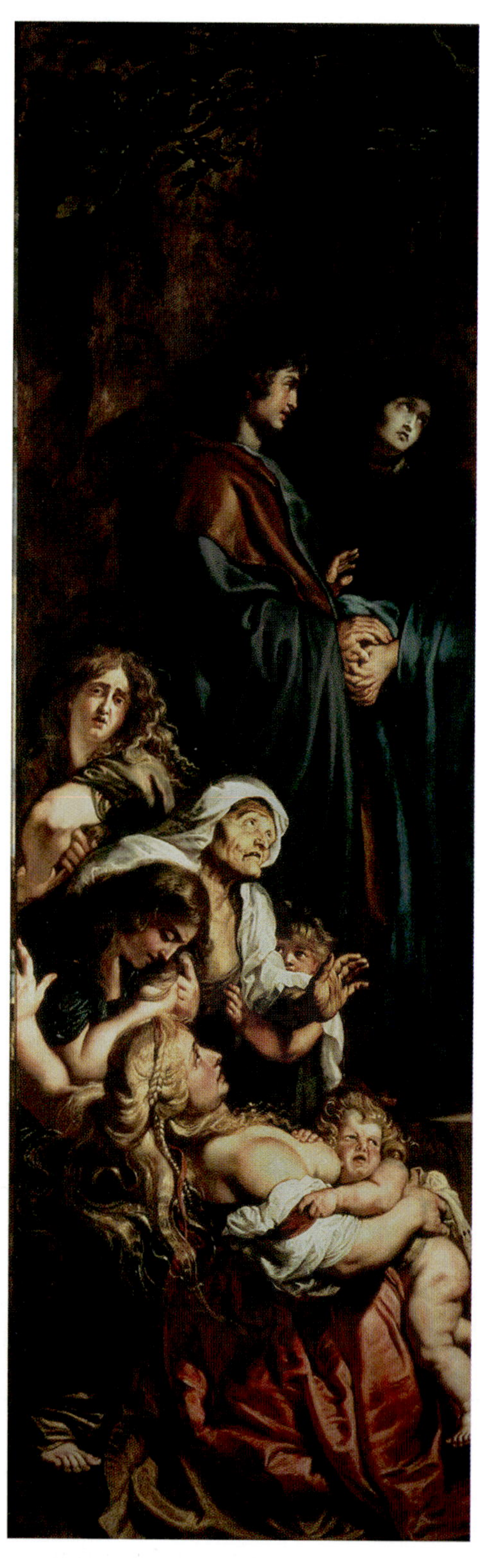

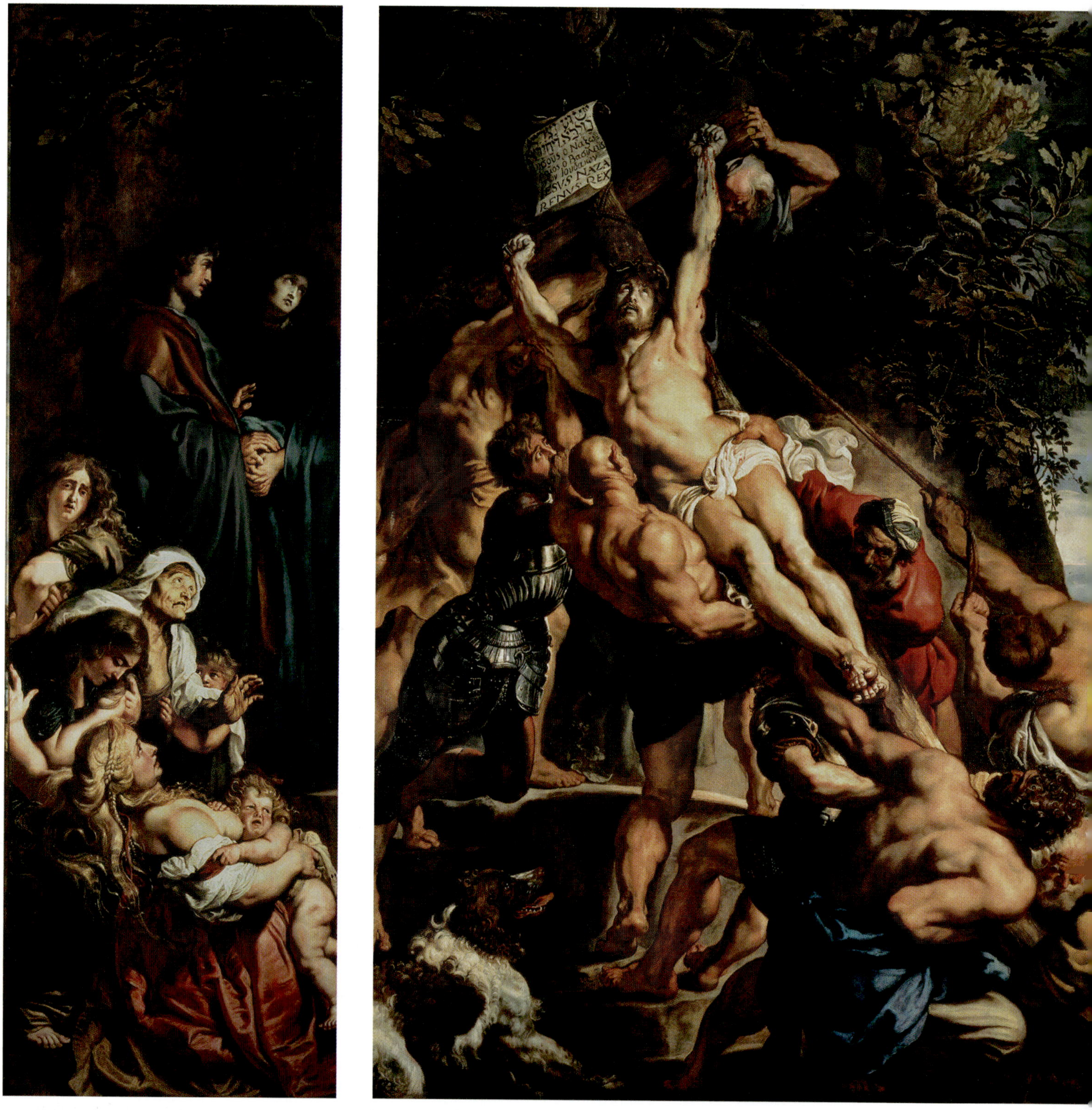

center of Antwerp, where the Spanish were enthusiastic patrons of the arts.

The art of Peter Paul Rubens (1577–1640) has become nearly synonymous with the Flemish Baroque style. Rubens was accepted into the Antwerp painters' guild at age 21, and shortly thereafter, in 1600, he left for Italy, where he obtained a post with the duke of Mantua. Other than designs for court entertainment and occasional portraits, the duke never acquired an original painting by Rubens. Instead, he had him copy famous paintings in collections all over Italy to enlarge the ducal collection, thus coincidentally providing the young painter with an excellent education.

In 1608, Rubens returned to Antwerp, where he accepted employment from the Habsburg governors of Flanders, the Spanish princess Isabel Clara Eugenia (daughter of Philip II) and her husband, Archduke Albert. His first major commission was a large canvas triptych for the main altar of the Church of Saint Walpurga, *The Raising of the Cross* (fig. **14–16**), painted in 1610–1611. Unlike many earlier triptychs, in which the wings contain related but independent images—as seen, for example, in Grünewald's *Isenheim Altarpiece* (see fig. 13–34)—Rubens extended the action and landscape of the central scene across all three panels. At the center, Herculean figures strain to haul upright the wooden cross with Jesus already stretched upon it. The followers of Jesus mourn at left, and indifferent soldiers on the right supervise the execution. In his paintings Rubens merges the drama and intense emotion of Caravaggio with the virtuoso technique of Annibale Carracci, but he transforms these qualities into a distinctive personal style. The heroic nude figures, dramatic lighting effects, dynamic diagonal composition, and intense emotions show the artist's debt to Italian art, but the rich colors and the careful description of surface textures reflect his native Flemish tradition.

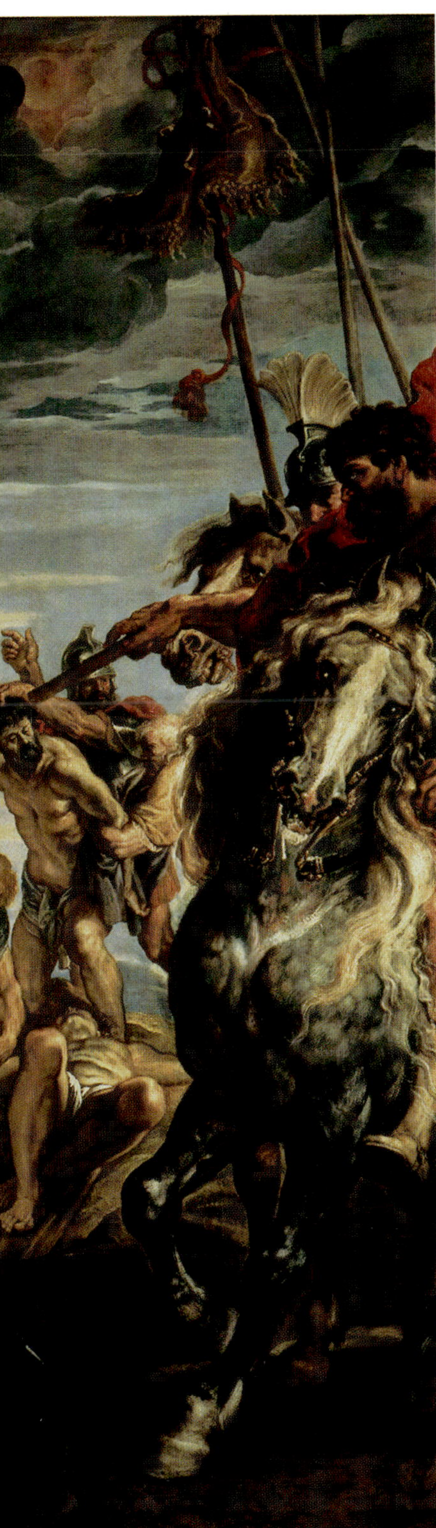

14–16 Peter Paul Rubens. ***The Raising of the Cross***, painted for the Church of Saint Walpurga, Antwerp, Belgium. 1610–1611. Oil on canvas, center panel 15' 1⅞" × 11' 1½" (4.62 × 3.39 m), each wing 15' 1⅞" × 4' 11⅞" (4.62 × 1.52 m). Cathedral of Our Lady, Antwerp

Rubens's intelligence, courtly manners, and personal charm made him a valuable and trusted courtier to royal patrons, including Philip IV of Spain, Marie de' Medici of France, and Charles I of England. In fact, he became the first international superstar of the European art world. In 1621, Marie de' Medici, widow of King Henry IV and regent for her young son, Louis XIII, asked Rubens to paint the story of her life. In 21 paintings, Rubens glorified her role in ruling France and also commemorated the founding of the Bourbon dynasty, which began with Henry IV. The lives and political careers of Marie and Henry appear as one continuous triumph overseen by ancient Roman gods. In the painting depicting the royal engagement (fig. **14–17**), Henry IV falls in love with Marie as he gazes at her portrait, shown to him—at the exact center of the composition—by Cupid and the god of marriage, Hymen. The supreme Roman god, Jupiter, and his wife, Juno, look down approvingly from the clouds. A personification of France encourages Henry, outfitted with steel breastplate and silhouetted against a landscape in which the smoke of battle lingers in the distance, to abandon war for love, as *putti* frolic below with pieces of his armor. The ripe colors, lavish textures, and dramatic diagonals give sustained visual excitement to these enormous canvases making them not only important works of art but political propaganda of the highest order.

Rubens accepted commissions from all over Europe and employed dozens of assistants as specialists in the painting of

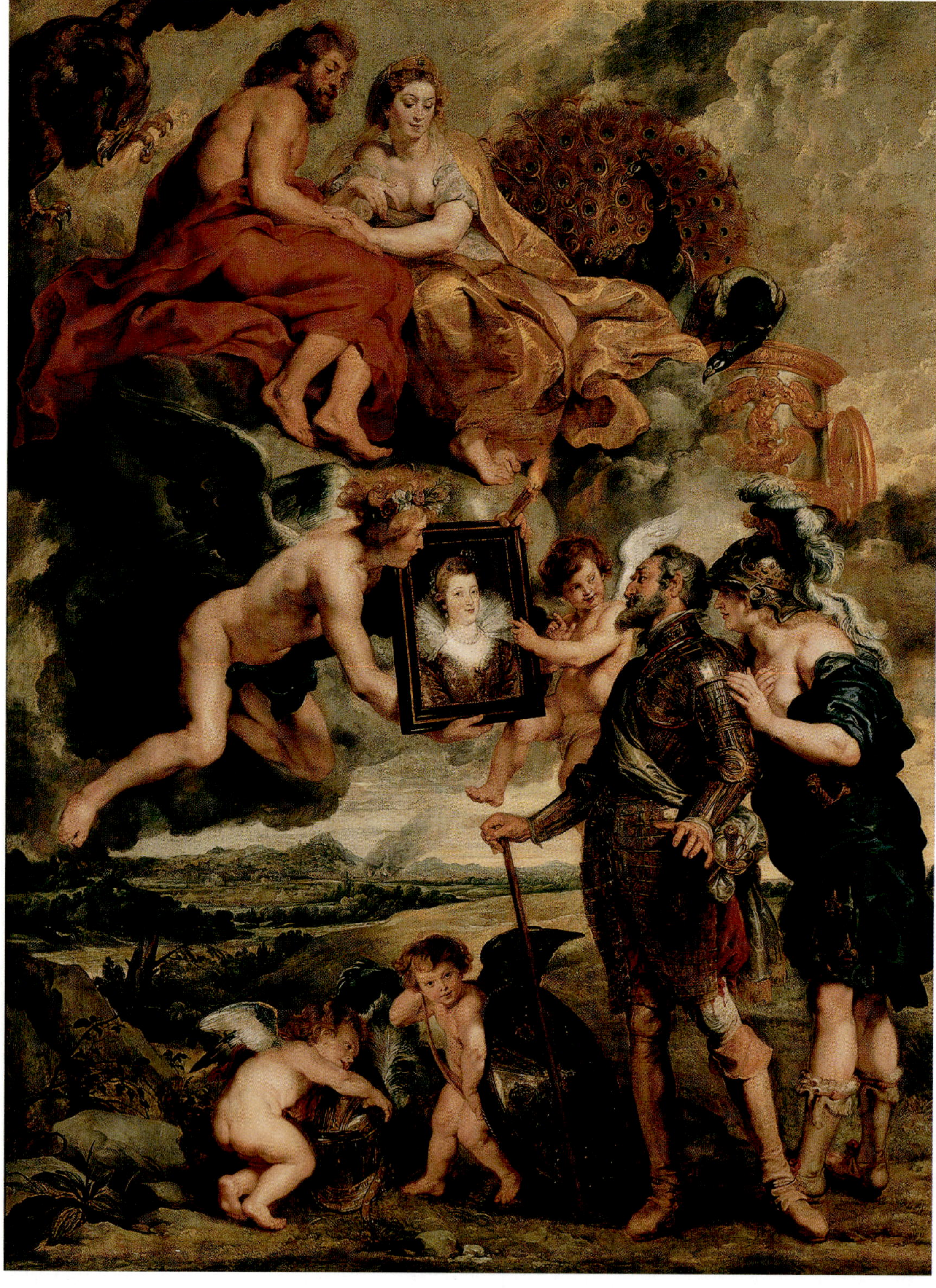

14–17 Peter Paul Rubens. ***Henry IV Receiving the Portrait of Marie de' Medici.*** 1621–1625. Oil on canvas, 12' 11⅛" × 9' 8⅛" (3.94 × 2.95 m). Musée du Louvre, Paris

portraits, textiles, landscapes, even fruits and flowers. Using workshop assistants was standard practice among major artists, but Rubens was particularly efficient and created something close to a painting factory. Working from his detailed sketches, his assistants completed giant canvases suitable for palatial rooms. Among these assistants were two artists who became, important painters in their own right: Jan Brueghel and Anthony van Dyck.

Jan Brueghel (1568–1625), the grandson of Pieter Bruegel (see fig. 13–41) (Jan added the "h" to the family name), was Rubens' neighbor in Antwerp. The two artists frequently collaborated, with Rubens painting the figures and Brueghel creating their settings. About 1617, Rubens and Brueghel worked together on a series of allegorical paintings on the theme of the senses, made for the Habsburg governors of the Netherlands, Princess Isabel Clara

CLOSER LOOK

Of the five paintings in the series of allegories on *The Five Senses*, painted for Archduke Albert and Princess Isabel Clara Eugenia, Habsburg rulers of the Netherlands, *Sight* (fig. **14–18**) is the most splendid. It is almost an illustrated catalog of the ducal collection. Gathered in a huge vaulted room are paintings, sculpture, furniture, objects in gold and silver, and scientific equipment—all under the magnificent double-headed eagle emblem of the Habsburgs (at the top of the chandelier). The viewer is encouraged to explore the painting inch by inch, as if reading a book or a palace inventory. There on the table are Brueghel's copies of Rubens' portraits of the royal couple; another portrait of the duke is on the floor. Besides the portraits, we can find Rubens' *Daniel in the Lions' Den* (upper left corner), *Lion and Tiger Hunt* (top center), and *Drunken Silenus* (lower right), as well as the popular subject *Madonna and Child in a Wreath of Flowers* (far right), for which Rubens painted the Madonna and Brueghel created the floral wreath. Brueghel also included Raphael's *Saint Cecilia* (behind the globe) and Titian's *Venus and Psyche* (over the door).

In the foreground, the Classical goddess Venus attended by Cupid (both painted by Rubens) has put aside her mirror to contemplate Jan Brueghel's painting *Christ Healing the Blind.* Venus is surrounded by the equipment needed to see and to study. The huge globe (the earth) at the right and the armillary sphere with its gleaming rings (the heavens) at the upper left represent the extent of Humanistic learning in symbolism that speaks to viewers of our time as clearly as it did to those during Rubens's and Brueghel's day. The books and prints, ruler, compasses, magnifying glass, and the more complex astrolabe, telescope, and eyeglasses may also refer to spiritual blindness—to those who look but do not see.

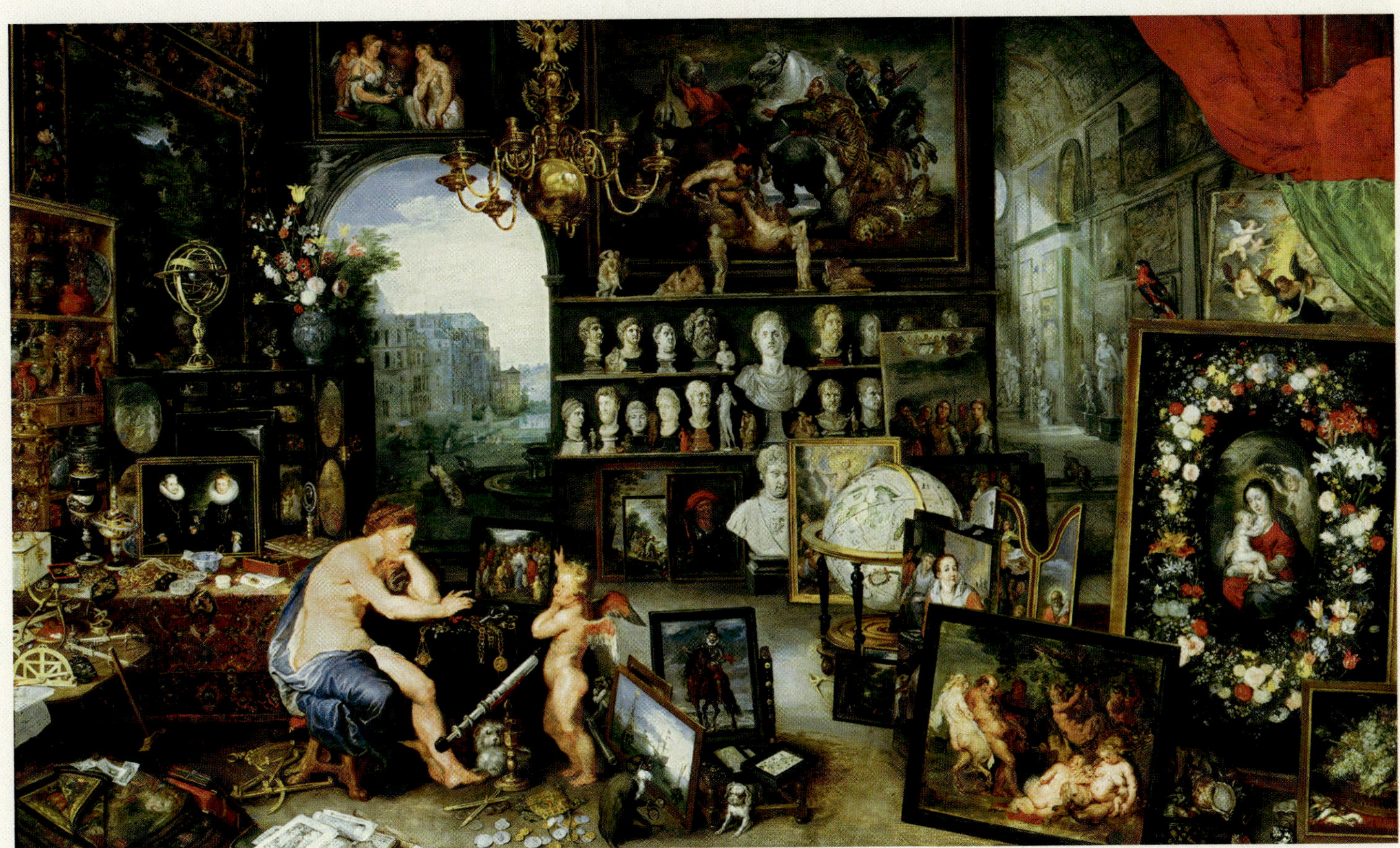

14–18 Jan Brueghel and Peter Paul Rubens. ***Sight***, one of the allegorical series *The Five Senses*. c. 1617–1618. Oil on panel, 25⅝" × 43" (65 × 109 cm). Museo del Prado, Madrid

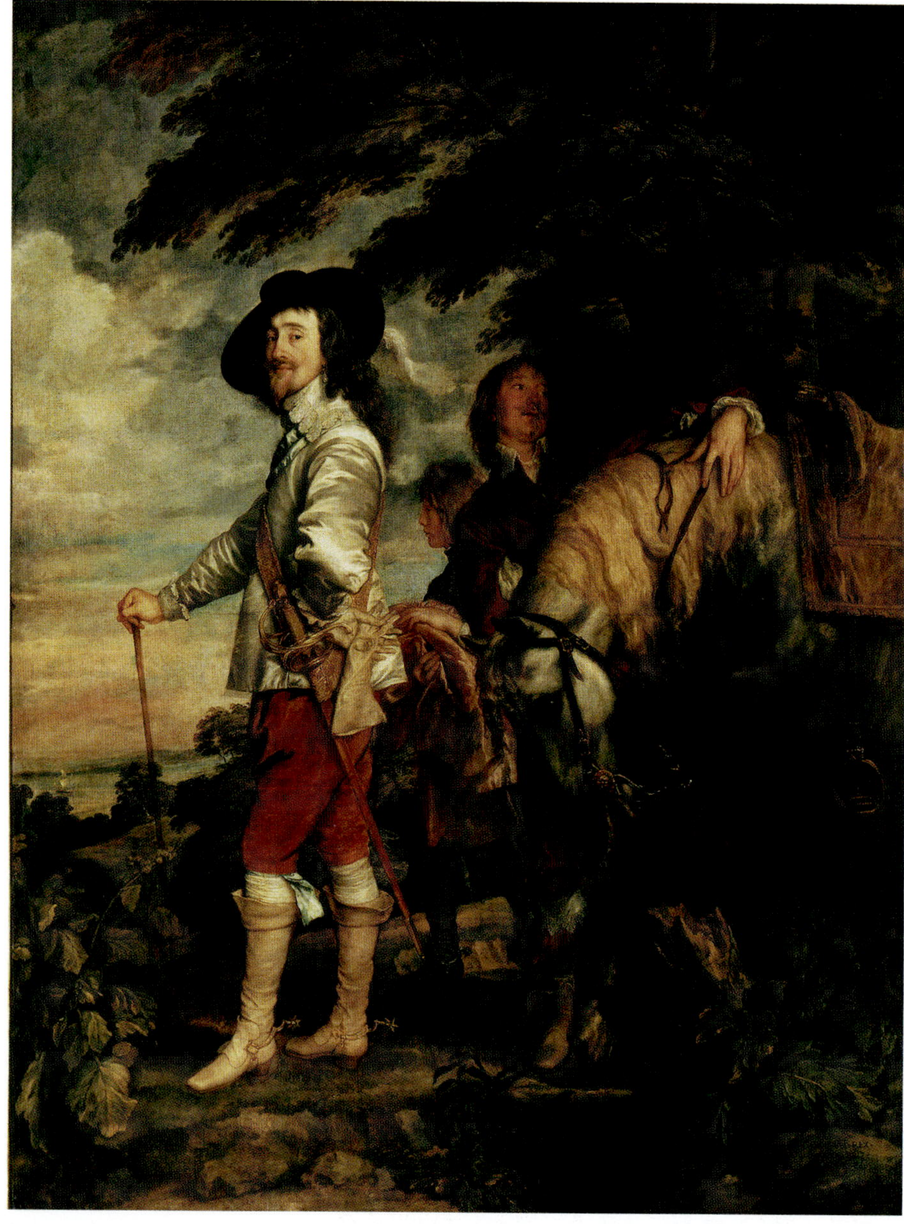

14–19 Anthony van Dyck. *Charles I at the Hunt.* 1635. Oil on canvas, 9' × 7' (2.75 × 2.14 m). Musée du Louvre, Paris

Eugenia and Archduke Albert, who were enthusiastic patrons of the arts and sciences. Indeed, it was their vast collection that inspired the painted allegory on *Sight* (fig. **14–18**).

Another of Rubens' collaborators, Anthony van Dyck (1599–1641), had an illustrious independent career as a portraitist. A precocious student at age 10, he had his own studio and a roster of pupils at age 16, although he did not become a member of the Antwerp painters' guild until 1618, the year after he began his association with Rubens as a specialist in painting heads. Later in his career, Van Dyck became court painter to Charles I of England, by whom he was knighted and given a studio, a large salary, and a summer home.

In *Charles I at the Hunt* (fig. **14–19**) of 1635, Van Dyck was able, by clever manipulation of the setting, to portray the king truthfully and yet as a quietly imposing figure. Dressed casually for the hunt and standing on a bluff overlooking a distant view, Charles, who was in fact very short, appears here taller than his pages and even than his horse, since the animal has lowered its head and its heavy body is partly off the canvas. The viewer's gaze is directed to the king's pleasant features, framed by his jauntily cocked hat. As if in decorous homage, the tree branches bow gracefully toward him, echoing the circular lines of the hat and the graceful cascade of his hair. Contrary to the appearance suggested by Van Dyck's portrait, Charles was not destined to rule his country successfully.

Religious and political tensions, particularly a conflict between Charles and the religious reformers known as Puritans, resulted in a series of civil wars, beginning in 1642. Charles lost his throne, and his head, in 1649. Once in power, the Puritans, led by Oliver Cromwell as lord protector, stifled artistic expression. However, austerity did not last, and in 1660, the restoration of the Stuart dynasty under Charles II brought renewed patronage of foreign artists, especially portrait painters.

The Protestant Netherlands

Spain recognized the sovereignty of the northern Netherlands in 1648. Even before this official recognition, the Dutch Republic—as the United Northern Provinces of the Low Countries was officially known—managed not only to maintain its hard-won freedom but also to prosper. Dutch artists found many eager patrons among the prosperous middle-class citizens of Amsterdam, Leiden, Haarlem, Delft, and Utrecht. Portraiture was especially popular and took many forms, ranging from pictures of single individuals in sparse settings to allegorical depictions in elaborate costumes and set in symbolic contexts. Group portraiture that documented the membership of corporate organizations became a Dutch specialty. These large canvases, filled with many individuals who shared the cost of the commission, challenged painters to present a coherent, interesting composition that also gave equal attention to each individual portrait.

Frans Hals (c. 1581/85–1666), the leading painter of Haarlem, developed a style grounded in the Netherlandish love of description and inspired by the Caravaggesque style. Yet like Velázquez, he tried to re-create the optical effects of light on the shapes and textures of objects, and he painted boldly, with slashing strokes and angular patches of paint. Only when seen at a distance do the colors merge into solid forms over which a flickering light seems to move. In Hals' hands, this seemingly effortless, loose technique suggests an infectious joy in life.

In his portrait of *Catharina Hooft and her Nurse* (fig. **14–20**), painted about 1620, Hals captured the vitality of a gesture caught within a fleeting moment in time. The portrait records for posterity the great pride of the parents in their child, but it also records their wealth in its study of rich fabrics, elaborate laces, and expensive toys (a golden rattle). Hals' depiction highlights the heartwarming delight of the child, who seems to be acknowledging the viewer as a loving family member, while her doting nurse attempts to distract her with an apple and at the same time looks out admiringly at the attention the viewer is directing to her charge.

The most important painter working in the Netherlands in the seventeenth century was Rembrandt van Rijn (1606–1669). After studying painting in Amsterdam and Leiden and working as an artist in both cities, Rembrandt established a busy studio in Amsterdam. He continued his studies with close observation of the art of his predecessors, witnessed by his drawing of Leonardo's *Last Supper* (see fig. Intro–22), as well as intense observation of the world

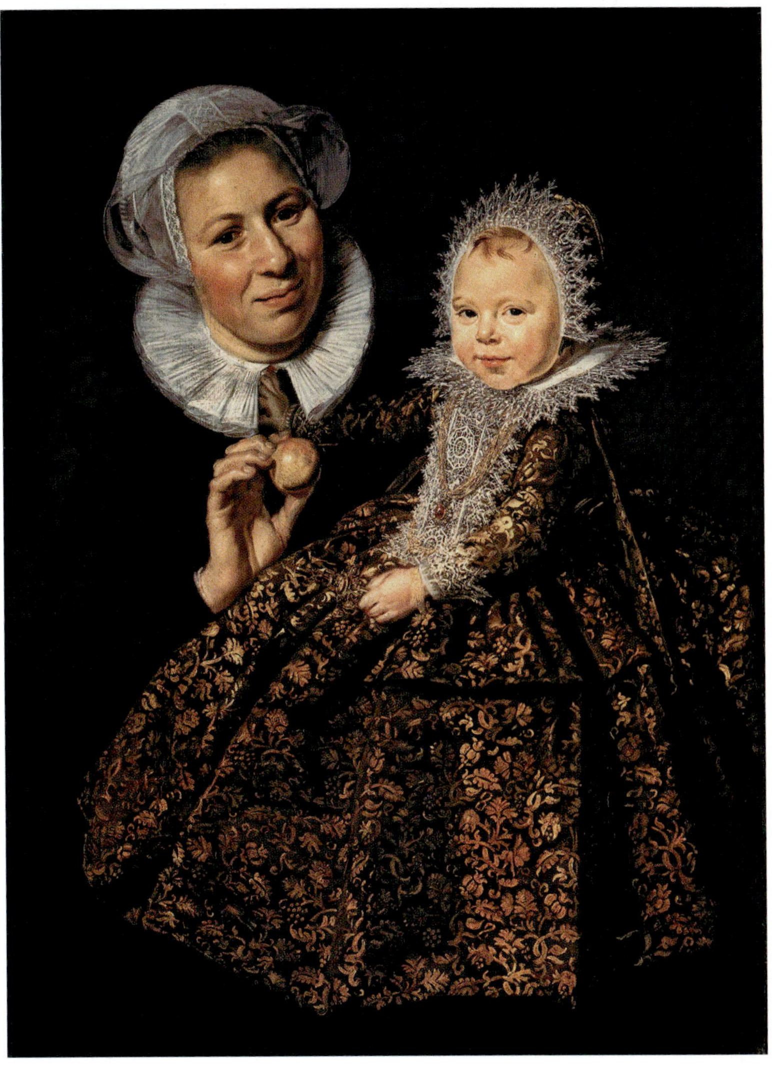

14–20 Frans Hals. *Catharina Hooft and her Nurse.* c. 1620. Oil on canvas, 33¾" × 25½" (85.7 × 64.8 cm). Staatliche Museen zu Berlin, Preussischer Kulturbesitz, Gemäldegalerie (INV. 801)

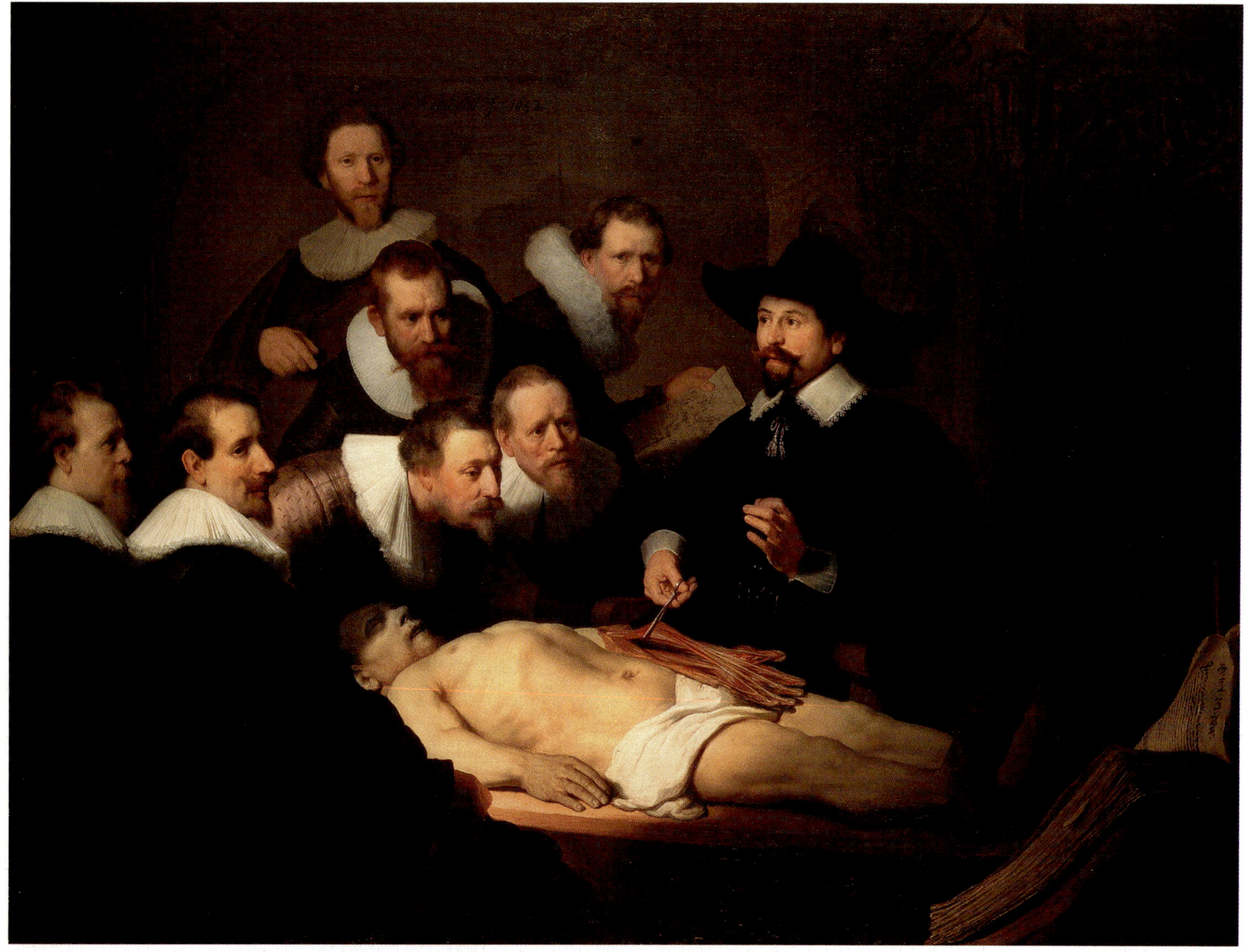

14–21 Rembrandt van Rijn. *The Anatomy Lesson of Dr. Nicolaes Tulp*. 1632. Oil on canvas, 5' 3¾" × 7' 1¼" (1.6 × 2.1 m). Mauritshuis, The Hague, Netherlands

around him. His repertoire included paintings and etchings of mythological subjects, religious scenes, and landscapes, but like many Dutch artists of the time his primary source of income was from portraiture.

The Anatomy Lesson of Dr. Nicolaes Tulp (fig. **14–21**) of 1632 was Rembrandt's first group portrait. Doctor Tulp, head of the surgeons' guild from 1628 to 1653, sits right of center, while a group of fellow doctors gathers to observe the cadaver and learn from the famed anatomist. Rembrandt built his composition on a sharp diagonal that pierces space from right to left, uniting the cadaver on the table, the calculated arrangement of speaker and listeners, and the open book into a dramatic narrative event. Rembrandt makes effective use of Caravaggio's tenebrist technique, as the figures emerge from a dark and undefined ambience, their attentive faces framed by brilliant white ruffs. Radiant light streams down to spotlight the ghostly flesh of the cadaver, drawing our attention to the extended arms of Dr. Tulp, who flexes his own left hand to demonstrate the action of the cadaver's arm muscles that he lifts up with silver forceps. Unseen by viewers are the illustrations of the huge book, presumably an edition of Andreas Vesalius's study of human anatomy, published in Basel in 1543, which was the first attempt at accurate anatomical illustrations in print. Rembrandt's painting has been seen as an homage to Vesalius and to science, as well as a group portrait of the members of the Amsterdam surgeons' guild.

In 1640, a civic guard company commissioned Rembrandt to create a large group portrait of its members for its new meeting hall. *Captain Frans Banning Cocq Mustering his Company* (fig. **14–22**) carries the idea of a group portrait as dramatic event even further. The painting has become known as *The Night Watch* because a layer of dirt and old varnish had so obscured its colors by the nineteenth century that viewers thought the scene took place at night. Since its cleaning and restoration during the 1970s, however, the painting glows with a golden light that ignites its palette of rich colors—browns, blues, olive green, orange, and red—around a central core

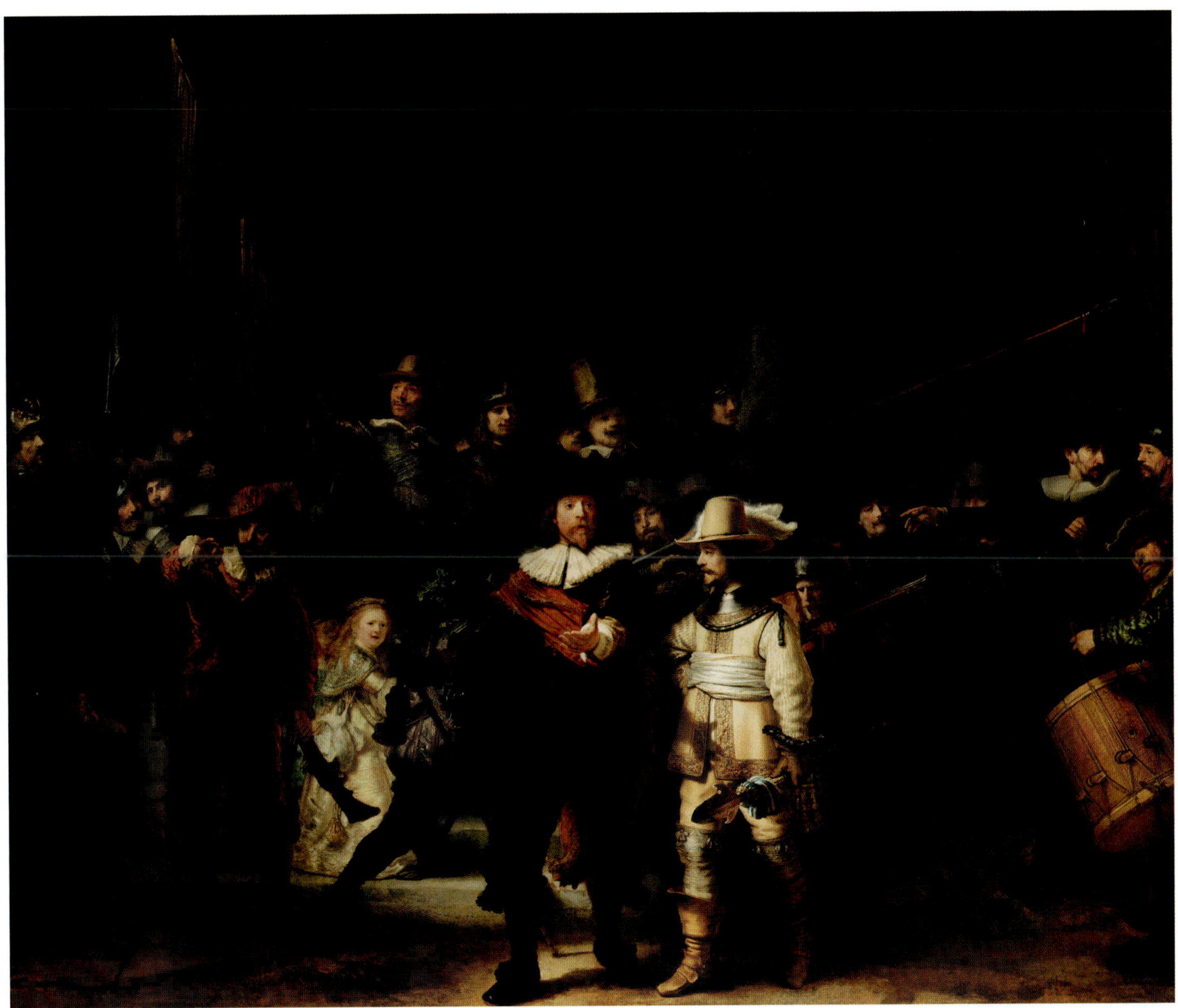

14–22 Rembrandt van Rijn. ***Captain Frans Banning Cocq Mustering his Company (The Night Watch).*** 1642. Oil on canvas (cut down from the original size), 11' 11" × 14' 4" (3.63 × 4.37 m). Rijksmuseum, Amsterdam

of lemon yellow. As the company takes up its ranks, a crowd, including children, mills around. The surprising, highlighted image in the left middle ground of a girl carrying a chicken with prominent claws (*klauw* in Dutch) may be a pun on the name of the guns (*klover*) that gave the name "The Kloveniers" to this company. The complex interactions of the figures and the vivid, individualized likenesses of the militiamen make this painting one of the greatest group portraits in the Dutch tradition.

Rembrandt also created profoundly moving religious art. His etchings and drypoints (see "Etching and Drypoint," page 403) were sought after, widely collected, and brought high prices even during his lifetime. As he grew older, Rembrandt seems to have experienced a deepening religious commitment based on his personal study of the Bible. In *The Three Crosses*, Rembrandt tried to capture the moment during the Crucifixion when Jesus cried out, "Father, into your hands I commend my spirit" (Luke 23:46). We can follow Rembrandt's creative process through four successive stages, from the relatively anecdotal depiction of the crosses and the surrounding crowd in the first state (fig. **14–23**) to the haunting blackness of the fourth and final state. As Jesus cries out, a mystical light, beyond

14–23 Rembrandt van Rijn. ***The Three Crosses*** **(first state).** 1653. Drypoint and etching, 15⅛" × 17¾" (38.5 × 45 cm). Rijksmuseum, Amsterdam

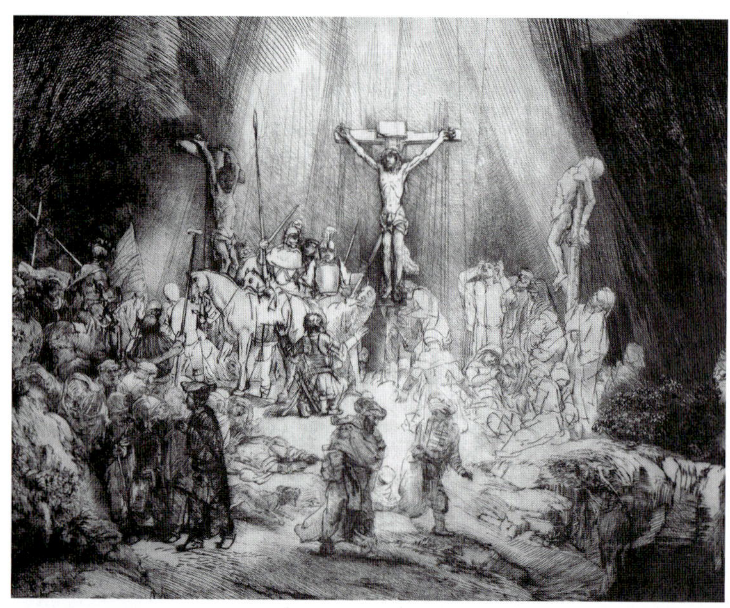

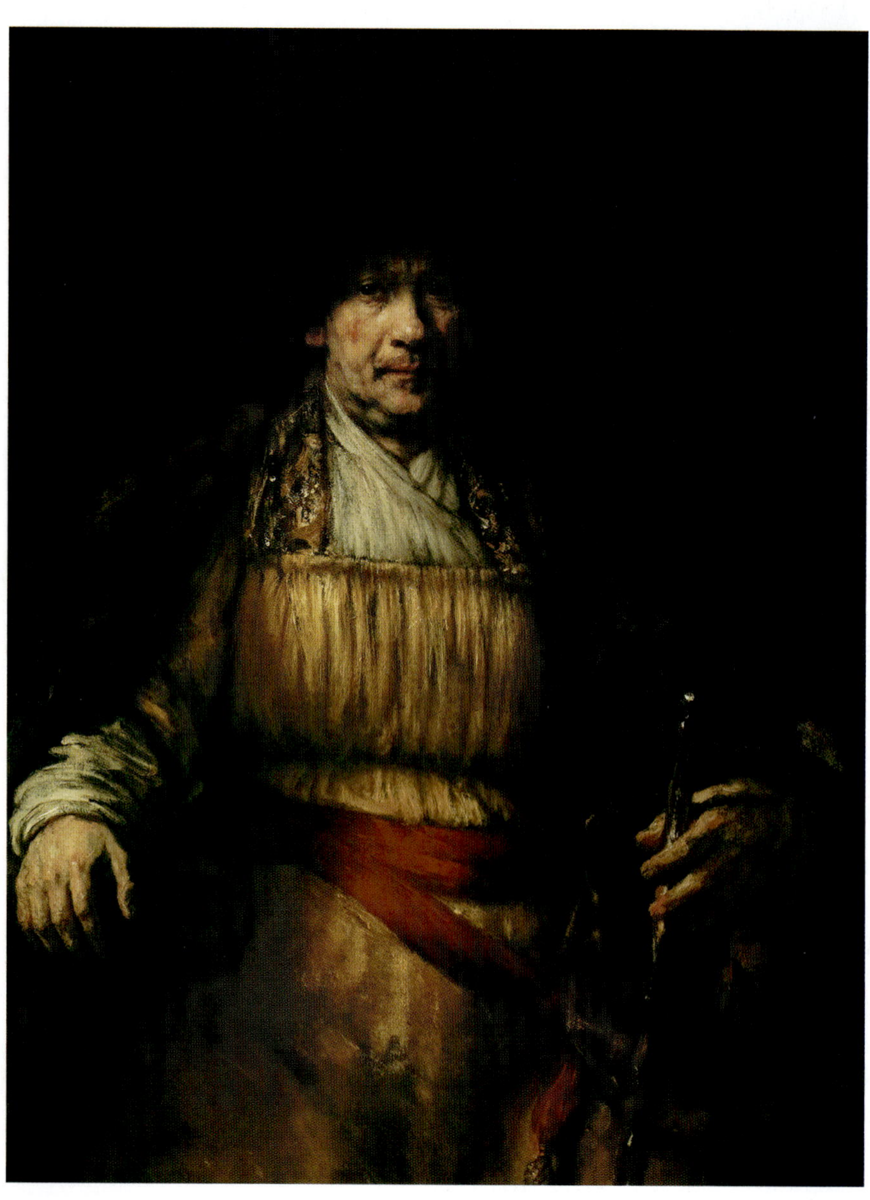

14–24 Rembrandt van Rijn. ***Self-Portrait.*** 1658. Oil on canvas, 52⅝" × 40⅞" (133.6 × 103.8 cm). The Frick Collection, New York

Technique

Etching and Drypoint

Rembrandt was the first artist to popularize etching as a major form of artistic expression. In the etching process, a metal plate is coated on both sides with an acid-resistant resin that dries hard without being brittle. Then, instead of laboriously cutting the lines of the desired image directly into the plate as in an engraving (see "Woodcuts and Engravings, page 315), the artist draws through the resin with a sharp needle to expose the metal. The plate is then immersed in acid, which eats into the metal exposed by the drawn lines. By controlling the time the acid stays on different parts of the plate, the artist can make fine, shallow lines or heavy, deep ones. After the resin covering is removed from the surface of the plate, an impression is taken. If changes need to be made, lines can be "erased" with a sharp metal scraper. Not surprisingly, a complex image with a wide range of tones requires many steps.

Another technique for registering images on a metal plate is called drypoint, in which a sharp needle is used to scratch lines in the metal. In drypoint, however, the burr, or metal pushed up by the drypoint needle, is left in place. Unlike engraving, in which the burr is scraped off, both the burr and the groove hold the ink. This creates a printed line with a rich black appearance that is impossible to achieve with engraving or etching alone. Unfortunately, drypoint burr is fragile, and no more than a dozen prints can be made before it flattens and loses its character. Rembrandt's earliest prints were entirely etched, but later he added drypoint to develop tonal richness.

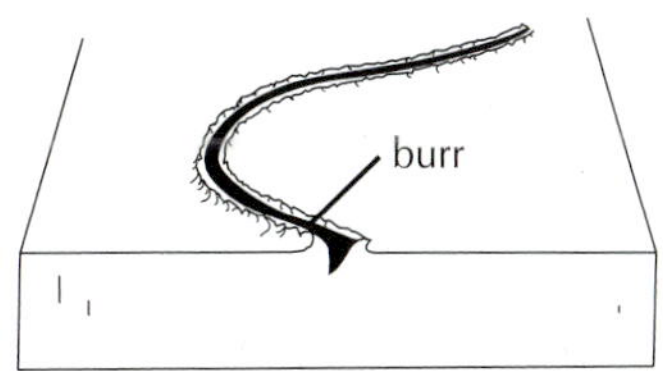

rational explanation, illuminates the darkened scene. The "realism" here is spiritual, conveying inner meaning not surface details. The eternal battle of dark and light, doom and salvation, evil and good, all seem to be waged anew.

Rembrandt painted many self-portraits, and as the artist aged, these personal images became more searching and, like many of his paintings, expressed a deepening internalized spirituality and psychological honesty new in the history of art. In a self-portrait of 1658 (fig. **14–24**), the artist assumes an almost regal pose, at ease with arms and legs spread, holding a staff as if it were a baton of authority. Yet his face and eyes seem weary and introspective. We know that he had reason to worry, since he declared bankruptcy in this same year. A few well-placed brushstrokes are sufficient to capture the tension in the fingers and the weariness in the deepset eyes, half in shadow. Mercilessly analytical, the portrait depicts the furrowed brow, sagging flesh, and prematurely aged face (he was only 53) of one who has suffered deeply but retained his dignity.

More typical of Dutch painters, Judith Leyster (c. 1609–1660) painted boisterous genre scenes categorized in their own time by descriptive titles such as "merry company" or "garden party." In her lively *Self-Portrait* (fig. **14–25**), Leyster displays on her easel the type of work on which her popularity was based. The subject, a man playing a violin, may also be a visual pun on the painter's instruments, the palette and brush. To let the viewer immediately see the difference between her painted portrait and the painted painting, she varied her technique, executing the image on her easel more loosely. The narrow range of colors sensitively dispersed in the composition and the warm spotlighting are typical of Leyster's mature style.

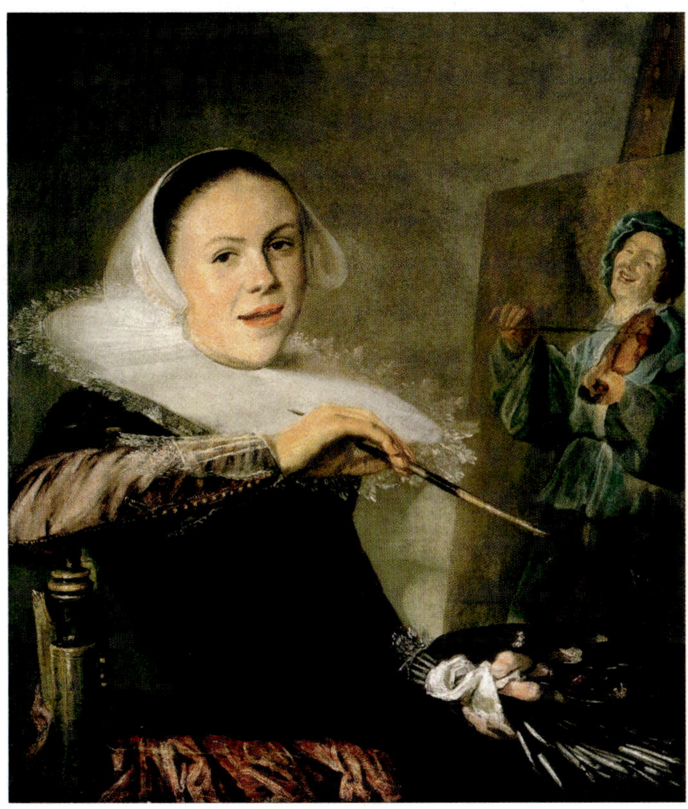

14–25 Judith Leyster. ***Self-Portrait.*** c. 1630. Oil on canvas, 29⅜" × 25⅝" (74.6 × 45.1 cm). National Gallery of Art, Washington, D.C.
GIFT OF MR. AND MRS. ROBERT WOODS BLISS

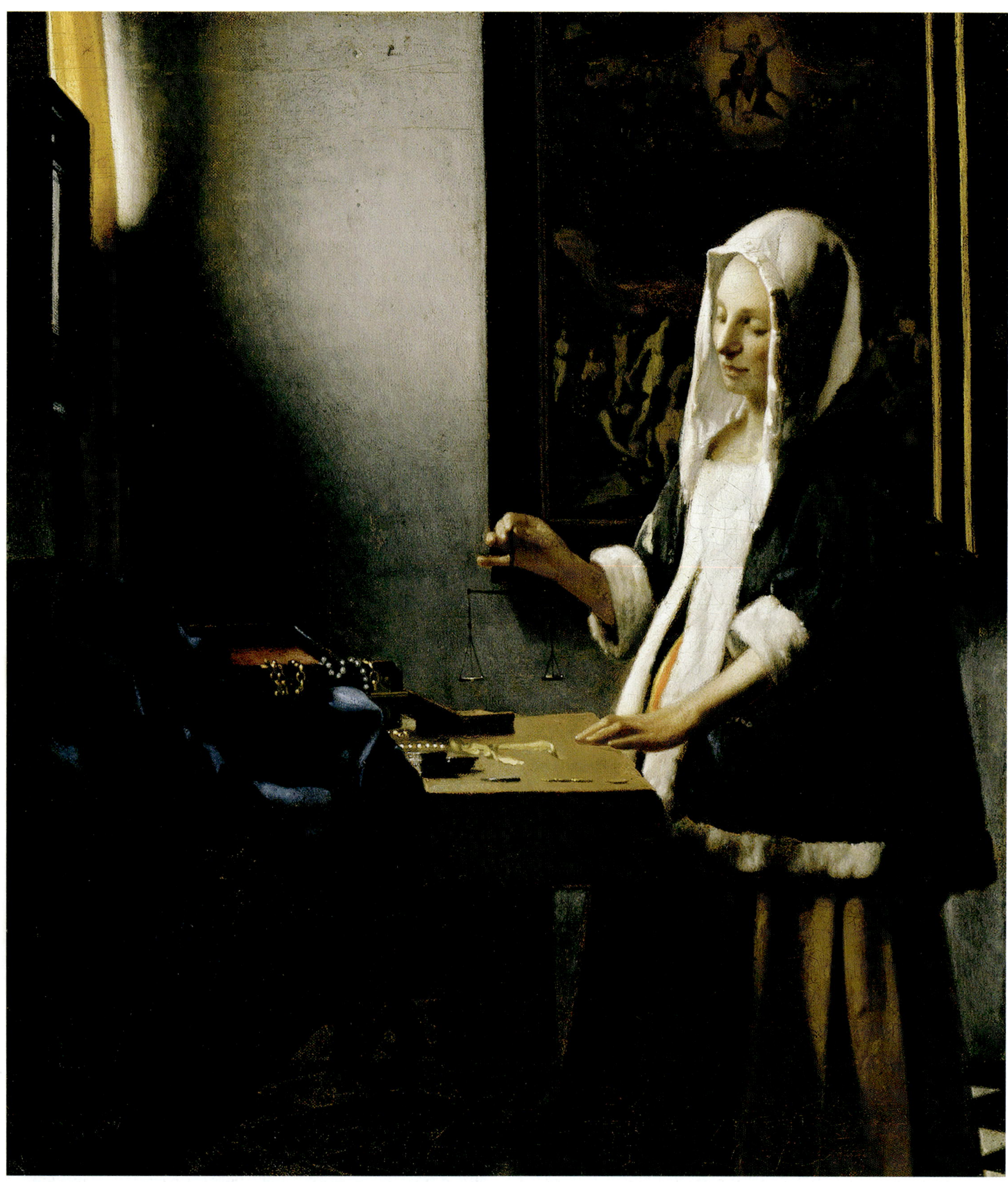

14–26 Jan Vermeer. ***Woman Holding a Balance.*** c. 1664. Oil on canvas, 16¾" × 15" (42.5 × 38.1 cm). National Gallery of Art, Washington, D.C. (14–26)

The artist's shift of viewpoint slightly to one side has created an interesting spatial composition, and strong contrasts of light and shade add drama to the simple interior.

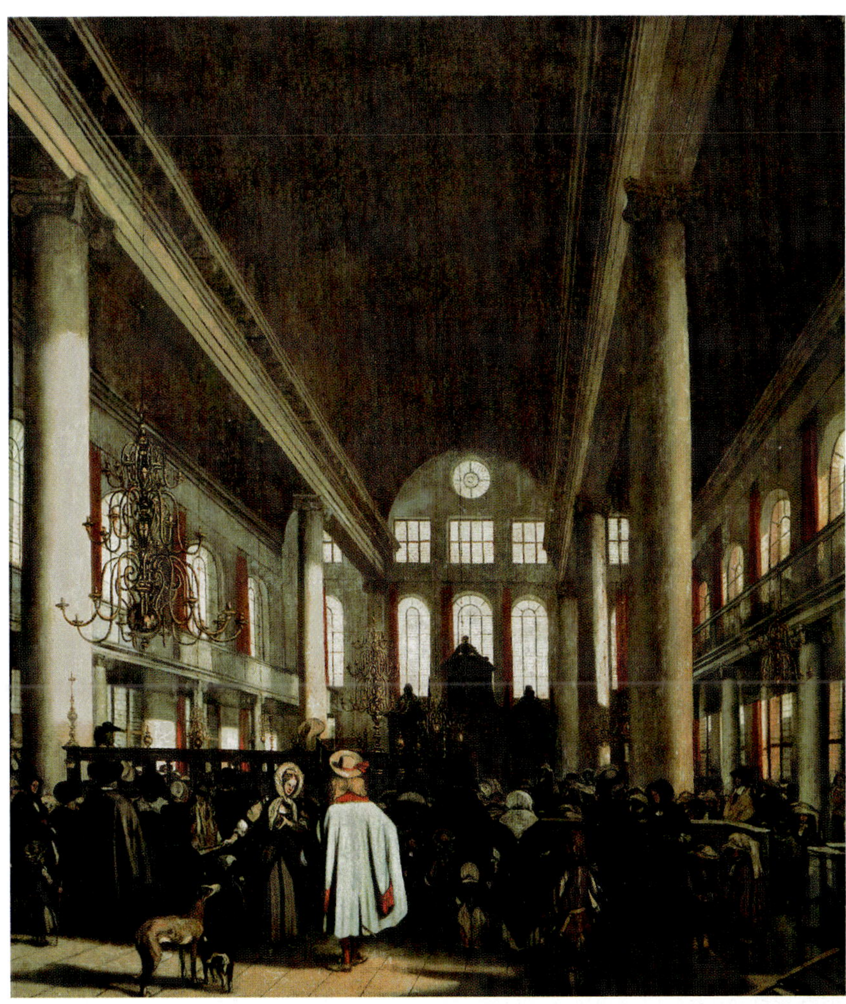

14–27 Emanuel de Witte. ***Portuguese Synagogue, Amsterdam.*** 1680. Oil on canvas, 43½" × 39" (110.5 × 99.1 cm). Rijksmuseum, Amsterdam

The art produced in the Netherlands during the seventeenth century shows that the Dutch delighted in depictions not only of themselves, but also of their country's landscape, cities, and scenes of daily life, known as genre paintings. Perhaps the most evocative painter of contemporary Dutch life was Jan (Johannes) Vermeer of Delft (1632–1675). Vermeer produced few works, and most concentrate on enigmatic scenes of women in their homes, occupied with some cultivated activity such as writing, reading letters, or making music. These are quiet interior scenes, low-key in color, asymmetrical but strongly geometric and balanced in organization. An even, pearly light from a window gives solidity to the figures and objects in the room. Emotion is subdued, evoking the stillness of meditation. The brushwork is so controlled that it becomes invisible, except where he paints his characteristic pools of reflected light as tiny, pearl-like droplets of color.

In *Woman Holding a Balance* (fig. **14–26**), painted about 1664, perfect compositional equilibrium creates a moment of supreme stillness. The woman contemplates the balance in her right hand, drawing our attention to the act of weighing and judging. Hung on the wall behind her, is a painting of the Last Judgment, highlighting the figure of Christ the Judge directly over her head. The juxtaposition seems to turn Vermeer's genre scene into a metaphor for eternal judgment, a sobering religious reference that may reflect the artist's own position as a Catholic living in a Protestant country. And the woman's moment of quiet introspection in front of the gold and pearls displayed on the table before her, shimmering with reflected light from the window, also evokes the ***vanitas*** theme (vanity of earthly things), inspiring spiritual reflections on the fleeting nature of beauty, youth, and riches.

Another type of genre painting that achieved great popularity in the Baroque period is the architectural interior. Buildings seem to have been painted for their own special beauty, just like landscapes, cities, and harbors. Emanuel de Witte (1617–1692) specialized in architectural painting, and many of his interiors depict actual buildings, such as his *Portuguese Synagogue, Amsterdam* (fig. **14–27**). The synagogue is shown as a rectangular hall with women's galleries on both sides, roofed by three wooden barrel vaults and lit by large glass windows. Standing within this space, the elegant couple in the foreground, the crowd behind them, and the dogs in the foreground provide a sense of scale and add human interest.

Today, this painting is interesting not only as a work of art, but also as a record of seventeenth-century synagogue architecture. It also reflects Dutch religious tolerance in an age when Jews were often persecuted. Expelled from Spain and Portugal beginning in the late fifteenth century, many Jews had settled in Amsterdam, where there was at this time a community of about 2,300, most of

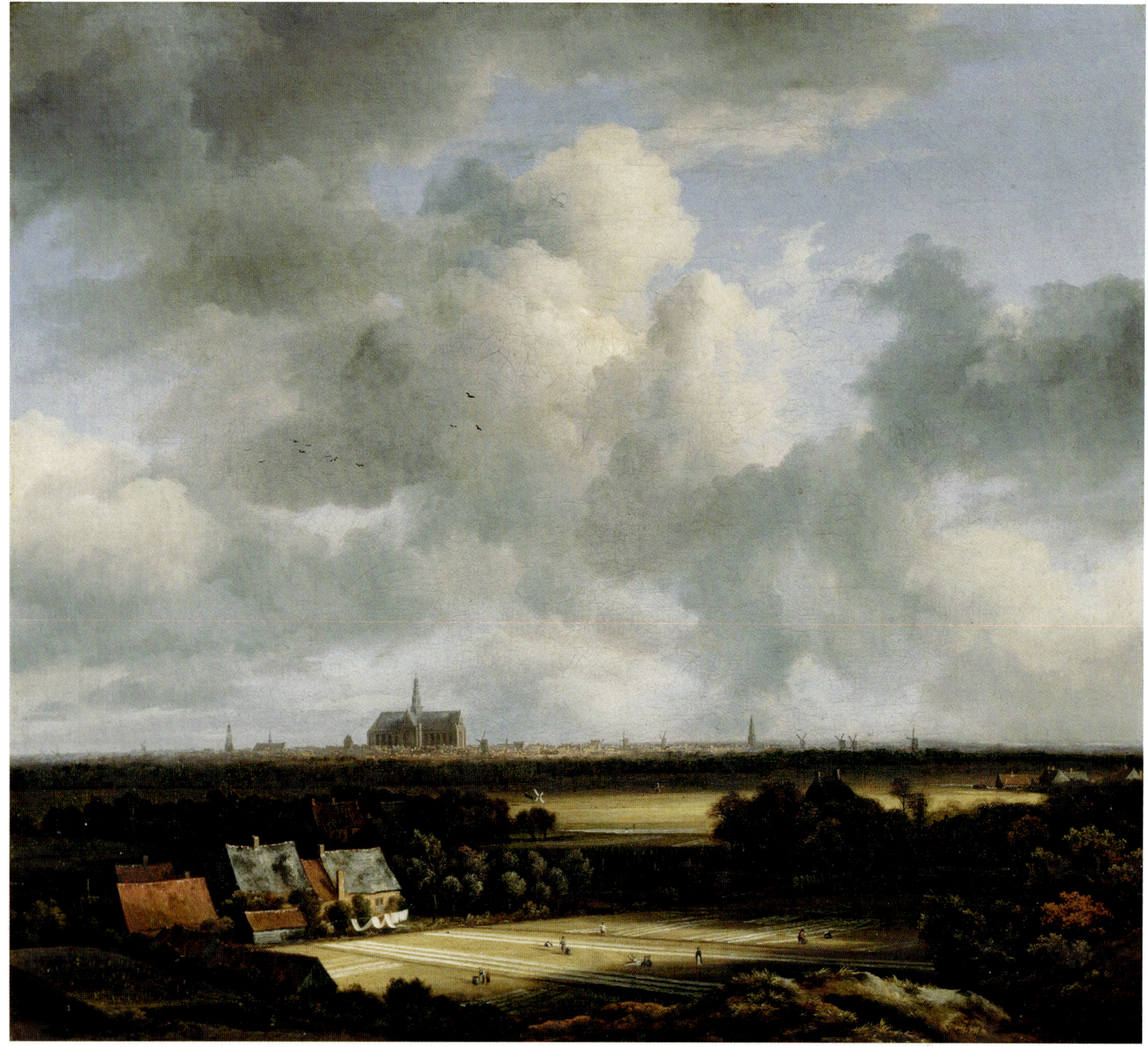

14–28 Jacob van Ruisdael. ***View of Haarlem from the Dunes at Overveen.*** c. 1670. Oil on canvas, 22" × 24¾" (55.8 × 62.8 cm). Mauritshuis, The Hague, Netherlands

whom were well-to-do merchants. Fund-raising for a new synagogue began in 1670, and in 1671 Elias Bouman won the building competition. With its classical architecture, Brazilian jacaranda-wood furniture, and 26 brass chandeliers, this was considered one of the most impressive buildings in Amsterdam. The synagogue was spared by the Nazis during World War II because the Germans planned to turn it into a museum of Jewish culture.

The Dutch loved the landscapes and vast skies of their country. Jacob van Ruisdael's *View of Haarlem from the Dunes at Overveen* (fig. **14–28**), painted about 1670, celebrates the flatlands outside Haarlem that had been reclaimed from the sea as part of a massive landfill project of 1650–1670 that the Dutch compared with God's restoration of the earth after Noah's flood. Such a religious interpretation may be referenced here in the prominent Gothic church of Saint Bavo, looming on the horizon. Devoting almost three-fourths of this painting to a glorious rendering of the powerfully cloudy sky gives it a spectacular monumentality, dwarfing the labor of the tiny humans spotlighted below, caught in the process of spreading white linen across the broad fields to bleach in the sun—a representation of the Protestant virtues of work and cleanliness.

The Dutch love of nature is also apparent in still-life paintings of artfully arranged everyday objects or flowers. The latter were

SCIENCE AND THE CHANGING WORLDVIEW

From the mid-sixteenth through the eighteenth centuries, new discoveries about the natural world brought a sense of both the grand scale and the microscopic detail of the universe. To publish their theories and research, early scientists learned to draw or depended on artists to draw what they discovered in the world around them. This practice would continue until the invention of photography in the nineteenth century.

Artist and scientist were seldom the same person, but Anna Maria Sibylla Merian (1647–1717) contributed to botany and entomology both as a researcher and as an artist. German by birth and Dutch by training, Merian was once described by a Dutch contemporary as a painter of worms, flies, mosquitoes, spiders, "and other filth." In 1699, the city of Amsterdam subsidized Merian's research on plants and insects in the Dutch colony of Surinam in South America, where she spent two years exploring the jungle and recording insects. On her return to the Dutch Republic, she published the results of her research as *Metamorphosis of Insects in Surinam*, illustrated with 72 large plates engraved after her watercolors (fig. **14–29**). For all her meticulous scientific accuracy, Merian carefully arranged her depictions of exotic insects and elegant fruits and flowers into skillful and harmonious compositions.

But interest in scientific exploration was not limited to the Netherlands. The writings of philosophers Francis Bacon (1561–1626) in England and René Descartes (1596–1650) in France helped establish a new method of studying the world by insisting on scrupulous objectivity and logical reasoning. Bacon argued that the only significant knowledge came from investigating the natural world, and he proposed that facts be gathered and studied systematically. Descartes, who was also a mathematician, is credited with inventing analytic geometry and the modern scientific method.

In 1543, the Polish scholar Nicolaus Copernicus (1473–1543) published *On the Revolutions of the Heavenly Spheres*, which contradicted the long-held view that Earth is the center of the universe (the Ptolemaic theory) by arguing instead that Earth and other planets revolve around the Sun. The Church viewed Copernican theory as a challenge to its doctrines, and in 1616 put Copernicus's work on its Index of Prohibited Books.

At the beginning of the seventeenth century, Johannes Kepler (1571–1630), court mathematician and astronomer to Holy Roman Emperor Rudolf II, demonstrated that the planets revolve around the Sun in elliptical orbits. Kepler noted a number of interrelated dynamic geometric patterns in the universe, the overall design of which he believed was an expression of divine order.

Galileo Galilei (1564–1642), an astronomer, philosopher, and physicist, was the first to develop a tool for observing the heavens: the telescope. As the first person to see moons traveling around Jupiter, his findings provided further confirmation of Copernican theory. After the Church prohibited the teaching of that theory, Galileo was tried for heresy by the Inquisition. Under duress, he publicly rejected his views, although at the end of his trial, according to legend, he muttered, "*Eppur si muove!*" ("Nevertheless it [Earth] does move").

The new seventeenth-century science turned to the study of the very small as well as to the vast reaches of space. This included the refinement of the microscope by the Dutch lens-maker and amateur scientist Anton van Leeuwenhoek (1632–1723). Leeuwenhoek perfected grinding techniques and increased the power of magnification in his lenses far beyond the requirements of a simple magnifying glass. Ultimately, he was able to study the inner workings of plants and animals and even see micro-organisms.

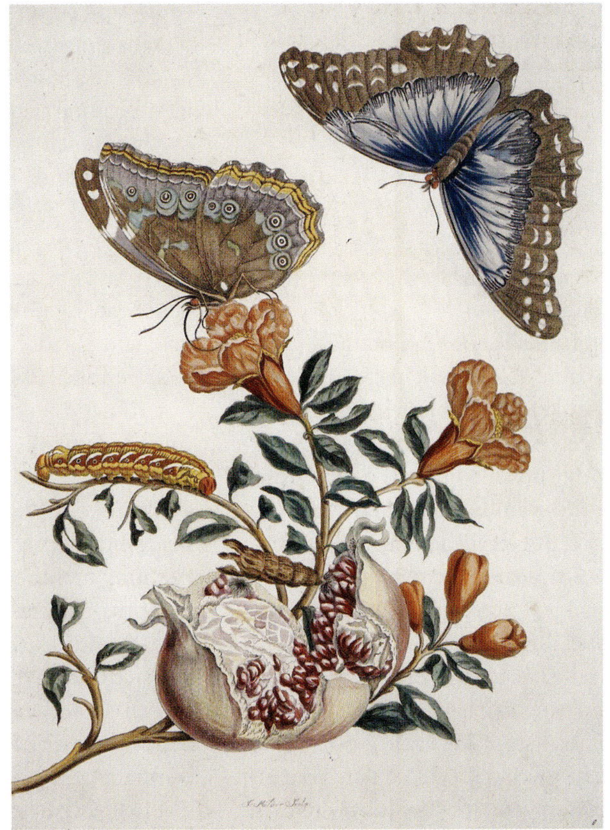

14–29 Anna Maria Sibylla Merian. *Plate 9* from *Metamorphosis of Insects in Surinam*. 1719 (printed posthumously). Bound volume of 72 hand-colored engravings (second edition), 18⅞" × 13" (47.9 × 33 cm). National Museum of Women in the Arts, Washington, D.C. GIFT OF WALLACE AND WILHELMINA HOLLADAY

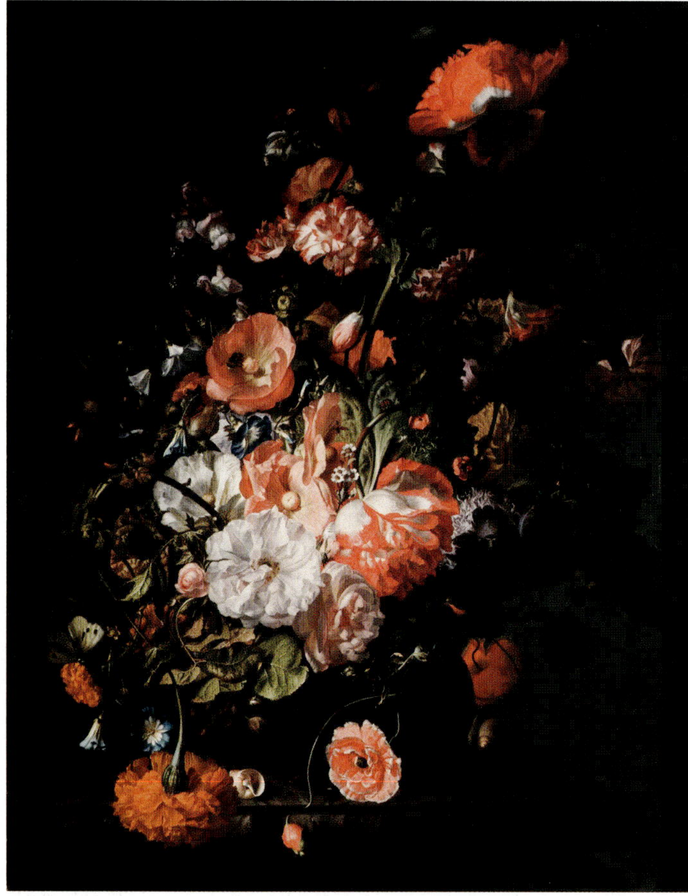

14–30 Rachel Ruysch. ***Flower Still Life.*** After 1700. Oil on canvas, 30" × 24" (76.2 × 61 cm). The Toledo Museum of Art, Ohio
PURCHASED WITH FUNDS FROM THE LIBBEY ENDOWMENT. GIFT OF EDWARD DRUMMOND LIBBEY

more than straightforward depictions of actual fresh flowers. Artists made color sketches of prime examples of each type of flower and studied scientifically accurate color illustrations in botanical publications (see "Science and the Changing Worldview," page 407). Once in the studio, they would use their sketches and notebooks to compose imaginary bouquets of perfect specimens, juxtaposing within their arrangements flowers that did not bloom at the same time. *Flower Piece with Curtain* by Adrien van der Spelt and Frans van Mieris (see fig. Intro–2) is a playful, but learned, example.

Rachel Ruysch (1663–1750) was one of the most sought-after and highest-paid flower painters in Amsterdam. During her 70-year career, her works were highly prized for their sensitive, free-form floral arrangements and their unusual and beautiful color harmonies (fig. **14–30**). Perhaps less daring than some of her peers, she was more "scientific" in outlook, transforming each flower in her still lifes into a botanical study. Ruysch had learned botany as a girl from her father, a professor of anatomy and botany in Amsterdam. Although married with 10 children, Ruysch never stopped painting. She achieved such fame in her lifetime that her paintings often brought higher prices than works by Rembrandt. Frequently she enlivened her compositions with reptiles or insects—in this case, two snail shells and a large gray moth—that lend an unsettling feeling to her paintings since such predators pose a potential threat to the fragile beauty of the flowers. And besides appreciating the sumptuousness of the natural world and the virtuosity with which it is captured by Ruysch, viewers may have also recognized the singularly expensive flaming tulip as a warning against the vanity of pride and greed, just as the short life of the cut flowers may have reminded them of the fleeting nature of beauty and human life. In the Protestant Netherlands, even art informed by science could carry a moral message.

Art for the State: France

Absolute monarchs were expected to be patrons of the arts in Baroque Europe. Many emulated the example of late seventeenth-century French King Louis XIV, striving to match his court at Versailles by building and rebuilding their own palaces, planting vast gardens dotted with richly sculptured fountains, and spending fortunes on paintings and the decorative arts. But, the early seventeenth century had actually been a difficult period in France, marked by almost continuous foreign and civil wars. King Henry IV was assassinated in 1610, and the country endured a long regency during the youth of Henry's 9-year-old heir, Louis XIII (ruled 1610–1643).

Louis XIV (ruled 1643–1715) also came to the throne as a youth, and began his personal rule only in 1661. His autocratic reign was the longest in European history. As he became known as *le Roi Soleil* ("the Sun King"), he was sometimes glorified in art through identification with the Classical sun god, Apollo. In a 1701 portrait by the French court painter Hyacinthe Rigaud (1659–1743), the richly costumed monarch is framed by a lavish, billowing curtain (fig. **14–31**). Proudly showing off his elegant legs, the 63-year-old Louis XIV poses in a blue robe of state, trimmed with gold fleurs-de-lys and lined with white ermine. He wears the high-heeled shoes he devised to compensate for his shortness. Despite his pompous pose and magnificent surroundings, the directness of the king's gaze and the frankness of his aging face make him surprisingly human.

Under Louis XIV's lavish patronage of the arts, the French court became the cultural center of Europe. The Royal Academy of Painting and Sculpture, founded in 1648, maintained strict national control over the arts, and membership ensured an artist lucrative royal and civic commissions. Although the French Academy was not the first in Europe, none before it had exerted such dictatorial authority—an authority that lasted in France until the late nineteenth century (see "Grading the Old Masters," page 409). Classicism enjoyed particular favor in the academy and permeated French Baroque painting, sculpture, and architecture. When the corresponding Royal Academy of Architecture was founded in 1671, its members developed guidelines for architectural design based on the belief that mathematics was the true basis of beauty, with Vitruvius (see "The Vitruvian Man," page 338) and Palladio (see figs. 13–24 and 13–25) as their models.

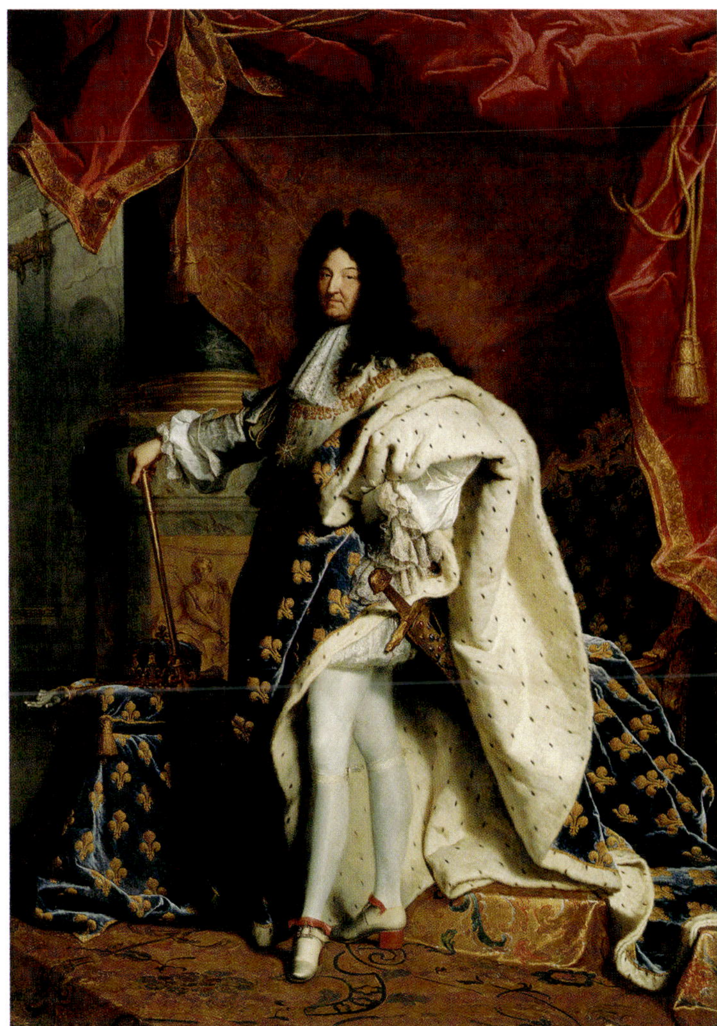

14–31 Hyacinthe Rigaud. ***Louis XIV.*** 1701. Oil on canvas, 9' 2" × 7' 10½" (2.79 × 2.4 m). Musée du Louvre, Paris

Louis XIV had ordered this portrait as a gift for his grandson, the future Philip V of Spain (ruled 1700–1746), but when Rigaud finished the painting, Louis liked it too much to give it away and only three years later he ordered a copy from Rigaud to give to his grandson. The request for copies of royal portraits was not unusual since the aristocratic families of Europe were linked through marriage. Paintings made appropriate gifts and at the same time memorialized important political alliances by recording them in visual form.

GRADING THE OLD MASTERS

The members of the French Royal Academy of Painting and Sculpture considered ancient Classical art the standard by which contemporary art should be judged. By the 1680s, however, younger artists began to argue that modern art might equal and even surpass the art of the ancients. A related debate arose over the relative merits of drawing and color in painting. Conservatives argued that drawing was superior because it appealed to the mind, while color appealed to the senses. They saw the work of Nicolas Poussin as the perfect embodiment of Classical principles. But younger artists preferred the vivid colors of Titian, Veronese, and Rubens, claiming that painting should deceive the eye, and since color achieves this deception more convincingly than drawing, color should be valued over drawing. The two factions were called *poussinistes* (in honor of Poussin) and *rubénistes* (for Rubens).

The portrait painter and critic Roger de Piles (1635–1709) took up the cause of the *rubénistes* in a series of published pamphlets. In *The Principles of Painting*, he evaluated painters on a scale of 0 to 20. He gave no score higher than 18, since no mortal could possibly achieve perfection. Caravaggio received the lowest grade, a 0 in expression and 6 in drawing, while Michelangelo and Leonardo both got a 4 in color and Rembrandt a 6 in drawing. Top grades (18) went to Titian for color, Rubens for composition, and Raphael for drawing and expression.

If we work out the "grades" using the traditional scale of 90% = A, 80% = B, and so forth, many important painters don't do very well. Raphael and Rubens get A's; but no one seems to get a B, although Van Dyck is close with a C+. Poussin and Titian earn solid C's, while Rembrandt slips by with a C-. Leonardo gets a D, but Michelangelo, Dürer, and Caravaggio are resounding failures in de Piles' view. Tastes change. Someday our ideas may seem just as misguided as those of the academicians.

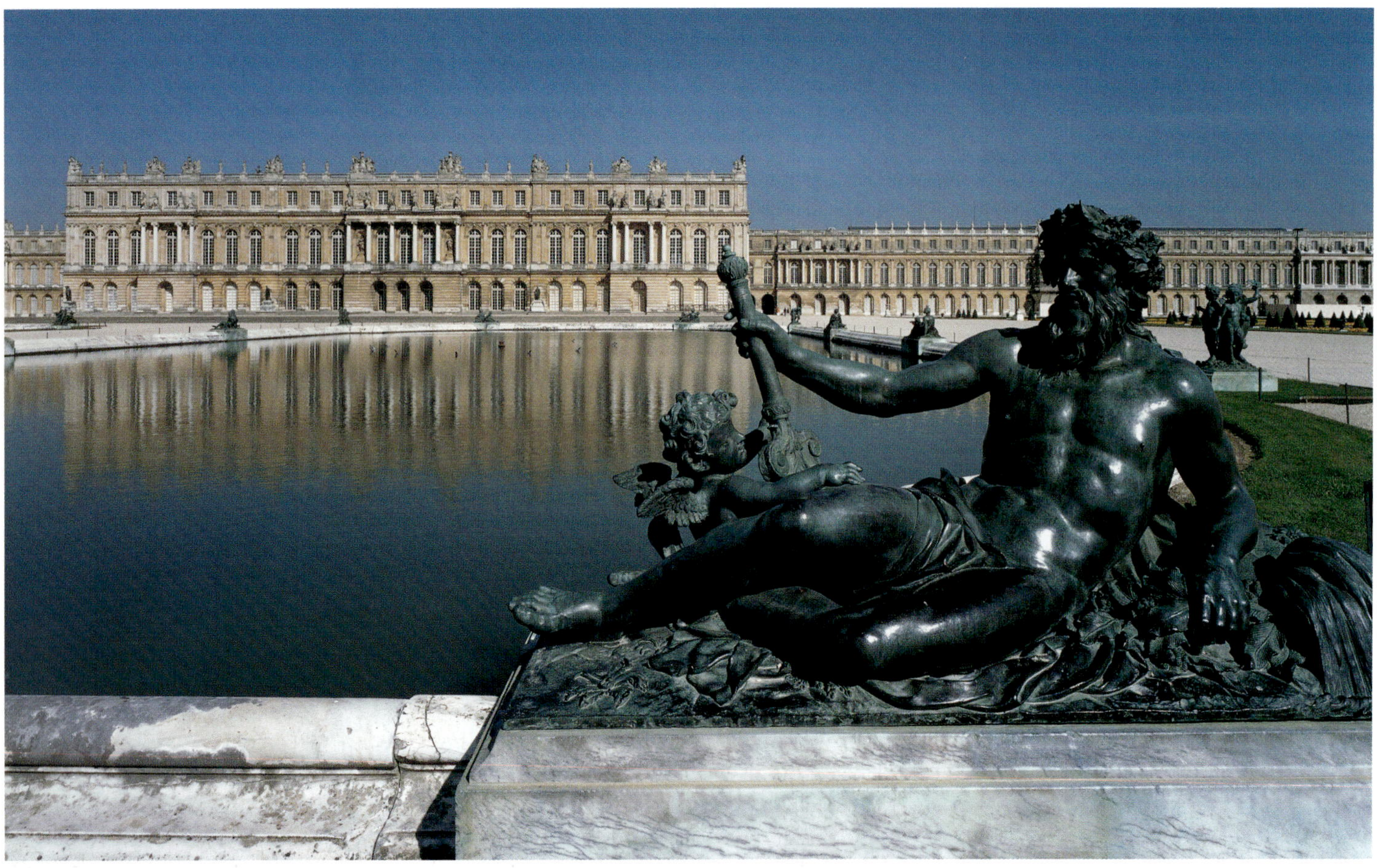

14–32 Jean-Baptiste Tuby. ***Neptune***, bronze statue by a reflecting pool in front of **Louis Le Vau and Jules Hardouin-Mansart. The Garden Façade, Palais de Versailles.** Gardens by André Le Nôtre, 1668–1685

In 1668, Louis XIV turned his attention to transforming a small hunting château at Versailles, built by his father Louis XIII, into the seat of his spectacular court of 5,000 aristocrats, supported by 14,000 resident soldiers and servants. This vast royal project consumed the energy of France's greatest painters, sculptors, designers, and architects for decades. The new architectural complex went up around the original château under the direction first of Louis Le Vau (1612–1670), beginning in 1668, and then after his death, of Jules Hardouin-Mansart (1646–1708) (fig. **14–32**). The three-story garden façade elevation has a lightly rusticated ground floor, a grand first or main floor (we would call it the second floor) lined with enormous arched windows separated by Ionic columns or pilasters, and a less lofty attic level with rectangular windows. The overall design is a sensitive balance of horizontals and verticals relieved by a restrained overlay of regularly spaced projecting blocks with open, colonnaded porches.

Concurrently, André Le Nôtre (1613–1700), who planned the gardens, turned the terrain around the palace into an extraordinary work of art, destined to have a powerful influence on urban as well as garden design. Neatly contained expanses of lawn and broad, straight vistas seem to stretch to the horizon, while the formal gardens, pools, fountains, and sculpture immediately behind the palace are an exercise in precise geometry. From these gardens, terraces descend to shaped, wooded areas and the mile-long Grand Canal. Classically harmonious and restful in their symmetrical, geometric design, the vast Versailles gardens extend into the surrounding countryside.

Residents and visitors to the château originally admired the gardens from an arcaded rear terrace, but in his renovations, Hardouin-Mansart enclosed this previously open space, turning it into an immense gallery known as the Hall of Mirrors (fig. **14–33**). He lit the 240-feet-long hall with 17 immense arched windows, lining the opposite wall with Venetian glass mirrors—enormously expensive in the seventeenth century—of exactly the same size and shape. The mirrors reflect the natural light from the windows and give the impression of an even larger space. In a tribute to Annibale Carracci's Farnese ceiling (see fig. 14–6), the painter Charles Le Brun (1619–1690), a founding member of the Royal Academy of Painting and Sculpture, decorated the vaulted ceiling with paintings glorifying the reign of Louis XIV and associating his military victories with the assistance of the deities of Classical antiquity.

As in the Netherlands, seventeenth-century painting in France was much affected by developments in Italian art. The important painter Nicolas Poussin (1594–1665) worked for French patrons but actually pursued his career in Italy. As a dedicated classicist, he did not paint the landscape as he saw it but instead organized nature,

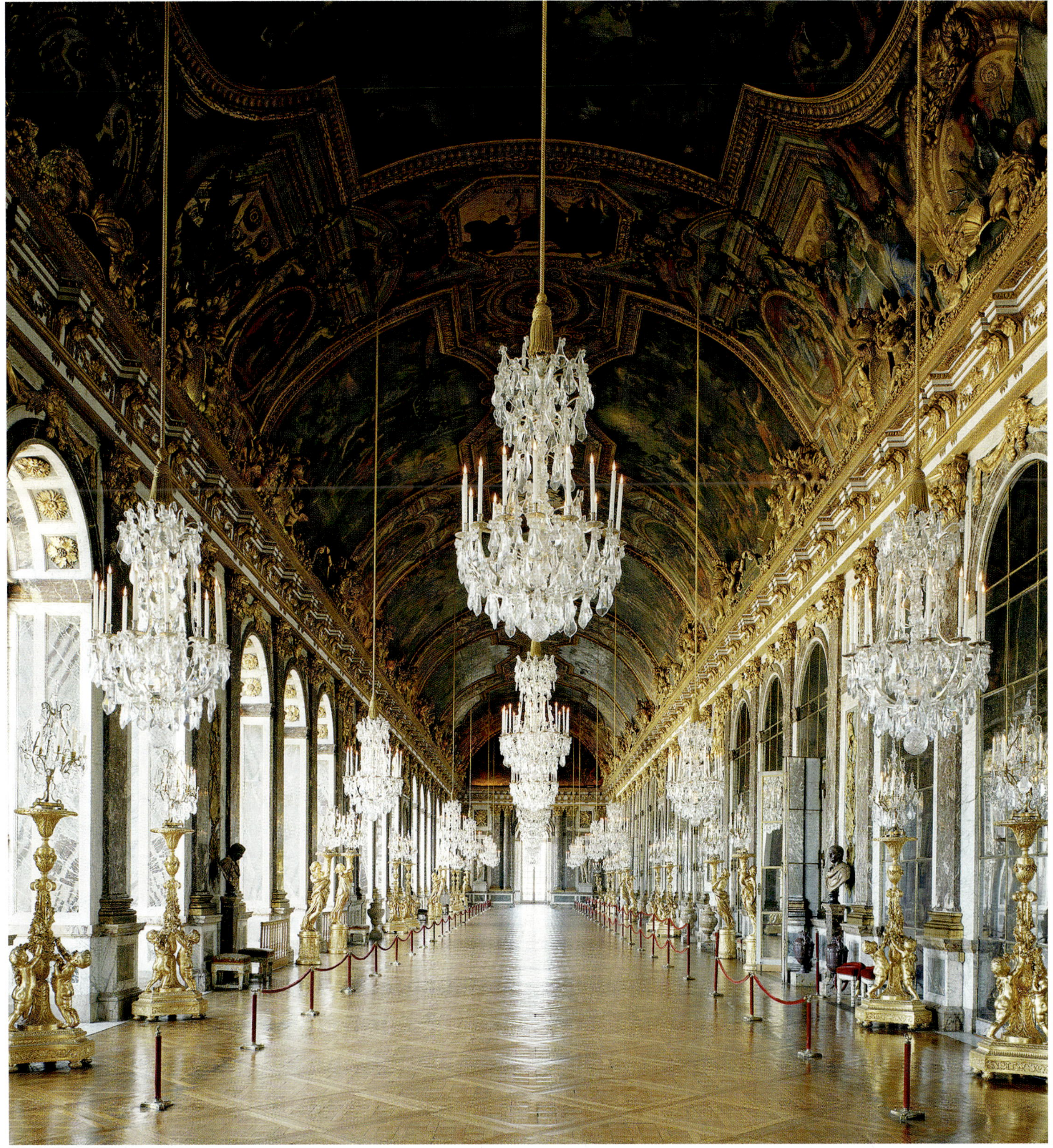

14–33 Jules Hardouin-Mansart (architecture) **and Charles Le Brun** (painting), Palais de Versailles. 1668–1685. Hall of Mirrors begun 1678

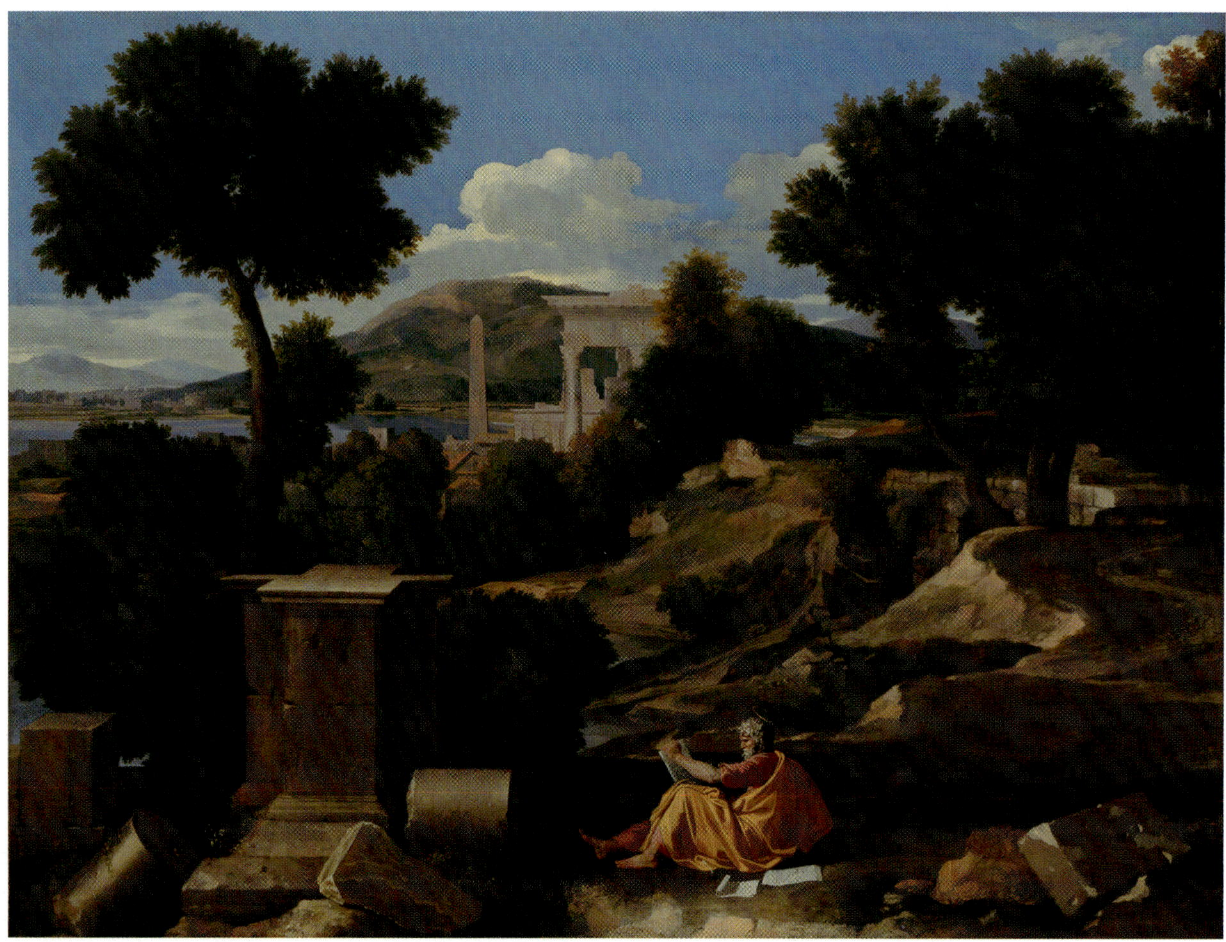

14–34 Nicolas Poussin. ***Landscape with Saint John on Patmos.*** 1640. Oil on canvas, 39½" × 53¾" (100.3 × 136.4 cm).
The Art Institute of Chicago

buildings, and figures into carefully ordered compositions such as his *Landscape with Saint John on Patmos* (fig. **14–34**), from 1640. The artist devised a consistently organized progression from the picture plane to the horizon through a clearly defined foreground, middle ground, and background. Receding zones are marked by alternating sunlight and shade, as well as by the placement of Classical architectural elements. Poussin incorporates both real and imaginary buildings. In the middle distance are an imaginary ruined temple and an obelisk, while across the lake on the left the round building is Hadrian's tomb from Rome. Precisely placed trees, hills, mountains, water, and even clouds have an almost architectural formal solidity. The reclining Saint John seems almost incidental, locked into this perfect landscape. The true subject of Poussin's painting is not an incident in the life of a saint, but the balance and order of the natural world.

Rococo

The Rococo style may be seen partly as a reaction at all levels of society, even among kings and bishops, against the Grand Manner of Baroque art, identified with the formality and rigidity of seventeenth-century court life. Rococo is characterized by pastel colors, delicately curving forms, dainty figures, and lightheartedness. The style began in French architectural decoration at the end of Louis XIV's reign and quickly spread across Europe.

The Duke of Orléans, regent for the boy-king Louis XV (ruled 1715–1774), made his home in Paris, and the royal court—delighted to escape Versailles—followed him there, building elegant townhouses (in French, *hôtels*), in whose small rooms the Rococo style flourished. The Salon de la Princesse in the Hôtel de Soubise in Paris (fig. **14–35**), designed by Germain Boffrand beginning in 1732, is typical. The glitter of silver or gold against expanses of white or pastel color, the visual confusion of mirror reflections, delicate ornament in sculpted stucco, carved wood panels called *boiseries*, and inlaid wood designs on furniture and floors were all part of the new look. In residential settings, pictorial themes were often taken from Classical love stories, and sculpted ornaments were rarely devoid of *putti*, cupids, and clouds. In these elegant rooms, Parisian intellectuals gathered for conversation and entertainments presided over by accomplished, educated women of the upper class.

In painting, the Rococo style emerged with the career of the French artist Jean-Antoine Watteau (1684–1721). Watteau worked for a time as a decorator of interiors. In 1717, he was elected to membership of the Royal Academy of Painting and Sculpture on the basis of a painting he submitted to secure his admission: *The Pilgrimage to Cythera* (fig. **14–36**). There was no established category for such a painting, so the academicians created a new classification for it: the ***fête galante***, or elegant outdoor entertainment. Watteau depicts a dreamworld in which beautifully dressed couples depart for, or perhaps take their leave from, dalliance on the mythical island of love. The lush landscape has no more reality than a painted theater backdrop. It would never soil the characters' shimmering satins and plush velvets, nor would a summer shower threaten their charmed reverie. Watteau's idyllic vision, with its overtones of wistful melancholy, had a powerful attraction in early eighteenth-century Paris and soon charmed most of Europe.

Tragically, Watteau died from tuberculosis while still in his 30s, but he left many followers. Jean-Honoré Fragonard (1732–1806) carried Watteau's French Rococo fantasies into the second half of the eighteenth century. Around 1771, Fragonard created 14 fanciful

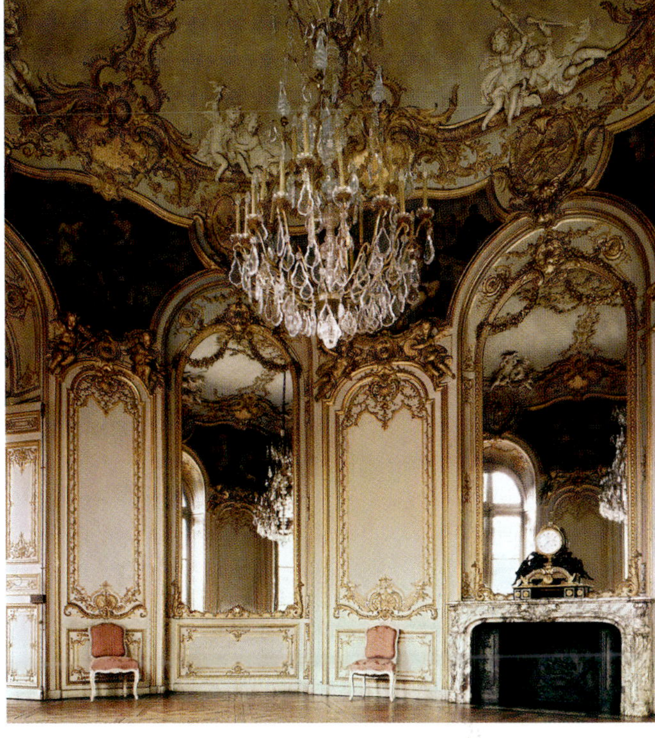

14–35 (RIGHT) **Germain Boffrand.** ***Salon de la Princesse***, Hôtel de Soubise, Paris. Begun 1732

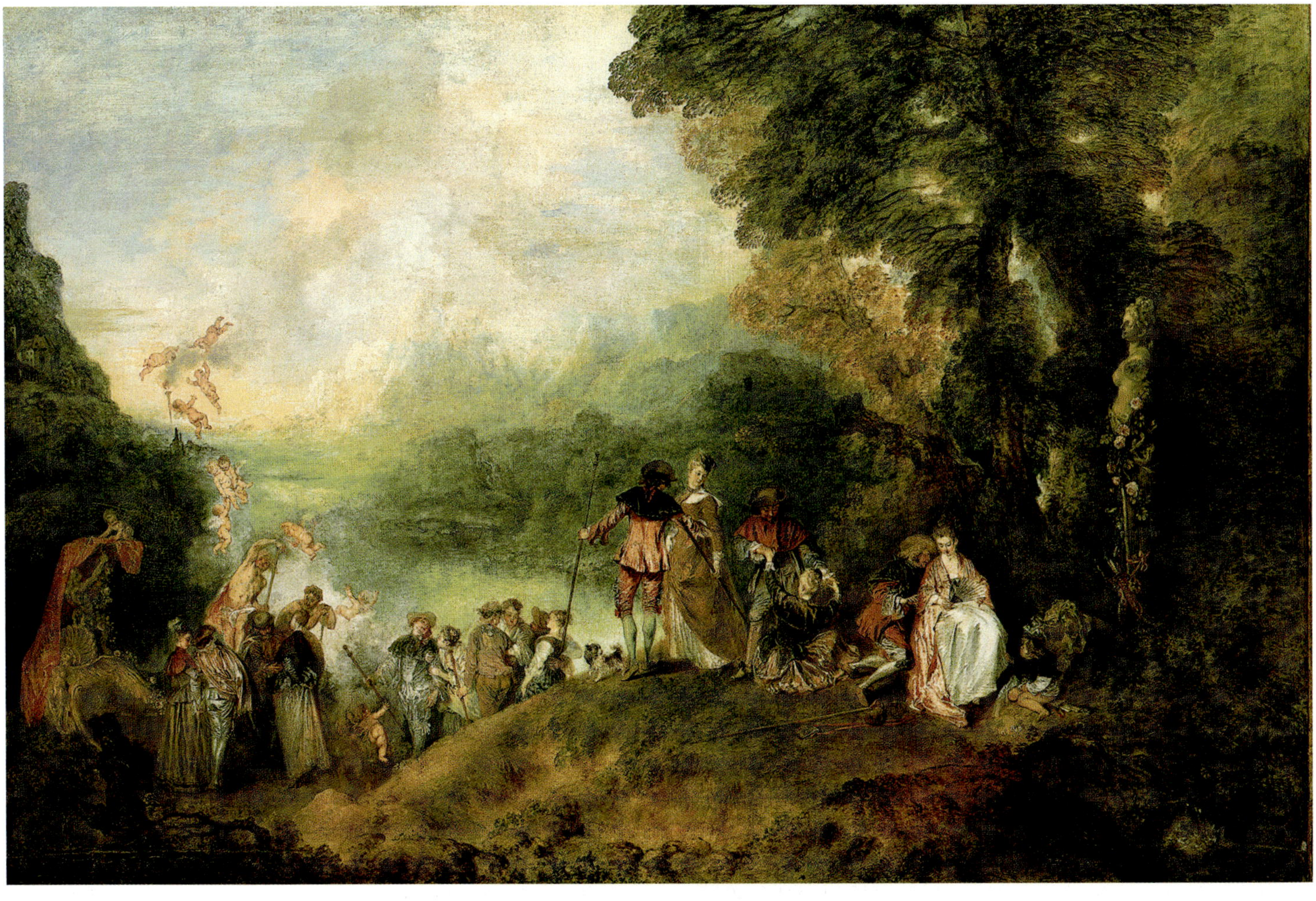

14–36 Jean-Antoine Watteau. ***The Pilgrimage to Cythera.*** 1717. Oil on canvas, 4' 3" × 6' 4½" (1.3 × 1.9 m). Musée du Louvre, Paris

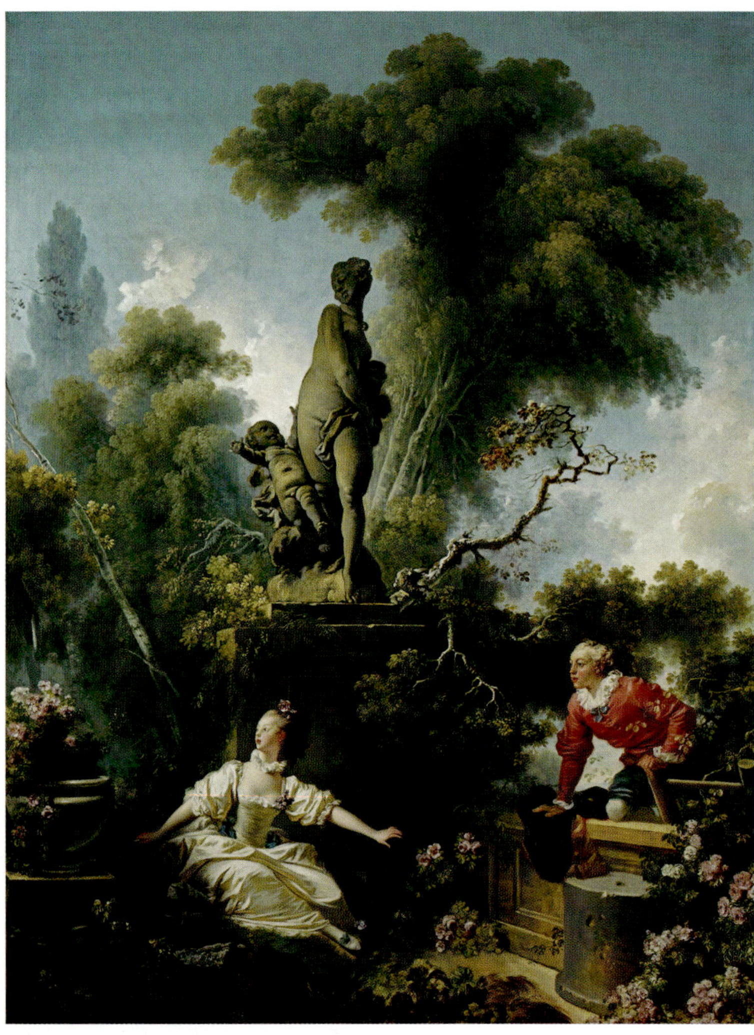

14–37 Jean-Honoré Fragonard. *The Meeting*, from *The Progress of Love*. 1771–1773.
Oil on canvas, 10' 5¼" × 7' ⅝" (3.18 × 2.15 m).
The Frick Collection, New York

visions of lovers for the château of Madame du Barry, Louis XV's last mistress. *The Meeting* (fig. **14–37**) shows a secret encounter between a young man and his sweetheart, who looks back anxiously over her shoulder to be sure she has not been followed, while clutching the letter arranging the tryst. These marvelously free and dynamic visions of lovers seem to explode in color and luxurious vegetation. The rapid brushwork that distinguishes Fragonard's technique is at its freest and most lavish here. Madame du Barry, however, rejected the paintings and commissioned another set in the newly fashionable Neoclassical style (see Chapter 17). Her dismissal of Fragonard's ravishing visions signals the end of the world of Rococo.

Looking Back

Sometimes Baroque art seems strangely familiar. In the seventeenth century, as today, many artists and their patrons were concerned with the uses of art, with "viewer response," and with "art theory." At a time when political and religious factions attacked each other with lethal fanaticism—even claimed God was on their side—works of art could play an important role in capturing the imagination and swaying the emotions of viewers.

Spectacular visions, brilliant state portraits, grandiose palaces and churches proclaimed the power of the Church and State. Some artists became international superstars; Rubens, whose home was in Antwerp, enjoyed the patronage of the kings of Spain, France, and England. Other artists, such as Caravaggio, played the role of disruptive, even violent, outsider, even though they too sought the patronage of the establishment. Patronage expanded to include not only the aristocracy and the Catholic Church but also the newly affluent middle class. In places like the Dutch Republic, art was democratized to such extent that the acquisition and collecting of works of art spread through all levels of society, from millers and tavern-keepers to bankers and civic guardsmen.

Many artists abandoned Renaissance ideals of beauty and grace. Seeking a new relationship with the natural world and influenced by the scientific interests of the day, they addressed new subjects, including landscape, still life, and scenes of daily life. But others, like today's Postmodernists, delighted in self-conscious references to the past, often turning to the art and architecture of ancient Rome for grand themes as well as decorative details. The ancient world provided the historical context and the "critical theory" for both works of art and the education of artists in official academies.

IN PERSPECTIVE

1600

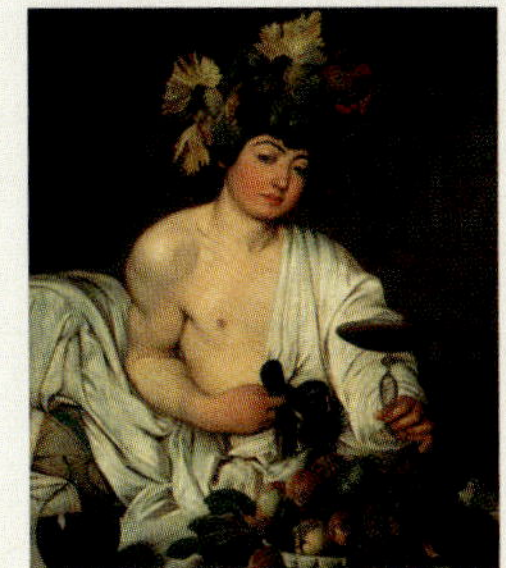

CARAVAGGIO,
BACCHUS,
1595–1596

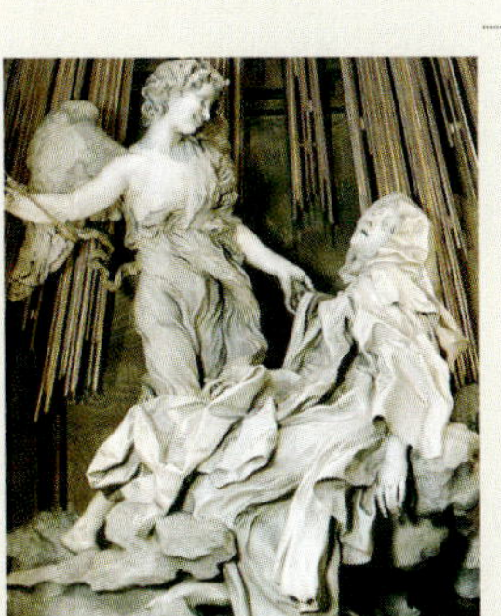

BERNINI,
SAINT TERESA OF ÁVILA IN ECSTASY,
1645–1652

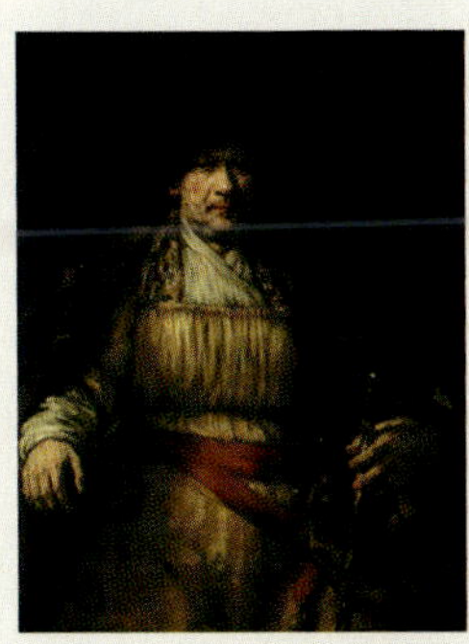

REMBRANDT,
SELF-PORTRAIT,
1658

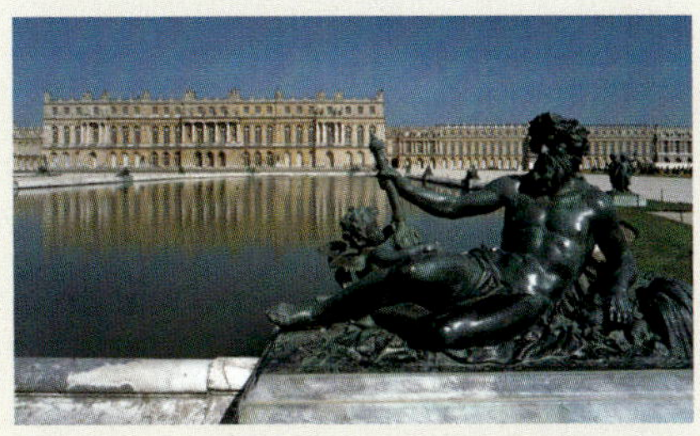

LE VAU AND HARDOUIN-MANSART,
PALAIS DE VERSAILLES,
1668–1685

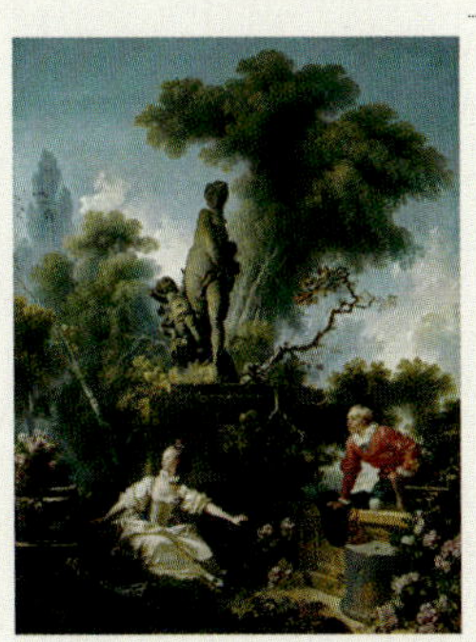

FRAGONARD,
THE MEETING,
1771–1773

- **Mayflower Lands in North America,** 1620
- **Galileo Forced to Recant,** 1633
- **Louis XIV, King of France,** ruled 1643–1715
- **Founding of French Royal Academy of Painting and Sculpture,** 1648
- **Spanish Habsburgs Recognize Independence of Dutch Republic,** 1648

1650

- **Founding of French Royal Academy of Architecture,** 1671
- **Newton Publishes His Laws of Gravity,** 1687

1700

- **Steam Engine Invented,** 1698
- **Louis XV, King of France,** ruled 1715–1774
- **Seven Years' War,** 1756–1763
- **Women Among Founding Members of English Royal Academy,** 1768
- **Louis XVI, King of France,** ruled 1774–1792
- **American Revolution Begins,** 1776
- **French Revolution Begins,** 1789

1800

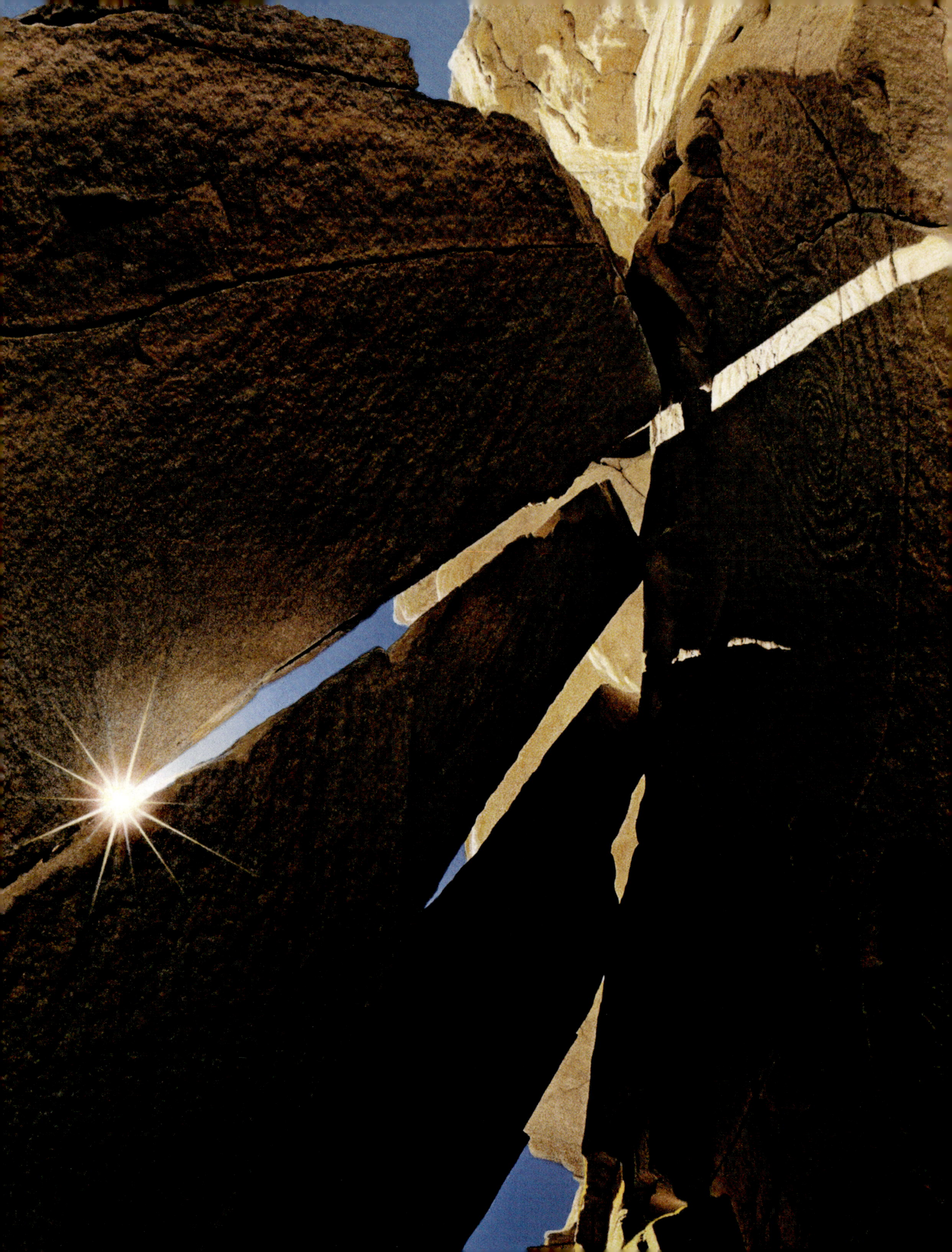

15
Art of the Americas

LOOKING FORWARD

On the morning of the summer solstice a streak of light strikes a high cliff in Chaco Canyon. Slowly this "Sun Dagger" descends, and by noontime it pierces the heart of a large spiral engraved into the rock by the Ancestral Puebloans who lived there (fig. **15–1**). The shaft of light framed by the openings between huge slabs of rock changes with the seasonal position of the sun. Only at the summer solstice in June does the Great Dagger appear. At the winter solstice two streaks frame the spiral petroglyph, and at both spring and fall equinoxes a small spike of light hits the center of the small spiral and a large shaft cuts through the large spiral but misses its center. "Sun Watchers" may have monitored these events and reported when the time had come to begin communal ceremonies or plant the life-sustaining corn. The rock formation that molds light from the seasonal sun is natural, but the spirals are human additions. Nature and art combine here, as they do in the work of a modern environmental artist.

The architectural and monumental center of Chaco Canyon is Pueblo Bonito (see fig. 15–22), a complex of rooms and corridors begun in the tenth century CE and continually enlarged. It stood at the hub of a network of straight roads that radiated out to some 70 other communities. Almost invisible today, the roads were only discovered through aerial photography. They make no detour to avoid topographic obstacles, becoming stairs when they encounter cliffs. Their undeviating course suggests that the roads were more than practical thoroughfares; they may have served as processional ways. Was Pueblo Bonito a cultural gathering place at specific times of year? Did people assemble there when called by the Sun Watchers? Was this Sun Marker, situated high above the living areas in the canyon, a pilgrimage shrine?

When the Ancient Puebloans were watching for their Sun Dagger in Chaco Canyon, men and women in Europe were also using light to honor and communicate with their God in churches filled with stained glass. Pueblo Bonito is contemporary with the great ceremonial centers of Saint-Denis (fig. 11–2) and Chartres (figs. 11–7 to 11–9). But for Chaco Canyon, we have no written texts and little living tradition to help understand how the Sun Dagger was used. For answers we turn directly to art and architecture.

15–1 Sun Dagger Solar Marker at Equinox, Fajada Butte, Chaco Canyon, New Mexico. 850–1250 CE

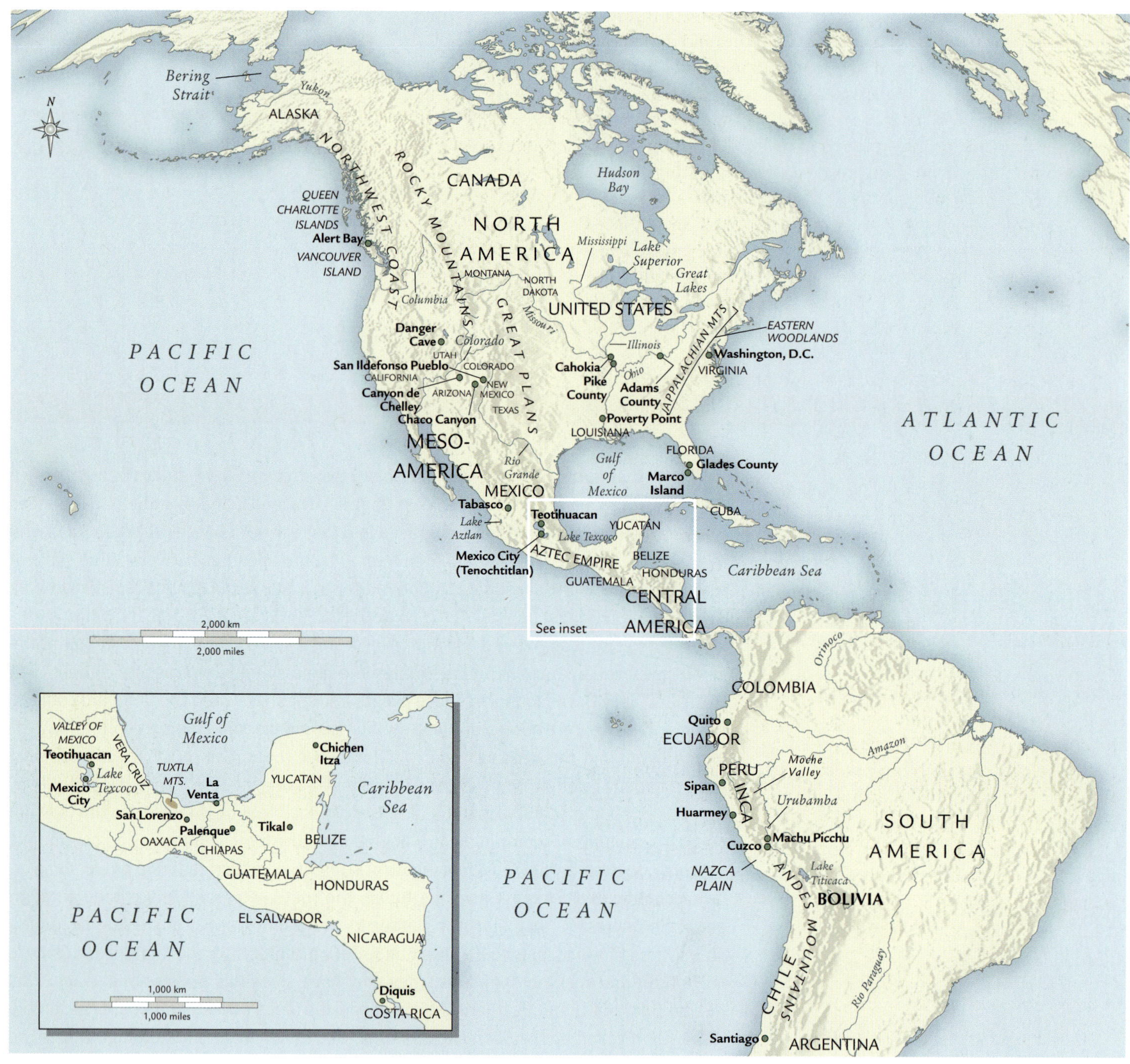

Map 15–1 The Americas

Traditionally, scholars have held that human beings first arrived in North and South America from Asia during the last Ice Age, when glacial growth lowered the level of the oceans to expose a land bridge across the Bering Strait, just south of the arctic circle. Perhaps as early as 20,000 to 30,000 years ago, Paleolithic hunter-gatherers would have crossed over this corridor and begun to spread out into two vast, uninhabited continents.

This view is now challenged by the early dates of some new archaeological finds and by evidence suggesting the possibility of new connections with Europe as well, perhaps along the Arctic coast of the north Atlantic. In any event, between 10,000 and 12,000 years ago, bands of hunters roamed throughout the Americas. After the ice had retreated and rising oceans had flooded the Bering Strait, the people of the Western Hemisphere were essentially cut off from those of Africa and Eurasia until they were overrun by European invaders beginning in the late fifteenth century CE (see map **15–1**).

In this isolation, the people of the Americas experienced transformations similar to those that followed the end of the Paleolithic era elsewhere. In most regions, they developed an agricultural way of life. A trio of native plants—corn, beans, and squash—was especially important, but people also cultivated potatoes, tobacco, cacao (chocolate), tomatoes, and avocados. As elsewhere, the shift to agriculture in the Americas was accompanied by population growth and, in some places, the rise of hierarchical societies and the appearance of ceremonial centers and towns with monumental architecture and the development of the arts. Cities such as Teotihuacan in the Basin of Mexico rivaled those of Europe in size and splendor. The people of Mesoamerica—the region that extends from central Mexico to northern Central America—developed writing, a complex and accurate calendar, and a sophisticated system of mathematics. Central and South American peoples had an advanced metallurgy and produced exquisite work in gold, silver, and copper. In the American Southwest, Native American people built multistoried, apartment-like villages and cliff dwellings, as well as elaborate irrigation systems with canals. Basketry and weaving became major art forms across the Americas.

The sudden incursion of Europeans from the fifteenth century onward had a dramatic and lasting impact on Native American people and their art. In some areas, highly advanced civilizations, such as those of the Aztec and Inca, were destroyed. In other regions, such as the North American plains, indigenous groups lost much of their land and saw their populations decimated by newly introduced diseases, yet they retained their traditions and still exist as distinct cultural entities today.

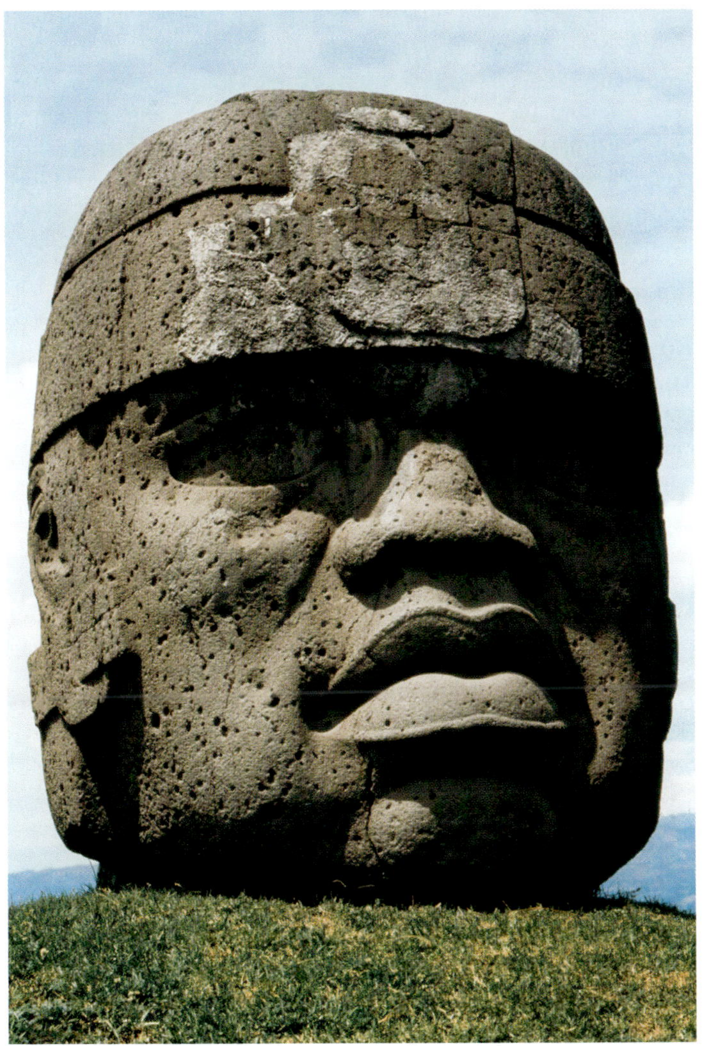

15–2 Colossal Head, San Lorenzo, Mexico. Olmec culture, c. 900–400 BCE. Basalt, height 65" (2.26 m)

The colossal heads found at La Venta and San Lorenzo were carved from basalt boulders that were transported to the Gulf Coast from the Tuxtla Mountains, more than 60 miles inland.

Mesoamerica

Ancient Mesoamerica encompassed the area from north of the Basin of Mexico (the location of Mexico City) to modern Belize, Honduras and western Nicaragua in Central America. The people of this environmentally diverse region, which included tropical rainforests and semiarid mountain plateaus, were linked by cultural similarities and trade. Among the shared features were a ritual ball game with religious and political significance, aspects of monumental ceremonial building construction, and a complex system of multiple calendars including a 260-day ritual cycle and a 365-day agricultural cycle. Mesoamerican society was also sharply divided into elite and commoner classes.

Archaeologists have traditionally divided Mesoamerican civilizations into three broad periods: Formative or Preclassic (1500 BCE–250 CE), Classic (250–900 CE), and Postclassic (900–1521 CE). The Classic period brackets the time during which the Maya erected dated stone monuments. The term reflects the view of early scholars that the Classic period was a kind of golden age, the equivalent of the Classical period in ancient Greece (see Chapter 5). Although this view is no longer current—and the periods are only roughly applicable to other parts of Mesoamerica—the terminology has endured.

The Olmecs

The first major Mesoamerican art, that of the Olmecs, emerged during the Preclassic period along the Gulf of Mexico. In the swampy coastal areas of the modern Mexican states of Veracruz and Tabasco, the Olmecs cleared farmland, drained fields, and raised earth mounds on which they constructed ceremonial centers. They also created monumental works of basalt sculpture, including colossal heads (fig. **15–2**), altars, and seated figures. The huge basalt blocks for the large works of sculpture were quarried at distant sites and transported to San Lorenzo, La Venta, and other centers. The colossal heads range in height from 5 to 12 feet and weigh from 5 to more than 20 tons. They portray adult males wearing close-fitting caps with chin straps and large, round earspools (cylindrical earrings that pierce the earlobe). The fleshy faces have almond-shaped eyes, flat, broad noses, thick protruding lips, and downturned mouths. Each face is different, suggesting that they may represent specific individuals. Twelve heads were found at San Lorenzo. All had been mutilated and buried about 900 BCE, about the time the site went into decline. At La Venta, 102 basalt monuments were found. The Olmecs also established trade contacts throughout Mesoamerica, importing goods not found in the Gulf region, such as obsidian, iron ore, and jade. Writing and calendrical systems first appeared around 600 to 500 BCE in areas with strong Olmec influence.

By 200 CE, forests and swamps began to reclaim Olmec sites, but Olmec civilization had spread widely throughout Mesoamerica and was to have an enduring influence on its successors. As the Olmec centers of the Gulf Coast faded, the great Classic-period centers at Teotihuacan in the Basin of Mexico as well as in the Maya region were beginning their ascendancy.

The Maya

The homeland of the Maya people is in southern Mesoamerica, which includes the Yucatán peninsula and the lands of several present-day countries, including Guatemala, Belize, and the western parts of Honduras and El Salvador. The Maya built imposing pyramids, temples, palaces, and administrative structures in densely populated cities. They developed the most advanced hieroglyphic writing in Mesoamerica and the most sophisticated version of the Mesoamerican calendrical system. In addition, they studied astronomy and the natural cycles of plants and animals, and they developed the mathematical concepts of zero and place value before such concepts were used in Europe.

An increasingly detailed picture of the Maya has emerged from recent archaeological research and from advances in deciphering their writing. It shows a society divided into competing centers, each with a hereditary ruler and an elite class of nobles and priests supported by a far larger class of farmer-commoners. Rulers established their legitimacy, maintained links with their divine ancestors, and venerated the gods through elaborate rituals, including ball games, bloodletting ceremonies, and human sacrifice. A complex pantheon of deities, many with several manifestations, presided over the Maya universe.

The Maya civilization, which had emerged during the late Preclassic period (250 BCE–250 CE), reached its peak in the southern lowlands of Guatemala during the Classic period (250–900 CE), and shifted to northern Yucatán during the Postclassic period (900–1521 CE). In Palenque, a prominent city of the Classic period, the major buildings are grouped on high ground. A central group of structures includes the so-called Palace (possibly an administrative and ceremonial center as well as a residential structure), the Temple of the Inscriptions, and two other temples (fig. **15–3**). Most of the structures in the three building complexes were commissioned by a powerful ruler, Lord Pakal (Maya for "shield"), who ruled from 615 to 683 CE, and his two sons, who succeeded him.

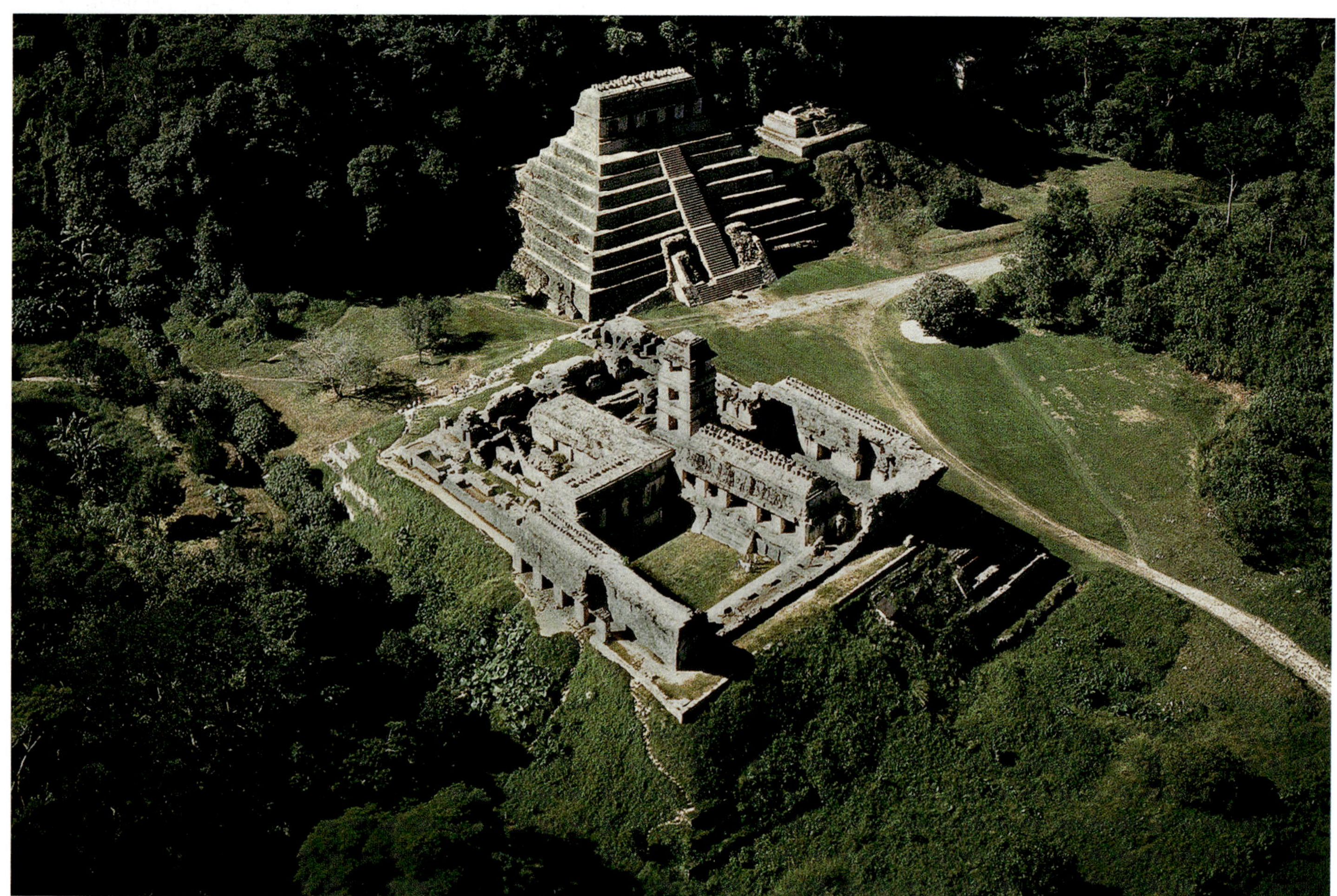

15–3 Palace (foreground) and **Temple of the Inscriptions** (tomb-pyramid of Lord Pakal). Palenque, Mexico. Maya culture, late 7th century CE

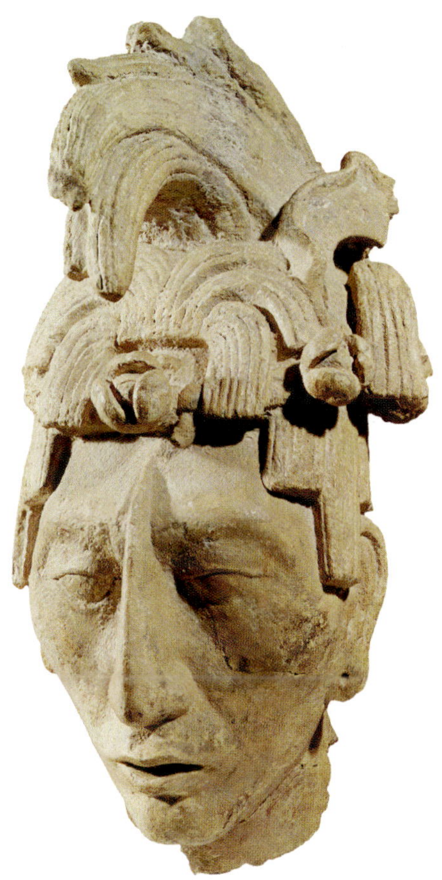

15–4 Portrait of Lord Pakal, from his tomb, Temple of the Inscriptions. Late 7th century CE. Stucco, height 16⅞" (43 cm). Museo Nacional de Antropologia, Mexico City

This portrait of the youthful Lord Pakal might have been placed in his tomb as an offering, or it might have formed part of the original exterior decoration of the Temple of the Inscriptions.

The Temple of the Inscriptions is a nine-level pyramid that rises to a height of about 75 feet. The consecutive layers probably reflect the belief, current among the Aztec and the Maya at the time of the Spanish Conquest, that the underworld had nine levels. Priests would climb the steep stone staircase on the exterior to reach the temple on top, which recalls the kind of pole-and-thatch houses the Maya still build in parts of Yucatán today. The roof of the temple was topped with a crest known as a **roof comb**, and its façade still retains much of its stucco sculpture. Inscriptions line the back wall of the outer chamber, giving the temple its name.

In 1948, a Mexican archaeologist cleared the rear chamber of the summit shrine and entered the corbel-vaulted stairwell that zigzagged 80 feet down to the tomb of Lord Pakal. After four years of work, the undisturbed tomb of the ruler was revealed. Covered in jade ornaments, Lord Pakal lay in a monumental sarcophagus with a lid carved in low relief that shows him balanced between the underworld and the earth. A stucco portrait found with the sarcophagus depicts the ruler as a young man wearing a diadem of jade and feathers (fig. **15–4**). His features reveal the characteristics of the Maya ideal of beauty: a sloping forehead and elongated skull (babies had their heads bound to produce this shape), a large curved nose (enhanced by an added ornamental bridge, perhaps of latex), and full lips. Traces of pigment indicate that this portrait, like much Maya sculpture, was colorfully painted.

As the focus of Maya civilization shifted northward in the Postclassic period, a northern Maya group called the Itzá rose to prominence. Their principal center, Chichén Itzá, which means "at the mouth of the well of the Itzá," flourished from the ninth to the thirteenth century CE, eventually covering about 6 square miles.

One of Chichén Itzá's most conspicuous structures is a massive, nine-level pyramid in the center of a large plaza with a stairway on each side leading to a square temple on the pyramid's summit (fig. **15–5**). At the spring and fall equinoxes, the setting sun casts an

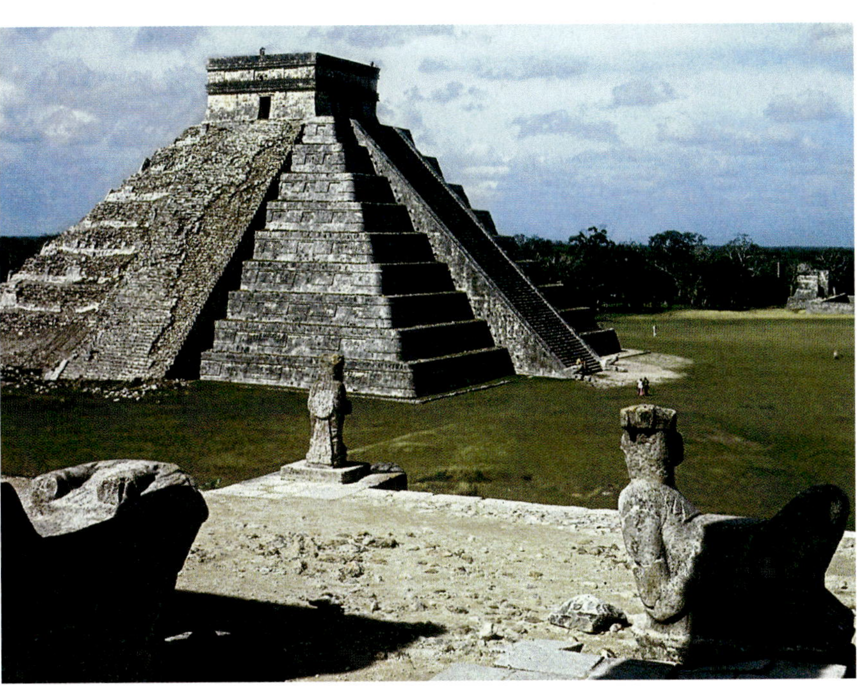

15–5 Pyramid ("**El Castillo**") with **Chacmool** in foreground, Chichén Itzá, Yucatán, Mexico. 9th–13th century; Chacmool 800–1000 CE

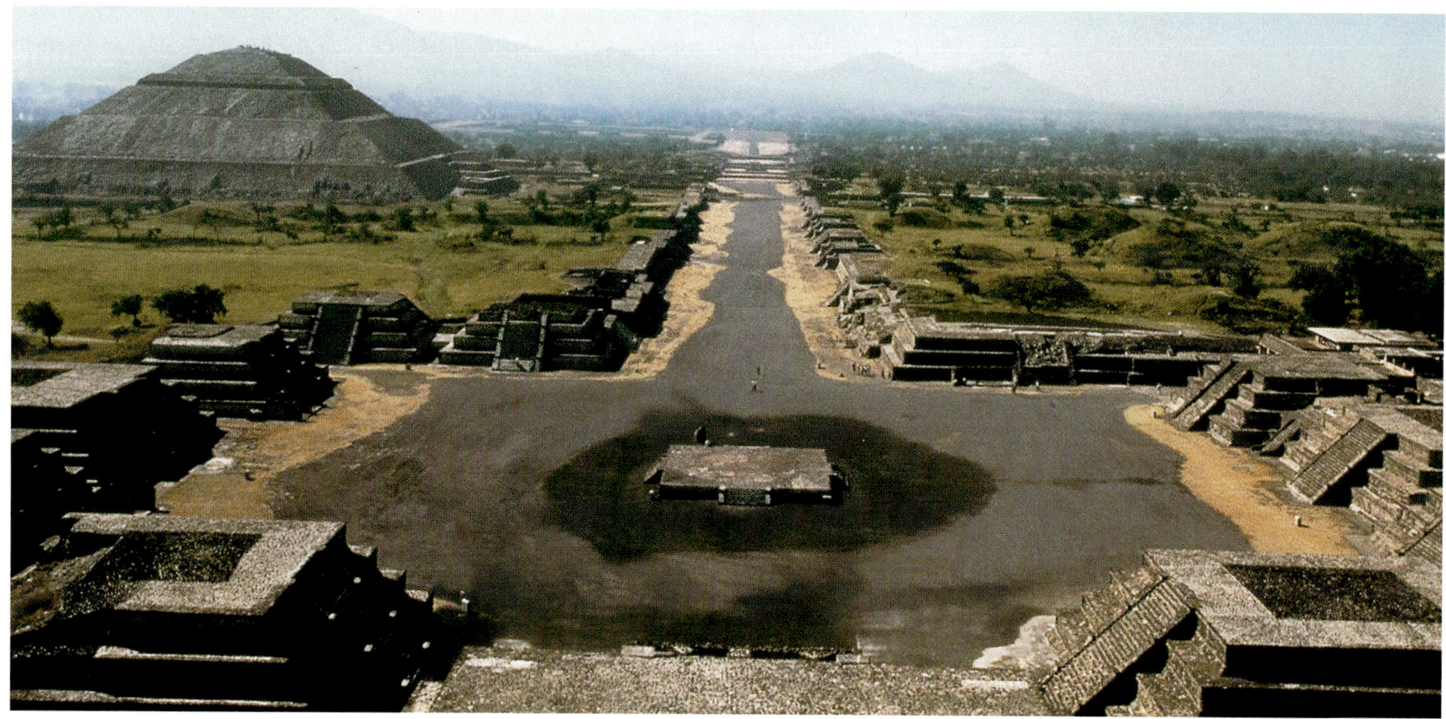

15–6 Ceremonial center of the city of Teotihuacan, Mexico. Teotihuacan culture, c. 350–650 CE

View from the Pyramid of the Moon down the Avenue of the Dead to the Ciudadela and the Temple of the Feathered Serpent. The Pyramid of the Sun is at the middle left. The avenue is over a mile long.

undulating, serpent-like shadow on the stairways forming bodies for the serpent heads carved at the bases of the balustrades. Sculpture at Chichén Itzá includes half-reclining figures known as **chacmools**, which have the sturdy forms, proportions, and angularity of architecture. The chacmools probably represent fallen warriors and were used to receive sacrificial offerings.

Teotihuacan

Located some 30 miles northeast of present-day Mexico City, Teotihuacan experienced a period of rapid growth early in the first millennium CE. By 200 CE, it had emerged as a significant center of commerce and manufacturing, the first large city-state in the Americas. At its height, between 350 and 650 CE, Teotihuacan covered nearly 9 square miles and had a population of about 200,000, making it one of the largest cities in the world at that time (figs. **15–6** and **15–7**). One reason for its dominance was its control of the market for high-quality obsidian. This volcanic stone, made into tools and vessels, was traded for luxury items such as the green feathers of the quetzal bird, used for priestly headdresses, and the spotted fur of the jaguar, used for ceremonial garments.

The people of Teotihuacan worshiped many deities that were recognizably similar to those worshiped by later Mesoamerican people, including the Aztecs, who dominated central Mexico at the time of the Spanish Conquest. Among these are the Rain or Storm God (god of fertility, war, and sacrifice), known to the Aztecs as Tlaloc, and the Feathered Serpent, known to the Maya as Kukulcan and to the Aztecs as Quetzalcoatl.

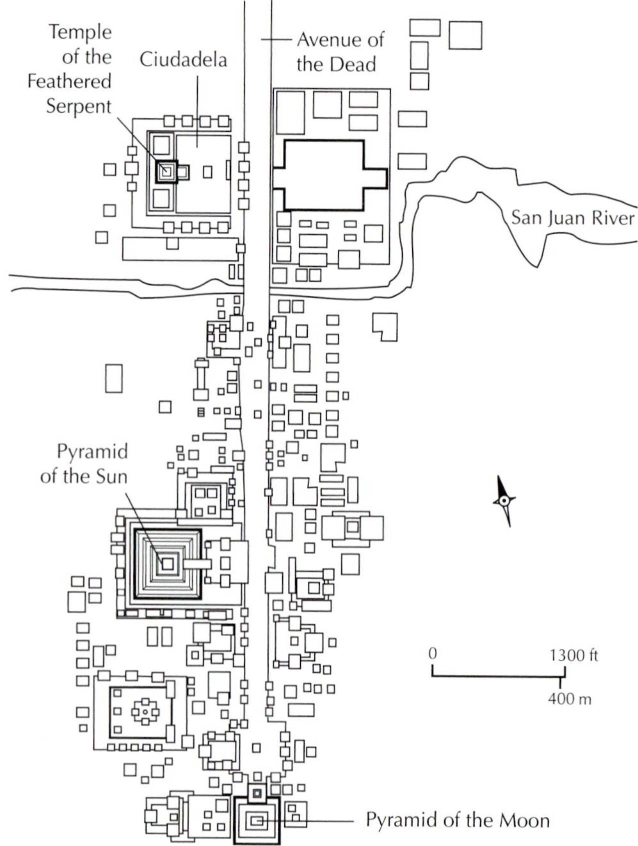

15–7 Plan of the ceremonial center of Teotihuacan

Teotihuacan's principal monuments include the Pyramid of the Sun, the Pyramid of the Moon, and the Ciudadela (Spanish for fortified city center), a vast sunken plaza surrounded by temple platforms. The city's principal religious and political center, the Ciudadela could accommodate an assembly of more than 60,000 people. Its focal point was the pyramidal Temple of the Feathered Serpent (fig. **15–8**). This seven-tiered structure exhibits the ***talud-tablero*** construction that is a hallmark of the Teotihuacan architectural style. The sloping base, or *talud*, of each platform supports a vertical *tablero*, or entablature, which is surrounded by a frame and filled with sculptural decoration. The Temple of the Feathered Serpent was enlarged several times, and—as was characteristic of Mesoamerican pyramids—each enlargement completely enclosed the previous structure, like the layers of an onion. Archaeological excavations of this temple's earlier-phase *tableros* (fig. 15–8) and a stairway balustrade have revealed painted heads of the Feathered Serpent, the goggle-eyed Rain or Storm God (or Fire God, according to some), and reliefs of aquatic shells and snails. The flat, angular, abstract style, typical of Teotihuacan art, is in marked contrast to the curvilinear style of Olmec art. The Rain God features a squarish, stylized head or headdress with protruding upper jaw, huge, round eyes originally inlaid with obsidian, and large, circular earspools. The fanged serpent heads, perhaps composites of snakes and other creatures, emerge from an aureole of stylized feathers. The Rain God and the Feathered Serpent may be symbols of regeneration and cyclical renewal, perhaps representing the alternating wet and dry seasons.

Sometime in the middle of the seventh century disaster struck Teotihuacan. The ceremonial center burned, and the city went into a permanent decline. Nevertheless, its influence continued as other centers throughout Mesoamerica and as far south as the highlands of Guatemala borrowed and transformed its imagery over the next several centuries. The site was never entirely abandoned, however, because it remained a legendary pilgrimage center. The much later

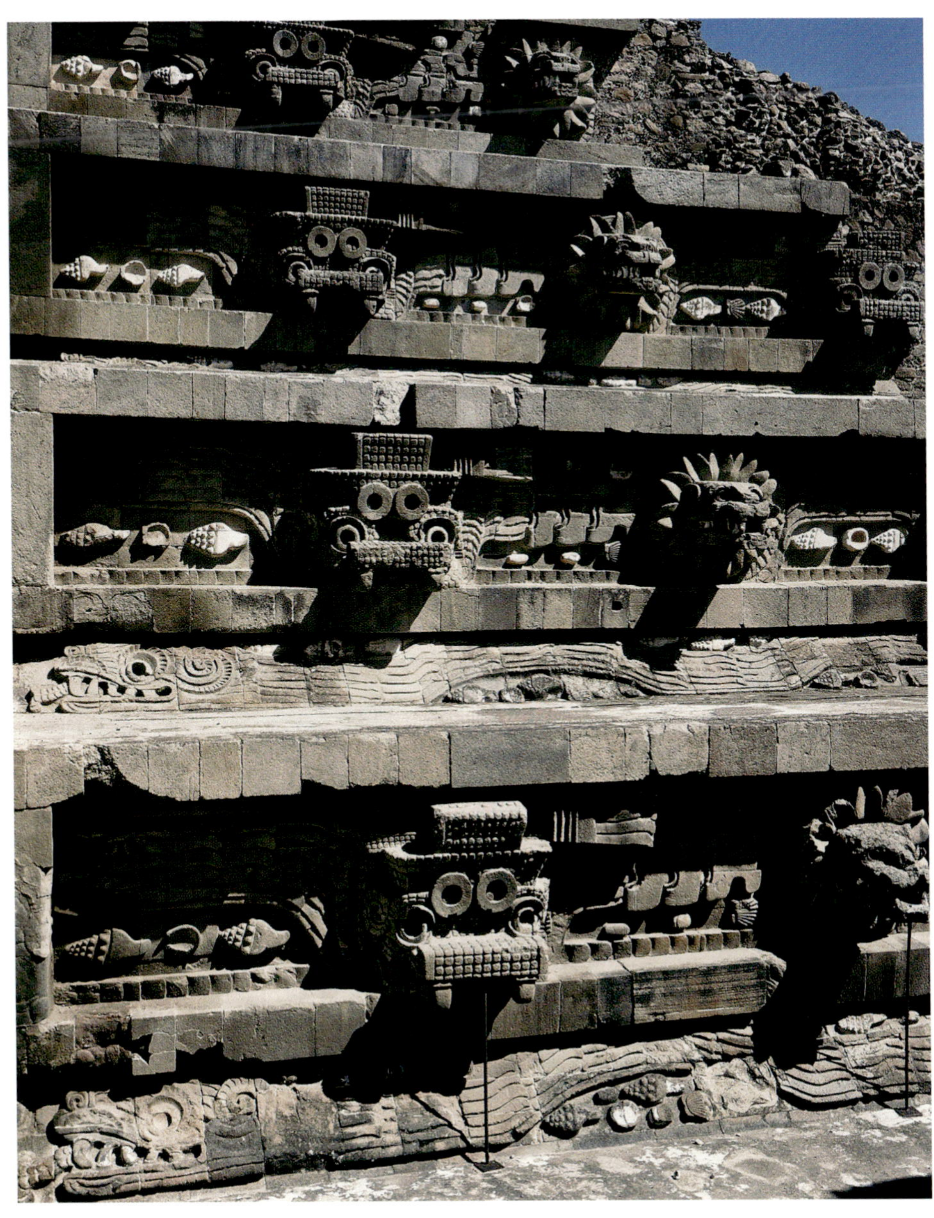

15–8 Temple of the Feathered Serpent, the Ciudadela, Teotihuacan, Mexico. Teotihuacan culture, c. 350 CE

Aztec people (c. 1300–1525 CE) revered the site, believing it to be the place where the gods created the sun and the moon. In fact, the name "Teotihuacan" is actually an Aztec word meaning "Gathering Place of the Gods."

The Aztecs

Maya civilization was in decline by the time of the Spanish Conquest in 1519. Already by the end of the fifteenth century, a people known as the Aztecs controlled much of Mexico. Their rise to power had been recent and swift. Only 400 years earlier, according to their own legends, they had been a nomadic people living on the shores of a mythical island called Aztlan (from which the word "Aztec" derives) somewhere to the northwest of the Basin of Mexico, where present-day Mexico City is located. They called themselves the Mexica, hence the name "Mexico."

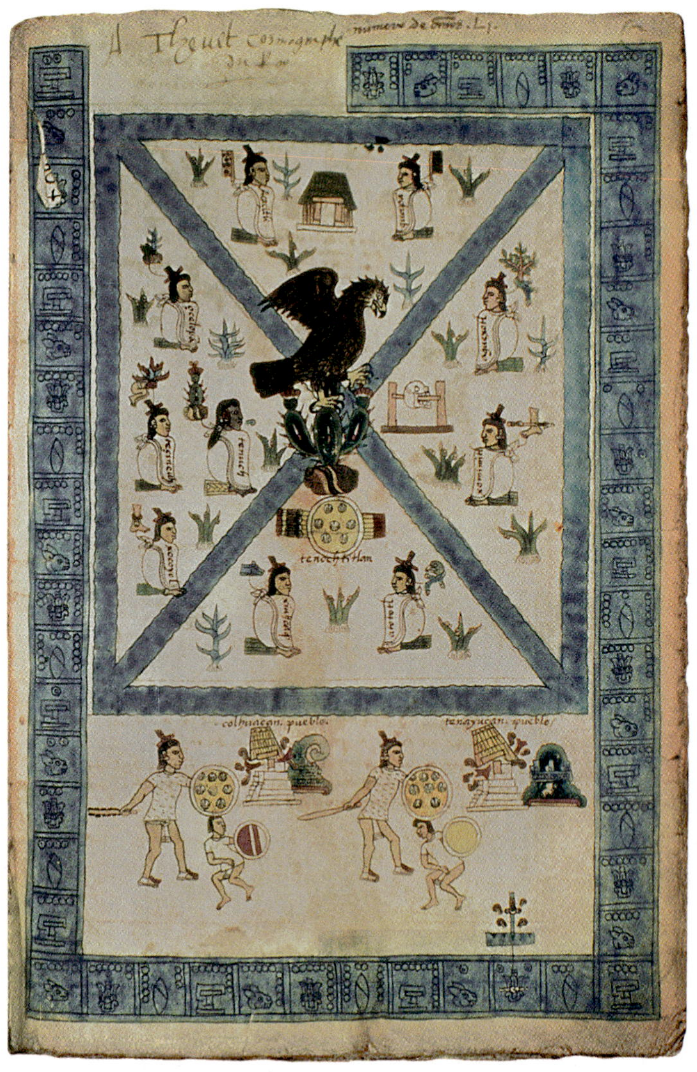

15–9 ***The Founding of Tenochtitlan***, page from *Codex Mendoza*. Aztec, 1540s CE. Ink and paint on paper, 8 7/16" × 12 3/8" (21.4 × 31.4 cm). The Bodleian Library, Oxford (MS. Arch Selden. A.1.fol. 2r)

After a period of migration, the Aztecs arrived in the Basin of Mexico in the thirteenth century. There they eventually settled on an island in Lake Texcoco, where they had seen an eagle perching on a prickly pear cactus (*tenochtli*), a sign that Huitzilopochtli, their patron god, told them would mark the end of their wandering. They called the place Tenochtitlan (meaning "the prickly pear cactus on a stone"). The city was situated on a collection of islands linked by human-made canals.

In the fifteenth century, the Aztecs, joined by allies in a triple alliance, began an aggressive campaign of expansion. The tribute they exacted from all over central Mexico transformed Tenochtitlan into a glittering capital. As the Spanish conquistador Hernán Cortés approached Tenochtitlan in November 1519, he and his soldiers marveled at the stone buildings, towers, and temples that seemed from a distance to rise from the water like a mirage.

Most Aztec books were destroyed in the wake of the Spanish invasion, but the work of Aztec scribes appears in several manuscripts created after the conquest. The first page of the *Codex Mendoza*, prepared for the Spanish viceroy in the 1540s, can be interpreted as an idealized representation of the city of Tenochtitlan (fig. **15–9**). An eagle perched on a prickly pear cactus—the symbol of the city—fills the center of the page. Waterways surround the city and divide it into four quarters, which are further subdivided into wards, as represented by the seated figures. The victorious warriors at the bottom of the page represent early Aztec conquests of nearby cities.

Tenochtitlan had a sacred precinct, possibly symbolized in figure 15–9 by the structure (a temple or house) at the top of the page. The focal point of the precinct was the Great Temple, a 130-foot-high stepped pyramid with dual temples on top, one of which was dedicated to Huitzilopochtli (an Aztec patron-god associated with the sun and warfare) and the other to Tlaloc (god of rain and fertility). The Great Temple was an important site for ritual sacrifice. Victims climbed stairs on the exterior to the Temple of Huitzilopochtli at the summit, where priests threw them over a stone, quickly cut open their chests, and pulled out their still-throbbing hearts, offering them to the gods. The bodies were then rolled down the stairs and dismembered. Hundreds of severed heads were said to have been kept on a skull rack in the plaza of the sacred precinct, represented in figure 15–9 with a single skull to the right of the eagle.

The Aztecs believed that human actions, including bloodletting and human sacrifice, were vital to the continued existence of the universe. Huitzilopochtli, son of the Earth Mother Coatlicue, was thought to require sacrificial victims so that he could, in a re-creation of the events surrounding his birth, drive the stars and the moon from the sky at the beginning of each day. The stars were his half-brothers, and the moon, Coyolxauhqui, his half-sister. According to the myth, when Coatlicue conceived Huitzilopochtli by placing a ball of hummingbird feathers (the soul of a fallen warrior) in her bosom, Huitzilopochtli's jealous siblings—the stars and moon—conspired to kill her. When they attacked, Huitzilopochtli emerged from her body fully grown and armed, drove off his brothers, and destroyed Coyolxauhqui. Aztec rituals recreated the mythic events surrounding his birth, and the Aztecs believed it was

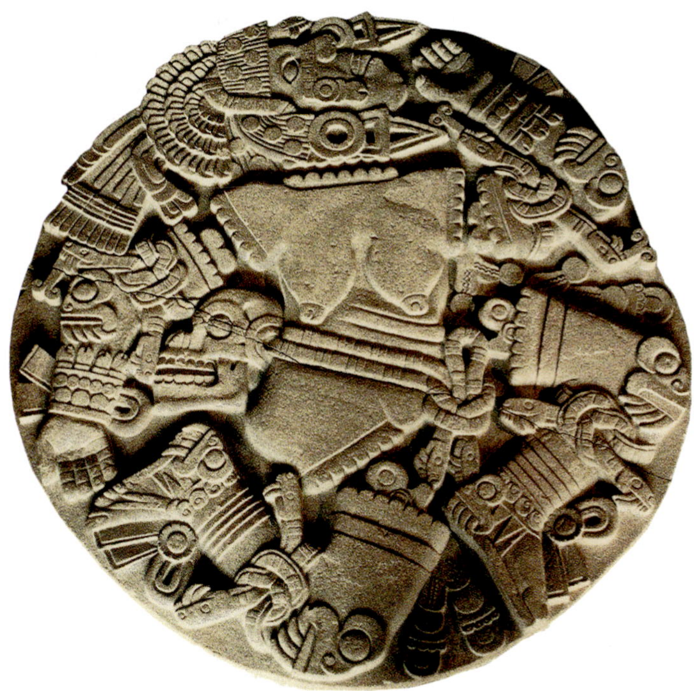

15–10 ***The Moon Goddess, Coyolxauhqui***, from Tenochtitlan. Aztec, 1469 (?) CE. Stone, diameter 10' 10" (3.33 m). Museo Templo Mayor, Mexico City

This disk was discovered accidentally in 1978 by workers from a utility company who were excavating at a street corner in downtown Mexico City.

reenacted each dawn as the sun god Huitzilopochtli fights off his siblings to allow the start of a new day.

A huge circular relief of Coyolxauhqui once lay at the foot of the Huitzilopochtli shrine, as if the enraged and triumphant god had cast her there like a sacrificial victim (fig. **15–10**). Her torso is in the center, surrounded by her decapitated head and dismembered limbs. The rope belt around her waist is attached to a skull. She wears bells on her cheeks, a magnificent feather headdress, and distinctive ear ornaments composed of disks, rectangles, and triangles. The powerful sculpture is two-dimensional in concept—shallow depth of pictorial relief emerging sharply from a deeply cut background. Inside the Temple of Huitzilopochtli, an imposing statue of Coatlicue (fig. **15–11**), mother of Huitzilopochtli, stood high above the vanquished Coyolxauhqui. One of the conquistadors who arrived at the site in 1520 described seeing such a statue covered with blood. Coatlicue means "she of the serpent skirt," and this broad-shouldered figure with clawed hands and feet wears a skirt of twisted snakes. A pair of serpents, symbols of gushing blood, rise from her neck to form her head. In the confronting profiles, their eyes are her eyes, their fangs her tusks. Around her neck hangs a necklace of sacrificial offerings: hands, hearts, and a skull pendant. Despite its intricate surface and its composite nature, the sculpture's simple, bold, and blocky form creates a commanding unified whole. The colors with which it was originally painted would no doubt have heightened its dramatic impact.

Central America

Unlike their neighbors in Mesoamerica who lived in complex hierarchical societies, the people of Central America generally lived in family groups led by chiefs. A notable example of these small chiefdoms was the Diquis culture (in present-day Costa Rica), which lasted from about 700 CE to about 1500 CE.

The Diquis occupied fortified villages and seem to have engaged in constant warfare with one another. They did not produce monumental sculpture or architecture, but they created fine featherwork, ceramics, textiles, and gold objects. This exquisite

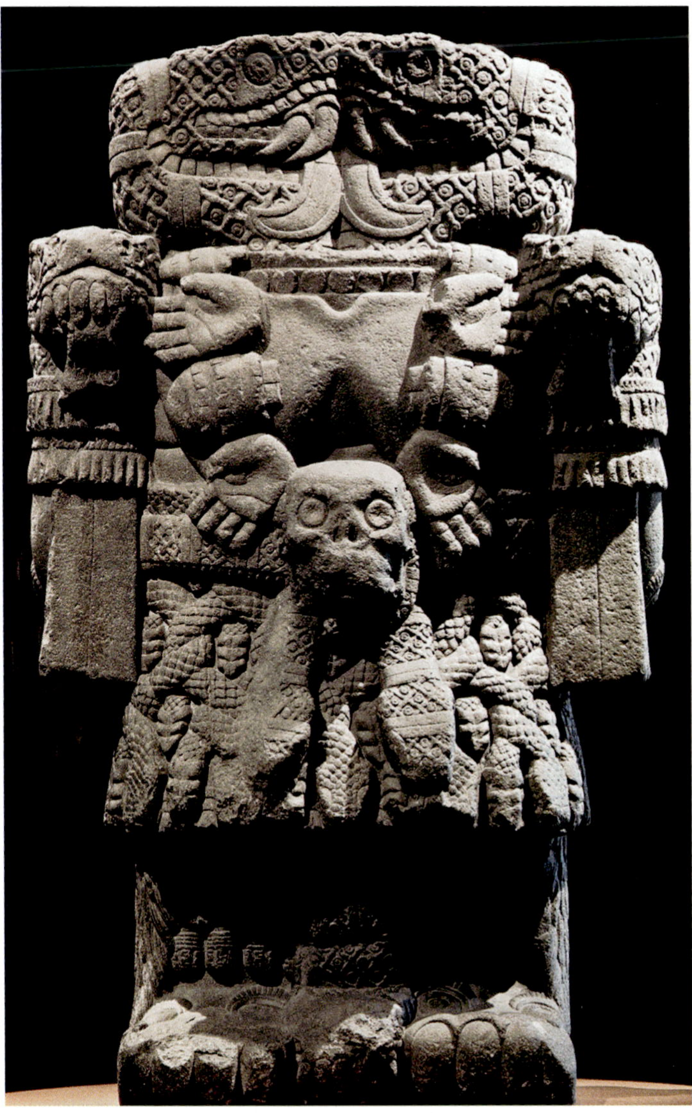

15–11 ***The Mother Goddess, Coatlicue.*** Aztec, 1487–1520 CE. Basalt, height 8' 6" (2.65 m). Museo Nacional de Antropologia, Mexico City

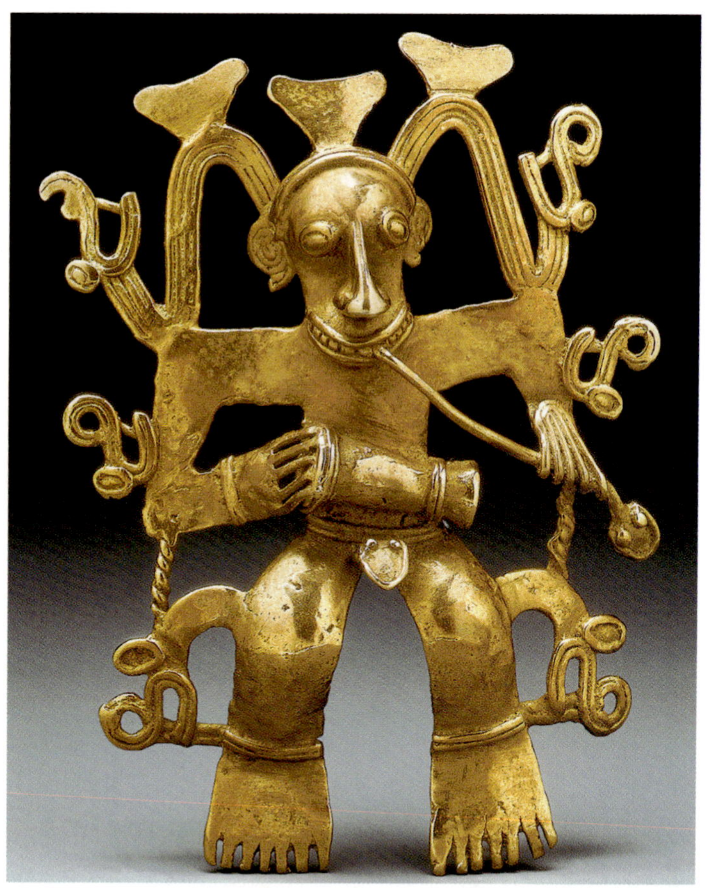

pendant (fig. **15–12**) illustrates the sophisticated design and technical facility of Diquis goldsmiths, working in the lost-wax technique (see page 446). The pendant depicts a male figure wearing bracelets, anklets, and a belt with a snake-headed penis sheath. He plays a drum while holding the tail of a snake in his teeth and its head in his left hand. The wavy forms with serpent heads emerging from his scalp suggest an elaborate headdress, and the creatures emerging from his legs suggest some kind of reptile costume. The inverted triangles on the headdress probably represent birds' tails.

In Diquis mythology, serpents and crocodiles inhabited a lower world; humans and birds a higher one. Diquis art depicts animals and insects as fierce and dangerous. Perhaps the man in the pendant is a shaman transforming himself into a composite serpent-bird or performing a ritual snake dance surrounded by serpents or crocodiles. The scrolls on the sides of his head could represent the shaman's power to hear and understand the speech of animals. Whatever its specific meaning, the pendant evokes a ritual of mediation between earthly and cosmic powers involving music, dance, and costume.

15–12 Shaman with Drum and Snake, from Costa Rica. Diquis culture, c. 13th–16th century CE. Gold, 4¼" × 3¼" (10.8 × 8.2 cm). Museos del Banco Central de Costa Rica, San José, Costa Rica

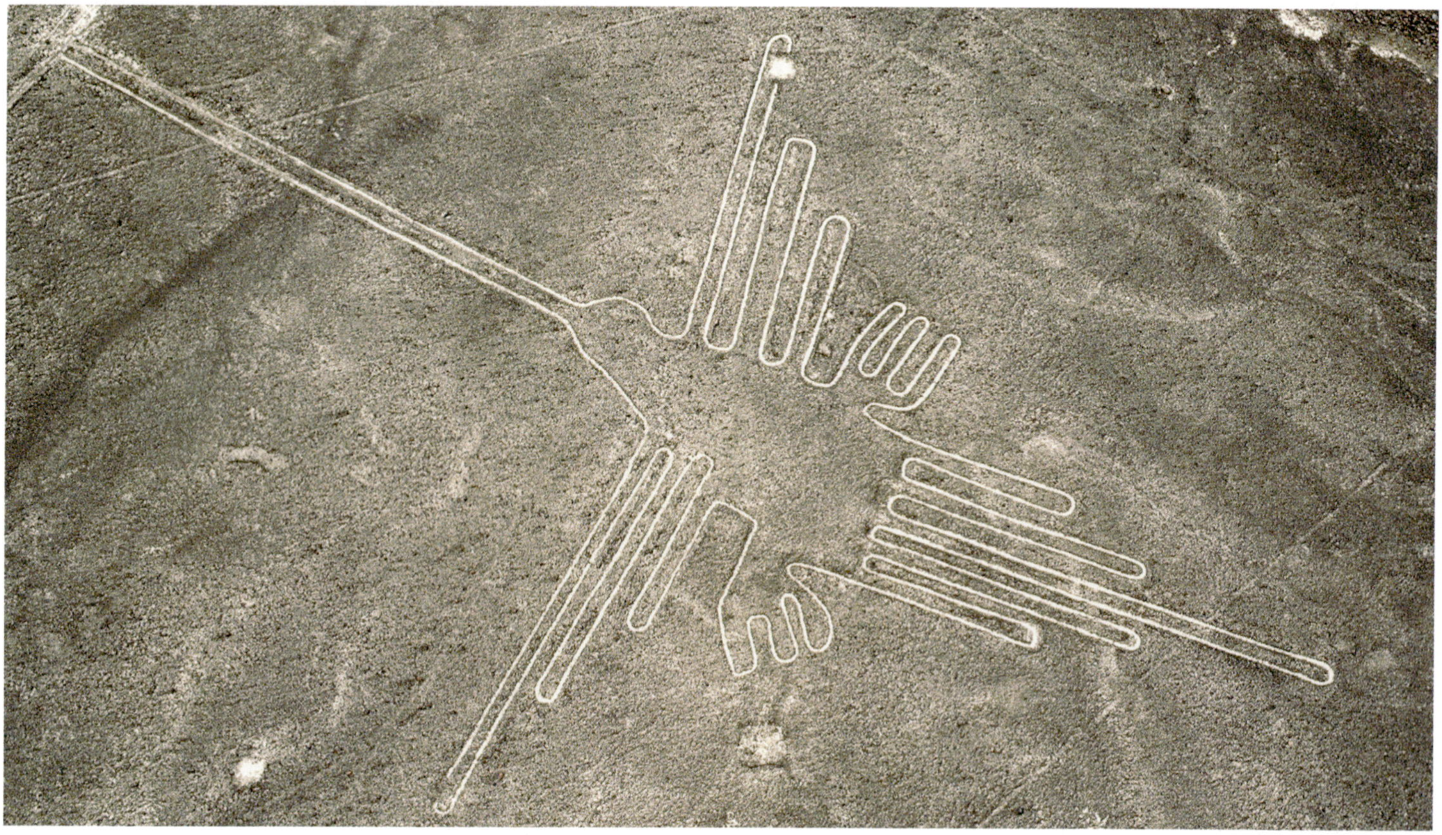

15–13 Geoglyph (earth drawing) **of a hummingbird**, Nazca Plain, southwest Peru. Nazca culture, c. 100 BCE–700 CE. Length approx. 450' (137 m); wingspan approx. 220' (60.9 m)

Whether gold figures of this kind were protective amulets or signs of high status, they were certainly more than personal adornment. Shamans and warriors wore gold to inspire fear, perhaps because gold was thought to capture the energy and power of the sun. This energy was also thought to allow shamans to leave their bodies and travel into cosmic realms.

South America: The Central Andes

Like Mesoamerica, the central Andes of South America—primarily present-day Peru and Bolivia—saw the development of complex hierarchical societies with rich and varied artistic traditions. The area is one of dramatic contrasts. The narrow coastal plain sandwiched between the Pacific Ocean and the soaring Andes is one of the driest deserts in the world. Life here depends on the rich marine resources of the Pacific and the rivers that descend from the Andes. The Andes themselves are a region of snowcapped peaks, fertile river valleys, and high plateaus, home to llamas, alpacas, vicuñas, and guanacos. The lush eastern slopes of the Andes descend to the tropical rainforest of the Amazon basin.

In the central Andes, the earliest evidence of monumental architecture dates to the third millennium BCE. Sites with ceremonial mounds and plazas were discovered near the sea, while early centers in the highlands consisted of multiroomed, stonewalled structures with sunken central fire pits in which ritual offerings were burned. Large, U-shaped ceremonial complexes with circular sunken plazas were built from the second millennium BCE. Some of the most enigmatic monumental constructions in Peru are the earthworks, or **geoglyphs**, first created by the people of the Nazca culture, who dominated the south coast of Peru from about 100 BCE to 700 CE. On great stretches of desert, the people literally drew in the earth. By removing a layer of dark gravel, they exposed the lighter underlying soil, then edged the resulting lines with stones. In this way, they created gigantic images, including a hummingbird with a beak 120 feet long (fig. **15–13**), a killer whale, a monkey, a spider, a duck, and other birds. They also made abstract patterns and configurations of straight, parallel lines that extend for up to 12 miles. Despite numerous theories, the purpose of these geoglyphs is not known. They dwarf even the most ambitious modern environmental sculpture and can only be seen fully from the air. Animals and plants in a similar style appear on a much smaller scale on multicolored pottery made by Nazca artisans.

The Moche Culture

The Moche culture dominated the north coast of what is now Peru, from the Piura Valley to the Huarmey Valley—a distance of some 370 miles—between about 200 BCE and 600 CE. Moche lords ruled each valley in this region from a ceremonial-administrative center. The largest of these, in the Moche Valley (from which the culture takes its name), contained the so-called Pyramids of the Sun and the Moon, both built entirely of adobe bricks. The Pyramid of the Sun, the largest ancient structure in South America, was originally a cross-shaped structure 1,122 feet long by 522 feet wide that rose in a series of terraces to a height of 59 feet. This site had been thought to be the capital of the entire Moche realm, but accumulating evidence indicates that the Moche maintained a decentralized social network.

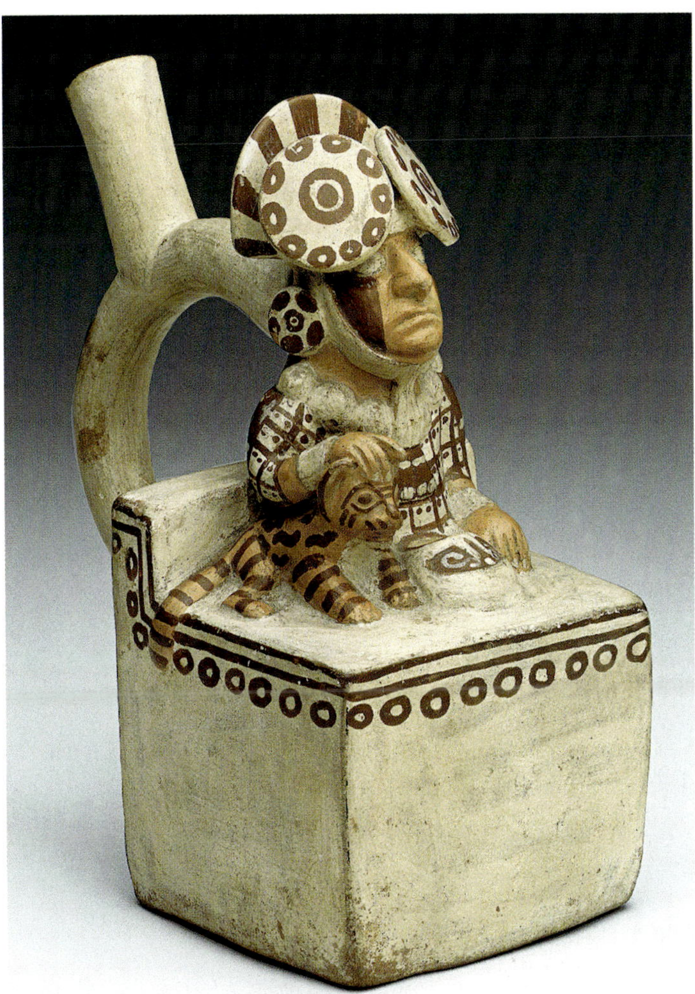

15–14 ***Moche Lord with a Feline,*** from Moche Valley, Peru. Moche culture, c. 100 BCE–500 CE. Painted ceramic, height 7½" (19 cm). Art Institute of Chicago
BUCKINGHAM FUND (1955–2281)

Behind the figure is the distinctive stirrup-shaped handle and spout. Vessels of this kind, used in Moche rituals, were also treasured as special luxury items and were buried with individuals of high status.

The Moche were exceptional potters and metalsmiths. They developed ceramic molds that allowed them to mass-produce forms. Some vessels were made in the forms of human beings, animals, and architectural structures. They also created portrait vessels and recorded in intricate fine-line painting mythological narratives and ritual scenes similar to those painted on the walls of temples and administrative buildings. Moche smiths, the most sophisticated in the central Andes, developed several innovative metal alloys. The ceramic vessel in figure **15–14** shows a Moche lord sitting in a throne-like structure associated with high office. He wears an elaborate headdress and large earspools and strokes a cat or perhaps a jaguar cub.

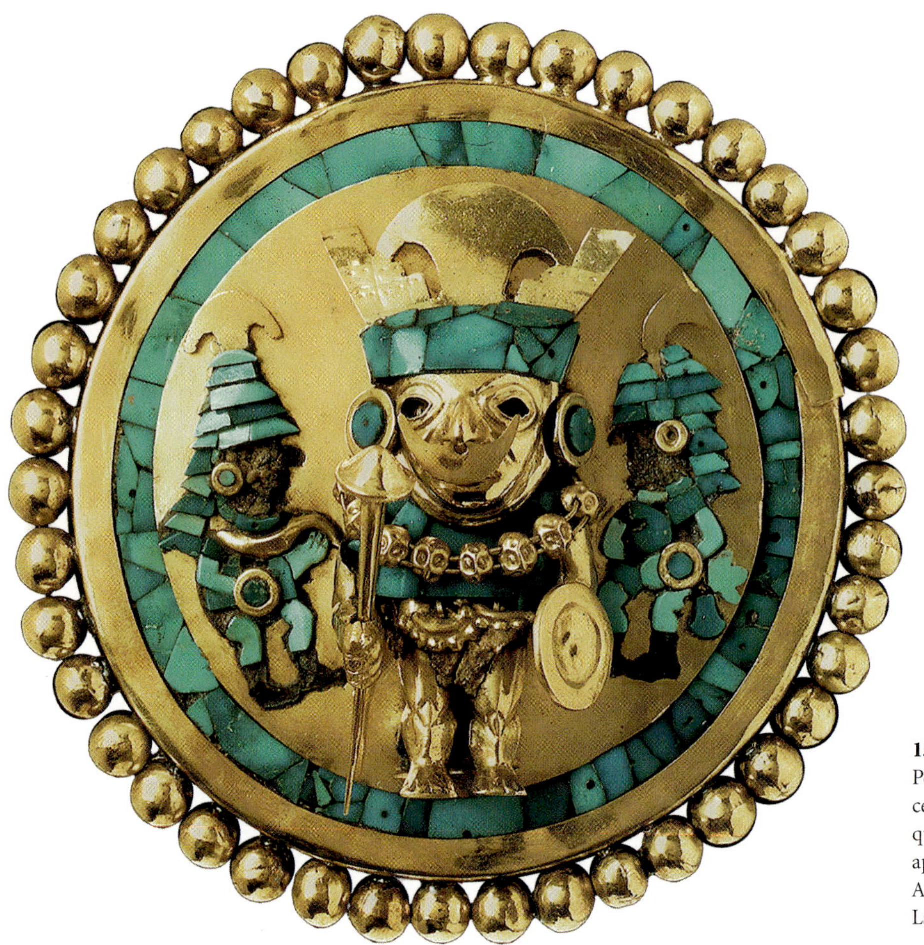

15–15 Earspool, from Sipan, Peru. Moche culture, 2nd–5th century CE. Gold, turquoise, quartz, and shell, diameter approx. 5" (12.7 cm). Bruning Archaeological Museum, Lambayeque, Peru

A central theme in Moche iconography is the ceremony in which prisoners captured in battle are sacrificed and elaborately dressed figures drink their blood. Archaeologists have labeled the principal figure in this ceremony as the Warrior Priest and other important figures as the Bird Priest and the Priestess. The recent discovery of a number of spectacularly rich Moche tombs indicates that the sacrifice ceremony was an actual Moche ritual performed by Moche lords. The occupant of a tomb at Sipan was buried with the regalia of a warrior priest. Among the riches accompanying him was a pair of exquisite gold-and-turquoise earspools, each of which depicts three Moche warriors (fig. **15–15**). The central figure is made of beaten gold and turquoise. He and his companions are adorned with tiny gold-and-turquoise earspools. They wear spectacular gold-and-turquoise headdresses topped with delicate sheets of gold that resemble the crescent-shaped knives used in sacrifices. The crests, like feathered fans of gold, would have swayed in the breeze as the wearer moved. The central figure has a crescent-shaped nose ornament and carries a gold club and shield. A necklace of owl's-head beads strung with gold thread hangs around his shoulders.

The Inca Empire

At the beginning of the sixteenth century, the Inca Empire was one of the largest states in the world, certainly the largest in the Andes region. It extended for more than 2,600 miles along western South America, encompassing most of present-day Ecuador, Peru, Bolivia, northern Chile, and part of Argentina. The Inca called their empire the Land of the Four Quarters. At its center was their capital, Cuzco, "the navel of the world," located high in the Andes Mountains. The early history of the Inca people is obscure, but in the fifteenth century, the Inca, like the Aztecs in the Basin of Mexico, began suddenly and rapidly to expand. Through conquest, alliance, and intimidation, they subdued most of their vast domain by 1500. To hold this linguistically and ethnically diverse empire together, the Inca relied on an overarching state religion, a hierarchical bureaucracy, and various forms of labor taxation, satisfied by a set amount of time spent performing tasks for the state. To speed transport and communication, the Inca built nearly 23,000 miles of roads, with more than 1,000 lodgings spaced a day's journey apart and a relay system of runners waiting to carry messages.

Inca builders created stonework structures of great refinement and durability (see "Inca Masonry," page 429). The most spectacular surviving example is Machu Picchu (fig. **15–16**). At 9,000 feet above sea level, the site straddles a ridge between two high peaks in the eastern slopes of the Andes. Machu Picchu, located near the eastern limits of the empire, was the ruler's summer home. Its temples and sacred stones imply it may also have had an important religious function.

The production of textiles is an ancient art in the Andes. Making cloth required a settled agricultural community where wool

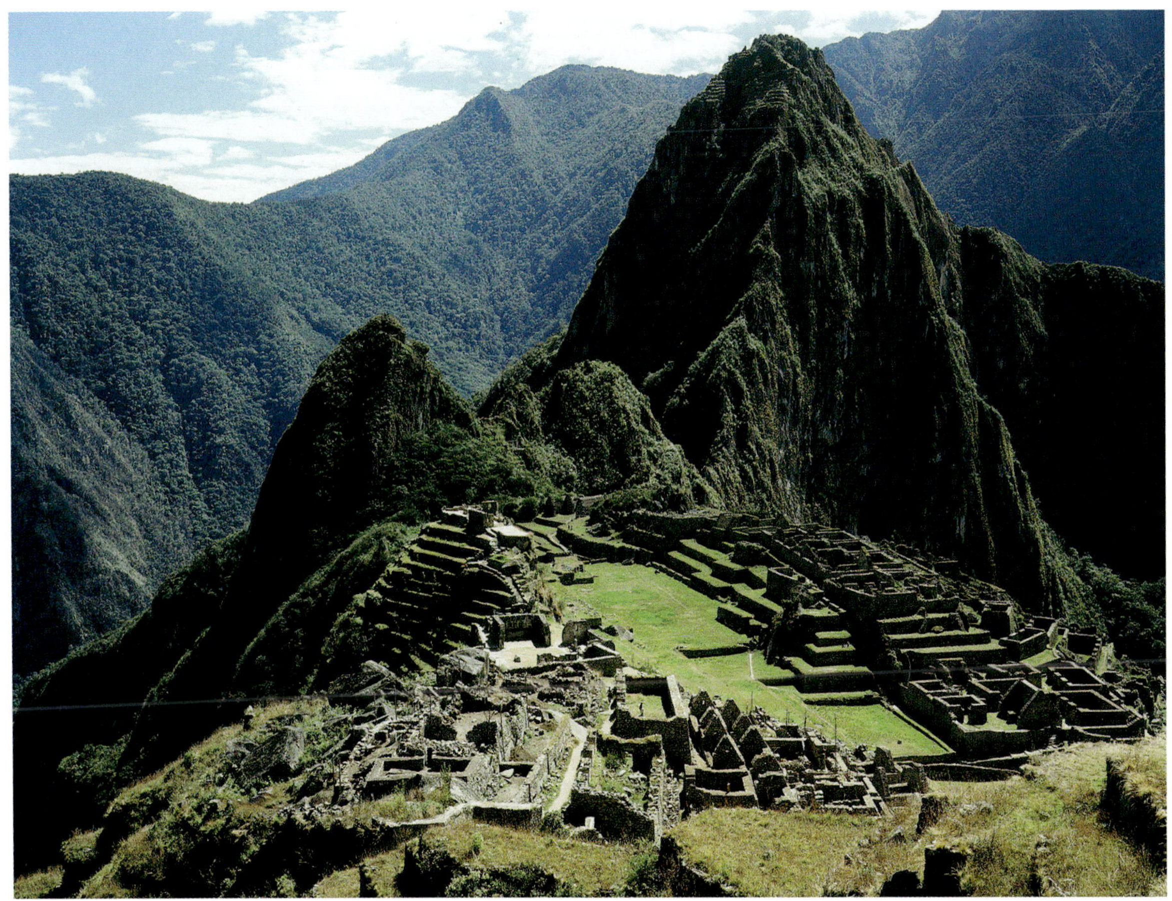

15–16 Machu Picchu, Peru.
Inca, 1450–1530 CE

ELEMENTS OF **Architecture**

Inca Masonry

Working with the simplest of tools—mainly heavy stone hammers—and using no mortar, Inca builders created superb stonework, built terraces for growing crops, and made structures both simple and elaborate, including roads that linked the empire together. At Machu Picchu (see fig. 15–16), all buildings and terraces were made of granite, the hard stone indigenous to the site. Commoners' houses and some walls were constructed of irregular stones and religious structures were erected using squared-off, smooth-surfaced stones laid in even rows. At a few Inca sites, the stones were boulder-size—up to 27 feet tall.

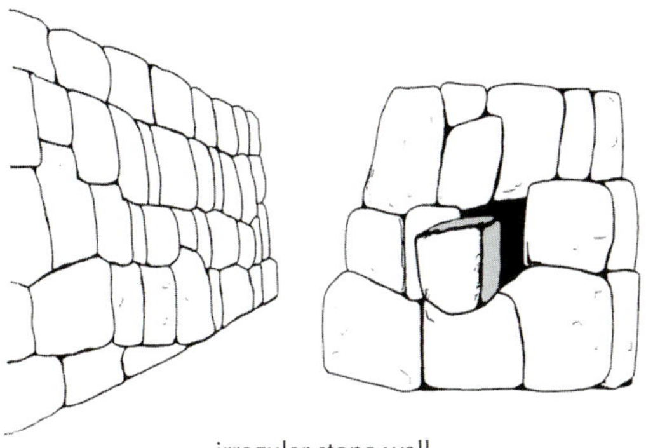

irregular-stone wall

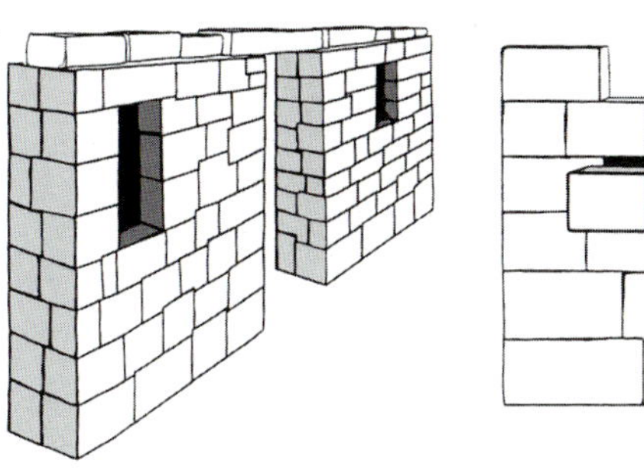

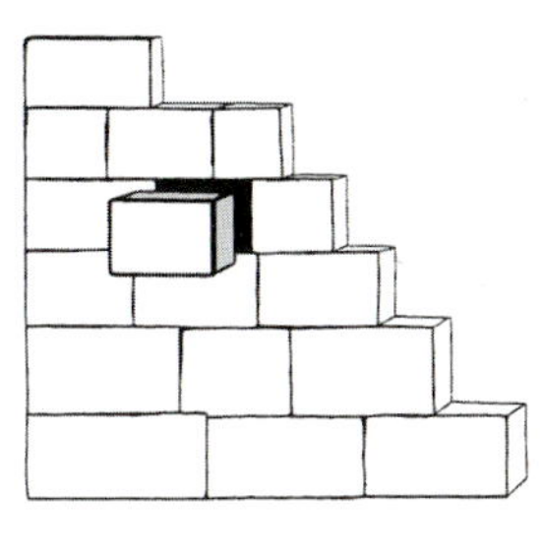

smooth-surfaced wall

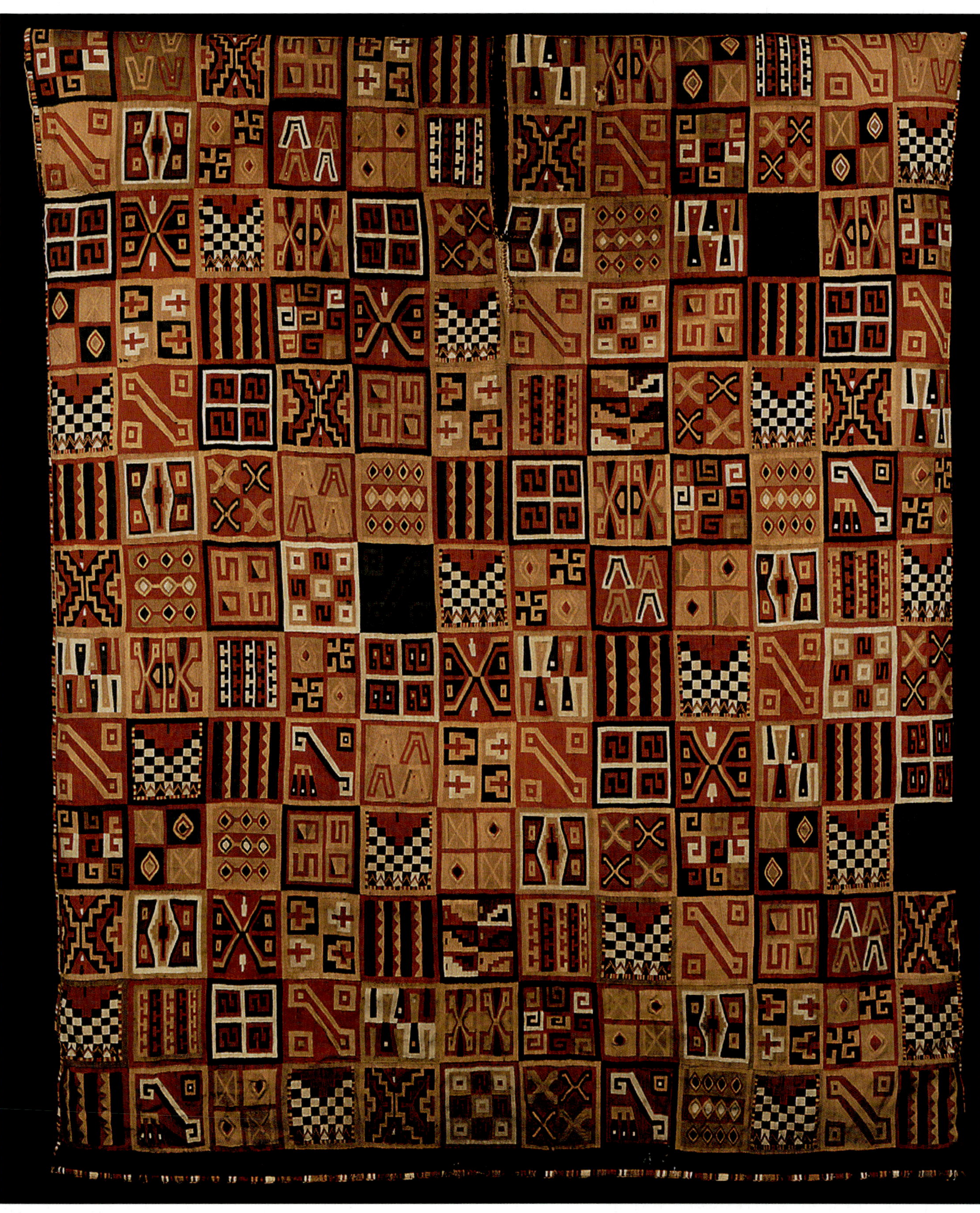

15–17 Tunic, from Peru. Inca, c. 1500 CE. Wool and cotton, 35⅞" × 30" (91 × 76.5 cm). Dumbarton Oaks Research Library and Collection, Washington, D.C.

(llama, alpaca and vicuña) and cotton could be produced, cleaned, dyed, and spun into yarn. Both men and women worked as weavers for the central government, paying their labor taxes by producing textiles. As one of the primary forms of wealth for the Inca, cloth was a fitting offering for the gods. Fine garments were draped around golden statues, and even three-dimensional images were constructed of cloth. Garments also carried important symbolic messages. Their patterns could indicate a person's ethnic identity and social rank. In the elaborate tunic in figure **15–17**, each square represents a miniature tunic, but the meaning of the individual patterns is not yet completely understood. The checkerboard pattern designated military officers and royal escorts. The four-part motifs may refer to the Land of the Four Quarters.

The Aftermath of the Spanish Conquest

Hernán Cortés arrived off the eastern coast of Mexico from the Spanish colony in Cuba in 1519. He forged alliances with the Aztecs' enemies and, within two years, took control of Tenochtitlan. Over the next several years, Spanish forces subdued much of the rest of what is today Mexico and established it as a colony of Spain. In 1532, Francisco Pizarro, following Cortés' example, led an expedition to South America. He and his men seized the Inca ruler, Atahualpa, held him for a huge ransom in gold, and then treacherously strangled him. They marched on to Cuzco and seized it in 1533.

The Spanish who conquered the Inca Empire were obsessed with amassing gold and silver. They melted down whatever they could find to enrich themselves and the royal coffers of Spain. The Inca, in contrast, valued gold and silver not as precious metals in themselves, but as symbols—the "sweat of the sun" and the "tears of the moon." Only a few small figures, buried as offerings, escaped the invaders' treasure hunt.

Native American populations in Mexico and Peru declined sharply after the conquest because of the exploitative policies of the conquerors and the ravages of smallpox and other newly introduced diseases, against which the indigenous people had no immunity. European missionaries suppressed local beliefs and practices and worked to spread Roman Catholicism throughout the Americas. Increasingly, Europeans began to settle the land.

North America

In America north of Mexico, from the upper reaches of Canada and Alaska to the southern tip of Florida, there existed many different peoples with widely varying cultures. In previous times their artworks—often small, portable, fragile, and impermanent—were collected as anthropological artifacts or curiosities rather than works of art. As a consequence, anthropology and natural history museums often have large collections of indigenous art. That this attitude has changed is signaled by the establishment of such prestigious institutions as the National Museum of the American Indian in Washington, D.C. And works of an increasing number of young Native American artists can be seen alongside Euro-American artists in mainstream art galleries.

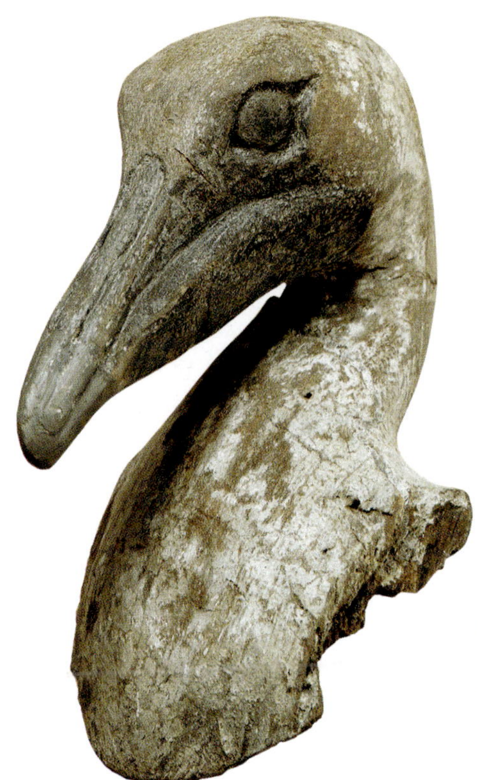

15–18 Pelican figurehead, Key Marco, Florida. Glades culture, c. 1000 CE. Wood and paint, 4⅜" × 2⅜" × 3⅛" (11.2 × 6 × 8 cm). Penn Museum, Philadelphia
PENN MUSEUM OBJECT 4078, IMAGE 150303

The Southeast

The indigenous culture of the southeast is only beginning to be understood. Archaeologists have shown that as early as 3400–3000 BCE people lived in communities formed around a central earthen mound—a platform that probably supported a chief's house, the shrines of ancestors, and a place for a sacred fire, tended by special guardians.

In 1895, excavators working in submerged mud and shell mounds off Key Marco on the west coast of Florida made a remarkable discovery from what has been named the Florida Glades culture. Painted wooden animal and bird heads, a human mask, and the figure of a kneeling cat-human were found in circumstances that suggested a ruined shrine. Carbon-14 dating of these items has confirmed a date of about 1000 CE. The sculptors show a remarkable power of observation in reproducing the creatures they saw around them, such as the pelican (fig. **15–18**). The surviving head, neck, and breast of the pelican are made of carved wood painted black, white, and gray (other pieces also included pink and blue). The bird's outstretched wings were discovered nearby, but the wood shrank and disintegrated as it dried. Also found were carved wooden wolf and deer heads that might have been attached to ceremonial furniture or posts. Such images could suggest the existence of a bird and animal cult or perhaps the use of birds and animals as clan symbols.

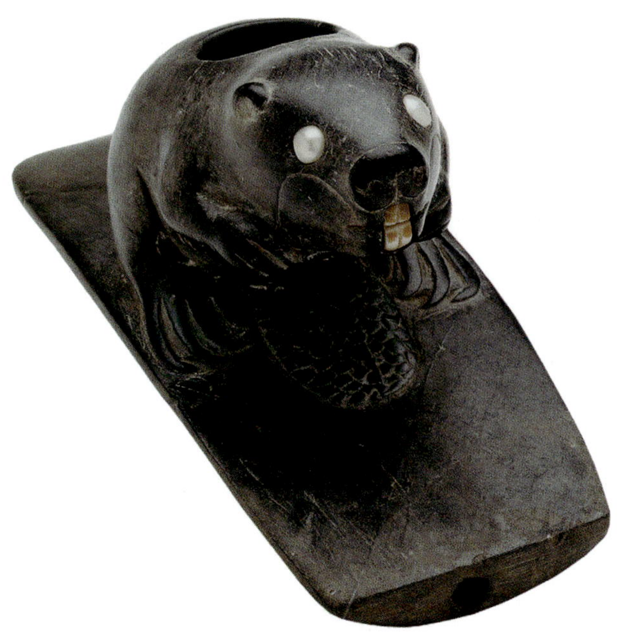

15–19 Beaver effigy platform pipe, from Bedford Mound, Pike County, Illinois. Hopewell culture, c. 100–200 CE. Pipestone, river pearl eyes, and bone teeth, length 4½" (11.4 cm). Gilcrease Museum, Tulsa, Oklahoma

Pipes like this may have been used for smoking hallucinatory plants, perhaps during rituals involving the animal carved on the pipe bowl. Could the beaver's shining pearl eyes suggest an association with the spirit world?

The Mound Builders In the fertile lands near the Ohio, Illinois, Mississippi, and Missouri rivers, the people of the Adena, Hopewell, and Mississippian cultures cultivated maize (corn) and other crops. Sometime before 1000 BCE, they began building monumental earthworks and burying their leaders with valuable grave goods. Objects discovered in these burials show that the people of the Mississippi and Ohio Valleys traded widely with other regions. For example, burials of the mound-building Adena (1000 BCE–200 CE) and Hopewell (c. 100 BCE–550 CE) cultures contained jewelry made with copper imported from the Upper Peninsula of present-day Michigan and silhouettes cut in sheets of mica from the Appalachian Mountains.

The Hopewell people also made pipes of fine-grain pipestone carved with lifelike representations of forest animals and birds, sometimes with inlaid eyes and teeth of freshwater pearls and bone. A pearl-eyed beaver crouching on a platform forms the bowl of a pipe found in present-day Illinois (fig. **15–19**). As in a modern pipe, the bowl—a hole in the beaver's back—could be filled with dried leaves (the Hopewell may not have grown tobacco), the leaves lighted, and smoke drawn through a hole in the stem. A second way to use these pipes was to blow smoke inhaled from another vessel through the pipe to envelop the animal carved on it. Hopewell pipes and pipestone have been found from Lake Superior to the Gulf of Mexico.

The people of the Mississippian culture (700–1550 CE) continued the mound-building tradition of the Adena, Hopewell, and other early southeastern cultures. One of the most impressive Mississippian-period earthworks is the Great Serpent Mound, nearly a quarter of a mile long, in present-day Ohio (fig. **15–20**). Carbon-14 dating of wood charcoal samples from the mound suggests that the earthwork was built about 1070 CE. There have been many interpretations of the twisting snake form, especially the "head" at the highest point, an oval enclosure that some see as opening its jaws to swallow a huge egg formed by a heap of stones.

The Mississippian peoples built a major urban center known as Cahokia near the juncture of the Illinois, Missouri, and Mississippi rivers (now East St. Louis, Illinois). Although the site may have been inhabited as early as circa 3000 BCE, Cahokia, as we know it, was begun about 900 CE, and most construction was complete by about 1500. At its height, the city had a population of about 20,000 people, with another 10,000 in the surrounding countryside (fig. **15–21**).

The most prominent feature of Cahokia is an enormous 100-foot earth mound called Monk's Mound covering 15 acres. A small, conical platform on its summit originally supported a wooden fence and a rectangular building, aligned with the sun at the equinox. Smaller rectangular and conical mounds in front of the principal mound surrounded a large, roughly rectangular plaza. The city's entire ceremonial center was protected by a stockade, or fence, of upright wooden posts—a sign of increasing insecurity or warfare. In all, the walled enclosure contained more than 500 mounds, platforms, wooden enclosures, and houses. The various earthworks functioned as tombs and as bases for palaces and temples, and perhaps also to make astronomical observations. One conical burial mound was located next to a platform that may have been used for sacrifices.

The Southwest

Farming cultures were slower to arise in the arid Southwest. The Hohokam culture, centered in the central and southern parts of present-day Arizona, emerged around 200 BCE and endured until sometime after 1200 CE. The Hohokam built large-scale irrigation systems, constructing deep and narrow canals to reduce evaporation and lining the canals with clay to reduce seepage.

Another early southwestern culture, the Ancestral Puebloans (formerly called Anasazi), emerged around 550 CE in what is now called the Four Corners region—where Colorado, Utah, Arizona, and New Mexico meet. They adopted the irrigation technology of the Hohokam to produce food for settled communities, and around 850 CE they began building elaborate, multistoried, apartment-like "great houses" with many rooms for specialized purposes, including communal food storage and rituals. The Spaniards called such communities "pueblos," or towns (see fig. 18–12).

The largest known great house is Pueblo Bonito in Chaco Canyon, New Mexico, which was built between c. 850 and 1350 CE

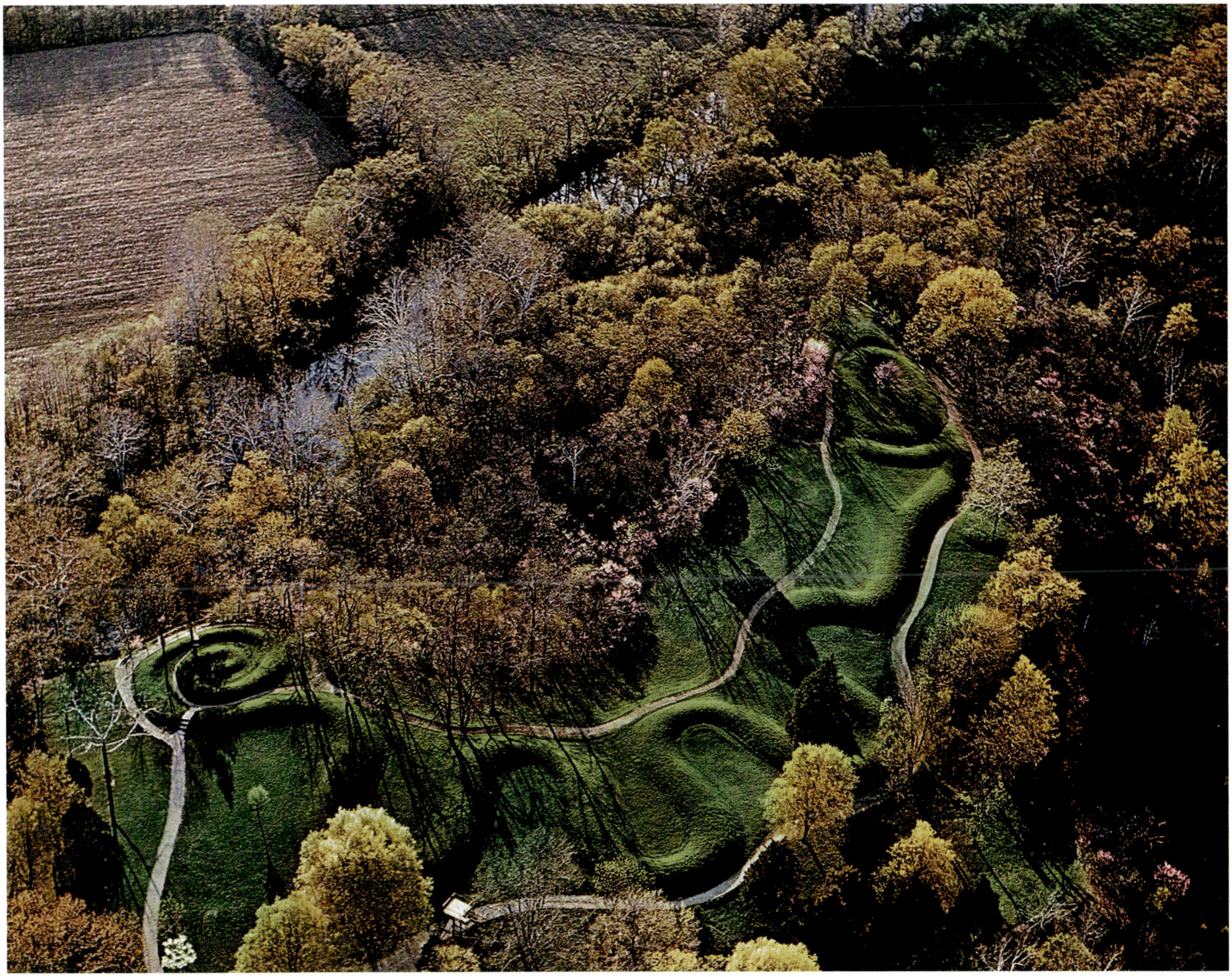

15–20 Great Serpent Mound, Adams County, Ohio. c. 1070 CE. Length 1,254' (328.2 m)
COURTESY OF CAHOKIA MOUNDS STATE HISTORIC SITE

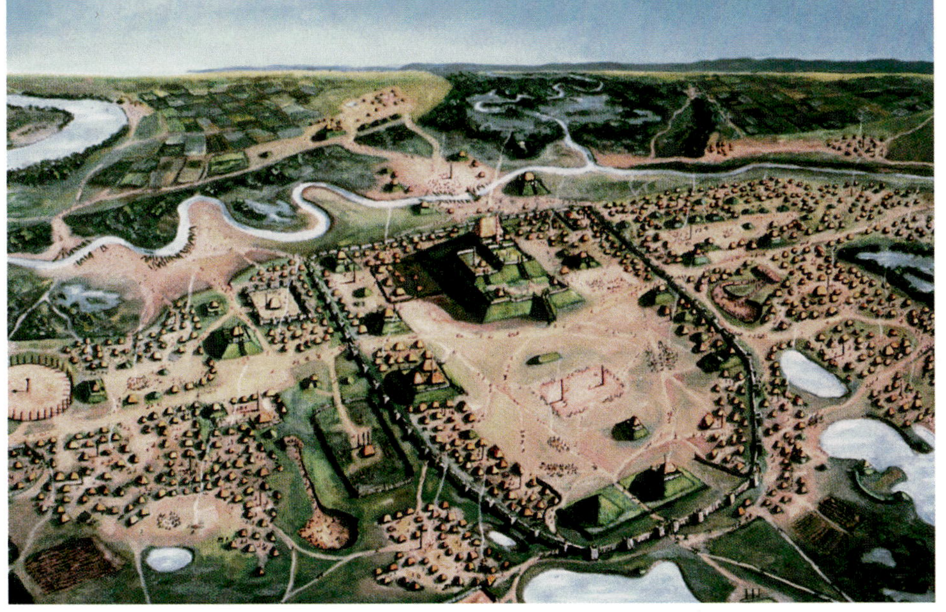

15–21 Reconstruction of central Cahokia as it would have appeared c. 1150 CE, East St. Louis, Illinois. Mississippian culture, c. 1150 CE. Earth mounds and wooden structures; east–west length approx. 3 miles (4.84 km), north–south length approx. 2¼ miles (3.63 km); base of great mound, 1,037' × 790' (316 × 241 m), height approx. 100' (30 m). Painting by William R. Iseminger

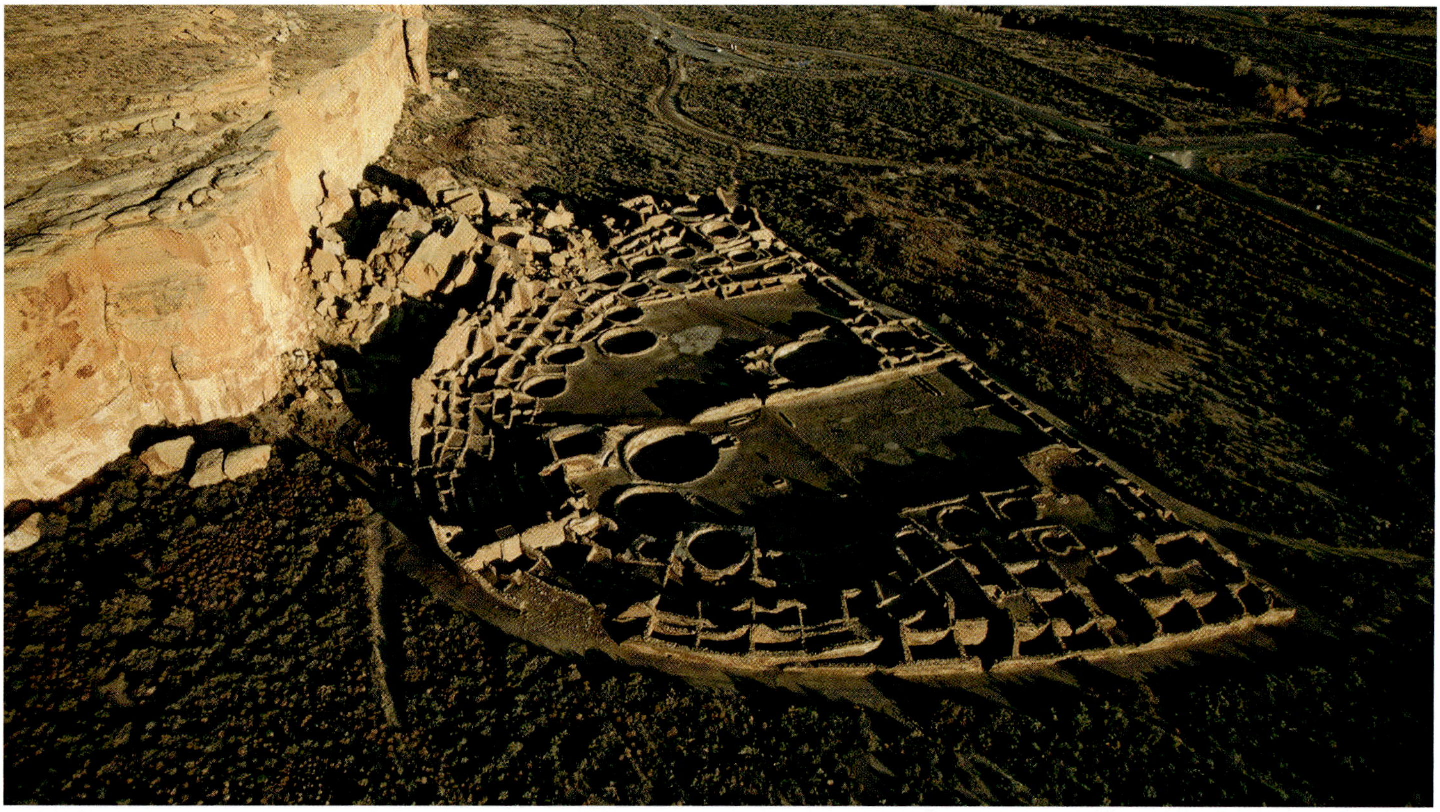

15–22 Pueblo Bonito, Chaco Canyon, New Mexico. Ancestral Pueblo culture, 850–1250 CE

(figs. 15–1 and **15–22**). This remarkable, D-shaped structure, one of nine great houses in Chaco Canyon, covered more than three acres. Some 800 rooms—including 30 **kivas** (subterranean circular rooms used as ceremonial centers)—rose four or five stories high. The sandstone masonry walls on the ground floor were 4 feet thick, and trunks of ponderosa pines transported from 50 miles away were used for roof beams. Amazingly, all aspects of construction, including quarrying, timber cutting, and transport, were done without draft animals, wheeled vehicles, or metal tools. The size of this complex has led some to speculate that it may have provided temporary housing for people on pilgrimage to a sacred site, especially since it sits at the center of a network of wide, straight roads. Perhaps many traveled to Chaco at the summer solstice, guided by "Sun Watchers" to witness the descent of the "Sun Dagger" high in the cliff walls above Pueblo Bonito (see fig. 15–1).

Ancestral Puebloans found aesthetic expression in their pottery, a craft perfected over generations and still alive today. Women were the potters in pueblo society. In the eleventh century, they perfected a functional, aesthetically engaging, coil-built earthenware fired at a low temperature. The wide-mouthed seed jar shown in figure **15–23** is painted with complex black-and-white dotted squares and zigzag patterns that conform to the body of the jar and, in spite of their angularity, enhance its curved shape. The intricate and inventive play of positive and negative space—represented by dark and light areas—suggests lightning flashing over a grid of irrigated fields.

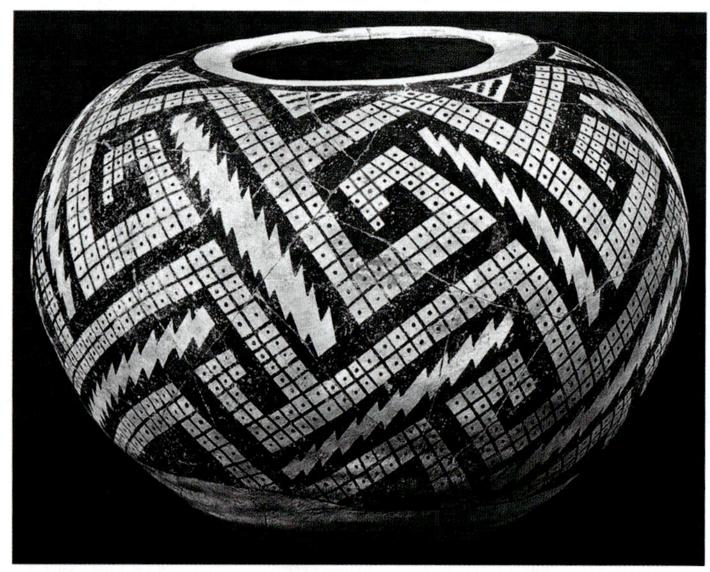

15–23 Seed jar. Ancestral Pueblo culture, c. 1150 CE. Earthenware and black-and-white pigment, diameter 14½" (36.8 cm). The St. Louis Art Museum, St. Louis, Missouri

PURCHASE: FUNDS GIVEN BY THE CHILDREN'S ART FESTIVAL 175:1981

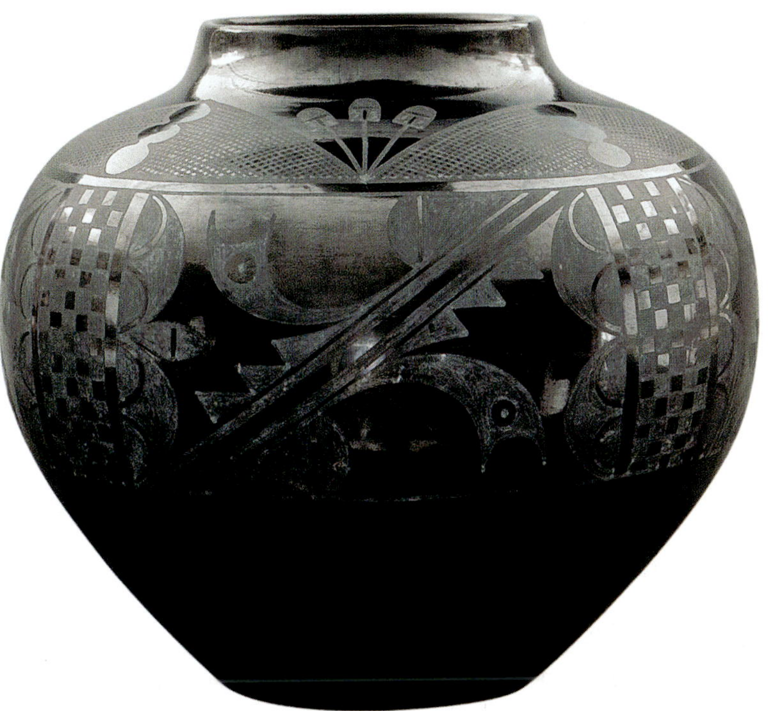

15–24 Maria Montoya Martinez and **Julian Martinez. Storage jar**, from San Ildefonso Pueblo, New Mexico. c. 1942 CE. Black on black ceramic, height 18¾" (47.6 cm), diameter 22½" (57.1 cm). Museum of Indian Arts and Culture/Laboratory of Anthropology, Museum of New Mexico, Santa Fe

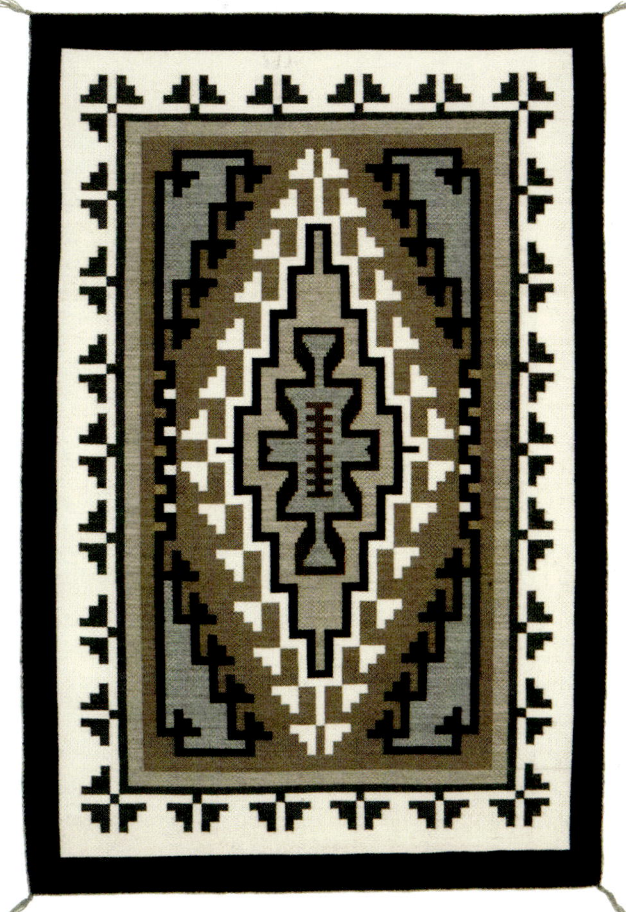

15–25 Julia Jumbo, Two Gray Hills Tapestry Weaving, Navajo. 2003 CE. Handspun wool, 36" × 24½" (91.2 × 62.1 cm). Wheelwright Museum of the American Indian, Santa Fe, New Mexico

The Pueblo people of the southwest still make fine ceramics in the traditional way, using traditional designs. One of the best-known twentieth-century Pueblo potters was Maria Montoya Martinez (1881–1980) of the San Ildefonso Pueblo in New Mexico. Inspired by prehistoric blackware pottery that was unearthed at nearby archaeological excavations, she and her husband, Julian Martinez (1885–1943), developed a distinctive ceramic style, reserving **matte** (non-gloss) black designs on a lustrous black background (fig. **15–24**). Their decorative patterns were inspired by traditional Pueblo imagery, but they also show the influence of the then-fashionable Euro-American Art Deco.

Navajo women have been renowned for their skill as weavers for centuries, both among fellow Native Americans and also Euro-American collectors. According to Navajo mythology, the universe itself is a weaving, its fibers spun by Spider Woman out of sacred cosmic materials. Spider Woman taught the art of weaving to Changing Woman (a Mother Earth figure), and she in turn taught it to Navajo women, who continue to keep this art vital to this day, many seeing its continuation as a sacred act. The earliest Navajo blankets had simple horizontal stripes, but over time, weavers developed finer techniques and introduced more intricate patterns in the creation of rugs. The tapestry weaving in figure **15–25**—designed in the Two Gray Hills style that developed during the early twentieth century around a trading post of that name in northwest New Mexico—was created in 2003 by Julia Jumbo (born 1928). This artist, who learned her art as a child and used her weaving to support her family, is renowned for the clarity of her traditional designs and the technical perfection of her fine weave. In this example she has restricted herself to the natural colors of the handspun wool.

Technique

Basketry

Basketry involves weaving reeds, grasses, or other materials to form containers. The three principal basket-making techniques are coiling, or sewing together a spiraling foundation of rods with some other material; twining, or sewing together a vertical warp of rods; and plaiting, which involves weaving strips over and under each other. In North America the earliest evidence of basketwork, found in Danger Cave, Utah, dates to as early as 8400 BCE. Over the subsequent centuries basket makers developed their craft into a veritable art form, producing objects whose ornamental design transcends the demands of their usefulness as containers.

The coiled basket shown here (fig. **15–26**) was made by the Pomo of northern California. According to Pomo legend, the earth was dark until their ancestral hero stole the sun and brought it to earth in a basket. He hung the basket first just over the horizon, but, dissatisfied with the light it gave, he kept suspending it in different places across the dome of the sky. He repeats this process every day, which is why the sun moves across the sky from east to west. In the Pomo basket, the structure of coiled willow and bracken fern root produces a spiral surface into which the artist worked sparkling pieces of clamshell, trade beads, and the soft tufts of woodpecker and quail feathers. Such baskets were treasured possessions, often cremated with their owners at death.

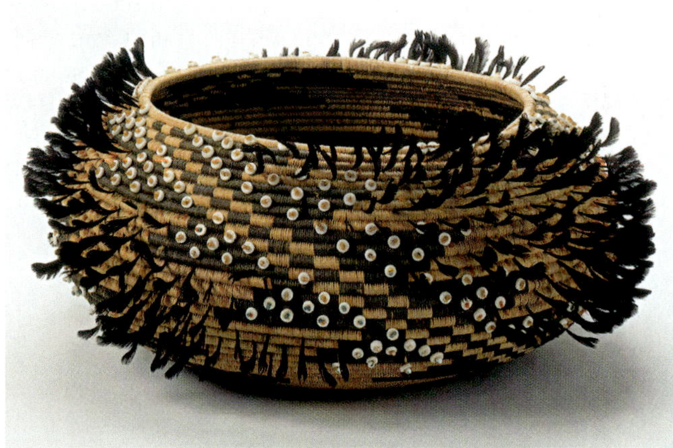

15–26 Feathered Bowl Wedding Basket. Pomo, c. 1877 CE. Willow, bulrush, fern, feather, shells, glass beads, height 5½" (14 cm), diameter 12" (30.5 cm). Philbrook Museum, Tulsa, Oklahoma
GIFT OF CLARK FIELD (1948.39.37)

The Eastern Woodlands and the Great Plains

When European settlement began in earnest in North America around the late 1500s to early 1600s, forests stretched from the Hudson Bay to the Gulf of Mexico and from the Atlantic coast to the Mississippi River and Missouri River watersheds. Between this Eastern Woodlands region and the Rocky Mountains to the west lay an area of prairie grasslands now known as the Great Plains.

In the Eastern Woodlands, most Native American peoples lived in stable villages and supported themselves by a combination of hunting and agriculture. They used waterproof birchbark to construct their homes and to make the watercraft known as the canoe. As European settlers on the eastern seaboard began to turn forests into farms, they put increasing pressure on the Eastern Woodlands peoples, seizing their lands and forcing them westward. The resulting interaction of Eastern Woodlands artists with one another and with Plains artists led to the emergence of a Prairie style among numerous groups.

Woodlands art focused on personal adornment—tattoos, body paint, elaborate dress—and fragile arts such as quillwork. Quillwork involved dyeing porcupine and bird quills with a variety of natural dyes, soaking the quills to soften them, and then working them into rectilinear, ornamental surface patterns on deerskin clothing and on birchbark items like baskets and boxes. A Sioux legend recounts how a mythical ancestor, Doublewoman ("double" because she was both beautiful and ugly, benign and dangerous), appeared to a woman in a dream and taught her the art of quillwork. As the legend suggests, like pottery and basketry, this was a woman's art form. The Sioux baby carrier in figure **15–27** is richly decorated with quillwork symbols of protection and well-being, including bands of antelopes in profile and thunderbirds flying with their heads turned and tails outspread. The thunderbird was an especially beneficent symbol, thought to be capable of protecting against both human and supernatural adversaries.

On the Great Plains, two differing ways of life developed, one traditional and sedentary, and the other (relatively recent and short-lived, 1700–1870) nomadic and dependent on the region's great migrating herds of buffalo for food, clothing, and shelter. Horses—introduced by Spanish explorers in the sixteenth century—and later firearms, made buffalo hunting vastly more efficient, increasing the appeal of the nomadic way of life.

The nomadic Plains peoples developed a light, portable dwelling known as a **tepee** (fig. **15–28**), which was sturdily constructed to withstand the wind, dust, and rain of the prairies. Buffalo hides (later, canvas) covered a framework of poles to form an almost conical structure that leaned slightly in the direction of the prevailing wind. The flap-covered door and smoke hole (the opening at the top above the central hearth) usually faced away from the wind. Designed and built by women, the typical tepee required about 18 buffalo hides, the largest about 38. An inner lining covered the lower part of the walls and part of the floor to protect the occupants from drafts. Women painted, embroidered, quilled, and beaded tepee linings, backrests, clothing, and equipment. Plains men recorded their exploits in symbolic and narrative form in paintings on tepee linings and covers and also on buffalo-hide robes.

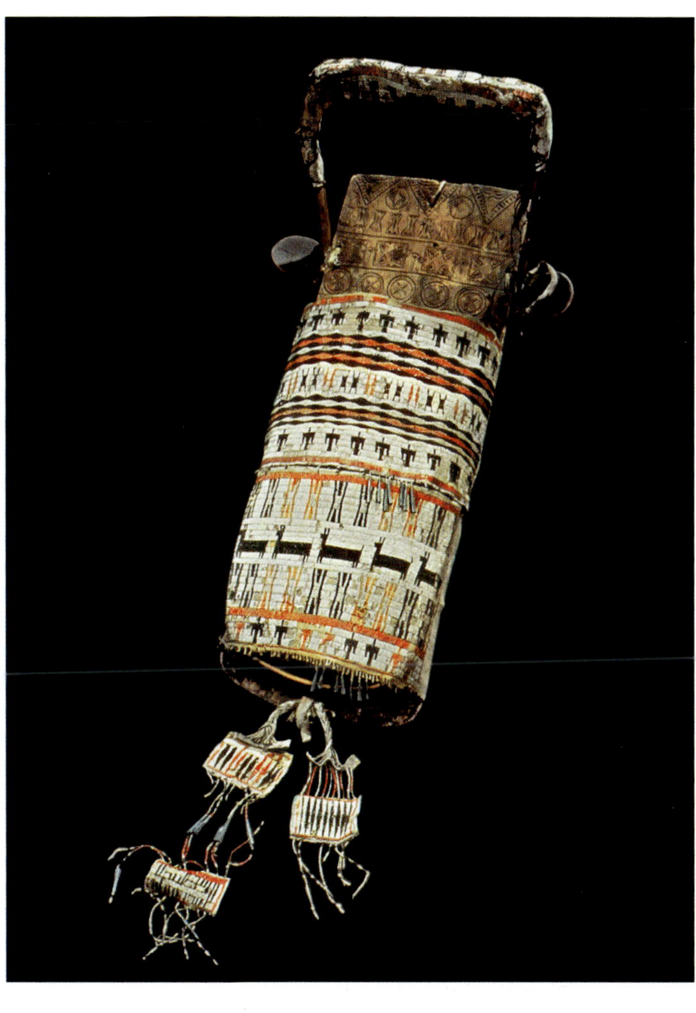

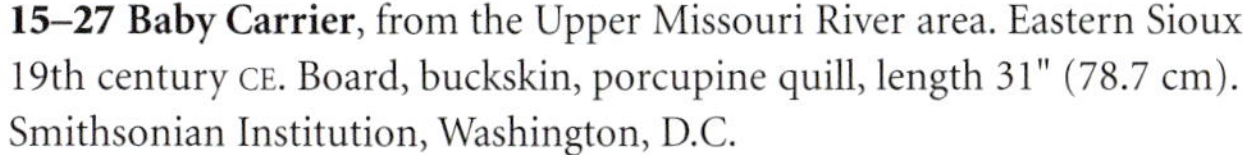

15–27 Baby Carrier, from the Upper Missouri River area. Eastern Sioux, 19th century CE. Board, buckskin, porcupine quill, length 31" (78.7 cm). Smithsonian Institution, Washington, D.C.

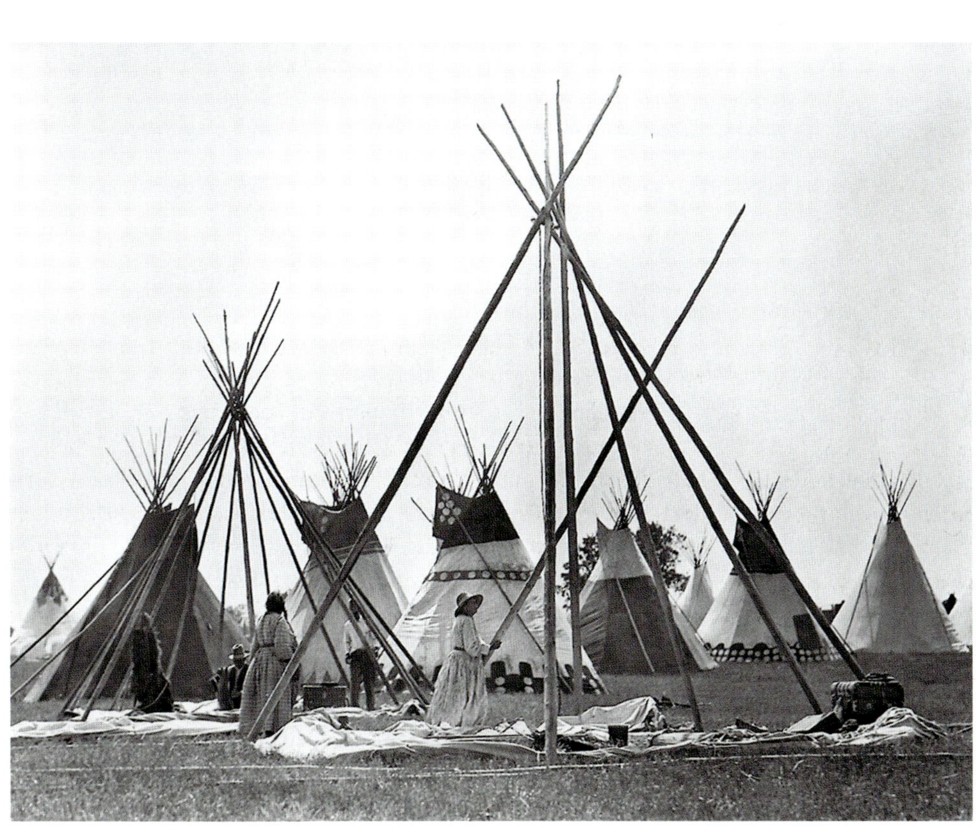

15–28 Blackfoot Women Raising a Tepee. Photographed c. 1900 CE. Montana Historical Society, Helena

When packed to be dragged by a horse, the tepee served as a platform for transporting other possessions as well. Tepees were the property and responsibility of women. Blackfoot women could set up their tepees in less than an hour.

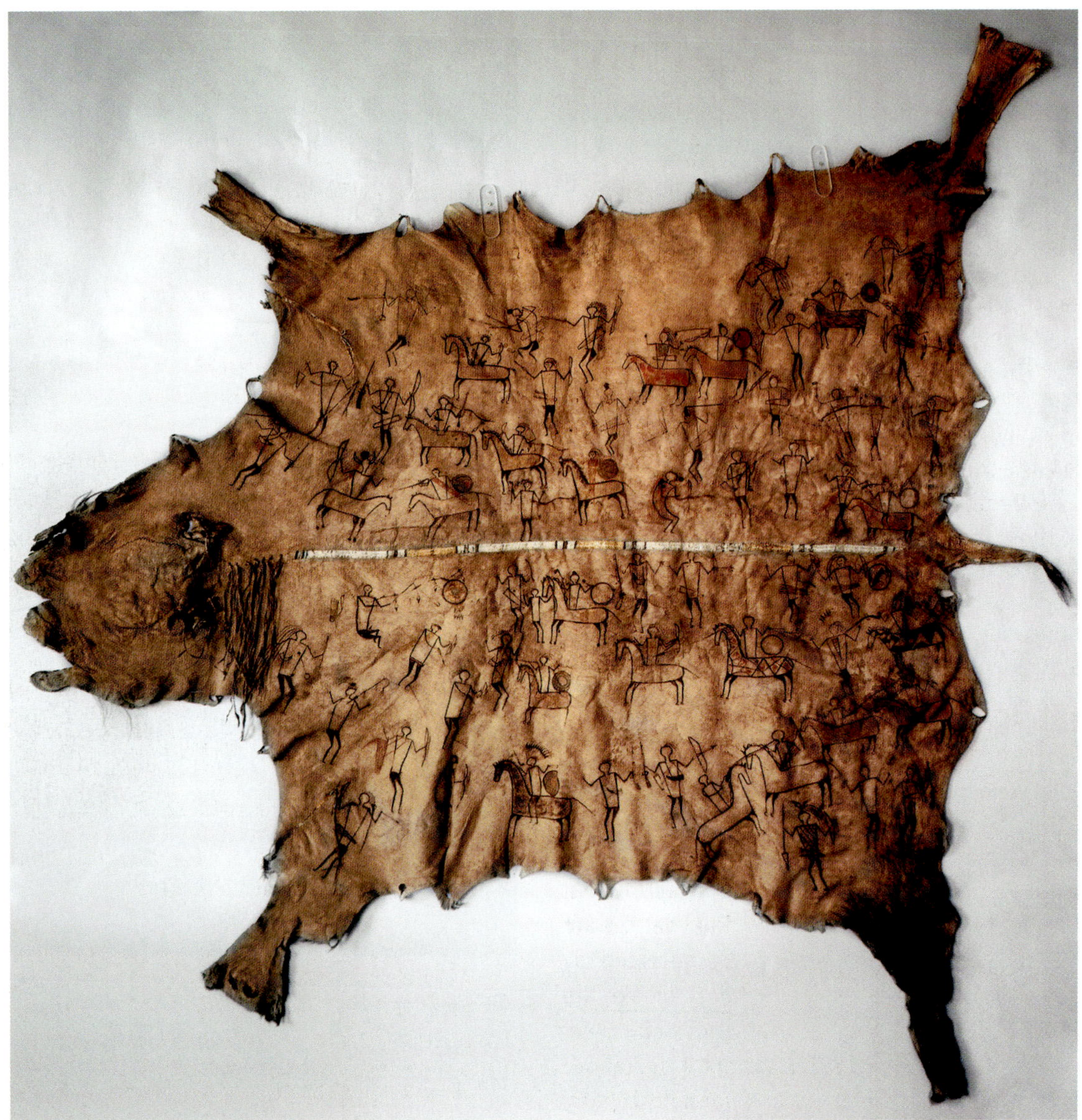

15–29 Battle-scene hide painting, from North Dakota. Mandan, 1797–1800 CE. Tanned buffalo hide, dyed porcupine quills, and black, red, green, yellow, and brown pigment, 7' 10" × 8' 6" (2.44 × 2.65 m). Peabody Museum of Archaeology, Harvard University, Cambridge, Massachusetts
(99-12-10/53121)

This painted hide was collected in 1804 by Meriwether Lewis and William Clark on their 1804–1806 expedition into western lands acquired by the United States in the Louisiana Purchase, making it the earliest documented example of Plains painting. Lewis and Clark presented it to President Thomas Jefferson, who displayed the robe in the entrance hall of Monticello, his home in Virginia.

The earliest known painted buffalo-hide robe illustrates a battle fought in 1797 by the Mandan (of what is now North Dakota) and their allies against the Sioux (fig. **15–29**). The painter, trying to capture the full extent of a conflict in which five nations took part, shows a party of warriors in 22 separate episodes. The party is led by a man with a pipe and an elaborate eagle-feather headdress, and the warriors are armed with bows and arrows, lances, clubs, and flintlock rifles. The lively, stylized figures of the warriors stand out clearly against the light-colored background of the buffalo hide. The painter pressed lines into the hide, then filled in with black, red, green, yellow, and brown pigments. A strip of colored porcupine quills runs down the "spine." The robe would have been worn draped over the shoulders of the powerful warrior whose deeds it commemorates. As he moved, the painted horses and warriors would appear to come alive, transforming him into a living representation of his exploits.

Life and art on the Plains changed abruptly in 1869, when the Euro-Americans finished the transcontinental railway, bringing increasing numbers of settlers into Native American lands. By 1890 these new settlers had killed off most of the buffalo while farmers and ranchers took over more and more of the land, thereby destroying the Native American way of life on the Great Plains.

CLOSER LOOK

During the harsh winter season, when spirits are thought to be most powerful, many northern people seek spiritual renewal through their ancient rituals—including the potlatch and the initiation of new members into the prestigious Hamatsa society. With snapping beaks and cries of "*Hap! Hap! Hap!*" ("Eat! Eat! Eat!"), Hamatsa, the people-eating spirit of the north, and his three assistants—horrible monster birds—begin their wild ritual dance (fig. **15–30**). The dancing birds threaten and even attack the Kwakwaka'wakw (Kwakiutl) people who gather for the Winter Ceremony. At this time, youths are captured, taught the Hamatsa lore, and then—in a spectacular theater-dance performance—are "tamed" and brought back into civilized life.

Afterward, the masked bird dancers appear—first Raven-of-the-North-End-of-the-World, then Crooked-Beak-of-the-End-of-the-World, and finally the untranslatable Huxshukw, who cracks open skulls with its beak and eats the brains of its victims. Snapping their beaks, these masters of illusion enter the room backward, their masks pointed up as though looking skyward. They move slowly counterclockwise around the floor. At each change in the music they crouch, snap their beaks, and let out wild cries of "*Hap! Hap! Hap!*" Essential to the ritual dances are the huge carved and painted wooden masks, operated by strings worked by the dancers. Among the finest masks are those by Willie Seaweed (1873–1967), a Kwakwaka'wakw chief (fig. **15–31**). Their brilliant colors and exuberantly decorative carving style determined the direction of twentieth-century Kwakwaka'wakw sculpture.

The Canadian government, abetted by missionaries, outlawed the Winter Ceremony and potlatches in 1885, claiming the event was injurious to health, encouraged prostitution, endangered children's education, damaged the economy, and was cannibalistic. But the Kwakwaka'wakw refused to give up their "oldest and best" festival, one that spoke powerfully to them in many ways, establishing social rank and playing an important role in arranging marriages. By 1936 the government and the missionaries, who called the Kwakwaka'wakw "incorrigible," gave up. But not until 1951 could the Kwakwaka'wakw people gather openly for Winter Ceremonies, including the initiation rites of the Hamatsa society.

The photographer Edward S. Curtis (1868–1952) devoted 30 years to documenting the lives of Native Americans and First Nations peoples. This 1914 photograph shows participants in a film he made about the Kwakwaka'wakw. For the film, his assistant, Richard Hunt (a member of the Kwakwaka'wakw), borrowed family heirlooms and commissioned many new pieces from the finest Kwakwaka'wakw artists. Most of the pieces are now in museum collections. The photograph shows carved and painted posts, masked dancers (including those representing people-eating birds), a chief at the left (holding a speaker's staff and wearing a cedar neck ring), and spectators at the far right.

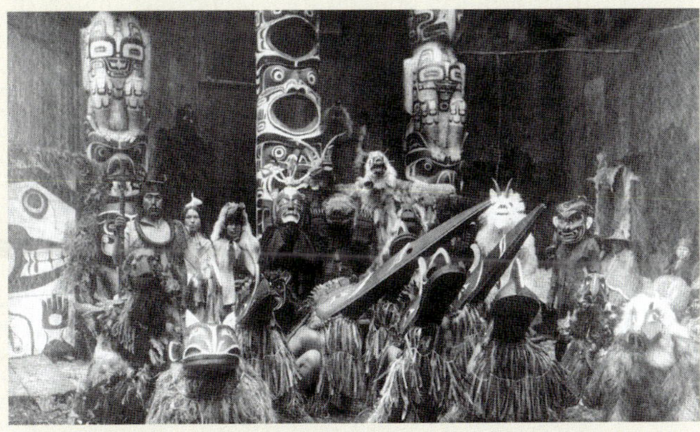

15–30 Hamatsa Dancers. Kwakwaka'wakw (Kwakiutl), Canada. Photographed in 1914 CE by Edward S. Curtis

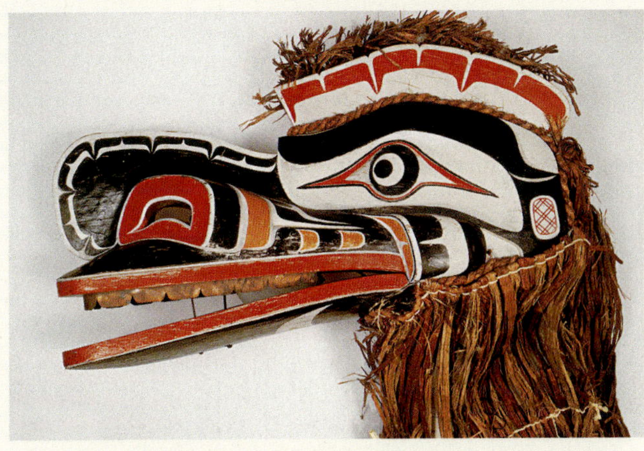

15–31 Attributed to Willie Seaweed. Kwakwaka'wakw (Kwakiutl) bird mask, from Alert Bay, Canada. Prior to 1951 CE. Cedar wood, cedar bark, feathers, and fiber, 10" × 72" × 15" (25.4 × 183 × 38.1 cm). Collection of the Museum of Anthropology, Vancouver, Canada

The name "Seaweed" is an Anglicization of the Kwakwaka'wakw name Siwid, meaning "Paddling Canoe," "Recipient of Paddling," or "Paddled to"—referring to a great chief whose guests paddle from afar to attend potlatches. Willie Seaweed was not only a sculptor; he was the chief of his clan and a great orator, singer, and tribal historian who kept the tradition of the potlatch alive during years of government repression.

The Northwest Coast

Before the arrival of European explorers, the Native American peoples composing the First Nations of the Northwest Coast—among them the Tlingit (of southern Alaska), the Haida (of southern Alaska and the Queen Charlotte Islands), and the Kwakwaka'wakw (formerly spelled Kwakiutl, of the central Canadian coast and Alert Bay)—lived on the Pacific coast of North America from what is today southern Alaska to as far south as what is today northern California. Their major food source was salmon from the region's many rivers. Harvested and dried, the fish could sustain large populations throughout the year.

People lived in extended family groups or clans in large, elaborately decorated communal houses made of massive timbers and thick planks. Clans claimed descent from a mythic animal or animal-human ancestor. Chiefs, who were in the most direct line of descent from the ancestor, validated their status and garnered prestige for themselves and their families by holding ritual feasts known as potlatches during which they gave valuable gifts to their guests. Shamans, both male and female, mediated between the human and spirit worlds.

The participants who danced in the Winter Ceremony of the Kwakwaka'wakw wore striking costumes and gigantic carved and painted masks (see "Closer Look," page 439). Among the most elaborate masks were those used by the elite Hamatsa society in their dances. Transformed into supernatural creatures, the dancers searched for "victims". By using strings inside the masks, they could snap the beaks open and shut with spectacular effect. Isolated in museums as "art," these masks lose the vivacity they command in performance.

Northwest Coast painters preferred a color scheme of black, white, and red—later adding yellow and blue-green. Although their designs are complex and difficult to interpret, the images consist of two basic elements: the ovoid (a slightly bent rectangle with rounded corners) and the **formline** (a continuous, shape-defining line).

The contemporary Haida artist Bill Reid (1920–1998) sought to sustain and revitalize the traditions of his Haida ancestors' art in his work. Trained as a wood carver, painter, and jeweler, Reid revived the art of carving dugout canoes and totem poles in the Haida homeland of Haida Gwaii ("Islands of the People"), known today as the Queen Charlotte Islands. Late in life he began to create large-scale sculpture in bronze. With their black patina, these works recall traditional Haida carvings in argillite, a shiny black stone. One of them, *The Spirit of Haida Gwaii*, now stands outside the Canadian Embassy in Washington, D.C. (fig. **15–32**). This sculpture, which Reid viewed as a metaphor for modern Canada's multicultural society, depicts a boatload of figures from the natural and mythic worlds of the First Nations struggling to paddle forward in a canoe. The dominant figure in the center is a shaman wearing a spruce-root basket hat and Chilikat blanket. He holds a speaker's pole, signaling authority. On the prow, the place reserved for the chief in a war canoe, sits the Bear, facing backward rather than forward and bitten by an Eagle, with patterned wings. The Eagle, in turn, is bitten by the Seawolf. In the stern, steering the canoe, is the Raven, the trickster in Haida mythology. The Raven is assisted by Mousewoman, the traditional guide and escort of humans in the spirit realms. According to Reid, the work represents a "mythological and environmental lifeboat," where "the entire family of living things ... whatever their differences, ... are paddling together in one boat, headed in one direction."

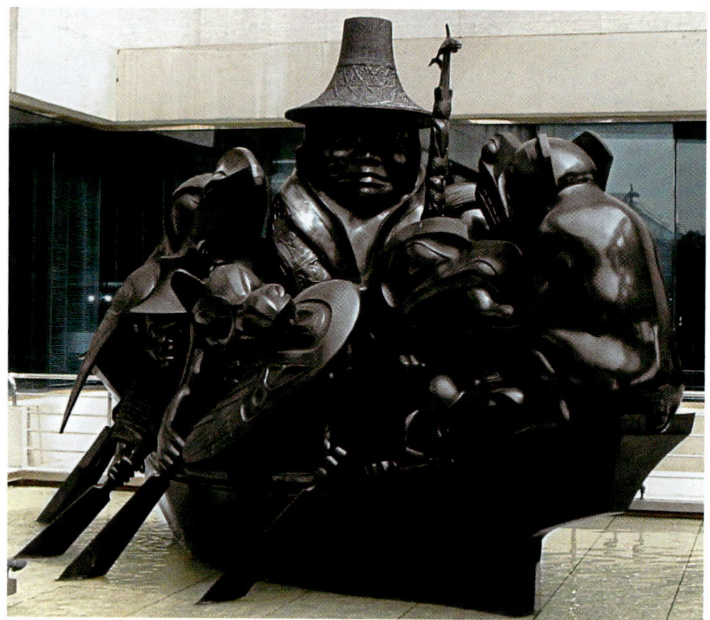

15–32 Bill Reid. ***The Spirit of Haida Gwaii.*** Haida, 1991. Bronze, approx. 13' × 20' (4 × 6 m). Canadian Embassy, Washington, D.C.

Looking Back

Although works of visual and symbolic power were central to their lives, the indigenous peoples of the Americas designated no special objects as "works of art." We are the ones who have given their material culture that label. In Mesoamerica, monumental sculpture covered buildings and, in the form of gods and goddesses, loomed over the devotees. In the river valleys of North America people shaped the earth into huge serpents, bears, and eagles, while in the Nazca Plain in Peru people engraved images of birds and insects into the surface of the earth. But Native American art could be small and fragile as well as large and enduring. The textiles of the Incas have been preserved in the desert climate, while in North America only relatively modern basketry, quillwork, weavings, and hide paintings survive. As we have seen in many cultures, ceramics outlast the damage of time and climate.

Having survived first as anthropological "curiosities" in natural history museums, and subsequently produced on a large scale as tourist souvenirs or objects of "interior decoration," the arts of the indigenous peoples of the Americas have at last been recognized for their distinctive visual and symbolic power, just as contemporary Native American artists are claiming their proper place within the current mainstream of an international art world (see fig. 20–31).

IN PERSPECTIVE

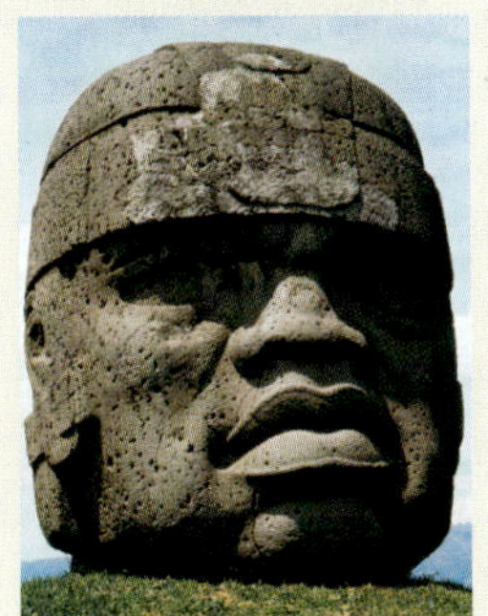

OLMEC HEAD, c. 900–400 BCE

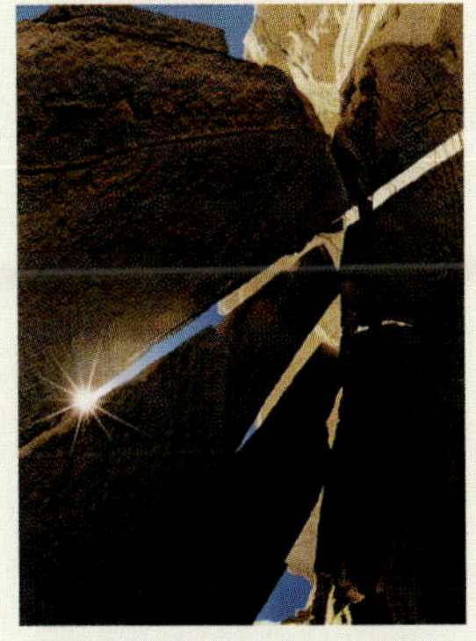

CHACO CANYON SUN DAGGER, 850–1250 CE

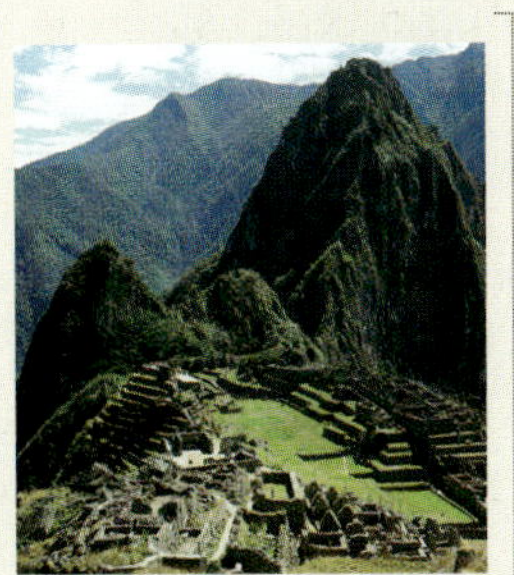

MACHU-PICCHU, 1450–1530 CE

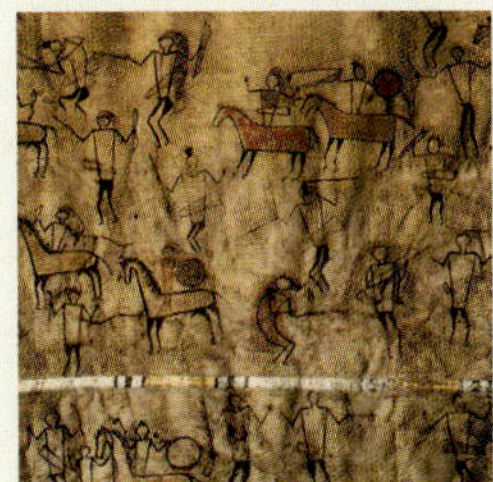

BATTLE-SCENE, HIDE PAINTING, 1797–1800 CE

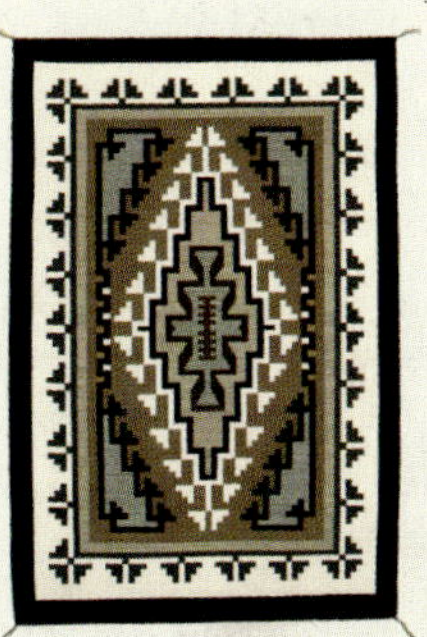

JUMBO, TWO GRAY HILLS TAPESTRY, 2003 CE

1200 BCE

- **Olmec Culture in Mexico,** c. 1200–400 BCE

500

- **Maya Culture in Southern Mesoamerica,** c. 250 BCE–1521 CE
- **Moche Culture in Peru,** c. 200 BCE–600 CE
- **Hohokam Culture in Southwest North America,** c. 200 BCE–1200 CE
- **Hopewell Culture in Central North America,** c. 100 BCE–550 CE

1 CE

- **Teotihuacan Culture in Mexico,** c. 1–750 CE
- **Mimbres/Mogollon Culture,** c. 200–1250 CE

500

- **Ancestral Puebloan in Southwest North America,** c. 550–1250 CE
- **Diquis in Costa Rica,** c. 700–1500 CE
- **Mississippian Culture of Central North America,** c. 700–1550 CE

1000

- **Navajo People Migrate to Southwest North America,** c. 1000–1200 CE
- **Aztec Empire in Mexico at its Height,** c. 1400–1519 CE
- **Inca Empire in the Andes at its height,** c. 1438–1532 CE

1500

- **Cortés Conquers Aztecs,** c. 1519–1524 CE
- **Pizarro Conquers Incas,** c. 1532 CE

1700

- **Plains Nomadic Culture in North America,** 1700–1870 CE
- **Louisiana Purchase,** 1803 CE
- **Transcontinental United States Railway Completed,** 1869 CE
- **Kwakwaka'wakw Winter Ceremony Outlawed,** 1885–1951 CE

2000

- **Opening of the National Museum of the American Indian in Washington, D.C.,** 2004 CE

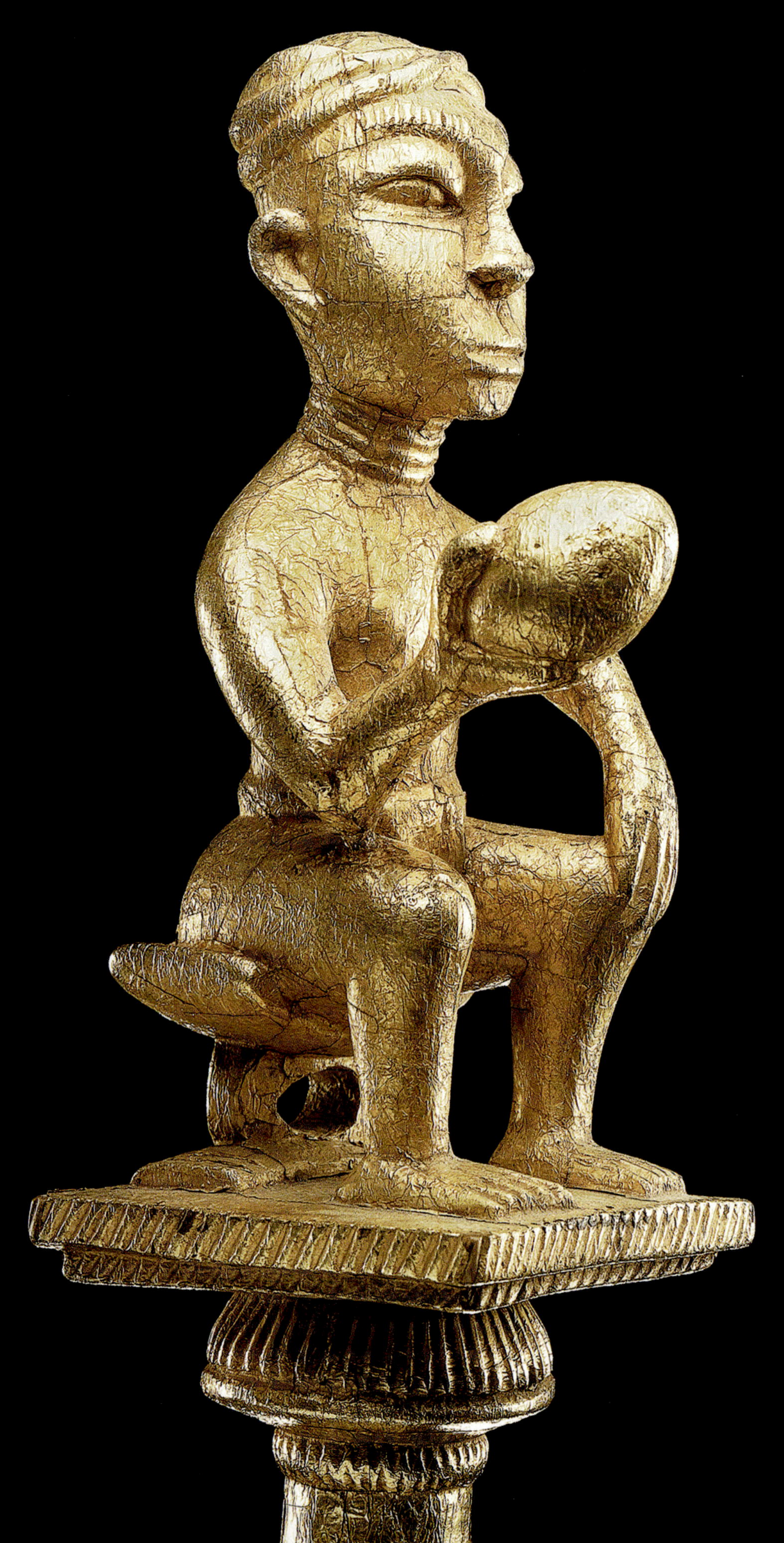

16
African Art

LOOKING FORWARD

"Political power is like an egg," says an Ashanti proverb. "Grasp it too tightly and it will shatter in your hand; hold it too loosely and it will slip from your fingers." Whenever the *okyeame*, or spokesperson, for one twentieth-century Ashanti ruler was conferring with that ruler or communicating the ruler's words to others, he held a staff with this symbolic caution on the use and abuse of power prominently displayed on the gold-leaf-covered finial (fig. **16–1**).

A staff or scepter is a nearly universal symbol of authority and leadership. Today in many colleges and universities a ceremonial mace is still carried by the leader of an academic procession, and it is often placed in front of the speaker's lectern, as a symbol of the speaker's authority. The Ashanti spokespersons who carry their image-topped staffs are part of this widespread and long-lived tradition.

Since the fifteenth century, when the first Europeans explored Africa, objects such as this staff have been shipped back to Western museums of natural history or ethnography, where they were catalogued as curious artifacts of "primitive cultures." Toward the end of the nineteenth century, however, changes in Western thinking about African culture gradually led more and more people to appreciate the inherent aesthetic qualities of these unfamiliar objects and at last to embrace them fully as art. In recent years scholars have further enhanced the appreciation of traditional African arts by exploring their meaning from the point of view of the people who made them.

If we are to understand African art such as this staff on its own terms, we must take it out of the glass case of the museum where we usually encounter it and imagine it playing a vital role in a human community, often in relationship to routine or ritual performance. Indeed, this is true of any work of art produced anywhere in the world. When we recognize how artwork was used as a pure expression of communal values and cherished beliefs, our imaginations can cross a bridge toward understanding.

16–1 Attributed to Kojo Bonsu. Finial of a spokesperson's staff *(okyeame poma)*, from Ghana. Ashanti culture, 1960s–1970s. Wood and gold, height 11¼" (28.57 cm). Sarah Da Vanzo Collection, Johannesburg, South Africa

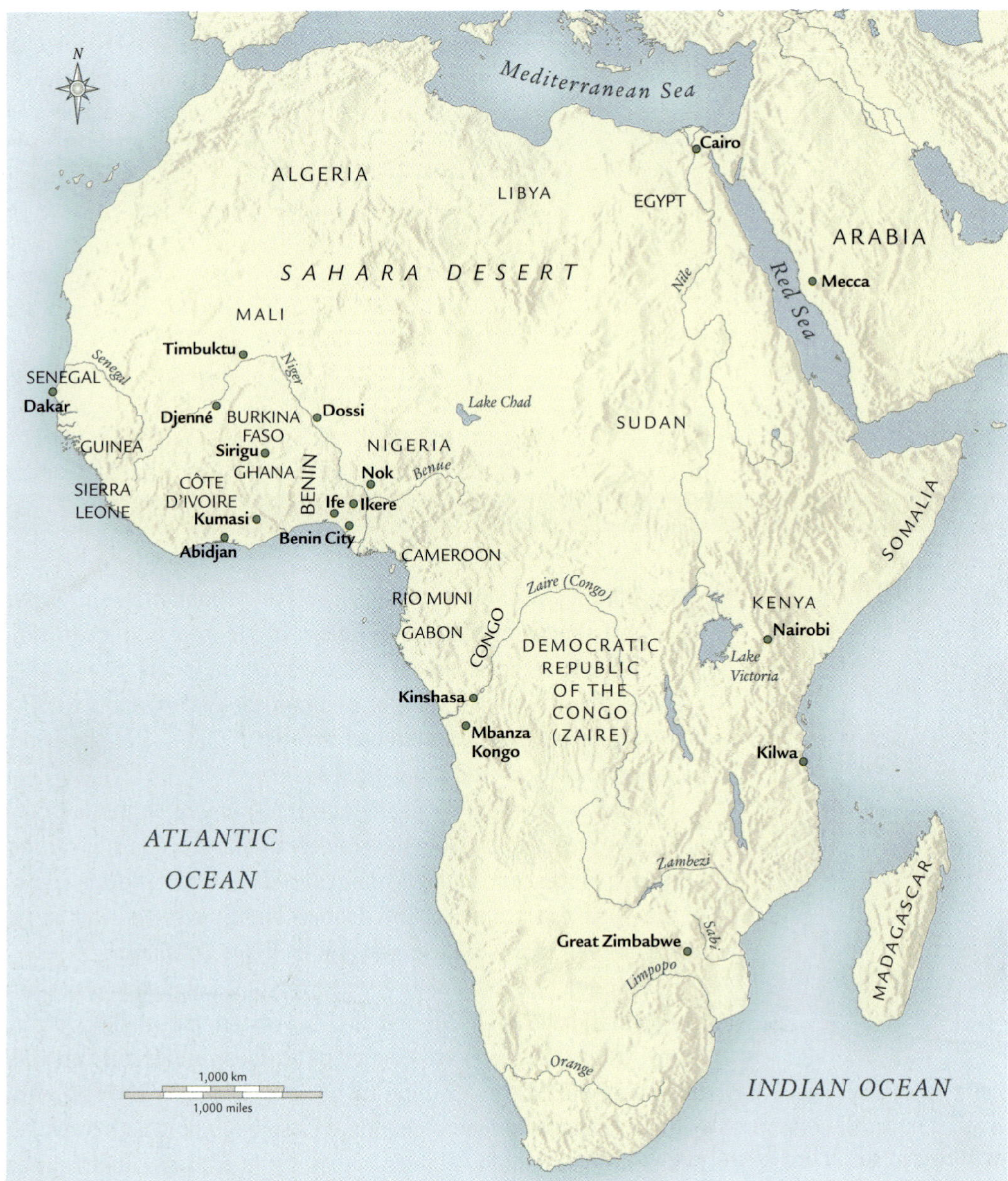

Map 16–1 Africa

Africa is a continent of enormous diversity (see map **16–1**). Geographically, it ranges from vast deserts to tropical rainforests, from flat grasslands to spectacular mountains and dramatic rift valleys. Human diversity is equally impressive. More than 1,000 major languages have been identified, representing a vast variety of cultures, each with its own history, customs, and art forms. Africa is the site of one of the great ancient civilizations, that of Egypt (see Chapter 3), and North Africa later contributed to the development of Islamic art and culture (see Chapter 8).

The history of African art begins in the Paleolithic era. Like prehistoric people around the world, early Africans painted and inscribed an abundance of images on the walls of caves and overhanging rocks. The mountains of the central Sahara have especially fascinating examples of rock art, with the earliest images dating from at least 8000 BCE. At that time, the Sahara was a great grassy plain, perhaps much like the game-park areas of modern East Africa. Vivid images of hippopotamuses, elephants, giraffes, antelope, and other animals incised into rock surfaces testify to the abundant wildlife that roamed the region.

By 4000 BCE, hunting had given way to herding as the Saharan climate became more arid. Remarkably lifelike paintings on rock surfaces from the herding period show scenes of cattle and the people who tended them. The desiccation of the Sahara coincided with the rise of Egyptian civilization along the Nile Valley to the east. As the Saharan grasslands dried up, some of their inhabitants may have migrated to the Nile Valley region in search of arable land and

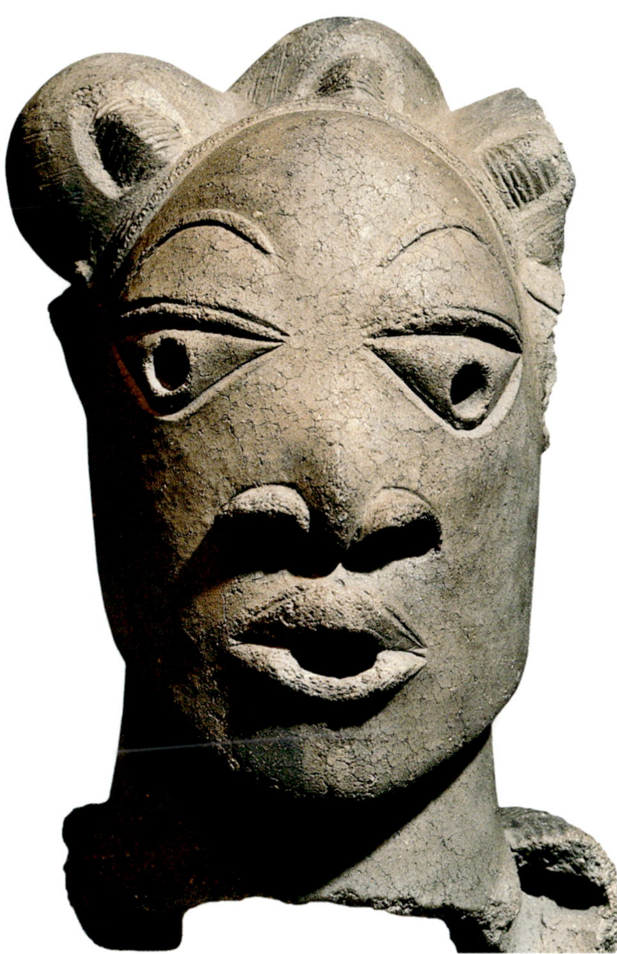

16–2 Head, from Nigeria. Nok, c. 500 BCE–200 CE. Terracotta, height 14³⁄₁₆" (36 cm). National Museum, Lagos, Nigeria

pasture. Perhaps this migration, by greatly expanding the population of the valley, contributed to the tensions that resulted in the emergence of complex forms of social organization there.

Saharan people presumably migrated southward as well, into the Sudan, the broad belt of grassland that stretches across Africa south of the Sahara desert, bringing with them knowledge of agriculture and animal husbandry. Agriculture reached the Sudan by at least 3000 BCE, and knowledge of ironworking spread across the area toward the middle of the first millennium BCE.

Some of the earliest evidence of iron technology in sub-Saharan Africa comes from the so-called Nok culture, which arose in the western Sudan (present-day Nigeria), as early as 500 BCE. The Nok people were farmers who grew grain and oil-bearing seeds; they were also smelters, using the technology for refining ore. In addition, they created the earliest known sculpture of sub-Saharan Africa, producing accomplished terracotta figures of human and animal subjects between about 500 BCE and 200 CE.

The Nok head shown here (fig. **16–2**), slightly larger than life-size, originally formed part of a complete figure. The triangular or D-shaped eyes are characteristic of Nok style and appear in Nok animal sculptures. Each large bun of the elaborate hairstyle is pierced with a hole that may have held ornamental feathers. Other Nok figures boast large quantities of beads and other prestige ornaments. Since the original context for these pieces is unknown—none of these sculptures was excavated by archaeologists—it is difficult to hypothesize what their original meaning and function might have been.

The city of Ife, a sacred site for the Yoruba people, had arisen in the southern, forested part of present-day Nigeria by about 800 CE, several centuries after the last Nok terracottas were produced. Yoruba myth tells how at Ife the gods descended from heaven on iron chains to create the world. Lifelike sculpted heads, created by the artists of this sacred city between about 1050 CE and 1400 CE are among the most remarkable works in the history of art.

A life-size bronze head of an *oni* (king) shows the extraordinary artistry achieved by Ife sculptors (fig. **16–3**). The modeling of the flesh is extremely sensitive, especially around the nose and mouth,

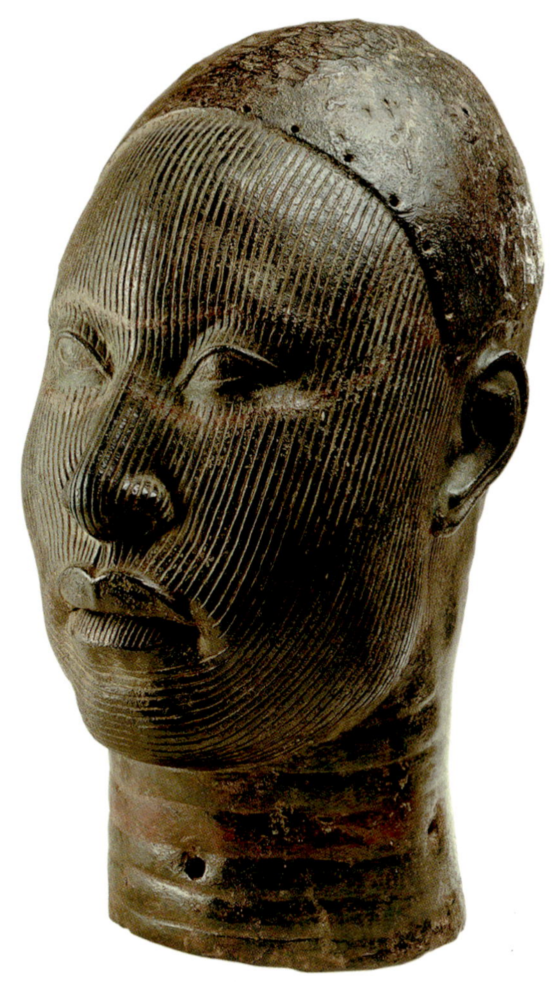

16–3 Head of a king, from Ife, Nigeria. Yoruba culture, c. 13th century CE. Zinc brass, height 11⁷⁄₁₆" (29 cm). Museum of Ife Antiquities, Ife, Nigeria

The lifelike presence of Ife sculpture contradicted everything Europeans thought they knew about African art. The German scholar who "discovered" Ife sculpture in 1910 suggested that it had been created not by Africans but by survivors from the legendary lost island of Atlantis. Later scholars speculated that influence from ancient Greece or Renaissance Europe must have reached Ife. But scientific dating methods have finally put such misleading comparisons and prejudices to rest.

and the face is covered with decorative parallel lines of scarification (patterns made by scarring the skin). Holes along the scalp apparently permitted the attachment of hair, a crown, or perhaps a beaded veil. The head might possibly have been attached to a wooden mannequin using the large holes at the base of the neck. If so, the mannequin may have been dressed in a deceased *oni*'s robe used for display during his memorial services.

Ife was the artistic parent of the great city-state of Benin, which arose some 150 miles to the southeast. According to oral histories, the earliest kings of Benin belonged to the Ogiso, or Skyking, dynasty. After a long period of misrule, however, the Edo people of Benin asked the *oni* of Ife for a new ruler. The *oni* sent Prince Oranmiyan, who founded a new dynasty in 1170 CE. Some two centuries later, the fourth king, or *oba*, of Benin decided to start a tradition of memorial sculpture like that of Ife (fig. **16–4**). He sent to Ife for master metal casters, and the practice of casting memorial heads for the shrines of the royal ancestors of Benin is still in the hands of their descendants to this day.

The Benin kings also commissioned important works in ivory. One example is a beautiful ornamental mask (fig. **16–5**) that represents an *iyoba*, or queen mother (the *oba*'s mother), the senior female member of the royal court. The mask was carved as a belt ornament worn at the *oba*'s hip. Its pupils were originally inlaid with iron, as were the scarification patterns on the forehead. This particular belt ornament may represent Idia, who was the mother of Esigie, a powerful *oba* who ruled from 1504 to 1550. Idia is

Technique

Lost-Wax Casting

The lost-wax process begins with a core on which the sculptor models an image in wax. A heat-resistant mold is then formed over the wax. The wax is melted and replaced with molten metal. Finally, the mold is broken away and the piece finished and polished by hand.

The usual metal used in this casting process was bronze, an alloy of copper and tin, although sometimes casters used brass, an alloy of copper and zinc. The progression of drawings here shows the steps used by the Benin sculptors of Africa. A heat-resistant "core" of clay approximating the shape of the sculpture-to-be (and eventually becoming the hollow inside the sculpture) was covered by a layer of wax having the thickness of the final sculpture. The sculptor carved or modeled the details in the wax. Rods and a pouring cup made of wax were attached to the model. A thin layer of fine, damp sand was pressed very firmly into the surface of the wax model, and then model, rods, and cup were encased in thick layers of clay. When the clay was completely dry, the mold was heated to melt out the wax. The mold was then turned upside down to receive the metal, heated to the point of liquification. The cast was placed in the ground. When the metal was completely cool, the outside clay cast and the inside core were broken up and removed, leaving the cast brass sculpture. Details were polished to finish the piece, which could not be duplicated because the mold had been destroyed in the process.

In the eighteenth century a second process came into use—the piece mold. As its name implies, the piece mold could be removed without breaking, allowing sculptors to make several copies (an edition) of each work.

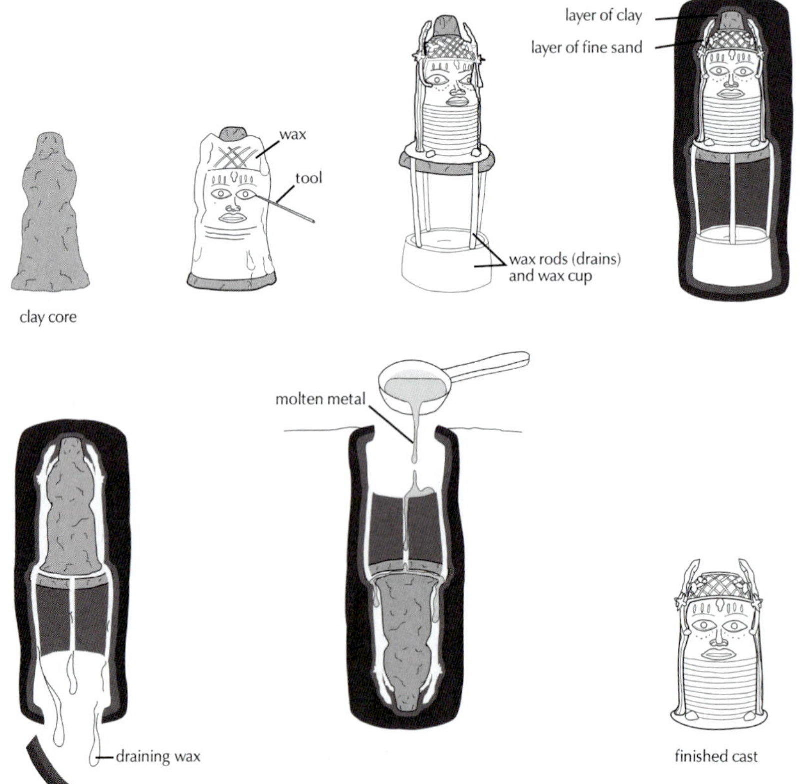

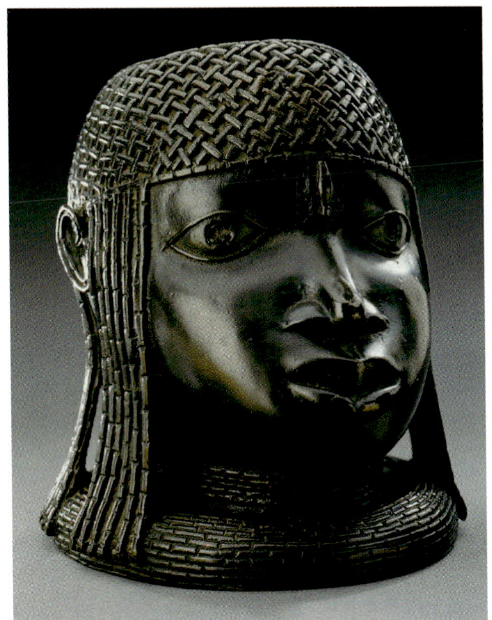

16–4 Memorial head of an *Oba* (king), from Benin, Nigeria. Early period, c. 16th century CE. Brass, height 9" (23 cm). The Nelson-Atkins Museum of Art, Kansas City, Missouri

This head belongs to a small group of rare early Benin sculptures called "rolled-collar" heads that are distinguished by the roll collar that serves as a firm base for the exquisitely modeled head.

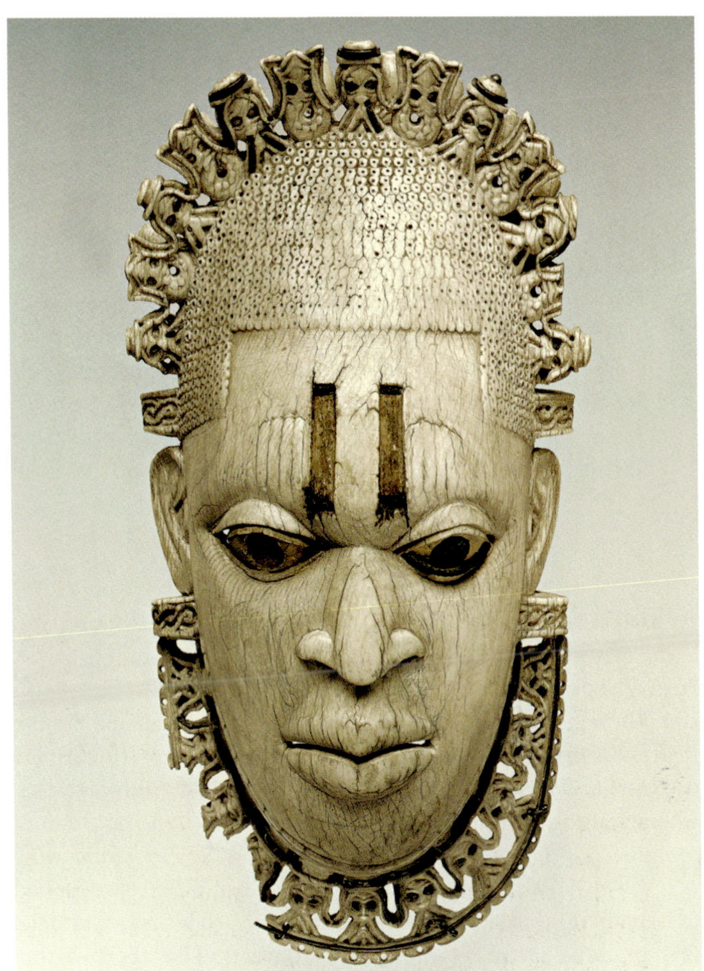

16–5 Hip mask representing an *Iyoba* ("queen mother"), from Benin, Nigeria. Middle Period, c. 1550 CE. Ivory, iron, and copper, height 9¼" (23.4 cm). The Metropolitan Museum of Art, New York

THE MICHAEL C. ROCKEFELLER MEMORIAL COLLECTION, GIFT OF NELSON A. ROCKEFELLER, 1972 (1978.412.323)

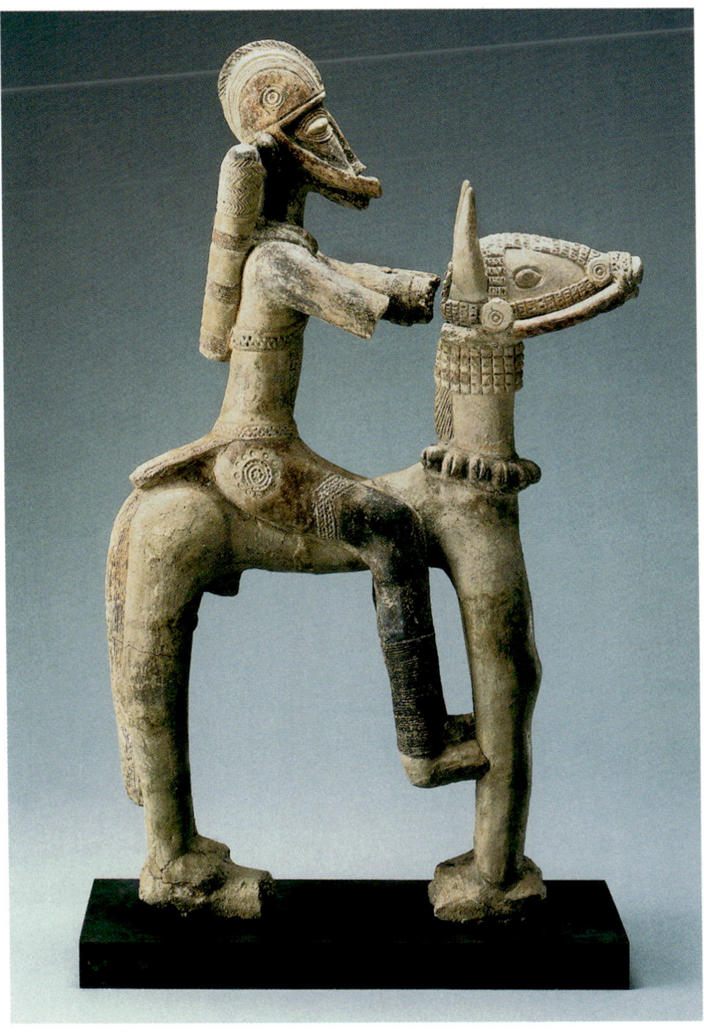

16–6 *Horseman*, from Old Jenné, Mali. 13th–15th century CE. Terracotta, height 27¾" (70.5 cm). The National Museum of African Art, Smithsonian Institution, Washington, D.C.

MUSEUM PURCHASE (86-12-2)

particularly remembered for raising an army and using magical powers to help her son defeat his enemies. Like Idia, the Portuguese helped Esigie expand his kingdom. The necklace represents heads of Portuguese soldiers with beards and flowing hair. In the crown, more Portuguese heads alternate with figures of mudfish, which symbolize Olokun, the Lord of the Great Waters. Mudfish live near riverbanks, mediating between water and land, just as the *oba*, who is viewed as semidivine, mediates between the human world and the supernatural world of Olokun.

Ife and Benin were only two of the many cities that arose in ancient Africa. At a site near Jenné, known as Jenné-Jeno or Old Jenné, excavations (by both archaeologists and looters) have uncovered hundreds of terracotta figures dating from the thirteenth to the sixteenth centuries. The figures were polished, covered with a red clay slip, and fired at a low temperature. A horseman, armed with quiver and arrows and a dagger, is an impressive example (fig. **16–6**). Man and horse are formed of rolls of clay on which details of faces, clothing, and harness are carved, engraved, and painted. The rider has a long oval head and jutting chin, pointed oval eyes set in

THE MYTH OF "PRIMITIVE" ART

The word "primitive" was once used by Western art historians to lump together the art of Africa, the Pacific Islands, and North, South, and Central America before the arrival of Columbus. The term itself means "early," and its very use implies that these civilizations are frozen at an early stage of development.

How did labels like "primitive" arise? Many historical attitudes were rooted in racism and colonialism. Criteria previously used to label a people primitive included the use of so-called Stone Age technology, the absence of written histories, and the failure to build "great" cities. These usages were extended to the creations of the cultures, and "primitive" art became the dominant label for the cultural products of these people. Yet the accomplishments of the people of Africa strongly belie this categorization: Africans south of the Sahara have smelted and forged iron since at least 500 BCE, and Africans in many areas made and used high-quality steel for weapons and tools. Many African people have recorded their histories in Arabic since at least the tenth century. The first European visitors to Africa admired politically and economically sophisticated urban centers such as Benin, Kilwa, Djenné, Great Zimbabwe, and Mbanza Kongo.

multiple framing lids, and a long straight nose. He wears short pants and a helmet with a chin strap, and his horse has an ornate bridle. Such elaborate military equipment suggests that the horseman could be a guardian figure, hero, or even a deified ancestor. Similar figures have been found in sanctuaries. Over time, urban life declined, and so did the arts. In the fifteenth and sixteenth centuries, when rivals began to raid these African cities, the long tradition of ceramic sculpture came to an end.

When Koi Konboro, the twenty-sixth king of Jenné, converted to Islam in the thirteenth century, he transformed his palace into the first of three successive mosques in the city. Like the two that followed, the first mosque was built of adobe brick. With its great surrounding wall and tall towers, it was said to have been more beautiful and more lavishly decorated than the Kaaba, the central shrine of Islam, at Mecca. In the early nineteenth century, the mosque was razed and a far more humble structure erected on a new site. This second mosque was in turn replaced by the current grand mosque, constructed between 1906 and 1907 on the ancient site and in the style of the original.

The mosque's eastern, or "marketplace," façade boasts three tall towers; the center of the façade contains the mihrab (fig. **16–7**). The finials, or crowning ornaments, at the top of each tower bear ostrich

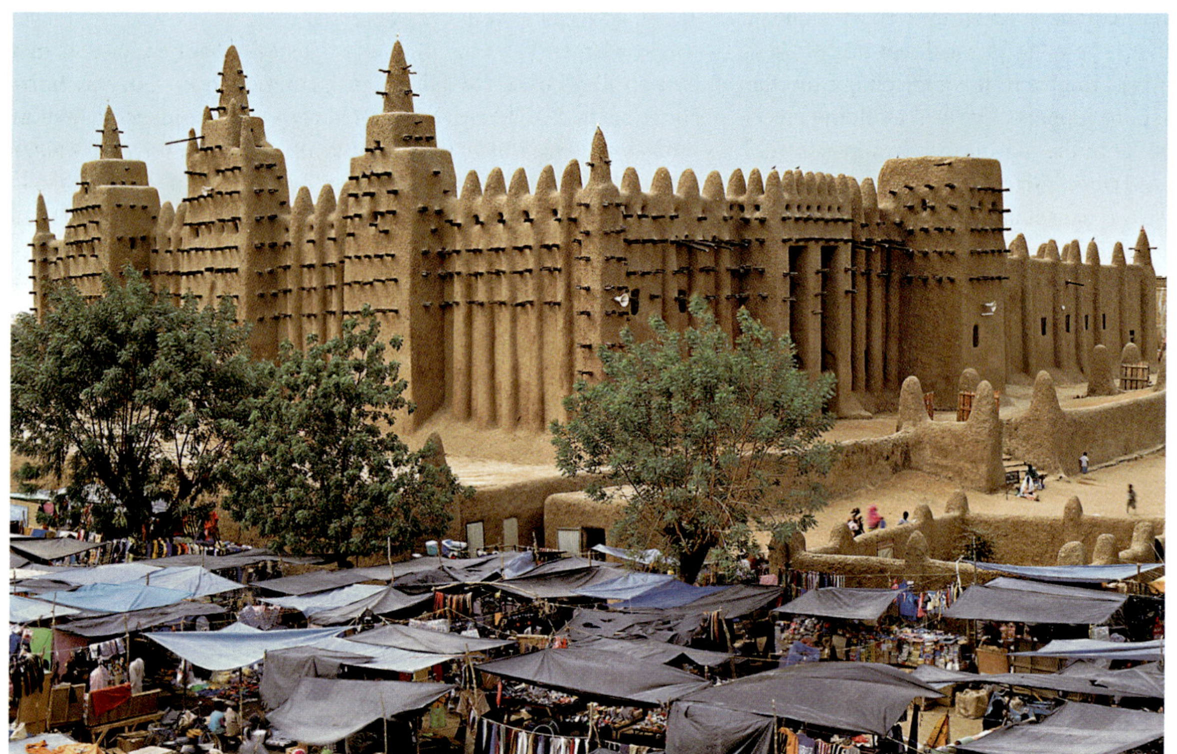

16–7 Great Friday Mosque, Jenné, Mali, showing the eastern and northern façades. Rebuilding of 1907 in the style of 13th-century CE original

The plan of the mosque is not quite rectangular. Inside, nine rows of heavy adobe columns, 33 feet tall and linked by pointed arches, support a flat ceiling of palm logs. An open courtyard on the west side is enclosed by a great double wall only slightly lower than the walls of the mosque itself. The main entrances to the prayer hall are in the north wall (to the right in the photograph).

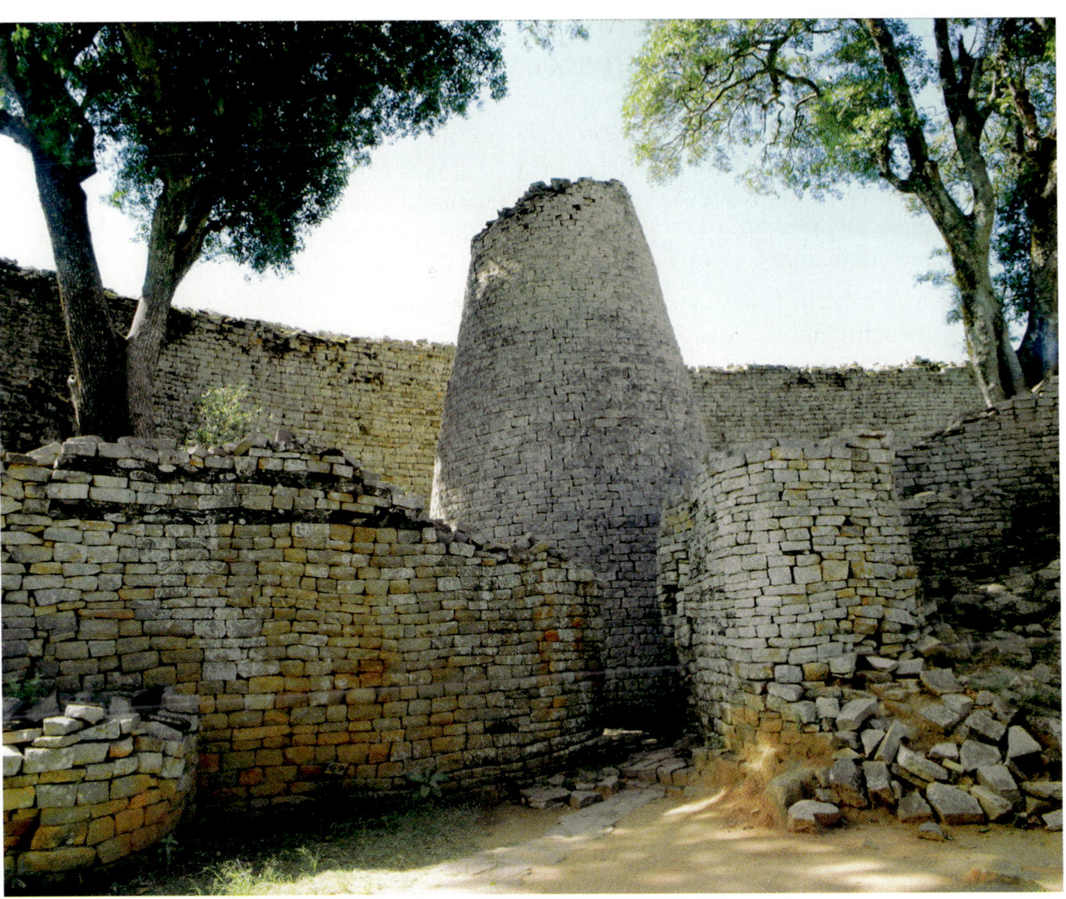

16–8 Conical Tower, Great Zimbabwe. c. 1200–1400 CE. Height of tower 30' (9.1 m)

eggs, symbols of fertility and purity. The façade and sides of the mosque are distinguished by tall, narrow, engaged columns, which act as buttresses. These columns are characteristic of West African mosque architecture, and their cumulative rhythmic effect is one of great verticality and grandeur. The most unusual features of West African mosques are the torons, wooden beams projecting from the walls. Torons provide permanent supports for the scaffolding erected each year so that the exterior of the mosque can be replastered.

In southeastern Africa, the city of Great Zimbabwe was home to the Shona people. Zimbabwe was part of an extensive trade network along the Zambezi, Limpopo, and Sabi Rivers. It funneled gold, ivory, and exotic skins to coastal trading towns of the Swahili peoples between 1000 and 1500 CE. It is estimated that at the height of its power in the fourteenth century, Great Zimbabwe and its environs housed a population of more than 10,000 people. A large cache of goods found there containing items such as Portuguese medallions, Persian pottery, and Chinese porcelain testifies to the extent of trade at Great Zimbabwe.

The word "Zimbabwe" derives from the Shona term for "venerated houses" or "houses of stone," and, indeed, much of Great Zimbabwe was built of stone. Scholars agree that the stone structures were built by the ancestors of the present-day Shona people, who still live in the region. Construction at the site took advantage of the enormous boulders abundant in the vicinity. Masons used the uniform granite blocks that split naturally from the boulders to build a series of tall enclosing walls. As the artisans grew more skillful, they used dressed, or smoothly finished, stones and laid them in fine, level courses. Each enclosure defined a ritual space or surrounded dwellings made of adobe (a sun-dried mixture of clay and straw) with conical thatched roofs.

The largest building complex at Great Zimbabwe is located in a broad valley below the hilltop enclosures. Known today as Imba Huru, or the Big House, it was probably a royal residence as well as a religious center. It is ringed by a massive masonry wall—more than 800 feet long, 32 feet high, and 17 feet thick at the base—constructed without mortar. Inside the outer wall are numerous smaller stone enclosures and adobe platforms. A fascinating structure known simply as the Conical Tower (fig. **16–8**) is some 18 feet in diameter and 30 feet high, and the tower was originally capped with three courses of ornamental stonework. Resembling a large version of a present-day Shona granary, it may have represented the good harvest and prosperity for which the ruler of Great Zimbabwe was held responsible.

During the twentieth century, African sculptures—wood carvings of astonishing formal inventiveness and power—found admirers around the world. Wood decays rapidly, however, and little wood sculpture from lands south of the Sahara remains from before the nineteenth century. As a result, much of ancient Africa's artistic heritage has been irretrievably lost. Yet the beauty of ancient African creations in such durable materials as terra cotta, stone, and bronze bear eloquent witness to the skill of ancient African artists and the splendor of the civilizations in which they worked.

African Art in the Modern Era: Living Traditions and New Trends

European exploration and subsequent colonization of the African continent brought Africa's flourishing and diverse societies into sudden and traumatic contact with the "modern" world. European ships first visited sub-Saharan Africa in the fifteenth century, and for the next several hundred years, European contact with Africa was almost entirely limited to coastal areas, where trade, including the devastating slave trade, was carried out. During the nineteenth century, however, as the trade in slaves to the West was gradually eliminated, European explorers and Christian missionaries, such as Sir Henry Morton Stanley and Dr. David Livingstone, began to investigate the unmapped African interior. Drawn by the potential wealth of Africa's natural resources, European governments began to seek territorial concessions from African rulers. Diplomacy soon

AFRICAN FURNITURE AND THE ART DECO STYLE

In some African cultures, elaborate stools or chairs were created not only to indicate their owners' status but also to serve as altars for their souls after death. Thrones and other important seats in Africa are often carved from a single block of wood. This is the case with a chair taken from the Ngombe people, who live along the Congo River. The back is cantilevered out from the seat, which is in turn supported by four massive, braced legs. The rich surface decoration consists of European brass carpet tacks and darker iron tacks arranged in parallel lines and diamond patterns. The use of the imported tacks indicates that the owner had access to the extensive trade routes linking people of the inland forest to people of the coast. Both copper and iron were precious materials in central Africa; they were used as currency long before contact with Europe, and they were associated with both high social status and spirituality. The chair was thus an object of both beauty and power.

France began to colonize Africa in the late nineteenth century, and African objects were brought to France by soldiers, administrators, and adventurers. Exhibitions held in France in 1919 and 1923 displayed trophies from the newly vanquished territories, including household objects and artworks from African courts.

Just as painters and sculptors such as Picasso and Matisse were inspired by the formal power of African masks, the French designer Pierre Legrain (1889–1929) recognized the aesthetic excellence of African sculpture and furniture. Legrain's Africa-inspired pieces appeared in the 1925 design exhibition "International Exposition of Modern Decorative and Industrial Arts," where the term *style moderne* was used to describe the new geometric simplicity that characterized many of the objects displayed there. The exhibition helped launch a popular commercial style called Art Deco (a label coined in the late 1960s).

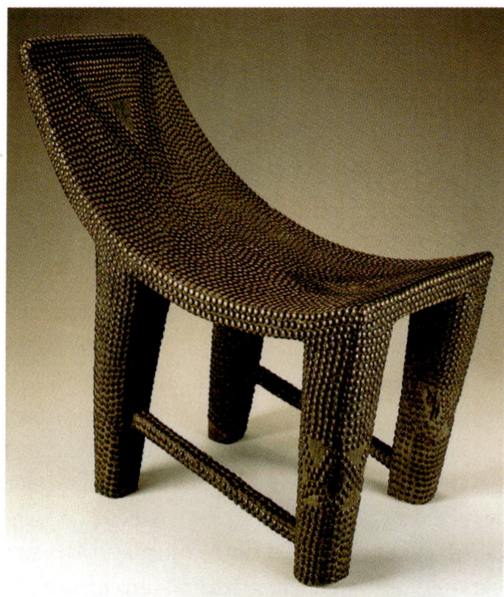

16–9 Chair, from Democratic Republic of Congo. Ngombe culture, 20th century CE. Wood, brass, and iron tacks, height at tallest point 25⅝" (65.1 cm). National Museum of African Art, Washington, D.C.
MUSEUM PURCHASE, 90-4-1

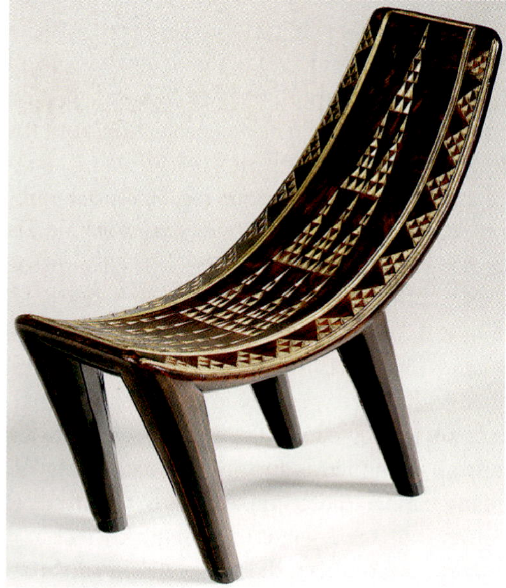

16–10 Pierre Legrain. *Tabouret*. c. 1923 CE. Lacquered wood, horn, gilding, length 20½" × 10½" × 25¼" (52 × 26.6 × 64.1 cm). Virginia Museum of Fine Arts, Richmond
THE SYDNEY AND FRANCES LEWIS ENDOWMENT FUND

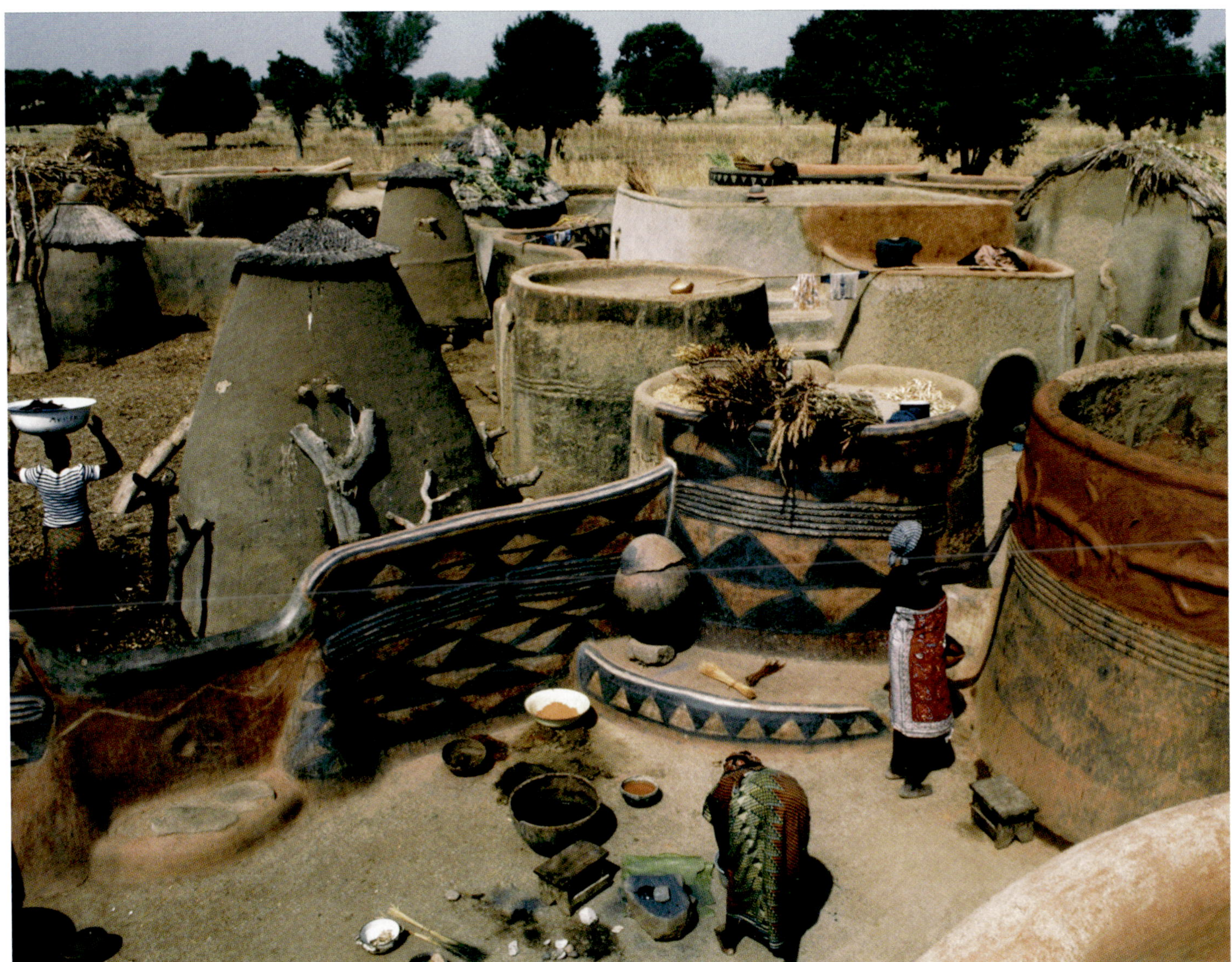

16–11 Nankani compound, Sirigu, Ghana. 1972 CE

Among the Nankani people, creating living areas is a cooperative but gender-specific project. Men build the structures, women decorate the surfaces. The structures themselves are also gender-specific. The round dwellings shown here are women's houses located in an interior courtyard; men occupy rectangular flat-roofed houses. The bisected lozenge design on the dwelling to the left is called zalanga, *the name for the braided sling that holds a woman's gourds and most treasured possessions.*

gave way to force, and, toward the end of the century, competition among rival European powers fueled the so-called Scramble for Africa, when European leaders raced to lay claim to whatever portion of the continent they were powerful enough to seize. By 1914, virtually all of Africa was under colonial rule. In the years following World War I, nationalistic movements arose across the continent; from 1945 through the mid-1970s, one colony after another gained its independence.

Art and Domestic Life

Shelter is a basic human concern, approached in distinct ways from culture to culture. The farming communities of the Nankani people in the border area between Burkina Faso and Ghana, in West Africa, developed a distinctive painted architecture. The mud and adobe buildings of their walled compounds are low and single-storied with either flat roofs that form terraces or conical roofs. Some buildings are used only by men, others by women. The Nankani men control an ancestral shrine by the entrance, a corral for cattle, and a granary, and they have rectangular houses. The inner courtyards, outdoor kitchen, and round houses are the women's areas (fig. **16–11**). Men build the compound; women paint the buildings inside and out.

The women decorate the walls with horizontal molded ridges called *yidoor*, meaning both "rows in a cultivated field" and "long eye" (long life) to express good wishes for the family. They paint the

CLOSER LOOK

In many West African cultures, fired ceramics are made exclusively by women. Among the Mande-speaking people of Mali, Burkina Faso, Guinea, and Ivory Coast, potters are *numumusow*, female members of *numu* lineages. Their husbands, fathers, and sons are the sculptors and blacksmiths of the Mande. In addition to being potters, women may also resolve disputes and initiate girls.

Numumusow make a wide selection of vessels, whose shapes reflect their intended use: wide bowls and cooking pots, narrow-necked stoppered water bottles, small eating dishes, and huge storage jars (fig. **16–12**). The *numumusow* form the soft and sticky clay by coiling and modeling with their fingers. They decorate their vessels by burnishing (polishing), engraving, adding pellets or coils of clay, or coloring with slip (a wash of colored clay). The vessels are fired at low temperatures in a shallow pit or in the open; this produces a ware that can be used to cook over an open fire without breaking.

Even though most urban Africans use metal and plastic dishes and cookware today, large earthenware jars still keep water cool and clean in areas where refrigeration is expensive. In the past, water-storage jars were public display pieces, standing near the entrance to the house, where a guest would be offered a drink of cool water as an essential part of hospitality. Mande vessels for drinking water are often decorated with incised lines and molded ridges. On older wares, such as this example, raised images of figures or lizards may refer to Mande myths or philosophical concepts.

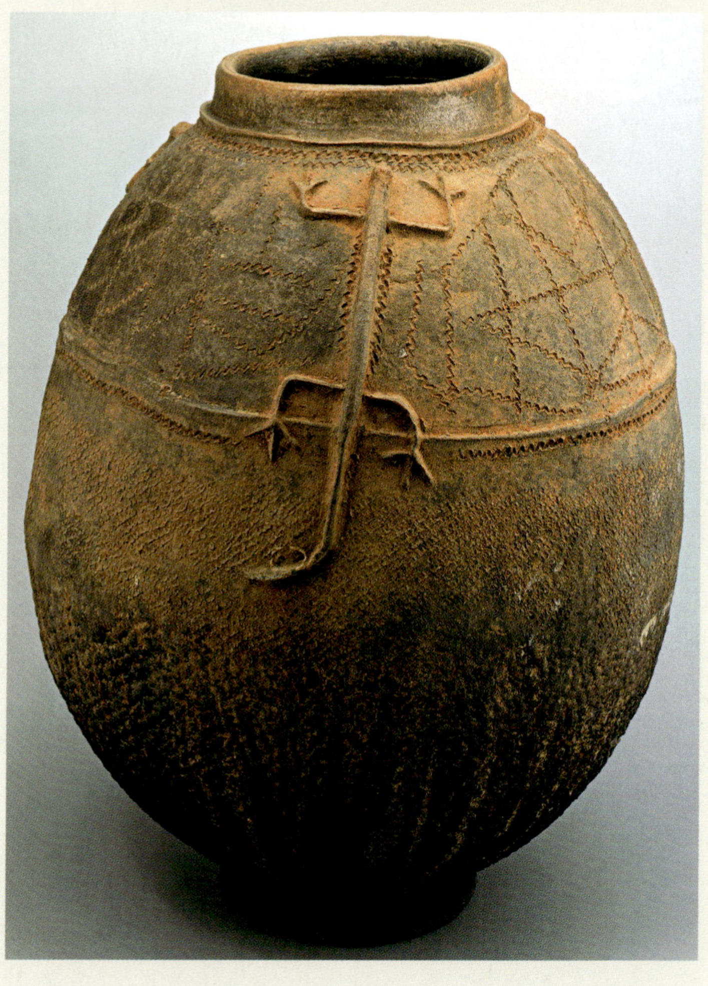

16–12 Jar, from Mali. Bamana culture, 20th century CE. Earthenware, 23½" × 18¾" (59.7 × 47.6 cm). The Nelson-Atkins Museum of Art, Kansas City, Missouri
PURCHASE: WILLIAM ROCKHILL NELSON TRUST THROUGH THE GEORGE H. AND ELIZABETH O. DAVIS FUND (96-36/1). PHOTOGRAPH: ROBERT NEWCOMBE

walls with rectangles and squares cut diagonally to create triangular patterns, a rectilinear surface decoration that contrasts with the curving walls. The painted patterns are called "braided sling," "broken pottery," and "broken gourd," and since the triangular motifs can be seen as pointing up or down, they are sometimes called "filed teeth." The same geometric motifs are used on pottery and baskets, and for scarification of the skin. When people decorate themselves, their homes, and their possessions with the same patterns, art is serving to embody a cultural identity.

Art and the Spirit World

Much traditional African art is devoted to dealings with the spirit world. Spirits are believed to inhabit the fields that produce crops, the rivers that provide fish, the bush and forests that are home to game, and the land that must be cleared in order to build a new village. A family, too, includes spirits—those of its ancestors as well as those of children yet unborn. In the blessing or curse of these myriad spirits lies the difference between success and failure in life. To communicate with these all-important spirits, many African

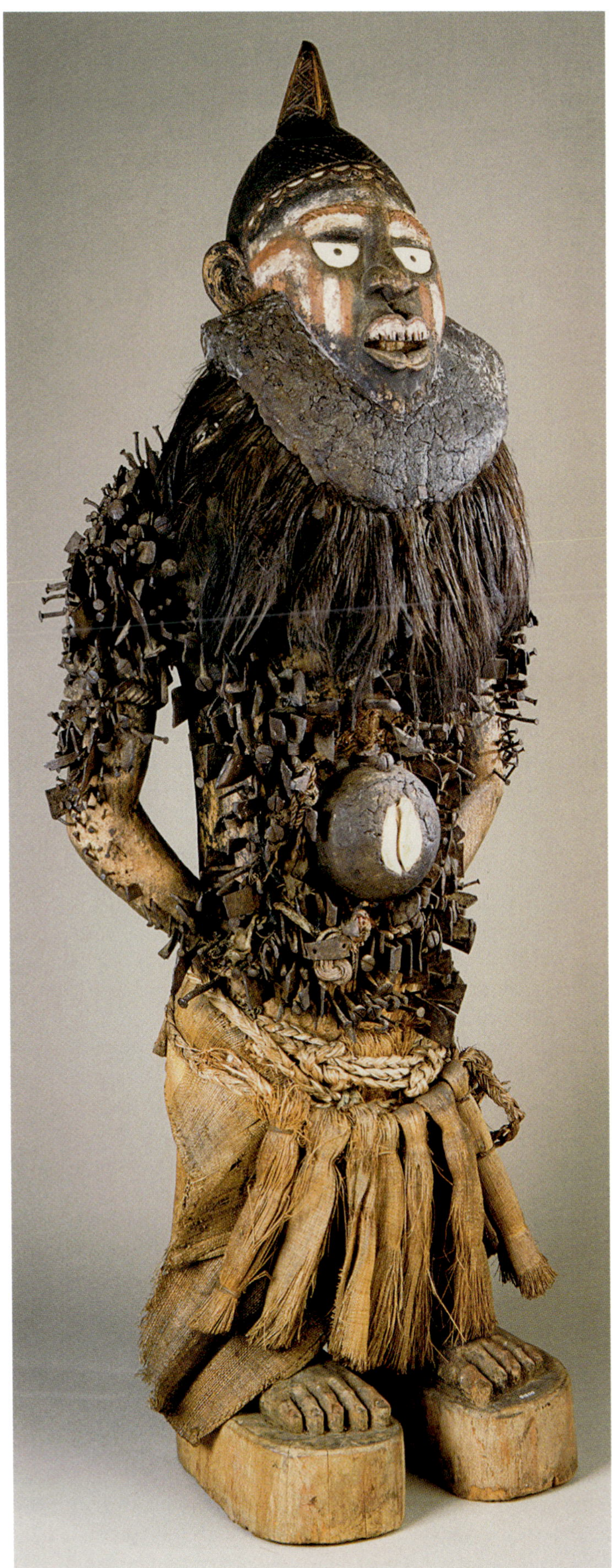

societies rely on a specialist in ritual—a person known as a diviner who opens the lines of communication between the supernatural and human worlds (see Introduction, page 10). Diviners use such techniques as prayer, sacrifice, offerings, magic, divination, and sometimes the creation of images that give visible identity and personality to what is imaginary and intangible.

Among the most potent images of spiritual power in Africa are the *nkisi*, or spirit figures of the Kongo and Songye peoples of the Democratic Republic of the Congo (formerly Zaire). These pieces enforce ethical behavior and regulate power. The best-known of the *nkisi* are the large wooden *nkonde* figures, which bristle with nails, pins, blades, and other sharp objects (fig. **16–13**). A *nkisi nkonde* begins its life as a simple, unadorned wooden figure. It may be purchased from a carver at a market or commissioned by a diviner adept at diagnosing supernatural ills on behalf of clients. Drawing on vast knowledge, the diviner prescribes certain magical/medicinal ingredients, called *bilongo*, that will help solve the client's problem. These *bilongo*, which may include human hair, nail clippings, and other animal, plant, or mineral ingredients, are added to the figure, either mixed with white clay and plastered directly onto the body or held in a packet suspended from the neck or waist.

The *bilongo* transform the *nkonde* into a powerful agent, ready to attack the forces of evil on behalf of a human client. Each *bilongo* ingredient has a specific role in activating the figure. For example, the Kongo people admire the quickness and agility of a particular species of mouse. Tufts of this mouse's hair included in the *bilongo* ensure that the *nkisi nkonde* will act rapidly when its powers are activated.

To mobilize the figure's powers, clients drive a nail or other pointed object into the *nkisi nkonde*, which may serve many private and public functions. Two warring villages might agree to end their conflict by swearing an oath of peace in the presence of the *nkonde* and then driving a nail into it to seal the agreement. A mother might invoke the power of the *nkonde* to heal her sick children. Two merchants might agree to a partnership by driving two small nails into the figure side by side and then make their pact binding by wrapping the nails together with a stout cord.

16–13 Power figure *(nkisi nkonde)*, from the Democratic Republic of the Congo. Kongo culture, 19th century CE. Wood, nails, pins, blades, and other materials, height 44" (111.7 cm). The Field Museum, Chicago (# A109979AC)

This sculpture provides a dramatic example of the ways in which works of African art are transformed by use. When first carved, the figure is "neutral," with no particular significance or use. Magical materials applied by a diviner transform the figure into a powerful being, at the same time modifying its form. While the object is empowered, nails may also be added as part of a healing or oath-taking process. And when the figure's particular powers are no longer needed, then additions may all be stripped away to be replaced with different magical materials that give the same figure a new function. The result is that many hands played a role in creating the nkisi nkonde *we see in a museum. The person we are likely to label as the "artist" is only the initial creator. Many others modify the work, and in their hands the figure becomes a visual document of the history of the conflicts and afflictions that have threatened the community.*

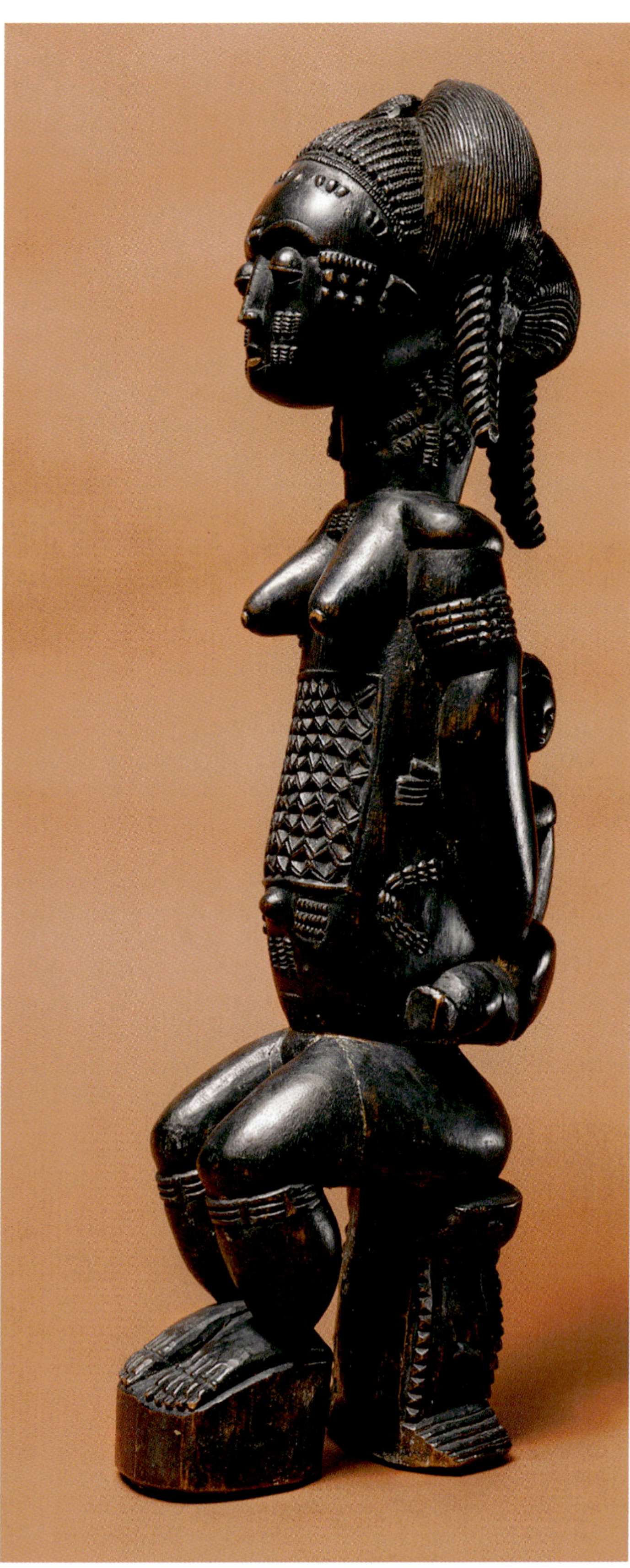

16–14 Spirit spouse *(blolo bla)*, from Ivory Coast. Baule culture, early 20th century CE. Wood, height 17⅛" (43.5 cm). Penn Museum, Philadelphia
PENN MUSEUM OBJECT 29-12-68, IMAGE 150827

Another ongoing artistic tradition is found among the Baule people of the Ivory Coast. They believe that each of us lived in the spirit world, a parallel realm, before we were born. While there, we had a spirit spouse, whom we left behind when we entered this life. A person who has difficulty assuming his or her gender-specific role as an adult Baule—a man who has not married, for example, or a woman who has not borne children—may dream of his or her spirit spouse. For such a person, the diviner may prescribe the commissioning of an image of the spirit spouse (fig. **16–14**)—either a female figure (*blolo bla*) for a man or a male figure (*blolo bian*) for a woman. The figures display the most admired and desirable marks of beauty so that the spirit spouses may be encouraged to enter and inhabit them. The owner keeps the figure in his or her room, dressing it in beautiful textiles and jewelry, washing it, anointing it with oil, feeding it, and caressing it. The Baule hope that pleasing their spirit spouse (by caring for the sculpture) will restore balance to their human life.

Art and Power

As in societies throughout the world, art in Africa is used to signify power in this world as well as power in the spirit world. In an Akan kingdom of Ghana or the Ivory Coast, for example, the spokesperson's staff indicates the eminence of the ruler's special advisors and identifies them as leaders. The finial of one such staff (see fig. 16–1) is an allegorical carving of a man holding an egg. It was probably made in the 1960s or 1970s by Kojo Bonsu, son of famous carver Osei Bonsu (1900–1976), who lives in the Ashante city of Kumasi and continues to carve prolifically. He embellished the staff with gold leaf to signal its importance. Gold was a major source of power for the Ashante, who traded it for centuries, first across the Sahara to the Mediterranean world, and then directly to Europeans on the West African coast.

Yoruba kings manifested their power through the large, complex palaces in which they lived. In the traditional palace plan, the principal rooms opened onto a veranda, where elaborate figured posts supported the roof, and dense, highly descriptive figure carvings covered the doors. Perhaps the finest architectural sculptor of modern times was Olówè of Isè, who carved doors and veranda posts for rulers of the Ekiti-Yoruba kingdoms in southwestern Nigeria.

The door of the royal palace in Ikéré illustrates Olówè's artistry (fig. **16–15**). Its asymmetrical composition combines narrative and symbolic scenes in horizontal, rectangular panels. Tall bodies carved in profile are topped with heads that face out to confront the viewer. Long necks and elaborate hairstyles make the figures appear even taller, unlike typical Yoruba sculpture, which uses short, static figures. The figures—which move energetically against an underlying decorative pattern—are carved in such high relief that their upper portions are actually carved in the round. The entire surface of the door is painted.

Olówè seems to have worked from the early 1900s until his death in 1938. He was famous throughout Yorubaland and called upon by patrons as distant as 60 miles from his home, though few written records of his activities remain. The art historian Philip Allison wrote of meeting Olówè and watching him work, and

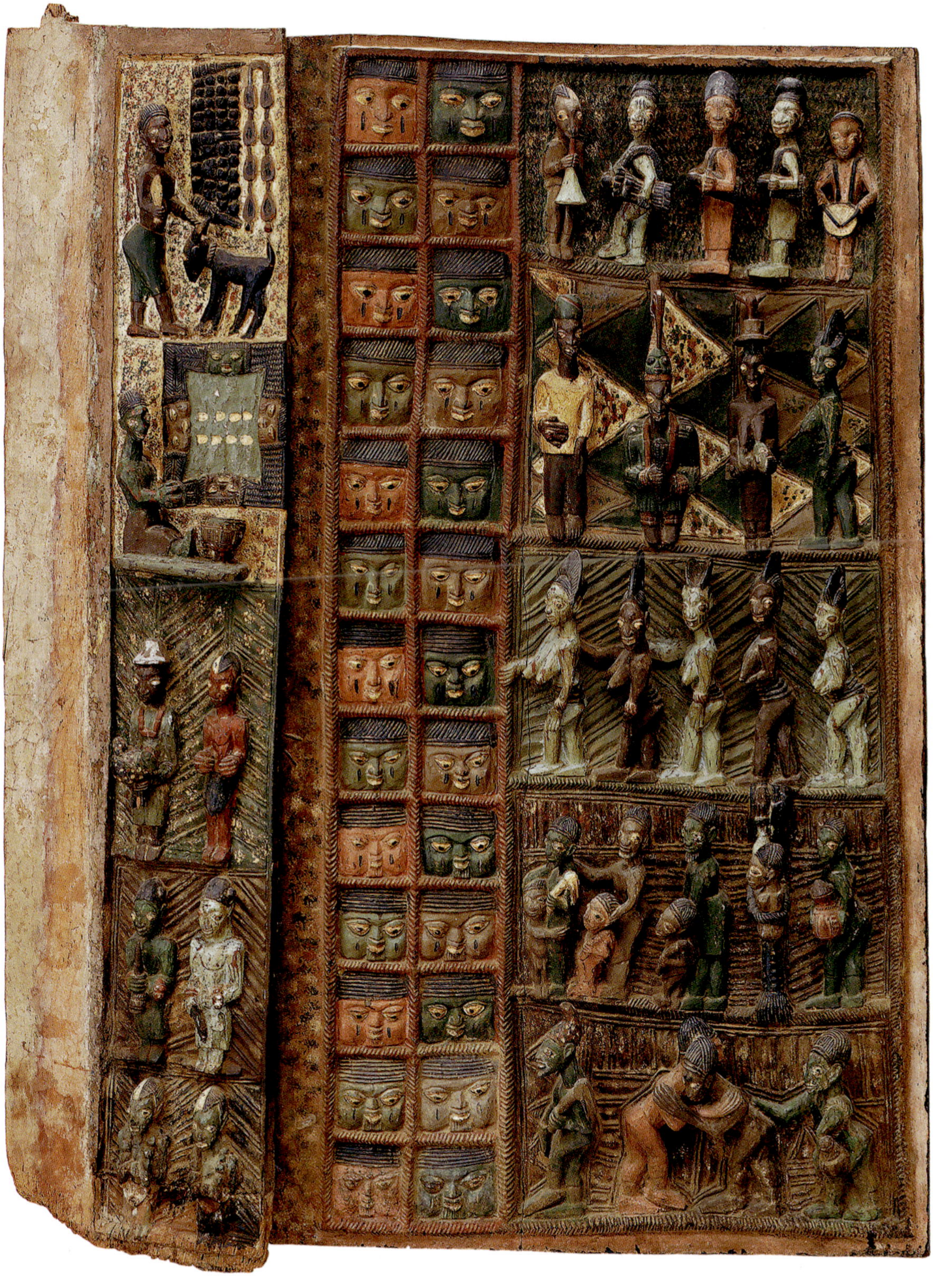

16–15 Olówè of Isè. Door from Yoruba royal palace in Ikéré, Nigeria. Yoruba culture, c. 1925 CE. Wood and pigment, height 72" (1.9 m). The Detroit Institute of the Arts. GIFT OF BETHEA AND IRWIN GREEN

The carvings on this door illustrate scenes from palace life, focusing on divination. On the left-hand panel, the future is foretold by reading oracles. At the top is a man with sacrificial animal and palm nuts. Below him, a diviner sits with a divination board and the ceremonial cup for the palm nuts, and lower still are messengers and assistants. To the right, two rows of faces introduce the court. The crowned king is represented in the second panel from the top, seated between his guard and two royal wives; the chief wife is nursing a child and wearing a European top hat, a symbol of power. Above the royals, musicians perform, while below, royal wives dance. The bottom two registers depict farm workers and a pair of wrestlers.

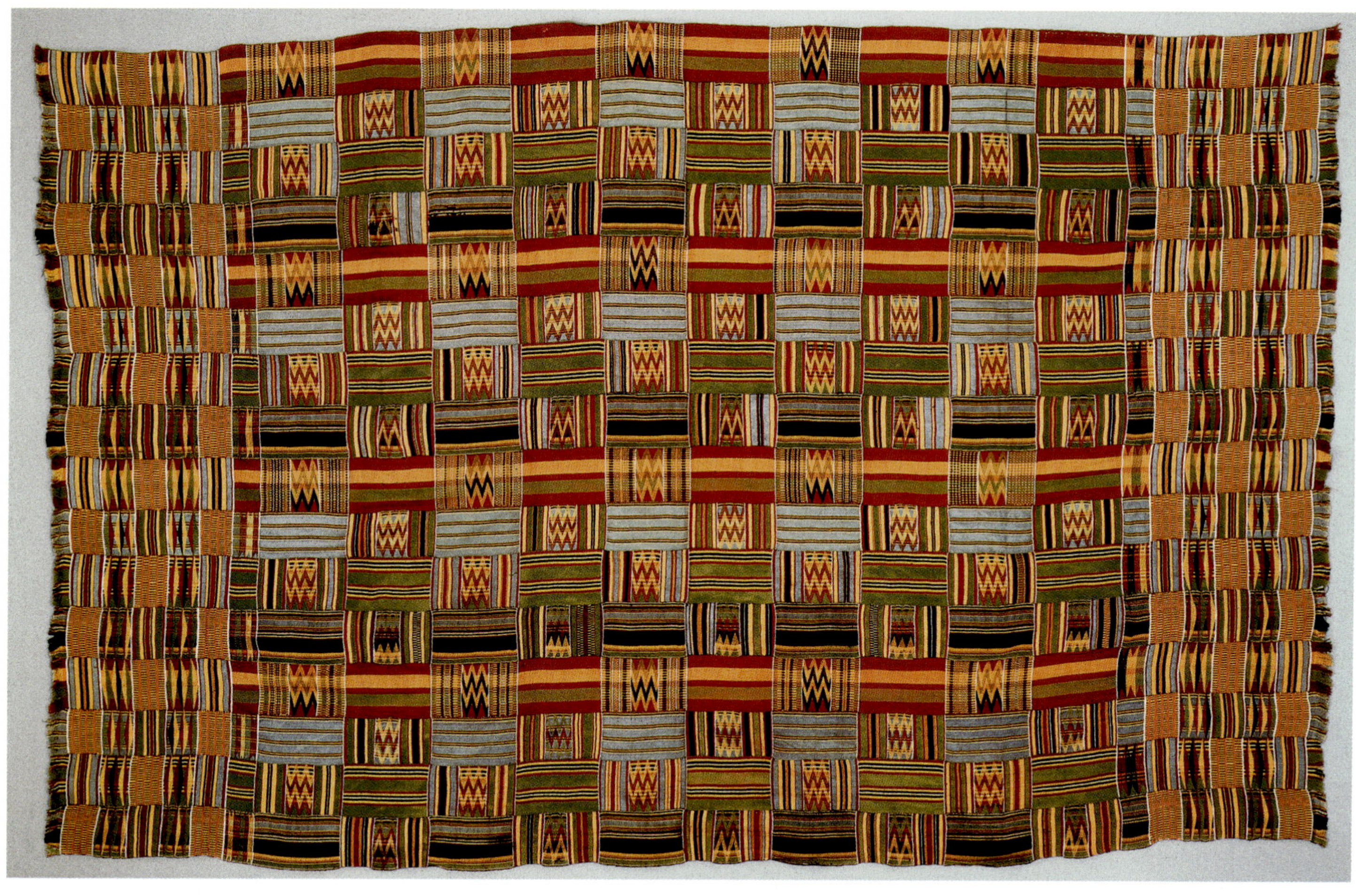

16–16 Kente cloth, from Ghana. Ashanti culture, 20th century CE. Silk, 6' 10⁹⁄₁₆" × 4' 3⁹⁄₁₆" (2.1 × 1.31 m). National Museum of African Art and National Museum of Natural History, Washington, D.C.
PURCHASED WITH FUNDS PROVIDED BY THE SMITHSONIAN COLLECTIONS ACQUISITION PROGRAM, 1983–85, EJ 10583

(echoing the praises of the Yoruba themselves) described Olówè carving the iron-hard African oak "as easily as [he would] a calabash [gourd]." Olówè also carved the divination bowl illustrated in Figure Intro–14.

Woven textiles, called **kente**, still signal status in the Akan kingdoms of Ghana (fig. **16–16**). The pattern of the Ashante kente cloth here, known as *oyokoman ogya da mu*—meaning "there is a fire between two factions of the Oyoko clan"—refers to the civil war that followed the death of the Ashante king Osei Tutu in about 1730. Traditionally, only the king of the Ashante was allowed to wear this pattern. Other patterns were reserved for members of the royal family or the court.

Kente cloth is made on small, light looms that produce long, narrow strips of fabric. Ashante weavers begin by laying out the long warp (vertical) threads in a brightly colored pattern. Today the threads are likely to be rayon. Formerly, however, they were silk, which the Ashante produced by unraveling Chinese cloth obtained through European trade. Weft threads woven through the warp produce complex patterns, including double weaves in which the front and back of the cloth display different patterns. The long strips produced on the loom are then cut to size and sewn together to form large rectangles of finished kente cloth. In present-day Ghana, the wearing of kente and other traditional textiles is encouraged, and patterns are no longer restricted to a particular person or group.

The Art of Masquerade

Among the best-known works of African art are masks. In many communities, masquerades no longer occur, and Kongo peoples rarely dance with masks today. However, the Bwa people of central Burkina Faso still use masks to depict spirits in seasonal ceremonies. When young Bwa men and women are initiated into adulthood following the onset of puberty, they are taught about the world of nature spirits and about the wooden masks that represent them in performance.

The initiates are first separated from younger playmates by older relatives who "kidnap" them, though they explain the youths' disappearance in the community by saying that they have been devoured by wild beasts. The initiates are stripped of their clothing and sleep on the ground without blankets. Isolated from the community, they are taught about the spirit world invoked by the masks. Although they have seen these masks all their lives, they learn for the first time that they are made of wood and have been worn by their older brothers and cousins. They learn of the spirit each mask represents, and they memorize the story of each spirit's encounter with the founding ancestors of the clan. They also learn how to construct the costumes worn with the masks, and they learn the songs that accompany them in performance. Returning to the community, the initiates display their new knowledge in a public ceremony. Each boy performs with one of the masks, in a dance that expresses the character and personality that the mask represents. The girls, who are not allowed to wear the masks, sing the songs that accompany each one. At the end of the ceremony, the young men and women rejoin their families as adults, ready to marry, start farms, and begin families of their own.

Most Bwa masks depict spirits that take human or animal forms. Among the most spectacular masks, however, are abstract examples crowned with a tall, narrow plank, which represent spirits that have taken neither animal nor human form (fig. **16–17**). The patterns of these abstract masks convey a message about the proper moral conduct of life. The white crescent at the top represents the quarter-moon, under which initiations are held. The large central X represents the scar that every initiated Bwa wears as a mark of their piety. The horizontal zigzags represent the path of ancestors and symbolize adherence to traditional ways, indicating that this path is difficult to follow. The curving red hook that projects above the face is said to represent the beak of the hornbill, a bird associated with the supernatural world and believed to be an intermediary between the living and the dead.

Art and Death

Africa also has a rich tradition of funerary art. That of ancient Egypt is probably best known in the West (see Chapter 3), but all over Africa, when death comes, special ceremonies and rituals help the community mourn. The death of a child is a particularly traumatic event. The Yoruba people of Nigeria have one of the highest rates of twin births in the world, and the birth of twins is a joyful occasion.

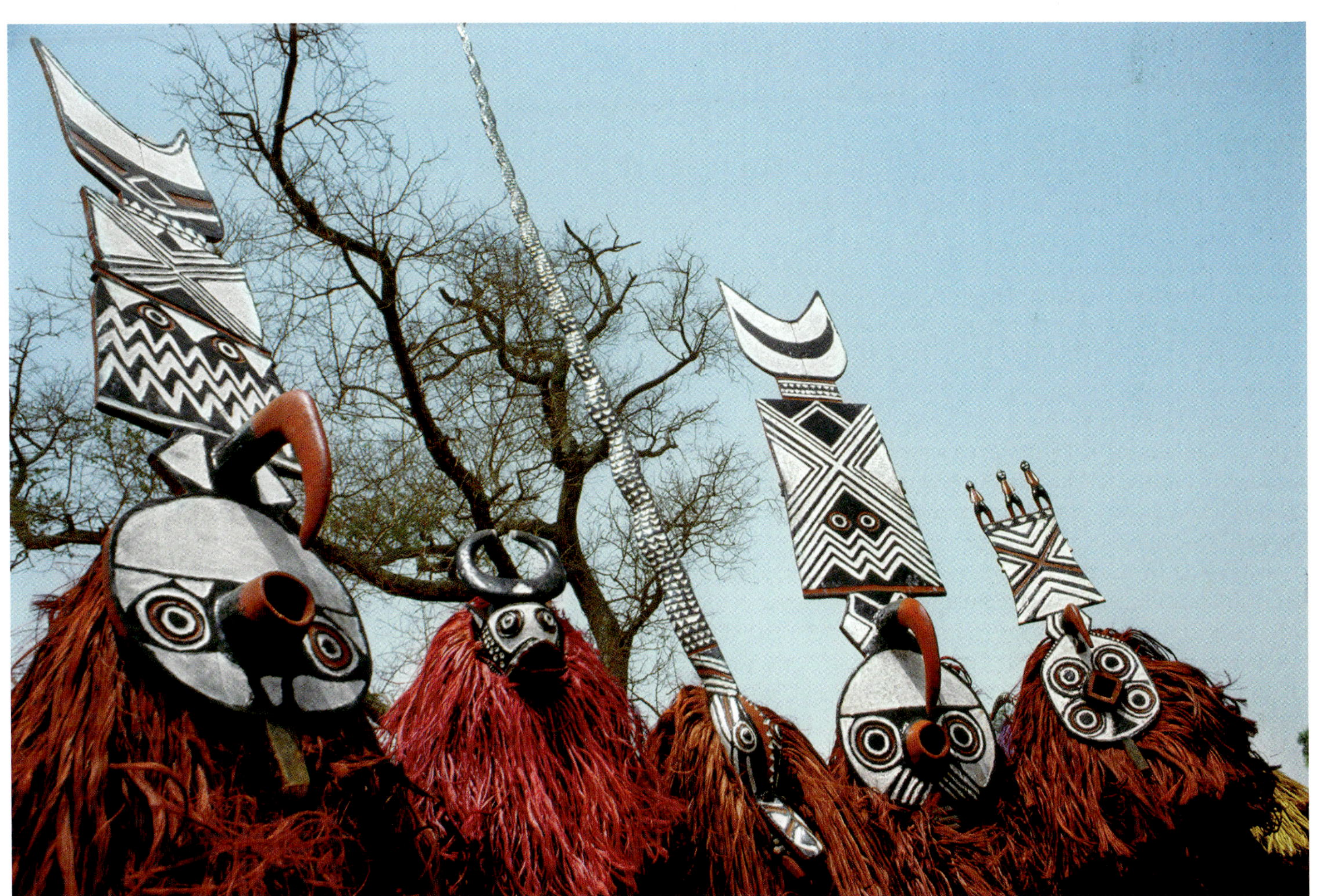

16–17 Masks in performance, from Dossi, Burkina Faso. Bwa culture, 1984 CE. Wood, mineral pigments, and fiber, height approx. 7' (2.13 m)

The use of such masks by the Bwa is a relatively recent practice. The elders of the family who own these masks state that they, like all Bwa, once followed the cult of the spirit of Do, who is represented by masks made of leaves. When during the last quarter of the nineteenth century, the Bwa were the targets of slave raiders, they acquired wooden masks from their neighbors, for such masks seemed a more effective and powerful way of communicating with spirits who could help them. Thus, faced with a new form of adversity, the Bwa imported a new tradition to cope with it.

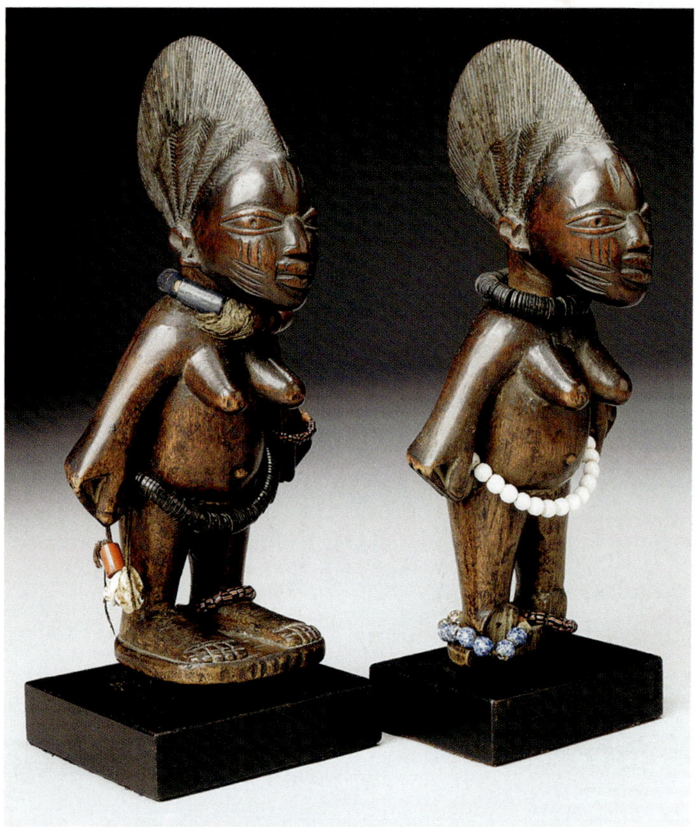

16–18 Twin figures ***(ere ibeji)***, from Nigeria. Yoruba culture, 20th century CE. Wood, height 7⅞" (20 cm). The University of Iowa Museum of Art, Iowa City
THE STANLEY COLLECTION

As with other African sculpture, patterns of use result in particular signs of wear. The facial features of ere ibeji *are often worn down or even obliterated by repeated feedings and washings. Camwood powder applied as a cosmetic builds to a thick crust in areas that are rarely handled, and the blue indigo dye regularly applied to the hair eventually builds to a thin layer.*

But since twins are more delicate than single babies, occasionally one or both may die. When this happens, Yoruba parents consult a diviner, who may tell them that an image of a twin, or *ere ibeji*, must be carved to serve as a dwelling place for the deceased twin's spirit (fig. **16–18**).

The mother cares for the "birth" of this image by sending the artist food while the image is being carved and gifts when it is finished. Then she dances home, carrying the figure as she would a living child, accompanied by the singing of neighborhood women. She places the figure in a shrine in her bedroom and lavishes care upon it, feeding it, dressing it richly, and anointing it with cosmetic oils. The Yoruba believe that the spirit of a dead twin thus honored is appeased and will look with favor on surviving family members.

The female *ibeji* figures in fig. 16–18, which may be the work of the Yoruba artist Akiode (died 1936), radiate health and well-being. Their beautiful, glossy surfaces and ample forms suggest that they are well fed. Full breasts, elaborate hairstyles, and scarification patterns signal the mature adulthood that they might one day have achieved. They represent hope for the future, for survival, and for prosperity.

Many African artists today have come of age in a postcolonial culture that mingles elements of American, European, and African traditions. Drawing on these diverse influences, they have established a place in the lively international art scene along with their European, American, and Asian counterparts, and their work is shown as readily in Paris, Tokyo, and Los Angeles as it is in the African cities of Abidjan, Kinshasa, and Dakar.

Looking Back

In many world cultures, the distinction between "fine art" and "craft" does not exist. The traditional Western academic hierarchy of materials, in which marble, bronze, oil, and fresco are valued more than terra cotta, wood, and watercolor, and the equally artificial hierarchy of subjects in which history painting, including religious history, stands supreme are irrelevant outside the European tradition. The indigenous peoples of Africa and the Americas did not produce ritual or political objects as works of art, but as utilitarian objects, adorned in ways that enhanced their ability to perform their cultural function. A work was valued for its effectiveness and for the role it played in society. And like art in other cultures, many pieces had great spiritual or magical power. Such works of art cannot be fully comprehended or appreciated when they are seen on pedestals or encased in glass boxes in museums. They must be imagined, or better yet seen, "living" within the societies that made and originally used them. How powerfully might our minds and emotions be engaged if we saw Kwakwaka'wakw (see fig. 15–31) or Bwa masks (see fig. 16–17) functioning in religious ritual, changing not only the outward appearance, but also the very essence of the performers themselves.

IN PERSPECTIVE

500 BCE

◀ **Nok,** c. 500 BCE–200 CE

0

500 CE

◀ **Ife,** c. 800 CE–Present

1000

◀ **Great Zimbabwe,** c. 1000–1500 CE

◀ **Benin,** c. 1170 CE–Present

◀ **Europeans Establish Contact with Coastal Sub-Saharan Africa,** c. 1400 CE

◀ **Portuguese First Encounter Kongo Culture,** 1482 CE

◀ **Cordial Relations Established between Benin and Portugal,** 1485 CE

1500

◀ **British Sack and Burn Benin Royal Palace,** 1897 CE

◀ **Oba of Benin Returns from Exile,** c. 1914 CE

◀ **Most of Africa Under Foreign Control,** c. 1914 CE

◀ **African Colonies Gain Independence,** 1950s–1980s CE

2000

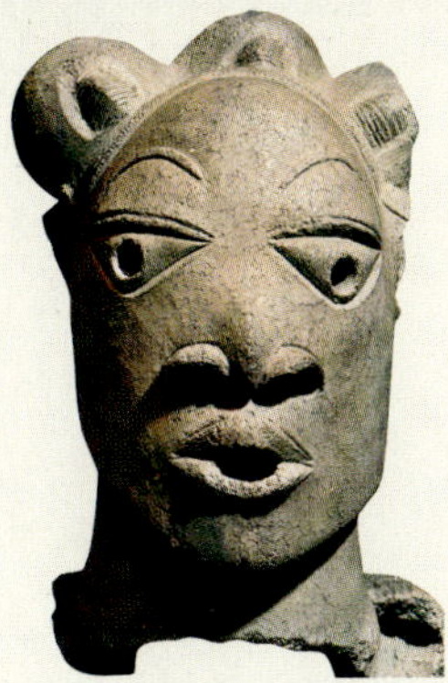

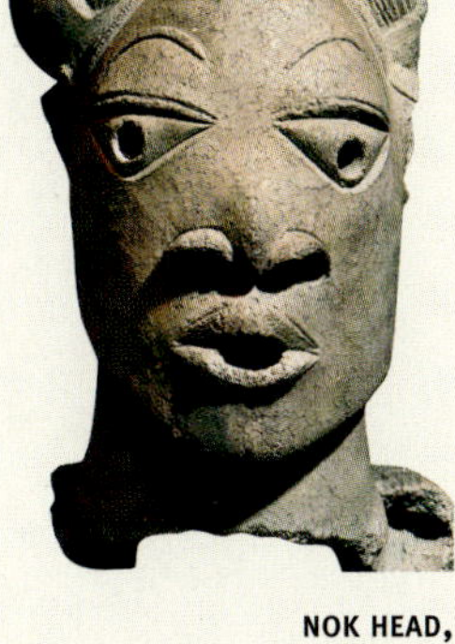

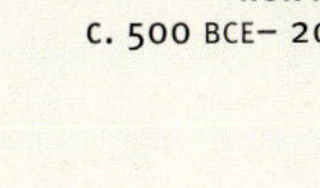

NOK HEAD, c. 500 BCE– 200 CE

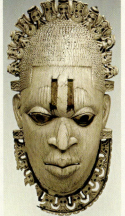

GREAT ZIMBABWE CONICAL TOWER, c. 1200–1400 CE

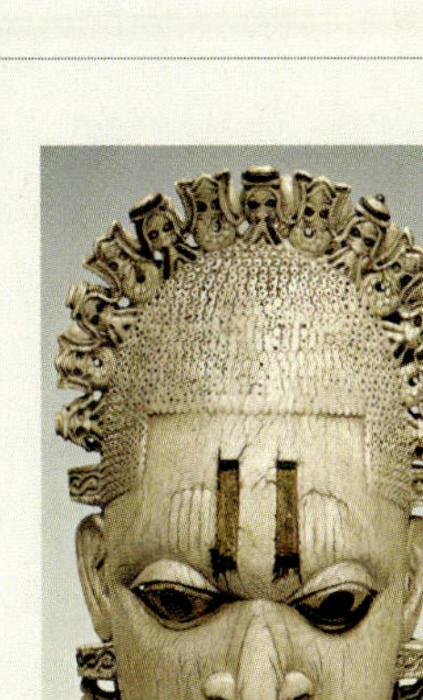

HIP MASK OF AN IYOBA, c. 1550 CE

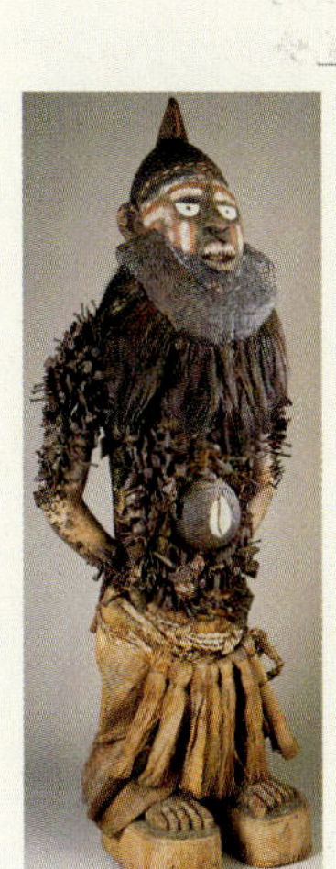

KONGO POWER FIGURE, 19TH CENTURY CE

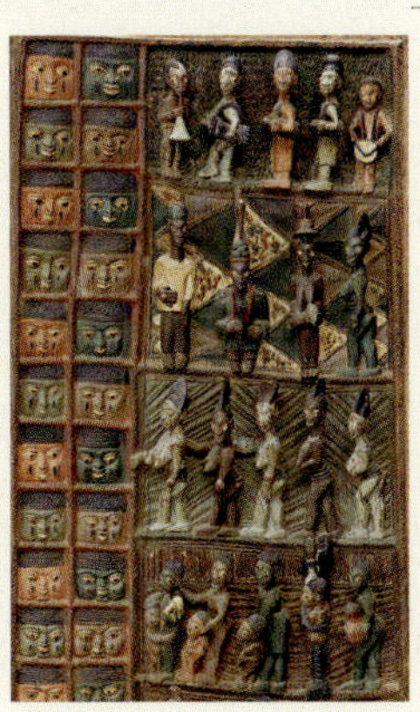

OLÓWÈ OF ISÈ, DOOR FROM YORUBA ROYAL PALACE, c. 1925 CE

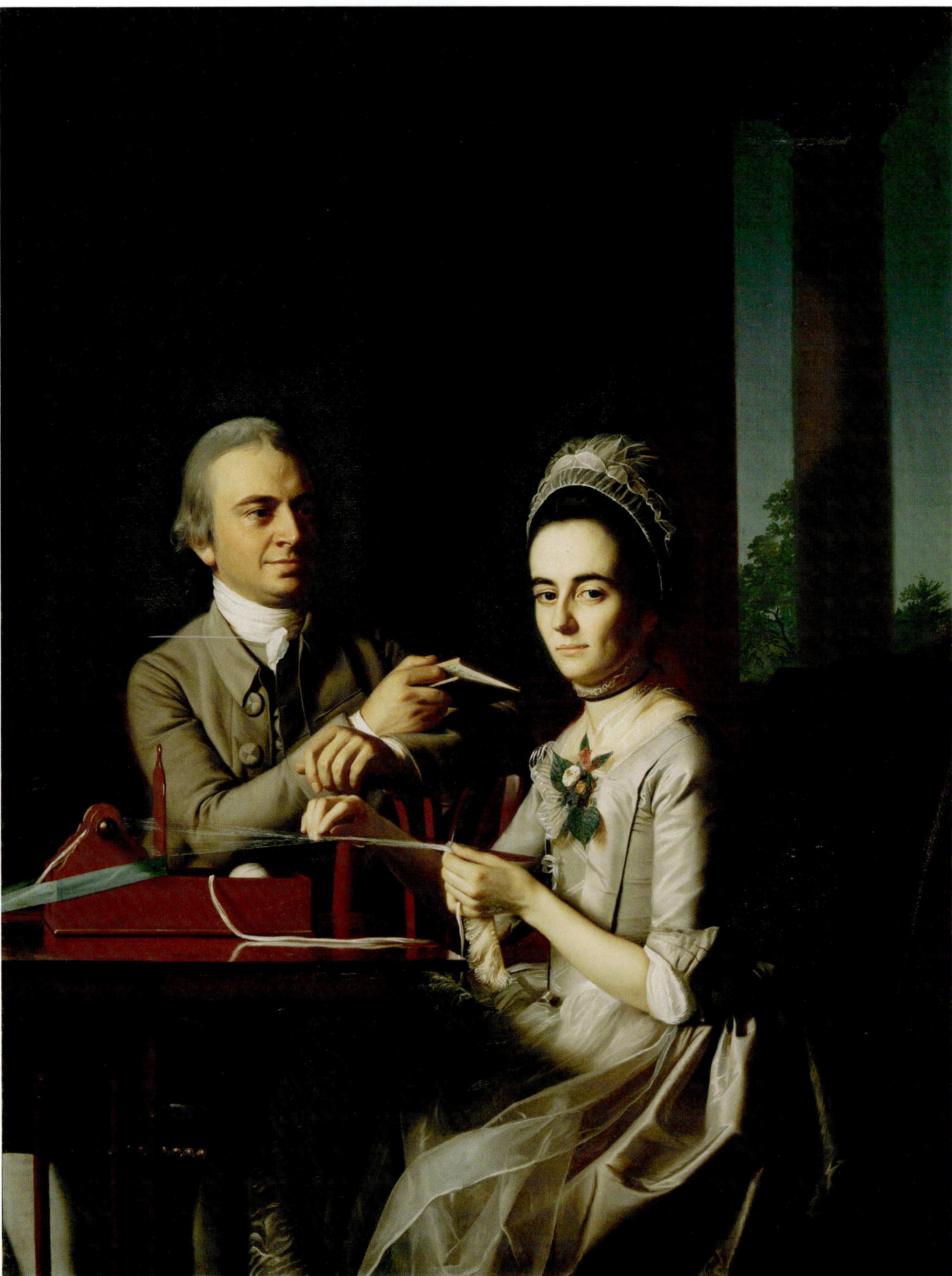

17 Neoclassicism, Romanticism, and Realism

LOOKING FORWARD

Our encounter with the Philadelphia couple portrayed in this arresting double portrait of 1773 by Boston painter John Singleton Copley (fig. **17–1**) is very different from our experience looking at the Arnolfinis in Jan van Eyck's signature work painted almost three and a half centuries earlier (see fig. 12–1). Here it is the spotlighted woman, Sarah Morris, who commands our attention. She turns to meet our gaze, and she is the focus not only for us, but for her husband, ardent patriot Thomas Mifflin. He is content to sit in the background of this picture, interrupting his reading to look admiringly at his beloved Sarah.

The couple was visiting Boston for a family funeral when they engaged Copley to paint their portrait. Thomas, a Quaker, had already established himself as a successful merchant. In 1775 he would be commissioned as a general in George Washington's army, and would eventually become a framer of the Constitution and the first governor of Pennsylvania. His intelligent and accomplished partner Sarah shared his conviction for the cause of American independence. Her political persuasions are emphasized in the painting by what she is doing: weaving homespun fringe on a portable loom to support the Colonial boycott on British imports. This double portrait's record of an affectionate marriage that was also an equal partnership seems curiously modern. But its veracity is confirmed by the historical record, and such unions were not unusual in the upper social echelons of eighteenth-century American society.

Copley (1738–1815) was at the pinnacle of artistic and commercial accomplishment when he painted this portrait. Born in Boston, the artist would flee the unsettled climate of the colonies the year after he painted the Mifflins to begin a second career in London. In America he was revered by his subjects for accurately rendering their faces and clothing, though they were occasionally annoyed by his exacting working habits; Sarah Morris sat 20 times while he painted her hands. Copley's painting of the Mifflins contains many elements that would become key features in the great explosion of artistic movements during the late eighteenth and nineteenth century. His structured compositions and stylistic finish evoke the calm decorum of Neoclassicism, while the psychological connection his subjects make with their viewers references Romanticism. And the powerful impression that this image captures the Mifflin's at a particular moment in their normal life together looks even further forward to Realism and its interest in the "unvarnished truth."

17–1 John Singleton Copley. ***Thomas Mifflin and Sarah Morris (Mr. and Mrs. Mifflin).*** 1773. Oil on canvas, 61⅝" × 48" (156.5 × 121.9 cm). Philadelphia Museum of Art

BEQUEST OF MRS ESTHER F. WISTAR TO THE HISTORICAL SOCIETY OF PENNSYLVANIA IN 1900 AND ACQUIRED BY MUTUAL AGREEMENT WITH THE SOCIETY THROUGH THE GENEROSITY OF MR. AND MRS. FITZ EUGENE DIXON, JR

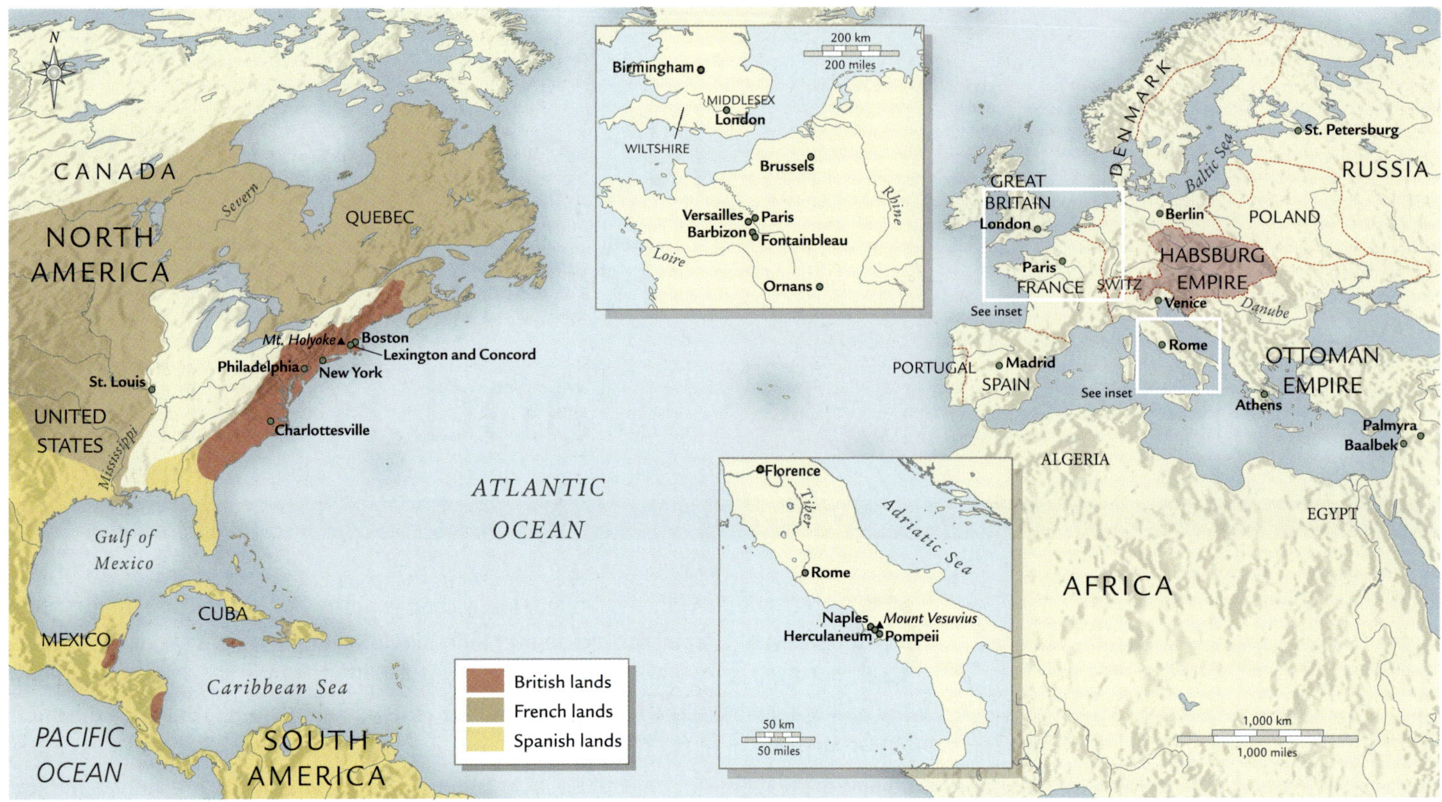

Map 17–1 Eighteenth-Century Europe and North America

Cultural historians call the eighteenth century the Age of Enlightenment or the Age of Reason. Reason certainly became the touchstone for evaluating nearly every civilized endeavor, including philosophy and politics, as well as art and architecture. An optimistic, even reverential attitude toward scientific inquiry developed, and this enthusiasm extended to historical and archaeological studies, as well as to investigations of the natural world. Nature, which was thought to embody reason, was invoked to corroborate the correctness—and goodness—of everything from political systems to architectural designs.

Neoclassicism and Romanticism

The period between the middle of the eighteenth and the middle of the nineteenth century in Europe, and its cultural extension in America (see map **17–1**), is characterized by a marked increase in stylistic variety in the visual arts. Art historians have focused their principal attention on two trends they have named Neoclassicism and Romanticism.

Neoclassicism is characterized by stylistic sources in ancient Greek or Roman art, by heroic nudity in sculpture and sometimes painting, by Classical orders in architecture, by the dominance of drawing over painterly effects in the visual arts, and by a general emphasis on what were perceived to be noble and serious modes of expression that often manifested themselves in subjects highlighting moral incorruptibility, patriotism, and courage. In paintings, brushstrokes are tightly controlled, compositions are ordered and balanced, figures are idealized beyond blemish, emotions are kept to a minimum.

Many see Italy—its wealth of antique ruins enhanced in 1748 by the archaeological discovery of the ancient city of Pompeii—as the birthplace of eighteenth-century Neoclassicism, led by Antonio Canova (1757–1822), the foremost Neoclassical sculptor in Europe. Born into a family of stonemasons near Venice, Canova settled in Rome in 1781, rapidly achieving accolades that compared him with Michelangelo. One of Canova's most admired works depicts the erotically charged mythological subject *Cupid and Psyche* (fig. **17–2**) in a way that recalls the ancient Classical sculpture that attracted artists and scholars to Rome. Condemned to a death-like sleep by a jealous Venus, Psyche revives at Cupid's kiss. His projecting wings offset the rounded forms of the two linked bodies and balance the downward diagonal extensions of the figures' legs. The lustrous finish of their marble skin shines against the contrasting textures of drapery and rocks. Although carved fully in the round, the work is meant to be experienced frontally, as a symmetrically stable composition of interlocking triangles and ovals. The effect is ordered, decorous, and calming, if somewhat titillating.

The mode of expression that art historians label Romanticism features loose, fluid brushwork, strong colors, dramatic contrasts of

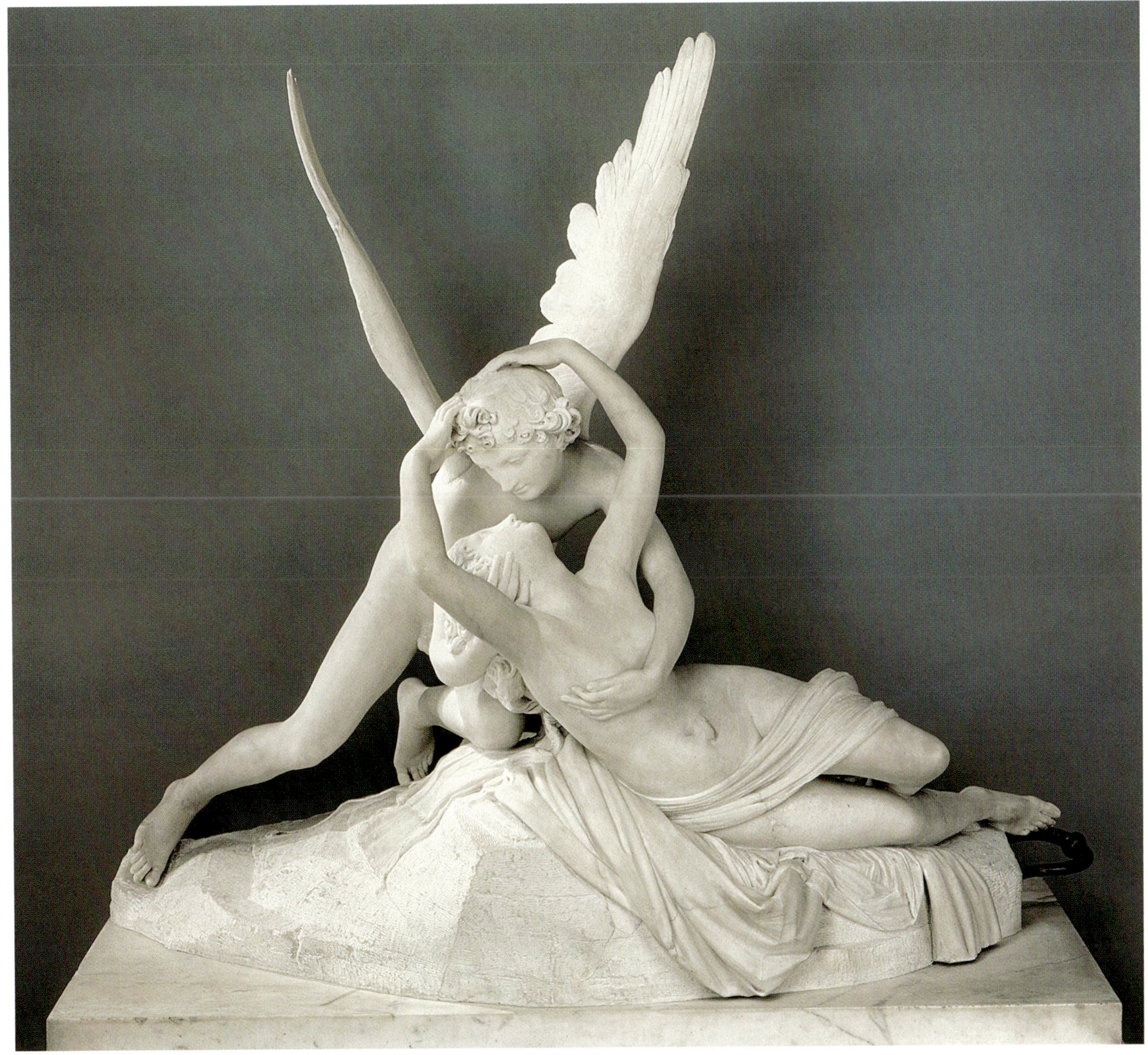

17–2 Antonio Canova. *Cupid and Psyche.* 1787–1793. Marble, 61" × 68" (1.55 × 1.73 cm).
Musée du Louvre, Paris

light and dark, complex compositions, and expressive poses and gestures, all reminiscent of the more dramatic aspects of the Baroque. Paintings and sculptures were often based on literary fantasies set in remote times or exotic places and infused with a spirit of sensationalism or melancholy. Romanticism was an imaginative approach to art, centering it in the strong feelings of artists and their attempts to inspire those same feelings in viewers. The Enlightenment's faith in reason and empirical knowledge was strongly challenged by Romanticism's celebration of the emotions and subjectivity.

Characteristic of this trend is the work of Swiss painter John Henry Fuseli (1741–1825), who glorified the irrational side of human nature that the Enlightenment sought to deny. Fuseli was raised in an intellectual household that celebrated originality,

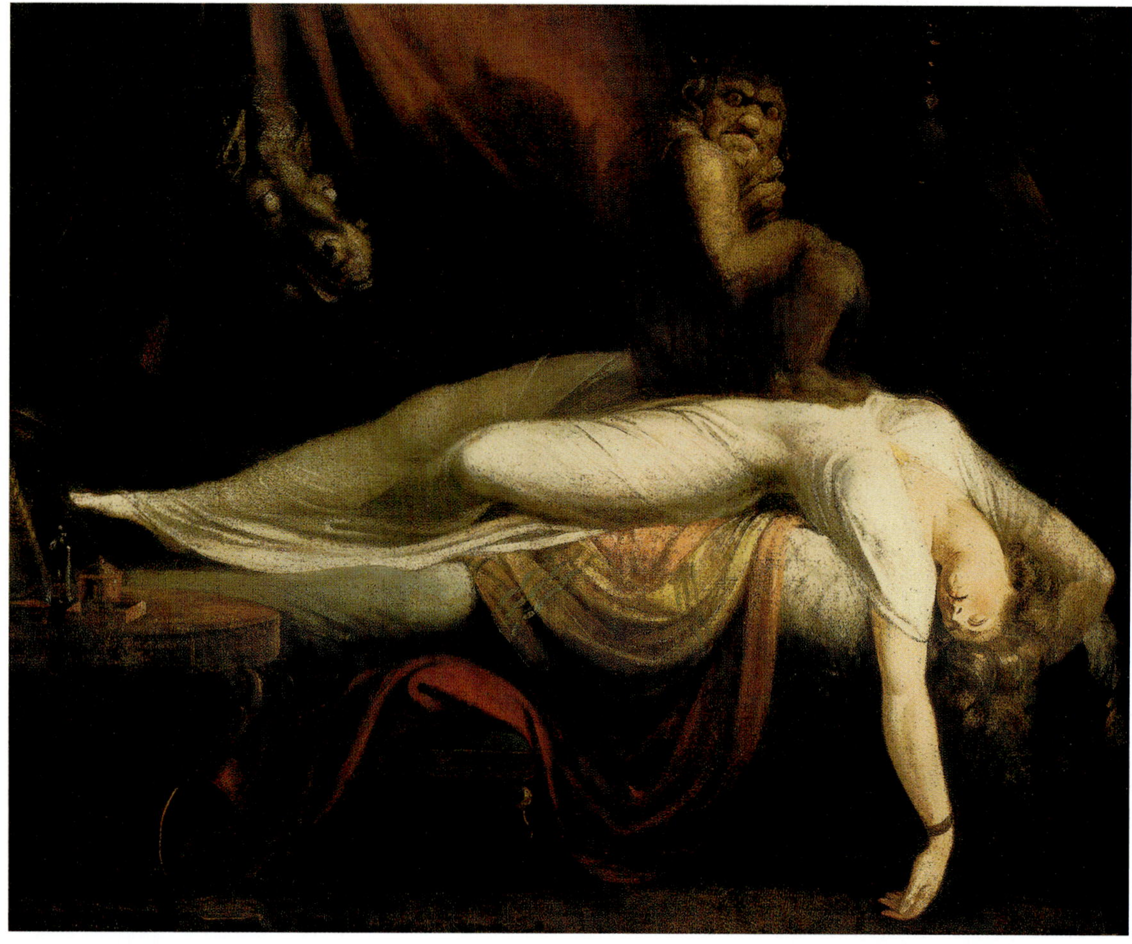

17–3 John Henry Fuseli. ***The Nightmare.*** 1781. Oil on canvas, 39¾" × 49½" (101 × 126 cm). The Detroit Institute of Arts
FOUNDERS SOCIETY PURCHASE WITH FUNDS FROM MR. AND MRS. BERT L. SMOKLER AND MR. AND MRS. LAWRENCE A. FLEISCHMANN

The Austrian psychoanalyst Sigmund Freud, who believed that dreams were manifestations of the dreamer's repressed desires, had a reproduction of The Nightmare *in his office. Romantic escape was as appealing in the eighteenth and nineteenth centuries as it is at the beginning of the twenty-first century.*

freedom of expression, and the imaginative power of the irrational. After studying in Rome (1770–1778), where he was drawn to Michelangelo rather than to Classical art, Fuseli settled permanently in London. By the early 1780s, with works such as *The Nightmare* (fig. **17–3**), he developed a reputation as a painter of the irrational and the erotic. Fuseli depicts a sleeping woman, sprawled across a divan, oppressed by an erotic dream brought on by the gruesome demon sitting on her chest. In comparison to Canova's calming configuration, the asymmetry of the heroine's offset position is particularly unsettling. The phosphorescent eyes of the horse who thrusts his head into the scene from the murky background at left heightens the frightening effect. And since Romantic art is often personally charged and subjectively felt, it is hardly surprising that Fuseli's *Nightmare* may be autobiographical. On the back of the painting, he sketched a portrait of Anna Landolt, a woman he loved and lost, and whom he confessed he often encountered in erotic dreams.

Art historians at times think of Neoclassicism and Romanticism as successive stylistic movements. Perhaps they have been overly influenced by the progression these two tendencies followed in French painting, moving from David and his followers from the 1780s onward to Géricault and Delacroix by the 1820s. But surveying the broader European landscape, we will discover that the stylistic progression, and even crisp stylistic differentiation, is not so tidy. The contrasting works of Canova and Fuseli, for example, are essentially contemporary, and by the end of the eighteenth century, many works of art combine elements of both Neoclassicism and Romanticism, though they still sometimes also reference Rococo, or even Baroque. By the middle of the nineteenth century, new interests in styles and subjects that more faithful evoke ordinary life and reproduce its frank visual appearance will mount a challenge to all these by-then-traditional artistic tendencies, rooted in past styles or escapist fantasies.

England and North America

Portraiture

During the eighteenth century, British patrons preferred pictures of themselves to grand scenes of Classical or religious history, and Thomas Gainsborough (1727–1788) grew into one of England's greatest portraitists by catering to the tastes of the rich and famous. The emphasis on setting in his early portrait of Robert Andrews and his wife Frances Carter (fig. **17–4**) almost turns this work into a landscape painting, and the shimmering satin of her skirt, the bench on which she sits, as well as the fluttering lyricism of the countryside and the casual elegance of the couple's poses recall the Rococo

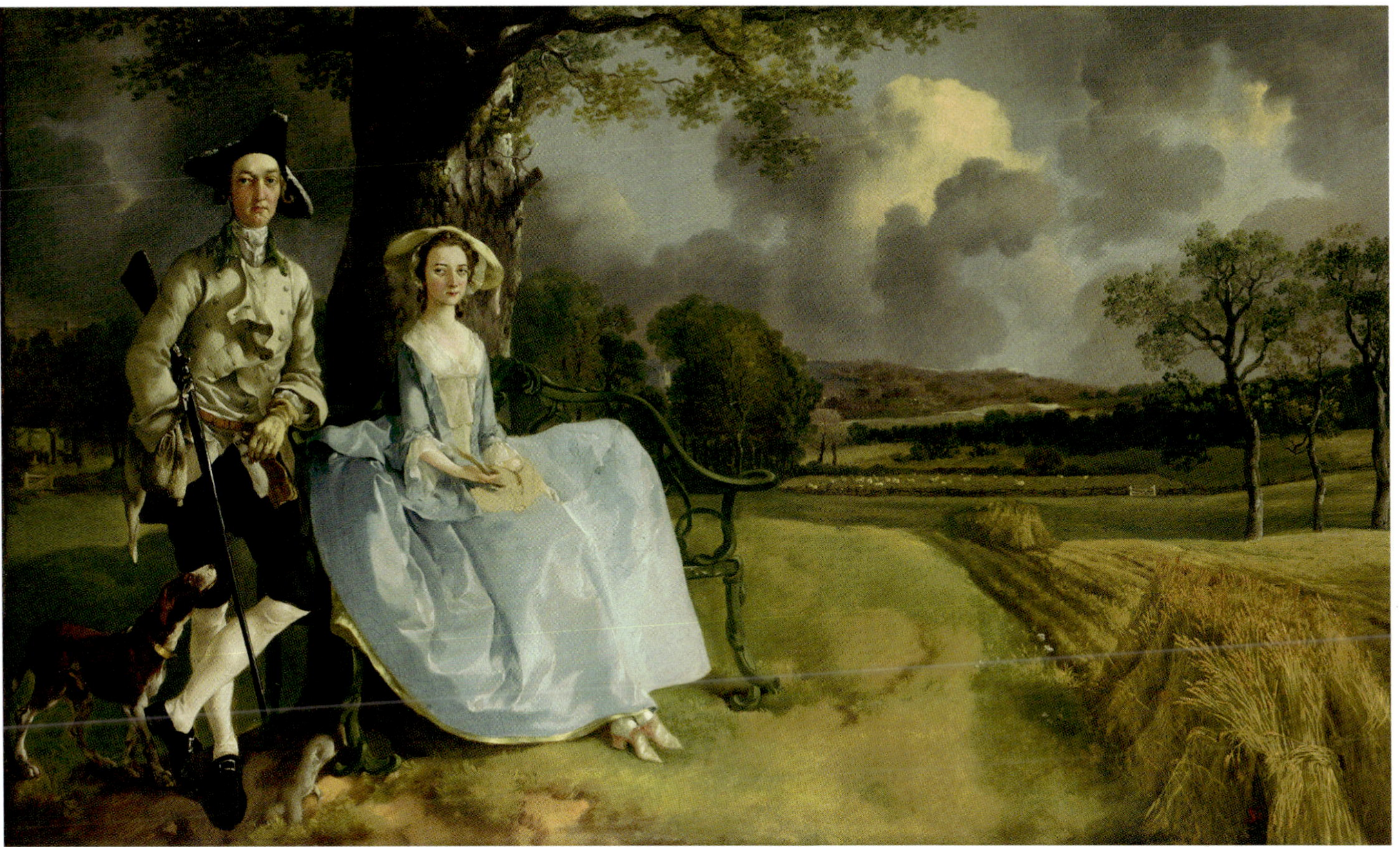

17–4 Thomas Gainsborough. *Robert Andrews and Frances Carter (Mr. and Mrs. Andrews)* . c. 1748–1750. Oil on canvas, 27½" × 47" (69.7 × 119.3 cm). The National Gallery, London

Gainsborough was engaged to paint this couple's portrait shortly after the 20-year-old Robert Andrews married 16-year-old Frances Carter in November 1748. An area of painting in Frances' lap has been left unfinished, perhaps anticipating the later addition of a child for her to hold.

of Watteau. But essentially this work is about the connection of the landed gentry with the estates that signaled their identity and provided their wealth and power. Andrews's land-holdings had just expanded as a result of his marriage, and the hunting rifle tucked casually under his arm is a clear sign of his dominion over the expansive landscape.

In Colonial America, self-taught portraitist John Singleton Copley (1738–1815) developed into what one art historian has called "America's First Old Master." Copley's training and experience were limited, but he was already drawing attention as a painter by the time he was 15. Copley's clients, who included notable patriots Sam Adams and Paul Revere, valued not only his technical skill, but also his ability to dignify them while recording their features with unflinching accuracy. The austere seriousness of his portrait of *Thomas Mifflin and Sarah Morris* (see fig. 17–1)—preoccupied as they both are with politics, leaving little leisure for noble diversions such as hunting—sharply contrasts with Gainsborough's lighthearted and pretty rendering of *Mr. and Mrs. Andrews.* Copley seems to capture something significant here about the nature of the Colonial American experience, soon to ignite in revolution. By that time, however, Copley himself would already be pursuing a second career as a history painter in London, where he moved in 1774 to escape political unrest in the colonies and was elected to the Royal Academy in 1779.

Moralized Genre Painting

Members of the growing English middle class, made up of newly prosperous merchants and professionals who had money to commission portraits, helped fuel the market for other types of painting, such as moralizing satire or scenes drawn from history or literature. Whatever their subject matter, many pictures reflected Enlightenment values, including an interest in promoting public virtue and social progress, a love of natural beauty, and a faith in reason and science.

British patrons tended to favor amusing and easily understandable satirical and moralizing scenes over high-minded history paintings with subjects drawn from mythology, the Bible, or Classical literature. By doing so, they contradicted art theorists of their time and earlier, who had long considered history painting the highest form of artistic endeavor. Following the discontinuation of

ART ACADEMIES IN THE EIGHTEENTH CENTURY

During the seventeenth century, the French king had founded royal academies for the instruction and encouragement of artists and architects, writers, scientists, musicians, and dancers. In 1667, the Royal Academy of Painting and Sculpture began to mount occasional exhibitions of members' recent work that came to be known as "Salons" because they were held in the Salon Carré in the Louvre Palace. From 1737, Salons were mounted every other year, with a jury of members selecting the works that would be shown. As the only public art exhibitions of any importance in Paris, the Salons were enormously influential in establishing officially approved styles and in molding public taste.

In England, the Royal Academy of Arts, founded in 1768, was significantly different. Since it was a private institution, it was independent of any interference from the Crown. It served only two functions: to operate an art school and to hold two annual exhibitions, one displaying art of the past and the other presenting contemporary art, open to any exhibitor on the basis of merit alone. The Royal Academy continues to function in this way today.

Besides the influential French and British academies, other art academies, public and private, sprang up throughout Europe in the eighteenth century. All primarily welcomed male artists. Some restricted the number of women members, while others welcomed women only as honorary members. In France only seven women were awarded the title of academician (full member) between 1648 and 1706. In 1770, when four women were members of the French Royal Academy, because the men worried that women members would become "too numerous," the academy declared that four women would be the limit at any one time. Women were not admitted to the academy's school nor allowed to compete for academy prizes, both of which were nearly indispensable for professional success.

Women fared even worse at the British Royal Academy in London. After the Swiss painters Angelica Kauffmann and Mary Moser were named founding members in 1768, no other women were elected until 1922, and then only as associates. In a 1771–1772 portrait of the London Academicians (fig. **17–5**), Johann Zoffany showed the men grouped around two nude male models. Propriety prohibited the presence of women in this setting, so Zoffany painted the portraits of the two female members hanging on the wall.

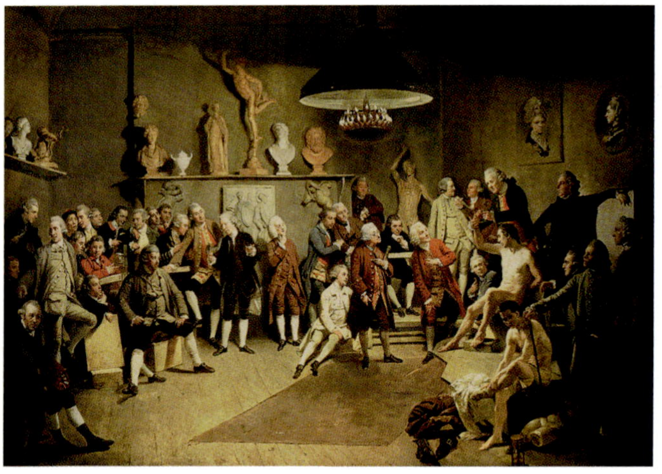

17–5 Johann Zoffany. *Academicians of the Royal Academy.* 1771–1772. Oil on canvas, 47½" × 59½" (120.6 × 151.2 cm). The Royal Collection, Windsor Castle, England

government censorship in 1695, there had emerged in Britain a flourishing culture of literary satire, directed at a variety of political and social targets. The first artist inspired by the work of these novelists and essayists was William Hogarth (1697–1764). Believing that art should contribute to the improvement of society, about 1730 Hogarth began illustrating moralizing tales of his own invention in sequences comprised of four to six paintings. He then reproduced the canvases as prints, to be sold as sets to the public, both maximizing his profits and disseminating his message as broadly as possible.

Hogarth's *Marriage à la Mode* series (1743–1745) was inspired by Joseph Addison's essay promoting the concept of marriage based on love. The opening scene, *The Marriage Contract* (fig. **17–6**), shows the gout-ridden Lord Squanderfield pointing proudly to his family tree as he arranges for his son to marry the daughter of a wealthy merchant. The merchant will be securing his family's entry into the aristocracy, while the lord gains the money he needs to complete his Palladian house, visible through the window. Sitting back to back are the loveless couple, who will be sacrificed for their fathers' pride and greed. The young Squanderfield admires himself in the mirror, while the lawyer Silvertongue whispers to the unhappy fiancée. The five subsequent scenes show the progressively disastrous results of such a union, culminating in murder and suicide. Stylistically, Hogarth's paintings combine the accumulated detail characterizing seventeenth-century Dutch genre painting (see fig. Intro–20) with the casual elegance of Rococo. His work became so popular that in 1745 he was able to abandon portrait painting altogether—an art he deplored as a form of vanity—and devote full time to moralizing satires.

The Italian-trained Swiss artist Angelica Kauffmann (1741–1807), a leading Neoclassical history painter, had been invited to

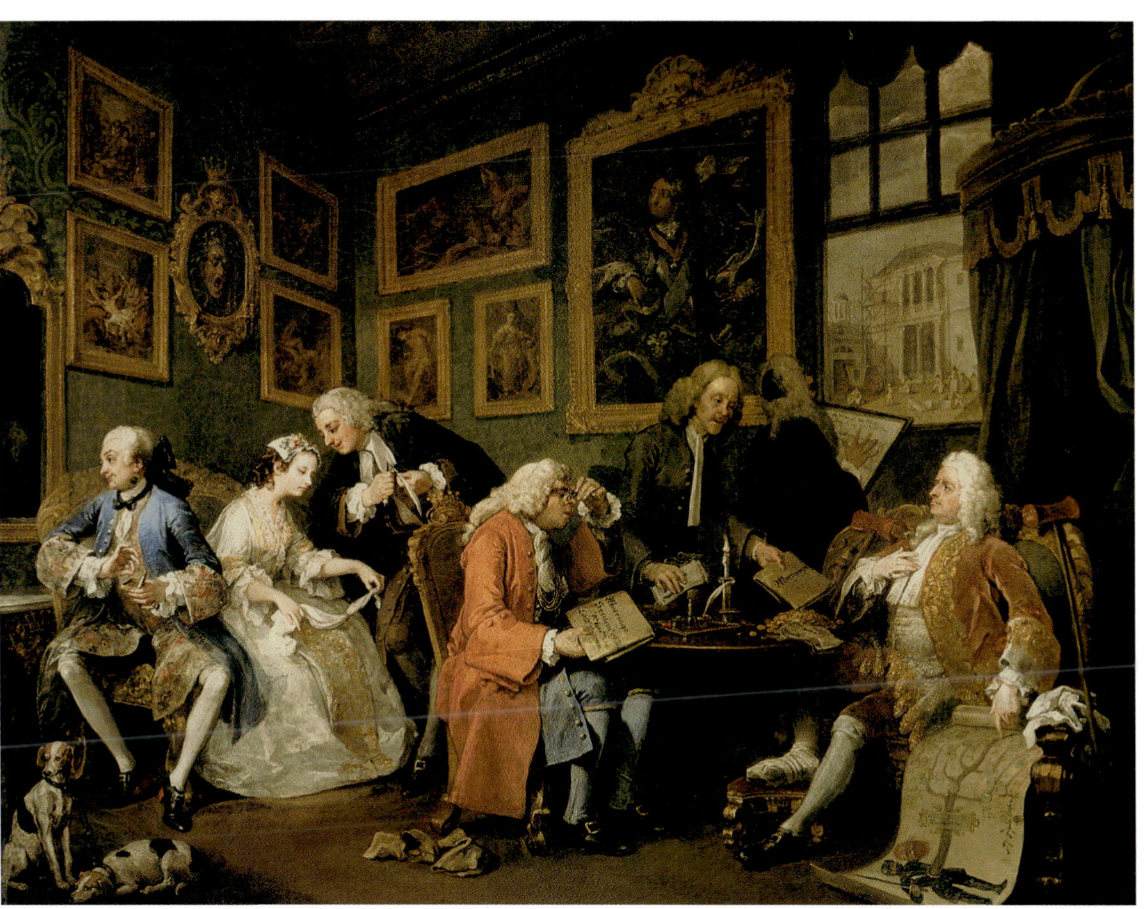

17–6 William Hogarth. *The Marriage Contract*, from *Marriage à la Mode.* 1743–1745. Oil on canvas, 27½" × 35¾" (69.9 × 90.8 cm). The National Gallery, London

"AM I NOT A MAN AND A BROTHER?"

For two centuries the name Wedgwood has been—and still remains—synonymous with fine English ceramics, especially tableware. But there was another side to Josiah Wedgwood. He was active in the international effort to abolish slavery. To publicize the abolitionist cause, he asked the sculptor William Hackwood to design an emblem for the British Committee to Abolish the Slave Trade, formed in 1787. In the compelling image created by Hackwood (fig. **17–7**), the legend, "Am I Not a Man and a Brother?" surrounds an African man kneeling in chains. Wedgwood sent copies of the medallion to Benjamin Franklin, then president of the Philadelphia Abolition Society, and to others in the movement. In the nineteenth century, the women's suffrage movement in the United States adapted the image by representing a woman in chains with the motto, "Am I Not a Woman and a Sister?"

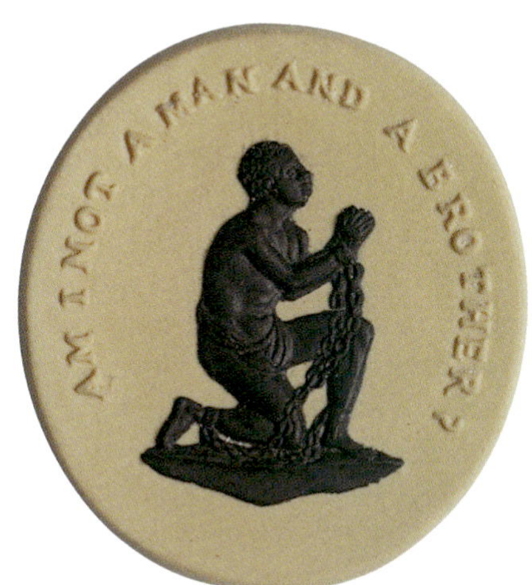

A work of art as explicitly political as this was unusual in the eighteenth century. Nevertheless, artists in both Europe and America responded to the tumultuous social changes and political events with powerful and courageous works of art.

17–7 William Hackwood, for Josiah Wedgwood. *"Am I Not a Man and a Brother?"* 1787. Black-and-white jasperware, 1⅜" × 1⅜" (3.5 x 3.5 cm). Wedgwood Museum Trust Limited, Barlaston, Staffordshire, England

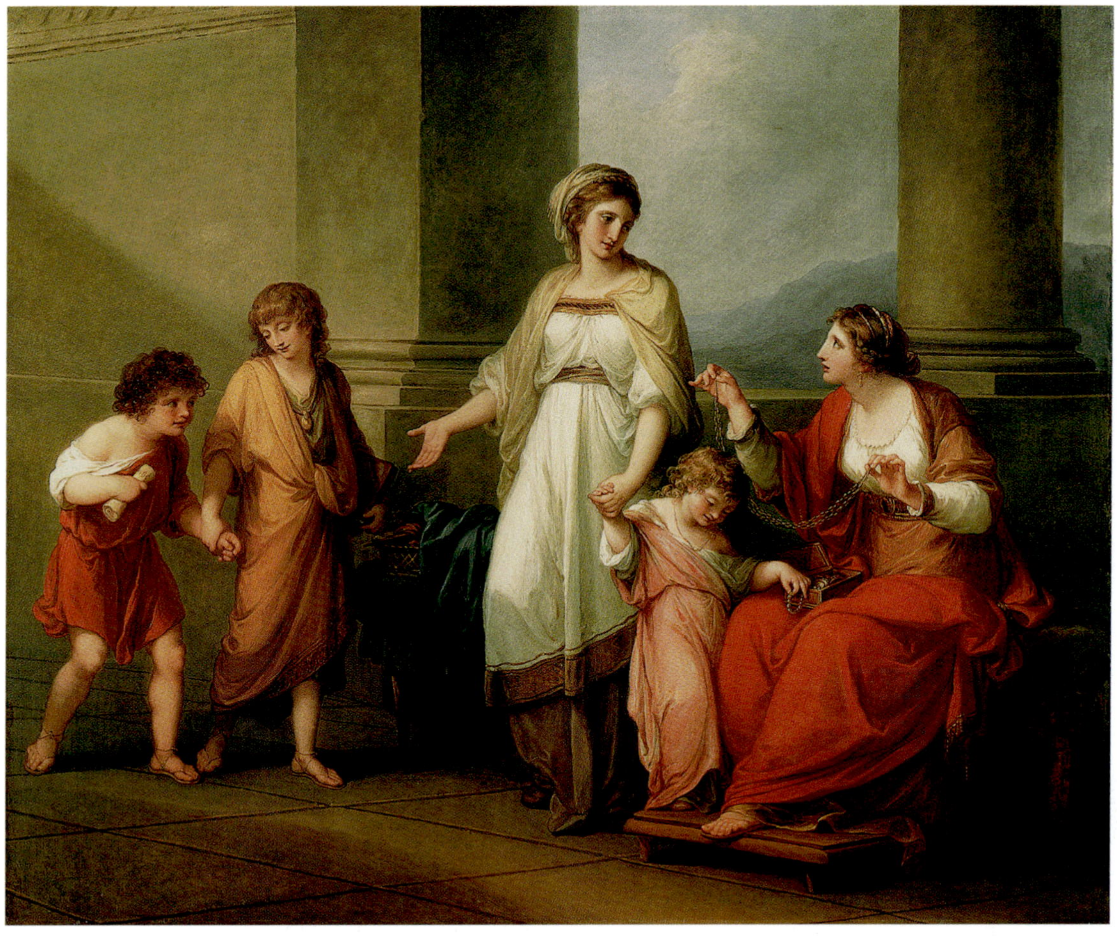

17–8 Angelica Kauffmann. ***Cornelia Pointing to her Children as her Treasures.*** c. 1785. Oil on canvas, 40" × 50" (101.6 × 127 cm). Virginia Museum of Fine Arts, Richmond, Virginia
THE ADOLPH D. AND WILKINS C. WILLIAMS FUND

Britain in 1766 by a wealthy client, and by 1768 she was one of only two women artists named among the founding members of the Royal Academy in London (see "Art Academies in the Eighteenth Century," page 466). In her painting *Cornelia Pointing to her Children as her Treasures* (fig. **17–8**), Kauffmann illustrated both an incident from ancient Republican Rome and a moral lesson. A woman visitor who has been showing Cornelia her jewels, requests to see those of her hostess. In response, Cornelia gestures to her children, saying, "These are my jewels." The setting is ordered and simple, and the figures are based loosely on ancient Roman paintings. The sentiment, however—the glorification and idealization of the "good mother"—belongs unmistakably to the eighteenth century.

Neoclassical Architecture

While Rococo remained popular on the continent, a group of British architects and wealthy amateurs took a stance against what they saw as its immoral extravagance. They advocated a return to the austerity and simplicity they saw in the architecture of Andrea Palladio, traveling to Italy to see it and then returning home to build magnificent Palladian villas set in extensive gardens on country estates.

In the art of garden design, the British could claim true originality. They created layouts that contrasted sharply not only with the rigid formality of seventeenth-century French gardens but also with the Classicism of English stately homes. Known throughout Europe as the English landscape garden, the sweeping lawns, winding paths, irregularly shaped pools and streams, and asymmetrically placed groves of trees imitated the appearance of the natural rural landscape, carefully and discreetly "improved" by human intelligence and skill.

An especially innovative British Neoclassical designer was the Scottish architect Robert Adam (1728–1792). When he made the Grand Tour (a trip through Europe with an extended stay in Rome) in 1754–1758, Adam largely ignored the great Roman civic architecture and focused instead on the applied ornament of Roman domestic buildings. When he returned to London to set up an architectural firm with his two younger brothers, he brought with him drawings and prints that provided a complete inventory of ancient decorative motifs, which he then modified to formulate his own elegant style. His designs proved ideally suited both to the evolving taste of wealthy clients and to the imperial aspirations of the new British king, George III, whose reign began in 1760.

Adam achieved wide renown for his interior designs, such as the renovations he carried out between 1760 and 1769 for the Duke of Northumberland at his country estate, Syon House, near London. The opulent colored marbles, gilded relief panels, classical statues,

CLOSER LOOK

An Enlightenment concern with developments in the natural sciences is at the center of the dramatic depiction of *An Experiment on a Bird in the Air-Pump* (fig. **17–9**) by Joseph Wright of Derby (1734–1797). Trained as a portrait painter, Wright made the Grand Tour in 1773–1775 and then returned to the English Midlands to paint local society. Many of those he painted were the self-made entrepreneurs of the first wave of the Industrial Revolution, which was centered there in towns such as Birmingham. Wright belonged to the Lunar Society, a group of industrialists (including Josiah Wedgwood), mercantilists, and progressive nobles who met in Derby. As part of the society's attempts to popularize science, Wright painted a series of "entertaining" scenes of scientific experiments, including this work.

The eighteenth century was an age of rapid technological advances and the development of the air pump was among its most innovative scientific achievements. Although it was employed primarily to study the property of gases, it was also widely used to promote the public's interest in science because of its dramatic possibilities. In the experiment shown here, air was pumped out of the large glass bowl until the small creature inside, a bird, collapsed from lack of oxygen; before the animal died, air was reintroduced by a simple mechanism at the top of the bowl. In front of an audience of adults and children, a lecturer is shown on the verge of reintroducing air into the glass receiver. Near the window at the right—through which a full moon references the Lunar Society—a boy stands ready to lower a cage when the bird revives. By delaying the reintroduction of air, the scientist has created considerable suspense, as the reactions of the two girls indicate. Their father attempts to dispel their fears with a voice of reason.

The dramatic lighting not only underscores the life-and-death issue of the bird's fate but also suggests that science brings light into a world of darkness and ignorance. The lighting adds a spiritual dimension as well. During the Baroque era, such intimate lighting effects had been used for religious scenes (see fig. 14–9). Here science replaces religion as humanity's great light and hope, a theme emphasized by the rapt expressions of some of the observers.

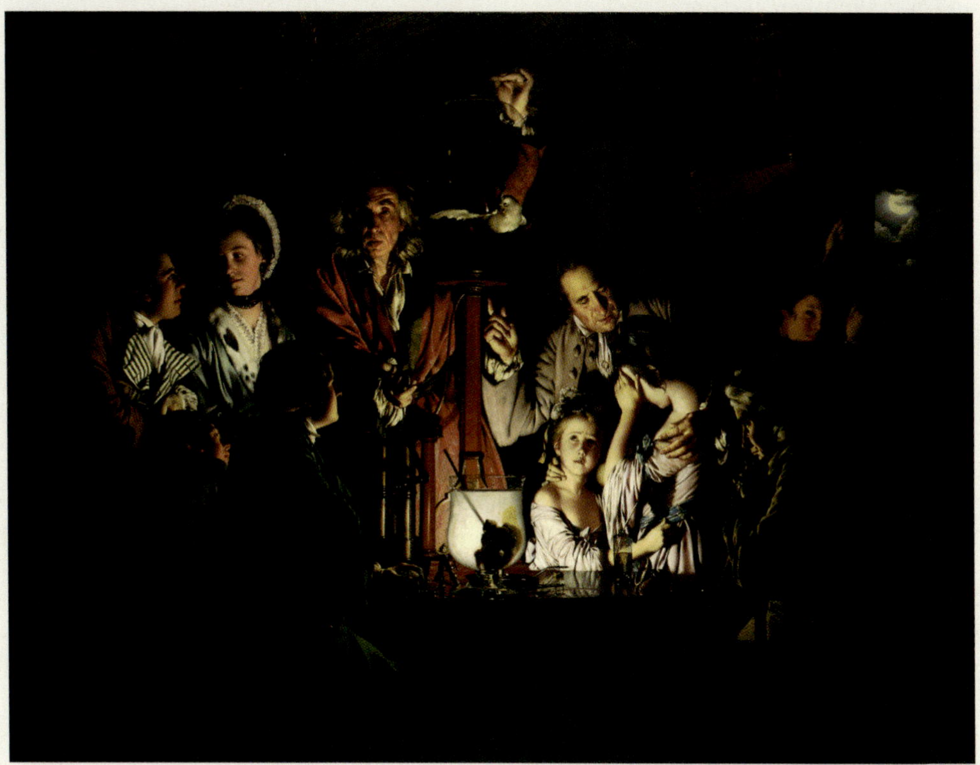

17–9 Joseph Wright. ***An Experiment on a Bird in the Air-Pump.*** 1768. Oil on canvas, 6' × 8' (1.83 × 2.44 m). The National Gallery, London

spirals, garlands, rosettes, and gilded moldings are luxuriously profuse yet are restrained by the strong geometric order imposed on them (fig. **17–10**). Adam's preference for bright pastel colors and small-scale decorative elements derives both from Rococo and the recently uncovered ruins of Pompeii (see Chapter 6). Such interiors were designed partly as settings for the art collections of British aristocrats, which included antiquities as well as a range of Neoclassical painting, sculpture, and decorative arts.

Neoclassicism continued as the dominant architectural style in the United States during the Federal Period (1783–1830) that followed the colonies' victory in their War of Independence. Thomas Jefferson (1743–1826), an enthusiastic amateur architect, had in the 1770s designed his Virginia residence, Monticello, in a style influenced by ancient Roman architecture and British Palladian villas, with direction from Palladio's *Four Books of Architecture*. But when Jefferson went to Paris as the American ambassador to France from 1785 to 1789, he discovered an elegant domestic architecture that made his home seem provincial. When he returned to Monticello in 1793, he completely redesigned Monticello, using French doors and tall narrow windows (fig. **17–11**), placing a balustrade above the unifying cornice to mask the second floor. Despite these French elements and his stated rejection of the British Palladian mode, the building's simplicity and combination of temple front and dome remain closer to English than to French buildings.

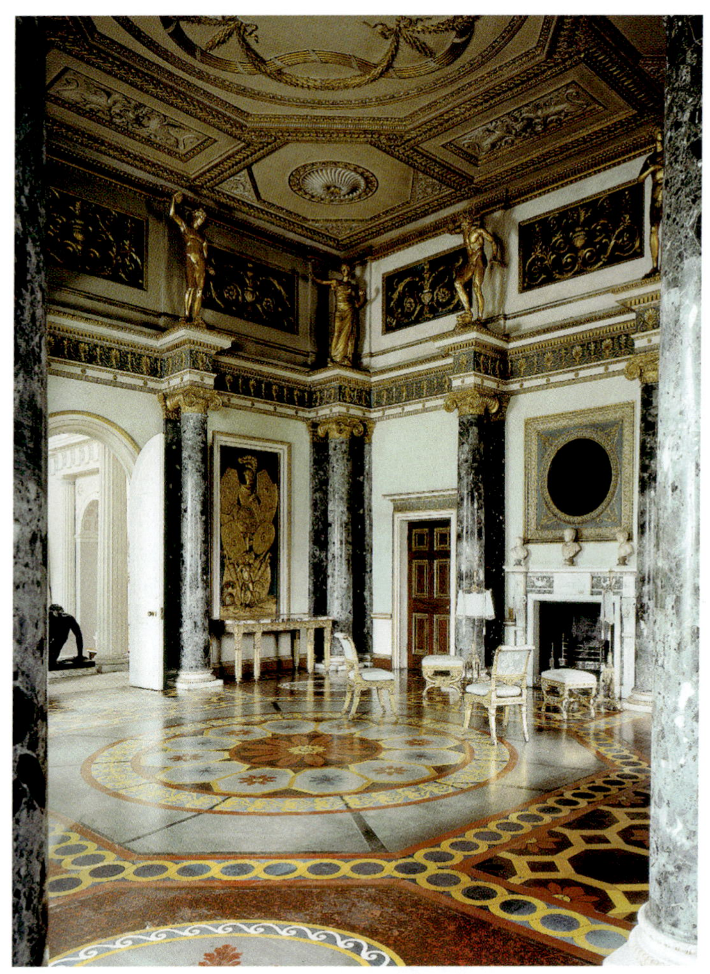

17–10 Robert Adam. Anteroom, Syon House, Middlesex, England. 1760–1769

Adam's conviction that it was acceptable to modify details of the Classical orders was generally opposed by the British architectural establishment. As a result of that opposition, Adam was never elected to the Royal Academy.

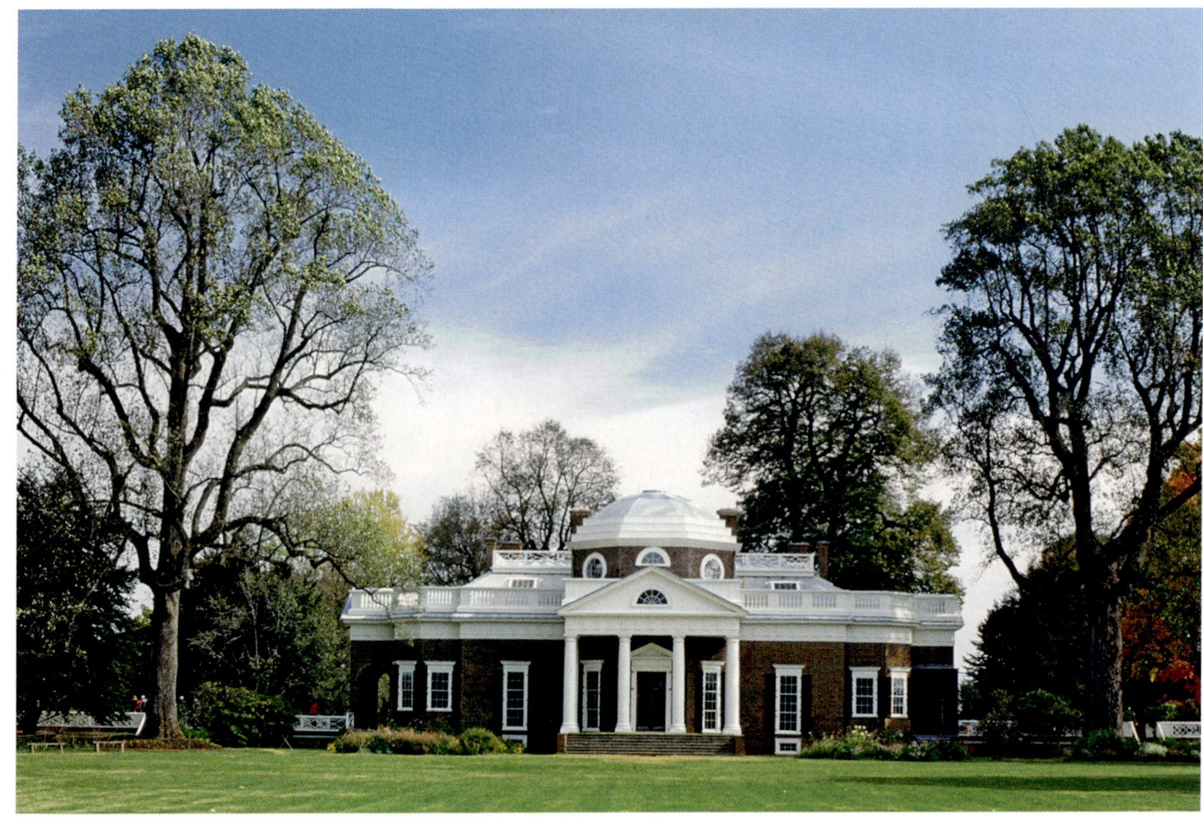

17–11 Thomas Jefferson. Monticello, near Charlottesville, Virginia. 1769–1782, 1796–1809

CLOSER LOOK

During the Georgian period, wealthy British families filled their homes with objects made of fine silver. The utensils and vessels they collected were not simply practical articles; they signified high social status.

Gentlefolk employed finely crafted silver vessels to serve and consume punch and drank from cups or simple but elegant goblets such as this one by Ann and Peter Bateman, which has a gilded interior to protect the silver from the acid present in alcoholic drinks. Hester Bateman's double beaker, also with a gilded interior, was made for use while traveling. The punch was served with a ladle such as the one shown here, by Elizabeth Morley, which has a twisted whalebone handle that floats, making it easy to retrieve from the punch bowl. Filled goblets would be offered on a flat salver like this one made by Elizabeth Cooke. Gentlemen also used silver containers to carry snuff, a pulverized tobacco that was inhaled by well-to-do members of both sexes. The flat snuffbox, by Alice and George Burrows, has curved sides for easy insertion into the pockets of a gentleman's tight-fitting trousers.

All the objects shown here bear the marks of silver shops run either wholly or partly by women, who played a significant role in the production of Georgian silver (fig. **17–12**). While some women served formal apprenticeships and went on to become members of the goldsmiths' guild (which included silversmiths), most women became involved with silver through their relation to a master silversmith—typically a father, husband, or brother—and they frequently specialized in a specific aspect of the craft, such as engraving, chasing, or polishing. The widows of silversmiths often took over their husbands' shops and ran them with the help of journeymen or partners.

Hester Bateman (1708–1794), the most famous woman silversmith in eighteenth-century Britain, inherited her husband's small spoon-making shop at age 52 and transformed it into one of the largest silver manufactories in the country. Adapting new technologies of mass production to the manufacture of silver, Bateman marketed her well-designed, functional, and relatively inexpensive wares to the newly affluent middle class, making no attempt to compete with those silversmiths who catered to the monarchy or the aristocracy. She retired when she was 82 after training her daughter-in-law Ann and her sons and grandson to carry on the family enterprise.

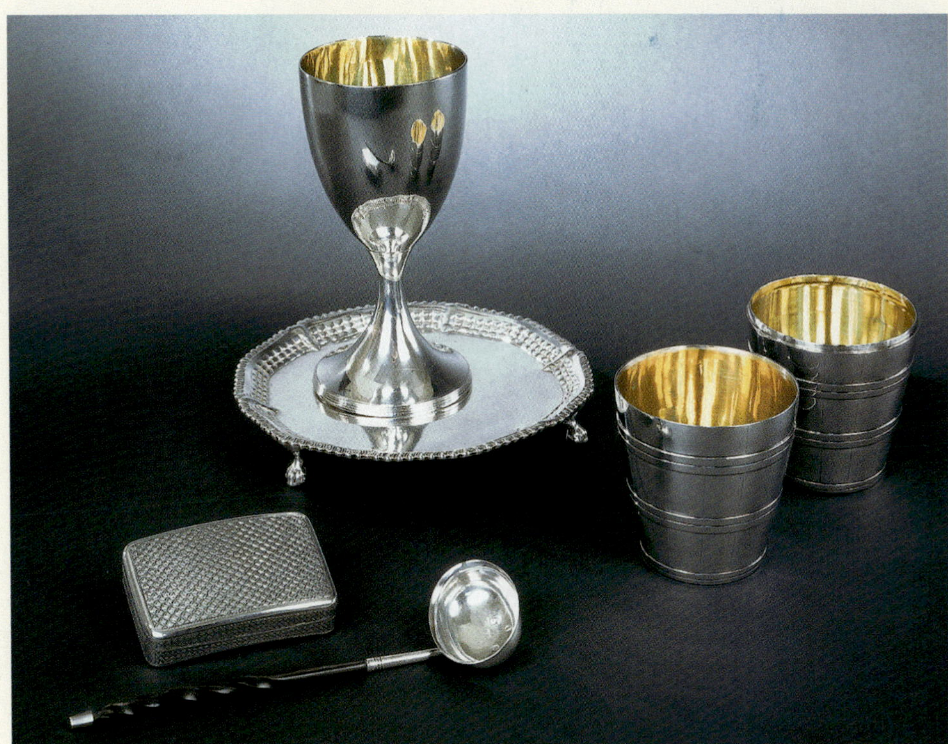

17–12 Elizabeth Morley. George III toddy ladle, 1802; **Alice and George Burrows. George III snuffbox,** 1802; **Elizabeth Cooke. George III salver,** 1767; **Ann and Peter Bateman. George III goblet,** 1797; **Hester Bateman. George III double beaker,** 1790. National Museum of Women in the Arts, Washington, D.C.

SILVER COLLECTION ASSEMBLED BY NANCY VALENTINE, PURCHASED WITH FUNDS DONATED BY MR. AND MRS. OLIVER GRACE AND FAMILY

France

Portraiture

In France a reaction against Rococo had solidified during the 1760s, and many French artists began to work in more classicizing modes. For some years they expressed their new sobriety through their choice of subject matter, while still retaining Rococo coloring and composition. Marie-Louise-Élisabeth Vigée-Lebrun's portrait of the French queen, Marie Antoinette, and her children falls into this mode (fig. **17–13**). Painted two years before the outbreak of the French Revolution, this work by the queen's favorite painter is a flagrant piece of royal propaganda. The court had hoped that the queen's depiction as the "good mother"—a theme already seen in Angelica Kauffman's painting of Cordelia (see fig. 17–8)—would counter her public image as immoral, extravagant, and conniving. Marie Antoinette's youngest son squirms on her lap, and her daughter leans affectionately against her. In a poignant touch, the older son points to the empty cradle of a recently deceased sibling. The image of Marie Antoinette as a loving mother surrounded by her children represented the ideal expounded by Enlightenment philosophers, especially the influential French-Swiss theorist Jean-Jacques Rousseau (1712–1778), who concluded that men and women should conform to the roles assigned to them by nature (i.e., biology), with women tending to the home and raising children, and men practicing learned professions, governing the state, and taking other active roles in public life.

In 1783, Vigée-Lebrun (1755–1842) was elected to one of the four places in the French Academy available to women (see "Art Academies in the Eighteenth Century," page 466). Also elected in that year was Adélaïde Labille-Guiard (1749–1803), who in 1790 successfully petitioned to end the restriction on entry for women. Labille-Guiard's commitment to increasing the number of women painters in France is reflected in a monumental but engaging self-portrait with two pupils (fig. **17–14**) that she submitted to the Salon of 1785. This image of the artist at her easel, although it flatters her conventional feminine charms in a manner derived from the Rococo tradition, was also meant to answer sexist rumors that her paintings and those by Vigée-Lebrun had actually been painted by men. In a witty role reversal, the only male to be seen is her father, and he is there only in a sculpted portrait bust at her side.

Neoclassicism: David and Ingres

In the 1770s, French history painter Jacques-Louis David (1748–1825) developed a truly Neoclassical style in paintings that have come to stand as ideal representatives of this artistic movement. In 1774, David had won the Prix de Rome, a competitive scholarship for study in Italy awarded to the top graduating students

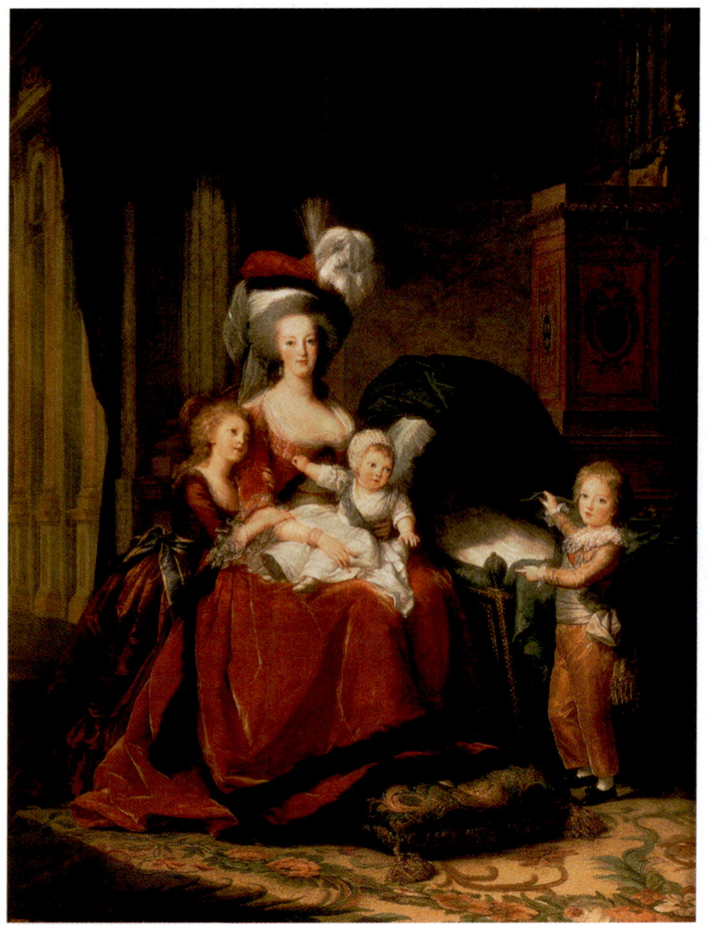

17–13 Marie-Louise-Élisabeth Vigée-Lebrun. ***Portrait of Marie Antoinette with her Children.*** 1787. Oil on canvas, 9' ¼" × 7' ⅝" (2.75 × 2.15 m). Musée Nationale du Château de Versailles

As the favorite painter of the queen, Vigée-Lebrun escaped from Paris with her daughter on the eve of the Revolution in 1789 and fled to Rome. After a very successful self-exile working in Italy, Austria, Russia, and England, the artist finally resettled in Paris in 1805 and again became popular with Parisian art patrons. Over her long career, she painted about 800 portraits in a vibrant style that changed very little over the decades.

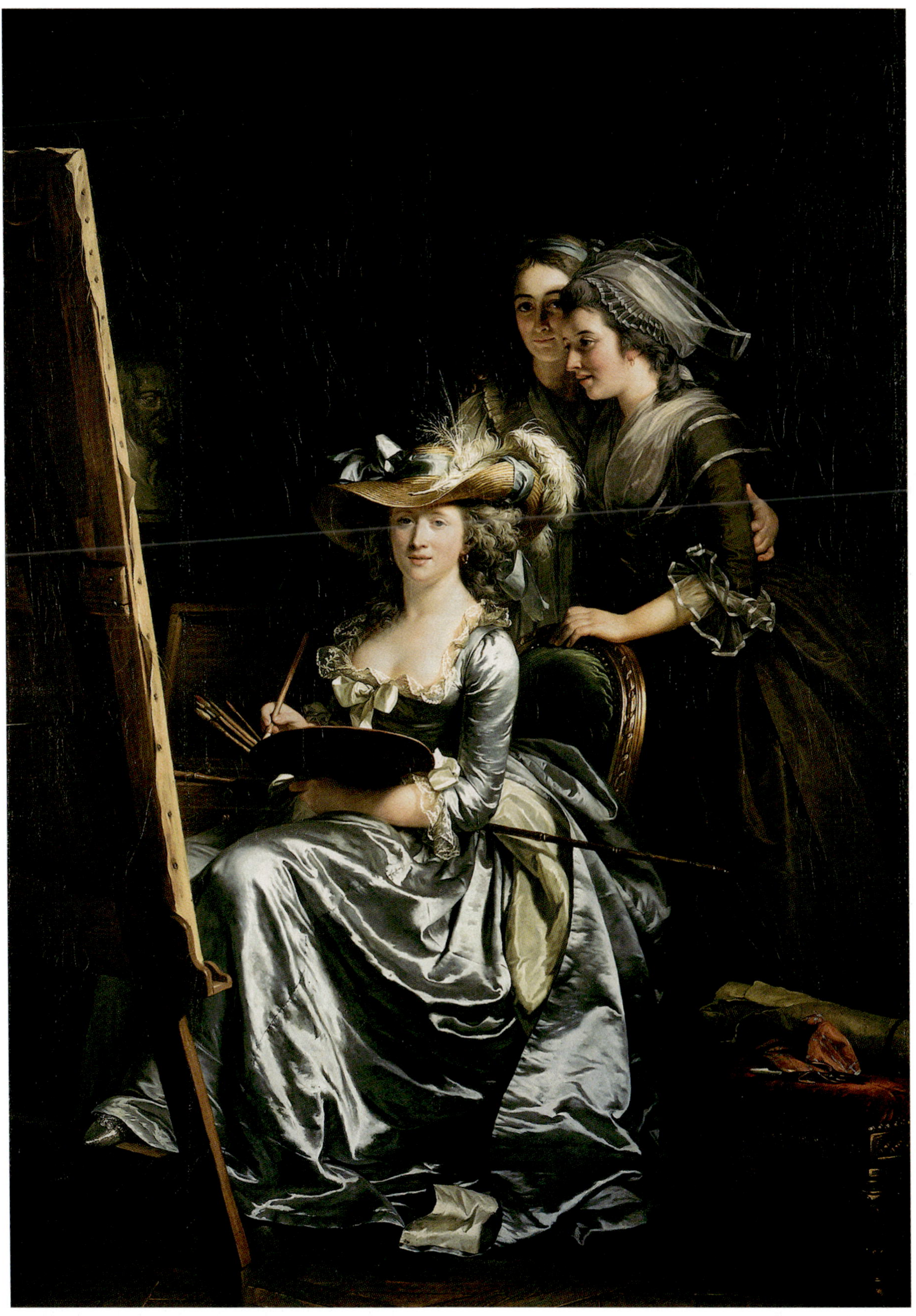

17–14 Adélaïde Labille-Guiard. ***Self-Portrait with Two Pupils, Mademoiselle Marie Gabrielle Capet (1761–1818) and Mademoiselle Carreaux de Rosemond (died 1788).*** 1785. Oil on canvas, 6' 11" × 4' 11½" (2.11 × 1.51 m). The Metropolitan Museum of Art, New York
GIFT OF JULIA A. BERWIND (53.2255)

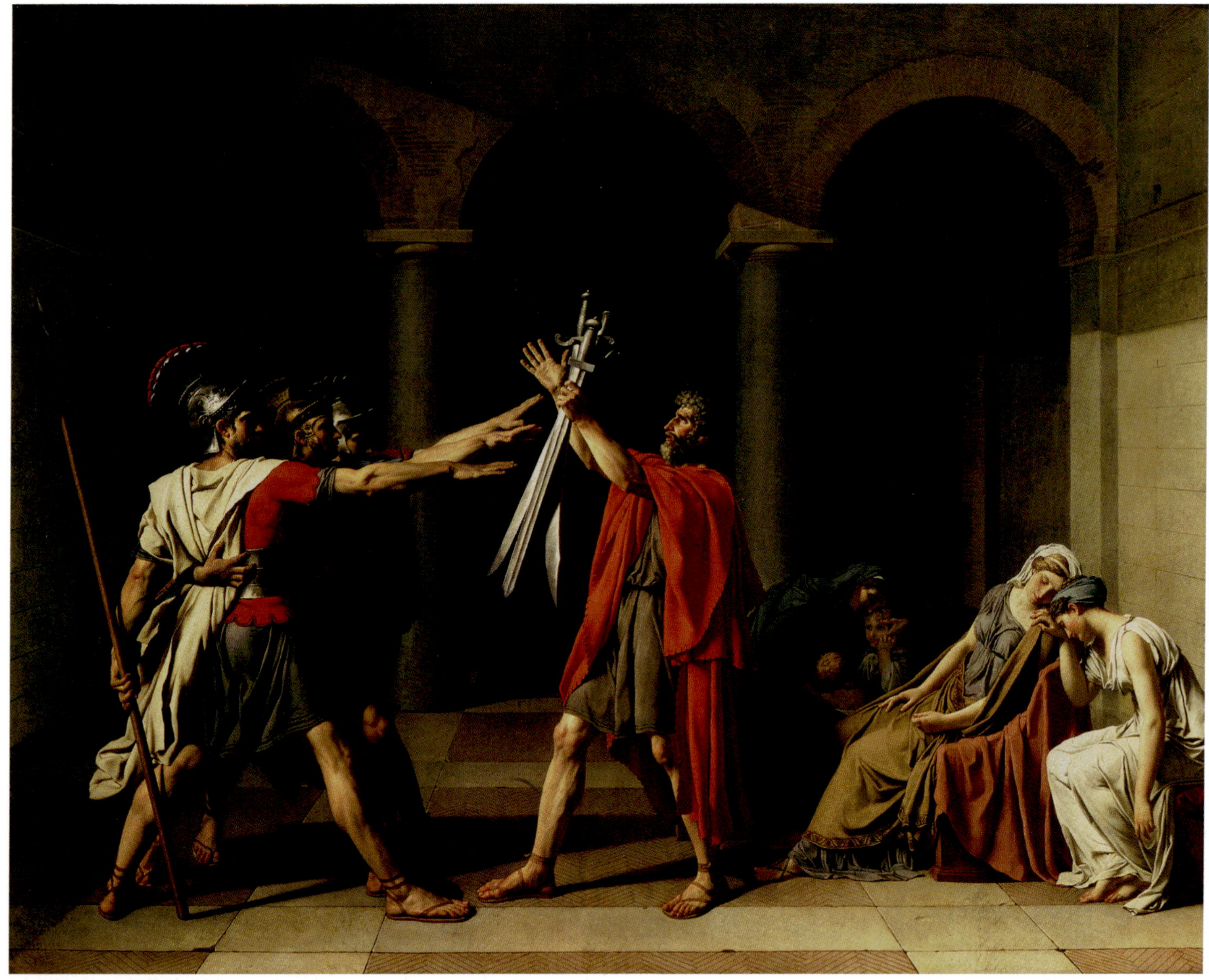

17–15 Jacques-Louis David. *Oath of the Horatii.* 1784–1785. Oil on canvas, 10' 8¼" × 14' (3.26 × 4.27 m). Musée du Louvre, Paris

from the French Academy's art school. During six years in Rome, David studied the art of Raphael and Michelangelo, the Baroque Classicism of Poussin and the Carracci, and above all, ancient Roman sculpture and frescoes. After his return to Paris, he produced a series of severe Classical paintings that extolled the antique virtues of moral incorruptibility, stoicism, courage, and patriotism. The first of these, painted as a royal commission, was the *Oath of the Horatii* of 1784–1785 (fig. **17–15**).

David's painting was inspired by Pierre Corneille's seventeenth-century drama *Horace*, that was itself based on ancient Roman history. David chose to invent for his painting, however, an incident—the Horatii taking an oath to fight to the death for Rome—that is not found in the play nor in any ancient text. The young men's father, Horace, standing at the center, administers the oath to his sons. To the right, Horace's daughter-in-law Sabina (from an enemy family) and his daughter Camilla (betrothed to Sabina's brother) both weep, knowing that whatever the outcome of the battle, they will inevitably lose someone dear to them. The tense, energetic young men with prominent glittering swords strike a powerful contrast to the limp swooning of the women, already mourning the tragedy to come, but the entire figural composition is stabilized by the interlocking of classical pyramidal groupings, coordinated with the measured rhythm of repeated arches in the background. The painting's moral message—valuing patriotic duty above personal interests and even family obligations—is expressed with such clarity and power that it created a sensation when David exhibited it in Rome and Paris in early 1785.

David's *Oath* became an emblem of the French Revolution of 1789, which, ironically, precipitated the downfall of the monarchy that had commissioned the work. Its harsh lesson in republican

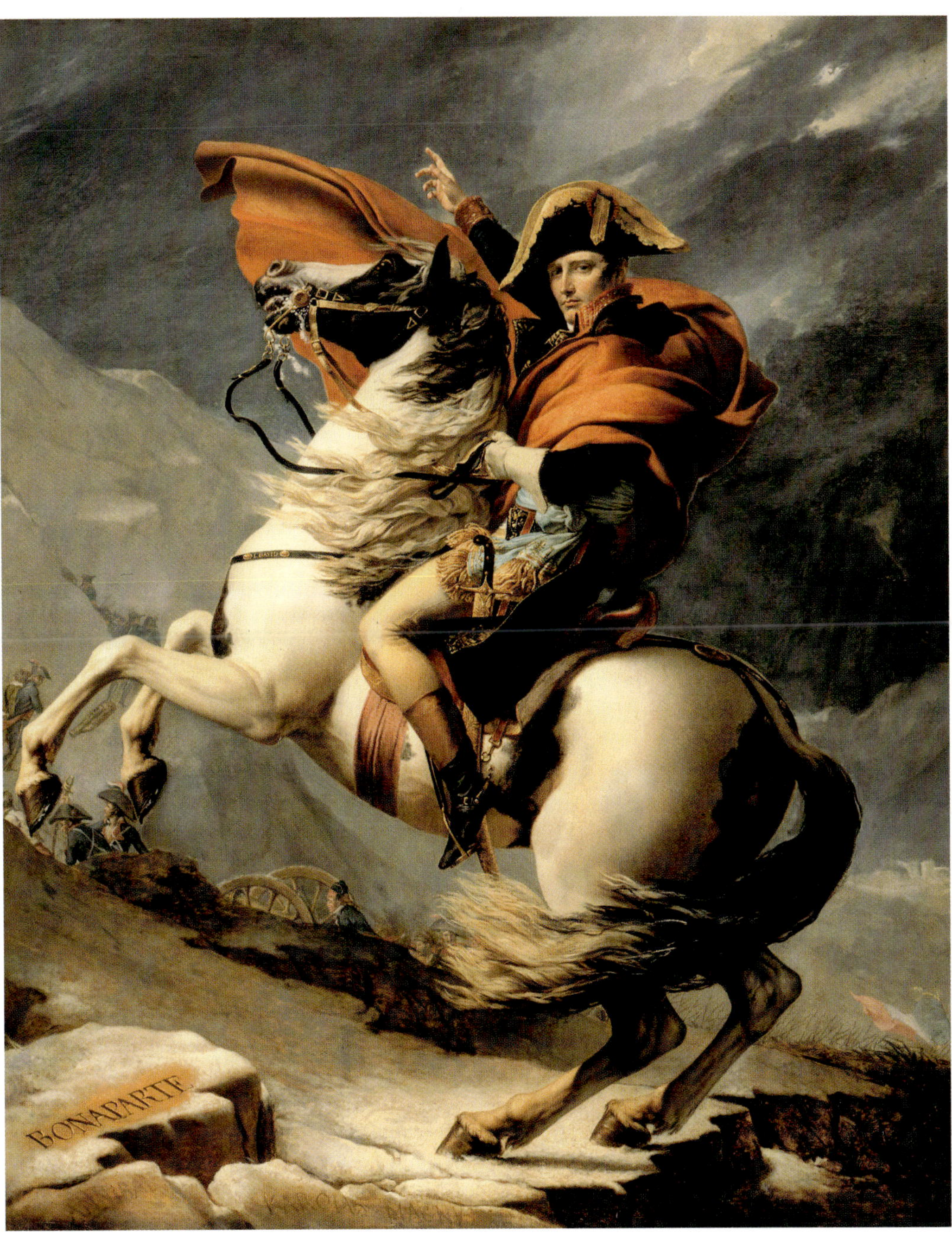

17–16 Jacques-Louis David. *Napoleon Crossing the Saint-Bernard*. 1800–1801. Oil on canvas, 8' 11" × 7' 7" (2.7 × 2.3 m). Musée National du Château de la Malmaison, Rueil-Malmaison

citizenship effectively captured the mood of the new leaders of the French state who came to power in 1793—especially the Jacobins, egalitarian democrats who abolished the monarchy and presided over the Reign of Terror in 1793–1794, unprecedented in its appetite for murderous vengeance. The initial French Republic ended in 1799 when the government was reorganized under Napoleon Bonaparte, a popular and successful general. After Napoleon was named emperor in 1804, David became his court painter.

Even before that time, David had produced canvases that turned Napoleon into an iconic, larger-than-life figure. *Napoleon Crossing the Saint-Bernard* (fig. **17–16**), painted during 1800–1801, is an idealized vision of the future emperor leading his troops across the Alps into Italy. Although Napoleon actually made the crossing on a donkey, here he charges up the mountain on a rearing horse, past rocks incised with his name and the names of his heroic predecessors, Hannibal and Charlemagne. While strongly Neoclassical in its firm drawing and crisp delineation of individual forms, the painting's sweeping diagonals and flowing draperies recall the idealized Grand Manner of the Baroque. David's career had become so closely linked with Napoleon that when Napoleon fell from power in 1814, David went into exile in Brussels, where he died in 1825.

As the leading force in French painting during the Revolutionary and Napoleonic eras, David trained many young artists, among them the highly talented Jean-Auguste-Dominique Ingres (1780–1867), who thoroughly absorbed his teacher's Neoclassicism yet interpreted it in a new manner. Inspired more by

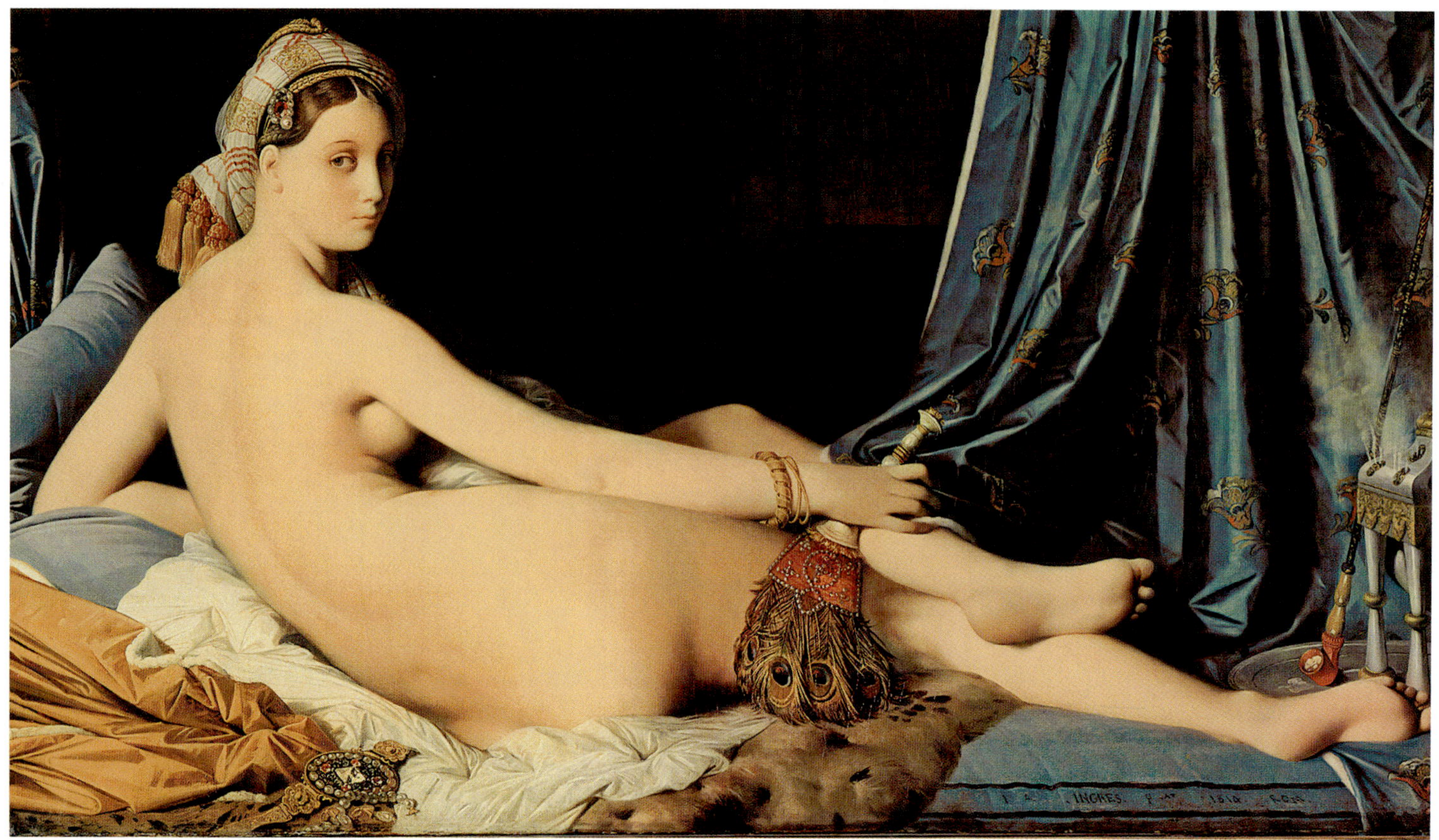

17–17 Jean-Auguste-Dominique Ingres. *Large Odalisque*. 1814. Oil on canvas, approx. 35" × 64" (88.9 × 162.5 cm). Musée du Louvre, Paris

During Napoleon's campaigns against the British in North Africa, the French discovered the exotic Near East. Upper-middle-class men were particularly attracted to the patriarchal institutions they encountered abroad, perhaps in part as a reaction against the demands for equality being made by French women inspired by the revolutions of the eighteenth century.

Raphael than by antique art, Ingres emulated the Renaissance artist's graceful lyricism, precise drawing, and idealized forms. Ingres won the Prix de Rome and lived in Italy from 1806 to 1824, ultimately returning in 1835 to serve as director of the French Academy in Rome until 1841.

Ingres most successful paintings were sultry portraits of aristocratic women and exotic, orientalizing fantasies featuring nude odalisques (female slaves or concubines living in a Turkish sultan's harem). In the *Large Odalisque* (fig. **17–17**) of 1814, the look the woman levels at her master, while turning her naked body away from what we assume is his gaze, makes her simultaneously erotic and aloof. The cool blues of the couch and the curtain at the right heighten the effect of the woman's warm skin, while the tight angularity of the crumpled sheets accentuates the languid, sensual contours of her body. Ingres' virtuosity in defining three-dimensional form and differentiating surface textures is so dazzling that we are hardly aware of the physical medium of paint that has brought them into being.

Although Ingres' commitment to fluid line and elegant postures was grounded in his Neoclassical training, he treated a number of fantasy themes, such as the odalisque, in a highly personal fashion that suggests Romanticism. Note the elongation of the woman's back (she seems to have several extra vertebrae); the widening of her hip; and her tiny, seemingly boneless feet. They may be anatomically incorrect, but they are aesthetically compelling. As a teacher and theorist, Ingres established the taste of a generation and helped ensure the dominance of Neoclassicism over a strong subcurrent of Romanticism in French painting well into the nineteenth century.

Romanticism: Géricault and Delacroix

Romanticism, already anticipated in French painting during Napoleon's reign, did not gain wide public acceptance until after 1830. Artists who painted in this style began to draw on new literary sources; they also added a new dimension of social criticism. Their dramatic presentations were intended to stir public emotions,

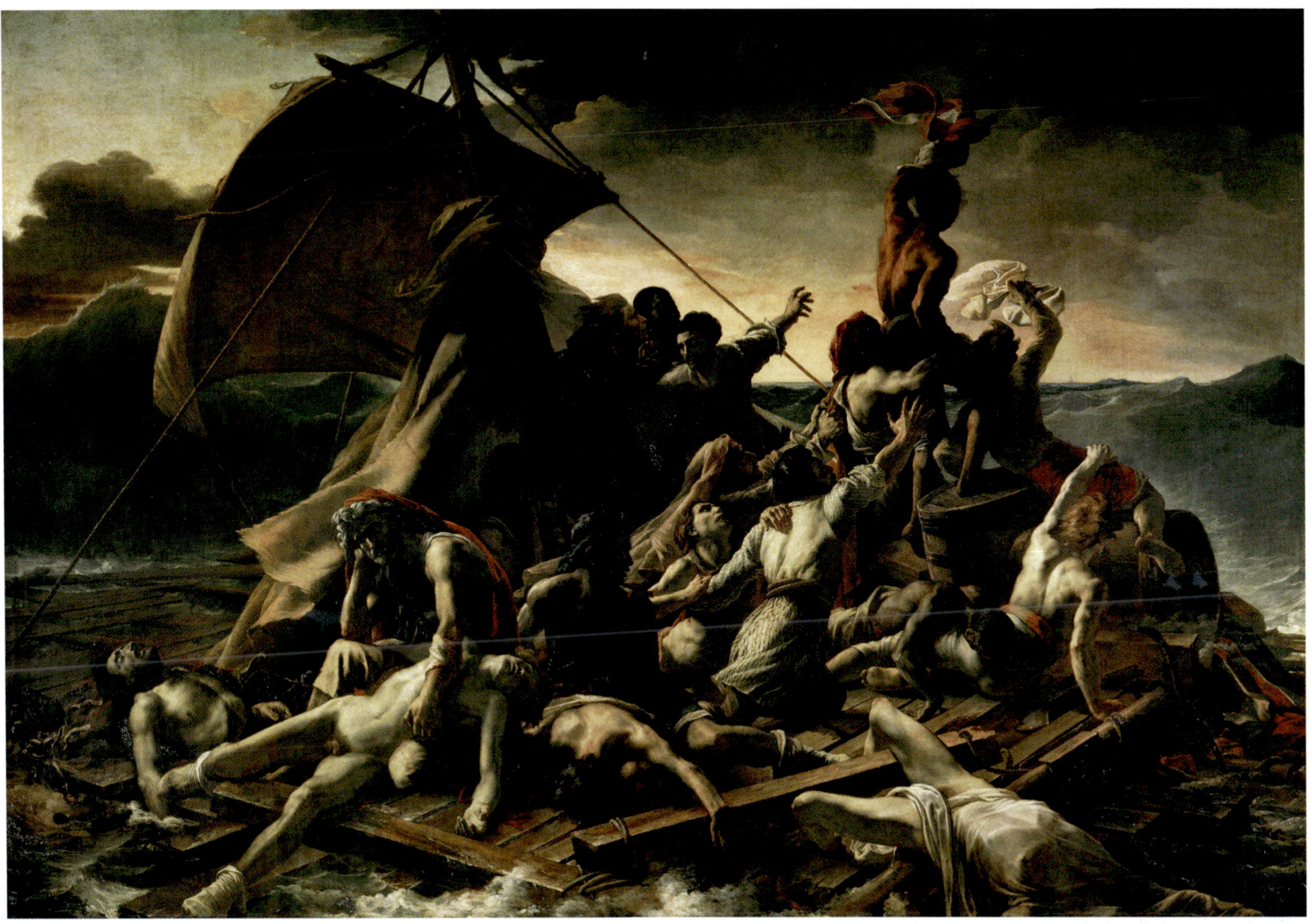

17–18 Théodore Géricault. *The Raft of the "Medusa."* 1818–1819. Oil on canvas, 16' 1" × 23' 6" (4.9 × 7.16 m). Musée du Louvre, Paris

especially in the work of Théodore Géricault (1791–1824) and Eugène Delacroix (1798–1863).

After a brief stay in Rome between 1816 and 1817, Géricault returned to Paris determined to make a great painting of a contemporary event, settling on the scandalous and sensational shipwreck of the *Medusa* for his subject (fig. **17–18**). In 1816, a ship carrying colonists headed for Madagascar ran aground near its destination; its captain was an incompetent aristocrat appointed by the newly restored monarchy for political reasons. Because there were insufficient lifeboats for all on board, the captain reserved them for himself and his officers, consigning the 152 passengers and crew to a hastily built raft, which tossed about on stormy seas for nearly two weeks before it was found. The 15 passengers who had managed to survive over this period had subsisted for the last days of their horrific voyage on human flesh. Géricault decided to show the moment when they first spotted their rescue ship, their survival not yet assured.

The artist's academic training underlies the painting's careful organization, constructed as a series of interlocking triangular figural groups. The outstretched arms of the victims lead viewers' eyes to the upper right, where the climactic figure of Jean Charles, an African survivor, is held aloft, waving a red cloth to attract the attention of a ship that is still only a speck on the stormy horizon. By placing a black man at the top of the pyramid of survivors and giving him the power to save his comrades by signaling the rescue ship, Géricault suggests that freedom for all will occur only when the most oppressed member of society is emancipated.

At the Salon of 1819, Géricault showed this painting under the neutral title *A Shipwreck Scene*, perhaps to downplay its contemporary political critique and deflect attention to a larger philosophical theme—the eternal struggle of humanity against the elements. Most contemporary French critics, however, were not fooled, and interpreted the painting as a political commentary. Liberals praised it for exposing the scandal, and royalists condemned it as sensationalist

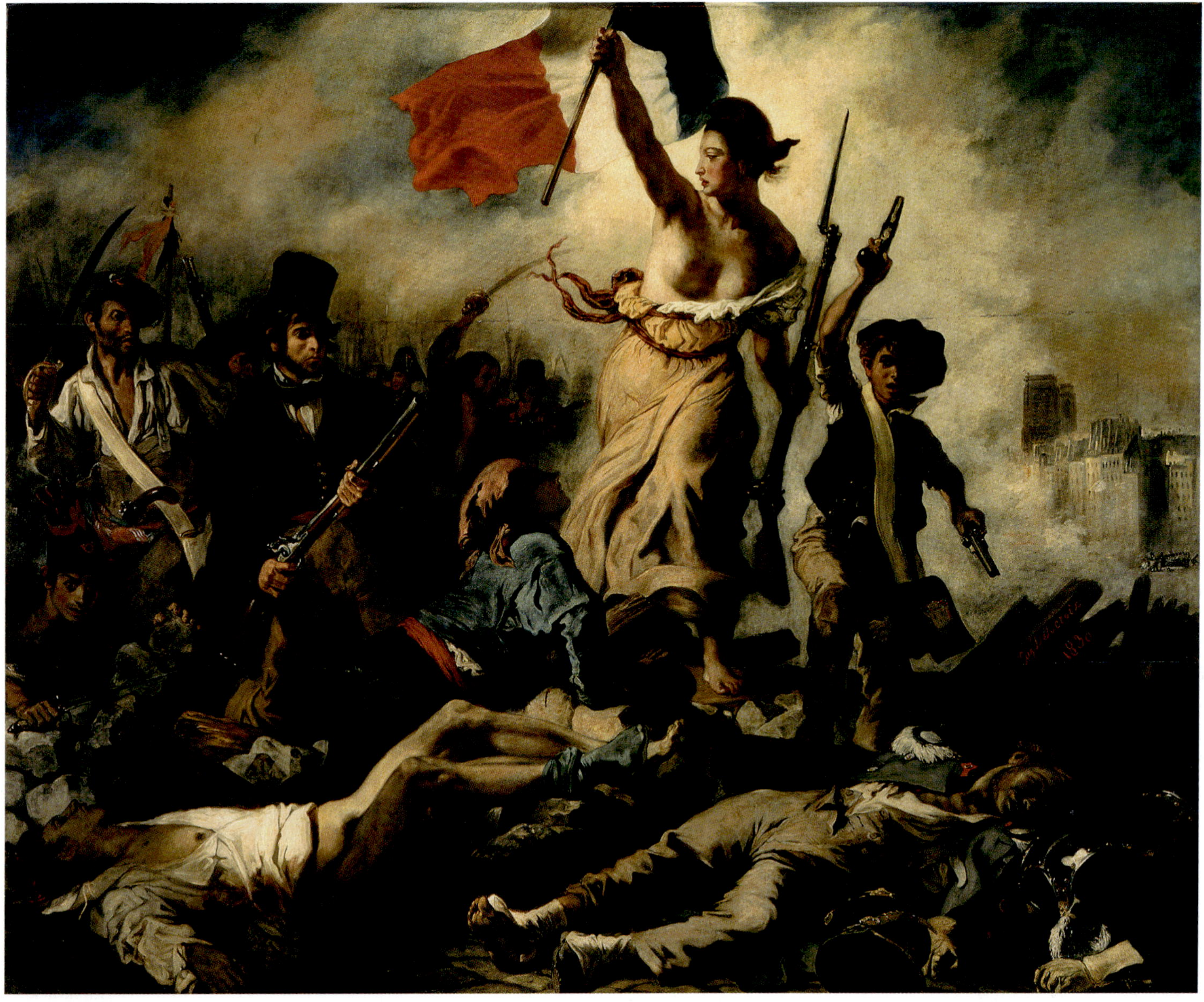

17–19 Eugène Delacroix. *Liberty Leading the People: July 28, 1830*. 1830. Oil on canvas, 8' 6½" × 10' 8" (2.6 × 3.25 m). Musée du Louvre, Paris

journalism rather than art. Because the monarchy refused to buy it, Géricault exhibited *The Raft of the "Medusa"* commercially on a two-year tour of Ireland and England, where the London exhibition attracted more than 50,000 paying visitors. Today, the work remains a masterful illustration of human tragedy, revealing the injustice that often causes it, and inspiring responses of indignant compassion.

Eugène Delacroix, who modeled for one of the nude victims on Géricault's raft, soon succeeded him as the inspirational leader of the Romantic movement. *Liberty Leading the People: July 28, 1830* (fig. **17–19**)—his most famous work, now as well as then—summarized for many the destiny of France after the fall of Napoleon in 1815. The new constitutional monarchy undid many reforms instituted after the Revolution, including the reinstatement of press censorship, the return of education to Church control, and the limitation of voting rights. Public resentment ignited in a massive uprising in July 1930, and Delacroix's painting memorialized this revolt a few months after it took place. An allegorical figure of Liberty leads the revolutionaries—a motley crew of students, laborers, children, and top-hatted lawyers—into the midst of battle. This is not the record of an actual event but an imaginative artistic recreation, faithful to the emotional climate of the moment as the artist himself felt it.

Spain

In Spain, Francisco Goya y Lucientes (1746–1828) became the major figure in the Romantic movement, famous as both painter and printmaker. In 1799, he published *Los Caprichos* (*The Caprices*), the first of several suites of etchings he created during his career. Setting the tone for the series of 80 etchings is its frontispiece, *The Sleep of Reason Produces Monsters* (fig. **17–20**). Although the text published with the print sounds a hopeful note ("Imagination abandoned by reason produces impossible monsters; united with her, she is the mother of the arts and the source of their wonders"), the images are an angry attack on contemporary Spanish manners and morals that make Hogarth's satire (see fig. 17–6) seem tame. This introductory print shows a slumbering personification of Reason, behind whom lurk dark creatures of the night—owls, bats, and a cat—that are let loose when Reason sleeps. The following prints enumerate specific follies of Spanish life. Goya hoped they would alert Spanish people to the errors of their foolish ways and reawaken them to reason. The premise may be hopeful, but Goya's portrait of human folly and cruelty is bitter and disturbing. Far from Enlightenment faith in the inherent rationality and goodness of humanity, Goya believed that the violence, greed, and foolishness of his society had to be examined mercilessly if it were to be changed in any way.

Goya had begun his career as a court painter producing Rococo tapestry designs for royal manufacture, but by the turn of the century, his study of Velázquez and Rembrandt inspired him to freer brushwork, richer colors, and more dramatic presentations. In his large portrait of the *Family of Charles IV* (fig. **17–21**), Goya openly acknowledges the influence of Velázquez's *Las Meninas* (see fig. 14–13) by inserting himself behind a leaning canvas in the left background, mimicking Velázquez's composition. Unlike *Las Meninas*,

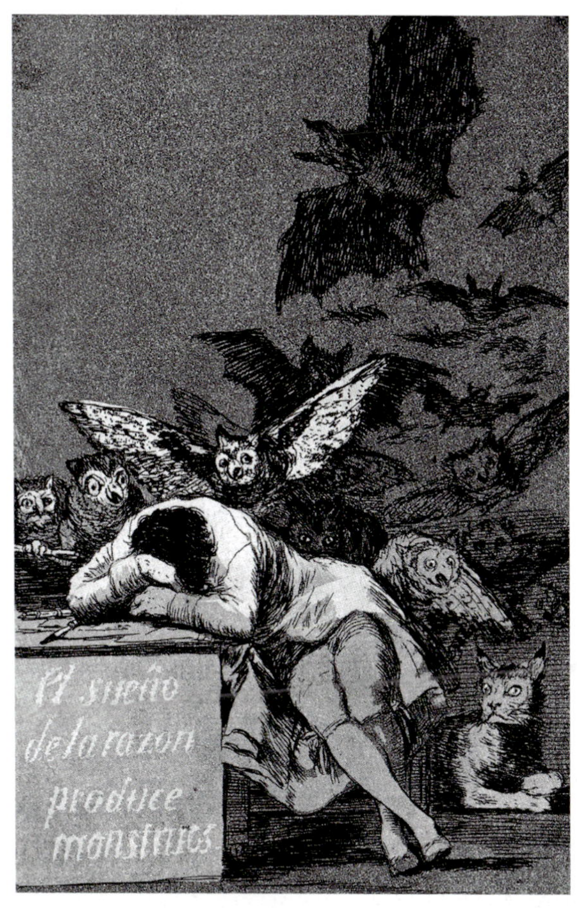

17–20 (ABOVE) **Francisco Goya.** ***The Sleep of Reason Produces Monsters,*** no. 43 from *Los Caprichos* (*The Caprices*). 1796–1798; published 1799. Etching and aquatint, 8½" × 6" (21.6 × 15.2 cm)
COURTESY OF THE HISPANIC SOCIETY OF AMERICA, NEW YORK

Goya offered the 300 sets of this series for sale in 1799 but withdrew them two days later without explanation. He was probably responding to a Church warning that if he did not, he might be called to appear before the Inquisition because of the unflattering portrayal of the Church in some of the etchings.

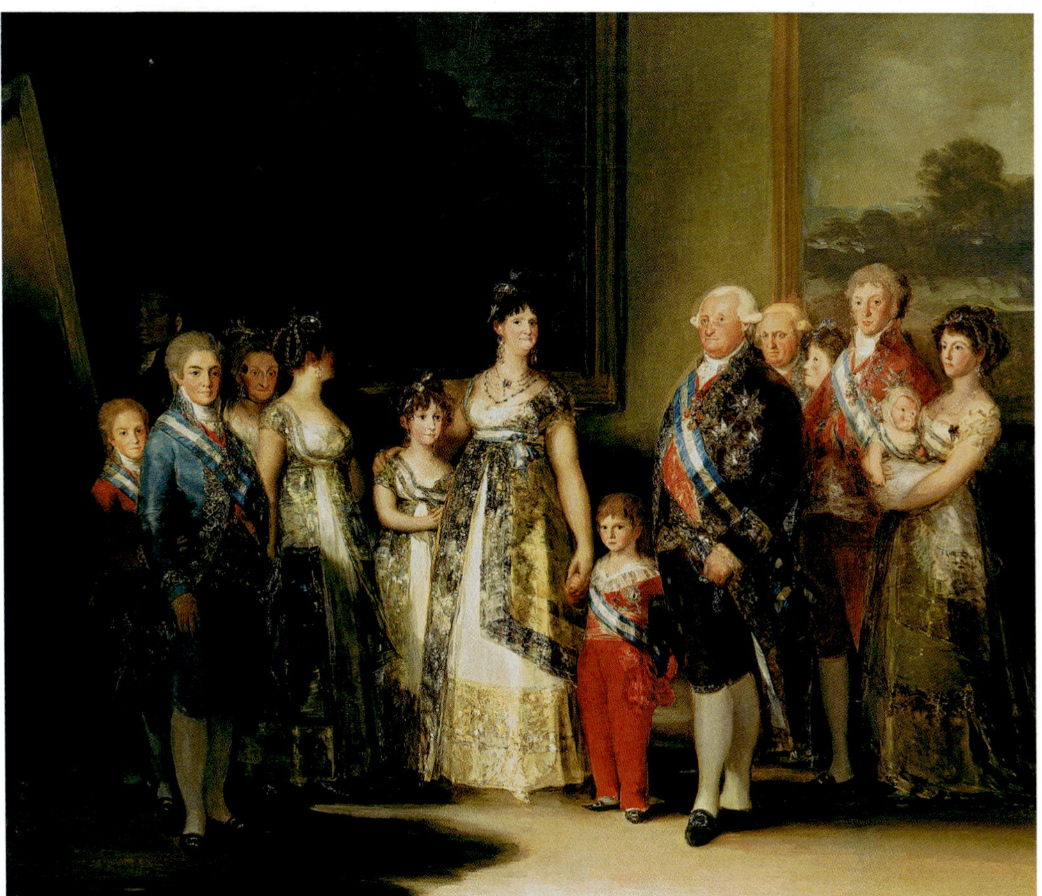

17–21 (LEFT) **Francisco Goya.** ***Family of Charles IV.*** 1800. Oil on canvas, 9' 2" × 11' (2.79 × 3.36 m). Museo del Prado, Madrid

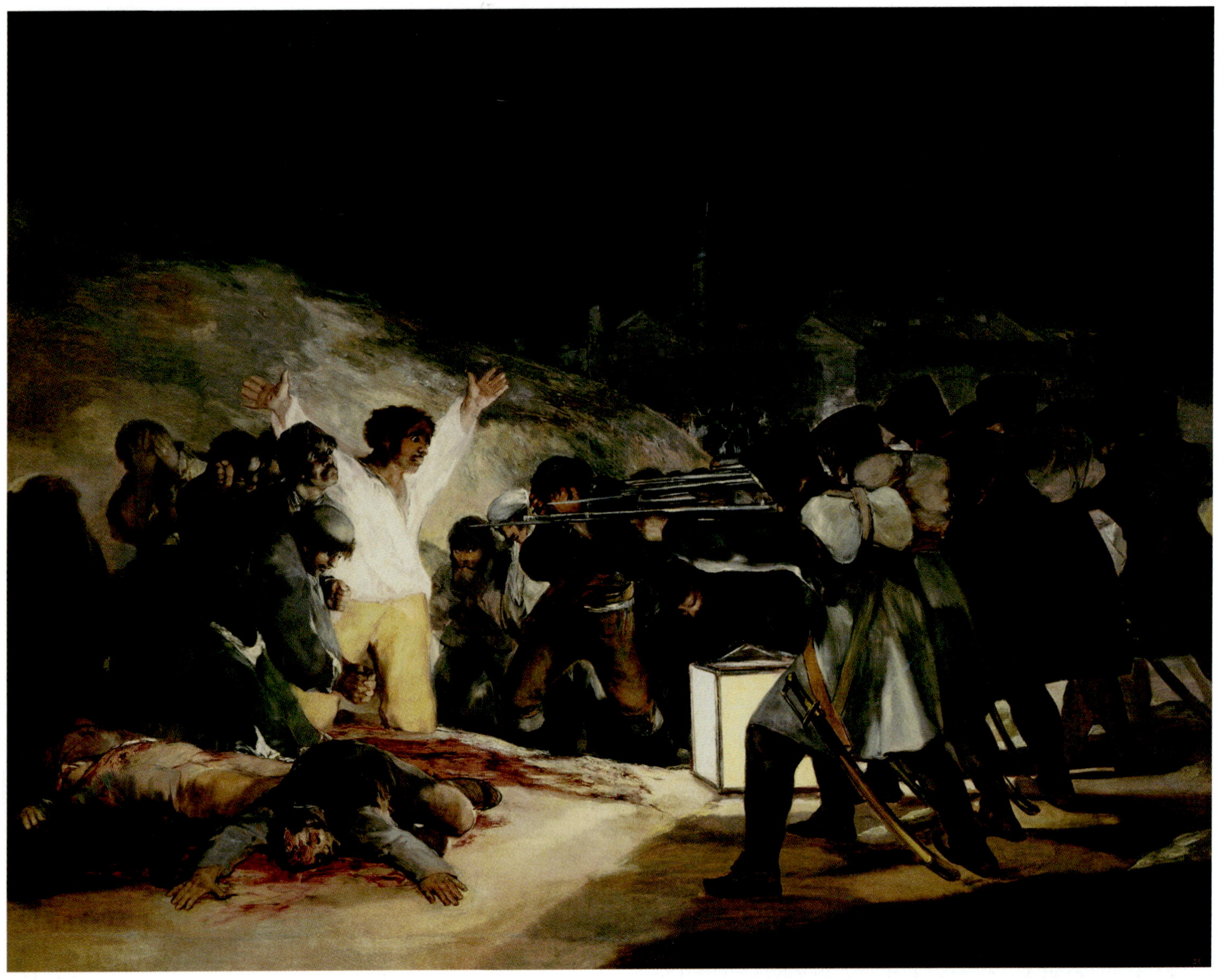

17–22 Francisco Goya. ***Third of May, 1808.*** 1814–1815. Oil on canvas, 8' 9" × 13' 4" (2.67 × 4.06 m). Museo del Prado, Madrid

however, Goya's painting is frank rather than flattering; some see the painting as a cruel exposé of the royal family as common, ugly, detached, and inept. Considering Goya's position as principal court painter, it is difficult to imagine him deliberately mocking his patrons in a royal commission. In fact, the family approved Goya's preparatory sketches for the painting. Viewers who first saw it in 1800 may have found it striking not because it was demeaning but because its candid representation was refreshingly modern.

In 1808, Napoleon conquered Spain and placed his brother Joseph Bonaparte on its throne. Many Spaniards, including Goya, at first welcomed the French because they hoped for liberal reforms, but the government soon turned despotic. On May 2, 1808, a rumor spread through Madrid that the French planned to kill the royal family. The populace rose up and a day of bloody street fighting ensued. Hundreds of Spanish people were herded into a convent and executed by a French firing squad in the pre-dawn hours of May 3rd. Goya commemorated the event in a painting (fig. **17–22**) where the violent gestures of the terrified rebels and the mechanical efficiency of the firing squad are like scenes from a nightmare. One man, spotlighted in a brilliant white shirt, confronts his faceless killers with outstretched arms recalling the crucified Jesus, an image of particular horror and pathos. This powerful work encapsulates the essence of Romanticism: the sensationalizing of a current event, the loose brushwork, the unbalanced composition, and the theatrical lighting. But Goya's painting is less an indictment of the French occupation than of the faceless and mechanical nature of war itself, unleashing dark impulses to destroy defenseless humanity. When asked why he painted such a brutal scene, Goya responded, "To warn men never to do it again."

Romantic Landscape Painting in England and America

Romanticism in England flourished in landscape painting. It took two forms—tranquil and dramatic. The tranquil style entailed closely observed representations of nature, meant to communicate reverence for the landscape as a spiritual precinct and to counteract the effects of industrialization and urbanization that were rapidly transforming it. In contrast, dramatic landscape painting emphasized turbulent or fantastic natural scenery, often shaken by natural disasters such as storms and avalanches, and aimed to stir viewers' emotions and arouse a feeling of the sublime. John Constable (1776–1837) specialized in carefully observed scenes of rural tranquility, while Joseph Mallord William Turner (1775–1851), focused on loosely painted studies of mood and drama.

Constable claimed that the landscape of his youth in southern England had made him a painter before he ever picked up a brush. In spite of his training at the Royal Academy, where landscape was considered an inferior subject for art, he was captivated by the landscapes of seventeenth-century Dutch artists, and decided to follow in their footsteps. *The White Horse* (fig. **17–23**) of 1819 draws on Constable's determination to base his paintings on careful studies of nature. Although he composed his paintings in his studio, he used sketches recorded on walking tours, insisting that art should be an objective record of things actually seen. His goal was to capture the time of day, the humidity in the air, the smell of wet earth. In this painting, a storm passes away to the right, while a farmer and his helpers ferry a workhorse across a river. Sunlight glistens off the water and foliage, an effect Constable achieved through tiny dabs of pure white paint.

Turner, Constable's contemporary, won public acclaim at an early age. By age 27, he was elected to full membership in the Royal

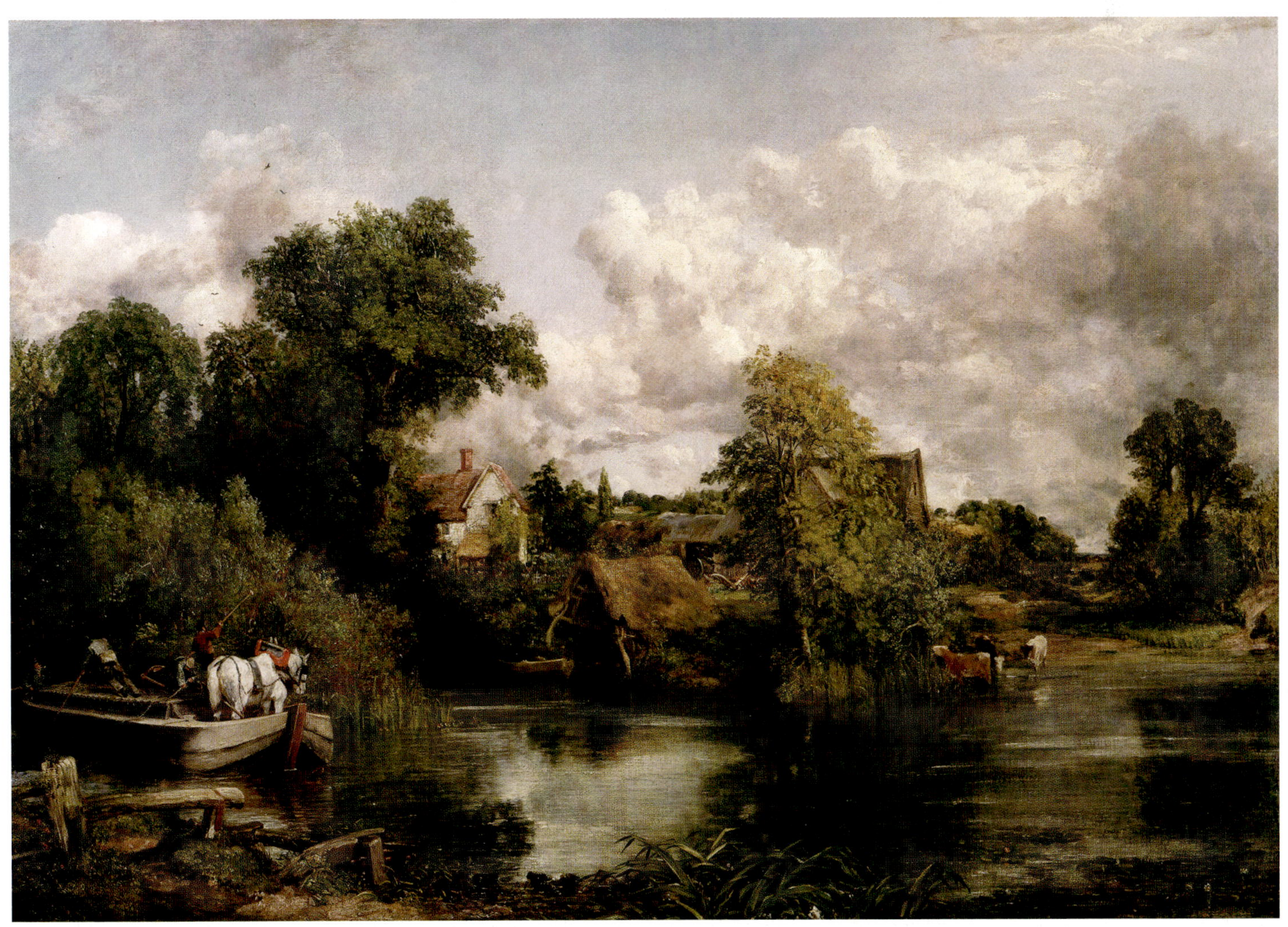

17–23 John Constable. *The White Horse.* 1819. Oil on canvas, 4' 3¾" × 6' 2⅛" (1.31 × 1.88 m). The Frick Collection, New York

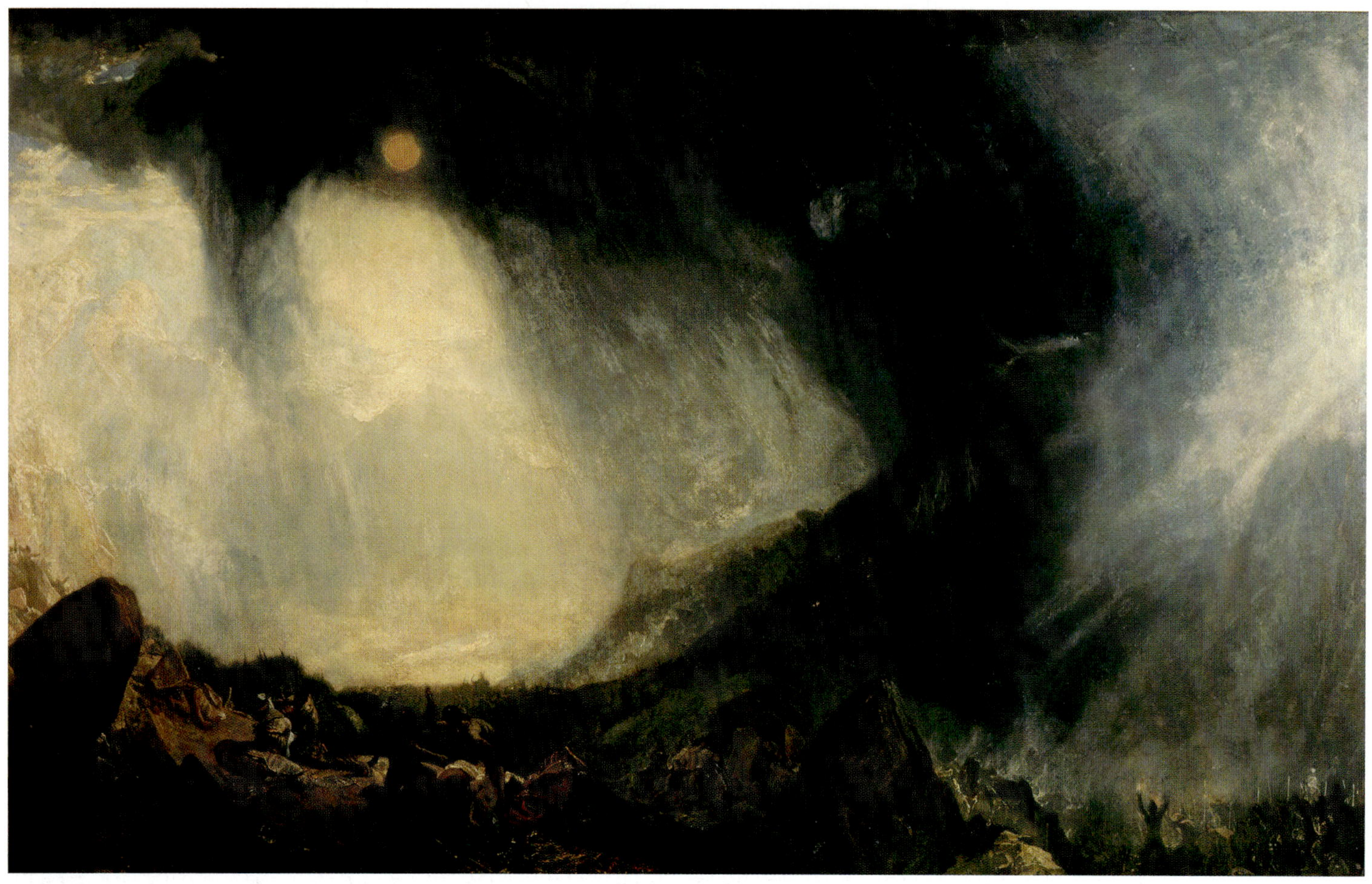

17–24 Joseph Mallord William Turner. ***Snowstorm: Hannibal and his Army Crossing the Alps.*** 1812.
Oil on canvas, 4' 9" × 7' 9" (1.46 × 2.39 m). Tate Gallery, London

Academy, eventually becoming a professor at the Royal Academy school. In his mature paintings, the phenomena of colored light and misty atmosphere became his true subject. To academicians, his works increasingly looked like sketches or preliminary underpainting of unfinished canvases, but to his admirers, including Constable, they were "golden visions, glorious and beautiful," painted with "tinted steam."

His *Snowstorm: Hannibal and his Army Crossing the Alps* (fig. **17–24**) epitomized Romanticism's view of the awesomeness of nature. An enormous vortex of wind, mist, and snow masks the sun and threatens to annihilate the soldiers marching below it. Barely discernible in the distance is the figure of Hannibal, mounted on an elephant to lead his troops through the Alps to meet the Roman army in 218 BCE. Turner probably meant his painting as an allegory of the Napoleonic Wars. Napoleon himself had crossed the Alps, an event celebrated by David in a laudatory portrait (see fig. 17–16). But while David's painting, which Turner saw in Paris in 1802, conceived Napoleon as a powerful figure, commanding not only his troops but nature itself, Turner reduced Hannibal to a speck on the horizon, threatened with his troops by natural disaster, as if foretelling their eventual defeat.

Turner's paintings also evoke notions of the **sublime**, an aesthetic category outlined by British writer Edmund Burke in an essay of 1756 that strongly influenced Romantic artists. According to Burke, when we witness something that instills fascination mixed with fear, or when we stand in the presence of something far larger than ourselves, our feelings will transcend those we encounter in normal life. The awe-inspiring aspect of savage grandeur, uncontrollable by mere humans, evokes the transcendent power of God. Turner translated this concept of the sublime into powerful paintings of turbulence in the natural world.

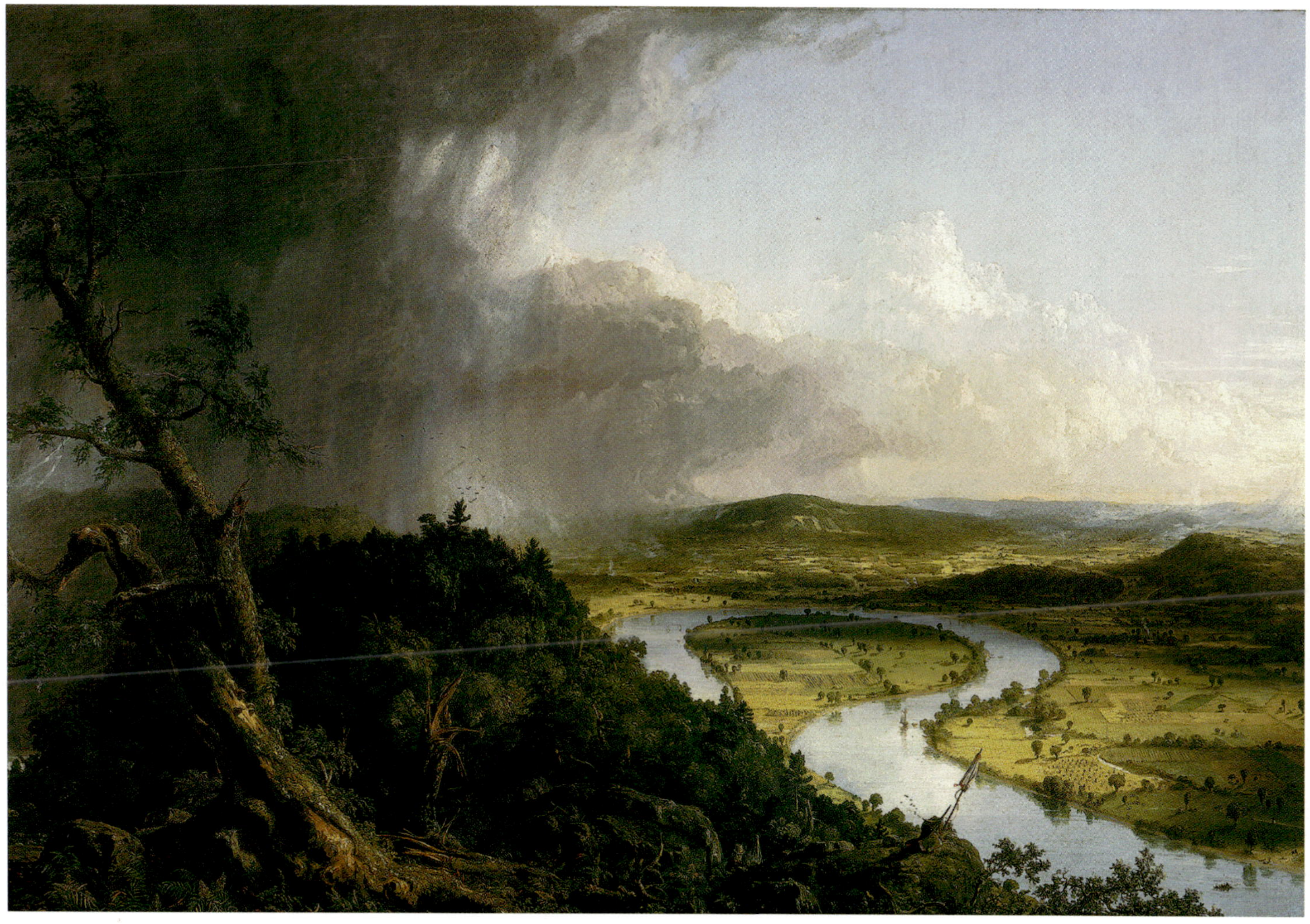

17–25 Thomas Cole. *The Oxbow*. 1836. Oil on canvas, 51½" × 76" (1.31 × 1.94 cm). The Metropolitan Museum of Art, New York
GIFT OF MRS. RUSSELL SAGE, 1908 (08.228)

If we place English Romantic landscape painters in a sequence, with those favoring imagination and drama at one end (Turner) and partisans of down-to-earth idylls on the other (Constable), we will find the middle ground occupied by American painters such as Thomas Cole (1801–1848). Cole emigrated from England to the United States at 17 and by 1820 was working as an itinerant portrait painter. On trips around New York state, he sketched and painted the landscape, which quickly became his chief interest as he launched what became known as the Hudson River School. Cole painted *The Oxbow* (fig. **17–25**) for exhibition at the National Academy of Design in New York. The monumental scale suits the dramatic view from the top of Mount Holyoke in western Massachusetts across a spectacular oxbow-shaped bend in the Connecticut River. To Cole, such ancient geological formations constituted America's "antiquities." Along a great sweeping arc produced by the departing dark clouds and the edge of the mountain, Cole contrasts two sides of the American landscape: dense, stormy wilderness and congenial pastoral valleys. The fading storm perhaps suggests that the wild will eventually give way to the civilized.

Along with such images of native scenery, pictures of everyday American life within the landscape were also popular. A leading American proponent was the first major painter to live and work in the western half of North America, Missouri artist George Caleb Bingham (1811–1879). With *Fur Traders Descending the Missouri*

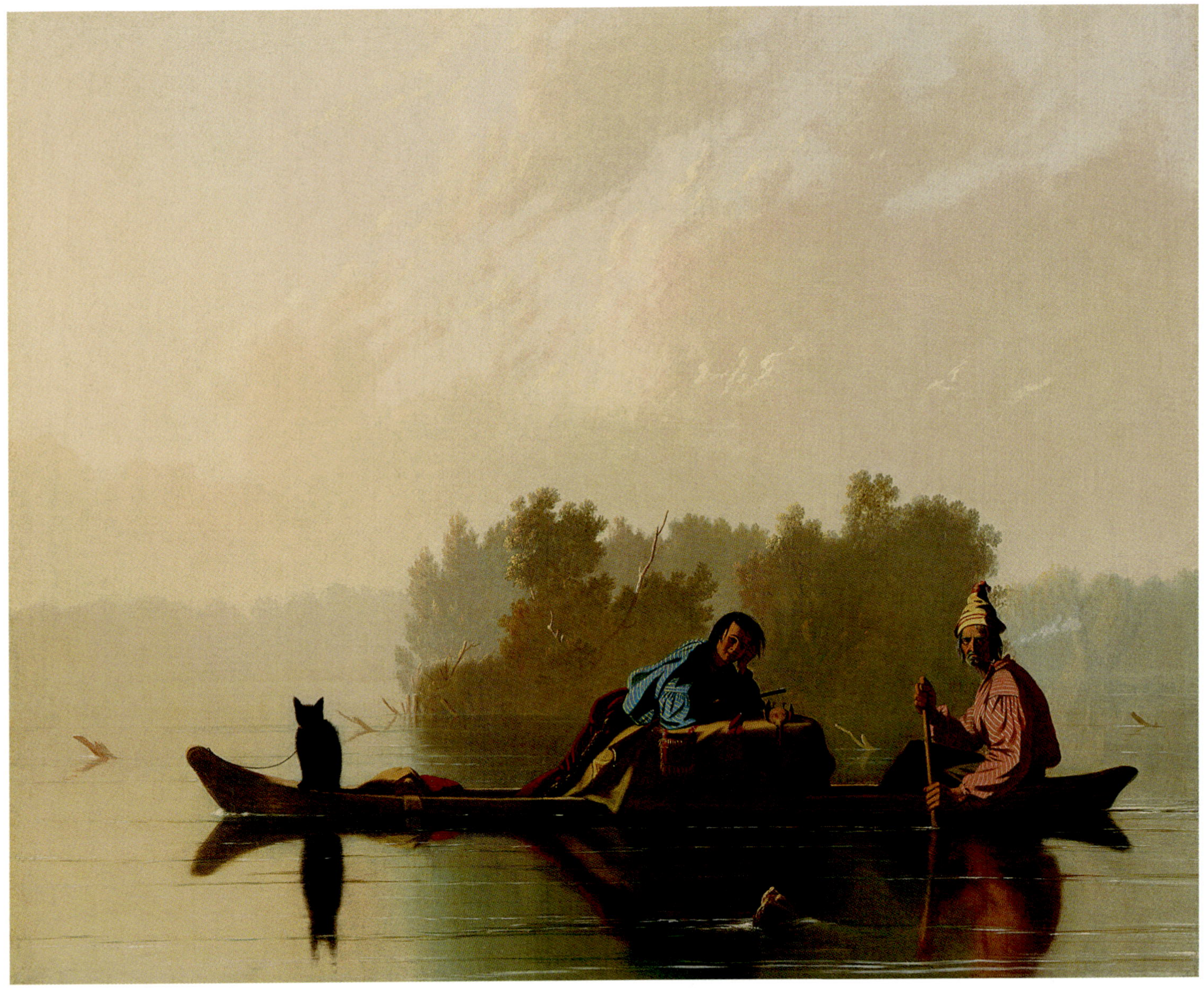

17–26 George Caleb Bingham. *Fur Traders Descending the Missouri.* c. 1845. Oil on canvas, 29" × 36½" (73.7 × 92.7 cm).
The Metropolitan Museum of Art, New York
MORRIS K. JESUP FUND, 1933 (33.61)

(fig. **17–26**), painted about 1845, Bingham began an association with the newly formed American Art Union in New York. To promote American painters, the Union purchased works for a flat fee, then reproduced prints of the paintings to be sold by subscription. Bingham sold this painting to the Union for $25. It is an idyllic scene of a French trapper and his son riding in a dugout canoe. As they glide through the early-morning stillness, the sun tinges the clouds with rosy gold and morning mists shroud the river landscape in mystery. Despite the peacefulness of the scene, there is an underlying ominous feeling. Branches and rocks stick out of the water, reminders of the hazards the boatmen faced, and the mysterious black shape of the chained pet mirrored in the glassy water surface produces an eerie effect. Bingham's scene is not only idealized but potentially nostalgic, for by the time it was painted the independent French voyageurs who had opened the fur trade using canoes had been replaced by trading companies using larger, more efficient craft. Bingham's painting records a vanished way of life with a sense of melancholy that seems to mourn its loss.

Early Photography

The development of photography in the early nineteenth century was a prime expression of the new, positivist interest in descriptive accuracy. Since the Renaissance, Westerners had been seeking a mechanical method for recording what is seen. One early device was the **camera obscura** (Latin for "dark chamber"). It consisted of a darkened room or box with a lens on one side through which light passed and projected onto the opposite side an upside-down image of the scene, which an artist could then trace. Photography was developed as a way to "fix"—that is, to make permanent—the visual impressions produced by a camera obscura, or camera, on light-sensitive material.

The first person to "fix" a photographic image was painter Louis-Jacques-Mandé Daguerre (1787–1851), who discovered that an exposure to light of only 20 to 30 minutes would produce a latent image on a silver-coated metal plate treated with iodine fumes, which could then be made visible through an after-process involving mercury vapor. By 1837, he had developed a method of fixing the image by bathing the plate in a strong solution of common salt after exposure. Daguerre's first picture of this type (**daguerreotype**), a still life of plaster casts and a framed drawing (fig. **17–27**), makes the earliest claim for photography as an art form through its specifically "artistic" subject matter.

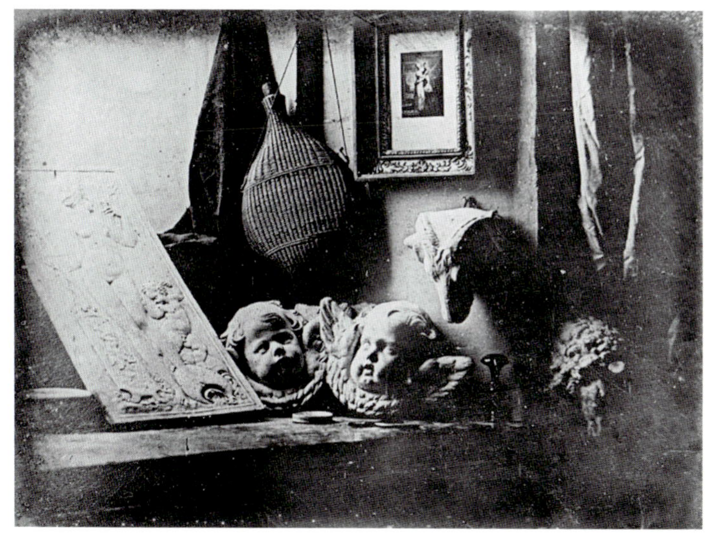

17–27 Louis-Jacques-Mandé Daguerre. *The Artist's Studio*. 1837. Daguerreotype, 6½" × 8½" (16.5 × 21.6 cm). Société Française de Photographie, Paris

Technique

How Photography Works

A camera is essentially a lightproof box with a hole, called the aperture (a), which is usually adjustable in size and regulates the amount of light that strikes the film (b). The aperture is covered with a lens (c), which focuses (d) the image on the film, and a shutter (e), a kind of door that opens for a controlled amount of time to regulate the length of time that the film is exposed to light—usually a small fraction of a second. In the example illustrated, the shutter is open, exposing the film to light. Modern cameras with viewfinders (f) and small single-lens reflex cameras are generally used at eye level, permitting the photographer to see virtually the same image that the film will capture.

In modern black-and-white photography, silver halide crystals (silver combined with iodine, chlorine, or other halogens) are suspended in a gelatin base to make an emulsion that coats the film (in early photography, before the invention of plastic, a glass plate was coated with a variety of emulsions). When the shutter is open, light reflected off objects enters the camera and strikes the film, exposing it. Pale objects reflect more light than do dark ones. The silver in the emulsion collects most densely where it is exposed to the most light, producing a "negative" image on the film. Later, when the film is placed in a chemical bath (developed), the silver deposits turn black, as if tarnishing. The more light the film receives, the denser the black tone created. A positive image is created from the negative in a darkroom, where the film negative is placed over a sheet of paper that, like the film, has been treated to be light-sensitive, and light is directed through the negative onto the paper. Through this process, a multiple number of positive prints can be generated from a single negative.

Today this traditional process in being replaced by the development of digital photography, which allows the creation of images without film and the manipulation of images on computers rather than in darkrooms. The artistic potential of the new photographic medium is only beginning to be explored.

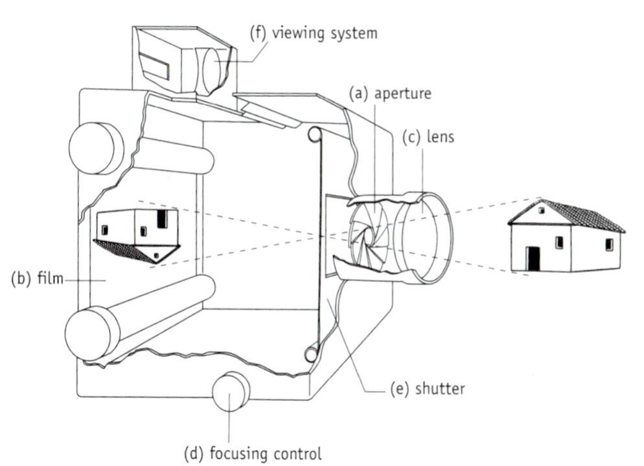

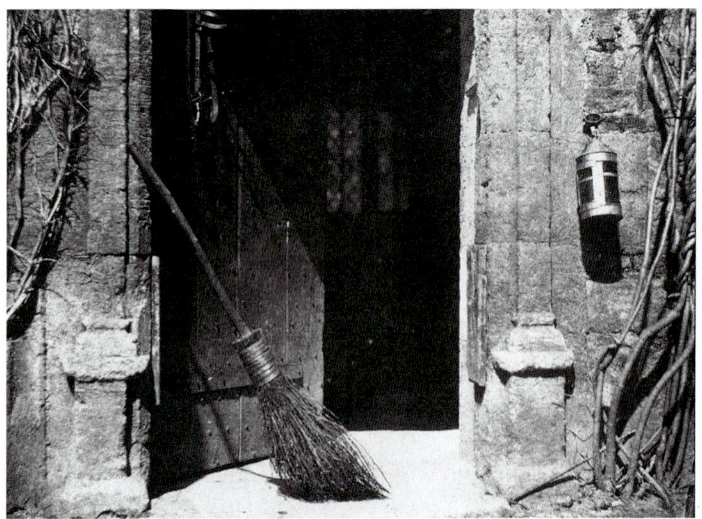

17–28 William Henry Fox Talbot. ***The Open Door.*** 1843. Salt-paper print from a calotype negative. Science Museum, London
FOX TALBOT COLLECTION

The 1839 announcement of Daguerre's invention prompted the English scientist William Henry Fox Talbot (1800–1877) to publish the results of his own work on what he called the **calotype** (from the Greek term for "beautiful image"). Beginning in the mid-1830s, Fox Talbot had made negative copies of engravings, pieces of lace, and leaves by placing them on paper impregnated with silver chloride and exposing them to light. By the summer of 1835, he was using this chemically treated paper in both large and small cameras. Then, in 1840, he discovered, independently of Daguerre, that latent images resulting from exposure to the sun for short periods of time could be developed chemically. Applying the technique he had earlier used with engravings and leaves, Fox Talbot was able to make positive prints from the calotype negatives. His process, even more than Daguerre's, became the basis of modern photography because, unlike daguerreotypes—which created a single, positive image—Talbot's calotype process produced a negative image from which an unlimited number of positives, or prints, could be made.

Fox Talbot's book *The Pencil of Nature* (issued in six parts, 1844–1846) was the first book to be illustrated with photographs. The subjects were often rural. In *The Open Door* (fig. **17–28**) the photographer evoked an agrarian way of life that was fast disappearing. A traditional, handcrafted broom of a type that mass production was beginning to make obsolete rests against the doorway of a timeworn cottage. In an attempt at artfulness, the photographer carefully positioned the broom's handle to parallel the shadows on the upper right of the door.

In 1851, Frederick Scott Archer, a British sculptor and photographer, took the final step in the development of early photography. Archer found that silver nitrate would adhere to glass if it was mixed with collodion, a combination of guncotton, ether, and alcohol used in medicinal bandages. When wet, this collodion–silver nitrate mixture needed only a few seconds' exposure to light to create an image. The result was a glass negative, from which countless positive proofs with great tonal subtleties could be made.

Once this practical photographic process had been invented, the question became how to make use of it. Those in the sciences agreed on its value for recording data, but artists were initially more skeptical. For some, photography was a convenience, replacing a live model; for others, it was a cheap substitute for, and therefore a threat to, the profession of painting, especially portraiture; but for Julia Margaret Cameron (1815–1879) it offered an exciting new creative medium.

This pioneer in the use of photography as an art form received her first camera as a gift from her daughters when she was 49. Her principal subjects became the great men of British arts, letters, and sciences, many of whom had long been family friends. Like many of Cameron's portraits, her likeness of famous British historian Thomas Carlyle is slightly out of focus on purpose (fig. **17–29**). By blurring details Cameron sought to call attention to the light that suffused her subjects—an artistic metaphor for creative genius. Carlyle's concentrated expression is so intense that the dramatic lighting of his hair, face, and beard almost seems to emanate from within. With regard to her medium Cameron said: "My aspirations are to ennoble Photography and to secure for it the character and uses of High Art by combining the real and ideal."

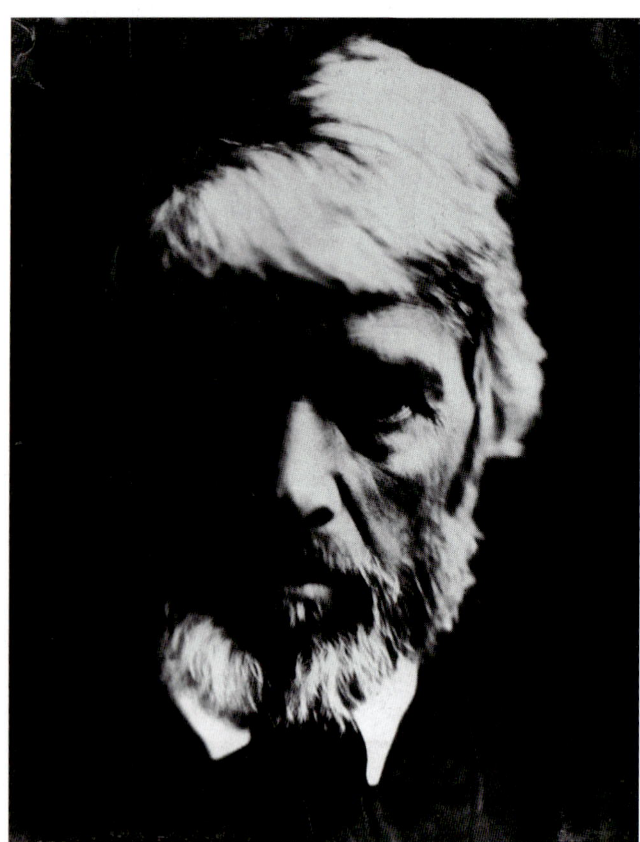

17–29 Julia Margaret Cameron. ***Portrait of Thomas Carlyle.*** 1867. Silver print, 10" × 8" (25.4 × 20.3 cm). The Royal Photographic Society, London

In her autobiography Cameron said, "When I have had such men before my camera my whole soul has endeavored to do its duty towards them in recording faithfully the greatness of the inner as well as the features of the outer man."

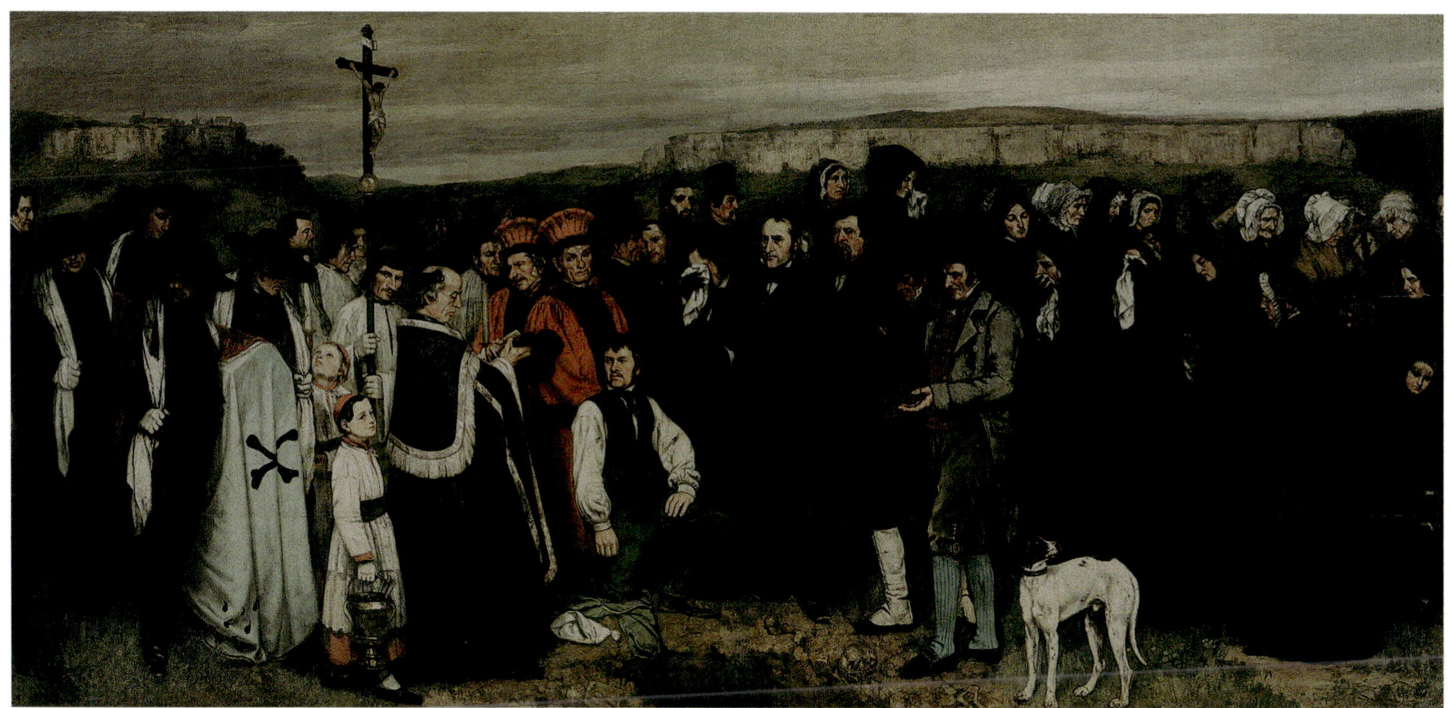

17–30 Gustave Courbet. *A Burial at Ornans*. 1849. Oil on canvas, 10' 2" × 21' 8" (3.1 × 6.6 m). Musée d'Orsay, Paris

A Burial at Ornans *was inspired by the 1848 funeral of Courbet's maternal grandfather, Jean-Antoine Oudot, a veteran of the Revolution of 1793. The painting is not meant as a record of that particular funeral, however, since Oudot is shown alive in profile at the extreme left of the canvas, his image adapted by Courbet from an earlier portrait. The two men to the right of the open grave, dressed not in contemporary but in late eighteenth-century clothing, are also revolutionaries of Oudot's generation, and their proximity to the grave suggests that one of their peers is being buried. In this way Courbet's picture appears to link the revolutions of 1793 and 1848, both of which sought to advance the cause of democracy in France.*

Realism

Toward the middle of the nineteenth century, both Neoclassicism and Romanticism were challenged by a new movement that art historians have labeled Realism. To a certain extent this new direction was motivated by a positivist rejection of Romantic subjectivism and imaginativeness on the one hand, and Neoclassical idealism and balance on the other, in favor of the accurate and seemingly unmitigated description of the ordinary, observable world, showcasing its "unvarnished truth." Some have seen this allegiance to factual accuracy in recording visual appearance as related to the advent of photography and its development into a new artistic medium. But at its inception, Realism carried a social critique, and often a political message. It is this new trend—encompassing new motivations, new subjects, and new modes of representing them—that propels the history of art forward toward Modernism.

A defining moment in French Realism was the Revolution of 1848. In February of that year, an uneasy Parisian coalition of socialists, anarchists, and workers overthrew the monarchy and established the Second Republic (1848–1851), whose founders' socialist goals, including collective ownership of the means of production and distribution, were abandoned when conservative factions won elections that summer. Fear of further disruptions continued to trouble many, while others, including the painter Gustave Courbet (1819–1877), became converts to the radicals' visions of social change.

Courbet was inspired by the events of 1848 to turn his attention to portraying poor and ordinary people. Born and raised in the town of Ornans near the Swiss border and largely self-taught as an artist, he moved to Paris in 1839, where the street fighting of 1848 radicalized him. Courbet proclaimed his political commitment in three large paintings he submitted to the Salon of 1850–1851. One of these, *A Burial at Ornans* (fig. **17–30**), is a monumental canvas commemorating (but not actually recording) the funeral of Courbet's grandfather Oudot, who had died in 1847. Instead of arranging figures in a conventional pyramid that would indicate a hierarchy of importance, Courbet lined them up in rows across the picture plane—an arrangement he considered more democratic. Through the work's grand scale, the artist accords the ordinary citizens aligned here the respect conventionally reserved for participants in major historical, religious, or mythological events. And the genuine sorrow of some mourners is contrasted with the apparent indifference of the two Church officials dressed in red behind the officiating priest. Conservative critics hated the work for its focus on common people, its disrespect for traditional standards of order and beauty. Critics also decried the absence of any suggestion of an afterlife; here death and burial are simply physical facts. Courbet relished the controversy.

Similar accusations of political radicalism were leveled against Jean-François Millet (1814–1875. This artist grew up on a farm and, despite living in Paris between 1837 and 1848, never felt comfortable with urban life. After the Revolution of 1848, Millet began to focus on paintings of peasant life, and a state commission allowed him to move from Paris to the village of Barbizon where he could be a closer observer of the difficulties and simple pleasures of rural life. Among his best-known mature works is *The Gleaners* (fig. **17–31**), showing three women gathering grain at harvest time. The warm colors and hazy atmosphere initially seem soothing, but the scene is one of extreme poverty; gleaning (the gathering of left-over grain) was a form of relief offered to the rural poor, requiring hours of backbreaking work to collect enough wheat for a single loaf of bread. When the painting was shown in 1857, critics accused Millet of attempting to rekindle the passions of 1848, and he was labeled a socialist. He denied the accusations, but his paintings contradict him.

Rosa Bonheur (1822–1899) was one of the most popular French painters to address farm life. Her success in what was then a male domain owed much to the socialist convictions of her parents, who belonged to a radical utopian sect that believed in the equality of women. In order to achieve accurate depictions of her beloved farm animals, she read zoology books and made detailed studies in stockyards and slaughterhouses. In fact, to gain access to these all-male preserves, Bonheur had to obtain police permission to dress in men's clothing. Her professional breakthrough came in the Salon of 1848, where she showed eight paintings and won a first-class medal. Shortly afterwards, she received a government commission to paint the monumental *Plowing in the Nivernais: The Dressing of the Vines* (fig. **17–32**). Powerful beasts and workers offer a reassuring image of

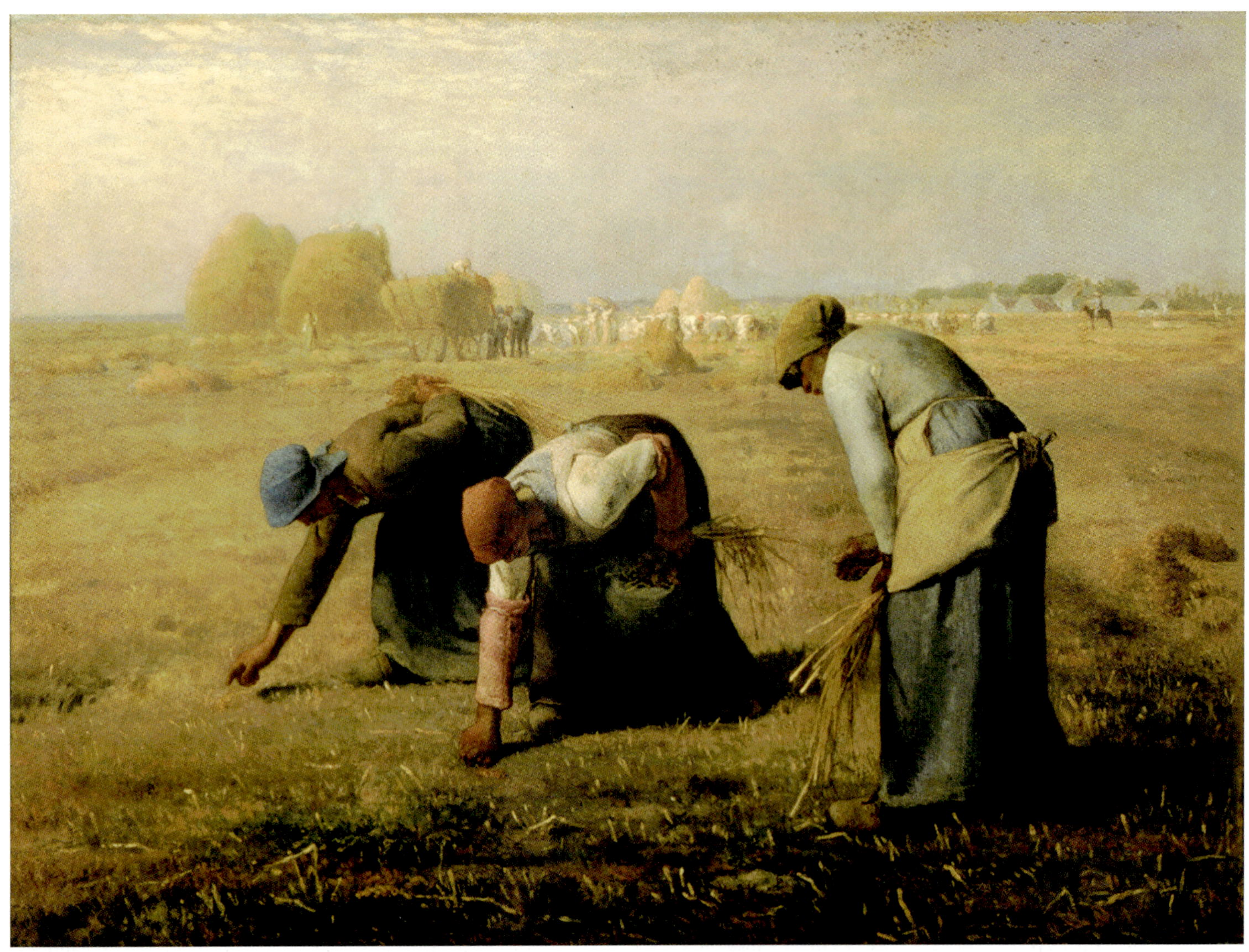

17–31 Jean-François Millet. *The Gleaners*. 1857. Oil on canvas, 33" × 44" (83.8 × 111.8 cm). Musée d'Orsay, Paris

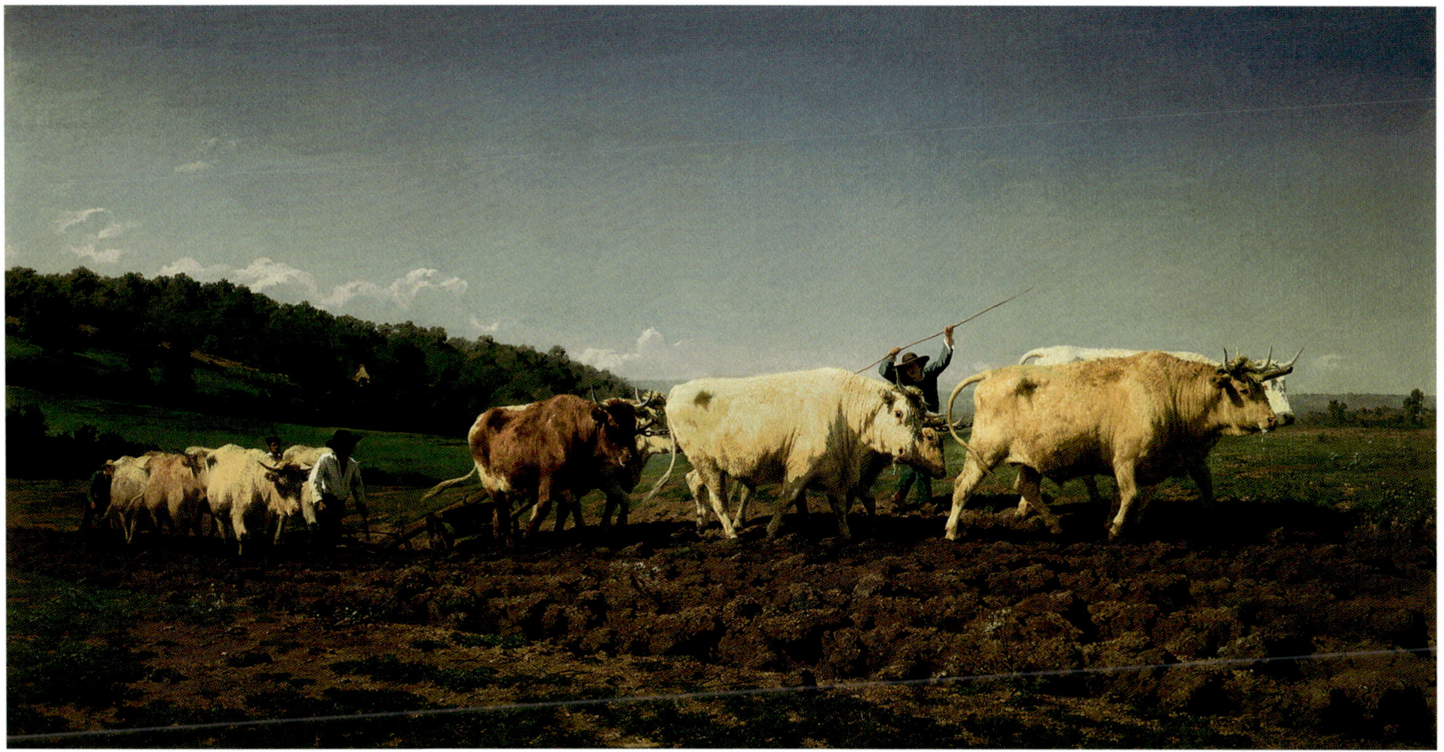

17–32 Rosa Bonheur. ***Plowing in the Nivernais: The Dressing of the Vines.*** 1849. Oil on canvas, 5' 9" × 8' 8" (1.75 × 2.64 m). Musée d'Orsay, Paris

Bonheur was often compared with Georges Sand, a contemporary woman writer who adopted a male name as well as male dress. Sand devoted several of her novels to the humble life of farmers and peasants. Critics at the time noted that Plowing in the Nivernais *may have been inspired by a passage in Sand's novel* The Devil's Pond *(1846) that begins: "But what caught my attention was a truly beautiful sight, a noble subject for a painter. At the far end of the flat ploughland, a handsome young man was driving a magnificent team [of] oxen."*

the continuity of agrarian life. The stately movement of men and animals reflects the carefully balanced compositional schemes taught in the academy and echoes scenes of processions found in Classical art. The painting's compositional harmony—the shape of the hill is answered by and continued in the general profile of the oxen and their handler on the right—as well as its smooth illusionism and conservative theme were very appealing to popular taste. Bonheur became so famous that in 1865 she received France's highest award, membership in the Legion of Honor, becoming the first woman to be awarded its Grand Cross.

Bonheur, Millet, Courbet, and other Realists who emerged in the 1850s are sometimes referred to as the "Generation of 1848" (named for the year of the Revolution). Because he had liberal political views and sympathized with urban working-class people, the somewhat older Honoré Daumier (1808–1879) is also grouped with this generation. Daumier believed that art and architecture must invent new forms and subject matter to speak to the realities of contemporary life (see fig. Intro–16). He used the new medium of lithography and the popular press to circulate biting satires of academic art and its upper-middle-class audience, producing powerful images that recall those of Goya.

Artists of other Western nations also embraced Realism and its politics in the period after 1850. In Russia, for example, the plight of the peasantry captured the attention of painters. In 1861, the czar abolished serfdom, emancipating Russia's peasants from the virtual slavery they had endured on the large estates of the aristocracy. Two years later, a group of painters inspired by the emancipation declared their allegiance to the peasant cause and to freedom from the St. Petersburg Academy of Art, which had controlled Russian art since 1754. Rejecting what they considered the escapist aesthetics of the academy, the members of the group, calling themselves the Wanderers, dedicated themselves to bringing a socially relevant art to the people in traveling exhibitions.

Ilya Repin (1844–1930), who attended the St. Petersburg Academy and won a scholarship to study in Paris, joined the Wanderers on his return to Russia in 1878. He had already painted a series of works illustrating the social injustices then prevailing in his homeland, the first and most famous of which was *Bargehaulers*

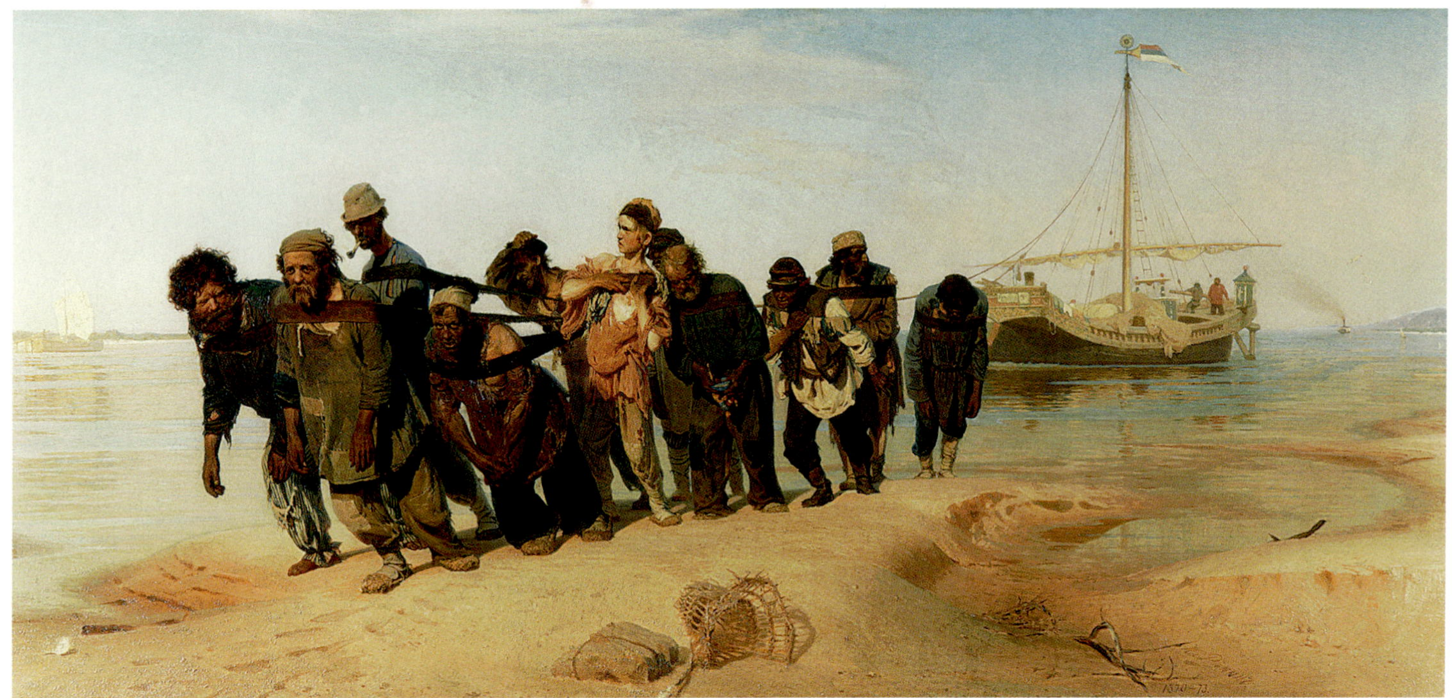

17–33 Ilya Repin. *Bargehaulers on the Volga.* 1870–1873. Oil on canvas, 4' 3 1/16" × 9' 2 5/8" (1.3 × 2.81 m). Russian State Museum, St. Petersburg

on the Volga (fig. **17–33**). The painting features a group of wretched peasants condemned to the brutal work of pulling ships up the Volga River. In order to heighten our sympathy for these workers, Repin placed a youth in the center of the group, a young man who will soon look as old and tired as his companions unless something is done to rescue him. Like much of Realist art, at its core this painting is more than a thing of beauty. It is a cry for action.

Looking Back

The eighteenth century marks a great divide in Western history. When the century opened, wealthy aristocrats owned or controlled the land worked by the largest and poorest class, the farmers. By the end of the century, the situation had changed dramatically. Revolutions were wrenching power away from the aristocracy, and new sources of wealth created an expanded affluent middle class while peasants continued to suffer.

Developments in politics and economics were themselves manifestations of a broader philosophical revolution known as the Enlightenment, espousing the optimistic view that humanity and its institutions could be reformed, if not perfected. Rejecting conventional notions that men and women were here to serve God or the ruling class, philosophers insisted that humans were born to pursue their own happiness and fulfillment. By the nineteenth century, such idealism had been challenged by the rise of capitalist societies.

Four artistic styles prevailed across this period: Rococo, Neoclassicism, Romanticism, and Realism. Severe and serious Neoclassicism arose in reaction to the playful and sensuous Rococo style that dominated the early eighteenth century. In its didactic manifestations, Neoclassicism was an important means for conveying Enlightenment ideals. In many ways its antithesis, Romanticism encompasses not only a style but an attitude. It concerned itself chiefly with imagination and emotions, and is often understood as a subjective reaction against the Enlightenment focus on rationality. Realism, in turn, was a reaction against all three earlier styles. It favored the accurate portrayal of the natural world, growing out of a nineteenth-century belief in close observation rooted in the scientific method. But it was founded on blatantly political values, drawing attention to the neglected plight of peasants and the urban poor. No longer the privileged preserve of aristocrats, art has become a means of engaging with the social complexities of a world in transition.

IN PERSPECTIVE

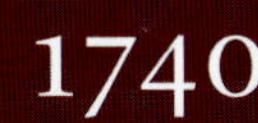

1740

◀ **Discovery of Pompeii,** 1748

1760

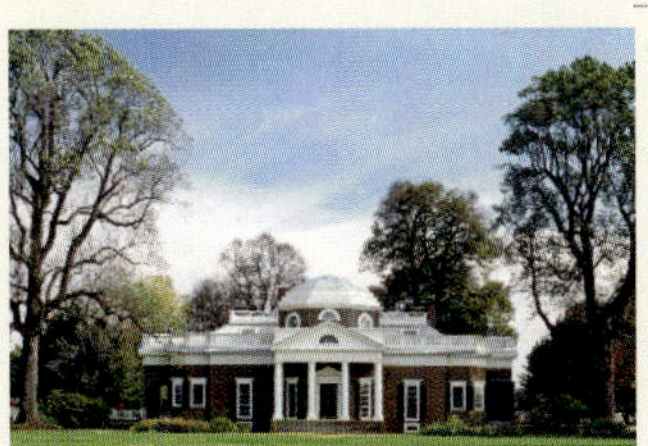

JEFFERSON,
MONTICELLO,
1769–1809

◀ **English Royal Academy of Arts Founded,** 1768

◀ **American Revolution Begins,** 1776

1780

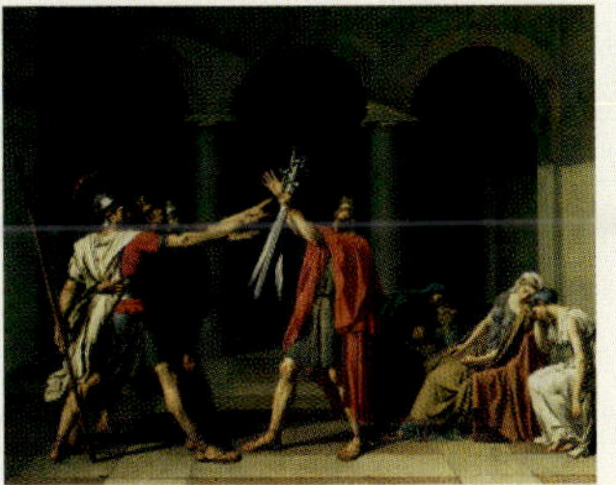

DAVID,
OATH OF THE HORATII,
1784–1785

◀ **Thomas Jefferson is American Ambassador to France,** 1785–1789

◀ **French Revolution Begins,** 1789

1800

◀ **Napoleon, Emperor of France,** 1804–1815

1820

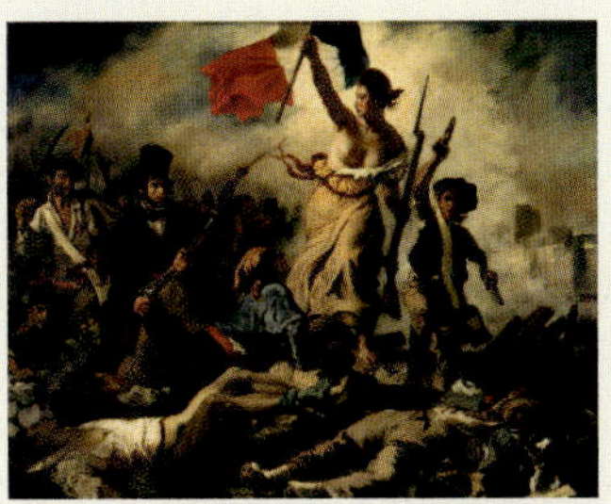

DELACROIX,
LIBERTY LEADING THE PEOPLE: JULY 28, 1830,
1830

1840

◀ **Beginning of Modern Photography,** c. 1840

◀ **French Revolution of 1848**

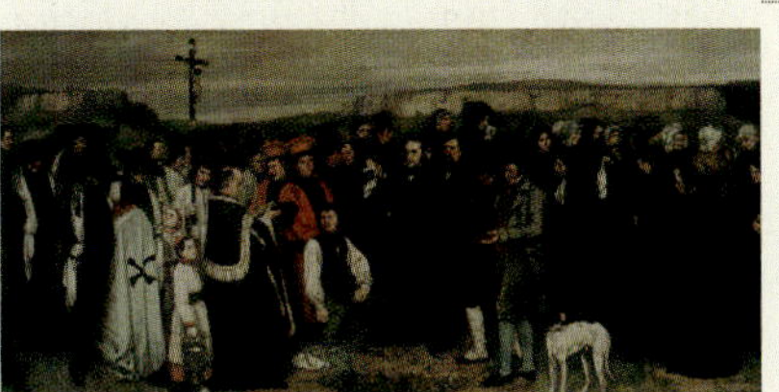

COURBET,
A BURIAL AT ORNANS,
1849

1860

◀ **American Civil War,** 1861–1865

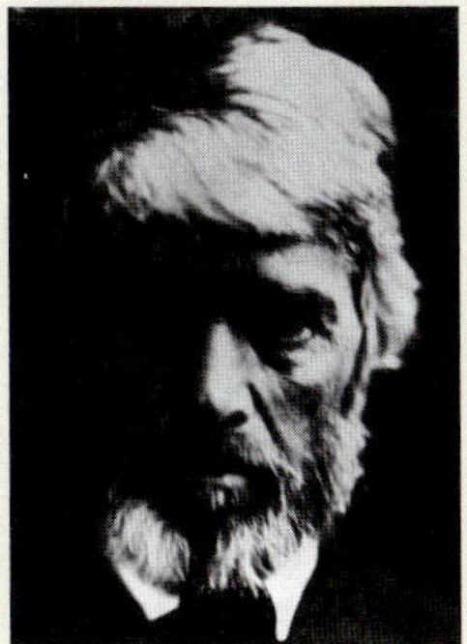

CAMERON,
PORTRAIT OF THOMAS CARLYLE,
1867

1880

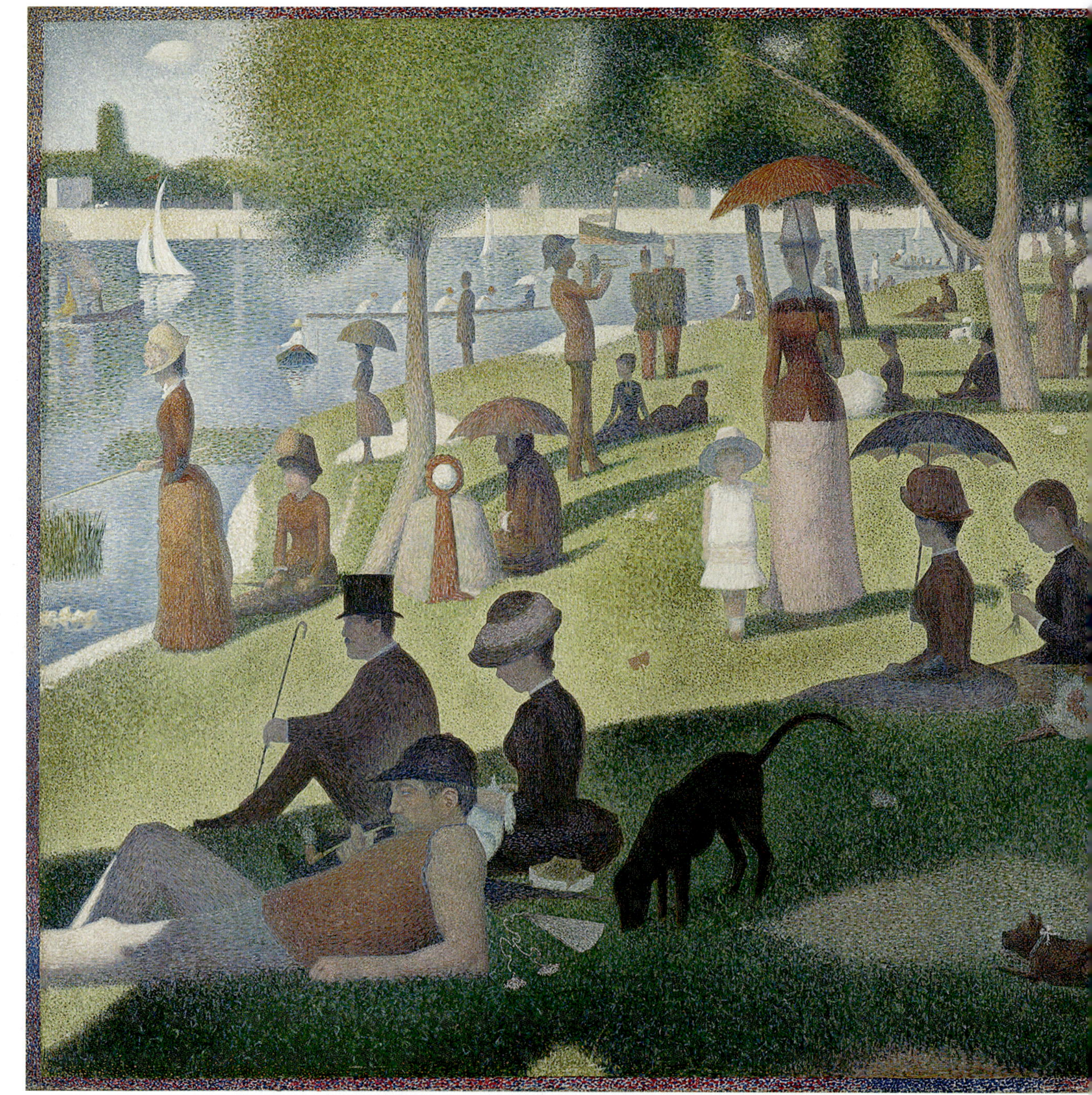

18–1 Georges Seurat. ***A Sunday Afternoon on the Island of La Grande Jatte.*** 1884–1886. Oil on canvas, 6' 9½" × 10' 1¼" (2.07 × 3.08 m). The Art Institute of Chicago

HELEN BIRCH BARTLETT MEMORIAL COLLECTION (1926.224)

18

Later Nineteenth-Century Art in Europe and the United States

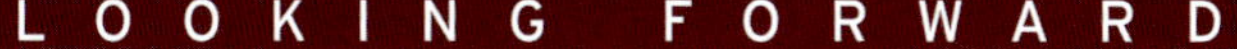

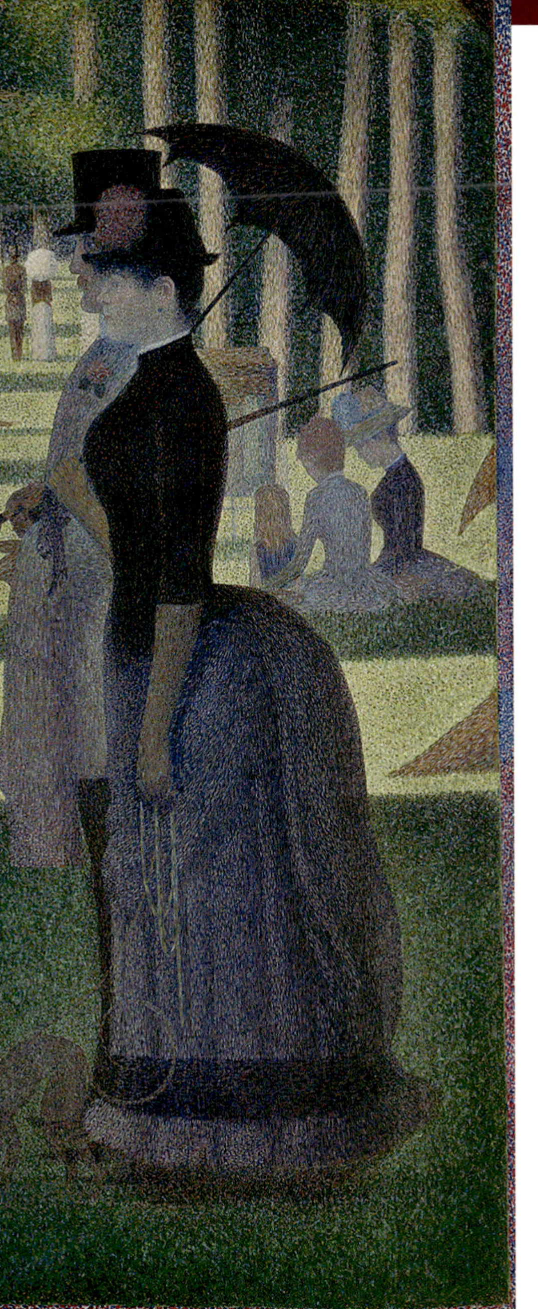

LOOKING FORWARD

In his painted evocation *A Sunday Afternoon on the Island of La Grande Jatte*, Georges Seurat (1859–1891) took a typical Impressionist subject—weekend leisure activities—and gave it an entirely new interpretation (fig. **18–1**). An avid reader of scientific color theory, Seurat applied his paint in small dots of pure color in the belief that when they are "mixed" in the eye—as opposed to being mixed on the palette—the result would be more luminous. He used upward moving lines (seen in the angle of the coastline, a tree branch and elsewhere) and warm bright colors, since according to another theory current at the time these elements created "happy" paintings. During the months Seurat spent visiting the island, he studied the individuals he found there and also the way the light fell on the people and the landscape. Each character in the final painting—even the woman with the monkey—was based on detailed observations made at the original site.

The technique of painting that Seurat developed, known as pointillism, was an aspect of the Neo-Impressionist style—just one among many techniques and styles that became popular at the end of the nineteenth century in both Western Europe and the United States. These various modes of painting—often consciously at odds with one another—are nevertheless grouped by writers and critics under a common label: "Modernism."

Modernism is an attitude, not a look. Artists began to foreground the process of making a work of art, including the materials chosen and the way they are handled, an approach that led to abstract and nonrepresentational art in the twentieth century. Some artists focused on self-expression, while others worked to suppress human feeling. Many artists saw the need to communicate deeply felt social concerns, while others looked on the world with unbridled utopianism, often in direct counterpoint to the political and social realities of the age. Some artists saw the artwork as a unique experience in which the materials and process of painting, or carving, or printmaking were primary, and subject matter became an irrelevant distraction.

Surely Seurat's Parisians felt as much rain and cold as sun, and the popular island of La Grand Jatte must have been littered with picnic refuse by the time crowds left on Sundays. But in his painting, Seurat transforms it into an island of perpetual tranquility, a place to escape from messy worldly problems. It is a perfect lazy day, and that feeling of relaxation is conveyed through the vivid warm colors and a composition of horizontals and verticals receding gently into the background. Is Seurat presenting his vision of an ideal society in this carefully calculated dream world of people in a sunny landscape? Or is he simply engaged in an intellectual exercise on the nature of art?

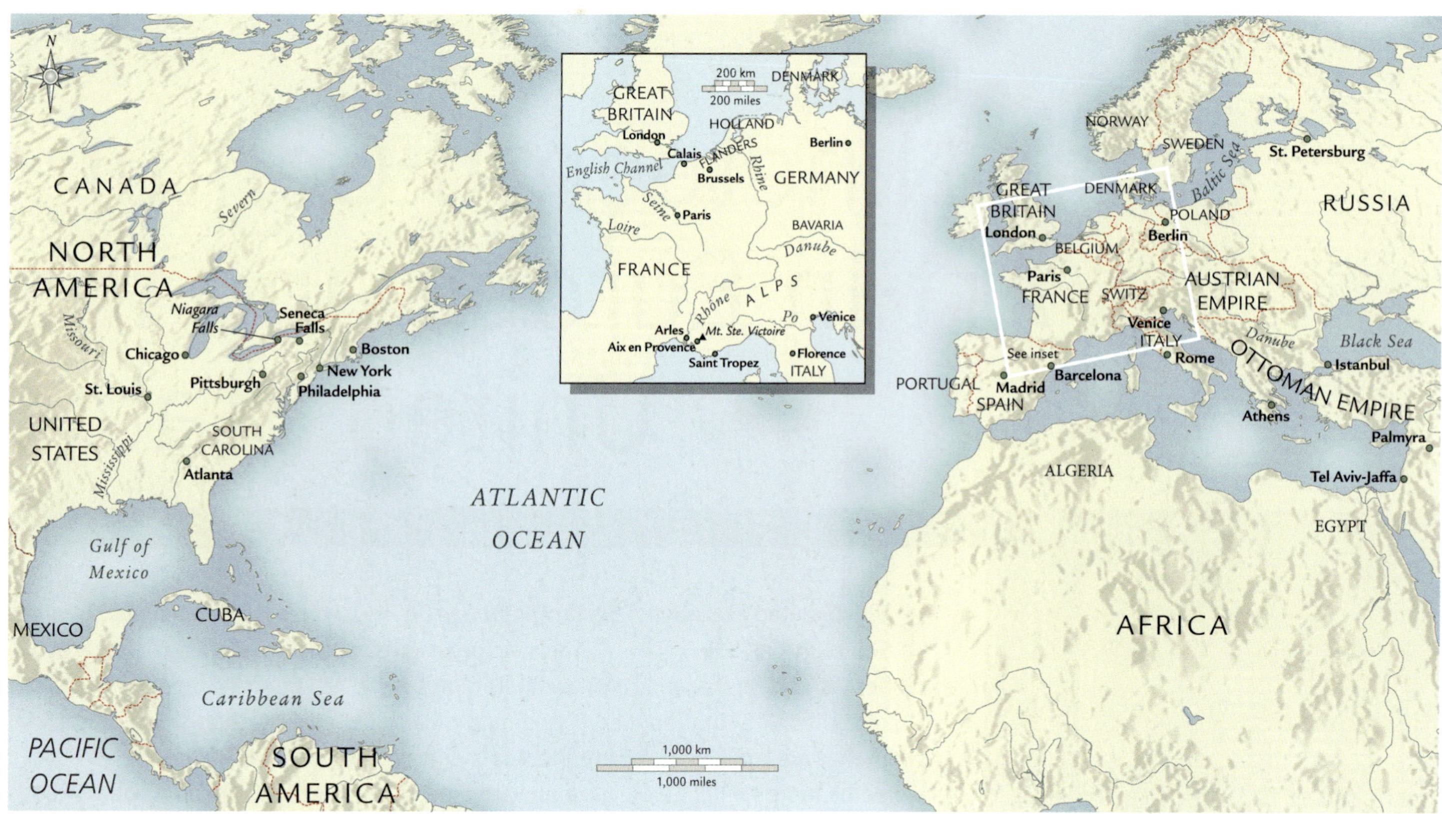

Map 18–1 Europe and North America in 1848

The Enlightenment set in motion powerful forces that would dramatically transform life in Europe and the United States during the nineteenth century (see Map **18–1**). Great advances in manufacturing, transportation, and communications created new products for consumers and new wealth for entrepreneurs, fueling the rise of urban centers and improving living conditions for many. Animating these developments was the widespread belief in "progress" and the ultimate perfectibility of human civilization—a belief rooted deeply in Enlightenment thought. But this so-called Industrial Revolution also condemned masses of workers to poverty and catalyzed new political movements that sought to reform society.

Technological developments in agriculture and manufacturing displaced many owners of small farms and cottage industries—as well as their employees—forcing people to move to new factory and mining towns in search of employment. Increasing numbers of industrial laborers suffered miserable working and living conditions. Socialist movements, in turn, condemned the exploitation of laborers by capitalist factory owners and advocated communal or state ownership of the means of production and distribution. The most radical of these movements was Communism, which called for the abolition of private property. In 1848, Karl Marx and Friedrich Engels published the *Communist Manifesto*, which predicted the violent overthrow of the property-holding bourgeoisie (middle class) by the proletariat (working class) and the creation of a classless society.

Also in 1848, the Americans Lucretia Mott and Elizabeth Cady Stanton held the country's first women's rights convention, in Seneca Falls, New York. In their fight to improve the status of women, they called for the equality of women and men before the law, property rights for married women, the acceptance of women into institutions of higher education, the admission of women to all trades and professions, equal pay for equal work, and women's suffrage (achieved only in 1920).

American suffragists were also active in the abolitionist movement, which sought to end slavery, but slavery in the United States was only finally eliminated as a result of the devastating Civil War (1861–1865). After this battle between the states, the United States became a major industrial power, and the American Northeast underwent rapid urbanization, fueled by millions of immigrants from Europe seeking economic opportunities.

The second half of the nineteenth century has been called the "positivist age" because of widespread faith in the affirmative consequences of rational thought and scientific progress. This was the period that brought us telephone and radio, vaccines and disinfectant, steel and electrical lighting. But some scientific discoveries challenged traditional religious beliefs and affected social philosophy. Geologists claimed that the earth was far older than the 6,000 years claimed by biblical fundamentalists, and Charles Darwin challenged the literal acceptance of the biblical account of creation, proposing that all life evolved from a common ancestor and changed through genetic mutation and natural selection. Religious

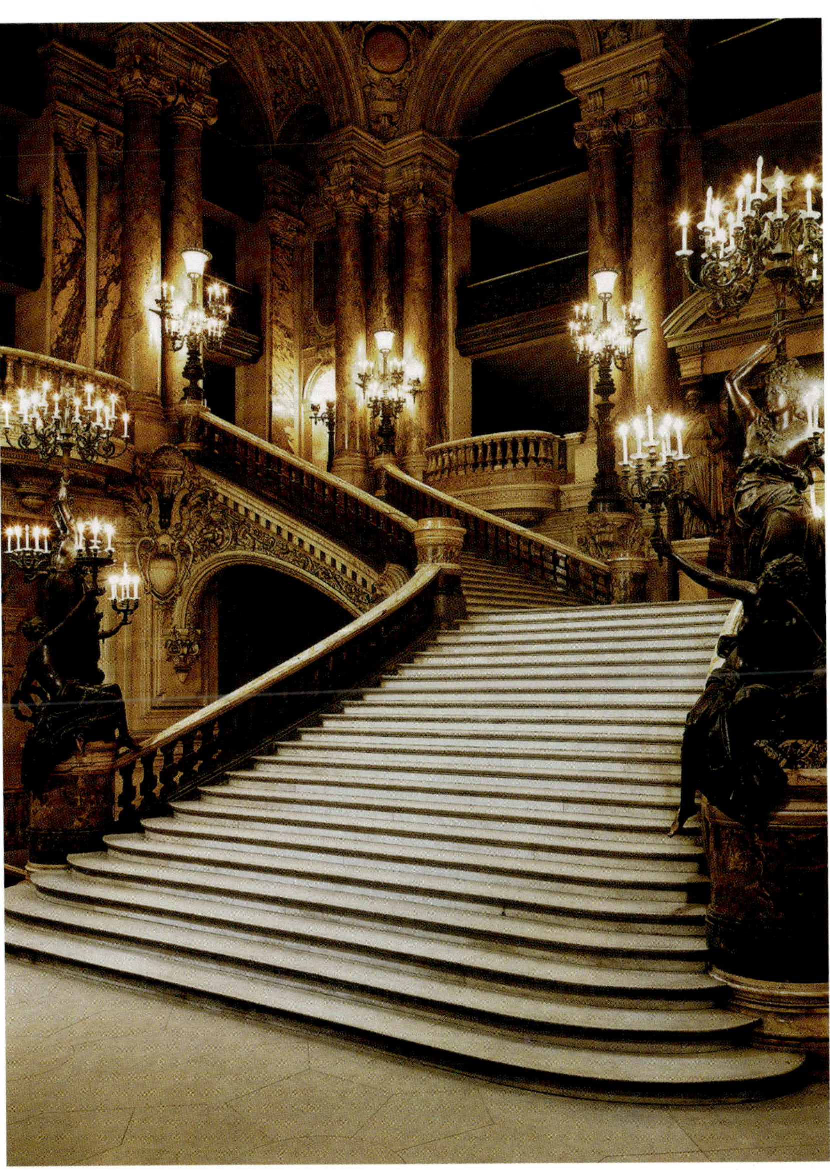

18–2 Charles Garnier. Grand Staircase, The Opéra, Paris. 1861–1874

The bronze figures holding the lights on the staircase are by Marcello, the pseudonym used by Adèle d'Affry, Duchess Castiglione-Colonna (1836–1879), as a precaution against the male chauvinism of the contemporary art world.

conservatives attacked Darwin's account of evolution, which they saw as a denial of the divine creation of humans and even the existence of God.

These developments parallel transformations in the visual arts. There was widespread rejection of Romanticism in favor of visualizing the ordinary, observable world, at times seeking scientific accuracy. There is a positivist component across the full range of artistic developments after 1850—from photography's ability to record certain aspects of the world with unprecedented accuracy, to Impressionism's quasi-scientific emphasis on the optical properties of light and color. In architecture, the application of new technologies also led gradually to the abandonment of the fashion for facing buildings with historicizing ornamentation, in favor of allowing structural systems and materials to emerge and create expressive qualities on their own.

But the emphasis on science, technology, and the modern world did not go unchallenged. Late in the nineteenth century, some artists began to turn to radically new abstract ways of expressing their personal feelings about their subjects or evoking affective states of mystery or spirituality. Like the Romantic artists before them, they shunned the depiction of the ordinary or the heroic in favor of exploring the realms of myth, fantasy, and imagination.

Architecture

Major works of public architecture in the nineteenth century were decorated, inside and out, with motifs drawn from historic models—a practice called **historicism**. The conventions of historicism were taught at the architecture school of the École des Beaux-Arts (School of Fine Arts) in Paris, which became an important training ground for European and American architects. A spectacular exponent of historicizing architecture is the Paris Opera House (fig. **18–2**), designed by Charles Garnier (1825–1898). The underlying cast-iron frame of the building is concealed by a lavish overlay of nonstructural "neo-Baroque" decoration, employed here to recall an

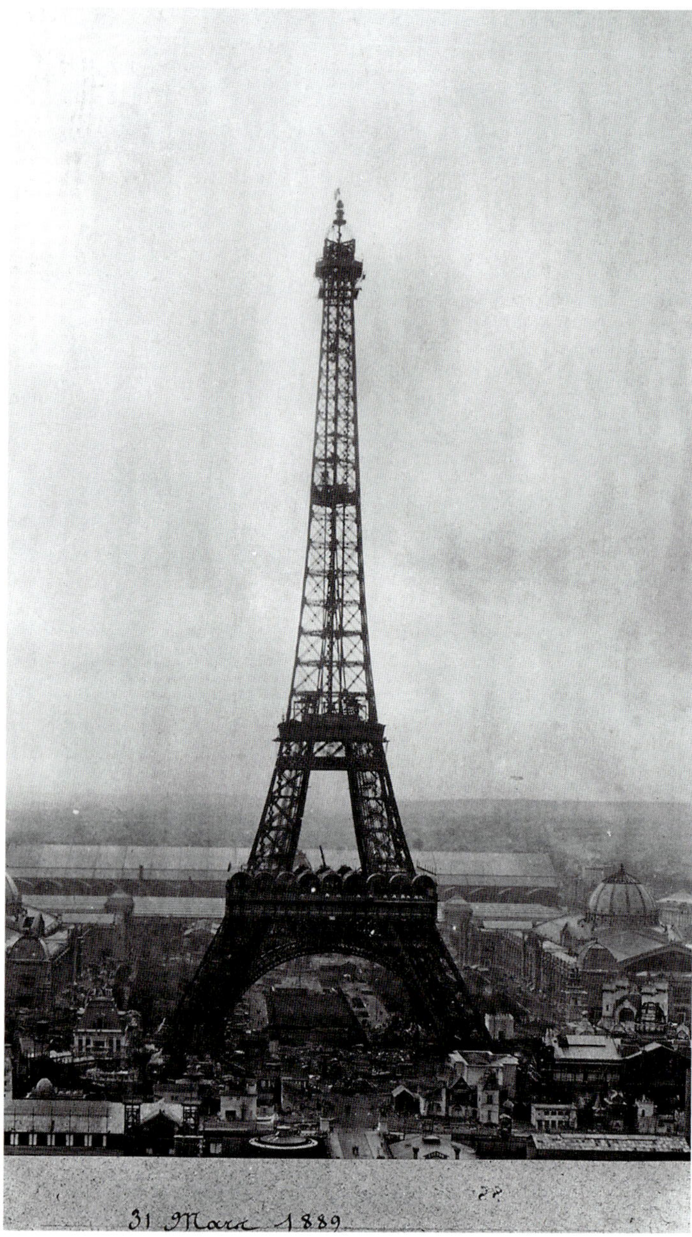

18–3 Gustave Eiffel. Eiffel Tower, Paris. 1887–1889. Height 984' (300 m)

earlier period of French greatness. The opulence is consistent with the building's primary function as the site of entertainment, showcasing the dedication to wealth and pleasure that characterized the period. Gilded decoration, exuberant sculpture, and a lavish mix of expensive, polychrome materials cover the foyer (entrance hall or lobby), where the great, sweeping neo-Baroque staircase served as a stage, rivaling the one inside where the operatic spectacles were performed, on which members of the Parisian elite—nobility and newly wealthy bourgeois—could display themselves. As Garnier himself said, the purpose of the Opera House was to fulfill the most basic of human desires: to hear, to see, and to be seen.

While historicism and revival styles were popular, modern conditions and materials had an increasing impact on architecture. Building techniques introduced in the late eighteenth and first half of the nineteenth centuries ultimately led to an emphasis on structure and the abandonment of any historicizing decorative overlay. It was engineers rather than architects who had pioneered the use of the most important new building materials: cast iron, wrought iron, and steel. They sought with these new materials to create skeletal structures—recalling those achieved in stone by builders of the Gothic period—that transformed the pure qualities of light, space, and movement into the aesthetic components of architectural design.

The Eiffel Tower (fig. **18–3**) is a prime example of this new design direction, dominating the skyline of modern Paris just as the towers of Notre-Dame had been the focus of the medieval city. Gustave Eiffel (1832–1923), a civil engineer, built his famous tower for the Paris Universal Exposition of 1889. He won a competition for the design of a monument that would symbolize French industrial progress. Composed of iron latticework, the tower stands on four huge legs reinforced by trussed (braced) arches similar to those used in railway bridges. Passenger elevators allowed fair-goers to ascend to the top of what was then, at 984 feet (300 meters), the tallest structure in the world. The French public loved the tower, but most architects, artists, and writers found it completely lacking in beauty; "monstrous," "ugly," and "useless" were but a few of the words they used to describe it. They dolefully predicted that it would have a brutalizing effect on the future of architecture in Paris.

Iron-framed buildings, however, have a fatal susceptibility to fire. Exposed to intense heat, iron will warp, buckle, collapse, or melt altogether. The immediate solution was to encase the internal iron supports in fireproof materials and return to masonry sheathing. In the early 1860s, the perfection of a technique for making inexpensive steel (an alloy of iron and carbon that is stronger and lighter than pure iron) introduced new architectural possibilities. Steel's combination of light weight and superior strength made taller buildings feasible, as did the introduction of passenger elevators, the first of which was installed in the United States in 1857.

Steel was first used for building in 1884 by young Midwestern architects who are now grouped under the label "the Chicago School." Equipped with the new technologies and eager to escape from Beaux-Arts historicism, the Chicago School architects produced a new kind of building: the skyscraper. An early example of their work, and evidence of its rapid spread throughout the Midwest, is the Wainwright Building in St. Louis, Missouri (fig. **18–4**), built by Louis Sullivan (1856–1924). Sullivan adapted the formal vocabulary and basic compositional rules of the Beaux-Arts tradition, dividing the ten-story office building into three parts—base, body, and crowning cornice—but he gave the building an entirely new vertical emphasis. The Wainwright Building is taller than it is wide, and its design emphasizes this; corner piers rise in uninterrupted lines to the cornice, their verticality echoed and reinforced between the windows by small piers, designed to suggest the steel framing beneath them. The Chicago School had found an American alternative to the Beaux-Arts tradition—an end to historicism and the invention of a new architectural style emphasizing scale and structural advances that was immanently appropriate to the modern age.

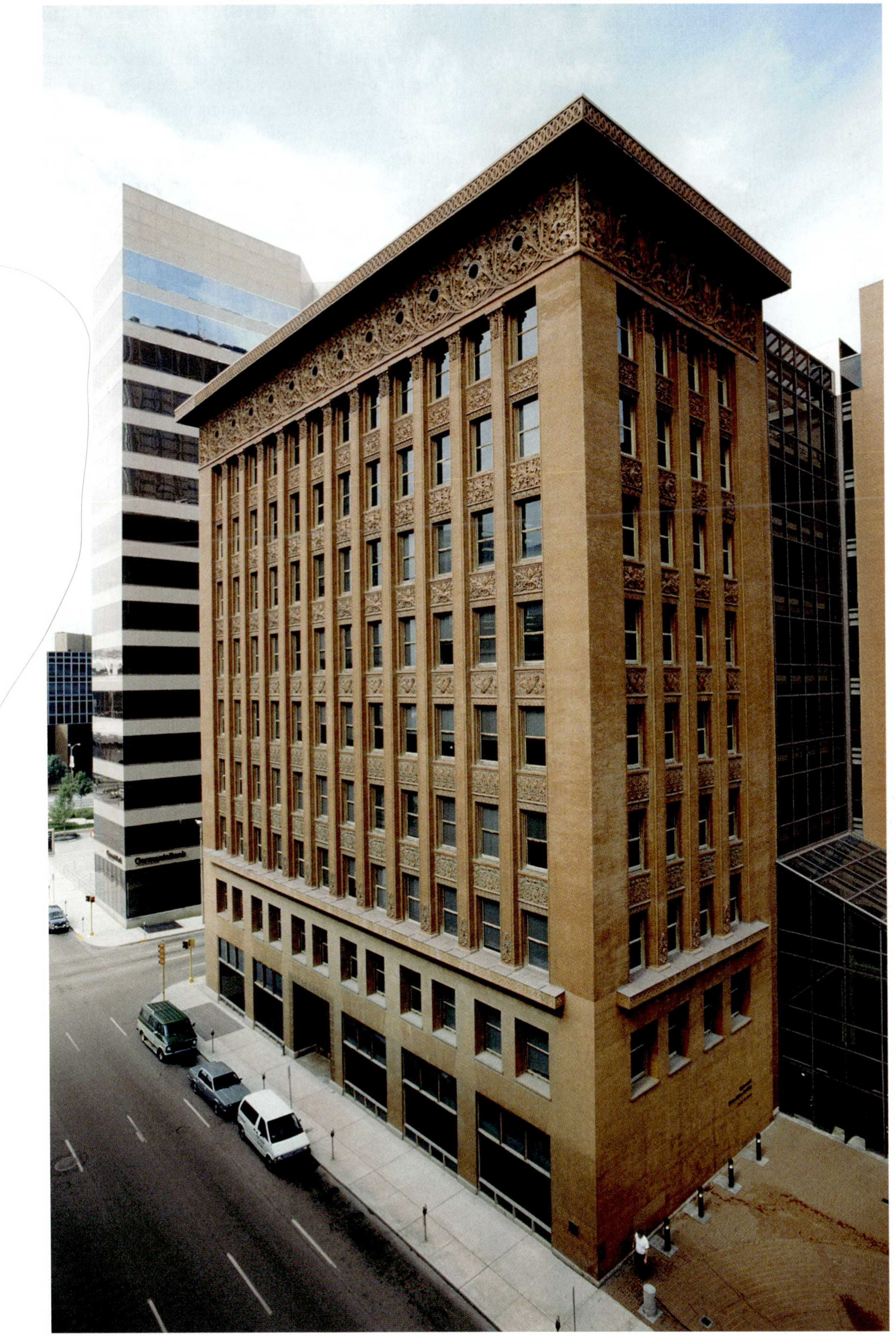

18–4 Louis Sullivan. Wainwright Building, St. Louis, Missouri. 1890–1891

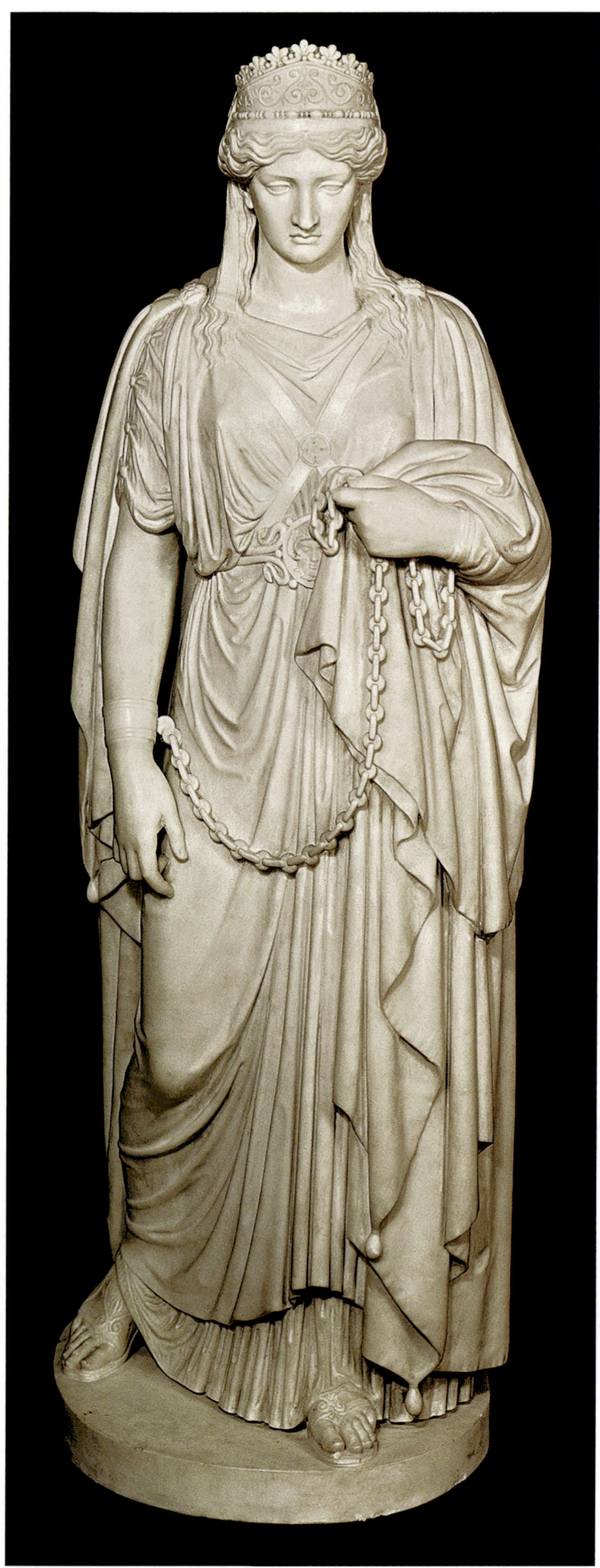

Enduring Neoclassicism in Academic Art

Historicism in nineteenth-century architecture had its counterpart in academic painting and sculpture conforming to the conservative principles of the French Academy, which continued to exert enormous international influence throughout the century. Students at the École des Beaux-Arts and comparable academic institutions began their training by copying prints and plaster casts of Classical and Renaissance sculpture; then they studied live models posed like Classical sculpture. When, in the opinion of their teachers, they had developed sufficient technical skill and detailed knowledge of the human form to make actual paintings or sculptures, they were expected to recall their earlier immersion in Classical art and "correct" ordinary nature, emulating higher Classical ideals.

As a sequel to study at the Academy, or sometimes as an alternative to it, young artists, and sculptors in particular, often visited or settled in Italy. Italy remained the wellspring of inspiration for artists. For sculptors it was also the source of the materials and skilled workers needed to work in fine white marble, the material associated with Classical sculpture. By the second half of the nineteenth century bustling artists' colonies in Rome and Florence even included women, whom the American author Henry James dubbed the "white, marmorean [marble] flock."

The most prominent of these women, Harriet Hosmer (1830–1908), had moved to Rome in 1852, rapidly mastering the Neoclassical mode and producing major exhibition pieces such as *Zenobia in Chains* (fig. **18–5**). Neoclassical in form but Romantic in content, the sculpture represents an exotic historical subject calculated to appeal to viewers' emotions. Zenobia, the heroic third-century queen of Palmyra, was defeated by the Romans and forced to march through the streets of Rome in chains. Hosmer presents her as a noble figure, resolute even in defeat. "I have tried to make her too proud to exhibit passion or emotion of any kind," wrote Hosmer of Zenobia, "not subdued, though a prisoner; but calm, grand, and strong within herself." Zenobia embodies an ideal of womanhood strikingly modern in its defiance of Victorian conventions of female submissiveness.

Edmonia Lewis (c. 1845–after 1911) likewise moved to Rome to become a sculptor. Born in New York State to a Chippewa mother and an African-American father, Lewis was orphaned at age 4 and raised by her mother's family. With the help of abolitionists, she attended Oberlin College, the first college in the United States to grant degrees to women, and then moved to Boston. Her highly successful busts and medallions of abolitionist leaders and Civil War heroes financed her move to Rome in 1867, where she was welcomed into Hosmer's circle.

Still inspired by the struggle of the recently freed slaves for equality, the newly arrived Lewis created *Forever Free* (fig. **18–6**)

18–5 Harriet Hosmer. *Zenobia in Chains*. 1859. Marble, height 4' (1.21 m). Wadsworth Atheneum, Hartford, Connecticut
GIFT OF MRS. JOSEPHINE M. J. DODGE

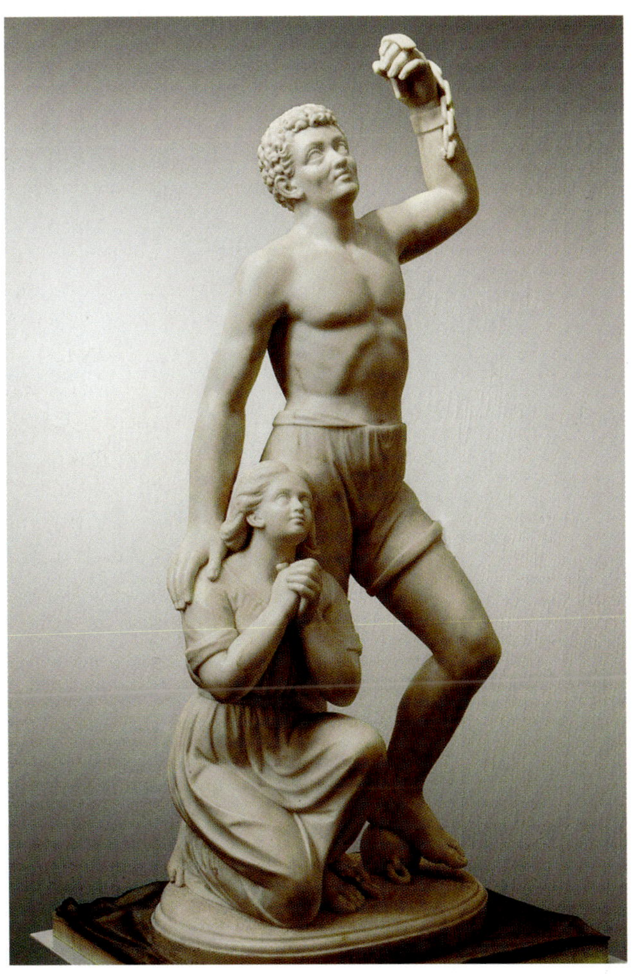

18–6 Edmonia Lewis. ***Forever Free.*** 1867. Marble, 41¼" × 22" × 17" (104.8 × 55 × 43.2 cm). Howard University Art Gallery, Washington, D.C.

in Rome to commemorate the Emancipation Proclamation (1862–1863). A woman kneels in grateful prayer, while her male companion boosts himself up on the ball that once bound his ankle, raising the broken chain in a gesture of triumphant liberation. Lewis's enthusiasm outran her financial abilities, so that she had to borrow money to pay for the marble for this work. She shipped it back to Boston hoping that a subscription drive among abolitionists would redeem her loan. The effort was only partially successful, but her steady income from the sale of commemorative medallions eventually paid it off.

Neoclassical idealism remained a powerful force in both sculpture and painting well into the nineteenth century, but an emerging new taste for more references to the real world reflected the positivist values of the times. Photography, with the camera's extraordinary ability to record some aspects of the seen world with accuracy, may also have contributed to this shift in taste. The bankers and businesspeople who came to dominate European and North American society and politics in the second half of the nineteenth century became less interested in art that idealized than in art that brought the ideal down to earth. Soon even art academies embraced this new desire for highly detailed depictions of nature. With a reporter's concern for the facts, Sir Lawrence Alma-Tadema (1836–1912) carefully researched Greek history and archaeology for his 1868 painting, *Phidias and the Frieze of the Parthenon, Athens* (see fig. Intro–26), even recording the color applied to the sculpted frieze in defiance of the Neoclassical delight in pure white marble (see fig. 17–2). Compared with Neoclassical artists such as Jacques-Louis David (see fig. 17–15), Sir Lawrence and his contemporaries began to think of history painting as diverting fantasies rooted in objective descriptions rather than as sober stories that teach moral lessons.

Reactions against the Academy

In England, reaction against academic art began building at mid-century as seven young artists formed the Pre-Raphaelite Brotherhood in 1848 to counter what they considered the misguided practices of contemporary British art. Instead of the idealized Raphaelesque conventions taught at the Royal Academy, they advocated the descriptive approach to the human body and to nature used by earlier Renaissance masters, especially those in Flanders. They also advocated moralizing subject matter in keeping with a long tradition in Britain, exemplified by Hogarth (see fig. 17–6), and they enriched their paintings with the type of symbolism found in medieval art.

Dante Gabriel Rossetti (1828–1882), a leading member of the Pre-Raphaelite Brotherhood, looked to the Middle Ages for a beauty

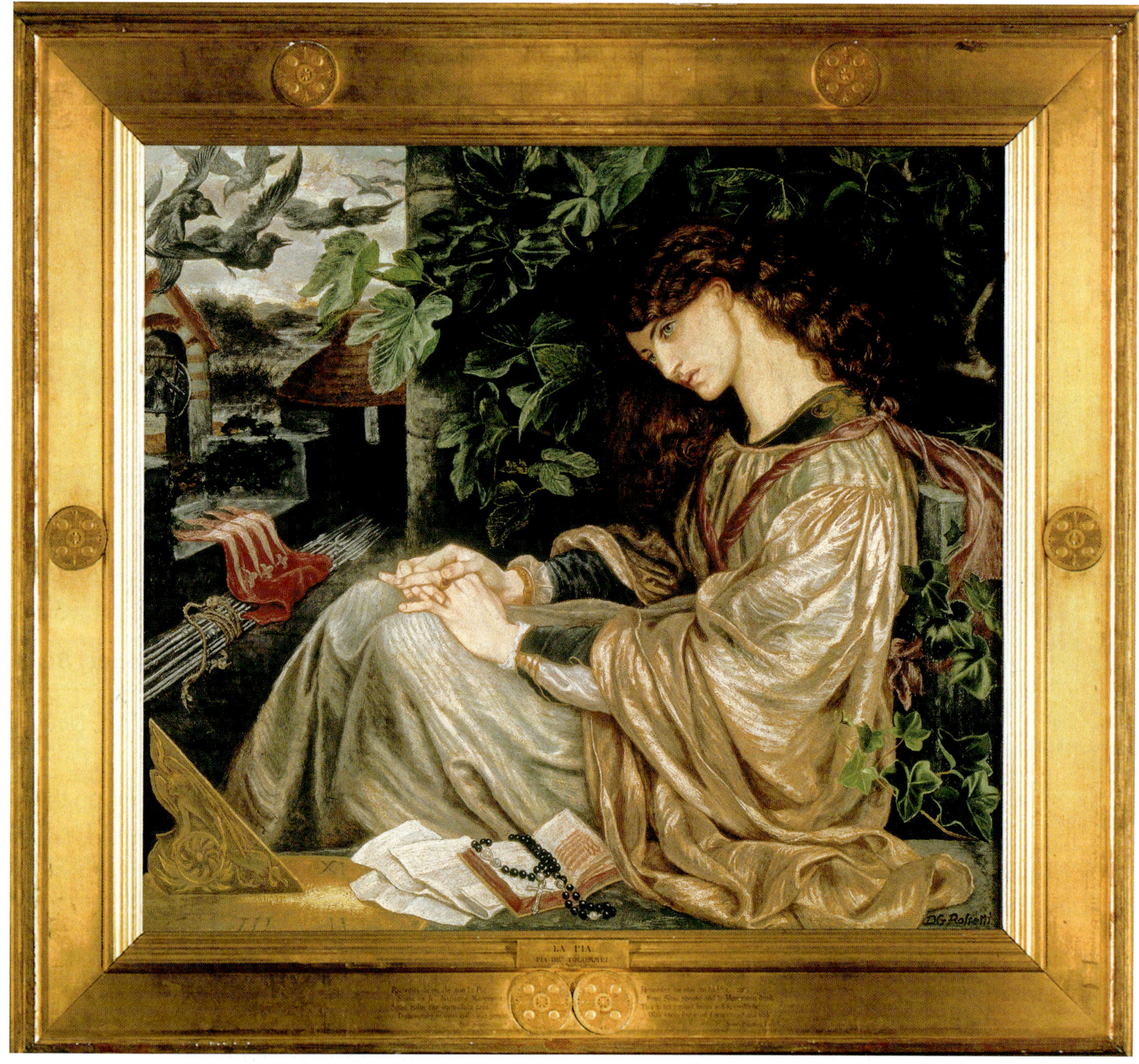

18–7 Dante Gabriel Rossetti. *La Pia de' Tolomei.* 1868–1869. Oil on canvas, 41½" × 47½" (105.4 × 119.4 cm). Spencer Museum of Art, The University of Kansas, Lawrence
MUSEUM PURCHASE: STATE FUNDS (1956.0031)

In addition to his work as a painter and poet, Rossetti created innovative and beautiful designs for picture frames, book bindings, wallpaper, and furniture, as well as architectural sculpture and stained glass. The massive gilded frame he designed for La Pia de' Tolomei *features simple moldings on either side of broad, sloping boards, into which are set a few large roundels. The title of the painting is inscribed above the paired roundels at the lower center. On either side of them appear four lines from Dante's* Purgatory *spoken by the spirit of La Pia, in Italian at the left and in Rossetti's English translation at the right: "Remember me who am La Pia,—me/From Siena sprung and by Maremma dead./This in his inmost heart well knoweth he/With whose fair jewel I was ringed and wed."*

and spirituality he found lacking in his own time. His painting *La Pia de' Tolomei* (fig. **18–7**) illustrates a story from Dante's *Purgatory*. La Pia (the Pious One), wrongly accused of infidelity and locked up by her husband in a castle, is dying. The rosary and prayer book at her side refer to the piety signaled by her name, while the sundial and ravens symbolize the passage of time and her impending death. La Pia's continuing love for her husband, whose letters lie under her prayer book, is also symbolized by the evergreen ivy behind her. The luxuriant fig leaves that surround her are traditionally associated with lust and original sin. They have no source in Dante's tale, but they had personal relevance for the artist. Jane Burden, who was Rossetti's model for this and many other paintings, was the wife of his friend William Morris, but she had become Rossetti's lover. Note that La Pia/Jane fingers her wedding ring, a captive not so much of her husband as of her marriage. In the context of the artist's personal history, the painting becomes a metaphor for Rossetti's own unhappy situation.

William Morris (1834–1896) was less interested in painting than in domestic design. His interest developed in the context of a widespread reaction against gaudy and shoddy industrially produced goods, and he sought to provide handcrafted alternatives to them, inspired by the medieval art he so revered. After marrying Jane Burden in 1859, Morris set out to decorate their new home. Unable to find satisfactory furnishings, with the help of some friends, he designed and made their furniture himself. He then founded a decorating firm to produce a full range of domestic products. Although many of the furnishings offered by Morris & Company were expensive, one-of-a-kind items, others, such as the rush-seated chair illustrated here (fig. **18–8**), were relatively inexpensive. Concerned with creating a "total" environment in which architecture and décor were styled in harmony, Morris and his colleagues designed not only furniture but also stained glass, tiles, wallpaper, and fabrics such as the Peacock and Dragon curtain seen here behind the Sussex chair.

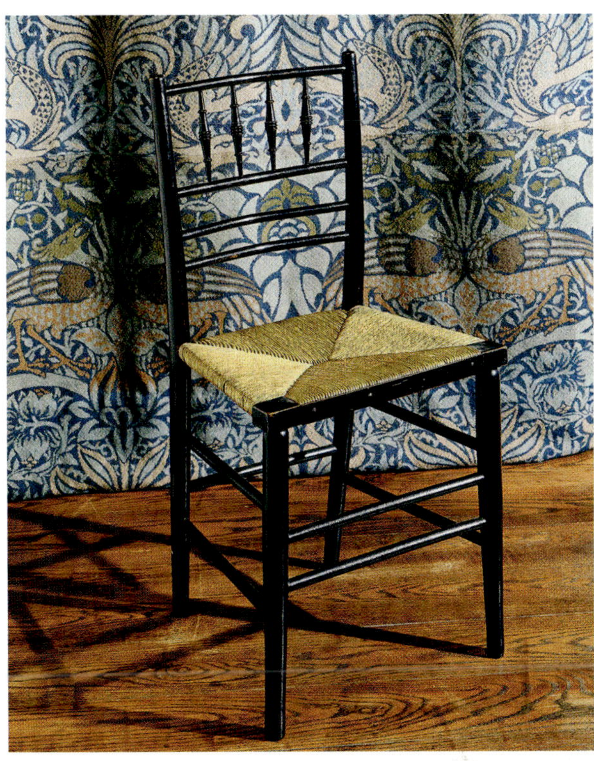

18–8 *(foreground in photo)* **Philip Webb. Single chair from the Sussex range.** In production from c. 1865. Ebonized wood with rush seat, 32⅝" × 19⅝" (83.8 × 35.6 cm). Manufactured by Morris & Company. William Morris Gallery (London Borough of Waltham Forest) *(background)* **William Morris. Peacock and Dragon curtain**. 1878. Handloomed jacquard-woven woolen twill, 12' 10½" × 11' 5⅛" (3.96 × 3.53 m). Manufactured at Queen Square and later at Merton Abbey

Morris and his principal furniture designer, Philip Webb (1831–1915), adapted the Sussex range from traditional rush-seated chairs of the Sussex region. The handwoven curtain in the background is typical of Morris's fabric designs in its use of flat patterning that affirms the two-dimensional character of the textile medium. The pattern's prolific organic motifs and soothing blue and green hues—the decorative counterpart to those of naturalistic landscape painting—were meant to provide relief from the stresses of modern urban existence.

Morris was a socialist who saw the pre-industrial era as a model for both economic and social reform, and he recognized a wholesome social component in the skilled work required to produce handcrafts. He sought to eliminate industrialization not only because he found factory-made products ugly but also because of mass production's deadening influence on the worker. Thus his aim was to benefit not just a few wealthy clients but his broader society. With craftwork, he maintained, the laborer would acquire as much satisfaction from creating a fine piece as the consumer did using it. He dreamed of a utopian future without class envy, where everyone participated in the enjoyment of art. Morris's work and ideas inspired what became known as the Arts and Crafts Movement.

Not all those who reacted against official academic art were motivated by a commitment to improving the conditions of modern life. Many, including the American expatriate James Abbott McNeill Whistler (1834–1903), simply saw the Arts and Crafts revival as a means to satisfy an elitist taste for beauty. Whistler had been one of the first to collect Japanese art when it became available in curio shops in London and Paris after the 1853 reopening of that nation to the West. The new vogue for Japanese art had fueled in him a growing dissatisfaction with the art of his time, and in 1859 he moved from Paris to London, in part to distance himself from Realist artists such as Gustave Courbet.

The simplified, elegant forms and subtle chromatic harmonies of Japanese art (see Chapter 9) had a profound influence on Whistler. In 1864, he exhibited three paintings that signaled this new direction. One of them, *Rose and Silver: The Princess from the Land of Porcelain* (see fig. Intro–24, left wall), shows a Caucasian woman dressed in a Japanese robe and posed amid a collection of Asian artifacts, Whistler's answer to the medieval costume pieces of the Pre-Raphaelites. Delicate organic shapes are shown against a rich orchestration of colors featuring silver and rose. By leaving his wet brushmarks visible, Whistler emphasized the paint itself over the depicted subject. Whistler's growing commitment to an art of purely aesthetic values, culminated in the dining-room decoration he called *Harmony in Blue and Gold: The Peacock Room*, a showcase for his painting *Rose and Silver*.

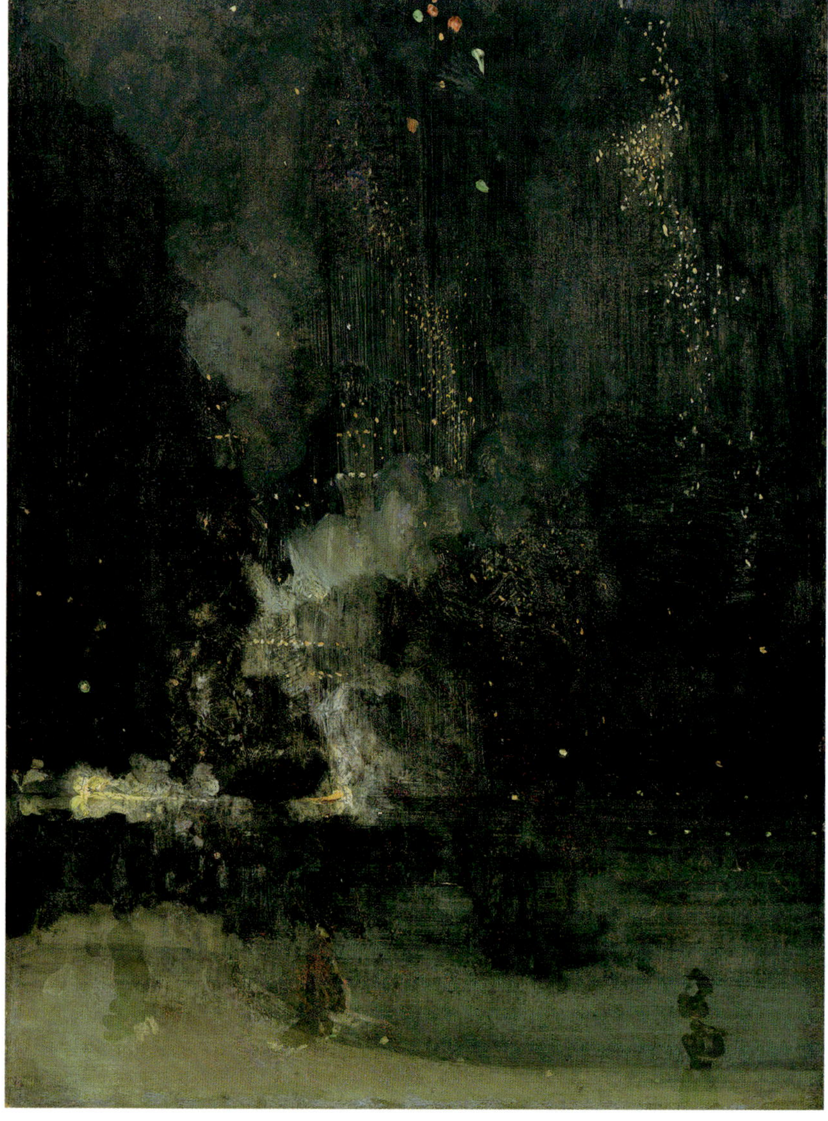

18–9 James Abbott McNeill Whistler. ***Nocturne in Black and Gold, The Falling Rocket.*** 1875. Oil on panel, 23¾" × 18⅜" (60.2 × 46.7 cm). Detroit Institute of Arts, Michigan
GIFT OF DEXTER M. FERRY, JR

In 1877, Whistler exhibited in London several night-time landscapes, including *Nocturne in Black and Gold, The Falling Rocket* (fig. **18–9**), depicting a fireworks show viewed over a lake by several observers dimly recognizable in the foreground. The exhibition inspired a vitriolic review from England's leading art critic, John Ruskin, a devotee of Pre-Raphaelite art. He found Whistler's work disturbingly unfinished and devoid of moral purpose, asking in print how the artist could demand such high prices "for flinging a pot of paint in the public's face." Whistler sued Ruskin for libel, defending on the witness stand his view that art has no higher purpose than creating visual delight, that it needs no identifiable subject matter to be successful, and that the prices he charged for his pictures compensated him not just for the two days it took to paint them but also for "knowledge gained through a lifetime." The trial was decided in Whistler's favor, but he was awarded only a farthing (a quarter of a penny) in damages, and his considerable legal expenses bankrupted him. While Whistler never made a completely abstract painting, his theories became important for justifying abstract art in the next century.

Art Nouveau

Whistler's commitment to seeing art as pure visual beauty anticipated a popular style known as Art Nouveau (literally "New Art"). Practitioners of Art Nouveau such as Belgian architect Victor Horta (1861–1947) rejected the values of modern industrial society and works such as the Eiffel Tower (see fig. 18–3) that showcased exposed structure as architectural style and sought new aesthetic forms that would recapture a pre-industrial sense of beauty, creating a stylistic vision that permeated European art in many media at the end of the nineteenth century. They applied fluid linear arabesques and stylized organic forms to all aspects of design, drawing inspiration from ancient Celtic art and from nature—vines, snakes, flowers, and winged insects—whose delicate and sinuous forms were the basis of their graceful and attenuated curvilinear designs. Following from this commitment to organic principles, they also sought to interrelate all aspects of design into a harmonized system, comparable to what they saw in nature itself. In 1892, Horta received his first independent commission, to design Tassel

House, a private residence in Brussels (fig. **18–10**). The result, especially the house's entry hall and staircase, was strikingly original. Horta laid out the wall decoration, floor mosaic, and ironwork (used instead of stone or wood) as an intricate series of long, graceful curves to integrate interior design and architecture into an exquisite and unified whole.

Almost ten years before Horta's decorative ironwork at Tassel House, the Catalan architect Antoní Gaudí (1852–1926) was already designing Art Nouveau buildings in Barcelona. His brilliantly creative Casa Batllò (fig. **18–11**), draws on indigenous Islamic, Gothic, and Baroque traditions as well as Art Nouveau aesthetic principles in a dynamic design, free from right angles. In 1904, wealthy industrialist Josep Batllò commissioned Gaudí to replace a nondescript building of the 1870s with a distinctive private residence to rival and surpass the lavish houses of other prominent local families. Gaudí convinced his patron to maintain the underlying structure of the existing building, but to reface it and reorganize its interior spaces. The resulting façade is a dreamlike fantasy of undulating sandstone sculpture and surfaces sheathed by multicolor glass and tile mosaic. The gaping lower-story windows brought the building the nickname "house of yawns," while the use of giant human tibia for upright supports led others to call it "house of bones." The roof resembles a recumbent dragon, with overlapping tiles as scales. A fanciful turret surfaces through its edge, recalling the sword of Saint George—patron of Catalunya—plunged into the back of his legendary foe. Gaudí's highly personal alternative to academic historicism and modern industrialization in urban buildings such as this, reflects his affinity for Iberian traditions as well as his concern to provide organic and fanciful surroundings to enrich the lives of city dwellers.

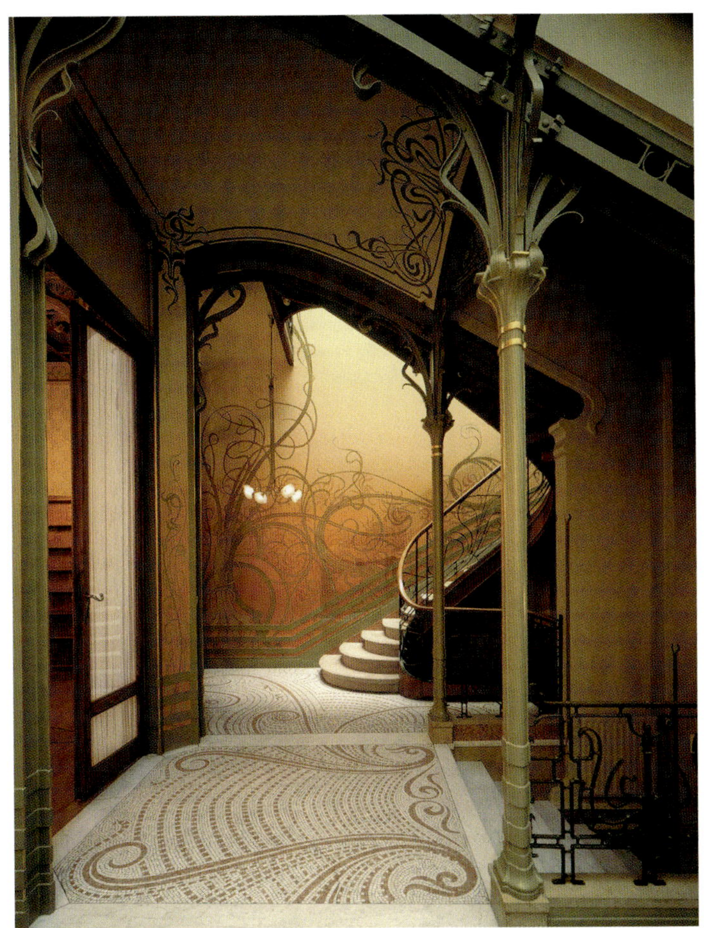

18–10 Victor Horta. Stairway, Tassel House, Brussels. 1892–1893

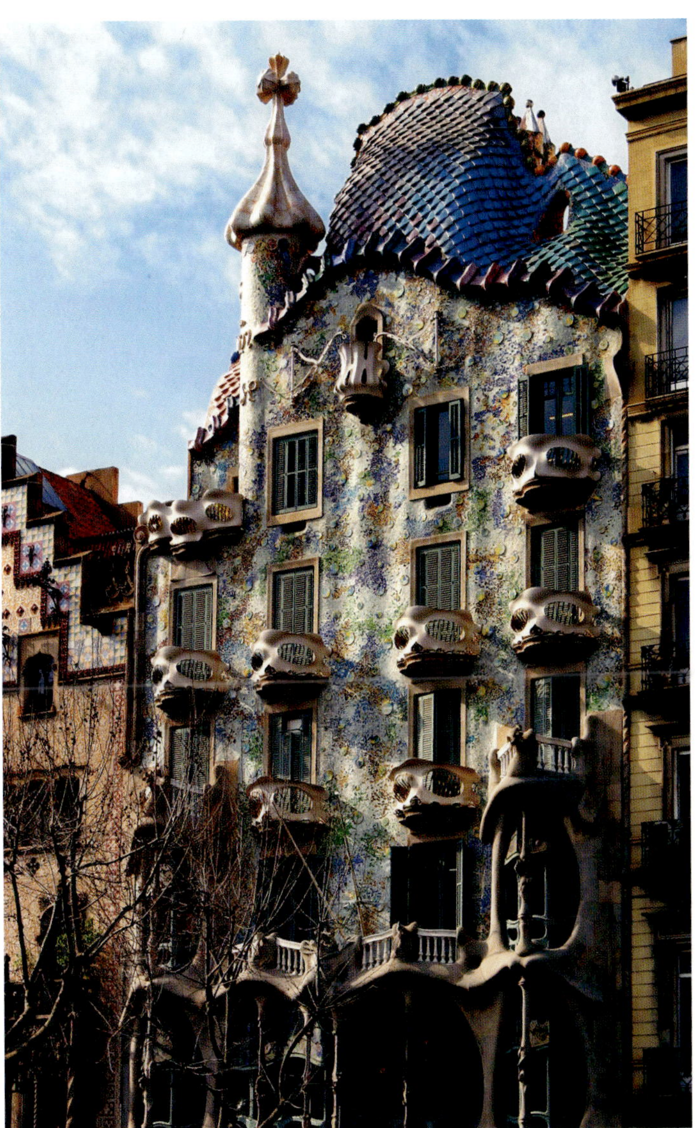

18–11 Antoní Gaudí. ***Casa Batllò***, 43 Passeig de Gràcia, Barcelona. 1904–1907

Realism

A Continuing American Tradition

In the United States, although Neoclassicism was prevalent in sculpture, Realism could trace its origins to an unbroken tradition in painting stretching back to Colonial portrait painters (see fig. 17–1). Advocates of the trend had long considered it distinctly American and democratic, and the Civil War (1861–1865) brought increasing attention to that most exactingly descriptive medium—photography.

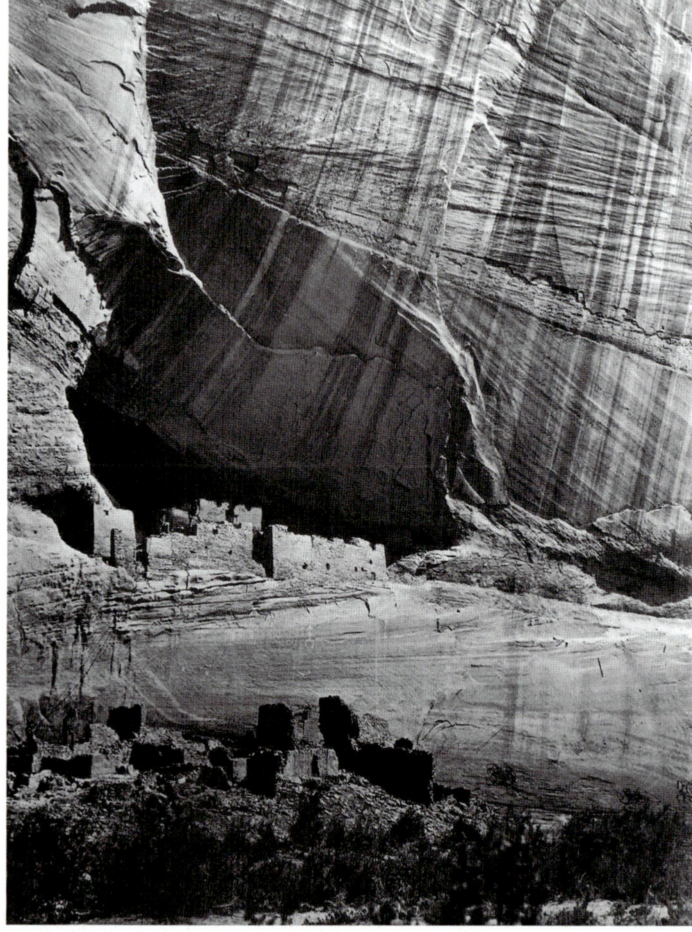

18–12 Timothy O'Sullivan. ***Ancient Ruins in the Cañon de Chelley, Arizona.*** 1873. Albumen print. National Archives, Washington, D.C.

The work of photographers came to public attention when Mathew B. Brady (1823–1896) gained permission from government officials to take a team and a darkroom wagon to the field of battle. Among his assistants was Timothy O'Sullivan (1840–1882), whose photographs of Western landscapes rival the finest paintings.

O'Sullivan accompanied Western survey expeditions to make what were ostensibly documentary photographs. But images like *Ancient Ruins in the Cañon de Chelley, Arizona* (fig. **18–12**) are infused with a Romantic sense of awe before the grandeur of nature that rivals the Hudson River School. The 700-foot canyon wall fills the composition, giving viewers no clear vantage point and scant visual relief. The bright, raking sunlight across the sheer rock face sharply reveals the cracks and striations formed over eons, as well as the gently diagonal striping of desert varnish (mineral deposits forming on stone surfaces in arid climates). The image suggests not only the immensity of geological time but also humanity's insignificant place within it. Like the Classical ruins that were a popular theme in European Romantic art and poetry, the Native American ruins suggest the inevitable passing of all civilizations. The four puny humans on the left, standing in this majestic yet barren place, reinforce the theme of human futility and insignificance, and the overall melancholic sensibility of the work may reflect the emotional impact of the Civil War.

Another artist who made his name recording images of the Civil War was Winslow Homer (1836–1910). Prior to the war, he had produced illustrations for books as well as popular weekly magazines. In his role as both reporter and illustrator for *Harper's Weekly*, Homer produced works that are considered to be among the finest pictorial reporting of the Civil War. In 1866–1867 he spent ten months in France, where the Realist art he saw may have inspired the rural subjects that he painted when he returned, but at heart he believed that unidealized Realism was the most appropriate style for a democratic society.

In the 1870s, Homer became a master of the difficult medium of watercolor (fig. **18–13**). In **watercolor**, pigments suspended in water are laid down with rapid, sure brushstrokes on absorbent white paper, creating an image that cannot be corrected or reworked. Colors are almost translucent, with whites, including highlights, produced by leaving the paper bare. Watercolor had become a popular medium for rapid sketching outdoors, but Homer used it to produce finished works of art that capture fleeting impressions of sparkling sunlight, wind-blown foliage, and water, with stunning freshness and spontaneity, as well as a distinct luminosity and saturation of color.

The most uncompromising American Realist was Philadelphia artist Thomas Eakins (1844–1916). Following academic training at the Pennsylvania Academy of the Fine Arts and anatomical study at the nearby Jefferson Medical College, supplemented by a stint at the École des Beaux-Arts in Paris, Eakins spent six months in Spain, where he encountered the highly descriptive works of Diego Velázquez (see fig. 14–12). Returning to Philadelphia in 1870, Eakins began painting frank portraits, often in everyday settings, whose lack of conventional charm generated little popular interest. But he was a charismatic teacher and was soon appointed director of the Pennsylvania Academy.

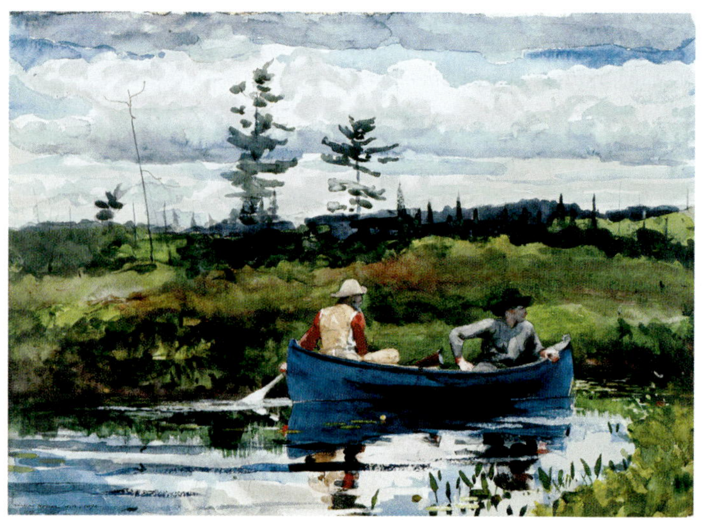

18–13 Winslow Homer. ***The Blue Boat.*** 1892. Watercolor over graphite, 15" × 21½" (38.5 × 54.7 cm). Museum of Fine Arts, Boston

OTIS NORCROSS FUND

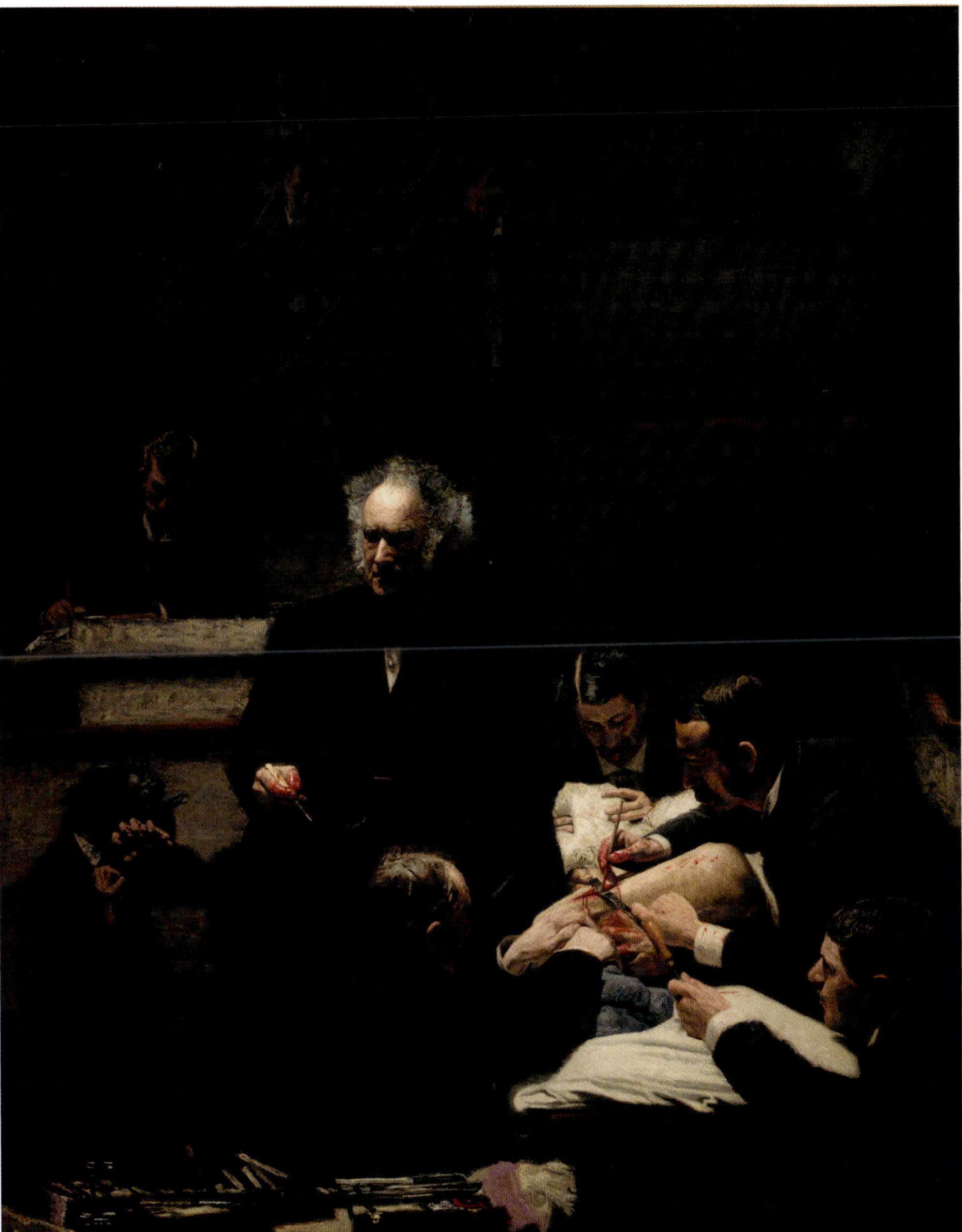

18–14 Thomas Eakins. ***The Gross Clinic (Portrait of Dr. Samuel D. Gross).*** 1875. Oil on canvas, 8' × 6' 6" (2.43 × 1.98 m). Pennsylvania Academy of the Fine Arts and The Philadelphia Museum of Art
GIFT OF THE ALUMNI ASSOCIATION TO JEFFERSON MEDICAL COLLEGE IN 1878 AND PURCHASED BY THE PENNSYLVANIA ACADEMY OF THE FINE ARTS IN 2007 WITH THE GENEROUS SUPPORT OF MORE THAN 3,500 DONORS

Eakins' career as a Realist artist developed in relationship to his association with the Pennsylvania Academy of the Fine Arts in Philadelphia, where he started teaching the year after he painted this work and was named director in 1882. But in 1886, when he removed the loincloth from a male model in a class where women were present, the scandalized Academy board offered him the choice of changing his teaching methods or resigning. He resigned.

One of his paintings, *The Gross Clinic* of 1875 (fig. **18–14**), did attract considerable attention, mostly negative. It was severely criticized and refused exhibition space at the 1876 Philadelphia Centennial because the jury did not consider surgery a fit subject for art. The monumental canvas shows Dr. Samuel David Gross performing an operation in the surgical amphitheater of Jefferson Medical College, assisted by famous associates and observed by young medical students in the background, as well as by Eakins himself, who included his portrait along the painting's right edge. A woman at left, presumably a relative of the patient, cringes in horror at the bloody spectacle. But the surgeon is portrayed as a heroic figure, spotlighted by beams of light on his forehead and bloodied right hand with glinting scalpel. Principal illumination, however, is reserved for the patient, presented here not as an entire body but a dehumanized jumble of thigh, buttock, socked feet, and bunches of cloth. In conceiving this portrait, Eakins must have had Rembrandt's famous Baroque painting of Dr. Tulp in mind (see fig. 14–21). Eakins used light not to stir emotions but to make a point: amid the darkness of ignorance and fear, modern science is the light of knowledge. The procedure showcased here, in fact, was an innovative surgery that allowed Dr. Gross to save a patient's leg that heretofore would have been routinely amputated.

Among Eakins' students at the Pennsylvania Academy of Fine Arts were women and African-Americans, groups often excluded from art schools. One of his star pupils was Henry Ossawa Tanner (1859–1937) who, from 1879 to 1885, absorbed Eakins' lessons of truthful representation and his focus on real-life subjects. In 1891, after working as a photographer and teacher in Atlanta, Tanner

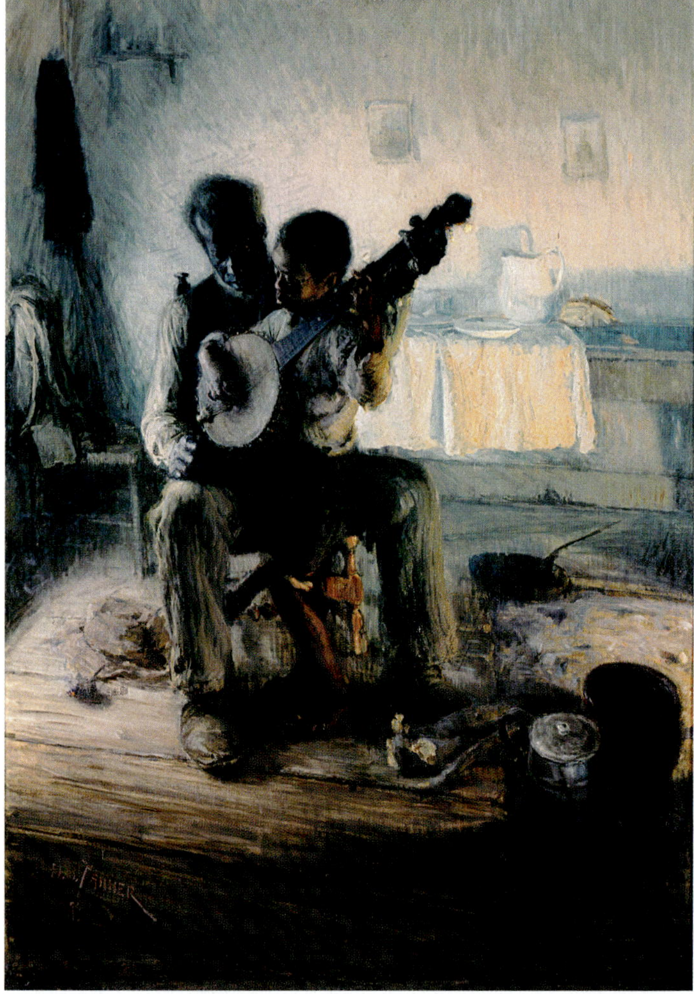

18–15 Henry O. Tanner. *The Banjo Lesson.* c. 1893. Oil on canvas, 48" × 35" (121.9 × 88.9 cm). Hampton University Museum, Hampton, Virginia

moved to Paris where his painting received favorable critical attention. In the 1890s, he painted scenes from African-American and rural French life in a style that combined Eakins' Realism with the delicate brushwork he had learned in France. With strongly felt, humanizing images like the *The Banjo Lesson* (fig. **18–15**), he sought to counter caricatures of African-American life created by other artists. The use of the banjo here is especially significant since it had become identified with images of minstrels—just the sort of patronizing paintings that Tanner sought to replace with his sympathetic genre scenes focused on the intimate interactions that brought meaning to family life. Ultimately Tanner dedicated himself to religious subjects, believing that Bible stories could illustrate the struggles and hopes of contemporary African-Americans.

"The Painter of Modern Life"

By the mid-1860s Parisian painter Édouard Manet (1832–1883) had become the unofficial leader of a group of progressive artists and writers who gathered at the Café Guerbois in the Montmartre district of Paris. These artists, who matured around 1870, pushed the French Realist tradition into new territory. Instead of continuing themes that had engaged Courbet, Millet, and Bonheur—the working classes and rural life—they generally moved to what they thought were more modern subjects: the city, the bourgeois (upper-middle class), and leisure. And although many of them also painted the countryside, their point of view was usually that of a city dweller on holiday.

Frustration among progressive artists with the exclusionary practices of the juries that decided which painting would hang in grand, official Salon exhibitions (see "Art Academies in the Eighteenth Century," page 466) reached a fever pitch in 1863 when the jury turned down nearly 3,000 submitted works. A storm of protest erupted, prompting French emperor Napoleon III to order an exhibition of the rejected work called the Salon des Refusés (Salon of the Rejected Ones). Featured in it was Manet's *Le Déjeuner sur l'herbe (The Luncheon on the Grass)* (fig. **18–16**), which scandalized viewers and helped establish Manet as a radical artist by provoking a critical avalanche that mixed shock with bewilderment.

Manet's strong commitment to Realism was fueled by his friendship with poet Charles Baudelaire. In his 1863 article "The Painter of Modern Life," Baudelaire called for an artist to be the painter of contemporary manners, "the painter of the passing moment and of all the suggestions of eternity that it contains." *Le Déjeuner sur l'herbe* seems to be Manet's response. To viewers accustomed to the traditional use of controlled gradations of shadow to model smoothly rounded forms, which were then nestled within spaces logically mapped by illusionistic perspective, this painting seemed a jarring rejection of the basic tenets of painting. Manet offered flat, sharply outlined and starkly lit figures who, rather than being integrated with their natural setting, seem to stand out sharply against it, like silhouetted cutouts propped up before a painted backdrop. The fact that Manet based his composition on Renaissance works, such as Titian's *Pastoral Concert* (fig. 13–18), a copy of which was hanging in his studio, and an engraving of a deeply Classical work by Raphael—the source for the pose of the naked woman's right arm as well as the broad gesture of the reclining man on the right—only made Manet's painting more unsettling.

Most disturbing to contemporary viewers, however, was the "immorality" of Manet's subject: a suburban picnic featuring a scantily clad bathing woman in the background and, in the foreground, a completely naked woman seated alongside two fully clothed bourgeois men. Manet's scandalized audience assumed that these women were prostitutes and the well-dressed men their clients. But what was fundamentally shocking was the work's modernity, presenting frank nudity not as part of historical or mythological narrative, but within the context of contemporary life. The underlying meanings of this radical painting are still the subject of art-historical debate. Some see it as a commentary on the alienation of modern life, for the figures do not connect with one another psychologically. Even if the man on the right gestures toward his companions, the other man looks off absently, while the nude turns her attention boldly toward the viewer, making us quite aware of our own estrangement from what is going on in the painting.

Shortly after completing *Le Déjeuner sur l'herbe*, Manet painted *Olympia* (fig. **18–17**), whose title alluded to a socially ambitious

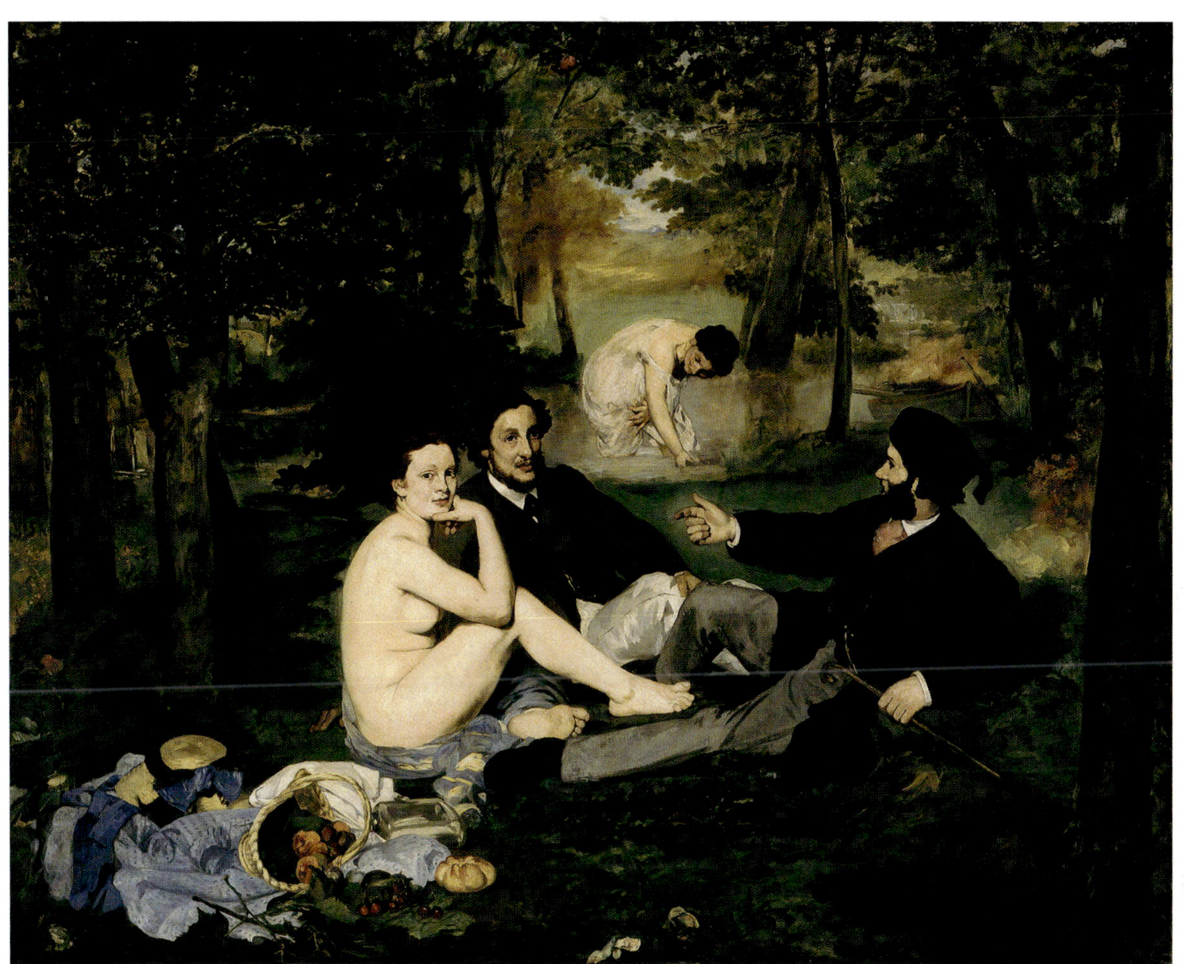

18–16 Édouard Manet. ***Le Déjeuner sur l'herbe (The Luncheon on the Grass).*** 1863. Oil on canvas, 7' × 8' 8" (2.13 × 2.64 m). Musée d'Orsay, Paris

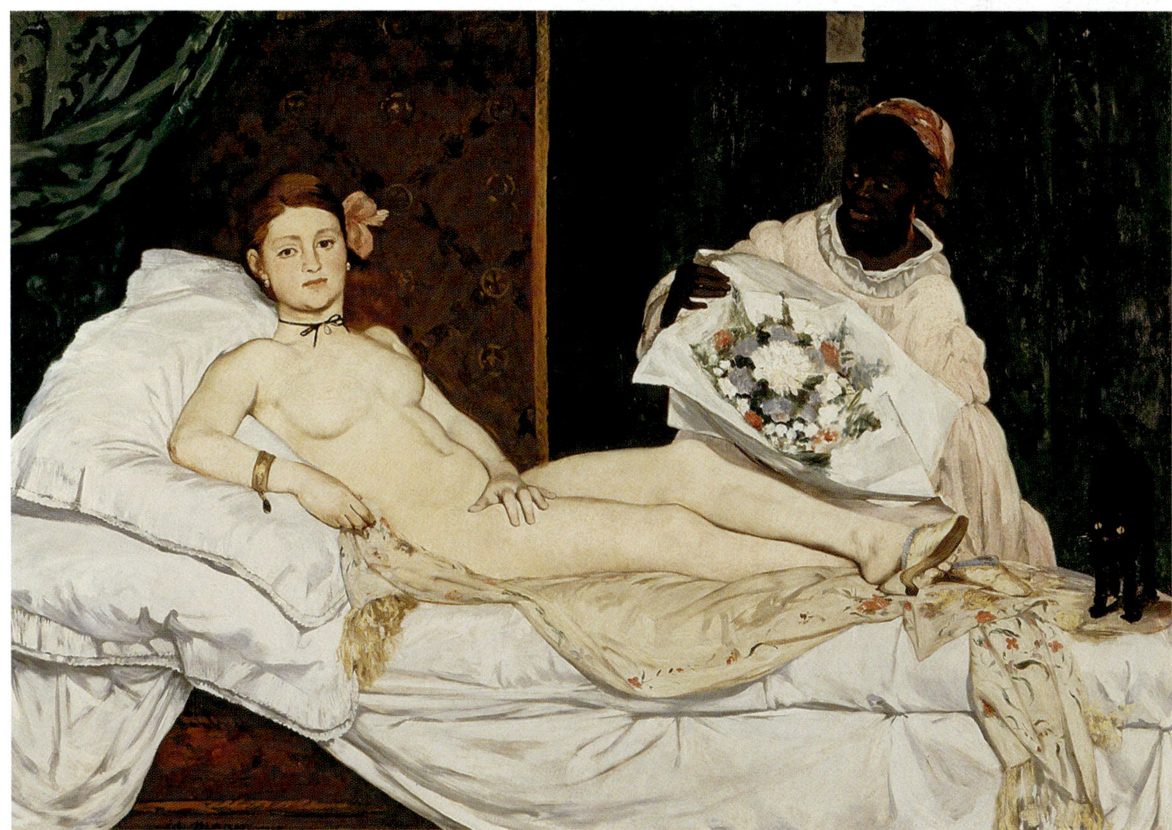

18–17 Édouard Manet. ***Olympia.*** 1863. Oil on canvas, 4' 3" × 6' 2¼" (1.31 × 1.91 m). Musée d'Orsay, Paris

prostitute of the same name in a novel and play by Alexandre Dumas *fils* (the son). Like *Le Déjeuner sur l'herbe, Olympia* was based on a painting by Titian, the so-called *Venus of Urbino* (fig. 13–21). At first glance, Manet appears to pay homage to the work's Venetian source, but Manet has made his modern counterpart the very antithesis of Titian's reclining nude. Whereas Titian's woman is curvaceous and softly rounded, Manet's is angular and flattened. Whereas Titian's looks lovingly at the male spectator, Olympia appears coldly indifferent, if not downright defiant. Our relationship with Olympia is underscored by the reaction of her cat, who—unlike the sleeping dog in Titan's painting—arches its back at us. Manet has subverted the entire tradition of the accommodating female nude, for Olympia stares down on us, indicating that she is in the position of power. Despite our offering of flowers, presented by her Caribbean servant arriving from the background, she may not surrender to our advances, a point underscored by the protective placement of her tensed left hand (compare fig. 13–21). Not surprisingly, conservative critics heaped scorn on the painting when it was displayed at the Salon of 1865.

Impressionism

Among the artists who frequented the Café Guerbois with Manet were Claude Monet, Edgar Degas, and Pierre-Auguste Renoir. With the exception of Degas—who, like Manet, remained a studio painter—they began to paint outdoors, ***en plein air*** ("in the open air"), in an effort to record directly the fleeting effects of light and atmosphere. *Plein-air* painting was greatly facilitated by the invention in 1841 of tin tubes for oil paint.

In April 1874, Monet, Degas, and Renoir, joined by Berthe Morisot, Camille Pissaro, Paul Cézanne, and others, exhibited together in Paris as the *Société Anonyme des Artistes Peintres, Sculpteurs, Graveurs, etc.* (Corporation of Artists Painters, Sculptors, Engravers, etc.), usually shortened to *Société Anonyme.* While the exhibition received some positive reviews, it was attacked by conservative critics. Louis Leroy seized on the title of a painting by Monet—*Impression, Sunrise* (1872) (fig. **18–18**)—and dubbed the entire exhibition *Impressionist.* While Leroy used the word to attack the seemingly haphazard technique and unfinished look of their paintings, Monet and many of his colleagues were pleased to accept the label, which spoke to their concern for capturing an instantaneous impression of a scene in nature. Seven more Impressionist exhibitions followed between 1876 and 1886, with the contributors varying slightly on each occasion. By the end of the century, these independent exhibitions effectively ended the French Academy's centuries-old stranglehold on the display of art and thus on artistic standards.

Claude Monet (1840–1926), after some early efforts at *plein-air* painting near his family home along the Normandy coast, developed his own technique of applying paint with strokes and touches of pure color, intended to describe flowers, leaves, and waves, but

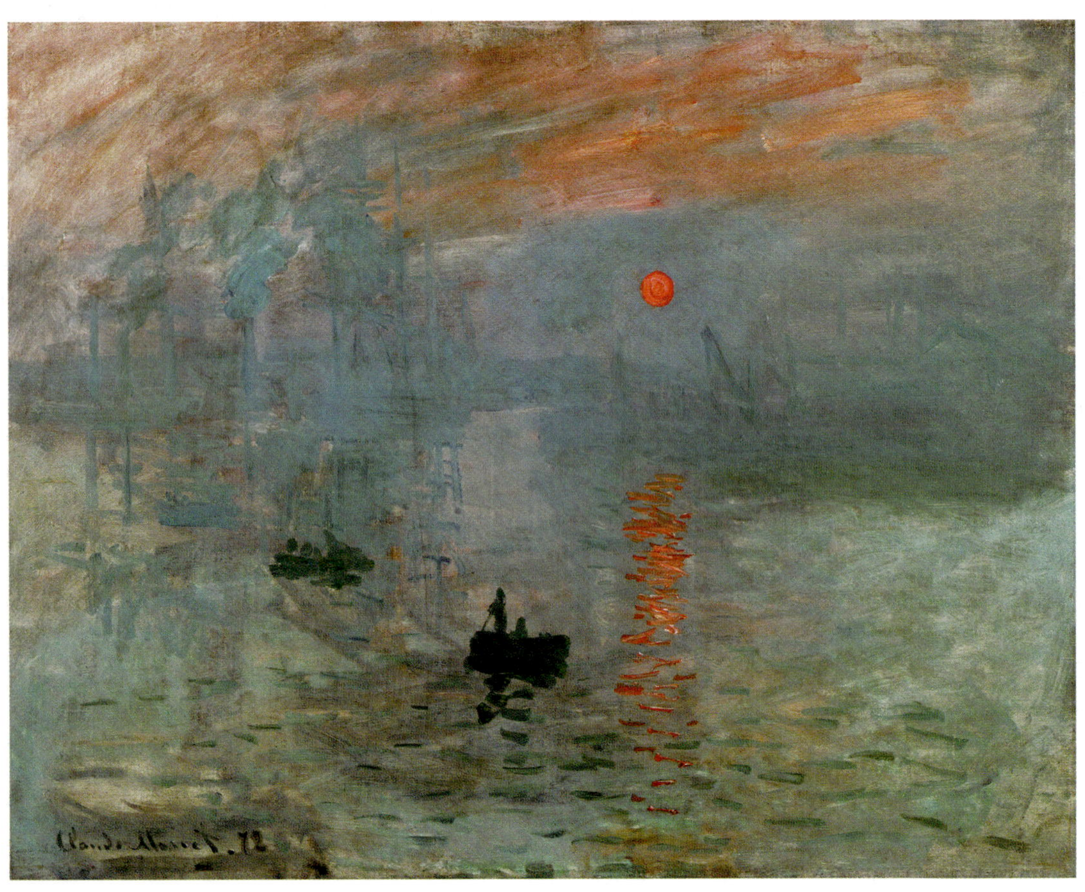

18–18 Claude Monet. *Impression, Sunrise.* 1872. Oil on canvas, 19½" × 25½" (49.5 × 64.7 cm). Musée Marmottan, Paris, France

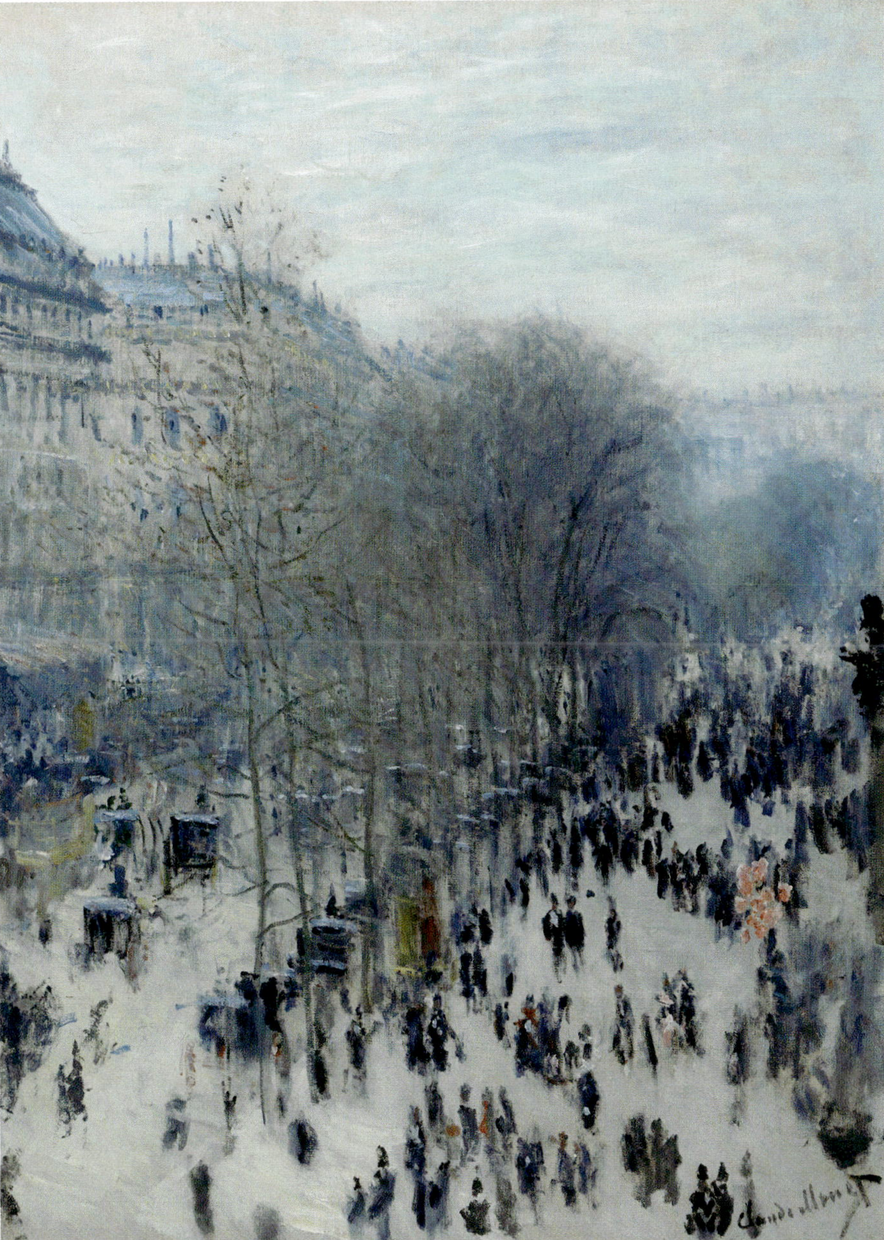

18–19 Claude Monet. *Boulevard des Capucines, Paris.* 1873–1874. Oil on canvas, 31¼" × 23¼" (79.4 × 59.1 cm). The Nelson-Atkins Museum of Art, Kansas City, Missouri
PURCHASE: THE KENNETH A. AND HELEN F. SPENCER FOUNDATION ACQUISITION FUND (F72–35)

Monet painted this picture from the balcony of Parisian photographer Nadar's studio at 35 Boulevard des Capucines, the site of the first Impressionist exhibition. In an appreciative review, critic Ernest Chesnau wrote: "The extraordinary animation of the public street, the crowd swarming on the sidewalks, the carriages on the pavement, and the boulevard's trees waving in the dust and light—never has movement's elusive, fugitive, instantaneous quality been captured and fixed in all its tremendous fluidity as it has in this extraordinary, marvelous sketch."

also to register simply as marks of paint on the surface of the canvas. Monet's fully Impressionist pictures of the 1870s and 1880s—such as *Impression, Sunrise* and *Boulevard des Capucines, Paris* (fig. **18–19**)—are made up almost entirely of flecks of color (Leroy sneeringly called them "tongue-lickings"). Using these discrete marks of paint, Monet recorded the shifting play of light on the surface of objects and the effect of that light on the eye, rather than the physical character of the objects.

The American painter Lilla Cabot Perry (1848–1933) recalled Monet telling her, "When you go out to paint, try to forget what objects you have before you—a tree, a house, a field, or whatever. Merely think, here is a little square of blue, here an oblong of pink, here a streak of yellow, and paint it just as it looks to you, the exact color and shape, until it gives your own naïve impression of the scene before you." Two important ideas are expressed here. One is that a quickly painted oil sketch provides the most accurate record. This view had been a part of academic training since the late eighteenth century, but such sketches had been considered merely part of the preparation for the final work. As a result, viewers did not see Monet's paintings as "finished." The second idea is fundamentally modern: that artists have a special ability see the world freshly, untainted by intellectual preconceptions or socially imposed patterns.

Monet's fellow Impressionist Berthe Morisot (1841–1895), who participated in seven of the Impressionists' eight exhibitions, married Manet's brother, Eugène, in 1874, and unlike most married women painters of the time, who gave up their art to devote themselves to domestic duties, Morisot continued painting even after the birth of their daughter in 1879. She dedicated her art to the lives of bourgeois women, which she depicted in a style that became

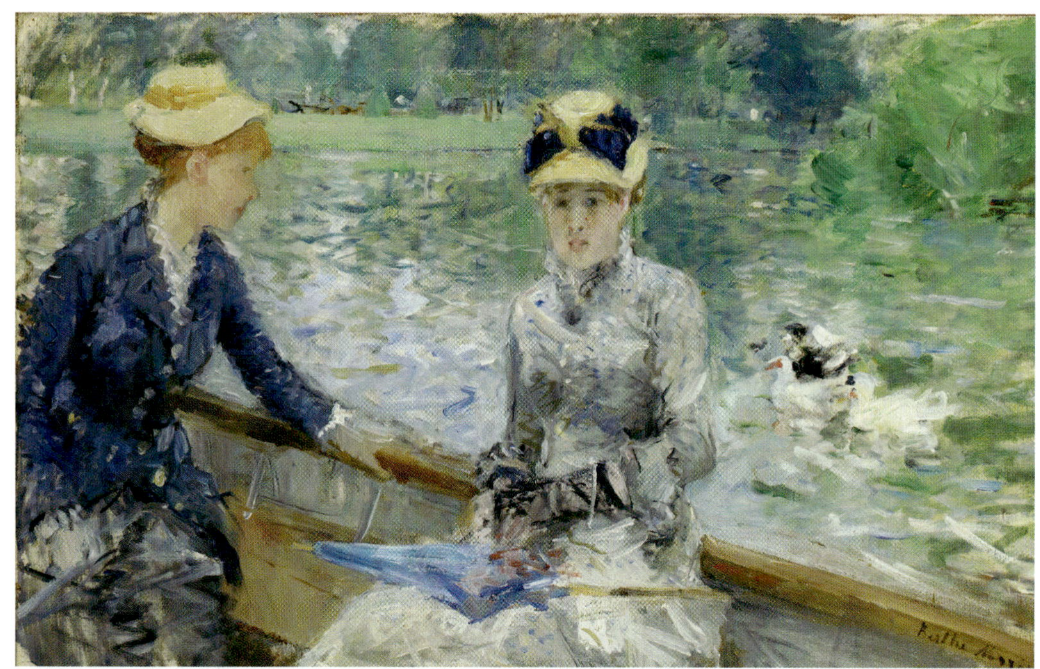

18–20 Berthe Morisot. *Summer's Day.* 1879. Oil on canvas, $17\frac{13}{16}$" × $29\frac{5}{16}$" (45.7 × 75.2 cm). The National Gallery, London

18–21 (BELOW) **Edgar Degas. *The Rehearsal of the Ballet on Stage.*** c. 1874. Pastel over brush-and-ink drawing on thin, cream-colored wove paper, laid on bristol board, mounted on canvas, $21\frac{3}{8}$" × $28\frac{3}{4}$" (54.3 × 73 cm). The Metropolitan Museum of Art, New York
BEQUEST OF MRS. H. O. HAVEMEYER COLLECTION, GIFT OF HORACE HAVEMEYER, 1929 (29.160.26)

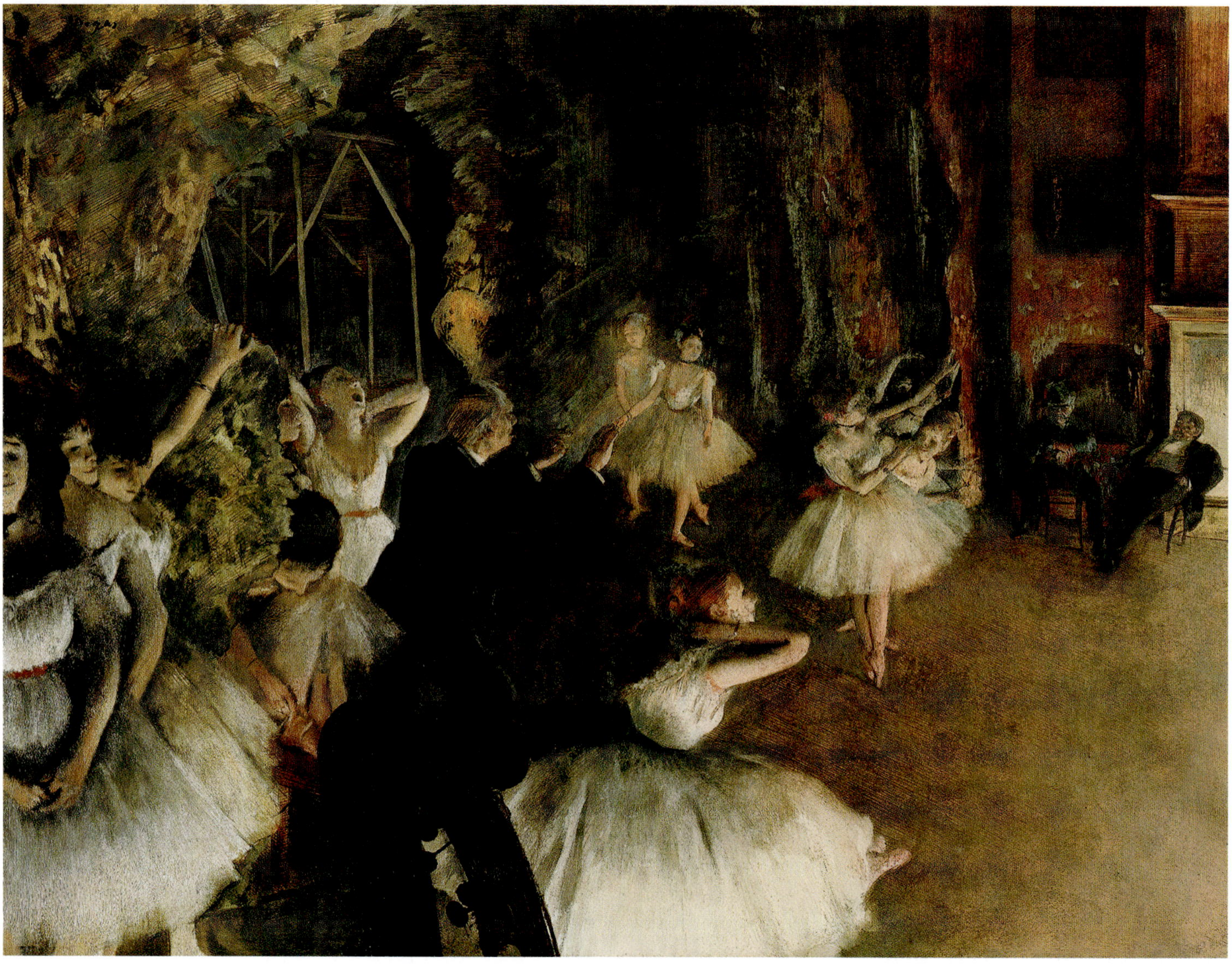

increasingly loose and painterly over the course of the 1870s. In works such as *Summer's Day* (fig. **18–20**) Morisot pushed the "sketch aesthetics" of Impressionism almost to their limit, dissolving forms into a flurry of feathery brushstrokes. In her painting, Morisot sought an equality for women that she felt men refused to cede. Late in life she commented, "I don't think there has ever been a man who treated a woman as an equal, and that's all I would have asked, for I know I'm worth as much as they" (Higonnet, page 19).

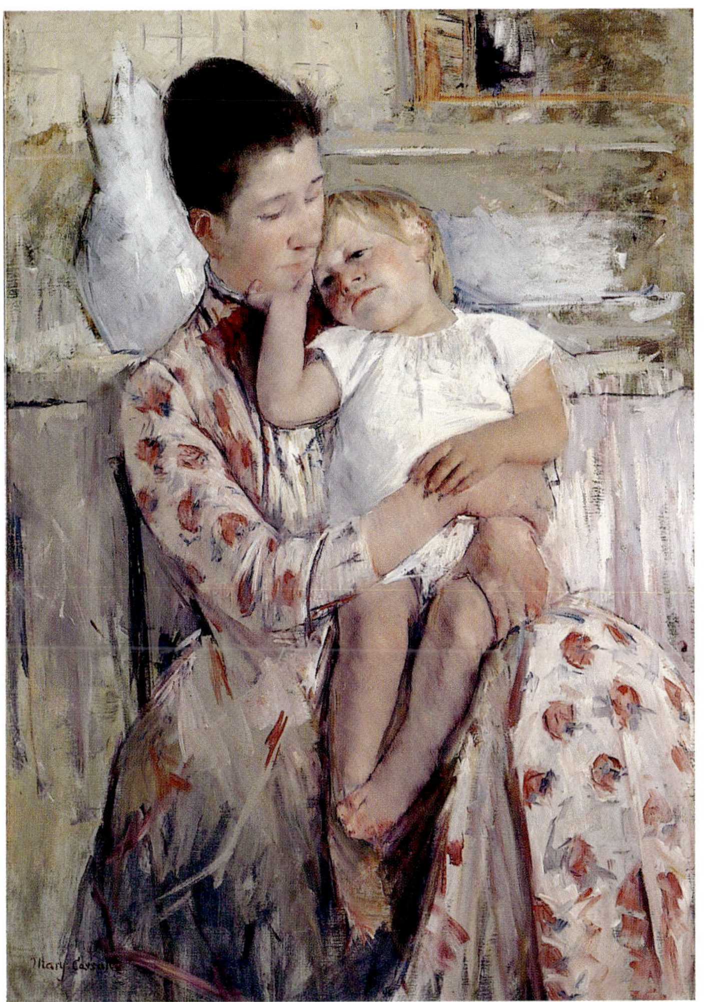

18–22 Mary Cassatt. *Mother and Child*. c. 1890. Oil on canvas, 35½" × 25⅜" (90.2 × 64.5 cm). Wichita Art Museum, Kansas

Unlike Morisot, not all the painters who are grouped with the Impressionists (because they participated in some or all of the exhibitions organized by Monet and his friends) truly worked in an Impressionist style. The artist whose work most severely tests the Impressionist label is Edgar Degas (1834–1917). His friendship with Manet, whom he met in 1862, and with the Realist critics in his circle, led him gradually away from the constrictions of his rigorous academic training and toward frank portrayals of contemporary life. After a period of painting psychologically probing portraits of friends and relatives, Degas turned in the 1870s to such Paris amusements as the music hall, opera, ballet, circus, and racetrack.

Degas was especially drawn to the ballet. From carefully observed studies of rehearsals and performances, he arranged his own visual choreography. *The Rehearsal of the Ballet on Stage* (fig. **18–21**) is not a factual record of something seen but a careful contrivance calculated to delight the idea but also to refocus the mind on the stern realities of modern life. In the right background slouch two well-dressed, middle-aged men, each probably a "protector" of one of the dancers. Because ballerinas generally came from lower-class families and exhibited their scantily clad bodies in public—something that "respectable" bourgeois women did not do—they were widely assumed to be sexually available, and they often attracted the attentions of wealthy men willing to support them in exchange for sexual favors. Several of Degas's ballet pictures include one or more of the dancers' mothers, who would accompany their daughters to rehearsals and performances in order to safeguard their virtue.

The rehearsal is viewed as if from an opera box close to the stage, creating an abrupt foreshortening of the scene emphasized by the dark scroll of the bass viols that juts up from the lower left. Degas's work shows two new important influences. The angular viewpoint from above in this and many of his other works reveals his knowledge of Japanese prints, which he collected, and the seemingly arbitrary cropping of figures, seen here in the ballerina at far left, shows the influence of photography, which he also practiced.

Another artist who exhibited with the Impressionists but whose art soon diverged from them in both style and technique—conditioned in part by her contact with Degas—was American expatriate Mary Cassatt (1844–1926). Born near Pittsburgh, raised in the cosmopolitan world of Philadelphia, and studying during the early 1860s at the Pennsylvania Academy of the Fine Arts, she moved to Paris in 1865 to further her academic training and lived there for most of the rest of her life. Cassatt focused her paintings on the world to which she had best access: the domestic and social life of bourgeois women. She is known for extraordinarily sensitive paintings of mothers with children, which, like the genre paintings of expatriate artist Henry Ossawa Tanner (see fig. 18–15), sought to counteract the clichéd conceptions of her age. In a painting of this theme from about 1890 (fig. **18–22**) she uses a contrast between the loosely painted, Impressionist treatment of clothing and setting and the solidly modeled forms of faces and hands to rivet viewers' attention on the tender connection between mother and child. And because the structured composition and traditional subject recall much earlier portrayals of the Virgin and Child (e.g., see figs. 11–17 and 13–5), she elevates this vignette of modern life to the level of heroic dialogue with the history of art.

In the years after 1880, Impressionism underwent what historians have termed a "crisis," as artists grew dissatisfied with their attempts to capture momentary perceptions through spontaneous brushwork and casual compositions. In response, more and more artists began to select subjects more carefully, work longer on their pictures, and develop styles that lent their imagery a greater sense of permanence and seriousness. Auguste Renoir (1841–1919) was strongly affected by this crisis. It was his exposure to the paintings of Old Masters during a trip to Italy in 1881 that caused him to reconsider his commitment to painting fleeting impressions of modern life. Consequently, although he continued to use sensual

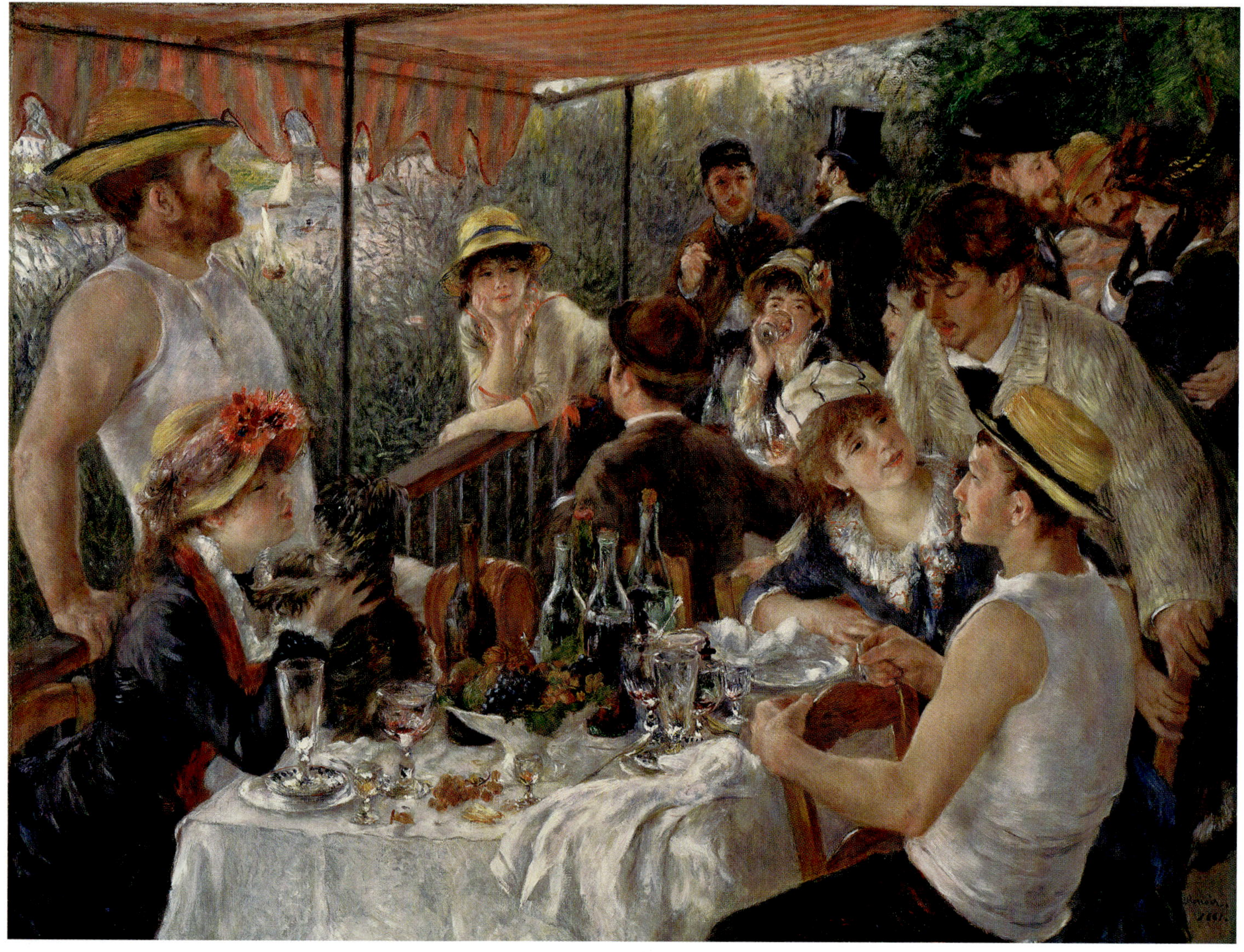

18–23 Pierre-Auguste Renoir. ***Luncheon of the Boating Party.*** 1881. Oil on canvas, 4' 3" × 5' 8" (1.29 × 1.73 m). The Phillips Collection, Washington, D.C.
ACQUIRED 1923

brushwork and lush color, he began to present firmly modeled figures and relatively traditional compositions.

In Renoir's *Luncheon of the Boating Party*, a variation on the traditional pyramidal structure advocated by the academies underlies the apparent informality of the summer scene (fig. **18–23**). A small triangle whose apex is the woman leaning on the rail is set within a larger, somewhat looser pyramid that culminates in the two men at the rear. Thus, instead of a moment quickly scanned in passing (an impression), Renoir composed a more stable and permanent grouping. But he has remained faithful to the traditional subject matter of Impressionism—already challenged in the work of Degas and Cassatt. Renoir has glamorized his young artist friends and their models, who constitute the gathering celebrated here, showing them in attitudes of relaxed congeniality, smiling, chatting, and flirting. This naïve image of a carefree life of innocent leisure, a kind of bourgeois paradise, nicely encapsulates Renoir's notion of art. He said, "For me a picture should be a pleasant thing, joyful and pretty—yes pretty! There are quite enough unpleasant things in life without the need to manufacture more." As we have seen, not everyone painting at this time agreed with him.

Post-Impressionism

The English critic Roger Fry coined the term "Post-Impressionism" in 1910 to identify a broad reaction against Impressionism in painting that was mounted during the late nineteenth and early twentieth centuries. Art historians recognize Paul Cézanne, Georges Seurat, Paul Gauguin, Vincent van Gogh, and Paul Signac as the principal artists united under this term; some also add Henri de Toulouse-Lautrec. Each of these painters moved through an Impressionist phase and continued to use the bright Impressionist palette in his mature work. But each also came to reject Impressionism's emphasis on the spontaneous recording of light

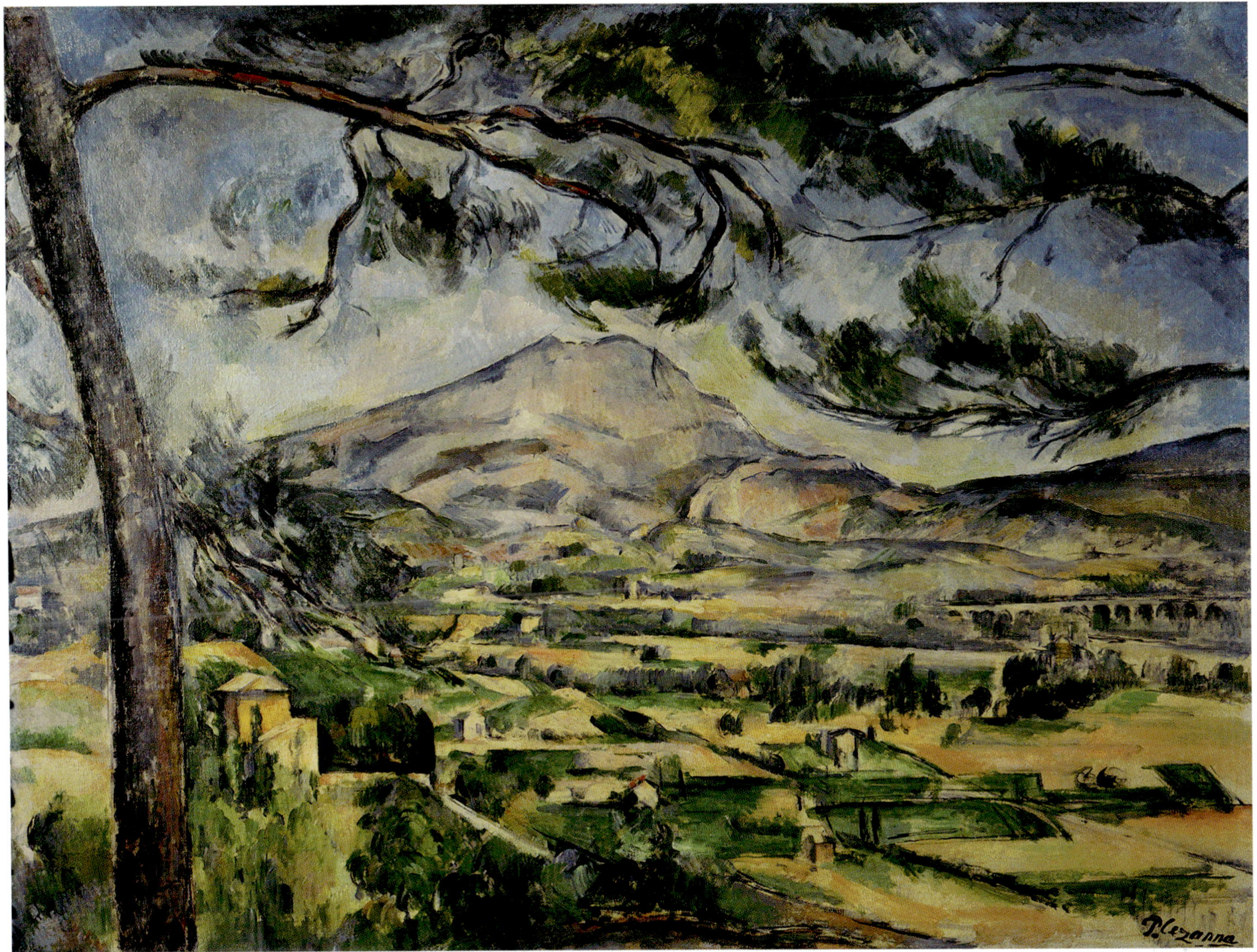

18–24 Paul Cézanne. ***Mont Sainte-Victoire.*** c. 1885–1887. Oil on canvas, 25½" × 32" (64.8 × 92.3 cm). Courtauld Gallery, London

On the one hand, recession into depth is suggested by elements such as the foreground tree that helps draw the eye into the valley, and by the gradual transition from the intense greens and orange-yellows of the foreground to the softer blues and pinks in the distant mountain range, which create an effect of atmospheric perspective. On the other hand, this illusion of consistent recession into depth is challenged by the inclusion of blues, pinks, and reds in the foreground foliage, which relate the foreground forms to the background mountain and sky, and by the tree branches in the sky, which follow the contours of the mountain, making the peak appear nearer and binding it to the foreground plane.

and color and instead sought to create art with a greater degree of formal order and structure. This goal led the Post-Impressionists to develop more abstract and expressive styles that would prove highly influential for the development of Modernist painting in the early twentieth century.

No artist had a greater impact on the next generation of Modern painters than Paul Cézanne (1839–1902), yet he was ignored or misunderstood in his own day by all but a few perceptive collectors and fellow artists. Son of a prosperous banker in the southern French city of Aix-en-Provence, Cézanne began his career painting unsettling Realist scenes of dramatic conflict and sexual violence (these were consistently rejected by the salon), but during the 1870s he discovered Impressionism and rededicated himself to the objective transcription of what he called his "sensations" of nature. Unlike the Impressionists, however, Cézanne did not seek to capture transitory effects of light and atmosphere but rather to create a sense of order in nature through a careful and methodical application of color that merged drawing and modeling into a single process. His professed aim was to "make of Impressionism something solid and durable, like the art of the museums."

Cézanne's tireless pursuit of this goal is exemplified in a series of paintings of Mont Sainte-Victoire, which he could view near his home in Aix-en-Provence. In this example (fig. **18–24**), the mountain rises above the valley, which is dotted with houses and trees and is traversed at the far right by an aqueduct. Framing the scene at the left is an evergreen tree, which echoes the contours of the mountain, creating harmony between the two principal elements of the composition. The even lighting, still atmosphere, and absence of human activity in the landscape communicate a sense of timeless endurance, at odds with the Impressionists' interest in capturing a momentary aspect of the ever-changing world. Cézanne's handling of paint is more deliberate and constructive than the Impressionists' spontaneous and sometimes random brushwork. His strokes, which vary from short, parallel hatchings to sketchy lines to broader swaths of flat color, weave every element of the landscape together into a unified surface design. That surface design coexists with the effect of spatial recession that the composition simultaneously creates, generating a fruitful tension between the illusion of three dimensions "behind" the picture plane and the physical reality and chromatic delight of its two-dimensional surface.

Although it is tempting to see in *Mont Sainte-Victoire* evidence of Cézanne's ultimate rejection of Impressionist principles for a renewed interest in solid form, this and works like it remain firmly grounded in the understanding of the individual brush mark as a record of the artist's immediate "sensation" of nature. In the middle section of the composition, for example, the solid rectangular strokes, generally applied according to a rigid grid of vertical and horizontal lines, nevertheless form dynamic and irregular contours. Shapes closed on one side are open on another so that they can merge with adjacent shapes. Such merging of shapes, along with the prominent juxtaposition of warm and cool colors creates a spatial tension, heightened by the contradiction between the presumed depth of the landscape and the flat painted surface of the canvas that the viewer actually sees, a contradiction that allowed Cézanne's paintings to evoke the essential tension in nature between permanence and change.

Spatial ambiguities of a different sort appear in Cézanne's late still lifes, in which many of the objects seem incorrectly drawn. In *Still Life with Basket of Apples* (fig. **18–25**), for example, the right side of the table is higher than the left, the wine bottle has two different silhouettes, and the pastries on the table next to it are tilted upward toward the viewer, while the apples below seem to be seen head-on. Such shifting viewpoints are not evidence of any incompetence, however, but of the artist's willful disregard for the rules of traditional perspective. Although scientific perspective mandates that the eye of the artist (and hence the viewer) occupy a fixed point relative to the scene being observed (see "Renaissance Perspective Systems, page 324), Cézanne studies the objects in his still lives from a variety of different positions just as we might move around or turn our heads to take everything in. The composition as a whole, assembled from multiple sightings, is more complex and dynamic, seeming at times on the verge of collapse. Instead of a faithful reproduction of static objects, Cézanne was re-creating, or reconstructing, nature, or at least our experience of it.

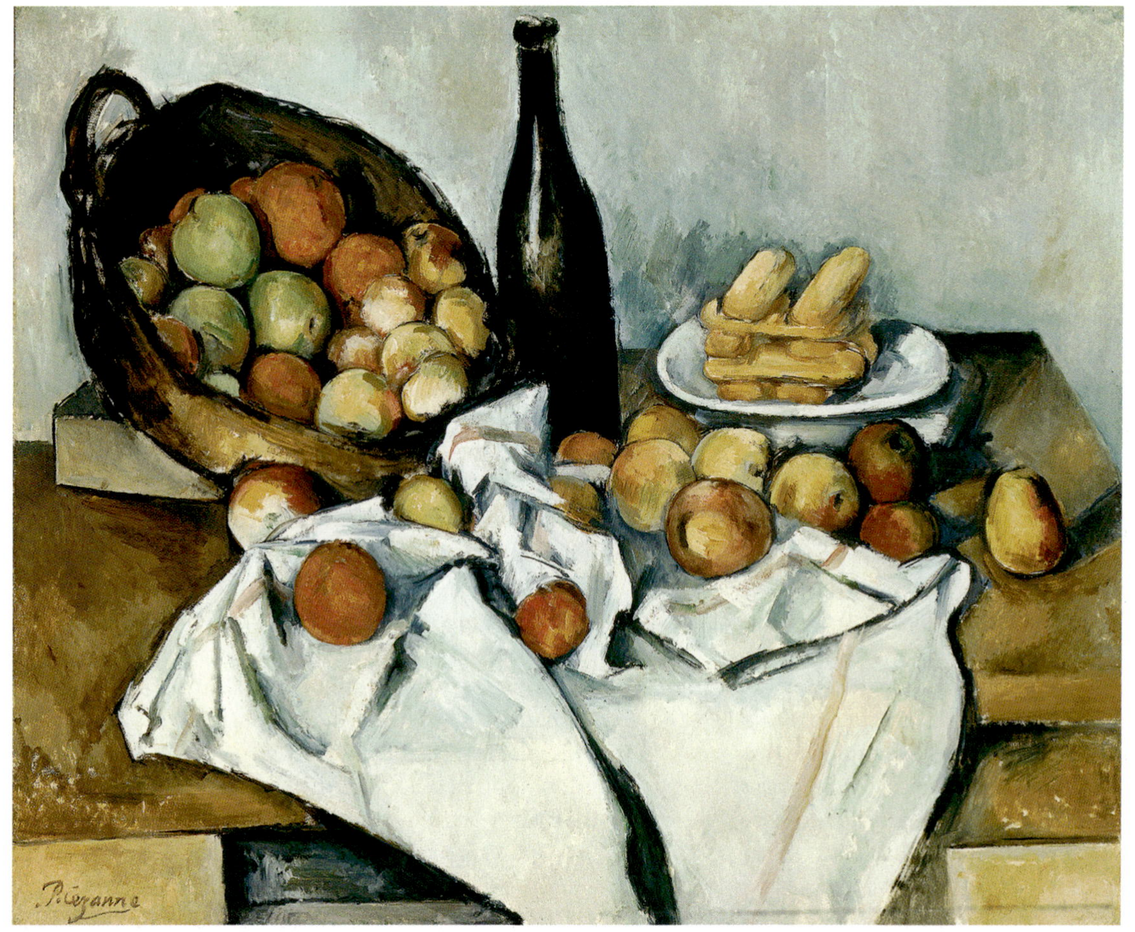

18–25 Paul Cézanne. *Still Life with Basket of Apples*. 1890–1894. Oil on canvas, 24⅜" × 31" (62.5 × 79.5 cm). The Art Institute of Chicago
HELEN BIRCH BARTLETT MEMORIAL COLLECTION

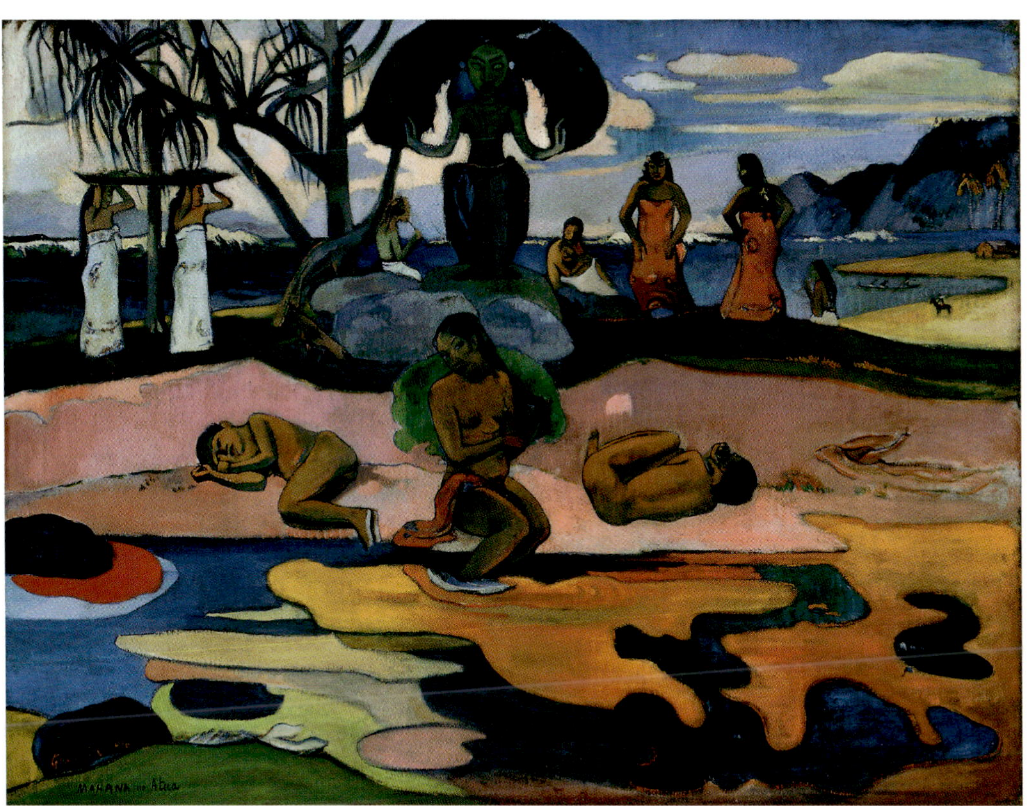

18–26 Paul Gauguin. ***Mahana no atua* (*Day of the God*).** 1894. Oil on canvas, 27⅜" × 35⅝" (69.5 × 90.5 cm). The Art Institute of Chicago
HELEN BIRCH BARTLETT MEMORIAL COLLECTION (1926.198)

Other Post-Impressionists had different objectives. Some saw art as a force for social commentary, even as a way to promote social change. The name that came into general use to describe such art was **avant-garde**. Originally a military term for an advance unit, it was used in 1825 by a French socialist, the Comte de Saint-Simon, to refer to those artists whose visual expression would prepare people to accept the social changes he and his colleagues envisioned. The idea of producing a socially revolutionary art had attracted such artists as Courbet and Millet, but the widespread popularity of this notion dates from the Post-Impressionist era. Eventually the term came to stand for the forward-looking aspect of Modern art conceived more broadly, the belief that Modernist artists are working ahead of the public's ability to comprehend developments within the art world. This promoted a sense on the part of artists that they stood in an elite and progressive position as harbingers of change and prophets of progress, set against the mundane preoccupations of the world around them.

Georges Seurat (1859–1891) was apparently one of the first in his generation to think of himself as an avant-garde artist. He devoted his energies to "correcting" Impressionism, which he found too intellectually shallow and too improvisational. Seurat belonged to a group of artists, intellectuals, and amateur scientists who were studying theories of vision, light, and color, and he applied their theories to his painting in a technique he called "divisionism" or "pointillism". The work that became the centerpiece of the new movement and made Seurat's reputation was *A Sunday Afternoon on the Island of La Grande Jatte* (see fig. 18–1), which Seurat first exhibited at the eighth and final Impressionist exhibition in 1886. The theme of weekend leisure is typically Impressionist, but the rigorous technique, the stiff formality of the figures, and the highly calculated geometry of the composition produce a solemn, abstract effect quite at odds with the casual naturalism of earlier Impressionism.

From its first appearance, the painting has been the subject of a number of conflicting interpretations. Contemporary accounts of the island indicate that on Sundays it was noisy, littered, and chaotic. By painting the island the way he did, Seurat may have intended to represent an ideal image of middle-class life and leisure—a model of how tranquil the island, and perhaps life, *should* be. On the other hand, some art historians see him satirizing the habits and attitudes of the growing Parisian middle class, since he was a known anarchist.

Certainly for one artist, the desire to escape modern life in Paris was a clear goal; the French painter Paul Gauguin (1848–1903) moved first to Brittany and then to Panama. At age 37, he had given up a conventional existence as a Paris stockbroker and left his wife and five children to pursue a full-time painting career. In 1888, he spent two months with van Gogh in Arles, and sailed for Tahiti in the South Pacific in 1891. Before Gauguin left for the South Pacific, he had found inspiration in the simplified drawing, flattened space, and antinaturalistic color of medieval stained glass, Breton folk art, and Japanese prints. He rejected Impressionism (although he had exhibited in the last four Impressionist exhibitions, 1880–1886) because it neglected subjective feelings. Gauguin called his anti-Impressionist style *synthetism*, because it synthesized observation of the subject in nature with the artist's feelings about that subject, expressed through abstracted line, shape, space, and color.

Very much a product of such synthesis is *Mahana no atua* (*Day of the God*) (fig. **18–26**), which, despite its Tahitian subject, was painted in France during Gauguin's return after two years in the South Pacific. Gauguin had gone to Tahiti hoping to find an unspoiled, pre-industrial paradise. He had imagined the Tahitians to be childlike and close to nature, but what he discovered, instead, was a thoroughly colonized country whose native culture was rapidly disappearing under the pressures of Westernization. In his paintings, Gauguin chose to ignore this reality and to depict the Edenic ideal of his imagination.

Gauguin divided *Mahana no atua* into three horizontal zones in styles of increasing abstraction. The upper zone, painted in the most lifelike manner, centers on the statue of a god, behind which extends a beach landscape populated by Tahitians. In the middle zone, directly beneath the statue, three figures occupy a beach divided into several bands of antinaturalistic color. The central female bather dips her feet in the water and looks coyly out at the viewer, while on either side of her two figures recline in fetus-like postures—perhaps symbolizing birth, life, and death. Filling the bottom third of the canvas is a strikingly abstract pool whose surface offers a dazzling array of bright colors, arranged in a puzzle-like pattern of flat, curvilinear shapes. By reflecting a strange and unexpected reality exactly where we expect to see a mirror image of the familiar world, this magic pool seems the perfect symbol of Gauguin's desire to evoke "the mysterious centers of thought."

Among the artists in Gauguin's circle before his departure for Tahiti was the Dutch painter Vincent van Gogh (1853–1890). Van Gogh had moved to Paris in 1886, where at first he came under the influence of the Impressionists and Neo-Impressionists. He quickly adapted Seurat's divisionist technique, but rather than laying down

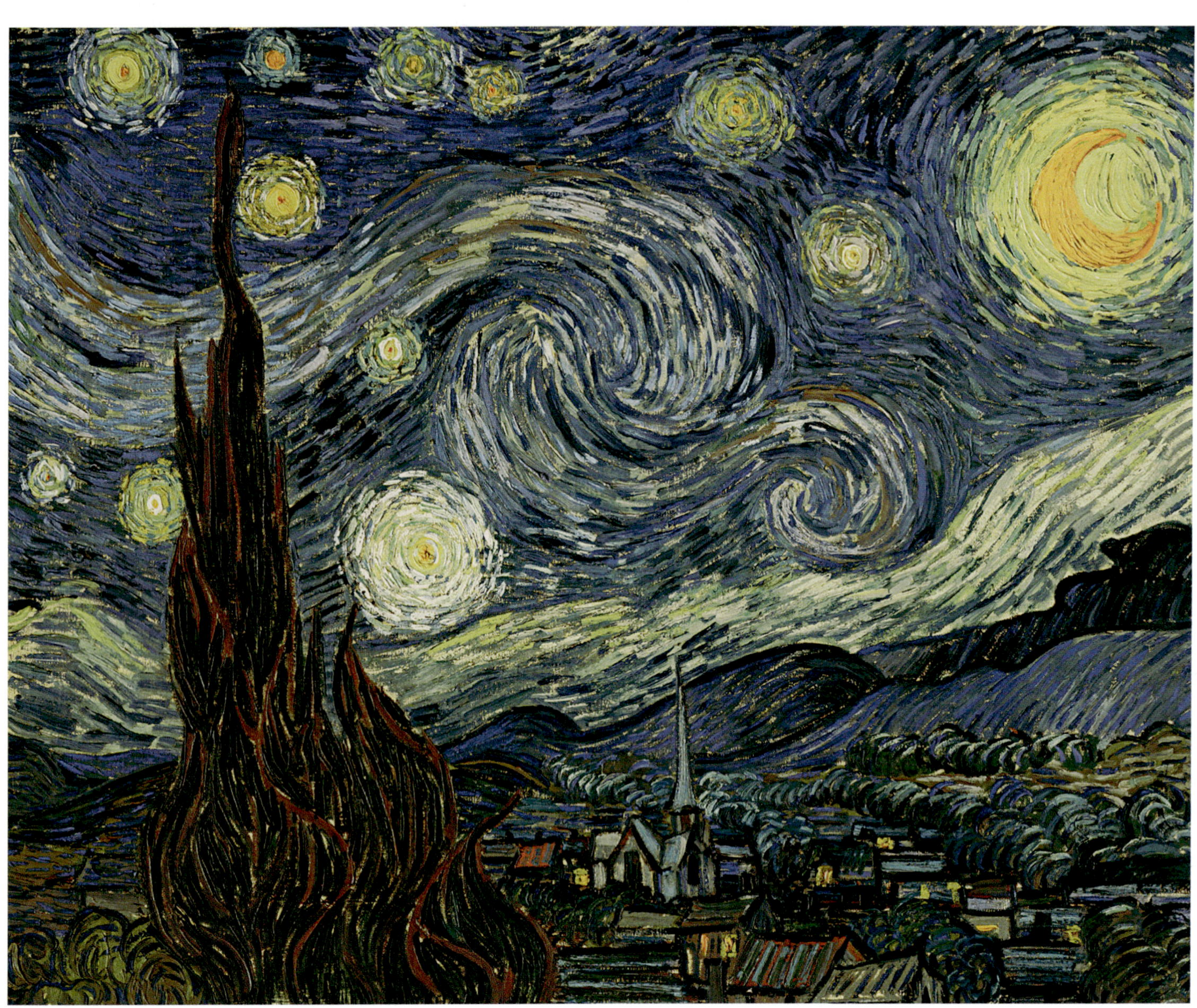

18–27 Vincent van Gogh. *The Starry Night*. 1889. Oil on canvas, 28¾" × 36¼" (73 × 92 cm)
THE MUSEUM OF MODERN ART, NEW YORK
ACQUIRED THROUGH THE LILLIE P. BLISS BEQUEST (472.1941).

his paint regularly in dots, he applied it freely in multidirectional dashes of **impasto** (thickly applied pigment), giving his pictures a sense of physical energy and a palpable surface texture. Van Gogh shared Gauguin's desire for a simple, preindustrial life, and the two planned to move to the south of France and establish a commune of like-minded artists. When Gauguin finally joined van Gogh, their constant quarrels soon led to violent confrontation and Gauguin's departure. Only a few close friends and his brother Theo stood by van Gogh to the end. After a series of psychological crises that led to his hospitalization, van Gogh shot himself in July 1890.

The paintings van Gogh produced during the last year and a half of his life testify to his heightened emotional state. At the same time, they contributed significantly to the emergence of an expressionistic tradition, in which the intensity of an artist's feelings overrides any desire for fidelity to the actual appearance of things. A prime example is *The Starry Night* (fig. **18–27**), which van Gogh completed near the asylum of Saint-Rémy, where the artist spent the last years of his life. The sky, pulsating with exploding stars high above the quiet town, is clearly more a record of what van Gogh felt than what he saw. Perhaps van Gogh ascribed to the then-popular

JAPONISME

Art created by cultures outside the European tradition has been a constant influence on Modern art. In some respects this is logical. If artists regard their own tradition as outmoded or in need of reform, they may naturally look to other cultures for inspiration.

The first wave of outside influence was from Japan, beginning shortly after the U.S. Navy forcibly opened that country to Western trade and diplomacy in 1853. Two years later, France, England, Russia, and the United States signed trade agreements that permitted regular exchange of goods. The first Japanese art to engage the attention of Modern artists was a sketchbook called *Manga* by Hokusai (1760–1849), which several Parisian artists eagerly passed around. Soon it became fashionable for those in the art world to collect Japanese objects for their homes. Édouard Manet, for example, painted a portrait of Émile Zola at his desk surrounded by a Japanese screen and some prints that he owned.

The Paris International Exposition of 1867 hosted the first exhibition of Japanese prints in Europe, and soon, Japanese lacquers, fans, bronzes, hanging scrolls, kimonos, ceramics, illustrated books, and ***ukiyo-e*** (prints of the "floating world," the realm of geishas and popular entertainment) began to appear in specialty shops, art galleries, and even some department stores. French interest in Japan and its arts reached such proportions by 1872 that the art critic Philippe Burty gave it a name: ***japonisme***.

Japanese art profoundly influenced Western painting, printmaking, applied arts, and eventually architecture. The tendency toward simplicity, flatness, and the decorative evident in much painting and graphic art in the West between roughly 1860 and 1900 is the clearest indication of the influence. Nevertheless, the impact of Japanese art was extraordinarily diverse. What individual artists took depended on their own interests. Whistler found encouragement for his decorative conception of art, while Edgar Degas discovered both realistic subjects and interesting compositional arrangements. Those interested in the reform of late nineteenth-century industrial design found in Japanese objects both fine craft and a smooth elegance lacking in the West. Vincent van Gogh enjoyed the bold design and handcrafted quality of Japanese prints. He both owned and copied Japanese prints, as can be seen by comparing figures **18–28** and **18–29**.

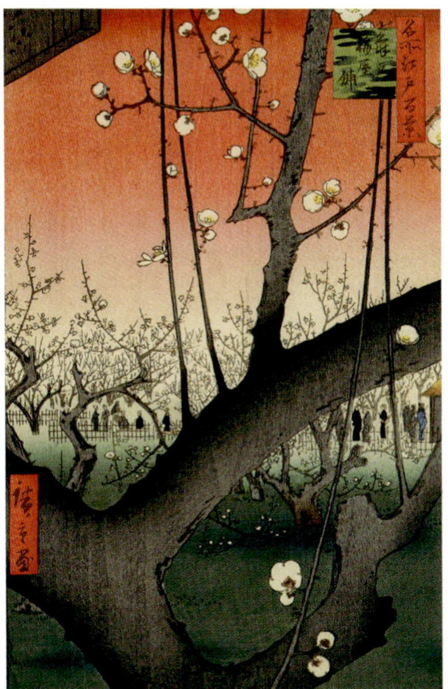

18–28 Hiroshige. *Plum Orchard, Kameido*, from *One Hundred Famous Views of Edo*. 1857. Woodblock print, 13¼" × 8⅝" (33.6 × 47 cm). The Brooklyn Museum, New York
GIFT OF ANNA FERRIS (30.1478.30)

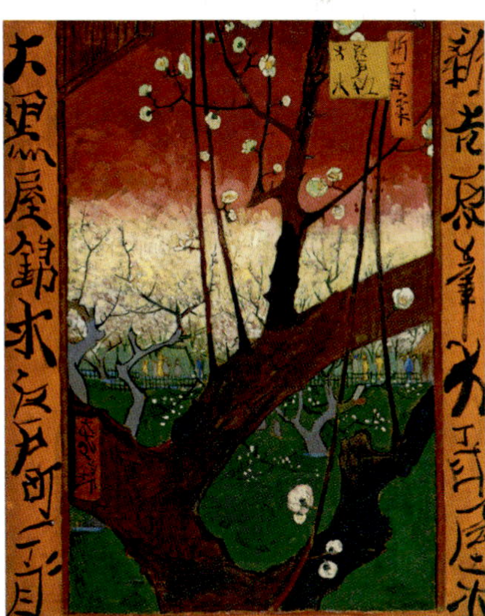

18–29 Vincent van Gogh. *Japonaiserie: Flowering Plum Tree*. 1887. Oil on canvas, 21½" × 18" (54.6 × 45.7 cm). Vincent van Gogh Museum, Amsterdam

idea that after death people journeyed to a star, where they continued their lives; he wrote, "Just as we take the train to get to Tarascon or Rouen, we take death to reach a star." In the painting, a cypress tree, a traditional symbol of both death and eternal life, dramatically links the terrestrial world with the heavens.

A more frightening image of the night sky can be seen in the painting of the Norwegian Edvard Munch (1863–1944). His famous work, *The Scream* (fig. **18–30**) is an unforgettable image of modern alienation that radiates Expressionist intensity of feeling. Munch recorded the painting's genesis in his diary: "one evening I was walking along a path; the city was on one side, and the fjord below. I was tired and ill. … I sensed a shriek passing through nature. … I painted this picture, painted the clouds as actual blood." The overwhelming anxiety that sought release in this primal scream was chiefly a dread of death, as the sky and the figure's skull-like head suggest, but the setting of the picture also suggests a fear of open spaces. The expressive abstraction of form and color in the painting reflects the influence of Gauguin and his Scandinavian followers, whose work Munch had encountered shortly before painting *The Scream.*

Expressionism was one way to communicate the psychological impact of the modern world. Another artistic response was to capture the emotive energy of modern life, a tactic followed by Henri de Toulouse-Lautrec (1864–1901) in his paintings and prints. From the late 1880s, Toulouse-Lautrec chronicled life in Montmartre—a section of Paris devoted to entertainment and inhabited by those who lived on the fringes of society—through his designs for lithographic posters used as advertisements for popular night spots and entertainers. His portrayal of the café dancer *Jane Avril* (fig. **18–31**) demonstrates the remarkable artistry that he brought to an essentially commercial project. The composition juxtaposes the dynamic figure of the dancer on a boldly foreshortened stage with the cropped arm of a bass viol player in the immediate foreground, suggesting the influence of Degas (see fig. 18–21). But Toulouse-Lautrec has extended the bass viol's head into a curving frame that surrounds Avril and connects her visually with her musical accompaniment. The radical simplification of form, suppression of modeling, flattening of space, and integration of blank paper into the composition all suggest the influence of Japanese woodblock prints

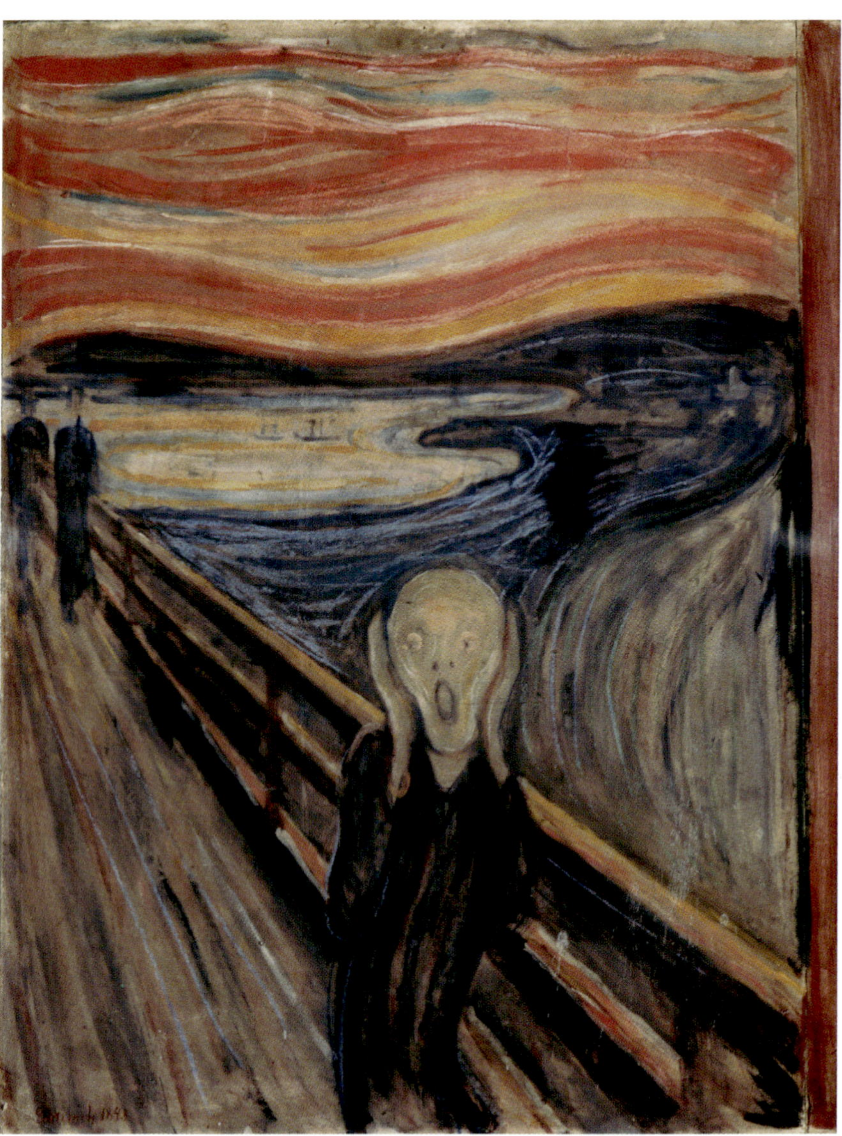

18–30 Edvard Munch. ***The Scream.*** 1893. Tempera and casein on cardboard, 36" × 29" (91.3 × 73.7 cm). Nasjonalgalleriet, Oslo

Munch derived his anxious, compelling visions from observation of the real world—the red and yellow lights in the sky actually occur in northern lands—however he transformed the visual record using acid colors, crude forms, and rough surface textures.

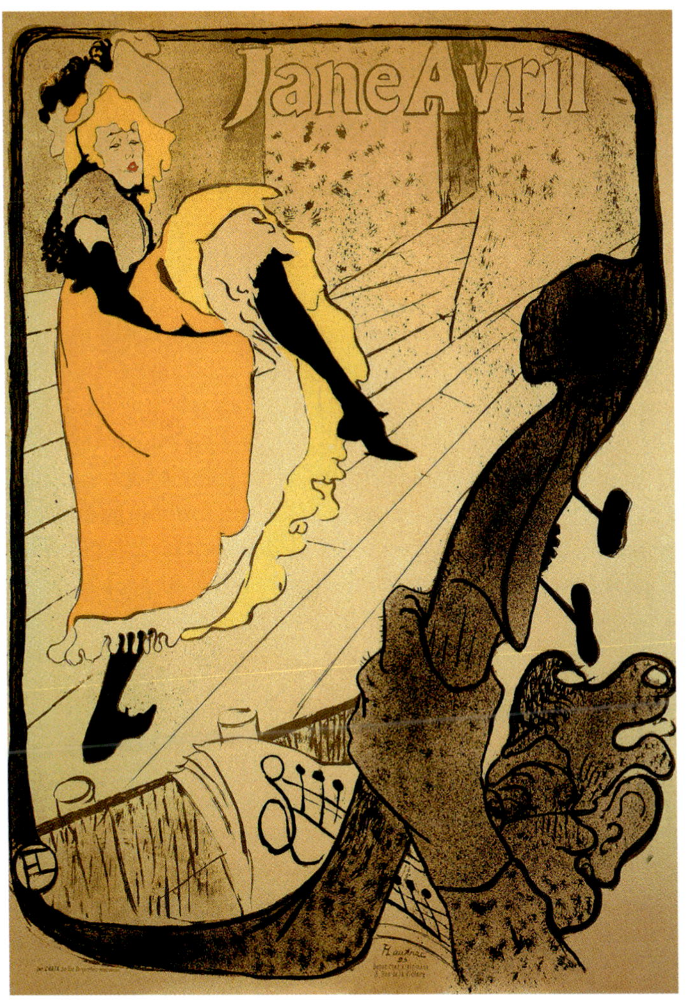

(see "Japonisme," page 517). The emphasis on curving lines and the incorporation of lettering into the total design also connect the poster with Art Nouveau. Ultimately, although they are energetic and colorful, many of Toulouse-Lautrec's images evoke the sad reality of the festivities at popular dance halls. Like Manet's paintings, they reveal the artist's sensitivity to a new kind of loneliness: the modern feeling of alienation.

Paul Signac (1863–1935) moved in the avant-garde intellectual and art circles of Paris. He was particularly fascinated by other painters' experiments with color and became close to people who (in retrospect) became leading Post-Impressionists and Expressionists—van Gogh, Gauguin, Toulouse-Lautrec, and Henri Matisse (see Chapter 19). But after he became enchanted by the landscape of the French Riviera, he acquired a house in Saint-Tropez on the coast, painting the harbor with its old houses and sailboats and occasionally painting the local inhabitants as well. From his outpost in the south, Signac emerged as the leading theorist in the Neo-Impressionist circle of the 1880s and 1890s, a group that included the critic Félix Fénéon (1861–1944) and the eccentric amateur scientist Charles Henry (1859–1926). In Fénéon's view, great art "sacrifices anecdote to arabesque, analysis to synthesis, fugitive to permanent" (Ferretti-Bocquillon, page 161). And this is precisely what Signac has done in his *Place des Lices, Saint-Tropez* (see "Closer Look," page 520). The work, to which Signac gave the alternate musical title of *Opus 242*, is an homage to the light and color of the south—and to the rhythms of the swaying plane trees.

18–31 Henri de Toulouse-Lautrec. ***Jane Avril.*** 1893.
Lithograph, 50½ × 37" (129 × 94 cm). San Diego Museum of Art
THE BALDWIN M. BALDWIN COLLECTION

Technique

Lithography

Aloys Senefelder invented **lithography** in Bavaria, Germany, in 1796 and registered for an exclusive right to the process the following year. Lithography is a planographic process—that is, the printing is done from a flat surface. It was the first wholly new printing process to be introduced since the fifteenth century, when the intaglio, or incising, process was developed (see "Woodcuts and Engravings," page 315).

Lithography, still popular today, is based on the natural antagonism between oil and water. Artists draw on a flat surface—traditionally, fine-grained stone—with a greasy crayon. The stone's surface is flooded with water, over which an oil-based ink is rolled. The ink adheres to the greasy areas but not to the damp ones. Then a sheet of paper is placed face-down on the inked stone, and the stone and paper, covered by a blanket for protection, are passed through a flatbed press. A scraper applies light pressure from above as the stone and paper pass under it, transferring ink from stone to paper. This makes lithography a direct method of creating a printed image. Francisco Goya, Honoré Daumier, and Toulouse-Lautrec exploited the medium to great effect.

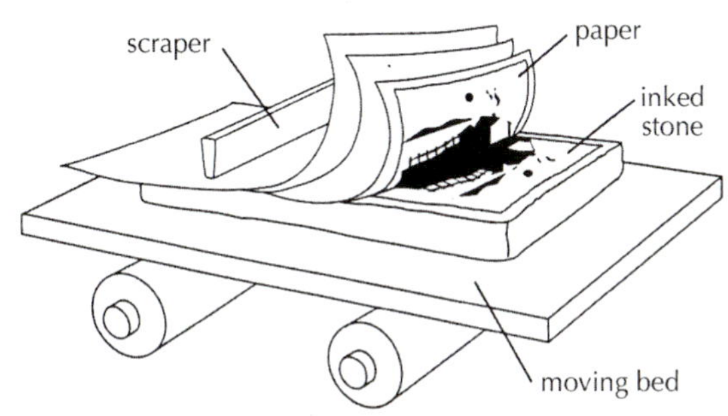

CLOSER LOOK

In the center of a park in Saint-Tropez, a man sits, framed by the undulating branches of plane trees (European sycamores) and the horizontal lines of the bench, the distant wall, and red-roofed buildings (fig. **18–32**). The trees defy the regularity of the rows in which they were planted and seem to dance rhythmically. Signac's painting reflects the avant-garde artist's interests in the abstract, decorative quality of Japanese prints and in the scientific study of light and perception. The subtle asymmetrical composition of dark branches against the setting sun recalls Hokusai's views of Mount Fuji (see fig. 9–27), and the brilliant contrasting purple/blue and yellow/orange paint reflects color theories being discussed in intellectual circles in Paris.

Artists like Seurat and Signac, whom in 1886 the critic Félix Fénéon dubbed Neo-Impressionists, knew Michel-Eugene Chevreul's "Law of the simultaneous contrast of colors" (1839). Chevreul (1786–1889) argued that not only do contrasting colors enhance each other's intensity, but that adjacent objects cast reflections of their own color onto their neighbors. Fénéon described the phenomenon: "Two adjacent colors exert a mutual influence, each imposing its own complementary on the other; for green a purple, for red a blue green, for yellow an ultramarine, for violet a greenish yellow, for orange a cyan blue" (Ferretti-Bocquillon, page 160).

The backlit trees, sun-dappled leaves, and areas of dazzling light breaking up the shadows on the ground reveal that Neo-Impressionists did not feel constrained to apply Chevreul's law systematically. They listened to people like the intellectual Charles Henry, too, who in 1889 devised a color wheel, which he called a chromatic circle. Henry studied the exact gradations of contrasting colors that, when placed side by side, not only intensify each other's effect but, when used in small dots, also "blend in the eye of the beholder." This phenomenon, known as optical mixture, creates a shimmering effect in the viewer's vision. Painters put this theory into practice, setting down hues in dots of pure color, one next to another, in what came to be known by various names: divisionism (the term preferred by Seurat), pointillism, and simply Neo-Impressionism. In theory, these juxtaposed dots would merge in the viewer's eye to produce the impression of other colors, more luminous and intense than if they had been mixed on the palette. In fact, this optical mixture is never complete, for the dots of color tend to remain separate, giving Neo-Impressionist paintings a speckled appearance.

In addition to illustrating Henry's *Chromatic Circle*, which was published as a monograph in 1890, Signac wrote his own book, *From Delacroix to Neo-Impressionism* (1899), in which he articulated the Neo-Impressionist aesthetic theory. The work is considered a landmark both in the study of color and in the appreciation of Delacroix.

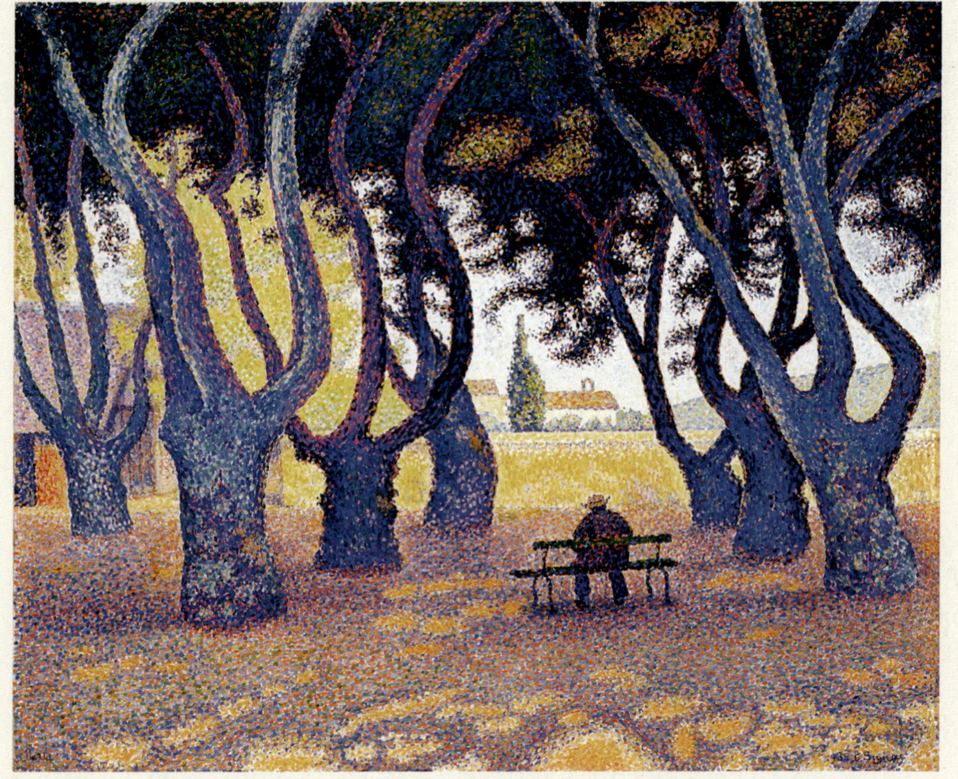

18–32 Paul Signac. *Place des Lices, Saint-Tropez.* 1893. Oil on canvas, 25¾" × 32³⁄₁₆" (65.4 × 81.8 cm). Carnegie Museum of Art, Pittsburgh
ACQUIRED THROUGH THE GENEROSITY OF THE SARAH MELLON SCALFE FAMILY

Late Nineteenth-Century French Sculpture

The most successful and influential sculptor of the Post-Impressionist era was Auguste Rodin (1840–1917). Rodin failed on three occasions to gain entrance to the École des Beaux-Arts and as a result spent the first 20 years of his career assisting other sculptors and decorators. It was only after a trip to Italy in 1875, where he saw the works of Donatello and Michelangelo, that he began to develop his mature style of vigorously modeled figures in unconventional poses, which were simultaneously scorned by critics and adored by the public. His status as a major sculptor was confirmed in 1884, when he won the competition for a monument, commissioned by the city of Calais, to commemorate an event from the Hundred Years' War: the *Burghers of Calais* (fig. **18–33**). In 1347, King Edward III of England had offered to spare the besieged city of Calais if six leading citizens (burghers) would surrender themselves to him for execution. Rodin shows the six volunteers—dressed in sackcloth with rope halters and carrying the keys to the city—marching out to what they assume will be their deaths. Though it is unknown to them at this point, the king would be so impressed by their courage, that he would spare them.

The Calais commissioners were not pleased with Rodin's conception of the event. Instead of calm, idealized heroes, Rodin presented ordinary-looking men in various attitudes of resignation and despair. He exaggerated their facial expressions, lengthened their arms, greatly enlarged their hands and feet, and swathed them in heavy fabric, showing not only how they may have looked but also how they must have felt as they forced themselves to take one difficult step after another. Rodin's willingness to stylize the human body for expressive purposes was a revolutionary move that opened the way for the more radical innovations of later sculptors. Nor were the commissioners pleased with Rodin's plan to display the figures

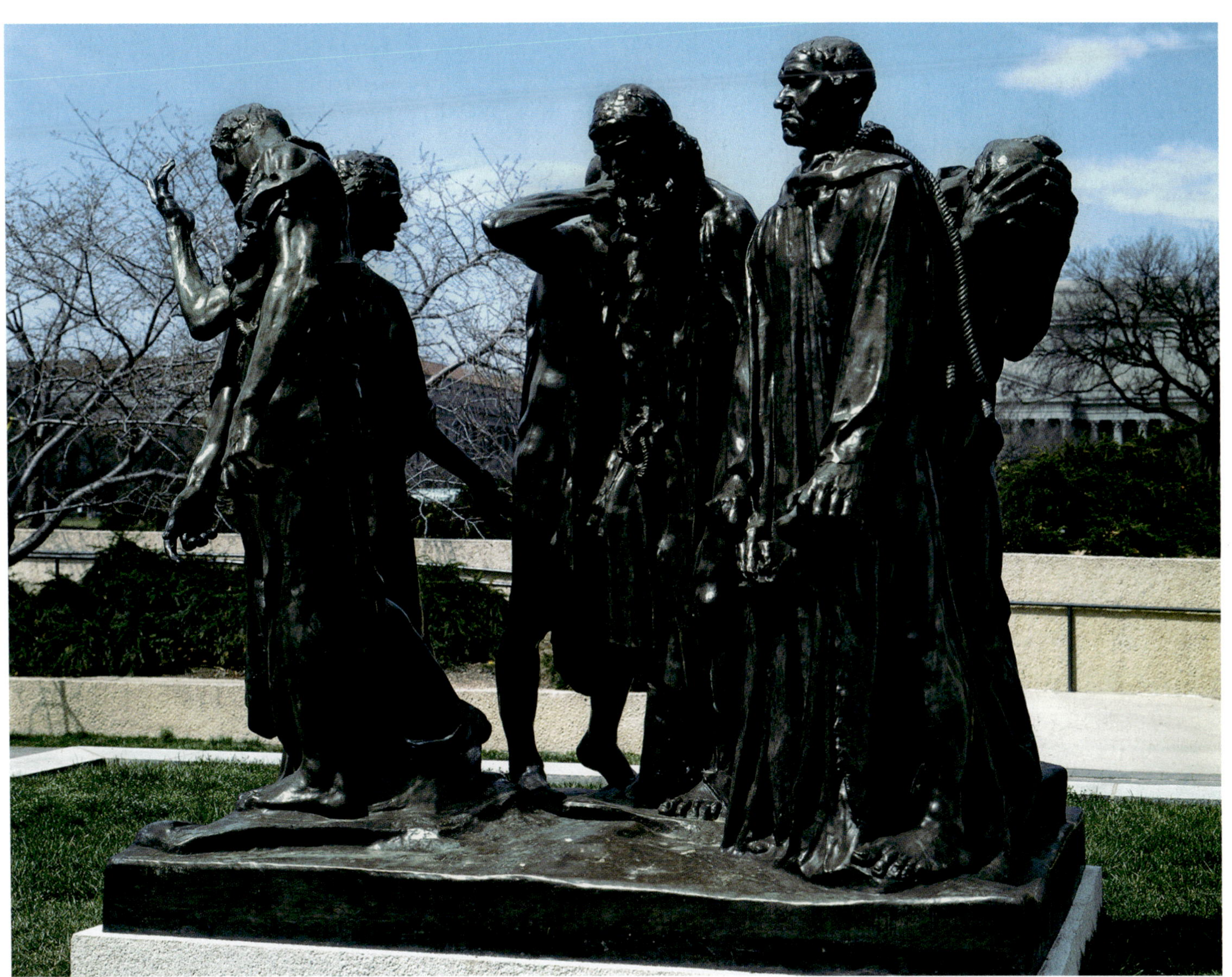

18–33 Auguste Rodin. ***Burghers of Calais***. 1884–1889. Bronze, 6' 10½" × 7' 11" × 6' 6" (2.1 × 2.4 × 2 m). Hirshhorn Museum and Sculpture Garden, Smithsonian Institution, Washington, D.C.

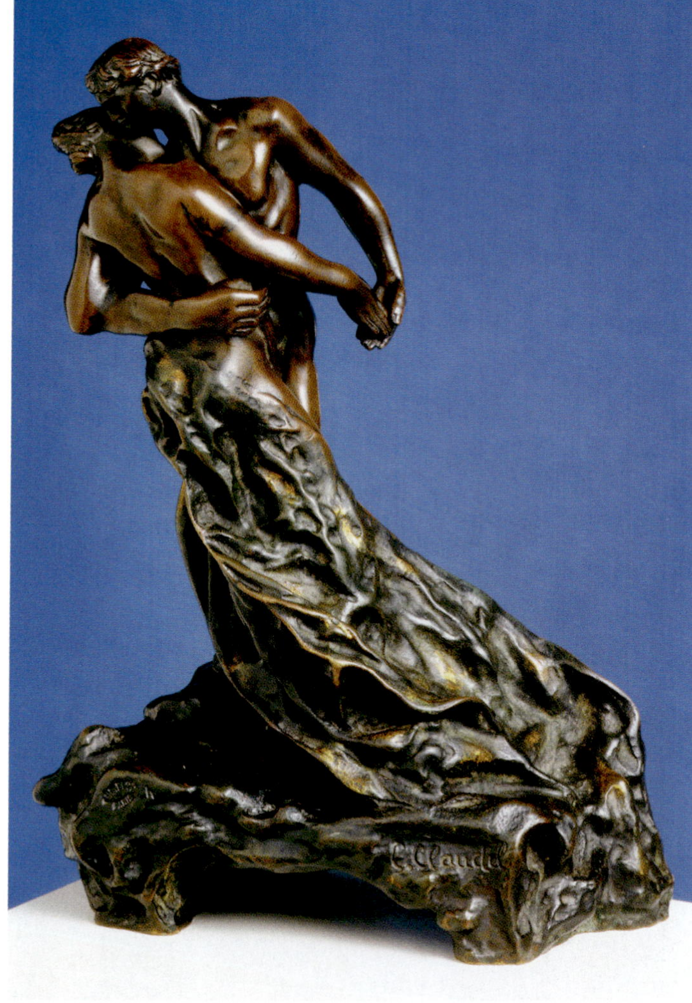

18–34 Camille Claudel. *The Waltz*. 1892–1905. Bronze, height 9⅞" (25 cm). Neue Pinakothek, Munich

Claudel's close friend, French composer Claude Debussy, whose innovative musical compositions were often influenced by art and literature, displayed a cast of this sculpture on his piano.

on a low base, almost at street level, to suggest to viewers that ordinary people like themselves were capable of noble acts. Rodin's removal of public sculpture from a high pedestal to a low base would lead, in the twentieth century, to the elimination of the pedestal itself and to the presentation of sculpture in the "real" space of the viewer.

Camille Claudel (1864–1943), an assistant in Rodin's studio who worked on the *Burghers of Calais*, was herself an accomplished sculptor whose work was long overshadowed by the dramatic story of her life. Claudel formally began to study sculpture in 1879 and became Rodin's pupil four years later. After she started working in his studio, she also became his mistress, and their often stormy relationship lasted 15 years. Both during and after her association with Rodin, Claudel enjoyed independent professional success, but she also suffered from psychological problems that eventually overtook her, and she spent the last 30 years of her life in a mental asylum.

Among Claudel's most celebrated works is *The Waltz* (fig. **18–34**). The sculpture depicts a dancing couple, the man unclothed and the woman seminude, her lower body enveloped in a long, flowing gown. In Claudel's original conception, both figures were entirely nude, but she had to add drapery to the female figure after a government inspector declared the piece to be indecent. The swirling drapery, which recalls the fluid lines of Art Nouveau, conveys an illusion of fluent motion as the dancing partners whirl in space. Despite the closeness of the pair, there is little actual physical contact between them, and their facial expressions reveal no passion or sexual desire. After violating decency standards with her first version of *The Waltz*, Claudel perhaps sought in this new rendition to portray love as a union more spiritual than physical.

Looking Back

As the nineteenth century began, Neoclassicism and Romanticism emerged as the principal directions in European art, with the former dominant in the academies, while the latter sought innovative portrayals of landscape, literature, or dramatic current events, rendered in dynamic, often unbalanced compositions and loose, painterly brushwork. The Realists that emerged in the 1840s challenged both of these stylistic currents with scenes of modern life—both in the country and the city—giving special attention to accurate descriptions of visual appearance and to the furthering of social and political change.

The Impressionists during the 1870s reacted to all three of these earlier nineteenth-century art movements. Some regard these painters as the founders of Modern art. Rejecting traditional rules and traditional techniques, they painted landscapes and scenes of urban life in pure, unmixed colors and loose brushstrokes as they tried to capture the fleeting play of light in an instantaneous "impression."

As Impressionism reached a crisis in the mid-1880s, artists went in several directions. Post-Impressionists like Cézanne and Seurat built on the Impressionist foundations but introduced more structured formal organization and deeper personal expression. Symbolists like Gauguin took refuge from the changing world around him in the creative realm of imagination. Vincent van Gogh sought to capture emotional states. In a variety of ways, throughout Europe, artists sought to become part of a cultural avant-garde, to innovate, to be modern.

IN PERSPECTIVE

1850

◀ **Pre-Raphaelite Brotherhood Founded,** 1848

◀ **United States Forcibly Opens Japan to Western Trade and Diplomacy,** 1853

1860

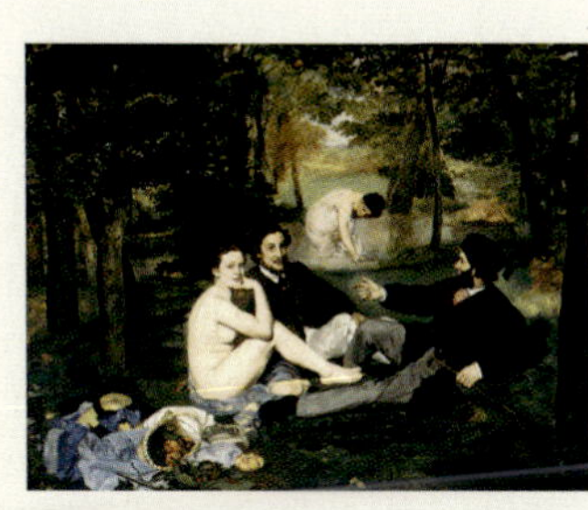

MANET,
LUNCHEON ON THE GRASS,
1863

◀ **American Civil War,** 1861–1865

◀ **Emancipation Proclamation,** 1862–1863

◀ **Salon des Refusés,** 1863

LEWIS,
FOREVER FREE,
1867

1870

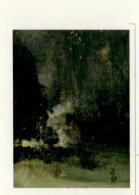

WHISTLER,
NOCTURNE IN BLACK AND GOLD, THE FALLING ROCKET,
1875

◀ **First Impressionist Exhibition of the *Société Anonyme*,** 1874

◀ **Artist James Abbott McNeill Whistler sues the Critic John Ruskin for Libel,** 1877

1880

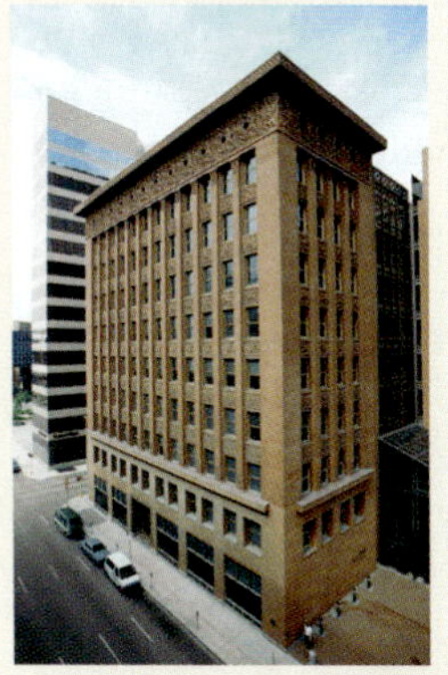

SULLIVAN,
WAINWRIGHT BUILDING,
1890–1891

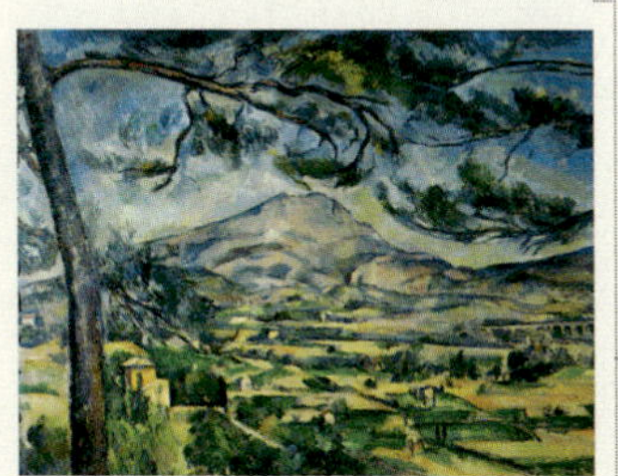

CÉZANNE,
MONT SAINTE-VICTOIRE,
c. 1885–1887

◀ **Paris Universal Exposition,** 1889

1890

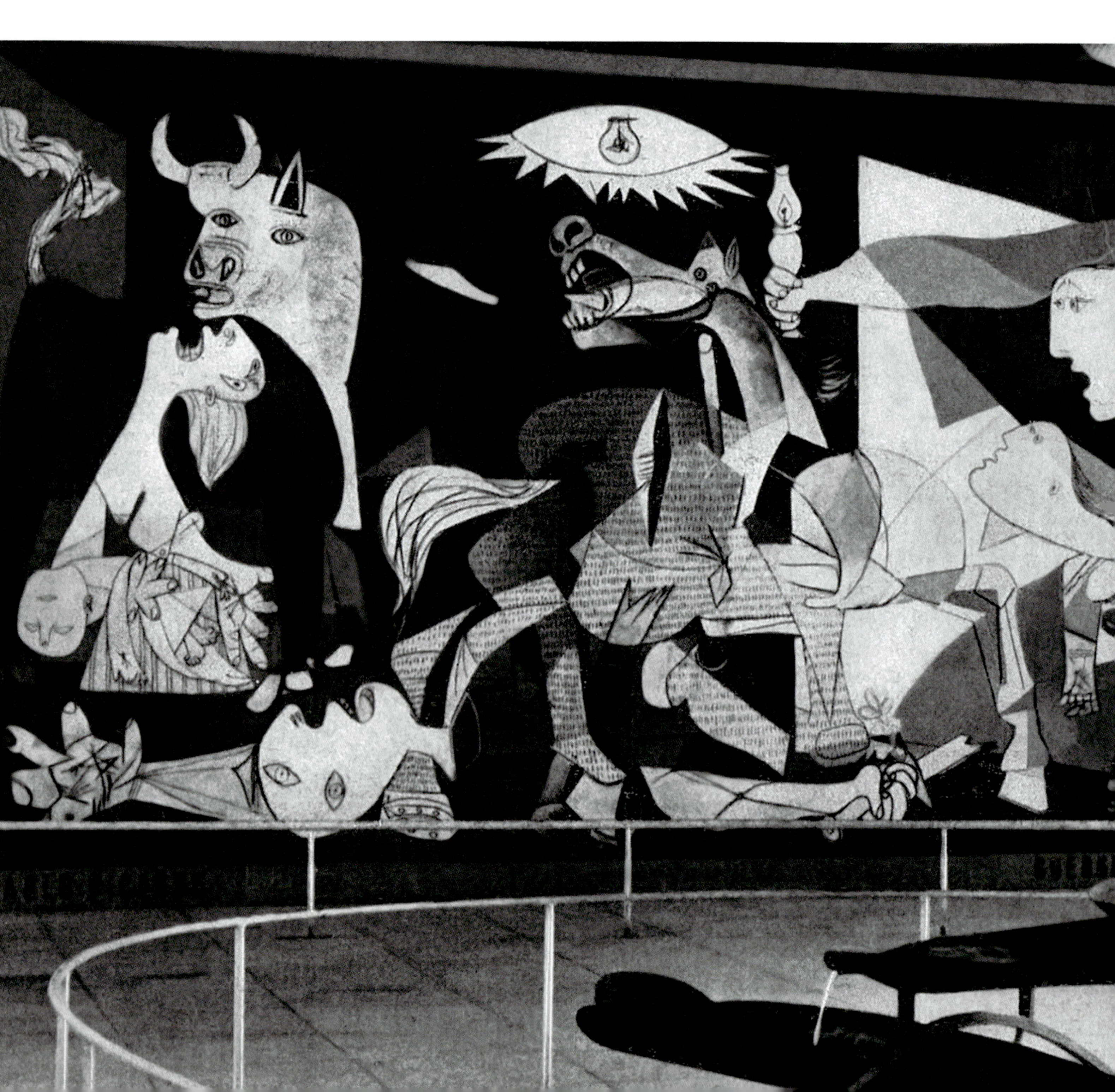

19 Modern Art: Europe and North America in the Early Twentieth Century

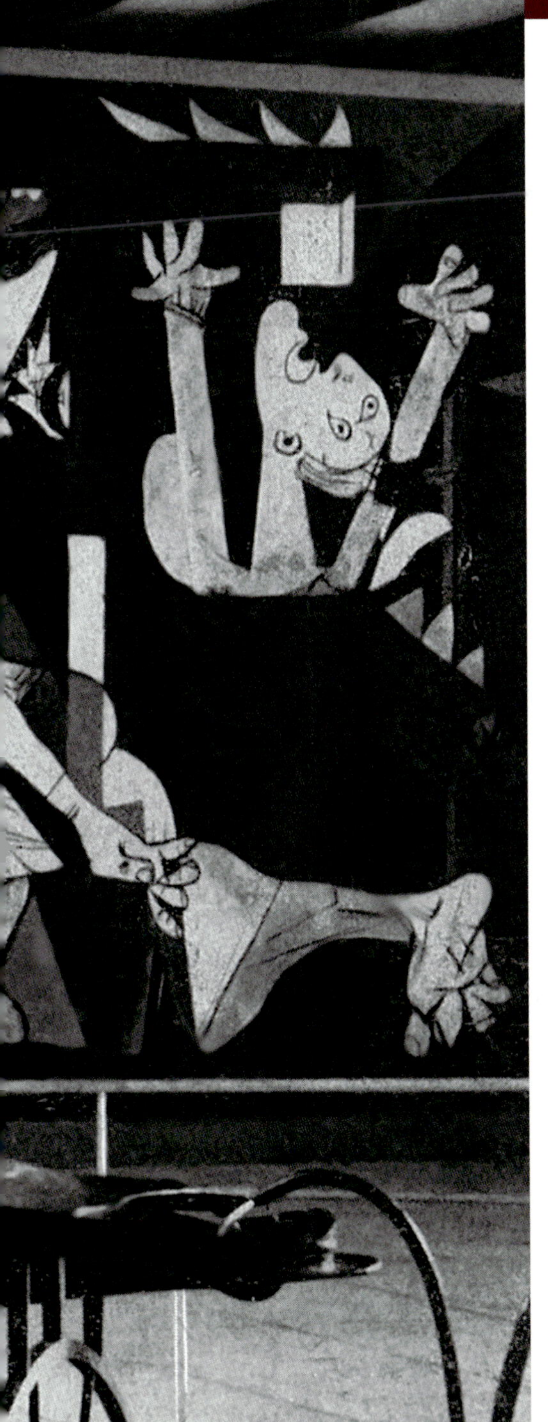

LOOKING FORWARD

In April 1937, during the Spanish Civil War, German pilots flying for Spanish fascist leader General Francisco Franco targeted the Basque city of Guernica. This act, the world's first intentional mass bombing of civilians, killed more than 1,600 people and shocked the world. The Spanish artist Pablo Picasso, living in Paris at the time, reacted to the massacre by painting *Guernica* (fig. **19–1**), a stark, hallucinatory nightmare that became as powerful a symbol of the brutality of war for the twentieth century as Goya's *Third of May, 1808* (see fig. 17–22) had been for the nineteenth.

Focusing on the victims, Picasso restricted his palette to black, gray, and white—the tones of the newspaper photographs that publicized the atrocity. Expressively distorted women, one holding a dead child and another trapped in a burning house, wail in desolation at the carnage. A screaming horse, an image of betrayed innocence, represents the suffering Spanish Republic, while a bull symbolizes either Franco or Spain. An electric light and a woman holding a lantern suggest Picasso's desire to reveal the event in all its horror.

The work excited widespread admiration when exhibited later that year in the short-lived Spanish Republic's pavilion at the International Exposition in Paris because the artist used the language of Modern art to comment in a heartfelt manner on what seemed an international scandal. That same summer Adolf Hitler held the infamous Nazi exhibition of "degenerate art" in Munich (see "Suppression of the Avant-Garde in Germany," page 548). Picasso spent World War II in Paris, and when a Nazi officer showed him a reproduction of *Guernica* and asked, "Is it you who did that?" Picasso is said to have replied, "No, it is you." Unfortunately, the tactic of bombing civilians became a common strategy employed by all sides in this brutal international war that left such a strong imprint on the developing history of Modern art.

19–1 Pablo Picasso. ***Guernica.*** 1937. Oil on canvas, 11' 6" × 25' 8" (3.5 × 7.8 m). Museo Nacional Centro de Arte Reina Sofia, Madrid. On permanent loan from the Museo del Prado, Madrid. Shown installed in the Spanish Pavilion of the Paris Exposition, 1937. In the foreground: Alexander Calder's *Fontaine de Mercure.* Mercury, sheet metal, wire rod, pitch, and paint, 44" × 115" × 77" (122 × 292 × 196 cm). Fundacio Joan Miró, Barcelona

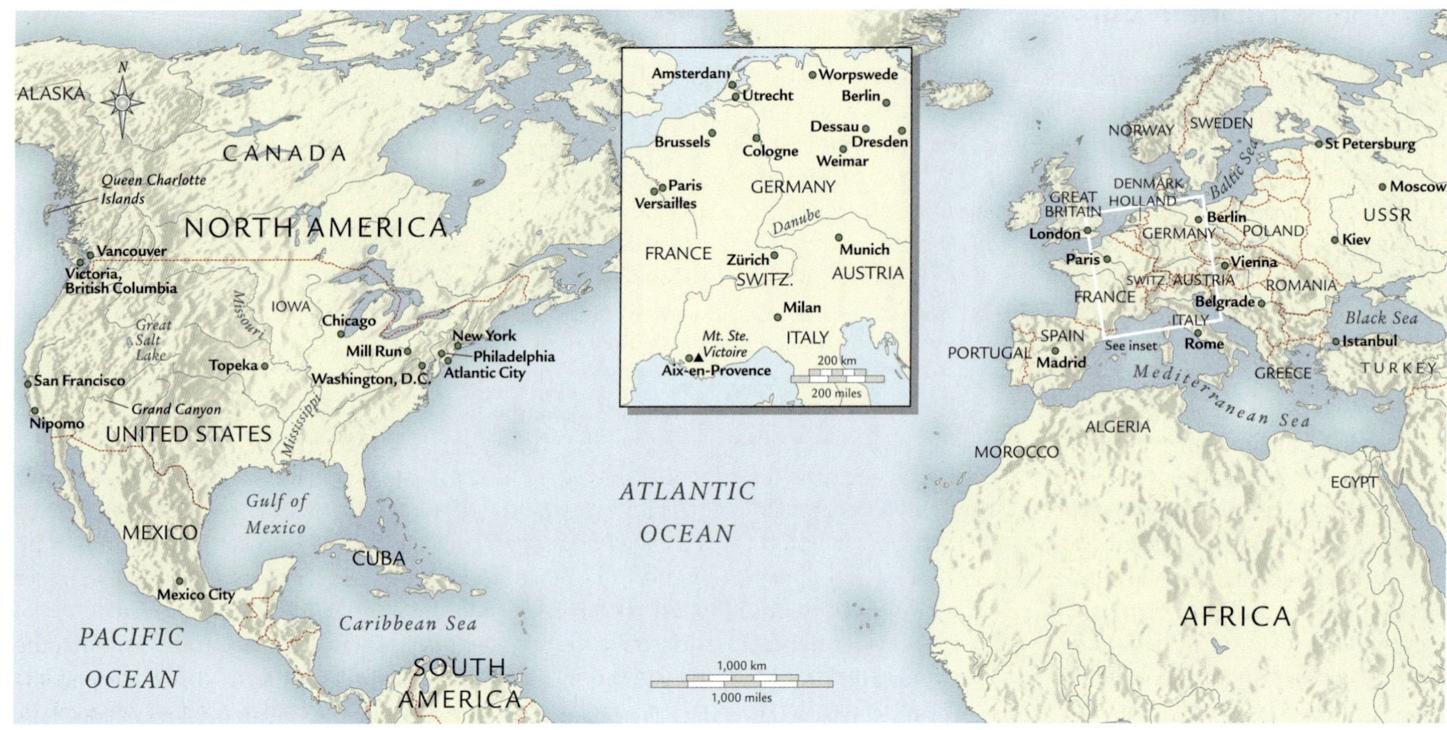

Map 19–1 Europe and North America in the 1920s and 1930s

The backdrop of politics, war, and technological change is critical to understanding twentieth-century art. As the century dawned, many Europeans and Americans believed optimistically that human society would "advance" through the spread of democracy, capitalism, and technological innovation. However, the competitive nature of colonialism, nationalism, and capitalism created great instability in Europe, and countries joined together in rival political alliances (see map **19–1**).

World War I erupted in August 1914, initially pitting Britain, France, and Russia (the Allies) against Germany and Austria (the Central Powers). The United States entered the war in 1917 and contributed to an Allied victory the following year. World War I significantly transformed European politics and economics, especially in Russia, which became the world's first Communist nation in 1917, when a popular revolution brought the Bolshevik (meaning "Majority") Communist party of Vladimir Lenin to power. In 1922, the Soviet Union, a Communist state encompassing Russia and neighboring states, was created.

American and Western European economies soon recovered from the war (with the exception of Germany, whose economy was weakened by reparations that the Allies demanded), but the 1929 New York stock-market crash plunged much of the world into the Great Depression. In 1933, U.S. President Franklin D. Roosevelt responded with the New Deal, an ambitious welfare program meant to provide jobs and stimulate the American economy. Britain and France instituted state welfare policies during the 1930s as well. Elsewhere in Europe, the economic crisis brought to power right-wing totalitarian regimes: Benito Mussolini in Italy, Adolf Hitler in Germany, and General Francisco Franco in Spain. Meanwhile, in the Soviet Union, Joseph Stalin succeeded Lenin in 1924.

German aggression toward Poland in 1939 led to the outbreak of World War II. The most destructive war in history, World War II claimed the lives of millions of soldiers and civilians from Asia, North America, and Europe, including 6 million European Jews who perished in the Nazi Holocaust. It ended in Europe in May 1945 and in the Pacific that August.

During the two great wars of the twentieth century, technological innovations resulted in such deadly devices as the fighter bomber and the atom bomb. Yet dramatic scientific developments and improvements in medicine, agriculture, communications, and transportation also transformed the daily life of millions of people, especially in Europe and North America. The first analog and digital computers, designed to process huge amounts of data and perform advanced calculations, were also introduced in the 1930s.

Accompanying the momentous changes in politics, economics, and science were equally revolutionary developments in art and culture, which scholars have gathered under the label of "Modernism." Although "modern" simply means "up-to-date," the term "Modernism" connotes a rejection of conventions and a commitment to radical innovation. Like scientists and inventors, Modernist artists engaged in a process of experimentation and discovery, exploring new possibilities of creativity and expression in a rapidly changing world.

Early Modernism in Europe

As the twentieth century progressed, the pace of artistic innovation within Modernism increased, producing a dizzying succession of movements, or "isms," including Fauvism, Cubism, Futurism, Dadaism, and Surrealism. Each movement had a charismatic leader or group who promoted a defining philosophy, often through written declarations of principles called manifestos. Although Modernism is characterized by tremendous diversity, several broad tendencies mark many Modernist artists across the boundaries created by the "isms." Foremost is a tendency toward abstraction, at times going as far as **nonrepresentational** art, which communicates exclusively through such formal means as line, shape, color, and texture, avoiding any reference to the natural world. A second feature of Modernism is a tendency to emphasize the physical process of artistic creation, for example, by highlighting the visibility of brushstrokes or chisel marks. A third feature is Modernism's continual questioning of the nature of art itself through the adoption of new techniques and ordinary materials that break down distinctions between art and everyday life.

The rise and spread of Modernism in the early twentieth century was driven by such exhibitions as the 1905 *Salon d'Automne* ("Autumn Exhibition") in Paris, which launched the Fauve movement; the first *Der Blaue Reiter* exhibition in Munich in 1911; and the 1913 New York Armory Show, the first large-scale introduction of European Modernism to American audiences. The Museum of Modern Art opened in New York in 1929, and state-supported museums dedicated to modern art also appeared in major European capitals, such as Paris, Rome, and Brussels, signaling the transformation of Modernism from an embattled fringe movement to an officially recognized vanguard of "high culture."

Les Fauves

The Salon system still operated in France, but the ranks of artists dissatisfied with its conservative precepts swelled. Early in the century, these malcontents launched the *Salon d'Automne* in opposition to the official Salon in the spring. Reviewing the exhibition in 1905, critic Louis Vauxcelles referred to some of the young painters contemptuously as *fauves* ("wild beasts"), a term that captured their paintings' sense of forceful color and impulsive brushwork, conveying a new intensity of visual experience—"like sticks of dynamite," as *fauve* painter André Derain remarked. Vauxcelle's derogatory characterization seemed more than fitting to those who admired these paintings, and art historians now group them under the label Fauvism.

The Joy of Life (fig. **19–2**), painted by one of Fauvism's leading painters Henri Matisse (1869–1954), transforms hedonistic pursuits in a pastoral landscape into a vibrant arrangement of luscious colors. Naked revelers dance, make love, commune with nature, or simply stretch out in their idyllic glade by the sea. Colors freed from naturalistic constraints contribute as much to the joyous mood as the uninhibited figures themselves. The long, flowing curves of the

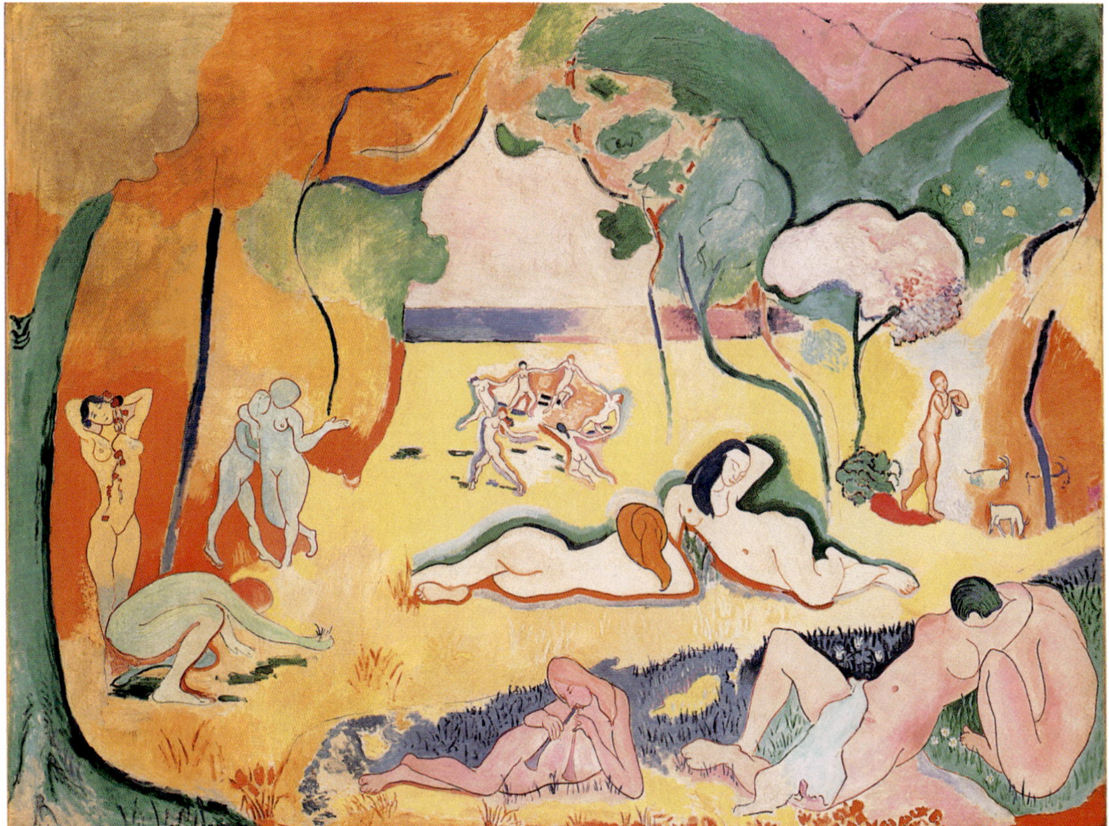

19–2 Henri Matisse. ***Le bonheur de vivre (The Joy of Life).*** 1905–1906. Oil on canvas, 5' 8½" × 7' 9¾" (1.74 × 2.38 m). The Barnes Foundation, Merion, Pennsylvania

The Joy of Life *was originally owned by the brother and sister Leo and Gertrude Stein, important American patrons of European avant-garde art in the early twentieth century. They hung their collection in their Paris apartment, where they hosted an informal salon that attracted leading literary, musical, and artistic figures, including Matisse and Picasso. In 1913, Leo moved to Italy while Gertrude remained in Paris, pursuing a career as a Modernist writer and continuing to host a salon with her partner, Alice B. Toklas.*

trees and the sinuous contours of the nude bodies animate the composition with continual movement. These undulating rhythms, in combination with the relaxed but stabilizing poses of the two reclining women at the center, establish the quality of "serenity, relief from the stress of modern life," as Matisse characterized his work from this period. In an essay titled "Notes of a Painter," which Matisse published in 1908, he expressed his allegiance to "an art … devoid of troubling or depressing subject matter … a mental comforter, something like a good armchair in which to rest."

Die Brücke

The German counterpart to Fauvism was *Die Brücke* ("The Bridge"). In 1905, three architecture students at the Dresden Technical College, including Ernst Ludwig Kirchner (1880–1938), formed what they called a brotherhood, rooted in their shared admiration for the writings of German philosopher Frederich Nietzsche. In *Thus Spoke Zarathustra*, Nietzsche used the metaphor of the bridge to explain how civilization is precariously balanced between two contradictory states of being in the evolutionary process; progress and degeneration, or modernity (the future) and barbarism (the past). With Nietzche, these artists perceived possibilities for rebirth and renewal in "primitive" states such as childhood or in animal instincts, and they believed that both modernity (as symbolized by the metropolis) and the "primitive" held connotations for regeneration, but that both could also signify and lead to regression. They associated large urban centers with fresh creativity and new beginnings, yet also acknowledged how the modern metropolis tended to breed a competitive climate that inspired a Darwinian struggle for the survival of the fittest. Seeing just below the surface of polite society a seething barbarism on the verge of being unleashed, Die Brücke artists were both excited by and wary of this precarious balance.

Kirchner's *Street, Berlin* (fig. **19–3**) captures this dynamic paradox in a sharp critique of urban life. Dominating the left half of the

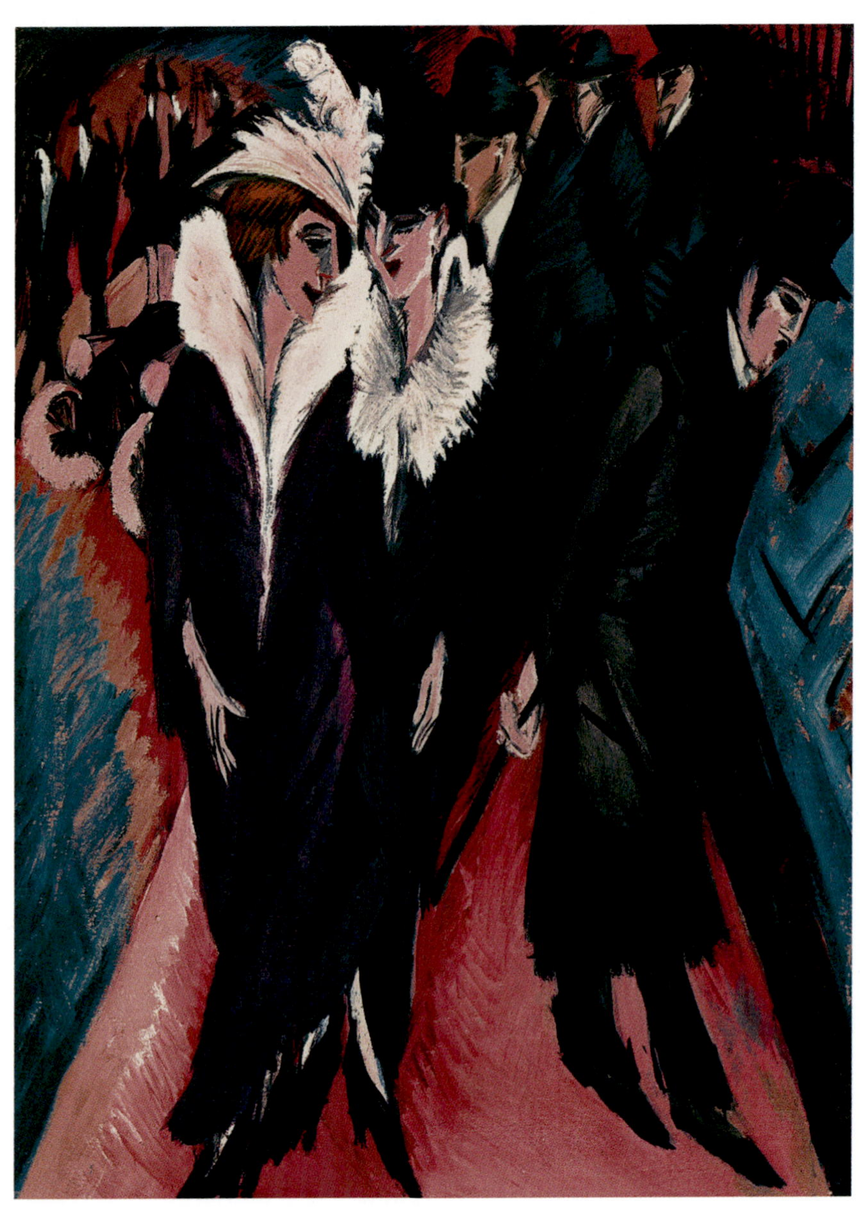

19–3 Ernst Ludwig Kirchner. *Street, Berlin*. 1913.
Oil on canvas, 47½" × 37⅞" (120.6 × 91 cm).
The Museum of Modern Art, New York
PURCHASE (274.39)

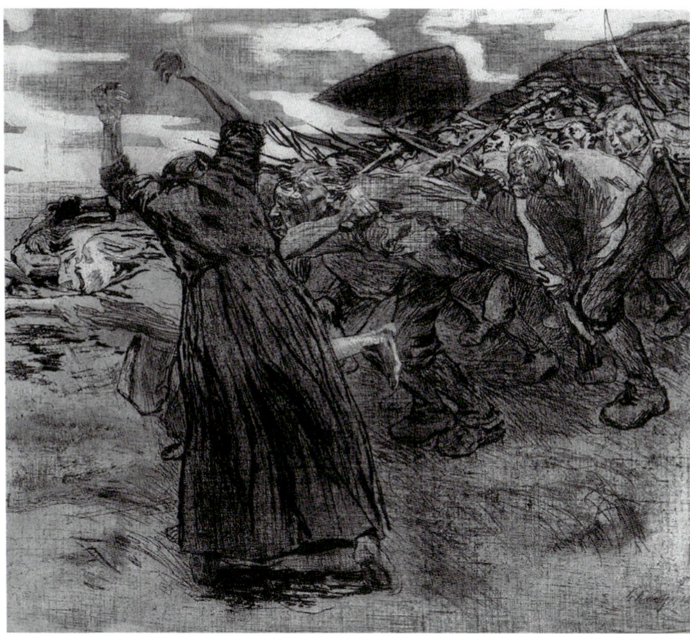

19–4 Käthe Kollwitz. *The Outbreak*, from the *Peasants' War* series. 1903. Etching, 20" × 23⅓" (50.7 × 59.2 cm). Staatliche Museen zu Berlin, Preussischer Kulturbesitz, Kupferstichkabinett

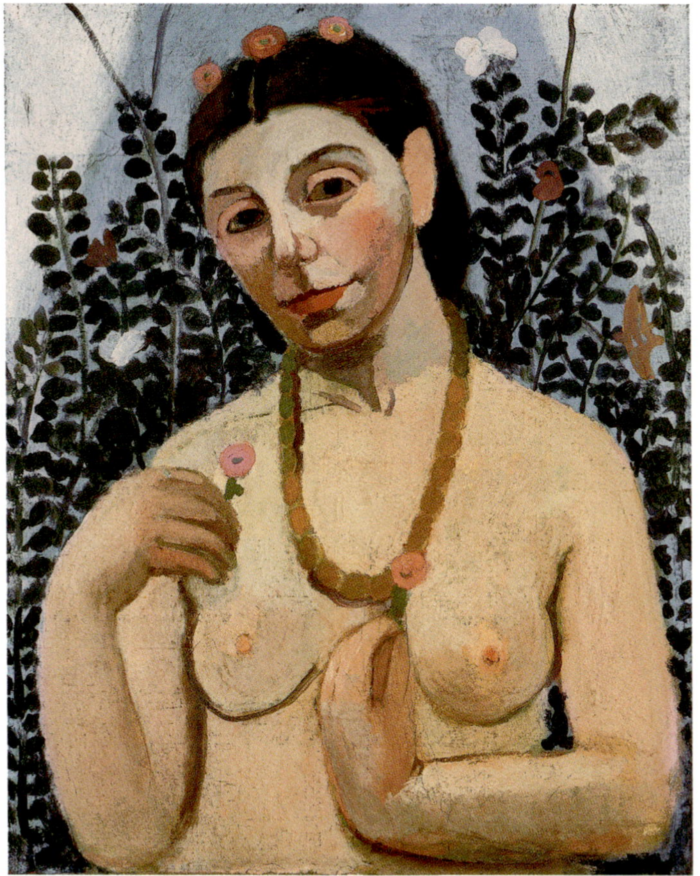

19–5 Paula Modersohn-Becker. *Self-Portrait with an Amber Necklace*. 1906. Oil on canvas, 24" × 19¾" (61 × 50 cm). Öffentliche Kunstsammlung, Kunstmuseum, Basel, Switzerland

painting are two prostitutes—identified by their lavish feathered hats and fur-trimmed coats—strutting past well-dressed bourgeois men, their potential clients. The immediacy of their hurried movement is conveyed through Kirchner's slashing brushstrokes. Although crowded together physically, the figures seem isolated from one another psychologically—artificial and dehumanized manikins, with mask-like faces and stiff gestures, victims of modern urban alienation. The raw colors, tilted perspective, and angular lines register Kirchner's response to a metropolis where savagery can be masked by seemingly civilized behaviors.

Käthe Kollwitz (1867–1945) was even more deeply involved with the ills of society, especially the plight of the working class. Raised in a socialist household, she studied at the Berlin School of Art for Women and at a similar school in Munich. In 1891, she married a doctor who shared her leftist political views, and they settled in a working-class neighborhood in Berlin. Art for her was a political tool, and to reach as many people as possible, she became a printmaker. Between 1902 and 1908, she produced the *Peasants' War* series, seven etchings that depict events of the sixteenth-century peasant rebellion in a stark graphic style. In *The Outbreak* (fig. **19–4**), Kollwitz takes full advantage of etching techniques to express the peasants' emotive energy exploding against their oppressors. Raw and jagged lines scratched into the plate communicate the peasants' built-up fury from years of mistreatment. In the front, with her back to us, is Black Anna, the leader of the revolt, who was modeled after the figure of the artist herself.

Paula Modersohn-Becker (1876–1907) also trained at the Berlin School of Art for Women, before moving in 1898 to the rustic village of Worpswede, an artist's colony in northern Germany. Dissatisfied with the local artists' naturalistic style, she made four trips to Paris between 1900 and her death in 1907 to see the latest developments in art and was particularly drawn to the work of Gauguin (see fig. 18–26). Her *Self-Portrait with an Amber Necklace* (fig. **19–5**), painted in 1906, shows his influence. The basic shapes and simple outlines of the self-portrait—with its prominent eyes as well as its nudity, her body decorated only with flowers and a necklace—suggest that she may have seen African sculpture as well as Post-Impressionist painting in Paris. By presenting herself against a screen of flowering plants and tenderly holding flowers that echo the shape and color of her breasts, she shows herself as a natural being at one with nature.

Der Blaue Reiter

An Expressionist group of painters formed in Munich around the Russian artist Vasily Kandinsky (1866–1944). In 1895, after being deeply moved by color in a painting by Monet, Kandinsky decided to devote himself to art. He left Moscow to study in Munich because of research under way there on the effects of color and form on the human psyche. In 1911, Kandinsky organized a group of nine artists sharing his interest in the power of color under the name *Der Blaue Reiter* ("The Blue Rider" or "The Blue Knight"), based on a popular Russian image of Saint George, mounted on a horse and slaying a dragon that appeared on the Moscow city emblem. Kandinsky considered the color blue symbolic of spirituality and the male principle.

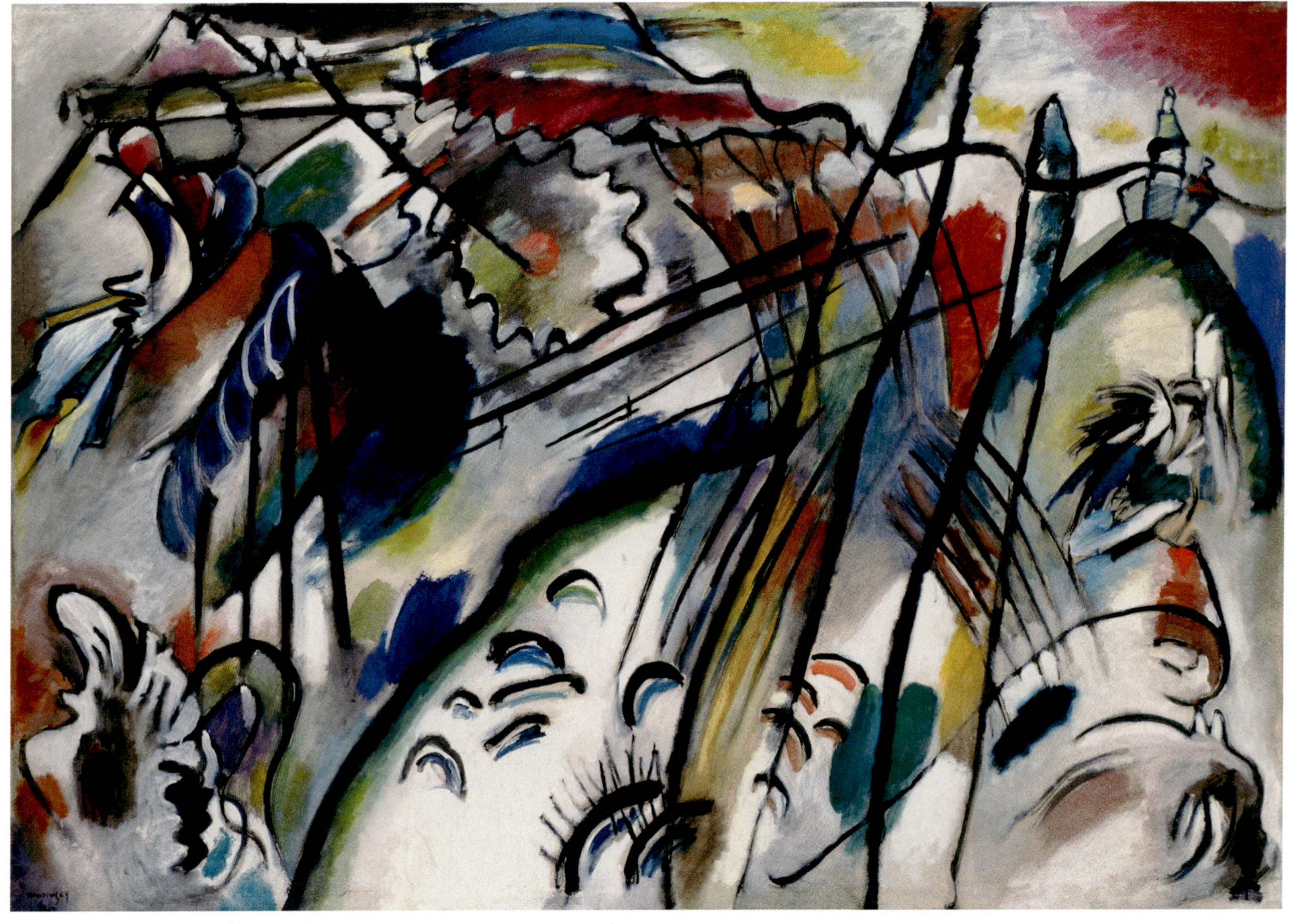

19–6 Vasily Kandinsky. ***Improvisation 28 (Second Version).*** 1912. Oil on canvas, 43⅞" × 63⅞" (111.5 × 162.3 cm). Guggenheim Museum, New York

Kandinsky explained the musical analogies evoked in paintings like this in a short book about his own working methods called Concerning the Spiritual in Art*: "Color directly influences the soul. Color is the keyboard, the eyes are the hammers, the soul is the piano with many strings. The artist is the hand that plays, touching one key or another purposively, to cause vibrations in the soul."*

Kandinsky's study of the work of Whistler (see fig. 18–9), inspired the Russian artist to see a strong relationship between the arts of painting and music, and his musical explorations led him to the work of Austrian composer Arnold Schoenberg, who in the years around 1910 was taking a momentous step in musical history. Since antiquity, Western music had been grounded in the use of scales or modes to create the "tonal center" of a musical composition. Schoenberg, however, treated all notes equally, denying listeners any sense of repose and prolonging tension indefinitely. After contacting the composer, Kandinsky wondered, if music can do without a tonal center, can painting do without subject matter? Sometime in 1910, Kandinsky painted his first completely abstract work. Typical of the paintings that followed is *Improvisation 28* (fig. **19–6**), the title itself indicative of the impact of musical thought on the evolution of his work. There is a vestige of landscape in this work; Kandinsky found references to the natural world the trickiest to transcend. But if we see buildings or faces here, we may be seeing the painting in an old-fashioned way, looking for correspondences between it and the world where none is intended. Kandinsky would have us look at his painting as if we were listening to a symphony, responding instinctively and freely to this or that passage, and then to the total experience, energized by dynamic linearity and enriched by vibrant patches of sensual color.

Cubism

Cubism, one of the most talked-about "isms" of twentieth-century art, was the joint invention of Pablo Picasso and Georges Braque.

Picasso (1881–1973) was born in Spain and educated in art academies in Barcelona and Madrid, but he moved to Paris in 1904. Initially drawn to the socially conscious tradition in French painting that included artists such as Daumier (see fig. Intro–16) and Toulouse-Lautrec (see fig. 18–31), Picasso went through an extraordinary and complex transformation between early 1905 and the winter of 1906–1907. In 1906, the Louvre installed a newly acquired collection of sculpture from Iberia (Spain and Portugal) that dated to the sixth and fifth centuries BCE, and these archaic figures became

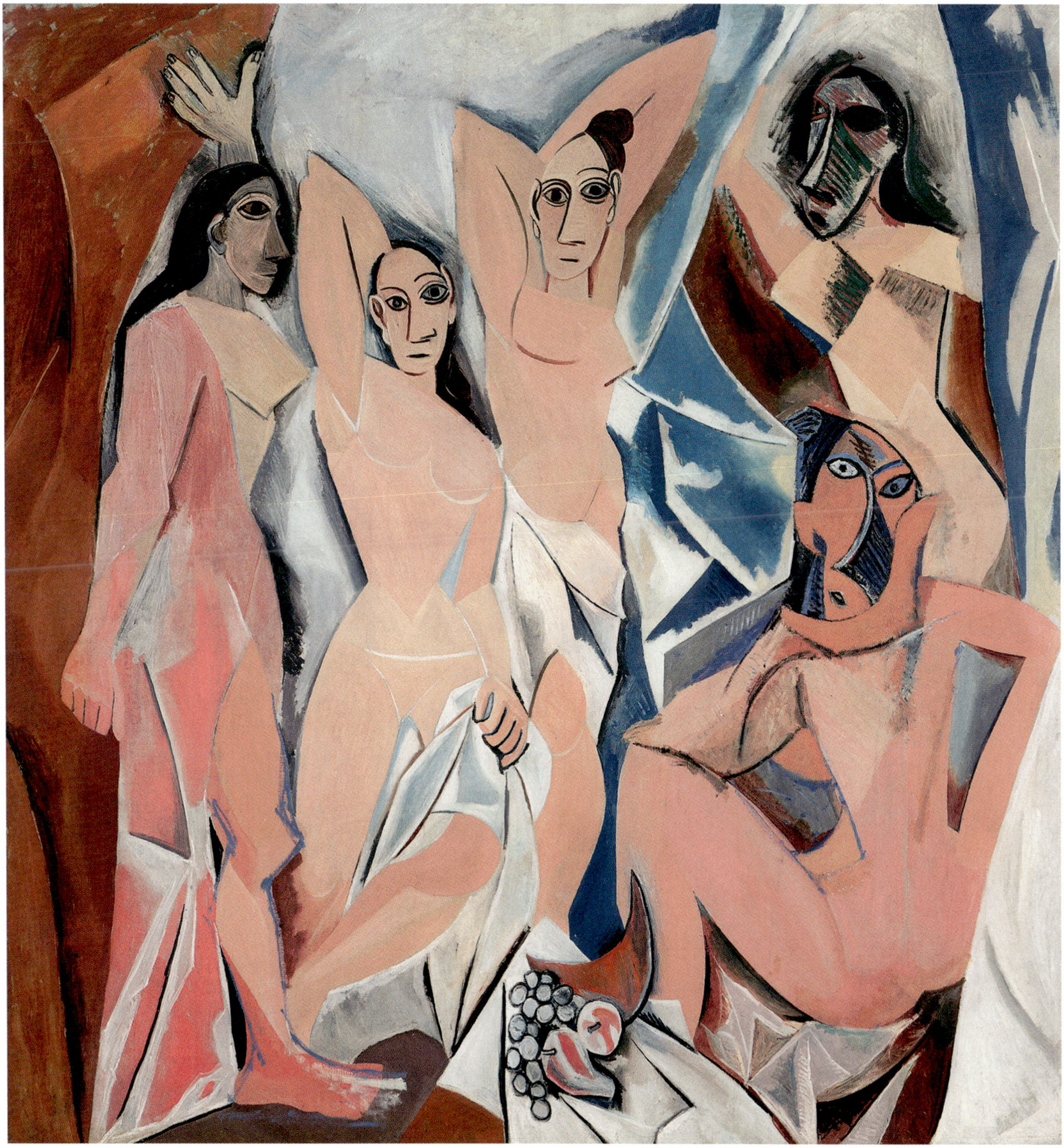

19–7 Pablo Picasso. ***Les Demoiselles d'Avignon.*** 1907. Oil on canvas, 8' × 7' 8" (2.43 × 2.33 m). The Museum of Modern Art, New York
ACQUIRED THROUGH THE LILLIE P. BLISS BEQUEST (333.1939)

a powerful influence on his work over the next year. Even more influential were his repeated visits to the ethnographic museum where African art from France's colonies was displayed. While he never stopped to study the cultures that produced this arresting art, Picasso was greatly stimulated by its expressive and formal power. He bought several pieces and kept them in his studio.

Picasso's wide-ranging studies culminated in 1907 in *Les Demoiselles d'Avignon* (fig. **19–7**). The simplified features and wide, almond-shaped eyes of the three figures on the left reflect the Iberian influence, while the two figures at the right were inspired by African masks. Given contemporary condescending attitudes toward such allegedly "primitive" cultures, Picasso's wholesale adoption and adaptation of Iberian and African art in a large, multifigure painting was an act of cultural rebellion. The painting might be viewed as Picasso's response to Matisse's *The Joy of Life* (see fig. 19–2), exhibited the year before, or more broadly to the French classical tradition as embodied in Ingres' paintings of odalisques (see fig. 17–17). Picasso, however, substituted a brothel for a harem. The term *demoiselles* (meaning "young ladies") was a euphemism for prostitutes, and "Avignon" refers not to the French town but to a street in the red-light district of Barcelona.

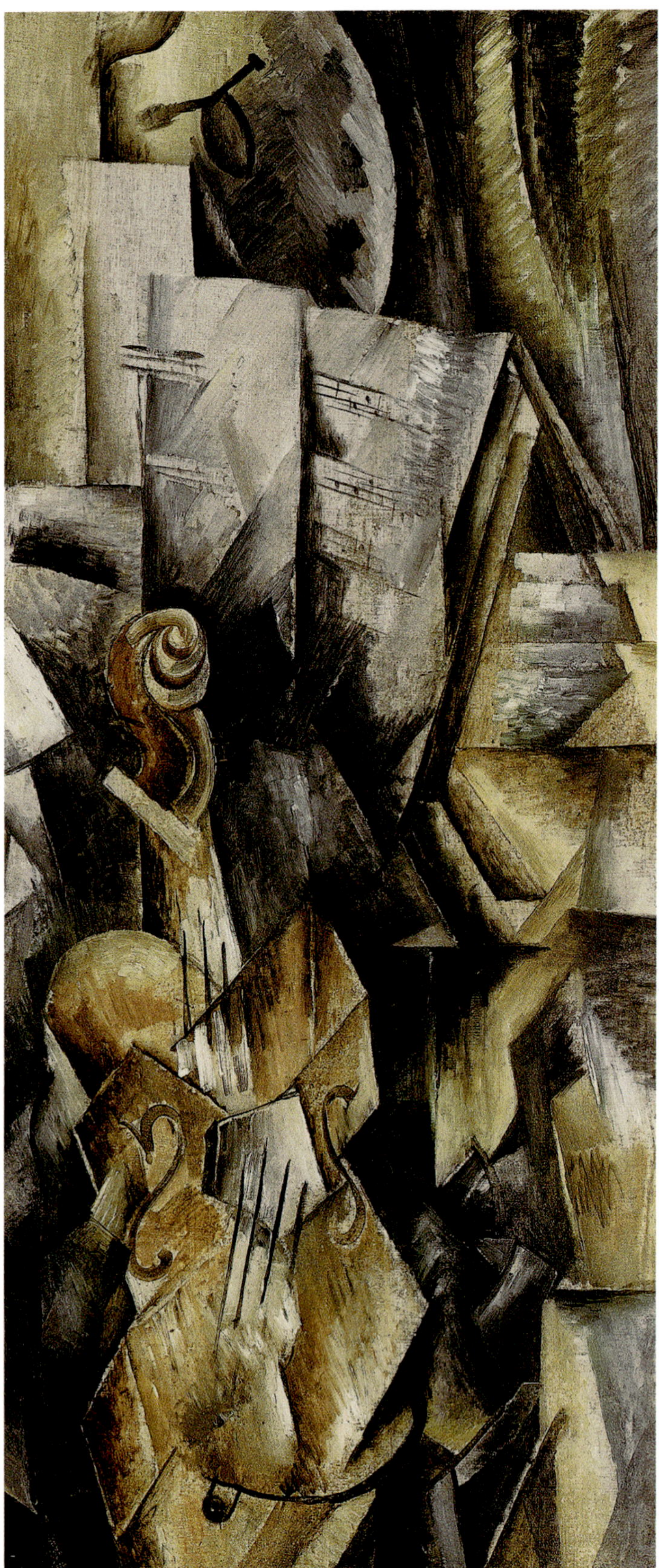

19–8 Georges Braque. ***Violin and Palette.*** 1909–1910. Oil on canvas, 36⅛" × 16⅞" (91.8 × 42.9 cm). Solomon R. Guggenheim Museum, New York (54.1412)

Picasso makes viewers looking at this painting uneasy. The women are shielded by masks, flattened and fractured into sharp angular shapes. The space they inhabit is incoherent and convulsive. The women pose for, and some look directly at, us—conventional cues of accessibility that are contradicted by their hard, piercing gazes and tight mouths, and what one art historian has called "a tidal wave of aggression." Even the fruit in the foreground, symbols of female sexuality, seems hard and dangerous. Women, Picasso suggests, are not the gentle and passive creatures men would like them to be. This viewpoint contradicts an enduring tradition of portraying sexual availability in the female nude, prevalent at least since the Renaissance, just as strongly as Picasso's treatment of space shatters the reliance on ordered linear perspective, equally standard since that same period.

Most of Picasso's friends were horrified by his new work. Matisse, for example, accused Picasso of making a joke of modern art and threatened to break off their friendship. Only one artist, the French painter Georges Braque (1882–1963), responded positively, and he saw in *Les Demoiselles d'Avignon* a potential that Picasso probably had not fully intended. Picasso has used expressionistic distortions to convey his view of women—branded by many as misogynistic—but what secured his place at the forefront of the Parisian avant-garde was the work's inauguration of a revolution in form. Braque responded eagerly to Picasso's formal innovations and set out, alongside Picasso, to develop them by exploring the flattening of pictorial space, by incorporating multiple perspectives within a single picture plane, and by fracturing form, all features that these artists had admired in Cézanne's late paintings.

Braque carried the formal experiment further during 1908. In his landscape painting, he reduced nature's complexity to its essential colors and basic geometric shapes, but his works were rejected that year from the Autumn Salon. Matisse dismissively referred to Braque's "little cubes." The critic Louis Vauxcelles picked up the phrase, claiming that Braque "reduced everything to cubes," and giving birth to the art-historical category of Cubism. Braque's painting also pointed Picasso in a new direction, and soon the two artists began an intimate working relationship that lasted until Braque went off to war in 1914. "We were like two mountain climbers roped together," Braque would later say.

The move toward abstraction and simplification continued in a series of still-life paintings Braque and Picasso produced over the next two-and-a-half years. In Braque's *Violin and Palette* (fig. **19–8**), the gradual abstraction of deep space and recognizable subject matter is well under way. The still-life items are not arranged in a measured recession from foreground to background but are pushed close to the picture plane, compressed into a shallow space. Braque knit

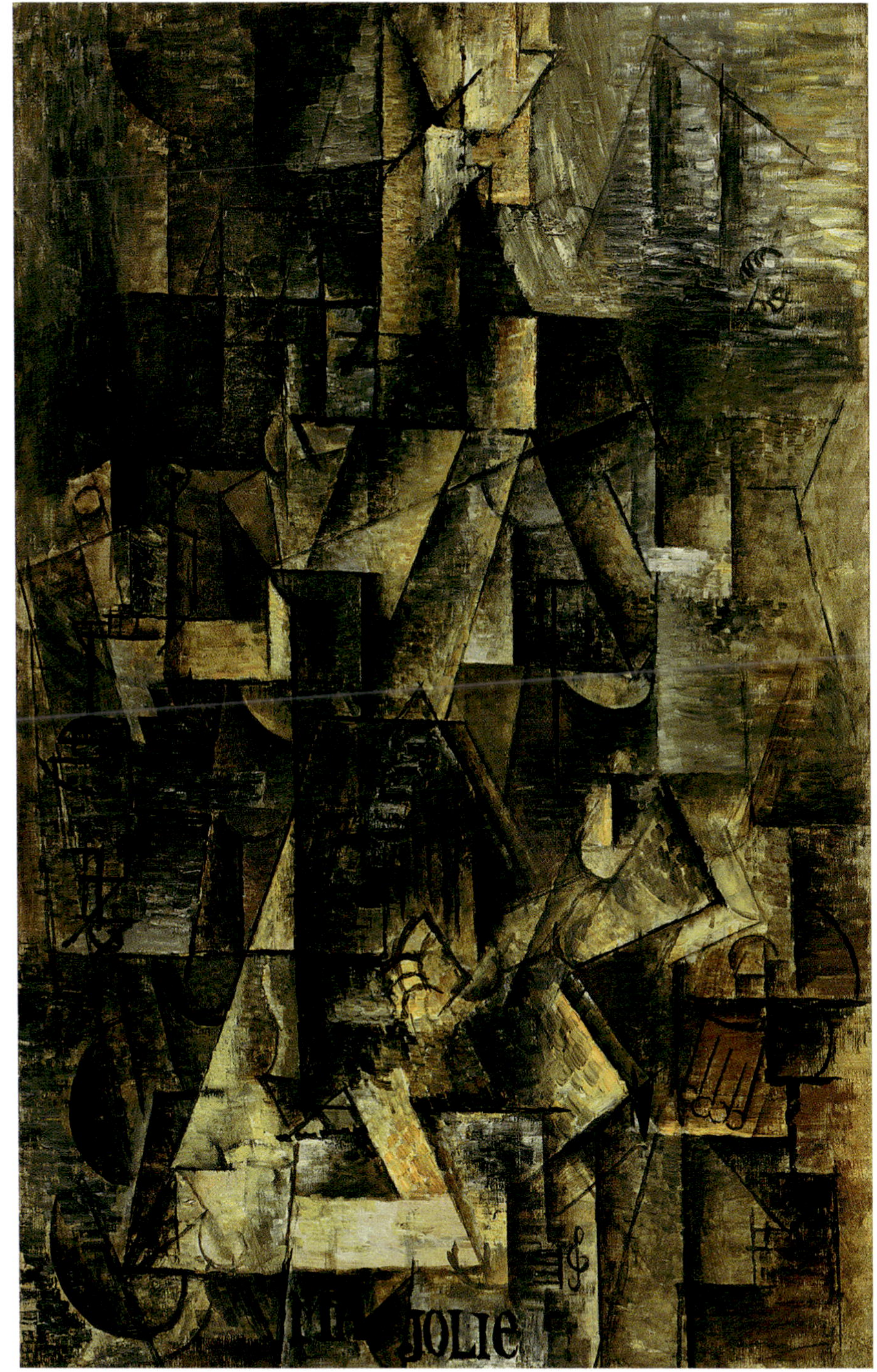

19–9 Pablo Picasso. ***Ma Jolie.*** 1911–1912. Oil on canvas, 39⅜" × 25¾" (100 × 65.4 cm). The Museum of Modern Art, New York

Picasso included a musical analogy in this painting—a treble clef and the words Ma Jolie ("My Pretty One"), a popular song. He seems to be suggesting that the viewer should approach the painting the way one would a musical composition, either by simply enjoying the arrangement of its elements or by analyzing it, but not by asking what it represents.

the various elements together into a single shifting surface of forms and colors. In some areas of the painting, formal elements lose not only their natural spatial relations but their identities as well. Where representational motifs remain—the violin, for example—Braque fragments them to facilitate their integration into the whole. Such paintings of 1909–1910 initiate what art historians call Analytic Cubism because of the way the artists broke objects into parts as if to analyze them.

Picasso and Braque's works of 1911 and early 1912 reflect a different approach to the breaking up of forms and the flattening of pictorial space. Instead of simply fracturing an object, they pick it apart and rearrange its elements. In this way, Analytic Cubism replicates the actual process of perception, during which we examine objects from various angles and then our brain reassembles our glances into a whole. Only Picasso and Braque reassemble their shattered subjects not according to our process of perception but conforming to principles of artistic composition. For example, remnants of the subject are evident throughout Picasso's *Ma Jolie* (fig. **19–9**), but any attempt to reconstruct from them the image of a woman with a stringed instrument would be misguided since the

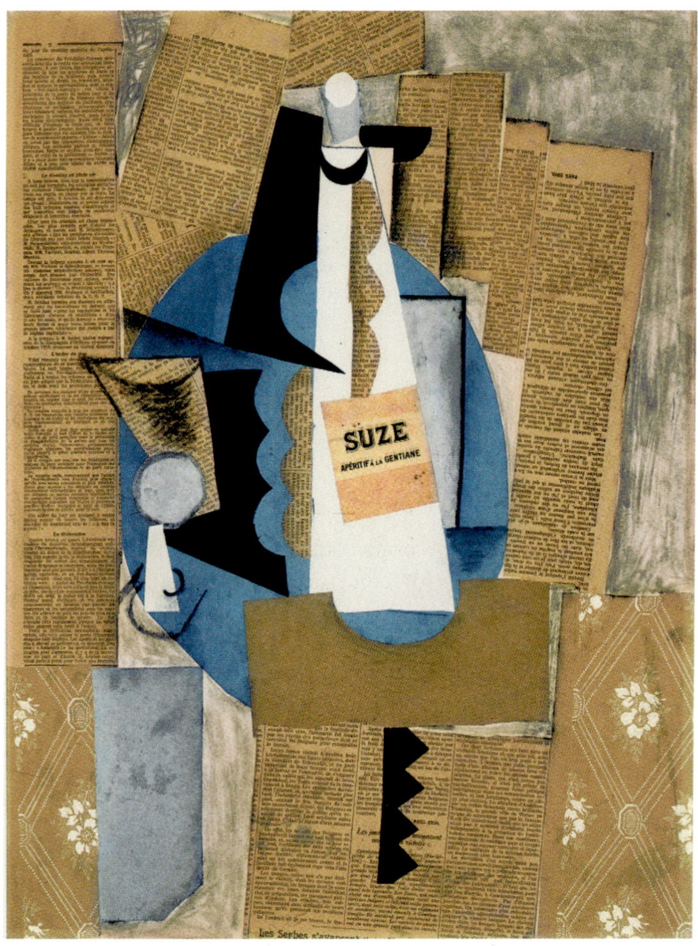

19–10 Pablo Picasso. ***Glass and Bottle of Suze*.** 1912. Pasted paper, gouache, and charcoal, 25¾" × 19¾" (65.4 × 50.2 cm). Mildred Lane Kemper Art Museum, Washington University, St. Louis, Missouri
UNIVERSITY PURCHASE, KENDE SALE FUND, 1946

subject provided only the raw material for a formal composition. *Ma Jolie* is not a representation of a woman, a place, or an event; it is simply a painting.

A subtle tension between order and disorder is maintained throughout the painting. For example, the shifting effect of the surface, a delicately patterned texture of grays and browns, is regularized through the use of short, horizontal brushstrokes that firmly establish a grid and effectively counteract the surface flux. What at first may seem a random assemblage of lines and muted colors is in fact a well-organized composition. The aesthetic satisfaction of such a work is thus heightened by the way chaos seems to resolve itself into order. In 1923, Picasso said, "Cubism is no different from any other school of painting. The same principles and the same elements are common to all. The fact that for a long time Cubism has not been understood … means nothing. I do not read English, [but] this does not mean that the English language does not exist, and why should I blame anyone … but myself if I cannot understand [it]?"

Works like *Ma Jolie* brought Picasso and Braque to the brink of nonrepresentation, but in the spring of 1912 they pulled back and began to create works that suggested more clearly discernible subjects. This second major phase of Cubism is known as Synthetic Cubism because of the way the artists created motifs by combining simpler elements, as in a chemical synthesis. Picasso's *Glass and Bottle of Suze* (fig. **19–10**), like many of the works he and Braque created from 1912 to 1914, is a **collage** (from *coller*, "to glue" in French), a technique in which paper or other material is pasted onto another surface. At the center, newsprint and construction paper suggest a tray or round table supporting a glass and a bottle of liquor with an actual label. Around this arrangement Picasso pasted larger pieces of newspaper and wallpaper. As in earlier Cubism, multiple perspectives are offered. We see the top of the blue table, tilted to face us, and simultaneously the side of the glass. The bottle stands on the table, its label facing us, while we can also see the round profile of its opening, as well as the top of the cork that plugs it. The elements together evoke not only a place—a bar—but also an activity: the viewer alone with a newspaper, enjoying a quiet drink. The newspaper clippings glued to this picture, however, disrupt the quiet mood. They reference the First Balkan War of 1912–1913, which contributed to the outbreak of World War I. Did Picasso want to underline the disorder in his art by comparing it with the disorder building in the world around him, or was he warning his viewers not to sit blindly and sip Suze while political events threatened to shatter the peaceful pleasures this work evokes?

Responses to Cubism

As Cubism evolved and emerged from the studios of Braque and Picasso, it became clear that something of great significance was happening in the art world. The radical innovations may have upset the general public and many critics, but members of the avant-garde saw in them the future of Modern art. Artists in many countries adopted various aspects of the Cubist style, broadening the impact of Cubism beyond the studio-based aesthetic of Braque and Picasso.

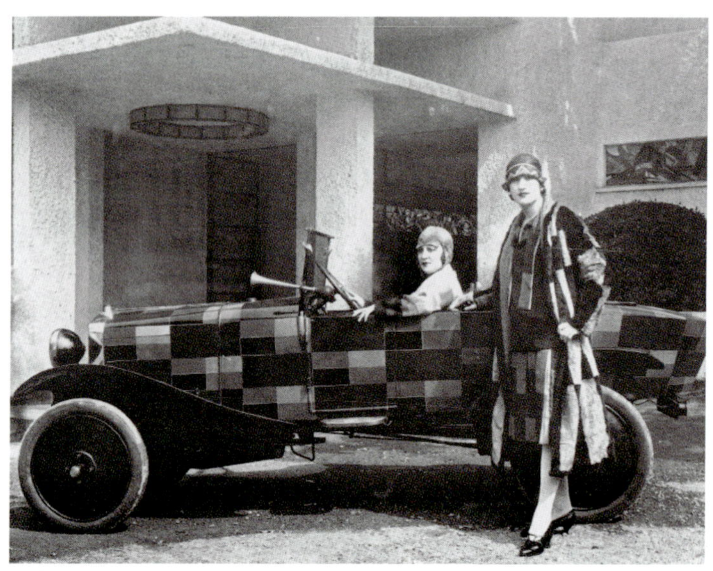

19–11 Sonia Delaunay-Terk. Clothes and customized Citroën B-12.
From *Maison de la Mode*, 1925

ART DECO

The 1925 International Exposition of Modern Decorative and Industrial Arts in Paris—at which Sonia Delaunay-Terk's fabric designs were displayed—helped launch a popular commercial style then considered *art moderne* and now called Art Deco (a label coined in a 1960s revival). The Art Deco label is loosely applied to describe variations on a modern design trend developed in Europe and the United States during the 1920s and 1930s that visually defined the "Machine Age," the era between World War I and World War II. Influenced by Cubism and abstract art, Art Deco objects and ornaments are characterized by angular or arched lines or forms rendered with an impersonal precision that recall the attributes of machines: flawless accuracy, speed, and automation. Ironically, many Art Deco objects that celebrate modern mechanization through their style are actually handcrafted luxury items. See "African Furniture and the Art Deco Style," page 450.

French Responses Robert Delaunay (1885–1941) and his wife, the Ukranian-born Sonia Delaunay-Terk (1885–1979), took monochromatic, static, Analytic Cubism into a wholly different direction by fusing it with Fauvist color in works celebrating the modern city and modern technology. The critic and poet Guillaume Apollinaire labeled the style "Orphism" (from Orpheus, the legendary Greek musician), implying an analogy between their painting and music. The Delaunays preferred to think of their work in terms of "simultaneity," a complicated concept connoting the collapse of spatial distance and temporal sequence into a simultaneous "here and now," and the creation of harmonic unity out of discordant elements.

Delaunay-Terk became a distinguished textile and fashion designer. Her greatest critical success came at the International Exposition of Modern Decorative and Industrial Arts in 1925, for which she decorated a Citroën sports car to match one of her textile designs (fig. **19–11**). Her bold geometric patterns seem to express the new modernity of the automobile age. Moreover, the small three-seater Citroën was specifically designed to appeal to the "new woman," who, like Delaunay-Terk, was more mobile, less tied to home and family, and less dependent on men than her predecessors.

Similarly fascinated by technology was Fernand Léger (1881–1955), who developed a version of Cubism based on machine forms. His artistic development was affected by his wartime experience. Drafted into the French army, he was almost killed by poison gas in 1916, and this experience led him to see more beauty in everyday objects, even those made by machines. *Three Women* (fig. **19–12**) is a machine-age version of the French odalisque tradition

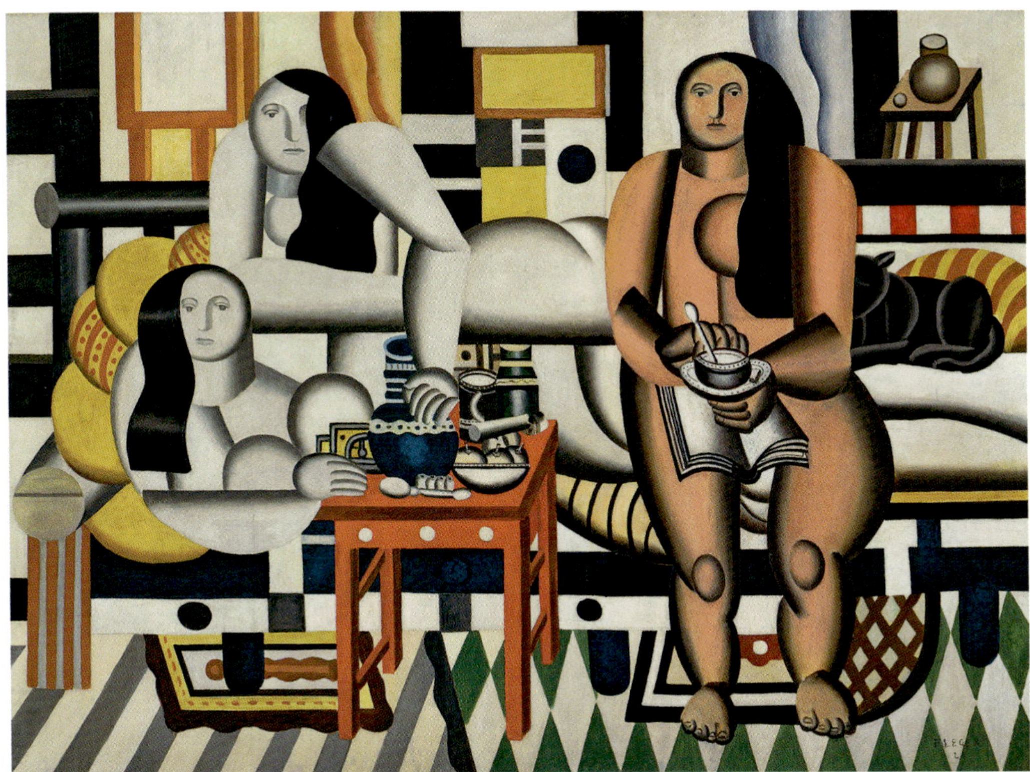

19–12 Fernand Léger. *Three Women*. 1921. Oil on canvas, 6' ½" × 8' 3" (1.84 × 2.52 m). The Museum of Modern Art, New York
MRS SIMON GUGGENHEIM FUND (189.1942)

initiated by Ingres (see fig. 17–17). The picture space is shallow and compressed but less radically shattered than in Analytic Cubism. The women, arranged within a geometric grid, stare out blankly at us with Classical calmness. They have identical faces, and their bodies seem assembled from standardized, interchangeable metal parts. The bright, exuberant colors and patterns that surround them, however, suggest a positive vision of an orderly industrial society.

Italian Responses In Italy, Cubism led to Futurism, which emerged on February 20, 1909, when a Milanese literary magazine editor, Filippo Marinetti, published his "Foundation and Manifesto of Futurism" in a Paris newspaper. An outspoken attack against everything old, dull, "feminine," and safe, Marinetti's manifesto promoted the supposedly exhilarating "masculine" experiences of warfare and reckless speed to liberate Italy from its outworn past and to celebrate the technological power of modern urban life.

Among the artists and poets who gathered around Marinetti was Umberto Boccioni (1882–1916), whose major sculptural work, *Unique Forms of Continuity in Space* (fig. **19–13**), seems to epitomize a revitalized Italy. Cubist figure studies, which Boccioni saw in Paris in 1911, inspired the exaggerated muscular curves and countercurves of this powerful sculpture, the stretched and inflated forms which express the figure's force and speed. The work personifies the new Italian man envisioned by the Futurists, a strong figure rushing headlong into the brave new Futurist world.

Russian Responses Since the time of Peter the Great (ruled 1682–1725), the Russian upper classes had turned to Western Europe for cultural models. Knowledge of Analytic Cubism and Futurism arrived in Moscow almost simultaneously, and since the two had some superficial similarities, Russian artists tended to link them. Natalia Goncharova (1881–1962) was one of many Russian artists who adopted French styles with some ambivalence. Among her creations were costumes and sets that she designed for the

19–13 Umberto Boccioni. *Unique Forms of Continuity in Space.* 1913. Bronze, 43⅞" × 34⅞" × 15¾" (111.4 × 88.6 × 40 cm). The Museum of Modern Art, New York
ACQUIRED THROUGH THE LILLIE P. BLISS BEQUEST (231.1948)

Boccioni and the Futurist architect Antonio Sant'Elia were both killed in World War I. The Futurists had ardently promoted Italian entry into the war on the side of France and England. After the war Marinetti's movement, still committed to nationalism and militarism, supported the rise of Fascism under Benito Mussolini, although a number of the original members of the group rejected this direction.

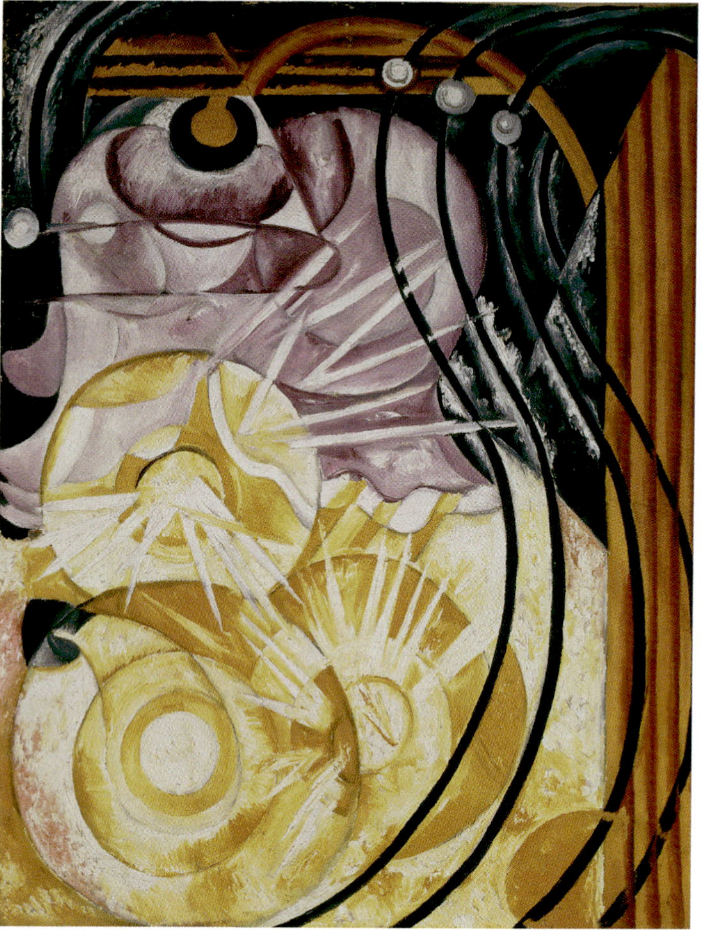

19–14 Natalia Goncharova. *Electric Light.* 1913. Oil on canvas, 41½" × 32" (105.5 × 81.3 cm). Musée National d'Art Moderne. Centre National d'Art et de Culture Georges Pompidou

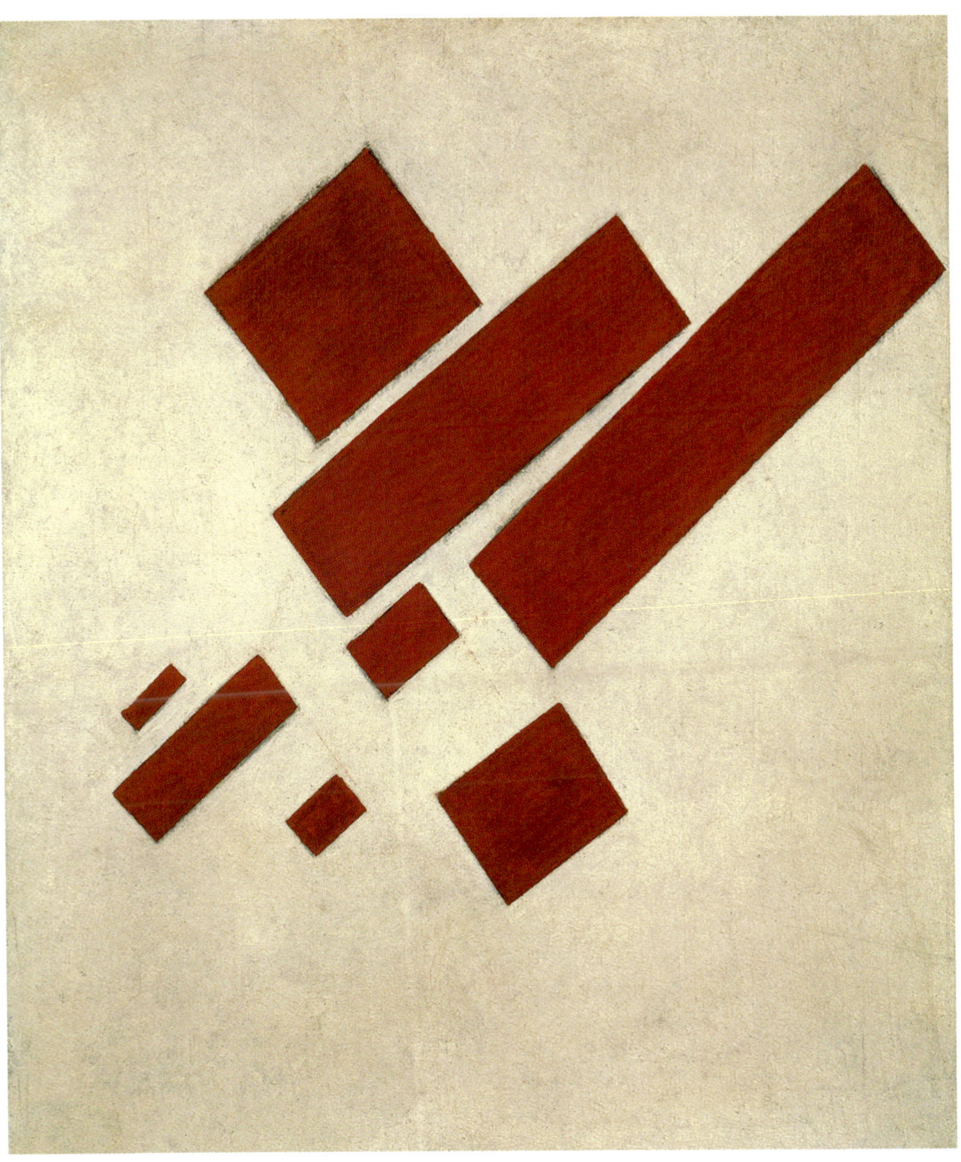

19–15 Kazimir Malevich. ***Suprematist Painting (Eight Red Rectangles).*** 1915. Oil on canvas, 22½" × 18⅞" (57 × 48 cm). Stedelijk Museum, Amsterdam

impresario Sergei Diaghilev's famed Ballets Russes, including the performances of *Le Coq d'or* (1914), *Night on Bald Mountain* (1923), and the 1926 revival of Stravinsky's *Firebird.*

Goncharova and her lifelong companion, Mikhail Larionov (1881–1964), were torn between the desire to develop a native, characteristically Russian art and the wish to keep up with Western European developments. Exposed to French and Italian art and also the Slavophile (pro-Russian) movement in Moscow, they created a new Russian style known as Cubo-Futurism. In her *Electric Light* (fig. **19–14**), Goncharova combines two styles: simplified Cubist shapes and a dynamic Futurist composition. Brilliant electric light bulbs almost explode into yellow disks and rays, energized by their swinging, snake-like cords and switches. The painting is at the same time a study in contrasting enhanced colors and a potent symbol of technological advance—of Russia's modernity.

After Goncharova and Larionov left for Paris in 1915, their colleague Kazimir Malevich (1878–1935) emerged as the leading figure of the Moscow avant-garde. Indeed, Malevich was the first Russian to go beyond Cubo-Futurism, and he did so unforgettably. Malevich is recognized as the first Modernist artist to produce a truly nonrepresentational work of art. According to his later reminiscences, "in the year 1913, in my desperate attempt to free art from the burden of the object, I took refuge in the square form and exhibited a picture which consisted of nothing more than a black square on a white field." Malevich exhibited 39 works in this radically new mode in St. Petersburg in the winter of 1915–1916. One, *Suprematist Painting* (*Eight Red Rectangles*) (fig. **19–15**), consists simply of rectangles arranged diagonally on a white painted ground. Malevich called this art "Suprematism," short for "the supremacy of pure feeling in creative art." By eliminating traditional subject matter and focusing entirely on formal issues, Malevich intended to "liberate" the essential beauty of all great art.

The Suprematist movement attracted many women, the most radical of whom was Liubov Popova (1889–1924). Born into a

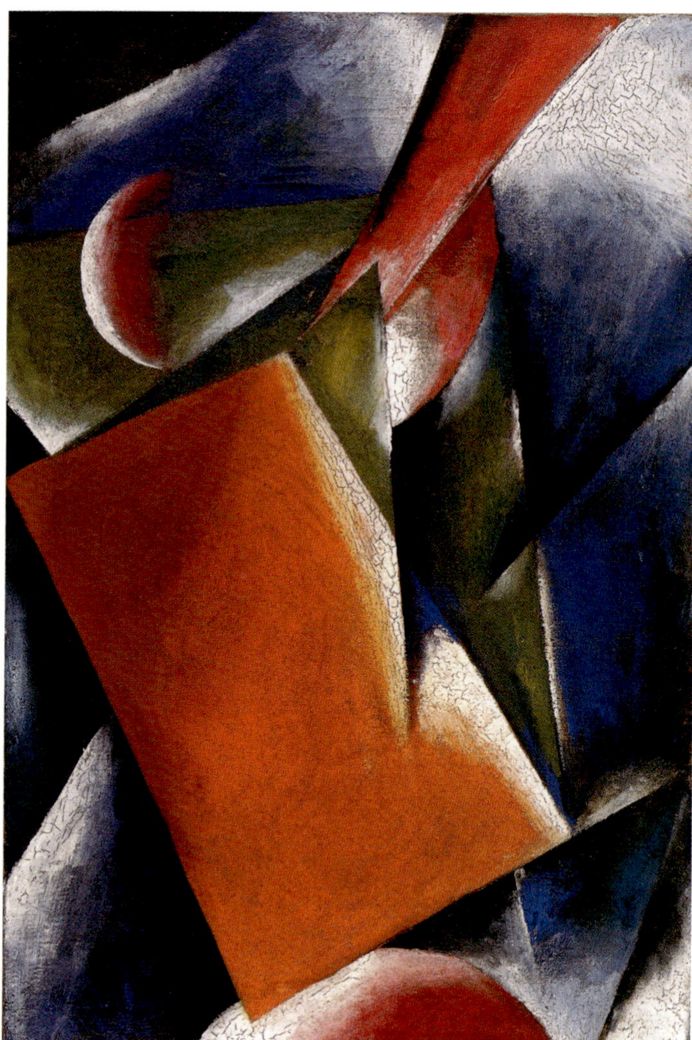

19–16 Liubov Popova. *Architectonic Painting*. 1917. Oil on canvas, 29 13/16" × 21" (75.57 × 53.34 cm). Los Angeles County Museum of Art

wealthy family, she studied Modern art in Paris in 1912–1913. On her return to Russia she gravitated toward the Suprematists, and she made her first completely abstract Cubist works in 1916. She titled all of these works *Architectonic Painting* (fig. **19–16**). They are more dynamic than Malevich's paintings since their forms are modeled and since they seem to project out of their shallow Cubist space and into the world of the viewer. The bright colors contribute to dynamism—warm reds and oranges seem to advance toward the viewer, while cool blues and blacks recede.

This Russian avant-garde enthusiastically supported the Revolution that broke out in 1917, thinking that their radical new form of art was appropriate for the new Russia that would emerge from the ashes of the czarist dictatorship. Into the 1920s it was. But eventually avant-garde art was branded "bourgeois" and "decadent" by the Soviet government, and a highly representational and heroic style called Socialist Realism became state policy in 1932 under dictator Joseph Stalin.

Dada

The Dada movement, which began with the opening of the Cabaret Voltaire in Zürich, Switzerland, on February 5, 1916, was a remarkable manifestation of the disillusioned mood of its time, as World War I, which had begun in 1914, spiraled out of control and settled into a stalemate during which the latest technologies for killing were piling up human casualties of unprecedented proportions. The cabaret's founders, the German actor and artist Hugo Ball (1886–1927) and his companion, Emmy Hennings, a nightclub singer, attracted a circle of avant-garde writers and artists who shared in Ball's and Hennings' disgust with the political culture that had visited such brutality on their world.

Ball's performance while reciting one of his sound poems, "Karawane" (fig. **19–17**), reflects the spirit of the cabaret. Ball encased his legs and body in blue cardboard tubes, and wore on his head a white-and-blue "witch-doctor's hat," as he called it. The huge gold-painted cardboard collar over his shoulders flapped when he moved his arms. Dressed in this manner, he slowly and solemnly

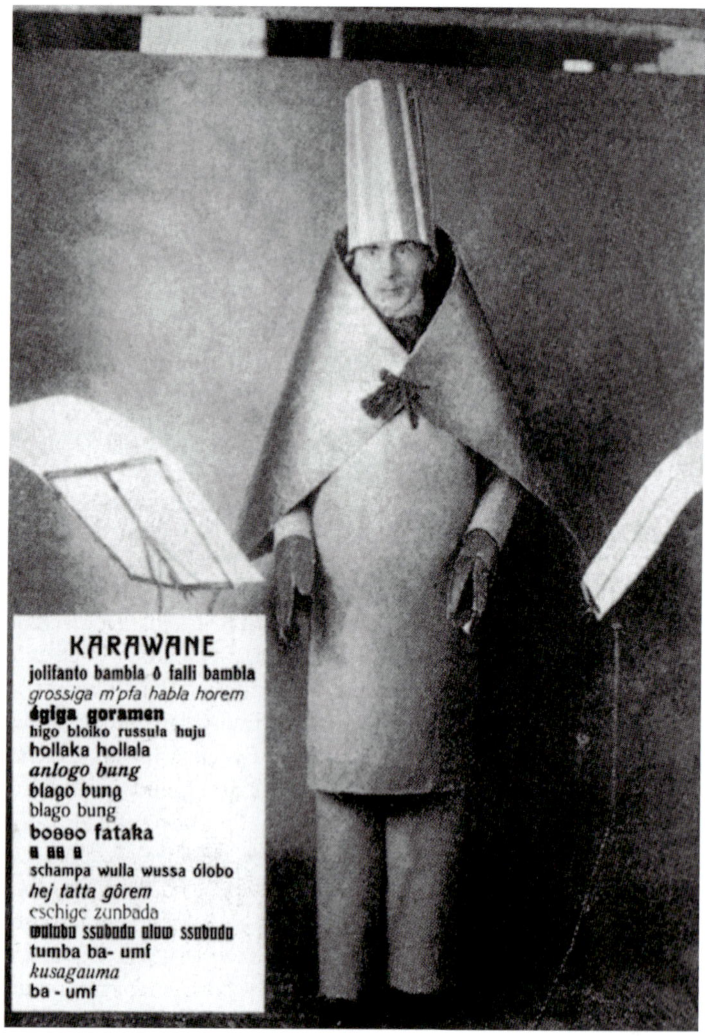

19–17 Hugo Ball reciting the sound poem "Karawane." Photographed at the Cabaret Voltaire, Zürich, 1916
KUNSTHAUS ZURICH DADA-ARCHIVE

19–18 Marcel Duchamp. ***Fountain (second version).*** 1950. Porcelain urinal, 12" × 15" × 18" (30.5 × 38.1 × 45.7 cm). Readymade: glazed sanitary china with black paint. Philadelphia Museum of Art
GIFT (BY EXCHANGE) OF MRS. HERBERT CAMERON MORRIS

An ordinary plumbing fixture signed by Duchamp with the pseudonym "R. Mutt" and presented as a "readymade" work of art, the original Fountain *mysteriously disappeared shortly after it was rejected by the jury of the American Society of Independent Artists exhibition in 1917. The appearance of this lost original is known only from a photograph by Alfred Stieglitz. The second version of* Fountain, *illustrated here, was selected in Paris by the art dealer Sidney Janis at Duchamp's request for an exhibition in New York in 1950. In 1964, Duchamp supervised the production of a small edition of replicas of the original* Fountain *based on the Stieglitz photograph. One of these replicas sold at auction in 1999 for $1.76 million, setting a record for a work by Duchamp.*

recited the poem, which consisted entirely of nonsense sounds. By retreating into sound alone, he avoided language, which he believed had been spoiled by the lies and excesses of journalism and advertising. But his goals were not all political and intellectual. Ball also wanted to introduce the healthy play of children back into restricted adult lives.The flexibility of interpretation inherent in Dada extended to its name, which, according to one account, was chosen at random from a dictionary. In German, "dada" signifies "baby talk"; in French, it means "hobbyhorse"; and in Russian, "yes, yes." The name, and the movement, could be defined as the individual wished.

Dada first spread from Zürich to New York and Barcelona, and then to Berlin (1918), Cologne, and Paris. The leading figure in New York was French artist Marcel Duchamp (1887–1968), who had moved to New York in 1915. Duchamp and his friends maintained that art should appeal to the mind rather than to the senses. This cerebral approach is exemplified in Duchamp's **readymades**—ordinary manufactured objects transformed into artworks simply through their selection by the artist. The most notorious readymade was *Fountain* (fig. **19–18**), a porcelain urinal turned through 90 degrees and signed with the pseudonym "R. Mutt," a play on the name of the fixture's manufacturer. Duchamp submitted *Fountain* anonymously in 1917 to the first exhibition of the American Society of Independent Artists, open to anyone who paid a $6 entry fee. Duchamp, a founding member of the society, entered the found object partly as a test. A majority of the society's directors declared that the *Fountain* was not a work of art, and, moreover, was indecent, so the piece was refused. Duchamp immediately resigned from the society.

Duchamp wrote, "The only works of art America has given are her plumbing and bridges." In a more serious vein, he added: "Whether Mr. Mutt with his own hands made the fountain or not has no importance. He CHOSE it. He took an ordinary article of life, placed it so that its useful significance disappeared under the new title and point of view—created a new thought for that object." Duchamp's philosophy of the readymade, succinctly expressed in these words, had a tremendous impact on later twentieth-century artists.

Modern Art Comes to the United States

At the end of the nineteenth century, American artists, led by the artist and teacher Robert Henri (1865–1929), sought a purely "American" style, as free from Impressionism as it was from European academic conventions. Henri told his students, "Paint what you see. Paint what is real to you." In 1908, he organized an exhibition of paintings by artists who came to be called "The Eight," five of whom became known as members of the Ashcan School because of their interest in depicting scenes of gritty urban life in New York City.

An outspoken opponent of the Ashcan School was the photographer Alfred Stieglitz (1864–1946), who chose a different approach in photographing the quintessentially modern city of New York (see fig. **19–19**). In 1905, Stieglitz opened a New York gallery where he exhibited contemporary art and photography, hoping to break down the artificial barrier between the two. Located at 291 Fifth Avenue, the Little Galleries of the Photo-Secession was soon simply called 291. In collaboration with another American photographer, Edward Steichen (1879–1973), who then lived in Paris, Stieglitz arranged exhibitions unlike any seen before in the United States, showing works by Cézanne, Toulouse-Lautrec, Rodin, Picasso, Braque, Matisse, and the Romanian sculptor Constantin Brancusi.

The event that climaxed Stieglitz's pioneering efforts on behalf of European Modernism (although he himself did not arrange it) was the so-called Armory Show, an "International Exhibition of Modern Art," which was held in 1913 at the 69th Regiment Armory in New York City. The aim of the exhibition was to call attention both to the outmoded views of the National Academy of Design and to the old-fashioned Realist tradition perpetuated by the Ashcan School.

Of the more than 1,300 works in the show, only about a quarter were by Europeans, but it was to these works that primary attention was paid. Critics claimed that Matisse, Kandinsky, Braque, and others were the agents of "universal anarchy." The American academic painter Kenyon Cox called them mere "savages." When a selection of works from the show was exhibited in Chicago, civic leaders there called for an investigation by a morals commission. Faculty and students at the School of the Art Institute were so enraged that they hanged Matisse in effigy.

A number of younger artists, however, responded positively. For example, Marsden Hartley (1877–1943), who had been a regular exhibitor at Stieglitz's gallery, and whose works were included in the Armory Show, showed every sign of becoming a pioneer of American Modernism (see "Closer Look," page 541). During an extended stay in Europe between 1912 and 1915, Hartley discovered Cubism in Gertrude Stein's circle in Paris and was drawn to Kandinsky's Expressionism in Berlin. But as a gay man seeking a place within an America marked by little tolerance for diversity, he spent most of the rest of his career wandering around Europe and North America, seeking a spiritual and cultural home, and restlessly moving between European Modernism and the American Realist traditions.

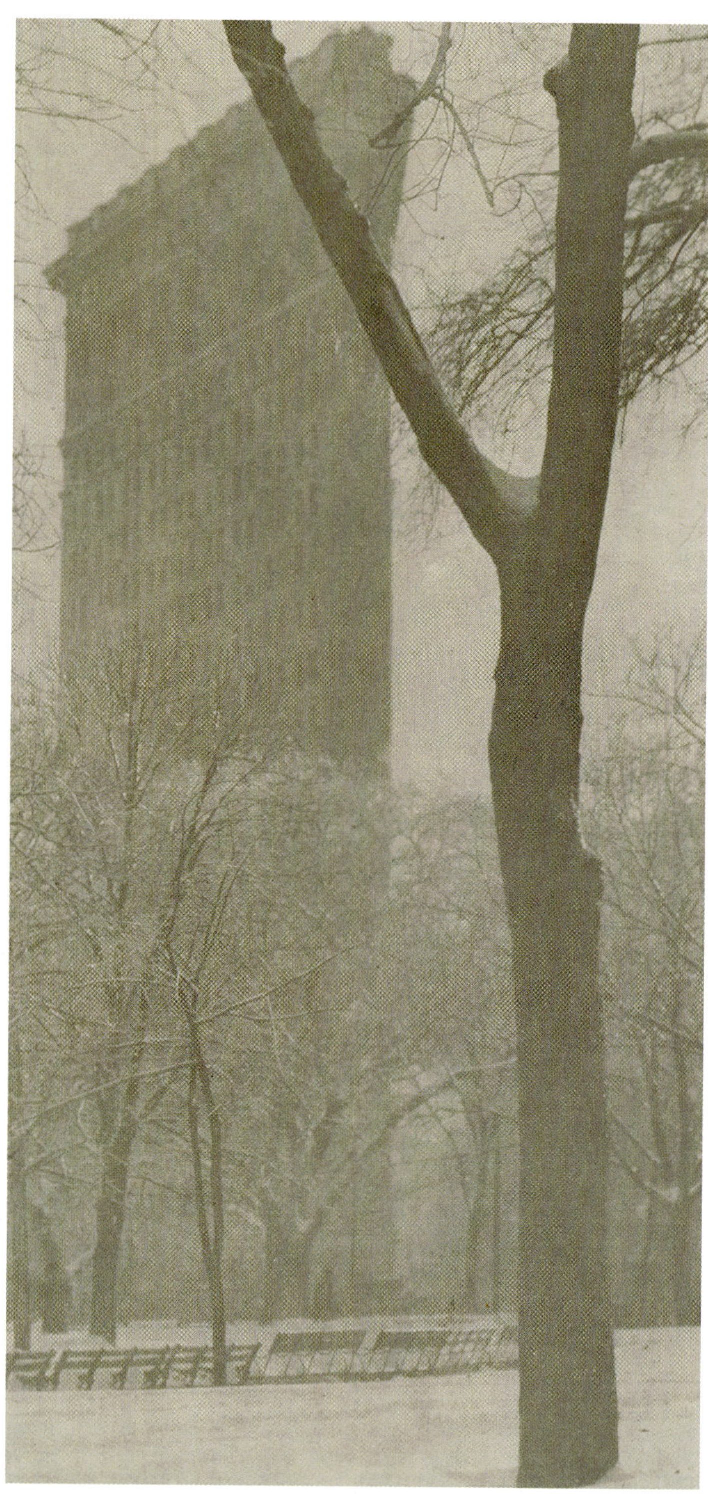

19–19 Alfred Stieglitz. ***The Flatiron Building.*** 1903. Photogravure, 6 11/16" × 3 5/16" (17 × 8.4 cm). The Metropolitan Museum of Art, New York
GIFT OF J.B. NEUMANN, 1958 (58.577.37)

CLOSER LOOK

Like the collage still lives of Synthetic Cubism (see fig. 19–10), American artist Marsden Hartley's Modernist painting *Portrait of a German Officer* (fig. **19–20**) does not literally represent its subject but speaks of him symbolically and indirectly through the use of numbers, letters, fragments of German military paraphernalia and insignia, heraldic motifs, and personal symbols. While living in Berlin in 1914, Hartley fell in love with a young Prussian lieutenant, Karl von Freyburg, whom he later described in a letter to his dealer, Alfred Stieglitz, as "in every way a perfect being—physically, spiritually and mentally, beautifully balanced—24 years young...." Freyburg's tragic death in combat during October 1914 devastated Hartley, and he mourned the fallen officer through this striking but eloquent painting.

The black background of *Portrait of a German Officer* heightens the intensity of its colors at the same time as it creates a solemn, funereal mood. The symbolic references to Freyburg include his initials ("Kv.F"), his age ("24"), his regiment number ("4"), epaulettes, lance tips, and the Iron Cross (a German military decoration) he was awarded the day before he was killed. The cursive "E" may refer to Hartley himself, whose given name was Edmund.

Even the seemingly abstract, geometric patterns carry symbolic meaning. The blue-and-white diamond pattern comes from the flag of Bavaria, while the black-and-white stripes are those of the historic flag of Prussia, and the red, white, and black bands constitute the flag of the German Empire, adopted in 1871. But some of the symbols are more personal. The black-and-white checkerboard evokes Freyburg's love of chess, a poignant reminder that at its core this Modernist painting is an artist's heartfelt expression of a personal loss.

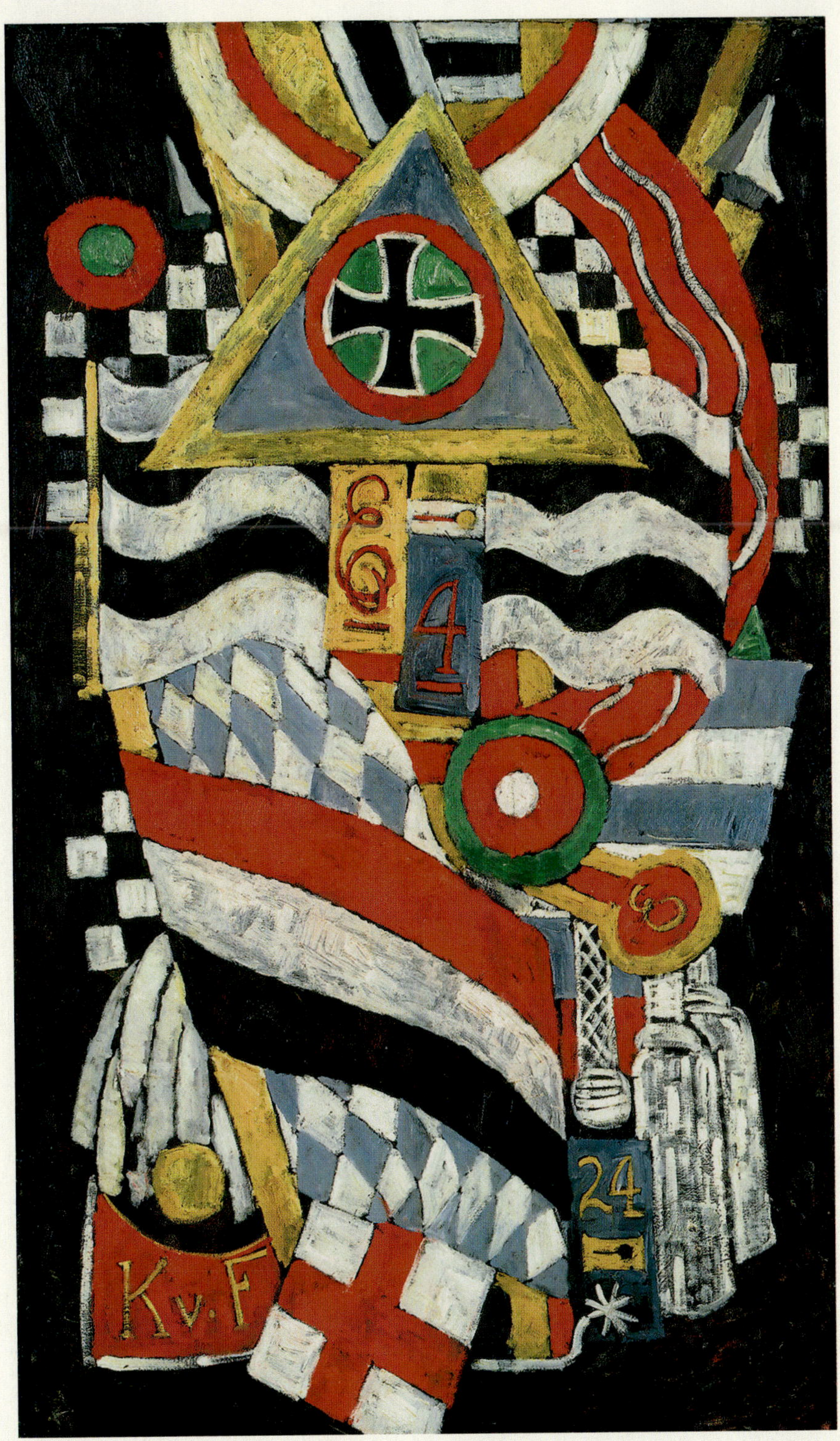

19–20 Marsden Hartley. ***Portrait of a German Officer.*** 1914.
Oil on canvas, 68¼" × 41⅜" (178 × 105 cm). The Metropolitan Museum of Art, New York
THE ALFRED STIEGLITZ COLLECTION, 1949 (49.70.42)

European Art between the Wars

The wars that ravaged Europe in the first half of the twentieth century had a profound effect on Western artists and architects. The dizzying array of "isms" that fragmented the European art world before World War I offered many formal options to postwar innovators. After the Great War, as World War I was then known, members of artists' groups such as the Dutch de Stijl and the German Bauhaus sought the basis for a new society in severely rational beauty and order. The Surrealists, in contrast, celebrated subjectivity, intuition, and chance.

Constructivism

In Russia, the most dynamic artistic achievements of the period immediately following World War I came from avant-garde artists who enthusiastically supported the Russian Revolution of 1917, during which the czar was overthrown, and the Bolsheviks (radical Socialists) rose to power under Vladimir Lenin. Among these artists were Constructivists, who were committed to the notion that artists should leave the studio and "go into the factory, where the real body of life is made." They envisioned politically engaged artists devoted to creating useful objects and promoting the aims of collective society.

One member of this socially visionary movement was engineer El Lissitzky (1890–1941). After the revolution, he taught architecture and graphic arts and soon came under the influence of Malevich, who was a fellow professor. By 1919, El Lissitzky was using Malevich's formal vocabulary for propaganda posters and for artworks he called *Prouns* (pronounced "pro-oon"), an acronym for "Project for the Affirmation of the New." Most Prouns were paintings or prints, but a few were spaces (fig. **19–21**), early examples of **installation art**—artworks created for a specific site, arranged to create a total environment. The engineered look of Lissitzky's art celebrates industrial technology, but more significantly, it encourages viewers to think with precision.

de Stijl

In the Netherlands, the counterpart to El Lissitzky's Constructivism was de Stijl ("The Style"), a movement led by Piet Mondrian (1872–1944). De Stijl was grounded in the conviction that there are two kinds of beauty: a sensual or subjective one and a higher, rational, objective, "universal" kind. In his mature works, Mondrian sought the essence of universal beauty, eliminating representational elements because of their subjective associations and curves because of their sensual appeal.

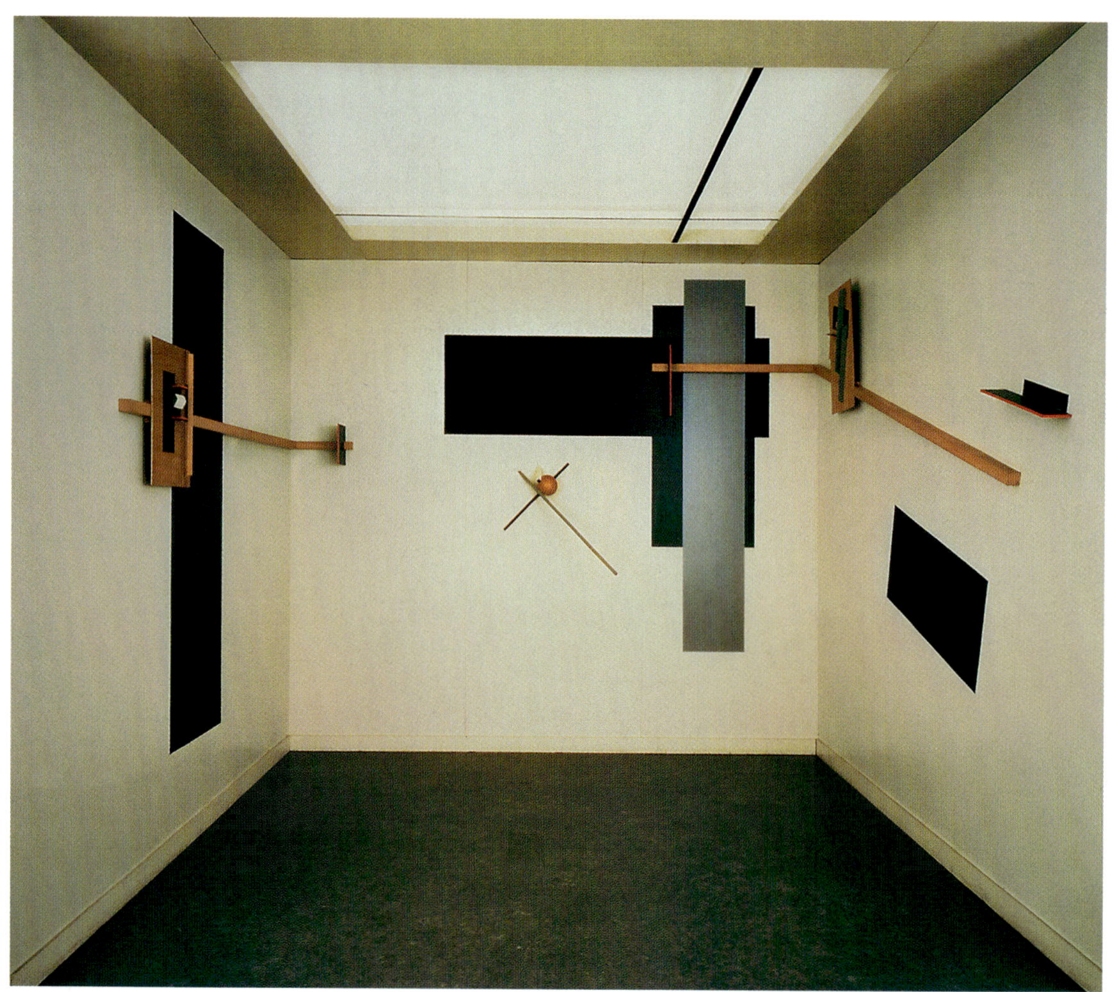

19–21 El Lissitzky. Proun space, created for the Great Berlin Art Exhibition. 1923, reconstruction 1965. Stedelijk Van Abbemuseum, Eindhoven, the Netherlands

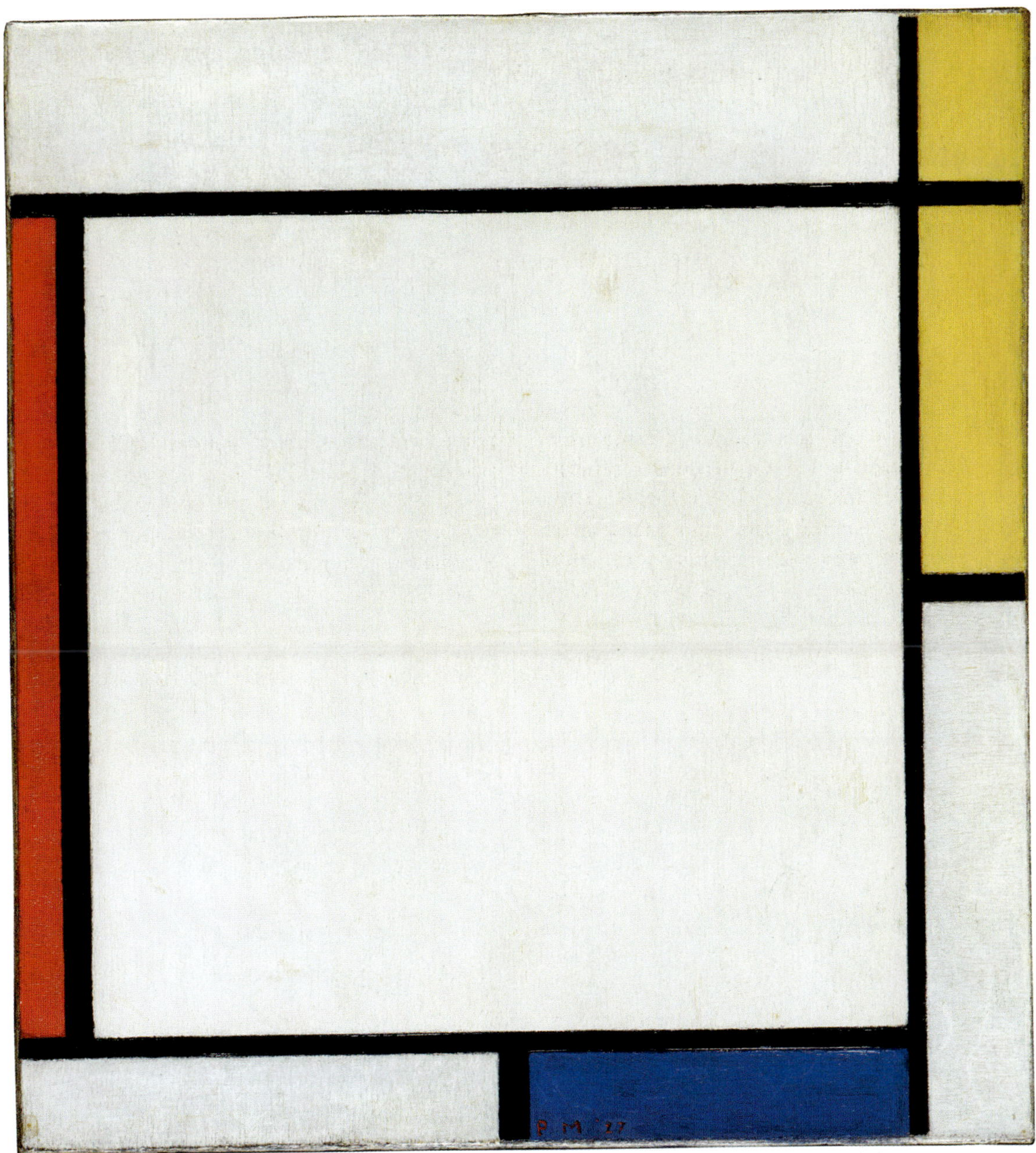

19–22 Piet Mondrian. *Composition with Yellow, Red, and Blue*. 1927. Oil on canvas, 14⅞" × 13¾" (37.8 × 34.9 cm). The Menil Collection, Houston

Mondrian so disliked the sight of nature, whose irregularities he held largely accountable for humanity's problems, that when seated at a restaurant table with a view of the outdoors, he would ask to be moved.

From about 1920, in paintings such as *Composition with Yellow, Red, and Blue* (fig. **19–22**), he restricted his formal vocabulary to the three **primary colors** (red, yellow, and blue), the three neutrals (black, gray, and white), and horizontal and vertical lines. The two linear directions are meant to symbolize the harmony of a series of opposites, including male versus female, individual versus society, and spiritual versus material. For Mondrian, the essence of higher beauty was resolved conflict or what he called "dynamic equilibrium." Here, in a typical composition, Mondrian achieved this equilibrium through the precise arrangement of color areas of different size, shape, and "weight," asymmetrically grouped around the edges of a canvas whose center is dominated by a large area of white. The ultimate purpose of such a painting is to demonstrate a universal style with applications beyond the realm of art. Mondrian hoped to be the world's last artist, believing that if art provided us with the beauty that was lacking in our world and inspired the incorporation of beauty into every aspect of daily life, there would be no need for artists to create special objects labeled "art."

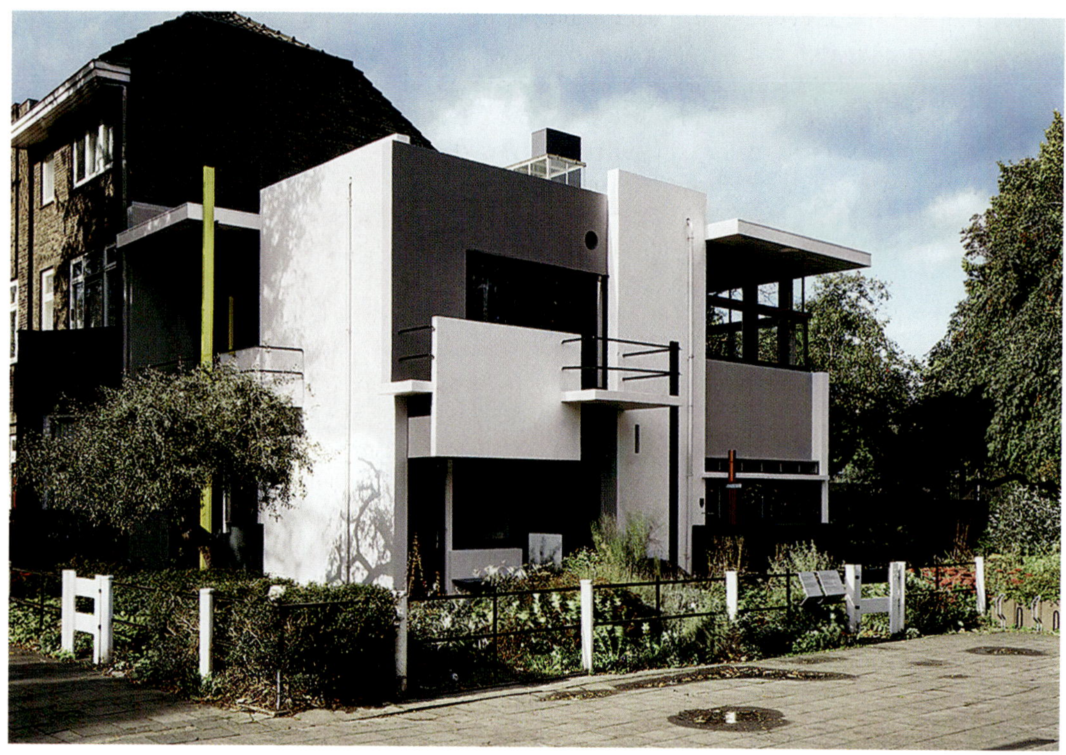

19–23 Gerrit Rietveld. Schröder House, Utrecht, the Netherlands. 1925

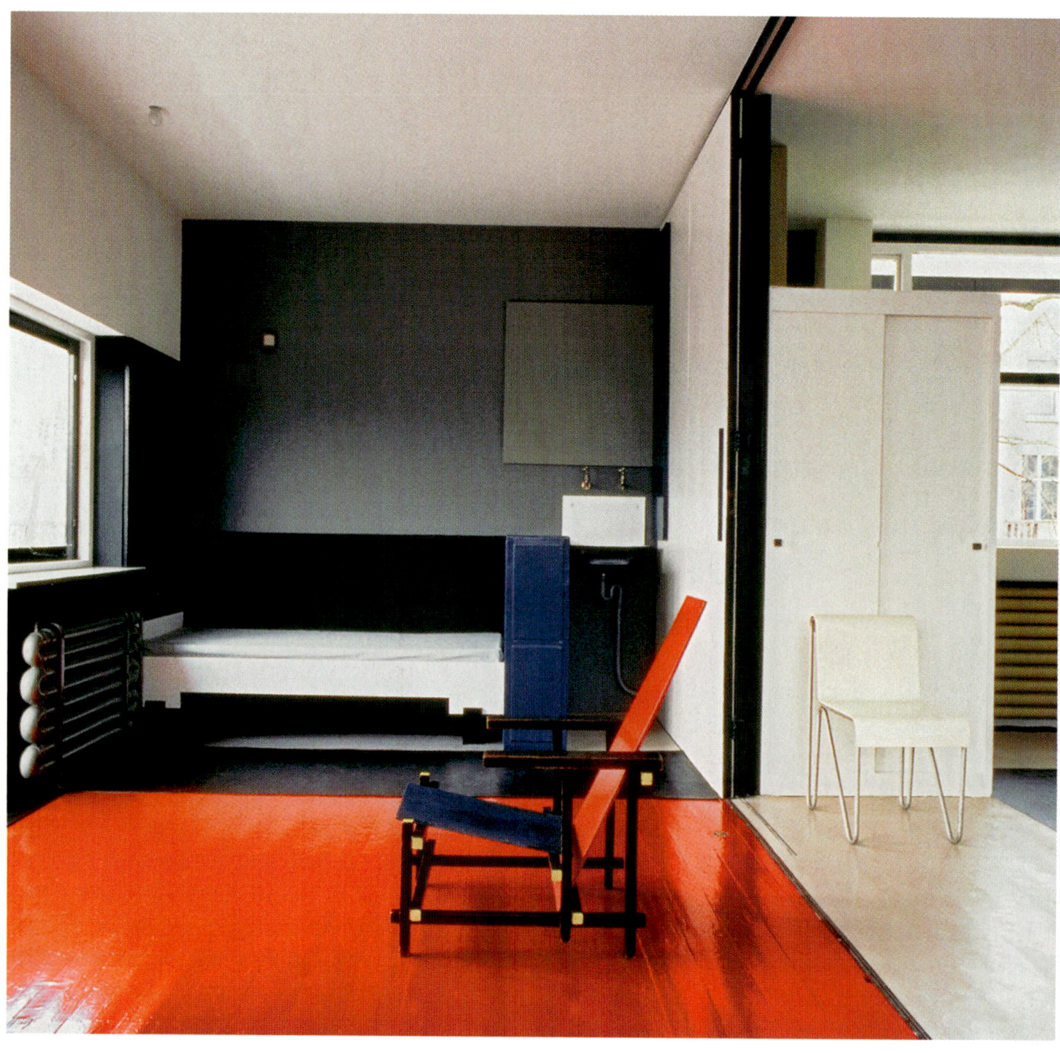

19–24 Gerrit Rietveld. Interior, Schröder House, with "Red-Blue" Chair. 1925

Given this perspective, it is hardly surprising that de Stijl developed in architectural design as well as painting. Architect and designer Gerrit Rietveld (1888–1964) took the lead with his design of the Schröder House in Utrecht (fig. **19–23**), a seminal monument in the development of the Modern architectural movement known as the International Style. Rietveld applied Mondrian's principle of dynamic equilibrium to the whole house. The radically asymmetrical exterior is composed of interlocking gray and white planes of varying sizes, combined with horizontal and vertical accents in primary colors and black. His famous "Red-Blue" Chair is shown here in the bedroom (fig. **19–24**), where his patron, Truus Schröder-Schräder, wanted sliding partitions to allow modifications in the spaces used for sleeping, working, and entertaining. She wanted her home to suggest an elegant austerity, with the basic necessities sleekly integrated into a meticulously restrained whole.

Architectural Purism

Like the Dutch proponents of de Stijl, followers of a French movement known as Purism firmly believed in the power of art to change the world. The leading Purist figure was the Swiss-born Charles-Édouard Jeanneret (1887–1965), a largely self-taught architect and designer who moved to Paris in 1917. Three years later, Jeanneret, partly to demonstrate his faith in the ability of individuals to remake themselves, renamed himself Le Corbusier, a play on the French word for crow (*corbeau*).

Le Corbusier's Villa Savoye (fig. **19–25**) has become an icon of the International Style (see "The International Style," page 546). This weekend retreat house near Versailles is the purest embodiment of his domino construction system, first elaborated in 1914, in which seemingly floating slabs of concrete reinforced with steel bars were positioned on free-standing steel posts. This elevation of the house allowed the owners, arriving from Paris, to drive right underneath it and into a three-car garage. The incorporation of flat-roof terraces, partition walls slotted between supports on the interior, and curtain walls on the exterior with ribbon windows running along their entire length, all became hallmarks of Modern architecture. Le Corbusier referred to this building as a "machine for living," meaning that it was as rationally designed as an automobile or an appliance.

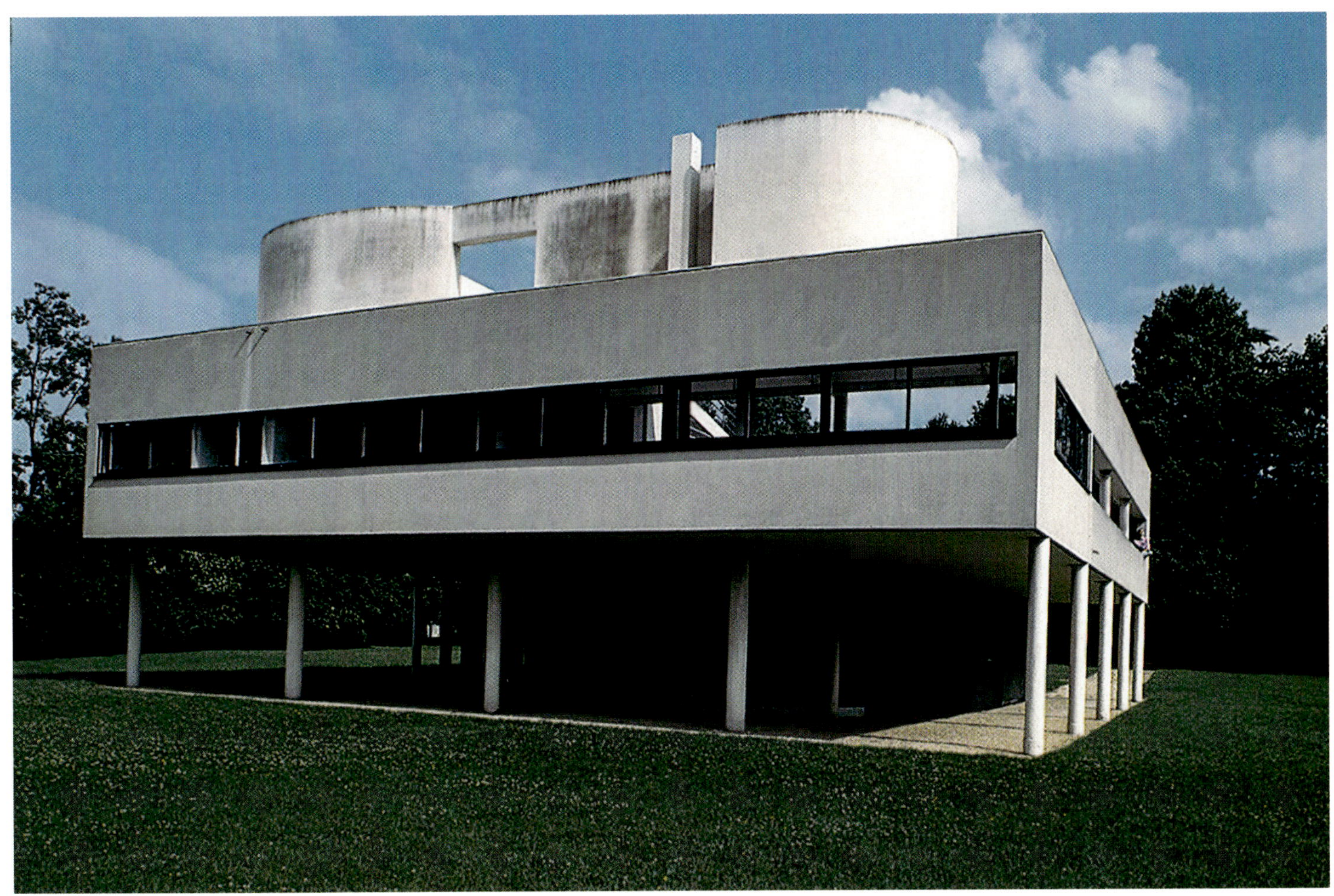

19–25 Le Corbusier. Villa Savoye, Poissy-sur-Seine, France. 1929–1930

The Bauhaus

The German counterpart to the total, rational planning envisioned by de Stijl and Le Corbusier was carried out at a school called the Bauhaus (loosely translated as "House of Building"). The Bauhaus (1919–1933) was the brainchild of Walter Gropius (1883–1969), another founder of Modern architecture. Gropius, who belonged to several utopian groups, admired the spirit of the medieval building guilds, or *Bauhütten*, that had erected the great German cathedrals. He sought to revive their cooperative spirit and bring together modern art and industry by combining the schools of art and craft in the German city of Weimar into this single institution.

At first the Bauhaus school had no formal training program in architecture. Gropius felt that students needed to demonstrate proficiency in workshop courses before going on to study architecture. The workshops—which included classes in pottery, metalwork, textiles, stained glass, furniture making, carving, and wall painting—were intended to teach both specific technical skills and basic design principles. Learning was rooted in doing. Since Gropius believed that art should serve a socially useful function, in 1922 the Bauhaus implemented a new emphasis on industrial design.

The next year the Hungarian-born László Moholy-Nagy (1895–1946) reoriented the Bauhaus workshops toward the creation of sleek, functional designs suitable for mass production. The elegant tea and coffee service by Marianne Brandt (1893–1983), for example (fig. **19–26**), though handcrafted in silver, was a prototype for mass production in a cheaper metal such as nickel silver. Several of Brandt's designs went into mass production, earning much-needed revenue for the school. After Gropius and Moholy-Nagy left the Bauhaus in 1928, Brandt directed the metal workshop. As a woman holding her own in the otherwise all-male metal workshop, she was exceptional at the Bauhaus. Although women were admitted to the school on an equal basis with men, Gropius opposed their education as architects and channeled them into pottery and textile workshops, which he deemed more appropriate for them.

When the Bauhaus moved to the German city of Dessau in 1925, Gropius designed the new building, built in 1925–1926 (fig. **19–27**). Since Gropius made no attempt to cover or decorate his building materials, the structure frankly acknowledges the reinforced concrete, steel, and glass of which it is built. Modern engineering methods made it possible to eliminate the need for walls to

ELEMENTS OF **Architecture**

The International Style

After World War I, increased exchanges between Modern architects led to the development of a common formal language, transcending national boundaries, which came to be known as the International Style. The term gained wide currency as a result of a 1932 exhibition at the Museum of Modern Art in New York, "The International Style: Architecture Since 1922," organized by the architectural historian Henry-Russell Hitchcock and the architect and curator Philip Johnson. Hitchcock and Johnson identified three fundamental principles of the style.

The first principle was "the conception of architecture as volume rather than mass." The use of a structural skeleton of steel and concrete made it possible to eliminate load-bearing walls on both the exterior and interior. Thus the building could be wrapped in a skin of glass, metal, or masonry, creating an effect of enclosed space (volume) rather than dense material (mass). And interiors could feature open, free-flowing plans providing maximum flexibility in the use of space.

The second principle was "regularity rather than symmetry as the chief means of ordering design." Regular distribution of structural supports and the use of standard building parts promoted rectangular regularity rather than the balanced axial symmetry of Classical architecture. The avoidance of Classical balance also encouraged an asymmetrical disposition of the building's components.

The third principle was the rejection of "arbitrary applied decoration." The new architecture depended upon the intrinsic elegance of its materials and the formal arrangement of its elements to produce harmonious aesthetic effects.

Pioneered in France, Germany, and the Netherlands, and spreading by the 1920s into other industrialized countries, the International Style remained influential in architectural design until the 1970s. It was particularly important in United States, where numerous architects sought refuge as they fled Germany during the 1930s, notably Walter Gropius and Mies van der Rohe.

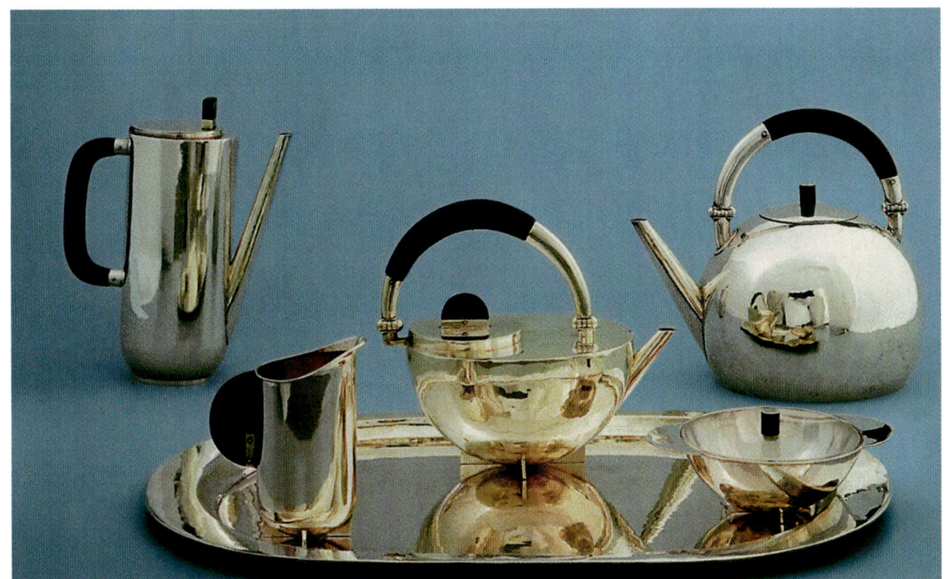

19–26 Marianne Brandt. ***Tea and Coffee Service.*** 1924. Silver and ebony, with Plexiglas cover for sugar bowl. Bauhaus Archiv, Berlin

The lid of Marianne Brandt's sugar bowl is made of Plexiglas, reflecting the Bauhaus's interest in incorporating the latest advances in materials and technology into the manufacture of utilitarian objects.

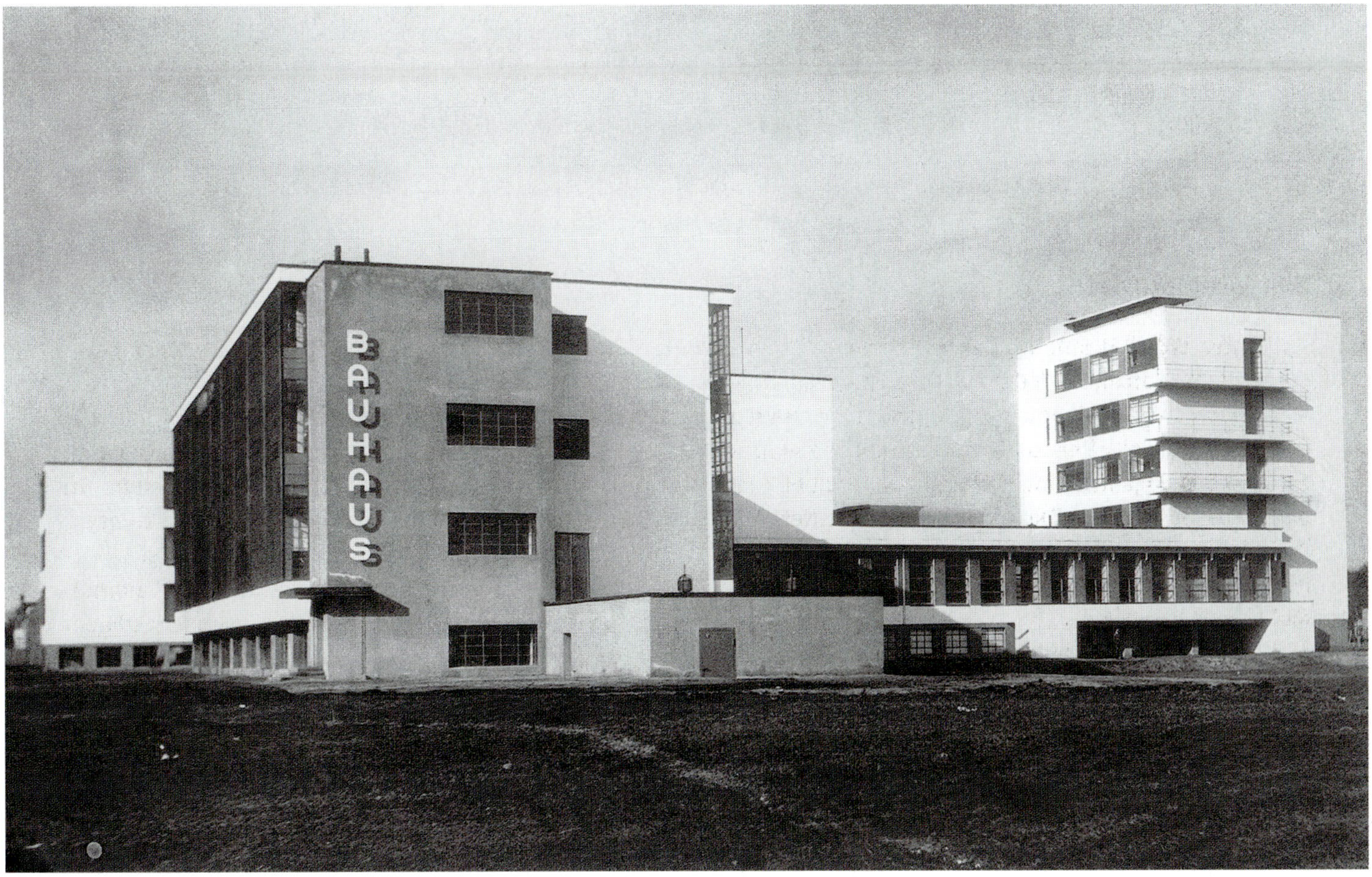

19–27 Walter Gropius. Bauhaus Building, Dessau, Germany. 1925–1926. View from northwest

One of the enduring contributions of the Bauhaus was graphic design. The sans-serif letters of the building's sign not only harmonize with the architecture's clean lines but also communicate the Bauhaus commitment to modernity. Sans-serif typography (that is, a typeface without serifs, the short lines at the end of the stroke of a letter) had been used since the early nineteenth century, but many new sans-serif typefaces were created in the 1920s.

SUPPRESSION OF THE AVANT-GARDE IN GERMANY

The 1930s in Germany witnessed a serious political reaction against avant-garde art and, eventually, a concerted effort to suppress it. One of the principal targets was the Bauhaus, the art and design school founded in 1919 by Gropius, where Mies van der Rohe, Paul Klee, Kandinsky, Josef Albers, and many other luminaries taught. Through much of the 1920s, the Bauhaus had struggled against an increasingly hostile and reactionary political climate. As early as 1924 conservatives had considered it not only educationally unsound but also politically subversive. To avoid having the school shut down by the opposition, Gropius accepted the invitation of the liberal mayor of Dessau to move it there in 1925, but he left soon after the relocation. Gropius' successors faced increasing political pressure, and this prime center of Modernist practice was again forced to move in 1932, this time to Berlin.

After Adolf Hitler came to power in 1933, the Nazi party mounted an aggressive campaign against Modern art. In his youth Hitler himself had been a mediocre academic painter, and he had developed an intense hatred of Modernism and the avant-garde. During the first year of his regime, the Bauhaus was forced to close for good. A number of the artists, designers, and architects who had been on its faculty, including Gropius, Mies, and Albers, emigrated to the United States.

The Nazis also launched attacks against Modernist painters, whose often intense depictions of German soldiers defeated in World War I and the economic depression following the war were considered unpatriotic. Most of all, the expressionistic exaggeration of human forms and facial features, was deemed offensive. The works of these and other artists were removed from museums, while the artists themselves were subjected to public ridicule and often forbidden to buy canvas or paint.

As a final move against the avant-garde, the Nazi leadership organized in 1937 a notorious exhibition of banned works. The "Degenerate Art" exhibition was intended to erase Modernism once and for all from the artistic life of the nation. Seeking to brand all the advanced movements of art as sick and degenerate, it presented Modern artworks as specimens of human pathology; the organizers printed derisive slogans and comments to that effect on the gallery walls (fig. **19–28**). The 650 paintings, sculptures, prints, and books confiscated from German public museums were viewed by 2 million people in the four months the exhibition was on view in Munich and by another million during its subsequent three-year tour of German cities.

By the time World War II broke out, the German authorities had confiscated countless "subversive" works from all over the country. Most were publicly burned, though the Nazi officials sold much of the looted art at public auction in Switzerland to obtain foreign currency. Among the many artists crushed by Nazi suppression was Ernst Ludwig Kirchner, whose *Street, Berlin* (see fig. 19–3) was included in "Degenerate Art." The state's open animosity was a factor in Kirchner's suicide in 1938.

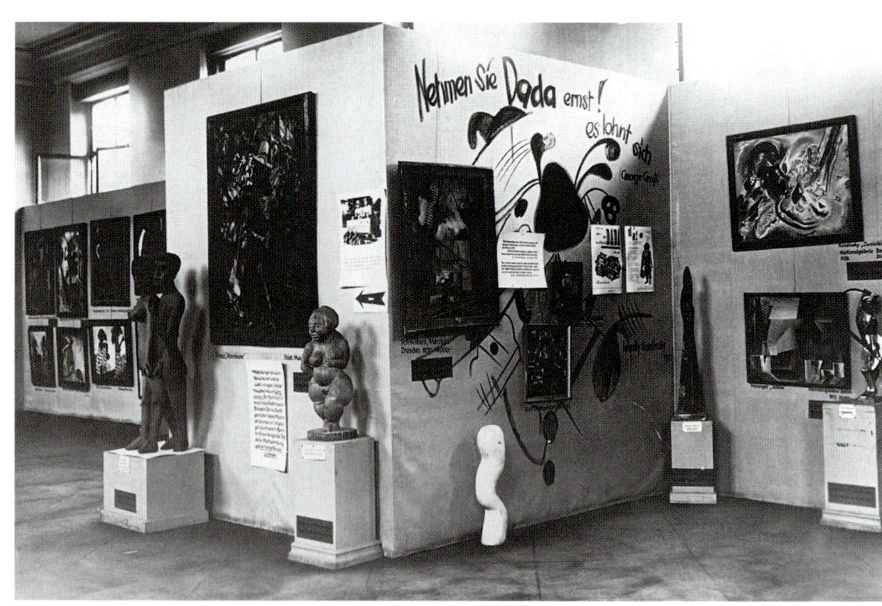

19–28 The Dada Wall, in Room 3 of the "Degenerate Art" (Entartete Kunst) Exhibition, Munich. 1937

be structural supports and replace them with glass panels and to create light, airy interior spaces. Even the sans-serif (without serifs) letters of the Bauhaus sign proclaim its sleek functional ideals.

Beginning in 1930, the Bauhaus was directed by the architect Ludwig Mies van der Rohe (1886–1969). Mies had a passion for realizing the subtle perfection of structure, proportion, and detail, using sumptuous materials such as travertine, richly veined marbles, tinted glass, and bronze. The school remained under his direction until 1933, when the Nazi party came to power. They closed the school.

Surrealism

The intellectual successor to Dada was Surrealism, a movement founded by French writer André Breton (1896–1966). Breton sought to free human behavior from the constrictions of reason and bourgeois morality. In 1924, he published his *Manifesto of Surrealism*, outlining his own view of the theory of Austrian psychiatrist Sigmund Freud (1856–1939) that the human psyche is a battleground where the rational forces of the conscious mind struggle against the irrational, instinctual urges of the unconscious. Breton and his followers employed a number of techniques for liberating the individual unconscious, including dream analysis, free association, automatic writing, word games, and hypnotic trances. Their aim was to help people discover the more intense reality, or "surreality," that lay beyond conventional notions of what was real.

Among the writers and artists around Breton was the Spanish painter and printmaker Salvador Dalí (1904–1989). Dalí contributed the "paranoid-critical method" to Surrealist practice. In this approach, sane artists cultivate the ability of the paranoid to misread ordinary appearances in order to free themselves from the shackles of conventional thought. Dalí demonstrated his method in *The Persistence of Memory* (fig. **19–29**) by placing limp timepieces in a very realistic view of the Bay of Rosas near his birthplace in Catalunya.

According to Dalí, the idea of the soft watches came to him one evening after dinner while he was meditating on a plate of ripe Camembert cheese. One of the limp watches drapes over an amoeba-like human head, its shape inspired by a large rock on the coast. The head, which Dalí identified as a self-portrait, appeared in several paintings and, in combination with the limp watches, may express the anxiety Dalí felt concerning his own sexuality. Another image of anxiety in the work is the ant-covered watchcase at the lower left, inspired by Dalí's childhood memories of seeing dead animals swarming with ants. The absurd yet compelling image of

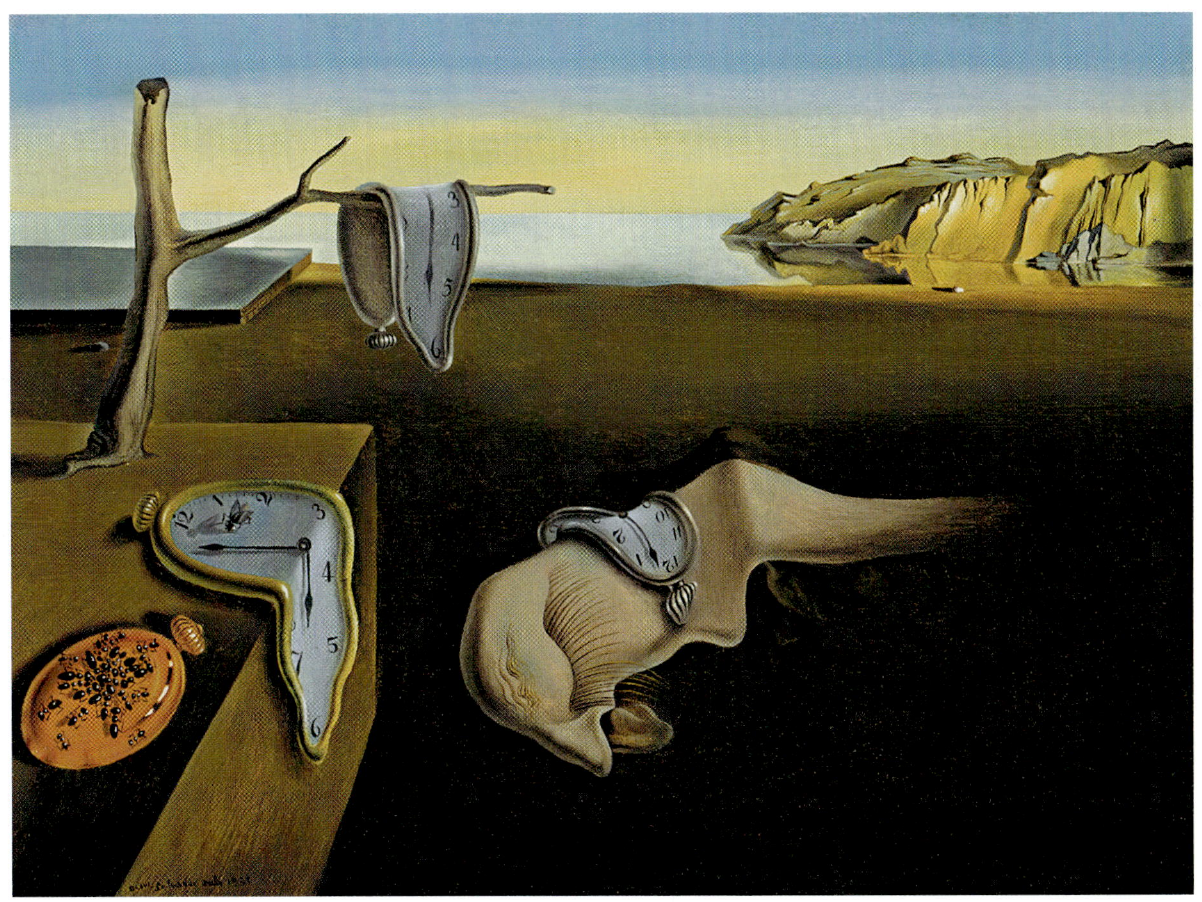

19–29 Salvador Dalí. *The Persistence of Memory*. 1931. Oil on canvas, 9½" × 13" (24.1 × 33 cm). The Museum of Modern Art, New York
GIVEN ANONYMOUSLY (162.1934)

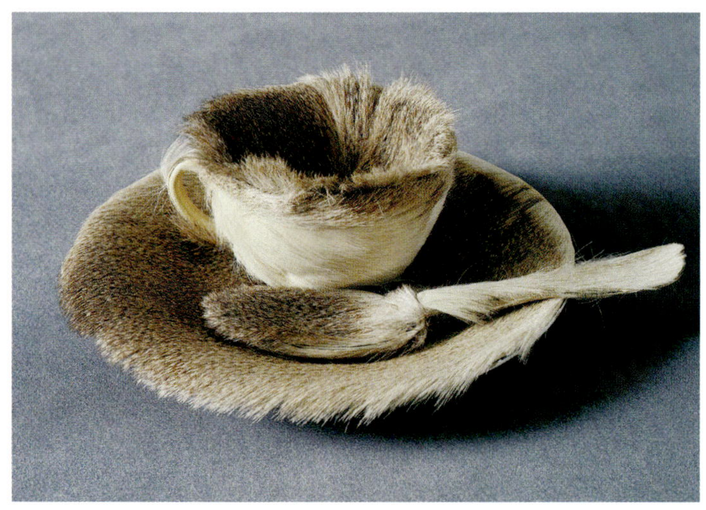

19–30 Meret Oppenheim. ***Object (Le Dejeuner en fourrure)/Luncheon in Fur.*** 1936. Fur-covered cup, diameter 4⅜" (10.9 cm); fur-covered saucer, diameter 9⅜" (23.7 cm); fur-covered spoon, length 8" (20.2 cm); overall height 2⅞" (7.3 cm). The Museum of Modern Art, New York (130.1946A-C)

Oppenheim's Object *was inspired by a café conversation with Picasso about her designs for jewelry made of fur-lined metal tubing. When Picasso remarked that one could cover just about anything with fur, Oppenheim replied, "Even this cup and saucer."*

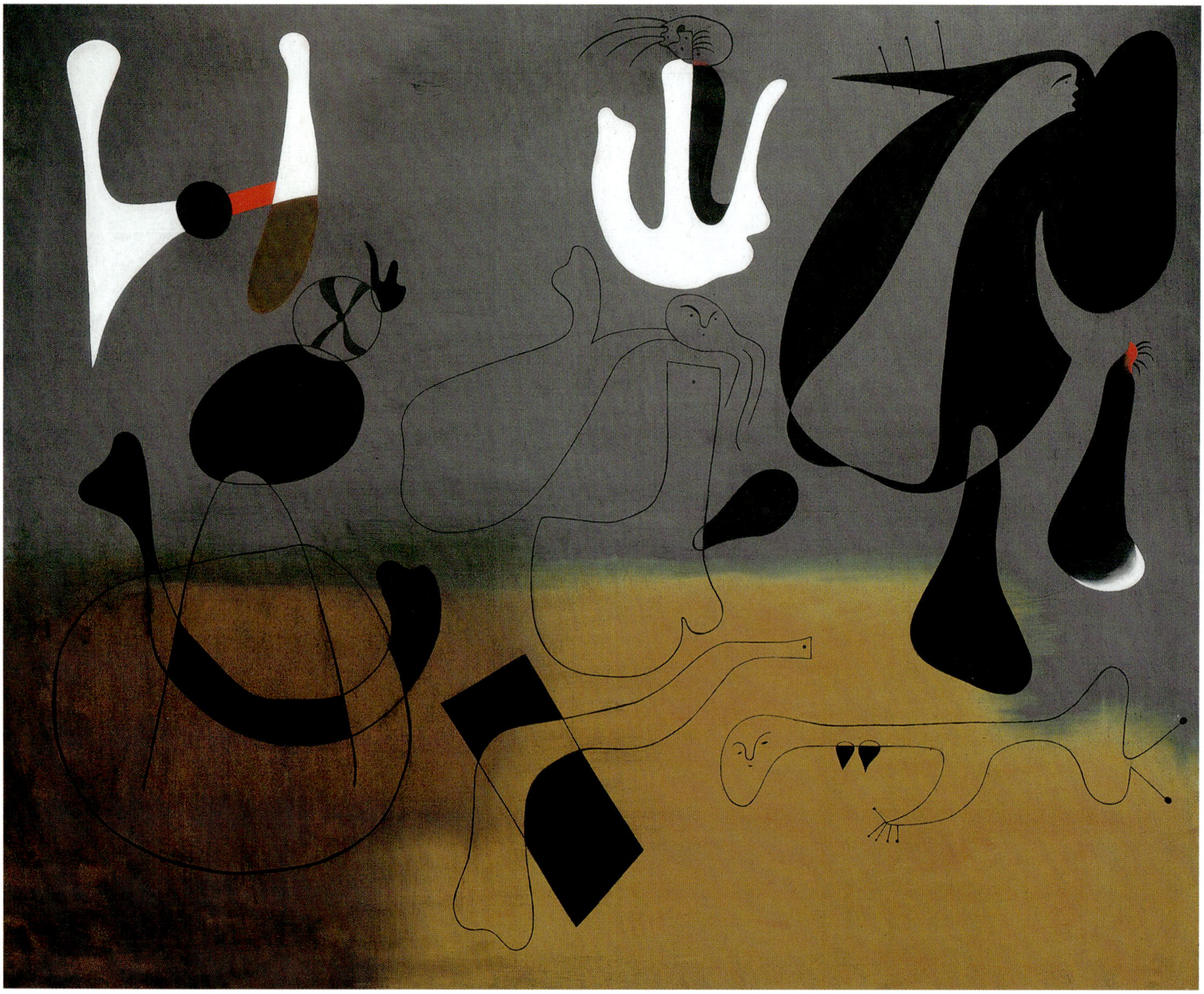

19–31 Joan Miró. ***Composition.*** 1933. Oil on canvas, 51¼" × 63½" (130.2 × 161.3 cm). Wadsworth Atheneum, Hartford, Connecticut

ants feeding on a metallic watch typifies the Surrealist interest in unexpected juxtapositions of disparate realities. Dalí's choice of a meticulously descriptive style makes his irrational world seem more convincing, thus more unsettling.

Building on Duchamp's earlier found objects, the Swiss artist Meret Oppenheim (1913–1985), one of the few female participants in the Surrealist movement, produced disquieting assemblages such as *Object* (*Le Dejeuner en fourrure*) (fig. **19–30**). Consisting of a cup, saucer, and spoon covered with the fur of a Chinese gazelle, Oppenheim's work transforms implements normally used for drinking tea into a hairy ensemble that simultaneously attracts and repels the viewer.

In contrast, a blithe and playful spirit animates the painting of Catalan artist Joan Miró (1893–1983), who exhibited on numerous occasions with the Surrealists, but who never officially joined the group or shared its theoretical interests. In *Composition* of 1933 (fig. **19–31**), he silhouettes shapes so sharply against a hazy background that the picture takes on the feeling of the collage Miró made as a preparatory study. The biomorphic, curving contours evoke organic forms—many rooted in features that recall human figures—that seem to be taking shape before our eyes. Their identity is in flux just as our thought process is always in flux. Are they ancestral spirits or menacing ghosts? Do they tell a story, express a struggle, embody an emotion? Although at its core this is an abstract composition commanded by a high degree of formal control, it seems at the same time evocative of primal or mythic meaning.

Sculpture

Constantin Brancusi (1876–1957) took a different approach to portraying "the essence of things." He arrived in Paris from his native Romania in 1904, and by 1907 was an assistant to Rodin (fig. 18–33). Soon, however, he rejected Rodin's modeling method for the technique of direct carving. In his mature sculpture, such as the *Torso of a Young Man* (fig. **19–32**), he emphasized formal and conceptual simplicity, distilling his subject into smooth and purified forms. He has turned this male human trunk into three cylinders, precariously balanced on two cubes and two trapezoids. Brancusi was motivated by his interest in the ancient Greek philosophy of Plato, who held that all natural forms are imperfect imitations of their perfect ideas, which exist only in the mind. Like Plato, Brancusi sought timeless essence, and he tried to capture the higher world of ideas through elegantly simplified forms.

During the 1920s and 1930s, British sculptor Henry Moore (1898–1986) also practiced direct carving in stone and wood to pursue his ideal of "truth to material." Moore's art developed in a series of massive, simplified reclining female figures, inspired by the

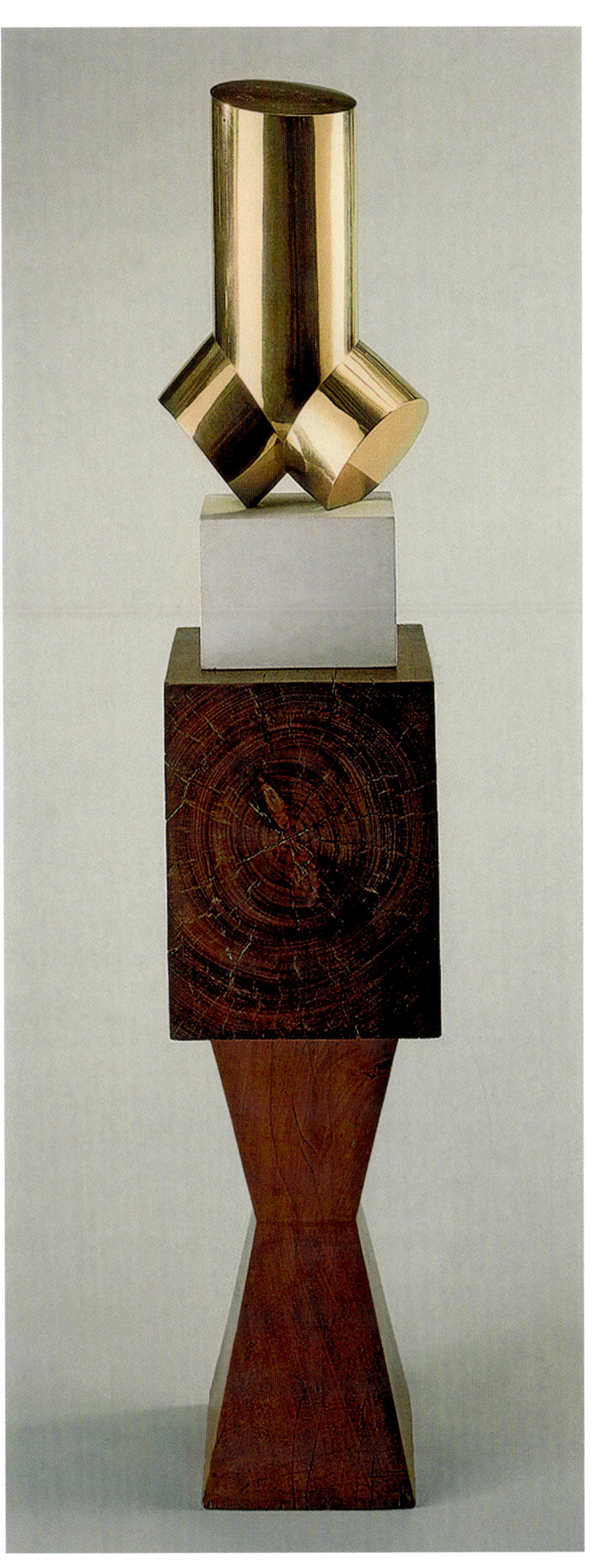

19–32 Constantin Brancusi. *Torso of a Young Man*. 1924. Bronze on stone and wood bases; combined figure and bases 40⅜" × 20" × 18¼" (102.4 × 50.5 × 46.1 cm). Hirshhorn Museum and Sculpture Garden, Smithsonian Institution
GIFT OF JOSEPH H. HIRSHHORN, 1966

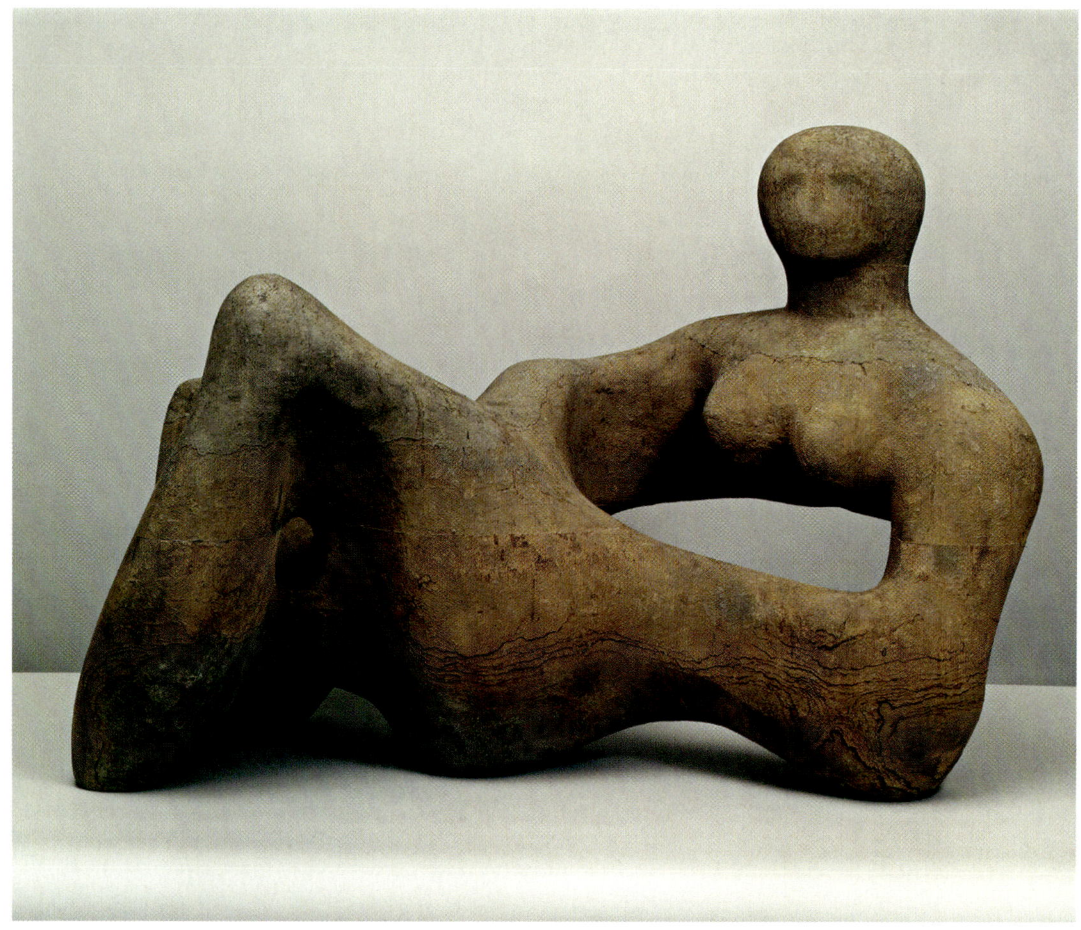

19–33 Henry Moore. *Recumbent Figure*. 1938. Hornton stone, 35" × 52" × 29" (88.9 × 132.7 × 73.7 cm). Tate Gallery, London

Originally carved for the garden of the architect Serge Chermayeff in Sussex, Moore's sculpture was situated next to a low-lying Modernist building with an open view of the gently rolling landscape. "My figure looked out across a great sweep of the Downs, and her gaze gathered at the horizon," Moore later recalled. "The sculpture had no specific relationship to the architecture. It had its own identity and did not *need to be on Chermayeff's terrace, but it so to speak* enjoyed *being there, and I think it introduced a humanizing element; it became a mediator between modern house and ageless land." (Marcel)*

chacmools of Toltec and Mayan art (see fig. 15–5). *Recumbent Figure* (fig. **19–33**) of 1938 reveals Moore's sensitivity to the inherent qualities of the stone, whose natural striations harmonize with the sinuous surfaces of the design. While certain elements of the body, such as the head, breasts, supporting elbow, and raised knee, are clearly defined, other parts flow together into an undulating mass more suggestive of a hilly landscape than of a human body. An open cavity penetrates the torso, emphasizing the relationship of solid and void fundamental to Moore's art. The sculptor wrote in 1937, "A hole can itself have as much shape-meaning as a solid mass."

North American Art between the Wars

The Armory Show of 1913 had marked an important turning point in American art, as artists began to assimilate the most recent developments of the European avant-garde. But many artists soon retreated from this imported Modernism, returning their focus to the American scene, realistically chronicling the life and landscape of their own world. Only in the late 1930s and 1940s did artists and architects fleeing Hitler's Europe renew American interest in nonrepresentational art.

The United States

The American sculptor and engineer Alexander Calder (1898–1976) made contact with members of the Dada and Surrealist groups on visits to Paris in the 1920s and 1930s. He also visited Mondrian's studio, where he was impressed by the rectangles of colored paper that Mondrian had tacked up everywhere on the walls. What would it be like, he wondered, if the flat shapes were moving freely in space, interacting in not just two but three dimensions? The experience inspired Calder to begin creating mobiles, sculptures like his *Lobster Trap and Fish Tail* (fig. **19–34**) in which the individual parts float and bob in response to shifting currents of air. At first, this mobile seems almost nonrepresentational, but Calder's title works on our imagination, helping us to find the oval trap awaiting unwary crustaceans. The delicate wires at the left suggest the backbone of a fish. The term "mobile," which in French means both "moving body" and "motive," or "driving force," came from Calder's friend Marcel Duchamp, who no doubt relished the double meaning of the word.

Alfred Stieglitz's gallery at 291 was one of the few places where American artists could see the more radical manifestations of contemporary European art and the work of pioneering American modernists such as Georgia O'Keeffe (1887–1986), who had her first

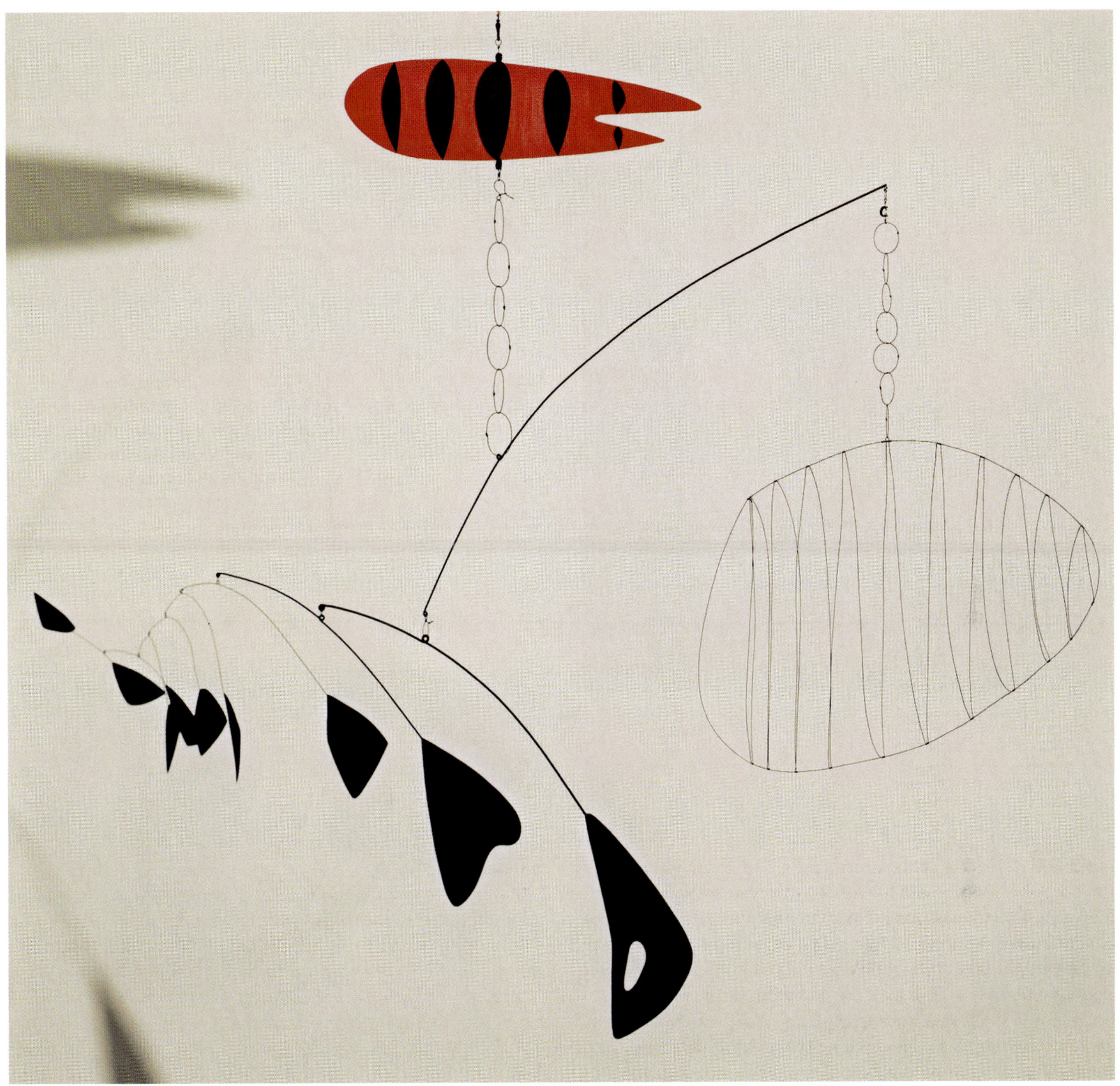

19–34 Alexander Calder. ***Lobster Trap and Fish Tail.*** 1939. Hanging mobile of painted steel wire and sheet aluminum, height 8' 6" (2.6 m). The Museum of Modern Art, New York

COMMISSIONED BY THE ADVISORY COMMITTEE FOR THE STAIRWELL OF THE MUSEUM (590.1939.A–D)

solo exhibition there in 1917. Beginning in 1924, the year of her marriage to Stieglitz, O'Keeffe focused on the innovative paintings of flowers (see fig. Intro–4) that remain her best-known works. These gigantic and distorted close-up views—perhaps rooted in a long American tradition of faithfully described paintings of nature—recall Surrealism in their blatant suggestion of female sexuality. By the late 1920s, O'Keeffe was already finding the New York art world claustrophobic and confining. In 1929, she began spending summers in New Mexico, and after Stieglitz's death in 1946, she moved there permanently, redirecting her painting to evocative images of the spectacular landscape of the American Southwest.

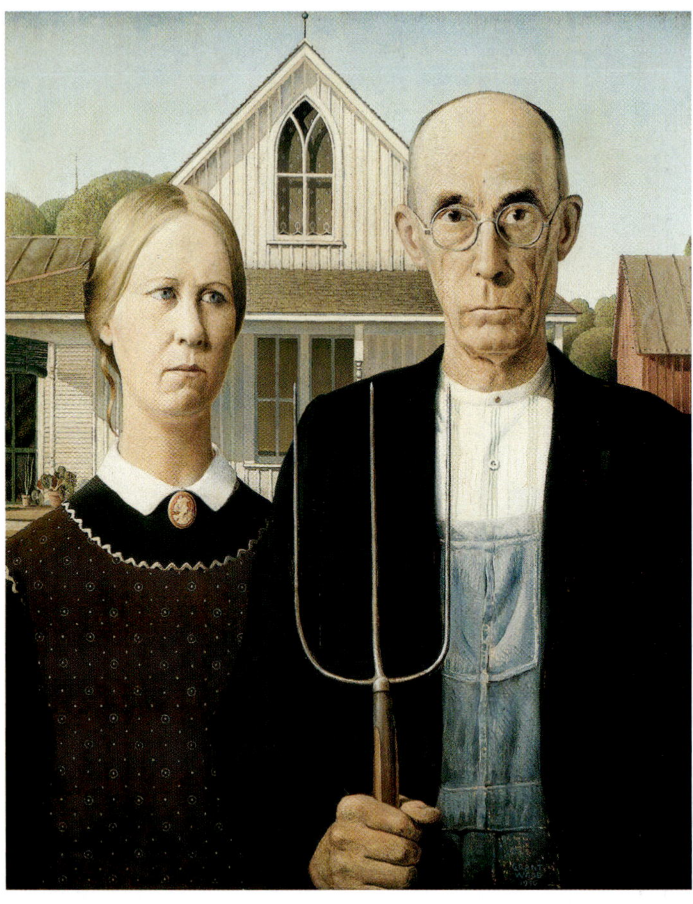

19–35 Grant Wood. *American Gothic*. 1930. Oil on beaverboard, 29⅞" × 24⅞" (74.3 × 62.4 cm). The Art Institute of Chicago
FRIENDS OF AMERICAN ART COLLECTION. 1930.934

O'Keeffe's artistic migration from New York to New Mexico reminds us that the American art scene between the wars was diverse geographically as well as stylistically. During the Great Depression, a flourishing group of artists across the United States documented the lives and circumstances of the American people and the American landscape, painting in styles that derived from native Realist traditions. Art historians refer to this movement as American Scene Painting.

One group of American Scene painters from the Midwest, called Regionalists, are characterized by their generally optimistic attitudes toward their subjects. Their leader was Iowa painter Grant Wood (1891–1942), who focused on the farms and small-town life of the American heartland. His *American Gothic* (fig. **19–35**) is usually mistaken for a picture of a husband and wife, but it was actually meant to show an aging Iowa farmer and his unmarried daughter (Wood's dentist and sister were the models). The stony-faced pair stands in front of their house, built in a Victorian style known as "Carpenter Gothic," which suggests the importance of religion in their lives. The farmer's pitchfork signifies his occupation while giving him a somewhat menacing air. The woman is associated with potted plants, seen behind her right shoulder, which symbolize traditionally feminine domestic and horticultural skills. Wood considered the painting to be a sincerely affectionate portrayal of the small-town Iowans he had grown up with—conservative, provincial, religious Midwesterners, descendants of the pioneers.

In spite of the largely positive visions of the Regionalists, the economic hardships of the Great Depression meant that many farmers faced bankruptcy, and rural regions suffered great poverty. In 1935, a newly established government agency, the Farm Securities Administration (FSA), began to hire photographers to document the problems of farmers and migrant workers. Dorothea Lange (1895–1965) played a major role in the formation of the FSA photography program. As a freelance photographer in San Francisco, Lange was touched by the struggles of the city's poor and unemployed, and she began to photograph their plight. In 1934, she collaborated on a report on migrant farm laborers in California, which helped persuade state officials to build migrant labor camps. Her photographs influenced the federal government to include a photographic unit in the FSA, and in 1935 Lange was hired as one of the

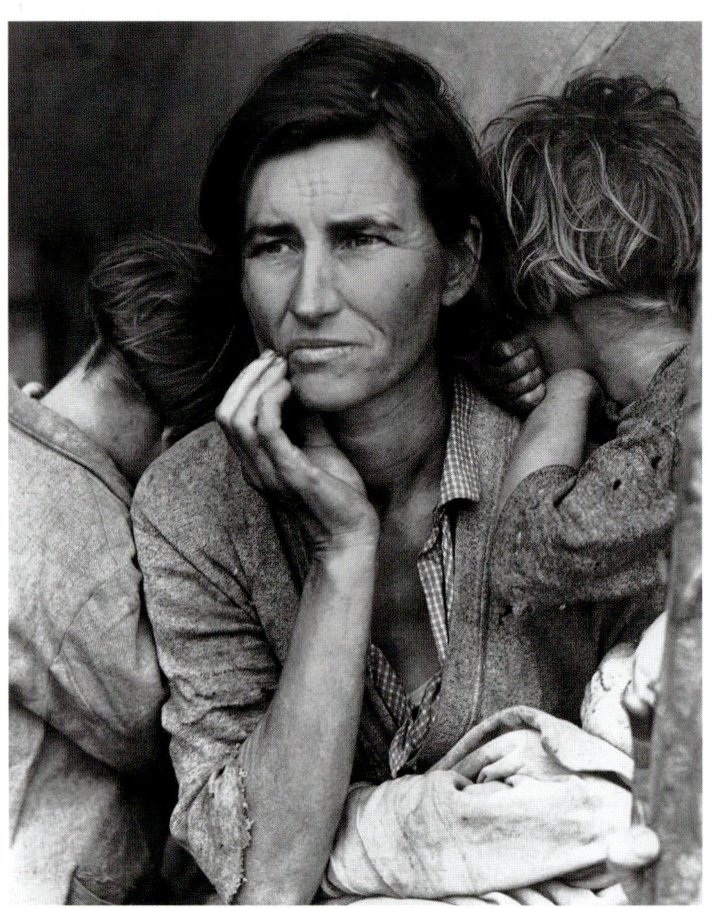

19–36 Dorothea Lange. *Migrant Mother, Nipomo, California*. February 1936. Gelatin-silver print. Library of Congress, Washington, D.C.

unit's first photographers. Her most famous photograph is *Migrant Mother, Nipomo, California* (fig. **19–36**). The woman in the picture is Florence Thompson, a 32-year-old mother of ten children. Drawn and prematurely aged, she gazes past the viewer into an uncertain future. The fears of all disenfranchised people, perpetually shunted to the margins of society, seem crystallized in her worried face.

The Harlem Renaissance

Between the wars, hundreds of thousands of African-Americans migrated from the rural South to the urban, industrialized North, fleeing racial and economic oppression and seeking greater social and economic opportunity. This transition gave rise to the so-called "New Negro" movement, which encouraged African-Americans to become politically progressive and racially conscious. It also stimulated a flowering of art and culture known as the Harlem Renaissance, which encouraged the work of musicians like Duke Ellington and poets like Langston Hughes. The intellectual leader of the movement was Alain Locke (1886–1954), a critic and philosophy professor who encouraged black artists and writers to seek their artistic roots in the traditional arts of Africa, rather than in the art of white America or Europe.

The first visual artist to answer Locke's call was Aaron Douglas (1898–1979), a native of Topeka, Kansas, who moved to New York City in 1925 and rapidly developed an abstract style of schematic, silhouetted figures influenced by African art. Douglas limited his palette to a few subtle hues, varying in value from light to dark and sometimes organized abstractly into concentric bands that suggest musical rhythms or spiritual emanations. In *Aspects of Negro Life: From Slavery Through Reconstruction* (fig. **19–37**), painted for the 135th Street branch of the New York Public Library under the sponsorship of the Public Works of Art Project, Douglas intended to awaken in African-Americans a sense of their place in history. At the right, they celebrate the Emancipation Proclamation of 1863, which freed the slaves. Concentric circles issue from the Proclamation, which is read by a figure in the foreground. At the center of the composition, an orator, symbolizing black leaders of the Reconstruction era, urges black freedmen, some still picking cotton, to cast their ballots, while he points to a silhouette of the U.S. Capitol on a distant hill. Concentric circles highlight the ballot in his hand. In the background, the fearsome Ku Klux Klan, hooded and on horseback, invades from the left while at the right the arts—a jazz trumpeter and a dancer—herald freedom. The heroic orator at the center of Douglas's panel remains the focus of the composition, inspiring contemporary viewers to continue the struggle for equality.

Like Douglas, photographer James VanDerZee (1886–1983) created positive, non-stereotypical images of African-Americans that proclaimed the racial pride and social empowerment promoted by the "New Negro" movement. The largely self-taught VanDerZee maintained a studio in Harlem for nearly 50 years, specializing in portraits of the neighborhood's middle- and upper-class

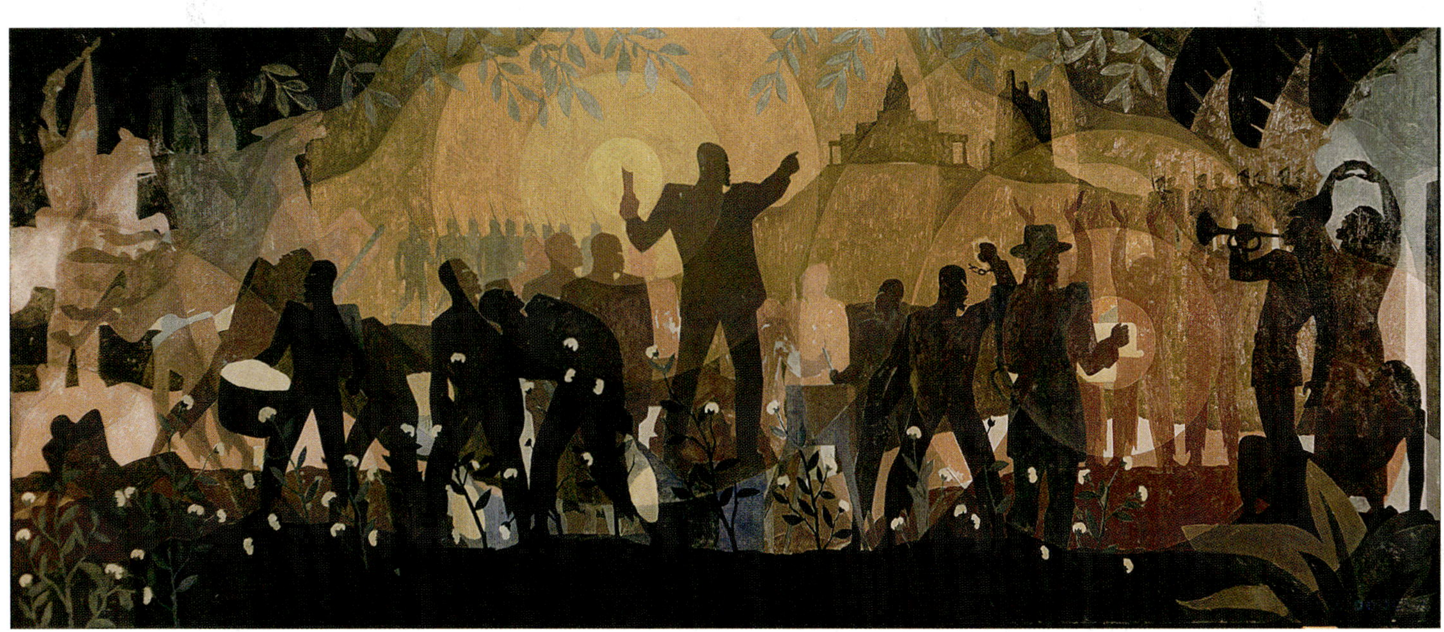

19–37 Aaron Douglas. *Aspects of Negro Life: From Slavery Through Reconstruction*. 1934. Oil on canvas, 5' × 11' 7" (1.5 × 3.5 m).
Schomburg Center for Research in Black Culture, New York Public Library

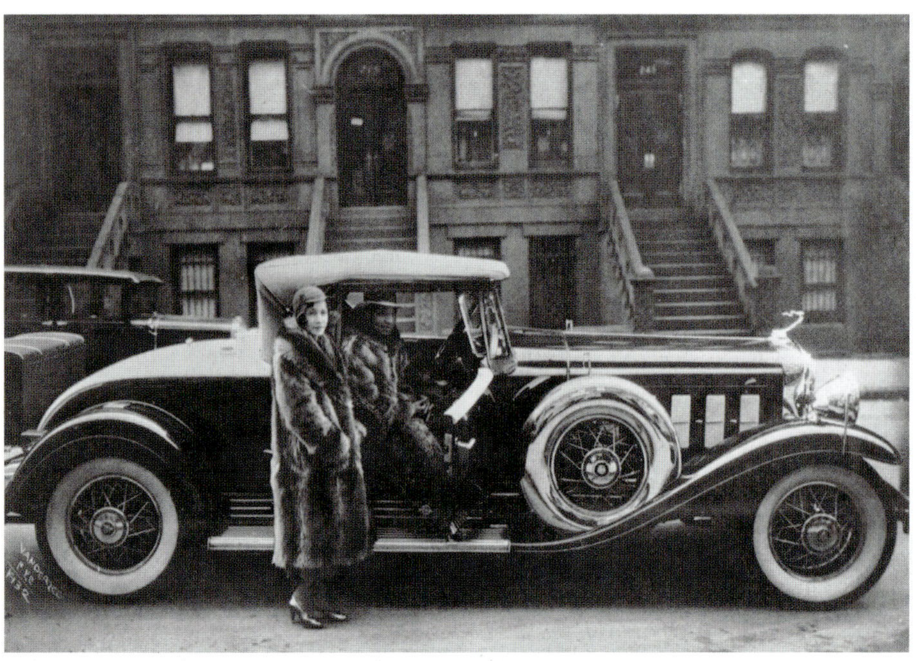

19–38 James VanDerZee. Detail of *Couple Wearing Raccoon Coats with a Cadillac, Taken on West 127th Street, Harlem, New York.* 1932. Gelatin-silver print

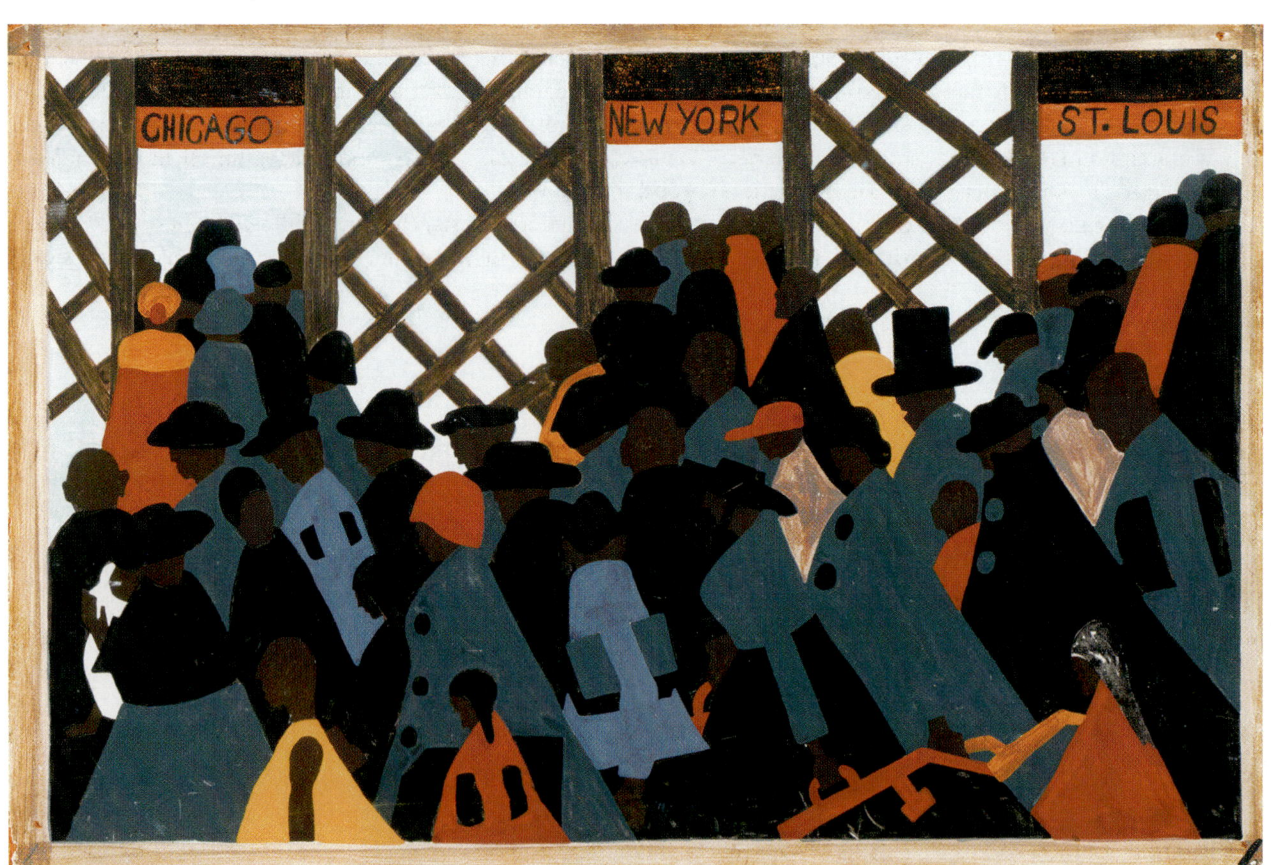

19–39 Jacob Lawrence. *During the World War There Was a Great Migration North by Southern Negroes*, panel 1 from ***The Migration Series***. 1940–1941. Casein tempera on hardboard, 12" × 18" (30.5 × 45.7 cm). The Phillips Collection, Washington. D.C.
ACQUIRED 1942

This is the first image in Lawrence's 60-panel cycle that tells the story of the migration of Southern African-Americans to the industrialized North in the decades between the two world wars. Edith Halpert exhibited the entire series in 1941 at her Downtown Gallery. Thus, at age 23 Lawrence became the first African-American artist to gain acclaim in the segregated New York art world. The next year, The Migration Series *was jointly acquired by the Phillips Collection in Washington, D.C., and the Museum of Modern Art in New York, each of which purchased 30 paintings.*

residents. His best-known photograph, *Couple Wearing Raccoon Coats with a Cadillac, Taken on West 127th Street, Harlem, New York* (fig. **19–38**), depicts the ideal "New Negro" man and woman: prosperous, confident, and cosmopolitan, thriving and living glamorously, even in the midst of the Depression.

Influenced by Aaron Douglas, the younger Harlem artist Jacob Lawrence (1917–2000) devoted much of his early work to chronicling black history, in carefully researched groups of small paintings conceived as cycles. In 1940–1941, Lawrence created his best-known cycle, *The Migration Series.* Sixty panels narrate the great twentieth-century exodus of African-Americans from the rural South to the urban North, an exodus that had brought Lawrence's own parents from South Carolina to Atlantic City, New Jersey, where he was born. The first panel (fig. **19–39**), depicts a train station filled with black migrants who stream through portals labeled with the names of Northern and Midwestern destinations. The boldly abstracted style, with its simple shapes and bright, flat colors, suggests the influence of Cubism, but is more likely based on Lawrence's own study of the African art that also influenced Cubist painters.

Mexico

Artists in Mexico also focused on local scenes and local concerns as they fulfilled government commissions to decorate public buildings with murals celebrating the history, life, and work of the Mexican people. Prominent in the new Mexican mural movement of the 1930s initiated by this public patronage, was Diego Rivera (1886–1957). Rivera had lived in Paris, painting in the Synthetic Cubist style, and in 1920–1921 he traveled to Italy to study the great frescoes of the Renaissance. On his return to Mexico, he fulfilled government commissions for a series of monumental murals, inspired by both Italian Renaissance art and the Pre-Columbian art of Mexico. In 1932, the Rockefeller family commissioned Rivera to paint a mural for the lobby of the Art Deco RCA Building in Rockefeller Center in New York City on the theme "Man at the Crossroads Looking with Hope and High Vision to the Choosing of a New and Better Future." When Rivera, a Communist, provocatively included a portrait of Lenin in the mural, the Rockefellers canceled his commission, paid him his fee, and had the unfinished mural destroyed. In response to what he called an "act of cultural vandalism," Rivera re-created the mural in the Palacio de Bellas Artes in Mexico City, under the new title *Man, Controller of the Universe* (fig. **19–40**).

At the center of the mural, a figure in overalls represents Man, who symbolically controls the universe through his manipulation of technology. Crossing behind him are two great ellipses that represent, respectively, the microcosm of living organisms as seen through the microscope at Man's right hand, and the macrocosm of outer space as viewed through the giant telescope above his head. Below, fruits and vegetables rise from the earth as a result of his agricultural efforts. To the viewer's right, Lenin joins the hands of several workers of different races; at the left, decadent capitalists debauch themselves in a nightclub. Rivera vengefully included in this section a portrait of the bespectacled John D. Rockefeller, Jr. At the sides of the mural, Rivera contrasts the peaceful socialist workers at right with the militarism and labor unrest of the capitalist world to the left.

While the muralists painted public messages, other Mexican artists made more private, introspective statements in easel

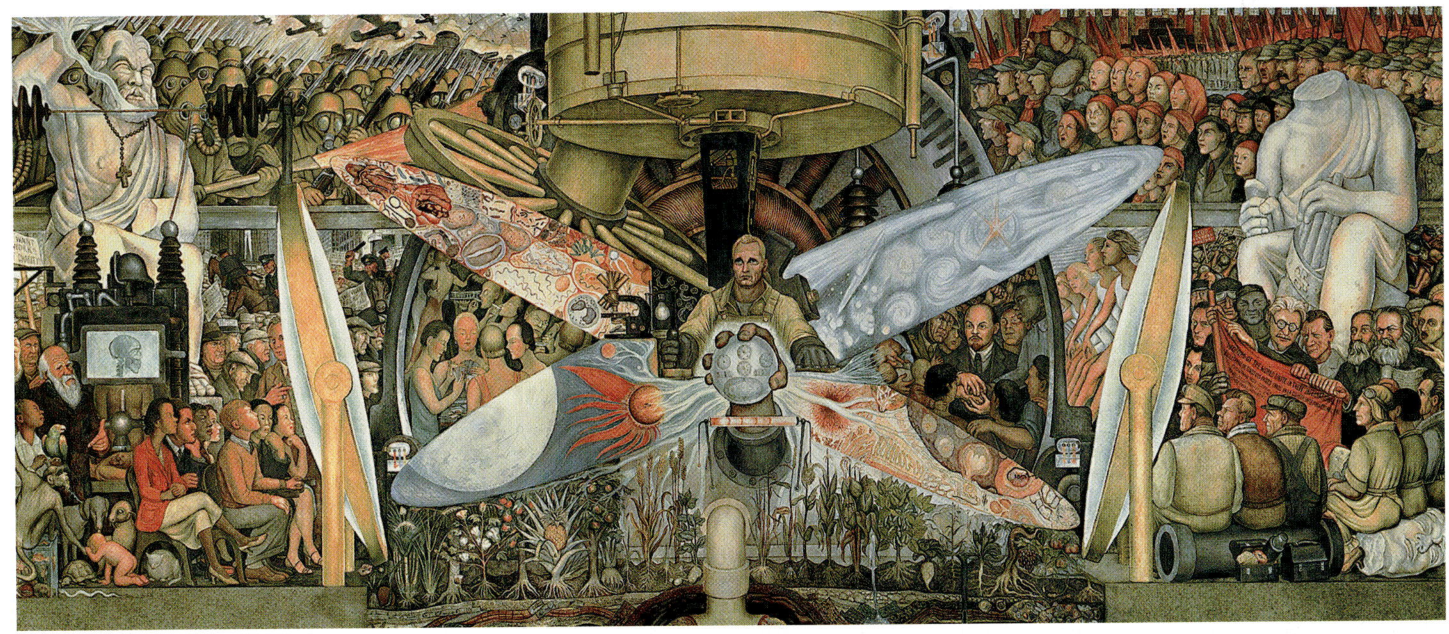

19–40 Diego Rivera. *Man, Controller of the Universe.* 1934. Fresco, 15' 9⅛" × 37' 2½" (4.85 × 11.45 m). Museo del Palacio de Bellas Artes, Mexico City

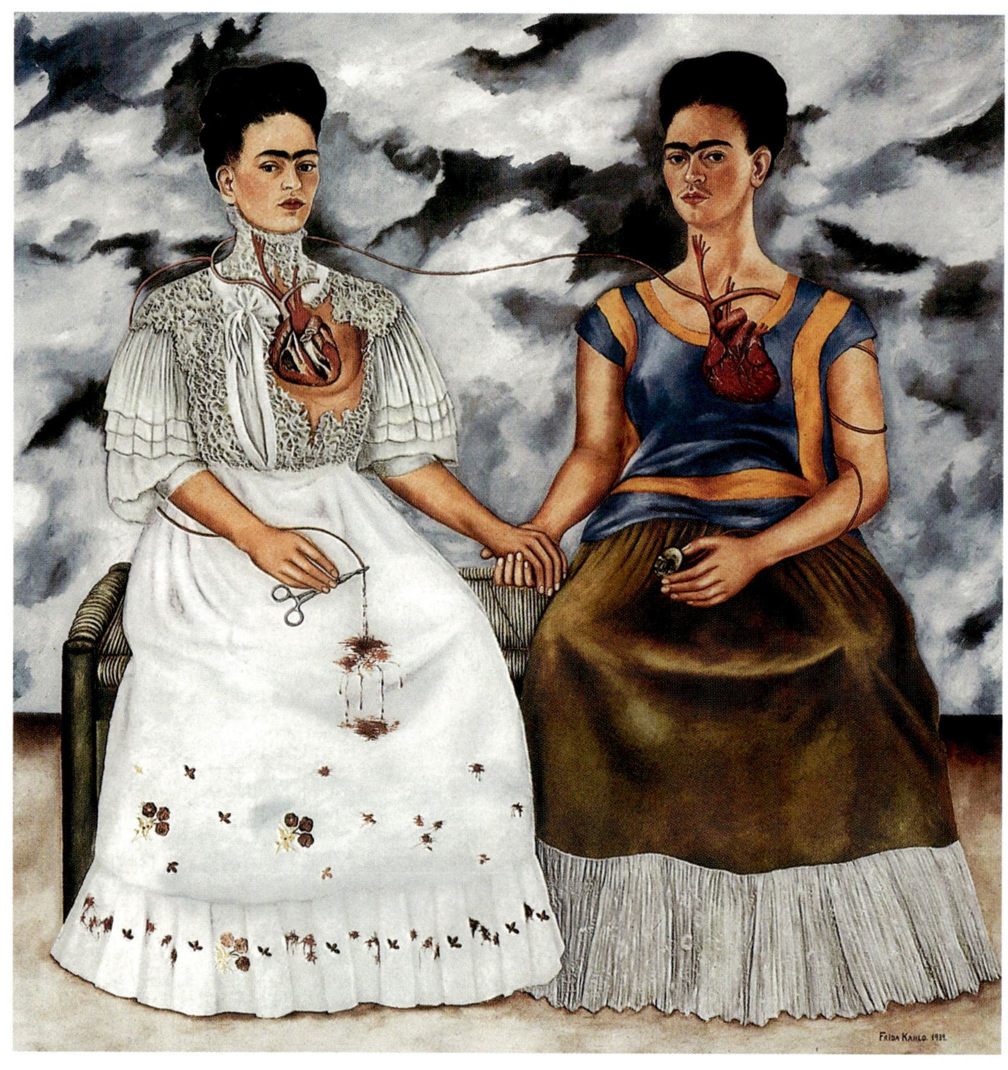

19–41 Frida Kahlo. ***The Two Fridas.*** 1939. Oil on canvas, 5' 8½" × 5' 8½" (1.74 × 1.74 m). Museo de Arte Moderno, Instituto Nacional de Bellas Artes, Mexico City

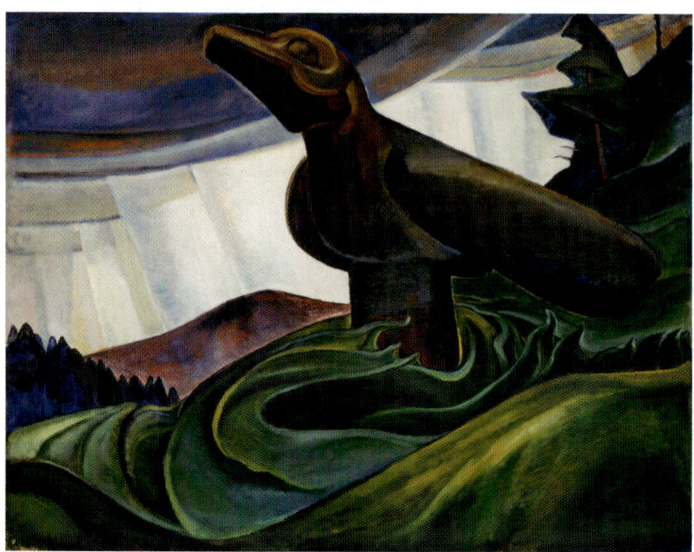

19–42 Emily Carr. ***Big Raven.*** 1931. Oil on canvas, 34" × 44⅝" (87.3 × 114.4 cm). The Vancouver Art Gallery, Canada
EMILY CARR TRUST

paintings. André Breton claimed Frida Kahlo (1910–1954) to be a natural Surrealist, although she herself said: "I never painted dreams. I painted my own reality." That reality included her mixed German and Mexican ancestry. In *The Two Fridas* (fig. **19–41**), Kahlo presented her two ethnic selves: the European one, in a Victorian dress; and the Mexican one, wearing a traditional Mexican skirt and blouse. The painting also reflects her stormy relationship with Diego Rivera. The two married in 1929 but were in the process of obtaining a divorce when Kahlo was painting *The Two Fridas* in 1939. She told an art historian at the time that the European image was the Frida whom Diego loved, and the Mexican image was the Frida he did not. The two Fridas join hands and the artery running between them begins at a miniature of Rivera as a boy held by the Mexican Frida and ends in the lap of the Europeanized Frida, who attempts without success to stem the flow of blood.

Canada

The artist Emily Carr (1871–1945) lived in Vancouver, British Columbia, where she taught art and became a founding member of the British Columbia Society of Art. On a 1907 trip to Alaska, she first saw the monumental carved poles of Northwest Coast Native Americans and resolved to document these "real art treasures of a passing race." Over the next 23 years Carr visited more than 30 villages across British Columbia, making drawings and watercolors, which became the basis for oil paintings.

As her art matured, Carr developed a dramatic and powerfully sculptural style full of dark and brooding energy. She painted *Big Raven* (fig. **19–42**) in 1931, basing it on a watercolor she made in 1912 in an abandoned village in the Queen Charlotte Islands. She had discovered a carved raven raised on a pole, the surviving member of a pair that had marked a mortuary house. In her autobiography Carr described the raven as "old and rotting," but in her painting the bird appears strong and majestic, thrusting dynamically above the swirling vegetation, a symbol of enduring spiritual power. Through its focus on a Native American artifact set in a recognizably northwestern Canadian landscape, Carr's *Big Raven* asserts a national pride comparable to the paintings of the Mexican muralists and the Harlem Renaissance.

Architecture

After 1900, New York had assumed leadership in the development of the skyscraper, whose height grew increasingly with technological advances in the steel-frame support skeleton (see "The Skyscrapers," page 560). New York clients, however, rejected the innovative style pioneered in Chicago by Louis Sullivan, who refused to disguise the lines of the structural grid with ornamental overlay when developing the modern skyscraper in the late nineteenth century (see fig. 18–4). They preferred the historicizing ornamental veneer exemplified by the Woolworth Building of 1911–1913 (fig. **19–43**), which, when it was completed was at 792 feet and 55 floors, the world's tallest building. In the 1930s it would be surpassed by an even more

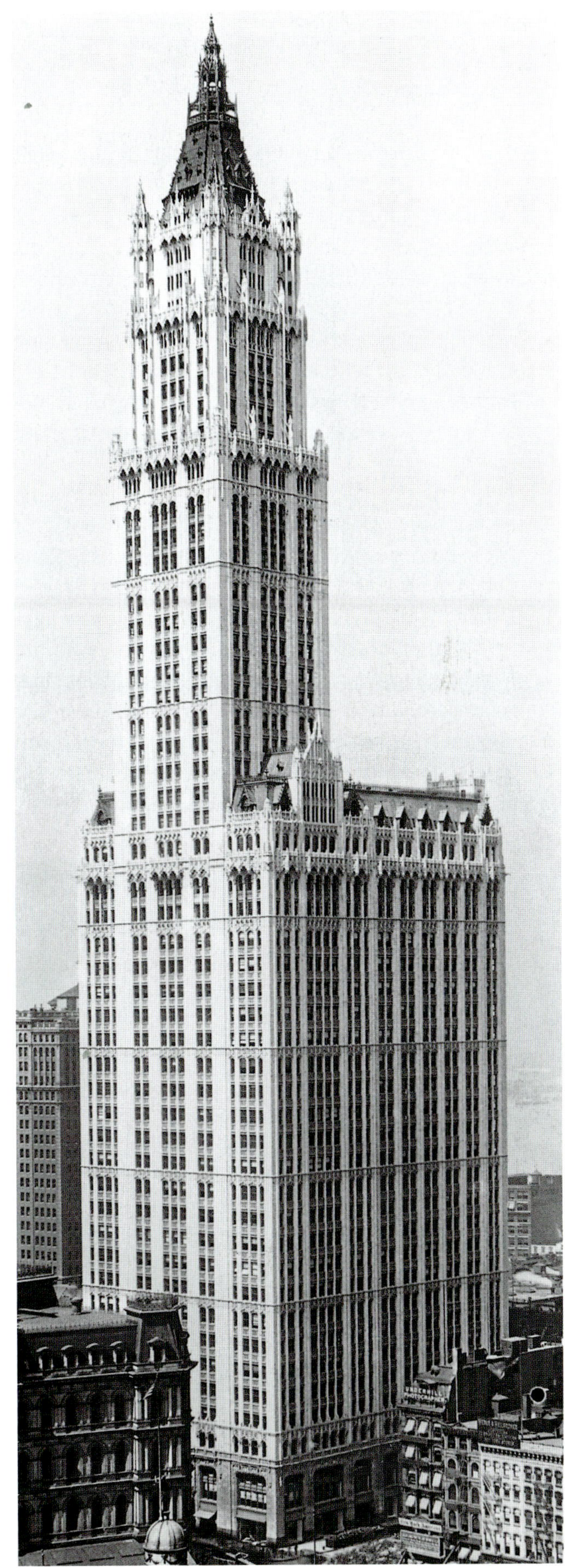

19–43 Cass Gilbert. Woolworth Building, New York. 1911–1913

ELEMENTS OF Architecture

The Skyscraper

The skyscraper depended on the development of these essentials: metal beams (or girders) and columns for the structural-support skeleton; the separation of the building-support structure from the enclosing layer (the cladding); fireproofing materials and measures; elevators; and plumbing, central heating, artificial lighting, and ventilation systems. First-generation skyscrapers, built between about 1880 and 1900, were concentrated in the Midwest, especially Chicago. Second-generation skyscrapers, with more than 20 stories, date from 1895.

At first the tall buildings were freestanding towers, sometimes with a base, like the Woolworth Building of 1911–1913 (fig. 19–43). But New York City's Building Zone Resolution of 1916 introduced mandatory setbacks—recessions from the ground-level building line—to ensure light and ventilation of adjacent sites. Built in 1931, the 1,250-foot setback form of the Empire State Building, diagrammed here, presents a streamlined Art Deco exterior cladding that conceals the great complexity of the internal structure and mechanisms that make its height possible. It is still one of the tallest buildings in the world.

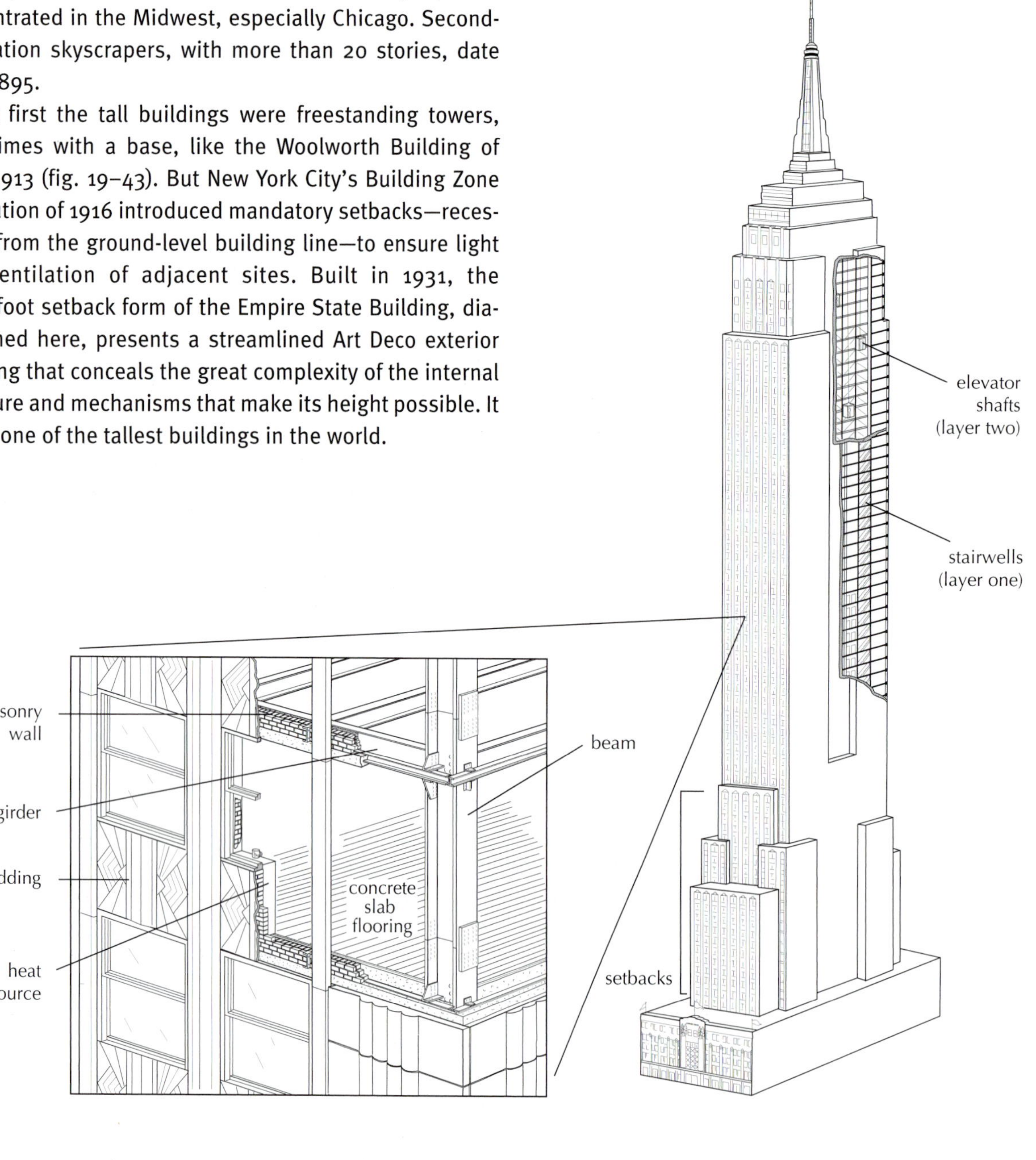

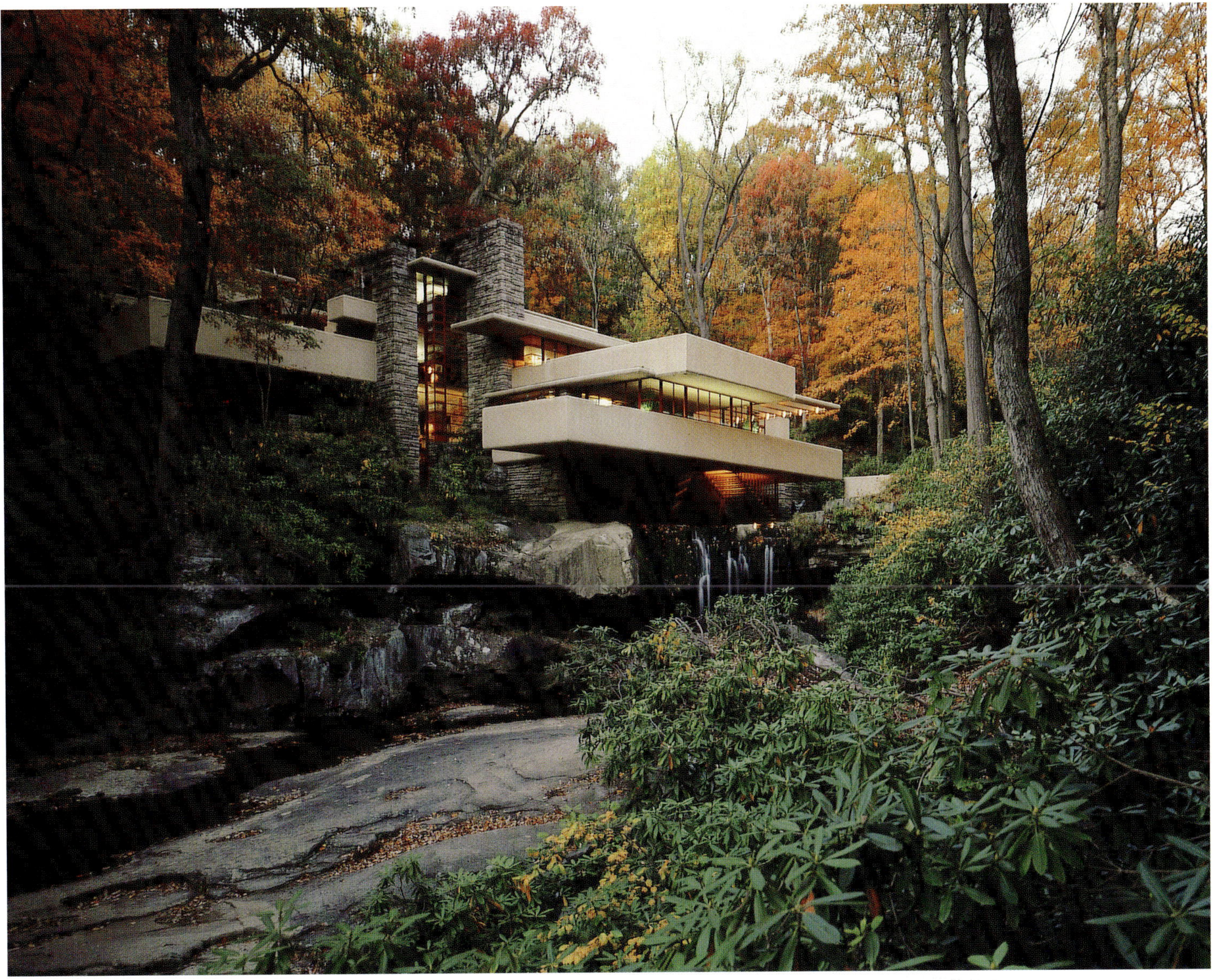

19–44 Frank Lloyd Wright. Edgar Kaufmann House (Fallingwater), Mill Run, Pennsylvania. 1937

famous skyscraper, the Empire State Building, whose structure is likewise covered by a veneer of applied ornamental panels, in this case Art Deco rather than classicizing in style. With the arrival of European Modernism, however, the International Style became the architectural movement embraced by American business leaders. It seemed to epitomize the efficiency, standardization, and impersonality that had become synonymous with the modern corporation itself.

But other architects and critics called for an American architecture that would provide spiritual nourishment to those starved by the severity of the International Style. As early as 1900, Frank Lloyd Wright (1867–1959) advocated an "organic" approach that integrated architecture with nature. The best-known expression of Wright's conviction that buildings ought to be not only on the landscape, but *in* it, is Fallingwater, in rural Pennsylvania (fig. **19–44**). The house was commissioned by Edgar Kaufmann, a Pittsburgh department-store owner, to replace a family summer cottage on a site that featured a waterfall into a pool where the Kaufmann children played. Wright decided to build the house into the cliff over the pool, allowing the water to flow around and under the house. In a daring engineering move, he cantilevered a series of broad concrete terraces out from the house, echoing the great slabs of natural rock. The rocks on which the family had once sunbathed by the waterfall became the hearthstone of their fireplace. Long bands of windows and glass doors offer spectacular views, uniting woods, water, and house. Such houses do not simply testify to the ideal of living in harmony with nature; they declare war on the modern industrial city. When asked what could be done to improve the city, Wright responded bluntly: "Tear it down."

An even stronger connection to the landscape, combined with a dose of Modernism's devotion to the integrity of building materials, is evident in the architecture of Mary Colter (1869–1958), which

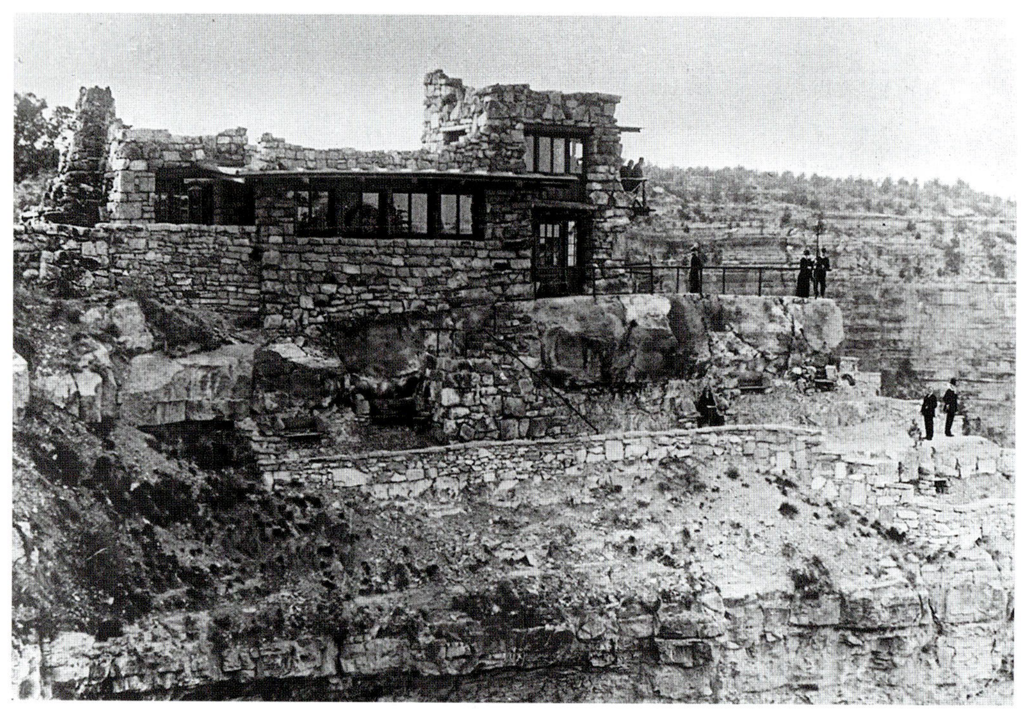

19–45 Mary Colter. Lookout Studio, Grand Canyon National Park, Arizona. 1914

developed concurrently and separately from that of Wright. Born in Pittsburgh and educated in San Francisco, she spent most of her career designing for the Fred Harvey Company, a firm in the American Southwest that catered to the tourist trade. Colter was an avid student of Native American arts, and her building quote liberally from the traditions of the Puebloan peoples. She designed several visitor facilities at Grand Canyon National Park, of which the most dramatic is the Lookout Studio (fig. **19–45**). Built on the edge of the canyon's south rim, the building's foundation is in natural rock, and the walls are built of local stone, making it seem an extension of the sheer natural wall beneath. The sole concession to Modernism is the liberal use of glass and the flat cement floor. Colter's designs for hotels and railway stations throughout the Southwest helped establish an architectural identity for that region as distinct as the skyscraper was for the far-away metropolis of New York.

Looking Back

The story of twentieth-century art recalls the title of Aldous Huxley's 1928 novel *Point Counter Point.* Artists and art movements reacted to each other with accelerating speed and vigor, as artistic innovation and public taste swung back and forth—a pattern that had begun in the nineteenth century between the poles of Rococo and Neoclassicism, Romanticism and Realism, then Impressionism and Post-Impressionism. This point-counterpoint relationship appears on a personal level, too, for example between Braque and Picasso, two artists who challenged and inspired each other to create Cubist paintings, prints, and collages. Their relationship exemplifies the way in which individual artists often propose, test, and revise their ideas and techniques within a broader artistic community.

Rapidly developing technology also had a profound impact on how people made and saw art. Futurism sought to capture the energy—the speed and light—of the Modern age, while Dada mocked and denied the very validity of the work of art itself. Surrealist artists turned inward as they explored a universal, symbolic dreamworld, while other artists glorified external appearances and celebrated their local heritage in Regionalism. Decades of technological innovation also underlay amazing achievements in architecture as engineering and aesthetic practice combined to permit architects to create new building forms, from skyscrapers to private homes, pitting city streamliners against regional naturalists—yet another point-counterpoint within the restless creativity characterizing twentieth-century culture.

IN PERSPECTIVE

1900

◀ **Wright Brothers' First Flight,** 1903

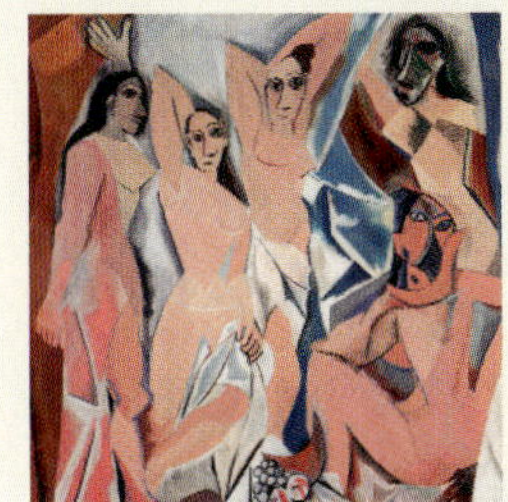
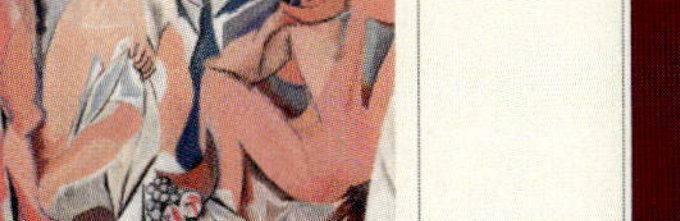

PICASSO,
LES DEMOISELLES D'AVIGNON,
1907

◀ **First Flight Across English Channel,** 1909

1910

◀ **Mexican Revolution,** 1910–1917

◀ **First Balkan War,** 1912–1913

◀ **Armory Show,** 1913

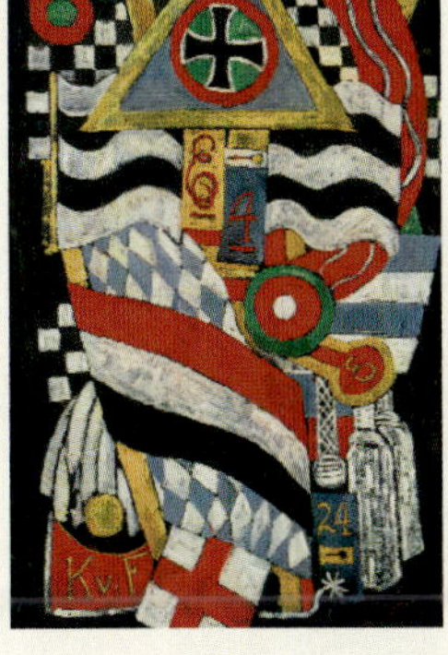

HARTLEY,
PORTRAIT OF A GERMAN OFFICER,
1914

◀ **World War I,** 1914–1918

◀ **Russian Revolution,** 1917

1920

◀ **Soviet Union Formed,** 1922

◀ **Stalin Comes to Power,** 1924

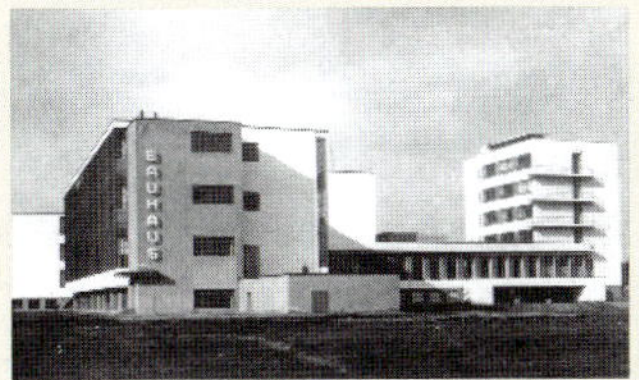

GROPIUS,
BAUHAUS BUILDING,
1925–1926

◀ **Great Depression Begins,** 1929

◀ **Museum of Modern Art (MOMA) in New York Opens,** 1929

1930

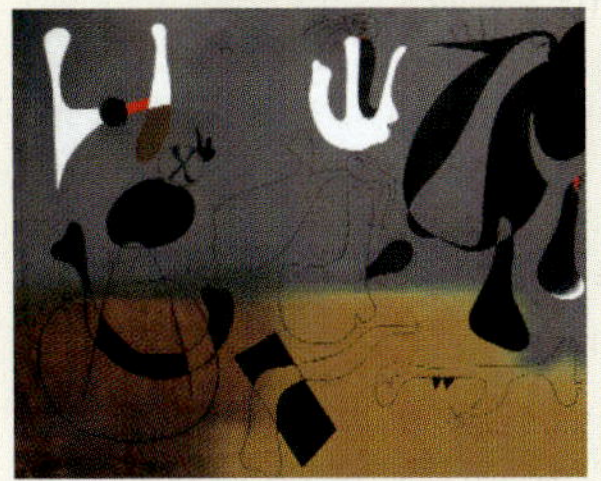

MIRÓ,
COMPOSITION,
1933

◀ **New Deal in U.S.; Hitler Comes to Power in Germany,** 1933

◀ **First Analog Computer,** 1935

◀ **Spanish Civil War,** 1936–1939

◀ **World War II,** 1939–1945

◀ **First Digital Computer,** 1939

1940

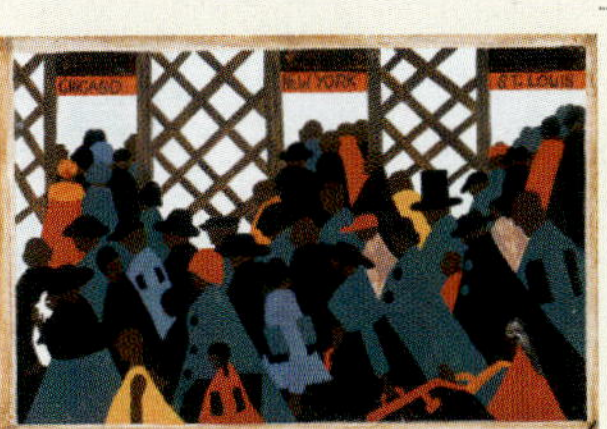

LAWRENCE,
THE MIGRATION SERIES,
1940–1941

◀ **Atomic Bomb Dropped on Hiroshima and Nagasaki,** 1945

1950

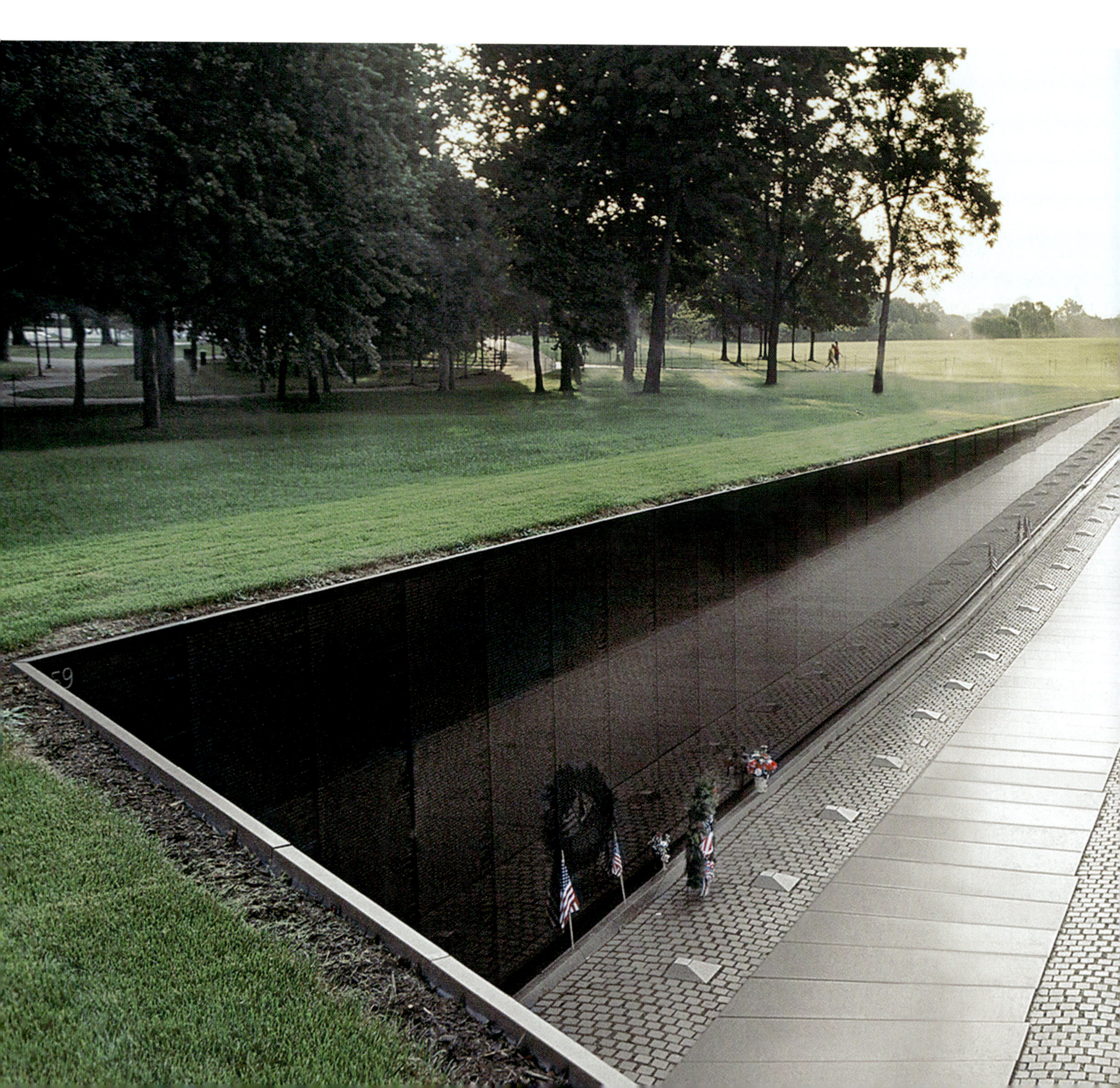

20
Art Since 1945

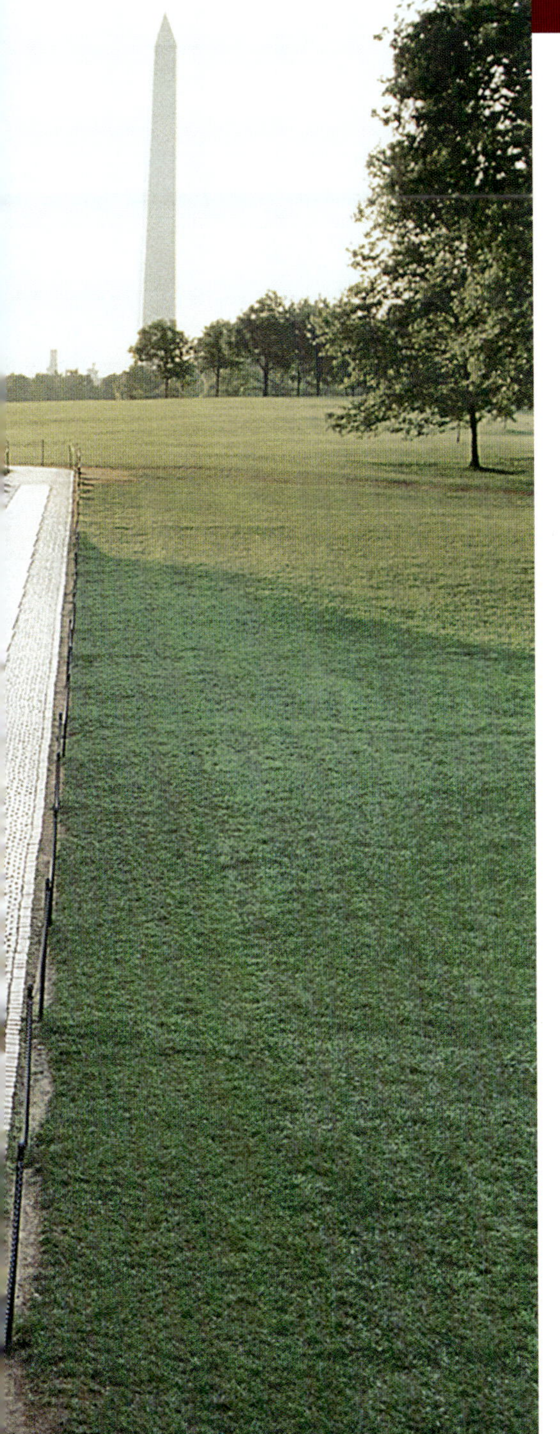

LOOKING FORWARD

"Cattle die. Kinfolk die. We all die. Only fame lasts," said the Vikings. Names remain. Flat, polished stone walls inscribed with thousands of names reflect back the images of the living as they contemplate the memorial to the Vietnam War's (1965–1973) dead and missing veterans (fig. **20–1**). The design is brilliant in its simplicity. The artist, Maya Ying Lin (born 1960), combined two basic ideas: the minimal grandeur of long, black granite walls and row upon row of engraved names—the abstract and the intimate conjoined. The power of Lin's monument lies in its understatement. It is a statement of loss, sorrow, and the futility of war; the names are so numerous that they lose individuality and become a surface texture. It is a timeless monument to suffering humanity, faceless in sacrifice, observed by viewers who must descend themselves into the earth to survey it. Maya Ying Lin said, "The point is to see yourself reflected in the names."

The walls also reflect more than visitors. One wall faces and reflects the George Washington Monument (constructed 1848–1884). Robert Mills, the architect of many public buildings at the beginning of the nineteenth century, chose the obelisk, a time-honored Egyptian sun symbol, for his memorial to the nation's founder. The other wall leads the eye to the Neoclassical-style Lincoln Memorial. By subtly incorporating the Washington and Lincoln memorials into its design, Lin's Vietnam Veterans Memorial reminds viewers of sacrifices made in defense of liberty throughout the nation's history.

Until the modern era, most public art celebrated and commemorated political and social leaders and certain consequences of war in large, freestanding monuments, sometimes motivated by patriotism and a sincere desire to honor heroes, at other times presenting political propaganda or seeking social intimidation. Lin's memorial in Washington, D.C., to the American men and women who died in or never returned from the Vietnam War was unique. Perhaps that is one reason it remains among the most visited works of public art and certainly among the most affecting war monuments ever conceived. As art critic Michael Kimmelman wrote in *The New York Times* (January 13, 2002), "Good art outlasts the events that prompted the artists to make it."

20–1 Maya Ying Lin. Vietnam Veterans Memorial.
1982. Black granite, length 500' (152 m).
The Mall, Washington, D.C.

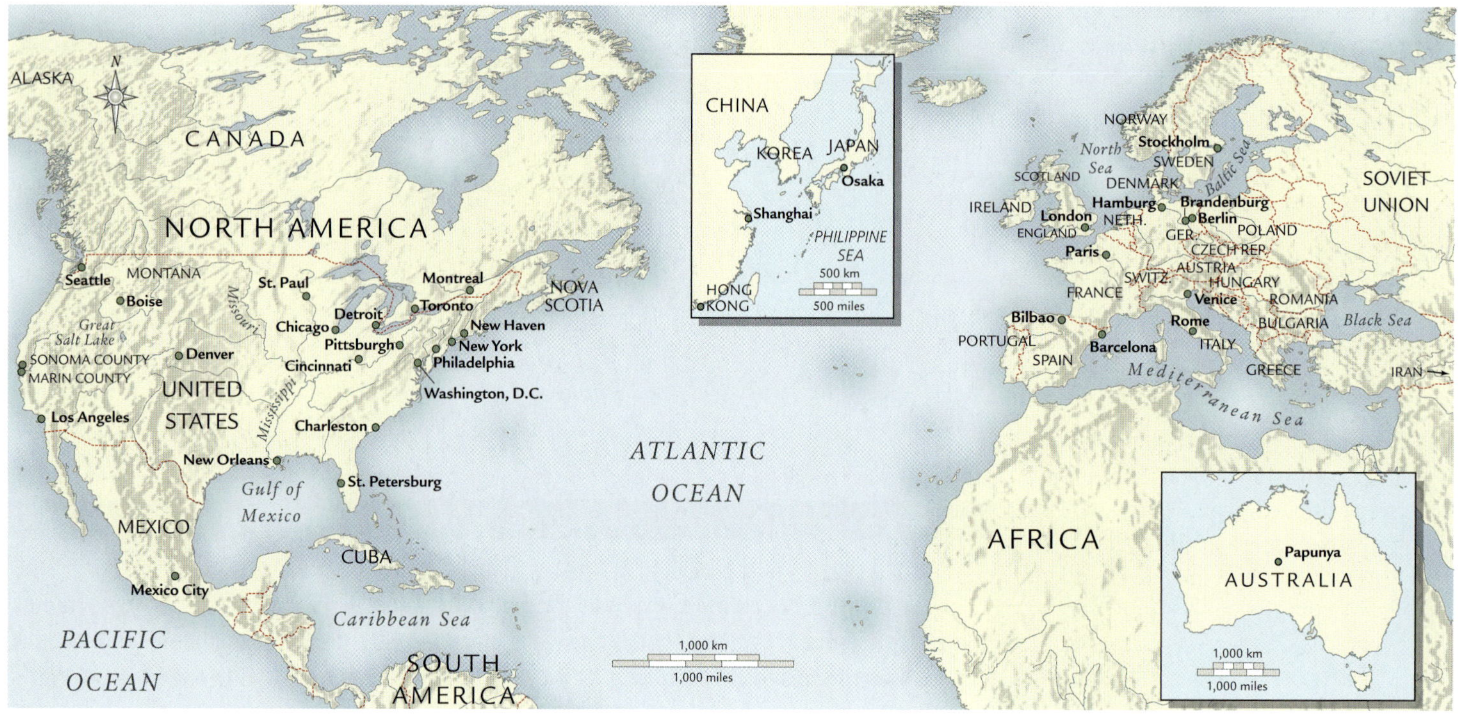

Map 20–1 Contemporary Europe and North America

The United States and the Soviet Union emerged from World War II as the world's most powerful nations and soon were engaged in the Cold War (see map **20–1**). The Soviets set up Communist governments in Eastern Europe and supported the development of Communism elsewhere. Meanwhile the United States, through financial aid and political support, sought to contain Communism's global spread. A second huge Communist nation emerged in 1949 when Mao Zedong established the People's Republic of China. The United States tried to prevent the further spread of Communism in Asia, intervening in the Korean War (1950–1953) and the Vietnam War (1965–1975). The United States and the Soviet Union built massive nuclear arsenals aimed at each other, effectively deterring either from aggression for fear of an apocalyptic retaliation. While the Soviet Union and the United States vied for world leadership, the old European states gave up their empires. The British led the way by withdrawing from India in 1947. Other European nations gradually granted independence to colonies in Asia and Africa.

The United States' stature after World War II as the most powerful democratic nation was soon reflected in the arts. American artists and architects assumed leadership in artistic innovation, and by the late 1950s the dominance of their work was acknowledged across the Atlantic, even in Paris. This dominance endured until around 1970, when the belief in the existence of an identifiable mainstream, or single dominant line of artistic development, began to wane (see "Clement Greenberg and the Idea of the Mainstream," page 572).

Although Realism had dominated American art in the period between the two world wars, some artists of the period had maintained an interest in abstract and nonrepresentational styles of art. America's living link with the European Modernist tradition was Hans Hofmann (1880–1966), a German-born teacher and painter who had come to the United States before World War II. The rise of Fascism in Europe and the outbreak of World War II stranded people like Hofmann and led a number of prominent European artists and writers to flee to the United States. By 1940 André Breton, Salvador Dalí, and Piet Mondrian were all living in New York. Although many of the émigrés kept to themselves, their very presence provoked fruitful discussions among American artists.

Abstract Expressionism

Deeply affected by the ideas of Surrealism and the teaching of Hans Hofmann, New York artists of the 1940s began working in a style collectively called Abstract Expressionism. This term designates a wide variety of work produced between 1940 and roughly 1960. Two major approaches to nonrepresentational art emerged: **action painting** or **gesturalism**, characterized by active paint handling; and **Color Field painting**, distinguished by broad sweeping expanses of color. Some art historians prefer to refer to the work of these artists simply as the New York School.

The Abstract Expressionists took from the Surrealists both a commitment to examining the unconscious and techniques for doing so, but whereas the European Surrealists had derived their notion of the unconscious from Sigmund Freud, many of the Americans subscribed to the thinking of Swiss psychoanalyst Carl Jung (1875–1961). His theory of the "collective unconscious" holds that beneath one's private memories is a storehouse of feelings and symbolic associations common to all humans.

A leading Jung-inspired Abstract Expressionist was the action painter Jackson Pollock (1912–1956). Undergoing Jungian analysis between 1939 and 1941, the alcoholic and self-destructive artist made little progress with his personal problems, but the sessions greatly affected his work, giving him a new vocabulary of signs and symbols and a belief in the therapeutic role of art in society.

In the mid-1940s, Pollock replaced Jungian painted symbols with freely applied paint. He began to employ enamel house paints along with conventional oils in the winter of 1946–1947, using sticks and brushes to drip them in a variety of fluid movements onto large canvases spread out on the floor (fig. **20–2**). The result over the next four years was a series of graceful linear abstractions such as *Autumn Rhythm (Number 30)* (fig. **20–3**). Delicate skeins of paint

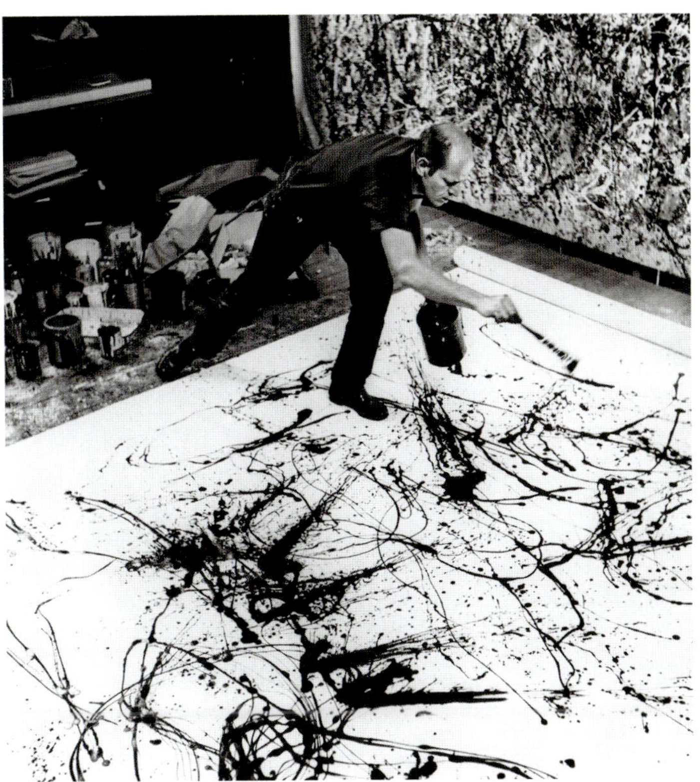

20–2 Hans Namuth. Photograph of Jackson Pollock Painting, The Springs, New York. 1950. COURTESY CENTER FOR CREATIVE PHOTOGRAPHY, UNIVERSITY OF ARIZONA. © 1991 HANS NAMUTH ESTATE

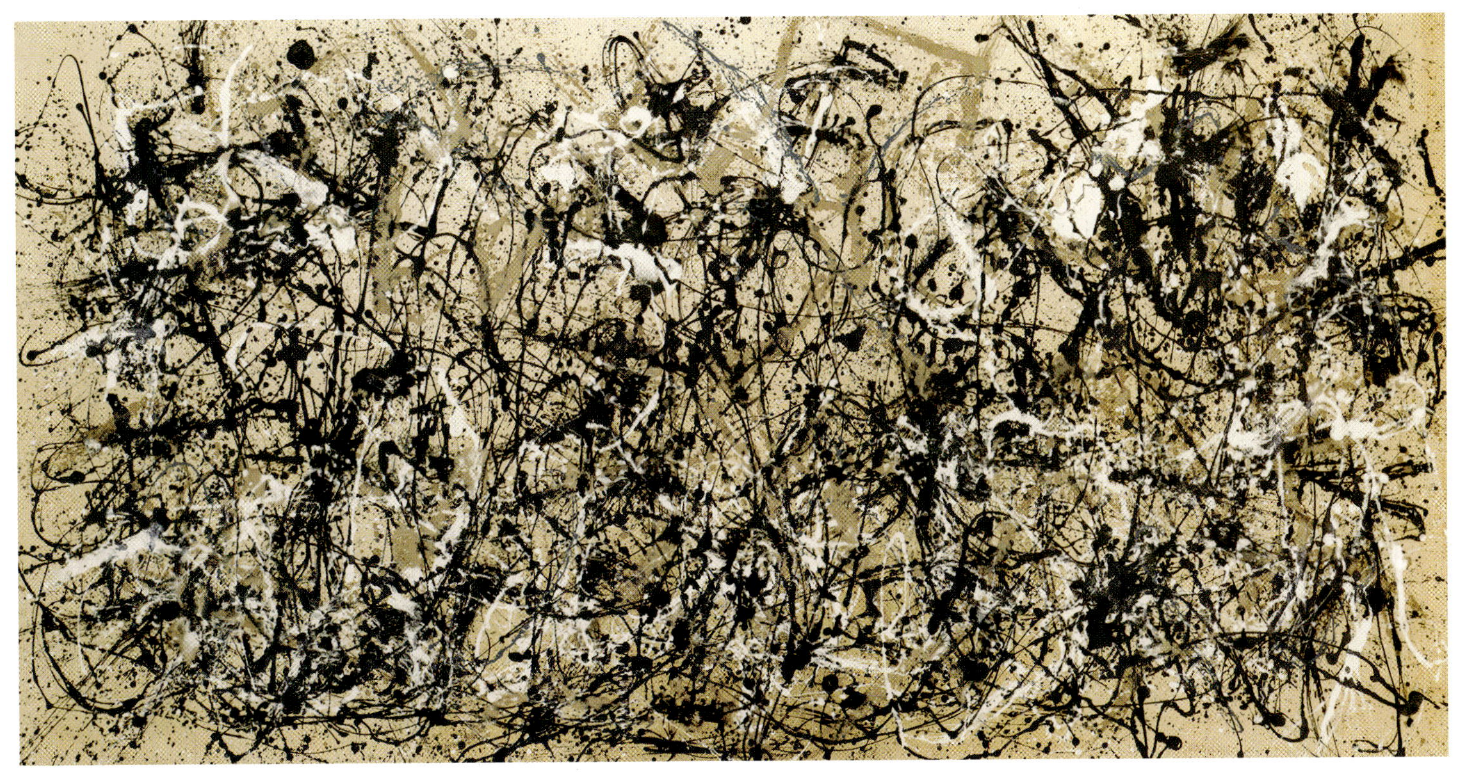

20–3 Jackson Pollock. *Autumn Rhythm (Number 30)*. 1950. Oil on canvas, 8' 9" × 17' 3" (2.66 × 5.25 m). The Metropolitan Museum of Art, New York
GEORGE A. HEARN FUND, 1957 (57.92)

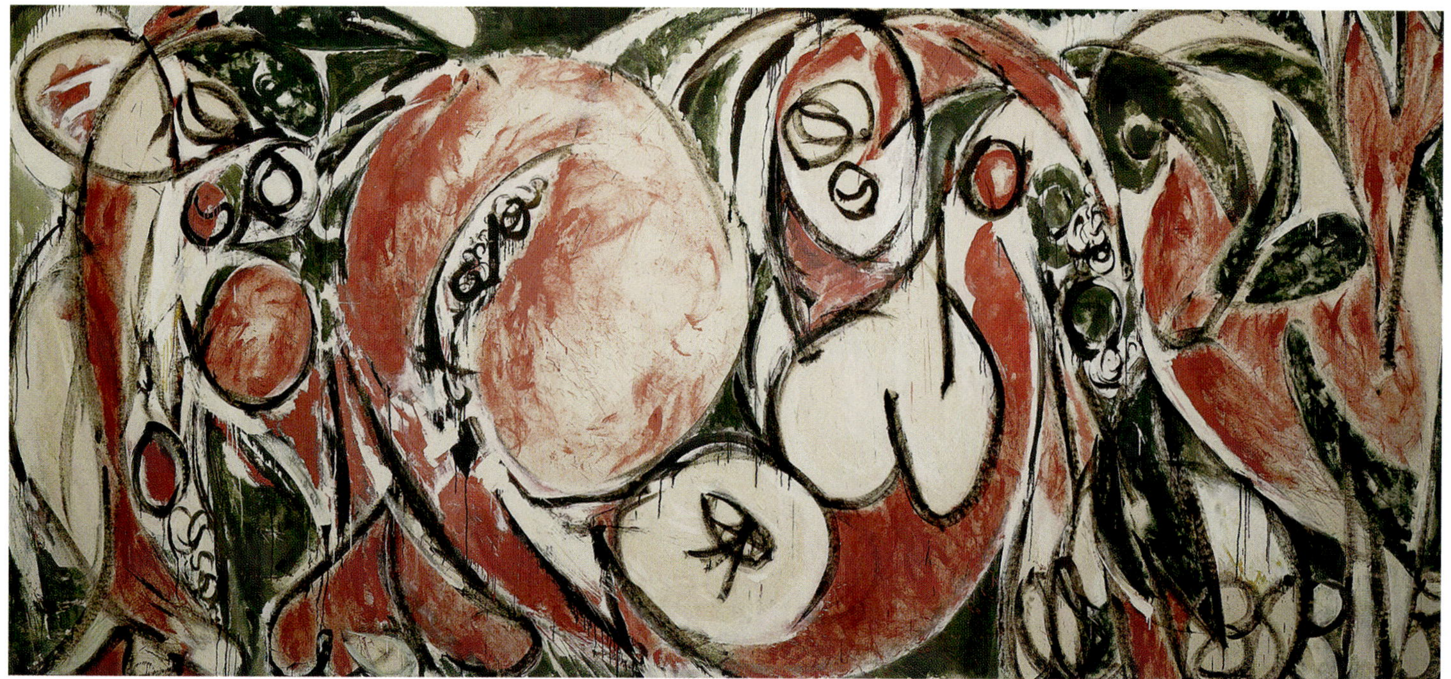

20–4 Lee Krasner. *The Seasons*. 1957. Oil on canvas, 7' 8¾" × 16' 11¾" (2.36 × 5.18 m). Whitney Museum of Art, New York

effortlessly loop over and under one another in a mesmerizing pattern that spreads across the surface of the canvas. As the title of this and other Pollock paintings suggest, the artist seems to have felt that in the free, unselfconscious act of painting he was giving vent to primal, natural forces. Pollock said that he was creating for "the age of the airplane, the atom bomb, and the radio," and the works do seem to embody something of the tensions of the Cold War period, as each side silently threatened the other with instant annihilation.

In 1945, Pollock married Lee Krasner (1908–1984), a student of Hofmann who produced fully nonrepresentational work several years before Pollock. When Krasner moved in with Pollock in 1942, she virtually stopped painting in order to devote herself to the conventional role of a supportive wife. But she soon resumed her art, and despite the problems that developed in their marriage—exacerbated by Pollock's alcoholism—she continued to paint. After Pollock's death in an automobile crash in 1956, Krasner took over his studio and during the next year and a half produced a dazzling group of monumental gestural paintings (fig. **20–4**), painted in bold sweeping curves that express not only her grief but also her identification with the forces of nature suggested by the bursting rounded forms and spring-like colors. "Painting, for me, when it really 'happens' is as miraculous as any natural phenomenon," she said, suggesting an attitude similar to that of Pollock, who found "pure harmony" in the act of painting.

In contrast, Willem de Kooning (1904–1997) insisted, "Art never seems to make me peaceful or pure." Immigrating from his native Netherlands to the United States in 1926, he initially painted nonrepresentationally, but he shocked the New York art world in the early 1950s by returning to the figure with a series of paintings of women. The first, *Woman I* (fig. **20–5**), took him almost two years to finish. De Kooning's wife, the artist Elaine de Kooning (1918–1989), said that he painted it, scraped it, and repainted it at least several dozen times. Part of de Kooning's dissatisfaction stemmed from the way his subject, a figure inspired by conventionally pretty images of women seen in American advertising, kept veering away from those models. What emerges in *Woman I* is not the elegant companion of advertising fantasy but a powerful adversary, more dangerous than alluring. The prettiness of the soft pastel colors and the luxuriousness of the painted surface are nearly lost in the furious slashing of his brush. "Liquefied Cubism" is the way one art historian described de Kooning's work. Its deeper roots, however, lie in the coloristic tradition of artists such as Titian and Rubens, who superbly transformed flesh into luscious layers of paint.

During the 1950s, de Kooning dominated the avant-garde in New York. Among the handful of Modernist painters who resisted his influence was Mark Rothko (1903–1970), a pioneering Color Field painter who used large rectangles of color to evoke states of transcendent contemplation. In works such as *No. 61 (Rust and*

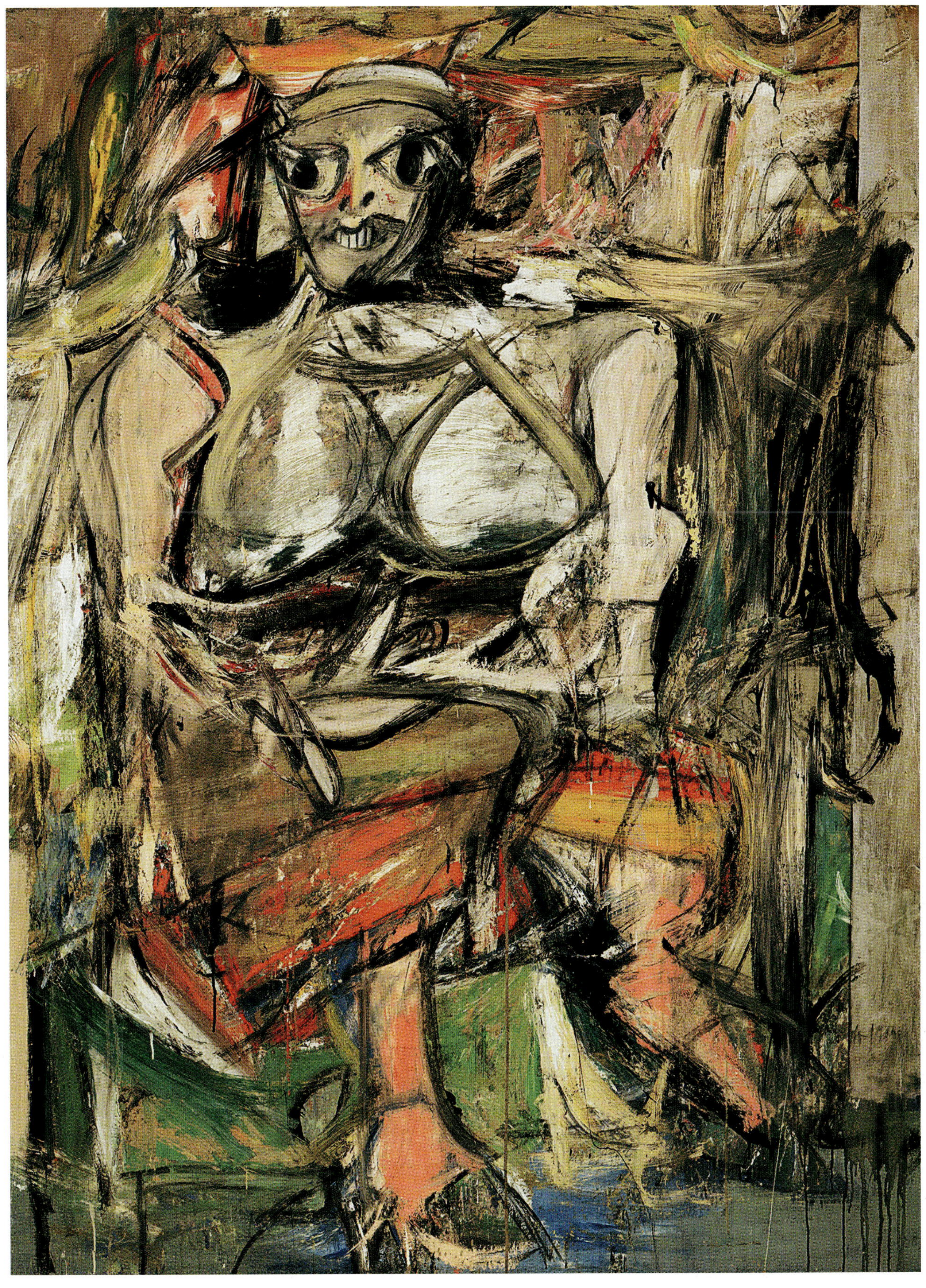

20–5 Willem de Kooning. ***Woman I.*** 1950–1952. Oil on canvas, 6' 3⅞" × 4' 10" (1.93 × 1.47 m). The Museum of Modern Art, New York (478.1953)

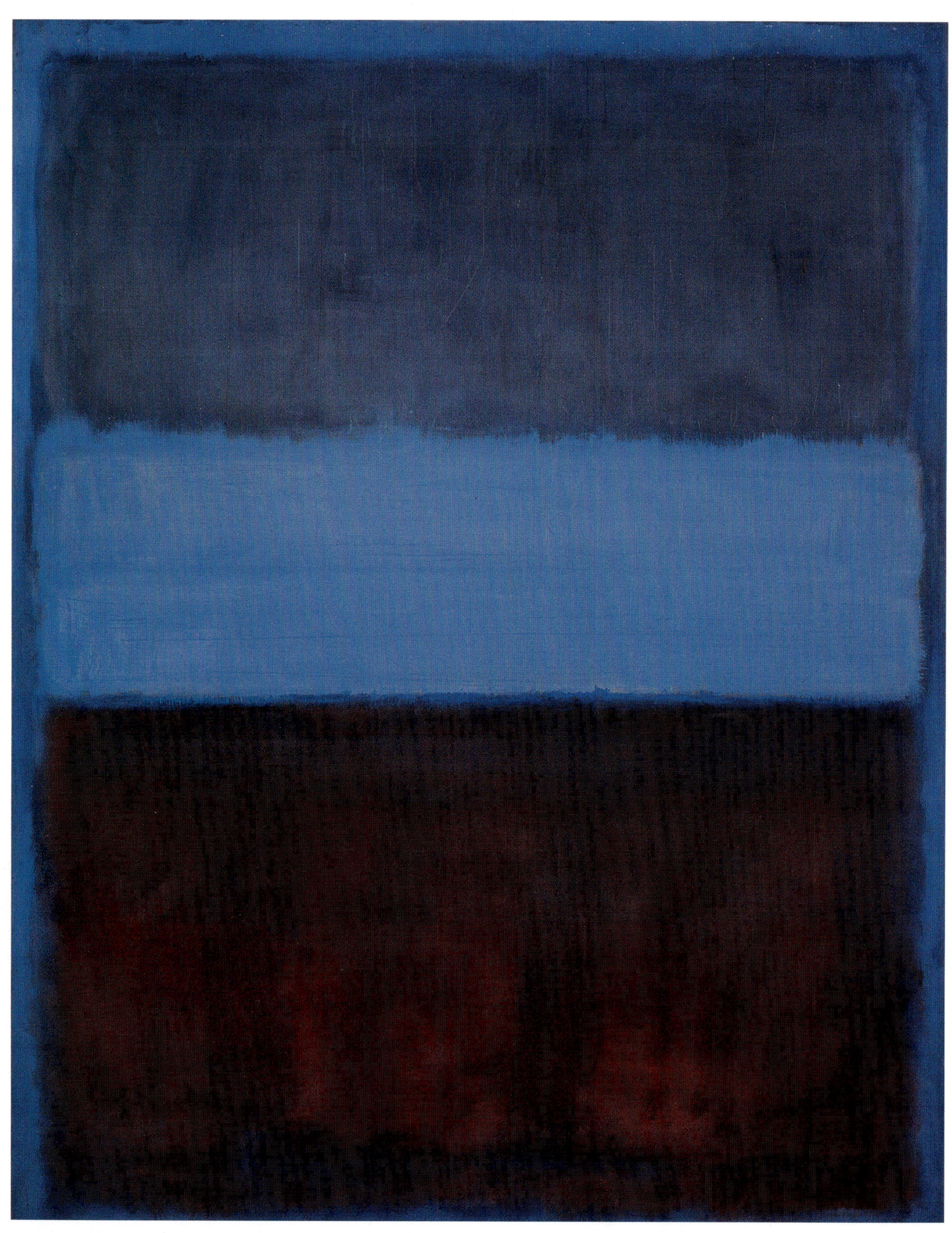

20–6 Mark Rothko. ***No. 61 (Rust and Blue) [Brown Blue, Brown on Blue]***. 1953. Oil on canvas, 9' 7¼" × 7' 10¼" (2.97 × 2.34 m). The Museum of Contemporary Art, Los Angeles

THE PANZA COLLECTION (80.9). KATE ROTHKO PRIZEL & CHRISTOPHER ROTHKO

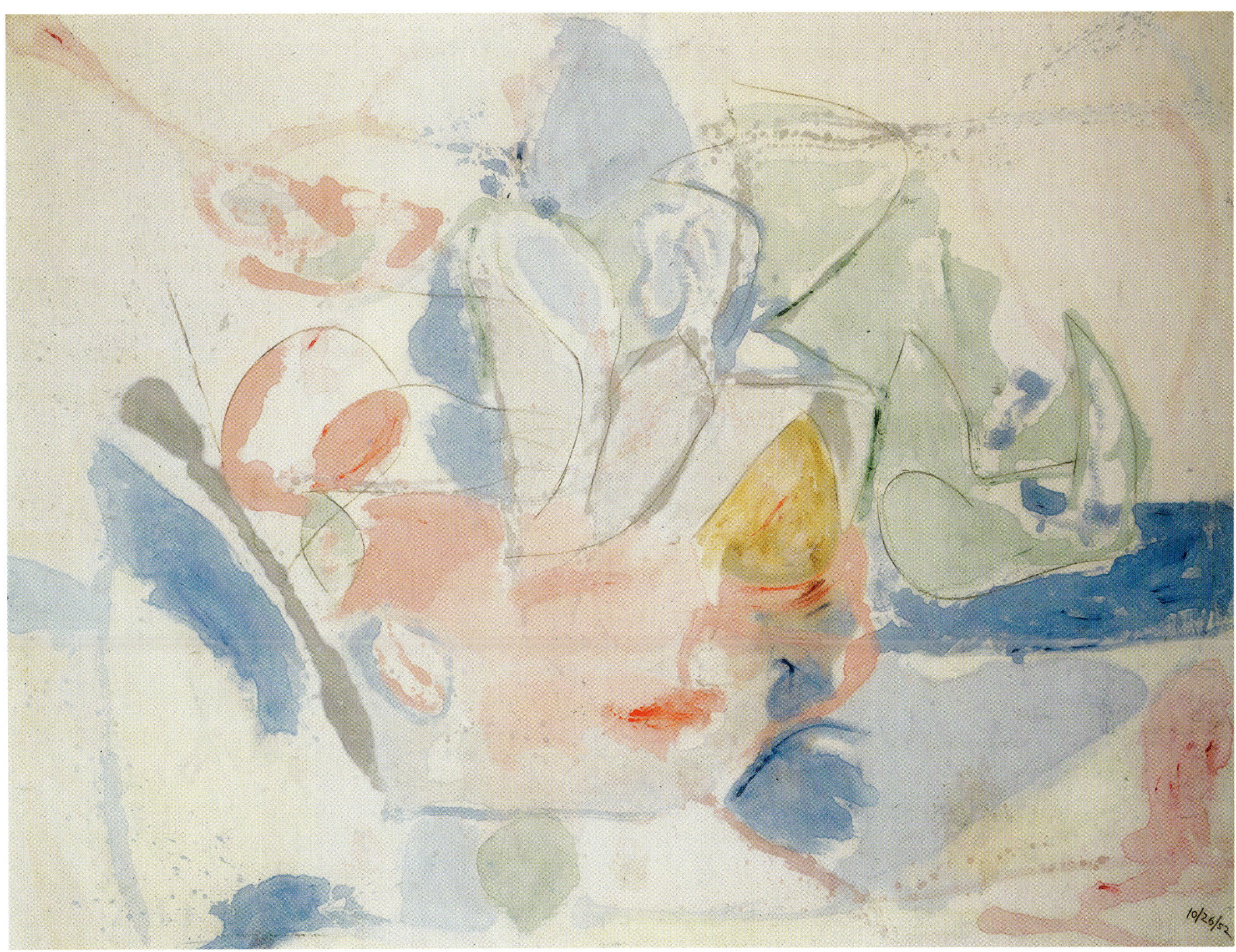

20–7 Helen Frankenthaler. ***Mountains and Sea.*** 1952. Oil on canvas, 7' 2¾" × 9' 8¼" (2.2 × 2.95 m). Collection of the artist on extended loan to the National Gallery of Art, Washington, D.C.

Blue) (fig. **20–6**), Rothko consciously sought to harmonize divergent human tendencies that German philosopher Friedrich Nietzsche (1844–1900) called the Dionysian (after the Greek god of wine, the harvest, and inspiration) and the Apollonian (after the Greek god of light, music, and truth). The painting's rich color is its Dionysian element, the emotional and instinctive side of human nature, while the simple compositional structure underlying the coloristic virtuosity is its rational and disciplined Apollonian counterpart. His mature paintings maintain a tension between the harmony they seem to seek and the fragmentation they regretfully acknowledge.

Elements from Color Field paintings like Rothko's intermingled with the gesturalism of action painting in the work of Helen Frankenthaler (b. 1928). Like Pollock, she worked on the floor, drawn to what she described as Pollock's "dancelike use of arms and legs." But rather than flinging or dripping full-strength paint, as Pollock did, Frankenthaler poured her thinned oil paints so that they soaked into the raw canvas, producing an effect in *Mountains and Sea* (fig. **20–7**) that resembles watercolor. A few delicate contour lines suggest not only the mountains of Nova Scotia referenced in the painting's title, but also less translatable, dream-inspired Surrealistic forms.

The New York School also included talented sculptors such as David Smith (1906–1965), who learned metalworking as a welder and riveter at an automobile plant in his native Indiana. During the last five years of his life, Smith turned to **formalism**—a shift partly inspired by his discovery of stainless steel as a medium. Smith explored both the relative lightness and the beauty of steel's polished surfaces in the Cubi series, monumental combinations of geometric units inspired by and offering homage to the formalism of Cubism. Like the Analytic Cubist works of Braque and Picasso, *Cubi XVII*, *XVIII*, and *XIX* (see fig. Intro–5) presents a finely tuned balance of elements that, though firmly welded together, seem ready to collapse at the slightest provocation. The viewer's aesthetic pleasure depends on this tension and on the dynamic curvilinear patterns formed by the play of light over the sculpture's burnished surfaces. These works were meant to be seen outdoors, not only because of the effect of sunlight, but also because of the way natural shapes and colors would complement and set off the inorganic form of the Cubi.

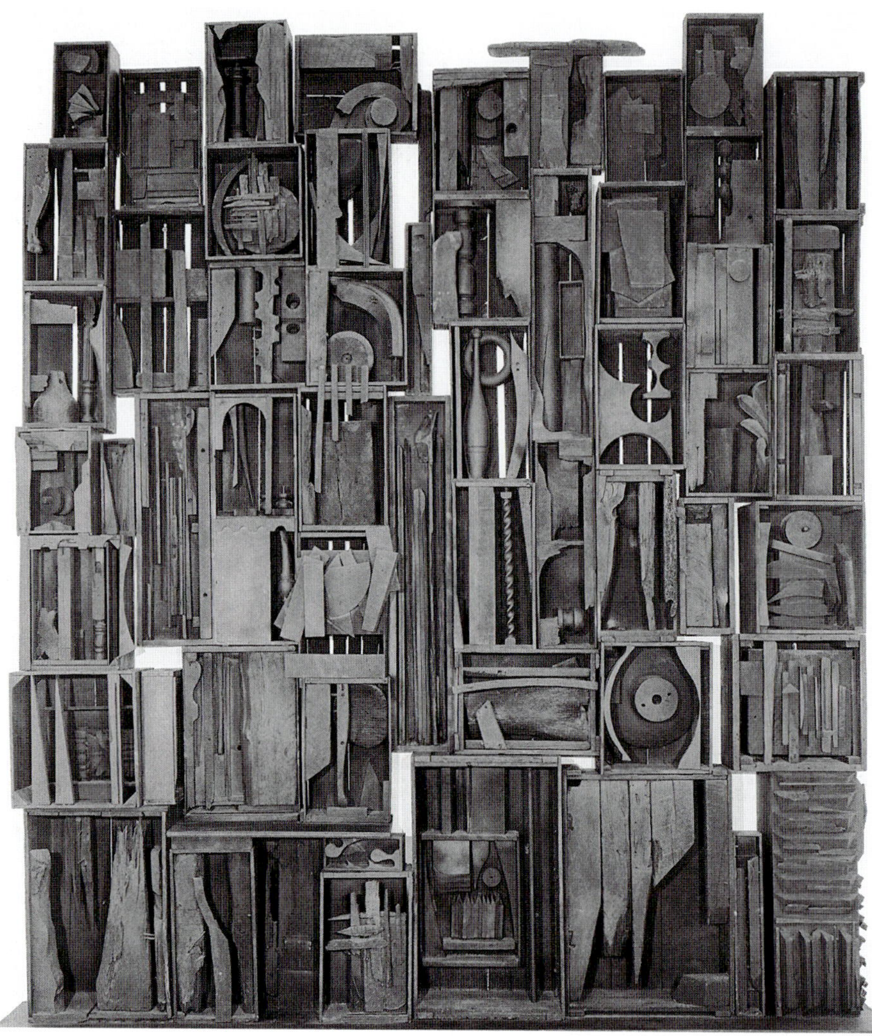

20–8 Louise Nevelson. ***Sky Cathedral.*** 1958. Assemblage of wood construction painted black, 11' 3½" × 10' ¼" × 18" (3.44 × 3.05 × 4.57 m). The Museum of Modern Art, New York
GIFT OF MR AND MRS BEN MILDWOFF (136.1958.1-57)

CLEMENT GREENBERG AND THE IDEA OF THE MAINSTREAM

A central conviction of Modernist artists, critics, and art historians has been the existence of an artistic mainstream, the notion that some artworks are more central and important than others because they participate in the progressive unfolding of some larger historical pattern. This type of art is often extolled as representing "high culture." According to this view, the overall evolutionary pattern is what confers value, and any art that does not fit within it, regardless of its appeal, can be for the most part ignored (see "'High' and 'Low' Culture in the Myth of Modernism," page 576).

The first significant discussions of what exactly constitutes the Modernist mainstream emerged after World War II, shaped by the critical writings of Clement Greenberg (1909–1994). Greenberg argued that beginning with the Realist paintings of Édouard Manet (see Chapter 18), Modern art charted the progressive elimination of narrative, figuration, and pictorial space from painting because art itself—regardless of what artists may have thought they were doing—was undergoing a "process of self-purification" in reaction to a deteriorating civilization.

Greenberg was famous for identifying Abstract Expressionism as the dominant style of the late 1940s and 1950s; he championed the New York School of painting. Inspired in part by Hofmann's teaching, he demanded close analysis of the work of art and critical judgments based on visual perception alone—a methodology called formalism. Belief in the concept of the mainstream gradually eroded, however, and a reaction against Greenberg's ideas began in the 1970s. Because Greenbergian formalism omitted so much of the history of recent art, observers began questioning whether a single, dominant mainstream had ever existed. The extraordinary proliferation of art styles and trends after the 1960s fueled those doubts.

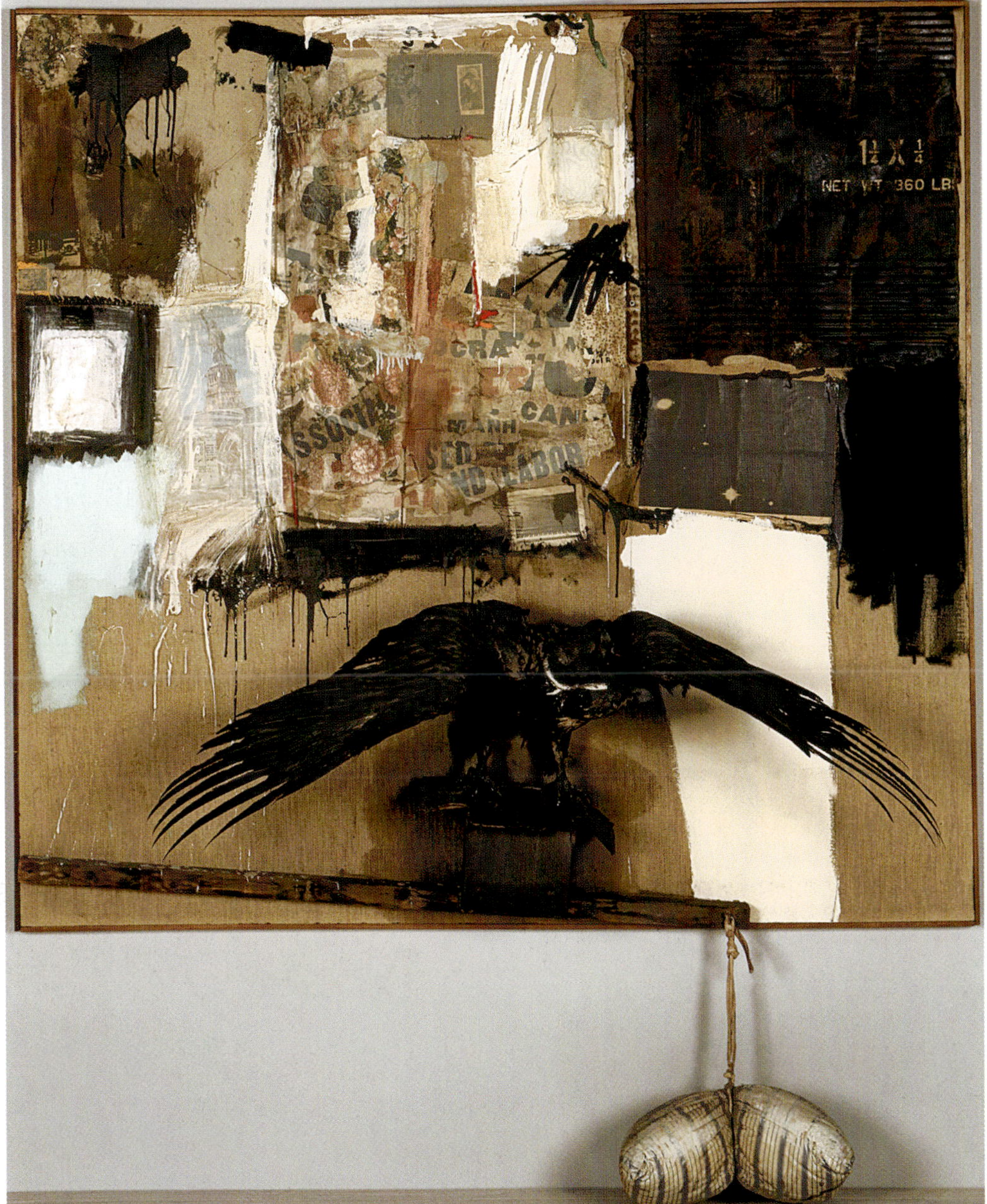

20–9 Robert Rauschenberg. ***Canyon.*** 1959. Combine painting with oil, pencil, paper, metal, photograph, fabric, wood, on canvas, plus buttons, mirror, stuffed eagle, cardboard box, pillow, paint tube, 6' 1" × 5' 6" × 2' ¾" (1.85 × 1.68 × 0.63 m)
COURTESY SONNABEND, NEW YORK. BALTIMORE MUSEUM OF ART

Avant-garde critics were not bothered by the fact that much of Rauschenberg's materials were drawn from popular culture. Many of the early twentieth-century collagists, including Picasso and Braque, had worked with similar materials. However, critics such as Hilton Kramer (at the New York Times*) and Thomas Hess (at* Artnews*) pointed out that whereas earlier artists had aesthetically coordinated such elements, transforming the crude materials of life into the finer ones of art, Rauschenberg and his associates left them in their raw, "unpurified" condition. In this view, such works were not art at all.*

Assemblage

By the end of the 1950s, many artists and critics were ready to move beyond Abstract Expressionism. One alternative path was **assemblage**, that is combining disparate elements to construct a work of art. By 1950, Louise Nevelson (1899–1988) had developed an Analytic Cubist-inspired version of assemblage. Prowling the streets of downtown Manhattan, she collected discarded packing boxes in which she would carefully arrange chair legs, broom handles, cabinet doors, spindles, and other wooden refuse. She painted her assemblages a matte black to obscure the identity of the individual elements, to integrate them formally, and to provide an air of mystery.

After stacking several of these boxes together against a studio wall, Nevelson realized that the accumulated effect was more powerful than viewing them individually. One of her first monumental wall assemblages was *Sky Cathedral* (fig. **20–8**). What she particularly liked about the new schema was the way it could transform ordinary space just as the prosaic elements she worked with had themselves been transformed into a work of art. To add a further poetic dimension, Nevelson first displayed *Sky Cathedral* bathed in soft blue light, recalling moonlight.

Robert Rauschenberg (1925–2008) developed a distinctive style of assemblage by chaotically mixing painted and found elements in artworks he called "combines." *Canyon* (fig. **20–9**) incorporates an assortment of old family photographs, public imagery (the Statue of Liberty), fragments of political posters (in the center), and various objects salvaged from the trash (the flattened steel drum at upper right), purchased, or donated by friends (the stuffed eagle). The rich disorder, enhanced by the seemingly sloppy application of paint, challenges viewers to make sense of what they see. In fact, Rauschenberg meant his work to be open to various readings, so he assembled material that each viewer might interpret differently. Cheerfully accepting the chaos and unpredictability of modern urban experience, he tried to find artistic metaphors for it. "I only consider myself successful," he said, "when I do something that resembles the lack of order I sense."

In 1961, the Museum of Modern Art organized an exhibition titled "The Art of Assemblage." Rauschenberg was one of two major American artists included in the show; the other was his close friend, and at times lover, Jasper Johns (born 1930). Inspired by the example of Marcel Duchamp (see fig. 19–18), Johns produced more controlled, cerebral, and puzzling works that seemed to bear on issues raised in contemporary art. For instance, art critics had praised the evenly dispersed, "nonhierarchical" quality of so much Abstract Expressionist painting, particularly Pollock's. The target in *Target with Four Faces* (fig. **20–10**), an emphatically hierarchical, organized image, can be seen as a response to and rebuttal of this position.

Target also has a psychological dimension that may stem from the artist's own anxieties and fears. Above the target are four faces, casts taken at different times from the same model. Cut off below

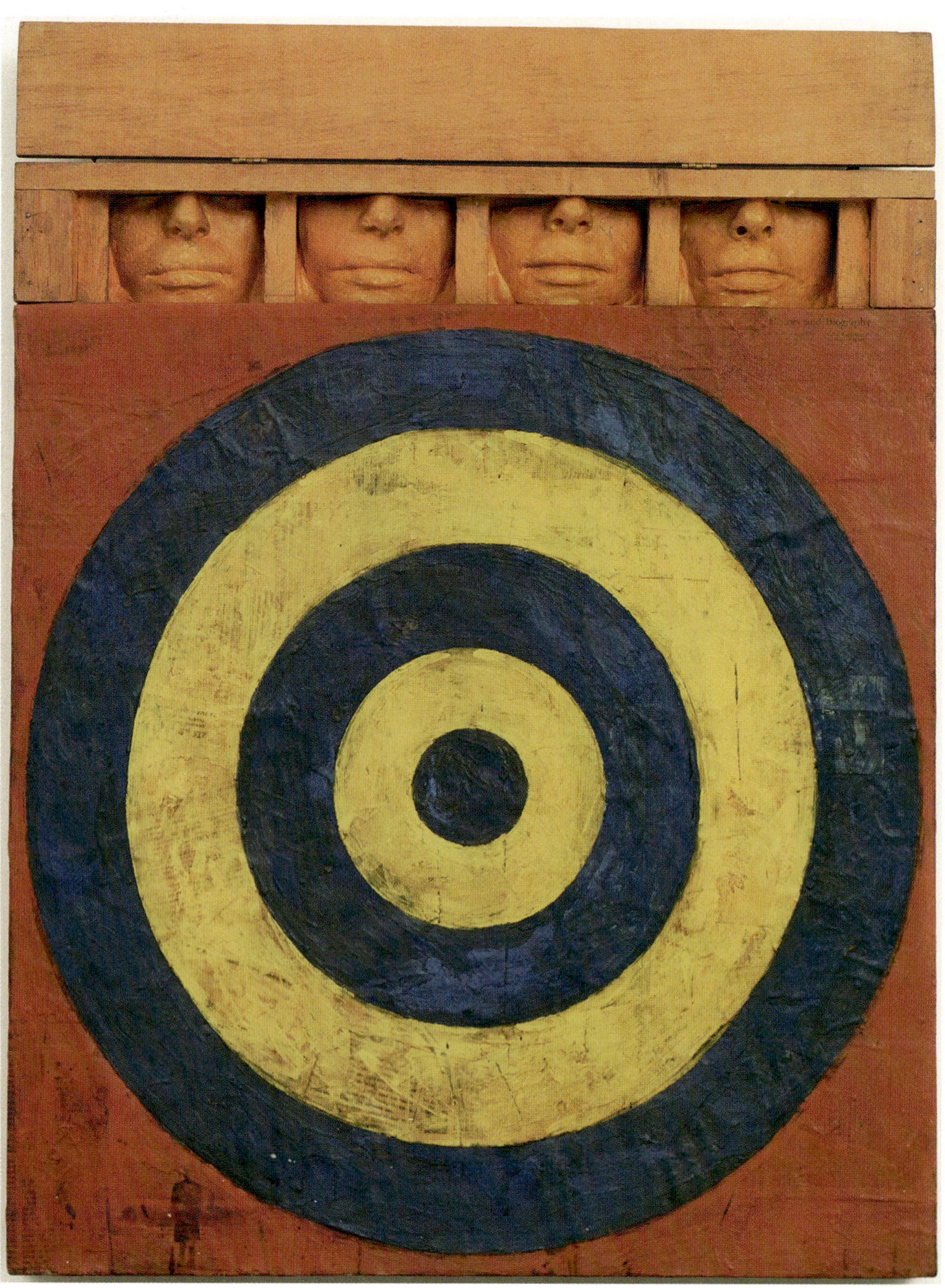

20–10 Jasper Johns. *Target with Four Faces*. 1955. Assemblage: encaustic on newspaper and cloth over canvas, surmounted by four tinted plaster faces in wood box with hinged front; overall, with box open, 33⅝" × 26" × 3" (85.4 × 66 × 7.6 cm). The Museum of Modern Art, New York
GIFT OF MR AND MRS ROBERT C. SCULL (8.1958)

CLOSER LOOK

On the evening of March 17, 1960, a distinguished group of guests, including Governor Nelson Rockefeller of New York, gathered in the sculpture garden of the Museum of Modern Art in New York City. Awaiting them was an unlikely construction: *Homage to New York* (fig. **20–11**) by the Swiss-born artist Jean Tinguely (1925–1991). The work was assembled from yards of metal tubing, several dozen bicycle and baby-carriage wheels, a washing-machine drum, an upright piano, a radio, several electric fans, a noisy old Addressograph machine, a bassinet, numerous small motors, two motor-driven devices that produced abstract paintings by the yard, several bottles of chemical inks, and assorted noisemakers. White paint covered everything except the crowning element—an inflated orange meteorological balloon.

The machine, designed to destroy itself when activated, was plugged in as the expectant guests watched. Smoke poured out of the machinery and covered the crowd. Parts of the contraption broke free and scuttled off in various directions, sometimes threatening onlookers. A device meant to douse the burning piano—which repeatedly played three notes—failed to work, and firefighters had to be called in. The firefighters extinguished the blaze and finished the work's destruction to boos from the crowd, which, with the exception of the museum officials present, had been delighted by the spectacle. The artist said the event was better than any he could have planned.

This new kind of art, dramatic but transitory, prefigured a question and answer raised by musician and philosopher John Cage (see page 581). Surveying art and music in 1961, he asked, "Where do we go from here," and his answer was, "Towards theater." Such questions about what art is and what role it plays in society have marked the richly innovative period since 1960.

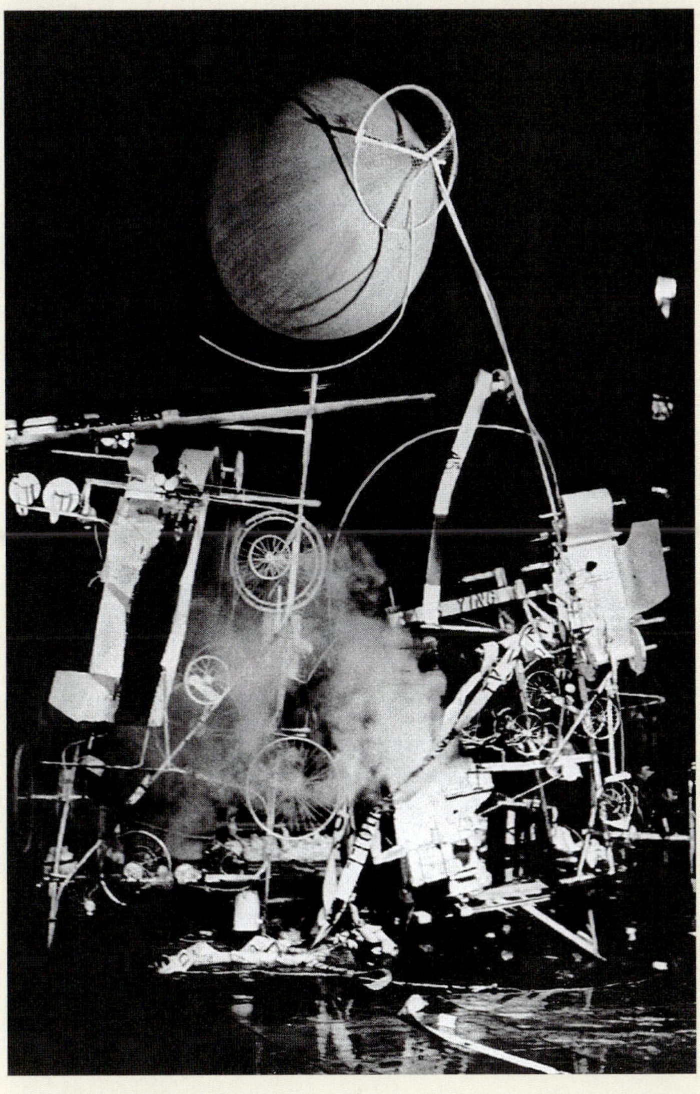

20–11 Jean Tinguely. Fragment from *Homage to New York*. 1960. Painted metal, wood, and cloth, 6' 8¼" × 29⅝" × 7' 3⅞" (203.7 × 75.1 × 223.2 cm). Self-destroying sculpture in the garden of the Museum of Modern Art, New York. Gift of the artist (227.1968)

eye level and thus made anonymous without these windows into the soul, these human heads are as blank and empty as the target itself. The viewer can complete the process of depersonalization by closing the hinged flap over the faces, obliterating the human presence. This juxtaposition of partially hidden faces and sharply defined target takes on richer meaning in the context of Johns' position as a gay artist in the restrictive, often paranoid, climate of Cold War America. Steadfastly silent but boldly present, in this painting personal identity remains elusive, masked, removed from the center and safely off target.

The work of Johns had a powerful effect on the artists who matured around 1960, and Johns' interest in Duchamp helped elevate that artist to a place of importance previously reserved for Picasso. And not since Dada had the art world seen sensationalism to compare with the kinetic sculptures of Jean Tinguely (1925–1991). In his *Homage to New York* (see fig. 20–11), this anarchist wanted to free the machine, to let it play. "Art hasn't been fun for a long time," Tinguely said. Like the creations of his Dada forebears, Tinguely's work was implicitly critical of an overly restrained and practical bourgeois mentality.

Pop Art

Pop art, as its name suggests, took its style and subject matter from popular culture: its sources were comic books, advertisements, movies, and television. Many critics were alarmed by Pop, fearful that open acknowledgment of already powerful commercial culture would threaten the survival of both Modernist art and "high culture"—meaning a civilization's most sophisticated, not its most representative, products (see "'High' and 'Low' Culture in the Myth of Modernism," below).

Pop art originated in London in the work of the Independent Group (IG), formed in 1952 by a few members of London's Institute of Contemporary Art (ICA). One of the IG's most prominent figures was artist Richard Hamilton (born 1922) whose collage *Just What Is It That Makes Today's Homes So Different, So Appealing?* (1956) satirizes modern life and especially American materialism (fig. **20–12**). American advertisements, whose utopian vision of a future of contented people with ample leisure time to enjoy cheap and plentiful material goods, was very appealing to people living amid the austerity of post-war Britain. Products of the American mass media and commercial culture—including Hollywood movies, Madison Avenue advertising, science fiction, and pop music—soon became the central subject matter of British Pop art.

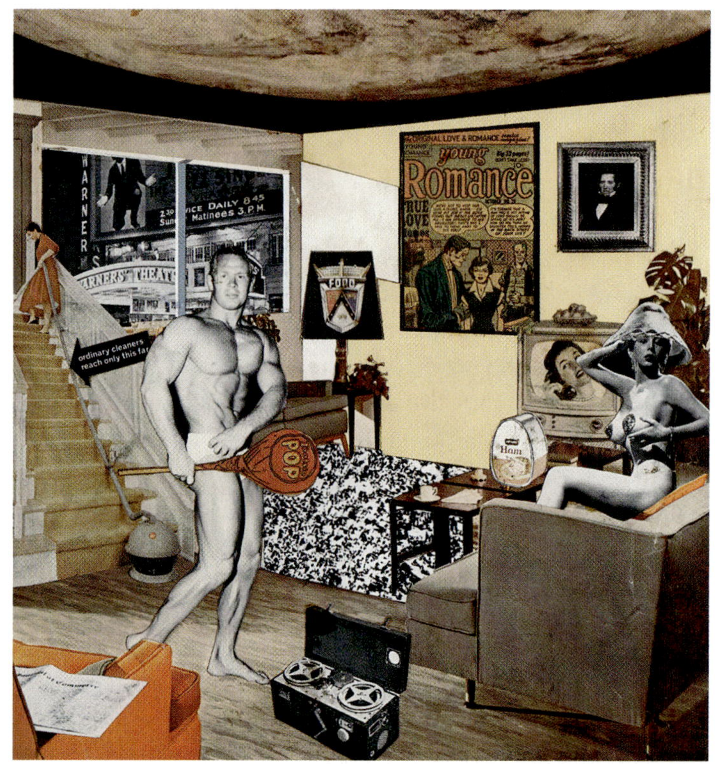

20–12 Richard Hamilton. *Just What Is It That Makes Today's Homes So Different, So Appealing?* 1956. Collage, 10¼" × 9¼" (26 × 23.5 cm). Kunsthalle, Tübingen, Germany

Hamilton's collage was part of a 1956 London exhibition titled "This Is Tomorrow."

"HIGH" AND "LOW" CULTURE IN THE MYTH OF MODERNISM

One of the prevailing ideals of the Modernist avant-garde was to distance itself intellectually and aesthetically from the banalities of everyday, middle-class life—what was sometimes referred to as "lowbrow" culture.

"Lowbrow" and "kitsch" are labels applied to the habits, tastes, artifacts (mostly mass-produced), and amusements of ordinary, popular culture, that is, any cultural expression that falls outside the parameters of what was considered elite, or "high" culture (see "Clement Greenberg and the Idea of the Mainstream," page 572). The term "kitsch" derives from the German word *verkitschen* (to make cheap). Mass-produced consumer goods have generally been given this label—a categorization that often has a pejorative sense when such goods are compared to "high," or fine, art. Kitsch has taken on a further connotation of vulgarity and "bad," cheap, or uneducated taste.

Boundaries between "high" and "low" began to blur when the Pop artists of the early 1960s began to champion imagery culled from "low" popular culture for incorporation into "high" art—similar to what Marcel Duchamp did when he exhibited a urinal as a work of art in 1917 (see fig. 19–18). Postmodern artists continue to question and obscure distinctions between "high" and "low" as a way of repudiating and/or critiquing what they see as the smugness of Modernism.

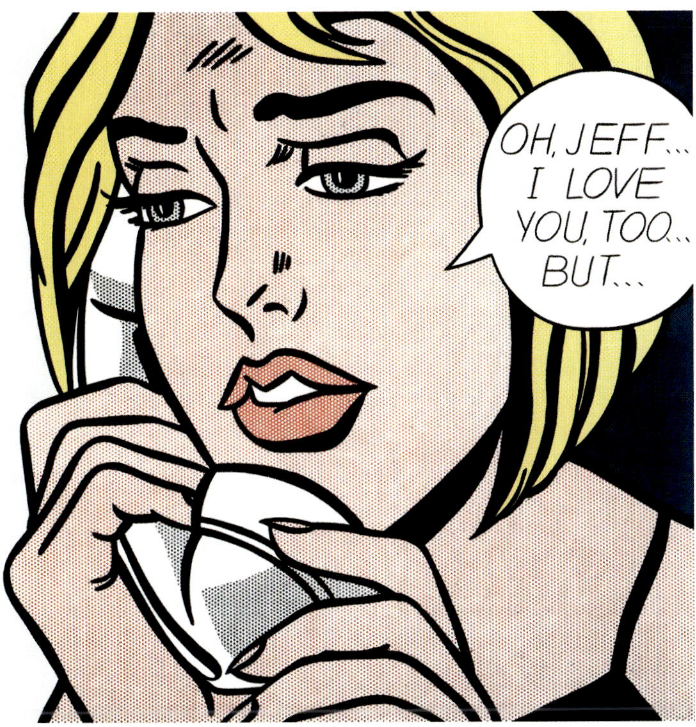

20–13 Roy Lichtenstein. *Oh, Jeff ... I Love You, Too ... But ...* 1964. Oil on Magna on canvas, 4' × 4' (1.22 × 1.22 m). Private collection

Even more attuned to popular culture, American artist Roy Lichtenstein (1923–1997) used imagery he found in cartoons and advertisements, even adopting the print medium's heavy outlines and the Benday dots used in offset printing. Although many people assume that he merely copied from the comics, in fact he made numerous subtle, important formal adjustments that tightened, clarified, and strengthened the final image. *Oh, Jeff...I Love You, Too...But...* (fig. **20–13**) compresses into a single frame the generic comic romance story line, in which two people fall in love, face a crisis that temporarily threatens their relationship, and then live happily ever after. But Lichtenstein plays games pitting illusion against reality. We know that comic-book emotions are unrealistically melodramatic, yet he presents them vividly, almost reverently, enshrined in a work of art. The issue of what is real and what is unreal in media culture was becoming a topic of concern and discussion in the early 1960s, and it is still with us today.

Another Pop artist who veiled personal meditations behind the impersonal veneer of American popular imagery was Andy Warhol (1928?–1987). A successful commercial illustrator in New York City during the 1950s, Warhol grew envious of Rauschenberg's and Johns' emerging "star status" and decided in 1960 to pursue a career as an artist. His decision to focus on popular culture was more than a careerist move, however; it also allowed him to celebrate the middle-class social and material values he had absorbed growing up in Pittsburgh amid the hardships of the Great Depression. In the *Marilyn Diptych* (fig. **20–14**), Warhol even celebrates its industrial mode of production.

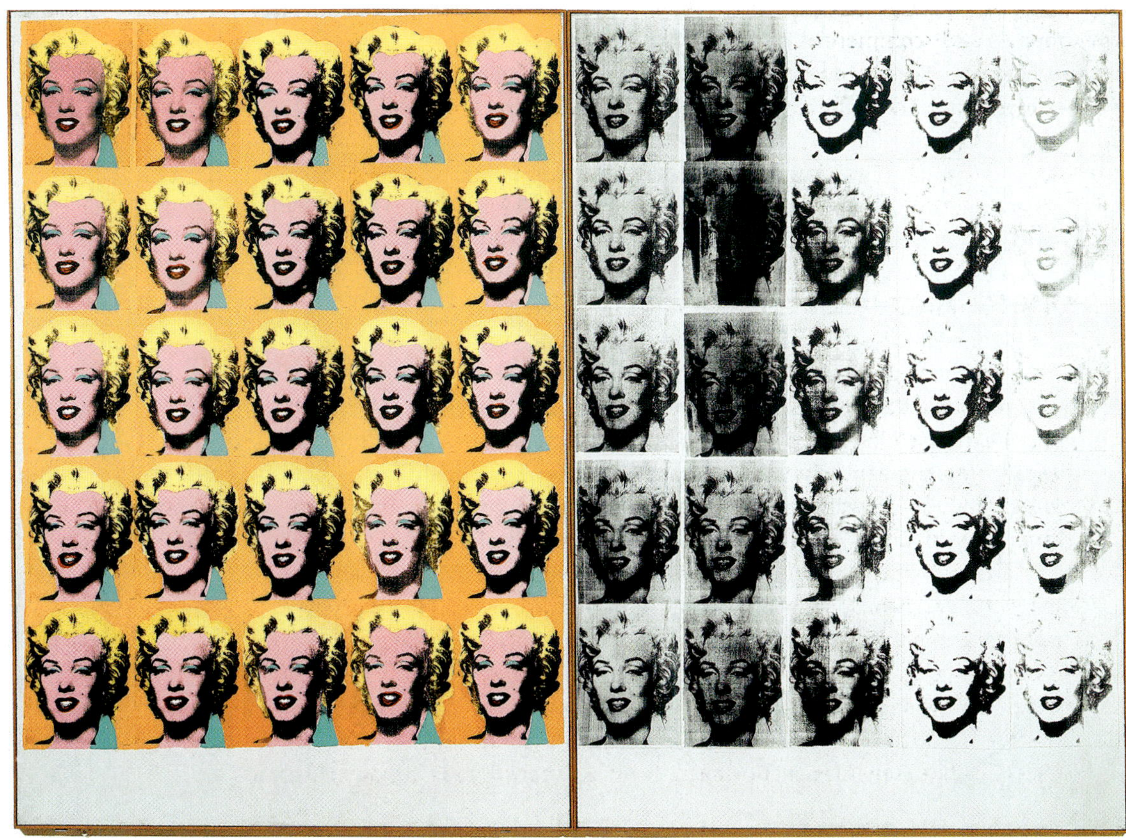

20–14 Andy Warhol. *Marilyn Diptych*. 1962. Oil, acrylic, and silk screen on enamel on canvas, two panels, each 6' 10" × 4' 9" (2.05 × 1.44 m). Tate Gallery, London

Warhol assumed that all Pop artists shared his affirmative view of ordinary culture. In his account of the beginnings of the Pop movement, he wrote: "The Pop artists did images that anybody walking down Broadway could recognize in a split second—comics, picnic tables, men's trousers, celebrities, shower curtains, refrigerators, Coke bottles—all the great modern things that the Abstract Expressionists tried so hard not to notice at all."

APPROPRIATION AND THE "DEATH OF THE AUTHOR"

During the late 1970s and 1980s, **appropriation** (an artist's incorporation of a preexisting image into a new creation) became a popular technique among American and European Postmodernists. The borrowing of figures or compositions, of course, has been a standard practice throughout the history of art, but the emphasis had centered in adapting or personalizing the source. A straightforward reuse was not considered legitimate until Marcel Duchamp changed the rules with his readymades (see fig. 19–18), insisting that the essence of an artwork was not its formal invention but its underlying ideas. Duchamp's own appropriations inspired Pop artists like Warhol and Lichtenstein (see figs. 20–13 and 20–14) to reuse imagery from popular culture, high art, ordinary commerce, and even tabloids, and they, in turn, paved the way for Postmodern artists of the 1970s and 1980s.

Critics and historians now use the term "appropriation" to describe the activities of two distinct groups. To the first belong artists such as Betye Saar (see fig. 20–25) and Jaune Quick-to-See Smith (see fig. 20–31), who combine and shape their borrowings in personal ways. Like Rauschenberg (see fig. 20–9), they might be called "collage appropriators." "Straight appropriators," on the other hand, are those who simply repaint or photograph imagery from commerce or the history of art and present it within their own, essentially unaltered.

The work of appropriators is grounded in the ideas of Post-Structuralist French literary criticism. In his essay "The Death of the Author" (1968), for example, Roland Barthes (1915–1980) argued that the meaning of a work of art depends not on its author's intent but on its reader's understanding. Furthermore, he questioned the Modernist notion of originality, and thus the idea of authors as individual creators of new meaning. According to Barthes, authors instead recycle meanings from other sources.

The painting, produced in Warhol's studio called the Factory, is one of the first in which Warhol turned from hand painting to the assembly-line technique of silk-screening photographic images onto canvas, allowing him to produce many versions of a single subject and increase his profits from the sale of his art. Like so many people, Warhol was fascinated by American movie stars such as Marilyn Monroe, especially after her apparent suicide in 1962, which prompted him to begin painting her. The strip of pictures in this work suggests the sequential images of film. Even the face Warhol portrays, taken from a publicity photograph (see "Appropriation," above), is not that of Monroe the person but of Monroe the star; Warhol was interested in her public mask, not in her personality or character. He borrowed the diptych format from the icons of saints he recalled from the Byzantine Catholic church he attended as a youth. By symbolically treating the famous actress as a saint, Warhol shed light on his own fascination with fame.

Unlike Warhol and Lichtenstein, Swedish-born Claes Oldenburg (born 1929) took a more critical, but also more humorous attitude toward popular culture. Oldenburg's humor—aimed at reanimating a dull, lifeless culture—is most evident in such large-scale public projects as his 1969 Lipstick Monument for his alma mater, Yale University (fig. **20–15**). The late 1960s were marked by

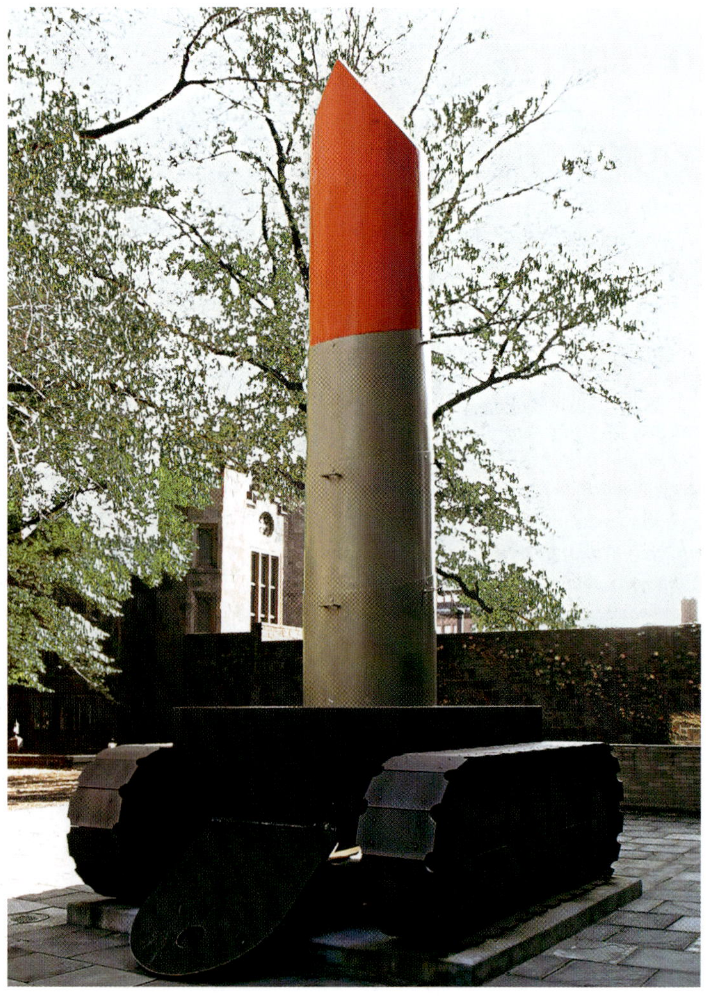

20–15 Claes Oldenburg. ***Lipstick (Ascending) on Caterpillar Tracks.*** 1969, reworked 1974. Painted steel body, aluminum tube, and fiberglass tip, 21' × 19' 5½" × 10' 11" (6.7 × 5.94 × 3.33 m). Installed at Beinike Plaza, Yale University, New Haven, Connecticut. Yale University Art Gallery
GIFT OF COLOSSAL KEEPSAKE CORPORATION

student demonstrations against the Vietnam War. By mounting a giant lipstick tube on tracks from a Caterpillar tractor, Oldenburg suggested a missile rising from a tank and simultaneously subverted the warlike reference by casting the missile in the eroticized form of a feminine cosmetic with blatant phallic overtones. Oldenburg thus urged his audience, in the vocabulary of the time, to "make love, not war." The university, offended by the work's irreverent humor, made Oldenburg remove it. In 1974, he reworked *Lipstick (Ascending) on Caterpillar Tracks* in fiber-glass, aluminum, and steel and donated it to the university, which this time accepted it.

Op Art and Minimalism

In contrast to the emphasis on image-based content of Pop art, other styles that emerged in the wake of Abstract Expressionism focused on stripping all external meanings from artworks and reducing them to technical essentials. Intense investigation of perception occurred in "optical art," popularly known as Op art, a nonobjective art that used precisely structured patterns of lines and colors to affect visual perception. *Current* (fig. **20–16**) by British artist Bridget Riley (born 1931) consists of tightly spaced, parallel, curved lines that produce an effect of fluctuating motion. Staring at Op art patterns can produce viewer discomfort.

Other artists, including the sculptor Donald Judd (1928–1994), turned to a style known as Minimalism. Convinced that Abstract Expressionism had deteriorated into a set of techniques for faking both the subjective and the transcendent, around 1960 Judd began to search for an art free of falsehood. He decided that sculpture offered a better medium than painting for creating such matter-of-fact art. Rather than *depicting* shapes, which Judd thought smacked of illusionism and therefore fakery, he produced *actual* shapes. Seeking simplicity and clarity, he soon evolved a formal vocabulary reduced to identical rectangular units arranged in rows and

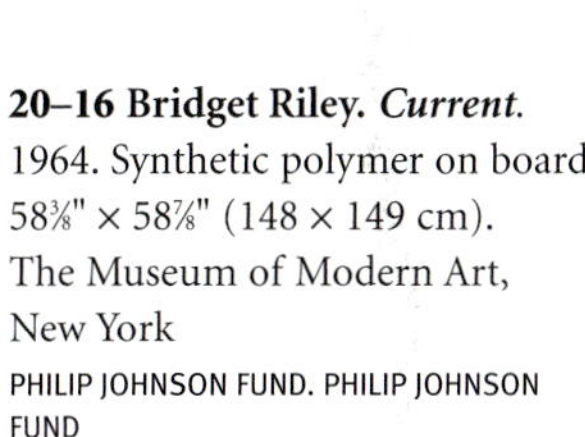

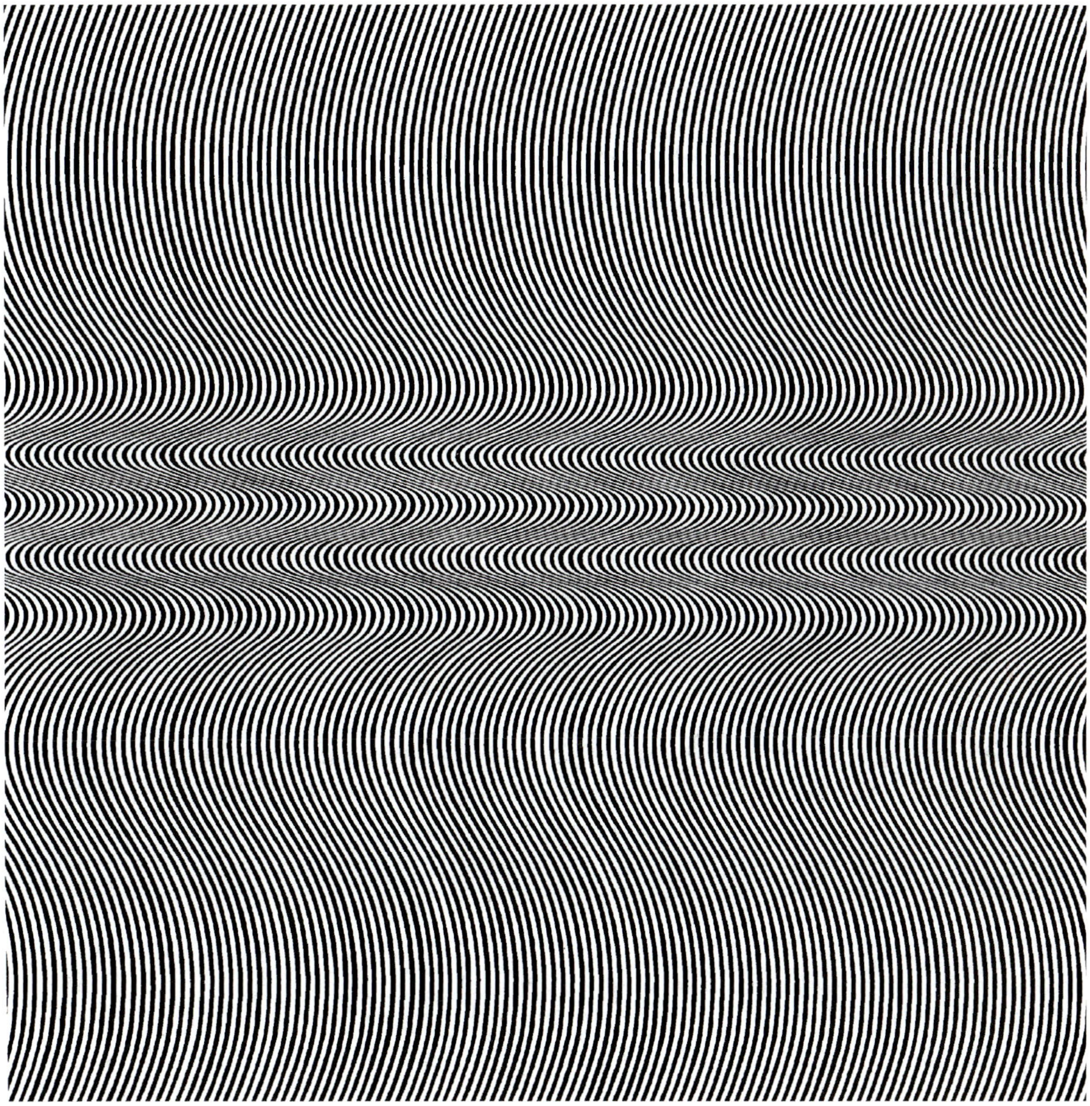

20–16 Bridget Riley. ***Current.*** 1964. Synthetic polymer on board, 58⅜" × 58⅞" (148 × 149 cm). The Museum of Modern Art, New York

PHILIP JOHNSON FUND. PHILIP JOHNSON FUND

While the American popular media loved Op art, most New York critics detested it, claiming it was too involved with investigating the processes of perception to qualify as serious art. Lucy Lippard called it "an art of little substance," depending "on purely technical knowledge of color and design theory which, when combined with a conventional geometric…framework, results in jazzily respectable jumping surfaces, and nothing more."

constructed of industrial materials, especially anodized aluminum and Plexiglas. *Untitled* (fig. **20–17**) is typical of Judd's mature work.

Although Judd passionately protested against the Vietnam War, he felt that his art should deal only with aesthetic issues, not personal convictions. Some Minimalists disagreed. For Eva Hesse (1936–1970), personal history was a central influence in artistic creation. Born in Hamburg, Germany, to Jewish parents, Hesse narrowly escaped the Nazi Holocaust when her family emigrated to New York City in 1939. Initially painting darkly Expressionistic self-portraits that reflected the emotional turbulence of her life, in 1964 she turned to abstract sculpture and adapted the vocabulary of Minimalism to a similarly self-expressive purpose. "For me ...," said Hesse, "art and life are inseparable. If I can name the content ... it's the total absurdity of life." The "absurdity" that Hesse pursued in her last works was the complete denial of fixed form and scale, so vital to Minimalists like Judd. Her *Rope Piece* (fig. **20–18**), for example, takes on a different shape and size each time it is installed. The work consists of several sections of rope, which Hesse and her assistant dipped in latex, knotted and tangled, and then hung from wires attached to the ceiling. The resulting linear web or "drawing in space" resembles a three-dimensional version of a dripped action painting by Jackson Pollock, and, like Pollock's work, it achieves a sense of structure despite its chaotic appearance. The Minimal art of Judd is tightly controlled by the artist, but Hesse allowed the natural force of gravity a much larger role.

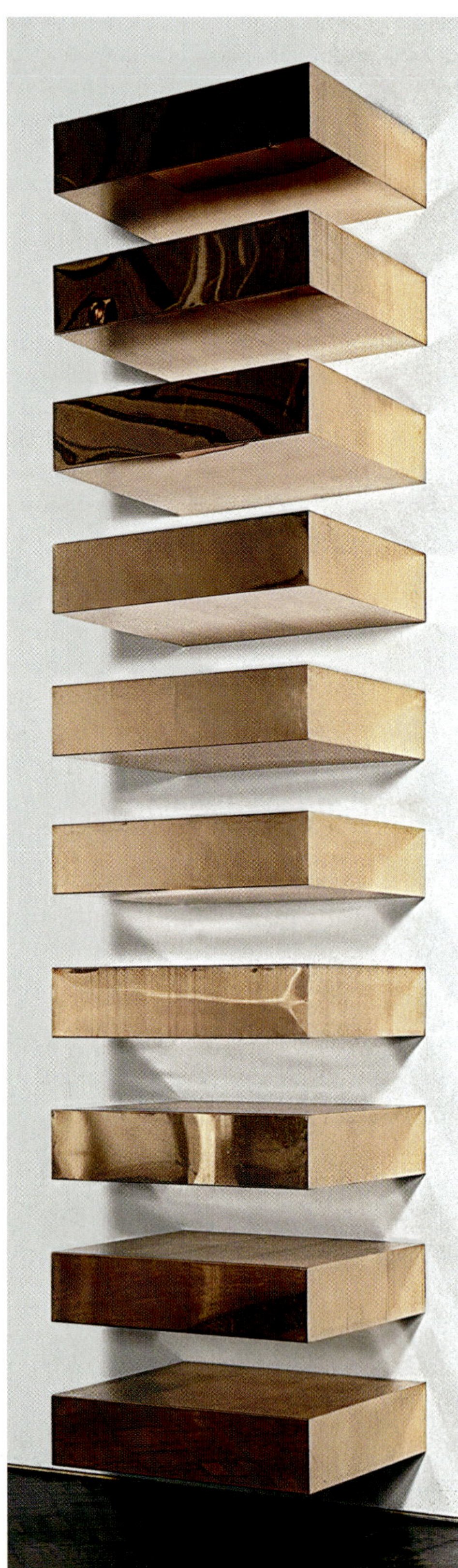

20–17 Donald Judd. ***Untitled.*** 1967. Stainless steel and Plexiglas, each of the ten units measures 6" × 27" × 24" (15.2 × 68.6 × 61 cm). Solomon R. Guggenheim Museum, New York

PANZA COLLECTION, 1991 (91.3713)

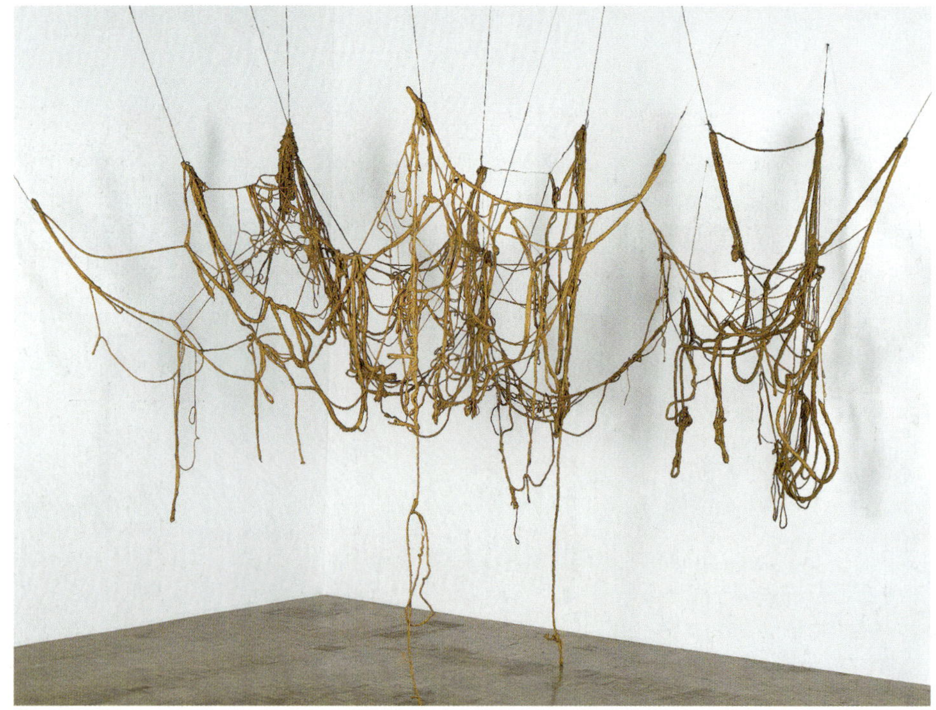

20–18 Eva Hesse. ***Rope Piece.*** 1969–1970. Latex over rope, string and wire; two strands, dimensions variable. Whitney Museum of American Art, New York

PURCHASE, WITH FUNDS FROM ELI AND EDYTHE L. BROAD, THE MRS. PERCY URIS PURCHASE FUND, AND THE PAINTING AND SCULPTURE COMMITTEE (88.17A–B)

Conceptual and Performance Art

While Judd and Hesse seemed radical, at least they were making things. The artists who came to be known as Conceptualists pushed Minimalism to its logical extreme by eliminating the art object itself. The ultimate root of Conceptual art is Marcel Duchamp and his assertion that making art should be a mental, not a physical, activity.

The most prominent American Conceptual artist, Joseph Kosuth (born 1945), abandoned painting in 1965 and began to work with language, which he believed, under the influence of philosopher Ludwig Wittgenstein (1889–1951), would direct art away from aesthetics and toward philosophical speculation. His *One and Three Chairs* (fig. **20–19**) presents an actual chair, a full-scale black-and-white photograph of the same chair, and a dictionary definition of the word "chair." The work thus leads the viewer from the physical chair to the purely linguistic ideal of "chairness" and invites the question, "Which is the most real?"

Many Conceptual artists used their own bodies as a medium and engaged in activities or performances that they considered works of art. Some had fallen under the spell of composer and philosopher John Cage (1912–1992) during the 1950s. Cage incorporated everyday experience and pure chance in his musical compositions. He advocated the unity of the arts—including theater, music, and dance as well as the visual arts. Under Cage's influence, Allan Kaprow (1927–2006) gave up painting for loosely scripted, multimedia Happenings. Meanwhile in Japan the Gutai group of artists produced dramatic displays they called Performance Art. In *Hurling Colors* of 1956, they smashed bottles of paint on a canvas laid on the floor. In Paris, Yves Klein (1928–1962)—who after 1957 worked only in blue, which he considered the most spiritual color—produced *Anthropometries of the Blue Period* in 1960. He covered three nude female models with blue paint and directed them to press their bodies against large sheets of paper covering the floor. Klein's *Monotone Symphony*—20 minutes of single notes followed by 20 minutes of silence—accompanied the performance. In part, this was a satire on the pretentiousness of Pollock's action painting (see fig. 20–2). In contrast, Klein's work was created by a sensuous and diverting display, without even touching it himself. "I dislike artists who empty themselves into their paintings," he wrote. "They spit out every rotten complexity as if relieving themselves, putting the burden on their viewers."

In 1966–1967, the American artist Bruce Nauman (born 1941) made a series of 11 color photographs based on wordplay and visual puns. In *Self-Portrait as a Fountain* (fig. **20–20**), for example, the bare-chested artist tips his head back, spurts water into the air, and, in the spirit of Duchamp, designates himself a work of art, even naming himself *Fountain*, after Duchamp's famous urinal (see fig. 19–18).

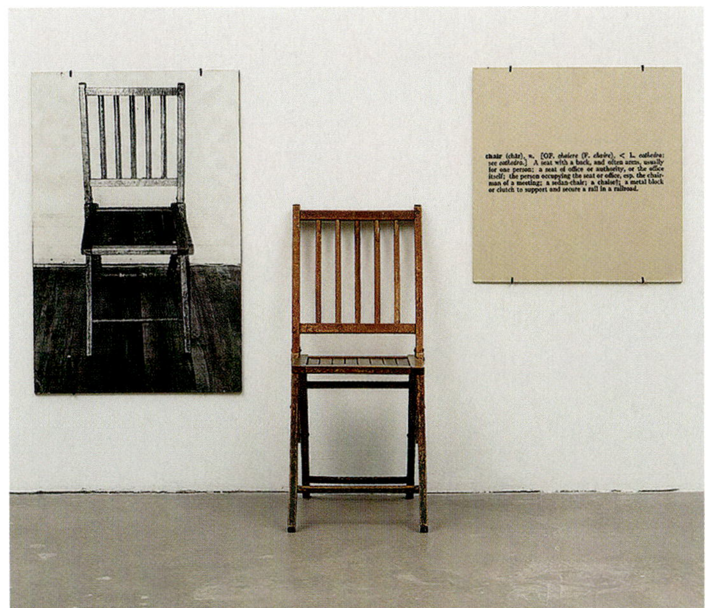

20–19 Joseph Kosuth. ***One and Three Chairs.*** 1965. Wood folding chair, photograph of chair, and photographic enlargement of dictionary definition of chair; chair, 32⅜" × 14⅞" × 20⅞" (82.2 × 37.8 × 53 cm); photo panel 36" × 24⅛" (91.4 × 61.3 cm); text panel 24⅛" × 24½" (61.3 × 62.2 cm). The Museum of Modern Art, New York
LARRY ALDRICH FOUNDATION (393.1970A-C)

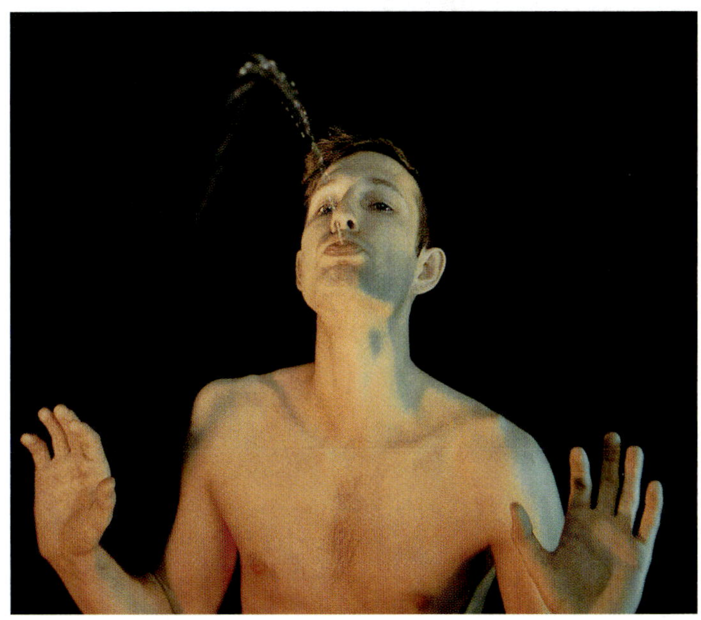

20–20 Bruce Nauman. ***Self-Portrait as a Fountain.*** 1966–1967. Color photograph, 19¾" × 23¾" (50.1 × 60.3 cm)
COURTESY LEO CASTELLI GALLERY, NEW YORK

Earthworks and Site-Specific Art

Conceptual and Performance artists seemed to have taken art to its limits, but most of their events happened in art galleries or museums. Some artists in the late 1960s and 1970s wondered if art could do without such traditional settings. Perhaps artists in the present—like some in the past (see figs. Intro–1, 1–9, and 15–20)—could take the earth itself as a medium and shape a site or do something on it. Sculptors began to work outdoors, using what they found at the site to fashion **earthworks**. They also pioneered a category of art called **site-specific sculpture**, designed for a particular outdoor location.

Robert Smithson (1938–1973) sought to illustrate what he called the "ongoing dialectic" in nature between the constructive forces that build and shape form and the destructive forces that destroy it. *Spiral Jetty* (fig. **20–21**), a 1,500-foot stone and earth platform spiraling into the Great Salt Lake in Utah, reflects these ideas. To Smithson, the salty water and the algae of the lake suggested the primordial ocean where life began, and the abandoned oil rigs dotting the lake shore brought to mind both prehistoric dinosaurs and a vanished civilization. He used the spiral because it is an archetypal shape that appears throughout the natural world, from galaxies to seashells. Also, unlike Modernist squares, circles, and straight lines, it is a "dialectical" shape, one that opens and closes, curls and uncurls endlessly, suggesting to Smithson the perpetual "coming and going of things." He hoped that the algae living in the lake would turn the water into a display of ephemeral colors, and that eventually the action of the water would cause the earthwork to erode and disappear.

Strongly committed to the realization of temporary, site-specific artworks in both rural and urban settings are Christo and Jeanne-Claude, both born on June 13, 1935. Christo Javacheff (who uses only his first name) emigrated from his native Bulgaria to Paris in 1958, where he met Jeanne-Claude de Guillebon. In 1964, they emigrated to New York with their son Cyril. Their artistic collaboration

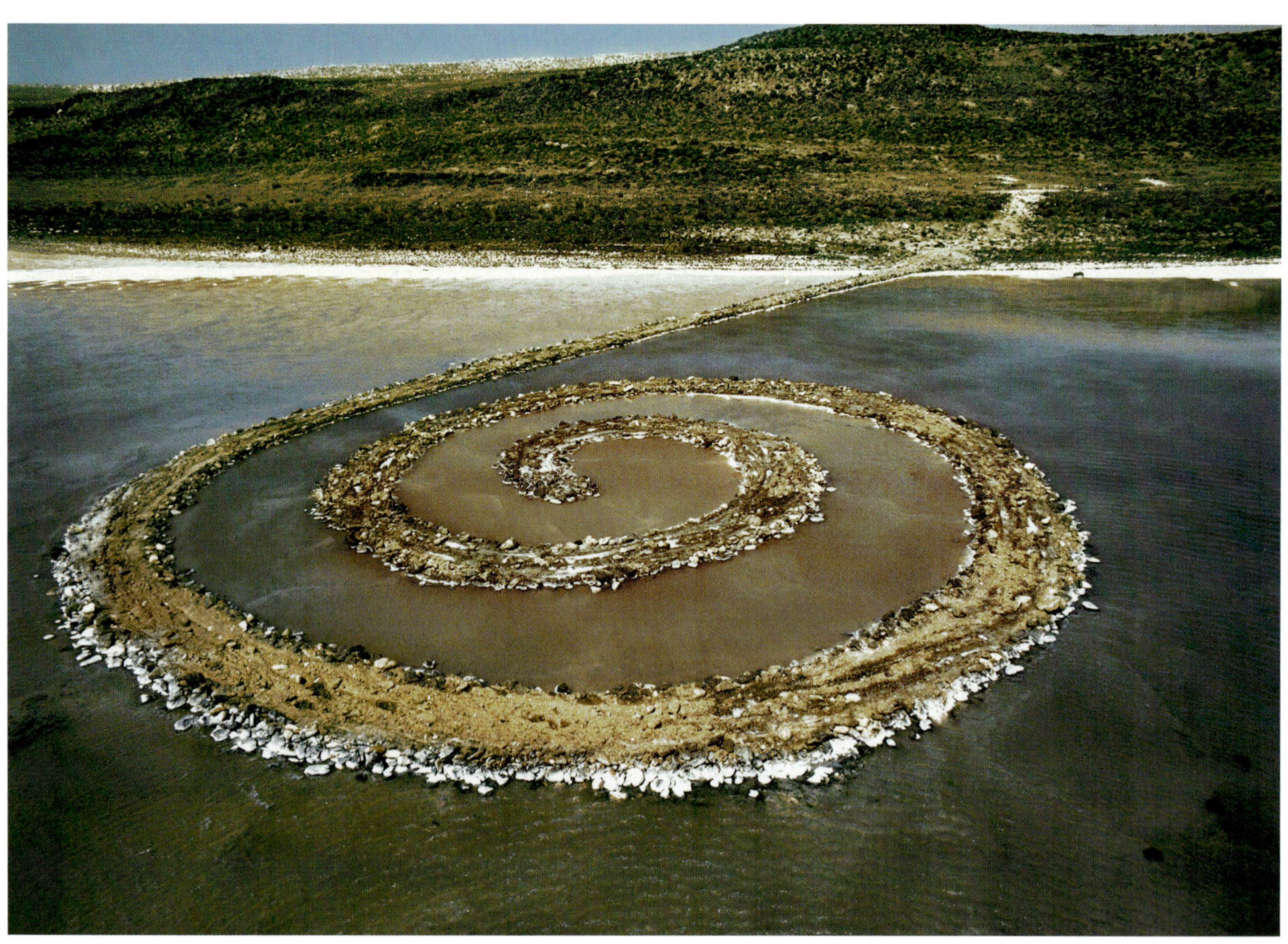

20–21 Robert Smithson. ***Spiral Jetty***. 1969–1970. Black rock, salt crystal, and earth spiral, length 1,500' (457 m). Great Salt Lake, Utah

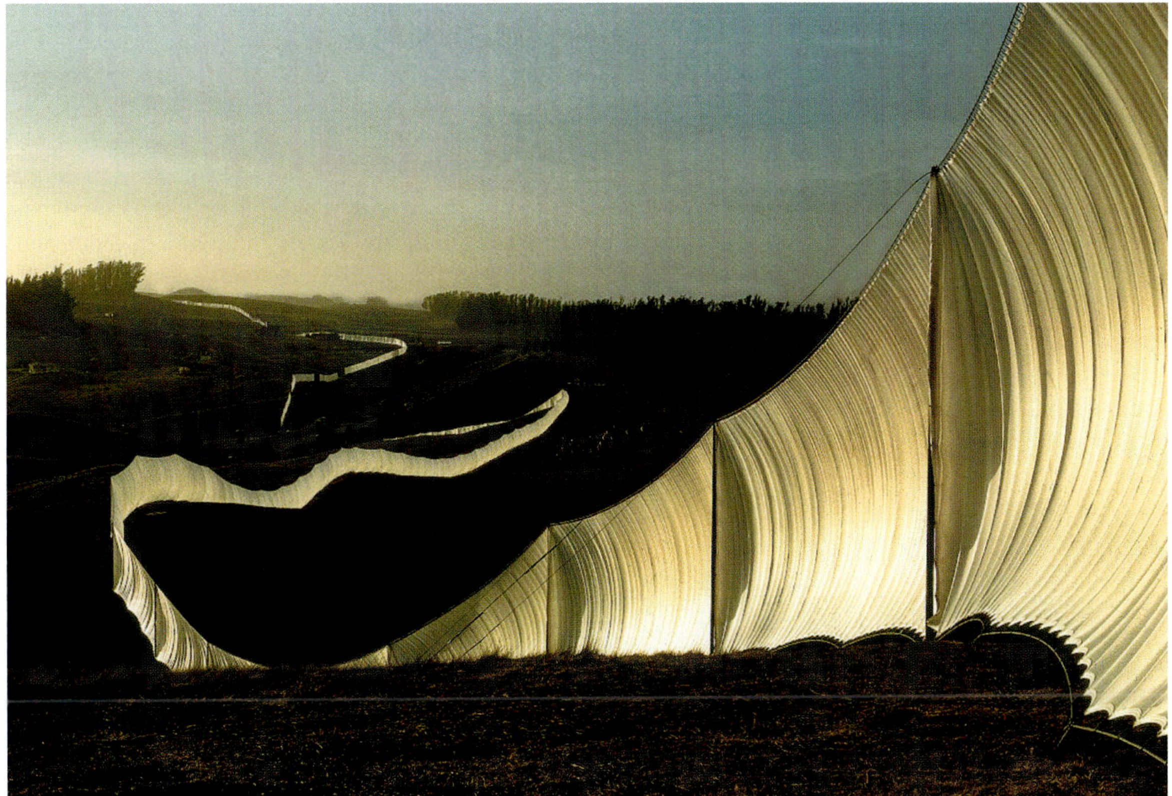

20–22 Christo and Jeanne-Claude. *Running Fence*. Sonoma and Marin Counties, California. 1972–1976. Nylon fence, height 18' (5.5 m), length 24½ miles (40 km)

"All the materials used in this project were recycled. We accept no sponsors and pay for our projects with our own money."
—Jeanne-Claude

began in 1961, obsessed with "wrapping" places or things in swaths of fabric. One of their best-known works from the 1970s, *Running Fence* (fig. **20–22**) consisted of a 24½-mile-long, 18-foot-high nylon "fence" that crossed two counties in northern California. The artists chose the location in Sonoma and Marin counties because they found it beautiful, as well as to call attention to the link between urban, suburban, rural spaces, and the ocean. At the same time, given the nature of their work, the conflict and collaborations between the artists and various social groups open the workings of the political system to scrutiny and invest their work with a sense of social space. For *Running Fence* they spent 42 months overcoming the resistance of county commissioners, as well as local opposition. To realize their massive projects, Christo and Jeanne-Claude usually rely on a diverse and devoted community of supporters and workers, including college students, ranchers, lawyers, and fellow artists. In a way this *Fence* broke down barriers that frequently separate social groups. The work remained in place for two weeks and then was taken down.

Feminist Art

The late 1960s and early 1970s also saw the rise of the feminist movement in the United States. Through Modernism feminists challenged one of the major unspoken facts in the history of art—the dominance of men—and discovered that women had contributed to most of the movements of Western art but were rarely even mentioned in accounts of its history. Feminists attacked the traditional Western hierarchy that valued some arts—easel and wall painting, sculpture, and architecture—over others—such as ceramics and textiles—and in the process relegated women's achievements to second-class status.

But the inequities were not restricted to art's past. In August 1970 (the fiftieth anniversary of the adoption of the Nineteenth Amendment to the Constitution, which guaranteed women the right to vote), women assessed their progress in various fields since 1920. They were disappointed by what they found. In the arts, women constituted about half the nation's practicing artists, but only 18 percent of commercial New York galleries carried any work by women. And of the 143 artists whose works were in the 1969 Whitney Annual (now Biennial)—one of the country's most important exhibitions of the work of living artists—only eight were women. Few women served as museum directors, and few achieved the rank of full professor in art history departments. To focus more attention on women in the arts, feminist artists began organizing women's cooperative galleries, while feminist art historians wrote about women artists. In 1971, Miriam Schapiro (born 1923) and Judy Chicago (born 1939) established the Feminist Art Program, dedicated to training women artists, at the California Institute of the Arts (CalArts).

Schapiro championed the theory that women have a distinct artistic sensibility that can be distinguished from that of men, and hence a specifically feminine aesthetic. During the late 1950s and 1960s she made explicitly female versions of the dominant

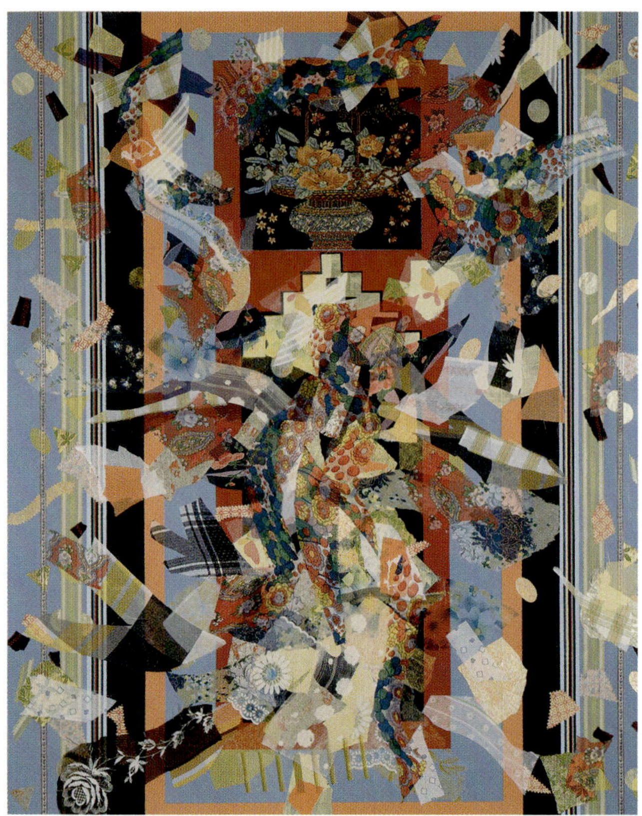

20–23 Miriam Schapiro. *Personal Appearance #3*. 1973. Acrylic and fabric on canvas, 60" × 50" (152.4 × 127 cm). Private collection

Modernist styles, including reductive, hard-edged abstractions of the female form: large X-shapes with openings at their centers. In 1973, she created *Personal Appearance #3* (fig. **20–23**), using underlying hard-edged rectangles and overlaying them with a collage of fabric and paper, materials associated with women's craftwork. She called her new technique *fem mage* (from *female* and *collage*). A founder of the P and D (Pattern and Decoration) movement, Schapiro said, "I dovetail my feminism with decoration" (cited in Gouma-Peterson and Schapiro, page 29). The formal and emotional richness of her work were meant to counter the Minimalist aesthetic of the 1960s, which Schapiro and other feminists considered typically male.

Judy Chicago's work *The Dinner Party* (fig. **20–24**) is perhaps the best-known work of feminist art from the 1970s. In 1970, she had adopted the surname Chicago (the city of her birth) to free herself from "all names imposed upon her through male social dominance." At CalArts, Chicago and Schapiro led a collective of 21 women students in the creation of *Womanhouse* (1971–1972), a collaborative art environment. From *Womanhouse* emerged *The Dinner Party* (1974–1979), a complex, mixed-media installation that fills an entire room with powerful proclamations of the accomplishments of women throughout history. Five years of collaborative effort went into the creation of the work, involving hundreds of women and several men who volunteered their talents as ceramists, needleworkers, and china painters to realize Chicago's designs.

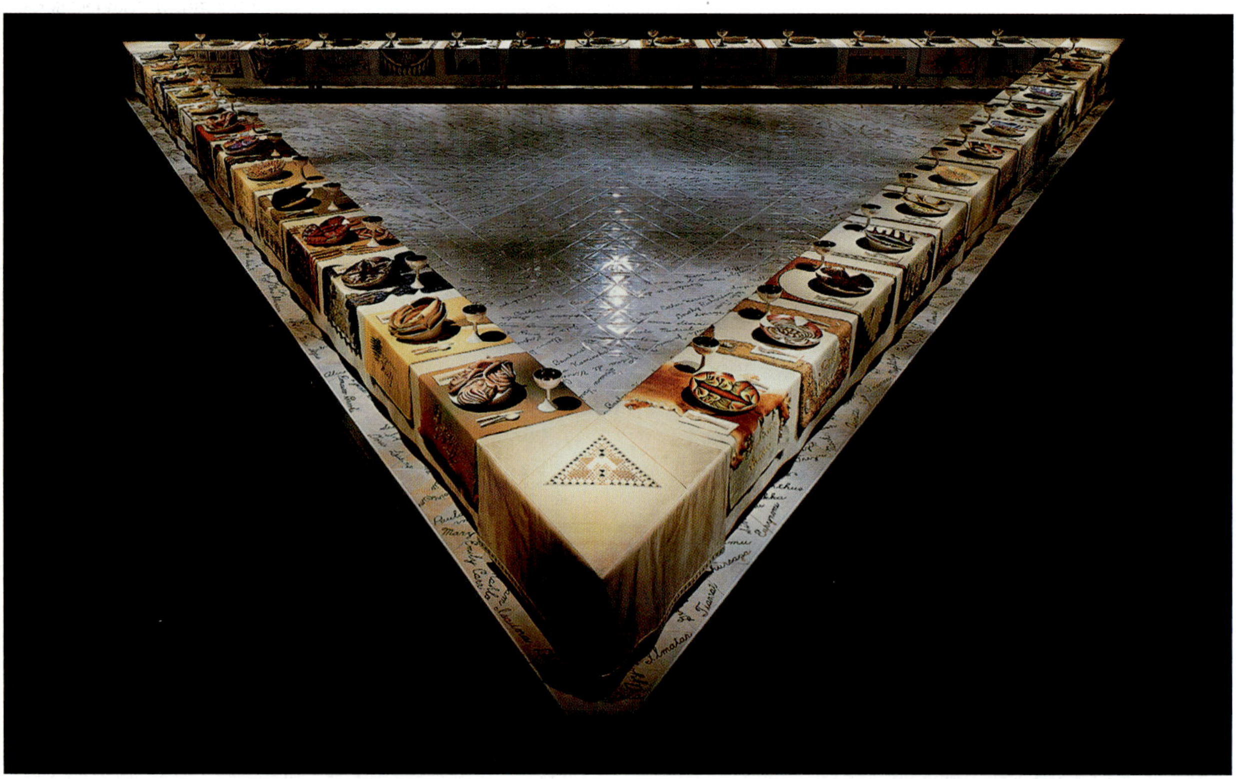

20–24 Judy Chicago. *The Dinner Party*. 1974–1979. Overall installation view. White tile floor inscribed in gold with 999 women's names; triangular table with painted porcelain, sculpted porcelain plates, and needlework. Mixed media, 48' × 42' × 3' (14.6 × 12.8 × 1 m)
COLLECTION OF THE BROOKLYN MUSEUM OF ART. GIFT OF THE ELIZABETH A. SACKLER FOUNDATION THROUGH THE FLOWER, NM

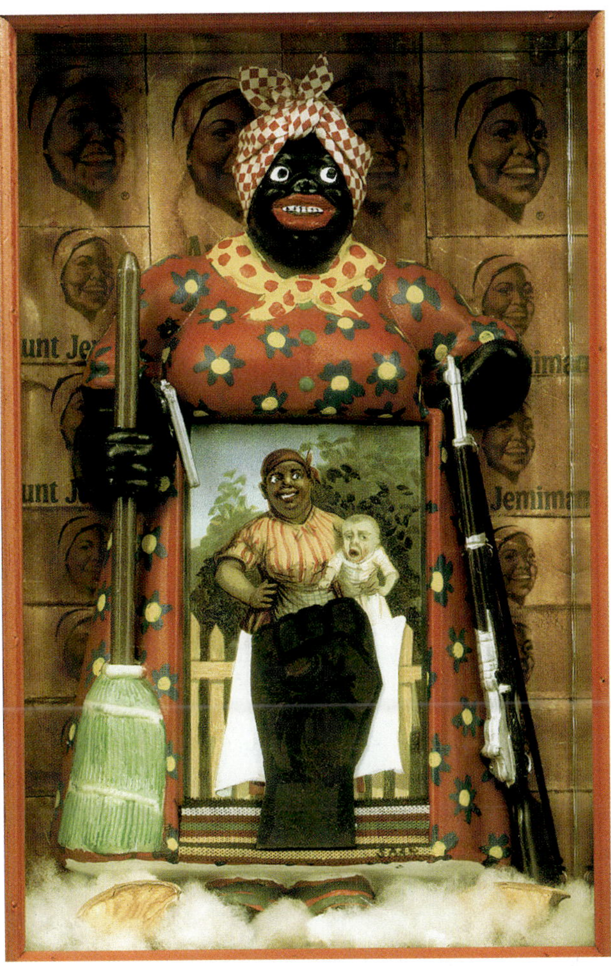

20–25 Betye Saar. ***The Liberation of Aunt Jemima.*** 1972. Mixed media, 8" × 11¾" × 2¾" (20.3 × 29.8 × 6.9 cm). University Art Museum, University of California, Berkeley
PURCHASED WITH THE AID OF FUNDS FROM THE NATIONAL ENDOWMENT OF ARTS (SELECTED BY THE COMMITTEE FOR THE ACQUISITION OF AFRO-AMERICAN ART)

The Dinner Party is composed of a large, triangular table, each side stretching 48 feet, which rests on a triangular platform covered with 2,300 triangular porcelain tiles. Chicago saw the equilateral triangle as a symbol of the equalized world sought by feminism and also identified it as one of the earliest symbols of the feminine. The porcelain "Heritage Floor" bears the names of 999 notable women from myth, legend, and history. Along each side of the table, 13 place settings each represent a famous woman. The 39 women thus honored include some that we have encountered in this book, including the ancient Egyptian pharaoh Hatshepsut (see fig. 3–13); the French poet and scholar Christine de Pizan (see fig. Intro–23); the Renaissance art patron Isabella d'Este (see fig. 13–19); and the painters Artemesia Gentileschi (see fig. 14–11) and Georgia O'Keeffe (see fig. Intro–4). Chicago emphasized china painting and needlework in *The Dinner Party* to celebrate craft media traditionally practiced by women and to argue for their consideration as "high" art forms equivalent to easel-painting and sculpture. This argument complemented her larger aim of raising awareness of the many contributions women have made to history, thereby fostering women's empowerment in the present.

Los Angeles-based artist Betye Saar (born 1926) only achieved widespread recognition with the arrival of the feminist movement, although she had been making assemblages for years, showing a political militancy rare in postwar American art. Her best-known work, *The Liberation of Aunt Jemima* (fig. **20–25**) is a box constructed of found objects. It appropriates the derogatory stereotype of the cheerfully servile "mammy" and transforms it into an icon of militant black feminist power. Aunt Jemima holds a broom and pistol in one hand and a rifle in the other and stands behind a large clenched fist, a symbol of "black power." Saar's armed Jemima liberates herself not only from racial oppression but also from traditional gender roles that had long relegated black women to subservient positions as domestic servants.

In the early 1970s, African-American artist Faith Ringgold (born 1930) began to paint on soft fabrics rather than stretched canvases and to frame her images with decorative quilted borders. In 1977, Ringgold began writing an autobiography, and, unable immediately to find a publisher, she decided to tell her story on quilts. Ringgold's story quilts are always narrated by women, and usually address themes related to women's lives. A splendid example is *Tar Beach* (fig. **20–26**) based on the artist's childhood memories of growing up in Harlem. The "Tar Beach" of the title is the roof of the apartment building where Ringgold's family slept on hot summer nights. The little girl, Cassie, describes sleeping on Tar Beach as a magical experience. She dreams that she can fly and that she owns everything she passes over. Ringgold's colorful painting in the center of the quilt shows Cassie and her brother lying on a blanket at the lower right while their parents and two neighbors play cards at

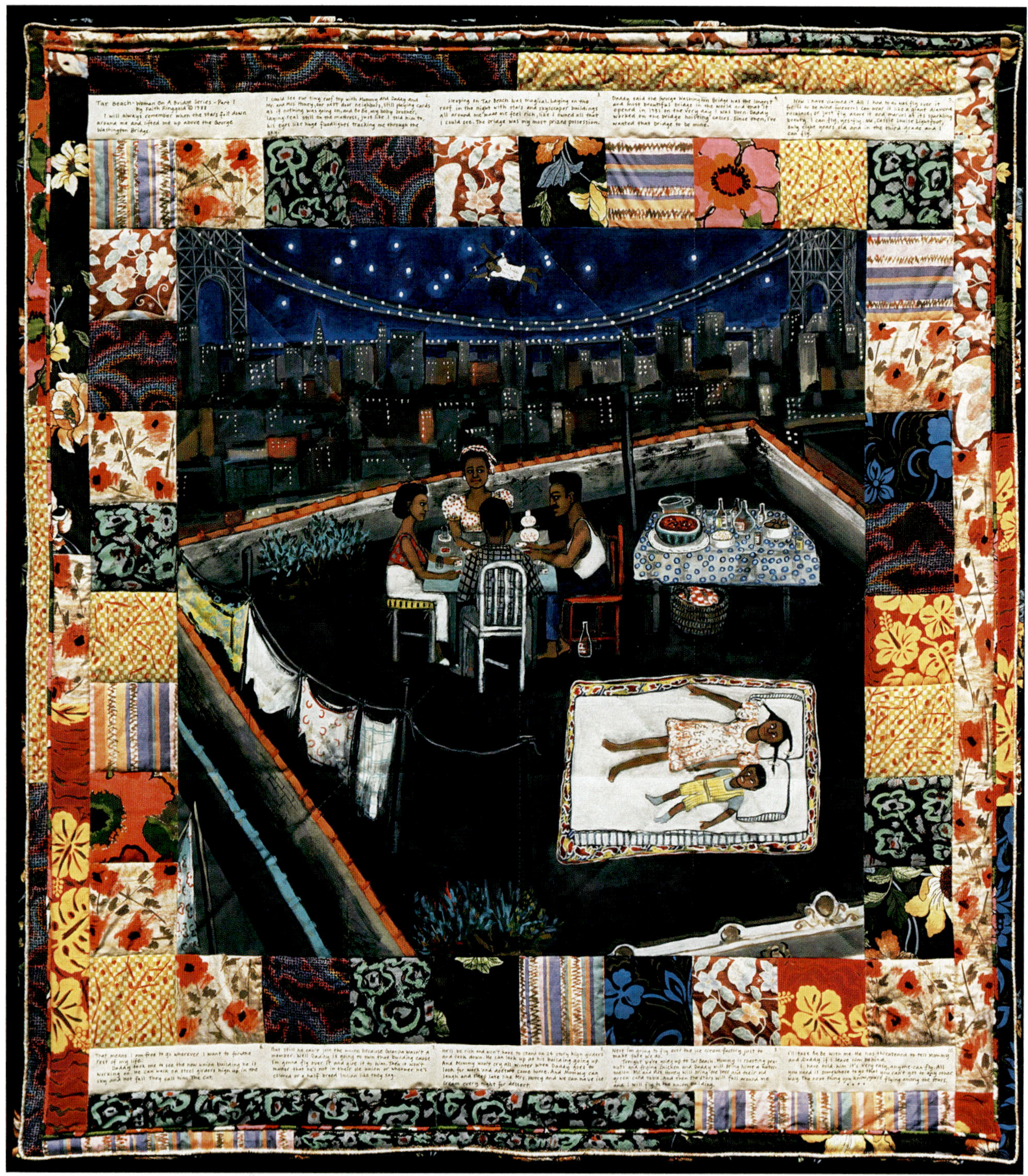

20–26 Faith Ringgold. ***Tar Beach*** (Part I from the *Woman on a Bridge* series). 1988. Acrylic on canvas, bordered with printed, painted, quilted, and pieced cloth, 74⅝" × 68½" (190.5 × 174 cm). Solomon R. Guggenheim Museum, New York
PHOTO © FAITH RINGGOLD

a table at center. Directly above the adults appears a second Cassie, flying over the George Washington Bridge against a star-dotted sky. Cassie's childish fantasy of achieving the impossible is charming but also delivers a serious message by reminding viewers of the real social and economic limitations that African-Americans have faced throughout American history.

In 1977, Cindy Sherman (born 1954), began work on a series of black-and-white photographs of herself in various assumed roles, modeled on publicity stills from B-movies of the 1940s and 1950s. In one of these photographs, Sherman plays a perplexed young innocent recently arrived in the big city, its buildings looming threateningly behind her (fig. **20–27**). The image suggests a host of

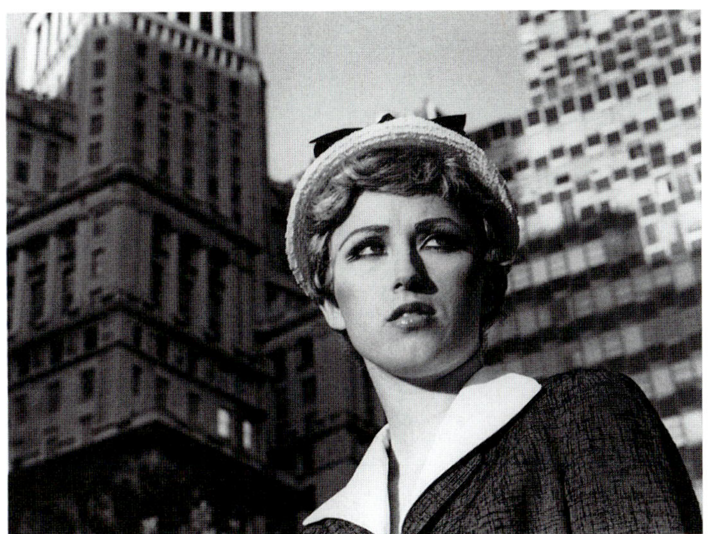

20–27 Cindy Sherman. ***Untitled Film Still.*** 1978. Black-and-white photograph, 8" × 10" (20.3 × 25.4 cm)
COURTESY CINDY SHERMAN AND METRO PICTURES, NEW YORK

films in which a similar character is overwhelmed by dangerous forces and is rescued by a hero. These works examine the roles that popular culture assigns to women, and Sherman demonstrates that she knows them well and plays them willingly. Perhaps she is saying that since her personality is the sum of all the movies she has seen, she does not know where the real Cindy Sherman starts and the movie persona stops.

Postmodernism

Many Minimalists, inspired by the theories of art critics such as Greenberg (see "Clement Greenberg and the Idea of the Mainstream," page 572), believe that art represents a pure realm outside ordinary existence and that the history of art has followed a coherent, progressive trajectory culminating in Modernism. To most of the artists who came after them, by contrast, the concepts of artistic purity and the mainstream seemed naïve. Critics and artists recognized that they lived in the midst of an age of artistic **pluralism** that accepted and fostered a simultaneous variety of artistic trends and styles.

The generation that grew to maturity around 1970 had been the first to accept pluralism as a manifestation of their culturally heterogeneous age. The decline of Modernism was neither uniform nor sudden. Its gradual erosion occurred over a long period and was the result of many individual transformations. The variety of approaches to art that emerged at the end of the twentieth century have been characterized by the umbrella term "postmodernism." Although there is no consensus on precisely what "postmodern" means, it involves rejection of the concept of the mainstream and embraces artistic pluralism.

The Persistence of Modernism

Despite declarations of the death of Modernism by Postmodern artists and critics, many artists remained committed to its central tenets: formal innovation and personal expression. Elizabeth Murray (born 1940), is just such a late Modernist painter, whose artistic breakthrough came in the late 1970s, when she began to work on irregularly shaped canvases. *Chaotic Lip* (fig. **20–28**) is an enormous, organically shaped canvas with rounded lobes that radiate out in several directions. Murray's bold and colorful style is inspired simultaneously by "high" Modernist art and "low" popular culture, combining Cubist-style fragmentation, Fauvist color, Surrealist biomorphism, and the gestural brushstrokes of Abstract Expressionism, while also drawing inspiration from cartoons and animated films.

The influence of American and European Modernism spread around the world during the second half of the twentieth century. In Australia, for example, Aborigine artists adopted canvas and acrylic paint for rendering traditional imagery once associated with more ephemeral media such as bark, sand, and body painting. In 1971, native experts in sand painting—an ancient ritual art form

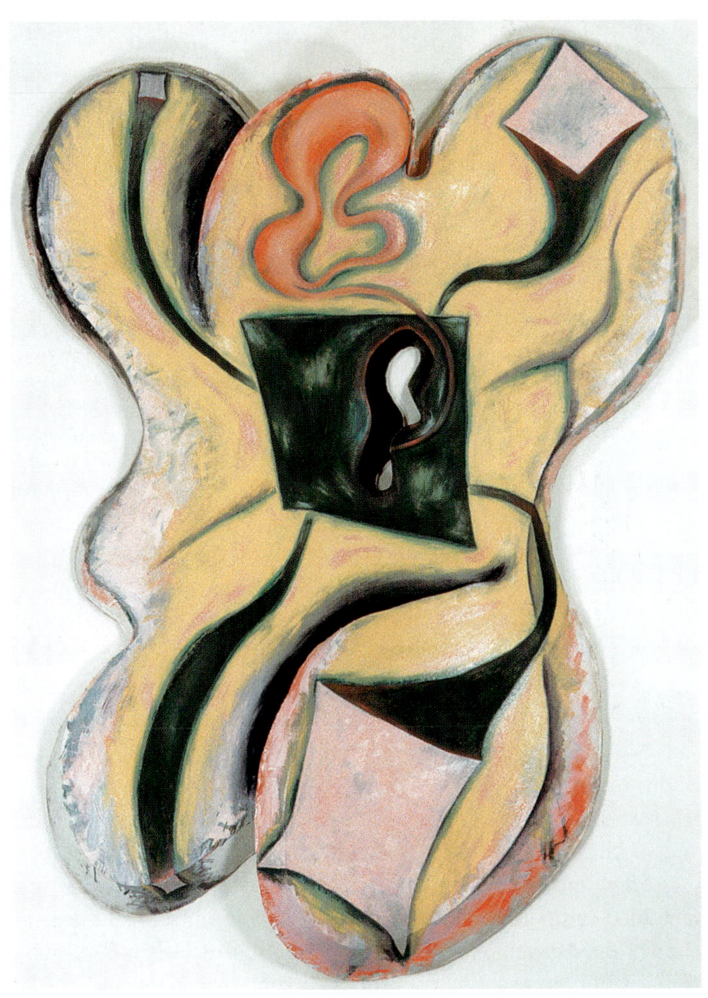

20–28 Elizabeth Murray. ***Chaotic Lip.*** 1986. Oil on canvas, 9' 9½" × 7' 2½" × 1' (3.01 × 2.22 × 0.31 m). Spencer Museum of Art, The University of Kansas, Lawrence

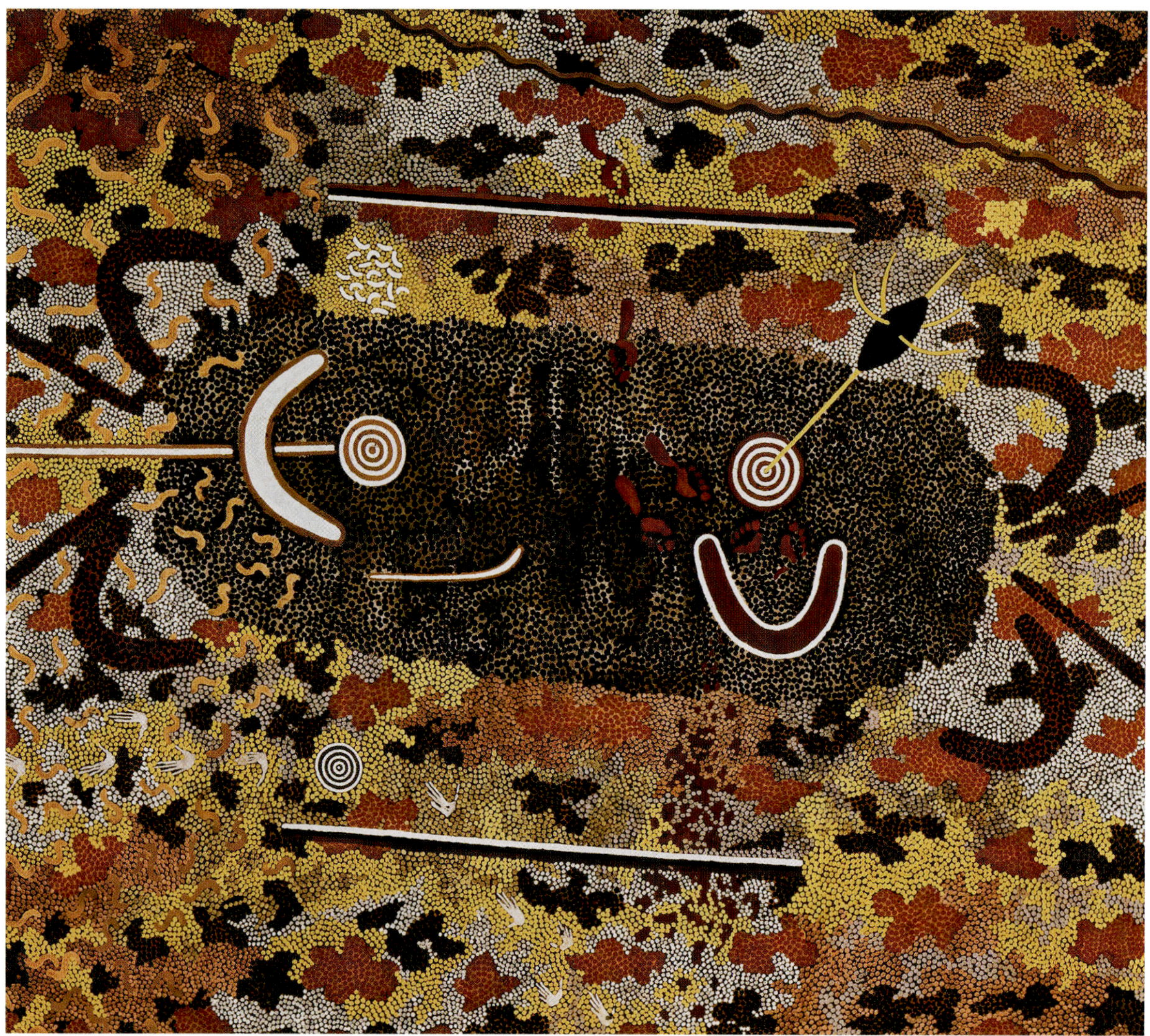

20–29 Clifford Possum Tjapaltjarri. ***Man's Love Story.*** 1978. Papunya, Northern Territory, Australia. Synthetic polymer paint on canvas, 6' 11¾" × 8' 4¼" (2.13 × 2.55 m). Art Gallery of South Australia, Adelaide
VISUAL ARTS BOARD OF THE AUSTRALIA COUNCIL CONTEMPORARY ART PURCHASE GRANT, 1980

that involves creating large colored designs on the ground—formed an art cooperative in Papunya, in central Australia, and painting soon became an economic mainstay in the region. After a 1988 exhibition of his paintings, Clifford Possum Tjapaltjarri (c. 1932–2002), one of the cooperative's founders, gained an international reputation. Following the traditions of sand painting, he worked with his canvas on the floor, painting traditional patterns, principally in the traditional red and yellow color. His work may at first seem nonrepresentational, but it tells stories rooted in complex myths, traditions, and social rules.

Man's Love Story (fig. **20–29**) involves two mythical ancestors. One man came to Papunya in search of honey ants. He appears as the white U-shape on the left, seated in front of a water hole with an ants' nest, represented by concentric circles. His digging stick lies to his right and white sugary leaves lie to his left. The straight white "journey line" represents his trek from the west. A second man, represented by the brown-and-white U-shaped form, came from the north, leaving footprints, and sat down by another water hole nearby. He began to spin a string made of human hair on a spindle (the form leaning toward the upper right of the painting), but he thought about the woman he loved, who belonged to a kinship group into which he could not marry. Distracted by her approach, he let his hair string blow away (represented by the brown flecks below him) and so lost all his work. Then four women (the dark, dotted U-shapes) whom he could marry came with their digging sticks and sat around the two men. A rich food supply surrounds them—wiggly shapes representing caterpillars and dots representing seeds. Thus, what seems to be a richly decorative surface pattern is in fact a visual record of the ephemeral impressions left on the earth by the figures—their tracks, direction lines, and the U-shaped marks they left when sitting. Though it seems Modernist to us in appearance and technique, Tjapaltjarri's painting hardly conforms to the focus solely on artistic forms and structure that had characterized the Modernist mainstream.

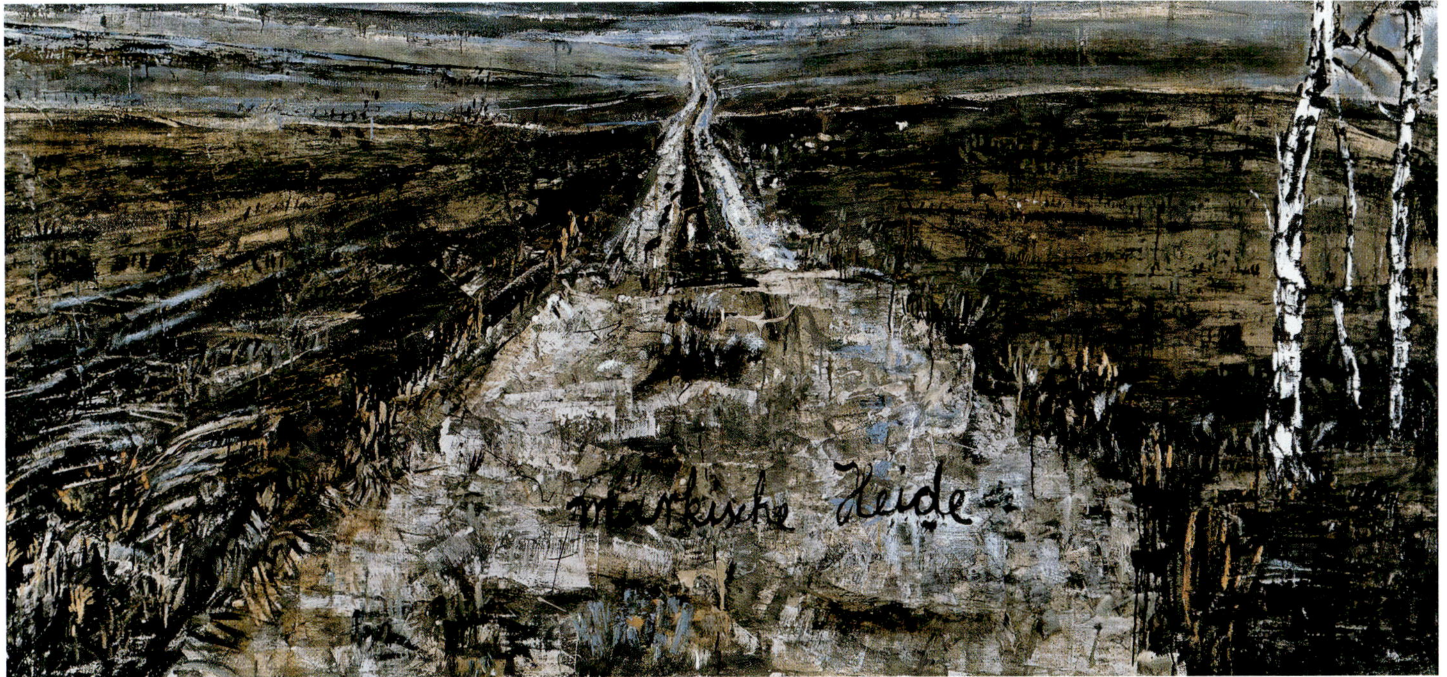

20–30 Anselm Kiefer. ***Märkische Heide.*** 1974. Oil, acrylic, and shellac on burlap, 3' 10½" × 8' 4" (1.18 × 2.54 m). Stedelijk Van Abbemuseum, Eindhoven, the Netherlands

Neo-Expressionism

Much contemporary art from around 1970 to the present, however, implicitly acknowledges the exhaustion of the old Modernist promotion of innovation—and what it implied about the "progressive" course of art history—by the revival of older styles. The names assigned to these styles often begin with the prefix "neo," denoting a new form of something that already exists, a practice we have already encountered in the eighteenth-century with "Neoclassicism." Leading New York art galleries in 1980 signaled the emergence of Neo-Expressionism, the first of these revival styles. About the same time, various European artists working in a similar vein gained critical recognition in the United States. One is German artist Anselm Kiefer (born 1945). In his work, Kiefer, who was born in the last weeks of World War II, revisits his country's Nazi past and the events of the war. The burned and barren landscape in *Märkische Heide* (The Heath of the Brandenburg March) (fig. **20–30**) evokes the ravages of war experienced in the Brandenburg area, near Berlin. The road that lures us into the landscape—a standard device used since the seventeenth century—invites us into the region's dark past. Kiefer's works compel viewers to ponder troubling historical and social realities, "in order," he said, "to understand the madness."

DERRIDA AND DECONSTRUCTION

Many artists since the 1980s have had an interest in the theory of Deconstruction developed by the French philosopher Jacques Derrida (1930–2004). Concerned mostly with the analysis of verbal texts, Deconstruction holds that no text possesses a single, intrinsic meaning, but rather its meaning is always "intertextual"—a product of its relationship to other texts—and is always "decentered," or "dispersed" along an infinite chain of linguistic signs whose meanings are themselves unstable. Deconstructivist art and architecture is, consequently, often "intervisual" in its use of design elements drawn from other traditions, including Modernism, and "decentered" in its denial of unified and stable meanings.

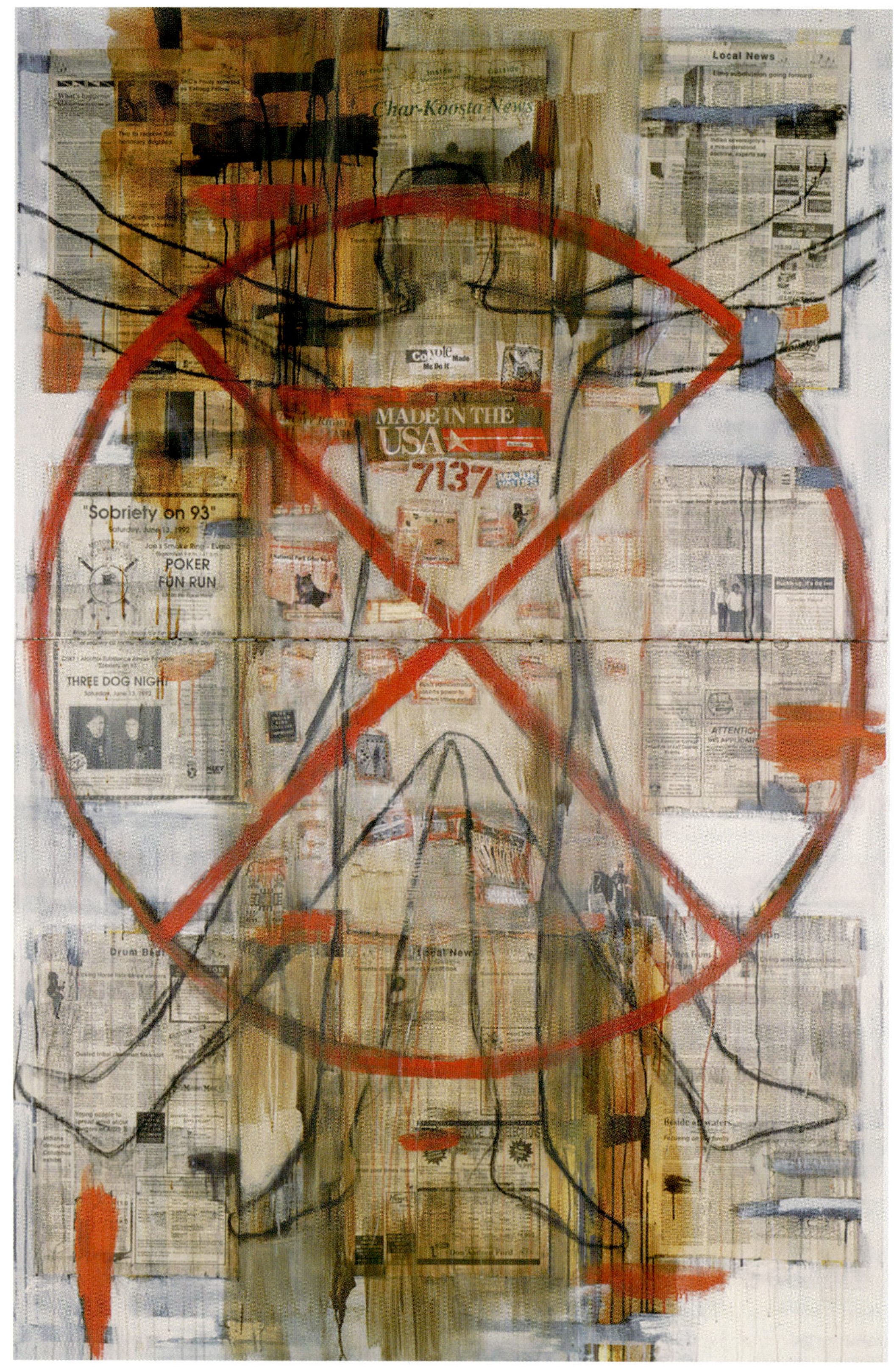

20–31 Jaune Quick-to-See Smith. ***The Red Mean: Self Portrait.*** 1992. Acrylic, newspaper collage, and mixed media on canvas, 90" × 60" (228.6 × 154.4 cm). Smith College Museum of Art, Northampton, Massachusetts
PARTIAL GIFT FROM JANET WRIGHT KETCHAM, CLASS OF 1953 AND PART PURCHASE FROM THE JANET WRIGHT KETCHAM, CLASS OF 1953, AQUISITION FUND

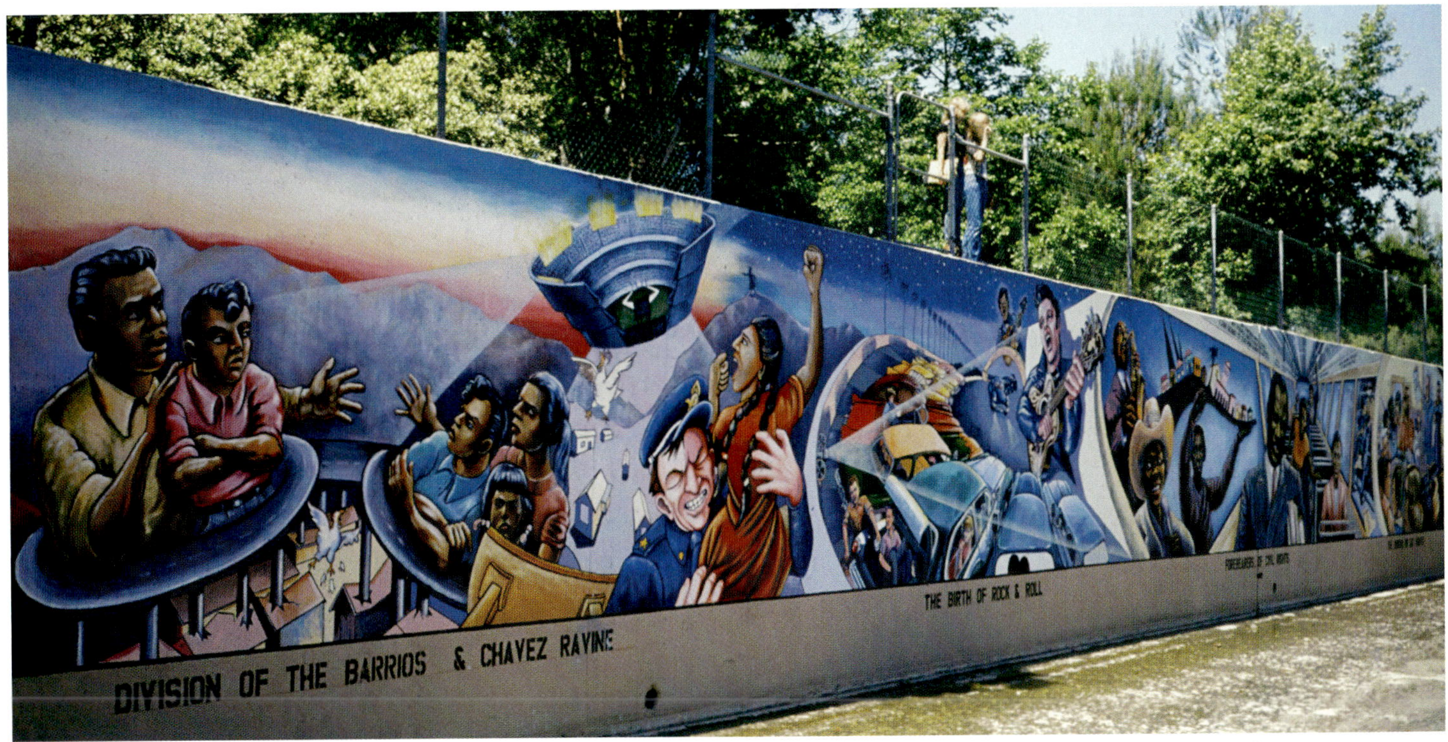

20–32 Judith F. Baca. Detail of *The Great Wall of Los Angeles*, showing the "Division of the Barrios and Chavez Ravine" from the section depicting the 1950s. San Fernando Valley Tujunga Wash, Van Nuys, California. Begun 1976 (the section in the detail painted summer 1983). Acrylic on cast concrete, Height 13' (4 m), overall length of mural 2,400' (731 m). © SPARC

Social Commentary and Ethnic Heritage

As a major form of communication, the visual arts have always been used to drive home ideas, and Postmodern artists often use their art to underline their own convictions and explore their own heritage. Roger Shimomura (born 1939) turned painting and prints into personal political statements in a series based on his grandmother's diary. His 1978 painting *Diary* (see fig. Intro–17), is based on his grandmother's account of the family's experience in an internment camp in Idaho, where U.S. citizens of Japanese ancestry were forcibly confined during World War II. Shimomura shows his grandmother writing while he (the toddler) and his mother stand by an open door that reveals a barbed-wire-enclosed compound. Shimomura melded two formal traditions—the Japanese art of color woodblock prints (see figs. Intro–8, 9–26, and 9–27) and American Pop art—into a personal style that expresses his own dual heritage at the same time as it presents a nuanced social commentary.

Jaune Quick-to-See Smith, who was born in 1940 on the Confederated Salish and Kootenai Nation Reservation in western Montana, also combines traditional and contemporary forms to convey political and social messages. Pasted across the chest of a human figure outlined at the center of *The Red Mean: Self Portrait* (fig. **20–31**) is a bumper sticker that reads "Made in the U.S.A." The background is a collage of Native American tribal newspapers, inviting viewers to do some reading. Thus even if the central figure itself quotes Leonardo da Vinci's *Vitruvian Man* (see fig. 13–3), the message here is autobiographical. Leonardo inscribed his human form within a geometric framework to emphasize its perfection, while Smith places her silhouette under the red *X* that signifies radiation. She alludes both to the uranium mines found on some Indian reservations and also to the lamentable fact that many have become temporary repositories for nuclear waste. In her self-portrait her ethnic identity is juxtaposed with commentaries on reservation life and the history of Western art. As Gerrit Henry wrote in *Art in America* (November 2001), Smith "looks at things Native and national through bifocals of the old and the new, the sacred and the profane, the divine and the witty."

Chicana artist Judith F. Baca (born 1946) followed Postmodern revivalist tendencies when she emulated the style of the Mexican mural movement of the early twentieth century (see fig. 19–40) to recount from a new perspective the history of California (fig. **20–32**). The resulting *Great Wall of Lost Angeles* extends almost 2,500 feet along a flood drainage canal, making it the world's longest mural. Baca's history of California emphasizes the role of ethnic minorities, including the deportation of Mexican-Americans during the Great Depression and the internment of Japanese-American citizens during World War II, but it concludes with more positive evocations of the opportunities gained during the 1960s. Like Judy Chicago's *Dinner Party* (see fig. 20–24), Baca's *Great Wall of Los Angeles* was a collaborative effort, involving professional artists and hundreds of young people, all of whom shared its painted execution under the artist's direction.

The African American painter Kerry James Marshall (born 1955) updated the pre-Modern genre of history paintings for the

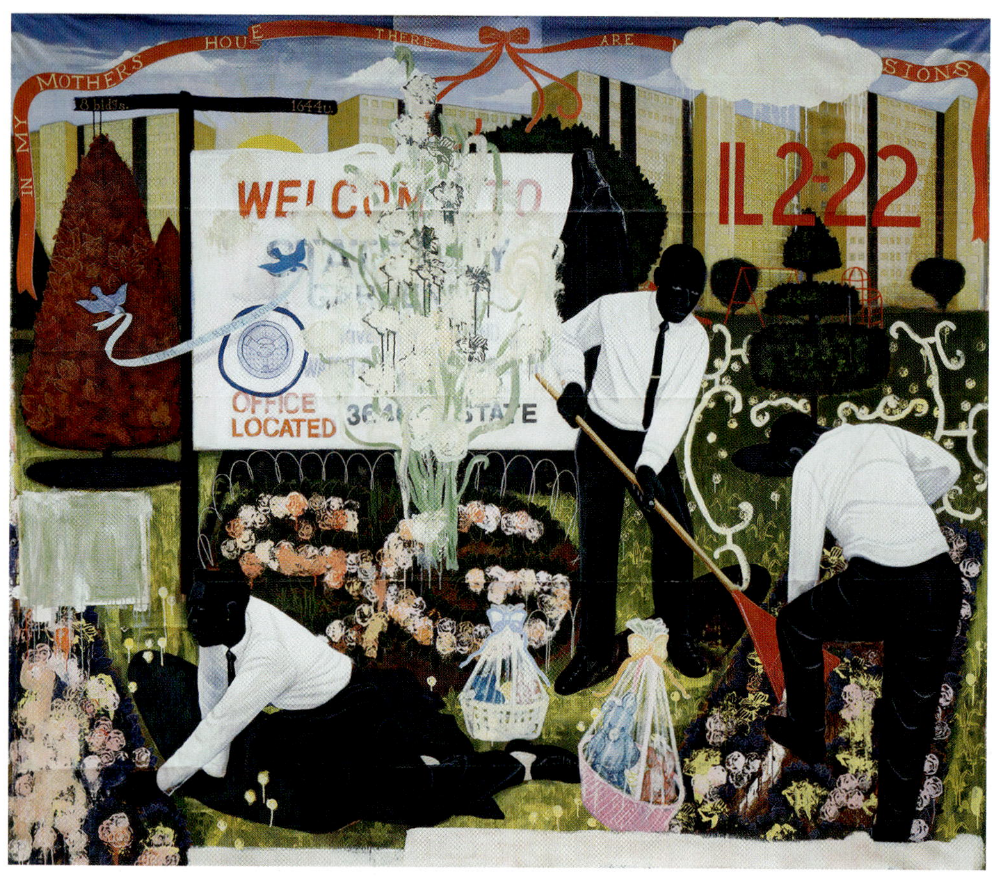

20–33 Kerry James Marshall. *Many Mansions*. 1994. Acrylic on paper mounted on canvas, 114¼" × 135⅛" (2.9 × 3.43 m). Art Institute of Chicago

contemporary era. In *Many Mansions* (fig. **20–33**), he painted a visual essay on life in public housing projects, like those in Alabama and California where he grew up. In the background we see the huge buildings of Stateway Gardens, one of America's largest housing projects, located in Chicago, and three well-dressed black men in the foreground actually plant a garden in order to help create a sense of community. They are arrayed in an off-center triangle that Marshall based on Géricault's *Raft of the "Medusa"* (see fig. 17–18). He told an interviewer from the PBS television network, "That whole genre of history painting, that grand narrative style of painting, was something that I really wanted to position my work in relation to." But overlying this weighty historical reference are touches of sentimentality, such as the red ribbon across the top with the adapted biblical quotation: "In my mother's house there are many mansions." Two bluebirds fly along at the left bearing another ribbon in their beaks. Such overtly cute features, juxtaposed with an impossibly florid garden, lend the work a sense of irony.

Shanghai-born Wenda Gu (born 1955) dedicates his art to bringing people together by creating metaphors for the mixture of races that he predicts will eventually unite humanity into "a brave new racial identity." In 1993, he began his *United Nations* series, consisting of installations made of human hair pressed or woven into bricks, carpets, and curtains. Many of his "monuments," such as *United Nations—Babel of the Millennium* (fig. **20–34**), incorporate invented scripts that, by frustrating viewers' ability to read them, "evoke the limitations of human knowledge" and help prepare them for entry into an "unknown world."

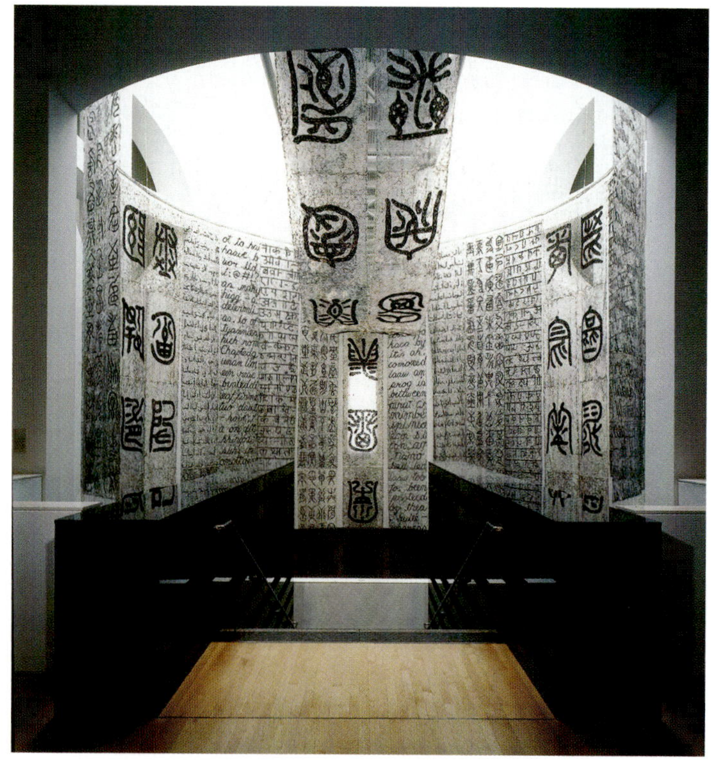

20–34 Wenda Gu. *United Nations—Babel of the Millennium*. 1999. Site-specific installation made of human hair, height 75' (22.9 m), diameter 34' (10.4 m). San Francisco Museum of Modern Art
FRACTIONAL AND PROMISED GIFT OF VIKI AND KENT LOGAN

Installation. Electronic and Video Art

The renewed realization of art's potential as an instrument of social change and the desire to make art meaningful to a larger public took on a new prominence approaching the 1990s. Artists experimented with new media like video, to connect with contemporary audiences living in a media-saturated culture. Jenny Holzer (born 1950) turned to some of advertising's more pervasive tools, including electronic signage, to reach out to people who do not usually go to galleries and museums. For example, using the Spectacolor board then in use in New York City's Times Square, she flashed a series of short, provocative messages—one-liners suited to the reading habits of Americans raised on advertising sound bites. And her use of signage as a medium emphasizes the Postmodern conviction that art consists of layered meanings that must be decoded (see "Derrida and Deconstruction," page 589).

In a spectacular installation of 1989–1990, Holzer wrapped her signboards in a continuous loop around the multilevel spiraling interior of Frank Lloyd Wright's Guggenheim Museum (fig. **20–35**). The words moved and flashed in red, green, and yellow colored lights, surrounding the visitor with Holzer's unsettling declarations ("You are a victim of the rules you live by") and disturbing commands ("Scorn Hope," "Forget Truths," and "Don't Try to Make Me Feel Nice"). The installation also included, on the ground floor and in a side gallery, spotlighted granite benches carved with more of Holzer's texts. The juxtaposition of cutting-edge technology, lights, and motion with the static, hand-carved benches, evocative of antiquity and mortality, was particularly striking.

A number of contemporary artists create installations with video, either using the video monitor itself as a visible part of their work or projecting video imagery onto walls, screens, or other surfaces. Korean-born Nam June Paik (1931–2006) was a pioneer in this medium. He proclaimed that just "as collage technique replaced oil paint, the cathode ray tube will replace the canvas." He began working with modified television sets in 1963 and bought his first video camera in 1965. Paik worked with live, recorded, and computer-generated images displayed on video monitors of varying sizes,

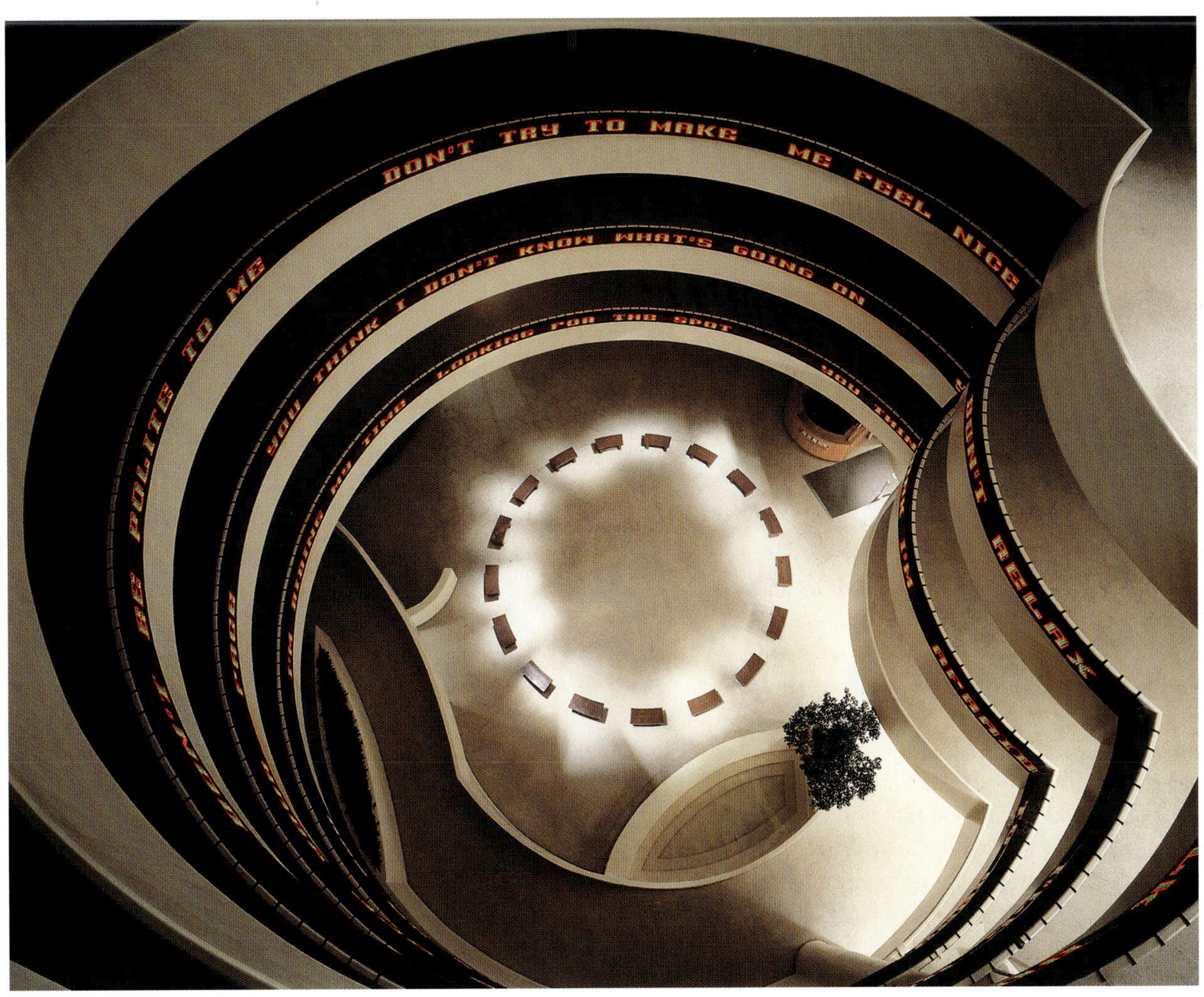

20–35 Jenny Holzer. ***Untitled (Selections from Truisms, Inflammatory Essays, The Living Series, The Survival Series, Under a Rock, Laments, and Mother and Child Text).*** Installation within the Guggenheim Museum, 1989. Extended helical tricolor LED electronic-display signboard; site-specific dimensions, 16½" × 162' × 6" (41.9 cm × 49 m × 15.2 cm)
SOLOMON R. GUGGENHEIM MUSEUM, NEW YORK (89.326). PARTIAL GIFT OF THE ARTIST, 1989

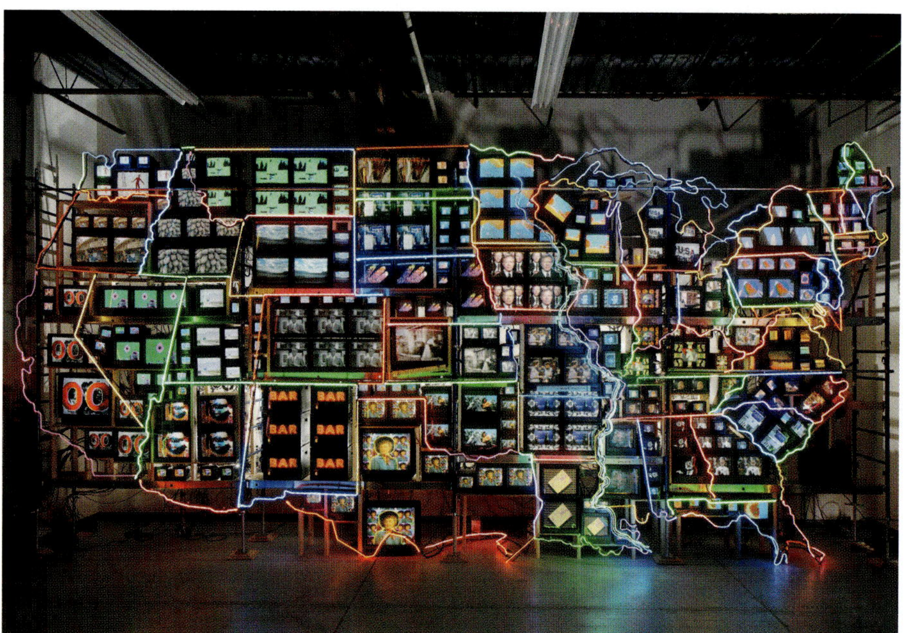

20–36 Nam June Paik. *Electronic Superhighway: Continental U.S.* 1995. 47-channel closed-circuit video installation with 313 monitors, neon, steel structure, color, and sound, approx. 15' × 32' (4.57 × 9.75 m). The Smithsonian American Art Museum, Washington, D.C.
GIFT OF THE ARTIST

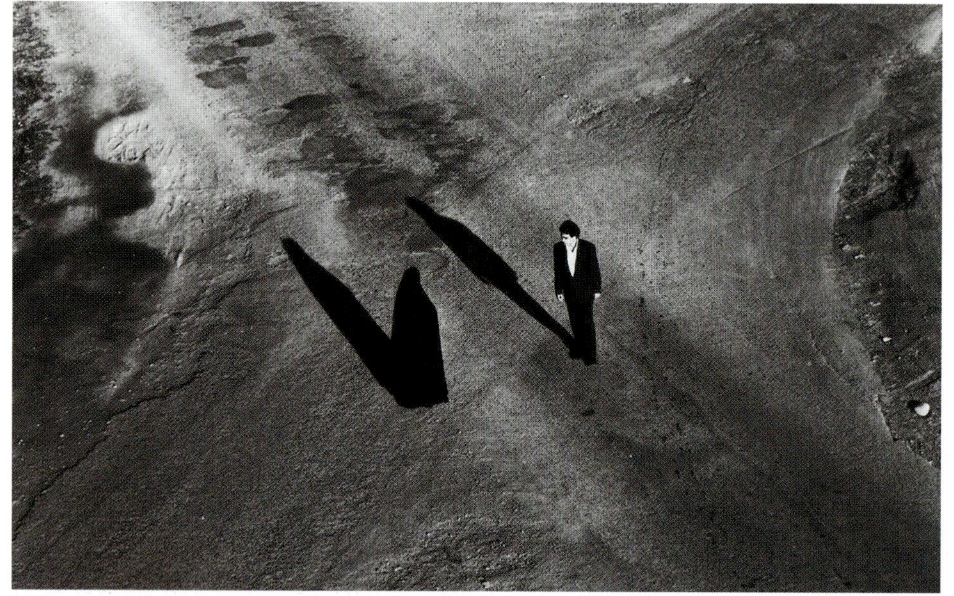

20–37 Shirin Neshat. Production still from *Fervor*. 2000. Video/sound installation with two channels of black-and-white video projected onto two screens, 10 minutes
COURTESY BARBARA GLADSTONE GALLERY

which he often combines into sculptural ensembles such as *Electronic Superhighway: Continental U.S.* (fig. **20–36**). Stretching across an entire wall, the work features a map of the continental United States (side walls featured Alaska and Hawaii) outlined in neon and backed by video monitors perpetually flashing with color and movement and accompanied by sound. The monitors within the borders of each state displayed images reflecting that state's culture and history, both past and present. New York State was the only exception. There monitors displayed live, closed-circuit images of the gallery visitors, placing them in the artwork and transforming them from passive spectators into active participants.

The videos of Shirin Neshat (born 1957) address universal themes within the specific context of modern-day Islamic society. Neshat was studying art in California when revolution shook her native Iran in 1979, and when she returned to Iran in 1990, she was shocked by the extent to which fundamentalist Islamic rule had transformed her homeland, particularly the requirement that women appear in public veiled from head to toe in the traditional *chador*. Upon her return to the United States, Neshat began using the black *chador* as the central motif of her work.

In the late 1990s, Neshat began to make visually arresting and poetically structured videos that subtly critique aspects of Islamic society. *Fervor*, in Neshat's words, "focuses on taboos regarding sexuality and desire" that "inhibit the contact between the sexes in public. A simple gaze, for instance, is considered a sin." Composed of two separate video channels projected simultaneously on two large, adjoining screens, *Fervor* presents a simple narrative. In the opening scene, a black-veiled woman and jacket-wearing man, viewed from

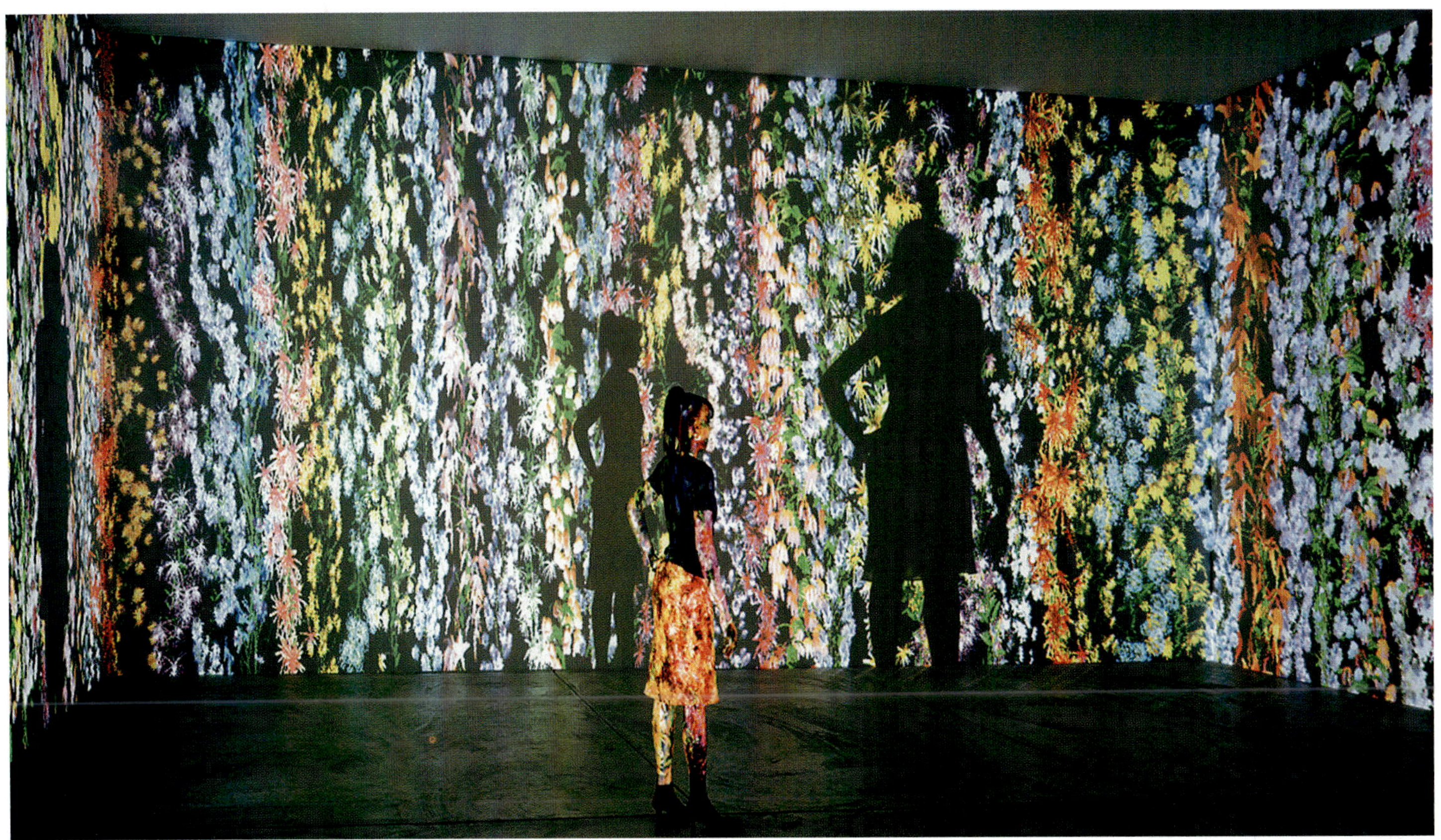

20–38 Jennifer Steinkamp. ***Jimmy Carter***. 2002. Site-specific computer-generated light projection installation with 3 projectors and 3 Mac G3 computers, 35' × 18' × 14' (10.6 × 5.5 × 4.3 m)
COURTESY ACME

above (fig. **20–37**), cross paths in an open landscape. The viewer senses a sexual attraction between them, but they go their separate ways. Later, they meet again while entering a public ceremony where men and women are divided by a large curtain. On a stage before the audience, a bearded man fervently recounts a story adapted from the Qur'an about Yusuf (Joseph in the Hebrew Bible) and Zolokha, who attempts to seduce Yusuf (her husband's slave), and when he resists her advances, falsely accuses him of having seduced her. The speaker passionately urges his listeners to resist such sinful desires. As the audience begins to chant in response to his exhortations, the male and female protagonists grow increasingly anxious, and the woman eventually rises and exits hurriedly. *Fervor* ends with the man and woman passing each other in an alley, again without verbal or physical contact. Neshat concentrates on dualisms and divisions—between East and West, male and female, individual desire and collective law.

The rapid development of computers in recent decades has provided artists with increasingly powerful tools. A rich creative alternative that soon developed was the digitization of scanned drawings, photographs, and video images, the tones of which were broken down into individual units (pixels) and the lines of which were translated into sine curves. These elements, rendered as sets of digits, could then be manipulated by the computer to create digital art. Jennifer Steinkamp's (born 1958) work *Jimmy Carter* (fig. **20–38**) is an impressive example. Thousands of multicolored flowers are projected in constant movement, destabilizing the walls, dematerializing the space, and suspending viewers between the real and the imagined. She named the piece to honor a man whose selfless and generous leadership she finds increasingly rare in the contemporary world.

New Ideas in Traditional Materials

Only since the Renaissance has there existed such a strict distinction between the so-called "high" or "fine" arts—architecture, sculpture, painting, prints, and, more recently, photography—and the so-called "minor" or "decorative" arts such as ceramics, textiles, glass, metalwork, furniture, and jewelry, which typically serve either a practical or an ornamental function. In the postwar decades of the twentieth century, however, a number of artists took up an initiative begun during the nineteenth-century Arts and Crafts movement (see fig. 18–8) to push the so-called crafts toward acceptance as "high" art. Ceramics, wood, and glass became media for the production of sculpture.

A major innovator in clay was the Montana-born Peter Voulkos (1924–2002), who came under the influence of de Kooning and other gestural painters in 1953. The radical American break from European and Asian traditions, sometimes called the "clay revolution," began with the ruggedly sculptural ceramic works Voulkos produced in the mid-1950s. By the late 1950s Voulkos had abandoned the pot form altogether and was making large ceramic works

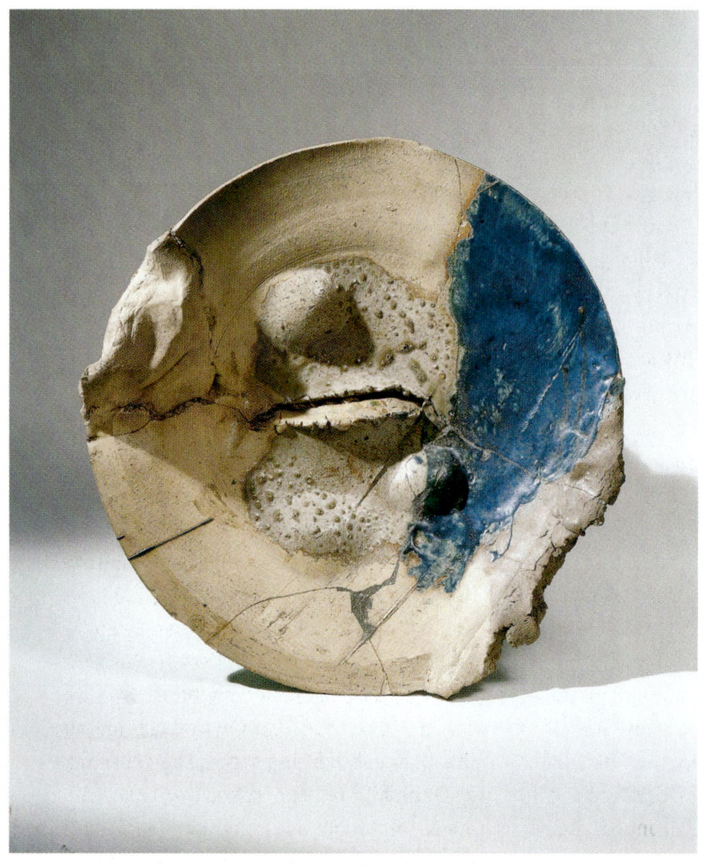

20–39 Peter Voulkos. ***Untitled Plate.*** 1962. Gas-fired stoneware with glaze, diameter 16¼" (41.3 cm). The Oakland Museum of California
GIFT OF THE ART GUILD OF TKE OAKLAND MUSEUM ASSOCIATION (62.87.4)

spontaneously assembled from numerous wheel-thrown and slab-built elements, their surfaces often covered with bright, freely applied glazes or epoxy paint. In the early 1960s, Voulkos returned to traditional ceramic forms but rendered them nonfunctional by tearing, gouging, and piercing them in the gestural fashion derived from Abstract Expressionism (fig. **20–39**).

A comparable revolution in using glass as a "high" art medium was initiated by Harvey Littleton (born 1922), who in 1963, established America's first studio program in glass at the University of Wisconsin. Other glass programs soon sprang up around the country, many of them led by Littleton's former students, including Dale Chihuly (born 1941) who established the famous Pilchuck Glass School in Seattle in 1971. Chihuly has become well known for glass sculptures (see fig. Intro–19) that draw on the natural forms of plants and sea life. Some are small enough to hold in the hand, but occasionally they cover entire ceilings or hang from them as massive chandeliers.

As with ceramics and glass, artists' use of traditional woodworking techniques also broke down barriers between decorative and fine arts. Martin Puryear (b. 1941) is a contemporary sculptor whose medium happens to be wood. Perhaps it was an early interest in biology that shaped Puryear's mature aesthetic, but his skills as a wood sculptor was certainly shaped by his experiences working with local carpenters as a Peace Corps volunteer in Sierra Leone and subsequently with cabinet makers in Sweden. His *Plenty's Boast* (fig. **20–40**), while hardly representational, suggests any number of things, including a strange sea creature or a fantastic musical instrument. Perhaps the most obvious reference is to the horn of plenty evoked in the sculpture's title. But the cone is empty, implying an

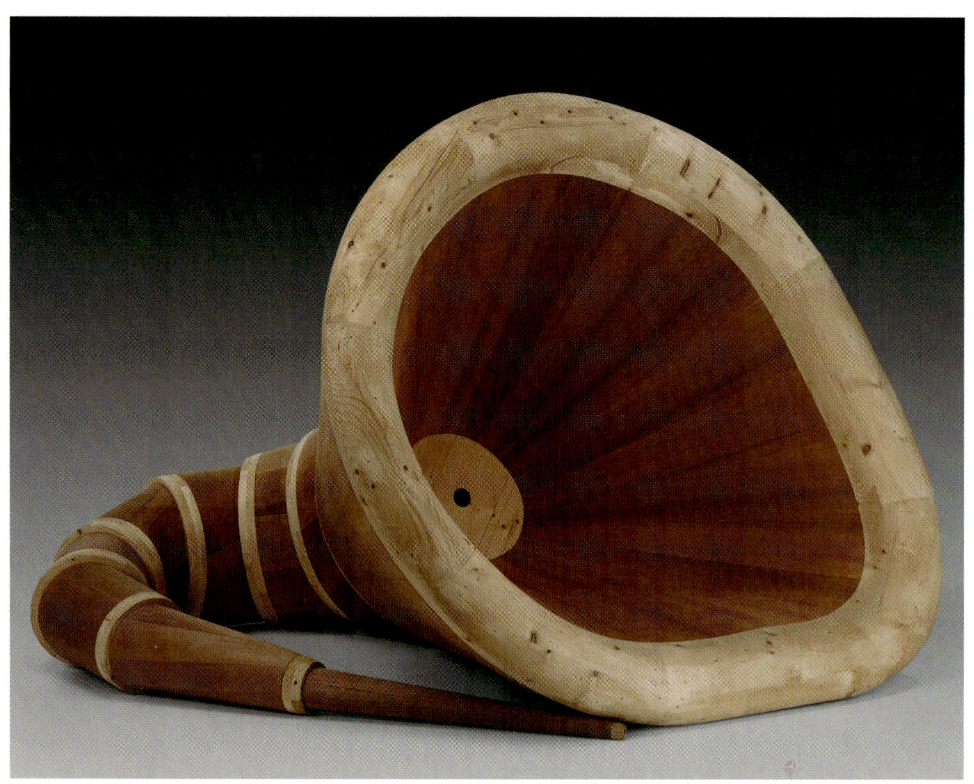

20–40 Martin Puryear. ***Plenty's Boast.*** 1994–1995. Red cedar and pine, 68" × 83" × 118" (1.73 × 2.11 × 3 m) The Nelson-Atkins Museum of Art, Kansas City, Missouri
PURCHASE OF THE RENÉE C. CROWELL TRUST (F95-16A-C)
PHOTO: ROBERT NEWCOMBE

CRITICAL THEORY

Since the ancient Greek Polykleitos wrote his canon (see page 126), theories of art and the creative process have proliferated. Leon Alberti (1404–1472) wrote on art and architecture in the Renaissance (see page 321), and Roger de Piles (1635–1709) established criteria for judging the masters in the seventeenth century (see page 409). Heinrich Wölfflin (1864–1945) called his binary formulation for distinguishing representational modes in Classic and Baroque art *Principles of Art History*, and in the mid-twentieth century Erwin Panofsky (1892–1968) sought the symbolic and cultural understanding of images through iconography and iconology. But these theorists maintained a close relationship between critical assessment and the works of art themselves, between artistic theory and artistic practice.

Postmodern critical theory evolved out of linguistics and literary theory. At the beginning of the twentieth century, Swiss linguist Ferdinand de Saussure (1857–1913) developed the "science of signs" (semiotics). He wrote of language and words, but by equating images with words, his theories and terminology were also employed to decode works of art, in a complex system of shifting meanings balanced between the "signifiers" and the "signified" (see fig. 20–19). Post-Structuralists—like Roland Barthes—argued that meaning lies not in the intention of the artist who creates art but in the understanding of art by those who view it (see "Appropriation and 'The Death of the Author,'" page 578). And in the theoretical position known as Deconstruction (see "Derrida and Deconstruction," page 589), developed by Jacques Derrida, meaning is suggested through pairings of opposites (light/dark, male/female) and becomes diffused, always related to other texts/ signs, which are equally fluid or "decentered."

Theorists have also looked at the social implications of art. Inspired by Marxist theory and focusing on class struggle, they have looked beneath such elite ideas as aesthetic quality, treating art as a social and economic commodity, not as the product of ineffable creative genius embodying spiritual values. Artistic patronage is sometimes seen as a vehicle of class oppression. As the arts are seen as one part of a broader "visual culture," all objects become equally useful in creating a social history of art.

Meanwhile, Sigmund Freud's theories of the irrational mind, further developed by Jacques Lacan (1901–1981), have formed the basis of psychoanalytic theories of art and its history. Feminist and gender theorists, and recently Post-colonial and Queer studies, have further extended the analysis of how the cultural politics of male-heterosexual-dominated societies and cultures have patterned the production and reception of art.

Not everyone has been happy with the impact of critical theory on Postmodern art history. Some have claimed that abandoning the traditional concept of the creative process makes the work of art seem simply "cooked up." Sculptor Michael Aurbach (born 1952) created a "machine" that he called *The Critical Theorist* (fig. **20–41**). In this playful but biting satire, the "Essence of Derrida" and the "Extract of Foucault" are cooked up in a big pot and then processed. Color and fragrance are added, and the mix goes into two stainless steel strainers ("Fact Removers") and from there into commercial condiment dispensers with freely spinning cranks (the "Spin Cycle of scholarly hype"). After passing by a meat cleaver (the "Cutting Edge") and through a teapot ("Art Evaporator") and a garbage disposal ("Object Disposal"), the product comes out on a conveyor belt as a book on critical theory. The book, however, proves to be only a wooden block. Aurbach's machine has gone to a lot of trouble creating an unreadable book.

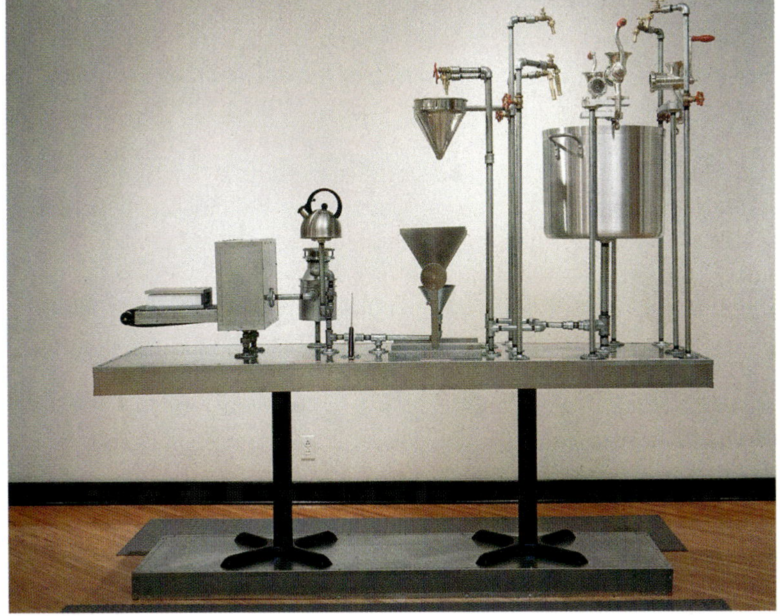

20–41 Michael Aurbach. *The Critical Theorist*. 2002. Mixed media (cooking equipment). 7½' × 6½' × 8' (2.29 × 1.98 × 2.44 m). Collection of the artist

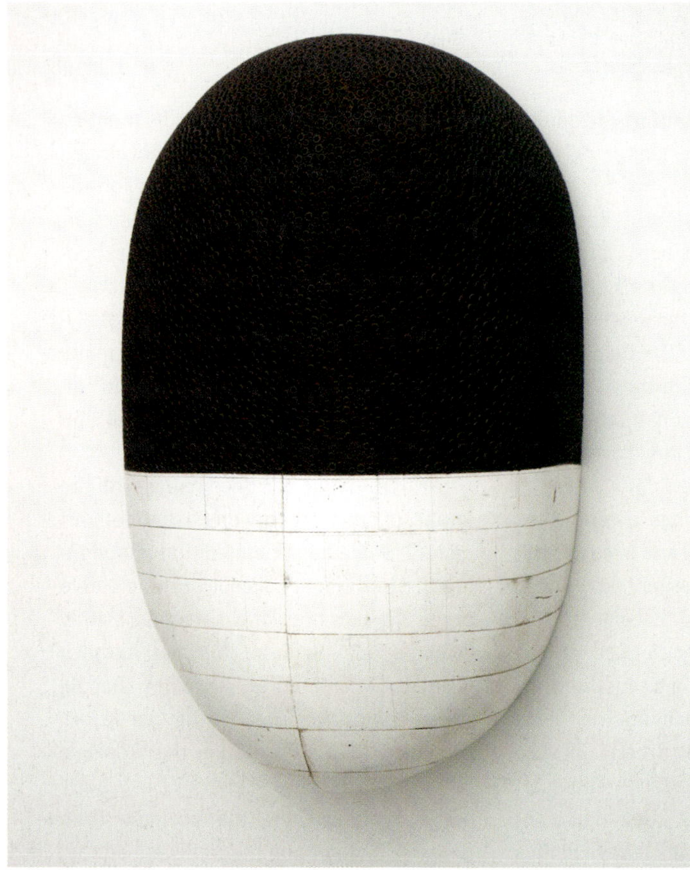

20–42 Hiroyuki Hamada. *#55*. 2005–2008. Enamel, oil, plaster, tar, and resin, over a wood and foam core, 44" × 24" × 12½" (112 × 61 × 32 cm). Collection of the artist

"empty boast"—another phrase suggested by the title. The richness of the sculpture lies not only in its multiple metaphorical references (a common Postmodern trait), but also in its superbly crafted, idiosyncratic yet elegant forms. As if clinging to his relationship to early twentieth-century Modernism, Puryear has said, "The task of any artist is to discover his own individuality at its deepest."

Japanese-born artist Hiroyuki Hamada (born 1968), who moved to the United States when he was 18, also creates highly individualized and powerfully elegant abstract forms. But his chosen medium is more complicated, and his fastidiously textured surfaces more intricate. Over a substructure of wood and foam, he applies a layer of plaster, which he refines and finishes over several years. In *#55* (fig. **20–42**), Hamada used drill bits to give the upper half of the form an intricately patterned surface, before staining it with resin and tar to add a complementary contrast in color. There is an archetypal quality to his elemental sculptural forms. They seem strange but at the same time hauntingly familiar, remaining open to a variety of viewer associations. Is this a fragment of a spacecraft, an ancient cocoon, an exotic fruit, or a barnacled buoy? Hamada prefers to leave the question of meaning open, naming his sculptures after their numerical position within a creative sequence. "A title would tell people how to interpret the work," he has said, "and I don't want that."

Postwar Architecture

The stripped-down, rectilinear industrial vocabulary pioneered by such Modernist architects as Gropius (see fig. 19–27) and Le Corbusier (see fig. 19–25) and known as the International Style dominated urban construction in much of the world after World War II (see "The International Style," page 546). Many of the finest examples were built in the United States by Bauhaus architects, including Ludwig Mies van der Rohe (1886–1969), who escaped Nazi Germany and assumed prestigious positions at American schools of architecture and design.

Whether designing housing, schools, or office buildings, Mies used the same sleek, rectiliniar system that came to signify the efficient culture of postwar capitalism. His buildings differ only in details. Because he had a large budget for the Seagram Building in New York City (fig. **20–43**), which he designed with Philip Johnson (1906–2005), he used custom-made bronze instead of standardized steel on the exterior. Mies would have preferred to leave the internal steel structure visible, but building codes required him to encase them in concrete, so the exterior bronze beams are only ornamental stand-ins for the functional girders inside. Tall, narrow windows with discreet dark glass emphasize the skyscraper's height and give it—and the Seagram Company that commissioned it—a discreet and dignified image. The clean lines and crisp design seemed to epitomize the efficiency, standardization, and impersonality that had become synonymous with the modern corporation itself, perhaps one of the reasons this particular Modernist style dominated corporate architecture after World War II.

Postmodernism manifested itself first in the work of Philadelphia architect Robert Venturi (born 1925), who rejected the abstract purity of the International Style by incorporating design elements drawn from vernacular (meaning ordinary or popular) buildings. Parodying Mies' famous aphorism "Less is more," Venturi claimed that "Less is a bore" in his pioneering 1966 book *Complexity and Contradiction in Architecture.* He argued that the problem with International Style architects was their impractical unwillingness to accept the modern city for what it is: a complex, contradictory, and heterogeneous collection of "high" and "low" architectural forms. Taking these ideas further in the book *Learning from Las Vegas* (1972), he suggested that rather than turning their backs in disdain on ordinary commercial buildings, architects should get in "the habit of looking nonjudgmentally" at them. "Main Street is almost all right," Venturi observed.

While writing *Complexity and Contradiction in Architecture,* Venturi designed a house for his mother (fig. **20–44**) that put many of his new ideas into practice. The building is both simple and complex. The shape of the façade returns to the archetypal "house" shape that Modernists (see figs. 19–23 and 19–25) had rejected because of its clichéd historical associations. Venturi's vocabulary of triangles and squares is also elementary, but the shapes are arranged in a playful asymmetry that skews the staid harmonies of Modernist design. The rounded moldings over the door have no structural function, a purely decorative flourish that would be heretical in the strict tenets of the International Style. But the most disruptive element of the façade is the deep cleavage over the door, which

20–43 Ludwig Mies van der Rohe and Philip Johnson. Seagram Building, New York. 1954–1958

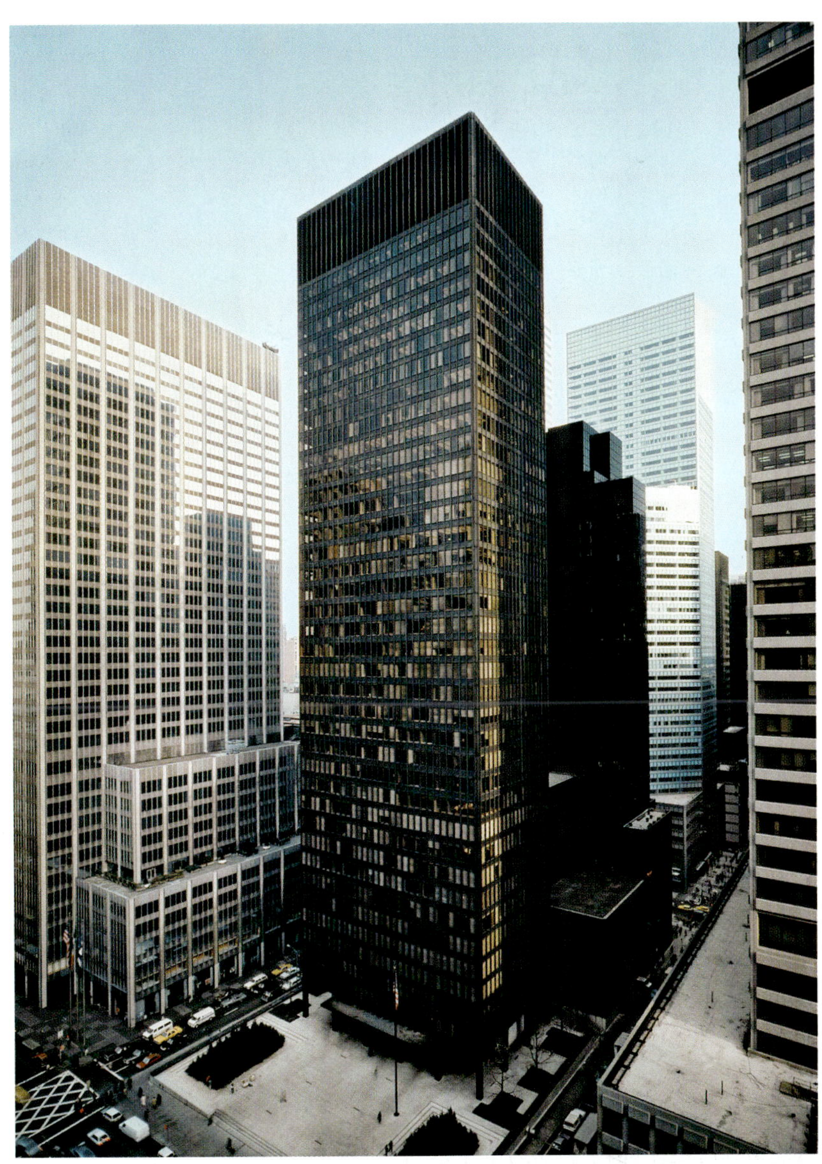

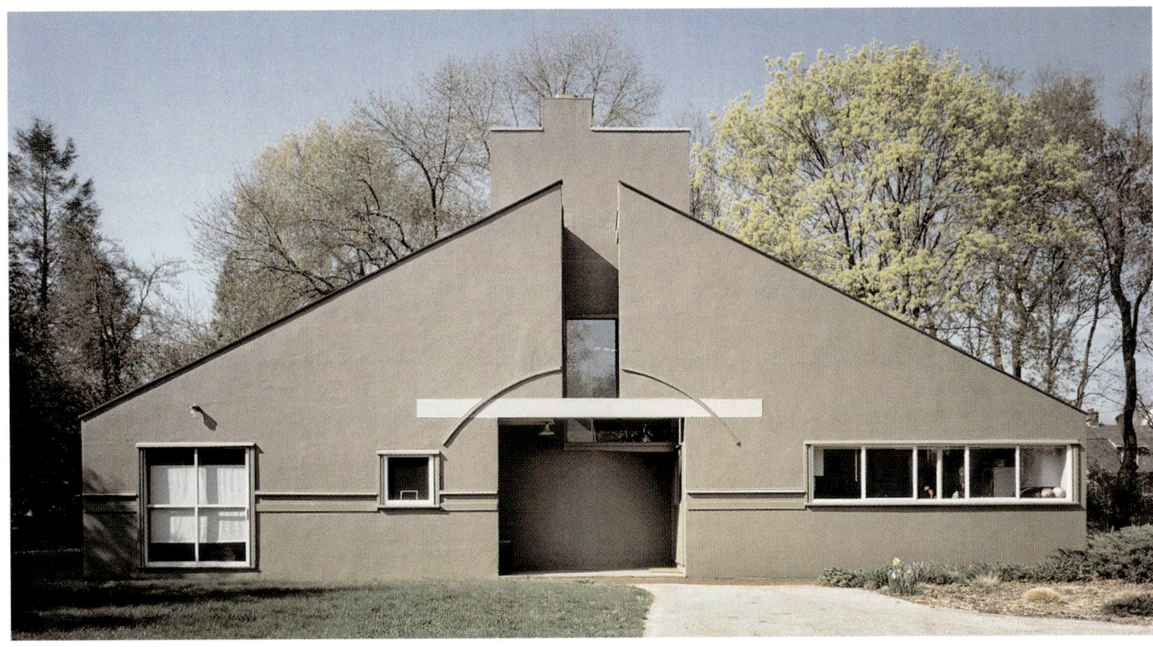

20–44 Robert Venturi. Vanna Venturi House, Chestnut Hill, Philadelphia, Pennsylvania. 1961–1964

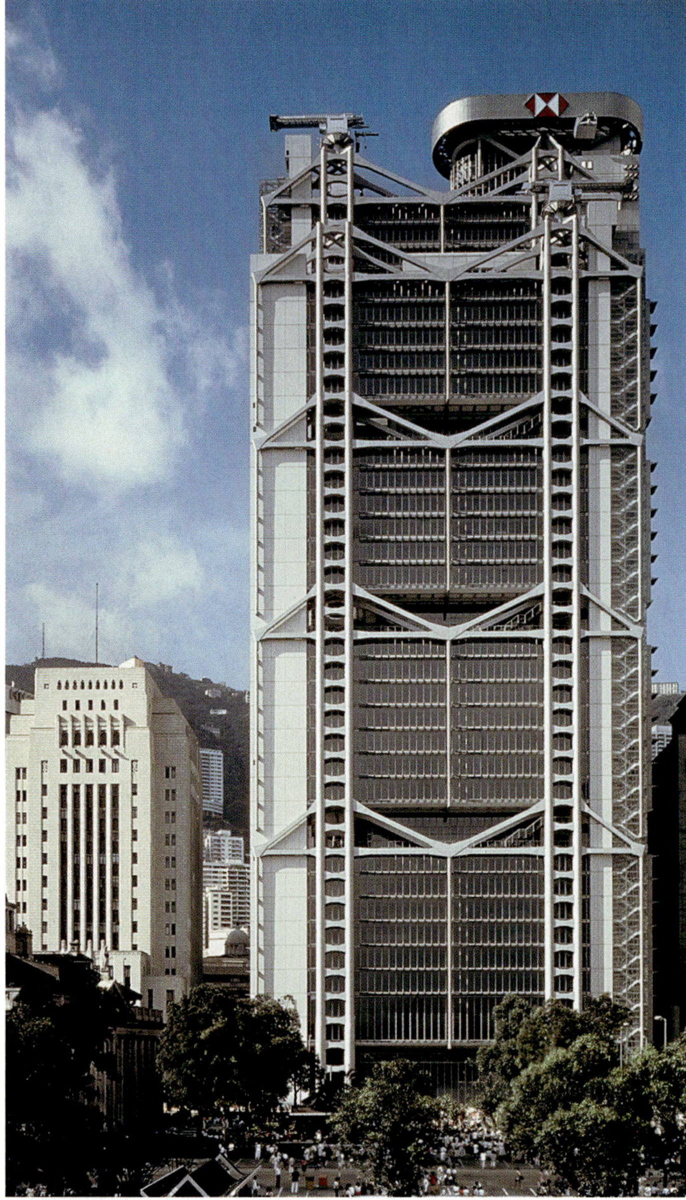

20–45 Norman Foster. Hong Kong & Shanghai Bank, Hong Kong. 1979–1986
FOSTER + PARTNERS. PHOTO: IAN LAMBOT

opens to reveal a mysterious upper wall and chimney top. On the inside, a highly irregular floor plan manifests the same complexity and contradiction.

Another reaction to mid-century Modernism in architecture is known as High Tech, characterized by the expressive use of exposed building materials, technology, and equipment, and components. Among the most spectacular examples is the Hong Kong & Shanghai Bank (fig. **20–45**) by English architect Norman Foster (born 1935). Invited by his client to design the most beautiful bank in the world, Foster spared no expense in the creation of this futuristic 47-story skyscraper. The rectangular plan features service towers at the east and west ends, eliminating the central service core typical of International Style skyscrapers. The load-bearing steel skeleton, composed of giant masts and girders, is on the exterior. The individual stories hang from this structure, allowing for uninterrupted façades and open working areas filled with natural light.

More recently, a tendency to disturb even further traditional architectural values of harmony, unity, and stability by using skewed, distorted, and dynamic geometry has been labeled Deconstructivist architecture because of its perceived relationship with the theories of Jacques Derrida (see "Derrida and Deconstruction," page 589). The Toronto-born, California-based architect Frank Gehry (born 1929) is one of the best-known proponents. In the 1990s, Gehry developed a powerfully organic, sculptural style, most famously exemplified in his dramatic Guggenheim Museum in the Basque city of Bilbao, Spain (fig. **20–46**), where he reconciled the client's needs for a museum and civic monument with his own interest in sculptural form. Gehry covered the building's complex steel skeleton with a thin skin of silvery titanium that shimmers gold or silver depending on the light. Seen from the north, the building resembles a giant ship, a reference to the shipbuilding and port facilities so important to the economy of Bilbao. This building initiated a trend of adventurous designs for art museums—such as the jagged projections of Daniel Libeskind's 2006 museum extension in Denver—that continues today. "Artists want to be in great buildings," Gehry claimed.

Public Memory and Art: The Memorial

Public memorials often engage our intellect, reminding us of important events in history, sometimes claiming their universal significance. But they can also appeal to our emotions, inspiring personal responses as well as encapsulating a collective consciousness. In recent years, art designed for public spaces—rather than for museum walls or private collectors—has provoked sensational controversies surrounding public funding, censorship, and individual rights.

The Vietnam Veterans Memorial (see fig. 20–1), now widely admired as a fitting and moving testament to the Americans who died in that conflict, was originally a lightning rod for contention. The request for design proposals for this monument stipulated that the memorial be without political or military content, that it be reflective in character, that it harmonize with its surroundings, and that it include the names of the more than 58,000 dead and missing. In 1981, the Vietnam Veterans Memorial Fund awarded the

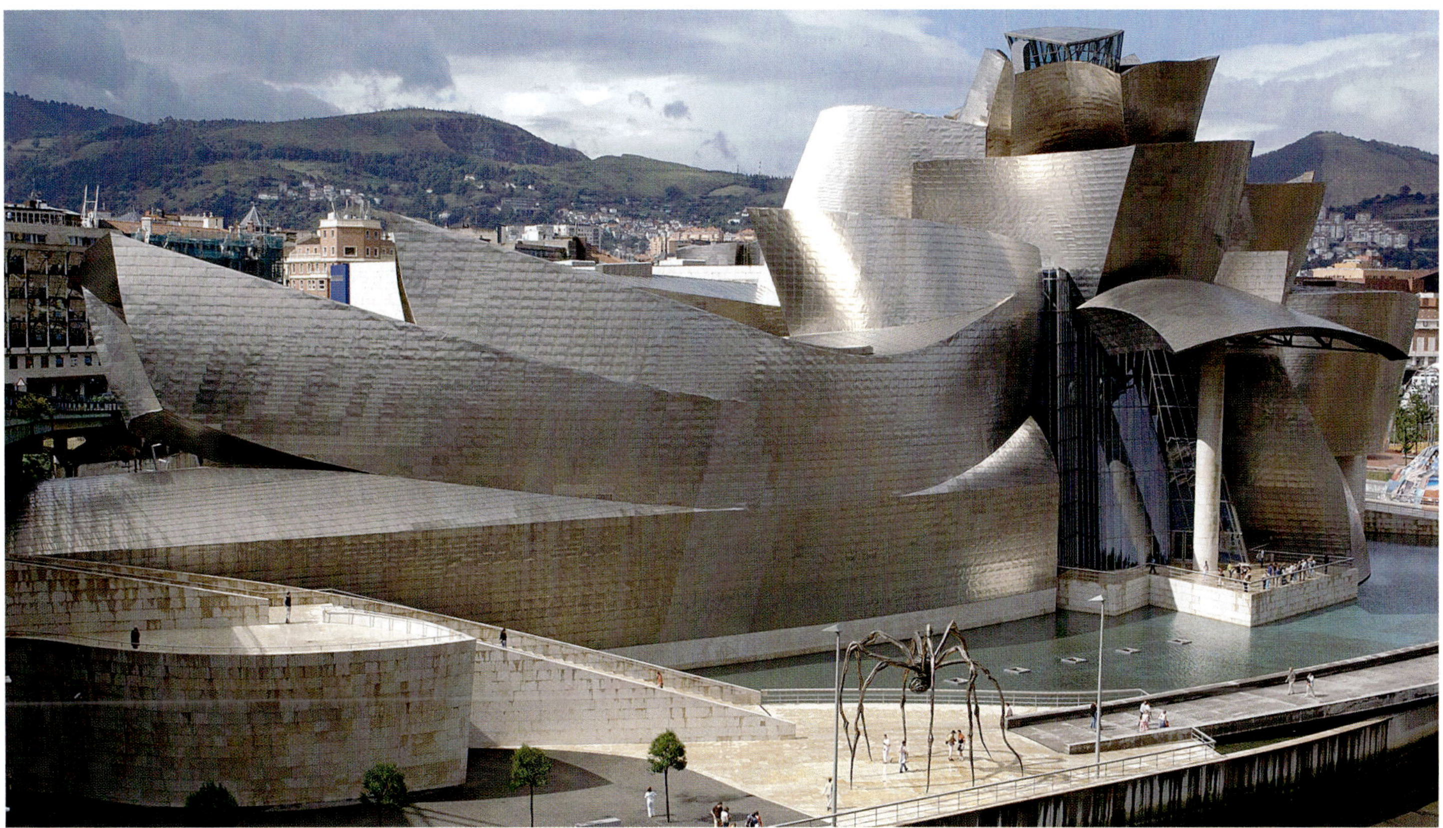

20–46 Frank O. Gehry. Guggenheim Museum, Bilbao, Spain. 1993–1997

This commission provided Gehry with an extraordinary opportunity. New York's Guggenheim Museum had become one of the most famous museums in the world, as much for Frank Lloyd Wright's innovative architecture (see figs. Intro–25 and 20–35) as for its collection of abstract art. Like Wright's spiraling design, Gehry's sprawling, organic plan resembles a living organism, like some gigantic metallic flower growing along the bank of the river.

commission to Maya Ying Lin, then an undergraduate in the architecture department at Yale University. Her Minimalist-inspired design called for two 200-foot-long walls (later expanded to almost 250 feet), sunk into rising ground. The names of the dead were to be incised into the walls in the order in which they died.

It seems somehow fitting that the Cold War ended in 1980, just before this memorial was erected. Soviet leader Mikhail Gorbachev's economic and political reforms, known as "glasnost," ultimately led to the dissolution of the Soviet Union, giving rise to a cluster of independent republics that turned to capitalism, many instituting democratic reforms on social, economic, and political levels. Global capitalism increased the economic interdependence among nations, and wealthy countries like the United States saw increasing prosperity. Thanks to remarkable advances in transportation and communication, including the Internet, the world has begun to seem smaller. And with enhanced global communication has come increased awareness of the grave problems that confront human beings in the twenty-first century. The devastating terrorist attacks on the United States at the World Trade Center in New York and the Pentagon in Washington on September 11, 2001, only escalated tension around the globe.

Soon after the World Trade Center was destroyed, artists, architects, government officials, and ordinary citizens sought to create a meaningful testament that would serve as a global statement against the horrors of terrorism. Conceived and executed during the Cold War, the Modernist World Trade Center reflected the United States' self-confidence as a global power. The Twin Towers stood 110 stories tall, dominating the Manhattan skyline. While their simplistic and brute form was not well received by some critics, their sheer size left all in awe of this major engineering accomplishment.

Most felt the World Trade Center site had to be rebuilt: as a memorial, as a symbol, and as a functional group of buildings. In February 2003, the Polish-born American architect Daniel Libeskind (born 1946) won an international competition to design the site. Libeskind's plans are centered around a sunken field incorporating the foundations of the destroyed towers and the concrete slurry wall that prevented the Hudson River from flooding the site—Libeskind's metaphor of tenacity and survival. This area also includes a memorial to the more than 2,500 people who died there. A skyscraper soaring to the patriotic height of 1776 feet would contain gardens which Libeskind calls "a constant affirmation of life."

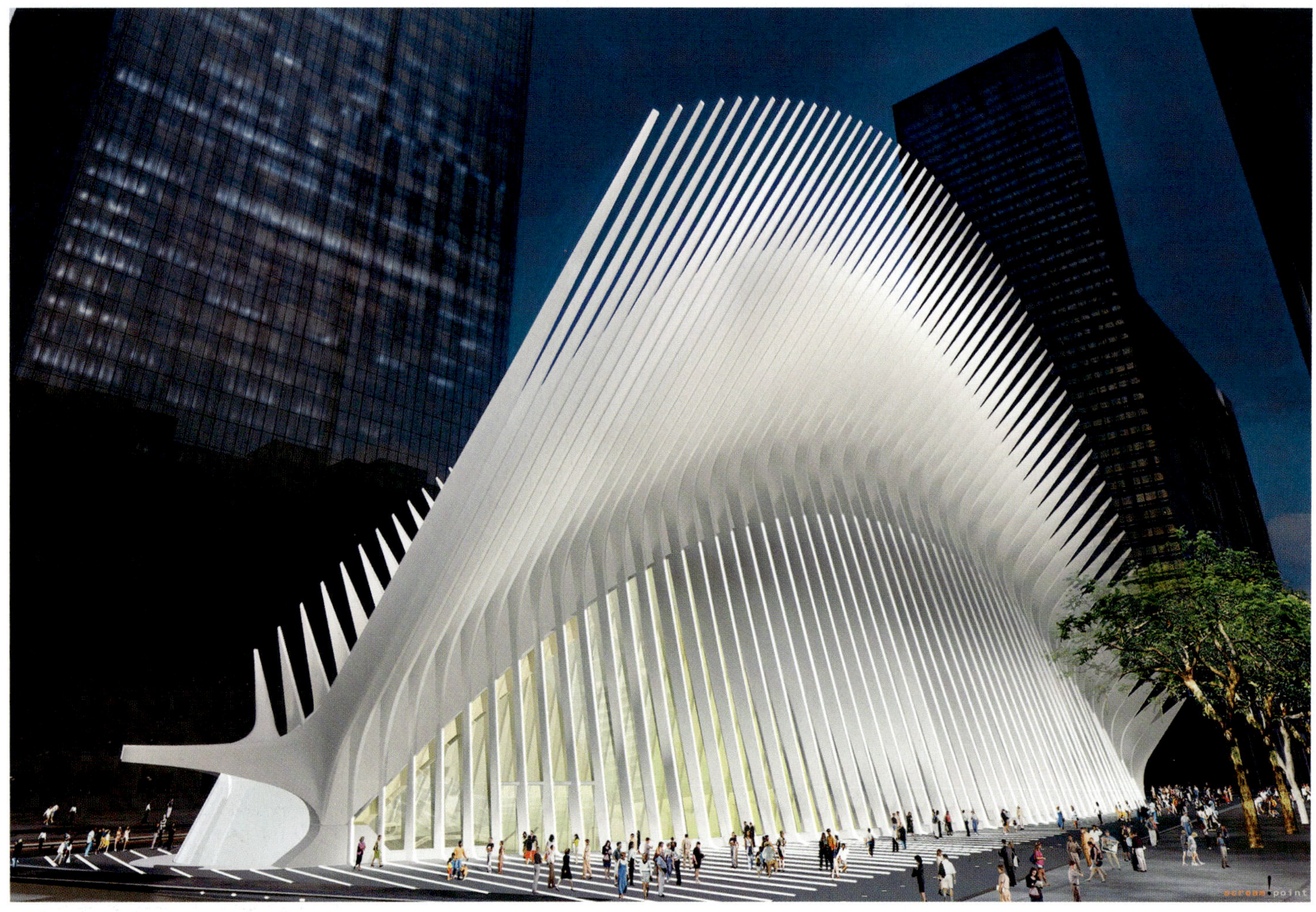

20–47 Santiago Calatrava. World Trade Center, Transportation Hub. Digital three-dimensional model. 2006–2009. New York City
PORT AUTHORITY OF NEW YORK AND NEW JERSEY

Libeskind sees the tower rising triumphant from the disaster of September 11, "an affirmation of vitality in the face of danger, an affirmation of life in the aftermath of tragedy."

As part of the the World Trade Center site, Spanish architect Santiago Calatrava (born 1951) designed a subway and train station (fig. **20–47**). The steel and glass terminal, now scheduled for completion in 2011, will comfortably handle 80,000 travelers a day. Calatrava has conceived a light, airy structure. Hinged wings of a retractable roof were originally intended to open each year on the anniversary of the attack, and Calatrava carefully positioned the terminal on the site to coordinate with the place of the sun at the time of the tragedy. This image of hope, built on the site of unfathomable loss, is charting new domains for communal commemorations in the twenty-first century. It continues the fundamental quest of artists throughout history to extend the boundaries of human perception, feeling, and thought in ways that express our deepest hopes and give form to our most powerful dreams.

Looking Back

During the 1950s, Modernist artists made assault after assault on traditions that dated back to the Renaissance. As in the earlier twentieth century, movements followed each other in quick succession, each claiming to be more radical than the last. Abstract Expressionists eliminated representation and narrative. Minimal artists eliminated personal feeling and social reference. Conceptual artists eliminated the art object itself. Performance artists refused to produce anything permanent. Feminists assaulted the unspoken tradition of male dominance.

By the 1970s there seemed to be no traditional rules of art left to break, and the avant-garde all but ceased to exist as a group separate from society at large. Postmodern artists ceased focusing inward on formal innovation and began looking outside, devoting more energy to reflections on the state of their larger world and opening new possibilities for interaction with their audience. As we, as members of that audience, become increasingly aware of the art of the past, we will enrich our ability to appreciate the as-yet-unimagined varieties of creativity that await us in the future.

IN PERSPECTIVE

1940

◀ **World War II Ends,** 1945

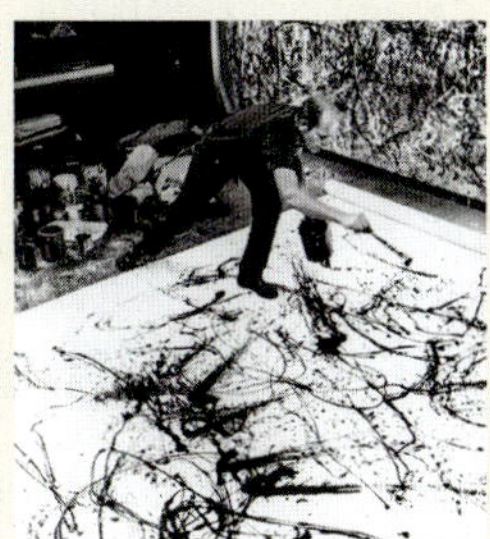

NAMUTH,
PHOTOGRAPH OF JACKSON POLLACK PAINTING,
1950

◀ **Britain Withdraws from India,** 1947

◀ **Israel Declares Independence,** 1948

◀ **People's Republic of China Established,** 1949

1950

◀ **Korean War,** 1950–1953

◀ **Civil Rights Movement Begins in U.S.,** 1954

◀ **USSR Launches First Satellite, Sputnik I,** 1957

1960

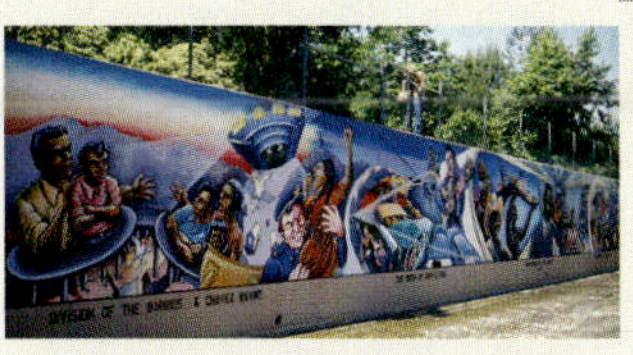

BACA,
THE GREAT WALL OF LOS ANGELES,
1968–1973

◀ **Soviet Yuri Gagarin is the First Human in Space,** 1961

◀ **President John F. Kennedy Assassinated,** 1963

◀ **U.S. Enters Vietnam War,** 1965

◀ **Martin Luther King, Jr. Assassinated,** 1968

1970

◀ **Apollo 11 Lands First Humans on the Moon,** 1969

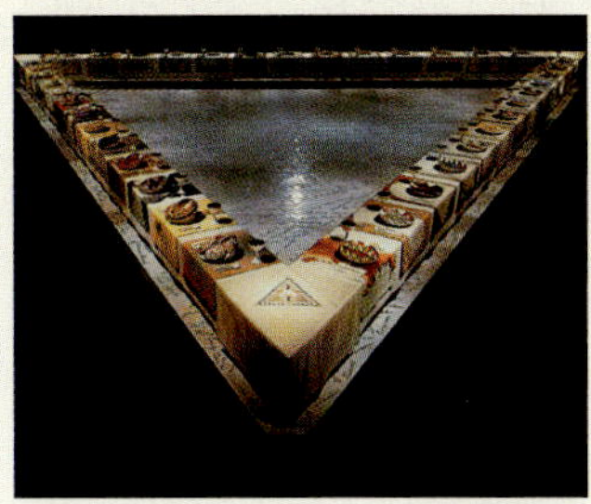

CHICAGO,
THE DINNER PARTY,
1974–1979

◀ **Stephen Hawking Proposes Black Hole Theory,** 1974

1980

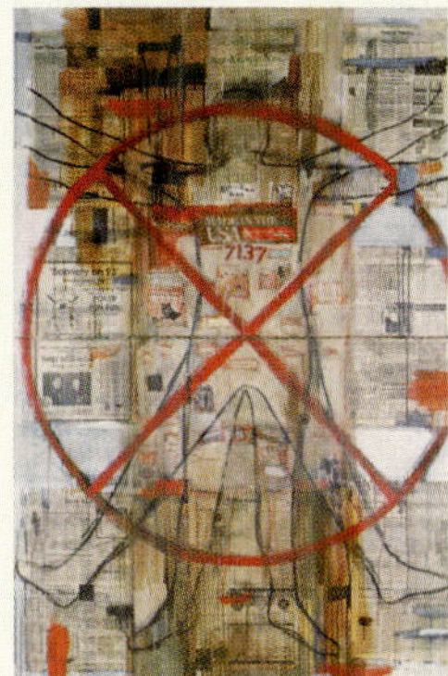

SMITH,
THE RED MEAN: SELF PORTRAIT,
1992

◀ **Tiananmen Square Protests in China,** 1989

1990

◀ **Nelson Mandela Released from Prison Signaling the end of Apartheid in South Africa,** 1990

◀ **Germany Reunited,** 1990

◀ **USSR Dissolved,** 1990

◀ **Advent of World Wide Web Early 1990s**

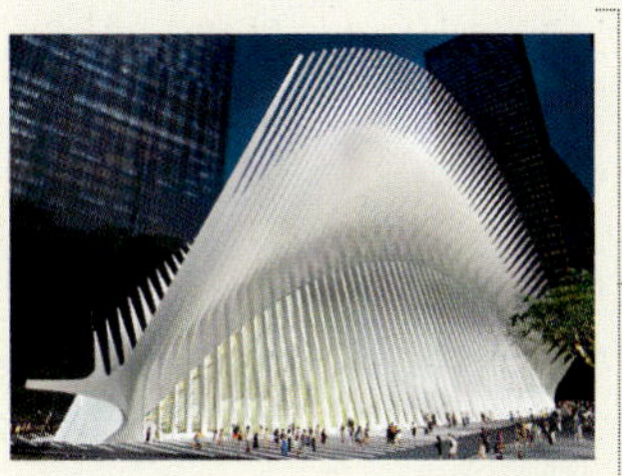

CALATRAVA,
WTC, TRANSPORTATION HUB,
2006–2009

◀ **First Cloned Mammal, Dolly the Sheep,** 1996

2000

◀ **Human Genome Sequence Decoded,** 2000

◀ **World Trade Center Attack,** 2001

◀ **U.S. War in Iraq Begins,** 2003

◀ **Barack Obama Elected President of U.S.,** 2008

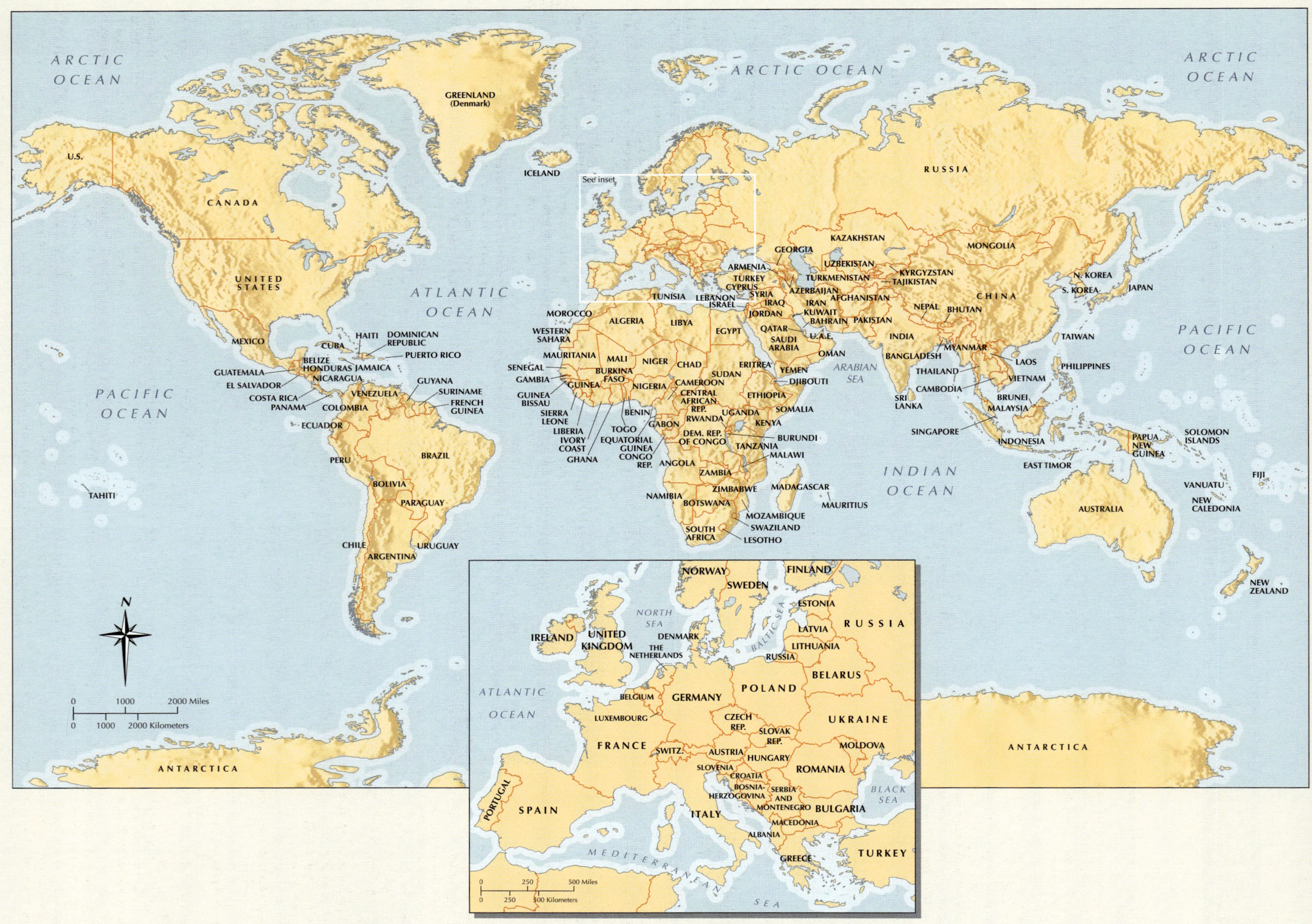

ARCTIC OCEAN
ARCTIC OCEAN
ARCTIC OCEAN
GREENLAND (Denmark)
ICELAND
U.S.
CANADA
UNITED STATES
MEXICO
CUBA
HAITI
DOMINICAN REPUBLIC
PUERTO RICO
BELIZE
HONDURAS
JAMAICA
GUATEMALA
NICARAGUA
EL SALVADOR
COSTA RICA
PANAMA
VENEZUELA
COLOMBIA
GUYANA
SURINAME
FRENCH GUIANA
ECUADOR
PERU
BRAZIL
BOLIVIA
PARAGUAY
CHILE
ARGENTINA
URUGUAY
PACIFIC OCEAN
TAHITI
ATLANTIC OCEAN
See inset
MOROCCO
WESTERN SAHARA
MAURITANIA
SENEGAL
GAMBIA
GUINEA BISSAU
GUINEA
SIERRA LEONE
LIBERIA
IVORY COAST
GHANA
MALI
BURKINA FASO
TOGO
BENIN
NIGERIA
NIGER
ALGERIA
TUNISIA
LIBYA
EGYPT
CHAD
SUDAN
CAMEROON
CENTRAL AFRICAN REP.
EQUATORIAL GUINEA
GABON
CONGO REP.
DEM. REP. OF CONGO
RWANDA
UGANDA
BURUNDI
KENYA
TANZANIA
ANGOLA
ZAMBIA
MALAWI
NAMIBIA
ZIMBABWE
BOTSWANA
MOZAMBIQUE
SWAZILAND
SOUTH AFRICA
LESOTHO
MADAGASCAR
MAURITIUS
ERITREA
ETHIOPIA
DJIBOUTI
SOMALIA
YEMEN
OMAN
U.A.E.
SAUDI ARABIA
QATAR
BAHRAIN
KUWAIT
JORDAN
ISRAEL
LEBANON
CYPRUS
SYRIA
IRAQ
IRAN
TURKEY
ARMENIA
GEORGIA
AZERBAIJAN
TURKMENISTAN
UZBEKISTAN
KAZAKHSTAN
KYRGYZSTAN
TAJIKISTAN
AFGHANISTAN
PAKISTAN
INDIA
NEPAL
BHUTAN
BANGLADESH
SRI LANKA
ARABIAN SEA
MYANMAR
THAILAND
LAOS
CAMBODIA
VIETNAM
BRUNEI
MALAYSIA
SINGAPORE
INDONESIA
EAST TIMOR
PHILIPPINES
TAIWAN
CHINA
MONGOLIA
RUSSIA
N. KOREA
S. KOREA
JAPAN
PACIFIC OCEAN
PAPUA NEW GUINEA
SOLOMON ISLANDS
VANUATU
NEW CALEDONIA
FIJI
AUSTRALIA
NEW ZEALAND
INDIAN OCEAN
N
0 1000 2000 Miles
0 1000 2000 Kilometers
ANTARCTICA
ANTARCTICA
NORWAY
SWEDEN
FINLAND
ESTONIA
RUSSIA
LATVIA
LITHUANIA
RUSSIA
BELARUS
NORTH SEA
BALTIC SEA
IRELAND
UNITED KINGDOM
DENMARK
THE NETHERLANDS
BELGIUM
GERMANY
POLAND
LUXEMBOURG
CZECH REP.
SLOVAK REP.
UKRAINE
MOLDOVA
ATLANTIC OCEAN
FRANCE
SWITZ.
AUSTRIA
HUNGARY
SLOVENIA
CROATIA
ROMANIA
BOSNIA-HERZOGOVINA
SERBIA AND MONTENEGRO
BULGARIA
BLACK SEA
PORTUGAL
SPAIN
ITALY
MACEDONIA
ALBANIA
GREECE
TURKEY
MEDITERRANEAN SEA
0 250 500 Miles
0 250 500 Kilometers

Glossary

abacus The flat slab at the top of a **capital**, directly under the **entablature**.

abstract, abstraction Any art that does not represent observable aspects of nature or transforms visible forms into a pattern resembling the original model. Also: the formal qualities of this process.

academy, academician An institutional group established for the training of artists. Most academies date from the Renaissance and after; they were particularly powerful state-run institutions in the seventeenth and eighteenth centuries. In general, academies replaced **guilds** as the venue where students learned the craft of art and were also provided with a complete education, including art theory and artistic rules. The academies helped artists to be seen as trained specialists, rather than as craftspeople, and promoted the change in the social status of the artist. An academician is an official academy-trained artist.

acanthus A leafy plant whose foliage inspired architectural ornamentation, used in the **Corinthian** and **Composite orders** and in the **relief** scroll known as the *rinceau.*

acropolis The citadel of an ancient Greek city, located at its highest point and consisting of temples, a treasury, and sometimes a royal palace. The most famous is the Acropolis in Athens, where the ruins of the Parthenon can be found.

action painting Using broad gestures to drip or pour paint onto a pictorial surface. Associated with mid-twentieth-century American Abstract Expressionists, especially Jackson Pollock.

adobe Sun-baked blocks made of clay mixed with straw. Also: the buildings made with this material.

aedicula (aediculae) A decorative architectural frame, usually found around a **niche**, door, or window. An aedicula is made up of a **pediment** and **entablature** supported by **columns** or **pilasters**.

aesthetics The philosophy of beauty.

aisle Passage or open corridor of a church, hall, or other building that parallels the main space, usually on both sides, and is delineated by a row, or **arcade**, of **columns** or **piers**. Called **side aisles** when they flank the **nave** of a church.

alabaster A soft, fine, translucent, white stone.

album A book consisting of blank pages (**album leaves**) on which typically an artist may sketch, draw, or paint.

allegory In a work of art, an image (or images) that illustrates an **abstract** concept, idea, or story, often suggesting a deeper meaning.

altar A tablelike structure where religious rites are performed. In Christian churches, the altar is the site of the rite of the **Eucharist**.

altarpiece A painted or carved panel or **winged** structure placed at the back of or behind and above an **altar**. Contains religious imagery, often specific to the place of worship for which it was made.

ambulatory The passage (walkway) around the **apse** in a **basilican** church or around the central space in a **centrally planned building**.

amphora An ancient Greek jar for storing oil or wine, with an egg-shaped body and two curved handles.

animal interlace Decoration made up of interwoven animals or serpents, often found in Celtic and early northern European art.

animal style A type of imagery used in Europe and western Asia during the ancient and medieval periods, characterized by animals or animal-like **forms** arranged in intricate patterns or combats.

apotheosis Deification of a person or thing. In art, often shown as an ascent to heaven or glory, borne by an eagle, angels, or **putti**.

apprentice A student artist or craftsperson in training. In a traditional system of art and craft training established under the **guilds** and still in use today, master artists took on apprentices (students) for a specific number of years. The apprentice was taught every aspect of the artist's craft, and he or she participated in the master's workshop or **atelier**.

appropriation Term used to describe an artist's practice of borrowing from another source for a new work of art. While in previous centuries artists often copied one another's figures, **motifs**, or **compositions**, in modern times the sources for appropriation extend from material culture to works of art.

apse, apsidal A large semicircular or polygonal (and usually vaulted) **niche** protruding from the end wall of a building. In a Christian church, it contains the **altar**. Apsidal is an adjective describing the condition of having such a semicircular or polygonal space.

aquatint A type of **intaglio** printmaking developed in the eighteenth century that produces an area of even **tone** without laborious **cross-hatching**. The aquatint is made by using a porous resin coating on a metal plate, which, when immersed in acid, allows an even, allover biting of the plate. The resulting printed image has a granular, textural effect.

aqueduct A trough to carry flowing water, if necessary, supported by **arches**.

arabesque A type of **linear** surface decoration based on foliage and **calligraphic forms**, usually characterized by flowing lines and swirling shapes.

arcade A series of arches, carried by **columns** or **piers** and supporting a common wall or **lintel**. In a **blind** arcade, the arches and supports are engaged (attached to the background wall) and have a decorative function.

arch In architecture, a curved structural element that spans an open space. Built from wedge-shaped stone blocks called **voussoirs**, which, when placed together and held at the top by a trapezoidal **keystone**, form an effective weight-bearing unit. Requires **buttresses** at either side to contain outward thrust caused by the weight of the structure. **Corbel arch**: arch or **vault** formed by **courses** of stones, each of which projects beyond the lower course until the space is enclosed; usually finished with a **capstone. Horseshoe arch**: an arch of more than a half-circle, often used in western Islamic architecture. Ogival arch: a pointed arch created by S-curves. **Relieving arch**: an arch built into a heavy wall just above a **post-and-lintel** structure (such as a gate, door, or window) to help support the wall above. Relieves some of the weight on the lintel by transferring the load to the side walls.

Archaic smile The curved lips of an ancient Greek statue, usually interpreted as an attempt to animate the features.

architrave The bottom element of an **entablature**, beneath the **frieze** and the **cornice**.

archivolt Curved **molding** formed by the **voussoirs** making up an **arch**.

assemblage An artwork created by gathering and manipulating two- and/or three-dimensional found objects.

atelier The studio or workshop of a master artist or craftsperson, often including junior associates and **apprentices**.

atmospheric perspective See **perspective**.

atrium An unroofed interior courtyard in a Roman house, sometimes having a pool. Also: the open courtyard in front of a Christian church, or an entrance area in modern architecture.

attic story The top story of a building. In **classical** architecture, the level above the **entablature**, often decorated or carrying an inscription.

attribute The symbolic object or objects that identify a particular deity, saint, or personification in art.

automatic writing, automatism A technique whereby the usual intellectual control of the artist over his or her brush or pencil is forgone. The artist's aim is to allow the subconscious to create the artwork without rational interference.

avant-garde A term derived from the French military word meaning "before the group," or "vanguard." Avant-garde denotes those artists or concepts of a strikingly new, experimental, or radical nature for the time.

axis mundi A concept of an axis of the world, which denotes important sacred sites and provides a link between the human and celestial realms. For example, in Buddhist art, the *axis mundi* can be marked by monumental freestanding decorated pillars.

background Within the depicted space of an artwork, the area of the image at the greatest distance from the **picture plane**.

bailey The outermost walled courtyard of a castle.

baldachin A canopy (whether suspended from the ceiling, projecting from a wall, or supported by **columns**) placed over an honorific or sacred space such as a throne or church **altar**.

balustrade A low barrier consisting of a series of short circular posts (called balusters), with a rail on top.

baptistry A building used for the Christian ritual of baptism. It is usually separate from the main church and often octagonal or circular in shape.

bar tracery See **tracery**.

barrel vault See **vault**.

base Any support. Masonry supporting a statue or the **shaft of a column**.

basilica A large rectangular building. Often built with a **clerestory**, **side aisles** separated from the center **nave** by **colonnades**, and an **apse** at one or both ends. Roman centers for administration, later adapted to Christian church use. Constantine's architects added a transverse aisle at the end of the nave called a **transept**.

bay A unit of space defined by architectural elements such as **columns**, **piers**, and walls.

beehive tomb A **corbel**-vaulted tomb, conical in shape like a beehive, and covered by an earthen mound.

bell krater An ancient Greek bell-shaped vessel for mixing wine and water.

Benday dots In modern printing and typesetting, the dots that make up lettering and images. Often machine- or computer-generated, the dots are very small and closely spaced to give the effect of density and richness of **tone**.

biomorphic Adjective used to describe forms that resemble shapes found in nature. Also, a **style** in art characterized by biomorphic shapes is called Biomorphism.

bird's-eye view A view from above.

black-figure A style of ancient Greek pottery in which black figures are painted on a red clay ground.

blackware A ceramic technique that produces pottery with a primarily black surface. Blackware has both matte and glossy patterns on the surface of the wares.

blind window See **blind**.

blind Decorative elements attached to the surface of a wall, with no openings.

block printing A printed image, such as a **woodcut** or wood engraving, made from a carved wooden block.

bodhisattva A deity that is far advanced in the long process of transforming itself into a buddha. While seeking enlightenment or emancipation from this world (*nirvana*), bodhisattvas help others attain this same liberation.

Book of Hours A private prayer book, having a calendar, services for the canonical hours, and sometimes, special prayers.

bracket, bracketing An architectural element that projects from a wall and that often helps support a horizontal part of a building, such as beams or the eaves of a roof.

bronze A metal made from copper alloy, usually mixed with tin. Also: any sculpture or object made from this substance.

burin A metal instrument used in **engraving** to cut lines into the metal plate. The sharp end of the burin is trimmed to give a diamond-shaped cutting point, while the other end is finished with a wooden handle that fits into the engraver's palm.

buttress, buttressing An architectural support, usually consisting of massive masonry built against an exterior wall to brace the wall and counter the thrust of the **vaults**. Transfers the weight of the vault to the ground. **Flying buttress**: An **arch** built on the exterior of a building that transfers the thrust of the roof vaults at important stress points through the wall to a detached buttress **pier** leading to the wall buttress.

cairn A pile of stones or earth and stones that served both as a prehistoric burial site and as a marker of underground tombs.

calligraphy The art of highly ornamental handwriting.

calotype The first photographic process utilizing negatives and paper positives. It was invented by William Henry Fox Talbot in the late 1830s.

came (cames) A lead strip used in the making of leaded or **stained-glass** windows. Cames have an indented vertical groove on the sides into which the separate pieces of glass are fitted to hold the design together.

cameo A low relief carving on a semiprecious stone or gemstone.

camera obscura An early cameralike device used in the Renaissance and later for recording images of nature. Made from a dark box (or room) with a hole in one side (sometimes fitted with a lens), the camera obscura operates when bright light shines through the hole, casting an upside-down image of an object outside onto the inside wall of the box.

canon Established rules or standards.

canon of proportions A set of ideal mathematical ratios in art based on measurements of the human body.

cantilever A beam or structure that is anchored at one end and projects horizontally beyond its vertical support, such as a wall or **column**. It can carry loads throughout the rest of its unsupported length. Or a bracket used to carry the **cornice** or extend the eaves of a building.

capital The sculpted block that tops a **column**. According to the conventions of the orders, capitals include different decorative elements. See **order**. Also: a **historiated capital** is one displaying a narrative.

capstone The final, topmost stone in a **corbel** arch or **vault**, which joins the sides and completes the structure.

cartoon A full-scale drawing used to transfer the outline of a design onto a surface (such as a wall, canvas, or panel) to be painted, carved, or woven.

cartouche A frame for a **hieroglyphic** inscription formed by a rope design surrounding an oval space. Used to signify a sacred or honored name. Also: in architecture, a decorative device or plaque used for inscriptions or epitaphs.

caryatid A sculpture of a draped female figure acting as a **column** supporting an entablature.

catacomb An underground burial ground consisting of tunnels on different levels, having **niches** for urns and **sarcophagi** and often incorporating rooms (**cubicula**).

cathedral The principal Christian church in a diocese, built in the bishop's administrative center and housing his throne *(cathedra)*.

cella The principal interior room in a Greek or Roman temple within which the cult statue was usually housed. Also called the **naos**.

centering A temporary structure that supports a masonry **arch** and **vault** or **dome** during construction until the mortar is fully dried and the masonry is self-sustaining.

central-plan building Any structure designed with a primary central space surrounded by symmetrical areas on each side. For example, **Greek-cross plan** (equal-armed cross).

ceramics Wares made of baked clay.

chacmool In Mayan sculpture, a half-reclining figure probably representing an offering bearer.

chasing The tooling of a metal surface to add decoration.

château (châteaux) A French country house or residential castle. A *château fort* is a military castle incorporating defensive works such as towers and battlements.

cherub (cherubim) The second-highest order of angels. Popularly, an idealized small child, usually depicted naked and with wings.

chevet In a French church the space beyond the **transepts** consisting of **apse**, **ambulatory**, and radiating chapels.

chevron A decorative motif made up of repeated inverted Vs; a zigzag pattern.

chiaroscuro An Italian word designating the contrast of dark and light in a painting, drawing, or print. Chiaroscuro creates spatial depth and **volumetric** forms through gradations in the intensity of light and shadow.

choir The section of a Christian church reserved for the clergy or the religious, either between the **crossing** and the **apse** or in the **nave** just before the crossing, screened or walled and fitted with stalls (seats). Also an area reserved for singers.

Classical A term referring to the art and architecture of ancient Greece between c. 480–323 BCE.

classical, classicism Any aspect of later art or architecture reminiscent of the rules, **canons**, and examples of the art of ancient Greece and Rome. Also: in general, any art aspiring to the qualities of restraint, balance, and rational order exemplified by the ancients. Also: the peak of perfection in any period.

clerestory The topmost zone of a wall with windows in a **basilica** extending above the **aisle** roofs. Provides direct light into the central interior space (the nave).

cloison See **cloisonné**.

cloisonné An enamel technique in which metal wire or strips are affixed to the surface to form the design. The resulting areas (**cloisons**) are filled with **enamel** (colored glass).

cloister An open space, part of a monastery, surrounded by an **arcaded** or **colonnaded** walkway, often having a fountain and garden, and dedicated to nonliturgical activities and the secular life of the religious. Members of a cloistered order do not interact with outsiders.

codex (codices) A book, or a group of manuscript pages (**folios**), held together by stitching or other binding on one side.

coffer A recessed decorative panel that is used to reduce the weight of and to decorate ceilings or **vaults**. The use of coffers is called coffering.

coiling A technique in basketry. In coiled baskets a spiraling structure is held in place by another material.

collage A technique in which cutout paper forms (often painted or printed), and/or found materials, are pasted onto another surface. Also: an image created using this technique.

colonnade A row of **columns**, supporting a straight **lintel** (as in a porch or **portico**) or a series of **arches** (an **arcade**).

colonnette A small **column** attached to a pier or wall.

colophon The data placed at the end of a book listing the book's author, publisher, **illuminator**, and other information related to its production.

Color Field painting A type of Abstract Expressionist painting in the 1950s and 1960s characterized by broad abstract sweeps of solid color that emphasize the surface of the picture plane and deemphasize gestural brushstrokes.

column An architectural element used for support and/or decoration. Consists of a rounded vertical **shaft** placed on a **base** topped by a decorative **capital**. May follow the rules of one of the architectural **orders**. Although usually freestanding, columns can be attached to a wall (engaged).

complementary color The primary and secondary colors across from each other on the color wheel (red and green, blue and orange, yellow and purple). When juxtaposed, the intensity of both colors increases.

Composite order See **order**.

composition The arrangement of **formal elements** in an artwork.

compound pier A **pier** or large **column** with **shafts**, **pilasters**, or **colonnettes** attached to it on one or all sides.

conch A half-**dome**.

concrete A building material developed by the Romans, made primarily from lime, sand, cement, and rubble mixed with water. Concrete is easily poured or **molded** when wet and hardens into a particularly strong and durable stonelike substance.

connoisseurship A term derived from the French word *connoisseur,* meaning "an expert," and signifying the study and evaluation of art based on formal, visual, and stylistic analysis. A **connoisseur** studies the **style** and technique of an object to deduce its relative quality and possible maker. This is done through visual association with other, similar objects and styles. See also **contextualism**.

content When discussing a work of art, the term can include all of the following: its subject matter; the ideas contained in the work; the artist's intention; and even its meaning for the beholder.

contextualism A methodological approach in art history that focuses on the cultural background of an art object. Contextualism utilizes the literature, history, economics, and social developments (among other things) of a period, as well as the object itself, to explain the meaning of an artwork. See also **connoisseurship**.

contrapposto A twisting body position. Also: a way of representing the human body so that its weight appears to be borne on one leg.

convention A traditional way of representing forms.

corbel, corbeling A roofing and arching technique in which each course of stone projects inward and slightly beyond the previous layer (a corbel) until the uppermost corbels meet. Results in a high, nearly pointed **arch** or **vault**. A corbel table is a table supported by corbels.

corbel arch See **arch**.

corbeled vault See **vault**.

Corinthian order See **order**.

cornice The uppermost section of a **Classical entablature**. More generally, a horizontally projecting element found at the top of a building wall or **pedestal**. A raking cornice is formed by the junction of two slanted cornices, most often found in **pediments**.

course A horizontal layer of stone used in building.

crenellation Alternating high and low sections of a wall, giving a notched appearance and creating permanent defensive shields in the walls of fortified buildings.

cross-hatching A technique primarily used in printmaking and drawing, in which a set of parallel lines (hatching) is drawn across a previous set, but from a differing (usually right) angle. Cross-hatching gives a great density of **tone** and allows the artist to create the illusion of shadows efficiently.

crossing The juncture of the **nave** and the **transept** in a church, often marked on the exterior by a tower or **dome**.

cruciform A term describing anything that is cross-shaped, as in the cruciform plan of a church.

cubiculum (cubicula) A small private room for burials in the **catacombs**.

cuneiform writing An early form of writing with wedge-shaped marks impressed into wet clay with a **stylus**; used primarily by ancient Mesopotamians.

curtain wall A wall in a building that does not support any of the weight of the structure. Also: the freestanding outer wall of a castle, usually encircling the inner **bailey** (yard) and **keep** (primary defensive tower).

cycle A series of images depicting a story or theme intended to be displayed together, and forming a visual narrative.

cyclopean construction A method of building utilizing huge blocks of rough-hewn stone. Any large-scale, **monumental** building project that impresses by sheer size. Named after one-eyed giants of legendary strength from Greek myth.

cylinder seal A small cylindrical stone decorated with **incised** patterns. When rolled across soft clay or wax, the resulting raised pattern or design (relief) served as an identifying signature.

dado (dadoes) The lower part of a wall, differentiated in some way (by a **molding** or different color) from the upper section.

daguerreotype An early photographic process named for Louis-Jacques Mandé Daguerre. A daguerreotype was a positive print made on a light-sensitized copper plate.

Daoism A Chinese philosophy that emphasizes the close relationship of humans and nature.

desert varnish In southwestern North America, a substance that turned cliff faces into dark surfaces. Neolithic artists would draw images by scraping through the dark surface.

diptych Two panels of equal size, usually decorated with paintings or **reliefs**, and hinged together.

dolmen A prehistoric structure made up of two or more large (often upright) stones supporting a large, flat, horizontal slab or slabs.

dome A round **vault**, usually over a circular space. Consists of a curved masonry vault of shapes and cross sections that can vary from hemispherical to bulbous to ovoidal. May use a supporting vertical wall (drum), from which the vault springs, and may be crowned by an open space (**oculus**) and/or an exterior **lantern**. When a dome is built over a square space, an intermediate element is required to make the transition to a circular drum. There are two types: A dome on **pendentives** (spherical triangles) incorporates **arched**, sloping intermediate sections of wall that carry the weight and thrust of the dome to heavily **buttressed** supporting **piers**. A dome on **squinches** uses an arch built into the wall (squinch) in the upper corners of the space to carry the weight of the dome across the corners of the square space below. A half-dome or conch may cover a semicircular space.

Doric order See **order**.

dressed stone Highly finished, precisely cut blocks of stone laid in even **courses**, creating a uniform face with fine joints. Often used as a facing on the visible exterior of a building, especially as a **veneer** for the **façade**. Also called ashlar.

drillwork The technique of using a drill for the creation of certain effects in sculpture.

drum The wall that supports a **dome**. Also: a segment of the circular **shaft of a column**.

drypoint An **intaglio** printmaking process by which a metal (usually copper) plate is directly inscribed by means of a pointed instrument (stylus). The resulting design of scratched lines is inked, wiped, and printed. Also: the print made by this process.

earthworks Artwork and/or sculpture, usually on a large scale, created by manipulating the natural environment. Also: the earth walls of a fort. See also **geoglyph**.

echinus A cushion-like circular element found below the **abacus** of a **Doric capital**. Also: a similarly shaped **molding** (usually with egg-and-dart **motifs**) underneath the **volutes** of an **Ionic** capital. Egg-and-dart is a **motif** used in decorative **molding**, and is made up of an alternating pattern of round (egg) and downward-pointing, tapered (dart) elements.

edition A single printing of a book or print. An edition includes only what is printed at a particular moment, usually pulled from the same press by the same publisher.

elevation The arrangement, proportions, and details of any vertical side or face of a building. Also: an architectural drawing showing an exterior or interior wall of a building.

embroidery The technique in needlework of decorating fabric by stitching designs and figures with threads. Also: the material produced by this technique.

en plein air A French term meaning "in the open air" describing the Impressionist practice of painting outdoors so artists could have direct access to the fleeting effects of light and atmosphere while working.

enamel A technique in which powdered glass is applied to a metal surface in a decorative design. After firing, the glass forms an opaque or transparent substance that is fixed to the metal background. Also: an object created with enamel technique. See **cloisonné**.

enamelwork See **enamel**.

encaustic A painting medium using pigment suspended in hot wax.

engaged column See **column**.

engraving An **intaglio** printmaking process of inscribing an image, design, or letters onto a metal or wood surface from which a print is made. An engraving is usually drawn with a sharp implement (**burin**) directly onto the surface of the plate. Also: the print made from this process.

entablature In the **Classical orders**, the horizontal elements above the **columns** and **capitals**. The entablature consists of, from top to bottom, a **cornice**, **frieze**, and **architrave**.

entasis A slight swelling of the **shaft** of a Greek **column**. The optical illusion of entasis makes the column appear from afar to be straight.

etching An **intaglio** printmaking process in which a metal plate is coated with acid-resistant resin and then inscribed with a **stylus** in a design, revealing the plate below. The plate is then immersed in acid, and the design of exposed metal is eaten away by the acid. The resin is removed, leaving the design etched permanently into the metal and the plate ready to be inked, wiped, and printed.

Eucharist The central rite of the Christian Church, from the Greek word "thanksgiving." Also known as the Mass or Holy Communion, it is based on the Last Supper. According to traditional Catholic Christian belief, consecrated bread and wine become the body and blood of Christ; in Protestant belief, bread and wine symbolize the body and blood.

exedra (exedrae) In architecture, a semicircular **niche**. On a small scale, often used as decoration, whereas larger exedrae can form interior spaces.

expressionism Terms describing a work of art in which forms are created primarily to evoke subjective emotions rather than to portray objective reality.

façade The face or front wall of a building.

fête galante A subject in painting depicting well-dressed people at leisure in a park or country setting. It is most often associated with eighteenth-century French Rococo painting.

fillet The flat surfaces separating the **flutes** on the **shaft** of a **column**.

finial A knoblike architectural decoration usually found at the top point of a spire, **pinnacle**, canopy, or **gable**. Also found on furniture.

flower piece Any painting with flowers as the primary subject; a **still life** of flowers.

fluting, fluted Shallow concave grooves running vertically on the **shaft** of a **column**, **pilaster**, or other surface.

flying buttress See **buttress**.

flying gallop Animals posed off the ground with legs fully extended backwards and forwards to signify that they are running.

folio A large sheet of paper, which, when folded and cut, becomes four separate or **parchment** pages in a book. Also: a page or leaf in a **manuscript** or book; more generally, any large book.

foreground Within the depicted space of an artwork, the area that is closest to the **picture plane**.

foreshortening The illusion created on a flat surface in which figures and objects appear to recede or project sharply into space. Accomplished according to the rules of **perspective**.

form In speaking of a work of art or architecture, the term refers to purely visual components: line, color, shape, texture, mass, spatial qualities, and **composition**—all of which are called **formal elements**.

formalism, formalist An approach to the understanding, appreciation, and valuation of art based almost solely on considerations of **form**. This approach tends to regard an artwork as independent of its time and place of making.

formline In Native American works of art, a line that defines a space or **form**.

forum A Roman town center; site of temples and administrative buildings and used as a market or gathering area for the citizens.

fresco A painting technique in which water-based pigments are applied to a surface of wet plaster (called *buon fresco*). ***Fresco secco*** is created by painting on dried plaster. **Murals** made by both these techniques are called frescoes.

frieze The middle element of an **entablature**, between the **architrave** and the **cornice**. Usually decorated with sculpture, painting, or **moldings**. Also: any continuous flat band with **relief** sculpture or painted decorations.

frontispiece An illustration opposite or preceding the title page of a book. Also: the primary **façade** or main entrance **bay** of a building.

fusuma Sliding doors covered with paper, used in a Japanese house. *Fusuma* are often highly decorated with paintings and colored **backgrounds**.

gable The triangular wall space found on the end wall of a building between the two sides of a pitched roof. Also: a triangular decorative panel that has a gablelike shape.

gallery In church architecture, the story found above the side aisles of a church, usually open to and overlooking the **nave**. Also: in secular architecture, a long room, usually above the ground floor in a private house or a public building, used for entertaining, exhibiting pictures, or promenading. Also, *galleria*.

genre A type or category of artistic form, subject, technique, **style**, or **medium**.

genre painting A term used to loosely categorize paintings depicting scenes of everyday life, including (among others) domestic interiors, parties, inn scenes, and street scenes.

geoglyphs Earthen designs on a colossal scale, often created in a landscape as if to be seen from an aerial viewpoint.

geometric A period in Greek art that flourished from about 900 to 700 BCE; the art is characterized by patterns of rectangles, squares, and other **abstract** shapes. Also: any **style** or art using primarily these shapes.

gesso A ground made from glue, gypsum, and/or chalk forming the ground or the priming layer of a wood panel or canvas. Provides a smooth surface for painting.

gesturalism Painting and drawing in which the brushwork or line visibly records the artist's physical gesture at the moment the paint was applied or the lines laid down. Associated especially with expressive styles, such as Zen painting and Abstract Expressionism.

gilding The application of paper-thin **gold leaf** or gold pigment to an object made from another **medium** (for example, a sculpture or painting). Usually used as a decorative finishing detail.

giornata (giornate) Adopted from the Italian term meaning "a day's work," a *giornata* is the section of a fresco plastered and painted in a single day.

glazing An outermost layer of vitreous liquid (glaze) that, upon firing, renders ceramics waterproof, and forms a decorative surface. In painting, a technique particularly used with oil **media** in which a transparent layer of paint (glaze) is laid over another, usually lighter, painted or glazed area.

gold leaf Paper-thin sheets of hammered gold that are used in **gilding**.

graffiti Decorative drawings scratched on rocks, walls, or objects. Also: drawings and/or text of an obscene, political, or violent nature.

Grand Manner A grand and elevated **style** of painting popular in the eighteenth century in which the artist looked to the ancients and to the Renaissance for inspiration.

granulation A technique for decorating gold in which tiny balls of the precious metal are fused to the main surface in a pattern.

graphic arts A term referring to those arts that are drawn or printed and that utilize paper as primary support.

graphic design A concern in the visual arts for shape, line, and two-dimensional patterning, often especially apparent in works including typography and lettering.

Greek-cross plan See **central-plan building**.

grid A system of regularly spaced horizontally and vertically crossed lines that gives regularity to an architectural **plan**. Also: in painting, a **grid** enables designs to be enlarged or transferred easily.

grisaille A painting executed primarily in shades of gray.

groin vault See **vault**.

ground line The solid baseline that indicates the ground plane on which the figure stands. In ancient representations, such as those of the Egyptians, the figures and the objects are placed on a series of groundlines to indicate depth (space in registers).

guild An association of craftspeople. The medieval guild had great economic power, as it controlled the selling and marketing of its members' products, and it provided economic protection, political solidarity, and training in the craft to its members. The painters' guild was usually dedicated to Saint Luke, their patron saint.

half-barrel vault See **vault**.

hall church A building with nave and side aisles of equal height, creating a spacious and open interior especially suited for preaching.

halo A circle that surrounds and frames the heads of emperors and Christian saints to signify power and/or sanctity. Also known as a **nimbus**.

handscroll A long, narrow, horizontal painting or text (or combination thereof) common in Chinese and Japanese art and of a size intended for individual use. A handscroll is stored wrapped tightly around a wooden pin and is unrolled for viewing or reading.

hanging scroll In Chinese and Japanese art, a vertically oriented painting or text mounted within sections of silk. At the top is a semicircular rod; at the bottom is a round dowel. Hanging scrolls are kept rolled and tied except for special occasions, when they are hung for display, contemplation, or commemoration.

haniwa Pottery forms (cylinders, buildings, and human

figures) that were placed on top of Japanese tombs or burial mounds.

Happening An art form developed in the 1960s incorporating performance, theater, and visual images. A Happening was organized without a specific narrative or intent; with audience participation, the event proceeded according to chance and individual improvisation.

hemicycle A semicircular interior space or structure.

henge A circular area enclosed by stones or wood posts set up by Neolithic peoples. It is usually bounded by a ditch and raised embankment.

hieratic scale The use of different sizes for significant or holy figures and those of the everyday world to indicate importance. The larger the figure, the greater the importance.

hieroglyphs Picture writing; words and ideas rendered in the form of pictorial symbols.

high relief See **relief sculpture**.

historicism The strong consciousness of and attention to the institutions, themes, **styles**, and forms of the past, made accessible by historical research, textual study, and archaeology.

historiated capital See **capital**.

history painting Paintings based on historical, mythological, or biblical narratives. Once considered the noblest form of art, history paintings generally convey a high moral or intellectual idea and are often painted in a grand pictorial **style**.

hollow-casting See **lost-wax casting**.

horizon line A horizontal "line" formed by the implied meeting point of earth and sky. In **linear perspective**, the **vanishing point** or points are located on this "line."

horseshoe arch See **arch**.

house-church A Christian place of worship located in a private home.

house-synagogue A Jewish place of worship located in a private home.

hue Pure color. The saturation or intensity of the hue depends on the purity of the color. Its **value** depends on its lightness or darkness.

hydria A large ancient Greek and Roman jar with three handles (horizontal ones at both sides and one vertical at the back), used for storing water.

hypostyle hall A large interior room characterized by many closely spaced **columns** that support its roof.

icon An image in any material representing a sacred figure or event in the Byzantine, and later the Orthodox, Church. Icons were venerated by the faithful, who believed them to have miraculous powers to transmit messages to God.

iconic image A picture that expresses or embodies an intangible concept or idea.

iconoclasm The banning or destruction of **icons** and religious art. Iconoclasm in eighth- and ninth-century Byzantium and sixteenth- and seventeenth-century Protestant territories arose from differing beliefs about the power, meaning, function, and purpose of imagery in religion.

iconography The study of the significance and interpretation of the **subject matter** of art.

iconostasis A screen covered with **icons** that separates the **sanctuary** from the congregational space in a Byzantine church.

idealization A process in art through which artists strive to make their **forms** and figures attain perfection, based on pervading cultural values or their own mental image of beauty.

illumination A painting on paper or **parchment** used as illustration and/or decoration for **manuscripts** or **albums**. Usually done in rich colors, often supplemented by gold and other precious materials. The illustrators are referred to as illuminators. Also: the technique of decorating manuscripts with such paintings.

illusionism, illusionistic An appearance of reality in art created by the use of certain pictorial means, such as **perspective** and **foreshortening**. Also: the quality of having this type of appearance.

impasto Thickly applied paint that gives a three-dimensional surface quality to a painting.

impost, impost block A block, serving to concentrate the weight above, imposed between the **capital** of a **column** and the springing of an **arch** above.

impression Any single printing of an **intaglio** print (**engraving**, **drypoint**, or **etching**). Each and every impression of a print is by nature different, given the possibilities for variation inherent in the printing process, which re-quires the plate to be inked and wiped between every impression.

incising A technique in which a design or inscription is cut into a hard surface with a sharp instrument.

ink painting A monochromatic **style** of painting developed in China using black ink with gray **washes**.

inlay A decorative process in which pieces of one material are set into the surface of an object fashioned from a different material.

installation art A term coined in the 1960s and 1970s to refer to works created for a specific site and arranged (usually temporarily) to create a total environment.

intaglio Term used for a technique in which the design is carved out of the surface of an object, such as an engraved seal stone. In the **graphic arts**, intaglio includes **engraving**, **etching**, and **drypoint**—all processes in which ink transfers to paper from **incised**, ink-filled lines cut into a metal plate.

intarsia Technique of **inlay** decoration using variously-colored woods.

interlace A type of **linear** decoration in which ribbonlike bands are **illusionistically** depicted as if woven under and over one another.

intuitive perspective See **perspective**.

Ionic order See **order**.

iwan A large, **vaulted** chamber with a **monumental arched** opening on one side.

jamb In architecture, the vertical element found on both sides of an opening in a wall, and supporting an **arch** or **lintel**.

japonisme **A style** in nineteenth-century French and American art that was highly influenced by Japanese art.

joined-wood sculpture A method of constructing large-scale wooden sculpture developed in Japan. The entire work is constructed from smaller hollow blocks, each individually carved and assembled when complete. The joined-wood technique allowed the production of larger sculpture, as the multiple joints alleviate the problems of drying and cracking found with sculpture carved from a single block.

kente A woven cloth made by the Ashanti peoples of Africa. Kente cloth is woven in long, narrow pieces in complex and colorful patterns, which are then sewn together.

key block A key block is the master block in the production of a colored **woodcut**, which requires different blocks for each color. The key block is a flat piece of wood with the entire design carved or drawn on its surface. From this, other blocks with partial drawings are made for printing the areas of different colors.

keystone The topmost **voussoir** at the center of an arch, and the last block to be placed. The pressure of this block holds the arch together. Often of a larger size and/or decorated.

keep Principal tower in a castle.

kiln An oven designed to produce the high temperature for the baking, or firing, of clay.

kinetic art Artwork that contains parts that can be moved either by hand, air, or motor.

kiva A subterranean, circular room used as a ceremonial center in Native American settlements.

***kore* (*korai*)** An archaic Greek statue of a young woman.

***kouros* (*kouroi*)** An archaic Greek statue of a young man or boy.

kylix A shallow Greek vessel or cup, used for drinking, with a wide mouth and small handles near the rim.

lacquer A hard, glossy surface varnish. Lacquer can be layered and manipulated or combined with pigments and other materials for various decorative effects.

lancet A tall, narrow window crowned by a sharply pointed **arch**, typically found in Gothic architecture.

lantern A turretlike structure situated on a roof, **vault**, or **dome**, with windows that allow light into the space below.

Latin-cross plan A cross-shaped building plan, incorporating a long arm (nave) and three shorter arms.

linear, linearity An emphasis on line, as opposed to mass or color.

linear perspective See **perspective**.

lintel A horizontal element of any material carried by two or more vertical supports to form an opening.

literati painting A style of painting that reflects the taste of the educated class of East Asian intellectuals and scholars. Aspects include an appreciation for the antique, small scale, and an intimate connection between maker and audience.

lithograph A print made from a design drawn on a flat stone block with greasy crayon. Ink is applied to a wet stone and, when printed, adheres only to the greasy areas of the design.

loggia Italian term for a covered open-air **gallery**. Often used as a corridor between buildings or around a courtyard, loggias usually have **arcades** or **colonnades**.

longitudinal-plan building Any structure designed with a rectangular shape. If a cross-shaped building, the main arm of the building would be longer than any arms that cross it. For example, **Latin-cross plan** buildings.

lost-wax casting A method of casting metal, such as bronze, by a process in which a wax mold is covered with clay and plaster, then fired, melting the wax and leaving a hollow form. Molten metal is then poured into the hollow space and slowly cooled. When the hardened clay and plaster exterior shell is removed, a solid metal form remains to be smoothed and polished.

low-relief See **relief sculpture**.

lunette A semicircular wall area, framed by an **arch** over a door or window. Can be either plain or decorated.

madrasa An Islamic institution of higher learning, where teaching is focused on theology and law.

majolica Pottery painted with a tin **glaze** that, when fired, gives a lustrous and colorful surface.

mandala A concentric cosmic diagram that positions Buddhist deities in schematic order.

mandorla An almond-shaped area in which a sacred figure, such as Christ, is represented.

Mannerist A sophisticated, elegant style characterized by elongated **forms**, irrational spatial relationships, unusual colors and lighting effects, and exquisite craft. These traits are associated with the style called Mannerism of the sixteenth century.

manuscript A handwritten book or document.

maqsura An enclosure for rulers or dignitaries in front of the ***mihrab*** of a mosque.

martyrium (martyria) In Christian architecture, a church, chapel, or shrine built over the grave of a martyr or the site of a great miracle.

mastaba A flat-topped, one-story building with slanted walls over an ancient Egyptian underground tomb.

mathematical perspective See **perspective**.

matte A smooth surface without shine or luster.

mausoleum A monumental building used as a tomb. Named after the tomb of Mausolos erected at Halikarnassos around 350 BCE.

medallion Any round ornament or decoration. Also: a large medal.

medium (media) In general, the material from which any given object is made. In painting, the liquid substance in which pigments are suspended.

megaron A "great room" or large audience hall in a Mycenaean Greek ruler's residence.

menorah A Jewish lamp-stand with seven or nine branches; the nine-branched menorah is used during the celebration of Hanukkah. Representations of the seven-branched menorah, once used in the Temple of Jerusalem, became a symbol of Judaism.

metope The carved, painted, or plain rectangular spaces between the **triglyphs** of a **Doric frieze**.

middle ground Within the depicted space of an artwork, the area that takes up the middle distance of the image. See also **foreground**.

mihrab A recess or **niche** that distinguishes the wall oriented toward Mecca *(qibla)* in a mosque.

millefiori A term derived from the Italian for "a thousand flowers" that refers to a glass-making technique in which rods of differently-colored glass are fused in a long bundle that is subsequently sliced to produce disks or beads with small-scale, multicolor patterns.

minaret A tall slender tower on the exterior of a mosque from which believers are called to prayer.

minbar A high platform or pulpit in an Islamic mosque.

modeling In painting, the process of creating the illusion of three-dimensionality on a two-dimensional surface by the use of light and **shade**. In sculpture, the process of **molding** a three-dimensional form out of a malleable substance.

module A basic unit of construction.

molding A shaped or sculpted strip with varying contours and patterns. Used as decoration on architecture, furniture, frames, and other objects.

monumental A term used to designate a project or object that, whatever its physical size, gives an impression of grandeur.

mosaic Images formed by small colored stone or glass pieces (**tesserae**), affixed to a hard, stable surface.

mosque An edifice used for communal Muslim worship.

motif Any recurring element of a design or composition. Also: a recurring theme or subject in artwork.

Mozarabic An eclectic style practiced in Christian medieval Spain while much of the Iberian peninsula was ruled by Muslim dynasties.

mudra A symbolic hand gesture in Buddhist art that denotes certain behaviors, actions, or feelings.

mullion A slender straight or curving bar that divides a window into subsidiary sections to create **tracery**.

muqarna Niche-like cells that mark the transition between decorative flat and rounded surfaces; usually found on the **vault** of a **dome**.

mural Wall-like. A large painting or decoration, created either directly on the wall, or created separately and affixed to the wall.

naos The principal room in a temple or church. In ancient architecture, known as the **cella**. In a Byzantine church, known as the **nave** and **sanctuary**.

narrative image A picture that recounts an event drawn from a story, either factual (e.g., biographical) or fictional.

narthex The vestibule or entrance porch of a church.

naturalism, naturalistic A **style** of depiction in which the physical appearance of the rendered image in nature is the primary inspiration. A naturalistic work appears to record the visible world.

nave The central **aisle of a basilica**, two or three stories high and flanked by aisles, and defined by the nave **arcade** or nave **colonnade**.

necropolis A large cemetery or burial area, literally a city of the dead.

niche A hollow or recess in a wall or other solid architectural element. Niches can be of varying size and shape, and may be intended for many different uses, from display of objects to housing of a tomb.

niello A metal technique in which a black sulfur alloy is rubbed into fine lines **engraved** into a metal (usually gold or silver). When heated, the alloy becomes fused with the surrounding metal and provides contrasting detail.

nimbus Another term for **halo**. A figure whose head is surrounded by a nimbus is referred to as nimbed.

nonobjective art See **nonrepresentational**.

nonrepresentational Abstract art that does not attempt to reproduce the appearance of objects, figures, or scenes in the natural world. Also called **nonobjective art**.

obelisk A tall, four-sided stone **shaft**, hewn from a single block, that tapers at the top and is completed by a pyramidion. A sun symbol erected by the ancient Egyptians in ceremonial spaces (such as entrances to temple complexes). Today used as a commemorative monument.

oculus (oculi) In architecture, a circular opening. Oculi are usually found either as windows or at the apex of a **dome**. When at the top of a dome, an oculus is either open to the sky or covered by a decorative exterior **lantern**.

oil painting Any painting executed with the pigments floating in a **medium** of oil. Oil paint has particular properties that allow for greater ease of working (among others, a slow drying time, which allows for corrections, and a great range of relative opaqueness of paint layers, which permits a high degree of detail and luminescence).

one-point perspective See **perspective**.

openwork Decoration, such as **tracery**, with open spaces incorporated into the pattern.

orant The representation of a standing figure praying with outstretched and upraised arms.

oratory A small chapel.

order A system of proportions in **Classical** architecture that includes every aspect of the building's **plan**, **elevation**, and decorative system. **Composite**: a combination of the Ionic and the Corinthian orders. The **capital** combines **acanthus** leaves with **volute** scrolls. **Corinthian**: the most ornate of the orders, the Corinthian includes a **base**, a **fluted** column **shaft** with a capital elaborately decorated with acanthus leaf carvings. Its **entablature** consists of an **architrave** decorated with **moldings**, a **frieze** often containing sculptured **reliefs**, and a **cornice** with dentils. **Doric**: the column shaft of the Doric order can be **fluted** or smooth-surfaced and has no base. The Doric capital consists of an undecorated **echinus** and **abacus**. The Doric entablature has a plain architrave, a frieze with **metopes** and **triglyphs**, and a simple cornice. **Ionic**: the column of the Ionic order has a base, a **fluted** shaft, and a capital decorated with volutes. The Ionic entablature consists of an architrave of three panels and moldings, a frieze usually containing sculpted relief ornament, and a cornice with dentils. **Tuscan**: a variation of Doric characterized by a smooth-surfaced column shaft with a base, a plain architrave, and an undecorated frieze. A colossal order is any of the above built on a large scale, rising through several stories in height and often raised from the ground by a **pedestal**.

orthogonal Any line running back into the represented space of a picture perpendicular to the imagined **picture plane**. In **linear perspective**, all orthogonals converge at a single **vanishing point** in the picture and are the basis for a **grid** that maps out the internal space of the image. An orthogonal **plan** is any plan for a building or city that is based exclusively on right angles, such as the grid plan of many modern cities.

pagoda An East Asian **reliquary** tower built with successively smaller, repeated stories. Each story is usually marked by an elaborate, projecting roof.

painterly A **style** of painting which emphasizes the techniques and surface effects of brushwork (also color, light, and shade).

palazzo Italian term for palace, used for any large urban dwelling.

palette A handheld support used by artists for the storage and mixing of paint during the process of painting. Also: the choice of a range of colors made by an artist in a particular work, or typical of his or her style.

palmette A fan-shaped petal design used as decoration on classical Greek vases.

panel painting Any painting executed on a wood support. The wood is usually planed to provide a smooth surface. A panel can consist of several boards joined together.

parapet A low wall at the edge of a balcony, bridge, roof, or other place from which there is a steep drop, built for safety. A parapet walk is the passageway, usually open, immediately behind the uppermost exterior wall or battlement of a fortified building.

parchment A writing surface made from treated skins of animals. Very fine parchment is known as **vellum**.

passage In painting, passage refers to any particular area within a work, often those where **painterly** brushwork or color changes exist.

passage grave A prehistoric tomb under a **cairn**, reached by a long, narrow, slab-lined access passageway or passageways.

passage technique A term used to describe Paul Cezanne's technique of blending adjacent shapes in which shapes closed on one side are open on another so that they can merge.

patron The group or person who commissions or supports a work of art.

pedestal A platform or **base** supporting a sculpture or other monument. Also: the block found below the base of a **classical column** (or **colonnade**), serving to raise the entire element off the ground.

pediment A triangular **gable** found over major architectural elements such as **Classical** Greek **porticoes**, windows, or doors. Formed by an **entablature** and the ends of a sloping roof or a raking **cornice**. A similar architectural element is often used decoratively above a door or window, sometimes with a curved upper **molding**. A broken pediment is a variation on the traditional pediment, with an open space at the center of the topmost angle and/or the horizontal **cornice**.

pendentive The concave triangular section of a **vault** that forms the transition between a square or polygonal space and the circular base of a **dome**.

Performance Art An artwork based on a live, sometimes theatrical performance by the artist.

peristyle A surrounding **colonnade** in Greek architecture. A peristyle building is surrounded on the exterior by a colonnade. Also: a peristyle court is an open colonnaded courtyard, often having a pool and garden.

perspective A system for representing three-dimensional space on a two-dimensional surface. **Atmospheric perspective**: A method of rendering the effect of spatial distance by subtle variations in color and clarity of representation. **Intuitive perspective**: A method of giving the impression of recession by visual instinct, not by the use of an overall system or program. Oblique perspective: An intuitive spatial system in which a building or room is placed with one corner in the picture plane, and the other parts of the structure recede to an imaginary **vanishing point** on its other side. Oblique perspective is not a comprehensive, mathematical system. **One-point** and multiple-point **perspective** (also called **linear**, **scientific**, or **mathematical perspective**): A method of creating the illusion of three-dimensional space on a two-dimensional surface by delineating a **horizon line** and multiple **orthogonal** lines. These recede to meet at one or more points on the horizon (called vanishing points), giving the appearance of spatial depth. Called scientific or mathematical because its use requires some knowledge of geometry and mathematics, as well as optics. Reverse perspective: A Byzantine perspective theory in which the orthogonals or rays of sight do not converge on a vanishing point in the picture, but are thought to originate in the viewer's eye in front of the picture. Thus, in reverse perspective the image is constructed with orthogonals that diverge, giving a slightly tipped aspect to objects.

pictograph A highly stylized depiction serving as a symbol for a person or object. Also: a type of writing utilizing such symbols.

picture plane The theoretical spatial plane corresponding with the actual surface of a painting.

picturesque A term describing the taste for the familiar, the pleasant, and the pretty, popular in the eighteenth and nineteenth centuries in Europe. When contrasted with the **sublime**, the picturesque stood for all that was ordinary but pleasant.

pier A masonry support made up of many stones, or rubble and concrete (in contrast to a column **shaft**, which is formed by a single stone or a series of **drums**), often square or rectangular in plan and capable of carrying very heavy architectural loads. See also **compound pier**.

pietà A devotional subject in Christian religious art. After the Crucifixion the body of Jesus was laid across the lap of his grieving mother, Mary. When others are present the subject is called the Lamentation.

pilaster An engaged **columnar** element that is rectangular in format and used for decoration in architecture.

pinnacle In Gothic architecture, a steep pyramid decorating the top of another element such as a **buttress**. Also: the highest point.

plaiting In basketry, the technique of weaving strips of fabric or other flexible substances under and over each other.

plan A graphic convention for representing the arrangement of the parts of a building.

plate tracery See **tracery**.

plinth The slablike base or pedestal of a column, statue, wall, building, or piece of furniture.

pluralism A social structure or goal that allows members of diverse ethnic, racial, or other groups to exist within society while continuing to practice the customs of their own divergent cultures. Also: an adjective describing the state of having many valid contemporary styles available at the same time to artists.

podium A raised platform that acts as the foundation for a building, or as a platform for a speaker.

polychrome The multicolored painted decoration applied to any part of a building, sculpture, or piece of furniture.

porcelain A type of extremely hard and fine ceramic made from a mixture of kaolin and other minerals. Porcelain is fired at a very high heat, and the final product has a translucent surface.

portal A grand entrance, door, or gate, usually to an important public building, and often decorated with sculpture.

portico In architecture, a projecting roof or porch supported by **columns**, often marking an entrance.

post-and-lintel construction An architectural system of construction with two or more vertical elements (posts) supporting a horizontal element (lintel).

predella The lower zone, or base, of an **altarpiece**, decorated with painting or sculpture related to the main **iconographic** theme of the altarpiece.

primary colors Blue, red, and yellow, the three colors from which all others are derived.

pronaos The enclosed vestibule of a Greek or Roman temple, found in front of the cella and marked by a row of **columns** at the entrance.

proscenium The stage of an ancient Greek or Roman theater. In modern theater, the area of the stage in front of the curtain. Also: the framing **arch** that separates a stage from the audience.

punch A handheld metal instrument used to stamp decorative designs onto a surface, such as metal or leather.

***putto* (putti)** A plump, naked little boy, often winged. In classical art, called a cupid; in Christian art, a **cherub**.

pylon A massive gateway formed by a pair of tapering walls of oblong shape. Erected by ancient Egyptians to mark the entrance to a temple complex.

qibla The mosque wall oriented toward Mecca indicated by the **mihrab**.

quadrant vault See **vault**.

quillwork A Native American decorative craft technique. The quills of porcupines and bird feathers are dyed and attached to material in patterns.

raku A type of ceramic pottery made by hand, coated with a thick, dark **glaze**, and fired at a low heat. The resulting vessels are irregularly shaped and glazed and are highly prized for use in the Japanese tea ceremony.

readymade An object from popular or material culture presented without further manipulation as an artwork by the artist.

realism, realistic A term first used in Europe around 1850 to designate a kind of **naturalism** with a social or political message, which soon lost its didactic import and became synonymous with naturalism.

red-figure A style of ancient Greek vase painting made in the sixth and fifth centuries BCE. Characterized by red-clay-colored figures on a black **background**.

register A device used in systems of spatial definition. In painting, a register indicates the use of differing **groundlines** to differentiate layers of space within an image. In sculpture, the placement of self-contained bands of **reliefs** in a vertical arrangement. In printmaking, the marks at the edges used to align the print correctly on the page, especially in multiple-block color printing.

relic See **reliquary**.

relief sculpture A sculpted image or design whose flat background surface is carved away to a certain depth, setting off the figure. Called high or low (bas) relief depending upon the extent of projection of the image from the background. Called sunken relief when the image is modeled below the original surface of the background, which is not cut away.

relieving arch See **arch**.

reliquary A container, often made of precious materials, used as a repository for sacred **relics** (venerated objects associated with a saint or martyr).

repoussé A technique of hammering metal from the back to create a protruding image. Elaborate **reliefs** are created with wooden armatures against which the metal sheets are pressed and hammered.

representational Any art that attempts to depict an aspect of the external, natural world in a visually understandable way.

rib vault See **vault**.

roof comb In a Mayan building, a masonry wall along the apex of a roof that is built above the level of the roof proper. Roof combs support the highly decorated false **façades** that rise above the height of the building at the front.

rose window A round window, often filled with **stained glass**, with **tracery** patterns in the form of wheel spokes. Large, elaborate, and finely crafted, rose windows are usually a central element of the **façade** of French Gothic cathedrals.

rosette A round or oval ornament resembling a rose.

rotunda Any building (or part thereof) constructed in a circular (or sometimes polygonal) shape, usually producing a large open space crowned by a **dome**.

roundel Any element with a circular format, often placed as a decoration on the exterior of architecture.

rustication, rusticated In building, the rough, irregular, and unfinished effect deliberately given to the exterior facing of a stone edifice. Rusticated stones are often large and used for decorative emphasis around doors or windows or across the entire lower floors of a building.

sacristy In a Christian church, the room in which the priest's robes and the sacred vessels are housed. Sacristies are usually located close to the **sanctuary** and often have a place for ritual washing.

Salon The annual display of art by French artists in Paris during the eighteenth and nineteenth centuries. Established in the seventeenth century as a venue to show the work of members of the French Academy, the Salon and its judges established the accepted official style of the time.

sanctuary A sacred or holy enclosure used for worship. In ancient Greece and Rome, consists of one or more temples and an **altar**. In Christian architecture, the space around the altar in a church called the chancel or presbytery.

sarcophagus (sarcophagi) A rectangular stone coffin. Often decorated with **relief** sculpture.

scientific perspective See **perspective**.

scribe A professional who wrote texts or maintained written records.

scriptorium (scriptoria) A room in a monastery for writing or copying **manuscripts**.

sculpture in the round Three-dimensional sculpture that is carved free of any background or block.

sfumato In painting, the effect of haze in an image. Resembling the color of the atmosphere at dusk, *sfumato* gives a smoky effect.

sgraffito A decoration produced by scratching through plaster or glaze.

shade Any area of an artwork that is shown through various technical means to be in shadow.

shading The technique of making such an effect.

shaft The main vertical section of a **column** between the **capital** and the **base**, usually circular in cross section.

shikhara In the architecture of northern India, a conical (or pyramidal) structure found atop a Hindu temple.

side aisle See **aisle**.

site-specific sculpture A sculpture commissioned and designed for a particular spot.

slip A mixture of clay and water applied to a ceramic object as a final decorative coat. Also: a solution that binds different parts of a vessel together, such as the handle and the main body.

spandrel The area of wall adjoining the exterior curve of an **arch** between its springing and the **keystone**, or the area between two arches, as in an **arcade**.

squinch An **arch** or **lintel** built over the upper corners of a square space. Allows a circular or polygonal **dome** to be more securely set above the walls, and converts the space to an octagon.

stained glass Molten glass is given a color that becomes intrinsic to the material. Additional colors may be fused to the surface (flashing). Stained glass is most often used in windows, for which small pieces of differently-colored glass are precisely cut and assembled into a design, held together by **cames**. Additional painted details may be added to create images.

statue column An elongated human figure often appearing on the columns of Gothic portal jambs.

stele (stelae) A stone slab placed vertically and decorated with inscriptions or **reliefs**. Used as a grave marker or memorial.

stave church A Scandanavian wooden structure with four huge timbers (staves) at its core.

stereobate The series of steep steps that form a platform for Greek temples.

still life A type of painting that has as its subject inanimate objects (such as food, dishes, fruit, or flowers).

stringcourse A continuous horizontal band, such as a **molding**, decorating the face of a wall.

stucco A mixture of lime, sand, and other ingredients into a material that can be easily molded or modeled. When dry, produces a very durable surface used for covering walls or for architectural sculpture and decoration.

stupa In Buddhist architecture, a bell-shaped or pyramidal religious monument, made of piled earth or stone and containing sacred **relics**.

style A particular manner, **form**, or character of representation, construction, or expression typical of an individual artist or of a certain school or period.

stylization, stylized A manner of representation that conforms to an intellectual or artistic idea rather than to **naturalistic** appearances.

stylobate In **Classical** architecture, the stone foundation on which a temple stands.

stylus An instrument with a pointed end (used for writing and printmaking), which makes a delicate line or scratch. Also: a special writing tool for **cuneiform** writing with one pointed end and one triangular wedge end.

subject matter See **content**.

sublime A concept, thing, or state of exceptional and awe-inspiring beauty and moral or intellectual expression. The sublime was a goal to which many nineteenth-century artists aspired in their artworks.

sunken relief See **relief sculpture**.

swag A decorative device in architecture or interior ornament (and in paintings) in which a loosely hanging garland is made to look like flowers or gathered fabric.

taludtablero A design characteristic of Mayan architecture at Teotihuacan in which a sloping *talud* at the base of a building supports a wall-like *tablero,* where ornamental painting and sculpture are usually placed.

tapestry A pictorial textile in which the colored **weft** threads that form the pattern or pictures are woven into an un-dyed **warp** during the process of making the fabric itself.

tempera A painting **medium** made by blending egg or egg yolks with water, pigments, and occasionally other materials, such as glue.

tenebrism The use of strong **chiaroscuro** and artificially illuminated areas to create a dramatic contrast of light and dark in painting.

tepee A portable dwelling constructed from hides (later canvas) stretched on a structure of poles set at the base in a circle and leaning against one another at the top. Tepees were typically found among the nomadic Native Americans of the North American plains.

terracotta A **medium** made from clay fired over a low heat and sometimes left unglazed. Also: the orange-brown color typical of this medium.

tessera (tesserae) The small piece of stone, glass, or other object that is pieced together with many others to create a **mosaic**.

tholos tombs Circular, vaulted structures (often underground) used as burial places in Mycenean culture.

tint The dominant color in an object, image, or pigment.

tondo A painting or **relief** of circular shape.

tone The overall degree of brightness or darkness in an artwork. Also: saturation, intensity, or **value** of color and its effect.

torana In Indian architecture, an ornamented gateway **arch** in a temple, usually leading to the **stupa**.

torc A circular neck ring worn by Celtic warriors.

tracery Linear networks within a window opening or applied to a flat surface that often create elaborate decorative patterns. In **plate tracery** these patterns are created by removing areas or punching holes in flat, solid surfaces, while in **bar tracery** they are formed by bars of stone or wood called **mullions**.

transept The arm of a **cruciform** church, perpendicular to the **nave**. The point where the nave and **transept** cross is called the **crossing**. Beyond the crossing lies the **sanctuary**, whether **apse**, **choir**, or **chevet**.

triforium The element of the interior **elevation** of a church, found directly below the **clerestory** and consisting of a series of arched openings. The triforium can be made up of openings from a passageway or **gallery** or can be a plain or decorated wall.

triglyph Rectangular blocks between the **metopes** of a **Doric frieze**. Identified by the three carved vertical grooves, which approximate the appearance of the ends of wooden beams.

triptych An artwork made up of three panels. The panels may be hinged together so the side segments (wings) fold over the central area.

triumphal arch A freestanding, massive stone gateway with a large central **arch**, built as urban ornament and/or to celebrate military victories (as by the Romans).

trompe l'oeil A manner of representation in which the appearance of natural space and objects is recreated with the express intention of fooling the eye of the viewer, who may be convinced that the subject actually exists as three-dimensional reality.

trumeau **A column, pier,** or **post** found at the center of a large **portal** or doorway, supporting the **lintel**.

tugras Imperial ciphers developed into a specialized art form by the Ottomans.

Tuscan order See **order**.

twining A basketry technique in which short rods are sewn together vertically. The panels are then joined together to form a vessel.

tympanum In **Classical** architecture, the vertical panel of the **pediment**. In medieval and later architecture, the area over a door enclosed by an **arch** and a **lintel**, often decorated with sculpture or **mosaic**.

ukiyo-e A Japanese term for a type of popular art that was favored from the sixteenth century, particularly in the form of color **woodblock** prints. *Ukiyo-e* prints often depicted the world of the common people in Japan, such as courtesans and actors, as well as landscapes and myths.

undercutting A technique in sculpture by which the material is cut back under the edges so that the remaining form projects strongly forward, casting deep shadows.

underglaze Color or decoration applied to a ceramic piece before glazing.

value The darkness or lightness of a color (hue).

vanishing point In a **perspective** system, the point on the **horizon line** at which **orthogonals** meet. A complex system can have multiple vanishing points.

vanitas An image, especially popular in Europe during the seventeenth century, in which all the objects symbolize the transience of life. *Vanitas* paintings are usually of **still lifes** or **genre** subjects.

vault An **arched** masonry structure that spans an interior space. **Barrel** or tunnel **vault**: an elongated or continuous semicircular vault, shaped like a half-cylinder. **Groin** or cross **vault**: a vault created by the intersection of two barrel vaults of equal size which creates four side compartments of identical size and shape. **Quadrant** or **half-barrel vault**: as the name suggests, a half-barrel vault. **Rib vault**: ribs (extra masonry) demark the junctions of a groin vault. Ribs may function to reinforce the groins or may be purely decorative. **Corbeled vault**: a vault made by projecting courses of stone. See also **corbeling**.

vellum A fine animal skin prepared for writing and painting. See **parchment**.

veneer In architecture, the exterior facing of a building, often in decorative patterns of fine stone or brick. In decorative arts, a thin exterior layer of finer material (such as rare wood, ivory, metal, and semiprecious stones) laid over the form.

verism A **style** in which artists concern themselves with capturing the exterior likeness of an object or person, usually by rendering its visible details in a finely executed, meticulous manner.

villa A country house, usually on a large estate.

volumetric A term indicating the concern for rendering the impression of three-dimensional volumes in painting, usually achieved through **modeling** and the manipulation of light and shadow (**chiaroscuro**).

volute A spiral scroll, as seen on an **Ionic capital**.

votive figure An image created as a devotional offering to a god or other deity.

voussoirs The oblong, wedge-shaped stone blocks used to build an **arch**. The topmost voussoir is called a **keystone**.

wall painting See **mural**.

ware A general term designating pottery produced and decorated by the same technique.

warp The vertical threads in a weaver's loom. Warp threads make up a fixed framework that provides the structure for the entire piece of cloth, and are thus often thicker than weft threads. See also **weft**.

wash A diluted watercolor or ink. Washes may be applied to drawings or prints to add **tone** or touches of color.

watercolor A painting technique in which pigments suspended in water are applied to absorbent paper, creating an image that cannot be corrected or reworked.

weft The horizontal threads in a woven piece of cloth. Weft threads are woven at right angles to and through the warp threads to make up the bulk of the decorative pattern. In carpets, the weft is often completely covered or formed by the rows of trimmed knots that form the carpet's soft surface. See also **warp**.

westwork The monumental, west-facing entrance section of a Carolingian, Ottonian, or Romanesque church. The exterior consists of multiple stories between two towers; the interior includes an entrance vestibule, a chapel, and a series of **galleries** overlooking the **nave**.

wing A side panel of a **triptych** or **polyptych** (usually found in pairs), which was hinged to fold over the central panel. Wings often held the depiction of the donors and/or subsidiary scenes relating to the central image.

woodblock print A print made from a block of wood that is carved in **relief** or **incised**.

woodcut A type of print made by carving a design into a wooden block. The ink is applied to the plate with a roller. As the ink remains only on the raised areas between the carved-away lines, these carved-away areas and lines provide the white areas of the print. Also: the process by which the woodcut is made.

x-ray style In Aboriginal art, a manner of representation in which the artist depicts a figure or animal by illustrating its outline as well as essential internal organs and bones.

ziggurat In Mesopotamia, a tall stepped tower of earthen materials, often supporting a shrine.

Selected Bibliography

Revised and updated by Mary Clare Altenhofen, Fine Arts Library, Harvard University.

General

30,000 Years of Art: The Story of Human Creativity Across Time and Space. London; New York: Phaidon, 2007.

Adams, Laurie Schneider. *Art across Time.* 3rd ed. New York: McGraw-Hill, 2007.

Andrews, Malcolm. *Landscape and Western Art.* Oxford History of Art. Oxford: Oxford Univ. Pr., 1999.

The Art Atlas. Ed. John Onians. New York: Abbeville, 2008.

Ball, Philip. *Bright Earth: Art and the Invention of Color.* Chicago: Univ. of Chicago Pr., 2003.

Bell, Julian. *Mirror of the World: A New History of Art.* London: Thames & Hudson, 2007.

Bearden, Romare. *A History of African American Artists: From 1792 to the Present.* New York: Pantheon, 1993.

Berlo, Janet Catherine, and Lee Ann Wilson. *Arts of Africa, Oceania, and the Americas: Selected Readings.* Englewood Cliffs, N.J.: Prentice Hall, 1993.

Breward, Christopher. *Fashion.* Oxford History of Art. Oxford; New York: Oxford Univ. Pr., 2003.

The Bulfinch Guide to Art History: A Comprehensive Survey and Dictionary of Western Art and Architecture. Ed. Shearer West. Boston: Little, Brown, 1996.

Büttner, Nils. *Landscape Painting: A History.* New York: Abbeville, 2006.

Chadwick, Whitney. *Women, Art, and Society.* 4th. ed. New York: Thames & Hudson, 2007.

A Concise History of Architecture Styles. Ed. Emily Clark. London: A & C Black, 2003.

The Concise Oxford Dictionary of Art and Artists. Ed. Ian Chilvers. 3rd ed. Oxford; New York: Oxford Univ. Pr., 2003.

Conway, Hazel. *Understanding Architecture: An Introduction to Architecture and Architectural History.* 2nd ed. London; New York: Routledge, 2005.

The Dictionary of Art. Ed. Jane Turner. 34 vols. New York: Grove's Dictionaries, 1996.

Dictionary of Women Artists. Ed. Delia Gaze. London; Chicago: Fitzroy Dearborn, 1997.

A Documentary History of Art. Ed. Elizabeth G. Holt. 3 vols. New Haven: Yale Univ. Pr., 1986.

Encounters: The Meeting of Asia and Europe, 1500-1800. Ed. Anna Jackson & Amin Jaffer. London: Victoria & Albert; New York: Abrams, 2004.

Encyclopedia of Gardens: History and Design. Ed. Candice Shoemaker. Chicago: Fitzroy Dearborn, 2001.

Encyclopedia of Comparative Iconography: Themes Depicted in Works of Art. Ed. Helene Roberts. 2 vols. Chicago: Fitzroy Dearborn, 1998.

Encyclopedia of World Art. 17 vols. New York: McGraw-Hill, 1972–87.

Fazio, Michael W. *A World History of Architecture.* 2nd ed. Boston: McGraw-Hill, 2008.

Gascoigne, Bamber. *How to Identify Prints: A Complete Guide to Manual and Mechanical Processes From Woodcut to Inkjet.* 2nd ed. New York: Thames & Hudson, 2004.

Gardner, Helen. *Gardner's Art through the Ages.* 12th ed. Eds. F. Kleiner & C. Mamiya. Fort Worth: Harcourt Brace College, 2005.

Griffiths, Antony. *Prints and Printmaking: An Introduction to the History and Techniques.* 2nd ed. London: British Museum, 1996.

Hall, James. *Dictionary of Subjects and Symbols in Art.* 2nd. ed. Boulder: Westview, 2008.

Heller, Nancy G. *Women Artists: An Illustrated History.* 4th ed. New York: Abbeville, 2003.

Honour, Hugh. *The Visual Arts: A History.* 7th ed. Upper Saddle River, NJ: Pearson Prentice Hall, 2005.

Hughes, Robert. *American Visions: The Epic History of Art in America.* New York: Knopf, 1997.

Hults, Linda C. *The Print in the Western World: An Introductory History.* Madison: Univ. of Wisconsin Pr., 1996.

Janson, H. W. *Janson's History of Art: the Western Tradition.* Penelope J.E. Davies et al. 8th ed., Upper Saddle River, NJ: Pearson Prentice Hall, 2010.

Johnson, Paul. *Art: A New History.* New York: HarperCollins, 2003.

Kemp, Martin. *The Oxford History of Western Art.* Oxford: Oxford Univ. Pr., 2000.

Kostof, Spiro. *A History of Architecture: Settings and Rituals.* 2nd ed. New York: Oxford Univ. Pr., 1995.

Langmuir, Erika. *Yale Dictionary of Art and Artists.* New Haven: Yale Univ. Pr., 2000.

Marien, Mary W. *Photography: A Cultural History.* 3rd ed. Upper Saddle River, NJ: Pearson Prentice Hall, 2010.

McConkey, Wilfred J. *Klee as in Clay: A Pronunciation Guide.* 3rd ed. Lantham, MD: Madison Books, 1992.

Morgan, Ann Lee. *The Oxford Dictionary of American Art and Artists.* Oxford; New York: Oxford Univ. Pr., 2007.

Ochoa, George, and Melinda Corey. *The Wilson Chronology of the Arts.* New York: H.W. Wilson, 1998.

The Oxford Companion to Western Art. Ed. Hugh Brigstocke. Oxford; New York: Oxford Univ. Pr., 2001.

Patton, Sharon F. *African-American Art.* Oxford; New York: Oxford Univ. Pr., 1998.

The Penguin Dictionary of Architecture and Landscape Architecture. John Fleming et al. 5th ed. New York: Penguin, 1998.

Pohl, Frances. *Framing America: A Social History of American Art.* 2nd ed. New York: Thames & Hudson, 2008.

Rosenblum, Naomi. *A World History of Photography.* 4th ed. New York: Abbeville, 2007.

Roth, Leland M. *Understanding Architecture: Its Elements, History, and Meaning.* New York: Icon Editions, 1993.

Shepherd, Rowena. *1000 Symbols.* New York: Thames & Hudson, 2002.

Slatkin, Wendy. *Women Artists in History: From Antiquity to the Present.* 4th ed. Upper Saddle River, NJ: Prentice Hall, 2001.

St. James Guide to Black Artists. Pref. H. Dodson. Detroit: St. James Pr., 1997.

Stokstad, Marilyn. *Art History.* 3rd ed. Upper Saddle River, NJ: Prentice Hall, 2008.

Sutton, Ian. Western *Architecture: From Ancient Greece to the Present.* World of Art. New York: Thames & Hudson, 1999.

Trachtenberg, Marvin, and Isabelle Hyman. *Architecture, from Prehistory to Postmodernity.* 2nd ed. New York: Abrams, 2002.

Watkin, David. *A History of Western Architecture.* 4th ed. New York: Watson-Guptill, 2005.

Wilkins, David, et al. *Art Past/Art Present.* 6th ed. Upper Saddle River, NJ: Prentice Hall, 2009.

Women Artists: The National Museum of Women in the Arts. Ed. Susan F. Sterling. New York: Abbeville, 1995.

Introduction

Acton, Mary. *Learning to Look at Paintings.* 2nd ed. New York: Routledge, 2009.

The Architecture Reader: Essential Writings from Vitruvius to the Present. Ed. A. Krista Sykes. New York: Braziller, 2007.

Arnold, Dana. *Art History: A Very Short Introduction.* Oxford; New York: Oxford Univ. Pr., 2004.

Art and History: Images and Their Meaning. Eds. Robert Rothberg & Theodore Rabb. Cambridge: Cambridge Univ. Pr., 1988.

Art in Theory 1648-1815: An Anthology of Changing Ideas. Eds. Charles Harrison et al. Oxford; Malden, MA: Blackwell, 2001.

Art in Theory, 1815-1900: An Anthology of Changing Ideas. Eds. Charles Harrison et al. Malden, MA: Blackwell, 1998.

The Art of Art History: A Critical Anthology. Ed. Donald Preziosi. Oxford; New York: Oxford Univ. Pr., 1998.

Baxandall, Michael. *Patterns of Intention: On the Historical Explanation of Pictures.* New Haven: Yale Univ. Pr., 1985.

A Companion to Art Theory. Eds. Paul Smith & Carolyn Wilde. Oxford: Blackwell, 2002.

Critical Terms for Art History. Eds. Robert S. Nelson & Richard Shiff. 2nd ed. Chicago: Univ. of Chicago Pr., 2003.

Freeland, Cynthia A. *Art Theory: A Very Short Introduction.* Oxford; New York: Oxford Univ. Pr., 2003.

Geertz, Clifford. "Art as a Cultural System." *Modern Language Notes* 91, 1976, pp. 1473-1499.

Glancey, Jonathan. *Architecture.* New York: DK Pub., 2006.

Langer, Suzanne. *Feeling and Form.* Upper Saddle River, NJ: Prentice Hall, 1978.

Leppert, Richard D. *The Nude: The Cultural Rhetoric of the Body in the Art of Western Modernity.* Boulder, CO: Westview, 2007.

MacGregor, Arthur. *Curiosity and Enlightenment: Collectors and Collections From the 16th to the 19th Century.* New Haven; London: Yale Univ. Pr., 2007.

Minor, Vernon Hyde. *Art History's History.* Upper Saddle River, NJ: Prentice Hall, 2001.

Panofsky, Erwin. *Meaning in the Visual Arts.* Phoenix ed. Chicago: Univ. of Chicago Pr., 1982, 1955.

Preble, Duane. *Artforms: An Introduction to the Visual Arts.* 8th ed. Upper Saddle River, NJ: Pearson Prentice Hall, 2008.

Recht, Roland, et al. *The Great Workshop: Pathways of Art in Europe, 5th to 18th Centuries.* Brussels: Mercatorfonds; Ithaca: Cornell Univ. Pr., 2007.

Sowers, Robert. *Rethinking the Forms of Visual Expression.* Berkeley: Univ. of California Pr., 1990.

Taylor, Joshua. *Learning to Look: A Handbook for the Visual Arts.* Chicago: Chicago Univ. Pr., 1981.

Williams, Robert. *Art Theory: An Historical Introduction.* Malden, MA: Blackwell, 2004.

Chapter 1 Prehistoric Art in Europe

Bahn, Paul G. *The Cambridge Illustrated History of Prehistoric Art.* Cambridge: Cambridge Univ. Pr., 1998.

Bataille, Georges. *The Cradle of Humanity: Prehistoric Art and Culture.* Ed. Stuart Kendall. New York: Zone Books; Cambridge, MA: MIT Pr., 2005.

Blocker, H. Gene. *The Aesthetics of Primitive Art.* Lantham, MD.: Univ. Pr. of America, 1994.

Boardman, John. *The World of Ancient Art.* London; New York: Thames & Hudson, 2006.

Chippindale, Christopher. *Stonehenge Complete.* New and exp. ed. New York: Thames & Hudson, 2004.

Clottes, Jean. *Cave Art.* London; New York: Phaidon, 2008.

______. *World Rock Art.* Los Angeles: Getty Conservation Institute, 2002.

Haywood, John. *The Cassell Atlas of the Ancient World: 4,000,000 - 500 BC.* London: Cassell, 1998.

Hill, Rosemary. *Stonehenge.* Cambridge, MA: Harvard Univ. Pr., 2008.

Leick, Gwendolyn. *A Dictionary of Ancient Near Eastern Architecture.* London; New York: Routledge, 1988.

McCarter, Susan Foster. *Neolithic.* New York; London: Routledge, 2007.

Price, T. Douglas. *Images of the Past.* 5th ed. Boston: McGraw-Hill, 2008.

Runnels, Curtis Neil. *Greece Before History: An Archaeological Companion and Guide.* Stanford, CA: Stanford Univ. Pr., 2001.

Sandars, N. K. *Prehistoric Art in Europe.* 2nd ed. Pelican History of Art. New Haven: Yale Univ. Pr., 1995.

Sura Ramos, Pedro A. *The Cave of Altamira.* New York: Abrams, 1999.

White, Randall. *Prehistoric Art: The Symbolic Journey of Mankind.* New York: Abrams, 2003.

Chapter 2 Art of the Ancient Near East

Beyond Babylon: Art, Trade, and Diplomacy in the Second Millennium B.C. Ed. Joan Aruz et al. New York: Metropolitan Museum of Art; New Haven: Yale Univ. Pr., 2008.

Black, Jeremy A. *Gods, Demons and Symbols of Ancient Mesopotamia: An Illustrated Dictionary.* London: British Museum, 1992.

Bottéro, Jean. *Ancestor of the West: Writing, Reasoning, and Religion in Mesopotamia, Elam, and Greece.* Chicago: Univ. of Chicago Pr., 2000.

Collon, Dominique. *Ancient Near Eastern Art.* Berkeley: Univ. of California Pr., 1995.

Curatola, Giovanni, et al. *The Art and Architecture of Mesopotamia.* New York: Abbeville, 2007.

______. *The Art and Architecture of Persia.* New York: Abbeville, 2007.

Curtis, John. *Ancient Persia.* Cambridge, MA: Harvard Univ. Pr., 1989.

Errington, Elizabeth. *From Persepolis to the Punjab: Exploring Ancient Iran, Afghanistan and Pakistan.* London: British Museum, 2007.

Forgotten Empire: The World of Ancient Persia. Ed. John Curtis & Nigel Tallis. Berkeley: Univ. of California Pr., 2005.

Fildes, Alan. *Alexander the Great: Son of the Gods.* Los Angeles: J. Paul Getty Museum, 2002.

Frankfort, Henri. *The Art and Architecture of the Ancient Orient.* 5th ed. Pelican History of Art. New Haven: Yale Univ. Pr., 1996.

Haywood, John. *Ancient Civilizations of the Near East and the Mediterranean.* London: Cassell, 1997.

Leick, Gwendolyn. *A Dictionary of Ancient Near Eastern Architecture.* London; New York: Routledge, 1988.

Roaf, Michael. *Cultural Atlas of Mesopotamia and the Ancient Near East.* New York: Facts on File, 1990.

Roux, Georges. *Ancient Iraq.* 3rd ed. London: Penguin, 1992.

Saggs, H. W. F. *Babylonians.* London: British Museum, 1995.

______. *Civilization before Greece and Rome.* New Haven: Yale Univ. Pr., 1989.

Winter, Irene. "Sex, Rhetoric and the Public Monument: The Alluring Body of the Male Ruler in Mesopotamia." In *Sexuality in Ancient Art,* Eds. N. B. Kampen et al. Cambridge & New York: Cambridge Univ. Pr., 1996, pp. 11-26.

Chapter 3 Art of Ancient Egypt

Aldred, Cyril. *The Egyptians.* 3rd ed. rev. and updated by Aidan Dodson. London: Thames & Hudson, 1998.

Andrews, Carol. *Ancient Egyptian Jewelry.* New York: Abrams, 1991.

Arnold, Dieter. *The Encyclopedia of Ancient Egyptian Architecture.* Princeton: Princeton Univ. Pr., 2003.

______. *Temples of the Last Pharaohs.* New York: Oxford Univ. Pr., 1999.

Brier, Bob. *Daily Life of the Ancient Egyptians.* 2nd ed. Westport, CT: Greenwood, 2008.

Egyptian Art in the Age of the Pyramids. New York: Metropolitan Museum of Art, 1999.

Egyptian Treasures from the Egyptian Museum in Cairo. Ed. Francesco Tiarditti. New York: Abrams, 1999.

Foster, John L., trans. *Love Songs of the New Kingdom.* New York: Charles Scribner's Sons, 1974.

Hellum, Jennifer. *The Pyramids.* Westport, CT: Greenwood, 2007.

Kozloff, Arielle P *Egypt's Dazzling Sun: Amenhotep III and His World.* Cleveland: Cleveland Museum of Art, 1992.

Lehner, Mar. *The Complete Pyramids.* New York: Thames & Hudson, 1997.

Malek, Jaromir. *Egyptian Art.* Art & Ideas. London: Phaidon, 1999.

_____. *Egypt: 4,000 Years of Art.* London: Phaidon, 2003.

Menu, Bernadette. *Ramesses II: Greatest of the Pharaohs.* Discoveries. New York: Abrams, 1999.

Montet, Pierre. *Everyday Life in Egypt in the Days of Ramesses the Great.* Trans. A. R. Maxwell-Hysop & Margaret S. Drower. Philadelphia: Univ. of Pennsylvania Pr., 1981.

Müller, Hans Wolfgang. *Gold of the Pharaohs.* Ithaca, NY: Cornell Univ. Pr., 1999.

The Pharaohs. Ed. Cristiane Ziegler. New York: Rizzoli, 2002.

Pharaohs of the Sun: Akhenaten, Nefertiti, Tutankhamen. Eds. Rita E. Freed, Yvonne J. Markowitz & Sue H. D'Auria. Boston: Museum of Fine Arts; Little, Brown, 1999.

Reeves, C.N. *The Complete Tutankhamun: The King, the Tomb, the Royal Treasure.* London: Thames & Hudson,1990.

______. *The Complete Valley of the Kings: Tombs and Treasures of Egypt's Greatest Pharaohs.* London: Thames & Hudson, 1996.

Robins, Gay. *The Art of Ancient Egypt.* Rev. ed. Cambridge, MA: Harvard Univ. Pr., 2008.

Russmann, Edna R. *Temples and Tombs: Treasures of Egyptian Art from the British Museum.* New York: American Federation of Arts; Seattle : Univ. of Washington Pr., 2006.

______. *Civilization before Greece and Rome.* New Haven: Yale Univ. Pr., 1989.

Stierlin, Henri. *The Pharaohs Master-Builders.* Paris: Terrail, 1995.

Walker, Susan. *Ancient Faces: Mummy Portraits from Roman Egypt.* 2nd ed. London: British Museum, 2000.

Wilkinson, Richard H. *Reading Egyptian Art: A Hieroglyphic Guide to Ancient Egyptian Painting and Sculpture.* London: Thames & Hudson, 1992.

Winstone, H. V. F. *Howard Carter and the Discovery of the Tomb of Tutankhamun.* Rev. ed. Manchester: Barzan, 2006.

Chapter 4 Early Asian Art

Ancient Sichuan: Treasures From a Lost Civilization. Ed. Robert Bagley. Seattle: Seattle Art Museum; Princeton: Princeton Univ. Pr., 2001.

Barnhart, Richard M. *Three Thousand Years of Chinese Painting.* New Haven: Yale Univ. Pr., 1997.

Behl, Benoy K. *The Ajanta Caves: Artistic Wonder of Ancient Buddhist India.* New York: Abrams, 1998.

Berkson, Carmel. *The Life of Form in Indian Sculpture.* New Delhi: Abhinav, 2000.

Brand, Michael. *The Vision of Kings: Art and Experience in India.* Canberra: National Gallery of Australia; New York: Thames & Hudson, 1995.

Clunas, Craig. *Art in China.* Oxford History of Art. Oxford: Oxford Univ. Pr., 1997.

Craven, Roy C. *Indian Art: A Concise History.* Rev. ed. World of Art. New York: Thames & Hudson, 1997.

The Crossroads of Asia: Transformation in Image and Symbol in the Art of Ancient Afghanistan and Pakistan. Ed. Elizabeth Errington. Cambridge: Ancient India and Iran Trust, 1992.

Dehejia, Vidya. *Indian Art.* Art & Ideas. London: Phaidon, 1997.

Ebrey, Patricia B. *The Cambridge Illustrated History of China.* 2nd ed. Cambridge: Cambridge Univ. Pr., 2010.

Eck, Diana L. *Darsan: Seeing the Divine Image in India.* 3rd ed. Chambersburg, PA: Anima, 1998.

Elisseeff, Danielle, and Vadime Elisseeff. *Art of Japan.* New York: Abrams, 1985.

Fang, Jing Pei. *Symbols and Rebuses in Chinese Art: Figures, Bugs, Beasts, and Flowers.* Berkeley, CA: Ten Speed Pr., 2004.

Frampton, Kenneth. *Japanese Building Practice: From Ancient Times to the Meiji Period.* New York: Van Nostrand Reinhold, 1997.

The Glory of the Silk Road: Art From Ancient China. Ed. Li Jian. Dayton, Ohio: Dayton Art Institute, 2003.

Harle, James C. *The Art and Architecture of the Indian Subcontinent.* 2nd ed. Pelican History of Art. New Haven: Yale Univ. Pr., 1994.

Heller, Amy. *Early Himalayan Art.* Oxford: Ashmolean Museum, 2008.

Khanna, Balraj. *Human and Divine: 2000 Years of Indian Sculpture.* London: Hayward Gallery; Berkeley, CA: Univ. of California Pr., 2000.

Lee, Sherman E. *A History of Far Eastern Art.* 5th ed. New York: Abrams, 1994.

_____. *China, 5,000 Years: Innovation and Transformation in the Arts.* New York: Solomon R. Guggenheim Museum, 1998.

Mason, Penelope. *History of Japanese Art.* 2nd. ed. Rev. by Donald Dinwiddie. Upper Saddle River, NJ: Pearson/Prentice Hall, 2005.

Michell, George. *Elephanta.* Bombay: India Book House, 2002.

Mitter, Partha. *Indian Art.* Oxford; New York: Oxford Univ. Pr., 2001.

Owyoung, Steven D. *Ancient Chinese Bronzes in the Saint Louis Art Museum.* St. Louis, MO: St. Louis Art Museum, 1997.

Paine, Robert Treat. *Art and Architecture of Japan.* 3rd ed. Pelican History of Art. Harmondsworth, UK: Penguin, 1981.

Pearson, Richard. *Ancient Japan.* Washington, DC: Sackler Gallery, 1992.

Possessing the Past: Treasures From the National Palace Museum. New York: Metropolitan Museum of Art; Taipei: National Palace Museum, 1996.

Rhie, Marylin M. *Early Buddhist Art of China and Central Asia.* 2 vols. in 3. Leiden; Boston: Brill, 1999-2002.

Shinto: The Sacred Art of Ancient Japan. Ed. Victor Harris. London: British Museum, 2001.

Stanley-Baker, Joan. *Japanese Art.* Rev. & exp. ed. World of Art. New York: Thames & Hudson, 2000.

Sullivan, Michael. *The Arts of China.* 4th ed. exp. & rev. Berkeley: Univ. of California Pr., 1999.

Thorp, Robert L.*Chinese Art and Culture.* New York: Abrams, 2001.

Tregear, Mary. *Chinese Art.* Rev. ed. World of Art. New York: Thames & Hudson, 1997.

Watson, William. *The Arts of China to AD 900.* Pelican History of Art. New Haven: Yale Univ. Pr., 1995.

Welch, Patricia B. *Chinese Art: A Guide to Motifs and Visual Imagery.* North Clarendon, VT: Tuttle, 2008.

Whitfield, Roderick, and Anne Farrer. *Caves of the Thousand Buddhas: Chinese Art from the Silk Route.* London: British Museum, 1990.

Chapter 5 Art of Ancient Greece and the Aegean World

Ashmole, Bernard. *Architect and Sculptor in Classical Greece.* Wrightsman Lectures. New York: New York Univ. Pr., 1972.

Barletta, Barbara A. *The Origins of the Greek Architectural Orders.* Cambridge; New York: Cambridge Univ. Pr., 2001.

Beard, Mary. *Classical Art: From Greece to Rome.* Oxford History of Art. Oxford: Oxford Univ. Pr., 2001.

Biers, William. *The Archaeology of Greece: An Introduction.* 2nd ed. Ithaca: Cornell Univ. Pr., 1996.

Boardman, John. *Greek Art.* Rev. and exp. 4th ed. World of Art. London: Thames & Hudson, 1997.

_____. Greek Sculpture: *The Archaic Period, A Handbook.* World of Art. New York: Oxford Univ. Pr., 1991.

_____. *The Greeks Overseas: Their Early Colonies and Trade.* Rev. ed. London: Thames & Hudson, 1999.

_____. Greek Sculpture: *The Classical Period, A Handbook.* London: Thames & Hudson, 1985.

Burn, Lucilla. *Hellenistic Art: From Alexander the Great to Augustus.* Los Angeles: J. Paul Getty Museum, 2004.

The Cambridge Companion to Archaic Greece. Ed. H.A. Shapiro. Cambridge; New York: Cambridge Univ. Pr., 2007.

The Cambridge Companion to the Aegean Bronze Age. Ed. Cynthia W. Shelmerdine. Cambridge; New York: Cambridge Univ. Pr., 2008.

The Cambridge Illustrated History of Ancient Greece. Ed. Paul Cartledge. Cambridge Illustrated History. Cambridge: Cambridge Univ. Pr., 1998.

Curl, James S. *Classical Architecture: An Introduction to its Vocabulary and Essentials.* New York: Norton, 2003.

Fitton, J. Lesley. *Cycladic Art.* 2nd ed. London: British Museum, 1999.

Fullerton, Mark D. *Greek Art.* Cambridge: Cambridge Univ. Pr., 2000.

Grant, Michael. *Atlas of Classical History.* 5th ed. New York: Oxford Univ. Pr., 1994.

______. *Myths of the Greeks and Romans.* New York: Meridian, 1995.

Great Moments in Greek Archaeology. Athens: Kapon Editions, 2007.

Greek Sculpture: Function, Materials, and Techniques in the Archaic and Classical Periods. Ed. Olga Palagia. New York: Cambridge Univ. Pr., 2006.

Hard, Robin. *The Routledge Handbook of Greek Mythology: Based on H.J. Rose's "Handbook of Greek Mythology."* London; New York: Routledge, 2004.

Higgins, Reynold. *Minoan and Mycenean Art.* Rev. ed. World of Art. New York: Thames & Hudson, 1997.

Hurwit, Jeffrey M. *The Acropolis in the Age of Pericles.* Cambridge; New York: Cambridge Univ. Pr., 2004.

Jenkins, Ian. *The Parthenon Sculptures.* Cambridge: Harvard Univ. Pr., 2007.

Kunze, Max. *The Pergamon Altar: Its Rediscovery, History, and Reconstruction.* Berlin: Staatliche Museen zu Berlin, Antikensammlung, 1991.

Lawrence, A. W. *Greek Architecture.* Rev. by R.A. Tomlinson. 5th ed. Pelican History of Art. New Haven: Yale Univ. Pr., 1996.
Neils, Jenifer. *The British Museum Concise Introduction to Ancient Greece.* Ann Arbor, MI: Univ. of Michigan Pr., 2008.
Osborne, Robin. *Archaic and Classical Greek Art.* Oxford History of Art. Oxford: Oxford Univ. Pr., 1998.
The Parthenon: From Antiquity to the Present. Ed. Jenifer Neils. Cambridge; New York: Cambridge Univ. Pr., 2005.
Pedley, John Griffiths. *Greek Art and Archaeology.* 4th ed. Upper Saddle River, NJ: Pearson/Prentice Hall, 2007.
Pollitt, J.J. *Art and Experience in Classical Greece.* Cambridge: Cambridge Univ. Pr., 1972.
____. *Art in the Hellenistic Age.* Cambridge: Cambridge Univ. Pr., 1986.
____. *The Art of Ancient Greece: Sources and Documents.* Cambridge; New York: Cambridge Univ. Pr., 1990.
Preziosi, Donald, and Louise Hitchcock. *Aegean Art and Architecture.* Oxford History of Art. Oxford: Oxford Univ. Pr., 1999.
Smith, R.R.R. *Hellenistic Sculpture: A Handbook.* World of Art. New York: Thames & Hudson, 1991.
Spivey, Nigel. *Greek Art.* Art & Ideas. London: Phaidon, 1997.
Stewart, Andrew F. *Greek Sculpture: An Exploration.* 2 vols. New Haven: Yale Univ. Pr., 1990.

Chapter 6 Etruscan and Roman Art

Allan, Tony. *Life, Myth and Art in Ancient Rome.* Los Angeles: J. Paul Getty Museum, 2005.
Art of the Classical World in the Metropolitan Museum of Art: Greece, Cyprus, Etruria, Rome. New York: Metropolitan Museum of Art; New Haven: Yale Univ. Pr., 2007.
Balsdon, J. P. V. D. *Roman Women.* London: The Bodley Head, 1962.
Borrelli, Federica. *The Etruscans: Art, Architecture, and History.* Los Angeles: J. Paul Getty Museum, 2004.
Breeze, David J. *Hadrian's Wall.* 4th ed. London: Penguin, 2000.
Brendel, Otto J. *Prolegomena to the Study of Roman Art.* New Haven, Yale Univ. Pr., 1979.
____. *Etruscan Art.* 2nd ed. Pelican History of Art. New Haven: Yale Univ. Pr., 1995.
Brown, Peter. *The World of Late Antiquity: A.D. 150-750.* New York: Norton, 1989.
D'Ambra, Eve. *Roman Art.* Cambridge: Cambridge Univ. Pr., 1998.
Dunabin, Katherine M.D. *Mosaics of the Greek and Roman World.* Cambridge: Cambridge Univ. Pr., 1999.
Elsner, Ja. *Imperial Rome and Christian Triumph: The Art of the Roman Empire, A.D. 100–450.* Oxford History of Art. Oxford: Oxford Univ. Pr., 1998.
Gabucci, Ada. *Ancient Rome: Art, Architecture, and History.* Los Angeles: J. Paul Getty Museum, 2002.
____. *Rome.* Berkeley: Univ. of California Pr., 2006.
Haynes, Sybille. *Etruscan Civilization: A Cultural History.* London: British Museum, 2000.
Hopkins, Keith. *The Colosseum.* London: Profile Books, 2005.
Kamm, Antony. *The Romans: An Introduction.* 2nd ed. London; New York: Routledge, 2008.
Kleiner, Fred S. *A History of Roman Art.* Australia: Thomson/Wadsworth, 2007.
Ling, Roger. *Ancient Mosaics.* Princeton: Princeton Univ. Pr., 1998.
MacDonald, William L. *The Architecture of the Roman Empire: An Introductory Study.* Rev. ed. 2 vols. Yale Publications in the History of Art. New Haven:Yale Univ. Pr., 1982.
____. *The Pantheon: Design, Meaning, and Progeny.* With a new foreword by John Pinto. Cambridge, MA: Harvard Univ. Pr., 2002.
Mazzoleni, Donatella. *Domus: Wall Painting in the Roman House.* Los Angeles: J. Paul Getty Museum, 2004.
Packer, James E. *The Forum of Trajan in Rome: A Study of the Monuments in Brief.* Berkeley: Univ. of California Pr., 2001.
Pollitt, J. J. *The Art of Rome, c. 753 B.C.–337 A.D.: Sources and Documents.* Englewood Cliffs, NJ: Prentice Hall, 1966.
Polybius. *The Histories.* Trans. W.R. Paton. 6 vols. Loeb Classical Library. Cambridge, MA: Harvard Univ. Pr., 1998.
Ramage, Nancy H. *The British Museum Concise Introduction to Ancient Rome.* Ann Arbor, MI: Univ. of Michigan Pr., 2008.
Ramage, Nancy H., and Andrew Ramage. *Roman Art: Romulus to Constantine.* 4th ed. Upper Saddle River, NJ: Prentice Hall, 2005.
Sear, Frank. *Roman Architecture.* London: Routledge, 1998.
Spivey, Nigel. *Etruscan Art.* World of Art. New York: Thames & Hudson, 1997.
Stewart, Peter. *Roman Art.* Oxford: Oxford Univ. Pr., 2004.
____. *The Social History of Roman Art.* Cambridge; New York: Cambridge Univ. Pr., 2008.
Strong, Donald. *Roman Art.* 2nd. rev. & annotated ed. Pelican History of Art. New Haven: Yale Univ. Pr., 1995.
Vitruvius, Pollio. *Vitruvius on Architecture.* Ed. Thomas G. Smith. New York: Monacelli, 2003.
Ward-Perkins, J.B. *Roman Imperial Architecture.* Pelican History of Art New Haven: Yale Univ. Pr., 1994, 1981.

Chapter 7 Jewish, Early Christian, and Byzantine Art

Age of Spirituality: A Symposium. Ed. Kurt Weitzmann. New York: Metropolitan Museum of Art; Princeton: Princeton Univ. Pr., 1980.
Age of Spirituality: Late Antique and Early Christian Art, Third to Seventh Century. New York: Metropolitan Museum of Art, 1979.
Byzantium, 330-1453. Eds. Robin Cormack & Maria Vassilaki. London: Royal Academy of Arts; New York: Abrams, 2008.
Byzantium: Faith and Power (1261-1557). Ed. Helen C. Evans. New York: Metropolitan Museum of Art; New Haven:Yale Univ. Pr., 2004.
Cioffarelli, Ada. *Guide to the Catacombs of Rome and Its Surroundings.* Rome: Bonsignori, 2000.
Cormack, Robin. *Byzantine Art.* Oxford History of Art. Oxford: Oxford Univ. Pr., 2000.
Cutler, Anthony. *The Hand of the Master: Craftsmanship, Ivory, and Society in Byzantium, 9th–11th Centuries.* Princeton: Princeton Univ. Pr., 1994.
Demus, Otto. *Mosaic Decoration of San Marco, Venice.* Chicago: Univ. of Chicago Pr., 1988.
Fine, Steven. *Art and Judaism in the Greco-Roman World: Toward a New Jewish Archaeology.* Cambridge; New York: Cambridge Univ. Pr., 2005.
Freely, John. *Byzantine Monuments of Istanbul.* Cambridge: New York: Cambridge Univ. Pr., 2004.
The Glory of Byzantium. Eds. Helen C. Evans & William D. Wixon. New York: Abrams, 1997.
Grant, Michael. *From Rome to Byzantium: The Fifth Century A.D.* London; New York: Routledge, 1998.
Holloway, R. Ross. *Constantine & Rome.* New Haven: Yale Univ. Pr., 2004.
Interpreting Late Antiquity: Essays on the Post-Classical World. Ed. G.W. Bowersock et al. Harvard University Press Reference Library. Cambridge, MA: Belknap Press of Harvard Univ. Pr., 2001.
Kitzinger, Ernst. *The Art of Byzantium and the Medieval West: Selected Studies.* Bloomington: Indiana Univ. Pr., 1976.
____. *Byzantine Art in the Making: Main Lines of Stylistic Development in Mediterranean Art 3rd to 7th Century.* Cambridge, MA: Harvard Univ. Pr., 1977.
Kleinbauer, W. Eugene. *Hagia Sophia.* London: Scala; Istanbul: Archaeology & Art Publications, 2004.
Koch, Guntram. *Early Christian Art and Architecture: An Introduction.* London: SCM Pr., 1996.
Krautheimer, Richard. *Early Christian and Byzantine Architecture.* 4th ed. Pelican History of Art. Harmondsworth: Penguin, 1986.
Lowden, John. *Early Christian and Byzantine Art.* Art & Ideas. London: Phaidon, 1997.
Mainstone, R.J. *Hagia Sophia: Architecture, Structure and Liturgy of Justinian's Great Church.* London: Thames & Hudson, 1988.
Mark, Robert, and Ahmet S. Cakmak. *Hagia Sophia from the Age of Justinian to the Present.* Cambridge: Cambridge Univ. Pr., 1992.
Mathews, Thomas F. *The Clash of Gods: A Reinterpretation of Early Christian Art.* Princeton: Princeton Univ. Pr., 1999.
____. *Byzantium: From Antiquity to the Renaissance.* New York: Abrams, 1998.
The Oxford History of Byzantium. Ed. Cyril Mango. Oxford; New York: Oxford Univ. Pr., 2002.
Picturing the Bible: The Earliest Christian Art. Ed. Jeffrey Spier New Haven: Yale Univ. Pr., 2007.
Rutgers, Leonard V. *Subterranean Rome: In Search of the Roots of Christianity in the Catacombs of the Eternal City.* Leuven: Peeters, 2000.
Sed-Rajna, Gabrielle. *Jewish Art.* New York: Abrams, 1997.
Teteriatnikov, Natalia. *Mosaics of Hagia Sophia, Istanbul: The Fossati Restoration and the Work of the Byzantine Institute.* Washington, DC: Dumbarton Oaks Research Library, 1998.
Tree of Paradise: Jewish Mosaics From the Roman Empire. Ed. Edward Bleiberg. Brooklyn: Brooklyn Museum, 2005.
Vio, Ettore, and Eunio Concina. *The Basilica of St. Mark in Venice.* New York: Riverside Pr., 1999.
Webb, Matilda. *The Churches and Catacombs of Early Christian Rome: A Comprehensive Guide.* Brighton: Sussex Academic Pr., 2001.
Weitzmann, Kurt. *Late Antique and Early Christian Book Illumination.* New York: Braziller, 1977.

Chapter 8 Islamic Art

Al-Andalus: The Art of Islamic Spain. Ed. Jerrilynn D. Dodds. New York: Metropolitan Museum of Art, 1992.
Asher, Catherine B. *Architecture of Mughal India.* New York: Cambridge Univ. Pr., 1992.
Atil, Esin. *The Age of Sultan Suleyman the Magnificent.* Washington, DC: National Gallery of Art, 1987.
Beach, Milo Cleveland. *Mughal and Rajput Painting.* New York: Cambridge Univ. Pr., 1992.
Blair, Sheila. *Islamic Calligraphy.* Edinburgh: Edinburgh Univ. Pr., 2006.
Blair, Sheila S., and Jonathan M. Brown. *The Art and Architecture of Islam 1250–1800.* New Haven: Yale Univ. Pr., 1994.
Brend, Barbara. *Islamic Art.* Cambridge, MA: Harvard Univ. Pr., 1991.
Canby, Sheila R. *Islamic Art in Detail.* London: British Museum, 2005.
Ettinghausen, Richard. *Islamic art and architecture, 650-1250.* 2nd ed. Pelican History of Art. New Haven: Yale Univ. Pr., 2001.
Frishman, Martin, and Hasan-Uddin Khan. *The Mosque: History, Architectural Development and Regional Diversity.* London: Thames & Hudson, 1994.
Grabar, Oleg. *The Alhambra.* Cambridge, MA: Harvard Univ. Pr., 1978.
____. *The Dome of the Rock.* Cambridge, MA: Harvard Univ. Pr., 2006.
____. *The Formation of Islamic Art.* New Haven: Yale Univ. Pr., 1987.
____. *Islamic Visual Culture, 1100-1800.* Constructing the Study of Islamic Art; 2. Aldershot, UK; Burlington, VT: Ashgate/Variorum, 2006.
____. *Mostly Miniatures: An Introduction to Persian Painting.* Princeton, NJ: Princeton Univ. Pr., 2000.
Grabar, Oleg, and Richard Ettinghausen. *The Art and Architecture of Islam, 650–1250.* Penguin History of Art. New Haven: Yale Univ. Pr., 2001.
Hillenbrand, Robert. *Islamic Art and Architecture.* London: Thames & Hudson, 1999.
Irwin, Robert. *The Alhambra.* Cambridge, MA: Harvard Univ. Pr., 2004.
____. *Islamic Art in Context: Art, Architecture, and the Literary World.* Perspectives. New York: Abrams, 1997.
Jenkins, Marilyn. "Islamic Glass: A Brief History." *Bulletin of the Metropolitan Museum of Art* 44/2, 1986.
Koch, Ebba. *The Complete Taj Mahal and the Riverfront Gardens of Agra.* London: Thames & Hudson, 2006.
The Koran: With a Parallel Arabic Text. Trans. With notes by N. J. Dawood. London; New York: Penguin Books, 2000.
Kossak, Steven. *Indian Court Painting, 16th-19th Century.* New York: Metropolitan Museum of Art, 1997.

Michell, George. *The Majesty of Mughal Decoration: The Art and Architecture of Islamic India.* London: Thames & Hudson, 2007.
Necipoglu, Gülru. *The Age of Sinan: Architectural Culture in the Ottoman Empire.* London: Reaktion, 2005.
Okada, Amina. *Indian Miniatures of the Mughal Court.* New York: Abrams, 1992.
Palace and Mosque: Islamic Art from the Near East. Ed. Tim Stanley. London: Victoria & Albert Museum 2004.
Sims, Eleanor. *Peerless Images: Persian Painting and Its Sources.* New Haven; London: Yale Univ. Pr., 2002.
Verma, Som Prakash. *Painting the Mughal Experience.* New Delhi; New York: Oxford Univ. Pr., 2005.
Welch, Stuart C. *From Mind, Heart, and Hand: Persian, Turkish, and Indian Drawings From the Stuart Cary Welch Collection.* New Haven: Yale Univ. Pr.; Cambridge, MA: Harvard Univ. Art Museums, 2004.

Chapter 9 Later Asian Art

Addiss, Stephen. *77 Dances: Japanese Calligraphy by Poets, Monks, and Scholars, 1568-1868.* Boston: Weatherhill, 2006.
______. *How to Look at Japanese Art.* New York: Abrams, 1996.
Andrews, Julia F. *A Century in Crisis: Modernity and Tradition in the Art of Twentieth-Century China.* New York: Guggenheim Museum, 1998.
Awakenings: Zen Figure Painting in Medieval Japan. Eds. Naomi N. Richard & Melanie B.D. Klein. New York: Japan Society; New Haven: Yale Univ. Pr., 2007.
Barnhart, Richard M., et al. *Three Thousand Years of Chinese Painting.* The Culture & Civilization of China. New Haven: Yale Univ. Pr.; Beijing: Foreign Languages Pr., 1997.
Blurton, T. Richard. *Hindu Art.* Cambridge, MA: Harvard Univ. Pr., 1993.
Calza, Gian Carlo. *Hokusai.* London; New York: Phaidon, 2003.
Chinese Architecture. Ed. and exp. by Nancy Steinhardt. New Haven: Yale Univ. Pr.; Beijing: New World Pr., 2002.
Chinese Calligraphy. Ouyang Zhongshi et al. New Haven: Yale Univ. Pr.; Beijing: Foreign Languages Pr., 2008.
Clunas, Craig. *Empire of Great Brightness: Visual and Material Cultures of Ming China, 1368-1644.* Honolulu: Univ. of Hawaii Pr., 2007.
Eight Dynasties of Chinese Painting: The Collections of the Nelson Gallery-Atkins Museum, Kansas City, and the Cleveland Museum of Art. Cleveland: Cleveland Museum of Art; Bloomington: Indiana Univ. Pr., 1980.
Fang, Jing Pei. *Treasures of the Chinese Scholar: Form, Function, and Symbolism.* New York: Weatherhill, 1997.
Fisher, Robert E. *Buddhist Art and Architecture.* World of Art. New York: Thames & Hudson, 1993.
Fong, Wen. *Landscapes Clear and Radiant: The Art of Wang Hui (1632-1717).* New York: Metropolitan Museum of Art; New Haven: Yale Univ. Pr., 2008.
Guth, Christine. *Art of Edo Japan: The Artist and the City, 1615–1868.* Perspectives. New York: Abrams, 1996.
Hearn, Maxwell K. *How to Read Chinese Paintings.* New York: Metropolitan Museum of Art; New Haven: Yale Univ. Pr., 2008.
Hickman, Money L. *Japan's Golden Age: Momoyama.* New Haven: Yale Univ. Pr., 1996.
Holdsworth, May. *The Forbidden City.* Hong Kong; New York: Oxford Univ. Pr., 1998.
Karetzky, Patricia E. *Chinese Buddhist Art.* New York: Oxford Univ. Pr., 2002.
Khanna, Balraj and Aziz Kurtha. *Art of Modern India.* London: Thames & Hudson, 1998.
Latter Days of the Law: Images of Chinese Buddhism, 850–1850. Ed. Marsha Weidner. Lawrence, KS: Spencer Museum of Art, 1994.
Losty, Jeremiah P. *The Art of the Book in India.* London: British Library, 1982.
Merritt, Helen and Nanako Yamada. *Guide to Modern Japanese Woodblock Prints, 1900–1975.* Honolulu: Univ. of Honolulu Pr., 1995.
Michell, George. *Hindu Art and Architecture.* New York: Thames & Hudson, 2000.
______. *The Royal Palaces of India.* London: Thames & Hudson, 1994.
Munroe, Alexandra. *Japanese Art after 1945: Scream Against the Sky.* New York: Abrams, 1994.
Murase, Miyeko. *Iconography of the Tale of Genji: Genji Monogatari Ekotoba.* New York: Weatherhill, 1983.
______. *Masterpieces of Japanese Screen Painting: The American Collections.* New York: Braziller, 1990.
Ng, So Kam. *Brushstrokes: Styles and Techniques of Chinese Painting.* San Francisco: Asian Art Museum of San Francisco, 1993.
Plutschow, Herbert E. *Rediscovering Rikyu and the Beginnings of the Japanese Tea Ceremony.* Folkestone, UK: Global Oriental, 2003.
Possessing the Past: Treasures From the National Palace Museum. New York: Metropolitan Museum of Art; Taipei: National Palace Museum,1996.
Rowland, Benjamin. *Art and Architecture of India: Buddhist, Hindu, Jain.* Pelican History of Art. Harmondsworth, UK: Penguin, 1977.
Seo, Audrey Yoshiko. *The Art of Twentieth-Century Zen: Paintings and Calligraphy by Japanese Masters.* Boston: Shambhala, 1998.
Singer, Jane C. *Divine Presence: Arts of India and the Himalayas.* Barcelona: Casa Asia; Milan: 5 Continents, 2003.
Sullivan, Michael. *Art and Artists of Twentieth-Century China.* Berkeley: Univ. of California Pr., 1996.
Thompson, Sarah E. *Undercurrents in the Floating World: Censorship and Japanese Prints.* New York: Asia Society, 1992.
Tillotson, G.H.R. *The Rajput Palaces: The Development of an Architectural Style, 1450–1750.* New York: Oxford Univ. Pr. 1999.
Tregear, Mary. *Chinese Art.* Rev. ed. New York: Thames & Hudson, 1997.
Vainker, S.J. *Chinese Paintings in the Ashmolean Museum.* Oxford: Ashmolean Museum, 2000.
______. *Chinese Pottery and Porcelain: From Prehistory to the Present.* London: British Museum, 1991.
Watson, William. *The Arts of China, 900–1620.* Pelican History of Art. New Haven: Yale Univ. Pr., 2000.
______. *The Arts of China after 1620.* Pelican History of Art. New Haven: Yale Univ. Pr., 2007.

Chapter 10 Early Medieval and Romanesque Art

Alexander, J.J.G. *Medieval Illuminators and Their Methods of Work.* New Haven: Yale Univ. Pr., 1992.
Backhouse, Janet. *The Golden Age of Anglo-Saxon Art, 966–1066.* Bloomington: Indiana Univ. Pr., 1984.
Bandmann, Günter. *Early Medieval Architecture as Bearer of Meaning.* New York: Columbia Univ. Pr., 2005.
Benton, Janetta R. *Art of the Middle Ages.* World of Art. New York: Thames & Hudson, 2002.
Braunfels, Wolfgang. *Monasteries of Western Europe: The Architecture of the Orders.* New York: Thames & Hudson, 1993.
Brown, Michelle. *Understanding Illuminated Manuscripts: A Guide to Technical Terms.* Malibu, CA: J. Paul Getty Museum and the British Library, 1994.
Cahn, Walter. *Studies in Medieval Art and Interpretation.* London, Pindar, 2000.
Calkins, Robert C. *Medieval Architecture in Western Europe: From A.D. 300–1500.* New York: Oxford Univ. Pr., 1998.
_____. *Monuments of Medieval Art.* New York: Dutton, 1979.
Caviness, Madeline H. "Hildegard as Designer of the Illustrations to her Works." In *Hildegard of Bingen: The Context of her Thought and Art.* Eds. Charles Burnett & Peter Dronke. London: Warburg Institute, 1998, pp. 29-63.
Coldstream, Nicola. *Masons and Sculptors.* Toronto; Buffalo: Univ. of Toronto Pr., 1991.
Conant, Kenneth J. *Carolingian and Romanesque Architecture, 800–1200.* 4th ed. Pelican History of Art. New Haven: Yale Univ. Pr., 1993.
Diebold, William J. *Word and Image: An Introduction to Early Medieval Art.* Boulder, CO: Westview, 2000.
A Documentary History of Art. Ed. Elizabeth G. Holt. New Haven: Yale Univ. Pr., 1986. Vol. 1.
Dodwell, C.R. *Pictorial Arts of the West, 800–1200.* Pelican History of Art. New Haven: Yale Univ. Pr., 1993.
Evans, Angela Care. *The Sutton Hoo Ship Burial.* Rev ed. London: British Museum, 1994.
Farr, Carol. *The Book of Kells: Its Function and Audience.* British Library Studies in Medieval Culture. London: British Library, 1997.
Forsyth, Ilene H. *The Throne of Wisdom: Wood Sculptures of the Madonna in Romanesque France.* Princeton: Princeton Univ. Pr., 1972.
From Attila to Charlemagne: Arts of the Early Medieval Period in the Metropolitan Museum of Art. Ed. Katharine R. Brown et al. New York: Metropolitan Museum of Art; New Haven: Yale Univ. Pr., 2000.
Harbison, Peter. *The Golden Age of Irish Art: The Medieval Achievement, 600–1200.* London: Thames & Hudson, 1999.
Klindt-Jensen, Ole. *Viking Art.* 2nd ed. Minneapolis: Univ. of Minnesota Pr., 1980.
Kubach, Hans E. *Romanesque Architecture.* History of World Architecture. New York: Electa/Rizzoli, 1988.
Laing, Lloyd. *Art of the Celts.* World of Art. New York: Thames & Hudson, 1992.
Lasko, Peter. *Ars Sacra, 800-1200.* 2nd ed. Pelican History of Art. New Haven: Yale Univ. Pr., 1994.
Lepage, Jean-Denis. *Castles and Fortifed Cities of Medieval Europe: An Illustrated History.* Jefferson, NC: McFarland, 2002.
Making Medieval Art. Ed. Phillip Lindley. Donington, UK: Shaun Tyas, 2003.
The Making of England: Anglo-Saxon Art and Culture, AD 600-900. Eds. Leslie Webster & Janet Backhouse. London: British Museum, 1991.
Megaw, Ruth. *Celtic Art: From Its Beginnings to the Book of Kells.* Rev. and exp. ed. New York: Thames & Hudson, 2001.
Mentre, Mirelle. *Illuminated Manuscripts of Medieval Spain.* New York: Thames & Hudson, 1996.
Minne-Sève, Viviane. *Romanesque and Gothic France: Architecture and Sculpture.* New York: Abrams, 2000.
Musset, Lucien. *The Bayeux Tapestry.* New ed. Woodbridge, UK; Rochester, NY: Boydell Pr., 2005.
Myer-Harting, Henry. *Ottonian Book Illumination: An Historical Study.* 2nd rev. ed. 2 vols. London: Harvey Miller, 1999.
Nees, Lawrence. *Early Medieval Art.* Oxford History of Art. Oxford: Oxford Univ. Pr., 2003.
Nordenfalk, Carl Adam Johan. *Studies in the History of Book Illumination.* London, Pindar, 1992.
Radding, Charles M. *Medieval Architecture, Medieval Learning: Builders and Masters in the Age of Romanesque and Gothic.* New Haven: Yale Univ. Pr., 1992.
Schapiro, Meyer. *Language of Forms: Lectures on Insular Manuscript Art.* Ed. Jane Rosenthal. New York: Pierpont Morgan Library, 2006.
_____. *Romanesque Architectural Sculpture.* Ed. Linda Seidel. Chicago: Univ. of Chicago Pr., 2006.
_____. *Romanesque Art.* New York: George Braziller, 1977.
Seidel, Linda. *Legends in Limestone: Lazarus, Gislebertus, and the Cathedral of Autun.* Chicago: Chicago Univ. Pr., 1999.
Sekules, Veronica. *Medieval Art.* Oxford History of Art. Oxford: Oxford Univ. Pr., 2001.
Shahar, Shulamith. *The Fourth Estate: A History of Women in the Middle Ages.* Rev. ed. London; New York: Routledge, 2003.
Snyder, James. *Art of the Middle Ages.* 2nd ed. Upper Saddle River, NJ: Prentice Hall, 2006.
Stalley, R. A. *Early Medieval Architecture.* Oxford History of Art. Oxford: Oxford Univ. Pr., 1999.
Stokstad, Marilyn. *Medieval Art.* 2nd ed. Boulder, CO: Westview Pr., 2004.
Stones, Alison. *The Pilgrim's Guide: A Critical Edition.* 2 vols. London: Harvey Miller, 1998.
Vikings: The North Atlantic Saga. Eds. William Fitzhugh & Elisabeth Ward. Washington, DC: Smithsonian Institution Pr., 2000.
Williams, John. *The Illustrated Beatus: Corpus of the Illumination of the Commentary on the Apocalypse.* 5 vols. London: Harvey Miller, 1994-2003.
Wilson, David M. *The Bayeux Tapestry: The Complete Tapestry in Color.* New York: Random House, 1985.

Wilson, David M., and Ole Klindt-Jensen. *Viking Art.* 2nd ed. Minneapolis: Univ. of Minnesota Pr., 1980.
Wolf, Norbert. *Romanesque Art.* Basic Genre. Köln: Taschen, 2007.

Chapter 11 Gothic Art

Bellosi, Luciano. *Cimabue.* New York: Abbeville, 1998.
Bony, Jean. *French Gothic Architecture of the 12th and 13th Centuries.* California Studies in the History of Art; 20. Berkeley: Univ. of California Pr., 1983.
Branner, Robert. *Gothic Architecture.* New York: George Braziller, 1961.
Camille, Michael. *Gothic Art: Glorious Visions.* Perspectives. New York: Abrams, 1996.
Cennini, Cennino d'Andrea. *The Craftsman's Handbook.* Trans. Daniel V. Thompson, Jr. New York: Dover Publications, 1960.
Clifton-Taylor, Alec. *The Cathedrals of England.* Rev. ed. London; New York: Thames & Hudson, 1986.
Coldstream, Nicola. *Masons and Sculptors.* Toronto; Buffalo: Univ. of Toronto Pr., 1991.
______. *Medieval Architecture.* Oxford History of Art. Oxford: Oxford Univ. Pr., 2002.
The Cambridge Companion to Giotto. Eds. Anne Derbes & Mark Sandona. Cambridge; New York: Cambridge Univ. Pr., 2004.
Clark, William W. *The Medieval Cathedrals.* Westport, CT: Greenwood, 2005.
Cole, Bruce. *Giotto: The Scrovegni Chapel, Padua.* New York: Braziller, 1993.
Crosby, Sumner M. *The Royal Abbey of Saint-Denis from Its Beginnings to the Death of Suger, 475–1151.* Yale Publications in the History of Art. New Haven: Yale Univ. Pr., 1987.
A Documentary History of Art. Ed. Elizabeth G. Holt. New Haven: Yale Univ. Pr., 1986. Vol. 1.
Enamels of Limoges, 1100–1350. Ed. John P. O'Neill. New York: Metropolitan Museum of Art, 1996.
Erlande Brandenburg, Alain. *Notre Dame de Paris.* New York: Abrams, 1998.
Frankl, Paul. *Gothic Architecture.* Rev. ed. New Haven: Yale Univ. Pr., 2000.
Gothic: Art for England 1400-1547. Eds. Richard Marks & Paul Williamson. London: V&A; New York: Abrams, 2003.
Grodecki, Louis, and Catherine Brisac. *Gothic Stained Glass, 1200–1300.* Ithaca, NY: Cornell Univ. Pr., 1985.
Grössinger, Christa. *Picturing Women in Late Medieval and Renaissance Art.* New York: St. Martin's, 1997.
Hyman, Timothy. *Sienese Painting: The Art of a City-Republic (1278-1477).* New York: Thames & Hudson, 2003.
Jordan, Alyce. *Visualizing Kingship in the Windows of the Sainte-Chapelle.* Turnhout: Brepols, 2002.
Limentani Virdis, Caterina. *Great Altarpieces: Gothic and Renaissance.* New York: Vendome, 2002.
Maginnis, Hayden B.J. *The World of the Early Sienese Painter.* University Park: Pennsylvania State Univ. Pr., 2001.
Panofsky, Erwin. *Abbot Suger on the Abbey Church of St. Denis and Its Art Treasures.* 2nd ed. Princeton, NJ: Princeton Univ. Pr., 1979.
Poeschke, Joachim. *Italian Frescoes, the Age of Giotto, 1280-1400.* New York: Abbeville, 2005.
Pope-Hennessy, John W. *An Introduction to Italian Sculpture.* 4th ed. 3 vols. London: Phaidon, 1996. Vol. 1. Italian Gothic sculpture.
Sauerlander, Willibald. Gothic *Sculpture in France, 1140–1270.* London: Thames & Hudson, 1972.
Scott, Robert A. *The Gothic Enterprise: A Guide to Understanding the Medieval Cathedral.* Berkeley: Univ. of California Pr., 2003.
Simson, Otto Georg von. *The Gothic Cathedral: Origins of Gothic Architecture and the Medieval Concept of Order.* 3rd ed. Bollingen Series. Princeton: Princeton Univ. Pr., 1988.
Strehlke, Carl B. *Italian paintings, 1250-1450 in the John G. Johnson Collection and the Philadelphia Museum of Art.* Philadelphia: Philadelphia Museum of Art, 2004.
White, John. *Art and Architecture in Italy, 1250 to 1400.* 3rd ed. Pelican History of Art. Harmondsworth: Penguin, 1993.
Williamson, Paul. *Gothic Sculpture, 1140–1300.* Pelican History of Art. New Haven: Yale Univ. Pr., 1995.
Wilson, Christopher. *The Gothic Cathedral: The Architecture of the Great Church, 1130–1530.* Repr. with revisions. New York: Thames & Hudson, 2000.

Chapter 12 Early Renaissance Art

Adams, Laurie. *Italian Renaissance Art.* Boulder, CO: Westview Pr., 2001.
Ames, Lewis F. *The Intellectual Life of the Early Renaissance Artist.* New Haven: Yale Univ. Pr., 2000.
Baxandall, Michael. *Painting and Experience in Fifteenth-Century Italy: A Primer in the Social History of Pictorial Style.* 2nd ed. Oxford; New York: Oxford Univ. Pr., 1988.
Black, C.F. *Cultural Atlas of the Renaissance.* New York: Prentice Hall, 1993.
Borchert, Till-Holger. *Jan van Eyck: Renaissance Realist.* Köln: Taschen, 2008.
The Cambridge Companion to Masaccio. Ed. Diana C. Ahl. New York: Cambridge Univ. Pr., 2002.
Campbell, Lorne. *Renaissance Faces: Van Eyck to Titian.* London: National Gallery; New Haven: Yale Univ. Pr., 2008.
Cavallo, Adolph S. *The Unicorn Tapestries at the Metropolitan Museum of Art.* New York: The Metropolitan Museum of Art; Abrams, 1998.
Christine de Pizan. *The Book of the City of Ladies.* Trans. Earl J. Richards. New York: Persea Books, 1982.
Cole, Bruce. *Studies in the History of Italian Art, 1250–1550.* London: Pindar, 1996.
The Gates of Paradise: Lorenzo Ghiberti's Renaissance Masterpiece. Ed. G.M. Radke. Atlanta: High Museum of Art, 2007.
Goldwater, Robert, and Marco Treves. *Artists on Art from the XIV to the XX Century.* New York: Pantheon Books, 1945.
Grössinger, Christa. *Picturing Women in late Medieval and Renaissance art.* Manchester: New York: Manchester Univ. Pr. and St. Martin's, 1997.
Hartt, Frederick, and David G. Wilkins. *History of Italian Renaissance Art: Painting, Sculpture, Architecture.* 6th ed. Upper Saddle River, NJ: Pearson Prentice Hall, 2007.
Heydenreich, Ludwig Heinrich. *Architecture in Italy, 1400 to 1500.* Rev. by P. Davies. Pelican History of Art. New Haven: Yale Univ. Pr., 1996.
Huizinga, Johan. *The Autumn of the Middle Ages.* Chicago: Univ. of Chicago Pr., 1996.
Limentani Virdis, Caterina. *Great Altarpieces: Gothic and Renaissance.* New York: Vendome and Rizzoli, 2002.
Lincoln, Evelyn. *The Invention of the Italian Renaissance Printmaker.* New Haven: Yale Univ. Pr., 2000.
Lubbock, Jules. *Storytelling in Christian Art from Giotto to Donatello.* New Haven; London: Yale Univ. Pr., 2006.
Making Renaissance Art. Ed. Kim Woods. New Haven: Yale Univ. Pr. and The Open University, 2007.
Nevola, Fabrizio. *Siena: Constructing the Renaissance City.* New Haven: Yale Univ. Pr., 2007.
Norman, Diana. *Painting in Late Medieval and Renaissance Siena (1260-1555).* New Haven: Yale Univ. Pr., 2003.
Pacht, Otto. *Early Netherlandish Painting: From Rogier van der Weyden to Gerard David.* London: Harvey Miller, 1997.
_____. *Van Eyck and the Founders of Early Netherlandish Painting.* London: Miller, 1994.
Pope-Hennessy, John W. *An Introduction to Italian Sculpture.* 4th ed. 3 vols. London: Phaidon, 1996. Vol. 2. Italian Renaissance Sculpture.
Saalman, Howard. *Filippo Brunelleschi: The Buildings.* University Park: Pennsylvania State Univ. Pr., 1993.
Smith, Jeffrey C. *The Northern Renaissance.* London; New York: Phaidon, 2004.
Snyder, James. Northern *Renaissance Art: Painting, Sculpture, and the Graphic Arts from 1350 to 1575.* 2nd ed. Upper Saddle River, NJ: Prentice Hall, 2005.
Welch, Evelyn S. *Art and Society in Italy, 1350–1500.* New ed. Oxford History of Art. Oxford: Oxford Univ. Pr., 2000, 1997.

Chapter 13 Art of the High Renaissance and Reformation

Bambach, Carmen. *Drawing and Painting in the Italian Renaissance Workshop: Theory and Practice, 1300–1600.* Cambridge: Cambridge Univ. Pr., 1999.
Baxandall, Michael. *The Limewood Sculptors of Renaissance Germany.* New Haven: Yale Univ. Pr., 1980.
Black, C.F. *Cultural Atlas of the Renaissance.* New York: Prentice Hall, 1993.
Blunt, Anthony. *Art and Architecture in France: 1500–1700.* 5th ed. Pelican History of Art. New Haven: Yale Univ. Pr., 1999.
Boucher, Bruce. *Andrea Palladio: The Architect in His Time.* 2nd ed. New York: Abbeville, 2007
Brambilla Barcilon, Pinin. *Leonardo: The Last Supper.* Chicago: Univ. of Chicago Pr., 2001.
Brown, Jonathan. *Painting in Spain, 1500–1700.* Pelican History of Art. New Haven: Yale Univ. Pr., 1998.
Brown, Patricia F. *Art and Life in Renaissance Venice.* Perspectives. New York: Abrams, 1997.
Burke, Peter. *The Italian Renaissance: Culture and Society in Italy.* 2nd ed. Princeton: Princeton Univ. Pr., 1999.
The Cambridge Companion to Raphael. Ed. Marcia B. Hall. Cambridge; New York: Cambridge Univ. Pr., 2008.
Chapuis, Julien. *Tilman Riemenschneider, Master Sculptor of the Late Middle Ages.* Washington, DC: National Gallery of Art; New York: Metropolitan Museum of Art,1999.
Chastel, Andre. *French Art.* 4 vols. Paris: Flammarion, 1995. Vol. 2: The Renaissance, 1430-1620.
Cole, Alison. *Virtue and Magnificence: Art of the Italian Renaissance Courts.* Perspectives. New York: Abrams, 1995.
Farago, Claire J. *Reframing the Renaissance: Visual Culture in Europe and Latin America, 1450–1650.* New Haven: Yale Univ. Pr., 1995.
Ferino Pagden, Sylvia. *Sofonisba Anguissola: A Renaissance Woman.* Washington, DC: National Museum of Women in the Arts, 1995.
Field, Judith V. *The Invention of Infinity: Mathematics and Art in the Renaissance.* Oxford: Oxford Univ. Pr., 1997.
Franklin, David. *Painting in Renaissance Florence, 1500-1550.* New Haven: Yale Univ. Pr., 2001.
Freedberg, S.J. *Painting in Italy, 1500 to 1600.* 3rd ed. Pelican History of Art. New Haven: Yale Univ. Pr., 1993.
The Genius of Venice, 1500–1600. Eds. Jane Martineau & Charles Hope. New York: Abrams, 1984.
Graham-Dixon, Andrew. *Renaissance.* Berkeley: Univ. of California Pr., 1999.
Hall, Marcia B. *After Raphael: Painting in Central Italy in the Sixteenth Century.* Cambridge; New York: Cambridge Univ. Pr., 1999
Harbison, Craig. *The Mirror of the Artist: Northern Renaissance Art in Its Historical Context.* Perspectives. New York: Abrams, 1995.
Hopkins, Andrew. *Italian Architecture: from Michelangelo to Borromini.* London; New York: Thames & Hudson, 2002.
Huizinga, Johan. *Waning of the Middle Ages: A Study of the Forms of Life, Thought, and Art in France and the Netherlands in the XIVth and XVth Centuries.* Updated ed. New York: St. Martins, 1985, 1924.
The Image of the Individual: Portraits in the Renaissance. Eds. Nicolas Mann & Luke Syson. London: British Museum Pr., 1998
Italian Women Artists: From Renaissance to Baroque. Ed. Elizabeth S.G. Nicholson et al. Milan: Skira; New York: Rizzoli, 2007.
Jestaz, Bertrand. *The Art of the Renaissance.* New York: Abrams, 1995.
Koerner, Joseph L. *The Reformation of the Image.* Chicago: Univ. of Chicago Pr., 2004.
Landau, David, and Peter Parshall. *The Renaissance Print: 1470–1550.* New Haven: Yale Univ. Pr., 1994.
Leonardo da Vinci, Michelangelo, and the Renaissance in Florence. Ed. David Franklin. Ottawa: National Gallery of Canada, 2005.
Looking at Italian Renaissance Sculpture. Ed. Sarah B. McHam. Cambridge: Cambridge Univ. Pr., 1998.
Lotz, Wolfgang. *Architecture in Italy, 1500–1600.* Pelican History of Art. New Haven: Yale Univ. Pr., 1995.
Markschies, Alexander. *Icons of Renaissance Architecture.* Munich; New York: Prestel, 2003.
Murray, Linda. *The High Renaissance and Mannerism: Italy, the North, and Spain, 1500–1600.* World of Art. London: Thames & Hudson, 1995.
Nash, Susie. *Northern Renaissance Art.* New York: Oxford Univ. Pr., 2008.

Paoletti, John T., and Gary M. Radke. *Art in Renaissance Italy*. 3rd ed. Upper Saddle River, NJ: Pearson Prentice Hall, 2005.
Partridge, Loren W. *The Art of Renaissance Rome, 1400–1600*. Perspectives. New York: Abrams, 1996.
______. *Michelangelo, the Last Judgment: A Glorious Restoration*. New York: Abrams, 1997.
Picturing Women in Renaissance and Baroque Italy. Eds. Geraldine A. Johnson and Sara F. M. Grieco. Cambridge; New York: Cambridge Univ. Pr., 1997.
Pope-Hennessy, John W. *An Introduction to Italian Sculpture*. 4th ed., 3 vols. London: Phaidon Pr., 1996. Vol. 3: Italian High Renaissance and Baroque Sculpture.
Renaissance Florence: A Social History. Eds. Roger J. Crum & John T. Paoletti. New York: Cambridge Univ. Pr., 2006.
Renaissance Venice and the North: Crosscurrents in the Time of Bellini, Dürer, and Titian. Eds. Bernard Aikema & Beverly Brown. New York: Rizzoli, 2000.
Richter, Gottfried. *The Isenheim Altar: Suffering and Salvation in the Art of Grünewald*. Edinburgh: Floris Books, 1998.
Rosand, David. *Painting in Cinquecento Venice: Titian, Veronese, Tintoretto*. Rev. ed. Cambridge: Cambridge Univ. Pr., 1997.
Rowland, Ingrid D. *The Culture of the High Renaissance: Ancients and Moderns in Sixteenth-Century Rome*. Cambridge: Cambridge Univ. Pr., 1998.
The Sistine Chapel: A Glorious Restoration. Eds. Pierluigi de Vecchi et al. New York: Abrams, 1994.
Sixteenth-Century Italian Art. Ed. Michael W. Cole. Malden, MA; Oxford: Blackwell, 2006.
Smith, Jeffrey Chipps. *German Sculpture of the Later Renaissance, c. 1520-1580: Art in an Age of Uncertainty*. Princeton: Princeton Univ. Pr., 1994.
______. *The Northern Renaissance*. London; New York: Phaidon, 2004.
Titian to Tiepolo: Three Centuries of Italian Art. Ed. Gilberto Algranti. New York: Rizzoli/St. Martin's, 2002.
Titian's Venus of Urbino. Ed. Rona Goffen. Cambridge: Cambridge Univ. Pr., 1997.
Turner, Richard. *Renaissance Florence: The Invention of a New Art*. Perspectives. New York: Abrams, 1997.
Vasari, Giorgio. *The Lives of the Artists*. Trans. Julia & Peter Bondanella. New York: Oxford Univ. Pr., 1991.
Wohl, Hellmut. *The Aesthetics of Italian Renaissance Art: A Reconsideration of Style*. Cambridge: Cambridge Univ. Pr., 1999.
Women Who Ruled: Queens, Goddesses, Amazons in Renaissance and Baroque Art. Ed. Annette Dixon. London: Merrell; Ann Arbor: Univ. of Michigan Museum of Art, 2002.
Wundram, Manfred. *Andrea Palladio, 1508-1580: Architect Between the Renaissance and Baroque*. Köln; Los Angeles: Taschen, 2004.
Zerner, Henri. *Renaissance Art in France: The Invention of Classicism*. Paris: Flammarion; London: Thames & Hudson, 2003.

Chapter 14 Baroque and Rococo Art

Alpers, Svetlana. *The Art of Describing: Dutch Art in the Seventeenth Century*. Chicago: Chicago Univ. Pr., 1983.
______. *The Making of Rubens*. New Haven: Yale Univ. Pr., 1995.
Antoine Watteau: Perspectives on the Artist and the Culture of His Time. Ed. Mary D. Sheriff. Newark: Univ. of Delaware, 2006.
Baroque Architecture, Sculpture, Painting. Ed. Rolf Toman. Köln: Könemann, 1998.
Blunt, Anthony. *Roman Baroque*. London: Pallas Athene, 2001.
Boucher, Bruce. *Italian Baroque Sculpture*. World of Art. New York: Thames & Hudson, 1998.
Brown, Jonathan. *Painting in Spain, 1500-1700*. Pelican History of Art. New Haven: Yale Univ. Pr., 1998.
Brown, Jonathan, and Carmen Garrido. *Velasquez: The Technique of Genius*. Hew Haven: Yale Univ. Pr., 1998.
The Cambridge Companion to Velázquez. Ed. Suzanne L. Stratton-Pruitt. Cambridge; New York: Cambridge Univ. Pr., 2002.
The Cambridge Companion to Vermeer. Ed. Wayne E. Franits. Cambridge: Cambridge Univ. Pr., 2001.
Chapman, H. Perry. *Rembrandt's Self-Portraits: a Study in 17th-Century Identity*. Princeton: Princeton Univ. Pr., 1990.
Chastel, Andre. *French Art*. 4 vols. Paris: Flammarion, 1995. Vol. 3: The Ancien Régime, 1620-1775; Vol. 4: The Age of Eloquence, 1775-1820.
Circa 1700: Architecture in Europe and the Americas. Ed. Henry A. Millon. Studies in the History of Art; 66. Washington, DC: National Gallery of Art; New Haven: Yale Univ. Pr., 2005.
Earls, Irene. *Baroque Art: A Topical Dictionary*. Westport, CT: Greenwood, 1996.
Franits, Wayne E. *Dutch Seventeenth-Century Genre Painting: Its Stylistic and Thematic Evolution*. New Haven: Yale Univ. Pr., 2004.
The Genius of Rome, 1592-1623. Ed. Beverly L. Brown. London: Royal Academy of Arts; New York: Abrams, 2001.
Italian Women Artists: From Renaissance to Baroque. Ed. Elizabeth S.G. Nicholson et al. Milano: Skira; New York: Rizzoli, 2007.
Judith Leyster: A Dutch Master and Her World. Eds. James Welu & Pieter Biesboer. New Haven: Yale Univ. Pr., 1993.
Keazor, Henry. *Nicolas Poussin, 1594-1665*. Köln; London: Taschen, 2007.
Kiers, Judikje. *Golden Age of Dutch Art: Painting, Sculpture, and Decorative Art*. London: Thames & Hudson, 2000.
Lagerlof, Margaretha R. *Ideal Landscape: Annibale Caracci, Nicolas Poussin, and Claude Lorrain*. New Haven: Yale Univ. Pr., 1990.
Lemerle, Frédérique. *Baroque Architecture 1600-1750*. Paris: Flammarion, 2008.
Liedtke, Walter. *Vermeer and the Delft School*. New York: Metropolitan Museum of Art, 2001.
Minor, Vernon H. *Baroque and Rococo: Art & Culture*. New York: Abrams, 1999.
Olson, Todd. *Poussin and France: Painting, Humanism, and the Politics of Style*. New Haven: Yale Univ. Pr., 2002.
Pérouse de Montclos, Jean-Marie. *Versailles*. New York: Abbeville, 1991.
Picturing Women in Renaissance and Baroque Italy. Eds. Geraldine A. Johnson & Sara F. M. Grieco. Cambridge; New York: Cambridge Univ. Pr., 1997.
Pope-Hennessy, John W. *An Introduction to Italian Sculpture*. 4th ed. 3 vols. London: Phaidon, 1996. Vol. 2. Italian Renaissance Sculpture; Vol. 3. Italian High Renaissance and Baroque Sculpture.
Rand, Richard. *Claude Lorrain, the Painter as Draftsman: Drawings from the British Museum*. New Haven: Yale Univ. Pr.; Williamstown, MA: Clark Art Institute, 2006.
Saints & Sinners: Caravaggio & the Baroque Image. Ed. Franco Mormando. Boston: McMullen Museum of Art and Univ. of Chicago Pr., 1999.
Slive, Seymour. *Dutch Painting 1600–1800*. Pelican History of Art. New Haven: Yale Univ. Pr., 1995.
Sutton, Peter. *The Age of Rubens*. Boston: Museum of Fine Arts, 1993.
Tomlinson, Janis. *From El Greco to Goya: Painting in Spain, 1561–1828*. Perspectives. New York: Abrams, 1997.
The Triumph of the Baroque: Architecture in Europe, 1600-1750. Ed. Henry A. Millon. New York: Rizzoli, 1999.
Varriano, John. *Caravaggio: The Art of Realism*. University Park, PA: The Pennsylvania State Univ. Pr., 2006.
Vlieghe, Hans. *Flemish Art and Architecture, 1585–1700*. Pelican History of Art. New Haven: Yale Univ. Pr., 1998.
Westermann, Mariët. *Art and Home: Dutch Interiors in the Age of Rembrandt*. Denver, CO: Denver Art Museum; Netherlands: Waanders, 2001.
______. *A Worldly Art: The Dutch Republic, 1585–1718*. Perspectives. New York: Abrams, 1996.
White, Christopher. *Rembrandt as an Etcher: A Study of the Artist at Work*. 2nd ed. New Haven: Yale Univ. Pr., 1999.
Wintermute, Alan. *Watteau and His World: French Drawing from 1700–1750*. New York: Rizzoli; St. Martin's, 1999.
Wittkower, Rudolf. *Art and Architecture in Italy, 1600 to 1750*. 6th rev. ed. 3 vols. Pelican History of Art. New Haven: Yale Univ. Pr., 1999.

Chapter 15 Art of the Americas

Art and Architecture of Spain. Ed. Xavier Barral i Altet. Boston: Little, Brown, 1998.
Art of the North American Indians: The Thaw Collection. Ed. Gilbert T. Vincent et al. Cooperstown, NY: Fenimore Art Museum and Univ. of Washington Pr., 2000.
Auger, Emily E. *The Way of Inuit Art: Aesthetics and History In and Beyond the Arctic*. Jefferson, NC: McFarland, 2005.
Berlo, Janet C., and Ruth B. Phillips. *Native North American Art*. Oxford History of Art. Oxford: Oxford Univ. Pr., 1998.
Broder, Patricia Janis. *Earth Songs, Moon Dreams: Paintings by American Indian Women*. New York: St. Martin's Pr., 1999.
Changing Hands: Art Without Reservation. Eds. David McFadden & Ellen Taubman. 2 vols. London: Merrell; New York: American Craft Museum, 2002.
Circa 1700: Architecture in Europe and the Americas. Ed. Henry A. Millon. Studies in the History of Art; 66. Washington, DC: National Gallery of Art; New Haven: Yale Univ. Pr., 2005.
Coe, Michael D. *Mexico: From the Olmecs to the Aztecs*. 6th ed. rev. and exp. London: Thames & Hudson, 2008.
______. *The Maya*. 7th ed. fully rev. and exp. Ancient Peoples and Places. New York: Thames & Hudson, 2005.
Fane, Diana. *Converging Cultures: Art and Identity in Spanish America*. New York: Brooklyn Museum, 1996.
Farago, Claire J. *Reframing the Renaissance: Visual Culture in Europe and Latin America, 1450–1650*. New Haven: Yale Univ. Pr., 1995.
First American Art: The Charles and Valerie Diker Collection of American Indian Art. Eds. Bruce Bernstein & Gerald McMaster.Washington, DC: National Museum of the American Indian, 2004.
Frank, Larry. *Historic Pottery of the Pueblo Indians, 1600-1880*. 2nd ed. West Chester, PA: Schiffer, 1990.
Hawthorn, Audrey. *Kwakiutl Art*. Seattle: Univ. of Washington Pr.; Vancouver: Douglas & McIntyre, 1994.
Horse Capture, Joseph D., and George P. *Beauty, Honor and Tradition: The Legacy of Plains Indian Shirts*. Washington, DC: National Museum of the American Indian; Minneapolis, MN: Univ. of Minnesota Pr., 2001.
Jonaitis, Aldona. *Art of the Northwest Coast*. Seattle: Univ. of Washington Pr.; Vancouver: Douglas & McIntyre, 2006.
Kubler, George. *The Art and Architecture of Ancient America: The Mexican, Maya, and Andean Peoples*. 3rd ed. Pelican History of Art. New Haven: Yale Univ. Pr., 1990.
Lucie-Smith, Edward. *Latin American Art of the 20th Century*. 2nd ed. World of Art. New York: Thames & Hudson, 2004.
McQuiston, Don. *Visions of the North: Native Art of the Northwest Coast*. San Francisco: Chronicle Books, 1995.
Master of the Americas: In Praise of the Pre-Columbian Artists: The Dora and Paul Janssen Collection. Ed. Geneviève Le Fort. Brussels: Mercatofonds; Milan: 5 Continents, 2005.
Mexico: Splendors of Thirty Centuries. New York: Metropolitan Museum of Art, 1990.
Miller, Mary Ellen. *The Art of Mesoamerica: from Olmec to Aztec*. 4th ed. World of Art. London: Thames & Hudson, 2006.
Monroe, Dan L., et al. *Gifts of the Spirit: Works of Nineteenth-Century and Contemporary Native American Artists*. Salem, MA: Peabody Essex Museum, 1996.
Olmec Art of Ancient Mexico. Eds. Elizabeth P. Benson & Beatriz de la Fuente. Washington, DC: National Gallery of Art, 1996.
Pasztory, Esther. *Pre-Columbian Art*. New York: Cambridge Univ. Pr., 1998.
Penney, David W. *North American Indian Art*. World of Art. London: Thames & Hudson, 2004.
Phillips, Charles. *The Art & Architecture of the Aztec & Maya: An Illustrated Encyclopedia of the Buildings, Sculptures and Art of the Peoples of Mesoamerica*. London: Southwater, 2007.
Rasmussen, Waldo, et al. *Latin American Artists of the Twentieth Century*. New York: Museum of Modern Art, 1993.
Raven Travelling: Two Centuries of Haida Art. Ed. Daina Augaitis et al. Vancouver: Vancouver Art Gallery, 2006.
Schobinger, Juan. *The Ancient Americans: A Reference Guide to the Art, Culture, and History of Pre-Columbian North and South America*. Armonk, NY: Sharp Reference, 2001.
Taíno: Pre-Columbian Art and Culture From the Caribbean.

Ed. Fatima Bercht et al. New York: El Museo del Barrio: Monacelli, 1997.
Trimble, Stephen. *Talking With the Clay: The Art of Pueblo Pottery in the 21st Century.* 20th Anniversary rev. ed. Santa Fe, NM: School for Advanced Research Pr., 2007.
Uncommon Legacies: Native American Art from the Peabody Essex Museum. Ed. John B Grimes et al. New York: American Federation and the Univ. of Washington Pr., 2002.
Wyatt, Gary. *Mythic Beings: Spirit Art of the Northwest Coast.* Vancouver: Douglas & McIntyre; Seattle: Univ. of Washington Pr., 1999.

Chapter 16 African Art

Africa, Arts and Cultures. Ed. John Mark. London: British Museum, 2000.
African Costumes and Textiles from the Berbers to the Zulus: The Zaira and Marcel Mis Collection. Anne-Marie Bouttiaux et al. Milan: 5 Continents, 2008.
African Seats. Ed. Sandro Bocola. Munich; New York: Prestel, 1995.
Art of the Senses: African Masterpieces from the Teel Collection. Ed. Suzanne P. Blier. Boston: MFA Publications; New York: D.A.P./Distributed Art Publishers, 2004.
Asante, Molefi K. *Spear Masters: An Introduction to African Religion.* Lanham, MD: Univ. Pr. of America, 2007.
Astonishment and Power. Washington, DC: National Museum of African Art, 1993.
Bacquart, Jean-Baptiste. *The Tribal Arts of Africa.* New York: Thames & Hudson, 1998.
Bargna, Ivan. *African Art.* Milan: Jaca; Wappingers' Falls, NY: Antique Collector's Club, 2000.
Bassani, Ezio. *African Art and Artifacts in European Collections: 1400–1800.* London: British Museum, 2000.
Bassani, Ezio, et al. *Arts of Africa: 7000 Years of African Art.* Milan: Skira; Monaco: Grimaldi Forum, 2005.
______. *The Power of Form: African Art From the Horstmann Collection.* Milan: Skira; New York: Rizzoli, 2002.
Berzock, Kathleen Bickford. *Benin: Royal Arts of a West African Kingdom.* Chicago: Art Institute of Chicago; New Haven; London: Yale Univ. Pr., 2008.
______. *For Hearth and Altar: African Ceramics From the Keith Achepohl Collection.* Chicago: Art Institute of Chicago; New Haven: Yale Univ. Pr., 2005.
Blauer, Ettagale. *African Elegance.* New York: Rizzoli, 1999.
Blier, Suzanne Preston. *Ritual Arts of Africa: The Majesty of Form.* Perspectives. New York: Abrams, 1998.
Cameron, Elisabeth L. *Art of the Lega.* Los Angeles: UCLA Fowler Museum of Cultural History; Seattle: Univ. of Washington Pr., 2001.
Cultural Atlas of Africa. Ed. Jocelyn Murray. New York: Facts on File, 1998.
Drewal, Henry J. *Beads, Body, and Soul: Art and Light in the Yorùbá Universe.* Los Angeles: Fowler Museum of Cultural History, 1998.
Eternal Ancestors: The Art of the Central African Reliquary. Ed. Alisa LaGamma. New York: Metropolitan Museum of Art; New Haven: Yale Univ. Pr., 2007.
Garlake, Peter S. *Early Art and Architecture of Africa.* Oxford History of Art. Oxford: Oxford Univ. Pr., 2002.
______. *The Hunter's Vision: The Prehistoric Art of Zimbabwe.* Seattle: Univ. of Washington Pr., 1995.
Gillow, John. *African Textiles.* San Francisco: Chronicle Books, 2003.
Hackett, Rosalind I.J. *Art and Religion in Africa.* Religion in the Arts Series. London; New York: Cassell, 1996.
Hair in African Art and Culture. Eds. Roy Sieber & Frank Herreman. New York: Museum for African Art; Munich; New York: Prestel, 2000.
Jenkins, Earnestine. *A Kingly Craft: Art and Leadership in Ethiopia: A Social History of Art and Visual Culture in Pre-Modern Africa.* Lanham, MD: Univ. Pr. of America, 2008.
Kasfir, Sidney L. *Contemporary African Art.* World of Art. London: Thames & Hudson, 2000.
Magnin, André. *African Art Now: Masterpieces from the Jean Pigozzi Collection.* New York: Merrell; Houston: Museum of Fine Arts, 2005.
Maurer, Evan, and Niangi Batulukisi. *Spirits Embodied: Art of the Congo: Selections From the Helmut F. Stern Collection.* Minneapolis, MN: Minneapolis Institute of Arts, 1999.
McClusky, Pamela. *Art from Africa: Long Steps Never Broke a Back.* Seattle: Seattle Art Museum; Princeton, NJ: Princeton Univ. Pr., 2002.
Meyer, Laure. *African Forms: Art and Rituals.* New York: Assouline, 2001.
______. *Art and Craft in Africa: Everyday Life, Ritual, and Court Art.* Paris: Terrail, 1995.
Morris, James, and Suzanne P. Blier. *Butabu: Adobe Architecture of West Africa.* New York: Princeton Architectural Pr., 2004.
Okediji, Moyosore B. *African Renaissance: New Forms, Old Images in Yoruba Art.* Boulder: Univ. Pr. of Colorado, 2002.
Perrois, Louis. *Fang.* Visions of Africa. Milan: 5 Continents, 2006.
Phillips, Tom. *Africa: The Art of a Continent.* London: Prestel, 1996.
Prussin, Labelle. *African Nomadic Architecture: Space, Place, and Gender.* Washington, DC: Smithsonian Institution; National Museum of African Art, 1995.
Roy, Christopher D. *Clay and Fire: Pottery in Africa.* Iowa Studies in African Art, 4. Iowa City: Univ. of Iowa School of Art & Art History, 2000.
Schuster, Carl, and Edmund Carpenter. *Patterns That Connect: Social Symbolism in Ancient & Tribal Art.* New York: Abrams, 1996.
Spring, Christopher. *Angaza Afrika: African Art Now.* London: Laurence King Publishing, 2008.
Stepan, Peter. *Africa.* London: Prestel, 2001.
______. *Spirits Speak: A Celebration of African Masks.* Munich; New York: Prestel, 2005.
Thompson, Robert F. *Face of the Gods: Art and Altars of Africa and the African Americas.* New York: Museum for African Art; Munich: Prestel, 1993.
Visonà, Monica B., et al. *A History of Art in Africa.* Upper Saddle River, NJ: Pearson Prentice Hall, 2007.
Vogel, Susan Mullin. *Baule: African Art, Western Eyes.* New Haven: Yale Univ. Art Gallery, 1997.
Wheelock, Thomas G.B. *Land of the Flying Masks: Art and Culture in Burkina Faso.* Munich; New York: Prestel, 2007.
Willett, Frank. *African Art: An Introduction.* 3rd ed. World of Art. New York: Thames & Hudson, 2003.

Chapter 17 Neoclassicism, Romanticism, and Realism

Angelica Kauffman: A Woman of Immense Talent. Ed. Tobias Natter. Ostfildern: Hatje Cantz, 2007.
Art and the Academy in the Nineteenth Century. Eds. Rafael Denis & Colin Trodd. New Brunswick, NJ: Rutgers Univ. Pr., 2000.
Barger, M. Susan, and William B. White. *The Daguerreotype: Nineteenth-Century Technology and Modern Science.* Washington, DC: Smithsonian Institution, 1991.
Bergdoll, Barry. *European Architecture 1750-1890.* Oxford History of Art. New York: Oxford Univ. Pr., 2000.
Boime, Albert. *Magisterial Gaze: Manifest Destiny and American Landscape Painting.* Washington, DC: Smithsonian Institution, 1991.
_____. *Art in an Age of Bonapartism, 1800–1815.* Chicago: Univ. of Chicago Pr., 1990.
Brown, David B. *Romanticism.* Arts & Ideas. London: Phaidon, 2001.
The Cambridge Companion to Delacroix. Ed. Beth S. Wright. Cambridge; New York: Cambridge Univ. Pr., 2001.
Clark, T.J. *The Absolute Bourgeois: Artists and Politics in France, 1848–1851.* Berkeley: Univ. of California Pr., 1999.
_____. *Image of the People: Gustave Courbet and the 1848 Revolution.* Berkeley: Univ. of California Pr., 1999.
Clarke, Graham. *The Photograph.* Oxford History of Art. Oxford: Oxford Univ. Pr., 1997.
Conrads, Margaret C. *Winslow Homer and the Critics: Forging a National Art in the 1870s.* Princeton, NJ: Princeton Univ. Pr. and the Nelson-Atkins Museum of Art, 2001.
Cooper, Wendy A. *Classical Taste in America 1800–1840.* Baltimore: Baltimore Museum of Art, 1993.
Denis, Rafael C., and Colin Trodd. *Art and the Academy in the Nineteenth Century.* New Brunswick, NJ: Rutgers Univ. Pr., 2000.
Eisenman, Stephen, and Thomas E. Crow. *Nineteenth-Century Art: A Critical History.* 3rd ed. London; New York: Thames & Hudson, 2007.
Gray, Michael, et al. *First Photographs: William Henry Fox Talbot and the Birth of Photography.* New York: PowerHouse Books and the Museum of Photographic Arts, San Diego, 2002.
Hallett, Mark. *Hogarth.* Art & Ideas. London: Phaidon, 2000.
Handlin, David P. *American Architecture.* 2nd ed. World of Art. London: Thames & Hudson, 2004.
Hemingway, Andrew, and William Vaughn. *Art in Bourgeois Society, 1790–1850.* Cambridge: Cambridge Univ. Pr., 1998.
Hofmann, Werner. *Goya: To Every Story There Belongs Another.* New York: Thames & Hudson, 2003.
Irwin, David. *Neoclassicism.* London: Phaidon, 1997.
Johns, Christopher M.S. *Antonio Canova and the Politics of Patronage in Revolutionary and Napoleonic Europe.* Berkeley: Univ. of California Pr., 1998.
King, David N. *Complete Works of Robert and James Adam and Unbuilt Adam.* Repr. with corrections and additions. Oxford: Architectural Pr., 2001.
Lewis, Michael J. *American Art and Architecture.* World of Art. London; New York: Thames & Hudson, 2006.
Lucie-Smith, Edward. *American Realism.* New York: Abrams, 1994.
Malpas, James. *Realism.* Cambridge: Cambridge Univ. Pr., 1997.
Miller, Angela L., et al. *American Encounters: Art, History and Cultural Identity.* Upper Saddle River, NJ: Pearson Education, 2008.
Mitchell, Timothy. *Art and Science in German Landscape Painting, 1770–1840.* New York: Oxford Univ. Pr., 1993.
Monneret, Sophie. *David and Neoclassicism.* Paris: Terrail, 1999.
Neoclassicism and Romanticism: Architecture, Sculpture, Painting, Drawing, 1750–1848. Ed. Rolf Toman. Köln: Könemann, 2000.
Nesterova, Yelena. *The Itinerants: The Masters of Russian Realism: Second Half of the 19th and Early 20th Centuries.* Bournemouth, UK: Parkstone; St. Petersburg: Aurora, 1996.
Newhall, Beaumont. *The History of Photography: From 1839 to the Present.* Rev. and enl. 5th ed. New York: Museum of Modern Art; Boston: Little, Brown, 1999.
Nineteenth-Century Theories of Art. Ed. Joshua C. Taylor. Berkeley: Univ. of California Pr., 1987.
Novak, Barbara. *American Painting of the Nineteenth Century: Realism, Idealism, and the American Experience.* 3rd ed., with a new pref. Oxford; New York: Oxford Univ. Pr., 2007.
Novotny, Fritz. *Painting and Sculpture in Europe, 1780–1880.* 2nd ed. Pelican History of Art. New Haven: Yale Univ. Pr., 1995.
Orvell, Miles. *American Photography.* Oxford History of Art. Oxford: New York: Oxford Univ. Pr., 2003.
The Oxford Companion to the Photograph. Ed. Robin Lenman. Oxford; New York: Oxford Univ. Pr., 2005.
Porterfield, Todd B. and Susan L. Siegfried. *Staging Empire: Napoleon, Ingres, and David.* University Park: Pennsylvania State Univ. Pr., 2006.
Prettejohn, Elizabeth. *Beauty and Art, 1750-2000.* Oxford History of Art. Oxford; New York: Oxford Univ. Pr., 2005.
Rosenblum, Naomi. *A World History of Photography.* 4th ed. New York: Abbeville,2007.
Rosenblum, Robert, and H. W. Janson. *19th-Century Art.* Rev. and updated ed. Upper Saddle River, NJ: Pearson Prentice Hall, 2005.
Russia!: Nine Hundred Years of Masterpieces and Master Collections. New York: Solomon R. Guggenheim Museum; London: Thames & Hudson, 2005.
Sewell, Darrel. *Thomas Eakins.* Philadelphia: Philadelphia Museum of Art, 2001.
Shelton, Andrew C. *Ingres.* London; New York: Phaidon, 2008.
Todd, Pamela. *Pre-Raphaelites at Home.* New York: Watson-Guptill, 2001.
Treuherz, Julian. *Dante Gabriel Rossetti.* London: Thames & Hudson, 2003.
Valkenier, Elizabeth K. *Ilya Repin and the World of Russian Art.* New York: Columbia Univ. Pr., 1990.
Vaughan, William, and Françoise Cachin. *Arts of the 19th Century.* 2 vols. New York: Abrams, 1998.
Viscomi, Joseph. *Blake and the Idea of the Book.* Princeton, NJ: Princeton Univ. Pr., 1993.

Werner, Marcia. *Pre-Raphaelite Painting and Nineteenth-Century Realism.* Cambridge; New York: Cambridge Univ. Pr., 2005.
West, Alison. *From Pigalle to Préault: Neoclassicism and the Sublime in French Sculpture, 1760–1840.* Cambridge: Cambridge Univ. Pr., 1998.

Chapter 18 Later Nineteenth-Century Art in Europe and the United States

Adams, Steven. *The Barbizon School and the Origins of Impressionism.* London: Phaidon, 1994.
Adler, Kathleen. *Impressionism.* New Haven: Yale Univ. Pr., 1999.
Adler, Kathleen, et al. *Americans in Paris, 1860-1900.* London: National Gallery, 2006.
Art and the Academy in the Nineteenth Century. Eds. Rafael Denis & Colin Trodd. New Brunswick, NJ: Rutgers Univ. Pr., 2000.
Art, Culture, and National Identity in Fin-de-Siècle Europe. Eds. Michelle Facos & Sharon L. Hirsh. Cambridge; New York: Cambridge Univ.Pr., 2003.
Baudelaire, Charles. *The Painter of Modern Life, and Other Essays.* Ed. Jonathan Mayne. 2nd ed. London: Phaidon, 1995.
Blakesley, Rosalind P. *The Arts and Crafts Movement.* London: Phaidon, 2006.
Boime, Albert. *The Academy and French Painting in the Nineteenth Century.* New Haven: Yale Univ. Pr., 1986.
Brettell, Richard R. *Impressionism: Painting Quickly in France, 1860-1890.* New Haven: Yale Univ. Pr. and the Clark Art Institute, 2000.
______. *Modern Art, 1851–1929: Capitalism and Representation.* Oxford History of Art. Oxford: Oxford Univ. Pr., 1999.
Broude, Norma. *World Impressionism: The International Movement, 1860–1920.* New York: Abrams, 1990.
_____. *Impressionism: A Feminist Reading: The Gendering of Art, Science, and Nature in the Nineteenth Century.* New York: Rizzoli, 1991.
Callen, Anthea. *The Art of Impressionism: Painting Technique and the Making of Modernity.* New Haven: Yale Univ. Pr., 2000.
Clark, T.J. *The Painting of Modern Life: Paris in the Time of Manet and His Followers.* Rev. ed. Princeton, NJ: Princeton Univ. Pr., 1999.
Critical Readings in Impressionism and Post-Impressionism: An Anthology. Ed. Mary T. Lewis. Berkeley: Univ. of California Pr., 2007.
Denvir, Bernard *Post-Impressionism.* World of Art. New York: Thames & Hudson, 1992.
Escritt, Stephen. *Art Nouveau.* Arts & Ideas. London: Phaidon, 2000.
Ferretti-Bocquillon, Marina, et al. *Signac, 1863–1935.* New York: Metropolitan Museum of Art; New Haven: Yale Univ. Pr., 2001.
The French Academy: Classicism and Its Antagonists. Ed. June Hargrove. Newark: Univ. of Delaware Pr., 1990.
Gerdts, William H. *American Impressionism.* 2nd ed. New York: Abbeville, 2001.
Gibson, Michael. *Symbolism.* Köln: Taschen, 1995.
Hamilton, George H. *Painting and Sculpture in Europe, 1880–1940.* 6th ed. Pelican History of Art. New Haven: Yale Univ. Pr., 1993.
Handlin, David P. *American Architecture.* 2nd ed. World of Art. London: Thames & Hudson, 2004.
Herbert, Robert L. *From Millet to Léger: Essays in Social Art History.* New Haven: Yale Univ.Pr., 2002.
_____. *Seurat: Drawings and Paintings.* New Haven. Yale Univ. Pr., 2001.
Higonnet, Anne. *Berthe Morisot's Images of Women.* Cambridge, MA: Harvard Univ. Pr., 1992.
Hornberg, Cornelia. *Vincent van Gogh and the Painters of the Petit Boulevard.* New York: St. Louis Art Museum; Rizzoli, 2001.
House, John. *Impressionism: Paint and Politics.* New Haven: Yale Univ. Pr., 2004.
Lewer, Debbie. *Post-Impressionism to World War II.* Malden, MA: Blackwell, 2006.
Lewis, Mary T. *Cézanne.* Arts & Ideas. London: Phaidon, 2000.
Lewis, Michael J. *American Art and Architecture.* World of Art. London; New York: Thames & Hudson, 2006.
Machotka, Pavel. *Cezanne: Landscape into Art.* New Haven: Yale Univ. Pr., 1996.
Masson, Raphaël. *Rodin.* Paris: Flammarion; Paris: Musée Rodin, 2004.
Miller, Angela L., et al. *American Encounters: Art, History and Cultural Identity.* Upper Saddle River, NJ: Pearson Education, 2008.
Nochlin, Linda. *Representing Women.* New York: Thames & Hudson, 1999.
Nord, Phillip. *Impressionists and Politics: Art and Democracy in the Nineteenth Century.* London: Routledge, 2000.
The Oxford Companion to the Photograph. Ed. Robin Lenman. Oxford; New York: Oxford Univ. Pr., 2005.
Post-Impressionism: Cross-currents in European and American Painting, 1880–1906. Washington, DC: National Gallery of Art, 1980.
Rapetti, Rodolphe. *Symbolism.* Paris: Flammarion; New York: Rizzoli, 2005.
Roos, Jane Mayo. *Early Impressionism and the French State, 1866–1874.* Cambridge: Cambridge Univ. Pr., 1996.
Rosenblum, Robert, and H.W. Janson. *19th-Century Art.* Rev. and updated ed. Upper Saddle River, NJ: Pearson Prentice Hall, 2005.
Rubin, James Henry. *Impressionism.* London: Phaidon, 1999.
______. *Impressionism and the Modern Landscape: Productivity, Technology, and Urbanization from Manet to Van Gogh.* Berkeley: Univ. of California Pr., 2008.
Schapiro, Meyer. *Impressionism: Reflections and Perceptions.* New York: George Braziller, 1997.
Smith, Paul. *Seurat and the Avant-Garde.* New Haven: Yale Univ. Pr., 1997.
_____. *Impressionism: Beneath the Surface.* Perspectives. New York: Abrams, 1995.
Thomson, Belinda. *Impressionism: Origins, Practice, Reception.* New York: Thames & Hudson, 2000.
_____. *Post-Impressionism.* Movements in Modern Art. Cambridge: Cambridge Univ. Pr., 1998.
Van Gogh's Imaginary Museum: Exploring the Artist's Inner World. Amsterdam: Van Gogh Museum; New York: Abrams, 2003
Walther, Ingo. *Impressionist Art, 1860–1920.* New York: Taschen, 1997.
Women in Impressionism: From Mythical Feminine to Modern Woman. Ed. Sidsel M. Søndergaard. Milan: Skira; New York: Rizzoli, 2006.

Chapter 19 Modern Art: Europe and North America in the Early Twentieth Century

The A-Z of Modern Architecture. Ed. Peter Gössel. Köln; Los Angeles: Taschen, 2007.
American Art in the 20th Century: Painting and Sculpture, 1913-1993. Ed. Christos M. Joachimides & Norman Rosenthal. Munich: Prestel; New York: te Neues, 1993.
Antliff, Mark. *Cubism and Culture.* World of Art. London: Thames & Hudson, 2001.
Arnason, H. H. *History of Modern Art: Painting, Sculpture, Architecture, Photography.* 6th ed. Upper Saddle River, NJ: Prentice Hall, 2009.
Art of the Forties. Ed. Riva Castleman. New York: Museum of Modern Art, 1991.
Art in Theory, 1900–1990: An Anthology of Changing Ideas. Eds. Charles Harrison & Paul Woods. New ed. Cambridge, MA: Blackwell, 2003.
Bauhaus Culture: From Weimar to the Cold War. Ed. Kathleen James-Chakraborty. Minneapolis: Univ. of Minnesota Pr., 2006.
Bearden, Romare. *A History of African-American Artists: From 1792 to the Present.* New York: Pantheon, 1993.
Behr, Shulamith. *Expressionism.* New York: Cambridge Univ. Pr., 1999.
Bois, Yves Alain. *Matisse and Picasso.* Paris: Flammarion, 1998.
Brown, Milton W. *The Story of the Armory Show: The 1913 Exhibition That Changed American Art.* 2nd ed. New York: Abbeville, 1988.
Chipp, Herschel B. *Theories of Modern Art: A Source Book by Artists and Critics.* California Studies in the History of Art, 11. Berkeley: Univ. of California Pr., 1996.
Colquhoun, Alan. *Modern Architecture.* Oxford History of Art. Oxford; New York: Oxford Univ. Pr., 2002.
Corn, Wanda. *The Great American Thing: Modern Art and National Identity, 1915–1935.* Berkeley: Univ. of California Pr., 1999.
Cowling, Elizabeth, et al. *Matisse, Picasso.* London: Tate; Paris: Réunion des Musées Nationaux; New York: Museum of Modern Art, 2002.
Craven, Wayne. *American Art: History and Culture.* Rev. 1st ed. New York: McGraw Hill, 2003.
Curtis, Penelope. *Sculpture, 1900–1945: After Rodin.* Oxford History of Art. Oxford: Oxford Univ. Pr., 1999.
Dachy, Marc. *Dada: The Revolt of Art.* New York: Abrams, 2006.
Dada. Ed. Rudolf Kuenzli. Themes and Movements. London; New York: Phaidon, 2006.
Degenerate Art: The Fate of the Avant-Garde in Nazi Germany. Ed. Stephanie Barron. Los Angeles: Los Angeles County Museum of Art, 1991.
Dickerman, Leah. *Dada: Zurich, Berlin, Hannover, Cologne, New York, Paris.* Washington, DC: National Gallery of Art and Distributed Art Publishers, 2005.
Droste, Magdalena. *Bauhaus, 1919–1939.* Köln: Taschen, 1990.
Duchamp, Man Ray, Picabia. Ed. Jennifer Mundy. London: Tate, 2008.
Elger, Dietmar. *Expressionism: A Revolution in German Art.* Köln: Taschen, 1998.
Folgarait, Leon. *Mural Painting and Social Revolution in Mexico, 1920–1940: Art of the New Order.* New York: Cambridge Univ. Pr., 1998.
Foster, Hal, et al. *Art Since 1900: Modernism, Antimodernism, Postmodernism.* New York: Thames & Hudson, 2004. Vol. 1, 1900-1944.
Frampton, Kenneth. *Modern Architecture: A Critical History.* World of Art. 4th ed. London; New York: Thames & Hudson, 2007.
Davies, Hugh M., et al. *Frida Kahlo, Diego Rivera, and Twentieth-Century Mexican Art: the Jacques and Natasha Gelman Collection.* San Diego: Museum of Contemporary Art, 2000.
German Expressionism: Art and Society. Eds. Stephanie Barron & Wolf-Dieter Dube. New York: Rizzoli, 1997.
Golding, John. *Paths to the Absolute: Mondrian, Malevich, Kandinsky, Pollock, Newman, Rothko, and Still.* Princeton, NJ: Princeton Univ. Pr., 2000.
Gooding, Mel. *Abstract Art.* Movements in Modern Art. Cambridge; New York: Cambridge Univ. Pr., 2001.
Gray, Camilla. *Russian Experiment in Art, 1863–1922.* Rev. and enl. ed. New York: Thames & Hudson, 1986.
Green, Christopher. *Picasso's Les demoiselles d'Avignon.* Cambridge: Cambridge Univ. Pr., 2001.
_____. *Art in France, 1900–1940.* Pelican History of Art. New Haven: Yale Univ. Pr., 2000.
Greenough, Sarah, et al. *Modern Art and America: Alfred Stieglitz and His New York Galleries.* Washington, DC: National Gallery of Art; New York: Bullfinch, 2000.
Harrison, Charles. *Primitivism, Cubism, Abstraction: The Early Twentieth Century.* New Haven: Yale Univ. Pr., 1993.
Haskell, Barbara. *The American Century: Art and Culture, 1900–1950.* New York: Whitney Museum of American Art, 1999.
Hunter, Sam. *Modern Art: Painting, Sculpture, Architecture.* 3rd ed. rev. and exp. Upper Saddle River, NJ: Prentice Hall, 2004.
Julier, Guy. *The Thames & Hudson Dictionary of Design Since 1900.* 2nd ed. London; New York: Thames & Hudson, 2005.
Klingsöhr-Leroy, Cathrin. *Surrealism.* Köln: Taschen, 2004.
Kovtun, E.F. The *Russian Avant-Garde in the 1920s-1930s: Paintings, Graphics, Sculpture, Decorative Arts from the Russian Museum in St. Petersburg.* Schools and Movements. Bournemouth, UK: Parkstone; St. Petersburg: Aurora, 1996.
Lewer, Debbie. *Post-Impressionism to World War II.* Malden, MA: Blackwell, 2006.
Levine, Neil. *The Architecture of Frank Lloyd Wright.* Princeton, NJ: Princeton Univ. Pr., 1996.
Lewis, Samella S. *African American Art and Artists.* Rev. and exp. ed. Berkeley: Univ. of California Pr., 2003.
Lloyd, Jill. *German Expressionism: Primitivism and Modernity.* New Haven: Yale Univ. Pr., 1991.
Lupfer, Gilbert. *Walter Gropius, 1883-1969: The Promoter of a New Form.* Köln: Taschen, 2004.

Miller, Angela L., et al. *American Encounters: Art, History and Cultural Identity.* Upper Saddle River, NJ: Pearson Education, 2008.
Murray, Joan. *Canadian Art of the Twentieth Century.* Toronto: Dundurn, 1999.
The Oxford Companion to the Photograph. Ed. Robin Lenman. Oxford; New York: Oxford Univ. Pr., 2005.
Overy, Paul. *De Stijl.* World of Art. New York: Thames & Hudson, 1991.
Parkinson, Gavin. *The Duchamp Book.* Essential Artists. London: Tate; New York: Abrams, 2008.
Patton, Sharon. *African-American Art.* Oxford History of Art. Oxford: Oxford Univ. Pr., 1998.
Potts, Alex. *The Sculptural Imagination: Figurative, Modernist, Minimalist.* New Haven: Yale Univ. Pr., 2000.
Powell, Richard J. *Black Art: A Cultural History.* 2nd ed. World of Art. London: Thames & Hudson, 2003.
Rickey, George. *Constructivism: Origins and Evolutions.* Rev. ed. New York: Braziller, 1995.
Rosenblum, Robert. *Cubism and Twentieth-Century Art.* Rev. ed. New York: Abrams, 2001.
Rubin, William. *Picasso and Braque: Pioneering Cubism.* New York: Museum of Modern Art, 1989.
The Sources of Surrealism: Art in Context. Ed. Neil Matheson. Aldershot,UK; Burlington, VT: Lund Humphries, 2006.
Surrealist Painters and Poets: An Anthology. Ed. Mary Ann Caws. Cambridge, MA: MIT Pr., 2001.
Udall, Sharyn R. *Carr, O'Keeffe, Kahlo: Places of Their Own.* New Haven: Yale Univ. Pr., 2000.
Weiss, Jeffrey S. *The Popular Culture of Modern Art: Picasso, Duchamp, and Avant-Gardism.* New Haven: Yale Univ. Pr., 1994.
Whitfield, Sarah. *Fauvism.* World of Art. New York: Thames & Hudson, 1996.
Whitford, Frank. *The Bauhaus: Masters and Students by Themselves.* Woodstock, NY: Overlook Pr., 1993.
Women Artists in the 20th and 21st Century. Ed. Uta Grosenick. Köln; New York: Taschen, 2001.
Wright, Alastair. *Matisse and the Subject of Modernism.* Princeton: Princeton Univ. Pr., 2004.
Yablonskaya, Miuda. *Women Artists of Russia's New Age, 1900-1935.* New York: Rizzoli, 1990.
Zafran, Eric, and Paul Paret. *Surrealism and Modernism: From the Collection of the Wadsworth Atheneum.* Hartford, CT: Wadsworth Atheneum, 2003.

Chapter 20 Art Since 1945

Anfam, David. *Abstract Expressionism.* World of Art. New York: Thames & Hudson, 1990.
American Art in the 20th Century: Painting and Sculpture, 1913-1993. Eds. Christos M. Joachimides & Norman Rosenthal. Munich: Prestel; New York: te Neues, 1993.
Archer, Michael. *Art Since 1960.* 2nd ed. New York: Thames & Hudson, 2002.
Art in Theory, 1900–1990: An Anthology of Changing Ideas. Eds. Charles Harrison & Paul Woods. New ed. Cambridge, MA: Blackwell, 2003.
Atkins, Robert. *Artspeak: A Guide to Contemporary Ideas, Movements, and Buzzwords.* 2nd ed. New York: Abbeville, 1997.
Broude, Norma, and Mary D. Garrard. *The Power of Feminist Art: The American Movement of the 1970s, History and Impact.* New York: Abrams, 1994.
Burton, Johanna, et al. *Pop Art: Contemporary Perspectives: Princeton University Art Museum.* Princeton: The Museum; New Haven: Yale Univ. Pr., 2007.
Conceptual Art: A Critical Anthology. Eds. Alexander Alberro & Blake Stimson. Cambridge, MA: MIT Pr., 1999.
Cotton, Charlotte. *The Photograph as Contemporary Art.* World of Art. London; New York: Thames & Hudson, 2004.
Deepwell, Katy. *Women Artists and Modernism.* New York: St. Martin's, 1998.
Discourses: Conversations in Postmodern Art and Culture. Ed. Russell Ferguson. Documentary Sources in Contemporary Art. Cambridge, MA: MIT Pr., 1990.
Fineberg, Jonathan. *Art since 1940: Strategies of Being.* 2nd. ed. New York: Abrams, 2000.
Foster, Hal, et al. *Art Since 1900: Modernism, Antimodernism, Postmodernism.* New York: Thames & Hudson, 2004. Vol. 2, 1945 to the present.
Goldberg, Rose L. *Performance Art: From Futurism to the Present.* Rev. ed. London: Thames & Hudson, 2001.
Gouma-Peterson, Thalia. *Miriam Schapiro.* New York: Abrams, 1999.
Greenberg, Clement. *Clement Greenberg, Late Writings.* Ed. Robert C. Morgan. Minneapolis: Univ. of Minnesota Pr., 2003.
Heartney, Eleanor, et al. *After the Revolution: Women Who Transformed Contemporary Art.* Munich; New York: Prestel, 2007.
Hertz, Richard. *Theories of Contemporary Art.* 2nd ed. Englewood Cliffs, NJ: Prentice Hall, 1993.
Holzer, Jenny. *Jenny Holzer.* Ostfildern, Germany: Hatje Cantz, 2008.
Julier, Guy. *The Thames & Hudson Dictionary of Design Since 1900.* 2nd ed. London; New York: Thames & Hudson, 2005.
Kingsley, April. *The Turning Point: The Abstract Expressionists and the Transformation of American Art.* New York: Simon & Schuster, 1992.
Madoff, Steven H. *Pop Art: A Critical History.* Berkeley: Univ. of California Pr., 1997.
Martin, Sylvia. *Video Art.* Basic Art Series. Köln; Los Angeles: Taschen, 2006.
Marzona, Daniel. *Conceptual Art.* Köln; Los Angeles: Taschen, 2005.
______. *Minimal Art.* Köln; Los Angeles: Taschen, 2004.
McCarthy, David. *Pop Art.* New York: Cambridge Univ. Pr., 2000.
Meyer, James. *Minimalism.* Themes and Movements. London: Phaidon, 2000.
Modern Contemporary: Art Since 1980 at MoMA. Eds. Kirk Varnedoe et al. 2nd ed. New York: Museum of Modern Art and Distributed Art Publishers, 2004.
New York, New York: Fifty Years of Art, Architecture, Cinema, Performance, Photography and Video. Eds. Germano Celant & Lisa Dennison. Milan: Skira; Monaco: Grimaldi Forum, 2006.
The Oxford Companion to the Photograph. Ed. Robin Lenman. Oxford; New York: Oxford Univ. Pr., 2005.
Pearlman, Alison. *Unpackaging Art of the 1980s.* Chicago: Univ. of Chicago Pr., 2003.
Phillips, Lisa. *The American Century: Art and Culture, 1950–2000.* New York: Whitney Museum of American Art, 2000.
Rexer, Lyle. *How to Look at Outside Art.* New York: Abrams, 2005.
Rush, Michael. *New Media in Art.* 2nd ed. World of Art. London: Thames & Hudson, 2005.
______. *Video Art.* Rev. ed. London: Thames & Hudson, 2007.
Rushing, Jackson W. *Native American Art in the Twentieth Century: Makers, Meanings, and Histories.* London: Routledge, 1999.
Sandler, Irving. *Art of the Postmodern Era: From the Late 1960s to the Early 1990s.* New York: IconEditions, 1996.
_____. *The New York School: The Painters and Sculptors of the Fifties.* New York: Harper & Row, 1978.
Shapiro, David, and Cecile Shapiro. *Abstract Expressionism: A Critical Record.* New York: Cambridge Univ. Pr., 1990.
Sparke, Penny. *An Introduction to Design and Culture: 1900 to the Present.* 2nd ed. London; New York: Routledge, 2004.
Theories and Documents of Contemporary Art: A Sourcebook of Artists' Writings. Eds. Kristine Stiles & Peter Selz. California Studies in the History of Art; 35. Berkeley: Univ. of California Pr., 1996.
Varnedoe, Kirk. *Pictures of Nothing: Abstract Art since Pollock.* Bollingen Series, 48. Princeton: Princeton Univ. Pr., 2006.
Wagner, Anne M. *Three Artists (Three Women): Modernism and the Art of Hesse, Krasner, and O'Keeffe.* Berkeley: Univ. of California Pr., 1996.
Waldman, Diane. *Collage, Assemblage, and the Found Object.* New York: Abrams, 1992.
Women Artists in the 20th and 21st Century. Ed. Uta Grosenick. Köln; New York: Taschen, 2001.
Word as Image: American Art, 1960–1990. Milwaukee: Milwaukee Art Museum, 1990.

Index

Boldface names refer to artists. Pages in italics refer to illustrations.

Credits

Credits and Copyrights

Introduction

Intro–1 Paul M.R. Maeyaert; Intro–2 © The Art Institute of Chicago; Intro–3 University of Arizona, Museum of Art; Intro–4 © Georgia O'Keeffe Museum / DACS, 2009; Intro–5 © Estate of David Smith / DACS, London / VAGA, New York 2009; Intro–6 © 1990. Photo Scala, Florence–courtesy of the Ministero Beni e Att. Culturali; Intro–9 Photograph: E. G. Schempf; Intro–10 © Estate of Duane Hanson//VAGA, New York/DACS, London 2009; Intro–11 John Decopoulos; Intro–12 © 2000 Smithsonian American Art Museum Washington DC / Art Resource/ Scala, Florence; Intro–13 Image courtesy of the of the Board of Trustees, National Gallery of Art, Washington D.C.; Intro–14 Photo:Franko Khoury; Intro–15 © 1997. Photo Scala, Florence; Intro–16 akg–images / Erich Lessing; Intro–20 The J. Paul Getty Museum; Intro–21 Index Ricerca Iconografica; Intro–22 © 2007. Image The Metropolitan Museum of Art/ Art Resource/Scala,Florence; Intro–23 British Library Board; Intro–26 The Bridgeman Art Library; Intro–27 Araldo De Luca, Rome; Intro–28 Hirmer Fotoarchiv; Intro–29 V & A Images; Intro–30 Fotografica Foglia, Naples.

Chapter 1

1–1 Rock Art Research Institute / Univ. of Witwatersrand; 1–3 National Geographic Image Collection; 1–4 akg–images / Erich Lessing; 1–5 National Geographic Image Collection; 1–6 Ministere de la Culture et des Communications; 1–7 National Geographic Image Collection; 1–8 Yvonne Vertut; 1–9 National Geographic Image Collection; 1–10 Yvonne Vertut; 1–11 Marilyn Stokstad; 1–12a akg–images / Erich Lessing; 1–12b akg–images / Erich Lessing; 1–14 David Lyons / Alamy; 1–15 The Heritage Service; 1–16 Aerofilms; 1–18 Nationalmuseet Danske Afdeling.

Chapter 2

2–1 Photo Josse, Paris; 2–3a akg–images / Erich Lessing; 2–3b akg–images / Erich Lessing; 2–3c akg–images / Erich Lessing; 2–5 Michael S. Yamashita/CORBIS; 2–6 University of Pennsylvania Museum of Archaeology and Anthropology; 2–7 University of Pennsylvania Museum of Archaeology and Anthropology; 2–8 The Metropolitan Museum of Art / Art Resource/Scala, Florence; 2–9 RMN / Arnaudet; 2–10 RMN / Hervé Lewandowski; 2–11 he Metropolitan Museum of Art / Art Resource/ Scala, Florence; 2–12 © The Trustees of the British Museum; 2–13 © The Trustees of the British Museum; 2–14 RMN / Hervé Lewandowski; 2–16 Photo Scala, Florence / BPK, Bildagentur fuer Kunst, Kultur und Geschichte, Berlin; 2–17 Gérard Degeorge / Corbis.

Chapter 3

3–1 The Egyptian Museum, Cairo; 3–2a Werner Forman Archive / Egyptian Museum, Cairo; 3–2b Werner Forman Archive / Egyptian Museum, Cairo; 3–3 Corbis/Bettmann; 3–5 Free Agents Limited/CORBIS; 3–7 Werner Forman Archive; 3–8 Araldo de Luca; 3–10 Araldo de Luca; 3–12 Araldo de Luca; 3–13 Scala /Art Resource / The Metropolitan Museum of Art; 3–14 Peter A. Clayton; 3–17 Yvonne Vertut; 3–18 Photo Scala, Florence; 3–19 © 2005 Photo Scala, Florence/BPK Bildagentur fuer Kunst, Kultur und Geschichte, Berlin; 3–20 © 2005 Photo Scala, Florence/BPK Bildagentur fuer Kunst, Kultur und Geschichte, Berlin; 3–21 © 2005 Photo Scala, Florence/BPK Bildagentur fuer Kunst, Kultur und Geschichte, Berlin; 3–22 Araldo de Luca; 3–23 © The Trustees of the British Museum; 3–24 © The Trustees of the British Museum.

Chapter 4

4–1 National Geographic Image Collection; 4–2 National Museum of New Delhi; 4–3 Jean–Louis Nou; 4–4 National Museum of New Delhi; 4–5 University of Michigan / Asian Art Archives; 4–6 National Museum of New Delhi; 4–7 Government Museum of Mathura; 4–8 Benoy K. Behl; 4–9 University of Michigan / Asian Art Archives; 4–10 University of Michigan / Asian Art Archives; 4–11 Panos Pictures; 4–12 Institute of History and Philology, Academia Sinica; 4–13 Cultural Relics Publishing House; 4–14 Cultural Relics Publishing House; 4–16 Wolfgang Kaehler/CORBIS; 4–17 Cultural Relics Publishing House; 4–18 Cultural Relics Publishing House; 4–19 Cultural Relics Publishing House; 4–20 National Palace Museum, Taipei, Taiwan; 4–21 National Museum of Korea; 4–22 Tokyo National Museum DNP Archives.Com Co., Ltd; 4–23 Japan National Tourist Organization; 4–24 Carmen Redondo/CORBIS; 4–25 Japan National Tourist Organization.

Chapter 5

5–1 Musei Vaticani; 5–2 Hellenic Republic Ministry of Culture; 5–3 McRae Books Srl; 5–4 The Archaeological Society at Athens; 5–5 Studio Kontos Photostock; 5–6 Craig & Marie Mauzy, Athens; 5–7 Studio Kontos Photostock; 5–8 akg–images / Nimatallah; 5–10 The Art Archive / Gianni Dagli Orti ; 5–12 Deutsches Archaologisches Institut, Athens; 5–13 © 2007 The Metropolitan Museum of Art/Art Resource / Scala, FlorenceScala; 5–14 © 2007 Image copyright The Metropolitan Museum of Art/Art Resource/Scala, FlorenceScala; 5–15a Fotografica Foglia, Naples; 5–16 Craig & Marie Mauzy, Athens; 5–17 Craig & Marie Mauzy, Athens; 5–21 Photo Scala, Florence/BPK, Bildagentur fuer Kunst, Kultur und Geschichte, Berlin; 5–22a Craig & Marie Mauzy, Athens; 5–22b Studio Kontos Photostock; 5–23 Studio Kontos Photostock; 5–24a © 1990. Photo Scala, Florence–courtesy of the Ministero Beni e Att. Culturali; 5–24b © Photo Scala/Museo Archeologico Nazoinale, Reggio, Calabria; 5–25 Royal Ontario Museum ROM; 5–26a Greek National Tourism Organization; 5–27a © The Trustees of the British Museum; 5–27b © The Trustees of the British Museum; 5–28 © The Trustees of the British Museum; 5–29 Giraudon / The Bridgeman Art Library; 5–30 Studio Kontos Photostock; 5–31 Wolfgang Kaehler/CORBIS; 5–32 Studio Kontos Photostock; 5–33 Canali Photobank; 5–34 Studio Kontos Photostock; 5–35 Musei Vaticani; 5–36 Canali Photobank; 5–37 © 1990 Photo Scala, Florence – courtesy of the Ministero Beni e Att. Culturali; 5–38 Studio Kontos Photostock; 5–40 Marvin Trachtenberg; 5–41 RMN / Hervé Lewandowski; 5–42 © 2007 Image copyright The Metropolitan Museum of Art/Art Resource/Scala, FlorenceScala; 5–43 RMN / Gérard Blot / Christian Jean; 5–44a Musei Capitolini, Rome; 5–44b Araldo de Luca/CORBIS; 5–45 © RMN/ Jean–Gilles Berizzi; 5–46 Tourist Organization of Greece; 5–47 Photo Scala, Florence/BPK, Bildagentur fuer Kunst, Kultur und Geschichte, Berlin.

Chapter 6

6–1 Vincenzo Pirozzi, Rome; 6–2 Vincenzo Pirozzi, Rome; 6–3a University of Rome; 6–4 © 1990. Photo Scala, Florence–courtesy of the Ministero Beni e Att. Culturali; 6–5 akg–images / Nimatallah; 6–6 Araldo De Luca, Rome; 6–7 Courtesy of the American Numismatic Society; 6–8 Canali Photobank; 6–9 Araldo de Luca; 6–10a © Vincenzo Pirozzi, Rome; 6–11 Danita Delimont Photography; 6–12 Araldo De Luca, Rome; 6–13 Ikona; 6–14 Ikona; 6–17 Index Ricerca Iconografica; 6–18 Musei Vaticani; 6–19 © 2004. Photo Scala, Florence / Luciano Romano; 6–20 Canali Photobank; 6–22 Canali Photobank; 6–23 Index Ricerca Iconografica; 6–24 Alinari Archives, Florence; 6–25 American Academy in Rome–Fototeca dell'Unione Internazionale; 6–26 Dr. James E. Packer; 6–27 Alamy Images; 6–28 Canali Photobank; 6–30a Araldo de Luca; 6–30b Araldo de Luca; 6–31a Ikona; 6–31b Ikona; 6–32 Gemeinnutzige Stiftung Leonard von Matt; 6–33 Canali Photobank; 6–34 Araldo de Luca; 6–35 Araldo de Luca; 6–36 Ikona; 6–38 Vincenzo Pirozzi, Rome ; 6–39 © Vincenzo Pirozzi, Rome ; 6–40 Ikona.

Chapter 7

7–1 Index Ricerca Iconografica; 7–2 Ikona; 7–3 Princeton University Press/ Art Resource, N.Y; 7–4 Israel Museum Jerusalem; 7–5 Yale University Art Gallery, Dura–Europos Collection; 7–6 Yale University Art Gallery, Dura–Europos Collection; 7–10 Index Ricerca Iconografica; 7–11 Canali Photobank; 7–12 Canali Photobank; 7–13 Achim Bednorz; 7–14b Reprinted with the permission of Perspecta, Yale School of Architecture; 7–15 Robert Harding/Getty Images; 7–17 Photo Scala, Florence; 7–18 Canali Photobank; 7–19 Canali Photobank; 7–20 Bildarchiv der Osterreichische Nationalbibliothek; 7–21 Studio Kontos Photostock; 7–23 Mario Carrieri Fotografo; 7–25 Cameraphoto Arte, Venice; 7–26 The Metropolitan Museum of Art/ Scala, Florence; 7–27 The Metropolitan Museum of Art / Scala, Florence; 7–28 The Getty Research Institute, Wim Swaan Collection (96.P.21); 7–29 Photo Scala, Florence.

Chapter 8

8–2a akg–images / A.F.Kersting; 8–2b Said Nuseibeh Photography; 8–3 © 1992 Said Nuseibeh Photography. All Rights Reserved; 8–4 Roger Wood/CORBI; 8–5A Raffaello Bencini ; 8–6 Raffaello Bencini ; 8–7 The Metropolitan Museum/ Scala, Florence; 8–8 RMN; 8–9A Werner Forman Archive Ltd; 8–10 © 2007.The Metropolitan Museum of Art / Art Resource / Scala, Florence; 8–11 John and Lisa Merrill/Corbis; 8–12 Peter Sanders Photography; 8–14 The Saint Louis Art Museum; 8–15 The Metropolitan Museum/ Scala, Florence; 8–16 British Library Board; 8–17 Austrian Museum of Applied Arts/ Contemporary Art, Vienna. Photograph© MAK / Georg Mayer; 8–18 © 1990. Photo Scala, Florence; 8–19 Sonia Halliday Photographs; 8–20 © 2007.The Metropolitan Museum of Art / Art Resource / Scala, Florence; 8–21 The Aga Khan Program for Islamic Architecture.

Chapter 9

9–1 Woodfin Camp & Associates, Inc.; 9–2 David Cumming; Eye Ubiquitous / Corbis; 9–4 Henri Stierlin; 9–5 Museum of Fine Arts, Boston; 9–6 Photo: Katherine Wetzel.; 9–7 Dave G. Houser / Corbis; 9–9 The National Palace Museum; 9–11 © The Trustees of the British Museum; 9–12 Tokyo National Museum DNP Archives.Com Co., Ltd; 9–13 The National Palace Museum; 9–15 The Palace Museum; 9–16 Robert Harding World Imagery; 9–17 Japan National Tourist Organization; 9–18 AKG–Images; 9–19 Japan National Tourist Organization; 9–21 The Tokugawa Reimeikai Foundation; 9–22 The Cleveland Museum of Art; 9–23 Japan National Tourist Organization; 9–24 Sunritz Hattori Museum of Arts; 9–26 Philadelphia Museum of Art / Scala.

Chapter 10

10–1 Trinity College, Dublin; 10–2 © The Trustees of the British Museum; 10–3 Trinity College Library; 10–4 Nationalmuseet Danske Afdeling; 10–5a © Bildarchiv Monheim / Arturimage / VIEW; 10–6 akg–images / Erich Lessing; 10–8 Achim Bednorz; 10–9a Stiftsbibliotjek, St. Gallen; 10–11 Giraudon / The Bridgeman Art Library; 10–12 Photo Pierpont Morgan Library/Art Resource/Scala, Florence; 10–13 © 2008. PhotoThe Pierpont Morgan Library/ Art Resource/Scala, Florence; 10–14 Rheinisches Bildarchiv, Museen Der Stadt Koln; 10–15 Dom–Museum Hildesheim; 10–16 Achim Bednorz; 10–17 Hessisches Landes– und Hochschulebibliothek; 10–18 Bayerische Staatsbibliothek; 10–19 Skyscan; 10–20 Achim Bednorz; 10–23 Achim Bednorz; 10–24a akg–images / A.F.Kersting; 10–25 Index Ricerca Iconografica; 10–26 Achim Bednorz; 10–27a The Bridgeman Art Library; 10–27b Cathedral Museum of St. Lazare, Autun, Burgundy, France/ The Bridgeman Art Library; 10–28 Museu Nacional d'Art de Catalunya; 10–29 Musee de la Tapisserie, Bayeux, France/ The Bridgeman Art Library; 10–30 Musee de la Tapisserie de Bayeux; 10–31 Corpus Christi College; 10–32 Thuringer Universitats– und Landesbibliothek Jena; 10–33 Wiesbaden Hessische Landesbibliothek; 10–34 © 2007.The Metropolitan Museum of Art / Art Resource / Scala, Florence.

Chapter 11

11–1 Sonia Halliday Photographs; 11–3 Achim Bednorz; 11–5 Achim Bednorz; 11–6 Achim Bednorz; 11–8 Achim Bednorz; 11–10 Angelo Hornak, London; 11–11 Corbis; 11–12 Paul Almasy/Corbis; 11–13 Foto Marburg / Art Resource, N.Y.; 11–15a © 2004 The Pierpont Morgan Library / Art Resource/Scala Florence; 11–15b © 2004 The Pierpont Morgan Library / Art Resource / Scala Florence; 11–16 © 2007.The Metropolitan Museum of Art / Art Resource / Scala, Florence; 11–17 RMN / Martine Beck–Coppola; 11–18 Walters Art Gallery, Baltimore; 11–20 Skyscan / Corbis; 11–21 akg–images / A.F.Kersting; 11–22 © 2004 The Pierpont Morgan Library / Art Resource / Scala Florence; 11–23 © 2007.The Metropolitan Museum of Art / Art Resource / Scala, Florence; 11–24 Achim Bednorz; 11–25 akg–images / Erich Lessing; 11–26a The Bridgeman Art Library; 11–26b The Bridgeman Art Library; 11–27 Quattrone, Florence; 11–28 Lew Minter; 11–29 © Kimbell Art Museum, Fort Worth, Texas/ Art Resource / Scala, Florence; 11–30 Index Ricerca Iconografica; 11–31 Galleria degli Uffizi; 11–32 Alinari Archives, Florence; 11–33 Alinari Archives, Florence.

Chapter 12

12–1 © 2009 The National Gallery, London/ Scala, Florence; 12–2 RMN / René–Gabriel Ojéda; 12–3 Bibliotheque Nationale de France; 12–4 © 2007. The Metropolitan Museum of Art / Art Resource / Scala, Florence; 12–5 Image courtesy of the Board of Trustees, National Gallery of Art, Washington; 12–7 © 2007.The Metropolitan Museum of Art / Art Resource / Scala, Florence; 12–8C © Quattrone, Florence; 12–8L © Quattrone, Florence; 12–8R © Quattrone, Florence; 12–9 © 2007.The Metropolitan Museum of Art / Art Resource / Scala, Florence; 12–10 John Rylands University Library of Manchester; 12–11 © The Metropolitan Museum of Art/Art Resource/Scala, Florence; 12–12 Cincinnati Art Museum; 12–13 Arte & Immagini srl / Corbis; 12–14 akg–images / Erich Lessing; 12–15 Vanni Archive/CORBIS; 12–16 © Quattrone, Florence; 12–17 Photo Scala, Florence; 12–18 Index Ricerca Iconografica; 12–19 Photo © The Walters Art Museum, Baltimore; 12–20 Nimatallah / Art Resource, NY; 12–21 The Bridgeman Art Library; 12–22 Quattrone, Florence; 12–23 Photo Scala, Florence; 12–24 Canali Photobank; 12–25 Photo Scala, Florence/Fondo Edifici di Culto – Min. dell'Interno; 12–26 © Quattrone, Florence; 12–27 akg–images / Erich Lessing; 12–28 © 2009 The National Gallery, London/ Scala, Florence; 12–29 akg–images / Erich Lessing; 12–30 Photo Scala, Florence – courtesy of the Ministero Beni e Att. Culturali; 12–31 © 1990. Photo Scala, Florence – courtesy of the Ministero Beni e Att. Culturali; 12–32 Canali Photobank.

Chapter 13

13–1 Musei Vaticani; 13–2 © Quattrone, Florence; 13–3 akg–images / Cameraphoto; 13–4 RMN / Hervé Lewandowski / Thierry Le Mage; 13–5 Image courtesy of the Board of Trustees, National Gallery of Art, Washington; 13–6 Musei Vaticani; 13–7 Musei Vaticani; 13–8 Araldo De Luca, Rome; 13–9 Quattrone, Florence; 13–10 Ikona; 13–11 Musei Vaticani; 13–12 Canali Photobank; 13–13 Musei Vaticani; 13–14 Canali Photobank; 13–15 Ikona; 13–16 The Cleveland Museum of Art ; 13–17 CAMERAPHOTO Arte, Venice; 13–18 akg–images / Erich Lessing; 13–20 Embassy of Italy; 13–21 Index Ricerca Iconografica; 13–22 © 1990. Photo Scala, Florence–courtesy of the Ministero Beni e Att. Culturali; 13–23 CAMERAPHOTO Arte, Venice; 13–24 CAMERAPHOTO Arte, Venice; 13–26 Index Ricerca Iconografica; 13–27 Canali Photobank; 13–28 © 2007.The Metropolitan Museum of Art / Art Resource / Scala, Florence; 13–30 Canali Photobank; 13–31 © RMN / Jean–Pierre Lagiewski; 13–33 akg–images / Erich Lessing; 13–34a Musee d'Unterlinden; 13–34b Musee d'Unterlinden; 13–35 © 1990. Photo Scala, Florence; 13–36 Photo The Philadelphia Museum of Art / Art Resource / Scala, Florence; 13–37 Artothek; 13–38 Image courtesy of the Board of Trustees, National Gallery of Art, Washington; 13–39 Index Ricerca Iconografica; 13–40 Museo Nacional del Prado; 13–41 akg–images / Erich Lessing; 13–42 Photo: Martin Buhler; 13–43 Marilyn Stokstad.

Chapter 14

14–1 Canali Photobank; 14–2 Achim Bednorz; 14–3 Alinari Archives / Corbis; 14–4 Photo Scala, Florence – courtesy of the Ministero Beni e Att. Culturali; 14–5 © Vincenzo Pirozzi, Rome; 14–6 Canali Photobank; 14–7 Photo Scala, Florence/Fondo Edifici di Culto – Min. dell'Interno; 14–8 © Quattrone, Florence; 14–9 Canali Photobank; 14–10 Canali Photobank; 14–11 The Bridgeman Art Library; 14–12 V & A Images; 14–14 The State Hermitage Museum; 14–15 Photography courtesy of the Denver Art Museum; 14–16C Institut Royal du Patrimoine Artistique (IRPA–KIK); 14–16L Institut Royal du Patrimoine Artistique (IRPA–KIK); 14–16R Institut Royal du Patrimoine Artistique (IRPA–KIK); 14–17 RMN / René–Gabriel Ojéda / Thierry Le Mage; 14–18 © 1994. Photo Scala; 14–19 Photo Scala, Florence; 14–20 © 2005 Scala, Florence/BPK Bildagentur fuer Kunst, Kultur und Geschichte, Berlin Photo: Joerg P. Anders; 14–21 © 1990. Photo Scala, Florence; 14–25 Image courtesy of the Board of Trustees, National Gallery of Art, Washington; 14–26 Image courtesy of the Board of Trustees, National Gallery of Art, Washington; 14–28 Stichting Vrienden van Het Mauritshuis; 14–29 National Museum of Women In the Arts; 14–31 RMN / Herve Lewandowski; 14–32 Paul M.R. Maeyaert; 14–33 Massimo Listri / CORBIS; 14–34 The Art Institute of Chicago; 14–35 The Getty Research Institut, Wim Swaan Collection (96.P.21); 14–36 RMN / Gérard Blot.

Chapter 15

15–1 © Corson Hirschfeld 1988; 15–2 Werner Forman Archive / Anthropology Museum, Veracruz University, Jalapa.; 15–3 © 2007. Photo Scala, Florence; 15–4 © 2005 Photo Scala, Florence; 15–5 The Getty Research Institute, Wim Swaan Collection (96.P.21); 15–6 Mexican Government Tourism Office; 15–8 The Art Archive / Gianni Dagli Orti; 15–9 Bodleian Library, University of Oxford; 15–10 Embassy of Mexico; 15–11 Werner Forman Archiv e/ National Museum of Anthropology, Mexico City. Location: 28; 15–12 John Bigelow Taylor; 15–13 Kevin Schafer / Corbis; 15–14 The Art Institute of Chicago; 15–15 UCLA Fowler Museum of Cultural History; 15–16 The Art Archive / Gianni Dagli Orti; 15–17 Dumbarton Oaks Pre–Columbian Collection, Washington DC.; 15–18 University of Pennsylvania Museum of Archaeology and Anthropology; 15–20 Ohio Dept. of Natural Resources; 15–21 Cahokia Mounds State Historic Site; 15–22 Richard A. Cooke/ Corbis; 15–24 Museum of Indian Arts & Culture; 15–25 Wheelwright Museum of the American Indian, Santa Fe, New Mexico; 15–27 Smithsonian National Museum of Natural History; 15–30 Northwestern University Library; 15–32 Embassy of Canada.

Chapter 16

16–2 Werner Forman Archive / National Museum, Lagos, Nigeria. Location: 02.; 16–3 Dirk Bakker; 16–4 Purchase: William Rockhill Nelson Trust through the generosity of Donald J. and Adele C. Hall, Mr. and Mrs. Herman Robert Sutherland, and an anonymous donor; The Nelson Gallery Foundation; and the exchange of a Trust property, 87–7. Photograph E. G. Schempt ; 16–5 © 2007 The Metropolitan Museum of Art / Art Resource / Scala, Florence; 16–7 Peter Adams/ Getty Images ; 16–8 Robert Harding World Imagery / Corbis; 16–9 Smithsonian Institution; 16–11 Margaret Courtney–Clarke / Corbis; 16–14 University of Pennsylvania Museum of Archaeology and Anthropology; 16–15 The Bridgeman Art Library; 16–17 Charles & Josette Lenars / Corbis.

Chapter 17

17–1 © 2007 Photo The Philadelphia Museum of Art/Art Resource / Scala, Florence; 17–2 RMN / Christian Jean; 17–3 The Bridgeman Art Library; 17–4 © 2009 The National Gallery, London/ Scala, Florence; 17–6 © 2009 The National Gallery, London/ Scala, Florence; 17–8 Photo: Katherine Wetzel; 17–9 © 2009 The National Gallery, London/ Scala, Florence; 17–10 Arcaid; 17–11 © David R. Frazier Photolibrary, Inc. / Alamy; 17–12 National Museum of Women In the Arts; 17–13 Caisse Nationale des Monuments Historique et des Sites; 17–14 © 2008. Image The Metropolitan Museum of Art / Art Resource / Scala, Florence; 17–15 RMN / Gérard Blot / Christian Jean; 17–16 RMN / Franck Raux; 17–17 RMN / Hervé Lewandowski; 17–18 RMN / Hervé Lewandowski; 17–19 RMN / Hervé Lewandowski; 17–21 akg–images / Erich Lessing; 17–22 Archivo Oronoz; 17–24 © Tate, London 2010; 17–25 © 2007 The Metropolitan Museum of Art/ Art Resource/ Scala, Florence; 17–26 © 2007 The Metropolitan Museum of Art/ Art Resource/ Scala, Florence; 17–28 Science & Society Picture Library; 17–29 Science & Society Picture Library; 17–30 RMN (Musée d'Orsay) / Gérard Blot / Hervé Lewandowski; 17–31 RMN (Musée d'Orsay) / Jean Schormans; 17–32 akg–images / Erich Lessing; 17–33 Corbis.

Chapter 18

18–1 The Art Institute of Chicago; 18–2 Giraudon / The Bridge-man Art Library; 18–3 Getty Images Inc. – Hulton Archive Photos; 18–4 ART on FILE / Corbis; 18–6 Photo Gregory R. Staley; 18–7 Spencer Museum of Art; 18–8 William Morris Gallery; 18–9 The Bridgeman Art Library; 18–10 Ch. Bastin & J. Evrard; 18–11 Vincent Abbey Photography; 18–16 RMN (Musée d'Orsay) / Hervé Lewandowski; 18–17 RMN (Musée d'Orsay) / Hervé Lewandowski; 18–18 akg–images / Erich Lessing; 18–19 Photograph: Jamison Miller; 18–20 © 2009 The National Gallery, London/ Scala, Flor-ence; 18–21 © 2008. Image The Metropolitan Museum of Art / Art Resource/ Scala, Florence; 18–24 The Bridgeman Art Library; 18–25 The Art Institute of Chicago; 18–26 The Art Institute of Chicago; 18–27 © 2008 Digital image The Museum of Modern Art, New York / Scala, Florence; 18–28 The Brooklyn Museum of Art; 18–29 Vincent Van Gogh Museum, Amsterdam; 18–30 Nasjonal-museet for Kunst / Nasjonalgalleriet, © Munch Museum/Munch – Ellingsen Group, BONO, Oslo / DACS, London 2009; 18–33 Hirsh-horn Museum and Sculpture Garden/Smithsonian Institution; 18–34 Artothek.

Chapter 19

19–1 The New York Public Library / Art Resource NY; 19–2 The Bridgeman Art Library; 19–3 © 2008 Digital image The Museum of Modern Art, New York / Scala, Florence; 19–4 © 2005 Scala, Florence/BPK Bildarchiv Preussischer Kulturbesitz / DACS 2009; 19–5 Photo: Martin Buhler; 19–6 The Solomon R. Guggenheim Museum, New York © ADAGP, Paris and DACS, London 2009; 19–7 © 2008 Digital image The Museum of Modern Art, New York / Scala, Florence. © Succession Picasso/DACS 2009; 19–8 The Solomon R. Guggenheim Museum © ADAGP, Paris and DACS, London 2009; 19–9 © 2008 Digital image The Museum of Modern Art, New York / Scala, Florence. © Succession Picasso/DACS 2009; 19–10 © Succession Picasso/DACS 2009; 19–11 © L & M SERVICES B.V., The Hague 20090706; 19–12 © 2008. Digital image, The Museum of Modern Art, New York / Scala, Florence / ADAGP, Paris and DACS, London 2009; 19–13 © 2008 Digtila image, The Museum of Modern Art, New York / Scala, Florence; 19–14 RMN (Centre National d'Art et de Culture. Georges Pompidou) © ADAGP, Paris and DACS, London 2009; 19–15 Stedelijk Museum; 19–16 © 2009 Museum Associates / LACMA; 19–18 © 2005. Photo The Philadelphia Museum of Art/ Art Resource/Scala, Florence / © Succession Marcel Duchamp/ ADAGP, Paris and DACS, London 2009; 19–19 Art Resource/The Metropolitan Museum of Art. © Georgia O'Keeffe Museum / DACS, 2009; 19–20 © 2007 The Metropolitan Museum of Art/ Art Resource/ Scala, Florence; 19–21 Van Abbemuseum; 19–22 Photo: Hickey–Robertson. The Menil Collection, Houston; 19–23 © Bildarchiv Monheim GmbH / Alamy; 19–24 Jannes Linders Photography © DACS 2009; 19–25 © 2008. White Images/ Scala, Florence. © FLC/ADAGP, Paris and DACS, London 2009; 19–26 Bauhausarchiv–Museum fur Gestaltung; 19–27 © 2008 Photo Scala, Florence / BPK, Bildagentur fuer Kunst, Kultur und Gesch-ichte, Berlin; 19–28 Akademie der Kunste / Archiv Bildende Kunst; 19–29 © 2008 Digital image The Museum of Modern Art, New York / Scala, Florence. © Salvador Dali, Gala–Salvador Dali Foun-dation, DACS, 2009; 19–30 © 2008 Digital image The Museum of Modern Art, New York / Scala, Florence/DACS 2009; 19–31 © Suc-cession Miro/ADAGP, Paris and DACS, London 2009; 19–32 © AD AGP, Paris and DACS, London 2009; 19–33 © The Henry Moore Foundation/Tate, London 2010; 19–34 © 2008 Digital image The Museum of Modern Art, New York / Scala, Florence. © Calder Foundation, New York / DACS London 2009; 19–35 The Art Institute of Chicago. All rights reserved by the Estate of Nan Wood Graham/by VAGA, New York, NY; 19–36 Library of Congress; 19–37 Art Resource; 19–38 © Donna Van Der Zee; 19–39 © ARS, NY and DACS, London 2009; 19–40 © 2005. Photo Art Resource / Scala, Florence. © 2009, Banco de Mexico Diego Rivera & Frida Kahlo Museums Trust, Me-xico D.F. / DACS; 19–41 © 2004. Photo Art Resource / Scala, Flor-ence. © 2009, Banco de Mexico Diego Rivera & Frida Kahlo Mus-eums Trust, Mexico D.F. / DACS; 19–42 Photo: Trevor Mills, Van-couver Art Gallery; 19–43 The New–York Historical Society; 19–44 Thomas A Heinz, AIA, Photographer © Copyright Western Penn-sylvania Conservancy 2007; 19–45 Grand Canyon National Park.

Chapter 20

20–01 Frank Fournier; 20–02 Scala. © The Pollock–Krasner Foundation ARS, NY and DACS, London 2009; 20–03 © 2007.The Metropolitan Museum of Art / Art Resource / Scala, Florence; 20–04 Photo Geoffrey Clements; 20–05 © 2008. Digital image, The Museum of Modern Art, New York/Scala, Florence / The Willem de Kooning Foundation, New York/ ARS, NY and DACS, London 2009; 20–06 © 1998 Kate Rothko Prizel & Christopher Rothko ARS, NY and DACS, London; 20–07 Image courtesy of the Board of Trustees, National Gallery of Art, Washington; 20–08 © 2008 Digital image The Museum of Modern Art, New York / Scala, Florence / ARS, NY and DACS, London 2009; 20–09 © Estate of Robert Rauschenberg /DACS, London / VAGA, New York 2009; 20–10 Digital image, The Museum of Modern Art, New York/Scala, Florence. © Jasper Johns / VAGA, New York / DACS, London 2009; 20–11 © 2008 Digital image The Museum of Modern Art, New York / Scala, Florence / ADAGP, Paris and DACS, London 2009; 20–12 © Richard Hamilton. All Rights Reserved, DACS 2009; 20–13 © The Estate of Roy Lichtenstein/ DACS 2009; 20–14 © The Andy Warhol Foundation for the Visual Arts / Artists Rights Society (ARS), New York / DACS, London 2009; 20–15 Scala/Art Resource/Yale University Art Gallery; 20–16 © 2008 Digital image The Museum of Modern Art, New York / Scala, Florence; 20–17 Photo by David Heald ©The Solomon R. Guggenheim Foundation / Judd Foundation. Licensed by VAGA, New York / DACS, London 2009; 20–18 © The Estate of Eva Hesse. Courtesy Hauser & Wirt, Photo Geoffrey Clements; 20–19 © 2008 Digital image The Museum of Modern Art, New York / Scala, Florence / ARS, NY and DACS, London 2009; 20–20 © ARS, NY and DACS, London 2009; 20–21 Dia Art Foundation; 20–22 Photo: Jeanne–Claude © Christo 1976; 20–23 Robert Hickerson; 20–24 © ARS, NY and DACS, London 2009; 20–25 Photo Benjamin Blackwell; 20–26 Faith Ringgold, Inc.; 20–28 Spencer Museum of Art, Museum purchase: Friends of the Art Museum and Helen Foresman Spencer Art Acquisition Fund, 1987.0035 © Estate of Elizabeth Murray, courtesy PaceWildenstein, New York. Photograph courtesy Paula Cooper Gallery, New York; 20–29 Art Gallery of South Australia; 20–30 Van Abbemuseum; 20–32 © SPARC www.sparcmurals.otg; 20–33 The Art Institute of Chicago; 20–35 © ARS, NY and DACS, London 2009; 20–36 © 2005 Smithsonian American Art Museum/Art Resource/ Scala; 20–37 Gladstone Gallery; 20–38 ACME. / Photo: Robert Wedemeyer; 20–39 The Oakland Museum; 20–41 Michael Lawrence Aurbach; 20–43 Andrew Garn; 20–44 Venturi, Scott Brown & Associates, Inc.; 20–45 Foster and Partners; 20–46 © AAD Worldwidw Travel Images / Alamy.